Ounces	9×12 envelope, 9×12 SASE number of pages	9×12 SASE (for return trips) number of pages	First Class ** Postage	Third Class ** Postage	Postage from U.S. to Canada **
under 2	…	1 to 2	$.43*	$.43*	$.63*
2	1 to 4	3 to 8	.55	.55	.73
3	5 to 10	9 to 12	.78	.78	.86
4	11 to 16	13 to 19	1.01	1.01	1.09
5	17 to 21	20 to 25	1.24	1.24	1.32
6	22 to 27	26 to 30	1.47	1.47	1.55
7	28 to 32	31 to 35	1.70	1.70	1.78
8	33 to 38	36 to 41	1.93	1.93	2.01
9	39 to 44	42 to 46	2.16	2.16	2.24
10	45 to 49	47 to 52	2.39	**	2.47
11	50 to 55	53 to 57	2.62	**	2.70
12-32	56 to 99	58 to 101	3.00	**	2.80

* This cost includes a 11¢ assessment for oversized mail that is light in weight.

** Third class postage over 9 ounces is determined by weight and distance.

1996
Writer's Market

Where & how
to sell what you write

Editor: Mark Garvey

Assistant Editor: Kirsten Holm

WRITER'S DIGEST BOOKS
Cincinnati, Ohio

Distributed in Canada by
McGraw-Hill Ryerson
300 Water St.
Whitby, Ontario L1N 9B6

Distributed in Australia by
Kirby Book Co.
Private Bag No. 19
Alexandria NSW 2015

Managing Editor, Market Books Department:
Constance J. Achabal
Production Editor: Richard D. Muskopf

This edition of Writer's Market *features a "self-
jacket" that eliminates the need for a separate dust
jacket. It provides sturdy protection for your book
while it saves paper, trees and energy.*

Library of Congress Catalog Number
31-20772
International Standard Serial Number
0084-2729
International Standard Book Number
0-89879-701-2

Cover illustration: Mercedes McDonald
U.S. Postage by the Page by Carolyn Lieberg
Canadian Postage by the Page by Barbara Murrin

Attention Booksellers: This is an annual directory of F&W Publications. Return deadline for
this edition is December 31, 1996.

Contents

Getting Published

Before Your First Sale *5*

This section will introduce you to the basics of writing for publication. Interviews with first-time book authors Jack White, Andrea Louie and Everett Weinberger offer inspiration and advice on finding success as a new writer.

Current Trends in Publishing, by Kirsten Holm *21*

This in-depth analysis of present trends in the book and magazine industries will bring you up to date on what's selling and what's not and help you pitch your ideas more effectively.

Magazine Editors' Roundtable, by Anne Bowling *28*

Five consumer magazine editors offer freelance writers their advice and insights on the subject of effective query letters, targeting markets, simultaneous submissions, working with magazine editors and more.

The Business of Writing

Minding the Details *34*

From contracts to subsidiary rights, copyright, money and taxes, this section will help you negotiate and secure fair agreements, manage your rights and handle earnings responsibly and legally. Magazine editor Michael Robbins talks about getting to know your magazine markets, and Ian Frazier discusses his role and goals as a nonfiction writer.

How Much Should I Charge? *44*

Setting freelance writing fees can be tricky. We help take some of the guesswork out of the process in our annually updated list of representative freelance writing jobs and typical pay ranges.

A Writer's Guide to New Media Publishing 56

Writers looking for new opportunities may want to consider the world of electronic publishing. This article will bring you up to speed on the present state of "new media" publishing and help you discern where the current and future opportunities may be found. Random House's President of New Media, Randi Benton, discusses the challenges of publishing and writing for this emerging art form.

The Markets

Hundreds of places to sell your book ideas. The introduction to this section helps you refine your approach to publishers and features an interview with veteran editor Pamela Strickler.

The introduction to this section covers how to submit your work to international markets and includes an interview with Canadian publisher Oliver Salzmann.

This section contains hundreds of listings for magazines on nearly every subject imaginable. The introduction offers tips on approaching consumer magazine markets and includes an interview with Atlantic Monthly *editor C. Michael Curtis.*

Trade, Technical and Professional Journals *681*

*Magazines listed in this section serve a wide variety of trades and professions. The introduction
tells how to break in and establish yourself in the trades*

Scriptwriting *817*

Companies seeking scripts for films, television and the stage are listed here. The introduction to this section includes valuable advice on breaking into this specialized field.

Syndicates *864*

Newspaper syndicates distribute writers' works around the nation and the world. The introduction offers advice for breaking into this market.

Greeting Cards & Gift Ideas *875*

Greeting card and gift markets provide outlets for a wide variety of writing styles. The introduction to this section tells you how to approach these companies professionally.

Resources

Contests and Awards *885*

Organizations of Interest *938*

Publications of Interest *940*

Glossary *942*

Book Publishers Subject Index *947*

General Index *981*

From the Editors

Seventy-five years ago, Warren G. Harding was president of the United States. The First World War had recently ended. Chaplin, Fairbanks, Valentino and Pickford were the hottest box office draws of the day. Fitzgerald was ushering in the jazz age; D.H. Lawrence had just published *Women in Love*; Hemingway was in France as a foreign correspondent for the Toronto *Star*; and here in Cincinnati the first edition of *Writer's Market* rolled off the press. That pragmatic, unassuming volume—a 100-page, 4×6″ hardbound guide offering "a convenient reference to the various firms and publishers in the market for manuscripts"—set the tone for the partnership between *Writer's Market* and the writing community that flourishes to this day.

Several of the publishing companies and periodicals listed in the first *Writer's Market* are still in business today—and are listed in our current edition. To pick one example, here is the 1921 listing for *The Saturday Evening Post*:

> SATURDAY EVENING POST, THE, The Curtis Publishing Company, Philadelphia, Pa. "We are always in the market for short fiction, preferably stories from 6,000 to 10,000 words in length, dealing with American characters and with life of today. At the present time we are rather plentifully supplied with longer stories and serial material. We do not use essays and only occasionally short verse. We suggest that the subjects of articles be brought to our attention in advance, rather than the articles submitted in their completed form. We will always reply promptly to queries in this field. We conduct no prize contests."

To get some idea not only of how things have changed at *The Saturday Evening Post*, but also of how the information-gathering process at *Writer's Market* has evolved, check out their listing this year in the Consumer Magazine section.

The majority of publishers and periodicals listed in the 1921 edition are, regrettably, no longer with us. Some, such as *American Blacksmith* and *American Hatter*, have gone the way of the technologies and fashions they served. Others no doubt fell victim to the vicissitudes of the marketplace and the vagaries of the reading public—thus we are no longer able to bring you periodicals such as *Little Story Magazine*, which excluded "no subject save the lewd," or *The Young People's Papers*, which cautioned writers against submitting stories involving theater, dancing, cards, tobacco, train wrecks, money troubles or "stories in which a fire provides the excitement."

Since 1921, *Writer's Market* has grown from a pamphlet-sized publication you could slip into the pocket of your racoon coat to the thousand-page tome you now hold in your hand and whose ancillary uses include everything from pressing wildflowers to boosting toddlers at the supper table. Its physical bulk aside, *Writer's Market* has grown into an essential marketing tool for thousands upon thousands of writers. For the past 75 years, we have kept our eye on the publishing industry and given our ear to the community of writers who rely on us for accurate, up-to-date information on where and how to publish their work.

In this, the 75th anniversary edition, we have added more than 800 new listings and completely updated those listings that are returning from last year. As always, we have supplemented the listings of freelance markets with helpful articles and interviews featuring advice and instruction from industry insiders and successful newcomers. If you're new to the world of magazine writing, be sure to read the Magazine Editors' Roundtable, on page 28, for an editor's-eye-view of queries and submissions and hints on breaking into magazine markets. For the latest trends in both book and magazine publishing, check out Current Trends in Publishing, on page 21. As always, you'll find "nuts and bolts" writing business information in Before Your First Sale, on page 5, and Minding the Details, on page 34.

You'll note an added emphasis on electronic media in this edition of *Writer's Market*. The emergence of multimedia and other "new media" formats is having a palpable effect on how writing is produced, edited, published and marketed—an effect that will only intensify with time. While some writers may be less than enthusiastic about the coming electronic wave, many others are gearing up to take advantage of this burgeoning market.

We have added a multimedia classification to our Book Publisher's Subject Index so you can track down publishers working in new media. For more information on this subject, be sure to read A Writer's Guide to New Media Publishing, on page 56 and the interview with Randi Benton, Vice President of New Media at Random House, on page 59.

We would appreciate hearing your thoughts on the subject of computers and the new media. How has the computer boom affected your writing? What new opportunities have you found? How can we best serve your needs as this technology evolves? Why not drop us a line—you guessed it—*electronically*, via e-mail, at wdigest@aol.com.

In his preface to the 1921 *Writer's Market*, the editor, Julius J. Hoffmann, promised his readers that "a market for practically every meritorious piece of literary work can be found in the following pages." With a nod to our predecessor and a wish for success to you, our writing readers, we are happy to be able to extend that same promise to you today.

Mark Garvey
Editor

Kirsten Holm
Assistant Editor

How to Get the Most Out of *Writer's Market*

Writer's Market is here to help you decide where and how to submit your writing to appropriate markets. Each listing contains information about the editorial focus of the market, how they prefer material to be submitted, payment information and other helpful tips.

Where to start

A quick look at the Table of Contents will familiarize you with the arrangement of *Writer's Market*. The three largest sections of the book are the market listings of Book Publishers; Consumer Magazines; and Trade, Technical and Professional Journals. You will also find sections for scriptwriting markets, syndicates and greeting card publishers. Be sure to read the introduction for each section before you turn to the listings. The section introductions contain specific information about trends, submission methods and other helpful resources for the material included in that section.

Narrowing your search

After you've identified the market categories you're interested in, you can begin researching specific markets within each section.

Publishers listed in the Book Publishers section are categorized, in the Book Publishers Subject Index, according to types of books they are interested in. If, for example, you plan to write a book on a religious topic, simply turn to the Book Publishers Subject Index and look under the Religion subhead in Nonfiction for the names and page numbers of companies that publish such books.

Consumer Magazines and Trade, Technical and Professional Journals are categorized by subject to make it easier for you to identify markets for your work. If you want to publish an article dealing with some aspect of retirement, you could look under the Retirement category of Consumer Magazines to find an appropriate market. You would want to keep in mind, however, that magazines in other categories might also be interested in your article (for example, women's magazines publish such material as well). Keep your antennae up while studying the markets: less obvious markets often offer the best opportunities.

Interpreting the markets

Once you've identified companies or publications that cover the subjects you're interested in, you can begin evaluating specific listings to pinpoint the markets most receptive to your work and most beneficial to you.

In evaluating an individual listing, first check the location of the company, the types of material it is interested in seeing, submission requirements, and rights and payment policies. Depending upon your personal concerns, any of these items could be a deciding factor as you determine which markets you plan to approach. Many listings also include a reporting time, which lets you know how long it will typically take for the publisher to respond to your initial query or submission. (We suggest that you allow an additional month for a response, just in case your submission is under further review or the publisher is backlogged.)

Check the Glossary at the back of the book for unfamiliar words. Specific symbols and abbreviations are explained in the table on page 64. The most important abbreviation is SASE—self-addressed, stamped envelope. Always enclose one when you send unsolicited queries, proposals or manuscripts. This requirement is not included in most of the individual market listings because it is a "given" that you must follow if you expect to receive a reply.

A careful reading of the listings will reveal many editors are very specific about their needs. Your chances of success increase if you follow directions to the letter. Often companies do not accept unsolicited manuscripts and return them unread. Read each listing closely, heed the tips given, and follow the instructions. Work presented professionally will normally be given more serious consideration.

Whenever possible, obtain writer's guidelines before submitting material. You can usually obtain them by sending a SASE to the address in the listing. You should also familiarize yourself with the company's publications. Many of the listings contain instructions on how to obtain sample copies, catalogs or market lists. The more research you do upfront, the better your chances of acceptance, publication and payment.

Additional help

This year's book contains articles on electronic publishing, current trends in book and magazine publishing and much more. "Insider Reports"—interviews with writers, editors and publishers—offer advice and an inside look at publishing. Some listings contain editorial comments, indicated by a bullet (●), that provide additional information discovered during our compilation of this year's *Writer's Market*.

Minding the Details offers valuable information about rights, taxes and other practical matters. New or unpublished writers should also read Before Your First Sale. There is also a helpful section titled How Much Should I Charge? that offers guidance for setting your freelance writing fees.

Getting Published

Before Your First Sale

Many writers new to the craft feel that achieving publication—and getting paid for their work—is an accomplishment so shrouded in mystery and magic that there can be little hope it will ever happen to *them*. Of course, that's nonsense. All writers were newcomers once. Getting paid for your writing is not a matter of learning a bit of privileged information or being handed the one "key" to success by an insider. There's not even a secret handshake.

Making money from your writing will require three things of you:
- Good writing;
- Knowledge of writing markets (magazines and book publishers) and how to approach them professionally;
- Persistence.

Good writing without marketing know-how and persistence might be art, but who's going to know if it never sells? A knowledge of markets without writing ability or persistence is pointless. And persistence without talent and at least a hint of professionalism is simply irksome. But a writer who can combine the above-mentioned virtues stands a good chance of not only selling a piece occasionally, but enjoying a long and successful writing career.

You may think a previously unpublished writer has a difficult time breaking into the field. As with any profession, experience is valued, but that doesn't mean publishers are closed to new writers. While it is true some editors prefer working with certain writers, most are open to professional submissions and good ideas from any writer, and quite a few magazine editors like to feature different styles and "voices" in their publications.

In nonfiction book publishing, experience in writing or in a particular subject area is valued by editors as an indicator of the author's ability and expertise in the subject. Again, as with magazines, the idea is paramount, and new authors break in every year with good, timely ideas.

As you work in the writing field, you may read articles or talk to writers and editors who give conflicting advice. There are some norms in the business, but they are few. You'll probably hear as many different routes to publication as writers you talk to.

The following information on submissions has worked for many writers, but it's not the *only* method you can follow. It's easy to get wrapped up in the specifics of submitting (should my name go at the top left or right of the manuscript?) and fail to consider weightier matters (is this idea appropriate for this market?). Let common sense and courtesy be your guides as you work with editors, and eventually you'll develop your own most effective submission methods.

Targeting your ideas

Writers often think of an interesting story, complete the manuscript and then begin the search for a suitable publisher or magazine. While this approach is common for fiction, poetry and screenwriting, it reduces your chances of success in many other writing areas. Instead, try choosing categories that interest you and study those sections in *Writer's Market*. Select several listings that you consider good prospects for your type of writing. Sometimes the individual listings will even help you generate ideas.

Next, make a list of the potential markets for each idea. Make the initial contact with markets using the method stated in the market listings. If you exhaust your list of possibilities, don't give up. Reevaluate the idea, revise it or try another angle. Continue developing ideas and approaching markets with them. Identify and rank potential markets for an idea and continue the process.

As you submit to the various periodicals listed in *Writer's Market*, it's important to remember that every magazine is published with a particular slant and audience in mind. Probably the number one complaint we hear from editors is that writers often send material and ideas that are completely wrong for their magazines. The first mark of professionalism is to know your market well. That knowledge starts here in *Writer's Market*, but you should also search out back issues of the magazines you wish to write for and learn what specific subjects they have published in past issues and how those subjects have been handled.

Prepare for rejection and the sometimes lengthy wait. When a submission is returned, check your file folder of potential markets for that idea. Cross off the market that rejected the idea and immediately mail an appropriate submission to the next market on your list. If the editor has given you suggestions or reasons as to why the manuscript was not accepted, you might want to incorporate these when revising your manuscript.

About rejection. Rejection is a way of life in the publishing world. It's inevitable in a business that deals with such an overwhelming number of applicants for such a limited number of positions. Anyone who has published has lived through many rejections, and writers with thin skin are at a distinct disadvantage. The key to surviving rejection is to remember that it is not a personal attack—it's merely a judgment about the appropriateness of your work for that particular market at that particular time. Writers who let rejection dissuade them from pursuing their dream or who react to each editor's "No" with indignation or fury do themselves a disservice. Writers who let rejection stop them do not publish. Resign yourself to facing rejection now. You will live through it, and you will eventually overcome it.

Query and cover letters

A query letter is a brief but detailed letter written to interest an editor in your manuscript. It is a tool for selling both nonfiction magazine articles and nonfiction books. With a magazine query you are attempting to interest an editor in your writing an article for her periodical. A book query's job is to get an editor interested enough to ask you to send in either a full proposal or the entire manuscript. [Note: Some book editors accept proposals on first contact. Refer to individual listings for contact guidelines.] Some beginners are hesitant to query, thinking an editor can more fairly judge an idea by seeing the entire manuscript. Actually, most editors of nonfiction prefer to be queried.

There is no query formula that guarantees success, but there are some points to consider when you begin. Queries should:

• Be limited to one page, single-spaced, and address the editor by name (Mr. or Ms. and the surname).

- Grab the editor's interest with a strong opening. Some magazine queries begin with a paragraph meant to approximate the lead of the intended article.
- Indicate how you intend to develop the article or book. Give the editor some idea of the work's structure and contents.
- Let the editor know if you have photos available to accompany your magazine article (never send original photos—send duplicates).
- Mention any expertise or training that qualifies you to write the article or book. If you've published before, mention it; if not, don't.
- End with a direct request to write the article (or, if you're pitching a book, ask for the go-ahead to send in a full proposal or the entire manuscript). Give the editor an idea of the expected length and possible delivery date of your manuscript.

Querying for fiction

Fiction is sometimes queried, but most fiction editors don't like to make a final decision until they see the complete manuscript. Most editors will want to see a synopsis and sample chapters for a book, and a complete manuscript of a short story. Consult individual listings for specific fiction guidelines. If a fiction editor does request a query, briefly describe the main theme and story line, including the conflict and resolution of your story.

Some writers state politely in their query letters that after a specified date (slightly beyond the listed reporting time), they will assume the editor is not currently interested in their topic and will submit the query elsewhere. It's a good idea to do this only if your topic is a timely one that will suffer if not considered quickly.

For more information about writing query letters, read *How to Write Irresistible Query Letters*, by Lisa Collier Cool (Writer's Digest Books).

A brief single-spaced cover letter enclosed with your manuscript is helpful in personalizing a submission. If you have previously queried the editor on the article or book, the cover letter should be a brief reminder, not a sales pitch. "Here is the piece on goat herding, which we discussed previously. I look forward to hearing from you at your earliest convenience."

If you are submitting to a market that considers unsolicited complete manuscripts, your cover letter should tell the editor something about your manuscript and about you—your publishing history and any particular qualifications you have for writing the enclosed manuscript.

Once your manuscript has been accepted, you may offer to get involved in the editing process, but policy on this will vary from magazine to magazine. Most magazine editors don't send galleys to authors before publication, but if they do, you should review the galleys and return them as soon as possible. Book publishers will normally involve you in rewrites whether you like it or not.

Book proposals

Most nonfiction books are sold by book proposal, a package of materials that details what your book is about, who its intended audience is, and how you intend to write it. Most fiction is sold either by complete manuscript, especially for first-time authors, or by two or three sample chapters. Take a look at individual listings to see what submission method editors prefer.

The nonfiction book proposal includes some combination of a cover or query letter, an overview, an outline, author's information sheet and sample chapters. Editors also want to see information about the audience for your book and about titles that compete with your proposed book.

If the listing does not specify, send as much of the following information as you can.

- The cover or query letter should be a short introduction to the material you include in the proposal.
- An overview is a brief summary of your book. For nonfiction, it should detail your book's subject and give an idea of how that subject will be developed. If you're sending a synopsis of a novel, cover the basic plot.
- An outline covers your book chapter by chapter. The outline should include all major points covered in each chapter. Some outlines are done in traditional outline form, but most are written in paragraph form.
- An author's information sheet should—as succinctly and clearly as possible—acquaint the editor with your writing background and convince her of your qualifications to write about the subject.
- Many editors like to see sample chapters, especially for a first book. In fiction it's essential. In nonfiction, sample chapters show the editor how well you write and develop the ideas from your outline.
- Marketing information—i.e., facts about how and to whom your book can be successfully marketed—is now expected to accompany every book proposal. If you can provide information about the audience for your book and suggest ways the book publisher can reach those people, you will increase your chances of acceptance.

Editors also want to know what books in the marketplace compete with yours. Look in the *Subject Guide* to *Books in Print* for titles on the topic of your book. They are your competition. Check out those titles and write a one- or two-sentence synopsis describing each. Be sure to mention how your book will be different from the other titles.

A word about agents

An agent represents a writer's work to publishers, often negotiates publishing contracts, follows up to see that contracts are fulfilled and generally handles a writer's business affairs while leaving the writer free to write. Effective agents are valued for their contacts in the publishing industry, their savvy about which publishers and editors to approach with which ideas, their ability to guide an author's career and their business sense.

While most book publishers listed in *Writer's Market* publish books by unagented writers, some of the larger ones are reluctant to consider submissions that have not reached them through a literary agent. Companies with such a policy are so noted in the listings.

For more information about finding and working with a literary agent, see *Guide to Literary Agents* (Writer's Digest Books). The *Guide* offers listings of agents as well as helpful articles written by professionals in the field.

Professionalism and courtesy

Publishers are as crunched for time as any other other business professionals. Between struggling to meet deadlines without exceeding budgets and dealing with incoming submissions, most editors find that time is their most precious commodity. This state of affairs means an editor's communications with new writers, while necessarily a part of his job, have to be handled efficiently and with a certain amount of bluntness.

But writers work hard too. Shouldn't editors treat them nicely? Shouldn't an editor take the time to point out the *good* things about the manuscript he is rejecting? Is that too much to ask? Well, in a way, yes. It *is* too much to ask. Editors are not writing coaches; much less are they counselors or therapists. Editors are in the business of

INSIDER REPORT

Award-winning first novelist advises: "Explore every avenue"

Jack McBride White's first book, *The Keeper of the Ferris Wheel*, is part coming-of-age tale, part portrait of the anti-Vietnam War movement. The book was a hard sell at first. White sent it to several agents who rejected it outright based on its subject matter and the period of recent history it covered. They said it was well written but they weren't sure how to sell it—it just didn't fit any prescribed categories.

There was enough positive feedback, however, to keep White going and he finally found an agent. She said she loved the book, but after a year hadn't sold it, and when she rejected his second book, White decided he just had to try something different.

Jack McBride White

"At that point I had two unpublished novels and it just occurred to me I ought to try to publish the first one myself," says White. "I didn't even know if that was possible, but I went to the library and got a few books on the subject of self-publishing. I knew I had a good book so I decided to do it."

White, with help from his future wife, Andrea, published 2,000 copies of the book in hard cover. Then he was faced with the formidable task of distributing and selling a first, self-published novel. It was another uphill battle—he was only able to place the book at some local bookstores and to sell a few books himself at readings in the Washington, D.C. area, where he was living.

He knew he needed to make something bigger happen—something to garner attention for his book—so he entered the book in the *Writer's Digest* 1993 Self-Publishing Awards competition and *The Keeper of the Ferris Wheel* became Grand Prize winner that year. Meanwhile, White had been trying other things to draw attention to the book. He sent the book and a letter to *Washington Post* book reviewer David Streitfeld, who wrote a column about the book. The column and the award worked; White eventually heard from two publishers interested in publishing his novel and he finally decided on Donald I. Fine, who brought the book out in hard cover in May 1995.

By the time Fine had expressed interest in the book, White had secured another agent who handled negotiations with the publisher on the first book and who is working on selling his second novel, a thriller set in Turkey. While White did not hear much from his first agent after he sent her the book, he finds the feedback he receives from his current agent very helpful. "I think you should be able to talk to your agent frequently and he should be patient with you and answer all your questions to give you a sense he really cares about the book."

Over all, White says he's learned a lot about publishing through his agent and with his self-publishing experience. "Self-publishing was satisfying to an extent, but it was frustrating because I needed to sell more books. I still wanted to launch a writing career. Winning the contest and then getting a publisher made it all pay off," White explains.

White actually lost money self-publishing the book and advises writers to be very careful should they decide to go that route. "I wouldn't necessarily advise it unless you're really sure it's a good book. You need to get positive feedback on the book and being able to attract an agent is a good sign. But, then, you have to realize you'll probably lose money and you're going to devote a lot of time trying to produce and sell the book. It's a very hard thing. For nonfiction it's much easier if you have a niche market you can sell to, but for fiction you're trying to reach everybody. Even big publishers have a tough time selling fiction."

Although he does not recommend self-publishing, White says writers should be prepared to do something—anything—to make things happen. "If you really believe in your work and you're really passionate about it, I think you should explore every possible avenue, like writing letters to guys at the *Washington Post*, entering contests, self-publishing, banging your head against whatever door you find and someday something will open up."

—*Robin Gee*

buying workable writing from people who produce it. This, of course, does not excuse editors from observing the conventions of common business courtesy. Good editors know how to be polite (or they hire an assistant who can be polite for them).

The best way for busy writers to get along with (and flourish among) busy editors is to develop professional business habits. Correspondence and phone calls should be kept short and to the point. Don't hound editors with unwanted calls or letters. Honor all agreements, and give every assignment your best effort. Pleasantness, good humor, honesty and reliability will serve you as well in publishing as they will in any other area of life.

You will occasionally run up against editors and publishers who don't share your standard of business etiquette. It is easy enough to withdraw your submissions from such people and avoid them in the future.

Writing tools

Typewriters and computers. For many years, *the* tool of the writer's trade was the typewriter. While many writers do continue to produce perfectly acceptable material on their manual or electric typewriters, more and more writers have discovered the benefits of writing on a computer. Editors, too, have benefited from the change; documents produced on a computer are less likely to present to the editor such distractions as typos, eraser marks or globs of white correction fluid. That's because writing composed on a computer can be corrected before it is printed out.

If you think computers are not for you, you should reconsider. A desktop computer, running a good word processing program, can be the greatest boon to your writing career since the dictionary. For ease of manipulating text, formatting pages and correcting spelling errors, the computer handily outperforms the typewriter. Many word processing programs will count words for you, offer synonyms from a thesaurus, construct an index and give you a choice of typefaces to print out your material. Some will even correct your grammar (if you want them to). When you consider that the personal computer is also a great way of tracking your submissions and staying on top of all the other business details of a writing career—and a handy way to do research if you have a modem—it's hard to imagine how we ever got along without them.

Many people considering working with a computer for the first time are under the mistaken impression that they face an insurmountable learning curve. That's no longer true. While learning computer skills may once have been a daunting undertaking, today's personal computers are specifically designed to be usable by beginners. They are much more user-friendly than they once were.

Whether you're writing on a computer or typewriter, your goal should be to produce pages of clean, error-free copy. Stick to standard typefaces, avoiding such unusual styles as script or italic. Your work should reflect a professional approach and consideration for your reader. If you are printing from a computer, avoid sending material printed from a low-quality dot-matrix printer, with hard-to-read, poorly shaped characters. Many editors are unwilling to read these manuscripts. New dot-matrix and ink jet printers, however, produce "near letter-quality" pages that *are* acceptable to editors. Readability is the key.

Electronic submissions. Many publishers are accepting or even requesting that final manuscript submissions be made on computer disk. This saves the magazine or book publisher the expense of having your manuscript typeset, and can be helpful in the editing stage. The publisher will simply download your finished manuscript into the computer system they use to produce their product. If a listing in *Writer's Market* specifies "Query for electronic submissions," you should inquire about what computer format they use and how they would like to receive your material.

Some publishers who accept submissions on disk also will accept electronic submissions by modem. Modems are computer components that can use your phone line to send computerized files to other computers with modems. It is an extremely fast way to get your manuscript to the publisher. You'll need to work out submission information with the editor before you send something via modem.

Fax machines and e-mail. We have included publishers' fax machine numbers and some e-mail addresses in the listings. Fax machines transmit copy across phone lines. E-mail addresses are for receiving and sending electronic mail over a computer network, most commonly the Internet. Those publishers who wanted to list their fax machine numbers and e-mail addresses have done so.

Between businesses, the fax has come into standard daily use for materials that have to be sent quickly. In addition, some public fax machines are being installed in airports, hotels, libraries and even grocery stores.

The fax and e-mail information we have included in listings is not to be used to transmit queries or entire manscripts to editors, unless they specifically request it. Writers should continue to use traditional means for sending manuscripts and queries and use the fax number or e-mail address we list only when an editor asks to receive correspondence by this method.

Letters and manuscripts sent to an editor for consideration should be presented in a neat, clean and legible format. That means typed (or computer-printed), double spaced, on 8½ × 11 inch paper. Handwritten materials will most often not be considered at all. The typing paper should be at least 16 lb. bond (20 lb. is preferred). Very thin papers and erasable bond papers are not recommended for manuscripts. Paper with a 25% cotton fiber content will provide a crisp, sharp surface for your typewritten words and

INSIDER REPORT

Journalist to novelist: Making the transition

Unlike many first-time authors, Andrea Louie was fairly used to seeing her name in print when her first novel, *Moon Cakes*, a story about a young Chinese-American woman coming to terms with her personal and ancestral past, was published under Ballantine's One World imprint in spring 1995. A working journalist for about nine years, she had most recently been a reporter for the *Akron Beacon Journal* before she decided to take the plunge and write fiction.

Although she admits she's slightly jaded by having been in the "writing business" for a time, publication of her novel was still a thrill—the culmination of a dream she'd had for a long while. In fact, when she sold her novel, she had been preparing

Andrea Louie

Photograph by Keith Jenkins

to leave journalism and move to New York City where, bolstered by temp jobs and any other employment she could find, she hoped to work on her fiction full-time.

Thanks to her reporting career, however, her plans got an unexpected jump start. She had done a story for her newspaper about "the new face of fiction," featuring interviews with authors Amy Tan and Cristina Garcia. She wanted to send Tan a copy of the final piece, so she mailed it to Tan's publicist at Ballantine who in turn handed it to Tan's editor. A few weeks later Louie got a call from Claire Ferraro at Ballantine, who was impressed with her writing and wanted to know if she had anything else—a novel-in-progress, perhaps?

"I just happened to have completed a proposal for *Moon Cakes* which I had sent to a friend's agent. When I decided I was ready to leave journalism, I thought I should find a contact, so I sent it to the agent, but he turned it down. I had the proposal all prepared, so I just sent a copy off to Ballantine and they bought it."

With contract in hand, Louie found another agent and moved to New York as planned. There she worked on her book while "pouring coffee and photocopying" at temp jobs.

Making the switch from writing nonfiction to writing fiction was not as difficult at one might think, says Louie, but she did discover some differences. "The most obvious difference is that in nonfiction you rely so much on your sources but in fiction you must rely on yourself. In terms of the actual writing process, though, what surprised me was the line between fiction and nonfiction is not all that wide. The actual creative process is very similar.

"A lot of the skills you must use in nonfiction definitely apply to fiction. You need to make the writing lively and engaging but you must also be clear—clear and accurate is, of course, one of the great paragons of writing nonfiction, but it applies just as well to writing stories. My approach to fiction is the same as to reporting—you're not successful unless you've gotten your point across."

Another similarity Louie finds is that "write what you know" applies in both fields. The challenge is the same, too, she says—to take what you know and write about it with a fresh perspective. "I think it's always important to keep writing but I also think it's important to go out and do things, keep meeting people. Go do some bizarre or funky things, volunteer, put yourself in different situations. I grew up in Wooster, Ohio, a tiny town, and lived a rather sheltered life, but journalism got me to do things I never thought I'd do. I rode an elephant, flew a plane, covered political races and I also had to talk to mothers after their children were killed in terrible rural accidents, I had to go into jails, talk to people I never imagined I'd be talking with. As writers, we need to open ourselves up to different experiences because that's where inspiration comes from."

Nonfiction writers can train themselves to write fiction, says Louie. "One way I found to make the transition is to start by writing about something that is real. For instance, I'd start with a description of a building I had actually seen. I was able to say 'this is what the building looked like; these are the people who were there; this is what the air felt like' and, once I started with something that I knew to be real and then I expanded on it, I could actually make this little switch in my head and start describing things that weren't there, people who weren't there, people I'd never met before."

As a reporter Louie was used to being edited and to rewriting, so when she was asked to rewrite some of her novel, she was not surprised. What did surprise her was that she was asked to double the size of the book. "This was one time when I had to be very, very disciplined about my writing. I basically locked myself in a room and wrote 2,000 words a day. I had the whole story there originally, but it needed to be aired out, made more palatable."

Another thing that surprised her about publishing was the importance of reviews and selling yourself after publication. "I found out there's a lot of industry milestones you have to pass in order to make it in terms of reviews in certain publications and how well your book moves in the stores. This is very much a business. It can be brutal and you have to be strong."

Because so much depends on timing and business, Louie says the real motivation behind writing fiction must be a love of the art rather than a longing for material gain. Not only is writing fiction more of a financial risk, it can also be emotionally draining. "Sometimes you really have to plumb emotional depths that can be very harrowing. You have to do it because you really love it."

She tries to write every day in her journal or at least every few days when she's working a temp job. "I have people from other fields come up to me and say they want to be a writer and they read a lot of books. I think the best thing they can do is to start writing. I think the most important thing a writer can do is keep the pen moving."

—*Robin Gee*

will stand up to the frequent handling many manuscripts receive. The first impression an editor has of your work is its appearance on the page. Why take the chance of blowing that impression with a manuscript or letter that's not as appealing as it could be?

You don't need fancy letterhead for your correspondence with editors. Plain bond paper is fine. Just type your name, address, phone number and the date at the top of the page—centered or in the right-hand corner. If you want letterhead, make it as simple and businesslike as possible. Many quick print shops have standard typefaces and can supply letterhead stationery at a relatively low cost. Never use letterhead for typing your manuscripts. Only the first page of queries, cover letters and other correspondence should be typed on letterhead.

Manuscript format

When submitting a manuscript for possible publication, you can increase its chances of making a favorable impression by adhering to some fairly standard matters of physical format. Many professional writers use the format described here. Of course, there are no "rules" about what a manuscript must look like. These are just guidelines— some based on common sense, others more a matter of convention—that are meant to help writers display their work to best advantage. Strive for easy readability in whatever method you choose and adapt your style to your own personal tastes and those of the editors to whom you submit. Complete information on formats for books, articles, scripts, proposals and cover letters, with illustrated examples, is available in *The Writer's Digest Guide to Manuscript Formats*, by Dian Dincin Buchman and Seli Groves (Writer's Digest Books).

Most manuscripts do not use a cover sheet or title page. Use a binder only if you are submitting a play or a television or movie script. Use a paper clip to hold pages together, not staples. This allows editors to separate the pages easily for editing.

The upper corners of the first page of an article manuscript contain important information about you and your manuscript. This information should be single-spaced. In the upper *left* corner list your name, address, phone number and Social Security number (publishers must have this to file accurate payment records with the government). If you are using a pseudonym for your byline, your legal name still must appear in this space. In the upper *right* corner, indicate the approximate word count of the manuscript, the rights you are offering for sale and your copyright notice (© 1996 Ralph Anderson). A handwritten copyright symbol is acceptable. (For more information about rights and copyright, see Minding the Details on page 34.) For a book manuscript include the same information with the exception of rights. Do not number the first page of your manuscript.

Center the title in capital letters one-third of the way down the page. Set your typewriter to double-space. Type "by" centered one double-space under your title, and type your name or pseudonym centered one double-space beneath that.

After the title and byline, drop down two double-spaces, paragraph indent, and begin the body of your manuscript. Always double-space your manuscript and use standard paragraph indentations of five spaces. Margins should be about 1½ inches on all sides of each full page of typewritten manuscript.

On every page after the first, type your last name, a dash and the page number in either the upper left or right corner. The title of your manuscript may, but need not, be typed on this line or beneath it. Page number two would read: Anderson—2. Follow this format throughout your manuscript.

If you are submitting novel chapters, leave the top one-third of the first page of each chapter blank before typing the chapter title. Subsequent pages should include the author's last name, the page number, and a shortened form of the book's title: Anderson—2—Skating. (In a variation on this, some authors place the title before the name on the left side and put the page number on the right-hand margin.)

When submitting poetry, the poems should be typed single-spaced (double-space between stanzas), one poem per page. For a long poem requiring more than one page, paper clip the pages together. You may want to write "continued" at the bottom of the page, so if the pages are separated, editors, typesetters and proofreaders won't assume your poem ends at the bottom of the first page.

Estimating word count

Many computers will provide you with a word count of your manuscript. Don't be surprised if your editor does another count after editing the manuscript. While your computer is counting characters, an editor or production editor is more concerned with the amount of space the text will occupy on a page. If you have several small headlines, or subheads, for instance, they will be counted the same by your computer as any other word of text. An editor may count them differently to be sure enough space has been estimated for larger type.

For short manuscripts, it's often quickest to count each word on a representative page and multiply by the number of pages. You can get a very rough count by multiplying the number of pages in your manuscript by 250 (the average number of words on a double-spaced typewritten page). Do not count words for a poetry manuscript or put the word count at the top of the manuscript.

To get a more precise count, add the number of characters and spaces in an average line and divide by six for the average words per line. Then count the number of lines of type on a representative page. Multiply the words per line by the lines per page to find the average number of words per page. Then count the number of manuscript pages (fractions should be counted as fractions, except in book manuscript chapter headings, which are counted as a full page). Multiply the number of pages by the number of words per page you already determined. This will give you the approximate number of words in the manuscript.

Photographs and slides

The availability of good quality photos can be a deciding factor when an editor is considering a manuscript. Many publications also offer additional pay for photos accepted with a manuscript. When submitting black-and-white prints, editors usually want to see 8×10 glossy photos, unless they indicate another preference in the listing. The universally accepted format for transparencies is 35mm; few buyers will look at color prints. Don't send any transparencies or prints with a query; wait until an editor indicates interest in seeing your photos.

On all your photos and slides, you should stamp or print your copyright notice and "Return to:" followed by your name, address and phone number. Rubber stamps are preferred for labeling photos since they are less likely to cause damage. You can order them from many stationery or office supply stores. If you use a pen to write this information on the back of your photos, be careful not to damage the print by pressing too hard or by allowing ink to bleed through the paper. A felt tip pen is best, but you should take care not to put photos or copy together before the ink dries.

Captions can be typed on a sheet of paper and taped to the back of the prints. Some writers, when submitting several transparencies or photos, number the photos and type captions (numbered accordingly) on a separate $8\frac{1}{2} \times 11$ sheet of paper.

Submit prints rather than negatives or consider having duplicates made of your slides or transparencies. Don't risk having your original negative or slide lost or damaged when you submit it.

Photocopies

Make copies of your manuscripts and correspondence before putting them in the mail. Don't learn the hard way, as many writers have, that manuscripts get lost in the mail and that publishers sometimes go out of business without returning submissions. You might want to make several copies of your manuscript while it is still clean. Some writers keep their original manuscript as a file copy and submit good quality photocopies.

Some writers include a self-addressed postcard with a photocopied submission and suggest in the cover letter that if the editor is not interested in the manuscript, it may be tossed out and a reply returned on the postcard. This practice is recommended when dealing with international markets. If you find that your personal computer generates copies more cheaply than you can pay to have them returned, you might choose to send disposable manuscripts. Submitting a disposable manuscript costs the writer some photocopy or computer printer expense, but it can save on large postage bills.

Mailing submissions

No matter what size manuscript you're mailing, always include sufficient return postage and a self-addressed envelope large enough to contain your manuscript if it is returned.

A manuscript of fewer than six pages may be folded in thirds and mailed as if it were a letter using a #10 (business-size) envelope. The enclosed SASE can be a #10 folded in thirds or a #9 envelope which will slip into the mailing envelope without being folded. Some editors also appreciate the convenience of having a manuscript folded into halves in a 6×9 envelope.

For manuscripts of six pages or longer, use 9×12 envelopes for both mailing and return. The return SASE may be folded in half.

A book manuscript should be mailed in a sturdy, well-wrapped box. Enclose a self-addressed mailing label and paper clip your return postage stamps or International Reply Coupons to the label.

Always mail photos and slides First Class. The rougher handling received by Fourth Class mail could damage them. If you are concerned about losing prints or slides, send them certified or registered mail. For any photo submission that is mailed separately from a manuscript, enclose a short cover letter of explanation, separate self-addressed label, adequate return postage and an envelope. Never submit photos or slides mounted in glass.

To mail up to 20 prints, you can buy photo mailers that are stamped "Photos—Do Not Bend" and contain two cardboard inserts to sandwich your prints. Or use a 9×12 manila envelope, write "Photos—Do Not Bend" and make your own cardboard inserts. Some photography supply shops also carry heavy cardboard envelopes that are reusable.

When mailing a number of prints, say 25-50 for a book with illustrations, pack them in a sturdy cardboard box. A box for typing paper or photo paper is an adequate mailer. If, after packing both manuscript and photos, there's empty space in the box, slip in enough cardboard inserts to fill the box. Wrap the box securely.

To mail transparencies, first slip them into protective vinyl sleeves, then mail as you would prints. If you're mailing a number of sheets, use a cardboard box as for photos.

Types of mail service
● First Class is the most expensive way to mail a manuscript, but many writers prefer it. First Class mail generally receives better handling and is delivered more quickly.

Mail sent First Class is also forwarded for one year if the addressee has moved, and is returned automatically if it is undeliverable.

● Fourth Class rates are available for packages, but be sure to pack your materials carefully because they will be handled roughly. To make sure your package will be returned to you if it is undeliverable, print "Return Postage Guaranteed" under your address.

● Certified Mail must be signed for when it reaches its destination. If requested, a signed receipt is returned to the sender. There is a $1 charge for this service, in addition to the required postage, and a $1 charge for a return receipt.

● Registered Mail is a high-security method of mailing. The package is signed in and out of every office it passes through, and a receipt is returned to the sender when the package reaches its destination. This service begins at $4.40 in addition to the postage required for the item. If you obtain insurance for the package, the cost begins at $4.50.

● United Parcel Service may be slightly cheaper than First Class postage if you drop the package off at UPS yourself. UPS cannot legally carry First Class mail, so your cover letter needs to be mailed separately. Check with UPS in your area for current rates. The cost depends on the weight of your package and the distance to its destination.

● If you're in a hurry to get your material to your editor, you have a lot of choices these days. In addition to fax and computer technologies mentioned earlier, overnight and two-day mail services are provided by both the U.S. Postal Service and several private firms. More information on next day service is available from the U.S. Post Office in your area, or check your Yellow Pages under "Delivery Services."

Other correspondence details

Use money orders if you are ordering sample copies or supplies and do not have checking services. You'll have a receipt, and money orders are traceable. Money orders for up to $35 can be purchased from the U.S. Postal Service for a 75¢ service charge; the cost is $1 for a maximum $700 order. Banks, savings and loans, and some commercial businesses also carry money orders; their fees vary. *Never* send cash through the mail for sample copies.

Insurance is available for items handled by the U.S. Postal Service but is payable only on typing fees or the tangible value of the item in the package—such as typing paper—so your best insurance when mailing manuscripts is to keep a copy of what you send. Insurance is 75¢ for $50 or less and goes up to a $5 maximum charge.

When corresponding with publications and publishers in other countries, International Reply Coupons (IRCs) must be used for return postage. Surface rates in other countries differ from those in the U.S., and U.S. postage stamps are of use only within the U.S. Currently, one IRC costs 95¢ and is sufficient for one ounce traveling at surface rate; two must be used for airmail return. Canadian writers pay $1.50 for an IRC.

Because some post offices don't carry IRCs (or because of the added expense), many writers dealing with international mail send photocopies and tell the publisher to dispose of them if the manuscript is not appropriate. When you use this method, it's best to set a deadline for withdrawing your manuscript from consideration, so you can market it elsewhere.

International money orders are also available from the post office for a $3 charge. See U.S. and Canadian Postage by the Page on the inside covers for specific mailing costs. All charges were current at press time but are subject to change during the year.

Recording submissions

Once you've begun submitting manuscripts, you'll need to manage your writing business by keeping copies of all manuscripts and correspondence, and by recording the dates of submissions.

Investment paying off for new writer

The difference between a "wannabe" and a "gonnabe" often boils down to an investment of time, energy, and sometimes money. As an investment banker, Everett Weinberger recognizes the potential rewards of taking risks. And he's willing to go out on a limb, whether he's trying to break into Hollywood, as he describes in his new book, *Wannabe* (Birch Lane Press), or developing his own supplementary marketing program to spread the word about his first published book.

Photograph by Selwyn Fund

Everett Weinberger

Weinberger left his Wall Street investment banking position to return to school, hoping a Stanford MBA would be helpful in pursuing his dream job of movie producer. After graduation he packed up and moved to Los Angeles to begin his job search. Months of unproductive interviews later he began temping in movie studio executives' offices to get his foot in the door. *Wannabe* lets others in on what's behind the door as well.

"I kept a diary throughout of what was happening to me out there," Weinberger says. "After half the time there, I realized I had great experiences to write. I wasn't sure whether it would be a guidebook or if I would write it in the first person. Once I decided that, it took a life of its own. It wasn't all that easy," he qualifies, "because I realized that even if it's nonfiction, it has to have a fiction type of read. It has to have a motivated character, a core conflict, there have to be changes in the character, an arc, and some transition. That isn't always apparent in real life.

"First, I wrote everything down in chapters based on major events. Making transitions between those events helped link the book throughout and draw the reader through it. Eventually, I decided to push the episode with Alec Baldwin and Kim Basinger up front, because I needed to draw the reader in. That was a marketing decision since I'm not a famous celebrity. I needed the drawing power of the most exciting episode in the first chapter. Then, once I have the readers' attention, they would realize it was more an emotional journey I was taking them on and I hopefully have interested them in reading further."

Weinberger has learned a lot about publishing. "It was a four-year experience. I wrote the book in two years. Getting an agent and finding a publisher took another year. And then having it printed took another year.

"For a first-time author, you have to find an agent who is willing to endure a lot of rejections and still stick by you. My agent isn't affiliated with a large agency; she's an independent and runs her own show. If she believes in something she is willing to really go forward. I was lucky—my agent got what I was trying to say in my book right away. The person who really gets it and understands is probably better than a more renowned agent who doesn't totally understand but is willing to take it on. I think when things get rough, it's going to be the person who believes in it that carries it through."

Weinberger discovered that finding a publisher for his work was tougher than finding an agent. "Getting a publisher was very difficult because a lot of publishers are owned by movie studios. They would say 'I love the book, but I can't touch this, I'm owned by Paramount.' It was really frustrating." Another problem was the window of opportunity in submitting to a publisher. "Each holiday period is a total loss. From late November until mid-January or February, the whole industry goes on holiday or on conventions. Then June through August, nobody is there either."

Eventually, Weinberger's manuscript made it to Kevin McDonough at Carol Publishing. "Again, he got it. He has my kind of sense of humor. Carol is owned by Steven Schragis, who is one of the founding investors in *Spy* magazine. That was a good sign, because it's a sarcastic book." The book was scheduled for a spring release, and with some editing, production began and marketing took shape.

"Luckily, this publisher is a very strong marketer. They won't pay for advertising, but they'll publicize the heck out of it through free media. In addition, I'm going to LA for a book signing and reading and some media interviews, and will be doing the same in New York."

Weinberger has also devised his own marketing effort to augment the publisher's. He sent a mass mailing of a postcard he had printed announcing the publication, with a short synopsis and the date and place of the signings. "I can send this to people I know, friends, family, colleagues. You would be amazed if you sat down and asked every member of your family to write up lists of people they know. I can also send it to people I don't know—graduates from other years of high school, college and business school. I have a little sticker next to my name that says, for instance, 'Columbia College, class of '86.' My feeling is that people may be more inclined to take note of something a fellow graduate has done."

In addition to the alumni lists, Weinberger prepared a mailing from the *Hollywood Creative Directory*, an authoritative list of production companies and their personnel. "I went through the *Directory* and singled out the most junior person, because they were the wannabes. I think the book will be of interest to them, and they'll spread the word. They'll know I'm targeting them because they're the low men on the totem pole."

Weinberger sees his own marketing efforts as seed money. "This will impact whatever I choose to do next. I feel I should spend an inordinate amount of time and money to publicize this book, and that will afford me opportunities in the future. It can't hurt. And I don't want to second-guess myself later and say, 'Gee, did I do everything I could to get this book out?' "

—*Kirsten Holm*

One way to keep track of your manuscripts is to use a record of submissions that includes the date sent, title, market, editor and enclosures (such as photos). You should also note the date of the editor's response, any rewrites that were done, and, if the manuscript was accepted, the publication date and payment information. You might want to keep a similar record just for queries.

Also remember to keep a separate file for each manuscript or idea along with its list of potential markets. You may want to keep track of expected reporting times on a calendar, too. Then you'll know if a market has been slow to respond and you can follow up on your query or submission. It will also also provide you with a detailed picture of your sales over time.

Current Trends in Publishing

by Kirsten Holm

Book publishing

Business, on the whole, is good. Book sales increased 5.7 percent in 1994 and were estimated to rise a slightly lower 5.1 percent in 1995. Adult hardcover sales were up 11 percent overall. According to *Publishers Weekly*, hardcover bestsellers set new sales records in 1994, often surpassing the previous years' high water mark by a considerable amount. Adult trade revenues were projected to increase 6.2% in 1995.

Juvenile books had mixed results. Paperbacks were up 18.3 percent, but hardcover sales fell 3.1 percent, the third consecutive downturn in that segment. However, good news may be on the horizon. A slightly higher increase in the juvenile population should allow children's publishing to post its first sales increase in 1995.

Religion sales grew a whopping 40 percent in 1994, reflecting one of publishing's major trends, but may be unable to sustain that level of growth. Sales were predicted to drop 4.1 percent in 1995.

Steep increases in the price of paper, however, threaten the publishing climate. Demand has outstripped supply, causing prices to skyrocket. Uncoated book stock rose 35 percent over the last six months of 1994, was predicted to rise an additional 15 to 30 percent through 1995 and supply is projected to be tight well into 1996. Paper represents between 40 and 60 percent of a publisher's production costs. A 20 percent increase in the price of paper would cause retail book prices to grow by up to 10 percent. Several mass market paperbacks have already hit $7.50, trade paperbacks are reaching $13, and hardcover prices are moving from the low $20s towards the mid-$20 level.

Many publishers have made production and design changes in an attempt to shorten books and use less paper, shrinking margins and typeface to squeeze more lines on a page, standardizing book sizes and in many cases switching to lower grade papers. Higher production costs mean that large print runs and decisions to reprint books are more carefully scrutinized. As a result, more books will be going out of print sooner.

A brave new world

While paper prices are cyclical, the recent upswing coincides with publishers' exploration of alternative ways of delivering their products. Chief among the options is electronic publishing. This can take the form of books on disk or may encompass video and computer technology in an interactive or multimedia format.

Multimedia (CD-ROM) is a technology in the throes of defining itself. Publishers are struggling to get a fix on how to operate in this brave new world. The opportunities, meanwhile, are both staggering and baffling. Staggering because it was estimated that by early 1995 nearly 15 million multimedia PCs would be in place, growing to 40

*****Editor's Note:** *Statistics for the publishing industry are compiled on a calendar year basis and released in late February for book publishing and late June for magazines. This article, written in July 1995, draws on collected statistics for 1994, projected estimates for 1995 and, where noted, actual numbers for the first quarter of 1995.*

million by 1998. The multimedia CD-ROM market grew 227% in 1994, according to Dataquest, an industry organization. Approximately 2,000 new CD-ROM titles were released in 1994, a number which was expected to double in 1995.

Multimedia is a baffling market as well, in which most publishers staking out a presence are losing money. Of the 3,500 to 10,000 CD-ROM products currently available, fewer than 200 have made a profit. Many publishers have learned, to their dismay, that producing a CD-ROM that sells is not as simple as dumping text into an electronic format and adding a few bells and whistles. There are also problems in marketing and distribution. CD-ROMs are not very "browsable," and the salesforces of publishers and bookstore buyers often know little about the products. Jonathan Newcomb, president of Simon & Schuster, estimates that no more than 1 percent of Simon & Schuster's multimedia products are sold in bookstores.

To that end, alliances with, investment in or outright purchase of software development companies bring creative staff to the publisher hoping to assemble a winning combination of quality content and innovative format. New technology and cross-media fertilization are redefining book distribution. Online bookstores, TV shopping networks and computer/electronic stores are all getting into the act. Publishers are cultivating relationships with computer stores and other media outlets. Simon & Schuster and Random House have each formed separate sales divisions to handle multimedia and electronic products, serving predominantly software and other non-bookstore outlets. "All-media" stores, such as Borders Books & Music and Media Play, are emerging, carrying books, music, video, software and multimedia products.

While CD-ROM is the future, the future is still several months away. And not every book will benefit from an interactive multimedia approach. There will always be paperbacks to take to the beach or read in the bathtub, and serious fiction and nonfiction will call for a substantive physical product. The aim of successful multimedia products is to involve the reader in new, exciting ways to learn and be entertained.

Writers and publishers view electronic rights differently

The battleground for writers in this area will be the disposition of electronic rights. On the one hand, writers and their representative organizations feel that, bottom line, the author controls her copyright, not the publisher. As multimedia becomes an industry in itself, electronic rights are up for negotiation as are other rights. The publisher may obtain them, if the price is right. On the other hand, publishers feel that holding electronic rights is vital to their survival. Many publishers believe they are entitled to a share of the rights (and resulting profits) of a multimedia application stemming from books they developed, published and established.

While both sides profess a willingness to negotiate, book sales from famous authors have fallen through because of a publisher's unwillingness to accept less than total control of a book's electronic rights. Last spring, the Association of American Publishers (AAP) began circulating a draft document intended as a general agreement within the association regarding publishers' interest in electronic rights. It sets forth why the association believes an author is better served by the publisher retaining these rights.

The Authors' Guild, American Society of Journalists and Authors, Dramatists Guild and Association of Authors' Representatives joined forces to form The Authors Registry, Inc., an "ASCAP"-style agency to provide a simple accounting system to pay royalties to registered authors when their work is accessed for such electronic formats as online services and CD-ROM products. It will also create a central directory of authors and their representatives so that foreign publishers, movie producers and multimedia developers can quickly identify the appropriate contact person for further rights sales.

Regardless of the format, successful books are a combination of good content and good marketing. One way to put yourself above the crowd is to stay abreast of what type of books are popular now. We will be focusing primarily on nonfiction; for a more thorough discussion of directions in fiction, see "Commercial Fiction Trends Report" in *Novel & Short Story Writer's Market*.

Nonfiction trends

The more things change, the more they stay the same. It's true in publishing as well. While there have been several significant developments in publishing in the past year, and new directions for the future are opening up, many of the last year's top sellers continued previous popular themes. General topics that are doing well are business, cooking, gardening, health, relationships and spirituality. Topics that seem to be on the way out are celebrity biographies, true crime and parenting.

"Mass market" media exposure on TV, radio and movies continues to be a powerful force in selling books. A new company, TV Books Inc., has been formed to publish titles that accompany and are derived from multi-hour cable, network and public TV programs. With Oprah as a walking advertisement, *In the Kitchen with Rosie* set a record for the fastest selling book of all time, with over 6 million copies in print. Infommercials and home shopping opportunities are also influential. QVC announcer Bob Bowersox's cookbook sold over 150,000 copies in one day on the TV shopping network. Nonfiction by comedians-turned-sitcom stars is very popular, as witnessed by Paul Reiser, Tim Allen, Jerry Seinfeld and a new book by Ellen DeGeneres. Movie tie-ins brought a number of books back to the bestseller list, such as *Forrest Gump*, *Schindler's List*, *Interview with the Vampire* and *Disclosure*. The market may be too saturated for *Bridges of Madison County* to sell much more, but two ancillary books are expected to do well.

With the continued growth of superstores and their need to fill increased shelf space, there is a strong movement to identify small niche markets and create titles to meet their needs. In the area of travel, for instance, *Music Lover's Guide to Great Britain and Ireland*, Fodor's *Kodak Guide to Shooting Great Travel Pictures* and Insight Guide's *The American Wild West* appeal to different vacationers. Retirement travel for those over 50 shares shelf space with cycling guides to Tasmania, which sit next to *On the Road Again with Man's Best Friend*.

The cross-fertilization of trends continues. Business and spirituality? *Meditations for Those Who Lead*. Health and multimedia? HarperCollins Interactive's *Health Desk*, personal wellness software with customized medical charts and interactive health reference information. Religion and multiculturalism? *The Holy Bible for Children of Color*. It seems there are any number of combinations and permutations of current trends. To differentiate your proposal from what has already been published and others being suggested, you must be able to show a prospective publisher why *your* book is special.

Healthy from the inside out

Books that deal with spiritual and inspirational themes or issues of morality and values are striking a responsive chord these days and will continue to do so for some time. "Spirituality" encompasses a wide-ranging field, from the doctrinal theology of the *Catechism of the Catholic Church* and approaches to prayer such as *Illuminata: Prayers for Everyday Living*, to the more esoteric *The Celestine Prophecy* and *Mutant Message Down Under*. Books geared to address the spiritual needs of every nook and cranny of the human experience are appearing, from overweight individuals (*Nothing to Lose*) to gay men (*Wrestling with the Angel*). Whether it is the concerns of aging baby boomers, the perceived breakdown of social order or the coming end of the millennium, people are searching for sources of meaning and purpose for their lives. Books offering insight and inspiration provide nourishment to feed a spiritual hunger.

While chicken soup may be good for the soul, a barrage of high-flavor, low-fat cookbooks is out to convince the general public that healthy alternatives can be tasty as well. Health concerns are dictating more cookbooks focusing on low-fat, low-salt seasonal cooking with an emphasis on vegetarian principles and fresh ingredients. The author of *High-Flavor, Low-Fat Cooking* has written *High-Flavor, Low-Fat Vegetarian Cooking*, with an emphasis on "big-flavored" ingredients such as herbs, spices and chiles. Even general cookbooks are including more recipes using grains and vegetables. Books exploring ethnic cuisines also fuel this drive, such as Sheila Lukins's great success, *All Around the World Cookbook*.

At the same time, homey comfort foods are highlighted as well. Some attempt to allow the reader to have her low-fat chocolate cake and eat it too, with titles such as *Healthy Homestyle Cooking*, but others make no apologies for the appeal of solid, familiar recipes, such as the dozens of bread pudding recipes in *Classic Home Desserts*.

Mixing spirituality and health is a winning combination. Holistic approaches to spiritual, mental and physical health have proven extremely popular. Thanks in large part to Deepak Chopra's *Ageless Body, Timeless Mind*, pathways to health using a mind/body approach have blossomed in the past several years. The PBS series, *Healing and the Mind*, helped shed light on alternative medicine and treatments. *Thoroughly Fit* has been on the Christian Booksellers Association bestseller list for months, and the editors of *Handbook for the Soul* have put together another essay collection entitled *Healers on Healing*.

Juvenile books on the upswing

After several years of struggle, children's hardcovers have good news to report. While juvenile paperbacks continue to thrive, hardcover sales are starting to recover. In 1994, 59 new hardcovers reported sales of over 75,000 copies compared to the previous year's 48, and 75 backlist hardcovers sold over 100,000 copies, compared to prior year's 47. Of those 59 top sellers, 18 were connected to movies (13 from *The Lion King* alone!) and another seven were tied to TV shows.

Juvenile paperbacks are up: 130 new paperback titles sold over 100,000 copies last year, compared to 90 from the year before. R.L. Stine, author of the middle-grade horror series Fear Street and Goosebumps, is enjoying incredible success, with almost 13.9 million copies of Goosebumps books sold last year and a TV show slated for fall 1995. Christopher Pike is also extremely popular, and other series books, such as The Babysitters Club, Sweet Valley University and American Girls hold strong appeal.

Computer products for children continue to be very strong sellers. Through exposure at school and at home, school-age children are computer literate and media savvy. Publishers are scrambling to enter this potentially lucrative market. The Walt Disney Company formed Disney Interactive to create a range of multimedia products from video games and entertainment to educational software. Publisher Dorling Kindersley has met with great success with its CD-ROM products. Random House has formed an alliance with Knowledge Adventure to copublish multimedia titles it will distribute along with Knowledge Adventure's existing line of educational software.

According to a Census Bureau report describing the changing American population, by the year 2020 Hispanics will be the second largest minority, and African-American and Asian populations will continue to grow. Multicultural publishing can mean many things, from including more minority characters in mainstream books to focusing on cultures that have been ignored, but it has become a major thrust of publishers' juvenile lists. A global approach to social studies curricula, combined with the whole language theory of reading, increases the need for trade children's works that examine different peoples and cultures.

Gathering market information

Many publishers stress inclusion of marketing information in book proposals they receive. How many other books are being published on this topic? What makes your take on the subject different (and better) than these others? Who *will* buy (not who *ought* to buy) this book? Publishers must answer these questions before they offer you a contract. By answering these questions for them upfront you give yourself an edge. But this edge takes research.

To keep up with trends in book publishing you can turn to several sources. One invaluable reference is your local bookseller, who is keenly aware of which subjects are running hot or cold. *Publishers Weekly*, *Library Journal* and *The American Bookseller* feature up-to-date news on publishing and bookselling, as well as chart book sales and trends. *Book Industry Trends* published by the Book Industry Study Group predicts how the industry will perform in the years ahead. Almost all writers' organizations offer newsletters with markets information. Check into the writers' organizations in your area, or contact national groups such as the American Society of Journalists and Authors or National Writers Union. All can offer invaluable market direction insights that help present your book proposal in its most favorable light.

Consumer magazines

The magazine market is more energetic than ever. Continuing a trend, ad pages and revenue are up in most categories. Print circulation is increasing and many magazines are busily exploring electronic opportunities.

1994 was another banner year for consumer magazines startups, 832 compared to 789 for the previous year, according to *Samir Husni's Guide to New Consumer Magazines*. Mr. Husni estimates that there are currently about 4,000 magazines in the United States. While there have been a number of notable acquisitions in the past year, with Hachette Filipacchi acquiring *Family Life* and *Mirabella*, for example, as well as magazines folding, forecasts predict increased startups, as publishers continue the search for lucrative niche markets. It's important to note, however, that half of all new magazines will be operating after one year, and only three out of ten will still be around ten years from now.

A storm cloud on the horizon, though, as with books, is the increased cost and shortage of paper. Increases for the fourth quarter of 1994 averaged 7 percent, an additional 8 to 10 percent rise was predicted for 1995, and annual increases around 3 percent are expected until 1999. In addition, postage increased January 1, 1995 and ink prices are beginning to creep up after three years of stability. The average cover price of new magazines rose to $4.15 last year, up from $4 the previous year. With the large increases in magazine materials, however, cover prices should climb well above that.

Most of the trends we will be examining are specific to the consumer magazine market. For more information on trade journals see the introduction to that section. Trade journals tend to be more stable and less susceptible to trends, since they exist to serve a specific industry or profession. While there may be less prestige in the trade and professional journal market, it is definitely a way to build your portfolio of clips and perhaps a career. Many writers with a particular professional expertise parlay that knowledge into a successful career writing for trade magazines.

Exploring the future now

Just as electronic publishing is exciting those in book publishing circles, magazine publishers are looking at new media as a mainstream way to deliver content to readers.

Many major magazine companies are establishing new media divisions to handle multi-media development. Magazines are mixing and matching new media elements to create their own electronic presence in the market.

A large number of magazines, such as *The Atlantic Monthly, Car and Driver, Elle, Smithsonian* and *Time*, as well as *The New York Times* and *Chicago Tribune*, exist on online services such as America Online. The science magazine *Omni* has recently reconfigured the print version to be a quarterly supplement to its primary version online.

Some magazines, wishing to exert more control over the presentation of their product, are going their own way rather than joining a network in progress. *The Utne Reader* will be launching a site on the World Wide Web, tentatively titled The Edge, and *The Paris Review*, in conjunction with the new media house Voyager Company, has established its own homepage. In an even more involved joint venture, Fodor's, a division of Random House, *Golf Digest* and *Condé Nast Traveler*, of Advance Publications, and the Sunday travel section of *The New York Times*, have together established a travel network on the Web, TravelConnect, with a joint homepage and links to move between the different services.

With all the new electronic media possibilities, many magazine publishers are exploring an existing electronic outlet—TV, notably cable. Some magazines help create TV shows, such as Cahners Publishing's long-running "American Baby Show" and "Healthy Kids Show" on The Family Channel. Some magazines license their names to independent production companies, such as "*Working Woman* Television Show." Some provide editorial authority in exchange for advertising, such as the contributions of *Travel & Leisure* to CNN Travel Guide's "Strategies." One magazine buys space outright from a cable network, while others create their own networks, such as Times Mirror's Outdoor Channel, drawing on the editorial content of its many outdoor and sporting titles. The visual medium of TV delivers a large audience, exposing many potential subscribers to print communications.

With all of these alternative avenues, some fear that new media products will draw readers away from the print version of a magazine. Some magazines exist in three different forms: print, online and as a CD-ROM. While the audience and editorial mission are the same, each product is different, with distinctive qualities. Print is portable and attractive to advertisers. An online format has the advantages of timeliness and capacity. A CD-ROM version incorporates many of the advantages of online, but currency takes a back seat to performance and interactivity. Ziff-Davis's *PC Magazine*, which exists in all three formats, has found that renewal rates for the print product have increased as more subscribers go online, and that many people subscribe to all three forms.

Keeping up with the trends

Many popular book subjects also make good magazine topics. This edition of *Writer's Market* contains an explosion in the number of religious magazines—30 new consumer titles for juveniles, teens and adults, as well as several trade magazines answering the needs of church personnel from youth leaders to music ministry.

The nesting trend of baby boomers influences a wide variety of magazine areas. As baby boomers settle in, home and shelter topics are doing well. A number of renovation and remodeling magazines are rolling out, as it is estimated that $180 billion will be spent on renovation by the year 2000, more money than on new construction. A part of this trend is an increased interest in gardening. Not satisfied with simple flats of impatiens at the grocery store, consumers are becoming educated in Latin names, native wildflowers and organic techniques. An offshoot of Rodale's *Organic Gardening, Or-*

ganic Flower Gardening has proven so popular in two trial issues that it may be launched as a quarterly.

The epicurean category is booming as people spend more time at home. Samir Husni identifies this category as the second largest, with 16 startups. Some titles aim at a market of busy people on the go, such as *Fast and Healthy*. There is also a trend that sees cooking as a leisure activity, rather than a chore. Titles such as *Fine Cooking* and *Bon Appetit* serve the food enthusiast. A slew of healthy food magazines such as *Eating Well* and *Cooking Light* are complemented by a number of vegetarian magazines emphasizing health and practicality.

Health and fitness continues to be a hot topic, with an emphasis on holistic well-being and strength. A number of new magazines have been created to fit the needs of specific demographic groups. *Heart and Soul* focuses on the health needs and interests of African-American Women, while *Remedy* covers the concerns of Americans 55 and older.

Magazines covering child care and parental guidance are holding their own. Baby boomers have general questions about everything from diapers to discipline, as well as more individual needs, but have a limited amount of time to look for answers. General magazines such as *FamilyFun* look for articles on "all the wonderful things families can do together." Magazines for niche markets are being created to meet specific needs. *Exceptional Parent*, for example, covers the special situations that parents of children and young adults with disabilities are faced with.

Magazines for children themselves mirror the depressed juvenile book market. Several teen magazines have started up and been shut down within a few issues, partly because the potential market is so lucrative (all those teen discretionary dollars) that the arena has become overcrowded.

We have added a section this year, *Gay and Lesbian Interest*, which reflects growing public recognition of these communities. Many of these magazines feature subjects similar to general interest magazines, covering topics such as arts and entertainment, politics and popular culture, as well as parenting, fitness and finance.

Know your markets

With magazines starting up and shutting down so rapidly, it's important for writers to stay on top of changes not only in the industry but also in the specific markets they target. Libraries, bookstores and newsstands are good sources for field research. Trade magazines such as *Folio*, *Advertising Age* and *Writer's Digest* offer information and analysis of trends in subject matter as well as the economics of advertising and circulation.

Perhaps the most important step in building a career in magazine writing is magazine reading. Check your local library's holdings or order a few sample copies for a market in which you are particularly interested. Peruse a few issues to get the flavor and perspective of a magazine, and gather a list of article ideas the editors might be interested in. Request a copy of the writer's guidelines and editorial calendar. Study the listing information closely and construct your query letter with care. Make your query impress the editor with your knowledge of the magazine's editorial mission and understanding of its audience. Presenting an editor with well-written, appropriately targeted material is the unchanging key to success in this changeable business.

Magazine Editors' Roundtable

by Anne Bowling

Most editors agree, freelancing is a tough business, whether you're writing to supplement a full-time income or striking out on your own. Theoretically, freelance writers should have no problem finding work in the national magazine market. Every month, editors rely on regular freelance writers for everything from brief news items to full-length features, sometimes for up to 90 percent of a magazine's copy. But in reality, the competition is stiff, and for every accepted query there are probably ten that don't make it past a cursory glance and form rejection letter. So how do you, as a writer untried in the national magazine market, work your way into the pool of freelance writers editors have come to count on?

Start with professionalism, tenacity and a taste for hard work. So say the editors gathered by *Writer's Market* to discuss what makes freelance writers succeed. For this roundtable discussion, we selected editors from five national magazines to share an inside look at the basics: what makes story ideas appealing, how to write attention-getting queries, how to target your submissions, and the importance of cultivating relationships with editors. Participating in this discussion were:

Steve Salerno, editor of *American Legion* magazine. Salerno spent more than 15 years freelance writing for national publications such as *The New York Times Magazine*, *Harper's*, *New Republic* and *Writer's Digest*. His editorial experience includes work for *America West* and *San Diego Executive* magazines.

Nancy Gagliardi, executive editor of *Weight Watchers* magazine. Starting out as a freelance writer concentrating in health, nutrition and fitness, Gagliardi's work has been published in *New Woman*, *Woman's Day*, *Redbook* and *McCall's*. Gagliardi also served as health editor for *New Woman*, fitness editor for *Good Housekeeping*, and editorial assistant for *Working Woman*.

Michael Scheibach, Ph.D. and editor-in-chief of *Grit*, America's Family Magazine. Before joining *Grit* in 1995, Scheibach was part-owner of two business publishing companies based in Topeka, Kansas. With some 20 years in magazines as both a publisher and editor, Scheibach has also worked as a part-time teacher of English and technical writing.

Nancy Clarke, deputy editor of *Family Circle*. With 25 years of experience in the freelance writing and editing business, Clarke also spent three years as features editor for *Child* magazine, and four years editing features for *Harper's Bazaar*.

Bruce Raskin, managing editor of *Parenting* magazine. An eight-year veteran of *Parenting*, Raskin has also served as managing editor of *Publish* magazine, and as executive editor and assistant publisher of *Learning* magazine.

Anne Bowling *is a Cincinnati-based freelance writer and a frequent contributor to Writer's Digest Books.*

How much of your publication is freelance written, and how easy is it for new writers to break into your market?

Gagliardi: Quite a bit of *Weight Watchers* is freelance written. It's about a 50-50 split of the book. If someone has sent us a really well-thought-out query, and they don't have clips, I'll definitely have an editor call and feel them out. We have given cover stories to writers who have maybe one good clip. But the idea has to be really good and really different, and the writer has to prove in the query letter that he's going to write us a great story.

Scheibach: Forty to fifty percent of any issue's freelance writers are what you would call unproven to us. In any one issue, if we have six features from freelancers, there's a good probability that two or three of those will be from people we have not used previously.

Clarke: Generally speaking, you do use the writers you have a relationship with, but there is the opportunity for a new person to break in. Out of fifteen articles per issue, one or two may be written by freelancers we haven't used before, maybe as many as five.

Raskin: We're always open to new people. We tend to use more of the regular writers, but in any given issue we usually use five to ten percent new writers.

From an editor's perspective, what are some of the advantages and disadvantages of working with freelance writers?

Salerno: One of the biggest problems we run into is writers not understanding the basic rules of journalism. One of the things I see a lot of from novices is people simply taking material that has appeared elsewhere, paraphrasing it or recycling it somehow, and considering that an article. There seems to be a lack of appreciation for doing new research. Writers will pick up a quote they read elsewhere rather than picking up the phone. They don't realize the legwork that goes on. It isn't just about style, it has a lot to do with substance, and the effort you're willing to put into the story.

Clarke: Especially for magazines like *Family Circle*, which has an enormous national reach, we need writers who are not New York-based. We need to find writers who speak to a different, non-urban experience, and who can come up with different stories that are happening somewhere else. The disadvantage, to be perfectly honest, is that people's clips don't necessarily represent how they write. So there are occasional disasters.

Raskin: The main risk in using freelancers is that they'll get the story completely wrong—they won't know the style we require, or the audience, or how to write for the readers of *Parenting*. Style is a big problem, from the small things like how we identify a Ph.D. versus a doctor to the voice and tone. Also, some people still use composites in doing their reporting, which we don't go for. Or in quoting sources, they may not have a wide enough distribution, or may rely on too few people. We try to alert them to that, in going through guidelines with new writers.

Which do you prefer that writers submit for initial contact, a query letter or unsolicited manuscript, and why?

Scheibach: It depends on the type of query or manuscript we get. We get a lot of manuscripts for our 250- to 800-word articles that we actually prefer, because they don't warrant queries. Those types of submissions are coming in from writers who receive *Grit*, they know the departments, they know the nature of our readership, and so they're pinpointing these shorter manuscripts extremely well. They know the style, the flavor and the content. When we get into the longer features, I would much rather receive a query so I know the nature of what someone wants to do before they do it, and I can give them a call and focus it even more for our readership.

Clarke: Generally speaking, we want queries. The exception to that is personal essays, and in those cases I do not assign. We have to see the whole thing. There are occasions when someone will submit a query, and it's a little marginal, and for someone who has not written for us before we might ask them to submit it on speculation. That does not happen very often, but people are generally willing to do that.

Raskin: We definitely want queries. I don't want someone sending me a reported piece because I don't know where it came from, or how that person came about writing that piece. Who was that person technically writing for when they reported it and called up all those sources? I sure don't want someone calling up and saying they're writing for *Parenting* if we haven't assigned it. Also, why put all that energy into a piece if it's dead wrong for us? If it's a first-person piece, I don't want a query, I want to see the piece.

What makes a query letter effective, and do you prefer writers incorporate a 'hook' into their queries, or use a more straightforward approach?

Salerno: Just tell me what the story is. Don't try to oversell the story, or be your own publicist. Tell me who you propose to go to as your sources, and tell me why it's important. If you can do that with some sort of flash, so much the better. But the basics have to be there. Being that we have so few slots to assign articles, it's a selection process that pretty much narrows it down to people who already have national magazine experience. On the other hand, if you write a really compelling query, and you show your willingness to do legwork, and show an understanding of who you're writing for at *American Legion*, you'd have a chance.

Scheibach: I like the more straightforward approach to query letters. The others almost appear too cute, and I tend to discount that. I'm looking at a query letter for the professionalism of the writer, so I look for someone who can write a very clear, concise query—identify the topic, perhaps recommend a working title, give me a synopsis paragraph on the angle, and attach a writing sample. The hook really is showing me you've studied the magazine and know our readers. It's very important to me that I get a good indication that someone has done a little bit of research about *Grit*. Make a phone call for a sample publication and writer's guidelines, and then tailor the query to *Grit*. When you send the query, always use my name. It really does make a difference.

Clarke: Give me the first paragraph, give me the lead, make me want to read it, and then describe the rest of the article. You really can do that without a lot of research. I think that kind of hook is what really works. A kind of dry, 'I would like to do an article for you, and I would talk to these experts,' is less effective. Yes, I need to know what experts you're going to talk to, and what sources you're going to quote, and what sort of anecdotal material you can come up with, but that dry letter is less grabby than something that actually puts me there.

Raskin: Personally, I like to see something that's pretty straightforward that also shows some style in the letter. But I don't really want to see the lead to the piece. Give me two or three paragraphs maximum, and make them read well. Also, make sure you know who our reader is. Show me in the query that you've got some interesting hook, something that's going to separate your take from the pack. I can't tell you how many queries we get from stay-at-home dads who want to tell you what their life is like. But if we get a query from a stay-at-home dad on how to create support groups for stay-at-home dads, I'm going to look at it. It's a difference in the sharpness of the angle. The other thing writers should think about as a way to break in is not to go for the features, but go for the departments. That's where you want to focus your queries. And ideally you want to find out the editor of that department, and send it right to that editor.

What qualities do you look for when reviewing a writer's clips?

Salerno: How do you define style? I don't know, but good writers have it. You look for a certain elegance in construction. Also, it drives me crazy when I see articles where every paragraph begins 'however,' and 'but,' and 'then again.' I call it the 'but-however' syndrome. Novice writers who don't know how to put a piece together structurally tend to fall back on that crutch. Instead of organizing their material so it all comes through in a nice, orderly flow, you have this constant back and forth. That identifies somebody who doesn't have too much magazine experience. And if I get an article that has no quotes in it from anyone, I tend to be skeptical and think they just read a few clips someplace, paraphrased them, and used them as the basis for the article. I like quotes, and from the highest-level people you can get.

Scheibach: I really look for a writer with an ability to do research. One of the reasons I like my current pool of writers is I know they're willing to do research. If I want them to do an article about older Americans going back to school, I know I have a writer who will call the Department of Education, and a local university, talk to continuing education experts. They'll interview people who are 50 and older who are going back, and go to the library. They have the capability and willingness to do research. There are many, many stories that I don't get a sense that the freelancers are willing to do the work. They'd rather sit at their typewriters and put together the words. So I think it's a quality a lot of editors are looking for, and you should tell me about it. Don't assume that I'm going to understand that you enjoy doing research. It should be part of the query. Some of the better clips I see have facts and figures, they show trends, they've really done enough homework to put together a quality article.

Clarke: In addition to showing me you can follow our tone or style, what I look for is a way of writing that involves the reader, so it really is a put-me-there kind of style. It's anecdotal. Obviously our articles are backed up by experts, but we need the hook that will draw the reader in, and they can say "oh, that might have happened to me." We really want something the reader can relate to.

Raskin: We're looking for smart, crisp writing that shows some style. A well-organized and reported piece that doesn't waste a lot of words. We're looking for writers who know how to use sources well, and don't use them gratuitously—they use a good variety of sources both geographically and in terms of what they have to say.

What is your policy on simultaneous submissions?

Salerno: They are fine, as long as they are identified as such, because we have a really long lead time. I hate a situation where it's not identified as simultaneous, and when you get back to the writer they've sold it to somebody else. If you're sending it around to everybody shotgun style, you have to let me know.

Scheibach: Personally, I don't like simultaneous manuscript submissions. We have had bad experiences with people who don't inform us that these are simultaneous, and I think any editor likes the notion that something is being written exclusively for that publication. I feel it's acceptable to have a *query* that goes to more than one publication; however, if the writer has done his or her homework, that query will be tailored for each publication.

Raskin: If they tell us, we don't care, because we're very good about getting back to people. Writers have to have a lot of queries out there at any given time if they're waiting four to eight weeks for four different publications to respond. I understand the dilemma of the freelancer.

If you were to develop a profile of the ideal freelancer, what characteristics would that writer have?

Salerno: Can you find me several of them? An ideal freelancer is somebody who's not intimidated by the idea of calling the president. You may not get the president on the phone, but you certainly make the effort. In other words, you start looking for your sources at the top, and as you are forced by necessity you work a little lower. Also, an ideal freelancer understands that the first draft frequently is not going to be on target, and there will be work required after the fact. They also understand that the facts are more important than writing in some florid, colorful, self-conscious way. They also don't miss deadlines. And accuracy, of course—an ideal freelancer isn't sloppy with the facts.

Gagliardi: I really look for professionalism in people. People who meet deadlines, and send their bills promptly. They also know an editor might call and say "Look, can you do a little more research?" This is how you develop a good working relationship. Look at yourself as a business. Once you do that, you start getting treated differently, as well.

Clarke: There are two kinds of ideal freelance writer for most magazines. The first is a generalist, probably someone with an English degree, with wide-ranging interests and enthusiasms, somebody with a real sense for the heartbeat of people, who can establish a background of experts and real people and sources that really can make a great article. The other ideal freelancer is an expert. Maybe they have a degree in nutrition, or public health or social work, and the trick is they can also write. Also, these writers have very specifically targeted ideas, and in addition to being really interesting and readable writers, they are utterly dependable. When push comes to shove, I can count on them to write that sidebar overnight.

Are there any pieces of parting advice you'd like to offer freelancers just breaking into the business?

Salerno: Don't be discouraged. You can figure that the odds are you'll be rejected 30 times for every one time you sell a piece. So if you're not prepared to deal with that, maybe you'd better find another business. Sooner or later, if you have the talent, you will start selling—but be willing to let people show you the ropes. If you want to write the great American novel your own way, that's one thing. But if you want to do magazine writing you're going to have to make concessions in terms of style and the type of material you want to write about. You're going to have to write to fit—to fit the publication, the topic, the space, and you're going to have to seem like you're easy to work with.

Scheibach: Never send a query or manuscript to a publication you don't have a good understanding of. A little bit of homework goes a long way. Many magazines have health, travel, lifestyle and food sections, so there are more than just up-front features you can query. Secondly, develop a specialty. If you can focus on an area you feel very strong in, and develop that, in the long run it will make you a much better writer.

Clarke: Develop a thick skin. Because when you get a rejection, it doesn't mean that your idea wasn't good. It could well mean that we have the story in inventory, or we did it last year, or it's an idea that really isn't for us. Also, realize that relationships are extremely important. I think sometimes it's difficult to establish them, especially for writers who are long-distance. But the writers I use are people that I have gotten to know—that's really how the business works. So once you've gotten an article placed, the next step is calling to say "Hey, I'm so glad you liked that one. Can I come and meet you, and talk about some other ideas I have?" The goal really has to be establishing a personal relationship with a variety of editors.

Raskin: Try to start small, in the departments. And pinpoint as much as possible the topic, the query, the editor, and get your foot in the door that way. After that, just stick with it.

The Business of Writing

Minding the Details

Writers who have had some success in placing their work know that the effort to publish requires an entirely different set of skills than does the act of writing. A shift in perspective is required when you move from creating your work to selling it. Like it or not, successful writers—*career* writers—have to keep the business side of the writing business in mind as they work.

Each of the following sections discusses a writing business topic that affects anyone selling his writing. We'll take a look at contracts and agreements—the documents that license a publisher to use your work. We'll consider your rights as a writer and sort out some potentially confusing terminology. We'll cover the basics of copyright protection—a topic of perennial concern for writers. And for those of you who are already making money with your writing, we'll offer some tips for keeping track of financial matters and staying on top of your tax liabilities.

Our treatment of the business topics that follow is necessarily limited. Look for complete information on each subject at your local bookstore or library—both in books (some of which we mention) and periodicals aimed at writers. Information is also available from the federal government, as indicated later in this article.

Contracts and agreements

If you've been freelancing even a short time, you know that contracts and agreements vary considerably from one publisher to another. Some magazine editors work only by verbal agreement; others have elaborate documents you must sign in triplicate and return before you begin the assignment. As you evaluate any contract or agreement, consider carefully what you stand to gain and lose by signing. Did you have another sale in mind that selling all rights the first time will negate? Does the agreement provide the publisher with a number of add-ons (advertising rights, reprint rights, etc.) for which they won't have to pay you again?

In contract negotiations, the writer is usually interested in licensing the work for a particular use but limiting the publisher's ability to make other uses of the work in the future. It's in the publisher's best interest, however, to secure rights to use the work in as many ways as possible, both now and later on. Those are the basic positions of each party. The negotiation is a process of compromise and capitulation on questions relating to those basic points—and the amount of compensation to be given the writer for his work.

A contract is rarely a take-it-or-leave-it proposition. If an editor tells you that his company will allow *no* changes on the contract, you will then have to decide how important the assignment is to you. But most editors are open to negotiation, and you should learn to compromise on points that don't matter to you while maintaining your stand on things that do.

When it's not specified, most writers assume that a magazine publisher is buying one-time rights. Some writers' groups can supply you with a sample magazine contract to use when the publisher doesn't supply one, so you can document your agreement in writing. Members of The Authors Guild are given a sample book contract and information about negotiating when they join. For more information about contracts and agreements, see *Business and Legal Forms for Authors & Self-Publishers*, by Tad Crawford (Allworth Press, 1990); *From Printout to Published*, by Michael Seidman (Carroll & Graf, 1992) or *The Writer's Guide to Contract Negotiations*, by Richard Balkin (Writer's Digest Books, 1985), which is out of print but should be available in libraries.

Rights and the writer

A creative work can be used in many different ways. As the originator of written works, you enjoy full control over how those works are used; you are in charge of the rights that your creative works are "born" with. When you agree to have your work published, you are giving the publisher the right to use your work in one or more ways. Whether that right is simply to publish the work for the first time in a periodical or to publish it as many times as he likes and in whatever form he likes is up to you—it all depends on the terms of the contract or agreement the two of you arrive at. As a general rule, the more rights you license away, the less control you have over your work and the more money you should be paid for the license. We find that writers and editors sometimes define rights in different ways. For a classification of terms, read Types of Rights, below.

Sometimes editors don't take the time to specify the rights they are buying. If you sense that an editor is interested in getting stories but doesn't seem to know what his and the writer's responsibilities are regarding rights, be wary. In such a case, you'll want to explain what rights you're offering (preferably one-time or first serial rights only) and that you expect additional payment for subsequent use of your work.

You should strive to keep as many rights to your work as you can from the outset, otherwise, your attempts to resell your writing may be seriously hampered.

The Copyright Law that went into effect January 1, 1978, said writers were primarily selling one-time rights to their work unless they—and the publisher—agreed otherwise in writing. Book rights are covered fully by the contract between the writer and the book publisher.

Types of rights

- First Serial Rights—First serial rights means the writer offers a newspaper or magazine the right to publish the article, story or poem for the first time in any periodical. All other rights to the material remain with the writer. The qualifier "North American" is often added to this phrase to specify a geographical limit to the license.

  When material is excerpted from a book scheduled to be published and it appears in a magazine or newspaper prior to book publication, this is also called first serial rights.
- One-Time Rights—A periodical that licenses one-time rights to a work (also known as simultaneous rights) buys the *nonexclusive* right to publish the work once. That is, there is nothing to stop the author from selling the work to other publications at the same time. Simultaneous sales would typically be to periodicals without overlapping audiences.
- Second Serial (Reprint) Rights—This gives a newspaper or magazine the opportunity

INSIDER REPORT

Ian Frazier on risks, road-building and defeating chaos

Writing full-time opens writers to a world of risks—including such unique and formative experiences as morale-numbing rejection and the standing threat of poverty—but according to Ian Frazier, such risks are the very best reasons for writing in the first place. Writers who don't take risks don't grow, and an art that's not pressed forward by its practitioners is not worthy of the name.

Frazier began his writing career in college, on the staff of the *Harvard Lampoon*. After graduation and a short stint at *Oui* as a staff writer, he went to work for the *New Yorker*, where he has been a regular contributor for more than 20 years. He has published two collections of short pieces, *Dating Your Mom* (1986, Farrar, Straus & Giroux) and

Ian Frazier

© Sigrid Estrada

Nobody Better, Better Than Nobody (1987, FSG); and two longer nonfiction works, *Great Plains* (1989, FSG) and *Family* (1994, FSG). Frazier is a nonfiction writer with a fiction writer's eye and ear for scene, setting and dialogue. His work is distinguished by dry, finely-tuned humor, delicately-rendered word pictures, meticulous research, and surprising moments of self-revelation.

"The more you risk in publication, the more you learn from it," says Frazier. "If you show a piece to a friend whose opinion you really value, you're risking something because the friend might not like it and that would hurt. If you send a piece away to a magazine where you very much want to appear and you are rejected, that hurts a lot; but if you are accepted, you feel great. I think writing will wither if you don't risk the most scary publication you can stand."

For Frazier, publication is the means by which writers take soundings of their audience—just as ships gauge their positions by bouncing sonar off the terrain submerged beneath their hulls. Frequent and accurate soundings give writers the feedback they need to keep their skills sharp and their incomes as steady as possible. The most telling feedback, Frazier asserts, reaches writers in the form of money. "If you get paid, then you believe that the people liked your book or they liked your piece. If someone comes up to you, at a writing program, for instance, and says 'Oh, I loved your piece,' I don't believe that. I don't believe it until they buy it." While writers work toward achieving economic equilibrium with the aid of this sonar, they must be prepared for the possibility of hardship along the way. "It's hard to make a living writing, but it is not impossible," says

Frazier. "All kinds of writers have gone through poverty, supporting themselves any way they could while they were writing. I've never been deeply poor, but having no money is not fun; it takes a certain kind of equanimity or discipline to live without it. But if you can stand it, you will get money eventually. If you stay with it you do get money eventually."

Another benefit of staying with it is a continual refinement of the writer's technique. Over the years, Frazier has developed an engaging, intimate voice and the ability to convincingly recreate bits and pieces of the real world for his readers. In attempting to convey experiences to his audience, Frazier looks first for the emotional core of each situation. "I try and find the moment of a particular scene that stuck with me the longest. Or there might have been a moment when my heart beat the fastest or when I was the most scared or the most excited or the most engaged by what was happening. Then, when I'm writing, I try and arrange impressions as they relate to that moment—they're either building to that moment or they're going away from that moment. As you do that, you follow what are sort of the basic rules; for instance, you don't say it was a 'fantastic moment'—things like that. You try to give the reader devices which *his* imagination can use. You try and stay out of the way of the reader's imagination. You don't kick it in any direction, you just give it the raw material, with which it can build an impression. It's sort of like you're building a really smooth, good road through a very complicated landscape so that the reader just goes wooosh, wooosh, wooosh, so that at each point he sort of effortlessly sees the important thing. As he comes around *this* turn there's *this* important thing, as he comes *this* way he sees *this* important thing, and as he comes out at the end he sees this *other* important thing. You don't ever want to have a sentence in there that the reader himself has to rewrite. Basically, you want it to be very pleasurable for the reader, at least that's my opinion."

Beyond crafting work that is pleasing to readers, what does Frazier hope to accomplish in his writing and his career? "What you want to do is . . . defeat chaos. You want to heal people; you want to make people know that heroism is possible and that it exists; you want people to read and just say, 'You know, life is glorious!' You're glorifying creation. Even if it's a tragedy, even if it's a nightmare, there's something glorious about it.

"More practically, though, what you're doing with any piece of writing is not only taking a shot at an audience that's around you but also aiming at an audience that doesn't exist yet. I'm reading a book by Dickens; I didn't exist when he wrote it. If I wrote something really great, my audience would not be born yet, not for 150 years. It's like you're making a little craft that might sail on and on and on in the future. And, to me, that's like sending a space probe or something— it's really an exciting thing to try and do. Just for the heck of it. Despite whatever your aspirations are, that particular practical goal, to me, seems like something worth doing."

to print an article, poem or story after it has already appeared in another newspaper or magazine. Second serial rights are nonexclusive—that is, they can be licensed to more than one market.

● All Rights—This is just what it sounds like. If you license away all rights to your work, you forfeit the right to ever use it again. If you think you'll want to use the material later, you must avoid submitting to such markets or refuse payment and withdraw your material. Ask the editor whether he is willing to buy first rights instead of all rights before you agree to an assignment or sale. Some editors will reassign rights to a writer after a given period, such as one year. It's worth an inquiry in writing.

● Subsidiary Rights—These are the rights, other than book publication rights, that should be covered in a book contract. These may include various serial rights; movie, television, audiotape and other electronic rights; translation rights, etc. The book contract should specify who controls these rights (author or publisher) and what percentage of sales from the licensing of these sub rights goes to the author.

● Dramatic, Television and Motion Picture Rights—This means the writer is selling his material for use on the stage, in television or in the movies. Often a one-year option to buy such rights is offered (generally for 10% of the total price). The interested party then tries to sell the idea to other people—actors, directors, studios or television networks, etc. Some properties are optioned over and over again, but most fail to become dramatic productions. In such cases, the writer can sell his rights again and again—as long as there is interest in the material. Though dramatic, TV and motion picture rights are more important to the fiction writer than the nonfiction writer, producers today are increasingly interested in nonfiction material; many biographies, topical books and true stories are being dramatized.

Selling subsidiary rights

The primary right in the world of book publishing is the right to publish the book itself. All other rights (such as movie rights, audio rights, book club rights, electronic rights and foreign rights) are considered secondary, or subsidiary, to the right to print publication. In contract negotiations, authors and their agents traditionally try to avoid granting the publisher subsidiary rights that they feel capable of marketing themselves. Publishers, on the other hand, typically hope to obtain control over as many of the sub rights as they can. Philosophically speaking, subsidiary rights will be best served by being left in the hands of the person or organization most capable of—and interested in—exploiting them profitably. Sometimes that will be the author and her agent, and sometimes that will be the publisher.

Larger agencies have experience selling foreign rights, movie rights and the like, and many authors represented by such agents prefer to retain those rights and let their agents do the selling. Book publishers, on the other hand, have subsidiary rights departments, which are responsible for exploiting all sub rights the publisher was able to retain during the contract negotiation. Cathy Fox, vice president and director of subsidiary rights for the Putnam Berkley Group in New York, says her department's mission is to "maximize our income [and, by extension, the author's income] by exploiting whatever rights we have." That job might begin with a push to sell foreign rights, which normally bring in advance money which is divided among author, agent and publisher. "Usually internationally is where things start to happen first," says Fox. "We can make foreign sales at the same time we're buying the book, or soon after we've bought it."

Further efforts then might be made to sell the right to publish the book as a paperback (although many book contracts now call for hard/soft deals, in which the original hardcover publisher buys the right to also publish the paperback version). "Most houses are buying many more titles hard/soft and selling less outside to paperback," Fox says. "Paperback used to be a place where you could make a lot of money, and now it seems there aren't many places on a paperback publisher's list. They'll buy something which they think they can put out in bestseller numbers and they'll buy category [romance, mystery, etc.]. But anything in between is very hard to sell today in paperback reprints."

Any other rights which the publisher controls will be pursued. "As soon as the manuscript's in and read, it goes to the book clubs," Fox says. "If we have first serial rights, it goes to the magazines. If we have audio rights, it goes to the audio publishers. Some very nice money is in selling large print rights." Publishers usually don't control movie rights to a work, as those are most often retained by author and agent.

The marketing of electronic rights to a work, in this era of rapidly expanding capabilities and markets for electronic material, can be tricky. With the proliferation of electronic and multimedia formats, publishers, agents and authors are going to great pains these days to make sure contracts specify exactly *which* electronic rights are being conveyed (or retained). For more on electronic and multimedia publishing, see A Writer's Guide to New Media Publishing, on page 56.

Copyright

Copyright law exists to protect creators of original works. It is engineered to encourage creative expression and aid in the progress of the arts and sciences by ensuring that artists and authors hold the rights by which they can profit from their labors.

Copyright protects your writing, unequivocally recognizes you (its creator) as its owner, and grants you all the rights, benefits and privileges that come with ownership. The moment you finish a piece of writing—whether it is a short story, article, novel or poem—the law recognizes that only you can decide how it is to be used.

The basics of copyright law are discussed here. More detailed information can be obtained from the Copyright Office and in the books mentioned at the end of this section.

Copyright law gives you the right to make and distribute copies of your written works, the right to prepare derivative works (dramatizations, translations, musical arrangements, etc.—any work based on the original) and the right to perform or publicly display your work. With very few exceptions, anything you write today will enjoy copyright protection for your lifetime plus 50 years. Copyright protects "original works of authorship" that are fixed in a tangible form of expression. Titles, ideas and facts can *not* be copyrighted.

Some people are under the mistaken impression that copyright is something they have to send away for, and that their writing is not properly protected until they have "received" their copyright from the government. The fact is, you don't have to register your work with the Copyright Office in order for your work to be copyrighted; any piece of writing is copyrighted the moment it is put to paper. Registration of your work does, however, offer some additional protection (specifically, the possibility of recovering punitive damages in an infringement suit) as well as legal proof of the date of copyright.

Registration is a matter of filling out a form (for writers, that's generally form TX) and sending the completed form, a copy of the work in question and a check for $20 to the Register of Copyrights, Library of Congress, Washington DC 20559. If the thought of paying $20 each to register every piece you write does not appeal to you, you can cut costs by registering a group of your works with one form, under one title for one $20 fee.

Most magazines are registered with the Copyright Office as single collective entities themselves; that is, the individual works that make up the magazine are *not* copyrighted individually in the names of the authors. You'll need to register your article yourself if you wish to have the additional protection of copyright registration. It's always a good idea to ask that your notice of copyright (your name, the year of first publication, and the copyright symbol ©) be appended to any published version of your work. You may use the copyright notice regardless of whether or not your work has been registered.

One thing writers need to be wary of is "work for hire" arrangements. If you sign an agreement stipulating that your writing will be done as work for hire, you will not control the copyright of the completed work—the person or organization who hired you will be the copyright owner. Work for hire arrangements and transfers of exclusive rights must be in writing to be legal, but it's a good idea to get every publishing agreement in writing before the sale.

You can obtain more information about copyright from the Copyright Office, Library of Congress, Washington DC 20559. To get answers to specific questions about copyright, call the Copyright Public Information Office at (202)707-3000 weekdays between 8:30 a.m. and 5 p.m. eastern standard time. To order copyright forms by phone, call (202)707-9100. A thorough (and thoroughly enjoyable) discussion of the subject of copyright law as it applies to writers can be found in Stephen Fishman's *The Copyright Handbook: How to Protect and Use Written Works* (Nolo Press, 1994). A shorter but no less enlightening treatment is Ellen Kozak's *Every Writer's Guide to Copyright & Publishing Law* (Henry Holt, 1990).

Finances and taxes

As your writing business grows, so will your obligation to keep track of your writing-related finances and taxes. Keeping a close eye on these details will help you pay as little tax as possible and keep you apprised of the state of your freelance business. A writing business with no systematic way of tracking expenses and income will soon be no writing business at all. If you dislike handling finance-related tasks, you can always hire someone else to handle them for a fee. If you do employ a professional, you must still keep the original records with an eye to providing the professional with the appropriate information.

If you decide to handle these tasks yourself—or if you just want to know what to expect of the person you employ—consider these tips:

Accurate records are essential, and the easiest way to keep them is to separate your writing income and expenses from your personal ones. Most professionals find that separate checking accounts and credit cards help them provide the best and easiest records.

Get in the habit of recording every transaction (both expenses and earnings) related to your writing. You can start at any time; you don't need to begin on January 1. Because you're likely to have expenses before you have income, start keeping your records whenever you make your first purchase related to writing—such as this copy of *Writer's Market*.

Any system of tracking expenses and income will suffice, but the more detailed it is, the better. Be sure to describe each transaction clearly—including the date; the source of the income (or the vendor of your purchase); a description of what was sold or bought; whether the payment was by cash, check or credit card; and the amount of the transaction.

The other necessary component of your financial record-keeping system is an orderly way to store receipts related to your writing. Check stubs, receipts for cash purchases, credit card receipts and similar paperwork should all be kept as well as recorded in your ledger. Any good book about accounting for small business will offer specific suggestions for ways to track your finances.

Freelance writers, artists and photographers have a variety of concerns about taxes that employees don't have, including deductions, self-employment tax and home office credits. Many freelance expenses can be deducted in the year in which they are incurred (rather than having to be capitalized, or depreciated, over a period of years). For details, consult the IRS publications mentioned later. Keep in mind that to be considered a

INSIDER REPORT

The art of targeting a market

Knowing the style and focus of the magazine you're submitting to is as important as knowing the subject you're writing about. Michael Robbins, editor of *Audubon* magazine, sees researching a possible market as one of the most important steps a writer can take in getting his work published.

Audubon, which Robbins calls a "nature magazine with an edge," is owned by the National Audubon Society and deals with nature conservation and the environment. Most of the articles in the magazine deal with issues that relate to nature—and a prospective writer for the magazine needs to know exactly what that means. Carefully reading past issues of *Audubon* will help you decide if you're submitting exactly what the magazine is looking for.

Photograph by Richard Frank

Michael Robbins

Many of the stories published in *Audubon* are assigned by the editorial staff, but a significant number come through queries from writers. "We make a strenuous effort to keep incorporating new voices in the magazine," Robbins says. The first thing Robbins looks for in a prospective writer is whether he or she has studied the magazine. "There's always a percentage of people trying to crack a magazine who don't do their homework," he says. "For instance, if they suggest a story on the Yellowstone River, it would be a dead giveaway that they have not read *Audubon*, because we did a story last year on the Yellowstone River. Obviously, they aren't paying a whole lot of attention."

Paying attention means carefully reading the articles that *Audubon* publishes, noting the style in which they are written and the audience they are written for. "I think anyone reading *Audubon* would find an awareness of the political aspects of things," Robbins says. As a membership circulation publication, it's important to note that readers of the magazine are also members of the National Audubon Society. "The magazine is pitched at an educated audience," Robbins continues. "There is a news aspect to our stories, but we also value graceful writing—it's not a newspaper. The stories are very fact-based, and we try to make the stories very timely. And we don't do a lot of musing, meditative essay pieces."

Knowing where the author of a piece fits in is an important element to consider when researching a potential market. "Reading *Audubon* should give you a sense of where the author is in a story," Robbins says. "A lot of times we're looking for reporting and may or may not want the author in the story, in a first person sense. In some magazines, the writer carries a great deal of importance as an in-the-story narrator. We tend not to do that unless the story is really defined by the experience of the writer. Usually the author is reporting rather than talking about himself."

All of this research into a market's style, voice and audience should be reflected in your query letter. "When I look at a query," Robbins says, "I look at a couple of things. First, is the query literate? Then I look for an authoritative voice. *Audubon* is a journalistic magazine, written by people who are professional writers rather than scientists trying to be writers. We look for some sense that the writer is grounded in the subject." For instance, Robbins suggests, if a query came in proposing a story on searching the Peruvian Amazon for unknown species of parrots, the query should reflect several things. One, that the writer is familiar with the territory; two, he knows his parrots; and three, he is capable of the type of independence it takes to travel and get the story. "It may be just an armchair query," Robbins explains, "but if it's a person who's a reasonably experienced world traveler, we're going to pay attention."

Indicating that your story proposal is actually a story, and not just an idea, is another important element Robbins looks for in a query. "We all look to see some sense that there is a story involved," he says. "A huge number of queries come from people who haven't formulated a story. They don't have a sense of events unfolding, who the characters might be—is there a beginning, middle and end? We get an alarming number of stories that say, 'I'm going to the Great Barrier Reef in Australia and I'd like to do an article about it.' Our response to that is, 'What's the story?' And a lot of people—even experienced writers— often don't have an answer. We can't afford to send people out just to nose around and see if there are any stories out there." Having a clear-cut story in mind is a must. "The people who are very successful as writers," Robbins says, "are successful because they come up with a lot of good ideas and are able to deliver on those ideas."

—*Cindy Laufenberg*

business (and not a hobby) by the IRS you need to show a profit in three of the past five years. Hobby losses are deductible only to the extent of income produced by the activity.

There also is a home office deduction that can be claimed if an area in your home is used *exclusively* and *regularly* for business. Contact the IRS for information on requirements and limitations for this deduction. If your freelance income exceeds your expenses, regardless of the amount, you must declare that profit. If you make $400 or more after deductions, you must pay Social Security tax and file Schedule SE, a self-employment form, along with your Form 1040 and Schedule C tax forms.

While we cannot offer you tax advice or interpretations, we can suggest several sources for the most current information.

● Call your local IRS office. Look in the white pages of the telephone directory under U.S. Government—Internal Revenue Service. Someone will be able to respond to your request for IRS publications and tax forms or other information. Ask about the IRS Tele-tax service, a series of recorded messages you can hear by dialing on a touch-tone phone. If you need answers to complicated questions, ask to speak with a Taxpayer Service Specialist.

● Obtain the basic IRS publications. You can order them by phone or mail from any

IRS office; most are available at libraries and some post offices. Start with *Your Federal Income Tax* (Publication 17) and *Tax Guide for Small Business* (Publication 334). These are both comprehensive, detailed guides—you'll need to find the regulations that apply to you and ignore the rest. There are many IRS publications relating to self-employment and taxes; Publication 334 lists many of these publications—such as *Business Use of Your Home* (Publication 587) and *Self-Employment Tax* (Publication 533).

● Consider other information sources. Many public libraries have detailed tax instructions available on tape. Some colleges and universities offer free assistance in preparing tax returns. And if you decide to consult a professional tax preparer, the fee is a deductible business expense on your tax return.

How Much Should I Charge?

Most freelance writers take on a variety of types of writing work. Knowing what to charge for each job is difficult, as many factors are involved in the decision. The size of the job is a primary concern, but other variables such as your level of experience, the nature of your client's business and even where you and your client are located can affect your fees.

The information supplied in this section will give you an idea of what other writers across the country are charging for various tasks. Yet, you will notice some of the ranges given are quite broad, taking location and other factors into account. To find out exactly what the market will bear in your area, networking with other writers is essential. Not only can contacts with others in your area give you an idea of what to charge, but you will also learn who uses freelance help and who the best clients are.

You'll want to make sure you aren't selling yourself short, of course, but you'll want to avoid pricing yourself out of the market. In preparing a bid, look at the range of fees listed for that particular service. Then, using what you've learned from other writers in your area, try to assess how much you think the client is willing to pay. If you are unsure, ask them what they have budgeted for the project and start from there.

Location has had a strong influence on fees in the past and it is still true that you can charge higher fees in larger metropolitan areas.

The nature of your client's business can also affect how much you may be able to charge. For example, work for business clients tends to bring higher fees than editorial work for magazines and newspapers. Nonprofit organizations do not generally pay rates as high as those paid by corporations. Smaller circulation publications tend to pay less than larger ones.

Your experience with a particular type of work will also affect what you will charge. If you will be working in an area new to you, you may want to begin by charging an hourly rate rather than a flat fee.

One way to figure an hourly fee is to determine how much a company might pay per hour for someone on staff to do the same job. If, for example, you think a buyer would have to pay a staff person $26,000 per year, divide that by 2,000 (approximately 40 hours per week for 50 weeks) and you arrive at $13 per hour.

Next, add another 33% to cover the cost of fringe benefits that an employer normally pays (but that you must now absorb) in Social Security, unemployment insurance, hospitalization, retirement funds, etc. This figure varies from employer to employer, but the U.S. Chamber of Commerce reports that the U.S. average paid by employers is 37.6% of an employee's salary.

Then add another dollars-per-hour figure to cover your actual overhead expense for office space, equipment, supplies; plus time spent on professional meetings, researching and writing unsuccessful proposals. (To get this figure, add one year's expenses and divide by the number of hours per year you have been freelancing.) In the beginning— when you may have large one-time expenses, such as a computer—you may have to adjust this figure to avoid pricing yourself out of the market. Finally, you may wish to figure in a profit percentage to be used for capital investments or future growth.

Here's an example:
$26,000 (salary) ÷ 2,000 (hours) = $13.00 **per hour**
+ 4.29 (33% to cover fringe benefits, taxes, etc.)
+ 2.50 (overhead based on annual expenses of $5,000)
+ 1.30 (10% profit margin)
———————
$21.09 **per hour charge**

We present this formula to help you determine what to charge based on what a client might expect to pay a staff person on a per-hour basis. Keep in mind, however, that few "fulltime" freelancers bill 2,000 hours per year. Most who consider themselves fulltime end up billing for about half that many hours. Using this formula, therefore, will probably not bring in the same amount of money as a fulltime staff position. Some experienced freelancers keep this in mind when setting rates and adjust their hourly charge upward to compensate. Again, this depends on the client's budget, your experience and what that particular market will bear.

Once you have worked repeatedly for a particular client or have established a specific area of expertise, you will get a feel for the time and effort involved. Then you may feel more comfortable charging a flat fee for projects rather than an hourly rate. Businesses are sometimes more likely to agree to flat fees because they like to know ahead of time how much a project will cost.

Reservations about hourly rates can be alleviated through effective communication. Be sure to get a letter of agreement signed by both parties covering the work to be done and the fee or rate to be paid. If there is any question about how long the project will take, be sure the agreement indicates that you are estimating the time and that your project fee is based on a certain number of hours. If you quote a flat fee, you should stipulate in your agreement that a higher rate might be charged for overtime hours or late changes in the project.

If you find that the project will take more time, be sure to let the client know right away and be certain the client understands and approves of the additional time and charges. Be sure to have any renegotiated fees put in writing. Some freelancers require a partial payment as parts of the job are completed, so both you and the client have a better idea of the time involved.

The rates given here are generally for "average" projects within a field. For translation, for example, translations from exotic languages into English or English into another language or translations of highly technical material will bring higher rates than the range listed. Whenever a project requires you to draw on your expertise in a technical area, you will be able to charge fees on the higher end of the range.

In markets where payment methods vary, both kinds of rates—hourly and per-project—are given so you have as many pricing options as possible. Please note that the categories often encompass a wide range due to responses from various locations and from writers at varying levels of experience.

Advertising, Copywriting & PR

Advertising copywriting: Advertising agencies and the advertising departments of large companies need part-time help in rush seasons. Newspapers, radio and TV stations also need copywriters for their small business customers who do not have agencies. Depending on the client, the locale and the job, the following rates could apply: $20-100 per hour, $250 and up per day, $500 and up per week, $1,000-2,000 as a monthly retainer. Flat-fee-per-ad rates could range from $100 and up per page depending upon size and kind of client. In Canada rates range from $40-80 per hour.

Book jacket copywriting: From $100-600 for front cover jacket plus flaps and back jacket copy summarizing content and tone of the book.

Brochures: $20-600 per published page or $100-7,500 and up per project depending on client (small nonprofit organization to large corporation), length and complexity of job.

Consultation for communications: *See Business & Technical Writing.*

Copyediting for advertising: $25 per hour.

Copywriting for book club catalogs: $85-200.

Direct-mail catalog copy: $75-200 per item; $150-1,000 per page.

Direct-mail packages: Copywriting direct mail letter, response card, etc., $500-30,000 depending on writer's skill, reputation and the client.

Direct response card on a product: $250-500.

Events promotion: $20-30 per hour. *See also Shopping mall promotion (this section).*

Fliers for tourist attractions, small museums, art shows: $50 and up for writing a brief bio, history, etc.

Fundraising campaign brochure: $5,000 for 20 hours' research and 30 hours to write a major capital campaign brochure, get it approved, lay out and produce with a printer. For a standard fundraising brochure, many fund-raising executives hire copywriters for $50-75 an hour to do research which takes 10-15 hours and 20-30 hours to write/produce.

New product release: $300-500 plus expenses.

News release: *See Press release (this section).*

Picture editing: *See Editorial/Design Packages.*

Political writing: *See Public relations and Speechwriting (this section).*

Press background on a company: $500-1,200 for 4-8 pages.

Press kits: $500-3,000.

Press release: 1-3 pages, $25-500.

Print advertisement: $200 per project. In Canada, $100-200 per concept.

Product literature: Usually paid per hour or day: $60 per hour; $400 per day. Per page, $100-300.

Promotional materials: *See Brochures (this section).*

Proofreading corporate publications and documents: $15-25 per hour.

Public relations for business: $250-600 per day plus expenses; up to $1,750 for large corporations.

Public relations for conventions: $500-2,500 flat fee.

Public relations for libraries: Small libraries, $5-10 per hour; larger cities, $35 per hour and up.

Public relations for nonprofit or proprietary organizations: Small towns, $100-500 monthly retainers.

Public relations for politicians: Small town, state campaigns, $10-50 per hour; incumbents, congressional, gubernatorial, and other national campaigns, $25-100 per hour; up to 10% of campaign budget.

Public relations for schools: $15-20 per hour and up in small districts; larger districts have full-time staff personnel.

Radio advertising copy: $20-100 per script; $200-225 per week for a four- to six-hour day; larger cities, $250-400 per week.

Recruiting brochure: 8-12 pages, $500-2,500.

Rewriting: Copy for a local client, $25-100 per hour, depending on the size of the project.

Sales brochure: 12-16 pages, $750-3,000. Up to $500 per page.

Sales letter for business or industry: $350-1,000 for one or two pages.

Services brochure: 12-18 pages, $1,250-2,000.

Shopping mall promotion: $500-1,000 monthly retainer up to 15% of promotion budget for the mall.

Speech, editing and evaluation: $18 per hour and up.

Speech for government official: $4,000 for 20 minutes plus up to $1,000 travel and miscellaneous expenses.

Speech for local political candidate: $250 for 15 minutes; for statewide candidate, $375-500.

Speech for national congressional candidate: $1,000 and up.

Speech for owner of a small business: $100 for 6 minutes.

Speech for owners of larger businesses: $500-3,000 for 10-30 minutes.

Speech for statewide candidate: $500-800.

Speechwriting (general): $20-75 per hour. In Canada, $70-125 per hour or $70-100 per minute of speech.

Trade journal ad copywriting: $250-500.

TV commercial: $60-375 per finished minute; $10-2,000 per finished project. In Canada, $3 per second of script.

TV home shopping: Local ad copy: $6 per hour. Writing, miscellaneous freelance: $15-85 per hour; 50¢-$1 per word.

Audiovisuals & Electronic Communications

Audiocassette scripts: $10-50 per scripted minute, assuming written from existing client materials, with no additional research or meetings; otherwise $75-100 per minute, $750 minimum.

Audiovisuals: For writing, $250-350 per requested scripted minute; includes rough draft, editing conference with client, and final shooting script. For consulting, research, producing, directing, soundtrack oversight, etc., $400-600 per day plus travel and expenses. Writing fee is sometimes 10% of gross production price as billed to client. Some charge flat fee of 1,500-2,100 per package.

Book summaries for film producers: $50-100 per book. *Note: You must live in the area where the business is located to get this kind of work.*

Copyediting audiovisuals: $20 per hour.

Industrial product film: $125-150 per minute; $500 minimum flat fee.

Novel synopsis for film producer: $150 for 5-10 pages typed, single-spaced.

Radio advertising copy: *See Advertising, Copywriting & PR.*

Radio continuity writing: $5 per page to $150 per week, part-time. In Canada, $40-80 per minute of script; $640 per show for a multi-part series.

Radio copywriting: *See Advertising, Copywriting & PR.*

Radio documentaries: $258 for 60 minutes, local station.

Radio editorials: $10-30 for 90-second to two-minute spots.

Radio interviews: For National Public Radio, up to 3 minutes, $25; 3-10 minutes, $40-75; 10-60 minutes, $125 to negotiable fees. Small radio stations would pay approximately 50% of the NPR rate; large stations, double the NPR rate.

Script synopsis for business: $40 per hour.

Script synopsis for agent or film producer: $75 for 2-3 typed pages, single-spaced.

Scripts for nontheatrical films for education, business, industry: Prices vary among producers, clients, and sponsors and there is no standardization of rates in the field.

Fees include $75-120 per minute for one reel (10 minutes) and corresponding increases with each successive reel; approximately 10% of the production cost of films that cost the producer more than $1,500 per release minute.

Screenwriting: $6,000 and up per project.

Slide presentation: Including visual formats plus audio, $150-600 for 10-15 minutes.

Slide/single image photos: $75 flat fee.

Slide/tape script: $75-100 per minute, $750 minimum.

TV commercial: *See Advertising, Copywriting & PR.*

TV copywriting: *See Advertising, Copywriting & PR.*

TV documentary: 30-minute 5-6 page proposal outline, $1,839 and up; 15-17 page treatment, $1,839 and up; less in smaller cities. In Canada research for a documentary runs about $6,500.

TV editorials: $35 and up for 1-minute, 45 seconds (250-300 words).

TV home shopping, local ad copy: *See Advertising, Copywriting & PR.*

TV information scripts: Short 5- to 10-minute scripts for local cable TV stations, $10-15 per hour.

TV instruction taping: *See Educational & Literary Services.*

TV news film still photo: $3-6 flat fee.

TV news story: $16-25 flat fee.

TV filmed news and features: From $10-20 per clip for 30-second spot; $15-25 for 60-second clip; more for special events.

TV, national and local public stations: $35-100 per minute down to a flat fee of $5,186 and up for a 30- to 60-minute script.

TV scripts: (Teleplay only), 60 minutes; network prime time, Writers Guild rates: $14,048; 30 minutes, $10,414. In Canada, $60-130 per minute of script.

Books

Abstracting and abridging: Up to $75/hour for nonfiction; $30/hour for reference material and professional journals.

Anthology editing: Variable advance plus 3-15% of royalties. Advance should cover reprint fees or fees handled by publisher. Flat-fee-per-manuscript rates could range from $500-5,000 or more if it consists of complex, technical material.

Book proposal consultation: $20-75 per hour, or flat rate, $100-250.

Book proposal writing: $175-3,000 depending on length and whether client provides full information or writer must do some research, and whether sample chapter is required. Also up to $150 per page.

Book query critique: $50 for letter to publisher and outline.

Book summaries for book clubs: $50-100 per book.

Consultant to publishers: $25-75 per hour.

Content editing: $15-50 per hour; $600-5,000 per manuscript, based on size and complexity of the project. *See also Manuscript criticism (this section).*

Copyediting: $10-35 per hour, $6 per 1,000 words or $2 per page. Rates generally on lower end of scale for juvenile books, mid-range for adult trade, and higher for reference material.

Ghostwriting a religious book: $6,000-15,000. 50% of flat fee in advance and 50% upon completion of accepted ms.

Ghostwriting, as told to: Author gets full advance and 50% of royalties; subject gets 50%. Hourly rate for subjects who are self-publishing ($25-50 per hour). In Canada, author also gets full advance and 50% of royalties or $10,000-20,000 plus research time (for a 200-300 page book).

Ghostwriting without as-told-to credit: For clients who are either self-publishing or have no royalty publisher lined up, $5,000 to $35,000 (plus expenses) with one-fourth down payment, one-fourth when book half finished, one-fourth at three quarters mark and last fourth of payment when manuscript completed; or chapter by chapter; or $100 per page.

Ghostwriting a corporate book: *See Business & Technical Writing.*

Indexing: $15-40 per hour; charge higher hourly rate if using computer indexing software programs that take fewer hours; $1.50-6 per printed book page; 40-70¢ per line of index; or flat fee of $250-500, depending on length.

Jacket copywriting: *See Advertising, Copywriting & PR.*

Manuscript criticism: $160 for outline and first 20,000 words; $300-500 for up to 100,000 words. Also $15-35 per hour for trade books, slightly lower for nonprofit. Some writers charge on a per-page basis of $1.30-2.50 per page.

Movie novelization: $3,500-15,000, depending on writer's reputation, amount of work to be done, and amount of time writer is given.

Novel synopsis for literary agent: $150 for 5-10 pages typed, single-spaced.

Packaging consultation: $75 per hour.

Picture editing: *See Editorial/Design Packages.*

Production editing: $22-30 per hour; for reference/professional books, up to $50 per hour.

Proofreading: $12-25 per hour and up; sometimes $1.50-3 per page.

Research for writers or book publishers: $15-40 an hour and up; $15-200 per day and all expenses. Some quote a flat fee of $300-500 for a complete and complicated job.

Rewriting: $18-50 per hour; sometimes $5 per page. Some writers have combination ghostwriting and rewriting short-term jobs for which the pay could be $350 per day and up. Some participate in royalties on book rewrites.

Science writing, textbook: *See Business & Technical Writing.*

Science writing, encyclopedias: *See Business & Technical Writing.*

Textbook copyediting: $15-20 per hour, depending on whether el-hi, college, technical or non-technical.

Textbook editing: $15-30 per hour.

Textbook proofreading: $13-20 per hour.

Textbook writing: $15-50 per hour.

Translation, literary: $25 per hour; also $95-125 per 1,000 English words.

Business & Technical Writing

Annual reports: A brief report with some economic information and an explanation of figures, $25-50 per hour; 12-page report, $600-1,500; a report that must meet Securities and Exchange Commission (SEC) standards and reports that use legal language could bill at $40-75 per hour. Some writers who provide copywriting and editing services charge flat fees ranging from $5,000-10,000.

Associations: Miscellaneous writing projects, small associations, $15-25 per hour; larger groups, up to $50 per hour; or a flat fee per project, such as $550-1,000 for 2,000-word magazine articles, or $1,200-1,800 for a 10-page booklet.

Audiovisuals/audiocassette scripts: *See Audiovisuals & Electronic Communications.*

Book, ghostwritten, as told to: *See Books.*

Book summaries for business people: 4-8 printed pages, $400.

Brochures: *See Advertising, Copywriting & PR.*

Business booklets, announcement folders: Writing and editing, $100-1,000 depending on size, research, etc.

Business content editing: $20-35 per hour.

Business facilities brochure: 12-16 pages, $1,000-4,000.

Business letters: Such as those designed to be used as form letters to improve customer relations, $100 per letter for small businesses; $500 and up per form letter for corporations.

Business meeting guide and brochure: 4 pages, $200; 8-12 pages, $400. *See also Advertising, Copywriting & PR.*

Business plan: $1 per word; $200 per manuscript page; or $100-1,500 per project.

Business writing: On the local or national level, this may be advertising copy, collateral materials, speechwriting, films, public relations or other jobs—see individual entries on these subjects for details. General business writing rates could range from $25-60 per hour; $100-200 per day, plus expenses. In Canada, $1-2 per word or $50-100 per hour.

Business writing seminars: $250 for a half-day seminar, plus travel expenses. *See also Educational & Literary Services.*

Catalogs for business: $25-40 per hour or $25-600 per printed page; more if many tables or charts must be reworked for readability and consistency. *See also Advertising, Copywriting & PR.*

Collateral materials for business: *See Catalogs for business (this section).*

Commercial reports for businesses, insurance companies, credit agencies: $6-10 per page; $5-20 per report on short reports.

Company newsletters and inhouse publications: Writing and editing 2-4 pages, $200-500; 4-8 pages, $500-1,000; 12-48 pages, $1,000-2,500. Writing, $20-100 per hour; editing, $15-40 per hour. *See also Editorial/Design Packages.*

Consultation on communications: $250 per day plus expenses for nonprofit, social service and religious organizations; $500 per day to others.

Consultation to business: On writing, PR, $25-60 per hour.

Consumer complaint letters: $25 each.

Copyediting for business: $20-50 per manuscript page or $15-25 per hour; up to $40 per hour for business proposals.

Copyediting for nonprofit organizations: $15-30 per hour.

Corporate comedy: Half-hour show, $300-800.

Corporate history: $1,000-20,000, depending on length, complexity and client resources.

Corporate periodicals, editing: $50-60 per hour.

Corporate periodicals, writing: $25-100 per hour, depending on size and nature of corporation. Also $1 per word. In Canada, $1-2 per word or $40-90 per hour.

Corporate profile: Up to 3,000 words, $1,250-2,500.

Editing/manuscript evaluation for trade journals: $20-25 per hour.

Executive biography: Based on a résumé, but in narrative form, $100.

Financial presentation for a corporation: 20-30 minutes, $1,500-4,500.

Fundraising campaign brochure: *See Advertising, Copywriting & PR.*

Ghostwriting, general: $25-100 per hour; $200 per day plus expenses.

Ghostwriting article for a physician: $2,500-3,000.

Ghostwriting a corporate book: 6 months' work, $20,000-40,000.

Government public information officer: Part-time, with local governments, $25 per hour; or a retainer for so many hours per period.

Government research: $35 per hour.

Government writing: In Canada $50-80 per hour.

Grant appeals for local non-profit organizations: $50 per hour or flat fee.

Grant proposals: $40-100 per hour. Also $500-1,000 each.

Handbooks: $50-100 per hour; $25 per hour for nonprofit.

Indexing for professional journals: $15-40 per hour.

Industrial manual: $50-100 per manuscript page or $4,000 per 50 pages.

Industrial product film: *See Audiovisuals & Electronic Communications.*

Industrial promotions: $15-40 per hour.

Job application letters: $20-40.

Manuals/documentation: $25-60 per hour.

Market research survey reports: $15-30 per hour; writing results of studies or reports, $500-1,200 per day; also $500-2,000 per project.

Medical editing: $25-65 per hour.

Medical proofreading: $12-30 per hour.

Medical writing: $25-100 per hour; manuscript for pharmaceutical company submitted to research journal, $4,500-5,000.

Newsletters, abstracting: $30 per hour.

Newsletters, editing: $50-500 per issue (up to $850 per issue if includes writing); also $25-150 per published page. Some writers who do this charge regularly on a monthly basis. *See also Company newsletters (this section) and Desktop publishing (Editorial/Design Packages).*

Newsletter writing: $10-800 per published page (depending on type of client); also $500-5,000 per issue. Also $250-400 per article. In Canada, $45-70 per hour. *See also Company newsletters and Retail business newsletters (this section) and Desktop publishing (Editorial/Design Packages).*

Opinion research interviewing: $4-6 per hour or $15-25 per completed interview.

Picture editing: *See Editorial/Design Packages.*

Production editing: $15-35 per hour.

Programmed instruction consultant fees: *See Educational & Literary Services.*

Programmed instruction materials for business: *See Educational & Literary Services.*

Proofreading: $15-50 per hour; $20 per hour limit for nonprofit.

Public relations for business: *See Advertising, Copywriting & PR.*

Résumé writing: $25-500 per résumé.

Retail business newsletters for customers: $175-300 for writing 4-page publications. Also $100 per page. Some writers work with a local printer and handle production details as well, billing the client for the total package. Some writers also do their own photography. *See also Editorial/Design Packages.*

Sales letter for business or industry: *See Advertising, Copywriting & PR.*

Science writing: For newspapers $150-600; magazines $2,000-5,000; encyclopedias $1 per line; textbook editing $40 per hour; professional publications $500-1,500 for 1,500-3,000 words.

Scripts for nontheatrical films for business & industry: *See Audiovisuals & Electronic Communications.*

Services brochure: *See Advertising, Copywriting & PR.*

Software manual writing: $35-50 per hour for research and writing.

Special news article for trade publication: *See Magazines & Trade Journals.*

Speech for business owner: *See Advertising, Copywriting & PR.*

Teaching business writing to company employees: *See Educational & Literary Services.*

Technical editing: $15-60 per hour.

Technical typing: $1-5 per double-spaced page.

Technical writing: $35 per ms page or $35-75 per hour, depending on degree of complexity and type of audience.

Translation, commercial: Final draft from one of the common European languages, $115-120 per 1,000 words.

Translation for government agencies: Up to $125 per 1,000 foreign words into English.

Translation through translation agencies: Agencies pay 33⅓% (average) less than end-user clients and mark up tranlators' prices as much as 100% or more.

Translation, technical: $125 per 1,000 words.

Editorial/Design Packages

Business catalogs: *See Business & Technical Writing.*

Demo software: $70 per hour.

Desktop publishing: For 1,000 dots-per-inch type, $10-15 per camera-ready page of straight type; $30 per camera-ready page with illustrations, maps, tables, charts, photos; $100-150 per camera-ready page for oversize pages with art. Also $20-40 per hour depending on graphics, number of photos, and amount of copy to be typeset. Packages often include writing, layout/design, and typesetting services.

Fundraising campaign brochure: *See Advertising, Copywriting & PR.*

Greeting cards ideas (with art included): Anywhere from $30-300, depending on size of company.

Newsletters: *See Desktop Publishing (this section) and Newsletters (Business & Technical Writing).*

Picture editing: $20-35.

Photo brochures: $700-15,000 flat fee for photos and writing.

Photo research: $12-25 per hour.

Photography: $10-150 per b&w photo; $25-300 per color photo; also $800 per day.

Printers' camera-ready typeset copy: Usually negotiated with individual printers. *See also Manuscript typing (Miscellaneous).*

Educational & Literary Services

Business writing seminars: *See Business & Technical Writing.*

Copyediting for theses/dissertations: $15-20 per hour.

Educational consulting and educational grant and proposal writing: $250-750 per day or $25-75 per hour.

English teachers, lay reading for: $6 per hour.

Lectures at national conventions by well-known authors: $2,500-20,000 and up, plus expenses; less for panel discussions.

Lectures at regional writers' conferences: $300 and up, plus expenses.

Lectures to local librarians or teachers: $50-100.

Lectures to school classes: $25-75; $150 per day; $250 per day if farther than 100 miles.

Indexing for scholarly journals: $12 per hour.

Manuscript evaluation for scholarly journals: $15 per hour.

Manuscript evaluation for theses/dissertations: $15-30 per hour.

Programmed instruction consultant fees: $300-700 per day; $50 per hour.

Programmed instruction materials for business: $50 per hour for inhouse writing and editing; $500-700 per day plus expenses for outside research and writing. Alternate method: $2,000-5,000 per hour of programmed training provided, depending on technicality of subject.

Public relations for schools: *See Advertising, Copywriting & PR.*

Readings by poets, fiction writers: $25-600 depending on the author.

Scripts for nontheatrical films for education: *See Audiovisuals & Electronic Communications.*

Short story manuscript critique: 3,000 words, $40-60.

Teaching adult education course: $10-60 per class hour; fee usually set by school, not negotiated by teachers.

Teaching adult seminar: $350 plus mileage and per diem for a 6- or 7-hour day; plus 40% of the tuition fee beyond the sponsor's break-even point. In Canada, $35-50 per hour.

Teaching business writing to company employees: $60 per hour.

Teaching college course or seminar: $15-70 per class hour.

Teaching creative writing in school: $15-70 per hour of instruction, or $1,500-2,000 per 12-15 week semester; less in recessionary times.

Teaching elementary and middle school teachers how to teach writing to students: $75-120 for a 1-1½ hour session.

Teaching home-bound students: $5-15 per hour.

Teaching journalism in high school: Proportionate to salary scale for full-time teacher in the same school district.

Tutoring: $25 per 1-1½ hour private session.

TV instruction taping: $150 per 30-minute tape; $25 residual each time tape is sold.

Writer-in-schools: Arts council program, $130 per day; $650 per week. Personal charges plus expenses vary from $25 per day to $100 per hour depending on school's ability to pay.

Writer's workshop: Lecturing and seminar conducting, $50-150 per hour to $750 per day plus expenses; local classes, $35-50 per student for 10 sessions.

Writing for scholarly journals: $75 per hour.

Magazines & Trade Journals

Abstracting: $20-30 per hour for trade and professional journals; $8 per hour for scholarly journals.

Article manuscript critique: 3,000 words, $40.

Arts reviewing: Regional arts events summaries for national trade magazines, $35-100.

Book reviews: $50-300.

Consultation on magazine editorial: $1,000-1,500 per day plus expenses.

Copyediting: $13-30 per hour.

Editing: General, $25-500 per day or $250-2,000 per issue; Religious publications, $200-500 per month or $15-30 per hour.

Fact checking: $17-25 per hour.

Feature articles: Anywhere from 20¢ to $4 per word; or $200-2,000 per 2,000 word article, depending on size (circulation) and reputation of magazine.

Feature article for an association: *See Business & Technical Writing.*

Ghostwriting articles (general): Up to $2 per word; or $300-3,000 per project.

Ghostwritten professional and trade journal articles under someone else's byline: $400-4,000.

Ghostwriting article for physician: $2,500-3,000.

Indexing: $15-40 per hour.

Magazine, city, calendar of events column: $150.

Magazine column: 200 words, $40; 800 words, $400. Also $1 per word. Larger circulation publications pay fees related to their regular word rate.

Manuscript consultation: $25-50 per hour.

Manuscript criticism: $40-60 per article or short story of up to 3,000 words. Also $20-25 per hour.

Picture editing: *See Editorial/Design Packages.*

Permission fees to publishers to reprint article or story: $75-500; 10-15 per word; less for charitable organizations.

Production editing: $15-25 per hour.

Proofreading: $12-20 per hour.

Poetry criticism: $25 per 16-line poem.

Research: $12-20 per hour.

Rewriting: Up to $80 per manuscript page; also $100 per published page.

Science writing for magazines: $2,000-5,000 per article. *See also Business & Technical Writing.*

Short story manuscript critique: 3,000 words, $40-60; $1.25 and up per page.

Special news article: For a business's submission to trade publication, $250-500 for 1,000 words. In Canada, 25-45¢ per word.

Stringing: 20¢-$1 per word based on circulation. Daily rate: $150-250 plus expenses; weekly rate: $900 plus expenses. Also $10-35 per hour plus expenses; $1 per column inch.

Trade journal ad copywriting: *See Advertising, Copywriting & PR.*

Trade journal feature article: For business client, $400-1,000. Also $1 per word.

Translation: $17 per hour.

Newspapers

Ads for small business: $25 for a small, one-column ad, or $10 per hour and up. *See also Advertising, Copywriting & PR.*

Arts reviewing: For weekly newspapers, $15-35; for dailies, $45 and up; for Sunday supplements, $100-400.

Book reviews: For small newspapers, byline and the book only; for larger publications, $35-200.

Column, local: $10-20 for a weekly; $15-30 for dailies of 4,000-6,000 circulation; $30-50 for 7,000-10,000 dailies; $40-75 for 11,000-25,000 dailies; and $100 and up for larger dailies.

Copyediting: $10-30 per hour; up to $40 per hour for large daily paper.

Copywriting: *See Advertising, Copywriting & PR.*

Dance criticism: $25-400 per article.

Drama criticism: Local, newspaper rates; non-local, $50 and up per review.

Editing/manuscript evaluation: $25 per hour.

Fact checking: *See Magazines & Trade Journals.*

Feature: $25-35 per article plus mileage for a weekly; $40-500 for a daily (depending on size of paper). Also 10-20¢ per word. In Canada $15-40 per word, but rates vary widely.

Feature writing, part-time: $2,000 a month for an 18-hour week.

Obituary copy: Where local newspapers permit lengthier than normal notices paid for by the funeral home (and charged to the family), $15-20. Writers are engaged by funeral homes.

Picture editing: *See Editorial/Design Packages.*

Proofreading: $20 per hour.

Science writing for newspapers: *See Business & Technical Writing.*

Stringing: Sometimes flat rate of $20-35 to cover meeting and write article; sometimes additional mileage payment.

Syndicated column, self-promoted: $5-10 each for weeklies; $10-25 per week for dailies, based on circulation.

Miscellaneous

Church history: $200-1,000 for writing 15 to 50 pages.

College/university history: $35 per hour for research through final ms.

Comedy writing for night club entertainers: Gags only, $5-25 each. Routines, $100-1,000 per minute. Some new comics may try to get a 5-minute routine for $150; others will pay $2,500 for a 5-minute bit from a top writer.

Comics writing: $35-50 per page and up for established comics writers.

Contest judging: Short manuscripts, $10 per entry; with one-page critique, $15-25. Overall contest judging: $100-500.

Copyediting and content editing for other writers: $10-50 per hour or $2-5 per page.

Craft ideas with instructions: $50-200 per project.

Encyclopedia articles: Entries in some reference books, such as biographical encyclopedias, 500-2,000 words; pay ranges from $60-80 per 1,000 words. Specialists' fees vary.

Greeting card verse: Anywhere from $25 up to $300 per sentiment, depending on the size of the company. Rates generally run higher for humorous material than for traditional. *See also Editorial/Design Packages.*

Genealogical research: $25 per hour.

Histories, family: Fees depend on whether the writer edits already prepared notes or does extensive research and writing; and the length of the work, $500-15,000.

Histories, local: Centennial history of a local church, $25 per hour for research through final manuscript for printer.

Manuscript criticism, poetry: $25 per 16 line poem.

Manuscript typing: Depending on ms length and delivery schedule, $1.25-2 per page with one copy; $15 per hour.

Party toasts, limericks, place card verses: $1.50 per line.

Research for individuals: $5-30 per hour, depending on experience, geographic area and nature of the work.

Restaurant guide features: Short article on restaurant, owner, special attractions, $20; interior, exterior photos, $25.

Special occasion booklet: Family keepsake of a wedding, anniversary, Bar Mitzvah, etc., $120 and up.

Writing for individual clients: $25-100 per hour for books; $15-20 per hour for thesis or dissertation.

A Writer's Guide to New Media Publishing

A revolution is afoot. Nearly 550 years after Gutenberg first liberated the written word from the tedium of hand copying, words have again been liberated—this time from the printed page itself. Again, it is a revolution of technology, made possible by the proliferation of faster, more capable desktop computers coupled with the development of new technologies for storing and displaying vast amounts of information in computer-readable form. Through the media of CD-ROM, commercial online services and the Internet, the home computer has become a new partner to both book and magazine publishers, a new means of expression for writers and artists of every kind, and a welcome source of information and entertainment in millions of homes.

The growth of new media

Consumers are delighted with all the wonderful new things their computers can do. No longer useful solely for crunching numbers and processing words, today's home computers are battling books and television for the family's leisure hours (and dollars). Most new computers being sold today are "multimedia capable," i.e., equipped with CD-ROM drives, enhanced sound- and video-handling capabilities and stereo speakers. It is estimated that by the beginning of 1996, in the home consumer market alone, more than 15 million multimedia personal computers will be in place. That number is expected to rise to 40 million by 1998. The upshot of this industry's growth has been the flowering of an entirely new market for digital information, and publishers unwilling to see consumer dollars diverted into revenue streams that don't flow directly to their doors have embraced multimedia technology enthusiastically. Publishing will never be the same.

Much of the growth of multimedia and electronic publishing has been fueled by consumer interest in computer games, children's products and reference works—all of which make good use of multimedia's interactivity and data-handling capacity. Early versions of electronic books tended to be less than satisfying, however; some publishers seemed to think all that was required to enter the electronic publishing arena was dumping existing texts onto a disk and marketing them to consumers. The purchaser was left with nothing more than text on her computer screen—readable, yes, but hardly an improvement over the portability and low cost of printed books. Such projects, known derisively as "shovelware," (large amounts of text simply "shoveled" onto a disk), are no longer considered viable, either commercially or artistically.

Titles that have performed the best in the marketplace are those which most effectively exploit the medium's unique capabilities. Publishers are giving more thought these days to the material they choose to release electronically. Most are attempting to ensure that the electronic products they market *make sense as electronic products*, i.e., that there are compelling reasons for these projects to be published electronically in addition to (or instead of) in a traditional print format.

Multimedia on CD-ROM

The word *multimedia* refers to the new technology's ability to combine a variety of types of media in one product. A CD-ROM (a computer-data disk the same size and

Tackling the terminology

CD-ROM—Compact Disc-Read Only Memory. A computer information storage medium capable of holding enormous amounts of data. Information on a CD-ROM cannot be deleted. A computer user must have a CD-ROM drive to access a CD-ROM.

E-mail—Electronic mail. Mail generated on a computer and delivered over a computer network to a specific individual or group of individuals. To send or receive e-mail, a user must have an account, which provides an e-mail address and electronic mailbox. Such accounts can be set up through online service providers.

Hardware—The actual computer equipment, as opposed to software, used by a computer operator. The monitor, keyboard, disk drive and printer are all examples of hardware.

Hypertext—Words or groups of words in an electronic document that are linked to other text, such as a definition or a related document. Hypertext can also be linked to illustrations.

Interactive—A type of computer interface that takes user input, such as answers to computer-generated questions, and then acts upon that input.

Internet— A worldwide network of computers that offers access to a wide variety of electronic resources.

Modem—MOdulator/DEModulator. A computer device used to send data from one computer to another via telephone line.

Multimedia—Computers and software capable of integrating text, sound, photographic-quality images, animation and video.

Network—A group of computers electronically linked to share information and resources.

Online Service Providers—Computer networks accessed via modem. These services provide users with various resources, such as electronic mail, news, weather, special interest groups and shopping. Examples of such providers include America Online and CompuServe.

Software—The computer programs that control computer hardware, usually run from a disk drive of some sort. Computers need software in order to run. These can be word processors, games, spreadsheets, etc.

World Wide Web (WWW)—An Internet resource that utilizes hypertext to access information. It also supports formatted text, illustrations and sounds, depending on the user's computer capabilities.

-by Richard Muskopf

---

shape as an audio CD), for instance, can deliver text, still photographs, animation, audio (both music and spoken word) and even video. Via CD-ROM, a multimedia encyclopedia can offer readers a text article about the Apollo 11 moon landing, an animated clip showing the trajectory of the space capsule and a video clip (with audio) of Neil Armstrong's descent from the lunar module.

Thanks to its large capacity (a CD-ROM can hold around 650 megabytes of information, the equivalent of over 150,000 pages of text), the CD-ROM is today's preferred format for delivery of memory-hungry computer games, large reference works and innovative audio/video/text products of every description. Computer games such as the phenomenally successful *Myst*, for instance, can incorporate sophisticated graphics, video and uncanny responsiveness to the person playing the game. Random House's Living Language series teaches foreign languages through tutorials, presentation of real-life speaking situations and the clever use of speech recognition technology to draw the user into conversation with the computer and give feedback on the user's pronunciation. Voyager's *With Open Eyes* lets users take a richly-detailed self-guided tour of the Art Institute of Chicago. And it's hard to imagine the preschooler who would not develop an alphabetic edge over her peers by spending a few minutes a day with Living Books' *Dr. Seuss's ABC.*

CD-ROM projects are most often put together by a team of specialists working under the direction of a project manager. Tracy Smith, editorial director of Random House Electronic Publishing, a reference and computer-information arm of the conglomerate, speaks of CD-ROMs as truly collaborative efforts. "They're complicated," she says. "A CD-ROM is usually comprised of a number of components that are contributed by different vendors or authors." Sometimes one author, or a team of authors, will handle the entire project. More often, though, authors work in collaboration with vendors, including specialists who translate the text into a searchable hypertext format and insert such elements as video clips and sound, and other specialists who design the interface for the project (what the consumer is faced with when the screen comes up). "Many publishers are doing it this way," says Smith, "because of the diverse set of talents needed to put these kinds of projects together."

Just as CD-ROMs are collaborative projects, some publishers themselves have been partnering with software development companies—as in Living Books, a partnership between Random House and Broderbund—in an effort to reach the marketplace in a financially viable way and with as much efficiency and expertise as possible.

Book and software publishers are not alone in offering their products on CD-ROM. Magazine publishers, too, are experimenting with the format. Some magazine CD-ROMs are being marketed with (or as supplemental to) the print magazines that spawned them (*Newsweek Interactive*, for example), while others, such as *NautilusCD* and *Medio*, are published *only* in CD-ROM format. While these CD-ROM periodicals are bravely exploring new frontiers and accomplishing marvelous things with the technology, it has yet to be proven that CD-ROM magazines can turn a substantial profit.

Online services and the Internet

Just as most computers sold today are multimedia capable, most also come equipped with modems, hardware components that enable computers to communicate via telephone lines with other computers. This capacity for interconnectivity, in case you've been off the planet for the last couple of years, has had an unprecedented impact on the flow of information worldwide. Whether you're navigating the Internet—the network of computer systems originally established by the U.S. government—or one of the popular commercial online services such as Prodigy, Compuserve or America Online, if you're online you have felt the impact of this new connectedness. Never before have so many people had at their fingertips the potential for accessing so much information. And never have so many people with widely divergent interests been able to find and share their enthusiasms with others of like mind. It's a global phenomenon that has publishers scrambling for potential profits.

While many magazines are experimenting with exposure on the Internet, especially on that portion of the Internet known as the World Wide Web, few have reported dramatic results with profitability. Condé Nast, the magazine conglomerate that publishes such periodicals as *Condé Nast Traveler*, *GQ*, *Vanity Fair* and *Vogue* recently

INSIDER REPORT

Authors should embrace multimedia as a new art form

One of the more time-honored elements of the act of reading literature has been the linear arrangement of the experience—you begin reading at the top of the first page and read each subsequent page, in order, until you reach the end of the book. Book authors create a certain order—a specific arrangement—of experiences for their readers, who, while they may dislike the author's orchestration of the facts, are powerless to alter them or to make a plot come out any other way than the one way in which the author put it to paper. That's all about to change.

Randi Benton, President of New Media at Random House, says that with the advent of multimedia publishing, we all might have to rethink what it means to write a story, to read a story and to derive

Photograph by Rex Miller

Randi Benton

satisfaction from literature. "I see it as a new art form," says Benton. "I think it's going to require writers who are able to think differently. We have yet to uncover the wonderful art of interactive story telling." The difference she's talking about is the difference between reading a story on the page, a story which can only be read one way, and *interacting* with a story on the computer, which, thanks to the free-form nature of CD-ROM and other multimedia content, can be read (more accurately, *experienced*) any number of ways. With sophisticated multimedia products, users don't so much read a story from one end to the other as they become immersed in a free-flowing series of situations. With a multitude of levels of story, the ability to move forward and backward in the story, and the ability to determine plot lines all left in the hands of the user, it is clear that all of us, writers and readers, are heading for a new experience of literature.

"We're starting to see some products which are interesting, but we have so much further to go," says Benton. "I think some people who write books are going to be able to write for this medium. I think this medium will also find a lot of people who are not writing linear stories, people who are writing in a very different way. I see the analogy as very similar to books and films. Some people write books and can also write screenplays, and a lot of people can't. The difference between writing books and writing for multimedia is like that, and maybe even more significant, because now you're not telling a linear story. Now you have a user, the consumer, sitting at the screen, who can stop and go—how do you develop an interesting experience with all of that? Authors are no longer totally in control of the timing, the pace of the story. When books and films are great they totally suspend our disbelief and take us to some place where we're not, and we believe we're there; it is about being controlled. And now, with multimedia, authors are giving some of that control to somebody else. It's a whole new way of thinking."

Multimedia writers are also going to have to get used to the idea of teamwork. Benton sees the best CD-ROM products of the future as being the result of collaborative efforts, and again she draws an analogy with the film industry: "Early on in this industry, you would have a programmer in his garage working on a title, producing the whole thing, from soup to nuts. But I think a much more appropriate and successful model is filmmaking, where you don't have one person doing the whole thing. You have a screenwriter, you have actors, you have a director and you have a score that's written by musical talent. Different people with different points of view are bringing their creative ideas to the product. That's what you're already starting to see on the very best multimedia titles. And I think the quality of the elements in the titles will just get better and better—the music, the writing, the voice-overs, the images, the whole thing."

Electronic publishing is an industry in its infancy, but it's maturing rapidly. One thing is certain: writers hoping to succeed in multimedia need to keep themselves informed. Profiting from the new technology will be the privilege of those who have troubled themselves to understand it. "The gap in our society is not necessarily going to be economical," says Benton, "it's going to be much more technology-driven. The gap will be between the people who really 'get' the technology and understand what to do with it and find the opportunities, and the people who don't."

announced it was forming a subsidiary—Condé Net—to develop material from its family of magazines for presentation on the World Wide Web. The move represents a substantial investment for Condé Nast, and seems to signal that publishers expect the Web will eventually be a profitable publishing medium. Other magazine publishers, among them Hearst, Hachette Filipacchi and Time Warner, are establishing Web sites as well. Some magazines, such as *Spin*, *Atlantic Monthly*, and *Scientific American* have chosen (at least for now) to team up with commercial online service providers and content themselves with receiving a portion of the service's profits calculated on the amount of time service users spend looking at their online publications. Microsoft's online service—still on the horizon at this writing—will offer magazine publishers a variety of ways to make money online, including charging users for attendance at special magazine-sponsored online events and allowing magazines to sell advertising space in their electronic publications.

It seems safe to speculate that magazines' use of the Internet as a medium of publication will continue to grow. Of course the key is profitability. As long as advertisers are willing to foot the bill, publications will feel justified in progressing with their explorations of new publishing media.

Joining the revolution

With the advent of multimedia and electronic publishing, writers are being handed a golden opportunity. Many will choose to let the opportunity pass them by, however. There is a learning curve associated with nearly every aspect of multimedia and electronic publishing, and plenty of writers still find all things computer-related either irrelevant to the art of writing, boring or vaguely upsetting. That's all right; print publishing is not going to disappear. Ignorance of computer publishing is not necessarily a dark cloud over a writer's career, but it does mean the loss of a wide array of new markets for one's work.

Mark Young is director of product development working to expand Facts on File's electronic publishing program. Multimedia publishing, says Young, offers writers a whole new world of opportunity. But writers hoping to work in multimedia must keep up with the technological developments driving the industry and they must think in terms of the capabilities of electronic publishing when they are conceiving projects. Says Young: "If you were planning to do a typical one-volume A-Z encyclopedia such as Facts on File might do, you [as the author] might think, 'Well, look, I can do it as just a book, but also in doing my research I can look out for any primary source materials that might go with it [if it were to be published as a CD-ROM].' With an electronic product you've got a lot of space, you can do so many things. If you're a writer who's interested in doing that kind of a project, you can say to the publisher, 'Look, I can do it in this format, but also it's very easy to expand this for electronic formats.' I think that's an opportunity for writers. Most people who are doing research end up with reams and reams of paper that they never use, and if they could think of a way that that can be used for an electronic format, then it's a definite opportunity."

A word about electronic rights

Electronic rights are part of the "bundle of rights" over which your copyright in an original work gives you control. With electronic publication now a tenable proposition, those rights have become an important bargaining chip between authors and publishers. Some publishers hold the position that electronic rights should be granted to them as a matter of course when an author signs the company's book contract. Those publishers argue that any success a work might be able to achieve in an electronic format is necessarily predicated on the success it first achieved in print, thanks to the publisher's efforts. Therefore, publishers should share, the argument goes, in profits derived from electronic publication. Writers and agents are, however, not necessarily buying that argument. Electronic rights, they say, belong to authors, and authors should be able to hang on to them until the best deal comes along. Authors should be wary of signing away electronic rights to a publishing company that might not be interested in or capable of exploiting those rights.

If you are interested in finding your place in publishing's new wave, you should start first by honing your computer literacy. Learn the capabilities of your computer and experiment with its modem. The next time one of the commercial online services offers you a free trial membership, which they undoubtedly will if you have made a recent computer purchase or subscribe to computer-related magazines, take them up on it. With your free online hours, spend time exploring available online magazines, many of which offer easy access to editors via e-mail; take advantage of that access to request submission guidelines and discuss article ideas with editors.

The best way to begin exploring writing opportunities in CD-ROM publishing is by exploring CD-ROMs themselves. Go to a bookstore or computer software retailer and ask to demo the available titles. Join a CD-ROM mail order club (advertised in magazines that cater to new media and computer enthusiasts) and familiarize yourself with the best new titles being published. The better acquainted you become with the possibilities of the technology, the more likely you'll be to find a place for your talents.

Mark Young suggests haunting your local library. "What I would advise for anybody is what I did when I was first considering getting involved in this: Go to the library and look at their CD-ROMS," says Young. "Some of the writers I work with get a little confused, a little intimidated by the process, because they don't quite see how this forms into the normal convention of a book—and of course it doesn't. So the thing to do is just go play with some CDs, whether in libraries or at home. Buy a few, take a look at them, and you'll begin to realize that you definitely have to have a little different mindset. Once you're working with them, though, they're not too intimidating. It's like going from a typewriter to a PC—at first you're wondering how you're ever going to work with it, but eventually it gets easier."

Educate yourself on an ongoing basis by reading computer and multimedia books and magazines. Keeping up with the changing technology is a challenge, but not impossible if your focus is on one or two niche areas. Some magazines that will keep you abreast of developments in the industry include *New Media* (P.O. Box 10639, Riverton NJ 08076-0639), *Internet World* (MecklerMedia Corporation, 20 Ketchum St., Westport CT 06880) and *CD-ROM Professional* (Pemberton Press, Inc., 462 Danbury Road, Wilton CT 06897-2126).

Important Listing Information

- *Listings are based on editorial questionnaires and interviews. They are not advertisements; publishers do not pay for their listings. The markets are not endorsed by* Writer's Market *editors.*
- *All listings have been verified before publication of this book. If a listing has not changed from last year, then the editor told us the market's needs have not changed and the previous listing continues to accurately reflect its policies. We require documentation in our files for each listing and never run a listing without its editorial office's approval.*
- Writer's Market *reserves the right to exclude any listing.*
- *When looking for a specific market, check the index. A market may not be listed for one of these reasons.*
  1. *It doesn't solicit freelance material.*
  2. *It doesn't pay for material.*
  3. *It has gone out of business.*
  4. *It has failed to verify or update its listing for the 1996 edition.*
  5. *It was in the middle of being sold at press time, and rather than disclose premature details, we chose not to list it.*
  6. *It hasn't answered* Writer's Market *inquiries satisfactorily. (To the best of our ability, and with our readers' help, we try to screen out fraudulent listings.)*
  7. *It buys few manuscripts, thereby constituting a very small market for freelancers.*
- *See the lists of changes at the end of each major section for specific information on individual markets not listed.*

Key to Symbols and Abbreviations

●—*Editorial comment offering additional market information from the editors of* Writer's Market

‡—*New listing in all sections*

*—*Subsidy book publisher in Canadian and International Book Publishers section*

□—*Cable TV market in Scriptwriting section*

ms—*manuscript;* **mss**-*manuscripts*

b&w—*black and white (photo)*

SASE—*self-addressed, stamped envelope*

SAE—*self-addressed envelope*

IRC—*International Reply Coupon, for use on reply mail in countries other than your own.*

See Glossary for definitions of words and expressions used in writing and publishing.

The Markets

Book Publishers...............................65

Book Publishers

The path to publication

The book business, for the most part, runs on hunches. Whether the idea for a book comes from a writer, an agent or the imagination of an acquiring editor, it is generally expressed in these terms: "This is a book that I *think* people will like. People will *probably* want to buy it." The decision to publish is mainly a matter of the right person, or persons, agreeing that those hunches are sound.

Ideas reach editors in a variety of ways. They arrive unsolicited every day through the mail. They come by phone, sometimes from writers but most often from agents. They arise in the editor's mind because of his daily traffic with the culture in which he lives. The acquiring editor, so named because he is responsible for securing manuscripts for his company to publish, sifts through the deluge of possibilities, waiting for a book idea to strike him as extraordinary, inevitable, profitable.

In some companies, acquiring editors possess the authority required to say, "Yes, we will publish this book." In most publishing houses, though, the acquiring editor must prepare and present the idea to a proposal committee made up of marketing and administrative personnel. Proposal committees are usually less interested in questions of extraordinariness and inevitability than they are in profitability. The editor has to convince them that it makes good business sense to publish this book.

Once a contract is signed, several different wheels are set in motion. The author, of course, writes the book if he hasn't done so already. While the editor is helping to assure that the author is making the book the best it can be, promotion and publicity people are planning mailings of review copies to influential newspapers and review periodicals, writing catalog copy that will help sales representatives push the book to bookstores, and plotting a multitude of other promotional efforts (including interview tours and bookstore signings by the author) designed to dangle the book attractively before the reading public's eye.

When the book is published, it usually receives a concerted promotional push for a month or two. After that, the fate of the book—whether it will "grow legs" and set sales records or sit untouched on bookstore shelves—rests in the hands of the public. Publishers have to compete with all of the other entertainment industries vying for the consumer's money and limited leisure time. Successful books are reprinted to meet the demand. Unsuccessful books are returned from bookstores to publishers and are sold off cheaply as "remainders" or are otherwise disposed of.

The state of the business

The book publishing business has remained healthy over the past year. Sales are up in almost every category. Much of publishing's success in recent years has been trace-able to the continuing growth of book superstores. Hundreds of the giant stores are now up and running all over the country, and many more are slated to be in place by the end of 1996. The superstore phenomenon—and the increased shelf space such stores offer—has allowed publishers to reach more customers with more books on a wider range of topics than ever before.

But that's not to say publishers are rushing to bring esoteric or highly experimental material to the marketplace. The blockbuster mentality—publishing's penchant for sticking with "name brand" novelists—still drives most large publishers. It's simply a less risky venture to continue publishing authors whom they know readers like. On the other hand, the prospects for nonfiction authors are perhaps better than they have been for years. The boom in available shelf space has provided entree to the marketplace for books on niche topics that heretofore would not have seen the light of day in most bookstores. The superstores position themselves as one-stop shopping centers for readers of every stripe. As such, they must carry books on a wide range of subjects.

Problems currently facing the publishing community include skyrocketing paper costs (which will eventually be at least partially passed along to consumers as higher book prices), and some ambivalence about if, when and how to enter the multimedia publishing market. For a full discussion of developments in multimedia and electronic publishing, see A Writer's Guide to New Media Publishing on page 56.

What's hot

The list of authors penning top-selling fiction over the past year includes few unfamiliar names. Blockbusters continued to issue forth from King, Clancy, Crichton, Clark, Grisham, Steel, Koontz and Rice, leaving little room for new blood at the top. Two books by bestseller-list newcomers that did achieve big sales were *The Celestine Prophecy*, by James Redfield, and *Politically Correct Bedtime Stories*, by James Finn Garner.

Nonfiction bestsellers were a mixed bag last year. Cooking (with celebrity tie-ins), dieting, relationships, biographies, spirituality, stereo computer images (e.g., the *Magic Eye* series) and the O.J. Simpson trial all proved of interest to large numbers of readers. Religious and spiritual topics in particular have enjoyed rapid growth lately—thought to be another baby boomer-induced phenomenon. Spiritual titles of note last year included *Crossing the Threshold of Hope*, *Catechism of the Catholic Church*, *Embraced by the Light*, and at least a half dozen angel-related titles.

How to publish your book

The markets in this year's Book Publishers section offer opportunities in nearly every area of publishing. Large, commercial houses are here as are their smaller counterparts; large and small "literary" houses are represented as well. In addition, you'll find university presses, industry-related publishers, textbook houses and more.

The Book Publishers Subject Index is the place to start. You'll find it in the back of the book, before the General Index. Subject areas for both fiction and nonfiction are broken out for the more than 900 total book publisher listings. Not all of them buy the kind of book you've written, but this Index will tell you which ones do.

When you have compiled a list of publishers interested in books in your subject area, read the detailed listings. Pare down your list by cross-referencing two or three subject areas and eliminating the listings only marginally suited to your book. When you have a good list, send for those publishers' catalogs and any writer's guidelines available. You want to make sure your book idea is not a duplicate of something they've already published. Visit bookstores and libraries to see if their books are well represented. When you find a couple of books they have published that are similar to yours, write or call the company to find out who edited these books. This last, extra bit of research could be the key to getting your proposal to precisely the right editor.

Publishers prefer different kinds of submissions on first contact. Most like to see a one-page query with SASE, especially for nonfiction. Others will accept a brief proposal package that might include an outline and/or a sample chapter. Some publishers will accept submissions from agents only. Virtually no publisher wants to see a complete manuscript on initial contact, and sending one when they prefer another method will

Ballantine Vice President and Senior Editor keeps her hands in the slush

Pamela Strickler knows that the simile concerning needles and haystacks might well have been coined by an editor searching for good, publishable material in the slush pile. But after more than 20 years in the publishing industry, she still makes it her business to look through incoming unsolicited proposals from hopeful writers.

A vice president and senior editor at Ballantine Books, Strickler is very much a hands-on editor. "I read the slush," she says, waving a hand in the direction of two three-foot-tall stacks of manuscripts and manila envelopes leaning against one wall of her office. "Those two piles are slush—about two weeks' worth. Sometimes I get seriously backed up, like four or five months; then I have

Pamela Dean Strickler

Photograph by Cori Wells Braun

trouble getting out of my office," she says, smiling. "I get a lot more slush than I get agented material, just by sheer volume. I get about 50 proposals or partial manuscripts a week, maybe a little more."

Of the unsolicited material that arrives in Strickler's office, much is interesting but, unfortunately, not right for Ballantine's program. "I get a lot of perfectly good novels that, 10 or 15 years ago, would have been fine mass-market, midlist originals," she says. "But now we really don't publish that many books in the midlist."

Opportunities in the midlist—that section of a publisher's list reserved for books that are not considered highly promotable or likely to become blockbusters, formerly a great route to publication for new writers trying to establish themselves—have shrunk dramatically, according to Strickler. While much "category" or genre fiction is still published in the midlist, fewer and fewer mainstream novels are. "We can't sell them," says Strickler. "The business has changed radically." Among the market forces that Strickler cites as being responsible for the change is price. "Our cover prices are much higher than they were 20 years ago," she says. "A lot of people cannot afford to go in and buy five romances at a time any more. And readers have become wary; they're not so willing to take a chance on an unknown author—and I don't blame them. Our customers want satisfaction for their dollars." The reader's quest for economic and aesthetic satisfaction leads many to forsake books by unknown writers in favor of sticking with old favorites. Fewer midlist readers—any way you figure it—means a decreased demand for midlist writers. Not only Ballantine, but many other publishers as well, have trimmed their midlists and are putting their marketing efforts and promotional dollars behind books they think stand a better-than-average chance in the marketplace.

Is this unreservedly bad news for writers? Not necessarily. Strickler sees small presses and university presses taking over some of the publication of books that would heretofore have been right for the larger publishers' midlist slots. "There are so many wonderful regional publishers and some university presses that are doing fiction very nicely now; they do business on a different scale than a huge place like Ballantine/Random House. They can do very nicely with regional books, selling them regionally, in a smart way. And I would suggest to some of these writers that after they've tried the New York publishers, look locally."

Before submitting to Ballantine, take a look at the company's listing on page 85. Then, through bookstore research, familiarize yourself with the books they are publishing. If, after your preliminary research, you're convinced you've got an idea that's right for them, here's what Strickler likes to see:

• A one- or two-page query letter. "Tell me what the book is in two sentences and a little about your background, especially if you have any kind of track record.

• The *first* 100 pages of text. "I especially *dis*like seeing selected chapters."

• A short synopsis of the story.

Once your proposal reaches Strickler, her decision whether to keep reading or to politely decline is based on a few clear and simple criteria. "I like fresh ideas and excellent writing. And pure storytelling talent; it's a rare gift."

---

signal to the publisher "this is an amateur's submission." Editors do not have the time to read an entire manuscript, even editors at small presses who receive fewer submissions. Perhaps the only exceptions to this rule are children's book manuscripts and poetry manuscripts, which take only as much time to read as an outline and sample chapter anyway.

In your one-page query, give an overview of your book, mention the intended audience, the competition (check *Books in Print* and local bookstore shelves), and what sets your book apart. Detail any previous publishing experience or special training relevant to the subject of your book. All of this information will help your cause; it is the professional approach.

Only one in a thousand writers will sell a book to the first publisher they query, especially if the book is the writer's first effort. Make a list of a dozen or so publishers that might be interested in your book. Try to learn as much about the books they publish and their editors as you can. Research, knowing the specifics of your subject area, and a professional approach are often the difference between acceptance and rejection. You are likely to receive at least a few rejections, however, and when that happens, don't give up. Rejection is as much a part of publishing, if not more, than signing royalty checks. Send your query to the next publisher on your list. You may be able to speed up the process at this early stage by sending simultaneous queries, but do so only to publishers who state they accept them.

Personalize your queries by addressing them individually and mentioning what you know about a company from its catalog or books you've seen. Never send a form letter as a query. Envelopes addressed to "Editor" or "Editorial Department" end up in the dreaded slush pile.

If a publisher offers you a contract, you may want to seek advice before signing and returning it. An author's agent will very likely take 15% if you employ one, but you could be making 85% of a larger amount. For more information on literary agents, contact the Association of Author's Representatives, 10 Astor Place, 3rd Floor, New York NY 10003, (212)353-3709. Also check the current edition of *Guide to Literary Agents* (Writer's Digest Books). Attorneys will only be able to tell you if everything is legal, not if you are getting a good deal, unless they have prior experience with literary contracts. If you have a legal problem, you might consider contacting Volunteer Lawyers for the Arts, 1 E. 53rd St., 6th Floor, New York NY 10022, (212)319-2787.

Special notice about subsidy publishing

Following the listings of Book Producers, you'll find listings of Subsidy/Royalty Publishers.

Subsidy publishing involves paying money to a publishing house to publish a book. The source of the money could be a government, foundation or university grant, or it could be the author of the book. When a book publisher has informed us that it considers author-subsidy arrangements, we have placed that publisher in the Subsidy/Royalty section. For more information on subsidy publishing, see the introduction to Subsidy/Royalty Book Publishers on page 276.

Writer's Market is primarily a reference tool to help you sell your writing, and we encourage you to work with publishers that pay a royalty. If one of the publishers in the Book Publishers section offers you an author-subsidy arrangement (sometimes called "cooperative publishing" or "co-publishing") or asks you to pay for all or part of the cost of any aspect of publishing (printing, advertising, etc.) or asks you to guarantee the purchase of any number of the books yourself, we would like you to let us know about that company immediately.

Publishers are offering more author-subsidy arrangements than ever before. Some publishers feel they must seek them to expand their lists beyond the capabilities of their limited resources. While this may be true, and you may be willing to agree to it, we would like to keep subsidy publishers and royalty publishers separate, so that you will be able to choose more easily between them.

Publishers that publish fewer than four books per year, but not more than 50% of them on an author-subsidy basis, are still listed in Small Presses with an asterisk (*). Author-subsidy publishers in Canada are also denoted with an asterisk (*), and are listed in Canadian and International Book Publishers.

For a list of publishers according to their subjects of interest, see the nonfiction and fiction sections of the Book Publishers Subject Index. Information on some book publishers and producers not included in this edition of *Writer's Market* can be found in Book Publishers and Producers/Changes '95-'96.

A.R.E. PRESS, 68th St. and Atlantic Ave., P.O. Box 656, Virginia Beach VA 23451-0656. (804)428-3588. Fax: (804)422-6926. Editor-in-Chief: Jon Robertson. Publishes hardcover and trade paperback originals. Publishes 14 titles/year. Receives 400 proposals and mss/year. 75% of books from first-time authors; 95% from unagented writers. Pays 10-15% royalty on net receipts after returns and discounts. Offers $2,000 advance. Publishes book 18 months after acceptance of ms. Reports in 2 months on queries. No unsolicited mss. Book catalog and author's guidelines for #10 SASE.

Nonfiction: "While we market books to the general public, proprosals must have a connection to the Edgar Cayce psychic material. We seek proposals for topical books that show how to apply the Cayce spiritual principles, and also strong stories of people who have applied them successfully in their lives. Mistakes are made when writers do not follow our Author Guidelines, and are not familiar with the thrust of the Cayce

material." Query or submit chapter outline with 3 sample chapters, including cover letter and brief synopsis.
Recent Nonfiction Title: *A Physician's Diary* by Dr. Dana Myatt.

Fiction: "We consider spiritual and metaphysical fiction that has an uplifting slant and is compatible with the Cayce philosophy. We are especially interested in novels that treat the topics of reincarnation and psychic phenomenon. We reject anything that could be considered 'dark' or 'occult'." Query first.

Tips: "Our audience is comprised of people of all ages, races and religious persuasions who are seeking deeper insights into themselves, their spirituality, and their connection to God. Keep your queries and proposals brief and to the point. Please don't send superfluous material with your proposal. Always send SASE."

ABBOTT, LANGER & ASSOCIATES, 548 First St., Crete IL 60417-2199. (708)672-4200. President: Dr. Steven Langer. Estab. 1967. Publishes trade paperback originals and loose-leaf books. Averages 25 titles/ year, mostly prepared inhouse. Receives 25 submissions/year. 10% of books from first-time authors; 90% of books from unagented writers. Pays 10-15% royalty. Publishes book 18 months after acceptance. Query for electronic submissions. Book catalog for 6×9 SAE with 2 first-class stamps. Reports in 1 month on queries, 3 months on mss.

Nonfiction: How-to, reference, technical on some phase of human resources management, security, sales management, etc. Especially needs "a very limited number (3-5) of books dealing with very specialized topics in the field of human resource management, wage and salary administration, sales compensation, recruitment, selection, etc." Publishes for human resources directors, wage and salary administrators, sales/ marketing managers, security directors, etc. Query with outline. Reviews artwork/photos.

Tips: "A writer has the best chance selling our firm a how-to book in human resources management, sales/ marketing management or security management."

ABC-CLIO, INC., 50 S. Steele St., Suite 805, Denver CO 80209-2813. (303)333-3003. Fax: (303)333-4037. Subsidiaries include ABC-CLIO Ltd. President: Heather Cameron. Editorial Director: Jeffrey Serena. Estab. 1955. Publishes hardcover originals. Averages 35 titles/year. Receives 500 submissions/year. 20% of books from first-time authors; 95% from unagented writers. Pays royalty on net receipts. Publishes ms 10 months after acceptance. Query for electronic submissions. Reports in 2 months on queries. Book catalog and ms guidelines free.

Nonfiction: Reference. Subjects include art/architecture, education, environmental issues, government/politics, history, literary studies, multicultural studies, mythology, science, women's issues/studies. "Looking for reference books on current world issues, women's issues, and for subjects compatible with high school curriculum. No monographs or textbooks." Query or submit outline and sample chapters.

Recent Nonfiction Title: *Encyclopedia of American Indian Costume.*

THE ABERDEEN GROUP, 426 S. Westgate St., Addison IL 60101. (708)543-0870. Fax: (708)543-3112. Managing Editor: Desiree Hanford. Publishes trade paperback originals. Publishes 6 titles/year. Receives 12 queries and 6 mss/year. 10% of books from first-time authors; 100% from unagented writers. Pays 6-18% royalty on retail price. Offers $1,000-3,000 advance. Publishes book 6 months after acceptance of ms. Accepts simultaneous submissions. Query for electronic submissions. Reports in 1 month on queries and proposals, 2 months on mss. Book catalog free on request.

Nonfiction: How-to, technical. Subjects include architecture, construction, general engineering and construction business. Query with outline, 2-3 sample chapters, definition of topic, features, market.

Recent Nonfiction Title: *Nondestructive Evaluation & Testing of Masonry Structures*, by Suprenant/Schullor (how-to/technical).

ABINGDON PRESS, Imprint of The United Methodist Publishing House, P.O. Box 801, Nashville TN 37202-0801. (615)749-6301. Fax: (615)748-6512. President/Publisher: Robert K. Feaster. Editorial Director/Vice President: Neil M. Alexander. Managing Director/Assistant Editorial Director: Michael E. Lawrence. Senior Editor General Interest Books & Resources Books: Mary Catherine Dean. Senior Editor Academic Books: Rex Mathews. Senior Editor United Methodist Newscope: J. Richard Peck. Lead Editor, Professional Books: Paul Franklyn. Lead Editor, Reference Books: Jack Keller. Estab. 1789. Publishes hardcover and paperback originals and reprints; church supplies. Average 100 titles/year. Receives approximately 2,500 submissions/ year. Few books from first-time writers; 90-95% of books from unagented writers. Average print order for a first book is 4,000-5,000. Pays royalty. Publishes book 2 years after acceptance. Query for electronic submissions. Manuscript guidelines for SASE. Reports in 3 months.

Nonfiction: Religious-lay and professional, children's religious books, academic texts. Length: 32-300 pages. Query with outline and samples only.

‡ABSEY & CO., 18351 Kuyendahl, #142, Spring TX 77379. Editorial Director: Jerry J. James. Publishes hardcover, trade paperback and mass market paperback originals. Publishes 15-25 titles/year. 50% of books from first-time authors; 50% from unagented writers. Pays 8-15% royalty on wholesale price. Publishes book 6 months after acceptance of ms. Accepts simultaneous submissions. Reports in 3 months on queries. Manuscript guidelines for #10 SASE.

Nonfiction: Children's/juvenile, cookbook (with a unique twist, e.g., cooking for busy teachers—something along those lines), how-to for teachers. Education subjects. "We are looking primarily for education books, especially those with teaching strategies based upon research. Often writers submit mss in which the voice isn't strong." Query with outline and 1-2 sample chapters. Reviews artwork/photos as part of ms package. Send photocopies, transparencies, etc.

Recent Nonfiction Title: *Jesus Didn't Use Worksheets*, by Dr. Joyce Carroll and Dr. Ron Habermas (education).

Fiction: Humor, juvenile, literary, mainstream/contemporary, short story collections. "Since we are a small, new press, we are looking for good manuscripts with a firm intended audience. As yet, we haven't explored this market. We feel more comfortable starting with nonfiction—educational. A mistake we often see in submissions is writers underwrite or overwrite—a lack of balance." Query with SASE.

Poetry: "We are primarily interested in narrative poems." Submit 6 sample poems or complete ms.

Recent Poetry Title: *Poems After Lunch*, edited by Joyce Armstrong Carroll and Edward E. Wilson (primarily narrative).

‡ACA BOOKS, 1 E. 53rd St., 3rd Floor, New York NY 10022. (212)223-2787. Publications Editor: Daniel Jones. Publishes trade paperback originals and reprints. Publishes 5-6 titles/year. Receives 40 queries and 15 mss/year. 100% of mss from unagented writers. Pays 10-12½% royalty. Publishes book 1 year after acceptance of ms. Accepts simultaneous submissions. Query for electronic submissions. Reports in 2 months on queries. Book catalog free on request.

Nonfiction: How-to, reference, textbook. Subjects include art/architecture, education and government/politics. "We do *not* publish art books (i.e. studies of artwork, coffee table books). We are most interested in books on careers in the arts, arts policy, arts education, arts fundraising and management. Query.

Recent Nonfiction Titles: *Arts Education for the 21st Century American Economy*, by Bruce O. Boston (arts education policy).

ACADEMY CHICAGO, 363 W. Erie St., Chicago IL 60610-3125. (312)751-7300. Fax: (312)751-7306. Editorial Director/Senior Editor: Anita Miller. Assistant Editor: Catherine Prendergast. Estab. 1975. Publishes hardcover and paperback originals and reprints. Averages 20 titles/year. Receives approximately 2,000 submissions/year. Average print order for a first book is 1,500-5,000. Pays 7-10% royalty. Modest advances. Publishes book 18 months after acceptance. Book catalog for 9×12 SAE with 5 first-class stamps. Manuscript guidelines for #10 SASE. Query with first 4 chapters and SASE. Reports in 2 months.

● The editor reports this press is cutting back on publishing fiction.

Nonfiction: Adult, biography, historical, travel, true crime, reprints. No how-to, cookbooks, self-help, etc. Query and submit first 4 consecutive chapters.

Recent Nonfiction Title: *No Tears for Mao*, by Niu-Nisi.

Fiction: Mainstream novels, mysteries. No romantic, children's, young adult, religious or sexist fiction; nothing avant-garde. Query with first 3 chapters.

Recent Fiction Title: *Sam and His Brother Len*, by John Mandarino.

Tips: "At the moment, we are looking for good nonfiction; we certainly want excellent original fiction, but we are swamped. No fax queries, no disks. We are always interested in reprinting good out of print books."

ACCENT ON LIVING, Subsidiary of Cheever Publishing, Inc., P.O. Box 700, Bloomington IL 61702. (309)378-2961. Fax: (309)378-4420. Editor: Betty Garee. Publishes 4 titles/year. Receives 300 queries and 150 mss/year. 70% of books from first-time authors; 100% from unagented writers. Pays 6% royalty or makes outright purchase. Publishes book 3 months after acceptance of ms. Accepts simultaneous submissions. Query for electronic submissions. Reports on queries in 1 month. Book catalog for 8×10 SAE with 2 first-class stamps. Manuscript guidelines for #10 SASE.

Nonfiction: How-to. Anything pertaining to physically disabled. Query. Reviews artwork/photos as part of ms package. Send snapshots or slides.

Recent Nonfiction Title: *If It Weren't for the Honor, I'd Rather Have Walked*, by Jan Little.

ACCENT PUBLICATIONS, P.O. Box 36640, Colorado Springs CO 80936-3664. (719)536-0100 ext. 337. Managing Editor: Mary B. Nelson. Estab. 1947. Publishes evangelical Christian education and church resource products. Pays royalty on cover price or purchases outright. Publishes book 1 year after acceptance. Query or submit 3 sample chapters, brief synopsis and chapter outline. Do not submit full ms unless requested. No phone calls, please. Reports in 8 months. Manuscript guidelines for #10 SASE.

● No longer considers fiction.

Nonfiction: "We are currently soliciting only nonfiction proposals in the areas of Christian education and Church Resources. C.E. products are teaching tools designed for the volunteer or professional Christian leadership to use in the church's education process. Church Resources are products that can be used in any aspect of the local church ministry. We would consider Bible studies, study guides, teacher helps, ministry aids, and other C.E. products. We do not consider fiction for children, youth, or adults. We do not consider

devotionals, poetry, biographies, autobiographies, personal experience stories, manuscripts with a charismatic emphasis, or general Christian living books."
Nonfiction Title: *Missions Made Fun for Kids.*

ACCORD COMMUNICATIONS, LTD., 18002 15th Ave. NE, Suite B, Seattle WA 98155. Managing Editor: Karen Duncan. Imprints are Evergreen Pacific Publishing, Larry Reynolds, Managing Editor; A.K.A. Seattle Books, Karen Duncan, Managing Editor. Publishes hardcover originals and trade paperback originals and reprints. Publishes 7 titles/year. Receives 200 queries and 350 mss/year. 80% of books from first-time authors; 100% from unagented writers. Pays royalty on wholesale price. Publishes ms 1 year after acceptance. Accepts simultaneous submissions. Reports in 3 months on proposals.
  • Due to a backlog of material, Accord Communications will not be reviewing manuscripts until mid-1996. Call before submitting.
Nonfiction: How-to (marine-related), reference, atlases and guides, hobbies, recreation, mystery criticism, history. Query. Reviews artwork/photos as part of ms package. Send photocopies.
Recent Nonfiction Title: *Cruising Guide to the West Coast of Vancouver Island*, by Don Watmough (text, photos and charts for boaters).
Fiction: Mystery. Submit synopsis with 3 sample chapters. "We plan to publish traditional detective/amateur sleuth mysteries, preferably with series characters."
Recent Fiction Title: *In Blacker Moments*, by S.E. Schenkel.

ACE SCIENCE FICTION, Imprint of The Berkley Publishing Group, 200 Madison Ave., New York NY 10016. (212)686-9820. Editor: Laura Anne Gilman. Estab. 1953. Publishes paperback originals and reprints. Averages 96 titles/year. Reports in 3-6 months. Manuscript guidelines for #10 SASE.
Fiction: Science fiction, fantasy. Query with synopsis and first 3 chapters.
Recent Fiction Title: *Spindoc*, by Steve Perry.

‡ACRES U.S.A., P.O. Box 8800, Metairie LA 70011. (504)889-2100. Publisher: Fred C. Walters. Imprint is Halcyon House Publishers, Inc. Publishes trade paperback originals. Publishes 6 titles/year. Pay negotiated—percentage of selling price. Publishes book 6 months after acceptance of ms. Accepts simultaneous submissions. Reports in 1 month on queries. Book catalog and ms guidelines free.
Nonfiction: Technical. "We only publish on sustainable agriculture. Writers often make the mistake of submitting work that is outside our area." Query.

‡ACROPOLIS SOUTH, 415 Wood Duck Dr., Sarasota FL 34236. (813)953-5214. Editor/Publisher: Alphons J. Hackl. Publishes hardcover originals. Publishes 6-8 titles/year. Receives 100 queries/year. 80% of books from first-time authors; 90% from unagented writers. Pays 10-18% royalty on net receipts. Offers $500-2,000 advance (only occasionally). Publishes book 8-10 months after acceptance of ms. Reports in 1 month on queries.
Nonfiction: Biography, how-to, self-help. Subjects include cooking/foods/nutrition, government/politics, health/medicine. "Books should be of social significance and have a promotional base." Query with outline, sample chapter and previous writings.
Recent Nonfiction Titles: *Staying Alive! Your Crime Prevention Guide*, by Richard A. Fike, Sr.

ACTA PUBLICATIONS, 4848 N. Clark St., Chicago IL 60640-4711. Co-Publishers: Gregory F. Augustine Pierce, Thomas R. Artz. Estab. 1958. Publishes trade paperback originals. Publishes 10 titles/year. Receives 50 queries and 15 mss/year. 50% of books from first-time authors; 90% from unagented writers. Pays 7½-12½% royalty on wholesale price. Publishes book 1 year after acceptance of ms. No simultaneous submissions. Reports in 2 months on proposals. Book catalog and author guidelines for SASE.
Nonfiction: Religion. "We publish non-academic, practical books aimed at the mainline religious market." Submit outline and 1 sample chapter. Reviews artwork/photos as part of ms package. Send photocopies.
Tips: "Don't send a submission unless you have read our catalog or one of our books."

ACTIVE PARENTING PUBLISHERS, INC., 810-B Franklin Court, Marietta GA 30067. Fax: (404)429-0334. Editorial Manager: Suzanne De Galan. Publishes 4 titles/year. Receives 100 queries and 25 mss/year. 75% of books from unagented writers. Pays 6-10% royalty on retail price. Publishes book 1 year after acceptance of ms. Accepts simultaneous submissions. Query for electronic submissions. Reports in 2 months on proposals. Book catalog for 8½×11 SAE with 4 first-class stamps.

 The double dagger before a listing indicates that the listing is new in this edition. New markets are often more receptive to freelance submissions.

Nonfiction: Self-help, textbook, educational. Subjects include child guidance/parenting, psychology, loss, self-esteem. Nonfiction work; mainly parent education and family issues. Submit outline and 2 sample chapters.

Recent Nonfiction Title: *Active Teaching Leader's Guide*, by Michael H. Popkin, Ph.D. (textbook).

ADAMS PUBLISHING, (formerly Bob Adams, Inc.), 260 Center St., Holbrook MA 02343. (617)767-8100. Fax: (617)767-0994. Managing Editor: Chris Ciaschini. Estab. 1980. Publishes hardcover and trade paperback originals. Averages 50 titles/year. Receives 1,000 submissions/year. 25% of books from first-time authors; 25% of books from unagented writers. Variable royalty "determined on case-by-case basis." Publishes book 12-18 months after acceptance. Reports in 6-8 weeks "if interested. We accept no responsibility for unsolicited manuscripts." Book catalog for 9 × 12 SAE with 10 first-class stamps.

Nonfiction: Reference books on careers, self-help, business. Query with SASE.

Recent Nonfiction Title: *101 Reasons Why A Cat Is Better Than a Man*, by Allen Zobel and Nicole Hollander.

ADAMS-BLAKE PUBLISHING, 8041 Sierra St., Fair Oaks CA 95628. (916)962-9296. Vice President: Paul Raymond. Senior Editor: Monica Blane. Publishes trade paperback originals and reprints. Publishes 10-15 titles/year. Receives 150 queries and 90 mss/year. 90% of books from first-time authors; 90% from unagented writers. Pays 10% royalty on wholesale price. Publishes book 6 months after acceptance of ms. Accepts simultaneous submissions. Reports in 1 month on mss.

Nonfiction: How-to, technical. Subjects include business and economics, computers and electronics, health/medicine, money/finance, software. "We are looking for business, technology and finance titles that can be targeted to older or retired members of the workforce. We also seek information on data that can be bound/packaged and sold to specific industry groups at high margins." Query with sample chapters or complete ms. Reviews artwork/photos as part of ms package. Send photocopies.

Recent Nonfiction Title: *Code 911: Emergency Procedures For Apartment Communities*, by John Macilta (real estate).

Tips: "We will take a chance on material the big houses reject. Since we sell the majority of our material directly, we can publish material for a very select market. Author should include a marketing plan. Sell us on the project!"

‡ADDICUS BOOKS, INC., P.O. Box 37327, Omaha NE 68137. President: Rod Colvin. Publishes trade paperback originals. Publishes 4-5 titles/year. 70% of books from first-time authors; 60% from unagented writers. Pays royalty on retail price. Publishes book 9 months after acceptance of ms. Accepts simultaneous submissions. Does not accept electronic submissions. Reports in 1 month on proposals. Book catalog and ms guidelines for #10 SASE.

Nonfiction: How-to, self-help. Subjects include Americana, business and economics, health/medicine, psychology, regional, true-crime. "We look for solidly written books with regional audiences; with true crime, we're looking for well-written, well-researched manuscripts with interesting stories behind the crimes." Query with outline and 3-4 sample chapters.

Recent Nonfiction Title: *Straight Talk About Breast Cancer*, by Suzanne Braddock, MD (health).

Fiction: Query with overview of book and author credentials; include proposal with chapter-by-chapter outline and 3-4 sample chapters; SASE.

AFRICAN AMERICAN IMAGES, 1909 W. 95th St., Chicago IL 60643. (312)445-0322. Publisher: Dr. Jawanza Kunjufu. Publishes trade paperback originals. Publishes 10 titles/year. Receives 520 queries and 520 mss/year. 90% of books from first-time authors; 95% from unagented writers. Pays 10% royalty on wholesale price. Publishes book 6 months after acceptance of ms. Accepts simultaneous submissions. Reports in 1 month on queries, 2 months on mss. Book catalog and ms guidelines free on request.

Nonfiction: Children's/juvenile. Subjects include education, ethnic, history, psychology. Submit complete ms.

Fiction: Juvenile.

ALASKA NORTHWEST BOOKS, Imprint of Graphic Arts Center Publishing. Editorial offices: Suite 300, 2208 NW Market St., Seattle WA 98107. (206)784-5071. Fax: (206)784-5316. Contact: Acquisitions Editor. Estab. 1959. Publishes hardcover and trade paperback originals and reprints. Averages 15 titles/year. Receives hundreds of submissions/year. 30% of books from first-time authors; 80% from unagented writers. Pays 10-15% royalty on wholesale price. Buys mss outright (rarely). Offers advance. Publishes book an average of 1 year after acceptance. Accepts simultaneous submissions. Reports in 6 months on queries. Book catalog and ms guidelines for 9 × 12 SAE with 6 first-class stamps.

● Editor reports this house is initating more of their own projects and publishing fewer unsolicited manuscripts.

Nonfiction: "All written for a general readership, not for experts in the subject." Subjects include nature and environment, travel, cookbooks, Native American culture, adventure, outdoor recreation and sports, the arts, children's books. "Our book needs are as follows: one-quarter Alaskan focus, one-quarter Northwest, one-quarter Pacific coast, one-quarter national (looking for logical extensions of current subjects)." Submit outline/synopsis and sample chapters.

Recent Nonfiction Title: *The Last Light Breaking: Living Among Alaska's Inupiat Eskimos,* by Nick Jans.

Tips: "Book proposals that are professionally written and polished, with a clear market receive our most careful consideration. We are looking for originality. We publish a wide range of books for a wide audience. Some of our books are clearly for travelers, others for those interested in outdoor recreation or various regional subjects. If I were a writer trying to market a book today, I would research the competition (existing books) for what I have in mind, and clearly (and concisely) express why my idea is different and better. I would describe the bookbuyers (and readers)—where they are, how many of them are there, how they can be reached (organizations, publications), why they would want or need my book."

THE ALBAN INSTITUTE, 4550 Montgomery Ave., Suite 433 North, Bethesda MD 20814-3341. (301)718-4407. Fax: (301)718-1958. Editor-in-Chief: Celia A. Hahn. Publishes trade paperback originals. Averages 9 titles/year. Receives 100 submissions/year. 100% of books from unagented writers. Pays 7-10% royalty on books; makes outright purchse of $50-100 on publication for 450-3,600 word articles relevant to congregational life—practical—ecumenical. Publishes book 1 year after acceptance. Reports in 4 months. Proposals must be submitted, no unsolicited mss. Book catalog and ms guidelines for 9×12 SAE with 3 first-class stamps.

Nonfiction: Religious—focus on local congregation—ecumenical. Must be accessible to general reader. Research preferred. Needs mss on the task of the ordained leader in the congregation, the career path of the ordained leader in the congregation, problems and opportunities in congregational life, and ministry of the laity in the world and in the church. No sermons, devotional, children's titles, novels, inspirational or prayers. Query for guidelines.

Tips: "Our audience is comprised of intelligent, probably liberal mainline Protestant and Catholic clergy and lay leaders, executives and seminary administration/faculty—people who are concerned with the local church at a practical level and new approaches to its ministry. We are looking for titles on problems and opportunities in congregational life, the clergy role and career, and the ministry of the laity in the church and in the world."

ALLEN PUBLISHING CO., 7324 Reseda Blvd., Reseda CA 91335. (818)344-6788. Owner/Publisher: Michael Wiener. Estab. 1979. Publishes mass market paperback originals. Averages 4 titles/year. Receives 50-100 submissions/year. 50% of books from first-time authors; 90% from unagented writers. Makes outright purchase for negotiable sum. Publishes book 6 months after acceptance. Accepts simultaneous submissions. Reports in 2 weeks. *Writer's Market* recommends allowing 2 months for reply. Book catalog and writer's guidelines for #10 SASE.

• This publisher reports having received many manuscripts outside its area of interest. Writers are encouraged to follow the publisher's subject matter guidelines.

Nonfiction: How-to, self-help. Subjects include how to start various businesses and how to improve your financial condition. "We want self-help material, 25,000 words approximately, aimed at wealth-builders, opportunity seekers, aspiring entrepreneurs. We specialize in material for people who are relatively inexperienced in the world of business and have little or no capital to invest. Material must be original and authoritative, not rehashed from other sources. All our books are marketed exclusively by mail, in soft-cover, 8½×11 format. We are a specialty publisher and will not consider anything that does not exactly meet our needs." Query. Reviews artwork/photos as part of ms package.

Recent Nonfiction Title: *How to Make Money In Your Own Home-Based Business.*

Tips: "We are a specialty publisher, as noted above. If your subject does not match our specialty, do not waste your time and ours by submitting a query we cannot possibly consider."

ALLWORTH PRESS, 10 E. 23rd St., New York NY 10010-4402. Editor: Ted Gachot. Estab. 1989. Publisher: Tad Crawford. Publishes trade paperback originals. Publishes 10 titles/year. Pays 6-7½% royalty (for paperback) on retail price. Reports in 1 month on queries and proposals. Book catalog and ms guidelines free on request.

Nonfiction: How-to, reference. Subjects include the business aspects of art, design, photography, writing, as well as legal guides for the public. "We are trying to give ordinary people advice to better themselves in practical ways—as well as helping creative people in the fine and commercial arts." Query.

ALMAR PRESS, 4105 Marietta Dr., Vestal NY 13850-4032. (607)722-0265. Fax: (607)722-3545. Editor-in-Chief: A.N. Weiner. Managing Editor: M.F. Weiner. Estab. 1977. Publishes hardcover and paperback originals and reprints. Averages 8 titles/year. Receives 200 submissions/year. 75% of books from first-time authors; 100% from unagented writers. Average print order for a first book is 2,000. Pays 10% royalty. No advance. Publishes book 6 months after acceptance. Prefers exclusive submissions; however, accepts simultaneous submissions, if so noted. Query for electronic submissions. Reports within 2 months. Book catalog for #10 SAE with 2 first-class stamps. Submissions *must* include SASE for reply.

Nonfiction: Publishes business, technical, regional, consumer books and reports. "These main subjects include general business, financial, travel, career, technology, personal help, Northeast regional, hobbies, general medical, general legal, how-to. *Almar Reports* are business and technology subjects published for management use and prepared in $8\frac{1}{2} \times 11$ book format. Reprint publications represent a new aspect of our business." Submit outline and sample chapters. Reviews artwork/photos as part of ms package.

Tips: "We're adding a new series of postcard books for various topics where the picture postcards are illustrated and the captions describe the scene on the postcard and the history related to it. Approximately 225 illustrations per book. We would like to expand our books on avoiding crime problems in business and personal life. We are open to any suggested topic. This type of book will be important to us. We look for timely subjects. The type of book the writer has the best chance of selling to our firm is something different or unusual—*no* poetry or fiction, also *no* first-person travel or family history. The book must be complete and of good quality."

‡ALPINE PUBLICATIONS, 225 S. Madison Ave., Loveland CO 80537. Publisher: Ms. B.J. McKinney. Imprint is Blue Ribbon Books. Publishes hardcover and trade paperback originals and reprints. Publishes 6-10 titles/year. 50% of books from first-time authors; 95% from unagented writers. Pays 7-15% royalty on wholesale price or occasionally makes outright purchase. Publishes book 1 year after acceptance of ms. Accepts simultaneous submissions. Reports in 1 month on queries; 3 months on mss. Book catalog free on request. Manuscript guidelines for #10 SASE.
Nonfiction: Coffee table book, how-to, illustrated book, reference. Animal subjects. "Alpine specializes in books that promote the enjoyment of and responsibility for companion animals with emphasis on dogs, cats and horses." Submit 2-3 sample chapters with SASE. Reviews artwork/photos as part of ms package. Send photocopies.
Recent Nonfiction Title: *The Mentally Sound Dog*, by Clark (dog behavior modification).
Fiction: "We publish fiction only occasionally. Must fit our established audience and markets."
Tips: Audience is pet owners, animal breeders and exhibitors, veterinarians, animal trainers, animal care specialists, judges. "We prefer to work directly with authors, not through agents. Look up some of our titles before you submit. See what is unique about our books. Write your proposal to suit our guidelines."

ALYSON PUBLICATIONS, INC., 40 Plympton St., Boston MA 02118-2425. (617)542-5679. Director: Alistair Williamson. Estab. 1979. Imprints are Lace, Alyson Wonderland and Perineum Press. Publishes trade paperback originals and reprints. Averages 30 titles/year. Receives 500 submissions/year. 40% of books from first-time authors; 80% from unagented writers. Average print order for a first book is 6,000. Pays 8-15% royalty on net price. Offers $1,000-3,000 advance. Publishes book 15 months after acceptance. Reports in 1 month. *Writer's Market* recommends allowing 2 months for reply. Book catalog and ms guidelines for 6×9 SAE with 3 first-class stamps.
Nonfiction: Gay/lesbian subjects. "We are especially interested in nonfiction providing a positive approach to gay/lesbian issues." Accepts nonfiction translations. Submit 2-page outline. Reviews artwork/photos as part of ms package with SASE.
Recent Nonfiction Title: *The Next Step*, edited by Jean Swallow.
Fiction: Gay novels. Accepts fiction translations. Submit 1-2 page synopsis with SASE.
Recent Fiction Title: *B-Boy Blues*, by James Earl Hardy.
Tips: "We publish many books by new authors. The writer has the best chance of selling to our firm well-researched, popularly-written nonfiction on a subject (e.g., some aspect of gay history) that has not yet been written about much. With fiction, create a strong storyline that makes the reader want to find out what happens. With nonfiction, write in a popular style for a non-academic audience. Actively soliciting manuscripts aimed at kids of lesbian and gay parents."

AMACOM BOOKS, Imprint of American Management Association, 135 W. 50th, New York NY 10020-1201. (212)903-8081. Managing Director: Weldon P. Rackley. Estab. 1923. Publishes hardcover and trade paperback originals and trade paperback reprints. Averages 68 titles/year. Receives 200 submissions/year. 50% of books from first-time authors; 90% from unagented writers. Pays 10-15% royalty on net receipts by the publisher. Publishes book 9 months after acceptance. Query for electronic submissions. Reports in 2 months. Free book catalog and proposal guidelines.
Nonfiction: Publishes business books of all types, including management, marketing, technology (computers), career, professional skills, small business. Retail, direct mail, college, corporate markets. Query. Submit outline/synopsis, sample chapters, résumé/vita.
Tips: "Our audience consists of people in the business sector looking for practical books on business issues, strategies, and tasks."

AMADEUS PRESS, Timber Press, Inc., 133 SW Second Ave., Suite 450, Portland OR 97204. (503)227-2878. Fax: (503)227-3070. Editorial Director: Karen Kirtley. Publishes hardcover originals and reprints and trade paperback originals. Publishes 8-10 titles/year. Receives 150 queries and 25 mss/year. 50% of books from first-time authors; 95% from unagented writers. Pays 10% royalty on net billings. Rarely offers advance. Accepts simultaneous submissions, if so noted. Query for electronic submissions. Reports in 2 months on proposals. Book catalog and ms guidelines for #10 SASE.

• Amadeus Press published *Bark*, by Prance & Sandued, winner of the Outstanding Reference Book Award from the American Library Association/Choice.

Nonfiction: Biography, reference. Subjects include music, classical music, opera. Submit outline, 2 sample chapters and sample illustrations. Reviews artwork/photos as part of ms package if appropriate. Send photocopies.

Recent Nonfiction Title: *Saturday Afternoons at the Old Met*, by Paul Jackson (music history and criticism).

Tips: "Our audience is discerning music lovers, opera and concert goers, amateur and professional musicians, music teachers, music scholars. We demand much of our authors—we expect them to make editorial changes on computer disks; to supply and pay for permissions, illustrations, music examples and index; and to proofread. In return we supply excellent editorial and pre-production support, and publish beautiful books."

AMERICA WEST PUBLISHERS, P.O. Box 3300, Bozeman MT 59772-3300. (406)585-0700. Fax: (406)585-0703. Review Editor: George Green. Estab. 1985. Publishes hardcover and trade paperback originals and reprints. Averages 20 titles/year. Receives 150 submissions/year. 90% of books from first-time authors; 90% from unagented writers. Pays 10% on wholesale price. Offers $300 average advance. Publishes book 6 months after acceptance. Accepts simultaneous submissions. Reports in 1 month. Book catalog and ms guidelines free.

Nonfiction: UFO—metaphysical. Subject includes health/medicine (holistic self-help), political (including cover-up), economic. Submit outline/synopsis and sample chapters. Reviews artwork/photos as part of ms package.

Recent Nonfiction Title: *Chaos In America*, by John King.

Tips: "We currently have materials in all bookstores that have areas of UFOs and also political and economic nonfiction."

‡AMERICAN & WORLD GEOGRAPHIC PUBLISHING, P.O. Box 5630, Helena MT 59604. (406)443-2842. Publications Director: Barbara Fifer. Publishes trade paperback originals. Publishes 12-15 titles/year. Receives 40 queries and 8 mss/year. 10% of books from first-time authors; 100% from unagented writers. Makes outright purchase of $3,500-7,000. Publishes book 1 year after acceptance of ms. Accepts simultaneous submissions. Reports in 4 months on proposals. Book catalog and ms guidelines free on request.

Nonfiction: Coffee table book, gift book, illustrated book. Subjects include recreation, regional. "Most of our titles are commissioned." Query with proposal package, including outline, sample chapter, photography with SASE. Reviews artwork/photos as part of ms package. Send transparencies; dupes acceptable.

Recent Nonfiction Titles: *Old San Juan*, by Rick Graetz (photography).

AMERICAN ASSOCIATION FOR STATE AND LOCAL HISTORY, 530 Church St., Suite 600, Nashville TN 37219-2325. (615)255-2971. Fax: (615)255-2979. Estab. 1940. Publishes paperback originals. Averages 6 titles/year. Receives 20-30 submissions/year. 50% of books from first-time authors; 100% from unagented writers. Query for royalty rates. Publishes book an average of 1 year after acceptance. Reports in 3 months on submissions. Book catalog free.

Nonfiction: How-to, reference, collections, preservation, textbook. "We publish books, mostly technical, that help people do effective work in historical societies, sites and museums, or do research in, or teach, history. No manuscripts on history itself—that is, on the history of specific places, events, people." Write for ms guidelines.

Recent Nonfiction Title: *Boats: A Manual for Their Documentation*, edited by Paul Lipke and Peter Spectre.

Tips: "The American Association for State and Local History provides leadership for and service to those who practice and support history in North America: historical societies, museums, historic sites, parks, libraries, archives, historic preservation organizations, schools, colleges, and other educational organizations."

AMERICAN ASTRONAUTICAL SOCIETY, Univelt, Inc., Publisher, P.O. Box 28130, San Diego CA 92198. (619)746-4005. Fax: (619)746-3139. Editorial Director: Robert H. Jacobs. Estab. 1970. Publishes hardcover originals. Averages 8 titles/year. Receives 12-15 submissions/year. 5% of books from first-time authors; 5% from unagented writers. Average print order for a first book is 600-2,000. Pays 10% royalty on actual sales. Publishes book 4 months after acceptance. Accepts simultaneous submissions. Reports in 1 month. *Writer's Market* recommends allowing 2 months for reply. Book catalog and ms guidelines for 9×12 SAE with 3 first-class stamps.

Nonfiction: Proceedings or monographs in the field of astronautics, including applications of aerospace technology to Earth's problems. "Our books must be space-oriented or space-related. They are meant for technical libraries, research establishments and the aerospace industry worldwide." Submit outline and 1-2 sample chapters. Reviews artwork/photos as part of ms package.

Recent Nonfiction Title: *Space-Flight Mechanics 1994*, edited by John Cochran, Jr., Charles Edwards Jr., Stephen Hoffman, Richard Holdaway.

AMERICAN ATHEIST PRESS, P.O. Box 2117, Austin TX 78768-2117. (512)458-1244. Fax: (512)467-9525 Editor: R. Murray-O'Hair. Estab. 1959. Imprints include Gusttav Broukal Press. Publishes trade paperback originals and reprints. Publishes 12 titles/year. Receives 200 submissions/year. 40-50% of books from first-time authors; 100% from unagented writers. Pays 5-10% royalty on retail price. Publishes book 2 years after acceptance. Accepts simultaneous submissions. Reports in 4 months on queries. Book catalog for 6½×9½ SAE. Writer's guidelines for 9×12 SAE.

Nonfiction: Biography, reference, general. Subjects include history (of religion and atheism, of the effects of religion historically); philosophy and religion (from an atheist perspective, particularly criticism of religion); politics (separation of state and church, religion and politics); atheism (particularly the lifestyle of atheism; the history of atheism; applications of atheism). "We are interested in hard-hitting and original books expounding the lifestyle of atheism and criticizing religion. We would like to see more submissions dealing with the histories of specific religious sects, such as the L.D.S., the Worldwide Church of God, etc. We are generally not interested in biblical criticism." Submit outline and sample chapters. Reviews artwork/photos.

Recent Nonfiction Title: *Manual of a Perfect Atheist*, by Rios.

Fiction: Humor (satire of religion or of current religious leaders); anything of particular interest to atheists. "We rarely publish any fiction. But we have occasionally released a humorous book. No mainstream. For our press to consider fiction, it would have to tie in with the general focus of our press, which is the promotion of atheism and free thought." Submit outline/synopsis and sample chapters.

Tips: We will need more how-to types of material—how to argue with creationists, how to fight for state/church separation, etc. We have an urgent need for literature for young atheists."

AMERICAN BAR ASSOCIATION, PUBLICATIONS PLANNING & MARKETING, 750 N. Lake Shore Dr., Chicago IL 60611. (312)988-6104. Fax: (312)988-6281. Executive Editor: Jane L. Johnston. Publishes hardcover and trade paperback originals and trade paperback reprints. Publishes 50 titles/year. Receives 100 queries/year. Pays royalties; "varies a great deal." Publishes book 6 months after acceptance of ms. Accepts simultaneous submissions. Query for electronic submission: prefers disk; WordPerfect or Microsoft Word software. Reports in 2 months on queries and proposals, 3 months on mss. Manuscript guidelines free on request.

Nonfiction: Law. Subjects include law practice. "All proposals should be for books that will help lawyers practice law better—no treatises, no memoirs, no philosophical meanderings. Writers should avoid not thinking of the audience; not meeting the needs of the reader; not writing well about practical matters." Query with outline and 1 sample chapter.

Tips: "We mainly serve lawyers. The best authors for us have an idea of what the law is about and, in fact, are probably practicing or teaching law."

AMERICAN CHEMICAL SOCIETY, 1155 16th St. NW, Washington DC 20036. (202)872-4564. Fax: (202)452-8913. Acquisitions: Cheryl Shanks. Publishes hardcover originals. Publishes 50 titles/year. Pays royalty. Publishes book 9-20 months after acceptance of ms. Accepts simultaneous submissions. Query for electronic submissions. Submissions not returned. Reports in 2 months on proposals. Book catalog free on request and available via gopher and WWW. Electronic catalog available.

Nonfiction: Technical, semi-technical. Science subjects. "Emphasis is on professional reference books." Submit outline and 2 sample chapters.

Recent Nonfiction Title: *Industry's Future: Changing Patterns of Industrial Research.*

AMERICAN CORRECTIONAL ASSOCIATION, 8025 Laurel Lakes Court, Laurel MD 20707-5075. (301)206-5100. Fax: (301)206-5061. Managing Editor: Alice Fins. Estab. 1870. Publishes hardcover and trade paperback originals. Averages 18 titles/year. Receives 40 submissions/year. 90% of books from first-time authors; 100% from unagented writers. Pays 10% royalty on net sales. Publishes book 1 year after acceptance. Query for electronic submissions. Reports in 3 months. Book catalog and ms guidelines free.

● This publisher advises out-of-town freelance editors and proofreaders to refrain from requesting work from them.

Nonfiction: How-to, reference, technical, textbook, correspondence courses. "We are looking for practical, how-to texts or training materials written for the corrections profession. No true-life accounts by current or former inmates or correctional officers, theses, or dissertations." Query. Reviews artwork/photos as part of ms package.

Tips: "People in the field want practical information, as do academics to a certain extent. Our audience is made up of criminal justice students and corrections professionals. If I were a writer trying to market a book today, I would contact publishers while developing my manuscript to get a better idea of the publishers' needs."

‡AMERICAN COUNSELING ASSOCIATION, 5999 Stevenson Ave., Alexandria VA 22304-3300. (703)823-9800. Acquisition and Development Editor: Carolyn C. Baker. Scholarly paperback originals. Publishes 10-15 titles/year. Receives 200 queries and 125 mss/year. 5% of books from first-time authors; 90% from unagented writers. Pays 10-15% royalty on wholesale price. Publishes book within 7 months after acceptance of ms. Accepts simultaneous submissions. Reports in 2 months on queries and proposals, 2-4 months on mss. Manuscript guidelines free on request.

Nonfiction: Reference, self-help, textbook. Subjects include education, gay/lesbian, health/medicine, psychology, religion, sociology, women's issues/studies. "All counseling topics." Query with proposal package, including outline, 2 sample chapters, vitae, outline.

Recent Nonfiction Title: *A Handbook for Developing Multicultural Awareness, 2 ed.*, by Pedersen (text).

Tips: "Target your market. Your books will not be appropriate for everyone across all disciplines."

AMERICAN EAGLE PUBLICATIONS INC., P.O. Box 1507, Show Low AZ 85901 . (520)367-1621. Publisher: Mark Ludwig. Estab. 1988. Publishes hardcover and trade paperback originals and reprints. Averages 8 titles/year. 50% of books from first-time authors; 100% from unagented writers. Pays 5-12% royalty on retail price. Offers $1,000 average advance. Publishes book 6 months after acceptance of ms. Accepts simultaneous submissions. Query for electronic submissions. Reports in 2 months. Catalog for #10 SASE.

● Publisher reports no interest in seeing *military or other autobiographies*.

Nonfiction: Historical biography, technical. Subjects include computers and electronics (security), military/war and science (computers and artificial intelligence). "We are highly specialized in nonfiction. Writers should call and discuss what they have first." Query. Reviews artwork/photos as part of freelance ms package. Send photocopies.

Recent Nonfiction Title: *Paul Schneider: The Witness of Buchenwald*, by Rudolf Wentorz.

Tips: Audience is "scholarly, university profs, (some used as textbooks) very technical programmers and researchers, military, very international."

AMERICAN FEDERATION OF ASTROLOGERS, P.O. Box 22040, Tempe AZ 85285. Fax: (602)838-8293. Publications Manager: Kris Brandt Riske. Publishes trade paperback originals and reprints. Publishes 15-20 titles/year. Receives 10 queries and 20 mss/year. 30% of books from first-time authors; 100% from unagented writers. Pays 10% royalty. Publishes book 10 months after acceptance of ms. Accepts simultaneous submissions. Query for electronic submissions. Reports in 3-6 months on mss. Book catalog for $2. Manuscript guidelines free on request.

Nonfiction: Astrology. Submit complete ms.

Recent Nonfiction Title: *Modern Horary Astrology*, by Doris Chase Doane.

AMERICAN HOSPITAL PUBLISHING, INC., American Hospital Association, 737 N. Michigan Ave., Chicago IL 60611-2615. (312)440-6800. Fax: (312)951-8491. Vice President, Books: Brian Schenk. Estab. 1979. Publishes trade paperback originals. Averages 20-30 titles/year. Receives 75-100 submissions/year. 20% of books from first-time authors; 100% from unagented writers. Pays 10-12% royalty on retail price. Offers $1,000 average advance. Publishes book 1 year after acceptance. Reports in 2-3 months. Book catalog and ms guidelines for 9×12 SAE with 7 first-class stamps.

Nonfiction: Reference, technical, textbook. Subjects include business and economics (specific to health care institutions); health/medicine (never consumer oriented). Need field-based, reality-tested responses to changes in the health care field directed to hospital CEO's, planners, boards of directors, or other senior management. No personal histories, untested health care programs or clinical texts. Query.

Tips: "The successful proposal demonstrates a clear understanding of the needs of the market and the writer's ability to succinctly present practical knowledge of demonstrable benefit that comes from genuine experience that readers will recognize, trust and accept. The audience is senior and middle management of health care institutions. These days we're a little more cautious in what we choose to publish."

AMERICAN SOCIETY OF CIVIL ENGINEERS, ASCE Press, 345 E. 47th St., New York NY 10017-2398. (212)705-7689. Fax: (212)705-7486. E-mail: jchau@ny.asce.org. Book Acquisitions Editor: Joy Chau. Estab. 1988. Averages 5-10 titles/year. 80% of books from first-time authors; 100% from unagented writers. Pays 10% royalty. No advance. Accepts simultaneous submissions. Query for electronic submissions. Request proposal guidelines.

Nonfiction: Civil engineering. "We are looking for topics that are useful and instructive to the engineering practitioner." Query with outline, sample chapters and cv.

Tips: "ASCE is a not-for-profit organization, so we've always been cost conscious. The recession has made us *more* conscious and much more cautious about our spending habits."

AMHERST MEDIA, INC., 418 Homecrest Dr., Amherst NY 14226-1219. (716)874-4450. Fax: (716)874-4508. Publisher: Craig Alesse. Estab. 1974. Publishes trade paperback originals and reprints. Publishes 10 titles/year. Receives 50 submissions/year. 80% of books from first-time authors; 100% from unagented

---

A bullet introduces comments by the editors of **Writer's Market** *indicating special information about the listing.*

writers. Pays 8% royalty on retail price. Publishes book 1 year after acceptance. Accepts simultaneous submissions. Reports in 2 months. Book catalog and ms guidelines free on request.
Nonfiction: How-to. Subjects include photography, astronomy, video. Looking for well-written and illustrated photo, video and astronomy books. Query with outline, 2 sample chapters and SASE. Reviews artwork/photos as part of ms package.
Recent Nonfiction Title: *Camcorder Tricks*, by Michael Stavros (how-to).
Tips: "Our audience is made up of beginning to advanced photographers and videographers. If I were a writer trying to market a book today, I would fill the need of a specific audience and self-edit in a tight manner."

‡THE AMWELL PRESS, P.O. Box 5385, Clinton NJ 08809-0385. (908)537-6888. President: James Rikhoff. Vice President: Monica Sullivan. Estab. 1976. Publishes hardcover originals. Averages 6 titles/year. Publishes book 18 months after acceptance. Reports in 1 month on queries. *Writer's Market* recommends allowing 2 months for reply.
• No longer considering fiction.
Nonfiction: Query. Hunting and fishing stories/literature (not how-to). Mostly limited editions.
Recent Nonfiction Title: *Where Spaniels Spring*, by Ken Roebuck.

ANCESTRY INCORPORATED, P.O. Box 476, Salt Lake City UT 84110-0476. (801)531-1790. Fax: (801)531-1798. E-mail: gbdc96a@prodigy.com. Managing Editor: Anne Lemmon. Estab. 1983. Publishes hardcover, trade and paperback originals. Averages 6-8 titles/year. Receives over 100 submissions/year. 70% of books from first-time authors; 100% from unagented writers. Pays 8-12% royalty or makes outright purchase. Advances discouraged. Publishes book 1 year after acceptance. Accepts simultaneous submissions. Reports in 2 months. Book catalog for 9×12 SAE with 2 first-class stamps.
Nonfiction: How-to, reference, genealogy. Subjects include Americana, historical methodology and genealogical research techniques. "Our publications are aimed exclusively at the genealogist. We consider everything from short monographs to book length works on immigration, migration, record collections and heraldic topics." No mss that are not genealogical or historical. Query, or submit outline/synopsis and sample chapters. Reviews artwork/photos.
Recent Nonfiction Title: *U.S. Miltary Records*, by James C. Neagles.
Tips: "Genealogical reference, how-to, and descriptions of source collections have the best chance of selling to our firm. Be precise in your description. Please, no family histories or genealogies."

ANCHORAGE PRESS, INC., P.O. Box 8067, New Orleans LA 70182-8067. (504)283-8868. Fax: (504)866-0502. Editor: Orlin Corey. Publishes hardcover originals. Estab. 1935. Averages 10 titles/year. Receives 450-900 submissions/year. 50% of books from first-time authors; 80% from unagented writers. Pays 10-15% royalty on retail price. Playwrights also receive 50-75% royalties. Publishes book 1 year after acceptance. Reports in 1 month on queries, 4 months on mss. Book catalog and ms guidelines free.
Nonfiction: Textbook, plays. Subjects include education, language/literature, plays. "We are looking for play anthologies; and texts for teachers of drama/theater (middle school and high school.)" Query. Reviews artwork/photos as part of ms package.
Recent Nonfiction Title: *Short Plays of Theatre Classics*, selected and edited by Aurand Harris (12 beloved plays from the Middle Ages to the 20th Century for students and readers).
Fiction: Plays of juvenile/young people's interest. Query.

ANDREWS AND McMEEL, 4900 Main St., Kansas City MO 64112. Editorial Director: Donna Martin. Publishes hardcover and paperback originals. Averages 100 titles/year. Pays royalty on retail price. Query only. No unsolicited mss. Areas of specialization include humor, how-to, and consumer reference books. Reports in 2 months.
Recent Nonfiction Title: *The Universal Almanac*, edited by John W. Wright.

‡ANOTHER CHICAGO PRESS, P.O. Box 11223, Chicago IL 60611. Publisher: Lee Webster. Publishes trade paperback originals and reprints. Publishes 4 titles/year. Receives 400 queries and 100 submissions/year. 10% of books from first-time authors; 50% from unagented writers. Pays 5-10% on retail price. Offers $500 average advance. Publishes book 2 years after acceptance of ms. Accepts simultaneous submissions. Reports in 2 months on queries, 6 months on proposals and mss.
Fiction: Ethnic, experimental, feminist, literary, short story collections. "Since we are such a small publisher and we receive so many queries, unless their writing has been accepted in other places (journals, magazines, etc.), writers' chances of publication by us are slim." Query with synopsis, 2 sample chapters and SASE.
Recent Fiction Title: *The Empty Lot*, by Mary Gray Hughes.
Poetry: Query with 2 sample poems. "We look for quality journal-published poets, especially award winners."
Recent Poetry Titles: *The Dangerous World*, by Naomi Replansky (feminist).
Tips: Audience is literary aficionados, people who enjoy reading good literature. "Queries and proposals that are not professional in tone and appearance have little chance of success. Do not phone to check on submissions."

APPALACHIAN MOUNTAIN CLUB BOOKS, 5 Joy St., Boston MA 02108. Editor: Gordon Hardy. Publishes trade paperback originals. Averages 6-10 titles/year. Receives 200 submissions/year. Receives 200 queries and 20 mss/year. 30% of books from first-time authors; 90% from unagented writers. Pays 6-12% royalty on retail price. Offers $1,000-4,000 advance. Publishes book 10 months after acceptance of ms. Accepts simultaneous submissions. Query for electronic submissions: ASCII text format; DOS or Apple Mac. Reports in 2-3 months on proposals. Book catalog for 8½ × 11 SAE with 4 first-class stamps. Manuscript guidelines for #10 SASE.

Nonfiction: How-to, guidebooks. Subjects include history (mountains, Northeast), nature/environment, recreation, regional (Northeast outdoor recreation). "We publish hiking guides, water-recreation guides (nonmotorized), nature, conservation and mountain-subject guides for America's Northeast. Writers should avoid submitting: proposals on Appalachia (rural southern mountains); not enough market research; too much personal experience—autobiography." Query. Reviews artwork/photos as part of ms package. Send photocopies and transparencies "at your own risk."

Recent Nonfiction Title: *Quiet Water Canoe Guide: MA/CT/RI*, by Alex Wilson (family canoe guidebook).

Tips: "Our audience is outdoor recreationalists, conservation—minded hikers and canoeists, family outdoor lovers, armchair enthusiasts. Always connect recreation with conservation—all our guidebooks have a strong conservation message."

AQUA QUEST PUBLICATIONS, INC., P.O. Box 700, Locust Valley NY 11560-0700. (516)759-0476. Fax: (516)759-4519. Associate Editor: John W. Bliss. Estab. 1989. Publishes trade paperback originals. Publishes 4-6 titles/year. Receives 1,000 queries and 60 mss/year. 60% of books from first-time authors; 100% from unagented writers. Pays 5-10% royalty on wholesale price. Offers up to 1,500 advance. Publishes books 1-2 years after acceptance of ms. Accepts simultaneous submissions. Query for electronic submissions. Reports in 1 month. Book catalog for 9 × 12 SAE with 2 first-class stamps.

Nonfiction: Children's/juvenile, how-to. Subjects include nature/environment, sports, travel. Query with SASE. Reviews artwork/photos after query.

Recent Nonfiction Title: *Guide to Marine Life*, by Wiseman & Snyderman.

Fiction: Adventure. Query with SASE.

ARCADE PUBLISHING, 141 Fifth Ave., New York NY 10010. (212)475-2633. Publisher: Richard Seaver. Publishes hardcover originals and trade paperback originals and reprints. Publishes 40 titles/year. 5% of books from first-time authors. Pays royalty on retail price. Offers $3,000-100,000 advance. Publishes book 12-18 months after acceptance of ms. Accepts simultaneous submissions. Query for electronic submissions: "via disk—but only if accompanied by a printout." Prefers Mac compatible. Reports in 2-3 months on queries.

Nonfiction: Biography, cookbook, general nonfiction. Subjects include cooking/foods/nutrition, government/politics, history, nature/environment and travel. Query. Reviews artwork/photos as part of freelance ms package. Writers should send photocopies.

Recent Nonfiction Title: *Images: My Life in Film*, by Ingmar Bergman (autobiography).

Fiction: Ethnic, historical, humor, literary, mainstream/contemporary, mystery, short story collections, suspense. Query. *Agented submissions only.*

Recent Fiction Title: *Dreams of Fair to Middling Women*, by Samuel Beckett.

Poetry: "We do not publish poetry as a rule; in our three-and-half years we have published only one volume of poetry." Query.

ARCHITECTURAL BOOK PUBLISHING CO., INC, 268 Dogwood Lane, Stamford CT 06903. (203)322-1460. President: Alan Frese. Estab. 1891. Averages 10 titles/year. Receives 400 submissions/year. 80% of books from first-time authors; 95% from unagented writers. Average print order for a first book is 5,000. Pays royalty on retail price. Publishes book 10 months after acceptance. Query with outlines and 2 sample chapters with number of illustrations. Reports in 2 weeks. *Writer's Market* recommends allowing 2 months for reply.

Nonfiction: Publishes architecture, decoration, and reference books on city planning and industrial arts. Accepts nonfiction translations. Also interested in history, biography, and science of architecture and decoration. Query with outline, 2 sample chapters and SASE for return of materials.

ARCHIVES PUBLICATIONS, 334 State St., Los Altos CA 94022. Contact: Phil Wycliff. Imprints are Archives Press. Contact: Phil Wycliff; Epona Media, Contact: Hazel Pethig. Publishes hardcover and trade paperback originals and reprints. Publishes 15 titles/year; each imprint publishes 2 titles/year. Receives 2,000 queries/year. 70% of books from first-time authors; 100% from unagented writers. Pays 7½-10% royalty on retail price or make outright purchase (negotiable). Offers $500-5,000 advance. Publishes book 16 months after acceptance of ms. No simultaneous submissions. Query for electronic submission. Reports in 4 months.

 • Archives Publications does not wish to see any unsolicited manuscripts without an initial query letter. If a full manuscript is requested, Archives requires a $25 reading and shipping fee at the time you send your manuscript. Contracts are only offered on completed manuscripts.

Nonfiction: Biography, cookbook, how-to, children's/juvenile, reference. Subjects include anthropology/archaeology, art/architecture, cooking/foods/nutrition, history (Irish only), music/dance, psychology, astronomy, literary. "We are deeply committed to excellence in literature, both fiction and nonfiction. If you're not a deep thinker don't bother us." Query by mail only. No response unless queried first. Do not send anything registered or certified mail.

Fiction: Historical, literary, occult, religious (no New Age), equestrian. "We take a serious look at all well presented mss *after* query." Query by mail only. "Include loose stamps, no envelope, and $2 to handle computer processing and reply." All unsolicited manuscripts are returned unread.

ARCHWAY PAPERBACKS/MINSTREL BOOKS, Imprint of Pocket Books, 1230 Avenue of the Americas, New York NY 10020. (212)698-7669. Vice President/Editorial Director: Patricia MacDonald. Send all submissions Attn: Manuscript Proposals. Publishes mass market paperback originals and reprints. Averages 80 titles/year. Receives over 1,000 submissions/year. Pays royalty. Publishes book an average of 2 years after acceptance. Reports in 3 months. SASE for all material necessary or query not answered.

Nonfiction: Middle grade, young adult. Subjects include current popular subjects or people, sports. Query with SASE. Submit outline/synopsis and 2 sample chapters. Reviews artwork/photos as part of ms package.

Fiction: Middle grade, young adult. Suspense thrillers and soap-opera romances for YA; mysteries, school stories, funny/scary stories, animal stories for middle grade readers. No picture books. Query with SASE. Submit outline/synopsis and sample chapters.

Recent Fiction Title: *I Left My Sneakers in Dimension X.*

ARDEN PRESS INC., P.O. Box 418, Denver CO 80201-0418. (303)697-6766. Publisher: Susan Conley. Estab. 1980. Publishes hardcover and trade paperback originals and reprints. 95% of books are originals; 5% are reprints. Averages 4-6 titles/year. Receives 600 submissions/year. 20% of books from first-time authors; 80% from unagented writers. Pays 8-15% royalty on wholesale price. Offers $2,000 average advance. Publishes book 6 months after acceptance. Accepts simultaneous submissions. Query for electronic submissions. Reports in 1 month on queries. Manuscript guidelines free on request.

Nonfiction: Biography, reference, textbooks. Subjects include women's issues/studies (history, biography, practical guides.) Query with outline/synopsis and sample chapters.

Tips: "Writers have the best chance selling us nonfiction on women's subjects. We sell to general and women's bookstores and public and academic libraries. Many of our titles are adopted as texts for college courses. If I were a writer trying to market a book today, I would learn as much as I could about publishers' profiles *then* contact those who publish similar works."

‡ARDSLEY HOUSE PUBLISHERS, INC., 320 Central Park West, New York NY 10025. (212)496-7040. Contact: Linda Jarkesy. Publishes hardcover and trade paperback originals and reprints. Publishes 5-8 titles/year. 25% of books from first-time authors; 100% from unagented writers (all are college professors). Pays generally by royalty. No advance. Publishes book 12-15 months after acceptance of ms. Reports in 1 month on queries, 1-2 months on proposals, 1-3 months on mss. Book catalog free on request.

Nonfiction: Textbook (college). Subjects include Americana, history, music/dance, philosophy, film. "We publish only college-level textbooks—particularly in the areas of music, philosophy, history, and film. We don't accept any other type of manuscript." Query with outline, 2-3 sample chapters, prospectus, author's résumé and SASE. Reviews artwork/photos as part of ms package. Send photocopies.

Recent Nonfiction Title: *Ethics in Thought and Action*, by Warren Cohen (college text).

‡ARMSTRONG PUBLISHING CORP., P.O. Box 1678, Greenwich CT 06836. (203)661-7602. Editor-in-Chief: George F. Johnson. Publishes hardcover and trade paperback originals and reprints. Publishes 8-12 titles/year. Receives 500 queries and 1,000 mss/year. 65% of books from first-time authors; 90% from unagented writers. Pays royalty or makes outright purchase. Publishes book 12-18 months after acceptance of ms. Accepts simultaneous submissions. Reports in 3-4 weeks. Book catalog and ms guidelines free on request.

Nonfiction: Children's/juvenile. Subjects include animals, child guidance/parenting, education. Query with proposal package, including ms, sample of artwork and SASE. Reviews artwork/photos as part of ms package. Send photocopies.

Fiction: Adventure, humor, juvenile, picture books. Query with full ms.

Recent Nonfiction Titles: *Wyatt The Whale* and *Rupert The Duck*, by Dan Slottje (picture book).

Tips: Audience is children ages 3 and up.

JASON ARONSON, INC., 230 Livingston St., Northvale NJ 07647-1726. (201)767-4093. Fax: (201)767-4330. Editor-in-chief: Arthur Kurzweil. Estab. 1967. Publishes hardcover and trade paperback originals and reprints. Averages 250 titles/year. 50% of books from first-time authors; 95% from unagented writers. Pays 10-15% royalty on retail price. Offers $250-$2500 advance. Publishes book an average of 1 year after acceptance. Reports in 1 month. Catalog and ms guidelines free on request. *Writer's Market* recommends allowing 2 months for reply.

Nonfiction: Subjects include history, philosophy, psychology, religion translation. "We publish in two fields: psychotherapy and Judaica. We are looking for high quality books in both fields." Query or submit outline and sample chapters. Reviews artwork/photos as part of ms packages. Send photocopies.
Recent Nonfiction Title: *Borderline Conditions*, by Otto Kernberg (psychotherapy).

ASIAN HUMANITIES PRESS, Imprint of Jain Publishing Co., P.O. Box 3523, Fremont CA 94539. (510)659-8272. Fax: (510)659-0501. Editor: M.K. Jain. Estab. 1976. Publishes hardcover and trade paperback originals and reprints. Averages 10 titles/year. Receives 200 submissions/year. 90% of books from unagented authors. Pays up to 6-10% royalty on net sale. Publishes book 1 year after acceptance. Query for electronic submissions. Reports in 3 months on mss. Book catalog for 6×9 SAE with 2 first-class stamps. Manuscript guidelines for #10 SASE.
   ● Publisher reports an increased emphasis on undergraduate level textbooks and culture-related books.
Nonfiction: Reference, textbooks, general trade books. Subjects include Asian classics (fiction and nonfiction), language/literature (Asian), philosophy/religion (Asian and East-West), psychology/spirituality (Asian and East-West), art/culture (Asian and East-West). Submit proposal package, including vita, list of prior publications and SASE. Reviews artwork/photos as part of ms package. Send photocopies.

ASQC, Imprint of ASQC Quality Press, 611 E. Wisconsin Ave., P.O. Box 3005, Milwaukee WI 53201-3005. (414)272-8575. Acquisitions Editor: Susan Westergarde. Publishes hardcover and paperback originals. Publishes 30 titles/year. Receives 300 queries and 120 mss/year. 65% of books from first-time authors; 100% from unagented writers. Pays 10% royalty on wholesale price. Publishes book 9 months after acceptance of ms. No simultaneous submissions. Reports in 2 months on proposals. Book catalog and ms guidelines free on request.
Nonfiction: Technical and business/manufacturing how-to. Subjects include business, education, government, healthcare, finance, software—all topics are dealt with only as they relate to quality. "Our primary focus is on quality in manufacturing, education, government, health care and finance." Submit proposal package, including outline, sample chapters, résumé, market analysis. Reviews artwork/photos as part of ms package. Send photocopies.
Recent Nonfiction Title: *Business Process Benchmarking*, by Robert C. Camp.

‡ASTRAGAL PRESS, P.O. Box 239, Mendham NJ 07945. (201)543-3045. President: Emil Pollak. Publishes hardcover and trade paperback originals and reprints. Publishes 10-15 titles/year. Receives 50 queries/year. Pays 10% royalty on net sales or 25% after direct costs (paid by Astragal Press) are recovered. Publishes book 6-12 months after acceptance of ms. Reports in 1 month. Book catalog and ms guidelines free on request.
Nonfiction: Books on early tools, trades or technology. Query. Reviews artwork/photos as part of ms package. Send photocopies.
Recent Nonfiction Titles: *Makers Of American Machinist Tools*, by Kenneth L. Cope.
Tips: "We sell to niche markets. We are happy to work with knowledgeable amateur authors in developing titles."

ASTRO COMMUNICATIONS SERVICES, INC., P.O. Box 34487, San Diego CA 92163-4487. (619)492-9919. Editorial Director: Maritha Pottenger. Estab. 1973. Publishes trade paperback originals and reprints. Averages 4-6 titles/year. Receives 400 submissions/year. 50% of books from first-time authors; 95% from unagented writers. Average print order for a first book is 3,000. Pays 10-12% royalty "on monies received through wholesale and retail sales." No advance. Publishes book 1 year after acceptance. Query for electronic submissions. Reports in 3 months. Book catalog and ms guidelines for 9×12 SAE with 2 first-class stamps.
Nonfiction: Astrology. "Our market is astrology. We are seeking pragmatic, useful, immediate applicable contributions to field; prefer psychological approach. Specific ideas and topics should enhance people's lives. Research also valued. No determinism ('Saturn made me do it.'). No autobiographies. No airy-fairy 'space cadet' philosophizing. Keep it grounded, useful, opening options (not closing doors) for readers." Query or submit outline and 3 sample chapters.
Tips: "The most common mistake writers make when trying to get their work published is to send works to inappropriate publishers. We get too many submissions outside our field or contrary to our world view."

ATHENEUM BOOKS FOR YOUNG READERS, Imprint of Simon & Schuster, 1230 Avenue of the Americas, New York NY 10020. (212)702-7894. Vice President/Editorial Director: Jonathan J. Lanman. Editors: Marcia Marshall, Sarah Caguiat, Ana Ceurro and Jean Karl. Estab. 1960. Publishes hardcover originals. Averages 60 titles/year. Receives 10,000 submissions/year. 8-12% of books from first-time authors; 50% from unagented writers. Pays 10% royalty on retail price. Offers $2,000-3,000 average advance. Publishes book 18 months after acceptance. Reports within 3 months. Manuscript guidelines for #10 SASE.
Nonfiction: Biography, how-to, humor, illustrated book, juvenile (pre-school through young adult), self-help, all for juveniles. Subjects include: Americana, animals, art, business and economics, cooking/foods, health, history, hobbies, music, nature, philosophy, photography, politics, psychology, recreation, religion, sociology, sports, and travel, all for young readers. "Do remember, most publishers plan their lists as much

as two years in advance. So if a topic is 'hot' right now, it may be 'old hat' by the time we could bring it out. It's better to steer clear of fads. Some writers assume juvenile books are for 'practice' until you get good enough to write adult books. Not so. Books for young readers demand just as much 'professionalism' in writing as adult books. So save those 'practice' manuscripts for class, or polish them before sending them." Query only.

Fiction: Adventure, ethnic, experimental, fantasy, gothic, historical, horror, humor, mainstream, mystery, science fiction, suspense, western, all in juvenile versions. "We have few specific needs except for books that are fresh, interesting and well written. Again, fad topics are dangerous, as are works you haven't polished to the best of your ability. (The competition is fierce.) We've been inundated with dragon stories (misunderstood dragon befriends understanding child), unicorn stories (misunderstood child befriends understanding unicorn), and variations of 'Ignatz the Egg' (Everyone laughs at Ignatz the egg [giraffe/airplane/accountant] because he's square [short/purple/stupid] until he saves them from the eggbeater [lion/storm/I.R.S. man] and becomes a hero). Other things we don't need at this time are safety pamphlets, ABC books, coloring books, board books, and rhymed narratives. In writing picture book texts, avoid the coy and 'cutesy.' " Query only for novels; complete ms for picture books. Reviews artwork as part of ms package. Send photocopies.

Recent Fiction Title: *Harper and Moon*, by Ramon Ross.

Poetry: "At this time there is a growing market for children's poetry. However, we don't anticipate needing any for the next year or two, especially rhymed narratives."

Tips: "Our books are aimed at children from pre-school age, up through high school. We no longer publish Argo Books."

AVALON BOOKS, Imprint of Thomas Bouregy & Co., Inc., 401 Lafayette St., New York NY 10003-7014. Vice President/Publisher: Marcia Markland. Estab. 1950. Publishes 60 titles/year. Reports in 3-6 months.

Fiction: "We publish wholesome romances, mysteries, westerns. Our books are read by adults as well as teenagers, and their characters are all adults. All the romances and mysteries are contemporary; all the westerns are historical." Length: 40,000-50,000 words. Submit first chapter, a brief, but complete summary of the book and SASE with sufficient postage.

Tips: "We are looking for love stories, heroines who have interesting professions, and we are actively seeking ethnic fiction. We do accept unagented manuscripts, and we do publish first novels. Right now we are concentrating on finding talented new mystery and romantic suspense writers."

AVANYU PUBLISHING INC., P.O. Box 27134, Albuquerque NM 87125. (505)266-6128. Fax: (505)821-8864. President: J. Brent Ricks. Estab. 1984. Publishes hardcover and trade paperback originals and reprints. Averages 4 titles/year. Receives 40 submissions/year. 30% of books from first-time authors; 90% from unagented writers. Pays 8% maximum royalty on wholesale price. No advance. Publishes book 1 year after acceptance. Query for electronic submissions. Reports in 6 weeks. *Writer's Market* recommends allowing 2 months for reply. Book catalog for #10 SASE.

Nonfiction: Biography, illustrated book, reference, Southwest Americana. Subjects include Americana, anthropology/archaeology, art/architecture, ethnic, history, photography, regional, sociology. Query. Reviews artwork/photos as part of ms package.

Fiction: Adventure, historical, Western. Query.

Tips: "Writers have the best chance selling us history oriented books with lots of pictures, or contemporary Indian/Western art. Our audience consists of libraries, art collectors and history students."

AVERY PUBLISHING GROUP, 120 Old Broadway, Garden City Park NY 11040. (516)741-2155. Fax: (516)742-1892. Contact: Managing Editor. Estab. 1976. Publishes hardcover and trade paperback originals. Averages 40 titles/year. Receives 200-300 submissions/year. 90% of books from first-time authors; 95% from unagented writers. Pays 10% royalty on wholesale price. Publishes book 1 year after acceptance. Accepts simultaneous submissions. Reports in 1 week. *Writer's Market* recommends allowing 2 months for reply. Book catalog free on request.

Nonfiction: Cookbook, how-to, reference, textbook. Subjects include business and economics, child guidance/parenting, cooking/foods/nutrition, health/medicine, history, military/war, nature/environment, childbirth, alternative health. Query.

AVON BOOKS, Division of the Hearst Corp., 1350 Avenue of the Americas, New York NY 10019. Send queries to Alice Webster-Williams. Estab. 1941. Publishes trade and mass market paperback originals and reprints. Averages 400 titles/year. Royalty and advance are negotiable. Publishes ms 2 years after acceptance. Accepts simultaneous submissions. Reports in 3 months. Guidelines for SASE.

Nonfiction: How-to, popular psychology, self-help, health, history, war, sports, business/economics, biography, politics. No textbooks. Query only with SASE.

Recent Nonfiction Title: *Don't Know Much About Geography* (trade).

Fiction: Romance (contemporary), historical romance, science fiction, fantasy, men's adventure, suspense/thriller, mystery, western. Query only with SASE.

Recent Fiction Title: *List of 7*, by Mark Frost.

AVON FLARE BOOKS, Young Adult Imprint of Avon Books, Division of the Hearst Corp., 1350 Avenue of the Americas, New York NY 10019. (212)261-6817. Fax: (212)261-6895. Editorial Director: Gwen Montgomery. Publishes mass market paperback originals and reprints. Imprint publishes 20-24 new titles/year. 25% of books from first-time authors; 15% from unagented writers. Pays 6-8% royalty. Offers $2,500 minimum advance. Publishes book 2 years after acceptance. Accepts simultaneous submissions. Reports in 4 months. Book catalog and ms guidelines for 8×10 SAE with 5 first-class stamps.
Nonfiction: General. Submit outline/synopsis and sample chapters. "*Very* selective with young adult nonfiction."
Fiction: Adventure, ethnic, humor, mainstream, mystery, romance, suspense, contemporary. "Very selective with mystery." Manuscripts appropriate to ages 12-18. Query with sample chapters and synopsis.
Recent Fiction Title: *Out of Control,* by Norma Fox Nazer.
Tips: "The YA market is not as strong as it was five years ago. We are very selective with young adult fiction. *Avon does not publish picture books,* nor do we use freelance readers."

AZTEX CORP., P.O. 50046, Tucson AZ 85703-1046. (608)882-4656. Estab. 1976. Publishes hardcover and paperback originals. Averages 10 titles/year. Receives 250 submissions/year. 100% of books from unagented writers. Average print order for a first book is 3,500. Pays 10% royalty. Publishes book 18 months after acceptance. Query for electronic submissions. Reports in 3 months. "Queries without return envelopes or postage are not responded to."
 • This company recently received the Thomas McKean Award from the Antique Automobile Club of America for outstanding research for *Tire Wars: Racing With Goodyear.*
Nonfiction: "We specialize in transportation subjects (how-to and history)." Accepts nonfiction translations. Submit outline and 2 sample chapters. Reviews artwork/photos as part of ms package.
Recent Nonfiction Title: *Tire Wars: Racing with Goodyear,* by William Neely.
Tips: "We look for accuracy, thoroughness and interesting presentation."

BAEN PUBLISHING ENTERPRISES, P.O. Box 1403, Riverdale NY 10471-0671. (718)548-3100. Consulting Editor: Josepha Sherman. Estab. 1983. Publishes hardcover, trade paperback and mass market paperback originals and reprints. Averages 120 titles/year. Receives 8,000 submissions/year. 10% of books from first-time authors; 50% from unagented writers. Pays royalty on retail price. Reports in 2 weeks on queries or proposals, 1-4 months on complete mss. Queries not necessary. Book catalog free on request. Manuscript guidelines for #10 SASE.
Fiction: Fantasy, science fiction. Submit outline/synopsis and sample chapters or complete ms.
Recent Fiction Title: *Field of Dishonor,* by David Weber (science fiction).
Tips: "See our books before submitting. Send for our writers' guidelines."

BAKER BOOK HOUSE COMPANY, P.O. Box 6287, Grand Rapids MI 49516-6287. Director of Publications: Allan Fisher. Assistant to the Director of Publications: Jane Schrier. Estab. 1939. Publishes hardcover and trade paperback originals. Averages 120 titles/year. 10% of books from first-time authors; 85% from unagented writers. Queries and proposals only. No unsolicited mss. Pays 14% royalty on net receipts. Publishes book within 1 year after acceptance. Accepts simultaneous submissions (if so identified). Reports in 2-3 months. Book catalog for 9×12 SAE with 6 first-class stamps.
Nonfiction: Contemporary issues, women's concerns, parenting, singleness, seniors' concerns, self-help, children's books, Bible study, Christian doctrine, reference books, books for pastors and church leaders, textbooks for Christian colleges and seminaries. Query with proposal.
Fiction: Literary novels focusing on women's concerns, mysteries. Query.
Tips: "Most of our authors and readers are evangelical Christians, and our books are purchased from Christian bookstores, mail-order retailers, and school bookstores."

‡BALDWIN & KNOWLTON BOOKS, 537 Newport Center Dr., Suite 264, Newport Beach CA 92660. (714)647-2495. Fax: (714)644-4329. 3023 N. Clark St., #859, Chicago IL 60657-5205. (312)854-5844. Fax: (312)281-4844. Editor: Marie DeVito. Publishes hardcover and trade and mass market paperback originals. Publishes 5-10 titles/year. 95% of books from first-time authors; 90% from unagented writers. Pays 10-12½% royalty. Negotiates advance. Publishes book 8 months after acceptance of ms. Accepts simultaneous submissions. Reports in 3 weeks on mss.
Nonfiction: Biography, how-to, humor, reference, self-help, technical. Subjects include Americana, animals, business and economics, child guidance/parenting, education, gay/lesbian, health/medicine, history, language/literature, money/finance, music/dance, nature/environment, philosophy, psychology, regional, sociology, women's issues/studies. "Writers don't use enough interspersement of dialogue and scene, thus we try to guide them in that direction if they are lacking." Submit outline or send complete ms with SASE.
Fiction: Adventure, erotica, ethnic, experimental, fantasy, feminist, gay/lesbian, gothic, historical, horror, humor, literary, mainstream/contemporary, mystery, occult, romance, science fiction, short story collections, suspense, western, young adult. "Intersperse dialogue and scene; play down flashbacks." Submit full ms with SASE.
Tips: "Our audience is educated, diverse, literary, Generation X."

BALE BOOKS, Division of Bale Publications, P.O. Box 2727, New Orleans LA 70176. Editor-in-Chief: Don Bale, Jr. Estab. 1963. Publishes hardcover and paperback originals and reprints. Averages 10 titles/year. Receives 25 submissions/year. 50% of books from first-time authors; 90% from unagented writers. Average print order for a first book is 1,000. Offers standard 10-12½-15% royalty contract on wholesale or retail price; sometimes makes outright purchases of $500. No advance. Publishes book 3 years after acceptance. Reports in 3 months. Book catalog for #10 SAE with 2 first-class stamps.

Nonfiction: Numismatics. "Our specialties are coin and stock market investment books; especially coin investment books and coin price guides. Most of our books are sold through publicity and ads in the coin newspapers. We are open to any new ideas in the area of numismatics. The writer should write for a teenage through adult level. Lead the reader by the hand like a teacher, building chapter by chapter. Our books sometimes have a light, humorous treatment, but not necessarily. We look for good English, construction and content, and sales potential." Submit outline and 3 sample chapters.

BALLANTINE BOOKS, Subsidiary of Random House, Inc., 201 E. 50th St., New York NY 10022. (212)572-2149. Vice President/Senior Editor: Pamela D. Strickler. Assistant Editor: Betsy Flagler.
● Also see the listing for Random House, Inc.
Nonfiction: How-to, humor, illustrated book (cartoons), reference, self-help. Subjects include animals, child guidance/parenting, cooking/foods/nutrition, health/medicine. Submit proposal and 100 ms pages. Reviews artwork/photos as part of ms package. Send photocopies.
Recent Nonfiction Title: *The Puppy Book*, by Larry Shook.
Fiction: Publishes originals (general fiction, mass market, trade paperback and hardcover). Needs: Historical fiction, women's mainstream, multicultural and general fiction. Submit query letter or brief synopsis, first 100 pages of ms and SASE of proper size to Pamela Strickler. Responds promptly to queries; 2-5 months on mss.
Recent Fiction Title: *An Imperfect Spy*, by Amanda Cross.

BANDANNA BOOKS, 319-B Anacapa St., Santa Barbara CA 93101. (805)962-9915. Fax: (805)504-3278. Publisher: Sasha Newborn. Ms Editor: Joan Blake. Publishes trade paperback originals and reprints. Publishes 3 titles/year. Receives 100 queries and 40 mss/year. 50% of books from first-time authors; 100% from unagented writers. Pays 5-10% royalty on retail price (a few books gratis). Offers $50-200 advance. Publishes book 9 months after acceptance. Accepts simultaneous submissions. Query for electronic submissions. Reports in 2 months on proposals.
Fiction and Nonfiction: General, textbook, some illustrated. Subjects include history, literature, language, non-sexist-oriented women's and men's issues/studies. "Bandanna Books seeks to humanize the classics, history, language-learning materials in non-sexist, modernized translations, using direct and plain language. Suitable for advanced high school, college classes, and general audiences. Interested in material expressing and inspiring progressive, independent thinking." Submit outline and 1-2 sample chapters. Reviews artwork/photos as part of ms package. Send photocopies.
Tips: "Our readers are age 16-22 and up, high school or college age, liberal arts orientation. A well-thought-out proposal is important, even if unconventional."

B&B PUBLISHING, INC., P.O. Box 96, Walworth WI 53184. Fax: (414)275-9530. Contact: Katy O'Shea. Publishes hardcover and trade paperback originals. Publishes 5-10 titles/year. Receives 1,000 queries and 100 mss/year. 10% of books from first-time authors; 90% from unagented writers. Pays 2½-5% royalty on net receipts or makes outright purchase for $2,000-5,000. Offers $2,000 advance. Publishes book 1 year after acceptance. Accepts simultaneous submissions. Accepts electronic submissions by disk only. Prefers Macintosh or PC in Microsoft Word. "Do not send entire manuscript unless requested to do so. Any submission or query without SASE will not be acknowledged." Reports in 2-3 months. Book catalog and ms guidelines free on request.
● Publisher would like to hear from journalists interested in writing/researching state trivia almanacs.
Nonfiction: Children's/juvenile, reference, Americana, trivia. "We are seeking innovative supplementary educational materials for grades K-12." Query. Reviews artwork/photos as part of ms package. Send photocopies.
Recent Nonfiction Title: *Serengeti Plain*, by Terri Wills.
Tips: Audience is general trade schools and public library.

BANKS-BALDWIN LAW PUBLISHING CO., 1904 Ansel Rd., Cleveland OH 44106. (216)721-7373. Fax: (216)721-8055. Affiliate of West Publishing of Eagan, Minnesota. Editor-in-Chief: P.J. Lucier. Managing Editor: Fred K. Gordon. Estab. 1804. Publishes law books and services in a variety of formats. Averages 10 new titles/year. Receives 10-15 submissions/year. 5% of books from first-time authors; 90% from unagented writers. "Most titles include material submitted by outside authors." Pays 8-16% royalty on net revenue, or fee. Offers advance not to exceed 25% of anticipated royalty or fee. Publishes book 18 months after acceptance, 3 months after receipt of ms. Query for electronic submissions. Reports in 3 weeks on queries. *Writer's Market* recommends allowing 2 months for reply. Book catalog and ms guidelines for SASE.

Nonfiction: Reference, law/legal. Query.
Tips: "We publish books for attorneys, government officials and professionals in allied fields. Trends in our field include more interest in handbooks, less in costly multi-volume sets; electronic publishing. A writer has the best chance of selling us a book on a hot new topic of law. Check citations and quotations carefully."

BANTAM BOOKS, Subsidiary of Bantam Doubleday Dell, Dept. WM, 1540 Broadway, New York NY 10036. (212)354-6500. Imprints are Spectra, Crime Lane, New Age, New Science, Domain, Fanfair, Bantam Classics, Bantam Wisdom Editions, Loveswept. Publishes hardcover, trade paperback and mass market paperback originals, trade paperback, mass market paperback reprints and audio. Publishes 350 titles/year. Publishes book an average of 8 months after ms is accepted. Accepts simultaneous submissions from agents.
Nonfiction: Biography, how-to, cookbook, humor, illustrated book, self-help. Subjects include Americana, business/economics, child care/parenting, diet/fitness, education, cooking/foods/nutrition, gay/lesbian, government/politics, health/medicine, history, language/literature, military/war, mysticism/astrology, nature, philosophy/mythology, psychology, religion/inspiration, science, sociology, spirituality, sports, true crime, women's studies.
Fiction: Adventure, fantasy, feminist, gay/lesbian, historical, horror, juvenile, literary, mainstream/contemporary, mystery, romance, science fiction, suspense, western. Query or submit outline/synopsis. All unsolicited mss returned unopened.

BANTAM DOUBLEDAY DELL, 1540 Broadway, New York NY 10036.
  • See separate listings for Bantam Books, Doubleday and Dell Publishing.

BARBOUR AND COMPANY, INC., P.O. Box 719, Uhrichsville OH 44683. Vice President Editorial: Stephen Reginald. Imprints are Barbour Books and Heartsong Presents (fiction). Publishes hardcover, trade paperback and mass market paperback originals and reprints. Publishes 75 titles/year. Receives 300 queries and 150 mss/year. 40% of books from first-time authors; 99% from unagented writers. Subsidy publishes .5% of books. Pays royalty on wholesale price or makes outright purchase of $1,000-2,500. Offers $250-500 advance. Publishes book 6 months after acceptance of ms. Accepts simultaneous submissions. Query for electronic submissions. Reports in 1 month on queries, 3 months on proposals, and mss. Book catalog for $2. Ms guidelines for #10 SASE.
Nonfiction: Biography, humor, children's/juvenile. Religious subjects. "We're a Christian evangelical publisher." Query.
Fiction: Historical, religious, romance "All these elements combined. We publish four inspirational romance titles per month. Two historical and two contemporary romances." Submit synopsis and 3 sample chapters.
Tips: "Having a great agent won't help here. A great idea or book will catch our attention."

BARRON'S EDUCATIONAL SERIES, INC., 250 Wireless Blvd., Hauppauge NY 11788. Fax: (516)434-3217. Director of Acquisitions: Grace Freedson. Publishes hardcover and paperback originals and software. Publishes 170 titles/year. 10% of books from first-time authors; 90% from unagented writers. Pays royalty based on both wholesale and retail price. Publishes book 1 year after acceptance. Accepts simultaneous submissions. Reports in 6-8 months. Book catalog free.
Nonfiction: Adult education, art, business, cookbooks, crafts, foreign language, review books, guidance, pet books, travel, literary guides, parenting, health, juvenile, young adult sports, test preparation materials and textbooks. Reviews artwork/photos as part of ms package. Query or submit outline/synopsis and 2-3 sample chapters. Accepts nonfiction translations.
Recent Nonfiction Title: _Gardening Wizardry for Kids_, by Pat Kire, illustrated by Yvette Banck.
Tips: "The writer has the best chance of selling us a book that will fit into one of our series."

BASELINE II, INC., (formerly New York Zoetrope, Inc.), 838 Broadway, 4th Floor, New York NY 10003. (212)420-0590. Fax: (212)529-3330. Contact: Olenthia Nelson. Publishes hardcover and trade paperback originals, reprints and software. Averages 10 titles/year. Receives 100 submissions/year. 25% of books from first-time authors; 75% from unagented writers. Nonauthor subsidy publishes 3% of books. Pays 10-20% royalty on wholesale prices or makes outright purchase of $500-1,000. Offers $1,000 average advance. Publishes book an average of 9 months after acceptance. Accepts simultaneous submissions. Query for electronic submissions. Reports in 2 months. Book catalog and guidelines for 6×9 SAE.
Nonfiction: Reference, technical, textbook. Subjects include film, TV, entertainment industry, media. Interested especially in film and television. No fiction. Query with synopsis and outline.
Tips: "Film- or media-oriented (academic and popular) subjects have the best chance of selling to our firm. Media books (reference) are our strongest line."

BAYWOOD PUBLISHING CO., INC., 26 Austin Ave., Amityville NY 11701. (516)691-1270. Fax: (516)691-1770. E-mail: Baywood@ix.netcom.com. Publishes 25 titles/year. Pays 7-15% royalty on retail price. E-mail: Baywood@ix.netcom.com. Publishes book within 1 year after acceptance of ms. Book list and ms guidelines free on request.

Nonfiction: Technical, scholarly. Subjects include anthropology/archaeology, computers and electronics, gerontology, imagery, labor relations, education, death and dying, drug, nature/environment, psychology, public health/medicine, sociology, technical communications, women's issues/studies. Submit outline/synopsis and sample chapters.

BEACON HILL PRESS OF KANSAS CITY, Book Division of Nazarene Publishing House, 6401 The Paseo, Kansas City MO 64131. Fax: (816)333-1748. Coordinator: Shone Fisher. Estab. 1912. Publishes hardcover and paperback originals. Averages 50 titles/year. Standard contract is 12% royalty on net sales for first 10,000 copies and 14% on subsequent copies. (Sometimes makes flat rate purchase.) Publishes book within 1 year after acceptance. Reports within 3 months. Accent on holy living; encouragement in daily Christian life. Query or proposal preferred. Average ms length: 30,000-60,000 words.
Nonfiction: Inspirational, Bible-based. Doctrinally must conform to the evangelical, Wesleyan tradition. No autobiography, poetry, short stories or children's picture books. Contemporary issues acceptable.
Fiction: Wholesome, inspirational. Considers historical and Biblical fiction, Christian romance, but no teen or children's.

BEACON PRESS, 25 Beacon St., Boston MA 02108-2892. (617)742-2110. Fax: (617)723-3097. Director: Wendy J. Strothman. Estab. 1854. Publishes hardcover originals and paperback reprints. Averages 50 titles/year. Receives 4,000 submissions/year. 10% of books from first-time authors; 70% from unagented writers. Average print order for a first book is 3,000. Pays royalty on net retail price. Advance varies. Publishes book 1 year after acceptance. Accepts simultaneous submissions. Reports in 3 months.
Nonfiction: General nonfiction including works of original scholarship, religion, women's studies, philosophy, current affairs, anthropology, environmental concerns, African-American studies, gay and lesbian studies. Query or submit outline/synopsis and sample chapters with SASE.
Recent Nonfiction Title: *Life Work*, Donald Hall.
Tips: "We probably accept only one or two manuscripts from an unpublished pool of 4,000 submissions per year. No fiction, children's book, or poetry submissions invited. Authors should have academic affiliation."

BEAR AND CO., INC., Aquisitions Dept., P.O. Box 600E, Lakeville CT 06039. (505)983-5968. Vice President, Editorial: Barbara Clow. Estab. 1978. Publishes trade paperback originals. Averages 12 titles/year. Receives 6,000 submissions/year. 20% of books from first-time authors; 90% from unagented writers. Pays 10% royalty on net. Publishes book 18 months after acceptance. Query for electronic submissions. Reports in 1 month on queries. *Writer's Market* recommends allowing 2 months for reply. "No response without SASE." Book catalog for 9×12 SAE with 3 first-class stamps.
Nonfiction: Illustrated books, science, theology, mysticism, religion, ecology. "We publish books to 'heal and celebrate the earth.' Our interest is in New Age, western mystics, new science, ecology. Our readers are people who are open to new ways of looking at the world. They are spiritually oriented but not necessarily religious; interested in healing of the earth, peace issues, and receptive to New Age ideas." Query or submit outline and sample chapters. Reviews artwork/photos as part of ms package.
Tips: "We have continued to publish 12 titles/year, instead of going to 15-20 at this point. We have *increased* publicity and marketing work, and our sales have not dropped."

BEHRMAN HOUSE INC., 235 Watchung Ave., West Orange NJ 07052-9827. (201)669-0447. Fax: (201)669-9769. Projects Editor: Adam Siegel. Managing Editor: Adam Bengal. Estab. 1921. Publishes Jewish nonfiction-history, Bible, philosophy, holidays, ethics—for children and adults. Averages 20 titles/year. Receives 200 submissions/year. 20% of books from first-time authors; 95% from unagented writers. Pays 2-10% on wholesale price or retail price. Buys some mss outright for $500-10,000. Offers $1,000 average advance. Publishes book 18 months after acceptance. Accepts simultaneous submissions. Reports in 2 months. Book catalog free.
Nonfiction: Juvenile (1-18), reference, textbook. Subjects include religion. "We want Jewish textbooks for the El-Hi market." Query with outline and sample chapters.

FREDERIC C. BEIL, PUBLISHER, INC., 609 Whitaker St., Savannah GA 31401. Phone/fax: (912)233-2446. E-mail: beilbook@delphi.com. Editor: Mary Ann Bowman. Publishes hardcover originals and reprints. Publishes 11 titles/year. Receives 700 queries and 9 mss/year. 15% of books from first-time authors; 100% from unagented writers. Pays 7½% royalty on retail price. Publishes book 20 months after acceptance. Accepts simultaneous submissions. Query for electronic submissions. Reports in 1 month on queries. Book catalog free on request.
Nonfiction: Biography, general trade, illustrated book, juvenile, reference. Subjects include art/architecture, history, language/literature, book arts, regional, religion. Query. Reviews artwork/photos as part of ms package. Send photocopies.
Fiction: Historical and literary. Query.

‡BELL TOWER, Imprint of Harmony, a division of the Crown Publishing Group, 201 E. 50th St., New York NY 10022. (212)572-2051. Editorial Director: Toinette Lippe. Publishes hardcover and trade paperback originals. Publishes 9 titles/year. 30% of books from first-time authors; 50% from unagented writers. Pays negotiable advance against royalties. Publishes book 1 year after acceptance of ms. Accepts simultaneous submissions. Reports in 1 week on queries and proposals, 2 weeks on mss. Book catalog free on request.

Nonfiction: Gift book, how-to, self-help, spiritual. Subjects include philosophy, psychology, religion, spiritual. Submit outline and 3 sample chapters with SASE. Reviews artwork/photos as part of ms package. Send photocopies.

Recent Nonfiction Title: *Chant: The Origins, Form, Practice, and Healing Power of Gregorian Chant,* by Katharine Le Mée (spiritual).

Fiction: Spiritual. Submit synopsis and 2 sample chapters with SASE.

Recent Fiction Title: *The Journal of Hildegard of Bingen,* by Barbara Lachman (spiritual).

ROBERT BENTLEY, INC., Automotive Publishers, 1033 Massachusetts Ave., Cambridge MA 02138. (617)547-4170. Publisher: Michael Bentley. Estab. 1949. Publishes hardcover and trade paperback originals and reprints. Publishes 15-20 titles/year. 20% of books are from first-time authors; 95% from unagented writers. Pays 10-15% royalty on net price or makes outright purchase. Advance negotiable. Publishes book 1 year after acceptance. Query for electronic submissions. Reports in 3-6 weeks. Book catalog and ms guidelines for 9×12 SAE with 4 first-class stamps.

Nonfiction: How-to, technical, theory of operation, coffee table. Automotive subjects only; this includes motor sports. Query or submit outline and sample chapters. Reviews artwork/photos as part of ms package.

Recent Nonfiction Title: *Ford F-series Pickup Truck Owners Bible.*

Tips: "We are excited about the possibilities and growth in the automobile enthusiast book market. Our audience is composed of serious, intelligent automobile, sports car, and racing enthusiasts, automotive technicians and high-performance tuners."

BERGH PUBLISHING, INC., Subsidiary of Bergh & Bergh Verlagsanstalt GmbH, Switzerland, Suite 715E, 20 E. 53rd St., New York NY 10022. (212)593-1040. Fax: (212)593-4638. Contact: Sven-Erik Bergh. Publishes hardcover originals and reprints. Publishes 10-15 titles/year. Receives 74 submissions/year. 40% of books from first-time authors; 60% from unagented writers. Pays 10-15% on wholesale price. Preliminary letter with SASE required.

Nonfiction: Biography, cookbook, illustrated book, juvenile. Subjects include animals, cooking/foods/nutrition, government/politics. Query.

Recent Nonfiction Title: *Ludmilla A. Pushkin Ruslan.*

THE BERKLEY PUBLISHING GROUP, Publishers of Berkley/Berkley Trade Paperbacks/Jove/Boulevard/Ace Science Fiction, Division of the Putnam Berkeley Group, 200 Madison Ave., New York NY 10016. (212)951-8800. Editor-in-Chief: Leslie Gelbman. Publishes paperback originals and reprints. Publishes approximately 800 titles/year. Pays 4-10% royalty on retail price. Offers advance. Publishes book 2 years after acceptance.

Nonfiction: How-to, family life, business, health, nutrition, true crime.

Fiction: Historical, mainstream, mystery, suspense, romance, science fiction, western. Submit outline/synopsis and first 3 chapters for Ace Science Fiction *only.* No other unagented mss accepted.

Tips: "No longer seeking adventure or occult fiction. Does not publish memoirs or personal stories."

BERKSHIRE HOUSE PUBLISHERS, INC., P.O. Box 297, Stockbridge MA 01262-0297. Fax: (413)298-5323. . President: Jean J. Rousseau. Estab. 1989. Publishes 12-15 titles/year. Receives 100 queries and 6 mss/year. 50% of books from first-time authors; 80% from unagented writers. Pays 5-10% royalty on retail price. Offers $500-5,000 advance. Publishes book 12-18 months after acceptance. Accepts simultaneous submissions. Query for electronic submissions. Reports in 1 month on proposals. Book catalog free on request.

Nonfiction: Biography, cookbook. Subjects include Americana, history, nature/environment, recreation (outdoors), wood crafts, regional. "All our books have a strong Berkshires or New England orientation—no others, please. To a great extent, we choose our topics then commission the authors, but we don't discourage speculative submissions. We just don't accept many. Don't overdo it; a well-written outline proposal is more useable than a full manuscript. Also, include a cv with other writing credits." Submit outline/proposal, cv and writing credits.

Tips: "Our readers are literate, active, prosperous, interested in travel, especially in selected 'Great Destinations' areas and outdoor activities and cooking."

BETHEL PUBLISHING, Subsidiary of Missionary Church, Inc., 1819 S. Main St., Elkhart IN 46516-4299. (219)293-8585. Fax: (800)230-8271. Executive Director: Rev. Richard Oltz. Estab. 1903. Publishes trade paperback originals and reprints. Averages 5 titles/year. Receives 250 submissions/year. 80% of books from first-time authors; 90% from unagented writers. Pays 5-10% royalties. Publishes book 1 year after acceptance. Accepts simultaneous submissions. Reports in 2 months. Book catalog for 9×12 SAE with 3 first-class stamps.

Nonfiction: Reference. Subjects include religion. Reviews artwork/photos as part of ms package. Query.
Fiction: Adventure, religious, suspense, young adult. Books must be evangelical in approach. No occult, gay/lesbian or erotica. Query.
Tips: "Our audience is made up of Christian families with children. If I were a writer trying to market a book today, I would find out what publisher specializes in the type of book I have written."

BETTERWAY BOOKS, Imprint of F&W Publications, 1507 Dana Ave., Cincinnati OH 45207. (513)531-2690. Editors: David Lewis, William Brohaugh. Estab. 1982. Publishes hardcover and trade paperback originals, and trade paperback reprints. Averages 30 titles/year. Pays 10-20% royalty on net receipts. Accepts simultaneous submissions if so noted. Publishes book 12-18 months after acceptance. Reports in 2 months. Book catalog for 9 × 12 SAE with 6 first-class stamps.
Nonfiction: How-to, illustrated book, reference and self-help in eight categories. Direct queries for these categories to David Lewis: home building and remodeling, woodworking, small business and personal finance, hobbies and collectibles. Direct queries for these categories to William Brohaugh: sports and recreation, reference books and handbooks (including genealogy), lifestyle (including home organization), theater and the performing arts. "Betterway books are instructional books that are to be *used*. We like specific step-by-step advice, charts, illustrations, and clear explanations of the activities and projects the books describe. We are interested mostly in original material, but we will consider republishing self-published nonfiction books and good instructional or reference books that have gone out of print before their time. Send a sample copy, sales information, and reviews, if available. If you have a good idea for a reference book that can be updated annually, try us. We're willing to consider freelance compilers of such works." No cookbooks, diet/exercise, psychology self-help, health or parenting books. Query or submit outline and sample chapters. Reviews artwork/photos as part of ms package.
Recent Nonfiction Title: *Kids, Money & Values,* by Patricia Schoff Estes and Irving Barocas.
Tips: "Keep the imprint name well in mind when submitting ideas to us. What is the 'better way' you're proposing? How will readers benefit *immediately* from the instruction and information you're giving them?"

BICYCLE BOOKS, INC., 1282 Seventh Ave., San Francisco CA 94122. (415)665-8214. Fax: (415)753-8572. Publisher/Editor: Rob van der Plas. Estab. 1985. Publishes hardcover and trade paperback originals. Averages 6 titles/year. Receives 20 submissions/year. 20% of books from first-time authors. 50% from unagented writers. Pays 15% of net royalty. Publishes book an average of 1 year after acceptance. Simultaneous submissions OK. Query for electronic submissions. Reports in 2 months. Book catalog free on request.
Nonfiction: How-to, technical. Subjects include bicycle-related titles only. "Bicycle travel manuscripts must include route descriptions and maps. Please, do not send anything outside the practical how-to field." Submit complete ms. Artwork/photos essential as part of the freelance ms package.
Tips: "Writers have a good chance selling us books with better and more illustrations and a systematic treatment of the subject. Our audience: sports/health/fitness conscious adults; cyclists and others interested in technical aspects. If I were a writer trying to market a book today, I would first check what is on the market and ask myself whether I am writing something that is not yet available and wanted."

BLACKBIRCH PRESS, INC., 1 Bradley Rd., Woodbridge CT 06525. Editorial Director: Bruce Glassman. Publishes hardcover and trade paperback originals. Publishes 30 titles/year. Receives 400 queries and 75 mss/year. 100% of books from unagented writers. Pays 4-8% royalty on wholesale price or makes outright purchase. Offers $1,000-5,000 advance. Publishes book 1 year after acceptance of ms. Accepts simultaneous submissions. Reports in 2 months.
Nonfiction Only: Biography, illustrated books, children's/juvenile, reference. Subjects include animals, anthropology/archeology, health/medicine, history, nature/environment, science, sports, women's issues/studies. No unsolicited mss or proposals. Cover letters and résumés are useful for identifying new authors. Query. Reviews artwork/photos as part of ms package. Send photocopies. No fiction or adult proposals, please.

JOHN F. BLAIR, PUBLISHER, 1406 Plaza Dr., Winston-Salem NC 27103-1470. (919)768-1374. Fax: (919)768-9194. Editor: Carolyn Sakowski. Estab. 1954. Publishes hardcover originals and trade paperbacks. Receives 2,000 submissions/year. 20-30% of books from first-time authors; 90% from unagented writers. Average print order for a first book is 5,000. Royalty negotiable. Publishes book 12-18 months after acceptance. Query for electronic submissions. Reports in 3 months. Book catalog and ms guidelines for 9 × 12 SAE with 5 first-class stamps.
Nonfiction: Especially interested in travel guides dealing with the Southeastern US. Also interested in Civil War, outdoors, travel and Americana; query on other nonfiction topics. Looks for utility and significance. Submit outline and first 3 chapters. Reviews artwork/photos as part of ms package.
Fiction: "We are interested only in material related to the Southeastern US." No category fiction, juvenile fiction, picture books or poetry.

BLUE BIRD PUBLISHING, 1739 E. Broadway, #306, Tempe AZ 85282. (602)968-4088. Fax: (602)831-1829. Publisher: Cheryl Gorder. Estab. 1985. Publishes trade paperback originals. Averages 6 titles/year. 50% of books from first-time authors; 100% from unagented writers. Pays 10% royalty on wholesale price;

15% on retail price. Publishes book 9 months after acceptance. Accepts simultaneous submissions. Reports in 3 months. Book catalog and ms guidelines for #10 SASE.

Nonfiction: How-to, reference. Subjects include child guidance/parenting, education (especially home education), sociology (current social issues). "The homeschooling population in the US is exploding. We have a strong market for anything that can be targeted to this group: home education manuscripts, parenting guides, curriculum ideas. We would also like to see complete nonfiction manuscripts in current issues, how-to topics." Submit complete ms. Reviews artwork/photos as part of ms package.

Recent Nonfiction Title: *Expanding Your Child's Horizons.*

Tips: "We are interested if we see a complete manuscript that is aimed toward a general adult nonfiction audience. We are impressed if the writer has really done his homework and the manuscript includes photos, artwork, graphs, charts, and other graphics." Please do not send fiction or short stories.

BLUE DOLPHIN PUBLISHING, INC., P.O. Box 1920, Nevada City CA 95959-1920. (916)265-6925. Fax: (916)265-0787. Imprint is Pelican Pond Publishing (mass market, contact Christopher Comins). Publisher: Paul M. Clemens. Estab. 1985. Publishes hardcover, trade and mass market paperback originals. Publishes 12-15 titles/year. Receives over 3,000 submissions/year. 65% of books from first-time authors; 90% from unagented writers. Pays 10-15% royalty on wholesale price. Publishes book 4-8 months after acceptance. Accepts simultaneous submissions. Query for electronic submissions. Reports in 2-3 months on queries; "longer with books we're considering more closely." Query with SASE. Book catalog and ms guidelines free.

• The publisher reports that sales have doubled in the past year.

Nonfiction: Biography, gift book, how-to, nature/environment, self-help. Subjects include anthropology/archaeology, foods/nutrition, ecology, education, health/medicine, psychology, comparative religion, women's issues/studies. "Blue Dolphin specializes in publishing books on comparative spiritual traditions, lay and transpersonal psychology, self-help, health, healing, and whatever helps people grow in their social conscience and conscious evolution." Submit outline, 3 sample chapters, synopsis, table of contents, author bio, with SASE. Reviews artwork as part of ms package. Send photocopies.

Recent Nonfiction Title: *What Do Women Want From Men?*, by Dan True.

Fiction: Ethnic, literary, mainstream/contemporary, religious. "Note: We are *not* fiction-based, but are publishing 1-2 year." Query with 2-page synopsis.

Recent Fiction Title: *The Gold-n-Quartz Crystal*, by Brian Jones.

Poetry: "We will only consider previously published authors of some merit or translations of noted works. Interested primarily in classical poetry or translations." Submit complete ms.

Tips: "Our audience is the concerned person interested in self-growth and awareness for oneself and the planet."

‡BLUE DOVE PRESS, P.O. Box 261611, San Diego CA 92196. (619)271-0490. Editor: Jeff Blom. Publishes hardcover and trade paperback originals and reprints. Publishes 12 titles/year. 20% of books from first-time authors; 50% from unagented writers. Pays 7.5-12% royalty on retail price. Offers $500-1,000 advance. Publishes book 8 months after acceptance of ms. Accepts simultaneous submissions. Reports in 3 months. Book catalog and ms guidelines free on request.

Nonfiction: Biography, spiritually oriented subjects. Subjects include religion, spiritually oriented. "We publish books on lives and message of saints and sages of all religions and spiritual and inspirational topics." Query with 2 sample chapters and SASE. Reviews artwork/photos as part of ms package. Send photocopies.

Recent Nonfiction Titles: *In Quest of God*, by Swami Ramdas (spiritual biography).

BLUE HERON PUBLISHING, 24450 NW Hansen Rd., Hillsboro OR 97124. (503)621-3911. President: Dennis Stovall. Vice President: Linny Stovall. Estab. 1985. Publishes trade paperback originals and reprints. Averages 6 titles/year. Reports in 6 weeks. Book catalog for #10 SASE.

Fiction: Young adult. "We are doing reprints of well known Northwest authors." Query with SASE.

Tips: "We publish Northwest writers *only*."

BLUE MOON BOOKS, INC., North Star Line, 61 Fourth Ave., New York NY 10003. Publisher/Editor: Barney Rosset. Publishes trade paperback and mass market paperback originals. Publishes 24-40 titles/year. Receives 700 queries and 500 mss/year. Pays 7½-10% royalty on retail price. Offers $500 and up advance. Publishes book 6-12 months after acceptance of ms. Accepts simultaneous submissions. Query for electronic submissions. Reports in 1-2 months. Book catalog free on request. Manuscript guidelines for #10 SASE.

Nonfiction: Query with outline and 3-6 sample chapters. Reviews artwork/photos as part of ms package if part of story. Color photocopies best but not necessary.

Recent Nonfiction Title: *Patrong Sisters: An American Woman's View of the Bangkok Sex World*, by Cleo Odzer.

Fiction: Erotica. Query or submit synopsis and 3-6 sample chapters.

BLUE POPPY PRESS, 1775 Linden Ave., Boulder CO 80304-1537. (303)442-0796. Fax: (303)447-8372. Editor-in-Chief: Bob Flaws. Publishes hardcover and trade paperback originals. Publishes 9-12 titles/year.

Receives 50-100 queries and 20 mss/year. 40-50% of books from first-time authors; 100% from unagented writers. Pays 10-15% royalty "of sales price at all discount levels." Publishes book 6-12 months after acceptance. Query for electronic submissions. Reports in 1 month. Book catalog and ms guidelines free on request.

Nonfiction: Self-help, technical, textbook related to acupuncture and Oriental medicine. "We only publish books on acupuncture and Oriental medicine by authors who can read Chinese and have a minimum of five years clinical experience. We also require all our authors to use Wiseman's *Glossary of Chinese Medical Terminology* as their standard for technical terms." Query or submit outline and 1 sample chapter with SASE.

Recent Nonfiction Title: *70 Essential TCM Formulas*, Bob Flaws (Chinese medicine).

Tips: Audience is "practicing accupuncturists, interested in alternatives in healthcare, preventive medicine, Chinese philosophy and medicine."

BLUE STAR PRODUCTIONS, (formerly Southwest Publishing Co. of Arizona), Division of Bookworld, Inc., 9666 E. Riggs Rd., #194, Sun Lakes AZ 85248. (602)895-7995. Editor: Barbara DeBolt. Publishes trade and mass market paperback originals. Publishes 10-12 titles/year. Receives 500 queries and 400-500 mss/year. 75% of books from first-time authors; 99% from unagented writers. Pays 10% royalty on wholesale or retail price. Reports in 1 month on queries, 2 months on proposals, 4-6 months on mss. Book catalog free on request. Manuscript guidelines for #10 SASE.

Nonfiction: Subjects include philosophy, ufology, religion (metaphysical). Reviews artwork/photos as part of the ms package. Send photocopies.

Recent Nonfiction Title: *We Have Watched You . . .*, by Anonymous (extraterrestrial).

Fiction: Fantasy, religious (metaphysical), UFO's "As a small press, we are doing everything possible for our authors with regard to distribution, etc. Some authors come to us knowing we are small yet expect large house results." Query or submit synopsis and the first 3 chapters.

Recent Fiction Title: *The Knowing*, by Al Bates (metal UFO).

Tips: "Know our no-advance policy beforehand and know our guidelines. No response ever without a SASE. Absolutely no phone queries. We have temporarily restricted our needs to those manuscripts whose focus is metaphysical, ufology, time travel and Native American. Query to see if this restriction has been lifted before submitting other material."

BNA BOOKS, Division of The Bureau of National Affairs, Inc., 1250 23rd St. NW, Washington DC 20037-1165. (202)833-7470. Fax: (202)833-7490. Contact: Acquisitions Manager. Estab. 1929. Publishes hardcover and softcover originals. Averages 35 titles/year. Receives 200 submissions/year. 20% of books from first-time authors; 95% from unagented writers. Pays 5-15% royalty on net cash receipts. Offers $500 average advance. Accepts simultaneous submissions. Publishes book 1 year after acceptance. Reports in 3 months on queries. Book catalog and ms guidelines free.

Nonfiction: Reference, professional/scholarly. Subjects include labor and unemployment law, environmental law, legal practice, labor relations and intellectual property law. No biographies, bibliographies, cookbooks, religion books, humor or trade books. Submit detailed table of contents or outline.

Tips: "Our audience is made up of practicing lawyers and business executives; managers, federal, state, and local government administrators; unions; and law libraries. We look for authoritative and comprehensive works that can be supplemented or revised every year or two on subjects of interest to those audiences."

THE BOLD STRUMMER LTD., 20 Turkey Hill Circle, P.O. Box 2037, Westport CT 06880-2037. (203)259-3021. Fax: (203)259-7369. Contact: Nicholas Clarke. Publishes hardcover and trade paperback originals and reprints. Publishes 6-8 titles/year. Receives 5 queries and 2 mss/year. 50% of books from first-time authors; 100% from unagented writers. Pays 10% royalty on retail price. Publishes book 9-12 months after acceptance of ms. Query for electronic submissions. Book catalog and ms guidelines free on request.

Nonfiction: Music with an emphasis on guitar and piano-related books. Query. Reviews artwork as part of ms package. Send photocopies.

Tips: "The Bold Strummer Ltd., or our associate publisher Pro/Am Music resources, publishes most good quality work that is offered in our field(s). BSL publishes guitar and related instrument books (guitar, violin, drums). Bold Strummer has also become a leading source of books about Flamenco. Pro/AM specializes in piano books, composer biography, etc. Very narrow niche publishers."

BONUS BOOKS, INC., 160 E. Illinois St., Chicago IL 60611. (312)467-0580. Editor: Anne Barthel. Estab. 1985. Publishes hardcover and trade paperback originals and reprints. Averages 30 titles/year. Receives 400-500 submissions/year. 40% of books from first-time authors; 60% from unagented writers. Royalties vary. Advances are not frequent. Publishes book 8 months after acceptance. Accepts simultaneous submissions, if so noted." Query for electronic submissions. Reports in 2 months on queries. Book catalog free on request. Manuscript guidelines for #10 SASE. All submissions and queries must include SASE.

Nonfiction: Biography, how-to. Subjects include business and economics, foods/nutrition, government/politics, health/medicine, money/finance, recreation, true crime, sports and women's issues/studies. Query with outline and sample chapters. Reviews artwork/photos as part of ms package.

BOOKCRAFT, INC., 1848 West 2300 South, Salt Lake City UT 84119. (801)972-6180. Editorial Manager: Cory H. Maxwell. Estab. 1942. Imprint is Parliament. Publishes mainly hardcover and trade paperback originals. Averages 40-45 titles/year. Receives 500-600 submissions/year. 20% of books from first-time authors; virtually 100% from unagented writers. Pays standard 7½-10-12½-15% royalty on retail price. Rarely gives advance. Publishes book 6 months after acceptance. Accepts simultaneous submissions. Reports in about 3 months. Book catalog and ms guidelines for #10 SASE.

• Volume 4 of *The Work and the Glory* received the 1994 Best Novel Award from the Association for Mormon Letters and the Frankie and John K. Orton Award for LDS Literature for 1995.

Nonfiction: "We publish for members of The Church of Jesus Christ of Latter-Day Saints (Mormons) and our books are closely oriented to the faith and practices of the LDS church, and we will be glad to review such mss. Those which have merely a general religious appeal are not acceptable. Ideal book lengths range from about 100-300 pages or so, depending on subject, presentation, and age level. We look for a fresh approach—rehashes of well-known concepts or doctrines not acceptable. Manuscripts should be anecdotal unless truly scholarly or on a specialized subject. We do not publish anti-Mormon works. We also publish short and moderate length books for children and young adults, and fiction as well as nonfiction. These reflect LDS principles without being 'preachy'; must be motivational. 30,000-45,000 words is about the right length, though good, longer manuscripts are not ruled out. We publish only 5 or 6 new juvenile titles annually. No poetry, plays, personal philosophizings, or family histories." Biography, childrens/juvenile, coffee table book, how-to, humor, reference, self-help. Subjects include: child guidance/parenting, history, religion. Query with full ms and SASE. Reviews artwork/photos as part of ms package. Send photocopies.

Recent Nonfiction Title: *Sunshine* by Elaine Cannon (inspirational).

Fiction: Should be oriented to LDS faith and practices. Adventure, historical, juvenile, literary, mainstream/contemporary, mystery, religious, romance, short story collections, suspense, western, young adult. Submit full ms with SASE.

Recent Fiction Title: *The Work and the Glory: A Season of Joy*, volume 5, by Gerald N. Lund.

Tips: "The competition in the area of fiction is much more intense than it has ever been before. We receive two or three times as many quality fiction manuscripts as we did even as recently as five years ago."

‡THE BORGO PRESS, P.O. Box 2845, San Bernardino CA 92406-2845. (714)884-5813. Fax: (909)888-4942. Publishers: Robert Reginald, Mary A. Burgess. Estab. 1975. Publishes hardcover and paperback originals. Averages 50 new titles/year, plus 150 new distributed books. Receives 500 submissions/year. 90% of books from first-time authors; 100% of books from unagented writers. Pays 10% royalty on retail price. No advance. Publishes book 3 years after acceptance. "99% of our sales go to the academic library market; we do not sell to the trade (i.e., bookstores)." Query for electronic submissions. Reports in 3 months. Book catalog for 9×12 SAE with 6 first-class stamps.

Nonfiction: Publishes literary critiques, bibliographies, historical research, film critiques, theatrical research, interview volumes, scholarly biographies, social studies, political science, and reference works for the academic library market only. Query with letter or outline/synopsis and 1 sample chapter. "All of our proprietary books, without exception, are published in open-ended, numbered, monographic series. Do not submit proposals until you have looked at actual copies of recent Borgo Press publications (*not our catalog*). We are *not* a market for fiction, poetry, popular nonfiction, artwork, or anything else except scholarly monographs in the humanities and social sciences. We discard unsolicited manuscripts from outside of our subject fields that are not accompanied by SASE. The vast majority of proposals we receive are clearly unsuitable and are a waste of both our time and the prospective author's."

Recent Nonfiction Title: *The Jewish Holocaust: An Annotated Guide To Books In English*, 2nd ed., by Marty Bloomberg and Buckley Barrett.

Tips: "We are currently buying comprehensive, annotated bibliographies of twentieth-century writers; these must be produced to a strict series format (available for SASE and 3 first-class stamps). Proposals for *The Milford Series: Popular Writers of Today* series of literary critiques (which has now reached Vol. 70) should go to the series editor, Dr. Dale Salwak, Dept. of English, Citrus College, 1000 W. Foothill Blvd., Glendora CA 91740. Many of our other series now have outside series editors."

BOWLING GREEN STATE UNIVERSITY POPULAR PRESS, Bowling Green State University, Bowling Green OH 43403-1000. (419)372-7866. Fax: (419)372-8095. Editor: Ms. Pat Browne. Estab. 1967. Publishes hardcover originals and trade paperback originals and reprints. Averages 25 titles/year. Receives 400 submissions/year. 50% of books from first-time authors; 100% from unagented writers. Pays 5-12% royalty on

---

Market conditions are constantly changing! If this is 1997 or later, buy the newest edition of Writer's Market *at your favorite bookstore or order directly from* Writer's Digest Books.

wholesale price or makes outright purchase. Publishes book 9 months after acceptance. Reports in 3 months. Book catalog and ms guidelines free on request.

Nonfiction: Biography, reference, textbook. Subjects include Americana, art/architecture, ethnic, history, language/literature, regional, sports, women's issues/studies. Submit outline and 3 sample chapters.

Recent Nonfiction Titles: *Steven King's America*, by Jonathan Davis.

Tips: "Our audience includes university professors, students, and libraries."

BOYDS MILLS PRESS, Subsidiary of *Highlights for Children*, 815 Church St., Honesdale PA 18431-1895. (717)253-1164. Imprint is Wordsong—publishes works of poetry. Manuscript Coordinator: Beth Troop. Estab. 1990. Publishes hardcover originals. Publishes 50 titles/year. Receives 10,000 queries and mss/year. 20% of books are from first-time authors; 75% from unagented writers. Pays varying royalty on retail price. Offers varying advance. Accepts simultaneous submissions. Reports in 1 month. *Writer's Market* recommends allowing 2 months for reply. Book catalog and ms guidelines free.

• Boyds Mills Press published two 1995 Junior Library Guild Selections, *The Long Silk Strand* and *The Case of the Mummified Pig*.

Nonfiction: Juvenile on all subjects. "Boyds Mills Press is not interested in manuscripts depicting violence, explicit sexuality, racism of any kind or which promotes hatred. We also are not the right market for self-help books." Submit outline and sample chapters. Reviews artwork/photos as part of ms package.

Recent Nonfiction Title: *Dinosaurs! Strange and Wonderful*, by Laurence Pringle

Fiction: Juvenile—picture book, middle grade, young adult, poetry. Submit outline/synopsis and sample chapters or complete ms.

Recent Fiction Title: *The Whispering Cloth*, by Pegi Deitz Shea.

Tips: "Our audience is pre-school to young adult. Concentrate first on your writing. Polish it. Then—and only then—select a market. We need primarily picture books with fresh ideas and characters—avoid worn themes of 'coming-of-age,' 'new sibling,' and self-help ideas. We are always interested in multicultural settings. Please—no anthropomorphic characters."

BRANDEN PUBLISHING CO., INC., 17 Station St., Box 843, Brookline Village MA 02147. Editor: Adolph Caso. Estab. 1965. Subsidiaries include International Pocket Library and Popular Technology, Four Seas and Brashear. Publishes hardcover and trade paperback originals, reprints and software. Averages 15 titles/year. Receives 1,000 submissions/year. 80% of books from first-time authors; 90% from unagented writers. Average print order for a first book is 3,000. Pays 5-10% royalty on net. Offers $1,000 maximum advance. Publishes book 10 months after acceptance. Query for electronic submissions. Reports in 1 month. *Writer's Market* recommends allowing 2 months for reply.

Nonfiction: Biography, illustrated book, juvenile, reference, technical, textbook. Subjects include Americana, art, computers, health, history, music, photography, politics, sociology, software, classics. Especially looking for "about 10 manuscripts on national and international subjects, including biographies of well-known individuals." No religion or philosophy. Paragraph query with author's vita and SASE. No unsolicited mss. No telephone inquiries. Reviews artwork/photos as part of ms package.

Recent Nonfiction Title: *We, the People*.

Fiction: Ethnic (histories, integration); religious (historical-reconstructive). No science, mystery or pornography. Paragraph query with author's vita and SASE. No unsolicited mss. No telephone inquiries.

Tips: "Branden publishes only manuscripts determined to have a significant impact on modern society. Our audience is a well-read general public, professionals, college students, and some high school students. If I were a writer trying to market a book today, I would thoroughly investigate the number of potential readers interested in the content of my book. We like books by or about women."

BRASSEY'S, INC., Division of Brassey's Ltd. (London), 1313 Dolley Madison Blvd., Suite #401, McLean VA 22101. (703)442-4535. Fax: (703)442-9848. Associate Director of Publishing: Don McKeon. Publishes hardcover and trade paperback originals and reprints. Publishes 30 titles/year. Receives 800 queries/year. 30% of books from first-time authors; 80% from unagented writers. Pays 6-12% royalty on wholesale price. Offers $50,000 maximum advance. Publishes book 9 months after acceptance of ms. Accepts simultaneous submissions. SASE required. Query for electronic submissions. Reports in 2 months on proposals. Book catalog and ms guidelines for 9×12 SASE.

Nonfiction: Biography, coffee-table book, reference, textbook. Subjects include government/politics, national and international affairs, history, military/war and intelligence studies. "We are seeking to build our biography, military history and national affairs lists." When submitting nonfiction, be sure to include sufficient biographical information (e.g., track records of previous publications), and "make clear in proposal how your work might differ from other such works already published and with which yours might compete." Submit proposal package, including outline, 1 sample chapter, bio, analysis of book's competition and return postage. Reviews artwork/photos as part of ms package. Send photocopies.

Fiction: "Submissions must be related to history, military, or intelligence topics, and authors must have previously published novels or have some special qualifications relevant to the topic." Submit synopsis and 1 sample chapter with SASE.

Tips: "Our audience consists of military personnel, government policymakers, and general readers with an interest in military history, biography, national and international affairs, defense issues and intelligence studies."

BREVET PRESS, INC., P.O. Box 1404, Sioux Falls SD 57101. Publisher: Donald P. Mackintosh. Managing Editor: Peter E. Reid. Estab. 1972. Publishes hardcover and paperback originals and reprints. Receives 40 submissions/year. 50% of books from first-time authors; 100% from unagented writers. Average print order for a first book is 5,000. Pays 5% royalty. Offers $1,000 average advance. Publishes book 1 year after acceptance. Accepts simultaneous submissions. Reports in 2 months. Book catalog free.
Nonfiction: Specializes in business management, history, place names, and historical marker series. Americana (A. Melton, editor); business (D.P. Mackintosh, editor); history (B. Mackintosh, editor); technical books (Peter Reid, editor). Query. "After query, detailed instructions will follow if we are interested." Reviews artwork/photos as part of ms package. Send photocopies.
Tips: "Write with market potential and literary excellence. Keep sexism out of the manuscripts."

BREWERS PUBLICATIONS, Division of Association of Brewers, 736 Pearl St., Boulder CO 80302. (303)447-0816. Publisher: Elizabeth Gold. Publishes trade paperback and mass market paperback originals. Publishes 8-10 titles/year. Receives 50 queries and 6 mss/year. 25% of books from first-time authors; 100% from unagented writers. Pays 2-15% royalty on net receipt. Offers $500 maximum advance. Publishes book within 18 months of acceptance of ms. Accepts simultaneous submissions. Reports in 3 months. Book catalog free on request.
Nonfiction: "We only publish books about beer and brewing—for professional brewers, homebrewers and beer enthusiasts." Query first, then submit outline if requested. Reviews artwork/photos only after a ms is accepted.
Recent Nonfiction Title: *Great American Beer Cookbook*, by Candy Schermerhorn (cookbook).

BRICK HOUSE PUBLISHING CO., #4 Limbo Lane, P.O. Box 266, Amherst NH 03031. (603)672-5112. President/publisher: Robert Runck. Estab. 1976. Publishes hardcover and trade paperback originals. Averages 8 titles/year. Receives 200 submissions/year. 20% of books from first-time authors; 100% of books from unagented writers. Pays 10% royalty on net price. Publishes book 6-12 months after acceptance. Accepts simultaneous submissions. Query for electronic submissions. Reports in 3-4 months on queries. *Writer's Market* recommends allowing 2 months for reply. Book catalog and ms guidelines for 9×12 SAE with 4 first-class stamps.
Nonfiction: How-to, reference, technical, textbook. "Subjects we are concentrating on now are renewable energy, energy conservationand environmental concerns. Other subjects include Northeast regional, business, selfhelp and sane public policy, but these are not being focused on as much.
Tips: "Authors should address the following questions in their query/proposals: What are my qualifications for writing this book? What distinguishes it from other books on the same topic. What can I do to promote the book?"

BRIGHTON PUBLICATIONS, INC., P.O. Box 120706, St. Paul MN 55112-0706. (612)636-2220. Editor: Sharon E. Dlugosch. Publishes trade paperback originals. Publishes 4 titles/year. Receives 20 queries and 4 mss/year. 50% of books from first-time authors; 100% from unagented writers. Pays 10% royalty on wholesale price. Publishes book 6 months after acceptance. Accepts simultaneous submissions. Query for electronic submissions. Reports in 3 months. Book catalog and ms guidelines for #10 SASE.
Nonfiction: How-to, business, tabletop, party themes, home making. "We're interested in topics telling how to live any part of life well. Specifically, we're developing business games for meetings, annual parties, picnics, etc., celebration themes, and party/special event planning." Query. Submit outline and 2 sample chapters.

BRISTOL PUBLISHING ENTERPRISES, INC., P.O. Box 1737, San Leandro CA 94577. (510)895-4461. Imprints include Nitty Gritty Cookbooks. Chairman: Patricia J. Hall. President: Brian Hall. Estab. 1988. Publishes 12-14 titles/year. Receives 750 proposals/year. 10% of books from first-time authors; 100% from unagented writers. Pays 6% royalty on wholesale price. Average advance $500. Publishes within 1 year of acceptance. Reports in 3-4 months. Book catalog for SAE with 2 first-class stamps.
Nonfiction: Cookbooks. Submit theme, outline and author's background.

‡BROADMAN & HOLMAN PUBLISHERS, (formerly Broadman & Holman Press) 127 Ninth Ave. N, Nashville TN 37234. Publishes hardcover and paperback originals. Averages 48 titles/year. Pays negotiable royalty. Reports in 2 months. Writer's guidelines for #10 SAE with 2 first-class stamps.
Nonfiction: Religion. "We are open to freelance submissions in all areas. Materials in these areas must be suited for an evangelical Christian readership. No poetry, biography, sermons, or art/gift books. Query with outline/synopsis and sample chapters.
Fiction: Religious. "We publish almost no fiction. For our occasional publication we want not only a very good story, but also one that sets forth Christian values. Nothing that lacks a positive Christian emphasis; nothing that fails to sustain reader interest."

Tips: "Textbook and family material are becoming an important forum for us—Bible study is very good for us. Preparation for the future and living with life's stresses and complexities are trends in the subject area."

BROADWAY PRESS, P.O. Box 1037, Shelter Island NY 11964-1037. (516)749-3266. Fax: (516)749-3267. Publisher: David Rodger. Estab. 1985. E-mail: drodger@acs.ucalgary.ca. Publishes trade paperback originals. Averages 2-3 titles/year. Receives 50-75 submissions/year. 50% of books from first-time authors; 75% from unagented writers. Pays negotiable royalty. Publishes book 18 months after acceptance. Accepts simultaneous submissions. Reports in 3 months on queries.
Nonfiction: Reference, technical. Subjects include theatre, film, television, performing arts. "We're looking for professionally-oriented and authored books." Submit outline and sample chapters.
Tips: "Our readers are primarily professionals in the entertainment industries. Submissions that really grab our attention are aimed at that market."

BUCKNELL UNIVERSITY PRESS, Lewisburg PA 17837. (717)524-3674. Fax: (717)524-3760. Director: Mills F. Edgerton, Jr. Estab. 1969. Publishes hardcover originals. Averages 25 titles/year. Receives 150 inquiries and submissions/year. 20% of books from first-time authors; 99% from unagented writers. Pays royalty. Publishes book 2 years after acceptance. Query for electronic submissions. Reports in 1 month on queries. *Writer's Market* recommends allowing 2 months for reply. Book catalog free.
Nonfiction: Subjects include scholarly art history, history, literary criticism, music, philosophy, political science, psychology, religion, sociology. "In all fields, our criterion is scholarly presentation; manuscripts must be addressed to the scholarly community." Query.
Tips: "An original work of high-quality scholarship has the best chance with us. We publish for the scholarly community."

BUSINESS McGRAW-HILL, The McGraw Hill Companies, 11 W. 19th St., New York NY 10011. (212)337-4098. Fax: (212)337-5999. Publisher: Philip Ruppel. Publishes hardcover and trade paperback originals. Publishes 100 titles/year. Receives 1,200 queries and 1,200 mss/year. 30% of books from first-time authors; 60% from unagented writers. Pays 5-17% royalty on net price. Offers $1,000-100,000 advance. Publishes book 6 months after acceptance of ms. Accepts simultaneous submissions. Query for electronic submissions. Reports in 2-3 months. Book catalog and ms guidelines free on request.
Nonfiction: How-to, reference, self-help, technical. Subjects include business and economics, government/politics, money/finance. "Current, up to date ideas, original ideas are needed. Good self promotion is key. We publish in a broad area of business." Submit proposal package, including outline, table of contents, concept.
Recent Nonfiction Title: *Buying Stock Without a Broker*, by C. Carlson (investing).

‡BUTTERWORTH-HEINEMANN, Division of Reed-Elsevier, 313 Washington St., Newton MA 02158-1626. Publishing Director: Karen Speerstra. Imprints are Focal Press (Marie Lee, editor); Digital Press (Frank Satlow, publisher); Butterworth-Heinemann (Karen Speerstra, publishing director); Medical (Susan Poli, publisher). Publishes hardcover and trade paperback originals. Publishes 100 titles/year. Each imprint publishes 25-30 titles/year. 25% of books from first-time authors; 95% from unagented writers. Pays 10-12% royalty on wholesale price. Offers modest advance. Publishes book 8-9 months after acceptance of ms. Reports in 1 month on proposals. Book catalog and ms guidelines free on request.
Nonfiction: How-to (in our selected areas), reference, technical, textbook. Subjects include business and economics, computers and electronics, health/medicine, photography, security/criminal justice, audio-video broadcast, communication technology. "We publish technical professional and academic books; no fiction." Submit outline, 1-2 sample chapters, competing books and how yours is different/better with SASE. Reviews artwork/photos as part of ms package. Send photocopies.

C Q INC., Imprint of Congressional Quarterly, Inc., 1414 22nd St. NW, Washington DC 20037. (202)887-8642 or 8645. Acquisitions Editors: Jeanne Ferris, Shana Wagger. Publishes 30-40 hardcover and paperback titles/year. 95% of books from unagented writers. Pays royalties on net receipts. Sometimes offers advance. Publishes book an average of 6-12 months after acceptance. Accepts simultaneous submissions. Reports in 3 months. Book catalog free.
Nonfiction: Reference books, information directories on federal and state governments, national elections, politics and governmental issues. Submit prospectus, writing sample and cv.
Tips: "Our books present important information on American government and politics, and related issues, with careful attention to accuracy, thoroughness and readability."

C Q PRESS, Imprint of Congressional Quarterly, Inc., 1414 22nd St. NW, Washington DC 20037. (202)887-8641. Acquisitions Editor: Brenda Carter. Publishes 20-30 hardcover and paperback titles/year. 95% of books from unagented writers. Pays standard college royalty on wholesale price. Offers college text advance. Publishes book 6 months after acceptance of final ms. Accepts simultaneous submissions. Reports in 3 months. Book catalog free.

Nonfiction: All levels of college political science texts. "We are interested in areas of American government, public administration, comparative government, and international relations." Submit proposal, outline and bio.

CADDO GAP PRESS, 3145 Geary Blvd., Suite 275, San Francisco CA 94118-3300. (415)750-9978. Fax: (415)750-9978. Publisher: Alan H. Jones. Estab. 1989. Publishes trade paperback originals and educational journals and newsletters. Publishes 4 titles/year. Receives 20 queries and 10 mss/year. 50% of books from first-time authors; 100% from unagented writers. Pays 10% royalty on wholesale price. Publishes book 1 year after acceptance of ms. Accepts simultaneous submissions. Query for electronic submissions. Reports in 2 months on proposals.
Nonfiction: Subjects limited to teacher education, social foundations of education, and multicultural education, with special interest in California education. Query.
Recent Nonfiction Titles: *The Los Angeles School Board vs. Frances Eisenberg*, by Martha Kransdorf.

CAMBRIDGE EDUCATIONAL, P.O. Box 2153, Charleston WV 25328-2153. (800)468-4227. Fax: (304)744-9351. Subsidiaries include: Cambridge Parenting and Cambridge Job Search. President: Edward T. Gardner, Ph.D. Estab. 1980. Publishes hardcover and trade paperback originals. Averages 12 titles/year. Receives 200 submissions/year. 20% of books from first-time authors; 90% from unagented writers. Makes outright purchase of $1,500-4,000. Occasional royalty arrangement. Publishes book 8 months after acceptance. Accepts simultaneous submissions. "No report unless interested." Book catalog and ms guidelines free.
● Publisher reports a greater focus on parenting and job search issues.
Nonfiction: How-to, young adult (13-24), self-help. Subjects include child guidance/parenting, cooking/foods/nutrition, education, health/medicine, money/finance and career guidance. "We need high quality books written for young adults (13-24 years old) on job search, career guidance, educational guidance, personal guidance, home economics, physical education, health, personal development, substance abuse. We are looking for scriptwriters in the same subject areas and age group. We only publish books written for young adults and primarily sold to libraries, schools, etc. We do not seek books targeted to adults or written at high readability levels." Query, submit outline/synopsis and sample chapters or send complete ms. Reviews artwork/photos as part of ms package.
Tips: "We encourage the submission of high-quality books on timely topics written for young adult audiences at moderate to low readibility levels. Call and request a copy of all our current catalogs, talk to the management about what is timely in the areas you wish to write on, thoroughly research the topic, and write a manuscript that will be read by young adults without being overly technical. Low to moderate readibility yet entertaining, informative and accurate."

CAMBRIDGE UNIVERSITY PRESS, 40 W. 20th St., New York NY 10011-4211. Editorial Director: Sidney Landau. Estab. 1534. Publishes hardcover and paperback originals. Publishes 1,300 titles/year. Receives 1,000 submissions annually. 50% of books from first-time authors; 99% from unagented writers. Pays 10% royalty on receipts; 8% on paperbacks. Publishes book an average of 1 year after acceptance. Query for electronic submissions. Reports in 4 months.
Nonfiction: Anthropology, archeology, economics, life sciences, medicine, mathematics, psychology, physics, art history, upper-level textbooks, academic trade, scholarly monographs, biography, history, and music. Looking for academic excellence in all work submitted. Department Editors: Frank Smith (history, social sciences); Mary Vaughn (English as second language); Deborah Goldblatt (English as a second language); Sidney Landau (reference); Lauren Cowles (mathematics, computer science); Scott Parris (economics); Julia Hough (developmental and social psychology, cognitive science); Alex Holzman (politics, history of science); Beatrice Rehl (fine arts, film studies); Richard Barling (medicine); Robin Smith (life sciences); Catherine Flack (earth sciences); Alan Harvey, (applied mathematics); Florence Padgett, (engineering, materials science); Terence Moore (philosophy); Susan Chang (American literature, Latin American literature); Elizabeth Neal (sociology, East Asian studies). Query. Reviews artwork/photos.

CAMELOT BOOKS, Children's Book Imprint of Avon Books, Division of the Hearst Corp., Dept. WM, 1350 Avenue of the Americas, New York NY 10019. (212)261-6817. Fax: (212)261-6895. Editorial Director: Gwen Montgomery. Publishes paperback originals and reprints. Averages 60-70 titles/year. Receives 1,000-1,500 submissions/year. 10-15% of books from first-time authors; 50% from unagented writers. Pays 6-8% royalty on retail price. Offers $2,000 minimum advance. Publishes book an average of 2 years after acceptance. Accepts simultaneous submissions. Reports in 10 weeks. Book catalog and ms guidelines for 8×10 SAE and 5 first-class stamps.
Fiction: Subjects include adventure, fantasy, humor, juvenile (Camelot, 8-12 and Young Camelot, 7-10) mainstream, mystery, ("very selective with mystery and fantasy") and suspense. Avon does not publish picture books. Submit entire ms or 3 sample chapters and a brief "general summary of the story, chapter by chapter."
Recent Fiction Title: *Crossroads*, by Paul Pitts.

CAMINO BOOKS, INC., P.O. Box 59026, Philadelphia PA 19102. (215)732-2491. Publisher: E. Jutkowitz. Estab. 1987. Publishes hardcover and trade paperback originals. Averages 5 titles/year. Receives 500 submissions/year. 20% of books from first-time authors. Pays 6-12% royalty on net price. Offers $1,000 average advance. Publishes book 1 year after acceptance. Reports in 2 weeks on queries. *Writer's Market* recommends allowing 2 months for reply.

Nonfiction: Biography, cookbook, how-to, juvenile. Subjects include agriculture/horticulture, Americana, art/architecture, child guidance/parenting, cooking/foods/nutrition, ethnic, gardening, government/politics, history, regional, travel. Query or submit outline/synopsis and sample chapters with SASE.

Tips: "The books must be of interest to readers in the Middle Atlantic states, or they should have a clearly defined niche, such as cookbooks."

CARADIUM PUBLISHING, 2503 Del Prado Blvd S., #435, Cape Coral FL 33904. Product Evaluation: Troy Dunn. Estab. 1989. Publishes hardcover, trade and mass market paperback originals. Publishes 15-20 titles/year. Receives 300 queries and 250 mss/year. 50% of books from first-time authors; 90% from unagented writers. Pays 15-20% royalty on retail price or makes outright purchase of $100 minimum. Offers $0-5,000 advance. Publishes book 3 months after acceptance of ms. Accepts simultaneous submissions. Does not return submissions; mss remain on file or destroyed. Reports on queries in 2 months.

Nonfiction: Business related: how-to, reference, self-help. Subjects include business and economics (motivation and how-to), money/finance. "We specialize in infomercials for our products." Query with outline and 3 sample chapters. Reviews artwork/photos as part of ms package. Send photocopies.

Tips: "Know the market you want to reach statistically and be creative in your submissions."

CARDOZA PUBLISHING, 132 Hastings St., Brooklyn NY 11235. (718)743-5229. Acquisitions Editor: Rose Swann. Imprints are Gambling Research Institute and Word Reference Library. Publishes trade paperback originals and mass market paperback originals and reprints. Publishes 175 titles/year. Receives 175 queries and 70 mss/year. 50% of books from first-time authors; 90% from unagented writers. Pays 5% royalty on retail price. Offers $500-2,000 advance. Publishes book 6 months after acceptance of ms. Accepts simultaneous submissions. Reports in 2 months on queries. Book catalog for 9 × 12 SAE with 3 first-class stamps.

Nonfiction: How-to, reference. Subjects include gaming, gambling, health/fitness, publishing, reference/word, travel. "The world's foremost publisher of gaming and gambling books is expanding into how-to books by qualified and knowledgeable writers. We're also seeking multimedia and software titles on all subjects for our sister company, Cardoza Entertainment." Submit outline, table of contents and 2 sample chapters.

Recent Nonfiction Title: *Complete Guide to Publishing*, by Avery Cardoza.

Tips: "The best manuscripts target the audience and appeal to readers in clear, easy-to-read writing."

CAREER PUBLISHING, INC., P.O. Box 5486, Orange CA 92613-5486. (714)771-5155. Fax: (714)532-0180. Editor-in-Chief: Marilyn M. Martin. Publishes paperback originals and software. Averages 6-20 titles/year. Receives 300 submissions/year. 80% of books from first-time authors; 90% of books from unagented writers. Average print order for a first book is 3,000-10,000. Pays 10% royalty on actual amount received. No advance. Publishes book 1 year after acceptance. Accepts simultaneous submissions (if informed of names of others to whom submissions have been sent). Query for electronic submissions. Reports in 2 months. Book catalog and ms guidelines for 9 × 12 SAE with 2 first-class stamps.

Nonfiction: Microcomputer material, educational software, work experience, allied health and medical, and transportation (trucking business, etc.) "Textbooks should provide core upon which class curriculum can be based: textbook, workbook or kit with 'hands-on' activities and exercises, and teacher's guide. Should incorporate modern and effective teaching techniques. Should lead to a job objective. We also publish support materials for existing courses and are open to unique, marketable ideas with schools (secondary and post secondary) in mind. Reading level should be controlled appropriately—usually 7th-10th grade equivalent for vocational school and community college level courses. Any sign of sexism or racism will disqualify the work. No career awareness masquerading as career training." Submit outline, 2 sample chapters and table of contents. Reviews artwork/photos as part of ms package. If material is to be returned, enclose SAE and return postage.

Recent Nonfiction Title: *Planning For Success On The Job*, by Rodger Busse.

Tips: "Authors should be aware of vocational/career areas with inadequate or no training textbooks and submit ideas and samples to fill the gap. Trends in book publishing that freelance writers should be aware of include education—especially for microcomputers."

CAROL PUBLISHING, 600 Madison Ave., New York NY 10022. (212)486-2200. Publisher: Steven Schragis. Imprints include Lyle Stuart (contact Allen Wilson), Birch Lane Press (contact Hillel Black), Citadel Press (contact Kevin McDonough) and University Books (contact Bruce Shostak). Publishes hardcover originals, and trade paperback originals and reprints. Averages 180 titles/year. Receives 2,000 submissions/year. 10% of books from first-time authors; 10% from unagented writers. Pays 5-15% royalty on retail price. Offers $1,000 advance. Publishes book 1 year after acceptance. Accepts simultaneous submissions. Reports in 2 months.

Nonfiction: Biography, cookbook, gift book, cookbook, gift book, how-to, humor, self-help. Subjects include Americana, animals, art/architecture, business and economics, computers and electronics, cooking/

foods/nutrition, education ethnic, gay/lesbian, government/politics, health/medicine, history, hobbies, language/literature, military/war, money/finance, music/dance, nature/environment, philosophy, psychology, recreation, regional, science, sports, travel, women's issues/studies. Submit outline/synopsis, sample chapters and SASE. Reviews artwork as part of ms package. Send photocopies.
Fiction: Very infrequently.

CAROLRHODA BOOKS, INC., 241 First Ave. N., Minneapolis MN 55401. (612)332-3344. Submissions Editor: Rebecca Poole. Estab. 1969. Publishes hardcover originals. Averages 50-60 titles/year. Receives 1,500 submissions/year. 15% of books from first-time authors; 95% from unagented writers. Makes outright purchase or negotiates payments of cents per printed copy. Publishes book 18 months after acceptance. Accepts simultaneous submissions. Include SASE for return of ms. Book catalog and ms guidelines for 9×12 SASE with 6 first-class stamps. No phone calls.
  ● Publisher reports a need for more multicultural stories and fewer issue-related stories for now.
Nonfiction: Publishes only children's books. Subjects include biography, animals, art, history, music, nature. Needs "biographies in story form on truly creative individuals—25 manuscript pages in length." Send full ms. Reviews artwork/photos separate from ms. Send color copies, no originals.
Recent Nonfiction Title: *Say It With Music: A Story About Irving Berlin*, by Tom Streissguth, illustrated by Jennifer Hagerman.
Fiction: Children's historical. No anthropomorphized animal stories. Submit complete ms.
Recent Fiction Title: *Jennifer Jean, the Cross-Eyed Queen*, by Phyllis Reynolds Naylor, illustrated by Jennifer Hagerman.
Tips: "Our audience consists of children ages four to eleven. We publish very few picture books. Nonfiction science topics, particularly nature, do well for us, as do biographies, photo essays, and easy readers. We prefer manuscripts that can fit into one of our series. Spend time developing your idea in a unique way or from a unique angle; avoid trite, hackneyed plots and ideas."

CARSTENS PUBLICATIONS, INC., Hobby Book Division, P.O. Box 700, Newton NJ 07860-0700. (201)383-3355. Fax: (204)383-4064. Publisher: Harold H. Carstens. Estab. 1933. Publishes paperback originals. Averages 8 titles/year. 100% of books from unagented writers. Pays 10% royalty on retail price. Offers advance. Publishes book 1 year after acceptance. Query for electronic submissions. *Writer's Market* recommends allowing 2 months for reply. Book catalog for SASE.
Nonfiction: Model railroading, toy trains, model aviation, railroads and model hobbies. "We have scheduled or planned titles on several railroads as well as model railroad and model airplane books. Authors must know their field intimately because our readers are active modelers. Our railroad books presently are primarily photographic essays on specific railroads. Writers cannot write about somebody else's hobby with authority. If they do, we can't use them." Query. Reviews artwork/photos as part of ms package.
Tips: "No fiction. We need lots of good photos. Material must be in model, hobby, railroad and transportation field only."

✓ **CASSANDRA PRESS**, P.O. Box 868, San Rafael CA 94915. (415)382-8507. Fax: (415)382-7758. President: Gurudas. Estab. 1985. Publishes trade paperback originals. Averages 6 titles/year. Receives 200 submissions/year. 50% of books from first-time authors; 50% from unagented writers. Pays 6-8% maximum royalty on retail price. Advance rarely offered. Publishes book 1 year after acceptance. Accepts simultaneous submissions. Reports in 3 weeks on queries, 2-3 months on mss. Book catalog and ms guidelines free.
Nonfiction: New Age, cookbook, how-to, self-help. Subjects include cooking/foods/nutrition, health/medicine (holistic health), philosophy, psychology, religion (New Age), metaphysical. "We like to do around six titles a year in the general New Age, metaphysical and holistic health fields so we continue to look for good material. No children's books." Submit outline and sample chapters. Reviews artwork/photos as part of ms package.
Tips: "Not accepting fiction or children's book submissions."

CATBIRD PRESS, 16 Windsor Rd., North Haven CT 06473-3015. (203)230-2391. E-mail: catbird@pipeline.com. Publisher: Robert Wechsler. Estab. 1987. Publishes hardcover and trade paperback originals and trade paperback reprints. Averages 5-6 titles/year. Receives 1,000 submissions/year. 10% of books from first-time authors. 100% from unagented writers. Pays 2½-10% royalty on retail price. Offers $1,500 average advance. Publishes book 1 year after acceptance. Accepts simultaneous submissions, if so noted. Reports in 1 month on nonfiction queries if SASE is included. *Writer's Market* recommends allowing 2 months for reply. Book catalog free on request. Manuscript guidelines for #10 SASE.
Nonfiction: Humor, reference. "We are looking for up-market prose humor and legal humor books. No joke or other small gift books." Submit outline and sample chapters with SASE.
Fiction: Humor, literary. "We are looking for well-written literature with a comic vision or style that takes a fresh approach and has a fresh, sophisitated style. No genre, wacky, or derivative mainstream fiction." Submit outline/synopsis and sample chapter with SASE.
Tips: "Our audience is generally up-market. If I were a writer trying to market a book today, I would learn about the publishing industry just as a musician learns about night clubs. If you play jazz, you should know

the jazz clubs. If you write children's books, you should learn the children's book publishers. Writing is just as much an art and a business as jazz."

CATHOLIC UNIVERSITY OF AMERICA PRESS, 620 Michigan Ave. NE, Washington DC 20064. (202)319-5052. Fax: (202)319-5802. E-mail: mcgonagle@cua.edu. Director: Dr. David J. McGonagle. Estab. 1939. Marketing Manager: Val Poletto. Averages 15-20 titles/year. Receives 100 submissions/year. 50% of books from first-time authors; 100% from unagented writers. Average print order for a first book is 750. Pays variable royalty on net receipts. Publishes book 1 year after acceptance. Query for electronic submissions. Reports in 3 months. Book catalog for SASE.
Nonfiction: Publishes history, biography, languages and literature, philosophy, religion, church-state relations, political theory. No unrevised doctoral dissertations. Length: 80,000-200,000 words. Query with outline, sample chapter, cv and list of previous publications.
Tips: "Freelancer has best chance of selling us scholarly monographs and works suitable for adoption as supplementary reading material in courses."

CATO INSTITUTE, 1000 Massachusetts Ave. NW, Washington DC 20001. (202)842-0200. Executive Vice President: David Boaz. Senior Editor: Sheldon Richman. Estab. 1977. Publishes hardcover originals, trade paperback originals and reprints. Averages 12 titles/year. Receives 50 submissions/year. 25% of books from first-time authors; 90% from unagented writers. Makes outright purchase of $1,000-10,000. Publishes book 9 months after acceptance. Accepts simultaneous submissions. Reports in 3 months. Book catalog free on request.
Nonfiction: Public policy *only*. Subjects include foreign policy, economics, education, government/politics, health/medicine, monetary policy, sociology. "We want books on public policy issues from a free-market or libertarian perspective." Query.

CAVE BOOKS, 756 Harvard Ave., St. Louis MO 63130-3134. (314)862-7646. Editor: Richard Watson. Estab. 1980. Publishes hardcover and trade paperback originals and reprints. Publishes 4 titles/year. Receives 20 queries and 10 mss/year. 75% of books from first-time authors; 100% from unagented writers. Pays 10% royalty on retail price. Publishes book 18 months after acceptance. Accepts simultaneous submissions. Reports in 3 months on mss. Book catalog free on request.
Nonfiction: Biography, technical (science), adventure. Subjects are Americana, animals, anthropology/archaeology, history, nature/environment, photography, recreation, regional, science, sports (cave exploration), travel. "We publish only books on caves, karst, and speleology." Send complete ms. Reviews artwork/photos as part of ms package. Send photocopies of illustrations.
Fiction: Adventure, historical, literary, mystery. "All must be realistic and related to cave exploration. No gothic, science fiction, fantasy, romance, or novels having nothing to do with caves. The cave and action in the cave must be central, authentic, and realistic." Send complete ms.
Tips: "Our readers are interested only in caves, karst, and speleology. Please do not send manuscripts on other subjects. Query with outline first."

THE CAXTON PRINTERS, LTD., 312 Main St., Caldwell ID 83605-3299. (208)459-7421. Fax: (208)459-7450. President: Gordon Gipson. General Editor: Pam Hardenbrook. Estab. 1895. Publishes hardcover and trade paperback originals. Averages 6-10 titles/year. Receives 250 submissions/year. 50% of books from first-time authors; 60% from unagented writers. Pays royalty. Offers advance of $500-2,000. Publishes book 18 months after acceptance. Accepts simultaneous submissions. Reports in 3 months. Book catalog for 9 × 12 SASE.
Nonfiction: Coffee table, Americana, Western Americana. "We need good Western Americana, especially the Northwest, preferably copiously illustrated with unpublished photos." Query. Reviews artwork/photos as part of ms package.
Tips: "Audience includes Westerners, students, historians and researchers."

CCC PUBLICATIONS, 1111 Rancho Conejo Blvd., Suite 411, Newbury Park CA 91320-1415. (805)375-7700. Contact: Editorial Director: Cliff Carle. Estab. 1983. Publishes trade paperback and mass market paperback originals. Averages 15-20 titles/year. Receives 400-600 mss/year. 50% of books from first-time authors; 50% of books from unagented writers. Pays 7-12% royalty on wholesale price. Publishes book an average of 6 months after acceptance. Accepts simultaneous submissions. Reports in 3 months. Catalog for 10 × 13 SAE with 2 first-class stamps.
• CCC is looking for shorter, punchier pieces with *lots* of cartoon illustrations.
Nonfiction: Humorous how-to/self-help. "We are looking for *original*, *clever* and *current* humor that is not too limited in audience appeal or that will have a limited shelf life. All of our titles are as marketable five years from now as they are today. No rip-offs of previously published books, or too special interest manuscripts." Query first with SASE. Reviews artwork/photos as part of ms package.
Tips: "Humor—we specialize in the subject and have a good reputation with retailers and wholesalers for publishing super-impulse titles. SASE is a must!"

CENTER PRESS, Box 16452, Encino CA 91416-6452. Managing Editor: Gabriella Stone. Publishes hardcover and trade paperback originals. Publishes 4-6 titles/year. Receives 600 queries and 300 mss/year. "We are no longer accepting unsolicited manuscripts. Only manuscripts received from agents, direct solicitation and through our sponsored literary contest will be read through 01/01/96." 25% of books from first-time authors. Pays 10-30% royalty on wholesale price or makes outright purchase of $500-5,000. "This depends largely on estimated sales." Offers $200-2,000 advance. Publishes book 6-10 months after acceptance. Accepts simultaneous submissions. Reports in 1-3 months on mss. Manuscript guidelines for #10 SASE.

Nonfiction: How-to, humor. Subjects include art/architecture, literature, money/finance, philosophy, photography. "We publish calendars and 'daily minders' that use photographs. We won't consider work which isn't *top* quality." Submit 1 sample chapter (maximum of 20 pages). Reviews artwork/photos as part of ms package. Send 3×5, 5×7 or 8×10 prints.

Fiction: Humor, literary, picture books. "We publish an annual collection of the winners of the "Masters Literary Award." Submit 1 sample chapter (up to 20 pages). "Will soon be joint venturing for an American version of an eastern European magazine similar to 'Vanity Fair' with a tinge of 'Playboy.' "

Poetry: Contemporary only, *very* professional, nothing saccharine, silly or sloppy. Don't confuse rhyming, metered jingles w/poetry. Submit 4-6 sample poems.

Tips: "Our readers are typically well-educated, tending to urbane, creative, middle income (mostly), eclectic and well-intended. *Read! Read! Read!* Then either have a list of sound publishing credits, or have taken several quality writing workshops from competent professionals."

CENTERSTREAM PUBLICATIONS, P.O. Box 5450, Fullerton CA 92635. (714)779-9390. Owner: Ron Middlebrook. Estab. 1980. Publishes hardcover and mass market paperback originals, trade paperback and mass market paperback reprints. Publishes 12 titles/year. Receives 15 queries and 15 mss/year. 80% of books from first-time authors; 100% from unagented writers. Pays royalty on wholesale price. Offers $300-3,000 advance. Publishes book 8 months after acceptance of ms. Accepts simultaneous submissions. Query for electronic submissions. Reports in 3 months on queries. Book catalog free on request.

Nonfiction: Currently publishing only music history.

CHAMPION BOOKS INC., P.O. Box 636, Lemont IL 60439. (800)230-1135. Contact: Rebecca Rush. Imprint is New Shoes Series. Publishes trade paperback originals. Publishes 5 titles/year. 100% of books from first-time authors; 100% from unagented writers. Pays 8-10% royalty on retail price. Publishes book 3-5 months after acceptance of ms. Accepts simultaneous submissions. Reports in 4 months on mss. Book catalog and ms guidelines free on request.

● This company reports that "we are seeking works that apply to or deal with contemporary American Society with an emphasis on counterculture and alternative lifestyles."

Fiction: Ethnic, feminist, gay/lesbian, literary, poetry, short story collections. Any finished/unfinished fiction works will be considered.

CHARLESBRIDGE PUBLISHING, 85 Main St., Watertown MA 02172. (617)926-0329. Managing Editor: Elena Dworkin Wright. Estab. 1980. Publishes school programs and hardcover and trade paperback originals. Receives 1,000 submissions/year. 10% of books from first-time authors; 100% from unagented writers. Publishes books 1 year after acceptance. Reports in 2 months.

Nonfiction: Picture books. "We look for nature/science books that teach about the world from a perspective that is relevant to a young child." Submit complete mss with written description proposing art.

Fiction: Multicultural and bilingual (English/Spanish) picture books.

Tips: "Markets through schools, book stores and specialty stores at museums, science centers, etc."

CHESS ENTERPRISES, 107 Crosstree Rd., Caraopolis PA 15108-2607. Fax: (412)262-2138. Owner: Bob Dudley. Estab. 1981. Publishes trade paperback originals. Publishes 10 titles/year. Receives 20 queries and 12 mss/year. 10% of books from first-time authors; 100% from unagented writers. Makes outright purchase of $500-3,000. Publishes book 4 months after acceptance of ms. Accepts simultaneous submissions. Query for electronic submissions. Reports in 1 month.

Nonfiction: Game of chess only. Query.

Tips: "Books are targeted to chess tournament players, book collectors."

‡CHICAGO PLAYS, 2632 N. Lincoln, Chicago IL 60614. (312)348-4658. President: Jill Murray. Publishes 35 titles/year. 75% of books from unagented writers. Pays royalty on retail price. No advance. Publishes book 6 months after acceptance of ms. Accepts simultaneous submissions. Reports in 6 month. Book catalog and ms guidelines free on request.

Nonfiction: Humor, theater. "We specialize in Chicago theater." Query.

Fiction: Plays.

CHICAGO REVIEW PRESS, 814 N. Franklin, Chicago IL 60610-3109. Editorial Director: Amy Teschner. Estab. 1973. Publishes hardcover and trade paperback originals and trade paperback reprints. Averages 25 titles/year. Receives 275 queries and 275 manuscripts annually. 30% of books from first-time authors; 50%

from unagented writers. Pays 7½-12½% royalty. Offers average $1,000 advance. Publishes book an average of 15 months after acceptance. Simultaneous submissions OK. Query for electronic submissions. Reports in 2 months on queriesm proposals or mss. Book catalog for 9×12 SAE with 10 first-class stamps. Ms. guidelines for #10 SASE.

Nonfiction: Children's/junvnile (activity books only), cookbooks (specialty only), how-to, child guidance/parenting/pregnancy, education, gardening (regional), history, hobbies, regional. "We're looking for intelligent nonfiction for educated readers (books for people with special interests in timely subjects). Submit outline and 1-2 sample chapters or proposal package (see our guidelines). Reviews artwork/photos.

Recent Nonfiction Title: *Kids Camp! Activities for the Backyard or Wilderness*, by Laurie Carlson and Judith Dammel.

Tips: "Please send for our guidelines and read them carefully."

CHILD WELFARE LEAGUE OF AMERICA, 440 First St. NW, Suite 310, Washington DC 20001. (202)638-2952. Director, Publications: Susan Brite. Publishes hardcover and trade paperback originals. Publishes 10-12 titles/year. Receives 60-100 submissions/year. 95% of books from unagented writers. 50% of books is nonauthor-subsidy published. Pays 0-10% royalty on net domestic sales. Publishes book 1 year after acceptance. Query for electronic submissions. Reports on queries in 3 months. Book catalog and ms guidelines free.

Nonfiction: Child welfare. Subjects include child guidance/parenting, sociology. Submit outline and sample chapters.

Tips: "Our audience is child welfare workers, administrators, agency executives, parents, etc. We also publish training curricula, including videos."

CHINA BOOKS & PERIODICALS, INC., 2929 24th St., San Francisco CA 94110-4126. (415)282-2994. Fax: (415)282-0994. Editor: James Wang. Estab. 1960. Publishes hardcover and trade paperback originals. Averages 5 titles/year. Receives 300 submissions/year. 10% of books from first-time authors; 95% from unagented writers. Pays 6-8% royalty on net receipts. Offers $1,000 average advance. Publishes book 1 year after acceptance. Accepts simultaneous submissions. Query for electronic submissions. Reports in 2-3 months on queries. *Writer's Market* recommends allowing 2 months for reply. Book catalog free on request. Manuscript guidelines for #10 SASE.

Nonfiction: "*Important*: *All* books *must* be on topics related to China or East Asia, or Chinese-Americans. Books on China's history, politics, environment, women, art, architecture; language textbooks, acupuncture and folklore." Biography, coffee table book, cookbook, how-to, juvenile, self-help, textbook. Subjects include agriculture/horticulture, art/architecture, business and economics, cooking/foods/nutrition, ethnic, gardening, government/politics, history, language/literature, nature/environment, religion, sociology, translation, travel, women's issues studies. Query with outline and sample chapters. Reviews artwork/photos as part of ms package.

Fiction: Ethnic, experimental, historical, literary. "*Must* have Chinese, Chinese-American or East Asian theme. We are looking for high-quality fiction with a Chinese or East Asian theme or translated from Chinese that makes a genuine literary breakthrough and seriously treats life in contemporary China or Chinese-Americans. No fiction that is too conventional in style or treats hackneyed subjects. No fiction without Chinese or Chinese-American or East Asian themes, please." Query with outline/synopsis and sample chapters.

Recent Fiction Title: *Outrageous Chinese*, by James Wang; *I Can Read That*, by Julie Sussman; and *A Dream of Red Mansions* (revised edition).

Tips: "We have a very much stronger need for writers and illustrators to work in children's nonfiction with a Chinese theme. We look for a well-researched, well-written book on China or East Asia that contains fresh insights and appeals to the intelligent reader. Our audience consists of educated and curious readers of trade books, academics, students, travelers, government officials, business people and journalists. I would also make sure to submit queries to the *smaller* publishers, especially those in your home region, because they will treat your work more seriously."

CHOSEN BOOKS PUBLISHING CO., LTD., Division of Baker Book House Company, 3985 Bradwater St., Fairfax VA 22031-3702. (703)764-8250. Fax: (703)764-3995. Editor: Jane Campbell. Estab. 1971. Publishes hardcover and trade paperback originals. Averages 8 titles/year. Receives 600 submissions/year. 15% of books from first-time authors; 99% from unagented writers. Pays royalty on net receipts. Publishes book an average of 1-2 years after acceptance. Accepts simultaneous submissions. Reports in 2-3 months. Manuscript guidelines for #10 SASE.

Nonfiction: Expositional books on narrowly focused themes. "We publish books reflecting the current acts of the Holy Spirit in the world, books with a charismatic Christian orientation." No New Age, poetry, fiction, autobiographies, academic or children's books. Submit synopsis, chapter outline, résumé and 2 sample chapters with SASE. No complete mss. No response without SASE.

Tips: "We look for solid, practical advice for the growing and maturing Christian from authors with professional or personal experience platforms. No conversion accounts or chronicling of life events, please. State the topic or theme of your book clearly in your cover letter."

CHRISTIAN EDUCATION PUBLISHERS, P.O. Box 2789, La Jolla CA 92038. (619)578-4700. Managing Editor: Carol Rogers. Publishes curriculum paperback originals. Publishes 64 titles/year. Receives 100 queries/year. 25% of books from first-time authors; 100% from unagented writers. Makes outright purchase of 2-3¢/word. Publishes book 1 year after acceptance of ms. Accepts simultaneous submissions. Query for electronic submissions. Reports in 1 month on queries. Book catalog for 9×12 SAE with 2 first-class stamps. Manuscript guidelines for #10 SASE.
Nonfiction: Curriculum, Bible studies, take-home papers. Subjects include curriculum for preschool-high school. "All writing is done on assignment. Writers should send a letter with the age level they'd like to write for (preschool-high school), and their qualifications." Query. "Freelance illustrators should send query and photocopies of artwork samples."
Recent Nonfiction Title: *Space Cubs Leader's Program Plans*, by Lynne Lepley (4-5 year-old curriculum).
Fiction: Juvenile, religious. "We publish juvenile fiction for take-home papers. All writing is on assignment and should be age appropriate—preschool through 6th grade." Query with age level preferred and qualifications.

CHRISTIAN PUBLICATIONS, INC., 3825 Hartzdale Dr., Camp Hill PA 17011. (717)761-7044. Associate Editor: David E. Fessenden. Imprints are Christian Publications, Inc., Horizon Books. Publishes hardcover originals and trade paperback originals and reprints. Publishes 40 titles/year (about 50% are reprints of classic authors). Receives 100 queries and 400 mss/year. 25% of books from first-time authors; 80% from unagented writers. Pays variable royalty or makes outright purchase. Publishes book 18 months after acceptance of ms. Accepts simultaneous submissions. Query for electronic submissions. Book catalog for 9×12 SAE with 3 first-class stamps. Manuscript guidelines for #10 SASE.
Nonfiction: Biography (missions-related preferred), how-to, reference (reprints *only*), self-help. Subjects include religion (Evangelical Christian perspective). "We are owned by the Christian and Missionary Alliance denomination; while we welcome and publish authors from various denominations, their theological perspective must be compatible with the Christian and Missionary Alliance. We are especially interested in fresh approaches to sanctification and the deeper life." Submit proposal package, including chapter synopsis, 2 sample chapters (including chapter 1), audience and market ideas, author bio.
Recent Nonfiction Title: *Just Call Me Mom! Practical Steps to Becoming a Better Mother-in-Law*, by Mary Tatern (marriage/family/parenting).
Fiction: Juvenile (missions-related *only*), religious. "Must be superbly written and incorporate biblical principles that dominate and are not secondary to the story line. We publish very little fiction; what we do publish must integrate the writer's faith." Submit synopsis and 2 sample chapters (include chapter 1).
Recent Fiction Title: *They Call Me AWOL*, by Bob Hosletler (young adult novel).
Tips: "Take time with your proposal—make it thorough, concise, complete. Authors who have done their homework regarding our message and approach have a much better chance of being accepted."

CHRONICLE BOOKS, Chronicle Publishing Co., 275 Fifth St., San Francisco CA 94103. (415)777-7240. Fax: (415)777-2289. Publisher: Jack Jensen. Associate Publishers: Nion McEvoy, Caroline Herter, Victoria Rock. Editor, fiction: Jay Schaefer. Editor, cookbooks: Bill LeBlond. Editor, general: Annie Barrows. Editor, children's: Victoria Rock. Editor, ancillary products: Debra Lande. Publishes hardcover and trade paperback originals. Averages 200 titles/year. Receives 2,500 submissions/year. 20% of books from first-time authors. 15% from unagented writers. Publishes book 18 months after acceptance. Accepts simultaneous submissions. Reports in 3 months on queries. Book catalog for 11×14 SAE with 5 first-class stamps.
Nonfiction: Coffee table book, cookbook, regional California, architecture, art, design, gardening, gift, health, nature, nostalgia, photography, recreation, travel. Query or submit outline/synopsis and sample chapters.
Fiction: Juvenile, picture books, novels, novellas, short story collections. Query or submit outline/synopsis and sample chapters. Picture books, submit ms, no query; middle grade, query first.

‡CHURCH GROWTH INSTITUTE, P.O. Box 7000, Forest VA 24551. (804)525-0022. Fax: (804)525-0608. Editor/Public Relations Coordinator: Cindy Spear. Director of Research and Development: Marvin Osborn. Estab. 1984. Publishes trade paperback originals. Publishes 10 titles/year. Pays 5% royalty on retail price or makes outright purchase. Publishes book 1 year after acceptance of ms. Accepts simultaneous submissions. Reports in 2 months on queries. Book catalog for 9×12 SAE with 4 first-class stamps. Manuscript guidelines given after query and outline is received.
Nonfiction: How-to, textbook. Subjects include religious education (church-growth related). "Material should originate from a conservative Christian view and cover topics that will help churches grow, through leadership training, new attendance or stewardship programs, and new or unique ministries. Accepted manuscripts will be adapted to our resource packet format. All material must be practical and easy for the *average* Christian to understand." Query or submit outline and brief explanation of what the packet will accomplish in the local church and whether it is leadership or lay-oriented. Reviews artwork/photos as part of ms package. Send photocopies or transparencies.

CIRCLET PRESS INC., P.O. Box 15143, Boston MA 02215-0143. Publisher/Editor: Cecilia Tan. E-mail: ctan@world.std.com. Publishes hardcover and trade paperback originals. Publishes 6-10 titles/year. Receives 50-100 queries and 200-300 mss/year. 50% of stories from first-time authors; 90% from unagented writers. Pays 4-12% royalty on retail price or makes outright purchase (depending on rights); also pays in books if author prefers. Publishes stories 3-12 months after acceptance. Accepts simultaneous submissions. Query for electronic submissions. Prefers Macintosh DD disk 3.5, queries via e-mail. Reports in 1 month on queries. Book catalog and ms guidelines for #10 SASE.

● Two stories published by Circlet Press have been nominated for the Best American Erotica 1995 volume. In 1994 they also had a winner in Best American Erotica.

Fiction: Erotic science fiction and fantasy short stories only. "Fiction must combine both the erotic and the fantastic. The erotic content needs to be an integral part of a science fiction story, and vice versa. Writers should not assume that any sex is the same as erotica." Submit full short stories up to 10,000 words. Queries only via e-mail.

Recent Fiction Title: *Techno Sex Anthology.*

Tips: "Our audience is adults who enjoy science fiction and fantasy, especially the works of Anne Rice, Storm Constantine, Samuel Delany, who enjoy vivid storytelling and erotic content. Seize your most vivid fantasy, your deepest dream and set it free onto paper. That is at the heart of all good speculative fiction. Then if it has an erotic theme as well as a science fictional one, send it to me. No horror, rape, death or mutilation! I want to see stories that *celebrate* sex and sexuality in a positive manner."

CITADEL PRESS, Imprint of Carol Publishing Group, 120 Enterprise, Secaucus NJ 07094. Fax: (201)866-8159. Editorial Director: Allan J. Wilson. Estab. 1945. Other imprints are Lyle Stuart, Birch Lane Press and University Books. Publishes hardcover originals and paperback reprints. Averages 60-80 titles/year. Receives 800-1,000 submissions/year. 7% of books from first-time authors; 50% from unagented writers. Average print order for a first book is 5,000. Pays 10% royalty on hardcover, 5-7% on paperback. Offers average $7,000 advance. Publishes book 1 year after acceptance. Accepts simultaneous submissions. Reports in 2 months. Book catalog for $1.

● Citadel Press also publishes books in conjunction with the Learning Annex, a popular adult education and self-improvement school in New York City. Recently published examples include *Starting Your Own Import-Export Business* and *Driving Your Woman Wild in Bed*.

Nonfiction and Fiction: Biography, film, psychology, humor, history. Also seeks "off-beat material, but no poetry, religion, politics." Accepts nonfiction and fiction translations. Query or submit outline/synopsis and 3 sample chapters. Reviews artwork/photos as part of ms package Send photocopies with SASE.

Tips: "We concentrate on biography, popular interest, and film, with limited fiction (no romance, religion, poetry, music)."

CLARION BOOKS, Imprint of Houghton Mifflin Company, 215 Park Ave. S., New York NY 10003. Editor/Publisher: Dorothy Briley. Executive Editor: Dinah Stevenson. Senior Editor: Nina Ignatowicz. Estab. 1965. Publishes hardcover originals. Averages 50 titles/year. Pays 5-10% royalty on retail price. Advances from $2,500. Prefers no multiple submissions. Reports in 2 months. Publishes book 2 years after acceptance. Manuscript guidelines for #10 SASE.

Nonfiction: Americana, biography, history, holiday, humor, nature, photo essays, word play. Prefers books for younger children. Query. Reviews artwork/photos as part of ms package. Send photocopies.

Fiction: Adventure, humor, mystery, strong character studies, suspense. "We would like to see more distinguished short fiction for readers seven to ten." Accepts fiction translations. Send complete ms.

Tips: Looks for "freshness, enthusiasm—in short, life" (fiction and nonfiction).

CLEAR LIGHT PUBLISHERS, 823 Don Diego, Santa Fe NM 87501-4224. (505)989-9590. Publisher: Harmon Houghton. Estab. 1981. Publishes hardcover and trade paperback originals. Publishes 12 titles/year. Receives 100 queries/year. 10% of books from first-time authors; 50% from unagented writers. Pays 10% royalty on wholesale price. Offers advance: 50% of gross potential. Publishes book 1 year after acceptance of ms. Accepts simultaneous submissions. Query for electronic submissions. Reports in 3 months on queries. Book catalog free on request.

Nonfiction: Biography, coffee table book, cookbook, humor. Subjects include Americana, anthropology/archaelogy, art/architecture, cooking/foods/nutrition, ethnic, history, nature/environment, philosophy, photography, regional (Southwest). Query. Reviews artwork/photos as part of ms package. Send photocopies.

A bullet introduces comments by the editors of Writer's Market indicating special information about the listing.

CLEIS PRESS, P.O. Box 14684, San Francisco CA 94114-0684. Fax: (415)864-3385. Acquisitions Coordinator: Frederique Delacoste. Estab. 1980. Publishes trade paperback originals and reprints. Publishes 10 titles/year. 20% of books are from first-time authors; 75% from unagented writers. Pays variable royalty on retail price. Publishes book 1 year after acceptance. Accepts simultaneous submissions "only if accompanied by an original letter stating where and when ms was sent." No electronic submissions. Reports in 2 months. Book catalog for #10 SAE with 2 first-class stamps.
Nonfiction: Subjects include feminist, gay/lesbian, queer human rights. "We are interested in books that: will sell in feminist and progressive bookstores, and will sell in Europe (translation rights). We are interested in books by and about women in Latin America; on lesbian and gay rights; on sexuality; and other feminist topics which have not already been widely documented. We do not want religious/spiritual tracts; we are not interested in books on topics which have been documented over and over, unless the author is approaching the topic from a new viewpoint." Query or submit outline and sample chapters.
Recent Nonfiction Title: *The Good Vibrations Guide to Sex*, edited by Anne Semens and Cathy Winks.
Fiction: Feminist, gay/lesbian, literary. "We are looking for high quality fiction by women. We are especially interested in translations of Latin American women's fiction. No romances!" Submit complete ms.
Recent Fiction Title: *Half a Revolution: Contemporary Fiction by Russian Women.*
Tips: "If I were trying to market a book today, I would become very familiar with the presses serving my market. More than reading publishers' catalogs, I think an author should spend time in a bookstore whose clientele closely resembles her intended audience; be absolutely aware of her audience; have researched potential market; present fresh new ways of looking at her topic; avoid 'PR' language in query letter."

CLEVELAND STATE UNIVERSITY POETRY CENTER, R.T. 1815, Cleveland State University, Cleveland OH 44115. (216)687-3986. Fax: (216)687-6943. Editor: Leonard M. Trawick. Estab. 1962. Publishes trade paperback and hardcover originals. Averages 3 titles/year. Receives 400 queries and 900 mss/year. 60% of books from first-time authors; 100% from unagented writers. 30% of titles subsidized by CSU, 20% by government subsidy. CSU Poetry Series pays one-time, lump-sum royalty of $200-400 plus 50 copies; Cleveland Poetry Series (Ohio poets only) pays 100 copies. $1,000 prize for best ms each year. No advance. Publishes book 1 year after acceptance. Accepts simultaneous submissions. Reports in 2 weeks on queries, 6-8 months on mss. Book catalog for 6×9 SAE with 2 first-class stamps. Manuscript guidelines for SASE.
Poetry: No light verse, "inspirational," or greeting card verse. ("This does not mean that we do not consider poetry with humor or philosophical/religious import.") Query—ask for guidelines. Submit only December-February. $15 reading fee. Reviews artwork/photos if applicable (e.g., concrete poetry).
Tips: "Our books are for serious readers of poetry, i.e. poets, critics, academics, students, people who read *Poetry, Field, American Poetry Review, Antaeus*, etc. Trends include movement away from 'confessional' poetry; greater attention to form and craftsmanship. Try to project an interesting, coherent personality; link poems so as to make coherent unity, not just a miscellaneous collection. Especially needs poems with *mystery*, i.e., poems that suggest much, but do not tell all."

CLIFFS NOTES, INC., P.O. Box 80728, Lincoln NE 68501. (402)423-5050. General Editor: Michele Spence. Notes Editor: Gary Carey. Studyware Editor: Chrissy Frye. Imprint is Centennial Press. Estab. 1958. Publishes trade paperback originals and educational software. Averages 20 titles/year. 100% of books from unagented writers. Pays royalty on wholesale price. Buys majority of mss outright; "full payment on acceptance of ms." Publishes book an average of 1 year after acceptance. Reports in 1 month. *Writer's Market* recommends allowing 2 months for reply. "We provide specific guidelines when a project is assigned."
Nonfiction: Self-help, textbook. "We publish self-help study aids directed to junior high through graduate school audience. Publications include *Cliffs Notes, Cliffs Test Preparation Guides, Cliffs Quick Reviews, Cliffs StudyWare*, and other study guides. Most authors are experienced teachers, usually with advanced degrees. Some books also appeal to a general lay audience. Query.
Recent Nonfiction Title: Cliffs *Quick Review Chemistry.*

CLINE/FAY INSTITUTE, INC., The Love and Logic Press, Inc., 2207 Jackson St., Golden CO 80401. (303)278-7552. Executive Vice President/Publisher: Nancy M. Henry. Publishes hardcover and trade paperback originals. Publishes 18 titles/year. Pays 5-7½ royalty. Offers $500-5,000 advance against royalties. Publishes book 1 year after acceptance of ms. Accepts simultaneous submissions. Query for electronic submissions. Reports in 2 months on queries, 3 months on proposals, 4 months on mss. Book catalog free on request.
Nonfiction: Self-help. Subjects include child guidance/parenting, education, health/medicine, psychology, sociology, current social issue trends. "We will consider any queries/proposals falling into the above categories (with the exception of parenting) but especially psychology/sociology and current social issues and trends." Please do not submit mss or proposal in New Age category, personal recovery stories, i.e., experiences with attempted suicide, drug/alcohol abuse, institutionalization or medical experiences. Query. Reviews artwork/photos as part of ms package. Send photocopies.
Recent Nonfiction Title: *Grandparenting With Love and Logic*, by Jim Fay and Foster W. Cline.

COBBLEHILL BOOKS, Affiliate of Dutton Children's Books, 375 Hudson St., New York NY 10014. (212)366-2000. Editorial Director: Joe Ann Daly. Executive Editor: Rosanne Lauer. Pays royalty. Publishes fiction and nonfiction for young readers, middle readers and young adults, and picture books. Query for mss longer than picture book length; submit complete ms for picture books. Reports in 1 month. Accepts simultaneous submissions, if so noted.

COFFEE HOUSE PRESS, 27 N. Fourth St., Suite 400, Minneapolis MN 55401. Editorial Assistant: Cheri Hickman. Estab. 1984. Publishes trade paperback originals. Publishes 15 titles/year. Receives 4,500 queries and mss/year. 95% of books are from unagented writers. Pays 8% royalty on retail price. Offers average $500 advance. Publishes book 18 months after acceptance. Reports in 2 months on queries, 6 months on mss. Book catalog and ms guidelines for #10 SAE with 2 first-class stamps.
  • Coffee House Press books received 13 nominations, awards and honors in 1994.
Fiction: Literary novels, short story collections, and short-short story-collections. No genre. Looking for prose by women and writers of color. Query first with samples and SASE.
Tips: Look for our books at stores and libraries to get a feel for what we like to publish. Please, no phone calls or faxes.

THE COLLEGE BOARD, Imprint of College Entrance Examination Board, 45 Columbus Ave., New York NY 10023-6992. (212)713-8000. Director of Publications: Carolyn Trager. Publishes trade paperback originals. Publishes 30 titles/year; imprint publishes 12 titles/year. Receives 50-60 submissions/year. 25% of books from first-time authors; 50% from unagented writers. Pays royalty on retail price of books sold through bookstores. Offers advance based on anticipated first year's earnings. Publishes book 9 months after acceptance. Reports in 1 month on queries. *Writer's Market* recommends allowing 2 months for reply. Book catalog free on request.
Nonfiction: Education-related how-to, reference, self-help. Subjects include college guidance, education, language/literature, science. "We want books to help students make a successful transition from high school to college." Query or send outline and sample chapters. Reviews artwork/photos as part of ms package.
Tips: "Our audience consists of college-bound high school students, beginning college students and/or their parents."

‡COLLEGE PRESS PUBLISHING CO., P.O. Box 1132, Joplin MO 64802. (417)623-6280. Publishes hardcover and trade paperback originals and reprints. Publishes 25-30 titles/year. 1-5% of books from first-time authors; 95% from unagented writers. Pays 5-12% royalty on wholesale price. Publishes book 6 months after acceptance of ms. Accepts simultaneous submissions. Reports in 2-3 months on proposals. Book catalog for 9 × 12 SAE with 5 first-class stamps. Manuscript guidelines free on request.
Nonfiction: Christian textbooks and small group studies. Subjects include religion. Submit help for Christian leaders, churches, and families . . . preparing people for the 21st Century. Query with outline, bio, 2 sample chapters and SASE.
  • A listing for this publisher also appears in the Subsidy/Royalty section.
Tips: Conservative Evangelical Christians. "Our affiliation is Christian Churches, Churches of Christ but appeal cross-denominationally. Submit conservative, Biblical expositions with an 'American' view/perspective. (We do not publish prophetic books.)"

‡COMBINED BOOKS, INC., 151 E. Tenth Ave., Conshohocken PA 19428. (610)828-2595. Senior Editor: Kenneth S. Gallagher. Publishes hardcover originals and trade paperback reprints. Publishes 12-14 titles/year. 30% of books from first-time authors; 100% from unagented writers. Pays 8-10% royalty on wholesale price. Offers $1,000-1,500 advance. Publishes book 1 year after acceptance of ms. Reports in 4 months. Book catalog free on request.
Nonfiction: Military history. "We publish a series called Great Campaigns. Authors should be aware of the editorial formula of this series." Submit outline and 1 sample chapter with SASE. Reviews artwork/photos as part of ms package. Send photocopies only.
Recent Nonfiction Title: *Gettysburg Campaign*, by Albert A. Nofi (trade military).

‡COMIC ART PUBLISHING CO., Imprint of Adventure Feature Syndicate, 329 Harvey Dr., Glendale CA 91206. (818)551-0077. Editor: Jo Bustamante. Publishes trade paperback originals and reprints. Publishes 6 titles/year. Receives 200 queries and 100 mss/year. 100% of books from first-time authors; 100% from unagented writers. Pays 30% royalty. Offers $1,500 advance. Publishes books 6 months after acceptance of ms. Accepts simultaneous submissions. Reports in 1-2 months on queries. Book catalog for #10 SASE. Guidelines for $2 and 2 first-class stamps.
Nonfiction: Children's/juvenile, how-to, illustrated book, textbook, art. Subjects include education, hobbies. Query. Reviews artwork/photos as part of ms package. Send photocopies.
Fiction: Adventure, fantasy, mystery, suspense, western. Submit synopsis and sample chapters.

‡COMMUNE-A-KEY PUBLISHING, P.O. Box 58637, Salt Lake City UT 84158. (801)581-9191. Editor-in-Chief: Caryn Summers. Publishes trade paperback originals and reprints and audiotapes. Publishes 4-6 titles/

year. 70% of books from first-time authors; 100% from unagented writers. Pays 7-8½ royalty on retail price. Publishes book 9-12 months after acceptance of ms. Accepts simultaneous submissions. Reports in 1 month on queries and proposals, 2 months on mss. Book catalog and ms guidelines free on request.

Nonfiction: Gift book/inspirational, humor, self-help/psychology, spiritual. Subjects include health/medicine, psychology, men's or women's issues/studies, recovery, Native American. "Commune-A-Key's mission statement is: 'Communicating Keys to Growth and Empowerment.' " Query. Reviews artwork/photos as part of ms package. Send photocopies.

Recent Nonfiction Title: *Inspirations for Caregivers*, by Caryn Summers, RN (inspirational/gift).

Fiction: Young adult, personal growth fiction. Must have psychological/personal growth/spiritual message. Query.

Recent Fiction Title: *The Girl, the Rock and the Water*, by C. Summers (book/audio package).

‡**COMMUNICATION/THERAPY SKILL BUILDERS**, Imprint of The Psychological Corporation, 3830 E. Bellevue, Tucson AZ 85718. (520)323-7500. Supervising Editor: Sarah Trotta. Imprints are Therapy Skill Builders (contact Pamela Prevost-Donison) and Communication Skill Builders (contact Patricia Hartmann). Publishes 60 titles/year; each imprint publishes 20-40/year. Receives 100 queries/year. 55% of books from first-time authors; 100% from unagented writers. Pays 6½-10% royalty. Offers $1,000-2,000 advance. Publishes book 1 year after acceptance of ms. Reports in 3 months. Book catalog and ms guidelines free on request.

Nonfiction: How-to, reference, therapy materials for SLPs, OTs and PTs. Subjects include education, language/literature, software. Submit outline. Reviews artwork as part of ms package. Reviews photocopies.

Recent Nonfiction Title: *Feeding and Nutrition for the Child with Special Needs: Handouts for Parents*, by Marsha Dunn Klein, M.Ed., OTR/L, and Tracy A. Delaney, Ph.D., RD.

‡**COMPUTER SCIENCE PRESS**, Imprint of W.H. Freeman and Company, 41 Madison Ave., New York NY 10010. (212)576-9451. Fax: (212)689-2383. Publisher: Richard T. Bonacci. Estab. 1974. Publishes hardcover and paperback originals. Averages 5 titles/year. 25% of books from first-time authors; 98% of books from unagented writers. All authors are recognized subject area experts. Pays royalty on net price. Publishes book 6-9 months after acceptance. Reports ASAP.

Nonfiction: "Technical books in all aspects of computer science, computer engineering, information systems and telecommunications. Both text and reference books. Also considers public appeal 'trade' books in computer science, manuscripts and diskettes." Query or submit complete ms. Looks for "technical accuracy of the material and an explanation of why this approach was taken. We would also like a covering letter stating what the author sees as the competition for this work and why this work is superior or an improvement on previous available material."

Recent Nonfiction Title: *Fundamentals of Data Structures in C++*, by Howowitz, Sahni, Mehta.

CONARI PRESS, 1144 65th St., Suite B, Emeryville CA 94608. (510)596-4040. Executive Editor: Mary Jane Ryan. Editorial Associate: Claudia Schaab. Estab. 1987. Publishes hardcover and trade paperback originals. Averages 17 titles/year. Receives 800 submissions/year. 50% of books from first-time authors; 50% from unagented writers. Pays 8-12% royalty on list price. Offers $1,500 average advance. Publishes book an average of 1 year after acceptance. Accepts simultaneous submissions. Query for electronic submissions. Reports in 3 months. Manuscript guidelines for #10 SASE.

Nonfiction: Psychology/self-help, spirituality, women's issues. Submit outline and sample chapters, attn: Claudia Schaab. Reviews artwork/photos as part of ms package.

Tips: "Writers should send us well-targeted, specific and focused manuscripts. No recovery issues."

‡**CONCORDIA PUBLISHING HOUSE**, 3558 S. Jefferson Ave., St. Louis MO 63118-3968. (314)268-1000. Fax: (314)268-1329. Family and Children's Editor: Ruth Geisler. Church Resources Director: Barry Bobb. Editorial Associate: Doris M. Schraer. Estab. 1869. Publishes hardcover and trade paperback originals. Averages 60 titles/year. Receives 2,000 submissions/year. 10% of books from first-time authors; 95% from unagented writers. Pays royalty or makes outright purchase. Publishes book 1 year after acceptance. Accepts simultaneous submissions. Query for electronic submissions. Reports in 2 months on queries. Manuscript guidelines for #10 SASE.

Nonfiction: Juvenile, adult. Subjects include child guidance/parenting (in Christian context), inspirational, how-to, religion. "We publish Protestant, inspirational, theological, family and juveniles. All manuscripts

Market conditions are constantly changing! If this is 1997 or later, buy the newest edition of Writer's Market at your favorite bookstore or order directly from Writer's Digest Books.

must conform to the doctrinal tenets of The Lutheran Church—Missouri Synod."
Fiction: Juvenile. "We will consider preteen and children's fiction and picture books. All books must contain Christian content. No adult Christian fiction."
Tips: "Our needs have broadened to include writers of books for lay adult Christians and of Christian novels (low-key, soft-sell) for pre-teens and teenagers."

CONFLUENCE PRESS, INC., Lewis-Clark State College, 500 Eighth Ave., Lewiston ID 83501-1698. (208)799-2336. Publisher/Director: James R. Hepworth. Publishes hardcover originals and trade paperback originals and reprints. Publishes 4-5 titles/year. Receives 500 queries and 150 mss/year. 50% of books from first-time authors; 50% from unagented writers. Pays 10-15% royalty on net sales price. Offers $100-2,000 advance. Publishes book 18 months after acceptance of ms. Accepts simultaneous submissions. Reports in 2 months on queries, 1 month on proposals, 3 months on mss. Book catalog and ms guidelines free on request.
Nonfiction: Reference, bibliographies. Subjects include Americana, ethnic, history, language/literature, nature/environment, regional, translation. Query.
Recent Nonfiction Title: *Norman Maclean*, edited by Ron McFarland and Hugh Nichols (literary criticism).
Fiction: Ethnic, literary, mainstream/contemporary, short story collections. Query.
Recent Fiction Title: *Cheerleaders From Gomorrah*, by John Rember.
Poetry: Submit 6 sample poems.
Recent Poetry Title: *Trace Elements From A Recurring Kingdom*, by William Pitt Root.

THE CONSULTANT PRESS, 163 Amsterdam Ave., #201, New York NY 10023-5001. (212)838-8640. Fax: (212)873-7065. Publisher: Bob Persky. Imprint is The Photographic Arts Center. Estab. 1980. Publishes trade paperback originals. Averages 7 titles/year. Receives 25 submissions/year. 20% of books from first-time authors; 75% from unagented writers. Pays 7-12% royalty on receipts. Offers $500 average advance. Publishes book 6 months after acceptance. No simultaneous submissions. Reports in 3 weeks. Book catalog free.
Nonfiction: How-to, reference, art/architecture, business and economics of the art world and photography. "Our prime areas of interest are books on the business of art and photography. Writers should check *Books In Print* for competing titles." Submit outline and 2 sample chapters.
Tips: "Artists, photographers, galleries, museums, curators and art consultants are our audience."

CONSUMER REPORTS BOOKS, Subsidiary of Consumers Union, 101 Truman Ave., Yonkers NY 10703-1057. Fax: (914)378-2902. Contact: Mark Hoffman. Estab. 1936. Publishes hardcover and trade paperback originals and reprints. Averages 15-20 titles/year. Receives 500 submissions/year. Pays variable royalty on retail price or makes outright purchase. Publishes book 18 months after acceptance. Accepts simultaneous submissions. Reports in 1 month on queries, 2 months on mss. Book catalog free on request.
Nonfiction: How-to, reference, self-help, automotive. Subjects include health and medicine, automotive, consumer guidance, home owners reference, money and finance. Submit outline/synopsis and 1-2 sample chapters.

‡CONSUMERTRONICS-TOP SECRET, 2011 Crescent Dr., P.O. Drawer 537, Alamogordo NM 88310-0537. (505)434-0234. CEO: John Williams. Publishes trade and mass market paperback originals. Publishes 15 titles/year. Receives 100 queries and 30 mss/year. 17% of books from first-time authors. Pays 10-50% royalty on retail price or makes outright purchase of $100-10,000. Publishes book 2 months after acceptance. Accepts simultaneous submissions. Reports in 1 month. Book catalog for $4. Manuscript guidelines free on request.
Nonfiction: How-to, illustrated book, self-help, technical. Subjects include computers, telephone and other electronics, security, surveillance, government/politics, health/medicine, hobbies, military/war, money/finance (economic survival), nature/environment, philosophy, science, software, hi-tech survivalism. Submit outline or proposal package, including entire ms. Reviews artwork/photos as part of ms package. Send photocopies (fully labeled).
Recent Nonfiction Title: *Phone Color Boxes*, by John Williams (how-to).
Tips: "Our readers are savvy, survival-oriented, with some hi-tech skills, particularly in computers, electronics and phones. Manuscripts should be complete, clear and comprehensive."

CONTEMPORARY BOOKS, INC., Two Prudential Plaza, Suite 1200, Chicago IL 60601. (312)782-9182. Editorial Director: Nancy J. Crossman. Estab. 1947. Publishes hardcover originals and trade paperback originals and reprints. Averages 75 titles/year. Receives 2,500 submissions/year. 10% of books from first-time authors; 25% of books from unagented writers. Pays 6-15% royalty on retail price. Publishes book 10 months after acceptance. Query for electronic submissions. Accepts simultaneous submissions. Reports in 3 weeks. *Writer's Market* recommends allowing 2 months for reply. Manuscript guidelines for SASE.
Nonfiction: Biography, cookbook, how-to, humor, reference, self-help. Subjects include business, finance, cooking, health/fitness, psychology, sports, real estate, nutrition, popular culture, women's studies. Submit outline and sample chapters. Reviews artwork/photos as part of ms package.

COOL HAND COMMUNICATIONS, INC., 1098 NW Second Ave., #1, Boca Raton FL 33432-2616. (407)750-9826. Fax: (407)750-9869. Publisher: Chris K. Hedrick. Editor: Peter D. Ackerman. Imprint is Cool

Kids Press. Publishes hardcover and trade paperback. Publishes 15-20 titles/year. Receives 1,000 queries/year. 40% of books from first-time authors; 80% from unagented writers. Pays 6-15% royalty on wholesale price. Advance varies. Publishes book 12-18 months after acceptance. Accepts simultaneous submissions. Reports in 6 weeks on queries, 3 months on mss. Catalog and ms guidelines for 9×12 SAE with 4 first-class stamps.

Nonfiction: Biography, cookbook, how-to, humor, self-help, books on important issues, subjects include cooking/foods/nutrition, health/medicine, travel, true crime. "We're looking for books that can make a positive difference in the lives of readers and society as a whole—novel, innovative approaches to the important issues of our times—the environment, poverty, race relations, animal and human abuse, drugs, crime, etc. We don't want to see anything so specialized that the subject matter limits the size of the potential audience. Nothing too esoteric—we prefer practical, useful information and material that offers concrete solutions to difficult problems. We seek positive, uplifting books that educate and entertain. We don't want lists of questions—we want answers." Query. Reviews artwork/photos as part of ms package.

Recent Nonfiction Title: *How to Figure Out A Man/Woman*, by Joella Cain (humor).

Fiction: Horror, maintream/contemporary, mystery. "We're in the market for fiction with great story lines and strong characters. Subject matter isn't nearly as important as the quality of the writing and whether the work has soul—it has to make the reader feel as well as think. And if the book succeeds in communicating a positive message, so much the better. No science fiction or fantasy, and we're not big for historical romance or *anything* with salacious sex, unwarranted violence or material intended to shock simply for shock's sake. The chance of our accepting a fiction manuscript is very slim—we've published one novel in two years. The writing must be of *superior* quality before we will even consider it."

‡COOL KIDS PRESS, Imprint of Cool Hand Communications, 1098 NW Boca Raton Blvd., Boca Raton FL 33432. (407)750-9826. Editorial Director: Lisa McCourt. Publishes hardcover original picture books. Publishes 10 titles/year. All contracts negotiated separately. Offers variable advance. Accepts multiple submissions and unsolicited mss. Send entire ms with SASE. No queries. Reports within 3 months.

Nonfiction: Juveniles (trade books). No textbooks.

Recent Nonfiction Title: *Bugs and Beasties ABC*, by Cheryl Nathan.

Fiction: Juveniles (trade books).

Recent Fiction Title: *Rockabye Rabbit*, by Kersten Hamilton.

‡COPPER CANYON PRESS, P.O. Box 271, Port Townsend WA 98368. (206)385-4925. Editor: Sam Hamill. Publishes trade paperback originals. Publishes 8 titles/year. Receives 900 queries/year and 500 mss/year. 10% of books from first-time authors; 95% from unagented writers. Pays 7-10% royalty on retail price. Offers $500-1,000 average advance. Publishes book 18 months after acceptance of ms. No simultaneous submissions. Reports in 1 month. Book catalog and ms guidelines free on request.

Poetry: Query with 5-7 sample poems.

Recent Poetry Titles: *The Book of Light*, by Lucille Clifton.

CORNELL MARITIME PRESS, INC., P.O. Box 456, Centreville MD 21617-0456. (410)758-1075. Fax: (410)758-6849. Managing Editor: Charlotte Kurst. Estab. 1938. Publishes hardcover originals and quality paperbacks for professional mariners and yachtsmen. Averages 7-9 titles/year. Receives 150 submissions/year. 41% of books from first-time authors; 99% from unagented writers. "Payment is negotiable but royalties do not exceed 10% for first 5,000 copies, 12½% for second 5,000 copies, 15% on all additional. Royalties for original paperbacks are invariably lower. Revised editions revert to original royalty schedule." Publishes book 1 year after acceptance. Query for electronic submissions. Query first, with writing samples and outlines of book ideas. Reports in 2 months. Book catalog for 10×13 SAE with 5 first-class stamps.

Nonfiction: Marine subjects (highly technical), manuals, how-to books on maritime subjects. Tidewater imprint publishes books on regional history, folklore and wildlife of the Chesapeake Bay and the Delmarva Peninsula.

Recent Nonfiction Title: *The Law of Tug, Tow, and Pilotage*, third ed., by Alex L. Parks and Edward V. Cattell, Jr.

CORWIN PRESS, INC., 2455 Teller Rd., Thousand Oaks CA 91320. (805)499-9734. Editor: Ann McMartin. Publishes hardcover and paperback originals. Publishes 40 titles/year. Pays 10% royalty on net sales. Publishes book 7 months after acceptance of ms. Accepts simultaneous submissions. Reports on queries in 1 month. *Writer's Market* recommends allowing 2 months for reply. Manuscript guidelines for #10 SASE.

Nonfiction: Professional-level publications. Subjects include educational policy, educational administration, educational evaluation, urban education reform, teacher development, classroom practice, primarily in K-12. Query.

COTTONWOOD PRESS, INC., 305 W. Magnolia, Suite 398, Fort Collins CO 80521. Editor: Cheryl Thurston. Publishes trade paperback originals. Publishes 2-8 titles/year. Receives 50 queries and 400 mss/year. 50% of books from first-time authors; 100% from unagented writers. Pays 10-12% royalty on net sales. Publishes book 1 year after acceptance. Accepts simultaneous submissions, if so noted. Reports in 1 month on queries and proposals, 3 months on mss. Book catalog for 6×9 SAE with 2 first-class stamps. Manuscript guidelines for #10 SASE.

Nonfiction: Textbook. Subjects include education, language/literature. "We publish *only* supplemental textbooks for English/language arts teachers, grades 5-12, with an emphasis upon middle school and junior high materials. Don't assume we publish educational materials for all subject areas. We do not. Never submit anything to us before looking at our catalog. We have a very narrow focus and a distinctive style. Writers who don't understand that are wasting their time." Query with outline and 1-3 sample chapters.

THE COUNTRYMAN PRESS, INC., P.O. Box 175, Woodstock VT 05091-0175. (802)457-1049. Managing Editor: Laura Jorstad. Estab. 1973. Imprints are Foul Play Press, Backcountry Publications. Publishes hardcover originals, trade paperback originals and reprints. Publishes 20-25 titles/year. Receives 2,500 submissions/year. 50% of books from first-time authors; 75% from unagented writers. Pays 6-10% royalty on retail price. Offers $1,000 average advance. Publishes book 1 year after acceptance. Accepts simultaneous submissions. Reports in 2 months. No material returned without SASE. No unsolicited mss. Book catalog free.

● This publisher recently received Vermont Book Publishers Association Special Merit Awards for *Perennials for the Backyard Gardner*, by Patricia Turcotte; *Full Duty*, by Howard Coffin; and *The Best of Libby Hillman's Kitchen*.

Nonfiction: Country living, how-to, travel and recreation guides. Subjects include history, nature/environment, recreation, fishing, regional (New England, especially Vermont), travel. "We want books related to nature/environmental issues; good 'how-to' books, especially those related to rural life; and regional guides to hiking, walking, bicycling, and fishing—especially fly-fishing—for all parts of the country." Submit outline and sample chapters. Reviews artwork/photos as part of ms package.

Fiction: Mystery. Query or submit outline and sample chapter with SASE. No unsolicited mss.

‡COUNTRYSPORT PRESS, 1515 Cass, P.O. Box 1856, Traverse City MI 49685. Editorial Director: Doug Truax. Publishes hardcover originals and reprints. Publishes 12 titles/year. 20% of books from first-time authors; 90% from unagented writers. Pays royalty on wholesale price. Advance varies by title. Publishes book 1 year after acceptance of ms. Accepts simultaneous submissions. Reports in 1 month on queries; 3 months on proposals and mss. Book catalog free.

Nonfiction: Coffee table book, illustrated book, other. Subjects include animals, hobbies, nature/environment, wing shooting, fly fishing, outdoor-related subjects. "We are looking for high-quality writing that is often reflective, anecdotal, and that offers a complete picture of an outdoor experience. Less interested in how-to." Query with outline and 3 sample chapters.

Recent Nonfiction Title: *Chasing Fish Tales*, by John Holt (fly fishing).

Tips: "Our audience is upscale sportsmen with interests in wing shooting, fly fishing, and other outdoor activities."

CRAFTSMAN BOOK COMPANY, 6058 Corte Del Cedro, Carlsbad CA 92009-9974. (619)438-7828 or (800)829-8123. Fax: (619)438-0398. Editorial Manager: Laurence D. Jacobs. Estab. 1957. Publishes paperback originals. Averages 12 titles/year. Receives 50 submissions/year. 85% of books from first-time authors; 98% from unagented writers. Pays 7½-12½% royalty on wholesale price or retail price. Publishes book 18 months after acceptance. Accepts simultaneous submissions. Query for electronic submissions. Reports in 1 month on queries. *Writer's Market* recommends allowing 2 months for reply. Book catalog and ms guidelines free.

Nonfiction: How-to, technical. All titles are related to construction for professional builders. Query. Reviews artwork/photos as part of ms package.

Tips: "The book should be loaded with step-by-step instructions, illustrations, charts, reference data, forms, samples, cost estimates, rules of thumb, and examples that solve actual problems in the builder's office and in the field. The book must cover the subject completely, become the owner's primary reference on the subject, have a high utility-to-cost ratio, and help the owner make a better living in his chosen field."

CREATION HOUSE, Strang Communications, 600 Rinehart Rd., Lake Mary FL 32746. (407)333-3132. Acquisitions Coordinator: Kelli Bass. Publishes hardcover and trade paperback originals. Publishes 18 titles/year. Receives 100 queries and 400 mss/year. 2% of books from first-time authors; 95% from unagented writers. Pays 5-20% royalty on wholesale price. Offers $500-3,000 advance. Publishes book 6-9 months after acceptance of ms. Accepts simultaneous submissions. Reports in 2 months on proposals. Manuscript guidelines for #10 SASE.

Nonfiction: Christian. "Our target market is Pentecostal/charismatic Christians." Submit outline, 3 sample chapters and author bio. Reviews artwork/photos as part of ms package. Send photocopies.

Recent Nonfiction Title: *The Truth About Angels*, by Terry Law.

‡CREATIVE BOOK COMPANY, 13920 Roscoe Blvd., Panorama City CA 91402-4213. (818)893-3565. President: Sol H. Marshall. Imprints are Edinburgh Castle Books, Ranchito del Sol Publications. Publishes trade and mass market paperback originals. Publishes 4-6 titles/year. 100% of books from first-time authors;

100% from unagented writers. Pays $100-500. Publishes book 8 months after acceptance of ms. Accepts simultaneous submissions. Reports in 2 months. Book catalog and ms guidelines for 9×12 SAE with 3 first-class stamps.

Nonfiction: Cookbook, how-to, humor, Jewish interest. Subjects include cooking/foods/nutrition, Judaism, gerontology, public relations. "Writers should know accepted procedures for submitting queries or proposals." Query. Reviews artwork/photos as part of ms package. Send photocopies.

Recent Nonfiction Title: *Public Relations Basics for Community Organizations*, by Sol H. Marshall (textbook).

Tips: Audience is beginning writers and publicists; cookbook collectors; gerontologists; individuals, students, teachers and others interested in Judaica; educators.

‡CRISP PUBLICATIONS, INC., 1200 Hamilton Ct., Menlo Park CA 94025-1427. (415)323-6100. Publisher: W. Philip Gerould. Publishes trade paperback originals. Averages 25-30 titles/year. Pays royalty on retail price. Publishes book 6 months after acceptance. Book catalog free.

Nonfiction: How-to, self-help. Subjects include art/architecture, business and economics, education, health/medicine and money/finance. Submit outline/synopsis and sample chapters.

CROSS CULTURAL PUBLICATIONS, INC., P.O. Box 506, Notre Dame IN 46556. Fax: (219)273-5973. General Editor: Cyriac Pullapilly. Publishes hardcover and software originals. Publishes 15-20 titles/year. Receives 3,000 queries and 1,000 mss/year. 25% of books from first-time authors; 99% from unagented writers. Pays 10% royalty on wholesale price. Publishes book 6 months after acceptance of ms. Accepts simultaneous submissions. Reports in 1 month on queries. *Writer's Market* recommends allowing 2 months for reply. Book catalog free on request.

Nonfiction: Biography. Subjects include government/politics, history, philosophy, religion, sociology, scholarly. "We publish scholarly books that deal with intercultural topics—regardless of discipline. Books pushing into new horizons are welcome, but they have to be intellually sound and balanced in judgement." Query.

THE CROSSING PRESS, 97 Hanger Way, Watsonville CA 95019. Co-Publishers: Elaine Goldman Gill, John Gill. Publishes hardcover and trade paperback originals. Averages 50 titles/year. Receives 1,600 submissions/year. 10% of books from first-time authors; 75% from unagented writers. Pays royalty. Publishes book 18 months after acceptance. Accepts simultaneous submissions. Reports in 6 weeks on queries. Book catalog free.

Nonfiction: Cookbook, how-to, women's interest. Subjects include health, New Age, gender issues, gay. Submit outline and sample chapter.

Recent Nonfiction Title: *Natural Remedy Book for Women*, by Diane Stein (health).

Recent Fiction Title: *When Warhol Was Alive*, by Margaret McMullen.

Tips: "Simple intelligent query letters do best. No come-ons, no cutes. It helps if there are credentials. Authors should research the press first to see what sort of books it publishes."

CROSSWAY BOOKS, Division of Good News Publishers, 1300 Crescent St., Wheaton IL 60187-5800. Fax: (708)682-4785. Editorial Director/Editor-in-Chief: Leonard G. Goss. Contact: Jill Carter. Estab. 1938. Publishes hardcover and trade paperback originals. Averages 50 titles/year. Receives 3,000 submissions/year. 5% of books from first-time authors; 90% from unagented writers. Average print order for a first book is 5,000-10,000. Pays negotiable royalty. Offers negotiable advance. Publishes book 1 year after acceptance. No phone queries. Reports in up to 9 months. Book catalog and ms guidelines for 9×12 SAE with 6 first-class stamps.

Nonfiction: Subjects include issues on Christianity in contemporary culture, Christian doctrine, church history. "All books must be written out of Christian perspective or world view." Query with outline.

Fiction: Contemporary, science fiction, fantasy (genuinely creative in the tradition of C.S. Lewis, J.R.R. Tolkien and Madeleine L'Engle), juvenile (10-14; 13-16). No formula romance, short stories, poetry, true stories, children's illustrated. Also, no horror novels or "issue" novels. Query with synopsis. "All fiction must be written from a genuine Christian perspective."

Tips: "The writer has the best chance of selling our firm a book which, through fiction or nonfiction, shows the practical relevance of biblical doctrine to contemporary issues and life."

CROWN PUBLISHING GROUP, Division of Random House, 201 E. 50th St., New York NY 10022. General interest publisher. This publisher did not respond to our request for information. Query before submitting.

‡CSLI PUBLICATIONS, Stanford University The Center for the Study of Language and Information, Stanford University, Ventura Hall, Stanford CA 94305. (415)723-1839. Editorial Associate: Tony Gee. Publishes hardcover and trade paperback originals. Publishes 10 titles/year. Receives 75-100 queries and 23-35 mss/year. 50% of books from first-time authors; 100% from unagented writers. Pays 5-10% royalty on retail price or makes outright purchase for books. Offers $150-250 advance. Publishes book 1 year after acceptance of ms. Accepts simultaneous submissions. Does not return submissions. Reports in 3 months on queries, 1 year on proposals and mss.

Nonfiction: Textbook, other academic books. Subjects include linguistics; computer science. "We only accept camera-ready copy and we prefer works recommended by professors and researchers in the field of linguistics." Query.

Recent Nonfiction Title: *Perspectives In Phonology*, by Jennifer Cole and Charles Kisseberth (linguistics text).

‡CYPRESS PUBLISHING GROUP, 11835 ROE #187, Leawood KS 66211. (913)681-9875. Vice President Marketing: Carl Heintz. Publishes hardcover and trade paperback originals. Publishes 10 titles/year. 80% of books from first-time authors; 90% from unagented writers. Pays 10-15% royalty on wholesale price. Publishes book 8 months after acceptance of ms. Reports in 2 weeks on queries, 1 month on proposals and mss. Book catalog free on request. Manuscript guidelines for #10 SASE.

Nonfiction: How-to, illustrated book, self-help, technical, textbook. Subjects include business and economics, computers and electronics (business related), hobbies (amateur radio, antique radio), money/finance, psychology (business related), software (business related). "We use America Online and CompuServe extensively. Our editorial plans change—we are always looking for outstanding submissions. Many writers fail to consider what other books on the topics are available. The writer must think about the fundamental book marketing question: Why will a customer *buy* the book?" Query with proposal package, including outline, 1-3 sample chapters, overview of book. Send photocopies.

Recent Nonfiction Title: *The Edison Effect*, by Ron Ploof (adapting to technological change).

DA CAPO PRESS, Plenum Publishing, 233 Spring St., New York NY 10013. Senior Editor: Yuval Taylor. Publishes trade paperback reprints. Publishes 60 titles/year. Pays 6% royalty on wholesale price. Offers $1,500-2,000 advance. Publishes book 6 months after acceptance of ms. Accepts simultaneous submissions. Reports in 3 months on queries. Book catalog free on request.

- Da Capo Press wishes to emphasize that it publishes only one or two paperback originals per year; the rest are reprints.

Nonfiction: Biography, history. Subjects include art/architecture, gay/lesbian, government/politics, military/war, music/dance, psychology, science, sports. Query.

Recent Nonfiction Title: *The Collapse of the Third Republic*, by William L. Shirer (history).

DAN RIVER PRESS, Imprint of The Conservatory of American Letters, P.O. Box 298, Thomaston ME 04861. (207)354-0998. Editor: Robert W. Olmsted. Publishes hardcover and trade paperback originals. Publishes 6-7 titles/year. Receives 600 queries and 200 mss/year. 100% of books from unagented writers. Pays 10-15% royalty on amount received by us. Offers $250-500 advance. Publishes book 1 year after acceptance of ms. Accepts simultaneous submissions, if so noted. Query for electronic submissions. Reports in 2 months on mss. Book catalog for 6×9 SAE with 2 first-class stamps. Manuscript guidelines for #10 SASE. Do not submit until you receive ms guidelines.

- Dan River Press requests a small reading fee donation to consider manuscripts for publication. It no longer publishes poetry.

Nonfiction: Biography. "We don't do much nonfiction." Query. Reviews artwork/photos as part of ms package. Send photocopies.

Fiction: Adventure, confession, erotica, experimental, fantasy, gothic, historical, horror, humor, literary, mainstream/contemporary, mystery, occult, plays, romance, science fiction, short story collections, suspense, western. Submit entire ms after reading guidelines and a book or two.

Recent Fiction Title: *The Bethvalen Road*, Sheldon Welinte (short story collection).

DANCE HORIZONS, Imprint of Princeton Book Co., Publishers, P.O. Box 57, 12 W. Delaware Ave., Pennington NJ 08534. (609)737-8177. Fax: (609)737-1869. Publicity Manager: Frank Bridges. Estab. 1976. Publishes hardcover and paperback originals and paperback reprints on dance only. Averages 10 titles/year. Receives 25-30 submissions/year. 50% of books from first-time authors; 98% of books from unagented writers. Pays 10% royalty on net receipts. No advance. Publishes book 10 months after acceptance. Accepts simultaneous submissions. Reports in 3 months. Book catalog free.

Nonfiction: Dance and children's movement subjects only.

Recent Nonfiction Title: *Duncan Dance*, by Julia Levien.

Tips: "We're very careful about the projects we take on. They have to be, at the outset, polished, original and cross-marketable."

‡DANCING JESTER PRESS, 3411 Garth Rd., Suite 208, Baytown TX 77521. (713)427-9560. Fax: (713)428-8685. Publisher/Editor: Glenda Daniel. Imprints are Gesture Graphic Design Books (Jane McClarney, editor); Dancing Dagger Publications (Dan L. Gilbert, mystery); Dancing Jester Poetry (Dorothy Lawson, poetry editor); *The Trickster Review of Cultural Censorship* (biannual periodical, Lierbag Nile Leinad, editor; Glenda Daniel, publisher); Dancing Jester Fiction (Shiloh Daniel, fiction). Publishes hardcover and trade paperback originals and reprints. Publishes 16 titles/year. Imprints publish 4 titles/year. 15% of books from first-time authors; 100% from unagented writers. Pays 4-12% royalty on retail price or makes outright purchase.

Advance negotiable. Publishes book 18 months after acceptance of ms. Accepts simultaneous submissions. Reports in 2 weeks on queries, 1 month on proposals, 3-6 months on mss. Book catalog for $1. Manuscript guidelines for #10 SASE.

• Dancing Jester Press also sponsors the "One Night in Paris Should Be Enough" prize. See the Contests and Awards section for more information.

Nonfiction: Autobiography, children's/juvenile, coffee table book, cookbook, how-to, humor, illustrated book, multimedia (CD-ROM), reference, self-help, textbook. Subjects include animals (rights), anthropology/ archaeology, art/architecture, cooking/foods/nutrition (vegan/low-fat only), ethnic, lesbian, government/politics, health/medicine, history (of censorship), language/literature/criticism/theory, music/dance, nature/environment, philosophy, photography, psychology, recreation, religion, science, sociology, software, translation, women's issues/studies. Query with outline and SASE. Reviews artwork/photos as part of ms package. Send photocopies or transparencies.

Recent Nonfiction Title: *The Third Millennium Spicery & Herbal Handbook: Low-low-fat Global Cooking*, by G.G. Thomson (audio-cookbook).

Fiction: Adventure, erotica, ethnic, experimental, feminist, gay/lesbian, historical, humor, juvenile, literary, mainstream/contemporary, mystery, picture books, plays, short story collections, suspense, western, young adult. "We are adding a children's mystery imprint next fall. We will consider 100-page manuscripts of books easily expandable into series." Query with synopsis, 3 sample chapters and SASE.

Recent Fiction Title: *Driver Without Malice*, by Clementine Mathis (novel/audio book).

Poetry: "I foresee a reemergence of love poetry in the tradition of *Another Birth* by Persian poet Fūrugh Farrukhzad (1967). A word of caution: I have little or no tolerance for the merely obscene attempting to pass itself off as erotic." Submit complete ms, e-mail address for a prompt response.

Recent Poetry Title: *Blue Atomic Heart-Eating Women & Quantum Blue Soul-Eating Men*, by Gabriel Thomson.

Tips: "I envision an audience with an insatiable desire to read, varied interests and deep pockets."

DANTE UNIVERSITY OF AMERICA PRESS, INC., P.O. Box 843, Brookline Village MA 02147-0843. President: Adolph Caso. Estab. 1975. Publishes hardcover and trade paperback originals and reprints. Averages 5 titles/year. Receives 50 submissions/year. 50% of books from first-time authors; 50% from unagented writers. Average print order for a first book is 3,000. Pays royalty. Negotiable advance. Publishes book 10 months after acceptance. No simultaneous submissions. Query for electronic submissions. Reports in 2 months.

Nonfiction: Biography, reference, reprints, translations from Italian and Latin. Subjects include general scholarly nonfiction, Renaissance thought and letter, Italian language and linguistics, Italian-American history and culture, bilingual education. Query first with SASE. Reviews artwork/photos as part of ms package.

Fiction: Translations from Italian and Latin. Query first with SASE.

Poetry: "There is a chance that we would use Renaissance poetry translations."

Recent Fiction Title: *Rogue Angel*, by Carol Damioli.

MAY DAVENPORT, PUBLISHERS, 26313 Purissima Rd., Los Altos Hills CA 94022. (415)948-6499. Editor/Publisher: May Davenport. Estab. 1976. Imprint is md Books (nonfiction and fiction). Publishes hardcover and trade paperback originals. Averages 4 titles/year. Receives 1,500 submissions/year. 95% of books from first-time authors; 100% from unagented writers. Pays 15% royalty on retail price. No advance. Publishes book 1 year after acceptance. Reports in 1 month. *Writer's Market* recommends allowing 2 months for reply. Book catalog and ms guidelines for #10 SASE.

Nonfiction: Juvenile (13-17). Subjects include: Americana language/literature, humorous memoirs for children/young adults. "For children. Stories to read with pictures to color. Either the writer can express himself in 500 words to make children laugh (and learn) or he can't. For young adults: humorous memoirs. Forget the Depression, WWII. Entertain an unseen audience with words. Query with SASE. Reviews artwork/photos as part of ms package. Send thumbnail sketches.

Recent Nonfiction Title: *Sumo, The Wrestling Elephant*, by Esther Mok (picture book to read and color).

Fiction: Humor, literary.

Recent Fiction Title: *Eyes in the Attic*, by Nadine McKinney (preteen humorous novel).

Tips: "Since the TV-oriented youth in schools today do not like to read or write, why not create books for that impressionable and captive audience. And if we can be successful with *Tug of War* as a textbook in Missouri middle schools, why not try to get it in the schools nationally? Great to work with talented writers. Perhaps we might motivate some youthful persons to become writers, to value the print media."

JONATHAN DAVID PUBLISHERS, INC., 68-22 Eliot Ave., Middle Village NY 11379-1194. Fax: (718)894-2818. Editor-in-Chief: Alfred J. Kolatch. Estab. 1948. Publishes hardcover and trade paperback originals and reprints. Publishes 20-25 titles/year. 50% of books from first-time authors; 90% from unagented writers. Pays royalty or makes outright purchase. Offers $1,000-5,000 advance. Publishes book 18 months after acceptance of ms. Reports in 2 months on queries. Book catalog for 6×9 SAE with 4 first-class stamps.

• This publisher has expressed an interest in seeing more projects geared toward children.

Nonfiction: Cookbook, how-to, reference, self-help. "We specialize in Judaica." Submit outline and 1 sample chapter with SASE.

HARLAN DAVIDSON, INC., 773 Glenn Ave., Wheeling IL 60090-6000. (708)541-9720. Fax: (708)541-9830. Editor-in-Chief: Maureen G. Hewitt. Estab. 1972. Additional Imprint is Forum Press, Inc. Publishes college texts, both hardcover and paperback. Publishes 15 titles/year. Receives 200 queries and 25 mss/year. 100% of books from unagented writers. Manuscripts contracted as work for hire. Pays royalty on net. Publishes book 10 months after acceptance of ms. Accepts simultaneous submissions. Query for electronic submissions. Reports in 3 months on proposals. Book catalog free on request.
Nonfiction: Subjects include business, education, ethnic history, government, history (main list), biographical history, literature, philosophy, regional state histories, sociology, women's issues/studies. "Because we are a college textbook publisher, academic credentials are extremely important. We usually find our own authors for a need in the field that we identify, but we are also receptive to ideas brought to us by qualified professionals, in history, especially." Submit proposal package, including outline, brief description of proposed book, its market and competition and a recent vita.

DAVIS PUBLICATIONS, INC., 50 Portland St., Worcester MA 01608. (508)754-7201. Fax: (508)753-3834. Managing Editor: Wyatt Wade. Acquisitions Editors: Claire M. Golding and Helen Ronan. Estab. 1901. Averages 5-10 titles/year. Pays 10-12% royalty. Publishes book 1 year after acceptance. Book catalog for 9×12 SAE with 2 first-class stamps. Write for copy of guidelines for authors.
Nonfiction: Publishes technique-oriented art, design and craft books for the educational market. Accepts nonfiction translations. "Keep in mind the intended audience. Our readers are visually oriented. All illustrations should be collated separately from the text, but keyed to the text. Photos should be good quality transparencies and black and white photographs. Well-selected illustrations should explain, amplify, and enhance the text. We average 2-4 photos/page. We like to see technique photos as well as illustrations of finished artwork, by a variety of artists, including students. Recent books have been on printmaking, clay sculpture, design, jewelry, drawing and watercolor painting." Submit outline, sample chapters and illustrations. Reviews artwork/photos as part of ms package.
Recent Nonfiction Title: *3-D Wizardry: Design in Papier-Mâché, Plaster and Foam*, by George Wolfe.

DAW BOOKS, INC., 375 Hudson St., 3rd Floor, New York NY 10014-3658. Submissions Editor: Peter Stampfel. Estab. 1971. Publishes science fiction and fantasy hardcover and paperback originals and reprints. Publishes 60-80 titles/year. Pays in royalties with an advance negotiable on a book-by-book basis. Sends galleys to author. Simultaneous submissions "returned unread at once, unless prior arrangements are made by agent." Reports in 6 weeks "or longer, if a second reading is required." Book catalog free.
Fiction: "We are interested in science fiction and fantasy novels only. We do not publish any other category of fiction. We accept both agented and unagented manuscripts. We are not seeking collections of short stories or ideas for anthologies. We do not want any nonfiction manuscripts." Submit complete ms.

‡DAWN PUBLICATIONS, 14618 Tyler Foote Rd., Nevada City CA 95959. (800)545-7475. Editor: Glenn J. Hovemann. Publishes hardcover and trade paperback originals. Publishes 6 titles/year. Receives 250 queries and 900 mss/year. 35% of books from first-time authors; 100% from unagented writers. Pays royalty on wholesale price. Publishes book 6-12 months after acceptance of ms. Accepts simultaneous submissions. Reports in 1-2 months. Book catalog and ms guidelines for #10 SASE.
Nonfiction: Children's/juvenile, cookbook. Subjects include animals, health/medicine, nature/environment, psychology. Query with SASE.
Recent Nonfiction Title: *The Tree In the Ancient Forest*, by Carol Reed-Jones (children's nature awareness).

W.S. DAWSON CO., P.O. Box 62823, Virginia Beach VA 23466. (804)499-6271. Fax: (804)497-0920. Publisher: C.W. Tazewell. Publishes hardcover and trade paperback originals. Publishes 10 titles/year. Receives 16 queries and 6 mss/year. Pays negotiated royalty. Publishes book 6 months after acceptance of ms. Accepts simultaneous submissions. Query for electronic submissions. Reports in 1 month on queries. *Writer's Market* recommends allowing 2 months for reply. Book catalog free on request.
Nonfiction: Biography, humor. Subjects include history, regional. "Most publications are Virginia local history, genealogy and biography, and in particular Eastern Virginia. Advance approval is requested before sending manuscripts, etc." Query. Reviews artwork/photos as part of ms package. Send photocopies.
Recent Nonfiction Title: *Health Freedom: Preventive Medicine Can Save your Life and Fortune.*

DEARBORN FINANCIAL PUBLISHING, INC., 155 N. Wacker Dr., Chicago IL 60606-1719. (312)836-4400. Fax: (312)836-1021. Senior Vice President: Anita Constant. Estab. 1959. Imprints are Dearborn/R&R Newkirk (contact Anne Shropshire), Enterprise/Dearborn (contact Caroline Carney), Real Estate Education Co. (contact Carol Luitjens), and Upstart Publishing Co. (contact Mr. Jere Calmes). Publishes hardcover and paperback originals. Averages 200 titles/year. Receives 200 submissions/year. 50% of books from first-time authors; 50% from unagented writers. Pays 1-15% royalty on wholesale price. Publishes book 6 months after

acceptance. Accepts simultaneous submissions. Query for electronic submissions. Reports in 1 month. *Writer's Market* recommends allowing 2 months for reply. Book catalog and ms guidelines free.
Nonfiction: How-to, reference, textbooks. Subjects include small business, real estate, insurance, banking, securities, money/finance. Query.
Tips: "People seeking real estate, insurance, broker's licenses are our audience; also professionals in these areas. Additionally, we publish for consumers who are interested in buying homes, managing their finances; and people interested in starting and running a small business."

IVAN R. DEE, INC., 1332 N. Halsted St., Chicago IL 60622-2632. (312)787-6262. Fax: (312)787-6269. President: Ivan R. Dee. Estab. 1988. Imprint is Elephant Paperbacks. Publishes hardcover originals and trade paperback originals and reprints. Averages 25 titles/year. 10% of books from first-time authors; 75% from unagented writers. Pays royalty. Publishes book 9 months after acceptance. Reports in 1 month on queries. *Writer's Market* recommends allowing 2 months for reply. Book catalog free on request.
Nonfiction: History, literature and letters, biography, politics, contemporary affairs, theater. Submit outline and sample chapters. Reviews artwork/photos as part of ms package.
Recent Nonfiction Title: *J. Edgar Hoover, Sex, and Crime*, by Athan Theoharis.
Tips: "We publish for an intelligent lay audience and college course adoptions."

DEL REY BOOKS, Imprint of Ballantine Books, Division of Random House, 201 E. 50th St., New York NY 10022-7703. (212)572-2856. Executive Editor: Shelly Shapiro. Senior Editor: Veronica Chapman. Estab. 1977. Publishes hardcover, trade paperback, and mass market originals and mass market paperback reprints. Averages 60 titles/year. Receives 1,900 submissions/year. 10% of books from first-time authors; 40% from unagented writers. Pays royalty on retail price. Offers competitive advance. Publishes book 1 year after acceptance. Reporting time 1-6 months, occasionally longer. Writer's guidelines for #10 SASE.
Fiction: Fantasy ("should have the practice of magic as an essential element of the plot"), science fiction ("well-plotted novels with good characterization, exotic locales, and detailed alien cultures"). Submit complete ms, outline and first 3 chapters.
Recent Fiction Title: *The Tangle Box*, by Terry Brooks.
Tips: "Del Rey is a reader's house. Our audience is anyone who wants to be pleased by a good, entertaining novel. Pay particular attention to plotting and a satisfactory conclusion. It must be/feel believable. That's what the readers like."

DELACORTE PRESS, Imprint of Dell Publishers, Division of Bantam Doubleday Dell, 1540 Broadway, New York NY 10036. (212)354-6500. Editor-in-Chief: Leslie Schnur. Publishes hardcover originals. Publishes 36 titles/year. Royalty and advance vary. Publishes book an average of 2 years after acceptance, but varies. Accepts simultaneous submissions. Reports in 2 months. Book catalog and guidelines for 9 × 12 SASE.
Nonfiction and Fiction: Query with outline, first 3 chapters or brief proposal. No mss for children's or young adult books accepted in this division.

DELL PUBLISHERS, division of Bantam Doubleday Dell, Inc., 1540 Broadway, New York NY 10036. Imprints include Delacorte, Delta Books and Laurel Books. General interest publisher of all categories of fiction and nonfiction. Publishes approximately 40 books/month. Query Editorial Department before submitting. Unsolicited and unagented mss will not receive a response for 3-4 months.

DELPHI PRESS, INC., P.O. Box 267990, Chicago IL 60626. (312)274-7910. Fax: (312)274-7912. Publisher: Karen Jackson. Estab. 1989. Publishes trade paperback originals and reprints. Publishes 10-12 titles/year. Receives 50-100 queries and 20-30 mss/year. 95% of books from first-time authors; 95% from unagented writers. Pays 7½-12% royalty on wholesale price. Publishes book within 2 years after acceptance of ms. Accepts simultaneous submissions. Reports in 2 months on proposals. Book catalog and ms guidelines free on request.
Nonfiction: Delphi Press focuses on women's spirituality, men's mysteries; Wicca, witchcraft and pagan practice; ritual, healing, divination and magick; nature/earth religions and deep ecology; sacred psychology and inner development especially utilizing magick or psychic techniques. Submit complete ms or outline and 3 sample chapters.
Tips: "Audience is educated-up-scale 30 + adults interested in alternative spirituality and personal power."

THE DENALI PRESS, P.O. Box 021535, Juneau AK 99802-1535. (907)586-6014. Fax: (907)463-6780. Editorial Director: Alan Schorr. Editorial Associate: Sally Silvas-Ottumwa. Estab. 1986. Publishes trade paperback originals. Averages 5 titles/year. Receives 120 submissions/year. 50% of books from first-time authors; 80% from unagented writers. Pays 10% royalty on wholesale price or makes outright purchase. Publishes book 9-12 months after acceptance. Accepts simultaneous submissions. Query for electronic submissions. Reports in 1 month. Prefer letter of inquiry. Book catalog free on request.
  • This publisher won an award from the Association of Jewish Libraries for "Outstanding Reference Book" in 1994.

Nonfiction: Reference. Subjects include Americana, Alaskana, anthropology, ethnic, government/politics, history, recreation. "We need reference books—ethnic, refugee and minority concerns." Query with outline and sample chapters. All unsolicited mss are tossed. Author must contact prior to sending ms.

Recent Nonfiction Title: *Building a New South*, edited by Wilkinson, Stoltz, Richards and Cox.

Tips: "We are looking for reference works suitable for the educational, professional and library market."

T.S. DENISON & CO., INC., 9601 Newton Ave. S., Minneapolis MN 55431-2590. (612)888-6404. Fax: (612)888-6318. Director of Product Development: Sherrill B. Flora. Acquisitions Editor: Danielle de Gregory. Estab. 1876. Publishes teacher aid materials. Receives 1,500 submissions/year. 20% of books from first-time authors; 100% from unagented writers. Average print order for a first book is 3,000. Makes outright purchase. Publishes book 1-2 years after acceptance. Reports in 2 months. Book catalog and ms guidelines for 9×12 SAE with 3 first-class stamps.

Nonfiction: Specializes in early childhood and elementary school teaching aids. Submit complete ms. *Writer's Market* recommends query with SASE first. Reviews artwork/photos as part of ms package. Send prints if photos are to accompany ms.

DEVYN PRESS, Subsidiary of Baron Barclay Bridge Supplies, Suite 230, 3600 Chamberlain Lane, Louisville KY 40241. (502)426-0410. President: Randy Baron. Publishes hardcover and trade paperback originals and reprints. Publishes 10 titles/year. Receives 40 queries and 20 mss/year. 50% of books from first-time authors; 90% from unagented writers. Pays 5-10% royalty on wholesale price. Offers $500-1,000 advance. Publishes book 6 months after acceptance of ms. Accepts simultaneous submissions. Query for electronic submissions. Reports in 2 months on queries. Book catalog and ms guidelines free on request.

Nonfiction: How-to, self-help. Subjects include sports and games/bridge. "We are the world's largest publisher of books on the game of bridge." Query. Reviews artwork/photos as part of ms package. Send photocopies.

DIAL BOOKS FOR YOUNG READERS, Division of Penguin USA Inc., 375 Hudson St., 3rd Floor, New York NY 10014. (212)366-2800. Imprints include Dial Easy-to-Read Books, Dial Very First Books. No unsolicited mss. Publishes hardcover originals. Averages 80 titles/year. Receives 8,000 submissions/year. 10% of books from first-time authors. Pays variable royalty and advance. Accepts simultaneous submissions, but not preferred. Reports in 4 months. Book catalog and ms guidelines for 9×12 SASE with 4 first-class stamps.

Nonfiction: Juvenile picture books, young adult books. Especially looking for "quality picture books and well-researched young adult and middle-reader manuscripts." Not interested in alphabet books, riddle and game books, and early concept books. Query with outline/synopsis and sample chapters. Reviews artwork/photos as part of ms package.

Fiction: Juvenile picture books, young adult books. Adventure, fantasy, historical, humor, mystery, romance (appropriate for young adults), suspense. Especially looking for "lively and well written novels for middle grade and young adult children involving a convincing plot and believable characters. The subject matter or theme should not already be overworked in previously published books. The approach must not be demeaning to any minority group, nor should the roles of female characters (or others) be stereotyped, though we don't think books should be didactic, or in any way message-y. No topics inappropriate for the juvenile, young adult, and middle grade audiences. No plays." Submit complete ms. Also publishes Pied Piper Book (paperback Dial reprints) and Pied Piper Giants (1½ feet tall reprints).

Tips: "Our readers are anywhere from preschool age to teenage. Picture books must have strong plots, lots of action, unusual premises, or universal themes treated with freshness and originality. Humor works well in these books. A very well thought out and intelligently presented book has the best chance of being taken on. Genre isn't as much of a factor as presentation."

DISCIPLESHIP RESOURCES, 1908 Grand Ave., Box 840, Nashville TN 37202-0840. (615)340-7068. Fax: (615)340-7006. Editor: Craig B. Gallaway. Publishes trade paperback originals and reprints. Publishes 30 titles/year. Receives 300 queries and 150 mss/year. 20% of books from first-time authors; 40% from unagented writers. Pays 5-10% royalty on retail price or makes outright purchase of $250-1,500. Offers $250 advance. Publishes book 6 months after acceptance of ms. Query for electronic submissions. Reports in 2 months on queries. Book catalog and ms guidelines for #10 SASE.

Nonfiction: Subjects include theology of ministry, evangelism, worship, stewardship, ministry of laity, family ministry, Christian education, ethnic (church), history (Methodist/church), music/dance (religious), nature/environment (ecology), recreation (leisure ministry), Christian biography (ecclesiastical). "Materials must be focused on specific ministries of the church, in particular the United Methodist Church, but we also work with ecumenical resources." Query or submit proposal package, including outline, sample chapter, description of audience. Reviews artwork/photos as part of ms package. Send photocopies.

Tips: "Focus on ministry, write simply, and do more research."

‡**DISCUS PRESS**, 3389 Sheridan St., #308, Hollywood FL 33021. (305)963-7134. Senior Editor: Karen Weiss. Publishes hardcover and trade and mass market paperback originals. Publishes 5 titles/year. 90% of books from first-time authors; 90% from unagented writers. Pays 10-12% royalty on retail price. Offers $2,500-10,000 advance. Publishes book 8 months after acceptance of ms. Accepts simultaneous submissions. Reports in 1 month.
Nonfiction: Biography, children's/juvenile, cookbook, how-to, humor, self-help, technical, textbook. Subjects include agriculture/horticulture, Americana, animals, art/architecture, business and economics, cooking/foods/nutrition, education, ethnic, gardening, government/politics, health/medicine, history, hobbies, language/literature, military/war, money/finance, nature/environment, philosophy, psychology, recreation, regional, science, sociology, sports, travel, women's issues/studies. Submit proposal including complete manuscript with SASE.
Fiction: Adventure, confession, erotica, ethnic, experimental, fantasy, feminist, gothic, historical, horror, humor, juvenile, mainstream/contemporary, mystery, occult, plays, religious, romance, science fiction, short story collections, suspense, western, young adult. Submit synopsis or complete ms with SASE.

DISTINCTIVE PUBLISHING CORPORATION, P.O. Box 17868, Plantation FL 33318-7868. (305)975-2413. Fax: (305)975-2413. Editor: D.P. Brown. Contact: C. Pierson. Estab. 1986. Publishes hardcover originals and trade paperback originals and reprints. Publishes 25 titles/year. Receives 1,200 submissions/year. 60% of books from first-time authors; 80% from unagented writers. Pays 6-10% royalty on retail price. Publishes book 1 year after acceptance. Averages simultaneous submissions. Reports within 3 months on queries. Book catalog and ms guidelines free on request.
Nonfiction: How-to, humor, reference, self-help, technical, textbook. Subjects include art/architecture, child guidance/parenting, education, health/medicine, music/dance, psychology, regional, sociology. Submit complete ms. Reviews artwork/photos as part of ms package.

‡**DORAL PUBLISHING, INC.**, 8560 SW Salish Lane, #300, Wilsonville OR 97070-9625. (503)682-3307. Fax: (503)682-2648. Editor-in-Chief: Luana Luther. Imprints are Golden Boy Press (Marketing Coordinator: Lynn Grey); Swan Valley Press (Editor: Joan Bailey); Adele Publications (Publisher: William Cusick). Publishes hardcover and trade paperback originals. Publishes 7 titles/year. Receives 16 queries and 12 mss/year. 60% of mss from first-time authors, 85% from unagented writers. Pays 10-17% royalty on wholesale price. Publishes book 4 months after acceptance of ms. Query for electronic submissions. *Writer's Market* recommends allowing 2 months for reply. Book catalog free on request. Manuscript guidelines for #10 SASE.
Nonfiction: How-to, children's/juvenile, reference. Subjects include animals (dogs). "We publish only books about Pure Bred Dogs. No flowery prose." Submit outline and 2 sample chapters. Reviews artwork/photos as part of the ms package. Send photocopies.

‡**DORLING KINDERSLEY PUBLISHING, INC.**, 95 Madison Ave., New York NY 10016. Editor, children's books: Camela Decaire. Executive Editor, adult books: Jeanette Mall. Publishes hardcover originals. Publishes 100 titles/year. Pays royalty. Only agented mss considered. Reports in 3 months. Book catalog and ms guidelines free on request.
Nonfiction: Coffee table book, cookbook, how-to, illustrated book, reference. Subjects include agriculture/horticulture, animals, art/architecture, guidance, cooking/foods/nutrition, gardening, health/medicine, hobbies, nature/environment, photography, recreation and travel. Submit proposal package. Reviews artwork/photos as part of ms package.
Recent Nonfiction Title: Eyewitness Science series.
Fiction: Juvenile division only.
Recent Fiction Title: *Bon Appetit, Bertie!*, by Joan Knight.

DOUBLEDAY, Division of Bantam Doubleday Dell, Inc., 1540 Broadway, New York NY 10036. (212)354-6500. Imprints are Anchor Books, Nan A. Talese, Image, Currency Books, Perfect Crime, Main Street Books, DD Western, Loveswept and Perfect Crime. General interest publisher of both fiction and nonfiction. Accepts only agented material. No unsolicited mss. Publishes everything but poetry and coffee table books.
Recent Nonfiction Title: *Schoolgirls*, by Peggy Orenstein.
Recent Fiction Title: *The Rainmaker*, by John Grisham.

DOWN EAST BOOKS, Division of Down East Enterprise, Inc., P.O. Box 679, Camden ME 04843-0679. Managing Editor: Karin Womer. Estab. 1954. Publishes hardcover and trade paperback originals and trade paperback reprints. Averages 10-14 titles/year. Receives 300 submissions/year. 50% of books from first-time authors; 90% from unagented writers. Average print order for a first book is 3,000. Pays 10-15% on receipts. Offers average $200 advance. Publishes book 1 year after acceptance. Accepts simultaneous submissions. Reports in 2 months. Manuscript guidelines for 9×12 SAE with 3 first-class stamps.
Nonfiction: Books about the New England region, Maine in particular. Subjects include Americana, history, nature, guide books, crafts, recreation. "All of our books must have a Maine or New England emphasis." Query. Reviews artwork/photos as part of ms package.
Fiction: "We generally publish no fiction except for an occasional juvenile title (average 1/year) but are now keeping alert for good general-audience novels—same regional criteria apply."

DRAMA BOOK PUBLISHERS, 260 Fifth Ave., New York NY 10001. (212)725-5377. Fax: (212)725-8506. E-mail: dramapub@aol.com or dramapub@etec.org. Managing Editor: Judith Durant. Estab. 1967. Publishes hardcover and paperback originals and reprints. Averages 4-15 titles/year. Receives 420 submissions/year. 70% of books from first-time authors; 90% from unagented writers. Royalty varies. Advance negotiable. Publishes book an average of 18 months after acceptance. Reports in 2 months.
Nonfiction: Texts, guides, manuals, directories, reference and multimedia—for and about performing arts theory and practice: acting, directing; voice, speech, movement, music, dance, mime; makeup, masks, wigs; costumes, sets, lighting, sound; design and execution; technical theatre, stagecraft, equipment; stage management; producing; arts management, all varieties; business and legal aspects; film, radio, television, cable, video; theory, criticism, reference; playwriting; theatre and performance history. Accepts nonfiction and technical works in translations also. Query with 1-3 sample chapters. No complete mss. Reviews artwork/photos as part of ms package.

‡DUKE PRESS, Subsidiary of Duke Communications International, 221 E. 29th St., Loveland CO 80538. (303)663-4700. Fax: (303)667-2321. E-mail: DBernard@newslink.com. Manager, Editorial Product Development: David R. Bernard. Publishes trade paperback originals. Publishes 8 titles/year. Receives 12 queries and 8 mss/year. Pays 8-12% royalty on retail price. Offers $500-2,000 advance. Publishes book 9 months after acceptance. Query for electronic submissions. Query with SASE. Reports in 1 month on proposals. Book catalog and ms guidelines free on request.
Nonfiction: How-to, technical, textbook. Subjects include IBM AS/400 midrange computer. Submit outline and 2 sample chapters.
Tips: "Readers are MIS managers, programmers, and system operators working on an IBM AS/400 midrange computer. Authors must have technical knowledge and experience on an IBM AS/400."

DUQUESNE UNIVERSITY PRESS, 600 Forbes Ave., Pittsburgh PA 15282-0101. (412)396-6610. Fax: (412)396-5780. Contact: Susan Wadsworth-Booth, Senior Editor. Estab. 1927. Averages 9 titles/year. Receives 400 submissions/year. 25% of books from first-time authors; 100% from unagented writers. Average print order for a first book is 1,000. Nonauthor subsidy publishes 20% of books. Pays 10% royalty on net sales. No advance. Publishes book 1 year after acceptance. Query for electronic submissions. Query. Reports in 3 months. Book catalog for 9×12 SAE with 2 first-class stamps. Manuscript guidelines for #10 SASE.
Nonfiction: Scholarly books in the humanities, social sciences for academics, libraries, college bookstores and educated laypersons. Looks for scholarship. No unsolicited mss in scholarly fields. Query. Also creative nonfiction by emerging writers. Looks for strong voice, interesting narrative. Unsolicited mss must include $20 reading fee.

DUSTBOOKS, Box 100, Paradise CA 95967. (916)877-6110. Publisher: Len Fulton. Publishes hardcover and paperback originals. Averages 7 titles/year. Offers 15% royalty. Accepts simultaneous submissions, if so noted. Reports in 2 months. Book catalog free. Writer's guidelines for #10 SASE.
Nonfiction: "Our specialty is directories of small presses, poetry publishers, and two monthly newsletters on small publishers (*Small Press Review* and *Small Magazine Review*)." Publishes annual *International Directory of Little Magazines & Small Presses.*

DUTTON, Imprint of Penguin USA, 375 Hudson St., New York NY 10014. (212)366-2000. Publisher: Elaine Koster. Estab. 1852. Publishes hardcover originals. Averages 90 titles/year. No unsolicited mss.
Nonfiction: Biography, self-help, serious nonfiction, politics, psychology, science.
Fiction: Mainstream/contemporary. "We don't publish genre romances or westerns."

‡DUTTON CHILDREN'S BOOKS, Division of Penguin USA, 375 Hudson St., New York NY 10014. (212)366-2000. Editor-in-Chief: Lucia Monfried. Estab. 1852. Publishes hardcover originals. Publishes 70 titles/year. 15% from first-time authors. Pays royalty on retail price. No unsolicited mss.
Nonfiction: For preschoolers to middle-graders; including animals/nature, US history, general biography, science and photo essays.

Recent Nonfiction Title: *Tundra Swans*, by Bianca Lavies.
Fiction: Dutton Children's Books has a complete publishing program that includes picture books; easy-to-read books; and fiction for all ages, from "first-chapter" books to young adult readers.
Recent Fiction Title: *The Arkadians*, by Lloyd Alexander.

EAGLE'S VIEW PUBLISHING, 6756 N. Fork Rd., Liberty UT 84310. Fax: (801)745-0903. Editor-in-Chief: Denise Knight. Estab. 1982. Publishes trade paperback originals. Publishes 4-6 titles/year. Receives 40 queries and 20 mss/year. 90% of books from first-time authors; 100% from unagented writers. Pays 8-10% royalty on wholesale price. Publishes book 1 year or more after acceptance of ms. Accepts simultaneous submissions. Query for electronic submissions. Reports in 6-12 months on proposals. Book catalog and ms guidelines for $1.50.
Nonfiction: How-to, Indian, mountain man and American frontier (history and craft). Subjects include anthropology/archaeology (native American crafts), ethnic (Native American), history (American frontier), hobbies (crafts, especially beadwork, earrings). "We are expanding from our Indian craft base to more general crafts." Submit outline and 1-2 sample chapters. Reviews artwork/photos as part of ms package. Send photocopies or sample illustrations. "We prefer to do photography in house."

EAKIN PRESS/SUNBELT MEDIA, INC., (formerly Sunbelt Media, Inc.), P.O. Box 90159, Austin TX 78709-0159. (512)288-1771. Fax: (512)288-1813. Imprints are Eakin Press and Nortex Press. Editorial Director: Edwin M. Eakin. Estab. 1978. Publishes hardcover and paperback originals and reprints. Averages 35 titles/year. Receives 1,500 submissions/year. 50% of books from first-time authors; 90% from unagented writers. Average print order for a first book is 2,000-5,000. Pays 10-12-15% royalty on net sales. Publishes book 12-18 months after acceptance. Accepts simultaneous submissions. Query for electronic submissions. Reports in 3 months. Book catalog and ms guidelines for #10 SAE with 4 first-class stamps.
Nonfiction: Adult nonfiction categories include Western Americana, African American studies, business, sports, biographies, Civil War, regional cookbooks, Texas history. Juvenile nonfiction includes biographies of historic personalities, prefer with Texas or regional interest, or nature studies. Easy read illustrated books for grades 1-3. Query with SASE.
Recent Nonfiction Title: *The Chow Dipper*, a personal and political odyssey by Pulitzer Prize winner Ken Towery.
Fiction: No longer publishes adult fiction. Juvenile fiction for grades 4-7, preferably relating to Texas and the southwest or contemporary. Query or submit outline/synopsis and sample chapters.

‡EASTLAND PRESS, P.O. Box 99749, Seattle WA 98199. (206)217-0204. Managing Editor: John O'Connor. Publishes hardcover and trade paperback originals. Publishes 4-6 titles/year. Receives 25 queries/year. 50% of books from first-time authors; 90% from unagented writers. Pays 8-15% royalty based on receipts. Offers $500-1,500 advance. Publishes book 12-18 months after acceptance of ms. Accepts simultaneous submissions. Reports in 1-2 months. Book catalog free on request.
Nonfiction: Reference, textbook, alternative medicine (Chinese and physical). Health/medicine subjects (alternative: Chinese & physical). "We are primarily interested in textbooks for practitioners of alternative medical therapies. We prefer that a manuscript be completed or close to completion before we will consider publication. Proposals are rarely considered, unless submitted by a published author or teaching institution." Submit outline and 2-3 sample chapters. Reviews artwork/photos as part of ms package. Send photocopies.
Recent Nonfiction Title: *Anatomy of Movement*, by Blandine Calais-Germain (musculoskeletal anatomy for bodyworkers, dancers, etc.).

THE ECCO PRESS, 100 W. Broad St., Hopewell NJ 08525. (609)466-4748. Editor-in-Chief: Daniel Halpern. Publishes hardcover and mass market paperback originals and reprints and trade paperback reprints. Publishes 40 titles/year. Receives 1,200 queries/year. Pays 7½-12% royalty. Offers $250-1,000 advance. Publishes book 1 year after acceptance of ms. No simultaneous submissions. Reports in 2 months on queries. Book catalog and ms guidelines free on request.
Nonfiction: Biography, coffee table book, cookbook. Subjects include Americana, art/architecture, cooking/foods/nutrition, government/politics, history, language/literature, music/dance, regional, translation, travel. Query. Reviews artwork/photos as part of ms package. Send transparencies.
Recent Nonfiction Title: *On Water*, by Thomas Farber (short essays).
Fiction: Ethnic, historical, literary, plays, short story collections.
Recent Fiction Title: *The American Story*, edited by Michael Rea (short story anthology).
Poetry: Submit 10 sample poems.
Recent Poetry Title: *Essential Haiku*, edited by Robert Hass (haiku anthology).

THE EDUCATION CENTER, INC., Product Development Division, 1607 Battleground Ave., Greensboro NC 27408. Fax: (910)230-1879. Development Manager: Kathryn Wolf. Estab. 1973. Publishes supplementary resource books for elementary teachers: preschool/grade 6. Publishes 25 titles/year. Receives 100 queries and 100 mss/year. Less than 5% of books from first-time authors; 100% from unagented writers. Pays 2-6% royalty on wholesale price (on books sold through dealers); 2-6% royalty on retail price (on books sold through direct mail). "Payment schedule and amount negotiated when contract signed." Publishes book 2-12 months after acceptance of ms (depending on condition of ms). Query for electronic submissions. Prefers Macintosh. Reports in 2 months on proposals. Book catalog and ms guidelines for 9×12 SASE.

- The Education Center is looking for seasonal/holiday and monthly teaching ideas as well as more preschool books in a series.

Nonfiction: Teacher resource/supplementary materials. Subjects include education P/K-6, language/literature. "We place a strong emphasis on materials that teach the basic language arts and math skills. We are also seeking materials for teaching science and geography, literature-based activities for the whole language classroom, cooperative learning ideas and multicultural materials. Technical, complex or comprehensive manuscripts (such as textbooks) are not accepted." Submit outline and 1 sample chapter.

Recent Nonfiction Title: *Arts & Crafts for Little Hands*, by Jennifer Overend.

‡ELDER BOOKS, P.O. Box 490, Forest Knolls CA 94933. (415)488-9002. Director: Carmel Sheridan. Publishes trade paperback originals. Publishes 6-10 titles/year. Receives 200 queries and 50 mss/year. 50% of books from first-time authors; 50% from unagented writers. Pays .7% royalty on retail price. Offers $500-2,000 advance. Publishes book 9 months after acceptance of ms. No simultaneous submissions. Reports in 3 months on queries. Book catalog free on request.

Nonfiction: Gift book, how-to, multimedia, self-help. Subjects include child guidance/parenting, education, health/medicine, money/finance, psychology, religion, senior issues, Alzheimer's disease, women's issues/studies. Submit outline and 2 sample chapters. Reviews artwork/photos as part of ms package. Send photocopies.

Recent Nonfiction Title: *Gone Without A Trace*, by Marianne Caldwell (guide book).

ELLIOTT & CLARK PUBLISHING, INC., P.O. Box 21038, Washington DC 20009. (202)387-9805. Fax: (202)483-0355. Publisher: Carolyn M. Clark. Publishes hardcover and trade paperback originals. Publishes 7 titles/year. 50% of books from first-time authors; 90% from unagented writers. Pays royalty on wholesale price. Offers $1,000-7,500 advance. Publishes book 15 months after acceptance. Accepts simultaneous submissions. Reports in 2 months on proposals. Book catalog and ms guidelines free on request.

- This publisher won the Fletcher Pratt Award for Best Civil War Book (given by Civil War Round Table of NY).

Nonfiction: Biography, coffee table book, self-help. Subjects include Americana, art/architecture, gardening, history, nature/environment, photography. "We specialize in illustrated histories—need to think of possible photography/illustration sources to accompany manuscript. Submit an analysis of audience or a discussion of possible sales avenues beyond traditional book stores (such as interest groups, magazines, associations, etc.)." Submit proposal package, including possible illustrations (if applicable), outline, sales avenues. Reviews artwork/photos as part of ms package. Send transparencies.

Recent Nonfiction Title: *Out Of Ireland*, Kerby Miller and Paul Wagner (American history hardcover).

Tips: "We prefer proactive authors who are interested in providing marketing and the rights leads."

ELYSIUM GROWTH PRESS, 5436 Fernwood Ave., Los Angeles CA 90027. (310)455-1000. Fax: (310)455-2007. Publishes hardcover and paperback originals and reprints. Averages 4 titles/year. Receives 20 submissions/year. 20% of books from first-time authors; 100% from unagented writers. Pays $3,000 average advance. Publishes book 18 months after acceptance. Query for electronic submissions. Reports in 1-2 months on queries; 2 months on submissions. Book catalog free on request.

Nonfiction: A nudist, naturist, special niche publisher. Needs books on "body self-image, body self-appreciation, world travel and subjects depicting the clothing-optional lifestyle." Illustrated book, self-help, textbook. Subjects include health, nature, philosophy, photography, psychology, recreation, sociology, travel. Query. All unsolicited mss are returned unopened. Reviews artwork/photos as part of ms package.

ENSLOW PUBLISHERS INC., 44 Fadem Rd., P.O. Box 699, Springfield NJ 07081. (201)379-8890. Editor: Brian D. Enslow. Estab. 1977. Publishes hardcover and paperback originals. Averages 90 titles/year. 30% require freelance illustration. Pays royalty on net price. Offers advance. Publishes book 1 year after acceptance. Reports in 2 weeks. *Writer's Market* recommends allowing 2 months for reply. Book catalog for $2 and 9×12 SAE with 3 first-class stamps. Writer's guidelines send SASE.

- This publisher is especially interested in ideas for series. It does not publish fiction, fictionalized history or educational materials.

Nonfiction: Interested in nonfiction mss for young adults and children. Some areas of special interest are science, social issues, biography, reference topics, recreation. Query with information on competing titles and writer's résumé.

EPICENTER PRESS INC., Box 82368, Kenmore WA 98028. (206)485-6822. Fax: (206)481-8253. E-mail: 74754.2040@compuserve.com. Publisher: Kent Sturgis. Associate Editor: Christine Ummel. Imprint is Umbrella Books. Publishes hardcover and trade paperback originals. Publishes 10 titles/year. Receives 200 queries and 100 mss/year. 90% of books from first-time authors; 90% unagented writers. Advance negotiable.

Publishes book 1-2 years after acceptance of ms. No simultaneous submissions. Reports in 2 months on queries. Book catalog and ms guidelines free on request.

• This publisher recently won the Western States Book Award and Pacific Northwest Bookseller Association Award for *Two Old Women*, by Velma Wallis.

Nonfiction: Biography, coffee table book, gift books humor. Subjects include animals, art/architecture, ethnic, history, nature/environment, photography, recreation, regional, travel, women's issues/studies. "Our focus is the Pacific Northwest and Alaska. We do not encourage nonfiction titles from outside Alaska and the Pacific Northwest, nor travel from beyond Arkansas, Washington, Oregon and California." Submit outline and 3 sample chapters. Reviews artwork/photos as part of ms package. Send photocopies.

Recent Nonfiction Title: *Flying Cold*, by Robert Merrill MacLean (aviation history).

‡EPM PUBLICATIONS, INC., Box 490, McLean VA 22101. Editor/Publisher: Evelyn P. Metzger. Publishes hardcover and trade paperback originals and reprints. Publishes 8-10 titles/year. Nearly all books from unagented writers. Pays 6-15% royalty on retail price. Publishes book 4 months after acceptance of ms. Reports within 1 month on queries, 1-2 months on mss.

Nonfiction: Biography, cookbook, gift book, how-to, humor, illustrated book, self-help. Subjects include Americana, art/architecture, child guidance/parenting, cooking/foods/nutrition, education, gardening, history, hobbies, language/literature, military/war (Civil War), nature/environment, recreation, regional, sports, travel, women's issues/studies. Query with outline and SASE. Reviews artwork/photos as part of ms package. Send photocopies.

PAUL S. ERIKSSON, PUBLISHER, P.O. Box 62, Forest Dale VT 05745-4210. (802)247-4210. Publisher/Editor: Paul S. Eriksson. Associate Publisher/Co-Editor: Peggy Eriksson. Estab. 1960. Publishes hardcover and paperback trade originals and paperback trade reprints. Averages 5 titles/year. Receives 1,500 submissions/year. 25% of books from first-time authors; 95% from unagented writers. Average print order for a first book is 3,000-5,000. Pays 10-15% royalty on retail price. Offers advance if necessary. Publishes book 6 months after acceptance. *Writer's Market* recommends allowing 2 months for reply. Catalog for #10 SASE.

Nonfiction: Americana, birds (ornithology), art, biography, business/economics, cookbooks/cooking/foods, health, history, hobbies, how-to, humor, nature, politics, psychology, recreation, self-help, sociology, sports, travel. Query with SASE.

Fiction: Serious, literary. Query with SASE. No simultaneous submissions.

Tips: "We look for intelligence, excitement and salability—serious, literary fiction."

ETC PUBLICATIONS, 700 E. Vereda Sur, Palm Springs CA 92262-4816. (619)325-5352. Editorial Director: LeeOna S. Hostrop. Senior Editor: Dr. Richard W. Hostrop. Estab. 1972. Publishes hardcover and paperback originals. Averages 6-12 titles/year. Receives 100 submissions/year. 75% of books from first-time authors; 90% from unagented writers. Average print order for a first book is 2,500. Offers 5-15% royalty, based on wholesale and retail price. No advance. Publishes book 9 months after acceptance. *Writer's Market* recommends allowing 2 months for reply.

Nonfiction: Educational management, gifted education, futuristics, textbooks. Accepts nonfiction translations in above areas. Submit complete ms with SASE. *Writer's Market* recommends query first with SASE. Reviews artwork/photos as part of ms package.

Tips: "ETC will seriously consider textbook manuscripts in any knowledge area in which the author can guarantee a first-year adoption of not less than 500 copies. Special consideration is given to those authors who are capable and willing to submit their completed work in camera-ready, typeset form."

M. EVANS AND CO., INC., 216 E. 49th St., New York NY 10017-1502. Fax: (212)486-4544. Editor-in-Chief: George C. deKay. Estab. 1960. Publishes hardcover originals. Royalty schedule to be negotiated. Averages 30-40 titles/year. 5% of books from unagented writers. Publishes book 8 months after acceptance. No unsolicited mss. Query. Reports in 2 months. Book catalog for 9×12 SAE with 3 first-class stamps.

Nonfiction and Fiction: "We publish a general trade list of adult fiction and nonfiction, cookbooks and semi-reference works. The emphasis is on selectivity because we publish only 30 titles a year. Our general fiction list, which is very small, represents an attempt to combine quality with commercial potential. We also publish westerns. Our most successful nonfiction titles have been related to health and the behavioral sciences. No limitation on subject. A writer should clearly indicate what his book is all about, frequently the task the writer performs least well. His credentials, although important, mean less than his ability to convince this company that he understands his subject and that he has the ability to communicate a message worth hearing." Reviews artwork/photos.

Tips: "Writers should review our book catalog before making submissions."

EXPLORER'S GUIDE PUBLISHING, 4843 Apperson Dr., Rhinelander WI 54501. Phone/fax: (715)362-6029. E-mail: 74220.610@compuserve.com. Managing Editor: Gary Kulibert. Publishes trade paperback originals. Publishes 6 titles/year. Receives 50 queries and 10 mss/year. 50% of books from first-time authors; 100% from unagented writers. Pays 7-15% royalty on wholesale price. Publishes book 9 months after acceptance of ms. Accepts simultaneous submissions. Query for electronic submissions. Reports in 2 months on queries. Book catalog for SASE.

Nonfiction: Outdoor cookbooks, outdoor-related children's/juvenile, guide books. Subjects include cooking, nature/environment, recreation, regional, travel. "Our main emphasis is outdoor recreation and related activities. We are looking for helpful and entertaining proposals with b&w photos, drawings, maps and other graphic elements. No coffee table books." Query with outline, 2 sample chapters, author qualifications, proposed market. Reviews artwork/photos as part of ms package. Send photocopies.

Recent Nonfiction Title: *From Blueberries to Wild Roses*, by Dottie Reeder (cookbook).

FABER & FABER, INC., Division of Faber & Faber, Ltd., London, England; 50 Cross St., Winchester MA 01890. (617)721-1427. Fax: (617)729-2783. Contact: Publishing Assistant. Estab. 1976. Publishes hardcover and trade paperback originals. Averages 30 titles/year. Receives 1,200 submissions/year. 10% of books from first-time authors; 25% from unagented writers. Pays royalty on retail price. Advance varies. Publishes book 1 year after acceptance. Accepts simultaneous submissions. Reports in 3 months on queries. Book catalog for 9×12 SAE with 4 first-class stamps. Writer's guidelines for #10 SASE.

Nonfiction: Anthologies, biography, contemporary culture, film and screenplays, history and natural history. Subjects include Americana, animals, pop/rock music, New England, sociology. Query with synopsis, outline and SASE. Reviews artwork/photos as part of ms package.

Recent Nonfiction Title: *The Gutenberg Elegies: the Fate of Reading in an Electronic Age*, by Sven Birkerts.

Fiction: Collections, ethnic, regional. No historical/family sagas, mysteries or thrillers, no children's. Query with synopsis, outline and SASE.

Recent Fiction Title: *Coconuts for the Saint*, by Debra Spark.

Tips: "Subjects that have consistently done well for us include popular culture; serious, intelligent rock and roll books; anthologies; and literary, somewhat quirky fiction. Please do not send entire manuscript; include SASE for reply."

FACTS ON FILE, INC., 460 Park Ave. S., New York NY 10016-7382. (212)683-2244. Editorial Director: Susan Schwartz. Estab. 1941. Publishes hardcover originals and reprints. Averages 135 titles/year. Receives approximately 2,000 submissions/year. 25% of books from unagented writers. Pays 10-15% royalty on retail price. Offers $10,000 average advance. Accepts simultaneous submissions. Query for electronic submissions. No submissions returned without SASE. Reports in 2 months on queries. Book catalog free.

Nonfiction: Reference, other informational books on economics, cooking/foods (no cookbooks), health, history, entertainment, natural history, philosophy, psychology, recreation, religion, language, sports, multicultural studies, science, popular culture. "We need serious, informational books for a targeted audience. All our books must have strong library interest, but we also distribute books effectively to the book trade." No computer books, technical books, cookbooks, biographies (except YA), pop psychology, humor, do-it-yourself crafts, fiction or poetry. Query or submit outline and sample chapter with SASE.

Tips: "Our audience is school and public libraries for our more reference-oriented books and libraries, schools and bookstores for our less reference-oriented informational titles."

FAIRLEIGH DICKINSON UNIVERSITY PRESS, 285 Madison Ave., Madison NJ 07940. (201)593-8564. Fax: (201)593-8543. Director: Harry Keyishian. Estab. 1967. Publishes hardcover originals. Averages 30 titles/year. Receives 300 submissions/year. 33% of books from first-time authors; 100% from unagented writers. Average print order for a first book is 1,000. "Contract is arranged through Associated University Presses of Cranbury, New Jersey. We are a *selection* committee only." Subsidy publishes (nonauthor) 2% of books. Publishes book an average of 1 year after acceptance. Reports in 2 weeks on queries. *Writer's Market* recommends allowing 2 months for reply.

Nonfiction: Reference, scholarly books. Subjects include art, business and economics, Civil War, film, history, Jewish studies, literary criticism, music, philosophy, politics, psychology, sociology, women's studies. Looking for scholarly books in all fields. No nonscholarly books. Query with outline and sample chapters. Reviews artwork/photos as part of ms package.

Tips: "Research must be up to date. Poor reviews result when authors' bibliographies and notes don't reflect current research. We follow *Chicago Manual of Style* style in scholarly citations."

FARRAR, STRAUS AND GIROUX, INC., 19 Union Square West, New York NY 10003. Imprints are Noonday Press, Hill and Wang, Sunburst Books, Aerial Fiction, Mirasol and North Point Press. Editor-in-Chief, Books for Young Readers: Margaret Ferguson. Publishes hardcover originals. Receives 5,000 submissions/year. Pays royalty. Offers advance. Publishes book 18 months after acceptance. Reports in 3 months. Catalog for 9×12 SAE with 3 first-class stamps.

Nonfiction and Fiction: "We are primarily interested in fiction picture books and novels for children and middle readers, but do some nonfiction—both picture book and longer formats." Submit outline/synopsis and sample chapters. Reviews copies of artwork/photos as part of ms package.

Recent Nonfiction Title: *Working River*, by Fred Powledge.
Recent Fiction Title: *The Examination*, by Malcolm Bosse.
Recent Picture Book Title: *Carl Makes a Scrapbook*, by Alexandra Day.
Tips: "Study our style and our list."

FAWCETT JUNIPER, Imprint of Ballantine/Del Rey/Fawcett/Ivy, Division of Random House, 201 E. 50th St., New York NY 10022. (212)751-2600. Editor-in-Chief, Vice President: Leona Nevler. Publishes 24 titles/ year. Pays royalty. Publishes book 1 year after acceptance. Accepts simultaneous submissions. Reports in 2 months on queries.
Nonfiction: Adult books.
Recent Nonfiction Title: *My Life: Magic Johnson*, by Magic Johnson.
Fiction: Mainstream/contemporary, young adult (12-18). No children's books. Query.
Recent Fiction Title: *The Secret History*, by Donna Tartt.

THE FEMINIST PRESS AT THE CITY UNIVERSITY OF NEW YORK, 311 E. 94th St., 2nd Floor, New York NY 10128. (212)360-5790. Fax: (212)348-1241. Senior Editor: Susannah Driver. Estab. 1970. Publishes hardcover and trade paperback originals and reprints. Publishes 8-10 titles/year. Receives 500 submissions/ year. 20% of books from first-time authors; 90% from unagented writers. Pays royalty on net price. Offers $100 average advance. Accepts simultaneous submissions. Query for electronic submissions. Reports in 4 months on proposals. Book catalog and ms guidelines free on request.
● The Feminist Press published *Songs My Mother Taught Me*, by Wahako Yamarchi, which received a Lila Wallace Readers Digest Award.
Nonfiction: "The Feminist Press's primary mission is to publish works committed to the eradication of gender-role stereotyping that are multicultural in focus. Persons should write for our guidelines for submission and catalog; note that we generally publish for the college classroom." Children's (ages 8 and up)/juvenile, primary materials for the humanities and social science classroom and general readers. Subjects include ethnic, gay/lesbian, government/politics, health/medicine, history, language/literature, music, sociology, translation, women's issues/studies and peace, memoir, international. Send proposal package, including materials requested in guidelines. Reviews artwork/photos as part of ms package. Send photocopies and SASE.
Recent Nonfiction Title: *Japanese Women: New Perspectives on the Past, Present and Future*, edited by Kumiko Fujimura-Fanselow and Atsuko Kameda.
Fiction: "The Feminist Press publishes fiction reprints only. No original fiction is considered."
Tips: "Our audience consists of college students, professors, general readers."

DONALD I. FINE, INC., 19 W. 21st St., New York NY 10010. (212)727-3270. Fax: (212)727-3277. Imprints include Primus Library of Contemporary Americana. Publishes hardcover originals and trade paperback originals and reprints. Averages 45-60 titles/year. Receives 1,000 submissions/year. 30% of books from first-time authors. Pays royalty on retail price. Advance varies. Publishes book 1 year after acceptance.
Nonfiction: Biography, cookbook, self-help. Subjects include history, military/war, sports. All unsolicited mss returned unopened. Reviews artwork/photos as part of ms package.
Recent Nonfiction Title: *Beyond All Reason*, by David James Smith.
Fiction: Adventure, ethnic, historical, horror, literary, mainstream/contemporary, mystery, suspense, Western. All unsolicited mss returned unopened.
Recent Fiction Title: *The 13th Juror*, by John T. Lescroart.

FIRE ENGINEERING BOOKS & VIDEOS, Division of PennWell Publishing Co., Park 80 W., Plaza 2, Saddle Brook NJ 07663. (201)845-0800. Fax: (201)845-6275. E-mail: 74677.1505@compuserve.com. Director, Book Publishing: Joanne Ezersky. Publishes hardcover originals. Publishes 10 titles/year. Receives 24 queries/ year. 75% of books from first-time authors; 100% from unagented writers. Pays 7-10% royalty on net sales. Publishes book 1 year after acceptance of ms. No simultaneous submissions. Query for electronic submissions. Reports in 3 months on proposals. Book catalog free on request.
Nonfiction: Reference, technical, textbook. Subjects include firefighter training, public safety. Submit outline and 2 sample chapters.
Recent Nonfiction Title: *Fire Chief's Handbook*, 5th Edition.

FIREBRAND BOOKS, 141 The Commons, Ithaca NY 14850. (607)272-0000. Publisher: Nancy K. Bereano. Estab. 1985. Publishes hardcover and trade paperback originals. Averages 8-10 titles/year. Receives 400-500 submissions/year. 50% of books from first-time authors; 90% from unagented writers. Pays 7-9% royalty on retail price, or makes outright purchase. Publishes book 18 months after acceptance. Accepts simultaneous submissions if notified. Reports in 1 month on queries. *Writer's Market* recommends allowing 2 months for reply. Book catalog free.
● This publisher recently won the Lambda Literary Award: Small Press Book for *Stone Butch Blues*.
Nonfiction: Personal narratives, essays. Subjects include feminism, lesbianism. Submit complete ms.
Fiction: Will consider all types of feminist and lesbian fiction.
Tips: "Our audience includes feminists, lesbians, ethnic audiences, and other progressive people."

FISHER BOOKS, 4239 W. Ina Road, Suite 101, Tucson AZ 85741. (602)744-6110. Fax: (602)744-0944. Contact: Editorial Submissions Director. Estab. 1987. Publishes trade paperback originals and reprints. Averages 16 titles/year. 25% of books from first-time authors; 75% from unagented writers. Pays 10-15% royalty on wholesale price. Accepts simultaneous submissions. Reports in 2 months. Book catalog for SAE with 3 first-class stamps.
Nonfiction: Subjects include automotive, cooking/foods/nutrition, regional gardening, family health, self-help. Submit outline and sample chapter, not complete ms. Include return postage.

‡THE FISHERMAN LIBRARY CORP., 1620 Beaver Dam Rd., Point Pleasant NJ 08742. (908)295-8600. Associate Publisher: Pete Barrett. Publishes hardcover and trade paperback originals. Publishes 6 titles/year. 75% of books from first-time authors; 100% from unagented writers. Makes outright purchase of $2,500-7,000. Offers $1,000-2,000 advance. Publishes book 12-18 months after acceptance of ms. Reports in 1 month on queries. Book catalog and ms guidelines free on request.
Nonfiction: How-to. Subjects include sport fishing only. "We are looking for potential titles to cover fishing on the East Coast." Query with outline. Reviews artwork/photos as part of ms package. Send transparencies.
Recent Nonfiction Title: *Fishing For Sailfish*, by Capt. Georgeo La Bonte (sport fishing how-to).

J. FLORES PUBLICATIONS, P.O. Box 830131, Miami FL 33283-0131. Editor: Eli Flores. Estab. 1982. Publishes trade paperback originals and reprints. Averages 10 titles/year. 99% of books from unagented writers. Pays 10-15% royalty on net sales. No advance. Publishes book 1 year after acceptance. Accepts simultaneous submissions. Reports in 1 month on queries. *Writer's Market* recommends allowing 2 months for reply. Book catalog for 9×12 SAE with 2 first-class stamps.
 • Publisher reports a special need for manuscripts on careers, starting your own business and credit and consumer matter. Previously published books will also be considered.
Nonfiction: How-to, illustrated book, self-help. "We need original nonfiction manuscripts on outdoor adventure, military science, weaponry, current events, self-defense, personal finance/careers. How-to manuscripts are given priority." Query with outline and 2-3 sample chapters. Reviews artwork/photos. "Photos are accepted as part of the manuscript package and are strongly encouraged."
Recent Nonfiction Title: *How To Be Your Own Detective*, by Kevin Sherlock.
Tips: "Trends include illustrated how-to books on a specific subject. Be thoroughly informed on your subject and technically accurate."

‡FLORICANTO PRESS, 16161 Ventura Blvd., Suite 830, Encino CA 91436. (818)990-1879. Publishes hardcover and trade paperback originals and reprints. Publishes 6 titles/year. Receives 200 queries/year. 60% of books from first-time authors; 5% from unagented writers. Pays 5% royalty on wholesale price. Offers $500-1,500 advance. Rejected mss destroyed. Reports in 3 months on queries, 7 months on mss. Book catalog for #10 SASE.
Nonfiction: Biography, cookbook, reference. Subjects include anthropology/archaeology, ethnic (Hispanic), health/medicine, history, language/literature, psychology, women's issues/studies. "We are looking primarily for nonfiction popular (but serious) titles that appeal the general public on Hispanic subjects: history, language, psychology, biography, cookbooks. Submit outline and sample chapter(s).
Recent Nonfiction Title: *Cinco de Mayo: A Symbol of Mexican Resistance.*
Fiction: Adventure, erotica, ethnic (Hispanic), literary, occult, romance, short story collections. "On fiction we prefer contemporary works and themes." Submit synopsis and 1 sample chapter.
Recent Fiction Title: *The Drug Lord*, by P. Neissa (novel).
Tips: Audience is general public interested in Hispanic culture. "Submit material as described, on DOS disk, graphic art for cover. We need authors that are willing to promote heavily their work."

FOCAL PRESS, Subsidiary of Butterworth Heinemann, Division of Reed Elsevier (USA) Inc., 313 Washington St., Newton MA 02158-1630. Publishing Director: Karen M. Speerstra. Estab. US, 1981; UK, 1938. Imprint publishes hardcover and paperback originals and reprints. Averages 30-35 UK-US titles/year; entire firm averages 100 titles/year. Receives 500-700 submissions/year. 25% of books from first-time authors; 90% from unagented writers. Pays 10-12% royalty on wholesale price. Offers $1,500 average advance. Publishes book 1 year after acceptance. Accepts simultaneous submissions. Reports in 2 months. Book catalog and ms guidelines free.
Nonfiction: How-to, reference, technical and textbooks in media arts: photography, film and cinematography, broadcasting, theater and performing arts. High-level scientific/technical monographs are also considered. "We do not publish collections of photographs or books composed primarily of photographs. Our books are text-oriented, with artwork serving to illustrate and expand on points in the text." Query preferred, or submit outline and sample chapters. Reviews artwork/photos as part of ms package.
Recent Nonfiction Title: *The Darkroom Cookbook* by Steve Ahchell.
Tips: "We are publishing fewer photography books. Our advances and royalties are more carefully determined with an eye toward greater profitability for all our publications."

FOCUS ON THE FAMILY BOOK PUBLISHING, 8605 Explorer Dr., Colorado Springs CO 80920. Managing Editor: Gwen Ellis. Publishes hardcover and trade paperback originals. Publishes 15-20 titles/year. 25% of books from first-time authors; 25% from unagented writers. Pays royalty. Offers advance. Publishes book 1 year after acceptance of ms. Accepts simultaneous submissions. Reports in 1 month on queries, 2 months on proposals. Book catalog free on request. Manuscript guidelines for #10 SASE.

Nonfiction: How-to, juvenile, self-help. Subjects include child guidance/parenting, money/finance and women's issues/studies. "We are the publishing arm of Focus on the Family, an evangelical Christian organization. Authors need to be aware that our book publishing is closely related to the focus of the organization, which is the strengthening and preservation of family and marriages." Query before submitting ms.

Tips: Our audience is "families and the people who make up families. Know what we publish before submitting query."

FOGHORN PRESS, 555 De Haro St., #220, San Francisco CA 94107. (415)241-9550. Fax: (415)241-9641. Acquisitions Editor: Judith Pynn. Publishes trade paperback originals and reprints. Publishes 20 titles/year. Receives 500 queries and 200 mss/year. 50% of books from first-time authors; 98% from unagented writers. Pays 10% royalty on wholesale price; occasional work for hire. Publishes book 1 year after acceptance of ms. Accepts simultaneous submissions. Query for electronic submissions. Reports in 1 month on queries, 2 months on proposals and mss. Book catalog and ms guidelines free on request.

• *Great Outdoor Getaways To the Bay Area and Beyond*, by T. Stiensha, was voted Best Outdoor Book of the Year 1993 in June 1994 by the Outdoor Writers Association of California.

Nonfiction: Guidebooks. Subjects include nature/environment, recreation, sports, outdoors, leisure. Submit proposal package, including outline or chapter headings, 2 or more sample chapters, marketing plan.

Recent Nonfiction Title: *California Hiking*, by Michael Hodgson and Tom Stienstra (hiking guidebook).

‡FORT DEARBORN PRESS, 1153 N. Dearborn, #1100, Chicago IL 60610. (312)235-8500. President: Gale Ahrens. Publishes hardcover, trade paperback and mass market paperback originals. Publishes 5 titles/year. Receives 1,000 queries and 1,000 mss/year. 95% of books from first-time writers; 90% from unagented writers. Pays 16% royalty on wholesale price. Publishes book 1 year after acceptance of ms. Reports in 1 month on queries, 3 months on proposals, 6 months on mss. Book catalog and ms guidelines for 4×11 SAE with 2 first-class stamps.

Nonfiction: Biography, children's/juvenile, coffee table book, cookbook, gift book, how-to, humor, illustrated book, reference, self-help, technical, textbook, (almost all). Subjects include agriculture/horticulture, Americana, animals, anthropology/archaeology, art/architecture, business and economics, child guidance/parenting, computers and electronics, cooking/foods/nutrition, education, ethnic, gardening, gay/lesbian, government/politics, health/medicine, history, hobbies, language/literature, military/war, money/finance, music/dance, nature/environment, philosophy, photography, psychology, recreation, regional, religion, science, soliology, software, sports, translation, travel, women's issues/studies (almost all). Query with SASE.

Recent Nonfiction Title: *God & Sex*, by Dr. Dean Daun (New Age).

Fiction: Adventure, confession, erotica, ethnic, experimental, fantasy, feminist, gay/lesbian, gothic, historical, horror, humor, juvenile, literary, mainstream/contemporary, mystery, occult, plays, religious, romance, science fiction, short story collections, suspense, Western, young adult, (almost all). Query with SASE.

Recent Fiction Title: *God & Sex, Too, The Novel*, by Dean C. Daun (mainstream).

Poetry: Query.

FORUM PUBLISHING COMPANY, 383 E. Main St., Centerport NY 11721. (516) 754-5000. Contact: Martin Stevens. Publishes trade paperback originals. Publishes 12 titles/year. Receives 200 queries and 25 mss/year. 75% of books from first-time authors; 75% from unagented writers. Makes outright purchase of $250-750. Publishes book 4 months after acceptance of ms. Accepts simultaneous submissions. Reports in 1 month on mss. Book catalog free on request.

Nonfiction: Subjects include business and economics, money/finance. "We only publish business titles." Submit outline. Reviews artwork/photos as part of ms package. Writers should send photocopies.

Recent Nonfiction Title: *Selling Information By Mail*, by Glen Gilcrest.

‡FORWARD MOVEMENT PUBLICATIONS, 412 Sycamore St., Cincinnati OH 45202. Senior Editor: Robert Horine. Publishes trade paperback originals. Publishes 12 titles/year. 50% of books from first-time authors; 100% from unagented writers. Pays one-time honorarium. No simultaneous submissions. Reports in 2 months on queries and proposals, 3 months on mss. Book catalog for #10 SAE with 3 first-class stamps.

Nonfiction: Essays. Religious subjects. "We publish a variety of types of books, but they all relate to the lives of Christians. We are an agency of the Episcopal Church." Query with SASE.

Recent Nonfiction Title: *Holy Days and Holidays*, by Lee Gibbs.

Tips: Audience is primarily members of mainline Protestant churches.

FOUR WALLS EIGHT WINDOWS, 39 W. 14th St., Room 503, New York NY 10011. Estab. 1987. Publishes hardcover originals, trade paperback originals and reprints. Averages 16 titles/year. Receives 2,000 submissions/year. 15% of books from first-time authors; 70% from unagented writers. Pays royalty on retail price. Offers $1,500 average advance. Publishes book 1 year after acceptance. Reports in 2 months on queries. Book catalog for 6×9 SAE with 3 first-class stamps.

● *Parable of the Sower*, by Octavia Butler was named a New York Times Notable Book of the Year.
Nonfiction: Political, investigative. Subjects include art/architecture, cooking/foods/nutrition, government/politics, history, language/literature, nature/environment, science, travel. "We do not want New Age works." Query first with outline and SASE. All sent without SASE discarded.
Recent Nonfiction Title: *Censored: The News That Didn't Make the News and Why*, by Carl Jensen and Project Censored, with introduction by Michael Crichton and cartoons by Tom Tomorrow.
Fiction: Ethnic, experimental, feminist, literary, mystery. "No romance, popular." Query first with outline/synopsis and SASE.
Recent Fiction Title: *Parable of the Sower*, by Octavia E. Butler.
Tips: No longer accepts unsolicited submissions.

‡FRANCISCAN UNIVERSITY PRESS, University Blvd., Steubenville OH 43952. Editor: Celeste Gregory. Publishes trade paperback originals and reprints. Publishes 7 titles/year. 5% of books from first-time authors; 100% from unagented writers. Pays 5-15% royalty on retail price. Publishes book 1 year after acceptance of ms. Reports in 3 months on proposals. Book catalog and ms guidelines free on request.
Nonfiction: Popular level Catholic theology. Subjects include religion, women's issues/studies, scripture, Catholic apologetics. Submit proposal package, including outline, 3 sample chapters, author cv.
Recent Nonfiction Title: *By Grief Refined: Letters to a Widow*, by Alice von Hildebrand (bereavement/women's issues).
Tips: "We seek to further the Catholic and Franciscan mission of Franciscan University of Steubenville by publishing quality popular-level Catholic apologetics and biblical studies. In this manner we hope to serve Pope John Paul II's call for a new evangelization of today's Catholics. 95% of our publications are solicited."

‡FREE SPIRIT PUBLISHING INC., 400 First Ave. N., Suite 616, Minneapolis MN 55401-1730. (612)338-2068. Editorial Assistant: M. Elizabeth Salzmann. Publishes trade paperback originals and reprints. Publishes 15-20 titles/year. 20% of books from first-time authors; 90% from unagented writers. Pays 5-12% royalty on net receipts. Offers $500-3,000 advance. Publishes book 18 months after acceptance of ms. Accepts simultaneous submissions. Reports in 3 months. Book catalog and ms guidelines free on request.
Nonfiction: Children's/juvenile, self-help (children's only). Subjects include child guidance/parenting, education (pre-K-12, but no textbooks or basic skills books like reading, counting, etc.), health (mental/emotional health—*not* physical health—for/about children), psychology (for/about children), sociology (for/about children). Query with outline, 2 sample chapters, resumé and SASE. Send photocopies. "But, we base our decisions on content. We don't require art to be part of the package, but will take author's wishes into consideration regarding illustration."
Recent Nonfiction Title: *What Kids Need To Succeed*, by Benson, Galbraith & Espeland (parenting/child rearing).
Fiction: Juvenile, young adult. "We only publish 1-2 fiction titles per year. Stories must be about humans and have an education or self-help focus." Query with synopsis, complete ms and SASE for return. Send complete ms with synopsis if the book is short.
Recent Fiction Title: *The Last Goodie*, by Stephen Schwardt (YA novel w/reading guide).
Tips: Audience is kids, teenagers, parents, teachers, counselors, youth workers. "Write or call and request a catalog and submission guidelines before submitting your work."

SAMUEL FRENCH, INC., 45 W. 25th St., New York NY 10010. (212)206-8990. Fax: (212)206-1429. Editor: Lawrence Harbison. Estab. 1830. Subsidiaries include Samuel French Ltd. (London); Samuel French (Canada) Ltd. (Toronto); Samuel French, Inc. (Hollywood); and Baker's Plays (Boston). Publishes paperback acting editions of plays. Averages 50-70 titles/year. Receives 1,500 submissions/year, mostly from unagented playwrights. 10% of publications are from first-time authors; 20% from unagented writers. Pays 10% book royalty on retail price. Publishes book an average of 6 months after acceptance. Accepts simultaneous submissions. Allow *minimum* of 3-4 months for reply. Catalog set $4.50. Manuscript submission guidelines $4.
Nonfiction: Acting editions of plays.
Tips: "Broadway and Off-Broadway hit plays, light comedies and mysteries have the best chance of selling to our firm. Our market is comprised of theater producers—both professional and amateur—actors and students. Read as many plays as possible of recent vintage to keep apprised of today's market; write plays with good female roles; and be one hundred percent professional in approaching publishers and producers (see Guidelines)."

FRIENDS UNITED PRESS, 101 Quaker Hill, Richmond IN 47374. (317)962-7573. Fax: (317)966-1293. Editor/Manager: Ardith Talbot. Estab. 1968. Publishes 12 titles/year. Receives 100 queries and 80 mss/year. 50% of books from first-time authors; 99% from unagented authors. Pays 7½% royalty. Publishes ms 1 year after acceptance of ms. Accepts simultaneous submissions. Query for electronic submissions. Reports in 12-16 months. Book catalog and ms guidelines free on request.

Nonfiction: Biography, humor, children's/juvenile, reference, textbook. Religious subjects. "Authors should be Quaker and should be familiar with Quaker history, spirituality and doctrine." Submit proposal package. Reviews artwork/photos as part of ms package. Send photocopies.

Fiction: Historical, juvenile, religious. "Must be Quaker-related." Query.

Tips: "Spirituality manuscripts must be in agreement with Quaker spirituality."

‡GARRETT PUBLISHING, INC., 384 S. Military Trail, Deerfield Beach FL 33442. Editor: Debra L. Franco. Publishes hardcover, trade paperback and mass market paperback originals and reprints. Publishes 10 titles/year. Receives 30 queries and 15 mss/year. 50% of books from first-time authors. Pays 10-15% royalty on wholesale price. Offers $1,000 average advance. Publishes book 3 months after acceptance of ms. Accepts simultaneous submissions. Reports in 1 month on queries and proposals, 3 months on mss.

Nonfiction: How-to, reference, self-help. Subjects include business and economics, law, money/finance. Query with outline.

Recent Nonfiction Title: *Asset Protection Secrets*, by Arnold S. Goldstein (personal finance).

Tips: Audience is business people, entrepreneurs, money-conscious individuals: the "do-it-yourself" person.

GASLIGHT PUBLICATIONS, 2809 Wilmington Way, Las Vegas NV 89102-5989. (702)221-8495. Fax: (702)221-8297. E-mail: 71604.511@compuserve.com. Publisher: Jack Tracy. Estab. 1979. Imprints include McGuffin Books. Publishes hardcover and paperback originals. Publishes 6 titles/year. Receives 15-20 submissions/year. 75% of books from first-time authors; 90% from unagented writers. Pays 10% royalty. Publishes book 1 year after acceptance. Accepts simultaneous submissions. Reports in 1 month. Book catalog free.

Nonfiction: "We publish specialized studies of the mystery genre and related fields: biography, criticism, analysis, reference, film, true crime. Submissions should be serious, well-researched, not necessarily for the scholar, but for readers who are already experts in their own right. 12,000 words minimum." Query with outline/synopsis and sample chapters or send complete ms. Reviews artwork/photos as part of ms package. "Please—we do *not* publish unsolicited fiction."

Recent Nonfiction Title: *Myth and Modern Man in Sherlock Holmes: Sir Arthur Conan Doyle and the Uses of Nostalgia*.

Tips: "Our purchasers tend to be public libraries and knowledgeable mystery aficionados."

GAY SUNSHINE PRESS and LEYLAND PUBLICATIONS, P.O. Box 410690, San Francisco CA 94141-0690. Editor: Winston Leyland. Estab. 1970. Publishes hardcover originals, trade paperback originals and reprints. Averages 6-8 titles/year. Pays royalty or makes outright purchase. Reports in 6 weeks on queries. Book catalog for $1.

Nonfiction: How-to and gay lifestyle topics. "We're interested in innovative literary nonfiction which deals with gay lifestyles." No long personal accounts, academic or overly formal titles. Query. "After query is returned by us, submit outline and sample chapters with SASE. All unsolicited manuscripts are returned unopened."

Fiction: Erotica, ethnic, experimental, historical, mystery, science fiction, gay fiction in translation. "Interested in well-written novels on gay themes; also short story collections. We have a high literary standard for fiction." Query. "After query is returned by us, submit outline/synopsis and sample chapters with SASE. All unsolicited manuscripts are returned unopened."

GEM GUIDES BOOK COMPANY, 315 Cloverleaf Dr., Suite F, Baldwin Park CA 91706-6510. (818)855-1611. Fax: (818)855-1610. Imprints include Gembooks. Editor: Robin Nordhues. Publishes trade paperback originals. Averages 6-8 titles/year. Receives 40 submissions/year. 30% of books from first-time authors; 100% from unagented writers. Pays 6-10% royalty on wholesale price. Offers $1,000 average advance. Publishes book 6-8 months after acceptance. Accepts simultaneous submissions. Reports in 1 month. *Writer's Market* recommends allowing 2 months for reply.

Nonfiction: Regional books for the Western US. Subjects include hobbies, Western history, nature/environment, recreation, travel. "We are looking for books on earth sciences, nature books, also travel/local interest titles for the Western US." Query. Submit outline/synopsis and sample chapters. Reviews artwork/photos as part of ms package.

Recent Nonfiction Title: *Discover Historic California*, by George and Jan Roberts.

Tips: "Authors have the best chance selling us books about rocks, minerals, and recreational opportunities in the Western US. We have a general audience of people interested in recreational activities. Publishers plan and have specific books lines in which they specialize. Learn about the publisher and submit materials compatible with that publisher's product line."

GLENBRIDGE PUBLISHING LTD., 6010 W. Jewell Ave., Denver CO 80232-7106. Fax: (303)987-9037. Editor: James A. Keene. Estab. 1986. Publishes hardcover originals and reprints, and trade paperback originals. Publishes 6-8 titles/year. Pays 10% royalty. Publishes book 1 year after acceptance. Accepts simultaneous submissions. Reports in 2 months on queries. Book catalog for 6×9 SASE. Manuscript guidelines for #10 SASE.

Nonfiction: General. Subjects include Americana, business and economics, history, music, philosophy, politics, psychology, sociology, cookbooks. Query with outline/synopsis, sample chapters and SASE.

THE GLOBE PEQUOT PRESS, INC., P.O. Box 833, Old Saybrook CT 06475-0833. (203)395-0440. Fax: (203)395-0312. Submissions Editor: Cindi Pietrzyk. Estab. 1947. Imprints are Voyager Books and East Woods Books. Publishes hardcover originals, paperback originals and reprints. Averages 80 titles/year. Receives 1,500 submissions/year. 30% of books from first-time authors; 60% from unagented writers. Average print order for a first book is 4,000-7,500. Makes outright purchase or pays 7½-10% royalty on net price. Offers advance. Publishes book 1 year after acceptance of ms. Accepts simultaneous submissions. Reports in 3 months. Book catalog for 9×12 SASE.
Nonfiction: Travel guidebooks (regional OK), outdoor recreation, home-based business, personal finance, gardening, how-to, cookbooks. No doctoral theses, fiction, genealogies, memoirs, poetry or textbooks. Submit outline, table of contents, sample chapter and résumé/vita. Reviews artwork/photos.

DAVID R. GODINE, PUBLISHER, INC., P.O. Box 9103, Lincoln MA 01773. President: David Godine. Editorial Director: Mark Polizzotti. Estab. 1970. Publishes hardcover and trade paperback originals and reprints. Publishes 30 titles/year. Pays royalty on retail price. Publishes book 3 years after acceptance of ms. Book catalog for 5×8 SAE with 2 first-class stamps.
Nonfiction: Biography, coffee table book, cookbook, illustrated book, children's/juvenile. Subjects include Americana, art/architecture, gardening, nature/environment, photography, literary criticism and current affairs.
Fiction: Literary, mystery, short story collection, young adult. "We are not currently considering unsolicited manuscripts."
Recent Fiction Title: *The Journalist*, by Harry Mathews.
Poetry: "Our poetry list is filled through 1996."
Recent Poetry Title: *The Stonecutter's Hand*, by Richard Tillinghast.

GOLDEN WEST BOOKS, Box 80250, San Marino CA 91118. (818)458-8148. Editor-in-Chief: Donald Duke. Managing Editor: Vernice Dagosta. Publishes hardcover and paperback originals. Averages 4 titles/year. Receives 50 submissions/year. 50% of books from first-time authors; 100% from unagented writers. Pays 10% royalty contract. No advance. Publishes book 3 months after acceptance. Accepts simultaneous submissions. Reports in 1 month.
Nonfiction: Publishes selected Western transportation Americana. Query or submit complete ms. "Illustrations and photographs will be examined if we like manuscript."

GOLD'N' HONEY BOOKS, Questar Publishers, Inc., P.O. Box 1720, Sisters OR 97759. Editorial Assistant: Brenda Saltzer. Publishes hardcover and trade paperback originals and reprints. Firm publishes 60 titles/year; imprint publishes 20 titles/year. Receives 300 queries and 200 mss/year. 5% of books from first-time authors; 100% from unagented writers. Pays 5-18% royalty on wholesale price. Publishes book 10 months after acceptance of ms. Reports in 2 months on queries.
Nonfiction: Illustrated book, children's/juvenile. Religious subjects. "Must reflect evangelical Christian world-view and values." Query.
Recent Nonfiction Title: *When Stars Come Out*, by L.J. Sattgast.
Fiction: Picture books, religious. Query.
Recent Fiction Title: *What Would Jesus Do?*, by Mack Thomas.

GOVERNMENT INSTITUTES, INC., 4 Research Place, Suite 200, Rockville MD 20850-3226. (301)921-2355. Fax: (301)921-0373. E-mail: giinc@aol.com. Acquisitions Editor: Alexander M. Padro (occupational and environmental safety and health) and Jeff Worsinger (environmental compliance and natural resources). Estab. 1973. Publishes hardcover and softcover originals and CD-ROM/disk products. Averages 45 titles/year. Receives 100 submissions/year. 50% of books from first-time authors; 100% from unagented writers. Pays royalty or makes outright purchase. No advance. Publishes book 2 months after acceptance. Accepts simultaneous submissions, if so noted. Reports in 1 month on queries. *Writer's Market* recommends allowing 2 months for reply. Book catalog available on request.
Nonfiction: Reference, technical. Subjects include environmental law, occupational safety and health, employment law, FDA matters, industrial hygiene and safety, real estate with an environmental slant. Needs professional-level titles in those areas. Also looking for international environmental topics. Submit outline and at least 1 sample chapter.
Recent Nonfiction Title: *1995 Environmental Guide to the Internet*, by Jon Schupp.
Tips: "We also conduct courses. Authors are frequently invited serve as instructors."

‡THE GRADUATE GROUP, 86 Norwood Rd., West Hartford CT 06117-2236. Vice President: Robert Whitman. Publishes trade paperback originals. Publishes 25 titles/year. Receives 100 queries and 70 mss/year. 60% of books from first-time authors; 90% from unagented writers. Pays 20% royalty on retail price. Publishes book 3 months after acceptance of ms. Accepts simultaneous submissions. Reports in 1 month. Book catalog and ms guidelines free on request.

● A listing for this publisher also appears in the Subsidy/Royalty section.

Nonfiction: Reference. Subjects include career/internships/law/medicine.

Tips: Audience is career planning offices, college and graduate school libraries and public libraries. "We are very open to all submittals, especially those involving career planning, internships and other nonfiction titles."

‡**GRANDIN BOOK COMPANY**, P.O. Box 2125, Orem UT 84059. Managing Editor: Robert Shawgo, Jr. Publishes hardcover originals and hardcover and trade paperback reprints. Publishes 20 titles/year. 20% of books from first-time authors; 80% from unagented writers. Pays 5-12½% royalty on retail price. Publishes book 9 months after acceptance of ms. Reports in 2 months on queries and proposals, 3 months on mss. Book catalog for 6×9 SAE with 3 first-class stamps. Manuscript guidelines for #10 SASE.

Nonfiction: Biography, children's/juvenile, reference, self-help. Subjects include history, religion. "Through our nonfiction, we seek to preserve and share the unique culture and history of the Mormon people. "Submit proposal package, including outline, 3 sample chapters, author time frame, previous publications with SASE. Reviews artwork/photos as part of ms package. Send 4×5 transparencies.

Recent Nonfiction Title: *William Law*, by Lyndon Cook (biography/Mormonism).

Fiction: Adventure, historical, humor, juvenile, literary, religious, Western. "Works do not need to be about Mormons or Mormonism but should reflect Mormon culture and beliefs." Submit synopsis and 3 sample chapters.

Recent Fiction Title: *Anna*, by Diane Sebra (juvenile fiction).

Tips: "Our audience consists of children, teenage, and adult members of the Church of Jesus Christ of Latter-day Saints. Writers should avoid sending manuscripts that address specific agendas or factional interests not held commonly among LDS people."

GRAPEVINE PUBLICATIONS, INC., P.O. Box 2449, Corvallis OR 97339-2449. (503)754-0583. Fax: (503)754-6508. Managing Editor: Christopher M. Coffin. Estab. 1983. Publishes trade paperback originals. Averages 2-4 titles/year. Receives 200-300 submissions/year. 20% of books from first-time authors; 100% from unagented writers. Pays 6-9% royalty on net sales. Publishes book 6 months after acceptance. Accepts simultaneous submissions. "Due to volume, we respond only if interested."

Nonfiction: Tutorials on technical subjects written for the layperson, innovative curricula or resources for math and science teachers. Subjects include math, science, computers, calculators, software, video, audio and other technical tools. Submit complete ms.

Recent Nonfiction Title: *Algebra/Precalculus on the HP48G/GX.*

Fiction: Children's picture books, juvenile fiction. Submit complete ms.

GRAPHIC ARTS CENTER PUBLISHING CO., 3019 NW Yeon Ave., P.O. Box 10306, Portland OR 97210-1519. (503)226-2402. Fax: (503)223-1410. General Manager: Douglas Pfeiffer. Managing Editor: Jean Andrews. Imprint is Alaska Northwest Books. Estab. 1968. Publishes hardcover originals. Makes outright purchase, averaging $3,000. Reports in 6 months. Book catalog for 9×12 SAE with 3 first-class stamps.

Nonfiction: "All titles are pictorials with text. Text usually runs separately from the pictorial treatment. Authors must be previously published and are selected to complement the pictorial essay." Query.

Recent Nonfiction Title: *America*, photography by Fred Huschman, text by Suzan Hall.

Tips: "Our subject areas include international, national, regional and state subjects. Working in conjunction with an established professional photographer to submit an idea is an excellent approach."

‡**GRAPHIC ARTS TECHNICAL FOUNDATION**, 4615 Forbes Ave., Pittsburgh PA 15213-3796. (412)621-6941. Fax: (412)621-3049. Editor-in-Chief: Thomas M. Destree. Technical Editor: Pamela J. Groff. Estab. 1924. Publishes trade paperback originals and hardcover reference texts. Averages 10 titles/year. Receives 15 submissions/year. 50% of books from first-time authors; 100% from unagented writers. Pays 5-15% royalty on average price. Publishes book 1 year after acceptance. Query for electronic submissions. Reports in 1 month on queries. *Writer's Market* recommends allowing 2 months for reply. Book catalog for 9×12 SAE with 2 first-class stamps. Manuscript guidelines for #10 SASE.

Nonfiction: How-to, reference, technical, textbook. Subjects include printing/graphic arts. "We want textbook/reference books about printing and related technologies, providing that the content does not overlap appreciably with any other GATF books in print or in production. Although original photography is related to printing, we do not anticipate publishing any books on that topic." Query or submit outline and sample chapters. Must include SAE with ample return postage for response. Reviews artwork/photos as part of ms package.

Tips: "Company has become more 'bottom-line' oriented. Thus we are less likely to accept manuscripts that require a lot of work. Recently, we had an author prepare the entire manuscript for us—all the way up to plate-ready films. The idea is to get it in and out as a marketable product as quickly as we can. We are more likely to work with authors who can bring a manuscript in quickly. More work is done inhouse. We are encouraged to spend less time on projects and authors."

GREAT QUOTATIONS PUBLISHING, 1967 Quincy Ct., Glendale Heights IL 60139. (708)582-2800. Editor/Publisher: Ringo Suek. Publishes 40 titles/year. Receives 400 queries and 300 mss/year. 50% of books from first-time authors; 80% from unagented writers. Pays 3-10% royalty on net sales or makes outright purchase of $300-3,000. Offers $200-1,200 advance. Publishes book 6 months after acceptance of ms. Accepts simultaneous submissions. Query for electronic submissions. "Usually we return submissions, but we do not guarantee 100% that they will be returned." Reports in 2 months. Book catalog for $1.50. Manuscript guidelines for #10 SASE.
Nonfiction: Humor, illustrated book, children's/juvenile, self-help, quotes. Subjects include business and economics, child guidance/parenting, nature/environment, religion, sports, women's issues/studies. "We look for subjects with identifiable markets, appeal to the general public." Submit outline and 2 sample chapters. Reviews artwork/photos as part of ms package. Send photocopies, transparencies.
Recent Nonfiction Title: *As A Cat Thinketh*, by Jim Proimos (humorous illustrated).
Poetry: "Presently, we would be most interested in upbeat and juvenile poetry."
Tips: "Our books are physically small, and generally a very quick read. These books are available at gift shops and book shops throughout the country. We are very aware that most of our books are bought on impulse and given as gifts. We need very strong, clever, descriptive titles; beautiful cover art; and brief, positive, upbeat text. Be prepared to submit final manuscript on computer disk, according to our specifications. (It is not necessary to try and format the typesetting of your manuscript to look like a finished book.)"

GREENHAVEN PRESS, INC., P.O. Box 289009, San Diego CA 92198-9009. Managing Editor: Katie de Koster. Estab. 1970. Publishes hard and softcover educational supplementary materials and (nontrade) nonfiction on contemporary issues for high school and college readers. Averages 8 mss/year; all anthologies are works for hire; 1-4 single titles are royalty contracts. Receives 100 submissions/year. 25% of books from first-time authors; 100% of books from unagented writers. Makes outright purchase of $1,000-3,000. Publishes ms 1 year after acceptance. No unsolicited mss. Book catalog for 9×12 SAE with 3 first-class stamps.
Nonfiction: "We produce tightly formatted anthologies on contemporary controversial issues for high school- and college-level readers. Each series has specific requirements. Potential writers should familiarize themselves with our catalog and senior high and college material."

‡GREENLEAF PRESS, 1570 Old La Guardo Rd., Lebanon TN 37087. Publisher: Rob Shearer. Publishes trade paperback originals and reprints. Publishes 4 titles/year. Receives 20 queries and 8 mss/year. 25% of books from first-time authors; 100% from unagented writers. Pays 5-10% royalty on wholesale price. Publishes book 6 months after acceptance of ms. Reports in 2 months on queries and proposals, 4 months on mss. Book catalog free on request.
Nonfiction: Biography, children's/juvenile. Subjects include education, history. Query with outline.
Recent Nonfiction Title: *Famous Men of Rome*, by Haaron (trade nonfiction).
Fiction: Historical, young adult. Query with synopsis.
Recent Fiction Title: *Ink on His Fingers*, by Vernon.
Tips: Audience is homeschooling parents and children.

GROSSET & DUNLAP PUBLISHERS, Imprint of the Putnam Berkley Publishing Group, 200 Madison Ave., New York NY 10016. President: Jane O'Connor. Editor-in-Chief: Judy Donnelly. VP/Art Director: Ronnie Ann Herman. Estab. 1898. Imprints are Tuffy Books and Platt & Munk. Publishes hardcover and paperback originals. Averages 75 titles/year. Receives more than 3,000 submissions/year. Publishes book 18 months after acceptance. Accepts simultaneous submissions. Reports in 2 months.
Nonfiction: Juveniles. Submit proposal or query first. Nature and science are of interest. Looks for new ways of looking at the world of a child.
Fiction: Juveniles, picture books for 3-7 age group and some higher. Submit proposal or query first.
Tips: "Nonfiction that is particularly topical or of wide interest in the mass market; new concepts for novelty format for preschoolers; and very well-written easy readers on topics that appeal to primary graders have the best chance of selling to our firm."

GROUP PUBLISHING, INC., 2890 N. Monroe Ave., Box 481, Loveland CO 80538. Fax: (303)669-3269. Book Acquisitions Editor: Mike Nappa. Publishes trade paperback originals. Publishes 20-30 titles/year. Receives 200-400 queries and 300-500 mss/year. 30% of books from first-time authors; 100% from unagented writers. Pays up to 10% royalty on wholesale price or makes outright purchase. Offers up to $1,000 advance. Publishes book 12-18 months after acceptance of ms. Accepts simultaneous submissions. Reports in 1-2 months on queries, 3-6 months on proposals. Book catalog for 9×12 SAE with 2 first-class stamps. Manuscript guidelines for #10 SASE.
Nonfiction: How-to, youth and children's ministry resources. Subjects include education, religion and any subjects pertinent to youth or children's ministry in a church setting. "We're an interdenominational publisher of resource materials for people who work with youth or children in a Christian church setting. We don't

publish materials for use directly by youth or children (such as devotional books, workbooks or stories). Everything we do is based on concepts of active and interactive learning as described in *Why Nobody Learns Much of Anything at Church: And How to Fix It* by Thom and Joani Schultz. We need new, practical, hands-on, innovative, out-of-the-box ideas—things that no one's doing . . . yet." Submit proposal package, including outline, 2 sample chapters, introduction to the book (written as if the reader will read it), and sample activities if appropriate.

Recent Nonfiction Title: *Fun Group Devotions for Children's Ministry* (programming).

GROVE/ATLANTIC, INC., 841 Broadway, New York NY 10003. General interest publisher of literary fiction and nonfiction. Query before submitting. No unsolicited mss.

Nonfiction: Subjects include current events, film, drama, social issues, arts. "An eclectic, varied list."

Fiction: Multicultural voice.

Recent Fiction Title: *The Lone Ranger and Tonto Fist Fight in Heaven*, by Sherman Alexie.

Tips: "Take a look at the list of what is published in the area you are interested in. Look at the acknowledgements page of the book to see who to send it to. Shots in the dark are just that. . . shots in the dark."

GRYPHON PUBLICATIONS, P.O. Box 209, Brooklyn NY 11228. Owner/Publisher: Gary Lovisi. Imprints are Paperback Parade Magazine, Hardboiled Magazine, Other Worlds Magazine, Gryphon Books, Gryphon Doubles. Publishes hardcover originals and trade paperback originals and reprints. Publishes 10 titles/year. Receives 500 queries and 1,000 mss/year. 60% of books from first-time authors; 90% from unagented writers. Makes outright purchase by contract, price varies. Publishes book 12-18 months after acceptance of ms. Query for electronic submissions. Reports in 2 weeks on queries. *Writer's Market* recommends allowing 2 months for reply. Book catalog and ms guidelines for #10 SASE.

Nonfiction: Reference, bibliography. Subjects include hobbies, literature and book collecting. "We need well-written, well-researched articles, but query first on topic and length. Mistakes writers often make when submitting nonfiction are submitting not fully developed/researched material." Query. Reviews artwork/photos as part of ms package. Send photocopies (slides, transparencies may be necessary later).

Fiction: Mystery, science fiction, suspense, urban horror, hardboiled fiction. "We want cutting-edge fiction, under 3,000 words with impact!" Query or submit complete ms.

Tips: "We are very particular about novels and book-length work. A first-timer has a better chance with a short story or article. On anything over 6,000 words *do not* send manuscript, send *only* query letter about the piece with SASE."

GYLANTIC PUBLISHING COMPANY, P.O. Box 2792, Littleton CO 80161-2792. (303)797-6093. Fax: (303)727-4279. Editor: Julie Baker. Estab. 1991. Publishes softcover and trade paperback originals. Publishes 5 titles/year. Receives 600 queries and mss/year. 50% of books from first-time authors; 100% from unagented writers. Pays 7½-12½% royalty on retail price. Publishes book 1 year after acceptance of ms. Accepts simultaneous submissions. Reports in 2 months. No unsolicited mss. Manuscript guidelines for #10 SASE.

Nonfiction: Subjects include parenting/young adult, women's and men's issues and social issues. No 'slice of life,' autobiographical, New Age, mystical, technically scientific, religious, art or music." Query.

Tips: "If I were a writer trying to market a book today, I would learn how to write a good proposal, have my work professionally edited, select an appropriate publisher for my subject, and study the market of my subject."

HALF HALT PRESS, INC., P.O. Box 67, Boonsboro MD 21713. (301)733-7119. Fax: (301)733-7408. Publisher: Elizabeth Carnes. Estab. 1986. Publishes 90% hardcover and trade paperback originals and 10% reprints. Averages 15 titles/year. Receives 50 submissions/year. 50% of books from first-time authors; 50% from unagented authors. Pays 10-12½% royalty on retail price. Offers advance by agreement. Publishes book an average of 1 year after acceptance. Reports in 1 month on queries. *Writer's Market* recommends allowing 2 months for reply. Book catalog for 6×9 SAE with 2 first-class stamps.

Nonfiction: Instructional: Horse and equestrian related subjects only. "We need serious instructional works by authorities in the field on horse-related topics, broadly defined." Query. Reviews artwork/photos as part of ms package.

Tips: "Writers have the best chance selling us well written, unique works that teach serious horse people how to do something better. If I were a writer trying to market a book today, I would offer a straightforward presentation, letting work speak for itself, without hype or hard sell. Allow publisher to contact writer, without frequent calling to check status. They haven't forgotten the writer but may have many different proposals at hand; frequent calls to 'touch base,' multiplied by the number of submissions, become an annoyance. As the publisher/author relationship becomes close and is based on working well together, early impressions may be important, even to the point of being a consideration in acceptance for publication."

ALEXANDER HAMILTON INSTITUTE, 70 Hilltop Rd., Ramsey NJ 07446-1119. (201)825-3377. Fax: (201)825-8696. Editor-in-Chief: Brian L.P. Zevnik. Estab. 1909. Publishes 3-ring binder and paperback originals. Averages 10-15 titles/year. Receives 50 queries and 10 mss/year. 25% of books from first-time authors; 95% from unagented writers. Pays 5-8% royalty on retail price or makes outright purchase ($3,500-

7,000). Offers $3,500-7,000 advance. Publishes book 10 months after acceptance. Accepts simultaneous submissions. Reports in 1 month on queries, 2 months on mss.

Nonfiction: Executive/management books for 2 audiences. The first is overseas, upper-level manager. "We need how-to and skills building books. *No* traditional management texts or academic treatises." The second audience is US personnel executives and high-level management. Subject is legal personnel matters. "These books combine court case research and practical application of defensible programs." Submit outline and 2 sample chapters. Preferred submission is outline, 3 paragraphs on each chapter, examples of lists, graphics, cases.

Tips: "We sell exclusively by direct mail to managers and executives around the world. A writer must know his/her field and be able to communicate practical systems and programs."

HANCOCK HOUSE PUBLISHERS LTD., 1431 Harrison Ave., Box 1, Blaine WA 98231-0959. (604)538-1114. Fax: (604)538-2262. Publisher: David Hancock. Estab. 1971. Publishes hardcover and trade paperback originals and reprints. Averages 12 titles/year. Receives 400 submissions/year. 50% of books from first-time authors; 100% from unagented writers. Pays 10% royalty. Accepts simultaneous submissions. Publishes book 6 months after acceptance. Reports in 6 months. Book catalog free on request.

● This publisher is planning more natural history books this year.

Nonfiction: Pacific Northwest history and biography, nature guides, native culture, and natural history.

‡HARCOURT BRACE & COMPANY, Trade Division, 525 B St., Suite 1900, San Diego, CA 92101. (619)699-6560. Contact: Marsha Brubaker.

Nonfiction: Publishes all categories except business/finance (university texts), cookbooks, self-help, sex.

Recent Nonfiction Title: *The Western Canon*, by Harold Bloom.

Recent Fiction Title: *Snow Falling on Cedars*, by David Guterson.

● *Snow Falling on Cedars* won the PEN/Faulkner Award for Fiction in 1995 among others.

HARPER SAN FRANCISCO, Division of HarperCollins, 1160 Battery St., 3rd Floor, San Francisco CA 94111-1213. (415)477-4400. Fax: (415)477-4444. Publisher: Thomas Grady. Estab. 1817. Publishes hardcover originals, trade paperback originals and reprints. Publishes 180 titles/year. Receives about 10,000 submissions/year. 5% of books from first-time authors; 50% from unagented writers. Pays royalty. Publishes book 12-18 months after acceptance. Accepts simultaneous submissions if notified. Reports in 2-3 months on queries. Ms guidelines free.

Nonfiction: Biography, how-to, reference, self-help. Subjects include philosophy, psychology, religion, women's issues/studies, ecology, anthropology, spirituality, gay and lesbian studies. Query or submit outline and sample chapters with SASE.

Recent Nonfiction Title: *Undercurrents*, by Martha Manning.

HARPERCOLLINS PUBLISHERS, 10 E. 53rd St., New York NY 10022. (212)207-7000. Executive Managing Editor: Tracy Behar. Imprints include Harper Adult Trade; Harper San Francisco (religious books only); Harper Perennial; Harper Reference; Harper Interactive; Basic Books; Harper Business; Harper Torchbooks; Harper Paperbacks; Harper Audio. Publishes hardcover and paperback originals and paperback reprints. Trade publishes more than 500 titles/year. Pays standard royalties. Advance negotiable. *No unsolicited queries or mss.* Reports on solicited queries in 6 weeks. *Writer's Market* recommends allowing 2 months for reply.

Nonfiction: Americana, animals, art, biography, business/economics, current affairs, cookbooks, health, history, how-to, humor, music, nature, philosophy, politics, psychology, reference, religion, science, self-help, sociology, sports, travel.

Recent Nonfiction Title: *Dolly.*

Fiction: Adventure, fantasy, gothic, historical, mystery, science fiction, suspense, western, literary. "We look for a strong story line and exceptional literary talent."

Recent Fiction Title: *Hostile Witness.*

Tips: "We do not accept any unsolicited material."

HARTLEY & MARKS, P.O. Box 147, Point Roberts WA 98281. (206)945-2017. Editorial Director: Vic Marks. Estab. 1973. Publishes hardcover and trade paperback originals. Averages 8-10 titles/year. Receives 700 submissions/year. 80% of books from first-time authors; 95% from unagented writers. Pays 7-10% royalty on retail price. Reports in 2 months. Book catalog for SASE.

Nonfiction: How-to, self-help, technical. Subjects include agriculture/gardening (organic), building, healthy lifestyles, preventive and holistic medicine, useful crafts, nature/environment (practical how-to), psychology self-help, typography, translations of aforementioned subjects. No metaphysical books, autobiography or recipe books. Query or submit outline and sample chapters.

THE HARVARD COMMON PRESS, 535 Albany St., Boston MA 02118-2500. (617)423-5803. Fax: (617)423-0679 or (617)695-9794. President: Bruce P. Shaw. Managing Editor: Dan Rosenberg. Imprint is Gambit Books. Estab. 1976. Publishes hardcover and trade paperback originals and reprints. Averages 8 titles/year. Receives 1,000 submissions/year. 50% of books from first-time authors; 75% of books from unagented writers. Average print order for a first book is $12,500. Pays royalty. Offers average $2,000 advance. Publishes book an average of 9 months after acceptance. Accepts simultaneous submissions. Reports in 2 months. Book catalog for 9 × 12 SAE with 3 first-class stamps. Manuscript guidelines for SASE.

● Harvard Common Press has changed subject focus from family matters to childcare.

Nonfiction: Cooking, childcare and parenting, travel. "We want strong, practical books that help people gain control over a particular area of their lives. An increasing percentage of our list is made up of books about cooking, child care and parenting; in these areas we are looking for authors who are knowledgeable, if not experts, and who can offer a different approach to the subject. We are open to good nonfiction proposals that show evidence of strong organization and writing, and clearly demonstrate a need in the marketplace. First-time authors are welcome." Accepts nonfiction translations. Submit outline and 1-3 sample chapters. Reviews artwork/photos.

Recent Nonfiction Title: *How to Take Great Trips With Your Kids*, by Sandy and Joan Portnoy.

HARVEST HOUSE PUBLISHERS, 1075 Arrowsmith, Eugene OR 97402-9197. (503)343-0123. Fax: (503)342-6410. Manager: LaRae Weikert. Estab. 1974. Publishes hardcover, trade paperback and mass market originals and reprints. Averages 70-80 titles/year. Receives 3,500 submissions/year. 10% of books from first-time authors; 90% from unagented writers. Pays 14-18% royalty on wholesale price. Publishes book 1 year after acceptance. Accepts simultaneous submissions. Reports in 10 weeks. Book catalog for 9 × 12 SAE with 2 first-class stamps. Manuscript guidelines for SASE.

● Harvest House is no longer interested in manuscripts dealing with counseling.

Nonfiction: Self-help, current issues, women's and family on Evangelical Christian religion. No cookbooks, theses, dissertations, music, or poetry. Query or submit outline and sample chapters.

Recent Nonfiction Title: *Angels Among Us*, by Ron Rhodes.

Fiction: Historical, mystery, religious. No short stories. Query or submit outline/synopsis and sample chapters.

Recent Fiction Title: *With an Everlasting Love*, by Kay Arthur.

Tips: "Audience is primarily women ages 25-40—evangelical Christians of all denominations."

HASTINGS HOUSE, Eagle Publishing Corp., 141 Halstead Ave., Mamaroneck NY 10543-2652. (914)835-4005. Fax: (914)835-1037. Editor/Publisher: Hy Steirman. Publishes hardcover and trade paperback originals and reprints. Publishes 12 titles/year. Receives 350 queries and 125 mss/year. 5% of books from first-time authors; 40% from unagented writers. Pays 8-10% royalty on retail price on trade paperbacks. Offers $1,000-10,000 advance. Publishes book 10 months after acceptance of ms. Reports in 1 month. *Writer's Market* recommends allowing 2 months for reply.

● Hastings House is putting less emphasis on children's titles.

Nonfiction: Biography, coffee table book, cookbook, how-to, humor, reference, self-help, consumer. Subjects include business and economics, cooking/foods/nutrition, health/medicine, psychology, travel, writing. "We are looking for books that address consumer needs." Query or submit outline.

Recent Nonfiction Title: *Lincoln's Unknown Private Life*.

THE HAWORTH PRESS, INC., 10 Alice St., Binghamton NY 13904-1580. (607)722-5857. Managing Editor: Bill Palmer. Estab. 1973. Imprints are Harrington Park Press, Food Products Press, Pharmaceutical Products Press, International Business Press, The Haworth Medical Press, The Haworth Pastoral Press. Publishes hardcover and trade paperback originals. Firm publishes 75 titles/year; each imprint publishes 5-10 titles/year. Receives 110 queries and 46 mss/year. 20% of books from first-time authors; 98% from unagented writers. Pays 7½-12% royalty on wholesale price. Publishes book 16 months after acceptance of ms. Reports in 3 months on mss. Book catalog and ms guidelines free on request.

Nonfiction: Reference, textbook, popular trade. Subjects include agriculture/horticulture, business and economics, cooking/foods/nutrition, gay/lesbian, health/medicine, psychology, religion, sociology, women's issues/studies, pharmacy. Submit outline and 3 sample chapters. Reviews artwork/photos as part of ms package. Send camera-ready artwork, b&w photos.

HAY HOUSE, INC., P.O. Box 6204, Carson CA 90749-6204. (310)605-0601. Editorial Director: Jill Kramer. Estab. 1985. Publishes hardcover originals, trade paperback originals and reprints. Publishes 12 titles/year. Receives approximately 900 submissions/year. 10% of books are from first-time authors; 25% from unagented writers. Pays 8-12% royalty. Offers $0-5,000 average advance. Publishes book 8-15 months after acceptance. Accepts simultaneous submissions. Reports in 2 months. Book catalog free on request. Absolutely no response or return of manuscripts without SASE.

● This publisher no longer produces children's books.

Nonfiction: Self-help, primarily. Subjects include ecology, nutrition, education, gardening/environment, health/medicine, money/finance, nature/environment, philosophy/New Age, psychology, recreation, religion, science, sociology, women's issues/studies. "Hay House is interested in a variety of subjects so long as they have a positive self-help slant to them. No poetry, children's books, or negative concepts that are not conducive to helping/healing ourselves or our planet." Query or submit outline and sample chapters with SASE.

Tips: "Our audience is concerned with our planet, the healing properties of love, and general self-help principles. Hay House has noticed that our reader is interested in taking more control of his/her life. A writer has a good chance of selling us a book with a unique, positive message. If I were a writer trying to market a book today, I would research the market thoroughly to make sure that there weren't already too many books on the subject I was interested in writing about. Then I would make sure that I had a unique slant on my idea. SASE a must!"

‡**HEALTH ADMINISTRATION PRESS**, Foundation of the American College of Healthcare Executives, 1021 E. Huron St., Ann Arbor MI 48104-9990. (313)764-1380. Fax: (313)763-1105. Director: Daphne M. Grew. Acquisitions Manager: S. Crump. Estab. 1972. Imprints are Health Administration Press, Association for Health Services Research/Health Administration Press, AUPHA Press/Health Administration Press, and ACHE Management Series. Publishes hardcover and trade paperback originals. Publishes 14 titles/year. Pays 10-15% royalty on net revenue from sale of book. Occasionally offers small advance. Publishes book 10 months after acceptance. Query for electronic submissions. Reports in 6 weeks on queries. *Writer's Market* recommends allowing 2 months for reply. Book catalog free on request.
Nonfiction: Professional or textbook. Subjects include business and economics, government/politics, health/ medicine, sociology, health administration. "We are always interested in good, solid texts and references, and we are adding to our management series; books in this series offer health services CEOs and top managers immediately useful information in an accessible format." Submit outline and sample chapters.
Tips: "We publish books primarily for an audience of managers of health care institutions and researchers and scholars in health services administration. The books we like to see have something to say and say it to our audience."

‡**HEALTH COMMUNICATIONS, INC.**, 3201 SW 15th St., Deerfield Beach FL 33442. Editorial Director: Christine Belleris. Publishes hardcover and trade paperback originals. Publishes 30 titles/year. 20% of books from first-time authors; 90% from unagented writers. Pays 15-20% royalty on retail price. Publishes book 9 months after acceptance of ms. Accepts simultaneous submissions. Reports in 1 month on queries, 3 months on proposals and mss. Book catalog for 8½×11 SASE. Manuscript guidelines for #10 SASE.
Nonfiction: Gift book, self-help. Subjects include child guidance/parenting, inspiration, psychology, spirituality, women's issues/studies. "We publish general self-help books, and are expanding to include new subjects such as business self-help and possibly alternative healing." Submit proposal package, including outline, 2 sample chapters, vita, marketing study and SASE. Reviews artwork/photos as part of ms package. Send photocopies.
Recent Nonfiction Title: *Chicken Soup for the Soul*, by Jack Canfield and Mark Victor Hansen (self-help/ inspiration).
Tips: Audience is composed primarily of women, aged 25-60, interested in personal growth and self-improvement. "Please do your research in your subject area. We need to know why there is a need for your book, how it might differ from other books on the market and what you have to offer in the way of promoting your work."

HEALTH PRESS, P.O. Box 1388, Santa Fe NM 87504. (505)982-9373. Fax: (505)983-1733. Editor: Corie Conwell. Publishes hardcover and trade paperback originals. Publishes 4 titles/year. Receives 80 queries and 20 mss/year. 90% of books from first-time authors; 90% from unagented writers. Pays standard royalty on wholesale price. Publishes book 1 year after acceptance of ms. Accepts simultaneous submissions. Reports in 2 weeks on proposals. *Writer's Market* recommends allowing 2 months for reply. Book catalog and ms guidelines free on request.
Nonfiction: Subjects include health/medicine, patient education. "We want books by health care professionals on cutting-edge patient education topics." Submit proposal package, including resume, outline and 3 complete chapters. Reviews artwork/photos as part of ms package. Send photocopies.
Recent Nonfiction Title: *Centenarians: The Bonus Years*, by Lynn Peters Adler, Jr.

HENDRICK-LONG PUBLISHING CO., INC., P.O. Box 25123, Dallas TX 75225-1123. (214)358-4677. Contact: Joann Long. Estab. 1969. Publishes hardcover and trade paperback originals and hardcover reprints. Averages 8 titles/year. Receives 500 submissions/year. 90% of books from unagented writers. Pays royalty on selling price. Publishes book 18 months after acceptance. Reports in 1 month on queries, 2 months if more than query sent. *Writer's Market* recommends allowing 2 months for reply. Book catalog for 8½×11 or 9×12 SAE with 4 first-class stamps. Manuscript guidelines for #10 SASE.
Nonfiction: Biography, juvenile. Subject mainly Texas and Southwest focused material for children and young adults. Query or submit outline and 2 sample chapters. Reviews artwork/photos as part of ms package; copies of material are acceptable. Do not send original art.
Recent Nonfiction Title: *Camels for Uncle Sam*, by Diane Yancey.
Fiction: Adventure, historical, mystery, western (all Texas juvenile). Query or submit outline/synopsis and 2 sample chapters.
Recent Fiction Title: *I Love You, Daisy Phew*, by Ruby C. Tolliver.

‡JOSEPH HENRY PRESS, Imprint of National Academy Press, 2101 Constitution Ave. NW, Washington DC 20418. Executive Editor: Stephen Mautner. Publishes hardcover and trade paperback originals and reprints. Publishes 15 titles/year. 20% of books from first-time authors; 90% from unagented writers. Pays 10-15% royalty on net. Offers $0-5,000 advance. Publishes book 9 months after acceptance of ms. Accepts simultaneous submissions. Reports in 1 month on queries and proposals, 2 months on mss. Book catalog and ms guidelines free on request.
Nonfiction: Subjects include health/medicine, science. Query with outline, 2 sample chapters and SASE.

VIRGIL HENSLEY PUBLISHING, 6116 E. 32nd St., Tulsa OK 74135-5494. (918)664-8520. Editor: Terri Kalfas. Estab. 1965. Publishes hardcover and paperback originals. Publishes 5-10 titles/year. Receives 800 submissions/year. 50% of books from first-time authors; 50% from unagented writers. Pays 5% minimum royalty on gross sales or makes outright purchase of $250 minimum for study aids. Publishes ms 18 months after acceptance. Reports in 2 months on queries. Manuscript guidelines for #10 SASE.
  • This publisher is no longer accepting fiction.
Nonfiction: Bible study curriculum. Subjects include child guidance, parenting, money/finance, men's and women's Christian education, prayer, prophecy, Christian living, large and small group studies, discipleship, adult development, parenting, personal growth, pastoral aids, church growth, family. "We do not want to see anything non-Christian." Actively seeking nonfiction other than Bible studies. No New Age, poetry, plays, sermon collections. Query with synopsis and sample chapters.
Recent Nonfiction Title: *Treasure Search for Godly Wisdom*, by Dorothy Hellstera.
Tips: "Submit something that crosses denominational lines directed toward the large Christian market, not small specialized groups. We serve an interdenominational market—all Christian persuasions."

HERALD PRESS, Imprint of Mennonite Publishing House, 616 Walnut Ave., Scottdale PA 15683-1999. (412)887-8500. Fax: (412)887-3111. Senior Editor: David Garber. Estab. 1908. Publishes hardcover and trade paperback originals and reprints. Averages 30 titles/year. Receives 1,000 submissions/year. 15% of books from first-time authors; 95% from unagented writers. Pays royalty of 10-12% retail. Advance seldom given. Publishes book 1 year after acceptance. Query for electronic submissions. Reports in 3 months. Book catalog for 50¢.
Nonfiction: Christian inspiration, Bible study, current issues, missions and evangelism, peace and justice, family life, Christian ethics and theology, ethnic (Amish, Mennonite), self-help, juvenile (mostly ages 8-14). No drama or poetry. Query or submit outline and 2 sample chapters. Reviews artwork/photos as part of ms package.
Recent Nonfiction Title: *Family Violence: The Compassionate Church Responds*, by Melissa A. Miller.
Fiction: Religious. Needs some fiction for youth and adults reflecting themes similar to those listed in nonfiction, also "compelling stories that treat social and Christian issues in a believable manner." No fantasy. Query or submit outline/synopsis and sample chapters.
Recent Fiction Title: *A Joyous Heart*, by Carrie Bender.
Tips: "We currently have a surplus of juvenile book proposals. We have been more selective to make sure of market for proposed book."

HERALD PUBLISHING HOUSE, Division of Reorganized Church of Jesus Christ of Latter Day Saints, 3225 South Noland Rd., P.O. Box 1770, Independence MO 64055. (816)252-5010. Fax: (816)252-3976. Editorial Director: Roger Yarrington. Estab. 1860. Imprints include Independence Press and Graceland Park Press. Estab. 1860. Publishes hardcover and trade paperback originals and reprints. Averages 30 titles/year. Receives 70 submissions/year. 20% from first-time authors; 100% of books from unagented writers. Pays 5% maximum royalty on retail price. Offers $400 average advance. Publishes book 14 months after acceptance. Reports in 3 weeks on queries, 2 months on mss. Book catalog for 9 × 12 SASE.
Nonfiction: Self-help, religious (RLDS Church). Subjects include Americana, history, religion. Herald House focus: history and doctrine of RLDS Church. Independence Press focus: regional studies (Midwest, Missouri). No submissions unrelated to RLDS Church (Herald House) or to Midwest regional studies (Independence Press). Query. Use *Chicago Manual of Style*. Reviews artwork/photos as part of ms package.
Tips: "The audience for Herald Publishing House is members of the Reorganized Church of Jesus Christ of Latter Day Saints; for Independence Press, persons living in the Midwest or interested in the Midwest; for Graceland Park Press, readers interested in academic and exploratory studies on religious topics."

HERITAGE BOOKS, INC., 1540-E Pointer Ridge Place, Bowie MD 20716-1859. (301)390-7708. Fax: (301)390-7193. Editorial Director: Karen Ackermann. Estab. 1978. Publishes hardcover and paperback originals and reprints. Averages 100 titles/year. Receives 300 submissions/year. 25% of books from first-time authors; 100% from unagented writers. Pays 10% royalty on list price. No advance. Publishes book 6 months after acceptance. Accepts simultaneous submissions. Reports in 1 month. *Writer's Market* recommends allowing 2 months for reply. Book catalog for SAE.
Nonfiction: "We particularly desire nonfiction titles dealing with history and genealogy including how-to and reference works, as well as conventional histories and genealogies. Ancestries of contemporary people are not of interest. The titles should be either of general interest or restricted to Eastern US and Midwest,

United Kingdom, Germany. Material dealing with the present century is usually not of interest. We prefer writers to query or submit an outline." Reviews artwork/photos.

Tips: "The quality of the book is of prime importance; next is its relevance to our fields of interest."

HEYDAY BOOKS, Box 9145, Berkeley CA 94709-9145. (415)549-3564. Publisher: Malcolm Margolin. Estab. 1974. Publishes hardcover originals, trade paperback originals and reprints. Averages 4-6 titles/year. Receives 200 submissions/year. 50% of books from first-time authors; 75% of books from unagented writers. Pays 8-15% royalty on net price. Publishes book 8 months after acceptance. Reports in 1 week on queries, 5 weeks on mss. Book catalog for 7×9 SAE with 2 first-class stamps.

Nonfiction: Books about California only: how-to, reference. Subjects include Americana, history, nature, travel. "We publish books about native Americans, natural history, history, and recreation, with a strong California focus." Query with outline and synopsis. Reviews artwork/photos.

Tips: "Give good value, and avoid gimmicks. We are accepting *only* nonfiction books with a California focus."

HIGH PLAINS PRESS, P.O. Box 123, 539 Cassa Rd., Glendo WY 82213. Fax: (307)735-4590. Publisher: Nancy Curtis. Publishes hardcover and trade paperback originals. Publishes 4 titles/year. Receives 300 queries and 200 mss/year. 80% of books from first-time authors; 95% from unagented writers. Pays 10-15% royalty on wholesale price. Offers $100-300 advance. Publishes book 2 years after acceptance. Accepts simultaneous submissions. Query for electronic submissions. Prefers Mac Word. Reports in 1 month on queries and proposals, 3 months on mss. Book catalog and ms guidelines for #10 SASE.

Nonfiction: Biography, Western Americana, Americana, art/architecture, history, nature/environment, regional, travel. "We plan to focus on books of the American West, particularly history." Submit outline. Reviews artwork/photos as part of ms package. Send photocopies.

Recent Nonfiction Title: *The Wyoming Lynching of Cattle Kate, 1889*, by George W. Hufsmith.

Poetry: "We only seek poetry closely tied to the Rockies. Poets should not submit single poems." Query with complete ms.

Recent Poetry Title: *The Red Drum*, by Jane Candia Coleman (free verse).

HIGHSMITH PRESS, P.O. Box 800, Fort Atkinson WI 53538-0800. (414)563-9571. Publisher: Donald J. Sager. Publishes hardcover and paperback originals. Publishes 20 titles/year. Receives 500-600 queries and 400-500 mss/year. 30% of books from first-time authors; 100% from unagented writers. Pays 10-12% royalty on net sales price. Offers $250-2,000 advance. Publishes book 6 months after acceptance of ms. Accepts simultaneous submissions. Query for electronic submissions. Reports in 1 month on queries, 2 months on proposals, 3 months on mss. Book catalog and ms guidelines free on request.

● This publisher recently won the PLA Notable Book for New Adult Readers for *From the Brothers Grimm*, by Tom Davenport and the Cooperative Children's Book Center Notable Children's Book on Contemporary Themes for *Working A-Z*, by Maria Kunstodter.

Nonfiction: Reference and professional. Subjects include education, language/literature, multicultural, professional (library science), teacher activity. "We are primarily interested in reference and library professional books, multicultural resources for youth, library and study skills, curricular and activity books for teachers and others who work with preschool through high school youth." Query with outline and 1-2 sample chapters. Reviews artwork/photos as part of ms package. Send transparencies.

Recent Nonfiction Title: *Women on the Brink of Divorce: A Guide to Self-Help Books*, by Cynthia David (reference).

Fiction: No longer accepting children's picture book ms. "Our current emphasis is on storytelling collections for children, preschool through grade 6. We prefer stories that can be easily used by teachers and children's libraries, multicultural topics, and manuscripts that feature fold and cut, flannelboard, tangram, or similar simple patterns that can be reproduced."

Recent Fiction Title: *Mystery-Fold Stories*, by Valene Marsh.

HIPPOCRENE BOOKS INC., 171 Madison Ave., New York NY 10016. (212)685-4371. President: George Blagowidow. Estab. 1971. Publishes hardcover and trade paperback originals. Averages 100 titles/year. Receives 250 submissions/year. 10% of books from first-time authors; 95% from unagented writers. Pays 6-10% royalty on retail price. Offers $2,000 advance. Publishes book 16 months after acceptance. Accepts simultaneous submissions. Reports in 2 months. Book catalog for 9×12 SAE with 5 first-class stamps. Manuscript guidelines for #10 SASE.

Nonfiction: Reference. Subjects include foreign language, Judaic reference, ethnic and special interest travel, military history, dictionaries and instruction. Submit outline and 2 sample chapters.

Recent Nonfiction Title: *Terrible Innocence*, by Mark Coburn.

Tips: "Our recent successes in publishing general books considered midlist by larger publishers is making us more of a general trade publisher. We continue to do well with reference books like dictionaries, atlases and language studies. We ask for proposal, sample chapter, and table of contents. We then ask for material if we are interested."

‡HIVE PUBLISHING CO., Imprint of Hive Management History Series, P.O. Box H, Easton PA 18042. (610)250-0615. Vice President/General Manager: John Halecky. Publishes hardcover and trade paperback originals and reprints. Publishes 5-10 titles/year. Receives 50 queries and 25 mss/year. 25% of books from first-time authors; 50% from unagented writers. Pays variable royalty. Offers $1,000-10,000 advance. Publishes book 18 months after acceptance of ms. Accepts simultaneous submissions. Reports in 2 months on queries and mss. Book catalog and ms guidelines free on request.

Nonfiction: Biography (exclusive to management and industry), reference, technical, textbook (all management, industrial engineering, business). Subjects include business and economics, history (business and industrial). "We maintain narrow focus on history of management science, historical management figures, histories of professions and industries. Also, reference books and bibliographies of management and industrial engineering." Query. Telephone contact OK. Reviews artwork/photos as part of ms package. Send photocopies.

Recent Nonfiction Title: *Hawthorne a Half-Century Later*, by A. Boulton (management history).

Tips: Audience is executives; management consultants; management historians; faculty; researchers; authors; graduate students in management, industrial engineering, economics, political economy studies.

‡HOLIDAY HOUSE, 425 Madison Ave., New York NY 10017. (212)688-0085. Editor-in-Chief: Margery Cuyler. Estab. 1935. Publishes hardcover originals, hardcover and trade paperback reprints. Averages 50 titles/year. Receives 3,000 submissions/year. 20% of books from first-time authors; 50% from unagented writers. Pays royalty. Publishes book an average of 1 year after acceptance. Accepts simultaneous submissions. Reports in 2 weeks on queries. *Writer's Market* recommends allowing 2 months for reply. Book catalog for 9 × 12 SAE with 7 first-class stamps. Manuscript guidelines for #10 SASE.

Nonfiction: Illustrated book, juvenile. Submit outline and sample chapters; submit complete ms for picture books only. Reviews artwork/photos as part of ms package.

Fiction: Adventure, ethnic, fantasy, historical, humor, juvenile, mystery, picture books, suspense. "We are interested in all juvenile fiction up to 8-12 year old novels. No young adult novels with sex, violence or drugs as subject matter." Submit outline/synopsis and 3 sample chapters; submit complete ms for picture books only.

Recent Fiction Title: *Dumbstruck*, by Sara Pennypacker.

Tips: "We are no longer interested in acquiring folktales or short-chapter books. We are interested in good picture book stories with strong plots. We do *not* publish board books or any books for toddlers."

‡HOLLOW EARTH PUBLISHING, P.O. Box 1355, Boston MA 02205-1355. (603)433-8735. Fax: (603)433-8735. E-mail: hep2@aol.com. Editor/Publisher: Helian Yvette Grimes. Publishes hardcover, trade and mass market paperback originals and reprints. Averages 6 titles/year. Receives 250 submissions/year. 30% of books from first-time authors. Pays 5-15% royalty on wholesale price. Publishes book 6 months after acceptance. No simultaneous submissions. Query first. Query for electronic submissions. Reports on queries in 3 weeks. *Writer's Market* recommends allowing 2 months for reply. Book catalog for 9 × 12 SAE with 3 first-class stamps. Manuscript guidelines for #10 SASE.

Nonfiction: How-to, reference, technical (computer), mythology. Subjects include architecture, computers and electronics, photography, religion/mythology and travel. "We are currently interested in books on technical aspects of photography and computer books on object-oriented programming." Query. All unsolicited mss are returned unopened. Reviews artwork/photos as part of ms package.

Fiction: Fantasy, literary, mystery, science fiction. Submit outline/synopsis and sample chapters. All unsolicited mss are returned unopened.

Tips: "Computer books are fairly easy to publish because they can be marketed specifically."

HOLMES & MEIER PUBLISHERS, INC., East Building, 160 Broadway, New York NY 10038. (212)374-0100. Fax: (212)374-1313. Publisher: Miriam H. Holmes. Editor: Sheila Friedling. Executive Editor: Katharine Turok. Estab. 1969. Imprint is Africana Publishing Co. Publishes hardcover and paperback originals. Publishes 20 titles/year. Pays royalty. Publishes book an average of 18 months after acceptance. Reports in up to 6 months. Query with SASE. Book catalog free.

Nonfiction: Africana, art, biography, business/economics, history, Judaica, Latin American studies, literary criticism, politics, reference and women's studies. Accepts translations. "We are noted as an academic publishing house and are pleased with our reputation for excellence in the field. However, we are also expanding our list to include books of more general interest." Query first and submit outline, sample chapters, cv and idea of intended market/audience.

HENRY HOLT & COMPANY, INC., 115 W. 18th St., New York NY 10011. Imprints include Owl Books, MIS: Press Inc. and Twenty-First Century Books. General interest publisher of both fiction and nonfiction. Query before submitting.

‡HOLT, RINEHARD & WINSTON, Division of Harcourt Brace. 6277 Sea Harbor Dr., Orlando FL 32887. Elementary school textbooks queries and proposals to Shannon Green, human resources manager. (407)345-

2000. Secondary school textbooks queries and proposals to Marilyn Jennings, human resource generalist, 1120 Capital of Texas, Highway South, Austin TX 78746. (512)314-6500.

HOME EDUCATION PRESS, P.O. Box 1083, Tonasket WA 98855. (509)486-1351. Fax: (509)486-2628. E-mail: hegener@aol.com. Publisher: Helen Hegener. Publishes trade paperback originals. Publishes 6-8 titles/year. Receives 20-40 queries and 10-12 mss/year. 95% of books from first-time authors; 95% from unagented writers. Pays 10% royalty on retail price. Publishes book 1 year after acceptance of ms. Query for electronic submissions. Reports in 1 month on queries. *Writer's Market* recommends allowing 2 months for reply. Book catalog free on request. Manuscript guidelines for #10 SASE.
Nonfiction: How-to, education; specifically homeschooling. Subjects include child guidance/parenting, education and homeschooling. Query. Reviews artwork/photos as part of ms package as appropriate. Send photocopies.
Tips: "We are not interested in any books not directly relating to homeschooling." Mistake writers often make when submitting nonfiction is "submitting curriculum or 'how to teach. . .' books. We are *not* interested in new ideas for teaching kids to read or write. We're more interested in real life experiences than academic expertise."

‡HOMESTEAD PUBLISHING, Box 193, Moose WY 83102. Editor: Carl Schreier. Publishes hardcover originals and trade paperback originals and reprints. Averages 10 titles/year. Receives 5,000 submissions/year. 30% of books from first-time authors; 90% of books from unagented writers. Pays 8-12% royalty on net receipts. Offers $1,000 average advance. Publishes book 1 year after acceptance. Query for electronic submissions. Reports in 2 months. Book catalog for #10 SAE with 2 first-class stamps.
Nonfiction: Biography, coffee table book, illustrated book, juvenile and reference. Subjects include animals, art, history, nature, photography and travel. Especially needs natural history and nature books for children. Query or submit outline and sample chapters with SASE. Reviews artwork/photos as part of ms package.
Tips: "Illustrated books on natural history are our specialty. Our audiences include professional, educated people with an interest in natural history, conservation, national parks, and western art. Underneath the visual aspects, a book should be well written, with a good grasp of the English language. We are looking for professional work and top quality publications."

‡HOUGHTON MIFFLIN CO., Adult Trade Division, 222 Berkeley St., Boston MA 02116-3764. (617)351-5000. Submissions Editor: Janice Harvey. General interest publisher of both fiction and nonfiction.
Nonfiction: Biography, current affairs, general nonfiction, juvenile, nature, popular science, reference.
Recent Nonfiction Title: *Strange Justice: The Selling of Clarence Thomas*, by Jane Mayer and Jill Abramson.
Recent Fiction Title: *Sabbath's Theater*, by Philip Roth.

HOUGHTON MIFFLIN CO., Children's Trade Books, 222 Berkeley St., Boston MA 02116-3764. E-mail: keller@hmcd.com.umc. Submissions Coordinator: Kimberly Keller. Estab. 1864. Publishes hardcover originals and trade paperback reprints (picture books and novels). Averages 60 titles/year. Pays standard royalty. Offers advance. Reports in 2 months. Enclose SASE to fit ms.
Nonfiction: Submit outline/synopsis and sample chapters. No dot-matrix print-outs. Reviews artwork/photos as part of ms package.
Fiction: Submit complete ms.

HOWELL PRESS, INC., 1147 River Rd., Suite 2, Charlottesville VA 22901-4172. (804)977-4006. President: Ross A. Howell Jr. Estab. 1985. Averages 6 titles/year. Receives 500 submissions/year. 10% of books from first-time authors; 80% from unagented writers. Pays 5-7% on net retail price. "We generally offer an advance, but amount differs with each project and is generally negotiated with authors on a case-by-case basis." Publishes book an average of 18 months after acceptance. Reports in 2 months. Book catalog for 9×12 SAE with 4 first-class stamps. Manuscript guidelines for #10 SASE.
Nonfiction: Illustrated books, historical texts. Subjects include aviation, military history, cooking, maritime history, motorsports, gardening. "Generally open to most ideas, as long as writing is accessible to average adult reader. Our line is targeted, so it would be advisable to look over our catalog before querying to better understand what Howell Press does." Query with outline and sample chapters. Reviews artwork/photos as part of ms package. Does not return mss without SASE.
Tips: "Focus of our program has been illustrated books, but we will also consider nonfiction manuscripts that would not be illustrated. Selections limited to history, transportation, cooking and gardening."

HOWELLS HOUSE, Box 9546, Washington DC 20016-9546. (202)333-2182. Publisher: W.D. Howells. Estab. 1988. Imprints are The Compass Press, Whalesback Books. Publishes hardcover and trade paperback originals and reprints. Firm publishes 4 titles/year; each imprint publishes 2-3 titles/year. Receives 2,000 queries and 300 mss/year. 50% of books from first-time authors; 60% from unagented writers. Pays 15% net royalty or makes outright purchase. May offer advance. Publishes book 8 months after ms development completed. Reports in 2 months on proposals.

● Howells House no longer publishes coffee table books or humorous fiction.

Nonfiction: Biography, illustrated book, textbook. Subjects include Americana, anthropology/archaeology, art/architecture, business and economics, education, government/politics, history, military/war, photography, science, sociology, translation. Query.

Fiction: Historical, literary, mainstream/contemporary. Query.

Tips: "Our interests will focus on institutions and institutional change."

HRD PRESS, INC., 22 Amherst Rd., Amherst MA 01002. (413)253-3488. Fax: (413)253-3490. Publisher: Robert W. Carkhuff. Estab. 1970. Publishes hardcover and trade paperback originals. Averages 15-20 titles/year. Receives 300-400 submissions/year. 25% of books from first-time authors; 100% from unagented writers. Pays 10-15% royalty on wholesale price. Offers $1,000 average advance. Publishes book an average of 6 months after acceptance. Accepts simultaneous submissions. Reports in 1 month on queries. *Writer's Market* recommends allowing 2 months for reply. Book catalog and ms guidelines free.

Nonfiction: Reference, software, technical. Subjects include business. "We are looking for mostly business oriented titles, training and the development of human resources. Submit outline and sample chapters.

Tips: "We are no longer seeking juvenile nonfiction or psychology titles."

HUDSON HILLS PRESS, INC., 230 Fifth Ave., Suite 1308, New York NY 10001-7704. (212)889-3090. Fax: (212)889-3091. President/Editorial Director: Paul Anbinder. Estab. 1978. Publishes hardcover and paperback originals. Averages 10 titles/year. Receives 50-100 submissions/year. 15% of books from first-time authors; 90% from unagented writers. Average print order for a first book is 3,000. Offers royalties of 4-6% on retail price. Offers $3,500 average advance. Publishes book an average of 1 year after acceptance. Accepts simultaneous submissions. Reports in 2 months. Book catalog for 6×9 SAE with 2 first-class stamps.

Nonfiction: Art, photography. "We are only interested in publishing books about art and photography, including monographs." Query first, then submit outline and sample chapters. Reviews artwork/photos as part of ms package.

HUMAN SERVICES INSTITUTE, INC., 165 W. 91st St, Suite 7-H, New York NY 10024-1357. (212)769-9738. Senior Editor: Dr. Lee Marvin Joiner. Estab. 1988. Publishes hardcover and trade paperback originals. Averages 10-12 titles/year. Receives 100 submissions/year. 95% of books are from first-time authors; 100% from unagented writers. Pays 7-15% royalty on wholesale price. Publishes book 9 months after acceptance. Query for electronic submissions. Reports in 1 month on queries, 2 months on mss. Book catalog and ms guidelines free.

Nonfiction: Self-help. Subjects include child guidance/parenting, psychology, women's issues/studies. "We are looking for books on divorce, cocaine, cults, sexual victimization, alternative medicine, mental health, secular recovery and violence. No autobiographical accounts." Query or submit outline/synopsis and sample chapters.

Tips: "Our audience is made up of clinics, hospitals, prisons, mental health centers, human service professionals and general readers."

‡HUMANICS PUBLISHING GROUP, 1482 Mecaslin St. NW, Atlanta GA 30309. (404)874-2176. Acquisitions Editor: W. Arthur Bligh. Imprints are Humanics Trade, Humanics Learning, Humanics Children's House. Publishes hardcover and trade paperback originals. Publishes 12 titles/year; each imprint publishes 4 titles/year. Receives 2,000 queries and 800 mss/year. 90% of books from first-time authors; 75% from unagented writers. Pays 10-20% royalty on wholesale price. Advance variable. Publishes book 5 months after acceptance of ms. Accepts simultaneous submissions only if specified. Reports in 1 month on queries and proposals; 3 months on mss. Book catalog for #10 SASE. Manuscript guidelines for 4×9 SASE.

Nonfiction: Children's/juvenile, cookbook, how-to, illustrated book (4-color for children only), self-help, activity books for parents and educators of young children. Subjects include anthropology, child guidance/parenting, cooking/foods/nutrition, education (for young children, elementary and before), ethnic (multicultural children's books), health/medicine, music/dance, philosophy, psychology, sociology, spirituality, women's issues/studies. "We are interested in books about growth—spiritual, emotional and physical. Submitting an entire manuscript is a mistake; query letters save time, energy and frustration." Query with SASE. Reviews artwork/photos as part of ms package. Send photocopies.

Recent Nonfiction Title: *Drama & Music: Creative Activities for Young Children*, by Janet Rubin and Margaret Merrion (nonfiction).

Tips: "For our activity books, audience is parents and educators looking for books which will enrich their children's lives. For our trade books, audience is anyone interested in positive, healthy self-development. We are looking for quality and creativity. As a small publisher, we don't waste our time or an author's time on books that are not of lasting importance or value."

‡HUMANITIES PRESS INTERNATIONAL INC., 165 First Ave., Atlantic Highlands NJ 07716. (908)872-1441. Editor: Cindy Kaufman-Nixon. Publishes hardcover originals and trade paperback originals and reprints. Publishes 35 titles/year. 25% of books from first-time authors; 99% from unagented writers. Pays 5-10% royalty on retail price. Offers $0-1,000 advance. Publishes book 15 months after acceptance of ms.

Reports in 1 month on queries and proposals, 3 months on mss. Book catalog and ms guidelines free on request.

Nonfiction: Textbook (college level). Subjects include political theory, history, philosophy, religion, sociology. "Junior/senior undergrad level up. All authors will be post doctoral, holding a current academic position."

Recent Nonfiction Title: *Protestant Politics*, by Thomas A. Brady Jr. (reformation history).

‡**HUNTER HOUSE**, P.O. Box 2914, Alameda CA 94501. Editor: Lisa E. Lee. Publishes hardcover and trade paperback originals and reprints. Publishes 12 titles/year. Receives 200-300 queries and 100 mss/year. 75% of books from first-time authors; 90% from unagented writers. Pays 12% royalty on net receipts, defined as selling price. Offers $0-3,000 advance. Publishes book 18-24 months after acceptance of final ms. Accepts simultaneous submissions. Reports in 2 months on queries, 3 months on proposals, 3-6 months on mss. Book catalog for 8½×11 SAE with 3 first-class stamps. Manuscript guidelines for #10 SASE.

Nonfiction: Reference, (only health reference); self-help, social issues. Subjects include education, ethnic, gay/lesbian, health/medicine, psychology, women's issues/studies, sexuality. "We are looking for manuscripts that will flesh out our 3 specific lines—health/women's health; specific issue-oriented self-help; social justice/social issues." Query with proposal package, including outline, 1 sample chapter, target audience info, relevant statistics, competition. Reviews artwork/photos as part of ms package. Send photocopies.

Recent Nonfiction Title: *The Menopause Industry*, by Sandra Coney (health/women's issues).

Tips: Audience is "relatively savvy, concerned and sensitive people who are looking to educate themselves and their community about real-life issues that affect them. Please send as much information about *who* your audience is, *how* your book addresses their needs, and *how* a publisher can reach the audience."

HUNTER PUBLISHING, INC., 300 Raritan Center Pkwy., Edison NJ 08818. President: Michael Hunter. Editor: Kim André. Estab. 1985. Averages 100 titles/year. Receives 300 submissions/year. 10% of books from first-time authors; 75% from unagented writers. Pays royalty. Offers $0-2,000 average advance. Publishes book 5 months after acceptance. Accepts simultaneous submissions. Query for electronic submissions. Prefers final text submission on IBM disk. Reports in 3 weeks on queries, 1 month on ms. *Writer's Market* recommends allowing 2 months for reply. Book catalog for #10 SAE with 4 first-class stamps.

Nonfiction: Reference. Subjects include travel. "We need travel guides to areas covered by few competitors: Caribbean Islands, South and Central America, Mexico, regional US from an active 'adventure' perspective." No personal travel stories or books not directed to travelers. Query or submit outline/synopsis and sample chapters. Reviews artwork/photos as part of ms package.

Tips: "Study what's out there, pick some successful models, and identify ways they can be made more appealing. We need active adventure-oriented guides and more specialized guides for travelers in search of the unusual."

HUNTINGTON HOUSE PUBLISHERS, P.O. Box 53788, Lafayette LA 70505-3788.(318)237-7049. Editor-in-Chief: Mark Anthony. Estab. 1982. Publishes hardcover, trade paperback and mass market paperback originals, trade paperback reprints. Averages 25-30 titles/year. Receives 1,500 submissions/year. 25% of books from first-time authors; 90% from unagented writers. Average print order for a first book is 5,000-10,000. Pays up to 10% royalty on sale price. Publishes book 1 year after acceptance. Accepts simultaneous submissions. Query for electronic submissions. Reports in 4 months. Book catalog and ms guidelines free.

Nonfiction: Current social and political issues, biographies, self-help, inspirational, children's books. Query with descriptive outline.

Tips: "Write clear, crisp and exciting manuscripts that grab the reader. The company's goal is to educate and keep readers abreast of critical current events. Published authors should expect a heavy publicity schedule."

HYPERION, a division of Disney Book Publishing, Inc., 114 Fifth Ave., New York NY 10011. General interest publisher of both fiction and nonfiction. This company did not respond to our request for information. Query before submitting. No unsolicited mss.

‡**ICS BOOKS, INC.**, 1370 E. 86th Pl., Merrillville IN 46410. (219)769-0585. Publisher/Editor: Thomas A. Todd. Publishes trade paperback originals. Publishes 8-10 titles/year. 40% of books from first-time authors; 95% from unagented writers. Pays 10% royalty on wholesale price. Publishes book 9 months after acceptance of ms. Accepts simultaneous submissions. Reports in 3 months on mss. Book catalog and ms guidelines free on request.

Nonfiction: Children's/juvenile, coffee table book, cookbook, gift book, how-to, humor, illustrated book. Subjects include animals, cooking/foods/nutrition, government/politics, health/medicine, nature/environment, photography, recreation, sports, travel, women's issues/studies. Send cover letter, proposal and outline with 3-5 sample chapters and SASE. Reviews artwork/photos as part of ms package.

Recent Nonfiction Title: *The National Parks Compromises*, by James Ridenaur (political science).

Fiction: Adventure, historical, horror, humor, juvenile, literary, picture books, short story collections. "We are looking for 15,000- to 18,000-word manuscripts on team sports and components of each sport (i.e., base stealing, hitting, passing, pitching, darts and billiards)." Query with SASE.

Recent Fiction Title: *Pale Moon*, edited by John Long (anthology).

Tips: "Send a thoughtful proposal with cover letter, table of contents and synopsis. Include number of words, submission date and retail preference."

ICS PUBLICATIONS, Institute of Carmelite Studies, 2131 Lincoln Rd. NE, Washington DC 20002. (202)832-8489. Fax: (202)832-8967. Editorial Director: Steven Payne, O.C.D. Publishes hardcover and trade paperback originals and reprints. Publishes 8 titles/year. Receives 10-20 queries and 10 mss/year. 10% of books from first-time authors; 90-100% from unagented writers. Pays 2-6% royalty on retail price or makes outright purchase. Offers $500 advance. Publishes book 1-2 years after acceptance. Accepts simultaneous submissions, if so noted. Query for electronic submissions. Reports in 2 months on proposals. Book catalog for 7×10 SAE with 2 first-class stamps. Writer's guidelines for #10 SASE.

Nonfiction: Religious (should relate to Carmelite spirituality and prayer). "We are looking for significant works on Carmelite history, spirituality, and main figures (Saints Theresa, John of the Cross, Therese of Lisieux, etc.). Also open to more general works on prayer, spiritual direction, etc. Too often we receive proposals for works that merely repeat what has already been done, or are too technical for a general audience, or have little to do with the Carmelite tradition and spirit." Query or submit outline and 1 sample chapter.

Tips: "Our audience consists of those interested in the Carmelite tradition or in developing their life of prayer and spirituality."

IDE HOUSE PUBLISHERS, 4631 Harvey Dr., Mesquite TX 75150. (214)686-5332. Senior Executive Vice President: Ryan Idol. Publishes hardcover and trade paperback originals. Publishes 10 titles/year. Receives 300 queries and 500 mss/year. 70% of books from first-time authors; 100% from unagented writers. Pays 1-7% royalty on retail price. Publishes book 4-12 months after acceptance of ms. No simultaneous submissions. Query for electronic submissions. Reports in 1 month on queries and proposals, 4 months on mss. Book catalog for 6×9 SAE with 5 first-class stamps. Manuscript guidelines for #10 SASE.

Nonfiction: Women's history. Subjects include gay/lesbian, government/politics (liberal only), history, women's issues/studies. "We accept only nonsexist/nonhomophobic scholarly works." Query with outline and 2 sample chapters. All unsolicited mss returned unopened.

Recent Nonfiction Title: *Politics of Women's Health*, by Karen Levy (women and politics).

IDEALS CHILDREN'S BOOKS, Imprint of Hambleton-Hill Publishing, Inc., 1501 County Hospital Rd., Nashville TN 37218. Contact: Copy Editor. Publishes children's hardcover and trade paperback originals. Publishes 40 titles/year. Receives 200 queries and 2,000-2,500 mss/year. 10% of books from first-time authors; 50% from unagented writers. Pay determined by individual contract. Publishes book 1 year after acceptance of ms. Accepts simultaneous submissions. Reports in 2 months on queries, 6 months on proposals and mss. Book catalog for 9×12 SASE with 11 first-class stamps. Manuscript guidelines for #10 SASE.

• *See the Ocean* was named American Bookseller Pick of the List.

Nonfiction: Children's. Subjects include Americana, animals, art/architecture, nature/environment, science, sports. Does not publish middle-grade or young adult novels. Submit proposal package; prefers to see entire ms. Reviews artwork/photos as part of ms package. Send photocopies.

Recent Nonfiction Title: *Children's Atlas of the World*, by Stephen Attmore.

Fiction: Prefers to see entire ms.

Recent Fiction Title: *See the Ocean*, by Estelle Condra (children's picture book).

Poetry: Submit complete ms.

Recent Poetry Title: *Just Open a Book*, by P.K. Hallinan (children's picture book).

Tips: Audience is children in the toddler to ten-year-old range.

‡IDYLL ARBOR, INC., P.O. Box 720, Ravensdale WA 98051. (206)432-3231. Contact: Tom Blaschko. Publishes hardcover and trade paperback originals and trade paperback reprints. Publishes 6 titles/year. 50% of books from first-time authors; 100% from unagented writers. Pays 8-20% royalty on wholesale price or retail price. Publishes book 6 months after acceptance of ms. Accepts simultaneous submissions. Reports in 1 month on queries, 2 months on proposals, 4 months on mss. Book catalog and ms guidelines free.

Nonfiction: Technical, textbook. Subjects include agriculture/horticulture (used in long term care activities or health care—therapy), health/medicine (for therapists, social service providers and activity directors), recreation (as therapy). "We look for manuscripts from authors with recent clinical experience. Good grounding in theory is required, but practical experience is more important." Query preferred with outline and 1 sample chapter. Reviews artwork/photos as part of ms package. Send photocopies.

Recent Nonfiction Title: *Long Term Care*, by Martini, Weeks and Wirth (health care text).

Tips: "Our books provide practical information on the current state and art of health care practice. We currently emphasize therapies (recreational, occupational, music, horticultural), activity directors in long term care facilities, and social service professionals. The books must be useful for the health practitioner who meets face to face with patients *or* the books must be useful for teaching undergraduate and graduate level classes. We are especially looking for therapists with a solid clinical background to write on their area of expertise."

ILR PRESS, A special imprint of Cornell University Press, Sage House, 512 E. State St., Cornell University Press, Ithaca NY 14850. (607)277-2338 ext. 232. Fax: (607)2374. Editor: E. Benson. Estab. 1945. Publishes hardcover and trade paperback originals and reprints. Averages 12-15 titles/year. Pays royalty. Reports in 2 months on queries. Book catalog free.
Nonfiction: All titles relate to industrial and labor relations, including relevant work in the fields of history, sociology, political science, economics, human resources, and organizational behavior. Needs for the next year include "manuscripts on workplace problems, employment policy, women and work, personnel issues, current history, and dispute resolution that will interest academics and practitioners." Query or submit outline and sample chapters.
Recent Nonfiction Title: *Gender and Racial Inequaity at Work*, by Donald Tomaskouk-Devy.
Tips: "We are interested in manuscripts that address topical issues in industrial and labor relations that concern both academics and the general public. These must be well documented to pass our editorial evaluation, which includes review by academics in the industrial and labor relations field."

INDEX PUBLISHING GROUP, INC., 3368 Governor Dr., Suite 273, San Diego CA 92122. (619)281-2957. Fax: (619)281-0547. E-mail: indexboox@aol.com. Publisher: Linton M. Vandiver. Publishes hardcover and trade paperback originals. Published 12 titles for 1994; will publish 20 for 1995. Receives 100 queries and 40 mss/year. 40% of books from first-time authors; 100% from unagented writers. Pays 6-20% royalty on price. Publishes book 4 months after acceptance of ms. Accepts simultaneous submissions. Query for electronic submissions. Reports in 1 week on queries, 2 weeks on proposals. Book catalog and ms guidelines free on request.
Nonfiction: Reference, technical, trade nonfiction. Subjects include computers and electronics, hobbies (consumer electronics: ham radio, scanners), electronic crime: cellular telephones, computer hacking, etc. "Index Publishing specializes in trade nonfiction (paper and hardcover) in three broad areas: (1) communication electronics, especially ham radio, scanning and radio monitoring, cellular telephones, computer hacking, etc.; (2) controversial topics such as eavesdropping, cable and satellite TV signal piracy, identity changes, electonic crime prevention; (3) gambling, especially casino gambling and gaming theory." Query.
Recent Nonfiction Title: *The Ultimate Scanner*, by Bill Cheek (radio scanner modifications).

INDIANA UNIVERSITY PRESS, 601 N. Morton St., Bloomington IN 47404-3797. (812)337-4203. Fax: (812)855-7931. Director: John Gallman. Estab. 1951. Publishes hardcover originals, paperback originals and reprints. Averages 175 titles/year. 30% of books from first-time authors; 98% from unagented writers. Average print order for a first book varies depending on subject. Nonauthor subsidy publishes 9% of books. Pays maximum 10% royalty on retail price. Offers occasional advance. Publishes book 1 year after acceptance. Reports in 2 months. Book catalog and ms guidelines free.
Nonfiction: Scholarly books on humanities, history, philosophy, religion, Jewish studies, Black studies, criminal justice, translations, semiotics, public policy, film, music, philanthropy, social sciences, regional materials, African studies, Russian Studies, women's studies, and serious nonfiction for the general reader. Also interested in textbooks and works with course appeal in designated subject areas. Query or submit outline and sample chapters. "Queries should include as much descriptive material as is necessary to convey scope and market appeal to us." Reviews artwork/photos.
Recent Nonfiction Title: *Charles Sanders Peirce: A Life*, by Joseph Brent.
Tips: "We have been a bit more cautious about specialized monographs."

INFORMATION RESOURCES PRESS, Division of Herner and Company, Suite 550, 1110 N. Glebe Rd., Arlington VA 22201. (703)558-8270. Fax: (703)558-4979. Vice President of Administration & Finance: Cameron McRae. Estab. 1970. Publishes hardcover originals. Averages 6 titles/year. Receives 25 submissions/year. 80% of books from first-time authors; 100% from unagented writers. Pays 10-15% royalty on net cash receipts after returns and discounts. Publishes book an average of 1 year after acceptance. Accepts simultaneous submissions. Query for electronic submissions. Reports in 2 months. Free book catalog available.
Nonfiction: Reference, technical, textbook. Subjects include health, library and information science. Needs basic or introductory books on information science, library science, and health planning that lend themselves for use as textbooks. Preferably, the mss will have been developed from course notes. No works on narrow research topics (nonbasic or introductory works). Submit outline and sample chapters.

 The double dagger before a listing indicates that the listing is new in this edition. New markets are often more receptive to freelance submissions.

Tips: "Our audience includes libraries (public, special, college and university); librarians, information scientists, college-level faculty; schools of library and information science; health planners, graduate-level students of health planning, and administrators; economists. Our marketing program is slanted toward library and information science and health planning, and we can do a better job of marketing in these areas."

INNER TRADITIONS INTERNATIONAL, P.O. Box 388, 1 Park St., Rochester VT 05767. (802)767-3174. Fax: (802)767-3726. Acquisitions Editor: (Ms.) Robin Dutcher-Bayer. Estab. 1975. Imprints are Inner Traditions, Destiny Books, Healing Arts Press, Park Street Press. Publishes hardcover and trade paperback originals and reprints. Averages 40 titles/year. Receives 2,000 submissions/year. 5% of books from first-time authors; 5% from unagented writers. Pays 8-10% royalty on net receipts. Offers $1,000 average advance. Publishes book 1 year after acceptance. Reports in 3 months on queries, 3-6 months on mss. Book catalog and ms guidelines free.
Nonfiction: Subjects include anthropology/archaeology, natural foods, cooking, nutrition, health/alternative medicine, history and mythology, indigenous cultures, music/dance, nature/environment, esoteric philosophy, psychology, world religions, women's issues/studies, New Age. Query or submit outline and sample chapters with return postage. Manuscripts without postage will not be returned. Reviews artwork/photos as part of ms package.
Tips: "We are interested in the spiritual and transformative aspects of the above subjects, especially as they relate to world cultures. We are not interested in autobiographical stories of self-transformation."

INSIGHT BOOKS, Imprint of Plenum Publishing Corp., 233 Spring St., New York NY 10013-1578. (212)620-8000. Fax: (212)463-0742. Editor: Frank K. Darmstadt. Estab. 1946. Publishes trade hardcover and paperback originals. Averages 12 titles/year. Receives 1,000 submissions/year. 50% of books from first-time authors; 75% from unagented writers. Pays royalty. Advance varies. Publishes book 18-24 months after acceptance. Accepts simultaneous submissions. Query for electronic submissions. Reports in 2 months. Book catalog free.
Nonfiction: Self-help, how-to, treatises, essays. Subjects include anthropology/archaeology, art/architecture, business and economics, education, ethnic, gay and lesbian studies, government/politics, health/medicine, language/literature, money/finance, nature/environment, parenting, psychology, science, sociology, women's issues/studies. Submit outline, sample chapters and résumé.
Recent Nonfiction Title: *HIV-Negative: How the Uninfected Are Affected by AIDS*, by William I. Johnston.
Tips: "Writers have the best chance selling authoritative, quality, well-written, serious information in areas of health, mental health, social sciences, education and contemporary issues. Our audience consists of informed general readers as well as professionals and students in human, life and social sciences. If I were a writer trying to market a book today, I would say something interesting, important and useful, and say it well."

‡INTERCULTURAL PRESS, INC., P.O. Box 700, Yarmouth ME 04096. (207)846-5168. Fax: (802)685-4842. E-mail: intercultural@mcimail.com. Contact Editor-in-Chief: David S. Hoopes, 130 North Rd., Vershire VT 05079. (802)685-4448. Estab. 1980. Publishes hardcover and trade paperback originals. Averages 10-15 titles/year. Receives 50-80 submissions/year. 50% of books from first-time authors; 95% of books from unagented writers. Pays royalty. Offers small advance occasionally. Publishes book 2 years after acceptance. Accepts simultaneous submissions. Reports in 2 months. Book catalog and ms guidelines free.
Nonfiction: How-to, reference, self-help, textbook and theory. Subjects include business and economics, philosophy, politics, psychology, sociology, travel, or "any book with an international or domestic intercultural, multicultural, diversity or cross-cultural focus, i.e., a focus on the cultural factors in personal, social, political or economic relations. We want books with an international or domestic intercultural or multicultural focus, especially those on business operations (how to be effective in intercultural business activities) and education (textbooks for teaching intercultural subjects, for instance). Our books are published for educators in the intercultural field, business people who are engaged in international business, managers concerned with cultural diversity in the workplace, and anyone else who works in an occupation where cross-cultural communication and adaptation are important skills. No manuscripts that don't have an intercultural focus." Accepts nonfiction translations. Query "if there is any question of suitability (we can tell quickly from a good query)," or submit outline. Do not submit mss unless invited.
Recent Nonfiction Title: *From Da to Yes: Understanding the East Europeans*, by Yale Richmond.

INTERLINK PUBLISHING GROUP, INC., 46 Crosby St., Northampton MA 01060. (413)582-7054. Fax: (413)582-7057. E-mail: interpg@aol.com. Publisher: Michel Moushabeck. Imprints are Interlink Books, Crocodile Books, USA, Olive Branch Press. Publishes hardcover and trade paperback originals. Averages 30 titles/year. Receives 200 submissions/year. 30% of books from first-time authors; 50% from unagented writers. Pays 5-7% royalty on retail price. Publishes book an average of 18 months after acceptance. Accepts simultaneous submissions. Reports in 1 month on queries. *Writer's Market* recommends allowing 2 months for reply. Book catalog and ms guidelines free.
 ● This publisher is looking for international fiction and folktales; also political/current affairs titles for new Voices & Visions series.

Nonfiction: Coffee table book, cookbook, how-to, illustrated book, juvenile. Subjects include art/architecture, child guidance/parenting, cooking/foods/nutrition, ethnic, gardening, government/politics, history, international and current affairs, nature/environment, religion, travel, women's issues/studies, third world literature, criticism. Submit outline and sample chapters for adult nonfiction; complete ms for juvenile titles. Reviews artwork/photos as part of ms package.

Fiction: Ethnic, international feminist, juvenile, picture books, short story collections (only third world). "Adult fiction—We are looking for translated works relating to the Middle East, Africa or Latin America. Juvenile/Picture Books—Our list is full for the next two years. No science fiction, romance, plays, erotica, fantasy, horror. Submit outline/synopsis and sample chapters.

Tips: "Any submissions that fit well in our International Folktale or Emerging Voices: New International Fiction Series will receive careful attention."

INTERNATIONAL FOUNDATION OF EMPLOYEE BENEFIT PLANS, P.O. Box 69, Brookfield WI 53008-0069. (414)786-6700. Fax: (414)786-2990. Senior Director of Publications: Dee Birschel. Estab. 1954. Publishes hardcover and trade paperback originals. Averages 10 titles/year. Receives 20 submissions/year. 15% of books from first-time authors; 80% from unagented writers. Pays 5-15% royalty on wholesale and retail price. Publishes book 1 year after acceptance. Reports in 3 months on queries. Book catalog free on request. Manuscript guidelines for SASE.

Nonfiction: Reference, technical, consumer information, textbook. Subjects limited to health care, pensions, retirement planning, and employee benefits. "We publish general and technical monographs on all aspects of employee benefits—pension plans, health insurance, etc." Query with outline.

Tips: "Be aware of interests of employers and the marketplace in benefits topics, for example, how AIDS affects employers, health care cost containment."

INTERNATIONAL INFORMATION ASSOCIATES, INC., P.O. Box 773, Morrisville PA 19067-0773. (215)493-9214. Vice President/Publisher: Richard Bradley. Publishes trade paperback originals. Publishes 4-6 titles/year. Receives 25 queries and 6 mss/year. 98% of books from first-time authors; 100% from unagented writers. Pays 10-12% royalty on retail price. Publishes book 12-14 months after acceptance. Accepts simultaneous submissions. Query for electronic submissions; prefers any major MS-DOS or ASCII. Reports in 3 weeks on queries. Book catalog free on request. Manuscript guidelines for #10 SASE.

• International Information Associates did not publish any new titles in 1994 nor in the first half of 1995.

Nonfiction: Technical, textbook. Subjects include business and economics, health/medicine, psychology, science. "Writers should be qualified in some way to write the text, if not by academic background then by experience." Query. Reviews artwork/photos as part of ms package. Send photocopies.

Tips: "Our audience is the professional at work in a particular field—on an international basis. Please remember that *anything* you write us will be used to judge *how* you write. Whether an author can write is as important as the topic."

INTERNATIONAL MARINE PUBLISHING CO., Division of TAB Books, Inc., The McGraw-Hill Companies, P.O. Box 220, Camden ME 04843-0220. Fax: (207)236-6314. Imprints are Seven Seas, Ragged Mountain Press. Acquisitions Editor: John J. Kettlewell. Editorial Director: Jonathan Eaton. Estab. 1969. Publishes hardcover and paperback originals. Averages 40 titles/year. Receives 500-700 mss/year. 30% of books from first-time authors; 80% from unagented writers. Pays standard royalties based on net price. Offers advance. Publishes book an average of 1 year after acceptance. Reports in 2 months. Book catalog and ms guidelines for SASE.

Nonfiction: "Marine nonfiction. A wide range of subjects include: boatbuilding, boat design, yachting, seamanship, boat maintenance, maritime history, etc." All books are illustrated. "Material in all stages welcome." Query first with outline and 2-3 sample chapters. Reviews artwork/photos as part of ms package.

Tips: "Freelance writers should be aware of the need for clarity, accuracy and interest. Many progress too far in the actual writing, with an unsaleable topic."

INTERNATIONAL MEDICAL PUBLISHING, 101 Pommander Walk, Alexandria VA 22314-3844. (703)519-0807. Fax: (703)519-0806. Editor: Thomas Masterson, MD. Publishes mass market paperback originals. Publishes 11 titles/year. Receives 20 queries and 2 mss/year. 5% of books from first-time authors; 100% from unagented writers. Pays royalty on gross receipts. Publishes book 8 months after acceptance. Query for electronic submissions. Prefers disk. Reports in 2 months on queries. Book catalog free on request.

Nonfiction: Reference, textbook. Health/medicine subjects. "We distribute only through medical and scientific bookstores. Look at our books. Think about practical material for doctors-in-training. We are interested in handbooks. Writers should avoid lack of clarity in writing. Keep prose simple when dealing with very technical subjects." Query with outline. Reviews artwork/photos as part of ms package. Send photocopies.

Tips: Audience is medical students and physicians.

INTERNATIONAL PUBLISHERS CO., INC., P.O. Box 3042, New York NY 10116-3042. (212)366-9816. Fax: (212)366-9820. President: Betty Smith. Estab. 1924. Publishes hardcover originals, trade paperback originals and reprints. Averages 10-15 titles/year. Receives 50-100 mss/year. 10% of books from first-time authors. Pays 5-7½% royalty on paperbacks; 10% royalty on cloth. No advance. Publishes book 6 months after acceptance. Accepts simultaneous submissions. Reports in 1 month on queries with SASE, 6 months on mss. Book catalog and ms guidelines for SAE with 2 first-class stamps.

Nonfiction: Biography, reference, textbook. Subjects include Americana, economics, history, philosophy, politics, social sciences, Marxist-Leninist classics. "Books on labor, black studies and women's studies based on Marxist science have high priority." Query or submit outline and sample chapters. Reviews artwork/photos as part of ms package.

Recent Nonfiction Title: *Dialectical Materialism and Modern Science*, by Kenneth Neill Cameron.

Tips: No fiction or poetry.

INTERNATIONAL WEALTH SUCCESS, P.O. Box 186, Merrick NY 11570-0186. (516)766-5850. Fax: (516)766-5919. Editor: Tyler G. Hicks. Estab. 1967. Averages 10 titles/year. Receives 100 submissions/year. 100% of books from first-time authors; 100% from unagented writers. Average print order for a first book "varies from 500 and up, depending on the book." Pays 10% royalty on wholesale or retail price. Buys all rights. Offers usual advance of $1,000, but this varies depending on author's reputation and nature of book. Publishes book 4 months after acceptance. Query for electronic submissions. Reports in 1 month. Book catalog and ms guidelines for 9 × 12 SAE with 3 first-class stamps.

Nonfiction: Self-help, how-to. "Techniques, methods, sources for building wealth. Highly personal, how-to-do-it with plenty of case histories. Books are aimed at the wealth builder and are highly sympathetic to his and her problems." Financing, business success, venture capital, etc. Length: 60,000-70,000 words. Query. Reviews artwork/photos as part of ms package.

Tips: "With the mass layoffs in large and medium-size companies there is an increasing interest in owning your own business. So we will focus on more how-to hands-on material on owning—and becoming successful in—one's own business of any kind. Our market is the BWB—Beginning Wealth Builder. This person has so little money that financial planning is something they never think of. Instead, they want to know what kind of a business they can get into to make some money without a large investment. Write for this market and you have millions of potential readers. Remember—there are a lot more people *without* money than *with* money."

INTERWEAVE PRESS, 201 E. Fourth St., Loveland CO 80537. (970)669-7672. Fax: (970)669-8317. Book Editor: Judith Durant. Estab. 1975. Publishes hardcover and trade paperback originals. Publishes 8-12 titles/year. Receives 50 submissions/year. 60% of books from first-time authors; 98% from unagented writers. Pays 10% royalty on net receipts. Offers $500 average advance. Publishes book 1 year after acceptance. Accepts simultaneous submissions, if so noted. Query for electronic submissions. Reports in 2 months. Book catalog and ms guidelines free.

Nonfiction: How-to, technical. Subjects limited to fiber arts—basketry, spinning, knitting, dyeing and weaving, and hebal topics—gardening, cooking, and lore. Submit outline/synopsis and sample chapters. Reviews artwork/photos as part of ms package.

Tips: "We are looking for very clear, informally written, technically correct manuscripts, generally of a how-to nature, in our specific fiber and herb fields only. Our audience includes a variety of creative self-starters who appreciate inspiration and clear instruction. They are often well educated and skillful in many areas."

IOWA STATE UNIVERSITY PRESS, 2121 S. State Ave., Ames IA 50014-8300. (515)292-0140. Fax: (515)292-3348. Acquisitions Editor: Laura Moran. Editor-in-Chief: Gretchen Van Houten. Estab. 1924. Publishes hardcover and paperback originals. Averages 55 titles/year. Receives 450 submissions/year. 98% of books from unagented writers. Average print order for a first book is 1,200. Nonauthor subsidy publishes some titles, based on sales potential of book and contribution to scholarship on trade books. Pays 10% royalty for trade books on wholesale price. No advance. Publishes book 1 year after acceptance. Accepts simultaneous submissions, if so noted. Query for electronic submissions. Reports in up to 6 months. Book catalog free. Manuscript guidelines for SASE.

• Iowa State University Press now publishes books with environmental themes.

Nonfiction: Publishes agriculture, environmental, engineering, history, scientific/technical textbooks, food and nutrition, economics, aviation, journalism, veterinary sciences. Accepts nonfiction translations. Submit outline and several sample chapters, preferably not in sequence; must be double-spaced throughout. Looks for "unique approach to subject; clear, concise narrative; and effective integration of scholarly apparatus." Send contrasting b&w glossy prints to illustrate ms.

ITALICA PRESS, 595 Main St., Suite 605, New York NY 10044-0047. (212)935-4230. Fax: (212)838-7812. E-mail: italica@aol.com. Publisher: Eileen Gardiner. Estab. 1985. Publishes trade paperback originals. Receives 75 queries and 20 mss/year. 50% of books from first-time authors; 100% from unagented writers. Pays 7-15% royalty on wholesale price. Publishes book 1 year after acceptance of ms. Accepts simultaneous submissions. Query for electronic submissions. Reports in 1 month on queries. *Writer's Market* recommends allowing 2 months for reply. Book catalog free.

Nonfiction: "We publish *only* English translations of medieval and Renaissance source materials and English translations of modern Italian fiction." Query. Reviews artwork/photos as part of ms package. Send photocopies.

Tips: "We are interested in considering a wide variety of medieval and Renaissance topics (not historical fiction), and for modern works we are only interested in translations from Italian fiction."

JAIN PUBLISHING CO., P.O. Box 3523, Fremont CA 94539. (510)659-8272. Fax: (510)659-0501. Editor-in-chief: M.K. Jain. Estab. 1987. Imprint is Asian Humanities Press. Publishes hardcover and trade paperback originals and reprints. Publishes 15 titles/year. Receives 500 queries/year. 20% of books from first-time authors; 100% from unagented writers. Pays 6-10% royalty on net sales or makes outright purchase of $500-2,000. Offers occasional $1,000-2,000 advance. Publishes book 1 year after acceptance. Query for electronic submissions. Reports in 3 months on mss. Book catalog for 6×9 SAE with 2 first-class stamps. Manuscript guidelines for #10 SASE.

* Jain is putting more emphasis on general purpose computer books and books dealing with business management. Continued emphasis on undergraduate textbooks.

Nonfiction: Self-help (motivational/inspirational), how-to, cooking/foods/nutrition (vegetarian), health/medicine (holistic/alternative), gift books, guides and handbooks, personal and organizational development, money and personal finance, computer books (general purpose), business/management, multicultural, reference, textbooks. "Manuscripts should be related to our subjects and written in an 'easy to read' and understandable format. Preferably between 40,000-80,000 words." Submit proposal package, including cv and list of prior publications with SASE. Reviews artwork/photos as part of ms package. Send photocopies.

Tips: "We're interested more in user-oriented books than general treatises."

‡JEWISH LIGHTS PUBLISHING, Division of Long Hill Partners Inc., P.O. Box 237, Sunset Farm Offices, Rte. 4, Woodstock VT 05091. Publishes hardcover originals and trade paperback originals and reprints. Publishes 12 titles/year. Receives 200 queries and 300-500 mss/year. Pays 10% royalty of net sales. Publishes book 6 months after acceptance of ms. Accepts simultaneous submissions. Reports in 4 months. Book catalog free on request. Manuscript guidelines for #10 SASE.

Nonfiction: Children's/juvenile, self-help, spirituality. Subjects include philosophy, religion, women's issues/studies, spirituality. "We publish a particular style of books. Find out about our books by looking at them or a catalog, before submitting. We don't publish 'Judaica' as it's typically defined. No biography or autobiography." Query with outline, sample chapter and SASE.

Tips: "Our audience includes people of all faiths, all backgrounds who yearn for books that attract, engage, educate and spiritually inspire."

‡JEWISH PUBLICATION SOCIETY, 1930 Chestnut St., Philadelphia PA 19103. (215)564-5925. Editor-in-Chief: Dr. Ellen Frankel. Publishes hardcover and trade paperback originals and trade paperback reprints. Publishes 12 titles/year. 20% of books from first-time authors; 75% from unagented writers. Pays 10-15% royalty on wholesale price. Offers $1,000-4,000 advance. Publishes book 18 months after acceptance. Accepts simultaneous submissions. Reports in 3 months on proposals. Book catalog free on request.

Nonfiction: Children's/juvenile, reference, trade books. Subjects include history, language/literature, religion, women's issues/studies. "We are interested in books of Judaica for a college-educated readership. No monographs or textbooks. We do not accept memoirs, biographies, art books, coffee-table books." Query with outline, proposal package including description and proposed table of contents, curriculum vitae with SASE.

Recent Nonfiction Title: *Reclaiming the Dead Sea Scrolls*, by Lawrence Schiffman (Jewish history).

Poetry: "We publish no original poetry in English. We would consider a topical anthology on a Jewish theme." Query.

Recent Poetry Title: *Modern Poems on the Bible*, edited by David Curzon (responses to biblical texts - 20 C.).

Tips: "Our audience is college-educated Jewish readers interested in Bible, Jewish history or Jewish practice."

JIST WORKS, INC., 720 N. Park Ave., Indianapolis IN 46202-3431. (317)264-3709. Fax: (317)264-3709. Managing Editor: Sara Hall. Estab. 1981. Publishes trade paperback originals and reprints. Receives 300 submissions/year. 60% of books from first time authors; 100% from unagented writers. Pays 5-12% royalty on wholesale price or makes outright purchase (negotiable). Publishes ms 6-12 months after acceptance. Accepts simultaneous submissions. Query for electronic submissions. Query with SASE. Reports in 3 months on queries. Book catalog and ms guidelines for 9×12 SAE with 6 first-class stamps.

For information on setting your freelance fees, see How Much Should I Charge?

• JIST Works has adopted a new imprint, Park Avenue Publications, to publish business and self-help manuscripts that fall outside of the JIST topical parameters.

Nonfiction: How-to, career, reference, self-help, software, textbook. Specializes in job search, self-help and career related topics. "We want text/workbook formats that would be useful in a school or other institutional setting. We also publish trade titles, all reading levels. Will consider books for professional staff and educators, appropriate software and videos." Reviews artwork/photos as part of ms package.

Tips: "Institutions and staff who work with people of all reading and academic skills, making career and life decisions or who are looking for jobs are our primary audience, but we're focusing more on business and trade topics for consumers."

JOHNSON BOOKS, Johnson Publishing Co., 1880 S. 57th Court., Boulder CO 80301. (303)443-9766. Fax: (303)443-1679. Editorial Director: Stephen Topping. Estab. 1979. Imprints are Spring Creek Press and Cordillera Press. Publishes hardcover and paperback originals and reprints. Publishes 10-12 titles/year. Receives 500 submissions/year. 30% of books from first-time authors; 90% from unagented writers. Average print order for a first book is 5,000. Royalties vary. Publishes book 1 year after acceptance. Reports in 2 months. Book catalog and ms guidelines for 9×12 SAE with 5 first-class stamps.

Nonfiction: General nonfiction, books on the West, environmental subjects, natural history, paleontology, geology, archaeology, travel, guidebooks, outdoor recreation. Accepts nonfiction translations. "We are primarily interested in books for the informed popular market, though we will consider vividly written scholarly works. As a small publisher, we are able to give every submission close personal attention." Query first or call. Submit outline/synopsis and 3 sample chapters. Looks for "good writing, thorough research, professional presentation and appropriate style. Marketing suggestions from writers are helpful." Reviews artwork/photos.

Tips: "We are looking for nature titles with broad national, not just regional, appeal. We are trying to include more outdoor recreation books in addition to our other areas listed."

‡JONES PUBLISHING, INC., P.O. Box 5000, Iola WI 54945. (715)445-5000. Publisher, Book Division: Gregory Bayer. Publishes trade paperback originals and reprints. Publishes 12 titles/year. 40% of books from first-time authors; 100% of books from unagented writers. Pays 8-10% royalty on "publisher's actual receipts," after discounts, returns, etc. Offers $100-5,000 advance. Publishes book 1 year after acceptance of ms. Reports in 2 weeks on queries and proposals, 2 months on mss. Author guidelines free on request.

Nonfiction: How-to, humor, illustrated book, reference, technical. Subjects include child guidance/parenting, hobbies (doll making, ceramics), military/war (aircraft), general aviation. Query with proposal package, including outline, 2 sample chapters, cover letter, author info, marketing info, possible competition. Reviews artwork/photos as part of ms package. Send photocopies.

Recent Nonfiction Title: *Hobby Ceramist's Guide to Finishing Products*, by Juanita Niemeyer (how-to).

Fiction: Humor (aviation), short story collections (aviation). Query with synopsis and 3 sample chapters.

Tips: "Our audience consists of very 'serious' hobbyists who are looking for how-to or reference books that will enhance their enjoyment of the hobby, whether it is doing ceramics, flying airplanes, or making dolls. Make sure that your proposal is complete and very detailed. Illustrations are very important when trying to sell books, so we'll always look at a manuscript that will employ author-provided photos/drawings first. Books that will help readers save or make money while engaging in their favorite hobby/activity are very desirable."

BOB JONES UNIVERSITY PRESS, Greenville SC 29614-0001. Acquisitions Editor: Ms. Gloria Repp. Estab. 1974. Publishes trade paperback originals and reprints. Publishes 10 titles/year. Receives 50 queries and 300 mss/year. 40% of books from first-time authors; 100% from unagented writers. Makes outright purchase of $500-1,250. Publishes book 1 year after acceptance. Accepts simultaneous submissions. Query for electronic submissions. Reports in 2 months on mss. Book catalog and ms guidelines free on request.

Nonfiction: Biography (for teens), children's/juvenile. Subjects include animals, gardening, health/medicine, history, nature/environment, sports. "We're looking for concept books on almost any subject suitable for children. We also like biographies." Submit outline and 3 sample chapters.

Fiction: Juvenile, young adult. "We're looking for well-rounded characters and plots with plenty of action." Submit synopsis and 5 sample chapters or complete ms.

Tips: "Our readers are children ages two and up, teens and young adults. We're looking for high-quality writing that reflects a Christian perspective and features well-developed characters in a convincing plot. Most open to: first chapter books; adventure; biography."

JUDSON PRESS, P.O. Box 851, Valley Forge PA 19482-0851. (610)768-2118. Fax: (610)768-2056. Publisher: Harold W. Rast. Acquisitions: Kristy Pullen. Editorial Manager: Mary Nicol. Estab. 1824. Publishes hardcover and paperback originals. Averages 15-20 titles/year. Receives 750 queries/year. Average print order for a first book is 5,000. Pays royalty or flat fee. Publishes book 15 months after acceptance. Accepts simultaneous submissions. Reports in 6 months. Enclose return postage. Book catalog for 9×12 SAE with 4 first-class stamps. Manuscript guidelines for #10 SASE.

• Judson Press has expanded its line from 10-15 titles/year to 15-20 titles/year.

Nonfiction: Adult religious nonfiction of 30,000-80,000 words. "Our audience is mostly church members who seek to have a more fulfilling personal spiritual life and want to serve Christ in their churches and other relationships." Query with outline and 1 sample chapter.
Tips: "Writers have the best chance selling us practical books assisting clergy or laypersons in their ministry and personal lives. Our audience consists of Protestant church leaders and members. Be sensitive to our workload and adapt to the market's needs. Books on multicultural issues are very welcome."

‡JUST US BOOKS, INC., 356 Glenwood Ave., 3rd Floor, East Orange NJ 07017. Submissions Manager: Allyson Sherwood. Imprint is Afro-Bets® (Cheryl Willis Hudson, publisher). Publishes hardcover and trade paperback and mass market paperback originals. Publishes 3-5 titles/year. Receives 300 queries and 500 mss/year. 33% of books from first-time authors; 33% from unagented writers. Pays royalty or makes outright purchase. Offers variable advance. Publishes book 18 months after acceptance of ms. Accepts simultaneous submissions. Reports in 2-4 weeks on queries and proposals, 1-3 months on mss. Book catalog and ms guidelines for 6×9 SAE with 2 first-class stamps.
Nonfiction: Biography, children's/juvenile, illustrated book, middle readers and young adult. Emphasis on African-American subjects. Concentrate on young adult readers—no picture books. Query with SASE. Reviews artwork/photos as part of ms package. Send photocopies, transparencies or color or b&w sketches.
Recent Nonfiction Title: *Book of Black Heroes, Vol. 2 Great Women in the Struggle*, by Toyomi Igus et. al. (biographical).
Fiction: Adventure, fantasy, historical, humor, multicultural, science fiction, suspense, young adult. Looking for "contemporary, realistic, appealing fiction for readers aged 9-12, especially stories involving boys. Stories may take the form of chapter books with a range of 5,000-20,000 words." Query with SASE. Unsolicited mss will be returned unread.
Recent Fiction Title: *Ziggy and the Black Dinosaurs*, by Sharon M. Draper (mystery).
Poetry: Not considering poetry at this time.

KALMBACH PUBLISHING CO., 21027 Crossroads Circle, P.O. Box 1612, Waukesha WI 53187-1612. Fax: (414)796-1142. Senior Acquisitions Editor: Terry Spohn. Estab. 1934. Publishes hardcover and paperback originals and paperback reprints. Averages 15-20 titles/year. Receives 100 submissions/year. 85% of books from first-time authors; 100% from unagented writers. Offers 10% royalty on net. Offers $1,500 average advance. Publishes book 18 months after acceptance. Reports in 2 months.
Nonfiction: Hobbies, how-to, amateur astronomy, railroading. "Our book publishing effort is in amateur astronomy, railroading and hobby how-to-do-it titles *only*." Query first. "I welcome telephone inquiries. They save me a lot of time, and they can save an author a lot of misconceptions and wasted work." In written query, wants to see a detailed outline of 2-3 pages and a complete sample chapter with photos, drawings, and how-to text. Reviews artwork/photos as part of ms package.
Recent Nonfiction Title: *The Guide to North American Steam Locomotives*, by George Drury.
Tips: "Our books are about half text and half illustrations. Any author who wants to publish with us must be able to furnish good photographs and rough drawings before we'll consider contracting for his book."

KAR-BEN COPIES INC., 6800 Tildenwood Lane, Rockville MD 20852-4371. (301)984-8733 or 1-800-4KARBEN. Fax: (301)881-9195. President: Judye Groner. Contact: Madeline Wikler. Estab. 1975. Publishes hardcover and trade paperback originals on Jewish themes for young children. Averages 8-10 titles/year. Receives 150 submissions/year. 25% of books from first-time authors; 100% from unagented writers. Average print order for a first book is 10,000. Pays 6-8% royalty on net receipts or makes negotiable outright purchase. Offers $1,000 average advance. Publishes book 1 year after acceptance. Reports in 2 months. Book catalog and ms guidelines for 9×12 SAE with 2 first-class stamps.
● This publisher recently received honors from the Jewish Book Awards for *The Kingdom of Singing Birds*, by Miriam Aroner and *Thank You, God!*, by Judy H. Groner and Madeline Wikler.
Nonfiction: Jewish juvenile (ages 1-12). Especially looking for books on Jewish life-cycle, holidays, and customs for children—"early childhood and elementary." Send only mss with Jewish content. Query with outline and sample chapters. Reviews artwork/photos as part of ms package.
Fiction: Adventure, fantasy, historical, religious (all Jewish juvenile). Especially looking for Jewish holiday and history-related fiction for young children. Submit outline/synopsis and sample chapters or complete ms.
Tips: "We envision Jewish children and their families, and juveniles interested in learning about Jewish subjects, as our audience."

KENT STATE UNIVERSITY PRESS, P.O. Box 5190, Kent OH 44242-0001. (216)672-7913. Fax: (216)672-3104. Director: John T. Hubbell. Senior Editor: Julia Morton. Estab. 1965. Publishes hardcover and paperback originals and some reprints. Averages 20-25 titles/year. Nonauthor subsidy publishes 20% of books. Standard minimum book contract on net sales. Offers advance rarely. "Always write a letter of inquiry before submitting manuscripts. We can publish only a limited number of titles each year and can frequently tell in advance whether or not we would be interested in a particular manuscript. This practice saves both our time and that of the author, not to mention postage costs. If interested we will ask for complete manuscript. Decisions based on inhouse readings and two by outside scholars in the field of study." Reports in 3 months. Enclose return postage. Book catalog free.

Nonfiction: Especially interested in "scholarly works in history and literary studies of high quality, any titles of regional interest for Ohio, scholarly biographies, archaeological research, the arts, and general nonfiction."

Tips: "We are cautious about publishing heavily-illustrated manuscripts."

MICHAEL KESEND PUBLISHING, LTD., 1025 Fifth Ave., New York NY 10028. (212)249-5150. Director: Michael Kesend. Editor: Judy Wilder. Estab. 1979. Publishes hardcover and trade paperback originals and reprints. Averages 4-6 titles/year. Receives 300 submissions/year. 20% of books from first-time authors; 40% from unagented writers. Pays 6% royalty on wholesale price. Advance varies. Publishes book 18 months after acceptance. Reports in 2 months on queries. Guidelines for #10 SASE.

• This publisher no longer accepts fiction.

Nonfiction: Biography, how-to, illustrated book, self-help, sports. Subjects include animals, health, history, hobbies, nature, sports, travel, the environment, guides to several subjects. Needs sports, health self-help and environmental awareness guides. No photography mss. Submit outline and sample chapters. Reviews artwork/photos as part of ms package.

Tips: "We are now more interested in nature-related topics, national guides, outdoor travel guides and sports nonfiction."

KINSEEKER PUBLICATIONS, P.O. Box 184, Grawn MI 49637-0184. (616)276-6745. Editor: Victoria Wilson. Estab. 1986. Publishes trade paperback originals. Averages 6 titles/year. 100% of books from unagented writers. Pays 10-25% royalty on retail price. Publishes book 8 months after acceptance. Accepts simultaneous submissions. Reports in 3 months. Book catalog and ms guidelines for #10 SASE.

Nonfiction: Reference books. Subjects are local history and genealogy. Query or submit outline and sample chapters. Reviews artwork/photos as part of ms package.

‡B. KLEIN PUBLICATIONS, P.O. Box 8503, Coral Springs FL 33075-8503. (305)752-1708. Fax: (305)752-2547. Editor-in-Chief: Bernard Klein. Estab. 1946. Publishes hardcover and paperback originals. Specializes in directories, annuals, who's who books, bibliography, business opportunity, reference books. Averages 5 titles/year. Pays 10% royalty on wholesale price, "but we're negotiable. Advance depends on many factors." Markets books by direct mail and mail order. Accepts simultaneous submissions. Reports in 2 months. Book catalog for #10 SASE.

Nonfiction: Business, hobbies, how-to, reference, self-help, directories and bibliographies. Query or submit outline and sample chapters.

Recent Nonfiction Title: *Guide to American Directories*, by Bernard Klein.

ALFRED A. KNOPF, INC., Division of Random House, 201 E. 50th St., New York NY 10022. (212)751-2600. Submit mss to Senior Editor or Children's Book Editor. Publishes hardcover and paperback originals. Averages 200 titles/yearly. 15% of books from first-time authors; 30% from unagented writers. Royalty and advance vary. Publishes book 1 year after acceptance. Accepts simultaneous submissions if so informed. Reports in 3 months. Book catalog for 7½×10½ SAE with 5 first-class stamps.

• Alfred A. Knopf received eight nominations for the 1994 National Book Critics Circle Awards.

Nonfiction: Book-length nonfiction, including books of scholarly merit. Preferred length: 50,000-150,000 words. "A good nonfiction writer should be able to follow the latest scholarship in any field of human knowledge, and fill in the abstractions of scholarship for the benefit of the general reader by means of good, concrete, sensory reporting." Query. Reviews artwork/photos as part of ms package.

Recent Nonfiction Title: *The Rape of Europa*, by Lynn Nicholas (art history).

Fiction: Publishes book-length fiction of literary merit by known or unknown writers. Length: 40,000-150,000 words. *Writer's Market* recommends writers query with sample chapters.

Recent Fiction Title: *Who Will Run the Frog Hospital?*, by Lorrie Moore.

‡KNOWLEDGE, IDEAS & TRENDS, INC. (KIT), 1131-0 Tolland Turnpike, Suite 175, Manchester CT 06040. (203)646-0745. Co-Publisher: Rita I. McCullough. Publishes hardcover and trade paperback originals. Publishes 4-5 titles/year. 80% of books from first-time authors; 100% from unagented writers. Pays royalty on wholesale price or advance against royalty. Advance varies. Publishes book 18 months after acceptance of ms. Accepts simultaneous submissions. Reports in 3 months on mss. Book catalog and ms guidelines free on request.

Nonfiction: Biography, how-to, humor, reference, self-help. Subjects include anthropology/archaeology, business and economics, ethnic, history, psychology, sociology, women's issues/studies. Send outline and 3 sample chapters to R.I. McCullough, 400 Prospect St., Glen Rock NJ 07452. Reviews artwork/photos as part of ms package. Send photocopies.

Tips: "Audience is general readers, academics, older women, sociologists."

KNOWLEDGE INDUSTRY PUBLICATIONS, INC., 701 Westchester Ave., White Plains NY 10604. (914)328-9157. Fax: (914)328-9093. Senior Vice President: Janet Moore. Publishes hardcover and paperback originals. Averages 10 titles/year. Receives 30 submissions/year. 60% of books from first-time authors; 100% from unagented writers. Average print order for a first book is 2,500. Offers negotiable advance. Publishes book 1 year after acceptance. Query for electronic submissions. Reports in 3 months. Book catalog free. Manuscript guidelines for SASE.

Nonfiction: Corporate, industrial video, interactive video, computer graphics. Especially needs TV and video. Query first, then submit outline and sample chapters. Reviews artwork/photos as part of ms package.

KODANSHA AMERICA, INC., 114 Fifth Ave., New York NY 10011. (212)727-6460. Fax: (212)727-9177. Contact: Editorial Department. Estab. 1989 (in US). Publishes 50% hardcover and trade paperback originals; 50% trade paperback originals and reprints in Kodansha Globe series. Averages 35-40 titles/year. Receives 3,000 submissions/year. 10% of books from first-time authors; 30% from unagented writers. Pays 6-15% royalty on retail price. Offers $2,000 (reprints), $10,000 (original) average advances. Publishes book an average of 9 months after acceptance. Accepts simultaneous submissions. Reports in up to 3 months. Book catalog for 9 × 12 SAE with 6 first-class stamps.

● Kodansha America published the extremely successful book, *Having Our Say,* by the Delany sisters, which spent 16 weeks on national bestseller lists and won an LMP award last year. *The Delany Sisters' Book of Wisdom* followed in the fall of 1994 with a first printing of over 350,000.

Nonfiction: Biography, anthropology/archaeology, business and economics, cooking, ethnic, gardening, history, craft, language, nature/environment, philosophy, psychology, religion, science, sociology, translation, travel, Asian subjects. Looking for distinguished critical books on international subjects. No pop psychology, how-to, true crime, regional. Query with sample chapters and SASE. Reviews artwork/photos as part of ms package.

Recent Nonfiction Title: *The Delany Sisters' Book of Everyday Wisdom.*

Tips: "Our focus is on nonfiction titles of an international and cross-cultural nature, well-researched, written with authority, bringing something of a world view to the general reading public. We are especially interested in titles with staying power, which will sell as well in five years' time as now. Potential authors should be aware of what comparable titles are on the market, and from whom."

KREGEL PUBICATIONS, Kregel, Inc., P.O. Box 2607, Grand Rapids MI 49501. Senior Editor: Dennis R. Hillman. Imprints are Kregel Publications, Kregel Resources, Kregel Classics. Publishes hardcover and trade paperback originals and reprints. Publishes 50 titles/year. Receives 100 queries and 30 mss/year. 5% of books from first-time authors; 100% from unagented writers. Pays 8-14% royalty on wholesale price or makes outright purchase of $500-1,000. Offers $1,000-2,000 advance. Publishes book 9 months after acceptance of ms. Accepts simultaneous submissions. Query for electronic submissions. Reports in 1 month on queries and proposals, 3 months on mss. Book catalog for 9 × 12 SAE with 3 first-class stamps. Manuscript guidelines for #10 SASE.

Nonfiction: Biography (Christian), reference, textbook. Subjects include religion. "We serve evangelical Christian readers and those in career Christian service." Query with outline, 2 sample chapters, bio and market comparison.

Recent Nonfiction Title: *Create & Celebrate*, by Harold Westing.

LAKE VIEW PRESS, P.O. Box 578279, Chicago IL 60657. Director: Paul Elitzik. Publishes hardcover and trade paperback originals. Publishes 5 titles/year. Receives 100 queries and 10 mss/year. 100% of books from unagented writers. Pays 6-10% royalty on wholesale price. Publishes book 1 year after acceptance of ms. No simultaneous submissions. Query for electronic submissions. Reports in 1 month on queries. Book catalog for #10 SASE.

Nonfiction: Biography, reference, technical. Subjects include government/politics, history, language/literature, sociology, women's issues/studies. "We are interested mainly in scholarly nonfiction which is written in a manner accessible to a nonprofessional reader." Query.

Recent Nonfiction Title: *Political Companion to American Film*, by Gary Crowdus (encyclopedia/film).

LANGENSCHEIDT PUBLISHING GROUP, 46-35 54th Rd., Maspeth NY 11378. (800)432-MAPS. Fax: (718)784-0640. Sales Director: Susan Pohja. Imprints are Hagstrom Map, American Map, Trakker Map, Arrow Map, Creative Sales. Publishes hardcover, trade paperback and mass market paperback originals. Publishes over 100 titles/year; each imprint publishes 20 titles/year. Receives 25 queries and 15 mss/year. 100% of books from unagented writers. Pays royalty or makes outright purchase. Offers advance of a percentage of the retail price/cost of the project. Publishes book 6 months after acceptance of ms. Accepts simultaneous submissions. Reports in 2 months on proposals. Book catalog free on request.

Nonfiction: Reference. Subjects include foreign language. "Any foreign language that fills a gap in our line is welcome." Submit outline and 2 sample chapters.

Recent Nonfiction Title: Laminated phrase cards, by R. Noble (travel companion).

LARK BOOKS, Altamont Press, 50 College St., Asheville NC 28801. Publisher: Rob Pulleyn. Estab. 1976. Imprints are: Lark Books; Sterling/Lark Books. Publishes hardcover and trade paperback originals and reprints. Publishes 40 titles/year. Sterling publishes 25; Lark publishes 5. Receives 400 queries and 300 mss/

year. 80% of books from first-time authors; 100% from unagented writers. Pays 5-20% royalty on gross income or makes outright purchase. Offers up to $2,500 advance. Publishes book 1 year after acceptance of ms. Accepts simultaneous submissions. Query for electronic submissions. Reports in 2 months.

Nonfiction: Coffee table book, cookbook, how-to, illustrated book, children's/juvenile. Subjects include cooking/foods/nutrition, gardening, hobbies, nature/environment, crafts. "We publish high quality, highly illustrated books, primarily in the crafts/leisure markets. We work closely with bookclubs. Our books are either how-to, 'gallery' or combination books." Submit outline and 1 sample chapter or proposal package, including sample projects, table of contents. Reviews artwork/photos as part of ms package. Send transparencies if possible.

‡LARSON PUBLICATIONS/PBPF, 4936 Rt. 414, Burdett NY 14818-9729. (607)546-9342. Director: Paul Cash. Estab. 1982. Publishes hardcover and trade paperback originals. Averages 4-5 titles/year. Receives 1,000 submissions/year. 5% of books from first-time authors. Pays 7½% royalty on retail price or 10% cash received. Rarely offers advance. Publishes book 1 year after acceptance. Accepts simultaneous submissions. Reports in 4 months on queries. Unsolicited mss not accepted; queries only. Book catalog for 9×12 SAE with 3 first-class stamps.

Nonfiction: Spiritual philosophy. Subjects include philosophy, psychology and religion. We are looking for studies of comparative spiritual philosophy or personal fruits of independent (transsectarian viewpoint) spiritual research/practice. Query or submit outline and sample chapters. Reviews artwork/photos as part of ms package.

Recent Nonfiction Title: *Visions of God from the Near Death Experience*, by Ken Vincent.

‡LAUREATE PRESS, P.O. Box 450597, Sunrise FL 33345. Editor-in-Chief/Publisher: Lance C. Lobo. Publishes trade paperback originals and reprints. Publishes 7 titles/year. 5% of books from first-time authors; 100% from unagented writers. Pays 6-10% royalty on wholesale price. Offers $100 advance. Publishes book 2 years after acceptance of ms. Reports in 2 months on queries.

Nonfiction: Fencing subjects only—biography, how-to, technical. Fencing books must be authored by diplomaed fencing masters. Query with outline and SASE.

Recent Nonfiction Title: *The Science of Foil Fencing*, by William M. Gaugler (fencing-technical).

Tips: Audience is recreational and competitive fencers worldwide.

MERLOYD LAWRENCE BOOKS, Imprint of Addison Wesley, 102 Chestnut St., Boston MA 02108. President: Merloyd Lawrence. Estab. 1982. Publishes hardcover and trade paperback originals. Averages 7-8 titles/year. Receives 400 submissions/year. 25% of books from first-time authors; 20% from unagented writers. Pays royalty on retail price. Publishes book an average of 1 year after acceptance. Accepts simultaneous submissions. Reports in 3 weeks on queries; no unsolicited ms read. All queries with SASE read and answered. Book catalog available from Addison Wesley.

Nonfiction: Biography. Subjects include child development/parenting, health/medicine, nature/environment, psychology. Query with SASE.

LAWYERS & JUDGES PUBLISHING CO., P.O. Box 30040, Tucson AZ 85751-0040. (602)751-1500. Fax: (602)751-1202. President: Steve Weintraub. Publishes professional hardcover originals. Publishes 15 titles/year. Receives 200 queries and 30 mss/year. 5% of books from first-time authors; 100% from unagented writers. Pays 7-10% royalty on retail price. Publishes book 5 months after acceptance of ms. Accepts simultaneous submissions. Query for electronic submissions. Reports in 2 months. Book catalog free.

Nonfiction: Reference. Legal/insurance subjects. "We are a highly specific publishing company, reaching the legal and insurance fields and accident reconstruction. Unless a writer is an expert in these areas, we are not interested." Submit proposal package, including full or *very* representative portion of ms. *Writer's Market* recommends query with SASE first.

Recent Nonfiction Title: *Train Accident Reconstruction and FELA Litigation*, 2nd Edition, by James R. Loumiet B.S.M.E. and William G. Jungbauer Esq.

LEADERSHIP PUBLISHERS, INC., Talented and Gifted Education, P.O. Box 8358, Des Moines IA 50301-8358. (515)278-4765. Fax: (515)270-8303. Editorial Director: Lois F. Roets. Estab. 1982. Publishes trade paperback originals. Publishes 5 titles/year. Receives 25 queries and 10 mss/year. Pays 10% royalty of sales. Publishes book 1 year after acceptance of ms. Reports in 3 months. Book catalog and ms guidelines for 9×12 SAE with 2 first-class stamps.

Nonfiction: Textbook. Education subjects. "We publish enrichment/supplementary educational programs and teacher reference books; our specialty is education of the talented and gifted." Submit outline and 2 sample chapters. Reviews artwork/photos as part of ms package. Send photocopies.

‡THE LEARNING WORKS, INC., P.O. Box 6187, Santa Barbara CA 93160. (805)964-4220. President: Linda Schwartz. Publishes trade paperback originals. Publishes 10 titles/year. Receives 75 queries and 50 mss/year. 5% of books from first-time authors; 95% from unagented writers. Makes outright purchase, amount varies according to author's experience. Publishes book within 1 year of acceptance of ms. Reports in 1 month. Book catalog and ms guidelines free on request.

Nonfiction: Children's/juvenile. Subjects include animals, anthropology/archaeology, art/architecture, child guidance/parenting, education, ethnic, health/medicine, history, language/literature, nature/environment, science, sports, travel, safety, arts/crafts, self-esteem, values clarification. "The Learning Works specializes in educational activity books for children, parents, and teachers. Subject matter ranges across the curriculum. Many are supplementary educational materials for ages preschool to 18. We do not publish story books or music." Query with outline, 10 sample activities and SASE.

Recent Nonfiction Title: *Gobble Up Math*, by Sue Mogard, Ginny McDonnell (math concepts/nutrition).

LEE & LOW BOOKS, 95 Madison Ave., New York NY 10016. (212)779-4400. Publisher: Philip Lee. Editor-in-Chief: Elizabeth Szabla. Estab. 1991. "We focus on multicultural children's books. Of special interest picture book are stories set in contemporary America. We are interested in fiction as well as nonfiction." Titles released include *Bein' With You This Way*, by W. Nikola-Lisa; *Zora Hurston and the Chinaberry Tree*, by William Motter; *Saturday at the New You*, by Barbara E. Barber.
- Awards Lee & Low have won include 1994 Reading Magic Award (Parenting Magazine); 1994 Washington Governor's Award; 1994 Pick of the Lists (American Bookseller Magazine).

LEHIGH UNIVERSITY PRESS, Linderman Library, 30 Library Dr., Lehigh University, Bethlehem PA 18015-3067. (610)758-3933. Fax: (610)974-2823. E-mail: inlup@lehigh.edu. Director: Philip A. Metzger. Estab. 1985. Publishes hardcover originals. Publishes 10 titles/year. Receives 30 queries and 25 mss/year. 70% of books from first-time authors; 100% from unagented writers. Pays royalty. Publishes book 18 months after acceptance of ms. Accepts simultaneous submissions. Reports in 3 months. Book catalog and ms guidelines free.

Nonfiction: Biography, reference, academic. Subjects include Americana, art/architecture, history, language/literature, science. "We are an academic press publishing scholarly monographs. We are especially interested in works on 18th century studies and the history of technology, but consider works of quality on a variety of subjects." Submit 1 sample chapter and proposal package.

LEISURE BOOKS, Division of Dorchester Publishing Co., Inc., Suite 1008, 276 Fifth Ave., New York NY 10001-0112. (212)725-8811. Editorial Assistant: Jennifer Eaton. Estab. 1970. Publishes mass market paperback originals and reprints. Averages 160 titles/year. Receives thousands of submissions/year. 20% of books from first-time authors; 20% from unagented writers. Pays royalty on retail price. Advance negotiable. Publishes book 18 months after acceptance. Reports in 1 month on queries. *Writer's Market* recommends allowing 2 months for reply. Book catalog and ms guidelines for #10 SASE.
- Love Spell, an imprint, publishes only romance titles.

Nonfiction: "Our needs are minimal as we publish perhaps two nonfiction titles a year." Query.

Fiction: Historical romance (115,000 words); time-travel romance (90,000 words); futuristic romance (90,000 words). "We are strongly backing historical romance. No sweet romance, gothic, science fiction, western, erotica, contemporary women's fiction, mainstream or male adventure." Query or submit outline/synopsis and sample chapters. "No material will be returned without SASE."

Tips: "Historical romance is our strongest category. We are also seeking time-travel and futuristic romances."

LERNER PUBLICATIONS COMPANY, 241 First Ave. N., Minneapolis MN 55401. (612)332-3344. Submissions Editor: Jennifer Martin. Estab. 1959. Imprints are Runestone Press, First Avenue Editions. Publishes hardcover originals. Averages 75-100 titles/year. Receives 1,000 queries and 300 mss/year. 50% of books from first-time authors; 90% from unagented writers. Pays negotiable royalty or makes outright purchase. Publishes book 18-24 months after acceptance of ms. Accepts simultaneous submissions. Query for electronic submissions. Reports in 2 months on proposals. Catalog for 9 × 12 SAE with 6 first-class stamps. Manuscript guidelines for #10 SAE.

Nonfiction: Children's/juvenile. Subjects include animals, anthropology/archaeology, art/architecture, business and economics, computers and electronics, cooking/foods/nutrition, ethnic, government/politics, health/medicine, history, language/literature, money/finance, multicultural, music/dance, nature/environment, recreation, science, sports, biography and geography. "We are interested in multicultural work by authors of the focus ethnic groups. Picture books or any work clearly intended for adults (parents and teachers) are not of interest to us. We also do not publish video or audio cassettes. Our main audience consists of children in grades 3-9." Submit proposal package, including introductory letter, outline, 1-2 sample chapters, résumé and SASE.

Fiction: Young adult, middle grade. "We publish very little fiction—usually only one or two titles per year—mainly in the mystery and/or multicultural issues areas. We do not publish adult fiction, picture books, 'Babysitters Club'-type series." Query.

Recent Fiction Title: *Ransom for a River Dolphin*, by Sarita Kendall (multicultural juvenile).

LEXINGTON BOOKS, Imprint of Paramount Publishing, Inc., 866 Third Ave., New York NY 10022. (212)702-3130. Senior Editor: Beth Anderson. Publishes hardcover originals. Imprint publishes 40 titles/

year. Receives 500 queries and 100 mss/year. 50% of books from first-time authors; 70% from unagented writers. Pays 10-15% royalty on wholesale or retail price. Publishes book 1-2 years after acceptance of ms. Accepts simultaneous submissions. Reports in 2 months on proposals. Book catalog and ms guidelines free on request.

Nonfiction: Reference, trade. Subjects include business, child guidance/parenting, gay/lesbian, psychology, sociology, women's issues/studies, criminology. "We publish practical books." Query.

THE LIBERAL PRESS, P.O. Box 140361, Las Colinas TX 75014. (214)686-5332. Executive Vice President: Rick Donovon. Publishes trade paperback originals. Publishes 4 titles/year. Receives 50 queries and 100 mss/year. 50% of books from first-time authors; 100% from unagented writers. Pays 4% royalty on retail price. Publishes book 1 year after acceptance of ms. No simultaneous submissions. Query for electronic submissions. Reports in 1 month on queries, 4 months on mss. Book catalog for 6×9 SAE with 5 first-class stamps. Manuscript guidelines for #10 SASE.

Nonfiction: Textbook. Subjects include gay/lesbian, government/politics (liberal only), history, women's issues/studies. "Work must be gender-free nonsexist, historical/factual with necessary bibliographic material (footnote/bibliography)." Query with outline and 2 sample chapters. All unsolicited mss returned unopened.

Recent Nonfiction Title: *An Ambitious Sort of Grief*, by Marion Cohen (neo-natal loss).

LIFETIME BOOKS, INC., 2131 Hollywood Blvd., Hollywood FL 33020. (305)925-5242. Fax: (305)925-5244. Senior Editor: Brian Feinblum. Imprints are Fell Publishers, Compact Books, Blockbuster Periodicals. Publishes hardcover and trade paperback originals and reprints. Publishes 25 titles/year. Receives 3,000 queries and 1,500 mss/year. 90% of books from first-time authors; 90% from unagented writers. Pays 6-15% royalty on retail price. Offers advance of $500-5,000. Publishes book 6-9 months after acceptance. Accepts simultaneous submissions. Reports in 3 months on mss. Book catalog and ms guidelines for 9×12 SAE with 5 first-class stamps.

Nonfiction: How-to, self-help. Subjects include business and sales, child guidance/parenting, foods/nutrition, education, history, hobbies, Hollywood bio/exposé money/finance, true crime. "We are interested in material on business, health and fitness, self-improvement and reference. We will not consider topics that only appeal to a small, select audience." Submit outline and 2 sample chapters. Reviews artwork as part of ms package. Send photocopies.

Recent Nonfiction Title: *Cholesterol Cure Made Easy*, by Sylvan R. Lewis, M.D. (health and diet).

Fiction: "We are currently publishing very little fiction." Submit outline/synopsis and sample chapters. No poetry.

Tips: "We are most interested in well-written, timely nonfiction with strong sales potential. Our audience is very general. Learn markets and be prepared to help with sales and promotion."

LIGUORI PUBLICATIONS, One Liguori Dr., Liguori MO 63057. (314)464-2500. Publisher: Thomas M. Santa, C.SS.R. Imprints are Liguori Books and Triumph Books™ (contact Robert Pagliari, editor-in-chief or Patricia Kossman, executive editor). Publishes hardcover originals and trade paperback originals and reprints. Publishes 20 titles/year; each imprint publishes 10 titles/year. Pays 9% royalty on retail price or makes outright purchase. Advance varies. Publishes book 2 years after acceptance of ms. No simultaneous submissions. Query for disk, CD ROM and Internet publishing. Reports in 2 months on queries and proposals, 3 months on mss. Author guidelines free on request.

Nonfiction: Children's/juvenile, self-help, devotional disk, CD ROM, Internet. Religious subjects. Query with outline, 1 sample chapter and SASE required.

LIMELIGHT EDITIONS, Imprint of Proscenium Publishers Inc., 118 E. 30th St., New York NY 10016. President: Melvyn B. Zerman. Publishes hardcover and trade paperback originals and trade paperback reprints. Publishes 14 titles/year. Receives 150 queries and 40 mss/year. 15% of books from first-time authors; 20% from unagented writers. Pays 7½ (on paperbacks)-10% (on hardcovers) royalty on retail price. Offers $500-2,000 advance. Publishes book 10 months after acceptance of ms. Query for electronic submissions. Reports in 1 month on queries and proposals, 3 months on mss. Book catalog and ms guidelines free on request.

Nonfiction: Biography, humor, illustrated book, music/dance, self-help, theater/film. "All books are on the performing arts *exclusively*." Query with proposal package, including 2-3 sample chapters, outline. Reviews artwork/photos as part of ms package. Send photocopies.

‡LION BOOKS, Subsidiary of Sayre Ross Co., 210 Melson Rd., Scarsdale NY 10583. (914)725-3372. Editor: Harriet Ross. Publishes hardcover originals and reprints and trade paperback reprints. Publishes 14 titles/year. Receives 40-60 queries and 20-30 mss/year. 30% of books from first-time authors. Pays 7-15% royalty on wholesale price or makes outright purchase $500-5,000. Publishes book 1 month after acceptance of ms. Reports in 1 week on queries, 1 month on mss.

Nonfiction: Biography, how-to. Subjects include Americana, ethnic, government/politics, history, recreation, sports. Submit complete mss with SASE

LITTLE, BROWN AND CO., CHILDREN'S BOOK DIVISION, 34 Beacon St., Boston MA 02108. (617)227-0730. Editorial Assistant: Erica Lombard. Only accepting submissions through literary agents and from previously published authors. Pays royalty on retail price. Offers advance to be negotiated individually. Publishes book 2 years after acceptance of ms. Accepts simultaneous submissions, if so noted. Reports in 1 month on queries, 3 months on proposals and mss. Book catalog for 8×10 SAE with 3 first-class stamps. Manuscript guidelines free on request.
   • Recent awards that Little, Brown & Company books have won include Christopher Award, ABA "Pick of the List," ALA Notable, Best Book, Texas Blue Bonnet, SLJ "Best Books," *NYT* Best Illustrated.
Nonfiction: Children's/juvenile. Subjects include animals, art/architecture, cooking/foods/nutrition, ethnic, gay/lesbian, history, hobbies, nature/environment, recreation, science, sports. "We have published and will continue to publish books on a wide variety of nonfiction topics which may be of interest to children and are looking for strong writing and presentation, but no predetermined topics." Writers should avoid "looking for the 'issue' they think publishers want to see, choosing instead topics they know best and are most enthusiastic about/inspired by." Submit outline and 3 sample chapters "including first and last if possible" or proposal package, including "most complete outline, possible samples and background info (if project is not complete due to necessary research)." Reviews artwork/photos as part of package. Send photocopies (color if possible).
Recent Nonfiction Title: *Tell Them We Remember*, by Susan D. Bachrach (middle reader nonfiction).
Fiction: All juvenile/young adult. Categories include adventure, ethnic, fantasy, feminist, gay/lesbian, historical, humor, mystery, picture books, science fiction and suspense. "We are looking for strong fiction for children of all ages in any area, including multicultural. We always prefer full manuscripts for fiction."
Recent Fiction Title: *Feliciana Feydra LeRoux: A Cajun Tall Tale*, by Tynia Thomassie (picture book).
Tips: "Our audience is children of all ages, from preschool through young adult. We are looking for quality material that will work in hardcover—send us your best."

LITTLE, BROWN AND CO., INC., Division of Time Warner Inc., 1271 Avenue of the Americas, New York NY 10020. (212)522-8700. Contact: Editorial Department, Trade Division. Estab. 1837. Imprint is Bulfinch Press. Publishes hardcover originals and paperback originals and reprints. Averages 100 titles/year. "Royalty and advance agreements vary from book to book and are discussed with the author at the time an offer is made. Submissions from literary agents only. No unsolicited mss or proposals."
Nonfiction: "Some how-to books, distinctive cookbooks, biographies, history, popular science and nature, and sports." Query *only*. No unsolicited mss or proposals.
Recent Nonfiction Title: *The Cat and the Curmudgeon*, by Cleveland Avery.
Fiction: Contemporary popular fiction as well as fiction of literary distinction. Query *only*. No unsolicited mss or proposals.
Recent Fiction Title: *The Last Voyage of Somebody the Sailor*, by John Barth.

‡LIVINGSTON PRESS, Station 22, University of West Alabama, Livingston AL 35470. Director: Joe Taylor. Imprint is Swallow's Tale Press. Publishes hardcover and trade paperback originals. Publishes 4-6 titles/year; imprint publishes 1 title/year. 20% of books from first-time authors; 90% from unagented writers. Pays 7.5% royalty on retail price or 12.5% of book run. Publishes book 15 months after acceptance of ms. Accepts simultaneous submissions. Reports in 1 month on queries; 1 year on mss.
Nonfiction: Local history, folklore only. "All unsolicited mss returned unopened."
Fiction: Experimental, literary, short story collections. Query with SASE.
Recent Fiction Title: *A Bad Piece of Luck*, by Tom Abrams (novel).
Poetry: "We publish very little poetry, mostly books we have asked to see." Query.
Recent Poetry Title: *Lizard Fever*, by Eugene Walter (literary).
Tips: "Our readers are interested in literature, often quirky literature."

LLEWELLYN PUBLICATIONS, Subsidiary of Llewellyn Worldwide, Ltd., P.O. Box 64383, St. Paul MN 55164-0383. (612)291-1970. Fax: (612)291-1908. Acquisitions Manager: Nancy J. Mostad. Estab. 1901. Publishes trade and mass market paperback originals. Averages 72 titles/year. Receives 500 submissions/year. 30% of books from first-time authors; 90% from unagented writers. Pays 10% royalty on moneys received both wholesale and retail. Publishes book 16 months after acceptance. Accepts simultaneous submissions. Query for electronic submissions. Reports in 3 months. Book catalog for 9×12 SAE with 4 first-class stamps. Manuscript guidelines for SASE.
   • Llewellyn has had a 20% growth rate each year for the past five years.
Nonfiction: How-to, self-help. Subjects include nature/environment, health and nutrition, metaphysical/magic, psychology, women's issues/studies. Submit outline and sample chapters. Reviews artwork/photos as part of ms package.
Recent Nonfiction Title: *Yoga for Every Day Athletes*, by Aladar Koglar Ph.D.
Fiction: Metaphysical/occult, which is authentic and educational, yet entertaining.

LOCUST HILL PRESS, P.O. Box 260, West Cornwall CT 06796-0260. (203)672-0060. Fax: (203)672-4968. Publisher: Thomas C. Bechtle. Publishes hardcover originals. Publishes 12 titles/year. Receives 150 queries and 20 mss/year. 100% of books from unagented writers. Pays 12-18% royalty on retail price. Publishes book 6 months after acceptance of ms. Accepts simultaneous submissions. Query for electronic submissions. Reports in 1 month on queries. Book catalog free.

• This publisher notes that it is *not* interested in fiction, poetry, how-to, or inspirational ms.

Nonfiction: Reference. Subjects include art/architecture, business and economics, ethnic, language/literature, music/dance, philosophy, psychology, religion, science, women's issues/studies. "Since our audience is exclusively college and university libraries (and the occasional specialist), we are less inclined to accept manuscripts in 'popular' (i.e., public library) fields. While bibliography has been and will continue to be a specialty, our Locust Hill Literary Studies is gaining popularity as a series of essay collections and monographs in a wide variety of literary topics." Query.

Tips: "Remember that this is a small, very specialized academic publisher with no distribution network other than mail contact with most academic libraries worldwide. Please shape your expectations accordingly. If your aim is to reach the world's scholarly community by way of its libraries, we are the correct firm to contact. But *please*: no fiction, poetry, popular religion, or personal memoirs."

LODESTAR BOOKS, Affiliate of Dutton Children's Books, Division of Penguin Books USA, 375 Hudson St., New York NY 10014. (212)366-2627. Fax: (212)366-2011. Editorial Director: Virginia Buckley. Senior Editor: Rosemary Brosnan. Publishes hardcover originals. Publishes juveniles, young adults, fiction, nonfiction and picture books. Averages 20-25 titles/year. Receives 1,000 submissions/year. 10-20% of books from first-time authors; 25-30% from unagented writers. Average print order for a first novel or nonfiction is 4,000-5,000; picture book print runs are higher. Pays royalty on invoice list price. Offers advance. Publishes book 18 months after acceptance. Reports in 3 months. Manuscript guidelines for SASE.

• Lodestar now only accepts queries (previously it would review chapters or complete mss) enabling it to cut reporting time from four months to three months.

Nonfiction: Query letters only. State availability of photos and/or illustrations. Reviews artwork/photos as part of ms package.

Recent Nonfiction Title: *Turn of the Century*, by Nancy Smiler Levinson.

Fiction: Publishes for young adults (middle grade) and juveniles (ages 5-17). Subjects include adventure, contemporary, fantasy, historical, humorous, multicultural, mystery, science fiction, suspense, western books, also picture books. Query only.

Recent Fiction Title: *Sound the Jubilee*, by Sandra Forrester.

Tips: "A young adult or middle-grade novel that is literary, fast-paced, well-constructed (as opposed to a commercial novel); well-written nonfiction on contemporary issues, photographic essays, and nonfiction picture books have been our staples. We do only a select number of picture books, which are very carefully chosen."

LONE EAGLE PUBLISHING CO., 2337 Roscomare Rd., Suite 9, Los Angeles CA 90077-1851. (310)471-8066. Toll Free: 1-800-FILMBKS. Fax: (310)471-4969. E-mail: filmbks@aol.com. Vice President: Joan V. Singleton. VP/Editorial: Beth Ann Wetzel. Estab. 1982. Publishes perfectbound and trade paperback originals. Averages 14 titles/year. Receives 20-30 submissions/year. 80% of books from unagented writers. Pays 10% royalty minimum on net income wholesale and retail. Offers $250-500 average advance. Publishes a book 1 year after acceptance. Accepts simultaneous submissions. Query for electronic submissions. Reports quarterly on queries. Book catalog for #10 SAE with 2 first-class stamps.

Nonfiction: Technical, how-to, reference. Film and television subjects. "We are looking for technical books in film and television. No unrelated topics or biographies." Submit outline and sample chapters. Reviews artwork/photos as part of ms package.

Tips: "A well-written, well-thought-out book on some technical aspect of the motion picture (or video) industry has the best chance: for example, script supervising, editing, special effects, costume design, production design. Pick a subject that has not been done to death, make sure you know what you're talking about, get someone well-known in that area to endorse the book and prepare to spend a lot of time publicizing the book."

LONELY PLANET PUBLICATIONS, 155 Filbert St., Suite 251, Oakland CA 94607-2538. Publishing Manager: Caroline Liow. Estab. 1973. Publishes trade paperback originals. Publishes 30 titles/year. Receives 500 queries and 100 mss/year. 5% of books from first-time authors; 50% from unagented writers. Makes outright purchase or negotiated fee—⅓ on contract, ⅓ on submission, ⅓ on approval. Publishes book 1-2 years after acceptance of ms. Accepts simultaneous submissions. Query for electronic submissions. Reports in 3 months on queries. Book catalog free.

Nonfiction: Travel guides and travel phrasebooks exclusively. "Writers should request our catalog first to make sure we don't already have a book similar to what they have written or would like to write. Also they should call and see if a similar book is on our production schedule. Lonely Planet publishes travel guides and phrasebooks, period." Submit outline or proposal package. Reviews artwork/photos as part of ms package. Send photocopies. "Don't send unsolicited transparencies!"

LONGSTREET PRESS, INC., 2140 Newmarket Parkway, Suite 118, Marietta GA 30067. (404)980-1488. Fax: (404)859-9894. Associate Editor: Suzanne Bell. Estab. 1988. Publishes hardcover and trade paperback originals. Averages 40 titles/year. Receives 2,500 submissions/year. 25-30% of books from first-time authors. Pays royalty. Publishes book 1 year after acceptance. Accepts simultaneous submissions. Reports in 3 months. Book catalog for 9×12 SAE with 4 first-class stamps. Manuscript guidelines for #10 SASE.
  • Longstreet now publishes children's books.
Nonfiction: Biography, coffee table book, cookbook, humor, illustrated book, reference. Subjects include Americana, cooking/foods/nutrition, gardening, history, language/literature, nature/environment, photography, regional, sports, women's issues/studies. "We want serious journalism-oriented nonfiction on subjects appealing to a broad, various audience. No poetry, how-to, religious or inspirational, scientific or highly technical, textbooks of any kind, erotica." Query or submit outline and sample chapters. Reviews artwork as part of ms package.
Fiction: Literary, mainstream/contemporary. Agented fiction only. "We are not interested in formula/genre novels, but we're open to popular fiction that's exceptionally well done."
Tips: "Midlist books have a harder time making it. The nonfiction book, serious or humorous, with a clearly defined audience has the best chance. The audience for our books has a strong sense of intellectual curiosity and a functioning sense of humor. If I were a writer trying to market a book today, I would do thorough, professional work aimed at a clearly defined and reachable audience."

LOOMPANICS UNLIMITED, P.O. Box 1197, Port Townsend WA 98368-0997. President: Michael Hoy. Editorial Director: Dennis P. Eichhorn. Estab. 1975. Publishes trade paperback originals. Publishes 15 titles/year. Receives 500 submissions/year. 40% of books from first-time authors; 100% from unagented writers. Average print order for a first book is 2,000. Pays 10-15% royalty on wholesale or retail price or makes outright purchase of $100-1,200. Offers $500 average advance. Publishes book 1 year after acceptance. Accepts simultaneous submissions. Reports in 2 months. Author guidelines free. Book catalog for $5, postpaid.
  • Loompanics is doing fewer books, (down from 20 to 15/year) but is putting more work into them and says their business is very, very good.
Nonfiction: How-to, reference, self-help. "In general, works about outrageous topics or obscure-but-useful technology written authoritatively in a matter-of-fact way." Subjects include the underground economy, crime, drugs, privacy, self-sufficiency, anarchism and "beat the system" books. "We are looking for how-to books in the fields of espionage, investigation, the underground economy, police methods, how to beat the system, crime and criminal techniques. We are also looking for similarly-written articles for our catalog and its supplements. No cookbooks, inspirational, travel, management or cutesy-wutesy stuff." Query or submit outline/synopsis and sample chapters. Reviews artwork/photos.
Tips: "Our audience is young males looking for hard-to-find information on alternatives to 'The System.' Your chances for success are greatly improved if you can show us how your proposal fits in with our catalog."

LOTHROP, LEE & SHEPARD BOOKS, Imprint of William Morrow & Company, 1350 Avenue of the Americas, New York NY 10019. (212)261-6500. Fax: (212)261-6648. Editor-in-Chief: Susan Pearson. Estab. 1859. Other children's imprints are Morrow Junior Books, Greenwillow Books and Tambourine Books. Publishes hardcover original children's books only. Royalty and advance vary according to type of book. Averages 30 titles/year. Fewer than 2% of books from first-time authors; 25% of books from unagented writers. Average print order for a first book is 6,000-10,000. Publishes book 2 years after acceptance. *No* unsolicitied mss. Reports in 3 months.
Fiction and Nonfiction: Publishes picture books, general nonfiction, and novels. Juvenile fiction emphasis is on picture books for the 8-12 age group. Looks for "organization, clarity, creativity, literary style." Query *only*. Does *not* read unsolicited mss.
Recent Nonfiction Title: *Kangaroos: On Location*, by Kathy Darling; photos by Tara Darling.
Tips: "Trends in book publishing that freelance writers should be aware of include the demand for books for children under age three and the shrinking market for young adult books, especially novels."

LOUISIANA STATE UNIVERSITY PRESS, Baton Rouge LA 70894-5053. (504)388-6294. Director: L.E. Phillabaum. Estab. 1935. Publishes hardcover originals, hardcover and trade paperback reprints. Averages 60-70 titles/year. Receives 800 submissions/year. 33% of books from first-time authors. 90% from unagented writers. Pays royalty on wholesale price. Publishes book 1 year after acceptance. Reports in 3 weeks on queries. *Writer's Market* recommends allowing 2 months for reply. Book catalog and ms guidelines free.
Nonfiction: Biography and literary poetry collections. Subjects include anthropology/archaeology, art/architecture, ethnic, government/politics, history, language/literature, military/war, music/dance, philosophy, photography, regional, sociology, women's issues/studies. Query or submit outline and sample chapters/poems.
Tips: "Our audience includes scholars, intelligent laymen, general audience."

‡THE LOVE AND LOGIC PRESS, INC., 2207 Jackson St., Golden CO 80401. Executive Vice President/Publisher: Nancy Henry. Publishes hardcover and trade paperback originals. Publishes 5-12 titles/year. 10% of books from first-time authors; 100% from unagented writers. Pays 7½-12% royalty on wholesale price.

Offers $500-5,000 advance. Publishes book 18 months after acceptance of ms. Accepts simultaneous submissions. Reports in 1 month on queries and proposals; 3 months on mss. Book catalog free on request.
Nonfiction: Self-help. Subjects include child guidance/parenting, education, health/medicine, psychology, sociology. "We are not accepting anything in the area of parenting at this time." Submit outline and several sample chapters. Reviews artwork/photos as part of ms package. Send photocopies.
Recent Nonfiction Title: *Conscienceless Acts, Societal Mayhem*, by Foster W. Cline, MD (psychology/sociology hardcover).

LOYOLA UNIVERSITY PRESS, 3441 N. Ashland Ave., Chicago IL 60657-1397. (312)281-1818 ext. 240. Fax: (312)281-0885. Editorial Director: Rev. Joseph F. Downey. Estab. 1912. Imprints are Campion Books, Values & Ethics, Chicago Books. Publishes hardcover and trade paperback originals and reprints. Averages 14 titles/year. Receives 150 submissions/year. 60% of books from first-time authors; 95% from unagented writers. Pays 10% royalty on net price, retail and wholesale. No advance. Publishes book 1 year after acceptance. Accepts simultaneous submissions. Query for electronic submissions. Reports in 2 months. Book catalog for 6×9 SASE.
Nonfiction: Biography, textbook. Subjects include art (religious), history (church), religion. The 3 subject areas of Campion Books include Jesuitica (Jesuit history, biography and spirituality); Literature-Theology interface (books dealing with theological or religious aspects of literary works or authors); contemporary Christian concerns (books on morality, spirituality, family life, pastoral ministry, prayer, worship, etc.) Chicago Books deal with the city of Chicago from historical, artistic, architectural, or ethnic perspectives, but with religious emphases. Values & Ethics Series favors mss of a more scholarly and interdisciplinary bent. Query before submitting ms. Reviews artwork/photos.
Recent Nonfiction Titles: *Resurrection Psychology*, by Margaret G. Alter.
Tips: "Our audience is principally the college-educated reader with a religious, theological interest."

LUCENT BOOKS, P.O. Box 289011, San Diego CA 92198-9011. (619)485-7424. Managing Editor: Bonnie Szumski. Estab. 1988. Publishes hardcover educational supplementary materials and (nontrade) juvenile nonfiction. Publishes 10 books/year. All are works for hire. Receives 100 submissions/year. 50% of books from first-time authors; 100% from unagented writers. Makes outright purchase of $1,000-3,000. Publishes book 1 year after acceptance. No unsolicited mss. Book catalog and ms guidelines for 9×12 SAE with 3 first-class stamps.
Nonfiction: Juvenile. "We produce tightly formatted books for young people grades 5-8. Each series has specific requirements. Potential writers should familiarize themselves with our material." No unsolicited mss.
Tips: "Please do not send material inappropriate to a company's list. In our case, no unsolicited manuscripts are accepted and no fiction is published. When writers send inappropriate material, they can make a lifetime enemy of the publisher."

LURAMEDIA, P.O. Box 261668, San Diego CA 92196-1668. (619)578-1948. Fax: (619)578-7560. Editorial Director: Lura Jane Geiger, Ph.D. Estab. 1982. Publishes trade paperback originals. Averages 6-8 titles/year. Receives 500 submissions/year. 60% of books from first-time authors; 90% from unagented writers. Pays 10% royalty on wholesale price. Publishes book 18 months after acceptance. Proposals only; no unsolicited mss. Reports in 3 months. Book catalog and ms guidelines for 9×12 SAE with 2 first-class stamps.
Nonfiction: "Books for healing and hope, balance and justice. We publish books that contribute to spiritual, emotional and physical renewal. Our subjects include health of body and mind, woman's issues, relationships, prayer/meditation, creativity, journaling, relational group work, creative biblical education, values for children/family, aging, justice, alternative life-styles, ecology, experience of minorities, social issues. We especially favor approaches that utilize self disclosure, personal reflection, journal writing, stories/fables/parables, essays, meditations, sermons and prayers. We are looking for books that are well-thought out, books that encourage creative thinking rather than giving all the answers." Query with proposal package, including outline, 2 sample chapters, competition, length, completion date, credentials, information on computer.
Recent Nonfiction Title: *Circle of Stones*, by Judith Duerck (women's growth book).
Tips: "Our audience includes people who want to grow and change; who want to get in touch with their spiritual side; who want to relax; who are creative and want creative ways to live."

LYONS & BURFORD, PUBLISHERS, INC., 31 W. 21st St., New York NY 10010. (212)620-9580. Fax: (212)929-1836. Publisher: Peter Burford. Estab. 1984. Publishes hardcover and trade paperback originals and reprints. Averages 40-50 titles/year. 50% of books from first-time authors; 75% from unagented writers. Pays varied royalty on retail price. Publishes book 1 year after acceptance. Accepts simultaneous submissions. Reports in 2 weeks on queries. *Writer's Market* recommends allowing 2 months for reply. Book catalog free.
Nonfiction: Subjects include agriculture/horticulture, Americana, animals, art/architecture, cooking/foods/nutrition, gardening, hobbies, nature/environment, science, sports, travel. Query.
Recent Nonfiction Title: *The Wold Almanac*, by Robert Busch.
Tips: "We want practical, well-written books on any aspect of the outdoors."

McDONALD & WOODWARD PUBLISHING CO., 6414 Riverland Dr., Fort Pierce FL 34982-7644. (407)468-6361. Fax: (407)468-6571. Managing Partner: Jerry N. McDonald. Estab. 1986. Publishes hardcover and trade paperback originals. Publishes 5 titles/year. Receives 30 queries and 10 mss/year. 50% of books from first-time authors; 100% from unagented writers. Pays 10% royalty on net receipts. Publishes book 1 year after acceptance of ms. Accepts simultaneous submissions. Query for electronic submissions. Reports in 2 months. Book catalog free.
Nonfiction: Biography, coffee table book, how-to, illustrated book, self-help. Subjects include Americana, animals, anthropology, ethnic, history, nature/environment, science, travel. "We are especially interested in additional titles in our 'Guides to the American Landscape' series. Should consult titles in print for guidance. We want well organized, clearly written, substantive material." Query or submit outline and sample chapters. Reviews artwork/photos as part of ms package. Send photocopies.

MARGARET K. McELDERRY BOOKS, Imprint of Macmillan Children's Book Group, Inc., 866 Third Ave., New York NY 10022. Fax: (212)605-3045. Vice President/Publisher: Margaret K. McElderry. Editor: Emma D. Dryden. Estab. 1971. Publishes hardcover originals. Publishes about 25 titles/year. Receives 4,000 submissions/year. 8% of books from first-time authors; 50% from unagented writers. Average print order is 6,000-7,500 for a first teen book; 10,000-15,000 for a first picture book. Pays royalty on retail price. Publishes book 18 months after acceptance. Reports in 4 months. Catalog for 9×12 SAE with 4 first-class stamps. Manuscript guidelines for #10 SASE.
 ● Margaret K. McElderry was named the 1993 recipient of the Association of American Publishers' Curtis Benjamin Award for Creative Publishing.
Nonfiction and Fiction: Quality material for preschoolers to 16-year-olds, but publishes only a few YAs. Looks for "originality of ideas, clarity and felicity of expression, well-organized plot and strong characterization (fiction) or clear exposition (nonfiction); quality." *Writer's Market* recommends query with SASE first. Reviews artwork/photos as part of ms package, but prefers to review texts only.
Recent Title: *My Dad*, by Niki Daly.
Tips: "There is not a particular 'type' of book that we are interested in above others, though we always look for humor. Rather, we look for superior quality in both writing and illustration. Freelance writers should be aware of the swing away from teen-age novels to books for younger readers and of the growing need for beginning chapter books for children just learning to read on their own."

McFARLAND & COMPANY, INC., PUBLISHERS, P.O. Box 611, Jefferson NC 28640. (919)246-4460. Fax: (919)246-5018. President and Editor-in-Chief: Robert Franklin. Vice President: Rhonda Herman. Editors: Lisa Camp, Steve Wilson. Estab. 1979. Publishes mostly hardcover and a few "quality" paperback originals; a non-"trade" publisher. Averages 120 titles/year. Receives 1,000 submissions/year. 70% of books from first-time authors; 95% from unagented writers. Average first printing for a book is 750. Pays 10-12½% royalty on net receipts. No advance. Publishes book 9 months after acceptance. Reports in 2 weeks. *Writer's Market* recommends allowing 2 months for reply.
 ● This publisher recently won the "Academic Book of the Year" by *Choice* magazine and "One of Year's 10 Best" by *Library Journal* for the *Journal of Information Ethics*.
Nonfiction: Reference books and scholarly, technical and professional monographs. Subjects include African American studies (very strong), art, business, chess, drama/theatre, cinema/radio/TV (very strong), health, history, librarianship (very strong), music, pop culture, sociology, sports/recreation (very strong) women's studies (very strong), world affairs (very strong). "We will consider *any* scholarly book—with authorial maturity and competent grasp of subject." Reference books are particularly wanted—fresh material (i.e., not in head-to-head competition with an established title). "We don't like manuscripts of fewer than 225 double-spaced pages. Our market consists mainly of libraries." No New Age material, memoirs, poetry, children's books, devotional/inspirational works or personal essays. Query or submit outline and sample chapters. Reviews artwork/photos as part of ms package.
Recent Nonfiction Title: *African Placenames: Origins and Meanings of the Names for Over 2000 Natural Features, Towns, Cities, Provinces and Countries*, by Adrian Room.
Tips: "We do *not* accept novels or fiction of any kind or personal Bible studies. What we want is well-organized *knowledge* of an area in which there is not good information coverage at present, plus reliability so we don't feel we have to check absolutely everything."

THE McGRAW-HILL COMPANIES, 1221 Avenue of the Americas, New York NY 10020. Divisions include College Division (Schaum), Regal Information Group (Shepard's/McGraw-Hill), Macmillan/McGraw-Hill School Publishing Group), McGraw-Hill Ryerson (Canada), Osborne/McGraw-Hill, Professional Book Group. General interest publisher of both fiction and nonfiction. Query before submitting.

‡THE McGRAW-HILL COMPANIES, Professional Book Group Division, 11 W. 19th St., New York NY 10011. Imprints are Engineering & Science (contact Sybil Parker); Business (contact Philip Ruppel); Trade Computer (contact Larry Leunsky); Professional Computing (contact Ron Powers); International Marine and Ragged Mountain Press (contact John Eaton); Tab Books (contact Kim Tabor). Publishes hardcover and trade paperback originals and reprints. Publishes 800 titles/year. 30% of books from first-time authors; 70% from unagented writers. Pays royalty. Offers $3,000 and up advance. Publishes book 10 months after acceptance of ms. Accepts simultaneous submissions. Reports in 1 month on queries. Book catalog and ms guidelines free on request.

Nonfiction: How-to, multimedia (disk and CD ROM), reference, self-help, technical, professional. Subjects include art/architecture, business and economics, computers and electronics, money/finance, science, software, sports, technical engineering, boating. Query with proposal package, including outline, sample chapters, author bio, marketing information. Reviews artwork/photos as part of ms package.

Recent Nonfiction Title: *How to Make Money in Stocks*, by William O'Neil (business-trade).

MCGUINN & MCGUIRE PUBLISHING INC., P.O. Box 20603, Bradenton FL 34203-0603. Managing Editor: Christopher Carroll. Estab. 1991. Publishes hardcover and trade paperback originals. Publishes 6 titles/year. Receives 500 queries and 75 mss/year. 50% of books from first-time authors; 100% from unagented writers. Pays 10-15% royalty on net receipts. Offers $250 advance. Publishes book 1 year after acceptance of ms. Accepts simultaneous submissions. Query for electronic submissions. Reports in 1 month on queries and proposals, 2 months on mss. Book catalog and ms guidelines for #10 SASE. Will not return submissions without SASE.

Nonfiction: Biography. Subjects include business, history. "We are not interested in religious materials, memoirs, books relating a personal philosophy, diet books, or investment books. Author should be able to demonstrate how his/her book fills a void in the market." Query or submit outline and 3 sample chapters. Reviews artwork/photos as part of the ms package. Send photocopies.

Recent Nonfiction Title: *The Making of a Manager*, by Donald A. Wellman (business/management).

Tips: "Always include a word count with queries and proposals. We will only consider books which are at least 50,000 words. Our audience consists of college-educated adults who look for books written by experts in their field. We are particularly interested in reviewing business books which help managers improve their business skills."

‡MACMURRAY & BECK, P.O. Box 150717, Lakewood CO 80215. Executive Editor: Frederick Ramey. Publishes hardcover and trade paperback originals. Publishes 5-8 titles/year. 90% of books from first-time authors; 20% from unagented writers. Pays 8-12% royalty on retail price. Offers $2,000-8,000 advance. Publishes book 18 months after acceptance of ms. Accepts simultaneous submissions. Reports in 1 month on queries and proposals, 2 months on mss. Book catalog and ms guidelines free.

Nonfiction: Health/medicine, men's issues, philosophy (non-academic), psychology (non-academic), sociology (non-academic), women's issues/studies. "We are looking for personal narratives and extraordinary perspectives." Submit outline and 2 sample chapters with SASE. Reviews artwork/photos as part of ms package. Send photocopies.

Recent Nonfiction Title: *Confessions of a Healer*, by O.T. Bennett (health).

Fiction: Literary. "We are most interested in debut novels of life in the contemporary west. But we select for voice and literary merit far more than for subject or narrative." Writers often make the mistake of "submitting genre fiction when we are in search of strong literary fiction." Submit synopsis and 3 sample chapters with SASE.

Recent Fiction Title: *Stygo*, by Laura Hendrie.

Tips: "Our books are for thinking readers in search of new ideas and new voices."

MADISON BOOKS, 4720 Boston Way, Lanham MD 20706. (301)459-3366. Fax: (301)459-2118. Publisher: James E. Lyons. Managing Editor: Julie Kirsch. Estab. 1984. Publishes hardcover originals, trade paperback originals and reprints. Averages 40 titles/year. Receives 1,200 submissions/year. 15% of books from first-time authors; 50% from unagented writers. Pays 10-15% royalty on net price. Publishes ms 1 year after acceptance. *Writer's Market* recommends allowing 2 months for reply. Book catalog and ms guidelines for 9×12 SAE with 4 first-class stamps.

Nonfiction: History, biography, contemporary affairs, trade reference. Query or submit outline and sample chapter. No complete mss.

‡MAISONNEUVE PRESS, P.O. Box 2980, Washington DC 20013-2980. (301)277-7505. Editor: Robert Merrill. Publishes hardcover and trade paperback originals. Publishes 4 titles/year. 5% of books from first-time authors; 100% from unagented writers. Pays 2-9% royalty on wholesale price or $2,000 maximum outright purchase. Publishes book 1 year after acceptance of ms. Accepts simultaneous submissions. Reports in 1 month on queries; 2 months on proposals; 5 months on mss. Book catalog free on request. Send letter for guidelines; individual response.

Nonfiction: Biography, philosophy, literary criticism, social theory. Subjects include education, ethnic, gay/lesbian, government/politics, history, language/literature, military/war, philosophy, psychology, sociology, translation, women's issues/studies, politics, economics, essay collections. "We make decisions on completed mss only. Will correspond on work in progress. Some books submitted are too narrowly focused; not marketable enough." Query; then send completed ms. Reviews artwork/photos as part of ms package. Send photocopies.

Recent Nonfiction Title: *Crisis Cinema: The Apocalyptic Idea in Postmodern Narrative Cinema*, edited by Christopher Sharrett.
Tips: Audience is serious adult readers: academics, political activists. "Need solid, first-hand information in the book."

MARKETSCOPE BOOKS, 119 Richard Court, Aptos CA 95003. (408)688-7535. Editor-in-Chief: Ken Albert. Estab. 1985. Publishes hardcover and trade paperback originals. Averages 10 titles/year. 50% of books from first-time authors; 50% from unagented writers. Pays 10-15% royalty on wholesale price. Publishes book 6-12 months after acceptance. Accepts simultaneous submissions. Reports in 1 week on queries. *Writer's Market* recommends allowing 2 months for reply.
Nonfiction: Biography, how-to, humor, self-help. Subjects include anthropology/archaeology, child guidance/parenting, sexuality, health/medicine, hobbies, money/finance, nature/environment, recreation, regional, religion, sociology. Query. Reviews artwork/photos as part of the ms package.

MARKOWSKI INTERNATIONAL PUBLISHERS, One Oakglade Circle, Hummelstown PA 17036-9525. (717)566-0468. Fax: (717)566-6423. Imprints are Success Publishers, Aviation Publishers and Markowski International Publishers. Editor-in-Chief: Marjorie L. Markowski. Estab. 1981. Publishes hardcover and trade paperback originals. Averages 12 titles/year. Receives 500 submissions/year. 90% of books from first-time authors; 100% from unagented writers. Average print order for a first book is 5,000. Royalty agreements vary or makes outright purchase. Publishes book 1 year after acceptance. Accepts simultaneous submissions. Reports in 2 months. Book catalog and ms guidelines for #10 SAE with 2 first-class stamps.
  ● Markowski is really focusing on the "people," success, motivation and self-help areas.
Nonfiction: Primary focus on popular health and fitness, marriage and human relations, career, personal development, self-help, personal growth, sales and marketing, leadership training, network marketing, motivation and success. Also publishes books on various aviation and model aviation topics. We are interested in how-to, motivational and instructionl books of short to medium length that will serve recognized and emerging needs of society." Query or submit outline and entire ms. Reviews artwork/photos as part of ms package.
Recent Nonfiction Title: *Brighten Your Day With Self-Esteem*, by W.J. McGrane II.
Tips: "We're very interested in publishing bestsellers."

MARLOR PRESS, INC., 4304 Brigadoon Dr., St. Paul MN 55126. (612)484-4600. Publisher: Marlin Bree. Estab. 1981. Publishes trade paperback originals. Averages 6 titles/year. Receives 100 queries and 25 mss/year. Pays 10% royalty on wholesale price. Publishes book an average of 8 months after final acceptance. Reports in 2 months on queries and proposals, 3 months on mss. Book catalog for 6×9 SAE with 2 first-class stamps. Manuscript guidelines for #10 SASE.
Nonfiction: General nonfiction, children's books. Subjects include boating, child guidance/parenting, travel. Query first; submit outline with sample chapters only when requested. Do not send full ms. Reviews artwork/photos as part of ms package.
Recent Nonfiction Title: *London for the Independent Traveler*, by Ruth Humleker.

MASTERS PRESS, 2647 Waterfront Pkwy., Suite 300, Indianapolis IN 46214-2041. (317)298-5706. Fax: (317)298-5604. Managing Editor: Holly Kondras. Estab. 1986. Imprint is Spalding Sports Library. Publishes hardcover and trade paperback originals. Publishes 30-40 titles/year; imprint publishes 20 titles/year. Receives 60 queries and 50 mss/year. 25% of books from first-time authors; 75% from unagented writers. Pays 10-15% royalty. Offers $1,000-5,000 advance. Publishes book 6-12 months after acceptance. Accepts simultaneous submissions. Query for electronic submission: prefers WordPerfect 5.1 or ASCII DOS. Reports in 2 months on proposals. Book catalog free on request.
Nonfiction: Biography, how-to, reference, self-help. Subjects include recreation, sports, fitness. Submit outline, 2 sample chapters, author bio and marketing ideas.
Recent Nonfiction Title: *Dickie V's Top 40 All-Everything Teams*, by Dick Vitale with Charlie Parker and Jim Angresano.
Tips: "Our audience is sports enthusiasts and participants, people interested in fitness."

MAVERICK PUBLICATIONS, P.O. Box 5007, Bend OR 97708. (503)382-6978. Fax: (503)382-4831. Publisher: Gary Asher. Estab. 1968. Publishes trade paperback originals and reprints. Averages 10 titles/year. Receives 100 submissions/year. Pays 15% royalty on wholesale price. Publishes book 1 year after acceptance. Accepts simultaneous submissions. Reports 2 months.
Nonfiction: Pacific Northwest only: aviation, cooking, history, hobby, how-to, marine, native American, nature and environment, recreation, reference, sports, travel. Submit proposal.

MAYFIELD PUBLISHING COMPANY, 1280 Villa St., Mountain View CA 94041. President: Richard Greenberg. Publishes 40-50 titles/year. Accepts simultaneous submissions. Reports in 2 months. Manuscript guidelines free on request.

Nonfiction: Textbook (college only). Subjects include anthropology/archaeology, art, child guidance/parenting, communications/theater, ethnic, health/physical education, language/literature, music/dance, philosophy, psychology, religion, sociology, women's studies. Submit proposal package including outline, table of contents, sample chapter, description of proposed market.

MEADOWBROOK PRESS, 18318 Minnetonka Blvd., Deephaven MN 55391. (612)473-5400. Fax: (612)475-0736. Contact: Submissions Editor. Estab. 1975. Publishes trade paperback originals and reprints. Averages 12 titles/year. Receives 500 queries/year. 25% of books from first-time authors; 75% from unagented writers. Publishes book 1 year after acceptance. Accepts simultaneous submissions. Reports in 3 months on queries. Book catalog and ms guidelines for #10 SASE.
• Meadowbrook has a greater need for children's poems and poetry in general and parenting titles (informative but easy to read), but no longer does travel or cookbook titles.
Nonfiction: How-to, humor, juvenile, illustrated book, reference. Subjects include baby and childcare, senior citizen's, children's activities, relationships. No academic, autobiography, semi-autobiography or fiction. Query with outline and sample chapters. "We prefer a query first; then we will request an outline and/or sample material."
Recent Nonfiction Title: *The Joy of Marriage*, by Monica and Bill Dodds.
Tips: "We like how-to books in a simple, accessible format and any new advice on parenting. We look for a fresh approach to overcoming traditional problems (e.g. potty training)."

‡MEDIA BRIDGE, 2280 Grass Valley Hwy., #181, Auburn CA 95603. (916)888-0690. Publisher: Rennie Mau. Imprints are Videobridge, Audiobridge, Family Media. Publishes trade paperback and mass market paperback originals. Publishes 6-10 titles/year. Each imprint publishes 4 titles/year. 50% of books from first-time authors; 75% from unagented writers. Pays 7-12% royalty on wholesale price. Publishes book 6 months after acceptance. Reports in 1 month on queries, 2 months on proposals, 3 months on mss.
Nonfiction: Children's/juvenile, cookbook, how-to, multimedia (CD ROM), self-help, textbook. Subjects include education, ethnic, music/dance, religion, multicultural. Submit outline and 2 sample chapters with SASE. Reviews artwork/photos as part of ms package. Send photocopies.
Fiction: Ethnic, juvenile, picture books, plays, religious, young adult. Submit synopsis and 2 sample chapters with SASE.

MEDICAL PHYSICS PUBLISHING, 4513 Vernon Blvd., Madison WI 53705. (608)262-4021. Fax: (608)265-2121. E-mail: mpp@macc.wisc.edu. Acquisitions Editor: John Cameron. Imprint is Cogito Books. Publishes hardcover and trade paperback originals and reprints. Publishes 10-15 titles/year; imprint publishes 3-5 titles/year. Receives 10-20 queries/year. 100% of books from unagented writers. Pays 10-20% royalty on wholesale price. Publishes book 6 months after acceptance of ms. Accepts simultaneous submissions. Reports in 2-6 months on mss. Book catalog free on request.
Nonfiction: Reference books, textbooks, and symposium proceedings in the fields of medical physics and radiology. Also distribute Ph.D. theses in these fields. "We publish a 'Focus on Health' and 'Focus on Science' series under our Cogito Books imprint. We need writers who are experts in general health and science fields to write books on issues such as AIDS, radon in the home, radiation, environmental policy, etc. with the public in mind." Submit entire ms. Reviews artwork/photos as part of ms package. Send disposable copies.

MERCURY HOUSE, INC., 201 Filbert St., Suite 400, San Francisco CA 94133. (415)433-7042. Assistant Editor: K. Janene-Nelson. Publishes hardcover originals and trade paperback originals and reprints. Averages 10 titles/year. Receives 1500 queries and 800 mss/year. 3-4% from first-time authors. 50% from unagented writers. Pays 10-20% royalty on retail price. Offers $3000-6000 advance. Publishes book 12 months after acceptance of ms. Query for electronic submissions. Reports in 1-4 weeks on queries, 2-3 months on proposals and mss. Catalog for 55¢ postage. Writers guidelines for #10 SASE. "No submissions accepted between June 1 and September 1. Manuscripts received during this period will be returned."
Nonfiction: Biography, essays, memoirs. Subjects include anthropology, ethnic, gay/lesbian, politics/current affairs, language/literature, literary current affairs, nature/environment, philosophy, translation, literary travel, women's issues/studies, human rights/indigenous peoples. "Within the subjects we publish, we are above all a literary publisher looking for a high quality of writing and innovative approach to book structure, research approach, etc." Query with outline, 1-2 sample chapters and SASE.

The double dagger before a listing indicates that the listing is new in this edition. New markets are often more receptive to freelance submissions.

Recent Nonfiction Title: *Temporary Homelands*, by Deming (nature essays).

Fiction: Ethnic, experimental, feminist, gay/lesbian, gothic, historical, literary, short story collections, literature in translation. "Very limited spots. We prefer sample chapters to determine writing style. It's very important to submit only if the subject is appropriate (as listed), though we do enjoy mutations/blending of genres (high quality, thoughtful work!). We do not publish mainstream, thrillers, sexy books. We look for a well-written cover letter, 1-2 dynamic sample chapters and SASE."

Recent Fiction Title: *In the Mountains of America*, by Willis.

Tips: "Our reader is a person who is discriminating about his/her reading material, someone who appreciates the extra care we devote to design, paper, cover, and exterior excellence to go along with the high quality of the writing itself. Be patient with us concerning responses: it's easier to reject the manuscript of a nagging author than it is to decide upon it. The manner in which an author deals with us (via letter or phone) gives us a sense of how it would be to work with this person for a whole project; good books with troublesome authors are to be avoided."

MERIWETHER PUBLISHING LTD., 885 Elkton Dr., Colorado Springs CO 80907-3557. (719)594-4422. Editors: Arthur or Theodore Zapel. Estab. 1969. Publishes hardcover and trade paperback originals and reprints. Publishes 45-60 books/year; 35-50 plays/year. Receives 1,200 submissions/year. 50% of books from first-time authors; 90% from unagented writers. Pays 10% royalty on retail price or makes outright purchase. Publishes book an average of 6 months after acceptance. Accepts simultaneous submissions. Reports in 2 months. Book catalog and ms guidelines for $2.
- Meriwether is looking for more books of short scenes and textbooks on directing, staging, make-up, lighting etc.

Nonfiction: How-to, reference, educational, humor, inspirational. Also textbooks. Subjects include art/theatre/drama, music/dance, recreation, religion. "We're looking for unusual textbooks or trade books related to the communication or performing arts and "how-to" books on staging, costuming, lighting, etc. We are not interested in religious titles with fundamentalist themes or approaches—we prefer mainstream religion titles." Query or submit outline/synopsis and sample chapters.

Fiction: Plays. "Plays only—humorous, mainstream, mystery, religious, suspense."

Tips: "Our educational books are sold to teachers and students at college and high school levels. Our religious books are sold to youth activity directors, pastors and choir directors. Our trade books are directed at the public with a sense of humor. Another group of buyers is the professional theatre, radio and TV category. We will focus more on books of plays and theater texts."

METAMORPHOUS PRESS, P.O. Box 10616, Portland OR 97210-0616. (503)228-4972. Fax: (503)223-9117. Publisher: David Balding. Editorial Director: Lori Stephens. Acquisitions Editor: Nancy Wyatt-Kelsey. Estab. 1982. Publishes trade paperback originals and reprints. Averages 4-5 titles/year. Receives 2,500 submissions/year. 90% of books from first-time authors; 90% from unagented writers. Average print order for a first book is 2,000-5,000. Pays minimum 10% profit split on wholesale prices. No advance. Publishes book 1 year after acceptance. Accepts simultaneous submissions. Query for ms and electronic submissions. Reports in 3 months. Book catalog and ms guidelines for 9×12 SAE with 3 first-class stamps.

Nonfiction: How-to, reference, self-help, technical, textbook—all related to behavioral science and personal growth. Subjects include business and sales, health, psychology, sociology, education, science and new ideas in behavioral science. "We are interested in any well-proven new idea or philosophy in the behavioral science areas. Our primary editorial screen is 'will this book further define, explain or support the concept that we are responsible for our reality or assist people in gaining control of their lives.' " Submit idea, outline, and table of contents only. Reviews artwork/photos as part of ms package.

MICHIGAN STATE UNIVERSITY PRESS, 1405 S. Harrison Rd., Suite 25, East Lansing MI 48823-5202. (517)355-9543. Fax: (800)678-2120; local/international (517)432-2611. E-mail: msp02@msu.edu (director), msp03@msu.edu (editor-in-chief). Director: Fred Bohm. Editor-in-Chief: Julie Loehr. Contact: Acquisitions Editor. Estab. 1947. Publishes hardcover and softcover originals. Averages 30 titles/year. Receives 400 submissions/year. 75% of books from first-time writers; 100% from unagented writers. Pays 10% royalty on net sales. Publishes ms 9 months after acceptance. Query for electronic submissions. Reports in 2 months. Book catalog and ms guidelines for 9×12 SASE.

Nonfiction: Reference, technical, scholarly. Subjects include African Studies, American history, American Studies, business and economics, Canadian Studies, Civil War history, communication and speech, literature, philosophy, politics, world religion. Looking for "scholarship that addresses the social and political concerns of the late 20th century." Query with outline and sample chapters. Reviews artwork/photos.

Recent Nonfiction Title: *Truman And The Hiroshima Cult*, by Robert Newman.

MID-LIST PRESS, Imprint of Jackson, Hart & Leslie, 4324 12th Ave S., Minneapolis MN 55407-3218. Contact: Lane Stiles. Estab. 1989. Publishes hardcover originals and reprints and trade paperback originals. Publishes minimum 4 titles/year. Pays 40-50% royalty of profits. Offers $500-1,000 advance. Mid-List Press is an independent press. In addition to publishing the annual winners of the Mid-List Press First Series Awards, Mid-List Press publishes general interest fiction and nonfiction by first-time and established writers.

Send SASE for First Series guidelines and/or general submission guidelines.
Recent Fiction Title: *Jump*, by John Prendergast (novel).

MILKWEED EDITIONS, Suite 400, 430 First Ave. N, Minneapolis MN 55401-1743. (612)332-3192. Editor: Emilie Buchwald. Estab. 1980. Publishes hardcover originals and paperback originals and reprints. Averages 12-14 titles/year. Receives 1,560 submissions/year. 30% of books from first-time authors; 70% from unagented writers. Pays 7½% royalty on list price. Advance varies. Publishes work 1 year after acceptance. Accepts simultaneous submissions. Reports in 1-6 months. Book catalog for $1. Manuscript guidelines for SASE.
   • This publisher has won numerous awards for several books, including ALA/YALSA, Best Books for Young Adults and Association Regional Book Award for *Montana 1948*, by Larry Watson and Mountains & Plains Booksellers for *I Am Lavina Cumming*, by Susan Lowell.
Nonfiction: Literary. Subjects include government/politics, history, language/literature, nature/environment, women's issues/studies, education. Query.
Recent Nonfiction Title: *Transforming a Rape Culture*, edited by Emilie Buchwald, Pamela Fletcher and Martha Roth.
Fiction: Literary. Query.
Recent Fiction Title: *Montana 1948*, by Larry Watson.
Children's: Novels and biographies for readers aged 8-14. High literary quality.
Tips: "We are looking for excellent writing in fiction, nonfiction, poetry and children's novels, with the intent of making a humane impact on society. Send for guidelines. Acquaint yourself with our books in terms of style and quality before submitting. Many factors influence our selection process, so don't get discouraged."

THE MILLBROOK PRESS INC., 2 Old New Milford Rd., Brookfield CT 06804. Manuscript Coordinator: Sarah DeCapua. Estab. 1989. Publishes hardcover and paperback originals. Publishes 120 titles/year. Pays varying royalty on wholesale price or makes outright purchase. Advance varies. Publishes book 1 year after acceptance of ms. Reports in 1 month on queries and proposals. Book catalog for 9 × 12 SAE with 4 first-class stamps. Manuscript guidelines for #10 SASE.
Nonfiction: Children's/juvenile. Subjects include animals, anthropology/archaeology, ethnic, government/politics, health/medicine, history, hobbies, nature/environment, science, sports. "We publish curriculum-related nonfiction for the school/library market. Mistakes writers most often make when submitting nonfiction are failure to research competing titles and failure to research school curriculum." Query or submit outline and 1 sample chapter.

MINNESOTA HISTORICAL SOCIETY PRESS, Minnesota Historical Society, 345 Kellogg Blvd. W., St. Paul MN 55102-1906. (612)297-4457. Managing Editor: Ann Regan. Imprint is Borealis Books (reprints only). Publishes hardcover and trade paperback originals and trade paperback reprints. Averages 10 titles/year (5 for each imprint). Receives 100 queries and 25 mss/year. 8% of books from first-time authors; 100% from unagented writers. Pays 5% royalty on net income. Publishes book 14 months after acceptance. Query for electronic submissions. Reports in 1 month on queries. *Writer's Market* recommends allowing 2 months for reply. Book catalog free on request.
   • Minnesota Historical Society Press is getting many inappropriate submissions from their listing. A regional connection is required.
Nonfiction: Regional works only: biography, coffee table book, cookbook, illustrated book, reference. Subjects include anthropology/archaeology, art/architecture, history, memoir, photography, regional, women's issues/studies, Native American studies. Query with proposal package including letter, outline, vita, sample chapter. Reviews artwork/photos as part of ms package. Send photocopies.
Recent Nonfiction Title: *Eggs in the Coffee, Sheep in the Corn: My Seventeen Years as a Farmwife*, by Marjorie Myers Douglas.

MIS PRESS, subsidiary of Henry Holt & Co., 115 W. 18th St., New York NY 10011. (212)886-9210. Fax: (212)807-6654. Associate Publisher: Paul Farrell. Publishes trade paperback originals. Publishes 60 titles/year. Receives 250 queries/year. 20% of books from first-time authors; 50% from unagented writers. Pays 5-15% royalty on net price received (receipts), or makes outright purchase of $5,000-20,000. Offers $5,000-10,000 advance. Publishes book an average of 4 months after acceptance. Accepts simultaneous submissions. Query for electronic submissions. Book catalog and ms guidelines free on request.
Nonfiction: Technical, computer, electronic. "Submissions should be about or related to computer software or hardware." Submit outline and proposal package.

MODERN LANGUAGE ASSOCIATION OF AMERICA, Dept. WM, 10 Astor Pl., New York NY 10003. (212)475-9500. Fax: (212)477-9863. Director of Book Acquisitions and Development: Joseph Gibaldi. Director of MLA Book Publications: Martha Evans. Estab. 1883. Publishes hardcover and paperback originals. Averages 15 titles/year. Receives 125 submissions/year. 100% of books from unagented writers. Pays 5-10%

royalty on net proceeds. Publishes book 1 year after acceptance. Query for electronic submissions. Reports in 2 months on mss. Book catalog free on request.
Nonfiction: Scholarly, professional. Subjects include language and literature. Publishes mss on current issues in literary and linguistic research and teaching of language and literature at postsecondary level. No critical monographs. Query with outline/synopsis.

MONUMENT PRESS, P.O. Box 140361, Las Colinas TX. 75014-0361. (214)686-5332. Contact: Mary Markal. Publishes trade paperback originals. Publishes 15 titles/year. Receives 100 queries and 50 mss/year. 100% of books from first-time authors; 100% from unagented writers. Pays 4% and up royalty on retail price. Publishes book 4-12 months after acceptance of ms. No simultaneous submissions. Query for electronic submissions. Reports in 4 months. Book catalog for 6×9 SAE with 6 first-class stamps. Manuscript guidelines for #10 SASE.
Nonfiction: Textbook. Subjects include gay/lesbian, government/politics, health/medicine, military/war, religion, women's issues/studies. Query with outline and 2 sample chapters. All unsolicited mss returned unopened.
Recent Nonfiction Title: *Military Secret*, by Robert Graham (homosexuality in Navy).

MOON PUBLICATIONS, INC., P.O. Box 3040, Chico CA 95927-3040. (916)345-3778. Fax: (916)345-6751. Executive Editor: Taran March. Senior Editor: Kevin Jeys. Estab. 1973. Publishes trade paperback originals. Publishes 15 titles/year. Receives 100-200 submissions/year. 50% from first-time authors; 95% from unagented writers. Pays royalty on net price. Offers advance of up to $10,000. Publishes book an average of 9 months after acceptance. Accepts simultaneous submissions. Query for electronic submissions. Reports in 2 months. Book catalog and proposal guidelines for 7½×10½ SAE with 2 first-class stamps.
● Moon is putting increased emphasis on acquiring writers who are experts in a given destination and demonstrate above-average writing ability. It has received several awards recently, including Lowell Thomas Best Guidebook for *Japan Handbook*, by J.D. Bisignani, Lowell Thomas Bronze Award and Pluma de Plata award for *Pacific Mexico Handbook*, by Bruce Whipperman.
Nonfiction: "We specialize in travel guides to Asia and the Pacific Basin, the United States, Canada, the Caribbean, Latin America and South America, but are open to new ideas. Our guides include in-depth cultural and historical background, as well as recreational and practical travel information. We prefer comprehensive guides to entire countries, states, and regions over more narrowly defined areas such as cities, museums, etc. Writers should write first for a copy of our guidelines. Proposal required with outline, table of contents, and writing sample. Author should also be prepared to provide photos, artwork and base maps. No fictional or strictly narrative travel writing; no how-to guides." Reviews artwork/photos as part of ms package.
Recent Nonfiction Title: *Northern Mexico Handbook*, by Joe Cummings.
Tips: "Moon Travel Handbooks are designed by and for independent travelers seeking the most rewarding travel experience possible. Our Handbooks appeal to all travelers because they are the most comprehensive and honest guides available."

MOREHOUSE PUBLISHING CO., 871 Ethan Allen Hwy., Ridgefield CT 06877-2801. Fax: (203)431-3964. Publisher: E. Allen Kelley. Senior Editor: Deborah Grahame-Smith. Estab. 1884. Publishes hardcover and paperback originals. Averages 20 titles/year. Receives 500 submissions/year. 40% of books from first-time authors; 75% from unagented writers. Pays 7-10% royalty on retail price. Offers $500-1,000 advance. Publishes book 8 months after acceptance. Accepts simultaneous submission. Reports in 1-4 months, "depending on material submitted." Book catalog for 9×12 SAE with 5 first-class stamps.
Nonfiction: Specializes in Christian publishing (with an Anglican emphasis). Theology, spirituality, ethics, church history, pastoral counseling, liturgy, religious education activity and gift books, and children's books (preschool-teen). No poetry or drama. Submit outline/synopsis and 1-2 sample chapters. Reviews artwork/photos as part of ms package. Send photocopies, color for color photos.
Recent Nonfiction Title: *Re-Inventing Marriage*, by Christopher L. Webber
Fiction: Juvenile, picture books, religious, young adult. Expanding children's list. Artwork essential. Query with synopsis, 2 chapters, intro and SASE.
Recent Fiction Title: *A Good Day for Listening*, Maryellen King.

WILLIAM MORROW AND CO., 1350 Avenue of the Americas, New York NY 10019. (212)261-6500. Fax: (212)261-6595. Editorial Director: Will Schwalbe. Managing Editor: Michael Beacon. Imprints include Beech Tree Books (juvenile), Paulette Kaufman, editor-in-chief. Greenwillow Books (juvenile), Susan Hirschman, editor-in-chief. Hearst Books (trade), Ann Bramson, editorial director. Hearst Marine Books (nautical), Ann Bramson, editor. Lothrop, Lee & Shepard (juvenile), Susan Pearson, editor-in-chief. Morrow Junior Books (juvenile), David Reuther, editor-in-chief. Mulberry Books (juvenile), Paulette Kaufmann, editor-in-chief. Quill Trade Paperbacks, Andrew Dutter, editor. Tambourine Books (juvenile), Amy Cohn, editor-in-chief. Estab. 1926. Publishes 200 titles/year. Receives 10,000 submissions/year. 30% of books from first-time authors; 5% from unagented writers. Payment is on standard royalty basis on retail price. Advance varies. Publishes book 1-2 years after acceptance. Reports in 3 months. Query letter on all books. *No unsolicited mss or proposals.*

Nonfiction and Fiction: Publishes adult fiction, nonfiction, history, biography, arts, religion, poetry, how-to books, cookbooks. Length: 50,000-100,000 words. Query only; mss and proposals should be submitted only through an agent.

MORROW JUNIOR BOOKS, Division of William Morrow and Co., 1350 Avenue of the Americas, New York NY 10019. (212)261-6691. Editor-in-Chief: David L. Reuther. Executive Editor: Meredith Charpentier. Senior Editor: Andrea Curley. Publishes hardcover originals. Publishes 50 titles/year. All contracts negotiated individually. Offers variable advance. Book catalog and guidelines for 9 × 12 SAE with 3 first-class stamps.
Nonfiction: Juveniles (trade books). No textbooks.
Fiction: Juveniles (trade books).
Tips: "We are no longer accepting unsolicited manuscripts."

‡MOTHER COURAGE PRESS, 1667 Douglas Ave., Racine WI 53404-2721. (414)637-2227. Fax: (414)637-8242. Publisher: Barbara Lindquist. Estab. 1981. Publishes trade paperback and hardcover originals. Averages 4 titles/year. Receives 800-900 submissions/year. 100% of books from first-time authors; 100% of books from unagented writers. Pays 10-15% royalty on wholesale. Offers $250 average advance. Publishes book 1 year after acceptance. Accepts simultaneous submissions. Query for electronic submissions. Reports in 3 months. Book catalog for #10 SASE.
Nonfiction: How-to, self-help. Subjects include sexual abuse, psychology, sociology and spirituality. "We are looking for books on women's spirituality, Native American with women's emphasis feminist issues, humor and books about courageous women." Submit outline and sample chapters. Reviews artwork/photos as part of ms package.
Fiction: Lesbian fiction of any genre. "Don't send male-oriented fiction of any kind." Submit outline/synopsis and sample chapters.
Tips: "We like to do books that have 'Women of Courage' as the theme. Do not send anything unsolicited by registered or certified mail. Call us with your proposal—we will give you our answer immediately."

MOUNTAIN PRESS PUBLISHING COMPANY, P.O. Box 2399, Missoula MT 59806-2399. (406)728-1900. Fax: (406)728-1635. History Editor: Daniel Greer. Natural History Editor: Kathleen Ort. Estab. 1948. Imprints are Roadside Geology Series, Roadside History Series, Classics of the Fur Trade. Publishes hardcover and trade paperback originals. Averages 15 titles/year. Receives 250 submissions/year. 50% of books from first-time authors; 90% from unagented writers. Pays 7-12% on wholesale price. Publishes book 2 years after acceptance. Query for electronic submissions. Reports in 2-3 months on queries. *Writer's Market* recommends allowing 2 months for reply. Book catalog free.
Nonfiction: Western history, Americana, nature/environment, regional, earth science, travel. "We are expanding our Roadside Geology and Roadside History series (done on a state by state basis). We are interested in how-to books (about horses) and well-written regional outdoor guides—plants, flowers and birds. No personal histories or journals." Query or submit outline and sample chapters. Reviews artwork/photos as part of ms package.
Tips: "It is obvious that small- to medium-size publishers are becoming more important, while the giants are becoming harder and less accessible. If I were a writer trying to market a book today, I would find out what kind of books a publisher was interested in and tailor my writing to them. Research markets and target my audience. Research other books on the same subjects. Make yours different. Don't present your manuscript to a publisher—*sell* it to him. Give him the information he needs to make a decision on a title."

THE MOUNTAINEERS BOOKS, 1011 SW Klickitat Way, Suite 107, Seattle WA 98134-1162. (206)223-6303. Director: Donna DeShazo. Editor-in-Chief: Margaret Foster. Estab. 1961. Publishes 95% hardcover and trade paperback originals and 5% reprints. Averages 40 titles/year. Receives 150-250 submissions/year. 25% of books from first-time authors; 98% from unagented writers. Average print order for a first book is 5,000-7,000. Pays royalty based on net sales. Pays advance. Publishes book 1 year after acceptance. Reports in 3 months. Book catalog and ms guidelines for 9 × 12 SAE with 3 first-class stamps.
● Mountain Books is looking for manuscripts with more emphasis on regional conservation and natural history. See the Contests and Awards section for information on the Barbara Savage/"Miles From Nowhere" Memorial Award offered by Mountain Books.
Nonfiction: Guidebooks for adventure travel, recreation, natural history, conservation/environment, non-competitive self-propelled sports, outdoor how-to, and some children's books. "We specialize in books dealing with mountaineering, hiking, backpacking, skiing, snowshoeing, canoeing, bicycling, etc. These can be either how-to-do-it or where-to-do-it (guidebooks)." Does *not* want to see "anything dealing with hunting, fishing or motorized travel." Submit author bio, outline and minimum of 2 sample chapters. Accepts nonfiction translations. Looks for "expert knowledge, good organization." Also interested in nonfiction adventure narratives. Ongoing award—The Barbara Savage/"Miles from Nowhere" Memorial Award for outstanding adventure narratives is offered.
Fiction: "We might consider an exceptionally well-done book-length manuscript on mountaineering." Does *not* want poetry or mystery. Query first.

Tips: "The type of book the writer has the best chance of selling our firm is an authoritative guidebook (*in our field*) to a specific area not otherwise covered; or a how-to that is better than existing competition (again, *in our field*)."

MUSTANG PUBLISHING CO., P.O. Box 3004, Memphis TN 38173-0004. (901)521-1406. Editor: Rollin Riggs. Estab. 1983. Publishes nonfiction hardcover and trade paperback originals. Averages 10 titles/year. Receives 1,000 submissions/year. 50% of books from first-time authors; 90% of books from unagented writers. Pays 6-8% royalty on retail price. Publishes book 1 year after acceptance. Accepts simultaneous submissions. Address proposals to Rollin Riggs. No electronic submissions. No phone calls, please. Reports in 1 month. *Writer's Market* recommends allowing 2 months for reply. Book catalog for $1 and #10 SASE.
Nonfiction: How-to, humor, self-help. Subjects include Americana, hobbies, recreation, sports, travel. "Our needs are very general—humor, travel, how-to, etc.—for the 18-to 40-year-old market." Query or submit outline and sample chapters with SASE.
Recent Nonfiction Title: *The Complete Book of Golf Betting Games*, by Scott Johnston.
Tips: "From the proposals we receive, it seems that many writers never go to bookstores and have no idea what sells. Before you waste a lot of time on a nonfiction book idea, ask yourself, 'How often have my friends and I actually *bought* a book like this?' Know the market, and know the audience you're trying to reach."

THE MYSTERIOUS PRESS, Subsidiary of Warner Books, 1271 Avenue of the Americas, New York NY 10020. (212)522-5144. Fax: (212)522-7990. Editor-in-Chief: William Malloy. Editorial Assistant: Sara Ann Freed. Editorial Assistant: Theresa Loong. Estab. 1976. Publishes hardcover and mass market paperback editions. Averages 70-90 titles/year. No unagented mss. Pays standard, but negotiable, royalty on retail price. Amount of advance varies widely. Publishes book an average of 1 year after acceptance. Reports in 2 months.
Fiction: Mystery, suspense. "We will consider publishing any outstanding crime/espionage/suspense/detective novel that comes our way. No short stories." Query with SASE.
Recent Fiction Title: *Fugitive Colors*, by Margaret Maron.
Tips: "We do not read unagented material. Agents only, please."

THE NAIAD PRESS, INC., P.O. Box 10543, Tallahassee FL 32302. (904)539-5965. Fax: (904)539-9731. Editorial Director: Barbara Grier. Estab. 1973. Publishes paperback originals. Averages 24 titles/year. Receives over 1,400 submissions/year. 20% of books from first-time authors; 99% from unagented writers. Average print order for a first book is 12,000. Pays 15% royalty on wholesale or retail price. No advance. Publishes book an average of 2 years after acceptance. Reports in 4 months. Book catalog and ms guidelines for 6×9 SAE and $1.50 postage and handling
Fiction: "We publish lesbian fiction, preferably lesbian/feminist fiction. We are not impressed with the 'oh woe' school and prefer realistic (i.e., happy) novels. We emphasize fiction and are now heavily reading manuscripts in that area. We are working in a lot of genre fiction—mysteries, short stories, fantasy—all with lesbian themes, of course. We have instituted an inhouse anthology series, featuring short stories only by our own authors (i.e. authors who have published full length fiction with us or those signed to do so)." Query.
Tips: "There is tremendous world-wide demand for lesbian mysteries from lesbian authors published by lesbian presses, and we are doing several such series. We are no longer seeking science fiction. Manuscripts under 60,000 words have twice as good a chance as over 60,000."

NASW PRESS, Division of National Association of Social Workers, 750 First St. NE, Suite 700, Washington DC 20002-4241. Fax: (202)336-8312. E-mail: lbeeb@cap.com. Executive Editor: Linda Beebe. Estab. 1956. Averages 10-12 titles/year. Receives 100 submissions/year. 20% of books from first-time authors; 100% from unagented writers. Pays 10-15% royalty on net prices. Publishes book an average of 8 months after acceptance of completed ms. Reports within 4 months on submissions. Book catalog and ms guidelines free.
  ● NASW is a growing company. They will be putting more emphasis on publishing health policy books.
Nonfiction: Textbooks of interest to professional social workers. "We're looking for books on social work in health care, mental health, multicultural competence and substance abuse. Books must be directed to the professional social worker and build on the current literature." Submit outline and sample chapters. Rarely reviews artwork/photos as part of ms package.
Tips: "Our audience includes social work practitioners, educators, students and policy makers. They are looking for practice-related books that are well grounded in theory. The books that do well are those that have direct application to the work our audience does. New technology, AIDS, welfare reform, and health policy will be of increasing interest to our readers. We are particularly interested in manuscripts for fact-based practice manuals that will be very user-friendly."

NATIONAL PRESS BOOKS, INC., 7200 Wisconsin Ave., Suite 212, Bethesda MD 20814. (301)657-1616. Fax: (301)657-8475. Editorial Director: G. Edward Smith. Estab. 1984. Publishes hardcover and trade paperback originals. Publishes 23 titles/year. Receives 1,500 submissions/year. 20% of books are from first-time

authors; 80% from unagented writers. Pays 5-10% royalty on wholesale or retail price or makes outright purchases. Offers variable advance. Publishes book 8 months after acceptance. Accepts simultaneous submissions. Reports in 4 months. Book catalog and ms guidelines for 7½×10½ SAE with 4 first-class stamps.
Nonfiction: Biography, cookbook, self-help. Subjects include business and economics, child guidance/parenting, government/politics, history, money/finance, psychology. Query or submit outline and sample chapters. Reviews artwork/photos as part of ms package.

NATIONAL TEXTBOOK CO., Imprint of NTC Publishing Group, 4255 W. Touhy Ave., Lincolnwood IL 60646. (708)679-5500. Fax: (708)679-2494. Publisher/CEO: Mark R. Pattis. Publishes originals for education and trade market, and software. Averages 100-150 titles/year. Receives 1,000 submissions annually. 10% of books from first-time authors. 75% from unagented writers. Manuscripts purchased on either royalty or fee basis. Publishes book 1 year after acceptance. Reports in 3 months. Book catalog and ms guidelines for 6×9 SAE and 2 first-class stamps.
Nonfiction: Textbooks. Major emphasis being given to foreign language and language arts classroom texts, especially secondary level material, and business and career subjects (marketing, advertising, sales, etc.). John T. Nolan, Language Arts Executive Editor; N. Keith Fry, Executive Editor/Foreign Language and ESL; Anne Knudsen, Executive Editor/NTC Business Books and Betsy Lancefield, Executive Editor/VGM Career Horizons, and Daniel Spinella, Associate Editor/Passport Books. Send sample chapter and outline or table of contents.

THE NAUTICAL & AVIATION PUBLISHING CO., 8 W. Madison St., Baltimore MD 21201. (410)659-0220. Fax: (410)539-8832. President/Publisher: Jan Snouck-Hurgronje. Editor: Robert Bischoff. Estab. 1979. Publishes hardcover originals and reprints. Averages 10-12 titles/year. Receives 125 submissions/year. Pays 10-15% royalty on net selling price. Rarely offers advance. Accepts simultaneous submissions. Book catalog free.
Nonfiction: Reference. Subjects include history, military/war. Query with synopsis and 3 sample chapters. Reviews artwork/photo as part of package.
Recent Nonfiction Title: *Southern Campaigns of the America Revolution*, by Dan Morrill.
Fiction: Historical. Submit outline/synopsis and sample chapters.
Recent Fiction Title: *Straits of Messina*, by William P. Mack.
Tips: "Please note that we are publishers of *military* history only—our name is misleading, and we often get inquiries on general nautical or aviation books. We generally do not publish fiction titles. We are primarily and increasingly a nonfiction publishing house."

NAVAL INSTITUTE PRESS, Imprint of U.S. Naval Institute, 118 Maryland Ave., Annapolis MD 21402-5035. Executive Editor: Paul Wilderson. Press Director: Ronald Chambers. Contact: Jean Tyson, acquisitions coordinator. Estab. 1873. Averages 50 titles/year. Receives 400-500 submissions/year. 60% of books from first-time authors; 75% from unagented writers. Average print order for a first book is 2,000. Pays 6-10% royalty based on net sales. Publishes book 1 year after acceptance. Query letter strongly recommended. *Writer's Market* recommends allowing 2 months for reply. Book catalog free. Manuscript guidelines for SASE.
Nonfiction: "We are interested in naval and maritime subjects and in broad military topics, including government policy and funding. Specific subjects include: tactics, strategy, navigation, military history, biographies, aviation and others."
Fiction: Limited fiction on military and naval themes.

NEAL-SCHUMAN PUBLISHERS, INC., 100 Varick St., New York NY 10013. (212)925-8650. Fax: (212)219-8916. Editorial Director: Margo Hart. Publishes hardcover originals. Publishes 30 titles/year. Receives 80 submissions/year. 75% of books from first-time authors; 80% from unagented writers. Pays 10% royalty on net sales. Publishes book 9-12 months after acceptance. Query for electronic submissions. Reports in 1 month on proposals. *Writer's Market* recommends allowing 2 months for reply. Book catalog and ms guidelines free.
Nonfiction: How-to, reference, software, technical, textbook, texts and professional books in library and information science. Subjects include business and economics, child guidance/parenting, computers and electronics, education, gay/lesbian, government/politics, health/medicine, language/literature, money/finance, recreation, software, travel. "We are looking for reference books in business and health-related sciences." Submit proposal package, including vita, outline, preface and sample chapters.
Recent Nonfiction Title: *A CD/ROM Primer*, by Cheryl LaGuardia.

‡NEGATIVE CAPABILITY, 62 Ridgelawn Dr. E., Mobile AL 36608. Editor/Publisher: Sue Walker. Publishes hardcover and trade paperback originals. Publishes 4 titles/year. Negotiates royalty. Publishes book 10 months after acceptance of ms. Reports in 2 months. Manuscript guidelines free.
Nonfiction: Self-help. Subjects include education, health/medicine, language/literature, women's issues/studies.

Recent Nonfiction Title: *Deeper Than Monday Night Football: Thoughts On High School & Beyond*, by James Brannan Walker (self-help advice for students).
Fiction: Feminist, historical, literary, short story collections. Query with SASE.
Recent Fiction Title: *Little Dragons*, by Michael Bugeja (short story collection).
Poetry: Submit 5 sample poems.
Recent Poetry Title: *The World's A Small Town*, by Roger Granet (free verse).

THOMAS NELSON PUBLISHERS, Nelson Place at Elm Hill Pike, P.O. Box 141000, Nashville TN 37214-1000. (615)889-9000. Contact: Submissions Editor. Estab. 1798. Imprints are Oliver-Nelson, Janet Thoma, and Jan Dennis Books. Publishes hardcover and paperback originals and reprints. Averages 250 titles/year. Pays royalty or makes outright purchase. Publishes book 1 year after acceptance. Send proposal to Book Editorial. Reports in 2 months.
Nonfiction: Adult inspirational/motivational Christian trade books and reference books on the Bible and Christianity. Submit outline/synopsis and 3 sample chapters with SASE.
Fiction: Seeking high quality novels with Christian themes for adults and teens.

‡NELSON-HALL PUBLISHERS, 111 N. Canal St., Chicago IL 60606. (312)930-9446. General Manager: Richard O. Meade. Estab. 1909. Publishes hardcover and paperback originals. Averages 30 titles/year. Receives 200 queries and 20 mss/year. 90% of books submitted by unagented writers. Pays 5-15% royalty on wholesale price. Publishes book 1 year after acceptance. Accepts simultaneous submissions. Reports in 1 month on queries.
Nonfiction: College textbooks and general scholarly books in the social sciences. Subjects include anthropology/archaeology, government/politics, music/dance, psychology, sociology. Query with outline, 2 sample chapters, cv.
Recent Nonfiction Title: *The Rich Get Richer*, by Denny Braun, Ph.D.

THE NEW ENGLAND PRESS, INC., P.O. Box 575, Shelburne VT 05482. (802)863-2520. Fax: (802)863-1510. President: Alfred Rosa. Managing Editor: Mark Wanner. Estab. 1978. Publishes hardcover and trade paperback originals and trade paperback reprints. Averages 6-12 titles/year. Receives 200 submissions/year. 25% of books from first-time authors; 90% from unagented writers. Publishes ms an average of 1 year after acceptance. Reports in 3 months. Catalog for 6×9 SAE with 4 first-class stamps.
Nonfiction: Biography, nature, photographic books. Subjects include Vermontiana and Northern New England topics; history (New England orientation); railroading (New England orientation). No juvenile or psychology. Query or submit outline and sample chapters. Reviews artwork/photos.
Fiction: Young adult historical (Vermont, Northern New England orientation). No original adult fiction. Query.

‡NEW HARBINGER PUBLICATIONS, 5674 Shattuck Ave., Oakland CA 94609. Aquisition Editors: Dana Landis, Kristin Beck. Publishes 16 titles/year. Receives 750 queries and 200 mss/year. 60% of books from first-time authors; 95% from unagented writers. Pays 12-13% royalty on wholesale price. Offers $0-3,000 advance. Publishes book 1 year after acceptance of ms. Accepts simultaneous submissions. Reports in 1 month on queries and proposals, 3 months on mss. Book catalog and ms guidelines free on request.
Nonfiction: Self-help (psychology/health), textbook. Subjects include child guidance/parenting, health/medicine, psychology. "Authors need to be a qualified psychotherapist or health practitioner to publish with us." Submit proposal package, including outline, 3 sample chapters, competing titles and why this one is special.
Recent Nonfiction Title: *Postpartum Survival Guide*, by Dunnwold/Sanford (psychology/medical self-help).
Tips: Audience includes psychotherapists and lay readers wanting step-by-step strategies to solve specific problems.

NEW HOPE, Woman's Missionary Union, P.O. Box 12065, Birmingham AL 34242-2065. (205)991-8100. Editorial Group Manager: Cindy McClain. Imprints are New Hope, Women's Missionary Union. Publishes 25 titles/year. Receives 25 queries and 60 mss/year. 50% of books from first-time authors; 100% from unagented writers. Pays 7-10% royalty on retail price or makes outright purchase. Publishes book 12-18 months after acceptance of ms. No simultaneous submissions. Reports in 6 months on mss. Book catalog for 9×12 SAE with 3 first-class stamps. Manuscript guidelines for #10 SASE.
Nonfiction: How-to, children's/juvenile (religion), personal growth, first person experience. Subjects include child guidance/parenting (from Christian perspective), education (Christian church), religion (Christian faith—must relate to missions work, culture, Christian concerns, Christian ethical issues, spiritual growth, etc.), women's issues/studies from Christian perspective. "We publish Christian education materials that focus on missions work or educational work in some way. Teaching helps, spiritual growth material, ideas for working with different audiences in a church, etc.—missions work overseas or church work in the US, women's spiritual issues, guiding children in Christian faith." Submit outline and 3 sample chapters for review. Submit complete ms for acceptance decision.

NEW READERS PRESS, Publishing Division of Laubach Literacy International, P.O. Box 131, Syracuse NY 13210-0131. Fax: (315)422-6369. Editorial Director: Mary MacKay. Estab. 1959. Publishes paperback originals. Averages 70 titles/year. Receives 500 submissions/year. 40% of books by first-time authors; 95% by unagented writers. Average print order for a first book is 5,000. "Most of our sales are adult basic education programs, volunteer literacy programs, private human services agencies, prisons, and libraries with literacy outreach programs." Pays royalty on retail price, or by outright purchase. Rate varies according to type of publication and length of ms. Advance is "different in each case, but does not exceed projected royalty for first year." Publishes book 1 year after acceptance. Query for electronic submissions. Reports in 3 months. Free book catalog and authors' brochure.

Nonfiction: "Our audience is adults with limited reading skills (12th grade level and below). We publish basic education and ESL literacy materials in reading and writing, math, social studies, health, science, and English as a second language. We are particularly interested in materials that fulfill curriculum requirements in these areas. Manuscripts must be not only easy to read (0 to 6th grade level) but mature in tone and concepts. We are not interested in anything at all written for children or teenagers." Write for guidelines or submit outline and 1-3 sample chapters.

Fiction: Short novels (7,500-10,000 words) at 3rd-5th grade reading level on themes of interest to adults and older teenagers. Write for guidelines or submit synopsis.

Tips: "We have a structured library of fiction and nonfiction titles for pleasure reading that need to follow specific guidelines."

NEW RIVERS PRESS, 420 N. Fifth St., Ste. 910, Minneapolis MN 55401. Managing Editor: Michelle Woster. Publishes trade paperback originals. Publishes 8-10 titles/year. Receives 100 queries and 450 mss/year. 95% of books from first-time authors; 99.9% from unagented writers. Pays 12-15% royalty or makes outright purchase. Publishes book 14 months after acceptance of ms. Query first with a synopsis of proposal. Reports in 6 months. Book catalog free on request. Manuscript guidelines for #10 SASE.

Nonfiction: Creative prose. "We publish memoirs, essay collections, and other forms of creative nonfiction." Query.

Recent Nonfiction Title: *Mykonos*, by Nancy Raeburn (memoir).

Fiction: Literary and short story collections. Query with synopsis and 2 sample chapters.

Poetry: Submit 10-15 sample poems.

‡NEW SOCIETY PUBLISHERS, 4527 Springfield Ave., Philadelphia PA 19143. Contact: Barbara Hirshkowitz. Publishes 12 titles/year. 20% of books from first-time authors; 90% from unagented writers. Pays 10-12% royalty on net sales. Offers $500-2,500 advance. Publishes book 9 months after acceptance of ms. Accepts simultaneous submissions. Reports in 1 month on queries, 6 months on proposals and mss. Book catalog and ms guidelines free on request.

Nonfiction: Subjects include teaching, alternative economics, ecology, women's issues/studies. "Look at our catalog and guidelines carefully." Query.

Recent Nonfiction Title: *Whole Life Economics*, by Barbara Brandt (alternative economics).

NEW VICTORIA PUBLISHERS, P.O. Box 27, Norwich VT 05055-0027. Phone/fax: (802)649-5297. E-mail: newvic@telecomp.com. Editor: Claudia Lamperti. Estab. 1976. Publishes trade paperback originals. Averages 8-10 titles/year. Receives 100 submissions/year. 50% of books from first-time authors; most books from unagented writers. Pays 10% royalty on wholesale price. Publishes book 1 year after acceptance. Reports on queries in 1 month. *Writer's Market* recommends allowing 2 months for reply. Book catalog free.

Nonfiction: History. "We are interested in feminist history or biography and interviews with or topics relating to lesbians. No poetry." Submit outline and sample chapters.

Fiction: Adventure, erotica, fantasy, historical, humor, mystery, romance, science fiction, western. "We will consider most anything if it is well written and appeals to lesbian/feminist audience." Submit outline/synopsis and sample chapters. Hard copy only—no discs.

Tips: "Try to appeal to a specific audience and not write for the general market."

‡NEW WORLD LIBRARY, Subsidiary of Whatever Publishing, Inc., 58 Paul Dr., San Rafael CA 94903. (415)472-2100. Publisher: Marc Allen. Imprint is Amber Allen Publishing (contact Janet Mills). Publishes hardcover and trade paperback originals and reprints. Publishes 25 titles/year. 10% of books from first-time authors; 50% from unagented writers. Pays 12-16% royalty on wholesale price. Offers $0-200,000 advance. Publishes book 9-12 months after acceptance of ms. Accepts simultaneous submissions. Reports in 2 months. Book catalog and ms guidelines free on request.

• New World Library also has an extensive audio program.

Nonfiction: Gift book, self-help. Subjects include business/prosperity, cooking/foods/nutrition, ethnic (African-American, Native American), money/finance, nature/environment, personal growth, psychology, religion, women's issues/studies. Query or submit outline, 1 sample chapter and author bio with SASE. Reviews artwork/photos as part of ms package. Send photocopies.

Recent Nonfiction Title: *The Seven Spiritual Laws of Success*, by Deepak Chopra (prosperity/career).

‡NEW YORK NICHE PRESS, 175 Fifth Ave., Suite 2646, New York NY 10010. (212)675-3699. Publisher: Michael Danowski. Publishes trade paperback originals and newsletters. Publishes 4 titles/year. Receives 4 queries/year. 50% of books from first-time authors; 100% from unagented writers. Accepts simultaneous submissions.
Nonfiction: Regional, travel. Subjects include New York City recreation and travel. "Timely information should be balanced with useful material that will not date the work. Should be street-smart in style." Submit outline with 1 sample chapter. Reviews artwork/photos as part of ms package. Send photocopies.
Recent Nonfiction Title: *Dim Sum: How About Some? A Guide to NYC's Liveliest Chinese Dining & How To Make A Day of It*, by Wanda Chin and Michael P. Danowski (New York restaurant/travel guide).
Tips: "Our readers are New York residents and enthusiastic visitors to NYC. We use material with the 'New York attitude.' We are considering children's fiction about and for New York."

THE NOBLE PRESS, INC., Suite 508, 213 W. Institute Place, Chicago IL 60610. (312)642-1168. Fax: (312)642-7682. Executive Editor: Janet Bell. Estab. 1988. Publishes hardcover and trade paperback originals. Publishes 8-12 titles/year. Receives 1,500 submissions/year. 50% of books from first-time authors; 70% from unagented writers; 30% agented. Pays 5-15% royalty on retail price. Advance varies. Publishes book an average of 8 months after acceptance. Accepts simultaneous submissions. Reports in 10 weeks. Manuscript guidelines for SASE.
• This publisher has launched a book club aimed at African-American readers called Black Literary Society. It will feature commercial titles but also focus on new writers, first novelists, works on race relations, art books and children's books as well as Caribbean and African history.
Nonfiction: Subjects should be multi-cultural. No cookbooks, technical manuals, or texts in full. Query or submit outline and 1 sample chapter.
Recent Nonfiction Title: *Volunteer Slavery*, by Jill Nelson.
Tips: "The writer has the best chance of selling us a nonfiction or fiction book that concerns African-Americans and would be of interest to multi-cultural readers."

‡NODIN PRESS, Imprint of Micawber's Inc., 525 N. Third St., Minneapolis MN 55401. (612)333-6300. President: Norton Stillman. Publishes hardcover and trade paperback originals. Publishes 4 titles/year. Receives 20 queries and 20 mss/year. 75% of books from first-time authors; 100% from unagented writers. Pays 10% royalty. Offers $250-1,000 advance. Publishes book 20 months after acceptance of ms. Accepts simultaneous submissions. Reports in 6 months on queries. Book catalog or ms guidelines free on request.
Nonfiction: Biography, regional guide book. Subjects include ethnic, history, sports, travel. Query.
Recent Nonfiction Title: *Golden Memories*, by Christensen (autobiography).

NORTH LIGHT BOOKS, Imprint of F&W Publications, 1507 Dana Ave., Cincinnati OH 45207. Editorial Director: David Lewis. Publishes hardcover and trade paperback originals. Averages 30-35 titles/year. Pays 10-20% royalty on net receipts. Offers $4,000 advance. Accepts simultaneous submissions. Reports in 2 months. Book catalog for 9×12 SAE with 6 first-class stamps.
Nonfiction: Art and graphic design instruction books. Interested in books on watercolor painting, oil painting, pastel, basic drawing, pen and ink, airbrush, crafts, decorative painting, basic design, computer graphics, desktop design, layout and typography. Do not submit coffee table art books without how-to art instruction. Query or submit outline and examples of artwork (transparencies and photographs).
Recent Nonfiction Title: *Timeless Techniques for Better Oil Paintings*.

NORTHERN ILLINOIS UNIVERSITY PRESS, DeKalb IL 60115-2854. (815)753-1826/753-1075. Fax: (815)753-1845. Director: Mary L. Lincoln (history). Acquisitions Editor: Dan Coran (literature, political science). Estab. 1965. Pays 10-15% royalty on wholesale price. Book catalog free.
Nonfiction: "The NIU Press publishes mainly history, political science, social sciences, philosophy, literary criticism and regional studies. We do not consider collections of previously published articles, essays, etc., nor do we consider unsolicited poetry." Accepts nonfiction translations. Query with outline and 1-3 sample chapters.

NORTHLAND PUBLISHING CO., INC., P.O. Box 1389, Flagstaff AZ 86002-1389. (602)774-5251. Fax: (602)774-0592. Editor: Erin Murphy. Estab. 1958. Publishes hardcover and trade paperback originals. Averages 25 titles/year. Receives 4,000 submissions/year. 30% of books from first-time authors; 95% from unagented writers. Pays 8-12% royalty on net receipts, depending upon terms. Offers $1,000-3,000 average advance. Publishes book 1-2 years after acceptance. Accepts simultaneous submissions if so noted. Reports in 1 month on queries, 2 months on mss. Book catalog and ms guidelines for 9×12 SAE with $1.50 in postage.
• This publisher has received the following awards in the past year: ASLA Arizona Young Reader Award (*The Three Little Javelivas*), ASLA Arizona Author Award (Susan Lowell), RUBPA Design Awards (*How Jackrabbit Got His Very Long Ears*, *Clowns of the Hopi*, and *Cattle, Horses, Sky, and Grass*).

Nonfiction: Subjects include animals, anthropology/archaeology, art/architecture, cooking, history, nature/ environment, photography and regional (American West/Southwest). "We are seeking authoritative, well-written manuscripts on natural history subjects. We do not want to see poetry; general fiction; mainstream, or New Age or science fiction material." Query or submit outline/synopsis and sample chapters. Reviews manuscripts and artwork/photos separately.

Recent Nonfiction Title: *Enduring Traditions: Art of the Navajo*, by Lois and Jerry Jacka.

Fiction: Unique children's stories, especially those with Southwest/West regional theme; Native American folktales (retold by Native Americans only, please). Manuscripts should be 350-1,500 words. Does not want to see chapter books or "mainstream" stories. Northland does not publish general trade fiction.

Recent Fiction Title: *Sunpainters: Eclipse of the Navajo Sun*, by Baje Whitethorn.

Tips: "Our audience is composed of general interest readers and those interested in specialty subjects such as Native American culture and crafts. It is not necessarily a scholarly market, but is sophisticated."

‡**NORTHWOODS PRESS**, Conservatory of American Letters, P.O. Box 298, Thomaston MA 04861. (207)354-0998. Editor: Robert W. Olmsted. Imprints are Northwoods Press, American History Press (division of Northwoods Press). Publishes hardcover and trade paperback originals. Publishes 6-8 titles/year. Northwoods Press publishes 2 titles/year. Receives 60 queries/year. 100% of books from unagented writers. Pays 10% royalty on "amount received by us." Offers $250-500 advance. Publishes book 1 year after acceptance of ms. Accepts simultaneous submissions, if so noted. Reports in 2-3 months on mss. Book catalog for 6×9 SAE with 2 first-class stamps. Manuscript guidelines for #10 SASE. Must request guidelines before submitting ms.

● Northwoods Press requests a reading donation to consider manuscripts.

Poetry: Request guidelines for #10 SASE. Then submit complete ms.

Recent Poetry Title: *Land of Four Quarters*, by Olivia Diamond/Joe Sarff (poetry of the Incas, illustrated).

NORTHWORD PRESS, INC., P.O. Box 1360, Minocqua WI 54548. (715)356-7644. Contact: Barbara K. Harold. Publishes hardcover and trade softcover originals for adults, teens, and children. Estab. 1984. Averages 25 titles/year. Receives 500 submissions/year. 50% of books are from first time authors; 90% are from unagented writers. Pays 10-15% royalty on wholesale price. Offers $2,000-20,000 advance. Publishes book an average of 1 year after acceptance. Accepts simultaneous submissions. Reports in 2 months on queries. Book catalog for 9×12 SASE with 7 first-class stamps. Manuscript guidelines for SASE.

● The editor reports rapid growth for this company.

Nonfiction: Coffee table books, introductions to natural history and wildlife, guidebooks, illustrated books, juvenile. Nature/wildlife/habitat subjects exclusively. "We are seeking nature topics only, with special attention to wildlife." Submit outline and sample chapters. Reviews artwork/photos as part of ms package.

Recent Nonfiction Titles: *Brother Wolf*, by Jim Brandenburg.

Fiction: Based on true-life wilderness experience and adventures—for teens and adults.

Tips: "Think nature and wildlife. That's exclusively what we publish."

W.W. NORTON CO., INC., 500 Fifth Ave., New York NY 10110. General trade publisher of fiction and nonfiction, educational and professional books. Subjects include biography, history, music, psychology, and literary fiction. Do not submit juvenile or young adult, religious, occult or paranormal, genre fiction (formula romances, science fiction or westerns), or arts and crafts. Query with outline, first 3 chapters and SASE.

‡**NOVA PRESS**, 11659 Mayfield Ave., Suite 1, Los Angeles CA 90049. (310)207-4078. President: Jeff Kolby. Publishes trade paperback originals. Publishes 5 titles/year. Pays 10-22½% royalty on retail price. Publishes book 6 months after acceptance of ms. Book catalog free on request.

Nonfiction: How-to, self-help, technical. Subjects include education, software.

Recent Nonfiction Title: *Master the LSAT*, by Jeff Kolby (test prep).

Tips: "Our readers are college students."

NOVA SCIENCE PUBLISHERS INC., 6080 Jericho Turnpike, Suite 207, Commack NY 11725-2808. (516)499-3103. Fax: (516)499-3146. E-mail: novasci1@aol.com. Subsidiary is Kroshka Books. Editor-in-Chief: Frank Columbus. Publishes hardcover and paperback originals. Publishes 150 titles/year. Receives 1,000 queries/year. Pays royalty. Publishes book 1 year after acceptance of ms. Accepts simultaneous submissions. Query for electronic submissions. Reports in 1 month.

A bullet introduces comments by the editors of *Writer's Market* **indicating special information about the listing.**

Nonfiction: Biography, novels, self-help, technical, textbook. Subjects include Americana, anthropology, business and economics, computers and electronics, nutrition, education, government/politics, health/medicine, history, money/finance, nature/environment, philosophy, psychology, recreation, religion, science, sociology, software, sports, childhood development. Query. Reviews artwork/photos as part of ms package. Send photocopies.
Recent Nonfiction Title: *Understanding Suicide*, by D. Lester.

NOYES DATA CORP., 120 Mill Rd., Park Ridge NJ 07656. Fax: (201)391-6833. Estab. 1959. Publishes hardcover originals. Averages 30 titles/year. Pays 12% royalty on net proceeds. Advance varies, depending on author's reputation and nature of book. Reports in 2 weeks. Book catalog free.
Nonfiction: Noyes Publications and Noyes Data Corp. publish technical books on practical industrial processing, science, economic books pertaining to chemistry, chemical engineering, food, textiles, energy, electronics, pollution control—primarily of interest to the business executive. Length: 50,000-250,000 words. Query the Editorial Department.

NTC PUBLISHING GROUP, 4255 W. Touhy Ave., Lincolnwood IL 60646-1975. (708)679-5500. Fax: (708)679-2494. Imprints include National Textbook Company, Passport Books, NTC Business Books, VGM Career Books, The Quilt Digest Press. Foreign Language and English as a Second Language Executive Editor: Keith Fry. Language Arts Executive Editor: John Nolan. Passport Books Editor: Dan Spinella. NTC Business Books Executive Editor: Anne Knudsen and VGM Career Books Executive Editor: Betsy Lancefield. Director of Dictionaries: Richard Spears. Estab. 1960. Publishes hardcover and trade paperback originals and reprints. Averages 150 titles/year. Receives 1,000 submissions/year. 90% of books from unagented writers. Pays royalty or acquires ms on fee basis. Offers varying advance. Publishes book 8 months after acceptance. Accepts simultaneous submissions. Query for electronic submissions. Reports in 2 months. Book catalog free on request.
Nonfiction: Textbook, travel, foreign language, reference, advertising and marketing business books. Subjects include business, education, language/literature, photography, travel, quilts and books related to the fiber arts. Query. Reviews artwork/photos as part of ms package.
Recent Nonfiction Title: *English Communication Skills for Professionals.*

OAK KNOLL PRESS, 414 Delaware St., New Castle DE 19720. (302)328-7232. Fax: (302)328-7274. E-mail: oakknoll@ssnet.com. Publishing Manager: Paul Wakeman. Publishes hardcover and trade paperback originals and reprints. Publishes 12 titles/year. Receives 25 queries and 5 mss/year. 5% of books from first-time authors; 100% from unagented writers. Pays 7-10% royalty on income. Publishes book 18 months after acceptance of ms. Accepts simultaneous submissions. Query for electronic submissions. Reports in less than 1 month on queries. Book catalog free on request.
Nonfiction: Book arts. Subjects include printing, papermaking, bookbinding, book collecting, etc. "We only specialize in books about books." Query. Reviews artwork/photos as part of ms package. Send photocopies.
Recent Nonfiction Title: *American Metal Typefaces of the Twentieth Century*, by Mac McGrew (typography/printing history).

OCEANA PUBLICATIONS, INC., 75 Main St., Dobbs Ferry NY 10522. (914)693-8100. Vice-President, Product Development: M.C. Susan De Maio. Publishes 200 looseleaf and clothbound titles/year. Receives 250 queries and 150 mss/year. 85% of books from first-time authors; 100% from unagented writers. Pays 10-15% royalty. Publishes book 3 months after acceptance of ms. Accepts simultaneous submissions. Query for electronic submissions. Reports in 1 month. Book catalog and ms guidelines free on request.
Nonfiction: Reference. Subjects include international law, business. "Most of Oceana's titles are looseleaf in format and should be structured accordingly." Query with outline, table of contents and 2 sample chapters.

OCTAMERON ASSOCIATES, 1900 Mt. Vernon Ave., Alexandria VA 22301. (703)836-5480. Editorial Director: Karen Stokstad. Estab. 1976. Publishes trade paperback originals. Averages 15 titles/year. Receives 100 submissions/year. 10% of books from first-time authors; 100% from unagented writers. Average print order for a first book is 8,000-10,000. Pays 7½% royalty on retail price. Publishes book 6 months after acceptance. Accepts simultaneous submissions. Query for electronic submissions. Reports in 2 months. Book catalog for #10 SAE with 2 first-class stamps.
Nonfiction: Reference, career, post-secondary education subjects. Especially interested in "paying-for-college and college admission guides." Query with outline and 2 sample chapters. Reviews artwork/photos as part of ms package.

‡OLDBUCK PRESS, INC., P.O. Box 1623, Conway AR 72033. Contact: Phillip A. Sperry. Publishes hardcover originals and trade paperback originals and reprints. Publishes 50 titles/year. Receives 5-10 queries/year. 75% of books from first-time authors; 100% from unagented writers. Pays 10-20% royalty. Publishes book 3-6 months after acceptance of ms. Accepts simultaneous submissions. Reports in 1 month. Book catalog and ms guidelines free on request.

Nonfiction: Biography, gift book, how-to, illustrated book, reference. Subjects include Americana, history, military/war, regional, religion, genealogical. Query with outline. Reviews artwork/photos as part of ms package. Send photocopies.
Tips: Audience is historians, genealogists, collectors.

ONE ON ONE COMPUTER TRAINING, Subsidiary of Mosaic Media, Suite 100, 2055 Army Trail Rd., Addison IL 60101. Manager Product Development: N.B. Young. Imprints are FlipTrack Learning Systems, OneOnOne Computer Training, Math House. Publishes 5-10 titles/year. 100% of books from unagented writers. Makes outright purchase of $2,000-12,000. Advance depends on purchase contract. Publishes book 2-4 months after acceptance of ms. Accepts simultaneous submissions. Query for electronic submissions. Reports in 2 months on proposals. Book catalog free on request.
Nonfiction: How-to, self-help, technical. Subjects include computers, software. Query. All unsolicited mss returned unopened.
Recent Nonfiction Title: *How to Use Access 2.0.*

OPEN COURT PUBLISHING COMPANY, Carus Publishing, Suite 2000, 332 S. Michigan Ave., Chicago IL 60604-9968. Editorial Director: David Ramsay Steele. Editor: Kerri Mommer. Assistant Editor: Edward Roberts. Estab. 1887. Publishes hardcover and trade paperback originals. Publishes 20 titles/year. Receives 400 queries and 200 mss/year. 20% of books from first-time authors; 85% from unagented writers. Pays royalty on wholesale price. Offers $1,000-2,000 advance. Publishes book 1-3 years after acceptance of ms. Reports in 6 months. Book catalog free on request.
Nonfiction: Textbook and academic philosophy. Tradebook subjects include education, philosophy, psychology, religious studies, women's issues/studies, Eastern thought. "We market to academic and intelligent lay readers. We are interested in manuscripts on social issues, cosmology, feminist thought, cognition, Eastern thought, comparative religion, Jungian psychology, academic philosophy, education and psychotherapy. When submitting nonfiction, writers often fail to specify the market for their books. It is not enough to list all the groups of people who *should* be interested." Submit proposal package, including prospectus, sample chapters, vita, outline and 2 sample chapters. Reviews artwork/photos as part of the freelance ms package. Writers should send photocopies.

OPEN ROAD PUBLISHING, P.O. Box 11249, Cleveland Park Station, Washington DC 20008. Contact: B. Borden. Publishes trade and mass market paperback originals. Publishes 15-17 titles/year. Receives 80 queries and 60 mss/year. 40% of books from first-time authors; 95% from unagented writers. Pays 5-6% royalty on retail price. Offers $500-2,000 advance. Publishes book 3 months after acceptance of ms. Accepts simultaneous submissions. Query for electronic submissions. Reports in 1 month on proposals. Book catalog free on request. Manuscript guidelines for #10 SASE.
Nonfiction: Travel guides. Subjects include sports. "We're looking for opinionated, selective travel guides that appeal to mainstream travelers in their mid-20s to early 50s. Our guides are fun, literate, and have a sense of adventure, offering readers solid cultural background and the opportunity to experience the country or city—not just visit it." Submit cover letter, outline and 2 sample chapters.
Recent Nonfiction Title: *Paris Guide*, by Robert F. Howe and Diane Huntley.

ORBIS BOOKS, P.O. Box 308, Maryknoll NY 10545-0308. (914)941-7590. Editor-in-Chief: Robert Ellsberg. Publishes hardcover and trade paperback originals. Publishes 50-55 titles/year. Receives 1,500 queries and 700 mss/year. 2% of books from first-time authors; 99% from unagented writers. Subsidy publishes 0-2% of books, depending on the year. Pays 10-15% royalty on wholesale price net. Offers $500-3,000 advance. Publishes book 15 months after acceptance of ms. Query for electronic submissions. Reports in 2 months on proposals. Book catalog and ms guidelines free on request.
Nonfiction: Reference. Subjects include religion. "Seeking books illuminating religious and social situation of Third World Christians and the lessons of Third World for the North." Submit proposal package, including outline, summary, 10-20 page chapter of intro."
Recent Nonfiction Title: *Is the Bible True?: Understanding the Bible Today*, by David Ord and Robert Coote.

ORCHARD BOOKS, Subsidiary of Grolier Inc., 95 Madison Ave., New York NY 10016. Contact: Submissions Committee. Imprints are Orchard Books, Richard Jackson Books, Melanie Kroupa Books. Publishes hardcover originals and trade paperback reprints. Publishes 60 titles/year. Receives 3,000 mss/year. 5-10% of books from first-time authors; 50% from unagented writers. Pays royalty within trade hardcover norms for children's publishers on retail price. Publishes book 1 year after acceptance of ms, longer for picture books. Reports in 3 months on mss, longer for novels. Book catalog for 8 × 10 SAE with 4 first-class stamps. Manuscript guidelines for #10 SASE.
Nonfiction: Children's/juvenile. "We publish very little nonfiction. Writers should review our list before submitting. Although we have done photo-illustrated nonfiction, we are moving away from it." Submit proposal package, including entire ms if picture-book length. Reviews artwork/photos as part of ms package. Writers should send photocopies.

Recent Nonfiction Title: *The Life and Times of the Apple*, by Charles Mizucci (picture book).
Fiction: All within children's category: adventure, ethnic, experimental, fantasy, feminist, gay/lesbian, gothic, historical, horror, humor, literary, mainstream/contemporary, mystery, picture books, romance, science fiction, suspense, young adult. "We publish a distinguished fiction list. There's room for variety within it, but writers should think about their submissions—an *unusual* genre novel may work for us—*not* a standard one." Submit entire ms.
Recent Fiction Title: *Toning the Sweep*, by Angela Johnson (middle grade fiction).
Poetry: "We publish very little. Poetry collections for children need a theme." Submit complete ms.
Recent Poetry Title: *Stardust Otel*, by Paul Janeczko

ORCHISES PRESS. P.O. Box 20602, Alexandria VA 22320-1602. (703)683-1243. Editor-in-Chief: Roger Lathbury. Estab. 1983. Publishes hardcover and trade paperback originals and reprints. Publishes 4-5 titles/year. Receives 200 queries and 100 mss/year. 1% of books from first-time authors; 95% from unagented writers. Pays 36% of receipts after Orchises has recouped its costs. Publishes book 1 year after acceptance of ms. Accepts simultaneous submissions. Query for electronic submissions. Reports in 3 months. Book catalog for #10 SASE.
Nonfiction: Biography, how-to, humor, reference, technical, textbook. No real restrictions on subject matter. Query. Reviews artwork/photos as part of the ms package. Send photocopies.
Poetry: Poetry must have been published in respected literary journals. Although publishes free verse, has strong formalist preferences. Query or submit 5 sample poems.
Recent Poetry Title: *Dreams of a Work*, by L.S. Asekoff.
Tips: "Audience is professional, literate and academic. Show some evidence of appealing to a wider audience than simply people you know."

OREGON HISTORICAL SOCIETY PRESS, Oregon Historical Society, 1200 SW Park, Portland OR 97205-2483. (503)222-1741. Fax: (503)221-2035. Managing Editor, Adair Law. Estab. 1873. Publishes hardcover originals, trade paperback originals and reprints and a quarterly historical journal, *Oregon Historical Quarterly*. Publishes 2-4 titles/year. Receives 150 submissions/year. 75% of books from first-time authors; 100% from unagented writers. Pays royalty on wholesale price or makes outright purchase. Publishes book 18 months after acceptance. Accepts simultaneous submissions. Query for electronic submissions. Reports in 6 months.
Nonfiction: Subjects include Americana, art/architecture, biography, business history, ethnic, government/politics, history, nature/environment, North Pacific Studies, photography, reference, regional juvenile, women's. Query with outline/synopsis and sample chapters. Reviews artwork/photos as part of ms package.
Recent Nonfiction Title: *Fire at Eden's Gate: Tom McCall and the Oregon Story*, by Brent Walth.

OREGON STATE UNIVERSITY PRESS, 101 Waldo Hall, Corvallis OR 97331-6407. (503)737-3166. Fax: (503)737-3170. Managing Editor: Jo Alexander. Estab. 1965. Publishes hardcover and paperback originals. Averages 6 titles/year. Receives 100 submissions/year. 75% of books from first-time authors; 100% of books from unagented writers. Average print order for a first book is 1,500. Pays royalty on net receipts. No advance. Publishes book 1 year after acceptance. Query for electronic submissions. Reports in 3 months. Book catalog for 6×9 SAE with 2 first-class stamps.
  ● This publisher recently won the Oregon Book Award for their Oregon Literature series.
Nonfiction: Publishes scholarly books in history, biography, geography, literature, life sciences and natural resource management, with strong emphasis on Pacific or Northwestern topics. Submit outline and sample chapters.

‡ORTHO INFORMATION SERVICES, The Solaris Group/Monsanto, P.O. Box 5006, San Ramon CA 94583. Editorial Director: Christine Jordan. Publishes 10 titles/year. Makes outright purchase.
Nonfiction: How-to. Subjects include gardening and home improvement. All unsolicited mss returned unopened.

ORYX PRESS, 4041 N. Central Ave., Suite 700, Phoenix AZ 85012. (602)265-2651. Fax: (602)265-6250. E-mail: info@oryxpress.com. President: Phyllis B. Steckler. Acquisitions Editors: Art Stickney (reference); Larry Mehren (electronic); Tracy Moore (K-12). Estab. 1975. Averages 50 titles/year. Receives 500-1,000 submissions/year. 40% of books from first-time authors; 80% from unagented writers. Average print order for a first book is 1,500. Pays 10% royalty on net receipts. No advance. Publishes book 9 months after

For information on book publishers' areas of interest, see the nonfiction and fiction sections in the Book Publishers Subject Index.

acceptance. Proposals via Internet welcomed. Reports in 6-12 weeks. Book catalog and author guidelines free.

Nonfiction: Directories, dictionaries, encyclopedias, other general reference works; special subjects: business, education, consumer health care, government information, gerontology, social sciences. Publishes print and/or electronic reference sources for public, college, K-12 school, business and medical libraries, and multicultural/literature-based/social studies resource materials for K-12 classroom use. Query or submit outline/rationale and samples. Queries/mss may be routed to other editors in the publishing group.

Recent Nonfiction Title: *Encyclopedia of Adult Development*, by Robert Kastenbaum.

OUR SUNDAY VISITOR, INC., 200 Noll Plaza, Huntington IN 46750-4303. (219)356-8400. Fax: (219)356-8472. President/Publisher: Robert Lockwood. Editor-in-Chief: Greg Erlandson. Acquistions Editor: Jacquelyn Lindsey. Estab. 1912. Publishes paperback and hardbound originals. Averages 20-30 titles a year. Receives over 100 submissions/year. 10% of books from first-time authors; 90% from unagented writers. Pays variable royalty on net receipts. Offers $1,000 average advance. Publishes book 1 year after acceptance. Query for electronic submissions. Reports in 3 months on most queries and submissions. Author's guide and catalog for SASE.

Nonfiction: Catholic viewpoints on current issues, reference and guidance, Bibles and devotional books, and Catholic heritage books. Prefers to see well-developed proposals as first submission with annotated outline, 3 sample chapters and definition of intended market. Reviews artwork/photos as part of ms package.

Tips: "Solid devotional books that are not first person, well-researched church histories or lives of the saints and catechetical books have the best chance of selling to our firm. Make it solidly Catholic, unique, without pious platitudes."

THE OVERLOOK PRESS, Distributed by Viking/Penguin, 149 Wooster St., New York NY 10012. Contact: Editorial Department. Imprint is Tusk Books. Publishes hardcover and trade paperback originals and hardcover reprints. Averages 40 titles/year. Receives 300 submissions/year. Pays 3-15% royalty on wholesale or retail price. Submissions accepted only through literary agents. Reports in 5 months. Book catalog free.

Nonfiction: Art, architecture, design, film, history, biography, current events, popular culture, New York State regional. No pornography.

Fiction: Literary fiction, fantasy, foreign literature in translation. "We tend not to publish commercial fiction."

RICHARD C. OWEN PUBLISHERS INC., P.O. Box 585, Katonah NY 10536. Contact: Janice Boland. Publishes hardcover and trade paperback originals. Publishes 3-12 titles/year. Receives 25 queries and 1,000 mss/year. 99% of books from first-time authors; 100% from unagented writers. Pays 5-8% royalty on wholesale price. Publishes book 3 years after acceptance of ms. Accepts simultaneous submissions, if so noted. Reports in 3-6 months on mss. Manuscript guidelines for #10 SASE.

Nonfiction: Children's/juvenile. Subjects include animals, nature/environment. "Our books are for 5-7-year-olds. The stories are very brief—under 100 words—yet well structured and crafted with memorable characters, language and plots." Send for ms guidelines, then submit complete ms.

Fiction: Picture books. "Brief, strong story line, real characters, natural language, exciting—child-appealing stories with a twist. No lists, alphabet or counting books." Submit full ms with SASE.

Poetry: Poems that excite children, fun, humorous, fresh. No jingles. Must rhyme without force or contrivance. Send for ms guidelines, then submit complete ms.

‡OWL CREEK PRESS, 1620 N. 45th St., #205, Seattle WA 98103. Editor: Rich Ives. Publishes hardcover originals, trade paperback originals and reprints. Publishes 4-6 titles/year. 50% of books from first time authors; 95% from unagented writers. Pays 10-15% royalty, makes outright purchase or with a percentage of print run. Publishes book 18-24 months after acceptance. No simultaneous submissions. Reports in 3 months. Book catalog for #10 SASE.

Fiction: Literary, short story collections. Submit 1 sample chapter.

Recent Fiction Title: *Beasts of the Forest*, by Matt Pavelish (short stories).

• Owl Creek Press holds two contests, the Owl Creek Poetry Prize and the Green Lake Chapbook Prize, and publishes the winners. See the Contests and Awards section for details.

Recent Poetry Title: *The Beginning of Responsibility*, by Mark Rubin.

‡OXFORD UNIVERSITY PRESS, 198 Madison Ave., New York NY 10016. (212)679-7300. Contact: Humanities (Helen McInnis, executive editor); Science (Don Jackson, executive editor); Trade (Laura Brown, director, trade publishing). Publishes hardcover and trade paperback originals and reprints. Publishes 1,500 titles/year. 40% of books from first-time authors; 80% from unagented writers. Pays 0-25% royalty on wholesale price or retail price. Offers $0-40,000 advance. Publishes book 10 months after acceptance of ms. Accepts simultaneous submissions. Reports in 2-3 months on proposals. Book catalog free on request.

Nonfiction: Biography, children's/juvenile, reference, technical, textbook. Subjects include anthropology/ archaeology, art/architecture, business and economics, computers and electronics, gay/lesbian, government/ politics, health/medicine, history, language/literature, military/war, music/dance, nature/environment, philos-

ophy, psychology, religion, science, sociology, women's issues/studies. Oxford is an academic, scholarly press. Submit outline and sample chapters. Reviews artwork/photos as part of ms package (but not necessary).
Recent Nonfiction Title: *Oxford Illustrated History of the American West*, by Clyde Milner (reference).

‡OZARK PUBLISHING, INC., P.O. Box 489, Mineral Wells TX 76068. (800)321-5671. Managing Editor: Michael Finkba. Publishes hardcover, trade and mass market paperback originals. Publishes 10-12 titles/year. Receives 60-100 queries and 60 mss/year. 75% of books from first-time authors; 100% from unagented writers. Pays 10% royalty on wholesale price. Authors receive a percentage of sales while visiting schools. Publishes book 6-9 months after acceptance of ms. Accepts simultaneous submissions. Reports in 1 month on queries, 3 months on mss. Book catalog free on request.
Nonfiction: Children's/juvenile, illustrated book. Subjects include animals, child guidance/parenting, education, nature/environment. Query with SASE. Reviews artwork/photos as part of ms package. Send photocopies.
Recent Nonfiction Title: *An Uphill Climb*, by Dave Sargent (autobiography).
Fiction: Adventure, historical, humor, juvenile, picture books, short story collections, young adult. Query with SASE.
Recent Fiction Title: *Barney the Bearkiller*, by Pat Sargent (juvenile).
Tips: "Our audience is children—elementary and junior high age. All authors must be available to visit schools on a full time basis. Promotional work and scheduling accomplished by Ozark Publishing."

‡PACIFIC VIEW PRESS, P.O. Box 2657, Berkeley CA 94702. Acquisitions Editor: Pam Zumwalt. Publishes hardcover and trade paperback originals. Publishes 4-6 titles/year. 50% of books from first-time authors; 100% from unagented writers. Pays 10% maximum royalty on retail price. Offers $1,000-5,000 advance. Publishes ms 6-12 months after acceptance. Accepts simultaneous submissions. Reports in 2 months on queries and proposals. Book catalog free on request. Writer's guidelines for #10 SASE.
Nonfiction: Children's/juvenile (Asia/multicultural only), reference, textbook (Chinese medicine only), contemporary Pacific Rim affairs. Subjects include business/economics (Asia and Pacific Rim only), health/medicine (Chinese medicine), history (Asia), regional (Pacific Rim), travel (related to Pacific Rim). Query with proposal package including outline, 1-2 chapters, target audience, with SASE.
Recent Nonfiction Title: *Vietnam: Business Opportunities and Risks*, Joseph Quinlan (Asian business).
Tips: Audience is "persons professionally/personally aware of growing importance of Pacific Rim and/or modern culture of these countries, especially China. Business people, academics, travelers, etc."

PALADIN PRESS, P.O. Box 1307, Boulder CO 80306-1307. (303)443-7250. Fax: (303)442-8741. President/Publisher: Peder C. Lund. Editorial Director: Jon Ford. Estab. 1970. Publishes hardcover and paperback originals and paperback reprints. Averages 36 titles/year. 50% of books from first-time authors; 100% from unagented writers. Pays 10-12-15% royalty on net sales. Publishes book 1 year after acceptance. Accepts simultaneous submissions. Reports in 2 months. Book catalog free.
Nonfiction: "Paladin Press primarily publishes original manuscripts on military science, weaponry, self-defense, personal privacy, financial freedom, espionage, police science, action careers, guerrilla warfare, fieldcraft and 'creative revenge' humor. How-to manuscripts are given priority. If applicable, send sample photographs and line drawings with complete outline and sample chapters." Query or submit outline and sample chapters.
Tips: "We need lucid, instructive material aimed at our market and accompanied by sharp, relevant illustrations and photos. As we are primarily a publisher of 'how-to' books, a manuscript that has step-by-step instructions, written in a clear and concise manner (but not strictly outline form) is desirable. No fiction, first-person accounts, children's, religious or joke books. We are also interested in serious, professional videos and video ideas (contact Michael Janich)."

‡PANTHEON BOOKS, Division of Random House, Inc., 25th Floor, 201 E. 50th St., New York NY 10022. Publishes quality fiction and nonfiction. Send query letter first, addressed to Adult Editorial Department.
Nonfiction: History, politics, autobiography, biography, interior design.
Recent Nonfiction Title: Autobiography of Richard Prior.
Recent Fiction Title: *Good Benito*, by Alan Lightman.

‡PAPER CHASE PRESS, 5721 Magazine St., #152, New Orleans LA 70115. (504)522-2025. Editor: Jennifer Osborn. Publishes hardcover and trade paperback originals and reprints. Publishes 5 titles/year. 90% of books from first-time authors; 100% from unagented writers. Pays royalty on retail price; varies from hardcover to trade. Publishes book 18 months after acceptance of ms. Accepts simultaneous submissions. Manuscripts will not be returned. Reports in 2 months on queries.
Nonfiction: How-to, self-help. Subjects include business and economics, hobbies, psychology, recreation, sports, women's issues/studies. "We look for enthusiasm about subject matter, fresh ideas, willingness of author to be involved in promotion of book (good speaking ability, willing to travel, etc.)." Send 1-page query letter only.

Recent Nonfiction Title: *Mock Rock: A Guide to Indoor Climbing*, by Sharon Urquhart (sports trade paperback).

Fiction: Mainstream/contemporary. "We don't want to see someone's first draft. Stay in tune with current trends in fiction. The beginning of the story should be strong enough to *immediately* generate interest in the whole book—sympathetic characters with depth and variety." Query; submit synopsis and 1-2 sample chapters.

Tips: Audience is "mainstream—people who read a lot and are open to all kinds of fiction, literary or otherwise. Relationship issues are particularly interesting to us, i.e., family relationhips, personal relationships. Make your characters and your story believable!"

‡PAPIER-MACHE PRESS, 135 Aviation Way, #14, Watsonville CA 95076. (408)763-1420. Acquisitions Editor: Shirley Coe. Publishes 6-8 titles/year. 90% of books from first-time authors; 95% from unagented writers. Pays royalty. Offers $500-1,000 advance. Publishes book 1 year after acceptance of ms. Accepts simultaneous submissions. Reports in 2 months on queries, 4 months on mss. Book catalog and ms guidelines free on request.

Nonfiction: Women's stories, essays, interviews, biography, gift book. Subjects include women's issues/studies, aging. Focus on women's issues; no technical or how-to books—creative nonfiction. Query with proposal package, including outline, 3-4 sample chapters, target audience, author's qualifications, similar books in marketplace and SASE.

Recent Nonfiction Title: *Learning to Sit in the Silence: A Journal of Caretaking*, by Elaine Marcus Starkmen (women's writings/self-help).

Fiction: Feminist, mainstream/contemporary (women), short story collections (women), aging. "We publish books about women's lives—primarily midlife women. We don't consider books with graphic sex or violence." Query with synopsis, 3-4 sample chapters and SASE.

Recent Fiction Title: *Late Summer Break*, by Ann B. Knox (short stories).

Poetry: Manuscripts must be 100-120 pages long. Prefers collections centered around 1 or 2 major themes. Accepts poetry in July and August only. Submit complete ms.

Recent Poetry Title: *Between One Future and the Next*, by Ruth Daigon.

Tips: Audience is women, 35-55 years old. Always request submission guidelines before submitting a ms.

PARADIGM PUBLISHING INC., Subsidiary of EMC Publishing Corporation, 280 Case St., St. Paul MN 55101. (612)771-1555. Fax: (612)772-5196. Publisher: Mel Hecker. Publishes 50 titles/year. Receives 40 queries and 20 mss/year. 20% of books from first-time authors; 100% from unagented writers. Pays 6-10% royalty on net. Offers $1,000-2,500 advance. Publishes book 1 year after acceptance of ms. Accepts simultaneous submissions. Query for electronic submissions. Reports in 2 months on proposals. Book catalog for 8×12 SAE with 4 first-class stamps. Manuscript guidelines free on request.

Nonfiction: Textbook. Subjects include business and office, communications, computers, psychology and software. "We focus on textbooks for business and office education marketed to proprietary business schools and community colleges." Submit outline and 2 sample chapters.

Recent Nonfiction Title: *WordPerfect 6.0 for Windows*, by Nita Rutkosky.

Tips: "With the cost of paper escalating, multimedia is a sure winner in educational publishing."

PASSPORT PRESS, P.O. Box 1346, Champlain NY 12919-1346. Publisher: Jack Levesque. Estab. 1975. Publishes trade paperback originals. Averages 4 titles/year. 25% of books from first-time authors; 100% from unagented writers. Pays 6% royalty on retail price. Publishes book 9 months after acceptance. Send 1-page query only. Does not return submissions.

Nonfiction: Travel books only, not travelogues. Especially looking for mss on practical travel subjects and travel guides on specific countries. Query. Reviews artwork/photos as part of ms package.

PAULINE BOOKS & MEDIA, (formerly St. Paul Books & Media), Daughters of St. Paul, 50 St. Paul's Ave., Boston MA 02130. (617)522-8911. Fax: (617)541-9805. Director, Editorial Department: Sister Mary Mark, FSP. Estab. 1948. Publishes hardcover and trade paperback originals and reprints. Average 35 titles/year. Receives approximately 1,300 proposals/year. Pays authors 8-12% royalty on net sales. Publishes ms an average of 1-2 years after acceptance. Reports in 3 months. Book catalog for 9×12 SAE with 4 first-class stamps.

Nonfiction: Biography, juvenile, spiritual growth and development. Subjects include child guidance/parenting, psychology, religion. "No strictly secular manuscripts." Query only. No unsolicited mss without prior query.

Recent Nonfiction Title: *When God Comes Close: A Journey Through Scripture*, by Rea McDonnell, S.S.N.D.

Fiction: Juvenile. Query only. No unsolicited mss, without prior query.

Tips: "We are more interested in books concerning faith and moral values, as well as in works on spiritual growth and development. Always interested in books of Christian formation for families. No New Age books, poetry or autobiographies please."

PAULIST PRESS, 997 Macarthur Blvd., Mahwah NJ 07430. (201)825-7300. Fax: (201)825-8345. Editor: Rev. Kevin A. Lynch. Managing Editor: Donald Brophy. Estab. 1865. Publishes hardcover and paperback originals and paperback reprints. Averages 90-100 titles/year. Receives 500 submissions/year. 5-8% of books from first-time authors; 95% from unagented writers. Nonauthor subsidy publishes 1-2% of books. Pays royalty on retail price. Usually offers advance. Publishes book 10 months after acceptance. Reports in 2 months. Query for electronic submissions.
Nonfiction: Philosophy, religion, self-help, textbooks (religious). Accepts nonfiction translations from German, French and Spanish. "We would like to see theology (Catholic and ecumenical Christian), popular spirituality, liturgy, and religious education texts." Submit outline and 2 sample chapters. Reviews artwork/photos as part of ms package.
Recent Nonfiction Title: *Paul VI: The First Modern Pope*, by Peter Hebblethwaite.

PBC INTERNATIONAL INC., 1 School St., Glen Cove NY 11542. (516)676-2727. Fax: (516)676-2738. Publisher: Mark Serchuck. Managing Editor: Susan Kapsis. Estab. 1980. Imprints are Library of Applied Design, Architecture & Interior Design Library, Great Graphics Series, Design In Motion Series, Showcase Edition. Publishes hardcover and paperback originals. Averages 18 titles/year. Receives 100-200 submissions/year. Most of books from first-time authors and unagented writers done on assignment. Pays royalty and/or flat fees. Accepts simultaneous submissions. Reports in 2 months. Book catalog for 9×12 SASE.
Nonfiction: Subjects include design, graphic art, architecture/interior design, packaging design, marketing design, product design. No submissions not covered in the above listed topics. Query with outline and sample chapters. Reviews artwork/photos as part of ms package.
Recent Nonfiction Title: *Rooms with a View: Two Decades of Outstanding American Interior Design from the Kips Bay Decorator Show Houses.*
Tips: "PBC International is the publisher of full-color visual idea books for the design, marketing and graphic arts professional."

PEACHPIT PRESS, 2414 Sixth St., Berkeley CA 94710. (510)548-4393. Fax: (510)548-8192. Contact: Roslyn Bullas. Estab. 1986. Publishes trade paperback originals. Publishes over 30 titles/year. Receives 250 queries and 6 mss/year. 10% of books from first-time authors; 80% from unagented writers. Pays 12-20% royalty on wholesale price. Offers $3,000-10,000 advance. Publishes book 6 months after acceptance of ms. Accepts simultaneous submissions. Query for electronic submissions. Reports in 3 months on proposals. Book catalog free on request.
Nonfiction: How-to, reference, technical. Subjects include computers and electronics. "We prefer no phone calls." Submit short, 1-page proposal (preferred) or outline. Reviews artwork/photos as part of the freelance ms package. Writers should send photocopies.
Recent Nonfiction Title: *The Little PC Book*, by Larry Magid (advice for computer novices).

PEACHTREE PUBLISHERS, LTD., 494 Armour Circle NE, Atlanta GA 30324-4888. (404)876-8761. Contact: Managing Editor. Estab. 1977. Publishes hardcover and trade paperback originals. Averages 15-20 titles/year. Between 25-50% of Peachtree's list consists of children's books. Receives up to 18,000 submissions/year. 25% of books from first-time authors; 75% from unagented writers. Average print order for a first book is 5,000-10,000. Publishes book 1-2 years after acceptance. Reports in 6 months on queries. Book catalog for 9×12 SAE with 3 first-class stamps.
Nonfiction: General and humor. Subjects include animals, children's titles and juvenile chapter books, cooking/foods/history, self-help, gardening, biography, general gift, recreation. No technical or reference. Submit outline and sample chapters. Reviews artwork/photos as part of ms package. No originals, please.
Recent Nonfiction Title: *Margaret Mitchell & John Marsh: The Love Story Behind Gone with the Wind,* by Marianne Walker (biography).
Fiction: Literary, juvenile, mainstream. "We are particularly interested in fiction with a Southern feel." No fantasy, science fiction or romance. Submit sample chapters.
Recent Fiction Title: *Jessie and Jesus and Cousin Claire*, by Raymond Andrews (fiction).
Tips: "Peachtree Publishers prefers to work with Southern writers, professional storytellers, and previously published authors."

PELICAN PUBLISHING COMPANY, 1101 Monroe St., P.O. Box 3110, Gretna LA 70053. (504)368-1175. Editor: Nina Kooij. Estab. 1926. Publishes hardcover, trade paperback and mass market paperback originals and reprints. Averages 40 titles/year. Receives 5,500 submissions/year. 5% of books from first-time authors; 60% from unagented writers. Pays royalty on publisher's actual receipts. Publishes book 18 months after acceptance. Reports in 1 month on queries. *Writer's Market* recommends allowing 2 months for reply. Writer's guidelines for SASE.
● Pelican continues to reduce the number of freelance projects it pursues, but their submissions are growing.
Nonfiction: Biography, coffee table book (limited), humor, illustrated book, juvenile, motivational, inspirational, Scottish. Subjects include Americana (especially Southern regional, Ozarks, Texas, Florida and Southwest); business and economics (popular motivational, if author is a speaker); health; history; music (American

artforms: jazz, blues, Cajun, R&B); politics (special interest in conservative viewpoint); recreation; religion (for popular audience mostly, but will consider others). *Travel*: Regional and international (especially areas in Pacific). *Motivational*: with business slant. *Inspirational*: author must be someone with potential for large audience. *Cookbooks*: "We look for authors with strong connection to restaurant industry or cooking circles, i.e. someone who can promote successfully." Query with SASE. "We require that a query be made first. This greatly expedites the review process and can save the writer additional postage expenses." No multiple queries or submissions. Reviews artwork/photos as part of ms package. Send photocopies only.

Recent Nonfiction Title: *Sam Okamoto's Incredible Vegetables*, by Osamu Okamoto.

Fiction: Historical, humor, Southern, juvenile. "We publish maybe one novel a year, ususally by an author we already have. Almost all proposals are returned. We are most interested in Southern novels." No young adult, romance, science fiction, fantasy, gothic, mystery, erotica, confession, horror, sex or violence. Submit outline/synopsis and 2 sample chapters with SASE.

Recent Fiction Title: *Why Cowboys Sleep With Their Boots On*, by Laurie Lazzaro Knowlton.

Tips: "We do extremely well with cookbooks, travel and popular histories. We will continue to build in these areas. The writer must have a clear sense of the market and this includes knowledge of the competition. A query letter should describe the project briefly, give the author's writing and professional credentials, and promotional ideas."

PENGUIN USA, 375 Hudson St., New York NY 10014. President: Peter Mayer. Imprints include Dial Books for Young Readers, NAL/Dutton, Penguin, Plume, Signet, Topaz and Viking. General interest publisher of both fiction and nonfiction. Query before submitting.

Recent Fiction: Stephen King.

PENNSYLVANIA HISTORICAL AND MUSEUM COMMISSION, Imprint of the Commonwealth of Pennsylvania, P.O. Box 1026, Harrisburg PA 17108-1026. (717)787-8099. Fax: (717)787-8312. Chief, Publications and Sales Division: Diane B. Reed. Estab. 1913. Publishes hardcover and paperback originals and reprints. Averages 6-8 titles/year. Receives 25 submissions/year. Pays 5-10% royalty on retail price. Makes outright purchase of mss or sometimes makes special assignments. Publishes book 18 months after acceptance. Accepts simultaneous submissions. Query for electronic submissions. Reports in 4 months. Manuscripts prepared according to the *Chicago Manual of Style*.

Nonfiction: All books must be related to Pennsylvania, its history or culture: biography, illustrated books, reference, technical and historic travel. "The Commission seeks manuscripts on Pennsylvania, specifically on archaeology, history, art (decorative and fine), politics, and biography." Query or submit outline and sample chapters. Guidelines and proposal forms available.

Recent Nonfiction Title: *J. Horace McFarland: A Thorn For Beauty*, by Ernest Morrison.

Tips: "Our audience is diverse—students, specialists and generalists—all of them interested in one or more aspects of Pennsylvania's history and culture. Manuscripts must be well researched and documented (footnotes not necessarily required depending on the nature of the manuscript) and interestingly written. Manuscripts must be factually accurate, but in being so, writers must not sacrifice style. We have a tradition of publishing scholarly and reference works, as well as more popularly styled books that reach an even broader audience."

PENNWELL BOOKS, PennWell Publishing, P.O. Box 1260, 1421 S. Sheridan Rd., Tulsa OK 74101-6619. Fax: (918)832-9319. Acquisitions Manager: Sue Rhodes Sesso. Estab. 1910. Publishes hardcover originals. Publishes 50 titles/year. Receives 200 queries and 75 mss/year. 50% of books from first-time authors; 99% from unagented writers. Pays 5-15% royalty on net receipts. Publishes book 6-9 months after acceptance of ms. Electronic submissions: IBM or Mac-compatible; must include 2 hard copies. Query with SASE, "but we expect all authors to keep their originals, and we cannot be held responsible for any submissions." Reports in 6 months on proposals. Book catalogs free on request; call 1-800-752-9764.

● This publisher received the Achievement Award from International Technical Publications and Art Competition.

Nonfiction: Technical. Subjects include petroleum, dental, environmental, power. "Texts must have practical application for professionals in the markets we serve. Study our catalogs first before submitting anything. Your expertise as a practitioner within the specific industry is an essential component. We do *not* publish theory or philosophy, nor do we publish texts for the general public. We *do* publish practical, how-to, reference-type books only for the industries we serve." Submit proposal package, including table of contents, chapter-by-chapter synopsis, résumé and sample chapter(s). Reviews artwork/photos as part of ms package. Send photocopies.

Recent Nonfiction Titles: *Creating the High Performance International Petroleum Company*, by John Treat.

Tips: Audiences include: Petroleum—engineers, geologists, chemists, geophysicists, economists, managers. Environmental—petroleum industry people needing information on hazardous materials, safety and crisis management. Power—professionals in electric utility industry. Dental—practicing dentists and their staffs.

THE PERMANENT PRESS/SECOND CHANCE PRESS, 4170 Noyac Rd., Sag Harbor NY 11963. (516)725-1101. Editor: Judith Shepard. Estab. 1978. Publishes hardcover originals. Permanent Press publishes literary fiction. Second Chance Press devotes itself exclusively to re-publishing fine books that are out of print and deserve continued recognition. Averages 12 titles/year. Receives 7,000 submissions/year. 60% of books from first-time authors; 60% from unagented writers. Average print order for a first book is 2,000. Pays 10-20% royalty on wholesale price. Offers $1,000 advance for Permanent Press books; royalty only on Second Chance Press titles. Publishes book 18 months after acceptance. Accepts simultaneous submissions. Reports in 3-4 months on queries. Book catalog for 8 × 10 SAE with 7 first-class stamps. Manuscript guidelines for #10 SASE.

- Permanent Press does not employ readers and the number of submissions it receives has grown (3,000 to 7,000) so much response time has had to increase (3 to 4 months). If the writer sends a query or manuscript that the press is not interested in, they may hear in two or three weeks. But if there is interest, it may take 3 to 6 months.

Nonfiction: Biography, autobiography, historical. No scientific and technical material, academic studies. Query.
Fiction: Literary, mainstream, mystery. Especially looking for high line literary fiction, "original and arresting." No genre fiction. Query with first 20 pages.
Recent Fiction Title: *Littlejohn*, by Howard Owen.
Tips: "We are interested in the writing more than anything and long outlines are a turn-off. The SASE is vital to keep track of things, as we are receiving ever more submissions. We aren't looking for genre fiction but a compelling, well-written story."

PERSPECTIVES PRESS, P.O. Box 90318, Indianapolis IN 46290-0318. (317)872-3055. Publisher: Pat Johnston. Estab. 1982. Publishes hardcover and trade paperback originals. Averages 4 titles/year. Receives 200 queries/year. 95% of books from first-time authors; 95% from unagented writers. Pays 5-15% royalty on net sales. Publishes book 1 year after acceptance. Accepts simultaneous submissions. Reports in 1 month on queries. *Writer's Market* recommends allowing 2 months for reply. Book catalog and writer's guidelines for #10 SAE with 2 first-class stamps.
Nonfiction: How-to, juvenile and self-help books on health, psychology and sociology. Must be related to infertility, adoption, alternative routes to family building. Query with SASE.
Fiction: Query with SASE.
Tips: "For adults we are seeking infertility and adoption decision-making materials, books dealing with adoptive or foster parenting issues, books to use with children, books to share with others to help explain infertility or adoption or foster care, third party reproductive assistance, special programming or training manuals, etc. For children we will consider adoption or foster care related fiction manuscripts that are appropriate for preschoolers and for early elementary children. We do not consider YA. Nonfiction manuscripts are considered for all ages. No autobiography, memoir, or adult fiction. While we would consider a manuscript from a writer who was not personally or professionally involved in these issues, we would be more inclined to accept a manuscript submitted by an infertile person, an adoptee, a birthparent, an adoptive parent, a professional working with any of these."

PETER PAUPER PRESS, INC., 202 Mamaroneck Ave., White Plains NY 10601-5376. Fax: (914)681-0389. Creative Director: Solomon M. Skolnick. Estab. 1928. Publishes hardcover originals. Averages 30-40 titles/year. Receives 450-500 queries and 150-200 mss/year. 5% of books from first-time authors; 99% from unagented writers. Publishes ms 9-15 months after acceptance. No simultaneous submissions. Reports in 1 month. *Writer's Market* recommends allowing 2 months for reply. Book catalog for $1. Manuscript guidelines for #10 SASE.
Nonfiction: Gift books, illustrated books, self-help. Subjects include gardening, nature/environment, psychology, special events and occasions (Valentines Day, Mother's Day, Christmas, etc.). "We do not publish extended narrative works. We publish, primarily, collections of brief quotes, aphorisms, and wise sayings. Do not send us prescriptive material, how-to, or practical material." Submit outline with SASE. Reviews artwork as part of ms package. Send photocopies or transparencies, not original art.
Tips: "Our readers are primarily female, 35 and over, who are likely to buy a 'gift' book in a stationery, gift or boutique store. Writers should become familiar with our previously published work. We publish primarily in three hardcover and one paperback format—56-80 pages depending upon format."

PETERSON'S, P.O. Box 2123, Princeton NJ 08543-2123. (800)338-3282. President: Peter W. Hegener. Publisher: Carole Cushmore. Editor-in-Chief: Jim Gish. Estab. 1966. Publishes trade and reference books. Averages 55-75 titles/year. Receives 200-250 submissions/year. 10% of books from first-time authors; 20% from unagented writers. Average print order for a first book is 10,000-15,000. Pays 10-12% royalty on net sales. Offers advance. Publishes book 1 year after acceptance. Reports in 2 months. Book catalog free.
Nonfiction: Business, careers, education, parenting and family books, as well as educational and career directories. Submit complete ms or detailed outline and sample chapters. *Writer's Market* recommends query with SASE first. Looks for "appropriateness of contents to our markets author's credentials, and writing style suitable for audience." Reviews artwork/photos as part of ms package.

Recent Nonfiction Title: *Why Teams Don't Work.*

PFEIFFER & COMPANY, 8517 Production Ave., San Diego CA 92121. (619)578-5900. Fax: (619)578-2042. President: J. William Pfeiffer. Estab. 1968. Publishes paperback and hardback originals and reprints. Averages 80 titles/year. Specializes in practical materials for human resource development professionals, consultants and general management. Pays 10% average royalty. No advance. Publishes book 6 months after acceptance. Markets books by direct mail and through bookstores. Accepts simultaneous submissions. Reports in 3 months. Book catalog and guidelines for SASE.
Nonfiction: JoAnn Padgett, managing editor. Publishes (in order of preference) human resource development and group-oriented material, management education, small business, career/self-help. No materials for grammar school or high school classroom teachers. Use *American Psychological Association Style Manual.* Query. Send prints or completed art or rough sketches to accompany ms.

PHB PUBLISHERS, 1 Washington St., Suite 304, Dover NH 03820. (603)743-4266. Senior Editor: P.H. Burr. Publishes 25 titles/year. Receives 50 queries/year. 50% of books from first-time authors. Pays royalty. Publishes book 6 months after acceptance of ms. Accepts simultaneous submissions. Query for electronic submissions. Reports in 3 months.
Nonfiction: Subjects include Americana, history, photography.

PHI DELTA KAPPA EDUCATIONAL FOUNDATION, P.O. Box 789, Bloomington IN 47402. (812)339-1156. Fax: (812)339-0018. Editor of Special Publications: Donovan R. Walling. Publishes hardcover and trade paperback originals. Publishes 24-30 titles/year. Receives 100 queries and 50-60 mss/year. 50% of books from first-time authors; 100% from unagented writers. Pays honorarium of $500-5,000. Publishes book 6-9 months after acceptance of ms. No simultaneous submissions. Query for electronic submissions. Reports in 1-3 months on proposals. Book catalog and ms guidelines free on request.
Nonfiction: How-to, reference, essay collections. Subjects include child guidance/parenting, education, and legal issues. "We publish books for educators—K-12 and higher ed. Our professional books are often used in college courses but are never specifically designed as textbooks." Query with outline and 1 sample chapter. Reviews artwork/photos as part of ms package.
Recent Nonfiction Title: *The State of the Nation's Public Schools*, edited by Elam (essay collection).

PHILOMEL BOOKS, Division of The Putnam Publishing Group, 200 Madison Ave., New York NY 10016. (212)951-8700. Editorial Director: Patricia Lee Gauch. Associate Editor: Michael Green. Editorial Assistant: David Briggs. Estab. 1980. Publishes hardcover originals. Publishes 25-30 titles/year. Receives 2,600 submissions/year. 15% of books from first-time authors; 30% from unagented writers. Pays standard royalty. Advance negotiable. Publishes book 1-2 years after acceptance. Reports in 1 month on queries, 3 months on unsolicited mss. Book catalog for 9 × 12 SAE with 4 first-class stamps. Request book catalog from marketing department of Putnam Publishing Group.
Nonfiction: Children's picture books (ages 4-8); middle-grade (ages 7-10); young adult novels/historical fiction (ages 10-15). Query with SASE.
Fiction: Children's picture books (ages 3-8); middle-grade fiction and illustrated chapter books (ages 7-10); and young adult novels (ages 10-15). Particularly interested in picture book mss with original stories and regional fiction with a distinct voice. Historical fiction OK. Unsolicited mss accepted for picture books only; query first for long fiction. Always include SASE. No series or activity books.
Tips: "We prefer a very brief synopsis that states the basic premise of the story. This will help us determine whether or not the manuscript is suited to our list. If applicable, we'd be interested in knowing the author's writing experience or background knowledge. We are always looking for beautifully written manuscripts with stories that engage. We try to be less influenced by the swings of the market than in the power, value, essence of the manuscript itself."

PICCADILLY BOOKS, P.O. Box 25203, Colorado Springs CO 80936-5203. (719)548-1844. Publisher: Bruce Fife. Estab. 1985. Publishes hardcover and trade paperback originals and trade paperback reprints. Publishes 3-8 titles/year. Receives 120 submissions/year. 70% of books from first-time authors; 95% from unagented writers. Pays 5-10% royalty on retail price. Offers $250 average advance. Publishes book 9 months after acceptance. Accepts simultaneous submissions. Responds only if interested. Manuscript guidelines for #10 SASE.
● Picadilly is no longer interested in any fiction or children's plays.
Nonfiction: How-to, humor, performing arts, business. "We are looking for how-to books on entertainment, humor, performing arts, small and/or home-based businesses and careers. We have a strong interest in subjects on clowning, magic, puppetry and related arts, including comedy skits and dialogs." Query with sample chapters.
Recent Nonfiction Title: *Clown Magic.*

PICTON PRESS, Imprint of Picton Corp., P.O. Box 250, Rockport ME 04856-0250. (207)236-6565. Imprints are Picton Press (contact Richard E. Lindahl, Jr.), Penobscot Press (contact Lew Rohrbach), Cricketfield

Press (contact Richard E. Lindahl, Jr.). Publishes hardcover and mass market paperback originals and reprints. Publishes 30 titles/year. Receives 30 queries and 15 mss/year. 50% of books from first-time authors; 100% from unagented writers. Pays 0-10% royalty on wholesale price or makes outright purchase. Publishes book 6 months after acceptance of ms. Reports in 2 months on queries and proposals, 3 months on mss. Book catalog free on request.

Nonfiction: Reference, textbook. Subjects include Americana, genealogy, history, vital records, outdoors subjects (especially place guides). Query with outline.

Recent Nonfiction Title: *Bibliography of Swiss Genealogies*, by Mario von Moos.

PILOT BOOKS, 103 Cooper St., Babylon NY 11702-2319. (516)422-2225. Fax: (516)422-2227. President: Sam Small. Estab. 1959. Publishes paperback originals. Averages 20-30 titles/year. Receives 100-200 submissions/year. 20% of books from first-time authors; 90% from unagented writers. Average print order for a first book is 3,000. Offers standard royalty contract based on wholesale or retail price. Offers $250 usual advance, but this varies, depending on author's reputation and nature of book. Publishes book an average of 8 months after acceptance. Reports in 1 month. *Writer's Market* recommends allowing 2 months for reply. Book catalog and guidelines for #10 SASE.

Nonfiction: Financial, business, travel, career, personal guides and training manuals. "Our training manuals are utilized by America's major corporations, as well as the government. Directories and books on travel and moneymaking opportunities. Wants clear, concise treatment of subject matter." Length: 8,000-30,000 words. Send outline. Reviews artwork/photos as part of ms package.

Recent Nonfiction Title: *The "I-See-It" Travel Game Book*, by Phil Philcox.

PINEAPPLE PRESS, INC., P.O. Box 16008, Southside Station, Sarasota FL 34239. (813)952-1085. Editor: June Cussen. Estab. 1982. Publishes hardcover and trade paperback originals. Averages 20 titles/year. Receives 1,500 submissions/year. 20% of books from first-time authors; 80% from unagented writers. Pays 6½-15% royalty on retail price. Seldom offers advance. Publishes book 1 year after acceptance. Accepts simultaneous submissions. Reports in 3 months. Book catalog for 9 × 12 SAE with $1.05 postage.

Nonfiction: Biography, how-to, reference, regional (Florida), nature. Subjects include animals, history, gardening, nature. "We will consider most nonfiction topics. We are seeking quality nonfiction on diverse topics for the library and book trade markets. Most, though not all, of our fiction and nonfiction deals with Florida." No pop psychology or autobiographies. Query or submit outline/brief synopsis and sample chapters with SASE.

Recent Nonfiction Title: *Search for the Great*.

Fiction: Literary, historical, mainstream, regional (Florida). No romance, science fiction, children's. Submit outline/brief synopsis and sample chapters.

Recent Fiction Title: *Death in Bloodhound Red*, by Virginia Lanier.

Tips: "If I were a writer trying to market a book today, I would learn everything I could about book publishing and book publicity and agree to actively participate in promoting my book. A query on a novel without a brief sample seems useless."

PIPPIN PRESS, 229 E. 85th St., P.O. Box 1347, Gracie Station, New York NY 10028. (212)288-4920. Fax: (212)563-5703. Publisher/President: Barbara Francis. Estab. 1987. Publishes hardcover originals. Publishes 4-6 titles/year. Receives 4,500 queries/year. 80% of queries from unagented writers. Pays royalty. Publishes book 18-24 months after acceptance. Reports in 3 weeks on queries. Query with SASE. Do *not* send mss. *Writer's Market* recommends allowing 2 months for reply. Book catalog for 6 × 9 SASE. Manuscript guidelines for #10 SASE.

Nonfiction: Children's books: biography, humor, picture books. Subjects include animals, history, language/literature, nature, science. General nonfiction for children ages 4-10. Query with SASE only. Reviews artwork/photos as part of ms package. Send photocopies.

Fiction: Adventure, fantasy, historical, humor, mystery, picture books, suspense. "We're looking for small chapter books with animal-fantasy themes, stories for 7-11 year olds, by people of many cultures." Wants humorous fiction for ages 7-11. Query with SASE only.

Recent Fiction Title: *The Spinner's Daughter*, by Amy Littlesugar, illustrated by Robert Quaekenbush.

Tips: "Read as many of the best children's books published in the last five years as you can. We are looking for multi-ethnic fiction and nonfiction for ages 7-10, as well as general fiction for this age group. I would pay particular attention to children's books favorably reviewed in *School Library Journal*, *The Booklist*, *The New York Times Book Review*, and *Publishers Weekly*."

‡PLANNERS PRESS, Imprint of American Planning Association, 1313 E. 60th St., Chicago IL 60637. Deputy Executive Director: Frank So. Publishes hardcover and trade paperback originals. Publishes 4-6 titles/year. Receives 20 queries and 6-8 mss/year. 50% of books from first-time authors; 100% from unagented writers. Pays 7½-12% royalty on retail price. Publishes book 1 year after acceptance of ms. Reports in 1 month on queries, 2 months on proposals and mss. Book catalog and ms guidelines free on request.

Nonfiction: Technical (specialty-public policy and city planning). Subjects include government/politics. "Our books have a narrow audience of city planners and often focus on the tools of city planning." Submit

2 sample chapters and table of contents. Reviews artwork/photos as part of ms package. Send photocopies.
Recent Nonfiction Title: *What Planners Do*, by Charles Hoch (essay).

‡PLANNING/COMMUNICATIONS, 7215 Oak Ave., River Forest IL 60305. (708)366-5200. President: Daniel Lauber. Publishes hardcover, trade and mass market paperback originals, trade paperback reprints. Publishes 3-8 titles/year. Receives 10 queries and 3 mss/year. 50% of books from first-time authors; 100% from unagented writers. Pays 15-20% royalty on wholesale price. Publishes book 6 months after acceptance of ms. Accepts simultaneous submissions. Reports in 2 months on queries, 3 months on proposals and mss. Book catalog for $1.95. Manuscript guidelines for #10 SASE.
Nonfiction: Self-help, careers. Subjects include business and economics (careers), education, government/politics, money/finance, sociology, software. Submit outline and 3 sample chapters with SASE. Reviews artwork/photos as part of ms package. Send photocopies.
Recent Nonfiction Title: *Professional's Private Sector Job Finder*, D. Lauber (trade).
Fiction: Mystery. Submit synopsis, 3 sample chapters and SASE.

PLAYERS PRESS, INC., P.O. Box 1132, Studio City CA 91614-0132. (818)789-4980. Vice President, Editorial: Robert W. Gordon. Estab. 1965. Publishes hardcover and trade paperback originals, and trade paperback reprints. Averages 25-35 titles/year. Receives 200-1,000 submissions/year. 10% of books from first-time authors; 80% from unagented writers. Pays royalty on wholesale price. Publishes book 20 months after acceptance. Reports on queries in 1 month, up to 1 year on mss. Book catalog and guidelines for 9×12 SAE with 4 first-class stamps.
Nonfiction: Juvenile and theatrical drama/entertainment industry. Subjects include the performing arts, costume, theater and film crafts. Needs quality plays and musicals, adult or juvenile. Query. Reviews artwork/photos as part of package.
Fiction: Subject matter of plays include adventure, confession, ethnic, experimental, fantasy, historical, horror, humor, mainstream, mystery, religious, romance, science fiction, suspense, western. Submit complete ms for theatrical plays only. "No novels or story books are accepted. We publish plays, musicals and books on theatre, film and television, only."
Tips: "Plays, entertainment industry texts, theater, film and television books have the only chances of selling to our firm."

‡PLAYGROUND BOOKS, P.O. Box 15039, Newark DE 19711. President: Ann B. Faccenda. Publishes hardcover, trade paperback and mass market paperback originals. Publishes 6-10 titles/year. 50% of books from first-time authors; 90% from unagented writers. Pays 5-15% royalty on retail price or invoice. Offers $0-500 advance. Publishes book 1 year after acceptance of ms. Accepts simultaneous submissions. Reports in 1 month. Book catalog for #10 SASE.
Nonfiction: Children's/juvenile, illustrated book. Query with SASE. Reviews artwork/photos as part of ms package. Send photocopies.
Fiction: Adventure, fantasy, historical, humor, juvenile, mystery, picture books, science fiction, short story collections, suspense, Western. Query with SASE.
Recent Fiction Title: *The Ghost of Brannock Hall*, by Ann Roede (paperback-historical fiction).
Poetry: Submit complete ms with SASE.

PLENUM PUBLISHING, 233 Spring St., New York NY 10013-1578. (212)620-8000. Senior Editor, Trade Books: Linda Greenspan Regan. Estab. 1946. Publishes hardcover originals. Averages 350 titles/year. Plenum Trade publishes 12. Receives 1,000 submissions/year. 25% of books from first-time authors; 20% from unagented writers. Publishes book 8-16 months after acceptance. Accepts simultaneous submissions. Query for electronic submissions. Reports in 6-8 months.
Nonfiction: Subjects include trade science, criminology, anthropology, sociology, psychology, health. "We are seeking high quality, popular books in the sciences and social sciences." Query only.
Tips: "Our audience consists of intelligent laymen and professionals. Authors should be experts on subject matter of book. They must compare their books with competitive works, explain how theirs differs, and define the market for their books."

PLEXUS PUBLISHING, INC., 143 Old Marlton Pike, Medford NJ 08055-8750. (609)654-6500. Fax: (609)654-4309. Editorial Director: Thomas Hogan. Estab. 1977. Publishes hardcover and paperback originals. Averages 4-5 titles/year. Receives 10-20 submissions/year. 70% of books from first-time authors; 90% from unagented writers. Pays 10-20% royalty on wholesale price; buys some booklets outright for $250-1,000. Offers $500-1,000 advance. Accepts simultaneous submissions/year. Reports in 3 months. Book catalog and guidelines for 10×13 SAE with 4 first-class stamps.
Nonfiction: Biography (of naturalists), reference. Subjects include plants, animals, nature, life sciences. "We will consider any book on a nature/biology subject, particularly those of a reference (permanent) nature that would be of lasting value to high school and college audiences, and/or the general reading public (ages 14 and up). Authors should have authentic qualifications in their subject area, but qualifications may be by experience as well as academic training." No gardening, philosophy or psychology; generally not interested

in travel but will consider travel that gives sound ecological information. Also interested in mss of about 20-40 pages in length for feature articles in *Biology Digest* (guidelines available with SASE). Query. Reviews artwork/photos as part of ms package.

Tips: "We will give serious consideration to well-written manuscripts that deal even indirectly with biology/ nature subjects. For example, *Exploring Underwater Photography* (a how-to for divers) and *The Literature of Nature* (an anthology of nature writings for college curriculum) were accepted for publication."

POCKET BOOKS, Division of Simon & Schuster, Dept. WM, 1230 Avenue of the Americas, New York NY 10020. Imprints include Pocket Star Books, Washington Square Press (high-quality mass market), Archway and Minstrel (juvenile/YA imprints), Folger Shakespeare Library, Star Trek. Publishes paperback originals and reprints, mass market and trade paperbacks and hardcovers. Averages 450 titles/year. Receives 5,000 submissions annually. 15% of books from first-time authors; 100% from agented writers. Pays royalty on retail price. Publishes book an average of 1 year after acceptance. *No unsolicited mss or queries.* "All submissions must go through a literary agent."

Nonfiction: History, biography, reference and general nonfiction, cookbooks, humor, calendars.

Fiction: Adult (mysteries, thriller, psychological suspense, Star Trek ® novels, romance, westerns).

POGO PRESS, INCORPORATED, 4 Cardinal Lane, St. Paul MN 55127-6406. Vice President: Leo J. Harris. Publishes trade paperback originals. Publishes 3 titles/year. Receives 20 queries and 20 mss/year. 100% of books from unagented writers. Pays royalty on wholesale price. Publishes book 6 months after acceptance. Query for electronic submissions. Reports in 2 months. Book catalog free on request.

● This publisher received a special award from the Minnesota Community of the Book, 1994 for Moira F. Harris' *Minnesota's Literary Visitors*.

Nonfiction: "We limit our publishing to Breweriana, history, art and popular culture. Our books are heavily illustrated." Query. Reviews artwork/photos as part of ms package. Send photocopies.

Recent Nonfiction Title: *North Star Statehouse*, by Thomas O'Sullivan.

POLYCHROME PUBLISHING CORPORATION, 4509 N. Francisco, Chicago IL 60625. (312)478-4455. Contact: Editorial Board. Publishes hardcover originals and reprints. Publishes 6 titles/year. Receives 500 queries and 1,250 mss/year. 50% of books from first-time authors; 100% from unagented writers. Pays royalty, "usually a combination of fee plus royalties." Advance "depends upon amount of editorial work necessary." Publishes book 1-2 years after acceptance of ms. Accepts simultaneous submissions. Query for electronic submissions. Reports in 6 months on mss. Book catalog and ms guidelines for #10 SASE.

Nonfiction: Children's/juvenile. Subjects emphasize ethnic, particularly multicultural/Asian American. Submit outline and 3 sample chapters. Reviews artwork/photos as part of ms package, but not necessary. Send photocopies.

Fiction: Multicultural, particularly Asian American. Ethnic, juvenile, picture books, young adult. "We do not publish fables, folktales, fairytales or anthropomorphic animal stories." Submit synopsis and 3 sample chapters; for picture books, submit whole ms.

Recent Fiction Title: *Stella: On The Edge of Popularity*, by Lauren Lee.

PRAKKEN PUBLICATIONS, INC., P.O. Box 8623, Ann Arbor MI 48107-8623. (313)769-1211. Fax: (313)769-8383. Publisher: George Kennedy. Managing Editor: Susanne Peckham. Estab. 1934. Publishes educational hardcover and paperback originals as well as educational magazines. Averages 4 book titles/ year. Receives 50 submissions/year. 20% of books from first-time authors; 95% from unagented writers. Pays 10% royalty on net sales of book (negotiable, with production costs). Publishes book 6 months after acceptance. Accepts simultaneous submissions. Reports in 2 months if reply requested and SASE furnished. *Writer's Market* recommends allowing 2 months for reply. Book catalog for #10 SASE.

Nonfiction: Industrial, vocational and technology education and related areas; general educational reference. "We are interested in manuscripts with broad appeal in any of the specific subject areas of industrial arts, vocational-technical education, and reference for the general education field." Submit outline and sample chapters. Reviews artwork/photos as part of ms package.

Recent Nonfiction Title: *High School to Employment Transition: Contemporary Issues.*

Tips: "We have a continuing interest in magazine and book manuscripts which reflect emerging issues and trends in education, especially vocational, industrial, and technical education."

PRECEPT PRESS, Subsidiary of Bonus Books, 160 E. Illinois St., Chicago IL 60611. (312)467-0424. Editor: Anne Barthel. Publishes hardcover and trade paperback originals. Publishes 20 titles/year. Receives 300 queries and 100 mss/year. 25% of books from first-time authors; 90% from unagented writers. Pays royalty. Publishes book 8 months after acceptance. Accepts simultaneous submissions if so noted. Query for electronic submissions. Reports in 3 months on proposals. Manuscript guidelines for #10 SASE.

Nonfiction: Reference, technical, textbook. Subjects include business and economics, health/medicine, science. Query with SASE.

‡PREP PUBLISHING, Subsidiary of PREP, Inc., 1110½ Hay St., Fayetteville NC 28305. (910)483-6611. Managing Editor: Anne McKinney. Imprints are Mysterious PREP (contact Anne McKinney); Religious/

spiritual PREP (contact Pat Mack); Young Adult (YA) PREP (contact Louise Jarvis); Nonfiction PREP (contact Anne McKinney). Publishes hardcover and trade paperback originals. Publishes 10 titles/year. Receives 500 queries/year. 50% of books from first-time authors; 90% from unagented writers. Pays 6-17% royalty on retail price. Publishes book 18 months after acceptance of ms. Accepts simultaneous submissions. Reports in 3 months on mss. Book catalog for $2. Manuscript guidelines free on request.

Nonfiction: Biography, children's/juvenile, how-to, humor, self-help, career advice. Subjects include Americana, business and economics, money/finance (self-help, how-to), philosophy, psychology, regional (especially the South), religion, women's issues/studies. Query with SASE. Reviews artwork/photos as part of ms package. Send photocopies.

Recent Nonfiction Title: *Résumés & Cover Letters for the 21st Century*, by Arthur Smith, edited by D.K. Doyle (self-help for people changing fields/jobs).

Fiction: Adventure, historical, horror, humor, juvenile, literary, mainstream/contemporary, mystery, religious, romance, science fiction, suspense, western, young adult. "We seek fiction for a wide general audience and fiction that encourages good values." Query with SASE.

Recent Fiction Title: *Second Time Around*, by Patty Sleem (spiritual fiction/religion).

Poetry: Submit complete ms.

Tips: Wide general audience of adults for most of our books (except YA books). "Rewrite and refine before submitting manuscript."

PRESIDIO PRESS, 505B San Marin Dr., Suite 300, Novato CA 94945-1340. (415)898-1081 ext. 125. Fax: (415)898-0383. Editor-in-Chief: Robert V. Kane. Estab. 1974. Imprint is Lyford Books. Publishes hardcover originals and reprints. Averages 24 titles/year. Receives 1,000 submissions/year. 35% of books from first-time authors; 65% from unagented writers. Pays 15-20% royalty on net receipts. Advance varies. Publishes book 12-18 months after acceptance. Reports within 1 month on queries. Book catalog and ms guidelines for 7½ × 10½ SAE with 4 first-class stamps.

Nonfiction: Subjects include military history and military affairs. Query. Reviews artwork/photos as part of ms package. Send photocopies.

Recent Nonfiction Title: *Firepower in Limited War*, by Robert H. Scales, Jr.

Fiction: Men's action-adventure, thriller, mystery, military, historical. Query.

Recent Fiction Title: *1901*, by Robert Conroy.

Tips: "Our audience consists of readers interested in military history and military affairs as well as general fiction. If I were a writer trying to market a book today, I would study the market. Find out what publishers are publishing, what they say they want and so forth. Then write what the market seems to be asking for, but with some unique angle that differentiates the work from others on the same subject. We feel that readers of hardcover fiction are looking for works of no less than 80,000 words."

PRICE STERN SLOAN, INC., Member of the Putnam & Berkley Group, New York, 11835 Olympic Blvd., 5th Floor, Los Angeles CA 90064-5006. Fax: (310)445-3933. Juvenile submissions to Assistant Editor: Michi Fujimoto. Adult trade/humor/calendars submissions to Editor: Bob Lovka. Estab. 1963. Imprint is Troubador Press. Publishes trade paperback originals. Averages 80 titles/year (90% children's). Receives 3,000 submissions/year. 20% of books from first-time authors; 20% from unagented writers. Pays royalty on wholesale price or makes outright purchase. Offers advance. Publishes book 1 year after acceptance. Reports in 3 months. Catalog for 9 × 12 SAE with 5 first-class stamps. Manuscript guidelines for SASE.

● Price Stern Sloan currently has smaller print runs and fewer titles per list.

Nonfiction: Subjects include humor, calendars and satire (limited). Juvenile fiction and nonfiction (all ages). Query *only*. Reviews artwork/photos as part of ms package. Do not send *original* artwork or ms. "Most of our titles are unique in concept as well as execution."

Tips: "We have been assigning a lot of work for hires for ongoing series. But writers must have a proven track record in those formats. As electronic technology flourishes, the lines between traditional publishing and new media blur. As our books tie in with movies, TV, toys, games, animated characters and more, I imagine our products will expand as the new media grows. We think it's fabulous."

PRIMA PUBLISHING, P.O. Box 1260, Rocklin CA 95677-1260. (916)768-0426. Publisher: Ben Dominitz, Lifestyles Division: Senior Acquisitions Editor, Jennifer Bayse-Sander. Computer Professional Reference Division: Senior Acquisitions Editor, Sherri Morningstar. Entertainment Division: Senior Acquisitions Editor, Hartley Lesser. Publishes hardcover originals and trade paperback originals and reprints. Publishes 300 titles/ year. Receives 750 queries/year. 10% of books from first-time authors; 30% from unagented writers. Pays 15-20% royalty on wholesale price. Advance varies. Publishes book 12 months after acceptance. Accepts simultaneous submissions. Query for electronic submissions. Reports in 3 months. Catalog for 9 × 12 SAE with 8 first-class stamps. Writer's guidelines for #10 SASE.

Nonfiction: Biography, cookbook, how-to, self-help, travel. Subjects include business and economics, cooking/foods, health, music, politics, psychology. "We want books with originality, written by highly qualified individuals. No fiction at this time." Query with SASE.

Recent Nonfiction Title: *Gooey Desserts*, by Elaine Corn (cookbook).

Tips: "Prima strives to reach the primary and secondary markets for each of its books. We are known for promoting our books aggressively. Books that genuinely solve problems for people will always do well if properly promoted. Try to picture the intended audience while writing the book. Too many books are written to an audience that doesn't exist."

PROFESSIONAL PUBLICATIONS, INC., 1250 Fifth Ave., Belmont CA 94002-3863. (415)593-9119. Fax: (415)592-4519. Acquisitions Editors: Gerald Galbo, Mary Fiala. Estab. 1975. Publishes hardcover and paperback originals. Averages 12 titles/year. Receives 100-200 submissions/year. Publishes book 6-18 months after acceptance. Accepts simultaneous submissions. Query for electronic submissions. Reports in 2 weeks on queries. *Writer's Market* recommends allowing 2 months for reply. Book catalog and ms guidelines free.
 • Professional Publications wants only professionals practicing in the field to submit material.

Nonfiction: Reference, technical, textbook. Subjects include mathematics, engineering, architecture, interior design, contracting and building. Especially needs "review books for all professional licensing examinations." Query or submit outline and sample chapters. Reviews artwork/photos as part of ms package.

Tips: "We specialize in books for working professionals: engineers, architects, contractors, interior designing, etc. The more technically complex the manuscript is the happier we are. We love equations, tables of data, complex illustrations, mathematics, etc. In technical/professional book publishing, it isn't always obvious to us if a market exists. We can judge the quality of a manuscript, but the author should make some effort to convince us that a market exists. Facts, figures, and estimates about the market—and marketing ideas from the author—will help sell us on the work. Besides our interest in highly technical materials, we will be trying to broaden our range of titles in each discipline. Specifically, we will be looking for career guides for interior designers and architects, as well as for engineers."

PROFESSIONAL RESOURCE PRESS, Imprint of Professional Resource Exchange, Inc., 2033 Wood St., Suite 215, Sarasota FL 34237. (813)366-7913. Managing Editor: Debra Fink. Publishes trade paperback originals. Publishes 15 titles/year. Receives 100 queries and 80 mss/year. 50% of books from first-time authors; 100% from unagented writers. Pays 6-10% royalty on wholesale price. Publishes book 1 year after acceptance of ms. No simultaneous submissions. Query for electronic submissions. Reports in 6 months. Book catalog and ms guidelines free on request.

Nonfiction: Reference, textbook; books for mental health professionals. "Authors must be mental health professionals and works must be highly applied and focused." Submit outline and 2-4 sample chapters.

Recent Nonfiction Title: *Writing Psychological Reports: A Guide for Clinicians*, by Greg J. Wolber and William F. Carne.

‡PROMPT PUBLICATIONS, Imprint of Howard W. Sams & Co., 2647 Waterfront Parkway E. Dr., Suite 300, Indianapolis IN 46214-2041. Contact: Acquisitions Department. Publishes trade paperback originals and reprints. Publishes 20 titles/year. Receives 30-40 queries and 25 mss/year. 60% of books from first-time authors; 90% from unagented writers. Pays negotiable royalty on wholesale price. Publishes book 1 year after acceptance of ms. Reports in 1 month on queries, 2 months on proposals, 4 months or more on mss. Book catalog free on request.

Nonfiction: How-to, reference, technical. Subjects include audio/visual, computers and electronics, electronics repair, science (electricity). "Books should be written for beginners *and* experts, hobbyists *and* professionals. Books on home electronics (stereos, etc.,) are a plus." Query with proposal package, including author bio, outline, 3 sample chapters and SASE. Reviews artwork/photos as part of ms package. Send photocopies or sketches ("we have technicians to produce illustrations if necessary").

Tips: Audience is electronics/technical hobbyists, professionals needing reference books, and technical schools. "Please keep in mind that most technical books have a short shelf life, and write accordingly. Remember, also, that it takes a while for a book to be published, so keep notes on updating some of your material when the book is ready to go to print. *When submitting:* Above all, *Be patient*. It can take up to a year for a publisher to decide whether or not to publish your book."

PRUETT PUBLISHING, 2928 Pearl St., Boulder CO 80301. (303)449-4919. Publisher: Jim Pruett. Editor: Mary Kay Scott. Estab. 1959. Publishes hardcover paperback and trade paperback originals and reprints. Averages 10-15 titles/year. 60% of books are from first-time authors; 100% from unagented writers. Pays 10-12% royalty on net income. Publishes book 18 months after acceptance. Accepts simultaneous submissions. Reports in 2 months on queries. Book catalog and ms guidelines free.
 • Pruett Publishing is no longer seeking coffee table books, child guidance/parenting books or railroad histories.

Nonfiction: Regional history, guidebooks, nature, biography. Subjects include Americana (Western), archaeology (Native American), history (Western), nature/environment, recreation (outdoor), regional/ethnic cooking/foods (Native American, Mexican, Spanish), regional travel, regional sports (cycling, hiking, fishing). "We are looking for nonfiction manuscripts and guides that focus on the Rocky Mountain West." Reviews artwork/photos and formal proposal as part of ms package.

Tips: "There has been a movement away from large publisher's mass market books and towards small publisher's regional interest books, and in turn distributors and retail outlets are more interested in small publishers. Author's don't need to have a big-name to have a good publisher. Look for similar books that you feel are well produced—consider design, editing, overall quality and contact those publishers. Get to know several publishers, and find the one that feels right—trust your instincts."

PSI RESEARCH, 300 N. Valley Dr., Grants Pass OR 97526. (503)479-9464. Fax: (503)476-1479. Contact: Acquisitions Editor. Estab. 1975. Imprint is Oasis Press. Publishes hardcover, trade paperback and binder originals. Publishes 20-30 books/year. Receives 90 submissions/year. 60% of books from first-time authors; 90% from unagented writers. Pays royalty. Publishes ms an average of 6-12 months after acceptance. Accepts simultaneous submissions. Reports in 2 months (initial feedback) on queries. Book catalog and ms guidelines free.
Nonfiction: How-to, reference, textbook. Subjects include business and economics, computers, education, money/finance, retirement, exporting, franchise, finance, marketing and public relations, relocations, environment, taxes, business start up and operation. Needs information-heavy, readable mss written by professionals in their subject fields. Interactive where appropriate. Authorship credentials less important than hands-on experience qualifications. Must relate to either small business or to individuals who are entrepreneurs, owners or managers of small business (1-300 employees). Query for unwritten material or to check current interest in topic and orientation. Submit outline/synopsis and sample chapters. Reviews artwork/photos as part of freelance ms package.
Recent Nonfiction Title: *Power Marketing*, by Jody Hornor.
Tips: "Best chance is with practical, step-by-step manuals for operating a business, with worksheets, check-lists. The audience is made up of entrepreneurs of all types: small businesses and those who would like to be; attorneys, accountants and consultants who work with small businesses; college students; dreamers. Make sure your information is valid and timely for its audience, also that by virtue of either its content quality or viewpoint, it distinguishes itself from other books on the market."

PUBLISHERS ASSOCIATES, P.O. Box 140361, Las Colinas TX 75014-0361. (214)686-5332. Senior Editor: Belinda Buxjom. Manuscript Coordinator: Mary Markal. Estab. 1974. Imprints are Hercules Press, The Liberal Press, Liberal Arts Press, Minuteman Press, Monument Press, Nichole Graphics, Scholars Books, Tagelwüld. Publishes trade paperback originals. Receives 1,500 submissions/year. 60% of books from first-time authors; 100% from unagented writers. Pays 4% and up royalty on retail price. Publishes book 4 months after acceptance. Reports in up to 4 months. Book catalog for 6×9 SAE with 4 first-class stamps. Manuscript guidelines for #10 SAE with 2 first-class stamps.
Nonfiction: Textbook (scholarly). Subjects include gay/lesbian, government politics (liberal), history, religion (liberation/liberal), women's issues/studies. "We are looking for gay/lesbian history, pro-choice/feminist studies and liberal politics. Quality researched gay/lesbian history will have beginning royalty of 7% and up. Academics are encouraged to submit. No biographies, evangelical fundamentalism/bible, conservative politics, New Age studies or homophobic. No fiction or poetry." Query. Reviews artwork/photos as part of ms package.
Tips: "Writers have the best chance with gender-free/nonsexist, liberal academic studies. We sell primarily to libraries and to scholars. Our audience is highly educated, politically and socially liberal, if religious they are liberational. If I were a writer trying to market a book today, I would compare my manuscript with books already published by the press I am seeking to submit to."

PURDUE UNIVERSITY PRESS, 1532 South Campus Courts, Bldg. E, West Lafayette IN 47907-1532. (317)494-2038. Director: David Sanders. Managing Editor: Margaret Hunt. Estab. 1960. Publishes hardcover and trade paperback originals and trade paperback reprints. Averages 12 titles/year. Receives 600 submissions/year. Royalties vary. No advance. Publishes book 15 months after acceptance. Reports in 2 months. Book catalog and ms guidelines for 9×12 SASE.
• This publisher has received Chicago Book Clinic design awards, the Association of American University Presses design award and the Chicago Women in Publishing design award.
Nonfiction: Biography, scholarly, regional. Subjects include Americana (especially Indiana), scholarly studies in history, philosophy, politics, sociology, biology, literary criticism, horticulture, history of technology. "The writer must present good credentials, demonstrate good writing skills, and above all explain how his/ her work will make a significant contribution to scholarship/regional studies. Our purpose is to publish scholarly and regional books. We are looking for manuscripts on these subjects: Balkan and Danubian studies, interdisciplinary, regional (Midwest) interest, horticulture, history, literature, history of philosophy, criticism, and effects of science and technology on society. No nonbooks, textbooks, theses/dissertations, manuals/ pamphlets, fiction, or books on how-to, fitness/exercise or fads. Submit prospectus."
Recent Nonfiction Title: *The Vienna Coffeehouse Wits, 1890-1938*, by Harold B. Segel.
Poetry: One poetry book a year selected by competition. Send SASE for guidelines.

THE PUTNAM BERKLEY GROUP, 200 Madison Ave., New York NY 10016. Divisions and imprints include the Berkley Publishing Group (including Ace Science Fiction & Fantasy), G.P. Putnam's Sons, Perigee

Books, Grosset & Dunlap, Philomel Books and Price Stern Sloan. Putnam did not respond to our request for information. Query before submitting.

‡QED PRESS, Subsidiary of Comp-Type, Inc., 155 Cypress St., Fort Bragg CA 95437. (707)964-9520. Senior Editor: John Fremont. Publishes hardcover and trade paperback originals. Publishes 10 titles/year. Receives 3,000 queries and 2,000 mss/year. 75% of books from first-time authors; 75% from unagented writers. Pays 7-15% royalty on retail price. Publishes book 16 months after acceptance of ms. Accepts simultaneous submissions. Reports in 1 month on queries, 3 months on mss. Book catalog for 9×12 SAE with 2 first-class stamps. Manuscript guidelines for #10 SASE.
Nonfiction: Biography, how-to, self-help. Subjects include business and economics, health/medicine, history, language/literature, psychology, translation. "We seek books on the aging process and health, coping with aging, careers for older people, investments, etc. No juvenile, illustrated, photography or travel or cookbooks." Query with outline, 3 sample chapters and SASE. Reviews artwork/photos as part of ms package. Send photocopies.
Recent Nonfiction Title: *Listening With Different Ears: Counseling People Over 60*, by James Warnick (counseling seniors).
Fiction: Ethnic, literary, mystery, suspense. "Our thrust will be the acquisition of translated fiction by contemporary European, African and South American authors." Query with synopsis, 3 sample chapters and SASE.
Recent Fiction Title: *Tales From the Mountain*, by Miguel Torga, tr. by Ivana Carlsen (short stories [Portugese]).
Poetry: "We have minimal needs for poetry. No traditional, religious, rhymed, or derivative poetry." Query with sample poems.
Recent Poetry Title: *Mendocino Portfolio*, by Cynthia Frank & Hannes Krebs (lyric).
Tips: "Our audience is older, literary, literate, involved and politically aware. Study the market, and think before you send."

‡QUEST BOOKS, Theosophical Publishing House, P.O. Box 270, Wheaton IL 60189. (708)665-0130. Executive Editor: Brenda Rosen. Publishes hardcover originals and trade paperback originals and reprints. Publishes 12-15 titles/year. Receives 400 queries and 150 mss/year. 25% of books from first-time authors; 50% from unagented writers. Pays 10% royalty on net minimum or 12% royalty on gross maximum. Offers $2,000-10,000 advance. Publishes book 20 months after acceptance of ms. Accepts simultaneous submissions. Reports in 1 month on queries and proposals, 3 months on mss. Book catalog and ms guidelines free on request.
Nonfiction: Biography, self-help, spiritual/metaphysical. Subjects include anthropology/archaeology, art/architecture, health/medicine, psychology, religion, science. Query.
Recent Nonfiction Title: *Tying Rocks to Clouds*, by Bill Elliott (interviews).

‡QUILL DRIVER BOOKS/WORD DANCER PRESS, 950 N. Van Ness, Fresno CA 93728. (209)497-0809. Publisher: Stephen Blake Mettee. Imprints are Quill Driver Books, Word Dancer Press. Publishes hardcover and trade paperback originals and reprints. Publishes 10-12 titles/year. (Quill Driver Books: 4/year, Word Dancer Press: 6-8/year). 20% of books from first-time authors; 95% from unagented writers. Pays 6-10% royalty on retail price. Offers $500-10,000 advance. Publishes book 9 months after acceptance of ms. Accepts simultaneous submissions. Reports in 1 month on queries and proposals, 3 months on mss. Book catalog and ms guidelines for #10 SASE.
Nonfiction: Biography, how-to, reference, general nonfiction. Subjects include Americana, regional, fundraising, writing. "We are interested in any well-written, well-researched nonfiction book with a large identifiable market." Query with proposal package. Reviews artwork/photos as part of ms package. Send photocopies.
Recent Nonfiction Title: *Black Bart: Boulevardier Bandit*, by George Hoeper (Western Americana).

RAGGED MOUNTAIN PRESS, Imprint of International Marine/The McGraw-Hill Companies, P.O. Box 220, Camden ME 04843-0220. (207)236-4837. Fax: (207)236-6314. Acquisitions Editor: John J. Kettlewell. Editorial Director: Jonathan Eaton. Estab. 1969. Publishes hardcover and trade paperback originals and reprints. Publishes 40 titles/year; imprint publishes 12, remainder are International Marine. Receives 200 queries and 100 mss/year. 30% of books from first-time authors; 90% from unagented writers. Pays 10-15% royalty on wholesale price. Offers advance. Publishes book 1 year after acceptance of ms. Accepts simultaneous submissions. Query for electronic submissions. Reports in 1 month on queries. *Writer's Market* recommends allowing 2 months for reply. Book catalog for 9×12 SAE with 10 first-class stamps. Manuscript guidelines for #10 SASE.
Nonfiction: Outdoor-related how-to, humor, essays. Subjects include outdoor cooking, fishing, camping, climbing and kayaking. "Ragged Mountain publishes nonconsumptive outdoor and environmental issues books of literary merit or unique appeal. Be familiar with the existing literature. Find a subject that hasn't been done, or has been done poorly, then explore it in detail and from all angles." Query with outline and 3 sample chapters. Reviews artwork/photos as part of ms package. Send photocopies.

Recent Nonfiction Title: *The Essential Outdoor Gear Manual*, by Annie Getchell.

RAINBOW PUBLISHERS, P.O. Box 2789, La Jolla CA 92038. (619)578-4700. Managing Editor: Carol Rogers. Publishes 8-12 titles/year. Receives 100 queries and 50 mss/year. 50% of books from first-time authors. Makes outright purchase of $500 maximum. Publishes book 12-18 months after acceptance of ms. Accepts simultaneous submissions. Query for electronic submissions. Reports in 3 months on queries and proposals, 3-6 months on mss. Book catalog for 9×12 SAE with 2 first-class stamps. Manuscript guidelines for #10 SASE.
Nonfiction: How-to, textbook. Subjects include religion and reproducible activity books for Sunday school teachers. "We publish 64-page reproducible activity books for teachers to use in teaching the Bible to children ages 2-12." Query with outline, sample pages, age level, introduction. "We do use freelance artists. Send a query and photocopies of art samples."
Recent Nonfiction Title: *52 Ways to Teach Children to Share the Gospel*, by Barbara Hibschman.

RANDOM HOUSE, INC., Subsidary of Advance Publications, 201 E. 50th St., 11th Floor, New York NY 10022. (212)751-2600. Random House Trade Division publishes 120 titles/year. Receives 3,000 submissions/year. Imprints include Random House, Alfred A. Knopf, Ballantine, Crown, Del Rey, Fawcett, Harmony, Modern Library, Pantheon, Clarkson N. Potter, Villard, and Vintage. Pays royalty on retail price. Accepts simultaneous submissions. Reports in 2 months. Free book catalog. Manuscript guidelines for #10 SASE.
Nonfiction: Biography, cookbook, humor, illustrated book, self-help. Subjects include Americana, art, business and economics, classics, cooking and foods, health, history, music, nature, politics, psychology, religion, sociology and sports. No juveniles or textbooks (separate division). Query with outline and at least 3 sample chapters.
Fiction: Adventure, confession, experimental, fantasy, historical, horror, humor, mainstream, mystery, and suspense. Submit outline/synopsis and at least 3 sample chapters.
Tips: Enclose SASE for reply or return of materials.

‡RANDOM HOUSE, INC. JUVENILE BOOKS, 201 E. 50th St., New York NY 10022. (212)572-2600. Subsidiaries include Random House Children's Books, Bullseye Books and Sprinter paperbacks, Crown and Knopf Children's Books, Apple Soup Books (an imprint of Alfred A. Knopf), and Dragonfly paperbacks. Juvenile Division: Random House/Bullseye: Kate Klimo, publishing director. Crown/Knopf: Simon Boughton, publishing director; Arthur Levine, editor-in-chief. Apple Soup Books: Anne Schwartz, publisher. Managing Editor (all imprints): Amy Nathanson. Publishes hardcover, trade paperback and mass market paperback originals, and mass market paperback reprints. Publishes 300 titles/year. *Unsolicited material no longer accepted by any imprint.*
Nonfiction: Biography, humor, illustrated books, juvenile. Subjects include animals, nature/environment, recreation, science, sports.
Fiction: Adventure, confession (young adult), fantasy, historical, horror, humor, juvenile, mystery, picture books, science fiction (juvenile/young adult), suspense, young adult.

‡RAWHIDE WESTERN PUBLISHING, P.O. Box 327, Safford AZ 85548. (520)428-5956. Publisher/Senior Editor: Tim R. Walters. Publishes hardcover originals, trade paperback originals and reprints. Publishes 4-6 titles/year. 50% of books from first-time authors; 100% from unagented writers. Pays 10-15% royalty on wholesale price. Publishes book 6 months after acceptance of ms. Accepts simultaneous submissions. Reports in 1 month on queries and mss. Book catalog and ms guidelines for #10 SASE.
Nonfiction: Grassroots informational. Subjects include Americana, government/politics, history, nature/environment, religion, sociology, constitutional rights/issues. "Books 50,000-80,000 words only." Query with 3 sample chapters and SASE. Reviews artwork/photos as part of ms package. Send photocopies.
Recent Nonfiction Title: *Surviving the Second Civil War: The Land Rights Battle . . . and How to Win It*, by Timothy Robert Walters.
Tips: "Don't hesitate to query about 'politically incorrect' material and ideas—intelligent, sound presentation valued over radical."

REFERENCE SERVICE PRESS, 1100 Industrial Rd., Suite 9, San Carlos CA 94070-4131. (415)594-0743. Fax: (415)594-0411. E-mail: rspstaff@aol.com. Acquisitions Editor: Stuart Hauser. Estab. 1977. Publishes hardcover originals. Publishes 5-10 titles/year. 100% of books from unagented writers. Pays 10% or higher royalty. Publishes book an average of 3-6 months after acceptance. Accepts simultaneous submissions. Query for electronic submissions. Reports in 2 months. Book catalog for #10 SASE.
● This publisher maintains databases on America Online and eWorld.
Nonfiction: Reference. Subjects include education, ethnic, military/war, women's issues/studies, disabled. "We are interested only in directories and monographs dealing with financial aid." Submit outline and sample chapters.
Tips: "Our audience consists of librarians, counselors, researchers, students, reentry women, scholars and other fundseekers."

REGNERY PUBLISHING, INC., 422 First St. SE, Suite 300, Washington DC 20003. Publisher: Alfred S. Regnery; Executive Editor: Richard Vigilante; Managing Editor: Jamila S. Abdelghani. Direct submissions to Managing Editor. Estab. 1947. Imprints are Gateway Editions and Tumbleweed Press. Publishes hardcover originals and paperback originals and reprints. Averages 30 titles/year. Pays 8-15% royalty on retail price. Offers $0-50,000 advance. Publishes book 9-12 months after acceptance of ms. Accepts simultaneous submissions. Reports in 4-6 months on proposals. Book catalog and ms guidelines free on request.
Nonfiction: Biography, business and economics, education, government/politics, health/medicine, history, military/war, nature/environment, philosophy, religion, science, sociology. Query with outline and 2-3 sample chapters. Reviews artwork/photos as part of ms package. Send photocopies.
Recent Nonfiction Title: *The Tragedy of American Compassion*, by Marvin Olasky.

‡RELIGIOUS EDUCATION PRESS, 5316 Meadow Brook Rd., Birmingham AL 35242-3315. (205)991-1000. Fax: (205)991-9669. Contact: Dr. Nancy J. Vickers. Estab. 1974. Publishes trade paperback and hardback originals. Averages 5 titles/year. Receives 280 submissions/year. 40% of books from first-time authors; 100% of books from unagented writers. Pays 10% royalty on retail price. No advance. Query for electronic submissions. Reports in 2 months. Book catalog free.
Nonfiction: Technical and textbook. Scholarly subjects in religion and religious education. "We publish serious, significant and scholarly books on religious education and pastoral ministry." Query with outline, 1 sample chapter and SASE. Reviews artwork/photos as part of ms package.
Recent Nonfiction Title: *Models of Confirmation and Baptismal Affirmation*, by Robert L. Browning and Roy A. Reed (religious education).
Tips: "Our books are written for an ecumenical audience, for pastors, religious educators, and persons interested in the field of religious education, on a serious, scholarly level."

RENAISSANCE HOUSE PUBLISHERS, Subsidiary of Jende-Hagan, Inc., 541 Oak St., P.O. Box 177, Frederick CO 80530-0177. (303)833-2030. Fax: (303)833-2030. Editor: Eleanor Ayer. Publishes an ongoing series of 48-page guidebooks of travel-related interest. Averages 8 titles/year. Receives 125 submissions/year. 60% of books from first-time authors; 75% of books from unagented writers. Pays 8-10% royalty on net receipts. Offers 10% average advance on anticipated first printing royalties. May consider work for hire by experts in specific fields of interest. Publishes book 18 months after acceptance. Query for electronic submissions. Reports in 1 month on queries. *Writer's Market* recommends allowing 2 months for reply.
Nonfiction: Regional guidebooks. No fiction, personal reminiscences, general traditional philosophy, books on topics totally unrelated to subject areas specified above. "Please—no inquiries outside the topic of regional guidebooks! We publish to a very specific formula." *Writer's Market* recommends query with SASE first.
Tips: "We rely exclusively on in-house generation of book concepts and then find authors who will write for hire to our specifications. We are continually adding to our American Traveler Guidebooks series."

REPUBLIC OF TEXAS PRESS, Imprint of Wordware Publishing, Inc., 1506 Capitol Ave., Plano TX 75074. (214)423-0090. Editor: Mary Goldman. Publishes trade and mass market paperback originals. Publishes 25-30 titles/year. Receives 400 queries and 300 mss/year. 80% of books from unagented writers. Pays 8-12% royalty on wholesale price. Publishes book 6-9 months after acceptance of ms. Reports in 1 month. Book catalog and ms guidelines for SASE.
Nonfiction: History (Old West and Southwest), general interest. Subjects include animals, cooking, government/politics, recreation and biography. Submit table of contents, 2 sample chapters, target audience and any competing books.
Recent Nonfiction Title: *Tragedy at Taos*, by James Crutchfield (historical nonfiction).

RESURRECTION PRESS, LTD., P.O. Box 248, Williston Park NY 11596. (516)742-5686. Fax: (516)746-6872. Publisher: Emilie Cerar. Imprint is Spirit Life Series. Publishes trade paperback originals and reprints. Publishes 10-12 titles/year; imprint publishes 6 titles/year. Receives 100 queries and 80 mss/year. 50% of books from first-time authors; 100% from unagented writers. Pays 5-10% royalty on retail price. Offers $250-2,000 advance. Publishes book 1 year after acceptance of ms. Accepts simultaneous submissions. Query for electronic submissions. Reports in 1 month on queries and proposals, 2 months on mss. Book catalog and ms guidelines free on request.
Nonfiction: Self-help. Religious subjects. Wants mss of no more than 200 double-spaced typewritten pages. Query with outline and 2 sample chapters. Reviews artwork/photos as part of ms package. Send photocopies.

FLEMING H. REVELL PUBLISHING, Subsidiary of Baker Book House, P.O. Box 6287, Grand Rapids MI 49516. Editorial Director: William J. Petersen. Imprint is Spire Books. Publishes hardcover, trade paperback and mass market paperback originals and reprints. Publishes 50 titles/year; imprint publishes 10 titles/year. Receives 750 queries and 1,000 mss/year. 10% of books from first-time authors; 75% from unagented writers. Pays royalty on wholesale price. Publishes book 1 year after acceptance of ms. Accepts simultaneous submissions. Query for electronic submissions. Reports in 2 months. Manuscript guidelines for #10 SASE.
Nonfiction: Biography, coffee table book, how-to, self-help. Subjects include child guidance/parenting, religion. Query with outline and 2 sample chapters.

Recent Nonfiction Title: *The Dual-Earner Marriage,* by Jack and Judith Balswick (family).
Fiction: Religious. Submit synopsis and 2 sample chapters.
Recent Fiction Title: *A Time to Laugh,* by Gilbert Morris (historical fiction).

RISING TIDE PRESS, 5 Kivy St., Huntington Station NY 11746-2020. (516)427-1289. Editor/Publisher: Lee Boojamra. Senior Editor: Alice Frier. Estab. 1991. Publishes trade paperback originals. Publishes 10-20 titles/year. Receives 500 queries and 150 mss/year. 75% of books from first-time authors; 100% from unagented writers. Pays 10-15% royalty on wholesale price. Publishes book 12-15 months after acceptance. Query for electronic submissions: prefers any major IBM compatible WP program on 5¼" or 3½" disk. Reports in 1 week on queries, 1 months on proposals, 2 months on mss. Book catalog for $1. Writer's guidelines for #10 SASE.
Nonfiction: Lesbian nonfiction. Query with outline, entire ms and *large* SASE. Reviews artwork/photos as part of ms package. Send photocopies.
Fiction: "Lesbian fiction only." Adventure, erotica, fantasy, historical, horror, humor, literary, mainstream/contemporary, mystery, occult, romance, science fiction, suspense, mixed genres. "Major characters must be lesbian. Primary plot must have lesbian focus and sensibility." Query with synopsis or entire ms and SASE.
Tips: "Our books are for, by and about lesbian lives. We welcome unpublished authors. We do *not* consider agented authors. Any material submitted should be proofed."

ROCKY TOP PUBLICATIONS, P.O. Box 5256, Albany NY 12205. President/Publisher: Joseph D. Jennings. Contact: Emerson Bach. Estab. 1982. Publishes hardcover and paperback originals. Averages 4-6 titles/year. 70% of books from first-time authors; 95% from unagented writers. Pays 4-10% royalty (may vary) on wholesale price. Publishes book 6 months after acceptance. Reports in up to 6 months.
Nonfiction: How-to, reference, self-help, technical. Subjects include animal health, health, hobbies (crafts), medical, nature, philosophy (Thoreau or environmental only), science. No autobiographies, biographies, business 'get rich quick' or fad books. Query. No unsolicited mss.

THE ROSEN PUBLISHING GROUP, 29 E. 21st St., New York NY 10010. (212)777-3017. Editor: Gina Strazzabosco. Publishes hardcover and trade paperback originals. Publishes 100 titles/year. Receives 150 queries and 75 mss/year. 10% of books from first-time authors; 95% from unagented writers. Pays 6-10% royalty on retail price or makes outright purchase of $300-1,000. Offers $500-1,000 advance. Publishes books 9 months after acceptance of ms. Reports in 2 months on proposals. Book catalog and ms guidelines free on request.
Nonfiction: Juvenile, self-help. Submit outline and 1 sample chapter.
  • The Rosen Publishing Group publishes young adult titles for sale to schools and libraries. Each book is aimed at teenage readers and addresses them directly. Books should be written to 4.0-9.0 grade reading level. Areas of particular interest include multicultural ethnographic studies, careers, coping with social and personal problems, values and ethical behavior, drug abuse prevention, self-esteem and social activism.
Recent Nonfiction Title: *Coping as a Survivor of Violent Crime,* by Barbara Mor.
Tips: "The writer has the best chance of selling our firm a book on vocational guidance or personal social adjustment, or high-interest, low reading level material for teens."

‡ROUTLEDGE, INC., Subsidiary of International Thompson Publishing, 29 W. 35th St., New York NY 10001-2299. (212)244-3336. Editorial Director (New York): William P. Germano. Imprint is Theatre Arts Books. Routledge list includes humanities, social sciences, business and economics, reference. Monographs, reference works, hardback and paperback upper-level texts, academic general interest. Averages 100 titles/year in New York. 10% of books from first-time authors; 95% of books from unagented writers. Pays royalty. Publishes book 1 year after acceptance. Accepts simultaneous submissions. Reports in 3 months on queries. Query with proposal package, including TOC, intro, sample chapter, overall prospectus, cv and SASE.
Nonfiction: Academic subjects include philosophy, literary criticism, psychoanalysis, social sciences, business and economics, history, psychology, women's studies, lesbian and gay studies, race and ethnicity, political science, anthropology, geography development, education, reference.
Recent Nonfiction Title: *Unequal Sisters,* by Vicki L. Ruiz and Ellen Carol DuBois, eds. (women's studies/race and ethnicity).

Market conditions are constantly changing! If this is 1997 or later, buy the newest edition of Writer's Market *at your favorite bookstore or order directly from* Writer's Digest Books.

Tips: "Audience is professors, graduates and undergratuate students and trade."

ROXBURY PUBLISHING CO., P.O. Box 491044, Los Angeles CA 90049. (213)653-1068. Executive Editor: Claude Teweles. Publishes hardcover and paperback originals and reprints. Averages 10 titles/year. Pays royalty. Accepts simultaneous submissions. Reports in 2 months.
Nonfiction: College-level textbooks only. Subjects include business and economics, humanities, speech, English, developmental studies, social sciences, sociology. Query, submit outline/synopsis and sample chapters, or submit complete ms.

‡ROYAL FIREWORKS PRESS, 1 First Ave., Unionville NY 10988. (914)726-3333. Editor: Charles Morgan. Publishes hardcover originals and reprints and trade paperback originals. Publishes 125 titles/year. 75% of books from first-time authors; 90% from unagented writers. Pays royalty. Publishes book 6 months after acceptance of ms. Reports in 3 months on mss. Book catalog for SAE with 4 first-class stamps. Manuscript guidelines for #10 SASE.
Nonfiction: Biography, children's/juvenile, how-to, humor, illustrated book, self-help, technical, textbook. Subjects include Americana, business and economics, child guidance/parenting, computers and electronics, education, ethnic, history, language/literature, software, women's issues/studies. Submit proposal package, including entire ms with SASE. Reviews artwork/photos as part of ms package. Send photocopies.
Recent Nonfiction Title: *African-American Experience*, by R. Beck (educational).
Fiction: Ethnic, juvenile, mystery, science fiction. "Most of our concentration will be on novels for middle school and young adult readers." Submit entire ms with SASE.
Recent Fiction Title: *Overmind*, by William Coffin (sci-fi).
Recent Poetry Title: *The Poetry Pad*, by Sue Thomas.

RUNNING PRESS, 125 South 22nd St., Philadelphia PA 19103. Publisher: Nancy Steele. Editor: Virginia Mattingly. General interest nonfiction publisher.
Recent Nonfiction Title: *Sisters*, by Sharon Wohlmuth and Carol Saline.

‡RUSSIAN INFORMATION SERVICES, 89 Main St., Suite 2, Montpelier VT 05602. (802)223-4955. Vice President: Stephanie Ratmeyer. Publishes trade paperback originals and reprints. Publishes 5-10 titles/year. Receives 5-10 queries and 5 mss/year. 50% of books from first-time authors; 100% from unagented writers. Pays 8-12% royalty on retail price. Publishes book 6-8 months after acceptance of ms. Accepts simultaneous submissions. Reports in 2 months on mss. Book catalog free on request.
Nonfiction: Reference, travel, business. Subjects include business and economics, language/literature, travel. "Our editorial focus is on (1) Russia and the NIS, and (2) newly emerging economies, ripe for foreign investment (China, Latin America, SE Asia). We currently are seeking authors for these latter regions." Submit proposal package, including ms, summary and cv. Reviews artwork/photos as part of ms package. Send photocopies.
Recent Nonfiction Title: *Russia Survival Guide: Business & Travel*, by Richardson (travel/business).
Tips: Audience is business people and independent travelers to Russia, NIS, China, SE Asia, L. America.

RUTGERS UNIVERSITY PRESS, 109 Church St., New Brunswick NJ 08901. (908)932-7762. Editor-in-Chief: Leslie Mitchner. Publishes hardcover and trade paperback originals and trade paperback reprints. Publishes 70 titles/year. Receives up to 1,500 queries and up to 300 books/year. Up to 30% of books from first-time authors; 70% from unagented writers. Pays 7½-15% royalty on retail price. Offers $1,000-10,000 advance. Publishes book 1 year after acceptance of ms. Accepts simultaneous submissions if so noted. Query for electronic submissions. Reports in 1 month on proposals. Book catalog free on request.
Nonfiction: Biography, textbook and books for use in undergraduate courses. Subjects include Americana, anthropology, Black studies, education, gay/lesbian, government/politics, health/medicine, history, language/literature, multicultural studies, nature/environment, regional, science, sociology, translation, women's issues/studies. "Our press aims to reach audiences beyond the academic community. Writing should be accessible." Submit outline and 2-3 sample chapters. Reviews artwork/photos as part of the ms package. Send photocopies.
Recent Nonfiction Title: *Frauen: German Women Recall the Third Reich*, by Alison Owings.
Tips: Both academic and general audiences. "Many of our books have potential for undergraduate course use. We are more trade-oriented than most university presses. We are looking for intelligent, well-written and accessible books. Avoid overly narrow topics."

RUTLEDGE HILL PRESS, 211 Seventh Ave. N., Nashville TN 37219-1823. (615)244-2700. Fax: (615)244-2978. President: Lawrence Stone. Editorial Secretary: Tracey Menges. Estab. 1982. Publishes hardcover and trade paperback originals and reprints. Averages 35 titles/year. Receives 600 submissions/year. 40% of books from first-time authors; 90% from unagented writers. Pays 10-20% royalty on wholesale price. Publishes book 1 year after acceptance. Reports in 3 months. Book catalog for 9×12 SAE with 4 first-class stamps.
Nonfiction: Biography, cookbook, humor, reference, self-help. "The book must have an identifiable market, preferably one that is geographically limited." Submit outline and sample chapters. Reviews artwork/photos as part of ms package.

‡SAFARI PRESS, Division of Woodbine Publishing Co., 15621 Chemical Lane, Building B, Huntington Beach CA 92649-1506. (714)894-9080. Editor: J. Neufeld. Publishes hardcover originals and reprints and trade paperback reprints. Publishes 6-15 titles/year. 50% of books from first-time authors; 99% from unagented writers. Pays 8-15% royalty on wholesale price. Accepts simultaneous submissions. Book catalog for $1.

Nonfiction: Biography, how-to. Subjects include hunting, firearms, wingshooting—"nothing else." Query with outline and SASE.

Recent Nonfiction Title: *Solo Safari*, by Cacek.

ST. ANTHONY MESSENGER PRESS, 1615 Republic St., Cincinnati OH 45210-1298. (513)241-5615. Fax: (513)241-0399. Publisher: The Rev. Jeremy Harrington, O.F.M. Managing Editor: Lisa Biedenbach. Estab. 1970. Publishes trade paperback originals. Averages 12-16 titles/year. Receives 200 queries and 50 mss/year. 5% of books from first-time authors; 100% from unagented writers. Pays 10-12% royalty on net receipts of sales. Offers $600 average advance. Publishes book 12-18 months after acceptance. No simultaneous submissions. Query for electronic submissions. Reports in 1 month on queries, 2 months on proposals and mss. Book catalog for 9×12 SAE with 4 first-class stamps. Manuscript guidelines free on request.

Nonfiction: History, religion, Catholic identity. Query with outline and SASE. Reviews artwork/photos as part of ms package.

● St. Anthony Messenger Press especially seeks books which will sell in bulk quantities to parishes, teachers, pastoral ministers, etc. They expect to sell at least 5,000 to 7,000 copies of a book.

Recent Nonfiction Title: *American and Catholic: A Popular History of Catholicism in the United States*, by Clyde F. Crews.

Tips: "Our readers are ordinary 'folks in the pews' and those who minister to and educate these folks. Writers need to know the audience and the kind of books we publish. Manuscripts should reflect best and current Catholic theology and doctrine."

ST. BEDE'S PUBLICATIONS, Subsidiary of St. Scholastica Priory, P.O. Box 545, Petersham MA 01366-0545. (508)724-3407. Fax: (508)724-3574. Editorial Director: Sr. Scholastica Crilly, OSB. Estab. 1978. Publishes hardcover originals, trade paperback originals and reprints. Averages 8-12 titles/year. Receives 100 submissions/year. 30-40% of books from first-time authors; 90% from unagented writers. Nonauthor subsidy publishes 10% of books. Pays 5-10% royalty on wholesale price or retail price. No advance. Publishes book 2 years after acceptance. Accepts simultaneous submissions. Query for electronic submissions. Unsolicited mss not returned unless accompanied by sufficient return postage. Reports in 2 months. Book catalog and ms guidelines for 9×12 SAE and 2 first-class stamps.

Nonfiction: Textbook (theology), religion, prayer, spirituality, hagiography, theology, philosophy, church history, related lives of saints. "We are always looking for excellent books on prayer, spirituality, liturgy, church or monastic history. Theology and philosophy are important also. We publish English translations of foreign works in these fields if we think they are excellent and worth translating." No submissions unrelated to religion, theology, spirituality, etc. Query or submit outline and sample chapters.

Tips: "There seems to be a growing interest in monasticism among lay people and we will be publishing more books in this area. For our theology/philosophy titles our audience is scholars, colleges and universities, seminaries, etc. For our other titles (i.e. prayer, spirituality, lives of saints, etc.) the audience is above-average readers interested in furthering their knowledge in these areas."

‡SALINA BOOKSHELF, 10250 Palomino Rd., Flagstaff AZ 86004. (602)527-0070. Publisher: Louise Lockard. Publishes trade paperback originals and reprints. No books from first-time authors; 100% from unagented writers. Pays 20% minimum royalty. Publishes book 6 months after acceptance of ms. Accepts simultaneous submissions. Reports in 3 months.

Nonfiction: Children's/juvenile, textbook (Navajo language). Ethnic subjects. "We publish childrens bilingual readers. Nonfiction should be appropriate to science and social studies curriculum grades 3-8." Query. Reviews artwork/photos as part of ms package. Send photocopies.

Fiction: Juvenile. "Submissions should be in English/a language taught in Southwest classrooms." Query.

Recent Fiction Title: *Who Wants to be a Prairie Dog?*, by Ann Nolan Clark (children's picture book).

Poetry: "We accept poetry in English/Southwest language for children." Submit 3 sample poems.

SAN FRANCISCO PRESS, INC., P.O. Box 42680, San Francisco CA 94142-6800. (510)524-1000. President: Terry Gabriel. Founded 1959. Publishes hardcover originals and trade paperback originals and reprints. Averages 5-10 titles/year. Receives over 100 submissions/year. 50% of books from first-time authors; 90% from unagented writers. Pays 10-15% on wholesale price. Publishes book 6 months after acceptance. Accepts simultaneous submissions. Reports in 1 week on queries. *Writer's Market* recommends allowing 2 weeks for reply. Book catalog for #10 SASE.

● This press has been overwhelmed with music-book manuscripts when their need is for musicology.

Nonfiction: Technical, college textbook. Subjects include electronics, biotechnology, public health, history of science and technology, musicology, science. Submit outline and sample chapters.

Tips: "Our books are aimed at specialized audiences; we do not publish works intended for the general public."

SARPEDON PUBLISHERS, 166 Fifth Ave., New York NY 10010. Contact: Janis Cakars. Publishes hardcover originals and trade paperback reprints. Publishes 6 titles/year. Receives 100 queries/year. 14% of books from first-time authors; 20% from unagented writers. Pays royalty. Offers $250-1,250 advance. Publishes book 6-9 months after acceptance of ms. Accepts simultaneous submissions. Reports in 1 months on queries, 2 months on proposals, 3 months on mss. Book catalog and ms guidelines for #10 SASE.
Nonfiction: Biography. Subjects include Americana, government, history, military/war. "We specialize in military history." Submit outline, 2 sample chapters and synopsis. Reviews artwork/photos as part of ms package. Send photocopies.

SCARECROW PRESS, INC., Division of University Press of America, 4720 Boston Way, Lanhau MD 20706. (301)459-3366. Fax: (301)459-2118. Contact: Editorial Dept. Estab. 1950. Publishes hardcover originals. Averages 110 titles/year. Receives 600-700 submissions/year. 70% of books from first-time authors; 100% from unagented writers. Average print order for a first book is 1,000. Pays 10% royalty on net of first 1,000 copies; 15% of net price thereafter. 15% initial royalty on camera-ready copy. Offers no advance. Publishes book 6-18 months after receipt of ms. Query for electronic submissions. Reports in 1 month. *Writer's Market* recommends allowing 2 months for reply. Book catalog for 9×12 SAE and 4 first-class stamps.
Nonfiction: Needs reference books and meticulously prepared annotated bibliographies, indexes and books on women's studies, music, movies and stage. Query. Occasionally reviews artwork/photos as part of ms package.
Tips: "Essentially we consider any scholarly title likely to appeal to libraries. Emphasis is on reference material, but this can be interpreted broadly, provided author is knowledgeable in the subject field."

‡SCHAUM, Division of The McGraw-Hill Companies, 1221 Avenue of the Americas, New York NY 10020. (212)512-3482. Sponsoring Editor: Jeanne Flagg. Publishes trade paperback originals and reprints. Imprint publishes 20-25 titles/year. 20% of books from first-time authors; 100% from unagented writers. Pays 10% royalty on net receipts. Offers $500-3,000 advance. Publishes book 1 year after acceptance of ms. Accepts simultaneous submissions. Reports in 2-3 months on proposals. Book catalog free on request. Manuscript guidelines provided "after our expression of interest."
Nonfiction: Self-help, technical, textbook, study aids. Subjects include business and economics, computers and electronics, government/politics, history, language, music, philosophy, science, accounting, finance, mathematics, writing, engineering. "We publish generic study aids, brief texts, and selected supplementary reading for 2- and 4-year college students—for course adoption and/or general trade sale. Publications include Schaum's Outline Series, Solved Problems Series, Interactive Outline Series, Foreign Language Series, and College Course and General Interest Paperbacks." Query or submit proposal package, including outline and rationale for project.
   ● At press time it was learned that Schaum has been restructured and placed under Business-McGraw Hill. See that listing for information.

SCHIFFER PUBLISHING LTD., 77 Lower Valley Rd., Atglen PA 19310. (610)593-1777. Fax: (610)593-2002. President: Peter Schiffer. Estab. 1972. Imprint is Whitford Press. Publishes hardcover and trade paperback originals and reprints. Firm averages 170 titles/year; imprint averages 2 titles/year. Receives 1,000 submissions/year. 90% of books from first-time authors; 95% from unagented writers. Pays royalty on wholesale price. Publishes book 6 months after acceptance. Reports in 1 month. Book catalog free.
Nonfiction: Coffee table book, how-to, illustrated book, reference, textbook. Subjects include Americana, art/architecture, aviation, history, hobbies, military/war, regional. "We want books on collecting, hobby carving, military, architecture, aeronautic history and natural history." Query with SASE or submit outline and sample chapters. Reviews artwork/photos as part of ms package.

SCHIRMER BOOKS, Imprint of Simon & Schuster, 866 Third Ave., New York NY 10022. (212)702-3445. Fax: (212)605-4850. Editor-in-Chief: Richard Carlin. Editor: Jonathan Wiener. Assistant Editor: Alicia Williamson. Publishes hardcover and paperback originals, related audio recordings, paperback reprints and some software. Averages 30 books/year. Receives 250 submissions/year. 25% of books from first-time authors; 75% of books from unagented writers. Submit photos and/or illustrations only "if central to the book, not if decorative or tangential." Publishes book 1 year after acceptance. Query for electronic submissions. Reports in 4 months. Book catalog and ms guidelines for SASE.
Nonfiction: Publishes college texts, biographies, scholarly, reference, and trade on the performing arts specializing in music, film and theatre. Submit outline/synopsis and sample chapters and current vita. Reviews artwork/photos as part of ms package.
Recent Nonfiction Title: *Black and Blue: The Life and Lyrics of Andy Razof*, by Barry Singer.
Tips: "The writer has the best chance of selling our firm a music book with a clearly defined, reachable audience, either scholarly or trade. Must be an exceptionally well-written work of original scholarship pre-

pared by an expert in the field who has a thorough understanding of correct manuscript style and attention to detail (see the *Chicago Manual of Style*)."

SCHOLASTIC, INC., 555 Broadway, New York NY 10012. (212)343-6100. Editorial Director: Bonnie Verburg. Estab. 1920. Publishes trade paperback originals and hardcovers. Pays royalty on retail price. Reports in 3 months. Manuscript guidelines for #10 SASE.
Nonfiction: Publishes general nonfiction. Query.
Recent Nonfiction Title: *Sojourner Truth: Ain't I a Woman*, by Patricia C. and Frederick McKissack.
Fiction: Family stories, mysteries, school, friendships for ages 8-12, 35,000 words. YA fiction, romance, family and mystery for ages 12-15, 40,000-45,000 words for average to good readers. Query. Not accepting unsolicited mss at this time.
Tips: Queries may be routed to other editors in the publishing group.

SCHOLASTIC PROFESSIONAL BOOKS, 411 Lafayette, New York NY 10003. Publishing Director: Claudia Cohl. Editor-in-Chief: Terry Cooper. Assistant Manager/Editor: Shawn Richardson. Buys 45-50 mss/year from published or unpublished writers. "Writer should have background working in the classroom with elementary or middle school children teaching pre-service students and developing quality, appropriate, and innovative learning experiences and/or solid background in developing supplementary educational materials for these markets." Offers standard contract. Reports in 2 months. Book catalog for 9×12 SAE.
Nonfiction: Elementary and middle-school level enrichment—all subject areas, whole language, theme units, integrated materials, writing process, management techniques, teaching strategies based on personal/professional experience in the classroom. Production is limited to printed matter: resource and activity books, professional development materials, reference titles. Length: 6,000-12,000 words. Query should include table of contents.

SERENDIPITY SYSTEMS, P.O. Box 140, San Simeon CA 93452. (805)927-5259. Internet e-mail: j.galuszka-@genie.geis.com. Publisher: John Galuszka. Imprints are Books-on-Disks, Eco-Books. Publishes electronic books for IBM-PC compatible computers. Publishes 6-12 titles/year; each imprint publishes 0-6 titles/year. Receives 600 queries and 150 mss/year. 100% of books from unagented writers. Pays 25-33% royalty on wholesale price or on retail price, "depending on how the book goes out." Publishes book 1-2 months after acceptance of ms. Accepts simultaneous submissions. Electronic submissions required. Queries by e-mail; mss, summaries with sample chapters, and long documents should be sent by postal mail. Reports in 1 month on mss. Book catalog on IBM-PC disk and in hypertext available for $1 (indicate 3½″ or 5¼″ disk). Manuscript guidelines for #10 SASE.
Nonfiction: Reference on literature, writing, publishing. Subjects include computers and electronics, language/literature, software. "We only publish nonfiction books on literature, writing and electronic publishing." Submit entire ms on disk in ASCII files.
Recent Nonfiction Title: *Electronic Books in Print - 1994* (reference).
Fiction: We want to see *only* works which use (or have a high potential to use) hypertext, multimedia, interactivity, or other computer-enhanced features. Submit entire ms on disk in ASCII files (unless author has already added hypertext, etc.).
Recent Fiction Title: *Force of Habit*, by M. Allen (science fiction novel).

‡SERGEANT KIRKLAND'S, Imprint of Sergeant Kirkland's Museum and Historical Society, Inc., 912 Lafayette Blvd., Fredericksburg VA 22401. (540)899-5565. Editor: Pat Gompper. Publishes hardover originals and reprints. Publishes 12-14 titles/year. Receives 20 queries and 15 mss/year. 60% of books from first-time authors; 100% from unagented writers. Pays 25% royalty on wholesale price. Publishes book 3 months after acceptance of ms. Accepts simultaneous submissions. Query for electronic submissions. Reports in 1 month. Book catalog and ms guidelines free on request.
Nonfiction: Subjects include Americana, archaeology, history, military/war (American Civil War). Mistake writers most often make is not including biography, index, footnotes and table of contents. Query with outline and 2-3 sample chapters. Reviews artwork as part of ms package. Send photocopies.
Recent Nonfiction Title: *A History of the 2nd South Carolina Infantry*, by MacWyckoff (military).

SERVANT PUBLICATIONS, 840 Airport Blvd., P.O. Box 8617, Ann Arbor MI 48107. (313)761-8505. Editorial Director: Bert Ghezzi. Estab. 1972. Imprints are Vine Books, "especially for evanglical Protestant readers"; and Charis Books, "especially for Roman Catholic readers." Publishes hardcover, trade and mass market paperback originals and trade paperback reprints. Averages 40 titles/year. 5% of books from first-time authors; 85% from unagented writers. Publishes book 1 year after acceptance. Reports in 2 months. Book catalog for 9×12 SASE.
Nonfiction: "We're looking for practical Christian teaching, self-help, scripture, current problems facing the Christian church, and inspiration." No heterodox or non-Christian approaches. Query or submit brief outline/synopsis and 1 sample chapter. All unsolicited queries and mss returned unopened. Only accepts queries from agents or from published authors.

Fiction: Historical fiction. Accepts unsolicited queries. Submit brief outline/synopsis and 1 sample chapter.
Recent Fiction Title: *Strike Midnight*, by D.M. Matera.

HAROLD SHAW PUBLISHERS, 388 Gundersen Dr., P.O. Box 567, Wheaton IL 60189. (708)665-6700.
Managing Editor: Joan Guest. Estab. 1967. Publishes mostly trade paperback originals and reprints. Averages
38 titles/year. Receives 4,000 submissions/year. 10% of books from first-time authors; 90% from unagented
writers. Offers 5-10% royalty on retail price. Sometimes makes outright purchase of $1,000-2,500. Publishes
book 12-15 months after acceptance. Reports in 6-8 weeks on queries. Book catalog and ms guidelines for
9×12 SAE with 7 first-class stamps.
Nonfiction: Subjects include marriage, family and parenting, self-help mental health, spiritual growth and
Bible study. "We are looking for general nonfiction, with different twists—self-help manuscripts with fresh
insight and colorful, vibrant writing style. No autobiographies or biographies accepted. Must have an evangelical Christian perspective for us even to review the manuscript." Query.
Tips: "Get an editor who is not a friend or a spouse who will tell you honestly whether your book is
marketable. It will save a lot of your time and money and effort. Then do an honest evaluation. Who would
actually read the book other than yourself? If it won't sell at least 5,000 copies, it's not very marketable and
most publishers wouldn't be interested."

‡SIBYL PUBLICATIONS, Subsidiary of Micro One, Inc., 123 NE Third Ave., #502, Portland OR 97232.
(503)235-8566. Publisher: Miriam Selby. Publishes trade paperback originals. Publishes 4-6 titles/year. 75%
of books from first-time authors; 100% from unagented writers. Pays 10-15% royalty on wholesale price.
Offers $500-1,000 advance. Publishes book 6-9 months after acceptance of ms. Accepts simultaneous submis-
sions. Reports in 1 month on queries, 2 months on proposals and mss. Book catalog and ms guidelines for
#10 SASE.
Nonfiction: Biography, gift book, self-help, textbook, book and card set. Subjects include psychology,
women's issues/studies, women's spirituality. "We publish nonfiction positive books by and about women."
Query with outline, 3 sample chapters and SASE.
Recent Nonfiction Title: *Mythmaking: Heal your Past, Claim Your Future*, by Patricia Montgomery, PhD
(writing your life story as myth).
Tips: Audience is women in midlife, ages 36-60, who are interested in spirituality, mythology, psychology,
women's studies, women's issues. "Make your writing unique and compelling. Give the reader a reason to
buy your books; something new, different, better. Characters who are positive women who can be role
models."

SIERRA CLUB BOOKS, Dept. WM, 100 Bush St., San Francisco CA 94104. (415)291-1600. Fax: (415)291-
1602. Senior Editor: James Cohee. Estab. 1962. Publishes hardcover and paperback originals and reprints.
Averages 30 titles/year. Receives 1,000 submissions/year. 50% of books from unagented writers. Royalties
vary by project. Offers $3,000-15,000 average advance. Publishes book 12-18 months after acceptance.
Reports in 2 months. Book catalog free.
• Sierra Club Books looks for literary nonfiction.
Nonfiction: A broad range of environmental subjects: outdoor adventure, descriptive and how-to, women
in the outdoors; landscape and wildlife pictorials; literature, including travel and works on the spiritual
aspects of the natural world; travel and trail guides; natural history and current environmental issues, including
public health and uses of appropriate technology; gardening; general interest; and children's books. "The
Sierra Club was founded to help people to explore, enjoy and preserve the nation's forests, waters, wildlife
and wilderness. The books program looks to publish quality trade books about the outdoors and the protection
of natural resources. Specifically, we are interested in literary natural history, environmental issues such as
nuclear power, self-sufficiency, politics and travel, and juvenile books with an ecological theme." Does *not*
want "proposals for large color photographic books without substantial text; how-to books on building things
outdoors; books on motorized travel; or any but the most professional studies of animals." Query first, then
submit outline and sample chapters. Reviews artwork/photos as part of ms package. Send photocopies.
Fiction: Adventure, historical, mainstream and ecological fiction. "We do very little fiction, but will consider
a fiction manuscript if its theme fits our philosophical aims: the enjoyment and protection of the environment." Query first, then submit outline/synopsis and sample chapters.

SIGNATURE BOOKS, 564 West 400 North, Salt Lake City UT 84116-3411. (801)531-1483. Fax: (801)531-
1488. Director of Publishing: Gary Bergera. Estab. 1981. Publishes hardcover, trade and mass market paper-
back originals. Publishes 12 titles/year. Receives 100 queries and 100 mss/year. 10% of books from first-
time authors; 100% from unagented writers. Pays royalty. Publishes book 1 year after acceptance of ms.
Accepts simultaneous submissions. Query for electronic submissions. Reports in 6 months on proposals.
Book catalog and ms guidelines free on request.
Nonfiction: Western Americana, biography, humor, essays. Subjects include history, religion (predominantly
Mormon), women's issues/studies. "We prefer manuscripts in Utah/Western studies. Familiarize yourself
with our backlist before submitting a proposal." Submit proposal package, including 2-3 sample chapters.
Reviews artwork/photos as part of ms package. Send photocopies.

Fiction: Western Americana: historical, humor, religious. Query or submit synopsis.
Poetry: Submit complete ms.
Tips: "We have a general adult audience that is somewhat Mormon-oriented."

SILHOUETTE BOOKS, 300 E. 42nd St., New York NY 10017. (212)682-6080. Fax: (212)682-4539. Editorial Director, Silhouette Books, Harlequin historicals: Isabel Swift. Estab. 1979. Publishes mass market paperback originals. Averages 350 titles/year. Receives 4,000 submissions/year. 10% of books from first-time authors; 25% from unagented writers. Pays royalty. Publishes book 1 year after acceptance. No unsolicited mss. Send query letter, 2 page synopsis and SASE to head of imprint. Manuscript guidelines for #10 SASE.
Imprints: Silhouette Romances (contemporary adult romances, 53,000-58,000 words), Anne Canadeo, senior editor. Silhouette Special Editions (contemporary adult romances, 75,000-80,000 words), Tara Gavin, senior editor. Silhouette Desires (contemporary adult romances, 55,000-60,000 words), Lucia Macro, senior editor. Silhouette Intimate Moments (contemporary adult romances, 80,000-85,000 words), Leslie Wainger, senior editor and editorial coordinator. Silhouette Yours Truly (contemporary adult romances), Melissa Senate, editor. Harlequin Historicals (adult historical romances, 95,000-105,000 words), Tracy Farrell, senior editor.
Fiction: Romance (contemporary and historical romance for adults). "We are interested in seeing submissions for all our lines. No manuscripts other than the types outlined above. Manuscript should follow our general format, yet have an individuality and life of its own that will make it stand out in the readers' minds."
Recent Fiction Title: *Maggie's Dad*, Diana Palmer.
Tips: "The romance market is constantly changing, so when you read for research, read the latest books and those that have been recommended to you by people knowledgeable in the genre. We are actively seeking new authors for all our lines, contemporary and historical."

‡SILVER BURDETT PRESS, Imprint of Simon & Schuster, 250 James St., Morristown NJ 07960-1918. (201)461-6257. Manager: David Vissoe. Imprints are Julian Messner, Silver Press (preschool and primary fiction and nonfiction), Crestwood House, Dillon Press and New Discovery. Publishes hardcover and paperback originals. Averages 65-80 titles/year. No unsolicited mss. Publishes book 1 year after acceptance. Offers variable advance. Book catalog free.
Nonfiction: Juvenile and young adult reference. Subjects include Americana, science, history, nature, and geography. "We're primarily intersted in nonfiction for students on subjects which supplement the classroom curricula, but are graphically appealing and, in some instances, have commercial as well as institutional appeal."
Recent Nonfiction Title: *History of the Civil Rights Movement*, introduction by Andrew Young.
Tips: "Our books are primarily bought by school and public librarians for use by students and young readers. Virtually all are nonfiction and done as part of a series."

SIMON & SCHUSTER, 1230 Avenue of the Americas, New York NY 10020. Imprints include Fireside, Touchstone, Simon & Schuster, Lisa Drew, Scribners, Scribner's Paperback Fiction, Free Press and Pocketbooks. Simon & Schuster Children's Publishing and New Media Division includes these imprints: Atheneum Books for Young Readers, Macmillan Books for Young Readers, Simon & Schuster Aguilar Libros en Español, Margaret K. McElderry Books. Simon & Schuster Books for Young Readers, Aladdin Paperbacks and Little Simon. General interest publisher of both fiction and nonfiction. Query before submitting to attn: Wendy Nicholson.

SJL PUBLISHING COMPANY, P.O. Box 152, Hanna IN 46340. (219)324-9678. Publisher/Editor: Sandra J. Cassady. Publishes hardcover and trade paperback originals. Publishes 8-10 titles/year. Receives 1,000 queries and 100 mss/year. 40% of books from first-time authors; 100% from unagented writers. Pays 10% royalty. Publishes book 1 year after acceptance of ms. Accepts simultaneous submissions. Reports in 1 month on queries and proposals, 2 months on mss. Manuscript guidelines for #10 SASE.
Nonfiction: Cookbook, children's/juvenile, reference, self-help, technical. Subjects include business and economics, computers and electronics, cooking/foods/nutrition, gardening, government/politics, science, sports. "Looking for good scientific publications." Query with synopsis and SASE. Reviews artwork/photos as part of ms package. Send photocopies.
Recent Nonfiction Title: *A Short Course in Permanent Magnet Materials*, by William A. Cassady (reference/science).
Fiction: Humor, juvenile, science fiction. Query with synopsis and SASE.

‡SKINNER HOUSE BOOKS, Imprint of The Unitarian Universalist Association, 25 Beacon St., Boston MA 02108. (617)742-2100, ext 601. Editorial Assistant: Marshall Hawkins. Publishes trade paperback originals and reprints. Publishes 8-10 titles/year. 50% of books from first-time authors; 100% from unagented writers. Pays 5-10% royalty on net sales. Offers $100 advance. Publishes book 1 year after acceptance of ms. Reports in 2 months on queries. Book catalog for 6×9 SAE with 3 first-class stamps. Manuscript guidelines for #10 SASE.
Nonfiction: Biography, children's/juvenile, self-help. Subjects include gay/lesbian, history, religion, women's issues/studies, inspirational. "We publish titles in Unitarian Universalist faith, history, biography, wor-

ship, and issues of social justice. We also publish a selected number of inspirational titles of poetic prose and at least one volume of meditations per year. Writers should know that Unitarian Universalism is a liberal religious denomination, committed to progressive ideals." Query. Reviews artwork/photos as part of ms package. Send photocopies.

Recent Nonfiction Title: *Telling Our Tales*, by Jeanette Ross (storytelling guide).

Fiction: Juvenile. "The only fiction we publish is for children, usually in the form of parables or very short stories (500 words) on liberal religious principles or personal development. Fiction for adults is not accepted." Query.

Tips: Audience is Unitarian Universalists, ministers, lay leaders, religious educators, feminists, gay and lesbian activists, and social activists. "From outside our denomination, we are interested in manuscripts that will be of help or interest to liberal churches, Sunday School classes, ministers and volunteers. Inspirational/spiritual titles must reflect liberal Unitarian Universalist values."

‡SLACK INC., 6900 Grove Rd., Thorofare NJ 08086. (609)848-1000. Acquisitions Editor: Amy E. Drummond. Publishes hardcover and softcover originals. Publishes 15 titles/year. Receives 60 queries and 20 mss/year. 75% of books from first-time authors; 100% from unagented writers. Pays 10% royalty. Publishes book 6 months after acceptance of ms. Accepts simultaneous submissions. Reports in 4 months on queries, 1 month on proposals and 2-3 months on mss. Book catalog and ms guidelines free on request.

Nonfiction: Textbook (medical). Subjects include ophthalmology, orthopaedics, physical therapy, occupational therapy. Submit proposal package, including outline, 2 sample chapters, market profile and cv. Reviews artwork/photos as part of ms package. Send photocopies.

Recent Nonfiction Title: *Incisional Keratotomy*, by J. Charles Casebeer, MD (medical).

THE SMITH, The Generalist Association, Inc., 69 Joralemon St., Brooklyn NY 11201-4003. (718)834-1212. Publisher: Harry Smith. Estab. 1964. Publishes hardcover and trade paperback originals. Averages 5 titles/year. Receives 2,500 queries/year. 50% of books from first-time authors; more than 90% from unagented writers. Pays royalty. Offers $500 advance. Publishes book 9 months after acceptance. Accepts simultaneous submissions. Reports in 3 months. Book catalog and guidelines on request for SASE.

Nonfiction: Literary essays, language and literature. "The 'how' is as important as the 'what' to us. Don't bother to send anything if the prose is not outstanding itself. We don't publish anything about how to fix your car or your soul." Query with proposal package including outline and sample chapter. Reviews artwork/photos as part of ms package. Send photocopies.

Fiction: Experimental, feminist, literary. "Emphasis is always on artistic quality. A synopsis of almost any novel sounds stupid." Query with 1 sample chapter. Do not send complete ms. Irregular hours preclude acceptance of registered mail.

Poetry: "No greeting card sentiments, no casual jottings." Do not send complete ms. Do not send registered mail. Submit 7-10 sample poems.

SOCIAL SCIENCE EDUCATION CONSORTIUM, 3300 Mitchell Lane, Suite 240, Boulder CO 80301-2296. (303)492-8154. Fax: (303)449-3925. Managing Editor: Laurel R. Singleton. Estab. 1963. Publishes trade paperback originals. Publishes 8 titles/year. 25% of books from first-time authors; 100% from unagented writers. Pays 8-12% royalty on net sales (retail price minus average discount). Publishes book 6 months after acceptance of ms. Accepts simultaneous submissions. Query for electronic submissions. Reports in 1 month on proposals. *Writer's Market* recommends allowing 2 months for reply.

Nonfiction: Teacher resources. Subjects include education, government/politics, history. "We publish titles of interest to social studies teachers particularly; we do not generally publish on such broad educational topics as discipline, unless there is a specific relationship to the social studies/social sciences." Submit outline and 1-2 sample chapters.

SOCIETY PUBLISHING, P.O. Box 66271, Auburndale Branch, Boston MA 02165. (617)965-7129. Contact: Editor. Publishes hardcover and trade paperback originals. Publishes 4 titles/year. Receives 6 queries/year. 50% of books from first-time authors; 100% from unagented writers. Pays on contract basis. Offers $500-1,500 advance. Publishes book 1 year after acceptance of ms. No simultaneous submissions. Query for electronic submissions. Reports in 2 months on queries.

Nonfiction: Self-help. Subjects include health/medicine, psychology. Query.

SOHO PRESS, INC., 853 Broadway, New York NY 10003. (212)260-1900. Editor-in-Chief: Juris Jurjevics. Estab. 1986. Publishes hardcover and trade paperback originals. Averages 25 titles/year. Receives 5,000 submissions/year. 75% of books from first-time authors; 50% from unagented writers. Pays 10-15% royalty on retail price. Publishes book 1 year after acceptance. Accepts simultaneous submissions. Reports in 1 month. Book catalog for 6×9 SAE with 2 first-class stamps.

Nonfiction: Biography. "We want literary nonfiction: travel, autobiography, biography, etc. No self-help." Submit outline and sample chapters.

Fiction: Adventure, ethnic, feminist, historical, literary, mainstream/contemporary, mystery, suspense. Submit complete ms with SASE. *Writer's Market* recommends query with SASE first.

SOUNDPRINTS, Division of Trudy Management Corporation, P.O. Box 679, Norwalk CT 06856. Fax: (203)866-9944. Assistant Editor: Dana M. Rau. Publishes hardcover originals. Publishes 9-12 titles/year. Receives 200 queries/year. 20% of books from first-time authors; 90% of books from unagented writers. Makes outright purchase. Publishes book 1-2 years after acceptance of ms. Accepts simultaneous submissions. Reports on queries in 2-3 months. Book catalog for 9×12 SASE. Manuscript guidelines for #10 SAE with 3 first-class stamps.

● This publisher creates multimedia sets for the Smithsonian Wild Heritage Collection, the Smithsonian Oceanic Collection and Smithsonian's Backyard. Sets include a book, read-a-long audiotape and realistic stuffed animal, combining facts about North American wildlife with stories about each animal's habits and habitats and have received the Parent's Choice Award for 1993 and 1994.

Nonfiction: Children's/juvenile, animals. "We focus on North American wildlife and ecology. Subject animals must be portrayed realistically and must not be anthropomorphic. Meticulous research is required." Query with SASE. Does not review artwork/photos as part of ms package. (All books are now illustrated in full color.)

Recent Nonfiction Title: *Chipmunk on Hollow Tree Lane* (winner of the 1994 Parent's Choice Award).

Fiction: Juvenile. "When we publish juvenile fiction, it will be about wildlife and all information in the book *must* be accurate." Query.

Tips: "Our books are written for children from ages 4-8. Our most successful authors can craft a wonderful story which is derived from authentic wildlife facts. First inquiry to us should ask about our interest in publishing a book about a specific animal or habitat."

SOURCEBOOKS, INC., P.O. Box 313, Naperville IL 60566. (708)961-3900. Fax: (708)961-2168. Publisher: Dominique Raccah. Associate Editor: Todd Stocke. Estab. 1987. Publishes hardcover and trade paperback originals. Averages 35 titles/year. 50% of books from first-time authors; 100% from unagented writers. Pays 6-15% royalty on wholesale price. Publishes book 6 months after acceptance. Accepts simultaneous submissions. Query for electronic submissions. Reports in 3 months on queries. No complete mss. Book catalog and ms guidelines for 9×12 SASE.

Nonfiction: *Small Business Sourcebooks:* books for small business owners, entrepreneurs and students. "A key to submitting books to us is to explain *how* your book helps the reader, *why* it is different from the books already out there (please do your homework) and the *author's credentials* for writing this book." *Sourcebook Trade:* gift books, self-help, general business, and how to. "Books likely to succeed with us are self-help, art books, parenting and childcare, psychology, women's issues, how-to, house and home, gift books or books with strong artwork." Query or submit outline and 2-3 sample chapters (not the first). Reviews artwork/photos as part of ms package.

Recent Nonfiction Titles: Sourcebooks Trade: *Finding Peace: Letting Go and Liking It*; Small Business Sourcebooks: *2-Minute Motivation*.

Tips: "We love to develop books in new areas or develop strong titles in areas that are already well developed. Our goal is to provide customers with terrific innovative books at reasonable prices."

SOUTHERN METHODIST UNIVERSITY PRESS, P.O. Box 415, Dallas TX 75275. Fax: (214)768-1428. Senior Editor: Kathryn Lang. Establ. 1937. Publishes hardcover and trade paperback originals and reprints. Publishes 10-15 titles/year. Receives 500 queries and 500 mss/year. 75% of books from first-time authors; 95% from unagented writers. Pays up to 10% royalty on wholesale price. Offers $500 advance. Publishes book 1 year after acceptance of ms. Query for electronic submissions. Reports in 1 month on queries and proposals, 6 months on mss.

● Southern Methodist University Press has been accepting fewer manuscripts.

Nonfiction: Subjects include medical ethics/human values and history (regional). "We are seeking works in the following areas: theology; film/theater; medical ethics/human values." Query with outline, 3 sample chapters, table of contents and author bio. Reviews artwork/photos as part of the ms package. Send photocopies.

Fiction: Literary novels and short story collections. Query.

Tips: Audience is general educated readers of quality fiction and nonfiction.

‡SOUTHFARM PRESS, Haan Graphic Publishing Services, Ltd., P.O. Box 1296, Middletown CT 06457. (203)346-8798. Publisher: Walter J. Haan. Estab. 1983. Publishes trade paperback originals. Publishes 5 titles/year. 50% from first-time authors; 100% from unagented writers. Pays 5-10% royalty on retail price. No advance. Publishes book 1 year after acceptance. Accepts simultaneous submissions. Reports in 1 month.

Nonfiction: Subjects include history, military/war and dog breeds. Submit outline/synopsis and sample chapters.

Recent Nonfiction Title: *Till War Do Us Part*, by Frank and Mary Bogart.

‡SPAN PRESS INC., 5722 S. Flamingo Rd., #277, Cooper City FL 33330. (305)434-4991. Director, Editorial Services: Barbara Teuten. Publishes trade paperback originals. Publishes 100 titles/year. Receives 75-80 queries and 50 mss/year. 75% of books from first-time authors; 100% from unagented writers. Pays 4-10%

royalty on wholesale price. Publishes book 12-18 months after acceptance of ms. Reports in 3 months on mss. Manuscript guidelines free on request.
Nonfiction: Spanish. Subjects include education, life of Hispanics in US. Submit 2 sample chapters. Reviews artwork/photos as part of ms package. Send photocopies.
Fiction: Spanish.

SPECTRUM PRESS INC., 3023 N. Clark St., #109, Chicago IL 60657. (312)281-1419. E-mail: specpress@aol.com. Editor-in-Chief: Dan Agin. Publishes floppy disk books. Publishes 50 titles/year. Receives 1,000 queries and 300 mss/year. 75% of books from first-time authors; 90% from unagented writers. Pays 10-15% royalty on retail price. Publishes book 3 months after acceptance of ms. Accepts simultaneous submissions. Electronic submissions preferred. Reports in 1 month on mss. Book catalog and ms guidelines for #10 SASE.
Nonfiction: Biography, reference. Subjects include Americana, anthropology/archaeology, art/architecture, ethnic, gay/lesbian, government/politics, history, language/literature, philosophy, sociology, translation, women's issues/studies. Query.
Fiction: Erotica, ethnic, experimental, feminist, gay/lesbian, literary, mainstream/contemporary, plays, short story collections. Submit complete work on floppy disk.
Recent Fiction Title: *Tell Me In Darkness*, by Julian Dacanay (contemporary novel).
Poetry: "Interested in new strong poetry." Submit 10 sample poems or complete ms.
Recent Poetry Title: *Song of the Sixties*, by Howard Rawlinson.

THE SPEECH BIN, INC., 1965 25th Ave., Vero Beach FL 32960-3062. (407)770-0007. Senior Editor: Jan Binney. Estab. 1984. Publishes trade paperback originals. Publishes 10-20 titles/year. Receives 500 mss/year. 50% of books from first-time authors; 90% from unagented writers. Pays negotiable royalty on wholesale price. Publishes ms average of 6 months after acceptance. Query for electronic submissions. Do NOT fax mss. Reports in up to 3 months. Book catalog for 9×12 SASE and $1.48 postage.
   • The Speech Bin is increasing the number of books published per year and is especially interested in reviewing treatment materials for adults and adolescents.
Nonfiction: How-to, illustrated book, juvenile (preschool-teen), reference, textbook, educational material and games for both children and adults. Subjects include health, communication disorders and education for handicapped persons. Query or submit outline and sample chapters. Reviews artwork/photos as part of ms package. Send photocopies only, no original artwork.
Recent Nonfiction Title: *Techniques for Aphasia Rehabilitation*, by Mary Jo Santo Pietro and Robert Goldfarb.
Fiction: "Booklets or books for children and adults about handicapped persons, especially with communication disorders." Query or submit outline/synopsis and sample chapters. "This is a potentially new market for The Speech Bin."
Tips: "Our audience is made up of special educators, speech-language pathologists and audiologists, parents, caregivers, and teachers of children and adults with developmental and post-trauma disabilities. Books and materials must be research-based, clearly presented, well written, competently illustrated, and unique. We'll be adding books and materials for use by occupational and physical therapists and other allied health professionals. We are also looking for more materials for use in treating adults and very young children with communication disorders. Please do not fax manuscripts to us."

SPINSTERS INK, 32 E. First St., #330, Duluth, MN 55802. (218)727-3222. Editor: Kelly Kager. Estab. 1978. Publishes trade paperback originals and reprints. Averages 6 titles/year. Receives 200 submissions/year. 50% of books from first-time authors; 95% from unagented writers. Pays 7-11% royalty on retail price. Publishes book 18 months after acceptance. Reports in 4 months. Book catalog free. Manuscript guidelines for SASE.
Nonfiction: Feminist analysis for positive change. Subjects include women's issues. "We are interested in books that not only name the crucial issues in women's lives, but show and encourage change and growth. We do not want to see work by men, or anything that is not specific to women's lives (humor, children's books, etc.)." Query. Reviews artwork/photos as part of ms package.
Recent Nonfiction Title: *Mother Journeys: Feminists Write About Mothering*, ed. by Maureen Reddy, Martha Roth and Amy Sheldon.
Fiction: Ethnic, women's, lesbian. "We do not publish poetry or short fiction. We are interested in fiction that challenges, women's language that is feminist, stories that treat lifestyles with the diversity and complexity they deserve. We are also interested in genre fiction, especially mysteries." Submit outline/synopsis and sample chapters.
Recent Fiction Title: *Fat Girl Dances With Rocks*, by Susan Stinson.

STACKPOLE BOOKS, 5067 Ritter Rd., Mechanicsburg PA 17055. Fax: (717)796-0412. Editorial Director: Judith Schnell. Estab. 1935. Publishes hardcover and paperback originals and reprints. Publishes 70 titles/year. Publishes book 1 year after acceptance. Reports in 1 month. *Writer's Market* recommends allowing 2 months for reply.

Nonfiction: Outdoor-related subject areas—fishing, hunting, wildlife, adventure, outdoor skills, gardening, decoy carving/woodcarving, outdoor sports, paddling, climbing, crafts, military guides, history. Submit proposal. Reviews artwork/photos as part of ms package.

Recent Nonfiction Title: *Camping and Backpacking with Children*, by Steven Boga.

Tips: "Stackpole seeks well-written, authoritative manuscripts for specialized and general trade markets. Proposals should include chapter outline, sample chapter and illustrations and author's credentials."

STANDARD PUBLISHING, Division of Standex International Corp., 8121 Hamilton Ave., Cincinnati OH 45231. (513)931-4050. Publisher/Vice President: Eugene H. Wigginton. Estab. 1866. Publishes hardcover and paperback originals and reprints. Specializes in religious books for children. Publishes book 18 months after acceptance. Reports in 3 months. Manuscript guidelines for #10 SASE; send request to Acquisitions Coordinator.

Nonfiction: Publishes crafts (to be used in Christian education), juveniles, Christian education (teacher training, working with volunteers), quiz, puzzle. All mss must pertain to religion. Query.

Recent Nonfiction Title: *Volunteer Ministries*, by Margie Morris.

Tips: "Children's books (picture books, ages 4-7), Christian education, activity books, and helps for Christian parents and church leaders are the types of books writers have the best chance of selling to our firm."

STANFORD UNIVERSITY PRESS, Stanford CA 94305-2235. (415)723-9598. Editor-in-Chief: Norris Pope. Estab. 1925. Averages 75 titles/year. Receives 1,500 submissions annually. 40% of books from first-time authors; 95% from unagented writers. Nonauthor subsidy publishes 65% of books. Pays up to 15% royalty ("typically 10%, often none"). Sometimes offers advance. Publishes book 16 months after receipt of final manuscript. Query for electronic submissions. Reports in 6 weeks.

Nonfiction: Scholarly books in the humanities, social sciences, and natural sciences: history and culture of China, Japan, and Latin America; European history; literature, criticism, and literary theory; political science and sociology; biology, natural history, and taxonomy; anthropology, linguistics, and psychology; archaeology and geology; and medieval and classical studies. Also high-level textbooks and books for a more general audience. Query. "We like to see a prospectus and an outline." Reviews artwork/photos as part of ms package.

Tips: "The writer's best chance is a work of original scholarship with an argument of some importance."

STARBURST PUBLISHERS, P.O. Box 4123, Lancaster PA 17604. (717)293-0939. Editorial Director: Ellen Hake. Estab. 1982. Publishes hardcover and trade paperback originals and trade paperback reprints. Averages 10-15 titles/year. Receives 1,000 submissions/year. 60% of books by first-time authors; 75% from unagented writers. Pays 6-15% royalty on net price to retailer. Publishes book 1 year after acceptance. Reports in 1 month on queries. Book catalog for 9×12 SAE with 4 first-class stamps. Manuscript guidelines for #10 SASE.

Nonfiction: General nonfiction, how-to, self-help, Christian. Subjects include business/economics, child guidance/parenting, cooking/foods/nutrition, counseling/career guidance, educational, gardening, health/medicine, juvenile (Bible-based teaching picture books), money/finance, nature and environment, psychology, real estate, recreation, religion. No poetry. "We are looking for contemporary issues facing Christians and today's average American." Submit outline, 3 sample chapters, bio and photo with SASE. Reviews artwork/photos as part of ms package.

Recent Nonfiction Title: *Dr. Kaplan's Lifestyle of the Fit & Famous*, by Dr. Eric Kaplan (health/weight loss/motivation).

Fiction: Adventure, fantasy, historical, mainstream/contemporary, romance, western. "We are looking for good, wholesome Christian fiction." Submit outline/synopsis, 3 sample chapters, bio and photo with SASE.

Recent Fiction Title: *The Far Fields Series, Book #2*, by Gilbert Morris (historical/fantasy).

Tips: "50% of our line goes into the Christian marketplace; 50% into the general marketplace. We are one of the few publishers that has *direct sales representation* into both the Christian and general marketplace (bookstore, library, health and gift). Write on an issue that slots you on talk shows and thus establish your name as an expert and writer."

STERLING PUBLISHING, 387 Park Ave. S., New York NY 10016. (212)532-7160. Acquisitions Manager: Sheila Anne Barry. Estab. 1949. Publishes hardcover and paperback originals and reprints. Averages 200 titles/year. Pays royalty. Offers advance. Publishes book 8 months after acceptance. Reports in 2 months. Guidelines for SASE.

Nonfiction: Alternative lifestyle, fiber arts, games and puzzles, health, how-to, hobbies, children's humor, children's science, nature and activities, pets, recreation, reference, sports, technical, wine, gardening, art, home decorating, dolls and puppets, ghosts, woodworking, crafts, history, medieval, Celtic subjects, new consciousness. Query or submit complete chapter list, detailed outline and 2 sample chapters with photos if applicable. Reviews artwork/photos as part of ms package.

Recent Nonfiction Title: *Nature Crafts with a Microwave*, by Dawn Cusick.

STILLPOINT PUBLISHING, Division of Stillpoint International, Inc., P.O. Box 640, Walpole NH 03608. (603)756-9281. Fax: (603)756-9282. Senior Editor: Dorothy Seymour. Publishes hardcover originals and trade paperback originals and reprints that awaken the human spirit. Averages 8-10 titles/year. Receives 500 submissions/year. 50% of books from first-time authors; 90% from unagented writers. Pays royalty. Publishes book 9-15 months after acceptance. Accepts simultaneous submissions. Reports in 6-8 weeks. Manuscript guidelines for SASE.

Nonfiction: Topics include personal growth and spiritual development; holistic health and healing for individual and global well-being; spirituality in business, work and community. Submit complete ms or query with table of contents and sample chapters.

Tips: "We are looking for manuscripts with a unique, clearly-stated theme supported by persuasive arguments and evidence. We publish nonfiction that offers a new perspective gained from life experience and/or research that addresses the spiritual foundations of a current aspect of personal, social or global change. The work needs to be insightful and practical, to reflect universal spiritual values."

STIPES PUBLISHING CO., 10-12 Chester St., Champaign IL 61824-9933. (217)356-8391. Contact: Robert Watts. Estab. 1925. Publishes hardcover and paperback originals. Averages 15-30 titles/year. Receives 150 submissions/year. 50% of books from first-time authors; 100% from unagented writers. Pays 15% maximum royalty on retail price. Publishes book 4 months after acceptance. Reports in 2 months.

Nonfiction: Technical (some areas), textbooks on business and economics, music, chemistry, agriculture/horticulture, environmental education, and recreation and physical education. "All of our books in the trade area are books that also have a college text market. No books unrelated to educational fields taught at the college level." Submit outline and 1 sample chapter.

STOEGER PUBLISHING COMPANY, 55 Ruta Court, S. Hackensack NJ 07606-1799. (201)440-2700. Fax: (201)440-2707. Vice President: David Perkins. Estab. 1925. Publishes trade paperback originals. Averages 12-15 titles/year. Royalty varies, depending on ms. Accepts simultaneous submissions. Reports in 1 month on queries. *Writer's Market* recommends allowing 2 months for reply. Book catalog for #10 SAE with 2 first-class stamps.

Nonfiction: Specializing in reference and how-to books that pertain to hunting, fishing and appeal to gun enthusiasts. Submit outline and sample chapters.

Recent Nonfiction Title: *Firearms Disassembly with Exploded Views.*

‡STONE BRIDGE PRESS, P.O. Box 8208, Berkeley CA 94707. (510)524-8732. Fax: (510)524-8711. Publisher: Peter Goodman. Imprints are The Rock Spring Collection of Japanese Literature. Publishes hardcover and trade paperback originals. Publishes 6 titles/year; imprint publishes 2 titles/year. Receives 100 queries and 75 mss/year. 15-20% of books from first-time authors; 90% from unagented writers. Pays royalty on wholesale price. Advance varies. Publishes book 18 months after acceptance of ms. Accepts simultaneous submissions. Reports in 1 month on queries and proposals, 3 months on mss. Book catalog free on request.

Nonfiction: How-to, reference. Subjects include art/architecture, business and economics, government/politics, language/literature, philosophy, translation, travel, women's issues/studies. "We publish Japan- (and some Asia-) related books only." Query with SASE. Reviews artwork/photos as part of ms package. Send photocopies.

Fiction: Experimental, fantasy, feminist, gay/lesbian, literary, mystery, science fiction, short story collections, translation. "Japan-related only based on author's first-hand experience, not Western exotic recreations." Query with SASE.

Poetry: Translations from Japanese only. Query.

Tips: Audience is "intelligent, worldly readers with an interest in Japan based on personal need or experience. No children's books. Realize that interest in Japan is a moving target. Please don't submit yesterday's trends or rely on a view of Japan that is outmoded. Stay current!"

STONEYDALE PRESS, 205 Main St., Stevensville MT 59870. (406)777-2729. Publisher: Dale A. Burk. Estab. 1976. Publishes hardcover and trade paperback originals. Publishes 4-6 titles/year. Receives 40-50 queries and 6-8 mss/year. 90% of books from unagented writers. Pays 12-15% royalty. Publishes book 18 months after acceptance of ms. Reports in 2 months. Book catalog available.

Nonfiction: How-to hunting books. "We are interested only in hunting books." Query.

STOREY COMMUNICATIONS/GARDEN WAY PUBLISHING, Schoolhouse Rd., Pownal VT 05261. (802)823-5200. Fax: (802)823-5819. Senior Editor/Director of Acquisitions: Gwen Steege. Estab. 1983. Publishes hardcover and trade paperback originals and reprints. Publishes 30 titles/year. Receives 300 queries and 150 mss/year. 25% of books from first-time authors; 80% from unagented writers. Pays royalty or makes outright purchase. Publishes book 2 years after acceptance of ms. Accepts simultaneous submissions. Query for electronic submissions. Reports in 1 month on queries, 3 months on proposals and mss. Book catalog and ms guidelines free on request.

Nonfiction: Cookbook, how-to, children's/juvenile. Subjects include agriculture/horticulture, animals, building, beer, cooking/foods/nutrition, crafts, gardening, hobbies, nature/environment. Submit proposal package, including outline, sample chapter, competitive books, author résumé. Occasionally reviews artwork/photos as part of the ms package.

SUCCESS PUBLISHING, P.O. Box 30965, Palm Beach Gardens FL 33420. (407)626-4643. Fax: (407)775-1693. President: Allan H. Smith. Submission Manager: Robin Garretson. Estab. 1982. Publishes trade paperback originals. Averages 6 titles/year. Receives 200 submissions/year. 75% of books from first-time authors; 100% from unagented writers. Pays 7% royalty. Publishes book 3 months after acceptance. Accepts simultaneous submissions. Reports in 2 months on queries. Book catalog and ms guidelines for #10 SAE with 2 first-class stamps.
  ● Success Publishing is looking for ghostwriters.
Nonfiction: How-to, humor, self-help. Subjects include business and economics, hobbies, money/finance. "We are looking for books on how-to subjects such as home business and sewing." Query.
Recent Nonfiction Title: *How To Write A "How To" Book*, by Smith (how-to).
Tips: "Our audience is made up of housewives, hobbyists and owners of home-based businesses. If I were a writer trying to market a book today, I would read books about how to market a self-written book."

SULZBURGER & GRAHAM PUBLISHING, LTD., 165 W. 91st St., New York NY 10024. Publisher: Neil Blond. Imprints are Human Services Institute, Blond's Law Guides, Carroll Press. Publishes hardcover and trade paperback originals and reprints. Publishes 35 titles/year. Publishes 10-15 imprint titles/year. Receives 400 queries and 100 mss/year. 80% of books from first-time authors; 95% from unagented writers. Pays 0-15% royalty on wholesale price. Offers $100-2,000 advance. Publishes book 6 months after acceptance of ms. Accepts simultaneous submissions. Query for electronic submissions. Reports in 2 months on queries and proposals, 4 months on mss. Book catalog for 8 × 11 SAE with 4 first-class stamps. Manuscript guidelines for #10 SASE.
Nonfiction: How-to, reference, self-help, technical, textbook. Subjects include business and economics, child guidance/parenting, computers and electronics, education, health/medicine, hobbies, money/finance, psychology, recreation, science, software, travel, women's issues/studies. Query with outline and 1 sample chapter. Reviews artwork/photos as part of ms package. Send photocopies.
Recent Nonfiction Title: *Gross Anatomy*, by John Tesoriero, Ph.D. (study guide).

‡SUMMERS PRESS, INC., Imprint of Business Publishing, 7035 Bee Caves Rd., Suite 203, Austin TX 78746. Editor: Mark Summers. Publishes hardcover originals. Publishes 5 titles/year. Several books from first-time authors; several from unagented writers. Pays 2-7½% royalty on retail price or makes outright purchase. Offers $1,000-2,500 advance. Accepts simultaneous submissions.
Nonfiction: Reference, technical, legal references for businesses. Subjects include business and economics, software. "Manuscript should be easily accessible, use short sentences, and attempt to convey complex information on a 10-12th grade reading level." Query with outline, 1 chapter and SASE.
Recent Nonfiction Title: *EPA Compliance Guide*, by Ray Kirk (reference book for businesses).

‡THE SUMMIT PUBLISHING GROUP, One Arlington Center, 112 E. Copeland, 5th Floor, Arlington TX 76011. Managing Editor: Mike Towle. Publishes hardcover and trade paperback originals and reprints. Publishes 25-30 titles/year. 50% of books from first-time authors; 75% from unagented writers. Pays 5-20% royalty on wholesale price. Offers 0-$15,000 advance. Publishes book 5 months after acceptance of ms. "We *attempt* to return submisions with accompanying SASE, but *no* promises." Reports in 3 months on mss.
Nonfiction: Biography, cookbook, gift book, how-to, humor, self-help. Subjects include child guidance/parenting, cooking, government/politics, health/medicine, money/finance, sports, women's issues/studies. "Books should have obvious national-distribution appeal, be of a contemporary nature and be marketing-driven: author's media experience and contacts a strong plus. Mistakes writers often make with submitting nonfiction: copying other successful concepts, with little or no marketing imagination; sending a regional book to a national publisher; and not being thorough enough in the proposal letter in providing marketing angles for the book—must sell the publisher on the benefits of spending tens of thousands of dollars in publishing the book." Submit outline, ½ of book, proposal marketing letter and resume with SASE. Reviews artwork/photos as part of ms package. Send photocopies.
Recent Nonfiction Title: *Byron Nelson: The Little Black Book*, Byron Nelson, golfer (personal diary and commentary).
Tips: National audience, mostly adults. "Don't use an agent with us and don't expect an advance."

For information on book publishers' areas of interest, see the nonfiction and fiction sections in the Book Publishers Subject Index.

SUNSTONE PRESS, Imprint of Sunstone Corp., P.O. Box 2321, Santa Fe NM 87504-2321. (505)988-4418. President: James C. Smith Jr. Estab. 1971. Other imprint is Sundial Publications. Publishes paperback originals; few hardcover originals. Averages 25 titles/year. Receives 400 submissions/year. 70% of books from first-time authors; 100% from unagented writers. Average print order for a first book is 2,000-5,000. Pays royalty on wholesale price. Publishes book 18 months after acceptance. Reports in 1 month. Book catalog for 9×12 SAE with 3 first-class stamps.

- The focus of this publisher is still the Southwestern U.S. but it receives many, many submissions outside this subject. It does not publish poetry.

Nonfiction: How-to series craft books. Books on the history and architecture of the Southwest. "Looks for strong regional appeal (Southwestern)." Query with SASE. Reviews artwork/photos as part of ms package.
Recent Nonfiction Title: *Dinetah: An Early History of the Navajo People*, by Dean Sundberg.
Fiction: Publishes material with Southwestern theme. Query with SASE.
Recent Fiction Title: *Heart of Stone*, by Anne Denton.

SWAN-RAVEN & CO., Imprint of Blue Water Publishing, Inc., P.O. Box 726, Newberg OR 97132. (503)538-0264. Fax: (503)538-8485. President: Pam Meyer. Contact: Amy E. Owen. Publishes trade paperback originals. Publishes 6 titles/year. Receives 25 queries and 15 mss/year. 80% of books from first-time authors; 90% from unagented writers. Pays 5-12% royalty on wholesale price. Publishes book 7-16 months after acceptance of ms. Accepts simultaneous submissions. Query for electronic submissions. Reports in 1 month on mss. Book catalog free on request. Manuscript guidelines for #10 SASE.
Nonfiction: Subjects include health, philosophy, software, women's issues/studies, spiritual, future speculation. Query with outline. Reviews artwork/photos as part of ms package. Send photocopies.
Recent Nonfiction Title: *Calling the Circle: The First and Future Culture*, by Christina Baldwin.
Fiction: Juvenile.

‡SWEDENBORG FOUNDATION, P.O. Box 549, West Chester PA 19381-0549. (610)430-3222. Fax: (610)430-7982. Imprints are Chrysalis Books, Swedenborg Foundation, Chrysalis Reader. Publishes hardcover and trade paperback originals and reprints. Publishes 6-10 titles/year; imprints publish 2-4 titles/year. Pays 5-10% royalty on net receipts or makes outright purchase. Offers $500 minimum advance. Reports in 3 months on queries, 6 months on proposals, 9 months on mss. Book catalog and ms guidelines free on request.
Nonfiction: Biography, spiritual growth, self-transformation, writings of Emanuel Swedenborg. Subjects include philosophy, psychology, religion. Query with proposal package, including synopsis, outline, sample chapter and SASE. Reviews artwork/photos as part of ms package. Send photocopies.
Recent Nonfiction Title: *Angels in Action*, by Robert Kirven (religion).
Tips: "The Swedenborg Foundation publishes books by and about Emanuel Swedenborg (1688-1772), his ideas, or how his ideas have influenced others, and related topics. Most readers of our books are thoughtful, well-read individuals seeking resources for their philosophical, spiritual, or religious growth. Prospective writers should be aware of how their work might serve as a bridge to key elements of Swedenborgian thought."

SYBEX, INC., 2021 Challenger Dr., Alameda CA 94501. (510)523-8233. Fax: (510)523-2373. Editor-in-Chief: Dr. Rudolph S. Langer. Acquisitions Editor and Manager: Kristine Plachy. Estab. 1976. Publishes paperback originals. Averages 120 titles/year. Royalty rates vary. Offers $3,000 average advance. Publishes book 3 months after acceptance. Accepts simultaneous submissions. Query for electronic submissions. Reports in up to 6 months. Free book catalog.
Nonfiction: Computers, computer software. "Manuscripts most publishable in the field of personal computers, desktop computer business applications, hardware, programming languages, and telecommunications." Submit outline and 2-3 sample chapters. Looks for "clear writing; technical accuracy; logical presentation of material; and good selection of material, such that the most important aspects of the subject matter are thoroughly covered; well-focused subject matter; and well-thought-out organization that helps the reader understand the material." Reviews artwork/photos as part of ms package.
Tips: Queries/mss may be routed to other editors in the publishing group.

SYRACUSE UNIVERSITY PRESS, 1600 Jamesville Ave., Syracuse NY 13244-5160. (315)443-5534. Fax: (315)443-5545. Executive Editor: Cynthia Maude-Gembler. Estab. 1943. Averages 30 titles/year. Receives 400 submissions/year. 40% of books from first-time authors; 95% from unagented writers. Nonauthor subsidy publishes 20% of books. Pays royalty on net sales. Publishes book an average of 15 months after acceptance. Simultaneous submissions discouraged. Book catalog and ms guidelines for 9×12 SAE with 3 first-class stamps.
Nonfiction: "Special opportunity in our nonfiction program for freelance writers of books on New York state. We have published regional books by people with limited formal education, but authors were thoroughly acquainted with their subjects, and they wrote simply and directly about them. Provide precise descriptions of subjects, along with background description of project. The author must make a case for the importance

of his or her subject." Query with outline and at least 2 sample chapters. Reviews artwork/photos as part of ms package.

‡SYSTEMS CO. INC., P.O. Box 339, Carlsborg WA 98324. (360)683-6860. President: Richard H. Peetz, Ph.D. Publishes hardcover and trade paperback originals. Publishes 3-5 titles/year. 50% of books from first-time authors; 100% from unagented writers. Pays 20% royalty on wholesale price after costs. Publishes book 6 months after acceptance of ms. Accepts simultaneous submissions. Reports in 2 months. Book catalog free on request. Manuscript guidelines for $1.
Nonfiction: Cookbook, how-to, self-help, technical, textbook. Subjects include business and economics, cooking/foods/nutrition, health/medicine, money/finance, nature/environment, science. "In submitting nonfiction, writers often make the mistake of picking a common topic with lots of published books in print." Submit outline and 2 sample chapters with SASE. Reviews artwork/photos as part of ms package. Send photocopies.
Recent Nonfiction Title: *Engineer's Guide to Autos* (technical).
Tips: "Our audience consists of people in technical occupations, people interested in doing things themselves."

TAB BOOKS, Imprint of The McGraw-Hill Companies, Blue Ridge, Summit PA 17294-0850. (717)794-2191. Fax: (717)794-5344. E-mail: Bschupp@pipeline.com. Editorial Director: Ron Powers. Estab. 1964. Contact: Brad Schepp. Publishes hardcover and paperback originals and reprints. Publishes 275 titles/year. Receives 600 submissions/year. 50% of books from first-time authors; 85% from unagented writers. Average print order for a first book is 10,000. Pays variable royalty or makes outright purchase. Offers advance. Query for electronic submissions. Reports in 3 months. Book catalog and ms guidelines free.
Nonfiction: TAB publishes titles in such fields as computer hardware, computer software, business, startup guides, with marine line, aviation, automotive, construction and mechanical trades, science, juvenile science, education, electronics, electrical and electronics repair, amateur radio, shortwave listening, calculators, robotics, telephones, TV servicing, audio, recording, hi-fi and stereo, electronic music, electric motors, electrical wiring, electronic test equipment, video programming, CATV, MATV and CCTV, broadcasting, appliance servicing and repair, license study guides, mathematics, reference books, schematics and manuals, small gasoline engines, two-way radio and CB. Accepts unsolicited proposals. Query with outline. Reviews artwork/photos as part of ms package.
Tips: "Many writers believe that a cover letter alone will describe their proposed book sufficiently; it rarely does. The more details we receive, the better the chances are that the writer will get published by us. We expect a writer to tell us what the book is about, but many writers actually fail to do just that."

TAMBOURINE BOOKS, Imprint of William Morrow & Co., Inc., 1350 Avenue of the Americas, New York NY 10019. (212)261-6661. Editorial Assistant: Chris Geissel. Estab. 1989. Publishes hardcover originals. Publishes 20 titles/year. Receives 120 queries and 2,000 mss/year. Accepts simultaneous submissions. Reports in 2 months on queries. Book catalog for 9 × 12 SASE. Manuscript guidelines for #10 SASE.
Nonfiction: Children's/juvenile. Subjects include history, hobbies, money/finance, science. Query with SASE. Reviews artwork/photos as part of ms package. Send color photocopies.
Recent Nonfiction Title: *Puppy Care and Critters, Too,* by Bill Fleming and Judy Petersen-Fleming.
Fiction: Juvenile, young adult. Primary emphasis on picture books and fiction. Query for novels, chapter books. For picture books send ms with SASE.
Recent Fiction Title: *No Milk,* by Jennifer Ericsson.

TAYLOR PUBLISHING COMPANY, 1550 W. Mockingbird Lane, Dallas TX 75235. (214)819-8560. Contact: Editorial Assistant, Trade Books Division. Estab. 1981. Publishes hardcover and softcover originals. Averages 30 titles/year. Receives 1,000 submissions/year. 25% of books from first-time authors; 25% from unagented writers. Publishes book 18 months after acceptance. Accepts simultaneous submissions. Reports in 2 months. Book catalog and ms guidelines for 10 × 13 SASE.
Nonfiction: Gardening, sports, popular culture, parenting, health, home improvement, how-to, celebrity biography, miscellaneous nonfiction. Submit outline and sample chapters, author bio as it pertains to proposed subject matter. Reviews artwork/photos as part of ms package.
• No longer seeking true crime, cookbooks, humor, self-help or trivia.
Recent Nonfiction Title: *Ty Cobb: His Tumultuous Life and Times.*

TEACHERS COLLEGE PRESS, 1234 Amsterdam Ave., New York NY 10027. (212)678-3929. Fax: (212)678-4149. Director: Carole P. Saltz. Executive Acquisitions Editor: Faye Zucker. Estab. 1904. Publishes hardcover and paperback originals and reprints. Averages 40 titles/year. Pays royalty. Publishes book an average of 1 year after acceptance. Reports in 2 months. Book catalog free.
Nonfiction: "This university press concentrates on books in the field of education in the broadest sense, from early childhood to higher education: good classroom practices, teacher training, special education, innovative trends and issues, administration and supervision, film, continuing and adult education, all areas of the curriculum, computers, guidance and counseling and the politics, economics, philosophy, sociology

and history of education. We have recently added women's studies to our list. The Press also issues classroom materials for students at all levels, with a strong emphasis on reading and writing and social studies." Submit outline and sample chapters.

TEMPLE UNIVERSITY PRESS, Broad and Oxford Sts., Philadelphia PA 19122. (215)204-8787. Fax: (215)204-4719. Editor-in-Chief: Michael Ames. Publishes 70 titles/year. Pays royalty of up to 10% on wholesale price. Publishes book 1 year after acceptance. Query for electronic submissions. Reports in 2 months. Book catalog free.
Nonfiction: American history, sociology, women's studies, health care, ethics, labor studies, photography, urban studies, law, Latin American studies, Afro-American studies, Asian-American studies, public policy and regional (Philadelphia area). "No memoirs, fiction or poetry." Uses *Chicago Manual of Style*. Reviews artwork/photos as part of ms package. Query.

TEN SPEED PRESS, P.O. Box 7123, Berkeley CA 94707. (510)559-1600. Address submissions to "Acquisitions Department." Estab. 1971. Imprints are Celestial Arts and Tricycle Press. Publishes trade paperback originals and reprints. Firm publishes 60 titles/year; imprint averages 20 titles/year. 25% of books from first-time authors; 50% from unagented writers. Pays 8-12% royalty on retail price. Offers $2,500 average advance. Publishes book 1 year after acceptance. Accepts simultaneous submissions. Reports in 2-3 months on queries. Book catalog for 9 × 12 SAE with 6 first-class stamps. Manuscript guidelines for #10 SASE.
Nonfiction: Cookbook, how-to, reference, self-help. Subjects include business and career, child guidance/parenting, cooking/foods/nutrition, gardening, health/medicine, money/finance, nature/environment, recreation, science. "We mainly publish innovative how-to books. We are always looking for cookbooks from proven, tested sources—successful restaurants, etc. *Not* 'grandma's favorite recipes.' Books about the 'new science' interest us. No biographies or autobiographies, first-person travel narratives, fiction or humorous treatments of just about anything." Query or submit outline and sample chapters.
Recent Nonfiction Title: *Running a One-Person Business*, by Claude Whitmyer, Salli Raspberry and Michael Phillips (business/career).
Tips: "We like books from people who really know their subject, rather than people who think they've spotted a trend to capitalize on. We like books that will sell for a long time, rather than nine-day wonders. Our audience consists of a well-educated, slightly weird group of people who like food, the outdoors and take a light but serious approach to business and careers. If I were a writer trying to market a book today, I would really study the backlist of each publisher I was submitting to, and tailor my proposal to what I perceive as their needs. Nothing gets a publisher's attention like someone who knows what he or she is talking about, and nothing falls flat like someone who obviously has no idea who he or she is submitting to."

TEXAS A&M UNIVERSITY PRESS, Drawer C, College Station TX 77843-4354. (409)845-1436. Fax: (409)847-8752. E-mail: fdl@tampress.tamu.edu. Editor-in-Chief: Noel Parsons. Editorial Assistant: Diana Vance. Estab. 1974. Publishes 38 titles/year. Nonauthor subsidy publishes 25% of books. Pays in royalties. Publishes book 1 year after acceptance. Query for electronic submissions. Reports in 1 month on queries. Book catalog free.
 • This publisher has won recent awards from the American Association for State and Local History, Presidio La Bahia Award, Liz Carpenter Award, H.L. Mitchell Award, San Antonio Conservation Society Publications Award and the STC Technical Publications Competition.
Nonfiction: Natural history, American history, environmental history, military history, women's studies, economics, regional studies. *Writer's Market* recommends query with SASE first.
Recent Nonfiction Title: *The Meaning of Nolan Ryan*, by Nick Trujillo.

TEXAS CHRISTIAN UNIVERSITY PRESS, P.O. Box 30783, TCU, Fort Worth TX 76129-0783. (817)921-7822. Director: Judy Alter. Editor: A.T. Row. Estab. 1966. Publishes hardcover originals, some reprints. Averages 8 titles/year. Receives 100 submissions/year. 10% of books from first-time authors; 75% from unagented writers. Nonauthor subsidy publishes 10% of books. Pays royalty. Publishes book 16 months after acceptance. Reports in 3 months on queries.
Nonfiction: American studies, juvenile (Chaparral Books, 10 and up), Texana, literature and criticism. "We are looking for good scholarly monographs, other serious scholarly work and regional titles of significance." Query. Reviews artwork/photos as part of ms package.
Fiction: Regional fiction. Manuscripts considered by invitation only. Please do not query.
Tips: "Regional and/or Texana nonfiction or fiction have best chance of breaking into our firm."

TEXAS STATE HISTORICAL ASSOCIATION, 2.306 Richardson Hall, University Station, Austin TX 78712. (512)471-1525. Assistant Director: George Ward. Publishes hardcover and trade paperback originals and reprints. Publishes 8 titles/year. Receives 50 queries and 50 mss/year. 10% of books from first-time authors; 95% from unagented writers. Pays 10% royalty of net cash proceeds. Publishes book 6-12 months after acceptance of ms. Query for electronic submissions. Reports in 2 months on mss. Book catalog and ms guidelines free on request.

Nonfiction: Biography, coffee table book, illustrated book, reference. Historical subjects. "We are interested primarily in scholarly historical articles and books." Query. Reviews artwork/photos as part of ms package. Send photocopies.

TEXAS TECH UNIVERSITY PRESS, Mail Stop 41037, Lubbock TX 79409-1037. (800)832-4042. Fax: (806)742-2979. Interim Director: Carole Young. Publishes hardcover and trade paperback originals and reprints. Publishes 20 titles/year. Receives 200 queries and mss/year. 10% of books from first-time authors; 80% from unagented writers. Subsidy publishes 50% of books. Decision to subsidy publish is based upon size of the market and cost of production. Pays 5-20% royalty on wholesale price. Publishes book 18 months after acceptance of ms. No multiple submissions. Query for electronic submissions. Reports in 1 month on queries, 6 months on mss. Book catalog free on request.
Nonfiction: "Coffee table" book, illustrated book, technical, memoirs, scholarly works; medical books. Subjects include Americana, animals, art/architecture, ethnic, health/medicine, history, language/literature, music/dance, nature/environment, regional (Texas/New Mexico), science. "We will consider all manuscripts that meet our requirements. Competition is stiff, however, and we suggest that authors present well-researched, amply documented, well-written manuscripts. No philosophy, psychology, or business and economics." Query with outline/synopsis and sample chapters or complete ms. Reviews artwork/photos as part of freelance ms package.
Recent Nonfiction Title: *Pumping Granite and Other Portraits of People at Play*, by Mike D'Orso (trade sports and recreation).
Poetry: "We only consider submissions that were finalists or winners in one of the national poetry contests. We also host an invitation-only poetry contest for first book authors." Submit complete ms.
Recent Poetry Title: *The Andrew Poems*, by Shelly Wagner (contemporary).
Tips: "Our trade books are for general audiences. Our scholarly books are directed toward specific disciplines."

TEXAS WESTERN PRESS, Imprint of The University of Texas at El Paso, El Paso TX 79968-0633. (915)747-5688. Fax: (915)747-5111. Director: John Bristol. Estab. 1952. Imprint is Southwestern Studies. Publishes hardcover and paperback originals. Publishes 7-8 titles/year. "This is a university press, 41 years old; we offer a standard 10% royalty contract on our hardcover books and on some of our paperbacks as well. We try to treat our authors professionally, produce handsome, long-lived books and aim for quality, rather than quantity of titles carrying our imprint." Reports in 2 months. Book catalog and ms guidelines free.
 • This publisher has won recent awards from the Border Regional Library Association, Ralph Emerson Twitchell Award, Western Writers of America Spur Award and The Lansing B. Bloom Award from the New Mexico Historical Association.
Nonfiction: Scholarly books. Historic and cultural accounts of the Southwest (West Texas, New Mexico, northern Mexico and Arizona). Occasional technical titles. "Our *Southwestern Studies* use manuscripts of up to 30,000 words. Our hardback books range from 30,000 words up. The writer should use good exposition in his work. Most of our work requires documentation. We favor a scholarly, but not overly pedantic, style. We specialize in superior book design." Query with outline. Follow *Chicago Manual of Style*.
Tips: "Texas Western Press is interested in books relating to the history of Hispanics in the US, will experiment with photo-documentary books, and is interested in seeing more 'popular' history and books on Southwestern culture/life."

THE THEOSOPHICAL PUBLISHING HOUSE, Subsidiary of The Theosophical Society in America, 306 W. Geneva Rd., Wheaton IL 60187-0270. (708)665-0130. Fax: (708)665-8791. Senior Editor: Brenda Rosen. Estab. 1968. Imprint is Quest Books. Publishes cloth and trade paperback originals. Averages 12 titles/year. Receives 750-1,000 submissions/year. 20% of books from first-time authors; 80% from unagented writers. Average print order for a first book is 5,000. Pays 12½% royalty on gross price. Offers $3,000 average advance. Publishes book 18 months after acceptance. Accepts simultaneous submissions. Reports in 2 months. Book catalog and ms guidelines for SASE.
 • Quest gives preference to writers with established reputations/successful publications. Manuscript required on disk if accepted for publication.
Nonfiction: Subjects include self-development, self-help, philosophy (holistic), psychology (transpersonal), Eastern and Western religions, theosophy, comparative religion, men's and women's spirituality, Native American spirituality, holistic implications in science, health and healing, yoga, meditation, astrology. "TPH seeks works that are compatible with the theosophical philosophy. Our audience includes the 'New Age' community, seekers in all religions, general public, professors, and health professionals. No submissions that do not fit the needs outlined above." Accepts nonfiction translations. Query or submit outline and sample chapters. Reviews artwork/photos as part of ms package.
Recent Nonfiction Title: *Tying Rocks to Clouds: Meetings and Conversations with Wise and Spiritual People*, by William Elliott.
Tips: "The writer has the best chance of selling our firm a book that illustrates a connection between spiritually-oriented philosophy or viewpoint and some field of current interest."

‡**THIRD SIDE PRESS, INC.**, 2250 W. Farragut, Chicago IL 60625. Editor/Publisher: Midge Stocker. Publishes 4-5 titles/year. 30% of books from first-time authors; 100% from unagented writers. Pays 6% royalty and up on wholesale price. Publishes book 18 months after acceptance of ms. Accepts simultaneous submissions (with nonfiction). Reports in 1 month on queries, 6 months on mss. Book catalog for 9 × 12 SAE with 2 first-class stamps. Manuscript guidelines for #10 SASE.
Nonfiction: Self-help. Subjects include business and economics (relating to women), health/medicine (women's only), language/literature, lesbian, psychology, women's issues/studies. "We are looking for manuscripts that approach women's health issues from a feminist perspective." Query with SASE.
Recent Nonfiction Title: *Alternatives for Women with Endometriosis*, Ruth Carol, editor (health).
Fiction: Contemporary, experimental, feminist, lesbian, literary. "We are not seeking collections of short stories by individual authors. We are actively seeking quality novels with lesbian main characters." Query with complete ms and SASE.
Recent Fiction Title: *The Sensual Thread*, by Beatrice Stone (lesbian first novel).

THIRD WORLD PRESS, P.O. Box 19730, Chicago IL 60619. (312)651-0700. Publisher: Haki R. Madhubuti. Publishes hardcover and trade paperback originals and reprints. Publishes 10 titles/year. Receives 200-300 queries and 200 mss/year. 20% of books from first-time authors; 80% from unagented writers. Pays 7% royalty on retail price. Publishes book 18 months after acceptance of ms. Accepts simultaneous submissions. Query for electronic submissions. Reports in 6 months. Book catalog and ms guidelines free on request.
Nonfiction: Illustrated book, children's/juvenile, reference, self-help, textbook. Subjects include anthropology/archaeology, Black studies, education, ethnic, government/politics, health/medicine, history, language/literature, literary criticism, philosophy, psychology, regional, religion, sociology, women's issues/studies. Query with outline and 5 sample chapters. Reviews artwork/photos as part of ms package. Send photocopies.
Recent Nonfiction Title: *Claiming Earth*.
Fiction: Ethnic, feminist, historical, juvenile, literary, mainstream/contemporary, picture books, plays, short story collections, young adult. Query with synopsis and 5 sample chapters.
Recent Fiction Title: *The Sweetest Berry On The Bush*.
Poetry: Submit complete ms.
Recent Poetry Title: *Hornman*.

THOMAS INVESTIGATIVE PUBLICATIONS, INC., Box 142226, Austin TX 78714. (512)719-3595. Fax: (512)719-3594. Contact: Ralph D. Thomas. Publishes trade paperback originals and reprints. Averages 8-10 titles/year. Receives 20-30 submissions/year. 90% of books from first-time authors; 90% from unagented writers. Pays 10-15% royalty on wholesale or retail price, or makes outright purchase of $500-2,000. Publishes book 1 year after acceptance. Accepts simultaneous submissions. Reports in 2 weeks on queries, 1 month on mss. Book catalog for $5.
Nonfiction: How-to, reference, textbook. Subjects include sociology, investigation and investigative techniques. "We are looking for hardcore investigative methods books, manuals on how to make more dollars in private investigation, private investigative marketing techniques, and specialties in the investigative professions." Query with outline/synopsis and sample chapters. Reviews artwork/photos as part of ms package.
Tips: "Our audience includes private investigators, those wanting to break into investigation, related trades such as auto repossessors, private process servers, news reporters, and related security trades."

THREE CONTINENTS PRESS, P.O. Box 38009, Colorado Springs CO 80937-8009. Fax: (719)576-4689. Publisher/Editor-in-Chief: Donald E. Herdeck. General Editor: Harold Ames, Jr. Estab. 1973. Publishes hardcover and paperback originals and reprints. Averages 20-30 titles/year. Receives 200 submissions/year. 15% of books from first-time authors; 99% from unagented writers. Average print order for a first book is 1,000. Nonauthor subsidy publishes 5% of books. Pays 10% royalty. Offers advance "only on delivery of complete manuscript which is found acceptable; usually $300." Accepts simultaneous submissions. State availability of photos/illustrations. Reports in 2 months.
Nonfiction, Fiction and Poetry: Specializes in African, Caribbean, Middle Eastern (Arabic and Persian) and Asian-Pacific literature, criticism and translation, Third World literature and history. Scholarly, well-prepared mss; creative writing. Fiction, poetry, criticism, history and translations of creative writing. "We search for books that will make clear the complexity and value of non-Western literature and culture, including bilingual texts (Arabic language/English translations). We are always interested in genuine contributions to understanding non-Western culture." Length: 50,000-125,000 words. Query. "Please do not submit manuscript unless we ask for it. We prefer an outline, and an annotated table of contents, for works of nonfiction; and a synopsis, a plot summary (one to three pages), for fiction. For poetry, five to ten sample poems." Reviews artwork/photos as part of ms package.
Tips: "We need a *polished* translation, or original prose or poetry by non-Western authors *only*. Critical and cross-cultural studies are accepted from any scholar from anywhere."

THUNDER'S MOUTH PRESS, 632 Broadway, 7th Floor, New York NY 10012. (212)780-0380. Publisher: Neil Ortenberg. Estab. 1982. Publishes hardcover and trade paperback originals and reprints, almost exclusively nonfiction. Averages 15-20 titles/year. Receives 1,000 submissions annually. 10% of books from unagented writers. Average print order for a first book is 7,500. Pays 5-10% royalty on retail price. Offers average $15,000 advance. Publishes book an average of 8 months after acceptance. Reports in 3 months on queries. No unsolicited mss.

Nonfiction: Biography, politics, popular culture. Query with SASE.

Fiction: Query only.

TIA CHUCHA PRESS, A Project of The Guild Complex, P.O. Box 476969, Chicago IL 60647. (312)252-5321. Fax: (312)252-5388. Director: Luis Rodriguez. Publishes trade paperback originals. Publishes 2-4 titles/year. Receives 60-70 queries and 25-30 mss/year. 100% of books from first-time authors; 100% from unagented writers. Pays 10% royalty on wholesale price. Publishes book 1 year after acceptance of ms. Query for electronic submissions. Reports in 3 months on mss. Book catalog and ms guidelines free on request.

Poetry: "We are a cross-cultural poetry press—not limited to style." Submit complete ms.

Recent Poetry Title: *Nightsong*, by Andres Rodriguez.

Tips: Audience is "those interested in strong, multicultural, urban poetry—the best of bar-cafe poetry."

TIARE PUBLICATIONS, P.O. Box 493, Lake Geneva WI 53147-0493. Fax: (414)248-8927. President: Gerry L. Dexter. Estab. 1986. Imprints are Limelight Books and Balboa Books. Publishes trade paperback originals. Publishes 6-12 titles/year. Receives 25 queries and 10 mss/year. 40% of books from first-time authors; 100% from unagented writers. Pays 15% royalty on retail/wholesale price. Publishes book 3 months after acceptance of ms. Query for electronic submission. Reports in 1 month on queries. Book catalog for $1.

Nonfiction: Technical, general nonfiction, mostly how-to, (Limelight); jazz/big bands (Balboa). "We are always looking for new ideas in the areas of amateur radio, shortwave listening, scanner radio monitoring, monitoring satellite transmissions—how to, equipment, techniques, etc." Query.

Recent Nonfiction Title: *Citizens Guide to Scanning*, by Laura E. Quarantello.

TIDEWATER PUBLISHERS, Imprint of Cornell Maritime Press, Inc., P.O. Box 456, Centreville MD 21617-0456. (410)758-1075. Fax: (410)758-6849. Managing Editor: Charlotte Kurst. Estab. 1938. Publishes hardcover and paperback originals. Averages 7-9 titles/year. Receives 150 submissions/year. 41% of books from first-time authors; 99% from unagented writers. Pays 7½-15% royalty on retail price. Publishes book 1 year after acceptance. Query for electronic submissions. Reports in 2 months. Book catalog for 10×13 SAE with 5 first-class stamps.

Nonfiction: Cookbook, history, illustrated book, juvenile, reference. Regional subjects. Query or submit outline and sample chapters. Reviews artwork/photos as part of ms package.

Recent Nonfiction Title: *Chesapeake Steamboats: Vanished Fleet*, by David C. Holly.

Fiction: Regional juvenile fiction only. Query or submit outline/synopsis and sample chapters.

Recent Fiction Title: *Awesome Chesapeake*, by David O. Bell, illustrated by Marcy Dunn Ramsey.

Tips: "Our audience is made up of readers interested in works that are specific to the Chesapeake Bay and Delmarva Peninsula area."

TIMBER PRESS, INC., 133 SW Second Ave., Suite 450, Portland OR 97204-3527. (503)227-2878. Fax: (503)227-3070. Publisher: Robert B. Conklin. Neal Maillet, acquisitions in horticulture and botany. Karen Kirtley, acquisitions in music. Estab. 1976. Imprints are Timber Press (horticulture), Amadeus Press (music). Publishes hardcover and paperback originals. Publishes 40 titles/year. Receives 300-400 submissions/year. 75% of books from first-time authors; 95% of books from unagented writers. Pays 10% royalty. Sometimes offers advance to cover costs of artwork and final ms completion. Publishes book 2 years after acceptance. Query for electronic submissions. Reports in 2 months. Book catalogs for 9×12 SAE with 5 first-class stamps.

● Timber Press published *The Nineteenth Century German Lied*, by Gorrall, which received Outstanding Reference Book Award from American Library Association/Choice.

Nonfiction: Horticulture, botany, plant sciences, natural history, Northwest regional material, classical and traditional music. Accepts nonfiction translations from all languages. Query or submit outline and 3-4 sample chapters. Reviews artwork/photos as part of ms package.

Recent Nonfiction Title: *Plant Propagation Made Easy*, by Alan Toogood.

Tips: "The writer has the best chance of selling our firm good books on botany, plant science, horticulture, or serious music."

TIME-LIFE BOOKS INC., Division of Time Warner Inc., 777 Duke St., Alexandria VA 22314. (703)838-7000. Fax: (703)838-7042. Managing Editor: Bobbie Conlan. Estab. 1960. Publishes hardcover originals. Publishes 40 titles/year. Books are almost entirely staff-generated and staff-produced, and distribution is primarily through mail order sale. TLB is always interested in freelance narrative and how-to writers. Submit résumé and clips to Managing Editor. No unpublished mss or book proposals.

Recent Nonfiction Title: *Perennials* (*The Complete Gardener* series).

TIMES BOOKS, Imprint of Random House, Inc., 201 E. 50 St., New York NY 10022. (212)872-8110. Vice President and Publisher: Peter Osnos. Editorial Director: Steve Wasserman. Publishes hardcover and paper-

back originals and reprints. Publishes 50-60 titles/year. Pays royalty. Offers average advance. Publishes book 1 year after acceptance. *Writer's Market* recommends allowing 2 months for reply.
Nonfiction: Business/economics, science and medicine, history, biography, women's issues, the family, cookbooks, current affairs. Accepts only solicited mss. Reviews artwork/photos as part of ms package.
Recent Nonfiction Title: *China Wakes: The Struggle for the Soul of a Rising Power*, by Nicholas Kristol and Sheryl WuDunn.

‡**TODD PUBLICATIONS**, 18 N. Greenbush Rd., West Nyack NY 10994. (914)358-6213. President: Barry Klein. Publishes hardcover and trade paperback originals. Publishes 5 titles/year. 1% of books from first-time authors. Pays 5-15% royalty on wholesale price. Publishes book an average of 6 months after acceptance of ms. Accepts simultaneous submissions. Reports in 2 months on proposals. Book catalog free. Manuscript guidelines for #10 SASE.
Nonfiction: How-to, reference, self-help. Subjects include business and economics, ethnic, health/medicine, money/finance, travel. Submit 2 sample chapters.

TOR BOOKS, Subsidiary of St. Martin's Press, 14th Floor, 175 Fifth Ave., New York NY 10010. (212)388-0100. Fax: (212)388-0191. Publisher: Tom Doherty. Editor-in-Chief: Robert Gleason. Estab. 1980. Publishes mass market, hardcover and trade paperback originals and reprints. Averages 250 books/year. Pays 6-8% royalty to unpublished authors (paperback); 8-10% to established authors (paperback). Hardback: 10% on first 5,000; 12½% on second 5,000; 15% thereafter. Offers negotiable advance. Reports in 4 months. Book catalog for 9×12 SAE with 2 first-class stamps.
 • TOR publishes selected nonfiction. Query first.
Fiction: Science fiction, fantasy, horror, techno-thrillers, "women's" suspense, American historicals, Westerns. "We prefer an extensive chapter-by-chapter synopsis and the first three chapters complete." Prefers agented mss or proposals.
Recent Fiction Title: *Zero Coupon*, by Paul Erdman.
Tips: "We're never short of good sci fi or fantasy, but we're always open to solid, technologically knowledgeable hard science fiction or thrillers by writers with solid expertise."

TRANSNATIONAL PUBLISHERS, INC., One Bridge St., Irvington NY 10533. (914)591-4288. Fax: (914)591-2688. Editor: Andrea Mastor. Publishes hardcover and trade paperback originals. Publishes 10 titles/year. Receives 60 queries and 30 mss/year. Pays 10% minimum royalty on wholesale or retail price; depends on contract. Publishes book 3-6 months after acceptance of ms. Accepts simultaneous submissions. Query for electronic submissions. Reports in 2 weeks on queries. Book catalog and ms guidelines free on request.
Nonfiction: Textbooks, law books. Subjects include law, environment, women's rights, human rights. Query with outline and 1 sample chapter.

TRANSPORTATION TRAILS, Imprint of National Bus Trader, Inc., 9698 W. Judson Rd., Polo IL 61064-9015. (815)946-2341. Fax: (815)946-2347. Editor: Larry Plachno. Estab. 1977. Publishes hardcover, trade paperback and mass market paperback originals. Publishes 8 titles/year. Receives 10 submissions/year. 50% of books from first-time authors; 100% from unagented writers. Pays 10-15% on retail price. Publishes book 1 year after acceptance. Accepts simultaneous submissions. Reports in 1 month. *Writer's Market* recommends allowing 2 months for reply. Book catalog and ms guidelines free.
Nonfiction: "We are interested in transportation history—prefer electric interurban railroads or trolley lines but will consider steam locomotives, horsecars, buses, aviation and maritime." Query. Reviews artwork/photos as part of ms package.
Tips: "We are not interested in travel nonfiction."

‡**TRILOGY BOOKS**, 50 S. DeLacey Ave., Suite 201, Pasadena CA 91105. (818)440-0669. Publisher: Marge Wood. Publishes trade paperback originals. Publishes 4 titles/year. Pays 6-10% royalty on retail price. Advance varies. Publishes book 1 year after acceptance of ms. Accepts simultaneous submissions. Reports in 1 month on queries. Book catalog and ms guidelines free on request.
Nonfiction: Biography and autobiography, self-help. Subjects include (women's) history, women's issues/studies. "We are seeking manuscripts that have mainstream as well as scholarly or academic appeal, and that focus on women's lives." Query.
Recent Nonfiction Title: *Sisters of the Wind: Voices of Early Women Aviators*, by Elizabeth S. Bell (women's history).
Tips: Audience is academic and well-educated mainstream women.

‡**TRIUMPH BOOKS**, Imprint of Liguori Publications, 333 Glen Head Rd., Old Brookville NY 11545. Executive Editor: Patricia A. Kossmann. Publishes hardcover originals and trade paperback originals and reprints. Publishes 75 titles/year; imprint publishes 20 titles/year. 10% of books from first-time authors; 75% from unagented writers. Pays 7-15% royalty on retail price. Offers $2,500-7,500 advance. Publishes book 10 months after acceptance of ms. Accepts simultaneous submissions. Reports in 1 month on queries and

proposals, 3 months on mss. Book catalog free to agents and published authors.

Nonfiction: Self-help, spirituality/inspiration. Subjects include religion (Catholic; mainline Protestant; inter-religious; some theology), women's issues/studies (from a religious or spiritual perspective. Serious, upscale, "thinking" books—well-grounded and well-written. Submit outline and 2 sample chapters with SASE. Reviews artwork/photos as part of ms package.

Recent Nonfiction Title: *Embodied Prayer*, by Celeste Schroeder (spirituality/self-development).

Tips: Audience is spiritual seekers (especially babyboomers) and the educated adult open to new thought and guidance.

TSR, INC., 201 Sheridan Spring Rd., Lake Geneva WI 53147. (414)248-3625. Estab. 1975. Executive Editor: Brian Thomsen. Imprints are TSR™ Books, Dungeons & Dragons Books, Dragonlance® Books, Forgotten Realms™ Books, Ravenloft™ Books, and Dark Sun™ Books. Publishes hardcover and trade paperback originals and trade paperback reprints. Publishes 40-50 titles/year. Receives 600 queries and 300 mss/year. 10% of books from first-time authors; 20% from unagented authors. Pays 4-8% royalty on retail price. Offers $4,000-6,000 average advance. Publishes book 6-12 months after acceptance. Accepts simultaneous submissions. Query for electronic submissions. Send to submissions editor. Reports in 2 months on queries.

Nonfiction: "All of our nonfiction books are generated inhouse."

Fiction: Fantasy, gothic, humor, science fiction short story collections, young adult. "We have a very small market for good science fiction and fantasy for the TSR Book line, but also need samples from writers willing to do work-for-hire for our other lines. No excessively violent or gory fantasy or science fiction." Query with outline/synopsis and 3 sample chapters.

Recent Fiction Title: *Elfsong*, by Elaine Cunningham.

Tips: "Our audience is comprised of highly imaginative 12-40 year-old males."

‡TUDOR PUBLISHERS, P.O. Box 38366, Greensboro NC 27438. (910)282-5907. Senior Editor: Pam Cox. Publishes hardcover and trade paperback originals. Publishes 4-6 titles/year. Receives 400 queries and 200 mss/year. 80% of books from first-time authors; 90% from unagented writers. Pays 10% royalty on wholesale price. No advance. Publishes book 9 months after acceptance of ms. Accepts simultaneous submissions. Reports in 1 month on queries and proposals, 3 months on mss. Book catalog and ms guidelines for #10 SASE.

Nonfiction: Biography, juvenile, cookbook, how-to, reference, self-help, technical, textbook. Subjects include Americana, child guidance/parenting, cooking/foods/nutrition, education, history, hobbies, military/war, psychology, regional, science, sports, women's issues/studies. Query with outline. "Writers should have a concise proposal statement on initial inquiry, author bio and publication credits with SASE. Upon request for outline, it should be detailed chapter by chapter, with SASE. Request for complete ms should result in accompanying SASE or postage." Reviews artwork as part of ms package.

Recent Nonfiction Title: *Who's Who on the Moon*, by Elijah E. Cocks and Josiah C. Cocks (astronomy/reference/biography).

Fiction: Adventure, ethnic, historical, humor, juvenile, mainstream/contemporary, mystery, romance, science fiction, short story collections, suspense, western, young adult. Query with synopsis.

Recent Fiction Title: *Mean Lean Weightlifting Queen*, by Mark Emerson (young adult).

‡TWENTY-FIRST CENTURY BOOKS, Imprint of Henry Holt and Company, Inc., 115 W. 18th St., New York NY 10011. Editorial Assistant: Tory Gillett. Publishes hardcover originals and imprints, trade paperback originals. Publishes 50 titles/year. Receives 100 queries and 50 mss/year. 20% of books from first-time writers; 75% from unagented writers. Pays 5-8% royalty on wholesale price. Offers $500-1,500 advance per title. Publishes book 10 months after acceptance of ms. Accepts simultaneous submissions. Reports in 3 months on proposals.

Nonfiction: Children's nonfiction. Subjects include animals, government/politics, health/medicine, history, military/war, nature/environment, science, current events and social issues. "We publish primarily in series of four or more titles, for ages 10 and up, grades 5 and up (middle grade). No picture books or adult books." Submit proposal package including outline, sample chapter and SASE. Does not review artwork.

Recent Nonfiction Title: The *Exploring Earth's Biomes* series.

TYNDALE HOUSE PUBLISHERS, INC., 351 Executive Dr., P.O. Box 80, Wheaton IL 60189-0080. (708)668-8300. Vice President, Editorial: Ronald Beers. Contact: Marilyn DellOrto. Estab. 1962. Publishes hardcover and trade paperback originals and mass paperback reprints. Averages 100 titles/year. 5-10% of books from first-time authors. Average first print order for a first book is 5,000-10,000. Royalty and advance negotiable. Publishes book 12-18 months after acceptance. Send query and synopsis, not whole ms. Reviews solicited mss only. Reports in up to 2 months. Book catalog and ms guidelines for 9×12 SAE with 9 first-class stamps.

● This publisher has received Book of the Year Award (CBA) and the *Campus Life* Book of the Year Award (2 titles).

Nonfiction: "Practical, user-friendly Christian books: home and family, Christian growth/self-help, devotional/inspirational, theology/Bible doctrine, children's nonfiction, contemporary/critical issues." Query.

Fiction: "Biblical, historical and other Christian themes. No short story collections. Youth books: character building stories with Christian perspective. Especially interested in ages 10-14." Query.

‡**THE TYRONE PRESS**, 348 Hartford Turnpike, Hampton CT 06247. (203)455-0039. Editor-in-Chief: Michael Donovan. Publishes hardcover and trade paperback originals and reprints. Publishes 6 titles/year. 30% of books from first-time authors; 60% from unagented writers. Pays royalty on wholesale price. Offers $500-1,000 advance. Publishes book 6 months after acceptance of ms. Accepts simultaneous submissions. Reports in 1 month on queries.
Nonfiction: Textbook, popular market general subjects. Subjects include anthropology/archaeology, ethnic, history, military/war, religion, sociology. "We are interested in serious subjects written for a general audience. Writers often make the mistake of writing in an academic style which assumes knowledge that the reader does not have. We prefer a simple and direct explanation of all concepts." Submit proposal package, including sample chapters.
Recent Nonfiction Title: *The Quest for the Galloping Hogan*, by M. J. Culligan-Hogan (popular history).

ULI, THE URBAN LAND INSTITUTE, 625 Indiana Ave. NW, Washington DC 20004-2930. (202)289-8500. Fax: (202)624-7140. Vice President/Publisher: Frank H. Spink, Jr. Estab. 1936. Publishes hardcover and trade paperback originals. Averages 15-20 titles/year. Receives 20 submissions/year. No books from first-time authors; 100% of books from unagented writers. Pays 10% royalty on gross sales. Offers $1,500-2,000 advance. Publishes book 6 months after acceptance. Query for electronic submissions. Book catalog and ms guidelines for 9×12 SAE.
Nonfiction: Technical books on real estate development and land planning. "The majority of manuscripts are created inhouse by research staff. We acquire two or three outside authors to fill schedule and subject areas where our list has gaps. We are not interested in real estate sales, brokerages, appraisal, making money in real estate, opinion, personal point of view, or manuscripts negative toward growth and development." Query. Reviews artwork/photos as part of ms package.
Recent Nonfiction Title: *Golf Course Development and Real Estate*, by Guy Rondo and Desmond Muirhead.

‡**ULTRAMARINE PUBLISHING INC.**, P.O. Box 303, Hastings-on-Hudson NY 10530. (914)478-2522. Publisher: C.P. Stephens. Publishes hardcover originals. Publishes 12 titles/year. No first-time or unagented writers. Pays 10% royalty. Publishes book 1 month after acceptance of ms. Accepts simultaneous submissions. Reports in 1 month. Book catalog free on request.
Nonfiction: Reference. Bibliographic subjects only. Query.
Recent Nonfiction Title: *A Checklist of Philip K. Dick*, (bibliography).
Fiction: Experimental, literary, science fiction. "We have never published an unsolicited manuscript." Agented submissions only.
Recent Fiction Title: *Renegades of Pern*, Anne McCaffrey.

ULYSSES PRESS, Suite 1, 3286 Adeline St., Berkeley CA 94703. (510)601-8301. Fax: (510)601-8307. Editorial Director: Leslie Henriques. Estab. 1982. Publishes trade paperback originals. Averages 39 titles/year. 25% of books from first-time authors; 75% from unagented writers. Pays 12-16% royalty on wholesale price. Offers $2,000-8,000 advance. Publishes book 6 months after acceptance. Accepts simultaneous submissions. Query for electronic submissions. Reports in 2 months on proposals. Book catalog free on request.
   • Ulysses is rapidly expanding its line of health books and is very interested in looking at proposals in this area.
Nonfiction: Travel, health. Submit proposal package including outline, 2 sample chapters, and market analysis. Reviews artwork/photos as part of freelance ms package. Writers should send photocopies.
Recent Nonfiction Title: Publishes three series of travel guidebooks—*Hidden, Ultimate* and the *The New Key to . . . .*

UMBRELLA BOOKS, Imprint of Epicenter Press Inc., Box 82368, Kenmore WA 98028-0368. (206)485-6822. Fax: (206)481-8253. E-mail: 74754.2040@compuserve.com. President: Kent Sturgis. Associate Editor: Christine Ummel. Estab. 1988. Publishes 4-6 titles/year. Pays royalty on net receipts. Publishes book 1 year after acceptance. Query for electronic submissions. Reports in 3 months on queries. Manuscript guidelines for #10 SASE.
   • Umbrella welcomes marketing and promotion ideas.
Nonfiction: Travel (West Coast and Alaska). Query. Do *not* send original photos or slides.

UNITY BOOKS, Unity School of Christianity, 1901 NW Blue Parkway, Unity Village MO 64065-0001. (816)524-3550 ext. 3190. Associate Editor: Gayle Revelle. Publishes hardcover and trade paperback originals and reprints. Publishes 16 titles/year. Receives 45 queries and 125-150 mss/year. 30% of books from first-time authors; 95% from unagented writers. Pays 10-11½% royalty on retail price. Publishes book 11 months after acceptance of ms. Accepts simultaneous submissions. Query for electronic submissions. Reports in 1 month on queries and proposals, 2 months on mss. Book catalog and ms guidelines free on request.

Nonfiction: Children's/juvenile, reference (spiritual/metaphysical), self-help. Subjects include health (nutrition/holistic), philosophy (perennial/New Thought), psychology (transpersonal), religion (spiritual/metaphysical Bible interpretation/modern Biblical studies). "Writers should be familiar with principles of metaphysical Christianity but not feel bound by them. We are interested in works in the related fields of holistic health, spiritual psychology as well as the philosophy of other world religions." Query with outline and 3 sample chapters. Reviews artwork/photos as part of ms package. Send photocopies.
Recent Nonfiction Title: *Finding Yourself in Transition*, by Robert Brumet (using life's changes for spiritual awakening).
Fiction: Picture books (spiritual/inspirational), metaphysical. Query with synopsis and 3 sample chapters.
Recent Fiction Title: *Ted Bear's Magic Swing*, by Dianne Baker (picture book).

UNIVELT, INC., P.O. Box 28130, San Diego CA 92198. (619)746-4005. Fax: (619)746-3139. Publisher: Robert H. Jacobs. Estab. 1970. Imprints are American Astronautical Society, National Space Society, Lunar & Planetary Institute. Publishes hardcover originals. Averages 8 titles/year. Receives 20 submissions/year. 5% of books from first-time authors; 5% from unagented writers. Nonauthor subsidy publishes 10% of books. Average print order for a first book is 1,000-2,000. Pays 10% royalty on actual sales. No advance. Publishes book 4 months after acceptance. Reports in 1 month. *Writer's Market* recommends allowing 2 months for reply. Book catalog and ms guidelines for SASE.
Nonfiction: Publishes in the field of aerospace, especially astronautics and technical communications, but including application of aerospace technology to Earth's problems, also astronomy. Submit outline and 1-2 sample chapters. Reviews artwork/photos as part of ms package.
Tips: "Writers have the best chance of selling manuscripts on the history of astronautics (we have a history series) and astronautics/spaceflight subjects. We publish for the American Astronautical Society. Queries may be routed to other editors in the publishing group."

UNIVERSITY OF ALABAMA PRESS, P.O. Box 870380, Tuscaloosa AL 35487-0380. Fax: (205)348-9201. Director: Malcolm MacDonald. Estab. 1945. Publishes hardcover and paperbound originals. Averages 40 titles/year. Receives 200 submissions/year. 80% of books from first-time authors; 100% from unagented writers. "Pays maximum 10% royalty on wholesale price. No advance." Publishes book 16 months after acceptance. Book catalog free. Manuscript guidelines for SASE.
● University of Alabama Press responds to an author immediately upon receiving the manuscript. If they think it is unsuitable for Alabama's program, they tell the author at once. If the manuscript warrants it, they begin the peer-review process, which may take two to four months to complete. During that process, they keep the author fully informed. This press has received The Jefferson Davis Award; The John Lyman Prize in Naval History; The Louis Brownlow Award; James F. Sulzby Award.
Nonfiction: Biography, history, politics, religion, literature, archaeology. Considers upon merit almost any subject of scholarly interest, but specializes in speech communication, political science and public administration, literary criticism and biography, and history. Accepts nonfiction translations. Reviews artwork/photos as part of ms package.
Tips: "The University Press does not commission projects with freelance writers. Some who submit their manuscripts to us are independent scholars who have written on speculation, but they are not freelancers in the commonly accepted meaning of that word."

UNIVERSITY OF ALASKA PRESS, P.O. Box 756240, 1st Floor Gruening Bldg., UAF, Fairbanks AK 99775-6240. (907)474-6389. Fax: (907)474-5502. Manager: Debbie Van Stone. Acquisitions: Pam Odom. Estab. 1967. Imprints are Ramuson Library Historical Translation Series, Lanternlight Library, Oral Biographies, and Classic Reprints. Publishes hardcover originals, trade paperback originals and reprints. Averages 5-10 titles/year. Receives 100 submissions/year. Pays 7½-10% royalty on net sales. Publishes book 2 years after acceptance. Query for electronic submissions. Reports in 2 months. Book catalog free on request.
Nonfiction: Biography, reference, technical, textbook, scholarly nonfiction relating to Alaska-circumpolar regions. Subjects include agriculture/horticulture, Americana (Alaskana), animals, anthropology/archaeology, art/architecture, education, ethnic, government/politics, health/medicine, history, language, military/war, nature/environment, regional, science, translation. Nothing that isn't northern or circumpolar. Query or submit outline. Reviews copies of artwork/photos as part of ms package.
Tips: "Writers have the best chance with scholarly nonfiction relating to Alaska, the circumpolar regions and North Pacific Rim. Our audience is made up of scholars, historians, students, libraries, universities, individuals."

UNIVERSITY OF ARIZONA PRESS, 1230 N. Park Ave., #102, Tucson AZ 85719-4140. (602)621-1441. Fax: (602)621-8899. Director: Stephen Cox. Senior Editor: Joanne O'Hare. Estab. 1959. Publishes hardcover and paperback originals and reprints. Averages 50 titles/year. Receives 300-400 submissions/year. 30% of books from first-time authors; 95% from unagented writers. Average print order is 1,500. Royalty terms vary; usual starting point for scholarly monograph is after sale of first 1,000 copies. Publishes book 1 year after acceptance. Query for electronic submissions. Reports in 3 months. Book catalog for 9×12 SAE. Manuscript guidelines for #10 SASE.

● *The Metropolitan Frontier*, by Carl Abbott, won Best Book of 1993 in North American Urban History from the Urban History Association. *Downcanyon: A Naturalist Explores the Colorado River Through the Grand Canyon*, by Ann Zwinger, was awarded the 1995 Book Award by the Western States Art Federation.

Nonfiction: Scholarly books about anthropology, Arizona, American West, archaeology, environmental science, global change, Latin America, Native Americans, natural history, space sciences and women's studies. Query with outline, list of illustrations and sample chapters. Reviews artwork/photos as part of ms package.

Tips: "Perhaps the most common mistake a writer might make is to offer a book manuscript or proposal to a house whose list he or she has not studied carefully. Editors rejoice in receiving material that is clearly targeted to the house's list, 'I have approached your firm because my books complement your past publications in . . .,' presented in a straightforward, businesslike manner."

THE UNIVERSITY OF ARKANSAS PRESS, 201 Ozark Ave., Fayetteville AR 72701-1201. (501)575-3246. Fax: (501)575-6044. Director: Kevin Brock. Acquisitions Editor: Kevin Brock. Estab. 1980. Publishes hardcover and trade paperback originals and reprints. Averages 36 titles/year. Receives 4,000 submissions/year. 30% of books from first-time authors; 90% from unagented writers. Pays 10% royalty on net receipts from hardcover; 6% on paper. Publishes book 1 year after acceptance. No simultaneous submissions. Accepted mss must be submitted on disk. Reports in up to 3 months. Book catalog for 9×12 SAE with 5 first-class stamps. Manuscript guidelines for #10 SAE with 2 first-class stamps.

Nonfiction: Americana, history, humanities, nature, general politics and history of politics, sociology. "Our current needs include literary criticism, history and biography. We won't consider manuscripts for texts, juvenile or religious studies, or anything requiring a specialized or exotic vocabulary." Query or submit outline and sample chapters.

Recent Nonfiction Title: *Rugged and Sublime: The Civil War in Arkansas*, edited by Mark Christ.

Fiction: Works of high literary merit; short stories. No genre fiction or novels. Query.

Recent Fiction Title: *Overgrown with Love*, short stories by Scott Ely.

Poetry: "Because of small list, query first." Arkansas Poetry Award offered for publication of first book. Write for contest rules.

Recent Poetry Title: *O Paradise*, by William Trowbridge.

UNIVERSITY OF CALIFORNIA PRESS, 2120 Berkeley Way, Berkeley CA 94720. Director: James H. Clark. Associate Director: Lynne E. Withey. Estab. 1893. Los Angeles office: 405 Hilgard Ave., Los Angeles CA 90024-1373. New York office: Room 513, 50 E. 42 St., New York NY 10017. UK office: University Presses of California, Columbia, and Princeton, 1 Oldlands Way, Bognor Regis, W. Sussex PO22 9SA England. Publishes hardcover and paperback originals and reprints. "On books likely to do more than return their costs, a standard royalty contract beginning at 7% on net receipts is paid; on paperbacks it is less." Publishes 180 titles/year. Queries are always advisable, accompanied by outlines or sample material. Accepts nonfiction translations. Send to Berkeley address. Reports vary, depending on the subject. *Writer's Market* recommends allowing 2 months for reply. Enclose return postage.

Nonfiction: "Most of our publications are hardcover nonfiction written by scholars." Publishes scholarly books including history, art, literary studies, social sciences, natural sciences and some high-level popularizations. No length preferences. *Writer's Market* recommends query with SASE first.

Fiction and Poetry: Publishes fiction and poetry only in translation.

UNIVERSITY OF IDAHO PRESS, 16 Brink Hall, Moscow ID 83844-1107. (208)885-5939. Fax: (208)885-9059. E-mail: uipress@raven.csrv.uidaho.edu. Imprints are: Northwest Folklife; Idaho Yesterdays; Northwest Naturalist Books. Director: Peggy Pace. Estab. 1972. Publishes hardcover and trade paperback originals and reprints. Publishes 8-10 titles/year. Receives 150-250 queries and 25-50 mss/year. 100% of books from unagented writers. Pays up to 10% royalty on net sales. Publishes book 1 year after acceptance of ms. Query for electronic submissions. Reports in 6 months. Book catalog and ms guidelines free on request.

Nonfiction: Biography, reference, technical, textbook. Subjects include agriculture/horticulture, Americana, anthropology/archaeology, ethnic, folklore, history, language/literature, nature/environment, recreation, regional, women's issues/studies. "Writers should contact us to discuss projects in advance and refer to our catalog to become familiar with the types of projects the press publishes. Avoid being unaware of the constraints of scholarly publishing, and avoid submitting queries and manuscripts in areas we don't publish in." Query or submit proposal package, including sample chapter, contents, vita. Reviews artwork/photos as part of the freelance ms package. Writers should send photocopies.

Tips: Audience is educated readers, scholars.

UNIVERSITY OF ILLINOIS PRESS, 1325 S. Oak St., Champaign IL 61820-6903. (217)333-0950. Fax: (217)244-8082. Director/Editor-in-Chief: Richard L. Wentworth. Contact: Janice Roney. Estab. 1918. Publishes hardcover and trade paperback originals and reprints. Averages 100-110 titles/year. 50% of books from first-time authors; 95% from unagented writers. Nonauthor subsidy publishes 20% of books. Pays 0-10% royalty on net sales; offers $1,000-1,500 average advance (rarely). Publishes book 1 year after acceptance. Query for electronic submissions. Reports in 1 month. *Writer's Market* recommends allowing 2 months for reply. Book catalog for 9×12 SAE with 2 first-class stamps.

Nonfiction: Biography, reference, scholarly books. Subjects include Americana, history (especially American history), music (especially American music), politics, sociology, philosophy, sports, literature. Always looking for "solid scholarly books in American history, especially social history; books on American popular music, and books in the broad area of American studies." Query with outline.

Recent Nonfiction Title: *Babe: The Life and Legend of Babe Didrikson Zaharias*, by Susan E. Cayleff.

Fiction: Ethnic, experimental, mainstream. "We are not presently looking at unsolicited collections of stories. We do not publish novels." Query.

Recent Fiction Title: *Middle Murphy*, by Mark Costello (stories).

Tips: "Serious scholarly books that are broad enough and well-written enough to appeal to non-specialists are doing well for us in today's market."

UNIVERSITY OF IOWA PRESS, 119 W. Park Rd., Iowa City IA 52242-1000. (319)335-2000. Fax: (319)335-2055. Director: Paul Zimmer. Estab. 1969. Publishes hardcover and paperback originals. Averages 35 titles/year. Receives 300-400 submissions/year. 30% of books from first-time authors; 95% from unagented writers. Average print order for a first book is 1,000-1,200. Pays 7-10% royalty on net price. "We market mostly by direct mailing of fliers to groups with special interests in our titles and by advertising in trade and scholarly publications." Publishes book 1 year after acceptance. Query for electronic submissions. Reports within 4 months. Book catalog and ms guidelines free.

Nonfiction: Publishes anthropology, archaeology, British and American literary studies, history (Victorian, US, regional Latin American), jazz studies, history of photography and natural history. Looks for evidence of original research; reliable sources; clarity of organization, complete development of theme with documentation and supportive footnotes and/or bibliography; and a substantive contribution to knowledge in the field treated. Query or submit outline. Use *Chicago Manual of Style*. Reviews artwork/photos as part of ms package.

Recent Nonfiction Title: *Reflecting A Prairie Town: A Year in Peterson*, by Drake Hohanson.

Fiction and Poetry: Currently publishes the Iowa Short Fiction Award selections and winners of the Iowa Poetry Prize Competition. Please query regarding poetry or fiction before sending manuscript.

Tips: "Developing a list of books on ornithology."

‡UNIVERSITY OF MAINE PRESS, 5717 Corbett Hall, Orono ME 04469-5717. (207)581-1408. Contact: Director. Publishes hardcover and trade paperback originals and reprints. Publishes 4 titles/year. Receives 50 queries and 25 mss/year. 10% of mss from first-time authors; 90% from unagented writers. Publishes book 1 year after acceptance of ms. Accepts simultaneous submissions. Query for electronic submissions. *Writer's Market* recommends allowing 2 months for reply.

Nonfiction: "We are an academic book publisher, interested in scholarly works on regional history, regional life sciences, Franco-American studies. Authors should be able to articulate their ideas on the potential market for their work." Query.

Fiction: Rarely. "The University of Maine Press publishes primarily regional fiction: Maine, New England, Canadian Maritimes." Query.

UNIVERSITY OF MASSACHUSETTS PRESS, P.O. Box 429, Amherst MA 01004-0429. (413)545-2217. Fax: (413)545-1226. Director: Bruce Wilcox. Senior Editor: Clark Dougan. Editoral Assistant: Chris Hammel. Estab. 1963. Publishes hardcover and paperback originals, reprints and imports. Averages 30 titles/year. Receives 600 submissions/year. 20% of books from first-time authors; 90% from unagented writers. Average print order for a first book is 1,500. Royalties generally 10% of net income. Advance rarely offered. No author subsidies accepted. Publishes book 1 year after acceptance. Query for electronic submissions. Preliminary report in 1 month. *Writer's Market* recommends allowing 2 months for reply. Book catalog free.

Nonfiction: Publishes African-American studies, art and architecture, biography, criticism, history, natural history, philosophy, poetry, public policy, sociology and women's studies in original and reprint editions. Accepts nonfiction translations. Submit outline and 1-2 sample chapters. Reviews artwork/photos as part of ms package.

Recent Nonfiction Title: *Black Legacy: America's Hidden Heritage*, by William D. Piersen.

‡THE UNIVERSITY OF MICHIGAN PRESS, P.O. Box 1104, Ann Arbor MI 48106-1104. Director: Colin Day. Publishes hardcover originals and trade paperback originals and reprints. Publishes 150 titles/year. 99.9% of books from unagented writers. Pays 5-10% royalty on wholesale price. Offers $200-1,000 advance. Publishes book 10 months after acceptance of ms. Accepts simultaneous submissions. Reports in 2 months on mss. Book catalog and ms guidelines free on request.

Nonfiction: Textbook, scholarly. Subjects include anthropology/archaeology, business and economics, ethnic, gay/lesbian, government/politics, history, language/literature, nature/environment, philosophy, regional, science, sociology, translation, women's issues/studies, classical studies, English as a second language. Query

with outline, 2 sample chapters and SASE. Reviews artwork/photos as part of ms package. Send photocopies.
Recent Nonfiction Title: *The Male Body: Features, Destinies, Exposure*, edited by Laurence Goldstein.

UNIVERSITY OF MISSOURI PRESS, 2910 LeMone Blvd., Columbia MO 65201. (314)882-7641. Director: Beverly Jarrett. Publishes hardcover and paperback originals and paperback reprints. Averages 150 titles/year. Receives 500 submissions/year. 25-30% of books from first-time authors; 90% from unagented writers. Average print order for a first book is 1,000-1,500. Pays up to 10% royalty on net receipts. No advance. Publishes book 1 year after acceptance. Reports in 6 months. Book catalog free.
Nonfiction: Scholarly publisher interested in history, literary criticism, political science, journalism, social science, some art history. Also regional books about Missouri and the Midwest. No mathematics or hard sciences. Query or submit outline and sample chapters. Consult *Chicago Manual of Style*.
Fiction: "Collections of short fiction are considered throughout the year; the press does not publish novels. Inquiries should be directed to Clair Willcox, acquisitions editor, and should include sample story, a table of contents, and a brief description of the manuscript that notes its length."

UNIVERSITY OF NEBRASKA PRESS, Dept. WM, 312 N. 14th St., P.O. Box 880484, Lincoln NE 68588-0484. (402)472-3581. Editor-in-Chief: Daniel J.J. Ross. Estab. 1941. Publishes hardcover and paperback originals and reprints. Specializes in scholarly nonfiction, some regional books; reprints of Western Americana; American history and culture. Averages 75 new titles, 75 paperback reprints (*Bison Books*)/year. Receives more than 1,000 submissions/year. 25% of books from first-time authors; 95% from unagented writers. Average print order for a first book is 1,000. Pays graduated royalty from 10% on wholesale price for original books. Occasional advance. Reports in 4 months. Book catalog and guidelines for 9 × 12 SAE with 5 first-class stamps.
Nonfiction: Publishes Americana, biography, history, military, nature, photography, psychology, sports, literature, agriculture, American Indian themes. Accepts nonfiction translations. Query with outline/synopsis, 2 sample chapters and introduction. Looks for "an indication that the author knows his/her subject thoroughly and interprets it intelligently." Reviews artwork/photos as part of ms package.
Recent Nonfiction Title: *Remember Laughter: A Life of James Thurber.*
● The University of Nebraska Press published *Making Bodies, Making History*, by Adelson, winner of the MLA Scaglione Prize.
Fiction: Accepts fiction translations but no original fiction.
Recent Fiction Title: *The Collected Stories of Max Brand.*

UNIVERSITY OF NEVADA PRESS, Reno NV 89557-0076. (702)784-6573. Fax: (702)784-6200. E-mail: radko@scs.unr.edu. Director: Thomas R. Radko. Editor-in-Chief: Margaret F. Dalrymple. Estab. 1961. Publishes hardcover and paperback originals and reprints. Averages 35 titles/year. 20% of books from first-time authors; 99% from unagented writers. Average print order for a first book is 2,000. Pays average of 10% royalty on net price. Publishes book 1 year after acceptance. Preliminary report in 2 months. Book catalog and ms guidelines free.
Nonfiction: Specifically needs regional history and natural history, literature, current affairs, ethnonationalism, gambling and gaming, anthropology, biographies, Basque studies. "We are the first university press to sustain a sound series on Basque studies—New World and Old World." No juvenile books. Submit complete ms. *Writer's Market* recommends query with SASE first. Reviews photocopies of artwork/photos as part of ms package.
Recent Nonfiction Title: *Cruising State: Growing Up in Southern California*, by Christopher Buckley.

UNIVERSITY OF NEW MEXICO PRESS, 1720 Lomas Blvd. NE, Albuquerque NM 87131-1591. (505)277-2346. Contact: Editor. Estab. 1929. Publishes hardcover originals and trade paperback originals and reprints. Averages 50 titles/year. Receives 500 submissions/year. 12% of books from first-time authors; 90% from unagented writers. Pays up to 15% royalty on wholesale price. Publishes book 1 year after acceptance. Reports in 2 weeks on queries. *Writer's Market* recommends allowing 2 months for reply. Book catalog free.
Nonfiction: Biography, illustrated book, scholarly books. Subjects include anthropology/archaeology, art/architecture, ethnic, history, photography. "No how-to, humor, juvenile, self-help, software, technical or textbooks." Query. Reviews artwork/photos as part of ms package. Prefers to see photocopies first.
Tips: "Most of our authors are academics. A scholarly monograph by an academic has a better chance than anything else. Our audience is a combination of academics and interested lay readers."

THE UNIVERSITY OF NORTH CAROLINA PRESS, P.O. Box 2288, Chapel Hill NC 27515-2288. (919)966-3561. Director: Kate Douglas Torrey. Publishes hardcover and paperback originals and occasionally, paperback reprints. Specializes in scholarly books and regional trade books. Averages 80 titles/year. 70% of books from first-time scholarly authors; 90% from unagented writers. Royalty schedule "varies." Occasional advances. Query for electronic submissions. Publishes book 1 year after acceptance. Reports in 5 months. Free book catalog. Manuscript guidelines for SASE.
Nonfiction: "Our major fields are American history, American studies and Southern studies." Also, scholarly books in legal history, Civil War history, literary studies, classics, gender studies, oral history, folklore,

political science, religious studies, historical sociology, Latin American studies. In European studies, focus is on history of the Third Reich, 20th-century Europe, and Holocaust history. Special focus on general interest books on the lore, crafts, cooking, gardening and natural history of the Southeast. Submit outline/synopsis and sample chapters; must follow *Chicago Manual of Style*. Looks for "intellectual excellence and clear writing. We do *not* publish poetry or original fiction." Reviews artwork/photos as part of ms package.

Recent Nonfiction Title: *Gastonia 1929: The Story of the Loray Mill Strike*, by John A. Salmond.

UNIVERSITY OF NORTH TEXAS PRESS, P.O. Box 13856, Denton TX 76203-3856. Fax: (817)565-4590. Director: Frances B. Vick. Editor: Charlotte Wright. Estab. 1987. Publishes hardcover and trade paperback originals and reprints. Publishes 15-20 titles/year. Receives 300 queries and mss/year. 99% of books from unagented writers. Pays 7½-10% royalty of net. Publishes book 1-2 years after acceptance of ms. Query for electronic submissions. Reports in 2-3 months on queries. Book catalog free on request.

Nonfiction: Biography, reference. Subjects include agriculture/horticulture, Americana, ethnic, government/politics, history, language/literature, military/war, nature/environment, regional. "We have a series called War and the Southwest; Environmental Philosophy Series; Texas Folklore Society Publications series, the Western Life Series. Literary biographies of Texas writers series." Query. Reviews artwork/photos as part of ms package. Send photocopies.

Fiction: Offers the Katherine Anne Porter Prize in Short Fiction.

Poetry: Offers the Vassar Miller Prize in Poetry, an annual, national competition resulting in the publication of a winning manuscript each fall. Query first.

UNIVERSITY OF OKLAHOMA PRESS, 1005 Asp Ave., Norman OK 73019-0445. (405)325-5111. Fax: (405)325-4000. Editor-in-Chief: John Drayton. Estab. 1928. Imprint is Oklahoma Paperbacks. Publishes hardcover and paperback originals and reprints. Averages 90 titles/year. Pays royalty comparable to those paid by other publishers for comparable books. Publishes book an average of 12-18 months after acceptance. Query for electronic submissions. Reports in 3 months. Book catalog for $1 and 9×12 SAE with 6 first-class stamps.

Nonfiction: Publishes American Indian studies, Western US history, literary theory, natural history, women's studies, classical studies. No unsolicited poetry and fiction. Query, including outline, 1-2 sample chapters and author résumé. Use *Chicago Manual of Style* for ms guidelines. Reviews artwork/photos as part of ms package.

UNIVERSITY OF PENNSYLVANIA PRESS, 418 Service Dr., Philadelphia PA 19104-6097. (215)898-6261. Fax: (215)898-0404. Editorial Director: Timothy Clancy. Estab. 1860. Publishes hardcover and paperback originals and reprints. Averages 70 titles/year. Receives 650 submissions/year. 10-20% of books from first-time authors; 99% from unagented writers. Decision to publish determined by evaluation obtained by the press from outside specialists and approval by Faculty Editorial Board. Royalty determined on book-by-book basis. Publishes book 10 months after delivery of final ms. Query for electronic submissions. Reports in 3 months or less. Book catalog for 9×12 SAE with 6 first-class stamps. No unsolicited mss.

Nonfiction: Publishes Americana, literary criticism, women's studies, cultural studies, medieval studies, business, economics, history, law, anthropology, folklore, art history, architecture. "Serious books that serve the scholar and the professional." Follow the *Chicago Manual of Style*. Query with outline, résumé or vita. Reviews artwork as part of ms package. Send photocopies. Do not send ms.

Recent Nonfiction Title: *Cultural Politics—Queer Reading*, by Alan Sinfield.

Tips: "Queries/manuscripts may be routed to other editors in the publishing group."

UNIVERSITY OF PITTSBURGH PRESS, Dept. WM, 127 N. Bellefield Ave., Pittsburgh PA 15260. (412)624-4110. Fax: (412)624-7380. E-mail: cmarsh+@pitt.edu. Editor-in-Chief: Catherine Marshall. Estab. 1936. Publishes hardcover and trade paperback originals and reprints. Averages 55 titles/year. 5% of books from first-time authors; 99% from unagented writers. Pays royalties on net sales (per contract). Publishes books 1 year after acceptance. Reports in 2 months. Book catalog free on request. Manuscript guidelines for contests for #10 SASE.

• See the Contests and Awards section for the Drue Heinz and Agnes Lynch Starrett prizes.

Nonfiction: Biography, reference, textbook, scholarly monographs. Subjects include anthropology/archaeology, art/architecture, business and economics, ethnic, government/politics, health/medicine, history, language/literature/culture, music/dance, philosophy, regional, Latin American studies, Russian and East European studies, social and labor history, Milton studies. Query. Reviews artwork/photos as part of ms package.

Recent Nonfiction Title: *Eating on the Street: Teacher Literacy in a Multicultural Society*, by David Schaafsma.

Fiction: Literary. "One title per year, winner of the Drue Heinz Literature Prize." No novels; short fiction (stories) only. Submit complete ms via contest; send SASE for rules.

Recent Fiction Title: *Departures*, by Jannifer C. Cornell.

Poetry: Seven titles/year; one from previously unpublished author. Also offers the Agnes Lynch Starrett Prize. Contest/submission guidelines for SASE. Authors with previous books send direct to press in September and October.

Recent Poetry Title: *School Figures*, by Cathy Sang.

UNIVERSITY OF SCRANTON PRESS, University of Scranton, Scranton PA 18510-4660. (717)941-7449. Fax: (717)941-4309. E-mail: rousseaur1@uofs.edu. Director: Richard Rousseau. Estab. 1981. Imprint is Ridge Row Press. Publishes hardcover paperbacks and originals. Publishes 5 titles/year. Receives 200 queries and 45 mss/year. 60% of books from first-time authors; 100% from unagented writers. Pays 10% royalty. Publishes book 1 year after acceptance of ms. Query for electronic submissions. Reports in 1 month on queries. *Writer's Market* recommends allowing 2 months for reply. Book catalog and ms guidelines free on request. Member of the Association of Jesuit University Presses.
Nonfiction: Scholarly monographs. Subjects include art/architecture, language/literature, philosophy, religion, sociology. Looking for clear editorial focus: theology/religious studies; philosophy/philosophy of religion; scholarly treatments; the culture of northeastern Pennsylvania. Query or submit outline and 2 sample chapters.
Poetry: Only poetry related to northeastern Pennsylvania.

THE UNIVERSITY OF TENNESSEE PRESS, 293 Communications Bldg., Knoxville TN 37996-0325. Fax: (615)974-3724. Acquisitions Editor: Meredith Morris-Babb. Estab. 1940. Averages 30 titles/year. Receives 450 submissions/year. 35% of books from first-time authors; 99% from unagented writers. Average print order for a first book is 1,000. Nonauthor subsidy publishes 10% of books. Pays negotiable royalty on net receipts. Publishes book 1 year after acceptance. Reports in 2 months. Book catalog for 12×16 SAE with 2 first-class stamps. Manuscript guidelines for SASE.
Nonfiction: American history, cultural studies, religious studies, vernacular architecture and material culture, literary criticism, African-American studies, women's studies, Caribbean, anthropology, folklore and regional studies. Prefers "scholarly treatment and a readable style. Authors usually have Ph.D.s." Submit outline, author vita and 2 sample chapters. No fiction, poetry or plays. Reviews artwork/photos as part of ms package.
Recent Nonfiction Title: *American Home Life, 1880-1930: A Social History of Spaces and Services*, edited by Jessica H. Foy and Thomas J. Schlereth.
Tips: "Our market is in several groups: scholars; educated readers with special interests in given scholarly subjects; and the general educated public interested in Tennessee, Appalachia and the South. Not all our books appeal to all these groups, of course, but any given book must appeal to at least one of them."

UNIVERSITY OF TEXAS PRESS, P.O. Box 7819, Austin TX 78713-7819. Fax: (512)320-0668. Executive Editor: Theresa May. Estab. 1952. Averages 80 titles/year. Receives 1,000 submissions/year. 50% of books from first-time authors; 99% from unagented writers. Average print order for a first book is 1,000. Pays royalty usually based on net income. Offers advance occasionally. Publishes book 18 months after acceptance. Query for electronic submissions. Reports in up to 3 months. Book catalog and ms guidelines free.
Nonfiction: General scholarly subjects: natural history, American, Latin American, Native American, Chicano and Middle Eastern studies, classics and the ancient world, film, biology, contemporary regional architecture, archeology, anthropology, geography, ornithology, environmental studies, linguistics, 20th-century and women's literature, literary biography (Modernist period). Also uses specialty titles related to Texas and the Southwest, national trade titles, and regional trade titles. Accepts nonfiction translations related to above areas. Query or submit outline and 2 sample chapters. Reviews artwork/photos as part of ms package.
Fiction: Latin American and Middle Eastern fiction only in translation.
Tips: "It's difficult to make a manuscript over 400 double-spaced pages into a feasible book. Authors should take special care to edit out extraneous material. Looks for sharply focused, in-depth treatments of important topics."

‡UNIVERSITY PRESS OF AMERICA, INC., 4720 Boston Way, Lanham MD 20706. (301)459-3366. Publisher: James E. Lyons. Estab. 1975. Publishes hardcover and paperback originals and reprints. Averages 450 titles/year. Pays 5-15% royalty on net receipts. Offers occasional advance. Reports in 6 weeks. Book catalog and guidelines for SASE.
Nonfiction: Scholarly monographs, college, and graduate level textbooks in anthropology, history, international studies, economics, business, psychology, political science, African studies, Black studies, philosophy, religion, sociology, music, art, literature, drama and educational research. No juvenile, elementary or high school material. Submit outline or request proposal questionnaire.
Recent Nonfiction Title: *The Use of Force: Military Power and International Politics*, fourth edition, edited by Robert J. Art and Kenneth N. Waltz (political science).

UNIVERSITY PRESS OF COLORADO, P.O. Box 849, Niwot CO 80544-0849. (303)530-5337. Fax: (303)530-5306. Director: Luther Wilson. Estab. 1965. Publishes hardcover and paperback originals. Averages 40 titles/year. Receives 1,000 submissions/year. 50% of books from first-time authors; 99% from unagented writers. Average print order for a first book is 1,500-2,000. Pays 10-12½-15% royalty contract on net price. No advance. Publishes book 10 months after acceptance. Electronic submissions mandatory. Reports in 3 months. Book catalog free.

Nonfiction: Scholarly, regional and environmental subjects. Length: 250-500 pages. Query first with table of contents, preface or opening chapter. Reviews artwork/photos as part of ms package.
Recent Nonfiction Title: *Our Guerillas, Our Sidewalks*, by Herbert Braun.
Fiction: New fiction series; works of fiction on the trans-Mississippi West, by authors residing in the region.
Recent Fiction Title: *Bluefeather Falling*, by Max Evans.
Tips: "Books should be solidly researched and from a reputable scholar, because we are a university press. We have new series on world resources and environmental issues, and on Mesoamerican worlds."

UNIVERSITY PRESS OF KENTUCKY, 663 S. Limestone, Lexington KY 40508-4008. (606)257-2951. Fax: (606)257-2984. Editor-in-Chief: Nancy Grayson Holmes. Estab. 1951. Publishes hardcover and paperback originals and reprints. Averages 50 titles/year. Payment varies. No advance. Publishes ms 1 year after acceptance. Reports in 2 months on queries. Book catalog free.
Nonfiction: Biography, reference, monographs. "We are a scholarly publisher, publishing chiefly for an academic and professional audience. Strong areas are history, literature, political science, international studies, folklore, sociology, Irish studies and military history. No textbooks, genealogical material, lightweight popular treatments, how-to books or books unrelated to our major areas of interest." The Press does not consider original works of fiction or poetry. Query. Reviews artwork/photos, but generally does not publish books with extensive number of photos.
Recent Nonfiction Title: *Women Editing Modernism: "Little" Magazine and Literary History*, by Jayne Marek.
Tips: "Most of our authors are drawn from our primary academic and professional audience. We are probably not a good market for the usual freelance writer."

UNIVERSITY PRESS OF MISSISSIPPI, 3825 Ridgewood Rd., Jackson MS 39211-6492. (601)982-6205. Fax: (601)982-6217. Director: Richard Abel. Associate Director and Editor-in-Chief: Seetha Srinivasan. Estab. 1970. Imprints are Muscadine Books (regional trade) and Banner Books (literary reprints). Publishes hardcover and paperback originals and reprints. Averages 50 titles/year. Receives 600 submissions/year. 20% of books from first-time authors; 90% from unagented writers. "Competitive royalties and terms." Publishes book 1 year after acceptance. Reports in up to 3 months. Book catalog for 9×12 SAE with 3 first-class stamps.
Nonfiction: Americana, biography, history, politics, folklife, literary criticism, ethnic/minority studies, natural sciences, popular culture with scholarly emphasis. Interested in southern regional studies and literary studies. Submit outline and sample chapters and curriculum vita to Acquisitions Editor. "We prefer a proposal that describes the significance of the work and a chapter outline." Reviews artwork/photos as part of ms package.
Fiction: Commissioned trade editions by prominent writers.

UNIVERSITY PRESS OF NEW ENGLAND, (Includes Wesleyan University Press), 23 S. Main St., Hanover NH 03755-2048. (603)643-7100. Fax: (603)643-1540. Director: Thomas L. McFarland. Acquisitions Editor: David Caffry. Editorial Director: Phil Pochoda. Estab. 1970. "University Press of New England is a consortium of university presses. Some books—those published for one of the consortium members—carry the joint imprint of New England and the member: Wesleyan, Dartmouth, Brandeis, Brown, Tufts, Universities of Connecticut, New Hampshire, Vermont, Rhode Island and Middlebury. Associate member: Salzburg seminar." Publishes hardcover and trade paperback originals and trade paperback reprints. Averages 70 titles/year. Nonauthor subsidy publishes 80% of books. Pays standard royalty. Offers advance occasionally. Query for electronic submissions. Reports in 2 months. Book catalog and guidelines for 9×12 SAE with 5 first-class stamps.
Nonfiction: Americana (New England), art, biography, history, music, nature, politics, psychology, reference, science, sociology, regional (New England). No festschriften, memoirs, unrevised doctoral dissertations, or symposium collections. Submit outline and 1-2 sample chapters.
Fiction: Regional (New England) novels and reprints.

UTAH STATE UNIVERSITY PRESS, Logan UT 84322-7800. (801)750-1362. Fax: (801)750-1541. Director: Michael Spooner. Estab. 1972. Publishes hardcover and trade paperback originals and reprints. Averages 10 titles/year. Receives 170 submissions/year. 8% of books from first-time authors. Average print order for a first book is 2,000. Nonauthor subsidy publishes 45% of books. Pays royalty on net price. No advance. Publishes book 18 months after acceptance. Query for electronic submissions. Reports in 1 month on queries. *Writer's Market* recommends allowing 2 months for reply. Book catalog free. Manuscript guidelines for SASE.

For explanation of symbols, see the Key to Symbols and Abbreviations. For unfamiliar words, see the Glossary.

• Utah State University Press is especially interested in supporting Native American writers with scholarly or creative manuscripts.
Nonfiction: Biography, reference and textbook on folklore, Americana (history and politics). "Particularly interested in book-length scholarly manuscripts dealing with folklore, Western history, Western literature. *Writer's Market* recommends query with SASE first. Reviews artwork/photos as part of ms package.
Poetry: "Accepting very few creative works at present. Query before sending manuscript."
Tips: "Marketability of work is more important than ever."

‡VALLEY OF THE SUN PUBLISHING, P.O. Box 38, Malibu CA 90265. President: Richard Sutphen. Publishes hardcover and trade paperback originals and trade paperback reprints. Publishes 6 titles/year. 80% of books from first-time authors; 100% from unagented writers. Pays 8-10% royalty on wholesale or retail price. "We have a large-circulation magalog and it's not unusual to sell half our books directly at full price. The 8-10% is based upon what we sell them for." Offers $1,500-2,000 advance. Publishes book 9 months after acceptance of ms. Accepts simultaneous submissions. Reports in 2 months. Book catalog free. Manuscript guidelines for #10 SASE.
Nonfiction: Self-help, New Age metaphysical. Submit outline with 2 sample chapters or complete ms. Reviews artwork/photos as part of ms package. Send photocopies.
Recent Nonfiction Title: *50 Spiritually Powerful Meditations*, by Margaret Rogers (New Age).

VANDAMERE PRESS, Imprint of ABI Associates, Inc., P.O. Box 5243, Arlington VA 22205. Acquisitions Editor: Jerry Frank. Publishes hardcover and trade paperback originals and reprints. Publishes 8 titles/year. Receives 750 queries and 2,000 mss/year. 50% of books from first-time authors; 90% from unagented writers. Pays royalty on revenues generated. Publishes book 6-24 months after acceptance of ms. Accepts simultaneous submissions. Reports in 3 months.
• Vandamere Press is looking for more history and geography manuscripts.
Nonfiction: Subjects include Americana, biography, child guidance/parenting, education, history, military/war, recreation, regional, career guide. Submit outline and 1-2 sample chapters. Reviews artwork/photos as part of ms package. Send photocopies.
Fiction: General fiction including adventure, erotica, humor, mystery, suspense. Submit synopsis and 5-10 sample chapters.
Tips: "Authors who can provide endorsements from significant published writers, celebrities, etc. will *always* be given serious consideration. Clean, easy-to-read, *dark* copy is essential. Patience in waiting for replies is essential. All unsolicited work is looked at but at certain times of the year our review schedule will stop." No response without SASE.

‡VANDERBILT UNIVERSITY PRESS, Box 1813, Station B, Nashville TN 37235. (615)322-3585. Director: Charles Backus. Among other titles, publishes Vanderbilt Library of American Philosophy (Herman J. Saatkamp, editor). Publishes hardcover originals and trade paperback originals and reprints. Publishes 10-12 titles/year. Receives 100-120 queries/year. 25% of books from first-time authors; 90% from unagented writers. Pays 15% maximum royalty on net income. Sometimes offers advance. Publishes 8-10 months after acceptance of ms. Accepts simultaneous submissions but prefers first option. Reports in 1-3 months on proposals. Book catalog and ms guidelines free on request.
Nonfiction: Biography, illustrated book, reference, textbook, scholarly. Subjects include Americana, anthropology/archaeology, art/architecture/ education, government/politics, health/medicine, history, language/literature, nature/environment, philosophy, regional, religion, translation, women's issues/studies. Submit outline, 1 sample chapter and cv. Reviews artwork/photos as part of ms package. Send photocopies.
Recent Nonfiction Title: *Rorty and Pragmatism: The Philosopher Responds to His Critics*, by Richard Rorty/Herman Saatkamp (philosophy).
Tips: "Our audience consists of scholars and educated general readers."

THE VESTAL PRESS, LTD., P.O. Box 97, Vestal NY 13851-0097. (607)797-4872. Fax: (607)797-4898. Editor: Elaine Stuart. Estab. 1961. Publishes hardcover and trade paperback originals and reprints. Averages 6-8 titles/year. Receives 50-75 submissions/year. 20% of books from first-time writers; 95% from unagented authors. Pays 10% maximum royalty on net sales. Publishes books 1 year after acceptance. Accepts simultaneous submissions. Reports in up to 6 months. Book catalog for $2 and 6×9 SAE with 2 first-class stamps.
Nonfiction: Technical antiquarian hobby topics in mechanical music (player pianos, music boxes, etc.), reed organs, carousels, cinema history, regional history based on postcard collections. Also publishes titles in woodcarving. Query or submit outline and sample chapters.
Recent Nonfiction Title: *Betty Grable: The Girl with the Million Dollar Legs*, by Tom McGee.

VICTOR BOOKS, Division of Scripture Press Publications, Inc. 1825 College Ave., Wheaton IL 60187-4498. Fax: (708)668-3806. Contact: Acquisitions Editor. Estab. 1934. Publishes hardcover and trade paperback originals. Averages 100 titles/year. Receives 1,500-2,000 submissions/year. Royalty on all books, advances on some. Accepts simultaneous submissions if specified. Reports in 1 month on queries. *Writer's Market* recommends allowing 2 months for reply. Manuscript guidelines for #10 SASE; specify general,

children's, adult novels or academic (BridgePoint). Catalog and guidelines for 4 first-class stamps.
Tips: "All books must in some way be Bible-related by authors who themselves are evangelical Christians with a platform. Victor, therefore, is not a publisher for everybody. Only a small fraction of the manuscripts received can be seriously considered for publication. Most books result from contacts that acquisitions editors make with qualified authors, though from time to time an unsolicited proposal triggers enough excitement to result in a contract. A writer has the best chance of selling Victor a well-conceived and imaginative manuscript that helps the reader apply Christianity to his/her life in practical ways. Christians active in the local church and their children are our audience."

‡**VIKING STUDIO BOOKS**, Imprint of Penguin USA, 375 Hudson St., New York NY 10014. (212)366-2191. Contact: Michael Fragnito, publisher. Publishes hardcover originals. Publishes 35-40 titles/year. Receives 200 submissions/year. Less than 10% of books are from first-time authors; less than 5% from unagented writers. Publishes book 1 year after acceptance. Accepts simultaneous submissions. Reports in 2 months.
Nonfiction: Coffee table book, cookbook, gift book, illustrated book. Subjects include Americana, animals, cooking/foods/nutrition, gardening, gay/lesbian, health/medicine, military/war, music/dance, photography, science, women's issues/studies, New Age/metaphysics. "We do not accept unsolicited material. We publish high-quality hardcover/trade books." Query. Agented submissions only. Reviews artwork as part of ms package. Send photocopies.
Recent Nonfiction Title: *Vision: The Life and Music of Hildegard von Bingen*, by Jane Bobko, with commentary by Matthew Fox and Barbara Newman.
Tips: "Often writers/agents misspell the publisher's name—be careful. It's hard to take someone seriously when those kinds of mistakes are the first thing the editor or publisher sees on a query letter or manuscript."

VILLARD BOOKS, Random House, 201 E. 50th St., New York NY 10022. (212)572-2780. Publisher: David Rosenthal. Executive Editor-in-Chief: Craig Nelson. Director of Publicity: Adam Rothberg. Estab. 1983. Publishes hardcover and trade paperback originals. Averages 55-60 titles/year. 95% of books are agented submissions. Pays varying advances and royalties; negotiated separately. Accepts simultaneous submissions. Query for electronic submissions. *Writer's Market* recommends allowing 2 months for reply.
Nonfiction and Fiction: Looks for commercial nonfiction and fiction. Submit outline/synopsis and up to 50 pages in sample chapters. No unsolicited submissions.

VOYAGEUR PRESS, 123 N. Second St., Stillwater MN 55082. (612)430-2210. Fax: (612)430-2211. Acquisitions Editor: Michael Dresni. Publishes hardcover and trade paperback originals. Publishes 20 titles/year. Receives 1,200 queries and 500 mss/year. 10% of books from first-time authors; 90% from unagented writers. Pays royalty. Publishes book 1 year after acceptance of ms. Accepts simultaneous submissions. Reports in 3 months. Book catalog and ms guidelines free on request.
Nonfiction: Coffee table book (and smaller format photographic essay books), cookbook, how-to (photography). Subjects include natural history, nature/environment, photography, outdoor recreation, regional, travel. Query or submit outline and proposal package. Reviews artwork/photos as part of the ms package. Photographers should send transparencies—duplicates only and tearsheets.
Tips: "Our audience includes readers interested in wildlife biology and natural history and tourists wishing to learn more about wilderness or urban areas. Please present as focused an idea as possible in a brief submission (one page cover letter; two page outline or proposal). Note your credentials for writing the book. Tell all you know about the market niche and marketing possibilities for proposed book."

‡**WADSWORTH PUBLISHING COMPANY**, Imprint of International Thompson Publishing Company, 10 Davis Dr., Belmont CA 94002. (415)595-2350. Fax: (415)592-3342. Editorial Director: Gary Carlson. Estab. 1956. Other divisions include Brooks/Cole Pub. Co., PWS/Kent Pub. Co. Heinle & Heinle Publishing Co., Delmar Publishing Company, Southwestern Publishing Company, Boyd & Fraser Publishing Company. Publishes hardcover and paperback originals and software. Publishes 350 titles/year. 35% of books from first-time authors; 99% of books from unagented writers. Pays 5-15% royalty on net price. Advances not automatic policy. Publishes ms an average of 1 year after acceptance. Accepts simultaneous submissions. Query for electronic submissions. Reports in 1 week. Book catalog (by subject area) and ms guidelines available.
Nonfiction: Textbooks and multimedia products: higher education only. Subjects include statistics, biology, astronomy, geology, music, social sciences, philosophy, religious studies, speech and mass communications, broadcasting, TV and film productions, English, history, and other subjects in higher education. "We need books and media products that use fresh teaching approaches to all courses taught at schools of higher education throughout the US and Canada. We specifically do not publish textbooks in art." Query or submit outline/synopsis and sample chapters.
Recent Nonfiction Title: *Sociology: A Global Perspective*, by Joan Ferrante.

WAITE GROUP PRESS, 200 Tamal Plaza, Corte Madera CA 94925. (415)924-2576. Fax: (415)924-2576. Editorial Director: John Crudo. Publishes trade paperback originals. Publishes 50 titles/year. Receives 50 queries and 35 mss/year. 50% of mss from first-time authors; 100% from unagented writers. Pays royalty on wholesale price or makes outright purchase. Publishes book 4 months after acceptance of ms. Query for electronic submissions. Reports in 2 months. Book catalog free on request.

Nonfiction: How-to, reference, self-help, technical. Subjects include computers and software. "We specialize in computer language and computer graphics." Query or submit outline.

Recent Nonfiction Title: *Visual Basic How-to*, by Zane Thomas.

Tips: Audience is "those interested in having fun and learning about their PC's and Macintoshes. We emphasize new technologies and graphics. Agents are not necessary or preferable. Know your subject and please be patient!"

J. WESTON WALCH, PUBLISHER, P.O. Box 658, Portland ME 04104-0658. (207)772-2846. Fax: (207)772-3105. Editor-in-Chief: Richard S. Kimball. Editor: Elizabeth Iselle. Math/Science Editor: Tom Cohn. Computer Editor: Robert Crepeau. Assistant Editor: Kate O'Halloran. Estab. 1927. Publishes paperback originals and software. Averages 75 titles/year. Receives 300 submissions/year. 10% of books from first-time authors; 95% from unagented writers. Average print order for a first book is 700. Offers 10-15% royalty on gross receipts or makes outright purchase of $100-2,500. No advance. Publishes book 18 months after acceptance. Query for electronic submissions. Reports in 4 months. Book catalog for 9 × 12 SAE with 5 first-class stamps. Manuscript guidelines for #10 SASE.

Nonfiction: Subjects include art, business, computer education, economics, English, foreign language, geography, government, health, history, literacy, mathematics, middle school, music, psychology, science, social studies, sociology, special education. "We publish only supplementary educational material for grades six to twelve in the US and Canada. Formats include books, posters, blackline masters, card sets, cassettes, microcomputer courseware, video and mixed packages. Most titles are assigned by us, though we occasionally accept an author's unsolicited submission. We have a great need for author/artist teams and for authors who can write at third- to tenth-grade levels. We do *not* want basic texts, anthologies or industrial arts titles. Most of our authors—but not all—have secondary teaching experience. *Query first.* Looks for sense of organization, writing ability, knowledge of subject, skill of communicating with intended audience." Reviews artwork/photos as part of ms package.

Recent Nonfiction Title: *The Walch Multicultural Art Series*, by Lucy Rosenfeld.

WALKER AND CO., Division of Walker Publishing Co., 435 Hudson St., New York NY 10014. Fax: (212)727-0984. Contact: Submissions Editor. Estab. 1959. Publishes hardcover and trade paperback originals and a few reprints of British books. Averages 100 titles/year. Receives 4,500 submissions/year. 30% of books from first-time authors; 30% from unagented writers. Pays varying royalty or makes outright purchase. Offers $1,000-3,000 average advance "but could be higher or lower." No phone calls. Material without SASE will not be returned. *Writer's Market* recommends allowing 3 months for reply. Book catalog and guidelines for 9 × 12 SAE with 3 first-class stamps.

Nonfiction: Biography, business, science and natural history, health, music, nature and environment, parenting, reference, popular science, sports/baseball, personal finance, some regional titles and self-help books. Query or submit outline and sample chapter. Reviews photos as part of ms package. Do not send originals.

Fiction: Mystery/suspense, western juvenile (ages 5 and up).

Tips: "We also need preschool to young adult nonfiction, biographies and middle-grade novels. Query."

WARD HILL PRESS, P.O. Box 04-0424, Staten Island NY 10304-0008. Editorial Director: Elizabeth Davis. Estab. 1989. Publishes trade paperback originals. Publishes 4-6 titles/year. Receives several hundred queries and mss/year. 75% of books from first-time authors; 90% from unagented writers. Pays 6-12% royalty on retail price. Offers $800-1,600 advance. Publishes book 6-12 months after acceptance. Query for electronic submissions. Prefers disk. Reports in 2 months on queries. Manuscript guidelines for #10 SASE.

● Ward Hill Press is looking for high-quality fiction for the following audience: middle readers and young adults (ages 10 and up). Fiction should focus on some aspect of US history (Civil War to present) or multiculturalism (US setting). Also nonfiction with the same themes and for the same age group.

Nonfiction and Fiction: Young adult, biography and multicultural fiction and nonfiction for the same age group. Query. Reviews artwork/photos as part of ms package. Send photocopies. "Query first. No phone calls please."

WARNER BOOKS, Warner Publishing Inc., Time & Life Bldg., 1271 Avenue of the Americas, New York NY 10020. General interest publisher of nonfiction and fiction. This publisher did not respond to our request for information. Query before submitting. No unsolicited mss.

WARREN PUBLISHING HOUSE, INC., P.O. Box 2250, Everett WA 98203-0250. (206)353-3100. Managing Editor: Kathleen Cubley. Estab. 1975. Publishes educational paperback originals, activity books and parenting books for teachers and parents of 2-6-year-olds. Publishes 20-30 titles/year. No complete mss. Considers activity book mss from early childhood education professionals. Considers single activity submissions from early childhood professionals. Considers parenting activity mss from parenting experts. 100% from unagented writers. Makes outright purchase plus copy of book/newsletter author's material appears in. Book catalog and ms guidelines free upon written request.

Nonfiction: Illustrated activity book for parents and teachers of 2-6-year olds. Subjects include animals, art, child guidance/parenting, cooking with kids, foods and nutrition, education, ethnic, gardening, hobbies, language/literature, music, nature/environment, science. "We consider activity ideas submitted by early childhood professionals. Manuscript and ideas must be appropriate for people (teacher/parents) who work with children two to six years old." Query. No fiction or poetry.

Recent Nonfiction Title: *A Year of Fun Just for Three's*, by Theodosia Spewock.

Tips: "Our audience is teachers and parents who work with children ages two to six. Write for submission requirements."

WASHINGTON STATE UNIVERSITY PRESS, Pullman WA 99164-5910. (800)354-7360. Fax: (509)335-8568. Director: Thomas H. Sanders. Editors: Glen Lindeman and Keith Petersen. Estab. 1928. Publishes hardcover originals, trade paperback originals and reprints. Averages 10 titles/year. Receives 75-150 submissions/year. 50% of books from first-time writers; 100% from unagented authors. Pays 5% minimum royalty, graduated according to sales. Publishes book 18 months after acceptance. Query for electronic submissions. Reports on queries in 2 months.

Nonfiction: Subjects include Americana, art, biography, economics, environment, ethnic studies history (especially of the American West and the Pacific Northwest), politics, essays. "Needs for the next year are quality manuscripts that focus on the development of the Pacific Northwest as a region, and on the social and economic changes that have taken place and continue to take place as the region enters the 21st century. No romance novels, how-to books, gardening books, or books specifically written as classroom texts." Submit outline and sample chapters. Reviews artwork/photos as part of ms package.

Tips: "Our audience consists of specialists and general readers who are interested in well-documented research presented in an attractive well-written format. Writers have the best chance of selling to our press completed manuscripts on regional history. We have developed our marketing in the direction of regional and local history and have attempted to use this as the base around which we hope to expand our publishing program. In regional history, the secret is to write a good narrative—a good story—that is substantiated factually. It should be told in an imaginative, clever way. Have visuals (photos, maps, etc) available to help the reader envision what has happened. Tell the local or regional history story in a way that ties it to larger, national, and even international events. Weave it into the large pattern of history."

FRANKLIN WATTS, INC., Division of Grolier, Inc., 95 Madison Ave., New York NY 10016. (212)686-7070. Fax: (212)689-7803. E-mail: jwself@aol.com. Publisher: John Selfridge. Contact: Submissions. Publishes both hardcover and softcover originals for middle schoolers and young adults. Firm publishes 150 titles/year. 10% of books from first-time authors; 90% from unagented writers. Reports in 2 months on queries with SASE. Book catalog for $3 postage.

Nonfiction: History, science, social issues, biography. Subjects include American and world history, politics, natural and physical sciences. Multicultural, curriculum-based nonfiction lists published twice a year. Strong also in the area of contemporary problems and issues facing young people. No humor, coffee table books, fiction, poetry, picture books, cookbooks or gardening books. Query. No calls or unsolicited mss.

WAYFINDER PRESS, P.O. Box 217, Ridgway CO 81432-0217. (303)626-5452. Owner: Marcus E. Wilson. Estab. 1980. Publishes trade paperback originals. Publishes 3 titles/year. Receives 80 submissions/year. 30% of books are from first-time authors; 90% from unagented writers. Pays 8-12% royalty on retail price. Publishes book 6 months after acceptance. Accepts simultaneous submissions. Reports in 2 weeks on queries. Return postage must be included.

• Wayfinder Press no longer accepts fiction or children manuscripts.

Nonfiction: Biography, illustrated book, reference. Subjects include Americana, government/politics, history, nature/environment, photography, recreation, regional, sociology, travel. "We are looking for books on western Colorado: history, sociology, nature, recreation, photo, and travel. No books on subjects outside our geographical area of specialization." Query or submit outline/synopsis and sample chapters. Reviews artwork/photos as part of ms package.

Tips: "Writers have the best chance selling us tourist-oriented books. The local population and tourists comprise our audience."

WEIDNER & SONS, PUBLISHING, P.O. Box 2178, Riverton NJ 08077. (609)486-1755. Fax: (609)486-7583. E-mail: jim.weidner@radiowave.com. President: James H. Weidner. Estab. 1967. Publishes hardcover and trade paperback originals and reprints. Imprints are Hazlaw Books, Medlaw Books, Bird Sci Books, Delaware Estuary Press, Tycooly Publishing USA and Pulse Publications. Publishes 10-20 titles/year; imprint publishes 10 titles/year. Receives 50 queries and 3 mss/year. 100% of books from first-time authors; 100% from unagented writers. Pays 10% maximum royalty on wholesale price. Average time between acceptance and publication varies with subject matter. Accepts simultaneous submissions. Query for electronic submissions. Reports in 1 month on queries. *Writer's Market* recommends allowing 2 months for reply. Book catalog for $1 (refundable with order).

Nonfiction: Reference, technical, textbook. Subjects include agriculture/horticulture, animals, business and economics, child guidance/parenting, computers and electronics, education, gardening, health/medicine, hobbies (electronic), language/literature, nature/environment, psychology, science and ecology/environment. "We are primarily science, text and reference books. Rarely fiction; never poetry. No topics in the 'pseudosciences': occult, astrology, New Age and metaphysics, etc." Query or submit outline and sample chapters. Reviews artwork/photos as part of the freelance ms package. Writers should send photocopies.
Recent Nonfiction Title: *At-Risk: The Vo-Tech Student in Suburban Society.*
Tips: "Our audience consists of scholars, college students and researchers."

SAMUEL WEISER, INC., P.O. Box 612, York Beach ME 03910-0612. (207)363-4393. Fax: (207)363-5799. Editor: Eliot Stearns. Estab. 1956. Publishes hardcover originals and trade paperback originals and reprints. Publishes 18-20 titles/year. Receives 200 submissions/year. 50% of books from first-time authors; 98% from unagented writers. Pays 10% royalty on wholesale or retail price. Offers $500 average advance. Publishes book 18 months after acceptance. Query for electronic submissions. Reports in 3 months. Book catalog free.
Nonfiction: How-to, self-help. Subjects include health, music, philosophy, psychology, religion. "We look for strong books in our specialty field—written by teachers and people who know the subject. Don't want a writer's rehash of all the astrology books in the library, only texts written by people with strong background in field. No poetry or novels." Submit complete ms. *Writer's Market* recommends query with SASE first. Reviews artwork/photos as part of ms package.
Recent Nonfiction Title: *Mysticism,* by Bruno Borchert.
Tips: "Most new authors do not check permissions, nor do they provide proper footnotes. If they did, it would help. We specialize in oriental philosophy, metaphysics, esoterica of all kinds (tarot, astrology, qabalah, magic, etc.). We look at all manuscripts submitted to us. We are interested in seeing freelance art for book covers."

‡WESTERN PUBLISHING, 850 Third Ave., 7th Floor, New York NY 10022. (212)753-8500. Vice President/ Publisher: Robin Warner.

‡WESTERNLORE PRESS, P.O. Box 35305, Tucson AZ 85740. Editor: Lynn R. Bailey. Publishes 6-12 titles/ year. Pays standard royalties on retail price "except in special cases." Query. Reports in 2 months. Query with return postage.
Nonfiction: Publishes Western Americana of a scholarly and semischolarly nature: anthropology, history, biography, historic sites, restoration, and ethnohistory pertaining to the greater American West. Re-publication of rare and out-of-print books. Length: 25,000-100,000 words.

WESTPORT PUBLISHERS, INC., Division of Trozzolo Resources, Inc., 1102 Grand, 23rd Floor, Kansas City MO 64106. (816)842-8111. Fax: (816)842-8188. Publisher: Paul Temme. Estab. 1982. Subsidiaries include Media Publishing, Midgard Press (author-subsidy division), Media Periodicals. Publishes trade paperback originals. Averages 5-6 titles/year. Receives 125 submissions/year. 50% of books from first-time authors; 100% from unagented writers. Pays royalty. Publishes book 1 year after acceptance. Reports in 2 months on queries.
Nonfiction: Subjects include child guidance/parenting, foods/nutrition, wellness and psychology. Query with outline and SASE. Reviews artwork/photos as part of ms package.
Recent Nonfiction Title: *Hugs from the Refrigerator,* by James McClearnan, Ed. D.
Tips: "Books with a well-defined audience have the best chance of succeeding. An author must have demonstrated expertise in the topic on which he or she is writing."

‡WHISPERING COYOTE PRESS, INC., 300 Crescent Court., Suite 1150, Dallas TX 75201. Publisher: Mrs. Lou Alpert. Publishes hardcover originals. Publishes 6 titles/year. 20% of books from first-time authors; 90% from unagented writers. Pays 8% royalty on retail price of first 10,000 copies, 10% after (combined author and illustrator). Offers $2,000-8,000 (combined author, illustrator, split 50/50). Publishes book 18-24 months after acceptance of ms. Accepts simultaneous submissions. Reports in 3 months. Book catalog and ms guidelines for #10 SASE.
Fiction: Adventure, fantasy, juvenile picture books. "We only do picture books." Submit complete ms. If author is illustrator also, submit complete package. Send photocopies, no original art.
Recent Fiction Title: *It's Raining,* by Kin Eagle (picture book).
Poetry: "We like poetry—see our catalog." Submit complete ms.
Recent Poetry Title: *Itsy Bitsy Spider,* by Iza Trapani (extended rhyme picture book).
Tips: Audience is children, 2-12.

‡WHITE CLIFFS MEDIA COMPANY, P.O. Box 433, Tempe AZ 85280-0433. (602)921-8039. Owner: Lawrence Aynesmith. Estab. 1985. Publishes hardcover and trade paperback originals. Averages 5-10 titles/year. 50% of books from first-time authors; 50% from unagented writers. Pays 5-12% royalty on retail price or makes outright purchase. Publishes book an average of 1 year after acceptance. No simultaneous submissions.

Query for electronic submissions. Reports in 2 months on queries, 4 months on proposals, 6 months on mss. Book catalog for #10 SASE.

Nonfiction: Biography, textbook. Subjects include anthropology, education, ethnic, music/dance, sociology. Query. Reviews artwork/photos as part of ms package. Send photocopies.

Recent Nonfiction Title: *Drum Damba: Talking Drum Lessons*, by Lock (musical instruction).

Tips: "Distribution is more difficult due to the large number of publishers. Writers should send proposals that have potential for mass markets as well as college texts, and that will be submitted and completed on schedule. Our audience reads college texts, general interest trade publications. If I were a writer trying to market a book today, I would send a book on music comparable in quality and mass appeal to a book like Stephen Hawking's *A Brief History of Time*."

WHITE PINE PRESS, 10 Village Square, Fredonia NY 14063. (716)672-5743. Director: Dennis Maloney. Imprint is Springhouse Editions. Publishes hardcover and trade paperback originals. Publishes 10 titles/year. Receives 200 queries and 150 mss/year. 20% of books from first-time authors; 99% from unagented writers. Pays 5-10% royalty on wholesale price. Offers $250 and up advance. Publishes book 18 months after acceptance of ms. Accepts simultaneous submissions. Query for electronic submissions. Reports in 2 months on queries. Book catalog free on request.

Nonfiction: Textbook. Subjects include ethnic, language/literature, translation, women's issues/studies. Query.

Recent Nonfiction Title: *Surviving Beyond Fear*, edited by Agosin (human rights).

Fiction: Ethnic, literary, short story collections. Query with synopsis and 2 sample chapters.

Recent Fiction Title: *Pleasure in the Word*, edited by Olmos and Gebert (anthology-Latin American literature).

Poetry: "We do a large amount of poetry in translation. We will be starting a poetry contest for US writers this year." Query.

Recent Poetry Title: *Anxious Moments*, by Debeljak (translation/Slovenian).

WHITFORD PRESS, Imprint of Schiffer Publishing, Ltd., 77 Lower Valley Rd., Atglen PA 19310. (610)593-1777. Managing Editor: Ellen Taylor. Estab. 1985. Publishes trade paperback originals. Averages 1-3 titles/year. Receives 400-500 submissions/year. 20% of books from first-time authors; 90% from unagented writers. Pays royalty on wholesale price; no advances. Publishes book 9-12 months after acceptance and receipt of complete ms. Accepts simultaneous submissions. Reports within 3 months. Book catalog free. Manuscript guidelines for SASE.

Nonfiction: How-to, self-help, reference. Subjects include astrology, metaphysics, New Age topics. "We are looking for well written, well-organized, originals books on all metaphysical subjects (except channeling and past lives). Books that empower the reader or show him/her ways to develop personal skills are preferred. New approaches, techniques, or concepts are best. No personal accounts unless they directly relate to a general audience. No moralistic, fatalistic, sexist or strictly philosophical books. Query first or send outline. Enclose SASE large enough to hold your submission if you want it returned.

Tips: "Our audience is knowledgeable in metaphysical fields, well-read and progressive in thinking. Please check bookstores to see if your subject has already been covered thoroughly. Expertise in the field is not enough; your book must be clean, well written and well organized. A specific and unique marketing angle is a plus. No Sun-sign material; we prefer more advanced work. Please don't send entire manuscript unless we request it, and be sure to include SASE. Let us know if the book is available on computer diskette and what type of hardware/software. Manuscripts should be between 60,000 and 110,000 words."

THE WHITSTON PUBLISHING CO., P.O. Box 958, Troy NY 12181-0958. Phone/fax: (518)283-4363. Editorial Director: Jean Goode. Estab. 1969. Publishes hardcover originals. Averages 15 titles/year. Receives 100 submissions/year. 50% of books from first-time authors; 100% from unagented writers. Pays 10% royalty on price of book (wholesale or retail) after sale of 500 copies. Publishes book 30 months after acceptance. Reports in up to 6 months. Book catalog for $1.

Nonfiction: "We publish scholarly and critical books in the arts, humanities and some of the social sciences. We will consider author bibliographies. We are interested in scholarly monographs and collections of essays." Query. Reviews artwork/photos as part of ms package.

‡MARKUS WIENER PUBLISHERS INC., 114 Jefferson Rd., Princeton, NJ 08540. (609)971-1141. Editor-in-Chief: Shelley Frisch. Imprint is Topics in World History. Publishes hardcover originals and trade paperback originals and reprints. Publishes 20-25 titles/year; imprint publishes 5 titles/year. Receives 50-150 queries and 50 mss/year. Pays 10% royalty on net sales. Publishes book 6-12 months after acceptance of ms. Reports in 1-2 months on queries and proposals. Book catalog free on request.

Nonfiction: Textbook. History subjects.

WILD FLOWER PRESS, Imprint of Blue Water Publishing, P.O. Box 726, Newberg OR 97132. (503)538-0264. Fax: (503)538-8485. President: Pam Meyer. Publishes hardcover originals and trade paperback originals and reprints. Publishes 6 titles/year. Receives 50 queries and 45 mss/year. 80% of books from first-time

authors; 90% from unagented writers. Pays royalty. Publishes book 6-16 months after acceptance of ms. Accepts simultaneous submissions. Query for electronic submissions. Reports in 2 months on mss. Book catalog and ms guidelines free on request.
Nonfiction: U.F.O. Submit outline. Reviews artwork/photos as part of ms package. Send photocopies.
Recent Nonfiction Title: *The Andreasson Affair & the Andreasson Affair, Phase Two*, by Raymond E. Fowler (reprints).

‡WILDE PUBLISHING, P.O. Box 4524, Albuquerque NM 87106. Editor: David Wilde. Publishes hardcover, trade paperback and mass market paperback originals. Publishes 4 titles/year. Pays 10% royalty on retail price. Offers negotiable advance.
Nonfiction: Biography, coffee table book, how-to (study-technique), technical, textbook (English/ESL), science. Subjects include agriculture/horticulture (eco-trails), Americana (travel-road-trips), computers and electronics (hacking), education (English text), government/politics, health/medicine (sports), history (American), language/literature (music-exice), music/dance (language of), nature/environment (eco-trails), philosophy (language), recreation (motivation), regional (Americana), science (quantum theory), software (hacking), sports (health), travel (route 66). "Americana is a first priority for first-time authors, and politics." Query with SASE.
Recent Nonfiction Title: *Monzano Trails, a Hiker's Guide*, by Steve Plumb (nature trails guide).
Fiction: Adventure (modern exploration), experimental (prose), historical (oil exploration), literary (essays/contemporary), mainstream/contemporary (20th C), occult (mysticism), plays (modern/American), romance (war), short story collections (rural), western (wildwest). "We would dearly like to see exciting writing, substantial plots, clearly recognized goals and structure, as well as good grammar, correct spelling and cadences—conclusions." Query with SASE.
Recent Fiction Title: *Classified Computer Hacker's Guide*, by Alexander Curry (cybernetics).
Poetry: "If we like it, we will publish it, especially pastoral/modern Greeks—existentialist/experimental."
Recent Poetry Title: *Teabags From England*, by David Wilde (romantic).

WILDERNESS ADVENTURE BOOKS, P.O. Box 217, Davisburg MI 48350-0217. Fax: (810)634-0946. Editor: Erin Sims Howarth. Estab. 1983. Publishes hardcover and trade paperback originals and reprints. Publishes 6 titles/year. Receives 250 submissions/year. 90% of books from first-time authors; 90% from unagented writers. Pays 5-10% royalty on retail price. Offers $100 average advance. Publishes book 16 months after acceptance. Accepts simultaneous submissions. Reports in 2 months.
Nonfiction: Biography, how-to, illustrated book. Subjects include Americana, animals, history, nature/environment, regional, non-competitive sports, travel. Query. Reviews artwork/photos as part of ms package.

WILDERNESS PRESS, 2440 Bancroft Way, Berkeley CA 94704-1676. (510)843-8080. Fax: (510)548-1355. E-mail: 74642.1147@compuserve.com. Editorial Director: Thomas Winnett. Estab. 1967. Publishes paperback originals. Averages 5 titles/year. Receives 150 submissions/year. 20% of books from first-time authors; 95% from unagented writers. Average print order for a first book is 5,000. Pays 8-10% royalty on retail price. Offers $1,000 average advance. Publishes book 8 months after acceptance. Reports in 1 month. *Writer's Market* recommends allowing 2 months for reply. Book catalog for 9×12 SASE.
Nonfiction: "We publish books about the outdoors. Most of our books are trail guides for hikers and backpackers, but we also publish how-to books about the outdoors. The manuscript must be accurate. The author must thoroughly research an area in person. If he is writing a trail guide, he must walk all the trails in the area his book is about. The outlook must be strongly conservationist. The style must be appropriate for a highly literate audience." Request guidelines for proposals.
Recent Nonfiction Title: *Bicycling the Connecticut River Valley*, by Robert Immler.

JOHN WILEY & SONS, INC., 605 Third Ave., New York NY 10158. Associate Publisher/Editor-in-Chief: Carole Hall. Publishes hardcover originals and trade paperback originals and reprints. Publishes 250 titles/year. Pays 10% royalty on wholesale price. Publishes book 1 year after acceptance of ms. Accepts simultaneous submissions. Query for electronic submissions. Book catalog free on request.
Nonfiction: Biography, how-to, children's/juvenile, reference, self-help, technical, textbook. Subjects include business and economics, child guidance/parenting, computers and electronics, gay/lesbian, government/politics, health/medicine, history, language/literature, military/war, psychology, science, sociology, software, women's issues/studies. Query.
Recent Nonfiction Title: *Janet Reno: Doing the Right Thing*, by Paul Anderson (biography).

WILLIAMSON PUBLISHING CO., P.O. Box 185, Church Hill Rd., Charlotte VT 05445. Editorial Director: Susan Williamson. Estab. 1983. Publishes trade paperback originals. Averages 12 titles/year. Receives 1,500 queries and 800 mss/year. 75% of books from first-time authors; 90% from unagented writers. Pays royalty on wholesale price. Advance negotiable. Publishes book 1 year after acceptance. Accepts simultaneous submissions, but prefers 1 month exclusivity. Reports in 3 months with SASE. Book catalog for 8½×11 SAE with 4 first-class stamps.
• Williamson's biggest success is their *Kids Can!* series with books like *The Kids' Nature Book* and

Kids Create. The Kids' Multicultural Art Book won the Parents' Choice Gold Award; *Kids Make Music* won Benjamin Franklin best juvenile nonfiction.

Nonfiction: Children's/juvenile, children's creative learning books on subjects ranging from science, art, to computer creations books. Adult books include psychology, cookbook, how-to, self-help. "Our children's books are geared toward 2-6 year olds and 4-10 year olds. They must incorporate learning through doing. No picture books please! Please don't call concerning your submission. It never helps your review, and it takes too much of our time. With an SASE, you'll hear from us." Submit outline, 2-3 sample chapters and SASE.

Recent Nonfiction Title: *The Kids' Science Book*, by White & Hirschfeld.

Tips: "Our children's books are used by kids, their parents, and educators. They encourage self-discovery, creativity and personal growth."

WILLOWISP PRESS, INC., Division of Pages, Inc., 801 94th Ave. N., St. Petersburg FL 33702-2426. (813)578-7600. Contact: Acquisitions Editor. Publishes trade paperback originals. 10% of books are from first-time authors; 80% from unagented writers. Pays royalty or makes outright purchase. Offers varying advance. Publishes book 9-18 months after acceptance. Accepts simultaneous submissions. Electronic submissions "only upon request." Reports in 5 weeks on queries, 2 months on mss. Book catalog for 9×12 SAE with 5 first-class stamps. Manuscript guidelines for #10 SASE.

• Willowisp plans to develop a line of pre-school books and welcomes submissions from qualified writers. Also they would like to see strong, tightly-written suspense titles for kids 10-13.

Nonfiction: Illustrated book, juvenile. Subjects include animals, science, sports, environmental, etc. Query with outline.

Recent Nonfiction Title: *Totally Useless Skills*, by Rick Davis.

Fiction: Pre-K through middle school only. Adventure, humor, juvenile, literary, contemporary, mystery, picture books, romance, science fiction, short story collections, suspense, young adult.

Recent Fiction Titles: *The Secret of Seaside*, by Linda Barr.

Tips: "Three to six grade level a prime market for both fiction and nonfiction. Nothing directed at high school; no poetry or religious orientation."

WILSHIRE BOOK CO., 12015 Sherman Rd., North Hollywood CA 91605-3781. (818)765-8579. Publisher: Melvin Powers. Senior Editor: Marcia Grad. Estab. 1947. Publishes trade paperback originals and reprints. Publishes 50 titles/year. Receives 3,000 submissions/year. 80% of books from first-time authors; 75% from unagented writers. Average print order for a first book is 5,000. Pays standard royalty. Offers variable advance. Publishes book 9 months after acceptance. Reports in 2 months.

Nonfiction: Self-help, motivation, inspiration, psychology, spirituality, recovery, how-to, entrepreneurship, mail order, how to get started doing business on computer bulletin boards, horsemanship. "We are always looking for books such as *Psycho-Cybernetics, The Magic of Thinking Big, Guide to Rational Living* and *Think and Grow Rich*. We also need manuscripts teaching mail order on computer bulletin boards and entrepreneur techniques. All we need is the concept of the book to determine if project is viable. We welcome phone calls to discuss manuscripts or book ideas with authors." Submit synopsis or detailed chapter outline, 3 sample chapters and SASE. Reviews artwork/photos as part of ms package.

Fiction: Adult fables that teach principles of psychological and/or spiritual growth or offer guidance in living.

Tips: "We are looking for such books as *Illusions, The Little Prince, The Greatest Salesman in the World* and *The Knight in Rusty Armor*. We are very interested in publishing books that tell you step-by-step how to do business on the computer bulletins especially for homebased businesses."

WINDWARD PUBLISHING, INC., P.O. Box 371005, Miami FL 33137-1005. (305)576-6232. Vice President: Jack Zinzow. Estab. 1973. Publishes trade paperback originals. Publishes 6 titles/year. Receives 50 queries and 10 mss/year. 35% of books from first-time authors; 100% from unagented writers. Pays 10% royalty on wholesale price. Publishes book 14 months after acceptance of ms. Accepts simultaneous submissions. Reports in 2 weeks on queries. *Writer's Market* recommends allowing 2 months for reply.

Nonfiction: Illustrated books, children's/juvenile natural history, handbooks. Subjects include agriculture/horticulture, animals, gardening, nature/environment, recreation (fishing, boating, diving, camping), science. Query. Reviews artwork/photos as part of the ms package.

WISDOM PUBLICATIONS, 361 Newbury St., 4th Floor, Boston MA 02115. (617)536-3358. Editorial Project Manager: Constance Miller. Publishes hardcover originals and trade paperback originals and reprints. Publishes 8-10 titles/year. Receives 150 queries and 50 mss/year. 50% of books from first-time authors; 95% from unagented writers. Pays 4-8% royalty on wholesale price (net). Publishes book 18-24 months after acceptance. Query for electronic submissions. Reports in 2-6 months on mss. Book catalog and ms guidelines free on request.

Nonfiction: Reference, self-help, textbook. Subjects include philosophy (Buddhist or Comparative Buddhist/Western), East-West, Buddhism, Buddhist texts and Tibet. Submit proposal package, including hard copy of ms. Reviews artwork/photos as part of ms package. Send photocopies.

WOODBINE HOUSE, 6510 Bells Mill Rd., Bethesda MD 20817. Editor: Susan Stokes. Estab. 1985. Publishes hardcover and trade paperback books. 90% of books from unagented writers. Pays royalty. Publishes book 18 months after acceptance. Accepts simultaneous submissions. Query for electronic submissions. Reports in 2 months. Book catalog and ms guidelines for 6×9 SAE with 3 first-class stamps.

 • Woodbine is less likely to publish illustrated children's books than other children's publishers.

Nonfiction: Primarily publishes books for and about children with disabilities, but will consider other nonfiction books that would appeal to a clearly defined audience. No personal accounts or general parenting guides. Submit outline and sample chapters. Reviews artwork/photos as part of ms package.

Recent Nonfiction Title: *Communication Skills in Children with Down Syndrome*, by Libby Kumin.

Tips: "Before querying, familiarize yourself with the types of books we publish and put some thought into how your book could be marketed (aside from in bookstores). Keep cover letters concise and to the point; if it's a subject that interests us, we'll ask to see more."

WOODBRIDGE PRESS, P.O. Box 209, Santa Barbara CA 93102. (805)965-7039. Editor: Howard Weeks. Estab. 1971. Publishes hardcover and trade paperback originals. Publishes 4-5 titles/year. Receives 300 submissions/year. 60% of books from first-time authors; 80% from unagented writers. Pays 10-15% on wholesale price. Publishes book 8 months after acceptance. Accepts simultaneous submissions. Reports as expeditiously as possible with SASE. *Writer's Market* recommends allowing 2 months for reply. Book catalog free.

Nonfiction: Cookbook (vegetarian), self-help. Subjects include agriculture/horticulture, cooking/foods/nutrition, gardening, health, psychology (popular). Query. Reviews artwork/photos as part of ms package.

Recent Nonfiction Title: *Your Good Health Garden*, by Pauline James.

‡**WOODLAND HEALTH BOOKS**, P.O. Box 160, Pleasant Grove UT 84062. Publisher: Mark Lisonbee. Publishes perfect bound and trade paperback originals. Publishes 8 titles/year. Receives 100 queries and 60 mss/year. 50% of mss from first-time authors; 100% from unagented writers. Publishes book 6 months after acceptance of ms. Accepts simultaneous submissions. Query for electronic submissions. Reports in 1 month on proposals. *Writer's Market* recommends allowing 2 months for reply. Book catalog free on request.

Nonfiction: Health/alternative medicine subjects. "Our readers are interested in herbs and other natural health topics. Most of our books are sold through health food stores." Query.

Recent Nonfiction Title: *The Complete Home Health Advisor*, by Rita Elkins.

WORKMAN PUBLISHING, 708 Broadway, New York NY 10003. General nonfiction publisher. This company did not respond to our request for information. Query before submitting.

‡**WRITE WAY PUBLISHING**, 3806 S. Fraser, Aurora CO 80014 Owner/Editor: Dorrie O'Brien. Publishes hardcover and trade paperback originals. Publishes 10 titles/year. Receives 300 queries and 600 mss/year. 50% of books from first-time authors; 95% from unagented writers. Pays 8-10% royalty on wholesale price. No advance. Publishes book 12-36 months after acceptance of ms. Accepts simultaneous submissions. Reports in 1 month on queries and proposals, in 5-6 months on mss. "We only consider completed works." Book brochure and ms guidelines free on request.

Nonfiction: Biography (of notable personages only). Subjects include government/politics (American or British only), history (American or British only), military, war (American or British only). No biographies of "unknowns." Query with short synopsis, 1-2 sample chapters and postage with proper-sized box or envelope. "Wait with material until we've determined if the manuscript is accepted for reading."

Fiction: Adventure, fantasy, historical, horror, humor, mainstream/contemporary, mystery, occult, science fiction, suspense. Query with short synopsis, 1-2 sample chapters and postage with proper-sized box or envelope.

Recent Fiction Title: *St. John's Bestiary*, by William Babula (detective).

Tips: "We find that lengthy outlines and/or synopsis are unnecessary and much too time-consuming for our editors to read. We prefer a very short plot review and 1-2 chapters to get a feel for the writer's style. If we like what we read, then we'll ask for the whole manuscript."

WRITER'S DIGEST BOOKS, Imprint of F&W Publications, 1507 Dana Ave., Cincinnati OH 45207. Editor: Jack Heffron. Estab. 1920. Publishes hardcover and paperback originals. Averages 16 titles/year. Pays 10-20% royalty on net receipts. Accepts simultaneous submissions if so advised. Publishes book 12-18 months after acceptance. Enclose return postage. *Writer's Market* recommends allowing 2 months for reply. Book catalog for 9×12 SAE with 6 first-class stamps.

Nonfiction: Instructional and reference books for writers. "Our instruction books stress results and how specifically to achieve them. Should be well-researched, yet lively and readable. Our books concentrate on writing techniques over marketing techniques. We do *not* want to see books telling readers how to crack specific nonfiction markets: *Writing for the Computer Market* or *Writing for Trade Publications*, for instance. Concentrate on broader writing topics. In the offices here we refer to a manuscript's 4T value—manuscripts must have information writers can Take To The Typewriter. We are continuing to grow our line of reference books for writers, such as *Modus Operandi* and *Malicious Intent* in our Howdunit series, and *A Writer's*

Guide to Everyday Life in the Middle Ages. References must be usable, accessible, and, of course, accurate. Query or submit outline and sample chapters. Be prepared to explain how the proposed book differs from existing books on the subject." No fiction or poetry. "Writer's Digest Books also publishes instructional books for photographers and songwriters but the main thrust is on writing books. The same philosophy applies to songwriting and photography books: they must instruct about the creative craft, as opposed to instructing about marketing."

Recent Nonfiction Title: *Elements of Fiction Writing: Style and Voice,* by Johnny Payne.

WRS PUBLISHING, 701 N. New Rd., Waco TX 76710. (817)776-6461. Fax: (817)757-1454. Acquisitions Director: Thomas Spence. Estab. 1967. Publishes hardcover, trade and mass market paperback originals. Publishes 30-35 titles/year. Receives 600 submissions/year. 20% of books from first-time authors; 50% from unagented writers. Pays 15% royalty on wholesale price. Advance negotiable. Publishes book 1 year after acceptance. Accepts simultaneous submissions if so noted. Query for electronic submissions. Reports in 1 month on queries. Book catalog and ms guidelines for SASE.

Nonfiction: Unique and compelling books relating to health, well being, character, ethics and moral values. Query or submit outlines and sample chapters. Submit artwork/photos as part of ms package with SASE.

Recent Nonfiction Title: *In Touch With Your Breasts,* by James Davidson, M.D.

Tips: "We are primarily interested in inspiring stories and health-related subjects which fit the bookstore market and library needs. Our books appeal primarily to educated persons with an interest in improving their general lifestyle."

ZEBRA and PINNACLE BOOKS, 850 Third Ave., New York NY 10022. (212)407-1500. Publisher: Lynn Brown. Publishes hardcover, trade paperback and mass market paperback originals, trade paperback and mass market paperback reprints. Zebra publishes 360 titles/year; Pinnacle publishes 120 titles/year. Pays royalty. Rarely makes outright purchase. Publishes book 2 years after acceptance of ms. Accepts simultaneous submissions. Reports in 3 months on proposals. Manuscript guidelines for #10 SASE.

Nonfiction: Biography, how-to, humor, self-help. Subjects include business and economics, health/medicine, military/war, money/finance. Submit outline with 3-5 sample chapters.

Fiction: Adventure, erotica, fantasy, gothic, historical, horror, humor, literary, mainstream/contemporary, mystery, occult, romance, short story collections, suspense, western, young adult. Submit synopsis with 3-5 sample chapters.

ZOLAND BOOKS, INC., 384 Huron Ave., Cambridge MA 02138. (617)864-6252. Fax: (617)661-4998. Publisher/Editor: Roland Pease, Jr. Marketing Associate: Junia MacNeil. Estab. 1987. Publishes hardcover and trade paperback originals. Averages 8-12 titles/year. Receives 400 submissions/year. 15% of books from first-time authors; 60% from unagented writers. Pays 7% royalty on retail price. Publishes book 18 months after acceptance. Reports in 4 months. Book catalog for 6½×9½ SAE with 2 first-class stamps.

● This publisher is more interested in nonfiction than it has been in the past.

Nonfiction: Biography, art book. Subjects include art/architecture, language/literature, nature/environment, photography, regional, translation, travel, women's issues/studies. Query. Reviews artwork/photos as part of ms package.

Fiction: Literary and short story collections. Submit complete ms.

Recent Fiction Title: *Matron of Honor,* by Sallie Bingham.

Tips: "We are most likely to publish books which provide original, thought-provoking ideas, books which will captivate the reader, and are evocative."

ZONDERVAN PUBLISHING HOUSE, 5300 Patterson Ave. SE, Grand Rapids MI 49530-0002. (616)698-6900. Contact: Editorial Coordinator. Estab. 1931. Publishes hardcover and trade paperback originals and reprints. Averages 130 titles/year. Receives 3,000 submissions/year. 20% of books from first-time authors; 80% from unagented writers. Average print order for a first book is 5,000. Pays royalty of 14% of the net amount received on sales of cloth and softcover trade editions and 12% of net amount received on sales of mass market paperbacks. Offers variable advance. Reports in 3 months on proposals. SASE required. Recommend ms guidelines for #10 SASE. To receive a recording about submission call (616)698-3447.

Nonfiction and Fiction: Biography, autobiography, self-help, devotional, contemporary issues, Christian living, Bible study resources, references for lay audience; some adult fiction; youth and children's ministry; teens and children. Academic and Professional Books: college and seminary textbooks (biblical studies, theology, church history, the humanities); preaching, counseling, discipleship, worship, and church renewal for pastors, professionals, and lay leaders in ministry; theological and biblical reference books. All from religious perspective (evangelical). Immediate needs listed in guidelines. Submit outline/synopsis, 1 sample chapter, and SASE for return of materials.

Recent Nonfiction Title: *False Assumptions,* by Dr. Henry Cloud and Dr. John Townsend.

Recent Fiction Title: *McKinney High, 1946,* by Ken Gire.

Canadian and International Book Publishers

Canadian book publishers share the same mission as their U.S. counterparts—publishing timely books on subjects of concern and interest to a targetable audience. Most of the publishers listed in this section, however, differ from U.S. publishers in that their needs tend toward subjects that are specifically Canadian or intended for a Canadian audience. Some are interested in submissions only from Canadian writers. There are many regional Canadian publishers that concentrate on region-specific subjects, and many Quebec publishers will consider only works in French.

U.S. writers hoping to do business with Canadian publishers should take pains to find out as much about their intended markets as possible. The listings will inform you about what kinds of books the companies publish and tell you whether they are open to receiving submissions from non-Canadians. To further target your markets and see very specific examples of the books they are publishing, send for catalogs from the publishers you are interested in.

There has always been more government subsidy of publishing in Canada than in the U.S. However, with the recent announcement of a 55% cut in such subsidies, government support appears to be on the decline. There still are a few author-subsidy publishers in Canada and writers should proceed with caution when they are made this offer. We have denoted partial author-subsidy publishers with an asterisk (*).

Despite a healthy book publishing industry, Canada is still dominated by publishers from the United States. Two out of every three books found in Canadian bookstores are published in the U.S. These odds have made some Canadian publishers even more determined to concentrate on Canadian authors and subjects. Writers interested in additional Canadian book publishing markets should consult *Literary Market Place* (R.R. Bowker & Co.), *The Canadian Writer's Guide* (Fitzhenry & Whiteside) and *The Canadian Writer's Market* (McClelland & Stewart).

International mail

U.S. postage stamps are useless on mailings originating outside of the U.S. When enclosing a self-addressed envelope for return of your query or manuscript from a publisher outside the U.S., you must include International Reply Coupons (IRCs). IRCs are available at your local post office and can be redeemed for stamps of any country. You can cut a substantial portion of your international mailing expenses by sending disposable proposals and manuscripts (i.e., photocopies or computer printouts which the recipient can simply throw away if he or she is not interested), instead of paying postage for the return of rejected material. Please note that the cost for items such as catalogs is expressed in the currency of the country in which the publisher is located.

For a list of publishers according to their subjects of interest, see the nonfiction and fiction sections of the Book Publishers Subject Index. Information on some book publishers and producers not included in this edition of *Writer's Market* can be found in Book Publishers and Producers/Changes '95-'96.

Approaching the Canadian marketplace

Reed Books Canada, a subsidiary of Reed International Books, publishes a wide variety of titles—both fiction and nonfiction—under its various imprints. Launched in 1991, Reed Books Canada, according to publisher Oliver Salzmann, is interested in "working with authors to develop the best possible books and using our marketing excellence to find them loyal readers. We want to publish profitably so that we can continue publishing."

If marketing expertise is one key to establishing and maintaining a successful publishing program, Salzmann comes well prepared to his position. Prior to his appointment as publisher, he was national sales manager for the company. His background includes other book sales positions, editorial work with John Wiley & Sons Canada, and clerking and management positions in retail bookstores. His multi-faceted experience in the Canadian book business gives him unique insight into the way that business works.

"Many who are unfamiliar with North American publishing overlook how the Canadian market differs from the American," says Salzmann. "The Canadian market is traditionally considered to be one tenth the size of the market in the United States. With a population spread out over greater distances, national marketing can be a challenge, but it can be accomplished. Canada is a country of many cultures, and very receptive to many different stories and voices. At Reed Canada we've seen many new writers find a loyal following after successful launches of their books in Canada. Often publishing well in Canada can help build a career in other countries."

Though a portion of its list is devoted to uniquely Canadian authors and subjects, Reed Canada is interested in hearing from Canadian *and* non-Canadian writers. "Reed Canada represents works by writers from all over the world through its numerous imprints and affiliate companies, so in that sense we have quite an international outlook," Salzmann says. "As a North American company, though, we are naturally interested in books with markets in the United States and Canada." Canadian writers enjoy an advantage, according to Salzmann, only when it comes to subjects with local Canadian appeal.

As the publisher at a new and growing publishing house, Salzmann keeps his hands in nearly every area of the company's operations. "Most of my workday is taken up with the details of books that are already under development: scheduling, coordinating, and suggesting changes that will improve a book. Because of my selling background, I tend to spend a lot of my time ensuring that the titles we are publishing are being sold through as many profitable market channels as possible."

Of course, a good portion of Salzmann's time is spent in finding new books to add to Reed Canada's list of successful titles. "Acquiring books is fairly straightforward," Salzmann says. "If you know what you're looking for, what fits with your lists, and if you have a developed—if personal—sense of what is good in its class, finding good books is not too difficult. Booksellers and other readers will introduce you to new writers, and the editors of the small presses and literary journals are generous about recommending new talents. Although most often one will pursue opportunities that come up this way, submissions that are professionally presented and interesting come in regularly both from agents, and unsolicited, from individuals."

Like many publishers, both in Canada and the U.S., Reed Canada appreciates hearing from writers who have given some thought to the marketing of the book they are proposing. "While we don't expect authors to be publishers, we welcome proposals that demonstrate some sense of the market for the writer's work," says Salzmann. "For publisher and author alike it is essential to know what other books have already been published that are similar to yours. These 'similar' books define the category you are writing or publishing for; amongst them you will most likely find your readers, your market. At the same time, you need to know why your book is unique amongst these other books, since that defines the special quality that will make your book succeed. Understanding this will help a writer present a better manuscript to a publisher, and it will also help a publisher develop a title that will capture the attention of book buyers as a title that is at once familiar, and yet new and different."

Beyond an awareness of marketing concerns, authors need to pay attention to a few other points when querying Reed Canada. "Since publishers receive so many submissions, brevity and clarity are always welcome. The proposal that is accompanied by a concise and compelling outline and a highly polished extract from the work will get the most attention. Both should reflect the very best that writer can achieve." Salzmann warns writers against sending a large manuscript just to show that they have completed a manuscript. "That's less important to us than knowing whether the writer can tell an engaging story, write a thoughtful paragraph, a gripping sentence, a memorable phrase," says Salzmann. "The submissions we look for reflect the work and the craft of a dedicated writer who has done her/his utmost to hint, briefly, at the depth of his skill, his care, and dedication to his work."

ARSENAL PULP PRESS, 100-1062 Homer St., Vancouver British Columbia V6B 2W9 Canada. (604)687-4233. Editor: Linda Field. Estab. 1980. Imprint is Tillacum Library. Publishes hardcover and trade paperback originals. Publishes 12-15 titles/year. Receives 400 queries and 200 mss/year. 25% of books from first-time authors; 100% from unagented writers. Pays 15% royalty on wholesale price. Advance varies. Publishes book 1 year after acceptance of ms. Accepts simultaneous submissions. Reports in 3-4 months on queries, with exceptions. Book catalog and ms guidelines free on request.
Nonfiction: Humor. Subjects include ethnic (Canadian, aboriginal issues), gay/lesbian, history (cultural), literature, regional (British Columbia), women's issues/studies. "We focus on Canadian or British Columbia issues." Submit outline and 2-3 sample chapters.
Recent Nonfiction Title: *Imagining Ourselves: An Anthology of Canadian Non-fiction*, edited by D. Francis (anthology).
Fiction: Experimental, feminist, gay/lesbian, literary and short story collections. "We only publish Canadian authors." Submit synopsis and 2-3 sample chapters.
Recent Fiction Title: *Lovely in Her Bones*, by J. Jill Robinson (short stories).

‡AURORA EDITIONS, 1184 Garfield St. N, Winnipeg, Manitoba R3C 2P1 Canada. Editor/Publisher: Roma Quapp. Publishes trade paperback originals. Publishes 5 titles/year. 20% of books from first-time authors; 100% from unagented writers. Pays 8-10% royalty, copies of work. Offers $50 advance. Publishes book 2 years after acceptance of ms. Accepts simultaneous submissions. Reports in 6 months on mss. Book catalog and ms guidelines for #10 SAE and IRC.

Nonfiction: Biography. Women's issues/studies subjects. "We are interested in short (maximum 15,000 words) literary biographies of Canadian women." Submit proposal package with 2 sample chapters or full ms and SAE and IRCs.
Recent Nonfiction Title: *A Slice of Life*, by Marie Barton (biography).
Fiction: Ethnic, experimental, feminist, literary, short story collections. "We publish very few titles, so chances are slim. But we do attempt to provide comments on all submissions." Submit full ms with SAE and IRCs.
Recent Fiction Title: *Tales of the Ex-Fire Eater*, by Sheila Dalton (literary).
Poetry: Publishes chapbooks of poetry by invitation only.
Recent Poetry Title: *Heartbeats*, by Joan McKay (modern).
Tips: "Audience is women and 'liberated men' (!), age 18-80; urban, professional."

BALLANTINE BOOKS OF CANADA, Division of Random House of Canada, Ltd., 1265 Aerowood Dr., Mississauga, Ontario L4W 1B9, Canada. General interest publisher of nonfiction and fiction. This publisher did not respond to our request for information. Query before submitting.

BANTAM BOOKS CANADA, INC., Subsidiary of Bantam Doubleday Dell Publishing Group, 105 Bond St., Toronto, Ontario M5B 1Y3, Canada. No unsolicited mss. Query with proposal letter and résumé to Submissions Editor. Reports in 2-3 months.

BOREALIS PRESS, LTD., 9 Ashburn Dr., Nepean, Ontario K2E 6N4 Canada. Editorial Director: Frank Tierney. Senior Editor: Glenn Clever. Estab. 1972. Publishes hardcover and paperback originals. Averages 10-12 titles/year. Receives 400-500 submissions/year. 80% of books from first-time authors; 95% from unagented writers. Pays 10% royalty on retail price. No advance. Publishes book 18 months after acceptance. "No multiple submissions or electronic printouts on paper more than 8½ inches wide." Reports in 2 months. Book catalog for $3 and SAE with IRCs.
Nonfiction: "Only material Canadian in content." Biography, children's/juvenile, reference. Subjects include government/politics, history, language/literature. Query with outline, 2 sample chapters and SASE. No unsolicited mss. Reviews artwork/photos as part of ms package. Looks for "style in tone and language, reader interest, and maturity of outlook."
Recent Nonfiction Title: *New Canadian Drama-6: Two Feminist Plays*, ed. Rita Much.
Fiction: "Only material Canadian in content and dealing with significant aspects of the human situation." Adventure, ethnic, historical, juvenile, literary, romance, short story collections, young adult. Query with synopsis, 1-2 sample chapters and SASE. No unsolicited mss.
Recent Fiction Title: *Margin of Error*, by Lesley Chayce.

THE BOSTON MILLS PRESS, 132 Main St., Erin, Ontario N0B 1T0 Canada. (519)833-2407. Fax: (519)833-2195. President: John Denison. Estab. 1974. Publishes hardcover and trade paperback originals. Averages 16 titles/year. Receives 100 submissions/year. 75% of books from first-time authors; 90% from unagented writers. Pays 10% royalty on retail price. Offers small advance. Publishes book 8 months after acceptance. Accepts simultaneous submissions. Query for electronic submissions. Reports in 2 months. Book catalog free.
Nonfiction: Illustrated book. Subjects include history. "We're interested in anything to do with Canadian or American history—especially transportation. We like books with a small, strong market." No autobiographies. Query. Reviews artwork/photos as part of ms package.
Recent Nonfiction Title: *Heartland*, by Greg McDonnell.
Tips: "We can't compete with the big boys so we stay with short-run specific market books that bigger firms can't handle. We've done well this way so we'll continue in the same vein."

THE CAITLIN PRESS, P.O. Box 2387 Station B, Prince George, British Columbia V2N 2S6 Canada. (604)964-4953. Contact: Cynthia Wilson. Estab. 1978. Publishes trade paperback and soft cover originals. Publishes 4-5 titles/year. Receives 105-120 queries and 50 mss/year. 100% of books from unagented writers. Pays 15% royalty on wholesale price. Publishes book 18 months after acceptance of ms. Accepts simultaneous submissions. Reports in 3 months on queries. Book catalog for #10 SASE.

ALWAYS submit unsolicited manuscripts or queries with a self-addressed, stamped envelope (SASE) within your country or a self-addressed envelope with International Reply Coupons (IRC) purchased from the post office for other countries.

Nonfiction: Biography, cookbook. Subjects include history, photography, regional. "We publish books about the British Columbia interior or by people from the interior. We are not interested in manuscripts that do not reflect a British Columbia influence." Submit outline and proposal package. Reviews artwork/photos as part of ms package. Send photocopies.

Fiction: Adventure, historical, humor, mainstream/contemporary, short story collections, young adult. Submit ms only. *Writer's Market* recommends query with SASE first.

Poetry: Submit sample poems or complete ms.

Tips: "Our area of interest is British Columbia and northern Canada. Submitted manuscripts should reflect our interest area."

CANADIAN INSTITUTE OF UKRAINIAN STUDIES PRESS, CIUS Toronto Publications Office, University of Toronto, Dept. of Slavic Languages and Literatures, 21 Sussex Ave., Toronto, Ontario M5S 1A1 Canada. (416)978-8240. Fax: (416)978-2672. E-mail: tarn@epas.utoronto.ca. Director: Maxim Tarnawsky. Estab. 1976. Publishes hardcover and trade paperback originals and reprints. Publishes 5-10 titles/year. Receives 10 submissions/year. Nonauthor subsidy publishes 20-30% of books. Pays 0-2% royalty on retail price. Publishes book 2 years after acceptance. Query for electronic submissions. Reports in 1 month on queries, 3 months on mss. Book catalog and ms guidelines free.

Nonfiction: Scholarly. Subjects include education, ethnic, government/politics, history, language/literature, religion, sociology, translation. "We publish scholarly works in the humanities and social sciences dealing with the Ukraine or Ukrainians in Canada." Query or submit complete ms. Reviews artwork/photos as part of ms package.

Recent Nonfiction Title: *Ukraine And Russia in Their Historical Encounter,* edited by Peter J. Potichny; Marc Raeff, Jaroslaw Pelenski, Gleb Žekulin.

Fiction: Ukrainian literary works. "We do not publish fiction that does not have scholarly value."

Recent Fiction Title: *Yellow Boots,* by Vera Lysenko.

Tips: "We are a scholarly press and do not normally pay our authors. Our audience consists of University students and teachers and the general public interested in Ukrainian and Ukrainian-Canadian affairs."

CANADIAN PLAINS RESEARCH CENTER, University of Regina, Regina, Saskatchewan S4S 0A2 Canada. (306)585-4795. Fax: (306)585-4699. Coordinator: Brian Mlazgar. Estab. 1973. Publishes scholarly paperback originals and some casebound originals. Averages 5-6 titles/year. Receives 10-15 submissions/year. 35% of books from first-time authors. Nonauthor subsidy publishes 80% of books. Publishes book 2 years after acceptance. Query for electronic submissions. Reports in 2 months. Book catalog and ms guidelines free. Also publishes *Prairie Forum,* a scholarly journal.

Nonfiction: Biography, illustrated book, technical, textbook, scholarly. Subjects include business and economics, history, nature, politics, sociology. "The Canadian Plains Research Center publishes the results of research on topics relating to the Canadian Plains region, although manuscripts relating to the Great Plains region will be considered. Material *must* be scholarly. Do not submit health, self-help, hobbies, music, sports, psychology, recreation or cookbooks unless they have a scholarly approach. For example, we would be interested in acquiring a pioneer manuscript cookbook, with modern ingredient equivalents, if the material relates to the Canadian Plains/Great Plains region." Submit complete ms. *Writer's Market* recommends query with SASE first. Reviews artwork/photos as part of ms package.

Recent Nonfiction Title: *The Records of the Department of the Interior and Research Concerning Canada's Western Frontier of Settlement,* by Irene M. Spry and Bennett McCardle.

Tips: "Pay great attention to manuscript preparation and accurate footnoting, according to the *Chicago Manual of Style.*"

‡CARSWELL THOMSON PROFESSIONAL PUBLISHING, Imprint of the Thomson Corp., One Corporate Plaza, 2075 Kennedy Rd., Scarborough, Ontario M1T 3V4 Canada. (416)298-5024. Senior Vice President, Publishing: Gary P. Rodrigues. Publishes hardcover originals. Publishes 150-200 titles/year. 30-50% of books from first-time authors. Pays 5-15% royalty on wholesale price. Offers $1,000-5,000 advance. Publishes book 4-6 months after acceptance of ms. Accepts simultaneous submissions. Reports in 1-3 months. Book catalog and ms guidelines free on request.

Nonfiction: Legal, tax and business reference. "Canadian information of a regulatory nature is our mandate." Submit proposal package, including résumé and outline.

Tips: Audience is Canada and persons interested in Canadian information; professionals in law, tax, accounting fields; business people interested in regulatory material.

‡CHEMTEC PUBLISHING, 38 Earswick Dr., Toronto-Scarborough, Ontario M1E 1C6 Canada. (416)265-2603. Fax: (416)265-1399. President: Anna Wypych. Publishes hardcover originals. Publishes 5 titles/year. Receives 8 queries and 5 mss/year. 20% of books from first-time authors. Pays 5-15% royalty on retail price. Publishes book 3-6 months after acceptance of ms. Accepts simultaneous submissions. Reports in 2 months on queries and 4 months on mss. Book catalog and ms guidelines free on request.

Nonfiction: Technical, textbook. Subjects include nature/environment, science, chemistry, polymers. Submit outline or sample chapter(s).

Recent Nonfiction Title: *Encyclopedic Dictionary of Commercial Polymer Blends*, by L.A. Utracki.
Tips: Audience is industrial research and universities.

COTEAU BOOKS, 2206 Dewdney Ave., Suite 401, Regina, Saskatchewan S4R 1H3 Canada. (306)777-0170. Fax: (306)522-5152. Managing Editor: Shelley Sopher. Estab. 1975. Publishes hardcover, trade paperback and mass market paperback originals. Publishes 11 titles/year. Receives approximately 1,000 queries and mss/year. 10% of books from first-time authors; 95% from unagented writers. Pays 12½% royalty on retail price or makes outright purchase of $50-200 for anthology contributors. Publishes book 18 months after acceptance. Reports in 2 months on queries, 4 months on mss. Book catalog free with SASE or IRC.
  • Coteau Books published *The Night You Called Me a Shadow*, by Barbara Klar, winner of the Gerald Lampert Award.
Nonfiction: Reference, desk calendars. Subjects include language/literature, regional studies. "We publish only Canadian authors."
Recent Nonfiction Title: *Many Patrols: Reminiscences of a Game Officer*, by R.D. Symons.
Fiction: Ethnic, feminist, humor, juvenile, literary, mainstream/contemporary, plays, short story collections. "No popular, mass market sort of stuff. We are a literary press." Submit complete ms. "We publish fiction and poetry only from Canadian authors."
Recent Fiction Title: *Teeth*, by Fred Stenson.
Tips: "We are not publishing children's picture books, but are still interested in juvenile and YA fiction from Canadian authors."

HARRY CUFF PUBLICATIONS LIMITED, 94 LeMarchant Rd., St. John's, Newfoundland, Labrador A1C 2H2 Canada. (709)726-6590. Fax: (709)726-0902. Publisher: Harry Cuff. Managing Editor: Robert Cuff. Estab. 1980. Publishes hardcover and trade paperback originals. Averages 10 titles/year. Receives 50 submissions/year. 50% of books from first-time authors; 100% from unagented writers. Pays 10% royalty on retail price. No advance. Publishes book 8 months after acceptance. Reports in 6 months on mss. Book catalog for 6×9 SASE.
Nonfiction: Biography, humor, reference, technical, textbook, all dealing with Newfoundland, Labrador. Subjects include history, photography, politics, sociology. Query.
Recent Nonfiction Title: *Coastal Cruising Newfoundland* by Rob Mills.
Fiction: Ethnic, historical, humor, mainstream. Needs fiction by Newfoundlanders or about Newfoundland, Labrador. Submit complete ms. *Writer's Market* recommends query with SASE first.
Recent Fiction Title: *The Burned Baby's Arm*, by Randy Lieb.
Tips: "We are currently dedicated to publishing books about Newfoundland, Labrador, but we will accept other subjects by Newfoundland, Labrador, authors. We will return 'mainstream' manuscripts from the US unread."

‡DOUBLEDAY CANADA LIMITED, 105 Bond St., Toronto, Ontario M5B 1Y3, Canada. No unsolicited mss. Query with proposal letter and résumé to Submissions Editor. Reports in 2-3 months.

DUNDURN PRESS LTD., 2181 Queen St. E., Toronto, Ontario M4E 1E5 Canada. (416)698-0454. Fax: (416)698-1102. Publisher: Kirk Howard. Senior Editor: Judith Turnbull. Estab. 1972. Publishes hardcover and trade paperback originals and reprints. Averages 35 titles/year. Receives 500 submissions/year. 45% of books from first-time authors; 90% from unagented writers. Average print order for a first book is 2,000. Pays 10% royalty on retail price; 8% royalty on some paperback children's books. Publishes book 1 year after acceptance. Query for electronic submissions. Reports in 3 months.
  • *Light for a Cold Land*, by Peter Larisey, was nominated for a Governor General's Nonfiction award.
Nonfiction: Biography, coffee table books, juvenile (12 and up), literary, reference. Subjects include Canadiana, art, history, hobbies, Canadian history, literary criticism. Especially looking for Canadian biographies. No religious or soft science topics. Query with outline and sample chapters. Reviews artwork/photos as part of ms package.
Tips: "Publishers want more books written in better prose styles. If I were a writer trying to market a book today, I would visit bookstores and watch what readers buy and what company publishes that type of book 'close' to my manuscript."

ECRITS DES FORGES, C.P. 335, 1497 Laviolette, Trois-Rivières, Quebec G9A 5G4 Canada. (819)379-9813. Fax: (819)376-0774. President: Gaston Bellemare. Publishes hardcover originals. Publishes 40 titles/year. Receives 30 queries and 1,000 mss/year. 10% of books from first-time authors; 90% from unagented writers. Pays 10-30% royalty. Offers 50% advance. Publishes book 6-9 months after acceptance of ms. Accepts simultaneous submissions. Query for electronic submissions. Reports in 6-9 months. Book catalog free on request.
Poetry: Poetry only and written in *French*. Submit 20 sample poems.
Recent Poetry Title: *Le rhythme des lieux*, by Claude Beausoleil.

ECW PRESS, 2120 Queen St. E., Suite 200, Toronto, Ontario M4E 1E2 Canada. (416)694-3348. Fax: (416)698-9906. President: Jack David. Estab. 1979. Publishes hardcover and trade paperback originals.

Publishes 30-40 titles/year. Receives 120 submissions/year. 50% of books from first-time authors; 80% from unagented writers. Nonauthor subsidy publishes up to 5% of books. Pays 10% royalty on retail price. Accept simultaneous submissions. Query for electronic submissions. Reports in 2 months. Book catalog free.

Nonfiction: Biography, directories, reference, Canadian literary criticism. "ECW is particularly interested in popular biography and all Canadian literary criticism aimed at the undergraduate and graduate university market." Query. Reviews artwork/photos as part of ms package.

Tips: "The writer has the best chance of selling reference works, biography, or literary criticism to our firm. ECW does not accept unsolicited fiction or poetry manuscripts."

ÉDITIONS LA LIBERTÉ INC., 3020 Chemin Ste-Foy, Ste-Foy, Quebec G1X 3V6 Canada. Phone/fax: (418)658-3763. Director of Operations: Pierre Reid. Publishes trade paperback originals. Publishes 4-5 titles/year. Receives 125 queries and 100 mss/year. 75% of books from first-time authors; 90% from unagented writers. Pays 10% royalty on retail price. Accepts only mss written in French. Publishes book 4 months after acceptance of ms. Accepts simultaneous submissions. Reports in 1 month on queries, 2 months on proposals, 3 months on mss. Book catalog free on request.

Nonfiction: Biography, children's/juvenile. Subjects include Americana, animals, anthropology/archaeology, child guidance/parenting, cooking/foods/nutrition, education, government/politics, history, hobbies, language/literature, music/dance, nature/environment, psychology, science, sociology. Submit proposal package, including complete ms.

Recent Nonfiction Title: *Cahiers Des Dix #49*, collective (history).

Fiction: Historical, juvenile, literary, mainstream/contemporary, short story collections, young adult. Query with synopsis.

Recent Fiction Title: *Basse-ville*, by Robert Fleury.

‡ÉDITIONS LOGIQUES/LOGICAL PUBLISHING, P.O. Box 10, Station D, Montreal, Quebec H3K 3B9 Canada. (514)933-2225. Fax: (514)933-2182. President: Louis-Philippe Hebert. Publishes hardcover, trade and mass market paperback originals and reprints. Publishes 30 titles/year. Receives 100 queries and 75 mss/year. 40% of books from first-time authors; 100% from unagented writers. Pays 6-10% royalty on retail price. Offers advance up to $1,000. Publishes book 6 months after acceptance of ms. Query for electronic submissions. Reports in 2 months. Book catalog free on request.

Nonfiction: Biography, coffee table book, cookbook, how-to, humor, illustrated book, children's/juvenile, reference, self-help, technical, textbook and computer books. "We aim to the contemporary man and women: technology, environment, learning, trying to cope and live a happy life. Writers should offer some insight on the reality of today." Submit outline, 2-3 sample chapters and pictures if required. Reviews artwork/photos as part of the ms package. Send photocopies.

Recent Nonfiction Title: *Les 4 Clés de l'Équilibre Personnel*, (self-help, health).

Fiction: Erotica, experimental, fantasy, literary, mainstream/contemporary and science fiction. "Be modern." Submit complete ms only. *Writer's Market* recommends query with SASE first.

Recent Fiction Title: *Les Bouquets de Noces* (romance).

Tips: "Our audience consists of contemporary men and women."

EKSTASIS EDITIONS, P.O. Box 8474, Main Post Office, Victoria, British Columbia V8W 3S1 Canada. Phone/fax: (604)385-3378. Publisher: Richard Olafson. Publishes hardcover and trade paperback originals and reprints. Publishes 8-12 titles/year. Receives 85 queries and 100 mss/year. 65% of books from first-time authors; 100% from unagented writers. Pays 10% royalty on wholesale price. Publishes book 6 months after acceptance of ms. Accepts simultaneous submissions. Query for electronic submissions. Reports in 5 months on mss. Book catalog free on request.

Nonfiction: Biography. Subjects include government/politics, nature/environment, psychology, translation. Query. Reviews artwork/photos as part of ms package. Send photocopies.

Recent Nonfiction Title: *Eternal Lake O'Hara*, by Carol Ann Sokoloff (history).

Fiction: Erotica, experimental, gothic, juvenile, literary, mainstream/contemporary, plays, science fiction, short story collections. Query with synopsis and 3 sample chapters.

Recent Fiction Title: *Bread of the Birds*, by André Carpentier (short story collection).

Poetry: "Ekstasis is a literary press, and is interested in the best of modern poetry." Submit 20 sample poems.

Recent Poetry Title: *From the Mouths of Angels*, by Richard Stevenson (lyric poetry).

‡EMPYREAL PRESS, P.O. Box 1746, Place Du Parc, Montreal, Quebec HZW 2R7 Canada. Publisher: Sonja Skarstedt. Publishes trade paperback originals. Publishes 1-4 titles/year. 50% of books from first-time authors; 90% from unagented writers. Pays 10% royalty on wholesale price. Offers $300 (Canadian) advance. Reports in 2 months. Book catalog for #10 SASE. No unsolicited mss.

Fiction: Experimental, feminist, gay/lesbian, literary, short story collections.

Recent Poetry Title: *The Compass*, by Stephen Morrissey.

Fiction: Experimental, feminist, gay/lesbian, literary, short story collections.

FITZHENRY & WHITESIDE, LTD., 195 Allstate Parkway, Markham, Ontario L3R 4T8 Canada. (905)477-9700. Fax: (905)477-9179. Senior Vice President: Robert Read. Estab. 1966. Publishes hardcover and paperback originals and reprints. Publishes 25 titles/year, text and trade. Royalty contract varies. Advance negotiable. Reports in 3 months. Enclose return postage.

● Fitzhenry & Whiteside, Ltd. recently won the Toronto Historical Society Award of Merit.

Nonfiction: "Especially interested in topics of interest to Canadians, and by Canadians." Textbooks for elementary and secondary schools, also biography, history, nature, fine arts, Native studies, and children's books. Submit outline and 1 sample chapter. Length: open.

Recent Title: *Seeing Canada Whole.*

GOOSE LANE EDITIONS, 469 King St., Fredericton, New Brunswick E3B 1E5 Canada. Acquisitions Editor: Laurel Boone. Estab. 1956. Averages 12-14 titles/year. Receives 500 submissions/year. 20% of books from first-time authors; 75-100% from unagented writers. Pays royalty on retail price. Reports in 6 months. Book catalog and ms guidelines for SASE (Canadian stamps or IRCs).

Nonfiction: Biography, illustrated book, literary history (Canadian). Subjects include art/architecture, history, language/literature, nature/environment, translation, women's issues/studies. No how-to, self-help or cookbooks. Query first.

Fiction: Experimental, feminist, historical, literary, short story collections. "Our needs in fiction never change: substantial, character-centred literary fiction (either as novel or collection of short stories) which shows more interest in the craft of writing (i.e. use of language, credible but clever plotting, shrewd characterization) than in cleaving to tired, mainstream genre-conventions. No children's, YA, mainstream, mass market, genre, mystery, thriller, confessional or sci-fi fiction." Query or submit complete ms.

Tips: "Writers should send us outlines and samples of books that show a very well-read author who has thought long and deeply about the art of writing and, in either fiction or nonfiction, has something of Canadian relevance to offer. We almost never publish books by non-Canadian authors. Our audience is literate, thoughtful, well-read, non-mainstream. If I were a writer trying to market a book today, I would contact the targeted publisher with a query letter and synopsis, and request a book catalog and manuscript guidelines. Purchase a recent book from the publisher in a relevant area, if possible. Never send a complete manuscript blindly to a publisher. **Never** send a manuscript or sample without IRC's or sufficient return postage in Canadian stamps."

GUERNICA EDITIONS, Box 117, Station P, Toronto, Ontario M5S 2S6 Canada. Fax: (416)657-8885. Editor/Publisher: Antonio D'Alfonso. Estab. 1978. Publishes trade paperback originals, reprints and software. Averages 20 titles/year. Receives 1,000 submissions/year. 5% of books from first-time authors. Average print order for a first book is 1,000. Nonauthor subsidy publishes 50% of titles. "Subsidy in Canada is received only when the author is established, Canadian-born and active in the country's cultural world. The others we subsidize ourselves." Pays 3-10% royalty on retail price or makes outright purchase of $200-5,000. Offers 10¢/word advance for translators. IRCs required. "American stamps are of no use to us in Canada." Reports in 3 months. Book catalog for SASE.

● Guernica Editions published *Aknos*, by Fulvio Caccia, winner of the Governor General Award.

Nonfiction: Biography, art, film, history, music, philosophy, politics, psychology, religion, literary criticism, ethnic history, multicultural comparative literature.

Fiction: Ethnic, translations. "We wish to open up into the fiction world and focus less on poetry. Also specialize in European, especially Italian, translations." Query.

Poetry: "We wish to have writers in translation. Any writer who has translated Italian poetry is welcomed. Full books only. Not single poems by different authors, unless modern, and used as an anthology. First books will have no place in the next couple of years." Submit samples.

Recent Poetry Title: *Where I Come From (New and Selected Poems)*, by Maria Mazziotti Gillan.

Tips: "We are seeking less poetry, more prose, essays, novels, and translations into English."

‡GUTTER PRESS, 50 Baldwin St., Suite 100, Toronto, Ontario M5T 1L4 Canada. (416)977-7187. Publisher: Sam Hiyate. Imprints are Ken Sparling Books, Eye Press, Kaleyard. Publishes trade paperback originals and reprints. Publishes 6 titles/year. Each imprint publishes 2 titles/year. 50% of books from first-time authors; 100% from unagented writers. Pays 10-15% royalty on retail price. Offers $500-1,500 (Canadian) advance. Publishes book 1-2 years after acceptance of ms. Accepts simultaneous submissions. Reports in 6 months. Manuscript guidelines for SAE and IRC.

Nonfiction: Biography, humor, literary theory. Subjects include art/architecture, education (theoretical), gay/lesbian, government/politics, history, language/literature, philosophy. Query.

Recent Nonfiction Title: *The Necrofile*, by Donna Lypchuk (humor/current affairs).

Fiction: Literary. "Ultimately, language is what has to be at issue, the issue you address with all your heart. Give us your heart and we'll give you ours back." Submit 3 sample chapters with SAE and IRC.

Recent Fiction Title: *Boys Night Out*, by James Wallen (literary).

Poetry: Submit 5 sample poems.

Recent Poetry Title: *The Small Words In My Body*, by Karen Connelly (award-winning).

Tips: "Our audience is people who care about language and what it can accomplish beyond what has already been accomplished."

‡**HARCOURT BRACE CANADA, INC.**, Subsidiary of Harcourt Brace & Company Canada, Ltd., 55 Horner Ave., Toronto, Ontario M8Z 4X6 Canada. Editorial Directors (School Division): Hans Mills and Wendy Cochran. Publishes educational material K-12.

HARPERCOLLINS PUBLISHERS LTD., 55 Avenue Rd., Suite 2900, Hazleton Lanes, Toronto, Ontario M5R 3L2 Canada. General interest publisher of trade, mass market paperback and children's books. This publisher did not respond to our request for information. Query before submitting.

HERALD PRESS CANADA, Subsidiary of Mennonite Publishing House, 490 Dutton Dr., Waterloo, Ontario N2L 6H7 Canada. (412)887-8500. Fax: (412)887-3111. Senior Editor: S. David Garber. Estab. 1908. Publishes hardcover and trade paperback originals and reprints. Publishes 30 titles/year. Receives 1,200 submissions/year. 15% of books are from first-time authors; 95% from unagented writers. Pays 10-12% royalty on retail price. Publishes book 1 year after acceptance. Accepts electronic submissions only with hard copy. Query with SASE. Reports in 1 month on queries. *Writer's Market* recommends allowing 2 months for reply. Book catalog for 60¢. Manuscript guidelines free on request.
Nonfiction: Coffee table book, cookbook, illustrated book, juvenile, reference, self-help, textbook. Subjects include child guidance/parenting, cooking/foods/nutrition, education, ethnic, Christian, Mennonite, Amish, history, language/literature, money/finance, stewardship, nature/environment, psychology, counseling, self-help, recreation, lifestyle, missions, justice, peace. "We will be seeking books on Christian inspiration, medium-level Bible study, current issues of peace and justice, family life, Christian ethics and lifestyle, and earth stewardship." Does not want to see war, politics, or scare predictions. Query or submit outline and 2 sample chapters. Reviews artwork/photos as part of ms package.
Recent Nonfiction Title: *Family Violence: The Compassionate Church Responds*, by Melissa A. Miller.
Fiction: Ethnic (Mennonite/Amish), historical (Mennonite/Amish), humor, juvenile (Christian orientation), literary, picture books, religious, romance (Christian orientation), short story collections, young adult. Does not want to see war, gangs, drugs, explicit sex, or cops and robbers. Query or submit outline/synopsis and sample chapters.
Recent Fiction Title: *A Joyous Heart*, by Carrie Bender.

‡**HIPPOPOTAMUS PRESS**, 22 Whitewell Rd., Frome, Somerset BA11 4EL United Kingdom. 0373-466653. Editor: R. John. Imprints Hippopotamus Press, *Outposts* Poetry Quarterly; distributor for University of Salzburg Press. Publishes hardcover and trade paperback originals. Publishes 6-12 titles/year. 90% of books from first-time authors; 90% from unagented writers. Pays 1.5-10% royalty on retail price. Rarely offers advance. Publishes book 10 months after acceptance of ms. Accepts simultaneous submissions. Reports in 1 month. Book catalog free on request.
Nonfiction: Poetry, essays, literary criticism. Subjects include language/literature, translation. Submit ms.
Recent Nonfiction Title: *Immigrants of Loss*, by G.S.Sharat Chandra (selected poems).
Poetry: "Read one of our authors! Poets often make the mistake of submitting poetry not knowing the type of verse we publish." Submit complete ms.
Recent Poetry Title: *A Cry from the Blue*, by Shaun McCarthy (third collection).
Tips: "We publish books for a literate audience. Read what we publish."

HMS PRESS, P.O. Box 340, Station B, London, Ontario N6A 4W1 Canada. (519)433-8994. E-mail: wayne.ray@onlinesys.com. President: Wayne Ray. Publishes books on disk only. Publishes 10-20 titles/year. Receives 30 queries and 10 mss/year. Pays 20% royalty on retail price. Publishes book 1 month after acceptance of ms. Accepts simultaneous submissions. Query for electronic submissions. Reports in 1 month on mss. Book catalog for #10 SASE.
Nonfiction: Biography, how-to, humor, children's/juvenile, reference, self-help, textbook. Subjects include agriculture/horticulture, Americana, Canadiana, animals, anthropology/archaeology, art/architecture, business and economics, child guidance/parenting, computers and electronics, cooking/foods/nutrition, education, ethnic, gardening, gay/lesbian, government/politics, health/medicine, history, hobbies, lanauge/literature, military/war, money/finance, music/dance, nature/environment, philosophy, photography, psychology, recreation, regional, religion, science, sociology, software, sports, translation, travel, women's issues/studies. Submit complete ms on diskette only in ASCII or IBM WP5.1.
Recent Nonfiction Title: *Titanic-Last Male Survivor*, by Lyle Bebeusee.
Fiction: Adventure, erotica, fantasy, feminist, gay/lesbian, historical, horror, humor, juvenile, literary, mainstream/contemporary, mystery, plays, religious, romance, science fiction, short story collections, suspense, young adult. Submit complete ms on diskette only.
Recent Fiction Title: *Desert*, by Robert McKay (science fiction).
Poetry: Well written, nothing maudlin, little to no rhyme. Submit all poems on diskette.
Recent Poetry Title: *Blowing Holes through the Everyday*, by Sheila Dalton (personal and life).

HORSDAL & SCHUBART PUBLISHERS LTD., 623-425 Simcoe St., Victoria, British Columbia V8V 4T3 Canada. (604)360-0829. Editor: Marlyn Horsdal. Publishes hardcover originals and trade paperback originals and reprints. Publishes 8-10 titles/year. 50% of books from first-time authors; 100% from unagented writers.

Pays 15% royalty on wholesale price. Negotiates advance. Publishes books 6 months after acceptance of ms. Accepts simultaneous submissions. Query for electronic submissions. Reports in 1 month on queries. Book catalog free on request.
Nonfiction: Biography, humor. Subjects include anthropology/archaeology, art/architecture, government/ politics, history, nature/environment, recreation, regional, sports, travel. Query with outline and 2-3 sample chapters. Reviews artwork/photos as part of ms package. Send photocopies.
Recent Nonfiction Title: *Seven-Knot Summers*, by Beth Hill (regional/travel/nature/history anthropology).

HOUNSLOW PRESS, Subsidiary of Dundurn Press Limited, 2181 Queen St., Suite 301, Toronto, Ontario M4E 1E5 Canada. Fax: (416)698-1102. General Manager: Tony Hawke. Estab. 1972. Publishes hardcover and trade paperback originals. Averages 8 titles/year. Receives 250 submissions/year. 10% of books from first-time authors; 95% from unagented writers. Pays 10-12½% royalty on retail price. Offers $500 average advance. Publishes book 1 year after acceptance. Reports in 2 months on queries. Book catalog free.
Nonfiction: Biography, coffee-table book, cookbook, how-to, humor, illustrated book, self-help. Subjects include animals, art/architecture, business and economics, child guidance/parenting, cooking/foods/nutrition, health/medicine, history, money/finance, photography, translation, travel. "We are looking for controversial manuscripts and business books." Query.
Fiction: Literary and suspense. "We really don't need any fiction for the next year or so." Query.
Tips: "If I were a writer trying to market a book today, I would try to get a good literary agent to handle it."

HYPERION PRESS, LTD.,, 300 Wales Ave., Winnipeg, Manitoba R2M 2S9 Canada. (204)256-9204. Publishes hardcover and trade paperback originals and reprints of children's picture books and how-to craft books for all ages. titles/year. Receives 500 queries and 1,000 mss/year. 30% of books from first-time authors; 100% from unagented writers. Pays royalty. Publishes book 6-12 months after acceptance of ms. Simultaneous submissions OK. Query for electronic submissions. Reports in 3-6 months on mss. Book catalog free on request.
Nonfiction: How-to, children's/juvenile. Subjects include ethnic. Reviews artwork/photos as part of free-lance ms package. Writers should send photocopies.
Recent Nonfiction Title: *Best Ever Paper Airplanes*, by Norman Schmidt.

KEY PORTER BOOKS LTD., 70 The Esplanade, Toronto, Ontario M5E 1R2 Canada. (416)862-7777. Editor-in-Chief: Susan Renou. Publishes hardcover originals and trade paperback originals and reprints. Publishes 50-60 titles/year. Receives 1,000 queries and 600 mss/year. 10% of books are from first-time authors; 5% from unagented writers. Pays 4-15% royalty on retail price. Offers $1,000-10,000 advance. Publishes book 1 year after acceptance of ms. Accepts simultaneous submissions. Reports in 2 months on proposals. Book catalog and ms guidelines free on request.
Nonfiction: Biography, coffee table book, cookbook, humor, illustrated book, children's/juvenile, self-help. Subjects include agriculture/horticulture, animals, business and economics, cooking/foods/nutrition, government/politics, health/medicine, military/war, money/finance, nature/environment, photography, sports, women's issues/studies. Submit outline and 2 sample chapters. Reviews artwork/photos as part of ms package. Send transparencies.
Recent Nonfiction Title: *A Life In Progress*, by Conrad Black (autobiography).
Fiction: Humor, mainstream/contemporary, picture books. Submit synopsis and 2 sample chapters.
Recent Fiction Title: *Don't Die Before You're Death*, by Yevgeny Yevtushenko.

‡KINDRED PRODUCTIONS, 4-169 Riverton Ave., Winnipeg, Manitoba R2L 2E5 Canada. (204)669-6575. Manager: Marilyn Hudson. Publishes trade paperback originals and reprints. Publishes 3 titles/year. 1% of books from first-time authors; 100% from unagented writers. Subsidy publishes 20% of books, "largely determined by the perceived general interest in the material." Pays 10-15% royalty on retail price. Publishes book 18 months after acceptance of ms. Accepts simultaneous submissions. Reports in 2 months on queries, 3 months on proposals. Book catalog and ms guidelines free on request.
Nonfiction: Biography (select) and Bible study. Religious subjects. "Our books cater primarily to our Mennonite Brethren denomination readers." Query with outline, 2-3 sample chapters and SASE.
Recent Nonfiction Title: *When the Church Was Young*, by David Ewert (Bible study).
Fiction: Historical (religious), juvenile, religious. "All our publications are of a religious nature with a high moral content." Submit synopsis, 2-3 sample chapters and SASE.
Tips: "Most of our books are sold to churches, religious bookstores and schools."

LES EDITIONS LA LIGNÉE, 140 Brunelle, Beloeil, Quebec J3H 2Z1 Canada. Phone/fax: (514)467-6641. Contact: Michel Paquin. Publishes hardcover originals and reprints. Publishes 3-4 titles/year. Receives 8 mss/year. 30% of books from first-time authors; 100% from unagented writers. Pays 10-14% royalty. Publishes book 30 months afer acceptance of ms. Accepts simultaneous submissions. Query for electronic submissions. Reports in 1 month. Book catalog free on request.

Nonfiction: Textbook. Subjects include language/literature. "Our publications concern post-secondary studies—French teaching." Submit 1 sample chapter.

LONE PINE PUBLISHING, 10426 81st Ave., #206, Edmonton, Alberta T6E 1X5 Canada. (403)433-9333. Fax: (403)433-9646. Editor-in-Chief: Glenn Rollans. Estab. 1980. Imprints are Lone Pine, Home World, Pine Candle and Pine Cone. Publishes hardcover and trade paperback originals and reprints. Averages 12-20 titles/year. Receives 200 submissions/year. 45% of books from first-time authors; 95% from unagented writers. Pays royalty. Accepts simultaneous submissions. Reports in 2 months on queries. Book catalog free.
● Lone Pine published *Knee-High Nature: Winter*, which was included on the Canadian Children's Book Centre's Our Choice list.
Nonfiction: Biography, how-to, juvenile, nature/recreation guide books. Subjects include animals, anthropology/archaeology, art/architecture, business and economics, gardening, government/politics, history, nature/environment ("this is where most of our books fall"), photography, sports, travel ("another major category for us). We publish recreational and natural history titles, and some historical biographies. Most of our list is set for the next year and a half, but we are interested in seeing new material." Submit outline and sample chapters. Reviews artwork/photos as part of ms package.
Recent Nonfiction Title: *Plants of Coastal British Columbia including Washington Oregon and Alaska*, by Pojar & Mackinnon.
Tips: "Writers have their best chance with recreational or nature guidebooks and popular history. Most of our books are strongly regional in nature. We are mostly interested in books for Western Canada, Ontario and the US Pacific Northwest."

JAMES LORIMER & CO., PUBLISHERS, 35 Britain St., Toronto, Ontario M5A 1R7 Canada. (416)362-4762. Publishing Assistant: Laura Ellis. Publishes trade paperback originals. Publishes 20 titles/year. Receives 150 queries and 50 mss/year. 10% of books from first-time authors; 100% from unagented writers. Pays 5-10% royalty on retail price. Publishes book 6 months after acceptance of ms. Query for electronic submissions. Reports in 4 months on proposals. Book catalog and ms guidelines for #10 SASE.
Nonfiction: Children's/juvenile. Subjects include business and economics, government/politics, history, sociology, women's issues/studies. "We publish Canadian authors only and Canadian issues/topics only." Submit outline, 2 sample chapters and résumé.
Recent Nonfiction Title: *Canadian Women's Issues Vol. 2*, by R. Pierson et al (college/university).
Fiction: Juvenile, young adult. "No fantasy, science fiction, talking animals; realistic themes only. Currently seeking chapter books for ages 7-11 and sports novels for ages 9-13 (Canadian writers only)." Submit synopsis and 2 sample chapters.
Recent Fiction Title: *Gallop for Gold*, by S. Siamon (chapter book-adventure).

‡M.A.P. PRODUCTIONS, Box 596, Station A, Fredericton NB, New Brunswick E3B 5A6 Canada. (506)454-5127. Publisher: Joe Blades. Imprints are Broken Jaw Press, Book Rat, BS Poetry Society, SparTime Editions. Publishes trade paperback originals and reprints. Publishes 8-12 titles/year. 50-75% of books from first-time authors; 100% from unagented writers. Pays 10-15% royalty on retail price, chapbook and 10% of print run. Offers $0-100 advance. Publishes book 1 year after acceptance of ms. Reports in 2-6 months on mss. Book catalog for 6½×9½ SAE with 2 first-class stamps. Manuscript guidelines for #10 SASE.
Nonfiction: Illustrated book. Subjects include history, language/literature, nature/environment, regional, translation, women's issues/studies, criticism, culture. Query with SASE. Reviews artwork/photos as part of ms package. Send photocopies, transparencies.
Recent Nonfiction Title: *A Lad From Brantford*, by David Adams Richards (essays).
Fiction: Fantasy, literary, science fiction. Query with bio and SASE.
Poetry: Submit complete ms.

McCLELLAND & STEWART INC., 481 University Ave., Suite 900, Toronto, Ontario M4P 2C4 Canada. (416)598-1114. Imprints are McClelland & Stewart, Stewart House, New Canadian Library. Publishes hardcover, trade paperback and mass market paperback originals and reprints. Publishes 80 titles/year. Receives thousands of queries/year. No unsolicited mss. 10% of books from first-time authors; 30% from unagented writers. Pays 10-15% royalty on wholesale price (hardcover rates). Publishes book 1 year after acceptance of ms. No simultaneous submissions. Query for electronic submissions. Reports in 3 months on proposals.
Nonfiction: Biography, coffee table book, how-to, humor, illustrated book, children's/juvenile, reference, self-help, textbook. Subjects include agriculture/horticulture, animals, art/architecture, business and economics, Canadiana, child guidance/parenting, cooking/foods/nutrition, education, gardening, gay/lesbian, government/politics, health/medicine, history, hobbies, language/literature, military/war, money/finance, music/dance, nature/environment, philosophy, photography, psychology, recreation, religion, science, sociology, sports, translation, travel, women's issues/studies. "We publish books by Canadian authors or on Canadian subjects." Submit outline; all unsolicited mss returned unopened.
Recent Nonfiction Title: *Memoirs*, by Pierre Trudeau (political memoirs).
Fiction: Experimental, historical, humor, literary, mainstream/contemporary, mystery, short story collections. "We publish quality fiction by prize-winning authors." Query. All unsolicited mss returned unopened.

Recent Fiction Title: *Open Secrets*, by Alice Munro (short stories).
Poetry: "Only Canadian poets should apply. We publish only 4 titles each year." Query.
Recent Poetry Title: *Stranger Music*, by Leonard Cohen.

MACMILLAN CANADA, Division of Canada Publishing Corporation, 29 Birch Ave., Toronto, Ontario M4V 1E2 Canada. (416)963-8830. Vice President/Publisher: Denise Schon. Publishes hardcover and trade paperback originals. Publishes 30-35 titles/year. Receives 100-200 queries/year. 30% of books from first-time authors; 90% from unagented writers. Pays royalty. Publishes book 1 year aftr acceptance of ms. Accepts simultaneous submissions. Query for electronic submissions. Reports in 2 months. Book catalog free on request.
Nonfiction: Biography, cookbook, humor, reference, self-help. Subjects include business and economics, Canadiana, cooking/foods/nutrition, health/medicine, history, military/war, money/finance, recreation, sports. Submit outline with 1-3 sample chapters, author bio, letter explaining rationale for book and SASE. Reviews artwork/photos as part of ms package. Writers should send photocopies.

MARCUS BOOKS, P.O. Box 327, Queensville, Ontario L0G 1R0 Canada. (905)478-2201. Fax: (905)478-8338. President: Tom Rieder. Publishes trade paperback originals and reprints. Publishes 3-4 titles/year. Receives 12 queries and 6 mss/year. 90% of books from first-time authors; 100% from unagented writers. Pays 10% royalty on retail price. Publishes book 6 months after acceptance of ms. No simultaneous submissions. Query for electronic submissions. Reports in 4 months on mss. Book catalog for $1.
Nonfiction: "Interested in alternative health and esoteric topics." Submit outline and 3 sample chapters.

THE MERCURY PRESS, Imprint of Aya Press, 137 Birmingham St., Stratford, Ontario N5A 2T1 Canada. Editor: Beverley Daurio. Estab. 1978. Publishes trade paperback originals and reprints. Averages 10 titles/year. Receives 200 submissions/year. 10% of books from first-time authors; 99% from unagented writers. Pays 10% royalty on retail price. Publishes book 1 year after acceptance. Query for electronic submissions. Reports in 2 months. Book catalog free. "We publish *only* Canadian writers."
Nonfiction: Biography. Subjects include art/architecture, government/politics, history, language/literature, music/dance, sociology, women's issues/studies. Query.
Recent Nonfiction Title: *Frontiers: Essays on Race and Culture*, by Marlene Nourbese Philip.
Fiction: Feminist, literary, short story collections. No genre fiction except Canadian murder mysteries, published under the Midnight Originals imprint. Submit complete ms with SASE.
Poetry: No unsolicited mss until 1997. No traditional, rhyme, confessional.
Tips: "Study markets objectively, listen to feedback, present manuscripts professionally."

‡NATURAL HERITAGE/NATURAL HERITAGE INC., P.O. Box 95, Station O, Toronto, Ontario M4A 2M8 Canada. (416)694-7907. Editor-in-Chief: Jane Gibson. Imprint is Natural Heritage. Publishes hardcover and trade paperback originals. Publishes 10-15 titles/year. 50% of books from first-time authors; 85% from unagented writers. Pays 10% royalty on retail price. Publishes book 2 years after acceptance of ms. Accepts simultaneous submissions. Reports in 3 months on queries; 6 months on proposals and mss. Book catalog free. Manuscript guidelines for #10 SAE and IRC.
Nonfiction: Biography, children's/juvenile, coffee table book, gift book. Subjects include agriculture/horticulture, animals, anthropology/archaeology, art/architecture, education, ethnic, health/medicine, history, military/war, nature/environment, photography, recreation, regional. "We are a Canadian publisher in natural heritage and history fields." Submit outline; don't include *details* of visuals.
Fiction: Historical, short story collections. Query.

NETHERLANDIC PRESS, Box 396, Station A, Windsor Ontario N9A 6L7 Canada. (519)944-2171. Editor: Hendrika Ruger. Publishes trade paperback originals 60-100 pages in length. Publishes 4 titles/year. Receives 60 queries and 40 mss/year. 2% of books from first-time authors; 100% from unagented writers. Pays 10% royalty on retail price. Publishes books 6 months after acceptance of ms. Accepts simultaneous submissions. Query for electronic submissions. Reports in 1 month on queries and proposals, 3 months on mss. Book catalog and ms guidelines free on request.
Nonfiction: Subjects include ethnic, history, language/literature. "Netherlandic Press publishes works with Netherlandic (Dutch, Belgian—Flemish) content or influences (circa 100 printed pages)." Query.
Recent Nontiction Title: *100 Years Ago*, by Jan Kryff (pioneer history).
Fiction: Literary and short story collections. "Should have Netherlandic aspect." Query.
Poetry: Query.

NEWEST PUBLISHERS LTD., 10359 Whyte Ave., #310, Edmonton, Alberta T6E 1Z9 Canada. (403)432-9427. Fax: (403)432-9429. General Manager: Liz Grieve. Editorial Coordinator: Eva Radford. Estab. 1977. Publishes trade paperback originals. Averages 8 titles/year. Receives 200 submissions/year. 40% of books from first-time authors; 90% from unagented writers. Pays 10% royalty. Publishes book 2 years after acceptance. Accepts simultaneous submissions. "We only publish Western Canadian authors." Reports in 6 weeks on queries. Book catalog for 9×12 SAE with 4 first-class Canadian stamps or US postal forms.

Nonfiction: Literary/essays (Western Canadian authors). Subjects include ethnic, government/politics (Western Canada), history (Western Canada), Canadiana. Query.
Fiction: Literary and short story collections. Submit outline/synopsis and sample chapters.
Recent Fiction Title: *Chorus of Mushrooms*, by Hiromi Goto.
Tips: "Our audience consists of people interested in the west and north of Canada; teachers, professors. Trend is towards more nonfiction submissions. Would like to see more full-length literary fiction."

‡OISE PRESS INC., 252 Floor W., Toronto, Ontario M5S 1V6 Canada. (416)923-6641, ext. 2403. Fax: (416)926-4725. Managing Editor: Ann Nicholson. Estab. 1965, incorporated 1994. Publishes paperback originals for the education market. Averages 25 titles/year. Receives 100 submissions/year. 20% of books from first-time authors; 90% from unagented writers. Nonauthor subsidy publishes 5% of books. Pays 10-15% royalty. Rarely offers an advance. No simultaneous submissions. Query for electronic submissions. Reports in up to 4 months. Book catalog and ms guidelines free.
Nonfiction: Textbooks and educational books. "Our audience includes educational scholars, educational administrators, principals and teachers and students. In the future, we will be publishing fewer scholarly books and more books for teachers and students." Submit complete ms. *Writer's Market* recommends query with SASE first. Reviews artwork/photos as part of ms package.
Recent Nonfiction Title: *Science Sense: An Introduction to Scientific Inquiry, Science Projects and Science Fairs*, by John Haysom.

‡OOLICHAN BOOKS, P.O. Box 10, Lantzville, British Columbia V0R 2H0 Canada. (604)390-4839. Publisher: Rhonda Bailey. Estab. 1974. Publishes hardcover originals and trade paperback originals and reprints. 99% of books are originals; 1% are reprints. Averages 10 titles/year. Receives 1,000 submissions/year. 40% of books from first-time authors; 90% from unagented writers. Pays 6-10% royalty on retail price. Publishes book 18 months after acceptance. "At present, we are booked two years in advance." Accepts simultaneous submissions. Query for electronic submissions. Reports in 2 months on queries. Book catalog for 9 × 12 SAE with 2 IRCs. Manuscript guidelines for #10 SASE.
Nonfiction: Biography, history. Subjects include ethnic, government/politics, history, language/literature, regional western Canadian, religion, translation and native issues. "We are interested in considering Western Canadian regional history and autobiography. However, our list is now booked to the end of 1995. Any manuscripts we accepted would not be published until at least 1996. No how-to books, including cookbooks; Americana, art/architecture, or business." Query or submit outline and sample chapters. Reviews artwork/photos as part of ms package occasionally.
Recent Nonfiction Title: *Twin Cities*, by Jan Peterson (regional history).
Fiction: Ethnic, experimental, feminist, humor, literary and short story collections. "Our list is now booked two years in advance. However, we are always interested in new fiction, either short story collections or novels. We publish only one children's book per year." Query or submit outline/synopsis and sample chapters.
Recent Fiction Title: *Visible Light*, by Carol Windley.
Poetry: "We are seeking contemporary poetry—poets should be aware of current aesthetics. Our list is booked in advance; any manuscripts considered would be for publication in 1996 or 1997. We do not want to see doggerel, card verse, or verse that proselytizes." Submit 10-15 samples.
Recent Poetry Title: *Tracks in the Snow*, by Ralph Gustafson.
Tips: "Oolichan is a literary press interested in fiction, poetry and regional history. Our decision to publish ultimately is based on the quality of the writing."

‡OPTIMUM PUBLISHING INTERNATIONAL, INC., Box 237, Victoria Station, Westmount, Quebec H3Y 2S5 Canada. (514)937-8822. Publisher: Michael Baxendale. Imprints are Hamdale, Atwater and Optimum. Publishes hardcover and trade paperback originals. Receives 500 queries and 50 mss/year. 15% of books from first-time authors; 20% from unagented writers. Pays royalty. Publishes book 1 year after acceptance of ms. No simultaneous submissions.
Nonfiction: Biography, children's/juvenile, coffee table book, cookbook, how-to, illustrated book. Subjects include animals, art/architecture, child guidance/parenting, cooking/foods/nutrition/ gardening, health/medicine, military/war, sports. Query with outline and 3 sample chapters.
Recent Nonfiction Title: *This Land is Our Land*, by McClean/Baxendale (Native American).

ORCA BOOK PUBLISHERS LTD., P.O. Box 5626 Station B, Victoria, British Columbia V8R 6S4 Canada. (604)380-1229. Publisher: R. Tyrrell. Children's Book Editor: Ann Featherstone. Estab. 1984. Publishes hardcover and trade paperback originals. Publishes 15-20 titles/year. Receives 500-600 submissions/year. 50% of books from first-time authors; 80% from unagented writers. Pays 10-12½% royalty on retail price. Offers $1,000 average advance. Publishes ms 9-12 months after acceptance. Reports in 3 weeks on queries. *Writer's Market* recommends allowing 2 months for reply. Book catalog for 9 × 12 SAE and $1 postage (Canadian). Manuscript guidelines for SASE or IRCs.
Nonfiction: Biography, illustrated book, travel guides, children's. Subjects include history, nature/environment, recreation, sports, travel. Needs history (*West Coast Canadian*) and young children's book. Query or

submit outline and sample chapters. Reviews artwork/photos as part of ms package. *Publishes Canadian material only.*
Fiction: Juvenile, literary, mainstream/contemporary. Needs west coast Canadian contemporary fiction; illustrated children's books, 4-8-year-old range older juvenile and YA. Query or submit outline/synopsis and sample chapters.
Recent Fiction Title: *Belle's Journey,* by Marilynn Reynolds.

OUTCROP, THE NORTHERN PUBLISHERS, Box 1350, Yellowknife, Northwest Territories X1A 2N9 Canada. (403)920-4652. Publisher: Ronne Heming. Publishes trade paperback originals. Publishes 4 titles/year. Receives 20 queries and 10 mss/year. 90% of books from first-time authors; 100% from unagented writers. Pays 8-10% on retail price. Publishes book 10 months after acceptance of ms. Reports in 3 months on queries and proposals. Book catalog free on request.
Nonfiction: Biography, cookbook, reference. Subjects include anthropology/archaelogy, business and economics, ethnic, government/politics, history, nature/environment, science, travel. Looking for books with "specific Northwest Territories/Yukon focus." Query or submit outline and 3 sample chapters. Reviews artwork/photos as part of freelance package. Writers should send photocopies.
Recent Nonfiction Title: *Barrenland Beauties*, by Page Burt.

PACIFIC EDUCATIONAL PRESS, Faculty of Education, University of British Columbia, Vancouver, British Columbia V6T 1Z4 Canada. Fax: (604)822-6603. E-mail: cedwards@unixg.ubc.ca. Director: Catherine Edwards. Publishes trade paperback originals. Publishes 6-8 titles/year. Receives 200 submissions/year. 15% of books from first-time authors; 100% from unagented writers. Accepts simultaneous submissions, if so noted. Query for electronic submissions. Reports in 3-6 months on mss. Book catalog free on request.
Nonfiction: Children's/juvenile, reference for teacher, textbook. Subjects for children: animals, Canadiana, history, language/literature. Subjects for children and teachers: art/architecture, education, ethnic (for children or professional resources for teachers), music/dance, nature/environment, regional (Pacific Northwest), science. "Our books often straddle the trade/educational line, but we make our selections based on educational potential (in classrooms or school libraries)." Submit outline and 3 sample chapters. Reviews artwork/photos as part of ms package. Send photocopies (color, if possible).
Recent Nonfiction Title: *It's Elementary! Investigating the Chemical World*, by Douglas Hayward and Gordon Bates. (nonfiction science activity book for 11 +).
Fiction: For children: ethnic, historical, juvenile, mystery, science fiction, young adult. For children or teachers: plays. "We select fiction based on its potential for use in language arts classes as well as its literary merit." Submit synopsis and 5 sample chapters; whole ms is best.
Recent Fiction Title: *Trapped by Coal*, by Constance Horne (historical fiction set in early 20th century coal-mining town for 8- to 11-year-olds).

PANDORA PRESS, Imprint of HarperCollins, 77-85 Fulham Palace Rd., Hammersmith, London W6 8JB England. Fax: 081-307-4440. Publishing Director: Eileen Campbell. Commissioning Editor: Belinda Budge. Publishes hardcover and paperback originals. Publishes 30 titles/year. Pays 7½-10% royalty. Reports in 2 months. Book catalog free.
  ● No longer publishes fiction.
Nonfiction: Wide-ranging list of feminist writing includes subjects on culture and media, health, lifestyle and sexuality, biography and reference, and women's issues/studies.

PEGUIS PUBLISHERS LIMITED, 318 McDermot Ave., Winnipeg, Manitoba R3A OA2 Canada. (204)987-3500. Fax: (204)947-0080. Acquisitions: Mary Dixon. Estab. 1967. Educational paperback originals. Publishes 8 titles/year. Receives 150 submissions/year. 50% of books from first-time authors; 100% from unagented writers. Pays 10% average royalty on educational net (trade less 20%). Publishes book 1-2 years after acceptance. Accepts simultaneous submissions. Reports in 3 months on queries, 1 month on mss if quick rejection, up to 1 year if serious consideration. Book catalog free.
Nonfiction: Educational (focusing on teachers' resource material for primary education, integrated whole language). Submit outline/synopsis and sample chapters or complete ms.
Recent Nonfiction Title: *A Stone in My Shoe: Teaching Literacy in Times of Change*, by Lorri Neilsen.
Tips: "Writers have the best chance selling us quality professional materials for teachers that help them turn new research and findings into classroom practice."

‡PENGUIN BOOKS CANADA LTD., Subsidiary of The Penguin Publishing Co., Ltd., Suite 300, 10 Alcorn Ave., Toronto, Ontario M4V 3B2 Canada.
Nonfiction: Sports, true crime and any Canadian subject by Canadian authors. No unsolicited mss.
Recent Nonfiction Title: *The Concubine's Children*, by Denise Chonge.
Recent Fiction Title: *The Lion's Al-Rossan*, by Guy Gavriel Kay.

PLAYWRIGHTS CANADA PRESS, Imprint of Playwrights Union of Canada, 54 Wolseley St., 2nd Floor, Toronto, Ontario M5T 1A5 Canada. (416)947-0201. Fax: (416)947-0159. Managing Editor: Tony Hamill.

Estab. 1972. Publishes paperback originals and reprints of plays by Canadian citizens or landed immigrants, whose plays have been professionally produced on stage. Receives 100 member submissions/year. 50% of plays from first-time authors; 50% from unagented authors. Pays 10% royalty on list price. Publishes 1 year after acceptance. No more than 2 simultaneous submissions. Reports in up to 1 year. Play catalog and ms guidelines free. Non-members should query. Accepts children's plays.

PRENTICE-HALL CANADA INC., Trade Division, Subsidiary of Simon & Schuster, 1870 Birchmount Rd., Scarborough, Ontario M1P 2J7 Canada. (416)293-3621. Fax: (416)293-3625. Editorial Manager: David Jolliffe. Estab. 1960. Publishes hardcover and trade paperback originals. Averages about 15 titles/year. Receives 750-900 submissions/year. 30% of books from first-time authors; 40% from unagented writers. Negotiates royalty and advance. Publishes book 9 months after acceptance. Query for electronic submissions. Reports in 3 months. Manuscript guidelines for #10 SAE with 1 IRC.
Nonfiction: Subjects of Canadian and international interest: politics and current affairs, sports, business, finance, health, food. Submit outline and sample chapters. Reviews artwork/photos as part of ms package.
Recent Nonfiction Title: *Ice Time: A Portrait of Figure Skating*, by Debbi Wilkes and Greg Cable.
Tips: "Present a clear, concise thesis, well-argued with a thorough knowledge of existing works with strong Canadian orientation. Need general interest nonfiction books on topical subjects."

‡PRESS GANG PUBLISHERS, Feminist Co-Operative, 225 E. 17th Ave., #101, Vancouver, British Columbia V5V 1A6 Canada. (604)876-7787. Fax: (604)876-7892. Editor: Barbara Kuhne. Publishes nonfiction, fiction and poetry, giving priority to Canadian women, women of color and lesbian writers.

PRODUCTIVE PUBLICATIONS, P.O. Box 7200 Station A, Toronto, Ontario M5W 1X8 Canada. E-mail: iain.williamson@canrem.com. Owner: Iain Williamson. Estab. 1985. Publishes trade paperback originals. Publishes 21 titles/year. Receives 30 queries and 20 mss/year. 80% of books from first-time authors; 100% from unagented writers. Pays 5-18% royalty on wholesale price. Publishes book 3 months after acceptance of ms. Query for electronic submissions. Reports in 1 month on queries and proposals, 3 months on mss. Book catalog free on request.
- Productive Publications is also interested in books on business computer software, the Internet for business purposes, investment, stock market and mutual funds, etc.
Nonfiction: How-to, reference, self-help, technical. Subjects include business and economics, health/medicine, hobbies, software (business). "We are interested in small business/entrepreneurship/employment/self-help (business)/how-to/health and wellness—100 pages." Submit outline. Reviews artwork as part of ms package. Send photocopies.
Recent Nonfiction Title: *The Online World: How to Profit From The Information Superhighway*, by Mike Weaver and Odd De Presno.
Tips: "We are looking for books written by *knowledgeable, experienced experts* who can express their ideas *clearly* and *simply.*"

‡PURICH PUBLISHING, Box 23032, Market Mall Post Office, Saskatoon, Saskatchewan S7J 5H3 Canada. (306)373-5311. Publisher: Donald Purich. Publishes trade paperback originals. Publishes 3-5 titles/year. 20% of books from first-time authors. Pays 8-12% royalty on retail price or makes outright purchase. Offers $100-1,500 advance. Publishes book 4 months after acceptance of ms. Accepts simultaneous submissions. Reports in 1 month on queries, 3 months on mss. Book catalog free on request.
Nonfiction: Reference, technical, textbook. Subjects include agriculture/horticulture, government/politics, history, law, Aboriginal issues. "We are a specialized publisher and only consider work in our subject areas." Query.
Recent Nonfiction Title: *Aboriginal Self-Government in Canada*, edited by John Hytton (reference and text).

‡QUARRY PRESS, P.O. Box 1061, Kingston, Ontario K7L-4Y5 Canada. Managing Editor: William Jake Klisivitch. Publishes hardcover originals and trade paperback originals and reprints. Publishes 30-40 titles/year. 10% of books from first-time authors; 90% from unagented writers. Pays 10% royalty on retail price. Publishes book 6-12 months after acceptance. Reports in 5-7 months. Book catalog for 9×12 SAE. Manuscript guidelines for #10 SASE.
Nonfiction: Biography, children's/juvenile (only by Canadians), gift book, humor. Subjects include art/architecture, education, gay/lesbian, history, language/literature, music/dance, photography, regional, religion, travel. "Our authors are generally Canadian." Query with SASE. Reviews artwork/photos as part of ms package. Send photocopies.
Recent Nonfiction Title: *Superman's Song: The Story of the Crash Test Dummies*, by Stephen Ostick (music/rock).
Fiction: Experimental, feminist, gay/lesbian, literary, mainstream/contemporary, science fiction, short story collections. Query with SASE.

Recent Fiction Title: *Under My Skin*, by Mary di Michele (fiction).
Poetry: "We publish Canadian poets only." Submit complete ms.
Recent Poetry Title: *Slow Reign of Calamity Jane*, by Gillian Robinson.

‡RAINCOAST BOOK DISTRIBUTION LIMITED, 8680 Cambie St., Vancouver British Columbia V6P 6M9 Canada. Imprint is Raincoast Books. Managing Editor: Michael Carroll. Publishes hardcover and trade paperback originals and reprints. Publishes 15-20 titles/year. Receives 800 queries and 500 mss/year. 1% of books from first-time authors; 80% from unagented writers. Pays 8-12% royalty on retail price. Offers $1,000-6,000 advance. Publishes book within 2 years after acceptance of ms. Reports in 1 month on queries, 2 months on proposals, 3 months on mss. Book catalog and ms guidelines for #10 SASE.
Nonfiction: Children's/juvenile, coffee table book, cookbook, gift book, humor, illustrated book. Subjects include animals, art/architecture, cooking/foods/nutrition, history, nature/environment, photography, recreation, regional, sports, travel, Canadian subjects and native studies/issues. "We are expanding rapidly and plan on publishing a great deal more over the next two or three years, particularly nonfiction. Proposals should be focused and include background information on the author. Include a market study or examination of competition. We like to see proposals that cover all the bases and offer a new approach to the subjects we're interested in. Query first. If we're interested, we will then ask for an outline, 3 sample chapters, author/artist bios, outline, sample chapters, market study with SASE." Reviews artwork/photos as part of ms package. Send color photocopies. Will request transparencies if interested.
Recent Nonfiction Titles: *Salmon of the Pacific*, by Adam Lewis (nature wildlife).
Fiction: Juvenile, literary, mystery, picture books, young adult. "Raincoast hopes to publish literary novels that have commercial appeal. Our interest is Canadian literary fiction or high-quality international literary fiction. Query first. If we're interested, we will then ask for a synopsis with SASE."
Recent Fiction Title: *If You're Not from the Prairie*, by Dave Bouchard, illustrated by Henry Ripplinger (children's).
Tips: "We have very high standards. Our books are extremely well designed and the texts reflect that quality. Be focused in your submission. Know what you are trying to do and be able to communicate it. Make sure the submission is well organized, thorough, and original. We like to see that the author has done some homework on markets and competition, particularly for nonfiction."

RANDOM HOUSE OF CANADA, Subsidiary of Random House, Inc., Suite 210, 33 Yonge St., Toronto, Ontario M5E 1G4 Canada. Imprint is Vintage Imprints. Publishes hardcover and trade paperback originals. No unsolicited mss.
Nonfiction: Biography, cookbook. Subjects include cooking/foods/nutrition, gardening, history, military/war, women's issues/studies. Agented submissions only.
Fiction: Literary. Agented submissions only. All unsolicited mss returned unopened.
Tips: "We are NOT a mass market publisher."

‡REED BOOKS CANADA, Subsidiary of Reed International Books, 204 Richmond St., #300, Toronto, Ontario L5V 1V6 Canada. (416)598-0045. Publisher: Oliver Salzmann. Imprints are Reed Books Canada; Secker & Warburg (Toronto); Minerva Canada; Methuen (Toronto); William Heinemann Canada; Sinclair Stevenson (Toronto). Publishes hardcover originals, trade paperback and mass market paperback originals and reprints. Publishes 300 titles/year; imprint publishes 50 titles/year. 10% of books from first-time authors; 10% from unagented writers. Pays 15% royalty on retail price or makes outright purchase of $5,000. Publishes book 1 year after acceptance of ms. Accepts simultaneous submissions. Reports in 1 months on queries, 2 months on proposals, 3 months on mss. Book catalog for $5. Manuscript guidelines for $2.
Nonfiction: Biography, children's/juvenile, coffee table book, cookbook, gift book, how-to, humor, illustrated book, multimedia, reference, self-help. Subjects include business and economics, child guidance/parenting, gardening, government/politics, history, language/literature, money/finance, nature/environment, recreation, software, travel, women's issues/studies. Query with proposal package including outline, 10 pages from a chapter, market analysis and SASE. Reviews artwork/photos as part of ms package. Send photocopies.
Recent Nonfiction Title: *See No Evil*, by Isabel Vincent (political science/biography).
Fiction: Ethnic, feminist, gay/lesbian, literary, mainstream/contemporary, mystery. Query with synopsis, 1 sample chapter and SASE.
Recent Fiction Titles: *Paddy Clarke Ha Ha Ha*, by Roddy Doyle; *How Late It Was, How Late*, by James Kelman.

REIDMORE BOOKS INC., 1200 Energy Square, 10109-106 Street, Edmonton, Alberta T5J 3L7 Canada. (403)424-4420. Fax: (403)441-9919. Director of Marketing/Sales: Cathie Crooks. Estab. 1979. Publishes hardcover originals and modular materials for elementary mathematics (grades 4, 5, 6). Publishes 10-12 titles/year. Receives 18-20 submissions/year. 60% of books from first-time authors; 100% from unagented writers. Subsidy publishes 5% of books. Pays royalty. Offers $1,500 average advance. Publishes book 12 months after acceptance. Query for electronic submissions. Reports in 1-3 months on queries. Book catalog free.

Nonfiction: Textbook. Subjects include ethnic, government/politics, history, elementary mathematics. Query. Most manuscripts are solicited by publisher from specific authors.

ROCKY MOUNTAIN BOOKS, #4 Spruce Centre SW, Calgary, Alberta T3C 3B3 Canada. Fax: (403)249-2968. E-mail: tonyd@cadvision.com. Publisher: Tony Daffern. Publishes trade paperback originals. Publishes 5 titles/year. Receives 30 queries/year. 75% of books from first-time authors; 100% from unagented writers. Pays 10% royalty. Offers $1,000-2,000 advance. Publishes books 1 year after acceptance of ms. No simultaneous submissions. Query for electronic submissions. Reports in 1 month on queries. Manuscript guidelines free on request.
Nonfiction: How-to. Subjects include nature/environment, recreation, travel. "Our main area of publishing is outdoor recreation guides to Western and Northern Canada." Query.
Recent Nonfiction Title: *Backcountry Biking in the Canadian Rockies*, by Eastcott & Lepp (outdoor recreation paperback).

RONSDALE PRESS, (formerly Cacanadadada Press), 3350 W. 21st Ave., Vancouver, British Columbia V6S 1G7 Canada. Director: Ronald B. Hatch. Publishes trade paperback originals. Publishes 6 titles/year. Receives 100 queries and 80 mss/year. 60% of books from first time authors; 95% from unagented writers. Pays 10% royalty on retail price. Publishes book 6 months after acceptance of ms. Accepts simultaneous submissions. Query for electronic submissions. Reports in 1 week on queries, 1 month on proposals, 3 months on mss. Book catalog for #10 SASE. Writers *must* be Canadian citizens or landed immigrants.
Nonfiction: Biography, children's/juvenile. Subjects include history, language/literature, nature/environment, regional.
Fiction: Experimental, novels, short story collections, children's literature. Query with at least 80 pages.
Poetry: "Poets should have published some poems in magazines/journals." Submit complete ms.

ROUSSAN PUBLISHERS INC., Division of Roussan Editeur Inc., 2110 Decarie Blvd., Suite 100, Montreal, Quebec H4A 3J3 Canada. (514)481-2985. Editors: Kathryn Rhoades, Jane Moore Frydenlund. Publishes trade paperback originals. Publishes 12 titles/year; each division publishes 6 titles/year. Receives 75 queries and 75 mss/year. 40% of books from first-time authors; 100% from unagented writers. Pays 8-10% royalty on retail price. Publishes book 6-8 months after acceptance of ms. Accepts simultaneous submissions. Query for electronic submissions. Reports in 3 months on proposals.
Fiction: Young adult and junior readers only—adventure, fantasy, feminist, historical, juvenile, mystery, science fiction. No picture books. Submit synopsis and 3 sample chapters.
Recent Fiction Title: *Summer of the Hand*, by Ishbel Moore (mystery/time travel).

‡SCHOLASTIC CANADA LTD., 123 Newkirk Rd., Richmond Hill, Ontario L4C 3G5 Canada. Editor, Children's Books: Diane Kerner. Imprints are: North Winds Press (contact Laura Peetoom); Les Éditions Scholastic (contact Maggy Thurston, Directrice du departement français). Publishes hardcover and trade paperback originals. Publishes 30 titles/year; imprint publishes 4 titles/year. 0.3% of books from first-time authors; 50% from unagented writers. Pays 5-10% royalty on retail price. Offers $1,000-5,000 (Canadian) advance. Publishes book 1 year after acceptance of ms. Accepts simultaneous submissions. Reports in 1 month on queries, 3 months on proposals. No unsolicited mss. Book catalog for 8½×11 SAE with 2 first-class stamps (IRC or Canadian stamps only).
Nonfiction: Children's/juvenile. Subjects include animals, history, hobbies, nature/environment, recreation, science, sports. Query with outline, 1-2 sample chapters and SASE. Reviews artwork/photos as part of ms package. Send photocopies.
Recent Nonfiction Title: *Take a Hike*, by Sharon Mackay and David Macleod (informal guide to hiking for kids).
Fiction: Children's/juvenile, young adult. Query with synopsis, 3 sample chapters and SASE.
Recent Fiction Title: *Daniel's Story*, by Carol Matas (juvenile novel).

SELF-COUNSEL PRESS, 1481 Charlotte Rd., North Vancouver, British Columbia V7J 1H1 Canada. (604)986-3366. Also 1704 N. State Street, Bellingham, WA 98225. (206)676-4530. Managing Editor: Ruth Wilson. Estab. 1970. Publishes trade paperback originals. Averages 15-20 titles/year. Receives 1,000 submissions/year. 80% of books from first-time authors; 95% from unagented writers. Average print run for first book is 6,000. Pays 10% royalty on net receipts. Publishes book 9 months after acceptance. Accepts simultaneous submissions. Query for electronic submissions. Reports in 2 months. Book catalog and ms guidelines for 9×12 SAE.
Nonfiction: How-to, self-help. Subjects include business, law, reference. Query or submit outline and sample chapters.
Recent Nonfiction Title: *Start and Run a Profitable Gift Basket Business* (self-help business).
Tips: "The self-counsel author is an expert in his or her field and capable of conveying practical, specific information to those who are not. We look for manuscripts full of useful information that will allow readers to take the solution to their needs or problems into their own hands and succeed. We do not want personal self-help accounts, however."

SHOESTRING PRESS, Edmonton Central Post Office, Box 1223, Edmonton, Alberta T5J 2M4 Canada. Fax: (403)426-0853. Editor: A. Mardon. Publishes hardcover and trade paperback originals and reprints. Averages 10 titles/year. Receives 150 submissions/year. 50% of books from first-time authors; 90% from unagented writers. Subsidy publishes 10% of books. Pays 3-15% royalty. Publishes book 6 months after acceptance. Accepts simultaneous submissions. Reports in 1 month.
Nonfiction: Biography, illustrated book, juvenile, reference, technical. Subjects include Canadiana/Americana, anthropology/archaeology, cooking/foods/nutrition, ethnic, government/politics (of Canada), history (of Alberta), military/war (theory and history), nature/environment, regional (Alberta, Western Canada and Western USA), science (for broad market), travel (accounts), Native Canadian. "We are interested in native American stories." Query. Submit outline with appropriate SASE with Canadian stamps or IRCs.
Fiction: Adventure, experimental, fantasy, general historical, juvenile, literary, picture books (Native American), religious, romance, science fiction, western. Submit complete ms with outline, Canadian SASE or IRCs.
Tips: "We have become a broad based publisher and need manuscripts in all categories and genres of nonfiction and fiction."

‡SHORELINE, 23 Ste.-Anne, Ste.-Anne-de-Bellevue, Quebec H9X 1L1 Canada. Editor: Judy Isherwood. Publishes trade paperback originals. Publishes 3 titles/year. Pays 10% royalty on retail price. Publishes book 1 year after acceptance. Reports in 1 month on queries, 4 month on ms. Book catalog for 50¢ postage.
Nonfiction: Biography, humor, illustrated book, reference. Subjects include Americana, art/architecture, Canadiana, education, ethnic, history, photography, regional, religion, travel. Query first.
Recent Nonfiction Title: *Stream of Memory*, by M. Laurel Buck (biography).
Fiction: Ethnic, literary, mainstream/contemporary, short story collections, young adult. Query first.
Poetry: Query first.
Recent Poetry Title: *Down to Earth*, by Judith Isherwood (contemporary).
Tips: Audience is "adults and young adults who like their nonfiction personal, different and special. Beginning writers welcome, agents unnecessary. Send your best draft (not the first!), make sure your heart is in it."

SONO NIS PRESS, 1745 Blanshard St., Victoria, British Columbia V8W 2J8 Canada. Editor: Angela Addison. Estab. 1976. Publishes hardcover and trade paperback originals and reprints. Receives hundreds of queries/year. 5-10% of books from first-time authors; 90% from unagented writers. Pays 10-12 royalty on retail price. Publishes book 8-14 months after acceptance of ms. Accepts simultaneous submissions. Query for electronic submissions. Reports in 2 months on queries. Book catalog for 9×12 SAE with 3 IRCs.
  • Sono Nis Press has published several books that have been awarded a number of prizes, including the Gerald Lampert Poetry Award, Alcuin Society Design Award, Stephen Leacock Award and the Arthur Ellis Nonfiction Crime Award.
Nonfiction: Biography, reference. Subjects include history (British Columbia), hobbies (trains), regional (British Columbia), maritime (British Columbia), transportation (Western Canada). Query or submit outline and 3 sample chapters. Reviews artwork/photos as part of the ms package. Send photocopies.
Recent Nonfiction Title: *Journey Back to Peshawar*, by Rona Murray.
Poetry: Query.
Recent Poetry Title: *Briefly Singing*, by Robin Skelton.

‡STODDARD PUBLISHING CO. LIMITED, 34 Lesmill Rd., Toronto, Ontario M3B 2T6 Canada. Managing Editor: Donald G. Bastian. Publishes hardcover originals, trade paperback and mass market paperback originals and reprints. Publishes 100 titles/year. 10% of books from first-time authors; 60% from unagented writers. Pays 6-15% royalty on retail price. Publishes book 6 months after acceptance of ms. Accepts simultaneous submissions. Reports in 1 month on queries and proposals; 2 months on mss.
Nonfiction: Biography, children's/juvenile, coffee table book, how-to, humor, illustrated book, reference, self-help. Subjects include business and economics, child guidance/parenting, cooking, gardening, Canadian government/politics, health/medicine, history, military/war, money/finance, nature/environment, psychology, recreation, sociology, translation, travel. Query with SAE, IRC.
Recent Nonfiction Title: *Good Fat, Bad Fat*, by Louise Lambert-Lagace and Michelle LaFlamme (health/nutrition).
Fiction: Juvenile, mainstream/contemporary. Submit synopsis and 2 sample chapters with SAE, IRCs.
Recent Fiction Title: *John A's Crusade*, by Richard Rohmer (novel).

‡SUNK ISLAND PUBLISHING, P.O. Box 74, Lincoln, Lincolnshire LN1 1QG United Kingdom. (+44)1522 575660. Managing Editor: Michael Blackburn. Imprint is Jackson's Arm (poetry). Publishes trade paperback originals and reprints. Publishes 4 titles/year; imprint publishes 2 titles/year. 99% of books from unagented writers. Pays 10% royalty on retail price; smaller titles, author receives 10% of print run. Offers $200-500 advance. Publishes book 15 months after acceptance of ms. Reports in 1 month on queries; 2 months on proposals and mss. Book catalog and ms guidelines for 2 IRCs.
Nonfiction: Self-help (starting 1996), books on 3.5 Disk (DOS). Subjects include language/literature, psychology (self-help), religion (New Age). "In 1996 we will launch a list in New Age and self-help titles.

Publication in UK and rest of Europe. Titles are to be made available on disk as well." Query with SAE/IRCs. Reviews artwork/photos as part of ms package. Send photocopies.
Recent Nonfiction Title: *The Constructed Space*, edited by Ronnie Duncan and Jonathan Davidson (collection of essays and memoirs).
Fiction: Literary, occult (commencing fall 1995). "Request catalog (also available on disk)." Query with SAE/IRCs.
Recent Fiction Title: *Hallowed Ground*, by Robert Edric (literary).
Poetry: "Submit poems to *Sunk Island Review*, our biannual literary magazine. Jackson's Arm runs a poetry pamphlet competition annually, with publication of winning title." Send 6 sample poems.
Recent Poetry Titles: *Singers Behind Glass*, James Brockway, editor/translator (modern Dutch).
Tips: "We publish books for intelligent and discerning readers with open minds."

THISTLEDOWN PRESS, 633 Main St., Saskatoon, Saskatchewan S7H 0J8 Canada. (306)244-1722. Fax: (306)244-1762. Editor-in-Chief: Patrick O' Rourke. Estab. 1975. Publishes trade paperback originals by resident Canadian authors *only*. Averages 10-12 titles/year. Receives 350 submissions/year. 10% of books from first-time authors; 90% from unagented writers. Average print order for a first poetry book is 500; fiction is 1,000. Pays standard royalty on retail price. Publishes book 18-24 months after acceptance. Reports in 2 months. Book catalog and guidelines for #10 SASE.
 ● *It's a Hard Cow* was shortlisted for the Governor General Award in 1994 and won the Saskatchewan First Book Award.
Fiction: Juvenile (ages 8 and up), literary. Interested in fiction mss from resident Canadian authors only. Minimum of 30,000 words. Accepts no unsolicited work. Query first.
Recent Fiction Title: *It's A Hard Cow*, by Terry Jordan (short fiction).
Poetry: "The author should make him/herself familiar with our publishing program before deciding whether or not his/her work is appropriate." No poetry by people *not* citizens and residents of Canada. Prefers poetry mss that have had some previous exposure in literary magazines. Accepts no unsolicited work. Query first.
Recent Poetry Title: *Angel Wings All Over*, by Anne Cample.
Tips: "We prefer to receive a query letter first before a submission. We're looking for quality, well-written literary fiction—for children and young adults and for our adult fiction list as well. Increased emphasis on fiction (short stories and novels) for young adults, aged 12-18 years."

THOMPSON EDUCATIONAL PUBLISHING INC., 14 Ripley Ave., Suite 105, Toronto, Ontario M6S 3N9 Canada. (416)766-2763. Fax: (416)766-0398. E-mail: canadabooks@ingenia.com. President: Keith Thompson. Publishes trade paperback originals. Publishes 10 titles/year. Receives 15 queries and 10 mss/year. 80% of books from first-time authors; 100% from unagented writers. Pays 10% royalty on wholesale price. Publishes book 1 year after acceptance of ms. Query for electronic submissions. Reports in 1 month on proposals. Book catalog free on request.
Nonfiction: Textbook. Subjects include business and economics, education, government/politics, sociology, women's issues/studies. Submit outline and 1 sample chapter.

‡THORSONS, Imprint of HarperCollins, 77-85 Fulham Palace Rd., Hammersmith, London W6 8JB England. Fax: 081-307-4440. Director: Eileen Campbell. Managing/Publishing Director: Jane Graham-Maw. Estab. 1930. Other imprint is Pandora. Publishes paperback originals. Averages 150 titles/year. Pays 7½-10% royalty. Reports in 2 months. Book catalog free.
Nonfiction: Publishes books on health and lifestyle, environmental issues, business, popular psychology, self-help and positive thinking, therapy, religion and spirituality, philosophy, new science, psychic awareness, astrology, divination, and Western tradition.

TITAN BOOKS LTD., 42-44 Dolben St., London SE1 0UP England. Editor: D. Barraclongh. Publishes trade and mass market paperback originals and reprints. Publishes 30-60 titles/year. Receives 1,000 queries and 500 mss/year. Less than 1% of books from first-time authors; 50% from unagented writers. Pays royalty of 6-8% on retail price. Advance varies. Publishes books 1 year after acceptance of ms. Accepts simultaneous submissions. Query for electronic submissions. Reports in 1 month on queries, 3 months on proposals, 6 months on mss. Manuscript guidelines for SASE with IRC.
Nonfiction: Biography, how-to, humor, illustrated book. Subjects include music, film and TV, true crime, comics. Query. Reviews artwork/photos as part of ms package. Send photocopies.
Recent Nonfiction Title: *Back to the Batcave*, by Adam West (biography).
Recent Fiction Title: *Star Trek: World Without End*, by Joe Maldean.

‡TREE FROG PRESS LIMITED, 10144 89th St., Edmonton, Alberta T5H 1P7 Canada. (403)429-1947. Editor/Publisher: Allan Shute. Publishes hardcover and trade paperback originals. Publishes 4 titles/year. 75% of books from first-time authors; 90% from unagented writers. Pays 7½-10% royalty on retail price. Offers $500 advance. Publishes book 9 months after acceptance of ms. Book catalog for $2 and 6½×9½ SAE with 2 first-class stamps. Manuscript guidelines for $2 and #10 SASE.

Nonfiction: Subjects include history (regional). "We only publish regional histories in cooperation with a sponsoring historical society." Query. Reviews artwork/photos as part of ms package. Send photocopies.
Recent Nonfiction Title: *Riverdale*, by Shute & Fortier (regional history).
Fiction: Juvenile, young adult. "We publish only Canadian authors." Query with complete ms and 9 × 12 SASE.
Recent Fiction Title: *The McIntyre Liar*, by David Bly (young adult-humor).

TURNSTONE PRESS, 607-100 Arthur St., Winnipeg, Manitoba R3B 1H3 Canada. (204)947-1555. Fax: (204)942-1555. E-mail: editor@turnstonepress.mb.ca. Managing Editor: James Hutchison. Estab. 1971. Publishes trade paperback originals. Publishes 8 titles/year. Receives 1,000 mss/year. Publishes Canadians and permanent residents only. 25% of books from first-time authors; 75% from unagented writers. Pays 10% royalty on retail price. Offers $100-500 advance. Publishes book 1 year after acceptance of ms. Query for electronic submissions. Reports in 4 months. Book catalog free on request.
• Turnstone Press would like to see more novels and nonfiction books.
Fiction: Adventure, ethnic, experimental, feminist, humor, literary, mainstream/contemporary, mystery, short story collections. Submit full ms. *Writer's Market* recommends query with SASE (Canadian postage) first.
Recent Fiction Title: *Days & Nights on the Amazon*, by Darlene Quaite.
Poetry: Submit complete ms.
Recent Poetry Title: *Animate Objects*, by Alan Wilson.
Tips: "We also publish one literary critical study per year and one general interest nonfiction book per year. Would like to see more ethnic writing, women's writing, gay and lesbian writing."

‡CHARLES E. TUTTLE PUBLISHING COMPANY, INC., 2-6 Suido 1-Chome, Tokyo 112, Japan. Fax: 03-5689-4926. President: Nicholas Ingleton. Imprint is Yenbooks (less serious Asia-related books). Publishes hardcover and trade paperback originals and reprints. Averages 36 titles/year. Receives 750 submissions/year. 10% of books from first-time authors; 80% from unagented writers. Subsidy publishes 5% of books. Pays 6-10% on wholesale price. Offers $1,000 average advance. Publishes book 8-12 months after acceptance. Accepts simultaneous submissions. Query for electronic submissions. Reports in 1 month. *Writer's Market* recommends allowing 2 months for reply. Book catalog and manuscript guidelines free.
Nonfiction: Cookbook, how-to, humor, illustrated book, reference. Subjects include art/architecture, business and economics, cooking/foods/nutrition, government/politics, history, language/literature, money/finance, philosophy, regional, religion, sports and travel. "We want Asia-related, but specifically Japan-related manuscripts on various topics, particularly business, martial arts, language, etc." Query with outline and sample chapters. Reviews artwork as part of ms package.
Recent Nonfiction Title: *Collecting Modern Japanese Prints*, by Norman Folman.
Fiction: Literature of Japan or Asia in English translation. Query with outline/synopsis and sample chapters.
Recent Fiction Title: *Autumn Winds*, trans. by Lane Dunlop.
Poetry: Submit samples.
Tips: "Readers with an interest in Japan and Asia—culture, language, business, foods, travel, etc.—are our audience."

THE UNITED CHURCH PUBLISHING HOUSE (UCPH), 3250 Bloor St. W., 4th Floor, Etobicoke, Ontario M8X 2Y4 Canada. (416)231-5931. Managing Editor: Ruth Bradley-St-Cyr. Publishes hardcover and trade paperback originals. Publishes Canadian authors only. Publishes 13 titles/year. Receives 30 queries and 20 mss/year. 80% of books from first-time authors; 99% from unagented writers. Pays 8-10% royalty on retail price. Offers $100-300 advance. Publishes books 4-6 months after acceptance of ms. No simultaneous submissions. Query for electronic submissions. Reports in 2 months on proposals. Book catalog and ms guidelines free on request.
Nonfiction: Biography, reference, self-help. Subjects include history, religion, sociology, women's issues/studies, theology and biblical studies. Submit outline and 1 sample chapter.

THE UNIVERSITY OF ALBERTA PRESS, 141 Athabasca Hall, Edmonton, Alberta T6G 2E8 Canada. (403)492-3662. Fax: (403)492-0719. Director: TBA. Mary Mahoney-Robson. Estab. 1969. Subsidiary/imprint is Pica Pica Press. Publishes hardcover and trade paperback originals and trade paperback reprints. Averages 10 titles/year. Receives 100 submissions/year. 60% of books from first-time authors; majority from unagented writers. Average print order for a first book is 1,000. Pays 10% royalty on retail price. Publishes book 1 year after acceptance. Query for electronic submissions. Reports in on queries, 3 months on mss. Book catalog and ms guidelines free.
• University of Alberta Press is looking for shorter works with minimum illustration.
Nonfiction: Scholarly or university textbook market. Preference given to Canadian authors or authors writing on Canadian topics. Subjects include art, history, nature, philosophy, politics, sociology. Submit table of contents and first chapter. No unrevised theses.
Tips: "We are interested in original research making a significant contribution to knowledge in the subject."

‡**UNIVERSITY OF CALGARY PRESS**, 2500 University Dr. NW, Calgary, Alberta T2N 1N4 Canada. (403)220-7578. Fax: (403)282-0085. Director: Shirley A. Onn. Estab. 1981. Publishes scholarly hardcover and paperback originals. Averages 12-15 titles/year. Receives 175 submissions/year. Less than 5% of books from first-time authors; 99% from unagented authors. "As with all Canadian University Presses, UCP does not have publication funds of its own. Money must be found to subsidize each project." Publishes book 1 year after acceptance. Pays negotiable royalties. "Manuscript must pass a two tier review system before acceptance." Query for electronic submissions. *Writer's Market* recommends allowing 2 months for reply. Book catalog and guidelines for 9×12 SAE with 2 IRCs.

Nonfiction: "UCP has developed an active publishing program that includes up to 15 new scholarly titles each year and 6 scholarly journals. (For UCP's purposes works of scholarship are usually required to be analytical in nature with unity of purpose and unfolding argument and aimed primarily at an audience of specialists.) UCP publishes in a wide variety of subject areas and is willing to consider any innovative scholarly manuscript. The intention is not to restrict the publication list to specific areas."

Recent Nonfiction Title: *Eternal Network: A Mail Art Anthology*, edited by Chuck Delch.

Tips: "If I were trying to interest a scholarly publisher, I would prepare my manuscript on a word processor and submit a completed prospectus, including projected market, to the publisher."

UNIVERSITY OF MANITOBA PRESS, 15 Gillson St., University of Manitoba, Winnipeg, Manitoba R3T 5V6 Canada. Director: Patricia Dowdall. Estab. 1967. Publishes hardcover and trade paperback originals. Publishes 4-6 titles/year. Pays 5-15% royalty on wholesale price. Reports in 3 months.

Nonfiction: Scholarly. Subjects include history, regional, religion, women's issues/studies, native. Query.

‡**UNIVERSITY OF MONTREAL PRESS**, P.O. Box 6128, Station Downtown, Montreal H3C 3J7 Canada. (514)343-6929. Editor-in-Chief: Marise Labrecque. Publishes hardcover and trade paperback originals. Publishes 20-25 titles/year. Subsidy publishes 25% of books. Pays 8-12 % royalty on wholesale price. Publishes book 6 months after acceptance of ms. Reports in 1 month on queries and proposals, 3 months on mss. Book catalog and ms guidelines free on request.

Nonfiction: Reference, textbook. Subjects include anthropology/archaeology, education, health/medicine, history, language/literature, philosophy, psychology, religion, sociology, translation. Submit outline and 2 sample chapters.

UNIVERSITY OF OTTAWA PRESS, 542 King Edward, Ottawa, Ontario K1N 6N5 Canada. (613)564-2270. Fax: (613)564-9284. Editor, English Publications: Suzanne Bossé. Estab. 1936. Publishes 25 titles/year; 12 titles/year in English. Receives 100 submissions/year. 20% of books from first-time authors; 95% from unagented writers. Determines subsidy by preliminary budget. Pays 5-10% royalty on net price. Publishes book 1 year after acceptance. Reports in 2 months on queries, 4 months on mss. Book catalog and author's guide free.

Nonfiction: Reference, textbook, scholarly. Subjects include criminology, education, Canadian government/politics, Canadian history, language/literature, nature/environment, philosophy, religion, sociology, translation, women's issues/studies. "We are looking for scholarly manuscripts by academic authors resident in Canada." No trade books. Submit outline/synopsis and sample chapters.

Recent Nonfiction Title: *When Science Becomes Culture: World Survey of Scientific Culture*, edited by Bernard Schiele.

Tips: "Envision audience of academic specialists and (for some books) educated public."

‡**UNIVERSITY OF TORONTO PRESS**, Suite 700, 10 St. Mary St., Toronto, Ontario M4Y 2W8, Canada. Manager of Human Resources: Susan Connor. Publishes approximately 130 nonfiction titles/year.

Nonfiction: Anthropology, scholarly, sociology.

Recent Nonfiction Title: *Ocean Bridge*, by Carl Christie (history of Ferry Command).

VANWELL PUBLISHING LIMITED, 1 Northrup Crescent, P.O. Box 2131, St. Catharines, Ontario L2M 6P5 Canada. (905)937-3100. Fax: (905)937-1760. General Editor: Angela Dobler. Estab. 1983. Publishes trade originals and reprints. Averages 5-7 titles/year. Receives 100 submissions/year. Publishes Canadian authors only. 85% of books from first-time authors; 100% from unagented writers. Pays 8-15% royalty on wholesale price. Offers $200 average advance. Publishes book 1 year after acceptance. Query for electronic submissions. Reports in 1 month on queries. *Writer's Market* recommends allowing 2 months for reply. Book catalog free.

● Vanwell Publishing Ltd. has received awards from Education Children's Book Centre and Notable Education Libraries Association. It is seeing increased demand for biographical nonfiction for ages 10-14.

Nonfiction: Biography. Subjects include military/war. All military/history related. *Writer's Market* recommends query with SASE first. Reviews artwork/photos as part of ms package.

Tips: "The writer has the best chance of selling a manuscript to our firm which is in keeping with our publishing program, well written and organized. Our audience: older male, history buff, war veteran; regional tourist; students. *Canadian* only military/aviation, military/history and children's nonfiction have the best chance with us."

VEHICULE PRESS, Box 125, Place du Parc Station, Montreal, Quebec H2W 2M9 Canada. (514)844-6073. Fax: (514)844-7543. President/Publisher: Simon Dardick. Estab. 1973. Imprints include Signal Editions (poetry) and Dossier Quebec (history, memoirs). Publishes trade paperback originals by Canadian authors *only*. Averages 13 titles/year. Receives 250 submissions/year. 20% of books from first-time authors; 95% from unagented writers. Pays 10-15% royalty on retail price. Offers $200-500 advance. Publishes book 1 year after acceptance. Query for electronic submissions. Reports in 4 months on queries. Book catalog for 9×12 SAE with IRCs.
Nonfiction: Biography, memoir. Subjects include Canadiana, feminism, history, politics, social history, literature. Especially looking for Canadian social history. Query. Reviews artwork/photos as part of ms package.
Recent Nonfiction Title: *The Strangest Dream*, by Merrily Weisbord.
Poetry: Michael Harris. Canadian authors *only*. Not accepting new material before 1997.
Recent Poetry Title: *The Signal Anthology*, edited by Michael Harris.
Tips: "We are only interested in Canadian authors."

VERSO, 6 Meard St., London WIV 3HR England. Fax: (71)734-0059. Commisioning Editor: Malcolm Imrie. Estab. 1970. Publishes hardcover and tradepaper originals. Publishes 60 titles/year. Receives 500 submissions/year. 15% of books from first-time authors; 80% from unagented writers. Pays 7-10% royalty on retail price. Offers $1,000 average advance. Publishes book 15 months after acceptance. Reports in 2 months.
Nonfiction: Academic, general. Subjects include economics, education, government/politics/social sciences, language/literature, nature/environment, philosophy, science, cultural and media studies, sociology, travel, women's issues/studies. Submit outline and sample chapters. Unsolicited mss not accepted.
Recent Nonfiction Title: *Deterring Democracy*, by Noam Chomsky (hardback).

WALL & EMERSON, INC., 6 O'Connor Dr., Toronto, Ontario M4K 2K1 Canada. (416)467-8685. Fax: (416)696-2460. President: Byron E. Wall. Vice President: Martha Wall. Estab. 1987. Imprints are Wall & Thompson and Wall & Emerson. Publishes hardcover and trade paperback originals and reprints. Publishes 5 titles/year. 50% of books from first-time authors; 100% from unagented writers. Nonauthor subsidy publishes 10% of books. (Only subsidies provided by external granting agencies accepted. Generally these are for scholarly books with a small market.) Pays royalty of 8-15% on wholesale price. Publishes book 1 year after acceptance. Accepts simultaneous submissions. Prefers electronic submissions. Reports in 2 months on queries.
Nonfiction: Reference, textbook. Subjects include adult education, health/medicine, philosophy, science, mathematics. "We are looking for any undergraduate college text that meets the needs of a well-defined course in colleges in the US and Canada." Submit outline and sample chapters.
Recent Nonfiction Title: *Cooperative Education and Experiential learning*, by Jeffrey A. Cantor.
Tips: "We are most interested in textbooks for college courses; books that meet well defined needs and are targeted to their audiences are best. Our audience consists of college undergraduate students and college libraries. Our ideal writer is a college professor writing a text for a course he or she teaches regularly. If I were a writer trying to market a book today, I would identify the audience for the book and write directly to the audience throughout the book. I would then approach a publisher that publishes books specifically for that audience."

WEIGL EDUCATIONAL PUBLISHERS LTD., 1902 11th St. SE, Calgary, Alberta T2G 3G2 Canada. (403)233-7747. Fax: (403)233-7769. Publisher: Linda Weigl. Estab. 1979. Publishes hardcover originals and reprints. Publishes 6-7 titles/year. Receives 50-100 submissions/year. 10% of books from first-time authors; 100% from unagented writers. Pays 5-12% royalty on retail price. Publishes book 2 years after acceptance. Query for electronic submissions. Reports in up to 6 months. Book catalog free.
Nonfiction: K-12 student and teacher materials: social studies, language arts, science/environmental studies, life skills, multicultural texts: Canadian focus. Submit outline and sample chapters with SASE or IRCs. Reviews artwork/photos as part of ms package.
Recent Nonfiction Title: *Alberta, It's People in History*.
Fiction: Juvenile educational: multicultural and environmental.
Tips: "Audience is school students and teachers. Curriculum fit is very important."

WHITECAP BOOKS LTD., 351 Lynn Ave., North Vancouver, British Columbia V7J 2C4 Canada. (604)980-9852. Fax: (604)980-8197. Editorial Director: Robin Rivers. Publishes hardcover and trade paperback originals. Publishes 24 titles/year. Receives 150 queries and 50 mss/year. 20% of books from first-time authors; 90% from unagented writers. Pays 10% royalty on retail price. Offers $500-2,000 advance. Publishes book 8 months after acceptance of ms. Simultaneous submissions OK. Query for electronic submissions. Reports in 2 months on proposals.
Nonfiction: Biography, coffee table book, cookbook, children's/juvenile. Subjects include animals, gardening, history, nature/environment, recreation, regional, travel. "We require an annotated outline. Writers should also take the time to parenting research our list through our catalogue." Submit outline, 2 sample chapters,

table of contents. Reviews artwork/photos as part of the freelance ms package. Writers should send photocopies, transparencies, relevant material.

Recent Nonfiction Title: *Guy to Goddess: An Intimate Look at Drag Queens*, photographs by Rosamond Norbury, text by Bill Richardson (photo essays).

Tips: "Our readership is a general audience."

‡WORDSTORM PRODUCTIONS INC., Box 49132, 7740 18th St. SE, Calgary, Alberta T2C 3W5 Canada. Phone/fax: (403)236-1275. Editor: Perry P. Rose. Publishes trade and mass market paperback originals. Publishes 3-5 titles/year. 90% of books from first-time authors; 95% from unagented writers. Pays 10-12% royalty on retail price. (Canadian works released in USA paid 66% of above.) Publishes book 1 year after acceptance of ms. Reports in 2 months on queries, 4 months on proposal, 6 months on mss. Manuscript guidelines for #10 SASE.

Nonfiction: Humor. Query with outline, 3 sample chapters and SASE. All unsolicited mss returned unopened. Reviews artwork/photos as part of ms package. Send photocopies.

Recent Nonfiction Title: *Tales From The Police Locker Room*, by Perry P. Rose (humor).

Fiction: Adventure, humor, mainstream/contemporary, mystery, short story collections, suspense. Query with synopsis, 3 sample chapters and SASE. All unsolicited mss returned unopened.

Recent Fiction Title: *Faxable Laughs Volumes 1* and *2*, by Perry P. Rose (office humor).

‡WORLDWIDE LIBRARY, Division of Harlequin Enterprises Ltd., 225 Duncan Mill Rd., Don Mills, Ontario M3B 3K9 Canada. (416)445-5860. Editorial Director: Randall Toye. Senior Editor/Editorial Coordinator: Feroze Mohammed. Estab. 1949. Imprints are Gold Eagle and Worldwide Mystery. Publishes mass market paperback originals. Mysteries are a reprint program. Averages 72 titles/year. Pays royalty on retail price. Offers $2,000-5,000 average advance. Publishes book 1 year after acceptance. Reports in 2 months.

Fiction: Paramilitary, law enforcement, action-adventure and near-future fiction. Query first or submit synopsis and first 3 chapters.

Recent Fiction Title: *Stakeout Squad*, by D.A. Hodgman.

Tips: "We are an excellent market for action-adventure and near-future fiction."

YORK PRESS LTD., P.O. Box 1172, Fredericton, New Brunswick E3B 5C8 Canada. (506)458-8748. General Manager/Editor: Dr. S. Elkhadem. Estab. 1975. Publishes trade paperback originals. Averages 10 titles/year. Receives 50 submissions/year. 10% of books from first-time authors; 100% from unagented writers. Pays 10-20% royalty on wholesale price. Publishes book 6 months after acceptance. Reports in 2 weeks. *Writer's Market* recommends allowing 2 months for reply.

Nonfiction and Fiction: Reference, textbook, scholarly. Especially needs literary criticism, comparative literature and linguistics and fiction of an experimental nature by well-established writers. Query.

Recent Nonfiction Title: *Tennessee Williams: Life, Work and Criticism*, by F. Londré.

Recent Fiction Title: *Red White & Blue*, by Ben Stoltzfus.

Tips: "If I were a writer trying to market a book today, I would spend a considerable amount of time examining the needs of a publisher *before* sending my manuscript to him. Scholarly books and creative writing of an experimental nature are the only kinds we publish. The writer must adhere to our style manual and follow our guidelines exactly."

Small Presses

"Small press" is a relative term. Compared to the dozen or so conglomerates, the rest of the book publishing world may seem to be comprised of small presses. Several of the publishers listed in the Book Publishers section consider themselves small presses and cultivate the image. For our purpose of classification, the publishers listed in this section are called small presses because they publish three or fewer books per year.

The publishing opportunities are slightly more limited with the companies listed here than with those in the Book Publishers section. Not only are they publishing fewer books, but small presses are usually not able to market their books as effectively as larger publishers. Their print runs and royalty arrangements are usually smaller. It boils down to money, what a publisher can afford, and in that area, small presses simply can't compete with conglomerates.

However, realistic small press publishers don't try to compete with Bantam or Random House. They realize everything about their efforts operates on a smaller scale. Most small press publishers get into book publishing for the love of it, not solely for the profit. Of course, every publisher, small or large, wants successful books. But small press publishers often measure success in different ways.

Many writers actually prefer to work with small presses. Since small publishing houses are usually begun based on the publisher's commitment to the subject matter, and since they necessarily work with far fewer authors than the conglomerates, small press authors and their books usually receive more personal attention than the larger publishers can afford to give them. Promotional dollars at the big houses tend to be siphoned toward a few books each season that they have decided are likely to succeed, leaving hundreds of "midlist" books underpromoted, and, more likely than not, destined for failure. Since small presses only commit to a very small number of books every year, they are vitally interested in the promotion and distribution of each title they publish.

Just because they publish three or fewer titles per year does not mean small press editors have the time to look at complete manuscripts. In fact, because most small presses are understaffed, the editors have even less time for submissions. The procedure for contacting a small press with your book idea is exactly the same as it is for a larger publisher. Send a one-page query with SASE first. If the press is interested in your proposal, be ready to send an outline or synopsis, and/or a sample chapter or two. Be patient with their reporting times; small presses are usually slower to respond than larger companies. You might consider simultaneous queries, as long as you note them, to compensate for the waiting game.

For more information on small presses, see *Novel & Short Story Writer's Market* and *Poet's Market* (Writer's Digest Books), and *Small Press Review* and *The International Directory of Little Magazines and Small Presses* (Dustbooks).

For a list of publishers according to their subjects of interest, see the nonfiction and fiction sections of the Book Publishers Subject Index. Information on some book publishers and producers not included in this edition of *Writer's Market* can be found in Book Publishers and Producers/Changes '95-'96.

ABELEXPRESS, 230 E. Main St., Carnegie PA 15106. Phone/fax: (412)279-0672. Owner: Ken Abel. Publishes trade paperback originals for unique markets in science and health.

ACME PRESS, P.O. Box 1702, Westminster MD 21158-1702. (410)848-7577. Managing Editor: Ms. E.G. Johnston. Estab. 1991. Publishes humor. "We accept submissions on any subject as long as the material is humorous; prefer full-length novels. No cartoons or art (text only). No pornography, poetry or children's material. SASE mandatory."

ADASTRA PRESS, 101 Strong St., Easthampton MA 01027. Contact: Gary Metras. Publishes 2-4 titles/year. Publishes poetry chapbooks (12-18 pages). Query with 5 samples in the fall; submit complete ms in February only.

ADVOCACY PRESS, Division of Girls Inc. of Greater Santa Barbara, P.O. Box 236, Santa Barbara CA 93102. (805)962-2728. Contact: Editor. Estab. 1983. Publishes hardcover children's illustrated books and trade paperback texts and workbooks for teens and young adults. All books have an equity/self-esteem focus. Does not publish young adult fiction. Children's books must focus on specific concepts, e.g. leadership, self-reliance, etc. Publishes 1-2 titles/year. Receives 300 submissions/year. Most from first-time authors; 100% from unagented writers. Accepts simultaneous submissions if so noted. Reports in 8-12 weeks. Texts, journal workbooks featuring self-awareness, personal planning for maximizing potential, gender equity. New series planned to feature job preparation and job analysis for specific industry (i.e., *Foodwork: Jobs in the Food Industry and How to Get Them*). Recent title: *Making Choices: Life Skills for Adolescents.*

AEGIS PUBLISHING GROUP, 796 Aquidneck Ave., Newport RI 02842-7202. (401)849-4200. Publisher: Robert Mastin. Estab. 1992. Reports in 2 months. "Our specialty is telecommunications books targeted to small businesses, entrepreneurs and telecommuters—how they can benefit from the latest telecom products and services. Author must be an experienced authority in the subject, and the material must be very specific with helpful step-by-step advice. No fiction."

AHSAHTA PRESS, Boise State University, Dept. of English, 1910 University Dr., Boise ID 83725-1525. (208)385-1999. Fax: (208)385-4373. E-mail: rentrusk@idbsu.idbsu.edu. Co-Editor: Tom Trusky. Estab. 1974. Publishes Western American poetry in trade paperback. Reads SASE samplers annually, January-March.

ALTA MIRA PRESS, INC., 96 Freneau Ave., Matawan NJ 07747-3436. Editor: Richard A. Herman. Estab. 1992. Publishes trade paperback originals. Publishes 3-4 titles/year. 100% of books from first-time authors; 100% from unagented writers. Publishes book 12-18 months after acceptance of ms. Query for electronic submissions. "We are looking for self-help, referrals, directories for the 45-year-old and older market only—no response without SASE!"

AMERICAN CATHOLIC PRESS, 16565 S. State St., South Holland IL 60473. (312)331-5845. Editorial Director: Rev. Michael Gilligan, Ph.D. Estab. 1967. Publishes hardcover originals and hardcover and paperback reprints. "Most of our sales are by direct mail, although we do work through retail outlets." Averages 4 titles/year. Pays by outright purchase of $25-100. No advance. "We publish books on the Roman Catholic liturgy—for the most part, books on religious music and educational books and pamphlets. We also publish religious songs for church use, including Psalms, as well as choral and instrumental arrangements. We are interested in new music, meant for use in church services. Books, or even pamphlets, on the Roman Catholic Mass are especially welcome. We have no interest in secular topics and are not interested in religious poetry of any kind."

AMIGADGET PUBLISHING COMPANY, P.O. Box 1696, Lexington SC 29071. Fax: (803)957-7495. E-mail: amigadget@cup.portal.com. Editor-in-Chief: Jay Gross. Publishes trade paperback originals. Averages 2 titles/year. "Do not send manuscript. Queries only. No books on Windows." Recent title: *How to Start Your Own Underground Newspaper*, by J. Gross (how-to).

ARCUS PUBLISHING COMPANY, P.O. Box 228, Sonoma CA 95476. (707)996-9529. Fax: (707)996-1738. Estab. 1983. Publishes personal growth and self-help books that are life-enchancing, useful, innovative and enduring. Send for quidelines. Query first.

ARIADNE PRESS, 4817 Tallahassee Ave., Rockville MD 20853-3144. (301)949-2514. President: Carol Hoover. Estab. 1976. Adventure, feminist, historical, humor, literary mainstream/contemporary fiction. "We look for exciting and believable plots, strong themes, and non-stereotypical characters who develop in fascinating and often unpredictable directions." Query with 1-2 page plot summary, bio and SASE. Pays 10% royalty. No advance. Recent title: *Lead Me to the Exit*, by Ellen Moore.

AUTO BOOK PRESS, P.O. Bin 711, San Marcos CA 92079-0711. (619)744-3582. Editorial Director: William Carroll. Estab. 1955. Publishes hardcover and paperback originals. Automotive material only: technical or definitive how-to.

AVIATION BOOK COMPANY, 25133 Anza Dr., Santa Clarita CA 91355. Fax: (805)294-0035. Editor: Walter P. Winner. Publishes hardcover and trade paperback originals and reprints. Publishes 2 titles/year. Specializes in all nonfiction civil and military aviation books.

BAY PRESS, INC., 115 W. Denny Way, Seattle WA 98119. Editor-in-Chief: Kimberly Barnett. Publishes trade paperback critical nonfiction originals on contemporary culture. Publishes 4-8 titles/year.

‡BEACHWAY PRESS, 9201 Beachway Lane, Springfield VA 22153. Publisher: Scott Adams. Publishes 1-2 titles/year. Pays 7-10% royalty on wholesale price. Publishes book 9 months after acceptance of ms. Reports in 2 months on queries and proposals. Manuscript guidelines for #10 SASE. Nonfiction: Guidebooks, maps. "Should be an avid outdoor enthusiast, knowledgeable in their area of interest, with a clear understanding of maps and terrain, and have an interest in local history. Please, no fiction or poetry." Query with outline, methods of research and SASE. Reviews artwork/photos as part of ms package. Send proof prints. Recent nonfiction title: *Mountain Bike Virginia*, by Scott Adams (guidebook).

BIDDLE PUBLISHING CO., #103, P.O. Box 1305, Brunswick ME 04011. President: Julie Zimmerman. Estab. 1990. Publishes general nonfiction, emphasizing peace and social concerns. Replies with SASE only.

‡BLACK BALL PRESS, P.O. Box 631561, Houston TX 77263-1561. (713)527-9227. Contact: Alex Velasquez, Paulie Grissom. Publishes trade paperback originals. Humor, illustrated book. Subjects include art/architecture, ethnic, government/politics, history, music/dance, philosophy, religion. Query or submit outline and 5 sample chapters. SASE. Recent Nonfiction Title:*Sheep Herder*, by Alex Velasquez (poetry/art). Poetry: "I like the 'spoken word' tours poetry/short stories." Query or submit 5 sample poems. Recent poetry title: *Re-Turn*, by Norman Ballinger (poetry/short stories).

BLACK HERON PRESS, P.O. Box 95676, Seattle WA 98145. (206)363-5210. Publisher: Jerry Gold. Publishes hardcover and trade paperback originals. "Only high quality fiction."

BLACK TIE PRESS, P.O. Box 440004, Houston TX 77244-0004. (713)789-5119. Publisher/Editor: Peter Gravis. Estab. 1986. Imprints are Deluxe, Matineé and Plain Editions. Publishes poetry. "We publish books, not individual poems, articles, or stories. We do not accept fiction manuscripts."

BLACK TOOTH PRESS, 768 N. 26th St., Philadelphia PA 19130. (215)232-6611. Contact: Jim Anderson. Publishes trade paperback originals. Averages 2 titles/year. Accepts only material of local interest to Philadelphia or material related to beer. Submit outline. Recent title: *So Sue Me!*, by Joe Kohut. "We're looking for work which conforms to our slogan: 'Quick reading for the short-attention-span 90s!' "

‡BLISS PUBLISHING CO., P.O. Box 920, Marlborough MA 01752. (508)779-2827. Publisher: Stephen H. Clouter. Publishes hardcover originals, trade paperback originals and reprints. Pays 10-15% royalty on wholesale price. Reports in 1 month. Manuscript guidelines for #10 SASE. Publishes biography, illustrated book, reference, textbook. Subjects include government/politics, history, music/dance, nature/environment, recreation, regional. Submit proposal package, including outline, table of contents, bio, 2 sample chapters and SASE. Recent nonfiction title: *The Charles River*, by Ron McAdow (guide).

BRETT BOOKS, INC., P.O. Box 290-637, Brooklyn NY 11229-0011. Publisher: Barbara J. Brett. Estab. 1993. Publishes general interest nonfiction books on timely subjects. Query only with SASE.

BRIGHT MOUNTAIN BOOKS, INC., 138 Springside Rd., Asheville NC 28803. (704)684-8840. Editor: Cynthia F. Bright. Imprint is Historical Images. Publishes hardcover and trade paperback originals and reprints. "Our current emphasis is on regional titles, which can include nonfiction by local writers."

BRIGHT RING PUBLISHING, P.O. Box 5768, Bellingham WA 98226. (206)734-1601. Owner: Mary Ann Kohl. Publishes trade paperback originals on creative ideas for children. No crafts, fiction, poetry or picture books. Publishes 1 title/year.
  • Bright Ring won the Benjamin Franklin Award for 1993 for Best Academic Educational Book.

CADMUS EDITIONS, P.O. Box 126, Tiburon CA 94920. Director: Jeffrey Miller. Publishes hardcover and trade paperback originals of literary fiction and poetry.

CALYX BOOKS, P.O. Box B, Corvallis OR 97339-0539. (503)753-9384. Also publishes *Calyx, A Journal of Art & Literature by Women*. Managing Editor: Margarita Donnelly. Estab. 1986 for Calyx Books; 1976 for Calyx, Inc. Publishes fine literature by women, fiction, nonfiction and poetry. Query with SASE for submission deadlines and guidelines.

CAROUSEL PRESS, P.O. Box 6061, Albany CA 94706-0061. (510)527-5849. Editor and Publisher: Carole T. Meyers. Estab. 1976. Publishes nonfiction, family-oriented travel and other travel books.

‡CARTER PRESS, P.O. Box 1136, Oakland CA 94604. (510)208-3654. Publisher: David Carter. Publishes 2-3 titles/year. "Carter Press specializes in quality fiction, usually character-driven works. We are not interested in genre pieces (i.e., mystery, suspense, detective, etc.)." Recent fiction title: *Eden's Apple*, by Patri Collins (Generation X).

CENTER FOR AFRO-AMERICAN STUDIES PUBLICATIONS, University of California at Los Angeles, 160 Haines Hall, 405 Hilgard Ave., Los Angeles CA 90024-1545. (310)825-3528. Managing Editor: Toyomi Igus. Publishes hardcover and trade paperback originals. "All manuscripts should be scholarly works about the African-American experience. Authors should be able to demonstrate a thorough knowledge of the subject matter. Not interested in autobiographies, poetry or fiction." Recent title: *Residential Apartheid: The American Legacy*, edited by Robert Bullard, J. Eugene Grigsby III and Charles Lee.

‡CFC PRODUCTIONS, P.O. Box 310-155, Franklin Square NY 11010-0310. (516)327-9155. Publisher: John Runion. Publishes trade paperback originals. Publishes 3 titles/year. Pays 10-15% royalty on retail price. Advance varies. Book catalog for #10 SASE. Coffee table book, self-help. Nonfiction: Subjects include psychology. Submit 3 sample chapters. Fiction: Confession. Submit 3-5 sample chapters. Poetry: Submit 3-5 sample poems. Recent poetry title: *Coming Full Circle, a Journey of Self-Discovery and Growth*, by Joe Ryan (self actualization psychology recovery). Tips: "We publish material that touches the soul, from poetry to new age, psychology, self-help, personal growth recovery, self actualization and beyond. Dedicated to finding ones true self."

CHAPEL STREET PUBLISHING, 43 Chapel St., Seneca Falls NY 13148. (315)568-2508. Publisher: Stephen Beals. Publishes trade paperback originals. Nonfiction and fiction material "must have strong New York State connection. Prefer Central New York/Finger Lakes."

‡CHARLES RIVER PRESS, 427 Old Town Court, Alexandria VA 22314-3544. (703)519-9197. Editor-in-Chief: Lynn Page Whittaker. Pays 5-10% royalty on retail price or makes outright purchase of $1,000-3,000. Offers $0-2,000 advance. Publishes biography and general nonfiction in these subject areas: Americana, education, ethnic, history, women's issues/studies. "I am especially interested in stories of individuals that illustrate historical events and social issues and in academic work that can be adapted to a general audience." Query with outline, 1 sample chapter and SASE. Recent title: *Until We Meet Again: A True Story of Love and Survival in the Holocaust*, by Michael Korenblit and Kathleen Janger (history/memoir).

CHRISTIAN MEDIA, Box 448, Jacksonville OR 97530. (503)899-8888. Sole Proprietor: James Lloyd. Publishes trade paperback originals. Also publishes a bimonthly newsletter, particularly interested in exposés of Christian organizations, ministries or artists (musicians, writers, etc.) that are behaving in a manner that brings the cause of Christ into disrepute.

CLARITY PRESS INC., 3277 Roswell Rd. NE, #469, Atlanta GA 30305. (404)231-0649. Fax: (404)231-3899. Editorial Committee Contact: Annette Gordon. Estab. 1984. Publishes mss on minorities, human rights in US, Middle East and Africa. No fiction. Responds *only* if interested, so do *not* enclose SASE.

CORKSCREW PRESS, INC., 2300 W. Victory, Suite C-313, Burbank CA 91506. Editorial Director: J. Croker Norge. Estab. 1988. Publishes trade humor and humorous how-to books. Reports in 6 months.

DELANCEY PRESS, P.O. Box 40285, Philadelphia PA 19106. (215)238-9103. E-mail: morrcomm@aol.com. Editorial Director: Wesley Morrison. Estab. 1990. "We are open to reviewing all types of nonfiction. Queries by *letter* only; no initial contact by phone."

‡DEPTH CHARGE, P.O. Box 7037, Evanston IL 60201. (708)733-9554. Editor: Eckhard Gerdes. Publishes trade paperback originals. Publishes 2-4 titles/year. Pays 10% royalty on retail price. Book catalog for 9 × 12 SAE with 2 first-class stamps. Manuscript guidelines for #10 SASE. Fiction: Experimental, literary fiction. "Familiarize yourselves with our publications and be aware that we publish 'subterficial' fiction. Be aware of what subterficial is." Recent fiction title: *Openings*, by Richard Kostelanetz (experimental fiction/interfaced with poetry). Poetry: "Note that the only poetry we publish is that which meets subterficial fiction at their interface area." Submit ms.

DIAMOND PRESS, Box 2458, Doylestown PA 18901. (215)345-6094. Fax: (215)345-6692. Marketing Director: Paul Johnson. Estab. 1985. Publishes trade paperback originals on softball and antiques. "We are now more interested in baseball, fast pitch softball and slow pitch softball books."

DICKENS PUBLICATIONS, 1703 Taylor St. NW, Washington DC 20011-5312. President: Nathaniel A. Dickens. Estab. 1982. Publishes nonfiction related to education, history, finance and various forms of fiction. Send query letter initially; manuscript only upon request.

DISKOTECH, INC., 7930 State Line, Suite 210, Prairie Village KS 66208. (913)432-8606. Fax: (913)432-8606 * 51. E-mail: 72754.2773@compuserve.com. Submissions Editor: Jane Locke. Estab. 1989. Publishes multimedia nonfiction and fiction for PC's on CD-ROM. Query first with SASE. Considers most nonfiction subjects. Considers all adult fiction genres. Recent nonfiction title: *How To Be Happily Employed in the 1990s*, by Janice Benjamin and Barbara Block. Recent fiction title: *Negative Space CVN*®, (computerized video novel) by Holly Franking.
 • Diskotech, Inc. is publishing a new form of the novel, a CVN® (computerized video novel), that combines print, software and video for CD-ROM.

DOWN THE SHORE PUBLISHING, Imprint of Cormorant Books & Calendars, 534 Cedar Run Dock Rd., Cedar Run NJ 08092. Publisher: Raymond G. Fisk. Publishes hardcover originals and trade paperback originals and reprints. "As a small regional publisher, we must limit our efforts and resources to our established market: New Jersey shore and mid-Atlantic. We specialize in regional histories and pictorial, coffee table books." Query with synopsis.

DUSTY DOG REVIEWS, 1904-A Gladden, Gallup NM 87301. (505)863-2398. Editor: John Pierce. Estab. 1991. Features honest and evaluative poetry book/chapbook reviews as well as literary magazine reviews from small and midrange presses in each issue. Subscription price: $4.50/yr/4 issues. Single copy price: $1.50. Each press editor and/or magazine editor will receive 1 free copy of the issue in which the review appears.

EARTH-LOVE PUBLISHING HOUSE LTD., 3440 Youngfield St., Suite 353, Wheat Ridge CO 80033. (303)233-9660. Fax: (303)233-9354. Director: Laodeciae Augustine. Publishes 1-2 trade paperback originals/year on metaphysics and minerals.

EASTERN PRESS, P.O. Box 881, Bloomington IN 47402-0881. Publisher: Don Lee. Estab. 1981. Publishes academic books on Asian subjects and pedagogy on languages.

‡EVRAS PRESS, P.O. Box 5692, Hercules CA 94547. Managing Editor: Tony Sakkis. Publishes mass market paperback originals. Pays 10-25% royalty on wholesale price. Offers $1,500-10,000 advance. Manuscript guidelines for SASE. Reference, technical. Subjects include ethnic, sports, translation, travel. "We are looking for work that can fill out our universal guide series as well as automotive- and motorsports-related works. We seek nonfiction in those areas that may be translated into Spanish or Italian." Recent nonfiction title: *A Racer's Guide to the Universe*, by T. Sakkis (sports/travel).

‡EXCALIBUR PUBLICATIONS, P.O. Box 36, Latham NY 12110-0036. Editor: Alan M. Petrillo. Pays royalty or makes outright purchase. "We publish works on military history, strategy and tactics, as well as the history of battles and firearms. We are seeking well-researched and documented works. Unpublished writers are welcome." Query with outline, 1st and 2 consecutive chapters with SASE. Recent title: *The Remington-Lee Rifle*, by Eugene Myszkowski (historical/technical).

EXCALIBUR PUBLISHING, 434 Avenue of Americas, #790, New York NY 10011. (212)777-1790. Publisher: Sharon Good. "We are interested in business, parenting and performing arts titles."

THE FAMILY ALBUM, Rt. 1, Box 42, Glen Rock PA 17327. (717)235-2134. Fax: (717)235-8042. E-mail: ronbiblio@delphi.com. Contact: Ron Lieberman. Estab. 1969. Publishes hardcover originals and reprints and software. Averages 2 titles/year. Average print order for a first book is 1,000. Pays royalty on wholesale price. "Significant works in the field of (nonfiction) bibliography. Worthy submissions in the field of Pennsylvania history, folk art and lore. We are also seeking materials relating to books, literacy, and national development. Special emphasis on Third World countries, and the role of printing in international development." No religious material. Submit outline and sample chapters.

FATHOM PUBLISHING COMPANY, P.O. Box 200448, Anchorage AK 99520-0448. (907)272-3305. E-mail: FathomPub@aol.com. Publisher: Constance Taylor. Publishes 1-2 trade paperback originals/year on Alaskana history, legal issues and reference. Prefers author participation in marketing efforts.

For explanation of symbols, see the Key to Symbols and Abbreviations. For unfamiliar words, see the Glossary.

J.G. FERGUSON PUBLISHING COMPANY, 200 W. Madison, Suite 300, Chicago IL 60606. Editorial Director: Holli Cosgrove. Estab. 1940. Publishes hardcover originals. Publishes 1 title/year. Pays by project. Reference. "We publish work specifically for the high school/college library reference market. Works are generally encyclopedic in nature. Our current focus is medical and career encyclopedias. No mass market, scholarly, or juvenile books, please." Query or submit outline and 1 sample chapter.

‡FIESTA CITY PUBLISHERS, ASCAP, P.O. Box 5861, Santa Barbara CA 93150. (805)733-1984. Publishes 2-3 titles/year. Pays 5-20% royalty on retail price. No advance. Reports in 1 month on queries. Book catalog and ms guidelines for #10 SASE. Publishes children's/juvenile, cookbook, how-to, humor nonfiction and musical plays. "Prefers material appealing to young readers, especially related to music: composing, performing, etc." Query with SASE. Recent nonfiction title: *Anything I Can Play, You Can Play Better* (self-teaching guitar method). Adventure, humor, juvenile fiction and plays, musical material. Query with SASE. Recent fiction title: *El Canon Perdido*, by Johnny Harris/Frank Cooke (musical play).

FILTER PRESS, P.O. Box 5, Palmer Lake CO 80133-0005. (719)481-2523. President: Gilbert L. Campbell. Estab. 1956. Publishes trade paperback originals and reprints. Publishes 2-3 titles/year. Pays 6-10% royalties on wholesale price. Publishes ms an average of 6-8 months after acceptance. Query with SASE. Cookbook, how-to. Subjects include Americana, anthropology/archaeology, cooking/foods/nutrition, ethnic, hobbies, regional, travel. "We will consider some Western Americana, up to 72 pages. We do not want family diaries. Most of our works are reprints of 19th century published things on Indians, Gold rushes, western exploration, etc. Very rarely do we use unsolicited material. I dream up a project, find an author in 90% of them." Reviews artwork/photos as part of ms package.

‡FLOWER VALLEY PRESS, INC., 7851-C Beechcraft Ave., Gaithersburg MD 20879. (301)990-6405. Editor: Seymour Bress. Publishes hardcover and trade paperback originals and reprints. Publishes 3 titles/year. Book catalog for #10 SASE. Nonfiction: Coffee table book, how-to nonfiction. Subjects include art, crafts and jewelry make with Polymer clay. "We look particularly for new and unique work of high quality (all of our recent books have been completely illustrated in color) and where the market for the book is relatively easy to identify and reach. Query. Reviews artwork/photos as part of ms package. Send transparencies. Recent nonfiction title: *The New Clay*, by Nan Roche (how-to). For fiction, "must catch us in the opening chapter or we'll never read beyond it." Submit synopsis and 1 sample chapter.

FRANCISCAN PRESS, Quincy University, 1800 College Ave., Quincy IL 62301-2670. (217)228-5670. Fax: (217)228-5672. Director: Dr. Terrence J. Riddell. Estab. 1991. Publishes nonfiction books on religion.

JOEL FRIEDLANDER, PUBLISHER, P.O. Box 3330, San Rafael CA 94912. (415)459-1311. Publisher: Joel Friedlander. Estab. 1985. Publishes hardcover and trade paperback originals on self-help and esoteric psychology. Subjects include history, philosophy and psychology. "We want popular manuscripts on East/West psychology. No economics, politics or how-to books."

FRONT ROW EXPERIENCE, 540 Discovery Bay Blvd., Byron CA 94514-9454. Phone/fax: (510)634-5710. Contact: Frank Alexander. Estab. 1974. Imprint is Kokono. Publishes teacher/educator edition paperback originals. Only wants submissions for "Movement Education," special education and related areas. Will accept submissions for parenting type books only from those people who are active in the field and can promote it through their activities.

GAFF PRESS, P.O. Box 1024, Astoria OR 97103-3051. (503)325-8288. Publisher: Paul Barrett. Publishes hardcover and trade paperback originals, poetry chapbooks. "Particularly interested in extraordinary ocean tales for next (third) book of sea stories and wondrous irresistible poems." Recent title: *I'll Be Home in Half-an-Hour-Essays*, by John Paul Barrett, author of *Sea Stories I & II*.

GAMBLING TIMES INCORPORATED, 16140 Valerio St., Suite B, Van Nuys CA 91406-2916. (818)781-9355. Fax: (818)781-3125. Publisher: Stanley R. Suudikoff. Publishes hardcover and trade paperback original how-to and reference books on gambling.

GEMINI PUBLISHING COMPANY, 14010 El Camino Real, Suite 120, Houston TX 77062-8024. (713)488-6866. E-mail: 74644,360@compuserve.com. President: Don Diebel. "We are seeking books, cassettes and videos on meeting, attracting and becoming intimate with women." Catalog for $1.

GILES ROAD PRESS, P.O. Box 212, Harrington Park NJ 07640. E-mail: gilesrdprs@aol.com. Publisher: Maria Langer. Publishes trade paperback originals. "Open to all nonfiction topics. We are a small publisher interested in doing limited interest books. Authors must have a clear understanding of the subject matter of their books and must provide marketing suggestions in their proposals." Guidelines for #10 SASE.

GOOD BOOK PUBLISHING COMPANY, 2747 S. Kihei Rd., D110, Kihei HI 96753. Phone/fax: (808)874-4876. Publisher: Richard G. Burns. Publishes trade paperback originals and reprints on the spiritual roots of Alcoholics Anonymous.

GRAPHIC ARTS PUB. INC., 3100 Bronson Hill Rd., Livonia NY 14487. (716)346-2776. Vice President: Donna Southworth. Publishes trade paperback originals on TQM and quality and color reproduction. Recent title: *Pocket Guide to Color Reproduction*, third edition, by Southworth and Southworth.

GREAT LAKES PRESS, P.O. Box 483, Okemos MI 48805. Managing Editor: Jeff Potter. Publishes hardcover and trade paperback originals. Publishes 2 titles/year. Pays 1-5% royalty or makes outright purchase of $500-5,000. Produces books on engineering test preparation.

‡GREAT OCEAN PUBLISHERS, 1823 N. Lincoln St., Arlington VA 22207-3746. President: Mark Esterman. Estab. 1975. Nonfiction: biography, how-to, illustrated book, reference, self-help technical and *educational*. "Main interest and focus is in area of *learning* as applied to school, home, workplace."

GRYPHON HOUSE, INC., P.O. Box 207, Beltsville MD 20704. (301)595-9500. Fax: (301)595-0051. Editor-in-Chief: Kathy Charner. Publishes trade paperback originals of how-to and creative educational activities for teachers to do with preschool children ages 1-5.

HARTWICK ELECTRONIC PRESS, P.O. Box 35, Grayling MI 49738. Fax: (808)672-9921. E-mail: bookstor-@lava.net. Editor: Robert W. Hanson. Publishes multimedia books on CD-ROM and FloppyBack® Books. Pays 10-50% royalty on net book revenue. "Our software, MultiMedia Bookstore™, contains graphics (photos, drawings, video clips) and sound effects, so writers are encouraged to make creative use of these features. Demo disk available for $5. Authors should submit complete ms on disk in any popular wordprocessing format, (i.e. MS-Word, MS-Works, ASCII, WordPerfect, RichText format)."

HEAVEN BONE PRESS, P.O. Box 486, Chester NY 10918. Editor: Steve Hirsch. Publishes mass market paperback originals of literary fiction and poetry. Reports in 10 months. Send SASE for guidelines. $6 for sample issue of *Heaven Bone Magazine*.

HELLS CANYON PUBLISHING, P.O. Box 646, Halfway OR 97834. Book Division Manager: David Light. Publishes hardcover and trade paperback originals. Publishes nonfiction, primarily business titles. Reports in 1 months on proposals. "We look for cutting edge issues."

HEMINGWAY WESTERN STUDIES SERIES, Boise State University, 1910 University Dr., Boise ID 83725. (208)385-1999. Fax: (208)385-4373. E-mail: rentrusk@idbsu.idbsu.edu. Editor: Tom Trusky. Publishes multiple edition artist's books which deal with Rocky Mountain political, social and environmental issues. Write for author's guidelines and catalog.

HERBAL STUDIES LIBRARY, 219 Carl St., San Francisco CA 94117. (415)564-6785. Fax: (415)564-6799. Owner: J. Rose. Publishes trade paperback originals and reprints. Averages 3 titles/year. How-to, reference and self-help. Subjects include gardening, health/medicine, herbs and aromatherapy. Query. Recent title: *Herbs & Aromatherapy for the Reproductive System (Men and Women)*, by Jeanne Rose (herbs/health).

W.D. HOARD & SONS CO., Imprint of Hoard's Dairyman, 28 Milwaukee Ave. W., Fort Atkinson WI 53538-0801. Editor: Elvira Kau. Estab. 1870. "We primarily are a dairy publishing company, but we have had success with a veterinarian who authored two James Herriott-type humor books for us, and we would consider regional (Wisconsin) titles as well. We also have published and would like to see submissions for agricultural science texts."

‡THE HOFFMAN PRESS, P.O. Box 2996, Santa Rosa CA 95405. Publisher: R.P. Hoffman. Publishes trade paperback and mass market paperback originals. Pays 5-10% royalty on retail price. No advance. Publishes book 10-24 months after acceptance of ms. Reports in 2 months. Publishes cookbook, how-to. "We publish cookbooks only." Query with 3 sample chapters and SASE. Reviews artwork/photos as part of ms package. Send photocopies. Recent nonfiction title: *California Wine Country Cookbook*

‡I.A.A.S. PUBLISHERS, 7676 New Hampshire Ave., Langley Park MD 20783. (301)499-6308. Senior Editor, New Manuscripts: Anthony Green. Publishes hardcover, trade paperback and mass market paperback originals. Manuscript guidelines free on request. Biography, children's/juvenile, how-to, illustrated book, textbook, Afro-America. Subjects include business and economics, child guidance/parenting, education, government/politics, health/medicine, history, military/war, money/finance, philosophy, psychology, sociology, Afro-American/African issues. Request "Guidelines for Authors" in advance of submission. Submit proposal package. Recent nonfiction title: *Critical Issues In Educating African-American Children*, by Norris Haynes.

IN PRINT PUBLISHING, 6770 W. State Route 89A, #46, Sedona AZ 86336-9758. Fax: (602)282-4631. Publisher/Editor: Tomi Keitlen. Estab. 1991. "We are interested in books that will give people hope: biographies of those that have overcome physical and mental disadvantages. No violence or sex or poetry. Particularly interested in metaphysical how-to books. Query letters must include SASE for answer or return of materials."

INDIANA HISTORICAL SOCIETY, 315 W. Ohio St., Indianapolis IN 46202-3299. (317)232-1882. Fax: (317)233-3109. Director of Publications: Thomas A. Mason. Estab. 1830. Publishes hardcover originals. Publishes 3 titles/year. Pays 6% royalty on retail price. "We seek book-length manuscripts that are solidly researched and engagingly written on topics related to the history of Indiana." Reports in 1 month on queries.

INTERTEXT, 2633 East 17th Ave., Anchorage AK 99508-3207. Editor: Sharon Ann Jaeger. Estab. 1982. Publishes poetry. Not currently accepting unsolicited mss.

INVERTED-A, INC., 401 Forrest Hill, Grand Prairie TX 75052. (214)264-0066. Editors: Amnon Katz. Estab. 1977. Publishes nonfiction books on a range of subjects, novellas, short story collections and poetry.

‡ITHACA PRESS, P.O. Box 853, Lowell MA 01853. General Editor: Charles E. Ziavras. Publishes historical and mainstream/contemporary fiction.

IVY LEAGUE PRESS, INC., P.O. Box 3326, San Ramon CA 94583-8326. 1-(800)IVY-PRESS or (510)736-0601. Fax: (510)736-0602. Editor: Maria Thomas. Publishes hardcover, trade paperback and mass market paperback originals. Subjects include health/medicine, Judaica and self-help nonfiction and medical suspense fiction. Recent nonfiction title: *Jewish Divorce Ethics*, by Bulka. Recent fiction title: *Allergy Shots*, by Litman.
  • Ivy League is focusing more on medical thrillers, although it still welcomes Judaica and other submissions.

‡JAMENAIR LTD., P.O. Box 241957, Los Angeles CA 90024-9757. (310)470-6688. Publisher: P.K. Studner. Estab. 1986. Publishes originals and reprints on business and economics, computers and electronics, education and career-advancement/job search.

JELMAR PUBLISHING CO., INC., P.O. Box 488, Plainview NY 11803. (516)822-6861. President: Joel J. Shulman. Publishes hardcover originals on how-to and technical subjects. Pays 25% royalty after initial production and promotion expenses of first printing. "The writer must be a specialist and recognized expert in the field." Query. Recent Title: *Design and Production of Corrugated Packaging and Displays*, by A. Howard Bessen.

‡JOHNSTON ASSOCIATES, INTERNATIONAL (JASI), P.O. Box 313, Medina WA 98039. (206)454-3490. Publisher: Ann Schuessler. Publishes trade paperback originals. Publishes 3-5 titles/year. Pays 12-17% royalty on wholesale price. Offers $1,000-1,500 advance. Publishes travel nonfiction and guidebooks. Query with outline. Recent nonfiction title: *Discover Washington With Kids*, by Rosanne Cohn and Suzanne Monson (regional guidebook).

‡KALI PRESS, P.O. Box 2169, Pagosa Springs CO 81147. (970)731-2363. Contact: Cynthia Olsen. Publishes trade paperback originals. Publishes 1-2 titles/year. Pays 8-12% royalty on retail price. Offers $1,000-1,500 advance. Children's/juvenile, natural health and spiritual nonfiction. Subjects include education (on natural health issues). Childrens books with a lesson and natural health (international topics also). Query with 3 sample chapters and SASE. Reviews artwork/photos as part of ms package. Send photocopies.

LAHONTAN IMAGES, 206 S. Pine St., Susanville CA 96130. (916)257-6747. Fax: (916)251-4801. Owner: Tim I. Purdy. Estab. 1986. Publishes nonfiction books pertaining to northeastern California and western Nevada.

LAWCO LTD., P.O. Box 2009, Manteca CA 95336-1209. (209)239-6006. Imprints are Money Tree and Que House. Senior Editor: Bill Thompson. Publishes nonfiction books on billiards industry. "We are looking for business books targeting the small business. We will also consider sports-related books."

LINCOLN SPRINGS PRESS, P.O. Box 269, Franklin Lakes NJ 07417. Contact: M. Gabrielle. Estab. 1987. Nonfiction: Americana, ethnic, government/politics, history, language/literature, military/war, sociology, women's issues/studies. Fiction: ethnic, feminist, gothic, historical, literary, mainstream/contemporary, mystery, romance, short story collections. Include SASE for reply or return of submission.

‡LION PRESS, LTD., 108-22 Queens Blvd, Suite 221, Forest Hills NY 11375. President: Leslie Diamond. Publishes hardcover and trade paperback originals. Publishes 2-3 titles/year. Pays 4-10% royalty on retail price or makes outright purchase of $500 and higher. Offers $500-up advance. Publishes book 12-18 months after acceptance of ms. Book catalog for 2 first-class stamps. Nonfiction: Biography, psychology subjects. Submit 3 sample chapters with SASE. Fiction: Adventure, fantasy, historical, humor, mainstream/contemporary, mystery, science fiction, young adult. "We seek new writers with growth potential." Query with synopsis, 3 sample chapters and SASE. Recent fiction titles: *Forest Wars*, by Graham Diamond (fantasy/adventure).

LORIEN HOUSE, P.O. Box 1112, Black Mountain NC 28711-1112. (704)669-6211. Owner/Editor: David A. Wilson. Estab. 1969. Publishes nonfiction. Subjects include Americana, history, nature/environment, philosophy, science. "I need only a few manuscripts at any time and therefore am very selective. I would like to see queries on the Appalachian region—nonfiction which can be technical or personal experience. I am 'fishing' for good material in what will be a new area for Lorien House."

‡McBOOKS PRESS, 908 Steam Mill Rd., Ithaca NY 14850. (607)272-2114. Publisher: Alexander G. Skutt. Publishes trade paperback originals and reprints. Pays 5-10% royalty on retail price. Offers $1,000-5,000 advance. Nonfiction: Coffee table book, how-to, illustrated book, reference. Subjects include child guidance/ parenting, cooking, regional, sports. "We are a small publishing house and we are only interested in queries within our narrow areas of interest: vegetarianism, parenting, regional books about upstate New York and (for a new imprint) sports history, records, and statistics." Query or submit outline and 2 sample chapters with SASE. Recent nonfiction title: *Vegetarian Pregnancy*, by Sharon Yntema (nutrition/parenting).

MADWOMAN PRESS, P.O. Box 690, Northboro MA 01532-0690. (508)393-3447. E-mail: 76620.460@compuserve.com. Editor/Publisher: Diane Benison. Estab. 1991. Publishes lesbian fiction and nonfiction. Query for further information.
   • Madwoman Press is looking for more mystery novels.

‡MARADIA PRESS, 228 Evening Star Dr., Naugatuck CT 06770-3548. (203)723-0758. Vice President: Peter A. Ciullo. Estab. 1990. Interested in well-researched works dealing with the effect of technology on American culture, any era from Colonial times to the present.

MASEFIELD BOOKS, 7210 Jordan Ave., Suite B-54, Canoga Park CA 91303. Fax: (818)703-6087. Publisher: M. Bloomfield. Estab. 1991. Publishes nonfiction: education, government/politics, history, psychology and sociology. A modest subsidy program is available for those books with extremely limited markets.

‡METAL POWDER INDUSTRIES FEDERATION, 105 College Rd. E., Princeton NJ 08540. (609)452-7700. Fax: (609)987-8523. Publications Manager: Cindy Jablonowski. Estab. 1946. "Contact Publications Manager before submittal of a manuscript; work must relate to powder metallurgy or particulate materials. We publish monographs, textbooks, handbooks, design guides, conference proceedings, standards, and general titles in this field."

MEYERBOOKS, PUBLISHER, P.O. Box 427, Glenwood IL 60425-0427. (708)757-4950. Publisher: David Meyer. Estab. 1976. Imprint is David Meyer Magic Books. History, reference and self-help works published on subjects of Americana, cooking and foods, health and herbal studies, history of stage magic. Reports in 3 months.

MIDDLE PASSAGE PRESS, 5517 Secrest Dr., Los Angeles CA 90043. (213)298-0266. Publisher: Barbara Bramwell. Estab. 1992. Publishes trade paperback and hardcover originals. "The emphasis is on contemporary issues that deal directly with the African-American Experience. No fiction."

MILLS & SANDERSON, PUBLISHERS, P.O. Box 833, Bedford MA 01730-0833. (617)275-1410. Fax: (617)275-1713. Publisher: Jan H. Anthony. Estab. 1986. Publishes trade paperback originals. Publishes 2 titles/year. Pays 10% royalty on net price. Offers standard $500 advance. Manuscript guidelines for #10 SASE. Nonfiction: Family problem solving. No religion or travel. Query first. Recent nonfiction title: *Surviving Your Crises, Reviving Your Dreams*, by Donald E. Watson, M.D. "We are currently publishing **only** nonfiction titles dealing with widely-shared, specific problems faced by today's families. Manuscript must cover an interesting subject with broad appeal, be written by an author whose credentials indicate he/she knows a lot about the subject. There must be a certain uniqueness about it."
   • Mills & Sanderson is going through restructuring and is planning to publish fewer books and pay less upfront.

MORTAL PRESS, 2315 N. Alpine Rd., Rockford IL 61107-1422. (815)399-8432. Editor/Publisher: Terry James Mohaupt. Publishes hardcover originals. Publishes 1 title/year. "We will consider only works related to the fine arts, specifically literary and graphic arts, poetry or words and pictures."

MOSAIC PRESS MINIATURE BOOKS, 358 Oliver Rd., Cincinnati OH 45215-2615. (513)761-5977. Publisher: Miriam Irwin. Estab. 1977. Publishes 1 nonfiction book/year. "Subjects range widely. Please query."

MOUNT IDA PRESS, 152 Washington Ave., Albany NY 12210. (518)426-5935. Fax: (518)426-4116. Publisher: Diana S. Waite. Publishes trade paperback original illustrated books on architecture.

MOUNTAIN AUTOMATION CORPORATION, P.O. Box 6020, Woodland Park CO 80866-6020. (719)687-6647. President: Claude Wiatrowski. Estab. 1976. Publishes illustrated souvenir books and videos for specific tourist attractions. "We are emphasizing videos more and books less."

MYSTIC SEAPORT MUSEUM, 75 Greenmanville Ave., Mystic CT 06355-0990. (203)572-0711. Fax: (203)572-5326. Imprint is American Maritime Library. Publications Director: Joseph Gribbins. Estab. 1970. "We need serious, well-documented biographies, studies of economic, social, artistic, or musical elements of American maritime (not naval) history; books on traditional boat and ship types and construction (how-to). We are now interested in all North American maritime history—not, as in the past, principally New England."

NATIONAL PUBLISHING COMPANY, P.O. Box 8386, Philadelphia PA 19101-8386. (215)732-1863. Fax: (215)735-5399. Editor: Peter F. Hewitt. Estab. 1863. Publishes Bibles, New Testaments and foreign language New Testaments.

NATUREGRAPH PUBLISHERS, INC., P.O. Box 1075, Happy Camp CA 96039. (916)493-5353. Fax: (916)493-5240. Editor: Barbara Brown. Estab. 1946. Publishes trade paperback originals. Primarily publishes nonfiction for the layman in 6 general areas: natural history (biology, geology, ecology, astronomy); American Indian (historical and contemporary); outdoor living (backpacking, wild edibles, etc.); land and gardening (modern homesteading); crafts and how-to; holistic health (natural foods and healing arts). Pays 8-10% royalty on wholesale price. Query with outline and 1 sample chapter. Recent title: *Wisdom of Nature*, by Dayton Foster (nature quotes).

‡**NEW ENGLAND CARTOGRAPHICS, INC.**, P.O. Box 9369, North Amherst MA 01059. (413)549-4124. President: Chris Ryan. Publishes trade paperback originals. Publishes 2-3 titles/year. Pays 10-15% royalty on retail price. Offers $250-500 advance expense only. Book catalog free on request. Outdoor recreation nonfiction subjects include nature/environment, recreation, regional. "We are interested in specific "where to" in the area of outdoor recreation guidebooks of the northeast US. Topics of interest are hiking/backpacking, skiing, canoeing etc. Query with outline. Reviews artwork/photos as part of ms package. Send photocopies. Recent nonfiction title: *High Peaks of the Northeast*.

‡**NEW JOY PRESS**, P.O. Box 1349, Ojai CA 93024. (805)640-0251. Fax: (805)640-1297. E-mail: njpublish @aol.com. Publisher: Joy Nyquist. Pays 10-15% royalty on retail price. Publishes self-help, travel. Subjects include travel, health, assertiveness/self-esteem, travelers' aid (not guidebooks), women's issues/studies with a feminist viewpoint. Recent title: *Strategic Marketing for Travel Agencies*, by Joy Nyquist.

‡**NICOLAS-HAYS**, Box 612, York Beach ME 03910. (207)363-4393. Publisher: B. Lundsted. Publishes trade paperback originals. Publishes 2 titles/year. Pays royalty on wholesale price. Offers $250-500 advance. Publishes Self-help; nonfiction. Subjects include philosophy (oriental), psychology (Jungian), religion (alternative), women's issues/studies. Recent nonfiction title; *Beginner's Guide to Revelation*, by Robin Robertson (psychology/millennium).

NIGHTSHADE PRESS, P.O. Box 76, Troy ME 04987-0076. (207)948-3427. Senior Editors: Carolyn Page. Estab. 1988. Publishes *Potato Eyes*, a semiannual literary arts journal and 10 poetry collections/year. Also publishes one novel or long nonfiction work per year and is often reading for the Nightshade Nightstand Reader, a collection of 25 previously unpublished short stories. Query first for info. Reports in 2 months.
● Poetry manuscript selection is based generally on the annual William & Kingman Page Chapbook competition conducted by the *Potato Eyes* Foundation *or* by invitation.

‡**OBERLIN COLLEGE PRESS**, Rice Hall Oberlin College, Oberlin OH 44074. (216)775-8407. Editors: Stuart Friebert, David Young, Alberta Turner, David Walker. Imprints are Field Magazine: Contemporary Poetry & Poetics, Field Translation Series, Field Poetry Series. Publishes hardcover and trade paperback originals. Publishes 2-3 titles/year. Pays 7½-10% royalty on retail price. Offers $500 advance. Query.Recent poetry title; *Selected Poems of Russell Edson*.

OHIO BIOLOGICAL SURVEY, Subsidiary of The Ohio State University College of Biosciences, Museum of Biological Diversity, 1315 Kinnear Rd., Columbus OH 43212-1192. (614)292-9645. Fax: (614)292-7774. Editor: Veda M. Cafazzo. Estab. 1912. "Subjects stress, but *not* limited to, information about Ohio's biota."

C. OLSON & CO., P.O. Box 5100, Santa Cruz CA 95063-5100. (408)458-3365. E-mail: 71054.1630@com-puserve.com. Owner: C. Olson. Estab. 1981. "We are looking for nonfiction manuscripts or books that can be sold at natural food stores and small independent bookstores on health and on how to live a life which improves the earth's environment." Query first with SASE only.

OMEGA PUBLICATIONS, RD 1 Box 1030E, New Lebanon NY 12125-9801. (518)794-8181. Fax: (518)794-8187. Contact: Abi'l-Khayr. Estab. 1977. "We are interested in any material related to sufism, and only that."

OUR CHILD PRESS, 800 Maple Glen Lane, Wayne PA 19087-4797. (610)964-0606. Fax: (610)293-9083. Editor: Carol Hallenbeck. Estab. 1984. "We publish only adoption-related materials. Query first." Recent titles: *Don't Call Me Marda* and *Blue Ridge*.

PACIFIC LEARNING COUNCIL, Suite 300, 251 Post St., San Francisco CA 94108. (415)391-4135. Contact: Richard Nodine. Publishes mass market paperback originals. Publishes how-to, self-help, technical books "designed to provide important lifeskills."

‡PACIFIC VIEW PRESS, P.O. Box 2657, Berkeley CA 94702. (510)849-4213. President: Pam Zumwalt. Publishes hardcover and trade paperback originals. Publishes 3-4 titles/year. Pays 6-12% royalty on wholesale or retail price. Offers $500-2,000 advance. Book catalog free on request. Children's/juvenile, reference. Subjects include business and economics, ethnic, health/medicine. "We are interested in Pacific Rim related issues." Query. Recent nonfiction title; *China: Business Strategies for the '90s*, by Arne de Kerjizer (business).

‡*PAIDEIA PRESS, P.O. Box 121303, Arlington TX 76012. (214)719-2629. Managing Editor: F.A. Nance. Publishes hardcover and trade paperback originals. Publishes 5-6 titles/year. 80% of books from first-time authors; 100% from unagented writers. Pays 5-15% royalty on retail price or makes outright purchase of $500. Publishes book 8 months after acceptance of ms. Accepts simultaneous submissions. Reports in 2 months on mss. Manuscript guidelines for #10 SASE.
Nonfiction: How-to, multimedia (CD-ROM, software), textbook. Subjects include education, philosophy, supplementary texts for education market, grades 5-college, women's issues/studies. "We are particularly interested in women's issues/studies and education texts dealing with the development of critical thinking skills." Submit proposal package, including full ms with SASE. Reviews artwork/photos as part of ms package. Send photocopies.
Recent Nonfiction Title: *An aMATHing Discovery*, by Sam Fiagome (education [math] text).
Tips: Audience is education/school market; retail and specialty shop (e.g., teacher supply); library. "Do not be discouraged if you are told your book's market is too narrow. Properly marketed texts to niche markets are profitable if the marketer knows what he/she is doing."

PARADISE PUBLICATIONS, 8110 SW Wareham, Portland OR 97223. (503)246-1555. President: Christie Stilson. Publishes specific location travel guides, primarily Hawaii related.

‡PARROT PRESS, 357 Sunnyslope Dr., Fremont CA 94536. (510)713-1154. Editor: Jennifer Warshaw. Publishes 3 titles/year. Pays 10-15% royalty on gross sales (wholesale, retail price). How-to, reference, self-help. Subject: pet birds only. "We publish nonfiction books written for pet bird owners. We are most interested in well-researched books on pet bird husbandry, health care, diet and species profiles. Good, clear, accessible writing is a requirement." Submit outline and 1-3 sample chapters with SASE.

PARTNERS IN PUBLISHING, P.O. Box 50374, Tulsa OK 74150-0374. Phone/fax: (918)835-8258. Editor: P.M. Fielding. Estab. 1976. Publishes biography, how-to, reference, self-help, technical and textbooks on learning disabilities, special education for youth and young adults.
● This press reports being deluged with submissions having nothing to do with learning disabilities.

PAX PUBLISHING, P.O. Box 22564, San Francisco CA 94122-2564. (415)759-5658. Senior Editor: Robert Black. Publishes nonfiction books; areas include how-to, humor, business, computers, health/medicine, money/finance. Submit table of contents and sample chapter. No complete mss without prior authorization. Will respond within 2 months only if interested.

PENDAYA PUBLICATIONS, INC., 510 Woodvine Ave., Metairie LA 70005. (504)834-8151. Manager: Earl J. Mathes. Estab. 1986. Publishes hardcover originals. Publishes 1-2 titles/year. Pays 4-8% royalty on retail price (varies). Offers $500-3,000 advance. Nonfiction: coffee table book; illustrated book. Subjects include anthropology/archaeology, art/architecture, photography, travel, design. Submit proposal package. Send sample transparencies.

PERMEABLE PRESS, 47 Noe St., #4, San Francisco CA 94114-1017. (415)255-9765. Publisher: Brian Clark. E-mail: bcclark@igc.apc.org. Publishes trade paperback originals. "Permeable publishes 'high risk' fiction that other publishers cannot stomach, but which is too good to go unpublished."

‡**PIGOUT PUBLICATIONS, INC.**, 4245 Walnut, Kansas City MO 64111. (816)531-3119. Marketing Director: Amy Winn. Publishes trade paperback originals. Publishes 2-4 titles/year. Pays 5-15% royalty on wholesale price. Offers $500-1,000 advance. BBQ & grill books only. Submit outline, 1-2 sample chapters and bio. Recent title: *Texas Barbecue*, by Paris Parmenier's John Bigley (cookbook and restaurant guide).

POLLARD PRESS, P.O. Box 19864, Jacksonville FL 32245. Owner: M.L. Lum. Publishes trade paperback and mass market paperback originals on cooking/foods/nutrition, education, hobbies, recreation and humor.

POPULAR MEDICINE PRESS, P.O. Box 1212, San Carlos CA 94070-1212. (415)593-3072. Fax: (415)594-1855. Vice President: John Bliss. Estab. 1986. Publishes books on nutrition, health and medicine. "We're less active this year and expect minimal activity in 1996."

POTENTIALS DEVELOPMENTS INC., 40 Hazelwood Dr., Suite 101, Amherst NY 14228. (716)691-6601. Fax: (716)691-6620. President: C.B. Seide. Estab. 1978. Publishes paperback originals. Averages 1 title/year. Average print order for a first book is 500. Pays at least 5% royalty on sales of first 3,000 copies; 8% thereafter. Book catalog and ms guidelines for 9×12 SASE.
 • This company has changed ownership and is looking to broaden its market.

PRAIRIE OAK PRESS, 821 Prospect Place, Madison WI 53703. (608)255-2288. Vice President: Kristin Visser. Estab. 1991. Imprint is Prairie Classics. Publishes nonfiction, history and travel books about the Upper Great Lakes region, especially Wisconsin, Michigan, Illinois, Minnesota.

‡**PRIMER PUBLISHERS**, 5738 N. Central Ave., Phoenix AZ 85012. (602)234-1574. Trade paperback books, mostly regional subjects; travel, outdoor recreation, history, etc. Query first.

PUBLISHERS SYNDICATION INTERNATIONAL, 1377 K Street NW, Suite 856, Washington DC 20005-3033. Fax: (405)364-4979. E-mail: APSam@aol.com. President/Editor: A.P. Samuels. Estab. 1971. Publishes books on military history.

PUCKERBRUSH PRESS, 76 Main St., Orono ME 04473-1430. (207)581-3832 or 866-4808. Publisher/Editor: Constance Hunting. Estab. 1971. Publishes trade paperback originals and reprints of literary fiction and poetry. Publishes 3-4 titles/year. Pays 10-15% royalty on wholesale price or makes outright purchase. Nonfiction: Belles lettres, translations. Recent title: *Welcome to a New World*, by Ernest Saunders (biblical analysis of gospel of John). Fiction: Literary and short story collections.

PURPLE FINCH PRESS, P.O. Box 758, Dewitt NY 13214. (315)445-8087. Publisher: Nancy Benson. Publishes hardcover and trade paperback originals. "I am interested in poetry, short stories, children's literature, adult mystery novels and cookbooks. Submissions should be written for an intelligent reader who is familiar with good literature, especially the classics. Submissions must be typewritten and include a SASE. Submissions must be original and previously unpublished."

REDBRICK PRESS, P.O. Box 1895, Sonoma CA 95476-1895. 707-996-2774. E-mail: JERedBRICK@aol.com. Publisher: Jack Erickson. Estab. 1987. "RedBrick Press currently is publishing only books on microbreweries and specialty beers. We are expanding in 1995 to include food and travel related titles."

‡**RESOLUTION BUSINESS PRESS**, 11101 NE Eighth St., Suite 208, Bellevue WA 98004. (206)455-4611. Fax: (206)455-9143. E-mail: rbpress@halcyon.com. Editor: Karen Strudwick. Estab. 1987. "We publish computer industry reference books, including *Northwest High Tech*, an annual guide to the computer industry of the Pacific Northwest and Western Canada, and *UNIX: An Open Systems Dictionary*, by William H. Holt and Rockie J. Morgan. Several Internet titles were planned for release in 1995."

RHOMBUS PUBLISHING CO., P.O. Box 806, Corrales NM 87048-0806. (505)897-3700. Submissions Editor: Benjamin Radford. Estab. 1984. Publishes nonfiction books on anthropology/archaeology, government/politics, nature/environment and Southwestern topics.

ROCKBRIDGE PUBLISHING CO., P.O. Box 351, Berryville VA 22611-0351. (703)955-3980. Fax: (703)955-4126. Publisher: Katherine Tennery. Estab. 1989. "We are developing a series of travel guides to the country roads in various Virginia counties. The self-guided tours include local history, identify geographic features, etc. We are also looking for material about the Civil War, especially biographies."

‡**ST. JOHN'S PUBLISHING, INC.**, 6824 Oaklawn Ave., Edina MN 55435. (612)920-9044. President: Donna Montgomery. Estab. 1986. Publishes nonfiction books on parenting.

SAND RIVER PRESS, 1319 14th St., Los Osos CA 93402. (805)528-7347. Publisher: Bruce Miller. Estab. 1987. Publishes mostly nonfiction titles on literature, Native Americans, regional (California) and some literary fiction.

SANDPIPER PRESS, P.O. Box 286, Brookings OR 97415-0028. (503)469-5588. Editor: Marilyn Riddle. Estab. 1979. Query.

SCOTS PLAID PRESS, 22-B Pine Lake Dr., Whispering Pines NC 28327-9388. Editor/Publisher: MaryBelle Campbell. Perfectbound, aesthetic paperback books, archival limited editions. Publishes biography, academic and textbooks. Subjects include anthropology/archaeology, philosophy, psychology. No unsolicited mss. Query with bio, vita, PC disc information and cover letter with concept and purposed use for book. Send opening page and contents page only. Enclose SASE.
  • This press reports being inundated with queries, but only accepts one in over 350 queries received.

SEA-LARK PRINT PRODUCTIONS, Subsidiary of Southwest Spirit Supply, 101 King's Lane, Commerce TX 75428-3710. (903)886-2729. Editor: Lisa Allen. Publishes hardcover and trade paperback originals. Publishes 2-3 titles/year. "We will be focusing on self-esteem, self-help books for youth and adult exceptional learners."

SIGNPOST BOOKS, 8912 192nd SW, Edmonds WA 98026. (206)776-0370. Publisher: Cliff Cameron. Publishes trade paperback originals. "We focus on self-propelled outdoor recreation in the Pacific Northwest (excluding hunting and fishing)."

SILVERCAT PUBLICATIONS, 4070 Goldfinch St., Suite C, San Diego CA 92103-1865. (619)299-6774. Fax: (619)299-9119. Editor: Robert Outlaw. Estab. 1988. Publishes consumer-oriented nonfiction on topics of current interest. Responds in 2 months.
  • Silvercat has expanded its interests to include books relating to quality-of-life issues.

16TH CENTURY JOURNAL PUBLISHERS, NMSU MC111L, Kirksville MO 63501. (816)785-4665. President: Robert V. Schnucker. Publishes hardcover and trade paperback originals. Scholarly monographs on art, history, language, religion.

‡**SOUND VIEW PRESS**, 170 Boston Post Rd., Madison CT 06443. President: Peter Hastings Falk. Estab. 1985. Publishes hardcover and trade paperback originals, dictionaries, exhibition records, and price guides on fine art.

SPECTACLE LANE PRESS INC., P.O. Box 34, Georgetown CT 06829. (203)762-3786. Editor: James A. Skardon. Publishes nonfiction trade paperback originals and reprints. Reports on queries in 2 weeks. Will do occasional title on subjects of import and strong current interest, but concentration is on sports and family-related humor books.

STONE BRIDGE PRESS, P.O. Box 8208, Berkeley CA 94707-8208. (510)524-8732. Fax: (510)524-8711. E-mail: sbp@netcom.com. Publisher: Peter Goodman. Estab. 1989. Publishes books on working and communicating with the Japanese, Japanese garden and design-related books, Japan related literary fiction, language learning, travel and translations. "No historical or genre fiction, please!"

‡**STORM PEAK PRESS**, 157 Yesler Way, Suite 413, Seattle WA 98104. (206)223-0162. Publisher: Mr. Loomis. Publishes trade paperback originals and reprints. Subsidy publishes 33% of books. Pays royalty on retail price. Biography, children's/juvenile. Subjects include Americana, health/medicine, history, travel. "We only consider high-quality, unique manuscripts." Recent Nonfiction Title: *As Long As Life*, by Mary C. Rowland, MD (autobiography).

Market conditions are constantly changing! If this is 1997 or later, buy the newest edition of Writer's Market *at your favorite bookstore or order directly from* Writer's Digest Books.

‡STORMLINE PRESS, P.O. Box 539, Urbana IL 61801. (217)328-2665. Publisher: Raymond Bial. Estab. 1985. "Publishes fiction and nonfiction, generally with a Midwest connection. Needs photography and regional works of the highest literary quality, especially those having to do with rural and small town themes. Stormline prefers works which are rooted in a specific place and time, such as *Silent Friends: A Quaker Quilt*, by Margaret Lacey. The Press considers queries (with SASE only) during November and December. We do not consider unsolicited manuscripts."

‡STUDENT COLLEGE AID PUBLISHING DIVISION, 7950 N. Stadium Dr. #229, Houston TX 77030. Fax: (713)796-9963. Owner: Edward Rosenwasser. "We publish books about college financial aid and careers. Any book that is informative and interesting will be considered."

STUDIO 4 PRODUCTIONS, P.O. Box 280400, Northridge CA 91328. (818)700-2522. Editor-in-Chief: Charlie Matthews. Publishes trade paperback originals. Reports on queries in 2 months. Subjects include character education (values, ethics and morals), child guidance, parenting, humor, self-help.

THE SUGAR HILL PRESS, 129 Sugar Hill Est. Rd., Weare NH 03281-4327. Publisher: L. Bickford. Estab. 1990. "We publish technical manuals for users of school administrative software *only*. (These are supplemental materials, not the manuals which come in the box.) A successful writer will combine technical expertise with crystal-clear prose."

THE SYSTEMSWARE CORPORATION, 973C Russell Ave., Gaithersburg MD 20879. (301)948-4890. Fax: (301)926-4243. Editor: Pat White. Estab. 1987. "We specialize in innovative books and periodicals on Knowledge Engineering or Applied Artificial Intelligence and Knowledge Based Systems. We also develop software packages."

TAMARACK BOOKS, INC., P.O. Box 190313, Boise ID 83719-0313. (208)387-2656. Fax: (208)387-2650. President/Owner: Kathy Gaudry. Publishes trade paperback originals and reprints. Cookbooks, illustrated books and nonfiction on the West for people living in the American West or interested in the West.

TAMBRA PUBLISHING, 4375 W. Desert Inn, Suite D-122, Las Vegas NV 89102-7678. Fax: (702)876-5252. Editor: Tambra Campbell. Publisher: Kate Stevens. Estab. 1985. Publishes how-to books on handwriting analysis; also accepts well-written screenplays and manuscripts with good storylines with some action that can be adapted into screenplays, as well as being published. Will consider works on psychology and on family relations, love stories. Include large SASE for return of ms or sp. Reports in 4 months.

‡TECHNICAL BOOKS FOR THE LAYPERSON, INC., P.O. Box 391, Lake Grove NY 11755. (703)877-1477. Contact: Mary Lewis. Publishes trade paperback originals. Publishes 3 titles/year. Pays 10-40% royalty on actual earnings. Book catalog and ms guidelines free on request. Publishes how-to, reference, self-help, technical, textbook. "Our primary goal is consumer-friendliness (Books by consumers for consumers.) All topics are considered." Submit 1 sample chapter. Reviews artwork/photos as part of ms package. Send photocopies.

TIMES CHANGE PRESS, P.O. Box 1380, Ojai CA 93024-1380. (805)646-8595. Publisher: Lamar Hoover. Estab. 1970. "Our books are small format (5½×7), and nondogmatic in their approach to such topics as ecology and earth-consciousness, personal liberation, feminism, etc. We are not considering any new manuscripts at this time."

TRAFALGAR SQUARE PUBLISHING, P.O. Box 257, N. Pomfret VT 05053-0257. (802)457-1911. Publisher: Caroline Robbins. Contact: Martha Cook, managing editor. Publishes nonfiction books about horses.

TURTLE PRESS, Subsidiary of S.K. Productions Inc., P.O. Box 290206, Wethersfield CT 06129-0206. (203)529-7770. Fax: (203)529-7775. E-mail: jcjv99a@prodigy.com. Editor: Cynthia Kim. Publishes trade paperback originals and reprints. Subjects include: how-to, martial arts, philosophy, self-help, sports, women's issues/studies.

T'WANDA BOOKS, P.O. Box 1227, Peralta NM 87042-1227. E-mail: twanda1@aol.com. Editor: Thelma Louise. Estab. 1992. Publishes 1 title/year. Payment arrived at by mutual agreement. Fantasy, feminist, science fiction. "Looking for experiences of women in nontraditional jobs that illuminate and educate." Query. SASE. Recent title: *Wild Justice*, by Ruth M. Sprague. "Our audience is all womankind and supporters who refuse to accept the definitions and limitations imposed by ancient conquerors."

‡TWO LANE PRESS, INC., 4245 Walnut, Kansas City MO 64111. (816)531-3119. Marketing Director: Amy Winn. Publishes trade paperback originals. Publishes 5 titles/year. Pays 5-15% royalty on wholesale price. Offers $500-1,000 advance. Book catalog and ms guidelines free on request. Regional cookbooks and regional travel guides. "We publish books for the heartland." Submit outline, 1-2 sample chapters and bio.

Recent title: *Pure Prairie: Farm Fresh and Wildly Delicious Foods from the Prairie*, by Judith Fertig. Audience: "people traveling to regions our books target or giving gifts about those regions. Do not call to pitch idea. Written proposals best. Do not handwrite."

UCLA-AMERICAN INDIAN STUDIES CENTER, UCLA, 3220 Campbell Hall, P.O. Box 951548, Los Angeles CA 90095-1548. (310)825-7315. Fax: (310)206-7060. E-mail: eji4rfk@mus.oac.ucla.edu. Editor: Duane Champagne. Estab. 1969. Publishes nonfiction how-to and reference books on anthropology, education, ethnic, government/politics, history, language/literature and sociology themes. Publishes poetry on Native American themes and an academic journal.

UNIVERSITY OF CALIFORNIA LOS ANGELES CENTER FOR AFRO-AMERICAN STUDIES PUBLICATIONS, 160 Haines Hall, 405 Hilgard Ave., Los Angeles CA 90024-1545. (310)825-3528. Fax: (310)206-3421. Managing Editor: Toyomi Igus. Estab. 1979. "Seeking nonfiction book-length manuscripts that have mainstream as well as scholarly or academic appeal and that focus on the African-American experience."

VALIANT PRESS, INC., P.O. Box 330568, Miami FL 33233. (305)665-1889. President: Charity Johnson. Estab. 1991. "We are interested in nonfiction books on Florida subjects."

VAN PATTEN PUBLISHING, 4204 SE Ogden St., Portland OR 97206. Phone/fax: (503)775-3815. E-mail: georgevp@teleport.com. Owner: George F. Van Patten. Publishes hardcover and trade paperback originals and reprints on gardening.

‡VISIONS COMMUNICATIONS, 50 Jayme Dr., York PA 17402. Publisher: Elise Oranges. Publishes hardcover originals and trade paperback originals and reprints. Publishes Children's/juvenile, how-to, reference, self-help, technical, textbook. Subjects include art/architecture, business and economics, computers and electronics, nature/environment, religion, science. Recent nonfiction title: *Illumination Engineering*, by Joseph Murdoch (engineering).

VISTA PUBLICATIONS, P.O. Box 661447, Miami Springs FL 33166-1447. Fax: (502)269-1003. Owner: Helen Brose. Estab. 1988. Publishes trade and mass market paperback originals. Publishes 2 titles/year. Subjects include anthropology/archaeology, government/politics, history, language/literature, regional, travel. "We specialize in books about Guatemala and Central America in English or Spanish. We are also open to works of fiction, as long as it relates to Guatemala." Submit synopsis.

VOLCANO PRESS, INC., P.O. Box 270, Volcano CA 95689-0270. (209)296-3445. Fax: (209)296-4515. Publisher: Ruth Gottstein. "We publish women's health and social issues, particularly in the field of domestic violence, and multicultural books for children that are non-racist and non-sexist."

WASATCH PUBLISHERS, 4460 Ashford Dr., Salt Lake City UT 84124-2506. (801)278-5826. Publisher: John Veranth. Estab. 1974. Publishes books on outdoor recreation in the intermountain west.
  ● Publisher has informed us they are "not taking on so many new books." Focus is on regional topics only.

‡WATERFRONT BOOKS, 85 Crescent Rd., Burlington VT 05401. Phone/fax: (802)658-7477. Publisher: Sherrill N. Musty. Estab. 1983. Publishes books on special issues for children: barriers to learning, mental health, prevention, family/parenting, and social/multicultural concerns.

WESTERN TANAGER PRESS, 1111 Pacific Ave., Santa Cruz CA 95060. (408)425-1111. Fax: (408)425-0171. Publisher: Hal Morris. Estab. 1979. Publishes historical biography, hiking and biking guides and regional history hardcover and trade paperback originals and reprints.

WHITEHORSE PRESS, 3424 N. Main St., P.O. Box 60, North Conway NH 03860-0060. (603)356-6556. Fax: (603)356-6590. Publisher: Dan Kennedy. Estab. 1988. "We are actively seeking nonfiction books to aid motorcyclists in topics such as motorcycle safety, restoration, repair and touring. We are broadening our editorial interests to include any aspect of motorcycling."

WHOLE NOTES PRESS, Imprint of *Whole Notes Magazine*, P.O. Box 1374, Las Cruces NM 88004-1374. (505)382-7446. Editor: Nancy Peters Hastings. Estab. 1988. Publishes poetry chapbooks. Submit a sampler of 3-8 poems, along with SASE.

WOMAN IN THE MOON, P.O. Box 2087, Cupertino CA 95015. Phone/fax: (408)738-4623(*). E-mail: sb02701@mercury.fhda.edu. Contact: Dr. SDiane A. Bogus. Publishes hardcover and trade paperback originals and trade paperback reprints. Publishes short stories and nonfiction. Reports on queries in 1 month. "We are very interested in New Age topics: angels, healing, ghosts, psychic phenomena, goddess worship, spiritual biography, etc."

● Woman in the Moon has a new subsidiary imprint, 2's Crow Magic, and a newsletter, *The Spirit.*

WORLD LEISURE, 177 Paris St., Boston MA 02128-3058. (617)569-1966. Fax: (617)561-7654. President: Charles Leocha. Reports in 2 months. "We will be publishing annual updates to *Ski Europe* and *Skiing America*. Writers planning any ski stories should contact us for possible add-on assignments at areas not covered by our staff. We also will publish general travel titles such as Travelers' Rights, Children's travel guides, guidebooks about myths and legends and self/help books such as *Getting To Know You*, and *ABCs of Life from Women Who Learned the Hard Way.*

‡**WRITER'S RESOURCES**, 15 Margaret's Way, Nantucket MA 02554. (508)325-0041. Editor: Barbara Cowper. Publishes trade paperback originals. Publishes 1-2 titles/year. Pays negotiable royalty. Manuscript guidelines for #10 SASE. How-to, reference, self-help nonfiction. Subjects include philosophy, religion, women's issues/studies, writing. Query with outline, 2 sample chapters and SASE. Recent nonfiction title: *New Choices for Writers* (writers' market guide).

XENOS BOOKS, Box 52152, Riverside CA 92517. (909)370-2229. Editor: Karl Kvitko. Interested chiefly in translations of 20th century literature, original experimental fiction and unusual memoirs. No children's literature, SF, PC, religious works or popular genres—detective, horror, romance, fantasy, political/espionage. "We want highly refined, strikingly original poetry and prose." Publishes 4-5 titles a year.

YMAA PUBLICATION CENTER, 38 Hyde Park Ave., Jamaica Plain MA 02130. (617)524-9673. Fax: (617)524-4184. Contact: David Ripianzi. Estab. 1982. "We publish exclusively Chinese philosophy, health, meditation, massage, martial arts. We no longer publish or solicit works for children. We also produce instructional videos to accompany our books on traditional Chinese martial arts, meditation, massage El Chi Kung."

‡**ZEPHYR PRESS**, 13 Robinson St., Somerville MA 02145. Co-director: Ed Hogan. Publishes hardcover originals and trade paperback originals and reprints. Publishes 3 titles/year. Pays 6-10% royalty on retail price. Offers $0-2,000 advance. Publishes book 18 months after acceptance of ms. Illustrated book, travel guides. Subjects include language/literature, translation, travel. "We focus on books concerning Russia: fiction, poetry, scholarly/general audience nonfiction and travel. We very rarely publish unsolicited proposals. It's essential that writers and translators be familiar with our books before considering making a proposal." Query with SASE. Recent nonfiction title; *An Explorer's Guide to Russia*, by Robert Greenall (travel).

Book Producers

Book producers provide services for book publishers, ranging from hiring writers to editing and delivering finished books. Most book producers possess expertise in certain areas and will specialize in producing books related to those subjects. They provide books to publishers who don't have the time or expertise to produce the books themselves (many produced books are highly illustrated and require intensive design and color-separation work). Some work with on-staff writers, but most contract writers on a per-project basis.

Most often a book producer starts with a proposal; contacts writers, editors and illustrators; assembles the book; and sends it back to the publisher. The level of involvement and the amount of work to be done on a book by the producer is negotiated in individual cases. A book publisher may simply require the specialized skill of a particular writer or editor, or a producer could put together the entire book, depending on the terms of the agreement.

Writers have a similar working relationship with book producers. Their involvement depends on how much writing the producer has been asked to provide. Writers are typically paid by the hour, by the word, or in some manner other than on a royalty basis. Writers working for book producers usually earn flat fees. Writers may not receive credit (a byline in the book, for example) for their work, either. Most of the contracts require work for hire, and writers must realize they do not own the rights to writing published under this arrangement.

The opportunities are good, though, especially for writing-related work, such as fact checking, research and editing. Writers don't have to worry about good sales. Their pay is secured under contract. Finally, writing for a book producer is a good way to broaden experience in publishing. Every book to be produced is different, and the chance to work on a range of books in a number of capacities may be the most interesting aspect of all.

Book producers most often want to see a query detailing writing experience. They keep this information on file and occasionally even share it with other producers. When they are contracted to develop a book that requires a particular writer's experience, they contact the writer. There are well over 100 book producers, but most prefer to seek writers on their own. The book producers listed in this section have expressed interest in being contacted by writers. For a list of more producers, contact the American Book Producers Association, 160 Fifth Ave., Suite 604, New York NY 10010, or look in *Literary Market Place* (R.R. Bowker).

For a list of publishers according to their subjects of interest, see the nonfiction and fiction sections of the Book Publishers Subject Index. Information on some book publishers and producers not included in this edition of *Writer's Market* can be found in Book Publishers and Producers/Changes '95-'96.

B&B PUBLISHING, INC., P.O. Box 96, Walworth WI 53125-0530. (414)275-9474. Fax: (414)275-9530. President: William Turner. Managing Editor: Katy O'Shea. Publishes supplementary educational materials for grades K-12. Publishes 5-10 titles/year. 10% of books from first-time authors, 90% from unagented writers. Pays 2½-5% royalty on net receipts, or makes outright purchase of $2,000-5,000. Offers $2,000 advance. Query for electronic submissions. Reports in 3 months. Book catalog and ms guidelines free on request.

• This company is also listed in Book Publishers.
Nonfiction: Query. Reviews artwork/photos as part of ms package.
Recent Nonfiction Title: *The Awesome Almanac of Wisconsin* (trade paperback).

‡**BEAR FLAG BOOKS**, P.O. Box 840, Arroyo Grande CA 93421-0840. Phone/fax: (805)473-1947. Editor: Lachlan P. MacDonald. Produces hardcover and trade paperback originals. Averages 6 titles/year. 80% of books from first-time authors; 95% from unagented writers. Pays 6-10% royalty. Advance varies. Reports in 6 weeks-6 months. Book catalog for $1 and 6×9 SAE. Manuscript guidelines for SAE with 2 first-class stamps.
Nonfiction: Juvenile, adult trade books and travel guides. Subjects include history, regional, travel. Query with proposal. Reviews artwork/photos as part of ms package.
Recent Nonfiction Title: *Columbia: Allistory of the Gem of the Southern Mines* (local history).
Fiction: Historical, juvenile (California settings and subjects preferred). Submit complete ms.
Recent Fiction Title: *Flower Tumbles: The Story of an Esselen Indian Boy* (juvenile).

THE BENJAMIN COMPANY, INC., 21 Dupont Ave., White Plains NY 10605-3537. (914)997-0111. Fax: (914)997-7214. President: Ted Benjamin. Estab. 1953. Produces custom-published hardcover and paperback originals. Averages 10 titles/year. 90-100% of books from unagented writers. "Usually commissions author to write specific book; seldom accepts proffered manuscripts." Publishes book 9-12 months after acceptance. Makes outright purchase. Offers advance. Accepts simultaneous submissions. Query for electronic submissions. Reports in 1 month.
Nonfiction: Business/economics, cookbooks, cooking/foods, health, hobbies, how-to, self-help, sports, consumerism. Query only. "Ours is a very specialized kind of publishing—for clients (industrial and association) to use in promotional, PR, or educational programs. If an author has an idea for a book and close connections with a company that might be interested in using that book, we will be very interested in working together with the author to 'sell' the program and the idea of a special book for that company. Once published, our books often get trade distribution through a distributing publisher, so the author generally sees the book in regular book outlets as well as in the special programs undertaken by the sponsoring company. *We do not encourage submission of manuscripts.* We usually commission an author to write for us. The most helpful thing an author can do is to let us know what he or she has written, or what subjects he or she feels competent to write about. We will contact the author when our needs indicate that the author might be the right person to produce a needed manuscript."
Recent Nonfiction Title: *McCormick/Schilling's New Spice Cookbook.*

‡**BLACKBIRCH GRAPHICS, INC.**, 1 Bradley Rd. #205, Woodbridge CT 06525. Fax: (203)389-1596. Editor-in-Chief: Bruce Glassman. Estab. 1979. Imprint is Blackbirch Press. Produces hardcover originals. Averages 70 titles/year. 20% of books from first-time authors; 85% from unagented writers. Pays 5-10% on net receipts. Makes outright purchase of $1,000-5,000. Offers $1,500 average advance. Query for electronic submissions. Does *not* return submissions, even those accompanied by SASE. Reports in 2 months. No phone calls, please.
Nonfiction: Only. Biography, how-to, illustrated books, juvenile, reference, self-help. Subjects include women, African-Americans, Native Americans, and nature/environment. Nonfiction only. Submit proposal. Reviews artwork/photos as part of ms package.
Tips: "Young adult publishing offers *series* work quite often. This means small advances and tight budgets on a *per book* basis, but can allow authors to get commitments on 4-8 titles at a time." Do not send fiction proposals or those not appropriate for young readers.

BOOKWORKS, INC., 119 S. Miami St., West Milton OH 45383. (513)698-3619. Fax: (513)698-3651. President: Nick Engler. Estab. 1984. Averages 6 titles/year. Receives 1-10 submissions/year. Less than 10% of books from first-time authors; 100% from unagented writers. Pays 2½-5% royalty on retail price. Makes outright purchase of $3,000-10,000. Advance varies. Publishes book 8-18 months after acceptance. Accepts simultaneous submissions. Reports in 6 weeks on queries, 2 months on mss.
Nonfiction: How-to. Subjects include woodworking, home improvement. Nothing other than woodworking/home improvement. Query or submit outline/synopsis and sample chapters. Reviews artwork/photos as part of ms package.
Tips: "We will not consider manuscripts unless written by experienced, competent craftsmen with firsthand knowledge of the subject. We publish how-to books for do-it-yourselfers, hobbyists and craftsmen."

A bullet introduces comments by the editors of **Writer's Market** *indicating special information about the listing.*

‡ALISON BROWN CERIER BOOK DEVELOPMENT, INC., 815 Brockton Lane N., Plymouth MN 55410. (612)449-9668. Fax: (612)449-9674. Produces hardcover and trade paperback originals. Averages 4 titles/year. 50% of books from first-time authors; 90% from unagented writers. Payment varies with the project. Reports in 3 weeks.
Nonfiction: Cookbook, how-to, reference, self-help. Subjects include business and economics, child guidance/parenting, cooking/foods/nutrition, health, psychology, sports. Query.
Recent Nonfiction Title: *The Cancer Recovery Eating Plan* (Random House hardcover).
Tips: "I often pair experts with writers and like to know about writers and journalists with co-writing experience."

‡CHAPELLE, LTD., Subsidiary of The Vanessa-Ann Collection, P.O. Box 9252, Ogden UT 84409. Contact: Lorin May. Imprint is Sterling/Chapelle, Ltd. (Jo Packham, president). Produces hardcover and trade paperback originals. Averages 12-16 titles/year. Receives 30 queries and 5 mss/year. 50% of books from first-time authors; 100% from unagented writers. Pays 1-2½% royalty or makes outright purchase. Offers $500-4,000 advance. Publishes book 4-12 months after acceptance of me. Accepts simultaneous submissions. Reports in 1 month. Book catalog free on request.
Nonfiction: How-to, children's/juvenile. Subjects include cooking/foods/nutrition, hobbies, crafts. "We package how-to books." Query with outline. Reviews artwork/photos as part of ms package. Send photocopies or transparencies, "any medium is fine."

‡COMPASS PRODUCTIONS, 211 E. Ocean Blvd., #360, Long Beach CA 90802. (310)432-7613. Fax: (310)495-0445. Vice President: Dick Dudley. Produces hardcover originals. Pays 2-8% royalty on wholesale price for total amount of books sold to publisher. Offers $2,000 advance for idea/text. Query for electronic submissions. Reports in 6 weeks. Query with SASE.
Nonfiction: Humor, illustrated book, juvenile, ("all our books are pop-up and novelty books"). Subjects include Americana, animals, child guidance/parenting, education, recreation, regional, religion, sports, travel (concept-early age books). Query.
Recent Nonfiction Title: *Dial Nature Note Books.*
Fiction: Adventure, fantasy, horror, humor, juvenile, mystery, picture books, plays, religious, science fiction. Query.
Recent Fiction Title: *Halloween Fright.*
Tips: "Keep in mind our books are *pop-up, dimensional,* or novelty *only!* Short verse, couplets or short nonfiction text for 6-7 spreads per book."

‡THE COUNTRYWOMAN'S PRESS, Box 840, Arroya Grande CA 93421-0840. Phone/fax: (805)473-1947. Publisher: Karen L. Reinecke. Produces hardcover and trade paperback originals. Averages 2-3 titles/year. 100% of books from first-time authors; 100% from unagented writers. Pays 6-10% royalty on retail price. Advance varies. Reports in 6 weeks-6 months. Catalog and ms guidelines for #10 SAE with 2 stamps.
Nonfiction: Cookbook, how-to (crafts), reference. Subjects include cooking/foods/nutrition, gardening, (crafts, food and beverage books; prefer single-subject approach). Submit proposal. Reviews artwork/photos as part of ms package.
Recent Nonfiction Title: *Earth Tones: Colors from Western Dye Plants* (crafts reference).

THE CREATIVE SPARK, 129 Avenida Victoria, San Clemente CA 92672. (714)366-8774. Fax: (714)366-2421. President: Mary Francis-Demarois. Produces hardcover originals. Averages 20-30 titles/year. Makes outright purchase. Offers advance. Query for electronic submissions. Reports in 3 months.
Nonfiction: Biography, juvenile, reference, self-help. Subjects include animals, child guidance/parenting, education, ethnic, government/politics, history, sociology, sports, women's studies. Submit résumé, publishing history and clips.
Recent Nonfiction Title: *Endangered Wildlife of the World*, by Marshall Cavendish (encyclopedia).

DESKTOP GRAFX, P.O. Box 520, Danville VA 24543-0520. E-mail: HilaryLL@aol.com. President: Hilary Levy. Designs hardcover, trade paperback and mass market paperback originals. Averages 1-2 titles/year. 90% of books from first-time authors; 10% from unagented writers. Pays 5-20% royalty. Query for electronic submissions.
Nonfiction: How-to, self-help, software, technical, textbook. Subjects include business and economics, computer/electronics, regional, translation. Submit proposal. Reviews artwork/photos as part of ms package. Now working on travel/tourism magazines.
Tips: "I will edit, proofread and design the book—including the cover design. Please submit your manuscript on disk. Call ahead for computer requirements, etc. I specialize in graphic design."

J.K. ECKERT & CO., INC., 3614 Webber St., Suite 107, Sarasota FL 34232-4413. (813)925-0468. Fax: (813)925-0272. Acquisitions Editor: William Marshall. Produces hardcover originals. Produces 12-18 titles/year. 80% of books from first-time authors; 90% from unagented writers. Pays 10-50% royalty on net receipts. Query for electronic submissions. Reports usually in 1-2 months. Manuscript guidelines free on request.

Nonfiction: Reference, software, technical, textbook. Subjects include computer science and electronic engineering. Submit proposal. Reviews artwork/photos as part of ms package.
Recent Nonfiction Title: *Electromagnetic Compatibility in Power Electronics*, E&C (professional).
Tips: "1.) Keep art and text separate—do not use page layout software. 2.) Save any artwork as EPS or TIFF; use a real art program like Adobe Illustrator—not something built into a word processor. 3.) Don't get creative with fonts—stick to Times and Helvetica. Avoid True-Type if humanly possible. 4.) Send synopsis, TOC, and sample chapter (preferably not Chapter 1). Include bio if you want, but if the book is good, we don't care who you are."

‡ERIAKO ASSOCIATES, 1380 Morningside Way, Venice CA 90291. (310)392-9019. Fax: (310)396-4307. Director: Erika Fabian. Produces hardcover and trade paperback originals. Averages 3-4 titles/year. 100% of books from unagented writers. Pays per contract agreement per individual artist. Reports in 4-6 weeks.
Nonfiction: Coffee table book, illustrated book, juvenile. Subjects include business and economics, ethnic, money/finance, photography, travel. Query with résumé, publishing history and clips. Reviews artwork/photos as part of ms package.
Recent Nonfiction Title: *Trade, Investment and Tourism in East Java (economy)*.
Fiction: Young adult (multi-ethnic, educational about a particular country and its culture, through the eyes of children). Submit résumé, publishing history and clips.
Recent Fiction Title: *Adventure in Splendid China* (juvenile, ages 9-12).
Tips: "We're interested in travel writers/photographers with a proven track record in professional photojournalism, and ability to function in foreign countries under all types of circumstances."

THE K S GINIGER COMPANY INC., 250 W. 57th St., Suite 519, New York NY 10107-0599. (212)570-7499. President: Kenneth S. Giniger. Estab. 1964. Produces hardcover, trade paperback and mass paperback originals. Averages 8 titles/year. Receives 250 submissions/year. 25% of books from first-time authors; 75% from unagented writers. Pays 5-15% royalty on retail price. Offers $3,500 average advance. Publishes book 18 months after acceptance. Reports in 6 weeks on queries.
Nonfiction: Biography, coffee table book, illustrated book, reference, self-help. Subjects include business and economics, health, history, travel. "No religious books, cookbooks, personal histories or personal adventure." Query with SASE. All unsolicited mss returned unread (if postage is enclosed).
Recent Nonfiction Title: *My Favorite Hymns*, by Norman Vincent Peale.
Tips: "We look for a book whose subject interests us and which we think can achieve success in the marketplace. Most of our books are based on ideas originating with us by authors we commission, but we have commissioned books from queries submitted to us."

GLEASON GROUP, INC., 12 Main St., Norwalk CT 06851. (203)854-5895. Fax: (203)838-5452. President: Gerald Gleason. Publishes textbooks. Work-for-hire.
Nonfiction: Textbook. Subjects include computer/software.
Recent Nonfiction Titles: *Desktop Publishing with PageMaker 5: A Professional Approach*, *Word 6 For Windows: A Professional Approach*; *MS-Excel 5.0: A Professional Approach* (all McGraw-Hill [Glencoe]).
Tips: "We are textbook packagers who occasionally use freelance tech writers to write portions of our texts. We need more freelance writers with experience writing about computer applications such as Microsoft Word, WordPerfect, Lotus, Excel, and PageMaker." No unsolicited mss.

GRABER PRODUCTIONS INC., 60 W. 15th St., New York MI 10011. (212)929-0154. Fax: (212-929-9630. President: Eden Graber. Produces hardcover and trade paperback originals. Averages 2 books/year. 50% from agented writers. Pay varies by project or makes outright purchase. Query for electronic submissions.
Nonfiction: Juvenile, reference, self-help. Subjects include child guidance/parenting, gardening, health, science, sports, travel. Query.
Recent Nonfiction Titles: *Staying Healthy In A Risky Environment: The NYU Medical Center Family Guide*.

‡HELM PUBLISHING, Box 840, Arroyo Grande CA 93421-0840. (805)473-1947. Fax: (805)473-1947. Editor: Lachlan MacDonald. Produces trade paperback originals. Averages 1 title/year. 100% of books from first-time authors; 100% from unagented writers. Pays 6-10% royalty on retail price. Advance varies. Reports in 6 weeks-6 months. Catalog and ms guidelines for #10 SAE with 2 first-class stamps.
Nonfiction: Reference. Subjects include history, regional, science, travel, natural history of marine life, nautical adventures. Submit proposal. Reviews artwork/photos as part of ms package.
Recent Nonfiction Title: *Dangerous Marine Animals of the Pacific Coast* (reference).

‡HILLER BOOK MANUFACTURING, 631 North 400 W., Salt Lake City UT 84103. (801)521-2411. President: Melvin Hiller. Publishes hardcover originals. Produces 10 titles/year. 10% of books from first-time authors; 20% from unagented writers. Pays royalty on net receipts. Query for electronic submissions. Reports in 1 month. Book catalog free.

Nonfiction: Coffee table book, cookbook, illustrated book, juvenile, reference, textbook. Subjects include cooking, education, religion. Submit proposal. Reviews artwork/photos as part of ms package.
Fiction: Historical, humor, juvenile, picture books, religious.

‡**INTERNATIONAL RESOURCES**, Box 840, Arroyo Grande CA 93421-0840. (805)473-1947. Fax: (805)473-1947. Editor: Lachlan MacDonald. Produces hardcover and trade paperback originals. Averages 3-4 titles/year. 80% of books from first-time authors; 90% from unagented writers. Pays 6-10% royalty on retail price. Advance varies. Reports in 6 weeks-6 months. Catalog and ms guidelines for #10 SAE with 2 first-class stamps.
Nonfiction: How-to, reference, travel. Subjects include anthropology, business and economics, history, photography, psychology, sociology, travel, directory and how-to guides. Query with proposal. Reviews artwork/photos as part of ms package.
Recent Nonfiction Title: *The Profits of Persuasion: Speaking Effectively for Your Company.*

JSA PUBLICATIONS, INC., 29205 Greening Blvd., Farmington Hills MI 48334-2945. (810)932-0090. Fax: (810)932-2659. Director: Joseph S. Ajlouny. Editor: Gwen Foss. Imprints are Push/Pull/Press, packagers of original illustrated humor books; Compositional Arts, packagers of creative nonfiction; Scrivener Press, packagers of history and travel. Packages trade paperback and mass market paperback originals. Averages 15-18 titles/year. Receives 400 queries and 100 mss/year. 95% of books from first-time authors; 100% from unagented writers. Negotiates fee and advance. Accepts simultaneous submissions. Reports in 1 month. Manuscript guidelines for #10 SASE.
• Formerly publishers, this group has shifted its focus to book packaging.
Nonfiction: Popular culture, popular reference, humor, how-to, music, Americana, history, hobbies, sports. Submit proposal package including illustration samples (photcopies) and SASE.
Recent Nonfiction Titles: *Here Kitty, Kitty: Practical Jokes To Play on your Cat*, by Richard Dommers (Pinnacle).
Tips: "Your submissions must be clever!"

‡**GEORGE KURIAN REFERENCE BOOKS**, Box 519, Baldwin Place NY 10505. Phone/fax: (914)962-3287. President: George Kurian. Produces hardcover originals. Averages 6 titles/year. 40% of books from first-time authors; 50% from unagented writers. Pays 10-15% royalty on net receipts. Query for electronic submissions. Reports in 2 months. Book catalog or ms guidelines for 8½×11 SAE with 2 first-class stamps.
Nonfiction: Reference. Subjects include Americana, business and economics, education, ethnic, government/politics, history, military/war, religion, travel. Query.
Recent Nonfiction Title: *World Encyclopedia of Cities.*

LAING COMMUNICATIONS INC., 16250 NE 80th St., Redmond WA 98052-3821. (206)869-6313. Fax: (206)869-6318. Vice President/Editorial Director: Christine Laing. Estab. 1985. Imprint is Laing Research Services (industry monographs). Produces hardcover and trade paperback originals. Averages 6-10 titles/year. 20% of books from first-time authors; 100% from unagented writers. Payment "varies dramatically since all work is sold to publishers as royalty-inclusive package." Reports in 1 month. *Writer's Market* recommends allowing 2 months for reply.
Nonfiction: History, biography, coffee table book, how-to, illustrated book, juvenile, reference, software, technical, textbook. Subjects include Americana, corporate histories, business and economics, computers/electronics, history. Query. Reviews artwork/photos as part of ms package. The company also manages book divisions for 3 firms, producing 8-12 titles annually in regional, technical and health care fields.
Recent Nonfiction Titles: *Reconstruction: American After the Civil War* and *For Home and Country: A Civil War Scrapbook* (Lodestar Books).

LAMPPOST PRESS INC., 1172 Park Ave., New York NY 10128-1213. (212)876-9511. President: Roseann Hirsch. Estab. 1987. Produces hardcover, trade paperback and mass market paperback originals. Averages 25 titles/year. 50% of books from first-time authors; 85% from unagented writers. Pays 50% royalty or makes outright purchase.
Nonfiction: Biography, cookbook, how-to, humor, illustrated book, juvenile, self-help. Subjects include child guidance/parenting, cooking/foods/nutrition, gardening, health, money/finance, women's issues. Query or submit proposal. Reviews artwork/photos as part of ms package.

LAYLA PRODUCTIONS, INC., 340 E. 74th St., New York NY 10021. (212)879-6984. Fax: (212)879-6399 949-6267. President: Lori Stein. Produces hardcover and trade paperback originals. Averages 6 titles/year. 50% of books from first-time authors; 50% from unagented writers. Pays 1-5% royalty or makes outright purchase, depending on contract with publisher. Offers $2,000-10,000 advance. Query for electronic submissions. Does not return submissions, even those accompanied by SASE. Reports in 6 months.
Nonfiction: Coffee table book, cookbook, how-to, humor, illustrated book, juvenile. Subjects include Americana, cooking/foods/nutrition, gardening, history, photography, recreation. Query. Reviews artwork/photos as part of ms package.

Recent Nonfiction Title: *The 50 Greatest Cartoons.*

MARKOWSKI INTERNATIONAL PUBLISHERS, One Oakglade Circle, Hummelstown PA 17036-9525. (717)566-0468. Fax: (717)566-6423. Editor-in-Chief: Marjorie L. Markowski. Guidelines for #10 SAE with 2 first-class stamps.
Nonfiction: How-to, self-help. Subjects include business, health, aviation, model aviation, money-finance, pop-psychology, sociology, success/motivation, career, relationships, sales, marketing, child development and Christian topics. Submit proposal with résumé, publishing history and clips.
Recent Nonfiction Title: *Designing & Building Composite R/C Model Aircraft.*
Tips: "Our focus is on publishing bestsellers!"

MEGA-BOOKS, INC., 116 E. 19th St., New York NY 10003. (212)598-0909. Fax: (212)979-5074. President: Pat Fortunato. Produces trade paperback and mass market paperback originals and fiction and nonfiction for the educational market. Averages 95 titles/year. Works with first-time authors, established authors and un-agented writers. Makes outright purchase for $3,000 and up. Offers 50% average advance. Manusript guide-lines free on request. No unsolicited mss.
Fiction: Juvenile, mystery, young adult. Submit résumé, publishing history and clips.
Recent Fiction Titles: Nancy Drew and Hardy Boys series; *Pocahantas* and *The Lion King* (Disney).
Tips: "Please be sure to obtain a current copy of our writers' guidelines before writing."

MENASHA RIDGE PRESS, INC., P.O. Box 43059, Birmingham AL 35243. (205)967-0566. Fax: (205)967-0580. Publisher: R.W. Sehlinger. Senior Acquisitions Editor: Budd Zehmer. Estab. 1982. Publishes hardcover and trade paperback originals. Averages 26 titles/year. Receives 600-800 submissions annually. 40% of books from first-time authors; 85% of books from unagented writers. Average print order for a first book is 4,000. Royalty and advances vary. Publishes book 1 year after acceptance. Accepts simultaneous submissions. Query for electronic submissions. Reports in 2 months. Book catalog for 9 × 12 SAE with 4 first-class stamps.
Nonfiction: How-to, humor, outdoor recreation, travel guides, small business. Subjects include business and economics, regional, recreation, adventure sports, travel. No fiction, biography or religious copies. Submit proposal, résumé and clips. Reviews artwork/photos.
Recent Nonfiction Title: *Unofficial Guides* (10 travel guides for Simon & Schuster).
Tips: "Audience: age 25-60, 14-18 years' education, white collar and professional, $30,000 median income, 75% male, 75% east of Mississippi River."

NEW ENGLAND PUBLISHING ASSOCIATES, INC., P.O. Box 5, Chester CT 06412. (203)345-READ. Fax: (203)345-3660. President: Elizabeth Frost Knappman. Vice President/Treasurer: Edward W. Knappman. Managing Editor: Larry Hand. Administrator: Susan Brainard Matterazzo. Editor: Victoria Harlow. Estab. 1982. Produces hardcover and trade paperback originals. 25% of books from first-time authors. Reports 2 months.
● Elizabeth Frost-Knappman's *ABC-Clio Companion to Women's Progress in America* was elected one of the outstanding academic reference books of 1994 by Choice, the Magazine of the American Library Association.
Recent Nonfiction Title: *The Gay and Lesbian Literary Heritage* (Holt).

OWL BOOKS, (formerly Greey De Pencier Books), 175 John St., Suite 500, Toronto, Ontario M5T 1A7 Canada. Editor-in-Chief: Sheba Meland. Estab. 1976. Produces hardcover and trade paperback originals. Averages 12 titles/year. Receives 100 queries and 500 mss/year. 15% of books from first-time authors; 80% from unagented writers. Pays royalty on retail price. Publishes book 18 months after acceptance of ms. Accepts simultaneous submissions. Query for electronic submissions. Reports in 3 months. Catalog and ms guidelines for #10 SAE with IRC. (No US stamps).
Nonfiction: Children's/juvenile. Subjects include animals, hobbies, nature/environment, science and science activities. "We are closely affiliated with the discovery-oriented children's magazines *Owl* and *Chickadee*, and concentrate on fresh, innovative nonfiction and picture books with nature/science themes, and quality children's craft/how-to titles." Submit proposal package, including outline, vita and 3 sample chapters. Reviews artwork/photos as part of ms package. Send photocopies or transparencies (not originals).
Fiction: Picture books. Submit complete ms.
Tips: "To get a feeling for our style of children's publishing, take a look at some of our recent books and at *Owl* and *Chickadee* magazines. We publish Canadian authors in the main, but will occasionally publish a work from outside Canada if it strikingly fits our list."

‡PARACHUTE PRESS, INC., 156 Fifth Ave., #325, New York NY 10010. (212)691-1421. Fax: (212)645-8769. Editoral Assistant: K. Pettit. Produces hardcover, trade paperback and mass market paperback originals. Averages 75 titles/year. Pays 3-4% royalty or makes outright purchase. Offers $3,500 average advance. Returns rejected submissions when time permits. Reports in 2 months.
● *Parachute Press* is specifically looking for middle grade writers, particularly middle grade horror.

Nonfiction: Juvenile. Subjects include animals, cooking/foods/nutrition and sports. Query. Reviews artwork/photos as part of ms package.
Fiction: Horror, juvenile and young adult. Submit proposal, résumé, publishing history and clips.

‡**THE PRESS OF MACDONALD & REINECKE**, Box 840, Arroya Grande CA 93421-0840. Phone/fax: (805)473-1947. Publisher: Karen L. Reinecke. Produces hardcover and trade paperback originals. Averages 3-4 titles/year. 80% of books from first-time authors; 70% from unagented writers. Advance varies. Reports in 6 weeks-6 months. Catalog and ms guidelines for #10 SAE with 2 first-class stamps.
Nonfiction: Biography, illustrated book, juvenile. Subjects include history, women's studies. Query.
Fiction: Historical, humor, juvenile, literary, plays, short stories, juveniles ages 8-14; no picture books or westerns. Query or submit complete ms.

PUBLICOM, INC., 409 Massachusetts Ave., Acton MA 01720. (508)263-5773. Fax: (508)263-7553. Vice President, Educational Materials: Patricia Moore. Packages textbooks, and produces hardcover and trade paperback originals under the imprint VanderWyke & Burnham. Averages 1-3 titles/year. 50% of books from first-time authors; 50% from unagented writers. "Work for hire" for textbooks; pays 3-10% royalty or makes variable outright purchase. Offers up to $3,000 advance for trade publishing. Query for electronic submissions. Reports in 6 months.
Nonfiction: Biography, how-to, illustrated book, juvenile, self-help, textbook. Subjects include business, child guidance/parenting, education, women's studies. Submit proposal, résumé, publishing history and clips.
Recent Nonfiction Title: *Something's Not Right: One Family's Struggle With Learning Disabilities*, by Nancy Lelewer.

SACHEM PUBLISHING ASSOCIATES, INC., P.O. Box 412, Guilford CT 06437-0412. (203)453-4328. Fax: (203)453-4320. President: Stephen P. Elliott. Estab. 1974. Produces hardcover originals. Averages 3 titles/year. 25% of books from first-time authors; 100% from unagented writers. Pays royalty or makes outright purchase. Query for electronic submissions. Reports in 1 month.
Nonfiction: Reference. Subjects include Americana, government/politics, history, military/war. Submit résumé and publishing history.

‡**SILVER MOON PRESS**, 126 Fifth Ave., #803, New York NY 10011. (212)242-6499. Fax: (212)242-6799. Editor: Eliza Booth. Produces hardcover originals. Produces 8-10 books/year. 10% of books from first-time authors; 90% from unagented writers. Book catalog free on request.
Nonfiction: Juvenile. Subjects include education, history, science, sports. Submit proposal. Reviews artwork/photos as part of ms package.
Recent Nonfiction Titles: *Melting Pots*, *Sportslab*, *Get Inside Baseball*.
Fiction: Historical, juvenile, mystery. Submit complete ms or submit proposal.
Recent Fiction Titles: *A Spy in the King's Colony*.

‡**SOMERVILLE HOUSE BOOKS LIMITED**, 3080 Yonge St., Suite 5000, Toronto Ontario M4N 3N1 Canada. Editorial Assistant: Anna Filippone. Produces trade paperback originals. Averages 6 titles/year. 5% of books from first-time authors; 5% from unagented writers. Reports in 4 months. Manuscript guidelines for #10 SASE with postage (Canadian or IRC).
Nonfiction: Subjects include religion, metaphysics. Query.
Recent Nonfiction Title: *Kids Are Worth It* (parenting).
Fiction: Literary, novels, short stories. Query.
Recent Fiction Title: *What You Need*, by Eliza Clark (romantic comedy).
Tips: "Remember that we publish very few adult fiction and nonfiction a year. And all those we have published have been agented, so far. Also, we do *not* accept manuscripts for children's books."

TENTH AVENUE EDITIONS, 625 Broadway, Suite 903, New York NY 10012. (212)529-8900. Fax: (212)529-7399. Managing Editor: Clive Giboire. Submissions Editor: Matthew Moore. Estab. 1984. Produces hardcover, trade paperback and mass market paperback originals. Averages 6 titles/year. Pays advance paid by publisher less our commission. Query for electronic submissions. Reports in 2 months.
Nonfiction: Biography, how-to, crafts, illustrated book, juvenile, catalogs. Subjects include music/dance, photography, women's issues/studies, art, children's. *Queries only.* Reviews artwork/photos as part of freelance ms package.
Tips: "Send query with publishing background. Return postage a must."

For information on setting your freelance fees, see How Much Should I Charge?

‡**THORSON & ASSOCIATES**, P.O. Box 94135, Washington MI 48094. (810)781-0907. Editorial Director: Timothy D. Thorson. Publishes hardcover and trade paperback originals. Produces 6-10 titles/year. 60% of books from first-time authors; 100% from unagented writers. Pays royalty or negotiates outright purchase on an individual basis. Query for electronic submissions. Reports in 1 month. Manuscript guidelines for #10 SAE with 2 first-class stamps.

Nonfiction: Illustrated book, juvenile, reference, software, technical. Subjects include Americana, anthropology, computer/electronics, history, hobbies, military/war, science. Specializes in architecture, history, automotive and military subjects. Query with résumé, publishing history and clips. Reviews artwork/photos as part of ms package.

Recent Nonfiction Titles: Three series of books: *Historic Horticulture*, *Masterpieces of Ancient Architecture*, *Automobiles in Profile*.

Tips: "Show us what you can do. We are very interested in working with experts in architecture, archeology, military and aviation history regardless of past writing experience."

2M COMMUNICATIONS LTD., 121 W. 27th St., New York NY 10001. (212)741-1509. Fax: (212)691-4460. Editorial Director: Madeleine Morel. Produces hardcover, trade paperback and mass market paperback originals. Averages 15 titles/year. 50% of books from first-time authors; 10% from unagented writers. Pays 7-15% royalty on wholesale price. Offers $15,000 advance. Reports in 2 weeks.

Nonfiction: Biography, coffee table book, cookbook, how-to, humor, illustrated book. Subjects include child guidance/parenting, cooking/foods/nutrition, ethnic, gay/lesbian, health, psychology, women's studies. Query or submit proposal with résumé and publishing history.

DANIEL WEISS ASSOCIATES, INC., 33 W. 17th St., 11th Floor, New York NY 10011. Fax: (212)645-3865. Editorial Assistant: Sigrid Berg. Estab. 1987. Produces mass market paperback originals. Averages 120 titles/year. 10% of books from first-time authors; 40% from unagented writers. Pays 1-4% royalty on retail price or makes outright purchase of $1,500-8,000 "depending on author's experience." Offers $1,500-8,000 advance. Reports in 2 months. Guidelines for #10 SASE.

Nonfiction: Adult, self-help. Submit outline, 2 sample chapters and SASE.

Fiction: Adventure, historical, horror, juvenile, romance, young adult. "All middle grade and YA. Mostly series fiction. Ask for guidelines prior to submission." Query with synopsis, 2 sample chapters and SASE.

THE WHEETLEY COMPANY, INC., 3201 Old Glenview Rd., Suite 300, Wilmette IL 60091-2942. (708)251-4422. Fax: (708)251-4668. Human Resources Manager: Linda Rogers. Estab. 1986. Produces hardcover originals for publishers of school, college and professional titles. Pays by the project. Query for electronic submissions. Does *not* return submissions, even those accompanied with SASE. Reports in 1 month.

Nonfiction: Technical, textbook. Subjects include animals, anthropology, art/architecture, business and economics, child guidance/parenting, computers/electronics, cooking/foods/nutrition, education, government/politics, health, history, language/literature, money/finance, music/dance, nature/environment, philosophy, psychology, recreation, regional, religion, science, sociology, sports, translation. Submit résumé and publishing history. Reviews artwork/photos as part of freelance ms package.

WIESER & WIESER, INC., 118 E. 25th St. New York NY 10010. (212)260-0860. Fax: (212)505-7186. Producer: George J. Wieser. Estab. 1976. Produces hardcover, trade paperback and mass market paperback originals. Averages 25 titles/year. 10% of books from first-time authors; 90% from unagented writers. Makes outright purchase of $5,000 or other arrangement. Offers $5,000 average advance. Reports in 2 weeks. *Writer's Market* recommends allowing 2 months for reply.

Nonfiction: Coffee table book. Subjects include Americana, cooking/foods/nutrition, gardening, health, history, hobbies, military/war, nature/environment, photography, recreation, sports, travel. Query. Reviews artwork/photos only as part of book package.

Tips: "Have an original idea and develop it completely before contacting us."

Subsidy/Royalty Book Publishers

In this section you'll find listings for U.S. book publishers that publish even a small percentage of their books on an author-subsidy basis.

Also known as "vanity presses," "co-publishers" or "cooperative publishers," they offer services ranging from editing and printing your book to distributing and promoting it. They are called "subsidy" publishers because they ask you, the author, to subsidize (pay for) all or part of the cost of publishing your book. Their prices can run as high as $25,000.

Letters making subsidy offers sometimes are the first and only encouraging correspondence writers receive about their book proposals. You should read with a grain of salt how much a publisher loves your book if they are asking you to pay for its production, marketing and/or distribution. Other letters express how much a publisher would like to publish a writer's book, if only they had sufficient funds. They ask if you, the author, would consider investing in a portion of the cost of the book's publication. These letters are often persuasive, and perhaps you will decide that co-publishing may be the route you want to take. Just be certain you know what you're getting into.

Full subsidy publishers often argue that the current economic climate necessitates authors paying the costs of publishing. Because subsidy publishers make a profit from authors by simply producing 1,000 or so bound books, they don't have a stake in marketing the books they publish. Royalty publishers, on the other hand, *must* sell books to make money because they have shouldered the publishing costs.

Before agreeing to a subsidy contract, ask yourself some questions. What would you do with 1,000 or even 500 copies of your book, if the distribution were left to you? How many do you realistically think you could sell? Few bookstores deal with individuals selling single books. Talk to a local bookstore owner before you sign a contract to see if they stock any titles by the publisher who wants to print your book.

In a co-publishing arrangement, the publisher will usually market its co-published books because it has paid part of the production cost, but writers have other concerns. How do you know the 50% you are paying is truly 50% of the total cost? If you are unsure, call a printer in your area and ask for an estimated cost of printing the type and number of books the publisher has proposed to you. If the printer's quote is significantly lower than the original figure you received, contact the publisher to discuss the matter.

Also at issue is your royalty arrangement. Often a writer is asked for up to half the cost to publish a book, and yet offered a royalty of less than 15%. Authors eager to have their books published find themselves adding up the number of sales they would need to break even. They forget that bookstores take 40-50% of the cover price for each copy they sell, and there are other charges: distributors, shippers and wholesalers all must be paid as well. Be realistic about what you think you could make back, and proceed cautiously.

Don't bow to pressure from any subsidy publisher who claims you must "act now" or the offer to publish may be withdrawn. Don't confuse subsidy publishers with royalty publishers. Unlike the relationship you might have with a royalty publisher, in which you attempt to earn their favor, you are a subsidy publisher's *customer*, not a supplicant.

And as a customer, you should approach the relationship as you would when considering the purchase of any other service—with a dose of skepticism and clear ideas about the contractual assurances you want to see. It is recommended that you consult with an attorney before signing any publishing contract.

If you are truly committed to your book and think there is a market for it, consider self-publishing as an option. It generally costs less than subsidy publishing for essentially the same services, and you have much more control over what is done with your book. For more information on self-publishing, take a look at *The Complete Guide to Self-Publishing*, by Tom and Marilyn Ross (Writer's Digest Books) or *The Publish It Yourself Handbook*, by Bill Henderson (Pushcart Press). In any case, proceed with caution any time a publisher is asking you to finance all or part of the cost of publication.

While we encourage writers to sell their work to royalty publishers, we have listed other book publishing options here. Publishers with full listings publish less than 50% of their books on a royalty basis. At the end of this section are the names and addresses of publishers producing more than 50% of their books on an author-subsidy basis.

For a list of publishers according to their subjects of interest, see the nonfiction and fiction sections of the Book Publishers Subject Index. Information on some book publishers and producers not included in this edition of *Writer's Market* can be found in Book Publishers and Producers/Changes '95-'96.

‡ACS PUBLICATIONS, Imprint of Astro Communications Services, Inc., 5521 Ruffin Rd., San Diego CA 92123. (619)492-9919. Editorial Director: Maritha Pottenger. Publishes trade paperback originals. Publishes 4 titles/year. Receives 200 queries and 20 mss/year. 20% of books from first-time authors; 90% from unagented writers. Subsidy publishes 5% of books. Pays 10-15% royalty on monies received. Publishes book 1 year after acceptance of ms. Accepts simultaneous submissions. Reports in 3 months on queries and proposals, 6 months on mss. Book catalog for #10 SAE and 2 first-class stamps. Manuscript guidelines free on request.
Nonfiction: Self-help, astrology. "Our focus is on personal empowerment through astrology. Forget 'Saturn made me do it.' An astrology of *choice* and *power*." Query with SASE.
Recent Nonfiction Title: *Your Magical Child*, by Maria Kay Simms (astrology/childcare).
Tips: Audience is general public, students and astrological professionals interested in enhancing their lives through use of astrology. "Be clear about whether your work fits the firm you're targeting. Read some of our books *before* submitting to us."

ALPINE PUBLICATIONS, INC., 225 S. Madison Ave., Loveland CO 80537-6514. (303)667-9317. Publisher: B.J. McKinney. Estab. 1975. Publishes hardcover and trade paperback originals. Averages 6 titles/year. Occasional advances. Pays 7-15% royalty. Publishes book 18 months after acceptance. Reports in 2-4 months. Writer's guidelines for #10 SASE.
● Alpine Publications, Inc. has published recent winners of the Dog Writers Association of America Best Breed, Best Care & Health and Best Juvenile Book Awards. Cat Writers Association nomination—Best Breed Book.
Nonfiction: How-to books about companion animals. "We need comprehensive dog breed books on the more popular AKC breeds, books on showing, breeding, genetics, gait, care, new training methods, and cat and horse books. No fiction or fictionalized stories; no books on reptiles; no personal experience stories except in case of well-known professional in field." Submit outline and sample chapters. Reviews artwork/photos as part of ms package.
Recent Nonfiction Title: *The Coloring Atlas of Horse Anatomy*, by Kainer, D.V.M. & McCracken.

‡M. ARMAN PUBLISHING, INC., P.O. Box 785, Ormond Beach FL 32175. (904)673-5576. Contact: Mike Arman. Estab. 1978. Publishes trade paperback originals, reprints and software. Averages 6-8 titles/year. Receives 20 submissions/year. 20% of books from first-time authors; 100% of books from unagented writers. Average print order for a first book is 2,500. Subsidy publishes 20% of books. Pays 10% royalty on wholesale price. No advance. Publishes book (on royalty basis) 8 months after acceptance; 6 weeks on subsidy basis. Query for electronic submissions. Reports in 3 weeks on mss. *Writer's Market* recommends allowing 2 months for reply. Book catalog for #10 SASE.
Nonfiction: How-to, reference, technical, textbook. "Motorcycle technical books only." Accepts nonfiction translations. Publishes for enthusiasts. Submit complete ms. Reviews artwork/photos as part of ms package.

Recent Nonfiction Title: *V-Twin Thunder*, by Carl McClanahan (motorcycle performance manual).
Tips: "The type of book a writer has the best chance of selling to our firm is how to fix motorcycles—specifically Harley-Davidsons. We have a strong, established market for these books."

ASHGATE PUBLISHING COMPANY, Old Post Rd., Brookfield VT 05036. (802)276-3651. Fax: (802)276-3837. President: James W. Gerard. Estab. 1978. Imprints include Ashgate, Avebury, Avebury Technical, Scolar, Varorium. Publishes hardcover originals and reprints and trade paperback originals. Averages 250 titles/year. Receives 100 submissions/year. 25% of books from first-time authors; 100% from unagented writers. Subsidy publishes 10% of books. Pays royalty on retail price or makes outright purchase. Publishes book 3 months after acceptance. Accepts simultaneous submissions. Query for electronic submissions. Reports in 2 months.
Nonfiction: Reference, technical, textbook. Subjects include art/architecture, business and economics, government/politics, money/finance, philosophy, sociology. Submit outline and sample chapters.

THE BOXWOOD PRESS, 183 Ocean View Blvd., Pacific Grove CA 93950. (408)375-9110. Fax: (408)375-0430. Editor: Dr. Ralph Buchsbaum. Imprints include Viewpoint Books, Free Spirit Books. Publishes hardcover and trade paperback originals. Averages 5 titles/year. Receives 25 submissions/year. Subsidy publishes 25% of books. Determines subsidy by high merit; low market. Pays 10% royalty. Publishes book 10 months after acceptance. Query for electronic submissions. Reports in 6 weeks on queries, 2 months on mss. Book catalog free on request.
Nonfiction: Biography, technical, textbook. Subjects include biology (plants and animals), health/medicine, history, nature/environment, philosophy, psychology, regional or area studies and other science. Submit complete ms. Reviews artwork/photos as part of ms package.
Tips: "Writers have the best chance selling us sound science and natural history books. Our audience is high school and college, general and educated. If I were a writer trying to market a book today, I would know my subject, readership and do my clearest writing."

‡BR ANCHOR PUBLISHING, P.O. Box 176, Hellertown PA 18055. (610)865-5331. Fax: (610)865-4021. Publisher: Beverly Roman. Publishes trade paperback and mass market paperback originals and reprints. Subsidy publishes 50% of books. " We publish primarily relocation books and newsletters. Authors pay for design, publishing and printing." Recent title: *A Winning Game Plan*, by Brent Williams (adult relocation).

BRIARCLIFF PRESS PUBLISHERS, 11 Wimbledon Ct., Jericho NY 11753. Editorial Director: Trudy Settel. Senior Editor: J. Frieman. Estab. 1977. Publishes hardcover and paperback originals. Averages 5-7 titles/year. Receives 250 submissions/year. 10% of books from first-time authors; 60% from unagented writers. Average print order for a first book is 5,000. Subsidy publishes 20% of books. Makes outright purchase of $4,000-5,000. Offers $1,000 average advance. Publishes book 6 months after acceptance. Reports in 3 months. Catalog for 9×12 SAE with 3 first-class stamps.
Nonfiction: How-to, cookbooks, sports, travel, fitness/health, business and finance, diet, gardening, crafts. "We want our books to be designed to meet the needs of specific businesses." Accepts nonfiction translations from French, German and Italian. Query or submit outline and 2 sample chapters. Reviews artwork/photos as part of ms package.
Tips: "We do not use unsolicited manuscripts. Ours are custom books prepared for businesses, and assignments are initiated by us."

BRIDGE PUBLISHING, 2500 Hamilton Blvd., South Plainfield NJ 07080. (908)754-0745. Editor: Catherine J. Barrier. Imprints are Logos, Bridge, Haven, Open Scroll. Publishes hardcover, trade paperback and mass market paperback originals and reprints. Publishes 50 titles/year; imprint publishes 12 titles/year. Receives 1,000 queries and 300 mss/year. 50% of books from first-time authors; 80% from unagented writers. Subsidy publishes 20% of books. Pays 10-20% royalty on net price. Offers $1,000-25,000 advance. Publishes book 4 months after acceptance of ms. Accepts simultaneous submissions. Query for electronic submissions. Reports in 3 months on proposals. Book catalog and ms guidelines free on request.
Nonfiction: Biography, coffee table books, juvenile, self-help, textbook, young adult/teen. Subjects include religion. "We are a flexible, dedicated Christian publisher. We are particularly interested in materials for Christian evangelism, spiritual growth, education and self-help." Query with brief synopsis (500-600 words), detailed and concise chapter-by-chapter outline, author bio information (including ministry involvements),

any marketing ideas and 3 sample chapters. Reviews artwork/photos as part of ms package. Send photocopies.
Recent Nonfiction Title: *An Instrument of Revival: The Complete Life of Evan Roberts*, by Brynmor Pierce Jones (biography)
Fiction: Religious. Query or submit synopsis and 3 sample chapters.

ARISTIDE D. CARATZAS, PUBLISHER, Box 210/30 Church St., New Rochelle NY 10801. (914)632-8487. Fax: (914)636-3650. Managing Editor: Evanthia Allen. Estab. 1975. Publishes hardcover originals and reprints. Averages 20 titles/year. Receives 100 submissions/year. 35% of books from first-time authors; 80% from unagented writers. Subsidy publishes 25% of books. "We seek grants/subsidies for limited run scholarly books; granting organizations are generally institutions or foundations." Pays royalty. Offers $1,500 average advance. Publishes book 18 months after acceptance. Accepts simultaneous submissions. Query for electronic submissions. Reports in 1 month on queries. *Writer's Market* recommends allowing 2 months for reply. Book catalog free.
Nonfiction: Reference, technical, textbook. Subjects include art, history (ancient, European, Russian), politics, religion, travel, classical languages (Greek and Latin), archaeology and mythology. Nonfiction book ms needs for the next year include "scholarly books in archaeology, mythology, ancient and medieval history, and art history." Query with sample chapters. Reviews artwork/photos as part of ms package.

‡CAREER ADVANCEMENT CENTER, P.O. Box 436, Woodmere NY 11598. Publicist: Arthur Van Dam. Publishes trade paperback originals. Publishes 2-3 titles/year. 50% of mss from first-time authors, 80% from unagented writers. Pays 6-10% royalty on retail price. Publishes book 8-10 months after acceptance. Accepts simultaneous submissions. Query for electronic submissions, but prefers hard copy. Book catalog and ms guidelines for #10 SASE.
Nonfiction: How-to, self-help. Subjects include business and economics, money/finance, career development. "Get in touch with the (intended) target market and make sure the book fits." Query with résumé, outline and 3 sample chapters, or send complete ms. Responds in 3 months. Reviews artwork/photos as part of ms package. Send photocopies "if applicable."
Recent Nonfiction Title: *Personal Budget Planner*, by Eric Gelb (how-to).
Tips: "Audience is mass market. We are a marketing firm. We publish general interest, user-friendly how-to books which are easy to read. Usually anecdotal! We expect our published authors to actively market their books through lectures, writing articles and radio appearances."

THE CENTER FOR WESTERN STUDIES, Augustana College, Box 727, Sioux Falls SD 57197. (605)336-4007. Managing Editor: Harry F. Thompson. Publishes hardcover and trade paperback originals and reprints. Publishes 2-3 titles/year. Receives 25-30 queries and 10-12 mss/year. 50% of books from first-time authors; 90% from unagented writers. Subsidy publishes 25% of books. Pays 7-10% royalty on wholesale price and copies of publication for resale. Publishes book 8 months after acceptance. Accepts simultaneous submissions. Reports in 2 months on queries, 4 months on proposals, 6-12 months on mss. Book catalog free on request.
Nonfiction: Biography, coffee table book, reference, textbook. Subjects include anthropology/archaeology, art/architecture, ethnic, history, regional, translation. "We are a small house, a program closely connected with the other activities of the Center for Western Studies, such as museum interpretation, archives, and Northern Plains/Western cultures. Most of our titles have foundation or commercial backing." Query with outline and 2 sample chapters.
Fiction: Historical, short story collections, western. "We are not especially interested in fiction, but would consider fiction that relates directly to the Northern Plains region." Query with synopsis and 3 sample chapters.

THE CHARLES PRESS, PUBLISHERS., P.O. Box 15715, Philadelphia PA 19103. (215)545-8933 or 545-8934. Fax: (215)545-8937. Also 1314 Chestnut St., Suite 200, Philadelphia, PA 19107. Editor-in-Chief: Lauren Meltzer. Estab. 1983. Publishes hardcover and trade paperback originals and reprints. Publishes 12-15 titles/year. Receives 300 queries and 100 mss/year. 20% of books from first-time authors; 100% from unagented writers. Subsidy publishes 1% of books "but we plan to increase this. If the project is for one reason or another, very high risk, then we would consider this." Pays 7½-10% royalty on gross monies received. Publishes book 6-12 months after acceptance of ms. Accepts simultaneous submissions. Query for electronic submission: prefers IBM-compatible—WordPerfect/MicroSoft Word, WordPerfect or Word for Windows. Reports in 3 months on proposals.
Nonfiction: How-to, coping. Subjects include health/medicine, psychology of illness, grief. Query.
Recent Nonfiction Title: *Now I Lay Me Down: Suicide in the Elderly*, by David Lester.

‡CHELSEA GREEN PUBLISHING CO., P.O. Box 428, #205 Gates-Briggs Bldg., White River Junction VT 05001. (802)295-6300. Editor-in-Chief: Jim Schley. Imprint is The Real Goods Independent Living Series. Publishes hardcover originals and trade paperback originals and reprints. Publishes 4-6 titles/year; imprint publishes 3-4 titles/year. Receives 1,000 queries and 600 mss/year. 10% of books from first-time authors; 60% from unagented writers. Pays royalty on publisher's net. Publishes book within 2 years after acceptance

of ms. Reports in 1-2 months on proposals and mss. Manuscript guidelines for 4×9 SASE.
Nonfiction: Biography, how-to, technical. Subjects include agriculture/horticulture, gardening, nature/environment. "Connection to environmental issues must be explicit and compelling." Query with outline, 2 sample chapters, clippings from previous publications and SASE.
Recent Nonfiction Title: *The Independent Home*, by Michael Potts (home ecology).

THE CHRISTOPHER PUBLISHING HOUSE, 24 Rockland St., Commerce Green, Hanover MA 02339-0024. (617)826-7474. Fax: (617)826-5556. Managing Editor: Nancy Lucas. Estab. 1910. Publishes hardcover and trade paperback originals. Averages 10-20 titles/year. Receives 400-500 submissions/year. 30% of books from first-time authors; 100% from unagented writers. Subsidy publishes 15% of books. Pays 5-30% royalty on net proceeds. No advance. Publishes book 12-15 months after acceptance. Accepts simultaneous submissions. Query for electronic submissions. Reports in 2 months. Book catalog for #10 SAE with 2 first-class stamps. Manuscript guidelines for SASE.
Nonfiction: Biography, how-to, reference, self-help, textbook. Subjects include Americana, animals, art, business and economics, cooking/foods/nutrition, health, history, philosophy, politics, psychology, religion, sociology, travel. "We will be glad to review all nonfiction manuscripts, particularly college textbook and religious-oriented." Submit complete ms. *Writer's Market* recommends query with SASE first. Reviews artwork/photos as part of ms package.
Poetry: "We will review all forms of poetry." Submit complete ms.
Recent Poetry Title: *Heartbeats*, by Ron J. Flemming.
Tips: "Our books are for a general audience, slanted toward college-educated readers. There are specific books targeted toward specific audiences when appropriate."

CLEANING CONSULTANT SERVICES, INC., P.O. Box 1273, Seattle WA 98111. (206)682-9748. President: William R. Griffin. Publishes trade paperback originals and reprints. Averages 4-6 titles/year. Receives 15 submissions/year. 75% of books from first-time authors; 100% from unagented writers. Subsidy publishes 5% of books. "If they (authors) won't sell it and won't accept royalty contract, we offer our publishing services and often sell the book along with our books." Pays 5-15% royalty on retail price or makes outright purchase of $100-2,500, depending on negotiated agreement. Publishes book 6-12 months after acceptance. Reports in 6 weeks on queries. Book catalog free. Manuscript guidelines for SASE.
Nonfiction: How-to, illustrated book, reference, self-help, technical, textbook, directories. Subjects include business, health, cleaning and maintenance. Needs books on anything related to cleaning, maintenance, self-employment or entrepreneurship. Query or submit outline and sample chapters. Reviews artwork/photos as part of ms package.
Tips: "Our audience includes those involved in cleaning and maintenance service trades, opportunity seekers, schools, property managers, libraries—anyone who needs information on cleaning and maintenance. How-to and self-employment guides are doing well for us in today's market. We are now seeking books on fire damage restoration and also technical articles for *Cleaning Business Magazine*, a quarterly. We are also interested in video or audio tapes, software and games that are specific to the cleaning industry."

COLLEGE PRESS PUBLISHING CO., INC., P.O. Box 1132, Joplin MO 64802-1132. (417)623-6280. Fax: (417)623-8250. Contact: John M. Hunter. Estab. 1958. Publishes hardcover and trade paperback originals and reprints. Publishes 25 titles/year. Receives 400 submissions/year. 25% of books from first-time authors; 95% from unagented writers. Subsidy publishes 5% of books. Subsidy considered "if we really want to publish a book, but don't have room in schedule at this time or funds available." Pays 10% royalty on net receipts. Publishes book 1 year after acceptance. Accepts simultaneous submissions. Reports on queries in 2 months. Book catalog for 9×12 SAE with 5 first-class stamps.
Nonfiction: Bible commentaries, topical Bible studies. (Christian Church, Church of Christ.) Query.
Recent Nonfiction Title: *Redeeming the Time: The Christian Walk in a Hurried World*, by Philip Patterson.
Fiction: Religious. No poetry. Query.
Tips: "Topical Bible study books have the best chance of being sold to our firm. Our audience consists of Christians interested in reading and studying Bible-based material."

‡COLONIAL PRESS, 3325 Burning Tree Dr., Birmingham AL 35226. (205)822-6654. President: Carl Murray. Estab. 1957. Publishes hardcover and trade paperback originals and reprints. Publishes 15-20 titles/year. Receives 800-1,000 queries/year. 90% of books from first-time authors; 100% from unagented writers. Subsidy publishes 25% of books. Pays 10-50% royalty net wholesale, based on percentage of author investment books. Publishes book 3 months after acceptance of ms. Accepts simultaneous submissions. Prefers camera ready copy. Reports in 3 months on queries.
Nonfiction: Biography, cookbook, humor, illustrated book, self-help, technical, textbook (pre-school to college). Subjects include business and economics, cooking/foods/nutrition, education, ethnic, government/politics, history, language/literature, music/dance, philosophy, psychology, regional, science, sociology, translation. Query.
Fiction: Ethnic, historical, humor, juvenile, picture books, plays, short story collections, young adult, gerontology, nutrition. "We are sympathetic and willing to look and see before we say no." Query.

Recent Fiction Title: *The Extinction of the Species,* by Robert Sims.
Poetry: "Just send us a little sample—two to five poems, short biographical sketch and telephone number."
Query.
Tips: "We publish several textbooks. We like lab manuals and worktext. We welcome good writers. If a good writer has a fresh idea and cannot find a publisher—contact us."

CONSORTIUM PUBLISHING, 640 Weaver Hill Rd., West Greenwich RI 02817-2261. Chief of Publications: John Carlevale. Estab. 1990. Publishes 10-12 titles/year. Receives 30 queries and 25 mss/year. 50% of books from first-time authors; 90% from unagented writers. Subsidy publishes 5% of books. Pays royalty. Publishes book 2-3 months after acceptance. Accepts simultaneous submissions. Query for electronic submissions. Reports in 1 month on queries, 1-2 months on proposals and mss. Book catalog and ms guidelines free on request.
Nonfiction: Biography, self-help, technical, textbook. Subjects include child guidance/parenting, education, health/medicine, language/literature, music/dance, psychology, science, sociology. Query.
Fiction: Juvenile. Query.

‡COVENANT COMMUNICATIONS, INC., P.O. Box 416, American Fork UT 84003. (801)756-9966. Managing Editor: JoAnn Jolley. Hardcover and trade paperback originals and reprints. Publishes 40 titles/year. Receives 200 queries/year. 80% of books from first-time authors; 100% from unagented writers. Subsidy publishes 5% of books. Pays 6½-10% royalty on retail price. Advance varies. Publishes book 6-8 months after acceptance of ms. Reports in 2 months on mss. Book catalog and ms guidelines free on request.
Nonfiction: Biography, Americana, child guidance/parenting, ethnic, history (Mormon), philosophy (Mormon), regional, religion, software, Mormon issues. "We began as strictly a publisher of Latter-day Saint (Mormon) material but are gradually expanding the scope while maintaining a highly moral emphasis." Query. Reviews artwork/photos as part of ms package. Send photocopies.
Recent Nonfiction Title: *As I Have Loved You,* by Kitty De Ruyter (inspirational wartime experiences).
Fiction: Adventure, ethnic, fantasy, historical, humor, juvenile, literary, mainstream/contemporary, mystery, religious, romance, science fiction, suspense, western, young adult. Submit synopsis and 3-5 sample chapters.
Recent Fiction Title: *First and Forever,* by Anita Stansfield (contemporary romance).
Tips: All of Covenant's publications are in harmony with principles of The Church of Jesus Christ of Latter-day Saints (Mormon Church).

CREATIVE ARTS BOOK COMPANY, 833 Bancroft Way, Berkeley CA 94710. (415)848-4777. Fax: (510)848-4844. Publisher: Donald S. Ellis. Senior Editor: George Samsa. Estab. 1976. Publishes hardcover and paperback originals and paperback reprints. Averages 20 titles/year. Receives 800-1,000 submissions/year. 10% from first-time authors; 20% from unagented writers. Subsidy publishes 5% of books. Pays 5-15% royalty on retail price. Offers $500 minimum advance. Publishes book 12-18 months after acceptance. Accepts simultaneous submissions. Reports in 2 months. Book catalog free.
Nonfiction: Biographies, essays. Especially interested in music, works on California and New York and minorities (African-Americans, Chicanos and Asians). *Writer's Market* recommends query with SASE first.
Recent Nonfiction Title: *Improvisation: Music From the Inside Out* (music).
Fiction: "Looking for serious literary fiction of broad appeal," especially books by and/or about women, crime and western fiction. *Writer's Market* recommends query with SASE first.
Recent Fiction Title: *Miss Coffin and Mrs. Blood* (poetry).

DISCOVERY ENTERPRISES, LTD., 134 Middle St., Suite 210, Lowell MA 01852-1815. (508)459-1720. Executive Director: JoAnne B. Weisman. Estab. 1989. Publishes hardcover and trade paperback originals. Publishes 10-12 titles/year. Receives 500 queries and 100 mss/year. 25% of books from first-time authors; 100% from unagented writers. Subsidy publishes 10% of books. Pays 6-10% royalty. Offers $500-750 advance. Publishes book 6-9 months after acceptance. Accepts simultaneous submissions. Reports in 6 months. Book catalog and ms guidelines for #10 SASE.
Nonfiction: History and science (inventors only) books for grades 5-12 and educational manuals; classroom plays for grades 5-8 (historical only). Subjects include education (teachers curriculum guides in social studies), history (American history series, including primary and secondary source materials—ages 10-18). Query with résumé and outline. Send photocopies.
Tips: "Query first, and then if asked, send sample chapters. Work must be neat, double-spaced, and must have a post-paid return envelope. We are only considering history and science writers for 1995-1997."

‡E.M. PRESS, INC., P.O. Box 4057, Manassas VA 22110. (703)439-0304. Publisher/Editor: Beth A. Miller. Publishes hardcover and trade paperback originals. Publishes 8 titles/year. Receives 3,000 queries and 1,000 mss/year. 50% of books from first-time authors; 100% from unagented writers. Subsidy publishes 10% of books. Pays 6-10% royalty on wholesale price. Offers $50-250 advance. Publishes book 1 year after acceptance of ms. Accepts simultaneous submissions. Reports in 2 months. Book catalog and ms guidelines for #10 SASE.

Nonfiction: Biography, children's/juvenile, humor, self-help. Subjects include Americana, animals, health/medicine, psychology, religion. Submit outline and 2 sample chapters with SASE. Reviews artwork/photos as part of ms package. Send photocopies.

Recent Nonfiction Title: *Merchants of Sex, Sin & Salvation*, by Jim Cornick (religious essay).

Fiction: Adventure, humor, literary, mainstream/contemporary, mystery, science fiction, young adult. "We are expanding and diversifying, within our budget." Query with synopsis, 2 sample chapters and SASE.

Recent Fiction Title: *Death Gods of Applevale*, by Tom O. Jones (folktale).

Poetry: Limited use of poetry. Query.

Recent Poetry Title: *Graves of the Poets*, by H.R. Coursen (traditional).

EDICIONES UNIVERSAL, P.O. Box 450353, Miami FL 33245-0353. (305)642-3355. Fax: (305)642-7978. Director: Juan M. Salvat. General Manager: Martha Salvat-Golik. Estab. 1965. Publishes trade paperback originals in Spanish. Publishes 50 titles/year. Receives 150 submissions/year. 40% of books from first-time authors; 90% from unagented writers. Subsidy publishes 10% of books. Pays 5-10% royalty on retail price. Publishes book 9 months after acceptance. Accepts simultaneous submissions. Reports in 1 month on queries. *Writer's Market* recommends allowing 2 months for reply. Book catalog free on request.

Nonfiction: Biography, cookbook, humor, reference. Subjects include cooking/foods, philosophy, politics, psychology, sociology. "We specialize in Cuban topics." All mss must be in Spanish. Submit outline and sample chapters. Reviews artwork/photos as part of ms package.

Fiction: "We will consider everything as long as it is written in Spanish." Submit synopsis and sample chapters.

Poetry: "We will consider any Spanish-language poetry." Submit 3 or more poems.

Tips: "Our audience is composed entirely of Spanish-language readers. This is a very limited market. Books on Cuban or Latin American topics have the best chance of selling to our firm."

WILLIAM B. EERDMANS PUBLISHING CO., 255 Jefferson Ave. SE, Grand Rapids MI 49503. (616)459-4591. Fax: (616)459-6540. Editor-in-Chief: Jon Pott. Assistant to the Editor: Anne Salsich. Managing Editor: Charles Van Hof. Children's Book Editor: Amy Eerdmans. Estab. 1911. Publishes hardcover and paperback originals and reprints. Averages 120-130 titles/year. Receives 1,500-2,000 submissions/year. 10% from first-time authors; 95% from unagented writers. Average print order for a first book is 4,000. Subsidy publishes 1% of books. Pays 7½-10% royalty on retail price. No advance usually. Publishes book 1 year after acceptance. Accepts simultaneous submissions if noted. Reports in 3-6 weeks for queries. *Writer's Market* recommends allowing 2 months for reply. Book catalog free.

Nonfiction: Religious, reference, textbooks, monographs, children's books. Subjects include ethics, religious literature, history, philosophy, psychology, religion, sociology, regional history, geography. "Approximately 80% of our publications are religious and largely of the more academic or theological variety (as opposed to the devotional, inspirational or celebrity-conversion books). Our history and social issues titles aim, similarly, at an educated audience. We prefer that writers take the time to notice if we have published anything at all in the same category as their manuscript before sending it to us." Accepts nonfiction translations. Query with outline, 2-3 sample chapters and SASE for return of ms. Reviews artwork/photos.

Recent Nonfiction Title: *Not the Way It's Supposed to Be: A Breviary of Sin*, by Cornelius Plantinga, Jr.

Tips: "We look for quality and relevance."

GARDNER PRESS, INC., 6801 Lake Worth Rd., #104, Lake Worth FL 33467. Phone/fax: (407)964-9700. Publisher: G. Spungin. Publishes hardcover and trade paperback originals and reprints. Publishes 20 titles/year. Receives 300 queries and 200 mss/year. 15% of books from first-time authors; 95% from unagented writers. Subsidy publishes 5% of books. Pays 5-10% royalty on wholesale price or makes outright purchase. Publishes book 8 months after acceptance. Accepts simultaneous submissions. Reports in 1 month on queries. Book catalog free. Manuscript guidelines for SAE with 2 first-class stamps.

Nonfiction: Biography, humor, reference, self-help, technical, textbook. Subjects include business and economics, child guidance/parenting, education, health/medicine, nature/environment, psychology, sociology, sports, women's issues/studies. Query with outline, 2 sample chapters and SASE.

Recent Nonfiction Title: *Chinese Fables & Wisdom*, by Tom Ma (self-help).

GENEALOGICAL PUBLISHING CO., INC., 1001 N. Calvert St., Baltimore MD 21202-3897. (410)837-8271. Fax: (410)752-8492. Editor-in-Chief: Michael H. Tepper, Ph.D. Estab. 1959. Imprint is Clearfield Co. Estab. 1959. Publishes hardcover originals and reprints. Subsidy publishes 10% of books. Averages 80 titles/year. Receives 400 submissions/year. 50% of books from first-time authors; 100% from unagented writers. Average print order for a first book is 2,000-3,000. Offers 10% royalty on retail price. Publishes book 6 months after acceptance. Reports in 3 months. Enclose SAE and return postage.

Nonfiction: Reference, genealogy, immigration records. "Our requirements are unusual, so we usually treat each author and his subject in a way particularly appropriate to his special skills and subject matter. Guidelines are flexible, but it is expected that an author will consult with us in depth. Most, though not all, of our original publications are offset from camera-ready typescript. Since most genealogical reference works are compilations of vital records and similar data, tabular formats are common. We hope to receive more manuscript material covering vital records and ships' passenger lists. We want family history compendia, basic methodology in genealogy, heraldry, and immigration records." Prefers query first, but will look at outline and sample chapter. Reviews artwork/photos as part of ms package.

THE GRADUATE GROUP, 86 Norwood Rd., West Hartford CT 06117-2236. (203)232-3100. President: Mara Whitman. Vice President: Robert Whitman. Estab. 1964. Publishes 25 titles/year. Receives 40 queries/ year. Subsidy publishes 5% of books. Reports in 1 month. Fliers free on request.
Nonfiction: Reference, career/internships. Subjects include career/internship. Query.
Tips: "Our audience is career planning offices and college and law school and medical and public libraries. We are a small publishing company that specializes in career planning and internship-related publications. Reference books that help students with their career. We are very anxious to get proposals from authors on books for use in public libraries, college career planning offices or college, law school, medical school libraries. Also books of interest to graduate students."

‡GUILD BINDERY PRESS, INC., P.O. 38099, Memphis TN 38183. (901)758-8577. President: Randall Bedwell. Publishes hardcover and trade paperback originals. Publishes 15 titles/year. 75% of books from first-time authors; 95% from unagented writers. Subsidy publishes 20% of books. Pays 8-18% royalty. Offers $2,000-5,000 advance. Publishes book 8 months after acceptance of ms. Accepts simultaneous submissions. Reports in 2 months on mss. Book catalog and ms guidelines free on request.
Nonfiction: Biography, coffee table book. Subjects include business and economics, history, regional. Query.
Recent Nonfiction Title: *In the Shadow of the Wall*, by Carsten Kaaz (history/cultural anthropology).
Fiction: Adventure, literary, mainstream/contemporary. "We're not looking for Southern writers, we're looking for writers from the South." Query.
Recent Fiction Title: *Intentional Harm*, by Stephen Gipson, MD.

HAMPTON ROADS PUBLISHING COMPANY, INC., 976 Norfolk Sq., Norfolk VA 23502-3209. (804)459-2453. Fax: (804)455-8907. Publisher: Robert S. Friedman. Vice President: Frank DeMarco. Estab.1989. Publishes hardcover and trade paperback originals and reprints. Publishes 20 titles/year. Receives 450 queries and 325 mss/year. 25% of books from first-time authors; 50% from unagented writers. Subsidy decision determined by market risk. Pays 8-15% royalty on wholesale/retail price. Offers advance. Publishes book 3-18 months after acceptance of ms. Accepts simultaneous submissions. Query for electronic submissions. Does not return submissions without SASE. Book catalog for 9×12 SAE with 3 first-class stamps.
Nonfiction: Concentration on "self-help metaphysics" (New Age and spiritual subjects in general). Query first. Reviews artwork/photos as part of ms package. Send photocopies.
Recent Nonfiction Title: *Magic and Loss*, by Greg Raver Lampman (inspirational).
Fiction: Literary, mainstream, metaphysical. Submit entire ms.

‡HARIAN CREATIVE BOOKS, 47 Hyde Blvd., Ballston Spa NY 12020-1607. (518)885-7397. Publisher: Dr. Harry Barba. Estab. 1967. Imprints include Barba-cue Specials, What's Cookin, The Harian Press. Estab. 1967. Publishes hardcover and trade paperback originals, mass market paperback originals and reprints. Publishes 3-5 titles/year. Receives 300-500 submissions/year. Subsidy publishes 10% of books. Pays 10-15% on retail price. Publishes book 1 year after acceptance. Accepts simultaneous submissions. Reports in 1 month on queries. *Writer's Market* recommends allowing 2 months for reply. Book catalog materials and sample copy of book $10. Manuscript guidelines for #10 SASE.
Nonfiction: Coffee table book, cookbook, humor, self-help. Subjects include Americana, education, language/literature, recreation and regional. Query with SASE.
Fiction: Adventure, experimental, humor, literary, mainstream/contemporary, contemporary romance, short story collections. Query with SASE.

HARMONY HOUSE PUBLISHERS, P.O. Box 90, Prospect KY 40026. (502)228-4446. Fax: (502)228-2010. Contact: William Strode. Estab. 1980. Publishes hardcover originals. Publishes 20 titles/year. Subsidy publishes 8% of books. Pays royalty. Offers advance. Publishes book 18 months after acceptance of ms. Accepts simultaneous submissions. Query for electronic submissions. Reports in 2 months on proposals.
Nonfiction: Coffee table book, cookbook, illustrated book. Subjects include animals, education, military/war, nature/environment, photography, sports. Query. Reviews artwork/photos as part of ms package. Send photocopies or transparencies.

HAWKES PUBLISHING, INC., 5947 South 350 West, Murray UT 84107. (801)266-5555. Fax: (801)266-5599. President: John Hawkes. Editor: Shanna J. Smith. Estab. 1965. Publishes mostly trade paperback originals. Averages 24 titles/year. Receives 200 submissions/year. 70% of books from first-time authors; 90% from unagented writers. Subsidy publishes 25-50% of books/year based on "how promising they are." Pays varying royalty of 10% on retail price to 10% on wholesale. No advance. Publishes book 6 months after acceptance. Submit complete ms. Reports in 3 weeks on queries. Book catalog free.
Nonfiction: Cookbook, how-to, self-help. Subjects include cooking/foods, health, history, hobbies, psychology. Query or submit complete ms. Reviews artwork/photos.

HEART OF THE LAKES PUBLISHING, P.O. Box 299, Interlaken NY 14847-0299. (607)532-4997. Fax: (607)532-4684. Contact: Walter Steesy. Estab. 1976. Imprints include Empire State Books, Windswept Press. Publishes hardcover and trade paperback originals and reprints. Averages 20-25 titles/year. Receives 20 submissions/year. 100% of books from unagented writers. Average print order for a first book is 500-1,000. Subsidy publishes 10% of books, "depending on type of material and potential sales." 15% author subsidized; 35% nonauthor subsidized. Payment is "worked out individually." Publishes book 1-2 years after acceptance. Accepts simultaneous submissions. Query for electronic submissions. Reports in 1 month. *Writer's Market* recommends allowing 2 months for reply. Current books flier for #10 SAE with 2 first-class stamps.
Nonfiction: New York state and regional, history, genealogy source materials. Query. Reviews artwork/photos.
Fiction: Done only at author's expense.

‡HONOR BOOKS, INC., P.O. Box 55388, Tulsa OK 74155. (918)496-9007. Acquisitions Assistant: Krista Dalrymple. Publishes hardcover, trade paperback and mass market paperback originals. Publishes 30 titles/year. 20% of books from first-time authors; 99% from unagented writers. Subsidy publishes 5% of books. Pays 5-15% royalty on wholesale price or negotiates outright purchase. Publishes book 18 months after acceptance. Accepts simultaneous submissions. Reports in 2 months. Manuscript guidelines free.
Nonfiction: Coffee table book, gift book, humor, inspirational, motivational. Subjects include business (Christian), child guidance/parenting, money/finance, religion (Christian). women's issues/studies. "Our goal is to publish quality, scriptually-based motivational and inspirational gift products that incorporate Christian values into every area of an individual's life. Send book proposals that can be formatted for a gift market, that inspires readers to apply biblical wisdom to their daily lives. No testimony, or chapter teaching books, but nuggets and devotional books are encouraged." Query or submit outline, table of contents, 1-2 sample pages and bio. SASE. Reviews artwork/photos as part of ms package. Send photocopies.
Recent Nonfiction Title: *Mama's Rules for Livin'*, by Mamie McCullough.
Tips: "Submit short and concise proposals stating what makes their topic different from other books on the same topic."

‡HUMANITIES PRESS INTERNATIONAL, INC., 165 First Ave., Atlantic Highlands NJ 07716-1289. (908)872-1441. Fax: (908)872-0717. President: Keith M. Ashfield. Contact: Cindy Nixon. Estab. 1951. Imprints are Humanities Press and The Caslon Company. Publishes hardcover originals and trade paperback originals and reprints. Averages 35-50 titles/year. Receives 500 submissions/year. 5% of books from first-time authors; 80% from unagented writers. Subsidy publishes 2% of books. Pays 5-12½% royalty on retail price. Offers $500 average advance. Publishes book 1 year after acceptance. Reports in 3 weeks on queries, 10 weeks on mss. Book catalog free.
● This publisher reports that recently the Jacques Barzun Prize in Cultural History was awarded to Roger Chickering for: *Karl Lamprecht! A German Academic Life.*
Nonfiction: Subjects include politics (international/theory), philosophy (continental, cultural theory), history (European Early Modern to Modern), and sociology. "We want books for senior level undergraduates and upward."
Recent Nonfiction Title: *Bad Faith and Antiblack Racism*, by Lewis R. Gordon.
Tips: "We want well-written contributions to scholarly investigation or syntheses of recent thought. Serious students and scholars are our audience."

‡INFO NET PUBLISHING, 34188 Coast Hwy., Suite C, Dana Point CA 92629. (714)489-9292. Fax: (714)489-9595. President: Herb Wetenkamp. Estab. 1985. Publishes trade and mass market paperback originals. Averages 4 titles/year. Receives 50-60 submissions/year. 85% of books from first-time authors; 85% from unagented writers. Subsidy publishes 5%, "determined case by case." Pays 5-10% on wholesale price. Makes outright purchase of $850 and up. Combination purchase/royalty. Publishes book 1 year after acceptance. Accepts simultaneous submissions. Reports in 2-4 months on queries.
Nonfiction: Cookbook, how-to, reference, self-help, bicycling, skiing and technical. Subjects include business and economics, cooking/foods/nutrition, history, hobbies, recreation, sports, travel, small retailer. "We are seeking specialty authors in vertical market how-tos, specific industry oriented overviews and senior how-tos and self-helps. No cookbooks without a theme, or travel books with too much goo. We are open to unique adventure and/or history first person accounts. No romance." Query or submit outline and sample chapters. Reviews artwork/photos as part of ms package.
Recent Nonfiction Title: *Principles of Bicycle Retailing III*, by Randy W. Kirk (retail how-to).
Tips: "We have noticed an increase in audience served by specialty pubishers, more targeted marketing, vertical publishing. If I were a writer trying to market a book today, I would expect to participate fully in

---

For explanation of symbols, see the Key to Symbols and Abbreviations. For unfamiliar words, see the Glossary.

marketing the book. No author can expect to be successful unless he/she *sells* the book after writing it."

INTERSTATE PUBLISHERS, INC., 510 N. Vermilion St., P.O. Box 50, Danville IL 61834-0050. (217)446-0050. Fax: (217)446-9706. Acquisitions/Vice President-Editorial: Ronald L. McDaniel. Estab. 1914. Hardcover and paperback originals and software. Publishes about 30 titles/year. 50% of books from first-time authors; 100% from unagented writers. Pays 10% royalty usually. No advance. Markets books by mail and exhibits. Publishes book 9-12 months after acceptance. Reports in 4 months. Book catalog for 9 × 12 SAE with 4 first-class stamps. "Our guidelines booklet is provided only to persons who have submitted proposals for works in which we believe we might be interested. If the booklet is sent, no self-addressed envelope or postage from the author is necessary."

• Interstate's interest at this time is in middle school and high school agricultural education materials into which science has been integrated: agriscience.

Nonfiction: Publishes middle school, high school, undergraduate college-level texts and related materials in agricultural education (production agriculture, agriscience and technology, agribusiness, agrimarketing, horticulture). "We wish to expand our line of *AgriScience* textbooks and related materials for grades 6-12." Also publishes items in correctional education (books for professional training and development and works for use by and with incarcerated individuals in correctional facilities). "We favor, but do not limit ourselves to, works that are designed for class-quantity rather than single-copy sale." Query or submit outline and 2-3 sample chapters. Reviews artwork/photos as part of ms package.

Recent Nonfiction Title: *The Earth and AgriScience*, by John R. Crankilton, et al.

Tips: "Freelance writers should be aware of strict adherence to the use of nonsexist language; fair and balanced representation of the sexes and of minorities in both text and illustrations; and discussion of computer applications and career opportunities wherever applicable. Writers commonly fail to identify publishers who specialize in the subject areas in which they are writing. For example, a publisher of textbooks isn't interested in novels, or one that specializes in elementary education materials isn't going to want a book on auto mechanics."

KUMARIAN PRESS, INC., 630 Oakwood Ave., Suite 119, W. Hartford CT 06110-1529. (203)953-0214. Fax: (203)953-8579. Editor: Trish Reynolds. Imprints are Kumarian Press Books for a World that Works and Kumarian Press Library of Management for Development. Estab. 1977. Publishes hardcover and paperback originals and paperback reprints. Averages 8-12 titles/year. Receives 100-150 submissions/year. 10% of books from first-time authors; 100% from unagented writers. Pays 0-10% royalty on net. Publishes book 9 months after acceptance. Query for electronic submissions. Reports in 2 months. Book catalog and ms guidelines free.

Nonfiction: "Kumarian Press Books for a World that Works are global in focus and appeal to the reader who is interested in world affairs, but who does not want an academic read. Subjects of interest include: global issues, environment, women, community development and travel. Kumarian Press Library of Management for Development is the professional, academic line. This line targets readers interested in international development and management. Subject areas include: nongovernmental organizations, people-centered development, women in development, international public administration, democratization, microenterprise, health and the environment."

Tips: "Please do not send a complete manuscript. Call and ask for a free copy of our writer's guidelines. The guidelines show you how to submit your book proposal for possible publication."

PETER LANG PUBLISHING, Subsidiary of Peter Lang AG, Bern, Switzerland, 62 W. 45th St., New York NY 10036-4208. (212)302-6740. Fax: (212)302-7574. Managing Director: Christopher S. Myers. Acquisitions Editor: Owen Lancer. Estab. 1952. Publishes mostly hardcover originals. Averages 300 titles/year. 75% of books from first-time authors; 98% from unagented writers. Publishes scholarly monographs in the Humanities and Social Sciences, as well as textbooks in selected fields of the Humanities and Social Sciences. Write or call for submission requirements. Pays 10-20% royalty on net price. Translators get flat fee plus percentage of royalties. No advance. Publishes book 1 year after acceptance. Reports in 2 months. Book catalog free.

Nonfiction: General nonfiction, reference works, scholarly monographs. Subjects include literary criticism, Germanic and Romance languages, art history, business and economics, American and European political science, history, music, philosophy, psychology, religion, sociology, biography. All books are scholarly monographs, textbooks, reference books, reprints of historic texts, critical editions or translations. No mss shorter than 200 pages. Submit complete ms. *Writer's Market* recommends query with SASE first. Fully refereed review process.

Fiction and Poetry: "We do not publish original fiction or poetry. We seek scholarly and critical editions only. Submit complete manuscript."

Tips: "Besides our commitment to specialist academic monographs, we are one of the few US publishers who publish books in most of the modern languages. A major advantage for Lang authors is international marketing and distribution of all titles. Translation rights sold for many titles."

LIBRA PUBLISHERS, INC., 3089C Clairemont Dr., Suite 383, San Diego CA 92117-6892. (619)571-1414. Contact: William Kroll. Estab. 1960. Publishes hardcover and paperback originals. Specializes in the behavioral sciences. Averages 15 titles/year. Receives 300 submissions/year. 60% of books from first-time authors; 85% from unagented writers. 10-15% royalty on retail price. No advance. "In addition, we will also offer our services to authors who wish to publish their own works. The services include editing, proofreading, production, artwork, copyrighting, and assistance in promotion and distribution." Publishes book 8 months after acceptance. Reports in 2 weeks. *Writer's Market* recommends allowing 2 months for reply. Book catalog for $1.50 postage. Writer's guidelines for #10 SASE.
Nonfiction: Manuscripts in all subject areas will be given consideration, but main interest is in the behavioral sciences. Prefers complete ms but will consider outline and 3 sample chapters. Reviews artwork/photos as part of ms package.

LIBRARY RESEARCH ASSOCIATES, INC., RD #6, Box 41, Dunderberg Rd., Monroe NY 10950-3703. (914)783-1144. President: Matilda A. Gocek. Editor: Dianne D. McKinstrie. Estab. 1968. Publishes hardcover and trade paperback originals. Averages 4 titles/year. Receives 300 submissions/year. 100% of books from first-time authors; 100% from unagented writers. Pays 10% maximum royalty on sales. Offers 20 copies of the book as advance. Publishes book 11 months after acceptance. Reports in 3 months. Book catalog free on request.
Nonfiction: Biography, how-to, reference, technical, American history. Subjects include Americana, business and economics, history, politics. "Our nonfiction book manuscript needs for the next year or two will include books about historical research of some facet of American history, and definitive works about current or past economics or politics." No astrology, occult, sex, adult humor or gay rights. Submit outline and sample chapters.
Recent Nonfiction Title: *P.O.W.: Tears That Never Dry.*
Tips: "Our audience is adult, over age 30, literate and knowledgeable in business or professions. The writer has the best chance of selling our firm historical nonfiction texts. Extremely selective in considering fiction. We are now also distributor of several other presses."

LONGSTREET HOUSE, P.O. Box 730, Hightstown NJ 08520-0730. (609)448-1501. Editor: Dr. David Martin. Estab. 1985. Publishes hardcover and paperback originals and reprints. Publishes 5 titles/year. Receives 30 queries and 20 mss/year. 40% of books from first-time authors; 100% from unagented writers. Subsidy publishes 25% of books. Pays 8-12% royalty on retail price. Publishes book 18 months after acceptance of ms. Accepts simultaneous submissions. Reports in 2 months on proposals. Book catalog free on request.
Nonfiction: Biography, history. Subjects include history, military/war (Civil War), regional. Submit outline. Reviews artwork/photos as part of ms package. Send photocopies.

‡MASTERMEDIA, 17 E. 89th St., New York NY 10128. (212)546-7650. Director of Marketing: Merry Clark. Imprint is The Heritage Imprint (contact Melinda Lambard). Publishes hardcover originals, trade paperback originals and reprints. Publishes 20 titles/year. 50% of books from first-time authors; 90% from unagented writers. Subsidy publishes 10% of books. Pays 10-15% royalty on wholesale price. Offers $2-10,000 advance. Publishes book 6 months after acceptance. Accepts simultaneous submissions. Reports in 1 month. Book catalog and ms guidelines for #10 SASE.
Nonfiction: Biography, children's/juvenile, how-to, reference, self-help. Subjects include business and economics, child guidance/parenting, computers and electronics, government/politics, health/medicine, money/finance, nature/environment, psychology, religion, women's issues/studies. "All authors must also be professional speakers. They must have received money for their knowledge. MasterMedia is the only company to combine publishing with speakers business." Submit outline and 1 sample chapter. Reviews artwork/photos as part of ms package.
Recent Nonfiction Title: *Office Biology*, by L. Borrin (ergonomics).

MAYHAVEN PUBLISHING, Subsidy imprint is Wild Rose. P.O. Box 557, Mahomet IL 61853. Contact: Doris R. Wenzel. Publishes hardcover, trade paperback and reprints. Publishes 4-11 titles/year. Receives 600 queries and 400 mss/year. 60% of books from first-time authors; 95% from unagented writers. Subsidy publishes 5% of books. Pays 6-12% royalty on wholesale price or retail price; subsidy author gets 40% of net sales. Offers $100-250 advance. Publishes book 18 months after acceptance. No simultaneous submissions. Reports in 6 months on queries and proposals, 9 months on mss. Book catalog for $1. Manuscript guidelines for $1 and #10 SASE.
Nonfiction: Cookbook, humor, illustrated book, children's/juvenile, reference, railroad history. Subjects include Americana, animals, art, computers, cooking, history, hobbies, nature/environment, regional. "We are seeking nonfiction (history, natural history, cookbooks, hobbies/reference)." Submit 3 sample chapters.
Recent Nonfiction Title: *America's Rural Hub*, by Stanley A. Changnon (railroading).
Fiction: Adventure, ethnic, gothic, historical, humor, juvenile, mainstream/contemporary, mystery, picture books, romance, science fiction, suspense, western, young adult. "Seeking more humor, mystery and young adult." Submit 3 sample chapters.
Recent Fiction Title: *Murder at the Strawberry Festival*, by Warren Carrier (mystery).

‡MICHAELIS MEDICAL PUBLISHING CORP., 2274 South 1300 East, #G 8-288, Salt Lake City UT 84106. (800)557-6672. Publisher: Nikos Linardakis. Publishes trade paperback originals. Publishes 4 titles/year. 50% of books from first-time writers; 100% from unagented writers. Subsidy publishes 20% of books. Pays 5-15% royalty on wholesale price or makes outright purchase of $1,000-3,000. Offers $500-1,000 advance. Publishes book 6-9 months after acceptance of ms. Accepts simultaneous submissions. Reports in 2 months on mss.

Nonfiction: Children's/juvenile, coffee table book, cookbook, how-to, self-help, textbook (medical). Subjects include business and economics, child guidance/parenting, cooking/foods/nutrition, education, health/medicine, money/finance, psychology, science, women's issues/studies. "New review series type books for the health professions, e.g., medicine, dentistry, pharmacy. Other areas including unique books will be highly considered." Submit proposal package, including ms.

Recent Nonfiction Title: *The World of Children's Sleep*, by Alexander Golbin, M.D., Ph.D.

Fiction: Historical, juvenile, picture books. "We are interested primarily with children's books that have meaning and real-life relationships to experiences that children are going to face." Submit ms.

MOUNT OLIVE COLLEGE PRESS, 634 Henderson St., Mount Olive NC 28365. (919)658-2502. Editor: Dr. Pepper Worthington. Publishes trade paperback originals. Averages 5 titles/year. Receives 500 queries/year. 60% of books from first-time authors; 100% from unagented writers. Subsidy publishes 35% of books. Publishes book 2 years after acceptance of ms. No simultaneous submissions. Reports in 6 months. Book catalog and ms guidelines free on request.

Nonfiction: Biography, coffee table book, cookbook, how-to, children's/juvenile. Subjects include cooking/foods/nutrition, education, language/literature, religion, travel. Submit outline and 1 sample chapter. Reviews artwork/photos as part of ms package. Send photocopies.

Fiction: Literary, mainstream/contemporary, plays, religious. Submit synopsis and 1 sample chapter.

Poetry: Submit 6 sample poems.

‡NACE INTERNATIONAL, 1440 S. Creek Dr., Houston TX 77084. (713)492-0535. Senior Editor: Aunee Pierce. Imprints are NACE International, National Association of Corrosion Engineers. Publishes hardcover and trade paperback originals. Publishes 12-20 titles/year; imprints publish 12 titles/year. Receives 10 queries and 20 mss/year. 5% of books from first-time authors; 100% from unagented writers. Subsidy publishes 5% of books. Pays 3-15% royalty on retail price. Offers $2,500 advance. Publishes 1-2 years after acceptance of ms. Reports in 6 months on proposals. Book catalog and ms guidelines free on request.

Nonfiction: Reference, technical, textbook. Subjects include science, engineering. Query for proposal form. Submit proposal package, including proposal form, outline, 2 sample chapters, résumé. Reviews artwork/photos as part of ms package. Send photocopies.

Recent Nonfiction Title: *Galvanic Corrosion Test Methods*, by Harvey P. Hack (textbook).

Tips: Audience is corrosion engineering professionals in a variety of industries including oil and gas, chemical process, pulp and paper, construction, restoration, etc.

NEW FALCON PUBLICATIONS, Subsidiary of J.W. Brown, Inc., 1739 E. Broadway Rd., Suite 1-277, Tempe AZ 85282. Phone/fax: (602)708-1409. Editor: Frank Martin. Estab. 1980. Publishes hardcover and trade paperback originals and reprints. Publishes 15-20 titles/year. Receives 800 queries and 400 mss/year. 30% of books from first-time authors; 90% from unagented writers. Subsidy publishes 10% of books. Pays 5-15% royalty on retail price or makes outright purchase; on subsidy—by agreement. Offers $0-5,000 advance. Publishes book 6-18 months after acceptance. Accepts simultaneous submissions. Query for electronic submissions. Reports in 2 months on queries. Book catalog and ms guidelines for 9×12 SAE with 3 first-class stamps.

Nonfiction: Biography, how-to, reference, self-help, textbook. Subjects include anthropology/archaeology, education, gay/lesbian, government/politics, health/medicine, philosophy, psychology, religion, science, sociology, occult, metaphysical, women's issues/studies. Query with outline, 3 sample chapters and SASE.

Recent Nonfiction Title: *The Game of Life*, by Timothy Leary (psychology).

Fiction: Erotica, experimental, fantasy, feminist gay/lesbian, horror, literary, occult, religious, science fiction. Query with 3 sample chapters and SASE.

Recent Fiction Title: *Illuminati of Immortality*, by Wayne Saalman (science fiction).

Tips: "Be polite, be timely, have patience, be neat. Include short résumé."

NORTH COUNTRY BOOKS, INC., 311 Turner St., Suite 217, Utica NY 13501-1729. Phone/fax: (315)735-4877. Publisher: Sheila Orlin. Imprints are Pine Tree Press, North Country Books. Publishes hardcover and trade paperback originals and reprints. Publishes 6-20 titles/year. Receives 300-500 queries and 200-300 mss/year. 80% of books from first-time authors; 99% from unagented writers. Pays 8-10% royalty on retail price. Publishes book 1-3 years after acceptance. Accepts simultaneous submissions. Reports in 6-9 months on mss. Book catalog free on request.

Nonfiction: New York State regional history, biography, field guides, stories, coffee table, children's, etc. Submit proposal package including completed ms, number of photos/artwork, any pertinent information.

Photocopies of photos/artwork helpful, but not imperative. An outline with 2-3 sample chapters would be read, but complete ms preferred.
Recent Nonfiction Title: *Guides of the Adironbacks: A History*, by Charles Brumley.
Fiction: Seldom publishes fiction.
Tips: "We are a New York State regional publisher appealing to a general trade market of people interested in NY State."

‡PACIFIC BOATING ALMANAC, 13468 Beach Ave., Marina Del Rey CA 90292. (310)577-9575. Fax: (310)577-9272. Editor: Peter L. Griffes. Publishes 4 annual boating guides along the West Coast. Estab. 1964.
Nonfiction: Almanacs include Coast Piloting, facilities information, history of harbors and miscellaneous information. Review photos and written material as it pertains to the areas.

PARADIGM PUBLISHING COMPANY, 2323 Broadway, Studio 202, San Diego CA 92102. (619)234-7115. Publisher: Deanna Leach. Publishes trade paperback originals. Averages 4-5 titles/year. Receives 100 queries and 50 mss/year. 95% of books from first-time authors; 100% from unagented writers. Pays 15% royalty on net proceeds after recovery of publishing cost. Publishes book 2 years after acceptance. No simultaneous submissions. Reports in 1 month on queries and proposals, 6 months on mss. Book catalog and ms guidelines ,free on request.
  ● This publisher has narrowed its focus to lesbian fiction and nonfiction.
Nonfiction: How-to, humor, personal. Lesbian subjects only. Query with outline. Reviews artwork/photos as part of ms package. Send photocopies.
Recent Nonfiction Title: *Hey Mom, Guess What!*, by Shelly Roberts (gay/lesbian humor).
Fiction: Lesbian only in the following genres: Adventure, humor, mystery, romance, science fiction, suspense. Submit entire ms, author bio, synopsis.
Recent Fiction Title: *Storm Front*, by Linda Kay Silva (lesbian mystery).

PARAGON HOUSE PUBLISHERS, 370 Lexington Ave., New York NY 10017. (212)953-5950. Fax: (212)953-5940. E-mail: MGiamp7@aol.com. Publisher: Michael Giampaoli. Estab. 1983. Publishes hardcover originals, trade paperback originals and reprints. Averages 25 titles/year. Receives 250 queries and 75 mss/year. 80% of books from first-time authors; 90% from unagented writers. Pays 10% royalty on wholesale price. Publishes book 9 months after acceptance of ms. Accepts simultaneous submissions. Query for electronic submissions. Reports in 2 months on queries. Book catalog free on request.
Nonfiction: Biography, reference, college textbook, scholarly monographs. Subjects include history, philosophy, religion. Query.
Poetry: No new or unestablished writers.

‡THE PARTHENON PUBLISHING GROUP, INC., One Blue Hill Plaza, P.O. Box 1564, Pearl River NY 10965. (914)735-9363. Editor-in-Chief: Nat Russo. Publishes hardcover originals. Publishes 50 titles/year. 10% of books from first-time authors; 100% from unagented writers. Subsidy publishes 5% of books. Pays 2-15% royalty on net sales price. Offers $1,000-1,500 advance. Publishes book 6 months after acceptance of ms. Reports in 2 months on queries and proposals. Manuscript guidelines for #10 SASE.
Nonfiction: Reference, textbook. Subjects include health/medicine, science. Query.

‡PATH PRESS, INC., 53 W. Jackson Boulevard, Suite 724, Chicago IL 60604-3610. (312)663-0167. President: Bennett J. Johnson. Vice President/Editorial Director: Herman C. Gilbert. Publishes hardcover, trade paperback and mass market paperback originals. Publishes 3 titles/year. Receives 100 queries and 50 mss/year. 50% of books from first-time authors; 95% from unagented writers. Subsidy publishes 10% of books. "If the quality is average or if the author does not want to wait for his turn in the queue." Pays 10-15% royalty on retail price. No advance. Publishes book 12-18 months after acceptance of ms. Accepts simultaneous submissions. Reports in 3-6 months. Book catalog and ms guidelines free on request.
Nonfiction: Biography, self-help. Subjects include Americana, business and economics, education, ethnic, government/politics, philosophy, women's issues/studies. "Path Press publishes books and poetry written for, by and about African-American Third World people and women." Query with sample chapters. Reviews artwork/photos as part of ms package.
Fiction: Adventure, ethnic, feminist, historical, humor, literary, mainstream/contemporary, short story collections, suspense. Query with sample chapters.
Poetry: Submit sample poems.

‡PICKWICK PUBLICATIONS, 4137 Timberlane Dr., Allison Park PA 15101-2932. Fax: (412)487-8862. Editorial Director: Dikran Y. Hadidian. Estab. 1982. Publishes paperback originals and reprints. Averages 6-8 titles/year. Receives 10 submissions/year. 50% of books from first-time authors; 90% from unagented writers. Subsidy publishes 10% of books. Publishes book 18-24 months after acceptance. Reports in 4 months. Book catalog for 6×9 SAE with 3 first-class stamps.

Nonfiction: Religious and scholarly mss in Biblical archeology, Biblical studies, church history and theology. Also reprints of outstanding out-of-print titles and original texts and translations. Accepts nonfiction translations from French or German. No popular religious material. Query or submit outline and 2 sample chapters. Consult *The Chicago Manual of Style.*
Recent Nonfiction Title: *Jesus the Parable of God: What Do We Really Know About Jesus?*, by Eduard Schweizer.

‡PINCUSHION PRESS, 6001 Johns Rd., Suite 148, Tampa FL 33634. (813)855-3071. Editor: Gregory Janson. Publishes hardcover and trade paperback originals and reprints. 25% of books from first-time authors; 50% from unagented writers. Subsidy publishes 10% of books. Pay varies from royalty to "joint venture" author subsidy. Publishes book 12-18 months after acceptance of ms. Accepts simultaneous submissions. Reports in 1-2 months. Book catalog for 9×12 SAE with 3 first-class stamps.
Nonfiction: Coffee table book, illustrated book. Subjects include art/architecture, hobbies. "We specialize in books on antiques and collectibles." Query. Reviews artwork/photos as part of ms package. Send transparencies.
Recent Nonfiction Title: *Collecting Toy Trains*, by Carlson.

‡PLATINUM PRESS INC., Subsidiary of Bobley Harmann Publishing and Marketing Co., 311 Crossways Park Dr., Woodbury NY 11797. President: Herbert Cohen. Publishes hardcover originals and reprints. Publishes 18 titles/year. Receives 50 queries and 10 mss/year. Subsidy publishes 20% of books. Pays royalty or makes outright purchase. Offers $1,000 advance. Publishes book 6 months after acceptance of ms. Reports in 1 month.
 • Platinum Press also owns and operates the Detective Book Club.
Nonfiction: Biography, cookbook, gift book. Subjects include anthropology/archaeology, cooking/foods/nutrition, health/medicine, history, military/war. Query. Reviews artwork/photos as part of ms package.
Recent Nonfiction Title: *Gettysberg*, by Beecham (American history).
Fiction: Mystery. Query.

PMN PUBLISHING, GFA Management, Inc., Box 47024, Indianapolis IN 46247. Fax: (317)791-8113. Publisher: George Allen. Estab. 1988. Publishes trade and mass market paperback originals and trade paperback reprints. Publishes 5-6 titles/year. Receives 24 queries and 24 mss/year. 50% of books from first-time authors; 75% from unagented writers. Subsidy publishes 25% of books. Subsidy determined by size of the market to which the work is targeted. Pays 5-10% royalty on retail price. Publishes book 18 months after acceptance of ms. Accepts simultaneous submissions. Reports in 2 months on queries and proposals. Book catalog free on request.
 • PMN is now publishing *The Allen Letter*, a monthly real estate management-oriented newsletter open to freelance submissions (300-500 words).
Nonfiction: How-to, reference, self-help, technical, textbook. Subjects include business and economics, military/war, money/finance, religion, real estate. "Strongest interest is in real estate management, mobile home park management." Query or submit outline.

PRINCETON ARCHITECTURAL PRESS, 37 E. Seventh St., New York NY 10003. (212)995-9620. Fax: (212)995-9454. Editor: Kevin Lippert. Estab. 1981. Publishes hardcover and trade paperback originals and hardcover reprints. Averages 30 titles/year. Receives 200 submissions/year. 50% of books from first-time authors; 100% from unagented writers. Pays 6-10% royalty on wholesale price. Accepts simultaneous submissions. Query for electronic submissions. Reports in 2-3 months. Book catalog and guidelines for 9×12 SAE with 3 first-class stamps. "Manuscripts will not be returned unless SASE is enclosed."
Nonfiction: Illustrated book, textbook. Subjects include architecture, landscape architecture, graphic design, urban planning and design. Needs texts on architecture, landscape architecture, architectural monographs, and texts to accompany a possible reprint, architectural history and urban design. Submit outline/synopsis and sample chapters or complete ms. Reviews artwork/photos as part of ms package.
Tips: "Our audience consists of architects, designers, urban planners, architectural theorists, and architectural-urban design historians, and many academicians and practitioners. We are still focusing on architecture and architectural history but would like to increase our list of books on graphic design and typography, as well as landscape architecture."

PROSTAR PUBLICATIONS, LTD., P.O. Box 67571, Los Angeles CA 90067. (310)577-1975. Fax: (310)577-9272. Editor: Peter L. Griffes. Publishes trade paperback originals and reprints. Publishes 15 titles/year. Receives 10 queries and 30 mss/year. 50% of books from first-time authors; 50% from unagented writers. Subsidy publishes 5% of books, depending on title, subject and time of publication. Pays 15% royalty on wholesale price. Offers advance under $5,000. Publishes book 6-12 months after acceptance of ms. Accepts simultaneous submissions. Query for electronic submissions. Reports in 2 months. Book catalog free on request. Manuscript guidelines for #10 SASE.

Nonfiction: How-to, multimedia, reference, technical, textbook (marine titles). Subjects include recreation (marine titles), sports (sailing), travel. Submit proposal package. Sometimes reviews artwork/photos as part of ms package. Send photocopies.

Recent Nonfiction Title: *Ultimate Air Travel Guide*, by Peter Griffes.

‡RAGGED EDGE PRESS, Imprint of White Mane Publishing Co., 63 W. Burd St., P.O. Box 152, Shippensburg PA 17257. (717)532-2237. Acquisitions Editor: Harold E. Collier. Publishes hardcover and trade paperback originals and reprints. Publishes 50-60 titles/year, imprint publishes 6-8 titles/year. 50% of books from first-time authors; 70% from unagented writers. Subsidy publishes 10% of books. Pays 7-13% royalty on wholesale and retail price. Publishes book 9 months after acceptance of ms. Accepts simultaneous submissions. Reports in 1 month on queries. Book catalog and ms guidelines free on request.

Nonfiction: Biography, self-help, textbook. Subjects include history, religion, sociology. Query. Reviews artwork/photos as part of ms package. Send photocopies.

Recent Nonfiction Title: *Celebrating Our Differences*, by Mary and Ned Rosenbaum (religion/self-help).

‡RESOURCE PUBLICATIONS, INC., 160 E. Virginia St., Suite 290, San Jose CA 95112-5876. Fax: (408)287-8748. E-mail: kenneth856@aol.com. Editorial Director: Kenneth E. Guentert. Estab. 1973. Publishes paperback originals. Publishes 14 titles/year. Receives 100-200 submissions/year. 30% of books from first-time authors; 99% of books from unagented writers. Average print order for a first book is 3,000. Subsidy publishes 10% of books. "If the author can present and defend a personal publicity effort or otherwise demonstrate demand and the work is in our field, we will consider it." Pays 8% royalty. Offers advance occasionally in the form of books. Publishes book 18 months after acceptance. Query for electronic submissions. Reports in 3 months.

Nonfiction: "We look for imaginative but practical books relating to ministry, counseling, and education. We are looking particularly for educational resources in the prevention field. Query or submit outline and sample chapters. Prepare a clear outline of the work and an ambitious schedule of public appearances to help make it known and present both as a proposal to the publisher." Accepts translations. Reviews artwork/photos as part of ms package.

Recent Nonfiction Title: *Tutoring and Mentoring: Two Peer Helping Programs for Elementary School.*

Fiction: "We are not interested in novels or collections of short stories in the usual literary sense. But we look for storytelling resources and collections of short works in the area of drama, dance, song, and visual art, especially if related to education or ministry." Query or submit outline/synopsis and sample chapters.

Tips: "Books that provide readers with practical, usable suggestions and ideas pertaining to worship, celebration, education, and the arts have the best chance of selling to our firm. We are hoping to build on a strong list of peer-helping books with additional resources on the prevention of drug abuse, domestic violence, and other social ills."

‡ST. VLADIMIR'S SEMINARY PRESS, 575 Scarsdale Rd., Crestwood NY 10707. (914)961-8313. Fax: (914)961-5456. Managing Director: Theodore Bazil. Publishes hardcover and trade paperback originals and reprints. Averages 15 titles/year. Subsidy publishes 20% of books. Market considerations determine whether an author should be subsidy published. Pays 8% royalty on retail price. Accepts simultaneous submissions. Reports in 3 months on queries, 9 months on mss. Book catalog and ms guidelines free.

Nonfiction: Religion dealing with Eastern Orthodox theology. Query. Reviews artwork/photos as part of ms package.

Tips: "We have an interest in books that stand on firm theological ground; careful writing and scholarship are basic."

SCHENKMAN BOOKS, INC., 118 Main St., Rochester VT 05767. (802)767-3702. Fax: (802)767-9528. Editor-in-Chief: Joe Schenkman. Contact: Kathryn Miles, managing editor. Publishes hardcover and trade paperback originals and trade paperback reprints. Publishes 8-10 titles/year. Receives 100 queries and 60 mss/year. 95% of books from unagented writers. Subsidy publishes 15% of books. Pays 5-15% royalty on wholesale price. Publishes book 10 months after acceptance of ms. Simultaneous submissions OK. Query for electronic submissions. Reports in 1 month on proposals. Book catalog and ms guidelines free on request.

Nonfiction: Reference, self-help, textbook. Subjects include anthropology/archaeology, business and economics, education, language/literature, nature/environment, psychology, science, sociology, women's issues/studies, "Third World" issues. Query with cover letter, résumé, table of contents, 1 sample chapter. Reviews artwork/photos as part of freelance ms package. Send photocopies.

Recent Nonfiction Title: *Spirituality and Communality*, by Dr. Donald Calhoun.

SKIDMORE-ROTH PUBLISHING, INC., 7730 Trade Center Dr., El Paso TX 79912. (915)877-4455. President: Linda Roth. Developmental Editor: Ross Todom. Estab. 1987. Publishes 40 titles/year. Receives 250 submissions/year. 50% of books from first-time authors; 100% from unagented writers. Pays 5-12½% royalty on wholesale price. Publishes book 9 months after acceptance. Accepts simultaneous submissions. Reports in 2 months.

• Skidmore-Roth also works with authors on a subsidy arrangement.

Nonfiction: Technical, textbook. Subjects include nursing, allied health and health/medicine. Currently searching for mss in nursing and allied health. Nothing on religion, history, music/dance, travel, sports, agriculture, computers, military, politics, gay/lesbian or literature. Query. Reviews artwork/photos as part of ms package.

Tips: "Anything on nursing is more likely to be published. Our audience is largely professionals in the field of medicine, nursing, allied health. If I were a writer trying to market a book today, I would look for an area that has been completely overlooked by other writers and write on that subject."

‡SOLUTION PUBLISHING, 1647 Willow Pass Rd., #101, Concord CA 94520. Editor: Dave West. Publishes hardcover, trade paperback and mass market paperback originals. Publishes 2-3 titles/year. Receives 12 queries/year. 80% of books from first-time authors; 100% from unagented writers. Subsidy publishes 30% of books. Pays 5-8% royalty on retail price. No advance. Publishes book 8 months after acceptance of ms. Accepts simultaneous submissions. Reports in 2 months on queries and proposals, 3 months on mss. Manuscript guidelines for #10 SASE.

Nonfiction: How-to, self-help. Subjects include business and economics, government/politics, science. "We look for books that challenge current myths about government, politics, science, how-to, etc. Writers should properly identify who might have an interest in the book." Query with SASE.

Recent Nonfiction Title: *Beat the Devil*, by R. Mackie (political).

Tips: "Our readers are active, involved, interested in learning new things and new ideas."

STARBOOKS PRESS, Imprint of Woldt Corp., P.O. Box 2737, Sarasota FL 34230-2737. (813)957-1281. Editor: Patrick J. Powers. Estab. 1980. Publishes trade paperback originals. Averages 10-12 titles/year. Receives 30-50 submissions/year. 10% of books from first-time authors; 100% from unagented writers. Subsidy publishes 10% of books. "Subsidy deals are based on marketability and quality of work. Poetry is in this category." Pays 15% royalty based on wholesale price or makes outright purchase. Offers 50% royalty average advance. Publishes book 2 months after acceptance. Accepts simultaneous submissions. Query for electronic submissions. Reports in up to 2 months. Book catalog free. Manuscript guidelines for 6×9 SAE with 2 first-class stamps.

Nonfiction: Gay subjects. Query or submit outline and sample chapters. Reviews artwork/photos as part of ms package.

Fiction: Erotica, gay. "We need to produce at least ten new titles per year. Only gay genre will be considered." Submit outline/synopsis and sample chapters (first and last pages vital).

Poetry: All poetry contracts are offered on a subsidy basis. Submit complete ms.

Tips: "Submission for one of our anthologies is in an ideal beginning. Our audience consists of gay males. If I were a writer trying to market a book today, I would keep trying to improve my work and recognize this is a business for the publisher; time is limited and suggestions should be accepted and acted upon. So often we get manuscripts which the author says cannot be edited in any way."

SUNFLOWER UNIVERSITY PRESS, Subsidiary of Journal of the West, Inc., 1531 Yuma, Box 1009, Manhattan KS 66502-4228. (913)539-1888. Publisher: Carol A. Williams. Publishes trade paperback originals and reprints. Averages 12 titles/year. Receives 250 submissions/year. 75% of books from first-time authors; 90% of books from unagented writers. Pays 10% royalty after first printing. Publishes book 8 months after acceptance and contract. Reports in 2 months. Book catalog free.

Nonfiction: Biography, illustrated books, reference. Subjects include agriculture/horticulture, Americana, anthropology/archaeology, business and economics, ethnic, government/politics, health/medicine, history, language/literature, military/war, money/finance, music/dance, nature/environment, photography, recreation, regional, religion, science, sociology, sports, women's issues/studies. "Our field of specialization lies in memoirs and histories of the West, and of the military, naval, and air fields; perhaps some specialized collectors' books." Query or submit 2-3 sample chapters. Reviews artwork/photos as part of the ms package. Send photocopies.

Fiction: Historical, western, military. "We publish a limited amount of fiction, based on an historical individual or event." No romance, X-rated, juvenile, stream of consciousness. Query or submit 2-3 sample chapters.

Tips: "Our audience is the informed aviation, military, or Western American history enthusiast."

‡TILBURY HOUSE, PUBLISHERS, 132 Water St., Gardiner ME 04345. (207)582-1899. Associate Publisher: Jennifer Elliott. Publishes hardcover and trade paperback originals and trade paperback reprints. Publishes 12 titles/year. 10% of books from first-time authors; 50% from unagented writers. Subsidy publishes 25% of books. Royalty negotiable. Publishes book 18 months after acceptance of ms. Accepts simultaneous submissions with notification. Reports in 2 months. Book catalog free. Manuscript guidelines for #10 SASE.

Nonfiction: Biography, children's/juvenile (multicultural, nature), history, poetry, regional. Subjects include agriculture/horticulture (regional), ethnic (multicultural for children), history, music/dance, nature/environment, photography, regional (New England), sports (maritime), women's issues/studies. Submit outline and sample chapters with SASE. Reviews artwork/photos as part of ms package.

Recent Nonfiction Title: *To the Third Power*, by Paul C. Larsen (about America's Cup Race).
Poetry: Submit sample poems.
Recent Poetry Title: *Green Notebook, Winter Road*, by Jane Cooper.

‡**TRANSACTION BOOKS**, Rutgers University, New Brunswick NJ 08903. (908)445-2280. Fax: (908)445-3138. President: I.L. Horowitz. Publisher: Scott Bramson. Book Division Director: Mary E. Curtis. Publishes hardcover and paperback originals and reprints. Specializes in scholarly social science books. Averages 135 titles/year. Receives 800 submissions/year. 15% of books from first-time authors; 85% of books from un-agented writers. Average print order for a first book is 1,000. Subsidy publishes 10% of books. "Royalty depends on individual contract; we've gone anywhere from 2% edited to 15% authored." No advance. Publishes book 10 months after acceptance. Electronic submissions OK, but requires hard copy also. Reports in 4 months. Book catalog and ms guidelines for SASE.
Nonfiction: Americana, biography, economics, history, law, medicine and psychiatry, music, philosophy, politics, psychology, reference, scientific, sociology, technical and textbooks. "All must be scholarly social science or related." Strong emphasis on applied social research. Query or submit outline. "Do not submit sample chapters. We evaluate complete manuscripts only." Accepts nonfiction translations. Use *Chicago Manual of Style*. Looks for "scholarly content, presentation, methodology, and target audience." State availability of photos/illustrations and send one photocopied example.

‡**CHARLES E. TUTTLE CO.**, 153 Milk St., 5th Floor, Boston MA 02109. Acquisition Editor: Michael Lewis. Publishes hardcover and trade paperback originals and reprints. Publishes 60 titles/year. Receives 200 queries/year. 20% of books from first-time authors; 60% from unagented writers. Subsidy publishes 20% of books. Pays 5-8% royalty on retail price. Offers $1,000-3,000 advance. Publishes book 18 months after acceptance of ms. Accepts simultaneous submissions. Reports in 6 weeks on proposals. Book catalog free on request.
Nonfiction: Self-help, eastern philosophy, alternative health. Subjects include cooking/foods/nutrition (Asian related), philosophy (Eastern-Buddhist, Taoist), religion (eastern). Submit query, outline and SASE. Cannot guarantee return of mss.
Recent Nonfiction Title: *Taoist Cookbook*, by Michael Saso (paperback).

UAHC PRESS, Union of American Hebrew Congregations, 838 Fifth Ave., New York NY 10021. (212)249-0100. Managing Director: Stuart L. Benick. Trade Acquisitions Editor: Aron Hirt-Manheimer. Text Acquisitions Editor: David Kasakove. Estab. 1873. Publishes hardcover and trade paperback originals. Averages 15 titles/year. 60% of books from first-time authors; 90% from unagented writers. Subsidy publishes 40% of books. Pays 5-15% royalty on wholesale price. Publishes book 9 months after acceptance. Accepts simultaneous submissions. Book catalog and ms guidelines for SASE.
Nonfiction: Illustrated, juvenile and Jewish textbooks. "Looking for authors that can share an enthusiasm about Judaism with young readers. We welcome first-time authors." Reviews artwork/photos as part of ms package.
Tips: "We publish books that teach values."

‡**UNIVERSITY PRESS OF GEORGIA, INC.**, 3316 S. Cobb Dr., Smyrna GA 30080. CEO: Ervin Williams. Vice President: Sherry Masters. Publishes 8-12 titles/year. 60% of books from first-time authors; 67% from unagented writers. Subsidy publishes 20% of books. Pays 3-7% royalty on retail price or makes outright purchase of $1,000-20,000. Offers $500-5,500 advance. Publishes book 4-6 months after acceptance of ms.
Nonfiction: Biography, technical, textbook. Subjects include Americana, business and economics, education, ethnic, money/finance, psychology, regional, science, travel. "We have an Author's Guidebook which answers most frequently asked questions." Query (always preferred) with outline and 2 sample chapters. Agented submissions preferred, but not required.
Recent Nonfiction Title: *The Renaissance Manager*, by Ervin Williams (general business).
Fiction: Adventure, confession, erotica, ethnic, fantasy, historical, literary, romance, science fiction, short story collections. Query with synopsis and 1-2 sample chapters. Agented submissions preferred, but not required.
Recent Fiction Title: *Ashes of the Red Heifer*, by Neil M. Shuman (life in rural Georgia).

‡**THE VIRTUAL PRESS (TVP)**, 408 Division St., Shwano WI 54166. Publisher: William Stanek. Imprints are Virtual Fantasy, Virtual Mystery, Virtual Science Fiction, Virtual Truth. Publishes trade paperback originals and electronic books. Publishes 16-20 titles/year. Receives 500 queries and 100 mss/year. 50% of books from first-time authors; 100% from unagented writers. Subsidy publishes 25% of books. Pays 8-25% royalty on wholesale price. Publishes book 9 months after acceptance of ms. No simultaneous submissions. Reports in 2-3 months on queries.
Nonfiction: Biography, how-to, multimedia (floppy disk), self-help, technical. Subjects include computers and electronics, hobbies, science, software. "Nonfiction needs are very limited. We are primarily interested in technical books on computers and electronics." Query with SASE. Reviews artwork as part of ms package. "We prefer images be scanned and put on floppy disk in PCX format. Please don't send disks, rather, tell us you have pictures (on floppy) available."

Fiction: Fantasy, mystery, science fiction, short story collections. "VF imprint tends toward high-fantasy and works written on a rich tapestry in believable world settings. VM imprint looks toward thrillers and away from the hard-boiled. VSF imprint prefers hard science fiction to soft, the publisher believes serious outlets for hard science fiction are an absolute necessity. We prefer serial fiction." Query with SASE.

Recent Fiction Title: *At Dream's End: A Kingdom In the Balance.*

Tips: "We are primarily a nontraditional press publishing high-quality electronic novels on disk. Electronic publishing enables us to offer a high-royalty percentage and give our books very long print lives. However, we don't sell in high-volume. Our e-books sell slowly over a long period of time."

VISTA PUBLISHING INC., 473 Broadway, Long Branch NJ 07740-5901. (908)229-6500. President: Carolyn Zagury. Publishes trade paperback originals. Estab. 1991. Publishes 10 titles/year. Receives 100 queries and 60 mss/year. 95% of books from first-time authors; 100% from unagented writers. Subsidy publishes 5% of books. "Decision to subsidy publish based on overall estimated market and shared risk factors." Pays 30-50% royalty on percentage of total net sales. Publishes book 1-2 years after acceptance. Accepts simultaneous submissions. Query for electronic submissions. Prefers hard copy. Reports in 3-4 months on mss. Book catalog and ms guidelines free on request.

   • This publisher reports that its current focus is on nurse authors.

Nonfiction: Biography, how-to, humor, reference, self-help, textbook. Subjects include business and economics, health/medicine, psychology, women's issues/studies. Query with complete ms and SASE. Reviews artwork/photos as part of ms package. Send photocopies.

Recent Nonfiction Title: *To Be a Nurse*, by Linda Strangio, RN MA CCRN (nursing experience short stories).

Fiction: Adventure, feminist, humor, mainstream/contemporary, mystery, short story collections, suspense. Query with complete ms and SASE.

Recent Fiction Title: *Dangerous Alibis*, by Carolyn Chambers Clark Ed.D, RN (mystery).

Poetry: "We prefer a mix of humor and serious poetry with reference to nursing." Submit complete ms.

Recent Poetry Title: *Signs of Life, Observations of Death*, by Craig E. Betson RN MHA (nursing).

Tips: Audience is nursing professionals, health care providers, women. "Be willing to take a chance and submit a manuscript for consideration. Our small press was developed to assist writers in successfully publishing. We seek the talent of nurses, healthcare providers and women authors."

WEATHERHILL, INC., 568 Broadway, Suite 705, New York NY 10012. (212)966-3080. President: Jeff Hunter. Imprints are Weatherhill Books, Tengu Books, Inklings. Editorial Director: Ray Furse. Publishes hardcover originals and trade paperback originals and reprints. Publishes 24 titles/year (20 Weatherhill, 4 Tengu). 50% of books from first-time authors; 70% from unagented writers. Subsidy publishes 5% of books. Pays 8-18% royalty on wholesale price. Offers $2,000-10,000 advance. Publishes book 1 year after acceptance of ms. Query for electronic submissions. Returns, postpaid, unsolicited mss if requested. Reports in 2 months. Book catalog and ms guidelines free on request.

Nonfiction: Biography, coffee table book, cookbook, how-to, humor, illustrated book, reference. Subjects include anthropology/archaeology, art/architecture, business and economics, cooking/foods/nutrition, gardening, government/politics, history, language/literature, nature/environment, philosophy, photography, sports, travel (all with Japanese or East Asian orientation). "Tengu Books is designed to afford a lighter, more irreverent look at Japan and the Far East. Our Weatherhill books are for the more discriminating general reader with an interest in Japan and the Far East (although we are *not* an academic publisher). Inklings are small-format gift books offering inklings of the enlightenment to be found in the great traditions of Asian wisdom and literature." Submit outline and 2 sample chapters or proposal package, including author bio/intended market. Reviews artwork/photos as part of ms package. Send transparencies—duplicates and description of complete illustration possibilities.

Recent Nonfiction Title: *Understanding Buddhism* (Weatherhill).

WESTERN BOOK/JOURNAL PRESS, Subsidiary of Journal Lithograph Co., 1470 Woodberry, San Mateo CA 94403. (415)573-8877. Executive Editor: Marie T. Mollath. Estab. 1960. Publishes hardcover and trade paperback originals and reprints. Publishes 16 titles/year. Receives 10 queries and 30 mss/year. 70% of books from first-time authors. Subsidy publishes 15% of books. Pays 10-22% royalty. Publishes book 14 months after acceptance of ms. Query for electronic submissions. Reports in 1 month on queries. *Writer's Market* recommends allowing 2 months for reply. Book catalog and ms guidelines free on request.

Nonfiction: Biography, self-help, technical. Subjects include architecture, government/politics, regional, science, historical biographies. Submit proposal package, including entire ms. *Writer's Market* recommends query with SASE first. Reviews artwork/photos as part of ms package. Send photocopies.

Recent Nonfiction Title: *Pioneer/Political Leader of Northeastern California*, by James Thomas Butler (California Gold Rush history).

Recent Fiction Title: *MAGMA: The Indestructible*, by Henry W. Crosby (about a whale).

‡B.L. WINCH & ASSOCIATES/JALMAR PRESS, 2675 Skypark Dr., Torrance CA 90505. (310)784-0016. General Manager: Jeanne Iler. Imprint is Sorrento Press (Bradley Winch Sr., President). Publishes hardcover and trade paperback originals. Publishes 80 titles/year. Receives 250 queries and 150 mss/year. 10% of books from first-time authors; 95% from unagented writers. Subsidy publishes 15% of books. Pays royalty. Offers $100-1,000 advance. Publishes book 1 year after acceptance of ms. Accepts simultaneous submissions. Reports in 3 months on proposals, 6 months on mss. Book catalog and ms guidelines for #10 SASE.

Nonfiction: Children's/juvenile, gift book, self-help. Subjects include child guidance/parenting, education, psychology, sociology. "We are pretty fully committed but open to ideas that fit our market. We do mostly books for educators about self esteem, peaceful conflict resolution, gender equity, etc. (not textbooks)." Query with outline and 1 sample chapter. Reviews artwork/photos as part of ms package. Send photocopies.

Recent Nonfiction Title: *Esteem Building Overview*, Dr. Michele Borba (teachers guide).

Fiction: Query.

Recent Fiction Title: *Someone Cries for the Children*, by Lisa Kent (child abuse).

WINDFLOWER COMMUNICATIONS, 123 N. Third St., P.O. Box 13544, Grand Forks ND 58208-3544. Winnipeg, Manitoba R2K 3N3 Canada. (204)668-7475. Fax: (204)661-8530. Editorial Director: Susan Braun Brandt. Publishes hardcover and trade paperback originals. Publishes 5 titles/year. Receives 250 queries and 125 mss/year. 85% of books from first-time authors; 100% from unagented writers. Subsidy publishes 30% of books. Pays 15% royalty on wholesale price. Publishes book 9 months after acceptance. Accepts simultaneous submissions. Query for electronic submissions. Reports in 1 month on queries, 3 months on proposals, 6 months on mss. Book catalog and ms guidelines free on request.

Nonfiction: Biography, children's juvenile, self-help. Subjects include ethnic, history, religion, sociology, women's issues/studies, Canadiana. "Must be family value-oriented; and be very carefully researched as to uniqueness for market. Often writers have not checked market, competition or have not been careful about sources." Submit proposal package, including outline, 4-6 chapters. Reviews artwork/photos as part of the ms package. Send photocopies.

Fiction: Adventure, fantasy, historical, juvenile, religious, Canadiana. "We are promoting Canadiana (Canadian historical fiction) and religious fiction of quality. Common mistakes are poor editing and re-writing. Submit synopsis with 4-6 sample chapters.

Poetry: Submit complete ms.

Tips: "Audience is family oriented people; religious (Christian) bent."

YE GALLEON PRESS, P.O. Box 287, Fairfield WA 99012-0287. (509)283-2422. Owner: Glen C. Adams. Estab. 1937. Publishes 25 titles/year. Subsidy publishes 25% of books. "Subsidy based on sales probabilities." Pays 5-10% royalties based on moneys actually received. No advance. Publishes book 9 months after acceptance. Reports in 2 weeks on queries. *Writer's Market* recommends allowing 2 months for reply. Book catalog free.

Nonfiction: Biography (if sponsored). Subjects include Americana, history. Query. Reviews artwork/photos as part of ms package.

Fiction: Historical. "I print historical fiction only if paid to do so, and even then it needs to be pretty good." Query.

Tips: "We are looking for books on native Americans written from an Indian point of view. Our audience is general. A probable reader is male, college-educated, middle-aged or past, wearing glasses or collector of rare western US history. We are not likely to take any more manuscripts on a royalty basis this year as we are offered more work than we can handle."

Subsidy Publishers

The following companies publish more than 50% of their books on an author-subsidy basis.

‡Aardvark Enterprises
204 Millbank Drive S.W.
Calgary, Alberta T26 2H9 Canada

Aegina Press, Inc
59 Oak Lane, Spring Valley
Huntington WV 25704

American Society for Nondestructive Testing
P.O. Box 28518
Columbus OH 43228

Authors' Unlimited
3324 Barham Blvd.
Los Angeles CA 90068

Automobile Quarterly
15040 Kutztown Rd., Box 348
Kutztown PA 19530

Barney Press
#60, 8300 Kern Canyon Rd.
Bakersfield CA 93306

Brunswick Publishing Company
P.O. Box 555
Lawrenceville VA 23868

‡Burch Street Press
63 W. Burch St., P.O. Box 152
Shippensburg PA 17257

Carlton Press, Inc.
11 W. 32nd St.
New York NY 10001

‡Common Courage Press
P.O. Box 702
Monroe ME 04951

Dorrance Publishing Co., Inc.
643 Smithfield St.
Pittsburgh PA 15222

Evanston Publishing, Inc.
1216 Hinman Ave.
Evanston IL 60202

Fairway Press
628 S. Main St.
Lima OH 45804

Fithian Press
P.O. Box 1525
Santa Barbara CA 93102

Give Books Away
2525 McKinnon Dr.
Decatur GA 30030

‡Golden Quill Press/Marshall Jones Co.
P.O. Box 2327, Barnumville Rd.
Manchester Center VT 05255-2327

The Golden Quill Press
Avery Rd.
Francestown NH 03043

Harbor House (West) Publishers, Inc.
40781 Smoke Tree Lane
Rancho Mirage CA 92270

Lucky Books
P.O. Box 1415
Winchester VA 22604

‡Pallas Press
P.O. Box 64921
Tucson AZ 85728

‡Perivale Press
13830 Erwin St.
Van Nuys CA 91401-2914

‡Only You Publications
1416 Eddingham
Lawrence KS 66046

Poetry On Wings, Inc.
P.O. Box 1000
Pear Blossom CA 93553

Prescott Press
Suite A3, 104 Row 2
Lafayette LA 70508.

Proclaim Publishing
#2610, 1117 Marquette Ave.
Minneapolis MN 55403

Peter Randall Publisher
P.O. Box 4726
Portsmouth NH 03802

Red Apple Publishing
P.O. Box 101
Gig Harbor WA 98335

Rivercross Publishing, Inc.
127 E. 59th St.
New York NY 10022

‡Todd Publishing
8383 E. Evans Rd.
Scottsdale AZ 85260

Treehaus Communications, Inc.
906 W. Loveland Ave.
Loveland OH 45140

Vantage Press
516 W. 34th St.
New York NY 10001

Whitman Publishing Inc.
383 Van Gordon St.
Lakewood CO 80228

Wildstar Publishing
1550 California St.
San Francisco CA 94109

Book Publishers and Producers/Changes '95-'96

The following book publishers and producers were listed in the 1995 edition but do not have listings in this edition of *Writer's Market*. The majority did not respond to our request to update their listings or return a questionnaire for a new listing. If a reason was given for the exclusion, we have included it in parentheses after the listing name.

A Capella Books (out of business)
Aardvark Publishing (removed by request)
Accelerated Development (removed by request)
Acorn Publishing
Advance Corp. (unable to contact)
Aegean Park
Afcom Publishing
Agrictech Publishing Group
Alaskan Viewpoint
American Assoc.
American Education Publishing
American Library Assoc.
American Media
American Press
American Psychiatric Press
American Veterinary Publications
Anaya Publishers
And Books
Anima Publications
Applause Books
Applezaba Press
Aqua Quest Publications
Art Direction Book Co.
Astarte Shell Press
Asylum Arts
Audio Entertainment (unable to contact)
Augsburg Books
Austin & Winfield
Backcountry Publications (removed by request)
Barricade Books
Beach Holme
Beaver Pond Publishing
Benjamin Publishing Co.
Bergh Publishing
Berwick Publishing
Better Homes and Gardens Books (no freelance)
Binford & Mort Publishing
Black Bear Publications
Black Hat Press (not accepting mss)
Black Sparrow Press (removed by request)
Blizzard Publishing
Blue Buddha Press
Blue Horizon Press
Book Creations
Border Books (out of business)
Bosco Multimedia, Don
Boyd & Fraser Publishing Co.
British American Publishing (no freelance)
Broadview Press
Brookings Institution (removed by request)
Buddha Rose (removed by request)
Bull Publishing Co.
Burning Gate Press

Business & Legal Reports
C&T Publishing
C.F.W. Enterprises
Camden House (no freelance)
Camden House
Capra Press (no freelance)
Capstone Press
Career Press
Cedi Pubilcations
Centering Corp. (removed by request for 1 year)
Chelsea Green
Christian Classics
Chronimed Publishing
Clark Co., Arthur H.
Clarkson Potter
Coach House Press
Compass American Guides
Compute Books
Computer Technology Research Corp.
Council for Indian Education (removed by request for 1 year)
Cracom Corp.
Creative Publishing Co.
CSS Publishing Co.
Deaconess Press
Delta Sales Publishing
Dimensions & Directions
East Coast Books (no longer does books)
Eastern Caribbean Inst.
Eastwind Publishing (out of business)
EES Pubilcations
Falcon Press Publishing Co.
Fall Creek Press (not accepting mss)
Fallen Leaf Press
Ford-Brown & Co.
Formac Publishing
Fox Chapel Publishing
FPMI Communications
Free Spirit Publishing
Friedman Publishing Group, Michael
Gallaudet Univ. Press (removed by request)
Garland Publishing
Garrett Park Press (removed by request)
Gibbs Smith
Gibson Co., C.R. (removed by request)
Global Professional Publications (unable to contact)
Golden Eagle Press
Golden West Publishers
Great Northwest Publishing and Distributing Co.
Green, Warren H.
Greenlawn Press
Group Hands-On Bible Curriculum (no freelance)

Hawkes Publishing
Helix Press
Hendrickson Publishers
Hope Publishing House
Horshoe Press (out of business)
Humdinger Books (removed by request)
Hunter House
Hyperion
ICAN Press
Ideals Publications
IEEE Press
Imagine
Incentive Publications
Industrial Press
Inst. of Psychological Research
Ishiyaku Euroamerica
Jacobs Publishing
James Books, Alice
Jefferson Univ. Press, Thomas
Jokes, Inc.
Judaica Press
K.I.P. Children's Books
Ketz Agency, Louse B.
Knowledge Book Publishers
Krieger Publishing
Larksdale
Lexikos
Libraries Unlimited
Life Survival Digest (unable to contact)
Literary Works Publishers (unable to contact)
Longman Publishing Group
Love Child Publishing
Lucas-Evans Books
M&T Books
Magicimage Filmbooks
Magna Publications
Mancorp Publishing
Marabou Publishing
Markgraf Publications Group
Masquerade Books (unable to contact)
Maupin House
Maupin House Publishing
McClanahan Book Co.
Media Forum International
Media Publishing/Midgard Press (subsidy)
Merry Men Press
Meteor Publishing Corporation
Mills & Sanders
Monitor Book Co.
Motorbooks Int'l
Museum of N. Arizona Press
New Leaf Press
Newsage Press
Nucleus Publications
O'Donnell Literary Services (complaints)
O'Reilly & Assoc.
Omni Books
Optimus Publishing

Orion Research
Ottenheimer Publishers
P&R Publishing
Pace Univ. Press
Pacific Press Publishing Assoc.
Pandemic Int'l Publishers
Pandora Press
Pantex Int'l
Parable Books
Parallax Press (removed by request)
Parenting Press (removed by request)
Peel Productions
Pennywhistle Press
Perfection Learning Corp.
Pickering Press (removed by request)
Pinter Publishers
Pleasant Co. Publications
Policy Studies Organization (essay collections only)
Preservation Press (removed by request for 1 year)
Princeton Book Co. (no freelance)
Probus Publishing (merged with Irwin Professional Publishing)
Prolingua Assoc.
Prove Books
QED Press
Quail Ridge Press
Rainbow Books (complaints)

Reference Publications
Revisionist Press (subsidy)
Richboro Press
Rock & Co., Andrew
Ross Books
S. Illinois Univ. Press
Sandhill Crane Press
Sandlapper Publishing
SAS Institute
Sasquatch Books
Sauvie Island Press
Savant Garde Workshop
Seacoast Publications of New England
Seaside Press
Severn House
Sevgo Press
Sheep Meadow Press
Sidran Press
Simon & Pierre Publishing Co.
Sky Publishing Corp.
South End Press
Southpark Publishing Group
Spheric House
St. Martin's Press
Star Books (out of business)
Star Song Publishing Group
Still Waters Press
Stonesong Press (removed by request)
Studio 4 Productions
Sunflower Univ. Press
Technical Analysis of Stocks &

Commodities
Ticket to Adventure
Trend Book Division
Tundra Books (removed by request)
Twayne Publishers
Twin Peaks Press (complaints)
Umbrella Press
Univ. of British Columbia Press (removed by request)
Venture Publishing
Vesta Publications
VGM Career Horizons
Victory House
Virginia State Library and Archives
Vortex Communications
Wake Forest Univ. Press
Webb Research Group (removed by request)
Wescott Publishing Co. (removed by request for 1 year)
Whitman and Co., Albert
Windsor Books
Wine Appreciation Guild
Wingbow Press (removed by request for 1 year)
Wolsak and Wynn
Women's Press (removed by request)
Wordware Publishing
YES Int'l (removed by request)

Consumer Magazines 299

Consumer Magazines

Approaching the consumer magazine market

Selling your writing to consumer magazines is as much an exercise of your marketing skills as it is of your writing abilities. Editors of consumer magazines are looking not simply for good writing, but for good writing which communicates pertinent information to a specific audience—their readers. Why are editors so particular about the readers they appeal to? Because it is only by establishing a core of faithful readers with identifiable and quantifiable traits that magazines attract advertisers. And with many magazines earning up to half their income from advertising, it is in their own best interests to know their readers' tastes and provide them with articles and features that will keep them coming back.

Marketing skills, in the case of freelance writers, have to do with successfully discerning a magazine's editorial slant and writing queries and articles that prove your knowledge of the magazine's readership to the editor. The one complaint we hear from magazine editors more than any other is that many writers don't take the time to become familiar with their magazine before sending a query or manuscript. Thus, editors' desks become cluttered with inappropriate submissions—ideas or articles that simply will not be of much interest to the magazine's readers.

You can gather clues about a magazine's readership—and thus establish your credibility with the magazine's editor—in a number of ways:

● Start with a careful reading of the magazine's listing in this section of *Writer's Market*. Most listings offer very straightforward information about their magazine's slant and audience.

● Send for a magazine's writer's guidelines, if available. These are written by each particular magazine's editors and are usually quite specific about their needs and their readership.

● If possible, talk to an editor by phone. Many will not take phone queries, particularly those working at the higher-profile magazines. But many editors of smaller publications will spend the time to help a writer over the phone.

● Perhaps most important, read several current issues of the target magazine. Only in this way will you see firsthand the kind of stories the magazine actually buys.

Writers who can correctly and consistently discern a publication's audience and deliver stories that speak to that target readership will win out every time over writers who simply write what they write and send it where they will.

Areas of current interest

Today's consumer magazines continue to parallel societal trends and interests. As baby boomers age and the so-called "Generation X" comes along behind, magazines arise to address concerns and cover topics of interest to various subsets of both of those wide-ranging demographic groups. Some areas of special interest now popular among consumer magazines include gardening, health & fitness, family leisure, computers, multimedia and interactive technology, travel, fashion and cooking. More information about magazine trends can be found in Current Trends in Publishing, on page 21.

As in the book publishing business, magazine publishers are experimenting with a variety of approaches to marketing their publications electronically, whether on the Internet, the World Wide Web or via CD-ROM. For more information about magazines in the electronic age, see Current Trends in Publishing, on page 21 and A Writer's Guide to New Media Publishing, on page 56.

What editors want

In nonfiction, editors continue to look for short feature articles covering specialized topics. They want crisp writing and expertise. If you are not an expert in the area about which you are writing, make yourself one through research.

Always query by mail before sending your manuscript package, but keep in mind that once a piece has been accepted, many publishers now prefer to receive your submission via disk or modem so they can avoid re-keying the manuscript.

Fiction editors prefer to receive complete short story manuscripts. Writers must keep in mind that marketing fiction is competitive and editors receive far more material than they can publish. For this reason, they often do not respond to submissions unless they are interested in using the story. Before submitting material, check the market's listing for fiction requirements to ensure your story is appropriate for that market. More comprehensive information on fiction markets can be found in *Novel & Short Story Writer's Market* (Writer's Digest Books).

When considering magazine markets, be sure not to overlook opportunities with Canadian and international publications. Many such periodicals welcome submissions from U.S. writers and can offer writers an entirely new level of exposure for their work.

Regardless of the type of writing you do, keep current on trends and changes in the industry. Trade magazines such as *Folio* and *Writer's Digest* will keep you abreast of start-ups and shut downs and other writing business trends.

Payment

Writers make their living by developing a good eye for detail. When it comes to marketing material, the one detail of interest to almost every writer is the question of payment. Most magazines listed here have indicated pay rates; some give very specific payment-per-word rates while others state a range. Any agreement you come to with a magazine, whether verbal or written, should specify the payment you are to receive and when you are to receive it. Some magazines pay writers only after the piece in question has been published. Others pay as soon as they have accepted a piece and are sure they are going to use it.

In *Writer's Market*, those magazines that pay on acceptance have been highlighted with the phrase—**"pays on acceptance"**—set in bold type. Payment from these markets should reach you faster than from those who pay "on publication." There is, however, some variance in the industry as to what constitutes payment "on acceptance"—some writers have told us of two- and three-month waits for checks from markets that supposedly pay "on acceptance." It is never out of line to ask an editor when you might expect to receive payment for an accepted article.

So what is a good pay rate? There are no standards; the principle of supply and demand operates at full throttle in the business of writing and publishing. As long as there are more writers than there are opportunities for publication, wages for freelancers will never skyrocket. Rates vary widely from one market to the next, however, and the news is not entirely bleak. One magazine industry source puts the average pay rate for consumer magazine feature writing at $1.25 a word, with "stories that require extensive reporting . . . more likely to be priced at $2.50 a word." In our opinion, those estimates are on the high side of current pay standards. Smaller circulation magazines and some departments of the larger magazines will pay a lower rate. As your reputation grows

INSIDER REPORT

C. Michael Curtis's search for 12 good stories

In 1963, C. Michael Curtis took a leave of absence from doctoral studies in political science at Cornell to work at the *Atlantic Monthly*. Thirty-two years later, he is still on leave from college and still at the *Atlantic*. For most of those years, Curtis has read and edited fiction for the magazine.

Since the *Atlantic* is a monthly magazine publishing one work of fiction in each issue, the competition is stiff among writers hoping to break in. The first challenge writers face is rising above the flood of incoming manuscripts. "We are dealing with a quantity of over 12,000 stories a year," says Curtis, "and we're printing only 12 so clearly a lot of our time is spent trying to winnow the very large pile down to something manageable. And this means,

C. Michael Curtis

inevitably, that an awful lot of material is sent back with a standard rejection slip. A good many of them, however, go back with a letter, typically from me, and those are stories that we think exhibit some talent and some promise from writers whom we want to hear from again." A rejection from the *Atlantic* is not, however, an indictment of a story's publishability. "We know perfectly well that we see a lot more publishable work than we can accommodate in this magazine. When we send a story back we aren't always saying it isn't a good story or it isn't worth our while or it isn't publishable—because it isn't any of those things. It may very well be publishable. A great many of the stories we see and turn away do wind up in other magazines."

Many of the incoming manuscripts are read by Curtis, but a system of screeners and interns helps in culling through the constant flow of material. The volume of stories being handled at the *Atlantic* requires the ability to quickly separate those with potential from those that miss the mark completely. Curtis says some of the problems that mitigate against a further consideration of a story include carelessness or awkwardness in use of grammar, punctuation and spelling; unnecessary emphasis indicated by an overabundant use of adjectives and adverbs; and inept writing of any kind. "There are other, somewhat more subtle signs of the beginning writer," says Curtis, "but they're complicated and they often occur in combination, and it's the combination that matters. One or two of these deficiencies by themselves aren't going to discourage us, but we're going to need pretty quickly a sign that the writer has an ear for language and a narrative purpose, some sign of artfulness."

The lack of a narrative purpose, according to Curtis, is a common cause for rejection of manuscripts at the *Atlantic*. "There is the question of whether the thing is a story at all, whether it really does have a narrative purpose and moves events toward some sort of conclusion. We do see an awful lot of writing, some of it quite good and some of it not so good, that doesn't take us anywhere. Given that we can only do 12 stories a year, that becomes a problem. So we tend to deflect a lot of very good writing that, in our sense of things, doesn't constitute an act of story telling."

Writers make it to publication in the *Atlantic* from a wide variety of backgrounds—there are no particular prerequisites of publication or experience that make acceptance more or less likely. Curtis says, "A great many writers whose work finally appeared in the *Atlantic* were working for years and years before we found something we wanted to publish. On the other hand we've also published a number of stories by people who say it was the first story they ever submitted to a magazine. All of which says that I don't see any consistent pattern. It's true, though, that even people whose first stories were published have said that they worked on the story over and over again for years and years before they finally decided it was ready to submit. Perhaps they were simply more patient or more reserved about their level of accomplishment than writers who send out everything they put on a piece of paper."

(along with your clip file), you may be able to command higher rates.

For more information on magazine industry trends, see Current Trends in Publishing, on page 21.

Information on some publications not included in *Writer's Market* may be found in Consumer Magazines/Changes '95-'96, located at the end of this section.

Animal

The publications in this section deal with pets, racing and show horses, and other pleasure animals and wildlife. Magazines about animals bred and raised for the market are classified in the Farm category of Trade, Technical and Professional Journals. Publications about horse racing can be found in the Sports section.

AKC GAZETTE, (formerly *Pure-bred Dogs/American Kennel Gazette*), American Kennel Club, 51 Madison Ave., New York NY 10010-1603. (212)696-8333. Executive Editor: Beth Adelman. 50% freelance written. Monthly association publication on purebred dogs. "Material is slanted to interests of fanciers of purebred dogs as opposed to commercial interests or pet owners." Estab. 1889. Circ. 58,000. **Pays on acceptance of final ms.** Publishes ms an average of 6 months after acceptance. Byline given. Buys first North American serial rights. Submit seasonal/holiday material 6 months in advance. Reports in up to 2 months. Writer's guidelines for #10 SASE.
Nonfiction: General interest, historical, how-to, humor, photo feature, profiles, dog art, travel. No poetry, tributes to individual dogs, or fiction. Buys about 75 mss/year. Query with or without published clips. Length: 1,000-2,500 words. Pays $200-350.
Photos: State availability of photos with submission. Reviews transparencies and prints. Offers $25-150/photo. Captions required. Buys one-time rights. Photo contest guidelines for #10 SASE.
Fiction: Annual short fiction contest only. Guidelines for #10 SASE.
Tips: "Contributors should be involved in the dog fancy or be expert in the area they write about (veterinary, showing, field trialing, obedience, training, dogs in legislation, dog art or history or literature). All submissions are welcome but the author must be a credible expert or be able to interview and quote the experts. Veterinary articles must be written by or with veterinarians. Humorous features are personal experiences relative to purebred dogs that have broader applications. For features generally, know the subject thoroughly and be conversant with jargon peculiar to the sport of dogs."

ANIMALS, Massachusetts Society for the Prevention of Cruelty to Animals, 350 S. Huntington Ave., Boston MA 02130. (617)522-7400. Fax: (617)522-4885. Editor: Joni Praded. Managing Editor: Paula Abend. 90% freelance written. Bimonthly magazine publishing "articles on wildlife (American and international), domestic animals, balanced treatments of controversies involving animals, conservation, animal welfare issues, pet health and pet care." Estab. 1868. Circ. 100,000. **Pays on acceptance.** Publishes ms an average of 5 months after acceptance. Byline given. Offers negotiable kill fee. Buys one-time rights or makes work-for-hire assignments. Submit seasonal/holiday material 6 months in advance. Reports in 6 weeks. Sample copy for $2.95 and 9×12 SAE with 4 first-class stamps. Writer's guidelines for #10 SASE.

Nonfiction: Exposé, general interest, how-to, opinion and photo feature on animal and environmental issues and controversies, plus practical pet-care topics. "*Animals* does not publish breed-specific domestic pet articles or 'favorite pet' stories. Poetry and fiction are also not used." Buys 50 mss/year. Query with published clips. Length: 2,200 words maximum. "Payment for features usually starts at $350." Sometimes pays the expenses of writers on assignment.

Photos: State availability of photos with submission, if applicable. Reviews contact sheets, 35mm transparencies and 5×7 or 8×10 prints. Payment depends on usage size and quality. Captions, model releases and identification of subjects required. Buys one-time rights.

Columns/Departments: Books (book reviews of books on animals and animal-related subjects), 300 words. Buys 18 mss/year. Query with published clips. Length: 300 words maximum. "Payment usually starts at $75."

Tips: "Present a well-researched proposal. Be sure to include clips that demonstrate the quality of your writing. Stick to categories mentioned in *Animals'* editorial description. Combine well-researched facts with a lively, informative writing style. Feature stories are written almost exclusively by freelancers. We continue to seek proposals and articles that take a humane approach. Articles should concentrate on how issues affect animals, rather than humans."

THE ANIMALS' AGENDA, Helping People Help Animals, P.O. Box 25881, Baltimore MD 21224. (410)675-4566. Fax: (410)675-0066. Editor: K.W. Stallwood. 80% freelance written. Bimonthly magazine covering animals, cruelty-free living, vegetarianism. "Dedicated to informing people about animal rights and cruelty-free living for the purpose of inspiring action for animals. We serve a combined audience of animal advocates, interested individuals and the entire animal rights movement." Estab. 1979. Circ. 20,000. Pays on publication. Publishes ms an average of 6 months after acceptance. Byline given. Offers 10% kill fee. Buys first North American serial rights. Editorial lead time 3 months. Submit seasonal material 8 months in advance. Accepts simultaneous and previously published submissions. Send photocopy of article. Does not pay for reprints. Reports in 2 months. Sample copy for $3. Writer's guidelines for #10 SASE.

Nonfiction: Book excerpts, exposé, general interest, interview/profile, opinion. Buys 1-10 mss/year. Query. Length: 1,000-3,000 words. Pays $100. Sometimes pays the expenses of writers on assignment.

Photos: State availability of photos with submissions. Reviews contact sheets. Offers no additional payment for photos accepted with ms; negotiates payment individually. Captions required. Buys one-time rights.

Columns/Departments: News (investigative news on animal abuse), 1,000-1,500 words; articles (in-depth writing/treatment), 1,000-3,000 words; News & Notes (news shorts, reports, updates) 500-750 words. Buys 1-10 mss/year. Query. Pays 10¢/word.

Tips: "Please read the magazine and understand how it is structured and organized and its focus. No phone calls. Every article must be accompanied by practical action you can take. Please remember we are a not-for-profit publication."

APPALOOSA JOURNAL, Appaloosa Horse Club, 5070 Hwy. 8 West, P.O. Box 8403, Moscow ID 83843-0903. (208)882-5578. Fax: (208)882-8150. Editor: Debbie Pitner Moors. 10-20% freelance written. Monthly magazine covering Appaloosa horses. Estab. 1946. Circ. 24,000. Pays on publication. Publishes ms an average of 3 months after acceptance. Byline given. Buys first North American serial rights. Query for electronic submissions. Reports in 1 month on queries; 2 months on mss. Free sample copy and writer's guidelines.

Nonfiction: Essays, historical/nostalgic, how-to, humor, interview/profile, horse health, personal experience, photo feature. Buys 6-7 mss/year. Query with or without published clips, or send complete ms. Length: 400-3,000 words. Pays $100-400. Sometimes pays expenses of writers on assignment.

Photos: Send photos with submission. Payment varies. Captions and identification of subjects required.

Columns: Horse racing, endurance riding, training.

Tips: "Articles by writers with horse knowledge, news sense and photography skills are in great demand. If it's a solid article about an Appaloosa, the writer has a pretty good chance of publication. Historical breed

 The double dagger before a listing indicates that the listing is new in this edition. New markets are often more receptive to freelance submissions.

features and "how-to" training articles are needed. A good understanding of the breed and the industry is helpful. Avoid purely sentimental, nostalgic horse owner stories. Make sure there's some substance and a unique twist."

‡AQUARIUM FISH MAGAZINE, Fancy Publications, Box 6050, Mission Viejo CA 92690. (714)855-8822. Fax: (714)855-3045. Editor: Edward Bauman. 100% freelance written. Monthly magazine on aquariums, tropical fish, ponds and pond fish. "We need well-written feature articles, preferably with color transparencies, dealing with all aspects of the hobby and directed toward novices and experienced hobbyists." Estab. 1988. Circ. 84,000. Pays on publication. Buys first North American serial rights. ASCII files by disk or modem. Reports in 1 month on queries; 2 months on mss. Sample copy for $4.50. Writer's guidelines free.
Nonfiction: "Articles on biology, care and breeding of aquarium and pond fish; pond and aquarium set-up and maintenance. No pet fish stories." Buys 60-75 mss/year. Query. Length: 1,500-3,500 words. Pays $100-300 for assigned articles.
Photos: Send slides with submission. Reviews contact sheets and transparencies. Offers $50-150 for color; up to $25 for b&w. Buys one-time rights.
Tips: "Know the subject; write tight, well-organized copy. Avoid 'my first aquarium' type of articles. Too many writers avoid adequate research. Many readers are knowledgeable about hobby and want solid information."

‡BIRD TALK, Dedicated to Better Care for Pet Birds, Fancy Publications, Box 6050, Mission Viejo CA 92690. (714)855-8822. Fax: (714)855-3045. Editor: Julie Rach. 85% freelance written. Monthly magazine covering the care and training of cage birds for men and women who own any number of pet or exotic birds. Pays latter part of month in which article appears. Byline given. Buys first North American serial rights. Submit seasonal/holiday material 7 months in advance. Accepts previously published submissions. No simultaneous submissions. Reports in 6 weeks on queries, 2 months on mss. Sample copy for $4.50. Writer's guidelines for #10 SASE.
Nonfiction: General interest (anything to do with pet birds); historical/nostalgic (of bird breeds, owners, cages); how-to (build cages, aviaries, playpens and groom, feed, breed, tame); humor; interview/profile (of bird and bird owners); how-to (live with birds—compatible pets, lifestyle, apartment adaptability, etc.); personal experience (with your own bird); photo feature (humorous or informative); travel (with pet birds or to see exotic birds); and articles giving behavioral guidelines, medical information, legal information, and description of species. No juvenile or material on wild birds not pertinent to pet care; everything should relate to *pet* birds. Buys 150 mss/year. Query. Length: 500-3,000 words. Pays 10-15¢/word.
Photos: State availability of photos or include in ms. Reviews b&w contact sheets; prefers slides. Pays $50-150 for color transparencies; $15 minimum for 5×7 b&w prints. Model release and identification of subjects preferred. Buys one-time rights.

CALIFORNIA HORSE REVIEW, P.O. Box 1238, Rancho Cordova CA 95741-1238. (916)638-1519. Fax: (916)638-1784. Editor: Diane Cranz. Monthly magazine covering equestrian interests. "*CHR* covers a wide spectrum—intensive veterinary investigation, trainer 'how-to' tips, breeding research updates and nutritional guidance. Editorial also devotes effort to reporting news and large state and national show results." Estab. 1963. Circ. 10,000. Pays on publication. Byline given. Buys first North American serial rights. Accepts previously published submissions. Send typed ms with rights for sale noted and information about when and where the article previously appeared. Reports in 2 months. Writer's guidelines with SASE.
Nonfiction: General interest (West Coast equine emphasis), how-to (training, breeding, horse care, riding) and technical (riding, training). "No fiction or anything *without* a strong focal point of interest for *West Coast equestrians* in the major performance/show English and Western disciplines." Buys 25-40 mss/year. Query with published clips. Length: 500-2,500 words. Pays $50-175 for assigned articles; $25-150 for unsolicited articles. Sometimes pays telephone expenses of writers on assignment.
Photos: Send photos with submission. Reviews 3×5 or larger prints. Offers no additional payment for photos accepted with ms. Captions required. Buys one-time rights.
Tips: "Be accurate, precise and knowledgeable about horses. Our readers are not beginners but sophisticated equestrians. Elementary, overly-basic how-to's are not appropriate for us."

CAT FANCY, Fancy Publications, Inc., Box 6050, Mission Viejo CA 92690. (714)855-8822. Editor: Debbie Phillips-Donaldson. 80-90% freelance written. Monthly magazine for men and women of all ages interested in all phases of cat ownership. Estab. 1965. Circ. 303,000. Pays on publication. Publishes ms an average of 6 months after acceptance. Buys first North American serial rights. Byline given. Absolutely no simultaneous submissions. Submit seasonal/holiday material 4 months in advance. Reports in 3 months. Sample copy for $5.50. Writer's guidelines for SASE.
Nonfiction: Historical, medical, how-to, humor, informational, personal experience, photo feature, technical; must be cat-oriented. Buys 5-7 mss/issue. *Query first*. Length: 500-3,000 words. Pays $35-400; special rates for photo/story packages.
Photos: Photos purchased with or without accompanying ms. Pays $35 minimum for 8×10 b&w glossy and $50 minimum for color prints; $50-200 for 35mm or 2¼×2¼ color transparencies; occasionally pays

more for particularly outstanding or unusual work. Send SASE for photo guidelines. Then send prints and transparencies. Model release required.

Fiction: Adventure, fantasy, historical, humorous. Nothing written with cats speaking or from cat's point of view. Buys 3-5 ms/year. *Query first.* Length: 500-3,000 words. Pays $50-400.

Fillers: Newsworthy or unusual; items with photos. Buys 5/year. Length: 500-1,000 words. Pays $35-100.

Tips: "Most of the articles we receive are profiles of the writers' own cats or profiles of cats that have recently died. We reject almost all of these stories. What we need are well-researched articles that will give our readers the information they need to better care for their cats. Please review past issues and notice the informative nature of articles before querying us with an idea. *Please query first.*"

CATS MAGAZINE, Cats Magazine Inc., P.O. Box 290037, Port Orange FL 32129-0037. (904)788-2770. Fax: (904)788-2710. Editor: Tracey Copeland. 85% freelance written. Monthly magazine for owners and lovers of cats. Estab. 1945. Circ. 149,000. Pays on publication. Byline given. Buys one-time rights. Submit seasonal/holiday material at least 6 months in advance. Reports in 3 months. Sample copy and writer's guidelines for $3 and 9×12 SAE.

Nonfiction: General interest (concerning cats); how-to (care, etc. for cats); health-related; humor; interview/profile (on cat-owning personalities); personal experience; stories about cats that live in remarkable circumstances, or have had a remarkable experience (can be historical). No talking cats, please. Send detailed query or complete ms with SASE. Length 400-2,000 words. Pays $25-450.

Photos: "Professional quality photographs that effectively illustrate the chosen topic are accepted with all submissions. However, it is the perogative of the art director to choose whether or not to use the photographs along with the printed piece." Photos that accompany an article should be in the form of color slides, 2¼×2¼ transparencies or glossy prints no smaller than 5×7. Pays $50-150 total depending on size used. To be considered for a cover shot, photos should be in the form of a transparency no smaller than 2¼×2¼. Pays $150-250. Clear, color prints are accepted for the Picture of the Month contest. Pays $25. Identification of subjects required. Buys one-time rights.

Fiction: Fantasy, historical, mystery, science fiction, slice-of-life vignettes and suspense are only used occasionally. All fiction must involve a cat or the relationship of a cat and humans, etc. No talking cats, please. Fiction should be believable. Send complete ms. Length: 800-1,500 words. Pays $30-50.

Poetry: Free verse, light verse, traditional. Length: 4-64 lines. Pays $5-30.

Tips: "Writer must show an affinity for cats. Extremely well-written, thoroughly researched, carefully thought out articles have the best chance of being accepted. Innovative topics or a new twist on an old subject are always welcomed."

THE CHRONICLE OF THE HORSE, P.O. Box 46, Middleburg VA 22117-0046. (703)687-6341. Fax: (703)687-3937. Editor: John Strassburger. Managing Editor: Nancy Comer. 80% freelance written. Weekly magazine about horses. "We cover English riding sports, including horse showing, grand prix jumping competitions, steeplechase racing, foxhunting, dressage, endurance riding, handicapped riding and combined training. We are the official publication for the national governing bodies of many of the above sports. We feature news, how-to articles on equitation and horse care and interviews with leaders in the various fields." Estab. 1937. Circ. 23,000. **Pays for features on acceptance**; news and other items on publication. Publishes ms an average of 4 months after acceptance. Byline given. Buys first North American rights and makes work-for-hire assignments. Submit seasonal/holiday material 3 months in advance. Reports in 1 month. Sample copy for $2 and 9×12 SAE. Writer's guidelines for #10 SASE.

Nonfiction: General interest; historical/nostalgic (history of breeds, use of horses in other countries and times, art, etc.); how-to (trailer, train, design a course, save money, etc.); humor (centered on living with horses or horse people); interview/profile (of nationally known horsemen or the very unusual); technical (horse care, articles on feeding, injuries, care of foals, shoeing, etc.); news (of major competitions, clear assignment with us first). Special issues: Steeplechasing, Grand Prix Jumping, Combined Training, Dressage, Hunt Roster, Junior and Pony, Christmas. No Q&A interviews, clinic reports, Western riding articles, personal experience or wild horses. Buys 300 mss/year. Query or send complete ms. Length: 300-1,225 words. Pays $25-200.

Photos: State availability of photos. Accepts prints or color slides. Accepts color for b&w reproduction. Pays $15-30. Identification of subjects required. Buys one-time rights.

Columns/Departments: Dressage, Combined Training, Horse Show, Horse Care, Racing over Fences, Young Entry (about young riders, geared for youth), Horses and Humanities, Hunting. Query or send complete ms. Length: 300-1,225 words. Pays $25-200.

Poetry: Light verse, traditional. No free verse. Buys 30/year. Length: 5-25 lines. Pays $15.

Fillers: Anecdotes, short humor, newsbreaks, cartoons. Buys 300/year. Length: 50-175 lines. Pays $10-25.

Tips: "Get our guidelines. Our readers are sophisticated, competitive horsemen. Articles need to go beyond common knowledge. Freelancers often attempt too broad or too basic a subject. We welcome well-written news stories on major events, but clear the assignment with us."

DOG FANCY, Fancy Publications, Inc., P.O. Box 6050, Mission Viejo CA 92690-6050. (714)855-8822. Editor: Kim Thornton. 75% freelance written. Eager to work with unpublished writers. "We'd like to see a balance of both new and established writers." Monthly magazine for men and women of all ages interested in all phases of dog ownership. Estab. 1970. Circ. 200,000. Pays on publication. Publishes ms an average of 6-12 months after acceptance. Buys one-time rights. Byline given. Submit seasonal/holiday material 6 months in advance. Reports in 2 months. Sample copy for $5.50. Writer's guidelines for #10 SASE.

Nonfiction: Historical, medical, how-to, humor, informational, interview, personal experience, photo feature, profile, technical. "We'll be looking for (and paying more for) high quality writing/photo packages. Interested writers should query with topics." Buys 5 mss/issue. Query. Length: 750-3,000 words. Payment depends on ms quality, whether photos or other art are included, and the quality of the photos/art.

Photos: For photos purchased *without* accompanying ms, pays $15 minimum for 8 × 10 b&w glossy prints; $50-200 for 35mm or 2¼ × 2¼ color transparencies. Send prints or transparencies. Model release required.

Tips: "We're looking for the unique experience that communicates something about the dog/owner relationship—with the dog as the focus of the story, not the owner. Medical articles are assigned to veterinarians. Note that we write for a lay audience (non-technical), but we do assume a certain level of intelligence: no talking down to people. If you've never seen the type of article you're writing in *Dog Fancy*, don't expect to. No 'talking dog' articles."

THE EQUINE MARKET, Midwest Outdoors, 111 Shore Dr., Hinsdale IL 60521. (708)887-7722. Fax: (708)887-1958. Editor: Midge Koontz. 90% freelance written. Monthly tabloid covering equestrian interests. Estab. 1970. Circ. 5,000. Pays on publication. Byline given. Buys all rights or makes work-for-hire assignments. Submit seasonal/holiday material 2 months in advance. Accepts previously published submissions. Send tearsheet or photocopy of article or typed ms with rights for sale noted and information about where and when the article previously appeared. For reprints, pays $25. Reports in 2 months. Free sample copy and writer's guidelines.

Nonfiction: Essays, general/interest, historical/nostalgic, how-to (horse care), inspirational, interview/profile, new product, opinion, personal experience, photo feature, show reporting technical, travel. Special issues: Holiday (November-December); Farm (June); Tack Shop (September). Buys 70 mss/year. Send complete ms. Length: 500-3,000 words. Pays $25 for assigned articles; $25 for unsolicited articles; or may trade articles for advertising.

Photos: Send photos with submission. Reviews negatives and 3 × 5 prints. Offers no additional payment for photos accepted with ms. Captions and identification of subjects required.

THE GREYHOUND REVIEW, P.O. Box 543, Abilene KS 67410. (913)263-4660. Fax: (913)263-4689. Editor: Gary Guccione. Managing Editor: Tim Horan. 20% freelance written. Monthly magazine covering greyhound breeding, training and racing. Estab. 1911. Circ. 6,000. **Pays on acceptance.** Byline given. Buys first rights. Submit seasonal/holiday material 2 months in advance. Accepts previously published material. Send photocopy of article. Pays 100% of the amount paid for an original article. Query for electronic submissions. Reports in 2 weeks on queries; 1 month on mss. *Writer's Market* recommends allowing 2 months for reply. Sample copy for $3. Free writer's guidelines.

Nonfiction: How-to, interview/profile, personal experience. "Articles must be targeted at the greyhound industry: from hard news, special events at racetracks to the latest medical discoveries." Do not submit gambling systems. Buys 24 mss/year. Query. Length: 1,000-10,000 words. Pays $85-150. Sometimes pays the expenses of writers on assignment.

Photos: State availability of photos with submission. Reviews 35mm transparencies and 8 × 10 prints. Offers $10-50/photo. Identification of subjects required. Buys one-time rights.

HOOF PRINT The Northeast's Equestrian Newspaper, Glens Falls Newspapers, Inc., P.O. Box 2157, Glens Falls NY 12801. (518)792-3131 ext. 3257. Managing Editor: Jennifer O. Bryant. 60% freelance written. Monthly tabloid covering equestrian (horse) news and features in the Northeast. "*Hoof Print* is an all-breed, all-discipline paper for Northeastern horse owners and horse lovers. We try to offer something for everyone at every experience level and produce an information-filled, colorful, easy-to-read paper." Estab. 1992. Circ. 15,000. Pays on publication. Publishes ms an average of 4 months after acceptance. Buys first North American serial or second serial (reprint) rights. Editorial lead time 2 months. Submit seasonal material 3 months in advance. Accepts simultaneous and previously published submissions. Query for electronic submissions. Reports in 1 month on queries; 2 months on mss. Sample copy for $2. Writer's guidelines free for SASE.

Nonfiction: How-to, humor, new product, personal experience (all must relate to horses). "No articles not pertinent to Northeast horse people." Buys 60 mss/year. Query or send complete ms. Length: 500-1,500 words. Pays $25 minimum. Sometimes pays expenses of writers on assignment.

Photos: Send photos with submission. Reviews negatives, transparencies and prints. Offers $15/photo. Captions and identification of subjects required. Buys one-time rights.

Columns/Departments: The Tail End (first-person experiences with horses) 800 words; Product reviews (products of interest to horse people) 500 words. Buys 12-24 mss/year. Query or send complete ms. Pays $25-40.

Poetry: Light verse. Buys 5 poems/year. Length: 5-20 lines. Pays $15-25.

Fillers: Facts, tips, short humor. Pays $5.

Tips: "Articles about events, people, horses, farms, etc., *in our area* and of interest to our readers are always needed. Knowledge of horses is necessary. We offer practical advice, how-to articles, plus news, information, and a variety of features in each issue. Send for writers' guidelines and study each month's theme. Query with ideas for theme-related articles. Cover photos that reflect monthly themes are needed as well."

HORSE ILLUSTRATED, The Magazine for Responsible Horse Owners, Fancy Publications, Inc., P.O. Box 6050, Mission Viejo CA 92690-6050. (714)855-8822. Fax: (714)855-3045. Editor: Audrey Pavia. 90% freelance written. Prefers to work with published/established writers but will work with new/unpublished writers. Monthly magazine covering all aspects of horse ownership. "Our readers are adults, mostly women, between the ages of 18 and 40; stories should be geared to that age group and reflect responsible horse care." Estab. 1976. Circ. 182,000. Pays on publication. Publishes ms an average of 8 months after acceptance. Byline given. Buys one-time rights; requires first North American rights among equine publications. Submit seasonal/holiday material 6 months in advance. Reports in 3 months. Sample copy for $3.50. Writer's guidelines for #10 SASE.

Nonfiction: How-to (horse care, training, veterinary care), photo feature. No "little girl" horse stories, "cowboy and Indian" stories or anything not *directly* relating to horses. "We are looking for longer, more authoritative, in-depth features on trends and issues in the horse industry. Such articles must be queried first with a detailed outline of the article and clips. We rarely have a need for fiction." Buys 100 mss/year. Query or send complete ms. Length: 1,000-2,500 words. Pays $100-300 for assigned articles; $50-300 for unsolicited articles.

Photos: Send photos with submission. Reviews 35mm transparencies, medium format transparencies and 5×7 prints. Occasionally offers additional payment for photos accepted with ms.

Tips: "Freelancers can break in at this publication with feature articles on Western and English training methods and trainer profiles (including training tips); veterinary and general care how-to articles; and horse sports articles. We rarely use personal experience articles. Submit photos with training and how-to articles whenever possible. We have a very good record of developing new freelancers into regular contributors/columnists. We are always looking for fresh talent, but certainly enjoy working with established writers who 'know the ropes' as well."

‡HORSEMEN'S YANKEE PEDLAR NEWSPAPER, 785 Southbridge St., Auburn MA 01501-1399. (508)832-9638. Fax: (508)832-6744. Publisher: Nancy L. Khoury. Managing Editor: Jane Sullivan. 40% freelance written. "All-breed monthly newspaper for horse enthusiasts of all ages and incomes, from one-horse owners to large commercial stables. Covers region from New Jersey to Maine." Circ. 15,000. Pays on publication. Buys all rights for one year. Accepts previously published submissions. Send photocopy of article or typed ms with rights for sale noted and information about when and where the article previously appeared. For reprints, pays 100% of the amount paid for an original article. Submit seasonal/holiday material 3 months in advance of issue date. Query for electronic submissions. Publishes ms an average of 5 months after acceptance. Reports in 1 month. Sample copy $3.75.

Nonfiction: Humor, educational and interview about horses and the people involved with them. Pays $2/published inch. Buys 100 mss/year. Query or submit complete ms or outline. Length: 1,500 words maximum.

Photos: Purchased with ms. Captions and photo credit required. Submit b&w prints; for return include SASE. Pays $5.

Columns/Departments: Area news column. Buys 85-95/year. Length: 1,200-1,400 words. Query.

Tips: "Query with outline of angle of story, approximate length and date when story will be submitted. Stories should be people-oriented and horse-focused. Send newsworthy, timely pieces, such as stories that are applicable to the season, for example: foaling in the spring or how to keep a horse healthy through the winter. We like to see how-tos, features about special horse people and issues affecting horsemen."

HORSEPLAY, Box 130, Gaithersburg MD 20884. (301)840-1866. Fax: (301)840-5722. Editor Emeritus: Cordelia Doucet. Managing Editor: Lisa Kiser. 50% freelance written. Works with published/established writers and a small number of new/unpublished writers each year. Monthly magazine covering horses and English horse sports for a readership interested in horses, show jumping, dressage, combined training, fox hunting and driving. 60-80 pages. Circ. 55,000. Pays at end of month following publication. Buys all, first North American serial and second serial (reprint) rights. Offers kill fee. Byline given. Deadline 2 months prior to issue date. Nothing returned without SASE. Rarely accepts previously published submissions. Send typed ms with rights for sale noted and, at query stage, information about when and where the article previously appeared. For reprints, pays 90% of the amount paid for an original article. Reports in 1 month. Sample copy for $3. Writer's and photographer's guidelines and house style sheet for #10 SASE.

• *Horse Play* is accepting fewer unsolicited manuscripts. The same amount of freelance material is published, but topics are assigned from editorial calendar.

Nonfiction: Instruction (various aspects of horsemanship, horse care, riding skills, stable management, shows, etc.), competitions, interviews, profiles, technical humorous essays. Query first. Preferred length: 2,500 words or less. Pays 10¢/word, all rights; 9¢/word, first North American serial rights; 7¢/word, second rights.

Photos: Purchased on assignment. Identify horse, rider, competition name, year on each image. Slides preferred, but sharp prints also accepted. Query or send contact sheet, prints or transparencies.

Tips: Don't send fiction, Western riding, or racing articles.

I LOVE CATS, I Love Cats Publishing, 950 Third Ave., 16th Floor, New York NY 10022-2705. (212)888-1855. Fax: (212)888-8420. Editor: Lisa Sheets. 85% freelance written. Bimonthly magazine covering cats. "*I Love Cats* is a general interest cat magazine for the entire family. It caters to cat lovers of all ages. The stories in the magazine include fiction, nonfiction, how-to, humorous and columns for the cat lover." Estab. 1989. Circ. 200,000. Pays on publication. Publishes ms an average of 1 year after acceptance. Byline given. No kill fee. Buys all rights. Must sign copyright consent form. Submit seasonal material 9 months in advance. Query for electronic submissions; IBM compatible. Reports in 2 months. Sample copy for $3. Writer's guidelines for #10 SASE.

Nonfiction: Essays, how-to, humor, inspirational, interview/profile, opinion, personal experience, photo feature. No poetry. Buys 200 mss/year. Send complete ms. Length: 100-1,000 words. Pays $40-250, contributor copies or other premiums "if requested." Sometimes pays expenses of writers on assignment. Send photos with submission. Offers no additional payment for photos accepted with ms. Identification of subjects required. Buys all rights.

Fiction: Adventure, fantasy, historical, humorous, mainstream, mystery, novel excerpts, slice-of-life vignettes, suspense. "This is a family magazine. No graphic violence, pornography or other inappropriate material. *I Love Cats* is strictly 'G-rated.' " Buys 50 mss/year. Send complete ms. Length: 500-1,200 words. Pays $40-250.

Fillers: Quizzes and short humor. Buys 20/year. Pays $10-35.

Tips: "Please keep stories short and concise. Send complete ms with photos, if possible. I buy lots of first-time authors. Nonfiction pieces w/color photos are always in short supply. With the exception of the standing columns, the rest of the magazine is open to freelancers. Be witty, humorous or take a different approach to writing."

LONE STAR HORSE REPORT, P.O. Box 14767, Fort Worth TX 76117-0767. (817)838-8642. Fax: (817)838-6410. Editor: Henry L. King. 15-20% freelance written. Monthly magazine on horses and horse people in Texas and Oklahoma. Estab. 1983. Circ. 10,000. Pays on publication. Publishes ms an average of 2 months after acceptance. Byline given. Buys first rights and second serial (reprint) rights. Submit seasonal/holiday material 2 months in advance. Accepts previously published submissions. Send tearsheet or photocopy of article or typed ms with rights for sale noted and information about when and where the article previously appeared. For reprints, pays 60% of amount paid for an original article. Reports in 2 months. Sample copy for $1. Writer's guidelines for #10 SASE.

Nonfiction: Interview/profile (horsemen living in trade area); photo feature (horses, farms, arenas, facilities, people in trade area). Buys 30-40 mss/year. Query with published clips or send complete ms. Length: 200-2,000 words. Pays $15-60. Sometimes pays the expenses of writers on assignment.

Photos: State availability of photos. Pays $5 for 5×7 b&w or color prints. Buys one-time rights.

Tips: "We need reports of specific horse-related events in Texas and Oklahoma such as trail rides, rodeos, play days, shows, etc., and also feature articles on horse farms, outstanding horses and/or horsemen."

‡MONKEY MATTERS, ILM Publishing Co., P.O. Box 62, Moraga CA 94556. (510)274-6210. Editor: Diane Sage. Managing Editor: Randy Helm. 20% freelance written. Bimonthly magazine covering monkey care and behavior. "Positive or informative articles on making life more positive for primates, accurate descriptions on the behavior of primates." Estab. 1995. Circ. 2,000. Pays on publication. Publishes ms an average of 3 months after acceptance. Byline given. Buys first or one-time rights. Editorial lead time 1 month. Submit seasonal material 4 months in advance. Accepts simultaneous and previously published submissions. Accepts electronic submissions. Reports in 1 month on queries; 2 months on mss. Sample copy for $2. Writer's guidelines for #10 SASE.

Nonfiction: Book excerpts, essays, general interest, historical/nostalgic, how-to, humor, inspirational, interview/profile, new product, opinion, personal experience, photo feature, technical, travel. Buys 24 mss/year. Send complete ms. Length: 500-2,500 words. Pays $5. Sometimes pays expenses of writers on assignment.

Photos: Send photos with submission. Offers $5/photo. Buys one-time rights.

Columns/Departments: Diane Sage. Primate Housing (description), 150 words; Zoo Reviews (description), 150 words; Nutrition (parallels to human nutrition), 200 words. Buys 12 mss/year. Send complete ms. Pays $5/year.

Fillers: Anecdotes, facts, gags to be illustrated by cartoonist, newsbreaks, short humor. Buys 6 mss/year. Length: 50-100 words. Pays $5.

Tips: "People who love animals can best describe their personalities and behavior. We are willing to work with beginning writers who wish to approach the subject of primates."

MUSHING, Stellar Communications, Inc., P.O. Box 149, Ester AK 99725-0149. (907)479-0454. Fax: (907)479-0454. Publisher: Todd Hoener. Managing Editor: Diane Herrmann. Bimonthly magazine on "all aspects of dog driving activities. We include information (how-to), nonfiction (entertaining), health, ethics, news and history stories." Estab. 1987. Circ. 6,000. Pays on publication. Publishes ms an average of 4 months after acceptance. Byline given. Buys first serial and second serial (reprint) rights. Submit seasonal/holiday material 4 months in advance. Query for electronic submissions. Reports in 8 months. Sample copy for $4. Writer's guidelines free. Call for information.

Nonfiction: Historical, how-to, humor, interview/profile, new product, personal experience, photo feature, technical, innovations, travel. Themes: Iditarod and long-distance racing (January/February); Expeditions (March/April); health and nutrition (May/June); musher and dog profiles, summer activities (July/August); equipment, fall training (September/October); races and places (November/December). Query with or without published clips, or send complete ms. Length: 500-3,000 words. Pays $50-250 for articles. Payment depends on quality, deadlines, experience. Sometimes pays expenses of writers on assignment.

Photos: Send photos with submission. Reviews contact sheets, transparencies, prints. Offers $20-150/photo. Captions, model releases, identification of subjects required. Buys one-time and second reprint rights. We look for good b&w and quality color for covers and specials.

Fillers: Anecdotes, facts, cartoons, newsbreaks, short humor, puzzles. Length: 100-250 words. Pays $20-35.

Tips: "Read our magazine. Know something about dog-driven, dog-powered sports."

PAINT HORSE JOURNAL, American Paint Horse Association, P.O. Box 961023, Fort Worth TX 76161-0023. (817)439-3400, ext. 210. Fax: (817)439-3484. Associate Editor: Dan Streeter. 10% freelance written. Works with a small number of new/unpublished writers each year. Monthly magazine for people who raise, breed and show Paint horses. Estab. 1966. Circ. 20,000. **Pays on acceptance.** Publishes ms an average of 3 months after acceptance. Buys first North American serial rights plus reprint rights occasionally. Pays negotiable kill fee. Byline given. Phone queries OK, but prefers written query. Submit seasonal/holiday material 3 months in advance. Accepts previously published articles. Send typed ms with rights for sale noted and information about when and where the article previously appeared. For reprints, pays 20-30% of the amount paid for an original article. Reports in 1 month. Writers guidelines available upon request. Sample copy $4.

Nonfiction: General interest (personality pieces on well-known owners of Paints); historical (Paint horses in the past—particular horses and the breed in general); how-to (train and show horses); photo feature (Paint horses). Now seeking informative well-written articles on recreational riding. Buys 4-5 mss/issue. Send complete ms. Pays $25-450.

Photos: Send photos with ms. Offers no additional payment for photos accepted with accompanying ms. Uses 3×5 or larger b&w or color glossy prints; 35mm or larger color transparencies. Captions required. Photos must illustrate article and must include Paint Horses.

Tips: "PHJ needs breeder-trainer articles, Paint horse marketing and timely articles from areas throughout the US and Canada. We are looking for more recreational and how-to articles. We are beginning to cover equine activity such as trail riding, orienteering and other outdoor events. Photos with copy are almost always essential. Well-written first person articles are welcomed. Submit items that show a definite understanding of the horse business. Be sure you understand precisely what a Paint horse is as defined by the American Paint Horse Association. Use proper equine terminology and proper grounding in ability to communicate thoughts."

THE QUARTER HORSE JOURNAL, P.O. Box 32470, Amarillo TX 79120. (806)376-4811. Fax: (806)376-8364. Editor-in-Chief: Audie Rackley. Editor: Jim Jennings. 20% freelance written. Prefers to work with published/established writers. Monthly official publication of the American Quarter Horse Association. Estab. 1948. Circ. 75,000. **Pays on acceptance.** Publishes ms an average of 3 months after acceptance. Buys first North American serial rights. Submit seasonal/holiday material 2 months in advance. Reports in 2 months. Free sample copy and writer's guidelines.

Nonfiction: Historical ("those that retain our western heritage"); how-to (fitting, grooming, showing, or anything that relates to owning, showing, or breeding); informational (educational clinics, current news); interview (feature-type stories—must be about established horses or people who have made a contribution to the business); personal opinion; and technical (equine updates, new surgery procedures, etc.). Buys 20 mss/year. Length: 800-2,500 words. Pays $150-300.

Photos: Purchased with accompanying ms. Captions required. Send prints or transparencies. Uses 5×7 or 8×10 b&w glossy prints, 2¼×2¼, 4×5 or 35 mm color transparencies. Offers no additional payment for photos accepted with accompanying ms.
Tips: "Writers must have a knowledge of the horse business."

THE RANCH DOG TRAINER, Stonehedge Publishing Co. Inc., 7686 State Route 17, West Plains MO 65775. (417)257-7376. Fax: (417)257-7376. E-mail: rdtkc@townsqr.com. Editor: Larry Conner. Managing Editor: Kathy Conner. 50% freelance written. Bimonthly magazine covering training and use of stock dogs. "Readers are farmers and ranchers who use dogs to handle livestock. Some readers are involved in competing in competitive events, working livestock with their dogs. Emphasis is made on practical use, covering all breeds of herding dogs." Estab. 1986. Circ. 3,000. Pays on publication. Byline given. Offers 25% kill fee. Buys first North American serial, all rights or makes work-for-hire assignments. Editorial lead time 4 months. Submit seasonal material 6 months in advance. Query for electronic submissions. Reports in 2 weeks on queries; 2 months on mss. Accepts previously published articles. Send typed ms with rights for sale noted and information about when and where the article previously appeared. Sample copy for $4. Writer's guidelines free on request.
Nonfiction: How-to train and use stockdogs, interview/profile, opinion, personal experience. "No articles about pets or show dogs." Buys 25-30 mss/year. Query with published clips. Length: 900-3,600 words. Pays minimum of $36 (4¢/word). Sometimes pays expenses of writers on assignment.
Photos: Send photos with submission. Reviews 3×5 or larger prints. Offers $5-50/photo. Identification of subjects required. Buys one-time rights.
Columns/Departments: Reviews (books or videos pertaining to stock-dog owners. Are they useful?) 900-1,800 words; Canine Health (information useful to layman) 1,800 words; Livestock Guardian Dogs (breed bio/use and training of quardian dogs—great Pyrenees, for example) 1,800 words. Buys 18-20 mss/year. Send complete ms. Pays $35-75 (4¢/word).
Tips: "Will work with authors who are willing to learn about stock dogs. Interviews with livestock producers who are using dogs—why a particular breed, how got started, detailed training info, etc.—are especially useful for us. Technical articles should be written by qualified professionals (i.e., canine health by veterinarians). All areas except reader-submitted sections (trial results, 'Liar's Tale,' letters to the editor) are open to freelancers. Generally, the more descriptive and detailed an article is, the better."

REPTILE & AMPHIBIAN MAGAZINE, RD3, Box 3709A, Pottsville PA 17901-9219. (717)622-6050. Fax: (717)622-5858. Editor: Erica Ramus. 80% freelance written. Full-color digest-size bimonthly magazine covering reptiles and amphibians. Devoted to the amateur herpetologist who is generally college-educated and familiar with the basics of herpetology. Estab. 1989. Circ. 15,000. **Pays on acceptance**. Publishes ms an average of 6 months after acceptance. Byline given. Buys first North American serial, one-time and (occasionally) second serial (reprint) rights. Accepts previously published material. Send photocopy of article and information about when and where the article previously appeared. For reprints pays 100% of the amount paid for an original article. Reports in 2 weeks. Sample copy for $4. Writer's guidelines for #10 SASE.
Nonfiction: General interest, photo feature, technical. Publishes articles on life cycles of various reptiles and amphibians, natural history, captive care and breeding. No first-person narrative, "me-and-Joe" stories or articles by writers unfamiliar with the subject matter. "Readers are already familiar with the basics of herpetology and are usually advanced amateur hobbyists." Buys 50 mss/year. Query or send complete ms. Length: 1,500-2,000 words. Pays $100. Sometimes pays expenses of familiar or regular writer on assignment.
Photos: Send photos with submission whenever possible. Reviews 35mm slide transparencies, 4×6, 5×7 and 8×10 glossy prints. Offers $10 for b&w, $25 for color photos. Captions, model releases and identification of subjects required. Animals should be identified by common and/or scientific name. Buys one-time rights.
Columns/Departments: Photo Dept./Herp●Art Dept., 500-750 words; Book Review, 500-750 words. Buys 12 mss/year. Send complete ms. Pays $50-75.
Tips: "Note your personal qualifications, such as experience in the field or advanced education. Writers have the best chance selling us feature articles—know your subject and supply high quality color photos."

TROPICAL FISH HOBBYIST, "The World's Most Widely Read Aquarium Monthly," TFH Publications, Inc., 211 W. Sylvania Ave., Neptune City NJ 07753. (908)988-8400. Fax: (908)988-9635. Editor: Ray Hunziker. Managing Editor: Neal Pronek. 90% freelance written. Monthly magazine covering the tropical fish hobby. "We favor articles well illustrated with good color slides and aimed at both the neophyte and veteran tropical fish hobbyist." Estab. 1952. Circ. 60,000. **Pays on acceptance.** Publishes ms an average of 15 months after acceptance. Byline given. Buys all rights. Submit seasonal/holiday material 4 months in advance. Accepts simultaneous and previously published submissions. Send tearsheet of article and information about when and where the article previously appeared. For reprints, pays 100% of the amount paid for an original article. Reports in 1 month. Sample copy for $3 and 9×12 SAE with 6 first-class stamps. Writer's guidelines for #10 SASE.
Nonfiction: General interest, how-to, personal experience, photo feature, technical, and articles dealing with beginning and advanced aspects of the aquarium hobby. No "how I got started in the hobby" articles that impart little solid information. Buys 40-50 mss/year. Length: 1,000-3,000 words. Pays $80-200.

Photos: State availability of or send photos with ms. Reviews contact sheets, transparencies, prints. Offers $10-15/photo. Identification of subjects required. Buys all rights.
Columns/Departments: Freshwater, saltwater, reptile, and amphibian sections (from a keeping standpoint), 1,000-2,000 words. Buys 10-20 mss/year. Pays $80-200.

THE WESTERN HORSEMAN, World's Leading Horse Magazine Since 1936, Western Horseman, Inc., P.O. Box 7980, Colorado Springs CO 80933-7980. (719)633-5524. Editor: Pat Close. 50% freelance written. Works with a small number of new/unpublished writers each year. Monthly magazine. Estab. 1936. Circ. 230,322. **Pays on acceptance.** Publishes ms an average of 5 months after acceptance. Buys one-time and North American serial rights. Byline given. Submit seasonal/holiday material 6 months in advance. Reports in 3 weeks. Sample copy for $5. Writer's guidelines for #10 SASE. No fax material accepted.
Nonfiction: How-to (horse training, care of horses, tips, ranch/farm management, etc.), informational (on rodeos, ranch life, historical articles of the West emphasizing horses). Buys 250 mss/year. Length: 500-2,500 words. Pays $35-500, "sometimes higher by special arrangement."
Photos: Send photos with ms. Offers no additional payment for photos. Uses 5×7 or 8×10 b&w glossy prints and 35mm transparencies. Captions required.
Tips: "Submit clean copy with professional quality photos. All copy, including computer copy, should be double-spaced. Stay away from generalities. Writing style should show a deep interest in horses coupled with a wide knowledge of the subject."

Art and Architecture

Listed here are publications about art, art history, specific art forms and architecture written for art patrons, architects, artists and art enthusiasts. Publications addressing the business and management side of the art industry are listed in the Art, Design and Collectibles category of the Trade section. Trade publications for architecture can be found in Building Interiors, and Construction and Contracting sections.

THE AMERICAN ART JOURNAL, Kennedy Galleries, Inc. 730 Fifth Ave., New York NY 10019. (212)541-9600. Fax: (212)977-3833. Editor-in-Chief: Jayne A. Kuchna. Prefers to work with published/established writers; works with a small number of new/unpublished writers each year. Semiannual scholarly magazine of American art history of the 17th, 18th, 19th and 20th centuries, including painting, sculpture, architecture, photography, cultural history, etc., for people with a serious interest in American art, and who are already knowledgeable about the subject. Readers are scholars, curators, collectors, students of American art, or persons with a strong interest in Americana. Circ. 2,000. **Pays on acceptance.** Publishes ms an average of 6 months after acceptance. Buys all rights, but will reassign rights to writer. Byline given. Reports in 2 months. Sample copy for $18.
Nonfiction: "All articles are about some phase or aspect of American art history." No how-to articles or reviews of exhibitions. No book reviews or opinion pieces. No human interest approaches to artists' lives. No articles written in a casual or "folksy" style. *Writing style must be formal and serious.* Buys 10-15 mss/year. Submit complete ms "with good cover letter." No queries. Length: 2,500-8,000 words. Pays $400-600.
Photos: Purchased with accompanying ms. Captions required. Uses b&w only. Offers no additional payment for photos accepted with accompanying ms.
Tips: "Articles *must be* scholarly, thoroughly documented, well-researched, well-written and illustrated. Whenever possible, all manuscripts must be accompanied by b&w photographs, which have been integrated into the text by the use of numbers."

AMERICAN INDIAN ART MAGAZINE, American Indian Art, Inc., 7314 E. Osborn Dr., Scottsdale AZ 85251-6417. (602)994-5445. Editor: Roanne P. Goldfein. 97% freelance written. Works with a small number of new/unpublished writers each year. Quarterly magazine covering Native American art, historic and contemporary, including new research on any aspect of Native American art north of the US/Mexico border. Estab. 1975. Circ. 20,000. Pays on publication. Publishes ms an average of 3 months after acceptance. Byline given. Buys one-time and first rights. Simultaneous queries OK. Reports in 3 weeks on queries; 3 months on mss. Writer's guidelines for #10 SASE.
Nonfiction: New research on any aspect of Native American art. No previously published work or personal interviews with artists. Buys 12-18 mss/year. Query. Length: 1,000-2,500 words. Pays $75-300.
Tips: "The magazine is devoted to all aspects of Native American art. Some of our readers are knowledgeable about the field and some know very little. We seek articles that offer something to both groups. Articles reflecting original research are preferred to those summarizing previously published information."

AMERICAN STYLE, Contemporary Crafts For Living and Giving, The Rosen Group, 3000 Chestnut Ave., Suite 304, Baltimore MD 21211. (410)889-3093. Fax: (410)243-7089. Editor: Laura Rosen. 50%

freelance written. Quarterly magazine covering handmade American Crafts, "designed to promote and educate consumers." Estab. 1994. Circ. 50,000. Pays on publication. Publishes ms an average of 6 months after acceptance. Byline given. Buys second serial (reprint) rights or all rights. Editorial lead time 4 months. Submit seasonal material 6 months in advance. Query for electronic submissions. Reports in 3 months. Sample copy for $3. Writer's guidelines for #10 SASE.

• *American Style* is especially interested in articles about the legend/storytelling aspect and cultural connections of contemporary craft arts.

Nonfiction: General interest, interview/profile, personal experience, photo feature. Buys 4 mss/year. Query with published clips. Length: 300-2,500 words. Pay rates vary. Sometimes pays expenses of writers on assignment.

Photos: Send photos with submission. Reviews oversized transparencies and 35mm slides. Negotiates payment individually. Captions required.

Columns/Departments: Laura Rosen. Home Decorating (collecting and decorating with American crafts), 700-1,000 words. Buys 4 mss/year. Query with published clips. Pay rates vary.

Tips: "Contact editor about upcoming issues, article ideas. Let us know what you are sending, follow-up. All departments will be open. Concentrate on contemporary American craft art, such as ceramics, wood, fiber, glass, etc., No popsicle sticks or macramé or other hobby crafts."

‡ART PAPERS, Atlanta Art Papers, Inc., P.O. Box 77348, Atlanta GA 30357. (404)588-1837. Editor: Glenn Harper. 75% freelance written. Bimonthly magazine covering contemporary art and artists. "*Art Papers*, a bimonthly magazine about regional and national contemporary art and artists, features a variety of perspectives on current art concerns. Each issue presents topical articles, interviews, reviews from across the US, and an extensive and informative artists' classified listings section. Our writers and the artists they cover represent the scope and diversity of the country's art scene." Estab. 1977. Circ. 4,000. Pays on publication. Publishes ms an average of 3 months after acceptance. Byline given. Buys all rights. Editorial lead time 2 months. Submit seasonal material 2 months in advance. Accepts simultaneous and previously published submissions. Query for electronic submissions. "Writers should contact us regarding manuscript status." Sample copy for $1.24. Writer's guidelines for #10 SASE.

Nonfiction: Interview/profile. See our editorial schedule. Buys 300 mss/year. "We rely on the initiatives of our writers for review coverage." Pays $35-100.

Photos: Send photos with submission. Reviews color slides, b&w prints. Offers no additional payment for photos accepted with ms. Identification of subjects required.

Columns/Departments: Contact: Barbara Schrieber, associate editor. Newsbriefs (current art concerns and news—call for scope). Buys 18-24 mss/year. Query. Pays $35.

Tips: "Write for a copy of our writer's guidelines and request a sample copy of *Art Papers*. Interested writers should call Glenn Harper to discuss intents."

‡ART REVUE MAGAZINE, 302 W. 13th St., Loveland CO 80537. (303)669-0625. Editor: Jan McNutt. 100% freelance written. Quarterly magazine covering fine art of sculpture and painting. "Articles are focused on fine art: how to, business of art, profiles on artists, museums, galleries, art businesses, art shows and exhibitions." Estab. 1990. Circ. 7,000. Pays on publication. Publishes ms an average of 3 months after acceptance. Byline given. Offers 25% kill fee or $25. Buys first rights. Editorial lead time 3 months. Submit seasonal material 3-6 months in advance. Accepts simultaneous submissions. Sample copy for $3. Writer's guidelines for #10 SASE.

Nonfiction: Essays, how-to, humor, interview/profile, new product, opinion, personal experience, photo feature, technical, travel. Does not want crafts, pottery, doll-making, inspirational, religious, tie-dying. Buys 12-20 mss/year. Query. Length: 1,000-2,500 words. Pays $100 and up.

Photos: Send photos with submission. Reviews 4×5 prints. Offers no additional payment for photos accepted with ms. Captions, identification of subjects required.

Columns/Departments: Art Matters (interesting art happenings), 100-200 words; Profiles (features) (famous, non-famous artists), 1,000-2,500 words; Profiles on Businesses (bronze foundries, art schools, etc.), 1,000-2,500 words; Covert (short profile on totally unknown artist), 50-150 words. Buys 12-20 mss/year. Query. Pays $100-200.

Fillers: Anecdotes, facts, gags to be illustrated by cartoonist, newsbreaks, short humor. Buys 10-12/year. Length: 50-250 words. Pays $25-100.

Tips: "Write a letter of inquiry to Jan McNutt. Present some ideas for articles."

ART TIMES, A Literary Journal and Resource for All the Arts, P.O. Box 730, Mount Marion NY 12456-0730. Phone/fax: (914)246-6944. Editor: Raymond J. Steiner. 10% freelance written. Prefers to work with published/established writers; works with a small number of new/unpublished writers each year. Monthly tabloid covering the arts (visual, theatre, dance, etc.). "*Art Times* covers the art fields and is distributed in locations most frequented by those enjoying the arts. Our copies are sold at newsstands and are distributed throughout upstate New York counties as well as in most of the galleries in Soho, 57th Street and Madison Avenue in the metropolitan area; locations include theaters, galleries, museums, cultural centers and the like. Our readers are mostly over 40, affluent, art-conscious and sophisticated. Subscribers are located across US and abroad (Italy, France, Germany, Greece, Russia, etc.)." Estab. 1984. Circ. 15,000. Pays on publication. Publishes ms an average of 1 year after acceptance. Byline given. Buys first serial rights. Submit seasonal/holiday material 8 months in advance. Accepts simultaneous submissions. Reports in 3 months on queries; 6 months on mss. Sample copy for 9 × 12 SAE with 6 first-class stamps. Writer's guidelines for #10 SASE.

Fiction: Raymond J. Steiner, fiction editor. "We're looking for short fiction that aspires to be *literary*. No excessive violence, sexist, off-beat, erotic, sports, or juvenile fiction." Buys 8-10 mss/year. Send complete ms. Length: 1,500 words maximum. Pays $25 maximum (honorarium) and 1 year's free subscription.

Poetry: Cheryl A. Rice, poetry editor. Poet's Niche. Avant-garde, free verse, haiku, light verse, traditional. "We prefer well-crafted 'literary' poems. No excessively sentimental poetry." Buys 30-35 poems/year. Submit maximum 6 poems. Length: 20 lines maximum. Offers contributor copies and 1 year's free subscription.

Tips: "Be advised that we are presently on an approximate two-year lead. We are now receiving 300-400 poems and 40-50 short stories per month. We only publish two to three poems and one story each issue. Be familiar with *Art Times* and its special audience. *Art Times* has literary leanings with articles written by a staff of scholars knowledgeable in their respective fields. Although an 'arts' publication, we observe no restrictions (other than noted) in accepting fiction/poetry other than a concern for quality writing—subjects can cover anything and not specifically arts."

THE ARTIST'S MAGAZINE, F&W Publications, Inc., 1507 Dana Ave., Cincinnati OH 45207-1005. Editor: Mary Magnus. 80% freelance written. Works with a small number of new/unpublished writers each year. Monthly magazine covering primarily two-dimensional art instruction for working artists. "Ours is a highly visual approach to teaching the serious amateur artist techniques that will help him improve his skills and market his work. The style should be crisp and immediately engaging." Circ. 250,000. **Pays on acceptance.** Publishes ms an average of 4 months after acceptance. Bionote given for feature material. Offers 20% kill fee. Buys first North American serial and second serial (reprint) rights. Accepts previously published articles "as long as noted as such." Reports in 2 months. Sample copy for $3 and 9 × 12 SAE with 3 first-class stamps. Writer's guidelines for #10 SASE.

● Writers must have working knowledge of art techniques. This magazine's most consistent need is for instructional articles written in the artist's voice.

Nonfiction: Instructional only—how an artist uses a particular technique, how he handles a particular subject or medium, or how he markets his work. "The emphasis must be on how the reader can learn some method of improving his artwork, or the marketing of it." No unillustrated articles; no seasonal/holiday material; no travel articles; no profiles of artists (except for "The Artist's Life," below). Buys 60 mss/year. Query first; all queries must be accompanied by slides, transparencies, prints or tearsheets of the artist's work as well as the artist's bio, and the writer's bio and clips. Length: 1,000-2,500 words. Pays $200-350 and up. Sometimes pays the expenses of writers on assignment.

Photos: "Transparencies are required with every accepted article since these are essential for our instructional format. Full captions must accompany these." Buys one-time rights.

Departments: Three departments are open to freelance writers. Strictly Business (articles dealing with the business and legal end of selling art; taxes, recordkeeping, copyright, contracts, etc.). Query first. Length: 1,800 word limit. Pays $150 and up. The Artist's Life and P.S. The Artist's Life (profiles and brief items about artists and their work; also, art-related games, puzzles and poetry). Query first with samples of artist's work for profiles; send complete ms for other items. Length: 600 words maximum. Pays $50 and up for profiles; up to $25 for brief items and poetry. P.S. (a humorous look at art from the artist's point of view, or at least sympathetic to the artist). Send complete ms. Pays $50 and up.

Tips: "Look at several current issues and read the author's guidelines carefully. Remember that our readers are fine and graphic artists."

EQUINE IMAGES, The National Magazine of Equine Art, Equine Images Ltd., P.O. Box 916, Fort Dodge IA 50501-3931. (800)247-2000, ext. 213. Fax: (800)247-2000, ext. 217. Editor: Susan J. Leman. Publisher: Susan Badger. 80% freelance written. Bimonthly magazine of equine art. "*Equine Images* serves collectors and equine art enthusiasts. We write for a sophisticated, culturally-oriented audience." Estab. 1986. Circ. 20,000. Pays on publication. Byline given. Buys first rights and makes work-for-hire assignments. Accepts previously published articles. Send photocopy of article and information about when and where the article previously appeared. For reprints pays 50% of amount paid for an original article. Reports in 2 months. Sample copy for $6.95 and 9 × 12 SAE. Writer's guidelines for #10 SASE.

Nonfiction: Historical/nostalgic (history of the horse in art), how-to (art collections), interview/profile (equine artists, galleries, collectors), personal experience (of equine artists and collectors), photo feature (artworks or collections). "No articles about horses in general—just horse art." Buys 8-10 mss/year. Query with published clips. Length: 500-3,000 words. Pays $150-300 for assigned articles; $100-300 for unsolicited articles.

Photos: State availability of photos with submission. Writer responsible for sending visuals with finished ms. Reviews contact sheets, transparencies, prints. Offers no additional payment for photos accepted with ms. Identification of subjects required. Buys one-time rights.

Tips: "We are interested only in art-related subjects. We are looking for stories that help art collectors better understand, expand or protect their collections. The most promising categories for writers are profiles of prominent artists and equine galleries or museums. Send a good query letter with accompanying visuals, along with published clips or writing samples."

‡JUXTAPOZ, New Magazine For New Art, High Speed Productions, Inc., P.O. Box 884570, San Francisco CA 99188-4570. (415)822-3083. Editor: Kevin J. Thatcher. Contact: Shay Nowick. 10% freelance written. Quarterly magazine covering new art, lowbrow art, weird art. "*Juxtapoz* features art in the form of surrealist paintings, underground comix, rock posters, side show freak banners, photography and sculpture and anything else that is weird, colorful, offbeat and fantastic. Audience is 15-34 years." Estab. 1994. Circ. 50,000. Pays on publication. Publishes ms an average of 6 months after acceptance. Byline given. Offers 10% kill fee. Buys first North American serial rights and one-time rights. Editorial lead time 4 months. Submit seasonal material 3 months in advance. Accepts previously published submissions. Query for electronic submissions. Reports in 2 weeks on queries; 1 month on mss. Sample copy for $4.95. Writer's guidelines free on request.
Nonfiction: Exposé, interview/profile, opinion, photo feature. Buys 4 mss/year. Query with published clips. Length: 250-3,000 words. Pays 10-25¢/word. Sometimes pays expenses of writers on assignment.
Photos: Send photos with submission and SASE. Offers $25-150/photo. Captions, model releases, identification of subjects required. Buys one-time rights.
Columns/Departments: Reviews (art shows, products, books, video, etc.), 250 words; Confusion (gossip, rumor, critique), 250 words; Art . . . & . . . (gallery listings), 10-50 words. Send complete ms. Pays 10-25¢/word.
Tips: "*Juxtapoz* covers artists with real talent and not just the latest trends. Each issue will feature something from the past, present and a hint to the future."

THE ORIGINAL ART REPORT, P.O. Box 15895, Loves Park IL 61132-5895. Editor/Publisher: Frank Salantrie. Newsletter emphasizing "visual art conditions from the visual artists' and general public's perspectives." Estab. 1967. Pays on publication. Reports in 2 weeks. Sample copy for $1.50 and #10 or #9 SASE.
Nonfiction: Investigative reports (art galleries, government agencies ripping off artists, or ignoring them); historical (perspective pieces relating to now); humor (whenever possible); informational (material that is unavailable in other art publications); interview (with artists, other experts; serious material on visual arts conditions; no profiles); personal opinion; technical (brief items to recall traditional methods of producing art); travel (places in the world where artists are welcomed and honored as well as unwanted and dishonored); philosophical, economic, aesthetic, and artistic. "We would like to receive investigative articles on government and private arts agencies, and nonprofits, too, perhaps hiding behind status to carry on for business entities. Exclusive interest in visual fine art condition as it affects individuals, society, and artists and as they affect it. Must take advocacy position. Prefer controversial subject matter and originality of treatment. Honesty and dedication to truth are absolute requirements. Also artist's position on non-art topics. No vanity profiles of artists, arts organizations and arts promoters' operations." Query or submit complete ms. Length: 1,000 words maximum. Pays 1¢/word.
Tips: "We have a stronger than ever emphasis on editorial opinion or commentary, based on fact and of the visual arts condition: economics, finances, politics and manufacture of art, and the social and individual implications of and to fine art."

SOUTHWEST ART, CBH Publishing, P.O. Box 460535, Houston TX 77256-8535. (713)850-0990. Fax: (713)850-1314. Editor-in-Chief: Susan H. McGarry. 60% freelance written. Monthly fine arts magazine "directed to art collectors interested in artists, market trends and art history of the American West." Estab. 1971. Circ. 64,000. **Pays on acceptance.** Publishes ms an average of 1 year after acceptance. Byline given. Offers $125 kill fee. Submit seasonal/holiday material 8 months in advance. Reports in 6 months. Free sample copy and writer's guidelines.
Nonfiction: Book excerpts, interview/profile, opinion. No fiction or poetry. Buys 70 mss/year. Query with published clips. Length 1,400-1,600 words. Pays $400 for assigned articles. Send photos with submission.
Photos: Reviews 35mm, 2¼, 4×5 transparencies and 8×10 prints. Captions and identification of subjects required. Negotiates rights.

THEDAMU, The Black Arts Magazine, Detroit Black Arts Alliance, 13217 Livernois, Detroit MI 48238-3162. (313)931-3427. Editor: David Rambeau. Managing Editor: Titilaya Akanke. Art Director: Charles Allen. 20% freelance written. Monthly literary magazine on the arts. "We publish Afro-American feature articles on local artists." Estab. 1965. Circ. 4,000. Pays on publication. Publishes 4 months after acceptance. Byline given. Buys one-time rights. Submit seasonal/holiday material 4 months in advance. Query for electronic submissions. Accepts simultaneous and previously published submissions. Send photocopy of article and information about when and where the article previously appeared. Pays 50% of their fee for an original article. Reports in 1 month on queries; 3 months on mss. Sample copy for $2 and 6×9 SAE with 4 first-class stamps. Writer's guidelines for #10 SASE.
Nonfiction: Essays, interview/profile. Buys 20 mss/year. Send complete ms. Length: 500-1,500 words. Pays $10-25 for unsolicited articles. Pays with contributor copies or other premiums if writer agrees.

Photos: State availability of photos with submission. Reviews 5×7 prints. Offers no additional payment for photos accepted with ms. Captions, model releases and identification of subjects required. Buys one-time rights.
Tips: "Send a résumé and sample manuscript. Query for fiction, poetry, plays and film/video scenarios. Especially interested in Afro-centric cartoonists for special editions and exhibitions."

U.S. ART: All the News That Fits Prints, MSP Communications, 220 S. Sixth St., Suite 500, Minneapolis MN 55402. (612)339-7571. Editor/Publisher: Frank Sisser. Managing Editor: Cathy Clauson. 75% freelance written. Magazine published 10 times/year, plus annual Wildlife Art Guide and Print Guide supplements. One artist profile per issue; service articles to inform limited-edition print collectors of trends and options in the market; round-up features spotlighting a particular genre (wildlife, western, fantasy art, etc.) All artists featured must be active in the market for limited-edition prints. National circulation 55,000. Distributed primarily through galleries as a free service to their customers. Writer byline given. Pays $450 for features. Offers 25% kill fee. Departments/columns are staff-written.
   ● *U.S. Art* has increased its coverage of original graphics (etchings, woodcuts, stone lithography) and is looking for more writers who understand these printmaking processes.

WESTART, P.O. Box 6868, Auburn CA 95604. (916)885-0969. Editor-in-Chief: Martha Garcia. Semimonthly 20-page tabloid emphasizing art for practicing artists and artists/craftsmen; students of art and art patrons. Estab. 1961. Circ. 5,000. Pays on publication. Buys all rights. Byline given. Phone queries OK. Free sample copy and writer's guidelines.
Nonfiction: Informational, photo feature, profile. No hobbies. Buys 6-8 mss/year. Query or submit complete ms. Include SASE for reply or return. Length: 700-800 words. Pays 50¢/column inch.
Photos: Purchased with or without accompanying ms. Send b&w prints. Pays 50¢/column inch.
Tips: "We publish information which is current—that is, we will use a review of an exhibition only if exhibition is still open on the date of publication. Therefore, reviewer must be familiar with our printing and news deadlines."

WOMEN ARTISTS NEWS BOOK REVIEW, (formerly *Women Artists News*), Midmarch Arts Press, 300 Riverside, New York NY 10025-5239. Editor: Judy Seigel. 70-90% freelance written. Eager to work with new/unpublished writers. Annual magazine for "artists and art historians, museum and gallery personnel, students, teachers, crafts personnel, art critics and writers." Estab. 1975. Circ. 5,000. "Token payment as funding permits." Publishes ms an average of 6 months after acceptance. Byline given. Submit seasonal material 6 months in advance. Reports in 3 months. Sample copy for $3.
Nonfiction: Features, historical, interview, book reviews, photo feature. Query or submit complete ms. Length: 500-2,500 words.
Photos: Used with or without accompanying ms. Query or submit contact sheet or prints. Pays $5 for 5×7 b&w prints when money is available. Captions required.

Associations

Association publications allow writers to write for national audiences while covering local stories. If your town has a Kiwanis, Lions or Rotary Club chapter, one of its projects might merit a story in the club's magazine. If you are a member of the organization, find out before you write an article if the publication pays members for stories; some associations do not. In addition, some association publications gather their own club information and rely on freelancers solely for outside features. Be sure to find out what these policies are before you submit a manuscript. Club-financed magazines that carry material not directly related to the group's activities are classified by their subject matter in the Consumer and Trade sections.

COMEDY WRITERS ASSOCIATION NEWSLETTER, P.O. Box 23304, Brooklyn NY 11202-0066. (718)855-5057. Editor: Robert Makinson. 10% freelance written. Semiannual newsletter on comedy writing for association members. Estab. 1989. **Pays on acceptance.** Publishes ms an average of 3 months after acceptance. Byline given. Buys all rights. Reports in 2 weeks on queries; 1 month on mss. Sample copy for $6. Writer's guidelines for #10 SASE.
Nonfiction: How-to, humor, opinion, personal experience. "No exaggerations about the sales that you make and what you are paid. Be accurate." Query. Length: 250-500 words. "You may submit articles and fillers and byline will be given if used. But at present payment is only made for jokes."
Photos: State availability of photos with submission. Offers no additional payment for photos accepted with ms.

Fillers: Facts. Length: 100 words maximum.
Tips: "The easiest way to be mentioned in the publication is to submit short jokes. (Payment is $1-3 per joke.)"

‡**THE ELKS MAGAZINE**, 425 W. Diversey, Chicago IL 60614-6196. Editor: Fred D. Oakes. Managing Editor: Judith L. Keogh. 50% freelance written. Prefers to work with published/established writers. Magazine published 10 times/year emphasizing general interest with family appeal. Estab. 1922. Circ. 1.5 million. **Pays on acceptance.** Buys first North American serial rights. Reports in 2 months. Sample copy and writer's guidelines for 9×12 SAE with 4 first-class stamps.
Nonfiction: Articles of information, business, contemporary life problems and situations, nostalgia, or just interesting topics, ranging from medicine, science and history to sports. "The articles should not just be a rehash of existing material. They must be fresh, thought-provoking, well-researched and documented." No fiction, political articles, travel, fillers or verse. Buys 2-3 mss/issue. Query; no phone queries. Length: 1,500-3,000 words. Pays from $150.
Tips: "Requirements are clearly stated in our guidelines. Loose, wordy pieces are not accepted. A submission, following a query letter go-ahead, should include several b&w prints if the piece lends itself to illustration. We offer no additional payment for photos accepted with manuscripts. We expect to continue targeting our content to an older (50+) demographic."

FEDCO REPORTER, A Publication Exclusively for FEDCO Members, Box 2605, Terminal Annex, Los Angeles CA 90051. (310)946-2511, ext. 3321. Editor: John Bregoli. 90% freelance written. Works with a small number of new/unpublished writers each year. Monthly catalog/magazine for FEDCO department store members. Estab. 1940. Circ. 2 million. **Pays on acceptance.** Publishes ms an average of 4 months after acceptance. Byline given. Offers $50 kill fee. Buys all rights. Query for electronic submissions. Reports in 6 weeks. Sample copy for 9×12 SAE with 4 first-class stamps. Writer's guidelines for SASE.
Nonfiction: The magazine publishes material on events, personalities, anecdotes, little-known happenings of historical significance relating to Southern California. No first person narrative. Buys 85 mss/year. Query with or without published clips or send complete ms. Length: 450 words. Pays $125.
Photos: State availability of photos. Reviews b&w and color slides. Pays $25.
Tips: "We publish tightly written, well-researched stories relating to the history of Southern California, regardless of prior writing experience."

KIWANIS, 3636 Woodview Trace, Indianapolis IN 46268-3196. Fax: (317)879-0204. Managing Editor: Chuck Jonak. 85% of feature articles freelance written. Buys about 40 mss/year. Magazine published 10 times/year for business and professional persons and their families. Estab. 1917. Circ. 275,000. **Pays on acceptance.** Buys first serial rights. Offers 40% kill fee. Publishes ms an average of 6 months after acceptance. Byline given. Reports within 2 months. Sample copy and writer's guidelines for 9×12 SAE with 5 first-class stamps.
Nonfiction: Articles about social and civic betterment, small-business concerns, science, education, religion, family, youth, health, recreation, etc. Emphasis on objectivity, intelligent analysis and thorough research of contemporary issues. Positive tone preferred. Concise, lively writing, absence of clichés, and impartial presentation of controversy required. When applicable, include information and quotations from international sources. Avoid writing strictly to a US audience. "We have a continuing need for articles of international interest. In addition, we are very interested in proposals that concern helping youth, particularly prenatal through age five: day care, developmentally appropriate education, early intervention for at-risk children, parent education, safety and health." Length: 2,000-2,500 words. Pays $600-1,000. "No fiction, personal essays, profiles, travel pieces, fillers or verse of any kind. A light or humorous approach is welcomed where the subject is appropriate and all other requirements are observed." Usually pays the expenses of writers on assignment. Query first. Must include SASE for response.
Photos: "We accept photos submitted with manuscripts. Our rate for a manuscript with good photos is higher than for one without." Model release and identification of subjects required. Buys one-time rights.
Tips: "We will work with any writer who presents a strong feature article idea applicable to our magazine's audience and who will prove he or she knows the craft of writing. First, obtain writer's guidelines and a sample copy. Study for general style and content. When querying, present detailed outline of proposed manuscript's focus, direction, and editorial intent. Indicate expert sources to be used for attribution, as well as article's tone and length. Present a well-researched, smoothly written manuscript that contains a 'human quality' with the use of anecdotes, practical examples, quotations, etc."

THE LION, 300 22nd St., Oak Brook IL 60521-8842. (708)571-5466. Fax: (703)571-8890. Senior Editor: Robert Kleinfelder. 35% freelance written. Works with a small number of new/unpublished writers each year. Monthly magazine covering service club organization for Lions Club members and their families. Estab. 1918. Circ. 600,000. **Pays on acceptance.** Publishes ms an average of 5 months after acceptance. Buys all rights. Byline given. Phone queries OK. Reports in 6 weeks. Free sample copy and writer's guidelines.
Nonfiction: Informational (issues of interest to civic-minded individuals) and photo feature (must be of a Lions Club service project). No travel, biography or personal experiences. Welcomes humor, if sophisticated

but clean; no sensationalism. Prefers anecdotes in articles. Buys 4 mss/issue. Query. Length: 500-2,200. Pays $100-750. Sometimes pays the expenses of writers on assignment.

Photos: Purchased with or without accompanying ms or on assignment. Captions required. Query for photos. Black and white and color glossies at least 5×7 or 35mm color slides. Total purchase price for ms includes payment for photos accepted with ms. "Be sure photos are clear and as candid as possible."

Tips: "Incomplete details on how the Lions involved actually carried out a project and poor quality photos are the most frequent mistakes made by writers in completing an article assignment for us. We are geared increasingly to an international audience. Writers who travel internationally could query for possible assignments, although only locally-related expenses could be paid."

THE OPTIMIST, (formerly *The Optimist Magazine*), Optimist International, 4494 Lindell Blvd., St. Louis MO 63108. (314)371-6000. Fax: (314)371-6006. Editor: Dennis R. Osterwisch. 10% freelance written. Magazine published 8 times/year about the work of Optimist clubs and members for members of the Optimist clubs in the United States and Canada. Circ. 165,000. **Pays on acceptance.** Publishes ms an average of 4 months after acceptance. Buys first North American serial rights. Submit seasonal material 3 months in advance. Accepts previously published submissions. Send photocopy of article and information about when and where the article previously appeared. Pays 50% of the amount paid for an original article. Reports in 1 week. Sample copy and writer's guidelines for 9×12 SAE with 4 first-class stamps.

Nonfiction: "We want articles about the activities of local Optimist clubs. These volunteer community-service clubs are constantly involved in projects, aimed primarily at helping young people. With over 4,000 Optimist clubs in the US and Canada, writers should have ample resources. Some large metropolitan areas boast several dozen clubs. We are also interested in feature articles on individual club members who have in some way distinguished themselves, either in their club work or their personal lives. Good photos for all articles are a plus and can mean a bigger check." Will also consider short (200-400 word) articles that deal with self-improvement or a philosophy of optimism. Buys 1-2 mss/issue. Query. "Submit a letter that conveys your ability to turn out a well-written article and tells exactly what the scope of the article will be." Length: up to 1,000 words. Pays $300 and up.

Photos: State availability of photos. Payment negotiated. Captions preferred. Buys all rights. "No mug shots or people lined up against the wall shaking hands."

Tips: "Find out what the Optimist clubs in your area are doing, then find out if we'd be interested in an article on a specific club project. All of our clubs are eager to talk about what they're doing. Just ask them and you'll probably have an article idea. We would like to see short pieces on the positive affect an optimistic outlook on life can have on an individual. Examples of famous people who overcame adversity because of their positive attitude are welcome."

PERSPECTIVE, Pioneer Clubs, P.O. Box 788, Wheaton IL 60189-0788. (708)293-1600. Fax: 708-293-3053. Editor: Rebecca Powell Parat. 15% freelance written. Works with a number of new/unpublished writers each year. Triannual magazine for "volunteer leaders of clubs for girls and boys ages 2 through grade 12. Clubs are sponsored by local churches throughout North America." Estab. 1967. Circ. 24,000. **Pays on acceptance.** Publishes ms an average of 6 months after acceptance. Buys full rights for assigned articles, first North American serial rights for unsolicited mss, and second serial (reprint) rights to material originally published elsewhere. Submit seasonal/holiday material 9 months in advance. Accepts previously published material. Send photocopy of article or typed ms with rights for sale noted. Reports in 6 weeks. Writer's guidelines and sample copy for $1.75 and 9×12 SAE with 6 first-class stamps.

Nonfiction: Informational (relationship skills, leadership skills); inspirational (stories of leaders and children in Pioneer Clubs); interview (Christian education leaders, club leaders); and personal experience (of club leaders). Buys 8-12 mss/year. Byline given. Length: 500-1,500 words. Pays $25-90.

Columns/Departments: Storehouse (game, activity, outdoor activity, service project suggestions—all related to club projects for ages 2 through grade 12). Buys 4-6 mss/year. Submit complete ms. Length: 150-250 words. Pays $8-15.

Tips: "We only assign major features to writers who have previously proven that they know us and our constituency. Submit articles directly related to club work, practical in nature, i.e., ideas for leader training in communication, discipline, teaching skills. Writers who have contact with a Pioneer Club program in their area and who are interested in working on assignment are welcome to contact us."

RECREATION NEWS, Official Publication of the League of Federal Recreation Associations, Inc., Icarus Publishers, Inc., P.O. Box 32335, Calvert Station, Washington DC 20007-0635. (202)965-6960. Editor: M.M. Ghannam. 85% freelance written. Monthly guide to leisure-time activities for federal workers covering outdoor recreation, travel, fitness and indoor pastimes. Estab. 1979. Circ. 104,000. Pays on publication. Publishes ms an average of 8 months after acceptance. Byline given. Buys first rights and second serial (reprint) rights. Submit seasonal/holiday material 10 months in advance. Accepts simultaneous and previously published submissions. Send tearsheet or photocopy of article, typed ms with rights for sale noted, with information about where and when it previously appeared. For reprints pays $50. Reports in 2 months. Sample copy and writer's guidelines for 9×12 SAE with 4 first-class stamps.

Nonfiction: Articles Editor. Leisure travel (no international travel); sports; hobbies; historical/nostalgic (Washington-related); personal experience (with recreation, life in Washington). Special issues: skiing (December); education (August). Query with clips of published work. Length: 800-2,000 words. Pays from $50-300.

Photos: Photo editor. State availability of photos with query letter or ms. Uses b&w prints. Pays $25. Uses color transparency on cover only. Pays $50-125 for transparency. Captions and identification of subjects required.

Tips: "Our writers generally have a few years of professional writing experience and their work runs to the lively and conversational. We like more manuscripts in a wide range of recreational topics, including the off-beat. The areas of our publication most open to freelancers are general articles on travel and sports, both participational and spectator, also historic in the DC area."

THE ROTARIAN, Rotary International, 1560 Sherman Ave., Evanston IL 60201-1461. (708)866-3000. Fax: (708)866-9732. Editor: Willmon L. White. Managing Editor: Charles W. Pratt. 40% freelance written. Monthly magazine for Rotarian business and professional men and women and their families, schools, libraries, hospitals, etc. "Articles should appeal to an international audience and in some way help Rotarians help other people. The organization's rationale is one of hope, encouragement and belief in the power of individuals talking and working together." Estab. 1911. Circ. 523,650. **Pays on acceptance**. Byline sometimes given. Kill fee negotiable. Buys one-time or all rights. Accepts previously published submissions. Send tearsheet or photocopy of article or typed ms with rights for sale noted and information about when and where the article previously appeared. Reports in 2 weeks. Sample copy for 9×12 SAE with 6 first-class stamps. Writer's guidelines for #10 SASE.

Nonfiction: Essays, general interest, humor, inspirational, photo feature, travel, business, environment. No fiction, religious or political articles. Query with published clips. Negotiates payment.

Photos: State availability of photos with submission. Reviews contact sheets and transparencies. Usually buys one-time rights.

Columns/Departments: Manager's Memo (business), Executive Health, Executive Lifestyle, Earth Diary and Trends. Length: 800 words. Query.

Tips: "Study issues, then query with SASE."

THE SAMPLE CASE, The Order of United Commercial Travelers of America, 632 N. Park St., Box 159019, Columbus OH 43215-8619. (614)228-3276. Editor: Megan Woitovich. Bimonthly magazine covering news for members of the United Commercial Travelers emphasizing fraternalism for its officers and active membership. Estab. 1891. Circ. 130,000. Pays on publication. Buys one-time rights. Reports in 3 months. Submit seasonal/holiday material 6 months in advance. Simultaneous queries and submissions OK. Accepts previously published material. Send tearsheet or photocopy of article or ms with rights for sale noted and information about where and when the article previously appeared. Pays same for reprints as for original articles.

Nonfiction: Articles on health/fitness/safety; family; hobbies/entertainment; fraternal/civic activities; business finance/insurance; travel in the US and Canada; food/cuisine.

Photos: David Knapp, Art Director. State availability of photos with ms. Prefers color prints. Pay negotiable. Captions required.

SCOUTING, Boy Scouts of America, 1325 W. Walnut Hill Lane, P.O. Box 75015, Irving TX 75015-2079. (214)580-2355. Fax: (214)580-2079. Editor: Jon C. Halter. Executive Editor: Scott Daniels. 90% freelance written. Bimonthly magazine on Scouting activities for adult leaders of the Boy Scouts. Estab. 1913. Circ. 1 million. **Pays on acceptance**. Accepts previously published submissions. Send photocopy of article and information about where and when the article previously appeared. Publishes ms an average of 4 months after acceptance. Byline given. Buys first North American serial rights. Submit seasonal/holiday material 4 months in advance. Reports in 2 weeks. Sample copy for $1 and #10 SAE with 4 first-class stamps. Writer's guidelines for #10 SASE.

• *Scouting* is looking for more articles about scouting families involved in interesting/unusual family-together activities/hobbies i.e. caving, bicycle touring, (two that they've done) and profiles of urban/inner-city scout leaders and packs or troop with successful histories.

Nonfiction: Buys 60 mss/year. Query with published clips. Length: 1,000-1,500 words. Pays $400-600 for assigned articles; $200-500 for unsolicited articles. Pays expenses of writers on assignment.

Photos: State availability of photos with submission. Reviews contact sheets and transparencies. Identification of subjects required. Buys one-time rights.

Columns/Departments: Family Quiz (quiz and puzzles on topics of family interest), 1,000 words; Way it Was (Scouting history), 1,200 words. Family Talk (family—raising kids, etc.), 1,200 words. Buys 6 mss/year. Query. Pays $200-400.

SONS OF NORWAY VIKING, Sons of Norway, 1455 W. Lake St., Minneapolis MN 55408. Fax: (612)339-5806. Editor: Karin B. Miller. 50% freelance written. Prefers to work with published/established writers. Monthly membership magazine for Sons of Norway, a fraternal and cultural organization, covering Norwegian culture, heritage, history, Norwegian-American topics, modern Norwegian society, genealogy and travel. "Our audience is Norwegian-Americans (middle-aged or older) with strong interest in their heritage and anything Norwegian. Many have traveled to Norway." Estab. 1903. Circ. 70,000. **Pays on acceptance.** Publishes ms an average of 8 months after acceptance. Byline given. Offers 25% kill fee. Buys first North American serial and second serial (reprint) rights. Submit seasonal/holiday material 6 months in advance. Reports in 4 months. Writer's guidelines on request.

Nonfiction: General interest, historical/nostalgic, interview/profile, youth-related and travel—all having a Norwegian angle. "Articles should not be personal impressions nor strictly factual but well-researched and conveyed in a warm and audience-involving manner. Does it entertain *and* inform?" Buys 30 mss/year. Query. Length: 1,500 words. Generally pays $100-350.

Photos: Reviews transparencies and prints. Generally pays $50/photo; $100 for cover color photo. Identification of subjects required. Buys one-time rights.

Tips: "Show familiarity with Norwegian culture and subject matter. Our readers are knowledgeable about Norway and quick to note misstatements. Articles about modern Norway and youth are most open to freelancers."

‡THE TOASTMASTER, Toastmasters International, 23182 Arroyo Vista, Rancho Santa Margarita CA 92688-7052 or P.O. Box 9052, Mission Viejo, CA 92690-7052. (714)858-8255. Fax: (714)858-1207. Editor: Suzanne Frey. Associate Editor: Kathy O'Connell. 50% freelance written. Monthly magazine on public speaking, leadership and club concerns. "This magazine is sent to members of Toastmasters International, a nonprofit educational association of men and women throughout the world who are interested in developing their communication and leadership skills. Members range from novice speakers to professional orators and come from a wide variety of backgrounds." Estab. 1932. Circ. 170,000. **Pays on acceptance.** Publishes ms an average of 8-10 months after acceptance. Byline given. Buys second serial (reprint), first-time or all rights. Submit seasonal/holiday material 3 months in advance. Accepts simultaneous and previously published submissions. Query for electronic submissions. Reports in 6 weeks on queries; 1 month on mss. Sample copy for 9×12 SAE with 4 first-class stamps. Writer's guidelines for #10 SASE.

Nonfiction: Book excerpts, how-to (communications related), humor (only if informative; humor cannot be off-color or derogatory), interview/profile (only if of a very prominent member or former member of Toastmasters International or someone who has a valuable perspective on communication and leadership). Buys 50 mss/year. Query. Length: 1,000-2,500 words. Pays $75-250. Sometimes pays expenses of writers on assignment. "Toastmasters members are requested to view their submissions as contributions to the organization. Sometimes asks for book excerpts and reprints without payment, but original contribution from individuals outside Toastmasters will be paid for at stated rates."

Photos: Reviews b&w prints. Offers no additional payment for photos accepted with ms. Captions are required. Buys all rights.

Tips: "We are looking primarily for 'how-to' articles on subjects from the broad fields of communications and leadership which can be directly applied by our readers in their self-improvement and club programming efforts. Concrete examples are useful. Avoid sexist or nationalist language."

VFW MAGAZINE, Veterans of Foreign Wars of the United States, 406 W. 34th St., Kansas City MO 64111. (816)756-3390. Fax: (816)968-1169. Editor: Rich Kolb. 40% freelance written. Monthly magazine on veterans' affairs, military history, patriotism, defense and current events. "*VFW Magazine* goes to its members worldwide, all having served honorably in the armed forces overseas from World War II through Haiti." Circ. 2.1 million. **Pays on acceptance.** Offers 50% kill fee on commissioned articles. Buys first rights. Submit seasonal/holiday material 6 months in advance. Submit detailed query letter, résumé and sample clips. Reports in 2 months. Sample copy for 9×12 SAE with 5 first-class stamps.

• *VFW Magazine* is becoming more current-events oriented.

Nonfiction: Interview/profile, veterans' affairs. Buys 25-30 mss/year. Query. Length: 1,500 words. Pays up to $500 maximum unless otherwise negotiated.

Photos: Send photos with submission. Reviews contact sheets, negatives, transparencies and prints. Captions, model releases and identification of subjects required. Buys first North American rights.

Astrology, Metaphysical and New Age

Magazines in this section carry articles ranging from shamanism to extraterrestrial phenomena. The following publications regard astrology, psychic phenomena, metaphysical experiences and related subjects as sciences or as objects of serious study. Each has an individual personality and approach to these phenomena. If you want to write for these publications, be sure to read them carefully before submitting.

FATE, Llewellyn Worldwide, Ltd., P.O. Box 64383, St. Paul MN 55164-0383. Fax: (612)291-1908. 70% freelance written. Estab. 1901. Buys all rights. Byline given. Pays after publication. Sample copy and writer's guidelines for $3 and 9×12 SAE with 5 first-class stamps. Query or submit completed ms. Reports in 3 months.

Nonfiction and Fillers: Personal psychic and mystical experiences, 400-600 words. Pays $25. Articles on parapsychology, Fortean phenomena, cryptozoology, parapsychology, spiritual healing, flying saucers, new frontiers of science, and mystical aspects of ancient civilizations, 2,000-5,000 words. Must include complete authenticating details. Prefers interesting accounts of single events rather than roundups. "We very frequently accept manuscripts from new writers; the majority are individual's first-person accounts of their own psychic/mystical/spiritual experiences. We do need to have all details, where, when, why, who and what, included for complete documentation. We ask for a notarized statement attesting to truth of the article." Pays 10¢/word. Fillers must be be fully authenticated also, and on similar topics. Length: 100-300 words.
Photos: Buys slides or prints with mss. Pays $10.
Tips: "We would like more stories about *current* paranormal or unusual events."

‡GNOSIS, A Journal of the Western Inner Traditions, Lumen Foundation, P.O. Box 14217, San Francisco CA 94114. (415)255-0400. Editor: Richard Smoley. 75% freelance written. Quarterly magazine covering esoteric spirituality. "*Gnosis* is a journal covering the esoteric, mystical, and occult traditions of Western civilization, including Judaism, Christianity, Islam, and Paganism." Estab. 1985. Circ. 16,000. Pays on publication. Publishes ms an average of 3 months after acceptance. Byline given. Buys first North American serial rights. Editorial lead time 5 months. Submit seasonal material 5 months in advance. Accepts electronic submissions by disk. Reports in 1 month on queries; 4 months on mss. Sample copy for $8. Writer's guidelines for #10 SASE.
Nonfiction: Book excerpts, essays, religious. Special issues: East Meets West (deadline November 1, 1995; Hermeticism (deadline February 1, 1996). Buys 32 mss/year. Query with published clips. Length: 1,000-5,000 words. Pays $100-300 for assigned articles; $50-200 for unsolicited articles. All contributors receive 4 contributor's copies plus a year's subscription in addition to payment.
Photos: State availability of photos with submissions. Reviews contact sheets, prints. Offers $50-125/photo. Captions, identification of subjects required. Buys one-time rights.
Columns/Departments: News & Notes (items of current interest in esoteric spirituality), 1,000 words; Book Reviews (reviews of new books in the field), 250-1,000 words. Buys 45 mss/year. Query with published clips. Pays $40-100.
Tips: "We give strong preference to articles related to our issue themes (available with writer's guidelines)."

NEW AGE JOURNAL, Rising Star Associates, 42 Pleasant St., Watertown MA 02172. Fax: (617)926-5021. Editor: Peggy Taylor. Editorial Manager: Lisa Horvitz. 35% freelance written. Works with a small number of new/unpublished writers each year. Bimonthly magazine emphasizing "personal fulfillment and social change. The audience we reach is college-educated, social-service/hi-tech oriented, 25-45 years of age, concerned about social values, humanitarianism and balance in personal life." Payment negotiated. Publishes ms an average of 5 months after acceptance. Byline given. Offers 25% kill fee. Buys first North American serial and reprint rights. Submit seasonal/holiday material 6 months in advance. Accepts simultaneous and previously published submissions. Send photocopy of article and information about when and where the article previously appeared. Does not pay for reprints. Reports in 2 months on queries. Sample copy for $5 and 9×12 SAE. Writer's guidelines for #10 SASE.
  ● *New Age Journal* received an Utne Reader Annual Alternative Press Award for Best publication (editorial excellence) 1994.
Nonfiction: Book excerpts, exposé, general interest, how-to (travel on business, select a computer, reclaim land, plant a garden, behavior, trend pieces, humor, inspirational, interview/profile, new product, food, sci-tech, nutrition, holistic health, education, personal experience. Buys 60-80 mss/year. Query with published clips. "Written queries only—no phone calls. The process of decision making takes time and involves more than one editor. An answer cannot be given over the phone." Length: 500-4,000 words. Pays $50-2,500. Pays the expenses of writers on assignment.
Photos: State availability of photos with submission. Model releases and identification of subjects required. Buys one-time rights.
Columns/Departments: Body/Mind; Reflections; First Person. Buys 60-80 mss/year. Query with published clips. Length: 750-1,500 words. Pays $100-400.
Tips: "Submit short, specific news items to the Upfront department. Query first with clips. A query is one to two paragraphs—if you need more space than that to *present* the idea, then you don't have a clear grip on it. The next open area is columns: First Person and Reflections often take first-time contributors. Read

The double dagger before a listing indicates that the listing is new in this edition. New markets are often more receptive to freelance submissions.

the magazine and get a sense of type of writing run in these two columns. In particular we are interested in seeing inspirational, first-person pieces that highlight an engaging idea, experience or issue. We are also looking for new cutting edge thinking."

NEW FRONTIER, Magazine of Transformation, New Frontier Education Society, P.O. Box 17397, Asheville NC 28806-2724. E-mail: swamiv@aol.com. Editor: Sw. Virato. 80% freelance written. Bimonthly New Age magazine. "*New Frontier* magazine writers should embody a sense of oneness with the universe. They should come from a basic spiritual model, and essentially be a New Age person. They should see the universe and all life from a holistic view." Estab. 1980. Circ. 60,000. Pays on publication. Publishes ms an average of 6 months after acceptance. Byline given. Offers 20% kill fee or $25. Buys first North American serial, first, one-time or second serial (reprint) rights or makes work-for-hire assignments. Editorial lead time 3 months. Submit seasonal material 4 months in advance. Accepts previously published articles. Send tearsheet, photocopy of article or typed ms with rights for sale noted and information about when and where the article previously appeared. For reprints, pays 20% of the amount paid for an original article. Query for electronic submissions. MicroSoft Word for windows, or any popular word processor program, 5.25 or 3.5 floppy. Reports in 6 weeks on queries. Sample copy for $2. Writer's guidelines for #10 SASE.
Nonfiction: Book excerpts, essays, expose, general interest, historical/nostalgic, how-to, humor, inspirational, interview/profile, new product, opinion, personal experience, photo feature and "anything with awareness. Nothing dealing with hate, violence, attack, war, crime, drugs, superficial sex, pornography, meat products or unconsciousness in general." Buys 15 mss/year. Query with published clips. Length: 1,500-4,000 words. Pays $100 minimum for assigned articles, $50 for unsolicited articles or 5¢/word or 10¢/word in advertising trade. Sometimes pays expenses of writers on assignment (limit agreed upon in advance).
Photos: State availability of photos with submission. Reviews contact sheets and 5×7 prints. Negotiates payment individually. Buys one-time rights.
Fillers: Newsbreaks. Buys 20/year. Length: 100-300 words. Pays $10-25.
Tips: "Our writers must have an awareness of the subject, and the subject must deal with a transformation of human consciousness in any of the following areas: astrology, ecology, spirituality, self-help, holistic health, metaphysics, health and natural food, Eastern philosophy, yoga, cosmic consciousness, social responsibility, altered states, and other areas of interest to a New Age reader."

‡NEW LIFESTYLES MAGAZINE, O'Connor Brokow Communications, 2314 Iowa Ave., Cincinnati OH 45206. Editor: Dennis O'Connor. 80% freelance written. Tabloid published 9 times/year covering New Age information. "Alternative health issues; New Age spirituality; environment; etc." Estab. 1980. Circ. 10,000. Pays on publication. No kill fee. Buys all rights. Editorial lead time 3 months. Submit seasonal material 6 months in advance. Accepts simultaneous and previously published submissions. Query for electronic submissions. Sample copy for $1. Writer's guidelines for #10 SASE.
Nonfiction: Inspirational, religious. Buys 20-30 mss/year. Query. Pays $30-50.
Photos: State availability of photos with submissions. Negotiates payment individually. Buys one-time rights.
Fillers: Facts, newsbreaks. Length: 50-200 words. Pays $5.
Tips: "Know the New Age market. No hocus pocus. Our writers already know our readership. Ask for copy of magazine and guidelines. Looking for short pieces on environment, aliens, angels, spirituality, etc."

PARABOLA, The Magazine of Myth and Tradition, The Society for the Study of Myth and Tradition, 656 Broadway, New York NY 10012-2317. (212)505-6200. Quarterly magazine on mythology, tradition and comparative religion. "*Parabola* is devoted to the exploration of the quest for meaning as expressed in the myths, symbols, and tales of the religious traditions. Particular emphasis is on the relationship between this wisdom and contemporary life." Estab. 1976. Circ. 40,000. Pays on publication. Publishes ms 3 months after acceptance. Byline given. Offers kill fee for assigned articles only (usually $100). Buys first North American serial, first, one-time or second serial (reprint) rights. Editorial lead time 4 months. Accepts simultaneous and previously published submissions. Send photocopy of article or short story (must include copy of copyright page) and information about when and where the article previously appeared. Publishes novel excerpts. Query for electronic submissions. IBM-compatible or Macintosh disks. Requires hard copy accompanying disk. Reports in 3 weeks on queries; on mss "variable—for articles directed to a particular theme, we usually respond the month before or the month of the deadline (so for an April 15 deadline, we are likely to respond in March or April). Articles not directed to themes may wait four months or more!" Sample copy for $6 current issue; $8 back issue. Writers guidelines and list of themes for SASE.
Nonfiction: Book excerpts, essays, inspirational, personal experience, photo feature and religious. Send for current list of themes. No articles not related to specific themes. Buys 4-8 mss/year. Query. Length: 2,000-4,000 words. Pays $200 minimum. Sometimes pays expenses of writers on assignment.
Photos: State availability of photos with submission. Reviews contact sheets, any transparencies and prints. Identification of subjects required. Buys one-time rights.
Columns/Departments: Contact: David Appelbaum (book reviews) (Tangents); Natalie Baan (Epicycles). Tangents (reviews of film, exhibits, dance, theater, video, music relating to theme of issue), 2,000-4,000 words; Book Reviews (reviews of current books in religion, spirituality, mythology and tradition), 500 words;

Epicycles (retellings of myths and folk tales of all cultures—no fiction or made-up mythology!), under 2,000 words. Buys 2-6 unsolicited mss/year. Query. Pays $75-300.
Fiction: "We *very* rarely publish fiction; must relate to upcoming theme. Query recommended." Query.
Poetry: Free verse, traditional. *No* concrete or experimental poetry (must relate to theme). Buys 2-4 poems/year. Pays $50-75.

‡THE SANTA FE SUN, New Mexico's Alternative Paper, Le Soleil de Santa Fe, Inc., P.O. Box 23168, Santa Fe NM 87502. (505)989-8381. Editor: Shawn Townsend. 80% freelance written. Monthly newspaper covering alternative/New Age, with a preference to articles with a northern New Mexico slant. Estab. 1988. Circ. 21,000. Pays on publication. Publishes ms an average of 2 months after acceptance. Byline given. Not copyrighted. Buys first rights. Editorial lead time 2 months. Submit seasonal material 1 month in advance. Accepts simultaneous and previously published submissions. Query for electronic submissions. Reports in 1 month on queries. Sample copy for $3. Writer's guidelines for #10 SASE.
Nonfiction: Book excerpts, essays, inspirational, interview/profile, opinion, personal experience, photo feature, religious, travel. Buys 12 mss/year. Query with published clips. Length: 600-2,200 words. Pays $50-200 for assigned articles; $42-176 for unsolicited articles. Sometimes pays expenses of writers on assignment.
Photos: State availability of photos with submission. Reviews contact sheets. Negotiates payment individually. Identification of subjects required. Buys one-time rights.
Columns/Departments: Pays 7¢/word.
Poetry: John Graham. Avant-garde, free verse, haiku, light verse, traditional.

SHAMAN'S DRUM, A Journal of Experiential Shamanism, Cross-Cultural Shamanism Network, P.O. Box 430, Willits CA 95490-0430. (707)459-0486. Editor: Timothy White. 75% freelance written. Quarterly educational magazine of cross-cultural shamanism. "*Shaman's Drum* seeks contributions directed toward a general but well-informed audience. Our intent is to expand, challenge, and refine our readers' and our understanding of shamanism in practice. Topics include indigenous medicineway practices, contemporary shamanic healing practices, ecstatic spiritual practices, and contemporary shamanic psychotherapies. Our overall focus is cross-cultural, but our editorial approach is culture-specific—we prefer that authors focus on specific ethnic traditions or personal practices about which they have significant firsthand experience. We are looking for examples of not only how shamanism has transformed individual lives but also practical ways it can help ensure survival of life on the planet. We want material that captures the heart and feeling of shamanism and that can inspire people to direct action and participation, and to explore shamanism in greater depth." Estab. 1985. Circ. 17,000. Publishes ms 6 months after acceptance. Buys first North American serial and first rights. Editorial lead time 1 year. Reports in 3 months. Occasionally accepts previously published articles. Send typed ms with rights for sale noted and information about when and where the article prevoiusly appeared. Pays 50% of the amount paid for an original article. Sample copy for $5. Writer's guidelines for #10 SASE.
Nonfiction: Book excerpts, essays, interview/profile (please query), opinion, personal experience, photo feature. *No fiction, poetry or fillers.* Buys 16 mss/year. Send complete ms. Length: 5,000-8,000. "We pay 5-10¢/word, depending on how much we have to edit. We also send two copies and tearsheets in addition to cash payment."
Photos: Send photos with submission. Reviews contact sheets, transparencies and all sizes prints. Offers $40-50/photo. Identification of subjects required. Buys one-time rights.
Columns/Departments: Contact: Judy Wells, Earth Circles Editor. Earth Circles (news format, concerned with issues, events, organizations related to shamanism, indigenous peoples and caretaking Earth. Relevant clippings also sought. Clippings paid with copies and credit line), 500-1,500 words. Buys 8 mss/year. Send complete ms. Pays 5-10¢/word. Reviews: contact Timothy White, Editor (in-depth reviews of books about shamanism or closely related subjects such as indigenous lifestyles, ethnobotany, transpersonal healing and ecstatic spirituality), 500-1,500 words. "Please query us first and we will send *Reviewer's Guidelines.*" Pays 5-10¢/word.
Tips: "All articles must have a clear relationship to shamanism, but may be on topics which have not traditionally been defined as shamanic. We prefer original material that is based on, or illustrated with, firsthand knowledge and personal experience. Articles should be well documented with descriptive examples and pertinent background information. Photographs and illustrations of high quality are always welcome and can help sell articles."

WHOLE LIFE TIMES, 21225 Pacific Coast Highway, Suite B, Malibu CA 90265. (310)317-4200. Contact: Editor. Monthly consumer tabloid covering holistic thinking. Estab. 1979. Circ. 55,000. Pays on publication. Buys first North American serial rights. Occasionally buys reprints. Query for electronic submissions. Accepts previously published articles. Send photocopy of article and information about when and where the article previously appeared. Pays 50% of the amount paid for an original article. Sample copy for $3. Writer's guidelines for #10 SASE.
Nonfiction: Exposé, general interest, how-to, humor, inspirational, interview/profile, spiritual, technical, travel, leading-edge information, book excerpts. Buys 25 mss/year. Query with published clips or send complete ms. Length: 1,600-2,000 words. Pays 5¢/word.

Tips: "Queries should show an awareness of current topics of interest in our subject area. We welcome investigative reporting and are happy to see queries that address topics in a political context."

Automotive and Motorcycle

Publications in this section detail the maintenance, operation, performance, racing and judging of automobiles and recreational vehicles. Publications that treat vehicles as means of shelter instead of as a hobby or sport are classified in the Travel, Camping and Trailer category. Journals for service station operators and auto and motorcycle dealers are located in the Trade Auto and Truck section.

AMERICAN IRON MAGAZINE, TAM Communications Inc., 6 Prowitt St., Norwalk CT 06855. (203)855-0008. Fax: (203)852-9980. Editor: Jonathan Gourlay. 60% freelance written. Monthly magazine covering Harley-Davidson and other US brands with a definite emphasis on Harleys. Circ. 80,000. Pays on publication. Publishes ms an average of 6 months after acceptance. Byline given. Query for electronic submissions. Reports in 1 month on queries with SASE. Sample copy for $3.
Nonfiction: "Clean and non-offensive. Stories include bike features, touring stories, how-to tech stories with step-by-step photos, historical pieces, profiles, events, opinion and various topics of interest to the people who ride Harley-Davidsons." No fiction. Buys 60 mss/year. Pays $250 for touring articles with slides to first-time writers. Payment for other articles varies.
Photos: Submit color slides or large transparencies. No prints. Send SASE for return of photos.
Tips: "We're not looking for stories about the top ten biker bars or do-it-yourself tattoos. We're looking for articles about motorcycling, the people and the lifestyle. If you understand the Harley mystique and can write well, you've got a good chance of being published."

AMERICAN MOTORCYCLIST, American Motorcyclist Association, 33 Collegeview Rd, Westerville OH 43081-6114. (614)891-2425. Executive Editor: Greg Harrison. Monthly magazine for "enthusiastic motorcyclists, investing considerable time and money in the sport. We emphasize the motorcyclist, not the vehicle." Estab. 1942. Circ. 175,000. Pays on publication. Rights purchased vary with author and material. Pays 25-50% kill fee. Byline given. Query with SASE. Submit seasonal/holiday material 4 months in advance. Reports in 1 month. Free sample copy and writer's guidelines.
Nonfiction: How-to (different and/or unusual ways to use a motorcycle or have fun on one); historical (the heritage of motorcycling, particularly as it relates to the AMA); interviews (with interesting personalities in the world of motorcycling); photo feature (quality work on any aspect of motorcycling); technical articles. No product evaluations or stories on motorcycling events not sanctioned by the AMA. Buys 20-25 mss/year. Query. Length: 500 words minimum. Pays minimum $7/published column inch.
Photos: Purchased with or without accompanying ms or on assignment. Captions required. Query. Pays $40/photo minimum.
Tips: "Accuracy and reliability are prime factors in our work with freelancers. We emphasize the rider, not the motorcycle itself. It's always best to query us first and the further in advance the better to allow for scheduling."

AMERICAN WOMAN MOTORSCENE, American Woman Motorscene, 1510 11th St., Suite 201B, Santa Monica CA 90401. (310)260-0192. Fax: (310)260-0175. Publisher: Courtney Caldwell. Editor-at-Large: Sue Elliott. Associate Editor: Steve Scott. 80% freelance written. Bimonthly magazine on women in automotive. "We are an automotive lifestyle magazine for women. Estab. 1988. Circ. 100,000. Pays on publication an average of 2 months after acceptance. Byline always given. Buys first rights and second serial (reprint) rights or makes work-for-hire assignments. Submit seasonal/holiday material 4 months in advance. Accepts previously published submissions. Send tearsheet or photocopy of article and information about when and where the article previously appeared. Query for electronic submissions. Reports in 2 months. Free sample copy.
Nonfiction: Humor, inspirational, interview/profile, new product, photo feature, travel, lifestyle. No articles depicting women in motorsports or professions that are degrading, negative or not upscale. Buys 30 mss/ year. Send complete ms. Length 250-1,000 words. Pays 10¢/word for assigned articles; 7¢ for unsolicited articles. Sometimes pays expenses of writers on assignment.
Photos: Send photos with submission. Reviews contact sheets. Black and white or Kodachrome 64 preferred. Offers $10-50/photo. Captions, model releases and identification of subjects required. Buys all rights.
Columns/Departments: Lipservice (from readers); Tech Talk: (The Mall) new products; Tale End (News); 100-150 words.
Fillers: Anecdotes, facts, gags to be illustrated by cartoonist, newsbreaks, short humor. Buys 12/year. Length: 25-100 words. Negotiable.
Tips: "It helps if the writer is into cars, trucks or motorcycles. It is a special sport. If he/she is not involved in motorsports, he/she should have a positive point of view of motorsports and be willing to learn more

about the subject. We are a lifestyle type of publication more than a technical magazine. Positive attitudes wanted."

‡AUTOMOBILE, 120 E. Liberty, Ann Arbor MI 48104. (313)994-3500. Fax: (313)994-1153. Deputy Editor: Jean Lindamoor.

AUTOMOBILE QUARTERLY, The Connoisseur's Magazine of Motoring Today, Yesterday, and Tomorrow, Kutztown Publishing Co., 15040 Kutztown Rd., Kutztown PA 19530-0348. (610)683-3169. Fax: (610)683-3287. Publishing Director: Jonathan Stein. Managing Editor: Karla Rosenbusch. Contact: John Heilig, associate editor. 85% freelance written. Quarterly magazine covering "automotive history, hardcover, excellent photography." Estab. 1962. Circ. 17,000. **Pays on acceptance.** Publishes ms an average of 1 year after acceptance. Byline given. Buys first international serial rights. Editorial lead time 9 months. Reports in 2 weeks on queries; 2 months on mss. Sample copy for $19.95.
 • *Automobile Quarterly* has recently won the Benz Award of Distinction for Nonfiction Auto Articles.
Nonfiction: Essays, historical/nostalgic, photo feature, technical. Buys 25 mss/year. Query. Length: typically 5,000-8,000 words. Pays approximately 30¢/word. Sometimes pays expenses of writers on assignment.
Photos: State availability of photos with submission. Reviews 4×5, 35mm and 120 transparencies and historical prints. Buys one-time rights.
Tips: "Study the publication, and stress original research."

BRACKET RACING USA, 299 Market St., Saddle Brook NJ 07663. (201)712-9300. Editor: Dale Wilson. Managing Editor: Diane Boccadoro. Magazine published 8 times/year covering bracket cars and bracket racing. Estab. 1989. Circ. 45,000. Pays on publication. Publishes ms 6 months after acceptance. Byline given. Buys first North American serial rights. Query for electronic submissions. Sample copy for $3 and 9×12 SAE with 5 first-class stamps.
Nonfiction: Automotive how-to and technical. Buys 35 mss/year. Query. Length: 500-1,500 words. Pays $150/page for all articles. Sometimes pays expenses of writers on assignment.
Photos: Send photos with submission.

BRITISH CAR, P.O. Box 9099, Canoga Park CA 91309. (818)710-1234. Fax: (818)710-1877. Editor: Dave Destler. 50% freelance written. Bimonthly magazine covering British cars. "We focus upon the cars built in Britain, the people who buy them, drive them, collect them, love them. Writers must be among the aforementioned. Written by enthusiasts for enthusiasts." Estab. 1985. Circ. 30,000. Pays on publication. Publishes ms an average of 3 months after acceptance. Byline given. Buys all rights, unless other arrangements made. Submit seasonal/holiday material 4 months in advance. Query for electronic submissions. Reports in 1 month. Sample copy for $5. Writer's guidelines for #10 SASE.
 • The editor is looking for more technical and restoration articles by knowledgeable enthusiasts and professionals.
Nonfiction: Historical/nostalgic; how-to (repair or restoration of a specific model or range of models, new technique or process); humor (based upon a realistic nonfiction situation); interview/profile (famous racer, designer, engineer, etc.); photo feature; technical. Buys 30 mss/year. Send complete ms. "Include SASE if submission is to be returned." Length: 750-4,500 words. Pays $2-5/column inch for assigned articles; $2-3/column inch for unsolicited articles.
Photos: Send photos with submission. Reviews transparencies and prints. Offers $15-75/photo. Captions and identification of subjects required. Buys all rights, unless otherwise arranged.
Columns/Departments: Update (newsworthy briefs of interest, not too timely for bimonthly publication), approximately 50-175 words. Buys 20 mss/year. Send complete ms.
Tips: "Thorough familiarity of subject is essential. *British Car* is read by experts and enthusiasts who can see right through superficial research. Facts are important, and must be accurate. Writers should ask themselves 'I know I'm interested in this story, but will most of *British Car's* readers appreciate it?' "

‡CAA'S AUTOPINION ANNUAL, Canadian Automobile Association, 1775 Courtwood Crescent, Ottawa, Ontario K2C 3J2 Canada. (613)226-7631. Editor: David Steventon. 75% freelance written. Annual magazine covering new and used car purchasing. "Contains features relating to what's new in cars and automotive technology, and to the car buying process including: leasing and factors to consider (size, intended use of vehicle, towing, etc); new vehicle profiles; results of annual vehicle durability survey." Estab. 1988. Circ. 48,000. Pays on publication. Byline given. No kill fee. Buys all rights. Accepts previously published submissions. Query for electronic submissions. Submission deadline September 1 for publication December 15.
Nonfiction: General interest (automotive), historical/nostalgic (auto), interview/profile, new product (automotive), and technical (automotive). Buys 5 mss/year. Query with or without published clips or send complete ms. Length: 2,500 words. Pays $250-500. Send photos with submission. Reviews transparencies. Offers no additional payment for photos accepted with ms. Captions, model releases and identification of subjects required. Buys one-time rights.
Tips: "Contact editor, submit clippings of recent work, verify type of material needed for next edition (topics, etc.)."

‡CANADIAN BIKER MAGAZINE, P.O. Box 4122, Victoria British Columbia V8X 3X4 Canada. (604)384-0333. Fax: (604)384-1832. Editor: Len Creed. 65% freelance written. Magazine covers motorcycling. "A family-oriented motorcycle magazine whose purpose is to unite Canadian motorcyclists from coast to coast through the dissemination of information in a non-biased, open forum. The magazine reports on new product, events, touring, racing, vintage and custom motorcycling as well as new industry information." Estab. 1980. Circ. 20,000. Publishes non-time sensitive mss an average of 6-12 months after acceptance. Byline given. Buys first rights and second serial (reprint) rights. Editorial lead time 3 months. Submit seasonal material 6-12 months in advance. Accepts simultaneous and previously published submissions. Query for electronic submissions. Reports in 6 weeks on queries; 6 months on mss. Sample copy for $5. Writer's guidelines free on request.
Nonfiction: General interest, historical/nostalgic, how-to, interview/profile (Canadian personalities preferred), new product, technical, travel. Buys 12 mss/year. All nonfiction must include photos and/or illustrations. Query with or without published clips, or send complete ms. Length: 500-1,500 words. Pays $100-200 (Canadian) for assigned article; $80-150 (Canadian) for unsolicited articles. Sometimes pays expenses of writers on assignment.
Photos: State availability of or send photos with submission. Reviews 4×4 transparencies, 3×5 prints. Negotiates payment individually. Captions, model releases, identification of subjects required. Buys one-time rights.
Columns/Departments: The Ladies Chronicle (women), 750-1,000 words; Fastlines (roadracing), 1,300-1,800 words; Dragracing, 1,000 words. Query with published clips.
Tips: Writers should be involved in the motorcycle industry and be intimately familiar with some aspect of the industry which would be of interest to readers. Observations of the industry should be current, timely and informative.

CAR AND DRIVER, 2002 Hogback Rd., Ann Arbor MI 48105-9736. (313)971-3600. Fax: (313)971-9188. Editor-in-Chief: Csaba Csere. Monthly magazine for auto enthusiasts; college-educated, professional, median 24-35 years of age. Estab. 1961. Circ. 1.1 million. **Pays on acceptance.** Rights purchased vary with author and material. Buys all rights or first North American serial rights. Reports in 2 months.
Nonfiction: Non-anecdotal articles about automobiles, new and old. Automotive road tests, informational articles on cars and equipment, some satire and humor and personalities, past and present, in the automotive industry and automotive sports. "Treat readers as intellectual equals. Emphasis on people as well as hardware." Informational, humor, historical, think articles and nostalgia. All road tests are staff-written. "Unsolicited manuscripts are not accepted. Query letters must be addressed to the Managing Editor. Rates are generous, but few manuscripts are purchased from outside."
Photos: Color slides and b&w photos sometimes purchased with accompanying mss.
Tips: "It is best to start off with an interesting query and to stay away from nuts-and-bolts ideas because that will be handled in-house or by an acknowledged expert. Our goal is to be absolutely without flaw in our presentation of automotive facts, but we strive to be every bit as entertaining as we are informative."

CAR AUDIO AND ELECTRONICS, Avcom Publishing, 21700 Oxnard St., Suite 1600, Woodland Hills CA 91367. (818)593-3900. Fax: (818)593-2274. Editor: William Neill. Managing Editor: Doug Newcomb. 80-90% freelance written. Monthly magazine on electronic products designed for cars. "We help people buy the best electronic products for their cars. The magazine is about electronics, how to buy, use and so on: *CA&E* explains complicated things in simple ways. Articles are accurate, easy, and fun." Estab. 1988. Circ. 122,000. **Pays on acceptance.** Publishes ms an average of 5 months after acceptance. Byline given. Buys all rights. Submit seasonal/holiday material 4 months in advance. Accepts simultaneous submissions. Query for electronic submissions. Reports in 1 month. Sample copy for $3.95 and 9×12 SAE with 4 first-class stamps.
Nonfiction: How-to (buy electronics for your car), interview/profile, new product, opinion, photo feature, technical. Buys 60-70 mss/year. Query with or without published clips, or send complete ms. Length: 500-1,700 words. Pays $300-1,000.
Photos: Send photos with submission. Review transparencies, any size.
Tips: "Write clearly and knowledgeably about car electronics."

CAR CRAFT, Petersen Publishing Co., 6420 Wilshire Blvd., Los Angeles CA 90048. (213)782-2320. Fax: (213)782-2263. Editor: Chuck Schifsky. Monthly magazine for men and women, 18-34, "enthusiastic owners of 1949 and newer muscle cars and street machines." Circ. 400,000. Study past issues before making submissions or story suggestions. Pays generally on publication, on acceptance under special circumstances. Buys all rights. Buys 2-10 mss/year. Query.
Nonfiction: How-to articles ranging from the basics to fairly sophisticated automotive modifications. Drag racing feature stories and some general car features on modified late model automobiles. Especially interested in do-it-yourself automotive tips, suspension modifications, mileage improvers and even shop tips and home-made tools. Length: open. Pays $100-200/page.
Photos: Photos purchased with or without accompanying text. Captions suggested, but optional. Reviews 8×10 b&w glossy prints, 35mm or 2¼×2¼ color. Pays $30 for b&w, color negotiable. "Pay rate higher

for complete story, i.e., photos, captions, headline, subtitle: the works, ready to go."

CHEVY HIGH PERFORMANCE, Petersen Publishing Co., 6420 Wilshire Blvd., Los Angeles CA 90048. (213)782-2000. Editor: Mike Magda. Managing Editor: Kim Ennis. 40% freelance written. Monthly magazine covering "all aspects of street, racing, restored high-performance Chevrolet vehicles with heavy emphasis on technical modifications and quality photography." Estab. 1985. Circ. 125,000. Pays on acceptance. Byline given. No kill fee. Buys all rights. Submit seasonal/holiday material 6 months in advance. Query for electronic submissions. Reports in 1 month. Sample copy for 9 × 12 SAE with 5 first-class stamps.
Nonfiction: How-to, new product, photo feature, technical. "We need well-researched and photographed technical articles. Tell us how to make horse-power on a budget." Buys 60 mss/year. Query. Length: 500-2,000 words. Pays $150-1,000. Sometimes pays expenses of writers on assignment.
Photos: Send photos with submission. Reviews contact sheets, any transparencies and any prints. Offers no additional payment for photos accepted with ms. Model releases required. Buys all rights.
Columns/Departments: Buys 24 mss/year. Query. Length: 100-1,500. Pays $150-500.
Tips: "Writers must be aware of the 'street scene.' Please read the magazine closely before query. We need well-photographed step-by-step how-to technical articles. No personality profiles, fluffy features and especially personal experiences. If you don't know the difference between Z/28 and Z28 Camaros, camel-hump and 18-degree heads or what COPO and RPO stand for, there's a good chance your background isn't what we're looking for."

CLASSIC AUTO RESTORER, Fancy Publishing, Inc., P.O. Box 6050, Mission Viejo CA 92690-6050. (714)855-8822. Fax: (714)855-3045. Editor: Dan Burger. Managing Editor: Ted Kade. 85% freelance written. Monthly magazine on auto restoration. "Our readers own old cars and they work on them. We help our readers by providing as much practical, how-to information as we can about restoration and old cars." Estab. 1988. Pays on publication. Publishes an average of 3 months after acceptance. Offers $50 kill fee. Buys first North American serial or one-time rights. Submit seasonal/holiday material 4 months in advance. Query for electronic submissions. Reports in 2 months. Sample copy for $5.50. Free writer's guidelines.
Nonfiction: How-to (auto restoration), new product, photo feature, technical, travel. Buys 120 mss/year. Query with or without published clips or send complete ms. Length: 200-5,000 words. Pays $100-500 for assigned articles; $75-500 for unsolicited articles.
Photos: Send photos with submission. Reviews contact sheets, transparencies and 5 × 7 prints. Offers no additional payment for photos accepted with ms.
Columns/Departments: Buys 12 mss/year. Send complete ms. Length: 400-1,000 words. Pays $75-200.
Tips: "Send a story. Include photos. Make it something that the magazine regularly uses. Do automotive how-tos. We need lots of them. We'll help you with them."

FOUR WHEELER MAGAZINE, 6728 Eton Ave., Canoga Park CA 91303. (818)992-4777. Fax: (818)992-4979. Editor: John Stewart. 20% freelance written. Works with a small number of new/unpublished writers each year. Monthly magazine covering four-wheel-drive vehicles, competition and travel/adventure. Estab. 1963. Circ. 355,466. Pays on publication. Publishes ms an average of 4 months after acceptance. Buys all rights. Submit seasonal/holiday material at least 4 months in advance. Query for electronic submissions. Writer's guidelines for #10 SASE.
Nonfiction: 4WD competition and travel/adventure articles, technical, how-tos, and vehicle features about unique four-wheel drives. "We like the adventure stories that bring four wheeling to life in word and photo: mud-running deserted logging roads, exploring remote, isolated trails, or hunting/fishing where the 4 × 4 is a necessity for success." See features by Gary Wescott and Matt Conrad for examples. Query with photos before sending complete ms. Length: 1,200-2,000 words; average 4-5 pages when published. Pays $100/ page minimum for complete package.
Photos: Requires professional quality color slides and b&w prints for every article. Captions required. Prefers Kodachrome 64 or Fujichrome 50 in 35mm or 2¼ formats. "Action shots a must for all vehicle features and travel articles."
Tips: "Show us you know how to use a camera as well as the written word. The easiest way for a new writer/photographer to break in to our magazine is to read several issues of the magazine, then query with a short vehicle feature that will show his or her potential as a creative writer/photographer."

4-WHEEL & OFF-ROAD, Petersen Publishing Co., 6420 Wilshire Blvd., Los Angeles CA 90048. (213)782-2360. Editor: David Freiburger. Monthly magazine covering four-wheel-drive vehicles, "devoted to new-truck tests, buildups of custom 4 × 4s, coverage of 4WD racing, trail rides and other competitions." Circ. 330,000. **Pays on acceptance.** Publishes ms an average of 4 months after acceptance. Byline given. Pays 20% kill fee. Buys first North American serial rights or all rights. Submit seasonal/holiday material 4 months in advance. Reports in 3 weeks. Writer's guidelines for #10 SASE.
Nonfiction: How-to (on four-wheel-drive vehicles—engines, suspension, drive systems, etc.), new product, photo feature, technical, travel. Buys 12-16 mss/year. Send complete ms. Length: 1,000-2,500 words. Pays $200-600.

Photos: Send photos with submission. Reviews transparencies and b&w prints. Offers no additional payment for photos accepted with ms. Captions, model releases and identification of subjects required. Buys all rights.
Fillers: Anecdotes, facts, gags, newsbreaks, short humor. Buys 12-16/year. Length: 50-150 words. Pays $15-50.
Tips: "Attend 4×4 events, get to know the audience. Present material only after full research. Manuscripts should contain *all* of the facts pertinent to the story. Technical/how-to articles are most open to freelancers."

HIGH PERFORMANCE PONTIAC, CSK Publishing Co., 299 Market St., Saddle Brook NJ 07663. (201)712-9300. Editor: Richard A. Lentinello. Managing Editor: Peter Easton. Bimonthly magazine covering Pontiac cars, events and technology. "Our writers must have a knowledge of automobiles in general, and of Pontiacs in particular." Estab. 1979. Circ. 45,000 nationwide. Pays on publication. Publishes ms an average of 3 months after acceptance. Byline given. Negotiable kill fee. Buys first North American serial rights. Query for electronic submissions. No previously published material. Length: 250-2,000 words. Pays $150/page for articles. Sometimes pays expenses of writers on assignment. Reports in 3 months. Sample copy for $4.50.
Nonfiction: Historical/nostalgic, how-to (hands-on Pontiac technical articles, e.g., how to do a 4-speed swap), interview/profile, new product, photo feature, technical. "We are not interested in articles about pre-'82 Pontiacs that have had Chevy engines installed (excluding Canadian Pontiacs, of course)." Buys 12 mss/year. Query with or without published clips or send complete ms.
Photos: Send photos with submission. Reviews contact sheets, negatives, transparencies, prints. Captions required. Buys one-time rights.

‡HOT ROD, Petersen Publishing Co., 6420 Wilshire Blvd., Los Angeles CA 90048-5515. (310)854-2280. Fax: (310)854-2223. Editor: Drew Hardin. 5% freelance written. Monthly magazine. Estab. 1948. Pays on publication. Publishes ms an average of 3 months after acceptance. Kill fee varies. Buys exclusive rights. Reports in 2 months. Send complete ms. Length and payment varies.

MUSCLE MUSTANGS & FAST FORDS, CSK Publishing Co., 299 Market St., Saddle Brook NJ 07663. (201)712-9300. Editor: Jim Campisano. Managing Editor: Diane Boccadoro. 40% freelance written. Magazine published 11 times/year covering late model 5-liter Mustangs and other high-performance Fords. Estab. 1988. Circ. 72,000. Pays on publication. Publishes ms an average of 6 months after acceptance. Byline given. Buys first North American serial rights. Query for electronic submissions. Reports in 3 weeks on queries; 6 weeks on mss. Sample copy for $3.50 and 9×12 SAE with 5 first-class stamps. Free writer's guidelines.
Nonfiction: How-to (automotive) and technical (automotive). Buys 50 mss/year. Query. Length: 500-1,500 words. Pays $150/magazine page for all articles. Sometimes pays expenses of writers on assignment.
Photos: Send photos with submission.

NATIONAL DRAGSTER, Drag Racing's Leading News Weekly, National Hot Rod Association, 2035 Financial Way, Glendora CA 91740. (818)963-8475. Fax: (818)335-4307. Editor: Phil Burgess. Managing Editor: Vicky Walker. 20% freelance written. Weekly tabloid of NHRA drag racing. "Covers NHRA drag racing—race reports, news, performance industry news, hot racing rumors—for NHRA members. Membership included with subscription." Estab. 1960. Circ. 80,000. Pays on publication. Publishes ms 1 month after acceptance. Byline given. Buys all rights. Submit seasonal/holiday material 2 months in advance. Accepts simultaneous submissions. Query for electronic submissions. Reports in 1 month. Free sample copy.
Nonfiction: General interest, historical/nostalgic, how-to, humor, interview/profile, new product, personal experience, photo feature, technical. Buys 20 mss/year. Query. Pay is negotiable. Sometimes pays expenses of writers on assignment.
Photos: State availability of photos with submission. Reviews 5×7 prints. Captions and identification of subjects required. Buys all rights.
Columns/Departments: On the Run (first-person written, ghost written by drag racers), 900-1,000 words. Buys 48 mss/year. Query. Pay is negotiable.
Tips: "Feature articles on interesting drag racing personalities or race cars are most open to freelancers."

RIDER, TL Enterprises, Inc., 3601 Calle Tecate, Camarillo CA 93012-5040. (805)389-0300. Editor: Mark Tuttle Jr.. Managing Editor: Donya Carlson. Contact: Mark Tuttle, Jr., Editor. 50% freelance written. Monthly magazine on motorcycling. "*Rider* serves owners and enthusiasts of road and street motorcycling, focusing on touring, commuting, camping and general sport street riding." Estab. 1974. Circ. 140,000. Pays on publication. Publishes ms an average of 6-12 months after acceptance. Byline given. Offers 25% kill fee. Buys first North American serial rights. Editorial lead time 4 months. Submit seasonal material 6 months in advance. Query for electronic submissions. Reports in 2 months. Sample copy for $2.95. Writer's guidelines for #10 SASE.
Nonfiction: General interest, historical/nostalgic, how-to (re: motorcycling), humor, interview/profile, personal experience. Does not want to see "fiction or articles on 'How I Began Motorcycling.' " Buys 30 mss/year. Query. Length: 500-1,500 words. Pays $100 minimum for unsolicited articles. Sometimes pays expenses of writers on assignment.

Photos: Send photos with submission. Reviews contact sheets, transparencies and 5×7 prints (b&w only). Offers no additional payment for photos accepted with ms. Captions required. Buys one-time rights.

Columns/Departments: Rides, Rallies & Clubs (favorite ride or rally), 800-1,000 words. Buys 15 mss/year. Query. Pays $100.

Tips: "We rarely accept manuscripts without photos (slides or b&w prints). Query first. Follow guidelines. We are most open to feature stories (must include excellent photography) and material for 'Rides, Rallies and Clubs.' Include information on routes, local attractions, restaurants and scenery in favorite ride submissions."

‡**ROAD & TRACK**, Hachette Filipacchi Magazines Inc., 1499 Monrovia Ave., Newport Beach CA 92663. (714)720-5300. Editor: Thomas L. Bryant. Contact: Ellida Maki. 25% freelance written. Monthly magazine covering automotive. Estab. 1947. Circ. 740,000. Pays on publication. Publishes ms an average of 6 months after acceptance. Kill fee varies. Buys first rights. Editorial lead time 3 months. No simultaneous or previously published submissions. Reports in 1 month on queries; 2 months on mss.

Nonfiction: Automotive interest. No how-to. Query. Length: 2,000 words. Pay varies. Pays expenses of writers on assignment.

Photos: State availability of photos with submissions. Reviews transparencies, prints. Negotiates payment individually. Model releases required. Buys one-time rights.

Columns/Department: Reviews (automotive), 500 words. Query. Pay varies.

Fiction: Automotive. Query. Length: 2,000 words. Pay varies.

Tips: "Because mostly written by staff or assignment, we rarely purchase unsolicited manuscripts—but it can and does happen! Writers must be knowledgeable about enthusiast cars."

STOCK CAR RACING MAGAZINE, General Media, Box 715, Ipswich MA 01938. Editor: Dick Berggren. 80% freelance written. Eager to work with new/unpublished writers. Monthly magazine for stock car racing fans and competitors. Circ. 400,000. Pays on publication. Publishes ms an average of 3 months after acceptance. Buys all rights. Byline given. Query for electronic submissions. Reports in 6 weeks. Free writer's guidelines.

Nonfiction: General interest, historical/nostalgic, how-to, humor, interviews, new product, photo features, technical. "Uses nonfiction on stock car drivers, cars and races. We are interested in the story behind the story in stock car racing. We want interesting profiles and colorful, nationally interesting features. We are looking for more technical articles, particularly in the area of street stocks and limited sportsman." Query with or without published clips or submit complete ms. Buys 50-200 mss/year. Length: 100-6,000 words. Pays up to $450.

Photos: State availability of photos. Pays $20 for 8×10 b&w photos; up to $250 for 35mm or larger transparencies. Captions required.

Fillers: Anecdotes, short humor. Buys 100 each year. Pays $35.

Tips: "We get more queries than stories. We just don't get as much material as we want to buy. We have more room for stories than ever before. We are an excellent market with 12 issues per year. Virtually all our features are submitted without assignment. An author knows much better what's going on in his backyard than we do. We ask that you write to us before beginning a story theme. If nobody is working on the theme you wish to pursue, we'd be glad to assign it to you if it fits our needs and you are the best person for the job. Judging of material is always a combination of a review of the story and its support illustration. Therefore, we ask for photography to accompany the manuscript on first submission."

‡**SUPER FORD**, Dobbs Publishing Group, 3816 Industry Blvd., Lakeland FL 33811-0322. (813)644-0449. Fax: (813)644-8373. Editor: Tom Wilson. Managing Editor: Steve Statham. 50% freelance written. Monthly magazine covering the Ford Motor Company automotive history and performance. Estab. 1987. Circ. 65,000. Pays on publication. Publishes ms an average of 5 months after acceptance. Byline given. Offers 20% kill fee. Buys one-time rights. Submit seasonal/holiday material 3 months in advance. Query for electronic submissions. Reports in 2 months. Free sample copy and writer's guidelines.

Nonfiction: Historical/nostalgic; how-to (automotive technical), interview/profile; new product; personal experience; photo features ("those on individual cars are our bread-and-butter"); technical. "We need more tech articles that are complete, in-depth and offer fresh information on Ford high-performance. Simple subjects areas desirable as complex stories." Buys 48 mss/year. Send complete ms. Length: 500-2,000 words. Pays $100-700 for unsolicited articles. Sometimes pays expenses of writers on assignment.

Photos: Reviews contact sheets and negatives and 2¼×2¼ transparencies. Soft box or umbrella lighting of b&w tech articles required. Offers $40/b&w photo, $150/color cover. Captions and identification of subjects required. Buys one-time rights.

Columns/Departments: Keepin' Track (Ford racing coverage), 50-1,000 words; In The Fast Lane (Ford automotive news), 100-200 words. Buys 15 mss/year. Query. Pays $50-150.

Tips: "We need more technical material. Our photography standards have risen."

VETTE MAGAZINE, CSK Publishing, Inc., 299 Market St., Saddle Brook NJ 07663. (201)712-9300. Fax: (201)712-9899. Editor-in-Chief: D. Randy Riggs. Managing Editor: Peter Easton. 75% freelance written. Monthly magazine covering all subjects related to the Corvette automobile. "Our readership is extremely knowledgeable about the subject of Corvettes. Therefore, writers must know the subject thoroughly and be good at fact checking." Estab. 1976. Circ. 65,000. Offers 50% kill fee. Buys first North American serial rights. Submit seasonal/holiday material 4 months in advance. Query for electronic submissions. Reports in 6 weeks. Sample copy for 9×12 SAE with 6 first-class stamps. Writer's guidelines for #10 SASE.

Nonfiction: General interest, historical/nostalgic, how-to, interview/profile, new product, personal experience, photo feature, technical, travel. Buys 120 mss/year. Query with published clips. Length: 400-2,700 words. Pays $150-750 for assigned articles; $100-350 for unsolicited articles. Sometimes pays expenses of writers on assignment.

Photos: State availability of photos with submission. Reviews contact sheets. Offers no additional payment for photos accepted with ms. Captions and model releases required. Buys one-time rights.

Columns/Departments: Reviews (books/videos), 400-500 words. Buys 12 mss/year. Query. Pays $50-150.

Fiction: Adventure, fantasy, slice-of-life vignettes. Buys 2 mss/year. Query with published clips. Length: 400-2,500 words. Pays $100-500.

Aviation

Professional and private pilots and aviation enthusiasts read the publications in this section. Editors want material for audiences knowledgeable about commercial aviation. Magazines for passengers of commercial airlines are grouped in the Inflight category. Technical aviation and space journals and publications for airport operators, aircraft dealers and others in aviation businesses are listed under Aviation and Space in the Trade section.

AIR & SPACE/SMITHSONIAN MAGAZINE, 370 L'Enfant Promenade SW, 10th Floor, Washington DC 20024-2518. (202)287-3733. Fax: (202)287-3163. Editor: George Larson. Managing Editor: Tom Huntington. 80% freelance written. Prefers to work with published/established writers. Bimonthly magazine covering aviation and aerospace for a non-technical audience. "Features are slanted to a technically curious, but not necessarily technically knowledgeable audience. We are looking for unique angles to aviation/aerospace stories, history, events, personalities, current and future technologies, that emphasize the human-interest aspect." Estab. 1985. Circ. 310,000. **Pays on acceptance.** Byline given. Offers kill fee. Buys first North American serial rights. Adapts from previously published or soon to be published books and other works. Send photocopy of article, including information about when and where the article previously appeared. Reports in 3 months. Sample copy for $3.50 and 9½×13 SASE. Free writer's guidelines.
  • The editors are actively seeking stories covering space and the history of the involvement of minorities in aviation and space.

Nonfiction: Book excerpts, essays, general interest (on aviation/aerospace), historical/nostalgic, how-to, humor, interview/profile, photo feature, technical. Buys 50 mss/year. Query with published clips. Length: 1,500-3,000 words. Pays $2,000 average. Pays the expenses of writers on assignment.

Photos: State availability of illustrations with submission. Reviews 35mm transparencies. Refuses unsolicited material.

Columns/Departments: Above and Beyond (first person), 1,500-2,000 words; Flights and Fancy (whimsy), approximately 1,200 words; From the Field (science or engineering in the trenches), 1,200 words; Collections (profiles of unique museums), 1,200 words. Buys 25 mss/year. Query with published clips. Pays $1,000 maximum. Soundings (brief items, timely but not breaking news), 500-700 words. Pays $300.

Tips: "Soundings is the section most open to freelancers."

AIR LINE PILOT, Air Line Pilots Association, 535 Herndon Parkway, P.O. Box 1169, Herndon VA 22070. (703)689-4176. Editor: Gary DiNunno, Jr. 10% freelance written. Prefers to work with published/established writers; works with a small number of new/unpublished writers each year. Monthly magazine for airline pilots covering commercial aviation industry information—economics, avionics, equipment, systems, safety—that affects a pilot's life in professional sense. Also includes information about management/labor relations trends, contract negotiations, etc. Estab. 1931. Circ. 62,000. **Pays on acceptance.** Publishes ms an average of 6 months after acceptance. Offers 50% kill fee. Buys all rights. Submit seasonal/holiday material 6 months in advance. Query for electronic submissions. Reports in 2 months. Sample copy for $2. Writer's guidelines for #10 SASE.

Nonfiction: Humor, inspirational, photo feature, technical. "We are backlogged with historical submissions and prefer not to receive unsolicited submissions at this time." Buys 20 mss/year. Query with or without published clips, or send complete ms. Length: 700-3,000 words. Pays $200-600 for assigned articles; pays $50-600 for unsolicited articles.

Photos: Send photos with submission. Reviews contact sheets, 35mm transparencies and 8×10 prints. Offers $10-35/photo. Identification of subjects required. Buys one-time rights.

Tips: "For our feature section, we seek aviation industry information that affects the life of a professional airline pilot from a career standpoint. We also seek material that affects a pilot's life from a job security and work environment standpoint. Any airline pilot featured in an article must be an Air Line Pilot Association member in good standing."

BALLOON LIFE, Balloon Life Magazine, Inc., 2145 Dale Ave., Sacramento CA 95815-3632. (916)922-9648. Fax: (916)922-4730. E-mail: 73232.1112@compuserve.com. Editor: Tom Hamilton. 75% freelance written. Monthly magazine for sport of hot air ballooning. Estab. 1986. Circ. 4,000. Pays on publication. Byline given. Offers 50-100% kill fee. Buys non-exclusive all rights. Submit seasonal/holiday material 3-4 months in advance. Accepts previously published submissions. Send photocopy of article or short story and information about when and where the article previously appeared. For reprints, pays 100% of amount paid for original article. Query for electronic submissions. Reports in 3 weeks on queries; 1 month on mss. *Writer's Market* recommends allowing 2 months for reply. Sample copy for 9×12 SAE with $2 postage. Writer's guidelines for #10 SASE.
Nonfiction: Book excerpts, general interest, how-to (flying hot air balloons, equipment techniques), interview/profile, new product, letters to the editor, technical. Buys 150 mss/year. Query with or without published clips, or send complete ms. Length: 800-5,000 words. Pays $50-75 for assigned articles; $25-50 for unsolicited articles. Sometimes pays expenses of writers on assignment.
Photos: Send photos with submission. Reviews transparencies, prints. Offers $15-50/photo. Identification of subjects required. Buys one-time rights.
Columns/Departments: Hangar Flying (real life flying experience that others can learn from), 800-1,500 words; Preflight (a news and information column), 100-500 words; Logbook (recent balloon events—events that have taken place in last 3-4 months), 300-500 words. Buys 60 mss/year. Send complete ms. Pays $15-50.
Fiction: Humorous. Buys 3-5 mss/year. Send complete ms. Length: 800-1,500 words. Pays $50.
Tips: "This magazine slants toward the technical side of ballooning. We are interested in articles that help to educate and provide safety information. Also stories with manufacturers, important individuals and/or of historic events and technological advances important to ballooning. The magazine attempts to present articles that show 'how-to' (fly, business opportunities, weather, equipment). Both our Feature Stories section and Logbook section are where most manuscripts are purchased."

CESSNA OWNER MAGAZINE, Jones Publishing, Inc., N7450 Aanstad Rd., P.O. Box 5000, Iola WI 54945. (715)445-5000. Fax: (715)445-4053. Editor: Frank Hamilton. 90% freelance written. Monthly magazine covering Cessna single and twin engine aircraft. "*Cessna Owner Magazine* is the official publication of the Cessna Owner Organization (C.O.O.). Therefore, our readers are Cessna aircraft owners, renters, pilots, and enthusiasts. Articles should deal with buying/selling, flying, maintaining, or modifying Cessnas. The purpose of our magazine is to promote safe, fun, and affordable flying." Estab. 1975. Circ. 5,555. Pays on publication. Publishes ms an average of 3 months after acceptance. Byline given. Buys first, one-time or second serial (reprint) rights or makes work-for-hire assignment on occasion. Editorial lead time 1 month. Submit seasonal material 3 months in advance. Accepts previously published submissions. Send typed ms with rights for sale noted and information about when and where the article previously appeared. Reports in 2 weeks on queries; 1 month on mss. Sample copy and writer's guidelines free on request.
Nonfiction: Historical/nostalgic (of specific Cessna models), how-to (aircraft repairs and maintenance), humor, interview/profile, new product, personal experience, photo feature, technical (aircraft engines and airframes), travel. "We are always looking for articles about Cessna aircraft modifications. We also greatly need articles on Cessna twin-engine aircraft. April, July, and November are always big issues for us, because we attend various airshows during these months and distribute free magazines. Feature articles on unusual, highly-modified, or vintage Cessnas are especially welcome during these months. Good photos are also a must for these special issues." Buys 24 mss/year. Query. Length: 1,500-3,500 words. Pays 8¢/word minimum for assigned articles; 5¢/word minimum for unsolicited articles.
Photos: Send photos with submission. Reviews 3×5 and larger prints. Offers no additional payment for photos accepted with ms or negotiates payment individually (on occasion). Captions and identification of subjects required.
Columns/Departments: Member's Corner (a feature article about a Cessna Owner Organization member and his/her plane), 1,000-1,500 words; Tailfeathers (humor/aviations "lighter" side), 1,500-3,000 words; Book Reviews, 1,000 words. Buys 6 mss/year. Query. Pays 5-12¢/word maximum.
Tips: "Always submit a hard copy and ASCII formatted computer disk (when possible). Color photos mean a lot to us, and manuscripts stand a much better chance of being published when accompanied by photos. Visit our booth at the major airshows (Osh Kosh, Sun 'n Fun, AOPA) and get to know our staff. Shows are also great places to find story leads. Freelancers can best get published by submitting articles on aircraft modifications, vintage planes, restorations, flight reports, twin-engine Cessnas, etc. We need articles on *women* who fly Cessna aircraft!"

GENERAL AVIATION NEWS & FLYER, N.W. Flyer, Inc., P.O. Box 39099, Tacoma WA 98439-0099. (206)471-9888. Fax: (206)471-9911. E-mail: 73200.126@compuserve.com. Editor: Dave Sclair. 30% freelance written. Prefers to work with published/established writers. Biweekly tabloid covering general aviation. Provides "coverage of aviation news, activities, regulations and politics of general and sport aviation with emphasis on timely features of interest to pilots and aircraft owners." Estab. 1949. Circ. 35,000. Pays 1 month after publication. Publishes ms an average of 3 months after acceptance. Byline given. Buys one-time and first North American serial rights; on occasion second serial (reprint) rights. Submit seasonal/holiday material 2 months in advance. Accepts previously published submissions from noncompetitive publications if so noted. Query for electronic submissions. Reports in 2 months. Sample copy for $3.50. Writer's and style guidelines for #10 SASE.

Nonfiction: Features of current interest about aviation businesses, developments at airports, new products and services, safety, flying technique and maintenance. "Good medium-length reports on current events—controversies at airports, problems with air traffic control, FAA, etc. We want solid news coverage of breaking stories. We don't cover airlines and military" Query first on historical, nostalgic features and profiles/interviews. Many special sections throughout the year; send SASE for list. Buys 100 mss/year. Query or send complete ms. Length: 500-2,000 words. Pays up to $3/printed column inch maximum. Rarely pays the expenses of writers on assignment.

Photos: "Good pics a must." Send photos (b&w or color prints preferred, no slides) with ms. Captions and photographer's ID required. Pays $10/b&w photo used.

Tips: "We always are looking for features about people and businesses using airplanes in unusual ways. Travel features must include information on what to do once you've arrived, with addresses from which readers can get more information. Get direct quotations from the principals involved in the story. We want current, first-hand information."

PIPERS MAGAZINE, Jones Publishing, Inc., N7450 Aanstad Rd., P.O. Box 5000, Iola WI 54945. (715)445-5000. Fax: (715)445-4053. Editor: Frank Hamilton. 90% freelance written. Monthly magazine covering Piper single and twin engine aircraft. "*Pipers Magazine* is the official publication of the Piper Owner Society (P.O.S.). Therefore, our readers are Piper aircraft owners, renters, pilots, mechanics and enthusiasts. Articles should deal with buying/selling, flying, maintaining, insuring, or modifying Pipers. The purpose of our magazine is to promote safe, fun and affordable flying." Estab. 1988. Circ. 3,158. Pays on publication. Publishes ms an average of 3 months after acceptance. Buys first, one-time or second serial (reprint) rights or makes work-for-hire assignment on occasion. Editorial lead time 1 month. Submit seasonal material 3 months in advance. Accepts previously published submissions. Send typed ms with rights for sale noted and information about when and where the article previously appeared. Query for electronic submissions. Reports in 2 weeks on queries;1 month on mss. Sample copy and writer's guidelines free on request.

Nonfiction: Historical/nostalgic (of specific models of Pipers), how-to (aircraft repairs & maintenance), humor, interview/profile (industry leaders), new product, personal experience, photo feature, technical (aircraft engines and airframes), travel. We are always looking for articles about Piper aircraft modifications. We also are in great need of articles on Piper twin engine aircraft, and late-model Pipers. April, July, and November are always big issues for us, because we attend airshows during these months and distribute free magazines. Feature articles on unusual, highly-modified, vintage, late-model, or ski/float equipped Pipers are especially welcome. Good photos are a must for these special "show issues." Buys 24 mss/year. Query. Length: 1,500-3,500 words. Pays 8¢/word for assigned articles, 5¢/word for unsolicited articles.

Photos: Send photos with submissions. Reviews transparencies, 3×5 and larger prints. Offers no additional payment for photos accepted with; or negotiates payment individually. Captions, identification of subjects required.

Columns/Departments: Member's Corner (feature article about a Piper Owner Society member and his/her plane), 1,000-1,500 words; Tailfeathers (humor/aviation's "lighter" side), 1,500-3,000 words; Book Reviews, 1,000 words. Buys 6 mss/year. Query. Pays 5-12¢ word.

Tips: "Always submit a hard copy and an ASCII formatted computer disk when possible. Color photos mean a lot to us, and manuscripts stand a much greater chance of being published when accompanied by photos. Visit our booth at the major airshows (OshKosh, Sun 'n Fun, AOPA) and get to know our staff. Shows are also great places to find story leads. Freelancers can best get published by submitting articles on aircraft modifications, vintage planes, late-model planes, restorations, twin-engine Pipers, etc. We need articles on *women* who fly Piper aircraft!"

PLANE AND PILOT, Werner Publishing Corp., 12121 Wilshire Blvd., Suite 1220, Los Angeles CA 90025. (310)820-1500. Fax: (310)826-5008. Editor: Steve Werner. Managing Editor: Alyson Behr. 100% freelance written. Monthly magazine that covers general aviation. "We think a spirited, conversational writing style is most entertaining for our readers. We are read by private and corporate pilots, instructors, students, mechanics and technicians—everyone involved or interested in general aviation." Estab. 1964. Circ. 130,000. Pays on publication. Publishes ms an average of 3 months after acceptance. Byline given. Kill fee negotiable. Buys all rights. Submit seasonal material 4 months in advance. Accepts previously published material. Send photocopy of article or typed ms with rights for sale noted and include information about when and where the article previously appeared. For reprints pays 50% of the amount paid for an original article. Query for electronic submissions. Reports in 2 months. Sample copy for $2.95. Free writer's guidelines.

Nonfiction: Book excerpts, essays, general interest, how-to, humor, inspirational, new product, personal experience, technical, travel, pilot proficiency and pilot reports on aircraft. Buys 150 mss/year. Send complete ms. Length: 1,000-2,500 words. Pays $200-500. Pays expenses of writers on assignment.

Photos: Send photos with submission. Reviews transparencies and prints. Offers $50-300/photo. Captions and identification of subjects required. Buys all rights.

Columns/Departments: Managing Editor: Alyson Behr. Associate Editor: Kristi Johnson. Readback (any newsworthy items on aircraft and/or people in aviation), 100-300 words; Flight To Remember (a particularly difficult or wonderful flight), 1,000-1,500 words; Jobs & Schools (a feature or an interesting school or program in aviation), 1,000-1,500 words; and Travel (any traveling done in piston-engine aircraft), 1,000-2,500 words. Buys 30 mss/year. Send complete ms. Length: 1,000-2,500 words. Pays $200-500.

PRIVATE PILOT, Fancy Publications Corp., P.O. Box 6050, Mission Viejo CA 92690-6050. (714)855-8822. Fax: (714)855-3045. Editor: J. Patrick O'Leary. Managing Editor: Chuck Stewart. 75% freelance written. Works with a small number of new/unpublished writers each year. For owner/pilots of private aircraft, for student pilots and others aspiring to attain additional ratings and experience. "We take a unique, but limited view within our field." Estab. 1964. Circ. 105,000. Buys first North American serial rights. Pays on publication. Publishes ms average of 6 months after acceptance. No simultaneous submissions. Query for electronic submissions. Reports in 2 months. Sample copy for $4. Writer's guidelines for SASE.
  • *Private Pilot* is looking for more concise treatments; better artwork and photos.

Nonfiction: Material on techniques of flying, developments in aviation, product and specific airplane test reports, travel by aircraft, and development and use of airports. All must be related to general aviation field. Buys about 60-90 mss/year. Query. Length: 1,000-4,000 words. Pays $75-300.

Photos: Pays $50 for 4-color prints or transparencies purchased with ms or on assignment. Pays $300 for color transparencies used on cover.

Tips: "Freelancer must know the subject about which he is writing and use good grammar; remember that we try to relate to the middle segment of the business/pleasure flying public. We see too many 'first flight' type of articles. Most writers do not do enough research on their subject. We would like to see more material on business-related flying, more on people involved in flying."

PROFESSIONAL PILOT, Queensmith Communications, 3014 Colvin St., Alexandria VA 22314. (703)370-0606. Fax: (703)370-7082. Editor: Mary F. Silitch. 75% freelance written. Monthly magazine on major and regional airline, corporate and various other types of professional aviation. "Our readers are commercial pilots with highest ratings and the editorial content reflects their knowledge and experience." Estab. 1967. Circ. 35,000. **Pays on acceptance.** Publishes ms an average of 3 months after acceptance. Byline given. Kill fee negotiable. Buys all rights. Free sample copy.
  • This publication is no longer in the market for articles concerning military aviation. It also has eliminated its column (Pireps) on aviation news.

Nonfiction: How-to (avionics and aircraft flight checks), humor, interview/profile, personal experience (if a lesson for professional pilots), photo feature, technical (avionics, weather, engines, aircraft). All issues have a theme such as regional airline operations, maintenance, jet aircraft, helicopters, etc. Buys 40 mss/year. Query. Length: 750-1,500. Pays $200-1,000. Sometimes pays expenses of writers on assignment.

Photos: Send photos with submission. Prefers transparencies. Offers no additional payment for photos accepted with ms. Captions and identification of subjects required. Buys all rights.

Tips: Query first. "Freelancer should be a professional pilot or have background in aviation that will make his articles believable to highly qualified pilots of commercial aircraft. We are placing a greater emphasis on airline operations, management and pilot concerns."

Business and Finance

Business publications give executives and consumers a range of information from local business news and trends to national overviews and laws that affect them. National and regional publications are listed below in separate categories. Magazines that have a technical slant are in the Trade section under Business Management, Finance or Management and Supervision categories.

National

BUSINESS START-UPS, Entrepreneur Group, Inc., 2392 Morse Ave., Irvine CA 92714. (714)261-2083. Editor: Will Swam. 20-25% freelance written. Monthly magazine on small business. "Provides how-to information for starting a small business, running a small business during the 'early' years and profiles of entrepreneurs who have started successful small businesses." Estab. 1989. Circ. 210,000. **Pays on accep-**

tance. Byline given. Offers 20% kill fee. Buys first time international rights. Submit seasonal/holiday material 6 months in advance. Reports in 2 months on queries. Sample copy for $3. Writer's guidelines for SASE. Please write: "Attn: Writer's Guidelines" on envelope.

Nonfiction: "We are especially seeking how-to articles for starting a small business. Please read the magazine and writer's guidelines before querying." Interview/profiles on entrepreneurs. Query. Length: 1,800. Pays $300.

Photos: State availability of photos with submission. Identification of subjects required.

BUSINESS TODAY, Meridian International, Inc., P.O. Box 10010, Ogden UT 84409. (801)394-9446. 40% freelance written. Bimonthly magazine covering all aspects of business. Particularly interested in tips to small/medium business managers. **Pays on acceptance.** Publishes ms an average of 3 months after acceptance. Byline given. Buys first rights, second serial (reprint) rights and nonexclusive reprint rights. Reports in 2 months with SASE. Sample copy for $1 and 9 × 12 SAE. Writer's guidelines for #10 SASE. All requests for samples and guidelines, and queries should be addressed Attn: Editorial Staff.

Nonfiction: General interest articles about employee relations, management principles, trends in finance, technology, ergonomics, and "how to do it better" stories. Articles covering up-to-date practical business information are welcome. Cover stories are often profiles of people who have expertise and success in a specific aspect of business. Buys 40 mss/year. Query. Length: 1,000 words. Pays 15¢/word for first rights plus non-exclusive reprint rights. Payment for second rights is 10¢/word.

Photos: Send photos with ms. Reviews 35mm or larger transparencies and 5 × 7 or 8 × 10 color prints. Pays $35 for inside photo; pays $50 for cover photo. Captions, model releases and identification of subjects required.

Tips: "We're looking for meaty, hard-core business articles with practical applications. Profiles should be prominent business-people, preferably Fortune-500 league. The key is a well-written query letter that: 1) demonstrates that the subject of the article is tried-and-true and has national appeal, 2) shows that the article will have a clear, focused theme, 3) gives evidence that the writer/photographer is a professional, even if a beginner."

BUSINESS WEEK, The McGraw Hill Companies, 1221 Avenue of the Americas, New York NY 10020. Weekly publication covering news and trends in the world of business. This magazine did not respond to our request for information. Query before submitting.

BUSINESS96, Success Strategies For Small Business, Group IV Communications, Inc., 125 Auburn Ct., #100, Thousand Oaks CA 91362-3617. (805)496-6156. Editor: Daniel Kehrer. Editorial Director: Don Phillipson. 75% freelance written. Bimonthly magazine for small and independent business. "We publish only practical articles of interest to small business owners all across America; also some small business owner profiles." Estab. 1993. Circ. 610,000. **Pays on acceptance.** Publishes ms an average of 4 months after acceptance. Byline given. Offers 25% kill fee. First and non-exclusive reprint rights. Reports in 6 months. Sample copy for $4. Writer's guidelines for #10 SASE.

• The editor notes that all submissions will also be considered for *Independent Business*, also published by Group IV.

Nonfiction: How-to articles for operating a small business. No "generic" business articles, articles on big business, articles on how to start a business or general articles on economic theory. Buys 80-100 mss/year. Query with résumé and published clips; do not send ms. Length: 1,000-2,000 words. Pays $500-1,500 for assigned articles. Pays expenses of writers on assignment.

Columns/Departments: Tax Tactics, Small Business Computing, Marketing Moves, Ad-visor, Banking & Finance, Business Cost-Savers, all 1,000-2,000 words. Buys 40-50 mss/year. Query with résumé and published clips. Pays $500-1,500.

Tips: "Talk to small business owners anywhere in America about what they want to read, what concerns or interests them in running a business. All areas open, but we use primarily professional business writers with top credentials in the field."

ENTREPRENEUR MAGAZINE, 2392 Morse Ave., Irvine CA 92714. Fax: (714)755-4211. Editor: Rieva Lesonsky. 40% freelance written. "Readers are small business owners seeking information on running a better business." Circ. 385,000. **Pays on acceptance.** Publishes ms an average of 5 months after acceptance. Buys first international rights. Byline given. Submit seasonal/holiday material 6 months in advance of issue date. Reports in 2 months. Sample copy for $3. Writer's guidelines for #10 SASE. Please write "Attn: Writer's Guidelines" on envelope.

Nonfiction: How-to (information on running a business, profiles of unique entrepreneurs). Buys 60-70 mss/year. Query with clips of published work and SASE. Length: 2,000 words. Payment varies.

Photos: "We use color transparencies to illustrate articles. Please state availability with query." Uses standard color transparencies. Buys various rights. Model release required.

Tips: "Read several issues of the magazine! Study the feature articles. (Columns are not open to freelancers.) It's so exciting when a writer goes beyond the typical, flat 'business magazine query'—how to write a press release, how to negotiate with vendors, etc.—and instead investigates a current trend and then develops a story on how that trend affects small business."

EXECUTIVE FEMALE, NAFE, 30 Irving Place, 5th Floor, New York NY 10003. (212)477-2200. Fax: (212)477-8215. Editor-in-Chief: Basia Hellwig. Executive Editor: Patti Watts. Managing Editor: Dorian Burden. 60% freelance written. Bimonthly magazine emphasizing "useful career, business and financial information for the upwardly mobile career woman." Prefers to work with published/established writers. Estab. 1975. Circ. 200,000. Byline given. **Pays on acceptance.** Publishes ms an average of 3 months after acceptance. Submit seasonal/holiday material 6 months in advance. Buys first rights, second serial (reprint) rights to material originally published elsewhere. Accepts previously published material. Send photocopy of article or typed ms with rights for sale noted and information about when and where the article previously appeared. Pays 25% of amount paid for an original article. Reports in 2 months. Sample copy for $2.50. Writer's guidelines for #10 SASE.

Nonfiction: "Articles on any aspect of career advancement and financial planning are welcomed." Needs how-tos for managers and articles about coping on the job, trends in the workplace, financial planning, trouble shooting, business communication, time and stress management, career goal-setting and get-ahead strategies. Written queries only. Submit photos with ms (b&w prints or transparencies) or include suggestions for artwork. Length: 800-2,000 words. Pays 50¢/word. Pays for local travel and telephone calls.

Columns/Departments: Your Money (savings, financial advice, economic trends, interesting tips); Managing Smart (tips on managing people, getting ahead); and Your Business (entrepreneurial stories). Buys 20 mss/year. Query with published clips or send complete ms. Length: 250-1,000 words. Pays 50¢/word.

INDEPENDENT BUSINESS: America's Small Business Magazine, Group IV Communications, Inc., 125 Auburn Ct., #100, Thousand Oaks CA 91362-3617. (805)496-6156. Editor: Daniel Kehrer. Editorial Director: Don Phillipson. 75% freelance written. Bimonthly magazine for small and independent business. "We publish only practical articles of interest to small business owners all across America; also some small business owner profiles." Estab. 1989. Circ. 630,000. **Pays on acceptance.** Publishes ms an average of 4 months after acceptance. Byline given. Offers 25% kill fee. First and non-exclusive reprint rights. Simultaneous queries OK. Reports in 3 months. Sample copy for $4. Writer's guidelines for #10 SASE.

• All submissions will also be considered for *Business96*, also published by Group IV.

Nonfiction: How-to articles for operating a small business. No "generic" business articles, articles on big business, articles on how to start a business or general articles on economic theory. Buys 80-100 mss/year. Query with résumé and published clips; do not send mss. Length: 1,000-2,000 words. Pays $500-1,500 for assigned articles. Pays expenses of writers on assignment.

Columns/Departments: Tax Tactics, Small Business Computing, Marketing Moves, Ad-visor, Banking & Finance, Business Cost-Savers, all 1,000-2,000 words. Buys 40-50 mss/year. Query with résumé and published clips. Pays $500-1,500.

Tips: "Talk to small business owners anywhere in America about what they want to read, what concerns or interests them in running a business. All areas open, but we use primarily professional business writers with top credentials in the field."

‡INTERNATIONAL, (formerly *Top Secret*), Detroit International Publishing, 5139 S. Clarendon Ave., Detroit MI 48204-2923. (313)438-0318. Editor: Mr. Shannon Roxborough. 100% freelance written. Monthly newsletter covering financial and personal privacy, international investing, offshore banking, tax havens, world business and related topics. Estab. 1992. Circ. 5,000. **Pays on acceptance**. Publishes ms an average of 1 month after acceptance. Byline given. Buys all rights. Submit seasonal material 6 months in advance. Accepts simultaneous submissions. Reports in 1 month. Sample copy $5 for SAE with 4 first-class stamps. Writer's guidelines for #10 SASE.

Nonfiction: General interest, historical/nostalgic, how-to, interview/profile and photo feature. "No technical pieces." Buys 25-35 mss/year. Query with or without published clips or send complete ms. Length: 500-1,800 words. Pays $10-50 for assigned articles; $5-35 for unsolicited articles.

Photos: Send photos with submission. Reviews negatives and prints. Offers $1-10/photo. Captions required. Buys all rights.

Fillers: Buys 25-35/year. Length: 100-500 words. Pays $5-25.

Tips: "New and unpublished writers are especially welcome. Exotic and lesser-known subjects are welcomed. We buy all rights. We're interested in new trends or new ways of looking at old topics."

MONEY, Time & Life Bldg., Rockefeller Center, New York NY 10020. (212)522-3292. Monthly publication covering investment and other money-related topics.

Nonfiction: Rich Eisenberg, assistant managing editor. Query with published clips.

Columns/Departments: Money Newsline (contact Nancy Perry, executive editor); Smart Spending (contact Joanna Krotz, executive editor).

Tips: "Know the magazine and know the readers. *Money Magazine* provides services for its readers—know how to do this."

OWNER-MANAGER, P.O. Box 1521, Wall St. Station, New York NY 10268-1521. (212)323-8056. Editor: Phil Chenery. Managing Editor: Jim Hill. Publisher: V. Ricasio. 20% freelance written. Bimonthly magazine for business and enterprise. "Our readers are owners who manage their own companies. The editorial mission is to provide them with information to manage their businesses, but not merely to become better businessmen but fulfilled individuals as well." Estab. 1992. Circ. 10,000. Pays on publication. Publishes ms an average of 4 months after acceptance. Byline given. Offers 30% kill fee. Buys first rights or second serial rights. Editorial lead time 2 months. Submit seasonal material 3 months in advance. Accepts previously published submissions. Send tearsheet of article and information about when and where the article previously appeared. For reprints, pays 60% of the amount paid for an original article. Query for electronic submissions. Sample copy for 8½ × 11 SAE with 2 first-class stamps. Writer's guideliines for #10 SASE.
Nonfiction: Book excerpts, essays, general interest, how-to (not detailed guide but why such actions are needed), interview/profile, opinion, technical. Buys 8 mss/year. Send complete ms. Length: 500-2,500 words. Pays $1,000 minimum for assigned articles, $350 minimum for unsolicited articles.
Photos: State availability of photos with submission. Reviews prints. Negotiates payment individually. Captions required. Buys one-time rights.
Columns/Departments: Buys 4 mss/year. Query. Pays $250-500.
Tips: "Cover stories are most open to freelancers."

REPORT ON BUSINESS MAGAZINE, Globe and Mail, 444 Front St. W., Toronto Ontario M5V 2S9 Canada. (416)585-5499. Editor: David Olive. 50% freelance written. Monthly "business magazine like *Forbes* or *Fortune* which tries to capture major trends and personalities." Circ. 300,000. **Pays on acceptance.** Publishes ms an average of 4 months after acceptance. Byline given. Offers 50% kill fee. Buys first North American serial rights. Query for electronic submissions. Reports in 3 weeks. Free sample copy.
Nonfiction: Book excerpts, exposé, interview/profile, new product, photo feature. Buys 30 mss/year. Query with published clips. Length: 2,000-4,000 words. Pays $200-3,000. Pays expenses of writers on assignment.
Tips: "For features send a one-page story proposal. We prefer to write about personalities involved in corporate events."

TECHNICAL ANALYSIS OF STOCKS & COMMODITIES, The Trader's Magazine, Technical Analysis, Inc., 4757 California Ave. SW, Seattle WA 98116-4499. (206)938-0570. Fax: (206)938-1307. Publisher: Jack K. Hutson. Editor: Thomas R. Hartle. 75% freelance written. Eager to work with new/unpublished writers. Magazine covers methods of investing and trading stocks, bonds and commodities (futures), options, mutual funds and precious metals. Estab. 1982. Circ. 45,000. Pays on publication. Publishes ms an average of 3 months after acceptance. Byline given. Offers 50% kill fee. Buys all rights; however, second serial (reprint) rights revert to the author, provided copyright credit is given. Accepts previously published submissions. Send tearsheet or photocopy of article or typed ms with rights for sale noted and information about when and where the article appeared. Query for electronic submissions. Reports in 3 weeks on queries; 1 month on mss. Sample copy for $5. Writer's guidelines for #10 SASE.
Nonfiction: Thomas R. Hartle, editor. Reviews (new software or hardware that can make a trader's life easier, comparative reviews of software books, services, etc.); how-to (trade); technical (trading and software aids to trading); utilities (charting or computer programs, surveys, statistics or information to help the trader study or interpret market movements); humor (unusual incidents of market occurrences, cartoons). "No newsletter-type, buy-sell recommendations. The article subject must relate to trading psychology, technical analysis, charting or a numerical technique used to trade securities or futures. Virtually requires graphics with every article." Buys 150 mss/year. Query with published clips if available or send complete ms. Length: 1,000-4,000 words. Pays $100-500. (Applies per inch base rate and premium rate—write for information). Sometimes pays expenses of writers on assignment.
Photos: Christine M. Morrison, art coordinator. State availability of art or photos. Pays $20-175 for b&w or color negatives with prints or positive slides. Captions, model releases and identification of subjects required. Buys one-time and reprint rights.
Columns/Departments: Buys 100 mss/year. Query. Length: 800-1,600 words. Pays $50-300.
Fillers: Karen Webb, fillers editor. Jokes and cartoons on investment humor. Must relate to trading stocks, bonds, options, mutual funds or commodities. Buys 20/year. Length: 500 words. Pays $20-50.
Tips: "Describe how to use technical analysis, charting or computer work in day-to-day trading of stocks, bonds, mutual funds, options or commodities. A blow-by-blow account of how a trade was made, including the trader's thought processes, is, to our subscribers, the very best received story. One of our prime considerations is to instruct in a manner that the lay person can comprehend. We are not hyper-critical of writing style. The completeness and accuracy of submitted material are of the utmost consideration. Write for detailed writer's guidelines."

YOUR MONEY, Consumers Digest Inc., 5705 N. Lincoln Ave., Chicago IL 60659. (312)275-3590. Editor: Dennis Fertig. 75% freelance written. Bimonthly magazine on personal finance. "We cover the broad range of topics associated with personal finance—spending, saving, investing earning, etc." Estab. 1979. Circ. 500,000. **Pays on acceptance.** Publishes ms an average of 2 months after acceptance. Byline given. Offers 50% kill fee. Buys first rights and second serial (reprint) rights. Reports in 3 months (or longer) on queries.

Do not send computer disks. Sample copy and writer's guidelines for 9×12 SAE with 4 first-class stamps. Writer's guidelines for #10 SASE.

• *Your Money* has been receiving more submissions and has less time to deal with them. Accordingly, they often need more than three months reporting time.

Nonfiction: How-to. "No first-person success stories or profiles of one company." Buys 25 mss/year. Send complete ms or query and clips. Include stamped, self-addressed postcard for more prompt response. Length: 1,500-2,500 words. Pays 50¢/word for assigned articles. Pays expenses of writers on assignment.

Tips: "Know the subject matter. Develop real sources in the investment community. Demonstrate a reader-friendly style that will help make the sometimes complicated subject of investing more accessible to the average person. Fill manuscripts with real-life examples of people who actually have done the kinds of things discussed—people we can later photograph."

Regional

‡ARIZONA BUSINESS MAGAZINE, 3111 N. Central Ave., Suite 230, Phoenix AZ 85012. (602)277-6045. Editor: Jessica McCann. 35% freelance written. Quarterly magazine covering business topics specific to Arizona: health care, banking, finance, legal issues, the environment, real estate and development, international, etc. "Our readers are primarily high-level executives and business owners. The magazine is recognized for our well-balanced articles and high-quality photography. We strive to offer readers well-researched, objective articles on the business issues facing our state." Estab. 1984. Circ. 80,000. Pays on completion of final draft for publication. Publishes ms an average of 3 months after acceptance. Byline given. Offers 100% kill fee. Buys first rights and makes work-for-hire assignments. Editorial lead time 2 months. Submit seasonal material 1 year in advance. Reports in 2 months on queries; 4 months on mss. Sample copy for 9×12 SAE with 6 first-class stamps. Writer's guidelines for #10 SASE.

Nonfiction: General interest, historical/nostalgic, interview/profile, new product, opinion, photo feature. No how-to articles. Buys 20-24 mss/year. Query with published clips. Length: 1,500-2,200 words. Pays $50-250. All articles are assigned. Sometimes pays expenses of writers on assignment.

Photos: State availability of photos with submissions. Reviews transparencies or slides. Negotiates payment individually. Captions, identification of subjects required. Buys one-time rights.

Columns/Departments: HealthWatch, High Finance, Power of Attorney, Environomics, Corporate Lifestyle, High Tech (all are general interest stories focusing on the industries mentioned), 1,500-2,000 words. Query with published clips. Pays $100-250.

Fillers: Personality profiles. Buys 8-12/year. Length: 400-600 words. Pays $25-100.

Tips: "Always begin with a one-page query letter/outline of the story idea and include one or two samples of your work. We rarely accept manuscripts. More often, we are impressed with the writer's presentation and respect for our time than with the story proposal. Grab us with one powerful point, fact or idea and you'll have your foot in the door for future assignments. The most important key is to be brief and to the point."

BOULDER COUNTY BUSINESS REPORT, 4865 Sterling Dr., Suite 200, Boulder CO 80301-2349. (303)440-4950. Fax: (303)440-8954. E-mail: jwlewis@bcbr.com. Editor: Jerry W. Lewis. 75% freelance written. Prefers to work with published/established writers; works with a small number of new/unpublished writers each year. Monthly newspaper covering Boulder County business issues. Offers "news tailored to a monthly theme and read primarily by Colorado businesspeople and by some investors nationwide. Philosophy: Descriptive, well-written articles that reach behind the scene to examine area's business activity." Estab. 1982. Circ. 18,000. Pays on publication. Publishes ms an average of 1 month after acceptance. Byline given. Buys one-time rights and second serial (reprint) rights. Query for electronic submissions. Reports in 1 month on queries; 2 weeks on mss. *Writer's Market* recommends allowing 2 months for reply. Sample copy for $1.44.

Nonfiction: Interview/profile, new product, examination of competition in a particular line of business. "All our issues are written around one or two monthly themes. No articles are accepted in which the subject has not been pursued in depth and both sides of an issue presented in a writing style with flair." Buys 120 mss/year. Query with published clips. Length: 250-2,000 words. Pays $50-300.

Photos: State availability of photos with query letter. Reviews b&w contact sheets. Pays $10 maximum for b&w contact sheet. Identification of subjects required. Buys one-time rights and reprint rights.

Tips: "Must be able to localize a subject. In-depth articles are written by assignment. The freelancer located in the Colorado area has an excellent chance here."

‡THE BUSINESS TIMES, Blackburn Magazine Group, 231 Dundas St., Suite 203, London, Ontario N6A 1H1 Canada. (519)679-4901. Editor: David Helwig. Contact: Nadia H. Shousher, assistant editor. 40% freelance written. Monthly glossy tabloid covering local business news, events and trends. "Local angle a must—aimed at business owners and executives." Estab. 1993. Circ. 10,000. Pays on publication. Publishes ms an average of 2 weeks after acceptance. Byline given. Offers $25 kill fee. Buys first North American serial rights. Editorial lead time 1-2 months, sometimes 1 week. Submit seasonal material 2 months in advance.

Accepts simultaneous submissions. Reports in 2 weeks on queries; 1 week on mss. Sample copy and writer's guidelines free.
Nonfiction: Book excerpts, exposé, new product, opinion, technical, timely news, industry trends and development. No advertorial, non-local news. Buys 200 mss/year. Query with published clips. Length: 150-600 words. Pays $50-150. Sometimes pays expenses of writers on assignment.
Photos: State availability of photos with submission. Offers $25-100/photo. Negotiates payment individually. Identification of subjects required. Buys one-time rights.
Columns/Departments: News (local emphasis), 100-500 words; Special Features (varies; to be assigned), 400-600 words. Query with published clips. Pays $50-150.
Tips: "Need local industry contacts to break news; need to know local sources, trends, events. Query by letter with sample news clips."

COLORADO BUSINESS, Wiesner Inc., 7009 S. Potomac St., Englewood CO 80112. (303)397-7600. Editor: Cynthia Evans. 75% freelance written. Monthly magazine covering Colorado-based businesses. Estab. 1973. Circ. 20,000. Pays on publication. Publishes ms an average of 3 months after acceptance. Byline given. Offers 50% kill fee. Buys first rights. Editorial lead time 3 months. Submit seasonal material 6 months in advance. Query for electronic submissions. Reports in 1 month on queries.
Nonfiction: Business, general interest, historical/nostalgic, how-to, interview/profile, new product, opinion, personal experience, photo feature, technical. Buys 40 mss/year. Query with published clips. Length: 700-3,000 words. Pays $200 for assigned articles; $50 for unsolicited articles. Sometimes pays expenses of writers on assignment.
Photos: State availability of photos with submission. Reviews contact sheets, transparencies. Negotiates payment individually. Captions, identification of subjects required. Buys one-time rights.
Columns/Departments: Buys 24 mss/year. Query with published clips. Pays $50-200.
Tips: "Know the magazine before you pitch me. Solid story ideas specifically geared to Colorado audience. No boring stories. No corporatese."

‡CRAIN'S DETROIT BUSINESS, Crain Communications Inc., 1400 Woodbridge Ave., Detroit MI 48207. (313)446-6000. Editor: Mary Kramer. Executive Editor: Cindy Goodaker. Contact: Chris Mead, special sections editor. 5% freelance written. Weekly tabloid covering business in the Detroit metropolitan area—specifically Wayne, Oakland, Macomb, Washtenaw and Livingston counties. Estab. 1985. Circ. 143,500. Pays on publication. Publishes ms an average of 1 month after acceptance. Byline given. Offers $150 kill fee. Buys all rights. Query for electronic submissions. Sample copy for $1.
Nonfiction: New product, technical, business. Buys 100 mss/year. Query with published clips. Length: 20-40 words/column inch. Pays $10/column inch. Pays expenses of writers on assignment.
Photos: State availability of photos with submissions.
Tips: "Contact special sections editor in writing with background and, if possible, specific story ideas relating to our type of coverage and coverage area."

‡DUPAGE BUSINESS LEDGER, Ledger Publishing Co., 709 Enterprise Dr., Oak Brook IL 60521. Editor: Don Kopriva. 50% freelance written. Monthly tabloid covering news and features focusing on the business environment of DuPage County, IL: trends, profiles, breaking news, instructional. Estab. 1993. Circ. 13,000. Pays on publication. Byline given. Editorial lead time 2 months. No simultaneous or previously published submissions. Query for electronic submissions. Reports in 2 weeks on queries. Sample copy for $3. Writer's guidelines for #10 SASE.
Nonfiction: Book excerpts, general interest, interview/profile. Buys 25 mss/year. Query. Length: 300-750 words. Pays $50-250. Sometimes pays expenses of writers on assignment.
Photos: State availability of photos with submissions. Reviews contact sheets, negatives. Offers $10-25/photo. Identification of subjects required. Buys one-time rights.

‡EXECUTIVE REPORT, Pittsburgh's Business Magazine, Riverview Pubications, 3 Gateway Center, 5th Floor, Pittsburgh PA 15222-1004. (412)471-4585. Editor: Jane A. Black. 80% freelance written. Monthly magazine covering business and industry of southwestern Pennsylvania. "All our writers (freelancers) are in southwestern Pennsylvania. This focus is our strength." Estab. 1981. Circ. 27,000. Pays on publication. Publishes ms an average of 4 months after acceptance. Byline given. Offers 60% kill fee. Buys first rights and second serial (reprint) rights. Editorial lead time 2-4 months. Query for electronic submissions. Writer's guidelines free.
Nonfiction: By assignment. Buys 24 mss/year. Query with published clips; wait for assignment go-ahead. No phone calls. Length: 700-3,000 words. Pays $130-600. Sometimes pays expenses of writers on assignment.
Photos: State availability of photos with submission. Reviews contact sheets, negatives, transparencies, prints. Negotiates payment individually. Captions and identification of subjects required.
Tips: "It helps to have written for business audience before. Must have published clips and references, must live in area, must be able to think and write clearly."

FLORIDA TREND, Magazine of Florida Business and Finance, Box 611, St. Petersburg FL 33731. (813)821-5800. Editor: John F. Berry. Monthly magazine covering business economics and public policy for

Florida business people and investors. Circ. 50,000. Pays on publication. Byline given. Buys first North American serial rights. Reports in 2 months. Sample copy for $2.95 plus tax and postage.
• *Florida Trend* has doubled the number of manuscripts it buys.
Nonfiction: Business, finance and public policy. Buys 20-25 mss/year. Query with or without published clips. Length: 1,200-2,500 words. Manuscripts not returned.

‡**HOMES TODAY**, Bartow Communications, 1568 Spring Hill Rd., Suite 102, McLean VA 22102. Editor: June Fletcher. 90% freelance written. Tabloid published 10 times/year covering real estate. "We are direct-mailed to households most likely to buy new homes. We provide practical, useful advice about mortgages, home shopping, working with an agent, landscaping, home improvement and interior design. All of our stories must have a local, metro-Washington, DC slant." Estab. 1994. Circ. 800,000. Pays on publication. Publishes ms an average of 3 months after acceptance. Byline given. Kill fee negotiated. Buys first North American serial rights and second serial (reprint) rights. Editorial lead time 3 months. Submit seasonal material 6 months in advance. Accepts previously published submissions. Query for electronic submissions. Reports in 1 month on queries; 3 months on mss. Sample copy for $5.
Nonfiction: Book excerpts, general interest (real estate), how-to (all of our publication is "how-to"), humor, new product, photo feature. "Our articles must be specific, detailed and keyed to local sources." Buys 30 mss/year. Query with published clips. Length: 1,000-2,500 words. Pays $100-500 for assigned articles; $25-500 for unsolicited articles. Sometimes pays expenses of writers on assignment.
Photos: Send photos with submission. Reviews 4×5 transparencies, 8×10 prints. Negotiates payment individually. Captions, model releases, identification of subjects required. Buys one-time rights.
Columns/Departments: How Can I Tell The Quality Of (a detailed description of a different product category, such as paint or carpeting each month; explain how to determine quality in that category when shopping for a new home or contemplating a home improvement), 1,250 words. Buys 10 mss/year. Pays $75.
Tips: "Write first with story ideas (at least five), and a short explanation of how you'd cover each topic. Read us first—all of our stories have a local slant. Send at least three published clips—we don't use beginners."

MONEY SAVING IDEAS, The National Research Bureau, P.O. Box 1, Burlington IA 52601-0001. (319)752-5415. Fax: (319)752-3421. Editor: Nancy Heinzel. 75% freelance written. Quarterly magazine that features money saving strategies. "We are interested in money saving tips on various subjects (insurance, travel, heating/cooling, buying a house, ways to cut costs and balance checkbooks). Our audience is mainly industrial and office workers." Estab. 1948. Pays on publication. Publishes ms an average of 1 year after acceptance. Byline given. Buys all rights. Sample copy and writers guidelines for #10 SAE with 2 first-class stamps. Writer's guidelines for #10 SASE.
Nonfiction: How-to (save on grocery bills, heating/cooling bills, car expenses, insurance, travel). Query with or without published clips, or send complete ms. Length: 500-700 words. Pays 4¢/word.
Tips: "Follow our guidelines. Keep articles to stated length, double-spaced, neatly typed. If writer wishes rejected manuscript returned include SASE. Name, address and word length should appear on first page."

ROCHESTER BUSINESS MAGAZINE, Rochester Business, Inc., 1600 Lyell Ave., Rochester NY 14606-2395. (716)458-8280. Fax: (716)458-9831. Editor: Kristina Hutch. 25% freelance written. Monthly magazine. "*RBM* is a colorful tutorial business publication targeted specifically toward business owners and upper-level managers in the Rochester metropolitan area. Our audience is comprised of upscale decision-makers with keen interest in the 'how-to' of business. Some features deal with lifestyle, golf, cultural focus, etc." Estab. 1984. Circ. 11,000. Pays on publication. Publishes ms an average of 6 months after acceptance. Byline given. Buys all rights. Accepts previously published submissions. Send tearsheet of article or typed ms with rights for sale noted and information about when and where the article previously appeared. For reprints pays 100% of the amount paid for an original article. Reports in 1 month. Sample copy and writer's guidelines for SAE with 6 first-class stamps.
Nonfiction: Essays, historical/nostalgic, how-to, humor, interview/profile, personal experience, all with business slant. Buys 12-24 mss/year. Query with published clips. Length: 1,500 words maximum. Pays $50-100.
Photos: State availability of photos with submission. Offers no additional payment for photos accepted with ms. Captions required.

‡**VERMONT BUSINESS MAGAZINE**, Lake Iroguois Publications, 2 Church St., Burlington VT 05401. (802)863-8038. Fax: (802)863-8069. Editor: Timothy McQuiston. 80% freelance written. Monthly tabloid covering business in Vermont. Circ. 8,000. Pays on publication. Publishes ms an average of 1 month after acceptance. Byline given. Offers kill fee. Accepts simultaneous and previously published submissions. Send tearsheet of article and information about when and where the article previously appeared. Not copyrighted. Buys one-time rights. Query for electronic submissions. Reports in 2 months. Sample copy for 11×14 SAE with 7 first-class stamps.
Nonfiction: Business trends and issues. Buys 200 mss/year. Query with published clips. Length: 800-1,800 words. Pays $100-200. Pays the expenses of writers on assignment.

Photos: Send photos with submission. Reviews contact sheets. Offers $10-35/photo. Identification of subjects required.

Tips: "Read daily papers and look for business angles for a follow-up article. We look for issue and trend articles rather than company or businessman profiles. Note: magazine accepts Vermont-specific material *only.* The articles *must* be about Vermont."

Career, College and Alumni

Three types of magazines are listed in this section: university publications written for students, alumni and friends of a specific institution; publications about college life for students; and publications on career and job opportunities. Literary magazines published by colleges and universities are listed in the Literary and "Little" section.

AMERICAN CAREERS, Career Communications, Inc., 6701 W. 64th St., Overland Park KS 66202. Editorial Consultant: Mary Pitchford. 10% freelance written. Middle school and high school student publication published 3 times during school year covering careers, career statistics, skills needed to get jobs. Most stories are provided at no charge by authors in business, education and government. Estab. 1990. Circ. 500,000. Payment depends on whether assignment or submission. Byline sometimes given. Buys first, one-time or second serial (reprint) rights and makes work-for-hire assignments. Accepts previously published submissions. Send tearsheet or photocopy of article and information about when and where the article previously appeared. Reprint payment is negotiable. Reports in 1 month. Sample copy and writer's guidelines free on request.

Nonfiction: Career and education features. Buys 6 mss/year. Query with published clips. Length: 350-750 words. Negotiates payment. Pays expenses of writers on assignment.

Photos: State availability of photos with submission. Reviews contact sheets. Negotiates payment individually. Captions, model releases and identification of subjects required. Buys one-time rights.

Columns/Departments: Reality Check (brief facts, statistics, how-to ideas on careers, job hunting and other career-related information.) Length: 25-100 words. Some reviewing of current related books, video software. Buys 6 mss/year. Negotiates payment.

Tips: "Letters of introduction or query letters with samples are ways we get to know writers. Samples should include how-to articles or career articles. Articles written for publication for teenagers also would make good samples. Short feature articles on careers, career-related how-to articles and self-assessment tools (10-20 point quizzes with scoring information) are primarily what we publish."

THE BLACK COLLEGIAN, The Career & Self Development Magazine for African American Students, Black Collegiate Services, Inc., 140 Carondelet St., New Orleans LA 70130. (504)523-0154. Fax: (504)523-0271. Editor: Sonya Stinson. 25% freelance written. Magazine published biannually (October and February) during school year for African-American college students and recent graduates with an interest in career and job information, African-American cultural awareness, personalities, history, trends and current events. Estab. 1970. Circ. 121,000. Buys one-time rights. Byline given. Pays on publication. Submit seasonal and special interest material 2 months in advance of issue date. Reports in 6 months. Sample copy $for 4 and 9×12 SAE. Writer's guidelines for #10 SASE.

• *The Black Collegian* has cut back the number of issues, now publishing biannually instead of bimonthly.

Nonfiction: Material on careers, sports, black history, news analysis. Articles on problems and opportunities confronting African-American college students and recent graduates. Book excerpts, exposé, general interest, historical/nostalgic, how-to (develop employability), opinion, personal experience, profile, inspirational. Buys 40 mss/year (6 unsolicited). Query with published clips or send complete ms. Length: 500-1,500 words. Pays $100-500.

Photos: State availability of or send photos with query or ms. Black and white photos or color transparencies purchased with or without ms. 8×10 prints preferred. Captions, model releases and identification of subjects required. Pays $35/b&w; $50/color.

‡CAMPUS CANADA, Canadian Controlled Media Communications, 287 MacPherson Ave., Toronto Ontario M4V 1A4 Canada. (416)928-2909. Managing Editor: Sarah Moore. 75% freelance written. Quarterly magazine covering student (university) life. "*Campus Canada* is written for the Canadian university student. Stories range in topic from current issues (date rape, etc.) to entertainment to collegiate sports." Estab. 1984. Circ. 125,000. Pays on publication. Byline given. Offers 50% kill fee. Buys first North American serial rights. Editorial lead time 3 months. Submit seasonal material 2 months in advance. Accepts simultaneous submissions. Query for electronic submissions. Reports in 2 months on queries. Sample copy on request.

Nonfiction: General interest, humor, interview/profile, opinion, personal experience, travel. Buys 15 mss/year. Query with published clips. Length: 1,000 words maximum. Pays $50-300.

Photos: State availability of photos with submissions. Identification of subjects required. Buys one-time rights.

Columns/Departments: Movies (upcoming releases), 800 words; Sports (Canadian university), 800 words; Music (Canadian pop/alternative), 500 words.

CAREER FOCUS, For Today's Rising Professional, Communications Publishing Group, Inc., 250 Mark Twain Tower, 106 W. 11th St., Kansas City MO 64105-1806. (816)221-4404. Fax: (516)273-8936. Editor: Neoshia Michelle Paige. 80% freelance written. Monthly magazine "devoted to providing positive insight, information, guidance and motivation to assist Blacks and Hispanics (ages 21-40) in their career development and attainment of goals." Estab. 1988. Circ. 250,000. Pays on publication. Byline often given. Buys second serial (reprint) rights and makes work-for-hire assignments. Submit seasonal/holiday material 6 months in advance. Accepts simultaneous and previously published submissions. Send tearsheet of article and information about when and where the article previously appeared. For reprints, pays 50% of the amount paid for an original article. Reports in 2 months. Sample copy for 9×12 SAE with 4 first-class stamps. Writer's guidelines for #10 SASE.

• The editor notes that if the writer can provide the manuscript on 3.25 disk, saved in generic ASCII, pay is $10 higher and chance of acceptance is greater.

Nonfiction: Book excerpts, general interest, historical, how-to, humor, inspirational, interview/profile, personal experience, photo feature, technical, travel. Length: 750-2,000 words. Pays $150-400 for assigned articles; 10¢/word for unsolicited articles. Sometimes pays expenses of writers on assignment.

Photos: State availability of photos with submission. Reviews transparencies. Pays $20-25/photo. Captions, model releases and identification of subjects required. Buys all rights.

Columns/Departments: Profiles (striving and successful Black and Hispanic young adult, ages 21-40). Buys 15 mss/year. Send complete ms. Length: 500-1,000 words. Pays $50-250.

Fiction: Adventure, ethnic, historical, humorous, mainstream, slice-of-life vignettes. Buys 3 mss/year. Send complete ms. Length: 1,500-5,000 words. Pays $100-400.

Poetry: Free verse. Buys 4/year. Length: 10-25 lines. Pays $10-50.

Fillers: Anecdotes, facts, gags to be illustrated by cartoonist, newsbreaks, short humor. Buys 10/year. Length: 25-250 words. Pays $25-100.

Tips: For new writers: Submit full ms that is double-spaced; clean copy only. If available, send clips of previously published works and résumé. Should state when available to write. Most open to freelancers are profiles of successful and striving persons including photos. Profile must be of a Black or Hispanic adult living in the US. Include on first page of ms name, address, phone number, Social Security number and number of words in article.

CAREER WOMAN, For Entry-Level and Professional Women, Equal Opportunity Publications, Inc., 150 Motor Pkwy., Suite 420, Hauppauge NY 11788-5145. (516)273-8643. Fax: (516)273-8936. Editor: Eileen Nester. Estab. 1973. 80% freelance written. Works with new/unpublished writers each year. Annual magazine covering career-guidance for college women. Strives to "bridge the gap between college life and the working world—with advice ranging from conducting an effective job search to surviving the first several years on the job to finding a balance between personal and professional lives." Audience is 60% college juniors and seniors, 40% working graduates. Circ. 10,500. Controlled circulation, distributed through college guidance and placement offices. Pays on publication. Publishes ms an average of 3-12 months after acceptance. Byline given. Buys first North American rights. Accepts simultaneous submissions. Reports in 2 months. Sample copy and writer's guidelines for 9×12 SAE with 5 first-class stamps.

• *Career Woman* no longer runs straight role model profile articles.

Nonfiction: "We want career-related articles describing for a college-educated woman the how-tos of obtaining a professional position and advancing her career." Looks for practical features detailing self-evaluation techniques, the job-search process and advice for succeeding on the job. Needs mss presenting information on professions offering opportunities to young women—especially the growth professions of the future. Special issues emphasize career opportunities for women in fields such as health care, communications, sales, marketing, banking, insurance, finance, science, engineering and computers. Query first.

Photos: Send with ms. Prefers 35mm color slides, but will accept b&w prints. Captions and identification of subjects required. Buys all rights.

Tips: "The best way to get published is to find a unique approach to common topics. Remember that you are addressing a group of women new to the workforce. They need advice on virtually every career-guidance topic."

CAREERS & COLLEGES MAGAZINE, E.M. Guild, Inc., 989 Avenue of Americas, 6th Floor, New York NY 10018. (212)563-4688. Fax: (212)967-2531. Editor-in-Chief/Publisher: June Rogoznica. Senior Editor: Don Rauf. 85-95% freelance written. Biannual magazine for education, careers and life choices for high school students. "*Careers & Colleges* is a magazine that believes in young people. It believes that they have the power—and responsibility—to shape their own futures. That is why each issue provides high school juniors and seniors with useful, thought-provoking reading on career choices, life values, higher education and other topics that will help them enjoy profitable and self-respecting work." Estab. 1980. Circ. 500,000.

Pays on acceptance. Byline given. Offers 20% kill fee. Buys first North American serial rights. Editorial lead time 6 months. Submit seasonal material 6 months in advance. Accepts previously published articles. Send photocopy of article. Reports in 1 month on queries. Sample copy for $2.50 and 9×12 SAE with 5 first-class stamps. Writer's guidelines for #10 SASE.

● This magazine has changed from quarterly to biannual publication and therefore reports they need fewer freelance articles.

Nonfiction: Book excerpts, how-to (job or college related), interview/profile (teen role models). May publish a Spring issue on summer jobs and other employment opportunities for young adults. "No personal essays, life experiences or fiction." Buys 36-52 mss/year. Query with published clips. Length: 600-1,500 words. Pays $150 minimum. Sometimes pays expenses of writers on assignment (limit agreed upon in advance).

Photos: State availability of photos with submission. Negotiates payment individually. Buys one-time rights.

Columns/Departments: MoneyWise (strategies and resources for financing education beyond high school), 600-800 words; Career Watch (profiles of growth careers/interview plus statistics), 800 words. Buys 18-24 mss/year. Query with or without published clips. Pays $150-350.

Tips: "Be sure to request writer's guidelines. Follow guidelines specifically. No unsolicited manuscripts are accepted. Send a one-page query and clips. Examine other teen magazines for current topic ideas. Many opportunities exist in our career profile section—pay is low, but it is a good testing ground for us to gauge a writer's ability—strong performance here can lead to bigger articles. Query about growth careers that we have not covered in the past (consult magazine's Career Watch Index)."

CAREERS & MAJORS (for College Students), Oxendine Publishing, Inc., P.O. Box 14081, Gainesville FL 32604-2081. (904)373-6907. Editor: W.H. "Butch" Oxendine Jr.. Managing Editor: Kay Quinn King. 35% freelance written. Quarterly magazine for college careers and job opportunities. Estab. 1983. Circ. 17,000. Pays on publication. Publishes ms an average of 2-3 months after acceptance. Byline given. Buys all rights. Submit seasonal/holiday material 4 months in advance. Accepts simultaneous and previously published submissions. Send tearsheet or photocopy of article or typed ms with rights for sale noted and information about when and where the article previously appeared. Query for electronic submissions; prefers IBM. Reports in 1 month on queries. Sample copy for 8×11 SAE with 3 first-class stamps. For query/response and/or writer's guidelines send SASE.

Nonfiction: How-to, humor, new product, opinion. "No lengthy individual profiles or articles without primary and secondary sources of attribution." Buys 10 mss/year. Query with published clips. Length: 250-1,000 words. Pays $35 maximum. Pays contributor copies to students or first-time writers. State availability of photos with submission. Reviews contact sheets, negatives and transparencies; size "doesn't matter." Offers $50/photo maximum. Captions, model releases and identification of subjects required. Buys all rights.

Fiction: Publishes novel excerpts.

Columns/Departments: College Living (various aspects of college life, general short humor oriented to high school or college students), 250-1,000 words; Buys 10 mss/year. Query. Length: 250-1,000 words. Pays $35 maximum.

Fillers: Facts, newsbreaks, short humor. Buys 10/year. Length: 100-500 words. Pays $35 maximum.

Tips: "Read other high school and college publications for current issues, interests. Send manuscripts or outlines for review. All sections open to freelance work. Always looking for lighter, humorous articles, as well as features on Florida colleges and universities, careers, jobs. Multi-sourced (5-10) articles best."

CARNEGIE MELLON MAGAZINE, Carnegie Mellon University, Bramer House, Pittsburgh PA 15213-3890. (412)268-2132. Fax: (412)268-6929. Editor: Ann Curran. Estab. 1914. Quarterly alumni publication covering university activities, alumni profiles, etc. Circ, 56,000. **Pays on acceptance.** Byline given. Copyrighted. Reports in 1 month.

● *Carnegie Mellon Magazine* is now copyrighted.

Nonfiction: Book reviews (faculty alumni), general interest, humor, interview/profile, photo feature. "We use general interest stories linked to Carnegie Mellon activities and research." No unsolicited mss. Buys 5 features and 5-10 alumni profiles/year. Query with published clips. Length: 800-2,000 words. Pays $100-400 or negotiable rate. Sample copy for $2 and 9×12 SAE.

Poetry: Avant-garde or traditional. No previously published poetry. No payment.

CIRCLE K MAGAZINE, 3636 Woodview Trace, Indianapolis IN 46268-3196. Fax: (317)879-0204. Executive Editor: Nicholas K. Drake. 60% freelance written. "Our readership consists almost entirely of above-average college students interested in voluntary community service and leadership development. They are politically and socially aware and have a wide range of interests." Published 5 times/year. Circ. 15,000. **Pays on acceptance.** Normally buys first North American serial rights. Byline given. Submit seasonal/holiday material 6 months in advance. Reports in 2 months. Sample copy and writer's guidelines for large SAE with 3 first-class stamps.

Nonfiction: Articles published in *Circle K* are of 2 types—serious and light nonfiction. "We are interested in general interest articles on topics concerning college students and their lifestyles, as well as articles dealing with careers, community concerns and leadership development. No first person confessions, family histories or travel pieces." Query. Length: 800-1,900 words. Pays $150-400.

Photos: Purchased with accompanying ms. Captions required. Total purchase price for ms includes payment for photos.

Tips: "Query should indicate author's familiarity with the field and sources. Subject treatment must be objective and in-depth, and articles should include illustrative examples and quotes from persons involved in the subject or qualified to speak on it. We are open to working with new writers who present a good article idea and demonstrate that they've done their homework concerning the article subject itself, as well as concerning our magazine's style. We're interested in college-oriented trends, for example, entrepreneur schooling is now a major shift; rising censorship on campus; high-tech classrooms; virtual reality; music; leisure; and health issues."

COLLEGE PREVIEW, A Guide for College-Bound Students, Communications Publishing Group, 250 Mark Twain Tower, 106 W. 11th St., Kansas City MO 64105-1806. (816)221-4404. Fax: (816)221-1112. Editor: Neoshia Michelle Paige. 80% freelance written. Quarterly educational and career source guide. "Contemporary guide designed to inform and motivate Black and Hispanic young adults, ages 16-21 years old about college preparation, career planning and life survival skills." Estab. 1985. Circ. 600,000. Pays on publication. Byline often given. Buys first serial and second serial (reprint) rights or makes work-for-hire assignments. Submit seasonal/holiday material 6 months in advance. Accepts simultaneous and previously published submissions. Send tearsheet or photocopy of article or short story or typed ms with rights for sale noted and information about when and where the article previously appeared. For reprints, pays 50% of the amount paid for an original article. Reports in 2 months. Sample copy for 9×12 SAE with 4 first-class stamps. Writer's guidelines for #10 SASE.
  • The editor notes that if the writer can provide the manuscript on 3.25 disk, saved in generic ASCII, pay is $10 higher and chance of acceptance is greater.

Nonfiction: Book excerpts or reviews, general interest, how-to (dealing with careers or education), humor, inspirational, interview/profile (celebrity or "up and coming" young adult), new product (as it relates to young adult market), personal experience, photo feature, technical, travel. Send complete ms. Length: 750-2,000 words. Pays $150-400 for assigned articles; 10¢/word for unsolicited articles. Sometimes pays expenses of writers on assignment.

Photos: State availability of photos with submission. Reviews transparencies. Offers $20-$25/photo. Captions, model releases and identification of subjects required. Will return photos—send SASE.

Columns/Departments: Profiles of Achievement (striving and successful minority young adults ages 16-35 in various careers). Buys 30 mss/year. Send complete ms. Length: 500-1,500. Pays 10¢/word.

Fiction: Adventure, ethnic, historical, humorous, mainstream, slice-of-life vignettes. Buys 3 mss/year. Send complete ms. Length: 1,000-5,000 words. Pays $100-400.

Poetry: Free verse. Buys 5 poems/year. Submit maximum 5 poems. Length: 10-25 lines. Pays $10-50.

Fillers: Anecdotes, facts, gags to be illustrated by cartoonist, newsbreaks, short humor. Buys 10/year. Length: 25-250 words. Pays $25-100.

Tips: For new writers—send complete ms that is double spaced; clean copy only. If available, send clips of previously published works and résumé. Should state when available to write. Include on first page of ms name, address, phone, Social Security number, word count and SASE.

DIRECT AIM, For Today's Career Strategies, Communications Publishing Group, #250, 106 W. 11th St., Kansas City MO 64105-1806. (816)221-4404. Fax: (816)221-1112. Editor: Neoshia Michelle Paige. 80% freelance written. Quarterly educational and career source guide for Black and Hispanic college students at traditional, non-traditional, vocational and technical institutions. "This magazine informs students about college survival skills and planning for a future in the professional world." Buys second serial (reprint) rights or makes work-for-hire assignments. Submit seasonal/holiday material 6 months in advance. Accepts simultaneous and previously published submissions. Send tearsheet of article or short story or typed ms with rights for sale noted and information about when and where the article previously appeared. For reprints pays 50% of the amount paid for an original article. Reports in 2 months. Sample copy for 9×12 SAE with 4 first-class stamps. Writer's guidelines for #10 SASE.
  • The editor notes that if the writer can provide the manuscript on 3.25 disk, saved in generic ASCII, pay is $10 higher and chance of acceptance is greater.

Nonfiction: Book excerpts or reviews, general interest, how-to (dealing with careers or education), humor, inspirational, interview/profile (celebrity or "up and coming" young adult), new product (as it relates to young adult market), personal experience, photo feature, technical, travel. Query or send complete ms. Length: 750-2,000 words. Pays $150-400 for assigned articles; 10¢/word for unsolicited articles. Sometimes pays expenses of writers on assignment.

Photos: State availability of photos with submission. Reviews transparencies. Offers $20-25/photo. Captions, model releases and identification of subjects required. Will return photos.

Columns/Departments: Profiles of Achievement (striving and successful minority young adult age 18-35 in various technical careers). Buys 25 mss/year. Send complete ms. Length: 500-1,500. Pays $50-250.

Fiction: Publishes novel excerpts. Adventure, ethnic, historical, humorous, mainstream, slice-of-life vignettes. Buys 3 mss/year. Send complete ms. Length: 1,000-5,000 words. Pays $100-400.

Poetry: Free verse. Buys 5 poems/year. Submit maximum 5 poems. Length: 10-25 lines. Pays $10-50.
Fillers: Anecdotes, facts, gags to be illustrated by cartoonist, newsbreaks, short humor. Buys 30/year. Length: 25-250 words. Pays $25-100.
Tips: For new writers—send complete ms that is double spaced; clean copy only. If available, send clips of previously published works and résumé. Should state when available to write. Include on first page of ms name, address, phone, Social Security number and word count. Photo availability is important."

‡**EEO BIMONTHLY, Equal Employment Opportunity Career Journal,** CASS Communications, Inc., 1800 Sherman Place, Suite 300, Evanston IL 60201-3769. (708)475-8800. Senior Editor: Robert Shannon. 80% freelance written. Bimonthly magazine covering career management, specifically for women, minorities and persons with disabilities. "Although our audience is specifically female and minority, much of our content applies to all white-collar professionals—career management tips, industry overviews and trends, and job search techniques. Anything job- or career-related (interviewing, résumé writing, relocating, communicating, automating, etc.) fits our publication. We're always looking for new trends and interesting profiles." Estab. 1969. Circ. 6,000. **Pays on acceptance.** Publishes ms an average of 4 months after acceptance. Byline given. Buys first North American serial rights. Editorial lead time 3 months. Accepts simultaneous submissions. Reports in 3 weeks on queries; 1 month on mss. Sample copy for 10×12 SAE with 6 first-class stamps.
Nonfiction: General interest (career/workplace related), how-to (career planning related), technical (industry trends/innovations). Buys 24-30 mss/year. Query with published clips. Length: 1,500-3,000 words. Pays $350-700 for assigned articles; $300-500 for unsolicited articles. Sometimes pays expenses of writers on assignment.
Photos: State availability of photos with submissions. Reviews contact sheets, transparencies, prints. Captions, model releases, identification of subjects required. Buys one-time rights.
Columns/Departments: Industry Focus (trends, rising players, etc. of various industries), 2,000 words; Success Stories (profiles of successful individuals either female, minority or disabled), 1,500 words. Buys 12-15 mss/year. Query with published clips. Pays $350-700.
Fillers: Robert Shannon. Anecdotes (How I Found My Job—unique job search stories). Buys 6/year. Length: 250-300 words. Pays $50.
Tips: "Your queries can be informal outlines; just show us that you can write and that you know your subject."

EQUAL OPPORTUNITY, The Nation's Only Multi-Ethnic Recruitment Magazine for Black, Hispanic, Native American & Asian American College Grads, Equal Opportunity Publications, Inc., 150 Motor Pkwy., Suite 420, Hauppauge NY 11788-5145. (516)273-0066. Fax: (516)273-8936. Editor: James Schneider. 50% freelance written. Prefers to work with published/established writers. Triannual magazine covering career guidance for minorities. "Our audience is 90% college juniors and seniors; 10% working graduates. An understanding of educational and career problems of minorities is essential." Estab. 1967. Circ. 15,000. Controlled circulation, distributed through college guidance and placement offices. Pays on publication. Publishes ms an average of 6 months after acceptance. Byline given. Buys first rights. Deadline dates: Fall (June 10); Winter (September 15); Spring (January 1). Accepts simultaneous queries and previously published submissions. Sample copy and writer's guidelines for 9×12 SAE with 5 first-class stamps.
Nonfiction: Book excerpts and articles (job search techniques, role models); general interest (specific minority concerns); how-to (job-hunting skills, personal finance, better living, coping with discrimination); humor (student or career related); interview/profile (minority role models); opinion (problems of minorities); personal experience (professional and student study and career experiences); technical (on career fields offering opportunities for minorities); travel (on overseas job opportunities); and coverage of Black, Hispanic, Native American and Asian American interests. Special issues include career opportunities for minorities in industry and government in fields such as banking, insurance, finance, communications, sales, marketing, engineering, computers, military and defense. Query or send complete ms. Length: 1,000-1,500 words. Sometimes pays expenses of writers on assignment. Pays 10¢/word.
Photos: Prefers 35mm color slides and b&w. Captions and identification of subjects required. Buys all rights. Pays $15/photo use.
Tips: "Articles must be geared toward questions and answers faced by minority and women students."

FIRST OPPORTUNITY, Today's Career Options, Communications Publishing Group, 250 Mark Twain Tower, 106 W. 11th St., Kansas City MO 64105-1806. (816)221-4404. Editor: Neoshia Michelle Paige. 80% freelance written. Biannual resource publication focusing on advanced vocational/technical educational opportunities and career preparation for Black and Hispanic young adults, ages 16-21. Circ. 500,000. Pays on publication. Byline sometimes given. Buys second serial (reprint) rights or makes work-for-hire assignments. Submit seasonal/holiday material 6 months in advance. Accepts simultaneous and previously published submissions. Send tearsheet of article or typed ms with rights for sale noted and information about when and where the article previously appeared. For reprints, pays 50% of the amount paid for an original article. Reports in 2 months. Sample copy for 9×12 SAE with 4 first-class stamps. Writer's guidelines for #10 SASE.

● The editor notes that if the writer can provide the manuscript on 3.25 disk, saved in generic ASCII, pay is $10 higher and chance of acceptance is greater.

Nonfiction: Book excerpts or reviews, general interest, how-to (dealing with careers or education), humor, inspirational, interview/profile (celebrity or "up and coming" young adult), new product (as it relates to young adult market), personal experience, photo feature, technical, travel. Length: 750-2,000 words. Pays $150-400 for assigned articles; 10¢/word for unsolicited articles. Sometimes pays expenses of writers on assignment.

Photos: State availability of photos with submission. Prefers transparencies. Offers $20-25/photo. Captions, model releases, identification of subjects required. Buys all rights.

Columns/Departments: Profiles of Achievement (striving and successful minority young adult, age 16-35 in various vocational or technical careers). Buys 15 mss/year. Send complete ms. Length: 500-1,500. Pays $50-250.

Fiction: Adventure, ethnic, historical, humorous, mainstream, slice-of-life vignettes. Buys 3 mss/year. Send complete ms. Length: 1,000-5,000 words. Pays $100-400.

Poetry: Free verse. Buys 5 poems/year. Submit maximum 5 poems. Length: 10-25 lines. Pays $10-50.

Fillers: Anecdotes, facts, gags to be illustrated by cartoonist, newsbreaks, short humor. Buys 10/year. Length: 25-250 words. Pays $25-100.

Tips: For new writers—send complete ms that is double spaced; clean copy only. If available, send clip of previously published works and résumé. Should state when available to write. Include on first page of ms name, address, phone, Social Security number and word count. Photo availability is important.

FLORIDA LEADER (for college students), P.O. Box 14081, Gainesville FL 32604. (904)373-6907. Fax: (904)373-8120. Publisher: W.H. "Butch" Oxendine, Jr. Editor: Kay Quinn King. 25% freelance written. Quarterly "college magazine, feature-oriented, especially activities, events, interests and issues pertaining to college students." Estab. 1981. Circ. 27,000. Publishes ms an average of 2 months after acceptance. Byline given. Submit seasonal/holiday material 6 months in advance. Accepts previously published submissions. Send tearsheet or phogocopy of article or typed ms with rights for sale noted and information about when and where the article previously appeared. Query for electronic submissions. Reports in 2 months on queries. Sample copy and writer's guidelines for 9×12 SAE with 5 first-class stamps.

Nonfiction: How-to, humor, interview/profile, feature—all multi-sourced and Florida college related. Special issues: Careers and Majors (January, June); Florida Leader high school edition (August, January, May); Transfer (for community college transfers, November, July); Returning Student (for nontraditional-age students, July); Student Leader (October, March—pays double). Query with SASE. Length: 500 words or less. Payment varies. Sometimes pays expenses of writers on assignment.

Photos: State availability of photos with submission. Reviews negatives and transparencies. Captions, model releases, identification of subjects requested.

Fiction: Publishes novel excerpts.

‡GW MAGAZINE, George Washington University, 2121 Eye St. NW, #512, Washington DC 20052. (202)994-6462. Editor: Robert Guldin. 30% freelance written. Bimonthly magazine covering aspects of George Washington University—its alumni, faculty, programs, students, campus life. Estab. 1990. Circ. 125,000. **Pays on acceptance.** Publishes ms an average of 4 months after acceptance. Byline given. Buys first North American serial rights. Editorial lead time 6 months. Submit seasonal material 4 months in advance. Accepts simultaneous and previously published submissions. Query for electronic submissions. Reports in 1 month. Sample copy free on request.

Nonfiction: Book excerpts, essays, general interest, historical/nostalgic, humor, interview/profile, personal experience, photo feature. Buys 8-10 mss/year. Query with published clips. Length: 1,000-3,000 words. Pays $500 minimum. Sometimes pays expenses of writers on assignment.

Photos: Send photos with submission. Reviews contact sheets, transparencies, prints. Identification of subjects required. Buys one-time rights.

Fiction: Confession, experimental, humorous, slice-of-life vignettes. Query. Length: 500-3,000 words. Pays $100-1,000.

Poetry: Avant-garde, free verse, Haiku, light verse, traditional. Buys 1 poem/year. Submit maximum 6 poems. Pays $50-100.

Tips: "Keep an eye open for alumni, faculty etc. from GW doing interesting things—then query us."

JOURNEY, A Success Guide for College and Career Bound Students, Communications Publishing Group, 250 Mark Twain Tower, 106 W. 11th St., Kansas City MO 64105-1806. (816)221-4404. Fax: (816)221-1112. Editor: Georgia Clark. 40% freelance written. Biannual educational and career source guide for Asian-American high school and college students (ages 16-25) who have indicated a desire to pursue higher education through college, vocational and technical or proprietary schools. Estab. 1982. Circ. 200,000. Pays on publication. Byline sometimes given. Buys second serial (reprint) rights or makes work-for-hire assignments. Submit seasonal/holiday material 6 months in advance. Accepts simultaneous and previously published submissions. Send typed ms with rights for sale noted and information about when and where the article previously appeared. For reprints pays 50% of the amount paid for an original article. Reports in 3 months. Sample copy for 9×12 SAE with 4 first-class stamps. Writer's guidelines for #10 SASE.

• The editor notes that if the writer can provide the manuscript on 3.25 disk, saved in generic ASCII, pay is $10 higher and chance of acceptance is greater.

Nonfiction: Book excerpts or reviews, general interest, how-to (dealing with careers or education), humor, inspirational, interview/profile (celebrity or "up and coming" young adult), new product (as it relates to young adult market), personal experience, photo feature, sports, technical, travel. First time writers with *Journey* must submit complete ms for consideration. Length: 750-2,000 words. Pays $150-400 for assigned articles; 10¢/word for unsolicited articles. Sometimes pays expenses of writers on assignment.

Photos: State availability of photos with submission. Prefers transparencies. Offers $20-25/photo. Captions, model releases and identification of subjects required. Buys all or one-time rights.

Columns/Departments: Profiles of Achievement (striving and successful minority young adult, age 16-35 in various careers). Buys 15 mss/year. Send complete ms. Length: 500-1,500. Pays $50-200.

Fiction: Publishes novel exerpts. Adventure, ethnic, historical, humorous, mainstream, slice-of-life vignettes. Buys 3 mss/year. Send complete ms. Length: 1,000-3,000 words. Pays $100-400.

Poetry: Free verse. Buys 5/year. Submit up to 5 poems at one time. Length: 10-25 lines. Pays $10-50.

Fillers: Anecdotes, facts, gags to be illustrated by cartoonist, newsbreaks, short humor. Buys 10/year. Length: 25-250 words. Pays $25-100.

Tips: For new writers—must submit complete ms that is double spaced; clean copy only. If available, send clippings of previously published works and résumé. Should state when available to write. Include on first page your name, address, phone, Social Security number and word count. Availability of photos enhances your chances. "We desperately need more material dealing with concerns of Asian-American students."

‡**LINK MAGAZINE, The College Magazine**, Creative Media Generations, Inc., 110 Greene St., #407, New York NY 10012. (212)966-1100. Editor-in-Chief: Ty Wenger. 50% freelance written. Quarterly magazine covering college news, issues and lifestyle. Estab. 1993. Circ. 1 million. Pays on publication. Publishes ms an average of 6 months after acceptance. Byline given. Offers 25% kill fee. Buys first or one-time rights. Editorial lead time 4 months. Submit seasonal material 4 months in advance. Accepts simultaneous and previously published material. Query for electronic submissions. Reports in 2 months on queries, 3 months on mss. Sample copy for $2. Writer's guidelines for #10 SASE.

Nonfiction: Book excerpts, essays, exposé, general interest, how-to (educational, financial, lifestyle, etc.), interview/profile, photo feature, travel. Special issues: Environmental, Job Hunting, Computers. Buys 50 mss/year. Query with published clips. Length: 400-3,000. Pays $150-500 for assigned articles; $100-200 for unsolicited articles. Pays expenses of writers on assignment.

Photos: Send photos with submission. Reviews contact sheets, transparencies, prints. Negotiates payment individually. Captions required. Buys one-time rights.

Columns/Departments: Get A Job (how-to job hunting), 700-800 words; It's Your Life (lifestyle articles), 700-800 words; Interview (national politicians and writers), 700-1,500 words. Buys 20 mss/year. Query with published clips. Pays $200-250.

Tips: "Research very informative, insightful or how-to articles and present completed ideas with clips in a query. Keep everything geared only to what college students would appreciate."

NOTRE DAME MAGAZINE, University of Notre Dame, Administration Bldg., Room 415, Notre Dame IN 46556-0775. (219)631-5335. Fax: (219)631-6947. Editor: Walton R. Collins. Managing Editor: Kerry Temple. 75% freelance written. Quarterly magazine covering news of Notre Dame and education and issues affecting the Roman Catholic Church. "We are interested in the moral, ethical and spiritual issues of the day and how Christians live in today's world. We are universal in scope, Catholic in viewpoint and serve Notre Dame alumni, friends and other constituencies." Estab. 1972. Circ. 120,000. **Pays on acceptance.** Publishes ms an average of 1 year after acceptance. Byline given. Kill fee negotiable. Buys first rights. Simultaneous queries OK. Query for electronic submissions. Reports in 1 month. Free sample copy.

Nonfiction: Opinion, personal experience, religion. Buys 35 mss/year. Query with clips of published work. Length: 600-3,000 words. Pays $250-1,500. Sometimes pays the expenses of writers on assignment.

Photos: State availability of photos. Reviews b&w contact sheets, transparencies and 8×10 prints. Model releases and identification of subjects required. Buys one-time rights.

OREGON QUARTERLY, The Magazine of the University of Oregon, University of Oregon, 130 Chapman Hall, Eugene OR 97403-5228. (503)346-5047. Fax: (503)346-2220. Executive Editor: Tom Hager. Managing Editor: Mike Lee. 50% freelance written. Quarterly university magazine of people and ideas at the University of Oregon and the Northwest. Estab. 1919. Circ. 95,000. Pays on publication. Publishes ms an average of 3 months after acceptance. Byline given. Offers 20% kill fee. Buys first North American serial rights. Accepts previously published submissions. Send photocopy of article and information about when and where the article previously appeared. For reprints, pays 50% of the amount paid for an original article. Query for electronic submissions. Reports in 2 months. Sample copy for 9×12 SAE with 4 first-class stamps.

Nonfiction: Northwest issues and culture from the perspective of UO alumni and faculty. Buys 30 mss/year. Query with published clips. Length: 250-2,500 words. Pays $50-500. Sometimes pays expenses of writers on assignment.

Fiction: Publishes novel excerpts.
Photos: State availability of photos with submission. Reviews 8×10 prints. Offers $10-25/photo. Identification of subjects required. Buys one-time rights.
Tips: "Query with strong, colorful lead; clips."

PORTLAND MAGAZINE, The University of Portland Quarterly, 5000 N. Willamette Blvd., Portland OR 97203. Editor: Brian Doyle. 70% freelance written. Quarterly magazine covering University of Portland news, issues, concerns. Generally features are about spirituality (esp. Catholicism), the Northwest, higher education, or the University itself. Estab. 1985. Circ. 25,000. Pays on publication. Publishes ms an average of 3 months after acceptance. Byline given. Buys first North American serial rights. Editorial lead time 8 months. Submit seasonal material 8 months in advance. Reports in 1 month on queries. Sample copy and writer's guidelines free on request.
Nonfiction: Book excerpts, essays, general interest, interview/profile, opinion, personal experience, religious. Buys 6 mss/year. Query with published clips or send complete ms. Length: 1,000-3,000 words. Pays $100-500. Sometimes pays expenses of writers on assignment.

THE PURDUE ALUMNUS, Purdue Alumni Association, Purdue Memorial Union 160, 101 N. Grant St., West Lafayette IN 47906-6212. (317)494-5184. Fax: (317)494-9179. Editor: Tim Newton. 75% freelance written. Prefers to work with published/established writers; works with small number of new/unpublished writers each year. Magazine published 9 times/year covering subjects of interest to Purdue University alumni. Estab. 1912. Circ. 65,000. Pays on publication. Publishes ms an average of 2 months after acceptance. Byline given. Buys first rights and makes work-for-hire assignments. Submit seasonal/holiday material 6 months in advance. Accepts simultaneous and previously published submissions. Reports in 2 weeks on queries; 1 month on mss. Sample copy for 9×12 SAE with 2 first-class stamps.
Nonfiction: Book excerpts, general interest, historical/nostalgic, humor, interview/profile, personal experience. Focus is on alumni, campus news, issues and opinions of interest to 65,000 members of the Alumni Association. Feature style, primarily university-oriented. Issues relevant to education. Buys 12-20 mss/year. Length: 1,500-2,500 words. Pays $250-500. Pays expenses of writers on assignment.
Photos: State availability of photos. Reviews b&w contact sheet or 5×7 prints.
Tips: "We have 280,000 living, breathing Purdue alumni. If you can find a good story about one of them, we're interested. We use local freelancers to do campus pieces."

RIPON COLLEGE MAGAZINE, P.O. Box 248, Ripon WI 54971-0248. (414)748-8364. Fax: (414)748-9262. Editor: Loren J. Boone. 15% freelance written. Quarterly magazine that "contains information relating to Ripon College and is mailed to alumni and friends of the college." Estab. 1851. Circ. 14,000. Pays on publication. Publishes ms an average of 3 months after acceptance. Byline given. Not copyrighted. Makes work-for-hire assignments. Query for electronic submissions. Reports in 2 weeks.
Nonfiction: Historical/nostalgic, interview/profile. Buys 4 mss/year. Query with or without published clips, or send complete ms. Length: 250-1,000 words. Pays $25-350.
Photos: State availability of photos with submission. Reviews contact sheets. Offers additional payment for photos accepted with ms. Captions and model releases are required. Buys one-time rights.
Tips: "Story ideas must have a direct connection to Ripon College."

‡RUTGERS MAGAZINE, Rutgers University, Alexander Johnston Hall, New Brunswick NJ 08903. (908)932-7315. Editor: Lori Chambers. 50% freelance written. Quarterly university magazine of "general interest, but articles must have a Rutgers university or alumni tie-in." Circ. 134,000. **Pays on acceptance.** Publishes ms an average of 4 months after acceptance. Byline given. Pays 30-35% kill fee. Buys first North American serial rights. Submit seasonal/holiday material 8 months in advance. Query for electronic submissions. Reports in 1 month. Sample copy for $3 and 9×12 SAE with 5 first-class stamps.
Nonfiction: Book excerpts, essays, general interest, historical/nostalgic, science/research, interview/profile, arts/humanities, and photo feature. No articles without a Rutgers connection. Buys 15-20 mss/year. Query with published clips. Pays competitively; pays expenses of writers on assignment.
Photos: State availability of photos with submission. Payment varies. Identification of subjects required. Buys one-time rights.
Columns/Departments: Business, Opinion, Sports, Alumni Profiles (related to Rutgers), 1,200-1,800 words. Buys 6-8 mss/year. Query with published clips. Pays competitively.
Tips: "Send ideas. We'll evaluate clips and topic for most appropriate use."

 A bullet introduces comments by the editors of Writer's Market *indicating special information about the listing.*

THE STUDENT, 127 Ninth Ave. N., Nashville TN 37234. Editor: Gina Howard. 10% freelance written. Works with a small number of new/unpublished writers each year. Publication of National Student Ministry of The Sunday School Board of the Southern Baptist Convention. Monthly magazine for college students. Estab. 1922. Circ. 40,000. Buys all rights. **Pays on acceptance.** Publishes ms an average of 10 months after acceptance. Manuscripts should be double-spaced on white paper with 50-space line, 25 lines/page. Sources for quotes and statistics should be given for verification. Reports usually within 2 months. Sample copy and guidelines for 9×12 SAE with 3 first-class stamps.
   • *The Student* has broadened its audience and no longer looks for material focusing on only freshman and sophomore levels.
Nonfiction: Contemporary questions, problems, and issues facing college students viewed from a Christian perspective to develop high moral and ethical values. Cultivating interpersonal relationships, developing self-esteem, dealing with the academic struggle, coping with rejection, learning how to love and developing a personal relationship with Jesus Christ. Prefers complete ms rather than query. Length: 1,000 words maximum. Pays 5½¢ after editing with reserved right to edit accepted material.
Fiction: Satire and parody on college life, humorous episodes; emphasize clean fun and the ability to grow and be uplifted through humor. Contemporary fiction involving student life, on campus as well as off. Length: 1,000 words. Pays 5½¢/word.

STUDENT LEADER (for college students), Oxendine Publishing Inc., P.O. Box 14081, Gainesville FL 32604-2081. (904)373-6907. Editor: W.H. "Butch" Oxendine Jr.. Managing Editor: Kay Quinn King. 30% freelance written. Semiannual magazine covering student government, leadership. Estab. 1993. Circ. 200,000. Pays on publication. Byline given. Buys all rights. Submit seasonal material 4 months in advance. Query for electronic submissions. Reports in 1 month on queries. Sample copy for #10 SAE with 3 first-class stamps. For query response and/or writer's guidelines send #10 SASE.
Nonfiction: How-to, humor, new product, opinion. "No lengthy individual profiles or articles without primary or secondary sources of attribution." Buys 10 mss/year. Query. Length: 250-1,000 words. Pays $100 maximum. Pays contributor copies to students or first-time writers.
Photos: State availability of or send photos with submission. Reviews contact sheets, negatives, transparencies. Offers $50 photo/maximum. Captions, model releases, identification of subjects required. Buys all rights.
Columns/Departments: Buys 10 mss/year. Query. Length: 250-1,000 words. Pays $100 maximum.
Fillers: Facts, newsbreaks, short humor. Buys 10/year. Length: 100 words minimum. Pays $35 maximum.
Tips: "Read other high school and college publications for current ideas, interests. Send outlines or manuscripts for review. All sections open to freelance work. Always looking for lighter, humorous articles, as well as features on colleges and universities, careers, jobs. Multi-sourced (5-10) articles are best."

TRANSFER STUDENT (for community college students), Oxendine Publishing, Inc., P.O. Box 14081, Gainesville FL 32604-2081. (904)373-6907. Editor: W.H. "Butch" Oxendine Jr.. Managing Editor: Kay Quinn King. 50% freelance written. Semiannual magazine "easing the transition from 2-year to 4-year schools." Estab. 1992. Circ. 20,000. Pays on publication. Publishes ms an average of 2-3 months after acceptance. Byline given. Buys all rights. Submit seasonal/holiday material 4 months in advance. Accepts previously published submissions. Send tearsheet or photocopy of article or typed ms with rights for sale noted and information about when and where the article previously appeared. Query for electronic submissions; prefers IBM. Reports in 1-2 months. Sample copy for 8×11 SAE with 3 first-class stamps. For query response and/or writer's guidelines send #10 SASE.
Nonfiction: How-to, humor, new product, opinion. "No lengthy individual's profiles, or articles without primary and secondary sources attribution." Buys 10 mss/year. Query. Length: 250-1,000 words. Pays $35 maximum. Pays with contributors copies to students or first-time writers.
Photos: State availability of photos with submission. Send photos with submission. Reviews contact sheets, negatives, transparencies. Offers $50/photo maximum. Captions, model releases, identification of subjects required. Buys all rights.
Columns/Departments: Transfer Student Trials, 250-1,000 words; Finding Financial Aid, 250-1,000 words. Query. Pays $35 maximum.
Fiction: Publishes novel excerpts.
Fillers: Facts, newsbreaks, short humor. Buys 10/year. Length: 100-500 words. Pays $35 maximum.
Tips: "Read other high school and college publications for current issues, interests. Send manuscripts or outlines for review. All sections open to freelance work. Always looking for lighter, humorous articles, as well as features on Florida colleges and universities, careers, jobs. Multi-sourced (5-10) articles are best."

VISIONS, A Success Guide for Native American Students, Communications Publishing Group, 250 Mark Twain Tower, 106 W. 11th St., Kansas City MO 64105-1806. (816)221-4404. Fax: (816)221-1112. Editor: Neoshia Michelle Paige. 80% freelance written. Biannual education and career source guide designed for Native American students who want to pursue a higher education through colleges, vocational and technical schools or proprietary schools, to focus on insight, motivational and career planning informations. For young adults, ages 16-25. Circ. 100,000. Pays on publication. Byline sometimes given. Buys second serial (reprint) rights or makes work-for-hire assignments. Submit seasonal/holiday material 6 months in advance. Accepts simultaneous and previously published submissions. Send typed ms with rights for sale noted and information about when and where the article previously appeared. For reprints, pays 50% of the amount paid for an original article. Reports in 2 months. Sample copy for 9×12 SAE with 4 first-class stamps. Writer's guidelines for #10 SASE.

• The editor notes that if the writer can provide the manuscript on 3.25 disk, saved in generic ASCII, pay is $10 higher and chance of acceptance is greater.

Nonfiction: Book excerpts or reviews, general interest, how-to, humor, inspirational, interview/profile, new product, personal experience, photo feature, technical, travel, sports. Query or send complete ms. Length: 750-2,000 words. Pays $150-400 for assigned articles; 10¢/word for unsolicited articles. Sometimes pays expenses of writers on assignment.

Photos: State availability of photos with submission. Reviews transparencies. Offers $20-25/photo. Captions, model releases, and identification of subjects required. Buys all rights.

Columns/Departments: Profiles of Achievement (striving and successful Native American young adults, age 16-35, in various careers). Length: 500-1,500 words. Buys 15 mss/year. Send complete ms. Pays $50-250.

Fiction: Adventure, ethnic, historical, humorous, mainstream, slice-of-life vignettes. Buys 3 mss/year. Send complete ms. Length: 1,000-5,000 words. Pays $100-400.

Poetry: Free verse. Buys 5 poems/year. Submit up to 5 poems at one time. Length: 10-25 lines. Pays $10-50.

Fillers: Anecdotes, facts, gags to be illustrated by cartoonist, newsbreaks, short humor. Buys 10 fillers/year. Length: 25-250 words. Pays $25-100.

Tips: For new writers—submit complete manuscript that is double spaced; clean copy only. If available, send clippings of previously published works and résumé. Should state when available to write. Include on first page of manuscript your name, address, phone, Social Security number and word count. Availability of photos will enhance your chances.

WHAT MAKES PEOPLE SUCCESSFUL, The National Research Bureau, Inc., P.O. Box 1, Burlington IA 52601-0001. (319)752-5415. Fax: (319)752-3421. Editor: Nancy Heinzel. 75% freelance written. Eager to work with new/unpublished writers and works with a small number each year. Quarterly magazine. Estab. 1948. Pays on publication. Publishes ms an average of 1 year after acceptance. Buys all rights. Submit seasonal/holiday material 8 months in advance of issue date. Sample copy and writer's guidelines for #10 SAE with 2 first-class stamps.

Nonfiction: How-to (be successful); general interest (personality, employee morale, guides to successful living, biographies of successful persons, etc.); experience; opinion. No material on health. Buys 3-4 mss/issue. Query with outline. Length: 500-700 words. Pays 4¢/word.

Tips: Short articles (rather than major features) have a better chance of acceptance because all articles are short.

Child Care and Parental Guidance

Some publications in this section are general interest parenting magazines while others for child care providers combine care information with business tips. Other markets that buy articles about child care and the family are included in the Religious and Women's sections and in the Trade Education section. Publications for children can be found in the Juvenile section.

ATLANTA PARENT/ATLANTA BABY, Suite 506, 4330 Georgetown Square II, Atlanta GA 30338-6217. (404)454-7599. Editor: Liz White. Managing Editor: Peggy Middendorf. 90% freelance written. Monthly tabloid covering parenting of children from birth-16 years old. Offers "down-to-earth help for parents." Estab. 1983. Circ. 65,000. Pays on publication. Publishes ms 3 months after acceptance. Byline given. Buys one-time rights. Submit seasonal material 6 months in advance. Accepts previously published articles. Send photocopy of article or typed ms with rights for sale noted and information about when and where the article previously appeared. For reprints pays 50-70% of the amount paid for an original article. Query for electronic submissions. Reports in 3 months. Sample copy for $2.

Nonfiction: General interest, how-to, humor, interview/profile, travel. Special issues: Private school (January); Birthday parties (February); Camp (March/April); Maternity and Mothering (May); Child care (July); Back-to-school (August); Drugs (October); Holidays (November/December). Does not want first person accounts or philosophical discussions. Buys 60 mss/year. Query with or without published clips, or send complete ms. Length: 700-2,100 words. Pays $15-30. Sometimes pays expenses of writers on assignment.

Photos: State availability of photos with submission and send photocopies. Reviews 3×5 photos "b&w preferably." Offers $5/photo. Buys one-time rights.

Columns/Departments: Pack up and go (travel). Buys 8-10 mss/year. Send complete ms. Length: 700-1,500 words. Pays $15-30.

Tips: "Articles should be geared to problems or situations of families and parents. Should include down-to-earth tips and clearly written. No philosophical discussions or first person narratives."

‡**BABY**, Beaudry Communications Inc., 5458 30th St. NW, Washington DC 20015. (202)682-0520. Contact: Ann Beaudry. 50% freelance written. Bimonthly magazine covering birth, first 2 years. "*Baby* is distributed by diaper services, doctor's offices and retail outlets to national circulation of 750,000. The primary recipients are women in the last trimester of pregnancy and new parents. Articles feature birth (*not* pregnancy) and baby/family issues of first two years." Estab. 1994. Circ. 750,000. Pays on publication. Publishes ms an average of 2 months after acceptance. Byline given. Buys first North American serial rights, one-time rights or second serial (reprint) rights. Editorial lead time 4 months. Submit seasonal material 4 months in advance. Accepts previously published submissions. Query for electronic submissions. Reports in 1 month. Sample copy for SAE with 3 first-class stamps.

Nonfiction: Essays (e.g. first-time dad), how-to (any topics of interest to new parents, e.g. baby care, photography, siblings, traveling, choosing doctor, breast feeding, etc.), personal experience, photo feature, professional or expert articles on baby care, family issues. Buys 18 mss/year. Send complete ms. Length: 900-2,000 words. Pays $400 and up for assigned articles; $200 and up for unsolicited articles.

Photos: Send photos with submission. Reviews 4×6 prints. Negotiates payment individually. Model releases, identification of subjects required. Buys one-time rights.

BAY AREA PARENT MAGAZINE, Bay Area Publishing Group Inc., 401 "A" Alberto Way, Los Gatos CA 95032-5404. Fax: (408)356-4903. Editor: Lynn Berardo. 80% freelance written. Works with locally-based published/established writers and some non-local writers. Monthly tabloid of resource information for parents and teachers. Circ 75,000. Pays on publication. Publishes ms an average of 3 months after acceptance. Byline given. Buys one-time rights. Submit seasonal/holiday material 3 months in advance. Accepts simultaneous and previously published submissions. Send typed ms with rights for sale noted and information about when and where the article previously appeared. Query for electronic submissions. Sample copy for 9×12 SAE with 6 first-class stamps. Writer's guidelines for #10 SASE.

Nonfiction: Book excerpts (related to our interest group); exposé (health, psychology); historical/nostalgic ("History of Diapers"); how-to (related to kids/parenting); humor; interview/profile; photo feature; travel (with kids, family). Special issues: Music (March); Art and Kid's Birthdays (April); Summer Camps and Vacations (May); Family Fun and Health and Medicine (June); Working Parents (July); Fashion and Sports (August); Back-to-School (September). No opinion or religious articles. Buys 45-60 mss/year. Query or send complete ms. Length: 150-1,500 words. Pays 6¢/word. Sometimes pays expenses of writers on assignment.

Photos: State availability of photos. Prefers b&w contact sheets and/or 3×5 b&w prints. Pays $5-25. Model release required. Buys one-time rights.

Columns/Departments: Child Care, Family Travel, Birthday Party Ideas, Baby Page, Toddler Page, Adolescent Kids. Buys 36 mss/year. Send complete ms. Length: 400-1,200 words. Pays $20-75.

Tips: "Submit new, fresh information concisely written and accurately researched. We also produce *Bay Area Baby Magazine*, a semiannual publication and *Valley Parent* Magazine, which focuses on central Contra Costa County and southern Alameda County."

‡**BIG APPLE PARENTS' PAPER**, Family Communications, Inc., 36 E. 12th St., New York NY 10003. (212)533-2277. Editor: Susan Hodara. Contact: Helen Freedman. 99% freelance written. Monthly tabloid covering New York City family life. Estab. 1985. Circ. 62,000. Pays on publication. Publishes ms an average of 3 months after acceptance. Byline given. Offers 50% kill fee. Buys first North American serial rights. Editorial lead time 1 month. Submit seasonal material 3 months in advance. Accepts simultaneous and previously published submissions. Query for electronic submissions. Reports in 2 weeks on queries; 1 month on mss. Sample copy and writer's guidelines free on request.

Nonfiction: Essays, exposé, general interest, how-to, humor, inspirational, interview/profile, opinion, personal experience, photo feature, travel. Buys 60-70 mss/year. Send complete ms. Length: 600-1,000 words. Pays $35-50. Sometimes pays expenses of writers on assignment.

Photos: State availability of or send photos with submission. Reviews contact sheets, prints. Offers $15-25/photo. Captions required. Buys one-time rights.

Columns/Departments; Dads (education); Reviews; Family Finance; Education; Travel. Buys 50-60 mss/year. Send complete ms. Pays $20-50.

Fillers: Anecdotes, facts, gags to be illustrated by cartoonist, newsbreaks, humor. Buys 20-30/year. Length: 50-300 words. Pays $10-25.

BIRACIAL CHILD, Interrace Publications, P.O. Box 12048, Atlanta GA 30355. (404)364-9690. Fax: (404)364-9965. Editor: Candy Mills. 60% freelance written. Quarterly magazine covering biracial/mixed-race and transracial adoption parenting. "Parenting issues specific to interracial families with biracial (mixed-race) children/teens. Also, transracial adoption and interracial step-families." Estab. 1994. Circ. 5,000. Pays on publication. Byline given. Buys first rights, second serial rights or makes work-for-hire assignments.

Submit seasonal material 3 months in advance. Accepts simultaneous and previously published submissions. Send tearsheet or photocopy of article. Query for electronic submissions. Reports in 2 months. Sample copy for $2 and 9×12 SAE with $1 postage. Writer's guidelines for #10 SASE.

Nonfiction: Essays, general interest, historical/nostalgic, how-to, humor, inspirational, interview/profile, new product, opinion, personal experience, photo feature. Buys 12-20 mss/year. Query. Length: 200-3,200 words. Pays $20-50 for assigned articles; $50-75 for cover stories. Sometimes pays expenses of writers on assignment.

Photos: State availability of photos with submission. Negotiates payment individually. Identification of subjects required. Buys one-time rights.

Columns/Departments: Buys 4 mss/year. Query. Pays $15.

Fiction: Ethnic, historical, humorous, slice-of-life vignettes. Buys 4 mss/year. Query. Length: 800-1,600 words. Pays $10-25.

CHILD, Gruner & Jahr, 110 Fifth Ave., New York NY 10011. (212)463-1000. Editor: Freddi Greenberg. Executive Editor: Mary Beth Jordan. 95% freelance written. Monthly magazine for parenting. Estab. 1986. Circ. 700,000. **Pays on acceptance.** Byline given. Offers 25% kill fee. Buys first North American serial, first, one-time and second serial (reprint) rights. Editorial lead time 3 months. Submit seasonal material 6 months in advance. Accepts simultaneous submissions. Reports in 2 months. Sample copy for $3.95. Writer's guidelines free on request.

Nonfiction: Book excerpts, general interest, interview/profile, new product, photo feature. No poetry. Query with published clips. Length: 250 words minimum. Payment negotiable. Pays expenses of writers on assignment.

Photos: State availability of photos with submission. Reviews transparencies. Negotiates payment individually. Buys one-time rights.

Columns/Departments: Articles editor: Miriam Arond. Love, Dad (fathers' perspective); Child of Mine (mothers' or fathers' perspective). Query with published clips.

CHRISTIAN PARENTING TODAY, Good Family Magazines, P.O. Box 36630, Colorado Springs CO 80936-3663. (719)531-7776. Fax: (719)535-0172. Editor: Brad Lewis. Assistant Editor: Erin Healy. 50% freelance written. Bimonthly magazine covering parenting today's children. "Between the covers of *Christian Parenting Today*, you'll find positive, practical articles that bring a Christian perspective to important family issues. Our ultimate goal: to affirm parents with a biblically based, inspirational, informative and authoritative magazine that guides them through all stages of their children's lives." Estab. 1988. Circ. 250,000. Pays on acceptance or publication. Byline given. Buys first North American serial or second serial (reprint) rights. Submit seasonal/holiday material 6 months in advance. Query for electronic submissions. Simultaneous submissions discouraged. Accepts previously published material. Send tearsheet or photocopy of article, or typed ms with rights for sale noted and information about when and where the article previously appeared. For reprints pays 7¢/word. Reports in 2 months. Sample copy for 9×12 SASE with 7 first-class stamps. Writer's guidelines for #10 SASE.

● This publication has changed its reprint payment from 25% of original payment to 7¢/word.

Nonfiction: Book excerpts, how-to, humor, inspirational, religious. Buys 50 mss/year. Query. Length: 750-2,000 words. Pays 15-25¢/word. Sometimes pays expenses of writers on assignment.

Photos: State availability of photos with submission. Do not submit photos without permission. Reviews transparencies. Model release required. Buys one-time rights.

Columns/Departments: Parent Exchange (family-tested parenting ideas from our readers), 25-100 words; Life In Our House (entertaining, true, humorous stories about your family), 25-100 words. Buys 120 mss/year. Send complete ms. Pays $25-40. No SASE required. Submissions become property of *CPT*.

‡EXCEPTIONAL PARENT, Parenting Your Child or Young Adult with a Disability, 209 Harvard St., Suite 303, Brookline MA 02146. (617)730-5800. Editor-in-Chief: Dr. Stan Klein. Contact: Kim Schive, associate editor. 75% freelance written (mostly reader and professionally written). Monthly magazine covering children and young adults with disabilities. Estab. 1971. Circ. 70,000. Pays on publication. Byline given. Buys first North American serial rights. Submit seasonal material 6 months in advance. Accepts previously published submissions. Query for electronic submissions. Reports in 6 months. Sample copy and writer's guidelines free.

Nonfiction: Book excerpts, essays, humor, inspirational, opinion, personal experience, religious, travel. Buys 50 mss/year. Query or send complete ms. Length varies. Pays $25 maximum and contributor copies.

Photos: Send photos with submission. Offers no additional payment for photos accepted with ms. Model releases and identification of subjects required. Buys all rights.

Columns/Departments: Fathers' Voices (fathers write about having child with disability), 600-1,000 words; Role Model (stories by and/or about role models who grew up with disability), 1,200 words; Children's Play (friends, siblings, children with disabilities write about their experiences), 300-500 words. Buys 40 mss/year. Send complete ms. Pays $25 maximum.

Tips: "Read back issues of magazine. Majority of the magazine is written by parents of children with disabilities and professionals. Pieces are usually advice from experience."

FAMILY LIFE, Hachette-Filipacchi Magazines, Inc., 1633 Broadway, New York NY 10019. Editor-in-Chief: Peter Herbst. Contact: Jennifer Cook. 90% freelance written. Bimonthly magazine for parents of children ages 3-12. Estab. 1993. Circ. 400,000. Pays on publication. Publishes ms an average of 4 months. Byline given. Offers 25% kill fee. Buys first North American rights. Editorial lead time 5 months. Submit seasonal material 8 months in advance. Accepts simultaneous submissions. Reports in 6 weeks on queries. Sample copy for $3, call (908)367-2900. Writer's guidelines for #10 SASE.

• *Family Life* has almost doubled its circulation since last year. It was recently bought by Hachette-Filipacchi Magazines.

Nonfiction: Book excerpts, essays, general interest, new product, photo feature, travel. Does not want to see articles about children under 3 or childbirth. Query with published clips. Pays $1/word. Pays expenses of writers on assignment.

Photos: State availability of photos with submission. Reviews transparencies. Negotiates payment individually. Buys one-time rights.

FAMILY TIMES, Family Times, Inc., 1900 SuperFine Lane, Wilmington DE 19802. (302)575-0935. Fax: (302)575-0933. Editor: Alison Garber. Assistant Editor: Dana Dillon. 25% freelance written. Monthly tabloid for parenting. "Our targeted distribution is to parents via a controlled network of area schools, daycares, pediatricians and places where families congregate. We only want articles related to parenting, children's issues and enhancing family life." Estab. 1990. Circ. 50,000. Pays on publication. Publishes ms an average of 5 months after acceptance. Byline given. Buys one-time or second serial (reprint) rights. Editorial lead time 5 months. Submit seasonal material 5 months in advance. Accepts simultaneous and previously published submissions. Query for electronic submissions. Prefers 3.5 text diskette. Reports in 3 months on mss. Sample copy for 3 first-class stamps.

• *Family Times* needs more material of national interest to run in online version.

Nonfiction: Book excerpts, how-to parenting, inspirational, interview/profile, new product, opinion, personal experience, photo feature, travel, children, parenting. Special issues: Schools (October); Camps (February); Maternity (July); Holiday (December); Fitness (March); Birthday (May); Back to School (August). Buys 60 mss/year. Send complete ms. Length: 350-1,200 words. Pays $30 minimum for assigned articles; $25 for unsolicited articles. Sometimes pays expenses of writers on assignment.

Photos: State availability of photos with submission. Negotiates payment individually. Identification of subjects required. Buys one-time rights.

Columns/Departments: Pays $25-50.

Tips: "Work with other members of PPA (Parenting Publications of America). Since we all share our writers and watch others' work. We pay little but you can sell the same story to 30 other publications in different markets. Online use (Internet) offers additional author credit and additional payment based on accesses. We are most open to general features."

‡FAMILYFUN, Disney Magazine Publishing Inc., 244 Main St., Northampton MA 01060. Editor: Alexandra Kennedy. Contact: Clare Ellis. Magazine published 10 times/year covering activities for families with kids ages 3-12. "*Family Fun* is about all the great things families can do together. Our writers are either parents or professionals in education." Estab. 1991. Circ. 675,000. **Pays on acceptance.** Publishes ms an average of 4 months after acceptance. Byline sometimes given. Offers 25% kill fee. Buys simultaneous rights or makes work-for-hire assignments. Editorial lead time 4 months. Submit seasonal material 6 months in advance. Accepts simultaneous submissions. Query for electronic submissions. Reports in 6-8 weeks on queries. Sample copies or back issues and writer's guidelines for $3 (call (800)289-4849).

Nonfiction: Book excerpts, essays, general interest, how-to (crafts, cooking, educational activities), humor, interview/profile, personal experience, photo feature, travel. Special issues: Crafts, Holidays, Back to School, Summer Vacations. Buys hundreds mss/year. Query with published clips. Length: 75-3,000 words. Pays 50¢-$1/word. Sometimes pays expenses of writers on assignment.

Photos: State availability of photos with submissions. Reviews contact sheets, negatives, transparencies. Offers $75-500/photo. Model releases, identification of subjects required. Buys all rights (simultaneous).

Columns/Departments: Family Ties (essay on family relationships and traditions), 1,500 words; Nature & Kids (essay on experiencing nature as a family), 1,500 words; My Great Idea (essay on a simple idea [usually a tradition] that is wonderful for families and is a proven hit with author's family), 600-800 words. Buys 20-25 mss/year. Query with published clips or send complete ms. Pays 75¢-$1/word.

Fiction: Deanna Cook. Children's read-aloud stories. Buys 4 mss/year. Send complete ms. Length: 200-500 words. Pays $1/word.

Tips: "Many of our writers break into *FF* by writing for either *Family Almanac* (front-of-book department with 75-300 word pieces on crafts, food, games, etc.) or *Family Traveler* (also a front-of-the-book department, but with 75-800 word pieces)."

GRAND RAPIDS PARENT MAGAZINE, Gemini Publications, 549 Ottawa NW, Grand Rapids MI 49503. (616)459-4545. Editor: Carole Valade Smith. 90% freelance written. Monthly magazine. "Written for parents in the West Michigan area." Estab. 1989. Circ. 12,000. Pays on publication. Byline given. Offers $25 kill fee. Buys first North American serial rights, simultaneous rights, all rights or makes work-for-hire assignments. Editorial lead time 2-3 months. Submit seasonal material 4 months in advance. Accepts simultaneous submissions. Query for electronic submissions. Reports in 2 months on queries; 6 months on mss. Writer's guidelines for #10 SASE.

Nonfiction: General interest, historical/nostalgic, how-to, inspirational, interview/profile, new product, opinion, personal experience, photo feature, religious, travel. Buys 20-30 mss/year. Query. Length: 500-1,500 words. Pays $25 and up. Sometimes pays expenses of writers on assignment.

Photos: State availability of photos with submission. Reviews contact sheets. Offers $25/photo. Captions, model releases and identification of subjects required. Buys one-time or all rights.

Columns/Departments: All local: law, finance, humor, opinion, mental health. Pays $25.

GROWING PARENT, Dunn & Hargitt, Inc., P.O. Box 620, Lafayette IN 47902-0620. (317)423-2624. Fax: (317)423-4495. Editor: Nancy Kleckner. 40-50% freelance written. Works with a small number of new/unpublished writers each year. "We do receive a lot of unsolicited submissions but have had excellent results in working with some unpublished writers. So, we're always happy to look at material and hope to find one or two jewels each year." Monthly newsletter which focuses on parents—the issues, problems, and choices they face as their children grow. "We want to look at the parent as an adult and help encourage his or her growth not only as a parent but as an individual." Estab. 1973. **Pays on acceptance.** Publishes ms an average of 6 months after acceptance. Byline given. Buys first North American serial rights; maintains exclusive rights for three months. Submit seasonal/holiday material 6 months in advance. Accepts previously published material. Send photocopy of article and information about when and where it previously appeared. Reports in 2 weeks. Sample copy and writer's guidelines for 5×8 SAE with 2 first-class stamps.

Nonfiction: "We are looking for informational articles written in an easy-to-read, concise style. We would like to see articles that help parents deal with the stresses they face in everyday life—positive, upbeat, how-to-cope suggestions. We rarely use humorous pieces, fiction or personal experience articles. Writers should keep in mind that most of our readers have children under three years of age." Buys 15-20 mss/year. Query. Length: 1,000-1,500 words; will look at shorter pieces. Pays 10-15¢/word (depends on article).

Tips: "Submit a very specific query letter with samples."

HEALTHY KIDS, Cahners Publishing, 249 W. 17th St., New York NY 10011. (212)463-6410. Managing Editor: Laura Broadwell. 90% freelance written. Bimonthly magazine covering children's health. Estab. 1989. Circ. 1.5 million. **Pays on acceptance.** Byline given. Buys first rights. Submit seasonal/holiday material at least 6 months in advance. Reports in 1 month on queries. Writer's guidelines for #10 SASE.

Nonfiction: How-to help your child develop as a person, keep safe, keep healthy. No poetry, fiction, travel or product endorsement. Buys 30 mss/year. Query. Length: 1,500-2,000 words. Pays $500-1,000. Pays expenses of writers on assignment. Does not accept unsolicited mss.

Columns/Departments: Buys 30 mss/year. Query. Length: 1,500-2,000 words. Pays $500-750.

HOME EDUCATION MAGAZINE, P.O. Box 1083, Tonasket WA 98855-1083. Editors: Mark J. Hegener and Helen E. Hegener. 80% freelance written. Eager to work with new/unpublished writers each year. Bimonthly magazine covering home-based education. "We feature articles which address the concerns of parents who want to take a direct involvement in the education of their children—concerns such as socialization, how to find curriculums and materials, testing and evaluation, how to tell when your child is ready to begin reading, what to do when homeschooling is difficult, teaching advanced subjects, etc." Estab. 1983. Circ. 10,000. Pays on publication. Publishes ms an average of 2 months after acceptance. Byline given. ("Please include a 30-50 word credit with your article.") Buys first North American serial, first, one-time rights. Submit seasonal/holiday material 6 months in advance. Query for electronic submission requirements. Reports in 2 months. Sample copy for $4.50. Writer's guidelines for #10 SASE.

Nonfiction: Book excerpts, essays, how-to (related to home schooling), humor, inspirational, interview/profile, personal experience, photo features, technical. Buys 40-50 mss/year. Query with or without published clips, or send complete ms. Length: 750-2,500 words. Pays 45¢/column inch. Sometimes pays expenses of writers on assignment.

Photos: Send photos with submission. Reviews 5×7, 35mm prints and b&w snapshots; color transparencies for covers $25 each. Write for photo rates. Identification of subjects required. Buys one-time rights.

Tips: SASE. "We would like to see how-to articles (that don't preach, just present options); articles on testing, accountability, working with the public schools, socialization, learning disabilities, resources, support groups, legislation and humor. We need answers to the questions that homeschoolers ask."

HOME LIFE, Sunday School Board, 127 9th Ave. N., Nashville TN 37234. Fax: (615)251-5008. Editor-in-Chief: Charlie Warren. Managing Editor: Leigh Neely. 50% freelance written. Prefers to work with published/established writers, but will work with new/unpublished writers. Monthly magazine emphasizing Christian marriage and family life for married adults of all ages, but especially newlyweds and middle-aged marrieds. Estab. 1947. Circ. 615,000. **Pays on acceptance.** Publishes ms an average of 15 months after acceptance. Buys first, first North American serial and all rights. Byline given. Query. Submit seasonal/holiday material 1 year in advance. Accepts previously published material. Send typed ms with rights for sale noted. For reprints, pays 75% of the amount paid for an original article. Reports in 2 weeks on queries; 3 months on mss. Sample copy for $1. Writer's guidelines for #10 SASE.

• *Home Life* no longer accepts complete manuscripts —send only queries.

Nonfiction: How-to (good articles on marriage and family life); informational (about some current family-related issue of national significance such as "Television and the Christian Family" or "Whatever Happened to Family Worship?"); personal experience (informed articles by people who have solved marriage and family problems in healthy, constructive ways). "No column material. We are not interested in material that will not in some way enrich Christian marriage or family life. We are interested in articles on fun family activities for a new department called Family Time." Buys 100-150 mss/year. Query only. "After query is accepted send disk copy." Pays $75-275.

Fiction: "Fiction should be family-related and should show a strong moral about how families face and solve problems constructively." Buys 12-20 mss/year. Submit complete ms. Length: 1,500-1,800 words. Pays from $150.

Tips: "Study the magazine to see our unique slant on Christian family life. We prefer a life-centered case study approach, rather than theoretical essays on family life. Our top priority is marriage enrichment material."

L.A. PARENT, The Magazine for Parents in Southern California, P.O. Box 3204, Burbank CA 91504. (818)846-0400. Fax: (818)841-4964. E-mail: 73311.514@compuserve.com. Editor: Jack Bierman. Article Editor: David Jamieson. 80% freelance written. Prefers to work with published/established writers, but works with a small number of new/unpublished writers each year. Monthly tabloid covering parenting. Estab. 1980. Circ. 200,000. **Pays on acceptance.** Publishes ms an average of 4 months after acceptance. Byline given. Buys first and reprint rights. Submit seasonal/holiday material 3 months in advance. Accepts simultaneous queries and previously published submissions. Send tearsheet of article and information about when and where the article previously appeared. For reprints pays 50% of the amount paid for an original article. Query for electronic submissions. Reports in 2 months. Sample copy and writer's guidelines for $2 and 11 × 14 SAE with 5 first-class stamps.

• *L.A. Parent* is looking for more articles pertaining to infants and early childhood. They have increased their reprint payment from 35 to 50% of the amount paid for the original article.

Nonfiction: David Jamieson, articles editor. General interest, how-to. "We focus on generic parenting for ages 0-10 and southern California activities for families, and do round-up pieces, i.e., a guide to private schools, art opportunities." Buys 60-75 mss/year. Query with clips of published work. Length: 700-1,200 words. Pays $200-300 plus expenses.

Tips: "We will be using more contemporary articles on parenting's challenges. If you can write for a 'city magazine' in tone and accuracy, you may write for us. The 'Baby Boom' has created a need for more generic parenting material. We look for a sophisticated tone in covering the joys and demands of being a mom or dad in the 90s."

LONG ISLAND PARENTING NEWS, RDM Publishing, P.O. Box 214, Island Park NY 11558. (516)889-5510. Fax: (516)889-5513. Editor: Pat Simms-Elias. Director: Andrew Elias. 70% freelance written. Free community newspaper published monthly covering parenting, children and family issues. "A publication for concerned parents with active families and young children. Our slogan is: 'For parents who care to know.' " Estab. 1989. Circ. 50,000. Pays on publication. Publishes ms an average of 3 months after acceptance. Byline given (also 1-3 line bio, if appropriate). Buys one-time rights. Accepts simultaneous and previously published submissions (sometimes). Send photocopy of article or typed ms with rights for sale noted and information about when and where the article previously appeared. Negotiates fee for an original article. Reports in 3 months. Sample copy for $3 and 9 × 12 SAE with 5 first-class stamps. Free writer's guidelines.

Nonfiction: Essays, general interest, humor, interview/profile, travel. Will need articles covering childcare, childbirth/maternity, schools, camps and back-to-school. Buys 20-30 mss/year. Query with or without published clips, or send complete ms. Length: 350-2,000 words. Pays $25-150. "Sometimes trade article for advertising space." Sometimes pays expenses of writers on assignment.

Photos: Send photos with submission. Reviews 4 × 5 prints. Offers $5-50/photo. Captions required. Buys one-time rights.

Columns/Departments: Off The Shelf (book reviews); Fun & Games (toy and game reviews); KidVid (reviews of kids' video); The Beat (reviews of kids' music); Monitor (reviews of computer hardware and software for kids); Big Screen (reviews of kids' films); Soon Come (for expectant parents); Educaring (parenting info and advice); Something Special (for parents of kids with special needs); Growing Up (family health issues); On the Ball (sports for kids); Perspectives (essays on family life); Words Worth (storytelling); Getaway (family travel). Buys 20-30 mss/year. Send complete ms. Length: 500-1,000 words. Pays 25-150.

Fillers: Facts and newsbreaks. Buys 1-10/year. Length: 200-500. Pays $10-25.

For explanation of symbols, see the Key to Symbols and Abbreviations. For unfamiliar words, see the Glossary.

METROKIDS MAGAZINE, The Resource for Delaware Valley Families, Kidstuff Publications, Inc., Riverview Plaza, 1400 S. Columbus Blvd., Philadelphia PA 19147. (215)551-3200. Fax: (215)551-3203. Editor: Nancy Lisagor. 80% freelance written. Monthly tabloid providing information for parents and kids in Philadelphia and surrounding counties. Estab. 1990. Circ. 70,000. Pays on publication. Byline given. Buys one-time rights. Submit seasonal material 4 months in advance. Accepts previously published submissions. Send tearsheet of article and information about when and where the article previously appeared. For reprints pays 75-80% of the amount paid for an original article. Query for electronic submissions. Reports in up to 8 months on queries. Sample copy for 9 × 12 SAE with 4 first-class stamps. Writer's guidelines for #10 SASE.
   ● *MetroKids* welcomes query letters or faxes. They especially want to hear from writers in their area.
Nonfiction: General interest, how-to, humor, new product, travel. "Each issue has a focus (for example: finance, extra-curricular lessons for kids, health and nutrition, new babies, birthdays, child care, etc.)." Buys 20 mss/year. Query with or without published clips. Length: 750 words maximum. Pays $1-50. Sometimes pays expenses of writers on assignment.
Photos: State availability of photos with submission. Captions required. Buys one-time rights.
Columns/Departments: Away We Go (travel), 500 words; On Call (medical), 500 words; Book Beat (book reviews), 500 words; SOS (In search of software), 500 words. Buys 25 mss/year. Query. Pays $1-50.
Tips: "Send a query letter several months before a scheduled topical issue; then follow-up with a telephone call. We are interested in receiving feature articles (on specified topics) or material for our regular columns (which should have a regional/seasonal base). 1996 editorial calendar available on request."

‡NEW MOON PARENTING: FOR ADULTS WHO CARE ABOUT GIRLS, New Moon Publishing, Inc., P.O. Box 3620, Duluth MN 55803. Editor: Joe Kelly. 10% freelance written. Bimonthly magazine covering adults (parents, teachers, others) who work with girls age 8-14. "*New Moon Parenting* is the companion publication to *New Moon: The Magazine For Girls and Their Dreams.* It is written by and for adults— parents, teachers, counselors and others—who are working to raise healthy, confident girls." Estab. 1992. Circ. 3,000. Pays on publication. Publishes ms an average of 2 months after acceptance. Byline given. Buys first rights and second serial (reprint) rights. Editorial lead time 3 months. Submit seasonal material 4 months in advance. Accepts simultaneous and previously published submissions. Query for electronic submissions. Reports in 1 month on queries; 2 months on mss. Sample copy for $6.50. Writer's guidelines free on request.
Nonfiction: Essays, general interest, historical/nostalgic, humor, inspirational, interview/profile, opinion, personal experience, photo feature, religious, technical, book reviews. Editorial calendar available. Buys 6 mss/year. Query. Length: 600-1,800 words. Pays 4-8¢/word.
Photos: State availability of photos with submissions. Reviews 4 × 5 prints. Negotiates payment individually. Captions, model releases, identification of subjects required. Buys one-time rights.
Columns/Departments: Mothering (personal experience), 900 words; Fathering (personal experience), 900 words; Current Research (girl-related), 900-1,800 words; Book Reviews, 900 words. Buys 3 mss/year. Query. Pays 4-8¢/word.
Fiction: Humorous, slice-of-life vignettes, multicultural/girl centered. Buys 1 mss/year. Query. Length: 900-1,800 words. Pays 4-8¢/word.
Tips: "Writers and artists who comprehend our goals have the best chance of publication. Refer to our guidelines and upcoming themes."

PARENTING MAGAZINE, 301 Howard, 17th Floor, San Francisco CA 94105. (415)546-7575. Fax: (415)546-0578. Executive Editor: Anne Krueger. Managing Editor: Bruce Raskin. Editor: Steve Reddicliffe. Contact: Articles Editor. Magazine published 10 times/year "for parents of children from birth to ten years old, with the most emphasis put on the under-sixes." Estab. 1987. **Pays on acceptance.** Byline given. Offers 25% kill fee. Buys first rights. Query for electronic submissions. Reports in 1 month. Sample copy for $1.95 and 9 × 12 SAE with 5 first-class stamps. Writer's guidelines for #10 SASE.
Nonfiction: Articles editor. Book excerpts, humor, investigative reports, personal experience, photo feature. Buys 20-30 features/year. Query with or without published clips, or send complete ms. Length: 1,000-3,500 words. Pays $500-2,000. Sometimes pays expenses of writers on assignment.
Columns/Departments: News and Views (news items relating to children/family), 100-400 words; Ages and Stages (health, nutrition, new products and service stories), 100-500 words; Passages (parental rites of passage), 850 words; Up in Arms (opinion, 850 words). Buys 50-60 mss/year. Pays $50-500.

PARENTLIFE, Baptist Sunday School Board, 127 Ninth Ave. N., Nashville TN 37234. (615)251-2229. Fax: (615)251-5008. Managing Editor: Michelle Hicks. 30% freelance written. Works with a small number of new/unpublished writers each year. Monthly magazine covering parenting issues for parents of infants through 12-year-olds, "written and designed from a Christian perspective." Estab. 1994. Circ. 120,000. **Pays on acceptance.** Byline given. "We generally buy all rights to manuscripts. First and reprint rights may be negotiated. Publishes novel excerpts." Submit seasonal/holiday material 1 year in advance. Accepts previously published submissions (on limited basis). Send photocopy of article or typed ms with rights for sale noted and information about when and where the article previously appeared. Résumés and queries only. Reports in 1 month on queries; 2 months on mss. Sample copy for 9 × 12 SASE. Free writer's guidelines.

PARENTS MAGAZINE, 685 Third Ave., New York NY 10017. Fax: (212)867-4583. Editor-in-Chief: Ann Pleshette Murphy. 25% freelance written. Monthly. Estab. 1926. Circ. 1,825,000. **Pays on acceptance.** Publishes ms an average of 8 months after acceptance. Usually buys first serial or first North American serial rights; sometimes buys all rights. Pays 25% kill fee. Reports in approximately 2 months. Sample copy for $2. Writer's guidelines for #10 SASE.

Nonfiction: "We are interested in well-documented articles on the development and behavior of preschool, school-age and adolescent children and their parents; good, practical guides to the routines of baby care; articles that offer professional insights into family and marriage relationships; reports of new trends and significant research findings in education and in mental and physical health; and articles encouraging informed citizen action on matters of social concern. Especially need articles on women's issues, pregnancy, birth, baby care and early childhood. We prefer a warm, colloquial style of writing, one which avoids the extremes of either slang or technical jargon. Anecdotes and examples should be used to illustrate points which can then be summed up by straight exposition." Query. Length: 2,500 words maximum. Payment varies. Sometimes pays the expenses of writers on assignment.

PARENTS' PRESS, The Monthly Newspaper for Bay Area Parents, 1454 Sixth St., Berkeley CA 94710. (510)524-1602. Editor: Dixie M. Jordan. 50% freelance written. Monthly tabloid for parents. Estab. 1980. Circ. 75,000. Pays within 60 days of publication. Publishes ms an average of 6 months after acceptance. Kill fee varies (individually negotiated). Buys first rights, second serial (reprint) and almost always Northern California Exclusive rights. Accepts previously published material. Send photocopy of article with rights for sale noted and information about when and where the article previously appeared. For reprints pays 10-25% of amount paid for an original article. Submit seasonal material 6 months in advance. Reports in 2 months. Sample copy for $3. Writer's guidelines for #10 SASE.

Nonfiction: Book excerpts (family, children), how-to (parent, raise children, nutrition, health, etc.), humor (family life, children), interview/profile (of Bay Area residents, focus on their roles as parents), travel (family), family resources and activities. "Annual issues include Pregnancy and Birth, Travel, Back-to-School, Children's Health. Write for planned topic or suggest one. We require a strong Bay Area focus where appropriate. Please don't send 'generic' stories. While we publish researched articles which spring from personal experience, we do not publish strictly personal essays. Please, no birth stories." Buys 30-50 mss/year. Query with or without published clips, or send complete ms. Length: 300-3,000 words; 1,500-2,000 average. Pays $50-150 for assigned articles; $25-125 for unsolicited articles. Will negotiate fees for special projects written by Bay Area journalists.

Photos: State availability of photos with submission. Reviews prints, any size, b&w only. Offers $10-15/photo. Model release and identification of subject required. Buys one-time rights.

Columns/Departments: Books (reviews of parenting and children's books, preferably by San Francisco Bay Area authors, publishers). Buys 12-24 mss/year. Send complete ms. Length: 100-750 words. Pays $15-25.

Tips: "All sections of Parents' Press are open to freelancers, but we are protective of our regular columnists' turf (children's health, women's health, infant and child behavior), so we ask writers to query whether a topic has been addressed in the last three years. Best bets to break in are family activities, education, nutrition, family dynamics and issues. While we prefer articles written by experts, we welcome well-researched journalism."

SAN DIEGO FAMILY PRESS, San Diego County's Leading Resource for Parents & Educators Who Care!, P.O. Box 23960, San Diego CA 92193-0960. Editor: Sharon Bay. 75% freelance written. Monthly magazine for parenting and family issues. "*SDFP* strives to provide informative, educational articles emphasizing positive parenting for our typical readership of educated mothers, ages 25-45, with an upper-level income. Most articles are factual and practical, some are humor and personal experience. Editorial emphasis is uplifting and positive." Estab. 1983. Circ. 72,000. Pays on publication. Byline given. Buys first, one-time or second serial (reprint) rights. Editorial lead time 2 months. Submit seasonal material 3 months in advance. Reports in 2 months on queries; 3 months on mss. Sample copy and writer's guidelines for $3.50 with 9×12 SAE.

Nonfiction: How-to, parenting, new baby help, enhancing education, family activities, interview/profile (influential or noted persons or experts included in parenting or the welfare of children) and articles of specific interest to or regarding San Diego (for California) families/children/parents/educators. "No rambling, personal experience pieces." Buys 75 mss/year. Send complete ms. Length: 1,000 maximum words. Pays $1.25/column inch. "Byline and contributor copies if writer prefers."

Photos: State availability of photos with submission. Reviews contact sheets and 3½×5 or 5×7 prints. Negotiates payment individually. Identification of subjects preferred. Buys one-time rights.

Columns/Departments: Kids' Books (topical book reviews), 800 words. Buys 12 mss/year. Query with published clips. Pays $1.25/column inch minimum.

Fillers: Facts and newsbreaks (specific to the family market). Buys 10/year. Length: 50-200 words. Pays $1.25/column inch minimum.

‡SAN FRANCISCO PENINSULA PARENT, Peninsula Parent Newspaper Inc., 1480 Rollins Rd., Burlingame CA 94010. (415)342-9203. Editor: Lisa Rosenthal. 25% freelance written. Monthly newsprint magazine geared to parents of children from birth to age 12. "We provide articles that empower parents with the essential parenting skills they need. We provide parents with local resource information." Estab. 1984. Circ. 60,000. Pays on publication. Publishes ms 3 months after acceptance. Byline given. Offers 50% kill fee. Buys first and second serial (reprint) rights. Editorial lead time 3-5 months. Submit seasonal material 4 months in advance. Accepts previously published submissions. Query for electronic submissions. Reports in 2 months on queries; 3 months on mss. Sample copy and writer's guidelines free.

Nonfiction: Humor, interview/profile, travel (family-related). No articles that preach to parents, no first-person memories. Buys 8 mss/year. Query with or without published clips. Length: 800-1,200 words. Pays $100-200 for assigned articles; $25-100 for unsolicited articles. Sometimes pays expenses of writers on assignment.

Photos: State availability of photos with submission. Offers $25-$50/photo; negotiates payment individually. Captions and model releases required. Buys one-time rights.

Columns/Departments: Upclose (profile), 1,000 words; Healthbeat (health news for families), 1,000 words. Buys 2 mss/year. Query with or without published clips. Pays $25-100.

‡SEATTLE'S CHILD, 2107 Elliott Ave., #303, Seattle WA 98121. (206)441-0191. Editor: Ann Bergman. Associate Editor: Rosi Williamson. 85% freelance written. Works with a small number of new/unpublished writers each year. Monthly tabloid of articles related to being a parent of children age 12 and under directed to parents and professionals. Circ. 25,000. Pays on publication. Publishes ms an average of 6 months after acceptance. Byline given. Offers 50% kill fee. Buys first North American serial rights or all rights. Submit seasonal/holiday material 6 months in advance. Accepts simultaneous and previously published submissions. Send tearsheet of article and information about when and where the article previously appeared. For reprints, pays 20% of the amount paid for an original article. Query for electronic submissions. Reports in 6 months. Sample copy for $1.50 and 10×13 SAE. Writer's guidelines for #10 SASE.

Nonfiction: Needs reports on political issues affecting families. Exposé, general interest, historical/nostalgic, how-to, humor, interview/profile, new product, opinion, personal experience, travel, record, tape and book reviews, and educational and political reviews. Articles must relate to parents and parenting. Buys 120 mss/year. Send complete ms (preferred) or query with published clips. Length: 400-2,500 words. Pays 10¢/word.

Tips: "We prefer concise, critical writing and discourage overly sentimental pieces. Don't talk down to the audience. Consider that the audience is sophisticated and well-read."

SESAME STREET PARENTS, Children's Television Workshop, 1 Lincoln Plaza, New York NY 10023. (212)595-3456. Fax: (212)875-6105. Editor-in-Chief: Ira Wolfman. Editorial Assistant: Kathryn Pottinger. 80% freelance written. Magazine published 10 times/year for parents of preschoolers that accompanies every issue of Sesame Street Magazine. Circ. 1.2 million. **Pays on acceptance.** Byline given. Offers 33% kill fee. Buys varying rights. Submit seasonal/holiday material 7 months in advance. Accepts previously published articles. Send typed ms with rights for sale noted and information about when and where the article previously appeared. For reprints pays 75% of the amount paid for an original article. Reports in 1 month on queries. Sample copy for 9×12 SAE with 6 first-class stamps. Writer's guidelines for #10 SASE.

● *Sesame Street Parents* won honors in the Parent's Choice awards and 1994 Parenting approval.

Nonfiction: Child development/parenting, how-to (practical tips for parents of preschoolers), interview/profile, personal experience, book excerpts, essays, photo feature, travel (with children). Buys 100 mss/year. Query with published clips, or send complete ms. Length: 500-2,000 words. Pays $300-2,000 for articles.

Photos: State availability of photos with submission. Model releases, identification of subjects required. Buys one-time or all rights.

TODAY'S FAMILY, P.O. Box 46112, Eden Prairie MN 55344. (612)975-2933. Editor: Jan Mars. 65% freelance written. Bimonthly magazine covering family social issues. Estab. 1991. Circ. 50,000. Pays on publication. Publishes ms 4 months after acceptance. Byline given. No kill fee. Buys first North American serial rights. Submit seasonal material 6 months in advance. Reports in 3 weeks on queries; 6 weeks on mss. Sample copy for $4. Writer's guidelines for #10 SASE.

Nonfiction: General interest, how-to, interview/profile, educational. "No fiction or personal essays." Buys 50 mss/year. Query. Length: 750-1,200 words. "Payment for assigned articles is negotiable." Pays $10-50 for unsolicited articles. Sometimes pays expenses of writers on assignment.

Photos: State availability of photos with submission. Reviews contact sheets and transparencies. Offers $5/photo minimum. Captions, model releases and identification of subjects required. Buys one-time rights.

Tips: "We like to see new ideas and new approaches to subjects of great concern to the family of today."

TWINS, The Magazine for Parents of Multiples, P.O. Box 12045, Overland Park KS 66282-2045. (913)722-1090. Fax: (913)722-1767. Editor-in-Chief: Barbara C. Unell. Managing Editor: Jean Cerne. Associate Editor: Bob Hart. 90% freelance written. Eager to work with new/unpublished writers. Bimonthly national magazine designed to give professional guidance to help multiples, their parents and those professionals who care for them learn about twin facts and research. Estab. 1984. Circ. 57,000. Pays on publication. Publishes ms an average of 6 months after acceptance. Byline given. Buys all rights. Accepts previously published submissions. Send tearsheet of article and information about when and where the article previously appeared. For reprints, pays 100% of the amount paid for an original article. Submit seasonal/holiday material 10 months in advance. Reports in 6 weeks on queries; 2 months on mss. Sample copy for $5. Writer's guidelines for #10 SASE.

● *Twins* is no longer in the market for fillers.

Nonfiction: General interest, how-to, humor, interview/profile, personal experience, photo feature. "No articles that substitute the word 'twin' for 'child'—those that simply apply the same research to twins that applies to singletons without any facts backing up the reason to do so." Buys 150 mss/year. Query with or without published clips, or send complete ms. Length: 1,250-3,000 words. Payment varies.

Photos: Send photos with submission. Reviews contact sheets, 4×5 transparencies, all size prints. Captions, model releases, identification of subjects required. Buys all rights.

Columns/Departments: Resources, Supertwins, Family Health, Family Finances, Twice as Funny, Double Focus (series from pregnancy through adolescence), Personal Perspective (first-person accounts of beliefs about a certain aspect of parenting multiples), Over the Back Fence (specific tips that have worked for the writer in raising multiples), Research, On Being Twins (first-person accounts of growing up as a twin), On Being Parents of Twins (first-person accounts of the experience of parenting twins), Double Takes (fun photographs of twins), Education Matters, Special Miracles (first-person accounts of life with physically, mentally or emotionally challenged twins). Buys 70 mss/year. Query with published clips. Length: 1,250-2,000 words. Payment varies.

Tips: "Features and columns are both open to freelancers. Columnists write for *Twins* on a continuous basis, so the column becomes their own. We are looking for a wide variety of the latest, well-researched practical information. There is no other magazine of this type directed to this market. We are interested in personal interviews with celebrity twins or celebrity parents of twins, tips on rearing twins from experienced parents and/or twins themselves and reports on national and international research studies involving twins."

WORKING MOTHER MAGAZINE, Lang Communications, 230 Park Ave., New York NY 10169. (212)551-9500. Editor: Judsen Culbreth. Executive Editor: Mary McLaughlin. Articles Editor: Linda Hamilton. 90% freelance written. Prefers to work with published/established writers; works with a small number of new/unpublished writers each year. Monthly magazine for women who balance a career with the concerns of parenting. Circ. 925,000. **Pays on acceptance.** Publishes ms an average of 4 months after acceptance. Byline given. Buys all rights. Pays 20% kill fee. Submit seasonal/holiday material 6 months in advance. Reports in 6 weeks. Sample copy for $1.95. Writer's guidelines for SASE.

● *Working Mother* has increased its payment but now buys all rights.

Nonfiction: Service, humor, child development, material pertinent to the working mother's predicament. Send query to attention of *Working Mother Magazine*. Buys 9-10 mss/issue. Length: 750-2,000 words. Pays $700-2,000. "We pay more to people who write for us regularly." Pays the expenses of writers on assignment.

Tips: "We are looking for pieces that help the reader. In other words, we don't simply report on a trend without discussing how it specifically affects our readers' lives and how they can handle the effects. Where can they look for help if necessary?"

Comic Books

Comic books aren't just for kids. Today, this medium also attracts a reader who is older and wants stories presented visually on a wide variety of topics. In addition, some instruction manuals, classics and other stories are being produced in a comic book format.

This doesn't mean you have to be an artist to write for comic books. Most of these publishers want to see a synopsis of one to two double-spaced pages. Be concise. Comics use few words and rely on graphics as well as words to forward the plot.

Once your synopsis is accepted, either an artist will draw the story from your plot, returning these pages to you for dialogue and captions, or you will be expected to write a script. Scripts run approximately 23 typewritten pages and include suggestions for artwork as well as dialogue. Try to imagine your story on actual comic book pages and divide your script accordingly. The average comic has six panels per page, with a maximum of 35 words per panel.

If you're submitting a proposal to Marvel, your story should center on an already established character. If you're dealing with an independent publisher, characters are often the property of their creators. Your proposal should be for a new series. Include a background sheet for main characters who will appear regularly, listing origins, weaknesses, powers or other information that will make your character unique. Indicate an overall theme or direction for your series. Submit story ideas for the first three issues. If you're really ambitious, you may also include a script for your first issue. As with all markets, read a sample copy before making a submission. The best markets may be those you currently read, so consider submitting to them even if they aren't listed in this section.

CARTOON WORLD, P.O. Box 30367, Lincoln NE 68503. Editor: George Hartman. 100% freelance written. Works with published/established writers and a small number of new/unpublished writers each year. "Monthly newsletter for professional and amateur cartoonists who are serious and want to utilize new cartoon markets in each issue." Buys only from paid subscribers. Circ. 150-300. **Pays on acceptance.** Publishes ms an average of 2 months after acceptance. Byline given. Buys second (reprint) rights to material originally published elsewhere. Accepts previously published submissions. Send photocopy of article with rights for sale noted and information about when and where the article previously appeared. For reprints pays 25% of the amount paid for an original article. Not copyrighted. Submit seasonal/holiday material 3 months in advance. Accepts simultaneous submissions. Reports in 1 month. Sample copy for $5.
Nonfiction: "We want only positive articles about the business of cartooning and gag writing." Buys 10 mss/year. Query. Length: 1,000 words. Pays $5/page.

COMICS SCENE, Starlog Group, 8th Floor, 475 Park Ave. S., New York NY 10016. (212)689-2830. Fax: (212)889-7933. Editor: David McDonnell. Magazine published bimonthly on comic books, strips, cartoons, those who create them and TV/movie adaptations of both. Estab. 1981. Pays on publication. Byline given. Offers 25% kill fee. Buys all rights. Submit seasonal/holiday material 6 months in advance. Absolutely *no* simultaneous submissions. Reports in 6 weeks on queries; 2 months on mss. Sample copy for $5. Writer's guidelines for #10 SASE. *No* queries by phone for *any* reason whatsoever.
  • *Comics Scene* is still looking for exciting stories—but fewer of them since it has cut back the frequency of publication.
Nonfiction: Historical, interview/profile, new product, personal experience. Buys 70 mss/year. Query with published clips. Length: 750-3,500 words. Pays $150-250. Sidebars $50-75. Does *not* publish fiction or comics stories and strips. Rarely buys reprints.
Photos: State availability of photos and comic strip/book/animation artwork with submission. Reviews contact sheets, transparencies and 8×10 prints. Offers $10-25 for original photos. Captions, model releases, identification of subjects required. Buys all rights.
Columns/Departments: The Comics Reporter ("newsy" mini-interview with writer, director, producer of TV series/movie adaptations of comic books and strips). Buys 10-12 mss/year. Query with published clips. Length: 100-750 words. Pays $15-50.
Tips: "This is *not* a magazine about comedians, comedy or stand-up improv. We *really* need coverage of independent comics companies' products and creators. We need interviews with specific comic strip creators. Most any writer can break in with interviews with hot comic book writers and artists (we really *need* more of the hot ones)—and with comic book creators who don't work for the big two companies. We do *not* want nostalgic items or interviews. Do not burden us with your own personal comic book stories or artwork. We don't have time to evaluate them and can't provide critiques or advice. Get interviews we can't get or haven't thought to pursue. Out-thinking overworked editors is an almost certain way to sell a story."

MARVEL COMICS, 387 Park Ave. S., New York NY 10016. (212)696-0808. Editor-in-Chief: John Lewandowski. 80% freelance written. Publishes 75 comics and magazines/month, 6-12 graphic novels/year, specials, paperbacks and industrials. Over 9 million copies sold/month. Pays a flat fee for most projects, plus a royalty type incentive based upon sales. Also works on advance/royalty basis on certain projects. **Pays on acceptance.** Publishes ms an average of 6 months after acceptance. Byline given. Offers variable kill fee. Rights purchased depend upon format and material. Submit seasonal/holiday material 1 year in advance. Accepts simultaneous submissions. Reports in 6 months. Writer's guidelines for #10 SASE. Additional guidelines on request.
  • Marvel Comics no longer accepts unsolicited mss.
Fiction: Super hero, action-adventure, science fiction, fantasy and other material. Only comics. Buys 600-800 mss/year. Query with brief plot synopses only. Do not send scripts, short stories or long outlines. A plot synopsis should be less than two typed pages; send two synopses at most. Pays expenses of writers on assignment.

Consumer Service and Business Opportunity

Some of these magazines are geared to investing earnings or starting a new business;

others show how to make economical purchases. Publications for business executives and consumers interested in business topics are listed under Business and Finance. Those on how to run specific businesses are classified by category in the Trade section.

JERRY BUCHANAN'S INFO MARKETING REPORT, TOWERS Club Press, Inc., P.O. Box 2038, Vancouver WA 98668-2038. (206)574-3084. Fax: (206)576-8969. Editor: Jerry Buchanan. 5-10% freelance written. Works with a small number of unpublished writers each year. Monthly of 10 or more pages on entrepreneurial enterprises, reporting especially on self-publishing of how-to reports, books, audio and video tapes, seminars, etc. "By-passing big trade publishers and marketing your own work directly to consumer (mail order predominantly)." Estab. 1974. Circ. 10,000. Pays on publication. Publishes ms an average of 2 months after acceptance. Byline given. Buys one-time rights. Fax submissions accepted of no more than 3 pages. Accepts previously published submissions. Send photocopy of article and information about when and where the article previously appeared. For reprints pays 50% of the amount paid for an original article. Reports in 2 weeks. Sample copy for $15 and 6×9 SASE.
Nonfiction: Exposé (of mail order fraud); how-to (personal experience in self-publishing and marketing); book reviews of new self-published nonfiction how-to-do-it books (must include name and address of author). "Welcomes well-written articles of successful self-publishing/marketing ventures. Must be current, and preferably written by the person who actually did the work and reaped the rewards. There's very little we will not consider, *if* it pertains to unique money-making enterprises that can be operated from the home." Buys 10 mss/year. Send complete ms. Length: 500-1,500 words. Pays $150-250. Pays extra for b&w photo and bonus for excellence in longer ms.
Tips: "The most frequent mistake made by writers in completing an article for us is that they think they can simply rewrite a newspaper article and be accepted. That is only the start. We want them to find the article about a successful self-publishing enterprise, and then go out and interview the principal for a more detailed how-to article, including names and addresses. We prefer that writer actually interview a successful self-publisher. Articles should include how idea first came to subject; how they implemented and financed and promoted the project; how long it took to show a profit and some of the stumbling blocks they overcame; how many persons participated in the production and promotion; and how much money was invested (approximately) and other pertinent how-to elements of the story. Glossy photos (b&w) of principals at work in their offices will help sell article."

CONSUMERS DIGEST MAGAZINE, for People who Demand Value, Consumers Digest, Inc., 5705 N. Lincoln Ave., Chicago IL 60659. (312)275-3590. Executive Editor: Elliott H. McCleary. Editor: John K. Manos. 70% freelance written. Bimonthly magazine offering "practical advice on subjects of interest to consumers: products and services, automobiles, health, fitness, consumer legal affairs, personal money management, etc." Estab. 1959. Circ. 1.3 million. **Pays on acceptance.** Publishes ms an average of 3 months after acceptance. Byline given. Offers 50% kill fee. Buys all rights. Submit seasonal material 6 months in advance. Accepts simultaneous submissions. Query for electronic submissions. Reports in 6 weeks on queries; 3 months on mss. Sample copy for 9×12 SAE with 6 first-class stamps. Free writer's guidelines.
Nonfiction: Elliott H. McCleary, articles editor. Exposé, general interest, how-to (financial, purchasing), new product, travel, health, fitness. Buys 50 mss/year. Query with published clips. Length: 1,000-3,500 words. Pays $400-3,500 for assigned articles; $400-1,700 for unsolicited articles. Sometimes pays expenses of writers on assignment.
Photos: State availability of photos with submission. Reviews transparencies. Pays $100-500/photo. Captions, model releases and identification of subjects required. Buys all rights.
Columns/Departments: Mary S. Butler, column editor. Consumerscope (brief items of general interest to consumers—auto news, travel tips, the environment, smart shopping, news you can use). Buys 10 mss/year. Query. Length: 100-500 words. Pays $75-200.
Tips: "Keep the queries brief and tightly focused. Read our writer's guidelines first and request an index of past articles for trends and to avoid repeating subjects. Focus on subjects of broad national appeal. Stress personal expertise in proposed subject area."

ECONOMIC FACTS, The National Research Bureau, Inc., P.O. Box 1, Burlington IA 52601-0001. (319)752-5415. Fax: (319)752-3421. Editor: Nancy Heinzel. 75% freelance written. Eager to work with new/unpub-

ALWAYS submit unsolicited manuscripts or queries with a self-addressed, stamped envelope (SASE) within your country or a self-addressed envelope with International Reply Coupons (IRC) purchased from the post office for other countries.

lished writers; works with a small number of new/unpublished writers each year. Published 4 times/year. Estab. 1948. Pays on publication. Publishes ms an average of 1 year after acceptance. Buys all rights. Byline given. Sample copy and writer's guidelines for #10 SAE with 2 first-class stamps.

Nonfiction: General interest (private enterprise, government data, graphs, taxes and health care). Buys 10 mss/year. Query with outline of article. Length: 500-700 words. Pays 4¢/word.

‡THE HOME BUSINESS ADVOCATE, The Alternate Press, R.R. 1, St. George, Ontario N0E 1N0 Canada. Editor: Wendy Priesnitz. 50% freelance written. Bimonthly tabloid covering home business for "people who are researching, starting or running a home-based business." Estab. 1986. Circ. 100,000. Pays on publication. Publishes ms 3-4 months after acceptance. Byline given. Buys first rights. Editorial lead time 4 months. Submit seasonal material 4 months in advance. Query for electronic submissions. Reports in 3 weeks on queries. Sample copy for $2.50. Writer's guidelines free on request.

Nonfiction: How-to, interview/profile, new product. Buys 20 mss/year. Query with published clips. Length: 500-800 words. Pays 10¢/word to $100; sometimes pre-arranged barter.

Photos: State availability with submission. Reviews prints. Offers no additional payment for photos accepted with ms. Captions and identification of subjects required. Buys one-time rights.

HOMEWORKING MOTHERS, Mothers' Home Business Network, Box 423, East Meadow NY 11554-0423. Attn: Editorial Submission. (516)997-7394. Fax: (516)997-0839. Editor: Georganne Fiumara. 25% freelance written. Will work with new/unpublished writers. Quarterly newsletter "written for mothers who have home businesses or would like to. These mothers want to work at home so that they can spend more time with their children." Circ. 10,000. Pays on publication. Publishes ms an average of 3-6 months after acceptance. Byline given. Buys one-time rights. Submit seasonal/holiday material 8 months in advance. Accepts simultaneous and previously published submissions. Send photocopy of article and information about when and where the article previously appeared. For reprints pays 100% of the amount paid for an original article. Reports in 1 month on queries; 6 weeks on mss. Sample copy for $5 and #10 SAE with 3 first-class stamps.

Nonfiction: Book excerpts, essays, how-to, humor, inspirational, personal experience, technical—*home business information* "all relating to working at home or home-based businesses." No articles about questionable home business opportunities. Buys 5-10 mss/year. Query with published clips, or send complete ms. Length: 300-1,000 words. Payment varies. Sometimes pays writers with contributor copies or in advertising or promoting a writer's business if applicable. "We will consider in-depth descriptions of one home business possibility, i.e., bookkeeping, commercial art, etc.—at least 3,000 words to be published in booklet form. (Pays $150 and buys all rights)."

Columns/Departments: It's My Business (mothers describe their businesses, how they got started, and how they handle work and children at the same time); Advice for Homeworking Mothers (business, marketing and tax basics written by professionals); Considering the Possibilities (ideas and descriptions of legitimate home business opportunities); A Look at a Book (excerpts from books describing some aspect of working at home or popular work-at-home professions). Length varies, but average 500 words. Buys 4 mss/year. Send complete ms.

Poetry: Free verse, light verse, traditional. "About being a mother working at home or home business." Submit maximum 5 poems. Pays $5.

Fillers: Facts and newsbreaks "about working at home for 'Marketing, Managing and More' page." Length: 150 words maximum. Pays $10.

Tips: "We prefer that the writer have personal experience with working at home or be an expert in the field when giving general home business information. It's My Business is most open to freelancers. Writers should read *HM* before trying to write for us. Only those submissions with SASE will receive response."

INCOME OPPORTUNITIES, IO Publications, 1500 Broadway, New York NY 10036-4015. (212)642-0600. Fax: (212)302-8269. E-mail: incomeed@aol.com. Editor: Stephen Wagner. Executive Editor: Linda Molnar. Managing Editor: Eric Barnes. 90% freelance written. Monthly magazine covering small business. Estab. 1956. Circ. 425,000. **Pays on acceptance.** Publishes ms an average of 5 months after acceptance. Byline given. Buys all rights and makes work-for-hire assignments. Submit seasonal/holiday material 6 months in advance. Query for electronic submissions. Reports in 3 weeks on queries, 1 month on mss. *Writer's Market* recommends allowing 2 months for reply. Free sample copy. Writer's guidelines for #10 SASE.

● *Income Opportunities* is no longer interested in buying reprints but it has increased its payment for original articles.

Nonfiction: How-to (start a small or home business), new product (for mail order, flea market sales). No purely inspirational articles. Buys 100 mss/year. Query. Length: 600-2,500 words. Pays $200-400. Sometimes pays expenses of writers on assignment.

Photos: Send photos with submission. Offers no additional payment for photos accepted with ms. Identification of subjects required. Buys all rights.

Tips: Areas most open to freelancers are "profiles of successful small-business operators. Details of how they started, start-up costs, how they operate, advertising methods, tools, materials, equipment needed, projected or actual earnings, advice to readers for success."

INCOME PLU$ MAGAZINE, Opportunity Associates, 73 Spring St., Suite 303, New York NY 10012. (212)925-3180. Fax: (212)925-3108. Editor: Donna Clapp. 75% freelance written. Monthly magazine on small business and money-making ideas. Provides "hands-on service to help small business owners, home office owners and entrepreneurs successfully start up and run their enterprises." Estab. 1989. Circ. 150,000. Pays on publication. Publishes ms 5 months after acceptance. Byline given. Offers 20% kill fee. Buys first North American serial or second serial rights. Query for electronic submissions. Reports in 6 weeks. Sample copy for $2.50. Writer's guidelines for #10 SASE.
Nonfiction: Book excerpts, how-to (business, finance, home office, technical start-up), interview/profile. Buys 48 mss/year. Query. Length: 900-2,000 words. Pays $200-300 for assigned articles; $100-200 for unsolicited articles. Sometimes pays expenses of writers on assignment.
Photos: State availability of photos with submission. Offers no additional payment for photos accepted with ms.
Columns/Departments: Sales and Marketing, 750-900 words; You the Boss (new biz how-to), 750-900 words; Money (taxes, financing, etc.), 750-900 words. Buys 24 mss/year. Query or send complete ms. Pays $50-100.
Tips: Write for editorial calendar as well as ms guidelines.

KIPLINGER'S PERSONAL FINANCE, (formerly *Changing Times*), 1729 H St. NW, Washington DC 20006. Editor: Ted Miller. Less than 10% freelance written. Prefers to work with published/established writers. Monthly magazine for general, adult audience interested in personal finance and consumer information. Estab. 1947. Circ. 1 million. **Pays on acceptance.** Publishes ms an average of 2 months after acceptance. Buys all rights. Reports in 1 month. Query for electronic submissions. Thorough documentation required for fact-checking.
Nonfiction: "Most material is staff-written, but we accept some freelance." Query with clips of published work. Pays expenses of writers on assignment.
Tips: "We are looking for a heavy emphasis on personal finance topics."

LIVING SAFETY, A Canada Safety Council publication for safety in the home, traffic and recreational environments, #6-2750 Stevenage Dr., Ottawa, Ontario K1G 3N2 Canada. (613)739-1535. Editor: Heather Totten. 65% freelance written. Quarterly magazine covering off-the-job safety. "Off-the job health and safety magazine covering topics in the home, traffic and recreational environments. Audience is the Canadian employee and his/her family." Estab. 1983. Circ. 105,000. **Pays on acceptance.** Publishes ms an average of 2 months after acceptance. Byline given. Buys all rights. Editorial lead time 4 months. Submit seasonal material 6 months in advance. Accepts simultaneous and previously published submissions. Reports in 1 month on queries. Sample copy and writer's guidelines free on request.
Nonfiction: General interest, how-to (safety tips, health tips), personal experience. Buys 24 mss/year. Query with published clips. Length: 1,000-2,500 words. Pays $500 maximum. Sometimes pays expenses of writers on assignment.
Photos: State availability of photos with submission. Reviews contact sheet, negatives, transparencies, prints. Offers no additional payment for photos accepted with ms. Identification of subjects required.
Tips: "Send intro letter, query, résumé and published clips (magazine preferable). Wait for a phone call from editor."

‡SPARE TIME MAGAZINE, The Magazine of Money Making Opportunities, Kipen Publishing Corp., 5810 W. Oklahoma Ave., Milwaukee WI 53219. (414)543-8110. Editor: Robert R. Warde. 60% freelance written. Monthly magazine published 9 times/year covering affordable money-making opportunities. "We publish information the average person can use to begin and operate a spare-time business or extra income venture. This is not the place for an expensive franchise opportunity. Our readers use these opportunities and businesses to earn money for college, vacation or retirement funds." Estab. 1955. Circ. 300,000. Pays on publication. Publishes ms an average of 3 months after acceptance. Byline given. Buys first North American serial rights. Editorial lead time 3 months. Submit seasonal material 4 months in advance. Accepts simultaneous and previously published submissions; query first. Query for electronic submissions. Reports in 1 month on queries; 2 months on mss. Sample copy for $2.50. Writer's guidelines for #10 SASE.
Nonfiction: Book excerpts (small business related), how-to (market, keep records, stay motivated, choose opportunity), interview/profile (small business related), personal experience (on running small business, not a franchise). Buys 24-54 mss/year. Query. Length: 500-1,500 words. Pays $75-300 for assigned articles; $50-250 for unsolicited articles. Sometimes pays expenses of writers on assignment.
Photos: State availability of photos with submission. Reviews contact sheets, 3×5 or larger prints. Negotiates payment individually. Captions, identification of subjects required. Buys one-time rights.
Tips: "It is always best to query. At all times keep in mind that the audience is the average person, not over-educated in terms of business techniques. The best pieces are written in lay language and relate to that type of person."

Contemporary Culture

These magazines combine politics, gossip, fashion and entertainment in a single package. Their approach to institutions is typically irreverent and the target is primarily a young adult audience. Although most of the magazines are centered in large metropolitan areas, some have a following throughout the country.

BOMB MAGAZINE, Artists Writers Actors Directors, New Art Publications, 594 Broadway, Suite 1002A, New York NY 10012. (212)431-3943. Editor-in-Chief: Betsy Sussler. 2% freelance accepted. Quarterly magazine covers literature, art, theater, film and music. "We are interested in interviews *between* professionals." Estab. 1981. Circ. 12,000. Pays on publication. Publishes ms an average of 6 months after acceptance. Byline given. Buys one-time rights. Reports in 4 months. Sample copy for $4 with 10 first-class stamps.
Nonfiction: Book excerpts. "Literature *only*." Length: 250-5,000 words. Pays $100 minimum.
Photos: Offers $100/photo minimum. Captions required. Buys one-time rights.
Fiction: Experimental and novel excerpts. "No commercial fiction." Buys 28 mss/year. Send complete ms. Length: 250-5,000. Pays $100 minimum. Publishes novel excerpts.
Poetry: Avant-garde. Buys 10 poems/year. Submit maximum 6 poems. Pays $50 minimum.

BRUTARIAN, The Magazine That Dares To Be Lame, Box 25222, Arlington VA 22202. Editor: Dominick Salemi. 100% freelance written. Quarterly magazine covering popular and unpopular culture. "A healthy knowledge of the great works of antiquity and an equally healthy contempt for most of what passes today as culture." Estab. 1991. Circ. 3,000. Pays on publication. Publishes ms an average of 3 months after acceptance. Byline given. Buys first or one-time rights. Editorial lead time 2 months. Submit seasonal material 6 months in advance. Accepts previously published submissions. Send typed ms with rights for sale noted and information about when and where the article previously appeared. For reprints, pays 100% of the amount paid for an original article. Reports in 1 week on queries; 2 months on mss. Sample copy for $4. Writer's guidelines free on request.
Nonfiction: Book excerpts, essays, exposé, general interest, humor, interview/profile, reviews of books, film and music. Buys 10-20 feature articles/year. Send complete ms. Length: 1,000-10,000 words. Pays $100-400, depending on length. Sometimes pays expenses of writers on assignment.
Photos: State availability of photos with submission. Reviews contact sheets. Offers no additional payment for photos accepted with ms. Caption, model releases, identification of subjects required. Buys one-time rights.
Columns/Departments: Celluloid Void (critiques of cult and obscure films), 500-1,000 words; Brut Library (critiques of books), 500-1,000 words; Audio Depravation (short critiques of odd and R&R music), 50-100 words. Buys "hundreds" of mss/year. Send complete ms. Pays $5-25.
Fiction: Adventure, confession, erotica, experimental, fantasy, horror, humorous, mystery, novel excerpts, science fiction, slice-of-life vignettes, suspense. Buys 4-10 mss/year. Send complete ms. Length: 1,000-10,000 words. Pays $100-500. Publishes novel excerpts.
Poetry: Avant-garde, free verse, traditional. Buys 10-15 poems/year. Submit maximum 10 poems. Length: 25-1,000. Pays $20-200.
Tips: "Send résumé with completed manuscript. Avoid dry tone and excessive scholasticism. Do not cover topics or issues which have been done to death unless you have a fresh approach or new insights on the subject."

CANADIAN DIMENSION, Dimension Publications Inc., #707-228 Notre Dame Ave., Winnipeg, Manitoba, R3B 1N7 Canada. Fax: (204)943-4617. E-mail: info@canadiandimension.mb.ca. 80% freelance written. Manager: Michelle Torres. Bimonthly magazine "that makes sense of the world. We bring a socialist perspective to bear on events across Canada and around the world. Our contributors provide in-depth coverage on popular movements, peace, labour, women, aboriginal justice, environment, third world and eastern Europe." Estab. 1963. Circ. 4,000. Pays on publication. Publishes ms an average of 6 months after acceptance. Copyrighted by CD after publication. Accepts simultaneous and previously published submissions. Send tearsheet of article (and "disk or electronic copy if accepted unless impossible"). Reports in 6 weeks on queries. Sample copy for $2. Writer's guidelines for #10 SAE with IRC.
Nonfiction: Interview/profile, opinion, reviews, political commentary and analysis, journalistic style. Buys 8 mss/year. Length: 500-2,000 words. Pays $25-100.

GRAY AREAS, Examining The Gray Areas of Life, Gray Areas, Inc., P.O. Box 808, Broomall PA 19008-0808. Editor: Netta Gilboa. 50% freelance written. Quarterly magazine covering music, popular culture, technology and law. "We are interested in exploring all points of view about subjects which are illegal, potentially illegal, immoral and/or controversial." Estab. 1991. Circ. 14,000. Pays on publication. Publishes ms 1 year after acceptance. Buys first North American serial, one-time and second serial (reprint) rights. Accepts previously published submissions. Send photocopy of article and information about when and where the article previously appeared. For reprints, pays in contributor's copies. Reports in 1 month on queries. Sample copy for $8.

Nonfiction: Essays, exposé, general interviews/profile, opinion, personal experience. "No poetry, short stories or fiction." Query. Pays with contributor copies if writer is a newcomer interested in building a portfolio.

Photos: State availability of photos with submission. Reviews prints only, any size. Negotiates payment individually. "We pay for one-time use of all photos published." Model releases and identification of subjects required. Buys one-time rights.

Columns/Departments: CD reviews (rock, pop, folk, world, alternative etc., no classical); concert reviews (no classical, country or opera); book reviews.

Tips: "1. We are actively looking for freelancers as we are writing most of *Gray Areas* ourselves. 2. We will answer all letters which include an SASE. 3. We use freelancers based on an ability to adhere to deadlines (which are loose as we are a quarterly) and based on their knowledge of our specialized subject matter. 4. We do not discriminate against freelancers for lack of prior publications, not having a computer or typewriter, etc. We need people with legal expertise, experience with criminals and/or law enforcement and with access to celebrities. We also need people whose tastes and political viewpoints differ from our own. Our readers have only one thing in common—an open mind. They want to read a broad spectrum of articles that disagree with each other. 5. Please read the magazine! We don't print fluff and have no word limits. In-depth articles are of more interest than traditional 750-2,000 word pieces."

HIGH TIMES, Trans High Corp., 235 Park Ave. S., 5th Floor, New York NY 10003-1405. (212)387-0500. Fax: (212)475-7684. E-mail: hightimes@echonyc.com. Editor: Steve Hager. News Editor: Bill Weinberg. 30% freelance written. Monthly magazine covering marijuana and the counterculture. Estab. 1974. Circ. 250,000. Pays on publication. Byline given. Offers 20% kill fee. Buys one-time or all rights or makes work-for-hire assignments. Submit seasonal/holiday material 6 months in advance. Accepts previously published and simultaneous submissions. Send tearsheet of article or typed ms with rights for sale noted. For reprints, pays in ad trade. Reports in 1 month on queries; 4 months on mss. Sample copy for $5 and #10 SASE. Writer's guidelines for SASE.

• No longer accepts fiction or poetry. Staff now writes more for each issue than freelancers.

Nonfiction: Book excerpts, exposé, humor, interview/profile, new product, personal experience, photo feature, travel. Buys 30 mss/year. Send complete ms. Length: 1,000-10,000 words. Pays $150-400. Sometimes pays in trade for advertisements. Sometimes pays expenses of writers on assignment.

Photos: Malcolm Mackinnon, photo editor. Send photos with submission. Pays $50-300. Captions, model release, identification of subjects required. Buys all rights or one-time use.

Columns/Departments: Steve Bloom, music editor. Gene Christian, cultivation editor. Peter Gorman, views editor. Drug related books; drug related news. Buys 10 mss/year. Query with published clips. Length: 100-2,000 words. Pays $25-300.

Fillers: Gags to be illustrated by cartoonist, newsbreaks, short humor. Buys 10 mss/year. Length: 100-500 words. Pays $10-50. Cartoon Editor: John Holmstrom.

Tips: "All sections are open to good, professional writers."

‡MOTHER JONES, Foundation for National Progress, 731 Market St., Suite 600, San Francisco CA 94103. (415)665-6637. Editor: Jeffrey Klein. Contact: Chris Orr, Sarah Pollock, senior editors. 80% freelance written. Bimonthly magazine covering politics, investigative reporting. "*Mother Jones* is a 'progressive' magazine— but the core of its editorial well is reporting (i.e., fact) based. No slant required." Estab. 1976. Circ. 120,000. Pays on publication. Publishes ms an average of 4 months after acceptance. Byline given. Offers 33% kill fee. Buys first North American serial rights, first rights, one-time rights or on-line rights (limited). Editorial lead time 4 months. Submit seasonal material 6 months in advance. Query only. Reports in 2 months. Sample copy for 9×12 SAE with 4 first-class stamps. Writer's guidelines for #10 SASE.

Nonfiction: Chris Orr, Sarah Pollock. Book excerpts, essays, exposé, humor, interview/profile, opinion, personal experience, photo feature, current issues, policy. Buys 70-100 mss/year. Length: 2,000-5,000 words. Pays 80¢/word. Sometimes pays expenses of writers on assignment.

Columns/Departments: Kerry Rauerman. Outfront (short, newsy and/or outrageous and/or humorous items), 200-500 words; Profiles of "Hellraisers," "Visionaries" (short interviews), 250 words. Pays 80¢/word.

Tips: "Send a great, short query and establish your credibility as a reporter."

‡ON THE ISSUES, The Progressive Woman's Quarterly, Choices Women's Medical Center, Inc., 97-77 Queens Blvd., Suite 1120, Forest Hills NY 33174. Contact: Ronni Sandroff. 90% freelance written. "*On The Issues* is a quarterly magazine for 'thinking feminists'—women and men interested in progressive social change, advances in feminist thought, and coverage of politics, society, economics, medicine, relationships, the media and the arts from a range of feminist viewpoints." Estab. 1983. Circ. 15,285. **Pays on acceptance.** Publishes ms an average of 5 months after acceptance. Byline given. Offers 20% kill fee. Buys first North American serial rights or all rights. Editorial lead time 3 months. Accepts simultaneous and previously published submissions, if so notified. Reports in 2 months. Sample copy and writer's guidelines free on request.

Nonfiction: Book excerpts, essays, exposé, general interest, historical/nostalgic, humor, interview/profile, opinion, personal experience, photo feature. Buys 40 mss/year. Query with published clips. Length: 75-2,500 words. Pays $25-400. Sometimes pays expenses of writers on assignment.

Photos: State availability of photos with submissions. Negotiates payment individually. Captions, identification of subjects required. Buys all rights.

Columns/Departments: Talking Feminist (personal experience), 1,500 words; Win Some Lose Some (briefs/news/humor), 200-500 words; Cutting Some Slack (Humor), 600 words; Book Reviews (query Nina Mehta, book review editor), 500 words. Buys 15 mss/year. Query with published clips. Pays $25-150.

Tips: "Always looking for investigative, newsworthy pieces. Query first. Our columns are also a good place to start. "Cutting Some Slack," on our last page, features a 600 word essay: humor or political satire with a feminist edge. "Talking Feminist" can be on any subject: a personal experience or editorial style essay. We're particularly interested in recruiting more writers for this column."

‡**SHEPHERD EXPRESS**, Alternative Publications, Inc., 1123 N. Water St., Milwaukee WI 53202. Editor: Doug Hissom. Contact: Scott Kerr, news editor. 50% freelance written. Weekly tabloid covering "news and arts with a progressive news edge and a hip entertainment perspective." Estab. 1982. Circ. 50,000. Pays on publication. Publishes ms an average of 2 weeks after acceptance. Byline given. No kill fee. Buys first, one-time or all rights or makes work-for-hire assignments. Editorial lead time 2 weeks. Submit seasonal material 1 month in advance. Accepts simultaneous and previously published submissions. Reports in 2 weeks on queries; 1 month on mss. Sample copy for $1.

Nonfiction: Book excerpts, essays, exposé, opinion. Buys 300 mss/year. Query with published clips or send complete ms. Length: 600-3,500 words. Pays $25-350 for assigned articles; $10-200 for unsolicited articles. Sometimes pays expenses of writers on assignment.

Photos: State availability of photos with submissions. Reviews prints. Negotiates payment individually. Captions, model releases, identification of subjects required. Buys one-time rights.

Columns/Departments: Opinions (social trends, politics, from progressive slant), 800-1,200 words; Books Reviewed (new books only: Social trends, environment, politics), 600-1,200 words. Buys 10 mss/year. Send complete ms.

Tips: "Include solid analysis with point of view in tight but lively writing. Nothing cute. Do not tell us that something is important, tell us why and what it will mean to us all down the road."

‡**TIKKUN MAGAZINE, A Bimonthly Jewish Critique of Politics, Culture and Society**, 251 W. 100th St., New York NY 10025. (212)864-4110. Editor: Michael Lerner. Contact: Alice Chasan, executive editor. 95% freelance written. Bimonthly magazine covering politics, culture, society. Estab. 1986. Circ. 25,000. Pays on publication. Publishes ms an average of 6 months after acceptance. Byline given. Kill fee varies. Buys first North American serial rights. Editorial lead time 2 months. Submit seasonal material 4 months in advance. Reports in 6 months. Sample copy for $8.

Nonfiction: Book excerpts, essays, general interest, historical/nostalgic, humor, opinion, personal experience, photo feature, religious, political analysis media and cultural analysis. Buys 25 mss/year. Send complete ms. Length: 2,000 words maximum. Pays $150.

Photos: State availability of photos with submissions. Reviews contact sheets or prints. Negotiates payment individually. Buys one-time rights.

Fiction: Contact: Melvin Jules Bukiet, fiction editor. Ethnic, historical, humorous, mystery, novel excerpts, religious, romance, slice-of-life vignettes. Buys 6 mss/year. Send complete ms.

Poetry: Contact: Marge Piercy, poetry editor. Avant-garde, free verse, Haiku, light verse traditional. We specifically reserve *Tikkun* for poetry with Jewish themes since there are so few places where such work can find a home. Submit maximum 5 poems. Long poems cannot be considered. Does not pay for poetry.

Tips: "Internships are available. Write to *Tikkun* for information. Enclose a résumé and self-revealing letter."

‡**UTNE READER**, 1624 Harmon Place, Suite 330, Minneapolis MN 55403. Fax: (612)338-6043. E-mail: editor@utnereader.com. Does *not* accept unsolicited material. Accepts previously published submissions. Send tearsheet or photocopy of article or typed ms with rights for sale noted and information about when and where the article previously appeared.

Detective and Crime

Fans of detective stories want to read accounts of actual criminal cases, detective work and espionage. The following magazines specialize in nonfiction, but a few buy some fiction. Markets specializing in crime fiction are listed under Mystery publications.

DETECTIVE CASES, Detective Files Group, 1350 Sherbrooke St. W., Montreal, Quebec H3G 2T4 Canada. Editor-in-Chief: Dominick A. Merle. Bimonthly magazine. See *Detective Files*.

DETECTIVE DRAGNET, Detective Files Group, 1350 Sherbrooke St. W., Montreal, Quebec H3G 2T4 Canada. Editor-in-Chief: Dominick A. Merle. Bimonthly 72-page magazine. See *Detective Files.*

DETECTIVE FILES, Detective Files Group, 1350 Sherbrooke St. W., Montreal, Quebec H3G 2T4 Canada. Editor-in-Chief: Dominick A. Merle. Estab. 1930. 100% freelance written. Bimonthly magazine; 72 pages. **Pays on acceptance.** Publishes ms an average of 3-6 months after acceptance. Buys all rights. Reports in 1 month. Sample copy and writer's guidelines for SAE with IRCs.
Nonfiction: True crime stories. "Do a thorough job; don't double-sell (sell the same article to more than one market); deliver, and you can have a steady market. Neatness, clarity and pace will help you make the sale." Query. Length: 3,500-6,000 words. Pays $250-350.
Photos: Purchased with accompanying ms; no additional payment.

HEADQUARTERS DETECTIVE, Detective Files Group, 1350 Sherbrooke St. W., Montreal, Quebec H3G 2T4 Canada. Editor-in-Chief: Dominick A. Merle. Bimonthly magazine; 72 pages. See *Detective Files.*

INSIDE DETECTIVE, Official Detective Group, R.G.H. Publishing Corp., 460 W. 34th St., New York NY 10001. (212)947-6500. Editor-in-Chief: Rose Mandelsberg. Managing Editor: Christofer Pierson. Magazine published 7 times/year. Circ. 90,000. **Pays on acceptance.** Publishes ms an average of 3 months after acceptance. Byline given. Buys first rights and one-time world rights. Query for electronic submissions. Reports in 2 weeks. Free writer's guidelines.
Nonfiction: Buys 120 mss/year. Query. Pays $250. Length: 5,000-6,000 words (approximately 20 typed pages).

P. I. MAGAZINE, America's Private Investigation Journal, 755 Bronx, Toledo OH 43609. (419)382-0967. Editor: Bob Mackowiak. 75% freelance written. "Audience includes professional investigators and mystery/private eye fans. Estab. 1988. Circ. 3,500. Pays on publication. Publishes ms an average of 3 months after acceptance. Buys one-time rights. Submit seasonal/holiday material 3 months in advance. Accepts simultaneous submissions. Reports in 3 months on queries; 4 months on mss. Sample copy for $5.75.
Nonfiction: Interview/profile, personal experience and accounts of real cases. Buys 4-10 mss/year. Send complete ms. Length: 1,500 words. Pays $50 for unsolicited articles.
Photos: Send photos with submission. May offer additional payment for photos accepted with ms. Model releases and identification of subjects required. Buys one-time rights.
Tips: "The best way to get published in *P.I.* is to write a detailed story about a professional private detective's true-life case."

STARTLING DETECTIVE, Detective Files Group, 1350 Sherbrooke St. W., Montreal, Quebec H3G 2T4 Canada. Editor-in-Chief: Dominick A. Merle. Bimonthly 72-page magazine. See *Detective Files.*

TRUE POLICE CASES, Detective Files Group, 1350 Sherbrooke St. W., Montreal, Quebec H3G 2T4 Canada. Editor-in-Chief: Dominick A. Merle. Bimonthly 72-page magazine. Buys all rights. See *Detective Files.*

Disabilities

These magazines are geared toward disabled persons and those who care for or teach them. A knowledge of disabilities and lifestyles is important for writers trying to break in to this field; editors regularly discard material that does not have a realistic focus. Some of these magazines will accept manuscripts only from disabled persons or those with a background in caring for disabled persons.

ACCENT ON LIVING, P.O. Box 700, Bloomington IL 61702-0700. (309)378-2961. Fax: (309)378-4420. Editor: Betty Garee. 75% freelance written. Eager to work with new/unpublished writers. Quarterly magazine for physically disabled persons and rehabilitation professionals. Estab. 1956. Circ. 20,000. Buys first and second (reprint) rights. Byline usually given. Buys 50-60 unsolicited mss/year. Pays on publication. Publishes ms an average of 6 months after acceptance. Accepts previously published submissions. Send tearsheet or photocopy of article and information about when and where the article previously appeared. Reports in 1 month. Sample copy and writer's guidelines $3 for #10 SAE with 7 first-class stamps. Writer's guidelines for #10 SASE.
Nonfiction: Articles about new devices that would make a disabled person with limited physical mobility more independent; should include description, availability and photos. Medical breakthroughs for disabled people. Intelligent discussion articles on acceptance of physically disabled persons in normal living situations; topics may be architectural barriers, housing, transportation, educational or job opportunities, organizations, or other areas. How-to articles concerning everyday living, giving specific, helpful information so the reader can carry out the idea himself/herself. News articles about active disabled persons or groups. Good strong

interviews. Vacations, accessible places to go, sports, organizations, humorous incidents, self improvement and sexual or personal adjustment—all related to physically handicapped persons. No religious-type articles. "We are looking for upbeat material." Query. Length: 250-1,000 words. Pays 10¢/word for article as it appears in magazine (after editing and/or condensing by staff).

Photos: Pays $10 minimum for b&w photos purchased with accompanying captions. Amount will depend on quality of photos and subject matter. Pays $50 and up for four-color slides used on cover. "We need good-quality transparencies or slides with submissions—or b&w photos."

Tips: "Ask a friend who is disabled to read your article before sending it to *Accent*. Make sure that he/she understands your major points and the sequence or procedure."

ARTHRITIS TODAY, Arthritis Foundation. 1314 Spring St. NW, Atlanta GA 30309. (404)872-7100. Fax: (404)872-9559. Editor: Cindy T. McDaniel. Managing Editor: Tracy Ballew. 70% freelance written. Bimonthly magazine about living with arthritis; latest in research/treatment. "*Arthritis Today* is written for the 37 million Americans who have arthritis and for the millions of others whose lives are touched by an arthritis-related disease. The editorial content is designed to help the person with arthritis live a more productive, independent and painfree life. The articles are upbeat and provide practical advice, information and inspiration." Estab. 1987. Circ. 500,000. Buys first North American serial rights but requires unlimited reprint rights in Arthritis Foundation publications. Submit seasonal/holiday material 6 months in advance. Accepts simultaneous and previously published submissions. Send photocopy of article with rights for sale noted and information about when and where the article previously appeared. For reprints, pays 25-50% of the amount paid for an original article. Reports in 1 month on queries; 2 months on mss. Sample copy for 9×11 SAE with 4 first-class stamps. Writer's guidelines for #10 SASE.

• *Arthritis Today* is looking for more general health and lifestyle topics.

Nonfiction: General interest, how-to (tips on any aspect of living with arthritis), inspirational, interview/profile, opinion, personal experience, photo feature, technical, nutrition, general health and lifestyle. Buys 45 mss/year. Query with published clips. Length: 1,000-3,500. Pays $450-1,500. Sometimes pays expenses of writers on assignment.

Photos: Submit slides, tearsheets or prints for consideration. Assignments range between $200-350/photo, reprints $50. Captions, model releases, identification of subjects required. Buy one-time North American serial rights.

Columns/Departments: Quick Takes (general news and information); Scientific Frontier (research news about arthritis), 200-600 words. Buys 16-20 mss/year. Query with published clips. Pays $150-400.

Tips: "In addition to articles specifically about living with arthritis, we look for articles to appeal to an older audience on subjects such as hobbies, general health, lifestyle, etc."

CAREERS & the disABLED, Equal Opportunity Publications, 150 Motor Pkwy., Suite 420, Hauppauge, NY 11788-5145. (516)273-0066. Fax: (516)273-8936. Editor: James Schneider. 60% freelance written. Triannual career guidance magazine that is distributed through college campuses for disabled college students and professionals. Deadline dates: April 1 (Fall); October 1 (Winter); January 1 (Spring). "The magazine offers role-model profiles and career guidance articles geared toward disabled college students and professionals." Pays on publication. Publishes ms an average of 6 months after acceptance. Estab. 1967. Circ. 15,000. Byline given. Buys first rights. Accepts simultaneous and previously published submissions. Reports in 2 weeks. Sample copy and writer's guidelines for 9×12 SAE with 5 first-class stamps.

Nonfiction: General interest, interview/profile, opinion, personal experience. Buys 15 mss/year. Query. Length: 1,000-1,500 words. Pays 10¢/word. Sometimes pays the expenses of writers on assignment.

Photos: State availability of photos with submission. Reviews prints. Offers $15/photo and/or color slides. Captions. Buys one-time rights.

Tips: "Be as targeted as possible. Role model profiles which offer advice to disabled college students are most needed."

DIABETES SELF-MANAGEMENT, R.A. Rapaport Publishing, Inc., 150 W. 22nd St., Suite 800, New York NY 10011-2421. (212)989-0200. Fax: (212)989-4786. Editor: James Hazlett. 20% freelance written. Bimonthly magazine about diabetes. "We publish how-to health care articles for motivated, intelligent readers who have diabetes and who are actively involved in their own health care management. All articles must have immediate application to their daily living." Estab. 1983. Circ. 285,000. Pays on publication. Publishes ms an average of 3 months after acceptance. Byline given. Offers 20% kill fee. Buys all rights. Submit seasonal/holiday material 6 months in advance. Query for electronic submissions. Reports in 1 month. Sample copy for $3.50 and 9×12 SAE with 6 first-class stamps. Writer's guidelines for #10 SASE.

Nonfiction: How-to (exercise, nutrition, diabetes self-care, product surveys), technical (reviews of products available, foods sold by brand name), travel (considerations and prep for people with diabetes). Buys 10-12 mss/year. Query with published clips. Length: 2,000-4,000 words. Pays $400-600 for assigned articles; $200-600 for unsolicited articles.

Tips: "The rule of thumb for any article we publish is that it must be clear, concise, useful and instructive, and it must have immediate application to the lives of our readers."

‡THE DISABILITY RAG & RESOURCE, The Advocado Press, P.O. Box 145, Louisville KY 40201. Editor: Barrett Shaw. Bimonthly magazine covering disability-related rights issues. "*The Rag* is a forum for discussion of issues related to living with a disability in American society today. It is interested in exploring and exposing the roots of discrimination, supporting positive change and developing disability community and culture. Its readers tend to be active, involved and informed, and want to be better informed." Estab. 1980. Circ. 3,200. Pays on publication. Publishes ms an average of 8 months after acceptance. Byline given. Buys first North American serial rights. Editorial lead time 2 months. Submit seasonal material 4-6 months in advance. Accepts electronic submissions by disk. Reports in 1 month on queries; 3 months on mss. Sample copy for $4.50. Writer's guidelines for #10 SASE.

Nonfiction: Book excerpts, essays, exposé, humor, opinion, reportage, analysis. Does not want to see inspirational, profile, personal experience except as part of or sidebar to broader piece. Buys 30 mss/year. Query. Length: 500-3,500 words. Pays $25-150 ($25 per printed page). Sometimes pays expenses of writers on assignment.

Photos: State availability of photos with submissions. Reviews contact sheets, prints. Offers $25/photo. Model releases, identification of subjects required. Buys one-time rights.

Columns/Departments: Reading (book reviews on disability, rights issues), 500-1,200 words; Myth and Media (film, TV, other media images of disability), 500-1,500 words; Views of Ourselves (disability identity), 500-1,500 words. Buys 12 mss/year. Query with published clips. Pays $25-75.

Fiction: Anne Finger, poetry/fiction editor. Erotica, ethnic, experimental, humorous, mainstream, novel excerpts, science fiction, slice-of-life vignettes, interested in work by writers with disabilities or treating disability themes. Buys 1-2 mss/year (but would like to use more). Send complete ms. Length: 500-3,500 words. Pays $25-150 ($25 for printed page).

Poetry: Anne Finger, poetry/fiction editor. Any contemporary form, by writers with disabilities or dealing with aspects of the disability experience. Buys 18 poems/year. Submit maximum 5 poems. Pays $25/poem (unless exceptionally long, multi-part).

Tips: "Be familiar with the disability rights movement and the issues that concern it."

‡DISABILITY TODAY, Disability Today Publishing Group, Inc., P.O. Box 237, Grimsby, Ontario L3M 3C4 Canada. Editor: Hilda Hoch. 70% freelance written. Quarterly magazine covering disability issues/profiles. "An awareness magazine for and about people with physical disabilities." Estab. 1990. Circ. 45,000. Pays on publication. Publishes ms an average of 3 months after acceptance. Byline given. Offers 75% kill fee. Buys one-time or second serial (reprint) rights. Editorial lead time 3 months. Submit seasonal material 6 months in advance. Accepts previously published submissions. Query for electronic submissions. Sample copy $5.50. Writer's guidelines for #10 SAE and IRC.

Nonfiction: Publisher: Jeffrey Tiessen. Book excerpts, general interest, humor, inspirational, interview/profile, new product, opinion, personal experience, photo feature, travel. Annual features: Acquired Brain Injury (August); Kids & Disability (November). Buys 12 mss/year. Query. Length: 1,000-2,500 words. Pays $100-400. Sometimes pays expenses of writers on assignment.

Photos: Send photos with submission. Reviews 4×6 prints. Offers no additional payment for photos accepted with ms. Model releases and identification of subjects required. Buys one-time rights.

Columns/Departments: Injury Prevention, 800 words; Newspage ("what's new"), 400 words; Sports (disabled sports), 800 words. Buys 24 mss/year. Query. Pays $50-200.

Tips: "Provide outline for a series of contributions; identify experience in field of disability."

INDEPENDENT LIVING PROVIDER, The Sales & Service Magazine for Home Dealers, Equal Opportunity Publications, Inc., 150 Motor Pkwy., Suite 420, Hauppauge NY 11788-5145. (516)-273-8743. Fax: (516)273-8936. Editor: Anne Kelly. 75% freelance written. Bimonthly magazine on home health care, rehabilitation, and disability issues as they relate to the home medical equipment dealer. *Independent Living* magazine is written for home care dealers to enhance their business through knowledge of health care issues, sales and marketing strategies and service to clients." Estab. 1968. Circ. 35,000. Pays on publication. Byline given. Buys First North American serial rights. Reports in 3 months. Free sample copy and writer's guidelines.

Nonfiction: Business, interview/profile, health care, new product, disability, chronic illness. Buys 40 mss/year. Query. Length: 500-1,500 words. Pays 10¢/word.

Photos: Send photos with submission. Reviews prints. Offers $15/photo. Prefers 35mm color slides. Captions and identification of subjects required. Buys all rights.

Tips: "The best way to have a manuscript published is to first send a detailed query on a subject related to home health care and home dealers. We also need articles on innovative ways that home health care dealers are meeting their clients needs, as well as profiles of successful dealers."

KALEIDOSCOPE: International Magazine of Literature, Fine Arts, and Disability, Kaleidoscope Press, 326 Locust St., Akron OH 44302-1876. (216)762-9755. Fax: (216)762-0912. Editor-in-Chief: Dr. Darshan Perusek. Senior Editor: Gail Willmott. Subscribers include individuals, agencies and organizations that assist people with disabilities and many university and public libraries. Estab. 1979. Circ. 1,500. 75% freelance written. Eager to work with new/unpublished writers. Byline given. Accepts previously published submissions. Send typed ms with rights for sale noted and information about when and where the article previously appeared. Publishes novel excerpts. Rights return to author upon publication. Appreciate work by established writers as well. Especially interested in work by writers with a disability. Features writers both with and without disabilities. Writers without a disability must limit themselves to our focus, while those with a disability may explore any topic (although we prefer original perspectives about experiences with disability). Submit photocopies with SASE for return of work. Please type submissions. All submissions should be accompanied by an autobiographical sketch. May include art or photos that enhance works, prefer b&w with high contrast. Reports in 3 weeks, acceptance or rejection may take 6 months. Pays $10-125 plus 2 copies. Sample copy for $4 prepaid. Guidelines free for SASE.

Nonfiction or Fiction: Publishes 8-14 mss/year. Maximum 5,000 words. Personal experience essays, book reviews and articles related to disability. Short stories, excerpts. Traditional and experimental styles. Works should explore experiences with disability. Use people-first language.

Poetry: Limit 5 poems/submission. Publishes 12-20 poems/year. Do not get caught up in rhyme scheme. High quality with strong imagery and evocative language. Will review any style.

Tips: Inquire about future themes of upcoming issues. Sample copy very helpful. Works should not use stereotyping, patronizing or offending language about disability. We seek fresh imagery and thought-provoking language.

MAINSTREAM, Magazine of the Able-Disabled, Exploding Myths, Inc., 2973 Beech St., San Diego CA 92102. (619)234-3138. Fax: (619)234-3155. E-mail: wstrothers@aol.com. Editor: Cyndi Jones. Managing Editor: William Strothers. 100% freelance written. Eager to develop writers who have a disability. Magazine published 10 times/year (monthly except January and June) covering disability-related topics, written for active and upscale disabled consumers. Estab. 1975. Circ. 19,400. Pays on publication. Publishes ms an average of 3 months after acceptance. Byline given. Buys all rights. Submit seasonal/holiday material 4 months in advance. Payment varies. Reports in 4 months. Sample copy for $5 or 9×12 SAE and $4 with 6 first-class stamps. Writer's guidelines for #10 SASE.

Nonfiction: Book excerpts, exposé, how-to (daily independent living tips), humor, interview/profile, personal experience (dealing with problems/solutions), photo feature, technology, computers, travel, politics and legislation. "All must be disability-related, directed to disabled consumers." *NO* articles on " 'my favorite disabled character', 'my most inspirational disabled person', 'poster child stories.' " Buys 65 mss/year. Query with or without published clips and send complete ms. Length: 8-12 pages. Pays $100-150. May pay subscription if writer requests.

Photos: State availability of photos with submission. Reviews contact sheets, 1½×¾ transparencies and 5×7 or larger prints. Offers $20-25/b&w photo. Captions and identification of subjects required. Buys all rights.

Columns/Departments: Creative Solutions (unusual solutions to common aggravating problems); Personal Page (deals with personal relations: dating, meeting people). Buys 10 mss/year. Send complete ms. Length: 500-800 words. Pays $75. "We also are looking for disability rights cartoons."

Tips: "It seems that politics and disability are becoming more important. Please include your phone number on cover page. We accept 5.25 or 3.5 floppy discs—ASCII, Wordperfect, Wordstar-IBM."

NEW MOBILITY, P.O. Box 8987, Malibu CA 90265-8987. (310)317-4522. Fax: (310)317-9644. Managing Editor: Jean Dobbs. 60% freelance written. Full color magazine for people who use wheelchairs, published 9 times a year. "*New Mobility* covers the lifestyles of *active* wheelchair users with articles on health and medicine; sports, recreation and travel; equipment and technology; relationships, family and sexual issues; personalities; civil rights and legal issues. Writers should address issues with solid reporting and strong voice." Estab. 1989. Circ. 25,000. Pays 30 days after publication (15¢/word). Publishes ms an average of 6 months after acceptance. Byline given. Offers 50% kill fee. Buys first North American serial rights. Editorial lead time 6 months. Accepts simultaneous and previously published submissions only if material does not appear in other disability publications and is rewritten. Send photocopy of article with rights for sale noted, information about when and where the article previously appeared. For reprints pays 100% of the amount paid for an original article "because we require additional work." Query for electronic submissions. Reports in 3 months. Sample copy $5. Writer's guidelines for #10 SASE.

● *New Mobility* has a new column, Back Spin, which is more literary than other departments. Writers should show panache and humor and should probably *have* a disability.

Nonfiction: Essays, exposé, humor, interview/profile, new product, opinion, photo feature, travel and medical feature. "No inspirational tear-jerkers." Buys 30 mss/year. Query with 1-2 published clips. Length: 700-2,000 words. Pays 15¢/word. Sometimes pays expenses of writers on assignment.

Always check the most recent copy of a magazine for the address and editor's name before you send in a query or manuscript.

Photos: State availability of photos with submission. Reviews contact sheets, transparencies and prints. Negotiates payment individually. Identification of subjects required. Buys one-time rights.

Columns/Departments: My Spin (opinion piece on disability-related topic), 700 words; Media (reviews of books, videos on disability), 300-400 words; People (personality profiles of people w/disabilities), 300-700 words. Buys 20 mss/year. Query with published clips. Send complete ms.

Tips: "Avoid 'courageous' or 'inspiring' tales of people who 'overcome' their disability. Writers don't have to be disabled to write for this magazine, but they should be familiar with the issues people with disabilities face. Most of our readers have disabilities, so write for this audience. We are most open to personality profiles, either for our short People department or as feature articles. In all of our departments, we like to see adventurous people, irreverent opinions and lively writing. Don't be afraid to let your *voice* come through."

Entertainment

This category's publications cover live, filmed or videotaped entertainment, including home video, TV, dance, theater and adult entertainment. In addition to celebrity interviews, most publications want solid reporting on trends and upcoming productions. Magazines in the Contemporary Culture section also use articles on entertainment. For those publications with an emphasis on music and musicians, see the Music section.

‡**ANGLOFILE, British Entertainment & Pop Culture**, The Goody Press, P.O. Box 33515, Decatur GA 30033. (404)633-5587. Fax: (404)321-3109. Editor: William P. King. Managing Editor: Leslie T. King. 15% freelance written. Bimonthly newsletter. "News and interviews on British entertainment, past and present, from an American point of view." Circ. 3,000. Accepts previously published submissions. Send information about when and where the article previously appeared. Pays on publication. Publishes ms an average of 6 months after acceptance. Byline given. Buys all rights. Reports in 2 months. Free sample copy.

Nonfiction: Justin Stonehouse articles editor. Book excerpts, essays, historical/nostalgic, interview/profile, opinion, personal experience, photo feature, and travel. "No articles written for general audience." Buys 5 mss/year. Send complete ms. Length: 1,500 words. Pays $25-250.

Photos: Send photos with submission. Reviews prints. Offers $10-25/photo. Identification of subjects required. Buys all rights.

CINEFANTASTIQUE MAGAZINE, The Review of Horror, Fantasy and Science Fiction Films, P.O. Box 270, Oak Park IL 60303. (708)366-5566. Editor: Frederick S. Clarke. 100% freelance written. Willing to work with new/unpublished writers. Bimonthly magazine covering horror, fantasy and science fiction films. Estab. 1970. Circ. 60,000. Pays on publication. Publishes ms an average of 6 months after acceptance. Byline given. Buys all magazine rights. Reports in 2 months or longer. Sample copy for $7 and 9 × 12 SAE. "Enclose SASE if you want your manuscript back."

Nonfiction: Historical/nostalgic (retrospects of film classics); interview/profile (film personalities); new product (new film projects); opinion (film reviews, critical essays); technical (how films are made). Buys 100-125 mss/year. Query with published clips. Length: 1,000-10,000 words. Sometimes pays the expenses of writers on assignment.

Photos: State availability of photos with query letter or ms.

Tips: "Study the magazine to see the kinds of stories we publish. Develop original story suggestions; develop access to film industry personnel; submit reviews that show a perceptive point of view."

COUNTRY AMERICA, Meredith Publishing Corporation, 1716 Locust, Des Moines IA 50309-3023. (515)284-2910. Fax: (515)284-3035. Editor: Danita Allen. Managing Editor: Bill Eftink. Magazine published 10 times/year covering country entertainment/lifestyle. Estab. 1989. Circ. 1,000,000. **Pays on acceptance.** Byline given. Buys all rights (lifetime). Submit seasonal/holiday material 8 months in advance. Accepts previously published submissions, if notified. Reports in 3 months. Free writer's guidelines.

Nonfiction: Garden/food, general interest, historical/nostalgic, how-to (home improvement), interview/profile (country music entertainers), photo feature, travel. Special issues: Christmas, travel, wildlife/conservation, country music. Buys 130 mss/year. Query. Pays $100-1,000 for assigned articles. Sometimes pays expenses of writers on assignment.

Photos: State availability of photos with submission. Reviews contact sheets, negatives, 35mm transparencies. Offers $50-500/photo. Captions and identification of subjects required. Buys all rights.

Fillers: Short humor. Country curiosities that deal with animals, people, crafts, etc.

Tips: "Think visually. Our publication will be light on text and heavy on photos. Be general; this is a general interest publication meant to be read by every member of the family. We are a service-oriented publication; please stress how-to sidebars and include addresses and phone numbers to help readers find out more."

DANCE CONNECTION, 815 First St. SW, #603, Calgary, Alberta T2P 1N3 Canada. Phone/fax: (403)237-7327. Editor: Heather Elton. 75% freelance written. Magazine published 5 times/year devoted to dance with a broad editorial scope reflecting a deep commitment to a view of dance that embraces its diversity of style and function. Articles have ranged in subject matter from the role of dance in Plains Indian culture, to an inquest into the death of Giselle, to postmodern dance. Estab. 1983. Circ. 5,000. Pays on publication. Byline given. Buys first rights or second serial (reprint) rights. Submit seasonal material 3 months in advance. Accepts simultaneous and previously published submissions. Send tearsheet or photocopy of article and information about when and where the article previously appeared. For reprints, pays 50% of the amount paid for an original article. Query for electronic submissions. Reports in 3 months. Sample copy for 9 × 12 SAE with 3 IRCs.

Nonfiction: A variety of writing styles including criticism, essay, exposé, general interest, historical/nostalgic, humor, opinion, interview, performance review, forum debate, literature and photo feature. Query with published clips or send complete ms. Length 800-2,500 words. Pays $5-250.

Fiction: Literature and poetry relating to dance. No poems about ballet. Publishes novel excerpts.

Columns/Departments: Performance Reviews, Book Reviews, Dance News, Calendar.

DANCE MAGAZINE, 33 W. 60th St., New York NY 10023. (212)245-9050. Fax: (212)956-6487. Editor-in-Chief: Richard Philp. 25% freelance written. Monthly magazine covering dance. Estab. 1927. Circ. 51,000. Pays on publication. Byline given. Offers up to $150 kill fee (varies). Makes work-for-hire assignments. Submit seasonal/holiday material 4 months in advance. Reports in "weeks." Sample copy and writer's guidelines for 9 × 12 SASE.

Nonfiction: Interview/profile. Buys 50 mss/year. Query with published clips or send complete ms. Length: 300-2,000 words. Pays $15-350. Sometimes pays expenses of writers on assignment.

Photos: State availability of photos with submission. Reviews transparencies and prints. Offers $25-285/photo. Captions and identification of subjects required. Buys one-time rights.

Columns/Departments: Presstime News (topical, short articles on current dance world events), 75-400 words. Buys 40 mss/year. Query with published clips. Pays $20-75. Teacher Talk (professional aspects of teaching dance to various categories of students); Jobs (where they are, how much they pay, what's expected); Personal You (multi-faceted coverage of issues of interest to professional dancers).

Tips: Writers must have "thorough knowledge of dance and take a sophisticated approach."

DRAMATICS MAGAZINE, Educational Theatre Association, 3368 Central Pkwy., Cincinnati OH 45225-2392. (513)559-1996. Editor-in-Chief: Donald Corathers. 70% freelance written. Works with small number of new/unpublished writers. For theater arts students, teachers and others interested in theater arts education. Magazine published monthly, September-May. Estab. 1929. Circ. 35,000. **Pays on acceptance.** Publishes ms an average of 3 months after acceptance. Buys first North American serial rights. Byline given. Submit seasonal/holiday material 3 months in advance. Accepts simultaneous and previously published submissions. Send tearsheet or photocopy of article or play, or typed ms with rights for sale noted and information about when and where the article previously appeared. Pays 50% of their fee for an original article. Query for electronic submissions. Reports in 3 months; may be longer on unsolicited mss. Sample copy for 9 × 12 SAE with 5 first-class stamps. Free writer's guidelines.

Nonfiction: How-to (technical theater, directing, acting, etc.), informational, interview, photo feature, humorous, profile, technical. Buys 30 mss/year. Submit complete ms. Length: 750-3,000 words. Pays $50-300. Rarely pays expenses of writers on assignment.

Photos: Purchased with accompanying ms. Uses b&w photos and transparencies. Query. Total purchase price for ms usually includes payment for photos.

Fiction: Drama (one-act and full-length plays). "No plays for children, Christmas plays or plays written with no attention paid to the conventions of theater." Prefers unpublished scripts that have been produced at least once. Buys 5-9 mss/year. Send complete ms. Pays $100-400.

Tips: "The best way to break in is to know our audience—drama students, teachers and others interested in theater—and to write for them. Writers who have some practical experience in theater, especially in technical areas, have a leg-up here, but we'll work with anybody who has a good idea. Some freelancers have become regular contributors. Others ignore style suggestions included in our writer's guidelines."

EAST END LIGHTS, The Quarterly Magazine for Elton John Fans ,Voice Communications Corp., P.O. Box 760, New Baltimore MI 48047. (810)949-7900. Fax: (810)949-2217. Editor: Tom Stanton. 70% freelance written. Quarterly magazine covering British rock star Elton John. "In one way or another, a story must relate to Elton John, his activities or associates (past and present). We appeal to discriminating Elton fans. No gushing fanzine material. No current concert reviews." Estab. 1990. Circ. 1,400. Pays 3 weeks after publication. Publishes ms an average of 2-3 months after acceptance. Byline given. Offers 100% kill fee. Buys first rights and second serial (reprint) rights. Submit seasonal material 2-3 months in advance. Accepts previously published submissions. Send information about when and where the article previously appeared. For reprints, pays 50% of the amount paid for an original article. Reports in 2 months. Sample copy for $2.

Nonfiction: Book excerpts, essays, exposé, general interest, historical/nostalgic, humor and interview/profile. Buys 20 mss/year. Query with or without published clips or send complete ms. Length: 400-1,000 words.

Pays $50-200 for assigned articles; $40-150 for unsolicited articles. Pays with contributor copies only if the writer requests. Sometimes pays the expenses of writers on assignment.

Photos: State availability of photos with submission. Reviews negatives and 5×7 prints. Offers $40-75/ photo. Identification of subjects required. Buys one-time rights and all rights.

Columns/Departments: Clippings (non-wire references to Elton John in other publications), maximum 200 words. Buys 12 mss/year. Send complete ms. Length: 50-200 words. Pays $10-20.

Tips: "Approach with a well-thought-out story idea. We'll provide direction. All areas equally open. We prefer interviews with Elton-related personalities—past or present. We are particularly interested in music/ memorabilia collecting of Elton material."

EMMY MAGAZINE, Academy of Television Arts & Sciences, 5220 Lankershim Blvd., North Hollywood CA 91601-3109. (818)754-2800. Fax: (818)761-2827. Editor/Publisher: Hank Rieger. Managing Editor: Gail Polevoi. 100% freelance written. Prefers to work with published established writers. Bimonthly magazine on television for TV professionals and enthusiasts. Circ. 12,000. Pays on publication or within 6 months. Publishes ms an average of 4 months after acceptance. Byline given. Offers 25% kill fee. Buys first North American serial rights. Reports in 1 month. Sample copy for 9×12 SAE with 6 first-class stamps.

Nonfiction: Articles on issues, trends, and VIPs (especially those behind the scenes) in broadcast and cable TV; programming; new technology; and important international developments. "We require TV industry expertise and clear, lively writing." Length: 2,000 words. Pay $750-950. Pays some expenses of writers on assignment.

Columns/Departments: Most written by regulars, but newcomers can break into CloseUps, Viewpoint or Innerviews. Length: 500-1,500 words, depending on department. Pays $250-600.

Tips: Study publication; query in writing with published clips. No fanzine or academic approaches, please.

‡EROTIC X-FILM GUIDE, Eton Publishing, P.O. Box 388, Hollywood CA 90078. Editorial Director: Marc Medoff. 25% freelance written. Monthly magazine covering erotic entertainment. "We cover all aspects of the adult entertainment/sex industry." Estab. 1984. Circ. 150,000. **Pays on acceptance.** Publishes ms an average of 3 months after acceptance. Byline given. Offers 25% kill fee. Buys first North American serial rights. Editorial lead time 3 months. Submit seasonal material 3 months in advance. Accepts simultaneous and previously published submissions. Reports in 1 month on queries; 2 months on mss. Sample copy and writer's guidelines for 10×13 SAE with $3.90 in postage.

Nonfiction: Book excerpts, essays, exposé, general interest, historical/nostalgic, how-to, humor, interview/ profile, new product, personal experience, photo feature, travel. Buys 6 mss/year. Query with published clips. Length: 500-4,000 words. Pays $50-750. Sometimes pays expenses of writers on assignment.

Photos: Send photos with submission. Reviews transparencies, prints. Negotiates payment individually. Captions, model releases, identification of subjects required. Buys one-time rights.

Columns/Departments: Video Reviews (porn films), 50-300 words; Q&A (porn stars), 300 words. Buys 6 mss/year. Query with published clips. Pays $50-750.

Fiction: Adventure, confession, erotica, fantasy, horror, humorous, romance, science fiction, suspense. Buys 6 mss/year. Query with published clips. Length: 250-3,000 words. Pays $100-600.

FILM COMMENT, Film Society of Lincoln Center, 70 Lincoln Center Plaza, New York NY 10023. (212)875-5610. Fax: (212)875-5636. Editor: Richard T. Jameson. 100% freelance written. Bimonthly magazine covering film criticism and film history. "*FC* publishes authoritative, personal writing (not journalism) reflecting experience of and involvement with film as an art form." Estab. 1962. Circ. 30,000. Pays on publication. Publishes ms an average of 2 months after acceptance. Byline given. Offers 50% kill fee (assigned articles only). Editorial lead time 1½ months. Accepts simultaneous submissions. Rarely accepts previously published submissions. Send typed ms with information about when and where the article previously appeared. For reprints, pays 50% of the amount paid for an original article. Query for electronic submissions. Reports in 2 weeks on queries. Writer's guidelines free on request.

Nonfiction: Essays, historical/nostalgic, interview/profile, opinion, personal experience. Buys 100 mss/year. Send complete ms. "We respond to queries, but rarely *assign* a writer we don't know." Length: 800-8,000 words. "We don't use a separate pay scale for solicited or unsolicited. There is no fixed rate, but roughly based on 3 words/$1."

Photos: State availability of photos with submission. Offers no additional payment for photos accepted with ms. Buys one-time rights.

Columns/Departments: Life With Video (impact of video on availability and experience of films; video as new imaginative dimension), 1,000-2,000 words. Pays $250 and up.

Tips: "Demonstrate ability and inclination to write *FC*-worthy articles. We read and consider everything we get, and we do print unknowns and first-timers. Probably the writer with a shorter submission (1,000-2,000 words) has a better chance than with an epic article that would fill half the issue."

‡HOME THEATER, The Ultimate Audio/Video Experience, Triple D Publishing, 1300 S. DeKalb St., Shelby NC 28152. Fax: (704)484-8558. E-mail: HomTheater@aol.com. Editor: David B. Melton. Monthly magazine covering home theater and entertainment. "Articles must be entertaining and informative as well as dirrectly related to home theater. *Home Theater* is a consumer publication to help readers understand and use home theater products." Estab. 1993. Circ. 60,000. Pays on publication. Publishes ms an average of 3-4 months after acceptance. Byline given. Offers 30% kill fee. Buys first North American serial rights. Editorial lead time 3 months. Submit seasonal material 4 months in advance. Query for electronic submissions. Reports in 1 month on queries; 2 months on mss. Sample copy and writer's guidelines free on request.

Nonfiction: General interest, historical/nostalgic, how-to, interview/profile, new product, photo feature, technical. Buys 80 mss/year. Query. Length: 1,200-2,000 words. Pays $150-450 for assigned articles; $50-250 for unsolicited articles. Pays expenses of writers on assignment.

Photos: Send photos with submission. Reviews 4×5 transparencies, 8×10 prints. Negotiates payment individually. Captions, model releases, identification of subjects required. Buys one-time rights.

Columns/Departments: Letters (Q & A), 150-400 words. Pays $50-200.

Tips: "A knowledgeable home theater or audio/video enthusiast with published writing already has a leg up."

KPBS ON AIR MAGAZINE, San Diego's Guide to Public Broadcasting, KPBS-TV/FM, 5200 Campanile Dr., San Diego CA 92182-5400. Mailing address: KPBS Radio/TV, San Diego CA 92182-5400. (619)594-3766. Fax: (619)265-6417. Editor: Michael Good. 15% freelance written. Monthly magazine on public broadcasting programming and San Diego arts. "Our readers are very intelligent, sophisticated and rather mature. Your writing should be, too." Estab. 1970. Circ. 63,000. Pays on publication. Publishes ms an average of 1 month after acceptance. Byline given. Pays 50% kill fee. Not copyrighted. Buys first North American serial rights. Submit seasonal/holiday material 3 months in advance. Accepts previously published submissions. Send tearsheet of article with rights for sale noted and information about when and where the article previously appeared. For reprints pays 25¢/word. Query for electronic submissions. Reports in 3 months. Sample copy for 9×12 SAE with 4 first-class stamps.

Nonfiction: Interview/profile of PBS personalities and/or artists performing in San Diego, opinion, profiles of public TV and radio personalities, backgrounds on upcoming programs. Nothing over 1,500 words. Buys 60 mss/year. Query with published clips. Length: 300-1,500 words. Pays 20¢/word; 25¢/word if the article is received via modem or computer disk. Sometimes pays expenses of writers on assignment.

Photos: State availability of photos with submission. Reviews transparencies and 5×7 prints. Offers $30-300/photo. Identification of subjects required. Buys one-time rights.

Columns/Departments: On the Town (upcoming arts events in San Diego), 800 words; Short Takes (backgrounds on public TV shows), 500 words; Radio Notes (backgrounders on public radio shows), 500 words. Buys 35 mss/year. Query or query with published clips. Length: 300-800 words. Pays 20¢/word; 25¢/word if the article is received via modem or computer disk.

Tips: "Feature stories for national writers are most open to freelancers. Arts stories for San Diego writers are most open. Read the magazine, then talk to me."

MOVIE MARKETPLACE, World Publishing, 990 Grove St., Evanston IL 60201. (708)491-6440. Editor: Robert Meyers. 90% freelance written. Bimonthly magazine featuring video and movie subjects. Estab. 1987. Circ. 100,000. **Pays on acceptance.** Byline given. Offers $75 kill fee. Buys first North American serial rights. Submit seasonal/holiday material 6 months in advance. Accepts simultaneous and previously published submissions. Reports in 3 weeks. Sample copy for $2.50 and 9×11 SASE.

Nonfiction: Interview/profile, movie-video topics. Query with published clips. Length: 350-500 words. Pays $150 for assigned articles.

Photos: State availability of or send photos (b&w only) with submission. Reviews contact sheets. Offers no additional payment for photos accepted with ms. Identification of subjects required. Buys first North American serial rights only.

NEW YORK/LONG ISLAND UPDATE, 990 Motor Pkwy., Central Islip NY 11722. (516)435-8890. Fax: (516)435-8925. Editor: Cheryl Ann Meglio. Managing Editor: Allison A. Whitney. 60% freelance written. Monthly magazine covering "regional entertainment interests as well as national interests." Estab. 1980. Circ. 60,000. Pays on publication. Publishes ms an average of 4 months after acceptance. Byline given. Buys all rights. Submit seasonal/holiday material 4 months in advance. Accepts previously published submissions. Send photocopy of article or short story and information about when and where the article previously appeared. Query for electronic submissions. Reports in 5 weeks on queries. Free sample copy and writer's guidelines.

Nonfiction: General interest, humor, interview/profile, new product, travel. Buys 60 mss/year. Query with published clips. Length: 250-1,500 words. Pays $25-125.

Columns/Departments: Nightcap (humor piece), 700 words. Query with published clips. Pays $50.

Fiction: Humorous. Buys 8 mss/year. Length: 700 maximum words. Pays $50 maximum.

PALMER VIDEO MAGAZINE, 1767 Morris Ave., Union NJ 07083. (908)686-3030. Fax: (908)686-2151. Editor: Susan Baar. 15% freelance written. Monthly magazine covering video and film related topics. "The *Palmer Video Magazine* is a 32-page magazine designed exclusively for Palmer Video members. It is both entertaining and informative as it pertains to film and video." Estab. 1983. Circ. 200,000. Pays 30 days after receipt of article. Publishes ms 1 month after acceptance. Makes work-for-hire assignments. Submit seasonal/holiday material 2 months in advance. Accepts simultaneous and previously published submissions. Send typed ms with rights for sale noted and information about when and where the article previously appeared. Reports in 2 months. Free sample copy and writer's guidelines.

Nonfiction: How-to (video related), interview/profile (film related), technical (video related). Buys 40 mss/year. Query with published clips. Length: 500-2,000 words. Pays $50-200 for assigned articles.

Photos: State availability of photos with submission. Offers no additional payment for photos accepted with ms.

Columns/Departments: Profile (interviews of profiles on actors/directors, etc.), 1,000 words; Cinemascope (article pertaining to film genre), 1,000-2,000 words. Buys 40 mss/year. Query with published clips. Pays $50-200.

PEOPLE MAGAZINE, Time-Warner, Inc., Time & Life Bldg., Rockefeller Center, New York NY 10020. Contact: Mary Reilly. Weekly publication covering popular culture for a general audience. Query. "Know the magazine well before submitting."

THE PLAY MACHINE, P.O. Box 330507, Houston TX 77233-0507. Editor: Norman Clark Stewart Jr. 90% freelance written. Quarterly tabloid of recreation/adult play. Estab. 1990. Circ. 1,000. Pays on publication. Byline given. Buys first North American, one-time or second serial (reprint) rights. Submit seasonal/holiday material 8 months in advance. Accepts simultaneous and previously published submissions. Reports in 8 months on mss. Sample copy for 9×12 SAE with 4 first-class stamps. Writer's guidelines for #10 SAE with 2 first-class stamps.

Nonfiction: How-to (play or have fun), humor (not satire—playful), interview/profile (with pranksters/jokers or genius in relation to fun), new product (recreational/hobby, etc.). Nothing that is not fun, playful or related to recreation—nothing serious. Buys 20-100 mss/year. Send complete ms. Length: 3,500 words maximum. Pays $50 maximum for unsolicited articles.

Photos: Send photos with submission. Offers no additional payment for photos accepted with ms. Model releases and identification of subjects required. Buys one-time rights.

Fillers: Anecdotes, facts, gags to be illustrated by cartoonist, short humor. Buys 200/year. Pays $5 maximum.

Tips: "Have fun writing the submissions."

PLAY MAGAZINE, Milor Entertainment Group, 3620 NW 43rd St., Gainesville FL 32606. (904)375-3705. Editor: Bill Stevenson. Editorial Consultant: Roy Parkhurst. 100% freelance written. Bimonthly consumer magazine covering educational entertainment products. "Interactive entertainment-oriented products. Geared towards parents. Cover music, video, software, travel, medical, toys." Estab. 1992. Circ. 120,000. Pays on publication. Byline given. Offers 50% kill fee. Buys first North American serial rights. Editorial lead time 6 months. Submit seasonal material 3 months in advance. Accepts simultaneous submissions. Query for electronic submissions. Reports in 2 months. Sample copy for 11×14 SAE with 10 first-class stamps. Writer's guidelines free on request.

Nonfiction: General interest, how-to (creative learning projects), interview/profile, new product (big one), technical, travel, medical (M.D.'s). "Virtually all freelance" material. Query with published clips. Length: 300-3,000 words. Pays 20¢/word. Sometimes pays expenses of writers on assignment.

Photos: Send photos with submission. Negotiates payment individually.

Columns/Departments: Play ground (review of new products), 100-300 words; Toys (seasonal), 1,000-2,000 words; Computers, music, video, 1,000-2,000 words. Buys 50 mss/year. Query with published clips. Pays 20-30¢/word.

Tips: "Query with clips. Edutainment is a relatively new concept. Find an interesting angle."

‡RIGHT ON!, Sterling's Magazines, 233 Park Ave. S., New York NY 10003. (212)780-3519. Editor: Cynthia Horner. 10% freelance written. Monthly black entertainment magazine for teenagers and young adults. Circ. 250,000. Pays on publication. Publishes ms an average of 3 months after acceptance. Byline given. Buys all rights. Submit seasonal/holiday material 4 months in advance. Reports in 1 month on queries.

Nonfiction: Interview/profile. "We only publish entertainment-oriented stories or celebrity interviews." Buys 15-20 mss/year. Query with or without published clips, or send ms. Length: 500-4,000 words. Pays $50-200. Sometimes pays the expenses of writers on assignment.

Photos: State availability of photos with submission. Reviews transparencies and 8×10 b&w prints. Offers no additional payment for photos accepted with ms. Identification of subjects required. Buys one-time rights or all rights.

‡ROLE MODEL MAGAZINE, P.O. Box 895, Lake Arrowhead CA 92352. (909)337-0759. Editor: Christine Coté. 30% freelance written. Quarterly magazine covering a Christian perspective on the fashion and entertainment and media/industries. Estab. 1994. Pays on publication. Publishes ms an average of 3 months after acceptance. Byline given. Buys all rights or makes work-for-hire assignments. Editorial lead time 3 months. Submit seasonal material 3 months in advance. Accepts previously published submissions. Reports in 1 month on queries. Sample copy for $3.75. Writer's guidelines for #10 SASE.

Nonfiction: Book excerpts, general interest, how-to, inspirational, interview/profile, opinion, personal experience, photo feature, religious, travel (relating to fashion industry only). Buys 25 mss/year. Query with published clips. Length: 300-2,500 words. Pays $50-150 for assigned articles; $25-100 for unsolicited articles.

Photos: Send photos with submission. Reviews contact sheets, transparencies, prints. Captions, identification of subjects required. Buys one-time rights.

Columns/Departments: Modeling, Entertainment, Music, Sports, Ministry, Career Spotlights, (spotlights are profiles of professionals, testimonies, inspirational interviews), 800-1,250 words. Buys 10-15 mss/year. Query with published clips. Pays $50-150.

Poetry: Free verse, traditional. Buys 4-6 poems/year. Pays $15-25.

Fillers: Anecdotes, facts, gags to be illustrated by cartoonist, newsbreaks, short humor. Buys 8/year. Length: 250 words maximum. Pays $15-25.

Tips: "Query first and tell us about yourself and why you're interested in writing for *Role Model Magazine*. Give us your phone number. If we're interested in working with you we'll call you and give you detailed information on exactly what we want in an article."

‡SCI-FI ENTERTAINMENT, Sovereign Media, 457 Carlisle Dr., Herndon VA 22070. (703)471-1556. E-mail: flixman@dorsai.org. Editor: Ed Flixman. Contact: Bob Martin, managing editor. 100% freelance written. Bimonthly magazine covering science fiction movies—old, new, upcoming fantasy. Estab. 1994. Circ. 46,500. Pays 30 days after acceptance. Publishes ms an average of 1 month after acceptance. Byline given. Offers 10% kill fee. Buys first world rights. Editorial lead time 1 month. Submit seasonal material 1 month in advance. Accepts simultaneous and previously published submissions. Query for electronic submissions. Reports in 2 weeks on queries; 1 month on mss. Sample copy for $4.95. Writer's guidelines for #10 SASE.

Nonfiction: General interest, historical/nostalgic, interview/profile, new product (games), opinion, personal experience. photo feature. Buys 54 mss/year. Query. Length: 2,300 words. Pays $100-400. Sometimes pays expenses of writers on assignment.

Photos: State availability of photos with submissions. Offers no additional payment for photos accepted with ms. Identification of subjects required. Buys one-time rights.

Columns/Departments: Infinite Channels (games), 2,300 words; Video (video reviews), 2,400 words; Books (books on movies), 2,500 words. Buys 6 mss/year. Query with published clips.

Tips: Query to Bob Martin via e-mail.

SOAP OPERA DIGEST, K-III Magazines, 45 W. 25 St., New York NY 10010. Editors: Lynn Leahey. Managing Editors: Jason Bonderoff, Roberta Caploe. 5% freelance written. Bimonthly magazine covering soap operas. "Extensive knowledge of daytime and prime time soap operas is required." Estab. 1975. Circ. 1,400,000. **Pays on acceptance.** Publishes ms an average of 3 months after acceptance. Byline given. Offers 30% kill fee. Buys first North American serial and second serial (reprint) rights. Submit seasonal/holiday material 4 months in advance. Reports in 1 month.

Nonfiction: Interview/profile. No essays. Buys 10 mss/year. Query with published clips. Length: 1,000-2,000 words. Pays $250-500 for assigned articles; $150-250 for unsolicited articles. Pays meal expenses of writers on assignment.

Photos: Offers no additional payment for photos accepted with ms. Buys all rights.

SOUND & IMAGE, Hachette Filipacchi Magazines, Inc., 1633 Broadway, 45th Floor, New York NY 10019. (212)767-6020. Fax: (212)767-5615. E-mail: soundimg@aol.com. Editor: Bill Wolfe. 80% freelance written. Quarterly magazine covering home entertainment and electronics. "*Sound & Image* reports on how average Americans can get the most entertainment value from home electronics systems, as well as emerging technologies, software, and lifestyle/cultural issues related to technology and media, audio, video, computers, etc." Estab. 1990. Circ. 50,000. **Pays on acceptance.** Publishes ms an average of 2 months after acceptance. Byline given. Offers 50% kill fee. Buys first North American serial rights. Editorial lead time 3 months. Submit seasonal material 3 months in advance. Accepts simultaneous submissions. Query for electronic submissions.

• *Sound & Image* has increased its publishing frequency to bimonthly and now requires electronic rights.

Nonfiction: Exposé (bad business deals, misuse of technology, etc.); how-to (buy and use electronic home-entertainment systems); humor (brief satires of TV, movies, etc.); interview/profiles (media/technology movers); new product (audio, video, computer, gadgets); opinion (technology and media's effect on society); technical (reviews of equipment, new technology). Buys 80 mss/year. Query with published clips. Length: 1,200-4,000 words. Pays $500-2,000. Sometimes pays expenses of writers on assignment.

Photos: State availability of photos at time of query. Reviews 4×5 transparencies. Negotiates payment individually. Model releases, identification of subjects required. Buys one-time rights.

Columns/Departments: Technology (new trends in home entertainment (5 per issue), 500-1,500 words; Preview (advance info on groundbreaking development), 200-300 words; Last Call (personal slant on elec. home ent, media, technology), 750 words. Buys 40 mss/year. Query with published clips. Pays $300-1,000.

Fiction: Fantasy (futurist science fiction); science fiction (how our lives/world will change as technology matures); slice-of-life vignettes (relating to electronic home entertainment). Will consider queries. Query with published clips. Length: 750-3,000 words. Pays $300-3,000.

Fillers: Facts, newsbreaks, celebrity blurbs. Buys 50/year. Length: 50-200 words. Pays $25-200.

Tips: "Discuss your subject from a position of expertise and write with a hip, pointed style. Queries should include a linear outline that demonstrates that the story will have a beginning, middle, and end. An ability to get quotes from appropriate luminaries is a big plus."

TDR; The Drama Review: The Journal of Performance Studies, New York University, 721 Broadway, 6th Floor, New York NY 10003. (212)998-1626. Managing Editor: Annemarie Bean. Editor: Richard Schechner. 95% freelance written. Works with a small number of new/unpublished writers each year. Quarterly magazine with "emphasis only on theater but also dance, ritual, musical performance, mime, and other facets of performative behavior. For avant-garde community, students and professors of anthropology, performance studies and related fields. Political material is welcome." Estab. 1954. Circ. 7,000. Pays on publication. Submit material 6 months in advance. Accepts previously published submissions (if published in another language). Reports in 3 months. Publishes ms an average of 6 months after acceptance. Sample copy for $10 (from MIT Press). Free writer's guidelines.

Nonfiction: Mariellen R. Sandford, associate editor. Buys 10 mss/issue. Query by letter only. Pay determined by page count. Submit both hard copy and disk (Word or WordPerfect).

Photos: State availability of photos and artwork with submission. Prefers 5×7 b&w photos. Captions required.

Tips: "*TDR* is a place where contrasting ideas and opinions meet. A forum for writing about performances and the social, economic and political contexts in which performances happen. The editors want interdisciplinary, intercultural, multivocal, eclectic submissions."

THEATREFORUM, International Theatre Journal, UCSD Department of Theatre, 9500 Gilman Dr., La Jolla CA 92093. (619)534-6598. Fax: (619)534-1080. E-mail: jcarmody@ucsd.edu. Editor: Jim Carmody. 75% freelance written. Semiannual magazine covering performance, theatrical and otherwise. "*TheatreForum* is an international journal of theater and performance art and dance theater and music theater and forms yet to be devised. We publish performance texts, interviews with artists on their creative process, and articles about innovative productions and groups. Written by and for members of both the academic and artistic community, we represent a wide variety of aesthetic and cultural interests." Estab. 1992. Circ. 2,000. Pays on publication. Byline given. Buys one-time rights or anthology rights for scripts. Editorial lead time 4 months. Query for electronic submissions. Reports in 1 month on queries; 2 months on mss. Sample copy for $5. Writer's guidelines for #10 SASE.

Nonfiction: Essays, interview/profile, photo feature, performance criticism. Buys 10-12 mss/year. Query with published clips. Length: 1,000-5,000 words. Pays 5¢/word.

Photos: State availability of photos with submission. Negotiates payment individually. Identification of subjects required. Buys one-time rights.

Fiction: Previously published plays are not considered. Buys 4-6 mss/year. Query with published clips. Pays $200 for fiction.

Tips: "We are interested in documenting, discussing, and disseminating innovative and provocative theater-works. Non-traditional and inventive texts (plays) are welcome. We also publish in-depth analyses of innovative theatrical productions. We are interested in finding artists who want to write about other artists."

TV GUIDE, 1211 Avenue of the Americas, New York NY 10036. Editor (National Section): Barry Golson. Managing Editor: Jack Curry. 50% freelance written. Prefers to work with published/established writers but works with a small number of new/unpublished writers each year. Weekly. Circ. 14 million. Publishes ms an average of 1 month after acceptance.

Nonfiction: Wants offbeat articles about TV people and shows. This magazine is not interested in fan material. Also wants stories on the newest trends of television, but they must be written in clear, lively English. Study publication. Length: 1,000-2,000 words.

Photos: Uses professional high-quality photos, normally shot on assignment by photographers chosen by *TV Guide*. Prefers color. Pays $350 day rate against page rates—$450 for 2 pages or less.

VIDEO, Hachette Filipacchi, 1633 Broadway, New York NY 10019. (212)767-6000. Fax: (212)767-5615. Editor-in-Chief: Bill Wolfe. 50% freelance written. Prefers to work with published/established writers; works with a small number of new/unpublished writers each year. Monthly magazine covering home video equipment, technology, CD-ROM, laser discs and prerecorded tapes. Circ. 350,000. **Pays on acceptance.** Publishes ms an average of 3 months after acceptance. Byline given. Buys first North American serial rights. Query for electronic submissions. Reports in 3 weeks on queries; 1 month on mss.

Nonfiction: Buys 50 mss/year. Query with published clips. Pays $300-1,000. Sometimes pays the expenses of writers on assignment.

Tips: "The entire feature area is open to freelancers. Write a brilliant query and send samples of published articles."

Ethnic/Minority

Ideas and concerns of interest to specific nationalities and religions are covered by publications in this category. General interest lifestyle magazines for these groups are also included. Many ethnic publications are locally-oriented or highly specialized and do not wish to be listed in a national publication such as *Writer's Market*. Query the editor of an ethnic publication with which you're familiar before submitting a manuscript, but do not consider these markets closed because they are not listed in this section. Additional markets for writing with an ethnic orientation are located in the following sections: Career, College and Alumni; Juvenile; Men's; Women's; and Teen and Young Adult.

AIM MAGAZINE, AIM Publishing Company, 7308 S. Eberhart Ave., Chicago IL 60620-0554. (312)874-6184. Editor: Ruth Apilado. Managing Editor: Dr. Myron Apilado. Estab. 1975. 75% freelance written. Works with a small number of new/unpublished writers each year. Quarterly magazine on social betterment that promotes racial harmony and peace for high school, college and general audience. Circ. 10,000. Pays on publication. Publishes ms an average of 3 months after acceptance. Offers 60% kill fee. Not copyrighted. Buys one-time rights. Submit seasonal/holiday material 6 months in advance. Accepts simultaneous submissions. Reports in 2 months on queries. Sample copy and writer's guidelines for $4 and 9×12 SAE with $1.31 postage.

Nonfiction: Exposé (education); general interest (social significance); historical/nostalgic (Black or Indian); how-to (create a more equitable society); profile (one who is making social contributions to community); book reviews and reviews of plays "that reflect our ethnic/minority orientation." No religious material. Buys 16 mss/year. Send complete ms. Length: 500-800 words. Pays $25-35.

Photos: Reviews b&w prints. Captions, identification of subjects required.

Fiction: Ethnic, historical, mainstream, suspense. "Fiction that teaches the brotherhood of man." Buys 20 mss/year. Send complete ms. Length: 1,000-1,500 words. Pays $25-35.

Poetry: Avant-garde, free verse, light verse. No "preachy" poetry. Buys 20 poems/year. Submit maximum 5 poems. Length: 15-30 lines. Pays $3-5.

Fillers: Jokes, anecdotes, newsbreaks. Buys 30/year. Length: 50-100 words. Pays $5.

Tips: "Interview anyone of any age who unselfishly is making an unusual contribution to the lives of less fortunate individuals. Include photo and background of person. We look at the nations of the world as part of one family. Short stories and historical pieces about Blacks and Indians are the areas most open to freelancers. Subject matter of submission is of paramount concern for us rather than writing style. Articles and stories showing the similarity in the lives of people with different racial backgrounds are desired."

‡ALBERTA SWEETGRASS, Aboriginal Multi-Media Society of Alberta, 15001 112th Ave., Edmonton, Alberta T5M 2V6 Canada. (403)455-2700. Contact: R. John Hayes, assistant editor. Monthly tabloid newspaper. Pays 10th of month following publication. Editorial lead time 1-2 months. Sample copy free. Writer's guidelines and production schedule for #10 SASE.

Nonfiction: Features, profiles, community-based stories, all with an Alberta angle (no exceptions). Usually runs 2-3 focus sections/month. Query with SASE. Length: 200-1,000 words (most often 500-800 words). Pays $3/published inch for one-source stories; $3.60 for multiple sources (reduced rate for excess editorial work). Pays expenses of writers by prior arrangement.

Photos: Reviews color or b&w prints or negatives. Offers $15/photo used; $50/cover photo.

‡AMERICAN JEWISH WORLD, AJW Publishing Inc., 4509 Minnetonka Blvd., Minneapolis MN 55416. (612)920-7000. Managing Editor: Marshall Hoffman. 1-5% freelance written. Weekly Jewish newspaper covering local, national and international stories. Estab. 1912. Circ. 6,500. Pays on publication. Publishes ms an average of 1-4 months after acceptance. Byline given. Publication copyrighted. Makes work-for-hire assignments. Submit seasonal/holiday material 3 months in advance. Query. No unsolicited mss. Accepts previously published and simultaneous submissions. Send typed ms with rights for sale noted. Accepts simultaneous submissions. Free sample copy and writer's guidelines.

For explanation of symbols, see the Key to Symbols and Abbreviations. For unfamiliar words, see the Glossary.

• *American Jewish World* is focusing move on Midwest and Minnesota angles.

Nonfiction: Essays, expose, general interest, historical/nostalgic, humor, inspirational, interview/profile, opinion, personal experience, photo feature, religious, travel. Buys 12-15 mss/year. Query with or without published clips. Length: 750 words maximum. Pays $10-75. Sometimes pays expenses of writers on assignment.

Fiction: Publishes novel excerpts.

Photos: State availability of photos with submission. Reviews prints. Pays $5/photo. Identification of subjects required. Buys one-time rights.

AMERICAN VISIONS, The Magazine of Afro-American Culture, 2101 S. Street, Washington DC 20008. (202)462-1779. E-mail: 72662.2631@compuserve.com. or Amvisions@ix.netcom.com. Managing Editor: Joanne Harris. 75% freelance written. Bimonthly magazine on African-American art, culture and history. "Editorial is reportorial, current, objective, 'pop-scholarly'. Audience is ages 25-54, mostly black, college educated." Estab. 1986. Circ. 125,000. Pays 30 days after publication. Publishes ms an average of 2 months after acceptance. Byline given. Offers 25% kill fee. Buys first North American, one-time and second serial (reprint) rights. Submit seasonal/holiday material 5 months in advance. Accepts simultaneous and previously published submissions. Query for electronic submissions. Reports in 2-3 months. Free sample copy and writer's guidelines with SASE.

Nonfiction: Book excerpts, general interest, historical/nostalgic, interview/profile literature, photo feature, travel. Publishes travel supplements—domestic, Africa, Europe, Canada, Mexico. No fiction, poetry, personal experience or opinion. Buys about 60-70 mss/year. Query with or without published clips or send complete ms. Length: 500-2,500 words. Pays $100-600 for assigned articles; $100-400 for unsolicited articles. Sometimes pays expenses of writers on assignment.

Photos: State availability of photos with submission. Reviews contact sheets, 3 × 5 transparencies, and 3 × 5 or 8 × 10 prints. Offers $15 minimum. Identification of subjects required. Buys one-time rights.

Columns/Departments: Books, Cuisine, Film, Music, Profile, Geneology, Computer Technology, Travel, 750-1,750 words. Buys about 40 mss/year. Query or send complete ms. Pays $100-400.

Tips: "Little-known but terribly interesting information about black history and culture is desired. Aim at an upscale audience. Send ms with credentials." Looking for writers who are enthusiastic about their topics.

THE B'NAI B'RITH INTERNATIONAL, JEWISH MONTHLY, 1640 Rhode Island Ave. NW, Washington DC 20036. (202)857-6645. Editor: Jeff Rubin. 50% freelance written. Magazine published 8 times/year covering Jewish affairs. Estab. 1886. Circ. 185,000. **Pays on acceptance.** Publishes ms an average of 3 months after acceptance. Byline given. Kill fee depends on rate of payment. Buys first North American serial rights. Submit seasonal/holiday material 6 months in advance. Query for electronic submissions. Reports in 1 month. Sample copy for $2 and 9 × 13 SAE with 2 first-class stamps. Free writer's guidelines.

Nonfiction: Book excerpts, essay, exposé, general interest, historical, interview/profile, photo feature. Buys 20-30 mss/year. Query with published clips. Length: 750-3,000 words. Pays $50-750 for assigned articles; $50-500 for unsolicited articles. Sometimes pays expenses of writers on assignment.

Photos: State availability of photos with submission. Reviews contact sheets, 2 × 3 transparencies and prints. Payment depends on quality and type of photograph. Identification of subjects required. Buys one-time rights.

• No longer publishes fiction.

Tips: "Writers should submit clips with their queries. The best way to break in to the *Jewish Monthly* is to submit a range of good story ideas accompanied by clips. We aim to establish relationships with writers and we tend to be loyal. All sections are equally open."

CLASS, R.E. John-Sandy Ltd., 900 Broadway, 8th Floor, New York NY 10003. (212)677-3055. Executive Editor: Denolyn Carroll. 25% freelance written. Monthly "general interest publication geared toward Caribbean, Latin and African Americans between ages 18-49." Estab. 1979. Circ. 250,000. Pays 45 days after publication. Byline given. Buys first North American serial and second serial (reprint) rights. Submit seasonal/ holiday material 3 months in advance. Reports in 6 weeks. Sample copy for 9 × 12 SAE with 4 first-class stamps. Writer's guidelines for #10 SASE.

Nonfiction: Exposé, general interest, historical/nostalgic, interview/profile, religious, travel. Query with published clips. Length: 500-1,300 words. Pays 10¢/word maximum. Sometimes pays expenses of writers on assignment.

Photos: Send photos with submission. Offers no additional payment for photos accepted with ms. Captions, model releases and identification of subjects required. Buys all rights.

Columns/Departments: Length: 500-1,300 words. Pays 10¢/word maximum.

Poetry: Buys 10-20 poems/year. Submit maximum 5 poems. Pays $10 maximum.

CONGRESS MONTHLY, American Jewish Congress, 15 E. 84th St., New York NY 10028. (212)879-4500. Editor: Maier Deshell. 90% freelance written. Magazine published 6 times/year covering topics of concern to the American Jewish community representing a wide range of views. Distributed mainly to the members of the American Jewish Congress. "Readers are intellectual, Jewish, involved." Estab. 1933. Circ. 35,000. Pays on publication. Publishes ms an average of 3 months after acceptance. Byline given. Buys one-time rights. Submit seasonal/holiday material 2 months in advance. No previously published submissions. Reports in 2 months.

Nonfiction: General interest ("current topical issues geared toward our audience"). No technical material. Send complete ms. Length: 2,000 words maximum. Pays $100-150/article.

Photos: State availability of photos. Reviews b&w prints. "Photos are paid for with payment for ms."

Columns/Departments: Book, film, art and music reviews. Send complete ms. Length: 1,000 words maximum. Pays $100-150/article.

EBONY MAGAZINE, 820 S. Michigan Ave., Chicago IL 60605. (312)322-9200. Publisher: John H. Johnson. Executive Editor: Lerone Bennett, Jr. 10% freelance written. For Black readers of the US, Africa and the Caribbean. Monthly. Circ. 1.8 million. Buys first North American serial and all rights. Buys about 10 mss/ year. Pays on publication. Publishes ms an average of 3 months after acceptance. Submit seasonal material 2 months in advance. Query the Ebony Editorial Committee. Reports in 1 month.

Nonfiction: Achievement and human interest stories about, or of concern to, Black readers. Interviews, profiles, humor pieces. Length: 1,500 words maximum. "Study magazine and needs carefully. Perhaps one out of 50 submissions interests us. Most are totally irrelevant to our needs and are simply returned." Pays $200 minimum. Sometimes pays the expenses of writers on assignment.

Photos: Purchased with mss, and with captions only. Buys 8 × 10 glossy prints, color transparencies, 35mm color. Submit negatives and contact sheets when possible. Offers no additional payment for photos accepted with mss.

EXITO, A magazine for all Filipinos, News and Sun Sentinel Company, #212, 8323 NW 12th St., Miami FL 33126. (305)597-5000. Editor: Humberto Cruz. 30% freelance written. Weekly tabloid that covers topics of general interest. "We reach bilingual, bicultural Hispanics, ages 25-54." Estab. 1991. Circ. 80,000. Pays on publication. Byline given. Buys one-time and second serial (reprint) rights. Submit seasonal/holiday material 6 months in advance. Accepts simultaneous submissions. Query for electronic submissions. Reports in 1 month. *Writer's Market* recommends allowing 2 months for reply. Sample copy for 9 × 12 SAE with 6 first-class stamps.

Nonfiction: Humberto Cruz (general interest and travel), Magaly Rubiera (lifestyle, health). General interest, how-to, interview/profile, new product, religious, travel. Buys 200 mss/year. Query with or without published clips or send complete ms. Length: 1,700 words. Pays $75 and up for articles.

Photos: State availability of photos with submission. Reviews transparencies. Captions and identification of subjects required. Buys one-time rights.

Tips: *Exito* only accepts mss written in Spanish. "We are particularly interested in articles on travel."

‡FILIPINAS, A magazine for all Filipinos, Filipinas Publishing, Inc., 655 Sutter St., Suite 333, San Francisco CA 94102. (415)563-5878. Editor: Rene Ciria-Cruz. Monthly magazine focused on Filipino American affairs. "*Filipinas* answers the lack of mainstream media coverage of Filipinos in America. It targets both Filipino immigrants and American-born Filipinos, gives in-depth coverage of political, social, cultural events in The Philippines and in the Filipino American community. Features role models, history, travel, food and leisure, issues and controversies." Estab. 1992. Circ. 25,000. Pays on publication. Publishes ms an average of 3 months after acceptance. Byline given. Offers $10 kill fee. Buys first rights or all rights. Editorial lead time 2 months. Submit seasonal material 4 months in advance. Query for electronic submissions. Reports in 5 weeks on queries; 18 months on mss. Sample copy for $5. Writer's guidelines for 9½ × 4 SAE with 1 first-class stamp.

Nonfiction: Exposé, general interest, historical/nostalgic, how-to, humor, interview/profile, personal experience, travel. No academic papers. Buys 80-100 mss/year. Query with published clips. Length: 800-1,500 words. Pays $50-100. Sometimes pays writers other than cash payment "per specific agreement with writer."

Photos: State availability of photos with submission. Reviews 2¼ × 2¼ and 4 × 5 transparencies. Offers $15-35/photo. Captions and model releases required. Buys one-time rights.

Columns/Departments: Entree (reviews of Filipino restaurants), 1,200 words; Cultural Currents (Filipino traditions, beliefs), 1,500 words. Query with published clips. Pays $50-75.

HADASSAH MAGAZINE, 50 W. 58th St., New York NY 10019. Executive Editor: Alan M. Tigay. 90% freelance written. Works with small number of new/unpublished writers each year. Monthly (except combined issues June/July and August/September). Circ. 334,000. Buys first rights (with travel and family articles, buys all rights). Sample copy and writer's guidelines for SASE.

Nonfiction: Primarily concerned with Israel, Jewish communities around the world and American civic affairs as relates to the Jewish community. "We are also open to art stories that explore trends in Jewish art, literature, theater, etc. Will not assign/commission a story to a first-time writer for Hadassah." Buys 10 unsolicited mss/year. No phone queries. Send query and writing samples. Length: 1,500-2,000 words. Pays— minimum $350, $75 for reviews. Sometimes pays the expenses of writers on assignment.

Photos: "We buy photos only to illustrate articles, with the exception of outstanding color from Israel which we use on our covers. We pay $175 and up for a suitable cover photo." Offers $50 for first photo; $35 for each additional. "Always interested in striking cover (color) photos, especially of Israel and Jerusalem."

Columns/Departments: "We have a Family column and a Travel column, but a query for topic or destination should be submitted first to make sure the area is of interest and the story follows our format."

Fiction: Joan Michel. Short stories with strong plots and positive Jewish values. No personal memoirs, "schmaltzy" or women's magazine fiction. "We continue to buy very little fiction because of a backlog." Length: 3,000 words maximum. Pays $300 minimum. "Require proper size SASE."

Tips: "We are interested in reading articles that offer an American perspective on Jewish affairs (1,500 words). For example, a look at the presidential candidates from a Jewish perspective. Send query of topic first."

‡HARMONY MAGAZINE, Pratt Station, Box 050081, Brooklyn NY 11205-0001. Editor: Shirley Ademu-John. Contact: Eku Ademu-John. 80% freelance written. Quarterly magazine covering multicultural experience. "Encourages multicultural understanding and acceptance of differences, African studies, Caribbean and African-American experiences. Our audience has an interest in other cultures." Estab. 1982. Circ. 5,000. Pays on publication. Buys one-time rights. Editorial lead time 2 months. Submit seasonal material 4 months in advance. Accepts simlultaneous and previously published submissions. Reports in 3-4 weeks on queries; 1 month on mss. Sample copy and writer's guidelines free on request.

Nonfiction: Book excerpts, essays, general interest, inspirational, interview/profile, opinion, personal experience, photo feature, travel. Buys 4 mss/year. Query with published clips. Length: 750-1,500 words. Pays $30.

Photos: Send photos with submission. Reviews negatives. Offers no additional payment for photos accepted with ms. Captions required. Buys one-time rights.

Columns/Departments: Family Corner (parenting information in a multicultural society), 750 words; Forum (idea exchange, opinions), 750 words; Arts & Culture (African, Caribbean, African-American), 750 words. Buys 4 mss/year. Query with published clips. Pays $30-100.

Fiction: Adventure (travel), condensed novels, historical, novel excerpts. Buys 4 mss/year. Query with published clips. Length: 2,500-3,500 words. Pays $30-100.

Poetry: Free verse, Haiku, light verse, traditional. Buys 4 poems/year. Submit maximum 3 poems. Length: 15-20 lines. Pays $15-30.

Fillers: Anecdotes, facts, gags to be illustrated by cartoonist, newsbreaks, short humor. Buys 10/year. Length: open.

Tips: "All areas are open to freelancers. Writers should send in query with work sample."

HERITAGE FLORIDA JEWISH NEWS, P.O. Box 300742, Fern Park FL 32730-0742. (407)834-8787. Fax: (407)831-0507. Associate Editor: Chris Allen. Publisher/Editor: Jeffrey Gaeser. 20% freelance written. Weekly tabloid on Jewish subjects of local, national and international scope, except for special issues. "Covers news of local, national and international scope of interest to Jewish readers and not likely to be found in other publications." Estab. 1976. Circ. 3,500. Pays on publication. Publishes ms an average of 2 months after acceptance. Byline given. Buys first North American serial, first, one-time, second serial (reprint) or simultaneous rights. Submit seasonal/holiday material 3 months in advance. Accepts previously published submissions. Send typed ms with rights for sale noted. Reports in 1 month. Sample copy for $1 and 9×12 SASE.

Nonfiction: General interest, interview/profile, opinion, photo feature, religious, travel. "Especially needs articles for these annual issues: Rosh Hashanah, Financial, Chanukah, Celebration (wedding and bar mitzvah), Passover, Health and Fitness, Education, Travel. No fiction, poems, first-person experiences." Buys 50 mss/year. Send complete ms. Length: 500-1,000 words. Pays 50¢/column inch.

Photos: State availability of photos with submission. Reviews b&w prints up to 8×10. Offers $5/photo. Captions and identification of subjects required. Buys one-time rights.

THE HIGHLANDER, Angus J. Ray Associates, Inc., P.O. Box 397, Barrington IL 60011-0397. (708)382-1035. Editor: Angus J. Ray. 50% freelance written. Works with a small number of new/unpublished writers each year. Bimonthly magazine covering Scottish history, clans, genealogy, travel/history, and Scottish/American activities. Estab. 1961. Circ. 40,000. **Pays on acceptance.** Publishes ms an average of 6 months after acceptance. Byline given. Buys first North American serial and second serial (reprint) rights. Submit seasonal/holiday material 6 months in advance. Accepts previously published submissions. Send tearsheet or photocopy of article. For reprints pays 50% of amount paid for an original article. Reports in 1 month. Sample copy for $3. Free writer's guidelines.

Nonfiction: Historical/nostalgic. "No fiction; no articles unrelated to Scotland." Buys 50 mss/year. Query. Length: 750-2,000 words. Pays $75-150.

Photos: State availability of photos. Pays $5-10 for 8×10 b&w prints or transparencies. Reviews b&w contact sheets. Identification of subjects required. Buys one-time rights.

Tips: "Submit something that has appeared elsewhere."

HISPANIC, 98 San Jacinto Blvd., Suite 1150, Austin TX 78701. (512)476-5599. Fax: (512)320-1943. Editor: Alfredo J. Estrada. Contact: Executive Editor. 90% freelance written. Monthly magazine for the Hispanic community. "HISPANIC is a general interest, lifestyle, entertainment, upbeat, role model publication." Estab.

1987. Circ. 250,000. Pays on publication. Publishes ms an average of 4 months after acceptance. Byline given. Offers 25% kill fee. Buys all rights. Submit seasonal/holiday material 4 months in advance. Free sample copy and writer's guidelines.

Nonfiction: General interest, historical/nostalgic, humor, interview/profile, opinion, personal experience, photo feature and travel. Buys 200 mss/year. Query. Length: 50-3,000 words. Pays $50-500. Pays writers phone expenses, "but these must be cleared with editors first."

Photos: State availability of photos with submission. Reviews transparencies. Offers $25-500/photo. Captions, model releases and identification of subjects required. Buys one-time rights.

Columns/Departments: Forum (political opinion and analysis), cars, money, career, business and reviews. All columns are approximately 500 words but vary in fee.

INSIDE, The Jewish Exponent Magazine, Jewish Federation of Greater Philadelphia, 226 S. 16th St., Philadelphia PA 19102. (215)893-5700. Fax: (215)546-3957. Editor: Jane Biberman. Managing Editor: Martha Ledger. 95% freelance written (by assignment). Works with published/established writers and a small number of new/unpublished writers each year. Quarterly Jewish community magazine for a general interest Jewish readership 25 years of age and older. Estab. 1979. Circ. 75,000. **Pays on acceptance.** Offers 20% kill fee. Publishes ms an average of 2 months after acceptance. Byline given. Buys first rights. Reprint possibilities with our licensees. Submit seasonal/holiday material 3 months in advance. Accepts previously published material. Send photocopy of article or short story. For reprints, pays 50% of the amount paid for an original article. Publishes novel excerpts. Reports in 2 weeks on queries; 1 month on mss. Sample copy for $5 and 9 × 12 SAE. Writer's guidelines for #10 SASE.

Nonfiction: Book excerpts, general interest, historical/nostalgic, humor, interview/profile, personal experience, religious. Philadelphia angle desirable. Buys 12 unsolicited mss/year. Query. Length: 1,000-3,500 words. Pays $100-1,000.

Photos: State availability of photos with submission. Identification of subjects required. Buys first rights.

Fiction: Short stories. Query.

Tips: "Personalities—very well known—and serious issues of concern to Jewish community needed."

INTERRACE MAGAZINE, Interrace Publications, P.O. Box 12048, Atlanta GA 30355. (404)364-9690. Fax: (404)364-9965. E-mail: 73424.1014@compuserve.com. Editor: Candy Mills. 70% freelance written. Bimonthly magazine covering interracial/multiracial topics. "We cover all aspects dealing with interracial couples and families; people who are mixed-race." Estab. 1989. Circ. 25,000. Pays on publication. Publishes ms an average of 1-3 months after acceptance. Byline given. Buys first rights or makes work-for-hire assignments. Submit seasonal material 3 months in advance. Accepts previously published submissions. Send tearsheet or photocopy of article or short story. Query for electronic submissions. Reports in 2 months on queries; 6 months on mss. Sample copy for $2 and 9 × 12 SAE with $1 postage. Writer's guidelines for #10 SASE.

Nonfiction: Essays, exposé, general interest, historical/nostalgic, humor, inspirational, interview/profile, new product, opinion, personal experience, travel. Buys 30-40 mss/year. Query. Length: 200-6,000 words. Pays $20-75 for assigned articles; $50-75 for cover stories. Sometimes pays expenses of writers on assignment. Freelancers should state availability of photos with submission. Negotiates payment individually. Identification of subjects required. Buys one-time rights.

Columns/Departments: Buys 3-5 mss/year. Query. Pays $20.

Fiction: Ethnic, historical, humorous, romance, slice-of-life vignettes. Buys 8 mss/year. Query. Length: 800-2,400 words. Pays $20-40.

JEWISH ACTION, Union of Orthodox Jewish Congregations of America, 333 Seventh Ave., 18th Floor, New York NY 10001-5072. (212)563-4000, ext. 146, 147. Fax: (212)564-9058. Editor: Charlotte Friedland. Assistant Editor: Elissa Feldman. 80% freelance written. "Quarterly magazine offering a vibrant approach to Jewish issues, Orthodox lifestyle and values." Circ. 45,000. Pays 4-6 weeks after publication. Byline given. Submit seasonal/holiday material 4 months in advance. Reports in 5 months. Sample copy and guidelines for 9 × 12 SAE with 5 first-class stamps.

Nonfiction: Current Jewish issues, history, biography, art, inspirational, humor, book reviews. Query with published clips. Length: 1,500-2,500 words. Pays $100-300 for assigned articles; $75-150 for unsolicited articles. Buys 30-40 mss/year.

Fiction: Must have relevance to Orthodox reader. Length: 1,000-2,000 words.

Poetry: Limited number accepted. Pays $25-75.

Columns/Departments: Student Voice (about Jewish life on campus), 1,000 words. Buys 4 mss/year. Just Between Us (personal opinion on current Jewish life and issues), 1,000 words. Buys 4 mss/year. Jewish Living (section pertaining to holidays, contemporary Jewish practices), 1,000-1,500 words. Buys 10 mss/year.

Photos: Send photos with submission. Identification of subjects required.

Tips: "Remember that your reader is well-educated and has a strong commitment to Orthodox Judaism. Articles on the Holocaust, holidays, Israel and other common topics should offer a fresh insight."

NA'AMAT WOMAN, Magazine of NA'AMAT USA, the Women's Labor Zionist Organization of America, NA'AMAT USA, 200 Madison Ave., New York NY 10016. (212)725-8010. Editor: Judith A. Sokoloff. 80% freelance written. Magazine published 5 times/year covering Jewish themes and issues; Israel; women's issues; Labor Zionism; and social, political and economic issues. Estab. 1926. Circ. 30,000. Pays on publication. Byline given. Not copyrighted. Buys first North American serial, one-time, first serial and second serial (reprint) rights to book excerpts and makes work-for-hire assignments. Reports in 3 months. Writer's guidelines for SASE.

Nonfiction: Exposé, general interest (Jewish), historical/nostalgic, interview/profile, opinion, personal experience, photo feature, travel (Israel), art and music. "All articles must be of particular interest to the Jewish community." Buys 35 mss/year. Query with clips of published work or send complete ms. Pays 10¢/word.

Photos: State availability of photos. Pays $10-30 for 4×5 or 5×7 prints. Captions, identification of subjects required. Buys one-time rights.

Columns/Departments: Film and book reviews with Jewish themes. Buys 20-25 mss/year. Query with clips of published work or send complete ms. Pays 10¢/word.

Fiction: Historical/nostalgic, humorous, women-oriented and novel excerpts. "Good intelligent fiction with Jewish slant. No maudlin nostalgia or trite humor." Buys 3 mss/year. Send complete ms. Length: 1,200-3,000 words. Pays 10¢/word.

NATIVE PEOPLES MAGAZINE, The Arts and Lifeways, 5333 N. Seventh St., Suite C-224, Phoenix AZ 85014-2804. (602)252-2236. Fax: (602)265-3113. Editorial Coordinator: Rebeca Withers. Editor: Gary Avey. Quarterly full-color magazine on Native Americans. "The primary purpose of this magazine is to offer a sensitive portrayal of the arts and lifeways of native peoples of the Americas." Estab. 1987. Circ. 120,000. Pays on publication. Byline given. Buys one-time rights. Query for electronic submissions. Reports in 1 month on queries; 2 months on mss. Sample copy for 9×12 SAE with 6 first-class stamps. Free writer's guidelines. "Extremely high quality reproduction with full-color throughout."

Nonfiction: Book excerpts, historical/nostalgic, interview/profile, personal experience, photo feature. Buys 45 mss/year. Query with published clips. Length: 1,800-2,200 words. Pays 25¢/word. Publishes nonfiction book excerpts.

Photos: State availability of photos with submission. Reviews transparencies (all formats). Offers $45-150 per page rates. Identification of subjects required. Buys one-time rights.

SCANDINAVIAN REVIEW, The American-Scandinavian Foundation, 725 Park Ave., New York NY 10021. (212)879-9779. Fax: (212)249-3444. Editor: Adrienne Gynongy. 75% freelance written. Triannual magazine for contemporary Scandinavia. Audience: members, embassies, consulates, libraries. Slant: popular coverage of contemporary affairs in Scandinavia. Estab. 1913. Circ. 3,500. Pays on publication. Publishes ms 2 months after acceptance. Byline given. Buys first North American serial and second serial (reprint) rights. Editorial lead time 3 months. Submit seasonal material 3 months in advance. Accepts previously published submissions. Query for electronic submissions. Reports in 6 weeks on queries. Sample copy and writer's guidelines free on request.

Nonfiction: General interest, interview/profile, photo feature, travel (must have Scandinavia as topic focus). Special issue on Scandinavian travel. *No pornography.* Buys 30 mss/year. Query with published clips. Length: 1,500-2,000 words. Pays $300 maximum. Pays contributor's copies (at writer's request).

Photos: State availability of photos with submission or send photos with submission. Reviews 3×5 transparencies or 3×5 prints. Pays $25-50/photo; negotiates payment individually. Captions required. Buys one-time rights.

‡THIRD FORCE MAGAZINE, Issues & Actions in Communities of Color, Center for Third World Organizing, 1218 E. 21st St., Oakland CA 94606. (510)533-7583. Editor/Publisher: John Anner. Contact: Andrea Lewis, senior editor. 65% freelance written. Bimonthly magazine covering communities of color, grassroots organizing, low-income communities. "Must reflect knowledge and understanding of issues in various communities of color. Writers of color are especially encouraged to submit queries. Approximately 70% of articles are written by authors of color." Estab. 1984. Circ. 3,000. Pays on publication. Publishes ms an average of 3 months after acceptance. Byline given. Offers 40% kill fee. Buys first North American serial rights. Editorial lead time 3 months. Submit seasonal material 4 months in advance. Accepts previously published submissions. Reports in 6 weeks on queries; 2 months on mss. Sample copy and writer's guidelines free on request.

Nonfiction: Essays, exposé, general interest, historical, interview/profile, opinion, photo feature. Special issues: 2 each year. Buys 40 mss/year. Query with published clips or writing samples. Length: 700-3,500 words. Pays $150 minimum plus 1 year subscription. Sometimes pays expenses of writers on assignment.

Photos: State availability of photos with submissions. Negotiates payment individually. Captions, identification of subjects required. Buys one-time rights.

Columns/Departments: Editorial/Commentary (political, cultural, social), 800 words; Historical (histories of organizing of other issues in communities of color), 1,000 words. Buys 6 mss/year. Query with published clips or send complete ms. Pays negotiable.

Fillers: Timely political/social cartoons (strip or single panel) or illustrations. Buys 6/year. Pay negotiable.
Tips: "The best way for writers to break in is to write or propose a short feature about a particular political struggle or grassroots campaign that the writer is familiar with. Authors of short features are often assigned longer features. Queries should be concise and clear and should include information on the writer's experience and expertise."

THE UKRAINIAN WEEKLY, Ukrainian National Association, 30 Montgomery St., Jersey City NJ 07302-3821. (201)434-0237. Editor-in-Chief: Roma Hadzewycz. 30% freelance written (mostly by a corps of regular contributors). Weekly tabloid covering news and issues of concern to Ukrainian community, primarily in North America but also around the world, and events in Ukraine. "We have a news bureau in Kyyiv, capital of Ukraine." Estab. 1933. Circ. 11,000. Pays on publication. Publishes ms an average of 1-2 months after acceptance. Byline given. Buys first North American serial and second serial (reprint) rights or makes work-for-hire assignments. Submit seasonal/holiday material 1 month in advance. Accepts previously published material. Send typed ms with rights for sale noted and information about when and where the article previously appeared. Pays 25-50% of amount paid for an original article. Reports in 1 month. Free sample copy for 9×12 SAE with 3 first-class stamps.
Nonfiction: Book excerpts, essays, exposé, general interest, historical/nostalgic, interview/profile, opinion, personal experience, photo feature, news events. Special issues: Easter, Christmas, anniversary of Ukraine's independence (August 24, 1991) (proclamation) and December 1, 1991 (referendum), student scholarships, anniversary of Chornobyl nuclear accident and year-end review of news. Buys 80 mss/year. Query with published clips. Length: 500-2,000 words. Pays $45-100 for assigned articles. Pays $25-100 for unsolicited articles. Sometimes pays the expenses of writers on assignment.
Photos: Send photos with submission. Reviews contact sheets, negatives and 3×5, 5×7 or 8×10 prints. Offers no additional payment for photos accepted with ms.
Columns/Departments: News & Views (commentary on news events), 500-1,000 words. Buys 10 mss/ year. Query. Pays $25-50.
Tips: "Become acquainted with the Ukrainian community in the US and Canada. The area of our publication most open to freelancers is community news—coverage of local events. We put more emphasis on events in Ukraine now that it has re-established its independence."

‡UPSCALE MAGAZINE, The Successful Black Magazine, Upscale Communications, Inc., 600 Bronner Brothers Way SW, Atlanta, GA 30310. (404)758-7467. Fax: (404)755-9892. Editor: Sheila Bronner. Senior Editor: Lee Bliss. Contact: Kimberly Nesbit, assistant editor. 75-80% freelance written. Monthly magazine covering topics that inspire, inform or entertain African-Americans. "*Upscale* is a general interest publication featuring a variety of topics—beauty, health and fitness, business news, travel, arts, relationships, entertainment and other issues that affect day to day lives of African-Americans." Byline given. Offers 25% kill fee. Buys all rights in published form. Editorial lead time 3 months. Submit seasonal material 4 months in advance. Accepts simultaneous submissions. Query for electronic submissions; Mac compatible. Sample copy for $2. Writer's guidelines free on request.
Nonfiction: Book excerpts/reviews, general interest, historical/nostalgic, inspirational, interview/profile, personal experience, religious, travel. Buys 135 mss/year. Query. Length varies. Pays $150 minimum. Sometimes pays expenses of writers.
Photos: State availability of photos with submission. Reviews contact sheets, transparencies, prints. Negotiates payment individually. Captions, model releases, identification of subjects required. Buys one-time rights.
Columns/Departments: Lee Bliss, senior editor. Positively You, Viewpoint, Perspective (personal experience/perspective). Buys 50 mss/year. Query. Pays $75.
Tips: "*Upscale* does not accept unsolicited fiction, poetry or essays. Unsolicited nonfiction is accepted for our Perspective, Positively You, and Viewpoint sections. Query letters for exciting and informative nonfiction story ideas are welcomed."

‡WINDSPEAKER, Aboriginal Multi-Media Society of Alberta, 15001-112 Ave., Edmonton Alberta T5M 2V6 Canada. (403)455-2700. Editor: Linda Caldwell. 75% freelance written. Monthly tabloid covering native issues. "Focus on events and issues that affect and interest native peoples." Estab. 1983. Circ. 12,500. Pays on publication. Publishes ms an average of 1 month after acceptance. Byline given. Offers $25 kill fee. Buys first rights. Editorial lead time 1 month. Submit seasonal material 2 months in advance. Accepts simultaneous submissions. Query for electronic submissions. Sample copy and writer's guidelines free on request.
Nonfiction: Humor, interview/profile, opinion, personal experience, photo feature, travel, reviews: books, music, movies. Special issues: Powwow (June); Travel supplement (May). Buys 200 mss/year. Query with published clips. Length: 300-1,000 words. Pays $3-3.60/published inch. Sometimes pays expenses of writers on assignment. "Query editor by phone with story ideas."
Photos: Send photos with submission. Reviews negatives, prints. Offers $15-50/photo. Identification of subjects required. Buys one-time rights.
Columns/Departments: Arts reviews (Aboriginal artists), 500-800 words. Buys 25 mss/year. Query with published clips. Pays $3-3.60/inch.

Food and Drink

Magazines appealing to gourmets, health-conscious consumers and vegetarians are classified here. Journals aimed at food processing, manufacturing and retailing are in the Trade section. Many magazines in General Interest and Women's categories also buy articles on food topics.

BEST RECIPES MAGAZINE, Stauffer Magazine Group, 1503 SW 42nd St., Topeka KS 66609-1265. (913)274-4300. Editor-in-Chief: Michael Scheibach. 20% freelance written. Bimonthly magazine with emphasis on recipes from a middle America perspective—*not* a high-income lifestyle or exotic cooking publication. Estab. 1987. Circ. 250,000. Pays on publication. Publishes average of 6 months after acceptance. Byline given. Buys first rights or makes work-for-hire assignments. Occasionally buys reprint rights if first publication was to extremely local or regional audience. Send tearsheet of article or typed ms with rights for sale noted and information about when and where the article previously appeared. For reprints pays 60% of the amount paid for an original article. Submit seasonal material one year in advance. Reports in 4 months on queries. Sample copy and writer's guidelines for $2.75 and 11 × 14 SAE with 5 first-class stamps.

Nonfiction: *Best Recipes* seeks articles about creative, interesting or famous people who cook or practical cooking advice, such as healthful ways to update grandma's recipes or adapting home cooking to the microwave. Top quality, professional color photography enhances acceptability of articles. Black and white line drawings also desirable for some stories, such as how-tos. Buys 4-6 mss a year. Length 800 words maximum. Pays $75 to $200 for unsolicited articles.

Tips: Do not send anything not related to foods, recipes, cooking tips. ALL stories (even tips, how-tos) should include practical, tested recipes.

BON APPETIT, America's Food and Entertaining Magazine, Condé Nast Publications, Inc., 6300 Wilshire Blvd., Los Angeles CA 90048. (213)965-3600. Fax: (213)937-1206. Executive Editor: Barbara Fairchild. Editor-in-Chief: William J. Garry. 10% freelance written. Monthly magazine that covers fine food, restaurants and home entertaining. "*Bon Appetit* readers are upscale food enthusiasts and sophisticated travelers. They eat out often and entertain four to six times a month." Estab. 1975. Circ. 1,331,853. **Pays on acceptance.** Byline given. Negotiates rights. Submit seasonal/holiday material 1 year in advance. No simultaneous or previously published submissions. Reports in 6 weeks on queries. Writer's guidelines for #10 SASE.

Nonfiction: Travel (restaurant or food-related), food feature, dessert feature. "No cartoons, quizzes, poetry, historic food features or obscure food subjects." Buys 45 mss/year. Query with published clips. Length: 750-2,000 words. Pays $500-1,800. Pays expenses of writers on assignment.

Photos: Never send photos.

Tips: "We are most interested in receiving travel or restaurant stories from freelancers. They must have a good knowledge of food (as shown in accompanying clips) and a light, lively style with humor. Nothing long and pedantic please."

CHILE PEPPER, The Magazine of Spicy Foods, Out West Publishing Company, 5106 Grand NE, P.O. Box 80780, Albuquerque NM 87198-0780. (505)266-8322. Fax: (505)266-2127. Managing Editor: Melissa Stock. 25-30% freelance written. Bimonthly magazine on spicy foods. "The magazine is devoted to spicy foods, and most articles include recipes. We have a very devoted readership who love their food hot!" Estab. 1986. Circ. 80,000. Pays on publication. Offers 50% kill fee. Buys first and second rights. Submit seasonal/holiday material 6 months in advance. Accepts previously published submissions. Send tearsheet or photocopy of article and information about when and where the article previously appeared. For reprints pays 25% of the amount paid for an original article. Query for electronic submissions. Reports in 2 months. Sample copy for 9 × 12 SAE with 5 first-class stamps. Writer's guidelines for #10 SASE.

Nonfiction: Book excerpts (cookbooks), how-to (cooking and gardening with spicy foods), humor (having to do with spicy foods), new product (hot products), travel (having to do with spicy foods). Buys 20 mss/year. Query. Length: 1,000-3,000 words. Pays $150 minimum for assigned articles; $100 for unsolicited articles. Sometimes pays expenses of writers on assignment.

Photos: State availability of photos with submission. Reviews contact sheets, negatives, transparencies and prints. Offers $25 minimum/photo. Captions and identification of subjects required. Buys one-time rights.

Market conditions are constantly changing! If this is 1997 or later, buy the newest edition of Writer's Market *at your favorite bookstore or order directly from Writer's Digest Books.*

Tips: "We're always interested in queries from *food* writers. Articles about spicy foods with six to eight recipes are just right. No fillers. Need exotic location travel/food pieces."

COOKING LIGHT, The Magazine of Food and Fitness, Southern Living, Inc. P.O. Box 1748, Birmingham AL 35201-1681. (205)877-6000. Editor: Douglas Crichton. Managing Editor: Nathalie Dearing. 75% freelance written. Bimonthly magazine on healthy recipes and fitness information. "*Cooking Light* is a positive approach to a healthier lifestyle. It's written for healthy people on regular diets who are counting calories or trying to make calories count toward better nutrition. Moderation, balance and variety are emphasized. The writing style is fresh, upbeat and encouraging, emphasizing that eating a balanced, varied, lower-calorie diet and exercising regularly do not have to be boring." Estab. 1987. Circ. 1.2 million **Pays on acceptance.** Publishes ms an average of 1 year after acceptance. Byline sometimes given. Offers 25% of original contract fee as kill fee. Submit seasonal/holiday material 1 year in advance. Reports in 1 year.
Nonfiction: Personal experience on nutrition, healthy recipes, fitness/exercise. Back up material a must. Buys 150 mss/year. Query with published clips. Length: 400-2,000 words. Pays $250-2,000 for assigned articles. Pays expenses of writers on assignment.
Columns/Departments: Try On a Sport (introducing readers to new sports as well as new ways to view old sports), 1,000 words; Attitudes (on the human mind at work; psychology, changing attitudes, trends and other issues involving the mind), 1,000 words; Health Matters (focuses on wide range of health issues), 1,000 words; Walk Talk (ways to make the most of our readers number one exercise), 1,000 words; Food for Thought (collection of food-related articles on the following topics—mini profile on a chef, restaurant and eating-out trends, food products and equipment, cooking tips and diet concerns) 250-350 words, short, 400-500 words, long. Buys 30 mss/year. Query. Pays $50-2,000.
Tips: "Emphasis should be on achieving a healthier lifestyle through food, nutrition, fitness, exercise information. In submitting queries, include information on professional background. Food writers should include examples of healthy recipes which meet the guidelines of *Cooking Light.*"

EATING WELL, The Magazine of Food and Health, Telemedia Communications (US) Inc., P.O. Box 1001, Charlotte VT 05445-1001. (802)425-3961. Fax: (802)425-3307. Editor: Jane Kirby. Food Editor: Susan Stuck. 90% freelance written. Bimonthly magazine covering food, health. Estab. 1989. Circ. 640,000. Pays 45 days after acceptance. Publishes ms an average of 6 months after acceptance. Byline given. Offers 25% kill fee. Buys first North American serial and second serial (reprint) rights. Submit seasonal/holiday material 1 year in advance. Reports in 2 months.
Nonfiction: Jane Kirby. Book excerpts, nutrition, cooking, interview/profile, food, travel. Query with published clips. Length: 2,000-4,000 words. Pays $1,500-3,500. Pays expenses of writers on assignment.
Columns/Departments: Mary Nowlan. Nutrition Report (timely nutrition research news), 150-400 words; and Marketplace (current news in the food world), 150-400 words. Buys 60 mss/year. Query. Pays $200-500.
Tips: "We invite experienced, published science writers to do a broad range of in-depth, innovative food-health-nutrition features. Read the magazine first."

‡FAST AND HEALTHY MAGAZINE, Pillsbury Co., 200 S. Sixth St., M.S. 28M7, Minneapolis MN 55402. Editor: Betsy Wray. 50% freelance written. Bimonthly digest covering food. "*Fast and Healthy* is a family-oriented food magazine with healthful recipes for active people. All recipes can be prepared in 30 minutes or less and meet the U.S. Dietary guidelines for healthful eating. The magazine's emphasis is on Monday through Friday cooking. Our readers are busy people who are looking for information and recipes that help them prepare healthy meals quickly." Estab. 1992. Circ. 200,000. **Pays on acceptance.** Publishes ms an average of 8 months after acceptance. Byline given. Offers 20% kill fee. Buys first North American serial rights or all rights. Editorial lead time 1 year. Submit seasonal material 18 months in advance. Query for electronic submissions. Reports in 6 weeks on queries. Sample copy for $3. Writer's guidelines for #10 SASE.
Nonfiction: Food topics related to health, nutrition, convenience. Buys 6 mss/year. Query with published clips. Length: 100-1,500 words. Pays $50-500.
Columns/Departments: Living Better (health, nutrition, healthy lifestyle news), 25-200 words. Buys 25 mss/year. Query with published clips. Pays $25-200.

FINE COOKING, The Taunton Press, P.O. Box 5506, 63 S. Main St., Newtown CT 06470. (203)426-8171. Editor: Martha Holmberg. Managing Editor: Jan Newberry. Bimonthly magazine focusing exclusively on cooking. "*Fine Cooking* is a magazine for people who are passionate about the craft of cooking. Most readers are avid home cooks, though many are professionals. Our writers are not necessarily professional writers. It is more important to us that they are experienced cooks with first-hand knowledge and information to share." Estab. 1993. Circ. 120,000. Pays on receiving corrected galleys. Byline given. Offers $150 kill fee or page rate. Buys one-time rights. Editorial lead time 6-9 months. Submit seasonal material 9 months in advance. Query for electronic submissions. Reports in 6 weeks on queries. Sample copy for $4.95. Writer's guidelines free on request.

Nonfiction: How-to, humor, personal experience. Buys approximately 40 mss/year. Query. Pays $150/page minimum. Sometimes pays expenses of writers on assignment.

Columns/Departments: Jan Newberry. Tidbits (humor), 500-600 words; Tips (shortcuts), 100 words; Basics (techniques), 400-500 words; Notes; New Products; Flavorings; Book Review; Food Science. Query. Pays $25-50.

Tips: "Our entire magazine is written by experienced cooks. We welcome submissions in all these areas. Unless you have first-hand experience, we're not the right magazine for you."

FOOD & WINE, American Express Publishing Corp., 1120 Avenue of the Americas, New York NY 10036. (212)382-5618. Editor: Dana Cowin. Managing Editor: Mary Ellen Ward. Monthly magazine for "active people for whom eating, drinking, entertaining, dining out and travel are central to their lifestyle." Estab. 1978. Circ. 725,000. **Pays on acceptance.** Byline given. Offers 25% kill fee. Buys first world rights. Submit seasonal/holiday material 9 months in advance. Reports in 3 weeks on queries; 2 weeks on mss. Sample copy for $5. Writer's guidelines for #10 SASE.

Nonfiction: Food trends and news, how-to, kitchen and dining room design, travel. Query with published clips. Buys 125 mss/year. Length: 1,000-3,000 words. Pays $800-2,000. Pays expenses of writers on assignment.

Photos: State availability of photos with submission. No unsolicited photos or art. Offers $100-450 page rate per photo. Model releases and identification of subjects required. Buys one-time rights.

Columns/Departments: Restaurants, Travel, Style, Selects-Food, Selects-Design, Health, Low-fat Cooking, Dinner in Under an Hour, Experts. Buys 120 mss/year. Query with published clips. Length: 800-3,000 words. Pays $800-2,000.

Tips: "Good service, good writing, up-to-date information, interesting article approach and appropriate point of view for *F&W*'s audience are important elements to keep in mind. Look over several recent issues before writing query."

GOURMET, 560 Lexington Ave., New York NY 10022. Executive Food Editor: Zanne Zakroff. Monthly publication covering cooking, entertaining, travel and culture. Query before submitting. Most sections of the magazine have inhouse staff writers.

‡JOURNAL OF ITALIAN FOOD & WINE, 609 W. 114th St., Suite 77, New York NY 10025. Managing Editor: J. Mimser Woggins. 80% freelance written. Bimonthly magazine. Estab. 1991. Circ. 50,000. Pays on publication. Publishes ms 2-4 months after acceptance. Byline given. Offers 25% kill fee or $100. Buys all rights. Editorial lead time 2-6 months. Submit seasonal material 4 months in advance. Simultaneous submissions OK. Query for electronic submissions. Reports in 2 weeks on queries; 2 months on mss. Sample copy $5.

Nonfiction: Book excerpts, essays, historical, how-to (cooking Italian), humor, interview/profile, new product, photo feature and travel. Special Christmas issue. "No first person, 'I remember when the smell of my mother's cooking came wafting into my room,' or 'ethnic' humor." Buys 12-18 mss/year. Query. Length: 500-2,500. Pays $350 minimum for assigned articles; $250 minimum for unsolicited articles. Sometimes pays expenses of writers on assignment.

Photos: Send photos with submission. Reviews 5×7 prints. Offers $35-200 but negotiates payment individually. Captions, model releases and identification of subjects required. Buys all rights.

Columns/Departments: J. Mimser Woggins, managing editor. Nota Bene (short, short on Italian food or wine ideas), 125-250 words. Buys 5-7 mss/year. Send complete ms. Pays $20-75.

Fiction: Ethnic, historical, slice-of-life vignettes. Buys 6 mss/year. Query. Length: 500-1,500 words. Pays $100-300.

Poetry: J. Mimser Woggins, managing editor. Facts, gags to be illustrated by cartoonist, short humor, cartoons. Buys 15/year. Length: 50-200 words. Pays $10-50.

Tips: "Writers should ignore *all* other food magazines. Articles should be long on hard facts and well-edited *before* we get them. It costs too much in human resources to edit the basics. And, don't try to recycle old material to us. It will be tossed back immediately."

KASHRUS MAGAZINE, The Bimonthly for the Kosher Consumer and the Trade, Yeshiva Birkas Reuven, P.O. Box 204, Parkville Station, Brooklyn NY 11204. (718)336-8544. Editor: Rabbi Yosef Wikler. 25% freelance written. Prefers to work with published/established writers, but will work with new/unpublished writers. Bimonthly magazine covering kosher food industry and food production. Estab. 1980. Circ. 10,000. Pays on publication. Publishes ms an average of 2 months after acceptance. Byline given. Offers 50% kill fee. Buys first or second serial (reprint) rights. Submit seasonal/holiday material 2 months in advance. Accepts simultaneous and previously published submissions. Send tearsheet or photocopy of article. Pays 25% of amount paid for an original article. Prefers submissions in major word processing programs on disk with accompanying hard copy. Reports in 1 week on queries, 2 weeks on mss. *Writer's Market* recommends allowing 2 months for reply. Sample copy for $3. Professional discount on subscription: $18/10 issues (regularly $33).

Nonfiction: General interest, interview/profile, new product, personal experience, photo feature, religious, technical and travel. Special issues feature; International Kosher Travel (October) and Passover (March). Buys 8-12 mss/year. Query with published clips. Length: 1,000-1,500 words. Pays $100-250 for assigned articles; pays up to $100 for unsolicited articles. Sometimes pays the expenses of writers on assignment.
Photos: State availability of photos with submission. Offers no additional payment for photos accepted with ms. Buys one-time rights.
Columns/Departments: Book Review (cook books, food technology, kosher food), 250-500 words; People in the News (interviews with kosher personalities), 1,000-1,500 words; Regional Kosher Supervision (report on kosher supervision in a city or community), 1,000-1,500 words; Food Technology (new technology or current technology with accompanying pictures), 1,000-1,500 words; Travel (international, national), must include Kosher information and Jewish communities, 1,000-1,500 words; Regional Kosher Cooking, 1,000-1,500 words. Buys 8-12 mss/year. Query with published clips. Pays $50-250.
Tips: "*Kashrus Magazine* will do more writing on general food technology, production, and merchandising as well as human interest travelogs and regional writing in 1996 than we have done in the past. Areas most open to freelancers are interviews, food technology, cooking and food preparation, dining, regional reporting and travel. We welcome stories on the availability and quality of Kosher foods and services in communities across the US and throughout the world. Some of our best stories have been by non-Jewish writers about kosher observance in their region. We also enjoy humorous articles. Just send a query with clips and we'll try to find a storyline that's right for you."

‡**RISTORANTE**, Foley Publishing, P.O. Box 73, Basking Ridge NJ 07920. (908)766-6006. Editor: Jaclyn Foley. 75% freelance written. Bimonthly magazine covering "Italian anything! *Ristorante—The magazine for the Italian Connoisseur.* For Italian restaurants and those who love Italian food, travel, wine and all things Italian!" Estab. 1994. Circ. 40,000. Pays on publication. Publishes ms an average of 3 months after acceptance. Byline sometimes given. Buys first North American and one-time rights. Editorial lead time 3 months. Submit seasonal material 3 months in advance. Accepts previously published submissions. Reports in 1 month on queries; 2 months on mss. Sample copy and writer's guidelines for 9×12 SAE and 4 first-class stamps.
Nonfiction: Book excerpts, general interest, historical/nostalgic, how-to (prepare Italian foods), humor, new product, opinion, personal experience, travel. Buys 25 mss/year. Send complete ms. Length: 100-1,000 words. Pays $100-350 for assigned articles; $75-300 for unsolicited articles. Sometimes pays expenses of writers on assignment.
Photos: Send photos with submission. Reviews 3×5 prints. Negotiates payment individually. Captions, model releases required. Buys one-time rights.
Columns/Departments: Send complete ms. Pays $50-200.
Fillers: Anecdotes, facts, short humor. Buys 10/year. Pays $10-50.

VEGETARIAN GOURMET, Chariot Publishing, Inc., 2 Public Ave., Montrose PA 18801. (717)278-1984. Fax: (717)278-2223. Editor: Jessica Dubey. 75% freelance written. Quarterly magazine on seasonal vegetarian cooking with additional low-fat issue. "An entertaining and practical how-to guide to cooking food that is delicious and healthful." Estab. 1991. Circ. 95,000. Pays on publication. Publishes ms an average of 1-3 months after acceptance. Byline given. Kill fee offered "depends on price ordinarily paid for accepted ms." Buys one-time rights and second serial (reprint) rights. Submit seasonal material 5-6 months in advance. Accepts previously published material. Send photocopy of article and information about when and where the article previously appeared. Query for electronic submissions. Reports in 3 weeks on queries; 6 weeks on mss. Sample copy free on request. Writer's guidelines for #10 SASE.
 • *Vegetarian Gourmet* prefers more how-to cooking articles which are shorter in length (500-800 words).
Nonfiction: How-to (cooking), book and restaurant reviews. "No previously published or non-vegetarian material; no articles not directly related to food or cooking." Buys approximately 40 mss/year. Send complete ms. Length: 400-800 words. Pays $175-250. Sometimes pays expenses of writers on assignment.
Photos: Send photos with submission. Reviews 2¼ transparencies. Offers $25-50/photo. Captions required. Buys one-time rights.
Columns/Departments: International fare (vegetarian cuisine of a foreign country), 800 words; desserts (vegetarian dessert made with natural sweeteners), 800 words; extraordinary vegetables (introduce one or more less familiar vegetables), 800 words; entertainment (unique ways of entertaining with vegetarian food), 800 words; *VG* visits (profile of a vegetarian restaurant), 500-700 words; cook for kids (fun ideas for vegetarian meals for kids), 400-600 words; fast foods (dishes that can be made quickly with a particular food), 400-500 words. Buys 40 mss/year. Send complete ms. Pays $75-250.
Tips: "Submit a completed ms along with recipe blurbs, photos (if available) and information on less familiar ingredients (what they are and how to obtain them). Include useful cooking tips and nutritional value of food(s) you are writing about. All departments open to freelance."

VEGETARIAN TIMES, P.O. Box 570, Oak Park IL 60303. (708)848-8100. Fax: (708)848-8175. 50% free-lance written. Prefers to work with published/established writers; works with small number of new/unpublished writers each year. Monthly magazine. Circ. 300,000. Buys first serial or all rights. Byline given unless extensive revisions are required or material is incorporated into a larger article. **Pays on acceptance.** Publishes ms an average of 4 months after acceptance. Submit seasonal material 6 months in advance. Reports in 3 months. Query. Writer's guidelines for #10 SASE.

Nonfiction: Features articles that inform readers about how vegetarianism relates to diet, cooking, lifestyle, health, consumer choices, natural foods, environmental concerns and animal welfare. "All material should be well-documented and researched, and written in a sophisticated and lively style." Informational, how-to, personal experience, interview, profile, investigative. Length: average 2,000 words. Pays flat rate of $100-1,000, sometimes higher, depending on length and difficulty of piece. Will also use 200-500-word items for news department. Sometimes pays expenses of writers on assignment.

Photos: Payment negotiated/photo.

Tips: "You don't have to be a vegetarian to write for *Vegetarian Times*, but it is vital that your article have a vegetarian perspective. The best way to pick up that slant is to read several issues of the magazine (no doubt a tip you've heard over and over). We are looking for stories that go beyond the obvious 'Why I Became a Vegetarian.' A well-written provocative query plus samples of your best writing will increase your chances of publication."

‡VEGGIE LIFE, Growing, Cooking, Eating Green, EGW Publishing, 1041 Shary Circle, Concord CA 94518. (510)671-9852. Editor: Margo M. Lemas. 90% freelance written. Bimonthly magazine covering vegetarian cooking. Estab. 1992. Circ. 200,000. **Pays on acceptance.** Publishes ms an average of 6 months after acceptance. Byline given. Offers 25% kill fee. Buys all rights or makes work-for-hire assignments. Editorial lead time 4 months. Submit seasonal material 4 months in advance. Query for electronic submissions. Reports in 1 month on queries; 2 months on mss. Writer's guidelines for #10 SASE.

Nonfiction: Margo Lemas. General interest, how-to, humor, interview/profile, travel. No animal rights issues/advocacy or religious/philosophical. Buys 30-50 mss/year. Query with or without published clips. Length: 1,000-2,000 words. Pays 25-35¢/word for assigned articles; 15-25¢/word for unsolicited articles.

Photos: State availability of photos with submission. Negotiates payment individually. Captions, model releases and identification of subjects required. Buys one-time rights.

Columns/Departments: Pays $25-100.

Tips: "Research back issues; be authoritative; no 'Why I Became a Vegetarian . . . ' stories."

WINE SPECTATOR, M. Shanken Communications, Inc., 387 Park Ave. S., New York NY 10016. (212)684-4224. Fax: (212)684-5424. Managing Editor: Jim Gordon. 20% freelance written. Prefers to work with published/established writers. Biweekly consumer news magazine covering wine. Estab. 1976. Circ. 150,000. Pays within 30 days of publication. Publishes ms an average of 2 months after acceptance. Byline given. Buys all rights and makes work-for-hire assignments. Submit seasonal/holiday material 4 months in advance. Query for electronic submissions. Reports in 3 months. Sample copy for $5. Free writer's guidelines.

Nonfiction: General interest (news about wine or wine events); interview/profile (of wine, vintners, wineries); opinion; travel, dining and other lifestyle pieces; photo feature. No "winery promotional pieces or articles by writers who lack sufficient knowledge to write below just surface data." Query. Length: 100-2,000 words average. Pays $50-500.

Photos: Send photos with ms. Pays $75 minimum for color transparencies. Captions, model releases and identification of subjects required. Buys all rights.

Tips: "A solid knowledge of wine is a must. Query letters essential, detailing the story idea. New, refreshing ideas which have not been covered before stand a good chance of acceptance. *Wine Spectator* is a consumer-oriented *news magazine*, but we are interested in some trade stories; brevity is essential."

Games and Puzzles

These publications are written by and for game enthusiasts interested in both traditional games and word puzzles and newer role-playing adventure, computer and video games. Additional home video game publications are listed in the Entertainment section. Other puzzle markets may be found in the Juvenile section.

bePUZZLED, Mystery Jigsaw Puzzles, 22 E. Newberry Rd., Bloomfield CT 06002. (203)769-5700. Fax: (203)286-8710. E-mail: malbepuzzd@aol.com. President: Mary Ann Lombard. Creative Director: Richard DeZinno. 100% freelance written. Mystery jigsaw puzzle using short mystery stories published 2-4 times/year. Covers mystery, suspense, adventure for children and adults. Estab. 1987. Pays on completion. Publishes ms an average of 9 months after acceptance. Byline given (sometimes pen name required). Buys all rights. Submit seasonal/holiday material 9 months in advance. Accepts simultaneous submissions. Accepts previously published submissions. Send photocopy of article or typed ms with rights for sale noted and information about when and where the article previously appeared. Reports in 2 weeks on queries, 3 months on mss. Writer's guidelines for SASE.

Fiction: Adventure, humorous, mainstream, mystery, suspense (*exact* subject within genre above is released to writers as available.) Buys 10 mss/year. Query. Length: 3,500-5,500 words. Pays $250-2,000.

Fillers: "Writers must follow submission format as outlined in writer's guidelines. We incorporate short mystery stories and jigsaw puzzles into a game where the clues to solve the mystery are cleverly hidden in both the short story and the puzzle picture. Writer must be able to integrate the clues in the written piece to these to appear in puzzle picture. Playing one of our games helps to clarify how we like to 'marry' the story clues and the visual clues in the puzzle."

CHESS LIFE, United States Chess Federation, 186 Route 9W, New Windsor NY 12553-7698. (914)562-8350. Fax: (914)561-2437. Editor: Glenn Petersen. 15% freelance written. Works with a small number of new/unpublished writers each year. Monthly magazine covering the chess world. Estab. 1939. Circ. 70,000. Pays variable fee. Publishes ms an average of 5 months after acceptance. Byline given. Offers kill fee. Buys first or negotiable rights. Submit seasonal/holiday material 8 months in advance. Accepts simultaneous and previously published submissions. Send typed ms with rights for sale noted and information about when and where the article previously appeared. Reports in 3 months. Sample copy and writer's guidelines for 9×11 SAE with 5 first-class stamps.
   • This publication won 1994 CJA awards for Best Independent Magazine and Best Layout.

Nonfiction: General interest, historical, interview/profile, technical—all must have some relation to chess. No "stories about personal experiences with chess." Buys 30-40 mss/year. Query with samples "if new to publication." Length: 3,000 words maximum. Sometimes pays the expenses of writers on assignment.

Photos: Reviews b&w contact sheets and prints, and color prints and slides. Captions, model releases and identification of subjects required. Buys all or negotiable rights.

Fiction: "Chess-related, high quality." Buys 2-3 mss/year. Pays variable fee.

Tips: "Articles must be written from an informed point of view—not from view of the curious amateur. Most of our writers are specialized in that they have sound credentials as chessplayers. Freelancers in major population areas (except New York and Los Angeles, which we already have covered) who are interested in short personality profiles and perhaps news reporting have the best opportunities. We're looking for more personality pieces on chessplayers around the country; not just the stars, but local masters, talented youths, and dedicated volunteers. Freelancers interested in such pieces might let us know of their interest and their range. Could be we know of an interesting story in their territory that needs covering."

COMPUTER GAMING WORLD, The #1 Computer Game Magazine, Ziff Davis Consumer Media Group, 135 Main St., 14th Floor, San Francisco CA 94105. (415)357-4900. Fax: (415)357-4977. E-mail: 76703.622@compuserve.com. Editor: Chris Lombardi. 75% freelance written. Works with a small number of new/unpublished writers each year. Monthly magazine covering computer games. "*CGW* is read by an adult audience looking for detailed reviews and information on strategy, adventure and action games." Estab. 1981. Circ. 145,000. Pays on publication. Publishes ms an average of 3 months after acceptance. Byline given. Buys all rights. Submit seasonal/holiday material 4 months in advance. Electronic submissions preferred, but not required. Query first. Reports in 4 months. Sample copy for $3.50. Free writer's guidelines.

Nonfiction: Reviews, strategy tips, industry insights. Buys 60 mss/year. Query. Length: 750-2,000 words. Pays 15-20¢/word. Sometimes pays the expenses of writers on assignment.

DRAGON MAGAZINE, TSR, Inc., 201 Sheridan Springs Rd., Lake Geneva WI 53147-0111. (414)248-3625. Fax: (414)248-0389. Editor: Wolfgang Baur. Monthly magazine of fantasy and science-fiction role-playing games. 90% freelance written. Eager to work with published/established writers as well as new/unpublished writers. "Most of our readers are intelligent, imaginative teenage males." Estab. 1976. Circ. about 100,000, primarily across the US, Canada and Great Britain. Byline given. Offers kill fee. Submit seasonal/holiday material 8 months in advance. Pays on publication for articles to which all rights are purchased; pays on acceptance for articles to which first/worldwide rights in English are purchased. Publishing dates vary from 1-24 months after acceptance. Reports in 3 months. Sample copy $4.50. Writer's guidelines for #10 SAE with 1 first-class stamp.

Nonfiction: Articles on the hobby of science fiction and fantasy role-playing. No general articles on gaming hobby. "Our article needs are *very* specialized. Writers should be experienced in gaming hobby and role-playing. No strong sexual overtones or graphic depictions of violence." Buys 120 mss/year. Query. Length: 1,000-8,000 words. Pays $50-500 for assigned articles; $5-400 for unsolicited articles.

Fiction: Barbara G. Young, fiction editor. Fantasy only. "No strong sexual overtones or graphic depictions of violence." Buys 12 mss/year. Send complete ms. Length: 2,000-8,000 words. Pays 6-8¢/word.

Tips: "*Dragon Magazine* is *not* a periodical that the 'average reader' appreciates or understands. A writer must *be* a reader and must share the serious interest in gaming our readers possess."

GAME INFORMER MAGAZINE, for Video Game Enthusiasts, Sunrise Publications, 10120 West 76th St., Eden Prairie MN 55344. (612)946-7245. Editor: Andy McNamara. 50% freelance written. Bimonthly magazine for video game industry. Estab. 1991. Circ. 200,000. Pays on publication. Publishes ms an average of 3 months after acceptance. Byline given. Offers 50% kill fee. Buys first and one-time rights. Editorial lead time 3 months. Submit seasonal material 3-4 months in advance. Accepts simultaneous submissions.

Query for electronic submissions. Sample copy and writer's guidelines free on request.

Nonfiction: Essays, general interest, historical/nostalgic, how-to, interview/profile, new product, opinion, technical, game strategies. Publishes year-end tip and strategy guide (deadline mid-October). No game reviews. Buys 4 mss/year. Query with published clips. Length: 500-2,000 words. Pays $50 for assigned articles.

Photos: State availability of photos with submission. Reviews 2×2 transparencies and 3×5 prints. Negotiates payment individually. Identification of subjects required. Buys one-time rights.

Columns/Departments: Query. Pays $25-150.

Fillers: Facts, gags to be illustrated by cartoonist, newsbreaks. Buys 6/year. Length negotiable. Pay negotiable.

Tips: "We appreciate queries prior to manuscript submissions, as we prefer to assign articles or discuss them first. It is best to call with one or two story ideas in mind. We are a very topic-specific publication and look for writers with expertise in a given area. However, the writing style must be open and appeal to a broad age range. We often look for special interest or focus articles on a given aspect of the very dynamic industry that we cover. Technical hardware features or company profiles are also welcome."

GIANT CROSSWORDS, Scrambl-Gram, Inc., Puzzle Buffs International, 1772 State Rd., Cuyahoga Falls OH 44223-1200. (216)923-2397. Editor: C.R. Elum. Submissions Editor: S. Bowers. 40% freelance written. Eager to work with new/unpublished writers. Quarterly crossword puzzle and word game magazine. Estab. 1970. **Pays on acceptance.** Publishes ms an average of 1 month after acceptance. No byline given. Buys all rights. Accepts previously published materials. Send information about when and where the article previously appeared. Reports in 1 month. "We offer constructors' kits, master grids, clue sheets and a 'how-to-make-crosswords' book for $37.50 postpaid." Send #10 SASE for details.

Nonfiction: Crosswords and word games only. Query. Pays according to size of puzzle and/or clues.

Tips: "We are expanding our syndication of original crosswords and our publishing schedule to include new titles and extra issues of current puzzle books."

SCHOOL MATES, United States Chess Federation, 186 Rte. 9W, New Windsor NY 12553-5794. (914)562-8350 ext. 152. Fax: (914)561-CHES (2437). Editor: Brian Bugbee. Contact: Judy Levine, assistant editor. 10% freelance written. Bimonthly magazine of chess for the beginning (some intermediate) player. Includes instruction, player profiles, chess tournament coverage, listings. Estab. 1987. Circ. 27,000. Pays on publication. Publishes ms an average of 6 months after acceptance. Byline given. Publication copyrighted "but not filed with Library of Congress." Buys first rights. Editorial lead time 2 months. Submit seasonal material 3 months in advance. Accepts simultaneous and previously published submissions. Send tearsheet, photocopy of article or typed ms with rights for sale noted and information about when and where the article previously appeared. For reprints, pays 100% of the amount paid for an original article. Query for electronic submissions. Reports in 1 week-6 months. Sample copy and writer's guidelines free on request.

Nonfiction: How-to, humor, personal experience (chess, but not "my first tournament"), photo feature, technical, travel and any other chess related item. "No poetry; no fiction; no sex, drugs, rock 'n roll." Buys 1-2 mss/year. Query. Length: 250-1,000 words. Pays $50/1,000 words. "We are not-for-profit; we try to make up for low $ rate with complimentary copies." Sometimes pays expenses of writers on assignment.

Photos: Send photos with submission. Reviews prints. Offers $25/photo for first time rights. Captions and identification of subjects required. Buys one-time rights, pays $15 for subsequent use.

Columns/Departments: Test Your Tactics/Winning Chess Tactics (explanation, with diagrams, of chess tactics; 8 diagrammed chess problems, e.g. "white to play and win in 2 moves"), 270 words; Basic Chess (chess instruction for beginners). Query with published clips. Pays $50/1,000 words.

Tips: "Know your subject; chess is a technical subject, and you can't fake it. Human interest stories on famous chess players or young chess players can be 'softer,' but always remember you are writing for children, and make it lively. We use the Frye readability scale (3rd-6th grade reading level), and items written on the appropriate reading level do stand out immediately! We are most open to human interest stories, puzzles, cartoons, photos. We are always looking for an unusual angle, e.g. (wild example) a kid who plays chess while surfing, or (more likely) a blind kid and how she plays chess with her specially-made chess pieces and board, etc."

Gay and Lesbian Interest

The magazines listed here cover a wide range of politics, culture, news, art, literature and issues of general interest to gay and lesbian communities. Magazines of a strictly sexual content are listed in the Relationships section.

BAY WINDOWS, New England's Largest Gay and Lesbian Newspaper, Bay Windows, Inc., 1523 Washington St., Boston MA 02118-2034. (617)266-6670. Fax: (617)266-0187. E-mail: jepperly@baywindows.com. Editor: Jeff Epperly. Arts Editor: Ruby Kikel. 30-40% freelance written. Weekly newspaper of gay news and concerns. "*Bay Windows* covers predominantly news of New England, but will print non-local news and features depending on the newsworthiness of the story. We feature hard news, opinion, news analysis, arts reviews and interviews." Estab. 1983. Publishes ms within 2 months of acceptance, pays within 2 months of publication. Byline given. Offers 50% kill fee. Rights obtained varies, usually first serial rights. Simultaneous submissions accepted if other submissions are outside of New England. Submit seasonal material 3 months in advance. Accepts previously published submissions. Send typed ms with rights for sale noted and information about when and where the article previously appeared. Pays 75% of their fee for an original article. Reports in 3 months. Sample copy for $5. Writer's guidelines for #10 SASE.

Nonfiction: Hard news, general interest with a gay slant, interview/profile, opinion, photo features. Publishes 200 mss/year. Query with published clips or send complete ms. Length: 500-1,500 words. Pay varies: $25-100 news; $10-60 arts.

Photos: $25/published photo, b&w photos only. Model releases and identification of subjects required.

Columns/Departments: Film, music, dance, books, art. Length: 500-1,500 words. Buys 200 mss/year. Pays $10-100.

● Looking for more humor.

Poetry: All varieties. Publishes 50 poems per year. Length: 10-30 lines. No payment.

Tips: "Too much gay-oriented writing is laden with the clichés and catch phrases of the movement. Writers must have intimate knowledge of gay community; however, this should not mean that standard English usage is not required. We look for writers with new—even controversial perspectives on the lives of gay men and lesbians. While we assume gay is good, we will print stories which examine problems within the community and movement. No pornography or erotica."

‡EVERGREEN CHRONICLES, A Journal of Gay And Lesbian Arts And Cultures, P.O. Box 8939, Minneapolis MN 55408. (612)649-4982. Editor: Jim Berg. Contact: Susan Raffo, managing editor. 75% freelance written. Triannual magazine covering gay, lesbian and bisexual communities. "*The Evergreen Chronicles* is a semi-annual journal dedicated to exploring gay and lesbian arts and cultures. We are interested in work that challenges and explores the meaning of 'gay' or 'lesbian,' especially as related to race, class, sexuality and gender." Estab. 1984. Circ. 2,000. Pays on publication. Publishes ms an average of 3 months after acceptance. Byline given. Buys first rights. Submit seasonal material 2 months in advance. Reports in 2 weeks on queries; 3 months on mss. Sample copy for $8. Writer's guidelines for #10 SASE.

Nonfiction: Book excerpts, essays, historical/nostalgic, interview/profile, opinion, personal experience. Buys 6 mss/year. Query or send complete ms. Length: up to 4,000 words. Pays $50.

Photos: State availability of photos with submissions. Reviews contact sheets. Captions required. Buys one-time rights.

Fiction: Erotica, ethnic, experimental, fantasy, historical, novel excerpts. Buys 20 mss/year. Send 4 copies of ms. Length: up to 4,000 words. Pays $50.

Poetry: All types. Buys 40 poems/year. Submit maximum 4 poems. Pays $50.

‡GIRLFRIENDS MAGAZINE, The Magazine of Lesbian Enjoyment, P.O. Box 713, Half Moon Bay CA 94019. Editor: Heather Findlay. Contact: Diane Anderson, managing editor. Bimonthly magazine covering lesbian culture, politics, and sexuality. "Hailed as 'the lesbian *Playboy*,' *Girlfriends* runs quality journalism, reviews, and photography covering lesbian culture, politics, and sexuality." Estab. 1994. Circ. 45,000. Pays on publication. Publishes ms an average of 2-6 months after acceptance. Byline given. Offers 25% kill fee. Buys first rights, use for advertising/promoting *Girlfriends*. Editorial lead time 3 months. Submit seasonal material 6 months in advance. Accepts simultaneous and previously published submissions. Query for electronic submissions. Reports in 3 weeks on queries; 3 months on mss. Sample copy for $4.95 plus $1.50 shipping and handling. Writer's guidelines for #10 SASE.

● *Girlfriends* is holding a contest for illustrators for the March/April 1996 issue cover.

Nonfiction: Book excerpts, essays, exposé, humor, interview/profile, personal experience, photo feature, travel. Buys 20-25 mss/year. Query with published clips. Length: 1,000-3,500 words. Pays 10¢/word.

Photos: Send photos with submissions. Reviews contact sheets, 4×5 or 2¼×2¼ transparencies, prints. Offers $30-250/photo. Captions, model releases, identification of subjects required. Buys one-time rights, use for advertising/promoting *GF*.

Columns/Departments: Crib Notes (lesbian parenting), 800 words; Out of Bounds (sports), 600 words; Playgrounds (travel), 1,000 words. Buys 20 mss/year. Query with published clips. Pays 10¢/word.

Fiction: Erotica, ethnic, experimental, fantasy, historical, humorous, mystery, novel concepts, science fiction. Buys 6-10 mss/year. Query with complete ms. Length: 1,000-3,000 words. Pays 10¢/word.

Poetry: Avant-garde, free verse, Haiku, light verse, traditional. Buys 6-10 poems/year. Submit maximum 5 poems. Length: 3-75 lines. Pays $50.

Fillers: Gags to be illustrated by cartoonist, short humor. Buys 6-10/year. Length: 500-800 words. Pays $50.

Tips: "Be unafraid of controversy—articles should focus on problems and debates raised around lesbian culture, politics, and sexuality. Fiction should be innovative and eyebrow-raising. Avoid being 'politically correct.' Photographers should aim for the suggestive, not the explicit."

THE GUIDE, To Gay Travel, Entertainment, Politics and Sex, Fidelity Publishing, P.O. Box 593, Boston MA 02199-0593. (617)266-8557. Fax: (617)266-1125. Editor: French Wall. 50% freelance written.

Monthly magazine on the gay and lesbian community. Estab. 1981. Circ. 30,000. **Pays on acceptance.** Publishes ms an average of 2 months after acceptance. Kill fee negotiable. Buys all rights. Submit seasonal material 2 months in advance. Accepts simultaneous submissions. Reports in 3 months. Sample copy for 9 × 12 SAE with 8 first-class stamps. Writer's guidelines for #10 SASE.

Nonfiction: Book excerpts (if yet unpublished), essays, exposé, general interest, historical/nostalgic, humor, interview/profile, opinion, personal experience, photo feature, religious. Buys 24 mss/year. Query with or without published clips or send complete ms. Length: 500-5,000 words. Pays $50-180.

Photos: Send photos with submission. Reviews contact sheets. Offers no additional payment for photos accepted with ms (although sometimes negotiable). Captions, model releases, identification of subjects prefered; releases required sometimes. Buys one-time rights.

Tips: "Brevity, humor and militancy appreciated."

LAMBDA BOOK REPORT, A Review of Contemporary Gay and Lesbian Literature, Lambda Rising, Inc., 1625 Connecticut Ave. NW, Washington DC 20009-1013. (202)462-7924. Fax: (202)462-7257. E-mail: lambdabookreport@his.com. Senior Editor: Jim Marks. Assistant Editor: Kanani Kauka. Managing Editor: Leslie Smith. 90% freelance written. Bimonthly magazine that covers gay/lesbian literature. "*Lambda Book Report* devotes its entire contents to the discussion of gay and lesbian books and authors. Any other submissions would be inappropriate." Estab. 1987. Circ. 11,000. Pays 30 days after publication. Byline given. Buys first rights. Query for electronic submissions. Reports in 2 months. Sample copy for $3.95 and 9 × 12 SAE with 5 first-class stamps. Free writer's guidelines.

● This editor sees an increasing need for writers familiar with economic and science/medical-related topics.

Nonfiction: Book excerpts, essays (on gay literature), interview/profile (of authors), book reviews. "No historical essays, fiction or poetry." Query with published clips. Length: 200-2,000 words. Pays $15-125 for assigned articles; $5-25 for unsolicited articles.

Photos: Send photos with submission. Reviews contact sheets. Offers $10-25/photo. Model releases required. Buys one-time rights.

Tips: "Assignments go to writers who query with 2-3 published book reviews and/or interviews. It is helpful if the writer is familiar with gay and lesbian literature and can write intelligently and objectively on the field. Review section is most open. Writers should demonstrate with clips their scope of knowledge, ability and interest in reviewing gay books."

MOM GUESS WHAT NEWSPAPER, 1725 L St., Sacramento CA 95814. (916)441-6397. Editor: Linda Birner. 80% freelance written. Works with small number of new/unpublished writers each year. Biweekly tabloid covering gay rights and gay lifestyles. Estab. 1978. Circ. 21,000. Publishes ms an average of 3 months after acceptance. Byline given. Buys all rights. Submit seasonal material 3 months in advance. Reports in 2 months. Sample copy for $1. Writer's guidelines for 10 × 13 SAE with 4 first-class stamps.

Nonfiction: Interview/profile and photo feature of international, national or local scope. Buys 8 mss/year. Query. Length: 200-1,500 words. Payment depends on article. Pays expenses of writers on special assignment.

Photos: Send photos with submission. Reviews 5 × 7 prints. Offers no additional payment for photos accepted with ms. Captions and identification of subjects required. Buys one-time rights.

Columns/Departments: News, Restaurants, Political, Health, Film, Video, Book Reviews. Buys 12 mss/year. Query. Payment depends on article.

‡OUT, 110 Greene St., Suite 600, New York NY 10012. Editors: Michael Goff, Sarah Pettit. 80% freelance written. Monthly "national gay and lesbian general-interest magazine. Our subjects range from current affairs to culture, from fitness to finance. Stories may be anywhere from 50-word items to 8,000-word investigative features." Estab. 1992. Circ. 120,000. Pays on publication. Publishes ms an average of 3 months after acceptance. Byline given. Offers 25% kill fee. Buys first North American serial rights, second serial (reprint) rights for anthologies (additional fee paid) and 30-day reprint rights (additional fee paid if applicable). Editorial lead time 3 months. Submit seasonal material 4-5 months in advance. Accepts simultaneous submissions and previously published submissions (infrequently). Reports in 6 weeks on queries; 2 months on mss. Sample copy for $6. Writer's guidelines. for #10 SASE.

Nonfiction: Book excerpts, essays, exposé, general interest, historical/nostalgic, humor, interview/profile, new product, opinion, personal experience, photo feature, travel, fashion/lifestyle. Buys 200 mss/year. Query with published clips. Length: 50-10,000 words. Pays 50¢/word. Sometimes pays expenses of writers on assignment.

Photos: State availability of photos with submission. Reviews contact sheets, transparencies, prints. Negotiates payment individually. Captions, model releases, identification of subjects required. Buys one-time rights.

Tips: "OUT's contributors include editors and writers from the country's top consumer titles: skilled reporters, columnists, and writers with distinctive voices and specific expertise in the fields they cover. But while published clips and relevant experience are a must, the magazine also seeks out fresh, young voices. The best guide to the kind of stories we publish is to review our recent issues—is there a place for the story you have in mind? Be aware of our long lead time."

‡**OUTSMART**, Up & Out Communications, 3406 Audubon Place, Houston TX 77006. (713)520-7237. Editor: Eric Roland. Contact: Greg Jeu, publisher. 70% freelance written. Monthly magazine covering gay and lesbian issues. *"OutSmart provides positive information to gay men, lesbians and their associates to enhance and improve the quality of our lives."* Estab. 1994. Circ. 15,000. Pays on publication. Publishes ms an average of 2 months after acceptance. Byline given. Buys one-time rights and simultaneous rights. Editorial lead time 2 months. Submit seasonal material 2 months in advance. Accepts simultaneous submissions and previously published submissions. Query for electronic submissions. Reports in 6 weeks on queries; 2 months on mss. Sample copy and writer's guidelines for SASE.
Nonfiction: Historical/nostalgic, interview/profile, opinion, personal experience, photo feature, travel. Buys 20 mss/year. Send complete ms. Length: 700-4,000 words. Pays $20-100.
Photos: State availability of photos with submission. Reviews 4×6 prints. Negotiates payment individually. Identification of subjects required. Buys one-time rights.

‡**TEN PERCENT**, Browning Grace Communications, 54 Mint St., Suite 200, San Francisco CA 94103. (415)905-8590. Editor: Sara Hart. Managing Editor: Anne-Marie Praetzel. Editorial Assistant: Daryl Lindsey. 75% freelance written. Bimonthly magazine covering gay and lesbians. Estab. 1992. Circ. 75,000. Pays on publication. Publishes ms an average of 3 months after acceptance. Byline given. Offers 25% kill fee. Buys first North American serial rights. Editorial lead time 4 months. Submit seasonal material 6 months in advance. Accepts simultaneous submissions. Query for electronic submissions. Reports in 2 weeks on queries; 1 month on mss. Sample copy and writer's guidelines free on request.
Nonfiction: David Thorpe. Book excerpts, essays, exposé, general interest, historical/nostalgic, humor, interview/profile, opinion, photo feature, travel. Buys 30 mss/year. Query with published clips. Length: 1,500-3,500 words. Pays 25-50¢/word. Sometimes pays expenses of writers on assignment.
Photos: State availability of photos with submissions. Reviews contact sheets, negatives, transparencies, prints. Negotiates payment individually. Buys one-time rights.
Columns/Departments: David Thorpe. Opinion, Travel, Food, Design, Humor (all with gay and lesbian focus), 1,200-1,500 words. Buys 18 mss/year. Query with published clips. Pays $300-600.
Fiction: Maria DeLao. Novel excerpts. Buys 3 mss/year. Query with published clips. Length: 2,000-3,000 words. Pays $600-800.
Fillers: Daryl Lindsay. Anecdotes, facts, short humor. Buys 25/year. Length: 150-750 wors. Pays 25-50¢/word.
Tips: "Detailed query letters. Some indication that writer is familiar with tone and attitude of *10 Percent.*"

THE WASHINGTON BLADE, Washington Blade, Inc., 1408 U St., NW, Washington DC 20009-3916. (202)797-7000. Fax: (202)797-7040. Senior Editor: Lisa M. Keen. 20% freelance written. Weekly news tabloid covering the gay/lesbian community. "Articles (subjects) should be written from or directed to a gay perspective." Estab. 1969. Circ. 43,000. Pays in 1 month. Publishes ms an average of 1 month after acceptance. Byline given. Offers $15 kill fee. Buys first North American serial rights. Submit seasonal material 1 month in advance. Reports in 2 months. Sample copy and writer's guidelines for 9×12 SAE with 6 first-class stamps.
Nonfiction: Exposé (of government, private agency, church, etc., handling of gay-related issues); historical/nostalgic; interview/profile (of gay community/political leaders; persons, gay or nongay, in positions to affect gay issues; outstanding achievers who happen to be gay; those who incorporate the gay lifestyle into their professions); photo feature (on a nationally or internationally historic gay event); travel (on locales that welcome or cater to the gay traveler). *The Washington Blade* basically covers 2 areas: news and lifestyle. News coverage of D.C. metropolitan area gay community, local and federal government actions relating to gays, as well as national news of interest to gays. Section also includes features on current events. Special issues: annual gay pride (early June). No sexually explicit material. Articles of interest to the community must include and be written for both gay men and lesbians. Buys 30 mss/year, average. Query with published clips and résumé. Length: 500-1,500 words. Pays 5-10¢/word. Sometimes pays the expenses of writers on assignment.
Photos: "A photo or graphic with feature/lifestyle articles is particularly important. Photos with news stories are appreciated." Send photos. Reviews b&w contact sheets and 5×7 glossy prints. Pays $25 minimum. Captions preferred; model releases required. On assignment, photographer paid mutually agreed upon fee, with expenses reimbursed. Publication retains all rights.
Tips: "Send good examples of your writing and know the paper before you submit a manuscript for publication. We get a lot of submissions which are entirely inappropriate. We're looking for more features, but fewer AIDS-related features. Greatest opportunity for freelancers resides in current events, features, interviews and book reviews."

THE JAMES WHITE REVIEW, A Gay Men's Literary Quarterly, P.O. Box 3356, Butler Quarter, Minneapolis MN 55403. (612)339-8317. Editor: Phil Willkie. 100% freelance written. Quarterly tabloid covering gay men. Estab. 1983. Circ. 4,500. Byilne given. Buys first North American serial rights. Editorial lead time 3 months. Submit seasonal material 3 months in advance. Query for electronic submissions. Reports in 3 months on queries. Sample copy for $3. Writer's guidelines for #10 SASE.

Nonfiction: Book excerpts and essays. Buys 4 mss/year. Send complete ms. Length: 2,000 words maximum. Pays $50 minimum.
Photos: Send photos with submission. Reviews prints. Negotiates payment individually. Buys one-time rights.
Fiction: Confession, erotica, experimental, fantasy, historical, novel excerpts and serialized novels. Buys 20 mss/year. Send complete ms. Length: 2,000 words maximum. Pays $50 maximum.
Poetry: Cliff Mayhood, poetry editor. Avant-garde, free verse, light verse and traditional. Buys 80 poems/year. Submit maximum 10 poems. Pays $20.

General Interest

General interest magazines need writers who can appeal to a broad audience—teens and senior citizens, wealthy readers and the unemployed. Each magazine still has a personality that suits its audience—one that a writer should study before sending material to an editor. Other markets for general interest material are in these Consumer categories: Ethnic/Minority, Inflight, Men's, Regional and Women's. General interest magazines that are geared toward a specific group (such as doctors) are listed in Trade in their respective sections.

THE AMERICAN LEGION MAGAZINE, P.O. Box 1055, Indianapolis IN 46206-1055. (317)635-8411. Editor: Steve Salerno. Monthly. 70% freelance written. Prefers to work with published/established writers, but works with a small number of new/unpublished writers each year. Estab. 1919. Circ. 2.9 million. Buys first North American serial rights. Reports on submissions "promptly." **Pays on acceptance.** Publishes ms an average of 6 months after acceptance. Byline given. Reports in 2 months. Sample copy for 9×12 SAE with 6 first-class stamps. Writer's guidelines for #10 SASE.
Nonfiction: Query first, considers some unsolicited ms. Query should explain the subject or issue, article's angle and organization, writer's qualifications and experts to be interviewed. Well-reported articles or expert commentaries cover issues/trends in world/national affairs, contemporary problems, general interest, sharply-focused feature subjects. Monthly Q&A with national figures/experts. Few personality profiles. No regional topics. Buys 75 mss/year. Length: 1,000-2,000 words. Pays $600-2,000. Pays phone expenses of writers on assignment.
Photos: On assignment.
Tips: "Queries by new writers should include clips/background/expertise; no longer than 1½ pages. Submit suitable material showing you have read several issues. *The American Legion Magazine* considers itself '*the* magazine for a strong America.' Reflect this theme (which includes economy, educational system, moral fiber, social issues, infrastructure, technology and national defense/security). We are a general interest, national magazine, not a strictly military magazine. No unsolicited jokes."

THE AMERICAN SCHOLAR, The Phi Beta Kappa Society, 1811 Q Street NW, Washington DC 20009-9974. (202)265-3808. Editor: Joseph Epstein. Managing Editor: Jean Stipicevic. 100% freelance written. Intellectual quarterly. "Our writers are specialists writing for the college-educated public." Estab. 1932. Circ. 26,000. Pays after author has seen edited piece in galleys. Byline given. Offers 50% kill fee. Buys first rights. Submit seasonal/holiday material 6 months in advance. Reports in 2 weeks on queries; 2 months on ms. Sample copy for $6.50. Writer's guidelines for #10 SASE.
Nonfiction: Book excerpts (prior to publication only), essays, historical/nostalgic, humor. Buys 40 mss/year. Query. Length: 3,000-5,000 words. Pays $500.
Columns/Departments: Buys 16 mss/year. Query. Length: 3,000-5,000 words. Pays $500.
Poetry: Sandra Costich, poetry editor. Buys 20/year. Submit maximum 3 poems. Length: 34-75 lines. Pays $50. "Write for guidelines."
Tips: "The section most open to freelancers is the book review section. Query and send samples of reviews written."

AMERICAN TIMES/PRIME TIMES, For The Ways We Live, Grote Publishing, 634 W. Main St., Suite 207, Madison WI 53703-2634. Editor: Barbara Walsh. 30% freelance written. Quarterly association-sponsored publication for financial institutions. "*American Times* is a topical magazine of broad appeal, available to the general public but mainly distributed to older adult club members of financial institutions. It offers investigative reporting, interviews, and timely articles on health, finance, travel, outdoor sports, consumer issues, lifestyle, home arts, science, and technology, specializing in articles that are quintessentially 'American' in flavor." Estab. 1979 (*Prime Times*), 1993 (*American Times*). Circ. 140,000. Pays on publication. Publishes ms an average of 3-7 months after acceptance. Byline given. Buys first North American serial rights, one-time rights, and second serial (reprint) rights. Editorial lead time 7 months. Submit seasonal material 7 months in advance. Accepts previously published submissions. Send photocopy of article or typed ms with rights for sale noted and information about when and where the article previously appeared. For reprints, pays $50-125, depending on length, quality and number of times published. Query for electronic submissions. Reports in 6 weeks on queries; 2 months on mss. Sample copy for $4, and 9×12 SAE with 5 first-class stamps. Writer's guidelines for #10 SASE.

Nonfiction: Book excerpts, general interest, travel, historical, humor, interview/profile, photo feature. "No nostalgia pieces, medical or financial pieces based solely on personal anecdotes, or personal opinion essays." Buys 4-10 mss/year. Prefers to see complete ms. Length: 1,200-2,000 words. Pays $250 minimum for full-length assigned articles; $100 minimum for unsolicited articles.

Photos: State availability of or send photos with submission. Reviews contact sheets, transparencies and prints. Negotiates payment individually. Model releases and identification of subjects required. Buys one-time rights.

Tips: "Articles that contain useful, well-documented, up-to-date information have the best chance of publication. Don't send personal essays, or articles that repeat information readily available in mainstream media. Articles on health and medical issues *must* be founded in sound scientific method and include current data. You must be able to document your research. Make it easy for us to make a decision on your submission. If the article is written, submit the entire thing—manuscript with professional-quality photos. If you query, be specific. Write part of it in the style in which you would write the article. Be sure to enclose clips. With every article we publish, something about the story must lend itself to strong graphic representation."

‡AMTRAK EXPRESS, Pace Communications, Inc., 1301 Carolina St., Greensboro NC 27401. (919)378-6065. Editor: Melinda Stovall. Associate Editor: Sarah Lindsay. Bimonthly magazine that covers life in the US (people, art, business, history, cultures). Estab. 1981. Circ. 250,000. **Pays on acceptance**. Publishes ms an average of 4 months after acceptance. Byline given. Offers 25% kill fee. Buys first North American serial rights. Submit seasonal/holiday material 4 months in advance. Query for electronic submissions. Reports in 6 weeks. Sample copy for $4. Writer's guidelines for SASE.

Nonfiction: General interest, business, sports, interview/profile, travel. "No fiction or reprints." Buys 12 mss/year. Query with published clips, or send complete ms. Length: 1,500-2,000 words. Pays $300-800.

Photos: State availability of photos with submission. Offers no additional payment for photos accepted with ms. Identification of subjects required. Buys one-time rights.

Columns/Departments: Features (sports and leisure, business, travel within Amtrak coverage area, health, American innovations and rail travel experiences), 1,500-2,000 words. Buys 36 mss/year. Query with published clips or send complete ms. Pays $300-500.

Tips: "We look for informed, energetic and keen writing to inform and entertain the mix of business and leisure travelers riding on Amtrak. Articles should be well-researched, current, lively, informative and balanced."

THE ATLANTIC, 745 Boylston St., Boston MA 02116. (617)536-9500. Editor: William Whitworth. Managing Editor: Cullen Murphy. Monthly magazine of arts and public affairs. Circ. 500,000. Pays on acceptance. Byline given. Buys first North American serial rights. Simultaneous submissions discouraged. Reporting time varies. All unsolicited mss must be accompanied by SASE.

● Writers should be aware that this is not a market for beginner's work (nonfiction and fiction), nor is it truly for intermediate work. Study this magazine before sending only your best, most professional work.

Nonfiction: Book excerpts, essays, general interest, humor, personal experience, religious, travel. Query with or without published clips or send complete ms. Length: 1,000-6,000 words. Payment varies. Sometimes pays expenses of writers on assignment.

Fiction: C. Michael Curtis, fiction editor. Buys 12-15 mss/year. Send complete ms. Length: 2,000-6,000 words preferred. Payment $2,500.

● See the interview with C. Michael Curtis in the introduction to this section.

Poetry: Peter Davison, poetry editor. Buys 40-60 poems/year.

CAPPER'S, Stauffer Communications, Inc., 1503 SW 42nd St., Topeka KS 66609-1265. (913)274-4346. Fax: (913)274-4305. Editor: Nancy Peavler. Associate Editor: Cheryl Ptacek. 25% freelance written. Works with a small number of new/unpublished writers each year. Biweekly tabloid emphasizing home and family for readers who live in small towns and on farms. Estab. 1879. Circ. 375,000. **Pays for poetry and fiction on acceptance;** articles on publication. Publishes ms an average of 6 months after acceptance. Buys first serial rights only. Submit seasonal/holiday material at least 2 months in advance. Accepts previously published submissions. Send typed ms with rights for sale noted and information about when and where the article previously appeared. For reprints, pays $1.50/column inch as printed. Reports in 4 months; 10 months for serialized novels. Sample copy for $1. Writer's guidelines for #10 SASE.

Nonfiction: Historical (local museums, etc.), inspirational, nostalgia, budget travel (Midwest slants), people stories (accomplishments, collections, etc.). Buys 50 mss/year. Submit complete ms. Length: 700 words maximum. Pays $1.65/inch.

Photos: Purchased with accompanying ms. Submit prints. Pays $10-15 for 8×10 or 5×7 b&w glossy prints. Total purchase price for ms includes payment for photos. Limited market for color photos (35mm color slides); pays $35-40 each.

Columns/Departments: Heart of the Home (homemakers' letters, recipes, hints); Hometown Heartbeat (descriptive). Submit complete ms. Length: 300 words maximum. Pays $1 gift certificate to $15 cash.

Fiction: "We buy very few fiction pieces—longer than short stories, shorter than novels." Adventure and romance mss. No explicit sex, violence or profanity. Buys 4-5 mss/year. Query. Pays $75-400 for 7,500-60,000 words.

Poetry: Free verse, haiku, light verse, traditional, nature, inspiration. "The poems that appear in *Capper's* are not too difficult to read. They're easy to grasp. We're looking for everyday events and down-to-earth themes." Buys 4-5/issue. Limit submissions to batches of 5-6. Length: 4-16 lines. Pays $5-15.

Tips: "Study a few issues of our publication. Most rejections are for material that is too long, unsuitable or out of character for our paper (too sexy, too much profanity, etc.). On occasion, we must cut material to fit column space."

THE CHRISTIAN SCIENCE MONITOR, 1 Norway St., Boston MA 02115. (617)450-2000. Contact: Submissions. International newspaper issued daily except Saturdays, Sundays and holidays in North America; weekly international edition. Estab. 1908. Circ. 95,000. Buys all newspaper rights worldwide for 3 months following publication. Buys limited number of mss, "top quality only." Publishes original (exclusive) material only. Pays on publication. Reports in 1 month. Submit complete original ms or letter of inquiry. Writer's guidelines for #10 SASE.

Nonfiction: Jane Lampmann, feature editor. In-depth features and essays. Please query by mail before sending mss. "Style should be bright but not cute, concise but thoroughly researched. Try to humanize news or feature writing so reader identifies with it. Avoid sensationalism, crime and disaster. Accent constructive, solution-oriented treatment of subjects." Home Forum page buys essays of 400-900 words. Pays $150 average. Education, arts, environment, food, science and technology pages will consider articles not usually more than 800 words appropriate to respective subjects. No medical stories." Pays $150-200.

Poetry: Traditional, blank and free verse. Seeks non-religious poetry of high quality and of all lengths up to 75 lines. Pays $35-75 average.

Tips: "We prefer neatly typed originals. No handwritten copy. Enclosing an SAE and postage with ms is a must."

‡DIVERSION, Hearst Business Publishing, 1790 Broadway, New York NY 10119. Almost 100% freelance written. Sample copy and writer's guidelines for SASE and 3 first-class stamps.

Tips: "Narrow the focus."

EQUINOX: Canada's Magazine of Discovery, Telemedia Communications, Inc., 25 Sheppard Ave. W., Suite 100, North York, Ontario M2N 6S7 Canada. (416)733-7600. Editor: Jim Cormier. Bimonthly magazine "publishing in-depth profiles of people, places and wildlife to show readers the real stories behind subjects of general interest in the fields of science and geography." Estab. 1982. Circ. 175,000. **Pays on acceptance.** Byline given. Offers 50% kill fee. Buys first North American serial rights only. Submit seasonal queries 1 year in advance. Reports in 2 months. Sample copy for $5 and #10 SAE with 50¢ Canadian postage. Writer's guidelines for #10 SASE.

Nonfiction: Book excerpts (occasionally), geography, science, art, natural history and environment, no travel articles. Should have Canadian focus. Query. Length: 1,500-5,000 words. Pays $1,750-3,000 negotiated.

Photos: Send photos with ms. Reviews color transparencies—must be of professional quality; no prints or negatives. Captions and identification of subjects required.

Columns/Departments: Nexus (current science that isn't covered by daily media); Habitat (Canadian environmental stories not covered by daily media). Buys 80 mss/year. Query with clips of published work. Length: 200-800 words. Pays $250-500.

Tips: "Submit ideas for short photo essays as well as longer features."

FRIENDLY EXCHANGE, The Aegis Group: Publishers, Friendly Exchange Business Office, P.O. Box 2120, Warren MI 48090-2120. Publication Office: (810)558-7226. Editor: (702)786-7419. Editor: Adele Malott. 80% freelance written. Works with a small number of new/unpublished writers each year. Quarterly magazine for policyholders of Farmers Insurance Group of Companies exploring travel and leisure topics of interest to active families. "These are traditional families (median adult age 39) who live primarily in the area bounded by Ohio on the east and the Pacific Ocean on the west. New states added recently include Tennessee, Alabama, and Virginia." Estab. 1981. Circ. 5.7 million. **Pays on acceptance.** Publishes ms an average of 5 months after acceptance. Offers 25% kill fee. Buys all rights. Submit seasonal/holiday material 1 year in advance. Query for electronic submissions. Reports in 2 months. Sample copy for 9×12 SAE with 5 first-class stamps. Writer's guidelines for #10 SASE.

● *Friendly Exchange* plans an article per issue devoted to the family's leisure hours.

Nonfiction: "Domestic travel and leisure topics of interest to the family can be addressed from many different perspectives, including health and safety, consumerism, heritage and education. Articles offer a service to readers and encourage them to take some positive action such as taking a trip. Style is colorful, warm and inviting, making liberal use of anecdotes and quotes. The only first-person articles used are those assigned; all others in third person. Only domestic travel locations are considered. Buys 8 mss/issue. Query. Length: 600-1,500 words. Pays $500-1,000/article, plus agreed-upon expenses.

Photos: Art director. Pays $150-250 for 35mm color transparencies; $50 for b&w prints. Cover photo payment negotiable. Pays on publication.

Columns/Departments: All columns and departments rely on reader-generated materials; none used from professional writers.

Tips: "We concentrate exclusively on the travel and leisure hours of our readers. Do not use destination approach in travel pieces—instead, for example, tell us about the people, activities, or events that make the location special. We prefer to go for a small slice rather than the whole pie, and we are just as interested in the cook who made it or the person who will be eating it as we are in the pie itself. Concentrate on what families can do together."

GRIT, America's Family Magazine, Stauffer Magazine Group, 1503 SW 42nd St., Topeka KS 66609-1265. (913)274-4300. Editor-in-Chief: Michael Scheibach. 60% freelance written. Open to new writers. "*Grit* is Good News. As a wholesome, family-oriented magazine published for more than a century and distributed nationally, *Grit* is characterized by old-fashioned friendliness. *Grit* features articles about family lifestyles, family traditions, our American heritage, social themes and family values. In short, *Grit* accents the best of American life and traditions—past and present. Our readers cherish family values and appreciate practical and innovative ideas. Many of them live in small towns and rural areas across the country; others live in cities but share many of the values typical of small-town America." Estab. 1882. Circ. 400,000. Pays on publication. Publishes ms an average of 2 months after acceptance. Byline given. Buys first rights. Occasionally buys reprint rights if first publication was to extremely local or regional audience. Submit seasonal material 8 months in advance. Reports in 2 months on queries. Accepts previously published submissions. Send typed ms with rights for sale noted and information about when and where article previously appeared. Sample copy and writer's guidelines for $2 and 11×14 SAE with 4 first-class stamps.

Nonfiction: Most in need of cover stories (timely, newsworthy, but with a *Grit* angle); Profile, Americana and human interest features, Home, and Health stories. Also need touching, humorous or off-beat shorts with art (color or b&w). Writers will best be able to successfully sell their work by becoming familiar with the publication. Pays minimum of 22¢/word for assigned articles (average $150-500 for a feature, more with photos), less for unsolicited mss or reprints. Main features run 1,500 to 2,500 words, sidebars often additional; department features average 500-1,000 words.

Fiction: Short stories, 2,500 words; may also purchase accompanying art if of high quality and appropriate occasionally publishes shorter or longer work also. Send complete ms with SASE. Note Fiction Dept. on envelope!

Photos: Professional quality photos (b&w prints or color slides) increase acceptability of articles. Black and white prints *required* with Profile submissions. Photos: $35-200 each, dependent on quality, placement and color/b&w.

Tips: "With the exception of Profile submissions, articles should be nationalized with several sources identified fully. Third-person accounts are preferred. Information in sidebar or graphic form is appropriate for many stories. *Grit* readers enjoy lists of tips, resources, or questions that help them understand the topic. *Grit* stories should be helpful and conversational with an upbeat approach. Preferred to queries: Submit a list of several brief but developed story ideas by department/feature along with a brief bio and examples of your published work."

HARPER'S MAGAZINE, 666 Broadway, 11th Floor, New York NY 10012. (212)614-6500. Fax: (212)228-5889. Editor: Lewis H. Lapham. 90% freelance written. Monthly magazine for well-educated, socially concerned, widely read men and women who value ideas and good writing. Estab. 1850. Circ. 205,000. Rights purchased vary with author and material. Accepts previously published submissions for its "Readings" section. Send tearsheet or photocopy of article, or typed ms with rights for sale noted and information about when and where the article previously appeared. Pays negotiable kill fee. **Pays on acceptance.** Reports in 2 weeks. Publishes ms an average of 3 months after acceptance. Sample copy for $2.95.

Nonfiction: "For writers working with agents or who will query first only, our requirements are: public affairs, literary, international and local reporting and humor." No interviews; no profiles. Complete ms and query must include SASE. No unsolicited poems will be accepted. Publishes one major report per issue. Length: 4,000-6,000 words. Publishes one major essay/issue. Length: 4,000-6,000 words. "These should be construed as topical essays on all manner of subjects (politics, the arts, crime, business, etc.) to which the author can bring the force of passionately informed statement."

Fiction: Publishes one short story/month. Generally pays 50¢-$1/word.

Photos: Angela Reichers, art director. Occasionally purchased with mss; others by assignment. Pays $50-500.

KNOWLEDGE, Official Publication of the World Olympiads of Knowledge, Knowledge, Inc., 3863 Southwest Loop 820, S 100, Ft. Worth TX 76133-2063. (817)292-4272. Fax: (817)294-2893. Editor: Dr.

O.A. Battista. Managing Editor: Elizabeth Ann Battista. 90% freelance written. Quarterly magazine for lay and professional audiences of all occupations. Estab. 1985. Circ. 3,000. Pays on publication. Publishes ms an average of 6 months after acceptance. Buys all rights. "We will reassign rights to a writer after a given period." Accepts previously published submissions. Send photocopy of article. Byline given. Submit seasonal/holiday material 6 months in advance. Reports in 1 month. Sample copy for $6. Writer's guidelines for #10 SASE.

Nonfiction: Informational—original new knowledge that will prove mentally or physically beneficial to all readers. Buys 30 unsolicited mss/year. Query. Length: 1,500-2,000 words maximum. Pays $100 minimum. Sometimes pays the expenses of writers on assignment.

Columns/Departments: Journal section uses maverick and speculative ideas that other magazines will not publish and reference. Payment is made, on publication, at the following minimum rates: Feature Articles $100. Why Don't They, $50; Salutes, $25; New Vignettes, $25; Quotes To Ponder, $10; and Facts, $5.

Tips: "The editors of *Knowledge* welcome submissions from contributors. Manuscripts and art material will be carefully considered but received *only* with the unequivocal understanding that the magazine will not be responsible for loss or injury. Material from a published source should have the publication's name, date and page number. Submissions cannot be acknowledged and will be returned only when accompanied by a SASE having adequate postage."

LEFTHANDER MAGAZINE, Lefthander International, P.O. Box 8249, Topeka KS 66608-0249. (913)234-2177. Managing Editor: Kim Kipers. 80% freelance written. Eager to work with new/unpublished writers. Bimonthly magazine for "lefthanded people of all ages and interests in 50 US states and 12 foreign countries. The one thing they have in common is an interest in lefthandedness." Estab. 1975. Circ. 26,000. Pays on publication. Publishes ms an average of 4 months after acceptance. Byline usually given. Offers 25% kill fee. Rights negotiable. Simultaneous queries OK. Reports on queries in 2 months. Sample copy for $2 and 9×12 SAE. Writer's guidelines for #10 SASE.

Nonfiction: Interviews with famous lefthanders; features about lefthanders with interesting talents and occupations; how-to features (sports, crafts, hobbies for lefties); research on handedness and brain dominance; exposé on discrimination against lefthanders in the work world; features on occupations and careers attracting lefties; education features relating to ambidextrous right brain teaching methods. Buys 50-60 mss/year. Length: 1,500-2,000 words for features. Pays $85-100. Buys 6 personal experience shorts/year. Pays $25. Pays expenses of writer on assignment. Query with SASE.

Photos: State availability of photos for features. Pays $10-15 for good contrast b&w glossies. Rights negotiable.

Tips: "All material must have a lefthanded hook. We prefer practical, self-help and self-awareness types of editorial content of general interest."

LEISURE WORLD, Ontario Motorist Publishing Company, 1253 Ouellette Ave., Box 580, Windsor, Ontario N8X 1J3 Canada. (519)971-3208. Fax: (519)977-1197. Editor: Douglas O'Neil. 30% freelance written. Bimonthly magazine distributed to members of the Canadian Automobile Association in southwestern and midwestern Ontario, the Niagara Peninsula and the maritime provinces. Editorial content is focused on travel, entertainment and leisure time pursuits of interest to CAA members." Estab. 1988. Circ. 321,000. Pays on publication. Publishes ms an average of 2 months after acceptance. Buys first rights and second serial (reprint) rights. Submit seasonal/holiday material 4 months in advance. Accepts previously published submissions. Send information about when and where the article previously appeared. Pays 100% of amount paid for original article. Reports in 2 months. Sample copy for $2. Free writer's guidelines.

Nonfiction: Lifestyle, humor, travel. Buys 20 mss/year. Send complete ms. Length: 800-1,500 words. Pays $50-200.

Photos: Reviews negatives. Offers $40/photo. Captions, model releases required. Buys one-time rights.

Columns/Departments: Query with published clips. Length: 800 words. Pays $50-100.

Tips: "We are most interested in travel destination articles that offer a personal, subjective and positive point of view on international (including US) destinations. Good quality color slides are a must."

LIFE, Time & Life Bldg., Rockefeller Center, New York NY 10020. (212)522-1212. Managing Editor: Daniel Okrent. Articles: Jay D. Lovinger, executive editor: 10% freelance written. Prefers to work with published/established writers; rarely works with new/unpublished writers. (*Life* used no previously unpublished writers in 1994.) Monthly general interest picture magazine for people of all ages, backgrounds and interests. Estab. 1936. Circ. 1.5 million. **Pays on acceptance.** Publishes ms an average of 3 months after acceptance. Byline given. Buys first North American serial rights. Submit seasonal material 4 months in advance. Accepts simultaneous submissions. Reports in 2 months.

• *Life* won the 1994 Clarion Awards for Most Improved Magazine.

Nonfiction: "We've done articles on anything in the world of interest to the general reader and on people of importance. It's extremely difficult to break in since we buy so few articles. Most of the magazine is pictures. We're looking for very high quality writing. We select writers whom we think match the subject they are writing about." Query with clips of previously published work. Length: 1,000-4,000 words.

MACLEAN'S, Canada's Weekly News Magazine, Maclean Hunter Ltd., 777 Bay St., Toronto, Ontario M5W 1A7, Canada. Weekly publication covering Canadian and international news. This magazine did not respond to our request for information. Query before submitting.

MERIDIAN'S LIFESTYLES, Meridian International, Inc., Box 10010, Ogden UT 84409. (801)394-9446. 40% freelance written. Bimonthly inhouse magazine featuring personality profiles. **Pays on acceptance.** Publishes ms an average of 8 months after acceptance. Byline given. Buys first rights, second serial (reprint) rights and non-exclusive reprint rights. Accepts simultaneous and previously published submissions (written query first). Query first. Reports in 2 months with SASE. Sample copy for $1 and 9×12 SAE. Writer's guidelines for #10 SASE. All requests for sample copies, guidelines and queries should be addressed Attn: Editorial Staff.

Nonfiction: Personality profiles of nationally recognized celebrities in sports, entertainment and fine arts. "Celebrities must have positive values and make a contribution, beyond their good looks, to society. These are cover features—photogenic appeal needed." Buys 40 mss/year. Query. Length: 1,000 words. Pays 15¢/word for first rights plus non-exclusive reprint rights. Payment for second rights is 10¢/word.

Photos: Send photos with ms. Pays $35/inside photo, $50/cover photo. Reviews 35mm or larger transparencies and 5×7 or 8×10 sharp color prints. Prefers transparencies. Captions, model releases and identification of subjects required.

Tips: "The key is a well-written query letter that: 1) demonstrates that the subject of the article has national appeal; 2) shows that a profile of the person interviewed will have a clear, focused theme; 3) gives evidence that the writer/photographer is a professional, even if a beginner."

NATIONAL GEOGRAPHIC MAGAZINE, 1145 17th St. NW, Washington DC 20036. (202)857-7000. Fax: (202)828-6667. Editor: William Allen. Approximately 50% freelance written. Prefers to work with published/established writers. Monthly magazine for members of the National Geographic Society. Estab. 1888. Circ. 9.5 million.

Nonfiction: *National Geographic* publishes general interest, illustrated articles on science, natural history, exploration, politics and geographical regions. Almost half of the articles are staff-written. Of the freelance writers assigned, some are experts in their fields; the remainder are established professionals. Fewer than 1% of unsolicited queries result in assignments. Query (500 words) by letter, not by phone, to Associate Editor Robert Poole. Do not send mss. Before querying, study recent issues and check a *Geographic Index* at a library since the magazine seldom returns to regions or subjects covered within the past 10 years. Pays expenses of writers on assignment.

Photos: Photographers should query in care of the Photographic Division.

THE NEW YORKER, 20 W. 43rd St., New York NY 10036-7441. Editor: Tina Brown. Weekly. Estab. 1925. Circ. 600,000. *The New Yorker* is one of today's premier markets for top-notch nonfiction, fiction and poetry. Query before submitting. To submit material, please direct your ms to the appropriate editor, (i.e., fact, fiction, poetry or humor) and enclose SASE. The editors deal with a tremendous number of submissions every week; writers hoping to crack this market should be prepared to wait at least two or three months for a reply.

‡NEWSWEEK, 251 W. 57th St., New York NY 10019. (212)445-4000. Contact: My Turn Editor. Although staff written, accepts unsolicited mss for My Turn, a column of personal opinion. The 1,000- to 1,100-word essays for the column must be original, not published elsewhere and contain verifiable facts. Payment is $1,000, on publication. Buys first rights. Reports in 2 months only on submissions with SASE.

OUT WEST, America's On the Road Newspaper, 408 Broad St., Suite 11, Nevada City CA 95959. (916)478-9080. Fax: (916)478-9082. E-mail: outwestcw@aol.com. Editor: Chuck Woodbury. 30% freelance written. Quarterly tabloid for general audience. Estab. 1988. Circ. 12,000. Pays on acceptance or publication (negotiated). Byline given. Buys one-time or reprint rights. Submit seasonal/holiday material 4 months in advance. Accepts simultaneous and previously published submissions. Send tearsheet or photocopy of article, or typed ms with rights for sale noted and information about when and where the article previously appeared. For reprints, pays 50-75% of the amount paid for an original article. Reports in 1 month. Sample copy for $2.50. Writer's guidelines for #10 SASE.

Nonfiction: Essays, historical, humor, photo feature, profiles, travel, but always relating to the rural West. Readers are travelers and armchair travelers interested in what's along the back roads and old 2-lane highways of the non-urban West. Articles about old cafes, motels, hotels, roadside trading posts, drive-in theaters, highways of yesteryear like Route 66 and good roadtrips are especially welcome. No foreign travel. Query or send complete ms. Length: 300-1,000 words. Pays $25-100.

Photos: Black and white only; prefers 5×7 or 8×10 prints. Buys stand-alone photos of funny things and signs along the road. Pays $5-30.

Columns/Departments: Western wildlife, roadfood, roadtrips, rural museums and attractions, tourist railroads, Alaska, Death Valley, ghost towns, western history, western tours and off-beat attractions. Length: 400-600 words. Pays $25-35.

Fillers: Anecdotes, short humor, unusual Western historical facts, funny small business slogans, cartoons, travel tips, book, video reviews. Length 25-150 words. Pays $2-20.

Tips: "It's very important to read the publication before submitting work. No how-to articles. *Out West* is not an RV or senior publication."

‡THE OXFORD AMERICAN, A Magazine From the South, The Oxford American, Inc., P.O. Drawer 1156, Oxford MS 38655. Editor: Marc Smirnoff. Managing Editors: Linda White, Sid Scott. Contact: Sid Scott. 30-50% freelance written. Bimonthly magazine covering the South. "*The Oxford American* is a general-interest literary magazine about the South." Estab. 1992. Circ. 4,000. Pays 30 days after publication. Publishes ms an average of 6 months after acceptance. Byline given. Offers 50% kill fee. Buys first North American serial rights and one-time rights. Editorial lead time 2 months. Submit seasonal material 4 months in advance. Reports in 3 weeks on queries; 3 months on mss. Sample copy for $6.50. Writer's guidelines for #10 SASE.

Nonfiction: Essays, general interest, humor, personal experience. Buys 6 mss/year. Query with published clips or send complete ms. Pay varies. Sometimes pays expenses of writers on assignment.

Photos: Negotiates payment individually. Captions required. Buys one-time rights.

Columns/Departments: Send complete ms. Pay varies.

Fiction: Buys 10 mss/year. Send complete ms. Pay varies.

Tips: "Like other editors, I stress the importance of being familiar with the magazine. Those submitters who know the magazine always send in better work because they know what we're looking for."

PARADE, Parade Publications, Inc., 711 Third Ave., New York NY 10017. (212)450-7000. Editor: Walter Anderson. Contact: Articles Editor. Weekly magazine for a general interest audience. 90% freelance written. Circ. 37 million. **Pays on acceptance.** Publishes ms an average of 3 months after acceptance. Kill fee varies in amount. Buys first North American serial rights. Reports in 6 weeks on queries. Writer's guidelines for #10 SASE.

Nonfiction: General interest (on health, trends, social issues or anything of interest to a broad general audience); interview/profile (of news figures, celebrities and people of national significance); and "provocative topical pieces of news value." Spot news events are not accepted, as *Parade* has a 6-week lead time. No fiction, fashion, travel, poetry, cartoons, nostalgia, regular columns, quizzes or fillers. Unsolicited queries concerning celebrities, politicians, sports figures, or technical are rarely assigned. Address single-page queries to Articles Correspondent; include SASE. Length of published articles: 800-1,500 words. Pays $2,500 minimum. Pays expenses of writers on assignment.

Tips: "Send a well-researched, well-written three-paragraph query targeted to our national market. Please, no phone or fax queries. Keep subject tightly focused—a writer should be able to state the point or theme of the query in three or four sentences."

‡RANDOM LENGTHS, Harbor Independent News, P.O. Box 731, San Pedro CA 90733-0731. (310)519-1016. Editor: James P. Allen. 60% freelance written. Biweekly tabloid covering alternative news/features. "*Random Lengths* follows Twain's dictum of printing news 'to make people mad enough to do something about it.' Our writers do exposés, scientific, environmental, political reporting and fun, goofy, insightful, arts and entertainment coverage, for a lefty, labor-oriented, youngish crowd." Estab. 1979. Circ. 30,000. Pays in 60 days. Byline given. Offers 50% kill fee. Buys all rights. Editorial lead time 1 month. Submit seasonal material 2 months in advance. Accepts simultaneous and previously published submissions. Reports in 6 weeks on queries. Sample copy for 9 × 13 SAE with 3 first-class stamps. Writer's guidelines free on request.

Nonfiction: Exposé, general interest, historical/nostalgic, interview/profile, opinion. Buys 150 mss/year. Query. Length: 300-2,500 words. Pays 5¢/word. Sometimes pays expenses of writers on assignment.

Photos: State availability of photos with submissions. Reviews prints. Offers $10/photo. Captions, identification of subjects required. Buys all rights.

Columns/Departments: Community News (local angle), 300-600 words; Commentary (national/world/opinion), 600-800 words; Feature (books/music/local events), 300-600 words. Buys 75 mss/year. Query. Pays 5¢/word.

Tips: "We use mostly local material and local writers, but we are open to current-event, boffo entertaining writing. Read other alternative weeklies for reference. We need local news most. Next, entertainment stuff with a local pitch."

READER'S DIGEST, Pleasantville NY 10570. Monthly. Circ. 15 million. Publishes general interest articles "as varied as all human experience." Does not read or return unsolicited mss. Address article queries and tearsheets of published articles to the editors. Original article rates begin at $3,000 and previously published material pays $1,200/*Reader's Digest* page for World Digest rights. (Usually split 50/50 between original publisher and writer.) Tearsheets of submitted article must include name of original publisher and date of publication.

Columns/Departments: "Original contributions become the property of *Reader's Digest* upon acceptance and payment. Life-in-These-United States contributions must be true, unpublished stories from one's own experience, revealing adult human nature, and providing appealing or humorous sidelights on the American scene." Length: 300 words maximum. Pays $400 on publication. True, unpublished stories are also solicited for Humor in Uniform, Campus Comedy, Tales Out of School and All in a Day's Work. Length: 300 words maximum. Pays $400 on publication. Towards More Picturesque Speech—the first contributor of each item used in this department is paid $50 for original material, $35 for reprints. For items used in Laughter, the Best Medicine, Personal Glimpses, Quotable Quotes, Notes From All Over, Points to Ponder and elsewhere in the magazine payment is as follows; to the *first* contributor of each from a published source, $35. For original material, $30/*Reader's Digest* two-column line. Previously published material must have source's name, date and page number. Please address your submission to the appropriate feature editor. Send complete anecdotes to *Reader's Digest*, Box LL, Pleasantville NY 10570, or fax to (914)238-6390. CompuServe address is notes:readersdigest or use readersdigest@notes.compuserve.com from other online services and the Internet."

READER'S DIGEST (CANADA), 215 Redfern, Westmount, Quebec H3Z 2V9 Canada. (514)934-0751. Fax: (514)935-4463. Editor-in-Chief: Alexander Farrell. Associate Editor: Ron Starr. 10-25% freelance written. Monthly magazine of general interest articles and subjects. Estab. 1948. Circ. 1.3 million. **Pays on acceptance** for original works. Pays on publication for "pickups." Byline given. Offers $500 (Canadian) kill fee. Buys one-time rights (for reprints), all rights (for original articles). Submit seasonal/holiday material 4-5 months in advance. Accepts previously published submissions. Send photocopy of article. Reprint payment is negotiable. Query for electronic submissions. Reports in 5 weeks on queries. Writer's guidelines for #10 SASE with Canadian postage or #10 SAE with 1 IRC.
Nonfiction: General interest, how-to (general interest), inspirational, personal experience. "No fiction, poetry or articles too specialized, technical or esoteric—read *Reader's Digest* to see what kind of articles we want." Query with published clips to Associate Editor: Ron Starr. Length: 3,000-5,000 words. Pays a minimum of $2,700 for assigned articles. Pays expenses of writers on assignment.
Photos: State availability of photos with submission.
Tips: "*Reader's Digest* usually finds its freelance writers through other well-known publications in which they have previously been published. There are guidelines available and writers should read *Reader's Digest* to see what kind of stories we look for and how they are written. WE DO NOT ACCEPT UNSOLICITED MANUSCRIPTS."

REAL PEOPLE, The Magazine of Celebrities and Interesting People, Main Street Publishing Co., Inc., 950 Third Ave. 16th Floor, New York NY 10022-2705. (212)371-4932. Fax: (212)838-8420. Editor: Alex Polner. 75% freelance written. Bimonthly magazine for ages 35 and up focusing on celebs and show business, but also interesting people who might appeal to a national audience. Estab. 1988. Circ. 125,000. Pays on publication. Byline given. Pays 33% kill fee. Buys all rights. Submit seasonal/holiday material 6 months in advance. Reports within 1 month. Sample copy for $3.75 and 8×11 SAE with 3 first-class stamps. Writer's guidelines for #10 SASE.
Nonfiction: Interview/profile. Buys 80 mss/year. Query with published clips (and SAE). Length: 500-2,000 words. Pays $200-500 for assigned articles; $100-250 for unsolicited articles.
Columns/Departments: Newsworthy shorts—up to 200 words. "We are doing more shorter (75-250 word) pieces for our 'Real Shorts' column." Pays $25-50. Submit to Brad Hamilton, editor.
Photos: State availability of photos with submissions. Reviews 5×7 prints and/or slides. Offers no additional payment for photos accepted with ms. Captions, model releases and identification of subjects required. Buys one-time rights.

‡REMEMBER, The People And News We Can't Forget, P.M. Publications, 6 Prowitt St., Norwalk CT 06855. (203)866-6688. Editor: Randall Beach. 75% freelance written. Bimonthly magazine covering events and people of 1920s-1980s. "We focus on reminiscences and reappraisals of past people and events in America. We concentrate on entertainment, sports and politics from 1920-1985." Estab. 1994. Circ. 100,000. **Pays on acceptance.** Publishes ms an average of 5 months after acceptance. Byline given. Offers 20% kill fee. Buys first North American serial and second serial (reprint) rights. Editorial lead time 5 months. Submit seasonal material 6 months in advance. Accepts simultaneous and previously published submissions. Query for electronic submissions. Reports in 2 months. Sample copy for $3.25. Writer's guidelines for #10 SASE.
Nonfiction: Book excerpts, general interest, historical/nostalgic, interview/profile, personal experience (remembrances of famous figures if writer had personal contact), photo feature. No personal nostalgic essays. Buys 50-60 mss/year. Query with published clips. Length: 400-2,500 words. Pays $200-500. Pays expenses of writers on assignment.
Photos: State availability of photos with submissions. Reviews 8×10 prints. Negotiates payment individually. Identification of subjects required. Buys one-time rights.
Columns/Departments: I Remember (remembrance of celebrity), 900 words; Where Are They Now? (what former stars doing now), 400 words; Puzzler Page (nostalgia quiz), 350 words. Buys 20-25 mss/year. Query with published clips. Pays $150-350.
Tips: "Be aware of anniversaries of big events that are at least 6 months down the road. Explain why you are the best person to write this story."

REUNIONS MAGAZINE, P.O. Box 11727, Milwaukee WI 53211-0727. (414)263-4567. Fax: (414)263-6331; (query first by fax). E-mail: reunionsl@aol.com or reunions@execpc.com. Managing Editor: Andi McKenna. 75% freelance written. Quarterly magazine covering reunions—all aspects, all types. *"Reunions Magazine* is primarily for those actively involved with class, family and military reunions or ongoing adoptive or genealogical searchers. We want easy, practical ideas about organizing, planning, researching/searching, attending or promoting reunions." Estab. 1990. Circ. 7,000. Pays on publication. Publishes ms an average of 9 months after acceptance. Byline given. Buys one-time rights. Editorial lead time 6 months. Submit seasonal material 9-12 months in advance. Accepts previously published submissions. Send tearsheet or photocopy of article or typed ms with rights for sale noted and information about when and where the article previously appeared. Query for electronic submissions. Reports in 3 months on queries. Sample copy free. Writer's guidelines for #10 SASE.

Nonfiction: Historical/nostalgic, how-to, humor, interview/profile, new product, personal experience, photo feature, travel, reunion recipes with reunion anecdote—all must be reunion-related. Special issues: African-American family reunions; reunions in various sections of the US; ethnic reunions. Buys 12 mss/year. Query with published clips. Length: 500-2,000 words. Pays $25 minimum. May pay expenses of writers on assignment.

Photos: State availability of photos with submission. Reviews contact sheets, negatives, 35mm transparencies and prints. Offers no additional payment for photos accepted with ms. Captions, model releases and identification of subjects required. Buys one-time rights.

Fillers: Anecdotes, facts, newsbreaks, short humor—must be reunion-related. Buys 8/year. Length: 50-250 words. Pays $5.

Tips: "Write a lively account of an interesting or unusual reunion, either upcoming or soon afterward while it's hot. Tell readers why reunion is special, what went into planning it and how attendees reacted. Our *Masterplan* section is a great place for a freelancer to start. Send us how-tos or tips on any aspect of reunions. Open your minds to different types of reunions—they're all around!"

ROBB REPORT, The Magazine for the Affluent Lifestyle, 1 Acton Place, Acton MA 01720. (508)263-7749. Fax: (508)263-0722. Editor: Robert Feeman. Managing Editor: Janice Stillman. 60% freelance written. Monthly magazine. "We are a lifestyle magazine geared toward active, affluent readers. Addresses upscale autos, luxury travel, boating, technology, lifestyles, personal style, sports, investments, collectibles." Estab. 1975. Circ. 80,000. Pays on publication. Byline given. Offers 50% kill fee. Buys all rights or first North American serial rights. Submit seasonal/holiday material 5 months in advance. Query for electronic submissions. Reports in 2 months on queries; 1 month on mss. Sample copy for $6. Writer's guidelines for #10 SASE.

Nonfiction: General interest (autos, lifestyle, etc.), interview/profile (business), new product (autos, boats, consumer electronics), travel (international and domestic). No essays, personal travel experiences, bargain travel. Buys 60 mss/year. Query with published clips if available. Length: 1,500-3,500 words. Pays $500-850. Sometimes pays expenses of writers on assignment.

Photos: State availability of photos with submission. Payment depends on article. Buys one-time rights.

Tips: "We have a continuing need for business/sports/celebrity profiles focusing on lifestyle. There are opportunities for new writers to break into departments. Study the magazine carefully. We have very specific needs and many queries are off base."

THE SATURDAY EVENING POST, The Saturday Evening Post Society, 1100 Waterway Blvd., Indianapolis IN 46202. (317)636-8881. Editor: Cory SerVaas, M.D. Managing Editor: Ted Kreiter. 30% freelance written. Bimonthly general interest, "family-oriented magazine focusing on physical fitness, preventive medicine." Estab. 1728. Circ. 500,000. Pays on publication. Publishes ms an average of 3 months after acceptance. Byline given. Buys second serial (reprint) and all rights. Submit seasonal/holiday material 4 months in advance. Accepts simultaneous and previously published submissions. Query for electronic submissions. Reports in 1 month on queries; 6 weeks on mss. Writer's guidelines for #10 SASE.

Nonfiction: Book excerpts, general interest, how-to (gardening, home improvement), humor, interview/profile, travel. "No political articles or articles containing sexual innuendo or hypersophistication." Buys 50 mss/year. Query with or without published clips, or send complete ms. Length: 750-2,500 words. Pays $200 minimum, negotiable maximum for assigned articles. Sometimes pays expenses of writers on assignment.

Photos: State availability of photos with submission. Reviews negatives and transparencies. Offers $50 minimum, negotiable maxmium per photo. Model release, identification required. Buys one-time or all rights.

Columns/Departments: Travel (destinations). Buys 16 mss/year. Query with published clips or send complete ms. Length: 750-1,500 words. Pays $200 minimum, negotiable maximum.

Fiction: Jack Gramling, fiction editor. Historical, humorous, mainstream, mystery, science fiction, western. "No sexual innuendo or profane expletives." Send complete ms. Length: 1,000-2,500 words. Pays $150 minimum, negotiable maximum.

Poetry: Light verse.

Fillers: PostScripts Editor: Steve Pettinga. Anecdotes, short humor. Buys 200/year. Length: 300 words. Pays $15.

Tips: "Areas most open to freelancers are Health, PostScripts and Travel. For travel we like text-photo packages, pragmatic tips, side bars and safe rather than exotic destinations. Query by mail, not phone. Send clips."

SELECTED READING, The National Research Bureau, Inc., P.O. Box 1, Burlington IA 52601-0001. (319)752-5415. Fax: (319)752-3421. Editor: Nancy Heinzel. 75% freelance written. Works with a small number of new/unpublished writers each year. Quarterly magazine. Estab. 1948. Pays on publication. Publishes ms an average of 1 year after acceptance. Buys all rights. Submit seasonal/holiday material 7 months in advance of issue date. Sample copy and writer's guidelines for #10 SAE with 2 first-class stamps.
Nonfiction: General interest (economics, health, safety, working relationships), how-to, travel (out-of-the way places). No material on car repair. Buys 10-12 mss/year. Query. Short outline or synopsis is best; lists of titles are no help. Length: 500-700 words. Pays 4¢/word.
Tips: "Writers have a better chance of breaking in at our publication with short articles."

SILVER CIRCLE, Home Savings of America, 4900 Rivergrade, Irwindale CA 91706. Editor: Jay A. Binkly. 80% freelance written. Consumer magazine published 3 times/year. "Despite the magazine's title, editorial is *not* the stereotypical senior fare. Articles that are aimed solely at *seniors* are rejected 99% of the time. Articles should have broad demographic appeal. Along with gardening and financial planning, subjects that have appeared in the magazine include computer software, heli-hiking tours, home fitness centers, high-tech new-car options, video cameras, investment scams, party planning, etc. Our editorial mission is to provide our readers with practical, relevant, upbeat consumer service information." Estab. 1974. Circ. 575,000. **Pays on acceptance.** Byline given. Offers 20% kill fee. Buys first North American serial rights. Editorial lead time 5 months. Submit seasonal material 5 months in advance. Accepts simultaneous and previously published submissions. Send tearsheet of article. Query for electronic submissions. Reports in 3 weeks on queries; 1 month on mss. Sample copy for 8½ × 11 SASE. Writer's guidelines for #10 SASE.
Nonfiction: How-to, new product, travel. Buys 15 mss/year. Query with published clips. Length: 800-3,000 words. Pays $150 minimum for assigned articles; $1,500 minimum for unsolicited articles. Sometimes pays expenses of writers on assignment.
Photos: Send photos with submissions. Offers $35-500/photo. Captions required. Buys one-time rights.
Columns/Departments: To Your Health (practical health items), 500 words; Minding Your Money (practical money items), 500 words; Travel Notes (practical travel items), 500 words. Buys 100 mss/year. Pays $35-100.

SMITHSONIAN MAGAZINE, 900 Jefferson Dr., Washington DC 20560. Articles Editor: Marlane A. Liddell. 90% freelance written. Prefers to work with published/established writers. Monthly magazine for "associate members of the Smithsonian Institution; 85% with college education." Circ. 3 million. Buys first North American serial rights. "Payment for each article to be negotiated depending on our needs and the article's length and excellence." **Pays on acceptance.** Publishes ms an average of 6 months after acceptance. Submit seasonal material 3 months in advance. Reports in 2 months. Sample copy for $3 % Judy Smith. Writer's guidelines for #10 SASE.
Nonfiction: "Our mandate from the Smithsonian Institution says we are to be interested in the same things which now interest or should interest the Institution: cultural and fine arts, history, natural sciences, hard sciences, etc." Query. Back Page humor: 1,000 words; full length article 3,500-4,500 words. Payment negotiable. Pays expenses of writers on assignment.
Photos: Purchased with or without ms and on assignment. Captions required. Pays $400/full color page.

THE STAR, 660 White Plains Rd., Tarrytown NY 10591. (914)332-5000. Fax: (914)332-5043. Editor: Richard Kaplan. Executive Editor: Steve LeGrice. 40% freelance written. Prefers to work with published/established writers. Weekly magazine "for every family; all the family—kids, teenagers, young parents and grandparents." Estab. 1974. Circ. 2.8 million. Publishes ms an average of 1 month after acceptance. Buys first North American serial, occasionally second serial book rights. Query for electronic submissions. Reports in 2 months. Pays expenses of writers on assignment.
Nonfiction: Exposé (government waste, consumer, education, anything affecting family); general interest (human interest, consumerism, informational, family and women's interest); how-to (psychological, practical on all subjects affecting readers); interview (celebrity or human interest); new product; photo feature; profile (celebrity or national figure); health; medical; diet. No first-person articles. Query or submit complete ms. Length: 500-1,000 words. Pays $50-1,500.
Photos: Alistair Duncan, photo editor. State availability of photos with query or ms. Pays $25-100 for 8 × 10 b&w glossy prints, contact sheets or negatives; $150-1,000 for 35mm color transparencies. Captions required. Buys one-time or all rights.

THE SUN, A Magazine of Ideas, The Sun Publishing Company, 107 N. Roberson St., Chapel Hill NC 27516. (919)942-5282. Editor: Sy Safransky. 90% freelance written. Monthly general interest magazine. "We are open to all kinds of writing, though we favor work of a personal nature." Estab. 1974. Circ. 27,000. Pays on publication. Publishes ms an average of 6 months after acceptance. Byline given. Buys first or one-time rights. Accepts previously published submissions. Send photocopy of article or short story and information about when and where the article previously appeared. For reprints, pays 50% of the amount paid for an original article. Reports in 1 month on queries; 3 months on mss. Sample copy for $3.50. Send SASE for writer's guidelines.

• *The Sun* no longer accepts simultaneous submissions.

Nonfiction: Book excerpts, essays, general interest, interview, opinion, personal experience, spiritual. Buys 24 mss/year. Send complete ms. Length: 8,000 words maximum. Pays $100-500. "Complimentary subscription is given in addition to payment (applies to payment for *all* works, not just nonfiction)."

Photos: Send b&w photos with submission. Offers $25-50/photo. Model releases preferred. Buys one-time rights.

Fiction: Experimental, humorous, literary, mainstream, novel excerpts. "We avoid stereotypical genre pieces like sci-fi, romance, western and horror. Read an issue before submitting." Buys 30 mss/year. Send complete ms. Length: 8,000 words maximum. Pays $200 for original fiction.

Poetry: Free verse, prose poems, short and long poems. Buys 24 poems/year. Submit 6 poems maximum. Pays $25.

TIME, Time & Life Bldg., Rockefeller Center, New York NY 10020-1393. Managing Editor: Jim Gaines. Weekly publication covering news and popular culture. This magazine did not respond to our request for information. Query before submitting.

TOWN AND COUNTRY, 1700 Broadway, New York NY 10019. (212)903-5000. Editor-in-Chief: Pamela Fiori. For upper-income Americans. Monthly. Circ. 530,000. **Pays on acceptance.** Not a large market for freelancers. Always query first.

Nonfiction: "We're looking for engaging service articles for a high-income, well educated audience." Length: 1,500-2,000 words. Pay varies. Also buys shorter pieces for which pay varies.

USA WEEKEND, Gannett Co., Inc., 1000 Wilson Blvd., Arlington VA 22229. Editor: Marcia Bullard. Contact: Leslie Ansley. 70% freelance written. Weekly Friday-Sunday newspaper magazine. Estab. 1985. Circ. 15 million. **Pays on acceptance.** Publishes ms an average of 3 months after acceptance. Byline given. Offers 25% kill fee. Buys first worldwide serial rights. Submit seasonal material 5 months in advance. Query for electronic submissions. Reports in 5 weeks.

Nonfiction: Food and Family Issues; Trends and Entertainment (contact: Gayle Carter); Recreation; Cover Stories (contact: Dan Olmsted). Also looking for book excerpts, general interest articles, how-to, interview/profile, travel, food, recreation. No first-person essays, historic pieces or retrospective pieces. Buys 200 mss/year. Query with published clips. No unsolicited mss accepted. Length: 50-2,000 words. Pays $75-2,000. Sometimes pays expenses of writers on assignment.

Photos: State availability of photos with submission.

Columns/Departments: Food, Travel, Entertainment, Books, Recreation. "All stories must be pegged to an upcoming event, must report new and refreshing trends in the field and must include high profile people." Length: 50-1,000 words. Query with published clips. Pays $250-500.

Tips: "We are looking for authoritative, lively articles that blend the author's expertise with our style. All articles must have a broad, timely appeal. One-page query should include peg or timeliness of the subject matter. We generally look for sidebar material to accompany each article."

THE WORLD & I, A Chronicle of Our Changing Era, News World Communications, Inc., 3600 New York Ave. NE, Washington DC 20002. (202)635-4000. Fax: (202)269-9353. Editor: Morton A. Kaplan. Executive Editor: Michael Marshall. Contact: Gary Rowe. 90% freelance written. Publishing more than 100 articles each month, this is a broad interest magazine for the thinking person. Estab. 1986. Circ. 30,000. Pays on publication. Publishes ms an average of 6 months after acceptance. Byline given. Offers 20% kill fee. Buys all rights. Submit seasonal material 5 months in advance. Accepts previously published material. Send tearsheet or photocopy of article, typed ms with rights for sale noted and information about when and where the article previously appeared. Query for electronic submissions. Reports in 6 weeks on queries; 10 weeks on mss. Sample copy for $5 and 9 × 12 SASE. Writer's guidelines for #10 SASE.

Nonfiction: "Description of Sections: Current Issues: Politics, economics and strategic trends covered in a variety of approaches, including special report, analysis, commentary and photo essay. The Arts: International coverage of music, dance, theater, film, television, design, architecture, photography, poetry, painting and sculpture—through reviews, features, essays and a 10-page Gallery of full-color reproductions. Life: Articles on well-known and respected people, cultural trends, adventure, travel, family and youth issues, education, consumer issues, gardens, home, health and food. Natural Science: Covers the latest in science and technology, relating it to the social and historical context, under these headings: At the Edge, Impacts, Nature Walk, Science and Spirit, Science and Values, Scientists: Past and Present, Crucibles of Science and Science Essay. Book World: Excerpts from important, timely books (followed by commentaries) and 10-12 scholarly reviews of significant new books each month, including untranslated works from abroad. Covers current affairs, intellectual issues, contemporary fiction, history, moral/religious issues and the social sciences. Currents in Modern Thought: Examines scholarly research and theoretical debate across the wide range of disciplines in the humanities and social sciences. Featured themes are explored by several contributors. Investigates theoretical issues raised by certain current events, and offers contemporary reflection on issues drawn from the whole history of human thought. Culture: Surveys the world's people in these subsections: Peoples (their unique characteristics and cultural symbols), Crossroads (changes brought by the meeting of cultures), Patterns (photo essay depicting the daily life of a distinct culture), Folk Wisdom (folklore and practical wisdom and their present forms), and Heritage (multicultural backgrounds of the American people and how they are bound to the world. Photo Essay: The 10-page Life and Ideals dramatizes a human story of obstacles overcome in the pursuit of an ideal. Three other photo essays appear each month: Focus (Current Issues), Gallery (The Arts), and Patterns (Culture). 'No *National Enquirer*-type articles.' " Buys 1,200 mss/year. Query with published clips. Length: 1,000-5,000 words. Pays 10-20¢/word. Sometimes pays expenses of writers on assignment. First-person work is discouraged.

Poetry: Query arts editor. Avant-garde, free verse, haiku, light verse, traditional. Buys 6-12 poems/year. Submit maximum 5 poems. Pays $25-50.

Photos: State availability of photos with submission. Reivews contact sheets, transparencies and prints. Payment negotiable. Model releases and identification of subjects required. Buys one-time rights.

Tips: "Send a short query letter with a viable story idea (no unsolicited mss, please!) for a specific section and/or subsection."

Health and Fitness

The magazines listed here specialize in covering health and fitness topics for a general audience. Many focus not as much on exercise as on general "healthy lifestyle" topics. Also see the Sports/Miscellaneous section where publications dealing with health and particular sports may be listed. For magazines that cover healthy eating, refer to the Food and Drink section. Many general interest publications are also potential markets for health or fitness articles. Magazines covering health topics from a medical perspective are listed in the Medical category of Trade.

AMERICAN HEALTH MAGAZINE, Fitness of Body and Mind, Reader's Digest Corp., 28 W. 23rd St., New York NY 10010. (212)366-8900. Fax: (212)366-8760. Editor: Carey Winfrey. Executive Editor: Judith Groch. 70% freelance written. General interest health magazine published 10 times/year covering both scientific and "lifestyle" aspects of health, including medicine, fitness, nutrition and psychology. Estab. 1982. Circ. 800,000. **Pays on acceptance.** Publishes ms an average of 6 months after acceptance. Byline or tagline given. Offers 25% kill fee. Buys first North American serial rights. Reports in 6 weeks. Sample copy for $3. Writer's guidelines for #10 SASE.
Nonfiction: Mail to Editorial/Features. News-based articles usually with a service angle; well-written pieces with an investigative or unusual slant; profiles (health or fitness related). No mechanical research reports, quick weight-loss plans or unproven treatments. "Stories should be written clearly, without jargon. Information should be new, authoritative and helpful to readers." Buys 60-70 mss/year (plus many more news items). Query with 2 clips of published work. Length: 1,000-3,000 words. Payment varies. Pays the expenses of writers on assignment.
Photos: Pays $100-600 for 35mm transparencies and 8×10 prints "depending on use." Captions and identification of subjects required. Buys one-time rights.
Columns/Departments: Mail to Editorial/News, Medicine, Fitness, Nutrition, The Mind, Environment, Family, Dental, Looking Good, First Person, Second Opinion. Other news sections included from time to time. Buys about 300 mss/year. Query with clips of published work. Pays $150-250 upon acceptance.
Tips: "*American Health* has no full-time staff writers; we rely on outside contributors for most of our articles. The magazine needs good ideas and good articles from experienced journalists and writers. Feature queries should be short (no longer than a page) and to the point. Give us a good angle and a paragraph of background. Queries only. We are not responsible for material not accompanied by a SASE."

COMMON GROUND MAGAZINE, Ontario's Quarterly Guide to Natural Foods & Lifestyles, New Age Times Ink, 356 Dupont St., Toronto, Ontario M5R 1V9 Canada. Editor: Julia Woodford. 50% freelance written. Quarterly magazine covering holistic health, nutritional medicine. "We give top priority to well-researched articles on nutritional medicine, healing properties of foods and herbs, environmental health issues, natural lifestyles, alternative healing for cancer, arthritis, heart disease, etc. Organic foods and issues. Estab. 1985. Circ. 50,000. Pays on publication. Publishes ms 3 months after acceptance. Byline given. Buys first rights, one-time rights or second serial (reprint) rights. Editorial lead time 3 months. Submit seasonal material 3 months in advance. Accepts simultaneous and previously published submissions. Reports "when we have time." Sample copy for $2. Writer's guidelines free on request by phone.
Nonfiction: Book excerpts, exposé, how-to (on self-health care), inspirational, personal experience. "Nothing endorsing drugs, surgery, pharmaceuticals. No submissions from public relations firms." Buys 8-12 mss/

year. Query with or without published clips. Length 1,000-1,800 words. Pays 10¢/word. Sometimes pays expenses of writers on assignment.

Photos: Send photos with submission. Offers $25-30/photo. Identification of subjects required. Buys one-time rights.

Fillers: Facts, newsbreaks.

Tips: "Must have a good working knowledge of subject area and be patient if not responded to immediately. Features are most open to freelancers. Write well, give me the facts, but do it in layman's terms. A sense of humor doesn't hurt. All material must be relevant to our *Canadian* readership audience."

COUNTDOWN, Juvenile Diabetes Foundation, 432 Park Ave. S., New York NY 10016-8013. (212)889-7575. Fax: (212)532-8791. Editor: Sandy Dylak. 75% freelance written. Quarterly magazine focusing on medical research. "*Countdown* is published for people interested in diabetes research. Written for a lay audience. Often, stories are interpretation of highly technical biomedical research." Estab. 1970. Circ. 150,000. **Pays on acceptance.** Byline given. Buys first rights. Editorial lead time 3 months. Submit seasonal material 3 months in advance. Accepts simultaneous and previously published submissions. Send photocopy of article. For reprints pays 50% of the amount paid for an original article. Query for electronic submissions. Prefers disc—any format. Reports in 1 month. Sample copy free on request.

Nonfiction: Essays, general interest, how-to, interview/profile, new product and personal experience. "All articles must relate to diabetes. 95% published freelance stories are assigned." Buys 15 mss/year. Query with published clips. Length: 500-2,500 words. Pays $500 minimum for assigned articles. Pays expenses of writers on assignment.

Photos: Send photos with submission. Reviews transparencies and prints. Negotiates payment individually. Captions, model releases and identification of subjects required. Buys one-time rights.

Tips: "Knowledge of biomedical research, specifically immunology and genetics, is necessary. We are most open to feature stories and profiles."

‡ENERGY TIMES, Enhancing Your Life Through Proper Nutrition, 548 Broadhollow Rd., Melville NY 11747. (516)777-7777. Editor: Gerard McIntee. Contact: Mike Finnegan. 90% freelance written. Bimonthly magazine covering nutrition, health and beauty aids, alternative medicinal, herbs (medicinal and culinary), natural foods. Estab. 1991. Circ. 575,000. **Pays on acceptance.** Publishes ms an average of 1 month after acceptance. Byline given. Offers 10% kill fee or $100. Buys all rights. Editorial lead time 2 months. Submit seasonal material 6 months in advance. Accepts simultaneous submissions and previously published submissions. Query for electronic submissions. Reports in 1 month on queries, 2 months on mss. Sample copy for $2.50. Writer's guidelines for #10 SASE.

Nonfiction: Book excerpts, how-to (food, natural beauty aids, homemade products), humor, inspirational, interview/profile, new product, photo feature, technical (science related to nutrition and alternative medicines), travel. Buys 36 mss/year. Query. Length: 1,500-2,500 words. Pays $300. Sometimes pays expenses of writers on assignment.

Photos: State availability of photos with submissions. Reviews negatives, transparencies, prints. Negotiates payment individually. Identification of subjects required. Buys one-time rights.

Columns/Departments: Nutritional news (current information on nutrition foods/supplements/vitamins), 250 words; university update (current research on nutrition, health related topics, herbs, vitamins), 250 words. Send complete ms. Pays $40.

Fillers: Uses anecdotes, facts, gags to be illustrated by cartoonist, newsbreaks, short humor, crossword puzzles, word games. Buys 12/year. Puzzles should fit on ½ page 4×5¼. Pays $75.

Tips: "Although we hire lay freelancers and professional journalists, we prefer to maintain an active group of professional medical/healthcare practitioners with accredited degrees. Queries should be brief (one page) and to the point. Show us why your article needs to be in our magazine."

FDA CONSUMER, 5600 Fishers Lane, Rockville MD 20857. (301)443-3220. Editor: Judith Levine Willis. 30% freelance written. Prefers to work with experienced health and medical writers. Monthly magazine (January/February and July/August issues combined) for general public interested in health issues. A federal government publication (Food and Drug Administration). Circ. 28,000. Pays after acceptance. Publishes ms an average of 3 months after acceptance. Byline given. Not copyrighted. Pays 50% kill fee. "All rights must be assigned to the USA so that the articles may be reprinted without permission." Query with résumé and clips only. Buys 15-20 freelance mss/year. "We cannot be responsible for any work by writer not agreed upon by prior contract." Free sample copy.

Nonfiction: "Upbeat feature articles of an educational nature about FDA regulated products and specific FDA programs and actions to protect the consumer's health and pocketbook. Articles based on health topics connected to food, drugs, medical devices, and other products regulated by FDA. All articles subject to clearance by the appropriate FDA experts as well as acceptance by the editor. All articles based on prior arrangement by contract." Length: 2,000-2,500 words. Pays $800-950 for "first-timers," $1,200 for those who have previously published in *FDA Consumer*. Pays phone and mailing expenses.

Photos: Black and white photos are purchased on assignment only.

Tips: "Besides reading the feature articles in *FDA Consumer,* a writer can best determine whether his/her style and expertise suit our needs by submitting a résumé and clips; story suggestions are unnecessary as most are internally generated."

‡FIT, The Magazine of Health & Fitness, (formerly *New Body*), GCR Publishing Group, Inc., 1700 Broadway, 34th Floor, New York NY 10019. (212)541-7100. Editor: Nicole Dorsey. Managing Editor: Sandra Kosherick. 75% freelance written. Works with a small number of new/unpublished writers each year. Bimonthly magazine covering fitness and health for active young, middle-class women. Circ. 125,000. Pays on publication. Publishes ms an average of 6 months after acceptance. Byline given. Offers 20% kill fee. Buys all rights. Submit seasonal/holiday material 6 months in advance. Accepts simultaneous and previously published submissions. Send tearsheet or photocopy of article and information about when and where the article previously appeared. Pays 50% of their fee for an original article. Reports in 3 months.

Nonfiction: Health, exercise, psychology, relationships, diet, celebrities, and nutrition. Please no telephone queries. No articles on "How I do exercises." Buys 75 mss/year. Query with published clips. Length: 800-1,500 words. Pays $100-300 for assigned articles; $50-150 for unsolicited articles.

Fiction: Publishes novel excerpts.

Photos: Reviews contact sheets, transparencies and prints. Model releases and identification of subjects required. Buys all rights.

Columns/Departments: Finally Fit! Contest. Readers can submit "before and after" success stories along with color slides or photos. Pays $100.

Tips: "We are moving toward more general interest women's material on relationships, emotional health, nutrition, etc. We look for a fresh angle—a new way to present the material. Celebrity profiles, fitness tips, and health news are good topics to consider. Make a clean statement of what your article is about, what it would cover—not why the article is important. We're interested in new ideas, new trends or new ways of looking at old topics."

HEALTH, Time Publishing Ventures, 301 Howard St., 18th Floor, San Francisco CA 94105. (415)512-9100. Editor: Barbara Paulsen. Send submissions to: Kate Lee, editorial assistant. Magazine published 7 times/year on health, fitness and nutrition. "Our readers are predominantly college-educated women in their 30s and 40s. Edited to focus not on illness, but on events, ideas and people." Estab. 1987. Circ. 900,000. **Pays on acceptance**. Byline given. Offers 25% kill fee. Buys first North American serial rights. Accepts simultaneous submissions. Reports in 2 months on queries. Sample copy for $5 to "Back Issues." Writer's guidelines for #10 SASE. "No phone calls, please."

• *Health* stresses that writers must send for guidelines before sending a query, and that only queries that closely follow the guidelines get passed on to editors.

Nonfiction: Buys 25 mss/year. No unsolicited mss. Query with published clips and SASE. Length: 1,200 words. Pays $1,800 for assigned articles. Pays the expenses of writers on assignment.

Departments: Food, Mind, Vanities, Fitness, Family, Money.

Tips: "We look for well-articulated ideas with a narrow focus and broad appeal. A query that starts with an unusual local event and hooks it legitimately to some national trend or concern is bound to get our attention. Use quotes, examples and statistics to show why the topic is important and why the approach is workable. We need to see clear evidence of credible research findings pointing to meaningful options for our readers. Stories should offer practical advice and give clear explanations."

‡HEART & SOUL, The African-American's Guide to Healthy Living, Rodale Press, 733 Third Ave., New York NY 10017. Editor-in-Chief: Stephanie Stokes Oliver. Managing Editor: Teresa L. Ridley. Contact: Claire McIntosh, senior editor. Bimonthly magazine covering how-to health, fitness, nutrition, weight loss, parenting, relationships; information researched and edited specifically for African-Americans. Estab. 1993. Circ. 200,000. **Pays on acceptance**. Publishes ms an average of 2 months after acceptance. Byline given. Offers 25% kill fee. Buys all rights or first North American serial rights. Editorial lead time 6 months. Submit seasonal material 6 months in advance. Accepts previously published submissions. Query for electronic submissions (upon assignment only). Reports in 6 weeks. Sample copy for 9 × 12 SAE with $1.93 postage. Writer's guidelines for #10 SASE.

Nonfiction: Book excerpts, how-to (health, fitness), interview/profile (champions), personal experience (My Body, weight loss, makeover). No non-health, celebrities. Buys 36 mss/year. Query with published clips. Length: 1,000-2,000 words. Pays 75¢-$1 for assigned articles; 75¢ for unsolicited articles. Sometimes pays expenses of writers on assignment.

Columns/Departments: Weight Loss (how-to); Mind (inspiration); Body (illness prevention). Length: 800-1,000 words. Buys 84 mss/year. Query with published clips. Pays 75¢-$1.

Tips: "Writers should be experienced in health writing and knowledgeable about the health of African-Americans, particularly Black women's health. We do not accept manuscripts; queries only."

LET'S LIVE MAGAZINE, Hilltopper Publications, Inc., 320 N. Larchmont Blvd., P.O. Box 74908, Los Angeles CA 90004-3030. (213)469-3901. Fax: (213)469-9597. Editor: Patty Padilla-Gallagher. Monthly magazine emphasizing nutrition. 15% freelance written. Works with a small number of new/unpublished writers each year. Estab. 1933. Circ. 850,000. Pays 1 month after publication. Publishes ms an average of 4 months after acceptance. Buys first world serial rights. Byline given. Submit seasonal/holiday material 6 months in advance. Reports in 2 months on queries; 3 months on mss. Sample copy for $3 for 10×13 SAE with 6 first-class stamps. Writer's guidelines for #10 SASE.

Nonfiction: General interest (effects of vitamins, minerals and nutrients in improvement of health or afflictions); historical (documentation of experiments or treatment establishing value of nutrients as boon to health); how-to (enhance natural beauty, exercise/body build, acquire strength and vitality, improve health of adults and/or children and prepare tasty health-food meals); interview (benefits of research in establishing prevention as key to good health); personal opinion (views of orthomolecular doctors or their patients on value of health foods toward maintaining good health); profile (background and/or medical history of preventive medicine, M.D.s or Ph.D.s, in advancement of nutrition). Manuscripts must be well-researched, reliably documented and written in a clear, readable style. Buys 2-4 mss/issue. Query with published clips. Length: 1,200-1,400 words. Pays $200. Sometimes pays expenses of writers on assignment.

Photos: Send photos with ms. Pays $50 for 8×10 color prints and 35mm transparencies. Captions and model releases required.

Tips: "We want writers with experience in researching nonsurgical medical subjects and interviewing experts with the ability to simplify technical and clinical information for the layman. A captivating lead and structural flow are essential. The most frequent mistakes made by writers are in writing articles that are too technical; in poor style; written for the wrong audience (publication not thoroughly studied), or have unreliable documentation or overzealous faith in the topic reflected by flimsy research and inappropriate tone."

‡**LISTEN MAGAZINE**, Review & Herald Publishing Association, 55 W. Oak Ridge Dr., Hagerstown MD 21740. (301)791-7000, ext. 2534. Fax: (301)790-9734. Editor: Lincoln Steed. Editorial Assistant: Anita Jacobs. 75% freelance written. Works with a small number of new/unpublished writers each year. Monthly magazine specializing in drug prevention, presenting positive alternatives to various drug dependencies. "*Listen* is used in many high school classes and by professionals: medical personnel, counselors, law enforcement officers, educators, youth workers, etc." Circ. 70,000. Buys first rights for use in *Listen*, reprints and associated material. Byline given. **Pays on acceptance.** Publishes ms an average of 6 months after acceptance. Accepts previously published submissions. Send tearsheet or photocopy of article or typed ms with rights for sale noted and information about when and where it previously appeared. For reprints, pays 50% of original article fee. Reports in 3 months. Sample copy for $1 and 9×12 SASE. Free writer's guidelines.

Nonfiction: Seeks articles that deal with causes of drug use such as poor self-concept, family relations, social skills or peer pressure. Especially interested in youth-slanted articles or personality interviews encouraging non-alcoholic and non-drug ways of life. Teenage point of view is essential. Popularized medical, legal and educational articles. Also seeks narratives which portray teens dealing with youth conflicts, especially those related to the use of or temptation to use harmful substances. Growth of the main character should be shown. "We don't want typical alcoholic story/skid-row bum, AA stories. We are also being inundated with drunk-driving accident stories. Unless yours is unique, consider another topic." Buys 15-20 unsolicited mss/year. Query. Length: 1,200-1,500 words. Pays 5-7¢/word. Sometimes pays the expenses of writers on assignment.

Photos: Purchased with accompanying ms. Captions required. Color photos preferred, but b&w acceptable.

Fillers: Word square/general puzzles are also considered. Pays $15.

Tips: "True stories are good, especially if they have a unique angle. Other authoritative articles need a fresh approach. In query, briefly summarize article idea and logic of why you feel it's good. Make sure you've read the magazine to understand our approach."

LONGEVITY, General Media International, Inc., 277 Park Ave., 4th Floor, New York 10172. (212)702-6000. Fax: (212)702-6262. Editor-in-Chief: Susan Millar Perry. Monthly magazine on medicine, health, fitness and life extension research. "*Longevity* is written for a baby-boomer audience who want to prolong their ability to lead a productive, vibrant, healthy life and to look as good as they feel at their best." Estab. 1989. Circ. 375,000. **Pays on acceptance.** Publishes ms an average of 2 months after acceptance. Byline given. Offers 25% kill fee. Makes work-for-hire assignments. Query for electronic submissions. Reports in 3 months. Sample copy for 10×13 SAE with 4 first-class stamps.

Nonfiction: Consumer trends in anti-aging, new products, health. Query. Length: 150-2,000 words. Pays $100-2,500. Pays expenses of writers on assignment.

Columns/Departments: Antiaging News; Outer Limits; Looks Savers; Childwise; Air, Earth & Water; Marketing Youth; Medicine; The Intelligent Eater; Mind Body Spirit; Love & Longevity; In Shape; Long Life Ideas; Health Style Setters.

MASSAGE MAGAZINE, Keeping Those Who Touch—In Touch, Noah Publishing Co., P.O. Box 1500, Davis CA 95617-1500. (916)757-6033. Fax: (916)757-6041. Publisher: Robert Calvert. Managing Editor: Karen Menehan. Southwest Editor: Melissa B. Mower. 80% freelance written. Prefers to work with published/

established writers, but works with a number of new/unpublished writers each year. Bimonthly magazine on massage-bodywork and related healing arts. Estab. 1985. Circ. 25,000. Pays 30 days after publication. Publishes ms an average of 6 months after acceptance. Byline given. Buys first North American rights. Accepts previously published submissions. Send photocopy of article or typed ms with rights for sale noted. For reprints, pays 50-75% of the amount paid for an original article. Reports in 1 month on queries; 2 months on mss. Sample copy for $5. Free writer's guidelines.

Nonfiction: General interest, historical/nostalgic, how-to, experiential, inspirational, interview/profile, new product, photo feature, technical, travel. Length: 600-2,000 words. Pays $25-250 for articles.

Photos: Send photos with submission. Offers $10-25/photo. Identification of subjects required. Buys one-time rights.

Columns/Departments: Touching Tales (experiential); Profiles, Insurance; Table Talk (news briefs); Practice Building (business); In Touch with Associations (convention highlights); In Review/On Video (product, book, and video reviews); Technique; Body/mind; Convention Calendar (association convention listings). Length: 800-1,200 words. Pays $35-75 for most of these columns.

Fillers: Facts, news briefs. Length: 100 words. Pays $25 maximum.

MEN'S FITNESS, Men's Fitness, Inc., 21100 Erwin St., Woodland Hills CA 91367-3712. (818)884-6800. Fax: (818)704-5734. Editor-in-Chief: Peter Sikowitz. Editorial Assistant: Ann Lien. 95% freelance written. Works with small number of new/unpublished writers each year. Monthly magazine for health-conscious men ages 18-45. Provides reliable, entertaining guidance for the active male in all areas of lifestyle. Pays 1 month after acceptance. Publishes ms an average of 4 months after acceptance. Offers 33% kill fee. Buys all rights. Submit seasonal material 4 months in advance. Reports in 2 months. Writer's guidelines for 9×12 SAE. Query before sending ms.

Nonfiction: Service, informative, inspirational and scientific studies written for men. Few interviews or regional news unless extraordinary. Query with published clips. Length: 1,200-1,800 words. Pays $500-1,000.

Columns/Departments: Nutrition, Mind, Appearance, Sexuality, Health. Length: 1,200-1,500 words. Pays $400-500.

Tips: "Be sure to know the magazine before sending in queries."

‡℞EMEDY MAGAZINE, Prescriptions for a Healthy Life, ℞ Remedy, Inc., 120 Post Rd., W., Westport CT 06880. Editor: Valorie G. Weaver. 95% freelance written. Bimonthly magazine covering health for people age 55 and older. "℞*EMEDY* covers everything that affects and improves the health of people 55 and up—nutrition and exercise, medicine and medications, mainstream and alternative approaches, agism in health care, hormones and hair loss, you name it—in an in-depth but reader-friendly way." Estab. 1993. Circ. 2 million households. **Pays on acceptance.** Publishes ms and average of 4 months after acceptance. Byline given. Offers 20% kill fee. Buys first North American serial rights. Editorial lead time 3 months. Submit seasonal material 6 months in advance. Accepts simultaneous submissions. Reports in 6 weeks on queries; 2 months on mss. Samples for $3 and SAE with 4 first-class stamps. Writer's guidelines free on request.

Nonfiction: Book excerpts, exposé (medical), how-to (exercise and nutrition for people age 55 and older), interview/profile (health); medical journalism/reporting for lay readers. Buys 30 mss/year. Query with published clips. Length: 600-2,500 words. Pays $1-1.25/word for assigned articles; 50¢-1.25/word for unsolicited articles. Sometimes pays expenses of writers on assignment.

Photos: State availability of photos with submission. Negotiates payment individually. Model releases, identification of subjects required. Buys one-time rights.

Columns/Departments: The Nutrition Prescription (How-to research), The Fitness Prescription (How-to research), Housecall (Interviews with top specialists), Mediew (Overviews of topical subject, i.e. "endless" menopause, see-better surgery), all 600-900 words. Buys 15 mss/year. Query. Pays 50¢-1.25/word.

Tips: "Query should include (ideally) specific doctors/practitioners likely to be interviewed for piece, and (again ideally) at least one clip showing writing/reporting familiarity with topic of query. Also an ability to write in a casual, friendly way about often complex material is essential."

SHAPE MAGAZINE, Weider Health & Fitness, 21100 Erwin St., Woodland Hills CA 91367. (818)595-0593. Fax: (818)704-5734. Editor-in-Chief: Barbara Harris. 70% freelance written. Prefers to work with published/established writers. Monthly magazine covering women's health and fitness. Estab. 1981. Circ. 900,000. **Pays on acceptance.** Offers 33% kill fee. Buys all rights and reprint rights. Submit seasonal/holiday material 8 months in advance. Reports in 2 months. Sample copy for 9×12 SAE and 4 first-class stamps.

• Weider Health Fitness also publishes *Living Fit*, covering health and fitness for women over 35.

Nonfiction: Book excerpts; exposé (health, fitness, nutrition related); how-to (get fit); interview/profile (of fit women); health/fitness. "We use some health and fitness articles written by professionals in their specific fields. No articles that haven't been queried first." Query with clips of published work. Length: 500-2,000 words. Pays negotiable fee. Pays expenses of writers on assignment.

SOBER TIMES, The Recovery Magazine, Recovery Communications of America, 6306 E. Green Lake Way N., Seattle WA 98103. (206)523-8005. Fax: (206)523-8085. Publisher: Gerauld D. Miller. 70% freelance written. Bimonthly tabloid on recovery from addictions. "*Sober Times* provides information about recovery from drug, alcohol and other addictive behavior, and it champions sober, sane and healthy lifestyles." Estab. 1987. Circ. 75,000. Pays on publication. Publishes ms an average of 2 months after acceptance. Byline given. Buys all rights and makes work-for-hire assignments. Submit seasonal/holiday material 3 months in advance. Reports in 2 months. Send SASE for writer's guidelines. Sample copy for $3 and 9×12 SAE with 4 first-class stamps.

Nonfiction: Essays, general interest, humor, interview/profile, opinion, personal experience, photo feature. "No fiction or poetry will be considered. No medical or psychological jargon." Buys 90 mss/year. Send complete ms. Length: 900-2,000 words. Pays $50+.

Photos: Send photos with submission. Reviews prints only. Offers no additional payment for photos accepted with ms. Identification of subjects required. Buys one-time rights.

Tips: "Send in finished ms with any prints. They will only be returned if accompanied by SASE. Most accepted articles are under 1,000 words. Celebrity interviews should focus on recovery from addiction."

STYLES, PERSONAL FITNESS, Fitness and Health for Adults over 30,, (formerly *Personal Fitness & Weight Loss Magazine*), International Recipe Collection, Inc., 4151 Knob Dr., Eagan MN 55122. (612)452-0571. Editor/Publisher: Russ Moore. 50% freelance written. Quarterly. "Articles should include what is new in health, fitness, and diet. Our audience is adults over 30 who want to stay young and fit, adults who want to take an active part in health and fitness. We review each and every submission." Estab. 1988. Circ. 150,000. Pays on publication. Byline given. Buys all rights. Submit seasonal material 3 months in advance. Accepts previously published submissions. Send photocopy of article or typed ms and information about when and where the article previously appeared. Writer's guidelines for #10 SAE with 4 first-class stamps.

Nonfiction: Book excerpts, general interest, how-to, exercise, health. Pays $200-300. Personal fitness, diet, lowfat cookbooks, and exercise are short single subjects that offer authors the opportunity to submit or write on a work-for-hire basis. Pays $650-2,000 for books.

Photos: State availability of photos with submission. Reviews transparencies. Offers $50-200/photo. Buys one-time rights.

TRAVELFIT, Magazine of Travel and Fitness, Publication Partners, Inc., 4151 Knob Dr., Eagan MN 55122. (612)452-0571. Editor/Publisher: Russ Moore. 50% freelance written. Quarterly magazine covering what is new in fitness and diet as it relates to travel. "Our audience is active adults of all ages who enjoy travel and desire active vacations that allow them to maintain their exercise and diet routines. Adventure and active vacation articles are requested. How-to travel and exercise should include photos." Estab. 1990. Circ. 150,000. Pays on publication. Byline given. Buys all rights. Submit seasonal material 6 months in advance. Accepts previously published submissions. Send photocopy of article, or typed ms with rights for sale noted and information about when and where the article previously appeared. Writer's guidelines for #10 SAE with 4 first-class stamps.

Nonfiction: Book excerpts, general interest, how-to, nutrition, health discussions. Length: 1,000-3,000 words. Pays $50-300.

Photos: State availability of photos with submission. Reviews transparencies. Offers $50-100/photo. Buys one-time rights.

VIBRANT LIFE, A Magazine for Healthful Living, Review and Herald Publishing Assn., 55 W. Oak Ridge Dr., Hagerstown MD 21740-7390. (301)791-7000. Fax: (301)790-9734. Contact: Editor. 20% freelance written. Enjoys working with published/established writers; works with a small number of new/unpublished writers each year. Bimonthly magazine covering health articles (especially from a prevention angle and with a Christian slant). Estab. 1845. Circ. 50,000. **Pays on acceptance.** "The average length of time between acceptance of a freelance-written manuscript and publication of the material depends upon the topics; some immediately used; others up to 2 years." Byline always given. Buys first serial, first World serial, or sometimes second serial (reprint) rights. Accepts previously published submissions. Send tearsheet of article and information about when and where the article previously appeared. For reprints, pays 50% of the amount paid for an original article. Submit seasonal/holiday material 6 months in advance. Reports in 2 months. Sample copy for $1. Writer's guidelines for #10 SASE.

Nonfiction: Interview/profile (with personalities on health). "We seek practical articles promoting better health and a more fulfilled life. We especially like features on breakthroughs in medicine, and most aspects of health." Buys 20-25 mss/year. Send complete ms. Length: 750-1,800 words. Pays $125-250.

Photos: Send photos with ms. Needs 35mm transparencies. Not interested in b&w photos.

Tips: "*Vibrant Life* is published for baby boomers, particularly women and young professionals, age 30-45. Articles must be written in an interesting, easy-to-read style. Information must be reliable; no faddism. We are more conservative than other magazines in our field. Request a sample copy, and study the magazine and writer's guidelines."

VIM & VIGOR, America's Family Health Magazine, Suite 400, 8805 N. 23rd Ave., Phoenix AZ 85021. (602)395-5850. Fax: (602)395-5853. Editor: Fred Petrovsky. 75% freelance written. Quarterly magazine covering health and healthcare. Estab. 1985. Circ. 900,000. **Pays on acceptance.** Publishes ms an average

of 3 months after acceptance. Byline given. Buys all rights. Query for electronic submissions. Reports in 2 weeks on queries. Sample copy for 9×12 SAE with 8 first-class stamps. Writer's guidelines for #10 SASE.
Nonfiction: Health, diseases and healthcare. "Absolutely no complete manuscripts will be accepted. All articles are assigned to freelance writers. Send samples of your style." Buys 4 mss/year. Query with published clips. Length: 2,000 words. Pays $500. Pays expenses of writers on assignment.
Photos: Send photos with submission. Reviews contact sheets and any size transparencies. Offers no additional payment for photos accepted with ms. Captions, model releases, identification of subjects required. Buys one-time rights.
Tips: "We rarely accept suggested story ideas."

WEIGHT WATCHERS MAGAZINE, 360 Lexington Ave., 11th Floor, New York NY 10017. (212)370-0644. Fax: (212)687-4398. Editor-in-Chief: Lee Haiken. Executive Editor: Nancy Gagliardi. Health Editor: Randi Rose. Food Editor: Joyce Hendley. Beauty & Fitness Editor: Geri Anne Fennessey. Features Editor: Catherine Censor. Approximately 80% freelance written. Monthly magazine for women interested in healthy lifestyle/behavior information/advice, including news on health, nutrition, fitness, psychology and food/recipes. Success and before-and-after stories also welcome. Estab. 1968. Circ. 1 million. Buys first North American rights. **Pays on acceptance**. Sample copy and writer's guidelines $1.95 for 9×12 SASE.
Nonfiction: "We are interested in general health, nutrition and behavorial/psychological articles (stories with a strong weight loss angle always a plus). Some fitness—everything from beginner to advanced ideas—freelanced out. Personal triumph/success stories of individuals who lost weight on the Weight Watchers plan also of interest. Back page a humorous look at some aspect of getting/staying in shape or achieving better health. Our articles have an authoritative yet friendly tone. How-to and service information crucial for all stories. To expedite fact-checking, we require a second, annotated manuscript including names, phone numbers, journal/newsletter citations of sources." Send detailed queries with published clips and SASE. Average article length: 700-1,200 words. Pay: $350-800.
Tips: "Well developed, tightly written queries always a plus, as are ideas that have a strong news peg. Trend pieces welcome and we're always on the lookout for a fresh angle on an old topic. Sources must be reputable; we prefer subjects to be medical professionals with university affiliations who are published in their field of expertise."

‡THE YOGA JOURNAL, California Yoga Teachers Association, 2054 University Ave., Berkeley CA 94704. (510)841-9200. Editor: Rick Fields. 75% freelance written. Bimonthly magazine covering yoga, holistic health, conscious living, spiritual practices and nutrition. "We reach a middle-class, educated audience interested in self-improvement and higher consciousness." Estab. 1975. Circ. 85,000. Pays on publication. Publishes ms an average of 10 months after acceptance. Byline given. Offers $50 kill fee. Buys first North American serial rights only. Reprints of previously published articles OK; submit tearsheet or photocopy of article and information about when and where the article previously appeared. Submit seasonal/holiday material 4 months in advance. Simultaneous queries OK. Reports in 3 months. Sample copy for $3.50. Free writer's guidelines.
Nonfiction: Book excerpts; how-to (exercise, yoga, massage, etc.); inspirational (yoga or related); interview/profile; opinion; photo feature; and travel (if about yoga). "Yoga is our main concern, but our principal features in each issue highlight other New Age personalities and endeavors. Nothing too far-out and mystical. Prefer stories about Americans incorporating yoga, meditation, etc., into their normal lives." Buys 40 mss/year. Query. Length: 750-3,500 words. Pays $150-800.
Photos: Tricia McGillis, art director. Send photos with ms. Pays $200-600 for cover transparencies; $25-100 for 8×10 b&w prints. Model release (for cover only) and identification of subjects required. Buys one-time rights.
Columns/Departments: Forum; Cooking; Nutrition; Natural Body Care; Bodywork; Meditation; Well-Being; Psychology; Profiles; Music (reviews of New Age music); and Book Reviews. Buys 12-15 mss/year. Pays $150-400 for columns; $50-100 for book reviews.
Tips: "We always read submissions. We are very open to freelance material and want to encourage writers to submit to our magazine. We're looking for out-of-state contributors, particularly in the Midwest and East Coast."

YOUR HEALTH, Globe Communications Corp., 5401 NW Broken Sound Blvd., Boca Raton FL 33487. (407)997-7733. Editor: Susan Gregg. Associate Editor: Lisa Rappa. 70% freelance written. Semimonthly magazine on health and fitness. "*Your Health* is a lay-person magazine covering the entire gamut of health, fitness and medicine." Estab. 1962. Circ. 50,000. Pays on publication. Byline given. Buys first North American serial and second serial (reprint) rights. Submit seasonal/holiday material 3 months in advance. Accepts previously published submissions. Send photocopy of article and information about when and where the article previously appeared. Pays $150-200 for reprints. Reports in 1 month on queries; 6 weeks on mss. Free sample copy and writer's guidelines.
Nonfiction: Book excerpts, general interest, how-to (on general health and fitness topics), inspirational, interview/profile, medical breakthroughs, natural healing and alternative medicine, new products. "Give us

something new and different." Buys 75-100 mss/year. Query with published clips or send complete ms. Length: 300-2,000 words. Pays $25-150.

Photos: Send photos with submission. Reviews contact sheets, negatives, transparencies, prints. Offers $50-100/photo. Captions, model releases, identification of subjects required. Buys one-time rights.

Tips: "Freelancers can best break in by offering us stories of national interest that we won't find through other channels, such as wire services. Well-written self-help articles, especially ones that focus on natural prevention and cures are always welcome."

YOUR HEALTH, Meridian International, Inc., Box 10010, Ogden UT 84409. (801)394-9446. 65% freelance written. Bimonthly inhouse magazine covering personal health, customized with special imprint titles for various businesses, organizations and associations. "Articles should be timeless, noncontroversial, upscale and positive, and the subject matter should have national appeal." Circ. 40,000. **Pays on acceptance.** Publishes ms an average of 3 months after acceptance. Byline given. Buys first rights, second serial (reprint) and non-exclusive reprint rights. Accepts simultaneous and previously published submissions. Reports in 2 months with SASE. Sample copy for $1 and 9×12 SAE. Writer's guidelines with #10 SASE. (All requests for sample copies and guidelines and queries should be addressed Attention: Editorial Staff.)

Nonfiction: "Health care needs, particularly for mature reader. Medical technology; common maladies and survey of preventitive or non-drug treatments; low-impact fitness activities; nutrition with recipes; positive aspects of hospital, nursing home, and home care by visiting nurse. Profiles on exceptional health care professionals or people coping with disability or illness. Photo support with healthy looking people is imperative. No chiropractic, acupuncture, podiatry or herbal treatments. Material must be endorsed by AMA or ADA. All articles are reviewed by a medical board for accuracy. Medical conclusions should be footnoted for fact-checking." Buys 40 mss/year. Query by mail. Length: 1,000 words. Pays 15¢/word for first rights plus non-exclusive reprint rights. Payment for second rights 10¢/word. Authors retain the right to resell material after it is printed by *Your Health*.

Photos: Send photos with ms. Reviews 35mm and 2¼×2¼ transparencies and 5×7 or 8×10 color prints. Offers $35/inside photo and $50/cover photo. Captions, model releases, identification of subjects required.

Tips: "The key for the freelancer is a well-written query letter that demonstrates that the subject of the article has national appeal; establishes that any medical claims are based on interviews with experts and/or reliable documented sources; shows that the article will have a clear, focused theme; top-quality color photos; and gives evidence that the writer/photographer is a professional, even if a beginner. The best way to get started as a contributor to *Your Health* is to prove that you can submit a well-focused article, based on facts, along with a variety of beautiful color transparencies to illustrate the story. Material is reviewed by a medical board and must be approved by them."

YOUR HEALTH & FITNESS, General Learning Corp., 60 Revere Dr., Northbrook IL 60062-1563. (708)205-3000. Senior Editor: Carol Lezak. 90-95% freelance written. Prefers to work with published/established writers. Quarterly magazine covering health and fitness. Needs "general, educational material on health, fitness and safety that can be read and understood easily by the layman." Estab. 1969. Circ. 1 million. Pays after publication. Publishes ms an average of 6 months after acceptance. No byline given (contributing editor status given in masthead). Offers 50% kill fee. Buys all rights. Reports in 1 year.

Nonfiction: General interest. "All article topics assigned. No queries; if you're interested in writing for the magazine, send a cover letter, résumé, curriculum vitae and writing samples. All topics are determined a year in advance of publication by editors; no unsolicited manuscripts." Buys approximately 65 mss/year. Length: 350-850 words. Pays $100-400 for assigned articles.

Tips: "Write to a general audience that has only a surface knowledge of health and fitness topics. Possible subjects include exercise and fitness, psychology, nutrition, safety, disease, drug data, and health concerns."

History

Listed here are magazines and other periodicals written for historical collectors, genealogy enthusiasts, historic preservationists and researchers. Editors of history magazines look for fresh accounts of past events in a readable style. Some publications cover an era, such as the Civil War, or a region, while others specialize in historic preservation.

AMERICAN HERITAGE, 60 Fifth Ave., New York NY 10011. (212)206-5500. Fax: (212)620-2332. Editor: Richard Snow. 70% freelance written. Magazine published 8 times/year. Circ. 300,000. Usually buys first North American rights or all rights. Byline given. **Pays on acceptance.** Publishes ms an average of 6-12 months after acceptance. Before submitting material, "check our index to see whether we have already treated the subject." Submit seasonal material 1 year in advance. Reports in 1 month. Writer's guidelines for #10 SASE.

Nonfiction: Wants "historical articles by scholars or journalists intended for intelligent lay readers rather than for professional historians." Emphasis is on authenticity, accuracy and verve. "Interesting documents, photographs and drawings are always welcome. Query. Style should stress readability and accuracy." Buys 30 unsolicited mss/year. Length: 1,500-5,000 words. Sometimes pays the expenses of writers on assignment.

Tips: "We have over the years published quite a few 'firsts' from young writers whose historical knowledge, research methods and writing skills met our standards. The scope and ambition of a new writer tell us a lot about his or her future usefulness to us. A major article gives us a better idea of the writer's value. Everything depends on the quality of the material. We don't really care whether the author is 20 and unknown, or 80 and famous, or vice versa."

AMERICAN HISTORY, P.O. Box 8200, Harrisburg PA 17105-8200. (717)657-9555. Fax: (717)657-9526. Editor: Ed Holm. 60% freelance written. Bimonthly magazine of cultural, social, military and political history published for a general audience. Estab. 1966. Circ. 160,000. **Pays on acceptance.** Byline given. Buys all rights. Query for electronic submissions. Reports in 10 weeks on queries. Writer's guidelines for #10 SASE. Sample copy and guidelines for $4.50 (includes 3rd class postage) or $4 and 9×12 SAE with 4 first-class stamps.

Nonfiction: Regular features include American Profiles (biographies of noteworthy historical figures); Artifacts (stories behind historical objects); Portfolio (pictorial features on artists, photographers and graphic subjects); Digging Up History (coverage of recent major archaeological and historical discoveries). "Material is presented on a popular rather than a scholarly level." Writers are required to query before submitting ms. "Query letters should be limited to a concise 1-2 page proposal defining your article with an emphasis on its unique qualities." Buys 10-15 mss/year. Length: 1,000-5,000 words depending on type of article. Pays $200-1,000. Sometimes pays the expenses of writers on assignment.

Photos: Welcomes suggestions for illustrations. Pays for the reproduced color illustrations that the author provides.

Tips: "Key prerequisites for publication are thorough research and accurate presentation, precise English usage and sound organization, a lively style, and a high level of human interest. Submissions received without return postage will not be considered or returned. Inappropriate materials include: fiction, book reviews, travelogues, personal/family narratives not of national significance, articles about collectibles/antiques, living artists, local/individual historic buildings/landmarks and articles of a current editorial nature."

AMERICA'S CIVIL WAR, Cowles History Group, 741 Miller Dr., SE, Suite D-2, Leesburg VA 22075. (703)771-9400. Fax: (703)779-8345. Editor: Roy Morris, Jr. Managing Editor: Roger Vance. 95% freelance written. Bimonthly magazine of "popular history and straight historical narrative for both the general reader and the Civil War buff." Estab. 1988. Circ. 125,000. Pays on publication. Publishes ms up to 2 years after acceptance. Byline given. Buys first North American serial rights. Query for electronic submissions. Reports in 3 months on queries; 6 months on mss. Sample copy for $3.95. Writer's guidelines for #10 SASE.

Nonfiction: Book excerpts, historical, travel. No fiction or poetry. Buys 48 mss/year. Query. Length: 4,000 words maximum. Pays $300 maximum.

Photos: Send photos with submission. Payment for photos negotiable. Captions and identification of subjects required. Buys one-time rights.

Columns/Departments: Personality (probes); Ordnance (about weapons used); Commands (about units); Travel (about appropriate historical sites). Buys 24 mss/year. Query. Length: 2,000 words. Pays up to $150.

THE ARTILLERYMAN, Cutter & Locke, Inc., Publishers, RR 1 Box 36, Tunbridge VT 05077. (802)889-3500. Fax: (802)889-5627. Editor: C. Peter Jorgensen. 60% freelance written. Quarterly magazine covering antique artillery, fortifications and crew-served weapons 1750 to 1900 for competition shooters, collectors and living history reenactors using artillery. "Emphasis on Revolutionary War and Civil War but includes everyone interested in pre-1900 artillery and fortifications, preservation, construction of replicas, etc." Estab. 1979. Circ. 2,200. Pays on publication. Publishes ms an average of 6 months after acceptance. Byline given. Not copyrighted. Buys one-time rights. Accepts simultaneous and previously published submissions. Send tearsheet or photocopy of article and information about when and where the article previously appeared. Reports in 3 weeks. Sample copy and writer's guidelines for 9×12 SAE with 4 first-class stamps.

Nonfiction: Historical; how-to (reproduce ordnance equipment/sights/implements/tools/accessories, etc.); interview/profile; new product; opinion (must be accompanied by detailed background of writer and include references); personal experience; photo feature; technical (must have footnotes); travel (where to find interesting antique cannon). Interested in "artillery *only*, for sophisticated readers. Not interested in other weapons, battles in general." Buys 24-30 mss/year. Send complete ms. Length: 300 words minimum. Pays $20-60. Sometimes pays the expenses of writers on assignment.

Photos: Send photos with ms. Pays $5 for 5×7 and larger b&w prints. Captions, identification of subjects required.

Tips: "We regularly use freelance contributions for Places-to-Visit, Cannon Safety, The Workshop and Unit Profiles departments. Also need pieces on unusual cannon or cannon with a known and unique history. To judge whether writing style and/or expertise will suit our needs, writers should ask themselves if they could knowledgeably talk *artillery* with an expert. Subject matter is of more concern than writer's background."

CHICAGO HISTORY, The Magazine of the Chicago Historical Society, Chicago Historical Society, Clark St. at North Ave., Chicago IL 60614-6099. (312)642-4600. Fax: (312)266-2077. Editor: Rosemary Adams. Editorial Assistant: Lydia Field. 100% freelance written. Works with a small number of new/unpublished writers each year. Triannual magazine covering Chicago history: cultural, political, economic, social and architectural. Estab. 1945. Circ. 9,500. Pays on publication. Publishes ms an average of 1 year after acceptance. Byline given. Buys all rights. Submit seasonal/holiday material 9 months in advance. Query for electronic submissions. Reports in 4 months. Sample copy for $3.50 and 9 × 12 SAE with 3 first-class stamps. Free writer's guidelines.

Nonfiction: Book excerpts, essays, historical, photo feature. Articles should be "analytical, informative, and directed at a popular audience with a special interest in history." No "cute" articles. Buys 8-12 mss/year. Query or send complete ms. Length: approximately 4,500 words. Pays $150-250.

Photos: Send photocopies with submission. Would prefer no originals. Offers no additional payment for photos accepted with ms. Identification of subjects required.

Tips: "A freelancer can best break in by 1) calling to discuss an article idea with editor; and 2) submitting a detailed outline of proposed article. All sections of *Chicago History* are open to freelancers, but we suggest that authors do not undertake to write articles for the magazine unless they have considerable knowledge of the subject and are willing to research it in some detail. We require a footnoted manuscript, although we do not publish the notes."

‡GOOD OLD DAYS, America's Premier Nostalgia Magazine, House of White Birches, 306 E. Parr Rd., Berne IN 46711. (219)589-8741. Editor: Ken Tate. 75% freelance written. Monthly magazine of first person nostalgia, 1900-1955. "We look for strong narratives showing life as it was in the first half of this century. Our readership is comprised of nostalgia buffs, history enthusiasts and the people who actually lived and grew up in this era." Pays on publication. Publishes ms an average of 8 months after acceptance. Byline given. Buys all, first North American serial or one-time rights. Reprints rarely accepted. Submit seasonal/holiday material 10 months in advance. Reports in 2 months. Sample copy for $2. Writer's guidelines for #10 SASE.

Nonfiction: Historical/nostalgic, humor, interview/profile, personal experience, favorite food/recipes and photo features. Buys 350 mss/year. Query or send complete ms. Length: 1,000-1,800 words maximum. Pays 2-4¢/word or more, depending on quality and photos. No fiction accepted.

Photos: Send photos or photocopies of photos with submission. Offers $5/photo. Identification of subjects required. Buys one-time or all rights.

HISTORIC PRESERVATION, (formerly *Preservation News*), National Trust for Historic Preservation, 1785 Massachusetts Ave. NW, Washington DC 20036. (202)673-4075. Editor-in-Chief: Anne Powell. 25-30% freelance written. Prefers to work with published/established writers. Bimonthly tabloid covering preservation of historic buildings in the US. "We cover proposed or completed preservation projects and controversies involving historic buildings and districts. Most entries are features, department or opinion pieces." Circ. 250,000. Pays on publication. Publishes ms an average of 1 month after acceptance. Byline given. Offers variable kill fee. Buys one-time rights. Reports in 2 months on queries.

Nonfiction: Features, news, profiles, opinion, photo feature, travel. Buys 16 mss/year. Query with published clips. Length: 500-3,500 words. Sometimes pays the expenses of writers on assignment, but not long-distance travel.

Tips: "Do not send or propose histories of buildings, descriptive accounts of cities or towns or long-winded treatises on any subjects."

LOUIS L'AMOUR WESTERN MAGAZINE, Dell Magazines, 1540 Broadway, New York NY 10036. (212)782-8532. Fax: (212)782-8338. Editor: Elana Lore. 100% freelance written. Bimonthly magazine covering western fiction. "*LLWM* publishes the best of new, never before published western fiction being written today. We focus on the traditional western, but consider modern, mystery-oriented Native American, and other types of western fiction. Our audience is 70% male, 35-64, living mostly in nonurban areas across the US and in Canada." Estab. 1993. **Pays on acceptance.** Publishes ms an average of 6 months after acceptance. Byline given. Buys first serial and anthology rights. Editorial lead time 6-8 months. Submit seasonal material 6-8 months in advance. Accepts simultaneous submissions. Reports in 1 month on queries; 2-3 months on mss. Sample copy for $3.95. Writer's guidelines for #10 SASE.

For information on setting your freelance fees, see How Much Should I Charge?

Nonfiction: Historical/nostalgic (profiles of western historical figures), interview/profile, travel (in the West). Buys 18 mss/year. Query with published clips. Length: 2,500-3,000 words. Pays 8¢/word. Sometimes pays expenses of writers on assignment.

Photos: State availability of photos with submission. Negotiates payment individually.

Columns/Departments: Interview (current western figures), 2,500-3,000 words; Frontier Profile (historical western figures), 2,500-3,000 words; Western Travel (combination of modern/historical information on locations, done by experts in the area), 2,500-3,000 words. Buys 18 mss/year. Query with published clips. Pays 8¢/word. Also publishes 1 Classic Western short story each issue—a Spur winner or story that has been made into a movie (must be notable in some way). Send photocopy of short story and information about when and where the article previously appeared. Pays 3¢/word.

Fiction: Western. Buys 50 mss/year. Send complete ms. Length: 12,000 words maximum. Pays 8¢/word.

Tips: "For fiction, do your historical research to make sure your story is accurate. Avoid writing about well-known historical figures in your work. For nonfiction, also, avoid querying us about well-known historical figures. We want people and places that aren't already well-known to our readership."

MILITARY HISTORY, Cowles History Group, 741 Miller Dr., SE, Suite D-2, Leesburg VA 22075. (703)771-9400. Fax: (703)779-8345. Editor: C. Brian Kelly. 95% freelance written. Circ. 200,000. "We'll work with anyone, established or not, who can provide the goods and convince us as to its accuracy." Bimonthly magazine covering all military history of the world. "We strive to give the general reader accurate, highly readable, often narrative popular history, richly accompanied by period art." Pays on publication. Publishes ms 1-2 years after acceptance. Byline given. Buys all rights. Submit anniversary material 1 year in advance. Reports in 3 months on queries; 6 months on mss. Sample copy for $3.95. Writer's guidelines for #10 SASE.

Nonfiction: Historical; interview (military figures of commanding interest); personal experience (only occasionally). Buys 18 mss, plus 6 interviews/year. Query with published clips. "To propose an article, submit a short, self-explanatory query summarizing the story proposed, its highlights and/or significance. State also your own expertise, access to sources or proposed means of developing the pertinent information." Length: 4,000 words. Pays $400.

Columns/Departments: Espionage, weaponry, perspectives, personality, travel (with military history of the place) and books—all relating to military history. Buys 24 mss/year. Query with published clips. Length: 2,000 words. Pays $200.

Tips: "We would like journalistically 'pure' submissions that adhere to basics, such as full name at first reference, same with rank, and definition of prior or related events, issues cited as context or obscure military 'hardware.' Read the magazine, discover our style, and avoid subjects already covered. Pick stories with strong art possibilities (*real* art and photos), send photocopies, tell us where to order the art. Avoid historical overview, focus upon an event with appropriate and accurate context. Provide bibliography. Tell the story in popular but elegant style."

PERSIMMON HILL, 1700 NE 63rd St., Oklahoma City OK 73111. Fax: (405)478-4714. Editor: M.J. Van Deventer. 70% freelance written. Prefers to work with published/established writers; works with a small number of new/unpublished writers each year. Quarterly magazine for an audience interested in Western art, Western history, ranching and rodeo, including historians, artists, ranchers, art galleries, schools, and libraries. Publication of the National Cowboy Hall of Fame and Western Heritage Center. Estab. 1970. Circ. 15,000. Buys first rights. Byline given. Buys 35-50 mss/year. Pays on publication. Publishes ms an average of 6 months-2 years after acceptance. Reports in 3 months. Sample copy for $8 and 10 first-class stamps. Writer's guidelines for #10 SASE.

• *Persimmon Hill* needs reviewers for book review column.

Nonfiction: Historical and contemporary articles on famous Western figures connected with pioneering the American West, Western art, rodeo, cowboys, etc. (or biographies of such people), stories of Western flora and animal life and environmental subjects. "We want thoroughly researched and historically authentic material written in a popular style. May have a humorous approach to subject. No broad, sweeping, superficial pieces; i.e., the California Gold Rush or rehashed pieces on Billy the Kid, etc." Length: 1,500 words. Query with clips. Pays $100-250; special work negotiated.

Photos: Black and white glossy prints or color transparencies purchased with ms, or on assignment. Pays according to quality and importance for b&w and color photos. Suggested captions required.

Tips: "Excellent illustrations for articles are essential! No telephone queries."

TIMELINE, Ohio Historical Society, 1982 Velma Ave., Columbus OH 43211-2497. (614)297-2360. Fax: (614)297-2411. Editor: Christopher S. Duckworth. 90% freelance written. Works with a small number of new/unpublished writers each year. Bimonthly magazine covering history, natural history, archaeology and fine and decorative arts. Estab. 1885. Circ. 17,500. **Pays on acceptance.** Publishes ms an average of 1 year after acceptance. Byline given. Offers $75 minimum kill fee. Buys first North American serial or all rights. Submit seasonal/holiday material 6 months in advance. Query for electronic submissions. Reports in 3 weeks on queries; 6 weeks on mss. Sample copy for $5 and 9 × 12 SAE. Writer's guidelines for #10 SASE.

Nonfiction: Book excerpts, essays, historical, profile (of individuals), photo feature. Buys 22 mss/year. Query. Length: 500-6,000 words. Pays $100-900.

Photos: Send photos with submission. Will not consider submissions without ideas for illustration. Reviews contact sheets, transparencies, 8×10 prints. Captions, model releases, and identification of subjects required. Buys one-time rights.

Tips: "We want crisply written, authoritative narratives for the intelligent lay reader. An Ohio slant may strengthen a submission, but it is not indispensable. Contributors must know enough about their subject to explain it clearly and in an interesting fashion. We use high-quality illustration with all features. If appropriate illustration is unavailable, we can't use the feature. The writer who sends illustration ideas with a manuscript has an advantage, but an often-published illustration won't attract us."

TRACES OF INDIANA AND MIDWESTERN HISTORY, Indiana Historical Society, 315 W Ohio St., Indianapolis IN 46202-3299. (317)232-1884. Fax: (317)233-3109. Executive Editor: Thomas A. Mason. Managing Editor: J. Kent Calder. 80% freelance written. Quarterly magazine on Indiana and Midwestern history. Estab. 1989. Circ. 11,000. **Pays on acceptance.** Publishes ms an average of 6 months after acceptance. Byline given. Buys one-time rights. Submit seasonal/holiday material 1 year in advance. Reports in 3 months on mss. Sample copy for $5 and 9×12 SAE with 6 first-class stamps. Writer's guidelines for #10 SASE.
   ● This publication was awarded with certificates of Design Excellence from *Print Magazine*.
Nonfiction: Book excerpts, historical essays, photo features. Buys 20 mss/year. Send complete ms. Length: 2,000-4,000 words. Pays $100-500.
Photos: Send photos with submission. Reviews contact sheets, photocopies, transparencies and prints. Pays "reasonable photographic expenses." Captions, model releases and identification of subjects required. Buys one-time rights.
Tips: "Freelancers should be aware of prerequisites for writing history for a broad audience. Should have some awareness of this magazine and other magazines of this type published by midwestern and western historical societies. Preference is given to subjects with an Indiana connection and authors who are familiar with *Traces*. Quality of potential illustration is also important."

TRUE WEST, Western Periodicals, Inc., P.O. Box 2107, Stillwater OK 74076-2107. (405)743-3370. Editor: John Joerschke. 100% freelance written. Works with a small number of new/unpublished writers each year. Magazine on Western American history before 1940. "We want reliable research on significant historical topics written in lively prose for an informed general audience." Estab. 1953. Circ. 30,000. **Pays on acceptance.** Publishes ms an average of 4 months after acceptance. Byline given. Buys first North American serial rights. Submit seasonal/holiday material 6 months in advance. Reports in 1 month on queries; 2 months on mss. Sample copy for $2 and 9×12 SAE. Writer's guidelines for #10 SASE.
Nonfiction: Historical/nostalgic, how-to, photo feature, travel. "We do not want rehashes of worn-out stories, historical fiction or history written in a fictional style." Buys 150 mss/year. Query. Length: 500-4,500 words. Pays 3-6¢/word.
Photos: Send photos with accompanying query or ms. Pays $10 for b&w prints. Identification of subjects required. Buys one-time rights.
Columns/Departments: Western Roundup—200-300-word short articles on historically oriented places to go and things to do in the West. Should include one b&w print. Buys 12-16 mss/year. Send complete ms. Pays $35.
Tips: "Do original research on fresh topics. Stay away from controversial subjects unless you are truly knowledgable in the field. Read our magazines and follow our guidelines. A freelancer is most likely to break in with us by submitting thoroughly researched, lively prose on relatively obscure topics. First person accounts rarely fill our needs."

WILD WEST, Cowles History Group, 741 Miller Dr. SE, Suite D-2, Leesburg VA 22075. (703)771-9400. Fax: (703)779-8345. Editor: William M. Vogt. Managing Editor: Roger Vance. 95% freelance written. Bimonthly magazine on history of the American West. "*Wild West* covers the popular (narrative) history of the American West—events, trends, personalities, anything of general interest." Estab. 1988. Circ. 125,000. Pays on publication. Byline given. Buys all rights. Submit seasonal/holiday material 1 year in advance. Query for electronic submissions. Sample copy for $3.95. Writer's guidelines for #10 SASE.
Nonfiction: Historical/nostalgic, humor, travel. No fiction or poetry—nothing current. Buys 24 mss/year. Query. Length: 4,000 words. Pays $300.
Photos: Send photos with submission. Captions, identification of subjects required. Buys one-time rights or all rights.
Columns/Departments: Travel; Gun Fighters & Lawmen; Personalities; Warriors & Chiefs; Artist West; Books Reviews. Buys 16 mss/year. Length: 2,000. Pays $150 for departments, by the word for book reviews.

Hobby and Craft

Magazines in this category range from home video to cross stitch. Craftspeople and hobbyists who read these magazines want new ideas while collectors need to know what is most valuable and why. Collectors, do-it-yourselfers and craftspeople look to these magazines for inspiration and information. Publications covering antiques and miniatures are also listed here. Publications covering the business side of antiques and collectibles are listed in the Trade Art, Design and Collectibles section.

‡THE AMERICAN MATCHCOVER COLLECTORS CLUB, The Retskin Report, P.O. Box 18481, Asheville NC 28814-0481. (704)254-4487. Fax: (704)254-1066. Editor: Bill Retskin. 70% freelance written. Quarterly newsletter for matchcover collectors and historical enthusiasts. Estab. 1986. Circ. 700. Pays on publication. Publishes ms an average of 3 months after acceptance. Byline given. Offers 20% kill fee. Buys first North American serial rights. Submit seasonal material 6 months in advance. Query for electronic submission. Sample copy for 9×12 SAE with 2 first-class stamps. Writer's guidelines for #10 SASE.
Nonfiction: General interest, historical/nostalgic, how-to (collecting techniques), humor, personal experience, photo feature; all relating to match industry, matchcover collecting hobby or ephemera. Buys 2 mss/year. Query with published clips. Length: 200-1,200 words. Pays $25-50 for assigned articles; $10-25 for unsolicited articles.
Photos: Send photos with submission. Reviews b&w contact sheets and 5×7 prints. Offers $2-5/photo. Captions and identification of subjects required.
Fiction: Historical (match cover related only). Buys 2 mss/year. Query with published clips. Length: 200-1,200 words. Pays $25-50.
Tips: "We are interested in clean, direct style with the collector audience in mind."

AMERICAN SQUARE DANCE MAGAZINE, Sanborn Enterprises, 661 Middlefield Rd., Salinas CA 93906. Editor: Jon Sanborn. 50% freelance written. Monthly magazine covering square, round, country-western, clogging, contra dance. Estab. 1945. Circ. 16,000. Pays on publication. Publishes ms an average of 4 months after acceptance. Byline given. Buys one-time rights. Editorial lead time 3 months. Submit seasonal material 6-8 months in advance. Accepts simultaneous and previously published submissions. Reports in 6 weeks on queries. Sample copy for $2. Writer's guidelines for #10 SASE.
Nonfiction: Book excerpts, exposé, personal experience, photo feature, travel. Buys 5 mss/year. Query with published clips. Length: 600-1,000 words. Pays $70 minimum for assigned articles; $25 minimum for unsolicited articles.
Columns/Departments: Pays $25-60.

AMERICAN WOODWORKER, Rodale Press, Inc., 33 E. Minor St., Emmaus PA 18098-0099. (610)967-5171. Fax: (610)967-8956. Editor/Publisher: David Sloan. Executive Editor: Ellis Wallentine. Managing Editor: Tim Snyder. 70% freelance written. Magazine published 7 times/year. "*American Woodworker* is a how-to magazine edited for the woodworking enthusiast who wants to improve his/her skills. We strive to motivate, challenge and entertain." Estab. 1985. Circ. 300,000. Pays on publication. Publishes ms an average of 6 months after acceptance. Byline given. Buys one-time and second serial (reprint) rights. Accepts previously published material. Send photocopy of article or typed ms with rights for sale noted. Submit seasonal material 8 months in advance. Query for electronic submissions. Reports in 1 month. Free sample copy and writer's guidelines.
Nonfiction: Essays, historical/nostalgic, how-to (woodworking projects and techniques), humor, inspirational, interview/profile, new product, personal experience, photo feature, technical. ("All articles must have woodworking theme.") Buys 30 mss/year. Query. Length: up to 2,500 words. Pays new authors base rate of $150/published page. Sometimes pays expenses of writers on assignment.
Photos: Send photos with submission. Reviews 35mm or larger transparencies. Offers no additional payment for photos accepted with ms. Model releases required. Buys one-time rights.
Columns/Departments: Offcuts (woodworking news and nonsense, 1,000 word max). Buys 10 mss/year. Send complete ms. Pays $100-300.
Poetry: Avant-garde, free verse, Haiku, light verse, traditional. "All poetry must have workworking or craftsmanship theme." Buys 1 poem/year. Submit maximum 5 poems. Pays $50-100.
Tips: "Reading the publication is the only real way to get a feel for the niche market *American Woodworker* represents and the needs and interests of our readers. Magazine editorial targets the serious woodworking enthusiast who wishes to improve his/her skills. Feature stories and articles most accessible for freelancers. Articles should be technically accurate, well organized and reflect the needs and interests of the amateur woodworking enthusiast."

‡THE ANTIQUE ALMANAC, Morgan Printing Co., P.O. Box 1616, 114 N. Mason, Bowie TX 76230. (817)872-5548. Fax: (817)872-3559. Editor: Judy Morgan. Contact: Jo Ellen Pennington. 25% freelance written. Biweekly tabloid covering antiques, collectibles, primitives, bed and breakfasts, tea rooms, historical sites. Estab. 1994. Circ. 10,000. Pays on publication. Publishes ms an average of 2 months after acceptance. Byline sometimes given. Buys all rights. Editorial lead time 2 months in advance. Submit seasonal material 3 months in advance. Accepts simultaneous and previously published submissions. Query for electronic

submissions. Reports in 3 weeks on queries, 2 months on mss. Sample copy and writer's guidelines free on request.

Nonfiction: Book excerpts, essays, general interest, historical/nostalgic, how-to, humor, inspirational, interview/profile, personal experience, photo feature, technical travel. Special issues: Antique Cars, Veterans Day, Dolls, Bed & Breakfasts. Buys 13 mss/year. Query with published clips. Length: 500-2,800 words. Pays $15-60.

Photos: State availability of photos with submission. Reviews contact sheets, 5×7 prints. Negotiates payment individually. Captions, model releases, identification of subjects required. Buys one-time rights.

Columns/Departments: Literary Spelunker (book reviews), 100 words; Antique Column (technical info), up to 500 words; Travel (B&Bs, tea rooms, specialty shops), up to 1,000 words. Buys 13 mss/year. Send complete ms. Pays $10-40.

Fiction: Ethnic, historical, humorous, slice-of-life vignettes, western. "Characters should revolve around Victorian period. Must have some relation to theme issues." Buys 3/year. Send complete ms. Length: 500-2,500 words. Pays $10-50.

Poetry: Free verse, haiku, traditional. Buys 13 mss/year. Submit batch of 5 poems at a time. Pays for poetry with 1-year subscription.

Fillers: Anecdotes, facts, short humor. Buys 10/year.

Tips: Query. If photo is to be included, need to see contact sheet to check quality. Need to be detail-oriented.

ANTIQUE REVIEW, P.O. Box 538, Worthington OH 43085-0538. Editor: Charles Muller. (614)885-9757. Fax: (614)885-9762. 60% freelance written. Eager to work with new/unpublished writers. Monthly tabloid for an antique-oriented readership, "generally well-educated, interested in Early American furniture and decorative arts, as well as folk art." Estab. 1975. Circ. 10,000. Pays on publication date assigned at time of purchase. Publishes ms an average of 3 months after acceptance. Buys first North American serial and second (reprint) rights to material originally published in dissimilar publications. Accepts previously published submissions if not first printed in competitive publications. Send tearsheet or photocopy of article or typed ms with rights for sale noted and information about when and where the article previously appeared. For reprints, pays 100% of the amount paid for an original article. Byline given. Phone queries OK. Reports in 3 months. Free sample copy and writer's guidelines for #10 SASE.

Nonfiction: "The articles we desire concern history and production of furniture, pottery, china, and other quality Americana. In some cases, contemporary folk art items are acceptable. We are also interested in reporting on antiques shows and auctions with statements on conditions and prices. We do not want articles on contemporary collectibles." Buys 5-8 mss/issue. Query with clips of published work. Query should show "author's familiarity with antiques, an interest in the historical development of artifacts relating to early America and an awareness of antiques market." Length: 200-2,000 words. Pays $100-200. Sometimes pays the expenses of writers on assignment.

Photos: Send photos with query. Payment included in ms price. Uses 3×5 or larger glossy b&w prints. Color acceptable. Captions required. Articles with photographs receive preference.

Tips: "Give us a call and let us know of specific interests. We are more concerned with the background in antiques than in writing abilities. The writing can be edited, but the knowledge imparted is of primary interest. A frequent mistake is being too general, not becoming deeply involved in the topic and its research. We are interested in primary research into America's historic material culture."

BANK NOTE REPORTER, Krause Publications, 700 E. State St., Iola WI 54990-0001. (715)445-2214. Fax: (715)445-4087. Editor: David Harper. Monthly tabloid for advanced collectors of US and world paper money. Estab. 1952. Circ. 5,600. Pays on publication. Buys first North American serial and reprint rights. Sample copy for 9×12 SAE and postage.

BECKETT BASEBALL CARD MONTHLY, Statabase, Inc., 15850 Dallas Pkwy., Dallas TX 75248. (214)991-6657. Fax: (214)991-8930. Editor: Dr. James Beckett. Editorial Directorial: Pepper Hastings. 85% freelance written. Monthly magazine on baseball card and sports memorabilia collecting. "Our readers expect our publication to be entertaining and informative. Our slant is that hobbies are fun and rewarding. Especially wanted are how-to-collect articles." Estab. 1984. Circ. 620,341. **Pays on acceptance.** Publishes ms an average of 4 months after acceptance. Byline given. Pays $50 kill fee. Buys first North American serial rights. Submit seasonal/holiday material 6 months in advance. No simultaneous submissions. Reports in 1 month. Sample copy for $2.95. Writer's guidelines free.

Nonfiction: Book excerpts, historical/nostalgic, how-to, humor, interview/profile, new product, opinion, personal experience, photo feature, technical. Special issues: Spring training (February); season preview (April); All-Star game (July); stay in school (August); World Series (October). No articles that emphasize speculative prices and investments. Buys 145 mss/year. Send complete ms. Length: 300-1,500 words. Pays $100-400 for assigned articles; $50-200 for unsolicited articles. Sometimes pays expenses of writers on assignment.

Photos: Send photos with submission. Reviews 35mm transparencies, 5×7 or larger prints. Offers $10-300/photo. Captions, model releases and identification of subjects required. Buys one-time rights.

Fiction: Humorous only.

Tips: "A writer for *Beckett Baseball Card Monthly* should be an avid sports fan and/or a collector with an enthusiasm for sharing his/her interests with others. Articles must be factual, but not overly statistic-laden. First person (not research) articles presenting the writer's personal experiences told with wit and humor, and emphasizing the stars of the game, are *always* wanted. Acceptable articles must be of interest to our two basic reader segments: teenaged boys and their middle-aged fathers who are re-experiencing a nostalgic renaissance of their own childhoods. Prospective writers should write down to neither group!"

BECKETT BASKETBALL MONTHLY, Statabase, Inc., 15850 Dallas Pkwy., Dallas TX 75248. (214)991-6657. Fax: (214)991-8930. Editor: Dr. James Beckett. Editorial Director: Pepper Hastings. 85% freelance written. Monthly magazine on basketball card and sports memorabilia collecting. "Our readers expect our publication to be entertaining and informative. Our slant is that hobbies are fun and rewarding. Especially wanted are articles dealing directly with the hobby of basketball card collecting." Estab. 1990. Circ. 392,854. **Pays on acceptance.** Publishes ms an average of 4 months after acceptance. Byline given. Pays $50 kill fee. Buys first North American serial rights. Submit seasonal/holiday material 6 months in advance. No simultaneous submissions. Reports in 1 month. Sample copy for $2.95. Writer's guidelines free.

Nonfiction: Book excerpts, historical/nostalgic, how-to, humor, interview/profile, new product, opinion, personal experience, photo feature, technical. Special issues: All Star game, stay in school (February); playoffs (June); new card sets (September). No articles that emphasize speculative prices and investments. Buys 145 mss/year. Send complete ms. Length: 300-1,500 words. Pays $100-400 for assigned articles; $100-200 for unsolicited articles. Sometimes pays expenses of writers on assignment.

Photos: Send photos with submission. Reviews 35mm transparencies, 5×7 or larger prints. Offers $10-300/photo. Captions, model releases and identification of subjects required. Buys one-time rights.

Fiction: Humorous only.

Tips: "A writer for *Beckett Basketball Monthly* should be an avid sports fan and/or a collector with an enthusiasm for sharing his/her interests with others. Articles must be factual, but not overly statistic-laden. First person (not research) articles presenting the writer's personal experiences told with wit and humor, and emphasizing the stars of the game, are *always* wanted. Acceptable articles must be of interest to our two basic reader segments: late teenaged boys and their fathers who are re-experiencing a nostalgic renaissance of their own childhoods. Prospective writers should write down to neither group!"

BECKETT FOCUS ON FUTURE STARS, Statabase, Inc., 15850 Dallas Pkwy., Dallas TX 75248. (214)991-6657. Fax: (214)991-8930. Editor: Dr. James Beckett. Editorial Director: Pepper Hastings. 85% freelance written. Monthly magazine offering superstar coverage of young, outstanding players in baseball (major-league rookies, minor league stars and college), basketball (college), football (college) and hockey (juniors and college), with an emphasis on collecting sports cards and memorabilia. "Our readers expect our publication to be entertaining and informative. Our slant is that hobbies are fun and rewarding. Especially wanted are how-to collect articles." Estab. 1991. Circ. 73,128. **Pays on acceptance.** Publishes ms an average of 4 months after acceptance. Byline given. Pays $50 kill fee. Buys first North American serial rights. Submit seasonal/holiday material 8 months in advance. No simultaneous submissions. Reports in 1 month. Sample copy for $2.95. Writer's guidelines free.

Nonfiction: Book excerpts, historical/nostalgic, how-to, humor, interview/profile, new product, opinion, personal experience, photo feature, technical. Special issues: card sets in review (January); stay in school (February); draft special (June). No articles that emphasize speculative prices and investments on cards. Buys 145 mss/year. Send complete ms. Length: 300-1,500 words. Pays $100-400 for assigned articles; $50-200 for unsolicited articles. Sometimes pays expenses of writers on assignment.

Photos: Send photos with submission. Reviews 35mm transparencies, 5×7 or larger prints. Offers $25-300/photo. Captions, model releases and identification of subjects required. Buys one-time rights.

Fiction: Humorous only

Tips: "A writer for *Beckett Focus on Future Stars* should be an avid sports fan and/or a collector with an enthusiasm for sharing his/her interests with others. Articles must be factual, but not overly statistic-laden. First person (not research) articles presenting the writer's personal experiences told with wit and humor, and emphasizing the stars of the game, are *always* wanted. Acceptable articles must be of interest to our two basic reader segments: teenaged boys and their middle-aged fathers who are re-experiencing a nostalgic renaissance of their own childhoods. Prospective writers should write down to neither group!"

BECKETT FOOTBALL CARD MONTHLY, Statabase, Inc., 15850 Dallas Pkwy., Dallas TX 75248. (214)991-6657. Fax: (214)991-8930. Editor: Dr. James Beckett. Editorial Director: Pepper Hastings. 85% freelance written. Monthly magazine on football card and sports memorabilia collecting. "Our readers expect our publication to be entertaining and informative. Our slant is that hobbies are fun and rewarding. Especially wanted are how-to collect articles." Estab. 1989. Circ. 206,194. **Pays on acceptance.** Publishes ms an average of 4 months after acceptance. Byline given. Pays $50 kill fee. Buys first North American serial rights. Submit seasonal/holiday material 6 months in advance. No simultaneous submissions. Reports in 1 month. Sample copy for $2.95. Writer's guidelines free.

Nonfiction: Book excerpts, historical/nostalgic, how-to, humor, interview/profile, new product, opinion, personal experience, photo feature, technical. Special issues: Super Bowl (January); Pro Bowl (February); NFL draft (April); stay in school (August) preview (September). No articles that emphasize speculative prices and investments. Buys 145 mss/year. Send complete ms. Length: 300-1,500 words. Pays $100-400 for assigned articles; $50-200 for unsolicited articles. Sometimes pays expenses of writers on assignment.
Photos: Send photos with submission. Reviews 35mm transparencies, 5×7 or larger prints. Offers $10-300/photo. Captions, model releases and identification of subjects required. Buys one-time rights.
Fiction: Humorous only.
Tips: "A writer for *Beckett Football Card Monthly* should be an avid sports fan and/or a collector with an enthusiasm for sharing his/her interests with others. Articles must be factual, but not overly statistic-laden. Acceptable articles must be of interest to our two basic reader segments: teenaged boys and their middle-aged fathers who are re-experiencing a nostalgic renaissance of their own childhoods. Prospective writers should write down to neither group!"

BECKETT HOCKEY MONTHLY, Statabase, Inc., 15850 Dallas Pkwy., Dallas TX 75248. (214)991-6657. Fax: (214)991-8930. Editor: Dr. James Beckett. Editorial Director: Pepper Hastings. 85% freelance written. Monthly magazine on hockey, hockey card and memorabilia collecting. "Our readers expect our publication to be entertaining and informative. Our slant is that hobbies are for fun and rewarding. Especially wanted are how-to collect articles." Estab. 1990. Circ. 159,346. **Pays on acceptance.** Publishes ms an average of 3 months after acceptance. Byline given. Pays $50 kill fee. Buys first North American serial rights. Submit seasonal/holiday material 6 months in advance. No simultaneous submissions. Reports in 1 month. Sample copy for $2.95. Writer's guidelines free.
Nonfiction: Book excerpts, historical/nostalgic, how-to, humor, interview/profile, new product, opinion, personal experience, photo feature, technical. Special issues: All-Star game (February); Stanley Cup preview (April); draft (June); season preview (October). No articles that emphasize speculative prices and investments. Buys 145 mss/year. Send complete ms. Length: 300-1,500 words. Pays $100-400 for assigned articles; $50-200 for unsolicited articles. Sometimes pays expenses of writers on assignment.
Photos: Send photos with submission. Reviews 35mm transparencies, 5×7 or larger prints. Offers $10-300/photo. Captions, model releases and identification of subjects required. Buys one-time rights.
Fiction: Humorous only.
Tips: "A writer for *Beckett Hockey Monthly* should be an avid sports fan and/or a collector with an enthusiasm for sharing his/her interests with others. Articles must be factual, but not overly statistic-laden. Acceptable articles must be of interest to our two basic reader segments: teenaged boys and their middle-aged fathers who are re-experiencing a nostalgic renaissance of their own childhoods. Prospective writers should write down to neither group!"

‡BECKETT RACING MONTHLY, Statabase, Inc., 15850 Dallas Pkwy., Dallas TX 75248. (214)991-6657. Fax: (214)991-8930. Editor: Dr. James Beckett. Editorial Director: Pepper Hastings. 85% freelance written. Monthly magazine on racing card, die cast and sports memorabilia collecting. "Our readers expect our publication to be entertaining and informative. Our slant is that hobbies are fun and rewarding. Especially wanted are articles dealing directly with the hobby of card collecting." Estab. 1994. Circ. 100,000 **Pays on acceptance**. Publishes ms an average of 4 months after acceptance. Byline given. Pays $50 kill fee. Buys first North American serial rights. Submit seasonal/holiday material 6 months in advance. No simultaneous submissions. Reports in 1 month Sample copy for $3.95. Writer's guidelines free.
Nonfiction: Book excerpts, historical/nostalgic, how-to, humor, interview/profile, new product, opinion, personal experience, photo feature, technical. No articles that emphasize speculative prices and investments. Send complete ms. Length: 300-1,500 words. Pays $100-400 for assigned articles; $100-200 for unsolicited articles. Sometimes pays expenses of writer on assignment.
Photos: Send photos with submission. Reviews 35mm transparencies, 5×7 or larger prints. Offers $10-300/photo. Captions, model releases and identification of subjects required. Buys one-time rights.
Fiction: Humorous only.
Tips: "A writer for *Beckett Racing Monthly* should be an avid sports fan and/or a collector with an enthusiasm for sharing his/her interests with others. Articles must be factual, but not overly statistic-laden. First person (not research) articles presenting the writer's personal experiences told with wit and humor, and emphasizing the stars of the sport, are always wanted."

THE BLADE MAGAZINE, Blade Publications, P.O. Box 22007, Chattanooga TN 37422. Fax: (615)479-3586. Publisher: Bruce Voyles. Editor: Steve Shackleford. 90% freelance written. Magazine published 8 times/year for knife enthusiasts who want to know as much as possible about quality knives and edged weapons. Estab. 1973. Pays on publication. Publishes ms an average of 6 months after acceptance. Buys all rights. Submit seasonal/holiday material 6 months in advance. Accepts previously published submissions if not run in other knife publications. Send photocopy of article or typed ms with rights for sale noted and information about when and where the article previously appeared. For reprints, pays 90% of the amount paid for an original article. Reports in 2 months. Sample copy for $3.25. Writer's guidelines for #10 SASE.

● *Blade Magazine* is putting more emphasis on new products, knife accessories, knife steels, knife handles, knives and celebrities, knives in the movies.

Nonfiction: How-to; historical (on knives and weapons); adventure on a knife theme; celebrities who own knives; knives featured in movies with shots from the movie, etc.; new product; nostalgia; personal experience; photo feature; profile; technical. "We would also like to receive articles on knives in adventuresome life-saving situations." No poetry. Buys 75 unsolicited mss/year. "We evaluate complete manuscripts and make our decision on that basis." Length: 500-1,000 words, longer if content warrants it. Pays $200/story minimum; more for "better" writers. "We will pay top dollar in the knife market." Sometimes pays the expenses of writers on assignment.

Photos: Send photos with ms. Pays $5 for 8 × 10 b&w glossy prints, $25-75 for 35mm color transparencies. Captions required. "Photos are critical for story acceptance."

Fiction: Publishes novel excerpts.

Tips: "We are always willing to read submissions from anyone who has read a few copies and studied the market. The ideal article for us is a piece bringing out the romance, legend, and love of man's oldest tool—the knife. We like articles that place knives in peoples' hands—in life saving situations, adventure modes, etc. (Nothing gory or with the knife as the villain.) People and knives are good copy. We are getting more and better written articles from writers who are reading the publication beforehand. That makes for a harder sell for the quickie writer not willing to do his homework."

‡BREW, The How-to Homebrew Beer Magazine, Niche Publications, 216 F Street, Suite 160, Davis CA 95616. (916)758-4596. Editor: Craig Bystrynski. 85% freelance written. Monthly magazine covering home brewing. Estab. 1995. Circ. 25,000. Pays on publication. Publishes ms 2-3 months after acceptance. Byline given. Buys all rights. Editorial lead time 2½ months. Submit seasonal material 2½ months in advance. Query for electronic submissions.

Nonfiction: How-to (home brewing), humor (related to home brewing), interview/profile, personal experience, technical. Query with published clips. Length: 800-3,000 words. Pays $50-250. Sometimes pays expenses of writers on assignment.

Photos: Send photos with submission. Reviews contact sheets, transparencies, 5×7 prints. Negotiates payment individually. Captions required. Buys all rights.

Columns/Departments: News (humorous, unusual news about home brewing), 50-250 words. Send complete ms. Pays $25-50.

‡CLASSIC TOY TRAINS, Kalmbach Publishing Co., 21027 Crossroads Circle, Waukesha WI 53187. (414)796-8776. Editor: Roger Carp. 75-80% freelance written. Magazine published 8 times/year covering collectible toy trains (O, S, Standard, G scale, etc.) like Lionel, American Flyer, Marx, Dorfan, etc. "For the collector and operator of toy trains, *CTT* offers full-color photos of layouts and collections of toy trains, restoration tips, operating information, new product reviews and information, and insights into the history of toy trains." Estab. 1987. Circ. 77,000. **Pays on acceptance.** Publishes ms an average of 1 year after acceptance. Byline given. Buys all rights. Editorial lead time 2 months. Submit seasonal material 6 months in advance. Accepts electronic submissions by disk, if accompanied by hard copy. Reports in 2 weeks on queries; 3 months on mss. Sample copy for $3.95 plus s&h. Writer's guidelines for #10 SASE.

Nonfiction: General interest, historical/nostalgic, how-to (restore toy trains; designing a layout; build accessories; fix broken toy trains), interview/profile, personal experience, photo feature, technical. Buys 90 mss/year. Query. Length: 500-5,000 words. Pays $75-500. Sometimes pays expenses of writers on assignment.

Photos: Send photos with submission. Reviews 4×5 transparencies; 5×7 prints preferred. Offers no additional payment for photos accepted with ms or $15-75/photo. Captions required. Buys all rights.

Fillers: Uses cartoons. Buys 6 fillers/year. Pays $30.

Tips: "It's important to have a thorough understanding of the toy train hobby; most of our freelancers are hobbyists themselves. One-half to two-thirds of *CTT*'s editorial space is devoted to photographs; superior photography is critical."

COINS, Krause Publications, 700 E. State St., Iola WI 54990-0001. (715)445-2214. Fax: (715)445-4087. Editor: Robert Van Rysin. 50% freelance written. Eager to work with new/unpublished writers. Monthly magazine about US and foreign coins for all levels of collectors, investors and dealers. Estab. 1952. Circ. 71,000. Reports in 2 months. Free sample copy and writer's guidelines.

Nonfiction: "We're looking for stories that will help coin collectors pursue their hobby in today's market. Stories should include what's available in the series being discussed, its value in today's market, and tips for buying that material." Buys 4 mss/issue. Query first. Length: 500-2,500 words. Pays 3¢/word to first-time contributors; fee negotiated for later articles.

Photos: Pays $5 minimum for b&w prints; $25 minimum for 35mm transparencies. Captions and model releases required. Buys first rights.

COLLECTOR EDITIONS, Collector Communications Corp., 170 Fifth Ave., New York NY 10010-5911. (212)989-8700. Fax: (212)645-8976. Editor: Joan Muyskens Pursley. 40% freelance written. Works with a small number of new/unpublished writers each year. Bimonthly magazine on porcelain and glass collectibles and limited-edition prints. "We specialize in contemporary (post-war ceramic and glass) collectibles, including reproductions, but also publish articles about antiques, if they are being reproduced today and are generally available." Estab. 1973. Circ. 96,000. Buys first North American serial rights. "First assignments are always done on a speculative basis." Pays within 30 days of acceptance. Publishes ms an average of 6 months after acceptance. Reports in 2 months. Sample copy for $2. Writer's guidelines for #10 SASE.

Nonfiction: "Short features about collecting, written in tight, newsy style. We specialize in contemporary (postwar) collectibles. Values for pieces being written about should be included." Informational, interview, profile, exposé, nostalgia. Buys 15-20 mss/year. Query with sample photos. Length: 500-1,500 words. Pays $200-400. Sometimes pays expenses of writers on assignment.

Columns/Departments: Staff written; not interested in freelance columns.

Photos: B&w and color photos purchased with accompanying ms with no additional payment. Captions are required. "We want clear, distinct, full-frame images that say something."

Tips: "Unfamiliarity with the field is the most frequent mistake made by writers in completing an article for us."

COLLECTORS NEWS & THE ANTIQUE REPORTER, P.O. Box 156, Grundy Center IA 50638-0156. (319)824-6981. Fax: (319)824-3414. Editor: Linda Kruger. 20% freelance written. Estab. 1959. Works with a small number of new/unpublished writers each year. Monthly magazine-size publication on newsprint covering antiques, collectibles and nostalgic memorabilia. Circ. 13,000. Byline given. Pays on publication. Publishes ms an average of 1 year after acceptance. Buys first rights and makes work-for-hire assignments. Submit seasonal/holiday material 3 months in advance. Reports in 2 weeks on queries; 6 weeks on mss. Sample copy for $3 for 9×12 SAE. Free writer's guidelines.

Nonfiction: General interest (any subject re: collectibles, antique to modern); historical/nostalgic (relating to collections or collectors); how-to (display your collection, care for, restore, appraise, locate, add to, etc.); interview/profile (covering individual collectors and their hobbies, unique or extensive; celebrity collectors, and limited edition artists); technical (in-depth analysis of a particular antique, collectible or collecting field); and travel (coverage of special interest or regional shows, seminars, conventions—or major antique shows, flea markets; places collectors can visit, tours they can take, museums, etc.). Special issues: show/flea market (January, June) and usual seasonal emphasis. Buys 100 mss/year. Query with sample of writing. Length: 800-1,000 words. Pays $1/column inch.

Photos: Reviews color or b&w prints. Payment for photos included in payment for ms. Captions required. Buys first rights.

Tips: Articles most open to freelancers are on farm/country/rural collectibles; celebrity collectors; collectors with unique and/or extensive collections; music collectibles; transportation collectibles; advertising collectibles; bottles; glass, china and silver; primitives; furniture; toys; black memorabilia; political collectibles; and movie memorabilia.

CRAFTING TODAY, M.S.C. Publishing, Inc., 243 Newton-Sparta Rd., Newton NJ 07860. (201)383-8080. Editor: Deborah McGowan. Contact: Linda Dunlap. Bimonthly magazine covering beginner to intermediate level crafts. Estab. 1989. Circ. 80,000. Pays on publication. Publishes ms an average of 3-6 months after acceptance. Byline given. Buys first rights and second serial (reprint) rights. Editorial lead time 6 months. Submit seasonal material 6 months in advance. No simultaneous submissions. Accepts previously published submissions occasionally. Writer's guidelines for #10 SASE.

Nonfiction: How-to (crafts). Special issues: Americana Designs cross stitch collectibles, Homestead Classics Christmas crafts. Buys 3 mss/year. Query. Length: 700-1,500 words. Pays 10¢/word.

CROCHET WORLD, House of White Birches, P.O. Box 776, Henniker NH 03242. Editor: Susan Hankins. 100% freelance written. Bimonthly magazine covering crochet patterns. "Crochet World is a pattern magazine devoted to the art of crochet. We also feature a Q&A column, letters (swap shop) column and occasionally non-pattern manuscripts, but it must be devoted to crochet." Estab. 1978. Circ. 75,000. Pays on publication. Byline given. Buys all rights. Editorial lead time 4 months. Submit seasonal material 6 months in advance. Query for electronic submissions. Reports in 1 month. Sample copy for $2. Writer's guidelines free on request.

Nonfiction: How-to (crochet). Buys 0-2 mss/year. Send complete ms. Length: 500-1,500 words. Pays $50.

Columns/Departments: Touch of Style (crocheted clothing); It's a Snap! (quick one-night simple patterns); Pattern of the Month, first and second prize each issue. Buys dozens of mss/year. Send complete pattern. Pays $40-300.

Poetry: Strictly crochet-related. Buys 0-10 poems/year. Submit maximum 2 poems. Length: 6-20 lines. Pays $10-20.

Fillers: Anecdotes, facts, gags to be illustrated by cartoonist, short humor. Buys 0-10/year. Length: 25-200 words. Pays $5-30.

Tips: "Be aware that this is a pattern generated magazine for crochet designs. I prefer the actual item sent along with the complete directions/graphs etc. over queries. In some cases a photo submission or good sketch will do. Crocheted designs must be well made and directions must be complete. Write for my Designer's

Guidelines which details how to submit designs. Non-crochet items, such as fillers, poetry *must* be crochet related, not knit, not sewing etc."

DECORATIVE ARTIST'S WORKBOOK, F&W Publications, Inc., 1507 Dana Ave., Cincinnati OH 45207-1005. Editor: Sandra Carpenter. Estab. 1987. 50% freelance written. Bimonthly magazine covering decorative painting projects and products of all sorts. Offers "straightforward, personal instruction in the techniques of decorative painting." Circ. 88,000. **Pays on acceptance.** Byline given. Offers 20% kill fee. Buys first North American serial rights. Submit seasonal/holiday material 8 months in advance. Reports in 1 month. Sample copy for $3.65 and 9×12 SAE with 5 first-class stamps.
Nonfiction: How-to (related to decorative painting projects), new products, techniques, artist profiles. Buys 30 mss/year. Query with slides or photos. Length: 1,200-1,800 words. Pays 10-12¢/word.
Photos: State availability of or send photos with submission. Reviews 35mm, 4×5 transparencies and quality photos. Offers no additional payment for photos accepted with ms. Captions required. Buys one-time rights.
Fillers: Anecdotes, facts, short humor. Buys 10/year. Length: 50-200 words. Pays $10-25.
Tips: "The more you know—and can prove you know—about decorative painting the better your chances. I'm looking for experts in the field who, through their own experience, can artfully describe the techniques involved. How-to articles are most open to freelancers. Be sure to query with slides or transparencies, and show that you understand the extensive graphic requirements for these pieces and are able to provide progressives—slides or illustrations that show works in progress."

DOLL COLLECTOR'S PRICE GUIDE, House of White Birches, 306 E. Parr Rd., Berne IN 46711. (219)589-8741. Editor: Cary Raesher. Quarterly magazine covering doll collecting. Audience is interested in informative articles about collecting and investing in dolls, museum exhibits, doll history, etc. Estab. 1991. Circ. 43,985. Pays pre-publication. Byline given. Buys first, one-time or all rights. Editorial lead time 6 months. Accepts previously published submissions. Reports in 3 months. Sample copy for $2. Writer's guidelines for #10 SASE.
Nonfiction: Historical/nostalgic. Buys 20 mss/year. Send complete ms. Pays $50.
Photos: Send photos with submission. Captions and identification of subjects required.

DOLL WORLD The Magazine for Doll Lovers, House of White Birches, 306 E. Parr Rd., Berne IN 46711. (219)589-8741. Fax: (219)589-8093. Editor: Cary Raesner. 90% freelance written. Bimonthly magazine covering doll collecting, restoration. "Interested in informative articles about doll history and costumes, interviews with doll artists and collectors, and how-to articles." Estab. 1978. Circ. 54,000. Pays pre-publication. Byline given. Buys first or one-time rights. Submit seasonal/holiday material 6 months in advance. Accepts previously published submissions. Reports in 2 months on queries; 4 months on mss. Sample copy for $2.95. Writer's guidelines for SASE.
Nonfiction: How-to, interview/profile. Buys 100 mss/year. Send complete ms. Pays $50.
Photos: Send photos with submission. Captions and identification of subjects required. Buys one-time or all rights.
Tips: "Choose a specific manufacturer and talk about his dolls or a specific doll—modern or antique—and explore its history and styles made."

DOLLS, The Collector's Magazine, Collector Communications Corp., 170 Fifth Ave., New York NY 10010-5911. (212)989-8700. Fax: (212)645-8976. Managing Editor: Marilyn A. Roberts. 75% freelance written. Works with a small number of new/unpublished writers each year. Magazine published 10 times/year covering doll collecting "for collectors of antique, contemporary manufacturer and artist dolls. We publish well-researched, professionally written articles illustrated with photographs of high quality, color or b&w." Estab. 1982. Circ. 120,000. Publishes ms an average of 9 months after acceptance. Byline given. "Almost all first manuscripts are on speculation. We rarely kill assigned stories, but kill fee would be about 33% of article fee." Buys first North American serial or second serial rights if piece has appeared in a non-competing publication. Submit seasonal/holiday material 6 months in advance. Accepts previously published material. Send typed ms with rights for sale noted and information about when and where the article previously appeared. For reprints pays 50% of the amount paid for an original article. Reports in 2 months. Sample copy for $2. Writer's guidelines for #10 SASE.
Nonfiction: Book excerpts; historical (with collecting angle); interview/profile (on doll artists); new product (just photos and captions; "we do not pay for these, but regard them as publicity"); technical (doll restoration advice by experts only); travel (museums and collections around the world). "No sentimental, uninformed 'my doll collection' or trade magazine-type stories on shops, etc. Our readers are knowledgeable collectors." Query with clips. Length: 500-2,500 words. Pays $100-350. Sometimes pays expenses of writers on assignment.
Photos: Send photos with accompanying query or ms. Reviews 4×5 transparencies; 4×5 or 8×10 b&w prints and 35mm slides. "We do not buy photographs submitted without manuscripts unless we have assigned them; we pay for the manuscript/photos package in one fee." Captions required. Buys one-time rights.

Columns/Departments: Doll Views—a miscellany of news and views of the doll world includes reports on upcoming or recently held events. "*Not* the place for new dolls, auction prices or dates; we have regular contributors or staff assigned to those columns." Query with clips if available or send complete ms. Length: 200-500 words. Pays $25-75. Doll Views items are given an endsig.

Fillers: "We don't use fillers but would consider them if we got something good. Hints on restoring, for example, or a nice illustration." Length: 500 words maximum. Pays $25-75.

Tips: "We need experts in the field who are also good writers. Freelancers who are not experts should know their particular story thoroughly and do background research to get the facts correct. Well-written queries from writers outside the NYC area are especially welcomed. Non-experts should stay away from technical or specific subjects (restoration, price trends). Editors want to know they are getting something from a writer they cannot get from anyone else. Good writing should be a given, a starting point. After that, it's what you know. We accept only written queries, no phone calls."

EARLY AMERICAN LIFE, Cowles Magazines, Inc., P.O. Box 8200, Harrisburg PA 17105-8200. Fax: (717)657-9552. Editor: Mimi Handler. 20% freelance written. Bimonthly magazine for "people who are interested in capturing the warmth and beauty of the 1600 to 1840 period and using it in their homes and lives today. They are interested in arts, crafts, travel, restoration and collecting." Estab. 1970. Circ. 150,000. Buys first North American serial rights. Buys 40 mss/year. **Pays on acceptance.** Publishes ms an average of 1 year after acceptance. Accepts previously published articles. Send typed ms with rights for sale noted and information about when and where the article previously appeared. Reports in 3 months. Sample copy and writer's guidelines for 9×12 SAE with 4 first-class stamps. Query or submit complete ms with SASE.

- The editor of this publication is looking for more on architecture, gardens and antiques and less on historic travel sites.

Nonfiction: "Social history (the story of the people, not epic heroes and battles), travel to historic sites, country inns, antiques and reproductions, refinishing and restoration, architecture and decorating. We try to entertain as we inform. While we're always on the lookout for good pieces on any of our subjects, the 'travel to historic sites' theme is most frequently submitted. Would like to see more on how real people did something great to their homes." Buys 40 mss/year. Query or submit complete ms. Length: 750-3,000 words. Pays $100-600. Pays expenses of writers on assignment.

Photos: Pays $10 for 5×7 (and up) b&w photos used with mss, minimum of $25 for color. Prefers $2\frac{1}{4} \times 2\frac{1}{4}$ and up, but can work from 35mm.

Tips: "Our readers are eager for ideas on how to bring early America into their lives. Conceive a new approach to satisfy their related interests in arts, crafts, travel to historic sites, and especially in houses decorated in the early American style. Write to entertain and inform at the same time, and be prepared to help us with illustrations, or sources for them."

ELECTRONICS NOW, Gernsback Publications, Inc., 500 B Bi-County Blvd., Farmingdale NY 11735. (516)293-3000. Editor: Brian C. Fenton. 75% freelance written. Monthly magazine on electronics technology and electronics construction. Estab. 1929. Circ. 175,000. **Pays on acceptance.** Publishes ms an average of 6 months after acceptance. Byline given. Buys all rights. Submit seasonal/holiday material 5-6 months in advance. Query for electronic submissions. Reports in 2 months on queries; 4 months on mss. Free sample copy and writer's guidelines.

Nonfiction: How-to (electronic project construction), humor (cartoons), new product. Buys 150-200 mss/year. Send complete ms. Length: 1,000-10,000 words. Pays $200-800 for assigned articles; $100-800 for unsolicited articles.

Photos: Send photos with submission. Offers no additional payment for photos accepted with ms. Captions, model releases and identification of subjects required. Buys all rights.

FIBERARTS, The Magazine of Textiles, Altamont Press, 50 College St., Asheville NC 28801. (704)253-0467. Fax: (704)253-7952. Editor: Ann Batchelder. 100% freelance written. Eager to work with new writers. Magazine published 5 times/year covering textiles as art and craft (weaving, quilting, surface design, stitchery, knitting, fashion, crochet, etc.) for textile artists, craftspeople, hobbyists, teachers, museum and gallery staffs, collectors and enthusiasts. Estab. 1975. Circ. 23,000. Pays 60 days after publication. Publishes ms an average of 4 months after acceptance. Byline given. Buys first rights. Editorial guidelines and style sheet available. Sample copy for $4.50 and 10×12 SAE with 2 first-class stamps. Writer's guidelines for #10 SAE with 2 first-class stamps.

Nonfiction: Historical, artist interview/profile, opinion, photo feature, technical, education, trends, exhibition reviews, textile news. Query. "Please be very specific about your proposal. Also an important consideration in accepting an article is the kind of photos—35mm slides and/or b&w glossies—that you can provide as illustration. We like to see photos in advance." Length: 250-2,000 words. Pays $60-350, depending on article. Rarely pays the expenses of writers on assignment or for photos.

Tips: "Our writers are very familiar with the textile field, and this is what we look for in a new writer. Familiarity with textile techniques, history or events determines clarity of an article more than a particular style of writing. The writer should also be familiar with *Fiberarts*, the magazine."

FINE WOODWORKING, The Taunton Press, P.O. Box 5506, Newtown CT 06470-5506. (203)426-8171. Fax: (203)426-3434. Editor: Scott Gibson. Bimonthly magazine on woodworking in the small shop. "All writers are also skilled woodworkers. It's more important that a contributor be a woodworker than a writer. Our editors (also woodworkers) will fix the words." Estab. 1975. Circ. 292,000. Pays on publication. Byline given. Kill fee varies; "editorial discretion." Buys first rights and rights to republish in anthologies and use in promo pieces. Submit seasonal/holiday material 6 months in advance. Accepts simultaneous submissions. Query for electronic submissions. Reports in 2 months. Sample copy for $5.50 and 10 first-class stamps. Free writer's guidelines.

Nonfiction: How-to (woodworking). Buys 120 mss/year. "No specs—our editors would rather see more than less." Pays $150/magazine page. Sometimes pays expenses of writers on assignment.

Photos: Send photos with submission. Reviews contact sheets, negatives, transparencies and prints. Captions, model releases and identification of subjects required. Buys one-time rights.

Columns/Departments: Notes & Comment (topics of interest to woodworkers); Question & Answer (woodworking Q & A); Follow-Up (information on past articles/readers' comments); Methods of Work (shop tips); Tool Forum (short reviews of new tools). Buys 400 items/year. Length varies. Pays $10-150/published page.

Tips: "Send for authors guidelines and follow them. Stories about woodworking reported by non-woodworkers *not* used. Our magazine is essentially reader-written by woodworkers."

FINESCALE MODELER, Kalmbach Publishing Co., 21027 Crossroads Circle, P.O. Box 1612, Waukesha WI 53187. (414)796-8776. Fax: (414)796-1383. Editor: Bob Hayden. 80% freelance written. Eager to work with new/unpublished writers. Magazine published 9 times/year "devoted to how-to-do-it modeling information for scale model builders who build non-operating aircraft, tanks, boats, automobiles, figures, dioramas, and science fiction and fantasy models." Circ. 85,000. **Pays on acceptance.** Publishes ms an average of 14 months after acceptance. Byline given. Buys all rights. Reports in 6 weeks on queries; 3 months on mss. Sample copy for 9×12 SAE with 3 first-class stamps. Free writer's guidelines.

Nonfiction: How-to (build scale models); technical (research information for building models). Query or send complete ms. Length: 750-3,000 words. Pays $40/published page minimum.

● This magazine is especially looking for how-to articles for car modelers.

Photos: Send photos with ms. Pays $7.50 minimum for transparencies and $5 minimum for 5×7 b&w prints. Captions and identification of subjects required. Buys one-time rights.

Columns/Departments: *FSM* Showcase (photos plus description of model); *FSM* Tips and Techniques (model building hints and tips). Buys 25-50 Tips and Techniques/year. Query or send complete ms. Length: 100-1,000 words. Pays $10-20.

Tips: "A freelancer can best break in first through hints and tips, then through feature articles. Most people who write for *FSM* are modelers first, writers second. This is a specialty magazine for a special, quite expert audience. Essentially, 99% of our writers will come from that audience."

GEM SHOW NEWS, Shows of Integrity, 19 River St., Cooperstown KY 13326. (607)547-2604. Publisher: Edward J. Tripp. Editor: Judi Tripp. Managing Editor: Stacy Hobbs. 50% freelance written. Annual newspaper on precious stones, mineral collecting and jewelry. "Slant should be gem/collectible investments including gold, gold coins, silver, silver jewelry and original silver designs." Estab. 1979. Circ. 30,000. **Pays on acceptance.** Publishes ms an average of 2 months after acceptance. Byline given. Publication not copyrighted. Buys first rights and makes work-for-hire assignments. Submit seasonal/holiday material 4 months in advance. Accepts simultaneous and previously published submissions. Send typed ms with rights for sale noted. For reprints, pays 50% of the amount paid for an original article. Reports in 4 months. Sample copy for 9×12 SAE with 5 first-class stamps. Writer's guidelines for #10 SASE.

Nonfiction: How-to (gem collecting; gem cutting/collecting), humor, interview/profile, new product, personal experience, photo feature, technical, travel. Buys 30 mss/year. Send complete ms; include word count for faster payment. Length: 1,000-3,000 words. Pays $50-150.

Photos: Send photos with submission. Reviews prints (3×5). Offers $5-10/photo. Captions, model releases and identification of subjects required. Buys one-time rights.

Fillers: Anecdotes, facts, gags to be illustrated by cartoonist, newsbreaks, short humor. Buys 30 mss/year. Length: 500 words maximum. Pays $10-25.

Tips: "Attend gem and jewelry shows to see the interest in this field. The gem and mineral collecting field is the second most popular hobby (second only to coin and stamp collecting) in the US. All areas are open, including current fads and trends such as articles on the current quartz crystals and crystal healing craze and related subjects. Since this is an annual issue publication (December/January), please submit articles in September or October only."

GOLD AND TREASURE HUNTER, 27 Davis Rd., P.O. Box 47, Happy Camp CA 96039-0047. (916)493-2062. Fax: (916)493-2095. Editor: Dave McCracken. Managing Editor: Janice Trombetta. Bimonthly magazine on small-scale gold mining and treasure hunting. "We want interesting fact and fiction stories and articles about small-scale mining, treasure hunting, camping and the great outdoors." Estab. 1987. Circ. 50,000. Pays on publication. Buys all rights. Submit seasonal/holiday material 4 months in advance. Accepts previously published articles. Send tearsheet, photocopy of article or typed ms with rights for sale noted and information about when and where the article previously appeared. For reprints, pays 50% of the amount paid for an original article. Query for electronic submissions. Reports in 1 month. Sample copy for 9×12 SAE with 5 first-class stamps. Writer's guidelines free.

Nonfiction: How-to, humor, inspirational, interview/profile, new product, personal experience, photo feature, travel. "No promotional articles concerning industry products." Buys 125 mss/year. Send complete ms. Length: 1,500-2,000 words. Pays 3¢/word.

Photos: Send photos with submission. Reviews any size transparencies and prints. Pays $10-50/photo. Captions are required. Buys all rights.

Fiction: Adventure, experimental, historical, horror, humorous, mystery, suspense, western—all related to gold mining/treasure hunting.

Tips: "Our general readership is comprised mostly of individuals who are actively involved in gold mining and treasure hunting, or people who are interested in reading about others who are active and successful in the field. True stories of actual discoveries, along with good color photos—particularly of gold—are preferred. Also, valuable how-to information on new and workable field techniques, preferably accompanied by supporting illustrations and/or photos."

‡**HANDWOVEN**, Interweave Press, 201 E. Fourth St., Loveland CO 80537. (303)669-7672. Fax: (303)667-8317. Editor: Jean Scorgie. 75% freelance written. Bimonthly magazine (except July) covering handweaving, spinning and dyeing. Audience includes "practicing textile craftsmen. Article should show considerable depth of knowledge of subject, although tone should be informal and accessible." Estab. 1975. Circ. 35,000. Pays on publication. Publishes ms an average of 10 months after acceptance. Byline given. Pays 50% kill fee. Buys first North American serial rights. Sample copy for $4.50. Writer's guidelines for #10 SASE.

Nonfiction: Historical and how-to (on weaving and other craft techniques; specific items with instructions); and technical (on handweaving, spinning and dyeing technology). "All articles must contain a high level of in-depth information. Our readers are very knowledgeable about these subjects." Query. Length: 500-2,000 words. Pays $35-200.

Photos: Send photos. Identification of subjects required.

Tips: "We prefer work written by writers with an in-depth knowledge of weaving. We're particularly interested in articles about new weaving and spinning techniques as well as applying these techniques to finished products."

HOME MECHANIX, 2 Park Ave., New York NY 10016. (212)779-5000. Fax: (212)725-3281. Editor: Michael Chotiner. Contact: Natalie Posner. 50% freelance written. Prefers to work with published/established writers. "If it's good, and it fits the type of material we're currently publishing, we're interested, whether writer is new or experienced." Magazine published 10 times/year for the active home and car owner. "Articles emphasize an active, home-oriented lifestyle. Includes information useful for maintenance, repair and renovation to the home and family car. Information on how to buy, how to select products useful to homeowners/car owners. Emphasis in home-oriented articles is on good design, inventive solutions to styling and space problems, useful home-workshop projects." Estab. 1928. Circ. 1 million. **Pays on acceptance.** Publishes ms an average of 6 months after acceptance. Byline given. Buys first North American serial rights. Reports in 3 months. Query.

Nonfiction: Feature articles relating to homeowner/car owner, 1,500-2,500 words. "This may include personal home-renovation projects, professional advice on interior design, reports on different or unusual construction methods, energy-related subjects, outdoor/backyard projects, etc. No high-tech subjects such as aerospace, electronics, photography or military hardware. Most of our automotive features are written by experts in the field, but fillers, tips, how-to repair, or modification articles on the family car are welcome. Articles on construction, tool use, refinishing techniques, etc., are also sought. Pays $300 minimum for features; fees based on number of printed pages, photos accompanying mss., etc." Pays expenses of writers on assignment.

Photos: Photos should accompany mss. Pays $600 and up for transparencies for cover. Inside color: $300/1 page, $500/2, $700/3, etc. Captions and model releases required.

Tips: "The most frequent mistake made by writers in completing an article assignment for *Home Mechanix* is not taking the time to understand its editorial focus and special needs."

THE HOME SHOP MACHINIST, 2779 Aero Park Dr., P.O. Box 1810, Traverse City MI 49685. (616)946-3712. Fax: (616)946-3289. Editor: Joe D. Rice. 95% freelance written. Bimonthly magazine covering machining and metalworking for the hobbyist. Circ. 29,400. Pays on publication. Publishes ms an average of 18 months after acceptance. Byline given. Buys first North American serial rights only. Accepts simultaneous submissions. Reports in 2 months. Free sample copy and writer's guidelines for 9×12 SASE.

Nonfiction: How-to (projects designed to upgrade present shop equipment or hobby model projects that require machining), technical (should pertain to metalworking, machining, drafting, layout, welding or foundry work for the hobbyist). No fiction. Buys 50 mss/year. Query or send complete ms. Length: open—"whatever it takes to do a thorough job." Pays $40/published page, plus $9/published photo.

Photos: Send photos with ms. Pays $9-40 for 5×7 b&w prints; $70/page for camera-ready art; $40 for b&w cover photo. Captions and identification of subjects required.

Columns/Departments: Book Reviews; New Product Reviews; Micro-Machining; Foundry. "Writer should become familiar with our magazine before submitting. Query first." Buys 25-30 mss/year. Length: 600-1,500 words. Pays $40-70/page.

Fillers: Machining tips/shortcuts. No news clippings. Buys 12-15/year. Length: 100-300 words. Pays $30-48.

Tips: "The writer should be experienced in the area of metalworking and machining; should be extremely thorough in explanations of methods, processes—always with an eye to safety; and should provide good quality b&w photos and/or clear drawings to aid in description. Visuals are of increasing importance to our readers. Carefully planned photos, drawings and charts will carry a submission to our magazine much farther along the path to publication."

KITPLANES, For designers, builders and pilots of experimental aircraft, Fancy Publications, P.O. Box 6050, Mission Viejo CA 92690. (714)855-8822. Fax: (714)855-3045. Editor: Dave Martin. Managing Editor: Keith Beveridge. 70% freelance written. Eager to work with new/unpublished writers. Monthly magazine covering self-construction of private aircraft for pilots and builders. Estab. 1972. Circ. 85,000. Pays on publication. Publishes ms an average of 3 months after acceptance. Byline given. Offers negotiable kill fee. Buys first North American serial rights. Submit seasonal/holiday material 6 months in advance. Query for electronic submissions. Reports in 2 weeks on queries; 6 weeks on mss. Sample copy for $3. Free writer's guidelines.

Nonfiction: How-to, interview/profile, new product, personal experience, photo feature, technical, general interest. "We are looking for articles on specific construction techniques, the use of tools, both hand and power, in aircraft building, the relative merits of various materials, conversions of engines from automobiles for aviation use, installation of instruments and electronics." No general-interest aviation articles, or "My First Solo" type of articles. Buys 80 mss/year. Query. Length: 500-5,000 words. Pays $100-400, including story photos.

Photos: State availability of or send photos with query or ms. Pays $250 for cover photos. Captions and identification of subjects required. Buys one-time rights.

Tips: "*Kitplanes* contains very specific information—a writer must be extremely knowledgeable in the field. Major features are entrusted only to known writers. I cannot emphasize enough that articles must be directed at the individual aircraft builder. We need more 'how-to' photo features in all areas of homebuilt aircraft."

THE LEATHER CRAFTERS & SADDLERS JOURNAL, 331 Annette Court, Rhinelander WI 54501-2902. (715)362-5393. Fax: (715)362-5391. Editor: William R. Reis. Managing Editor: Dorothea Reis. 100% freelance written. Bimonthly craft magazine. "Aid to craftsmen using leather as the base medium. All age groups and skill levels from beginners to master carvers and artisans." Estab. 1990. Circ. 6,000. Pays on publication. Publishes ms an average of 2 months after acceptance. Byline given. "All assigned articles subject to review for acceptance by editor." Buys first North American serial and second serial (reprint) rights. Submit seasonal/holiday material 6 months in advance. Accepts simultaneous and previously published submissions. Send tearsheet or photocopy of article. Pays 50% of original article fee. Reports in 1 month. Sample copy for $5. Writer's guidelines for #10 SASE.

Nonfiction: How-to (crafts and arts and any other projects using leather). "I want only articles that include hands-on, step-by-step, how-to information." Buys 75 mss/year. Send complete ms. Length: 500-2,500 words. Pays $20-200 for assigned articles; $20-150 for unsolicited articles. Send good contrast color print photos and full size patterns and/or full-size photo-carve patterns with submission. Lack of these reduces payment amount. Captions required.

Columns/Departments: Beginners, Intermediate, Artists, Western Design, Saddlemakers, International Design and Letters (the open exchange of information between all peoples). Length: 500-2,500 on all. Buys 75 mss/year. Send complete ms. Pays 5¢/word.

Fillers: Anecdotes, facts, gags illustrated by cartoonist, newsbreaks. Length: 25-200 words. Pays $3-10.

Tips: "We want to work with people who understand and know leathercraft and are interested in passing on their knowledge to others. We would prefer to interview people who have achieved a high level in leathercraft skill."

LINN'S STAMP NEWS, Amos Press, 911 Vandemark Rd., P.O. Box 29, Sidney OH 45365. (513)498-0801. Fax: (513)498-0814. Editor: Michael Laurence. Managing Editor: Elaine Boughner. 50% freelance written. Weekly tabloid on the stamp collecting hobby. "All articles must be about philatelic collectibles." Estab. 1928. Circ. 70,000. Pays on publication. Publishes ms an average of 1 month after acceptance. Byline given. Buys first North American serial rights. Submit seasonal/holiday material 2 months in advance. Reports in 2 weeks on mss. Free sample copy. Writer's guidelines for #10 SAE with 2 first-class stamps.

Nonfiction: General interest, historical/nostalgic, how-to, interview/profile, technical. "No articles merely giving information on background of stamp subject. Must have philatelic information included." Buys 300 mss/year. Send complete ms. Length: 500 words maximum. Pays $10-50. Rarely pays expenses of writers on assignment.

Photos: Send photos with submission. Prefers glossy b&w prints. Offers no additional payment for photos accepted with ms. Captions required. Buys all rights.

LIVE STEAM, Live Steam, Inc., 2779 Aero Park Dr., Box 629, Traverse City MI 49685. (616)946-3712. Fax: (616)946-3289. Editor: Joe D. Rice. 90% freelance written. Eager to work with new/unpublished writers. Bimonthly magazine covering steam-powered models and full-size engines (i.e., locomotives, traction, cars, boats, stationary, etc.) "Our readers are hobbyists, many of whom are building their engines from scratch. We are interested in anything that has to do with the world of live steam-powered machinery." Circ. 12,800. Pays on publication. Publishes ms an average of 18 months after acceptance. Byline given. Buys first North American serial rights only. Reports in 3 weeks. Free sample copy and writer's guidelines.
Nonfiction: Historical/nostalgic, how-to (build projects powered by steam), new product, personal experience, photo feature, technical (must be within the context of steam-powered machinery or on machining techniques). No fiction. Buys 50 mss/year. Query or send complete ms. Length: 500-3,000 words. Pays $30-500/published page. Sometimes pays the expenses of writers on assignment.
Photos: Send photos with ms. Pays $50/page of finished art. Pays $8 for 5×7 b&w prints; $40 for color cover. Captions and identification of subjects required.
Columns/Departments: Steam traction engines, steamboats, stationary steam, steam autos. Buys 6-8 mss/year. Query. Length: 1,000-3,000 words. Pays $20-50.
Tips: "At least half of all our material is from the freelancer. Requesting a sample copy and author's guide will be a good place to start. The writer must be well-versed in the nature of live steam equipment and the hobby of scale modeling such equipment. Technical and historical accuracy is an absolute must. Often, good articles are weakened or spoiled by mediocre to poor quality photos. Freelancers must learn to take a *good* photograph."

LOST TREASURE, INC., P.O. Box 1589, Grove OK 74344. Fax: (918)786-2192. Managing Editor: Grace Michael. 75% freelance written. Monthly, bimonthly and annual magazines covering lost treasure. Estab. 1966. Circ. 55,000. Buys all rights. Byline given. Buys 225 mss/year. Queries welcome. Length: 1,200-1,500 words. Pays on publication (4¢/word). No simultaneous submissions. Reports in 2 months. Queries welcome. Writers guidelines for #10 SASE. Sample copies (all 3 magazines) and guidelines for 10×13 SAE with $1.47 postage.
  • This editor needs more stories since the bimonthly magazine (*Treasure Facts*) has gone monthly.
Nonfiction: 1) *Lost Treasure*, a monthly publication, is composed of lost treasure stories, legends, folklore, and how-to articles. 2) *Treasure Facts*, a monthly publication, consists of how-to information for treasure hunters, treasure hunting club news, who's who in treasure hunting, tips, etc. 3) *Treasure Cache*, an annual publication, contains stories about documented treasure caches with a sidebar from the author telling the reader how-to search for the cache highlighted in the story.
Photos: Black and white or color prints with mss help sell your story. Pays $5/published photo. Cover photos pay $100/published photo; must be 35mm color slides, vertical. Captions required.
Tips: "We are only interested in treasures that can be found with metal detectors. Queries welcome but not required. If you write about famous treasures and lost mines, be sure we haven't used your selected topic recently and story must have a new slant or new information. Source documentation required. How-To's should cover some aspect of treasure hunting and how-to steps should be clearly defined. If you have a *Treasure Cache* story we will, if necessary, help the author with the sidebar telling how to search for the cache in the story."

MINIATURE QUILTS, Chitra Publications, 2 Public Ave., Montrose PA 18801. (717)278-1984. Fax: (717)278-2223. Contact: Editorial Team. 40% freelance written. Bimonthly magazine on miniature quilts. "We seek articles of an instructional nature (all techniques), profiles of talented quiltmakers and informational articles on all aspects of miniature quilts. Miniature is defined as quilts made up of blocks smaller than five inches." Estab. 1990. Circ. 50,000. Pays on publication. Publishes ms an average of 6 months after acceptance. Byline given. Buys second serial (reprint) rights. Submit seasonal/holiday material 6-8 months in advance. Query for electronic submissions. Reports in 2 months on queries and mss. Writer's guidelines for SASE.
  • This magazine was previously published quarterly; it is now published bimonthly.
Photos: Send photos with submission. Reviews 35mm slides and larger transparencies. Offers $20/photo. Captions, model releases and identification of subjects required. Buys all rights, unless rented from a museum.
Tips: "Publication hinges on good photo quality. Query with ideas; send samples of prior work."

MODEL RAILROADER, P.O. Box 1612, Waukesha WI 53187. Editor: Andy Sperandeo. Monthly for hobbyists interested in scale model railroading. Buys exclusive rights. "Study publication before submitting material." Reports on submissions within 1 month.
Nonfiction: Wants construction articles on specific model railroad projects (structures, cars, locomotives, scenery, benchwork, etc.). Also photo stories showing model railroads. Query. First-hand knowledge of subject almost always necessary for acceptable slant. Pays base rate of $90/page.

Photos: Buys photos with detailed descriptive captions only. Pays $10 and up, depending on size and use. Pays double b&w rate for color; full color cover earns $200.

MONITORING TIMES, Grove Enterprises Inc., P.O. Box 98, Brasstown NC 28902-0098. (704)837-9200. Fax: (704)837-2216. Managing Editor: Rachel Baughn. Publisher: Robert Grove. 20% freelance written. Monthly magazine for radio hobbyists. Estab. 1982. Circ. 35,000. Pays 30-60 days before date of publication. Publishes ms an average of 4 months after acceptance. Byline given. Buys first North American serial rights and limited reprint rights. Submit seasonal/holiday material 4 months in advance. Accepts previously published submissions. Send photocopy of article and information about when and where the article previously appeared. For reprints, pays 25% of amount paid for an original article. Reports in 1 month. Sample copy and writer's guidelines for 9×12 SAE and 9 first-class stamps.
Nonfiction: General interest, how-to, humor, interview/profile, personal experience, photo feature, technical. Buys 72 mss/year. Query. Length: 1,000-2,500 words. Pays $150-200.
Photos: Send photos with submission. Captions required. Buys one-time rights.
Columns/Departments: "Query managing editor."

NUTSHELL NEWS, For creators and collectors of scale miniatures, Kalmbach Publishing Co., 21027 Crossroads Circle, Waukesha WI 53187-9951. (414)796-8776. Fax: (414)796-1383. Editor: Sybil Harp. 50% freelance written. Monthly magazine covering dollhouse scale miniatures. "*Nutshell News* is aimed at serious, adult hobbyists. Our readers take their miniatures seriously and do not regard them as toys. We avoid 'cutesiness' and treat our subject as a serious art form and/or an engaging leisure interest." Estab. 1971. Circ. 40,000. Pays advance fee on acceptance and balance on publication. Byline given. Offers $25 kill fee. Buys all rights but will revert rights by agreement. Submit seasonal/holiday material 1 year in advance. Reports in 3 weeks on queries; 2 months on mss. Sample copy for $3.50. Writer's guidelines for #10 SASE.
Nonfiction: How-to miniature projects in 1", ½", ¼" scales, interview/profile (artisans or collectors), photo feature (dollhouses, collections, museums). Special issues: smaller scales annual—½", ¼" or smaller scales (May); kitcrafting—customizing kits or commercial miniatures, a how-to issue (August). No articles on miniature shops or essays. Buys 120 mss/year. Query. Length: 1,000-1,500 words for features, how-to's may be longer. "Payment varies, but averages $150 for features, more for long how-to's." Sometimes pays expenses of writers on assignment.
Photos: Send photos with submission. Requires 35mm slides and larger, 3×5 prints. "Photos are paid for with manuscript. Seldom buy individual photos." Captions preferred; identification of subjects required. Buys all rights.
Tips: "It is essential that writers for *Nutshell News* be active miniaturists, or at least very knowledgeable about the hobby. Our readership is intensely interested in miniatures and will discern lack of knowledge or enthusiasm on the part of an author. A writer can best break in to *Nutshell News* by convincing me that he/she knows and is interested in miniatures, and by sending photos and/or clippings to substantiate that. Photographs are extremely important. They must be sharp and properly exposed to reveal details. For articles about subjects in the Chicago/Milwaukee area, we can usually send our staff photographer."

POPULAR ELECTRONICS, Gernsback Publications, Inc., 500B Bi-County Blvd., Farmingdale NY 11735-3918. (516)293-3000. Fax: (516)293-3115. Editor: Carl Laron. 80% freelance written. Monthly magazine covering hobby electronics—"features, projects, ideas related to audio, radio, experimenting, test equipment, computers, antique radio, communications, consumer electronics, state-of-the-art, etc." Circ. 81,000. **Pays on acceptance.** Byline given. Buys all rights. Submit seasonal/holiday material 6 months in advance. Query for electronic submissions. Reports in 1 month. Free sample copy, "include mailing label." Writer's guidelines for #10 SASE.
Nonfiction: General interest, how-to, photo feature, technical. Buys 200 mss/year. Query or send complete ms. Length: 1,000-3,500 words. Pays $100-500.
Photos: Send photos with submission. "Wants b&w glossy photos." Offers no additional payment for photos accepted with ms. Captions required. Buys all rights.
Tips: "All areas are open to freelancers. Project-type articles and other 'how-to' articles have best success."

POPULAR ELECTRONICS HOBBYISTS HANDBOOK, Gernsback Publications, Inc., 500 B Bi-County Blvd., Farmingdale NY 11735-3918. (516)293-3000. Fax: (516)293-3115. Editor: Julian S. Martin. 95% freelance written. Semiannual magazine on hobby electronics. Estab. 1989. Circ. 125,000. **Pays on acceptance.** Byline given. Buys all rights. Submit seasonal/holiday material 6 months in advance. Query for electronic submissions. Reports in 2 weeks.
Nonfiction: General interest, historical/nostalgic, how-to (build projects, fix consumer products, etc., all of which must be electronics oriented), photo feature, technical. "No product reviews!" Buys 20-30 mss/year. Send complete ms. Length: 1,000-5,000 words. Pays $100-500 for assigned articles; $100-500 for unsolicited articles.
Photos: Send photos with submission. "We want b&w glossy photos." Reviews 5×7 or 8×10 b&w prints. Offers no additional payment for photos accepted with ms. Captions and model releases are required. Buys all rights.

Tips: "Read the magazine. Know and understand the subject matter. Write it. Submit it."

POPULAR MECHANICS, Hearst Corp., 3rd Floor, 224 W. 57th St., New York NY 10019. (212)649-2000. Editor: Joe Oldham. Managing Editor: Deborah Frank. 50% freelance written. Monthly magazine on automotive, home improvement, science, boating, outdoors, electronics. "We are a men's service magazine that tries to address the diverse interests of today's male, providing him with information to improve the way he lives. We cover stories from do-it-yourself projects to technological advances in aerospace, military, automotive and so on." Estab. 1902. Circ. 1.6 million. **Pays on acceptance**. Publishes ms an average of 6 months after acceptance. Byline given. Offers 25% kill fee. Buys all rights. Submit seasonal/holiday material 6 months in advance. Query. Reports in 2 weeks on queries; 1 month on mss. Sample copy and writer's guidelines for 9 × 12 SASE.
Nonfiction: General interest, how-to (shop projects, car fix-its), new product, technical. Special issues: Design and Engineering Awards (January); Boating Guide (February); Home Improvement Guide (April); Car Care Guide (May); Automotive Parts & Accessories Guide (October); Woodworking Guide (November). No historical, editorial or critique pieces. Buys 24 mss/year. Query with or without published clips or send complete ms. Length: 500-3,000 words. Pays $500-1,500 for assigned articles; $150-1,000 for unsolicited articles. Sometimes pays expenses of writers on assignment.
Photos: Send photos with submission. Reviews 5 × 7 transparencies and prints. Offers no additional payment for photos accepted with ms. Captions, model releases and identification of subjects required. Buys first and exclusive publication rights in the US during on-sale period of issue in which photos appear plus 90 days after.
Columns/Departments: New Cars (latest and hottest cars out of Detroit and Europe), Car Care (Maintenance basics, How It Works, Fix-Its and New products: send to Don Chaikin. Electronics, Audio, Home Video, Computers, Photography: send to Frank Vizard. Boating (new equipment, how-tos, fishing tips), Outdoors (gear, vehicles, outdoor adventures): send to Joe Skorupa. Home & Shop Journal: send to Steve Willson. Science (latest developments), Tech Update (breakthroughs) and Aviation (sport aviation, homebuilt aircraft, new commercial aircraft, civil aeronautics): send to Greg Pope. All columns are about 1,000 words.

POPULAR WOODWORKING, F&W Publications, 1507 Dana Ave., Cincinnati OH 45207. (513)531-2690, ext. 238. Fax: (513)531-2902. E-mail: wudworker@aol.com. Editor: Steve Shanesy. 60% freelance written. Eager to work with new/unpublished writers. Bimonthly magazine covering woodworking. "Our readers are the woodworking hobbyist and small woodshop owner. Writers should have a knowledge of woodworking, or be able to communicate information gained from woodworkers." Estab. 1981. Circ. 284,000. **Pays on acceptance**. Publishes ms an average of 10 months after acceptance. Byline given. Buys first North American serial rights. Submit seasonal/holiday material 6 months in advance. Reports in 2 months. Accepts previously published submissions. Send photocopy of article or typed ms with rights for sale noted and information about when and where the article previously appeared. For reprints, pays 100% of amount paid for an original article. Sample copy and writer's guidelines for $4.50 and 9 × 12 SAE with 6 first-class stamps.
Nonfiction: How-to (on woodworking projects, with plans); humor (woodworking anecdotes); technical (woodworking techniques). Buys 75 mss/year. Query with or without published clips or send complete ms. Pays up to $125/published page. "The project must be well-designed, well constructed, well built and well finished. Technique pieces must have practical application."
Photos: Send photos with submission. Reviews color only, slides and transparencies, 3 × 5 glossies acceptable. Offers no additional payment for photos accepted with ms. Photographic quality may affect acceptance. Need sharp close-up color photos of step-by-step construction process. Captions and identification of subjects required.
Columns/Departments: Tricks of the Trade (helpful techniques), Out of the Woodwook (thoughts on woodworking as a profession or hobby, can be humorous or serious), 500-1,500 words. Buys 6 mss/year. Query.
Fillers: Anecdotes, facts, short humor, shop tips. Buys 15/year. Length: 50-500 words.
Tips: "Submissions should include materials list, complete diagrams (blue prints not necessary), and discussion of the step-by-step process."

QST, American Radio Relay League, Inc., 225 Main St., Newington CT 06111-1494. (203)666-1541. Fax: (203)665-7531. Editor: Mark Wilson. Managing Editor: Albert Brogdon. 60% freelance written. Monthly magazine covering amateur radio interests and technology. "Ours are topics of interest to radio amateurs and persons in the electronics and communications fields." Estab. 1914. Circ. 175,000. Pays on publication. Publishes ms an average of 4 months after acceptance. Byline given. Usually buys all rights. Submit seasonal/holiday material 5 months in advance. Query for electronic submissions. Reports in 3 weeks on queries. Free sample copy and writer's guidelines for 10 × 13 SAE with 5 first-class stamps.
Nonfiction: General interest, how-to, humor, new products, personal experience, photo feature, technical (anything to do with amateur radio). Buys 50 mss/year. Query with or without published clips, or send complete ms. Length: no minimum or maximum. Pays $65/published page. Sometimes pays expenses of writers on assignment.

Photos: Send photos with submission. Sometimes offers additional payment for photos accepted with ms or for cover. Captions, model releases and identification of subjects required. Usually buys all rights.

Columns/Departments: Hints and Kinks (hints/time saving procedures/circuits/associated with amateur radio), 50-200 words. Buys 100 mss/year. Send complete ms. Pays $20.

Tips: "Write with an idea, ask for sample copy and writer's guide. Technical and general interest to amateur operators, communications and electronics are most open."

QUILTER'S NEWSLETTER MAGAZINE, P.O. Box 394, Wheatridge CO 80034-0394. Fax: (303)420-7358. Editor: Bonnie Leman. Senior Features Editor: Marie Shirer. Magazine published 10 times/year. Estab. 1969. Circ. 200,000. Buys first North American serial rights or second rights. Buys about 15 mss/year. Pays on publication, sometimes on acceptance. Accepts previously published submissions. Send tearsheet of article or typed ms with rights for sale noted and information about when and where the article previously appeared. Reports in 2 months. Free sample copy.

Nonfiction: "We are interested in articles on the subject of quilts and quiltmakers *only*. We are not interested in anything relating to 'Grandma's Scrap Quilts' but could use fresh material." Submit complete ms. Pays 10¢/word minimum, usually more.

Photos: Additional payment for photos depends on quality.

Fillers: Related to quilts and quiltmakers only.

Tips: "Be specific, brief, and professional in tone. Study our magazine to learn the kind of thing we like. Send us material which fits into our format but which is different enough to be interesting. Realize that we think we're the best quilt magazine on the market and that we're aspiring to be even better, then send us the cream off the top of your quilt material."

QUILTING TODAY MAGAZINE, Chitra Publications, 2 Public Ave., Montrose PA 18801. (717)278-1984. Fax: (717)278-2223. Contact: Editorial Team. 80% freelance written. Bimonthly magazine on quilting, traditional and contemporary. "We seek articles that will cover one or two full pages (800 words each); informative to the general quilting public, present new ideas, interviews, instructional, etc." Estab. 1986. Circ. 90,000. Pays on publication. Publishes ms an average of 6 months after acceptance. Byline given. Buys second serial (reprint) rights. Submit seasonal/holiday material 6-8 months in advance. Occasionally accepts previously published submissions. Send photocopy of article or typed ms with rights for sale noted and information about when and where the article previously appeared. For reprints, pays $75/published page. Query for electronic submissions. Reports in 1 month on queries; 2 months on mss. Writer's guidelines for SASE.

• *Quilting Today Magazine* has a new department appearing occasionally—"History Lessons," featuring a particular historical style or period in quiltmaking history.

Nonfiction: Book excerpts, essays, how-to (for various quilting techniques), humor, interview/profile, new product, opinion, personal experience, photo feature. "No articles about family history related to a quilt or quilts unless the quilt is a masterpiece of color and design, impeccable workmanship." Buys 20-30 mss/year. Query with or without published clips or send complete mss. Length: 800-1,600 words. Pays $50-75/page.

Photos: Send photos with submission. Reviews 35mm slides and larger transparencies. Offers $20/photo. Captions, identification of subjects required. Buys all rights unless rented from a museum.

Columns/Departments: Quilters Lesson Book (instructional), 800-1,600 words. Buys 10-12 ms/year. Send complete ms. Pays up to $75/column.

Tips: "Query with ideas; send samples of prior work so that we can assess and suggest assignment. Our publications appeal to traditional quilters (generally middle-aged) who use the patterns in each issue. Must have excellent photos."

RAILROAD MODEL CRAFTSMAN, Box 700, Newton NJ 07860. (201)383-3355. Fax: (201)383-4064. Editor: William C. Schaumburg. 75% freelance written. Works with a small number of new/unpublished writers each year. Monthly magazine for model railroad hobbyists, in all scales and gauges. Circ. 87,000. Buys all rights. Buys 50-100 mss/year. Pays on publication. Publishes ms an average of 9 months after acceptance. Submit seasonal material 6 months in advance. Sample copy for $2. Writer's and photographer's guidelines for SASE.

Nonfiction: "How-to and descriptive model railroad features written by persons who did the work are preferred. Almost all our features and articles are written by active model railroaders. It is difficult for non-modelers to know how to approach writing for this field." Pays minimum of $1.75/column inch of copy ($50/page).

Photos: Purchased with mss. Buys sharp 8×10 glossy prints and 35mm or larger transparencies. Pays minimum $5/diagonal inch. $200 for covers, which must tie in with article in that issue. Caption information required.

Tips: "We would like to emphasize modeling based on actual prototypes of equipment and industries as well as a model railroad design and operation."

SEW NEWS, The Fashion Magazine for People Who Sew, PJS Publications, Inc., News Plaza, P.O. Box 1790, Peoria IL 61656. (309)682-6626. Fax: (309)682-7394. Editor: Linda Turner Griepentrog. 90%

freelance written. Works with a small number of new/unpublished writers each year. Monthly magazine covering fashion-sewing. "Our magazine is for the beginning home sewer to the professional dressmaker. It expresses the fun, creativity and excitement of sewing." Estab. 1980. Circ. 261,000. **Pays on acceptance.** Publishes ms an average of 6 months after acceptance. Byline given. Buys all rights. Submit seasonal/holiday material 6 months in advance. Reports in 2 months. Sample copy for $3.95. Writer's guidelines for #10 SAE with 2 first-class stamps.

• All stories submitted to *Sew News Magazine* must be on disk.

Nonfiction: How-to (sewing techniques), interview/profile (interesting personalities in home-sewing field). Buys 200-240 ms/year. Query with published clips if available. Length: 500-2,000 words. Pays $25-500. Rarely pays expenses of writers on assignment.

Photos: Send photos. Prefers b&w, color photographs or slides. Payment included in ms price. Identification of subjects required. Buys all rights.

Tips: "Query first with writing sample and outline of proposed story. Areas most open to freelancers are how-to and sewing techniques; give explicit, step-by-step instructions plus rough art."

‡THE SEWING ROOM, LynnCarthy Industries, Inc., P.O. Box 2780, Boise ID 83701. (203)383-0300. Editor: Mia Crosthwaite. Contact: Andrea Simmonsen, assistant editor. 90% freelance written. Magazine published 10 times/year covering home sewing. "*The Sewing Room* is a hobby magazine for home sewers that focuses on all aspects of garment construction. To a lesser degree, it covers sewing crafts and quilting." Estab. 1994. Circ. 100,000. **Pays on acceptance.** Publishes ms an average of 4 months after acceptance. Byline given. Buys first North American serial rights and one-time rights. Editorial lead time 4 months. Submit seasonal material 4-6 months in advance. Accepts simultaneous submissions. Query for electronic submissions. Reports in 3 weeks on queries; 2 months on mss. Sample copy for $3.95 and 9 × 10 SAE with 4 first-class stamps. Writer's guidelines for #10 SASE.

Nonfiction: General interest, how-to, humor, inspirational, interview/profile, new product, opinion, personal experience, photo freature, technical. Buys 100 mss/year. Query. Length: 500-3,000 words. Pays $100-700.

Photos: Send photos with submission. Reviews contact sheets, negatives or prints. Offers no additional payment for photos accepted with ms. Captions and identification of subjects required. Buys one-time rights.

Columns/Departments: Small Stitches (projects for children), 500-2,000 words; Fabric (educational), 250-2,000 words; Wardrobe Makeover (reconstruction and/or embellishment), 500-2,000 words. Buys 100 mss/year. Query. Pays $100-600.

Fiction: Humorous. Buys 10 mss/year. Query. Length: 500-2,000. Pays $100-600.

Poetry: Avant-garde, free verse, haiku, light verse, traditional. Buys 10 poems/year. Submit maximum 2 poems. Length: 30 lines. Pays $50-200.

Fillers: Anecdotes, facts, gags to be illustrated by cartoonist, newsbreaks, short humor. Buys 30/year. Length: 50-300 words. Pays $50-250.

Tips: "Submit how-to articles with good supporting photos that have love-of-sewing attitude. No 1950s attitudes or 'sewing because I have to.' "

SHUTTLE SPINDLE & DYEPOT, Handweavers Guild of America, 2402 University Ave., Suite 702, St. Paul MN 55114. (612)646-0802. Fax: (612)646-0806. E-mail: 73744.202 CompuServe.com. Editor: Sandra Bowles. 60% freelance written. Quarterly magazine covering handweaving, spinning and dyeing and related fiber art. "We take the practical and aesthetic approach to handweaving, handspinning, and related textile arts." Estab. 1969. Pays on publication. Publishes ms 15 months after acceptance. Byline given. Buys first North American serial rights. Submit seasonal material 1 year in advance. Rarely accepts previously published submissions. Send photocopy of article on computer disk with rights for sale noted. Reports in 2 months. Sample copy for $6.50. Free writer's guidelines.

• This publication accepts/considers only those manuscripts sent on a computer disk.

Nonfiction: How-to, interview/profile, personal experience, photo feature, technical. "We want interesting, practical, technical information in our field." Buys 30 mss/year. Query with or without published clips, or send complete ms. Length: 500-1,200 words. Pays $25-125.

Photos: State availability of slides or transparencies or b&w photos with submission. Reviews contact sheets and transparencies.

SPORTS COLLECTORS DIGEST, Krause Publications, 700 E. State St., Iola WI 54990. (715)445-2214. Fax: (715)445-4087. Editor: Tom Mortenson. Estab. 1952. 50% freelance written. Works with a small number of new/unpublished writers each year. Weekly sports memorabilia magazine. "We serve collectors of sports memorabilia—baseball cards, yearbooks, programs, autographs, jerseys, bats, balls, books, magazines, ticket stubs, etc." Circ. 52,000. Pays after publication. Publishes ms an average of 3 months after acceptance. Byline given. Buys first North American serial rights only. Submit seasonal/holiday material 3 months in advance. Accepts previously published submissions. Send tearsheet of article. For reprints, pays 100% of amount paid for an original article. Reports in 5 weeks on queries; 2 months on mss. Free sample copy. Writer's guidelines for #10 SASE.

Nonfiction: General interest (new card issues, research on older sets); historical/nostalgic (old stadiums, old collectibles, etc.); how-to (buy cards, sell cards and other collectibles, display collectibles, ways to get autographs, jerseys and other memorabilia); interview/profile (well-known collectors, ball players—but must focus on collectibles); new product (new card sets); personal experience ("what I collect and why"-type stories). No sports stories. "We are not competing with *The Sporting News*, *Sports Illustrated* or your daily paper. Sports collectibles only." Buys 100-200 mss/year. Query. Length: 300-3,000 words; prefers 1,000 words. Pays $50-125.

Photos: Unusual collectibles. Send photos. Pays $5-15 for b&w prints. Identification of subjects required. Buys all rights.

Columns/Departments: "We have all the columnists we need but welcome ideas for new columns." Buys 100-150 mss/year. Query. Length: 600-3,000 words. Pays $70-90.

Tips: "If you are a collector, you know what collectors are interested in. Write about it. No shallow, puff pieces; our readers are too smart for that. Only well-researched articles about sports memorabilia and collecting. Some sports nostalgia pieces are OK. Write only about the areas you know about."

STAMP COLLECTOR, For People Who Love Philately, Division of Van Dahl Publications, Capital Cities/ABC, Inc., P.O. Box 10, Albany OR 97321-0006. (503)928-3569. Fax: (503)967-7262. Editor: Ken Palke. 55% freelance written. Weekly tabloid covering philately. "Stamp Collector is dedicated to promoting the growth and enjoyment of philately through the exchange of information and ideas. All shades of opinion are published to provide the widest possible view of the hobby." Estab. 1931. Circ. 18,500. Pays on publication. Byline given. Buys all rights. Submit seasonal/holiday material 1½ months in advance. Query for electronic submissions. Call for details. Reports in 2 months. Sample copy and writer's guidelines upon request for 9×12 SAE with 4 first-class stamps.

Nonfiction: "No general articles on world history, world geography, lengthy articles about one particular stamp, puzzles, games, quizzes, etc." Buys 500 mss/year. Query. Pays $25-50. Sometimes pays the expenses of writers on assignment. Send photos, stamps or clear photocopies with submission. Buys all rights. Send SASE with unsolicited mss.

Columns/Departments: Guest Editorials, 1,000 words. Buys 15 mss/year. Send complete ms. Pays $30.

Tips: "Be a stamp collector or stamp dealer with some specific area of interest and/or expertise. Find a subject (stamps of a particular country, time period, designer, subject matter portrayed, printing method, etc.) that you are interested in and knowledgeable about, and in which our average reader would be interested. Our average reader is well-educated, intelligent, professional with diverse interests in postal services, printing methods, politics, geography, history, anthropology, economics, arts, etc."

SUNSHINE ARTIST, America's Premier Show & Festival Publication, Palm House Publishing Inc., 422 W. Fairbanks Ave., #300, Winter Park FL 32789. (407)539-3939. Fax: (407)539-0533. Publisher: David F. Cook. Editor: Kristine Petterson. Monthly magazine covering art shows in the United States. "We are the premier marketing/reference magazine for artists and crafts professionals who earn their living through art shows nationwide. We list more than 4,000 shows annually, critique many of them and publish articles on marketing, selling and other issues of concern to professional show circuit artists." Estab. 1972. Circ. 12,000. Pays on publication. Publishes ms an average of 3 months after acceptance. Byline given. Buys first North American serial rights. Reports within 2 months. Sample copy for $5.

Nonfiction: "We publish articles of interest to artists and crafts professionals who travel the art show circuit. Current topics include marketing, computers and RV living." No how-to. Buys 5-10 freelance mss/year. Query or ms. Length: 1,000-2,000 words. Pays $50-150 for accepted articles.

Photos: Send photos with submission. Offers no additional payment for photos accepted with ms. Captions, model releases and identification of subjects required.

TEDDY BEAR REVIEW, Collector Communications Corp., 170 Fifth Ave., New York NY 10010. (212)989-8700. Editor: Stephen L. Cronk. 75% freelance written. Works with a small number of new/unpublished writers each year. Bimonthly magazine on teddy bears. Estab. 1985. Pays 30 days after acceptance. Byline given. Buys first North American serial rights. Submit seasonal/holiday material 6 months in advance. Sample copy and writer's guidelines for $2 and 9×12 SAE.

Nonfiction: Book excerpts, historical, how-to, interview/profile. No nostalgia on childhood teddy bears. Buys 30-40 mss/year. Query with published clips. Length: 500-1,500 words. Pays $75-200. Sometimes pays the expenses of writers on assignment "if approved ahead of time."

Photos: Send photos with submission. Reviews transparencies and b&w prints. Offers no additional payment for photos accepted with ms. Captions required. Buys one-time rights.

Tips: "We are interested in good, professional writers around the country with a strong knowledge of teddy bears. Historical profile of bear companies, profiles of contemporary artists and knowledgeable reports on museum collections are of interest."

TRADITIONAL QUILTWORKS, The Pattern Magazine for Creative Quilters, Chitra Publications, 2 Public Ave., Montrose PA 18801. (717)278-1984. Fax: (717)278-2223. Contact: Editorial Team. 50% freelance written. Bimonthly magazine on quilting. "We seek articles of an instructional nature, profiles of talented teachers, articles on the history of specific areas of quiltmaking (patterns, fiber, regional, etc.)." Estab. 1988. Circ. 90,000. Pays on publication. Publishes ms an average of 6 months after acceptance.

Byline given. Buys second serial (reprint) rights. Submit seasonal/holiday material 6-8 months in advance. Occasionally buys previously published submissions. Send photocopy of article or typed ms with rights for sale noted and information about when and where the article previously appeared. For reprints, pays $75/ published page. Query for electronic submissions. Reports in 2 months. Writer's guidelines for SASE.

Nonfiction: Historical, instructional, quilting education. "No light-hearted entertainment." Buys 12-18 mss/ year. Query with or without published clips, or send complete ms. Length: 1,600 words maximum. Pays $75/page.

Photos: Send photos with submission. Reviews 35mm slides and larger transparencies (color). Offers $20 per photo. Captions, model releases and identification of subjects required. Buys all rights.

Tips: "Query with ideas; send samples of prior work so that we can assess and suggest assignment. Our publications appeal to traditional quilters, generally middle-aged and mostly who use the patterns in the magazine. Publication hinges on good photo quality."

TREASURE CHEST, The Information Source & Marketplace for Collectors and Dealers of Antiques and Collectibles, Venture Publishing Co., 2112 Broadway, Suite 414, New York NY 10023. (212)496-2234. Editor: Howard E. Fischer. 100% freelance written. Monthly newspaper on antiques and collectibles. Estab. 1988. Circ. 50,000. Pays on publication. Publishes ms an average of 3 months after acceptance. Byline given. Buys first rights and second serial (reprint) rights. Accepts previously published submissions. Send tearsheet or photocopy of article and information about when and where the article previously appeared. For reprints, pays 60% of the amount paid for original article. Reports in 2 months on mss. Sample copy for 9×12 SAE with $2. Writer's guidelines for #10 SASE.

Nonfiction: How-to (detect reproductions, find new sources of items, etc.), humor, personal experience, photo feature. Primarily interested in feature articles on a specific field of antiques or collectibles which includes a general overview of that field. Buys 35 mss/year. Send complete ms. Length: 1,000 words. Pays $30 with photo. Payment in contributor copies or other premiums negotiable.

Fillers: Anecdotes, facts, gags to be illustrated by cartoonist, short humor. Buys 12/year. Length: 100-350 words. Pays $10.

Tips: "Learn about your subject by interviewing experts—appraisers, curators, dealers."

VIDEOMAKER, Camcorders, Editing, Desktop Video, Audio and Video Production, Videomaker Inc., P.O. Box 4591, Chico CA 95927. (916)891-8410. Fax: (916)891-8443. E-mail: videoma340@aol.com. Editor: Stephen Muratore. Managing Editor: Loren Alldrin. 75% freelance written. Monthly magazine on video production. "Our audience encompasses video camera users ranging from broadcast and cable TV producers to special-event videographers to video hobbyists . . . labeled professional, industrial, 'prosumer' and consumer. Editorial emphasis is on video*making* (production and exposure), *not* reviews of commercial videos. Personal video phenomenon is a young 'movement'; readership is encouraged to participate—get in on the act, join the fun." Estab. 1986. Circ. 90,000. Pays on publication. Publishes ms an average of 4-6 months after acceptance. Byline given. Buys all rights. Submit seasonal/holiday material 6 months in advance. Accepts simultaneous and previously published submissions. Send information about when and where the article previously appeared. For reprints, payment is negotiable. Query for electronic submissions. Reports in 3 months. Sample copy for 9×12 SAE with 9 first-class stamps. Free writer's guidelines.

Nonfiction: How-to (tools, tips, techniques for better videomaking); interview/profile (notable videomakers); product probe (review of latest and greatest or innovative); personal experience (lessons to benefit other videomakers); technical (state-of-the-art audio/video). Articles with comprehensive coverage of product line or aspect of videomaking preferred. Buys 70 mss/year. Query with or without published clips, or send complete ms. Length: open. Pays 10¢/word.

Photos: Send photos and/or other artwork with submissions. Reviews contact sheets, transparencies and prints. Captions required. Payment for photos accepted with ms included as package compensation. Buys one-time rights.

Columns/Departments: Desktop Video (state-of-the-art products, applications, potentials for computer-video interface); Profile (highlights videomakers using medium in unique/worthwhile ways); Quick Focus (brief reviews of current works pertaining to video production); Camera Work (tools and tips for beginning videomakers); Video Entrepeneur (money-making opportunities); Edit Points (tools and techniques for successful video editions). Buys 40 mss/year. Pays 10¢/word.

Tips: "Comprehensiveness a must. Article on shooting tips covers *all* angles. Buyer's guide to special-effect generators cites *all* models available. Magazine strives for an 'all-or-none' approach. Most topics covered once (twice tops) per year, so we must be thorough. Manuscript/photo package submissions helpful. *Videomaker* wants videomaking to be fulfilling and fun."

VOGUE KNITTING, Butterick Company, 161 Sixth Ave., New York NY 10013-1205. Fax: (212)620-2731. Editors: Carla Scott, Margery Winter. Associate Managing Editor: Ruth Tobacco. 100% freelance written. Quarterly magazine that covers knitting. "High fashion magazine with projects for knitters of all levels. In-depth features on techniques, knitting around the world, interviews, bios and other articles of interest to well-informed readers." Estab. 1982. Circ. 200,000. **Pays on acceptance**. Publishes ms an average of 4 months after acceptance. Buys all rights. Editorial lead time 6 months. Submit seasonal material 6 months in advance.

Accepts simultaneous submissions. Query for electronic submissions; prefers IBM WordPerfect or Microsoft Word. Requires hard copy with electronic submission. Writer's guidelines free on request.

Nonfiction: Essays, general interest, historical/nostalgic, how-to, interview/profile, personal experience, photo feature, technical, travel. Buys 25 mss/year. Query. Length: 600-1,200 words. Pays $250 minimum.

Photos: Send photos with submission. Reviews 3×5 transparencies. Negotiates payment individually. Captions, model releases and identification of subjects required. Buys all rights.

WOMEN'S HOUSEHOLD CROCHET, House of White Birches, Inc., 306 E. Parr Rd., Berne IN 46711-0776. Editor: Susan Hankins. 99% freelance written. Quarterly magazine for "crochet lovers—young and old, city and country, thread and yarn lovers alike. Our readers crochet for necessity as well as pleasure. Articles are 99% pattern-oriented. We need patterns for all expertise levels—beginner to expert. No knit patterns please." Estab. 1962. Circ. 25,000. Pays on publication. Publishes ms an average of 3-12 months after acceptance. Byline given. Buys all rights. Submit seasonal/holiday material 6 months in advance. Reports in 1 month on queries; 6 weeks on mss. Sample copy for $2 with 9×12 SAE and 3 first-class stamps. Free writer's guidelines.

Photos: Buys no photos. Must send crocheted item for staff photography.

Columns/Departments: Editor's Choice Contest (1st prize chosen each issue for crochet design). Buys 8 mss/year. Send complete ms. Length: 500-2,000 words. Pays competitive designer rates.

Poetry: Light verse, traditional (all related to crochet!). "No long poems over 20 lines. Nothing of a sexual nature." Buys 6 poems/year. Submit maximum 2 poems. Length: 5-20 lines. Pays $5-20.

Fillers: Anecdotes, crochet cartoons, facts, short humor. Buys 4-6/year. Length: 35-70 words. Pays $5-20.

Tips: "We only buy crochet patterns. No longer interested in non-pattern mss."

WOODSHOP NEWS, Soundings Publications Inc., 35 Pratt St., Essex CT 06426-1185. (203)767-8227. Fax: (203)767-1048. Editor: Ian C. Bowen. Senior Editor: Thomas Clark. 20% freelance written. Monthly tabloid "covering woodworking for professionals and hobbyists. Solid business news and features about woodworking companies. Feature stories about interesting amateur woodworkers. Some how-to articles." Estab. 1986. Circ. 100,000. Pays on publication. Publishes ms an average of 2-3 months after acceptance. Byline given. Offers 25% kill fee. Buys first North American serial rights. Submit seasonal/holiday material 4 months in advance. Accepts simultaneous submissions. Query for electronic submissions. Reports in 3 weeks on queries; 1 month on mss. Free sample copy and writer's guidelines.

• *Woodshop News* needs writers in major cities in all regions except the Northeast. Also looking for more editorial opinion pieces.

Nonfiction: How-to (query first), interview/profile, new product, opinion, personal experience, photo feature. No general interest profiles of "folksy" woodworkers. Buys 50-75 mss/year. Query with published clips. Length: 100-1,800 words. Pays $30-400 for assigned articles; $30-250 for unsolicited articles. Pays expenses of writers on assignment.

Photos: Send photos with submission. Reviews contact sheets and prints. Offers $20-35/photo. Captions and identification of subjects required. Buys one-time rights.

Columns/Departments: Pro Shop (business advice, marketing, employee relations, taxes etc. for the professional written by an established professional in the field). Length: 1,200-1,500 words. Buys 12 mss/year. Query. Pays $200-350.

Tips: "The best way to start is a profile of a business or hobbyist woodworker in your area. Find a unique angle about the person or business and stress this as the theme of your article. Avoid a broad, general-interest theme that would be more appropriate to a daily newspaper. Our readers are woodworkers who want more depth and more specifics than would a general readership. If you are profiling a business, we need standard business information such as gross annual earnings/sales, customer base, product line and prices, marketing strategy, etc. Black and white 35 mm photos are a must. We need more freelance writers from the Mid-Atlantic, Midwest and West Coast."

WOODWORK, A magazine for all woodworkers, Ross Periodicals, P.O. Box 1529, Ross CA 94957-1529. (415)382-0580. Fax: (415)382-0587. Editor: John McDonald. Publisher: Tom Toldrian. 90% freelance written. Bimonthly magazine covering woodworking. "We are aiming at a broad audience of woodworkers, from the home enthusiast/hobbyist to more advanced." Estab. 1986. Circ. 100,000. Pays on publication. Byline given. Buys first North American serial and second serial (reprint) rights. Accepts previously published material. Send tearsheet or photocopy of article or typed ms with rights for sale noted and information about when and where the article previously appeared. Pays 25% of amount paid for an original article. Reports in 2 months. Sample copy for $3 and 9×12 SAE with 6 first-class stamps. Writer's guidelines for #10 SASE.

Nonfiction: How-to (simple or complex, making attractive furniture), interview/profile (of established woodworkers that make attractive furniture), photo feature (of interest to woodworkers), technical (tools, techniques). "Do not send a how-to unless you are a woodworker." Buys 40 mss/year. Query first. Length: 1,500-3,000 words. Pays $150/published page.

Photos: Send photos with submission. Reviews 35mm slides. Offers no additional payment for photos accepted with ms. Captions and identification of subjects required. Buys one-time rights.

Columns/Departments: Feature articles 1,500-3,000 words. From non-woodworking freelancers, we use interview/profiles of established woodworkers. Bring out woodworker's philosophy about the craft, opinions about what is happening currently. Good photos of attractive furniture a must. Section on how-to desirable. Query with published clips. Pays $600-1,500 at $150/published page.

Tips: "If you are not a woodworker, the interview/profile is your best, really only chance. Good writing is essential as are good photos. The interview must be entertaining, but informative and pertinent to woodworkers' interests."

‡**WOODWORKER**, F&W Publications, 1507 Dana Ave., Cincinnati, OH 45207. (513)531-2222. Editor: Jim Ryder. Managing Editor: Christine Antolik. 70% freelance written. Bimonthly magazine covering woodworking. "*Woodworker* provides the developing woodworker with rewarding, quick-completion projects and clear technique instruction, employing easy-to-follow color photos and illustrations, all aimed at helping the reader master the efficient use of time, tools and materials." Estab. 1961. Circ. 107,171. Pays on publication. Publishes ms an average of 4 months after acceptance. Byline given. Offers 25% kill fee. Buys first rights and second serial (reprint) rights. Editorial lead time 6 months. Submit seasonal material 7 months in advance. Accepts simultaneous submissions. Query for electronic submissions. Reports in 1 month on queries; 2 months on mss. Sample copy and writer's guidelines for #10 SASE.

Nonfiction: How-to (projects, techniques), humor, inspirational, new product, personal experience, photo feature. "We only want to see unique and enterprising projects built for beginning to intermediate level woodworkers." Buys 30 mss/year. Query with picture of finished project. Length: 1,500-3,000 words. Pays $125/published page. Sometimes pays expenses of writers on assignment.

Photos: Send photos with submission. Reviews transparencies. Captions, model releases, identification of subjects required. Buys one-time rights.

Columns/Departments: Christine Antolik. Second Measure (humorous anecdotes on woodworking), 800 words; The Idea File (quick project ideas), 75 words with diagrams and photo; Shop Tips (helpful hints to improve skills), 100 words. Buys 35 mss/year. Query. Pays $25-250.

Tips: "The more original the project is, the better chance of it being published. We're looking for new ideas, with good project designs, complemented by step-by-step, clear illustrations and interesting, helpful text."

WORKBASKET, The World's Largest Needlework and Crafts Magazine, KC Publishing, 700 W. 47th St., Suite 310, Kansas City MO 64112. (816)531-5730. Executive Editor: Kay M. Olson. Editor: Sarah Johnson. 75% freelance written. Bimonthly magazine covering needlework and crafts. "A variety of needlework patterns and craft projects for all levels, beginners to experienced." Estab. 1935. Circ. 750,000. **Pays on acceptance.** Byline given. Buys first rights. Editorial lead time 6-12 months. Submit seasonal material 18-24 months in advance. Accepts previously published submissions occasionally. Reports in 4 months. Sample copy for $2.95. Writer's guidelines free on request.

• *Workbasket* has carefully themed issues and wants projects to have a fit with those themes.

Nonfiction: How-to. Buys 50 mss/year. Query. Payment varies depending on complexity of the project.

Tips: "Bazaar-type items are accepted for $25 payment of project idea."

WORKBENCH, 700 W. 47th St., Suite 310, Kansas City MO 64112. (816)531-5730. Fax: (816)531-3873. Executive Editor: A. Robert Gould. 75% freelance written. Prefers to work with published/established writers; but works with a small number of new/unpublished writers each year. For woodworkers and home improvement do-it-yourselfers. Estab. 1957. Circ. 750,000. **Pays on acceptance.** Publishes ms an average of 1 year after acceptance. Byline given. Buys all rights. Reports in 3 months. Sample copy for 9×12 SAE with 6 first-class stamps. Free writer's guidelines.

Nonfiction: "We have continued emphasis on do-it-yourself woodworking, home improvement and home maintenance projects. We provide in-progress photos, technical drawings and how-to text for all projects. We are very strong in woodworking, cabinetmaking and classic furniture construction. Projects range from simple toys to reproductions of furniture now in museums. We would like to receive woodworking projects that can be duplicated by both beginning do-it-yourselfers and advanced woodworkers." Query. Pays $175/published page or more depending on quality of submission. Additional payment for good color photos. "If you can consistently provide good material, including photos, your rates will go up and you will get assignments."

Columns/Departments: Shop Tips bring $25 with a line drawing and/or b&w photo.

Tips: "Our magazine focuses on woodworking, covering all levels of ability, and home improvement projects from the do-it-yourselfer's viewpoint, emphasizing the most up-to-date materials and procedures. We would like to receive articles on home improvements and remodeling, and/or simple contemporary furniture. We place a heavy emphasis on projects that are both functional and classic in design. We can photograph projects worthy for publication, so feel free to send snapshots."

Home and Garden

Some magazines here concentrate on gardens; others on the how-to of interior design.

Still others focus on homes and gardens in specific regions of the country. Be sure to read the publication to determine its focus before submitting a manuscript or query.

‡**THE ALMANAC FOR FARMERS & CITY FOLK**, Greentree Publishing, Inc., 850 S. Rancho, #2319, Las Vegas NV 89106. (702)387-6777. Editor: Lucas McFadden. Managing Editor: Thomas Alexander. 40% freelance written. Annual almanac of farm, garden, animal, anecdotes, etc. "Down-home, folksy material pertaining to farming, gardening, animals, etc." Estab. 1983. Circ. 1 million. Pays on publication. Publishes ms 6 months after acceptance. Byline given. Buys first North American serial rights. Deadline: January 31. Reports in 2 weeks on queries; 1 month on mss. Sample copy for $2.95.
Nonfiction: Essays, general interest, how-to, humor. No fiction or controversial topics. Buys 30 mss/year. Send complete ms. Length: 350-1,400 words. Pays $45/page.
Poetry: Buys 1 poem/year. Pays $45.
Fillers: Anecdotes, facts, short humor. Buys 60/year. Length 125 words maximum. Pays $10-45.
Tips: "Typed submissions essential as we scan in manuscript before editing. Short, succinct material is preferred. Material should appeal to a wide range of people and should be on the 'folksy' side, preferably with a thread of humor woven in."

AMERICAN HORTICULTURIST, Publication of the American Horticultural Society, 7931 E. Blvd. Dr., Alexandria VA 22308-1300. (703)768-5700. Fax: (703)765-6032. Editor: Kathleen Fisher. 90% freelance written. Bimonthly magazine covering gardening. Estab. 1922. Circ. 25,000. Pays on publication. Publishes ms an average of 6 months after acceptance. Byline given. Buys first North American serial rights. Submit seasonal/holiday material 6 months in advance. Reports in 3 months on queries, if SASE included. Sample copy for $3. Free writer's guidelines.
• *American Horticulturist* is putting greater stress on environmentally-responsible gardening. They are using fewer photos, trying to do more writing inhouse.
Nonfiction: Book excerpts, historical, children and nature, plants and health, city gardening, humor, interview/profile, personal experience, technical (explain science of horticulture to lay audience). Buys 30-40 mss/year. Query with published clips. Length: 1,000-2,500 words. Pays $100-400. Pays with contributor copies or other premiums when other horticultural organizations contribute articles.
Photos: Send photos with query. Pays $50-75/photo. Captions required. Buys one-time rights.
Tips: "We are read by sophisticated gardeners, but also want to interest beginning gardeners. Subjects should be unusual plants, recent breakthroughs in breeding, experts in the field, translated for lay readers."

‡**ARCHITECTURAL DIGEST**, Knapp Communications, 6300 Wilshire Blvd., Suite 1100, Los Angeles CA 90048. Executive Editor: Michael Wollager. Query with ideas and published clips.

ATLANTA HOMES AND LIFESTYLES, 5775-B Glenridge Dr., Suite 580, Atlanta GA 30328. (404)252-6670. Fax: (404)252-6673. Editor: Barbara S. Tapp. 65% freelance written. Bimonthly magazine on shelter design, lifestyle in the home. "*Atlanta Homes and Lifestyles* is designed for the action-oriented, well-educated reader who enjoys his/her shelter, its design and construction, its environment, and living and entertaining in it." Estab. 1983. Pays on publication. Byline given. Publishes ms an average of 6 months after acceptance. Pays 25% kill fee. Buys all rights. Accepts previously published material. Send tearsheet or photocopy of article and information about where and when it previously appeared. For reprints, pays 50% of amount paid for original article. Reports in 3 months. Sample copy for $2.95.
Nonfiction: Historical, interview/profile, new products, well-designed homes, antiques (then and now), photo features, gardens, local art, remodeling, food, preservation, entertaining. "We do not want articles outside respective market area, not written for magazine format, or that are excessively controversial, investigative or that cannot be appropriately illustrated with attractive photography." Buys 35 mss/year. Query with published clips. Length: 500-750 words. Pays $350 for features. Sometimes pays expenses of writers on assignment "if agreed upon in advance of assignment."
Photos: Send photos with submission; most photography is assigned. Reviews transparencies. Offers $40-50/photo. Captions, model releases, and identification of subjects required. Buys one-time rights.
Columns/Departments: Antiques, Quick Fix (simple remodeling ideas), Cheap Chic (stylish decorating that is easy on the wallet), Digging In (outdoor solutions from Atlanta's gardeners), Big Fix (more extensive remodeling projects), Short Takes (news and finds about the people and products in home-related businesses in and around Atlanta), Home Eco, Home Tech, Real Estate News, Interior Elements (hot new furnishings on the market), Weekender (long or short weekend getaway subjects). Query with published clips. Buys 25-30 mss/year. Length: 350-500 words. Pays $50-200.

BACKHOME: Hands On & Down to Earth, Wordsworth Communications, Inc., P.O. Box 70, Hendersonville NC 28792. (704)696-3838. Editor: Lorna K. Loveless. 80% freelance written. Quarterly magazine covering self-sufficiency in home, garden, shop and community. "*BackHome* encourages readers to take more control over their lives by doing more for themselves: productive organic gardening; building and repairing their homes; utilizing alternative energy systems; raising crops and livestock; building furniture;

toys and games and other projects; creative cooking. *BackHome* promotes respect for family activities, community programs and the environment." Estab. 1990. Circ. 19,000. Pays on publication. Publishes ms 3-12 months after acceptance. Byline given. Offers $25 kill fee at publisher's discretion. Buys first North American serial rights. Editorial lead time 3 months. Submit seasonal material 3-6 months in advance. Accepts previously published submissions. Send tearsheet or photocopy of article or typed ms with rights for sale noted and information about when and where the article previously appeared. For reprints, pays 100% of the amount paid for an original article. Query for electronic submissions. Prefers ASCII WordPerfect, Wordstar, MS Word, MacWrite. Reports in 6 weeks on queries; 2 months on mss. Sample copy for $4.50. Writer's guidelines with SASE.

• *The Millennium Whole Earth Catalog*, 1995, stated that *BackHome* contains "the most effective, practical, and appropriate tools and ideas for thinking and acting independently for the 21st century."

Nonfiction: How-to (gardening, construction, energy, home business), interview/profile, personal experience, technical, self-sufficiency. Buys 80 mss/year. Query. Length: 350-5,000 words. Pays $25 (approximately) for printed page.

Photos: Send photos with submission. Reviews 5×7 prints. Offers additional payment for photos published. Identification of subjects required. Buys one-time rights.

Columns/Departments: FeedBack (new products; book, tape and video reviews), 250 words. Buys 4 mss/year. Query. Pays $25-50.

Tips: "Very specific in relating personal experiences in the areas of gardening, energy, and homebuilding how-to. Third-person approaches to others' experiences are also acceptable but somewhat less desireable. Clear b&w or color photo prints help immensely when deciding upon what is accepted, especially those in which people are prominent."

BACKWOODS HOME MAGAZINE, INC., 1257 Siskiyou Blvd., #213, Ashland OR 97520. Editor: Dave Duffy. Senior Editor: John Silveira. 80% freelance written. Bimonthly magazine covering house building, alternate energy, gardening, health and self-sufficiency. "We write for the person who values independence above all else. Our readers want to build their own homes, generate their own electricity, grow their own food and in general stand on their own two feet." Estab. 1989. Circ. 85,000. **Pays on acceptance.** Publishes ms an average of 2 months after acceptance. Byline given. Offers 15% kill fee. Buys first rights and second serial (reprint) rights or makes work-for-hire assignments. Submit seasonal/holiday material 6 months in advance. Accepts previously published submissions. Send typed ms with rights for sale noted and information about when and where the article previously appeared. For reprints, pays 50% of the amount paid for an original article. Query for electronic submissions. Reports in 2 weeks. Sample copy for $2 and 9×12 SAE with 6 first-class stamps. Writer's guidelines for #10 SASE.

Nonfiction: Historical/nostalgic, how-to (about country things, alternate energy), humor, interview/profile (of independent people), new product (alternate energy), personal experience, photo feature (about country things), technical (about alternate energy production, building a house). "No opinion, exposé or religious articles." Buys 50 mss/year. Query with or without published clips or send complete ms. Length: 300-3,000 words. Pays $15-300.

Photos: Send photos with submission. Reviews 3×5 or larger prints. Identification of subjects required. Buys one-time rights.

Columns/Departments: Book Review (alternate energy/house building/gardening), 300-400 words; Recipes (country cooking), 150 words; Alternate Energy (solar cells, hydro, generator), 600-3,000 words; Gardening (organic), 600-1,800 words; Home Building (do-it-yourself), 600-2,800 words. Buys 30-40 mss/year. Send complete ms. Pays up to $300.

Poetry: Free verse, haiku, light verse, traditional. Buys 15 poems/year. Length: 3-25 lines. Pays $5.

Tips: "We insist on accuracy in nonfiction articles. Writers must know the subject. We are basically a country magazine that tries to show people how to do things that make country life more pleasant."

BETTER HOMES AND GARDENS, 1716 Locust St., Des Moines IA 50309-3023. (515)284-3000. Editor-in-Chief: Jean Lemmon. Editor (Building): Joan McCloskey. Editor (Foods): Nancy Byal. Editor (Garden/Outdoor Living): Mark Kane. Editor (Health & Education): Martha Miller. Editor (Money Management, Automotive, Features, Regional Travel): Margaret Daly. 10-15% freelance written. **Pays on acceptance.** Buys all rights. "We read all freelance articles, but much prefer to see a letter of query rather than a finished manuscript."

Nonfiction: Travel, education, health, cars, money management, home entertainment. "We do not deal with political subjects or with areas not connected with the home, community, and family." Pays rates "based on estimate of length, quality and importance." No poetry.

• Most stories published by this magazine go through a lengthy process of development involving both editor and writer. Some editors will consider *only* query letters, not unsolicited manuscripts.

Tips: Direct queries to the department that best suits your story line.

‡**CANADIAN GARDENING**, Camar Communications, 130 Spy Court, Markham, Ontario L3R 5H6 Canada. (905)475-8440. Editor: Liz Primeau. Contact: Rebecca Fox, managing editor. 99% freelance written. Magazine published 7 times/year covering home gardening. "We cover garden design, growing, projects for the

garden, products, regional information (pests, growing, etc.) for the Canadian gardener. Fundamental plants are the focus, but each issue contains at least one vegetable piece, usually with recipes." Estab. 1990. Circ. 130,000. **Pays on acceptance.** Publishes ms 3-18 months after acceptance. Byline given. Offers 25-50% kill fee. Buys first North American serial rights. Editorial lead time 3 months. Submit seasonal material 5 months in advance. Query for electronic submissions. Reports in 2 months. Sample copy and writer's guidelines free.

Nonfiction: Book excerpts, how-to (gardening, garden projects, pruning, pest control, etc.), personal experience and photo feature (as they relate to gardening). No US gardens or growing; no *public* gardens. Buys about 70 mss/year. Query with published clips. Length: 300-2,000 words. Pays $100-700. Sometimes pays expenses of writers on assignment.

Photos: State availability of photos with submission. Offers $50-250/photo. Identification of subjects required. Buys one-time rights.

Columns/Departments: Gardeners' Journal (garden facts, how-tos—homemade pest sprays, e.g.—and personal experience), 300-500 words; Green Gardening (organic practices), 800-1,000 words; Techniques (gardening techniques), 800-1,000 words. Buys 50 mss/year. Query. Pays $50-200.

Tips: "We prefer to use untried (to us) writers on small items for Gardeners' Journal, the upfront section. Short outlines that are already well focused receive the most attention. Consider, please, that our readers are Canadian gardeners dealing with Canadian conditions."

‡COLONIAL HOMES, Hearst Magazines, 1790 Broadway, 14th Floor, New York NY 10019. Editor: Jason Kontos. Contact: Roberta Dell Aquilo, chief copy editor. 40% freelance written. Bimonthly magazine. "*Colonial Homes* is a shelter book that celebrates 17th, 18th and 19th century design, architecture, decorative arts and decorating." Estab. 1975. Circ. 600,000. Pays on publication. Byline given. Offers 20% kill fee. Buys all rights. Editorial lead time 3 months. Submit seasonal material 6 months in advance. Accepts simultaneous submissions. Reports in 2 weeks on queries; 1 month on mss. Sample copy for #10 SASE. Writer's guidelines free on request.

Nonfiction: Contact: Individual department editors. General interest, historical/nostalgic, new product, travel. Buys 2 mss/year. Query with pubished clips. Length: 500-1,500 words. Pays $500-1,000. Pays expenses of writers on assignment.

Photos: Send photos with submission. Negotiates payment individually. Identification of subjects required. Buys all rights.

Columns/Departments: Masterworks (craftsperson), 750 words; Genealogy (colonial-era) 750 words. Buys 4 mss/year. Query. Pays $500-800.

Tips: "As we accept few unsolicited story ideas, the best way to propose an idea is with an outline and snapshots."

COLORADO HOMES & LIFESTYLES, 7009 S. Potomac St., Englewood CO 80112-4029. (303)397-7600. Fax: (303)397-7619. Editor: Evelyn McGraw. Assistant Editor: Lori Tobias. Publisher: Pat Cooley. 50% freelance written. Bimonthly magazine covering Colorado homes and lifestyles for upper-middle-class and high income households as well as designers, decorators and architects. Circ. 30,000. **Pays on acceptance.** Publishes ms an average of 4 months after acceptance. Byline given. Buys all rights. Submit seasonal/holiday material 6 months in advance. Simultaneous queries OK. Query for electronic submissions. Reports in 3 months.

Nonfiction: Fine homes and furnishings, regional interior design trends, interesting personalities and lifestyles, gardening and plants—all with a Colorado slant. Buys 30 mss/year. Send complete ms. Length: 1,000-1,500 words. "For unique, well-researched feature stories, pay is $150-200. For regular departments, $125-140." Sometimes pays the expenses of writers on assignment.

Photos: Send photos with ms. Reviews 35mm, 4×5 and 2¼ color transparencies and b&w glossy prints. Identification of subjects required. Please include photographic credits.

Tips: "The more interesting and unique the subject the better. A frequent mistake made by writers is failure to provide material with a style and slant appropriate for the magazine, due to poor understanding of the focus of the magazine."

COTTAGE LIFE, Quarto Communications, 111 Queen St. E., Suite 408, Toronto, Ontario M5C 1S2 Canada. (416)360-6880. Fax: (416)360-6814. E-mail: cottage life@magic.ca. Editor: Ann Vanderhoof. Managing Editor: David Zimmer. 80% freelance written. Bimonthly magazine covering waterfront cottaging. "*Cottage Life* is written and designed for the people who own and spend time at cottages throughout Canada and bordering U.S. states." Estab. 1988. Circ. 70,000. **Pays on acceptance.** Publishes ms an average of 2 months after acceptance. Byline given. Buys first North American serial rights. Query for electronic submissions.

Nonfiction: Book excerpts, exposé, historical/nostalgic, how-to, humor, interview/profile, personal experience, photo feature, technical. Buys 90 mss/year. Query with published clips. Length: 150-3,500 words. Pays $100-2,200 for assigned articles. Pays $50-1,000 for unsolicited articles. Sometimes pays expenses of writers on assignment. Query first.

Columns/Departments: Cooking, Real Estate, Fishing, Nature, Watersports, Personal Experience and Issues. Length: 150-1200 words. Query with published clips. Pays $100-750.

‡COUNTRY FOLK ART MAGAZINE, Long Publications, 8393 E. Holly Rd., Holly MI 48442. Editor: Cheryl Anderson. Contact: Judith Karns, managing editor. Monthly magazine covering Country Decorating. "We cater to those who have an interest in country decorating, how-to crafts, gardening, recipes, artist profiles." Estab. 1988. Circ. 250,000. **Pays on acceptance**; photography paid on publication. Publishes ms 10 months after acceptance. Byline given. Buys first North American serial rights. Editorial lead time 6 months. Submit seasonal material 1 year in advance. Query for electronic submissions. Reports in 6 weeks on queries. Sample copy and writer's guidelines free on request.
Nonfiction: Historical/nostalgic, how-to craft, interview/profile, photo feature, home decorating. Buys 100 mss/year. Query with published clips. Length: 700-1,000 words. Pays $200-300 for assigned articles. Pays expenses of writers on assignment.
Photos: State availability of photos or send photos with submission. Reviews ($2\frac{1}{4} \times 2\frac{1}{4}$, 4×5, 35mm) transparencies. Offer $25/photo. Captions, identification of subjects required. Buys one-time rights.
Tips: "Solid writing background is preferred. Be prepared to work with editor for clean, concise copy."

‡COUNTRY HOME, Meredith Corp., 1716 Locust St., Des Moines IA 50309-3023. (515)284-5000. Fax: (515)284-3684. Editor-in-Chief: Molly Culbertson. Managing Editor: Beverly Hawkins. Bimonthly magazine "for people interested in the country way of life." Circ. 1.1 million. "Although the majority of articles are staff written, approximately two or three full-length features per issue are assigned to freelance writers. *Country Home* magazine is a lifestyle publication created for readers who share passions for American history, style, craftsmanship, tradition, and cuisine. These people, with a desire to find a simpler, more meaningful lifestyle, live their lives and design their living spaces in ways that reflect those passions." Reports in 4-6 weeks. Sample copy for $4.95 (includes postage); make check payable to Kathy Stevens.
Nonfiction: Architecture and Design, Families at Home, Travel, Food and Entertaining, Art and Antiques, Gardens and Outdoor Living, Personal Reflections. Query with writing samples and SASE. "We are not responsible for unsolicited manuscripts, and we do not encourage telephone queries." Length: features, 750-1,500 words; columns or departments, 500-750 words. Pays $500-1,500 for features, $300-500 for columns or departments. Pays on completion of assignment.

COUNTRY HOME AND GARDENS, Magazine for Beautiful Homes and Bountiful Gardens, Prestige Publications, Inc., 4151 Knob Dr., Eagan MN 55122. (612)452-0571. Editor: Carla Waldemar. Publisher: Russ Moore. 40% freelance written (mainly reprints). Bimonthly magazine. "Articles should include what's new in decorating, collectibles, do-it-yourself home projects, crafts, gardening tips and new products. Our audience is men and women 25-50 who are interested in making the most of their home experience." Estab. 1993. Circ. 200,000. Pays on publication. Byline given. Buys all rights. Submit seasonal material 3 months in advance. Accepts previously published submissions. Send photocopy of article or typed ms with rights for sale noted and information about when and where the article previously appeared. For reprints pays $50-100.
Photos: State availability of photos with submission. Reviews transparencies. Offers $50-200/photo. Buys one-time rights.

COUNTRY LIVING, Hearst Corp., 224 W. 57th St., New York NY 10019. Featuares Editor: Marjorie Gage. Monthly publication covering country lifestyles. Query with proposal or article. Writer's guidelines for SASE.
Tips: "Make sure it's a 'country article'; no 'grandmother' stories."

DESIGN TIMES, Beautiful Interiors of the Northeast, Regis Publishing Co., Inc., 1 Design Center Place, Suite 828, Boston MA 02210. (617)443-0636. Managing Editor: Emily Crawford. 60% freelance written. Bimonthly magazine covering residential interior design in Northeast. "Show, don't tell. Readers want to look over the shoulders of professional interior designers. Avoid cliché. Love design." Estab. 1988. Circ. 15,000. Pays on publication. Publishes ms an average of 4 months after acceptance. Byline given. Offers 10% kill fee. Buys all rights. Editorial lead time 3 months. Submit seasonal material 6 months in advance. Accepts simultaneous submissions. Query for electronic submissions. Reports in 1 month. Sample copy for 10×13 SAE with 10 first-class stamps.
Nonfiction: Residential interiors (Northeast only). Buys 25 mss/year. Query with published clips. Length: 1,200-3,000 words. Pays $100. Sometimes pays the expenses of writers on assignment.
Photos: State availability of photos with submission. Reviews 4×5 transparencies, 9×10 prints. Negotiates payment individually. Caption, model releases, identification of subject required. Buys one-time rights.
Columns/Departments: Pays $100-150.
Tips: "A Northeast home owned by a well-known personality or designer would be a good feature query."

FINE GARDENING, Taunton Press, 63 S. Main St., P.O. Box 5506, Newtown CT 06470-5506. 1-800-243-7252. Fax: (203)426-3434. Editor: Carole Turner. Bimonthly magazine on gardening. "Focus is broad subject of landscape and ornamental gardening. Articles written by avid gardeners—first person, hands-on-gardening experiences." Estab. 1988. Circ. 175,000. Pays on publication. Byline given. Buys first North American serial rights. Receipt of work notice sent immediately. Decision made within a few months. Free writer's guidelines.

Nonfiction: Book review, essays, how-to, opinion, personal experience, photo feature. Buys 50-60 mss/year. Query. Length: 1,000-3,000 words. Pays $150/page.

Photos: Send photos with submission. Reviews 35mm transparencies. Buys serial rights.

Columns/Department: Book, video and software reviews (on gardening); Gleanings (news items directly related to gardening, other miscellaneous tidbits. No product reviews); Last Word (essays/serious, humorous, fact or fiction). Query. Length: 250-1,000 words. Pays $25-150.

Tips: "It's most important to have solid first-hand experience as a gardener. Tell us what you've done with your own landscape and plants."

FLOWER AND GARDEN MAGAZINE, 700 W. 47th St., Suite 310, Kansas City MO 64112. Fax: (816)531-3873. Editor: Kay Melchisedech Olson. 50% freelance written. Works with a small number of new/unpublished writers each year. Bimonthly picture magazine for home gardeners. Estab. 1957. Circ. 750,000. Buys first time nonexclusive reprint rights. Sometimes accepts previously published articles. Send typed ms with rights for sale noted, including information about when and where the article previously appeared. Byline given. **Pays on acceptance.** Publishes ms an average of 1 year after acceptance. Reports in 2 months. Sample copy for $2.95 and 10×13 SAE. Writer's guidelines for #10 SASE.

 ● The editor of this publication tells us good quality photos accompanying articles are more important than ever.

Nonfiction: Interested in illustrated articles on how to do certain types of gardening and descriptive articles about individual plants. Flower arranging, landscape design, house plants and patio gardening are other aspects covered. "The approach we stress is practical (how-to-do-it, what-to-do-it-with). We emphasize plain talk, clarity and economy of words. An article should be tailored for a national audience." Buys 20-30 mss/year. Query. Length: 500-1,500 words. Rates vary depending on quality and kind of material.

Photos: Buys transparencies, 35mm and larger. Photos are paid for on publication.

Tips: "The prospective author needs good grounding in gardening practice and literature. Offer well-researched and well-written material appropriate to the experience level of our audience. Use botanical names as well as common. Photographs help sell the story. Describe special qualifications for writing the particular proposed subject."

THE HERB COMPANION, Interweave Press, 201 E. Fourth St., Loveland CO 80537-5655. (303)669-7672. Fax: (303)667-8317. Editor: Kathleen Halloran. Managing Editor: Trish Faubion. 80% freelance written. Bimonthly magazine about herbs: culture, history, culinary use, crafts and some medicinal. Audience includes a wide range of herb enthusiasts. Circ. 110,000. Pays on publication. Byline given. Buys first North American serial rights. Reports in 2 months. Query in writing. Length: 6-12 pages. Typical payment is $100/published page. Sample copy for $4. Writer's guidelines for #10 SASE.

Photos: Send photos.

Tips: "Articles must show depth and working knowledge of the subject, though tone should be informal and accessible."

HERB QUARTERLY, P.O. Box 689, San Anselmo CA 94960-0689. Fax: (415)455-9541. E-mail: herbquart @aol.com. Publisher: James Keough. 80% freelance written. Quarterly magazine for herb enthusiasts. Estab. 1979. Circ. 35,000. Pays on publication. Publishes ms an average of 6 months after acceptance. Buys first North American serial and second (reprint) rights. Query for electronic submissions. Query letters recommended. Reports in 2 months. Sample copy for $5 and 9×12 SASE. Writer's guidelines for #10 SASE.

Nonfiction: Gardening (landscaping, herb garden design, propagation, harvesting); medicinal and cosmetic use of herbs; crafts; cooking; historical (folklore, focused piece on particular period—*not* general survey); interview of a famous person involved with herbs or folksy herbalist; personal experience; photo essay ("cover quality" 8×10 b&w or color prints). "We are particularly interested in herb garden design, contemporary or historical." No fiction. Send double-spaced ms. Length: 1,000-3,500 words. Pays $75-250.

Tips: "Our best submissions are narrowly focused on herbs with much practical information on cultivation and use for the experienced gardener."

HOME MAGAZINE, The Magazine of Remodeling and Decorating, 1633 Broadway, 44th Floor, New York NY 10019. Fax: (212)489-4576. E-mail: homell@aol.com. Editor/Director: Gale C. Steves. Articles Editor: Linda Lentz. 80% freelance written. Monthly magazine covering remodeling, decorating, architecture, entertaining, building and gardens. Estab. 1981. Circ. 1 million. **Pays on acceptance.** Publishes ms an average of 6 months after acceptance. Offers negotiable kill fee. Buys all rights, including electronic. Submit seasonal/holiday material 6-13 months in advance. Reports immediately. Free sample copy and writer's guidelines.

 ● *Home* is online with America Online and is currently using about half of its monthly articles in this media extension of the magazine.

Nonfiction: Linda Lentz, articles editor. Essays, how-to, interview/profile, personal experience, photo feature, technical. Buys 100-120 mss/year. Query with published clips. Length: 500-1,500 words. Negotiates payment.

‡HOMES & COTTAGES, The In-Home Show Ltd., 6557 Ississauga Rd., Suite D, Ississauga, Ontario L5N 1A6 Canada. (905)567-1440. Editor: Janice Naisby. Contact: Lisa Gardiner, Editorial Assistant. 80% freelance written. Magazine published 8 times/year covering building and renovating: "technically comprehensible articles." Estab. 1989. Circ. 54,000 Pays on publication. Publishes mss average of 2 months after acceptance. Byline given. Offers $100 kill fee. Buys first North American serial rights. Editorial lead time 3 months. Submit seasonal material 3 months in advance. Sample copy for SAE. Writer's guidelines free on request.

Nonfiction: Humor (building and renovation related), new product, technical. Buys 32 mss/year. Query. Length: 1,500-2,000 words. Pays $600-750. Sometimes pays expenses of writers on assignment.

Photos: State availability of photos with submission. Reviews transparencies. Negotiates payment individually. Captions and identification of subjects required. Buys one-time rights.

ISLAND HOME MAGAZINE, The Showcase of Island Architecture, Design & Lifestyle, Island Productions, Inc., 1221 Kapiolani Blvd., Penthouse 40, Honolulu HI 96814. Fax: (808)593-2900. Contact: Editorial Department. 50% freelance written. Bimonthly magazine. "We write about the uniqueness of island living, both in Hawaii and throughout the world. Our sections include Private Places (luxury homes on islands), Interiors (outstanding interior design in island residences), Travel (international island destinations and resorts), Dining (island restaurants), and Art/Collectibles (island artists/handicrafts). About half our readers are in Hawaii. Readers are either island dwellers, island travelers . . . or wish they were." Estab. 1990. Circ. 30,000. Pays within 30 days after publication. Byline given. Kill fee negotiable. Buys one-time rights. Editorial lead time 5-6 months. Submit seasonal material 6 months in advance. Accepts previously published submissions. Query for electronic submissions. Reports in 2 months. Sample copy for 10×13 SAE with 10 first-class stamps. Writer's guidelines for #10 SASE.

Nonfiction: Travel, island dining features, island home features (focus on architecture and design as well as location), island artist features. "Our annual golf issue is every March/April, in which we feature homes, restaurants and travel destinations with a golf or golf course focus. No articles that do not fall into our categories, which are Private Places, Interiors, Dining, Travel and Art/Collectibles. Nothing else will be considered as our categories do not change." Buys 3-4 mss/year from new freelancers; the rest are from existing pool of Hawaii freelance writers. Query with published clips. Length: 1,200-1,700 words. Pays 20¢/word.

Photos: State availability of photos or send photos with submission—preferable. Reviews contact sheets, 2¼×2¼ and 4×5 transparencies and 8×10 prints. Negotiates payment individually. Captions required—after acceptance only. Buys one-time rights.

LOG HOME LIVING, Home Buyer Publications Inc., P.O. Box 220039, Chantilly VA 22022. (703)222-9411. Editor: Roland Sweet. Less than 20% freelance written. Bimonthly magazine "for people who own or are planning to build contemporary manufactured and handcrafted kit log homes. Our audience is married couples 35-50 years old." Estab. 1989. **Pays on acceptance.** Publishes ms an average of 1 year after acceptance. Byline given. Buys one-time rights. Submit seasonal/holiday material 9-12 months in advance. Accepts previously published submissions. Send photocopy of article. Pays 50% of amount paid for an original article. Reports in 6 months. Sample copy for $3.50. Writer's guidelines for #10 SASE.

Nonfiction: How-to (buy or build log home), interview/profile (log home owners), photo feature (log homes), technical (design/decor topics). "We do not want historical/nostalgic material." Buys 4-6 mss/year. Query with published clips. Length: 750-1,500 words. Pays $100-500. Sometimes pays expenses of writers on assignment.

Photos: Send photos with submission. Reviews contact sheets, 2½×2½ transparencies and 4×5 transparencies. Offers $50-100/photo. Captions, model releases and identification of subjects required. Buys one-time rights.

Tips: "Owner profiles are most open to freelancers. Reveal how they planned for, designed and bought/built their dream home; how they decorated it; how they like it; advice for others thinking of buying."

MIDWEST LIVING, Meredith Corp., 1912 Grand Ave., Des Moines IA 50309. Contact: Barbara Humeston. Bimonthly publication covering lifestyle, travel, food and home subjects of interest to Midwestern readers. Query with outline and SASE; explain why article would be suitable for *Midwest Living*. The magazine often requests essays; guidelines can be found in the magazine.

NATIONAL GARDENING, National Gardening Association, 180 Flynn Ave., Burlington VT 05401. (802)863-1308. Fax: (802)863-5962. Editor: Michael MacCaskey. Managing Editor: Vicky Congdon. 80% freelance written. Willing to work with new/unpublished writers. Bimonthly magazine covering all aspects of food gardening and ornamentals. "We publish not only how-to garden techniques, but also news that affects home gardeners, like breeding advancements and new variety releases. Detailed, experienced-based articles with carefully worked-out techniques for planting, growing, harvesting and using garden fruits and vegetables sought as well as profiles of expert gardeners in this country's many growing regions. Our material is for both experienced and beginning gardeners." Estab. 1979. Circ. 250,000. **Pays on acceptance.** Publishes ms an average of 9 months after acceptance. Byline given. Buys first serial and occasionally second (reprint) rights to material originally published elsewhere. Reports in 2 months. Sample copy for $3. Writer's guidelines for #10 SASE.

Nonfiction: How-to, humor, interview/profile, pest profiles, opinion, personal experience, recipes. Buys 50-60 mss/year. Query first. Length: 500-2,500 words. Pays 25¢/word. Sometimes pays the expenses of writers on assignment; must have prior approval.

Photos: Vicky Congdon, managing editor. Send photos with ms. Pays $20-40 for b&w photos; $50 for color slides. Captions, model releases and identification of subjects required.

Tips: "Take the time to study the style of the magazine—the focus of the features and the various departments. Keep in mind that you'll be addressing a national audience."

ORGANIC GARDENING, Rodale Press, 33 E. Minor, Emmaus PA 18098. (610)967-5171. Managing Editor: Vicki Mattern. 30% freelance written. Published 9 times/year. Pays between acceptance and publication. Buys all rights. Reports in 2 months on queries; 1 month on mss.

Nonfiction: "Our title says it all. We seem to put more emphasis on the gardening aspect." Query with published clips and outline. Pays 50¢/word.

PLANT & GARDEN, Canada's Practical Gardening Magazine, Gardenvale Publishing Co. Ltd., 1 Pacifique, Ste. Anne de Bellevue, Quebec H9X 1C5 Canada. (514)457-2744. Editor: Michael Spillane. 95% freelance written. Quarterly magazine covering gardening in Canada. "We are a *practical* gardening magazine focusing on how-to, step-by-step type articles on all aspects of garden and houseplant care. Readers are both novice and experienced Canadian gardeners." Estab. 1988. Circ. 36,000. Pays on publication. Publishes ms 4 months after acceptance. Byline given. Offers 50% kill fee. Buys first North American serial rights. Editorial lead time 4 months. Submit seasonal material 4 months in advance. Accepts simultaneous submissions. Query for electronic submissions. Reports in 2 months. Sample copy free on request. Writer's guidelines for SAE and IRC or, preferably, SAE with 43¢ first-class Canadian stamp.

Nonfiction: Historical/nostalgic, how-to, humor, interview/profile, new product, personal experience—garden-related topics only. No religious/travel outside Canada. Buys 60 mss/year. Query with published clips. Length: 600-1,800 words. Pays $75 minimum (600 words). Sometimes pays expenses of writers on assignment.

Photos: Send photos with submission. Reviews negatives and 4×5 transparencies. Offers no additional payment for photos accepted with ms. Captions required. Buys one-time rights.

Columns/Departments: Profile (profiles of gardens and/or gardeners); Hydroponics (how-to for home gardener); Junior Gardener (how-to/ideas for kids and gardening); Down to Earth (humor/essay on gardening); Herb Garden (herb profiles). Length: 600-800 words. Buys 16 mss/year. Query with published clips. Pays $75-150.

Tips: "Please be knowledgeable about gardening—not just a freelance writer. Be accurate and focus on plants/techniques that are appropriate to Canada and be as down to earth as possible. We want good quality writing and interesting subject matter. Areas most open to freelancers are Down to Earth and Profile. We are especially looking for garden profiles from outside Ontario and Quebec (West Coast and Maritimes)."

TEXAS GARDENER, The Magazine for Texas Gardeners, by Texas Gardeners, Suntex Communications, Inc., P.O. Box 9005, Waco TX 76714-9005. (817)772-1270. Editor: Chris S. Corby. Managing Editors: Gloria Gonzales. 80% freelance written. Works with a small number of new/unpublished writers each year. Bimonthly magazine covering vegetable and fruit production, ornamentals and home landscape information for home gardeners in Texas. Estab. 1981. Circ. 37,000. Pays on publication. Publishes ms an average of 4 months after acceptance. Byline given. Buys first North American serial and all rights. Submit seasonal/holiday material 6 months in advance. Query for electronic submissions. Reports in 2 months. Sample copy for $2.75 and SAE with 5 first-class stamps. Writer's guidelines for #10 SASE.

Nonfiction: How-to, humor, interview/profile, photo feature. "We use feature articles that relate to Texas gardeners. We also like personality profiles on hobby gardeners and professional horticulturists who are doing something unique." Buys 50-100 mss/year. Query with clips of published work. Length: 800-2,400 words. Pays $50-200.

Photos: "We prefer superb color and b&w photos; 90% of photos used are color." Send photos. Pays negotiable rates for 2¼ or 35mm color transparencies and 8×10 b&w prints and contact sheets. Model release and identification of subjects required.

Tips: "First, be a Texan. Then come up with a good idea of interest to home gardeners in this state. Be specific. Stick to feature topics like 'How Alley Gardening Became a Texas Tradition.' Leave topics like 'How to Control Fire Blight' to the experts. High quality photos could make the difference. We would like to add several writers to our group of regular contributors and would make assignments on a regular basis. Fillers are easy to come up with in-house. We want good writers who can produce accurate and interesting copy. Frequent mistakes made by writers in completing an article assignment for us are that articles are not slanted toward Texas gardening, show inaccurate or too little gardening information or lack good writing style. We will be doing more 'people' features and articles on ornamentals."

Humor

Publications listed here specialize in gaglines or prose humor, some for readers and others for performers or speakers. Other publications that use humor can be found in nearly every category in this book. Some have special needs for major humor pieces; some use humor as fillers; many others are interested in material that meets their ordinary fiction or nonfiction requirements but also has a humorous slant. The majority of humor articles must be submitted as complete manuscripts on speculation because editors usually can't know from a query whether or not the piece will be right for them.

FUNNY TIMES, A Monthly Humor Review, Funny Times, Inc., P.O. Box 18530, Cleveland Heights OH 44118. (216)371-8600. Editors: Raymond Lesser, Susan Wolpert. 10% freelance written. Monthly tabloid for humor. "*Funny Times* is a monthly review of America's funniest cartoonists and writers. We are the *Reader's Digest* of modern American humor with a progressive/peace oriented/environmental/politically activist slant." Estab. 1985. Circ. 43,000. Pays on publication. Publishes ms an average of 3 months after acceptance. Byline given. Buys one-time or second serial (reprint) rights. Editorial lead time 2 months. Accepts simultaneous and previously published submissions. Reports in 3 months on mss. Sample copy for $3 or 9×12 SAE with 4 first-class stamps. Writer's guidelines for #10 SASE.
Nonfiction: Essays (funny), humor, interview/profile, opinion (humorous), personal experience (absolutely funny). "We only publish humor or interviews with funny people (comedians, comic actors, cartoonists, etc.). Everything we publish is very funny. If your piece isn't extremely funny then don't bother to send it. Don't send us anything that's not outrageously funny. Don't send anything that other people haven't already read and told you they laughed so hard they peed their pants." Buys 36 mss/year. Send complete ms. Length: 1,000 words. Pays $50 minimum for unsolicited articles.
Fiction: Humorous. Buys 6 mss/year. Query with published clips. Length: 5,000 words. Pays $50-150.
Fillers: Short humor. Buys 6/year. Pays $20.
Tips: "Send us a small packet (1-3 items) of only your very funniest stuff. If this makes us laugh we'll be glad to ask for more. We particularly welcome previously published material that has been well-received elsewhere."

LAF!, Scher Maihem Publishing, Ltd., P.O. Box 313, Avilla IN 46710-0313. Submissions Editor: Fran Glass. 100% freelance written. Bimonthly tabloid that features modern life cooperative humor. Estab. 1991. Circ. 1,000. Pays within 30 days of publication. Buys first or second serial (reprint) rights. Submit seasonal/holiday material 6 months in advance. Limit 3 simultaneous submissions. Reports in 3 months. Sample copy for 9×12 SASE with 2 first-class stamps. Writer's guidelines for #10 SASE.
 • *Laf!* also sponsors the Loudest Laf! Laurel contest. See the Contests and Awards section for information.
Fiction: Humor, cartoons. "No religious, political, sexually or racially offensive humor. No poems." Buys 60 mss/year; 35 cartoons/year. Send complete ms. Length: 250-600 words. Pays $5-15. No series.
Tips: "If your humor writing appeals to people ages 45 and younger and spoofs modern living, send it. Our audience is broad, so the writing and subject must have wide appeal. We highly suggest writers take a look at the tabloid and guidelines first."

LATEST JOKES, P.O. Box 23304, Brooklyn NY 11202-0066. (718)855-5057. Editor: Robert Makinson. Estab. 1974. 20% freelance written. Bimonthly newsletter of humor for TV and radio personalities, comedians and professional speakers. **Pays on acceptance.** Byline given. Buys all rights. Submit seasonal/holiday material 3 months in advance. Reports in 2 months. Sample copy for $3 and SASE.
Nonfiction: Humor (short jokes). No "stupid, obvious, non-funny vulgar humor. Jokes about human tragedy also unwelcome." Send complete ms. Pays $1-3/joke.
Fiction: Humorous jokes. Pays $1-3.
Poetry: Light verse (humorous). Submit maximum 3 poems at one time. Line length: 2-8 lines. Pays 25¢/line.
Tips: "No famous personality jokes. Clever statements are not enough. Be original and surprising. Our emphasis is on jokes for professional speakers."

‡LIGHTER TIMES, Lighter Times Publishing, 2929 Second Ave. N., Seattle WA 98109. (206)283-8384. Editor: Stan Snow. 30% freelance written. Magazine published 10 times/year covering "true news with humorous content." Estab. 1994. Pays on publication. Publishes ms an average of 3 months after acceptance. Byline given. Buys one-time rights. Editorial lead time 2 months. Submit seasonal material 3 months in advance. Accepts simultaneous submissions and previously published submissions. Query for electronic

submissions. Reporting time varies. Sample copy $5. Writer's guidelines for SASE.
Nonfiction: General interest, humor, opinion—all with humorous news value. Buys 40 mss/year. Send complete ms. "Mail only—no phone inquiries." Length: 50-500 words. Pays $35-200 for assigned articles; $15-100 for unsolicited articles.
Columns/Departments: Op-Ed (humorous opinion on current events), 50-100 words. Send complete ms. Pays 15-50.
Poetry: Light verse. Buys 8 poems/year. Submit maximum 3 poems. Pays $10-25.
Tips: "We are interested *only* in factual news with humorous content and void of murder, rape, sordid gossip, etc. Must be verifiable with sources listed. Also interested in humorous opinion and occasional verse relating to newsworthy topics and events. News journalism reported with use of clever puns and metaphors a plus."

MAD MAGAZINE, 1700 Broadway, New York NY 10019. (212)506-4850. Editors: Nick Meglin, John Ficarra. 100% freelance written. Magazine published 8 times/year. Estab. 1952. Circ. 1 million. **Pays on acceptance.** Publishes ms an average of 6 months after acceptance. Byline given. Buys all rights. Submit seasonal/holiday material 6 months in advance. Reports in 6-10 weeks. Writer's guidelines for #10 SASE.
Nonfiction: Satire, parody. "We're always on the lookout for new ways to spoof and to poke fun at hot trends. We're *not* interested in formats we're already doing or have done to death like 'what they say and what they really mean.' " Buys 400 mss/year. "Submit a premise with three or four examples of how you intend to carry it through, describing the action and visual content. Rough sketches not necessary. One-page gags: two to eight panel cartoon continuities at minimum very funny, maximum hilarious!" Pays minimum of $400/*MAD* page. "*Don't* send riddles, advice columns, TV or movie satires, book manuscripts, top ten lists, articles about Alfred E. Neuman, poetry, essays, short stories or other text pieces."
Tips: "Have fun! Remember to think visually! Surprise us! Freelancers can best break in with nontopical material. Include SASE with each submission. Originality is prized. We like outrageous, silly and/or satirical humor."

THE RAGAMUFFIN, The Best of College Humor, P.O. Box 21707, Cleveland OH 44121-0707. (216)932-7923. E-mail: ximinez@aol.com. Editor: Ima S. Finkter. Managing Editor: Eileen Dover. Contact: Margaret O'Shae-Vyorass, managing stapler. 75% college humor publication reprints, 25% freelance. Quarterly tabloid covering college humor from around the country. Estab. 1989. Circ. 65,000. Pays on publication. Publishes ms an average of 4 months after acceptance. Byline sometimes given. Buys all, one-time rights and second serial (reprint) rights. Editorial lead time 4 months. Accepts simultaneous and previously published submissions. Send typed ms with rights for sale noted. Query via e-mail for electronic submissions. Reports in 6 months on mss. Sample copy for 9×12 SAE and 4 first-class stamps. Writer's guidelines free on request.
Nonfiction: Humor. Query. Pays 10¢/word for feature or articles; $6/classified, letter to the editor, or horoscope published; $30/cartoon published.
Photos: State availability of photos with submission. Negotiates payment individually. Buys one-time rights.
Columns/Departments: Letters to Editor (parody), 3-50 words; Newswire (75-150 words); Classifieds (parody), 25 words. Buys 150 mss/year. Send complete ms.
  • *The Ragamuffin* no longer accepts freelance fiction.
Poetry: Parody. "No serious poetry." Buys 6 poems/year. Submit maximum 5 poems. Pays 15¢/word.
Fillers: Buys 20/year. Length: 5-300 words. Pays $12-45.
Tips: "We are 90% parody. The most popular pieces are either the sublimely stupid, or mind-bendingly contradictory. Or better yet, something that cleverly flames on the real-life situation of college life. What is suggested to new writers is that they begin with the fillers, letters to the editor, classifieds, or horoscopes. Once they publish ten of these, they become a contributing editor, and we work with them on assignments."

Inflight

Most major inflight magazines cater to business travelers and vacationers who will be reading, during the flight, about the airline's destinations and other items of general interest.

AL BURAQ, The Inflight Magazine for Kuwait Airways, Fortune Promoseven, P.O. Box 5989, Manama, Bahrain. (973)250148 ext. 635. Fax: (973)210672. Editor: Gregory O. Jones. 60% freelance written. Monthly magazine covering travel, general interest. "*Al Buraq* exists to promote Kuwait Airways and travel to destinations served by Kuwait Airways. Remember to keep stories brief and interesting; remember that one half the magazine is in Arabic for a Middle Eastern audience." Estab. 1989. Circ. 50,000. Pays on publication. Publishes ms an average of 3 months after acceptance. Byline given. Offers 50% kill fee. Buys first, one-time, second serial (reprint) or Arabic language rights. Editorial lead time 4 months. Submit seasonal material 4 months in advance. Accepts previously published submissions. Send photocopy of article or typed ms with rights for sale noted. For reprints, pays 50% of the amount paid for an original article. Query for electronic submissions. Reports in 1 month. Sample copy for 8½×12 SAE with 2 IRCs. Writer's guidelines free on request.

Nonfiction: General interest, interview/profile, photo feature, travel. "No humor, politics, sex or religious overtones. Humor translates poorly, the rest are not usable." Buys 40 mss/year. Query with published clips. Length: 400-1,200 words. Pays $120. Sometimes pays expenses of writers on assignment.

Photos: Ideally, send photos with submission. Reviews contact sheets, transparencies and prints (5×7 minimum). Offers $50-200/photo. Captions required. Buys one-time rights.

Tips: "Send for contributor notes and sample copy. Remember where we are published. The article may be published in Arabic, and will definitely be read by non-Americans; therefore, all American slang or 'in-terms' should either be avoided or explained. Write internationally, appeal personally. Stories complete with pictures and on diskettes go to the head of the queue. Always welcome well-written, competently-illustrated, succinct feature articles pertinent to our readers. *Al Buraq* is a good market for the fledgling writer."

AMERICA WEST AIRLINES MAGAZINE, Skyword Marketing, Inc., 4636 E. Elwood St., Suite 5, Phoenix AZ 85040-1963. (602)997-7200. Editor: Michael Derr. 90% freelance written. Works with small number of new/unpublished writers each year. Monthly "general interest magazine, with substantial business editorial, emphasizing the western and southwestern US. Some Midwestern, Northwestern and Eastern subjects also appropriate. We look for innovative, newsworthy and unconventional subject matter." Estab. 1986. Pays on publication. Publishes ms an average of 4 months after acceptance. Byline given. Offers 15% kill fee. Buys first North American rights. Submit seasonal/holiday material 8 months in advance. Accepts simultaneous submissions, if indicated. Reports in 1 month on queries; 5 weeks on mss. Sample copy for $3. Writer's guidelines for 9×12 SAE with 3 first-class stamps.

● This publication is not accepting unsolicited queries or manuscripts at this time.

Nonfiction: General interest, creative leisure, profile, photo feature, science, sports, business issues, entre-preneurs, nature, arts, travel, trends. Also considers essays and humor. No puzzles, reviews or highly contro-versial features. Buys 130-140 mss/year. Length: 300-2,200. Pays $150-900. Pays some expenses.

Photos: State availability of original photography. Offers $50-250/photo. Captions, model releases and identification of subjects required. Buys one-time rights.

AMERICAN WAY, P.O. Box 619640, Dallas/Fort Worth Airport TX 75261-9640. (817)967-1804. Fax: (817)967-1571. Editor-in-Chief: John H. Ostdick. Managing Editor: Elaine Srnka. 98% freelance written. Prefers to work with published/established writers. Biweekly inflight magazine for passengers flying with American Airlines. Estab. 1966. **Pays on acceptance.** Publishes ms an average of 4 months after acceptance. Buys first serial rights. Reports in 5 months.

● *American Way* increased its writer base during the past year, making it more difficult for a new writer to crack the lineup.

Nonfiction: Trends in business, the arts and entertainment industries, sports, technology, food, science, medicine, travel, Q&As with interesting people. "We are amenable to almost any subject that would be interesting, entertaining or useful to a passenger of American Airlines." Also humor, trivia, trends, and will consider a variety of ideas. Buys 450 mss/year. Query with published clips. Length: 1,000-3,500 words. Pays $850 and up. Usually pays some expenses for writers on assignment.

Fiction: Jeff Posey, editor. Length: 2,500 words maximum. Payment varies. Publishes novel excerpts.

THE AUSTRALIAN WAY, Qantas Inflight Magazine, David Syme & Co. Ltd., 250 Spencer St., Mel-bourne Victoria 3000 Australia. Fax: (03)6420852. Editor: Brian Courtis. 80% freelance written. Monthly magazine. "*The Australian Way* caters to Qantas Airways passengers travelling on both internal Australian routes and overseas. It provides articles on international events, travel, the arts, science and technology, sport, natural history and humor. The focus is on elegant writing and high-quality photography." Estab. 1993. Circ. 900,000. Pays on publication. Publishes ms an average of 3 months after acceptance. Byline given. Buys first rights. Editorial lead time 3 months. Submit seasonal material 4 months in advance. Query for electronic submissions.

Nonfiction: General interest, historical/nostalgic, interview/profile, photo feature, travel. Query with pub-lished clips. Buys 200 mss/year. Length: 800-2,000 words. Pays $500 (Australian) for assigned articles; $400 (Australian) for unsolicited articles.

Photos: State availability of photos with submission. Reviews transparencies and prints. Negotiates payment individually. Captions and identification of subjects required. Buys all rights if commissioned; one-time rights if unsolicited.

Columns/Departments: Contact: Emily Ross. Carousel (unusual news, facts, happenings that interest travellers—trends or personalities etc.) 150 words. Query. Pays $100-250 Australian.

Tips: "Writers should entertain as well as inform both an Australian and international readership. Features can be of general interest, about personalities, or on cultural, business or sporting interests. The magazine tends to avoid travel 'destination' pieces *per se*, though it carries appropriate stories that use these locations as backdrops."

GOLDEN FALCON, Fortune Promoseven, P.O. Box 5989, Manama, Bahrain. (973)250148 ext. 635. Fax: (973)271451. Managing Editor: Kamilia Ahmed. 60% freelance written. Monthly magazine covering travel, general interest for Gulf Air. Estab. 1988 (relaunched January 1993). Circ. 50,000. Pays on publication.

Publishes ms an average of 4 months after acceptance. Byline given. Offers 50% kill fee. Buys first, one-time, or Arabic language rights. Editorial lead time 4 months. Submit seasonal material 5 months in advance. Accepts previously published submissions. Send typed ms with rights for sale noted and information about when and where the article previously appeared. For reprints, pays 50% of the amount paid for an original article. Query for electronic submissions. Reports in 1 month. Sample copy for 8½ × 12 SAE with 2 IRCs. Writer's guidelines free on request.

Nonfiction: General interest, historical/nostalgic, interview/profile, photo feature, travel. "No humor, politics, sex or religion. Humor translates poorly, the other three are unusable." Buys 50 mss/year. Query with published clips. Length: 800-1,300 words. Pays $250-500. Sometimes pays the expenses of writers on assignment.

Photos: State availability of photos with submission. Reviews contact sheets, transparencies and prints (5 × 7 minimum). Offers $50-200/photo. Captions required. Buys one-time rights.

Columns/Departments: Technology (popular science, new gadgets), 300-500 words and photos; Business (no bad news—upbeat and optimistic), 300-500 words and photos; The Arts/Music/Show Biz (personalities, history, mini-articles), 300-500 words and photos. Buys 48 mss/year. Query with published clips. Pays $110-140.

Tips: "Read contributor notes carefully. Remember where we are published. National and religious sensibilities must be observed. The articles will be read by non-Americans, so avoid American-isms and slang. Write internationally, appeal individually. Stories which are complete with captioned photos and computer disk go to the head of the queue. Send for destination list and produce stories from places where travel companies do *not* send writers for 'familiarization trips.' Short columns, easily researched, complete with one picture, can be produced quickly. We have a prodigious appetite for them and they can be assembled from assorted manufacturers' and companies' press releases. Motoring, Business, Fashion, etc. columns must refrain from mention of a single company. Prefer three or more."

HEMISPHERES, Pace Communications for United Airlines, 1301 Carolina St., Greensboro NC 27401. (910)378-6065. Editor: Kate Greer. 95% freelance written. Monthly magazine for inflight passengers covering travel and business—a global perspective with information for the professional who travels frequently. Estab. 1992. Circ. 500,000. **Pays on acceptance**. Publishes ms 4-12 months after acceptance. Byline given. Offers 20% kill fee. Buys first, worldwide rights. Editorial lead time 4-8 months. Submit seasonal material 6-8 months in advance. Reports in 10 weeks on queries; 4 months on mss. Sample copy for $5. Writer's guidelines for #10 SASE.

● In 1994, this magazine won an "Editorial Excellence" award from *Magazine Week* and a Best Inflight magazine award from *Folio: The Magazine of Magazine Management*.

Nonfiction: Book excerpts, general interest, humor, personal experience. No "What I did (or am going to do) on a trip to . . ." Query with published clips. Length: 500-3,000 words. Negotiates payment individually.

Photo: State availability of photos with submission. Reviews transparencies "only when we request them." Negotiates payment individually. Captions, model releases and identification of subjects required. Buys one-time rights.

Columns/Departments: Making a Difference (Q&A interview with world leaders, movers and shakers); On Location (1-sentence "25 Fun Facts" about a city, state, country or destination); Executive Secrets (things that top executives know—e.g., business strategies); Case Study (business strategies of international companies or organizations); Weekend Breakway (physically active getaway—hiking, windsurfing, etc.—just outside a major city); Roving Gourmet (insider's guide to interesting eating in major city, resort area, or region; Collecting (photo with lengthy caption or occasional 800-word story on collections and collecting with emphasis on travel); Eye on Sports (global look at anything of interest in sports); Vintage Traveler (options for mature, experienced travelers); Savvy Shopper (insider's tour of best places in the world to shop); Science and Technology alternates with Computers (substantive, insightful story); Aviation Journal (for those fascinated with aviation); Of Grape And Grain (wine and spirits with emphasis on education); Show Business (films, music and entertainment); Musings (humor or just curious musings); Quick Quiz (tests to amuse and educate); Travel News (brief, practical, invaluable, trend-oriented tips). Length: 800-1,400 words. Query with published clips.

Fiction: Adventure, humorous, mainstream, slice-of-life vignettes. Buys 4 mss/year. Query. Length: 500-2,000 words. Negotiates payment individually.

Tips: "We increasingly require writers of 'destination' pieces or departments to 'live whereof they write.' Increasingly want to hear from U.S., U.K. or other English speaking/writing journalists (business & travel) who reside outside the U.S. in Europe, South America, Central America and the Pacific Rim—all areas that United flies."

Always check the most recent copy of a magazine for the address and editor's name before you send in a query or manuscript.

‡LATITUDES SOUTH, Caribbean Travel & Life, Inc., 8403 Colesville Rd., Suite 830, Silver Spring MD 20910. (301)588-2300. Editor: Laura Randall. 50% freelance written. Quarterly magazine covering travel in Florida and the Caribbean. Estab. 1991. Circ. 60,000. Pays on publication. Publishes ms an average of 6-12 months after acceptance. Byline given. Buys first North American serial rights. Submit seasonal material 9 months in advance. Accepts simultaneous and previously published submissions. Query for electronic submissions. Reports in 1 month on queries; 2 months on mss. Sample copy for 9×12 SAE with 5 first-class stamps. Writer's guidelines for #10 SASE.

Nonfiction: Travel. Query with published clips. Length: 2,000-3,000. Pays $250 minimum. Sometimes pays expenses of writers on assignment.

Photos: State availability of photos with submission. Reviews slides. Offers $75-250/photo. Buys one-time rights.

Columns/Departments: Tropical Party (food/dining in the Caribbean and Florida i.e., "St. Thomas Dining"), Island Buys (i.e., "Palm Beach Shopping"), all 1,000-1,500 words. Buys 1-2 mss/year. Query. Pays $150.

Fillers: Brief descriptions of new or interesting attractions and festivals in Florida and the Caribbean. Buys 10-12/year. Length 300-800 words. Pays $75 minimum.

MIDWEST EXPRESS MAGAZINE, Paradigm Communications Group, 2701 First Ave., Suite 250, Seattle WA 98121. Editor: Eric Lucas. 90% freelance written. Bimonthly magazine for Midwest Express Airlines. "Positive depiction of the changing economy and culture of the U.S., plus travel and leisure features." Estab. 1993. Circ: 32,000. Pays on publication. Byline given. Offers 33% kill fee. Buys first North American serial rights. Editorial lead time 9 months. Reports in 6 weeks on queries. Do not phone or fax. Sample copy for SASE. Writer's guidelines free on request.

● *Midwest Express* continues to look for sophisticated travel writing.

Nonfiction: Business, travel, sports and leisure. No humor or how-to. "Need good ideas for golf articles in spring." Buys 20-25 mss/year. Query with published clips and résumé. Length: 250-3,000 words. Pays $100 minimum. Sometimes pays expenses of writers on assignment.

Columns/Department: Todd Powell, associate editor. Preview (arts and events), 200-400 words; Portfolio (business-queries to Eric Lucas), 200-500 words. Buys 12-15 mss/year. Query with published clips. Pays $100-150.

Tips: "Article ideas *must* encompass areas within the airline's route system. We buy quality writing from reliable writers. Editorial philosophy emphasizes innovation and positive outlook. Do not send manuscripts unless you have no clips."

SKY, Inflight Magazine of Delta Air Lines, 600 Corporate Dr., Ft. Lauderdale FL 33334. (305)776-0066. Editor: Lidia De Leon. Managing Editor: Barbara Whelehan. 90% freelance written. Monthly magazine. "Delta *SKY* is a general interest, nationally/internationally-oriented magazine with the main purpose to entertain and inform business and leisure travelers aboard Delta Air Lines." Estab. 1971. Circ. 500,000. **Pays on acceptance.** Publishes ms an average of 2 months after acceptance. Byline given. Offers 100% kill fee when cancellation is through no fault of the writer. Buys one-time rights. Submit seasonal/holiday material 9 months in advance. Accepts simultaneous submissions. Query for electronic submissions. Reports in 1 month. Sample copy for 9×12 SAE. Writer's guidelines for #10 SASE.

Nonfiction: General interest, photo feature. "No opinion, religious, reviews, poetry, fiction or fillers." Buys 200-250 mss/year. Query with published clips. Length: 1700-2500 words. Pays $500-700 for assigned articles; $400-500 for unsolicited articles. Pays expenses of writers on assignment.

Photos: State availability of photos with submission. Reviews 4×5 transparencies and 5×7 prints. Offers varying rates on photos. Captions, model releases and identification of subject required. Buys one-time rights.

Columns/Departments: Management (managerial techniques, methods of topical nature); Living (subjects of topical, contemporary interest); Finance (personal finance, tips). Buys 50-60 mss/year. Query. Length: 1500-1700 words. Pays $400-500.

Tips: "Send a well detailed query tied in to one of the feature or column categories of the magazine. Since our lead times call for planning of editorial content 6-9 months in advance, that should also be kept in mind when proposing story ideas. All feature story and column/department categories are open to freelancers, with the exceptions of Travel (areas are predetermined by the airline) and the executive Profile Series (which is also predetermined)."

‡USAIR MAGAZINE, NYT Custom Publishing, 122 E. 42nd St., New York NY 10168. Editor: Catherine Sabino. Contact: Justin D. McCarthy, assistant editor. 95% freelance written. Monthly magazine covering travel/lifestyle. Estab. 1979. Circ. 450,000. **Pays on acceptance.** Publishes ms an average of 6 months after acceptance. Byline given. Offer 25% kill fee. Editorial lead time 3 months. No simultaneous submissions. Reports in 3 weeks on queries. Sample copy for $5. Writer's guidelines for #10 SASE.

Nonfiction: General interest, interview/profile, travel, lifestyle, essays. Buys 120-150 mss/year. Query with published clips. Length: 850-2,200. Pays approximately $1/word. Sometimes pays expenses of writers on assignment.

Photos: State availability of photos with submission. Reviews contact sheets, negatives, transparencies. Negotiates payment individually. Model releases, identification of subjects required. Buys one-time rights.
Columns/Departments: Buys 80-100 mss/year. Query with published clips. Pays approximately $1/word.
Tips: "Study the magazine—offer a clear, intelligent writing style. Queries for story ideas should be short and well-thought out. Any correspondence should include SASE."

Juvenile

Just as children change and grow, so do juvenile magazines. Children's magazine editors stress that writers must read recent issues. This section lists publications for children ages 2-12. Magazines for young people 13-19 appear in the Teen and Young Adult category. Many of the following publications are produced by religious groups and, where possible, the specific denomination is given. A directory for juvenile markets, *Children's Writer's and Illustrator's Market*, is available from Writer's Digest Books.

BOYS' LIFE, Boy Scouts of America, P.O. Box 152079, Irving TX 75015-2079. Editor: Scott Stuckey. 75% freelance written. Prefers to work with published/established writers; works with small number of new/unpublished writers each year. Monthly magazine covering activities of interest to all boys ages 8-18. Most readers are Scouts or Cub Scouts. Estab. 1911. Circ 1.3 million. **Pays on acceptance.** Publishes ms an average of 6-12 months after acceptance. Buys one-time rights. Reports in 6 weeks. Sample copy for $2.50 and 9×12 SAE. Writer's guidelines for #10 SASE.
Nonfiction: Major articles run 750-1,500 words; preferred length is about 1,000 words including sidebars and boxes. Pays minimum $500 for major article text. Uses strong photo features with about 500 words of text. Separate payment or assignment for photos. "Much better rates if you really know how to write for our market." Buys 60 major articles/year. Also needs how-to features and hobby and crafts ideas. Query all nonfiction ideas in writing with SASE. Pays expenses of writers on assignment. Also buys freelance comics pages and scripts. Query first in writing, not by phone.
Columns: "Food, Health, Pets, Bicycling, Sports, Electronics, Space and Aviation, Science, Entertainment, Music, History, Cars and Magic are some of the columns for which we use 400-600 words of text. This is a good place to show us what you can do. Query first in writing." Pays $150-350. Buys 75-80 columns/year.
Fiction: Short stories 1,000-1,500 words; rarely longer. Send complete ms with SASE. Pays $500 minimum. Buys 15 short stories/year.
Tips: "We strongly recommend reading at least 12 issues of the magazine before you submit queries. We are a good market for any writer willing to do the necessary homework."

CALLIOPE: The World History Magazine for Young People, Cobblestone Publishing, Inc., 7 School St., Peterborough NH 03458-1454. (603)924-7209. Fax: (603)924-7380. Editors: Rosalie and Charles Baker. 50% freelance written. Prefers to work with published/established writers. Magazine published 5 times/year covering world history through 1800 AD for 8- to 14-year-olds. Articles must relate to the issue's theme. Pays on publication. Byline given. Buys all rights. Accepts simultaneous submissions. Previously published submissions rarely accepted. Sample copy for $4.50 and 7½×10½ SASE with 4 first-class stamps. Writer's guidelines for SASE.
Nonfiction: Essays, general interest, historical/nostalgic, how-to (activities), recipes, humor, interview/profile, personal experience, photo feature, technical, travel. Articles must relate to the theme. No religious, pornographic, biased or sophisticated submissions. Buys approximately 30-40 mss/year. Query with published clips. Feature articles 700-800 words. Pays 20-25¢/printed word. Supplemental nonfiction 300-600 words. Pays 20-25¢/printed word.
Photos: State availability of photos with submission. Reviews contact sheets, color slides and b&w prints. Buys one-time rights. Pays $15-100 for b&w (color cover negotiated).
Fiction: All fiction must be theme-related. Buys 10 mss/year. Query with published clips. Length: up to 800 words. Pays 20-25¢/word.
Poetry: Light verse, traditional. No religious or pornographic poetry or poetry not related to the theme. Submit maximum 1 poem. Pays on individual basis. Poetry, up to 100 lines.
Columns/Departments: Puzzles and Games (no word finds); crossword and other word puzzles using the vocabulary of the issue's themes; mazes and picture puzzles that relate to the theme. Pays on an individual basis.
Tips: "Writers must have an appreciation and understanding of world history. Writers must not condescend to our readers."

CHICKADEE MAGAZINE, For Young Children from *OWL*, Owl Communications, 179 John St., Suite 500, Toronto, Ontario M5T 3G5 Canada. (416)971-5275. Editor: Lizann Flatt. 25% freelance written. Magazine

published 10 times/year (except July and August) for 3- to 8-year-olds. "We aim to interest young children in the world around them in an entertaining and lively way." Estab. 1979. Circ. 110,000 Canada and US. **Pays on acceptance.** Byline given. Buys all rights. Reports in 2 months. Sample copy for $3.50 and SAE ($1 money order or IRC's). Writer's guidelines for SAE.
Nonfiction: How-to (easy and unusual arts and crafts); personal experience (real children in real situations). No articles for older children; no religious or moralistic features.
Photos: Send photos with ms. Reviews 35mm transparencies. Identification of subjects required.
Fiction: Adventure (relating to the 3-8-year-old), humor. No talking animal stories or religious articles. Send complete ms with $1 money order for handling and return postage. Pays $210 (US).
Tips: "A frequent mistake made by writers is trying to teach too much—not enough entertainment and fun."

CHILD LIFE, Children's Better Health Institute, P.O. Box 567, Indianapolis IN 46206-0567. (317)636-8881. Fax: (317)684-8094. Editor: Lise Hoffman. 80% freelance written. Magazine (published 8 times/year) covering "general topics of interest to children—emphasis on health preferred but not necessary." Pays on publication. Byline given. Buys all rights. Submit seasonal/holiday material 8 months in advance. Reports in 2 months. Sample copy for $1.25. Writer's guidelines for #10 SASE.
Nonfiction: Profiles of child and adult athletes or those with active hobbies, accompanied by professional quality slides suitable for the cover, how-to (simple crafts), anything children might like—health topics preferred. Buys 20 mss/year. Send complete ms. Length: 400-800. Pays up to 12¢/word.
Photos: Send photos only with accompanying editorial material. Reviews transparencies. Offers $20-30 for inside color photo, $50 for front cover. Please, no snapshots; professional-quality slides or photos only. Captions, model releases and identification of subjects required. Buys one-time rights.
Columns/Departments: Regular columns especially hospitable to freelancers include "One World, Fun World: Games from the Global Village," "Odd Jobs," "Odd Hobbies" and "Snack Attack," (a recipe column). Query for descriptions with #10 SASE.
Fiction: Adventure, fantasy, historical, humorous, multicultural, mystery, science fiction, suspense. All must be geared to children (9-11 years old). Buys 20-25 mss/year. Send complete ms. Length: 400-800 words. Pays up to 12¢/word.
Poetry: Free verse, haiku, light verse, traditional. No long "deep" poetry not suited for children. Buys 8 poems/year. Submit maximum 5 poems. Pays $20-30.
Fillers: "Constant, ongoing demand for puzzles, games, mazes, etc." Variable pay.
Tips: "Present health-related items in an interesting, non-textbook manner. The approach to health fiction can be subtle—tell a good story first. We also consider non-health items—make them fresh and enjoyable for children."

CHILDREN'S DIGEST, Children's Better Health Institute, P.O. Box 567, Indianapolis IN 46206-0567. (317)636-8881. Fax: (317)684-8094. Editor: Layne Cameron. 85% freelance written. Works with a small number of new/unpublished writers each year. Magazine published 8 times/year covering children's health for preteen children. Estab. 1950. Pays on publication. Publishes ms an average of 1 year after acceptance. Byline given. Buys all rights. Submit seasonal/holiday material 8 months in advance. Submit *only* complete mss. "No queries, please." Reports in 2 months. Sample copy for $1.25. Writer's guidelines for #10 SASE.
• *Children's Digest* would like to see more photo stories about environmental topics and concerns and more nonfiction in general.
Nonfiction: Historical, interview/profile (biographical), craft ideas, health, nutrition, fitness and sports. "We're especially interested in factual features that teach readers about fitness and sports or encourage them to develop better health habits. We are *not* interested in material that is simply rewritten from encyclopedias. We try to present our health material in a way that instructs *and* entertains the reader." Buys 15-20 mss/ year. Send complete ms. Length: 500-1,000 words. Pays up to 12¢/word. Sometimes pays the expenses of writers on assignment.
Photos: State availability of full color or b&w photos. Payment varies. Model releases and identification of subjects required. Buys one-time rights.
Fiction: Adventure, humorous, mainstream, mystery. Stories should appeal to both boys and girls. "We need some stories that incorporate a health theme. However, we don't want stories that preach, preferring instead stories with implied morals. We like a light or humorous approach." Buys 15-20 mss/year. Length: 500-1,500 words. Pays up to 12¢/word.
Poetry: Pays $20 minimum.
Tips: "Many of our readers have working mothers and/or come from single-parent homes. We need more stories that reflect these changing times while communicating good values."

CHILDREN'S PLAYMATE, Children's Better Health Institute, P.O. Box 567, Indianapolis IN 46206-0567. (317)636-8881. Editor: Sandy Grieshop. 75% freelance written. Eager to work with new/unpublished writers. Magazine published 8 times/year. "We are looking for articles, stories, and activities with a health, sports, fitness or nutritionally oriented theme. We also publish general interest fiction and nonfiction. We try to present our material in a positive light, and we try to incorporate humor and a light approach wherever possible without minimizing the seriousness of what we are saying." For children ages 6-8. Estab. 1928.

Buys all rights. Byline given. Pays on publication. Publishes ms an average of 1 year after acceptance. Submit seasonal material 8 months in advance. Reports in 3 months. Sometimes may hold mss for up to 1 year, with author's permission. "Material will not be returned unless accompanied by a SASE." Sample copy for $1.25. Writer's guidelines for #10 SASE.

Nonfiction: 500 words maximum. "A feature may be an interesting presentation on animals, people, events, objects or places, especially about good health, exercise, proper nutrition and safety. Include word count. Buys 40 mss/year. "We would very much like to see more nonfiction features on nature and gardening. We do not consider outlines. Reading the whole manuscript is the only way to give fair consideration." No queries. Pays up to 17¢/word.

Fiction: Short stories for beginning readers, not over 700 words. Seasonal stories with holiday themes. Humorous stories, unusual plots. "We are interested in stories about children in different cultures and stories about lesser-known holidays (not just Christmas, Thanksgiving, Halloween, Hanukkah)." Vocabulary suitable for ages 6-8. Submit complete ms. Pays up to 17¢/word. Include word count with stories.

Fillers: Recipes, puzzles, dot-to-dots, color-ins, hidden pictures, mazes. Buys 30 fillers/year. Payment varies. Prefers camera-ready activities. Activity guidelines for #10 SASE.

Tips: Especially interested in features, stories, poems and articles about special holidays.

‡CLUB KIDSOFT, The Software Magazine for Kids, Kidsoft, Inc., 414 Jackson St., Suite 304, San Francisco CA 94111. Managing Editor: Lana Olson. 50% freelance written. Quarterly magazine. "We publish features and activities that encourage children ages 4-14 to use software." Estab. 1992. Circ. 100,000. Pays on publication. Publishes ms an average of 2-4 months after acceptance. Byline given sometimes. Kill fee varies. Buys all rights. Editorial lead time varies. Query for electronic submissions. Sample copy available in computer stores. Writer's guidelines free on request.

Nonfiction: Kids and computers—written for kids. "We assign everything and accept only solicited manuscripts." Buys 20 mss/year. Query with published clips. Length: 200-1,000 words. Pay varies.

Photos: "We arrange for photos."

Tips: "Send us a resume and five published sample articles, written for kids, all nonfiction. Don't send article ideas or manuscripts."

COBBLESTONE: The History Magazine for Young People, Cobblestone Publishing, Inc., 7 School St., Peterborough NH 03458-1457. (603)924-7209. Fax: (603)924-7380. Editor: Meg Chorlian. 100% (except letters and departments) freelance written (approximately 1 issue/year is by assignment only). Prefers to work with published/established writers. Monthly magazine (September-May) covering American history for children ages 8-14. "Each issue presents a particular theme, from different angles, making it exciting as well as informative. Half of all subscriptions are for schools." Circ. 36,000. Pays on publication. Publishes ms an average of 4 months after acceptance. Byline given. Offers 50% kill fee. Buys all rights. All material must relate to monthly theme. Editorial lead time 9 months. Accepts simultaneous and previously published submissions. Query for electronic submissions. Reports in 4 months. Sample copy for $4.50 and 7½ × 10½ SAE with 4 first-class stamps. Writer's guidelines and query deadlines for SASE.

Nonfiction: Historical, interview, plays, biography, recipes, activities, personal experience. "Request a copy of the writer's guidelines to find out specific issue themes in upcoming months." No material that editorializes rather than reports. Buys 80 mss/year. Query with published clips, outline and bibliography. Length: Feature articles 600-800 words. Supplemental nonfiction 300-500 words. Pays 20-25¢/printed word.

Photos: State availability of photos with submission. Reviews contact sheets, transparencies, prints. Offers $15 for non-professional quality, $100 for professional quality. Captions, identification of subjects required. Buys one-time rights.

Fiction: Adventure, ethnic, historical, biographical fiction. "Has to be very strong and accurate." Buys 5 mss/year. Length: 500-800 words. Query with published clips. Pays 20-25¢/printed word.

Poetry: Free verse, light verse, traditional. Buys 5 poems/year. Length: up to 100 lines. Pays on an individual basis. Must relate to theme.

Columns/Departments: Puzzles and Games (no word finds); crossword and other word puzzles using the vocabulary of the issue's theme.

Tips: "All material is considered on the basis of merit and appropriateness to theme. Query should state idea for material simply, with rationale for why material is applicable to theme. Request writer's guidelines (includes themes and query deadlines) before submitting a query. Include SASE. In general, please keep in mind that we are a magazine for children ages 8-14. We want the subject to be interesting and historically accurate, but not condescending to our readers. Queries should include a detailed outline and a bibliography."

CRICKET, Carus Publishing Co., P.O. Box 300, Peru IL 61354-0300. (815)224-6656. Editor-in-Chief: Marianne Carus. Monthly magazine. Estab. 1973. Circ. 100,000. Pays on publication. Byline given. Buys first publication rights in the English language. Submit seasonal/holiday material 1 year in advance. Accepts previously published submissions. Send typed ms with rights for sale noted and information about when and where the article previously appeared. For reprints pays 50% of the amount paid for original article. Reports in 3 months. Sample copy and writer's guidelines for $4 and 9 × 12 SAE. Writer's guidelines only for #10 SASE.

• *Cricket* is looking for more fiction and nonfiction for the older end of its age range.

Nonfiction: Adventure, biography, foreign culture, geography, history, science, social science, sports, technology, travel. (A short bibliography is required for *all* nonfiction articles.) Send complete ms. Length: 200-1,200 words. Pays up to 25¢/word.

Fiction: Adventure, ethnic, fairy tales, fantasy, historical, humorous, mystery, novel excerpts, science fiction, suspense, western. No didactic, sex, religious or horror stories. Buys 24-36 mss/year. Send complete ms. Length: 200-1,500 words. Pays up to 25¢/word.

Poetry: Buys 8-10 poems/year. Length: 50 lines maximum. Pays up to $3/line on publication.

CRUSADER MAGAZINE, P.O. Box 7259, Grand Rapids MI 49510-7259. Fax: (616)241-5558. Editor: G. Richard Broene. 40% freelance written. Works with a small number of new/unpublished writers each year. Magazine published 7 times/year. "*Crusader Magazine* shows boys (9-14) how God is at work in their lives and in the world around them." Estab. 1958. Circ. 14,000. Buys 20-25 mss/year. **Pays on acceptance.** Byline given. Publishes ms an average of 8 months after acceptance. Rights purchased vary with author and material; buys first serial, one-time, second serial (reprint) and simultaneous rights. Submit seasonal material (Christmas, Easter) at least 5 months in advance. Accepts simultaneous submissions. Reports in 2 months. Sample copy and writer's guidelines for 9×12 SAE with 3 first-class stamps.

Nonfiction: Articles about young boys' interests: sports, outdoor activities, bike riding, science, crafts, etc., and problems. Emphasis is on a Christian multi-racial perspective, but no simplistic moralisms. Informational, how-to, personal experience, interview, profile, inspirational, humor. Submit complete ms. Length: 500-1,500 words. Pays 2-5¢/word.

Photos: Pays $4-25 for b&w photos purchased with mss.

Fiction: "Considerable fiction is used. Fast-moving stories that appeal to a boy's sense of adventure or sense of humor are welcome. Avoid preachiness. Avoid simplistic answers to complicated problems. Avoid long dialogue and little action." Length: 900-1,500 words. Pays 2¢/word minimum.

Fillers: Uses short humor and any type of puzzles as fillers.

CURRENT HEALTH 1, The Beginning Guide to Health Education, General Learning Corporation, 60 Revere Dr., Northbrook IL 60062-1563. (708)205-3000. Fax: (708)564-8197. Senior Editor: Carole Rubenstein. 95% freelance written. An educational health periodical published monthly, September-May. "Our audience is 4th-7th grade health education students. Articles should be written at a 5th grade reading level. As a curriculum supplementary publication, info should be accurate, timely, accessible and highly readable." Estab. 1976. Circ. 200,000. Pays on publication. Publishes ms an average of 9 months after acceptance. Buys all rights.

Nonfiction: Health curriculum. Buys 70 mss/year. "We accept no unsolicited mss. *Articles are on assignment only.* Send introductory letter, résumé and clips." Length: 800-2,000 words. Pays $100-400 for assigned articles.

Tips: "We are looking for good writers with an education and health background preferably, who can write for the age group in a firm, accessible, and medically/scientifically accurate way. Ideally, the writer should be an expert in the area in which he or she is writing. Topics open to freelancers are disease, drugs, fitness and exercise, psychology, nutrition, first aid and safety, environment and personal health."

DISCOVERIES, 6401 The Paseo, Kansas City MO 64131. Fax: (816)333-4439. Editor: Rebecca S. Raleigh. Assistant Editor: Jennifer Stone. Mostly freelance written but "we are in recycle and need much less." For boys and girls ages 8-9. Weekly. Estab. 1974. Publishes ms an average of 1 year after acceptance. Buys all rights. "Minimal comments on pre-printed form are made on rejected material." Reports in 3 months. Sample copy and guidelines for #10 SASE.

Fiction: Stories with Christian emphasis on high ideals, wholesome social relationships and activities, right choices, Sabbath observance, church loyalty and missions. *Discoveries* extends the Sunday School lesson with life-related stories of 3rd and 4th grade children. Informal style. Submit complete ms. Length: 500-700 words. Pays 5¢/word.

DOLPHIN LOG, The Cousteau Society, 870 Greenbrier Circle, Suite 402, Chesapeake VA 23320-2641. (804)523-9335. Editor: Elizabeth Foley. 30-40% freelance written. Prefers to work with published/established writers; works with a small number of new/unpublished writers each year. Bimonthly nonfiction magazine covering marine biology, ecology, natural history and the environment. "*Dolphin Log* is an educational publication for children ages 7-13 offered by The Cousteau Society. Subject matter encompasses all areas related to our global water system. The philosophy of the magazine is to delight, instruct and instill an environmental ethic and understanding of the interconnectedness of living organisms, including people." Estab. 1981. Circ. 80,000. Pays on publication. Publishes ms an average of 1 year after acceptance. Byline given. Buys one-time, reprint and translation rights. Reports in 3 months. Sample copy for $2 and 9×12 SAE with 3 first-class stamps. Writer's guidelines for SASE. (Make checks payable to The Cousteau Society.)

Nonfiction: General interest (per guidelines); how-to (water-related crafts or science); photo feature (marine subject). "Of special interest are articles on specific marine creatures, and games involving an ocean/water-related theme which develop math, reading and comprehension skills. Experiments that can be conducted at home and demonstrate a phenomenon or principle of science are wanted, as are clever crafts or art projects which also can be tied to an ocean theme. No 'talking' animals. First-person accounts are discouraged, as are fictional narratives and articles that address the reader." Buys 8-12 mss/year. Query or send complete ms. Length: 400-600 words. Pays $50-150.

Photos: Send photos with query or ms (duplicates only). Prefers underwater animals, water photos with children, photos that explain text. Pays $25-200/photo. Identification of subjects required. Buys one-time and translation rights.

Columns/Departments: Discovery (science experiments or crafts a young person can easily do at home), 50-250 words; Creature Feature (lively article on one specific marine animal), 200-300 words. Buys 1 mss/year. Send complete ms. Pays $25-100.

Poetry: No "talking" animals or dark or religious themes. Buys 1-2 poems/year. Pays $10-100.

Tips: "Find a lively way to relate scientific facts to children without anthropomorphizing. We need to know material is accurate and current. Articles should feature an interesting marine creature and contain factual material that's fun to read. We are especially interested in material that draws information from current scientific research."

‡**FACES, The Magazine About People**, Cobblestone Publishing Co. Inc., 7 School St., Peterborough NH 03458. (603)924-7209. Editor: Carolyn P. Yoder. 90-100% freelance written. Monthly magazine published during school year. "*Faces* stands apart from other children's magazines by offering a solid look at one subject and stressing strong editorial content and black-and-white photographs and original illustrations. *Faces* offers an equal balance of feature articles and activities, as well as folktales and legends." Estab. 1984. Circ. 15,000. Pays on publication. Publishes ms an average of 4 months after acceptance. Byline given. Offers 50% kill fee. Buys all rights. Editorial lead time 10-12 months. Accepts simultaneous submissions. Query for electronic submissions. Sample copy for $4.50 and 7½×10½ SAE with 4 first-class stamps. Writer's guidelines for #10 SASE.

Nonfiction: Historical/nostalgic, humor, interview/profile, personal experience, photo feature, travel, recipes, activities (puzzles, mazes). All must relate to theme. Buys 45-50 mss/year. Query with published clips. Length: 300-1,000. Pays 20-25¢/word.

Photos: State availability of photos with submission or send copies of related images for photo researcher. Reviews contact sheets, transparencies, prints. Offers $15-100 (for professional). Negotiates payment individually (for non-professional). Captions, model releases, identification of subjects required. Buys one-time rights.

Fiction: Ethnic, historical, retold legends or folktales. Depends on theme. Query with published clips. Length: 500-1,000. Pays 20-25¢/word.

Poetry: Avant-garde, free verse, haiku, light verse, traditional. Length: 100 words maximum. Pays on individual basis.

Tips: "Freelancers should send for a sample copy of magazine and a list of upcoming themes and writer's guidelines. The magazine is based on a monthly theme (upcoming themes include Canada, Snakes, Taboos, The Meaning of Ornaments). We appreciate professional queries that follow our detailed writer's guidelines."

THE FRIEND, 50 E. North Temple, Salt Lake City UT 84150. Managing Editor: Vivian Paulsen. 50% freelance written. Eager to work with new/unpublished writers as well as established writers. Appeals to children ages 3-11. Monthly publication of The Church of Jesus Christ of Latter-Day Saints. Circ. 280,000. **Pays on acceptance.** Buys all rights. Submit seasonal material 8 months in advance. Sample copy and writer's guidelines for 75¢ and 9×12 SAE with 4 first-class stamps.

Nonfiction: Subjects of current interest, science, nature, pets, sports, foreign countries, things to make and do. Special issues: Christmas, Easter. "Submit only complete manuscript—no queries, please." No simultaneous submissions. Length: 1,000 words maximum. Pays 9¢/word minimum.

Fiction: Seasonal and holiday stories, stories about other countries and their children. Wholesome and optimistic; high motive, plot and action. Character-building stories preferred. Length: 1,200 words maximum. Stories for younger children should not exceed 250 words. Pays 9¢/word minimum.

Poetry: Serious, humorous, holiday. Any form with child appeal. Pays $25.

Tips: "Do you remember how it feels to be a child? Can you write stories that appeal to children ages 3-11 in today's world? We're interested in stories with an international flavor and those that focus on present-day problems. Send material of high literary quality slanted to our editorial requirements. Let the child solve the problem—not some helpful, all-wise adult. No overt moralizing. Nonfiction should be creatively presented—not an array of facts strung together. Beware of being cutesy."

‡**GIRL'S LIFE**, Monarch Publishing, 4517 Harford Rd., Baltimore MD 21214. Editor: Karen Bokram. Contact: Kelly A. White. Bimonthly magazine covering girls ages 7-14. Estab. 1994. Circ. 200,000. Pays on publication. Publishes ms an average of 3 months after acceptance. Byline sometimes given. Buys first North American serial rights. Editorial lead time 3 months. Submit seasonal material 4-6 months in advance. Reports in 3 months. Sample copy for $2.95. Writer's guidelines for #10 SASE.

Nonfiction: Book excerpts, essays, general interest, historical/nostalgic, how-to (crafts), humor, inspirational, interview/profile, new product, personal experience, photo feature, travel. Buys 20 mss/year. Query with published clips, Length: 700-2,000 words. Pays $150-800 for assigned articles.

Photos: State availability of photos with submission. Reviews contact sheets, negatives, transparencies. Negotiates payment individually. Captions, model releases, identification of subjects required.

Columns/Departments: Outta here! (travel information); Crafts (how-to, cheap); Try It! (new stuff to try); all 1,200 words. Buys 12 mss/year. Query with published clips. Pays $150-450.

Fillers: Gags to be illustrated by cartoonist, short humor. Buys 12/year. Pays $25-100.

Tips: Send queries with published writing samples and detailed résumé.

‡GUIDEPOSTS FOR KIDS, Guideposts Associates, Inc., P.O. Box 538A, Chesterton IN 46304. Editor: Mary Lou Carney. Contact: Sailor Metts. 30% freelance written. Bimonthly magazine. "Value centered—fun to read kids magazine for 7- to 12-year-olds (emphasis on upper end of age bracket). Issue oriented, thought provoking. No preachy stories." Estab. 1990. Circ. 190,000. **Pays on acceptance.** Byline given. Offers 25% kill fee. Buys all rights. Editorial lead time 6 months. Submit seasonal material 6 months in advance. Reports in 6 weeks. Sample copy for $3.25. Writer's guidelines for #10 SASE.

Nonfiction: Issue-oriented features, general interest, historical/nostalgic, humor, inspirational, interview/profile, technical (technology), travel. Does not want articles with adult voice/frame of reference. No Sunday-School-type articles. Buys 12 mss/year. Query. (Send complete ms if under 300 words.) Length: 300-1,500 words. Pays $100-400. Sometimes pays expenses of writers on assignment.

Photos: State availability of or send photos with submission. Negotiates payment individually. Identification of subjects required. Buys one-time rights.

Columns/Departments: Tips from the Top (Christian celebrities), 650 words; Featuring Kids (Profiles of interesting Kids), 300 words; Building a Better Me (value-centered how-to), 300 words. Buys 8 mss/year. Query. Send complete ms. Pays $100-350.

Fiction: Adventure, fantasy, historical, humorous, mystery, suspense, western. Buys 8 mss/year. Send complete ms. Length: 700-1,300 words. Pays $200-400.

Fillers: Facts, newsbreaks, short humor. Buys 4/year. Length: 250 words maximum. Pays $25-100.

Tips: "Before you submit to one of our departments, study the magazine. In most of our pieces, we look for a strong kid voice/viewpoint. We do not want preachy or overtly religious material. Looking for value-driven stories and profiles. In the fiction arena, we are very interested in historical and mysteries. In nonfiction, we welcome tough themes and current issues."

HIGHLIGHTS FOR CHILDREN, 803 Church St., Honesdale PA 18431-1824. Fax: (717)253-0179. Editor: Kent L. Brown Jr. Manuscript Coordinator: Beth Troop. 80% freelance written. Monthly magazine for children ages 2-12. Estab. 1946. Circ. 2.8 million. **Pays on acceptance.** Buys all rights. Reports in about 2 months. Free sample copy. Writer's guidelines for #10 SASE.

  • *Highlights* has a growing need for nonfiction articles geared to young readers (ages 6-8).

Nonfiction: "We need articles on science, technology and nature written by persons with strong backgrounds in those fields. Contributions always welcomed from new writers, especially engineers, scientists, historians, teachers, etc., who can make useful, interesting facts accessible to children. Also writers who have lived abroad and can interpret the ways of life, especially of children, in other countries in ways that will foster world brotherhood. Sports material, biographies and articles of general interest to children. Direct, original approach, simple style, interesting content, not rewritten from encyclopedias. State background and qualifications for writing factual articles submitted. Include references or sources of information." Length: 900 words maximum. Pays $125 minimum. Also buys original party plans for children ages 7-12, clearly described in 300-600 words, including drawings or samples of items to be illustrated. Also, novel but tested ideas in crafts, with clear directions and made-up models. Projects must require only free or inexpensive, easy-to-obtain materials. Especially desirable if easy enough for early primary grades. Also, fingerplays with lots of action, easy for very young children to grasp and to dramatize. Avoid wordiness. We need creative-thinking puzzles that can be illustrated, optical illusions, brain teasers, games of physical agility and other 'fun' activities." Pays minimum $35 for party plans; $20 for crafts ideas; $25 for fingerplays.

Fiction: Unusual, meaningful stories appealing to both girls and boys, ages 2-12. "Vivid, full of action. Engaging plot, strong characterization, lively language." Prefers stories in which a child protagonist solves a dilemma through his or her own resources. Seeks stories that the child ages 8-12 will eagerly read, and the child ages 2-7 will begin to read and/or will like to hear when read aloud (400-900 words). "We publish stories in the suspense/adventure/mystery, fantasy and humor category, all requiring interesting plot and a number of illustration possiblities. Also need rebuses (picture stories 125 words or under), stories with urban settings, stories for beginning readers (100-400 words), sports and horse stories and retold folk tales. We also would like to see more material of 1-page length (300-500 words), both fiction and factual. War, crime and violence are taboo." Pays $120 minimum.

Tips: "We are pleased that many authors of children's literature report that their first published work was in the pages of *Highlights*. It is not our policy to consider fiction on the strength of the reputation of the author. We judge each submission on its own merits. With factual material, however, we do prefer that writers be authorities in their field or people with first-hand experience. In this manner we can avoid the encyclopedic article that merely restates information readily available elsewhere. We don't make assignments. Query with simple letter to establish whether the nonfiction *subject* is likely to be of interest. A beginning writer should first become familiar with the type of material that *Highlights* publishes. Include special qualifications, if any, of author. Write for the child, not the editor."

HOPSCOTCH, The Magazine for Girls, Bluffton News Publishing & Printing Co., P.O. Box 164, Bluffton OH 45817-0164. (419)358-4610. Fax: (419)358-5027. Editor: Marilyn B. Edwards. Editor's Assistant: Becky Jackman. 90% freelance written. Bimonthly magazine on basic subjects of interest to young girls. "*HOP-SCOTCH* is a digest-size magazine with a four-color cover and two-color format inside. It is designed for girls ages 6-12 and features pets, crafts, hobbies, games, science, fiction, history, puzzles, careers, etc." Estab. 1989. Pays on publication. Byline given. Buys first and second rights. Submit seasonal/holiday material 6-8 months in advance. Accepts simultaneous and previously published submissions. Send tearsheet or photocopy of article or typed ms with rights for sale noted. For reprints, pays 100% of the amount paid for original article. Reports in 3 weeks on queries; 2 months on mss. Sample copy for $3. Writer's guidelines, current theme list and needs for #10 SASE.

• *Hopscotch* has a new magazine, *Boys' Quest*, for ages 6-13. It has the same old-fashioned principles that *Hopscotch* has and is a good market for freelance writers. Send $3 for copy and guidelines.

Nonfiction: Book excerpts, general interest, historical/nostalgic, how-to (crafts), humor, inspirational, interview/profile, personal experience, pets, games, fiction, careers, sports, cooking. "No fashion, hairstyles, sex or dating articles." Buys 60 mss/year. Send complete ms. Length: 400-1,100 words. Pays $30-100.

Photos: Send photos with submission. Prefers b&w photos, but color photos accepted. Offers $7.50-10/photo. Captions, model releases and identification of subjects required. Buys one-time rights.

Columns/Departments: Science—nature, crafts, pets, cooking (basic), 400-1,000 words. Send complete ms. Pays $25-60.

Fiction: Adventure, fantasy, historical, humorous, mainstream, mystery, novel excerpts, suspense. Buys 15 mss/year. Send complete ms. Length: 600-1,000 words. Pays $30-70.

Poetry: Free verse, light verse, traditional. "No experimental or obscure poetry." Submit maximum 6 poems. Pays $10-30.

Tips: "Almost all sections are open to freelancers. Freelancers should remember that *HOPSCOTCH* is a bit old-fashioned, appealing to *young* girls (6-12). We cherish nonfiction pieces that have a young girl or young girls directly involved in unusual and/or worthwhile activities. Any piece accompanied by decent photos stands an even better chance of being accepted."

HUMPTY DUMPTY'S MAGAZINE, Children's Better Health Institute, P.O. Box 567, Indianapolis IN 46206-0567. Editor: Janet Hoover. 90% freelance written. "We try not to be overly influenced by an author's credits, preferring instead to judge each submission on its own merit." Bimonthly magazine (monthly March, June, September, December) covering health, nutrition, hygiene, exercise and safety for children ages 4-6. Pays on publication. Publishes ms at least 8 months after acceptance. Buys all rights (but will return one-time book rights if author has name of interested publisher and tentative date of publication). Submit seasonal material 8 months in advance. Reports in 3 months. Sample copy for $1.25. Writer's guidelines for #10 SASE.

Nonfiction: "We are open to nonfiction on almost any age-appropriate subject, but we especially need material with a health theme—nutrition, safety, exercise, hygiene. We're looking for articles that encourage readers to develop better health habits without preaching. Very simple factual articles that creatively teach readers about their bodies. We use simple crafts, some with holiday themes. We also use several puzzles and activities in each issue—dot-to-dot, hidden pictures and other activities that promote following instructions, developing finger dexterity and working with numbers and letters. Submit complete ms with word count. Length: 500 words maximum. Pays up to 22¢/word.

Fiction: "We use some stories in rhyme and a few easy-to-read stories for the beginning reader. All stories should work well as read alouds. Currently we need sports/fitness stories and seasonal stories with holiday themes. We use contemporary stories and fantasy, some employing a health theme. We try to present our health material in a positive light, incorporating humor and a light approach wherever possible. Avoid stereotyping. Characters in contemporary stories should be realistic and up-to-date. Remember, many of our readers have working mothers and/or come from single-parent homes. We need more stories that reflect these changing times but at the same time communicate good, wholesome values." Submit complete ms with word count. Length: 500 words maximum. Pays up to 22¢/word.

Poetry: Short, simple poems. Pays $20 minimum.

Tips: "Writing for *Humpty Dumpty* is similar to writing picture book manuscripts. There must be a great economy of words. We strive for at least 50% art per page (in stories and articles), so space for text is limited. Because the illustrations are so important, stories should lend themselves well to visual imagery."

JACK AND JILL, Children's Better Health Institute, P.O. Box 567, Indianapolis IN 46206-0567. (317)636-8881. Editor: Daniel Lee. 70% freelance written. Magazine published 8 times/year for children ages 7-10. Pays on publication. Publishes ms an average of 8 months after acceptance. Buys all rights. Byline given. Submit seasonal material 8 months in advance. Reports in 10 weeks. May hold material being seriously considered for up to 1 year. "Material will not be returned unless accompanied by SASE with sufficient postage." Sample copy for $1.25. Writer's guidelines for #10 SASE.

Nonfiction: "Because we want to encourage youngsters to read for pleasure and for information, we are interested in material that will challenge a young child's intelligence *and* be enjoyable reading. Our emphasis is on good health, and we are in particular need of articles, stories, and activities with health, safety, exercise and nutrition themes. We try to present our health material in a positive light—incorporating humor and a light approach wherever possible without minimizing the seriousness of what we are saying." Straight factual articles are OK if they are short and interestingly written. "We would rather see, however, more creative alternatives to the straight factual article. For instance, we'd be interested in seeing a health message or facts presented in articles featuring positive role models for readers. Many of the personalities children admire— athletes, musicians, and film or TV stars—are fitness or nutrition buffs. Many have kicked drugs, alcohol or smoking habits and are outspoken about the dangers of these vices. Color slides, transparencies or b&w photos accompanying this type of article would greatly enhance salability." Buys 10-15 nonfiction mss/year. Length: 500-800 words. Pays a minimum of 15¢/word.

Photos: When appropriate, photos should accompany ms. Reviews sharp, contrasting b&w glossy prints. Sometimes uses color slides, transparencies or good color prints. Pays $20 for b&w, $35 for color, minimum of $50 for cover. Buys one-time rights.

Fiction: May include, but is not limited to, realistic stories, fantasy adventure—set in past, present or future. "All stories need a well-developed plot, action and incident. Humor is highly desirable. Stories that deal with a health theme need not have health as the primary subject." Length: 500-800 words (short stories). Pays 10¢/word minimum. Buys 20-25 mss/year.

Fillers: Puzzles (including various kinds of word and crossword puzzles), poems, games, science projects, and creative craft projects. Instructions for activities should be clearly and simply written and accompanied by models or diagram sketches. "We also have a need for recipes. Ingredients should be healthful; avoid sugar, salt, chocolate, red meat and fats as much as possible. In all material, avoid references to eating sugary foods, such as candy, cakes, cookies and soft drinks."

Tips: "We are constantly looking for new writers who can tell good stories with interesting slants—stories that are not full of out-dated and time-worn expressions. Our best authors are writers who know what today's children are like. Keep in mind that our readers are becoming 'computer literate', living in an age of rapidly developing technology. They are exploring career possibilities that may be new and unfamiliar to our generation. They are faced with tough decisions about drug and alcohol use. Many of them are latch-key children because both parents work or they come from single-parent homes. We need more stories and articles that reflect these changing times but that also communicate good, wholesome values. Obtain *current* issues of the magazines and *study* them to determine our present needs and editorial style."

LADYBUG, the Magazine for Young Children, Carus Publishing Co., P.O. Box 300, Peru IL 61354-0300. (815)224-6643. Editor-in-Chief: Marianne Carus. Editor: Paula Morrow. Monthly general interest magazine for children (ages 2-6). "We look for quality writing—quality literature, no matter the subject." Estab. 1973. Circ. 130,000. Pays on publication. Byline given. All accepted mss are published. Buys first publication rights in the English language. Submit seasonal/holiday material 1 year in advance. Accepts simultaneous submissions. Do not query; send completed ms. Reports in 3 months. Sample copy and guidelines for $4 and 9×12 SAE. Guidelines only for #10 SASE.

● *Ladybug* needs even more activities based on concepts (size, color, sequence, comparison, etc.) and interesting, appropriate nonfiction. Also needs articles and parent-child activities for its parents' section. See sample issues for what they like.

Columns/Departments: Can You Do This?, 2-3 pages; The World Around You, 2-4 pages; activities based on concepts (size, color, sequence, comparison, etc.), 1-2 pages. Buys 35 mss/year. Send complete ms. "Most *Ladybug* nonfiction is in the form of illustration. We'd like more simple science, how-things-work and behind-the-scenes on a preschool level. Maximum length 250-300 words."

Fiction: Adventure, ethnic, fantasy, folkore, humorous, mainstream, mystery. Buys 30 mss/year. Send complete ms. Length: 850 maximum words. Pays up to 25¢/word.

Poetry: Light verse, traditional, humorous. Buys 20 poems/year. Submit *maximum* 5 poems. Length: 20 lines maximum. Pays up to $3/line.

Fillers: Anecdotes, facts, short humor. Buys 10/year. Length: 250 (approximately) maximum words. Pays up to 25¢/word. We welcome interactive activities: rebuses, up to 100 words; *original* fingerplays and action rhymes (up to 8 lines).

Tips: "Reread a manuscript *before* sending it in. Be sure to keep within specified word limits. Study back issues before submitting to learn about the types of material we're looking for. Writing style is paramount. We look for rich, evocative language and a sense of joy or wonder. Remember that you're writing for preschoolers—be age-appropriate but not condescending. A story must hold enjoyment for both parent and child through repeated read-aloud sessions. Remember that we live in a multicultural world. People come in all colors, sizes, physical conditions and have special needs. Be inclusive!"

‡NEW MOON: THE MAGAZINE FOR GIRLS & THEIR DREAMS, New Moon Publishing, Inc., P.O. Box 3620, Duluth MN 55803. Managing Editor: Joe Kelly. 10% freelance written. Bimonthly magazine covering girls ages 8-14, edited by girls aged 8-14. "In general, all material should be pro-girl and feature girls and women as the primary focus. *New Moon* is for every girl who wants her voice heard and her dreams taken seriously." Estab. 1992. Circ. 25,000. Pays on publication. Publishes ms 2 months after acceptance. Byline given. Buys first rights and second serial (reprint) rights. Editorial lead time 6 months. Submit seasonal material 10 months in advance. Accepts simultaneous and previously published submissions. Query for electronic submissions. Reports in 2 months on queries; 3 months on mss. Sample copy for $6.50. Writer's guidelines free on request.

Nonfiction: General interest, humor, inspirational, interview/profile, opinion, personal experience, photo feature, religious, technical, travel, multicultural/girls from other countries. Buys 6 mss/year. Query. Length: 300-900 words. Pays 4-8¢/word.

Photos: State availability of photos with submission. Reviews 4×5 prints. Negotiates payment individually. Captions, model releases, identification of subjects required. Buys one-time rights.

Columns/Departments: Global Village (girl's life in another country), 600-900 words; Women's Work (profile of a woman's career), 600-900 words; She Did It (real girls doing real things), 300-600 words. Buys 3 mss/year. Query. Pays 4-8¢/word.

Fiction: Adventure, experimental, fantasy, historical, humorous, mystery, religious, romance, science fiction, serialized novels (on occasion), slice-of-life vignettes, suspense, girl centered. Buys 3 mss/year. Query. Send complete ms. Length: 300-900 words. Pays 4-8¢/word.

Poetry: Avant-garde, free verse, haiku, light verse. Buys 1 poem/year. Does not pay for poetry.

Tips: "Writers and artists who comprehend our goals have the best chance of publication. Refer to our guidelines and upcoming themes."

ON THE LINE, Mennonite Publishing House, 616 Walnut Ave., Scottdale PA 15683-1999. (412)887-8500. Fax: (412)887-3111. Editor: Mary Clemens Meyer. 90% freelance written. Works with a small number of new/unpublished writers each year. Weekly magazine for children ages 10-14. Estab. 1908. Circ. 6,500. **Pays on acceptance.** Publishes ms an average of 1 year after acceptance. Byline given. Buys one-time rights. Submit seasonal/holiday material 6 months in advance. Accepts simultaneous and previously published submissions. Reports in 1 month. Sample copy for 9×12 SAE with 2 first-class stamps.

Nonfiction: How-to (things to make with easy-to-get materials); informational (350-500 word articles on wonders of nature, people who have made outstanding contributions). Buys 95 unsolicited mss/year. Send complete ms. Pays $10-30.

Photos: Photos purchased with or without ms. Pays $25-50 for 8×10 b&w photos. Total purchase price for ms includes payment for photos.

Fiction: Adventure, humorous, religious. Buys 52 mss/year. Send complete ms. Length: 1,000-1,500 words. Pays 2-4¢/word.

Poetry: Light verse, religious. Length: 3-12 lines. Pays $5-15.

Tips: "Study the publication first. We need short well-written how-to and craft articles. Don't send query; we prefer to see the complete manuscript."

OUTSIDE KIDS, Mariah Media Inc., Outside Plaza, 400 Market St., Santa Fe NM 87501. (505)989-7100. Editor: Lisa Twyman Bessone. Contact: John Alderman. 100% freelance written. Quarterly magazine covering the outdoors for kids 15 and under. "*Outside Kids* is targeted to readers 8-15. We cover adventure travel, outdoor sports, wildlife, the environment, etc. Most of our subjects are kids. Quite a few of our pieces are written by kids." Estab. 1993. Circ. 150,000. Pays on publication. Publishes ms an average of 2 months after acceptance. Byline given. Offers 20% kill fee. Buys first North American serial rights, electronic rights. Editorial lead time 6 months. Submit seasonal material 8 months in advance. Query for electronic submissions. Writer's guidelines for #10 SASE.

Nonfiction: Buys 30 mss/year. Query with published clips. Length: 1,000-1,500 words.

Photos: State availability of photos with submission. Reviews transparencies. Negotiates payment individually. Buys one-time rights.

OWL MAGAZINE, The Discovery Magazine for Children, Owl Communications, 179 John St., Suite 500, Toronto, Ontario M5T 3G5 Canada. (416)971-5275. Editor: Nyla Ahmad. Managing Editor: Keltie Thomas. 25% freelance written. Works with small number of new writers each year. Magazine published 10 times/year (no July or August issues) covering science and nature. Aims to interest children in their environment through accurate, factual information about the world presented in an easy, lively style. Estab. 1976. Circ. 160,000. **Pays on acceptance.** Publishes ms an average of 3 months after acceptance. Byline given. Buys all rights. Submit seasonal/holiday material 1 year in advance. Reports in 10 weeks. Sample copy for $4.28. Writer's guidelines for SAE (large envelope if requesting sample copy) and money order for $1 postage (no stamps please).

Nonfiction: Personal experience (real life children in real situations); photo feature (natural science, international wildlife, and outdoor features); science and environmental features. No problem stories with drugs, sex or moralistic views, or talking animal stories. Query with clips of published work.

Photos: State availability of photos. Reviews 35mm transparencies. Identification of subjects required. Send for photo package before submitting material.

Tips: "Write for editorial guidelines first. Review back issues of the magazine for content and style. Know your topic and approach it from an unusual perspective. Our magazine never talks down to children. We would like to see more articles about science and technology that aren't too academic."

POCKETS, The Upper Room, P.O. Box 189, Nashville TN 37202-0189. (615)340-7333. Fax: (615)340-7006. Editor: Janet R. Knight. Associate Editor: Lynn Gilliam. 60% freelance written. Eager to work with new/unpublished writers. Monthly magazine (except January/February issues) covering children's and families spiritual formation. "We are a Christian, non-denominational publication for children 6 to 12 years of age." Estab. 1981. Circ. 94,000. **Pays on acceptance.** Byline given. Offers 4¢/word kill fee. Buys first North American serial rights. Submit seasonal/holiday material 1 year in advance. Accepts previously published submissions. Send typed ms with rights for sale noted and information about when and where the article previously appeared. For reprints, pays 100% of amount paid for original article. Reports in 10 weeks on mss. Sample copy for 7½×10½ SAE with 4 first-class stamps. Writer's guidelines and themes for #10 SASE.

• *Pockets* has expanded to 48 pages and is needing more fiction and poetry.

Nonfiction: Interview/profile, religious (retold scripture stories), personal experience. List of themes for special issues available with SASE. No violence or romance. Buys 5 mss/year. Send complete ms. Length: 600-1,500 words. Pays 12¢/word.

Photos: Send photos with submission. Prefer no photos unless they accompany an article. Reviews contact sheets, transparencies and prints. Offers $25-50/photo. Buys one-time rights.

Columns Departments: Refrigerator Door (poetry and prayer related to themes), 25 lines; Pocketsful of Love (family communications activities), 300 words; Activities/Games ($25 and up); Peacemakers at Work (profiles of people, particularly children, working for peace, justice and ecological concerns), 300-800 words. Buys 20 mss/year. Send complete ms. Pays 12¢/word; recipes $25.

Fiction: Adventure, ethnic, slice-of-life. "Stories should reflect the child's everyday experiences through a Christian approach. This is often more acceptable when stories are not preachy or overtly Christian." Buys 44 mss/year. Send complete ms. Length: 750-1,600 words. Pays 12¢/word and up.

Poetry: Buys 22 poems/year. Length: 4-25 lines. Pays $25-50.

Tips: "Theme stories, role models and retold scripture stories are most open to freelancers. We are also looking for nonfiction stories about children involved in peace/justic/ecology efforts. Poetry is also open, but we rarely receive an acceptable poem. It's very helpful if writers send for our themes. These are *not* the same as writer's guidelines."

POWER AND LIGHT, 6401 The Paseo, Kansas City MO 64131. Fax: (816)333-4439. Editor: Beula Postlewait. Associate Editor: Melissa Hammer. Mostly freelance written. Weekly magazine for boys and girls ages 11-12 using WordAction Sunday School curriculum. Estab. 1992. Publishes ms an average of 1 year after acceptance. Buys multiple use rights. "Minimal comments on pre-printed form are made on rejected material." Accepts previously published submissions. Send tearsheet or photocopy of article or typed ms with rights for sale noted and information about when and where article previously appeared. For reprints pays 3½¢/word. Reports in 3 months. Sample copy and guidelines for SASE.

Fiction: Stories with Christian emphasis on high ideals, wholesome social relationships and activities and right choices. Informal style. Submit complete ms. Length: 500-700 words. Pays 5¢/word.

Tips: "All themes and outcomes should conform to the theology and practices of the Church of the Nazarene."

‡PRIMARY STREET AND PRESCHOOL PLAYHOUSE, Urban Ministries, Inc., 1350 W. 103rd St., Chicago IL 60643. (312)233-4499. Editor: Judith Hull. 25% freelance written. Sunday School curriculum; quarterly magazine covering Bible lessons for African-American children. Estab. 1975. Circ. 40,000. Pays 2 months after acceptance. Publishes ms an average of 9 months after acceptance. No byline. Buys all rights. Submit seasonal material 9 months in advance. Query for electronic submissions. Reports in 26 weeks. Sample copy and writer's guidelines free.

Nonfiction: Religious. "We only publish assigned manuscripts, but writers may send sample of their work." Buys 32 mss/year. Query. Pays $80 maximum.

Photos: Offers $25 minimum/photo. Model releases required. Buys all rights.

Columns/Departments: Sunday School lesson, 13 pages. Buys 32 mss/year. Query. Pays $80 minimum.

Tips: "Look at our publication and guidelines. Then submit a sample lesson."

R-A-D-A-R, 8121 Hamilton Ave., Cincinnati OH 45231. (513)931-4050. Fax: (513)931-0904. Editor: Elaina Meyers. 75% freelance written. Prefers to work with published/established writers; works with a small number of new/unpublished writers each year. Weekly for children in grades 3-6 in Christian Sunday schools. Estab. 1866 (publishing house). Rights purchased varies with author and material; prefers buying first serial rights, but will buy second (reprint) rights. Occasionally overstocked. **Pays on acceptance.** Publishes ms an average of 6-12 months after acceptance. Submit seasonal material 1 year in advance. Accepts previously published submissions. Send tearsheet or photocopy of article or short story or typed ms with rights for sale noted and information about when and where article previously appeared. Reports in 2 months. Free sample copy and writer's guidelines for #10 SASE.

Nonfiction: Articles on hobbies and handicrafts, nature, famous people, seasonal subjects, etc., written from a Christian viewpoint. No articles about historical figures with an absence of religious implication. Length: 500-1,000 words. Pays 3-7¢/word.

Fiction: Short stories of heroism, adventure, travel, mystery, animals, biography. "True or possible plots stressing clean, wholesome, Christian character-building ideas, but not preachy. Make prayer, church attendance and Christian living a natural part of the story. We correlate our fiction and other features with a definite Bible lesson. Writers who want to meet our needs should send a #10 SASE for a theme list." No talking animal stories, science fiction, Halloween stories or first-person stories from an adult's viewpoint. Length: up to 1,000 words. Pays 3-7¢/word.

RANGER RICK, National Wildlife Federation, 1400 16th St. NW, Washington DC 20036. (703)790-4274. Editor: Gerald Bishop. 40% freelance written. Works with a small number of new/unpublished writers each year. Monthly magazine for children from ages 6-12, with the greatest concentration in the 7-10 age bracket. Buys all world rights unless other arrangements made. Byline given "but occasionally, for very brief pieces, we will identify author by name at the end. Contributions to regular columns usually are not bylined." Estab. 1967. **Pays on acceptance.** Publishes ms an average of 18 months after acceptance. Reports in 6 weeks. "Anything written with a specific month in mind should be in our hands at least 10 months before that issue date." Writer's guidelines for #10 SASE.

Nonfiction: "Articles may be written on anything related to nature, conservation, the outdoors, environmental problems or natural science. Please avoid articles about animal rehabilitation, unless the species are endangered." Buys 25-35 unsolicited mss/year. Query. Pays from $50-575, depending on length, quality and content (maximum length, 900 words). Unless you are an expert in the field or are writing from direct personal experience, all factual information must be footnoted and backed up with current, reliable references.

Fiction: "Same categories as nonfiction plus fantasy and science fiction. The attributing of human qualities to animals is limited to our regular feature, 'The Adventures of Ranger Rick,' so please do not humanize wildlife. We discourage keeping wildlife as pets."

Photos: "Photographs, when used, are paid for separately. It is not necessary that illustrations accompany material."

Tips: "In your query letter, include details of what manuscript will cover; sample lead; evidence that you can write playfully and with great enthusiasm, conviction and excitement (formal, serious, dull queries indicate otherwise). Think of an exciting subject we haven't done recently, sell it effectively with query, and produce a manuscript of highest quality. Read past issues to learn successful styles and unique approaches to subjects.

SHOFAR MAGAZINE, 43 Northcote Dr., Melville NY 11747-3924. (516)643-4598. Fax: (516)643-4598. Managing Editor: Gerald H. Grayson. 80-90% freelance written. Monthly children's magazine on Jewish subjects. Estab. 1984. Circ. 17,000. Pays on publication. Byline given. Buys one-time rights. Submit seasonal/holiday material 6 months in advance. Accepts simultaneous submissions. Reports in 2 months. Sample copy and writer's guidelines for 9×12 SAE with 4 first-class stamps.

Nonfiction: Dr. Gerald H. Grayson, publisher. Historical/nostalgic, humor, inspirational, interview/profile, personal experience, photo feature, religious, travel. Buys 15 mss/year. Send complete ms. Length: 750-1,000 words. Pays 7-10¢/word. Sometimes pays the expenses of writers on assignment.

Photos: State availability of or send photos with submission. Offers $10-50/photo. Identification of subjects required. Buys one-time rights.

Fiction: Adventure, historical, humorous, religious. Buys 15 mss/year. Send complete ms. Length: 750-1,000 words. Pays 7-10¢/word.

Poetry: Free verse, light verse, traditional. Buys 4-5 poems/year. Length: 8-50 words. Pays 7-10¢/word.

Tips: "Submissions must be on a Jewish theme and should be geared to readers who are 8 to 12 years old."

SPORTS ILLUSTRATED FOR KIDS, Time-Warner, Time & Life Building, 1271 Sixth Ave., New York NY 10020. (212)522-5437. Fax: (212)522-0120. Managing Editor: Craig Neff. 20% freelance written. Monthly magazine on sports for children 8 years old and up. Content is divided 50/50 between sports as played by kids, and sports as played by professionals. Estab. 1989. **Pays on acceptance.** Publishes ms an average of 3 months after acceptance. Byline given. Offers 25% kill fee. Buys all rights. For sample copy call (800)992-0196. Writer's guidelines for #10 SASE.

Nonfiction: Patricia Berry, articles editor. Games, general interest, how-to, humor, inspirational, interview/profile, photo feature, puzzles. Buys 15 mss/year. Query with published clips. Length: 100-1,500 words. Pays $75-1,000 for assigned articles; $75-800 for unsolicited articles. Pays expenses of writers on assignment.

Photos: State availability of photos with submission. Buys one-time rights.

Columns/Departments: The Worst Day I Ever Had (tells about day in pro athlete's life when all seemed hopeless), 500-600 words; Hotshots (young [8-13] athlete getting good things out of sports), 100-250 words; Sports Shorts (short, fresh news about kids doing awaiting things, on and off the field), 100-250 words. Buys 10-15 mss/year. Query with published clips. Pays $75-600.

STONE SOUP, The Magazine by Young Writers and Artists, Children's Art Foundation, P.O. Box 83, Santa Cruz CA 95063-0083. (408)426-5557. Fax: (408)426-1161. Editor: Ms. Gerry Mandel. 100% freelance written. Bimonthly magazine of writing and art by children, including fiction, poetry, book reviews, and art by children through age 13. Estab. 1973. Audience is children, teachers, parents, writers, artists. "We have a preference for writing and art based on real-life experiences; no formula stories or poems." Pays on publication. Publishes ms an average of 3 months after acceptance. Buys all rights. Submit seasonal/holiday material 6 months in advance. Accepts previously published submissions. Send photocopy of article or story and information about when and where the article or story previously appeared. Reports in 1 month. Sample copy for $4. Writer's guidelines with SASE.

Nonfiction: Book reviews. Buys 10 mss/year. Query. Pays $15 for assigned articles.

Fiction: Adventure, ethnic, experimental, fantasy, historical, humorous, mystery, science fiction, slice-of-life vignettes, suspense. "We do not like assignments or formula stories of any kind." Accepts 55 mss/year. Send complete ms. Pays $10 for stories. Authors also receive 2 copies and discounts on additional copies and on subscriptions.

Poetry: Avant-garde, free verse. Accepts 20 poems/year. Pays $10/poem. (Same discounts apply.)

Tips: "All writing we publish is by young people ages 13 and under. We do not publish any writing by adults. We can't emphasize enough how important it is to read a couple of issues of the magazine. We have a strong preference for writing on subjects that mean a lot to the author. If you feel strongly about something that happened to you or something you observed, use that feeling as the basis for your story or poem. Stories should have good descriptions, realistic dialogue and a point to make. In a poem, each word must be chosen carefully. Your poem should present a view of your subject and a way of using words that are special and all your own."

STORY FRIENDS, Mennonite Publishing House, 616 Walnut Ave., Scottdale PA 15683-1999. (412)887-8500. Fax: (412)887-3111. Editor: Marjorie Waybill. 80% freelance written. Monthly story paper in weekly parts for children ages 4-9. "*Story Friends* is planned to provide wholesome Christian reading for the 4- to 9-year-old. Practical life stories are included to teach moral values and remind the children that God is at work today. Activities introduce children to the Bible and its message for them." Estab. 1905. Circ. 7,000. **Pays on acceptance.** Publishes ms an average of 1 year after acceptance. Byline given. Publication not copyrighted. Buys one-time and second serial (reprint) rights. Submit seasonal/holiday material 6 months in advance. Accepts simultaneous and previously published submissions. Send photocopy or typed ms with rights for sale noted and information about when and where the article previously appeared. For reprints, pays 50% of amount paid for an article. Reports in 1 month. Sample copy for 9 × 12 SAE with 2 first-class stamps. Writer's guidelines for #10 SASE.

Nonfiction: How-to (craft ideas for young children), photo feature. Buys 20 mss/year. Send complete ms. Length: 300-500 words. Pays 3-5¢/word.

Photos: Send photos with submission. Reviews 8½ × 11 b&w prints. Offers $20-25/photo. Model releases required. Buys one-time rights.

Fiction: See writer's guidelines for *Story Friends*. Buys 50 mss/year. Send complete ms. Length: 300-800 words. Pays 3-5¢/word.

Poetry: Traditional. Buys 20 poems/year. Length: 4-16 lines. Pays $5-10/poem.

Tips: "Send stories that children from a variety of ethnic backgrounds can relate to; stories that deal with experiences similar to all children. For example, all children have fears but their fears may vary depending on where they live."

TOUCH, P.O. Box 7259, Grand Rapids MI 49510. Editor: Jan Boone. Publications Coordinator: Carol Smith. 80% freelance written. Prefers to work with published/established writers. Monthly magazine "to show girls ages 7-14 how God is at work in their lives and in the world around them. The May/June issue annually features material written by our readers." Estab. 1972. Circ. 15,500. **Pays on acceptance.** Publishes ms an average of 1 year after acceptance. Byline given. Buys second serial (reprint) and first North American serial rights. Submit seasonal/holiday material 9 months in advance. Accepts simultaneous and previously published submissions. Send typed ms with rights for sale noted. Reports in 2 months. Sample copy and writer's guidelines for 9 × 12 SAE with 3 first-class stamps.

Nonfiction: How-to (crafts girls can make easily and inexpensively); informational (write for issue themes); humor (need much more); inspirational (seasonal and holiday); interview; multicultural materials; travel; personal experience (avoid the testimony approach); photo feature (query first). "Because our magazine is published around a monthly theme, requesting the letter we send out twice a year to our established freelancers would be most helpful. We do not want easy solutions or quick character changes from bad to good. No pietistic characters. Constant mention of God is not necessary if the moral tone of the story is positive. We do not want stories that always have a good ending." Buys 36-45 unsolicited mss/year. Submit complete ms. Length: 100-1,000 words. Pays 2½-5¢/word, depending on the amount of editing.

Photos: Purchased with or without ms. Reviews 5 × 7 or 8 × 10 clear b&w glossy prints. Appreciate multicultural subjects. Pays $20-50 on publication.

Fiction: Adventure (that girls could experience in their hometowns or places they might realistically visit); humorous; mystery (believable only); romance (stories that deal with awakening awareness of boys are appreciated); suspense (can be serialized); religious (nothing preachy). Buys 30 mss/year. Submit complete ms. Length: 300-1,000 words. Pays 2½-5¢/word.

Poetry: Free verse, haiku, light verse, traditional. Buys 10/year. Length: 30 lines maximum. Pays $5-15 minimum.

Fillers: Puzzles, short humor, cartoons. Buys 3/issue. Pays $7-15.

Tips: "Prefers not to see anything on the adult level, secular material or violence. Writers frequently oversimplify the articles and often write with a Pollyanna attitude. An author should be able to see his/her writing style as exciting and appealing to girls ages 7-14. The style can be fun, but also teach a truth. The subject should be current and important to *Touch* readers. We would like to receive material that features a multicultural slant."

TURTLE MAGAZINE FOR PRESCHOOL KIDS, Children's Better Health Institute, P.O. Box 567, Indianapolis IN 46206-0567. (317)636-8881. Editor: Janet F. Hoover. 90% freelance written. Bimonthly magazine (monthly March, June, September, December). General interest, interactive magazine with the purpose of helping preschoolers develop healthy minds and healthy bodies. Pays on publication. May hold mss for up to 1 year before acceptance/publication. Byline given. Buys all rights. Submit seasonal/holiday material 8 months in advance. Reports in 3 months. Sample copy for $1.25. Writer's guidelines for #10 SASE.

Nonfiction: "Uses very simple science experiments. Would like to see some short, simple nature articles.

Fiction: Fantasy, humorous, realistic stories. All should have single-focus story lines and work well as readalouds. "Most of the stories we use will have a character-building bent, but they should not be preachy or overly moralistic. We are in constant need of stories that will help a preschooler grow to a greater appreciation of his/her body and what it can do; stories that encourage active, vigorous play; stories that teach fundamental lessons about good health without being too heavy-handed. We're no longer buying many stories about 'generic' turtles, as we now have PokeyToes, our own turtle character. All stories should 'move along' and lend themselves well to illustration. Writing should be energetic, enthusiastic and creative—like preschoolers themselves."

Poetry: We're especially looking for action rhymes to foster creative movement in preschoolers. We also use original finger plays, stories in rhyme and short verse.

Tips: "We are trying to include more material for our youngest readers. We'd like to see some well-executed ideas for teaching basic concepts to 2- and 3-year-olds. We're open to counting and alphabet stories, but they must be handled in a new, fresh way. All material must first be entertaining; otherwise all efforts to teach will be wasted."

VENTURE, Christian Service Brigade, P.O. Box 150, Wheaton IL 60189-0150. (708)665-0630. Fax: (708)665-0372. Editor: Deborah Christensen. 30% freelance written. Works with a small number of new/unpublished writers each year. Bimonthly company publication "published to support and compliment CSB's Stockade program. We aim to provide wholesome, entertaining reading for boys ages 8-11." Estab. 1959. Circ. 21,000. Pays on publication. Publishes ms an average of 6 months after acceptance, sometimes longer. Byline given. Offers $35 kill fee. Buys first North American serial, one-time and second serial (reprint) rights. Submit seasonal/holiday material 6 months in advance. Accepts previously published submissions. Send typed ms with rights for sale noted. For reprints, pays 75% of amount paid for original article. Reports in 1 week. Sample copy for $1.85 and 9×12 SAE with 4 first-class stamps. Writer's guidelines for #10 SASE.

● *Venture* has been redesigned. It's smaller (16 pages), full color and geared to a younger audience (8-11 years old).

Nonfiction: General interest, humor, inspirational, interview/profile, personal experience, photo feature, religious. Buys 18-20 mss/year. Send complete ms. Length: 500-1,000 words. Pays $75-150 for assigned articles; $40-100 for unsolicited articles. Sometimes pays expenses of writers on assignment.

Photos: Send photos with submission. Reviews color slides. Offers $50/photo. Buys one-time rights.

Fiction: Adventure, humorous, mystery, religious. Buys 10-12 mss/year. Send complete ms. Length: 500-1,000 words. Pays $40-100.

Tips: "Talk to young boys. Find out the things that interest them and write about those things. We are looking for material relating to our theme: Building Men to Serve Christ. We prefer shorter (1,000 words) pieces. Writers *must* weave Christianity throughout the story in a natural way, without preaching or token prayers. How does a boy's faith in Christ influence the way he responds to a situation."

WONDER TIME, 6401 The Paseo, Kansas City MO 64131. (816)333-7000. Fax: (816)333-4439. Editor: Lois Perrigo. 75% freelance written. "Willing to read and consider appropriate freelance submissions." Published weekly by WordAction for children ages 6-8. Correlates to the Bible Truth in the weekly Sunday School lesson. Pays on publication. Publishes ms an average of 1 year after acceptance. Byline given. Buys rights to reuse and all rights for curriculum assignments. Reports in 1 month. Sample copy and writer's guidelines for 9×12 SAE with 2 first-class stamps.

● *Wonder Time* is developing new curriculum for release in 1999. A new theme list and curriculum calendar is available in 1996.

Fiction: Buys stories portraying Christian attitudes without being preachy. Uses stories for special days—stories teaching honesty, truthfulness, kindness, helpfulness or other important spiritual truths, and avoiding symbolism. Also, stories about real life problems children face today. "God should be spoken of as our Father who loves and cares for us; Jesus, as our Lord and Savior." Buys 52/mss year. Length: 250-350 words. Pays $25 on publication.

Poetry: Uses verse which has seasonal or Christian emphasis. Length: 4-8 lines. Pays 25¢/line, minimum $3.

Tips: "Any stories that allude to church doctrine must be in keeping with Wesleyan beliefs. Any type of fantasy must be in good taste and easily recognizable."

Literary and "Little"

Fiction, poetry, essays, book reviews and scholarly criticism comprise the content of the magazines listed in this section. Some are published by colleges and universities, and many are regional in focus.

Everything about "little" literary magazines is different than other consumer magazines. Most carry few or no ads, and many do not even seek them. Circulations under 1,000 are common. And sales often come more from the purchase of sample copies than from the newsstand.

The magazines listed in this section cannot compete with the pay rates and exposure of the high-circulation general interest magazines also publishing fiction and poetry. But most "little" literary magazines don't try. They are more apt to specialize in publishing certain kinds of fiction or poetry: traditional, experimental, works with a regional sensibility, or the fiction and poetry of new and younger writers. For that reason, and because fiction and poetry vary so widely in style, writers should *always* invest in the most recent copies of the magazines they aspire to publish in.

Many "little" literary magazines pay contributors only in copies of the issues in which their works appear. *Writer's Market* lists only those that pay their contributors in cash. However, *Novel & Short Story Writer's Market* includes nonpaying fiction markets, and has in-depth information about fiction techniques and markets. The same is true of *Poet's Market* for nonpaying poetry markets (both books are published by Writer's Digest Books). There are also more literary opportunities listed in the Contests and Awards section.

ACM (Another Chicago Magazine), Left Field Press, 3709 N. Kenmore, Chicago IL 60613. Editor: Barry Silesky. 98% freelance written. Open to new/unpublished writers. Biannual literary journal. Estab. 1977. Circ. 2,500. **Pays on acceptance.** Publishes ms an average of 6 months after acceptance. Byline given. Buys first serial rights. Accepts simultaneous queries and submissions. Reports in 3 months. Sample copy for $7. Writer's guidelines for #10 SASE.

Nonfiction: Interview (contemporary poets and fiction writers), essays (contemporary literature), reviews of small press publications. Buys 5-6 mss/year. Query. Length: 1,000-20,000 words. Pays $5-25.

Fiction: Sharon Solwitz, fiction editor. Serious ethnic and experimental fiction. Buys 10-20 mss/year. Send complete ms. Length: 50-10,000 words. Pays $5-25.

Poetry: Serious poetry. No light verse or inspirational. Buys 50 poems/year. Length: 1-1,000 lines. Pays $5-25.

AGNI, Dept. WM, Boston University, 236 Bay State Rd., Boston, MA 02215. (617)353-5389. Fax: (617)353-7136. Editor: Askold Melnyczuk. Managing Editor: Erin Belieu. Book Review Editor: Joe Osterhaus. Semiannual literary magazine. "*AGNI* publishes poetry, fiction and essays. Also regularly publishes translations and is committed to featuring the work of emerging writers. We have published Derek Walcott, Joyce Carol Oates, Sharon Olds, John Updike, and many others, including then unknown writers: Sven Birkerts, Carolyn Chute, Tom Sleigh and Mary Morris." Estab. 1972. Circ. 2,000. Pays on publication. Publishes ms an average of 6 months after acceptance. Byline given. Buys first North American serial rights and rights to reprint in *AGNI* anthology (with author's consent). Editorial lead time 6 months. Accepts simultaneous submissions. Reports in 2 weeks on queries; 4 months on mss. Sample copy for $7. Writer's guidelines for #10 SASE.

• The $1 reading fee has been abolished! Send only a SASE with submission.

Fiction: Short stories. Buys 6-12 mss/year. Send complete ms. Pays $20-150.
Poetry: Buys more than 140/year. Submit maximum 5 poems. Pays $20-150.
Tips: "We suggest writers read *AGNI* first, and if they feel their work is compatible, send story or 1-5 poems for consideration. We read from October 1 through April 30. Manuscripts sent at other times will be returned unread."

ALABAMA LITERARY REVIEW, 253 Smith Hall, Troy State University, Troy AL 36082. (205)670-3286. Fax: (205)670-3519. Editor: Theron Montgomery. 80% freelance written. Semiannual magazine, "state literary medium for local and national submissions in contemporary, leading edge fiction, poetry, essays, drama, reviews and photography." Estab. 1987. Circ. 940. Pays on publication. Byline given. Editorial lead time 6 months. Submit seasonal material 6 months in advance. Accepts simultaneous submissions. Reports in 2 weeks on queries; 3 months on mss. Sample copy for $4.50. Writer's guidelines for #10 SASE.
Nonfiction: Steve Cooper. Essays, interview/profile (critical and academic). Buys 6-8 mss/year. Send complete ms. Length: 2,000-3,500 words.
Photos: Reviews 8×10, b&w prints only. Model releases required. Buys one-time rights.
Fiction: Jim Davis. Condensed novels, experimental, historical, mainstream, novel excerpts, science fiction, literary, contemporary. Buys 12 mss/year. Send complete ms. Length: 2,000-5,000 words. Pays honorarium when available.
Poetry: Ed Hicks. All kinds. Buys 12-15 poems/year. Submit maximum 5 poems. Pays honorarium when available.
Tips: "Query. Be sure of a literary on contemporary bent. Good writing a must. We pride ourselves in being open and in finding established as well as new writers."

ALASKA QUARTERLY REVIEW, College of Arts & Sciences, University of Alaska Anchorage, 3211 Providence Dr., Anchorage AK 99508. (907)786-4775. Executive Editor: Ronald Spatz. 95% freelance written. Prefers to work with published/established writers; eager to work with new/unpublished writers. Semiannual magazine publishing fiction and poetry, both traditional and experimental styles, literary criticism and reviews, with an emphasis on contemporary literature. Estab. 1982. Circ. 1,400. Pays honorariums on publication when funding permits. Publishes ms an average of 6 months after acceptance. Byline given. Buys first North American serial rights. Upon request, rights will be transferred back to author after publication. Reports in 4 months. Sample copy for $5. Writer's guidelines for SASE.
Nonfiction: Literary nonfiction: essays and memoirs. Buys 0-5 mss/year. Query. Length: 1,000-20,000 words. Pays $50-100 subject to funding; pays in copies and subscriptions when funding is limited.
Fiction: Experimental and traditional literary forms. No romance, children's or inspirational/religious. Publishes novel excerpts. Buys 20-26 mss/year. Send complete ms. Length: Up to 20,000 words. Pays $50-150 subject to funding; pays in contributor's copies and subscriptions when funding is limited.
Drama: Experimental and traditional one-act plays. Buys 0-2 mss/year. Query. Length: Up to 20,000 words but prefers short plays. Pays $50-150 subject to funding; contributor's copies and subscriptions when funding is limited.
Poetry: Avant-garde, free verse, traditional. No light verse. Buys 10-30 poems/year. Submit maximum 10 poems. Pays $10-50 subject to availability of funds; pays in contributor's copies and subscriptions when funding is limited.
Tips: "All sections are open to freelancers. We rely almost exclusively on unsolicited manuscripts. *AQR* is a non-profit literary magazine and does not always have funds to pay authors."

AMELIA MAGAZINE, Amelia Press, 329 E St., Bakersfield CA 93304. (805)323-4064. Editor: Frederick A. Raborg Jr. Estab. 1983. 100% freelance written. Eager to work with new/unpublished writers. "*Amelia* is a quarterly international magazine publishing the finest poetry and fiction available, along with expert criticism and reviews intended for all interested in contemporary literature. *Amelia* also publishes three supplements each year: *Cicada*, which publishes only high quality traditional or experimental haiku and senryu plus fiction, essays and cartoons pertaining to Japan; *SPSM&H*, which publishes the highest quality traditional and experimental sonnets available plus romantic fiction and essays pertaining to the sonnet; and the annual winner of the Charles William Duke long poem contest." Circ. 1,500. **Pays on acceptance.** Publishes ms an average of 6 months after acceptance. Byline given. Offers 50% kill fee. Buys first North American serial rights. Submit seasonal/holiday material 2 months in advance. Reports in 3 months on mss. Sample copy for $8.95 (includes postage). Sample copy of any supplement for $4.95. Writer's guidelines for #10 SASE.

A bullet introduces comments by the editors of **Writer's Market** *indicating special information about the listing.*

● An eclectic magazine, open to greater variety of styles—especially genre and mainstream stories unsuitable for other literary magazines. Receptive to new writers.

Nonfiction: Historical/nostalgic (in the form of belles lettres); humor (in fiction or belles lettres); interview/profile (poets and fiction writers); opinion (on poetry and fiction only); personal experience (as it pertains to poetry or fiction in the form of belles lettres); travel (in the form of belles lettres only); criticism and book reviews of poetry and small press fiction titles. "Nothing overtly slick in approach. Criticism pieces must have depth; belles lettres must offer important insights into the human scene." Buys 8 mss/year. Send complete ms. Length: 1,000-2,000 words. Pays $25 or by arrangement. Sometimes pays the expenses of writers on assignment.

Fiction: Adventure, book excerpts (original novel excerpts only), erotica (of a quality seen in Anais Nin or Henry Miller only), ethnic, experimental, fantasy, historical, horror, humorous, mainstream, mystery, novel excerpts, science fiction, suspense, western. "We would consider slick fiction of the quality seen in *Esquire* or *Vanity Fair* and more excellent submissions in the genres—science fiction, wit, Gothic horror, traditional romance, stories with complex *raisons d'être*; avant-garde ought to be truly avant-garde." No pornography ("good erotica is not the same thing"). Buys 24-36 mss/year. Send complete ms. Length: 1,000-5,000 words. Pays $35 or by arrangement for exceptional work.

Poetry: Avant-garde, free verse, haiku, light verse, traditional. "No patently religious or stereotypical newspaper poetry." Buys 100-160 poems/year depending on lengths. Prefers submission of at least 3 poems. Length: 3-100 lines. Pays $2-25; additional payment for exceptional work, usually by established professionals. *Cicada* pays $10 each to 3 "best of issue" poets; *SPSM&H* pays $14 to 2 "best of issue" sonnets; winner of the long poem contest receives $100 plus copies and publication.

Tips: "*Have something to say* and say it well. If you insist on waving flags or pushing your religion, then do it with subtlety and class. We enjoy a good cry from time to time, too, but sentimentality does not mean we want to see mush. Read our fiction carefully for depth of plot and characterization, then try very hard to improve on it. With the growth of quality in short fiction, we expect to find stories of lasting merit. I also hope to begin seeing more critical essays which, without sacrificing research, demonstrate a more entertaining obliqueness to the style sheets, more 'new journalism' than MLA. In poetry, we also often look for a good 'storyline' so to speak. Above all we want to feel a sense of honesty and value in every piece."

AMERICAN SHORT FICTION, University of Texas Press, University of Texas at Austin, Dept. of English, Austin TX 78712-1164. (512)471-1772. Editor: Joseph Kruppa. 100% freelance written. Quarterly fiction magazine. "*American Short Fiction* carries fiction of all lengths up to and including the novella, and is aimed at a general readership. No special slant or philosophy is required in writing for our readers." Estab. 1990. **Pays on acceptance.** Publishes ms an average of 1 year after acceptance. Buys first serial rights. Reports in 4 months. Sample copy for $7.95 and $2 for foreign postage if necessary.

Fiction: "Stories are selected for their originality and craftsmanship. No condensed novels or slice-of-life vignettes, please." Publishes novel excerpts. Buys 20-30 mss/year. Send complete ms. Pays $400.

Tips: "Manuscripts are only accepted September 1-May 31."

ANTIETAM REVIEW, 7 W. Franklin St., Hagerstown MD 21740-4804. (301)791-3132. Editors: Susanne Kass and Ann Knox. 100% freelance written. Annual magazine of fiction (short stories), poetry and b&w photography. Estab. 1982. Circ. 1,500. Pays on publication. Byline given. Reports in 2 months. Sample copy for $3.15 (back issue), $5.25 (current issue). Writer's guidelines for SASE.

Fiction: Novel excerpts (if work as independent pieces), short stories of a literary quality. No religious, romance, erotica, confession, horror or condensed novels. Buys 9 mss/year. Query or send complete ms. Length: 5,000 words. Pays $100.

Poetry: Crystal Brown. Avant-garde, free verse, traditional. Does not want to see haiku, religious and most rhyme. Buys 15-20 poems/year. Submit 5 poems maximum. Pays $20.

Tips: "Writers must live in or be native of, Maryland, Pennsylvania, Delaware, Virginia, West Virginia or District of Columbia. We consider materials from September 1 to February 1 each year."

ANTIOCH REVIEW, P.O. Box 148, Yellow Springs OH 45387-0148. Editor: Robert S. Fogarty. Quarterly magazine for general, literary and academic audience. Estab. 1941. Copyright held by *Antioch Review*; reverts to author upon publication. Byline given. Pays on publication. Publishes ms an average of 10 months after acceptance. Reports in 2 months. Sample copy for $6. Writer's guidelines for #10 SASE.

Nonfiction: "Contemporary articles in the humanities and social sciences, politics, economics, literature and all areas of broad intellectual concern. Somewhat scholarly, but never pedantic in style, eschewing all professional jargon. Lively, distinctive prose insisted upon." Length: 2,000-8,000 words. Pays $10/published page.

Fiction: Quality fiction only, distinctive in style with fresh insights into the human condition. No science fiction, fantasy or confessions. Pays $10/published page.

Poetry: No light or inspirational verse. Contributors should be familiar with the magazine before submitting.

THE ATLANTEAN PRESS REVIEW, P.O. Box 7336, Golden CO 80403. Editor: Patricia LeChevalier. E-mail: 4889616@mcimail.com. 95% freelance written. Quarterly literary magazine. "The Romantic-Realist school of literature and art is our focus. The essence of this kind of writing is choice—in fiction, the characters have free will and there is no sense that they are predestined; choice is also reflected in the fact that the writer exercises great selectivity in details, themes and characters." Estab. 1993. Circ. 500. Pays 50% on acceptance, 50% on publication. Byline given. Offers 50% kill fee. "We haven't made a practice of registering it, but each piece carries a copyright notice." Buys one-time rights. Editorial lead time 3 months. Submit seasonal material months at least 4 months in advance. Accepts simultaneous and previously published submissions. Query for electronic submissions. Reports in 2-8 weeks on queries, within 10 weeks on mss. Sample copy for $5. Writer's guidelines for SAE with 1 first-class stamp.

Nonfiction: Essays, interview/profile, photo feature, all pertaining to Romantic art or artist/writer. "Don't send anything not directly relevant to Romantic art." Buys 6 mss/year. Query. Length: 1,500-25,000 words. Pays $15 and up. Sometimes pays expenses of writers on assignment.

● *The Atlantean Press Review* reports an increased need for more nonfiction—essays, reviews and profiles.

Photos: Send photos with submissions. Reviews contact sheets and prints. Negotiates payment individually. Model releases required. Buys one-time rights.

Columns/Departments: Atlantean Favorites, reviews of Romantic literature and art (books, films, music, visual art), 250 words (can be much longer). Buys 12 mss/year. Query. Pays $10-50.

Fiction: Adventure, fantasy (alternate world OK, but no supernaturalism), historical, mystery, novel excerpts, romance, science fiction, suspense, western. "No erotica, confession, horror, religious, slice of life." Buys 20 mss/year. Send complete ms. Length: 1,000-25,000 words. Pays $15-125.

Poetry: Please study a sample issue. We rarely publish poems that don't rhyme. Espesially interested in translations of 19th century Romantic works (eg. Victor Hugo). "No work that depends on the appearance of the poem rather than its sound; nothing obscene, vulgar or malevolent." Buys 15 poems/year. Submit maximum 10 poems. Length: 4-300 lines. Pays $15-75.

Tips: "Our focus is strictly on the Romantic school of art, so the best way to break in is to learn about this school. The best introduction is Ayn Rand's book *The Romantic Manifesto*, available at most bookstores or from us. If you've studied and understand the Romantic school, we'll be very interested in your work. If you haven't, it's unlikely your work would be right for us. For nonfiction writers, reviews of of articles about little known Romantic works or writers and artists would be welcome."

AUTHORS, 501 Cambridge St. S.E., Medicine Hat, Alberta T1A 0T3 Canada. Editor: Philip Murphy. 100% freelance written. Monthly magazine providing a competitive platform that will both enhance professional skills as well as develop the novice. Estab. 1992. Circ. 300. Pays for assignments on publication. Byline given. Offer 50% kill fee. Buys one-time rights. Editorial lead time 2 months. Submit seasonal material 3 months in advance. Accepts simultaneous and previously published submissions. Reports in 2 weeks on queries; 1 month on mss. Sample copy and writer's guidelines free on request.

Nonfiction: Book excerpts, essays, general interest, historical/nostalgic, humor, inspirational, interview/profile, opinion, personal experience, religious, travel. Buys 6 mss/year. Query. Length: 1,500-10,000 words. Pays $150-250 for assigned articles and 1 free copy; $100 for unsolicited articles. Sometimes pays expenses of writers on assignment.

Fiction: Adventure, condensed novel, confession, ethnic, experimental, fantasy, historical, horror, humorous, mainstream, mystery, novel excerpts, religious, romance, science fiction, serialized novels, slice-of-life vignettes, suspense, western. Buys 12 mss/year. Query. Length: 300-10,000 words. Pays $100.

Poetry: Avant-garde, free verse, haiku, light verse, traditional. Buys 12 poems/year. Length: 1-1,000 lines. Pays $100.

Fillers: Anecdotes, facts, short humor. Pays free copy.

Tips: "*Authors* is reluctant to send out rejection slips. Since its purpose is to provide a platform for both novice and professional writers, it will endeavour to publish all serious non-controversial inquiries, either on a non-monetary or monetary basis, affording them both exposure and feedback, limited only by the subscriber base."

BANGTALE INTERNATIONAL, P.O. Box 83984, Phoenix AZ 85071-3984. Editor: William Dudley. 75% freelance written. Semiannual magazine. "We have only published poetry in the past. We are now moving towards short stories and essays that are creative and thought provoking." Estab. 1989. Circ. 250. Pays on publication. Publishes ms 1 year after acceptance. Byline given. Buys one-time rights. Editorial lead time 6 months. Accepts previously published submissions. Reports in 6 months. Sample copy $5.

Nonfiction: Book excerpts, essays, general interest, humor, interview/profile, opinion, personal experience. Buys 4 mss/year. Send complete ms. Length: 100-300 words. Pays $10-25.

Photos: Send photos with submission. Reviews 3×5 prints. Negotiates payment individually.

Fiction: Experimental, humorous, novel excerpts, slice-of-life vignettes. Buys 4 mss/year. Send complete ms. Length: 100-300 words. Pays $10-25.

Poetry: Avant-garde, free verse, light verse. Submit maximum 15 poems. Length: 10-20 lines. Pays 1 contributor's copy.

Tips: "Please be original, creative and thought provoking (include humor and/or irony when you can)."

BLACK WARRIOR REVIEW, P.O. Box 2936, Tuscaloosa AL 35486-2936. (205)348-4518. Editor: Mindy Wilson. Managing Editor: Tom McDougle. 95% freelance written. Semiannual magazine of fiction and poetry. Estab. 1974. Circ. 2,000. Pays on publication. Publishes ms an average of 6 months after acceptance. Byline given. Buys first rights. Reports in 2 weeks on queries; 3 months on mss. Sample copy for $6. Writer's guidelines for #10 SASE.
- Consistently excellent magazine. Placed stories and poems in recent *Best American Short Stories*, *Best American Poetry* and *Pushcart Prize* anthologies.

Nonfiction: Interview/profile, book reviews. Buys 5 mss/year. Query or send complete ms. No limit on length. Payment varies.

Photos: State availability of photos with submission. Offers no additional payment for photos accepted with ms. Identification of subjects required. Buys one-time rights.

Fiction: Mitch Wieland. Buys 10 mss/year. Publishes novel excerpts. One story/chapter per envelope, please.

Poetry: Madeline Marcotte. Submit 3-6 poems. Long poems encouraged. Buys 50 poems/year.

Tips: "Read the *BWR* before submitting; editor changes each year. Send us your best work. Submissions of photos and/or artwork is encouraged. We sometimes choose unsolicited photos/artwork for the cover. Address all submissions to the appropriate genre editor."

BOHEMIAN CHRONICLE, Bohemian Enterprises, P.O. Box 387, Largo FL 34649. Publisher: Emily Skinner. 90% freelance written. Monthly literary magazine/newsletter. "*Bohemian Chronicle* is an international publication dedicated to promoting sensitivity in the arts." Estab. 1991. Pays on publication. Publishes ms an average of 6-9 months after acceptance. Byline given. Buys first rights or all rights. Editorial lead time 4 months. Submit seasonal material 6 months in advance. Reports in 1 month on queries; 2 months on mss. Sample copy for $1 and #10 SASE. Writer's guidelines for #10 SASE.

Nonfiction: Essays, humor, inspirational, interview/profile, opinion, personal experience, photo feature, experimental. Awards "Bohos" each May (the "best of . . " the previous year's published works. Buys 10-20 mss/year. Send complete ms. Length: 1,500 words maximum. Pays $5 plus 5 copies.

Photos: Send photos with submission. (No slides.) Offers no additional payment for photos accepted with ms. Identification of subjects required. Buys one-time or all rights.

Fiction: Adventure, ethnic, experimental, historical, humorous, mystery, slice-of-life vignettes, suspense. Buys 60 mss/year. Send complete ms. Length: 500-1,500 words. Pays $5 plus 5 copies.

Poetry: Avant-garde, free verse. Buys 20 poems/year. Submit maximum 3 poems. Length: 1 page maximum. Pays $2 plus 2 copies.

BOULEVARD, Opojaz, Inc., P.O. Box 30386, Philadelphia PA 19103-4326. Editor: Richard Burgin. 100% freelance written. Triannual literary magazine covering fiction, poetry and essays. "*Boulevard* is a diverse triquarterly literary magazine presenting original creative work by well-known authors, as well as by writers of exciting promise." Estab. 1985. Circ. 3,000. Pays on publication. Publishes ms an average of 3-12 months after acceptance. Byline given. No kill fee. Buys first North American serial rights. Accepts simultaneous submissions. Reports in 2 weeks on queries; 2 months on mss. Sample copy for $7. Writer's guidelines for #10 SASE.
- *Boulevard* has received grants from the National Endowment for the Arts, and the Pennsylvania Council on the Arts, and work first published in *Boulevard* has appeared in *Best American Poetry*, the Pushcart Prize anthology, and the Best of the Pushcart Prize anthology.

Nonfiction: Book excerpts, essays, interview/profile. "No pornography, science fiction, children's stories or westerns." Buys 8 mss/year. Send complete ms. Length: 8,000 words maximum. Pays $50-150 (sometimes higher).

Fiction: Confession, experimental, mainstream, novel excerpts. "We do not want erotica, science fiction, romance, western or children's stories." Buys 20 mss/year. Send complete ms. Length: 8,000 words maximum. Pays $50-150 (sometimes higher).

Poetry: Avant-garde, free verse, haiku, traditional. "Do not send us light verse." Buys 80 poems/year. Submit maximum 5 poems. Length: up to 200 lines. Pays $25-150 (sometimes higher).

Tips: "Read the magazine first. The work *Boulevard* publishes is generally recognized as among the finest in the country. We continue to seek more good literary or cultural essays. Send only your best work."

CANADIAN LITERATURE, #225-2029 West Mall, University of British Columbia, Vancouver, British Columbia V6T 1Z2 Canada. (604)822-2780. E-mail: cdnlit@unixg.ubc.ca. Editor: W.H. New. 70% freelance written. Works with "both new and established writers depending on quality." Quarterly. Estab. 1959. Circ.

Always check the most recent copy of a magazine for the address and editor's name before you send in a query or manuscript.

2,000. Not copyrighted. Buys first Canadian rights only. Pays on publication. Publishes ms an average of 2 years after acceptance. Reports in 2 months. Sample copy and writer's guidelines for $15 (Canadian) plus postage (include SASE).
Nonfiction: Articles of high quality only on Canadian books and writers written in French or English. Articles should be scholarly and readable. Query "with a clear description of the project." Length: 2,000-5,500 words. Pays $5/printed page.

THE CAPILANO REVIEW, The Capilano Press Society, 2055 Purcell Way, North Vancouver, British Columbia V7J 3H5 Canada. Editor: Robert Sherrin. 100% freelance written. Triannual journal of fresh, original writing. Estab. 1972. Circ. 1,000. Pays on publication. Publishes ms 2 months after acceptance. Byline given. Buys first North American serial rights. No simultaneous or previously published submissions. Reports in 1 week on queries; 4 months on mss. Sample copy for $9. Writer's guidelines free on request.
Nonfiction: Essays, interview/profile, personal experience, creative nonfiction. Buys 1-2 mss/year. Query. Pays $50-200 plus 2 copies and 1 year subscription. Sometimes pays expenses of writers on assignment.
Fiction: Literary. Buys 10-15 mss/year. Send complete ms. Pays $50-200.
Poetry: Avant-garde, free verse. Buys 40 poems/year. Submit maximum 10 poems. Pays $50-200.

THE CHARITON REVIEW, Northeast Missouri State University, Kirksville MO 63501-9915. (816)785-4499. Fax: (816)785-7486. Editor: Jim Barnes. 100% freelance written. Semiannual (fall and spring) magazine covering contemporary fiction, poetry, translation and book reviews. Circ. 600. Pays on publication. Publishes ms an average of 6 months after acceptance. Byline given. Buys first North American serial rights. Reports in 1 week on queries; 1 month on mss. *Writer's Market* recommends allowing 2 months for reply. Sample copy for $2.50 and 7×10 SAE with 4 first-class stamps.
Nonfiction: Essays, essay reviews of books. Buys 2-5 mss/year. Send complete ms. Length: 1,000-5,000. Pays $15.
Fiction: Ethnic, experimental, mainstream, novel excerpts, traditional. Publishes novel excerpts if they can stand alone. "We are not interested in slick material." Buys 6-10 mss/year. Send complete ms. Length: 1,000-6,000 words. Pays $5/page.
Poetry: Avant-garde, free verse, traditional. Buys 50-55 poems/year. Submit maximum 5 poems. Length: open. Pays $5/page.
Tips: "Read *Chariton*. Know the difference between good literature and bad. Know what magazine might be interested in your work. We are not a trendy magazine. We publish only the best. All sections are open to freelancers. Know your market or you are wasting your time—and mine. Do *not* write for guidelines; the only guideline is excellence in all matters."

CHELSEA, Chelsea Associates, P.O. Box 773, Cooper Station, New York NY 10276. Editor: Richard Foerster. 70% freelance written. Semiannual literary magazine. "We stress style, variety, originality. No special biases or requirements. Flexible attitudes, eclectic material. We take an active interest, as always, in cross-cultural exchanges, superior translations, and are leaning toward cosmopolitan, interdisciplinary techniques, but maintain no strictures against traditional modes." Estab. 1958. Circ. 1,350. Pays on publication. Publishes ms an average of 6 months after acceptance. Byline given. Buys first North American serial rights. Reports in 3 months on mss. Include SASE. Sample copy for $6.
● A poem from a recent issue of *Chelsea* was included in the current Best American Poetry Anthology. The 1993 recipient of its fiction award received an O'Henry nomination. *Chelsea* also sponsors fiction and poetry contests. Write for guidelines.
Nonfiction: Essays, book reviews (query first with sample). Buys 6 mss/year. Send complete ms. Length: 6,000 words. Pays $10/page.
Fiction: Mainstream, literary. Buys 12 mss/year. Send complete ms. Length: 5-6,000 words. Pays $10/page.
Poetry: Avant-garde, free verse, traditional. Buys 60-75 poems/year. Pays $5/page.
Tips: "We are looking for more super translations, first-rate fiction and work by writers of color."

CICADA, *Amelia Magazine*, 329 E St., Bakersfield CA 93304. (805)323-4064. Editor: Frederick A. Raborg, Jr. 100% freelance written. Quarterly magazine covering Oriental fiction and poetry (haiku, etc.). "Our readers expect the best haiku and related poetry forms we can find. Our readers circle the globe and know their subjects. We include fiction, book reviews and articles related to the forms or to the Orient." Estab. 1984. Circ. 600. Pays on publication. Publishes ms an average of 6 months after acceptance. Byline given. Offers 50% kill fee. Buys first North American serial rights. Editorial lead time 2 months. Submit seasonal material 3 months in advance. Accepts simultaneous submissions. Reports in 2 weeks on queries, 3 months on mss. Sample copy for $4.95. Writer's guidelines for #10 SASE.
Nonfiction: Essays, general interest, historical/nostalgic, humor, interview/profile, opinion, personal experience, travel. Buys 1-3 mss/year. Send complete ms. Length: 500-2,500 words. Pays $10.
Photos: Send photos with submission. Reviews 5×7 or 8×10 prints. Offers $10-25/photo. Model releases required. Buys one-time rights.

Fiction: Adventure, erotica, ethnic, experimental, fantasy, historical, horror, humorous, mainstream, mystery, romance, science fiction, slice-of-life vignettes, suspense. Buys 4 mss/year. Send complete ms. Length: 500-2,500 words. Pays $10-20.
Poetry: Buys 400 poems/year. Submit maximum 12 poems. Length: 1-50 lines. Pays 3 "best of issue" poets $10.
Fillers: Anecdotes, short humor. Buys 1-4/year. Length: 25-500 words. No payment for fillers.
Tips: "Writers should understand the limitations of contemporary Japanese forms particularly. We also use poetry based on other Asian ethnicities and on the South Seas ethnicities. Don't be afraid to experiment within the forms. Be professional in approach and presentation."

CIMARRON REVIEW, Oklahoma State University, 205 Morrill Hall, OSU, Stillwater OK 74078-0135. (405)744-9476. Editor: Gordon Weaver. 85% freelance written. Quarterly literary magazine. "We publish short fiction, poetry, and essays of serious literary quality by writers often published, seldom published and previously unpublished. We have no bias with respect to subject matter, form (traditional or experimental) or theme. Though we appeal to a general audience, many of our readers are writers themselves or members of a university community." Estab. 1967. Circ. 500. Pays on publication. Published ms an average of 1 year after acceptance. Byline given. Buys all rights (reprint permission freely granted on request). Reports in 1 week on queries; 3 months on mss. Sample copy for $3 and 7×10 SASE. Writer's guidelines for #10 SASE.
Nonfiction: E.P. Walkiewicz, nonfiction editor. Essays, general interest, historical, interview/profile, opinion, personal experience, travel, literature and arts. "We are not interested in highly subjective personal reminiscences, obscure or arcane articles, or short, light 'human interest' pieces." Buys 9-12 mss/year. Send complete ms. Length: 1,000-7,500 words. Pays $50 plus one year's subscription.
Fiction: Mainstream, literary. No juvenile or genre fiction. Buys 12-17 mss/year. Send complete ms. Length: 1,250-7,000 words. Pays $50.
Poetry: Free verse, traditional. No haiku, light verse or experimental poems. Buys 55-70 poems/year. Submit maximum 6 poems. Pays $15/poem.
Tips: "For prose, submit legible, double-spaced typescript with name and address on manuscript. Enclose SASE and brief cover letter. For poetry, same standards apply, but single-spaced is conventional. Be familiar with high quality, contemporary mainstream writing. Evaluate your own work carefully."

CLOCKWATCH REVIEW, (a journal of the arts), Dept. of English, Illinois Wesleyan University, Bloomington IL 61702-2900. (309)556-3352. Editor: James Plath. 85% freelance written. Semiannual literary magazine. Estab. 1983. Circ. 1,400. **Pays on acceptance.** Byline given. Buys first North American serial rights. Submit seasonal/holiday material 6 months in advance. Reports in 6 months. Sample copy for $4. Writer's guidelines for #10 SASE.
Nonfiction: Literary essays, criticism (MLA style), interviews with writers, musicians, artists. Buys 4 mss/ year. Query with or without published clips. Length: 1,500-4,000 words. Pays up to $25.
Photos: State availability of photos with submission. Reviews contact sheets, negatives, transparencies. Offers no additional payment for photos accepted with ms. Buys one-time rights.
Fiction: Experimental, humorous, mainstream, novel excerpts. "Also literary quality genre stories that break the mold. No straight mystery, fantasy, sci-fi, romance or western." Buys 8 mss/year. Send complete ms. Length: 1,500-4,000 words. Pays $25.
Poetry: Avant-garde, free verse, light verse, traditional. Buys 30 poems/year. Submit maximum 6 poems. Length: 32 lines maximum. Pays $5.

CONFRONTATION, A Literary Journal, Long Island University, Brookville NY 11548. (516)299-2391. Fax: (516)299-2735. Editor: Martin Tucker. Assistant to Editor: Emily Berkowitz. 75% freelance written. Semiannual literary magazine. "We are eclectic in our taste. Excellence of style is our dominant concern." Estab. 1968. Circ. 2,000. Pays on publication. Publishes ms an average of 6-12 months after acceptance. Byline given. "We rarely offer kill fee." Buys first North American serial, first, one-time or all rights. Accepts simultaneous submissions. Reports in 3 weeks on queries; 2 months on mss. Sample copy for $3.
Nonfiction: Essays, personal experience. Buys 15 mss/year. Send complete ms. Length: 1,500-5,000 words. Pays $100-300 for assigned articles; $15-300 for unsolicited articles.
Photos: State availability of photos with submission. Offers no additional payment for photos accepted with ms. Buys one-time rights.
Fiction: Katherine Hill-Miller. Experimental, mainstream, science fiction, slice-of-life vignettes, novel excerpts (if they are self-contained stories). "We judge on quality, so genre is open." Buys 60-75 mss/year. Send complete ms. Length 6,000 words maximum. Pays $25-250.
Poetry: Joseph Cosenza. Avant-garde, free verse, haiku, light verse, traditional. Buys 60-75 poems/year. Submit maximum 6 poems. Length open. Pays $10-100.
Tips: "Most open to fiction and poetry."

CRAZYHORSE, Crazyhorse Association at UALR, English Dept., University of Arkansas, Little Rock AR 72204. (501)569-3161. Managing Editor: Zabelle Stodola. 100% freelance written. Semiannual magazine of short fiction and poetry. "*Crazyhorse* publishes quality poetry and short fiction; no special slant." Estab.

1960. Circ. 1,000. Pays on publication. Publishes ms 6-12 months after acceptance. Buys first North American serial rights. Editorial lead time 12-18 months. Reports in 3 weeks on queries; 6 months on mss. Sample copy for $5 and #10 SASE.

Nonfiction: Criticism Editor: Dennis Vannatta. Interview/profile, reviews of contemporary poetry and short fiction. Buys 3 mss/year. Send complete ms. Length 1,000-6,000 words. Pays $10/printed page and 2 contributor's copies.

Fiction: Judy Troy, fiction editor. Mainstream; short fiction only. Buys 10 mss/year. Send complete ms. Length: 500-10,000 words. Pays $10/printed page.

Poetry: Poetry Editor: Ralph Burns. Traditional. Buys 50-60 poems/year. Submit maximum 6 poems. Pays $10/printed page.

Tips: "Buy a sample copy to see the kind of work we publish. We do not have any guideline for poetry or short fiction."

THE CREAM CITY REVIEW, University of Wisconsin-Milwaukee, English, P.O. Box 413, UWM, Milwaukee WI 53201. (414)229-4708. Editors: Mark Drechsler, Andrew Rivera. Semiannual magazine. "*TCCR* seeks to publish an eclectic array of quality contemporary fiction, poetry and nonfiction. Our audience consists of writer, students and critics of literature. Our only criterion for publishing submitted manuscripts is quality." Estab. 1975. Circ. 1,000. Pays on publication. Publishes ms 6 months after acceptance. Byline given. Buys first North American serial rights. Editorial lead time 3 months. Submit seasonal material 4 months in advance. Accepts simultaneous submissions. Reports in 8-12 months on mss; 1 month on queries. Sample copy for $5. Writer's guidelines for #10 SASE.

Nonfiction: Nonfiction Editors. Essays, interview/profile, personal experience, cultural criticism, literary criticism, book reviews. Buys 20-25 mss/year. Send complete ms. Length: 500-5,000. Pays $5/page.

Photos: Send photos with submission. Offers $5/photo.

Fiction: Fiction Editors. Erotica, ethnic, experimental, historical, novel excerpts, romance, literary fiction of nearly any genre considered. Buys 15-20 mss/year. Send complete ms. Length: 500-5,000. Pays $5/page.

Poetry: Poetry Editors. Avant-garde, free verse, traditional, prose poems, long poems. Buys 100-125 poems/year. Submit maximum 5 poems. Pays $5/page.

Tips: "Submissions which do not include an SASE with sufficient postage for reply/return of manuscript will not be considered. Error-free, neatly-presented manuscripts are a plus. A brief cover letter, including a brief bio and publication history encouraged. *TCCR* has a reputation for publishing an eclectic array of work from both new writers and established talent. As always, reading a sample issue is the best way to see the types of work *TCCR* is publishing."

DANDELION, Dandelion Magazine Society, 922 Ninth Ave. SE, Calgary, Alberta T2G 0S4 Canada. (403)265-0524. Managing Editor: Bonnie Bennoit. 90% freelance written. Semiannual magazine. Reviews Alberta book authors—showcases Alberta visual artists. "*Dandelion* is a literary and visual arts journal with an international audience. There is no restriction on subject matter or form, be it poetry, fiction, visual art or review." Estab. 1975. Circ. 1,000. Pays on publication. Publishes ms an average of 3 months after acceptance. Byline given. Buys one-time rights. Editorial lead time 3 months. Query for electronic submissions. Reports in 3 weeks on queries; 3 months on mss. Sample copy for $7. Writer's guidelines for #10 SAE and IRC.

Nonfiction: Interview/profile, review. "We can only use book-related interviews, book reviews and literary essays." Buys 4 mss/year. Query with published clips. Length: 500-1,000 words. Pays $125 for assigned articles; $40 for unsolicited articles. Sometimes pays expenses of writers on assignment.

Photos: Send photos with submission. Reviews contact sheets. Negotiates payment individually. Captions required. Buys one-time rights.

Fiction: Judy Miller, fiction editor. Adventure, condensed novels, erotica, ethnic, experimental, historical, humorous, mainstream, novel excerpts, religious, epiphanic. Buys 6 mss/year. Send complete ms. Length: 3,500 words maximum. Pays $125.

Poetry: Contact poetry editor. Avant-garde, free verse, haiku, traditional, long poem. Buys 50 poems/year. Submit maximum 10 poems. Pays $15/poem.

Tips: "The mandate is so large and general, only a familiarity with literary journals and reviews will help. Almost all our material comes unsolicited; thus, find out what we publish and you'll have a means of 'breaking in.' "

THE DENVER QUARTERLY, University of Denver, Dept. of English, Denver CO 80208. (303)871-2892. Fax: (303)871-2853. Editor: Bin Ramke. 100% freelance written. Works with a small number of new/unpublished writers. Quarterly magazine for generally sophisticated readership. Estab. 1966. Circ. 1,000. Pays on publication. Publishes ms an average of 6-12 months after acceptance. Buys first North American serial rights. Reports in 5 months. Sample copy for $5.

● *The Denver Quarterly* has received two Pushcart Prizes for poetry.

Nonfiction: "Most reviews are solicited; we do publish a few literary essays in each number. Use nonsexist language, please." Send complete ms. Pays $5/printed page.

Fiction: Buys 10 mss/year. Send complete ms. Pays $5/printed page.
Poetry: Buys 50 poems/year. Send poems. Pays $5/printed page.
Tips: "We decide on the basis of quality only. Prior publication is irrelevant. Promising material, even though rejected, may receive some personal comment from the editor; some material can be revised to meet our standards through such criticism. I receive more good stuff than *DQ* can accept, so there is some subjectivity and a good deal of luck involved in any final acceptance. *DQ* is becoming interested in issues of aesthetics and *lucid* perspectives and performances of the avant-garde. We are also interested in topics and translations in the literature of Eastern Europe. Please look at a *recent* issue before submitting. Reading unsolicited mss during academic year only; we do *not* read between May 15 and September 15."

DESCANT, Descant Arts & Letters Foundation, P.O. Box 314, Station P, Toronto, Ontario M5S 2S8. (416)603-0223. Editor: Tracy Jenkins. Managing Editor: Janice Zawerbny. Quarterly literary journal. Estab. 1970. Circ. 1,200. Pays on publication. Publishes ms 8-16 months after acceptance. Editorial lead time 4 months. Submit seasonal material 4 months in advance. Query for electronic submissions. Sample copy for $8. Writer's guidelines for SASE.
Nonfiction: Book excerpts, essays historical/nostalgic, interview/profile, personal experience, photo feature, travel. Special issues: The Book (summer 1995). Query or send complete ms. Pays $100 honorarium plus 1 year's subscription. Sometimes pays the expenses of writers on assignment.
Photos: State availability of photos with submission. Reviews contact sheets and prints. Offers no additional payment for photos accepted with ms. Buys one-time rights.
Fiction: Send complete ms. Pays $100.
Poetry: Free verse, light verse, traditional. Submit maximum 10 poems. Pays $100.
Tips: "Familiarize yourself with our magazine before submitting."

EAGLE'S FLIGHT, P.O. Box 465, Granite OK 73547. (405)535-2452. Editor: Shyamkant Kulkarni. 60% freelance written. Quarterly literary tabloid "read by young and new writers with talent for writing. They should understand networking." Estab. 1989. Circ. 300. Pays on publication. Publishes ms an average of 1 year after acceptance. Buys first North American serial, first or one-time rights. Editorial lead time 3 months. Submit seasonal material 3 months in advance. Accepts simultaneous submissions. Reports in 6 weeks on queries; 6 months on mss. Sample copy for $1.25 and #10 SASE. Writer's guidelines for #10 SASE.
Fiction: Contact: Rekha Kulkarni. Adventure, condensed novels, humorous, mainstream, mystery, romance, slice-of-life vignettes, suspense. Buys 4-8 mss/year. Send complete ms. Length: 500-2,500 words. Pays $5-20.
Poetry: Avant-garde, free verse, haiku, light verse, traditional. Buys 8-10 poems/year. Submit maximum 10 poems. Length: 5-30. Pays $5 maximum (mostly contributors copies or 1 year subscription).
Tips: "A writer should be ready to read and appreciate other writers as well. One needs to read and read successful writers, develop their own style and form, search their heart and try to reach the truth."

EROTIC FICTION QUARTERLY, EFQ Publications, P.O. Box 424958, San Francisco CA 94142-4958. Editor: Richard Hiller. 100% freelance written. Small literary magazine (published irregularly) for thoughtful people interested in a variety of highly original and creative short fiction with sexual themes. Estab. 1983. **Pays on acceptance.** Byline given. Buys first rights. Reports in 1 month. Writer's guidelines for #10 SASE.
Fiction: "Heartfelt, intelligent erotica, any style. Also, stories—not necessarily erotic—about some aspect of authentic sexual experience. No standard pornography or men's magazine-type stories; no contrived or formula plots or gimmicks; no broad satire or parody. We do not publish poetry." Send complete ms. Length: 500-2,000 words. Pays $50 minimum.
Tips: "What we especially need and do not see enough of is truly interesting and original erotica, whether graphic or subtle, as well as literary-quality fiction that depends on sexual insight. No particular 'slant' is required. Stories should reflect real life, not media ideas."

EVENT, Douglas College, P.O. Box 2503, New Westminster, British Columbia V3L 5B2 Canada. Fax: (604)527-5095. Assistant Editor: Bonnie Bauder. 100% freelance written. Works with a small number of new/unpublished writers each year. Triannual magazine (April, August and December) for "those interested in literature and writing." Estab. 1970. Circ. 1,000. Buys 80-100 mss/year. Small payment and contributor's copy only. Publishes ms an average of 6 months after acceptance. Buys first North American serial rights. Byline given. Reports in 4 months. Submit complete ms with IRCs.
• *Event* won the 1993 National Magazine Gold Award for Poetry and the 1993 Western Magazine Award for Fiction.
Nonfiction: "High quality work." Reviews of Canadian books and essays.
Fiction: Short stories.
Poetry: Submit no more than 10 poems at a time. "We are looking for high quality modern poetry."

THE FIDDLEHEAD, Campus House, University of New Brunswick, P.O. Box 4400, Fredericton, New Brunswick E3B 5A3 Canada. (506)453-3501. Fax: (506)453-4599. Editor: Don MacKay. 90% freelance written. Eager to work with new/unpublished writers. Quarterly magazine covering poetry, short fiction and book reviews. Estab. 1945. Circ. 1,100. Pays on publication. Publishes ms an average of 1 year after acceptance. Not copyrighted. Buys first North American serial rights. Submit seasonal material 6 months in advance. Reports in 4 months. Sample copy $8.

Fiction: Banny Belyea, Ted Colson, fiction editors. "Stories may be on any subject—acceptance is based on quality alone. Because the journal is heavily subsidized by the Canadian government, some preference is given to Canadian writers." Buys 30 mss/year. Send complete ms. Length: 50-3,000 words. Pays $10/page.

Poetry: Robert Gibbs, Robert Hawkes, Don MacKay, Demetres Tryphonopoulos, poetry editors. Avant-garde, free verse, light verse. "Poetry may be on any subject—acceptance is based on quality alone. Because the journal is heavily subsidized by the Canadian government, some preference is given to Canadian writers." Buys 100 poems/year. Submit maximum 10 poems. Pays $12/page; $100 maximum.

Tips: "Quality alone is the criterion for publication. Canadian return postage or IRCs should accompany all manuscripts."

FIELD MAGAZINE, Contemporary Poetry & Poetics, Rice Hall, Oberlin College, Oberlin OH 44074-1095. (216)775-8407/8. Fax: (216)775-8124. Editors: Stuart Friebert, David Young, David Walker, Alberta Turner. Managing Editor: Dolorus Nevels. 60% freelance written. Semiannual magazine of poetry, poetry in translation, and essays on contemporary poetry by poets. Estab. 1969. Circ. 2,300. Pays on publication. Byline given. Buys first rights. Editorial lead time 4 months. Reports in 1 month on mss. Sample copy for $7.

Poetry: Buys 100 poems/year. Submit maximum 10 poems. Pays $15-25 minimum/page.

THE GETTYSBURG REVIEW, Gettysburg College, Gettysburg PA 17325. (717)337-6770. Editor: Peter Stitt. Managing Editor: Emily Ruark Clarke. Quarterly literary magazine. "Our concern is quality. Manuscripts submitted here should be extremely well written." Estab. 1988. Circ. 4,000. Pays on publication. Byline given. Buys first North American serial rights. Editorial lead time 6-12 months. Submit seasonal material 9 months in advance. Reports in 1 month on queries; 3 months on mss. Sample copy for $7. Writer's guidelines for #10 SASE. No simultaneous submissions.

Nonfiction: Essays. Buys 20/year. Send complete ms. Length: 3,000-7,000. Pays $25/page.

Fiction: High quality, literary. Publishes novel excerpts. Buys 20 ms/year. Send complete ms. Length: 2,000-7,000, Pays $25/page.

Poetry: Buys 50 poems/year. Submit maximum 3 poems. Pays $2/line.

GLIMMER TRAIN STORIES, Glimmer Train Press, Inc., 812 SW Washington St., #1205, Portland OR 97205. (503)221-0836. Editors: Linda Davies, Susan Burmeister-Brown. 90% freelance written. Quarterly magazine covering short fiction. "We are interested in well-written, emotionally-moving short stories published by unknown, as well as known, writers." Estab. 1991. Circ. 16,000. **Pays on acceptance.** Byline given. Buys first rights. Accepts simultaneous submissions. Reports in 3 months on mss. Sample copy for $9. Writer's guidelines for #10 SASE.

Fiction: "We are not restricted to any types (other than erotica or condensed novels)." Buys 32 mss/year. Send complete ms. Length: 1,200-8,000 words. Pays $500.

Tips: "Manuscripts should be sent to us in the months of January, April, July and October. Be sure to include a sufficiently-stamped SASE. We are particularly interested in receiving work from new writers." See *Glimmer Train's* Short Story Award for New Writers' listing in Contest and Awards section.

GRAIN LITERARY MAGAZINE, Saskatchewan Writers Guild, P.O. Box 1154, Regina, Saskatchewan S7K 2Z4 Canada. Editor: J. Jill Robinson. Business Manager: Steven Smith. 100% freelance written. Quarterly literary magazine covering poetry, fiction, creative nonfiction, drama. "*Grain* publishes writing of the highest quality, both traditional and nontraditional in nature. *The Grain* editors aim: To publish work that challenges its readers; to encourage promising new writers; and to produce a well-designed, visually exiciting magazine." Estab. 1971. Circ. 1,800. Pays on publication. Publishes ms an average of 11 months after acceptance. Byline given. Buys first, Canadian, serial rights. Editorial lead time 6 months. Reports in 1 month on queries; 3 months on mss. Sample copy for $6.95. Writer's guidelines free on request.

Nonfiction: Interested in creative nonfiction.

Fiction: Literary fiction of all types. "No romance, confession, science fiction, vignettes, mystery." Buys 40 mss/year. Query or send complete ms. Pays $30-100. Publishes novel excerpts.

Poetry: Avant-garde, free verse, haiku, traditional. "High quality, imaginative, well-crafted poetry. No sentimental, end-line rhyme, mundane." Buys 78 poems/year. Submit maximum 10 poems. Pays $30-100.

Tips: "Submit your best unpublished work."

HIGH PLAINS LITERARY REVIEW, 180 Adams St., Suite 250, Denver CO 80206. (303)320-6828. Editor: Robert O. Greer, Jr. Managing Editor: Phyllis A. Harwell. 80% freelance written. Triannual literary magazine. "The *High Plains Literary Review* publishes short stories, essays, poetry, reviews and interviews, bridging the gap between commercial quarterlies and academic reviews." Estab. 1986. Circ. 1,200. Pays on publication. Byline given. Buys first North American serial rights. Accepts simultaneous submissions. Reports in 12 weeks. Sample copy for $4. Writer's guidelines for #10 SASE.

● Its unique editorial format—between commercial and academic—makes for lively reading. Could be good market for that "in between" story.

Nonfiction: Essays, reviews. Buys 20 mss/year. Send complete ms. Length: 10,000 words maximum. Pays $5/page.

Fiction: Ethnic, historical, humorous, mainstream. Buys 12 mss/year. Send complete ms. Length: 10,000 words maximum. Pays $5/page.

Poetry: Buys 45 poems/year. Pays $10/page.

THE HOLLINS CRITIC, P.O. Box 9538, Hollins College, Roanoke VA 24019. Editor: John Rees Moore. 18% freelance written. "Non-specialist periodical published 5 times/year with artist's cover sketch and an essay on work of a contemporary poet, fiction writer or dramatist. Brief book review section and a few poems. *The Hollins Critic* owns the copyright." Estab. 1964. Circ. 488. Pays on publication. Buys all rights. Sample copy for $1.25. Writer's guidelines for #10 SASE.

Nonfiction: Essays. Buys 3 mss/year. Query with published clips and SASE. Length: 4,500-5,000 words. Pays $200 for feature essay.

INDIANA REVIEW, Indiana University, 316 N. Jordan, Bloomington IN 47405. (812)855-3439. Editor: Shirley Stephenson. Associate Editor: Geoffry Polluck. 100% freelance written. Semiannual magazine. "We publish innovative fiction and poetry. We're interested in energy, originality and careful attention to craft. While we publish many well-known writers, we also welcome new and emerging poets and fiction writers." Estab. 1982. **Pays on acceptance.** Byline given. Buys first North American serial rights. Reports within 4 months. Sample copy for $7. Free writer's guidelines.

Nonfiction: Essays. No pornographic or strictly academic articles dealing with the traditional canon. Buys 8 mss/year. Query. Length: 7,500 maximum. Pays $25-200.

Fiction: Experimental, mainstream. No pornography. Buys 18 mss/year. Send complete ms. Length: 250-15,000. Pays $5/page.

Poetry: Avant-garde, free verse. Looks for inventive and skillful writing. Buys 80 mss/year. Submit up to 5 poems at one time only. Length: 5 lines minimum. Pays $5/page.

Tips: "Read us before you submit. Often reading is slower in summer months."

THE IOWA REVIEW, 369 EPB, The University of Iowa, Iowa City IA 52242. (319)335-0462. Fax: (319)335-2535. Editor: David Hamilton. Associate Editor: Mary Hussmann, with the help of colleagues, graduate assistants. Triannual magazine. Estab. 1970. Buys first serial rights. Reports in 3 months. Sample copy for $6.

Nonfiction, Fiction and Poetry: "We publish essays, reviews, stories and poems and would like for our essays not always to be works of academic criticism." Buys 65-85 unsolicited mss/year. Submit complete ms with SASE. Pays $1/line for verse; $10/page for prose.

● This magazine's reading period is September-April.

IOWA WOMAN, Iowa Woman Endeavors, Inc., P.O. Box 680, Iowa City IA 52244-0680. Editor: Marianne Abel. Managing Editor: Rebecca Childers. Quarterly magazine of "award-winning fiction, poetry, essays, reviews, interviews and visual art by women everywhere. For readers of fine literature anywhere. As the publication of a nonprofit educational organization, we steer away from rhetoric and polemics." Estab. 1979. Circ. 2,500. Pays on publication. Publishes ms an average of 6-8 months after acceptance. Byline given. Buys first North American serial rights. Submit seasonal material 8-12 months in advance. Reports in 2 weeks on queries, 3 months on mss. Sample copy for $6. Writer's guidelines for #10 SASE.

Nonfiction: Essays, historical, humor, interview/profile articles, personal experience. "No rhetorical slant on current political or environmental causes." Buys 16 mss/year. Query or send complete ms. Length: 2,000-6,000. Pays $5/page and 2 copies. Sometimes pays expenses of writers on assignment.

Photos: State availability of or send photos with submission. Reviews contact sheets. Offers no additional payment for photos accepted with ms. Captions, model releases and identification of subjects required. Buys one time rights.

Columns/Departments: Under 21 (younger writers, any genre); As We Were (the good-?-!-old days); Crossings (culture shock in this society or others); First Person (a general category); Stopped Moments (incidents, environment, place); Genealogies (personal, historical, intergenerational); New Writers (never before published, any genre). Buys 12-15 mss/year. Pays $5/page.

Fiction: Adventure, ethnic, experimental, fantasy, historical, humorous, mystery, science fiction, slice-of-life vignettes, women, novel excerpts. "Nothing raunchy or maudlin." Buys 12 mss/year. Send complete ms. Length: 6,500 words maximum. Pays $5/page.

Poetry: Sandra Adelmund, poetry editor. Free verse, traditional. "No greeting card types or predictable rhymes or rhythms." Buys 25-40 poems/year. Submit maximum 5 poems. Pays $5/poem.

Tips: "We publish many writers and artists each year for their first time and welcome new and emerging writers who submit quality work in any sector of the magazine. Submissions have a better chance through the year; don't necessarily wait for the annual writing contest which is quite competitive."

JAPANOPHILE, P.O. Box 223, Okemos MI 48864-0223. Editor: Earl Snodgrass. 80% freelance written. Works with a small number of new/unpublished writers each year. Quarterly magazine for literate people who are interested in Japanese culture anywhere in the world. Estab. 1974. Pays on publication. Publishes ms an average of 3 months after acceptance. Buys first North American serial rights. Accepts previously published submissions. Send information about when and where article previously published. For reprints, pays up to 100% of amount paid for original article. Reports in 3 months. Sample copy for $4, postpaid. Writer's guidelines for #10 SASE.

• *Japanophile* would like to receive more haiku and more humorous articles and fillers. It needs more book reviews. It would also like to find one or more columnists to cover: California, Hawaii, New York. This column would probably be like "Tokyo Topics."

Nonfiction: "We want material on Japanese culture in *North America or anywhere in the world*, even Japan. We want articles, preferably with pictures, about persons engaged in arts of Japanese origin: a Michigan naturalist who is a haiku poet, a potter who learned raku in Japan, a vivid 'I was there' account of a Go tournament in California. We would like to hear more about what it's like to be a Japanese in the US. Our particular slant is a certain kind of culture wherever it is in the world: Canada, the US, Europe, Japan. The culture includes flower arranging, haiku, sports, religion, travel, art, photography, fiction, etc. It is important to study the magazine." Buys 8 mss/issue. Query preferred but not required. Length: 1,600 words maximum. Pays $8-20.

Photos: Pays $10-20 for 5× or 8×10 b&w glossy prints. "We prefer people pictures."

Fiction: Experimental, mainstream, mystery, adventure, humorous, romance, historical. Themes should relate to Japan or Japanese culture. Length: 1,000-4,000 words. Annual contest pays $100 to best short story (contest entry fee $5). Should include one or more Japanese and non-Japanese characters in each story.

Columns/Departments: Regular columns and features are Tokyo Topics and Japan in North America. "We also need columns about Japanese culture in various American cities." Query. Length: 1,000 words. Pays $20 maximum.

Poetry: Traditional, avant-garde and light verse related to Japanese culture or any subject in a Japanese form such as haiku. Length: 3-50 lines. Pays $1-20.

Fillers: Newsbreaks, clippings and short humor of up to 200 words. Pays $1-5.

Tips: "We prefer to see more articles about Japanese culture in the US, Canada and Europe. Lack of convincing fact and detail is a frequent mistake."

THE JOURNAL, Ohio State University, 421 Denney Hall, 164 W. 17th Ave., Columbus OH 43210. (614)292-4076. Editors: Kathy Fagan, Michelle Herman. Associate Editor: Stephen Spoerl. 100% freelance written. Semiannual literary magazine. "We're open to all forms; we tend to favor work that gives evidence of a mature and sophisticated sense of the language." Estab. 1972. Circ. 1,200. Pays on publication. Byline given. Buys first North American serial rights. Reports in 2 weeks on queries; 2 months on mss. Sample copy for $5. Writer's guidelines for #10 SASE.

Nonfiction: Essays, interview/profile. Buys 2 mss/year. Query. Length: 2,000-4,000 words. Pays $25 maximum and contributor's copies.

Photos: State availability of photos with submission. Offers no additional payment for photos accepted with ms. Identification of subjects required. Buys one-time rights.

Columns/Departments: Reviews of contemporary poetry, 2,000-4,000 words. Buys 2 mss/year. Query. Pays $25.

Fiction: Novel excerpts, literary short stories.

Poetry: Avant-garde, free verse, traditional. Buys 100 poems/year. Submit maximum 5 poems/year. Pays $25.

KALLIOPE, a journal of women's art, Florida Community College at Jacksonville, 3939 Roosevelt Blvd., Jacksonville FL 32205. (904)381-3511. Editor: Mary Sue Koeppel. 100% freelance written. Triannual magazine. "*Kalliope* publishes poetry, short fiction, reviews, and black and white art, and one act plays usually by women artists. We look for artistic excellence." Estab. 1978. Circ. 1,600. Pays on publication. Publishes ms an average of 3 months after acceptance. Buys first rights. Reports in 1 week on queries. Sample copy for $7 (recent issue) or $4 (back copy). Writer's guidelines for #10 SASE.

Nonfiction: Essays, interview/profile, reviews of new works of poetry and fiction. Buys 6 mss/year. Send complete ms. Length: 500-2,000 words. Pays $10 honorarium.

Fiction: Ethnic, experimental, fantasy, humorous, mainstream, slice-of-life vignettes, suspense. Buys 12 mss/year. Send complete ms. Length: 100-3,000 words. Pays $10 honorarium.

Poetry: Avant-garde, free verse, haiku, light verse, traditional. Buys 75 poems/year. Submit maximum 6 poems. Length 2-120 lines. Pays $10 honorarium.

Tips: "Women should send us their fine poetry and fiction. We publish the best of the material submitted to us each issue. (We don't build a huge backlog and then publish from that backlog for years.) We look for new writers and ususally publish several with each issue alongside already established writers. We love it when established writers send us their work. We've published Marge Piercy, E.M. Bruner and Colette (works published in English for the first time). Send a bio with all submissions."

THE KENYON REVIEW, Kenyon College, Gambler OH 43022. (614)427-3339. Editor: David H. Lynn. 100% freelance written. Triannual magazine covering contemporary literature and criticism. "An international journal of literature culture and the arts dedicated to an inclusive representation of the best in new writing, interviews and criticism from established and emerging writers." Estab. 1939. Circ. 4,500. Pays on publication. Publishes ms 9-12 months after acceptance. Byline given. Buys first or one-time rights. Editorial lead time 9-12 months. Submit seasonal material 1 year in advance. No simultaneous or previously published submissions. Reports in 2 weeks on queries; 3 months on mss. Sample copy for $8. Writer's guidelines for 4×9 SASE.
Nonfiction: Book excerpts (before publication), essays, interview/profile (query first), translations. Buys 12 mss/year. Query. Length: 7,500 words maximum. Pays $10/published page.
Fiction: Experimental, humorous, mainstream, novel excerpts (before publication), science fiction, slice-of-life vignettes. Buys 30 mss/year. Send complete ms. Length: 7,500 words maximum. Pays $10/published page.
Poetry: Avant-garde, free verse, haiku, light verse, traditional. Buys 60 poems/year. Submit maximum 6 poems. Pays $15/published page.

LINES IN THE SAND, LeSand Publications, 890 Southgate Ave., Daly City CA 94015-3741. Editor: Nina Z. Sanders. Managing Editor: Barbara J. Less. 100% freelance written. Bimonthly magazine. "Stories should be well-written, entertaining and suitable for all ages. No particular slant or philosophy. We strive to have 'something for everybody.' " Estab. 1992. Circ. 125. Pays on publication. Publishes ms an average of 4 months after acceptance. Buys first North American serial or second serial (reprint) rights. Editorial lead time 4 months. Submit seasonal material 4 months in advance. Accepts simultaneous and previously published submissions. Send typed ms with rights for sale noted and information about when and where the article previously appeared. Reports in 4 months. Sample copy for $3.50. Writer's guidelines for #10 SASE.
Fiction: Adventure, fantasy, horror, humorous, mainstream, mystery, science fiction, suspense, western. "No erotica." Buys 50-60 mss/year. Send complete ms. Length: 100-2,000 words. Pays $3-10.
Poetry: Free verse, haiku, light verse and traditional. "No erotica and avant-garde." Buys 12 poems/year. Submit maximum 5 poems. Length: 4-25 lines. Pays $1-3.
Tips: "Use a fresh, original approach. Show, don't tell. Conform to guidelines. Stories should have some type of conflict. Use dialogue, when appropriate. The entire publication is open to freelancers."

LITERARY MAGAZINE REVIEW, English Dept., Kansas State University, Manhattan KS 66506. (913)532-6706. Editor: G.W. Clift. 98% freelance written. Quarterly literary magazine devoted almost exclusively to reviews of the current contents of small circulation serials publishing some fiction or poetry. "Most of our reviewers are recommended to us by third parties." Estab. 1981. Circ. 500. Pays on publication. Publishes ms an average of 1 month after acceptance. Byline given. Buys first rights. Query for electronic submissions. Reports in 2 weeks. *Writer's Market* recommends allowing 2 months for reply. Sample copy for $5.
Nonfiction: Buys 60 mss/year. Query. Length: 1,500 words. Pays $25 maximum and 2 contributor's copies for assigned articles. Sometimes pays expenses of writers on assignment.
Photos: State availability of photos with submission. Identification of subjects required.
Tips: "Interested in omnibus reviews of magazines sharing some quality, editorial philosophy, or place of origin and in articles about literary magazine editing and the literary magazine scene."

LITERARY SKETCHES, P.O. Box 810571, Dallas TX 75381-0571. (214)243-8776. Editor: Olivia Murray Nichols. 33% freelance written. Willing to work with new/unpublished writers. Monthly newsletter for readers with literary interests of all ages. Estab. 1961. Circ 500. Byline given. Pays on publication. Publishes ms an average of 1 year after acceptance. Reports in 2 months. Occasionally accepts previously published material. Send copy of article or typed ms with rights for sale noted and information on when and where article previously appeared. Pays 100% of amount paid for an original article. Sample copy for #10 SASE.
Nonfiction: Interviews of well-known writers and biographical material of more than common knowledge on past writers. Concise, informal style. Centennial pieces relating to a writer's birth, death or famous works. Buys 4-6 mss/year. Submit complete ms. Length: up to 1,000 words. Pays ½¢/word, plus copies.
Tips: "Articles need not be footnoted, but a list of sources should be submitted with the manuscript. We appreciate fillers of 100 words or less if they concern some little known information on an author or book."

MAGIC REALISM, Pyx Press, P.O. Box 922648, Sylmar CA 91392-2648. Editor: C. Darren Butler. Managing Editor: Julie Thomas. 75% freelance written. Quarterly literary magazine of magic realism, literary fantasy and related fictions. Estab. 1990. Circ. 1,200. **Pays on acceptance**. Publishes ms an average of 6-18 months after acceptance. Buys first North American serial, one-time rights, non-exclusive (reprint) rights or Spanish language rights. Editorial lead time 4 months. Accepts simultaneous and previously published submissions. Reports in 1 month on queries, 6 months on mss. Sample copy for $4.95 (back issue); $5.95 (current issue). Writer's guidelines for #10 SASE.

• *Magic Realism* also offers a short fiction contest. See the Contest and Awards section.

Nonfiction: Book excerpts, essays, interview/profile, translations. Buys 2 mss/year. Query. Length: 8,000 words maximum. Pays 1¢/4 words.

Photos: State availability of photos with submission. Reviews contact sheets, prints. Offers $2-100/photo. Model releases required. Buys one-time rights.

Fiction: Experimental, fantasy, magic realism. Buys 70-80 mss/year. Send complete ms. Length: 8,000 words. Pays 1¢/4 words.

Poetry: All styles considered. Buys 25 poems/year. Submit maximum 8 poems. Pays $3/magazine page.

Tips: "We prefer a short cover letter with bio and/or credits. We especially need short-short fiction of 200-2,000 words."

THE MALAHAT REVIEW, The University of Victoria, P.O. Box 1700, Victoria, British Columbia V8W 2Y2 Canada. Contact: Editor. 100% freelance written. Eager to work with new/unpublished writers. Quarterly covering poetry, fiction, drama and criticism. Estab. 1967. Circ. 1,700. **Pays on acceptance.** Publishes ms up to 1 year after acceptance. Byline given. Offers 100% kill fee. Buys first serial rights. Reports in 2 weeks on queries; 3 months on mss. Sample copy for $7.

Nonfiction: Interview/profile (literary/artistic). Buys 2 mss/year. Query first. Length: 1,000-8,000. Pays $35-175.

Photos: Pays $25 for b&w prints. Captions required. Pays $100 for color print used as cover.

Fiction: Buys 20 mss/year. Send complete ms. Length: no restriction. Pays $40/1,000 words.

Poetry: Avant-garde, free verse, traditional. Buys 100/year. Pays $25/page.

MANOA, A Pacific Journal of International Writing, University of Hawaii Press, 1733 Donaghho Rd., Honolulu HI 96822. (808)956-3070. Fax: (808)956-3083. Editor: Frank Stewart. Associate Editor: Darlaine Dudoit. Managing Editor: Patricia Matsueda. Assistant Managing Editor: Charlene Gilmore. Semiannual literary magazine. "No special slant. Just high quality literary fiction, poetry, essays, personal narrative, reviews. About half of each issue is devoted to US writing, and half translations of new work from Pacific Rim nations. Our audience is primarily in the US, although expanding in Pacific Rim countries. US writing need not be confined to Pacific settings or subjects." Estab. 1989. Circ. 2,500. Pays on publication. Byline given. Buys first North American serial or non-exclusive, one-time reprint rights. Editorial lead time 6 months. Submit seasonal material 8 months in advance. Reports in 3 weeks on queries; 2 months on poetry mss, 4 months on fiction. Sample copy for $7. Writer's guidelines free on request.

Nonfiction: Frank Stewart, editor. Book excerpts, essays, interview/profile, creative nonfiction or personal narrative related to literature or nature. No Pacific exotica. Charlene Gilmore, reviews editor. Buys 3-4 mss/year, excluding reviews. Query or send complete ms. Length: 1,000-5,000 words. Pays $25/printed page, plus contributor copies.

Fiction: Ian MacMillan, fiction editor. "We're potentially open to anything of literary quality, though usually not genre fiction as such." Publishes novel excerpts. No Pacific exotica. Buys 12-18 mss/year in the US (excluding translation). Send complete ms. Length: 1,000-7,500. Pays $100-500 normally ($25/printed page).

Poetry: Frank Stewart, editor. No light verse. Buys 40-50 poems/year. Pays $25.

Tips: "Although we are a Pacific journal, we are a general interest US literary journal, not limited to Pacific settings or subjects. Translations are least open to freelancers, since these are usually solicited by a special guest editor for a special feature."

THE MASSACHUSETTS REVIEW, Memorial Hall, University of Massachusetts, Amherst MA 01003-9934. (413)545-2689. Editors: Mary Heath, Jules Chametzky, Paul Jenkins. Quarterly magazine. Estab. 1959. Pays on publication. Publishes ms 6-18 months after acceptance. Buys first North American serial rights. Reports in 3 months. Manuscripts will not be returned unless accompanied by SASE. Sample copy for $5 with 3 first-class stamps.

• *Massachusetts Review* no longer considers plays.

Nonfiction: Articles on literary criticism, women, public affairs, art, philosophy, music and dance. Length: 6,500 words average. Pays $50.

Fiction: Short stories or chapters from novels when suitable for independent publication. Length: 25 pages maximum. Pays $50.

Poetry: Pays 35¢/line or $10 minimum.

Tips: "No fiction manuscripts are considered from June to October."

MICHIGAN QUARTERLY REVIEW, 3032 Rackham Bldg., University of Michigan, Ann Arbor MI 48109-1070. Editor: Laurence Goldstein. 75% freelance written. Prefers to work with published/established writers. Quarterly. Estab. 1962. Circ. 1,500. Publishes ms an average of 1 year after acceptance. Pays on publication. Buys first serial rights. Reports in 2 months. Sample copy for $2.50 with 2 first-class stamps.

Nonfiction: "*MQR* is open to general articles directed at an intellectual audience. Essays ought to have a personal voice and engage a significant subject. Scholarship must be present as a foundation, but we are not interested in specialized essays directed only at professionals in the field. We prefer ruminative essays, written in a fresh style and which reach interesting conclusions. We also like memoirs and interviews with significant historical or cultural resonance." Length: 2,000-5,000 words. Pays $100-150.

Fiction and Poetry: No restrictions on subject matter or language. "We publish about 10 stories a year and are very selective. We like stories which are unusual in tone and structure, and innovative in language." Send complete ms. Pays $10/published page.

Tips: "Read the journal and assess the range of contents and the level of writing. We have no guidelines to offer or set expectations; every manuscript is judged on its unique qualities. On essays—query with a very thorough description of the argument and a copy of the first page. Watch for announcements of special issues, which are usually expanded issues and draw upon a lot of freelance writing. Be aware that this is a university quarterly that publishes a limited amount of fiction and poetry; that it is directed at an educated audience, one that has done a great deal of reading in all types of literature."

MID-AMERICAN REVIEW, Dept. of English, Bowling Green State University, Bowling Green OH 43403. (419)372-2725. Editor-in-Chief: George Looney. Willing to work with new/unpublished writers. Semiannual literary magazine of "the highest quality fiction, poetry and translations of contemporary poetry and fiction." Also publishes critical articles and book reviews of contemporary literature. Estab. 1972. Pays on publication. Publishes ms an average of 3-6 months after acceptance. Byline given. Buys one-time rights. Reports in 4 months. Sample copy for $7 (current issue), $5 (back issue); rare back issues $10.

Fiction: Character-oriented, literary. Buys 12 mss/year. Send complete ms; do not query. Pays $10/page up to $50.

Poetry: Strong imagery, strong sense of vision. Buys 60 poems/year. Pays $10/page up to $50.

Tips: "We are seeking translations of contemporary authors from all languages into English; submissions must include the original."

THE MISSOURI REVIEW, 1507 Hillcrest Hall, University of Missouri, Columbia MO 65211. (314)882-4474. Editor: Speer Morgan. Managing Editor: Greg Michalson. 100% freelance written. Triannual literary magazine. "We publish contemporary fiction, poetry, interviews, personal essays, cartoons, special features—such as 'History as Literature' series and 'Found Text' series—for the literary and the general reader interested in a wide range of subjects." Estab. 1978. Circ. 6,500. Pays on signed contract. Byline given. Buys first rights or one-time rights. Editorial lead time 6 months. Reports in 2 weeks on queries; 3 months on mss. Sample copy for $6. Writer's guidelines for #10 SASE.

Nonfiction: Evelyn Somers, associate editor. Book excerpts, essays. "No literary criticism." Buys 10 mss/year. Send complete ms. Pays approximately $15-20/printed page up to $750.

Fiction: Mainstream. Buys 25 mss/year. Send complete ms. Pays $15-20 per printed page up to $750.

Poetry: Greg Michalson, poetry editor. Publishes 3-5 poetry features of 6-12 pages each per issue. "Please familiarize yourself with the magazine before submitting poetry." Buys 50 poems/year. Pays $125-250.

MODERN HAIKU, P.O. Box 1752, Madison WI 53701-1752. Editor: Robert Spiess. 90% freelance written. Triannual magazine of haiku. "*Modern Haiku* is the foremost international English language haiku journal. We are open to all schools of haiku but do not publish sentimental, pretty-pretty, striving-for-effect or to-startle work." Estab. 1969. Circ. 675. **Pays on acceptance.** Byline given. Buys first North American serial rights. Editorial lead time 3 months. Reports in 2 weeks. Sample copy for $5.

Nonfiction: Essays. Buys 50 mss/year. Send complete ms. Pays $5/printed page.

Poetry: Haiku. "Send poems that can be recited in one breath length." Pays $1/haiku.

Tips: "A haiku is a poem written from the body's center of gravity, not from the head—written through the intelligence of the heart, not the mind. Forget the idea that a haiku must be 17 syllables; a haiku is an up-to-a-breath length *poem*, not an exercise in arithmetic."

MYSTIC FICTION, P.O. Box 40625, Bellevue WA 98015-4625. Editor: Su Llewellyn. 100% freelance written. Quarterly magazine "publishing stories about transformation (psychological or emotional). Story subject matter can include small but significant events in the lives of the fictional characters. (No addiction recovery stories, please)." Estab. 1993. Circ. 100. Pays in the quarter before the issue is due out. Byline given. Buys first North American serial or one-time rights. Editorial lead time 1 year. Submit seasonal material 1 year in advance. Accepts previously published submissions. Send typed ms with rights for sale noted and information about when and where the article previously appeared. For reprints, pays 100% of the amount paid for an original article. Query for electronic submissions. Reports in 2 weeks on queries, 1-2 months on mss. Sample copy for $5. Writer's guidelines for #10 SASE.

Fiction: Ethnic, historical, mainstream, slice-of-life vignettes, folklore/faerie tale, limited science fiction/fantasy. Buys 28-50 mss/year. Send complete ms. Length: 500-5,000 words. Pays $5-20 or in contributor's copies.

ALWAYS enclose a self-addressed, stamped envelope (SASE) with all your queries and correspondence.

Tips: "Read our guidelines, better yet, read an issue of *MF*."

NEGATIVE CAPABILITY, 62 Ridgelawn Dr. E., Mobile AL 36608-6116. Fax: (205)344-8478. Editor: Sue Walker. Managing Editor: Richard Beyer. 99% freelance written. Triannual literary journal. "Negative capability seeks work that lingers in the mind after the pages of the book have been closed. We want work that acts as an axe that breaks the frozen sea within us." Estab. 1981. Circ. 1,000. Pays on publication. Byline given. Buys first North American serial rights. Submit seasonal material 6 months in advance. Query for electronic submissions. Reports in 2 months on mss. Sample copy for $5. Writer's guidelines free on request.
Nonfiction: Essays, general interest, humor, interview/profile, opinion, personal experience, photo feature, religious. Upcoming issue on literature and law, literature and aging. Buys 6-8 mss/year. Send complete ms. Pays in contributor copies for nonfiction.
Photos: State availability of photos with submissions. Reviews 5×7 prints. Offers no additional payment for photos. Captions and identification of subjects required. Buys one-time rights.
Fiction: No pornography. Buys 20 mss/year.
Poetry: Avant-garde, free verse, haiku, light verse, traditional. Buys 200 poems/year. Submit maximum 5 poems.
Fillers: Anecdotes, gags to be illustrated by cartoonist, short humor.

THE NORTH AMERICAN REVIEW, University of Northern Iowa, Cedar Falls IA 50614-0516. (319)273-6455. Editor: Robley Wilson. 50% freelance written. Bimonthly. Circ. 5,000. Buys first rights. Pays on publication. Publishes ms an average of 1 year after acceptance. Sample copy for $4.
  • Now published six times per year rather than quarterly, this is one of the oldest and most prestigious literary magazines in the country. Also one of the most entertaining—and a tough market for the young writer.
Nonfiction: No restrictions, but most nonfiction is commissioned. Query. Rate of payment arranged.
Fiction: No restrictions; highest quality only. Length: open. Pays minimum $15/published page. Fiction department closed (no mss read) from April 1-December 31.
Poetry: Peter Cooley. No restrictions; highest quality only. Length: open. Pays 50¢/line; $20 minimum/poem.

NORTH CAROLINA LITERARY REVIEW: A Magazine of Literature, Culture, and History, English Dept., East Carolina University, Greenville NC 27858-4353. (919)328-4876. Fax: (919)328-4889. Editor: Alex Albright. 80% freelance written. Annual literary magazine published in spring covering North Carolina/Southern writers, literature, culture, history. "Articles should have North Carolina-related slant; essays by writers associated with North Carolina may address any subject. First consideration is always for quality of work. Although we treat academic and scholarly subjects, we do not wish to see jargon-laden prose; our readers, we hope, are found as often in bookstores and libraries as in academia. We seek to combine best elements of magazine for serious readers with best of scholarly journal." Estab. 1992. Circ. 1,500. Pays on publication. Publishes ms 6-9 months after acceptance. Byline given. Offers 25% kill fee. Buys first North American serial rights. (Rights returned to writer on request.) Editorial lead time 6 months. Query for electronic submissions. Reports in 10 weeks on queries, 2 months on mss, 8 months on unsolicited mss. Sample copy for $10. Writer's guidelines free on request.
Nonfiction: Book excerpts, essays, exposé, general interest, historical/nostalgic, humor, interview/profile, opinion, personal experience, photo feature, travel, reviews, short narratives; surveys of archives. "No reviews that treat single books by contemporary authors or jargon-laden academic articles." Buys 30-50 mss/year. Query with published clips. Length: 500-5,000 words. Pays $50 minimum. (Pay usually is in $100-300 range, sometimes higher, depending on article.)
Photos: State availability of photos with query. Reviews 5×7 or 8×10 prints; snapshot size or photocopy OK. Negotiates payment individually. Captions and identification of subjects required. (Releases when appropriate.) Buys one-time rights.
Columns/Departments: Archives (survey of North Carolina-writer archives), 500-1,500 words; Thomas Wolfe (Wolfe-related articles/essays), 1,000-2,000 words; Readers/Writers Places (bookstores or libraries, or other places readers and writers gather), 500-1,500; Reviews (essay reviews of North Carolina-related literature (fiction, creative nonfiction, poetry). Buys 10 mss/year. Send complete ms. Pays $50-150.
Fiction: Adventure, ethnic, experimental, fantasy, historical, horror, humorous, mainstream, mystery, novel excerpts, romance, science fiction, slice-of-life vignettes, suspense, western. "No unsolicited manuscripts; fiction and poetry are published in thematic sections or by invitation." Buys 3-4 mss/year. Query. Length: 5,000 words maximum. Pays $100-300.
Poetry: Solicited by editor only. *No unsolicited submissions, please.* Buys 8-10 poems/year. Length: 30-150 lines. Pays $30-150.
Fillers: Buys 2-10/year. Length: 50-300 words. Pays $10-25.
Tips: "By far the easiest way to break in is with departments; we are especially interested in reports on conferences, readings, meetings that involve North Carolina writers; and personal essays or short narratives with strong sense of place to use in loosely defined Readers/Writers Places department. We are more interested in essays that use creative nonfiction approaches than in straight articles of informational nature. See back

issues for other departments. These are the only areas in which we encourage unsolicited manuscripts; but we welcome queries and proposals for all others. Interviews are probably the other easiest place to break in; no discussions of poetics/theory, etc., except in reader-friendly (accessible) language; interviews should be personal, more like conversations, that explore connections between a writer's life and his/her work."

THE NORTHWOODS JOURNAL, A Magazine for Writers, Conservatory of American Letters, P.O. Box 298, Thomaston ME 04861. (207)354-0998. Managing Editor: Robert Olmsted. 80% freelance written. Quarterly literary magazine. Estab. 1993. Circ. 500. **Pays on acceptance**. Byline given. Buys first American serial rights. Editorial lead time 6 months. Submit seasonal material 9 months in advance. Query for electronic submissions. Sample copy for $5 (current) issue, $7.50 (back issue). Writer's guidelines for #10 SASE.
Nonfiction: Essays exposé, general interest, historical/nostalgic, opinion. "No porn or evangelical Christian material." Send complete ms. Length: 480-2,000 or so. Pays $4/page and up for unsolicited articles.
Photos: Offers $5. Model releases required. Buys one-time rights.
Columns/Departments: Reviews, 800 words; Contest, 800-1,000 words. Buys 8 mss/year. Query with clips. Pays $4 and up.
Fiction: Adventure, erotica, experimental, fantasy, historical, horror, humorous, mainstream, mystery, science fiction, slice-of-life vignettes, suspense, western. "No brilliantly written stuff without a plot." Buys 10 mss/year. Send complete ms. Length: 400-2,500 words. Pays $5-25.
Poetry: Avant-garde, free verse, haiku, light verse, traditional. "No religious poetry."Buys 30-40 poems. Pays $2.50-25.
Fillers: Anecdotes, facts, newsbreaks, short humor. Pays $2-5.
Tips: "Keep in mind that we are a magazine for writers, We consider it a showcase not a 'how-to.' We're not interested in sloppy writing or writing for information. We seek writing as art. Be nit picky. You have lots of competition, especially in fiction."

NOSTALGIA, A Sentimental State of Mind, Nostalgia Publications, P.O. Box 2224, Orangeburg SC 29116. Editor: Connie L. Martin. 100% freelance written. Semiannual magazine for poetry and true short stories. "True, personal experiences that relate faith, struggle, hope, success, failure and rising above problems common to all." Estab. 1986. Circ. 1,000. Pays on publication. Publishes ms an average of 1 year after acceptance. Byline given. Buys one-time rights. Submit seasonal material 6 months in advance. Reports in 6 weeks on queries. Sample copy for $3. Writer's guidelines for #10 SASE.
Nonfiction: General interest, historical/nostalgic, humor, inspirational, opinion, personal experience, photo feature, religious and travel. Does not want to see "anything with profanity or sexual references." Buys 10 or more stories/year. Send complete ms. Length: 1,000 words. Pays $25 minimum. Pays contributor copies "if copies are preferred." Short Story Award $100 plus publication.
Photos: State availability of photos with submission. Offers no additional payment for photos with ms.
Poetry: Free verse, haiku, light verse, traditional and modern prose. "No ballads—no profanity—no sexual references." Submit 3 poems maximum. Length: no longer than 45-50 lines preferably. Pays $100 (/semiannual Nostalgia Poetry Award).

OASIS, P.O. Box 626, Largo FL 34649-0626. (813)584-3461. Editor/Publisher: Neal Storrs. 100% freelance written. Quarterly magazine. "*Oasis* is not slanted toward any particular audience, unless it's an audience of people interested in what I hope will be high-quality contemporary fiction, nonfiction and poetry." Estab. 1992. Circ. 300. Pays on publication. Publishes ms an average of 4 months after acceptance. Byline given. Buys one-time rights. Editorial lead time 4 months. Accepts simultaneous and previously published submissions. Send photocopy of article or short story or typed ms with rights for sale noted and information about when and where the article previously appeared. For reprints, pays 100% of the amount paid for an original article. No electronic submissions. Reports in 1 week. Sample copy for $7.50. Writer's guidelines for #10 SASE.
Nonfiction: Book excerpts, essays, exposé, general interest, historical/nostalgic, humor, interview/profile. "No articles in which quality of writing is not a primary concern." Buys 8 mss/year. Send complete ms. Length: 1,000-7,000 words. Pays $15-50 for unsolicited articles.
Fiction: Quality literature only. No children's. Buys 30 mss/year. Send complete ms. Length: 1,000-7,000 words. Pays $15-50.
Poetry: Highly musical free verse. Buys 30. Pays $5/poem.
Tips: "I prefer well-written prose and poetry that feels authentic as well as original. Doesn't everybody? Professionalism in packaging predisposes me to expect a better product, and it usually is. No specific tips: take your best shot and let it fly. And remember that I'm on your side; I want to love your submission as much as you want me to."

THE OHIO REVIEW, 209C Ellis Hall, Ohio University, Athens OH 45701-2979. (614)593-1900. Editor: Wayne Dodd. 40% freelance written. Triannual magazine. "A balanced, informed engagement of contemporary American letters, with special emphasis on poetics." Circ. 3,000. Publishes ms an average of 8 months after acceptance. Rights acquired vary with author and material; usually buys first serial or first North American serial rights. Unsolicited material will be read only September-May. Reports in 10 weeks.

Nonfiction, Fiction and Poetry: Buys essays of general intellectual and special literary appeal. Not interested in narrowly focused scholarly articles. Seeks writing that is marked by clarity, liveliness and perspective. Interested in the best fiction and poetry. Submit complete ms. Buys 75 unsolicited mss/year. Pays minimum $5/page, plus copies.
Tips: "Make your query very brief, not gabby—one that describes some publishing history, but no extensive bibliographies. We publish mostly poetry—essays, short fiction, some book reviews."

THE PARIS REVIEW, 45-39 171st Place, Flushing NY 11358. Submit mss to 541 E. 72nd St., New York NY 10021. Editor: George A. Plimpton. Quarterly. Buys all rights. Pays on publication. Reporting time varies. Address submissions to proper department. Sample copy for $10. Writer's guidelines for #10 SASE (from Flushing Office). Reporting time often 6 months or longer.
Fiction: Study the publication. No length limit. Pays up to $600. Makes award of $1,000 in annual Aga Khan Fiction Contest.
Poetry: Richard Howard, poetry editor. Study the publication. Pay varies according to length, $35 minimum. Awards $1,000 in Bernard F. Conners Poetry Prize contest.

THE PINEHURST JOURNAL, P.O. Box 360747. Milpitas CA 95036-0747. (510)440-9259. Editor: Michael K. McNamara. Contributing Editor: Kathleen M. McNamara. 90% freelance written. Quarterly magazine of distinctive fiction, nonfiction and poetry. "For an educated audience appreciative of polished, thought-provoking work. Audience is 25-75." Estab. 1990. Circ. 300. Pays on publication. Publishes ms an average of 1-6 months after acceptance. Byline given. Buys one-time rights. Submit seasonal/holiday material 6 months in advance. Accepts simultaneous submissions, if identified as such. Offers 100% kill fee. Reports in 2 months. Sample copy for $6. Writer's guidelines for #10 SASE.
Nonfiction: Book or theater reviews, essays, historical/nostalgic, profile, general interest. No Op-ed. Buys 2-4 mss/year. Query for reviews and profiles; otherwise send complete ms. Length: 1,500-3,500 words. Pays $5 plus 1 contributor copy. Needs b&w artwork, no photos. Pays 1 contributor copy for artwork.
Fiction: Experimental, light fantasy, historical, horror, wry humor, mainstream, mystery, suspense. No formula romance or western. No hard sci-fi, occult, swords and sorcery, slasher, porno, travel or religious. Buys 60-70 mss/year. Send complete ms. Length: 750-4,000 words. Pays $5 plus 1 contributor copy.
   • *Pinehurst Press* prefers true fiction.
Poetry: Avant-garde, free verse, haiku, light verse, traditional. Buys 90-110 poems/year. Submit maximum 6 poems. Length: 2-24 lines. Pays contributor copy.
Tips: "Try to make each word pull its own weight but not at the expense of warmth. Spend the extra 25 words, but don't overly embellish. Polish and punctuation are very important to us. Please enclose a 20-40 word bio. This can be publishing success or whatever you're comfortable with. All areas are equally open although nonfiction might be the hardest to crack because of the limited number of topics."

PLOUGHSHARES, Emerson College, Dept. M, 100 Beacon St., Boston MA 02116. Editor: Don Lee. Triquarterly magazine for "readers of serious contemporary literature." Circ. 6,000. Pays on publication, $40 minimum/title, $200/author maximum, with 2 copies and 1-year subscription. Publishes ms an average of 6 months after acceptance. Buys first North American serial rights. Reports in 5 months. Sample copy for $6 (back issue). Writer's guidelines for SASE. Reading period: August 1-March 31.
   • A competitive and highly prestigious market. Rotating and guest editors make cracking the line-up even tougher, since it's difficult to know what is appropriate to send.
Nonfiction: Personal and literary essays (accepted only occasionally). Length: 5,000 words maximum. Pays $10/printed page. Reviews (assigned). Length: 500 words maximum. Pays $30/printed page, $50 maximum.
Fiction: Literary and mainstream. Buys 25-35 unsolicited mss/year. Length: 300-6,000 words. Pays $10/printed page.
Poetry: Traditional forms, blank verse, free verse and avant-garde. Length: open. Pays $20/printed page.
Tips: "We no longer structure issues around preconceived themes. If you believe your work is in keeping with our general standards of literary quality and value, submit at anytime during our reading period."

POETRY, The Modern Poetry Association, 60 W. Walton St., Chicago IL 60610. (312)255-3703. Editor: Joseph Parisi. Managing Editor: Helen Lothrop Klaviter. 100% freelance written. Monthly poetry magazine. Estab. 1912. Circ. 7,500. Pays on publication. Byline given. Buys all rights. "Copyright assigned to author on request." Submit seasonal/holiday material 6 months in advance. Reports in 3 months. Sample copy for $3.50. Writer's guidelines for #10 SASE.
Poetry: All styles and subject matter. Buys 180-250 poems/year. Submit maximum 4 poems. All lengths considered. Pays $2/line.

PRISM INTERNATIONAL, Department of Creative Writing, Buch E462, 1866 Main Mall, University of British Columbia, Vancouver, British Columbia V6T 1Z1 Canada. Fax: (604)822-3616. E-mail: prism@unix-g.ubc.ca. Editor-in-Chief: Leah Postman. Executive Editor: Andrew Gray. 100% freelance written. Eager to work with new/unpublished writers. Quarterly magazine emphasizing contemporary literature, including translations, for university and public libraries, and private subscribers. Estab. 1959. Circ. 1,200. Pays on publication. Publishes ms an average of 4 months after acceptance. Buys first North American serial rights. Reports in 3 months. Sample copy for $5. Writer's guidelines for #10 SAE with 1 first-class Canadian stamp (Canadian entries) or 1 IRC (US entries).

Nonfiction: *"Creative* nonfiction that reads like fiction." No reviews, tracts or scholarly essays.

Fiction: Annabel Lyon, fiction editor. Experimental, traditional, novel excerpts. Buys 3-5 mss/issue. Send complete ms. Length: 5,000 words maximum. Pays $20/printed page and 1-year subscription. Publishes novel excerpts, maximum length: 25 double-spaced pages.

Poetry: Jennifer Herbison, poetry editor. Avant-garde, traditional. Buys 20 poems/issue. Submit maximum 6 poems. Pays $20/printed page and 1-year subscription.

Drama: One-acts preferred. Pays $20/printed page and 1-year subscription.

Tips: "We are looking for new and exciting fiction. Excellence is still our number one criterion. As well as poetry, imaginative nonfiction and fiction, we are especially open to translations of all kinds, very short fiction pieces and drama which works well on the page."

PULPHOUSE: A Fiction Magazine, Pulphouse Publishing, Inc., Box 1227, Eugene OR 97440. Editor: Dean Wesley. 80% freelance written. Quarterly magazine featuring all short fiction."We like short stories that have an edge and are well written." Estab. 1987. Circ. 5,000. **Pays on acceptance.** Publishes ms an average of 16 months after acceptance. Byline given. Buys first North American serial rights. Editorial lead time 1 year. Submit seasonal material 1 year in advance. Reports in 2 months on mss. Occasionally accepts reprints of previously published material. Send photocopy of short story and information about when and where the article previously appeared. Sample copy for $4.95. Writer's guidelines for #10 SASE.

• *Pulphouse* has received its third nomination for the Hugo Award.

Fiction: Adventure, erotica, experimental, fantasy, historical, horror, humorous, mainstream, mystery, romance, science fiction, suspense, western. Pays 4-7¢/word.

QUARTERLY WEST, University of Utah Publications Council, 317 Olpin Union, University of Utah, Salt Lake City UT 84108. (801)581-3938. Co-editors: M.L. Williams and Lawrence Coates. Semiannual magazine. "We publish fiction, poetry, and nonfiction in long and short formats, and will consider experimental as well as traditional works." Estab. 1976. Circ. 1,100. Pays on publication. Publishes ms an average of 6 months after acceptance. Buys first North American serial and all rights. Accepts simultaneous submissions if so notified. Query for electronic submissions. Reports in 2-6 months on mss. Sample copy for $6.50. Writer's guidelines for #10 SASE.

Nonfiction: Essays, interview/profile, book reviews. Buys 2-3 mss/year. Send complete ms. Length: 10,000 words maximum. Pays $25.

Fiction: Wendy Mai Rawlings. Ethnic, experimental, humorous, mainstream, novel excerpts, short shorts, slice-of-life vignettes, translations. Buys 20-30 mss/year. Send complete ms. Pays $25-500.

Poetry: Margot Schilpp, short stories. Avant-garde, free verse, traditional. Buys 30-50 poems/year. Submit maximum 5 poems. Pays $15-100.

Tips: "Don't write long-winded cover letters. Strikingly original work speaks for itself."

QUEEN'S QUARTERLY, A Canadian Review, Queen's University, Kingston, Ontario K7L 3N6 Canada. (613)545-2667. Fax: (613)545-6822. E-mail: qquartrly@qucon.bitnet. Editor: Boris Castel. Estab. 1893. Quarterly magazine covering a wide variety of subjects, including science, humanities, arts and letters, politics and history for the educated reader. 15% freelance written. Circ. 3,000. Pays on publication. Publishes ms an average of 3 months after acceptance. Byline given. Buys first North American serial rights. Requires 1 double-spaced hard copy and 1 copy on disk in WordPerfect. Reports in 1 month on mss. *Writer's Market* recommends allowing 2 months for reply. Sample copy $6.50.

• No longer accepting fantasy fiction.

Fiction: Historical, humorous, mainstream and science fiction.

Buys 8-12 mss/year. Send complete ms. Length: 4,000 words maximum. Pays $80-150.

Poetry: Avant-garde, free verse, haiku, light verse, traditional. No "sentimental, religious, or first efforts by unpublished writers." Buys 25/year. Submit maximum 6 poems. Length: open. Pays $20-35.

Tips: "Poetry and fiction are most open to freelancers. Don't send less than the best. No multiple submissions. No more than 6 poems or one story per submission. We buy very few freelance submissions."

RARITAN, A Quarterly Review, 31 Mine St., New Brunswick NJ 08903. (908)932-7887. Editor: Richard Poirier. Contact: Suzanne Katz Hyman, managing editor. Quarterly magazine covering literature, general culture. Estab. 1981. Circ. 3,500. Pays on publication. Publishes ms 1 year after acceptance. Byline given. Buys first North American serial rights. Editorial lead time 5 months. Accepts simultaneous submissions.

Nonfiction: Book excerpts, essays. Buys 50 mss/year. Send complete ms. Length 15-30 pages. Pays $100.

THE RIALTO, 32 Grosvenor Rd., Norwich, Norfolk NR2 2PZ England. Co-Editors: Michael Mackmin, John Wakeman. 100% freelance written. Magazine of new poetry published 3 times/year. "We are looking for excellence. Writers must have an awareness of contemporary poetry." Estab. 1984. Circ. 1,500. Pays on publication. Pulishes ms an average of 10 months after acceptance. Byline sometimes given. Buys one-time rights. Reports in 2 months. Sample copy for 6 pounds sterling.

Poetry: "We buy from poets; not from people who are 'writing poetry.'" Buys 150 poems/year. Submit maximum 6 poems with SAE and IRCs. Pays 10 pounds sterling/poem.

RIVER STYX, Big River Association, 3207 Washington, Louis MO 63103. (314)533-4541. Senior Editors: Quincy Troupe and Michael Castro. Managing Editor: Richard Newman. Triannual literary magazine. "*River Styx* publishes the highest quality fiction, poetry, interviews, essays and visual art. We are an internationally distributed multicultural literary magazine." Estab. 1975. Pays on publication. Manuscripts read in September and October. Publishes ms an average of 1 year after acceptance. Byline given. Buys one-time rights. Accepts simultaneous submissions if so noted. Reports in 4 months on mss. Sample copy for $7. Writer's guidelines for #10 SASE.

Nonfiction: Essays, interview. Buys 2-5 mss/year. Send complete mss. Pays $8/page plus contributor copy.

Photos/Art: Send with submission. Reviews 5×7 or 8×10 b&w prints. Pays $8/page. Buys one-time rights.

Fiction: Mainstream, literary, novel excerpts. Buys 6 mss/year. Send complete ms. Pays $8/page.

Poetry: Avant-garde, free verse, traditional. No religious. Buys 40-50 poems/year. Submit maximum 6 poems. Pays $8/page.

ROOM OF ONE'S OWN, A Space for Women's Writing, West Coast Feminist Literary Magazine Society, P.O. Box 46160, Station D, Vancouver, British Columbia V6J 5G5 Canada. Contact: Growing Room Collective. Quarterly literary journal of feminist literature. Estab. 1975. Circ. 1,000. **Pays on acceptance.** Publishes ms an average of 8 months after acceptance. Byline given. Buys first North American serial rights. Editorial lead time 9 months. Query for electronic submissions. Reports on acceptance only. Sample copy for $7. Writer's guidelines for #10 SAE with 2 IRCs (US postage not valid in Canada).

Nonfiction: Creative documentary. Buys 6-10 mss/year. Send complete ms. Length: 3,500 words maximum. Pays $25 (option to get copies instead of Canadian-issued check).

Photos: Send photos with submission. Reviews prints. Offers no additional payment for photos accepted with ms. Buys one-time rights.

Fiction: Experimental, fantasy, historical, humorous, slice-of-life vignettes, feminist literature. No mainstream, popular. Buys 30 mss/year. Length: 3,500 words maximum. Pays $25.

Poetry: Avant-garde, free verse, haiku, traditional. "Nothing light, undeveloped." Buys 35 poems/year. Submit maximum 6 poems. Length: 3-80 lines. Pays $25 maximum/group per issue.

ROSEBUD, For People Who Enjoy Writing, Rosebud, Inc., P.O. Box 459, Cambridge WI 53523. (608)423-9609. Editor: Rod Clark. 100% freelance written. Quarterly magazine "for people who love to read and write. Our readers like good storytelling, real emotion, a sense of place and authentic voice." Estab. 1993. Circ. 6,500. Pays on publication. Publishes ms an average of 2 months after acceptance. Byline given. Buys one-time or second serial (reprint) rights. Editorial lead time 3 months. Submit seasonal material 3 months in advance. Accepts simultaneous submissions and previously published submissions. Reports in 2 months. Sample copy for $5.50. Writer's guidelines for SASE.

Nonfiction: Book excerpt, essays, general interest, historical/nostalgic, humor, interview/profile, personal experience, travel. "No editorializing." Buys 6 mss/year. Send complete ms. Length: 1,200-1,800 words. Pays $45-195 and 2 contributor's copies.

Photos: State availability of photos with submission. Offers no additional payment for photos accepted with ms. Captions, model releases and identification of subjects required. Buys one-time rights.

Fiction: Ethnic, experimental, historical, humorous, mainstream, novel excerpts, slice-of-life vignettes, suspense. "No contrived formula pieces." Buys 80 mss/year. Send complete ms. Length: 1,200-1,800 words. Pays $45-195.

Poetry: Avant-garde, free verse, traditional. No inspirational poetry. Buys 12 poems/year. Submit maximum 5 poems. Length: open. Pays $45-195.

Tips: "Something has to 'happen' in the pieces we choose, but what happens inside characters is much more interesting to us than plot manipulation."

SENSATIONS MAGAZINE, % 2 Radio Ave., A5, Secaucus NJ 07094. Editor: David Messineo. Semiannual magazine publishing contemporary poetry and fiction, and first collection of American poetry: 1565-1700. "*Sensations Magazine* requires writers to subscribe before allowing submission of material to our judges." Publication is not guaranteed with purchase. Cost of issue $20-30. We pay up to $125 per accepted poem up to $50/accepted story. **Pays on acceptance.** Publishes ms an average of 1 month after acceptance. Byline given. Buys one-time rights. Editorial lead time 2 months. Submit seasonal material 2 months in advance. Accepts simultaneous and previously published submissions. Query for electronic submissions. Reports in 3 weeks on queries. Sample copy for $10. Writer's guidelines for #10 SASE. Deadline: December 30, 1995.

● *Sensations Magazine* was the First Place Design Winner of the 1993-94 American Literary Magazine Awards.

Fiction: Adventure, ethnic, experimental, fantasy, historical, horror, humorous, mystery, science fiction, slice-of-life vignettes, suspense, western. Length: 5-15 pgs. Pays up to $50.

Poetry: Avant-garde, free verse, traditional. Buys 10-15 poems/year. Submit maximum 2 poems. Length: 12-80 lines. Pays up to $125.

Tips: "Read the magazine. Follow guidelines. Especially interested in mysteries, science fiction, good comedy, and historical fiction. March 1996 issue, general theme.

SHORT STUFF, for Grown-ups, Bowman Publications, P.O. Box 7057, Loveland CO 80537. (303)669-9139. Editor: Donna Bowman. 98% freelance written. Monthly magazine. "We are perhaps an enigma in that we publish only clean stories in any genre. We'll tackle any subject, but don't allow obscene language or pornographic description. Our magazine is for grown-ups, *not* x-rated 'adult' fare." Estab. 1989. Circ. 5,400. Pays on publication. Publishes ms an average of 6 months after acceptance. Byline given. Buys first North American serial rights. Editorial lead time 3 months. Submit seasonal material 3 months in advance. Reports in 3-6 months on mss. Sample copy for 11 × 14 SAE with 5 first-class stamps. Writer's guidelines for #10 SASE.

Nonfiction: Humor. Special issues: Celebrate February Valentine Issue (copy needed by November). Buys 20 mss/year. Send complete ms. Length: 500-1,800 words. Pays $10-50.

Photos: Send photos with submission. Offers no additional payment for photos accepted with ms. Identification of subjects required. Buys one-time rights.

Fiction: Adventure, historical, humorous, mainstream, mystery, romance, science fiction (seldom), slice-of-life vignettes, suspense, western. Buys 144 mss/year. Send complete ms. Length: 500-1,800 words. Pays $10-50.

Fillers: Anecdotes, short humor. Buys 200/year. Length: 20-500 words. Pays $5.

SING HEAVENLY MUSE!, Women's Poetry and Prose, Sing Heavenly Muse! Inc., Box 13320, Minneapolis MN 55414. (612)729-4266. Contact: Editorial Circle. 100% freelance written. Annual journal of women's literature. Circ. 1,500. Pays on publication. Publishes ms an average of 1 year after acceptance. Byline given. Buys first North American serial rights. Reports in 3 months. Sample copy for $4. Writer's guidelines for #10 SASE.

• Manuscripts that pass the first screening may be held longer.

Fiction: Women's literature, journal pieces, memoir and novel excerpts. Buys 15-20 mss/year. Length: 5,000 words maximum. Pays $15-25; contributors receive 2 free copies. Publishes novel excerpts.

Poetry: Avant-garde, free verse, haiku, light verse, traditional. Accepts 75-100 poems/year. No limit on length. Pays $15-25.

Tips: "To meet our needs, writing must be feminist and women-centered. Reading periods vary. Issues are often related to a specific theme; *writer should always query for guidelines and upcoming themes and reading periods before submitting manuscripts.*"

THE SOUTHERN REVIEW, 43 Allen Hall, Louisiana State University, Baton Rouge LA 70803-5001. (504)388-5108. Fax: (504)388-5098. Editors: James Olney and Dave Smith. 75% freelance written. Works with a moderate number of new/unpublished writers each year. Quarterly magazine for academic, professional, literary, intellectual audience. Estab. 1965. Circ. 3,100. Buys first serial rights only. Byline given. Pays on publication. Publishes ms an average of 18 months after acceptance. No queries. Reports in 3 months. Sample copy for $6. Writer's guidelines for #10 SASE.

Nonfiction: Essays with careful attention to craftsmanship, technique and to seriousness of subject matter. "Willing to publish experimental writing if it has a valid artistic purpose. Avoid extremism and sensationalism. Essays exhibit thoughtful and sometimes severe awareness of the necessity of literary standards in our time." Emphasis on contemporary literature, especially Southern culture and history. Minimum number of footnotes. Buys 25 mss/year. Length: 4,000-10,000 words. Pays $12/page for prose.

Fiction and Poetry: Short stories of lasting literary merit, with emphasis on style and technique. Length: 4,000-8,000 words. Pays $12/page for prose; $20/page for poetry.

SOUTHWEST REVIEW, 307 Fondren Library West, Box 374, Southern Methodist University, Dallas TX 75275-0374. (214)768-1036. Editor: Willard Spiegelman. 100% freelance written. Works with a small number of new/unpublished writers each year. Quarterly magazine for "adults and college graduates with literary interests and some interest in the Southwest, but subscribers are from all over America and some foreign countries." Circ. 1,500. Pays on publication. Publishes ms an average of 1 year after acceptance. Buys first North American serial rights. Byline given. Reports in up to 3 months. Sample copy for $6.

Nonfiction: "Literary essays, social and political problems, history (especially Southwestern), folklore (especially Southwestern), the arts, etc. Articles should be appropriate for a literary quarterly; no feature stories. Critical articles should consider writer's whole body of work, not just one book. History should use new primary sources or new perspective, not syntheses of old material." Interviews with writers, historical articles. Query. Length: 3,500-7,000 words.

Fiction: No limitations on subject matter for fiction; high literary quality is only criterion. Prefers stories of experimental and mainstream. Submit complete ms. Length: 1,500-7,000 words. The John H. McGinnis

Memorial Award of $1,000 made annually for fiction and nonfiction pieces that appeared in *SWR* during preceding year.

Poetry: No limitations on subject matter. Not particularly interested in broadly humorous, religious or sentimental poetry. Free verse, some avant-garde forms; open to all serious forms of poetry. "There are no arbitrary limits on length, but we find shorter poems are easier to fit into our format." The Elizabeth Matchett Stover Memorial Award of $150 made annually for a poem published in *SWR*.

Tips: "The most frequent mistakes we find in work that is submitted for consideration are lack of attention to grammar and syntax and little knowledge of the kind of thing we're looking for. Writers should look at a couple of issues before submitting."

SPARROW, Sparrow Press, 103 Waldron St., West Lafayette IN 47906. Editor: Felix Stefanile. 60% freelance written. Annual magazine covering poetry, the sonnet, articles on craft, criticism. "Writers who admire and are loyal to the lyric tradition of the English language enjoy our magazine. We are not affiliated with any group or ideology, and encourage poetry that uses meter, rhyme and structured verse, mainly the sonnet. We are not a 'school of resentment' publication." Estab. 1954. Circ. 1,000. Pays on publication. Publishes ms 8 months after acceptance. Byline given. Offers 100% kill fee. Buys first North American serial rights and second serial (reprint) rights. Editorial lead time up to 6 months. Reports in 2-6 weeks. Sample copy for $5 for back issue, $6 for current issue. Writer's guidelines for #10 SASE.

Poetry: Traditional, 90% sonnets. No free verse. Purchased over 100 poems for our 1995 issue, plus prose matter. Submit maximum 5 poems. Length: 14 lines. Pays $3/poem; $25 prize, best of the issue.

Tips: "We are interested in seeing material from poets and critics with a serious commitment to the lyric tradition of the English language, with emphasis on the formal sonnet of a contemporary accent. Our yearbook is used in classes, an audience we aim for. We are not for 'poets' who think the sonnet is passé. Neither do we consider ourselves part of any creative writing program network."

SPECTRUM, Spectrum/Anna Maria College, Box 72-F, Sunset Lane, Paxton MA 01612-1198. (508)849-3450. Editor: Robert H. Goepfert. "*Spectrum* is a multidisciplinary national publication aimed particularly at scholarly generalists affiliated with small liberal arts colleges." Estab. 1985. Circ. 1,000. Pays on publication. Publishes ms an average of 6 months after acceptance. Byline given. Publication copyrighted. Buys first North American serial rights. Reports in 2 months. Sample copy $3. Writer's guidelines for #10 SASE.

Nonfiction: Essays, general interest, historical/nostalgic, inspirational, opinion and interdisciplinary. Buys 8 mss/year. Send complete ms. Length: 3,000-15,000 words. Pays $20 for unsolicited articles.

Photos: State availability of photos with submission. Black and white 8 × 10 prints only. Offers no additional payment for photos accepted with ms. Model releases and identification of subjects required. Buys one-time rights.

Columns/Departments: Reviews (books/recordings/audiovisual aids), 300-500 words; (educational computer software), up to 2,000 words. Buys 2 mss/year. Send complete ms. Length: 300-2,000 words. Pays $20.

Fiction: Ethnic, experimental, fantasy, historical, humorous, mainstream, romance and slice-of-life vignettes. "No erotica, mystery, western or science fiction." Buys 2 ms/year. Send complete ms. Length: 3,000 words. Pays $20.

Poetry: Avant-garde, free verse, light verse and traditional. No long poems (over 100 lines). Buys 8 poems/year. Submit maximum 6 poems.

Tips: "We welcome short fiction and poetry, as well as short- to medium-length articles that are interdisciplinary or that deal with one discipline in a manner accessible to the scholarly-generalist reader. Articles referring to or quoting work of other authors should be footnoted appropriately. All areas are equally open to freelancers. In general, originality and relative brevity are paramount, although we will occasionally publish longer works (e.g., articles) that explore ideas not subject to a briefer treatment."

THE SPIRIT THAT MOVES US, The Spirit That Moves Us Press, Inc., P.O. Box 720820, Jackson Heights NY 11372-0820. (718)426-8788. Editor: Morty Sklar. Annual book of literary works. "We don't push any 'schools'; we're open to many styles and almost any subject matter. We favor work that expresses feeling, whether subtle or passionate. Irregularly we publish *Editor's Choice: Fiction, Poetry & Art from the U.S. Small Press*, which consists of selections from nominations made by other small literary publishers. When writers see our open call for nominations for this anthology, they should encourage their publishers to nominate their and other people's work." Estab. 1975. Pays on publication. Publishes ms an average of 3 months after acceptance. Byline given. Buys first North American serial and/or second serial (reprint) rights. Accepts simultaneous submissions, if so noted, and previously published submissions ("only for those collections that we specify"). Send tearsheet or photocopy of article or short story and information about when and where piece previously appeared. For reprints pays 100% of amount paid for original article. Reports in 2 weeks on queries; 3 months after deadline date on mss (nothing is accepted until everything is read). Sample copy for $5.75 for *15th Anniversary Issue*, $10.75 for *Editor's Choice* to readers of *Writer's Market*.

Nonfiction: Book excerpts, essays, interview/profile, personal experience. Upcoming special issue: *Hunting the Shark*, by Robert Peters. Buys 20-30 mss for special issues. Query; "or if you've seen our call for mss and know the theme, send the ms." Length: 8,500 words maximum. Pays $15-25 plus a free copy and offers extra copies at 40% discount. Pays in contributor copies if so requested by author. "Royalty set-up for single-author books, with a cash advance."

Photos: Reviews contact sheets and 8 × 10 prints. Offers $15/photo; $100 for cover photos plus a free copy and 40% off additional copies. Buys one-time rights. "Photos are considered for artistic merit, and not just illustrative function. All art that we use has to stand on its own."

Fiction: "Nothing slick or commercial." Buys 15-30 mss/year. Query; "or if you know our theme and time frame, send complete ms." Length: 8,500 words maximum. Pays $15-25 plus a free copy and 40% off additional copies.

Poetry: "Not interested in work that just tries to be smart, flashy, sensational; if it's technically skilled but conveys no feeling, we don't care about it for publication. We were the first US publisher to bring out a collection by the Czech poet Nobel Laureate of 1984—and before he won the Nobel prize." Buys 50-100 poems/year. Pays $15 (depending on length and funding/sales obtained) plus a free copy and 40% off additional copies.

Tips: "Writers and visual artists should query first to see what we're working on if they haven't seen our latest call for manuscripts in *Poets & Writers* magazine or elsewhere. Send #10 SASE for themes and time frames."

SPSM&H, *Amelia Magazine*, 329 E St., Bakersfield CA 93304. (805)323-4064. Editor: Frederick A. Raborg, Jr., 100% freelance written. Quarterly magazine featuring fiction and poetry with Romantic or Gothic theme. "SPSM&H (Shakespeare, Petrarch, Sidney, Milton and Hopkins) uses one short story in each issue and 20-36 sonnets, plus reviews of books and anthologies containing the sonnet forms and occasional articles about the sonnet form or about some romantic of Gothic figure or movement. We look for contemporary aspects of the sonnet form." Estab. 1984. Circ. 600. Pays on publication. Publishes ms an average of 6 months after acceptance. Byline given. Offers 50% kill fee. Buys first North American serial rights. Editorial lead time 2 months. Submit seasonal material 3 months in advance. Accepts simultaneous submissions. Reports in 2 weeks on queries; 2-12 weeks on mss. Sample copy for $4.95. Writer's guidelines for #10 SASE.

Nonfiction: Essays, general interest, historical/nostalgic, humor, interview/profile, opinion and anything related to sonnets or to romance. Buys 1-4 mss/year. Send complete ms. Length: 500-2,000 words. Pays $10.

Photos: Send photos with submission. Reviews 8 × 10 or 5 × 7 prints. Offers $10-25/photo. Model releases required. Buys one-time rights.

Fiction: Confession, erotica, experimental, fantasy, historical, humor, humorous, mainstream, mystery, romance, slice-of-life vignettes. Buys 4 mss/year. Send complete ms. Length: 500-2,500 words. Pays $10-20.

Poetry: Sonnets, sonnet sequences. Buys 140 poems/year. Submit maximum 10 poems. Length: 14 lines. Two "best of issue" poets each receive $14.

Fillers: Anecdotes, short humor. Buys 2-4/year. Length: 25-500 words. No payment for fillers.

Tips: "Read a copy certainly. Understand the limitations of the sonnet form and, in the case of fiction, the requirements of the romantic or Gothic genres. Be professional in presentation, and realize that neatness does count. *Be contemporary and avoid Victorian verse forms and techniques. Avoid convolution and forced rhyme.* Idiomatics ought to be contemporary. Don't be afraid to experiment. We consider John Updike's 'Love Sonnet' to be the extreme to which poets may experiment."

STAND MAGAZINE, 179 Wingrove Rd., Newcastle Upon Tyne NE4 9DA United Kingdom. Phone/fax: (091)273-3280. Editors: Jon Silkin, Lorna Tracy, Rodney Pybus. Managing Editor: Philip Bomford. 99% freelance written. Quarterly magazine covering short fiction, poetry, criticism and reviews. "*Stand Magazine* was given this name because it was begun as a stand against apathy towards new writing and in social relations." Estab. 1952. Circ. 4,500 worldwide. Pays on publication. Publishes ms an average of 2 years after acceptance. Byline given. Buys first rights. Editorial lead time 2 months. Reports in 1 week on queries, 2 months on mss. Sample copy for $7. Writer's guidelines for sufficient number of IRCs.

Nonfiction: Essays, interview/profile, reviews of poetry/fiction. "Reviews are commissioned from known freelancers." Buys 8 mss/year. Query. Length: 200-5,000 words. Pays $30.

Fiction: "No genre fiction." Buys 8-10 mss/year. Send complete ms. Length: 8,000 words maximum. Pays $45/thousand words.

Poetry: Avant-garde, free verse, traditional. Buys 30-40 poems/year. Submit maximum 6 poems. Pays $45/poem.

Tips: "Poetry/fiction areas are most open to freelancers." Submissions should be accompanied by UK SAE or sufficient IRCs.

STORY, F&W Publications, Inc., 1507 Dana Ave., Cincinnati OH 45207-1005. (513)531-2222. Fax: (513)531-1843. Editor: Lois Rosenthal. 100% freelance written. Quarterly literary magazine of short fiction. "We want short stories and self-inclusive novel excerpts that are extremely well written. Our audience is sophisticated and accustomed to the finest imaginative writing by new and established writers." Estab. 1931. Circ. 34,000. **Pays on acceptance.** Byline given. Buys first North American serial rights. Reports in 1 month. Sample copy for $6.95 and 7½ × 10½ SAE with 5 first-class stamps. Writer's guidelines for #10 SASE.

● *Story* won the National Magazine Award for Fiction in 1992, was nominated in 1994 and won again in 1995.

Fiction: No genre fiction. Buys 40-50 mss/year. Send complete ms. Length: up to 8,000 words. Pays $750.
Tips: "No replies without SASE."

THE STRAIN, Interactive Arts Magazine, Box 330507, Houston TX 77233-0507. Editor: Norman Clark Stewart Jr. 80% freelance written. Monthly literary compilation. Estab. 1987. Circ. 200-1,000. Pays on publication. Publishes ms an average of 3 years after acceptance. Byline given. Buys first, one-time or second serial rights. Makes work-for-hire assignments. Accepts previously published submissions. Send typed ms with rights for sale noted and information about when and where article previously appeared. Reports in up to 2 years.
● The primary purpose for this magazine is the exchange of ideas and criticism among its contributors and to develop or find material suitable for collections and anthologies.
Nonfiction: Alicia Alder, articles editor. Essays, exposé, how-to, humor, photo feature, technical. Buys 2-20 mss/year. Send complete ms. Pays $5 minimum.
Photos: Send photos with submissions. Reviews transparencies and prints. Model releases and identification of subjects required. Buys one-time rights.
Columns/Departments: Charlie Mainze, editor. Multi-media performance art. Send complete ms. Pays $5 minimum.
Fiction: John Peterson, editor. Buys 1-35 mss/year. Send complete ms. Pays $5 minimum. Rarely publishes novel excerpts.
Poetry: Michael Bond, editor. Avant-garde, free verse, light verse, traditional. Buys 100. Submit maximum 5 poems. Pays $5 minimum.

TAMAQUA, Tamaqua Press, Parkland College, 2400 W. Bradley Ave., C120, Champaign IL 61821-1899. (217)351-2217. Fax: (217)373-3899. Editor-in-Chief: Bruce Morgan. 100% freelance written. Semiannual magazine of literary and fine arts. "We are dedicated to being as open a forum as possible, publishing the best fiction, poetry, nonfiction, photography and artwork that we receive. We are particularly sensitive to emerging writers and artists." Estab. 1989. Circ. 2,000. Pays on publication. Byline given. Buys first North American serial rights. Accepts simultaneous submissions. Query for electronic submissions. Reports in 3 weeks on queries; 3 months on mss. Sample copy for $6 and 9 × 12 SAE with 7 first-class stamps. Writer's guidelines for #10 SASE.
Nonfiction: Essays, historical/nostalgic, humor, opinion, personal experience, photo feature, travel, book reviews. Buys 6 mss/year. Query or send complete ms. Length: 10,000 words maximum. Pays $25-50.
Photos: State availability of or send photos with submission. Reviews contact sheets, transparencies and 5 × 5 or 6 × 10 prints. Offers $5-10/photo. Captions, model releases and identification of subjects required. Buys one-time rights.
Columns/Departments: Reviews (reviews/critiques/meditations on literary works, films, and art which go beyond the work itself. We seek personal/theoretical slant.), 2,000-10,000 words. Buys 2-6 mss/year. Query. Pays $25-50.
Fiction: "We are interested in all types of fiction, but we do not want to see stupid writing in any form." Buys 15 mss/year. Send complete ms. Length: 1,000-12,000 words. Pays $25-75.
Poetry: "We are interested in all types of poetry, but as in fiction, we do not want to see any stupid writing." Buys 125 poems/year. Pays $10-75.
Tips: "Nothing replaces knowledge of the market; hence, *study Tamaqua* and similar magazines to discern the difference between good, solid, intelligent literature and that which is not. All areas are equally open to freelancers."

THEMA, Box 74109, Metairie LA 70033-4109. (504)887-1263. Editor: Virginia Howard. 100% freelance written. Triannual literary magazine covering a different theme for each issue. "*Thema* is designed to stimulate creative thinking by challenging writers with unusual themes, such as 'laughter on the steps' and 'jogging on ice.' Appeals to writers, teachers of creative writing and general reading audience." Estab. 1988. Circ. 350. **Pays on acceptance.** Byline given. Buys one-time rights. Reports in 4 months on mss (after deadline for particular issue). Sample copy for $8. Writer's guidelines for #10 SASE. Query with SASE for upcoming themes.
Fiction: Adventure, ethnic, experimental, fantasy, historical, humorous, mainstream, mystery, religious, science fiction, slice-of-life vignettes, suspense, western, novel excerpts. "No alternate lifestyle or erotica." Buys 33 mss/year. Send complete ms and *specify theme* for which it is intended. Pays $10-25.
Poetry: Avant-garde, free verse, haiku, light verse, traditional. No erotica. Buys 27 poems/year. Submit maximum 3 poems. Length: 4-50 lines. Pays $10.
Tips: "Be familiar with the themes. *Don't submit* unless you have an upcoming theme in mind. Specify the target theme on the first page of your manuscript or in a cover letter. Put your name on *first* page of manuscript only. (All submissions are judged in blind review after the deadline for a specified issue.) Most open to fiction and poetry. Don't be hasty when you consider a theme—mull it over and let it ferment in your mind. We appreciate interpretations that are carefully constructed, clever, subtle, well thought out."

360 DEGREES, Art & Literary Review, Hunting Creek Publishing, 980 Bush St., Suite 200, San Francisco CA 94109. City Managing Editor: Karen Kinnison. 100% freelance written. Quarterly literary magazine covering the arts—literature and artwork. "We are interested in writing and art which we feel contributes to civilization, that moves us forward. More like a museum than a magazine, we want to preserve the best from our times so readers in the future will seek us as a rare source." Estab. 1993. Circ. 1,000. Pays on publication. Publishes ms an average of 3 months after acceptance. No byline. Buys one-time rights and second serial (reprint) rights. Editorial lead time 6 months. Submit seasonal material 3 months in advance. Accepts simultaneous submissions. Reports in 2 weeks on queries, 1 month on mss. Sample copy for $3.60. Writer's guidelines free on request.

Nonfiction: Book excerpts, essays, personal experience. "No technical or religious submissions." Buys 2 mss/year. Send complete ms. Length: no minimum or maximum. Pays $10.

Photos: Send photos with submission. Reviews contact sheets, negatives, 3×5 prints. Offers no additional payment for photos accepted with ms. Identification of subjects required. Buys one-time rights with secondary reprint rights.

Fiction: Experimental, historical, mainstream, novel excerpts, stories by children or young writers. No religious or erotica. Buys 4 mss/year. Send complete ms. Pays $10-20.

Poetry: Avant-garde, free verse, haiku, traditional, poetry by children or young writers. No light verse. Buys 40 poems/year. Pays $5-10.

Tips: "For writers, write well. For artists, send clear photographs of artwork. The poetry department is most open to freelancers. Most of the poems we accept not only show mastery of words, but present new ideas. The mastery of language is something we expect from freelancers, but the content of the idea being presented is the selling point."

THE THREEPENNY REVIEW, P.O. Box 9131, Berkeley CA 94709. (510)849-4545. Editor: Wendy Lesser. 100% freelance written. Works with small number of new/unpublished writers each year. Quarterly literary tabloid. "We are a general interest, national literary magazine with coverage of politics, the visual arts and the performing arts as well." Estab. 1980. Circ. 9,000. **Pays on acceptance.** Publishes ms an average of 1 year after acceptance. Byline given. Buys first North American serial rights. Reports in 1 month on queries; 2 months on mss. Does *not* read mss in summer months. No simultaneous submissions. Sample copy for $6 and 10×13 SAE with 5 first-class stamps. Writer's guidelines for SASE.

Nonfiction: Essays, exposé, historical, personal experience, book, film, theater, dance, music and art reviews. Buys 40 mss/year. Query with or without published clips, or send complete ms. Length: 1,500-4,000 words. Pays $200.

Fiction: No fragmentary, sentimental fiction. Buys 10 mss/year. Send complete ms. Length: 800-4,000 words. Pays $200.

Poetry: Free verse, traditional. No poems "without capital letters or poems without a discernible subject." Buys 30 poems/year. Submit maximum 5 poems. Pays $100.

Tips: "Nonfiction (political articles, memoirs, reviews) is most open to freelancers."

TRIQUARTERLY, 2020 Ridge Ave., Northwestern University, Evanston IL 60208-4302. (312)491-3490. Editors: Reginald Gibbons, Susan Hahn. 70% freelance written. Eager to work with new/unpublished writers. Triannual magazine of fiction, poetry and essays, as well as artwork. Estab. 1964. Pays on publication. Publishes ms an average of 1 year after acceptance. Buys first serial and nonexclusive reprint rights. Reports in 3 months. Study magazine before submitting. Sample copy for $4. Writer's guidelines for #10 SASE.

● *Triquarterly* has had several stories published in the *O. Henry Prize* anthology and *Best American Short Stories* as well as *Best American Poetry.*

Nonfiction: Query before sending essays (no scholarly or critical essays except in special issues).

Fiction and Poetry: No prejudice against style or length of work; only seriousness and excellence are required. Buys 20-50 unsolicited mss/year. Pays $20/printed page.

UNIVERSITY OF TORONTO QUARTERLY, University of Toronto Press Inc., 10 St. Mary St., Suite 700, Toronto, Ontario M4Y 2W8 Canada. Editor: Alan Bewell. 66% freelance written. Works with new/unpublished writers. Quarterly magazine focused on interdisciplinary theory and criticism in literature and the humanities for the university community. Estab. 1933. Publishes ms an average of 1 year after acceptance. Acquires all rights. Byline given. Reports in 2 months. Sample copy for $8.95 and SAE with IRCs.

Nonfiction: Scholarly articles on the humanities, literary criticism, intellectual discussion.

VIRGINIA QUARTERLY REVIEW, University of Virginia, One West Range, Charlottesville VA 22903. (804)924-3124. Editor: Staige D. Blackford. Managing Editor: Janna Olson Gies. Quarterly magazine. "A national journal of literature and thought." Estab. 1925. Circ. 4,000. Pays on publication. Publishes ms an average of 1 year after acceptance. Byline given. Buys first rights. Editorial lead time 6 months. Submit season material 6 months in advance. Reports in 2 weeks on queries; 2 months on mss. Sample copy $5. Writer's guidelines for #10 SASE.

Nonfiction: Book excerpts, essays, general interest, historical/nostalgic, humor, inspirational, personal experience, travel. Send complete ms. Length: 2,000-4,000 words. Pays $10/page maximum.

Fiction: Adventure, ethnic, historical, humorous, mainstream, mystery, novel excerpts, romance. Send complete ms. Length: 2,000-4,000 words. Pays $10/page maximum.
Poetry: Gregory Orr, poetry editor. All types. Submit maximum 5 poems. Pays $1/line.

WEST COAST LINE, A Journal of Contemporary Writing & Criticism, West Coast Review Publishing Society, 2027 EAA. Simon Fraser University, Burnaby, British Columbia V5A 1S6 Canada. (604)291-4287. Fax: (604)291-5737. Managing Editor: Jacqueline Larson. Triannual magazine of contemporary literature and criticism. Estab. 1990. Circ. 500. Pays on publication. Buys one-time rights. Editorial lead time 4 months. Submit seasonal material 4 months in advance. Query for electronic submissions. Reports in 2 weeks on queries; 3 months on mss. Sample copy for $10. Writer's guidelines free on request.
Nonfiction: Essays (literary/scholarly), experimental prose. "No journalistic articles or articles dealing with nonliterary material. Buys 3-4 mss/year. Send complete ms. Length: 1,000-5,000 words. Pays $8/page. All contributors receive a year's free subscription to supplement cash payment."
Fiction: Experimental, novel excerpts. Buys 2-3 mss/year. Send complete ms. Length: 1,000-7,000 words. Pays $8/page.
Poetry: Avant-garde. "No light verse, traditional." Buys 6-8 poems/year. Length: 5-6 pages maximum. Pays $8/page.
Tips: "Submissions must be either scholarly or formally innovative. Contributors should be familiar with current literary trends in Canada and the US. Scholars should be aware of current schools of theory. All submissions should be accompanied by a brief cover letter; essays should be formatted according to the MLA guide. The publication is not divided into departments. We accept poetry, fiction, experimental prose and scholarly essays."

WILLOW SPRINGS, 526 Fifth St., MS-1, Eastern Washington University, Cheney WA 99004. (509)458-6429. Editor: Nance Van Winckel. 100% freelance written. Semiannual literary magazine. "We publish quality contemporary poetry, fiction, nonfiction and works in translation." Estab. 1977. Circ. 1,500. Pays on publication. Publishes ms an average of 10 months after acceptance. Byline given. Buys first publication rights. Editorial lead time 2 months. Reports in 2 months. Sample copy for $4.50. Writer's guidelines for #10 SASE.
 • A magazine of growing reputation. Takes part in the AWP Intro Award program.
Nonfiction: Essays. Buys 4 mss/year. Send complete ms. Pays $35.
Fiction: Literary fiction only. "No genre fiction, please." Buys 5-8 mss/year. Send complete ms. Pays $35 minimum.
Poetry: Avant-garde, free verse. "No haiku, light verse or religious." Buys 50-80 poems/year. Submit maximum 6 poems. Length: 12 pages maximum. Pays $10.
Tips: "We do not read manuscripts in June, July and August."

WINDSOR REVIEW, Windsor, Ontario N9B 3P4 Canada. (519)253-4232. ext. 2332. Fax: (519)973-7050. E-mail: uwrevu@uwindsor. ca. Editor: Wanda Campbell. Biannual for "the literate layman, the old common reader." Estab. 1965. Circ. 300. Buys first North American serial rights. Reports in 6 weeks. Sample copy for $5 and postage. Enclose SAE with Canadian postage or IRCs only.
Fiction: Alistair MacLeod. Mainstream prose with open attitude toward themes. Length: 2,000-6,000 words. Pays $50.
Poetry: John Ditsky. Accepts traditional forms, blank verse, free verse, avant-garde. No epics. Pays $15.

WITNESS, Oakland Community College, 27055 Orchard Lake Rd., Farmington Hills MI 48334. (313)471-7740. Editor: Peter Stine. 100% freelance written. Semiannual literary magazine. "*Witness* highlights the role of writer as witness. Alternate issues are thematic: holocaust, writings from prison, sixties, nature writing, sports in America, etc." Estab. 1987. Circ. 2,800. Pays on publication. Publishes ms an average of 1 year after acceptance. Byline given. Buys first North American serial rights. Editorial lead time 6 months. Accepts simultaneous submissions. Reports in 1 month on queries; 3 months on mss. Sample copy for $5. Writer's guidelines free on request.
 • A rising and energetic magazine. The frequent theme issues require more work from the writer in studying this market.
Nonfiction: Essays. Buys 10 mss/year. Send complete ms. Length: 1,000-8,000 words. Pays $6/page.
Fiction: Experimental, humorous, mainstream, literary. Buys 40 mss/year. Send complete ms. Length: 1,000-8,000 words. Pays $6/page.
Poetry: Avant-garde, traditional. Buys 15 poems/year. Submit maximum 4 poems. Pays $10/page.

WRITER'S KEEPER, P.O. Box 922648, Sylmar CA 91392-2648. Editor: C. Darren Butler. 100% freelance written. Quarterly newsletter covering writing and poetry. "All works must have writing fiction or poetry as subject matter." Estab. 1993. Circ. 800. Pays on publication. Publishes ms an average of 4 months after acceptance. Byline given. Sample copy free for #10 SASE.
Nonfiction: How-to, humor, inspirational. Buys 2-6 mss/year. Send complete ms. Length: 50-300 words maximum. Pays $1.

Fiction: Fantasy, humorous, mainstream. (All must be writing related). Buys 0-4 mss/year. Send complete ms. Length: 50-300 words. Pays $1.
Poetry: All styles used. Buys 10 poems/year. Submit maximum 8 poems. Length: 15 lines. Pays $1.
Fillers: Anecdotes, facts, short humor. Buys 0-10/year. Length: 200 words. Pays $1.
Tips: *"Writer's Keeper* is a newsletter for poets and writers. All submitted works must have writing-related subject matter."

THE YALE REVIEW, Yale University, P.O. Box 208243, New Haven CT 06520-8243. Editor: J.D. McClatchy. Managing Editor: Susan Bianconi. 20% freelance written. Buys first North American serial rights. Estab. 1911. Pays prior to publication. Responds in 2 months. Publishes in 5-12 months. "No writer's guidelines available. Consult back issues."
  • *The Yale Review* has published work chosen for the Pushcart anthology, *The Best American Poetry*, and the O. Henry Award.
Nonfiction and Fiction: Authoritative discussions of politics, literature and the arts. Buys quality fiction. Length: 3,000-5,000 words. Pays $100-500.

YELLOW SILK: Journal of Erotic Arts, verygraphics, Box 6374, Albany CA 94706. (510)644-4188. Editor: Lily Pond. 90% freelance written. Prefers to work with published/established writers. Quarterly magazine of erotic literature and visual arts. "Editorial policy: All persuasions; no brutality. Our publication is artistic and literary, not pornographic or pandering. Humans are involved: heads, hearts and bodies—not just bodies alone; and the quality of the literature is as important as the erotic content." Circ. 16,000. Pays on publication. Publishes ms an average of 6 months after acceptance. Byline given. Buys all publication rights for 1 year, at which time they revert to author; and reprint and anthology rights for duration of copyright. Reports in 3 months on mss. Sample copy for $7.50.
Nonfiction: Book excerpts, essays, humor, reviews. "We often have theme issues, but non-regularly and usually not announced in advance. No pornography, romance-novel type writing, sex fantasies. No first-person accounts or blow-by-blow descriptions. No articles. No novels." Buys 5-10 mss/year. Send complete ms. All submissions should be typed, double-spaced, with name, address and phone number on each page; always enclose SASE. No specified length requirements. Pays $1/printed column inch, 3 contributor copies and subscription.
Photos: Photos may be submitted independently, not as illustration for submission. Reviews photocopies, contact sheets, transparencies and prints. We accept 4-color and b&w artwork. Offers varying payment for series of 8-20 used, plus copies. Buys one-time rights and reprint rights.
Columns/Departments: Reviews (book, movie, art, dance, food, music, anything). "Erotic content and how it's handled is focus of importance. Old or new does not matter. We want to bring readers information of what's out there." Buys 8-10 mss/year. Send complete ms or query. Pays $1/printed column inch plus copies.
Fiction: Erotica, including ethnic, experimental, fantasy, humorous, mainstream, novel excerpts, science fiction. See "Nonfiction." Buys 12-16 mss/year. Send complete ms. Pays $1/printed column inch, plus copies.
Poetry: Avant-garde, free verse, haiku, light verse, traditional. "No greeting-card poetry." Buys 80-100 poems/year. No limit on number of poems submitted, "but don't send book-length manuscripts." Pays .375¢/line, plus copies.
Tips: "The best way to get into *Yellow Silk* is produce excellent, well-crafted work that includes eros freshly, with strength of voice, beauty of language, and insight into character. I'll tell you what I'm sick of and have, unfortunately, been seeing more of lately: the products of 'How to Write Erotica' classes. This is not brilliant fiction; it is poorly written fantasy and not what I'm looking for."

ZYZZYVA, The Last Word: West Coast Writers & Artists, 41 Sutter St., Suite 1400, San Francisco CA 94104-4987. (415)255-1282. Fax: (415)255-1144. E-mail: zyzzyva@&mn.com. Editor: Howard Junker. 100% freelance written. Works with a small number of new/unpublished writers each year. Quarterly magazine. "We feature work by West Coast writers only. We are essentially a literary magazine, but of wide-ranging interests and a strong commitment to nonfiction." Estab. 1985. Circ. 4,800. **Pays on acceptance.** Publishes ms an average of 3 months after acceptance. Byline given. Buys first North American serial rights and one-time anthology rights. Reports in 1 week on queries; 1 month on mss. Sample copy for $10.
Nonfiction: Book excerpts, general interest, historical/nostalgic, humor, personal experience. Buys 15 mss/year. Query. Length: open. Pays $50-250.
Fiction: Ethnic, experimental, humorous, mainstream. Buys 20 mss/year. Send complete ms. Length: open. Pays $50-250.
Poetry: Buys 20 poems/year. Submit maximum 5 poems. Length: 3-200 lines. Pays $50-250.

Men's

Many, though not all, magazines in this section typically focus on pictorial layouts accompanied by stories and aritcles of a sexual nature. Most also offer non-sexual features on topics of interest to men. Magazines that also use material slanted toward men can be found in Business and Finance, Child Care and Parental Guidance, Gay & Lesbian Interest, General Interest, Relationships, Military and Sports sections.

CHIC MAGAZINE, HG Publications, 9171 Wilshire Blvd., Suite 300, Beverly Hills CA 90210-5530. Executive Editor: Doug Oliver. 40% freelance written. Monthly magazine for men, ages 20-35 years, college-educated and interested in current affairs, entertainment and sex. Estab. 1976. Circ. 50,000. Pays 1 month after acceptance. Publishes ms an average of 3 months after acceptance. Buys all rights. Offers 20% kill fee. Byline given unless writer requests otherwise. Reports in 2 months. Writer's guidelines for #10 SASE.
Nonfiction: Sex-related topics of current national interest, interview (off-beat personalities in news and entertainment), celebrity profiles. Buys 12-18 mss/year. Query. Length: 3,000 words. Pays $750. Sometimes pays the expenses of writers on assignment.
Columns/Departments: Third Degree (short Q&As with unusual people), 2,000 words. Pays $350. My Confession (first-person sexual experiences), 1,000 words. Pays $25.
Fiction: Length: 3,000 words. Pays $500. "We buy stories with emphasis on erotic themes. These may be adventure, action, mystery, horror or humorous stories, but the tone and theme must involve sex and eroticism. The erotic nature of the story should not be subordinate to the characterizations and plot; the main graphically depicted sex slant should be 1½ pages in length, and must grow logically from the people and the plot, not be contrived or forced."
Tips: "We do not buy poetry or non-erotic science fiction. Refrain from stories with drug themes, sex with minors, male homosexuality, incest and bestiality."

‡COWBOY MAGAZINE, Range Writer, Inc., P.O. Box 126, LaVeta CO 81055-0126. (719)742-5250. Editor: Darrell Arnold. 80% freelance written. Quarterly magazine that covers all aspects of the cowboy lifestyle. "People who read our magazine are interested in cowboys. They want truth, not glorified, innacurate imaginings. If you've never worked on a ranch, or seen the West from horseback, you probably can't write for us." Estab. 1990. Circ. 15,500. Pays on publication. Publishes ms an average of 6 months after acceptance. Byline given. Buys first rights or one-time rights. Submit seasonal/holiday material 6 months in advance. Reports in 2 months on queries; 4 months on mss. Sample copy for $5.50. Writer's guidelines for #10 SASE.
• *Cowboy Magazine* has doubled its response time for responding to queries as well as to manuscripts.
Nonfiction: Essays, exposé, general interest, historical/nostalgic, humor, interview/profile, opinion and photo feature. "We are not another horse magazine. We don't want articles on horse care or horse training or horse shows. We do not want fiction except that pertaining to the life of a working cowboy." Buys 60 mss/year. Query. Length: 1,500 words maximum. Pays $200 maximum. Sometimes pays expenses of writers on assignment.
Photos: Send photos with submission. Reviews 5×7 prints. Offers $5/photo. Captions and identification of subjects required. Buys one-time rights.
Columns/Departments: Legacies (issues concerning the lives of cowboys and ranchers and others who value the use of public lands), 1,500 words. Buys 4 mss/year. Send complete ms. Pays $200 maximum.
Fiction: Historical, humorous, slice-of-life vignette and western. "No shoot-em-ups or romanticized visions of the West." Buys 4 mss/year. Send complete ms. Length: 1,500 words maximum. Pays $200 maximum.
Poetry: Traditional. "No verse that is not carefully rhymed, metered or constructed." Buys 4 poems/year. Submit maximum 5 poems. Length: 40 lines maximum. Pays $15 maximum.
Fillers: Facts, newsbreaks and short humor. Buys 4/year. Length: 200 words maximum. Pays $20 maximum.
Tips: "If you can write an honest, clear, account of some aspect of cowboy life, you can probably write for us. You must know the inside story on being a cowboy, on ranching life. You can do profiles of people who are cowboys or cowboy artists, or western (not country) musicians, or cowboy craftsmen. Don't make anything up. We can spot a phony. What we need the very most are articles about particular aspects of life as a working cowboy—how he does his work, where he lives, why he does it, etc. Good articles of this type are the hardest for us to get. They require spending some time on the ranch with a working cowboy or being one."

ESQUIRE, 250 W. 55th St., New York NY 10019. (212)649-4020. Editor-in-Chief: Edward Kosner. Articles Editor: Bill Tonelli. Men's monthly. Estab. 1933. General readership is college educated and sophisticated, between ages 30 and 45. Written mostly by contributing editors on contract. Rarely accepts unsolicited mss. **Pays on acceptance.** Publishes ms an average of 2 months after acceptance. Retains first worldwide periodical publication rights for 90 days from cover date. Queries must be sent by letter.
Nonfiction: Columns average 1,500 words; features average 6,000 words. Focus is on the ever-changing trends in American culture. Topics include current events and politics, social criticism, sports, celebrity profiles, the media, art and music, men's fashion.
Photos: Marianne Butler, photo editor. Uses mostly commissioned photography. Payment depends on size and number of photos.

Fiction: Will Blythe, literary editor. "Literary excellence is our only criterion." Accepts work chiefly from literary agencies. Publishes short stories, some poetry, and excerpts from novels, memoirs and plays.
Tips: "A writer has the best chance of breaking in at *Esquire* by querying with a specific idea that requires special contacts and expertise. Ideas must be timely and national in scope."

FLING INTERNATIONAL, Relim Publishing Co., Inc., 550 Miller Ave., Mill Valley CA 94941. (415)383-5464. Editor: Arv Miller. 80% freelance written. Prefers to work with published/established writers. Quarterly men's sophisticate magazine. Young male audience of adults ages 18-34. Estab. 1957. Circ. 125,000. Pays before publication. Publishes ms an average of 6 months after acceptance. Buys first North American serial and second serial (reprint) rights or makes work-for-hire assignments. Does not consider multiple submissions. Reports in 3 weeks on queries; 1 month on mss. Sample copy for $5. Writer's guidelines for SASE.
  • *Fling* has more than doubled its use of freelance writing.
Nonfiction: Exposé, how-to (better relationships with women, better lovers), interview/profile, sports, taboo sex articles. Buys 15 mss/year. Query. Length: 1,500-3,000 words. Pays $150-350. Sometimes pays expenses of writers on assignment.
Photos: Send photos with query. Reviews 35mm color transparencies. Pays $10-25 for single b&w; $125-500 for color layouts. Model releases required. Buys one-time rights.
Columns/Departments: Buys 12 mss/year. Query or send complete ms. Length: 100-200 words. Pays $35-150.
Fiction: Sexually oriented, strong male-female relationship. Lots of written detail about female's abundant chest-size a must. Buys 6 mss/year. Send complete ms. Length: 2,000-3,000 words. Pays $135-200.
Tips: "Nonfiction and fiction are wide open areas to freelancers. Always query with one-page letter to the editor before proceeding with any writing. Also send a sample photocopy of published material, similar to suggestion."

GALLERY MAGAZINE, Montcalm Publishing Corp., 401 Park Ave. S., New York NY 10016-8802. (212)779-8900. Fax: (212)725-7215. Editorial Director: Barry Janoff. Managing Editor: Rich Friedman. 50% freelance written. Prefers to work with published/established writers. Monthly magazine "focusing on features of interest to the young American man." Estab. 1972. Circ. 500,000. Pays 50% on acceptance, 50% on publication. Byline given. Pays 25% kill fee. Buys first North American serial rights or makes work-for-hire assignments. Submit seasonal/holiday material 6 months in advance. Reports in 1 month on queries; 2 months on mss. Sample copy for $6.95 (add $2 for Canadian and foreign orders). Writer's guidelines for SASE.
  • *Gallery* works on Macintosh Performa 475, so it accepts material on Mac or compatible disks if accompanied by hard copy.
Nonfiction: Investigative pieces, general interest, how-to, humor, interview, new products, profile. "We *do not* want to see pornographic articles." Buys 4-5 mss/issue. Query or send complete mss. Length: 1,000-3,000 words. Pays $300-1,500. "Special prices negotiated." Sometimes pays expenses of writers on assignment.
Photos: Send photos with accompanying mss. Pay varies for b&w or color contact sheets and negatives. Buys one-time rights. Captions preferred; model release required.
Fiction: Adventure, erotica (special guidelines available), experimental, humorous, mainstream, mystery, suspense. Buys 1 ms/issue. Send complete ms. Length: 1,000-3,000 words. Pays $350-500.

GENESIS, 110 E. 59th St., Suite 3100, New York NY 10022. (212)644-8800. Fax: (212)644-9212. Managing Editor: Steve Glassman. 85% freelance written. Men's magazine published 14 times/year. "We are interested in headline and behind-the-headlines articles on sexual or controversial subjects of interest to men." Estab. 1973. Circ. 425,000. Pays 60 days after acceptance. Publishes ms an average of 3 months after acceptance. Byline given. Offers 25% kill fee. Buys second serial (reprint) and English worldwide rights (may revert to writer upon request). Submit seasonal material 6 months in advance. Accepts simultaneous submissions. Reports in 3 months. Writer's guidelines for #10 SASE.
Nonfiction: Exposé; humor; interview/profile; photo feature; erotica; film, music and book reviews; comment on contemporary relationships; automotive. "With the exception of the entertainment reviews, one exposé-style piece and one automotive piece/issue, all editorial in *Genesis* has a sexual orientation." Buys 60 mss/year. Query with published clips. First-time writers must submit ms on spec. Length: 1,500-2,000 words. Pays $300-700 for assigned articles; $100-500 for unsolicited articles.
Photos: Send photos with submission. Reviews transparencies (no fixed size requirements) and prints. Offers $50-100/photo. Model releases and identification of subjects required. Buys English worldwide and second serial (reprint) rights.
Columns/Departments: Film, music and book reviews, 500-750 words; 'On the Couch' (sexual confessions from woman's point of view), 750-1,000 words. Buys 65 mss/year. Query with published clips. First-time writers must submit ms on spec. Pays $75-350.
Tips: "Because we accept only a small number of nonsex-related articles, freelancers' best chance to break in is to write sex features or contribute to the entertainment pages; we have a partciular need for 300-500 word articles on film and TV. When writing about sexual issues or lifestyles, writers should offer their own opinions on the subject rather than provide drably objective overviews. First-person point-of-view is strongly

recommended. Writing must be sexually explicit with a minimum amount of 'lead in.' "

GENT, "Home of the D-Cups," Dugent Publishing Corp., 2600 Douglas Rd., Suite 600, Coral Gables FL 33134. Managing Editor: Steve Dorfman. 80% freelance written. Monthly men's sophisticate magazine with emphasis on big breasts. Estab. 1960. Circ. 150,000. Pays on publication. Byline given. Buys first North American serial or second serial (reprint) rights. Editorial lead time 4 months. Submit seasonal material 6 months in advance. Accepts previously published submissions. Reports in 2 weeks on queries; 3 months on mss. Sample copy for $5. Writer's guidelines for #10 SASE.
Nonfiction: How-to ("anything sexually related"), personal experience ("any and all sexually related matters"). Buys 13 mss/year. Query. Length: 2,000-3,500 words. Pays $250.
Photos: Send photos with submission. Reviews 35mm transparencies. Negotiates payment individually. Model releases and identification of subjects required. Buys first North American with reprint rights.
Fiction: Erotica, fantasy. Buys 26 mss/year. Send complete ms. Length: 2,000-3,500 words. Pays $200-250.

GENTLEMEN'S QUARTERLY, Condé Nast, 350 Madison Ave., New York NY 10017. (212)880-8800. Editor-in-Chief: Arthur Cooper. Managing Editor: Martin Beiser. 60% freelance written. Circ. 650,000. Monthly magazine emphasizing fashion, general interest and service features for men ages 25-45 with a large discretionary income. **Pays on acceptance.** Byline given. Pays 25% kill fee. Submit seasonal/holiday material 6 months in advance. Reports in 1 month.
Nonfiction: Politics, personality profiles, lifestyles, trends, grooming, nutrition, health and fitness, sports, travel, money, investment and business matters. Buys 4-6 mss/issue. Query with published clips. Length: 1,500-4,000 words. Pay varies.
Columns/Departments: Martin Beiser, managing editor. Query with published clips. Length: 1,000-2,500 words. Pay varies.
Tips: "Major features are usually assigned to well-established, known writers. Pieces are almost always solicited. The best way to break in is through the columns, especially Contraria, Enthusiasms or First Person."

HEARTLAND USA, % PeakMedia, P.O. Box 925, Hailey ID 83333-0925. (208)788-4500. Fax: (208)788-5098. Editor: Brad Pearson. 50% freelance written. Bimonthly magazine for working people. "*Heartland USA* is a general interest, lifestyle magazine for working people 18 to 53. It covers spectator sports (primarily motor sports, football, baseball and basketball, hunting, fishing, how-to, travel, music, gardening, the environment, human interest, etc.), emphasizing the upbeat or humorous." Estab. 1991. Circ. 1 million. **Pays on acceptance**. Byline given. Offers 20% kill fee. Buys first North American serial and second serial (reprint) rights. Submit seasonal material 6 months in advance. Accepts simultaneous and previously published submissions. Send photocopy of article and information about when and where the article previously appeared. For reprints, pays $200. Query for electronic submissions. Reports in 1 month on queries. Sample copy for 9 × 12 SAE with $3 or 10 first-class stamps. Free writer's guidelines.
Nonfiction: Book excerpts, general interest, historical/nostalgic, how-to, humor, inspirational, interview/profile, new product, personal experience, photo feature, technical, travel. "No fiction or dry expository pieces." Buys 30 mss/year. Query with or without published clips or send complete ms. Length: 350-1,200 words. Pays 50-80¢/word for assigned articles; 25-80¢/word for unsolicited articles. Sometimes pays expenses of writers on assignment.
Photos: Send photos with submission. Reviews transparencies. Identification of subjects required. Buys one-time rights.
Tips: "Features with the possibility of strong photographic support are open to freelancers, as are our shorter departments. We look for a relaxed, jocular, easy-to-read style, and look favorably on the liberal use of anecdote or interesting quotations."

HUSTLER, HG Inc., 9171 Wilshire Blvd., Suite 300, Beverly Hills CA 90210. Fax: (310)275-3857. Editor: Allan MacDonell. Articles Editor: Lisa Jenio. 60% freelance written. Magazine published 13 times/year. "*Hustler* is the no-nonsense men's magazine. Our audience does not need to be told whether to wear their trousers cuffed or plain. The *Hustler* reader expects honest, unflinching looks at hard topics—sexual, social, political, personality profile, true crime." Estab. 1974. Circ. 750,000. Pays as boards ship to printer. Publishes ms an average of 3 months after acceptance. Byline given. Offers 20% kill fee. Buys all rights. Editorial lead time 4 months. Submit seasonal material 6 months in advance. Reports in 2 weeks on queries; 1 month on mss. Writer's guidelines for #10 SASE.
  ● *Hustler* is most interested in profiles of dynamic ground-breaking, indomitable individuals who don't mind "flipping a bird" at the world in general.
Nonfiction: Book excerpts, exposé, general interest, how-to, interview/profile, personal experience, trends. Buys 30 mss/yer. Query. Length: 3,500-4,000 words. Pays $1,500 for assigned articles; $1,000 for unsolicited articles. Sometimes pays expenses of writers on assignment.
Columns/Departments: Lisa Jenio. Sex Play (some aspect of sex that can be encapsulated in a limited space), 2,500 words. Buys 13 mss/year. Send complete ms. Pays $500.
Fiction: Lisa Jenio. "Difficult fiction market. Must have two sex scenes; yet not be rote or boring." Buys 2 mss/year. Send complete ms. Length: 3,000-3,500. Pays $700-1,000.

Fillers: Pays $50-100. Jokes and "Graffilthy," bathroom-wall humor.

Tips: "Don't try and mimic the *Hustler* style. If a writer needs to be molded into our voice, we'll do a better job of it than he or she will."

HUSTLER BUSTY BEAUTIES, America's Breast Magazine, HG Publications, Inc., 9171 Wilshire Blvd., Suite 300, Beverly Hills CA 90210. (213)858-7100. Fax: (213)275-3857. Associate Publisher: N. Morgen Hagen. 40% freelance written. Men's monthly sophisticate magazine. "*Hustler Busty Beauties* is an adult title that showcases attractive large-breasted women with accompanying erotic fiction, reader letters, humor." Estab. 1974. Circ. 180,000. Pays on publication. Publishes ms an average of 6 months after acceptance. Byline given. Buys all rights. Reports in 1 month. Sample copy for $6 and 9×12 SAE. Free writer's guidelines.

Columns/Departments: LewDDD Letters (erotic experiences involving large-breasted women from first-person point-of-view), 500-1,000 words. Buys 24-36 mss year. Send complete ms. Pays $50-75.

Fiction: Adventure, erotica, fantasy, humorous, mystery, science fiction, suspense. "No violent stories or stories without a bosomy female character." Buys 12 mss year. Send complete ms. Length: 750-2,500 words. Pays $250-500.

Jokes: Appropriate for audience. Pays $10-25.

‡MEN AS WE ARE, A Celebration of Men, Men As We Are Publishing, P.O. Box 150615, Brooklyn NY 11215-0007. (718)499-2829. Editor: Jonathan Running Wind. Managing Editor: David Teisler. 75% freelance written. Quarterly magazine covering men's issues. "Honest, vulnerable illumination of the masculine experience." Estab. 1991. Circ. 600. Pays on publication. Publishes ms an average of 9 months after acceptance. Byline given. Offers 50% kill fee. Buys first North American serial rights, one-time rights, or second serial (reprint) rights. Editorial lead time 6 months. Submit seasonal material 6 months in advance. Accepts simultaneous submissions and previously published submissions. Query for electronic submissions. Reports in 6 months on mss, 3 months on queries. Sample copy for $4.01. Writer's guidelines for #10 SASE.

Nonfiction: Book excerpts, essays, humor, interview/profile, opinion, personal experience. "No how-to, hunting stories!!" Buys 8 mss/year. Query or send complete ms. Length: 500-6,000 words. Pays $5-100 for assigned articles; $5-25 for unsolicited articles. Sometimes pays in contributor copies when cash not available. Sometimes pays expenses of writers on assignment.

Photos: State availability of photos with submission. Reviews 3×5 prints. Negotiates payment individually. Identification of subjects required. Buys one-time rights.

Columns/Departments: Man & Nature (depict an aspect of man's mutually enhancing relationship with nature), 2,500 words; Fathering (share your struggles, hopes, failures and triumphs in being a father), 1,500 words; Men in the Mass Media (description of and commentary on the way the media has interpreted a particular man or the male experience, written in the first personal plural), 1,500 words; Man Is A Giddy Thing (a sequence of unbylined short-short true stories about men acting in unexpected, often wonderful ways). Buys 16 mss/year. Send complete ms. Pays $5-25.

Fiction: Ethnic, novel excerpts, slice-of-life vignettes, literary. No hunting, science fiction. Buys 8 mss/year. Send complete ms. Length: 500-6,000 words. Pays $5-25.

Poetry: Free verse, haiku, traditional. Buys 20 poems/year. Submit maximum 3 poems. Pays $5-25.

Fillers: Anecdotes, facts. Buys 4/year. Length: 10-100 words. No payment.

Tips: "Be honest, authentic. We especially appreciate writing from Men of Color or writing with a multicultural slant."

NUGGET, Dugent Publishing Corp., 2600 Douglas Rd., Suite 600, Coral Gables FL 33134. Managing Editor: Nye Willden. Editor-in-Chief: Christopher James. 100% freelance written. Men's/adult magazine published 9 times a year covering fetish and kink. "*Nugget* is a one-of-a-kind publication which appeals to daring, open-minded adults who enjoy all forms of both kinky, alternative sex (catfighting, transvestism, fetishism, bi-sexuality, etc.) and conventional sex." Estab. 1960. Circ. 30,448. Pays on publication. Publishes ms an average of 1 year after acceptance. Byline given. Buys first North American serial rights. Editorial lead time 5 months. Submit seasonal material 1 year in advance. Accepts simultaneous submissions. Reports in 2 weeks on queries; 2 months on mss. Sample copy for $3.50. Writer's guidelines free on request.

Nonfiction: Interview/profile, sexual matters/trends (fetish and kink angle). Buys 4 mss/year. Query. Length: 2,000-3,000 words. Pays $200 minimum.

Photos: Send photos with submission. Reviews transparencies. Offers no additional payment for photos accepted with ms. Model releases required. Buys one-time second rights.

Fiction: Erotica, fantasy. Buys 20 mss/year. Send complete ms. Length: 2,000-3,000 words. Pays $200-250.

Tips: Most open to fiction submissions. (Follow readers guidelines for suitable topics.)

For explanation of symbols, see the Key to Symbols and Abbreviations. For unfamiliar words, see the Glossary.

OPTIONS, AJA Publishing, P.O. Box 470, Port Chester NY 10573. (914)939-2111. Editor: Don Stone. Associate Editor: Diana Sheridan. Mostly freelance written. Sexually explicit magazine for and about bisexuals and homosexuals, published 10 times/year. "Articles, stories and letters about bisexuality. Positive approach. Safe-sex encounters unless the story clearly pre-dates the AIDS situation." Estab. 1977. Circ. 100,000. Pays on publication. Publishes mss an average of 10 months after acceptance. Byline given, usually pseudonymous. Buys all rights. Submit seasonal material 8 months in advance; buys very little seasonal material. Reports in 3 weeks. Sample copy for $2.95 and 6×9 SAE with 5 first-class stamps. Writer's guidelines for SASE.
Nonfiction: Essays (occasional), how-to, humor, interview/profile, opinion, personal experience (especially). All must be bisexually or gay related. Does not want "anything not bisexually/gay related, anything negative, anything opposed to safe sex, anything dry/boring/ponderous/pedantic. Write even serious topics informally if not lightly." Buys 10 nonfiction mss/year. Send complete ms. Length: 2,000-3,000. Pays $100.
Photos: Reviews transparencies and prints. Pays $20 for b&w photos; $200 for full color. Black and white or color sets $150. Previously published photos acceptable.
Fiction: "We don't usually get enough true first-person stories and need to buy some from writers. They must be bisexual, usually man/man, hot and believable. They must not read like fiction." Buys 70 fiction mss/year. Send complete ms. Length: 2,000-3,000. Pays $100.
Tips: "We use many more male/male pieces than female/female. Use only one serious article per issue. A serious/humorous approach is good here, but only if it's natural to you; don't make an effort for it. No longer buying 'letters'. We get enough real ones."

PENTHOUSE, General Media, 277 Park Ave., 4th Floor, New York NY 10172-0003. (212)702-6000. Fax: (212)702-6279. Contact: Editorial Department. Monthly publication covering style, culture and fashion for men. Query before submitting.
Tips: "Read at least three copies of the magazine to know what types of articles freelancers are writing."

PLAYBOY, 680 N. Lakeshore Dr., Chicago IL 60611. Contact: Articles Editor or Fiction Editor. Monthly publication covering fashion, style and popular culture for men. Writer's guidelines for SASE. Query before submitting.

SWANK, Swank Publications, 210 Route 4 East, Suite 401, Paramus NJ 07652. (201)843-4004. Fax: (201)843-8636. Editor: Paul Gambino. Assistant Editor: Rob Ruvo. 75% freelance written. Works with new/unpublished writers. Monthly magazine on "sex and sensationalism, lurid. High quality adult erotic entertainment." Audience of men ages 18-38, high school and some college education, medium income, skilled blue-collar professionals, union men, some white-collar. Estab. 1954. Circ. 400,000. Pays on publication. Publishes ms an average of 4 months after acceptance. Byline given, pseudonym if wanted. Buys first North American serial rights. Submit seasonal material 6 months in advance. Reports in 3 weeks on queries; 1 month on mss. Sample copy for $5.95. Writer's guidelines for SASE.
Nonfiction: Exposé (researched), adventure must be accompanied by color photographs. "We buy articles on sex-related topics, which don't need to be accompanied by photos." Interested in lifestyle (unusual) pieces. Buys photo pieces on autos, action, adventure. Buys 34 mss/year. Query with or without published clips. Pays $350-500. Sometimes pays the expenses of writers on assignment. "It is strongly recommended that a sample copy is reviewed before submitting material."
Photos: Bruce Perez, photo editor. Send photos. "If you have good photographs of an interesting adventure/ lifestyle subject, the writing that accompanies is bought almost automatically." Model releases required.

‡XO, Man At Large, TMI, 22761 Pacific Coast Hwy., Suite 100, Malibu CA 90265. Editor: Tom Kagy. Bimonthly magazine covering sex, health, success for Asian men. "We publish articles of interest to success-oriented, free-thinking professional Asian American men with an active interest in self-improvement, vitality and sex." Estab. 1994. Circ. 18,000. Pays on publication. Publishes ms an average of 2 months after acceptance. Byline sometimes given. Offers 25% kill fee. Buys all rights or makes work-for-hire assignments. Editorial lead time 2½ months. Submit seasonal material 3 months in advance. Accepts simultaneous submissions. Query for electronic submissions. Reports in 1 month on queries, 3 months on mss. Sample copy for $9. Writers guidelines free.
Nonfiction: Book excerpts, essays, expose, general interest, how-to, humor, interview/profile, new product, opinion, personal experience, photo feature, travel. Buys 20-30 mss/year. Query with or without published clips or send complete ms. Length: 1,200-3,500 words. Pays $100-275 for assigned articles; $50-150 for unsolicited articles.
Photos: State availability of photos with submission or send photos with submission. Reviews transparencies.
Columns/Departments: Query with or without published clips or send complete ms.
Tips: "Be familiar with attitudes and interests of successful Asian American professional men aged 25-39."

Military

These publications emphasize military or paramilitary subjects or other aspects of military life. Technical and semitechnical publications for military commanders, personnel and planners, as well as those for military families and civilians interested in Armed Forces activities are listed here. Publications covering military history can be found in the History section.

AMERICAN SURVIVAL GUIDE, McMullen & Yee Publishing, Inc., 774 S. Placentia Ave., Placentia CA 92670-6832. Fax: (714)572-1864. Editor: Jim Benson. Managing Editor: Scott Stoddard. 50% freelance written. Monthly magazine covering "self-reliance, defense, meeting day-to-day and possible future threats—survivalism for survivalists." Circ. 72,000. Pays on publication. Publishes ms up to 1 year after acceptance. Byline given. Submit seasonal material 5 months in advance. Sample copy for $3.50. Writer's guidelines for SASE. Articles should be submitted on computer floppy disk, either 3.5 or 5.25 floppy with hard copy included. Microsoft Word files are preferred but other software text files will work such as WordPerfect.
• This staff is always looking for more good material with quality artwork (photos). They want articles on recent events and new techniques, etc. giving the latest available information to their readers.
Nonfiction: Exposé (political); how-to; interview/profile; personal experience (how I survived); photo feature (equipment and techniques related to survival in all possible situations); emergency medical; health and fitness; communications; transportation; food preservation; water purification; self-defense; terrorism; nuclear dangers; nutrition; tools; shelter; etc. "No general articles about how to survive. We want specifics and single subjects." Buys 60-100 mss/year. Query or send complete ms. Length: 1,500-2,000 words. Pays $140-350. Sometimes pays some expenses of writers on assignment.
Photos: Send photos with ms. "One of the most frequent mistakes made by writers in completing an article assignment for us is sending photo submissions that are inadequate." Captions, model releases and identification of subjects mandatory. Buys all rights.
Tips: "Prepare material of value to individuals who wish to sustain human life no matter what the circumstance. This magazine is a text and reference."

ARMY MAGAZINE, 2425 Wilson Blvd., Arlington VA 22201-3385. (703)841-4300. Fax: (703)525-9039. Editor: Mary Blake French. 70% freelance written. Prefers to work with published/established writers. Monthly magazine emphasizing military interests. Estab. 1904. Circ. 130,000. Pays on publication. Publishes ms an average of 5 months after acceptance. Buys all rights. Byline given except for back-up research. Submit seasonal/holiday material 3 months in advance. Sample copy and writer's guidelines for 9 × 12 SAE with $1 postage.
Nonfiction: Historical (military and original); humor (military feature-length articles and anecdotes); interview; new product; nostalgia; personal experience dealing especially with the most recent conflicts in which the US Army has been involved (Desert Storm, Panama, Grenada); photo feature; profile; technical. No rehashed history. "We would like to see more pieces about little-known episodes involving interesting military personalities. We especially want material lending itself to heavy, contributor-supplied photographic treatment. The first thing a contributor should recognize is that our readership is very savvy militarily. 'Gee-whiz' personal reminiscences get short shrift, unless they hold their own in a company in which long military service, heroism and unusual experiences are commonplace. At the same time, Army readers like a well-written story with a fresh slant, whether it is about an experience in a foxhole or the fortunes of a corps in battle." Buys 12 mss/issue. Submit complete ms. Length: 2,000 words, but shorter items, especially in 1,000 to 1,500 range, often have better chance of getting published. Pays 12-18¢/word. No unsolicited book reviews.
Photos: Submit photo material with accompanying ms. Pays $25-50 for 8 × 10 b&w glossy prints; $50-350 for 8 × 10 color glossy prints or 2¼ × 2¼ transparencies; will also accept 35mm. Captions preferred. Buys all rights. Pays $35-50 for cartoon with strong military slant.
Columns/Departments: Military news, books, comment (*New Yorker*-type "Talk of the Town" items). Buys 8/issue. Submit complete ms. Length: 1,000 words. Pays $40-150.

FAMILY MAGAZINE, The Magazine for Military Wives, PABCO, 169 Lexington Ave., New York NY 10016. (212)545-9740. Fax: (212)779-3080. Executive Editor: Liz DeFranco. 85% freelance written. Monthly magazine covering military family life. "All subjects covered must be germane to the military family or the military wife. All services mentioned must be accessible to military families. Any products or services should tie in with the PX/BX or commissary." Estab. 1958. Circ. 500,000. Pays on publication. Publishes ms an average of 4 months after acceptance. Byline given. Buys first North American serial rights and makes work-for-hire assignments. Editorial lead time 3 months. Submit seasonal material 6 months in advance. Accepts simultaneous submissions. Query for electronic submissions. Reports in 6 weeks on queries; 2 months on mss. Sample copy for $1.25 and 9 × 12 SASE. Writer's guidelines for #10 SASE.
Nonfiction: General interest, humor, interview/profile, new product, personal experience, photo feature, travel, military/family. Special issues: military retirees, active duty military women. Buys 35 mss/year. Send complete ms. Length: 1,000-3,000 words. Pays $50-200.
Photos: State availability of photos with submission. Reviews transparencies and prints. Negotiates payment individually. Buys one-time rights.

Columns/Departments: Comstore Cookery (recipes), 10-15 recipes plus text; Travel (things to do with children), 2,000-3,000 words; FAMILY Kid (children's puzzles, games, etc.), graphics (1 page). Buys 30 mss/year. Send complete ms. Pays $50-200.
Fillers: Short humor, travel tips, cooking tips. Buys 2 mss/year. Length: 50-250 words. Pays $25.
Tips: "Request a copy of the magazine before submitting. Don't send manuscripts that have made the rounds and are over-photocopied and messy. Have someone else read it for feedback before sending it out. Know the military market or the subject well."

‡**NAVAL HISTORY**, U.S. Naval Institute, 118 Maryland Ave., Annapolis MD 21402-5035. (410)268-6110. Editor: Fred L. Schultz. Contact: Bruce Gibson. 90% freelance written. Bimonthly magazine covering naval and maritime history, worldwide. "We are committed, as a publication of the 121-year-old US Naval Institute, to presenting the best and most accurate short works in international naval and maritime history. We do find a place for academicians, but they should be advised that a good story generally wins against a dull topic, no matter how well-researched." Estab. 1988. Circ. 34,000. **Pays on acceptance**. Publishes ms an average of 1-2 years after acceptance. Byline given. Buys first North American serial rights; occasionally allow rights to revert to authors. Editorial lead time 6 months. Submit seasonal material 6 months in advance. No simultaneous or previously published submissions. Query for electronic submissions. Reports in 1 month on queries; 2 months on mss. Sample copy for $3.50 and SASE. Writer's guidelines free on request.
Nonfiction: Book excerpts, essays, historical/nostalgic, humor, inspirational, interview/profile, personal experience, photo feature, technical. Buys 80-100 mss/year. Query. Send complete ms. Length: 1,000-3,000 words. Pays $300-500 for assigned articles; $75-400 for unsolicited articles.
Photos: State availability of photos with submission. Reviews contact sheets, transparencies, 4×6 or larger prints. Offers $10 minimum. Captions, model releases, identification of subjects required. Buys one-time rights.
Fillers: Anecdotes, news breaks (naval-related), short humor. Buys 40-50/year. Length: 50-1,000 words. Pays $10-50.
Tips: "A good way to break in is to write a good, concise, exciting story supported by primary sources and substantial illustrations. Naval history-related news items (ship decommissionings, underwater archaeology, etc.) are also welcome."

NAVY TIMES, Times Journal, 6883 Commercial Dr., Springfield VA 22159. (703)750-8636. Fax: (703)750-8622. Editor: Tobias Naegele. Managing Editor: Jean Reid Norman. Weekly newspaper covering sea services. News and features of men and women in the Navy, Coast Guard and Marine Corps. Estab. 1950. Circ. 90,000. **Pays on acceptance.** Byline given. Buys first North American serial or second serial (reprint) rights. Submit seasonal material 2 months in advance. Reports in 2 months. Free writer's guidelines.
Nonfiction: Historical/nostalgic, opinion. No poetry. Buys 100 mss/year. Query. Length: 500-1,000 words. Pays $50-500. Sometimes pays expenses of writers on assignment.
Photos: Send photos with submission. Offers $20-100/photo. Captions and identification of subjects required. Buys one-time rights.

OFF DUTY MAGAZINE, 3303 Harbor Blvd., Suite C-2, Costa Mesa CA 92626-1500. (714)549-7172. Fax: (714)549-4222. Editorial Director: Jim Shaw. Managing Editor: Gary Burch. 30% freelance written. Monthly magazine covering the leisure-time activities and interests of the military community. "Our audience is solely military members and their families; many of our articles could appear in other consumer magazines, but we always slant them toward the military; i.e. where to get a military discount when traveling." Estab. 1970. Circ. 570,000. **Pays on acceptance.** Publishes ms an average of 3 months after acceptance. Byline given. Buys one-time rights. Submit seasonal material at least 4 months in advance. Accepts simultaneous and previously published submissions. Send photocopy of article and information about when and where the article previously appeared. For reprints, pays 50% of the amount paid for an original article. Reports in 2 months on queries. Sample copy for 9×12 SAE with 6 first class stamps. Writer's guidelines for SASE.
Nonfiction: Humor (military), interview/profile (music and entertainment), travel, finance, lifestyle (with a military angle). "Must be familiar with *Off Duty* and its needs." Buys 30-40 mss/year. Query. Length: 800-2,100 words. Pays $160-420 for assigned articles.
   ● Publisher is not interested in seeing World War II reminiscences.
Photos: Send photos with submission. Reviews contact sheets and 35mm transparencies. Offers $50-300 (cover)/photo. Captions and identifiction of subjects required. Buys one-time rights. Unsolicited photos not returned without SASE.
Tips: "Get to know the military community and its interests beyond the stereotypes. Travel—query with the idea of getting on our next year's editorial calendar. We choose our primary topics at least 6 months prior to its start."

PARAMETERS: U.S. Army War College Quarterly, U.S. Army War College, Carlisle Barracks PA 17013-5050. (717)245-4943. Editor: Col. John J. Madigan, U.S. Army Retired. 100% freelance written. Prefers to work with published/established writers or experts in the field. Readership consists of senior leadership of US defense establishment, both uniformed and civilian, plus members of the media, government, industry and academia interested in national and international security affairs, military strategy, military leadership and management, art and science of warfare, and military history (provided it has contemporary relevance). Most readers possess a graduate degree. Estab. 1971. Circ. 12,000. Not copyrighted; unless copyrighted by author, articles may be reprinted with appropriate credits. Buys first serial rights. Byline given. Pays on publication. Publishes ms an average of 6 months after acceptance. Reports in 6 weeks. Free sample copy and writer's guidelines.

Nonfiction: Articles are preferred that deal with current security issues, employ critical analysis and provide solutions or recommendations. Liveliness and verve, consistent with scholarly integrity, appreciated. Theses, studies and academic course papers should be adapted to article form prior to submission. Documentation in complete endnotes. Submit complete ms. Length: 4,500 words average, preferably less. Pays $150 average (including visuals).

Tips: "Make it short; keep it interesting; get criticism and revise accordingly. Tackle a subject only if you are an authority."

PERIODICAL, Journal of America's Military Past, 10206 Lariston Lane, Silver Spring MD 20903-1311. Editor-in-Chief: Logan C. Osterndorf. 90% freelance written. Works with a small number of new/unpublished writers each year. Quarterly magazine emphasizing old and abandoned forts, posts and military installations; military subjects for a professional, knowledgeable readership interested in one-time defense sites or other military installations. Circ. 1,500. Pays on publication. Publishes ms an average of 6 months after acceptance. Buys one-time rights. Accepts simultaneous and previously published submissions (if published a long time ago). Reports in 3 weeks. Writer's guidelines for #10 SASE.

Nonfiction: Historical, personal experience, photo feature, technical (relating to posts, their construction/operation and military matters). Buys 4-6 mss/issue. Query or send complete ms. Length: 300-4,000 words. Pays $2/published page minimum.

Photos: Purchased with or without ms. Query. Reviews glossy, single-weight b&w prints. Offers no additional payment for photos accepted with accompanying ms. Captions required.

Tips: "We plan more emphasis on appeal to professional military audience and military historians."

SOLDIER OF FORTUNE, The Journal of Professional Adventurers, Omega Group, Ltd., P.O. Box 693, Boulder CO 80306-0693. (303)449-3750. Fax: (303)444-5617. Managing Editor: Tom Slizewski. Assistant Editor: Lynne Robertson. 50% freelance written. Monthly magazine covering military, paramilitary, police, combat subjects and action/adventure. "We are an action-oriented magazine; we cover combat hot spots around the world such as Afghanistan, El Salvador, Angola, etc. We also provide timely features on state-of-the-art weapons and equipment; elite military and police units; and historical military operations. Readership is primarily active-duty military, veterans and law enforcement." Estab. 1975. Circ. 175,000. Byline given. Offers 25% kill fee. Buys all rights; will negotiate. Accepts previously published submissions. Send photocopy of article and information about when and where it previously appeared. For reprints, pays 25% of their fee for an original article. Submit seasonal material 5 months in advance. Reports in 3 weeks on queries; 1 month on mss. Sample copy for $5. Writer's guidelines for #10 SASE. Send mss to articles editor; queries to managing editor.

Nonfiction: Exposé; general interest; historical/nostalgic; how-to (on weapons and their skilled use); humor; profile; new product; personal experience; novel excerpts; photo feature ("number one on our list"); technical; travel; combat reports; military unit reports and solid Vietnam and Operation Desert Storm articles. "No 'How I won the war' pieces; no op-ed pieces *unless* they are fully and factually backgrounded; no knife articles (staff assignments only). *All* submitted articles should have good art; art will sell us on an article." Buys 75 mss/year. Query with or without published clips or send complete ms. Length: 2,000-3,000 words. Pays $150-250/page. Sometimes pays the expenses of writers on assignment.

Photos: Send photos with submission (copies only, no originals). Reviews contact sheets and transparencies. Offers no additional payment for photos accepted with ms. Pays $500 for cover photo. Captions and identification of subjects required. Buys one-time rights.

Columns/Departments: Lynne Robertson, articles editor. Combat craft (how-to military and police survival skills) and I Was There (first-person accounts of the arcane or unusual based in a combat or law enforcement environment), both 600-800 words. Buys 16 mss/year. Send complete ms. Length: 600-800 words. Combat craft pays $200; I was There $100.

Fillers: Bulletin Board editor. Newsbreaks; military/paramilitary related, "*has* to be documented." Length: 100-250 words. Pays $25.

Tips: "Submit a professionally prepared, complete package. All artwork with cutlines, double-spaced typed manuscript with 5.25 or 3.5 IBM-compatible disc, if available, cover letter including synopsis of article, supporting documentation where applicable, etc. Manuscript must be factual; writers have to do their homework and get all their facts straight. One error means rejection. We will work with authors over the phone or by letter, tell them if their ideas have merit for an acceptable article, and help them fine-tune their work. I Was There is a good place for freelancers to start. Vietnam features, if carefully researched and art heavy, will always get a careful look. Combat reports, again, with good art, are number one in our book and stand the best chance of being accepted. Military unit reports from around the world are well received as are law enforcement articles (units, police in action). If you write for us, be complete and factual; pros read *Soldier* *of Fortune*, and are *very* quick to let us know if we (and the author) err. We will be Operation Desert Storm-oriented for years to come, in terms of first-person accounts and incisive combat reports. Read a current issue to see where we're taking the magazine in the 1990s."

TIMES NEWS SERVICE, Army Times Publishing Co., Springfield VA 22159-0200. (703)750-8125. Fax: (703)750-8781. E-mail: mconews@aol.com. Deputy Editor: Margaret Roth. Managing Editor: Kent Miller. Travel Editor: Maureen Rhea. 15% freelance written. Willing to work with new/unpublished writers. Manages weekly lifestyle section of Army, Navy and Air Force Times covering current lifestyles and problems of career military families around the world. Circ. 300,000. **Pays on acceptance.** Publishes ms an average of 2 months after acceptance. Byline given. Buys first worldwide rights. Submit seasonal material 3 months in advance. Query for electronic submissions. Reports in about 1 month. Writer's guidelines for #10 SASE.
  ● *Times News Service* accepts few exposé-type articles from freelancers but it is always interested in seeing queries. If you have news, they will accept it from a freelancer, but staff writers generally get the news before any freelancers can.
Nonfiction: Exposé (current military); interview/profile (military); personal experience (military only); travel (of military interest). Buys about 200 mss/year. Query with published clips. Length: 500-2,000 words. Pays $100-275. Sometimes pays the expenses of writers on assignment.
Photos: Send photos or send photos with ms. Reviews 35mm color contact sheets and prints. Captions, model releases and identification of subjects required.
Tips: "In your query write a detailed description of story and how it will be told. A tentative lead is nice. A military angle is crucial. Just one good story 'breaks in' a freelancer. Follow the outline you propose in your query letter and humanize articles with quotes and examples."

VIETNAM, Cowles History Group, 741 Miller Dr. SE, #D-2, Leesburg VA 22075-8920. (703)771-9400. Editor: Colonel Harry G. Summers, Jr. Managing Editor: Roger L. Vance. 80-90% freelance written. Bimonthly magazine that "provides in-depth and authoritative accounts of the many complexities that made the war in Vietnam unique, including the people, battles, strategies, perspectives, analysis and weaponry." Estab. 1988. Circ. 110,000. Pays on publication. Publishes ms up to 2 years after acceptance. Byline given. Buys all rights. Query for electronic submissions. Reports in 3 months on queries; 6 months on mss. Sample copy for $3.95. Writer's guidelines for #10 SASE.
Nonfiction: Book excerpts (if original), historical, interview, personal/experience, military history. "Absolutely no fiction or poetry; we want straight history, as much personal narrative as possible, but not the gung-ho, shoot-em-up variety, either." Buys 50 mss/year. Query. Length: 4,000 words maximum. Pays $300 for features.
Photos: Send photos with submission. Identification of subjects required. Buys one-time rights.
Columns/Departments: Arsenal (about weapons used, all sides); Personality (profiles of the players, all sides); Fighting Forces (about various units or types of units: air, sea, rescue); Perspectives. Query. Length: 2,000 words. Pays $150.

WORLD WAR II, Cowles History Group, 741 Miller Dr., SE, Suite D-2, Leesburg VA 22075. (703)771-9400. Fax: (703)779-8345. Editor: Michael Haskew. Managing Editor: Roger L. Vance. 95% freelance written. Prefers to work with published/established writers. Bimonthly magazine covering "military operations in World War II—events, personalities, strategy, national policy, etc." Estab. 1983. Circ. 220,000. Pays on publication. Publishes ms an average of 1-2 years after acceptance. Byline given. Buys all rights. Submit anniversary-related material 1 year in advance. Reports in 3 months on queries; 6 months or more on mss. Sample copy for $4. Writer's guidelines for #10 SASE.
Nonfiction: World War II military history. No fiction. Buys 24 mss/year. Query. Length: 4,000 words. Pays $200.
Photos: State availability of art and photos with submission. (For photos and other art, send photocopies and cite sources. "We'll order.") Sometimes offers additional payment for photos accepted with ms. Captions and identification of subjects required. Buys one-time rights.
Columns/Department: Undercover (espionage, resistance, sabotage, intelligence gathering, behind the lines, etc.); Personalities (WW II personalities of interest); Armaments (weapons, their use and development), all 2,000 words. Book reviews, 300-750 words. Buys 18 mss/year (plus book reviews). Query. Pays $100.
Tips: "List your sources and suggest further readings in standard format at the end of your piece—as a bibliography for our files in case of factual challenge or dispute. All submissions are on speculation. When the story's right, but the writing isn't, we'll pay a small research fee for use of the information in our own style and language."

Music

Music fans follow the latest industry news in these publications. Types of music and musicians or specific instruments are the sole focus of some magazines. Publications geared to the music industry and professionals can be found in the Trade Music section. Additional music and dance markets are found in the Entertainment section.

THE ABSOLUTE SOUND, The Journal of The High End, P.O. Box 360, Sea Cliff NY 11579. (516)676-2830. Fax: (516)676-5469. Editor-in-Chief: Harry Pearson, Jr. Managing Editor: Frank Doris. 10% freelance written. Works with a small number of new/unpublished writers each year. Magazine published 8 times/year covering the music reproduction business, audio equipment and records for "up-scale, high tech men and women, ages 20-100, serious music lovers." Estab. 1973. Pays on publication. Byline given. Buys all rights. Accepts previously published submissions. Send tearsheet or photocopy of article and information about when and where the article previously appeared. Pays 25-50% of their fee for an original article. Reports in 4 months. Query for electronic submissions. Sample copy for $7.50.
  • *The Absolute Sound* would like more industry reporting, as well as interviews with industry people. This magazine has increased its frequency from 6-8 issues/year. They report they need more queries.
Nonfiction: Exposé (of bad commercial audio practices); interview/profile (famous recording engineers, famous conductors); new product (audio); opinion (audio and record reviews); technical (how to improve your stereo system). Special Recordings issue. No puff pieces about industry. No newspaper clippings. Query with published clips. Length: 250-5,000 words. Pays $125-1,000. Sometimes pays the expenses of writers on assignment.
Columns/Departments: Audio Musings (satires), Reports from Overseas (audio shows, celebrities, record companies). Buys 8 mss/year. Length: 250-750 words. Pays $125-200.
Tips: "Writers should know about audio, recordings and the engineering of same, as well as live music. The approach is *literate*, witty, investigative, good journalism."

AMERICAN SONGWRITER, 121 17th Ave. S., Nashville TN 37203-2707. (615)244-6065. Fax: (615)742-1123. Editor: Vernell Hackett. Managing Editor: Deborah Price. 30% freelance written. Bimonthly magazine educating amateur songwriters while informing professionals. Estab. 1984. Circ. 5,000. Pays on publication. Publishes ms an average of 2 months after acceptance. Offers $10 kill fee. Buys first North American serial rights. Accepts simultaneous and previously published submissions. Send photocopy of article or typed ms with rights for sale noted and information about when and where the article previously appeared. For reprints, pays 50% of amount paid for an original article. Query for electronic submissions. Reports in 2 months. Sample copy for $3. Writer's guidelines for SAE.
Nonfiction: General interest, interview/profile, new product, technical. "No fiction." Buys 20 mss/year. Query with published clips. Length: 300-1,200 words. Pays $25-50 for assigned articles.
Photos: Send photos with submission. Reviews 3×5 prints. Offers no additional payment for photos accepted with ms. Identification of subjects required. Buys one-time rights.

‡BBC MUSIC MAGAZINE, Compete Guide to Classical Music, BBC Magazines, 80 Wood Lane, London W12 0TT England. (181)576-3283. Editor: Fiona Maddocks. Managing Editor: Jessica Gibson. 90% freelance written. Monthly magazine covering all aspects of classical music, including CDs, composers etc., for all levels of interest and knowledge. Estab. 1992. Circ. 250,000. Pays on publication. Publishes ms 3-4 months after acceptance. Byline given. Buys all rights. Editorial lead time 3 months. Submit seasonal material 1 year in advance. Query for electronic submissions.
Nonfiction: Essays, exposé, how-to (understand aspects of music better), interview/profile, opinion. Does not want to see interviews, profiles. Buys 300 mss/year. Query. Length: 500-2,500 words. Pays $150-1,500. Sometimes pays expenses of writers on assignments.
Photos: State availability of photos with submissions. Negotiates payment individually.
Fillers: Newsbreaks. Buys 100/year. Length: 100-200 words. Pays $50.
Tips: Send brief letter outlining idea(s) to editor.

BLUEGRASS UNLIMITED, Bluegrass Unlimited, Inc., P.O. Box 111, Broad Run VA 22014-0111. (703)349-8181 or (800)BLU-GRAS. Fax: (703)341-0011. Editor: Peter V. Kuykendall. Managing Editor: Sharon Watts. 80% freelance written. Prefers to work with published/established writers. Monthly magazine on bluegrass and old-time country music. Estab. 1966. Circ. 24,500. Pays on publication. Publishes ms an average of 4 months after acceptance. Byline given. Kill fee negotiated. Buys first North American serial, one-time, all rights and second serial (reprint) rights. Accepts previously published submissions. Send photocopy or typed ms with rights for sale noted and information about when and where the article previously appeared. Negotiates amount paid for reprints. Submit seasonal material 4 months in advance. Reports in 2 weeks on queries; 2 months on mss. Free sample copy and writer's guidelines for #10 SASE.
Nonfiction: General interest, historical/nostalgic, how-to, interview/profile, personal experience, photo feature, travel. No "fan" style articles. Buys 75-80 mss/year. Query with or without published clips. No set word length. Pays 6-8¢/word.
Photos: State availability of or send photos with query. Reviews 35mm transparencies and 3×5, 5×7 and 8×10 b&w and color prints. Pays $50-150 for transparencies; $25-50 for b&w prints; $50-250 for color prints. Identification of subjects required. Buys one-time and all rights.

Fiction: Ethnic, humorous. Buys 3-5 mss/year. Query. No set word length. Pays 6-8¢/word.
Tips: "We would prefer that articles be informational, based on personal experience or an interview with lots of quotes from subject, profile, humor, etc."

B-SIDE MAGAZINE, P.O. Box 15921, Philadelphia PA 19103. Editor: Carol L. Schutzbank. Managing Editor: Sandra Garcia. Contact: Carol Schutzbank. 60% freelance written. Bimonthly magazine covering music and related subjects of interest. "*B-Side* bridges the gap between "home-grown" fanzines and the more slick, commercial music magazines." Estab. 1986. Circ. 30,000. Pays varies according to assignment. Byline given. Buys first rights. Accepts previously published submissions. Send photocopy of article and information about when and where the article previously appeared. For reprints, pay varies. Query for electronic submissions. Reports in 2 months on queries; 4 months on mss. Sample copy for $5. Writer's guidelines for #10 SASE.
Nonfiction: Exposé, general interest, new product, interviews, reviews. Pay varies.
Photos: State availability of photos with submission. Reviews contact sheets. Negotiates payment indivi-aully. Identification of subjects required. Buys one-time rights.
Tips: "Read our magazine and learn who we are. Too many writers 'scan' us without paying attention to what sets us apart from our competitors. Read the magazine thoroughly. Good for breaking in are small profile pieces on emerging acts, topics, issues."

COUNTRY SONG ROUNDUP, Country Song Roundup, Inc., 210 Route 4 East, Suite 401, Paramus NJ 07652-5116. (201)843-4004. Fax: (201)843-8636. Editor: Celeste R. Gomes. Assistant Editor: Jennifer Fusco-Giacobbe. Contact: Celeste R. Gomes. 10% freelance written. Monthly magazine covering country music. "Our magazine is for the country music fan and songwriter. The slant of our articles is on the music, the songs; the artistic side. At times, we cover the private side of an artist." Estab: 1949. Circ. 200,000. Pays on publication. Publishes ms an average of 6 months after acceptance. Byline given. Offer 50% kill fee or $50. Buys first rights and second serial (reprint) rights. Editorial lead time 3 months. Submit seasonal material 6 months in advance. Query for assignments. "No phone calls please." Reports in 2 weeks on queries; 2 months on mss. Sample copy for $3.50. Writer's guidelines for #10 SASE.
Nonfiction: Interview/profile of country artists. "No profiles on new artists—they're done inhouse. No personal experience articles, reviews of any kind or Question and Answer articles." Buys 25-30 mss/year. Query with published clips. Length: 1,200-1,500 words. Pays $100 minimum. "Besides regular fee ($100) a copy of the issue in which article appears is sent to the writer."

GUITAR PLAYER MAGAZINE, GPI Publications, Suite 100, 411 Borel Ave., San Mateo CA 95112. (415)358-9500. Fax: (415)358-9216. Editor: Joe Gore. 70% freelance written. Monthly magazine for persons "interested in guitars, guitarists, manufacturers, guitar builders, bass players, equipment, careers, etc." Circ. 150,000. Buys first serial and limited reprint rights. **Pays on acceptance.** Publishes ms an average of 3 months after acceptance. Byline given. Reports in 6 weeks. Writer's guidelines for #10 SASE.
Nonfiction: Publishes "wide variety of articles pertaining to guitars and guitarists: interviews, guitar crafts-men profiles, how-to features—anything amateur and professional guitarists would find fascinating and/or helpful. On interviews with 'name' performers, be as technical as possible regarding strings, guitars, tech-niques, etc. We're not a pop culture magazine, but a magazine for musicians." Also buys features on such subjects as a guitar museum, role of the guitar in elementary education, personal reminiscences of past greats, technical gadgets and how to work them, analysis of flamenco, etc. Buys 30-40 mss/year. Query. Length: open. Payment varies. Sometimes pays expenses of writers on assignment.
Photos: Reviews b&w glossy prints. Buys 35mm color transparencies. Payment varies. Buys one time rights.

HIT PARADER, #220, 63 Grand Ave., River Edge NJ 07661. (201)843-4004. Editor: Andy Secher. Managing Editor: Anne Leighton. 5% freelance written. Monthly magazine covering heavy metal music. "We look for writers who have access to the biggest names in heavy metal music." Estab. 1943. Circ. 200,000. Pays on publication. Publishes ms an average of 4 months after acceptance. Byline given. Buys all rights. Submit seasonal material 4 months in advance. Reports in 2 months on queries. Sample copy for 9×12 SAE with 5 first-class stamps.
Nonfiction: General interest, interview/profile. Buys 3-5 mss/year. Query with published clips. Length: 600-800 words. Pays $75-140. Lifestyle-oriented and hardball pieces. "Study and really know the bands to get new angles on story ideas."
Photos: Reviews transparencies, 5×7 and 8×10 b&w prints and Kodachrome 64 slides. Offers $25-200/photo. Buys one-time rights. "We don't work with new photographers."
Tips: "Interview big names in metal, get published in other publications. We don't take chances on new writers."

ILLINOIS ENTERTAINER, 124 W. Polk, Suite 103, Chicago IL 60605. (312)922-9333. Fax: (312)922-9369. Editor: Michael C. Harris. 95% freelance written. Prefers to work with published/established writers but open to new writers with "style." Monthly tabloid covering music and entertainment for consumers within

100-mile radius of Chicago. Estab. 1974. Circ. 80,000. Pays on publication. Publishes ms an average of 2 months after acceptance. Byline given. Offers 10% kill fee. Buys one-time rights. Accepts previously published articles. Send tearsheet or photocopy of article and information about when and where the article previously appeared. For reprints, pays publication's standard *IE* freelance rate. Reports in 2 months. Sample copy for $5.

Nonfiction: Interview/profile (of entertainment figures). Buys 75 mss/year. Query with published clips. Length: 500-2,000 words. Pays $15-100. Sometimes pays expenses of writers on assignment.

Photos: Send photos. Pays $20-30 for 5×7 or 8×10 b&w prints; $125 for color cover photo, both on publication only. Captions and identification of subjects required.

Columns/Departments: Spins (record reviews stress record over band or genre). Buys 200 mss/year. Query with published clips. Length: 150-250 words. Pays $10-40.

Tips: "Send clips (published or unpublished) with phone number, and be patient. Full staff has seniority, but if you know the ins and outs of the entertainment biz, and can balance that knowledge with a broad sense of humor, then you'll have a chance. Also, *IE* is more interested in alternative music than the pop-pap you can hear/read about everywhere else."

INTERNATIONAL MUSICIAN, American Federation of Musicians, Paramount Building, 1501 Broadway, Suite 600, New York NY 10036. (212)869-1330. Fax: (212)302-4374. Editor: Stephen R. Sprague. Managing Editor: Jessica Roe. 10% freelance written. Prefers to work with published/established writers. Monthly magazine for professional musicians. Estab. 1900. **Pays on acceptance.** Publishes ms an average of 3 months after acceptance. Byline given. Accepts previously published material. Send typed ms with rights for sale noted. Pays 60% of amount paid for an original article. Reports in 3 months.

Nonfiction: Articles on prominent instrumentalists (classical, jazz, rock or country) who are members of the American Federation of Musicians. Send complete ms. Length: 1,500 words maximum.

‡JAZZ TIMES MAGAZINE America's Jazz Magazine, #303, 7961 Eastern Ave., Silver Spring MD 20910. Fax: (301)588-2009. Editor: Mike Joyce. 10% freelance written. Magazine published 10 times/year covering jazz. Estab. 1970. Circ. 71,000. Pays on publication. Publishes ms an average of 3 months after acceptance. Byline given. Offers 50% kill fee. Buys first rights. Editorial lead time 3-4 months. Query. Sample copy for $4. Writer's guidelines free on request.

Nonfiction: Interview/profile, reviews of CDS, books and videos. Query. Length: 250-2,000 words. Sometimes pays expenses of writers on assignment.

Photos: Send photos with submission. Reviews prints. Negotiates payment individually. Identification of subjects required. Buys one-time rights.

Tips: "We are interested in writers who are knowledgeable about jazz and who are already being published in newspapers or other music magazines. No beginners please. Get published in local papers or magazines first."

JAZZIZ MAGAZINE, Jazziz Magazine Inc., 3620 NW 43rd St., Gainesville FL 32606. (904)375-3705. Editor: Bill Stevenson. Managing Editor: Roy Parkhurst. 100% freelance written. Monthly magazine featuring adult oriented music—jazz, world beat, New Age, blues, what's new and innovative. Estab. 1984. Circ. 150,000. Pays on publication. Publishes ms an average of 2 months after acceptance. Byline given. Offers 50% kill fee. Buys first North American serial rights. Editorial lead time 6 months. Submit seasonal material 3 months in advance. Accepts simultaneous submissions. Query for electronic submissions. Reports in 2 weeks on queries; 2 months on mss. Sample copy for $2.90 and 11×14 SAE. Writers guidelines free on request.

Nonfiction: General interest (music), historical/nostalgic, interview/profile, new product, opinion, technical. Buys 100 mss/year. Query with published clips. Length: 300-4,000 words. Pays 12¢/word. Sometimes pays expenses of writers on assignment.

Photos: Send photos with submission. Negotiates payment individually.

Columns/Departments: Prelude (new artist release), 300 words; Coda (short artist profiles), 800 words; various topical review columns, 300-1,200 words. Buys 300 mss/year. Query with published clips. Pays 12¢/word.

Tips: "Query us. Get our writer's guidelines. Call or write us *after* you've become familiar with our publication and have definate ideas to discuss. All areas open to freelancers. Know what you're talking (writing) about."

MODERN DRUMMER, 12 Old Bridge Rd., Cedar Grove NJ 07009. (201)239-4140. Fax: (201)239-7139. Editor-in-Chief: Ronald Spagnardi. Features Editor: William F. Miller. Managing Editor: Rick Van Horn. Monthly magazine for "student, semi-pro and professional drummers at all ages and levels of playing ability, with varied specialized interests within the field." 60% freelance written. Circ. 95,000. Pays on publication. Publishes ms an average of 3 months after acceptance. Buys all rights. Accepts previously published submissions. Reports in 2 weeks. Sample copy for $3.95. Free writer's guidelines.

Nonfiction: How-to, informational, interview, new product, personal experience, technical. "All submissions must appeal to the specialized interests of drummers." Buys 20-30 mss/year. Query or submit complete ms. Length: 5,000-8,000 words. Pays $200-500.

Photos: Purchased with accompanying ms. Reviews 8×10 b&w prints and color transparencies.

Columns/Departments: Jazz Drummers Workshop, Rock Perspectives, In The Studio, Show Drummers Seminar, Teachers Forum, Drum Soloist, The Jobbing Drummer, Strictly Technique, Book Reviews, Record Reviews, Video Reviews, Shop Talk. "Technical knowledge of area required for most columns." Buys 40-50 mss/year. Query or submit complete ms. Length: 500-2,500 words. Pays $25-150.

MUSICIAN, Billboard Publications, 11th Floor, 1515 Broadway, New York NY 10036. (212)536-5208. Editor: Bill Flanagan. Senior Editors: Keith Powers, Ted Greenwald, Mark Rowland. 85% freelance written. Monthly magazine covering contemporary music, especially rock, pop and jazz. Estab. 1976. Circ. 170,000. Pays on publication. Byline given. Offers 25-33% kill fee. Buys first world serial rights. Submit seasonal material 3 months in advance.

Nonfiction: All music-related: book excerpts, exposé, historical, how-to (recording and performing), humor, interview/profile, new product, technical. Buys 150 mss/year. Query with published clips. Length: 300-10,000 words. Payment negotiable. Pays expenses of writers on assignment.

Photos: Assigns photo shoots. Uses some stock. Offers $50-300/photo.

Columns/Departments: Jazz (jazz artists or works), 1,000-5,000 words; Reviews (record reviews), 300-500 words; Rough Mix (short, newsy stories), 300 words; Working Musician (technical "trade" angles on musicians), 1,000-3,000 words. Query with published clips. Length 300-1,500 words.

Tips: "Be aware of special music writers' style; don't gush, be somewhat skeptical; get the best quotes you can and save the arcane criticism for reviews; know and apply Strunk and White; be interesting. Please send *published* clips; we don't want to be anyone's first publication. Our writing is considered excellent (in all modesty), even though we don't pay as much as we'd like. We recognize National Writers Union."

RELIX MAGAZINE, Music for the Mind, P.O. Box 94, Brooklyn NY 11229. Editor: Toni A. Brown. Fax: (718)692-4345. 60% freelance written. Eager to work with new/unpublished writers. Bimonthly magazine covering rock 'n' roll music and specializing in Grateful Dead and other San Francisco and 60s related groups for readers ages 15-65. Estab. 1974. Circ. 60,000. Pays on publication. Publishes ms an average of 6 months after acceptance. Byline given. Buys all rights. Reports in 1 year. Accepts previously published submissions. Send photocopy of article and information about when and where the article previously appeared. Sample copy for $4.

Nonfiction: Historical/nostalgic, interview/profile, new product, personal experience, photo feature, technical. Special issues: year-end special. Query with published clips if available or send complete ms. Length open. Pays $1.75/column inch.

Fiction: Publishes novel excerpts.

Columns/Departments: Query with published clips, if available, or send complete ms. Pays variable rates.

Tips: "The most rewarding aspects of working with freelance writers are fresh writing and new outlooks."

SOUNDTRACK, The Journal of the Independent Music Association, SoundTrack Publishing, P.O. Box 609, Ringwood NJ 07456. (201)831-1317. Fax: (201)831-8672. Editor: Don Kulak. 60% freelance written. Bimonthly music and business magazine. Estab. 1988. Circ. 10,000. Pays on publication. Publishes ms an average of 2-3 months after acceptance. Byline sometimes given. Buys first rights and second serial (reprint) rights. Submit seasonal/holiday material 4 months in advance. Accepts simultaneous and previously published submissions. Send photocopy of article. For reprints, pays 50% of the amount paid for an original article. Reports in 1 week on queries; 3 weeks on mss. Free sample copy and writer's guidelines for 9×12 SAE with $2 postage.

- *Soundtrack* now has an investigative reporting section on political, social, economic and environmental topics.

Nonfiction: Book excerpts, exposé, how-to, interview/profile, opinion, technical. Buys 36 mss/year. Query with published clips. Length: 1,000-2,000 words. Pays $50-200 for assigned articles. No unsolicited mss. Sometimes pays writers with contributor copies or other premiums rather than cash by "mutually beneficial agreement." Sometimes pays expenses of writers on assignment.

Photos: Send photos with submissions. Offers $10-20/photo. Buys all rights.

Columns/Departments: The Business of Music (promotion, distribution, forming a record label; alternative markets—film scores, jingles, etc.; how-to's on generating more income from own music). Buys 24 mss/year. Query with published clips. Length: 1,000-2,000 words.

Tips: "Write a letter explaining background, interests, and areas of special study and what you hope to get out of writing for our publication. All sections are open to freelancers. Writing should be fluid and direct. We especially need more how-to information on record marketing and distribution."

STEREO REVIEW, Hachette Filipacchi Magazines, Inc., 1633 Broadway, New York NY 10019. (212)767-6000. Editor-in-Chief: Louise Boundas. Executive Editor: Michael Riggs. Classical Music Editor: Robert Ripps. Popular Music Editor: Steve Simels. 65% freelance written, almost entirely by established contributing editors, and on assignment. Monthly magazine. Estab. 1958. Circ. 500,000. **Pays on acceptance.** Publishes ms an average of 5 months after acceptance. Byline given. Buys first North American serial or all rights. Reports in 5 months. Sample copy for 9×12 SAE with 11 first-class stamps.

Nonfiction: Equipment and music reviews, how-to-buy, how-to-use, stereo, interview/profile. Buys approximately 25 mss/year. Query with published clips. Length: 1,500-3,000 words. Pays $500-1,000 for assigned articles.

Tips: "Send proposals or outlines, rather than completed articles, along with published clips to establish writing ability. Publisher assumes no responsibility for return or safety of unsolicited art, photos or manuscripts."

Mystery

These magazines buy fictional accounts of crime, detective work and mystery. Skim through other sections to identify markets for fiction; some will consider mysteries. For nonfiction crime markets, refer to the Detective section. Also see the second edition of *Mystery Writer's Sourcebook* (Writer's Digest Books).

‡HARDBOILED, Gryphon Publications, P.O. Box 209, Brooklyn NY 11228. Editor: Gary Lovisi. 100% freelance written. Quarterly magazine covering crime/mystery fiction and nonfiction. "Hard-hitting crime fiction and columns/articles and reviews on hardboiled crime writing and private-eye stories—the newest and most cutting-edge work and classic reprints." Estab. 1988. Circ. 1,000. Pays on publication. Publishes ms an average of 6-18 months after acceptance. Byline given. Offers 100% kill fee. Buys one-time rights. Editorial lead time 2 months. Submit seasonal material 6 months in advance. Accepts simultaneous submissions. Query first for previously published submissions. Query for electronic submissions. Reports in 2 weeks on queries; 2 months on mss. Sample copy for $6. Writer's guidelines for #10 SASE.

Nonfiction: Book excerpts, essays, exposé. Query first. Buys 8-10 mss/year. Length: 500-3,000 words. Pays 1 copy for nonfiction.

Photos: State availability of photos with submission.

Columns/Departments: "Various review columns/articles on hardboiled writers—query first." Buys 16-24 mss/year. Query.

Fiction: Mystery, hardboiled crime and private-eye stories *all* on the cutting-edge. Buys 60 mss/year. Send complete ms. Length: 500-3,000 words. Pays $5-50, depending on length and quality.

ALFRED HITCHCOCK MYSTERY MAGAZINE, Bantam Doubleday Dell Magazines, 1540 Broadway, New York NY 10036. Editor: Cathleen Jordan. Magazine published 13 times/year featuring new mystery short stories. Circ. 215,000. **Pays on acceptance.** Byline given. Buys first, first anthology and foreign rights. Submit seasonal/holiday material 7 months in advance. Reports in 2 months. Writer's guidelines for SASE.

Fiction: Original and well-written mystery and crime fiction. Length: up to 14,000 words.

‡THE MYSTERY REVIEW, A Quarterly Publication for Mystery Readers, C. von Hessert & Associates, P.O. Box 233, Colborne, Ontario K0K 1S0 Canada. (613)475-4440. Editor: Barbara Davey. 80% freelance written. Quarterly magazine covering mystery and suspense. "Our readers are interested in mystery and suspense books, films. All topics related to mystery—including real life unsolved mysteries." Estab. 1992. Circ. 4,500 (70% of distribution is in US). Pays on publication. Publishes ms an average of 3-6 months after acceptance. Byline given. Buys first North American serial rights or second serial (reprint) rights. Editorial lead time 6 months. Submit seasonal material 6 months in advance. Accepts simultaneous and previously published submissions. Query for electronic submissions. Reports in 6 weeks on queries; 1 month on mss. Sample copy for $5. Writer's guidelines free on request.

Nonfiction: Interview/profile. Query. Length: 2,000-5,000 words. Pays $50 maximum for assigned articles.

Photos: Send photos with submission. Reviews 5×7 b&w prints. Offers no additional payment for photos accepted with ms. Model releases, identification of subjects required. Buys all rights.

Columns/Departments: Book reviews (mystery/suspense titles only), 500-700 words; True "unsolved" mysteries (less generally known cases), 2,000-5,000 words; Bookstore profiles (mystery bookstores only), 500 words. Buys 50 mss/year. Query with published clips. Pays $10-30.

Poetry: Only poems with a mystery theme. Buys 3 poems/year. Submit maximum 2 poems. Pays $10-20.

Fillers: Puzzles, items related to mystery/suspense. Buys 4/year. Length: 100-500 words. Pays $10-20.

NEW MYSTERY, The World's Best Mystery, Crime and Suspense Stories, 175 Fifth Ave., 2001 The Flatiron Bldg., New York NY 10010. Editor: Charles Raisch III. 100% freelance written. Quarterly magazine featuring mystery short stories and book reviews. Estab. 1989. Circ. 80,000. **Pays on acceptance.** Publishes ms an average of 6 months after acceptance. Byline given. Does not return mss. Buys first North American serial or all rights. Editorial lead time 6 months. Submit seasonal material 1 year in advance. Accepts simultaneous submissions. Query for electronic submissions. Reports in 2 months on mss. Sample copy for $5 and 9×12 SAE with 4 first-class stamps.

Nonfiction: New product, short book reviews. Buys 40 mss/year. Send complete ms. Length: 250-2,000 words. Pays $20-50.

Fiction: Mystery, crime, noire, police procedural, hardboiled, child-in-jeopardy, suspense. Buys 50 mss/year. Send complete ms. Length: 2,000-6,000 words. Pays $50-500.

Fillers: Acrostic or crossword puzzles. Pays $25-50.

Nature, Conservation and Ecology

These publications promote reader awareness of the natural environment, wildlife, nature preserves and ecosystems. Many of these "green magazines" also concentrate on recycling and related issues. They do not publish recreation or travel articles except as they relate to conservation or nature. Other markets for this kind of material can be found in the Regional; Sports; and Travel, Camping and Trailer categories, although magazines listed there require that nature or conservation articles be slanted to their specialized subject matter and audience. Some juvenile and teen publications also buy nature-related material for young audiences. For more information on recycling publications, turn to the Resources and Waste Reduction section in Trade.

AMC OUTDOORS, The Magazine of the Appalachian Mountain Club, Appalachian Mountain Club, 5 Joy St., Boston MA 02108. (617)523-0655 ext. 312. Fax: (617)523-0722. E-mail: ancontdoors@mcimail. com. Editor/Publisher: Catherine K. Buni. 90% freelance written. Monthly magazine covering outdoor recreation and conservation issues. Estab. 1907. Circ. 66,000. Pays on publication. Publishes ms an average of 3 months after acceptance. Byline given. Offers 25% kill fee. Buys all rights. Editorial lead time 3 months. Submit seasonal material 4 months in advance. Query for electronic submissions. Reports in 1 month on queries; 2 months on mss. Sample copy for #10 SASE. Writer's guidelines free on request.

Nonfiction: Book excerpts, essays, exposé, general interest, historical/nostalgic, how-to, interview/profile, opinion, personal experience, photo feature, technical, travel. Special issues: Northern Forest Report (April) featuring the northern areas of New York, New Hampshire, Vermont, and Maine, and protection efforts for these areas. Buys 10 mss/year. Query with or without published clips. Length: 500-3,000 words. Sometimes pays expenses of writers on assignment.

Photos: State availability of photos with submission. Reviews contact sheets, transparencies and prints. Model releases and identification of subjects required.

Columns/Departments: Contact: Kimberly Ridley. News (environmental/outdoor recreation coverage of northeast), 1,300 words. Buys 20 mss/year. Query. Pays $50-500.

AMERICAN FORESTS, American Forests, 1516 P St. NW, Washington DC 20005. (202)667-3300. Fax: (202)667-7751. Editor: Bill Rooney. 70% freelance written. Bimonthly magazine "of trees and forests, published by a nonprofit citizens' organization for the advancement of intelligent management and use of our forests, soil, water, wildlife and all other natural resources necessary for an environment of high quality." Estab. 1895. Circ. 30,000. **Pays on acceptance.** Publishes ms an average of 4-8 months after acceptance. Byline given. Buys one-time rights. Accepts previously published articles. Send tearsheet of article or typed ms with rights for sale noted and information about when and where the article previously appeared. For reprints, pays 50% of the amount paid for an original article. Written queries preferred. Submit seasonal material 5 months in advance. Reports in 2 months. Sample copy for $1.20. Writer's guidelines for SASE.

• This magazine is looking for more urban and suburban-oriented pieces.

Nonfiction: General interest, historical, how-to, humor, inspirational. All articles should emphasize trees, forests, forestry and related issues. Buys 7-10 mss/issue. Query. Length: 2,000 words. Pays $300-700.

Photos: Send photos. Offers no additional payment for photos accompanying ms. Uses 8×10 b&w glossy prints; 35mm or larger transparencies, originals only. Captions required. Buys one-time rights.

Tips: "Query should have honesty and information on photo support."

THE AMICUS JOURNAL, Natural Resources Defense Council, 40 W. 20th St., New York NY 10011. (212)727-2700. Editor: Kathrin Day Lassila. 80% freelance written. Quarterly magazine covering national and international environmental issues. "*The Amicus Journal* is intended to provide the general public with a journal of thought and opinion on environmental affairs, particularly those relating to policies of national and international significance." Estab. 1979. Estab. 170,000. Pays on publication. Publishes ms an average of 6 months after acceptance. Offers 25% kill fee. Buys first North American serial rights (and print/electronic reprint rights). Submit seasonal material 6 months in advance. Reports in 3 months on queries. Sample copy for $4 with 9×12 SAE. Writer's guidelines for SASE.

• This publication is now accepting occasional literary (personal) essays on environmental issues or with environmental themes. (The editor stresses that submissions must be of the highest quality only and must be grounded in thorough knowledge of subject.)

Nonfiction: Exposé, interview/profile, essays, reviews. Query with published clips. Length: 200-3,500 words. Pay negotiable. Sometimes pays expenses of writers on assignment. Buys 35 mss/year.

Photos: State availability of photos with submission. Reviews contact sheets, color transparencies, 8×10 b&w prints. Negotiates payment individually. Captions, model releases, identification of subjects required. Buys one-time rights.

Columns/Departments: News & Comment (summary reporting of environmental issues, usually tied to topical items), 700-2,000 words; International Notebook (new or unusual international environmental stories), 700-2,000 words; People, 2,000 words; Reviews (in-depth reporting on issues and personalities, well-informed essays on books of general interest to environmentalists interested in policy and history), 500-1,000 words. Query with published clips. Pay negotiable.

Poetry: Brian Swann. Avant-garde, free verse, haiku, others. All poetry should be rooted in nature. Must submit with SASE. Buys 16 poems/year. Pays $50 plus a year's subscription.

Tips: "Please stay up to date on environmental issues, and review *The Amicus Journal* before submitting queries. Except for editorials all departments are open to freelance writers. Queries should precede manuscripts, and manuscripts should conform to the Chicago Manual of Style."

APPALACHIAN TRAILWAY NEWS, Appalachian Trail Conference, P.O. Box 807, Harpers Ferry WV 25425-0807. (304)535-6331. Fax: (304)535-2667. Editor: Judith Jenner. 50% freelance written. Bimonthly magazine. Estab. 1925. Circ. 26,000. **Pays on acceptance.** Byline given. Buys first North American serial or second serial (reprint) rights. Accepts previously published submissions. Send photocopy of article or typed ms with rights for sale noted and information about when and where the article previously appeared. Reports in 2 months. Sample copy for $2.50 includes guidelines. Writer's guidelines only for SASE.

• Articles must relate to Appalachian Trail.

Nonfiction: Essays, general interest, historical/nostalgic, how-to, humor, inspirational, interview/profile, photo feature, technical, travel. No poetry or religious materials. Buys 15-20 mss/year. Query with or without published clips, or send complete ms. Length: 250-3,000 words. Pays $25-300. Pays expenses of writers on assignment. Publishes, but does not pay for "hiking reflections."

Photos: State availability of b&w photos with submission. Reviews contact sheets, negatives and 5×7 prints. Offers $25-125/photo. Identification of subjects required. Negotiates future use by Appalachian Trail Conference.

Tips: "Contributors should display an obvious knowledge of or interest in the Appalachian Trail. Those who live in the vicinity of the Trail may opt for an assigned story and should present credentials and subject of interest to the editor."

‡THE ATLANTIC SALMON JOURNAL, The Atlantic Salmon Federation, P.O. Box 429, St. Andrews, New Brunswick E0G 2X0 Canada. Fax: (506)529-4985. Editor: Harry Bruce. 50-68% freelance written. Works with a small number of new/unpublished writers each year. Quarterly magazine covering conservation efforts for the Atlantic salmon, catering to "affluent and responsive audience—the dedicated angler and conservationist." Circ. 15,000. Pays on publication. Publishes ms an average of 3-6 months after acceptance. Byline given. Buys first serial rights to articles and one-time rights to photos. Submit seasonal material 3 months in advance. Accepts simultaneous submissions. Query for electronic submissions. Reports in 2 months. Sample copy for 9×12 SAE with $1 (Canadian), or IRC. Free writer's guidelines.

Nonfiction: Exposé, historical/nostalgic, how-to, humor, interview/profile, new product, opinion, personal experience, photo feature, technical, travel, conservation, cuisine, science, research and management. "We are seeking articles that are pertinent to the focus and purpose of our magazine, which is to inform and entertain our membership on all aspects of the Atlantic salmon and its environment, preservation and conservation." Buys 15-20 mss/year. Query with published clips and state availability of photos. Length: 1,500-2,500 words. Pays $200-400. Sometimes pays the expenses of writers on assignment.

Photos: Send photos with query. Pays $50 for 3×5 or 5×7 b&w prints; $50-100 for 2¼×3¼ or 35mm color slides. Captions and identification of subjects required.

Columns/Departments: Adventure Eating (cuisine) and First Person (nonfiction, anecdotal, from first-person viewpoint, can be humorous). Buys about 6 mss/year. Length: 1,000-1,500 words. Pays $150.

 A bullet introduces comments by the editors of Writer's Market *indicating special information about the listing.*

Fillers: Clippings, jokes, anecdotes and short humor. Length: 100-300 words average. Does not pay.

Tips: "Articles must reflect informed and up-to-date knowledge of Atlantic salmon. Writers need not be authorities, but research must be impeccable. Clear, concise writing is essential, and submissions must be typed. Anecdote, River Log and photo essays are most open to freelancers. The odds are that a writer without a background in outdoors writing and wildlife reporting will not have the 'informed' angle I'm looking for. Our readership is well-read and critical of simplification and generalization."

AUDUBON, The Magazine of the National Audubon Society, National Audubon Society, 700 Broadway, New York NY 10003-9501. Fax: (212)477-9069. Editor: Michael W. Robbins. 85% freelance written. Bimonthly magazine. Estab. 1887. Circ. 430,000. **Pays on acceptance.** Byline given. Buys first North American serial rights, second serial (reprint) rights on occasion. Query before submission. Reports in 3 months. Sample copy for $4 and 9×12 SAE with 10 first-class stamps or $5 for magazine and postage. Writer's guidelines for #10 SASE.

Nonfiction: Essays, investigative, historical, humor, interview/profile, opinion, photo feature, book excerpts (well in advance of publication). Length: 250-4,000 words. Pays $250-4,000. Pays expenses of writers on assignment.

Photos: Query with photographic idea before submitting slides. Reviews 35mm transparencies. Offers page rates per photo on publication. Captions and identification of subjects required. Write for photo guidelines.

BIRD WATCHER'S DIGEST, Pardson Corp., P.O. Box 110, Marietta OH 45750. Editor: William H. Thompson III. 60% freelance written. Works with a small number of new/unpublished writers each year. Bimonthly magazine covering natural history—birds and bird watching. "*BWD* is a nontechnical magazine interpreting ornithological material for amateur observers, including the knowledgeable birder, the serious novice and the backyard bird watcher; we strive to provide good reading and good ornithology." Estab. 1978. Circ. 85,000. Pays on publication. Publishes ms an average of 1 year after acceptance. Byline given. Buys one-time, first serial and second serial (reprint) rights. Submit seasonal material 6 months in advance. Accepts previously published submissions. Reports in 2 months. Sample copy for $3. Writer's guidelines for #10 SASE.

Nonfiction: Book excerpts, how-to (relating to birds, feeding and attracting, etc.), humor, personal experience, travel (limited—we get many). "We are especially interested in fresh, lively accounts of closely observed bird behavior and displays and of bird watching experiences and expeditions. We often need material on less common species or on unusual or previously unreported behavior of common species." No articles on pet or caged birds; none on raising a baby bird. Buys 75-90 mss/year. Send complete ms. All submissions must be accompanied by SASE. Length: 600-3,500 words. Pays from $50.

Photos: Send photos with ms. Pays $10 minimum for b&w prints; $50 minimum for transparencies. Buys one-time rights.

Poetry: Avant-garde, free verse, light verse, traditional. No haiku. Buys 12-18 poems/year. Submit maximum 3 poems. Length 8-20 lines. Pays $10.

Tips: "We are aimed at an audience ranging from the backyard bird watcher to the very knowledgeable birder; we include in each issue material that will appeal at various levels. We always strive for a good geographical spread, with material from every section of the country. We leave very technical matters to others, but we want facts and accuracy, depth and quality, directed at the veteran bird watcher and at the enthusiastic novice. We stress the joys and pleasures of bird watching, its environmental contribution, and its value for the individual and society."

E THE ENVIRONMENTAL MAGAZINE, Earth Action Network, P.O. Box 5098, Westport CT 06881-5098. (203)854-5559. Fax: (203)866-0602. Editor: Doug Moss. Contact: Jim Motavalli, managing editor. 80% freelance written. Bimonthly magazine on environmentalism. "*E Magazine* was formed for the purpose of acting as a clearinghouse of information, news and commentary on environmental issues." Estab. 1990. Circ. 70,000. Pays on publication. Byline given. Offers 50% kill fee. Buys first North American serial rights. Editorial lead time 3 months. Submit seasonal material 3-6 months in advance. Accepts simultaneous submissions and occasionally previously published articles. Send tearsheet or photocopy of article or typed ms with rights for sale noted and information about when and where the article previously appeared. Query for all submissions. Sample copy for $4. Writer's guidelines for #10 SASE.

Nonfiction: Exposé (environmental), how-to (the "Environmentalist" section), interview/profile, new product, opinion. No fiction or poetry. Buys 100 mss/year. Query with published clips. Length: 100-5,000 words. Pays 20¢/word, negotiable. On spec or free contributions welcome. Sometimes pays telephone expenses of writers on assignment.

Photos: Mention photo availability, but send only when requested. Reviews printed samples, e.g., magazine tearsheet, postcards, etc. to be kept on file. Negotiates payment individually. Identification of subjects required. Buys one-time rights.

Columns/Departments: In Brief/Currents (environmental news stories/trends), 400-1,000 words; Consumer News (environmentally sound products/trends), 1,200 words; Food and Health (ecological and health impacts of dietary choices), 1,200 words; the Environmentalist (how-to eco lifestyle tips), 1,000 words;

Interviews (environmental leaders), 2,000 words. Buys 100 mss/year. Query with published clips. Pays 20¢/word, negotiable. On spec or free contributions welcome.

Tips: "Contact us to obtain writer's guidelines and back issues of our magazine. Tailor your query according to the department/section you feel it would be best suited for. Articles must be lively, well-researched, and relevant to a mainstream, national readership."

HIGH COUNTRY NEWS, High Country Foundation, P.O. Box 1090, Paonia CO 81428-1090. (303)527-4898. Editor: Betsy Marston. 80% freelance written. Works with a small number of new/unpublished writers each year. Biweekly tabloid covering environment and natural resource issues in the Rocky Mountain states for environmentalists, politicians, companies, college classes, government agencies, etc. Estab. 1970. Circ. 15,000. Pays on publication. Publishes ms an average of 2 months after acceptance. Byline given. Buys one-time rights. Accepts previously published submissions. Send tearsheet of article. Reports in 1 month. Free sample copy and writer's guidelines.

Nonfiction: Reporting (local issues with regional importance); exposé (government, corporate); interview/profile; opinion; personal experience; centerspread photo feature. Special issues include those on states in the region. Buys 100 mss/year. Query. Length: 3,000 words maximum. Pays 20¢/word minimum. Sometimes pays expenses of writers on assignment.

● This magazine has increased its pay rates since last being listed.

Photos: Send photos with ms. Prefers b&w prints. Captions and identification of subjects required.

Tips: "We use a lot of freelance material, though very little from outside the Rockies. Familiarity with the newspaper is a must. Start by writing a query letter."

INTERNATIONAL WILDLIFE, National Wildlife Federation, 8925 Leesburg Pike, Vienna VA 22184-0001. (703)790-4000. Editor: Jonathan Fisher. 85% freelance written. Prefers to work with published/established writers. Bimonthly magazine for persons interested in natural history and the environment in countries outside the US. Estab. 1971. Circ. 380,000. **Pays on acceptance.** Publishes ms an average of 4 months after acceptance. Usually buys all rights to text. "We are now assigning most articles but will consider detailed proposals for quality feature material of interest to a broad audience." Reports in 6 weeks. Writer's guidelines for #10 SASE.

Nonfiction: Focuses on world wildlife, environmental problems and peoples' relationship to the natural world as reflected in such issues as population control, pollution, resource utilization, food production, etc. Stories deal with non-US subjects. Especially interested in articles on animal behavior and other natural history, first-person experiences by scientists in the field, well-reported coverage of wildlife-status case studies which also raise broader themes about international conservation and timely issues. Query. Length: 2,000-2,500 words. Also in the market for short, 750-word "one pagers." Examine past issue for style and subject matter. Pays $1,500 minimum for long features. Sometimes pays expenses of writers on assignment.

Photos: Purchases top-quality color photos; prefers packages of related photos and text, but single shots of exceptional interest and sequences also considered. Prefers Kodachrome or Fujichrome transparencies. Buys one-time rights.

MICHIGAN NATURAL RESOURCES MAGAZINE, Kolka & Robb, Inc, Suite 1401, 30700 Telegraph Rd., Bingham Farms MI 48025. (810)642-9580. Editor: Richard Morscheck. 50% freelance written. Works with a small number of new/unpublished writers each year. Bimonthly magazine covering natural resources in the Great Lakes area. Estab. 1931. Circ. 100,000. **Pays on acceptance.** Publishes ms an average of 9 months after acceptance. Byline given. Buys first rights. Submit seasonal/holiday material 1 year in advance. Reports in 2 months. Sample copy for $4 and 9×12 SAE. Writer's guidelines for #10 SASE.

Nonfiction: "All material must pertain to this region's natural resources: lakes, rivers, wildlife, flora and special features. No personal experience." Buys 15 mss/year. Query with clips of published work. Length: 800-2,500 words. Pays $100-400. Sometimes pays expenses of writers on assignment.

Photos: Photos submitted with an article will help sell it, but they must be of professional quality and razor sharp in focus. Send photos with ms. Pays $50-250 for 35mm transparencies; Fuji or Kodachrome preferred. Identification of subjects required. Buys one-time rights.

Tips: "We hope to exemplify why Michigan's natural resources are valuable to people and vice versa. We also strongly suggest that prospective writers familiarize themselves with past issues of the magazine before sending us material to review."

NATIONAL PARKS, 1776 Massachusetts Ave. NW, Washington DC 20036. (202)223-6722. Fax: (202)659-0650. E-mail: editornp@aol.com. Editor: Sue Dodge. Associate Editor: Linda Rancourt. 85% freelance written. Prefers to work with published/established writers. Bimonthly magazine for a highly educated audi-

---

For information on setting your freelance fees, see How Much Should I Charge?

ence interested in preservation of National Park System units, natural areas, and protection of wildlife habitat. Estab. 1919. Circ. 450,000. **Pays on acceptance.** Publishes ms an average of 5 months after acceptance. Buys first North American serial and second serial (reprint) rights. Very rarely accepts previously published submissions. Send query. Reports in 3 months. Sample copy for $3 and 9×12 SAE. Writer's guidelines for #10 SASE.

Nonfiction: Exposé (on threats, wildlife problems in national parks); descriptive articles about new or proposed national parks and wilderness parks; natural history pieces describing park geology wildlife, or plants. All material must relate to national parks. No poetry, philosophical essays or first person narratives. "Queries are welcome, but unsolicited manuscripts are not accepted." Length: 2,000-2,500 words. Pays $800 for full-length features; $350 for serial articles.

Photos: $100-250 for transparencies. Captions required. Buys first North American serial rights.

NATIONAL WILDLIFE, National Wildlife Federation, 8925 Leesburg Pike, Vienna VA 22184-0001. (703)790-4524. Editor-in-Chief: Bob Strohm. Editor: Mark Wexler. 75% freelance written, "but assigns almost all material based on staff ideas. Assigns few unsolicited queries." Bimonthly magazine on wildlife, natural history and environment. "Our purpose is to promote wise use of the nation's natural resources and to conserve and protect wildlife and its habitat. We reach a broad audience that is largely interested in wildlife conservation and nature photography. We avoid too much scientific detail and prefer anecdotal, natural history material." Estab. 1963. Circ. 660,000. **Pays on acceptance.** Publishes ms an average of 1 year after acceptance. Offers 25% kill fee. Buys all rights. Submit seasonal material 8 months in advance. Reports in 6 weeks. Writer's guidelines for #10 SASE.

Nonfiction: General interest (2,500-word features on wildlife, new discoveries, behavior, or the environment); how-to (an outdoor or nature related activity); personal experience (outdoor adventure); photo feature (wildlife); short 700-word features on an unusual individual or new scientific discovery relating to nature. Buys 50 mss/year. Query with or without published clips. Length: 750-2,500 words. Pays $500-2,000. Sometimes pays expenses of writers on assignment.

Photos: John Nuhn, photo editor. Send photos or send photos with query. Prefers Kodachrome or Fujichrome transparencies. Buys one-time rights.

Tips: "Writers can break in with us more readily by proposing subjects (initially) that will take only one or two pages in the magazine (short features)."

NATURAL HISTORY, Natural History Magazine, Central Park W. at 79th St., New York NY 10024. (212)769-5500. Editor: Alan P. Ternes. 15% freelance written. Monthly magazine for well-educated, ecologically aware audience: professional people, scientists and scholars. Circ. 500,000. Pays on publication. Publishes ms an average of 3 months after acceptance. Byline given. Buys first serial rights and becomes agent for second serial (reprint) rights. Submit seasonal material at least 6 months in advance.

Nonfiction: Uses all types of scientific articles except chemistry and physics—emphasis is on the biological sciences and anthropology. Prefers professional scientists as authors. "We always want to see new research findings in almost all the branches of the natural sciences—anthropology, archeology, zoology and ornithology. We find that it is particularly difficult to get something new in herpetology (amphibians and reptiles) or entomology (insects), and we would like to see material in those fields. We lean heavily toward writers who are scientists. We expect high standards of writing and research. We favor an ecological slant in most of our pieces, but do not generally lobby for causes, environmental or other. The writer should have a deep knowledge of his subject, then submit original ideas either in query or by manuscript. Acceptance is more likely if article is accompanied by high-quality photographs." Buys 60 mss/year. Query or submit complete ms. Length: 1,500-3,000 words. Pays $750-1,000, plus additional payment for photos used.

Photos: Rarely uses 8×10 b&w glossy prints; pays $125/page maximum. Much color is used; pays $300 for inside and up to $500 for cover. Buys one-time rights.

Tips: "Learn about something in depth before you bother writing about it."

NATURE CANADA, Canadian Nature Federation, 1 Nicholas St., Suite 520, Ottawa, Ontario KIN 7B7 Canada. Fax: (613)562-3371. Editor: Barbara Stevenson. Quarterly membership magazine covering conservation, natural history and environmental/naturalist community. "*Nature Canada* is written for an audience interested in nature. Its content supports the Canadian Nature Federation's philosophy that all species have a right to exist regardless of their usefulness to humans. We promote the awareness, understanding and enjoyment of nature." Estab. 1971. Circ. 20,000. Pays on publication. Publishes ms an average of 3 months after acceptance. Byline given. Offers $100 kill fee. Buys one-time rights. Editorial lead time 3 months. Submit seasonal material 6 months in advance. Reports in 3 months on mss. Sample copy for $5. Writer's guidelines free on request.

Nonfiction: Canadian environmental issues and natural history. Buys 20 mss/year. Query with published clips. Length: 2,000-4,000 words. Pays 25¢/word (Canadian).

Photos: State availability of photos with submission. Offers $40-100/photo (Canadian). Identification of subjects required. Buys one-time rights.

Columns/Departments: The Green Gardener (naturalizing your backyard), 1,200 words; Small Wonder (on less well-known species such as invertebrates, nonvascular plants, etc.), 800-1,500 words; Connections

(Canadians making a difference for the environment), 1,000-1,500 words. Buys 16 mss/year. Query with published clips. Pays 25¢/(Canadian)/word.

Tips: "Our readers are knowledgeable about nature and the environment so contributors should have a good understanding of the subject. We also deal exclusively with Canadian issues and species."

PACIFIC DISCOVERY, California Academy of Sciences, Golden Gate Park, San Francisco CA 94118-4599. (415)750-7116. Fax: (415)750-7106. Editor: Keith Howell. 100% freelance written. Prefers to work with published/established writers. "Quarterly journal of nature and culture in California, the West, the Pacific and Pacific Rim countries read by scientists, naturalists, teachers, students, and others having a keen interest in knowing the natural world more thoroughly." Estab. 1948. Circ. 30,000. Buys first North American serial rights. Pays on publication. Query for electronic submissions. Reports within 2 months. Sample copy for 9×12 SAE with 5 first-class stamps. Writer's guidelines for #10 SASE.

Nonfiction: "Subjects of articles include behavior and natural history of animals and plants, ecology, evolution, anthropology, indigenous cultures, geology, paleontology, biogeography, taxonomy and related topics in the natural sciences. Occasional articles are published on the history of natural science, exploration, astronomy and archaeology. Emphasis is on current research findings. Authors need not be scientists; however, all articles should be based, at least in part, on firsthand fieldwork. Accuracy is crucial." Query with 100-word summary of projected article for review before preparing finished ms. Length: 800-4,000 words. Pays 25¢/word.

Photos: Send photos with submission "even if an author judges that his own photos should not be reproduced. Referrals to professional photographers with coverage of the subject will be greatly appreciated." Reviews 35mm, 4×5 or other transparencies or 8×10 b&w glossy prints. Offers $75-175 and $200 for the cover. Buys one-time rights.

SIERRA, 730 Polk St., San Francisco CA 94109-7813. (415)923-5656. Fax: (415)776-4868. Editor-in-Chief: Joan Hamilton. Senior Editors: Reed McManus, Paul Rauber. Managing Editor: Marc Lecard. Works with a small number of new/unpublished writers each year. Bimonthly magazine emphasizing conservation and environmental politics for people who are well educated, activist, outdoor-oriented and politically well informed with a dedication to conservation. Estab. 1893. Circ. 500,000. **Pays on acceptance.** Publishes ms an average of 4 months after acceptance. Byline given. Buys first North American serial rights. Query for electronic submissions. Accepts previously published submissions. Send typed ms with rights for sale noted and information about when and where the article previously appeared. Reports in 2 months.

● A new department, "Food For Thought," has been launched and is open to freelancers. "Good Going" and "Whereabouts" departments have been discontinued.

Nonfiction: Exposé (well-documented on environmental issues of national importance such as energy, wilderness, forests, etc.); general interest (well-researched nontechnical pieces on areas of particular environmental concern); photo feature (photo essays on threatened or scenic areas); journalistic treatments of semi-technical topics (energy sources, wildlife management, land use, waste management, etc.). No "My trip to . . . " or "why we must save wildlife/nature" articles; no poetry or general superficial essays on environmentalism; no reporting on purely local environmental issues. Buys 5-6 mss/issue. Query with published clips. Length: 800-3,000 words. Pays $450-2,000. Pays limited expenses of writers on assignment.

Photos: Naomi Williams, art and production manager. Send photos. Pays $300 maximum for transparencies; more for cover photos. Buys one-time rights.

Tips: "Queries should include an outline of how the topic would be covered and a mention of the political appropriateness and timeliness of the article. Statements of the writer's qualifications should be included."

SUMMIT, 1221 May St., Hood River OR 97031. (503)387-2200. Editor: John Harlin. 100% freelance written. Bimonthly magazine covering highcountry life, sports, exploration and travel. "Sophisticated, inspired, introspective and passionate writing for an educated audience with high literary standards. The writing must relate to the mountain world, but this can be treated broadly." Estab. 1990. Pays 3 months prior to publication or on acceptance. Publishes ms an average of 3-9 months after acceptance. Byline given. Offers 25% kill fee. Buys first North American serial, first, second serial (reprint) or simultaneous rights. Submit seasonal material 3-12 months in advance. Accepts simultaneous submissions. Reports in 6 months. Sample copy for $6 and 9×12 SAE with 10 first-class stamps "or send $8 w/SAE and we'll stamp." Writer's guidelines for #10 SASE.

Nonfiction: Book excerpts, essays, exposé, general interest, historical/nostalgic, humor, inspirational, interview/profile, opinion, personal experience, photo feature, travel. "No what-I-did stories that don't have strong literary content." Buys 30 mss/year. Query with or without published clips or send complete ms. Length: 100-4,000 words. Pays $50-800.

Photos: Send photos with query or ms. Send photos with submission. Reviews contact sheets, transparencies and prints. Offers $50-175/photo, $300 for cover. Identification of subjects required. Buys one-time rights.

Columns/Departments: Gazette and Scree (news and essays on mountain world), 50-1,500 words. Buys 25 mss/year. Query with published clips or send complete ms. Pays $50-300. The Summit Guide (mountain travel guide to destinations and techniques). Query stating fields of expertise. 50-1,500 words. Pays $50-700.

Poetry: Pays $50-200. Buys only occasionally. Must be mountain-related.

Fillers: Facts and short humor. Pays $50 minimum.

Tips: "If we don't know the writer, submitting complete manuscripts or partial manuscripts helps. Published clips help, but we distrust them because they've already been edited. Know the magazine, *know your subject* and *know your writing*. Scree news pieces and essays can be about any place and anything in the mountain world but must be entertaining or provocative. Previously published material from non-competing magazines is welcome. Send published piece with date and source."

WILDLIFE CONSERVATION MAGAZINE, Wildlife Conservation Society, 185th St. and Southern Blvd., Bronx NY 10460-1068. (212)220-5121. Editor: Joan Downs. 90% freelance written. Bimonthly magazine covering wildlife. Estab. 1895. Circ. 206,000. **Pays on acceptance.** Publishes ms an average of 1 year or more after acceptance. Byline given. Buys first North American serial rights. Submit seasonal material 1 year in advance. Accepts simultaneous submissions. Reports in 2 months on queries; 3 months on mss. Sample copy for $3.95 and 9×12 SAE with 7 first-class stamps. Writer's guidelines for SASE.

Nonfiction: Nancy Simmons, senior editor. Essays, personal experience, wildlife articles. No pet or any domestic animal stories. Buys 12 mss/year. Query. Length 1,500-2,500 words. Pays $500-2,000 for assigned articles; $500-1,000 for unsolicited articles.

Photos: Send photos with submission. Reviews transparencies. Buys one-time rights.

Personal Computers

Personal computer magazines continue to evolve. The most successful have a strong focus on a particular family of computers or widely-used applications and carefully target a specific type of computer use. Be sure you see the most recent issue of a magazine before submitting material.

BYTE MAGAZINE, 1 Phoenix Mill Lane, Peterborough NH 03458-0809. (603)924-9281. Fax: (603)924-2550. Editor: Rafe Needleman. Monthly magazine covering personal computers for professional users of computers. 50% freelance written. Estab. 1975. Circ. 515,000. **Pays on acceptance.** Byline given. Buys all rights. Reports on rejections in 6 weeks; 3 months if accepted. Electronic submissions accepted, IBM or Macintosh compatible. Sample copy for $3.50. Writer's guidelines for #10 SASE.

Nonfiction: News, reviews, in-depth discussions of topics related to microcomputers or technology. Buys 160 mss/year. Query. Length: 1,500-5,000 words. Pay is $350-1,000 for assigned articles; $500-750 for unassigned.

Tips: "Always interested in hearing from freelancers who are technically astute users of personal computers. Especially interested in stories on new computing technologies, from anywhere in the world. Read several issues of *Byte* to see what we cover, and how we cover it. Read technical journals to stay on the cutting edge of new technology and trends. Send us a proposal with a short outline of an article explaining some new technology, software trend, and the relevance to advanced business users of personal computers. Our readers want accurate, useful, technical information; not fluff and not meaningless data presented without insight or analysis."

COMPUSERVE MAGAZINE, 5000 Arlington Centre Blvd., Columbus OH 43220. (614)457-8600. Fax: (614)538-1004. Editor-in-Chief: Kassie Rose. 50% freelance written. Monthly membership magazine covering how to get the most from the CompuServe Information Service. "The editorial content shows members how to use the CompuServe Information Service. Departments address how the online connection can benefit them in using hardware and software, managing business (whether corporate or home-based), and pursuing hobbies, travel or other interests. The audience is 90% male (74% of whom are married) with an average annual income of $86,200. Ninety percent are professionals, managers, executives or proprietors." Estab. 1981. Circ. 1.5 million. Pays on publication. Publishes ms an average of 4 months after acceptance. Byline given. Offers 50% kill fee. Buys first North American serial rights. Editorial lead time 4 months. Query for electronic submissions. Reports in 1 month on queries. Sample copy free on request.

• *CompuServe* is using approximately 25% less freelance writing than last year.

Nonfiction: Technical, travel. "Each article relates to how members can use CIS to accomplish something, whether planning a trip or getting advice on buying hardware." Buys 120 mss/year. Query with published clips. Length: 1,000-4,000 words. Pay varies.

Photos: Send photos with submission. Reviews transparencies and prints up to 5×7. Model releases, identification of subjects required. Buys all rights.

Columns/Departments: Cathryn Conroy. Book Reviews (computer industry books), 300 words. Buys 100 mss/year. Query with published clips. Pays $75.

Tips: "Freelancers should familiarize themselves with the magazine's focus and style and, if possible, with the information service itself. They should then send a cover letter, résumé and appropriate clips to the editor, outlining areas of technical or other expertise. The magazine's departments (Computing Services, Personal

Enterprise and Random Access) are the most open to new freelancers. In all cases, the stories are heavily driven by member examples, with supporting advice from 'experts' who belong to the information service."

COMPUTOREDGE, San Diego's Computer Magazine, The Byte Buyer, Inc., P.O. Box 83086, San Diego CA 92138. (619)573-0315. Fax: (619)573-0205. E-mail: layneedge@aol.com. Executive Editor: Leah Steward. Editor: Ken Layne. 90% freelance written. Weekly magazine on computers. "We cater to the novice/beginner/first-time computer buyer. Humor is welcome." Estab. 1983. Circ. 90,000. Pays on publication. Net 30 day payment after publication. Byline given. Offers $15 kill fee. Buys first North American serial rights. Submit seasonal material 2 months in advance. Query for electronic submissions. Reports in 2 months. Writer's guidelines and an editorial calendar for #10 SASE "or call (619)573-1675 with your modem and download writer's guidelines. Read sample issue on-line." Sample issue for SAE with 7 first-class stamps.
 • *ComputorEdge* is no longer interested in seeing photos with submissions.
Nonfiction: General interest (computer), how-to, humor, personal experience. Buys 80 mss/year. Send complete ms. Length: 900-1,200 words. Pays 8-10¢/word for assigned articles. Pays 5-10¢/word for unsolicited articles.
Columns/Departments: Beyond Personal Computing (a reader's personal experience). Buys 80 mss/year. Send complete ms. Length: 500-1,000 words. Pays $50.
Fiction: Confession, fantasy, slice-of-life vignettes. No poetry. Buys 20 mss/year. Send complete ms. Length: 900-1,200 words. Pays 8-10¢/word.
Tips: "Be relentless. Convey technical information in an understandable, interesting way. We like light material, but not fluff. Write as if you're speaking with a friend. Avoid the typical 'Love at First Byte' article. Avoid the 'How My Grandmother Loves Her New Computer' article. We do not accept poetry. Avoid sexual innuendoes/metaphors. Reading a sample issue is advised."

‡DIEHARD, The Flyer for Commodore 8bitters, LynnCarthy Industries, Inc., 816 W. Bannock St., Suite 502, Boise ID 83702-5850. (208)383-0300. Editor: Brian L. Crosthwaite. Contact: Mia C. Crosthwaite, managing editor. 80% freelance written. Magazine published 10 times/year covering Commodore computer software, hardware and information. "Writing must be Commodore-related and must have a positive outlook." Estab. 1992. Circ. 12,000. **Pays on acceptance.** Byline given. Buys all rights. Editorial lead time 3 months. Submit seasonal material 4 months in advance. Query for electronic submissions. Sample copy for $2.95. Writer's guidelines free on request.
Nonfiction: General interest, how-to, humor, new product, opinion, technical. Buys 100 mss/year. Send complete ms. Pays $20. Pays writer with contributor copies at writer's request.
Photos: Send photos with submission. Reviews negatives, prints. Offers $1-10/photo. Buys all rights.
Columns/Departments: Review!; Archaic Computer; PRG. Buys 100 mss/year. Send complete ms. Pays $20-250.
Fiction: Humorous. Buys 10 mss/year. Pays $20-250.
Fillers: Anecdotes, facts, gags to be illustrated by cartoonist, newsbreaks, short humor. Buys 10/year. Pays $20-250.

ELECTRONIC ENTERTAINMENT, the #1 Interactive Entertainment Magazine, IDG Communications, 951 Mariners Island Blvd., #700, San Mateo CA 94404. (415)349-4300. Fax: (415)349-7482. E-mail: cgrech@iftw.com. Senior Editor: Christine Grech. 40% freelance written. Monthly magazine covering PC and Mac games, multimedia entertainment. CD-based game systems, virtual reality, interactive TV, on the entertainment and edutainment. Estab. 1993. Circ. 150,000. **Pays on acceptance.** Publishes ms an average of 3 months after acceptance. Byline given. Buys all rights. Editorial lead time 3-4 months. Submit seasonal material 6 months in advance. Query for electronic submissions.
 • No longer publishing fiction.
Nonfiction: Exposé, general interest, historical/nostalgic, how-to, humor, interview/profile, new product, opinion, personal experience, photo feature, technical. Query with published clips. Length: 100-4,000 words. Pays $50-1,000.
Photos: Send photos with submission. Reviews negatives, transparencies or computer files. Offers no additional payment for photos accepted with ms. Captions required. Buys all rights.
Columns/Departments: State of the Game (game reviews), 400-600 words. Buys 12 mss/year. Query with published clips. Pays $50-150.
Fillers: Contact: Ann Marcus. Anecdotes, facts, short humor. Length: 25-100 words. Pays $25.
Tips: "Read the magazine, know something about the field, have proven writing skills, and propose ideas with fresh angles."

‡HOME OFFICE COMPUTING, Scholastic Inc., 411 Layfayette, New York NY 10003. Fax: (212)505-4260. E-mail: 76703.2025@compuserve.com. Managing Editor: Michael Espindle. Editor: Gail Gabriel. 75% freelance written. Monthly magazine on home/small business and computing. Estab. 1983. Circ. 440,000. **Pays on acceptance.** Publishes ms an average of 3 months after acceptance. Byline given. Offers 25% kill fee. Buys all rights or makes work-for-hire assignments. Submit seasonal/holiday material 6 months in advance. Accepts simultaneous submissions. Query for electronic submissions. Sample copy and writer's guidelines for 9×12 SAE.

Nonfiction: How-to, interview/profile, new product, technical, reviews. "No fiction, humor, opinion." Buys 30 mss/year. Query with published clips. Length: 200-4,000 words. Pays $100-2,000. Sometimes pays the expenses of writers on assignment.

Photos: Send photos with submission.

Columns/Departments: Sales & Marketing, Desktop Publishing, Business Opportunities, Resources, Profiles, Hardware/Software Reviews. Length: 500-1,000 words. Pays $100-2,000.

Tips: "Submission must be on disk or telecommunicated."

LINK-UP, The Newsmagazine for Users of Online Services and CD-ROM, Information Today, Inc., 2222 River Dr., King George VA 22485. E-mail: 72105.1753@compuserve.com. Editor: Loraine Page. 70% freelance written. Bimonthly tabloid covering online communications and electronic information. "Our readers have modems or CD-ROM drives. We need articles on what they can do with them. Our primary audience is business users. What databases can they log onto to gain a business edge? What new CD-ROM titles are worthy of investing in? We also cover personal and educational use." Estab. 1980. Circ. 10,000. Pays on publication. Publishes ms an average of 2 months after acceptance. Byline given. Offers 50% kill fee. Buys first rights. Editorial lead time 2 months. Query first. Reports in 3 months. Sample copy for $2. "Study a few issues to determine types of articles used."

• *Link-up* has a new Education Link section. It is looking for stories dealing with the educational aspects of online services, the Internet and CD-ROM.

Nonfiction: Features, how-to, humor, personal experience. Buys 40 mss/year. Query with published clips. Length: 500-1,500 words. Pays $90-220. Sometimes pays half the phone expenses of writers on assignment, but only by special arrangment.

Tips: "Be on target. Please, no 'How I bought my first computer' stories! Our readers are way beyond that."

MACPOWER MAGAZINE, The Magazine for the Macintosh PowerBook and Newton, Hollow Earth Publishing, P.O. Box 1355, Boston MA 02205-1355. Editor: Heilan Yvette Grimes. 95% freelance written. Monthly magazine covering PowerBooks and Newton. "We offer helpful information about the PowerBook and Newton." Estab. 1994. Circ. 35,000. **Pays on acceptance.** Byline given. Buys all rights and makes work-for-hire assignments. Editorial lead time 2 months. Submit seasonal material 5 months in advance. Query for electronic submissions. Reports in 2 weeks on queries; 1 months on mss. Sample copy for 9×12 SAE with 3 first-class stamps. Writer's guidelines for #10 SASE.

Nonfiction: Book excerpts, general interest, historical/nostalgic, how-to, humor, interview/profile, new product, personal experience, technical. Query. Length: 300 or more words. Pays per page, negotiated. Sometimes pays expenses of writers on assignment.

Photos: Send photos with submission. Reviews transparencies. (Prefer electronic PICT of TIFF files.) Negotiates payment individually. Captions, model releases and identification of subjects required. Buys all rights.

Columns/Departments: "We are interested in Help columns on individual topics. Check the magazine for an idea of what we publish." Buys 60 mss/year. Query with published clips.

Fillers: Anecdotes, facts, gags to be illustrated by cartoonist, newsbreaks, short humor. Length: 20-50 words.

Tips: "Contact us in writing first. Know your subject and have something interesting to say. Reviews and new ideas are most open to freelancers."

‡MACWEEK, Ziff-Davis, 301 Howard St., 15th Floor, San Francisco CA 94105. (415)243-3500. Editor-in-Chief: Mark Hall. Managing Editor: Brenda Benner. 35% freelance written. Weekly tabloid covering Macintosh market and products. "Reaches sophisticated buyers of Macintosh-related products for large organizations." Estab. 1986. Circ. 100,000. **Pays on acceptance.** Publishes ms an average of 1 month after acceptance. Byline given. Offers 25% kill fee. Buys all worldwide rights. Editorial lead time news: 10 days; reviews: 2 months; features: 1 month. Submit seasonal material 2 months in advance. Query for electronic submissions. Reports in 1 month on mss. Writer's guidelines free on request.

Columns/Departments: Andrew Gore (news); Bob O'Donnell (reviews); Anita Malnig (features). Business Watch (business stories), 300 words; Reviews (new product testing), 500-1,200 words; Solutions (case histories), 1,000 words. Buys 30 mss/year. Query with published clips. Pays 65-90¢/word.

Tips: "Knowledge of the Macintosh market is essential. Know which section you would like to write for and submit to the appropriate editor."

MICROCOMPUTER JOURNAL, The Practical Magazine for Personal Computers & Microcontrollers, CQ Communications, 76 N. Broadway, Hicksville NY 11801. (516)681-2922. Fax: (516)681-2926. 90% freelance written. Editor: Art Salsberg. Managing Editor: Alex Burawa. Bimonthly magazine covering single-board computers, microcontrolled electronic devices, software, personal computers, electronic circuitry, construction projects and technology for readers with a technical affinity. Estab. 1984. Circ. 50,000. Pays on publication. Publishes ms an average of 3 months after acceptance. Byline given. Offers 25% kill fee. Buys first North American serial rights. Reports in 2 weeks on queries; 3 weeks on mss. *Writer's Market* recom-

mends allowing 2 months for reply. Sample copy for $1 and 9×12 SAE. Writer's guidelines for #10 SASE.
Nonfiction: How-to (construction projects, applications, computer enhancements, upgrading and trouble-shooting); new product (reviews); opinion (experiences with computer products); technical (features and tutorials: circuits, applications). "Articles must be technically accurate. Writing should be 'loose,' not textbookish." No long computer programs. Buys 90 mss/year. Query. Length: 500-4,000 words. Pays $90-150/published page. Sometimes pays expenses of writers on assignment.
Photos: Send photos with query or ms. Reviews transparencies and 5×7 b&w prints. Captions, model releases, and identification of subjects required. Buys first North American rights.
Tips: "The writer must have technical or applications acumen and well-researched material. Articles should reflect the latest products and technology. Sharp, interesting photos are helpful, as are rough, clean illustrations for re-drawing. Cover useful improvements to existing personal computers. Areas most open to freelancers include feature articles, technical tutorials, and projects to build. Some writers exhibit problems with longer pieces due to limited technical knowledge and/or poor organization. We can accept more short pieces. For electronic submissions, use Electronic mailbox, 'Computercraft' on MCI Mail."

ONLINE ACCESS, Chicago Fine Print, Inc., 900 N. Franklin, Suite 310, Chicago IL 60610. Fax: (312)573-0520. E-mail: 70324.343@compuserve.com. Editor-in-Chief: Kathryn McCabe. Managing Editor: Carol Freer. 75% freelance written. *Online Access* is a monthly international publication covering the entire online world from online services to bulletin board services to the Internet. The magazine is in its tenth year of publication." Pays on publication. Publishes ms an average of 2 months after acceptance. Byline given. Offers $50 kill fee. Buys first rights or second serial (reprint) rights. Submit seasonal/holiday material 6 months in advance. "Query for electronic submissions." Reports in 1 month on queries; 3 weeks on mss. *Writer's Market* recommends allowing 2 months for reply. Sample copy for $9.95.
Nonfiction: General interest (online industry); how-to (use a particular online service); humor; interview/profile (of major industry figures); new product (but *not* hardware!); opinion (about current online industry issues); personal experience (if relevant); photo feature. Query with published clips. Length: 1,500-2,500 words. Pays $100-500. Pays in contributor copies by mutual agreement before assignment is given. Sometimes pays expenses of writers on assignment.
Photos: Send photos with submission. Reviews 5×7 transparencies and prints. Offers no additional payment for photos accepted with ms. Captions, model releases and identification of subjects required. Buys one-time rights.
Tips: "We are seeking more articles about bulletin board systems."

PC GRAPHICS & VIDEO, Advanstar Communications, 201 E. Sandpointe Ave., Suite 600, Santa Ana CA 92707. Fax: (714)513-8612. E-mail: jveditor@aol.com. Editor: Gene Smarte. 50% freelance written. Monthly magazine covering Intel platform personal computer graphics and video. "*PC Graphics & Video* addresses hardware, software, techniques, resources, isssues in personal computer industry and use of IBM compatibles for graphics, video, multimedia, desktop publishing." Estab. 1992 (formerly *High Color*). Circ. 75,000. **Pays on acceptance**. Publishes ms an average of 2-3 months after acceptance. Negotiable contract and kill fee. Buys first and collateral rights. Editorial lead time 6-12 weeks depending on content. Query for electronic submissions. Sample copy and writer's guidelines free on request.
Nonfiction: How-to, technology update, new product, technical. Query with published clips. Length: 750-3,000 words. Pays approximately $250 per published page including photos.
Photos: Send photos with submission. Reviews digital prints. Captions, model releases and identification of subjects required. Buys one-time and collateral rights.

PC WORLD, PCW Communications, Inc., 501 2nd St., San Francisco CA 94107. (415)243-0500. Editor-in-Chief: Phil Lemmons. 60% freelance written. Monthly magazine covering IBM Personal Computers and compatibles. Circ. 915,000. **Pays on acceptance.** Byline given. Offers negotiable kill fee. Buys all rights. Query for electronic submissions. Free writer's guidelines.
Nonfiction: *PC World* is composed of 4 departments: News, How-tos, Review and Features. Reviews critically and objectively analyzes new hardware and software. How-tos gives readers instructions for improving their PC productivity. Features help readers understand the impact of PC technology on their business lives. News keeps readers apprised of new products, trends and industry events." Articles must focus on the IBM PC or compatibles. Query with or without published clips or send complete ms. Buys 50 mss/year. Length: 1,500-2,500 words. Pays $50-2,000. Does not accept unsolicited mss.
Tips: "Familiarity with the IBM PC or technical knowledge about its operations—coupled with a solid understanding of business needs—often determines whether we accept a query. Send all queries to the attention of Proposals—Editorial Department."

PC/COMPUTING, Ziff-Davis Publishing Co., 950 Tower Lane, 19th Floor, Foster City CA 94404-2121. (415)578-7000. Fax: (415)578-7029. Editor-in-Chief: Jon Zilber. Monthly magazine for business users of desktop computers. Estab. 1988. Circ. 850,000. **Pays on acceptance.** Byline given. Offers negotiable kill fee. Makes work-for-hire assignments. Query for electronic submissions. Reports in 1 month. Sample copy for $2.95. Writer's guidelines for #10 SASE.

• Ziff-Davis Publishing Company has created an electronic information service called the Interchange Online Network that draws on the contents of its various computer magazines, includes *PC Magazine*, *PC Computing*, *PC Week*, *Mac User*, *Mac Week*, *Computer Shopper* and *Computer Gaming World*.

Nonfiction: Book excerpts, how-to, new product and technical. Query with published clips. Payment negotiable. Sometimes pays expenses of writers on assignment.

Tips: "We're looking for helpful, specific information that appeals to advanced users of PCs. No novice material. Writers must be knowledgeable about personal computers."

WIRED MAGAZINE, 520 Third St., 4th Floor, San Francisco CA 94107-1815. (415)222-6200. Editor/Publisher: Louis Rossetto. Contact: John Battelle, Managing Editor. 95% freelance written. Monthly magazine covering technology and digital culture. "We cover the digital revolution and related advances in computers, communications and lifestyles." Estab. 1993. Circ. 180,000. Pays on publication. Publishes ms an average of 2 months after acceptance. Byline given. Offers 25% kill fee. Buys first North American serial rights, global rights with 25% payment. Editorial lead time 3 months. Query for electronic submissions. Reports in 3 weeks on queries. Sample copy for $4.95. Writer's guidelines for #10 SASE or e-mail to guidelines@wired.com.

Nonfiction: Essays, interview/profile, opinion. "No poetry or trade articles." Buys 85 features, 130 short pieces, 200 reviews, 36 essays and 50 other mss/year. Query. Pays expenses of writers on assignment.

WORDPERFECT DOS MAGAZINE, WordPerfect Publishing Corp., 270 W. Center St., Orem UT 84057-4683. (801)226-5555. Fax: (801)226-8804. Editorial Director: Clair F. Rees. Editor-in-Chief: Lisa Bearnson. 70% freelance written. Monthly magazine of "how-to" articles for users of various WordPerfect computer software. Estab. 1988. Circ. 275,000. Publishes ms an average of 6-8 months after acceptance. Byline given. Negotiable kill fee. Buys first and secondary world rights. Submit seasonal/holiday material 8 months in advance. Query for electronic submissions only. Reports in 2 months. Sample copy for 9×12 SAE with 7 first-class stamps. Free writer's guidelines.

• Articles should cover both WordPerfect 5.1 for DOS and WordPerfect 6.0 for DOS. When discussing a feature, keystrokes should be provided for both versions.

Nonfiction: How-to, step-by-step applications (with keystrokes), humor, interview/company profile, new product, technical. "Easy-to-understand articles written with *minimum* jargon. Articles should provide readers good, useful information about word processing and other computer functions." Buys 120-160 mss/year. Query with or without published clips. Length: 800-1,800 words.

Photos: Send photos with submission. Reviews transparencies (35mm or larger). Offers no additional payment for photos accepted with ms. Captions and identification of subjects required. Buys one-time rights.

Columns/Departments: Advanced Macro (WordPerfect macros), 1,000-1,400 words; Basics (tips for beginners), 1,000-1,400 words; Home Office, 1,000-1,400 words; Desktop Publishing, 1,000-1,400 words; Final Keystrokes (humor), 800 words. Buys 90-120 mss/year. Query with published clips. Pays $400-700, on acceptance.

Tips: "Studying publication provides best information. We're looking for writers who can both inform *and* entertain our specialized group of readers."

WORDPERFECT FOR WINDOWS MAGAZINE, Novell, 270 W. Center St., Orem UT 84057-4683. (801)226-5555. Fax: (801)226-8804. Editorial Director: Jeff Hadfield. Editor-in-Chief: Scott Larson. 60% freelance written. Monthly magazine of "how-to" articles for users of WordPerfect for Windows and compatible software. Estab. 1991. Circ. 200,000. Publishes ms an average of 6-8 months after acceptance. Byline given. Pays negotiable kill fee. Buys first and secondary world rights. Submit seasonal material 8 months in advance. Query. Reports in 2 months. Sample copy for 9×12 SAE with 7 first-class stamps. Free writers guidelines.

Nonfiction: How-to, step-by-step applications (with keystrokes and screenshots in PCX format), interview/company profile, new product, technical. "Easy-to-understand articles written with *minimum* jargon. Articles should provide readers good, useful information about word processing and other computer functions." Buys 120-160 mss/year. Query with or without published clips. Length: 800-1,800 words.

Columns/Departments: Desktop Publishing, Printing, Basics (tips for beginners), Advanced Macros, Help, all 1,000-1,400 words. Buys 90-120 mss/year. Query with published clips. Pays $400-700 on acceptance.

Tips: "Studying publication provides best information. We're looking for writers who can both inform *and* entertain our specialized group of readers."

Photography

Readers of these magazines use their cameras as a hobby and for weekend assignments. To write for these publications, you should have expertise in photography. Magazines geared to the professional photographer can be found in the Photography Trade section.

BLACKFLASH, P.G. Press, 12 23rd St. E., 2nd Floor, Saskatoon, Saskatchewan S7K 0H5 Canada. (306)244-8018. Fax: (306)665-6568. Editor: Wallace Polsom. Managing Editor: Monte Greenshields. Publications Coordinator: R.D. Funk. Quarterly magazine covering issues in contemporary photography. Estab. 1982. Circ. 1,700. **Pays on acceptance.** Byline given. Offers 50% kill fee. Editorial lead time 6 months. Submit seasonal material 6 months in advance. Query for electronic submissions. Prefers WordPerfect 5.1. Reports in 1 month on queries; 2 months on mss. Sample copy for $3.75. Writer's guidelines for #10 SASE.
Nonfiction: Richelle D. Funk. Essays, opinion. Send complete ms. Length: 2,500-3,000 words. Pays $350 minimum for assigned articles; $150 for unsolicited articles.
Photos: Send photos with submission. Offers no additional payment for photos accepted with ms.
Columns/Departments: Richelle D. Funk. Articles on photographic artists, book reviews, exhibition reviews, all 2,500-3,000 words. Articles are assigned. Query with published clips or send complete ms.
Tips: "All articles written to date have been assigned. We are interested in articles about contemporary photography to use if a deadline has been blown. Writers should submit an article (sample) and a cv for review. We are in the process of building a writers' file for assignments."

‡CAMERA & DARKROOM MAGAZINE, 9171 Wilshire Blvd., Suite 300, Beverly Hills CA 90210. (213)858-7100. Fax: (213)274-7985. Editor-in-Chief: Ana Jones. Editorial Assistant: Carrie Ryan. A photography magazine with darkroom coverage, published 12 times/year for both professional and amateur photographers. Estab. 1979. Circ. 80,000. Pays on publication. Byline given. Buys one-time rights. Query for electronic submissions. Reports in 6 weeks. Sample copy and writer's guidelines for $5 and 9×12 SASE.
Nonfiction: Historical/nostalgic (some photo-history pieces); how-to; interview/profile; and technical product reviews (articles on darkroom techniques, tools, tricks, shooting techniques, strobes, lighting, or in-camera image manipulation). Query or send complete ms. Pays 20¢/word; $25-100/page photos.
Photos: Send photos with query or ms. Reviews transparencies and prints. "Supporting photographs are considered part of the manuscript package."
Columns/Departments: Darkroom 101, Tools & Tricks, Special Effects. Query. Length: 800-3,000 words. "Published darkroom-related 'tips' receive free one-year subscriptions." Length: 100-150 words.

NATURE PHOTOGRAPHER, Nature Photographer Publishing Co., Inc., P.O. Box 2037, West Palm Beach FL 33402-2037. (407)586-3491. Fax: (407)586-9521. Editor: Evamarie Mathaey. 65% freelance written. Bimonthly magazine "emphasizing nature photography that uses low-impact and local less known locations, techniques and ethics. Articles include how-to, travel to world-wide wilderness locations and how nature photography can be used to benefit the environment and environmental education of the public." Estab. 1990, Circ. 20,000. Pays on publication. Buys one-time rights. Submit seasonal material 8 months in advance. Accepts simultaneous and previously published submissions. Send photocopy of article and information about when and where the article previously appeared. For reprints, pays 75% of the amount paid for an original article. Reports in 2 months. Sample copy for 9×12 SAE with 6 first-class stamps. Writer's guidelines for #10 SASE.
Nonfiction: How-to (underwater, exposure, creative techniques, techniques to make photography easier, low-impact techniques, macro photography, large-format, wildlife), photo feature, technical, travel. No articles about photographing in zoos or on game farms. Buys 12-18 mss/year. Query with published clips or writing samples. Length: 750-2,500 words. Pays $75-150.
Photos: Send photos upon request. Do not send with submission. Reviews 35mm, 2¼ and 4×5 transparencies. Offers no additional payment for photos accepted with ms. Identification of subjects required. Buys one-time rights.
Tips: "Query with original, well-thought out ideas and good writing samples. Make sure you send SASE. Areas most open to freelancers are travel, how-to and conservation. Must have good, solid research and knowledge of subject. Be sure to obtain guidelines by sending SASE with request before submitting query. If you have not requested guidelines within the last year, request an updated version of guidelines."

‡POPULAR PHOTOGRAPHY, 1633 Broadway, New York NY 10019. Editor: Jason Schneider. All articles must include photographs. Looking for specialty, different unusual photos. Do not send originals—dupes or prints. Most articles are written by staff. "Good photos are more important than good articles."

SHUTTERBUG MAGAZINE, Patch Communications, 5211 S. Washington Ave., Titusville FL 32780. (407)268-5010. Editor: Bob Shell. Managing Editor: Bonnie Paulk. Contact: Bob Shell. 100% freelance written. Monthly magazine covering photography. "Provides how-to articles for advanced amateur to professional photographers." Estab. 1970. Circ. 100,000. Byline given. Buys first rights and second serial (reprint) rights. Editorial lead time 6 months. Submit seasonal material at least 6 months in advance. Accepts previously published submissions. Reports in 6-8 weeks on queries. Sample copy free on request. Writer's guidelines for #10 SASE.
Nonfiction: Historical/nostalgic (photography), how-to (photography), humor, interview/profile, new product, photo feature, technical. "All photo related." *No unsolicited articles.* Buys 60+ mss/year. Query. Pays $300 minimum for assigned articles; $200 minimum for unsolicited articles. Pays expenses of writers on assignment.

Photos: Send photos with submission. Reviews any transparencies, 8×10 prints. Offers no additional payment for photos accepted with ms. Captions and model releases required. Buys one-time rights.
Tips: "Submit only material similar in style to that in our magazine. All sections open to freelancers."

WILDLIFE PHOTOGRAPHY, P.O. Box 224, Greenville PA 16125. (412)588-3492. Editor: Randy Ferguson. 90% freelance written. Eager to work with new/unpublished writers. Bimonthly magazine "dedicated to the pursuit and capture of wildlife on film. Emphasis on how-to." Estab. 1985. Circ. 3,000. Pays on publication. Publishes ms an average of 1 year after acceptance. Byline given. Buys first, one-time or second serial (reprint) rights. Submit seasonal/holiday material 4 months in advance. Accepts simultaneous and previously published submissions. Send tearsheet or photocopy of article, and information about when and where the article previously appeared. Reports in 6 weeks on queries; 2 months on mss. Sample copy for $3. Free writer's guidelines.
Nonfiction: Book excerpts, how-to (work with animals to take a good photo), interview/profile (of professionals), new product (of particular interest to wildlife photography), personal experience (with cameras in the field), travel (where to find superb photo opportunities of plants and animals). No fiction or photography of pets, sports and scenery. Buys 30 mss/year. Query. Length: 500-3,000 words. Pays $30-100.
Photos: Send sharp photos with submission. Reviews contact sheets, negatives, transparencies, 5×7 prints as part of ms package. Photos accepted only with ms. Offers no additional payment for photos. Captions and identification of subjects required. Buys one-time rights.
Fillers: Anecdotes, facts. Buys 12/year. Length: 50-200 words. Pays $5-15.
Tips: "Give solid how-to info on how to photograph a specific species of wild animal. Send photos, not only of the subject, but of the photographer and his gear in action. The area of our publication most open to freelancers is feature articles."

Politics and World Affairs

These publications cover politics for the reader interested in current events. Other publications that will consider articles about politics and world affairs are listed under Business and Finance, Contemporary Culture, Regional and General Interest. For listings of publications geared toward the professional, see Government and Public Service in the Trade section.

AFRICA REPORT, 833 United Nations Plaza, New York NY 10017. (212)949-5666. Fax: (212)682-6036. Editor: Margaret A. Novicki. 60% freelance written. Prefers to work with published/established writers. A bimonthly magazine for U.S. citizens and residents with a special interest in African affairs for professional, business, academic or personal reasons. Not tourist-related. Circ. 10,500. Pays on publication. Publishes ms an average of 2 months after acceptance. Rights purchased vary with author and material; usually buys all rights, very occasionally first serial rights. Byline given unless otherwise requested. Sample copy for $6.75; free writer's guidelines.
Nonfiction: Interested in "African political, economic and cultural affairs, especially in relation to U.S. foreign policy and business objectives. Style should be journalistic but not academic or light. Articles should not be polemical or long on rhetoric but may be committed to a strong viewpoint. I do not want tourism articles." Would like to see in-depth topical analyses of lesser known African countries, based on residence or several months' stay in the country. Buys 5 unsolicited mss/year. Pays $150-250.
Photos: Photos purchased with or without accompanying mss with extra payment. Reviews b&w only. Pays $25. Submit 12×8 "half-plate."
Tips: "Read *Africa Report* and other international journals regularly. Become an expert on an African or Africa-related topic. Make sure your submissions fit the style, length and level of *Africa Report*."

CALIFORNIA JOURNAL, 2101 K St., Sacramento CA 95816. (916)444-2840. E-mail: editor@statenet.com. Editor: Richard Zeiger. Managing Editor: A.G. Block. 20% freelance written. Prefers to work with published/established writers. Monthly magazine that emphasizes analysis of California politics and government. Estab. 1970. Circ. 20,000. Pays on publication. Publishes ms an average of 2 months after acceptance. Byline given. Buys all rights. Query for electronic submissions. Writer's guidelines for #10 SASE.
Nonfiction: Profiles of state and local government and political analysis. No outright advocacy pieces. Buys 25 unsolicited mss/year. Query. Length: 900-3,000 words. Pays $150-1,000. Sometimes pays the expenses of writers on assignment.

CHURCH & STATE, Americans United for Separation of Church and State, 1816 Jefferson Place, NW, Washington DC 20036. (202)466-3234. Fax: (202)466-2587. Managing Editor: Joseph Conn. 10% freelance written. Prefers to work with published/established writers. Monthly magazine emphasizing religious liberty and church/state relations matters. Strongly advocates separation of church and state. Readership "includes the whole spectrum, but is predominantly Protestant and well-educated." Estab. 1947. Circ. 33,000.

Pays on acceptance. Publishes ms an average of 2 months after acceptance. Buys all rights. Accepts simultaneous and previously published submissions. Send tearsheet or photocopy or typed ms with rights for sale noted and information about when and where the article previously appeared. Reports in 2 months. Sample copy and writer's guidelines for 9×12 SAE with 3 first-class stamps.

Nonfiction: Exposé, general interest, historical, interview. Buys 11 mss/year. Query. Length: 3,000 words maximum. Pays negotiable fee.

Photos: Send photos with query. Pays negotiable fee for b&w prints. Captions preferred. Buys one-time rights.

Tips: "We're looking for feature articles on underreported local church-state controversies. We also consider 'viewpoint' essays that offer a unique or personal take on church-state issues."

COMMONWEAL, A Review of Public Affairs, Religion, Literature and the Arts, Commonweal Foundation, 15 Dutch St., New York NY 10038. (212)732-0800. Editor: Margaret O'Brien Steinfels. Contact: Patrick Jordan, managing editor. Biweekly magazine. Estab. 1924. Circ. 18,000. **Pays on acceptance.** Byline given. Buys all rights. Submit seasonal material 2 months in advance. Reports in 2 months. Free sample copy.

Nonfiction: Essays, general interest, interview/profile, personal experience, religious. Buys 20 mss/year. Query with published clips. Length: 1,200-3,000 words. Pays $75-100.

Poetry: Rosemary Deen, poetry editor. Free verse, traditional. Buys 25-30 poems/year. Pays 75¢/line.

EMPIRE STATE REPORT, The magazine of politics and public policy in New York State, 4 Central Ave., 3rd Floor, Albany NY 12210. (518)465-5502. Fax: (518)465-9822. Editor: Jeff Plungis. 50% freelance written. Monthly magazine providing "timely political and public policy features for local and statewide public officials in New York State. Anything that would be of interest to them is of interest to us." Estab. 1983. Circ. 10,000. Pays 2 months after publication. Byline given. Buys first North American serial rights. Query for electronic submissions. Reports in 1 month on queries; 2 months on mss. Sample copy for $3.95 with 9×12 SASE.

Nonfiction: Essays, exposé, interview/profile and opinion. "Writers should send for our editorial calendar." Buys 48 mss/year. Query with published clips. Length: 500-3,000 words. Pays $50-400 for assigned articles. Sometimes pays expenses of writers on assignment.

Photos: Send photos with submission. Reviews any size prints. Offers $50-100/photo. Identification of subjects required. Buys one-time rights.

Columns/Departments: New York Digest (short news stories about state politics), 300-900 words; Perspective (opinion pieces), 750-800 words. Buys 24 mss/year. Query. Length: 750-1,000 words. Pays $50-100.

Tips: "Send us a query. If we are not already working on the idea, and if the query is well written, we might work something out with the writer. Writers have the best chance selling something for New York Digest."

EUROPE, 2300 M St. NW, 7th Floor, Washington DC 20037. (202)862-9555. Fax: (202)429-1766. Editor: Robert Guttman. Managing Editor: Peter Gwin. 75% freelance written. Magazine published 10 times/year for anyone with a professional or personal interest in Europe and European/US relations. Estab. 1963. Circ. 75,000. Pays on publication. Publishes ms an average of 2 to 3 months after acceptance. Buys first serial and all rights. Submit seasonal material 3 months in advance. Reports in 6 months.

Nonfiction: Interested in current affairs (with emphasis on economics, business and politics), the Single Market and Europe's relations with the rest of the world. Publishes monthly cultural travel pieces, with European angle. "High quality writing a must. We publish articles that might be useful to people with a professional interest in Europe." Query or submit complete ms or article outline. Include résumé of author's background and qualifications. Length: 500-2,000 words. Pays $150-500.

● This magazine is accepting more freelance articles and has increased its pay rates for them. The editor is encouraging more queries.

Photos: Photos purchased with or without accompanying mss. Buys b&w and color. Pays $25-35 for b&w print, any size; $100 for inside use of transparencies; $450 for color used on cover; per job negotiable.

‡THE FREEMAN, 30 S. Broadway, Irvington-on-Hudson NY 10533. (914)591-7230. Fax: (914)591-8910. Managing Editor: Beth Hoffman. 85% freelance written. Eager to work with new/unpublished writers. Monthly for "the layman and fairly advanced students of liberty." Buys all rights, including reprint rights. Estab. 1946. Pays on publication. Byline given. Publishes ms an average of 5 months after acceptance. Accepts previously published submissions. Send tearsheet or photocopy of article and information about when and where the article previously appeared. For reprints, pays 50% of amount paid for an original article. Sample copy for 7½×10½ SASE with 4 first-class stamps.

Nonfiction: "We want nonfiction clearly analyzing and explaining various aspects of the free market, private enterprise, limited government philosophy. Though a necessary part of the literature of freedom is the exposure of collectivistic cliches and fallacies, our aim is to emphasize and explain the positive case for individual responsibility and choice in a free economy. Especially important, we believe, is the methodology of freedom—self-improvement, offered to others who are interested. We try to avoid name-calling and personality clashes and find satire of little use as an educational device. Ours is a scholarly analysis of the principles underlying a free market economy. No political strategy or tactics." Buys 100 mss/year. Length: 3,500 words maximum. Pays 10¢/word. Sometimes pays expenses of writers on assignment.

Tips: "It's most rewarding to find freelancers with new insights, fresh points of view. Facts, figures and quotations cited should be fully documented, to their original source, if possible."

THE NATION, 72 Fifth Ave., New York NY 10011-8046. Fax: (212)463-9712. Editor: Katrina Vanden Heuvel. Assistant to Editor: Dennis Selby. 75% freelance written. Estab. 1865. Works with a small number of new/unpublished writers each year. Weekly. Buys first serial rights. Query for electronic submissions. Free sample copy and writer's guidelines for 6×9 SASE.

Nonfiction: "We welcome all articles dealing with the social scene, from an independent perspective." Queries encouraged. Buys 100 mss/year. Length: 2,500 words maximum. Modest rates. Sometimes pays expenses of writers on assignment.

Tips: "We are firmly committed to reporting on the issues of labor, national politics, business, consumer affairs, environmental politics, civil liberties and foreign affairs."

‡THE NEIGHBORHOOD WORKS, Building Alternative Visions for the City, Center for Neighborhood Technology, 2125 W. North Ave., Chicago, IL 60647. (312)278-4800 ext. 113. Fax: (312)278-3840. E-mail: tnwedit@cnt.org. Editor: Patti Wolter. Managing Editor: Carl Vogel. 50% freelance written. Bimonthly magazine covering community organizing, urban environmentalism. "We write to, for and about community organizers in low and middle-income neighborhoods specifically areas of environmentalism, energy transportation, housing and economic development." Estab. 1978. Circ. 2,000. Pays on publication. Publishes ms an average of 4 months after acceptance. Byline given. Kill fee negotiable. Buys all rights. Editorial lead time 2 months. Submit seasonal material 4 months in advance. Accepts simultaneous and previously published submissions. Query for electronic submissions. Reports in 2 months. Sample copy for 8½×11 SAE with 4 first-class stamps. Writer's guidelines free on request.

Nonfiction: Exposé, general interest, how-to (related to organizing and technical assistance to urban communities), interview/profile, opinion. Buys 10-20 mss/year. Query with published clips. Length: 800-2,000 words. Pays $250-500 for assigned articles; $150-300 for unsolicited articles. "We don't pay students and policy people for writing articles, but will give them a subscription." Sometimes pays expenses of writers on assignment.

Photos: State availability of photos with submission. Reviews contact sheets, 5×7 prints. Negotiates payment individually. Identification of subjects required. Buys one-time rights.

Columns/Departments: Reproducible feature (how-to), 1,400 words. Buys 4 mss/year. Query with published clips. Pay varies.

NEW JERSEY REPORTER, A Journal of Public Issues, The Center for Analysis of Public Issues, 16 Vandeventer Ave., Princeton NJ 08542. (609)924-9750. Fax: (609)924-0363. E-mail: njreporter@aol.com. Managing Editor: Bob Narus. 90% freelance written. Prefers to work with published/established writers but will consider proposals from others. Bimonthly magazine covering New Jersey politics, public affairs and public issues. "*New Jersey Reporter* is a hard-hitting and highly respected magazine published for people who take an active interest in New Jersey politics and public affairs, and who want to know more about what's going on than what newspapers and television newscasts are able to tell them. We publish a great variety of stories ranging from analysis to exposé." Estab. 1970. Circ. 2,200. Pays on publication. Byline given. Buys all rights. Reports in 1 month. Sample copy available on request.

• This magazine continues to increase its use of freelance writing.

Nonfiction: Book excerpts, exposé, interview/profile, opinion. "We like articles from specialists (in planning, politics, economics, corruption, etc.)—particularly if written by professional journalists—but we reject stories that do not read well because of jargon or too little attention to the actual writing of the piece. Our magazine is interesting as well as informative." Buys 18-25 mss/year. Query with published clips. Length: 1,800-4,500 words. Pays $100-500.

Tips: "Queries should be specific about how the prospective story is an issue that affects or will affect the people of New Jersey and its government. The writer's résumé should be included. Stories—unless they are specifically meant to be opinion—should come to a conclusion but avoid a 'holier than thou' or preachy tone. Allegations should be scrupulously substantiated. Our magazine represents a good opportunity for freelancers to acquire great clips. Our publication specializes in longer, more detailed, analytical features. The most frequent mistake made by writers in completing an article for us is too much personal opinion versus reasoned advocacy. We are less interested in opinion than in analysis based on sound reasoning and fact. *New Jersey Reporter* is a well-respected publication, and many of our writers go on to nationally respected newspapers and magazines."

POLICY REVIEW, The Heritage Foundation, 214 Massachusetts Ave. NE, Washington DC 20002. (202)546-4400. Editor: Adam Meyerson. Managing Editor: D.W. Miller. Deputy Editor: Joe Loconte. Quarterly magazine for conservative ideas about politics and policy. "We have been described as 'the most thoughtful, the most influential and the most provocative publication of the intellectual right.' " Estab. 1977. Circ. 30,000. Pays on publication. Byline given.

Nonfiction: "We are especially interested in freelance articles on how public policies affect families and communities." Buys 4 mss/year. Send complete ms. Length: 2,000-6,000 words. Average payment of $500 per article.

THE PROGRESSIVE, 409 E. Main St., Madison WI 53703-2899. (608)257-4626. Fax: (608)257-3373. Editor: Matthew Rothschild. 75% freelance written. Monthly. Estab. 1909. Pays on publication. Publishes ms an average of 6 weeks after acceptance. Byline given. Buys all rights. Reports in 1 month. Sample copy for 9 × 12 SAE with 4 first-class stamps. Writer's guidelines for #10 SASE.

Nonfiction: Primarily interested in articles which interpret, from a progressive point of view, domestic and world affairs. Occasional lighter features. "*The Progressive* is a *political* publication. General-interest material is inappropriate." Query. Length: 3,000 words maximum. Pays $100-300.

Tips: "Display some familiarity with our magazine, its interests and concerns, its format and style. We want query letters that fully describe the proposed article without attempting to sell it—and that give an indication of the writer's competence to deal with the subject."

TOWARD FREEDOM, A progressive perspective on world events, Toward Freedom Inc., 209 College St., Burlington VT 05401. (802)658-2523. Fax: (802)658-3738. Editor: Greg Guma. 75% freelance written. Political magazine published 8 times/year covering politics/culture, focus on third world, Europe and global trends. "*Toward Freedom* is an internationalist journal with a progressive perspective on political, cultural, human rights and environmental issues around the world. Also covers the United Nations, the post-nationalist movements and US foreign policy." Estab. 1952. Byline given. Circ. 3,500. Pays on publication. Kill fee "rare–negotiable." Buys first North American serial and one-time rights. Editorial lead time 1 month. Query for electronic submissions. Reports in 1 month on queries and mss. *Writer's Market* recommends allowing 2 months for initial reply. Sample copy for $3. Writer's guidelines free on request.

Nonfiction: Features, essays, book reviews, interview/profile, opinion, personal experience, travel, foreign, political analysis. Special issues: media environment, women and others. No how-to, fiction. Buys 80-100 mss/year. Query. Length: 700-2,500 words. Pays 10¢/word for all used.

Photos: Send photos with submission, if available. Reviews any prints. Offers $35 maximum/photo. Identification of subjects required. Buys one-time rights.

Columns/Departments: *TF* Reports (from foreign correspondents), UN, Population, Art and Book Reviews, 800-1,200 words. Buys 20-30 mss/year. Query. Pays 10¢/word. Last Word (creative commentary), 900 words. Buys 8/year. Pays $100.

Tips: "Except for book or other reviews, writers should have first-hand knowledge of country, political situation, foreign policy, etc., on which they are writing. Occasional cultural 'travelogues' accepted, especially those that would enlighten our readers about a different way of life. Writing must be professional."

‡WORLD VISION, World Vision, Inc., 919 W. Huntington Blvd., Monrovia CA 91016. Editor: Terry Madison. Contact: Larry Wilson. Up to 50% freelance written. "*World Vision*, a Christian humanitarian relief and development agency working in 100 countries." Bimonthly magazine covering world humanitarian issues for opinion leaders. Estab. 1955. Circ. 80,000. **Pays on acceptance**. Byline given. Kill fee varies. Buys multiple-use international rights and makes work-for-hire assignments. Editorial lead time 6 months. Submit seasonal material 6 months in advance. Reports in 3 weeks on queries; 2 weeks on mss. Sample copy and writer's guidelines free on request.

Nonfiction: Essays, general interest, inspirational, interview/profile, photo feature, religious, global issues. Buys 8 mss/year. Query with published clips. Send complete ms. Length: 700-3,000. Pays $1,500 maximum for assigned articles; $850 maximum for unsolicited articles. Sometimes pays expenses of writers on assignment.

Photos: State availability of photos with submissions. Reviews contact sheets, transparencies, 3 × 5 prints. Offers no additional payment for photos accepted with ms. Captions, identification of subjects required. Negotiable rights bought.

Tips: "As a nonprofit humanitarian agency aiding the poor worldwide, we give assignments to accomplished journalistic writers and photographers who travel the globe. We cover world issues with a humanitarian slant, such as: 'Are We Trashing Our Third-World Neighbors?' 'Homeless With Children,' and 'The Human Cost of the Small Arms Trade.' We invite traveling journalists to check with us for pick-a-back assignments."

The double dagger before a listing indicates that the listing is new in this edition. New markets are often more receptive to freelance submissions.

Psychology and Self-Improvement

These publications focus on psychological topics, how and why readers can improve their own outlooks, and how to understand people in general. Many General Interest, Men's and Women's publications also publish articles in these areas.

THE HEALING WOMAN, The monthly newsletter for women survivors of childhood sexual abuse, P.O. Box 3038, Moss Beach CA 94038. (415)728-0339. Fax: (415)728-1324. Editor: Margot Silk Forrest. Submissions Editor: Brenda Anderson. 70% freelance written. Monthly newsletter covering recovery from childhood sexual abuse. "Submissions accepted only from writers with personal or professional experience with childhood sexual abuse. We are looking for intelligent, honest and compassionate articles on topics of interest to survivors. We also publish first-person stories, poetry, interviews and book reviews." Estab. 1992. Circ. 5,000. **Pays on acceptance.** Publishes ms an average of 5-12 months after acceptance. Byline given. Offers 50% kill fee. Buys first North American serial rights. Editorial lead time 4 months. Submit seasonal material 4 months in advance. Accepts previously published submissions. Send photocopy of article and information about when and where the article previously appeared. For reprints pays 100% of the amount paid for an original article. Query for electronic submissions. Submit no more than 3 pieces at a time. Reports in 1 month on queries. Writer's guidelines for #10 SASE.
Nonfiction: Book excerpts, essays, general interest, interview/profile, opinion, personal experience. "No articles on topics with which the writer has not had first-hand experience. If you've been there, you can write about it for us. If not, don't write about it." Buys 30 mss/year. Query with published clips. Length: 300-1,500 words. Pays $25-50. "Pays in copies for poems, short first-person pieces."
Photos: Send photos with submission. Negotiates payment for photos individually. Identification of subjects required. Buys one-time rights.
Columns/Departments: Book Reviews (books or accounts of incest survivors, therapy for incest survivors), 500-600 words; and Survivors Speak Out (first-person stories of recovery), 300-500 words.
Poetry: No *long* poems preoccupied with painful aspects of sexual abuse. Buys 25 poems/year, but pays only in copies.
Tips: "Although our subject matter is painful, *The Healing Woman* is not about suffering—it's about healing. Our department called 'Survivors Speak Out' features short, honest, insightful first-person essays with a conversational tone. We are happy to work with unpublished writers in this department."

ROSICRUCIAN DIGEST, Rosicrucian Order, AMORC, Rosicrucian Park, San Jose CA 95191-0001. (408)947-3600. Editor-in-Chief: Robin M. Thompson. 50% freelance written. Works with a small number of new/unpublished writers each year. Quarterly magazine emphasizing mysticism, science and the arts for "men and women of all ages, seeking answers to life's questions." **Pays on acceptance.** Publishes ms an average of 5-6 months after acceptance. Buys first serial and second serial (reprint) rights. Byline given. Submit seasonal material 5 months in advance. Accepts previously published submissions. Reports in 2 months. Free sample copy. Writer's guidelines for #10 SASE.
Nonfiction: How to deal with life—and all it brings us—in a positive and constructive way. Informational articles—new ideas and developments in science, the arts, philosophy and thought. Historical sketches, biographies, human interest, psychology, philosophical and inspirational articles. No religious, astrological or political material or articles promoting a particular group or system of thought. Buys variable amount of mss/year. Query. Length: 1,000-1,500 words. Pays 6¢/word.
Photos: Purchased with accompanying ms. Send prints. Pays $10/8×10 b&w glossy print.
Fillers: Short inspirational or uplifting (not religious) anecdotes or experiences. Buys 6/year. Query. Length: 22-250 words. Pays 2¢/word.
Tips: "We are looking for well-written articles with a positive, constructive approach to life in these trying times. This seems to be a time of indecision and apathy in many areas, and we are encouraged when we read an article that lets the reader know that he/she can get involved, take positive action, make a change in his/her life. We are also looking for articles about how other cultures outside our own deal with the big questions, problems, and changes in life, i.e., the questions of 'Who am I?' 'Where do I fit in?', the role of elders in passing on culture to new generations, philosophical aspects of other cultures that can help us grow today."

SCIENCE OF MIND MAGAZINE, 3251 W. Sixth St., P.O. Box 75127, Los Angeles CA 90075. (213)388-2181. Fax: (213)388-1926. Editor: Sandra Sarr. 30% freelance written. Monthly magazine that features articles on spirituality, self-help and inspiration. "Our publication centers on oneness of all life and spiritual empowerment through the application of Science of Mind principles." Pays on publication. Publishes ms an average of 5 months after acceptance. Byline given. Buys first North American serial rights. Submit seasonal material 6 months in advance. Reports in 6 weeks on queries; 3 months on mss. Free writer's guidelines.
Nonfiction: Book excerpts, inspirational, personal experience of Science of Mind, spiritual. Buys 35-45 mss/year. Query or send complete ms. Length: 750-2,000 words. Pays $25/printed page. Pays in contributors copies for some special features written by readers.

Photos: Reviews 35mm transparencies and 5×7 or 8×10 b&w prints. Buys one-time rights.
Poetry: Inspirational and Science of Mind oriented. "We are not interested in poetry not related to Science of Mind principles." Buys 10-15 poems/year. Length: 7-25 lines. Pays $25.
Tips: "We are interested in first person experiences of a spiritual nature having to do with the Science of Mind."

Regional

Many regional publications rely on staff-written material, but others accept work from freelance writers who live in or know the region. The best regional publication to target with your submissions is usually the one in your hometown, whether it's a city or state magazine or a Sunday supplement in a newspaper. Since you are familiar with the region, it is easier to propose suitable story ideas.

Listed first are general interest magazines slanted toward residents of and visitors to a particular region. Next, regional publications are categorized alphabetically by state, followed by Canada. Publications that report on the business climate of a region are grouped in the regional division of the Business and Finance category. Recreation and travel publications specific to a geographical area are listed in the Travel, Camping and Trailer section. Keep in mind also that many regional publications specialize in specific topics, and are listed according to those sections (for example, *Grand Rapids Parent Magazine*, Child Care and Parental Guidance section). Regional publications are not listed if they only accept material from a select group of freelancers in their area or if they did not want to receive the number of queries and manuscripts a national listing would attract. If you know of a regional magazine that is not listed, approach it by asking for writer's guidelines before you send unsolicited material.

General

BLUE RIDGE COUNTRY, Leisure Publishing, P.O. Box 21535, Roanoke VA 24018-9900. (703)989-6138. Fax: (703)989-7603. Editor: Kurt Rheinheimer. 75% freelance written. Bimonthly magazine on the Blue Ridge region from Maryland to Georgia. "The magazine is designed to celebrate the history, heritage and beauty of the Blue Ridge region. It is aimed at the adult, upscale readers who enjoy living or traveling in the mountain regions of Virginia, North Carolina, West Virginia, Maryland, Kentucky, Tennessee, South Carolina and Georgia." Estab. 1972. Circ. 75,000. Pays on publication. Publishes ms an average of 8 months after acceptance. Byline given. Offers $50 kill fee for commissioned pieces only. Buys first and second serial (reprint) rights. Submit seasonal material 6 months in advance. Query for electronic submissions. Reports in 2 months. Sample copy for 9×12 SAE with 6 first-class stamps. Writer's guidelines for #10 SASE.
Nonfiction: General interest, historical/nostalgic, interview/profile, personal experience, photo feature, travel, history. Buys 25-30 mss/year. Query with or without published clips or send complete ms. Length: 500-1,800 words. Pays $50-250 for assigned articles; $25-250 for unsolicited articles.
   • This magazine is looking for more regional short pieces.
Photos: Send photos with submission. Prefers transparencies. Offers $10-25/photo and $100 for cover photo. Identification of subjects required. Buys all rights.
Columns/Departments: Country Roads (stories on people, events, ecology, history, antiques, books). Buys 12-24 mss/year. Query. Pays $10-40.
Tips: "Freelancers needed for regional departmental shorts and 'macro' issues affecting whole region. Need field reporters from all areas of Blue Ridge region. Also, we need updates on the Blue Ridge Parkway, Appalachian Trail, national forests, ecological issues, preservation movements."

NORTHWEST PARKS & WILDLIFE, Educational Publications Foundation, P.O. Box 18000, Florence OR 97439-0130. (800)348-8401. Fax: (503)997-1124. Editor: Dave Peden. Managing Editor: Judy Fleagle. 75% freelance written. Bimonthly regional magazine for Washington, Oregon, British Columbia, Idaho and occasionally Alaska. Estab. 1991. Circ. 25,000. Pays after publication. Publishes ms an average of 6-12 months after acceptance. Byline given. Offers 33% kill fee. Buys first North American serial rights. Submit seasonal material 6 months in advance. Accepts previously published submissions. Send tearsheet or photocoy of article and information about when and where the article previously appeared. For reprints, pays 65% of the amount paid for an original article. Query for electronic submissions. Reports on queries in 6 weeks and ms in 3 months. Sample copy for $4.50. Writer's guidelines for #10 SASE.

• *Northwest Parks & Wildlife* no longer buys manuscripts related to Montana or California.

Nonfiction: General interest, interview/profile, personal experience, photo feature, wildlife and wilderness areas, profiles of parks. "Any article not related to Pacific Northwest will be returned." Buys 60 mss/year. Query with published clips. Length: 500-2,000 words. Pays $50-350 plus 2-5 contributor's copies.

Photos: Send photos with submission. Reviews 35mm or larger transparencies. Prefers to buy photo-text packages. Captions, model releases, photo credits and identification of subjects required. Buys one-time rights.

Fillers: Newsbreaks. Uses 45/year. Length: 300-500 words. No payment for fillers.

Tips: "Slant articles for readers not living in Pacific Northwest. Keep articles informative rather than travel oriented. Do give directions and contact information for 'GettingThere' section at end of article; include a map with submission. An articulate query of one page is appreciated rather than a ms. Articles of 800-1,000 words with photos are easiest to fit in. Articles of 400 words with good horizontal photo are needed for back page section. Accurate captions and photo credits on separate sheet from photos are appreciated."

NORTHWEST TRAVEL, Northwest Regional Magazines, P.O. Box 18000, Florence OR 97439. (503)997-8401. Editor: Dave Peden. Managing Editor: Judy Fleagle. 50% freelance written. Bimonthly consumer magazine covering the Pacific Northwest. "We like energetic writing about popular activities and destinations in the Northwest. *Northwest Travel* aims to give readers practical ideas on where to go in the region. Magazine covers Oregon, Washington, Idaho, B.C.; occasionally Alaska and western Montana." Estab. 1991. Circ. 50,000. Pays after publication. Publishes ms an average of 8 months after acceptance. Offers 33% kill fee. Buys first North American serial rights or second serial (reprint) rights. Submit seasonal material 6 months in advance. Query for electronic submissions. Reports in 6 weeks on queries. Sample copy for $4.50. Writer's guidelines for #10 SASE.

• *Northwest Travel* now emphasizes day trips in the Pacific Northwest area.

Nonfiction: Book excerpts, general interest, historical/nostalgic, interview/profile (rarely), photo feature, travel (only in Northwest region). "No cliche-ridden pieces on places that everyone covers." Buys 40 mss/year. Query with or without published clips. Length: 300-2,500 words. Pays $125 minimum for assigned articles; $50 minimum for unsolicited articles.

Photos: State availability of photos with submission. Reviews transparencies (prefer dupes). Negotiates payment individually. Captions, model releases, credits and identification of subjects required. Buys one-time rights.

Columns/Departments: Restaurant Features, 1,000 words. Pays $125. Worth a Stop (brief items describing places "worth a stop"), 300-500 words. Buys 25-30 mss/year. Send complete ms. Pays $50. "A new department is Back Page, a photo and text package keyed to a specific season or festival"; 300 words and 1 photo. Pays $75.

Fillers: Anecdotes, facts. Length: 50-200 words. Pays $25-50.

Tips: "Write fresh, lively copy (avoid cliches) and cover exciting travel topics in the region that haven't been covered in other magazines. A story with stunning photos will get serious consideration. Areas most open to freelancers are Worth a Stop and the Restaurant Feature. Take us to fascinating, interesting, fun places we might not otherwise discover."

‡SOUTHERN EXPOSURE, A Journal of Politics and Culture, Institute for Southern Studies, P.O. Box 531, Durham NC 27702. (919)419-8311. Editor: Pat Arnow. 80% freelance written. Quarterly magazine covering southern politics and culture. "With special focus sections, investigative journalism, features, fiction, interviews, and news, *Southern Exposure* covers the wide range of Southern life today—and puts events and trends in perspective. Our goal is to provide information, ideas, and historical understanding of southern social struggles that will help bring about progressive change." Estab. 1973. Circ. 4,000. Pays on publication. Publishes ms an average of 6 months after acceptance. Byline given. Buys first rights, one-time rights, second serial (reprint) rights or all rights. Editorial lead time 6 months. Accepts simultaneous submissions. Query for electronic submissions. Reports in 3 months on queries; 6 months on mss. Sample copy for $5. Writer's guidelines for #10 SASE.

Nonfiction: Book excerpts, essays, exposé, how-to (build a grass roots organization, how-to conduct a citizen's campaign), humor, interview/profile, personal experience, photo feature. "Everything we publish has to have something to do with the South." Special issues: Women & Health, Timber, building community—community breakdown. Buys 50 mss/year. Query with published clips. Length: 250-3,500 words. Pays $50-250. Sometimes pays expenses of writers on assignment.

Photos: Send photos with submission. Reviews contact sheets, transparencies, prints. Offers $50 maximum/photo. Negotiates payment individually. Captions, identification of subjects required. Buys one-time rights.

Columns/Departments: Blueprint (how to change the South—from a person or organization's experience), 1,400 words; Voices (stories by or about people who have developed a point of view, strong feelings, actions), 2,100 words; Roundup (anecdotes and news from the region), 250-700 words; Still the South (information and statistics on some aspect of southern life), 650 words; Reviews (essay on one or more related books and/or other media), 2,100 words. Buys 15 mss/year. Query with published clips or send complete ms. Pays $50-100.

Fiction: Erotica, ethnic, experimental, historical, horror, humorous, novel excerpts. Buys 4 mss/year. Send complete ms. Length: 3,500 words maximum. Pays $100-250.

Tips: "Lively writing and original thinking are what we're after, new ways to look at events, people, places. Give a new perspective on arts, politics, local struggles, corruption, movements. We like in-depth reporting, plenty of specific information—quotes!—and everything we publish must pertain to the South in some way."

THE SOUTHERN JOURNAL/THE APPALACHIAN LOG, Appalachian Log Publishing Company, P.O. Box 20297, Charleston WV 25362-1297. (304)342-5789. Editor: Ron Gregory. 50% freelance written. Works with new/unpublished writers. Monthly magazine covering Southern mountain region. "We are dedicated to promoting the people and places of the Southern mountains. We publish only 'positive' articles concerning our region. We are *not* interested in religious or political material." Estab. 1992. Circ. 5,000. Pays 30 days from publication. Publishes ms an average of 9 months after acceptance. Byline given. Offers 10% kill fee or $10. Not copyrighted. Buys first, one-time, second serial (reprint) or simultaneous rights. Editorial lead time 2 months. Submit seasonal material 2 months in advance. Accepts simultaneous and previously published submissions. Query for electronic submissions. Reports in 6 weeks on queries; 6 months on mss. Sample copy for $1.50. Writer's guidelines for #10 SASE.

Nonfiction: Book excerpts, essays, historical/nostalgic, humor, inspirational, interview/profile, personal experience, photo feature, travel, genealogy. Special issues include snow skiing in the South, festivals in the South, whitewater Rafting in the South. "No religious, exposé or opinion pieces. (We are no longer interested in political/opinion articles.") Buys 20 mss/year. Send complete ms. Length: 300 words minimum. Pays $50 minimum for assigned articles; $10 minimum for unsolicited articles. Sometimes pays expenses of writers on assignment.

Photos: Send photos with submission. Reviews contact sheets. Captions required. Buys one-time rights.

Columns/Departments: Betty Gregory, publisher. Family History (genealogy), 1,000-2,000 words. Buys 4 mss/year. Query. Pays $20-50.

Fiction: Condensed novels, historical, humorous, mainstream, slice-of-life vignettes. No religious or erotic material. Buys 5 mss/year. Send complete ms. Length: 500-5,000 words. Pays $25-200.

Poetry: Betty Gregory, publisher. Avant-garde, free verse, light verse, traditional. Buys 20 poems/year. Length: 10-80 lines. Pays $7.50-30.

Fillers: Anecdotes, facts, short humor. Buys 15/year. Length: 25-250 words. Pays $5-50.

Tips: "Cover letters that give some indication of the author's knowledge of our region are helpful. All articles and submissions should, likewise, display the author's familiarity with the Southern mountains. Details—particularly nostalgic ones—must be authentic and correct. Fiction and nonfiction short stories or longer works that can be serialized appeal to us. Writers in this area should be clear in their storyline (no 'hidden' meanings) and should keep in mind that our magazine loves the South and its people."

‡SOUTHERN LIVING, Southern Progress Corp., 2100 Lakeshore Dr., Birmingham AL 35209. (205)877-6000. Editor: John A. Floyd, Jr. Managing Editor: Clay Nordan. Contact: Dianne Young. Monthly magazine covers travel, foods, homes, gardens, Southern lifestyle. Estab. 1966. Circ. 2,461,416. **Pays on acceptance.** Publishes ms an average of 1 year after acceptance. 25% kill fee. Buys all rights or other negotiated rights. Editorial lead time 6 months. Submit seasonal material 1 year in advance. Reports in 1 month on queries, 2 months on mss. Sample copy and writer's guidelines free on request.

Nonfiction: Essays, humor. Accepts unsolicited freelance only for personal, nonfiction essays about Southern life. Buys 45-50 mss/year. Query with or without published clips, but prefers completed mss. Length: 800 words minimum. Payment negotiated individually. Sometimes pays expenses of writers on assignment.

Photos: State availability of photos with submissions. Reviews 4×5 transparencies. Negotiates payment individually. Captions, model releases, identification of subjects required. Buys one-time rights.

Columns/Departments: Southern Journal (Southern lifestyle and subjects), 800 words. Buys 12 mss/year. Query with published clips.

‡SUNSET, Sunset Publishing Corp., 80 Willow Rd., Menlo Park CA 94025-3691. Freelance articles should be timely and *only about the 13 Western States*. Departments open to freelancers are: Building & Crafts, Food, Garden, Travel. Direct queries to the specific editorial department. Guidelines for freelance travel items for #10 SASE addressed to Editorial Services.

YANKEE, Yankee Publishing Inc., P.O. Box 520, Dublin NH 03444-0520. (603)563-8111. Fax: (603)563-8252. Editor: Judson D. Hale, Sr. Managing Editor: Tim Clark. Assistant Editor: Don Weafer. 50% freelance written. Monthly magazine that features articles on New England. "Our mission is to express and perhaps, indirectly, preserve the New England culture—and to do so in an entertaining way. Our audience is national, and has one thing in common—they love New England." Estab. 1935. Circ. 700,000. Pays within 30 days of acceptance. Byline given. Offers 33% kill fee. Buys first rights. Submit seasonal material 5 months in advance. Accepts simultaneous submissions. Send tearsheet, photocopy of article or short story, typed ms with rights for sale noted and information about when and where the material previously appeared. For reprints, pays 100% of the amount paid for an original article. Query for electronic submissions." Reports in 2 months on queries. Writer's guidelines for #10 SASE.

● In 1994 *Yankee* won The White Award for Public Affairs Reporting from the William Allen White School of Journalism.

Nonfiction: Don Weafer, assistant editor. Essays, general interest, historical/nostalgic, humor, interview/profile, personal experience. "No 'good old days' pieces, no dialect humor and nothing outside New England!" Buys 30 mss/year. Query with published clips. Length: 250-2,500 words. Pays $50-2,000 for assigned articles; $50-500 for unsolicited articles. Sometimes pays expenses of writers on assignment.

Photos: Send photos with submission. Reviews contact sheets and transparencies. Offers $50-150/photo. Identification of subjects required. Buys one-time rights.

Columns/Departments: New England Sampler (short bits on interesting people, anecdotes, lost and found), 100-400 words; Yankee's Home Companion (short pieces about home-related items), 100-400 words; I Remember (nostalgia focused on specific incidents), 400-500 words. Buys 80 mss/year. Query with published clips. Pays $50-400.

Fiction: Edie Clark, fiction editor. "We publish high-quality literary fiction that explores human issues and concerns in a specific place—New England." Publishes novel excerpts. Buys 6 mss/year. Send complete ms. Length: 500-2,500 words. Pays $1,000.

Poetry: Jean Burden, poetry editor. "We don't choose poetry by type. We look for the best. No inspirational, holiday-oriented, epic, limericks, etc." Buys 40 poems/year. Submit maximum 3 poems. Length: 2-20 lines. Pays $50.

Tips: "Submit lots of ideas. Don't censor yourself—let *us* decide whether an idea is good or bad. We might surprise you. Remember we've been publishing for 60 years, so chances are we've already done every 'classic' New England subject. Try to surprise us—it isn't easy. These departments are most open to freelancers: New England Sampler; Home Companion; I Remember. Study the ones we publish—the format should be apparent. Surprise us!"

Alabama

ALABAMA LIVING, Alabama Rural Electric Assn., P.O. Box 244014, Montgomery AL 36124. (334)215-2732. Editor: Darryl Gates. 10% freelance written. Monthly magazine covering rural electric consumers. "Our magazine is an editorially balanced, informational and educational service to members of rural electric cooperatives. Our mix regularly includes Alabama history, nostalgia, gardening, outdoor and consumer pieces." Estab. 1948. Pays on publication. Publishes ms an average of 3 months after acceptance. Byline given. Publication is not copyrighted. Buys second serial (reprint) rights. Editorial lead time 3 months. Submit seasonal material 4 months in advance. Accepts simultaneous and previously published submissions. Send tearsheet or photocopy of article or typed ms with rights for sale noted. Pays 100% of the amount paid for an original article. Reports in 1 month on queries. Sample copy free on request.

Nonfiction: Historical/nostalgic, rural-oriented. Buys 6 mss/year. Send complete ms (copy). Length: 300-750 words. Pays $100 minimum for assigned articles; $40 minimum for unsolicited articles.

Tips: "The best way to break into *Alabama Living* is to give us a bit of history or nostalgia about Alabama or the Southeast."

Alaska

ALASKA, The Magazine of Life on the Last Frontier, 808 E St., Suite 200, Anchorage AK 99501-9963. (907)272-6070. Publisher: Dana Brockway. Acting Editor: Tricia Brown. Editorial Assistant: Donna Rae Thompson. 80% freelance written. Eager to work with new/unpublished writers. Monthly magazine covering topics "uniquely Alaskan." Estab. 1935. Circ. 235,000. **Pays on acceptance.** Publishes ms an average of 6 months after acceptance. Byline given. Buys first or one-time rights. Submit seasonal material 1 year in advance. Query for electronic submissions. Reports in 2 months. Sample copy for $3 and 9×12 SAE with 7 first-class stamps. Writer's guidelines for #10 SASE.

Nonfiction: Historical/nostalgic, adventure, how-to (on anything Alaskan), humor, interview/profile, personal experience, photo feature. Also travel articles and Alaska destination stories. Does not accept fiction or poetry. Buys 60 mss/year. Query. Length: 100-2,500 words. Pays $100-1,250 depending upon length. Pays expenses of writers on assignment.

Photos: Send photos with submission. Reviews 35mm or larger transparencies. Captions and identification of subjects required.

Tips: "We are placing even more emphasis on natural history, adventure and profiles."

Arizona

ARIZONA HIGHWAYS, 2039 W. Lewis Ave., Phoenix AZ 85009-9988. (602)258-6641. Fax: (602)254-4505. Managing Editor: Richard G. Stahl. 90% freelance written. Prefers to work with published/established writers. State-owned magazine designed to help attract tourists into and through the state. Estab. 1925. **Pays on acceptance.** Reports in up to 3 months. Writer's guidelines for SASE.

Nonfiction: Feature subjects include narratives and exposition dealing with history, anthropology, nature, wildlife, armchair travel, out of the way places, small towns, old west history, Indian arts and crafts, travel, etc. Travel articles are experience-based. All must be oriented toward Arizona and the Southwest. Buys 6 mss/issue. Buys first serial rights. Query with "a lead paragraph and brief outline of story. We deal with professionals only, so include list of current credits." Length: 600-2,000 words. Pays 35-55¢/word. Sometimes pays expenses of writers on assignment.

Photos: "We will use transparencies of 2¼, 4×5 or larger, and 35mm when they display exceptional quality or content. We prefer 35mm Kodachrome. Each transparency *must* be accompanied by information attached to each photograph: where, when, what. No photography will be reviewed by the editors unless the photographer's name appears on *each* and *every* transparency." Pays $80-350 for "selected" transparencies. Buys one-time rights.

Columns/Departments: New departments in the magazine include Focus on Nature, Along the Way, Back-Road Adventure, Legends of the Lost, Hike of the Month and Arizona Humor. "Back Road and Hikes also must be experience-based."

Tips: "Writing must be of professional quality, warm, sincere, in-depth, well-peopled and accurate. Avoid themes that describe first trips to Arizona, the Grand Canyon, the desert, Colorado River running, etc. Emphasis is to be on Arizona adventure and romance as well as flora and fauna, when appropriate, and themes that can be photographed. Double check your manuscript for accuracy."

PHOENIX, Media America Corporation, 5555 North Seventh Ave., #B-200, Phoenix AZ 85013-1755. (602)207-3750. Fax: (602)207-3777. Editor/Publisher: Richard S. Vonier. Managing Editor: Beth Deveny. 70% freelance written. Monthly magazine covering southwest, state of Arizona, metro Phoenix. Estab. 1966. Circ. 50,000. Pays on acceptance or publication. Publishes ms an average of 5 months after acceptance. Byline given. Negotiable kill fee. Buys first North American serial rights and one-time rights. Submit seasonal material 4 months in advance. Accepts simultaneous and previously published submissions. Send tearsheet or photocopy of article and/or typed ms with rights for sale noted and information about when and where the article previously appeared. Pays 50% of their fee for an original article. Query for electronic submissions. Reports in 2 months. Sample copy for $1.95 and 9×12 SAE with 5 first-class stamps.

Nonfiction: Book excerpts, essays, investigative, general interest, historical/nostalgic, how-to, humor, inspirational, interview/profile, opinion, personal experience, photo feature, religious, technical, travel, other. "No material dealing with travel outside the region or other subjects that don't have an effect on the area." Buys 35-65 mss/year. Query with published clips. Pays $50-1,500 for assigned articles; $50-500 for unsolicited articles. Sometimes pays expenses of writers on assignment.

Photos: Send photos with submissions. Reviews contact sheets, negatives, transparencies, prints. Offers $25-100/photo. Captions, model releases and identification of subjects required. Buys one-time rights.

Tips: "We have no published guidelines. Articles should be of local or regional interest with vivid descriptions that put the reader in the story and present new information or a new way of looking at things. We are not afraid of opinion."

California

BUZZ, The Talk of Los Angeles, 11835 W. Olympic Blvd., Suite 450, Los Angeles CA 90064-5000. (310)473-2721. E-mail: buzzmag@aol.com. Editor-in-Chief: Allan Mayer. Deputy Editor: Greg Critser. 80% freelance written. Monthly magazine for Los Angeles. "We are looking for lively, provocative, insightful journalism, essays and fiction that reflect an L.A. sensibility." Estab. 1990. Circ. 100,000. Pays within 30 days of acceptance. Byline given. Offers 25% kill fee. Buys first North American serial rights. Submit seasonal material 4 months in advance. Query for electronic submissions. Reports in 3 months. Sample copy for $3 and 10×13 SAE with 10 first-class stamps.

Nonfiction: Greg Critser, deputy editor. Book excerpts, essays, general interest, interview/profile. "No satirical essays, book/movie/theater reviews or personal memoirs." Buys 30 mss/year. Query with published clips. Length: 2,500-4,000 words. Pays $2,000-5,000. Sometimes pays expenses of writers on assignment.

Photos: Send photos with submission. Photos are assigned separately. Model releases and identification of subjects required. Buys one-time rights.

Columns/Departments: Susan Gordon, senior editor. "What's the Buzz" (witty, "Talk of the Town"-like pieces on personalities, trends and events in L.A.), 300-1,000 words. Buys 20 mss/year. Query with published clips. Pays $200-1,000.

Fiction: Renee Vogel, fiction editor. "We are interested in any type fiction by L.A. writers, and in fiction relevant to L.A. by non-L.A.-based writers. No fiction that has no connection with L.A." Publishes novel excerpts. Buys 10 mss/year. Send complete ms. Length: 1,500-4,000 words. Pays $1,000-2,500.

Tips: "The 'What's the Buzz' section is the best place to break into *Buzz*. Freelancers should keep in mind that we're looking for national-quality works."

LOS ANGELES MAGAZINE, ABC/Capital Cities, 1888 Century Park East, Los Angeles CA 90067. (310)557-7569. Fax: (310)557-7517. Executive Editor: Rodger Claire. Editor: Lew Harris. 98% freelance written. Monthly magazine about southern California. "The primary editorial role of the magazine is to aid a literate, upscale audience in getting the most out of life in the Los Angeles area." Estab. 1963. Circ. 174,000. Pays on publication. Publishes ms an average of 4 months after acceptance. Byline given. Offers 30% kill fee. Buys first North American serial rights. Submit seasonal material 6 months in advance. Reports in 3 months. Sample copy for $5. Writer's guidelines for #10 SASE.

• *Los Angeles Magazine* continues to do stories with local angles but it is expanding its coverage to include topics of interest on a national level.

Nonfiction: Book excerpts (about L.A. or by famous L.A. author); exposé (any local issue); general interest; historical/nostalgic (about L.A. or Hollywood); interview/profile (about L.A. person). Buys up to 100 mss/year. Query with published clips. Length: 250-3,500 words. Pays $50-2,000. Sometimes pays expenses of writers on assignment.

Photos: Nancie Clare, photo editor. Send photos.

Columns/Departments: Buys 170 mss/year. Query with published clips. Length: 250-1,200 words. Pays $50-600.

LOS ANGELES READER, 5550 Wilshire Blvd., Suite 301, Los Angeles CA 90036-3389. (213)965-7430. Fax: (213)933-0281. Editor: James Vowell. Managing Editor: Erik Himmelsbach. 85% freelance written. Weekly tabloid of features and reviews for "intelligent young Los Angelenos interested in politics, the arts and popular culture." Estab. 1978. Circ. 90,000. Pays on publication. Publishes ms an average of 60 days after publication. Byline given. Buys first North American serial rights. Submit seasonal material 3 months in advance. Accepts simultaneous queries and submissions. Reports in 2 months. Sample copy and writer's guidelines free.

Nonfiction: General interest, journalism, interview/profile, personal experience, photo features—all with strong local slant. Buys "scores" of mss/year. Send complete ms or query. Length: 200-3,500 words. Pays $25-300.

Tips: "Break in with submissions for our Cityside page which uses short (400-800 word) news items on Los Angeles happenings, personalities and trends. Try to have some conflict in submissions: 'x exists' is not as good a story as 'x is struggling with y over z.' Stories must have Los Angeles angle. We much prefer submissions in electronic form."

LOS ANGELES TIMES MAGAZINE, *Los Angeles Times*, Times Mirror Sq., Los Angeles CA 90053. (213)237-7000. Fax: (213)237-7386. Editor: John Lindsay. 50% freelance written. Weekly magazine of regional general interest. Circ. 1,164,388. Payment schedule varies. Publishes ms an average of 2 months after acceptance. Byline given. Buys first North American serial rights. Submit seasonal material 3 months in advance. Accepts simultaneous submissions. Reports in 1-2 months. Sample copy and writer's guidelines free.

Nonfiction: General interest, investigative and narrative journalism, interview/profiles and reported essays. Covers California, the West, the nation and the world. Written queries only. Queries must include clips. Length: 2,500-4,500 words. Pays agreed upon expenses.

Photos: Query first; prefers to assign photos. Reviews color transparencies and b&w prints. Payment varies. Captions, model releases and identification of subjects required. Buys one-time rights.

Tips: "Prospective contributors should know their subject well and be able to explain why a story merits publication. Previous national magazine writing experience preferred."

ORANGE COAST MAGAZINE, The Magazine of Orange County, Orange Coast Kommunications Inc., 245-D Fischer Ave., Suite 8, Costa Mesa CA 92626-4514. (714)545-1900. Editor: Martin J. Smith. Managing Editor: Allison Joyce. 95% freelance written. Monthly magazine "designed to inform and enlighten the educated, upscale residents of Orange County, California; highly graphic and well-researched." Estab. 1974. Circ. 40,000. **Pays on acceptance.** Publishes ms an average of 4 months after acceptance. Byline given. Buys first serial rights. Submit seasonal material at least 6 months in advance. Accepts simultaneous and previously published submissions. Send tearsheet or photocopy of article or typed ms with rights for sale noted and information about when and where the article previously appeared. Reports in 2 months. Sample copy for $2.95 and 10×12 SAE with 8 first-class stamps. Writer's guidelines for SASE.

• *Orange Coast Magazine* has increased its payment for nonfiction.

Nonfiction: Exposé (Orange County government, politics, business, crime), general interest (with Orange County focus),; historical/nostalgic, guides to activities and services, interview/profile (prominent Orange County citizens), local sports, travel. Special issues: Dining and Entertainment (March); Health and Fitness (January); Resort Guide (November); Home and Garden (June); Holiday (December). Buys 100 mss/year. Query or send complete ms. Absolutely no phone queries. Length: 1,000-3,000 words. Pays $400-800.

Columns/Departments: Business statistics. Most departments are not open to freelancers. Buys 200 mss/year. Query or send complete ms. Length: 1,000-2,000 words. Pays $200 maximum.

Fiction: Buys only under rare circumstances. Send complete ms. Length: 1,000-5,000 words. Pays $250.
Tips: "Most features are assigned to writers we've worked with before. Don't try to sell us 'generic' journalism. *Orange Coast* prefers articles with specific and unusual angles focused on Orange County. A lot of freelance writers ignore our Orange County focus. We get far too many generalized manuscripts."

PALO ALTO WEEKLY, Embarcadero Publishing Co., 703 High St., P.O. Box 1610, Palo Alto CA 94302. (415)326-8210. Fax: (415)326-3928. Editor: Paul Gullixson. 5% freelance written. Semiweekly tabloid focusing on local issues and local sources. Estab. 1979. Circ. 48,000. Pays on publication. Publishes ms an average of 1 month after acceptance. Byline given. Offers 50% kill fee. Buys first rights. Submit seasonal/holiday material 2 months in advance. Accepts previously published submissions. For reprints, payment is negotiable. Reports in 2 weeks. Sample copy for 9×12 SAE with 2 first-class stamps.
 • *Palo Alto Weekly* is now doing sports and has expanded its arts and entertainment coverage. It is still looking for stories in Palo Alto area or features on people from the area.
Nonfiction: General interest, historical/nostalgic, interview/profile, photo feature. Special issues: Together (weddings—mid February); Interiors (May, October). Nothing that is not local; no travel. Buys 25 mss/year. Query with published clips. Length: 700-1,000 words. Pays $35-60.
Photos: Send photos with submission. Reviews contact sheets and 5×7 prints. Offers $10 minimum/photo. Captions, model releases and identification of subjects required. Buys one-time rights.
Tips: "Writers have the best chance if they live within circulation area and know publication and area well. DON'T send generic, broad-based pieces. The most open sections are food, interiors and sports. Longer 'cover story' submissions may be accepted, but very rare. Keep it LOCAL."

SACRAMENTO MAGAZINE, 4471 D St., Sacramento CA 95819. Fax: (916)452-6061. Editor: Krista Minard. Managing Editor: Darlena Belushin. 100% freelance written. Works with a small number of new/unpublished writers each year. Monthly magazine emphasizing a strong local angle on politics, local issues, human interest and consumer items for readers in the middle to high income brackets. Estab. 1975. Pays on publication. Publishes ms an average of 3 months after acceptance. Rights vary; generally buys first North American serial rights, rarely second serial (reprint) rights. No reprints. Reports in 2 months. Sample copy for $4.50. Writer's guidelines for #10 SASE.
Nonfiction: Local issues vital to Sacramento quality of life. Buys 5 unsolicited feature mss/year. Query first in writing. Length: 1,500-3,000 words, depending on author, subject matter and treatment. Sometimes pays expenses of writers on assignment.
Photos: Send photos. Payment varies depending on photographer, subject matter and treatment. Captions (including IDs, location and date) required. Buys one-time rights.
Columns/Departments: Business, home and garden, media, parenting, first person essays, regional travel, gourmet, profile, sports, city arts (1,000-1,800 words); and Do it or Don't (250-400 words).

‡SAN FRANCISCO FOCUS, The City Magazine for the San Francisco Bay Area, 2601 Mariposa St., San Francisco CA 94110-1400. (415)553-2800. Fax: (415)553-2470. Editor: Amy Rennert. Managing Editor: Rick Clogher. 80% freelance written. Prefers to work with published/established writers. Monthly city/regional magazine. Estab. 1968. Circ. 180,000. Pays on publication. Publishes ms an average of 2 months after acceptance. Byline given. Offers 25% kill fee. Buys one-time rights. Submit seasonal material 5 months in advance. Query for electronic submissions. Reports in 2 months. Sample copy for $2.50. Free writer's guidelines with SASE.
Nonfiction: Exposé, interview/profile, the arts, politics, public issues, sports, consumer affairs and travel. All stories should relate in some way to the San Francisco Bay Area (travel excepted). Query with published clips. Length: 750-4,000 words. Pays $75-750. Sometimes pays the expenses of writers on assignment.

VENTURA COUNTY & COAST REPORTER, VCR Inc., 1567 Spinnaker Dr., Suite 202, Ventura CA 93001. (805)658-2244. Fax: (805)658-7803. Editor: Nancy Cloutier. 12% freelance written. Works with a small number of new/unpublished writers each year. Weekly tabloid covering local news. Circ. 35,000. Pays on publication. Publishes ms an average of 2 weeks after acceptance. Byline given. Buys first North American serial rights. Reports in 3 weeks.
Nonfiction: General interest (local slant), humor, interview/profile, travel (local—within 500 miles). Local (Ventura County) slant predominates. Length: 2-5 double-spaced typewritten pages. Pays $10-25.
Photos: Send photos with ms. Reviews b&w contact sheet.
Columns/Departments: Entertainment, Sports, Dining News, Real Estate, Boating Experience (Southern California). Send complete ms. Pays $10-25.
Tips: "As long as topics are up-beat with local slant, we'll consider them."

‡WEST, 750 Ridder Park Dr., San Jose CA 95190. (408)920-5796. Fax: (405)288-8060. E-mail: westmail@a ol.com. Editor: Fran Smith. 50% freelance written. Prefers to work with published/established writers. Weekly newspaper/magazine published with the *San Jose Mercury News*. Circ. 320,000. **Pays on acceptance.** Publishes ms an average of 3 months after acceptance. Byline given. Buys first serial rights and occasionally second serial (reprint) rights. Submit seasonal material (skiing, wine, outdoor living) 3 months in advance.

Will consider simultaneous (if the simultaneous submission is out of the area) and previously published submissions. Send information about when and where the article previously appeared. For reprints, pays $100-200. Reports in 1 month.

• *West* now accepts personal essays.

Nonfiction: A general newspaper-magazine requiring that subjects be related to California (especially the Bay Area) and the interests of California. Length: 1,000-4,000 words. Query with published clips. Pays $250-1,500. Sometimes (but infrequently) pays expenses of writers on assignment.

Photos: Tracy Cox, art director. Payment varies for b&w and color photos purchased with or without mss. Captions required.

Colorado

ASPEN MAGAZINE, Ridge Publications, P.O. Box G-3, Aspen CO 81612. (303)920-4040. Fax: (303)920-4044. Editor: Janet C. O'Grady. Associate Editors: Laura Smith and Kara Skouck. 85% freelance written. "We rarely accept submissions by new freelance writers." Bimonthly magazine covering Aspen and the Roaring Fork Valley. Estab. 1974. Circ. 16,000. Pays within 30 days of publication. Byline given. Kill fee varies. Buys first North American serial rights. Query for electronic submissions. Reports in 6 months. Sample copy for 9 × 12 SAE with 10 first-class stamps. Writer's guidelines for #10 SASE.

Nonfiction: Essay, historical, interview/profile, photo feature, enrivonmental and local issues, architecture and design, sports and outdoors, arts. "We do not publish general interest articles without a strong Aspen hook. We do not publish 'theme' (skiing in Aspen) or anniversary (40th year of Aspen Music Festival)." Buys 30-60 mss/year. Query with published clips. Length: 50-4,000 words. Pays $50-1,000.

Photos: Send photos with submission. Reviews contact sheets, negatives, transparencies, prints. Model release and identification of subjects required.

Columns/Departments: Town and mountain news, sports, business, travel, health, beauty, fitness, art news. "We rarely accept freelance travel stories. Virtually all travel is written in-house." Query with published clips. Length: 200-1,500. Pays $50-150.

FLATIRONS, The Boulder Magazine, Mac Media, Inc., 5775 Flatiron Pkwy., Suite 205, Boulder CO 80301-5730. (303)449-1847. Fax: (303)879-4650. Contact: Leland Rucker, Managing Editor. 80% freelance written. Semiannual magazine covering Boulder and Boulder County region. "*Flatirons—The Boulder Magazine* showcases the people, events, lifestyles, interests and history of Boulder and Boulder County. Our readers are generally well-educated, well-traveled, active people in the area or visiting the region from all 50 states and many foreign countries. Writing should be fresh, entertaining and informative." Estab. 1993. Circ. 30,000. Pays on publication. Publishes ms an average of 6 months after acceptance. Byline given. Offers 100% kill fee. Buys one-time rights. Editorial lead time 8-12 months. Submit seasonal material 8-12 months in advance. Accepts simultaneous and previously published submissions. Send photocopy of article with information about when and where the article previously appeared. Query for electronic submissions. Reports in 1 month on queries; 2 months on mss. Sample copy for $5.95 and SASE. Writer's guidelines free on request.

Nonfiction: Essays, general interest, historical/nostalgic, humor, interview/profile, personal experience, photo feature. "No poetry." Buys 10-15 mss/year. Query with published clips. Length: 500-3,000 words. Pays $100-500 for assigned articles; $50-300 for unsolicited articles. Sometimes pays expenses of writers on assignment.

Photos: State availability of photos with submission. Reviews transparencies. Offers $50-250/photo. Captions, model releases and identification of subjects required. Buys one-time rights.

Tips: "(1) It is essential for writers to study current and past issues of our magazine to become familiar with type and balance of subject matter and angles. (2) It is also helpful for writers to have visited our region to capture the unique 'sense of place' aspects we try to share with readers. (3) We try to make subjects and treatments 'timeless' in nature because the magazine is a 'keeper' with a multi-year shelf life. Western lifestyles and regional history are very popular topics for our readers. So are nature (including environmental subjects), sports and recreation. Please query first with ideas to make sure subjects are fresh and appropriate."

STEAMBOAT MAGAZINE, Mac Media Inc., 2955 Village Dr., P.O. Box 4328, Steamboat Springs CO 80477. (303)879-5250 ext. 12. Fax: (970)879-4650. E-mail: rwahl@csn.net. Editor: Rolly Wahl. 80% free-lance written. Semiannual magazine covering Steamboat Springs and Northwest Colorado region. "Steamboat Magazine showcases the history, people, lifestyles and interests of Northwest Colorado. Our readers are generally well educated, well travelled, active people visiting our region to ski in winter and recreate in summer. They come from all 50 states and many foreign countries. Writing should be fresh, entertaining and informative." Estab. 1978. Circ. 20,000. Pays on publication. Publishes ms an average of 6 months after acceptance. Byline given. Offers 100% kill fee. Buys one-time rights. Editorial lead time 8-12 months. Submit seasonal material 6-12 months in advance. Accepts simultaneous and previously published submissions. Send tearsheet or photocopy of article. For reprints, pays 50-75% of the amount paid for an original article. Query for electronic submissions. Reports in 1 month on queries; 2 months on mss. Sample copy for $5.95 and SAE with 10 first-class stamps. Writer's guidelines free on request.

Nonfiction: Essays, general interest, historical/nostalgic, humor, interview/profile, personal experience, photo feature. Buys 10-15 mss/year. Query with published clips. Length: 500-3,000 words. Pays $100-500 for assigned articles; $50-300 for unsolicited articles. Sometimes pays expenses of writers on assignment.

Photos: State availability of photos with submission. Reviews transparencies. Offers $50-250/photo. Captions, model releases, identification of subjects required. Buys one-time rights.

Tips: "Western lifestyles and regional history are very popular topics for our readers. So is nature (including environmental subjects) and sports and recreation. Please query first with ideas to make sure subjects are fresh and appropriate. We try to make subjects and treatments "timeless" in nature, because our magazine is a "keeper" with a multi-year shelf life."

VAIL/BEAVER CREEK MAGAZINE, Flatirons/Vail L.L.C., P.O. Box 4328, Steamboat Springs CO 80477. (970)476-6600. Editor: Don Berger. 80% freelance written. Semiannual magazine covering Vail, Central Rocky Mountains, and mountain living. "*Vail/Beaver Creek Magazine* showcases the lifestyles and history of the Vail Valley. We are particularly interested in personality profiles, home and design features, the arts, winter and summer recreation and adventure stories, and environmental articles." Estab. 1975. Circ. 30,000. Pays on publication. Publishes ms an average of 6 months after acceptance. Byline given. Offers 100% kill fee. Buys one-time rights. Editorial lead time 8-12 months. Submit seasonal material 8-12 months in advance. Accepts simultaneous submissions. Query for electronic submissions. Reports in 1 month on queries; 2 months on mss. Sample copy for $5.95 and SAE with 10 first-class stamps. Writer's guidelines free on request.

Nonfiction: Essays, general interest, historical/nostalgic, humor, interview/profile, personal experience, photo feature. Buys 20-25 mss/year. Query with published clips. Length: 500-3,000 words. Pays $100-500 for assigned articles; $50-300 for unsolicited articles. Sometimes pays expenses of writers on assignment.

Photos: State availability of photos with submission. Reviews transparencies. Offers $50-250/photo. Captions, model releases and identification of subjects required. Buys one-time rights.

Tips: "Be familiar with the Vail Valley and its 'personality.' Approach a story that will be relevant for several years to come. We produce a magazine that is a 'keeper.' "

Connecticut

CONNECTICUT MAGAZINE, Communications International, 789 Reservoir Ave., Bridgeport CT 06606. (203)374-3388. Fax: (203)371-0318. Editor: Charles Monagan. Managing Editor: Dale Salm. Editorial Assistant: Danielle McLeod. 80% freelance written. Prefers to work with published/established writers who know the state and live/have lived here. Monthly magazine covering the state of Connecticut "for an affluent, sophisticated, suburban audience. We want only articles that pertain to living in Connecticut." Estab. 1971. Circ. 93,000. Pays on publication. Publishes ms an average of 4 months after acceptance. Byline given. Offers 20% kill fee. Buys first North American serial rights. Submit seasonal/holiday material 4 months in advance. Reports in 6 weeks on queries. Writer's guidelines for #10 SASE.

Nonfiction: Book excerpts, exposé, general interest, interview/profile, other topics of service to Connecticut readers. No personal essays. Buys 50 mss/year. Query with published clips. Length: 2,500-4,200 words. Pays $600-1,200. Sometimes pays the expenses of writers on assignment.

Photos: Joan Barrow, art director. Send photos with submission. Reviews contact sheets and transparencies. Offers $50 minimum/photo. Model releases and identification of subjects required. Buys one-time rights.

Columns/Departments: Business, Health, Politics, Connecticut Guide, Arts, Gardening, Environment, Education, People, Sports, Media. Buys 50 mss/year. Query with published clips. Length: 1,500-2,500 words. Pays $300-600.

Fillers: Around and About editor—Valerie Schroth, senior editor. Short pieces about Connecticut trends, curiosities, interesting short subjects, etc. Buys 50/year. Length: 150-400 words. Pays $75.

Tips: "Make certain that your idea is not something that has been covered to death by the local press and can withstand a time lag of a few months. Freelancers can best break in with Around and About; find a Connecticut story that is offbeat and write it up in a fun, lighthearted, interesting manner. Again, we don't want something that has already received a lot of press."

NORTHEAST MAGAZINE, *The Hartford Courant*, 285 Broad St., Hartford CT 06115-2510. (203)241-3700. Editor: Lary Bloom. 50% freelance written. Eager to work with new/unpublished writers. Weekly magazine for a Connecticut audience. Estab. 1982. Circ. 300,000. **Pays on acceptance.** Publishes ms an average of 10 months after acceptance. Byline given. Buys one-time rights. Reports in 3 months.

Nonfiction: General interest (has to have strong Connecticut tie-in); in-depth investigation of stories behind news (has to have strong Connecticut tie-in); historical/nostalgic; interview/profile (of famous or important people with Connecticut ties); personal essays (humorous or anecdotal). No poetry. Buys 50 mss/year. Length: 750-2,500 words. Pays $200-1,500.

Photos: Most assigned; state availability of photos. "Do not send originals."

Fiction: Well-written, original short stories and (rarely) novel excerpts. Length: 750-1,500 words.

Tips: "Less space available for all types of writing means our standards for acceptance will be much higher. We can only print three to four short stories a year."

District of Columbia

THE WASHINGTON POST, 1150 15th St. NW, Washington DC 20071. (202)334-7750. Travel Editor: Linda L. Halsey. 60% freelance written. Prefers to work with published/established writers. Weekly newspaper travel section (Sunday). Pays on publication. Publishes ms an average of 3-6 months after acceptance. Byline given. "We are now emphasizing staff-written articles as well as quality writing from other sources. Stories are rarely assigned; all material comes in on speculation; there is no fixed kill fee." Buys only first North American serial rights. Travel must not be subsidized in any way. Usually reports in 1 month. *Writer's Market* recommends allowing 2 months for reply.

Nonfiction: Emphasis is on travel writing with a strong sense of place, color, anecdote and history. Query with published clips. Length: 1,500-2,500 words, plus sidebar for practical information.

Photos: State availability of photos with ms.

THE WASHINGTONIAN MAGAZINE, 1828 L St. NW, Suite 200, Washington DC 20036-5169. Editor: John A. Limpert. Assistant Editor: Courtney Denby. 20% freelance written. Prefers to work with published/established writers who live in the Washington area. Monthly magazine for active, affluent and well-educated audience. Estab. 1965. Circ. 157,055. Buys first rights only. Pays on publication. Publishes ms an average of 2 months after acceptance. Accepts simultaneous submissions. Reports in 3 months. Sample copy for $5 and 9 × 12 SAE. Writer's guidelines for #10 SASE.

● The editors have specified that they do not take much freelance work.

Nonfiction: *"The Washingtonian* is written for Washingtonians. The subject matter is anything we feel might interest people interested in the mind and manners of the city. The only thing we ask is thoughtfulness and that no subject be treated too reverently. Audience is literate. We assume considerable sophistication about the city and a sense of humor." Buys how-to, personal experience, interview/profile, humor, think pieces, exposés. Buys 40 mss/year. Length: 1,000-7,000 words; average feature 4,000 words. Pays 50¢/word. Sometimes pays the expenses of writers on assignment. Query or submit complete ms.

Photos: Photos rarely purchased with mss.

Fiction: Publishes novel excerpts.

Florida

BOCA RATON MAGAZINE, JES Publishing, Suite 100, 6413 Congress Ave., Boca Raton FL 33487. (407)997-8683. Fax: (407)997-8909. Editor: Marie Speed. 70% freelance written. Bimonthly magazine covering Boca Raton lifestyles. "Ours is a lifestyle magazine devoted to the residents of South Florida, featuring fashion, interior design, food, people, places and issues that shape the affluent South Florida market." Estab. 1981. Circ. 20,000. **Pays on acceptance.** Publishes ms an average of 3 months after acceptance. Byline given. Offers $50 kill fee. Buys second serial (reprint) rights. Submit seasonal material 7 months in advance. Accepts simultaneous and previously published submissions. Send tearsheet of article. Pays 50% of amount paid for an original article. Query for electronic submission. Reports in 1 month. Sample copy for $3.95 for 10 × 13 SAE with 10 first-class stamps. Writer's guidelines for #10 SASE.

● No longer publishes fiction.

Nonfiction: General interest, historical/nostalgic, humor, interview/profile, photo feature, travel. Query with or without published clips, or send complete ms. Length: 800-2,500 words. Pays $50-500 for assigned articles; $50-300 for unsolicited articles. Sometimes pays expenses of writers on assignment.

Photos: Send photos with submission.

Columns/Departments: Body & Soul (health, fitness and beauty column, general interest), 1,000 words; Family Room (family and social interactions), 1,000 words; Humor (South Florida topics), 600-1,200 words. Buys 6 mss/year. Query with published clips or send complete ms. Length: 600-1,500 words. Pays $50-250.

FLORIDA KEYS MAGAZINE, Gibbons Publishing, Inc., P.O. Box 6524, Key West FL 33040. (800)273-1026. Fax: (305)296-7300. Editor: Gibbons D. Cline. Contact: Laura Watts, associate editor. 75% freelance written. Bimonthly magazine for lifestyle in the Florida Keys. "*FKM* caters to full-time residents of the Florida Keys. These are people with a unique lifestyle and a rich, colorful history." Estab. 1978. Circ. 10,000. Pays on publication. Publishes ms an average of 4-6 months after acceptance. Byline given. Buys first North American serial, first or all rights. Editorial lead time 4-6 months. Submit seasonal material at least 6 months in advance. Query for electronic submissions. Reports in 1 month weeks on queries; 2 months on mss. Sample copy for $2.50. Writer's guidelines free on request.

Nonfiction: General interest, historical/nostalgic, how-to (water sports, home improvement, gardening, crafts), humor, interview/profile (keys residents *only*), travel. Special issues: Fantasy Fest-Key West (Halloween); Home & Garden; Gourmet. "No erotica or personal experiences in the Keys . . . please do not send Hemingway-related stories or stories regarding your Keys vacation!" Buys 20-30 mss/year. Query with published clips. Length: 500-2,000 words. Pays $2/column inch, $100 maximum per story.

Photos: Send photos with submissions. Reviews transparencies (any size), prints, slides. Offers no additional payment for photos accepted with ms. Model releases and identification of subjects required. Buys all rights.

Columns/Departments: Dining Guide (Keys recipes, restaurant reviews), 1,200 words; Weekend Escapes (trips in our own backyards); Key Nomics (bargain and important economic issues); Nature of the Keys (environmental issues); Fact or Fishin'? (Fishing tales, tips, tournaments and recipes); History of the Keys; Health Matters (easy-to-use info on health and fitness).

Tips: "It is difficult to write about Keys unless writer is resident of Monroe County, Florida, or frequent visitor. Must be familiar with unique atmosphere and lifestyle of Florida Keys. Request résumé to be submitted with query and/or mss. If author is unfamiliar with Keys, massive research is suggested (strongly). We are most open to new and unusual angles on fishing, boating, diving, snorkeling, sailing, shelling, sunbathing and Keys special events."

FLORIDA LIVING, North Florida Publishing Co. Inc., 102 NE Tenth Ave., Suite 6, Gainesville FL 32601-2322. Fax: (904)372-3453. Editor: E. Douglas Cifers. Monthly lifestyle magazine covering Florida subjects for Floridians and would be Floridians. Estab. 1981. Circ. 41,000. Publishes ms an average of 3-6 months after acceptance. Byline given. No kill fee. Buys one-time rights. Submit seasonal/holiday material 3-12 months in advance. Reports in 2 months. Writer's guidelines sent on request with SASE.

Nonfiction: General Florida interest, historical/nostalgic, interview/profile, personal experience, travel, out-of-the-way Florida places. Buys 50-60 mss/year. Query. Length: 500-1,500 words. Pays $25-200 for assigned articles; $25-100 for unsolicited articles.

Photos: Send photos with submission. Reviews 3 × 5 color prints. Offers up to $10/photo. Captions required. Buys one-time rights.

Fiction: Historical. Buys 2-3 mss/year. Send complete ms. Length: 1,000-3,000 words. Publishes novel excerpts. Pays $50-200.

‡GULFSHORE LIFE, 2975 S. Horseshoe Dr., Suite 100, Naples FL 33942. (813)643-3933. Fax: (813)643-5017. Editor: Amy Bennett. 75% freelance written. Lifestyle magazine published 11 times/year for southwest Florida. Estab. 1970. Circ. 26,000. Pays on publication. Publishes ms an average of 4 months after acceptance. Byline given. Offers 25-33% kill fee. Buys first North American serial rights. Submit seasonal/holiday material 8 months in advance. Accepts simultaneous and previously published submissions. Sample copy for 9 × 12 SAE with 10 first-class stamps.

Nonfiction: Historical/nostalgic (SW Florida), interview/profile (SW Florida), issue/trend (SW Florida). All articles must be related to SW Florida. Buys 100 mss/year. Query with published clips. Length: 500-3,000 words. Pays $100-1,000 for assigned articles. Accepts previously published submissions. Send photocopy of article or tearsheet and information about when and where the article previously appeared. Fee negotiated.

Photos: Send photos with submission, if available. Reviews 35mm transparencies and 5 × 7 prints. Pays $25-50. Model releases and identification of subjects required. Buys one-time rights.

Tips: "We buy superbly written stories that illuminate southwest Florida personalities, places and issues. Surprise us!"

JACKSONVILLE, White Publishing Co., 1650 Prudential Dr., Suite 300, Jacksonville FL 32207. (904)396-8666. Editor-in-Chief: Larry Marscheck. 80% freelance written. Consumer magazine published 10 times/year covering life and business in Northeast Florida. "City/regional magazine for Jacksonville and the Beaches, Orange Park, St. Augustine and Amelia Island, Florida." Targets upwardly mobile residents. Estab. 1985. Circ. 25,000. Pays on publication. Byline given. Offers 25-33% kill fee. Buys first North American serial rights or second serial (reprint) rights. Editorial lead time 3 months. Submit seasonal 4 months in advance. Accepts previously published submissions. Send photocopy of article and include information about when and where it first appeared. For reprints, pays 33% of the amount paid for an original article. Query for electronic submissions. Reports in 4-6 weeks on queries; 1 month on mss. Sample copy for $5 (includes postage). Writer's guidelines free on request.

● This regional publication won 13 awards in 1994 for general excellence, writing and design from the Florida Magazine Association.

Nonfiction: Book excerpts, exposé, general interest, historical/nostalgic, how-to (service articles), humor, interview/profile, personal experience, photo feature, travel, local business successes, trends, personalities, how institutions work. "First Coast Guide is July/August issue—essentially a city guide for Northeast Florida region." All articles must have relevance to Jacksonville and Florida's First Coast (Duval, Clay, St. Johns, Nassau, Baker counties). Buys 50 mss/year. Query with published clips. Length: 1,200-3,000 words. Pays $50-500 for feature-length pieces. Sometimes pays expenses of writers on assignment.

Photos: State availability of photos with submission. Reviews contact sheets, transparencies. Negotiates payment individually. Captions, model releases required. Buys one-time rights.

Columns/Departments: Business (trends, success stories, personalities), 1,200-1,500 words; Health (trends, emphasis on people, hopeful outlooks, 1,200-1,500 words; Smart Money (practical personal financial/advice using local people, anecdotes and examples), 1,200-1,500 words; Real Estate/Home (service, trends, home photo features), 1,000-1,200 words; Hot Shot (local person worth noting), 300 words. Buys 40 mss/year. Pays $200-300.

Fiction: Adventure, condensed novels, historical, humorous, mainstream, mystery, novel excerpts, science fiction, slice-of-life vignettes, but *all* must have Jacksonville or Northeast Florida setting and/or characters. Buys 1 or more mss/year. Send complete ms. Length: 1,200-3,000 words. Pays $250-500. "It should be noted that we have bought only a few fiction pieces since publication began. We are open to buying more, if they are well-written and relevant to our area."

Tips: "We are a writer's magazine, therefore we demand writing that tells a story with flair. While the whole magazine is open to freelancers, new writers can break in via 'Short Takes'—50-300 word stories about trends, phenomena and people in the First Coast area."

ORLANDO MAGAZINE, Abarto Metro Publishing, 260 Maitland Ave., Suite 2000, P.O. Box 2207, Altamonte Springs FL 32701. (407)539-3939. Fax: (407)539-0533. 90% freelance written. Monthly magazine covering the greater Orlando area and its people, features include profiles, business, food, interiors, travel. Estab. 1946. Circ. 33,000. Pays on publication. Publishes ms an average of 4 months after acceptance. Byline given. Offers kill fee. Submit seasonal/holiday material 8 months in advance. Accepts simultaneous submissions. Reports in 2 months. Sample copy for $5. Writer's guidelines for #10 SASE..

Nonfiction: Buys 12-15 mss/year. Send complete ms. Length: 1,500-2,500 words. Pays $100-450 for articles. "Looking for insightful and entertaining articles that create a sense of community pride by informing readers about people, issues and businesses that impact their lives. Publishes 6-10 issue-oriented stories per year."

Photos: Send photos with submission. Reviews transparencies. Offers $5/photo. Captions and identification of subjects required. Buys one-time rights.

Columns/Departments: Food, Interiors, City Life, Neighborhood Life. All submissions should have local slant. Length: 1,200 words. Buys 5-10 mss/year. Pays $200-300.

PALM BEACH LIFE, Palm Beach Newspapers Inc./Cox Enterprises, 265 Royal Poinciana Way, Palm Beach FL 33480-4063. (407)820-3800. Fax: (407)655-4594. Contact: Leta Barnes. 100% freelance written. Semiannual magazine, a regional publication for Palm Beach County and South Florida. Estab. 1906. Circ. 26,000. **Pays on acceptance.** Publishes ms an average of 3 months after acceptance. Byline given. Buys first North American serial rights. Submit seasonal/holiday material 6 months in advance. Query for electronic submission. Reports in 1 month.

Nonfiction: Essays, exposé, general interest, historical/nostalgic, humor, interview/profile, photo feature, travel. Buys 100 mss/year. Query with published clips. Length: 900-5,000 words. Pays $150-700 for assigned articles; $75-400 for unsolicited articles. Sometimes pays expenses of writers on assignment (depending on agreed-upon fee).

Photos: Send photos with submission. Reviews transparencies. Offers $35-200 per photo. Captions, model releases, identification of subjects required. Buys one-time rights.

Columns/Departments: Travel (specifically focused topical travel pieces), 1,500 words; High Profile (profiles of people of interest to readers in our region), 2,500 words. Buys 36 mss/year. Query with published clips. Pays $75-400.

PENSACOLA MAGAZINE, PEC Printing and Publishing, 2101 W. Government St., Pensacola FL 32501. (904)438-5421. Fax: (904)434-2785. Editor: Donna Peoples. 100% freelance written. Magazine published 11 times/year for news about city of Pensacola. Estab. 1983. Pays on publication. Publishes ms an average of 2 months after acceptance. Byline given. Buys one-time or second serial (reprint) rights or makes work-for-hire assignments. Editorial lead time 2 months. Submit seasonal material 4 months in advance. Accepts simultaneous and previously published submissions. Send photocopy of article and information about when and where the article previously appeared. For reprints, pays 100% of the amount paid for an original article. Query for electronic submissions. Reports in 3 weeks on queries; 1 month on mss. *Writer's Market* recommends allowing 2 months for reply. Sample copy for $3.

Nonfiction: General interest, historical/nostalgic, how-to, humor, interview/profile (of Pensacola residents), photo feature, travel. Rarely runs stories that don't relate to Pensacola other than travel articles. Buys 80 mss/year. Query with published clips. Length: 800-1,500 words. Pays 7¢/word.

Photos: Send photos with submission. Reviews contact sheets, transparencies and prints. Offers $35/photo minimum. Negotiates payment individually. Captions, model releases and identification of subjects required. Buys one-time rights.

SENIOR VOICE OF FLORIDA, Florida's Leading Newspaper for Active Mature Adults, Suncoast Publishing Group, 6281 39th St. N., Suite F, Pinellas Park FL 34665-6040. Publisher: Donna Castellanos. Editor: Nancy Yost. 25% freelance written. Prefers to work with published/established writers. Monthly newspaper for mature adults 50 years of age and over. Estab. 1981. Circ. 70,000. Pays on publication.

Publishes ms an average of 3 months after acceptance. Byline given. Buys one-time rights. Submit seasonal material 3 months in advance. Accepts simultaneous and previously published submissions. Send typed ms with rights for sale noted. For reprints, pays flat fee. Reports in 2 months. Sample copy for $1 and 10×13 SAE with 6 first-class stamps.

Nonfiction: Exposé, general interest, historical/nostalgic, how-to, humor, inspirational, interview/profile, opinion, photo feature, travel, health, finance, all slanted to a senior audience. Buys 10 mss/year. Query or send complete ms. Length: 300-600 words. Pays $15.

Photos: Send photos with submission. Reviews 3×5 color and 5×7 b&w prints. Identification of subjects required.

Columns/Departments: Travel (senior slant) and V.I.P. Profiles (mature adults). Buys 10 mss/year. Send complete ms. Length: 300-600 words. Pays $15.

Fillers: Anecdotes, facts, cartoons short humor. Buys 10/year. Length: 150-250 words. Pays $10.

Tips: "Our service area is the Florida Gulf Coast, an area with a high population of resident retirees and repeat visitors who are 50 plus. We are interested primarily in serving their needs. In writing for that readership, keep their interests in mind. What they are interested in, we are interested in. We like a clean, concise writing style. Photos are important."

‡SOUTH FLORIDA, Florida Media Affiliates, 800 Douglas Rd., Suite 500, Coral Gables FL 33134. (305)445-4500. Fax: (305)445-4600. Editor: Jerry Renninger. 50% freelance written. Monthly general interest magazine for Miami, Fort Lauderdale, the Florida Keys and Palm Beach County. *Editor's note: This magazine has a new editorial focus—more topical, more newsy, harder edged; fewer soft articles.* Estab. 1975. Circ. 70,000. Pays 30-45 days after acceptance. Publishes ms an average of 3 months after acceptance. Byline given. Buys first North American serial rights. Submit seasonal material 4 months in advance. Query for electronic submissions. Reports in 2 month on queries. Sample copy for $3 plus 5 first-class stamps. Florida residents add 6% sales tax. Writer's guidelines for #10 SASE.

Nonfiction: Exposé, general interest, interview/profile, lifestyle. Buys 120 mss/year. Query with published clips. Length: 3,500 words maximum. Pays $100-750 for assigned articles. Sometimes pays expenses of writers on assignment.

Photos: Send photos with submission. Identification of subjects required. Buys one-time rights.

SUNSHINE: THE MAGAZINE OF SOUTH FLORIDA, The Sun-Sentinel Co., 200 E. Las Olas Blvd., Fort Lauderdale FL 33301-2293. (305)356-4685. Editor: John Parkyn. 60% freelance written. Prefers to work with published/established writers, but works with a small number of new/unpublished writers each year. General interest Sunday magazine "for the *Sun-Sentinel's* 800,000 readers in South Florida." Circ. 360,000. Pays within 1 month of acceptance. Publishes ms an average of 2 months after acceptance. Byline given. Offers 25% kill fee for assigned material. Buys first serial rights or one-time rights in the state of Florida. Submit seasonal/holiday material 2 months in advance. Accepts simultaneous and previously published submissions. Send tearsheet or photocopy of article or typed ms with rights for sale noted and information about when and where the article previously appeared. Reports in 1 month on queries; 2 months on mss. Free sample copy and writer's guidelines.

Nonfiction: General interest, interview/profile, travel. "Articles must be relevant to the interests of adults living in South Florida." Buys about 150 mss/year. Query with published clips. Length: 1,000-3,000 words; preferred length 2,000-2,500 words. Pays 25¢/word to $1,000 maximum.

Photos: Send photos. Pays negotiable rate for 35mm and 2¼ color slides. Captions and identification of subjects required; model releases required for sensitive material. Buys one-time rights for the state of Florida.

Tips: "Do not phone, but do include your phone number on query letter. Keep your writing tight and concise—readers don't have the time to wade through masses of prose. We are always in the market for first-rate profiles, human-interest stories and travel stories (which usually spotlight destinations within easy access of South Florida, e.g. Southeastern US, Caribbean, Central America). Freelancers should also consider our 1,000-word 'First Person' feature, which describes personal experiences of unusual interest."

TROPIC MAGAZINE, Sunday Magazine of the Miami Herald, Knight Ridder, 1 Herald Plaza, Miami FL 33132-1693. (305)376-3432. Editor: Bill Rose. Executive Editor: Tom Shroder. 20% freelance written. Works with small number of new/unpublished writers each year. Weekly magazine covering general interest, locally oriented topics for local readers. Circ. 500,000. Pays on publication. Publishes ms an average of 2 months after acceptance. Byline given. Buys first serial rights. Submit seasonal material 2 months in advance. Accepts previously published submissions. Send photocopy of article and information about when and where the article previously appeared. Pays 50% of the amount paid for an original article. Reports in 3 months. Sample copy for 11 × 14 SAE.

Nonfiction: General interest, interview/profile (first person), personal experience. No fiction or poetry. Buys 20 mss/year. Query with published clips or send complete ms with SASE. Length: 1,500-3,000 words. Pays $200-1,000/article.

Photos: Janet Santelices, art director. Send photos.

‡**WEEKLY PLANET**, (formerly *Creative Loafing/Tampa*), 402 Reo St., Suite 218, Tampa FL 33609. (819)286-1600. Editor: Susan Dix Tibbits. 75% freelance written. Alternative newsweekly tabloid covering news, arts and entertainment. "We welcome thoughtful and provocative pieces responsibly reported for well-read audience ages 25-44." Estab. 1988. Circ. 70,000. Pays on publication. Byline given. Offers 35% kill fee. Buys first rights. Editorial lead time 2 months. Submit seasonal material 3 months in advance. Query for electronic submissions. Reports in 3 weeks on queries; 1 month on mss.

Nonfiction: Exposé, interview/profile, opinion and photo feature. "No puff or promotional pieces." Buys 52 mss/year. Query with published clips or send complete ms. Length: 2,000-3,000 words. Pays $200 minimum. Sometimes pays expenses of writers on assignment.

Photos: Send photos with submission. Reviews 3 × 5 min. prints. Offers $25-50/photo. Buys all rights.

Columns/Departments: Opinion (local, timely), 500 words; art review (local,timely), 500-800 words. Buys 200 mss/year. Query with published clips or send complete ms. Pays $75-100.

Georgia

GEORGIA JOURNAL, The Indispensable Atlanta Co., Inc., P.O. Box 1604, Decatur GA 30031-1604. (404)377-4275. Fax: (404)377-1820. Editor: David R. Osier. 90% freelance written. Works with a small number of new/unpublished writers each year. Quarterly magazine covering the state of Georgia. Estab. 1980. Circ. 15,000. Please query first. Pays on publication. Publishes ms an average of 6-12 months after acceptance. Byline given. Buys first serial rights. Submit seasonal material 6 months in advance. Reports in 6 months. Sample copy for $4.50. Writer's guidelines for #10 SASE.

Nonfiction: "*Georgia Journal* primarily is interested in *authoritative* nonfiction articles with a *well-defined point of view* on any aspect of Georgia's human and natural history. Included among these are articles on the roles historic personalities played in shaping our state, important yet sometimes overlooked historical/political events, archaeological discoveries, unsolved mysteries (both natural and human), flora and fauna, and historic preservation. Sidebars are encouraged, such as interesting marginalia and bibliographies. We also are looking for adventures that explore the Georgia landscape. These can range from weekend antique hunting, camping, walking tours, arts & crafts festivals, and auto trips to more strenuous activities such as biking, boating, rafting, back-packing, rock climbing and caving. Adventures should also have a well-defined point of view, and be told through the author's personal experience. Articles should be accompanied by detailed map data and other pertinent location information, such as tips on access, lodging and camping. *Georgia Journal* has a place for authoritative topical articles as well, ranging from those about Georgia's environment, mysteries and trends in Georgia living to profiles of Georgia authors, adventurers, artisans, artists, sports figures and other personalities." Buys 30-40 mss/year. Query. Length: 200-5,000 words. Pays 10¢/word.

Columns/Departments: Books and writers; interesting or historic houses/buildings for sale; Commentary section; Pure Georgia—uses shorter pieces; Calendar of events; reviews of restaurants, B&Bs and historic inns.

Fiction: See submission guidelines. *Georgia Journal* does publish a limited amount of fiction, but while it encourages promising new writers, it is not looking for first-time or unpublished authors. Optimum length is 4,000 words. Stories must have a Georgia theme or Georgia setting. Payment varies, depending on publishing history. Unless mss are submitted with a return envelope with sufficient postage, they will not be returned.

Poetry: Janice Moore. Free verse, haiku, light verse, traditional. Uses poetry from or dealing with the South which is suitable for a general audience. Uses 20 poems/year. Submit maximum 4 poems. Length: 25 lines. Pays in copies.

‡**NORTH GEORGIA JOURNAL**, Legacy Communications, Inc., P.O. Box 127, Roswell GA 30077. Editor: Olin Jackson. 70% freelance written. Quarterly magazine covering travel and history, "designed for readers interested in travel, history, and mountain lifestyles of the North Georgia region." Estab. 1987. Circ. 17,000. Pays on publication. Publishes ms an average of 5 months after acceptance. Byline given. Offers 25% kill fee. Buys first and all rights. Editorial lead time 6 months. Submit seasonal material 6 months in advance. No simultaneous or previously published submissions. Sample copy for 9 × 12 SAE and 8 first-class stamps. Writer's guidelines for #10 SASE.

Nonfiction: Historical/nostalgic, how-to (survival techniques; mountain living; do-it-yourself home construction and repairs, etc.), interview/profile (celebrity), personal experience (anything unique or unusual pertaining to north Georgia mountains), photo feature (any subject of a historic nature which can be photographed in a seasonal context, i.e.—old mill with brilliant yellow jonquils in foreground), travel (subjects highlighting travel opportunities in North Georgia). Query with published clips. Pays $75-350 for assigned articles.

Photos: Send photos with submission. Reviews contact sheets, transparencies. Negotiates payment individually. Captions, model releases, identification of subjects required. Buys all rights.

Tips: "Good photography is crucial to the acceptance of all articles. Send written queries then *wait* for a response. *No telephone calls please*. The most useful material involves a first person experience of an individual who has explored a historic site or scenic locale and *interviewed* a person or persons who were involved with or have first-hand knowledge of a historic site/event. Interviews and quotations are crucial to acceptance. Articles should be told in the writer's own words."

Hawaii

ALOHA, THE MAGAZINE OF HAWAII AND THE PACIFIC, Davick Publications, P.O. Box 3260, Honolulu HI 96801. (808)593-1191. Fax: (808)593-1327. Editorial Director: Cheryl Tsutsumi. 50% freelance written. Bimonthly regional magazine of international interest. "Most of our readers do not live in Hawaii, although most readers have been to the Islands at least once. The magazine is directed primarily to residents of Hawaii in the belief that presenting material to an immediate critical audience will result in a true and accurate presentation that can be appreciated by everyone. Travelers to Hawaii will find *Aloha* shares vignettes of the real Hawaii. Estab. 1977. Circ. 65,000. Pays on publication. Publishes ms an average of 6 months after acceptance; unsolicited ms can take a year or more. Byline given. Offers variable kill fee. Buys first rights. Submit seasonal material 1 year in advance. Reports in 2 months. Sample copy for $3.95 with SAE and 10 first-class stamps. Free writer's guidelines.

Nonfiction: Book excerpts, historical/nostalgic (historical articles must be researched with bibliography), interview/profile, photo features. Subjects include the arts, business, flora and fauna, people, sports, destinations, food, interiors, history of Hawaii. "We don't want stories of a tourist's experiences in Waikiki or odes to beautiful scenery." Buys 24 mss/year. Query with published clips. Length: 1,000-4,000 words. Pay ranges from $200-500. Sometimes pays expenses of writers on assignment.

Photos: Send photos with query. Pays $25 for b&w prints; prefers negatives and contact sheets. Pays $60 for 35mm (minimum size) color transparencies used inside; $125 for double-page bleeds; $250 for color transparencies used as cover art. "*ALOHA* features Beautiful Hawaii, a collection of photographs illustrating that theme, in every issue. A second photo essay by a sole photographer on a theme of his/her own choosing is also published occasionally. Queries are essential for the sole photographer essay." Model releases and identification of subjects required. Buys one-time rights.

Fiction: Ethnic, historical. "Fiction depicting a tourist's adventures in Waikiki is not what we're looking for. As a general statement, we welcome material reflecting the true Hawaiian experience." Buys 2 mss/year. Send complete ms. Length: 1,000-2,500 words. Pays $300.

Poetry: Haiku, light verse, traditional. No seasonal poetry or poetry related to other areas of the world. Buys 6 poems/year. Submit maximum 6 poems. Prefers "shorter poetry"—20 lines or less. Pays $30.

Tips: "Read *ALOHA*. Be meticulous in your research and have good illustrative material available to accompany your text."

HAWAII MAGAZINE, Fancy Publications, Inc., 1400 Kapiolani Blvd., A-25, Honolulu HI 96814. (808)942-2556. Fax: (808)947-0924. Editor: Jim Borg. Managing Editor: Julie Applebaum. 60% freelance written. Bimonthly magazine covering The Islands of Hawaii. "*Hawaii Magazine* is written for residents and frequent visitors who enjoy the culture, people and places of the Hawaiian Islands." Estab. 1984. Circ. 71,000. Pays on publication. Byline given. Buys first North American serial rights. Submit seasonal material 6 months in advance. Query for electronic submissions. Reports in 1 month on queries; 6 weeks on mss. Sample copy for $3.95. Free writer's guidelines.

Nonfiction: General interest, historical/nostalgic, how-to, interview/profile, personal experience, photo feature, travel. "No articles on the following: first trip to Hawaii—How I discovered the Islands, the Hula, Poi, or Luaus." Buys 66 mss/year. Query with or without published clips or send complete ms. Length: 4,000 words maximum. Pays $100-500 for assigned articles.

Photos: Send photos with submission. Reviews contact sheets and transparencies. Offers $35-250 per photo. Identification of subjects preferred. Buys one-time rights.

Columns/Departments: Backdoor Hawaii (a light or nostalgic look at culture or history), 800-1,200 words; Hopping the Islands (news, general interest items), 100-200 words. Buys 6-12 mss/year. Query. Length: 800-1,500 words. Pays $100-200.

Tips: "Freelancers must be knowledgeable about Island subjects, virtual authorities on them. We see far too many first-person, wonderful-experience types of gushing articles. We buy articles only from people who are thoroughly grounded in the subject on which they are writing."

HONOLULU, Honolulu Publishing Co., Ltd., 36 Merchant St., Honolulu HI 96813. (808)524-7400. Fax: (808)531-2306. Publisher: John Alves. Editor: John Heckathorn. Managing Editor: Janice Otaguro. 50% freelance written. Prefers to work with published/established writers. Monthly magazine covering general interest topics relating to Hawaii. Estab. 1888. Circ. 75,000. **Pays on acceptance.** Publishes ms an average of 4 months after acceptance. Byline given. Buys first serial rights. Submit seasonal material 5 months in advance. Accepts simultaneous submissions. Reports in 2 months. Sample copy for $2 and 9×12 SAE with 8 first-class stamps. Free writer's guidelines.

• *Honolulu* has more than doubled its need for freelance writing.

Nonfiction: Exposé, general interest, historical/nostalgic, photo feature—all Hawaii-related. "We write for Hawaii residents, so travel articles about Hawaii are not appropriate." Buys 30 mss/year. Query with published clips if available. Length: 2,000-4,000 words. Pays $100-700. Sometimes pays expenses of writers on assignment.

Photos: Teresa Black, photo editor. Send photos. Pays $15 maximum for b&w contact sheet; $25 maximum for 35mm transparencies. Captions and identification of subjects required. Buys one-time rights.

Columns/Departments: Calabash ("newsy," timely, humorous column on any Hawaii-related subject). Buys 15 mss/year. Query with published clips or send complete ms. Length: 50-750 words. Pays $35-100. First Person (personal experience or humor). Buys 10 mss/year. Length: 1,500 words. Pays $200.

Illinois

CHICAGO LIFE, P.O. Box 11311, Chicago IL 60611-0311. E-mail: chgolife@mcs.com. Editor: Pam Berns. Managing Editor: Paula Lyon. 95% freelance written. Bimonthly magazine on Chicago life. Estab. 1984. Circ. 60,000. Pays on publication. Byline given. Kill fee varies. Submit seasonal/holiday material 8 months in advance. Accepts simultaneous and previously published submissions. Send photocopy of article and information about when and where the article previously appeared. Pays 100% of the amount paid for an original article. Reports in 3 months. Sample copy for 9×12 SAE with 7 first-class stamps.

Nonfiction: Book excerpts, essays, exposé, how-to, photo feature, travel. Buys 50 mss/year. Send complete ms. Length: 400-1,200 words. Pays $30 for unsolicited articles. Sometimes pays the expenses of writers on assignment.

Photos: Send photos with submission. Reviews contact sheets, negatives, transparencies, prints. Offers $15-30/photo. Buys one-time rights.

Columns/Departments: Law, Book Reviews, Travel. Send complete ms. Length: 500 words. Pays $30.

Fillers: Facts. Pays $15-30.

Tips: "Please send finished work with visuals (photos, if possible). Topics open include travel, self improvement, how-to-do almost anything, entrepreneurs, how to get rich, beautiful, more well-informed."

CHICAGO MAGAZINE, 414 N. Orleans, Chicago IL 60610-4409. Fax: (312)222-0699. Managing Editor: Shane Tritsch. 40% freelance written. Prefers to work with published/established writers. Monthly magazine for an audience which is "95% from Chicago area; 90% college educated; upper income, overriding interests in the arts, politics, dining, good life in the city and suburbs. Most are in 25-50 age bracket, well-read and articulate." Estab. 1968. Circ. 165,000. Buys first serial rights. **Pays on acceptance.** Publishes ms an average of 6 months after acceptance. Submit seasonal material 4 months in advance. Reports in 1 month. Query; indicate "specifics, knowledge of city and market, and demonstrable access to sources." For sample copy, send $3 to Circulation Dept. Writer's guidelines for #10 SASE.

Nonfiction: "On themes relating to the quality of life in Chicago: past, present, and future." Writers should have "a general awareness that the readers will be concerned, influential longtime Chicagoans reading what the writer has to say about their city. We generally publish material too comprehensive for daily newspapers." Personal experience and think pieces, profiles, humor, spot news, historical articles, exposés. Buys about 50 mss/year. Length: 500-6,000 words. Pays $100-$2,500. Pays expenses of writers on assignment.

Photos: Reviews b&w glossy prints, 35mm color transparencies or color prints. Usually assigned separately, not acquired from writers.

Tips: "Submit detailed queries, be business-like and avoid clichéd ideas."

THE CHICAGO TRIBUNE MAGAZINE, Chicago Tribune Newspaper, 435 N. Michigan Ave., Chicago IL 60611. (312)222-3573. Editor: Denis Gosselin. Managing Editor: Douglas Balz. 50% freelance written. Weekly Sunday magazine. "We look for unique, compelling, all-researched, eloquently written articles on subjects of general interest." Circ. 1.3 million. Pays on publication. Publishes ms an average of 2 months after acceptance. Offers $250 kill fee. Buys one-time rights. Submit seasonal/holiday material 6 months in advance. Query for electronic submissions. Reports in 1 month on queries; 6 weeks on mss.

Nonfiction: Book excerpts, exposé, general interest, interview/profile, photo feature, technical, travel. Buys 35 mss/year. Query or send complete ms. Length: 2,500-5,000 words. Pays $750-1,000. Sometimes pays the expenses of writers on assignment.

Photos: Send photos with submission. Payment varies for photos. Captions and identification of subjects required. Buys one-time rights.

Columns/Departments: First Person (Chicago area subjects only, talking about their occupations), 1,000 words; Chicago Voices (present or former high-profile Chicago area residents with their observations on or reminiscences of the city of Chicago), 1,000 words. Buys 40 mss/year. Query. pays $250. Buys 52 mss/year. Query. Pays $250.
Fiction: Length: 1,500-2,000 words. Pays $750-1,000.

‡NEAR WEST GAZETTE, Near West Gazette Publishing Co., 1660 W. Ogden Ave., Suite 301, Chicago IL 60612. (312)243-4288. Editor: Mark J. Valentino. Associate Editor: William S. Bike. 50% freelance written. Eager to work with new/unpublished writers. Monthly neighborhood newspaper covering Near West Side of Chicago and South Loop/Dearborn Park community. News and issues for residents, students and faculty of the neighborhood west of the University of Illinois of Chicago. Estab. 1983. Circ. 10,000. Pays on publication. Publishes ms an average of 1 month after acceptance. Byline given. Not copyrighted. Buys one-time or simultaneous rights. Submit seasonal material 2 months in advance. Accepts simultaneous and previously published submissions. Send photocopy of article and information about when and where the article previously appeared. For reprints, pays $40. Reports in 5 weeks. Sample copy for 11 × 14 SAE with 4 first-class stamps.
Nonfiction: Essays, exposé, general interest, historical/nostalgic, humor, inspirational, interview/profile, opinion, personal experience, religious or Near West Side's sports. Publishes a special Christmas issue. Doesn't want to see product promotions. Buys 60 mss/year. Length: 300-1,800 words. Pays $40. Sometimes pays the expenses of writers on assignment.
Photos: Send photos with submission. Reviews 5×7 prints. Offers no additional payment for photos accepted with ms. Identification of subjects required. Buys one-time rights.
Columns/Departments: To Your Health (health/exercise tips), 600 words; Forum (opinion), 750 words; Streets (Near West Side/South Loop history), 500 words. Buys 12 mss/year. Query. Pays $40.

‡NEW CITY, Chicago's News and Arts Weekly, New City Communications, Inc., 770 N. Halsted, Suite 208, Chicago IL 60622. (312)243-8786. Editor: Brian Hieggelke. 30% freelance written. Weekly magazine. Estab. 1986. Circ. 64,000. Pays 30 days after publication. Publishes ms an average of 1 month after acceptance. Byline given. Offers 20% kill fee. Buys first rights. Editorial lead time 2 months. Submit seasonal material 2 months in advance. Reports in 1 month. Sample copy for $3. Writer's guidelines for #10 SASE.
Nonfiction: Book excerpts, essays, exposé, general interest, historical/nostalgic, humor, interview/profile, personal experience. Buys 20 mss/year. Query with published clips. Length: 100-4,000 words. Pays $10-300. Sometimes pays expenses of writers on assignment.
Photos: State availability of photos with submissions. Reviews contact sheets. Captions, model releases, identification of subjects required. Buys one-time rights.
Columns/Departments: Lit (literary supplement), 300-2,000 words; Music, Film, Arts (arts criticism), 150-800 words; Chow (food writing), 300-2,000 words. Buys 50 mss/year. Query with published clips. Pays $10-300.

NORTH SHORE, The Magazine of Chicago's North and Northwest Suburbs, PB Communications, 874 Green Bay Rd., Winnetka IL 60093. (708)441-7892. Publisher: Asher Birnbaum. Senior Editor: Craig Keller. 75% freelance written. Monthly magazine. "Our readers are a diverse lot, from middle-class communities to some of the country's wealthiest zip codes. But they all have one thing in common—our proximity to Chicago." Pays on publication. Publishes ms an average of 3 months after acceptance. Byline given. Offers 50% kill fee. Buys first North American serial rights. Submit seasonal material 5 months in advance. Accepts previously published submissions. Reports in 3 months. Free writer's guidelines for #10 SASE.
Nonfiction: Book excerpts, exposé, general interest, how-to, interview/profile, photo feature, travel. Special issues: Weddings (January, July); Fitness (February); Homes/Gardens (March, June, September, December); Weekend Travel (May); Nursing/Retirement Homes (August); Dining and Nightlife (October). Buys 50 mss/ year. Query with published clips. Length: 500-4,000 words. Pays $100-800. Sometimes pays expenses of writers on assignment.
Photos: Send photos with submission. Reviews contact sheets, negatives, transparencies, prints. Offers $25-100/photo. Identification of subjects required. Buys one-time rights.
Fiction: Publishes novel excerpts.
Columns/Departments: "Prelude" (shorter items of local interest), 250 words. Buys 12 mss/year. Query with published clips. Pays $50.
Tips: "We're always looking for something of local interest that's fresh and hasn't been reported elsewhere. Look for local angle. Offer us a story that's exclusive in the crowded Chicago-area media marketplace. Well-written feature stories have the best chance of being published. We cover all of Chicago's north and northwest suburbs together with some Chicago material, not just the North Shore."

3RD WORD, Third Word Publishing, Inc., 1840 Hubbard St., Suite 3A, Chicago IL 60622. (312)666-3076. E-mail: the3rdword@aol.com. Editor: Michael G. Glab. 100% freelance written. Bimonthly consumer magazine covering general interest topics including culture, politics, style, the arts, fashion and entertainment. "We aim to be the one magazine published in Chicago that people actually *read*." Estab. 1993. Circ. 30,000.

Pays on publication. Publishes ms an average of 2 months after acceptance. Byline given. Buys first North American serial rights. Editorial lead time 2 months. Submit seasonal material 4 months in advance. Accepts simultaneous submissions. Query for electronic submissions. Reports in 3 weeks on queries. Sample copy for $3. Writer's guidelines free on request.

● *3rd Word* sponsors yearly fiction and poetry contests.

Nonfiction: Exposé, humor, interview/profile, personal experience. Buys 80 mss/year. Query with published clips. Length: 350-4,000 words. Pays $15-100. Sometimes pays expenses of writers on assignment.

Photos: State availability of photos with submission. Reviews contact sheets. Negotiates payment individually. Identification of subjects required. Buys one-time rights.

Fiction: Eclectic, experimental, humorous. Send complete ms. Length: 500-1,200 words. Pays $50.

Poetry: Avant-garde, free verse, light verse, traditional. Length: 20-60 lines. Pays $50.

Tips: "We want *3rd Word* to be a collection of voices. We want to inform and amuse. We'll shatter plaster saints and tout talented newcomers."

Indiana

ARTS INDIANA, Arts Indiana, Inc. 47 S. Pennsylvania, Suite 701, Indianapolis IN 46204-3622. (317)632-7894. Editor: Hank Nuwer. Assistant Editor: Elizabeth Weiner. 90% freelance written. Monthly (September-June) magazine on artists, writers, performers and arts organizations working in Indiana—literary, visual and performing. Estab. 1978. 11,000 printed. **Pays on acceptance.** Publishes ms an average of 3 months after acceptance. Byline given. Offers 20% kill fee. Buys first North American serial rights. Submit seasonal material 4 months in advance. Reports in 3 weeks. Sample copy available for $3.50 plus postage

Nonfiction: Indiana-linked essays, historical/nostalgic, interview/profile, opinion, photo feature, interviews with reviews (Q & A format), scenic. Query with published clips. Length: 1,000-3,000 words. Pays $50-300 for articles. Sometimes pays expenses of writer on assignment.

Photos: Send b&w photos with submission. Reviews 5×7 or larger prints. Sometimes offers additional payment for photos accepted with ms. Captions and identification of subjects required. Buys one-time rights.

Fiction: Publishes novel excerpts (if by an Indiana author).

Tips: "We are looking for people-oriented and issue-oriented articles. Articles about people should reveal personality as well as describe work. Remember this magazine is geared toward the arts."

INDIANAPOLIS MONTHLY, Emmis Publishing Corp., 950 N. Meridian St., Suite 1200, Indianapolis IN 46204. (317)237-9288. Fax: (317)237-9496. Editor-in-Chief: Deborah Paul. Editor: Sam Stall. 50% freelance written. Prefers to work with published/established writers. Monthly magazine of "upbeat material reflecting current trends. Heavy on lifestyle, homes and fashion. Material must be regional (Indianapolis and/or Indiana) in appeal." Estab. 1977. Circ. 42,000. Pays on publication. Publishes ms an average of 2 months after acceptance. Byline given. Offers 50% kill fee in some cases. Buys first North American serial rights. Submit seasonal material 3 months in advance. Accepts previously published submissions if published in a non-competing market. Send photocopy of article or typed ms with rights for sale noted and information about when and where the article previously appeared. Pays 100% of the amount paid for an original article. Reports in 2 months. Sample copy for $6.10 and 9×12 SAE. Writers' guidelines for #10 SASE.

Nonfiction: General interest, interview/profile, photo feature, but only with a strong Indianapolis or Indiana angle. No poetry, fiction or domestic humor; no "How Indy Has Changed Since I Left Town" or "An Outsider's View of the 500" stories. Buys 50 mss/year. Query with published clips or send complete ms. Length: 200-6,000 words. Pays $50-500.

● This magazine is using more first-person essays, but they must have a strong Indianapolis or Indiana tie. It will consider nonfiction book excerpts of material relevant to its readers.

Columns/Departments: Around the Circle; 9 to 5 (profile of person with intriguing job); Sport (star athletes and trendy activities); Health (new technology; local sources); Controversy; Hoosiers at Large; Peoplescape; Coping (overcoming adversity). "Again, a local angle is the key." Query with published clips or send complete mss. Pays $150-300.

Tips: "Tell us something we didn't know about Indianapolis. Find a trendy subject with a strong Indianapolis (or Indiana) angle and sell it with a punchy query and a few of your best clips. Don't confuse 'general interest' with 'generic interest'—all material must focus sharply on Indianapolis and/or Indiana. Topics, however, can vary from serious to wacky: Recent issues have included everything from a feature story about Indiana basketball star Damon Bailey to a two-paragraph piece on an Indiana gardening supply house that sells insects by mail. Best breaking-in topics for freelancers are Around the Circle (short takes on trendy local topics); Hoosiers at Large (Indiana natives relate first-person experiences); Peoplescape (one-paragraph back page feature about interesting resident). Fax queries OK; no phone queries please."

Kansas

KANSAS!, Kansas Department of Commerce and Housing, 700 SW Harrison, Suite 1300, Topeka KS 66603-3957. (913)296-3479. Editor: Andrea Glenn. 90% freelance written. Quarterly magazine emphasizing Kansas "people and places for all ages, occupations and interests." Estab. 1945. Circ. 48,000. **Pays on acceptance.** Publishes ms an average of 1 year after acceptance. Byline given. Buys one-time rights. Submit seasonal material 8 months in advance. Reports in 2 months. Sample copy and writer's guidelines available.

Nonfiction: General interest, interview, photo feature, travel. "Material must be Kansas-oriented and have good potential for color photographs. We feature stories about Kansas people, places and events that can be enjoyed by the general public. In other words, events must be open to the public, places also. People featured must have interesting crafts, etc. Query letter should clearly outline story in mind. I'm especially interested in Kansas freelancers who can supply their own photos." Length: 750-1,250 words. Pays $150-250. Sometimes pays expenses of writers on assignment.

Photos: "We are a full-color photo/manuscript publication." Send photos (original transparencies only) with query. Pays $50-75 (generally included in ms rate) for 35mm or larger format transparencies. Captions required.

Tips: "History and nostalgia stories do not fit into our format because they can't be illustrated well with color photography."

Kentucky

BACK HOME IN KENTUCKY, Greysmith Publishing Inc., P.O. Box 681629, Franklin TN 37068-1629. (615)794-4338. Fax: (615)790-6188. Managing Editor: Nanci P. Gregg. 50% freelance written. Bimonthly magazine covering Kentucky heritage, people, places, events. We reach Kentuckians and "displaced" Kentuckians living outside the state. Estab. 1977. Pays on publication. Publishes ms an average of 8 months after acceptance. Byline given. Buys first North American serial rights. Submit seasonal material 8 months in advance. Rarely accepts previously published submissions ("but rarely"). Send photocopy of article, typed ms with rights for sale noted and information about when and where the article previously appeared. Pays 25% of amount paid for an original article. Query for electronic submissions. Reports in 2 months. Sample copy for $3 and 9×12 SAE with 5 first-class stamps. Writer's guidelines for #10 SASE.

● This magazine is shifting to an emphasis on the "Back Home." It is interested in profiles of Kentucky gardeners, Kentucky cooks, Kentucky craftspeople, all with a flavor of the way things were.

Nonfiction: Historical (Kentucky related eras or profiles), profiles (Kentucky cooks, gardeners and craftspersons), photo feature (Kentucky places and events), travel (unusual/little known Kentucky places). No inspirational or religion—all must be Kentucky related. Buys 25 mss/year. Query with or without published clips or send complete ms. Length: 500-2,000 words. Pays $50-150 for assigned articles; $15-75 for unsolicited articles. "In addition to normal payment, writers receive 4 copies of issue containing their article." Sometimes pays expenses of writers on assignment.

Photos: Send photos with submission. Reviews transparencies and 4×6 prints. Offers no additional payment for photos accepted with ms. Model releases and identification of subjects required. Rights purchased depends on situation. Also looking for color transparencies for covers. Vertical format. Pays $50-150.

Columns/Departments: Kentucky travel, Kentucky crafts, Kentucky gardeners. Buys 10-12 mss/year. Query with published clips. Length: 500-750 words. Pays $15-40.

Tips: "We work mostly with unpublished writers who have a feel for Kentucky—its people, places, events, etc. The areas most open to freelancers are little known places in Kentucky, unusual history, and profiles of interesting, unusual Kentuckians."

KENTUCKY LIVING, P.O. Box 32170, Louisville KY 40232-0170. (502)451-2430. Fax: (502)459-1611. Editor: Donna Bunch Miller. Mostly freelance written. Prefers to work with published/established writers. Monthly feature magazine primarily for Kentucky residents. Estab. 1948. Circ. 400,000. **Pays on acceptance.** Publishes ms on average of 4-12 months after acceptance. Byline given. Buys first serial rights for Kentucky. Submit seasonal material at least 6 months in advance. Will consider previously published and simultaneous submissions (if previously published and/or submitted outside Kentucky). Reports in 1 month. Sample copy for 9×12 SAE with 4 first-class stamps. Writer's guidelines for #10 SASE.

● *Kentucky Living* is putting greater emphasis on personality profiles and Kentucky-travel. In addition, they have increased use of energy-use articles.

Nonfiction: Prefers Kentucky-related profiles (people, places or events), recreation, travel, leisure, lifestyle articles, book excerpts. Buys 18-24 mss/year. Query or send complete ms. Pays $75 to $125 for "short" features (600-800 words) used in section known as "Kentucky Fare." For major articles (800-2,000 words) pays $150 to $350. Sometimes pays the expenses of writers on assignment.

Photos: State availability of or send photos with submission or advise as to availability. Reviews color slides and b&w prints. Identification of subjects required. Payment for photos included in payment for ms. Pays extra if photo used on cover.

Tips: "The quality of writing and reporting (factual, objective, thorough) is considered in setting payment price. We prefer general interest pieces filled with quotes and anecdotes. Avoid boosterism. Well-researched, well-written feature articles are preferred. All articles must have a Kentucky connection."

‡**LOUISVILLE MAGAZINE**, 137 W. Muhammad Ali Blvd., Louisville KY 40202-1438. (502)625-0100. Editor: John Filiatreau. 67% freelance written. Monthly magazine "for and generally about people of the Louisville Metro area. Routinely covers arts, entertainment, business, sports, dining and fashion. Features range from news analysis/exposé to silly/funny commentary. We like lean, clean prose, crisp leads." Estab. 1950. Circ. 20,000. Publishes ms an average of 2-3 months after acceptance. Byline given. Offers 50% kill fee. Buys first North American serial rights. Editorial lead time 6 weeks. Submit seasonal material 6 months in advance. Query for electronic submissions. Reports in 3 months. Sample copy for $2.
Nonfiction: Book excerpts, essays, exposé, general interest, historical, interview/profile, photo feature. Special issues: Kentucky Derby (May). Buys 75 mss/year. Query. Length: 500-3,500 words. Pays $100-500 for assigned articles; $100-400 for unsolicited articles.
Photos: State availability of photos with submissions. Reviews transparencies. Offers $25-50/photo. Identification of subjects required. Buys one-time rights.
Columns/Departments: End Insight (essays), 850 words. Buys 10 mss/year. Send complete ms. Pays $100-150.

Louisiana

SUNDAY ADVOCATE MAGAZINE, P.O. Box 588, Baton Rouge LA 70821-0588. (504)383-1111, ext. 350. Fax: (504)388-0351. Newsfeatures Editor: Freda Yarbrough. 5% freelance written. "We are backlogged but still welcome submissions." Byline given. Estab. 1925. Pays on publication. Publishes ms up to 3 months after acceptance. Accepts previously published submissions. Send tearsheet or typed ms with rights for sale noted and information about when and where the article previously appeared. Query for electronic submissions.
Nonfiction and Photos: Well-illustrated, short articles; must have local, area or Louisiana angle, in that order of preference. Also interested in travel pieces. Photos purchased with mss. Pays $100-200.
Tips: "Styles and subject matter may vary. Local interest is most important. No more than 4-5 typed, double-spaced pages."

Maine

ISLESBORO ISLAND NEWS, HC60 Box 227, Islesboro ME 04848. (207)734-6745. Fax: (207)734-6519. Publisher: Agatha Cabaniss. 10% freelance written. Monthly tabloid on Penobscot Bay islands and people. Estab. 1985. **Pays on acceptance.** Byline given. Buys one-time rights. Accepts previously published submissions or short stories. Send typed ms with rights for sale noted. For reprints, payment varies. Sample copy for $2. Writer's guidelines for #10 SAE with 3 first-class stamps.
Nonfiction: Articles about contemporary issues on the islands, historical pieces, personality profiles, arts, lifestyles and businesses on the islands. Any story must have a definite Maine island connection. No travel pieces. Query or send complete ms. Pays $20-50.
Photos: Send photos with submission.
Tips: "Writers must know the Penobscot Bay Islands. We are not interested in pieces of a generic island nature unless they relate to development problems, or the viability of the islands as year round communities. We do not want 'vacation on a romantic island,' but we are interested in island historical pieces."

Maryland

BALTIMORE MAGAZINE, 16 S. Calvert St., Suite 1000, Baltimore MD 21202. (410)752-7375. Editor: Ramsey Flynn. Deputy Editor: Margaret Guroff. 30-40% freelance written. Monthly magazine covering the Baltimore area. "Pieces must address an educated, active, affluent reader and must have a very strong Baltimore angle." Estab. 1907. Circ. 50,000. Pays within 60 days of acceptance. Byline given. Offers 30% kill fee. Buys first rights. Submit seasonal/holiday material 4 months in advance. Query for electronic submissions. Reports in 2 months on queries; 2 weeks on assigned mss; 3 months on unsolicited mss. Sample copy for $2.05 and 9 × 12 SAE with 10 first-class stamps. Writer's guidelines for a business-sized SASE.
Nonfiction: Margaret Guroff. Book excerpt (Baltimore subject or Baltimore author), essays (Baltimore subject), exposé (Baltimore subject), humor (Baltimore focus), interview/profile (w/Baltimorean), personal experience (Baltimore focus), photo feature, travel (local and regional to Maryland *only*). "Nothing that lacks a strong Baltimore focus or angle." Query with published clips or send complete ms. Length: 200-4,500 words. Pays $25-2,500 for assigned articles; $25-500 for unsolicited articles. Sometimes pays expenses of writers on assignment.
Tips: "Writers who live in the Baltimore area can send résumé and published clips to be considered for first assignment. Must show an understanding of writing that is suitable to an educated magazine reader and show ability to write with authority, describe scenes, help reader experience the subject. Too many writers send us newspaper-style articles, instead. We are seeking: 1) *Human interest features*—strong, even dramatic

profiles of Baltimoreans of interest to our readers. 2) *First person accounts* of experience in Baltimore, or experiences of a Baltimore resident. 3) *Consumer*—according to our editorial needs, and with Baltimore sources." Writers new to us have most success with small humorous stories and 1,000-word personal essays that exhibit risky, original thought.

WARM WELCOMES MAGAZINE, Warm Welcomes Inc., P.O. Box 1066, Hagerstown MD 21741-1066. (301)797-9276. Fax: (301)797-1065. Editor: Winnie Wagaman. 25% freelance written. Monthly magazine that covers history, culture, events and people of the areas surrounding the state of Maryland. Our audience consists of upper- and middle-income professionals in Maryland, South Central Pennsylvania, Virginia, Washington, D.C. and West Virginia. Estab. 1989. Circ. 20,000. Pays on publication. Publishes ms an average of 3 months after acceptance. Byline given. Kill fee varies. Buys exclusive rights. Submit seasonal material 6 months in advance. Accepts simultaneous and previously published submissions. Send photocopy of article or typed ms with rights for sale noted and information about when and where the article previously appeared. Query for electronic submissions. Reports in 3 months. Sample copy for 6×9 SAE with 4 first-class stamps. Writer's guidelines for #10 SASE.
Nonfiction: General interest, historical/nostalgic, interview/profile. "We accept only material related to our area's history, people and locations." Buys 12 mss/year. Query with or without published clips or send complete ms. Length: 600-1,200 words. Pays $25-75 for assigned articles; $25-50 for unsolicited articles.
Photos: Send photos with submission. Reviews contact sheets and 5×7 b&w prints. Pays $10-25. Identification of subjects required. Buys one-time rights.
Tips: "Writers can best approach our publication with a well-written query or ms pertaining to the area— something that shows they know their subject and the audience they are writing for."

Massachusetts

BOSTON GLOBE MAGAZINE, *Boston Globe,* Boston MA 02107. Editor-in-Chief: Evelynne Kramer. Assistant Editor: Julie Michaels. 50% freelance written. Weekly magazine. Circ. 805,099. **Pays on acceptance**. Publishes ms an average of 2 months after acceptance. No reprints of any kind. Buys first serial rights. Submit seasonal material 3 months in advance. SASE must be included with ms or queries for return. Reports in 1 month. Sample copy for 9×12 SAE with 2 first-class stamps.
Nonfiction: Exposé (variety of issues including political, economic, scientific, medical and the arts), interview (not Q&A), profile, book excerpts (first serial rights only). No travelogs. Buys up to 100 mss/year. Query. Length: 2,000-5,000 words. Payment negotiable.
Photos: Purchased with accompanying ms or on assignment. Reviews contact sheets. Pays standard rates according to size used. Captions required.

‡BOSTON MAGAZINE, Metrocorp, 300 Massachusetts Ave., Boston MA 02115. (617)262-9700. Editor: Art Jahnke. Contact: Karen Levine. 50% freelance written. Monthly magazine covering the city of Boston. Estab. 1972. Circ. 114,476. Pays on publication. Publishes ms an average of 3 months after acceptance. Byline given. Offers 20% kill fee. Buys first North American serial rights. Editorial lead time 2 months. Submit seasonal material 4 months in advance. Reports in 2 weeks on queries; 1 month on mss. Writer's guidelines free on request.
Nonfiction: Book excerpts, exposé, general interest, historical/nostalgic, how-to, interview/profile, new product, personal experience, travel. Buys 40 mss/year. Query. Length: 1,200-5,000 words. Pays $400-5,000. Sometimes pays expenses of writers on assignment.
Photos: State availability of photos with submissions. Negotiates payment individually. Buys one-time rights.
Columns/Departments: Sports, Dining, Finance, City Life, Personal Style, Politics. Query. Pays $400-1,200.

THE BOSTON PHOENIX, 126 Brookline Ave., Boston MA 02215. (617)536-5390. Fax: (617)859-8201. Editor: Peter Kadzis. Contacts: Vicki Sanders (news); Caroline Knapp (features); Ted Drozdowski (arts). 40% freelance written. Weekly alternative newspaper for 18-40 age group, educated post-counterculture. Estab. 1966. Circ. 139,000. Buys first serial rights. Pays on publication. Offers kill fee. Publishes ms an average of 1 month after acceptance. Byline given. Accepts previously published submissions. Send tearsheet of article and information about when and where the article previously appeared. For reprints, payment varies. Reports in 2 months. Sample copy for $4.50.
   • *Boston Phoenix* has a monthly supplement (*One in Ten*) on gay and lesbian issues, edited by Robert Sullivan. The monthly *Phoenix Literary Section* (*PLS*) is edited by Marsha Pomerantz.
Nonfiction: News (local coverage, national, some international affairs, features, think pieces and profiles), lifestyle (features, service pieces, consumer-oriented tips, medical, food, some humor if topical, etc.), arts (reviews, essays, interviews), supplements (coverage of special-interest areas, e.g., skiing, seasonal, recreation, education). Query section editor. "Liveliness, accuracy, and great literacy are absolutely required."

No fiction. Query letter preferable to ms. Pays 4¢/word and up. Sometimes pays the expenses of writers on assignment.
Poetry: Contact: Lloyd Schwartz.

‡BOSTONIA, The Magazine of Culture & Ideas, Boston University, 10 Lenox St., Brookline MA 02146. (617)353-3081. Fax: (617)353-6488. Editor: Jerrold Hickey. 90% freelance written. Quarterly magazine on culture and ideas. Estab. 1900. Circ. 185,000. **Pays on acceptance.** Publishes ms an average of 2 months after acceptance. Byline given. Buys first rights. Reports in 2 months. Sample copy and writer's guidelines for $3.50.
Nonfiction: National, international issues, the arts, profiles, social issues. Primarily commissioned but will consider queries with published clips. Length: 2,000-5,000 words. Pays up to $1,250 plus expenses.
Photos: Portfolios with proposals to Art Director. All must be identified.
Columns/Departments: Commonwealth Avenue and In our Backyard, 300-1,000 words. Pays $150 on acceptance.
Fiction: No length restrictions, internationally known writers are preferred but will read new writers. Pays up to $1,500. Publishes novel excerpts.
Tips: "Freelancers' best way in is Commonwealth Avenue column."

CAPE COD LIFE, Including Martha's Vineyard and Nantucket, Cape Cod Life, Inc., P.O. Box 767, Cataumet MA 02534-0767. (508)564-4466. Fax: (508)564-4470. Editor: Brian F. Shortsleeve. 80% freelance written. Bimonthly magazine focusing on "area lifestyle, history and culture, people and places, business and industry, and issues and answers." Readers are "year-round and summer residents of Cape Cod as well as non-residents who spend their leisure time on the Cape." Circ. 35,000. Pays 30 days after publication. Byline given. Offers 20% kill fee. Buys first North American serial rights or makes work-for-hire assignments. Submit seasonal/holiday material 6 months in advance. Reports in 6 months on queries and ms. Sample copy for $3.75. Writer's guidelines for #10 SASE.
Nonfiction: General interest, historical, gardening, interview/profile, photo feature, travel, marine, nautical, nature, arts, antiques. Buys 20 mss/year. Query with or without published clips. Length: 1,000-4,000 words. Pays $100-400.
Photos: Send photos with query. Pays $25-200 for photos. Captions and identification of subjects required. Buys first rights with right to reprint.
Tips: "Freelancers submitting *quality* spec articles with a Cape Cod angle have a good chance at publication. We do like to see a wide selection of writer's clips before giving assignments. We accept more spec work written about Cape and Islands history than any other area."

PROVINCETOWN ARTS, Provincetown Arts, Inc., 650 Commercial St., Provincetown MA 02657. (508)487-3167. Editor: Christopher Busa. 90% freelance written. Annual magazine for contemporary art and writing. "*Provincetown Arts* focuses broadly on the artists and writers who inhabit or visit the Lower Cape, and seeks to stimulate creative activity and enhance public awareness of the cultural life of the nation's oldest continuous art colony. Drawing upon a 75-year tradition rich in visual art, literature, and theater, *Provincetown Arts* offers a unique blend of interviews, fiction, visual features, reporting, and poetry." Estab. 1985. Circ. 8,000. Pays on publication. Publishes ms an average of 4 months after acceptance. Offers 50% kill fee. Buys one-time and second serial (reprint) rights. Editorial lead time 4-6 months. Submit seasonal material 6 months in advance. Query for electronic submissions. Reports in 3 weeks on queries; 2 months on mss. Sample copy for $10. Writer's guidelines for #10 SASE.
Nonfiction: Book excerpts, essays, humor, interview/profile. Buys 40 mss/year. Send complete ms. Length: 1,500-4,000 words. Pays $150 minimum for assigned articles; $125 minimum for unsolicited articles. Sometimes pays expenses of writers on assignment.
Photos: Send photos with submission. Reviews 8×10 prints. Offers $20-100/photo. Identification of subjects required. Buys one-time rights.
Fiction: Mainstream. Also publishes novel excerpts. Buys 7 mss/year. Send complete ms. Length: 500-5,000 words. Pays $75-300.
Poetry: Buys 25 poems/year. Submit maximum 3 poems. Pays $25-150.

Michigan

ABOVE THE BRIDGE MAGAZINE, 120 McLaughlin Rd., Skandia MI 49885. Editor: Lynn DeLoughary St. Arnaud. 100% freelance written. Quarterly magazine on the Upper Peninsula of Michigan. "All material, including fiction, has an Upper Peninsula of Michigan slant. Our readership is past and present Upper Peninsula residents." Circ. 2,000. Pays on publication. Publishes ms an average of 1 year after acceptance. Byline given. Buys one-time rights. Submit seasonal/holiday material 6 months in advance. Accepts previously published submissions. Send typed ms with rights for sale noted and information about when and where the article previously appeared. For reprints, pays 100% of the amount paid for an original article.

Query for electronic submissions. Reports in 1 year. Sample copy for $3.50. Writer's guidelines for #10 SASE.

Nonfiction: Book excerpts (books on Upper Peninsula or UP writer), essays, historical/nostalgic (UP), interview/profile (UP personality or business), personal experience, photo feature (UP). Note: Travel by assignment only. "This is a family magazine; therefore, no material in poor taste." Buys 60 mss/year. Send complete ms. Length: 1,000-2,000 words. Pays 2¢/word.

Photos: Send photos with submission. Reviews prints (5×7 or larger). Offers $5 ($15-20 if used for cover). Captions, model releases, identification of subjects required. Buys one-time rights.

Fiction: Ethnic (UP heritage), humorous, mainstream, mystery. No horror or erotica. "Material set in UP has preference for publication." Buys 12 mss/year. Send complete ms. Length: 1,000-2,000 words. Pays 2¢/word.

Poetry: Free verse, haiku, light verse, traditional. No erotica. Buys 20 poems/year. Shorter poetry preferred. Pays $5.

Fillers: Anecdotes, short humor. Buys 25/year. Length: 100-500 words. Pays 2¢/word maximum.

Tips: "Material on the shorter end of our requirements has a better chance for publication. We're very well-stocked at the moment. We can't use material by out-of-state writers with content not tied to Upper Peninsula of Michigan. Know the area and people, read the magazine. Most material received is too long. Stick to our guidelines. We love to publish well written material by previously unpublished writers."

ANN ARBOR OBSERVER, Ann Arbor Observer Company, 201 E. Catherine, Ann Arbor MI 48104. Fax: (313)769-3375. Editor: John Hilton. 50% freelance written. Works with a small number of new/unpublished writers each year. Monthly magazine featuring stories about people and events in Ann Arbor. Estab. 1976. Circ. 58,000. Pays on publication. Publishes ms an average of 2 months after acceptance. Byline given. Query for electronic submissions. Reports in 3 weeks on queries; "several months" on mss. Sample copy for 12½×15 SAE with $3 postage. Free writer's guidelines.

Nonfiction: Historical, investigative features, profiles, brief vignettes. Must pertain to Ann Arbor. Buys 75 mss/year. Length: 100-7,000 words. Pays up to $1,000/article. Sometimes pays expenses of writers on assignment.

Tips: "If you have an idea for a story, write a 100-200-word description telling us why the story is interesting. We are most open to intelligent, insightful features of up to 5,000 words about interesting aspects of life in Ann Arbor."

MICHIGAN COUNTRY LINES, Michigan Electric Cooperative Association, 2859 W. Jolly Rd., Okemos MI 48864. (517)351-6322. Fax: (517)351-6396. Editor: Michael Buda. Managing Editor: Gail Knudtson. 10% freelance written. Bimonthly magazine covering rural Michigan. Estab. 1980. Circ. 170,000. Pays on publication. Publishes ms an average of 4 months after acceptance. Byline given. Buys one-time and second serial (reprint) rights. Submit seasonal material 3 months in advance. Accepts previously published submissions. Send tearsheet of article and information about when and where the article previously appeared. For reprints, 75% of the amount paid for an original article. Query for electronic submissions. Reports in 2 months. Free sample copy.

Nonfiction: Personalities, how-to (rural living), photo feature. No product or out-of-state. Buys 6 mss/year. Send complete ms. Length: 700-1,500 words. Pays $200 for assigned articles; $150 unsolicited articles. Pays expenses of writers on assignment.

Photos: Send photos with submission. Reviews contact sheets, 35mm transparencies and 3×5 prints. Offers $10-15/photo. Captions, model releases and identification of subjects required. Buys one-time rights.

Tips: "Features are most open to freelancers. We no longer need historical/nostalgic articles."

‡TRAVERSE, Northern Michigan's Magazine, Prism Publications, Inc., 121 S. Union St., Traverse City MI 49684. (616)941-8174. Editor: Deborah W. Fellows. Contact: Ellyn Tarrant. 40% freelance written. Monthly magazine covering Northern Michigan. Estab. 1981. Circ. 15,000. Pays on publication. Publishes ms an average of 6 months after acceptance. Offers 100% kill fee. Buys first North American serial rights. Editorial lead time 6 months. Submit seasonal material 6 months in advance. Accepts simultaneous submissions. Query for electronic submissions. Reports in 3 weeks on queries; 1 months on mss. Sample copy for $3.50 and SAE. Writer's guidelines for #10 SASE.

Nonfiction: Book excerpts, essays, exposé, general interest, historical/nostalgic, how-to, humor, interview/profile, personal experience. Buys 25-35 mss/year. Query with published clips or send complete ms. Length: 700-3,500 words. Pays $75-500 for assigned articles; $50-400 for unsolicited articles. Sometimes pays expenses of writers on assignment.

Columns/Departments: Up in Michigan (profiles, or first person accounts of elements of life in Northern Michigan), 750 words; Your Environment (what *you* can do to help the Northern environment—i.e., from land use to nature preservation, etc. Also can detail a hike or other natural experience as a destination.), 750 words. Buys 9-12 mss/year. Query with published clips or send complete ms. Pays $50-175.

Fiction: Adventure, historical, humorous, novel excerpts, slice-of-life vignettes. Buys 5 mss/year. Query with published clips or send complete ms. Length: 1,000-3,500 words. Pays $150-350.

Tips: "We're very writer-friendly! We encourage submissions on spec. We will review and accept, or return with comments/suggestions where applicable."

Minnesota

LAKE SUPERIOR MAGAZINE, Lake Superior Port Cities, Inc., P.O. Box 16417, Duluth MN 55816-0417. (218)722-5002. Fax: (218)722-4096. Editor: Paul L. Hayden. 60% freelance written. Works with a small number of new/unpublished writers each year. Bimonthly regional magazine covering contemporary and historic people, places and current events around Lake Superior. Estab. 1979. Circ. 20,000. Pays on publication. Publishes ms an average of 10 months after acceptance. Byline given. Offers $25 kill fee. Buys first North American serial and some second rights. Submit seasonal material 1 year in advance. Query for electronic submissions. Reports in 2 months. Sample copy for $3.95 and 5 first-class stamps. Writer's guidelines for #10 SASE.
Nonfiction: Book excerpts, general interest, historic/nostalgic, humor, interview/profile (local), personal experience, photo feature (local), travel (local), city profiles, regional business, some investigative. Buys 45 mss/year. Query with published clips. Length 300-2,200 words. Pays $80-400. Sometimes pays the expenses of writers on assignment.
Photos: Quality photography is our hallmark. Send photos with submission. Reviews contact sheets, 2×2 transparencies, 4×5 prints. Offers $20 for b&w and $35 for color. $75 for covers. Captions, model releases, identification of subjects required.
Columns/Departments: Current events and things to do (for Events Calendar section), short, less than 300 words; Around The Circle (media reviews and short pieces on Lake Superior or Great Lakes environmental issues and themes and letters and short pieces on events and highlights of the Lake Superior Region); I Remember (nostalgic lake-specific pieces), up to 1,100 words; Life Lines (single personality profile with b&w), up to 900 words. Other headings include Destinations, Nature, Wilderness Living, Heritage, Shipwreck, Chronicle, Lake Superior's Own, House for Sale. Buys 20 mss/year. Query with published clips. Pays $90.
Fiction: Ethnic, historic, humorous, mainstream, novel excerpts, slice-of-life vignettes, ghost stories. Must be regionally targeted in nature. Buys only 2-3 mss/year. Query with published clips. Length: 300-2,500 words. Pays $1-125.
Tips: "Well-researched queries are attended to. We actively seek queries from writers in Lake Superior communities. We prefer manuscripts to queries. Provide enough information on why the subject is important to the region and our readers, or why and how something is unique. We want details. The writer must have a thorough knowledge of the subject and how it relates to our region. We prefer a fresh, unused approach to the subject which provides the reader with an emotional involvement. Almost all of our articles feature quality photography, color or black and white. It is a prerequisite of all nonfiction. All submissions should include a *short* biography of author/photographer. Blanket submissions need not apply."

Missouri

PITCH WEEKLY, News and Entertainment for Metro Kansas City, Pitch Publishing, Inc., 3535 Broadway, Suite 400, Kansas City MO 64111-2826. (816)561-6061. Fax: (816)756-0502. E-mail: pitch@tyrell.net. Editor: Bruce Rodgers. 75% freelance written. Weekly alternative newspaper that covers arts, entertainment, politics and social and cultural awareness in Kansas City. Estab. 1980. Circ. 70,000. Pays 1 month from publication. Buys first or one-time rights or makes work-for-hire assignments. Editorial lead time 1 month. Submit seasonal material 2 months in advance. *Query first!* Accepts previously published submissions. Send photocopy of article or typed ms with rights for sale noted and information about when and where the article previously appeared. Pays 50% of the amount paid for an original article. Reports in 2 months on queries.
Nonfiction: Exposé, humor, interview/profile, opinion, news, photo feature. Buys 40-50 mss/year. Query with published clips. Length: 700. Pays $25-250. Sometimes pays expenses of writers on assignment. Prefer nonfiction with local hook.
Photos: Send photos with submission. Reviews contact sheets. Offers no additional payment for photos accepted with ms. Captions and identification of subjects required. Buys one-time rights.
Fiction: Holiday-theme fiction published on Christmas, Thanksgiving, Valentine's Day. "Must be slightly off-beat and good." Length: 1,500-2,000 words. Payment $75-125.
Tips: "Approach us with unusual angles on current political topics of responsible social documentary. Send well-written, clear, concise query with identifiable direction of proposed piece and SASE for reply or return. Previous publication in AAN paper a plus. We're looking for features and secondary features: current events in visual and performing arts (include new trends, etc.); social issues (OK to have an opinion as long as facts are well-documented); liberal politics."

RIVER HILLS TRAVELER, Todd Publishing, Route 4 Box 4396, Piedmont MO 63957. (314)223-7143. Editor: Bob Todd. 60% freelance written. Monthly consumer tabloid covering fishing, hunting, camping and southern

Missouri. "We are about outdoor sports and nature in the southeast quarter of Missouri. Topics like those in *Field & Stream* and *National Geographic*." Estab. 1973. Circ. 7,500. Pays on publication. Publishes ms an average of 2 months after acceptance. Byline given. Buys one-time rights. Editorial lead time 2 months. Submit seasonal material 1-12 months in advance. Accepts simultaneous and previously published submissions. Send typed ms with rights for sale noted and information about when and where the article previously appeared. Query for electronic submissions. Reports in 1 month. Sample copy and writer's guidelines free on request.

Nonfiction: Historical/nostalgic, how-to, humor, opinion, personal experience. photo feature, technical, travel. "No stories about other geographic areas." Buys 80 mss/year. Query with writing samples. Length: 1,500 maximum words. Pays $25. Sometimes pays expenses of writers on assignment.

Photos: Send photos with submission. Reviews contact sheets and prints. Negotiates payment individually. Identification of subjects required. Buys one-time rights.

Fillers: Gags. Pays $10.

Tips: "We are a 'poor man's version' of *Field & Stream* and *National Geographic*—about the eastern Missouri Ozarks."

SPRINGFIELD! MAGAZINE, Springfield Communications Inc., P.O. Box 4749, Springfield MO 65808-4749. (417)882-4917. Editor: Robert C. Glazier. 85% freelance written. Works with a small number of new/unpublished writers each year; eager to work with new/unpublished writers. Monthly magazine. "This is an extremely local and provincial magazine. No *general* interest articles." Estab. 1979. Circ. 10,000. Pays on publication. Publishes ms an average of 6 months after acceptance. Byline given. Buys first serial rights. Submit seasonal/holiday material 6-12 months in advance. Reports in 3 months on queries; 6 months on mss. Sample copy for $5 and 9½×12½ SAE.

Nonfiction: Book excerpts (by Springfield authors only), exposé (local topics only), historical/nostalgic (top priority but must be local history), how-to (local interest only), humor (if local angle), interview/profile (needs more on females than on males), personal experience (local angle), photo feature (local photos), travel (1 page/month). No material that could appeal to any other magazine anywhere else. Buys 150 mss/year. Query with published clips or send complete ms. Length: 500-5,000 words. Pays $25-250. Sometimes pays expenses of writers on assignment.

 • They need more photo features of a nostalgic bent.

Photos: Send photos or send photos with query or ms. Reviews b&w and color contact sheets, 4×5 color transparencies, 5×7 b&w prints. Pays $5-35 for b&w, $10-50 for color. Captions, model releases, identification of subjects required. Buys one-time rights.

Columns/Departments: Buys 250 mss/year. Query or send complete ms. Length varies widely but usually 500-2,500 words.

Tips: "We prefer that a writer read eight or ten copies of our magazine prior to submitting any material for our consideration. The magazine's greatest need is for features which comment on these times in Springfield. We are overstocked with nostalgic pieces right now. We also are much in need of profiles about young women and men of distinction."

Montana

MONTANA MAGAZINE, American Geographic Publishing, P.O. Box 5630, Helena MT 59604-5630. (406)443-2842. Fax: (406)443-5480. Editor: Beverly R. Magley. 90% freelance written. Bimonthly "strictly Montana-oriented magazine that features community and personality profiles, contemporary issues, travel pieces." Estab. 1970. Circ. 69,000. Publishes ms an average of 8-12 months after acceptance. Byline given. Offers $50-100 kill fee on assigned stories only. Buys one-time rights. Submit seasonal material at least 6 months in advance. Accepts simultaneous submissions. Send information about when and where the article previously appeared. Pays 50% of their fee for an original article. Reports in 2 months. Sample copy for $3. Writer's guidelines for #10 SASE.

Nonfiction: Essays, general interest, interview/profile, photo feature, travel. Special features on summer and winter destination points. Query by January for summer material; July for winter material. No 'me and Joe' hiking and hunting tales; no blood-and-guts hunting stories; no poetry; no fiction; no sentimental essays. Buys 30 mss/year. Query. Length: 300-4,500 words. Pays 15¢/word for articles. Sometimes pays the expenses of writers on assignment.

Photos: Send photos with submission. Reviews contact sheets, 35mm or larger format transparencies, 5×7 prints. Offers additional payment for photos accepted with ms. Captions, model releases, identification of subjects required. Buys one-time rights.

Columns/Departments: Memories (reminisces of early-day Montana life) 800-1,000 words; Small Towns (profiles of communities) 1,500 words; Over the Weekend (destination points of interest to travelers, family weekends and exploring trips to take), 500-1,000 words plus b&w or color photo; Food and Lodging (great places to eat; interesting hotels, resorts, etc.), 700-1,000 words plus b&w or color photo; Made in MT (successful cottage industries), 700-1,000 words plus b&w or color photo. Humor 800-1,000 words. Query.

Nevada

NEVADA MAGAZINE, 1800 E. Hwy. 50, Carson City NV 89710-0005. (702)687-5416. Fax: (702)687-6159. Publisher: Rich Moreno. Editor: David Moore. Associate Editor: Carolyn Graham. 50% freelance written. Works with a small number of new/unpublished writers each year. Bimonthly magazine published by the state of Nevada to promote tourism in the state. Estab. 1936. Circ. 100,000. Pays on publication. Publishes ms an average of 6 months after acceptance. Byline given. Buys first North American serial rights. Accepts phone queries. Submit seasonal material at least 6 months in advance. Query for electronic submissions. Word processing and page layout on Macintosh. Reports in 1 month. Sample copy for $1. Free writer's guidelines.
Nonfiction: Nevada topics only. Historical, nostalgia, photo feature, people profile, recreational, travel, think pieces. "We welcome stories and photos on speculation." Publishes nonfiction book excerpts. Buys 40 unsolicited mss/year. Submit complete ms or queries to Associate Editor, Carolyn Graham. Length: 500-2,000 words. Pays $75-300.
Photos: Paul AílLée, art director. Send photo material with accompanying ms. Pays $10-50 for 8 × 10 glossy prints; $15-75 for color transparencies. Name, address and caption should appear on each photo or slide. Buys one-time rights.
Tips: "Keep in mind that the magazine's purpose is to promote tourism in Nevada. Keys to higher payments are quality and editing effort (more than length). Send cover letter; no photocopies. We look for a light, enthusiastic tone of voice without being too cute; articles bolstered by amazing facts and thorough research; and unique angles on Nevada subjects."

New Jersey

ATLANTIC CITY MAGAZINE, P.O. Box 2100, Pleasantville NJ 08232-1924. (609)272-7912. Fax: (609)272-7910. Editor: Ken Weatherford. 80% freelance written. Works with small number of new/unpublished writers each year. Monthly regional magazine covering issues pertinent to the Jersey Shore area. Estab. 1978. Circ. 50,000. Pays on publication. Publishes ms an average of 4 months after acceptance. Byline given. Buys one-time rights. Offers variable kill fee. Accepts previously published submissions. Send typed ms with rights for sale noted and information about when and where the article previously appeared. For reprints, pays 50% of amount paid for original article. Submit seasonal material 6 months in advance. Reports in 6 weeks. Sample copy for $3 and 9 × 12 SAE with 6 first-class stamps. Writer's guidelines for SASE.
Nonfiction: Entertainment, general interest, recreation, history, lifestyle, interview/profile, photo feature, trends. "No hard news or investigative pieces. No travel pieces or any article without a South Jersey shore area/Atlantic City slant." Query. Length: 100-3,000 words. Pays $50-700 for assigned articles; $50-500 for unsolicited articles. Sometimes pays the expenses of writers on assignment.
Photos: Send photos. Reviews contact sheets, negatives, 2¼ × 2¼ transparencies, 8 × 10 prints. Pay varies. Captions, model releases, identification of subjects required. Buys one-time rights.
Columns/Departments: Art, Business, Entertainment, Sports, Dining, History, Style, Real Estate. Query with published clips. Length: 500-2,000 words. Pays $150-400.
Tips: "Our readers are a broad base of local residents and visiting tourists. We need stories that will appeal to both audiences."

NEW JERSEY MONTHLY, P.O. Box 920, Morristown NJ 07963-0920. (201)539-8230. Editor: Jenny De Monte. 50% freelance written. Monthly magazine covering "almost anything that's New Jersey related." Estab. 1976. Circ. 87,000. Pays on completion of fact-checking. Byline given. Offers 10-30% kill fee. Buys first rights. Submit seasonal material 6 months in advance. Reports in 3 months. Sample copy for $2.95 (% Back Issue Dept.); writer's guidelines for #10 SASE.
   ● This magazine continues to look for strong investigative reporters with novelistic style and solid knowledge of New Jersey issues.
Nonfiction: Book excerpts, essays, exposé, general interest, historical, humor, interview/profile, opinion, personal experience, travel. Special issues: Dining Out (February and August); Real Estate (March); Home & Garden (April); Great Weekends (May); Shore Guide (June); Fall Getaways (October); Holiday Shopping & Entertaining (November). "No experience pieces from people who used to live in New Jersey or general pieces that have no New Jersey angle." Buys 96 mss/year. Query with published magazine clips and SASE. Length: 200-3,000 words. Pays 30¢/word and up. Pays reasonable expenses of writers on assignment with prior approval.
Photos: Send photos with submission. Payment negotiated. Identification of subjects and return postage required. "Submit dupes only. Drop off for portfolios on Wednesdays only. The magazine accepts no responsibility for unsolicited photography, artwork or cartoons." Buys exclusive first serial or one-time rights.

Columns/Departments: Business (company profile, trends, individual profiles); Health & Fitness (trends, personal experience, service); Home & Garden (homes, gardens, trends, profiles, etc.); Travel (in and out-of-state). Buys 36 mss/year. Query with published clips. Length: 750-1,500 words. Pays 30¢ and up/word.
Tips: "To break in, we suggest contributing briefs to our front-of-the-book section, 'Garden Variety' (light, off-beat items, trends, people, things; short service items, such as the 10 best NJ-made ice creams; short issue-oriented items; gossip; media notes). We pay a flat fee, from $50-150."

THE SANDPAPER, Newsmagazine of the Jersey Shore, The SandPaper, Inc., 1816 Long Beach Blvd., Surf City NJ 08008-5461. (609)494-2034. Fax: (609)494-1437. Editor: Curt Travers. Freelance Submissions Editor: Gail Travers. 50% freelance written. Weekly tabloid covering subjects of interest to Jersey shore residents and visitors. "*The SandPaper* publishes three editions covering many of the Jersey Shore's finest resort communities including Long Beach Island, Cape May and Ocean City, New Jersey. Each issue includes a mix of news, human interest features, opinion columns and entertainment/calendar listings." Estab. 1976. Circ. 60,000. Pays on publication. Publishes ms an average of 1 month after acceptance. Byline given. Offers 100% kill fee. Buys first or all rights. Submit seasonal material 3 months in advance. Accepts simultaneous and previously published submissions. Send photocopy of article and information about when and where it previously appeared. Pays 25-50% of their fee for an original article. Reports in 1 month. Sample copy for 9×12 SAE with 8 first-class stamps.
Nonfiction: Essays, general interest, historical/nostalgic, humor, opinion, environmental submissions relating to the ocean, wetlands and pinelands. Must pertain to New Jersey shore locale. Also, arts, entertainment news, reviews if they have a Jersey shore angle. Buys 10 mss/year. Send complete ms. Length: 200-2,000 words. Pays $25-200. Sometimes pays the expenses of writers on assignment.
Photos: Send photos with submission. Offers $8-25/photo. Buys one-time or all rights.
Columns/Departments: SpeakEasy (opinion and slice-of-life; often humorous); Commentary (forum for social science perspectives); both 1,000-1,500 words, preferably with local or Jersey shore angle. Buys 50 mss/year. Send complete ms. Pays $30.
Tips: "Anything of interest to sun worshippers, beach walkers, nature watchers, water sports lovers is of potential interest to us. There is an increasing coverage of environmental issues. The opinion page and columns are most open to freelancers. We are steadily increasing the amount of entertainment-related material in our publication. Articles on history of the shore area are always in demand."

New Mexico

NEW MEXICO MAGAZINE, Lew Wallace Bldg., 495 Old Santa Fe Trail, Santa Fe NM 87503. (505)827-7447. Editor-in-Chief: Emily Drabanski. Editor: Jon Bowman. Associate Editors: Walter K. Lopez, Camille Flores-Turney. 80% freelance written. Monthly magazine emphasizing New Mexico for a college-educated readership, above average income, interested in the Southwest. Estab. 1922. Circ. 125,000. **Pays on acceptance.** Publishes ms an average of 6 months to a year after acceptance. Buys first North American serial rights. Submit seasonal material 1 year in advance. Reports in 2 months. Sample copy for $2.95. Free writer's guidelines.
Nonfiction: New Mexico subjects of interest to travelers. Historical, cultural, informational articles. "We are looking for more short, light and bright stories for the 'Asi Es Nuevo Mexico' section." No columns, cartoons, poetry or non-New Mexico subjects. Buys 5-7 mss/issue. Query with 3 published writing samples. No phone or fax queries. Length: 250-2,000 words. Pays $100-500.
   ● This magazine rarely publishes reprints but sometimes publishes excerpts from novels and nonfiction books.
Photos: Purchased with accompanying ms or on assignment. Query or send contact sheet or transparencies. Pays $50-80 for 8×10 b&w glossy prints; $50-150 for 35mm—prefers Kodachrome. Photos should be in plastic-pocketed viewing sheets. Captions and model releases required. Mail photos to Art Director John Vaughan. Buys one-time rights.
Tips: "Send a superb short (300 words) manuscript on a little-known person, event, aspect of history or place to see in New Mexico. Faulty research will ruin a writer's chances for the future. Good style, good grammar. No generalized odes to the state or the Southwest. No sentimentalized, paternalistic views of Indians or Hispanics. No glib, gimmicky 'travel brochure' writing. No first-person vacation stories. We're always looking for well-researched pieces on unusual aspects of New Mexico history. Lively writing."

New York

ADIRONDACK LIFE, P.O. Box 97, Jay NY 12941-0097. Fax: (518)946-7461. Editor: Tom Hughes. 70% freelance written. Prefers to work with published/established writers. Emphasizes the Adirondack region and the North Country of New York State in articles concerning outdoor activities, history, and natural history directly related to the Adirondacks. Publishes 7 issues/year, including special Annual Outdoor Guide. Estab. 1970. Circ. 50,000. Pays 45 days after acceptance. Publishes ms an average of 6 months after acceptance.

Buys one-time rights. Byline given. Submit seasonal material 1 year in advance. Reports in 1 month. Sample copy for 9 × 12 SAE with 8 first-class stamps. Writer's guidelines for #10 SASE.

Nonfiction: "*Adirondack Life* attempts to capture the unique flavor and ethos of the Adirondack mountains and North Country region through feature articles directly pertaining to the qualities of the area and through department articles examining specific aspects. Example: Barkeater: personal essay; Special Places: unique spots in the Adirondacks; Working: careers in the Adirondacks and Wilderness: environmental issues, personal experiences." Buys 20-25 unsolicited mss/year. Query. Length: for features, 5,000 words maximum; for departments, 1,800 words. Pays up to 25¢/word. Sometimes pays expenses of writers on assignment.

● Also considers novel excerpts in its subject matter.

Photos: All photos must have been taken in the Adirondacks. Each issue contains a photo feature. Purchased with or without ms or on assignment. All photos must be identified as to subject or locale and must bear photographer's name. Submit color slides or b&w prints. Pays $25 for b&w prints; $50 for transparencies; $300 for cover (color only, vertical in format). Credit line given.

Tips: "We are looking for clear, concise, well-organized manuscripts, that are strictly Adirondack in subject."

BUFFALO SPREE MAGAZINE, Spree Publishing Co., Inc., Dept. WM, 4511 Harlem Rd., Buffalo NY 14226-3859. (716)839-3405. Editor: Johanna V. Hall Van De Mark. Contact: Alyssa Chase, associate editor. 90% freelance written. Quarterly literary, consumer-oriented, city magazine. Estab. 1967. Circ. 21,000. Pays on publication. Publishes ms an average of 6-12 months after acceptance. Byline given. Buys first North American serial rights. Submit seasonal material 9-12 months in advance. Reports in 6 months on mss. Sample copy for $2 and 9 × 12 SAE with 9 first-class stamps.

Nonfiction: Essays, interview/profile, historical/nostalgic, humor, personal experience, regional, travel. Buys 50 mss/year. Send complete ms. Length: 1,000-2,000 words. Pays $100-150 for unsolicited articles.

Fiction: Original pieces with a strong sense of story. Literary humorous, mainstream and occasionally experimental pieces. No pornographic or religious mss. Buys 60 mss/year. Send complete ms. Ideal length: 2,000 words. Pays $100-150.

Poetry: Janet Goldenberg, poetry editor. Buys 24 poems/year. Submit maximum 4 poems. Length: 50 lines maximum. Pays $25.

CITY LIMITS, City Limits Community Information Service, Inc., 40 Prince St., New York NY 10012. (212)925-9820. Fax: (212)996-3407. Editor: Andrew White. Senior Editor: Jill Kirschenbaum. Associate Editor: Kim Nauer. 50% freelance written. Works with a small number of new/unpublished writers each year. Monthly magazine covering housing and related urban issues. "We cover news and issues in New York City as they relate to the city's poor, moderate and middle-income residents." Estab. 1976. Circ. 5,000. Pays on publication. Publishes ms an average of 2 months after acceptance. Byline given. Buys first North American serial, one-time, or second serial (reprint) rights. Query for electronic submissions. Reports in 3 weeks. Sample copy for $4.

Nonfiction: Exposé, interview/profile, opinion, hard news, community profile. "No fluff, no propaganda." Length: 1.500-3,500 words. Pays $125-300. Sometimes pays expenses of writers on assignment.

Photos: Reviews contact sheets and 5 × 7 prints. Offers $20-40/photo, cover only. Identification of subjects required. Buys one-time rights. By assignment only.

Columns/Departments: Briefs (brief news items on programs, policies, events, etc.), 250-400 words; Book Reviews (housing, urban development, planning, environment, criminal justice etc.), 950 words; Pipeline (covers community organizations, new programs, government policies, etc.), 1,200-1,700 words; Profile (organizations, community groups, etc.), 1,200-1,700 words; PlanWatch (analysis of a particular urban or economic planning proposal); CityView (op-ed piece on current political affairs, city policy, or other community-related issues). Buys 50-75 mss/year. Query with published clips. Pays $25-200.

Tips: "We are open to a wide range of story ideas in the community development field. If you don't have particular expertise in housing, urban planning etc., start with a community profile or pertinent book or film review. Briefs is also good for anyone with reporting skills. We're looking for writing that is serious and informed but not academic or heavy handed."

HUDSON VALLEY MAGAZINE, Suburban Publishing, P.O. Box 429, Poughkeepsie NY 12601-3109. (914)485-7844. Fax: (914)485-5975. Editor-in-Chief: Susan Agrest. Monthly magazine. Estab. 1971. Circ. 30,000. Pays on publication. Byline given. Offers 25% kill fee. Buys first North American serial rights or first rights. Submit queries 3 months in advance. Query for electronic submissions. Accepts previously published submissions. Send tearsheet, photocopy of article or short story and information about when and where the material previously appeared. Reports in 6 months. Sample copy for $1 and 11 × 14 SAE with 4 first-class stamps.

Nonfiction: Only articles related to the Hudson Valley. Book excerpts, exposé, general interest, historical/nostalgic, how-to, humor, interview/profile, new product, opinion, photo feature, travel, business. Buys 150 mss/year. Query with published clips. Length: 300-3,500 words. Pays $25-800 for assigned articles.

Photos: Send photos with submission. Captions, model releases, identification of subjects required.

Columns/Departments: Open Season (advocacy/editorial); Environs (environmental); Pleasure Grounds (places to go); Charmed Places (homes); Slice of Life (essays) and Table Talk (restaurant reviews). Query with published clips. Length: 1,200-1,500 words. Pays $75-200.

Fiction: Novel excerpts rarely accepted.

Fillers: Anecdotes, facts, newsbreaks. Buys 36/year. Length: 300-500 words. Pays $25-50.

Tips: "Send a letter, résumé, sample of best writing and queries. No manuscripts. Factual accuracy imperative."

NEW YORK MAGAZINE, K-III Magazine Corp., 755 Second Ave., New York NY 10017-5998. (212)880-0700. Editor: Kurt Andersen. Managing Editor: Sarah Jewler. 25% freelance written. Weekly magazine focusing on current events in the New York metropolitan area. Circ. 433,813. **Pays on acceptance.** Offers 25% kill fee. Buys first world serial and electronic rights. Submit seasonal material 2 months in advance. Reports in 1 month. Sample copy for $3.50. Writer's guidelines for SASE.

Nonfiction: Exposé, general interest, profile, new product, personal experience, travel. Query. Pays $1/word. Pays expenses of writers on assignment.

Tips: "Submit a detailed query to Sarah Jewler, *New York*'s managing editor. If there is sufficient interest in the proposed piece, the article will be assigned."

‡NEW YORK SPORTSCENE, Sportscene Enterprises, Inc., 990 Motor Parkway, Central Islip NY 11722. (516)435-8890. Editor: Mark Sosna. 80% freelance written. Monthly magazine covering sports. "We cover professional and major college teams in New York State, along with other notable events in the region (i.e.—Belmont Stakes, U.S. Open, NYC Marathon, etc.). Features include Interviews, Fan-in-the-street questions, trivia, calendar of upcoming games, etc." Estab. 1995. Circ. 125,000. Pays on publication. Publishes ms an average of 3 months after acceptance. Byline given. Makes work-for-hire assignments. Editorial lead time 4 months. Submit seasonal material 3 months in advance. Accepts simultaneous submissions. Sample copy free on request.

Nonfiction: General interest, humor, interview/profile, new product, photo feature. Buys 90 mss/year. Query with published clips. Length: 500-1,500 words. Pays $25-75. Sometimes pays expenses of writers on assignment.

Photos: State availability of photos with submission. Reviews transparencies. Negotiates payment individually. Captions, identification of subjects required.

Columns/Departments: Sports Cap (humorous take on NY sports), 750 words; Goat/Month/Penalty Box (those who ruin sports/give it a bad image), 750 words; Health/Fitness, 750 words. Buys 25 mss/year. Query with published clips. Pays $25-75.

Fiction: "As a new publication, we are looking for writers with solid contacts and creative story ideas. Obviously, a sports background is beneficial. We are especially interested in writers who can cover the lesser-covered sports—horse racing, tennis, golf, bowling, skiing, etc. Send résumé and clips for consideration."

NEWSDAY, Melville NY 11747-4250. Viewpoints Editor: Noel Rubinton. Opinion section of daily newspaper. Byline given. Estab. 1940.

Nonfiction: Seeks "opinion on current events, trends, issues—whether national or local, government or lifestyle. Must be timely, pertinent, articulate and opinionated. Preference for authors within the circulation area including New York City." Length: 700-800 words. Pays $150-200.

● At press time it was announced that *New York Newsday* will cease publication.

SPOTLIGHT MAGAZINE, Meadown Publications Inc., 126 Library Lane, Mamaroneck NY 10543. (914)381-4740. Fax: (914)381-4641. Editor: Marcia Hecht. 10% freelance written. Monthly magazine of general interest. Audience is "upscale, educated, 18-60, in the NY-NJ-CT tristate area. We try to appeal to a broad audience throughout our publication area." Estab. 1977. Circ. 73,000. Pays on publication. Byline given. Buys first rights. Editorial lead time 3 months. Submit seasonal material 5 months in advance. Accepts previously published submissions. Send tearsheet or photocopy of article and typed ms with rights for sale noted and information about when and where the article previously appeared. Reprint payment is negotiated. Reports in 3 weeks on queries; 2 months on mss. Sample copy for $3.

● *Spotlight* is looking for human interest articles woven around New York, New Jersey and Connecticut.

Nonfiction: Book excerpts, essays, exposé, general human interest, historical/nostalgic, how-to, humor, inspirational, interview/profile, new product, photo feature, travel, illustrations. Publishes annual special-interest guides: Wedding (February, June, September); Dining (December); Home Design (March, April, October); Home Technology (May); Travel (June); Health (July, January); Education (January, August); Holiday Gifts (November); Corporate (March, July, October). Does not want to see fiction or poetry. Buys 5-10 mss/year. Query. Pays $150 minimum.

Photos: State availability of or send photos with submission. Reviews transparencies and prints. Negotiates payment individually. Captions, model releases, identification of subjects required (when appropriate). Buys one-time rights.

SYRACUSE NEW TIMES, A. Zimmer Ltd., 1415 W. Genesee St., Syracuse NY 13204. Fax: (315)422-1721. E-mail: 71632.43@compuserve.com. Editor: Mike Greenstein. 50% freelance written. Weekly tabloid covering news, sports, arts and entertainment. *"Syracuse New Times* is an alternative weekly that can be topical, provocative, irreverent and intensely local." Estab. 1969. Circ. 45,000. Pays on publication. Publishes ms an average of 1 month after acceptance. Byline given. Buys one-time rights. Editorial lead time 3 months. Submit seasonal material 3 months in advance. Accepts simultaneous and previously published submissions. Query for electronic submissions. Reports in 2 weeks on queries; 1 month on mss. Sample copy for 9 × 11 SAE with 2 first-class stamps. Writer's guidelines for #10 SASE.
Nonfiction: Essays, general interest. Buys 200 mss/year. Query with published clips. Length: 250-2,500 words. Pays $25-200.
Photos: State availability of photos or send photos with submission. Reviews 8 × 10 prints. Offers $10-25/photo or negotiates payment individually. Identification of subjects required. Buys one-time rights.
Tips: "Move to Syracuse and query with strong idea."

North Carolina

‡**CAROLINA STYLE MAGAZINE**, Carolina Style, Inc., 3975-B Market St., Wilmington NC 28403. (910)341-3033. Editor: Anthony S. Policastro. 100% freelance written. Bimonthly magazine. *"Carolina Style Magazine* is an upscale four-color, magazine covering the people, the culture, the rich history, and the overall high quality of life on the North and South Carolina coasts." Estab. 1991. Circ. 100,000. Pays on publication. Byline given. Offers 50% kill fee. Buys first North American serial rights and electronic rights. Editorial lead time 3 months. Submit seasonal material 3 months in advance. Accepts simultaneous and previously published submissions. Query for electronic submissions. Reports in 3-6 weeks on queries. Sample copy for $5. Writer's guidelines for #10 SASE.
Nonfiction: Book excerpts, general interest, historical/nostalgic, humor, interview/profile, personal experience, photo feature, travel. Special issues: Holiday (November, deadline September 15). Buys 100 mss/year. Query. Length: 500-2,500 words. Pays 10¢/word. Sometimes pays expenses of writers on assignment.
Photos: State availability of photos with submission. Reviews 35mm or 4 × 5 transparencies. Offers $25-50/photo. Captions, identification of subjects required. Buys one-time rights and electronic rights.
Columns/Departments: Beach Bag (short items), 500 words; There You Go (unique photo run as full page). Buys 12 mss/year. Query. Pays 10¢/word.
Fiction: Adventure, condensed novels, historical, horror, humorous, mainstream, mystery, novel excerpts, romance, slice-of-life vignettes, suspense. Buys 6 mss/year. Send complete ms. Length: 1,000-4,000 words. Pays 10¢/word.
Poetry: Buys 6 poems/year. Submit maximum 5 poems. Length: 10-20 lines. Pays $25-50.
Fillers: Facts, short humor. Buys 12/year. Length: 500-750 words. Pays 10¢/word.

THE STATE, Down Home in North Carolina, 128 S. Tryon St., Suite 2200, Charlotte NC 28202. Fax: (704)375-8129. Managing Editor: Scott Smith. 80% freelance written. Monthly. Circ. 25,000. Publishes ms an average of 6-12 months after acceptance. Byline given. No kill fee. Buys first serial rights. Pays on publication. Submit seasonal material 8-12 months in advance. Reports in 2 months. Sample copy for $2.50.
Nonfiction: General articles about places, people, events, history, nostalgia, general interest in North Carolina. Emphasis on travel in North Carolina. Will use humor if related to region. Length: 700-2,000 words average. Pays $125-150 for assigned articles; $75-125 for unsolicited articles.
Photos: Send photos with submission if possible. Reviews contact sheets and transparencies. Offers additional payment for photos. Captions and identification of subjects required. Buys one-time rights.
Fiction: Publishes novel excerpts.
Columns/Departments: The State We're In (newsbriefs about current events in NC; most have travel, historic or environmental slant), 150-500 words. Buys 10 mss/year. Pays $25.

Ohio

BEND OF THE RIVER MAGAZINE, P.O. Box 39, Perrysburg OH 43552-0039. (419)874-7534. Publisher: R. Lee Raizk. 90% freelance written. Eager to work with new/unpublished writers. "We buy material that we like whether it is by an experienced writer or not." Monthly magazine for readers interested in northwestern Ohio history, antiques, etc. Estab. 1972. Circ. 5,000. Pays on publication. Publishes ms an average of 6 months after acceptance. Byline given. Buys one-time rights. Accepts previously published submissions. Send tearsheet of article and information about when and where the article previously appeared. For reprints, pays 100% of the amount paid for an original article. Submit seasonal material 2 months in advance; deadline for holiday issue is November 1. Reports in up to 6 months. Sample copy for $1.50.
Nonfiction: "We deal heavily in Northwestern Ohio history and nostalgia. We are looking for old snapshots of the Toledo area to accompany articles, personal reflection, etc. Buys 75 unsolicited mss/year. Submit complete ms or send query. Length: 1,500 words. Pays $10-25.

Photos: Purchases b&w or color photos with accompanying mss. Pays $1 minimum. Captions required.

Tips: "Any Toledo area, well-researched nostalgia, local history will be put on top of the heap. If you send a picture with manuscript, it gets an A +! We pay a small amount but usually use our writers often and through the years. We're loyal."

CINCINNATI MAGAZINE, 409 Broadway, Cincinnati OH 45202-3340. (513)421-4300. Editorial Director: Felix Winternitz. Homes Editor: Linda Vaccariello. Food Editor: Lilia F. Brady. Monthly magazine emphasizing Cincinnati living. Circ. 32,000. **Pays on acceptance.** Byline given. Buys first rights. Submit seasonal material 4 months in advance. Accepts simultaneous and previously published submissions. Send photocopy of article and information about when and where the article previously appeared. For reprints pays, 33% of the amount paid for an original article. Reports in 2 months.

Nonfiction: Profiles of Cincinnati celebrities, local business, trend stories. Buys 1 ms/issue. Query. Length: 2,000-4,000 words. Pays $150-400.

Columns/Departments: Cincinnati dining, media, arts and entertainment, people, politics, sports. Buys 2 mss/issue. Query. Length: 750-1,500 words. Pays $75-150.

Tips: "We do special features each month. January (Homes); February (Dining out, restaurants); March (Health, Personal finance); April (Home and Fashion); May (Environment and Golf); June (Health); July (Food and Homes); August (Fashion); September (Homes); October (Best and Worst); November (Automotive Guide and Fashion); December (City guide). We also have a special issue in August where we feature a local fiction contest."

‡CLEVELAND MAGAZINE, City Magazines, Inc., 1422 Euclid Ave., #730Q, Cleveland OH 44115. Editor: Liz Ludlow. 70% freelance written, mostly by assignment. Monthly magazine with a strong Cleveland/NE Ohio angle. Estab. 1972. Circ. 45,000. Pays on publication. Publishes ms an average of 3 months after acceptance. Byline given. Offers 50% kill fee. Buys first rights and second serial (reprint) rights. Editorial lead time 4-6 months. Submit seasonal material 6-8 months in advance. Accepts simultaneous submissions. No previously published submissions. Reports in 2 months. Sample copy for $3. Writer's guidelines for #10 SASE.

Nonfiction: Book excerpts, general interest, historical/nostalgic, humor, interview/profile. Buys 1 ms/year. Query with published clips. Length: 800-5,000 words. Pays $200-800. Sometimes pays expenses of writers on assignment.

Columns/Departments: City Life (Cleveland trivia/humor/info briefs), 200 words. Buys 2 mss/year. Query with published clips. Pays $50.

NORTHERN OHIO LIVE, LIVE Publishing Co., 11320 Juniper Rd., Cleveland OH 44106. (216)721-1800. Fax: (216)721-2525. E-mail: nohiolive@aol.com. Managing Editor: Shari M. Sweeney. Editor: Michael von Glahn. 70% freelance written. Monthly magazine covering Northern Ohio's arts, entertainment, education and dining. "*Live*'s reader demographic is mid-30s to 50s, though we're working to bring in the late 20s. Our readers are well-educated, many with advanced degrees. They're interested in Northern Ohio's cultural scene and support it." Estab. 1980. Circ. 32,000. Pays 20th of publication month. Publishes ms an average of 1 month after acceptance. Byline given. Offers 50% kill fee. Buys first North American serial rights. Editorial lead time 2 months. Submit seasonal material 4 months in advance. Query for electronic submissions. Reports in 3 weeks on queries; 2 months on mss. Sample copy for $2.

Nonfiction: Essays, exposé, general interest, humor, interview/profile, photo feature, travel. All should have a Northern Ohio slant and preferably an arts focus. Special issues: Gourmet Guide (restaurants), (May); Gallery Tour (May, October); After 5 (nightlife), (November). "No business/corporate articles, stories outside Northern Ohio." Buys 100 mss/year. Query with published clips. Length: 1,000-3,500 words. Pays $100-350. Sometimes pays expenses of writers on assignment.

Photos: State availability of photos with submission. Reviews contact sheets, 4×5 transparencies and 3×5 prints. Negotiates payment individually. Identification of subjects required. Buys one-time rights.

Columns/Departments: News & Reviews (arts previews, personality profiles, general interest), 800-1,800 words. Buys 60-70 mss/year. Query with published clips. Pays $100-150.

OHIO MAGAZINE, Ohio Magazine, Inc., Subsidiary of Dispatch Printing Co., 62 E. Broad St., Columbus OH 43215-3522. (614)461-5083. Editor: Casandra Ring. 40% freelance written. Works with a small number of new/unpublished writers each year. Monthly magazine emphasizing news and feature material of Ohio for an educated, urban and urbane readership. Estab. 1978. Circ. 100,000. Pays on publication. Publishes ms an average of 5 months after acceptance. Buys all, second serial (reprint), one-time, first North American serial or first serial rights. Byline given except on short articles appearing in sections. Submit seasonal material minimum 6 months in advance. Accepts previously published submissions. Send tearsheet or photocopy of article and information about when and where it previously appeared. For reprints, pays 50% of amount paid for an original article. Reports in 2 months. Sample copy for $3 and 9×12 SAE. Writer's guidelines for #10 SASE.

Nonfiction: Features: 2,000-8,000 words. Pays $800-1,400. Cover pieces $650-1,200. Sometimes pays expenses of writers on assignment.

Columns/Departments: Ohioans (should be offbeat with solid news interest; 1,000-2,000 words, pays $300-500); Business (covering business related news items, profiles of prominent people in business community, personal finance—all Ohio angle; 1,000 words and up, pays $300-500); Environment (issues related to Ohio and Ohioans, 1,000-2,000 words, pays $400-700). Buys minimum 40 unsolicited mss/year.

Photos: Brooke Wenstrup, art director. Rate negotiable.

Tips: "Freelancers should send all queries in writing, not by telephone or fax. Subject matter should be global enough to appeal to readers outside of Ohio, but regional enough to call in our own."

‡OVER THE BACK FENCE, South Central Ohio's Own Magazine, Back Fence Publishing, Inc., P.O.Box 756, Chillicothe OH 45601. (614)772-2165. Editor-in-Chief: Ann Zalek. Quarterly magazine covering regional history, people, events, etc. "We are a regional magazine serving 15 counties in south central Ohio. *Over the Back Fence* has a wholesome, neighborly style. It appeals to readers from young adults to seniors, often encouraging reader participation through replies." Estab. 1994. Circ. 15,000. Pays on publication. Byline given. Buys one-time rights, simultaneous rights, makes work-for-hire assignments. Editorial lead time 6-12 months. Submit seasonal material 6-12 months in advance. Accepts simultaneous submissions and previously published submissions—must be identified and described. Query for electronic submissions. Reports in 3 months. Sample copy for $4 and SASE. Writer's guidelines for #10 SASE.

Nonfiction: General interest, historical/nostalgic, humor, inspirational, interview/profile, personal exprience, photo feature, travel. Buys 9-12 mss/year. Query with or without published clips or send complete ms. Length: 750-2,000 words. Pays 10¢/word minimum, negotiable depending on experience. Sometimes pays expenses of writers on assignment.

Photos: State availability of photos with submission or send photos with submission. Reviews b&w contact sheets, transparencies (35mm or larger), 3⅓×5 prints. Offers $25-100/photo. Captions, model releases and identification of subjects required. Buys one-time rights.

Columns/Departments: Art, 750-2,000 words; History (relevant to one county), 750-2,000 words; Health, 750-2,000 words; Inspirational (poetry or short story), no minimum for poetry, short story 200-1,500 words; Recipes, 750-2,000 words; Profiles From Our Past, approx. 200-750 words (1 page). All must be relevant to south central Ohio. Buys 24 mss/year. Query with or without published clips or send complete ms. Pays 10¢/word minimum, negotiable depending on experience; 10¢/word or minimum $25 whichever is greater for poetry.

Fiction: Humorous. Buys 4 mss/year. Query with published clips. Length: 250-1,500 words. Pays 10¢/word minimum, negotiable depending on experience.

Poetry: Free verse, light verse, traditional. Buys 4-6 poems/year. Submit maximum 6 poems. Length: open ("we may have to restructure"). Pays $25 or 10¢/word.

Fillers: Anecdotes, short humor. Buys 0-8/year. Length: 100 words maximum. Pays $25-10¢/word.

Tips: "Our approach can be equated to a friendly and informative conversation with a neighbor about interesting people, places and events in south central Ohio (counties: Adams, Athens, Fayette, Fairfield, Gallia, Highland, Hocking, Jackson, Lawrence, Meigs, Pickaway, Pike, Ross, Scioto and Vinton)."

PLAIN DEALER MAGAZINE, Plain Dealer Publishing Co., 1801 Superior Ave., Cleveland OH 44114. (216)344-4546. Fax: (216)999-6354. Editor: Anne Gordon. 30% freelance written. Sunday weekly/general interest newspaper magazine focusing on Cleveland and northeastern Ohio. Circ. 550,000. Pays on publication. Publishes ms an average of 3 months after acceptance. Byline given. Buys first or one-time rights. Submit seasonal/holiday material 3 months in advance. Occasionally accepts previously published submissions. Send typed ms with rights for sale noted and information about when and where the article previously appeared. Reports in 1 month on queries; 2 months on mss. Sample copy for $1.

Nonfiction: Profiles, in-depth features, essays, exposé, historical/nostalgic, humor, personal experience. Must focus on northeast Ohio, people, places and issues of the area. Buys 20 mss/year. Query with published clips or send complete ms. Manuscripts must be double-spaced and should include a daytime telephone number. Length: 800-3,000 words. Pays $150-500.

Photos: Send photos with submission. Buys one-time rights.

Tips: "We're always looking for good writers and good stories."

Oklahoma

OKLAHOMA TODAY, P.O. Box 53384, Oklahoma City OK 73152-9971. Fax: (405)521-3992. Editor: Jeanne M. Devlin. 80% freelance written. Works with a small number of new/unpublished writers each year. Bimonthly magazine covering people, places and things Oklahoman. "We are interested in showing off the best Oklahoma has to offer; we're pretty serious about our travel slant but regularly run history, nature and personality profiles." Estab. 1956. Circ. 45,000. **Pays on final acceptance.** Publishes ms an average of 6 months after acceptance. Byline given. Buys first serial rights. Submit seasonal material 1 year in advance "depending on photographic requirements." Accepts previously published submissions. Send tearsheet of article or typed ms with rights for sale noted and information about when and where the article previously appeared. For reprints, pays varying amounts. Reports in 4 months. Sample copy for $2.50 and 9×12 SASE. Writer's guidelines for #10 SASE.

- *Oklahoma Today* recently won Magazine of the Year, awarded by the International Regional Magazine Association.

Nonfiction: Book excerpts (pre-publication only, on Oklahoma topics); photo feature and travel (in Oklahoma). Buys 40-60 mss/year. Query with published clips; no phone queries. Length: 1,000-3,000 words. Pays $25-750.

Photos: High-quality transparencies, b&w prints. "We are especially interested in developing contacts with photographers who either live in Oklahoma or have shot here. Send samples and price range." Free photo guidelines with SASE. Pays $50-100 for b&w and $50-750 for color; reviews 2¼ and 35mm color transparencies. Model releases, identification of subjects, other information for captions required. Buys one-time rights plus right to use photos for promotional purposes.

Tips: "The best way to become a regular contributor to *Oklahoma Today* is to query us with one or more story ideas, each developed to give us an idea of your proposed slant. We're looking for *lively*, concise, well-researched and reported stories, stories that don't need to be heavily edited and are not newspaper style. We have a two-person editorial staff, and freelancers who can write and have done their homework get called again and again."

Oregon

CASCADES EAST, P.O. Box 5784, Bend OR 97708-5784. (503)382-0127. Fax: (503)382-7057. Editor: Geoff Hill. Associate publisher: Kim Hogue, 90% freelance written. Prefers to work with published/established writers. Quarterly magazine for "all ages as long as they are interested in outdoor recreation in central Oregon: fishing, hunting, sight-seeing, golf, tennis, hiking, bicycling, mountain climbing, backpacking, rockhounding, skiing, snowmobiling, etc." Estab. 1972. Circ. 10,000 (distributed throughout area resorts and motels and to subscribers). Pays on publication. Publishes ms an average of 6 months after acceptance. Buys all rights. Byline given. Submit seasonal material 6 months in advance. Accepts previously published submissions. Send information about when and where the article previously appeared. Reports in 3 months. Sample copy and writer's guidelines for $5 and 9×12 SAE.

- *Cascades East* now accepts and prefers manuscripts along with a 3.5 disk. They can translate most word processing programs.

Nonfiction: General interest (first person experiences in outdoor central Oregon—with photos, can be dramatic, humorous or factual), historical (for feature, "Little Known Tales from Oregon History," with b&w photos), personal experience (needed on outdoor subjects: dramatic, humorous or factual). "No articles that are too general, sight-seeing articles that come from a travel folder, or outdoor articles without the first-person approach." Buys 20-30 unsolicited mss/year. Query. Length: 1,000-3,000 words. Pays 5-10¢/word.

Photos: "Old photos will greatly enhance chances of selling a historical feature. First-person articles need b&w photos, also." Pays $10-25 for b&w; $15-100 for transparencies. Captions preferred. Buys one-time rights.

Tips: "Submit stories a year or so in advance of publication. We are seasonal and must plan editorials for summer '97 in the spring of '96, etc., in case seasonal photos are needed."

OREGON COAST, The Bi-Monthly Magazine of Coastal Living, 1525 12th St., Florence OR 97439-0130. (800)348-8401. Managing Editor: Judy Fleagle. Senior Editor: Dave Peden. 65% freelance written. Bimonthly magazine covering the Oregon Coast. Estab. 1982. Circ. 65,000. Pays after publication. Publishes ms an average of 6-12 months after acceptance. Byline given. Offers 33% kill fee. Buys first North American serial rights. Submit seasonal material 6 months in advance. Sometimes accepts previously published submissions. Send tearsheet or photocopy of article and information about when and where the article previously appeared. For reprints, pays 65% of the amount paid for an original article. Query for electronic submissions. Reports in 1 month on queries; 3 months on mss. Sample copy for $4.50. Writer's guidelines for #10 SASE.

- This magazine is using fewer freelancers because its staff is doing more writing inhouse.

Nonfiction: "A true regional with general interest, historical/nostalgic, humor, interview/profile, personal experience, photo feature, travel and nature as pertains to Oregon Coast." Buys 60 mss/year. Query with published clips. Length: 500-2,000 words. Pays $75-350 plus 2-5 contributor copies.

Photos: Send photos with submission. Reviews 35mm or larger transparencies and 3×5 or larger prints. Photo submissions with no ms for stand alone or cover photos. Captions, model releases, photo credits, identification of subjects required. Buys one-time rights.

Fillers: Newsbreaks (no-fee basis) and short articles. Buys 12/year. Length: 300-500 words. Pays $35-50.

Tips: "Slant article for readers who do not live at the Oregon Coast. At least one historical article is used in each issue. Manuscript/photo packages are preferred over mss with no photos. List photo credits and captions for each print or slide. Check all facts, proper names and numbers carefully in photo/ms packages."

OREGON PARKS, Educational Publications Foundation, P.O. Box 18000, Florence OR 97439. (503)997-8401. Editor: Dave Peden. Managing Editor: Judy Fleagle. 50% freelance written. Consumer publication.

Bimonthly trade magazine covering parklands in Oregon/other public lands. "The magazine, which was begun with the active participation of the state parks department, aims to inform Oregonians and visitors about the parks and public lands in Oregon, their facilities, services, and issues." Estab. 1993. Circ. 25,000. Pays after publication. Byline given. Offers 33% kill fee. Buys first North American serial rights (for ms and ms/photo packages). Editorial lead time 4-6 months. Submit seasonal material 6 months in advance. "We haven't done reprints in *Oregon Parks*, but might be willing to consider it." Send photocopy of article or typed ms with rights for sale noted and information about when and where the article previously appeared. For reprints, pays 65% of the amount paid for an original article. Query for electronic submissions. Reports in 6 weeks on queries. Sample copy for $4.50. Writer's guidelines for #10 SASE.

Nonfiction: General interest, historical/nostalgic, photo feature, travel. "No interest in non-Oregon articles, or articles on wilderness areas in Oregon. Don't need spotted owl stories." Buys 40-45 mss/year. Query with or without published clips. Length: 500-2,000 words. Pays $75 minimum for unsolicited articles.

Photos: State availability of photos with query. Reviews transparencies. Captions, model releases (if person is readily identifiable) and credits required.

Tips: "Looking for interesting activity-oriented articles placed in parks (not necessarily state parks) and forestlands in Oregon. Lively writing and great photos are the best entree to the magazine. Pick a city or county park that you think is great, but not well known outside of your local area. Query first and have photos available—transparencies if possible."

‡PDXS, Art, Music, Politics, PDXS Publications Inc., 2305 NW Kearney, Portland OR 97210. (503)224-7316. Editor: Jim Redden. 90% freelance written. Biweekly tabloid covering alternative politics, deviant subcultures. Estab. 1991. Circ. 12,000. Pays on publication. Publishes ms an average of 2 months after acceptance. Byline given. Offers 50% kill fee for commissioned stories. Buys first rights and one-time rights. Editorial lead time 1 month. Submit seasonal material 2 months in advance. Accepts simultaneous and previously published submissions. Query for electronic submissions. Reports in 1 month on queries; 3 months on mss. Writer's guidelines for 9×11 SAE with 4 first-class stamps.

Nonfiction: Exposé, interview/profile, investigative. Buys 60 mss/year. Send complete ms. Length: 1,000-2,000 words. Pays $40-60. Sometimes pays expenses of writers on assignment.

Photos: Send photos with submission. Reviews prints. Offers $15-30/photo. Identification of subjects required. Buys one-time rights.

Columns/Departments: Films (pro-violence), 500 words; Record Reviews (honest), 250 words. Buys 100 mss/year. Send complete ms. Pays $15-30.

‡WILLAMETTE WEEK, Portland's Newsweekly, City of Roses Co., 822 SW Tenth Ave., Portland OR 97205. (503)243-2122. Editor: Mark Zusmon. 50% freelance written. Weekly alternative newsweekly focusing on local news. Estab. 1974. Circ. 75,000. Pays on publication. Byline given. Offers 25% kill fee. Buys first North American serial rights. Editorial lead time 2 months. Submit seasonal material 2 months in advance. Accepts simultaneous and previously published submissions. Query for electronic submissions. Reports in 1 month. Sample copy and writer's guidelines for #10 SASE.

Nonfiction: Exposé, interview/profile. Special issues: Summer Guide, Best of Portland, Fall Arts, 21st Anniversary. Buys 30 mss/year. Query. Length: 400-3,000 words. Pays 10-30¢/word. Sometimes pays expenses of writers on assignment.

Photos: State availability of photos with submission. Reviews contact sheets. Negotiates payment individually. Model releases, identification of subjects required. Buys one-time rights.

Pennsylvania

‡THE GAZETTE, Pittsburgh Post-Gazette, 34 Boulevard of the Allies, Pittsburgh, PA 15222. (412)263-2579. Editor: Mark S. Murphy. 10% freelance written. Weekly general interest newspaper magazine for Western Pennsylvania. Circ. 470,000. Pays on publication. Byline given. Buys first serial rights in circulation area. Query for electronic submissions.

Nonfiction: Regional or local interest, humor and interview/profile. No hobbies, how-to or timely events. Buys 40-50 mss/year. Length: 2,500-5,000 words. Pays $500.

PENNSYLVANIA, Pennsylvania Magazine Co., P.O. Box 576, Camp Hill PA 17001-0576. (717)761-6620. Publisher: Albert E. Holliday. Managing Editor: Matt Holliday. 90% freelance written. Bimonthly magazine. Estab. 1981. Circ. 40,000. Pays on acceptance except for articles (by authors unknown to us) sent on speculation. Publishes ms an average of 6-12 months after acceptance. Byline given. Offers 25% kill fee for assigned articles. Buys first North American serial or one-time rights. Accepts previously published submissions. Send photocopy of article, typed ms with rights for sale noted and information about when and where the article previously appeared. Pays 50% of amount paid for an original article. Reports in 1 month. Sample copy for $2.95. Writer's guidelines for #10 SASE.

Nonfiction: General interest, historical/nostalgic, photo feature, travel—all dealing with or related to Pennsylvania. Nothing on Amish topics, hunting or skiing. Buys 50-75 mss/year. Query. Length: 250-2,500 words.

Pays $50-400. Sometimes pays the expenses of writers on assignment. All articles must be illustrated; send photocopies of possible illustrations with query or mss. *Will not consider without illustrations.*

Photos: Reviews 35mm and 2¼ color transparencies (no originals) and 5×7 to 8×10 color and b&w prints. Do not send original slides. Pays $15-25 for inside photos; up to $100 for covers. Captions required. Buys one-time rights.

Columns/Departments: Panorama (short items about people, unusual events, family and individually owned consumer-related businesses); Almanac (short historical items). All must be illustrated.

Tips: "Our publication depends upon freelance work—send queries."

PENNSYLVANIA HERITAGE, Pennsylvania Historical and Museum Commission, P.O. Box 1026, Harrisburg PA 17108-1026. (717)787-7522. Fax: (717)787-8312. Editor: Michael J. O'Malley III. 90% freelance written. Prefers to work with published/established writers. Quarterly magazine. "*Pennsylvania Heritage* introduces readers to Pennsylvania's rich culture and historic legacy, educates and sensitizes them to the value of preserving that heritage and entertains and involves them in such as way as to ensure that Pennsylvania's past has a future. The magazine is intended for intelligent lay readers." Estab. 1974. Circ. 10,000. **Pays on acceptance.** Publishes ms an average of 6-12 months after acceptance. Byline given. Buys all rights. Accepts simultaneous queries and submissions. Reports in 6 weeks on queries; 6 months on mss. Sample copy for $4.50 and 9×12 SAE; writer's guidelines for #10 SASE.

● *Pennsylvania Heritage* is now considering freelance submissions that are shorter in length—2,000 to 2,500 words—and liberally illustrated articles devoted to Pennsylvania's objects, artifacts, and traditions, as well as full-color travel pieces devoted *exclusively* to the historic sites and museums administered by the Pennsylvania Historical and Museum Commission. Also a new addition is interviews.

Nonfiction: Art, science, biographies, industry, business, politics, transportation, military, historic preservation, archaeology, photography, etc. No articles which in no way relate to Pennsylvania history or culture. "Our format requires feature-length articles. Manuscripts with illustrations are especially sought for publication. We are now looking for shorter (2,000 words) manuscripts that are heavily illustrated with *Publication-quality* photographs or artwork." Buys 20-24 mss/year. Prefers to see mss with suggested illustrations. Length: 2,000-3,500 words. Pays $300-750.

Photos: State availability of, or send photos with ms. Pays $25-100 for transparencies; $5-10 for b&w photos. Captions and identification of subjects required. Buys one-time rights.

Tips: "We are looking for well-written, interesting material that pertains to any aspect of Pennsylvania history or culture. Potential contributors should realize that, although our articles are popularly styled, they are not light, puffy or breezy; in fact they demand strident documentation and substantiation (sans footnotes). The most frequent mistake made by writers in completing articles for us is making them either too scholarly or too nostalgic. We want material which educates, but also entertains. Authors should make history readable and enjoyable."

PITTSBURGH MAGAZINE, QED Communications, Inc., 4802 5th Ave., Pittsburgh PA 15213. (412)622-1360. Fax: (412)622-7066. No phone queries. Send queries to Michelle Pilecki, Managing Editor. 60% freelance written. Prefers to work with published/established writers. The magazine is purchased on newsstands and by subscription and is given to those who contribute $40 or more a year to public TV in western Pennsylvania. Estab. 1970. Circ. 65,000. Pays on publication. Publishes ms an average of 2 months after acceptance. Buys first North American serial rights and second serial (reprint) rights. Offers kill fee. Byline given. Submit seasonal material 6 months in advance. Query for electronic submissions. Reports in 2 months. Sample copy for $2 (old back issues).

● Editor reports a need for more hard news and more stories geared to young readers.

Nonfiction: Exposé, lifestyle, sports, informational, service, business, medical, profile. Must have regional angle. Query with outline. Length: 2,500 words or less. Pays $100-1,200.

Photos: Query for photos. Model releases required. Sometimes pays the expenses of writers on assignment.

‡**THE PITTSBURGH PRESS SUNDAY MAGAZINE**,The Pittsburgh Press Co., 34 Boulevard of the Allies, Pittsburgh PA 15230. (412)263-1510. Editor: Ed Wintermantel. 10% freelance written. Prefers to work with published/established writers. A weekly general interest newspaper magazine for a general audience. Circ. 544,402. Pays on publication. Publishes ms an average of 2 months after acceptance. Byline given. Not copyrighted. Buys first serial rights in circulation area. Rarely accepts previously published submissions. Send photocopy of article and information about when and where the article previously appeared. Query for electronic submissions. Reports in 1 month. Writer's guidelines for #10 SASE.

Nonfiction: Regional or local interest, humor and interview/profile. No hobbies, how-to or timely events. Buys 40-50 mss/year. Query. "When submitting a manuscript, writer must include his or her social security number. This is a requirement of the Internal Revenue Service since payments for published stories must be reported." Length: 1,000-3,000 words. Pays $100-400.

‡**SEVEN ARTS**, A.C. Publishers, 260 S. Broad St., 3rd Floor, Philadelphia PA 19106. Editor: Virginia Moles. Managing Editor: Judith West. 25% freelance written. Monthly magazine covering arts and culture. "*Seven*

Arts magazine aims to stimulate interest in the arts in the Philadelphia region." Estab. 1993. Circ. 135,000. Pays on publication. Publishes ms an average of 3 months after acceptance. Byline given. Offers 20% kill fee. Buys first North American serial rights. Editorial lead time 2 months. Submit seasonal material 6 months in advance. Accepts simultaneous submissions and previously published submissions. Query for electronic submissions. Reports in 3 months. Sample copy free.

Nonfiction: Book excerpts, essays, interview/profile, photo feature. No non-arts related material. Buys 25 mss/year. Query with published clips. Length: 800-2,000 words. Pays $200-700. Sometimes pays expenses of writers on assignment.

Photos: State availability of photos with submission. Reviews contact sheets. Negotiates payment individually. Captions, model releases and identification of subjects required. Buys one-time rights.

Columns/Departments: Theater, Music, Dance, Art; 800-1,500 words. Buys 25 mss/year. Query with published clips. Pays $200-400.

Tips: "Consider breaking in with small, front-of-the-book pieces; pitch ideas for specific sections of the magazine; hook to specific cultural events."

Rhode Island

‡NEWPORT LIFE, 174 Bellevue Ave., Suite 207, Newport RI 02840. Editor: Susan Ryan. Contact: Lynne Tungett. 90% freelance written. Quarterly magazine covering Newport County's people, history and general interest. "*Newport Life* is a community magazine focusing on the people, issues, history and events that make Newport County unique." Estab. 1993. Circ. 10,000. Pays on publication. Publishes ms an average of 3 months after acceptance. Byline given. Offers 20% kill fee. Buys one-time rights. Editorial lead time 1 year. Submit seasonal material 6 months in advance. Accepts simultaneous and previously published submissions. Query for electronic submissions. Reports in 1 month. Sample copy free on request. Writer's guidelines for #10 SASE.

Nonfiction: General interest, historical/nostalgic, interview/profile, opinion, photo feature. Buys 20 mss/ year. Query with published clips. Length: 500-3,000 words. Pays $50-300 for assigned articles. Sometimes pays expenses of writers on assignment.

Photos: State availability of photos with submission. Reviews 3×5 prints. Negotiates payment individually. Captions, model releases, identification of subjects required. Buys one-time rights.

Columns/Departments: Historical Newport (person or aspect of Newport County's history), 750-1,000 words; In Our Midst (local individuals who've made contribution to community), 500 words; At The Helm (significant person in the boating industry), 500 words; Arts Marquee (local artisans), 500 words. Buys 24 mss/year. Query with published clips. Pays $50-100.

Fillers: Anecdotes, facts, gags to be illustrated by cartoonist, short humor. Length: 20-50 words. Pays $10-25.

Tips: "Articles should be specific, informative and thoroughly researched. Historical information and quotes are encouraged. New/unpublished writers welcome. Query with lead paragraph and outline of story."

THE RHODE ISLANDER MAGAZINE, Providence Journal Co., 75 Fountain St., Providence RI 02902. (401)277-7349. Fax: (401)277-7346. Editor: Elliot Krieger. 50% freelance written. Weekly Sunday supplement magazine about news of Rhode Island and New England. Estab. 1946. Circ. 250,000. Pays on publication. Byline given. Buys first North American serial rights. Submit seasonal/holiday 3 months in advance. Accepts simultaneous and previously published submissions. Send tearsheet or typed ms with rights for sale noted. For reprints, pays 50% of the amount paid for an original article. Query for electronic submissions. Reports in 1 month on queries.

● This magazine is currently seeking more short pieces, containing less than 500 words.

Nonfiction: Book excerpts, exposé, general interest, historical/nostalgic, interview/profile, photo feature. "We are strictly a regional news magazine." No fiction or poetry. Buys 100 mss/year. Query. Length: 250-5,000. Pays $50-500.

Photos: Send photos with submission. Offers $25-100/photo. Captions and identification of subjects required.

South Carolina

CHARLESTON MAGAZINE, P.O. Box 21770, Charleston SC 29413-1770. (803)971-9811. Fax: (803)971-0121. Editor: Dawn Leggett. Assistant Editor: Patrick Sharbaugh. 95% freelance written. Bimonthly magazine covering the Lowcountry in South Carolina and the South as a region. "Consumer magazine with a general focus; each issue reflects an essential element of Charleston life and Lowcountry living." Estab. 1986. Circ. 20,000. Pays on publication. Publishes ms an average of 3 months after acceptance. Byline given. Buys one-time rights. Submit seasonal material 4 months in advance. Query for electronic submissions. Reports in 2 months. Sample copies for 9×12 SAE with 5 first-class stamps. Free writer's guidelines.

Nonfiction: Book excerpts, essays, general interest, historical/nostalgic, humor, food, architecture, sports, interview/profile, opinion, personal experience, photo feature, travel, current events, art. "Not interested in general interest articles. Must pertain to the Charleston area or, at their broadest scope, the South as a region." Buys 50 mss/year. Query with published clips. Length: 150-1,500 words. Pays 10¢/published word. Sometimes pays expenses of writers on assignment.

Photos: Send photos with submission if available. Reviews contact sheets, transparencies, slides. Offers $35 maximum/photo. Captions and identification of subjects required. Buys one-time rights.

Columns/Departments: Channel Markers (general local interest), 50-150 words; Hindsight (historical perspectives and local Lowcountry interest), 1,000-1,200 words; First Person (profile—people of local interest), 1,000-1,200 words; Art (features a successful or innovative artist), 1,000-1,200 words; Architecture (renovations, restorations or new constructions of Lowcountry houses), 1,000 words; Sporting Life (humorous, adventurous tales of life outdoors), 1,000-1,200 words; Southern View (expanded editorial page in which a person expresses his or her view on the South), 750 words; Good Tastes (thought-provoking pieces on regional food), 1,000-1,200 words.

Tips: "Follow our writer's guidelines. Areas most open to freelancers are Columns/Departments and features. Should be of local interest. We're looking for the freshest stories about Charleston—and those don't always come from insiders, but outsiders who are keenly observant."

SANDLAPPER, The Magazine of South Carolina, The Sandlapper Society, Inc., P.O. Box 1108, Lexington SC 29071-1108. (803)359-9954. Fax: (803)957-8226. Executive Director: Dolly Patton. Editor: Robert P. Wilkins. Managing Editor: Daniel E. Harmon. 35% freelance written. Quarterly feature magazine focusing on the positive aspects of South Carolina. Estab. 1989. Circ. 5,000. Pays during the dateline period. Publishes ms an average of 4 months after acceptance. Byline given. Buys first North American serial rights and the right to reprint. Submit seasonal material 6 months in advance. Query for electronic submissions. Free writer's guidelines.

Nonfiction: Feature articles and photo essays about South Carolina's interesting people, places, cuisine, things to do. Occasional history articles. Query. Length: 600-5,000 words. Pays $50-500. Sometimes pays the expenses of writers on assignment.

Tips: "We're not interested in articles about topical issues, politics, crime or commercial ventures. Humorous angles are encouraged. Avoid first-person nostalgia and remembrances of places that no longer exist."

South Dakota

DAKOTA OUTDOORS, South Dakota, Hipple Publishing Co., P.O. Box 669, 333 W. Dakota Ave., Pierre SD 57501-0669. (605)224-7301. Fax: (605)224-9210. Editor: Kevin Hipple. Managing Editor: Rachel Engbrecht. 50% freelance written. Monthly magazine on Dakota outdoor life. Estab. 1975. Circ. 6,500. Pays on publication. Publishes ms an average of 2 months after acceptance. Byline given. Submit seasonal material 3 months in advance. Accepts simultaneous and previously published submissions (if notified). Send typed ms with rights for sale noted and information about when and where the article previously appeared. Pays 50% of their fee for an original article. Query for electronic submissions. Reports in 3 months. Sample copy for 9 × 12 SAE with 3 first-class stamps.

Nonfiction: General interest, how-to, humor, interview/profile, new product, opinion, personal experience, photo feature, technical (all on outdoor topics—prefer in Dakotas). Buys 50 mss/year. Query with or without published clips, or send complete ms. Length: 200-1,000 words. Pays $5-50 for assigned articles; $40 maximum for unsolicited articles. Sometimes pays in contributor copies or other premiums (inquire).

Photos: Send photos with submission. Reviews 5 × 7 prints. Offers no additional payment for photos accepted with ms. Identification of subjects preferred. Buys one-time rights.

Fiction: Occasionally publishes novel excerpts.

Fillers: Anecdotes, facts, gags to be illustrated by cartoonist, newsbreaks, short humor. Buys 10/year. Also publishes line drawings of fish and game. Prefers 5 × 7 prints.

Tips: "Submit samples of manuscript or previous works for consideration; photos or illustrations with manuscript are helpful."

Tennessee

MEMPHIS, Contemporary Media, P.O. Box 256, Memphis TN 38101-0256. (901)521-9000. Fax: (901)521-0129. Editor: Tim Sampson. 60% freelance written. Works with a small number of new/unpublished writers. Estab. 1976. Circ. 21,917. Pays on publication. Publishes ms an average of 3 months after acceptance. Byline given. Buys first North American serial rights. Offers 20% kill fee. Accepts simultaneous submissions. Reports in 2 months. Sample copy for 9 × 12 SAE with 9 first-class stamps. Writer's guidelines for SASE.

Nonfiction: Exposé, general interest, historical, how-to, humor, interview, profile. "Virtually all of our material has strong Memphis area connections." Buys 25 freelance mss/year. Query or submit complete ms or published clips. Length: 500-5,000 words. Pays $50-500. Sometimes pays expenses of writers on assignment.

Tips: "The kinds of manuscripts we most need have a sense of story (i.e., plot, suspense, character), an abundance of evocative images to bring that story alive, and a sensitivity to issues at work in Memphis. The most frequent mistakes made by writers in completing an article for us are lack of focus, lack of organization, factual gaps and failure to capture the magazine's style. Tough investigative pieces would be especially welcomed."

Texas

TEXAS PARKS & WILDLIFE, 3000 South I.H. 35, Suite 120, Austin TX 78704. (512)912-7000. Fax: (512)707-1913. Editor: David Baxter. Managing Editor: Mary-Love Bigony. Senior Editor: Jim Cox. 80% freelance written. Monthly magazine featuring articles about Texas hunting, fishing, outdoor recreation, game and nongame wildlife, state parks, environmental issues. All articles must be about Texas. Estab. 1942. Circ. 180,000. **Pays on acceptance.** Publishes ms an average of 6 months after acceptance. Byline given. Kill fee determined by editor, usually $200-250. Buys first rights. Submit seasonal material 6 months in advance. Query for electronic submissions. Reports in 1 month on queries; 3 months on mss. Free sample copy and writer's guidelines.
   • *Texas Parks & Wildlife* needs more hunting and fishing material.
Nonfiction: Jim Cox, articles editor. General interest (Texas only), historical/nostalgic, how-to (outdoor activities), interview/profile, photo feature, travel (state parks). Buys 60 mss/year. Query with published clips. Length: 250-2,500 words. Pays $600 maximum.
Photos: Send photos with submission. Reviews transparencies. Offers $65-350 maximum/photo. Captions and identification of subjects required. Buys one-time rights.
Columns/Departments: Buys 6 mss/year. Query with published clips. Pays $100-300. Monthly departments: hunting and fishing, the environment, photo column, places to go. Maximum 1,000 words.
Tips: "Read outdoor pages of statewide newspapers to keep abreast of news items that can lead to story ideas. Feel free to include more than one story idea in one query letter. All areas are open to freelancers. All articles must have a Texas focus."

‡UPTOWN EXPRESS, Up & Out Communications, 3406 Audubon Place, Houston TX 77006. (713)520-7237. Editor: Eric Roland. Contact: Greg Jeu, publisher. 70% freelance written. Bimonthly magazine covering holistic community. "*Uptown Express* provides information for personal growth and awareness; information on Houston's holistic community, human potential, spirituality and creativity." Estab. 1985. Circ. 32,000. Pays on publication. Publishes ms an average of 2 months after acceptance. Byline given. Buys one-time rights and simultaneous rights. Editorial lead time 2 months. Submit seasonal material 2 months in advance. Accepts simultaneous submissions and previously published submissions. Query for electronic submissions. Reports in 6 weeks on queries, 2 months on mss. Sample copy and writer's guidelines for SASE.
Nonfiction: Book excerpts, inspirational, interview/profile, new product. Buys 20 mss/year. Send complete ms. Length: 700-4,000 words. Pays $20-100.
Photos: State availability of photos with submission. Reviews 4×6 prints. Negotiates payment individually. Identification of subjects required. Buys one-time rights.

Utah

SALT LAKE CITY, 1270 West 2320 S., Suite A, Salt Lake City UT 84119-1449. (801)975-1927. Fax: (801)975-1982. Editor: Michael Phillips. 60% freelance written. Bimonthly magazine. "Ours is a lifestyle magazine, focusing on the people, issues and places that make Utah and the Intermountain West unique. Our audience is mainly educated, affluent, ages 25-55. Our pieces are generally positive, or at the very least suggestive of solutions. Again, we focus heavily on people." Estab. 1989. Circ. 15,000. Pays on publication. Publishes ms an average of 3-6 months after acceptance. Byline given. Offers $25 kill fee. Buys first North American serial or second serial (reprint) rights. Submit seasonal material 6 months in advance. Accepts simultaneous and previously published submissions. Send photocopy or typed ms with rights for sale noted and information about when and where material previously appeared. Query for electronic submissions. Reports in 3 months on mss. Free sample copy and writer's guidelines. AP style.

Always check the most recent copy of a magazine for the address and editor's name before you send in a query or manuscript.

Nonfiction: Essays (health, family matters, financial), general interest, historical/nostalgic (pertaining to Utah and Intermountain West), humor, interview/profile (famous or powerful people associated with Utah business, politics, media), personal experience, photo feature (fashion available in Utah stores or cuisine of anywhere in world), travel (anywhere exotic in the world). "No movie reviews or current news subjects, please." Even essays need a tight local angle. Buys 5 mss/year. Query with published clips or send complete ms. Length: 800-2,000 words. Pays $75-400 for assigned articles; $75-250 for unsolicited articles. "A major feature is negotiable."

Photos: Send photos with submission. Reviews transparencies (size not important). Captions, model releases, identification of subjects required. Payment and rights negotiable. Don't send original negs/transparencies unless requested.

Columns/Departments: Up Close (standard personality profile), 1,200-1,500 words; Q & A of famous person, 1,200-1,500 words; Executive Signature (profile, business slant of major Utah entrepeneur); and Food (recipes must be included), 1,000-1,500 words. Buys 5-10 mss/year. Query with published clips or send complete ms. Pays $75-250.

● No longer accepting unsolicited fiction and poetry. Also writing more articles inhouse. They are overstocked in travel pieces, and are only considering stories from well-known Utah writers.

Tips: "Well-written, neatly typed, well-researched, complete manuscripts that come across my desk are most likely to be published if they fit our format. They are a godsend. Writers have the best chance of selling us humor, eye-openers, family topics and small features on topics of general interest to Utahns and American western living. For example, we have covered mountainwest recreation, child abuse, education, earthquakes, air pollution, Native American issues. Every story is tightly angled to a local audience. Please write for a free sample copy if you have never read our magazine."

Vermont

VERMONT LIFE MAGAZINE, 6 Baldwin St., Montpelier VT 05602-2109. (802)828-3241. Editor-in-Chief: Thomas K. Slayton. 90% freelance written. Prefers to work with published/established writers. Quarterly magazine. Estab. 1946. Circ. 90,000. Publishes ms an average of 9 months after acceptance. Byline given. Offers kill fee. Buys first serial rights. Submit seasonal material 1 year in advance. Reports in 1 month. *Writer's Market* recommends allowing 2 months for reply. Writer's guidelines for #10 SASE.

Nonfiction: Wants articles on today's Vermont, those which portray a typical or, if possible, unique aspect of the state or its people. Style should be literate, clear and concise. Subtle humor favored. No "Vermont clichés"—maple syrup, town meetings or stereotyped natives. Buys 60 mss/year. Query by letter essential. Length: 1,500 words average. Pays 20¢/word. Seldom pays expenses of writers on assignment.

Photos: Buys photographs with mss; buys seasonal photographs alone. Prefers b&w contact sheets to look at first on assigned material. Color submissions must be 4×5 or 35mm transparencies. Pays $75-150 inside color; $200 for cover. Gives assignments but only with experienced photographers. Query in writing. Captions, model releases, identification of subjects required. Buys one-time rights, but often negotiates for re-use rights.

Fiction: Publishes novel excerpts.

Tips: "Writers who read our magazine are given more consideration because they understand that we want authentic articles about Vermont. If a writer has a genuine working knowledge of Vermont, his or her work usually shows it. Vermont is changing and there is much concern here about what this state will be like in years ahead. It is a beautiful, environmentally sound place now and the vast majority of residents want to keep it so. Articles reflecting such concerns in an intelligent, authoritative, non-hysterical way will be given very careful consideration. The growth of tourism makes *Vermont Life* interested in intelligent articles about specific places in Vermont, their history and attractions to the traveling public."

VERMONT MAGAZINE, P.O. Box 288, Bristol VT 05443-0288. (802)453-3200. Managing Editor: Julie Kirgo. Bimonthly magazine about Vermont. Estab. 1989. Buys first North American serial rights. Submit all material 6 months in advance; must query first. Reports in 2 weeks. Writer's guidelines for #10 SASE.

Nonfiction: Journalism and reporting, book excerpts (pre- or post-book publication), essays, exposé, general interest, how-to, humor, interview/profile, photo feature, calendar. All material must be about contemporary Vermont. Buys 30 mss/year but most are assigned by the editor. Query with published clips. Length: 900-3,500 words. Pays $200-800. Sometimes pays expenses of writers on assignment. Rarely publishes reprints.

Photos: Vermont subjects a must. Send photos and illustrations to Susan Romanoff, art director. Reviews contact sheets, 35mm transparencies, 8×10 b&w prints. Captions, model releases (if possible), identification of subjects required. Buys one-time rights.

Fiction: Publishes novel excerpts and stories about Vermont (1-2/year, maximum).

Tips: "Our readers *know* their state well, and they know the 'real' Vermont can't be slipped inside a glib and glossy brochure. We're interested in serious journalism on major issues, plus coverage of arts, outdoors, living, nature, architecture."

Virginia

THE ROANOKER, Leisure Publishing Co., 3424 Brambleton Ave., P.O. Box 21535, Roanoke VA 24018-9900. (703)989-6138. Fax: (703)989-7603. Editor: Kurt Rheinheimer. 75% freelance written. Works with a small number of new/unpublished writers each year. Magazine published 10 times/year covering people and events of Western Virginia. "*The Roanoker* is a general interest city magazine edited for the people of Roanoke, Virginia and the surrounding area. Our readers are primarily upper-income, well-educated professionals between the ages of 35 and 60. Coverage ranges from hard news and consumer information to restaurant reviews and local history." Estab. 1974. Circ. 14,000. Pays on publication. Publishes ms an average of 4 months after acceptance. Byline given. Buys all rights; makes work-for-hire assignments. Submit seasonal material 4 months in advance. Reports in 2 months. Sample copy for $2 and 9×12 SAE with 5 first-class stamps.

Nonfiction: Exposé, historical/nostalgic, how-to (live better in western Virginia), interview/profile (of well-known area personalities), photo feature, travel (Virginia and surrounding states). "Were looking for more photo feature stories based in western Virginia. We place special emphasis on investigative and exposé articles." Periodic special sections on fashion, real estate, media, banking, investing. Buys 60 mss/year. Query with published clips or send complete ms. Length: 1,400 words maximum. Pays $35-200.

● This magazine is looking for shorter pieces than before.

Photos: Send photos with ms. Reviews color transparencies. Pays $5-10 for 5×7 or 8×10 b&w prints; $10 maximum for 5×7 or 8×10 color prints. Captions and model releases required. Rights purchased vary.

Tips: "It helps if freelancer lives in the area. The most frequent mistake made by writers in completing an article for us is not having enough Roanoke-area focus: use of area experts, sources, slants, etc."

Washington

SEATTLE, The Magazine for the Pacific Northwest, Adams Publishing of the Pacific Northwest, 701 Dexter Ave. N, Suite 101, Seattle WA 98109. (206)284-1750. Fax: (206)284-2550. Editor: Giselle Smith. 90% freelance written. Monthly magazine serving the Seattle area and the Pacific Northwest. Articles for the magazine should be written with our readership in mind. They are interested in the arts, social issues, their homes, gardens, travel and in maintaining the region's high quality of life. Estab. 1992. Circ. 65,000. Pays on publication. Publishes ms an average of 4 months after acceptance. Byline given. Offers 33% kill fee. Buys first rights or second serial (reprint) rights. Editorial lead time 3 months. Submit seasonal material 6 months in advance. Reports in 6 weeks on queries; 2 months on mss. Sample copy and writer's guidelines for #10 SASE.

● *Seattle* is now a monthly and will be assigning somewhat more freelance articles than when it was bimonthly.

Nonfiction: Book excerpts, general interest, interview/profile, photo feature, local interest. Buys 60-75 mss/ year. Query with published clips. Length: 200-2,500 words. Pays $75 minimum for assigned articles; $50 minimum for unsolicited articles. Sometimes pays expenses of writers on assignment.

Fiction: Publishes novel excerpts.

Photos: State availability of photos with submission. Negotiates payment individually. Buys one-time rights.

Columns/Departments: Home and Garden, Nightlife, Dining, Style, Neighborhood, Private Eye. Query with published clips. Pays $150-300.

SEATTLE WEEKLY, Sasquatch Publishing, 1008 Western Ave., Suite 300, Seattle WA 98104. (206)623-0500. Fax: (206)467-4377. Editor: Knute Berger. 20% freelance written. Eager to work with new/unpublished writers, especially those in the region. Weekly tabloid covering arts, politics, food, business and books with local and regional emphasis. Estab. 1976. Circ. 37,000. Pays 1 week after publication. Publishes ms an average of 1 month after acceptance. Byline given. Offers variable kill fee. Buys first North American serial rights. Submit seasonal material minimum 2 months in advance. Accepts previously published articles. Send tearsheet of article. For reprints, pay varies. Reports in 1 month. *Writer's Market* recommends allowing 2 months for reply. Sample copy for $2. Writer's guidelines for #10 SASE.

Nonfiction: Book excerpts, exposé, general interest, historical/nostalgic (Northwest), humor, interview/ profile, opinion, arts-related essays. Buys 6-8 cover stories/year. Query with résumé and published clips. Length: 700-4,000 words. Pays $75-800. Sometimes pays the expenses of writers on assignment.

Tips: "The *Seattle Weekly* publishes stories on Northwest politics and art, usually written by regional and local writers, for a mostly upscale, urban audience; writing is high-quality magazine style."

Wisconsin

MILWAUKEE MAGAZINE, 312 E. Buffalo St., Milwaukee WI 53202. (414)273-1101. Fax: (414)273-0016. E-mail: milmag@qgraph.com@inet#. Editor: John Fennell. 40% freelance written. Monthly magazine covering Milwaukee and surrounding region. "We publish stories about Milwaukee, of service to Milwaukee-area residents and exploring the area's changing lifestyle, business, arts, politics and dining." Circ. 40,000. Pays on publication. Publishes ms an average of 2 months after acceptance. Byline given. Offers 20% kill fee. Buys first rights. Submit seasonal material 6 months in advance. Query for electronic submissions.

Reports in 6 weeks on queries. *Writer's Market* recommends allowing 2 months for reply. Sample copy for $4.

Nonfiction: Book excerpts, essays, exposé, general interest, historical/nostalgic, interview/profile, photo feature, travel, food and dining and other services. "No articles without a strong Milwaukee or Wisconsin angle." Buys 30-50 mss/year. Query with published clips. Length: 1,500-5,000 words. Pays $600-1,000. Sometimes pays expenses of writers on assignment.

Photos: Send photos with submission. Reviews contact sheets, negatives, any transparencies and any prints. Offers no set rate per photo. Identification of subjects required. Buys one-time rights.

Columns/Departments: Steve Filmanowicz, departments editor. Insider (inside information on Milwaukee), 200-700 words. Buys 60 mss/year. Query with published clips. Pays $30-125.

Tips: "Pitch something for the Insider, or suggest a compelling profile we haven't already done and submit clips that prove you can do the job. The department most open is Insider. Think short, lively, offbeat, fresh, people-oriented."

WISCONSIN, *The Milwaukee Journal Magazine*, P.O. Box 661, Milwaukee WI 53201-0661. (414)224-2341. Fax: (414)224-2047. Editor: Brian Lovett. 20% freelance written. Prefers to work with published/established writers. Weekly general interest magazine appealing to readers living in Wisconsin. Estab. 1969. Circ. 500,000. Pays on publication. Publishes ms an average of 4 months after acceptance. Byline given. Buys first serial rights. Submit seasonal material 4 months in advance. Simultaneous queries OK. Reports in 2 months on queries; 6 months on mss. Sample copy and writer's guidelines for 9 × 12 SAE with 2 first-class stamps.

Nonfiction: Exposé, general interest, humor, interview/profile, opinion, personal experience, photo feature, with Wisconsin angles in most cases. Buys 50 mss/year. Query. Length: 500-2,500 words. Pays $75-600. Sometimes pays expenses of writers on assignment.

Photos: Send photos.

Columns/Departments: Opinion, Humor, Essays. Buys 50 mss/year. Length: 300-1,000 words. Pays $100-200. Published novel excerpts.

Tips: "We are primarily Wisconsin-oriented and are becoming more news-oriented."

WISCONSIN OUTDOOR JOURNAL, Krause Publications, 700 E. State St., Iola WI 54990-0001. (715)445-2214. Fax: (715)445-4087. Editor: Brian Lovett. 95% freelance written. Magazine published 8 times/year. "*Wisconsin Outdoor Journal* is more than a straight hook-and-bullet magazine. Though *WOJ* carries how-to and where-to information, it also prints narratives, nature features and state history pieces to give our readers a better appreciation of Wisconsin's outdoors." Estab. 1987. Circ. 48,000. **Pays on acceptance.** Byline given. Buys first North American serial rights. Submit seasonal material 1 year in advance. Reports in 6 weeks. *Writer's Market* recommends allowing 2 months for reply. Sample copy for 9 × 12 SAE with 7 first-class stamps. Writer's guidelines for #10 SASE.

Nonfiction: Book excerpts, essays, historical/nostalgic, how-to, humor, interview/profile, personal experience, photo feature. No articles outside of the geographic boundaries of Wisconsin. Buys 80 mss/year. Query. Send complete ms. "Established writers may query, otherwise I prefer to see the complete ms." Length: 1,500-2,000 words. Pays $100-250.

Photos: Send photos with submission. Reviews 35mm transparencies. Offers no additional payment. Captions required. Buys one-time rights. Photos without mss pay from $10-150. Credit line given.

Fiction: Adventure, historical, humorous, novel excerpts. "No eulogies of a good hunting dog." Buys 10 mss/year. Send complete ms. Length: 1,500-2,000 words. Pays $100-250.

Tips: "Writers need to know Wisconsin intimately—stories that appear as regionals in other magazines probably won't be printed within *WOJ*'s pages."

Canada

CANADIAN GEOGRAPHIC, 39 McArthur Ave., Ottawa, Ontario K1L 8L7 Canada. (613)745-4629. Fax: (613)744-0947. Editor: Ian Darragh. Managing Editor: Eric Harris. 90% freelance written. Works with a small number of new/unpublished writers each year. Estab. 1930. Circ. 246,000. Bimonthly magazine. **Pays on acceptance.** Publishes ms an average of 3 months after acceptance. Buys first Canadian rights; interested only in first-time publication. Reports in 1 month. Sample copy for $3.95 (Canada.) and 9 × 12 SAE. Free writer's guidelines.

Nonfiction: Buys authoritative geographical articles, in the broad geographical sense, written for the average person, not for a scientific audience. Predominantly Canadian subjects by Canadian authors. Buys 30-45 mss/year. *Always query first in writing and enclose a SASE.* Cannot reply personally to all unsolicited proposals. Length: 1,500-3,000 words. Pays 80¢/word minimum. Usual payment for articles ranges between $1,000-3,000. Higher fees reserved for commissioned articles. Sometimes pays the expenses of writers on assignment.

• They need articles on earth sciences.

Photos: Pays $75-400 for color photos, depending on published size.

‡THE COTTAGE MAGAZINE, Country Living in B.C. and Alberta, Harrison House Publishing, 4611 William Head Rd., Victoria, British Columbia V9B 5T7 Canada. (604)478-9209. Editor: Peter Chetteburgh. 60% freelance written. Bimonthly magazine covering recreational property in British Columbia and Alberta. Estab. 1992. Circ. 10,000. Pays on publication. Publishes ms an average of 2 months after acceptance. Byline given. Offers 50% kill fee. Not copyrighted. Buys first North American serial rights. Editorial lead time 2 months. Submit seasonal material 3 months in advance. Accepts simultaneous and previously published submissions. Query for electronic submissions. Reports in 1 month on queries; 2 months on mss. Sample copy for $2. Writer's guidelines free on request.

Nonfiction: General interest, historical/nostalgic, how-to, humor, interview/profile, new product, personal experience, technical. Buys 30 mss/year. Query. Length: 200-2,000 words. Pays $50-500. Sometimes pays expenses of writers on assignment (telephone expenses mostly).

Photos: State availability of photos with submission. Reviews contact sheets, transparencies and prints. Offers no additional payment for photos accepted with ms. Buys one-time rights.

Columns/Departments: Utilities (solar and/or wind power), 650-700 words; Cabin Wit (humor), 650 words. Buys 10 mss/year. Query. Pays $100-200.

Fillers: Anecdotes, facts, gags to be illustrated by cartoonist, newsbreaks. Buys 12/year. Length: 50-200 words. Pays 20¢/word.

THE GEORGIA STRAIGHT, Vancouver Free Press Publishing Corp., 1235 W. Pender St., 2nd Floor, Vancouver, British Columbia V6E 2V6 Canada. (604)681-2000. Fax: (604)681-0272. Managing Editor: Charles Campbell. 90% freelance written. Weekly tabloid on arts, entertainment, lifestyle and civic issues. Estab. 1967. Circ. 100,000. Pays on publication. Byline given. Offers 50-100% kill fee. Buys first North American serial or second serial (reprint) rights. Accepts simultaneous and previously published submissions. Send typed ms with rights for sale noted and information about when and where the article previously appeared. Pays 50-100% of their fee for an original article. Reports in 1 month. *Writer's Market* recommends allowing 2 months for reply. Sample copy for $1 and 9 × 12 SAE.

Nonfiction: General interest, humor, interview/profile, travel, arts and entertainment. Buys 600 mss/year. Query with published clips. Length: 250-4,000 words. Pays $40-1,500. Sometimes pays expenses of writers on assignment.

Photos: Send photos with submission. Offers $35-150/photo. Captions, model releases and identification of subjects required. Buys one-time rights.

Tips: "Be aware of entertainment events in the Vancouver area and expansion of our news coverage. We don't return manuscripts."

‡ONTARIO OUT OF DOORS, Dept. WM, 227 Front St. E., Toronto, Ontario M5A 1E8 Canada. (416)368-0185. Fax: (416)941-9113. Editor-in-Chief: Burton J. Myers. 80% freelance written. "We prefer a blend of both experienced and new writers." Magazine published 10 times/year emphasizing hunting, fishing, camping, and conservation. Estab. 1968. Circ. 89,000. **Pays on acceptance.** Publishes ms an average of 6 months after acceptance. Buys first North American serial rights. Phone queries OK. Submit seasonal material 5 months in advance of issue date. Reports in 2 months. Sample copy and writer's guidelines for SASE; mention *Writer's Market* in request.

Nonfiction: Exposé of conservation practices; how-to (improve your fishing and hunting skills); humor; photo feature (on wildlife); travel (where to find good fishing and hunting); and any news on Ontario. "Avoid 'Me and Joe' articles or funny family camping anecdotes." Buys 20-30 unsolicited mss/year. Query. Length: 150-3,500 words. Pays $35-500. Sometimes pays the expenses of writers on assignment.

Photos: Submit photo material with accompanying query. No additonal payment for b&w contact sheets and 35mm color transparencies. "Should a photo be used on the cover, an additional payment of $350-700 is made."

Fillers: Outdoor tips. Buys 100 mss/year. Length 20-50 words. Pays $15-35.

Tips: "It's rewarding for us to find a freelancer who reads and understands a set of writer's guidelines, but it is annoying when writers fail to submit supporting photography."

‡OUTDOOR CANADA MAGAZINE, 703 Evans Ave., Suite 202, Toronto Ontario M9C 5E9 Canada. (416)695-0311. Fax: (416)695-0381. Editor-in-Chief: Teddi Brown. 90% freelance written. Works with a small number of new/unpublished writers each year. Magazine published 8 times/year emphasizing noncompetitive outdoor recreation in Canada *only*. Estab. 1972. Circ. 95,000. Pays on publication. Publishes ms an average of 6-8 months after acceptance. Buys first rights. Submit seasonal/holiday material 1 year in advance of issue date. Byline given. *Enclose SASE or IRCs or material will not be returned.* Reports in 1 month. *Writer's Market* recommends allowing 2 months for reply. Mention *Writer's Market* in request for editorial guidelines.

Nonfiction: Fishing, hiking, canoeing, hunting, adventure, outdoor issues, exploring, outdoor destinations in Canada, some how-to. Buys 35-40 mss/year, usually with photos. Length: 1,000-2,500 words. Pays $100 and up.

Photos: Emphasize people in the outdoors. Pays $35-225 for 35mm transparencies; and $400/cover. Captions and model releases required.

Fillers: Short news pieces. Buys 70-80/year. Length: 200-500 words. Pays $6/printed inch.

‡TORONTO LIFE, 59 Front St. E., Toronto, Ontario M5E 1B3 Canada. (416)364-3333. Editor: John Macfarlane. 95% freelance written. Prefers to work with published/established writers. Monthly magazine emphasizing local issues and social trends, short humor/satire, and service features for upper income, well educated and, for the most part, young Torontonians. **Pays on acceptance.** Publishes ms an average of 4 months after acceptance. Byline given. Buys first North American serial rights. Pays 50% kill fee "for commissioned articles only." Phone queries OK. Reports in 3 weeks. Sample copy for $2.50 with SAE and IRCs.
Nonfiction: Uses most types of articles. Buys 17 mss/issue. Query with published clips. Buys about 40 unsolicited mss/year. Length: 1,000-5,000 words. Pays $800-3,000.
Photos: Send photos with query. Uses good color transparencies and clear, crisp b&w prints. Seldom uses submitted photos. Captions and model release required.
Columns/Departments: "We run about five columns an issue. They are all freelanced, though most are from regular contributors. They are mostly local in concern and cover politics, money, fine art, performing arts, movies and sports." Length: 1,800 words. Pays $1,500.

UP HERE, Life in Canada's North, OUTCROP The Northern Publishers, Box 1350, Yellowknife, Northwest Territories X1A 2N9 Canada. (403)920-4652. Fax: (403)873-2844. Editorial Assistant: Chris Fournier. 50% freelance written. Bimonthly magazine covering general interest about Canada's North. "We publish features, columns and shorts about people, wildlife, native cultures, travel and adventure in Northern Canada, with an occasional swing into Alaska. Be informative, but entertaining." Estab. 1984. Circ. 37,500. Pays on publication. Publishes ms an average of 4 months after acceptance. Buys first North American serial rights. Editorial lead time 4 months. Submit seasonal material 6 months in advance. Query for electronic submissions. Reports in 4 months. Sample copy for $3 (Canadian). Writer's guidelines free on request.
• This publication was a finalist for Best Editorial Package, National Magazine Awards.
Nonfiction: Historical/nostalgic, interview/profile, personal experience, photo feature, travel. Buys 40 mss/year. Send complete ms. Length: 750-3,000 words. Pays $150-750 (Canadian). Sometimes pays expenses of writers on assignment.
Photos: Send photos with submission. Reviews transparencies and prints. Offers $35-150/photo (Canadian). Captions required. Buys one-time rights.
Columns/Departments: Photography (how-to for amateurs), 1,250 words; Natural North (wildlife—the land, environment), 1,250-1,800 words; On the Road (driving in Northern regions, RV, etc.), 750-1,800 words. Buys 12 mss/year. Send complete ms. Pays $150-350.
Tips: "You must have lived in or visited Canada's North (the Northwest Territories, Yukon, the extreme north of British Columbia, Alberta, etc.). We like well-researched, concrete adventure pieces, insights about Northern people and lifestyles, readable natural history. Features are most open to freelancers—travel, adventure and so on. Top-quality photos can sell a piece better than any other factor."

‡UPTOWN, Regina's City Magazine, Concept Media Ltd., 3030 Victoria Ave., Regina, Saskatchewan S4T 1K9 Canada. Editor: Pat Rediger. 50% freelance written. Monthly tabloid covering issues, events, and people of downtown Regina. "*Uptown* profiles the people, places and events of Regina's Market Square. It is intended to showcase all the things that are good within the city. We place a special emphasis on the downtown." Estab. 1992. Circ. 35,000. Pays on publication. Publishes ms an average of 3 months after acceptance. Byline given. Offers 10% kill fee. Buys first rights. Editorial lead time 3 months. Submit seasonal material 3 months in advance. Query for electronic submissions. Reports in 2 weeks on queries. Sample copy and writer's guidelines for #10 SASE.
Nonfiction: General interest, historical/nostalgic, how-to, humor, interview/profile, personal experience, photo feature. Special issues: The Financial Times of Regina (February), Fiction (September). Buys 15-20 mss/year. Query with published clips. Length: 1,000-2,500 words. Pays $125-150 for assigned articles; $75-100 for unsolicited articles. Pays expenses of writers on assignment.
Photos: Send photos with submission. Reviews contact sheets. Negotiates payment individually. Identification of subjects required. Buys one-time rights.
Columns/Departments: Upfront (off-beat stories), 300 words; After Five (entertainment), 300 words; Lunch Hour (humor), 100 words. Buys 10 mss/year. Query with published clips. Pays $50-75.
Fiction: "We only accept fiction as part of our literary issue." Buys 3 mss/year. Send complete ms. Length: 500-1,000 words. Pays $25-100.
Fillers: Anecdotes, gags to be illustrated by cartoonist, short humor. Buys 25/year. Length: 50-200 words. Pays $5-10.
Tips: "The magazine mainly profiles people and issues that pertain specifically to Regina. Very little freelance material from outside the city is required. However, we do purchase fillers, cartoons and jokes. We're also open to new ideas. If you think you've got a good one, let us know."

‡WESTWORLD MAGAZINE, Canada Wide Magazines, 4180 Lougheed Hwy., #401, Burnaby, British Columbia V5C 6A7 Canada. Editor: Ms. Robin Roberts. 30% freelance written. Quarterly association magazine. "Magazine is distributed to members of The Canadian Automobile Association, so we require automotive and travel-related topics of interest to members." Estab. 1983. Circ. 500,000. Pays on publication. Byline given. Offers 50% kill fee. Buys first North American serial rights; second serial (reprint) rights at reduced rate. Editorial lead time 6 months. Submit seasonal material 6-12 months in advance. Accepts simultaneous submissions and previously published submissions. Query for electronic submissions. Reports in 1 month on queries; 4 months on mss. Writer's guidelines for #10 SAE and IRC.

Nonfiction: Automotive. "No purple prose." Buys 12 mss/year. Query with published clips. Length: 1,000-1,500 words. Pays 35-50¢/word.

Photos: State availability of photos with submission. Reviews transparencies and prints. Offers $35-75/photo. Captions, model releases and identification of subjects required. Buys one-time rights.

Columns/Departments: Buys 8 mss/year. Query with published clips. Pays 35-50¢/word.

Tips: "Don't send gushy, travelogue articles. We prefer stories that are informative with practical, useful tips that are well written and researched. Approach an old topic/destination in a fresh/original way."

WHERE VICTORIA/ESSENTIAL VICTORIA, Key Pacific Publishers Co. Ltd., 1001 Wharf St., 3rd Floor, Victoria, British Columbia V8W 1T6 Canada. (604)388-4324. Editor: Kirsten Meincke. Editorial Director: Janice Strong. 20% freelance written. Monthly magazine on Victoria and Vancouver Island. Estab. 1975. Circ. 30,000. Pays on publication. Publishes ms an average of 1-2 months after acceptance. Byline given. Buys first North American serial and all rights. Query for electronic submissions. Accepts previously published submissions. Send photocopy of article and information about when and where the article previously appeared. For reprints, pays 25-50% of the amount paid for an original article.

• This publication has cut its purchase of freelance material as well as its payment rate.

Nonfiction: General interest, travel. Essential Victoria. Query with published clips. Length: 500-2,500 words. Pays 15¢/word.

Photos: Send photos with submission. Reviews contact sheets, transparencies, prints. Offers $50-150/photo. Model releases and identification of subjects required. Buys one-time rights.

Relationships

These publications focus on lifestyles and relationships. They may offer writers a forum for unconventional views or serve as a voice for particular audiences or causes.

ATLANTA SINGLES MAGAZINE, Hudson Brooke Publishing, Inc., 180 Allen Rd., Suite 304N, Atlanta GA 30328. (404)256-9411. Fax: (404)256-9719. Editor: Shannon V. McClintock. 10% freelance written. Works with a small number of new/unpublished writers each year. Bimonthly magazine for single, widowed or divorced adults, medium to high income level, many business and professionally oriented; single parents, ages 25-55. Estab. 1977. Circ. 15,000. Pays on publication. Publishes ms an average of 6 months after acceptance. Byline given. Buys one-time, second serial (reprint) and simultaneous rights. Submit seasonal material 6 months in advance. Accepts simultaneous and previously submissions. Send tearsheet or photocopy of article and information about when and where the article previously appeared. For reprints, pays 50% of amount paid for an original article. Reports in 1 month. Sample copy for $2 and 8 × 10 SAE with 7 first-class stamps. Writer's guidelines for #10 SASE.

Nonfiction: General interest, humor, personal experience, photo feature, travel. No fiction or pornography. Buys 5 mss/year. Send complete ms. Length: 600-1,200 words. Pays $50-150 for unsolicited articles; sometimes trades for personal ad.

Photos: Send photos with submission. Cover photos also considered. Reviews prints. Offers no additional payment for photos accepted with ms. Model releases and identification of subjects required. Buys one-time rights.

Columns/Departments: Will consider ideas. Query. Length: 600-800 words. Pays $25-150/column or department.

Tips: "We are open to articles on *any* subject that would be of interest to singles. For example, travel, autos, movies, love stories, fashion, investments, real estate, etc. Although singles are interested in topics like self-awareness, being single again, and dating, they are also interested in many of the same subjects that married people are, such as those listed."

‡BLISS, Journal of Spiritual Sexuality, New Frontier Education Society, P.O. Box 17397, Asheville NC 28806. (704)251-0109. Editor: Swami Virato. 80% freelance written. Quarterly magazine covering sex. "We publish materials dealing with sexuality and sensuality as it relates to spirituality and metaphysics. Not pornographic, yet explicit. Estab. 1993. Circ. 10,000. Pays on publication. Publishes ms an average of 6 months after acceptance. Byline given. Offers 15% kill fee. Buys first North American serial rights, first rights, one-time rights and second serial (reprint) rights. Editorial lead time 3 months. Submit seasonal material 6 months in advance. Accepts simultaneous and previously published submissions. Reports in 2 months on queries; 3 months on mss. Sample copy for $3. Writer's guidelines for #10 SASE.

Nonfiction: Book excerpts, essays, exposé, general interest, humor, inspirational, interview/profile, opinion, personal experience, photo feature, religious. Buys 10 mss/year. Send complete ms. Length: 1,500-4,000 words. Pays $50-250 for assigned articles; $50-150 for unsolicited articles. Pays expenses of writers on assignment.

Photos: Send photos with submission. Reviews contact sheets, transparencies and 8 × 10 prints. Offers $10-100/photo. Captions, model releases, identification of subjects required. Buys all rights.

Columns/Departments: Getting Personal (personal sexual experiences); What's Hot (current spiritual/sexual), both 1,500-2,000 words. Buys 6 mss/year. Send complete ms. Pays $50-100.

Fiction: Confession, erotica, experimental, fantasy, religious. Buys 6 mss/year. Send complete ms. Length: 1,500-4,000 words. Pays $50-150.

Tips: "We regard human sexuality as sacred and want a writer to see it the same way. However, we are not prudes and seek explicit material."

‡THE BLOWFISH CATALOG, 2261 Market St., #284, San Francisco CA 94114. E-mail: blowfish@blowfish.com. 20% freelance written. Retail catalog published 3 times/year covering erotica and adult material. Estab. 1994. Circ. 4,000. Pays on publication. Publishes ms an average of 1-3 months after acceptance. Byline given. Offers 100% kill fee. Buys one-time rights. Editorial lead time 2 months. Submit seasonal material 3 months in advance. Accepts simultaneous and previously published submissions. Query for electronic submissions. Reports in 1 month on queries; 2 months on mss. Sample copy for $3. Writer's guidelines for #10 SASE.

Fiction: Erotica. All work must be under 500 words. Buys 12-15 mss/year. Send complete ms. Length: 500 words. Pays $25-75.

Poetry: Avant-garde, free verse, haiku, light verse, traditional. We buy only erotica. Buys 1-3 poems/year. Submit maximum 3 poems at a time. Length: 10 lines. Pays $25-75.

FIRST HAND, Experiences For Loving Men, Firsthand, Ltd., 310 Cedar Lane, Teaneck NJ 07666. (201)836-9177. Fax: (201)836-5055. Editor: Bob Harris. Publisher: Jackie Lewis. 75% freelance written. Eager to work with new/unpublished writers. Monthly magazine of homosexual erotica. Estab. 1980. Circ. 70,000. Pays 6 months after acceptance or on publication, whichever comes first. Publishes ms an average of 8 months after acceptance. Byline given. Buys all rights (exceptions made) and second serial (reprint) rights. Submit seasonal material 10 months in advance. Reports in 4 months. Sample copy for $5. Writer's guidelines for #10 SASE.

Columns/Departments: Survival Kit (short nonfiction articles, up to 1,000 words, featuring practical information on safe sex practices, health, travel, psychology, law, fashion, and other advice/consumer/lifestyle topics of interest to gay or single men). "For this section, we sometimes also buy reprint rights to appropriate articles previously published in local gay newspapers around the country." Infotainment (short reviews up to 1,000 words on books, film, TV, video, theater, performance art, museums, etc.). Reviews must have a gay slant. Query; include photocopy if previously published article. Pays $35-70, depending on length, if original; if reprint, pays half that rate.

Fiction: Erotic fiction up to 5,000 words, average 2,000-3,000 words. "We prefer fiction in the first person which is believable—stories based on the writer's actual experience have the best chance. We're not interested in stories which involve underage characters in sexual situations. Other taboos include bestiality, rape—except in prison stories, as rape is an unavoidable reality in prison—and heavy drug use. Writers with questions about what we can and cannot depict should write for our guidelines, which go into this in more detail. We print mostly self-contained stories; we will look at novel excerpts, but only if they stand on their own."

Poetry: Free verse and light verse. Buys 12/year. Submit maximum 5 poems. Length: 10-30 lines. Pays $25.

Tips: "*First Hand* is a very reader-oriented publication for gay men. Half of each issue is made up of letters from our readers describing their personal experiences, fantasies and feelings. Our readers are from all walks of life, all races and ethnic backgrounds, all classes, all religious and political affiliations, and so on. They are very diverse, and many live in far-flung rural areas or small towns; for some of them, our magazines are the primary source of contact with gay life, in some cases the only support for their gay identity. Our readers are very loyal and save every issue. We return that loyalty by trying to reflect their interests—for instance, by striving to avoid the exclusively big-city bias so common to national gay publications. So bear in mind the diversity of the audience when you write."

FORUM, The International Journal of Human Relations, General Media Inc., 277 Park Ave., New York, NY 10172. (212)496-6100. Editor: V.K. McCarty. 100% freelance written. Works with small number of new/unpublished writers each year. Monthly magazine. "*Forum* is the only serious publication in the US to cover human sexuality in all its aspects for the layman—not only the erotic, but the medical, political, legal, etc." Circ. 300,000. **Pays on acceptance.** Publishes ms an average of 6-12 months after acceptance. Byline given. "Pseudonym mandatory for first-person sex stories." Buys all rights. Submit seasonal/holiday material 6 months in advance. Reports in 2 months on mss.

Nonfiction: Book excerpts, personal experience, essays or scientifically researched articles on all aspects of sex and sexuality. Buys 100 mss/year. Query or send complete ms. Length: 2,000-3,000 words. Pay varies.

Fiction: "Excellent erotic fiction is considered. Letters detailing sexual adventures are sent in by our readers, and we make no payment for them. We do not publish poetry."

Tips: "We expect, as always, for writers to strive for excellence with rich, accurate, erotic observations. They must put names and addresses *on* their manuscripts—and double-space them."

GUYS, First Hand Ltd., P.O. Box 1314, Teaneck NJ 07666-3441. (201)836-9177. Fax: (201)836-5055. Editor: William Spencer. 80% freelance written. Monthly magazine of erotica for gay men. "A positive, romantic approach to gay sex." Estab. 1988. Circ. 60,000. Pays on publication. Publishes ms an average of 1 year after acceptance. Byline given. Buys first North American serial or all rights. Submit seasonal material 10 months in advance. Accepts previously published submissions. Send photocopy of article or short story or typed ms with rights for sale noted. Pays 50% of their fee for an original article. Reports in 2-6 months. Sample copy for $5. Writer's guidelines for #10 SASE.

Columns/Departments: Starstruck (arts and entertainment with a gay angle), 1,250-1,500 words. Buys 12 mss/year. Query. Pays $75-100.

Fiction: Erotica. Buys 72 mss/year. Length: 1,000-10,000 words. Pays $75-250.

IN TOUCH FOR MEN, In Touch International, Inc., 13122 Saticoy St., North Hollywood CA 91605-3402. (818)764-2288. Fax: (818)764-2307. Editor: D. Roberts. 80% freelance written. Works with a small number of new/unpublished writers each year. Monthly magazine covering the gay male lifestyle, gay male humor and erotica. Estab. 1973. Circ. 70,000. Pays on publication. Byline given, pseudonym OK. Buys one-time rights. Accepts simultaneous submissions. Reports in 2 months. Sample copy for $5.95. Writer's guidelines for #10 SASE.

Nonfiction: Buys 36 mss/year. Send complete ms. Length: 3,000-3,500 words. Pays $25-75.
  • Needs more lifestyle features.

Photos: Send photos with submission. Reviews contact sheets, transparencies, prints. Offers $35/photo. Captions, model releases, identification of subjects required. Buys one-time rights.

Fiction: Erotica, all must be gay male erotica. Buys 36 mss/year. Send complete ms. Length: 3,000-3,500 words. Pays $75 maximum.

Fillers: Short humor. Buys 12/year. Length: 1,500-3,500 words. Pays $50-75.

Tips: "Our publication features male nude photos plus three fiction pieces, several articles, cartoons, humorous comments on items from the media, photo features. We try to present the positive aspects of the gay lifestyle, with an emphasis on humor. Humorous pieces may be erotic in nature. We are open to all submissions that fit our gay male format; the emphasis, however, is on humor and the upbeat. We receive many fiction manuscripts but not nearly enough articles and humor."

LIBIDO, The Journal of Sex & Sensibility, Libido, Inc., 5318 N. Paulina St., Chicago IL 60640, Fax: (312)275-0752. E-mail: rune@mcs.com. Co-editors: Marianna Beck and Jack Hafferkamp. Submissions Editor: J.L. Beck. 50% freelance written. Quarterly magazine covering literate erotica. "*Libido* is about sexuality. Orientation is not an issue, writing ability is. The aim is to enlighten as often as it is to arouse. Humor—sharp and smart—is important, so are safer sex contexts." Estab. 1988. Circ. 9,000. Pays on publication. Byline given. Kill fee "rare, but negotiable." Buys one-time or second serial (reprint) rights. Editorial lead time 3 months. Submit seasonal material 4 months in advance. Accepts previously published submissions. Send tearsheet of article or short story and information about when and where the material previously appeared. Payment negotiable. Reports in 3-6 months. Sample copy for $7. Writer's guidelines for #10 SASE.

Nonfiction: Book excerpts, essays, historical/nostalgic, humor, photo feature, travel. "No violence, sexism or misty memoirs." Buys 10-20 mss/year. Send complete ms. Length: 300-2,500 words. Pays $50 minimum for assigned articles; $15 minimum for unsolicited articles. Pays contributor copies "when money isn't an issue and copies or other considerations have equal or higher value." Sometimes pays expenses of writers on assignment.

Photos: Send photos with submission. Reviews contact sheets and 5×7 and 8×10 prints. Negotiates payment individually. Model releases required. Buys one-time rights.

Fiction: Erotica, novel excerpts. Buys 10 mss/year. Send complete ms. Length: 800-2,500 words. Pays $20-50.

Poetry: Uses humorous short erotic poetry. No limericks. Buys 10 poems/year. Submit maximum 3 poems. Pays $15.

Tips: "Send us a manuscript—make it short, sharp and with a lead that makes us want to read. If we're not hooked by paragraph three, we reject the manuscript."

Religious

Religious magazines focus on a variety of subjects, styles and beliefs. Many are publishing articles relating to current topics such as AIDS, cults, or substance abuse. Fewer religious publications are considering poems and personal experience articles, but many emphasize special ministries to singles, seniors or other special interest groups. Such diversity makes reading each magazine essential for the writer hoping to break in. Educational and inspirational material of interest to church members, workers and leaders within a denomination or religion is needed by the publications in this category. Religious magazines for children and teenagers can be found in the Juvenile and Teen and Young Adult classifications. Other religious publications can be found in the Ethnic/ Minority section as well. Publications intended to assist professional religious workers in teaching and managing church affairs are classified in Church Administration and Ministry in the Trade section.

THE ANNALS OF SAINT ANNE DE BEAUPRÉ, Redemptorist Fathers, P.O. Box 1000, St. Anne De Beaupré, Quebec G0A 3C0 Canada. (418)827-4538. Fax: (418)827-4530. Editor: Roch Achard C.Ss.R. 80% freelance written. Works with a small number of new/unpublished writers each year. Monthly magazine on religion. "Our aim is to promote devotion to St. Anne and Catholic family values." Estab. 1878. Circ. 45,000. **Pays on acceptance.** Publishes ms an average of 1-2 years after acceptance. Byline given. Buys first North American rights only. Submit seasonal material 6 months in advance. Reports in 3 weeks. Free sample copy and writer's guidelines. "We never accept simultaneous submissions or reprints."
Nonfiction: Exposé, general interest, inspirational, personal experience. No articles without spiritual thrust. Buys 30 mss/year. Send complete ms. Length: 500-1,500 words. Pays 3-4¢/word.
Fiction: Religious. Buys 15 mss/year. Send complete ms. Length: 500-1,500 words. Pays 3-4¢/word.
Poetry: "Our poetry 'bank' is full and we will not be accepting any new items for the next year or so."
Tips: "We would like to see more articles about religious places or events of a religious interest. We are already 'rich' in the short-story type of submission. Also, we have been overrun with articles where the rights aren't clearly indicated. This has caused us numerous problems and may delay publication. These rights should be clearly indicated on each manuscript."

‡AREOPAGUS, A Living Encounter with Today's Religious World, Tao Fong Shan Christian Centre, P.O. Box 33, Shatin, New Territories, Hong Kong. (852)691-1904. Fax: (852)265-9885. Editor: John G. LeMond. Managing Editor: Eric Bosell. Contact: Editor. 75% freelance written. Quarterly magazine for interreligious dialogue. "*Areopagus* is a Christian periodical that seeks to engage its readers in a living encounter with today's religious world. Respecting the integrity of religious communities, *Areopagus* provides a forum for dialog between the good news of Jesus Christ and people of faith both in major world religious and new religious movements." Estab. 1987. Circ. 1,000. Pays on publication. Publishes ms an average of 6 months after acceptance. Offers 50% kill fee. Buys first-time rights. Editorial lead time 6 months. Submit seasonal material 6 months in advance. Accepts simultaneous and previously published submissions. Send typed ms with rights for sale noted and information about when and where the article previously appeared. Query for electronic submissions. Reports in 6 weeks on queries; 3 months on mss. Sample copy for $4. Writer's guidelines free on request.
    • *Areopagus* no longer solicits poetry.
Nonfiction: Book excerpts, essays and exposé (all on religious themes), humor (of a religious nature), inspirational (interreligious encounter), interview/profile (w/religious figures), opinion (on religious subjects), personal experience (of spiritual journey), photo feature and religious. Issue themes under consideration: birth rites, death, family, sex, aging, suffering, war, hope, healing. "We are not interested in articles that seek to prove the superiority or inferiority of a particular religious tradition." Buys 40 mss/year. Send complete ms. Length: 1,000-5,000 words. Pays $50 minimum.
Photos: Send photos with submission. Offers $15-50/photo. Identification of subjects required. Buys one-time rights.
Columns/Departments: Getting to Know (objective description of major world religions), 4,000 words; Pilgrimage (stories of personal faith journies), 3,000 words; and People and Communities (description of faith communities), 3,000 words. Buys 30 mss/year. Send complete ms. Pays $50-100.
Fillers: Facts, newsbreaks. Buys 5/year. Length: 100-400 words. Pays $10-25.
Tips: "Articles that reflect a balanced approach to interreligious dialogue are the most likely candidates. Followers of all faiths are encouraged to write about personal experience. Articles about religious conspiracy and arcane religious conjecture are of little interest. Virtually all of our departments are open to freelancers. In general, we look for compassionate, direct and unself-conscious prose that reflects a writer firmly rooted in his or her own tradition but unafraid to encounter other traditions."

THE ASSOCIATE REFORMED PRESBYTERIAN, Associate Reformed Presbyterian General Synod, 1 Cleveland St., Suite 110, Greenville SC 29601-3696. (803)232-8297. Editor: Ben Johnston. 5% freelance written. Works with a small number of new/unpublished writers each year. Christian magazine serving a conservative, evangelical and Reformed denomination, most of whose members are in the Southeast US. Estab. 1976. Circ. 6,300. **Pays on acceptance.** Publishes ms an average of 4 months after acceptance. Byline given. Not copyrighted. Buys first, one-time, or second serial (reprint) rights. Submit seasonal material 4 months in advance. Accepts simultaneous and previously published submissions. Send tearsheet or photocopy of article or short story or typed ms with rights for sale noted and information about when and where the article previously appeared. For reprints, pays 100% of the amount paid for an original article. Reports in 1 month. Sample copy for $1.50. Writer's guidelines for #10 SASE.

Nonfiction: Book excerpts, essays, inspirational, opinion, personal experience, religious. Buys 10-15 mss/ year. Query. Length: 400-2,000 words. Pays $70 maximum.

Photos: State availability of photos with submission. Reviews 5×7 reprints. Offers $25 maximum/photo. Captions and identification of subjects required. Buys one-time rights.

Fiction: Religious and children's. Pays $50 maximum.

Tips: "Feature articles are the area of our publication most open to freelancers. Focus on a contemporary problem and offer Bible-based solutions to it. Provide information that would help a Christian struggling in his daily walk. Writers should understand that we are denominational, conservative, evangelical, Reformed and Presbyterian. A writer who appreciates these nuances would stand a much better chance of being published here than one who does not."

BAPTIST LEADER, P.O. Box 851, Valley Forge PA 19482-0851. (610)768-2143. Editor: Don Ng. For pastors, teachers lay leaders and Christian education staff in churches. 5% freelance written. Works with several new/unpublished writers each year. Quarterly magazine. Estab. 1939. Pays on publication. Publishes ms an average of 8 months after acceptance. Editorial lead time 8 months. Accepts previously published submissions. Send typed ms with rights for sale noted and information about when and where the article previously appeared. For reprints, pays 100% of amount paid for an original article. Sample copy for $1.50. Writer's guidelines for #10 SASE.

Nonfiction: Educational topics. How-to articles and programs for local church teachers and leaders. Length: 1,500-2,000 words. Pays $25-75.

Tips: "Emphasis on Christian education administration and planning and articles for all church leaders."

‡CATHOLIC DIGEST, University of St. Thomas, P.O. Box 64090, St. Paul MN 55164. (612)962-6739. Editor: Richard J. Reece. Managing Editor: Kathleen Stauffer. Contact: Articles Editor. 15% freelance written. Monthly magazine covering Catholic life. Estab. 1936. Circ. 540,000. **Pays on acceptance** for articles. Publishes ms an average of 4 months after acceptance. Byline given. Buys first rights, one-time rights or second serial (reprint) rights. Editorial lead time 4 months. Submit seasonal material 5 months in advance. Accepts previously published submissions. Reports in 2 months on mss. Sample copy and writer's guidelines free on request.

Nonfiction: Book excerpts, essays, general interest, historical/nostalgic, how-to, humor, inspirational, interview/profile, personal experience, religious, travel. Buys 60 mss/year. Send complete ms. Length: 500-3,000 words. Pays $150-400.

Photos: State availability of photos with submission. Reviews contact sheets, transparencies, prints. Negotiates payment individually. Captions, model releases, identification of subjects required.

Columns/Departments: Buys 75 mss/year. Send complete ms. Pays $4-50.

Fillers: Contact: Susan Schaefer, Filler Editor. Anecdotes, short humor. Buys 200/year. Length: 1 line minimum, 500 words maximum. Pays $2-50 on publication.

CATHOLIC HERITAGE, Our Sunday Visitor, Inc., 200 Noll Plaza, Huntington IN 46750. (219)356-8400. Fax: (219)359-9117. E-mail: 76440.3571@compuserve.com. Managing Editor: Richard Beemer. Editor: Robert P. Lockwood. 25% freelance written. Bimonthly magazine covering the Catholic faith. "Explores the history and heritage of the Catholic faith with special emphasis on its impact on culture." Estab. 1991. Circ. 25,000. **Pays on acceptance.** Publishes ms an average of 1 year after acceptance. Byline given. Offers 33% or $50-75 kill fee. Buys first North American serial rights. Editorial lead time 6 months. Submit seasonal material 6 months in advance. Accepts previously published submissions. Send tearsheet and information about when and where the article previously appeared. For reprints, payment is negotiated. Reports in 3 weeks on queries; 1 month on mss. Sample copy free on request.

● This editor prefers manuscript on computer disks or submitted through CompuServe.

Nonfiction: Book excerpts, general interest, humor, interview/profile, photo feature, religious, travel, Church history. "No nostalgia pieces about what it was like growing up Catholic or about life in the Church prior to Vatican II." Buys 15 mss/year. Query. Length: 1,000-2,000 words. Pays $200. Sometimes pays expenses of writers on assignment.

Photos: State availability of photos with submission. Reviews prints. Negotiates payment individually. Captions required. Buys one-time rights.

Tips: "Write solid queries that take an aspect of the Catholic heritage and apply it to developments today. Show a good knowledge of the Church and a flair for historical writing. General features are most open to freelancers."

CATHOLIC NEAR EAST MAGAZINE, Catholic Near East Welfare Association, 1011 First Ave., New York NY 10022-4195. (212)826-1480. Fax: (212)838-1344. Editor: Michael La Città. 50% freelance written.

Bimonthly magazine for a Catholic audience with interest in the Near East, particularly its current religious, cultural and political aspects. Estab. 1926. Circ. 100,000. **Pays on acceptance.** Publishes ms an average of 4 months after acceptance. Byline given. Buys all rights. Reports in 2 months. Sample copy and writer's guidelines for 7½×10½ SAE with 2 first-class stamps.

Nonfiction: "Cultural, devotional, political, historical material on the Near East, with an emphasis on the Eastern Christian churches. Style should be simple, factual, concise. Articles must stem from personal acquaintance with subject matter, or thorough up-to-date research." Length: 1,200-1,800 words. Pays 20¢/word.

Photos: "Photographs to accompany manuscript are welcome; they should illustrate the people, places, ceremonies, etc. which are described in the article. We prefer color transparencies but occasionally use b&w. Pay varies depending on use—scale from $50-300."

Tips: "We are interested in current events in the regions listed above as they affect the cultural, political and religious lives of people."

‡CHRISTIAN COURIER, Calvinist Contact Publishing, 4-261 Martindale Rd., St. Catharines, Ontario L2W 1A1 Canada. (905)682-8311. Editor: Bert Witvoet. 20% freelance written. Weekly newspaper covering news of importance to Christians, comments and features. "We assume a Christian perspective which acknowledges that this world belongs to God and that human beings are invited to serve God in every area of society." Estab. 1945. Circ. 5,000. Pays a month after publication. Publishes ms an average of 2 months after acceptance. Byline given. Offers 50% kill fee. Buys all rights. Editorial lead time 1 month. Submit seasonal material 6 months in advance. Accepts simultaneous and previously published submissions. Accepts electronic submissions by disk. Reports in 1 week on queries; 1 month on mss. Sample copy for #10 SASE and writer's guidelines free on request.

Nonfiction: Interview/profile, opinion. Buys 40 mss/year. Send complete ms. Length: 500-1,200 words. Pays $35-60 for assigned articles; $25-50 for unsolicited articles. Sometimes pays expenses of writers on assignment.

Photos: State availability of photos with submission.

CHRISTIAN EDUCATION COUNSELOR, General Council of the Assemblies of God, 1445 Boonville, Springfield MO 65802-1894. (417)862-2781. Editor: Sylvia Lee. 60% freelance written. Works with small number of new/unpublished writers each year. Monthly magazine on religious education in the local church— the official Sunday school voice of the Assemblies of God channeling programs and help to local, primarily lay, leadership. Estab. 1994. Circ. 35,000. **Pays on acceptance.** Publishes ms an average of 9 months after acceptance. Byline given. Offers variable kill fee. Buys first North American serial, one-time, all, simultaneous, first serial or second serial (reprint) rights or makes work-for-hire assignments. Submit seasonal material 7 months in advance. Accepts simultaneous and previously published submissions. Send tearsheet of article or typed ms with rights for sale noted and information about when and where the article previously appeared. For reprints, pays 50% of amount paid for an original article. Reports in 1 month. Sample copy and writer's guidelines for SASE.

Nonfiction: How-to, inspirational, interview/profile, personal experience, photo feature. All related to religious education in the local church. Buys 100 mss/year. Send complete ms. Length: 300-1,800 words. Pays $25-150.

Photos: Send photos with ms. Reviews b&w and color prints. Model releases and identification of subjects required. Buys one-time rights.

• Looking for more photo-illustrated mss.

CHRISTIAN HOME & SCHOOL, Christian Schools International, 3350 East Paris Ave. SE, Grand Rapids MI 49512. (616)957-1070, ext. 234. Executive Editor: Gordon L. Bordewyk. Senior Editor: Roger Schmurr. 30% freelance written. Works with a small number of new/unpublished writers each year. Bimonthly magazine published 6 times/year covering family life and Christian education. "For parents who support Christian education. We feature material on a wide range of topics of interest to parents." Estab. 1922. Pays on publication. Publishes ms an average of 4 months after acceptance. Byline given. Buys first North American serial rights. Submit seasonal material 4 months in advance. Reports in 1 month. Sample copy for 9×12 SAE with 4 first-class stamps. Writer's guidelines for #10 SASE.

Nonfiction: Book excerpts, interview/profile, opinion, personal experience, articles on parenting and school life. "We publish features on issues which affect the home and school and profiles on interesting individuals, providing that the profile appeals to our readers and is not a tribute or eulogy of that person." Buys 40 mss/year. Send complete ms. Length: 500-2,000 words. Pays $75-150. Sometimes pays the expenses of writers on assignment.

Photos: "If you have any color photos appropriate for your article, send them along."

Tips: "Features are the area most open to freelancers. We are publishing articles that deal with contemporary issues that affect parents. Use an informal easy-to-read style rather than a philosophical, academic tone. Try to incorporate vivid imagery and concrete, practical examples from real life."

‡**CHRISTIAN PARENTING TODAY**, Good Family Magazines, P.O. Box 36630, Colorado Springs CO 80936-3663. Editor: Brad Lewis. Contact: Erin Healy, assistant editor. 90% freelance written. Bimonthly magazine."*CPT* readers are Christian parents who look to us for articles that are biblically based, authoritative, informative and inspirational—articles that can guide them through various stages of their children's lives and through the challenges that come from rearing children in the 90s." Estab. 1988. Circ. 225,000. Pays on publication. Publishes unsolicited ms an average of 8-12 months after acceptance. Byline given. Buys first North American serial rights. Editorial lead time 6 months. Submit seasonal material 10-12 months in advance. Accepts previously published submissions. Send typed ms with photocopy, include information about when and where the article appeared. Accepts electronic submissions by disk (when accompanied by a hard copy). Sample copy for 9×12 SAE with 10 first-class stamps. Writer's guidelines for #10 SASE.
Nonfiction: All types of articles should be family and/or parenting focused. Book excerpts, general interest, how-to, humor, new product, (Colin Miller, associate editor), personal experience. Buys 8-12 unsolicited mss/year. Query with a detailed outline. Exceptions: humor and personal experience (please send whole manuscript). Length: 750-2,500 words. Pays 15-25¢/word plus contributors tearsheets and a copy of the issue. Sometimes pays expenses of writers on assignment.
Columns/Departments: Life In Our House (humorous anecdotes of home life), 25-200 words; Parent Exchange (parent-tested tips), 25-200 words; Parents' Almanac (newsy, practical parenting tidbits), 300-500 words. Buys 60-70 mss/year. "We do *not* acknowledge or return submissions to Life in Our House and Parent Exchange. Please do not send SASE to these 2 departments. Original true submissions only." Send complete ms. Pays $25 for Life in Our House, $40 for Parent Exchange.
Tips: "Send a *detailed* outline of your proposed article along with your query."

CHRISTIAN SINGLE, Baptist Sunday School Board, 127 9th Ave. N., MSN 140, Nashville TN 37234. (615)251-5721. Fax: (615)251-5008. Editor-in-Chief: Stephen Felts. Contact: Ivey Harrington, managing editor. 30% freelance written. Prefers to work with published/established writers. Monthly "contemporary Christian magazine that offers substantive information to singles for living the abundant life. It seeks to be constructive and creative in approach." Estab. 1979. Circ. 73,000. **Pays on acceptance.** Byline given. Buys first rights or makes work-for-hire assignments. Submit seasonal material 6 months in advance. Reports in 2 months. Accepts previously published submissions. Send photocopy of article and typed ms and disk with rights for sale noted and information about when and where article previously appeared. Pays 75% of their fee for an original article. Sample copy and writer's guidelines for 9×12 SASE with 4 first-class stamps.
● They want more experienced writers and want submissions on disk, with accompanying hard copy.
Nonfiction: Humor (good, clean humor that applies to Christian singles), how-to (specific subjects which apply to singles), inspirational (of the personal experience type), high adventure personal experience (of single adults), photo feature (on outstanding Christian singles), financial articles targeted to single adults. Buys 60-75 unsolicited mss/year. Query with published clips. Length: 600-1,200 words. Payment negotiable.
Fiction: "We are also looking for fiction suitable for our target audience." Publishes novel excerpts.
Tips: "We are looking for people who experience single living from a positive, Christian perspective."

CHRYSALIS READER, P.O. Box 549, West Chester PA 19381-0549. Fax: (804)983-1074. Send inquiries and mss directly to the editorial office: Route 1, Box 184, Dillwyn VA 23936-9616. Editor: Carol S. Lawson. Managing Editor: Susanna van Rensselaer. 50% freelance written. Biannual literary magazine on spiritually related topics. "*It is very important to send for writer's guidelines and sample copies before submitting.* Content of fiction, articles, reviews, poetry, etc., should be directly focused on that issue's theme and directed to the educated, intellectually curious reader." Estab. 1985. Circ. 3,000. Pays at page-proof stage. Publishes ms an average of 9 months after acceptance. Byline given. Buys first rights and makes work-for-hire assignments. Reports in 1 month on queries; 3 months on mss. Sample copy for $10 and 9×12 SAE. Writer's guidelines and copy deadlines for SASE.
Nonfiction: Essays and interview/profile. Upcoming themes: Play (Autumn 1995); The Good Life (Spring 1996); Symbols (Autumn 1996). Buys 30 mss/year. Query. Length: 1,500-3,500 words. Pays $50-250 for assigned articles; $50-150 for unsolicited articles.
Photos and Illustrations: Send suggestions for illustrations with submission. Offers no additional payment for photos accepted with ms. Captions and identification of subjects required. Buys original artwork for cover and inside copy; b&w illustrations related to theme; pays $25-150. Buys one-time rights.
Fiction: Phoebe Loughrey, fiction editor. Adventure, experimental, historical, mainstream, mystery, science fiction, related to theme of issue. Buys 6 mss/year. Query. Length: 500-2,500 words. Short fiction more likely to be published. Pays $50-150.
Poetry: Rob Lawson, poetry editor. Avant-garde and traditional *but not religious*. Buys 15 poems/year. Pays $25. Submit maximum 6.

THE CHURCH HERALD, 4500 60th St. SE, Grand Rapids MI 49512-9642. Editor: Jeffrey Japinga. Managing Editor: Terry De Young. 5% freelance written. Prefers to work with published/established writers. Monthly magazine covering contemporary Christian life. "*The Church Herald* is the denominational publication of the Reformed Church in America, a Protestant denomination in the Presbyterian-Reformed family of churches. We will consider carefully researched and well-written articles on almost any subject, but they all must have a distinctively Christian perspective and must have a specific connection with our intended denominational audience." Circ. 108,000. **Pays on acceptance.** Publishes ms an average of 3 months after acceptance. Byline given. Offers 50% kill fee. Buys first, one-time, second serial (reprint), simultaneous and all rights. Submit seasonal material 6 months in advance. Accepts simultaneous and previously published submissions. Query for electronic submissions. Reports in 1 month on queries; 2 months on mss. Sample copy and writer's guidelines for $2 and 9 × 12 SAE.

Nonfiction: Essays, general interest, humor, inspirational, personal experience, religious. Buys 15 mss/year. Queries only; unsolicited mss returned. Length: 400-1,500 words. Pays $50-200 for assigned articles. Pays $50-150 for unsolicited articles. Pays expenses of writers on assignment.

Photos: State availability of photos with submission. Reviews color transparencies and 8 × 10 b&w prints. Offers $25-50/photo. Model releases required. Buys one-time rights.

Fiction: Religious. "We consider good fiction written from a Christian perspective. Avoid pious sentimentality and obvious plots." Buys 1 ms/year. Send complete ms. Length: 400-1,500 words. Pays $45-120.
- No longer considering poetry.

Tips: "Research articles carefully. Superficial articles are immediately recognizable; they cannot be disguised by big words or professional jargon. Also, what our readers want are new solutions to recognized problems; be specific. If a writer doesn't have any, he or she should try another subject. Section most open to freelancers is feature articles on issues of faith or Christian living. Finally, and most importantly—if you cannot tie your article in some way to the denomination we serve, we probably can't use it."

COLUMBIA, 1 Columbus Plaza, New Haven CT 06507. (203)772-2130. Editor: Richard McMunn. Monthly magazine for Catholic families. Caters particularly to members of the Knights of Columbus. Estab. 1921. Circ. 1.5 million. **Pays on acceptance.** Buys first serial rights. Free sample copy and writer's guidelines.
- *Columbia* is buying slightly fewer articles.

Nonfiction and Photos: Fact articles directed to the Catholic layman and his family dealing with current events, social problems, Catholic apostolic activities, education, ecumenism, rearing a family, literature, science, arts, sports and leisure. Color glossy prints, transparencies or contact prints with negatives are required for illustration. Articles without ample illustrative material are not given consideration. Pays up to $500, including photos. Buys 30 mss/year. Query. Length: 1,000-1,500 words.

COMPASS: A JESUIT JOURNAL, Jesuit Fathers of Upper Canada, 10 St. Mary St., #300, Toronto, Ontario M4Y 1P9 Canada.(416)921-0653. Fax: (416)921-1864. Editor: Robert Chodos. 80% freelance written. Bimonthly magazine covering religious affairs, "directed at an informed general audience, made up primarily but by no means exclusively of Canadian Catholics. It provides an ethical perspective on contemporary social and religious affairs." Estab. 1983. Circ. 3,500. Pays on publication. Byline given. Offers 50% kill fee. Buys first rights. Editorial lead time 4 months. Submit seasonal material 4 months in advance. Query for electronic submissions. Reports in 3 months. Sample copy and writer's guidelines for $2.

Nonfiction: Essays, general interest, opinion, personal experience, religious. Query for special issues. Buys 50 mss/year. Query with published clips. Length: 750-2,000 words. Pays $100.

Photos: State availability of photos with submission. Offers no additional payment for photos accepted with ms. Identification of subjects required. Buys one-time rights.

Columns/Departments: Testament (commentary on Scripture); Colloquy (relationship between theology and daily life); Disputation (comment on articles previously appearing in *Compass*). Length: 750 words. Buys 18 mss/year. Query. Pays $50-150.

Fiction: Mainstream, religious. Buys 2 mss/year. Send complete ms. Length: 1,000-2,500 words. Pays $100-350.

Poetry: Free verse, traditional. Buys 1 poem/year. Submit maximum 10 poems. Length: 50 lines maximum. Pays $50-100.

Fillers: Jack Costello, SJ, Points editor. Anecdotes, short humor. Buys 12/year. Length: 20-100 words. Pays 1 year subscription to *Compass*.

Tips: "*Compass* publishes theme issues. The best chance of being published is to get a list of upcoming themes and gear proposals to them. All sections are open to freelancers."

CONSCIENCE, A Newsjournal of Prochoice Catholic Opinion, Catholics for a Free Choice, 1436 U St. NW, Suite 301, Washington DC 20009-3997. (202)986-6093. Editor: Maggie Hume. 80% freelance written. Sometimes works with new/unpublished writers. Quarterly newsjournal covering reproductive health and rights, including but not limited to abortion rights in the church, and church-state issues in US and worldwide. "A feminist, pro-choice perspective is a must, and knowledge of Christianity and specifically Catholicism is helpful." Estab. 1980. Circ. 12,000. Pays on publication. Publishes ms an average of 4 months after acceptance. Byline given. Buys first North American serial rights; makes work-for-hire assignments. Sometimes accepts previously published submissions. Send tearsheet or photocopy of article or typed manuscript with rights for sale noted and information about when and where the article previously appeared. Pays 20-30% of their fee for an original article. Query for electronic submissions. Reports in 4 months. Sample copy for 9 × 12 SAE with 4 first-class stamps. Writer's guidelines for #10 SASE.
- This magazine is increasingly international in focus.

Nonfiction: Book excerpts, interview/profile, opinion, issue anaylsis, a small amount of personal experience. Especially needs material that recognizes the complexity of reproductive issues and decisions, and offers original, honest insight. Buys 8-12 mss/year. Query with published clips or send complete ms. Length: 1,000-3,500 words. Pays $25-150. "Writers should be aware that we are a nonprofit organization."

Photos: State availability of photos with query or ms. Prefers b&w prints. Identification of subjects required.

Columns/Departments: Book reviews. Buys 6-10 mss/year. Length: 600-1,200 words. Pays $25-50.

Fillers: Newsbreaks. Uses 6/year. Length: 100-300 words. $25-35.

Tips: "Say something new on the issue of abortion, or sexuality, or the role of religion or the Catholic church, or women's status in the church. Thoughtful, well-researched and well-argued articles needed. The most frequent mistakes made by writers in submitting an article to us are lack of originality and wordiness."

CORNERSTONE, Cornerstone Communications, Inc., 939 W. Wilson, Chicago IL 60640-5718. Editor: Dawn Mortimer. Submissions Editor: Jean Erickson. 10% freelance written. Eager to work with new/unpublished writers. 4 issues/year. Magazine covers contemporary issues in the light of Evangelical Christianity. Estab. 1972. Circ. 50,000. Pays after publication. Byline given. Buys first serial rights. Submit seasonal material 6 months in advance. Accepts simultaneous and previously published submissions. Manuscripts *not* returned. "Send copies, not originals. We will contact you *only* if your work is considered for publication. Manuscripts not accepted will be discarded." Do not send a SASE. We *encourage* simultaneous submissions because we take so long to get back to people! We prefer actual manuscripts to queries. (SASE must accompany queries.) Sample copy and writer's guidelines for 8½×11 envelope with 5 first-class stamps.

Nonfiction: Essays, personal experience, religious. Buys 1-2 mss/year. Query. 2,700 words maximum. Pays negotiable rate, 8-10¢/word. Sometimes pays the expenses of writers on assignment.

Photos: Send photos with accompanying ms. Reviews 8×10 b&w and color prints and 35mm slides. Identification of subjects required. Buys negotiable rights.

Columns/Departments: Music (interview with artists, mainly rock, focusing on artist's world view and value system as expressed in his/her music), Current Events, Personalities, Film and Book Reviews (focuses on meaning as compared and contrasted to biblical values). Buys 1-4 mss/year. Query. Length: 100-2,500 words (negotiable). Pays negotiable rate, 8-10¢/word.

Fiction: "Articles may express Christian world view but should not be unrealistic or 'syrupy.' Other than porn, the sky's the limit. We want fiction as creative as the Creator." Buys 1-4 mss/year. Send complete ms. Length: 250-2,500 words (negotiable). Pays negotiable rate, 8-10¢/word.

Poetry: Tammy Boyd, poetry editor. Avant-garde, free verse, haiku, light verse, traditional. No limits *except* for epic poetry ("We've not the room!"). Buys 10-50 poems/year. Submit maximum 5 poems. Payment negotiated. 1-15 lines: $10. Over 15 lines: $25.

Tips: "A display of creativity which expresses a biblical world view without clichés or cheap shots at non-Christians is the ideal. We are known as one of the most avant-garde magazines in the Christian market, yet attempt to express orthodox beliefs in language of the '90s. *Any* writer who does this may well be published by *Cornerstone*. Creative fiction is begging for more Christian participation. We anticipate such contributions gladly. Interviews where well-known personalities respond to the gospel are also strong publication possibilities."

‡COUNSELOR, Scripture Press Publications, Inc., 1825 College Ave., Wheaton IL 60187. Editor: Janice K. Burton. 60% freelance written. Quarterly Sunday School take-home paper with 13 weekly parts. "Our readers are 8-12 years old. All materials attempt to show God's working in the lives of children. Must have a true Christian slant, not just a moral implication." **Pays on acceptance.** Publishes ms an average of 1-2 years after acceptance. Byline given. Buys first North American serial rights, first rights, one-time rights, second serial (reprint) rights or all rights. Editorial lead time 1 year. Submit seasonal material 1 year in advance. Accepts previously published submissions. Reports in 2 months on mss. Sample copy and writer's guidelines for #10 SASE.

Nonfiction: Inspirational (stories), Interview/profile, personal experience, religious. All stories, etc., must have a spiritual perspective. Show God at work in a child's life. Buys 10-20 mss/year. Send complete ms. Length: 900-1,100 words. Pays 7-10¢/word.

Columns/Departments: God's Wonders (seeing God through creation and the wonders of science), Kids in Action (kids doing unusual activities to benefit others), World Series (missions stories from child's perspective), all 300-500 words. Send complete ms. Pays 7-10¢/word.

Fiction: Adventure, ethnic, religious. Buys 10-15 mss/year. Send complete ms. Length: 900-1,100 words. Pays 7-10¢/word.

Fillers: Buys 8-12 puzzles, games, fun activities/year. Length: 150 words maximum. Pays 7-10¢/word.

Tips: "Show a real feel for the age level. Know your readers and what is age appropriate in terms of concepts and vocabulary. Submit only best quality manuscripts."

THE COVENANT COMPANION, Covenant Publications of the Evangelical Covenant Church, 5101 N. Francisco Ave., Chicago IL 60625. (312)784-3000. Fax: (312)784-1540. Editor: John E. Phelan, Jr. 10-15% freelance written. "As the official monthly organ of The Evangelical Covenant Church, we seek to inform, stimulate and gather the denomination we serve by putting members in touch with each other and assisting them in interpreting contemporary issues. We also seek to inform them on events in the church. Our background is evangelical and our emphasis is on Christian commitment and life." Circ. 22,000. Publishes ms an average of 2 months after acceptance. Byline given. Buys first or all rights. Submit seasonal material 4 months in advance. Accepts simultaneous and previously published submissions. Send tearsheet, photocopy of article or typed ms with rights for sale noted. Query for electronic submissions. Sample copy for $2.25 and 9 × 12 SASE. Writer's guidelines for #10 SASE. Unused mss returned only if accompanied by SASE.

Nonfiction: Humor, inspirational, religious. Buys 20-25 mss/year. Send complete ms. Length: 500-2,000 words. Pays $15-50 for assigned articles; pays $15-35 for unsolicited articles.

Photos: Send photos with submissions. Reviews prints. Offers no additonal payment for photos accepted with ms. Identification of subjects required. Buys one-time rights.

Poetry: Traditional. Buys 10-15 poems/year. Submit maximum 10 poems. Pays $10-15.

Tips: "Seasonal articles related to church year and on national holidays are welcome."

‡THE CRITIC, A Journal of American Catholic Culture, Thomas More Association, 205 W. Monroe St., 6th Floor, Chicago IL 60606. Editor: Julie Bridge. 90% freelance written. Quarterly magazine. "*The Critic* is a cultural, literary journal written from a primarily American Catholic perspective. Considered liberal to moderate regarding Catholic doctrine. Our emphasis is on spirituality and literature; also feature serious theological material." Estab. 1985. Circ. 2,000. **Pays on acceptance.** Publishes ms an average of 3 months after acceptance. Byline given. Buys first North American serial rights. Editorial lead time 3 months. Submit seasonal material 4 months in advance. Query for electronic submissions. Reports in 10 weeks on queries; 2 months on mss. Sample copy for $5. Writer's guidelines for #10 SASE.

Nonfiction: Essays, humor, interview/profile, opinion, religious. Buys 20-30 mss/year. Query. Length: 750-4,500 words. Pays $50-400.

Photos: State availability of photos with submission. Reviews contact sheets. Offers $10-40/photo. Identification of subjects required. Buys one-time rights.

Fiction: Ethnic, humorous, mainstream, religious. Buys 20-30 mss/year. Send complete ms. Length: 6,000 words maximum. Pays $50-400.

Poetry: Free verse, haiku, light verse, traditional. Buys 20-30 poems/year. Pays $15-75.

Tips: "*The Critic* is a serious literary, cultural journal devoted primarily to American Catholic culture with an emphasis on Catholic authors/literature. Any quality spiritual fiction/nonfiction considered, as well as theological reflection and commentary. We are tailored to a literary, not an academic, audience. Do not use academic writing style in academic material. Material need not be overtly Catholic, but keep in mind our religious character when submitting."

DAILY MEDITATION, Box 2710, San Antonio TX 78299. Editor: Ruth S. Paterson. Quarterly. Byline given. Buys first North American serial rights only. **Pays on acceptance.** Submit seasonal material 6 months in advance. Sample copy for $2 or SASE for Guidelines only.

• This magazine is no longer accepting poetry submissions.

Nonfiction: "Inspirational, self-improvement and nonsectarian religious articles, showing the path to greater spiritual growth." Length: 750-1,600 words. Pays 1½-2¢/word.

Fillers: Length: 400 words maximum.

Tips: "All our material is freelance except our meditations, which are staff written. We buy approximately 100 manuscripts per year. Review our guidelines before submitting. Checking copy is sent upon publication."

‡DECISION, Billy Graham Evangelistic Association, 1300 Harmon Place, Minneapolis MN 55403-1988. (612)338-0500. Fax: (612)335-1299. Editor: Roger C. Palms. 25-40% freelance written. Works each year with small number of new/unpublished writers, as well as a solid stable of experienced writers. Magazine published 11 times/year, "to set forth to every reader the Good News of salvation in Jesus Christ with such vividness and clarity that he or she will be drawn to make a commitment to Christ; to encourage, teach and strengthen Christians." Estab. 1960. Circ. 1.6 million. Pays on publication. Byline given. Buys first rights and assigns work-for-hire manuscripts, articles, projects. Include telephone number with submission. Submit seasonal material 10 months in advance; other mss published up to 18 months after acceptance. Reports in 3 months on mss. Sample copy for 9 × 12 SAE with 4 first-class stamps. Writer's guidelines for #10 SASE.

Nonfiction: How-to, motivational, personal experience and religious. "No personality-centered articles or articles that are issue-oriented or critical of denominations." Buys approximately 75 mss/year. Send complete ms. Length: 400-1,800 words. Pays $30-250. Pays expenses of writers on assignment.

Photos: State availability of photos with submission. Reviews prints. Captions, model releases and identification of subjects required. Buys one-time rights.

Poetry: Accepting submissions. No queries.

Tips: "We are seeking personal conversion testimonies and personal experience articles that show how God intervened in a person's daily life and the way in which Scripture was applied to the experience in helping to solve the problem. The conversion testimonies describe in first person what author's life was like before he/she became a Christian, how he/she committed his/her life to Christ and what tangible difference He has made since that decision. We also are looking for vignettes on various aspects of personal evangelism. SASE required with submissions."

‡**DISCIPLESHIP JOURNAL**, NavPress, a division of The Navigators, P.O. Box 35004, Colorado Springs CO 80935-0004. (719)531-3529. Fax: (719)598-7128. Editor: Susan Maycinik. 90% freelance written. Works with a small number of new/unpublished writers each year. Bimonthly magazine on Christian discipleship. "The mission of *Discipleship Journal* is to help believers develop a deeper relationship with Jesus Christ, and to provide practical help in understanding the scriptures and applying them to daily life and ministry." Estab. 1981. Circ. 95,000. **Pays on acceptance.** Publishes ms an average of 6 months after acceptance. Byline given. Buys first North American serial rights and second serial (reprint) rights. Submit seasonal material 6 months in advance. Accepts previously published submissions. Send tearsheet of article and information about when and where the article previously appeared. Query for electronic submissions. Reports in 6 weeks. Sample copy and writer's guidelines for $2.24 and 9×12 SAE.

Nonfiction: Book excerpts (rarely); how-to (grow in Christian faith and disciplines; help others grow as Christians; serve people in need; understand and apply the Bible); inspirational; interview/profile (focusing on one aspect of discipleship); and interpretation/application of the Bible. No personal testimony; humor; anything not directly related to Christian life and faith; politically partisan articles. Buys 80 mss/year. Query with published clips only. Length: 500-3,000 words. Pays 5¢/word for reprint; 20¢/word for first rights. Sometimes pays the expenses of writers on assignment.

Tips: "Our articles are meaty, not fluffy. Study writer's guidelines and back issues and try to use similar approaches. Don't preach. Polish before submitting. About half of the articles in each issue are related to one theme. Freelancers should write to request theme list. We are looking for more practical articles on ministering to others and more articles dealing with world missions."

EVANGEL, Free Methodist Publishing House, P.O. Box 535002, Indianapolis IN 46253-5002. (317)244-3660. Fax: (317)244-1247. Editor: Carolyn Smith. 100% freelance written. Weekly take-home paper. Estab. 1897. Circ. 26,000. Pays on publication. Publishes ms an average of 1 year after acceptance. Buys simultaneous, second serial (reprint) or one-time rights. Submit seasonal material 9 months in advance. Accepts previously published submissions. Send photocopy of article and information about when and where the article previously appeared. For reprints, pays 4% of the amount paid for an original article. Reports in 1 month. Sample copy and writer's guidelines for 6×9 SAE with 2 first-class stamps.

Nonfiction: Interview (with ordinary person who is doing something extraordinary in his community, in service to others), profile (of missionary or one from similar service profession who is contributing significantly to society), personal experience (finding a solution to a problem common to young adults; coping with handicapped child, for instance, or with a neighborhood problem. Story of how God-given strength or insight saved a situation). Buys 100 mss/year. Submit complete ms. Length: 300-1,000 words. Pays 4¢/word.

Photos: Purchased with accompanying ms. Captions required. Send prints. Pays $10 for 8×10 b&w glossy prints.

Fiction: Religious themes dealing with contemporary issues dealt with from a Christian frame of reference. Story must "go somewhere." Buys 50 mss/year. Submit complete ms.

Poetry: Free verse, haiku, light verse, traditional, religious. Buys 50 poems/year. Submit maximum 6 poems. Length: 4-24 lines. Pays $10.

Tips: "Seasonal material will get a second look (won't be rejected so easily). Write an attention grabbing lead followed by an article that says something worthwhile. Relate the lead to some of the universal needs of the reader—promise in that lead to help the reader in some way. Lack of SASE brands author as a nonprofessional; I seldom even bother to read the script." Prefers non-justified righthand margin.

EVANGELIZING TODAY'S CHILD, Child Evangelism Fellowship Inc., Box 348, Warrenton MO 63383-0348. (314)456-4321. Editor: Elsie Lippy. 50% freelance written. Prefers to work with published/established writers. Bimonthly magazine. "Our purpose is to equip Christians to win the world's children to Christ and disciple them. Our readership is Sunday school teachers, Christian education leaders and children's workers in every phase of Christian ministry to children up to 12 years old." Estab. 1942. Circ. 22,000. Pays within 90 days of acceptance. Publishes ms an average of 6 months after acceptance. Byline given. Pays a kill fee if assigned. Buys first serial rights. Submit seasonal material 6 months in advance. Accepts previously published submissions. Send photocopy of article and information about when and where the article previously appeared. For reprints, pays 35% of amount paid for original article. Reports in 2 months. Sample copy for 9×12 SAE with 5 first-class stamps. Writer's guidelines for SASE.

Nonfiction: Unsolicited articles welcomed from writers with Christian education training or current experience in working with children. Buys 35 mss/year. Query. Length: 1,200-1,500. Pays 8-12¢/word.

Photos: Submissions of photos on speculation accepted. Needs photos of children or related subjects. Pays $45 for inside color prints or transparencies, $125 for cover transparencies.

‡**FAITH TODAY, Canada's Evangelical News/Feature Magazine**, Evangelical Fellowship of Canada, 175 Riviera Dr., #1, Markham Ontario L3R 5V6 Canada. (905)479-5885. Editor: Brian C. Stiller. Bimonthly magazine covering evangelical Christianity. "*FT* is an interdenominational, evangelical news/feature magazine that informs Canadian Christians on issues facing church and society, and on events within the church community. It focuses on corporate faith interacting with society rather than on personal spiritual life. Writers should have a thorough understanding of the *Canadian evangelical* community." Estab. 1983. Circ. 18,000.

Pays on publication. Publishes ms an average of 6 months after acceptance. Byline given. Offers 30-50% kill fee. Buys first rights. Editorial lead time 4 months. Reports in 6 weeks. Sample copy and writer's guidelines free on request.

Nonfiction: Religious, news feature. Buys 75 mss/year. Query. Length: 1,000-2,000 words. Pays $250-600. Sometimes pays expenses of writers on assignment.

Photos: State availability of photos with submission. Reviews contact sheets, prints. Identification of subjects required. Buys one-time rights.

Tips: "Query should include brief outline and names of the sources you plan to interview in your research. Use Canadian postage on SASE."

THE FAMILY—A Catholic perspective, Daughters of St. Paul, 50 St. Paul's Ave., Boston MA 02130. (617)522-8911. Editor: Sr. Mary Lea Hill. Contact: Sr. Theresa Frances, managing editor. Monthly magazine on Catholic family life. "*The Family* magazine stresses the special place of the family within society as an irreplaceable center of life, love and faith. Articles on timely, pertinent issues help families approach today's challenges with a faith perspective and a spirit of commitment to the Gospel of Jesus Christ." Estab. 1952. Pays on publication. Publishes ms an average of 12 months after acceptance. Byline given. Buys first and second serial (reprint) rights. Submit seasonal material 9 months in advance. Accepts previously published submissions. Send typed ms with rights for sale noted and information about when and where material previously appeared. For reprints, pays $50. Reports in 3 months. Sample copy for $3 and 9×12 SAE. Writer's guidelines for #10 SASE. "No simultaneous submissions. We do not review manuscripts in the months of July or August. No queries."

• *The Family* is buying less freelance material.

Nonfiction: Humor, inspirational, interview/profile, religious. Buys 20 mss/year. Send complete ms. Length: 500-1,500 words. Pays $50-125. Also may pay in contributor's copies.

Photos: Send photos with submission. Captions, model releases, identification of subjects required. Buys one-time rights.

Fiction: Humorous, religious, slice-of-life vignettes, family. Buys 8 mss/year. Send complete ms. Length: 800-1,200 words. Pays $50-125.

Fillers: Anecdotes, short humor. Buys 15/year. Length: 50-200 words. Pays $10-20.

THE FAMILY DIGEST, P.O. Box 40137, Fort Wayne IN 46804. Editor: Corine B. Erlandson. 95% freelance written. Bimonthly digest-sized magazine. "*The Family Digest* is dedicated to the joy and fulfillment of the Catholic family, and its relationship to the Catholic parish." Estab. 1945. Circ. 150,000. Pays within one month of acceptance. Publishes ms usually within 1 year after acceptance. Byline given. Buys first North American rights. Submit seasonal material 7 months in advance. Occasionally accepts previously published submissions. Send typed ms with rights for sale noted and information about when and where the article previously appeared. For reprints, pays 5¢/word. Reports in 2 months. Sample copy and writer's guidelines for 6×9 SAE with 2 first-class stamps.

Nonfiction: Family life, parish life, how-to, seasonal, inspirational, prayer life, Catholic traditions. Send ms with SASE. No poetry or fiction. Buys 55 unsolicited mss/year. Length: 750-1,100 words. Pays 5¢/word.

Fillers: Anecdotes, tasteful humor based on personal experience. Buys 5/issue. Length: 25-125 words maximum. Cartoons: Publishes 5-8 cartoons/issue, related to family and Catholic parish life. Pays $20/cartoon, on acceptance.

Tips: "Prospective freelance contributors should be familiar with the publication, and the types of articles we accept and publish. We are especially looking for upbeat articles which affirm the simple ways in which the Catholic faith is expressed in our daily life. Articles on family and parish life, including seasonal articles, how-to pieces, inspirational prayer, spiritual life and church traditions, will be gladly reviewed for possible publication."

‡FOURSQUARE WORLD ADVANCE, International Church of the Foursquare Gospel, 1910 W. Sunset Blvd., Suite 200, P.O. Box 26902, Los Angeles CA 90026-0176. Editor: Ronald D. Williams. 5% freelance written. Bimonthly magazine covering Devotional/Religious material, denominational news. "*Foursquare World ADVANCE* magazine is the official publication of the International Church of the Foursquare Gospel. It is published bimonthly and distributed, without charge, to members and friends of the Foursquare Church. Estab. 1917. Circ. 98,000. Pays on publication. Publishes ms an average of 2 months after acceptance. Byline given. Buys first rights, one-time rights, second serial (reprint) rights and simultaneous rights. Editorial lead time 6 months. Submit seasonal material 6 months in advance. Accepts simultaneous and previously published submissions. Reports in 2 weeks on queries. Sample copy and writer's guidelines free on request.

Nonfiction: Inspirational, interview/profile, personal experience, religious. Buys 2-3 mss/year. Send complete ms. Length: 800-1,200 words. Pays $75.

Photos: State availability of photos with submission. Reviews 4×6 prints. Offers no additional payment for photos accepted with ms. Captions, model releases, identification of subjects required. Buys one-time rights.

GROUP MAGAZINE, P.O. Box 481, Loveland CO 80538. (303)669-3836. Fax: (303)669-3269. Editor: Rick Lawrence. Publisher: Bob Fibkins. Departments Editor: Barbara Beach. 60% freelance written. Magazine published 6 times/year covering youth ministry. "Writers must be actively involved in youth ministry. Articles we accept are practical, not theoretical, and focused for local church youth workers." Estab. 1974. Circ. 57,000. **Pays on acceptance.** Publishes ms an average of 6 months after acceptance. Byline given. Offers $20 kill fee. Buys all rights. Submit seasonal material 7 months in advance. Reports in 2 months. Sample copy for $2 and 9×12 SAE. Writer's guidelines for SASE and 1 first-class stamp.
Nonfiction: How-to (youth ministry issues). No personal testimony, theological or lecture-style articles. Buys 50-60 mss/year. Query. Length: 500-1,800 words. Pays $75-200. Sometimes pays for phone calls on agreement.
    ● Looking for more mini-articles that are practical and tip-oriented; no more than 250 words.
Photos: State availability of photos with submission. Model releases and identification of subjects required. Buys all rights.

GUIDEPOSTS MAGAZINE, 16 E. 34th St., New York NY 10016-4397. Editor: Fulton Oursler, Jr. 30% freelance written. "Works with a small number of new/unpublished writers each year. *Guideposts* is an inspirational monthly magazine for people of all faiths, in which men and women from all walks of life tell in first-person narrative how they overcame obstacles, rose above failures, handled sorrow, learned to master themselves and became more effective people through faith in God." Estab. 1945. Publishes ms an "indefinite" number of months after acceptance. Pays 25% kill fee for assigned articles. "Most of our stories are ghosted articles, so the writer would not get a byline unless it was his/her own story." Buys all rights and second serial (reprint) rights. Reports in 2 months.
Nonfiction and Fillers: Articles and features should be written in simple, anecdotal style with an emphasis on human interest. Short mss of approximately 250-750 words (pays $50-200) considered for such features as Quiet People and general one-page stories. Address short items to Celeste McCauley. For full-length mss, 750-1,500 words, pays $200-400. All mss should be typed, double-spaced and accompanied by SASE. Annually awards scholarships to high school juniors and seniors in writing contest. Buys 40-60 unsolicited mss/year. Pays expenses of writers on assignment.
Tips: "Study the magazine before you try to write for it. Each story must make a single spiritual point. The freelancer would have the best chance of breaking in by aiming for a one- or two-page article. Sensitively written anecdotes are extremely useful. And it is much easier to just sit down and write them than to have to go through the process of preparing a query. They should be warm, well written, intelligent and upbeat. We like personal narratives that are true and have some universal relevance, but the religious element does not have to be driven home with a sledge hammer. A writer succeeds with us if he or she can write a true article in short-story form with scenes, drama, tension and a resolution of the problem presented. We are over-stocked with medical-type, personal experience stories, but we're in need of stories in which faith in God helps people succeed in business or with other life challenges."

HOME TIMES, A Good Little Newspaper, Neighbor News, Inc., 3676 Collin Dr., #12, West Palm Beach FL 33406. (407)439-3509. Editor: Dennis Lombard. 80% freelance written. Monthly tabloid of conservative, pro-Christian news and views. "*Home Times* is a conservative newspaper written for the general public but with a pro-Christian, family-values slant. It is not religious or preachy." Estab. 1988. Circ. 10,000. Pays on publication. Publishes ms an average of 2 months after acceptance. Byline given. No kill fee. Buys one-time rights or makes work-for-hire assignments. Editorial lead time 1 month. Submit seasonal material 1 month in advance. Accepts simultaneous and previously published submissions. Send tearsheet or photocopy of article or short story and information about when and where the material previously appeared. Pays up to 50% of amount paid for an original article. Reports in 2 weeks. *Writer's Market* recommends allowing 2 months for reply. Sample copy for $3 and 9×12 SASE with 4 first-class stamps. Writer's guidelines for #10 SASE.
    ● *Home Times* wants material for Human Heroes, Fatherhood, and The Children—People features with photos.
Nonfiction: Current events, essays, general interest, historical/nostalgic, how-to, humor, inspirational, interview/profile, opinion, personal experience, photo feature, religious, travel. "Nothing preachy, moralistic, religious or with churchy slant." Buys 50 mss/year. Send complete ms. Length 900 maximum words. Pays $5 minimum. Pays contributor's copies on mutual agreement. Sometimes pays expenses of writers on assignment.
Photos: Send photos with submission. Reviews 4×5 prints. Offers $5-10/photo. Captions, model releases, identification of subjects required. Buys one-time rights.
Columns/Departments: Buys 50 mss/year. Send complete ms. Pays $5-15.
Fiction: Historical, humorous, mainstream, religious, issue-oriented contemporary. "Nothing preachy, moralistic." Buys 5 mss/year. Send complete ms. Length: 500-1,200 words. Pays $5-25.
Poetry: Free verse, light verse, traditional. Buys 10 poems/year. Submit maximum 3 poems. Lines: 2-24 lines. Pays $5-10.

Fillers: Anecdotes, facts, newsbreaks, short humor. Uses 25/year. Length: to 100 words.

Tips: "We encourage new writers. We are different from ordinary news or religious publications. We strongly suggest you read guidelines and sample issues. (3 issues for $3 and 9×12 SASE with 4 stamps; writer's subscription 12 issues plus 3 samples for $9.) We are most open to material for new columns; journalists covering hard news in major news centers—with Conservative slant. Also, lots of letters and op-eds though we don't always pay for them."

‡KALEIDOSCOPE, A Magazine About Today's Christians, Baltimore-Washington Conf., UMC, 5124 Greenwich Ave., Baltimore MD 21229. (410)362-4700. Editor: J. E. Skillington. 95% freelance written. Bimonthly magazine covering United Methodists and other mainstream Christians. "*Kaleidoscope* is a lifestyle magazine about today's United Methodists facing challenges and together building a church for future generations. It includes inspiring articles and photos about mission work, faith in action, new ideas for personal ministries, and the history of our church. It also explores current faith topics from a United Methodist perspective. Our audience is primarily lay persons in The United Methodist Church." Estab. 1993. Circ. 110,000. Pays on publication. Publishes ms 6 months after acceptance. Byline given. Offers $75 kill fee. Buys first North American serial rights. Editorial lead time 6 months. Submit seasonal material 9 months in advance. Query for electronic submissions. Reports in 6 weeks on queries; 2 months on mss. Sample copy for 9×12 SAE. Writer's guidelines free.

Nonfiction: General interest, historical/nostalgic, interview/profile, personal experience, photo feature, religious. Special issues: Christmas and Easter. No poetry, no general articles without any Christian angle. Buys 75 mss/year. Query with published clips. Length: 1,500-2,300 words. Pays $150. Pays expenses of writers on assignment.

Photos: Send photos with submission. Reviews transparencies. Offers $75-150/article. Captions, model releases and identification of subjects required. Buys all rights.

Columns/Departments: Query. Pays $75-100.

LIGHT AND LIFE MAGAZINE, Free Methodist Church of North America, P.O. Box 535002, Indianapolis IN 46253-5002. Fax: (317)244-1247. Editor: Bob Haslam. 35% freelance written. Works with a small number of new/unpublished writers each year. Monthly magazine emphasizing evangelical Christianity with Wesleyan slant for a cross section of adults. Estab. 1868. Circ. 30,000. Pays on publication. Publishes ms an average of 6 months after acceptance. Byline given. Prefers first serial rights; rarely buys second serial (reprint) rights. Submit seasonal material 6 months in advance. Reports in 6 weeks. Sample copy and guidelines for $1.50. Writer's guidelines for SASE.

• *Light and Life* was named Denominational Magazine of the Year by the Evangelical Press Association.

Nonfiction: "We need fresh, upbeat articles showing the average layperson how to be Christ-like at home, work and play." Submit complete ms. Buys 50-60 unsolicited ms/year. Pays 4¢/word. Length: 500-600 or 1,000-1,200 words.

Photos: Purchased without accompanying ms. Send prints or slides. Pays $5-35 for color or b&w photos.

LIGUORIAN, Liguori MO 63057-9999. Fax: (314)464-8449. Editor: Rev. Allan Weinert. Managing Editor: Cheryl Plass. 25% freelance written. Prefers to work with published/established writers. Monthly magazine for families with Catholic religious convictions. Estab. 1913. Circ. 400,000. **Pays on acceptance.** Byline given "except on short fillers and jokes." Buys all rights but will reassign rights to author *after* publication upon written request. Submit seasonal material 6 months in advance. Query for electronic submissions. Reports in up to 6 months. Sample copy and writer's guidelines for 6×9 SAE with 3 first-class stamps.

Nonfiction: "Pastoral, practical and personal approach to the problems and challenges of people today. No travelogue approach or unresearched ventures into controversial areas. Also, no material found in secular publications—fad subjects that already get enough press, pop psychology, negative or put-down articles." Buys 60 unsolicited mss/year. Buys 12 fiction mss/year. Length: 400-2,000 words. Pays 10-12¢/word. Sometimes pays expenses of writers on assignment.

Photos: Photographs on assignment only unless submitted with and specific to article.

LIVE, 1445 Boonville Ave., Springfield MO 65802-1894. (417)862-2781. Fax: (417)862-6059. Adult Editor: Paul W. Smith. 100% freelance written. Works with several new/unpublished writers each year. Weekly magazine for adults in Assemblies of God Sunday schools. Circ. 160,000. **Pays on acceptance.** Publishes ms an average of 1 year after acceptance. Not copyrighted. Submit seasonal material 12-18 months in advance of publication. "Do not mention Santa Claus, Halloween or Easter bunnies." Accepts previously published submissions. Send tearsheet or photocopy of article or short story or typed ms with rights for sale noted and information about when and where the material previously appeared. Pays 75% (2¢/word) of the amount of their fee for original material. Reports in 6 weeks. Free sample copy and writer's guidelines for 7½×10½ SAE with 2 first-class stamps. Letters without SASE will not be answered. Buys 120-150 mss/year.

Nonfiction: In the narrative mode emphasizing some phase of Christian living presented in a down-to-earth manner. Biography or missionary material using narrative techniques, but must include verification. Historical, scientific, nature, humorous material with spiritual lesson. "Be accurate in detail and factual material.

Writing for Christian publications is a ministry. The spiritual emphasis must be an integral part of your material." Prefers not to see material on highly controversial subjects but would appreciate stories on contemporary issues and concerns (e.g. substance abuse, AIDS, euthanasia, cults, integrity, etc.). Length: 1,000-1,600 words. Pays 3¢/word for first serial rights; 2¢/word for second serial (reprint) rights, according to the value of the material and the amount of editorial work necessary.

Photos: Color photos or transparencies purchased with mss. Pay open.

Fiction: "Present believable characters working out their problems according to Bible principles; in other words, present Christianity in action without being preachy. The stories (fictional or true) should tell themselves without moral lessons tacked on. We want multinational, ethnic, urban and intercultural characters. Use action, suspense, humor! Stories should be true to life but not what we would feel is a sinful pattern for living. Stories should not put parents, teachers, ministers or other Christian workers in a bad light. Setting, plot and action should be realistic, with strong motivation. Characterize so that the people will live in your story. Construct your plot carefully so that each incident moves naturally and suspensefully toward crisis and conclusion. *An element of conflict is necessary in fiction.* We do not accept fiction based on incidents in the Bible." Length: 1,000-1,500 words. Pays 3¢/word for first serial rights; 2¢/word for second serial (reprint) rights.

Poetry: Traditional, free verse, blank verse. Length: 12-20 lines. "Please do not send large numbers of poems at one time." Pays $10-15/poem.

Fillers: Brief and humorous, usually containing an anecdote, and always with a strong evangelical emphasis. Length: 200-600 words.

LIVING WITH TEENAGERS, Baptist Sunday School Board, 127 Ninth Ave. N., Nashville TN 37234. (615)251-2229. Fax: (615)251-5008. Editor: Ellen Oldacre. 30% freelance written. Works with a number of new/unpublished writers each year. Monthly magazine about teenagers for parents of teenagers. Estab. 1978. Circ. 50,000. Pays within 2 months of acceptance. Publishes ms an average of 10-12 months after acceptance. Buys all or first rights. Accepts previously published submissions. Send photocopy of previously published article along with information about where and when it previously appeared. Submit seasonal material 1 year in advance. Reports in 2 months. Sample copy for 9 × 12 SAE with 4 first-class stamps. Writer's guidelines for #10 SASE. Résumés and queries only.

THE LOOKOUT, 8121 Hamilton Ave., Cincinnati OH 45231-9981. (513)931-4050. Fax: (513)931-0904. Editor: Simon J. Dahlman. 50-60% freelance written. Often works with new/unpublished writers. Weekly magazine for Christian adults, with emphasis on spiritual growth, family life, and topical issues. Audience is mainly conservative Christians. Estab. 1894. **Pays on acceptance.** Publishes ms an average of 6 months after acceptance. Byline given. Buys first serial, one-time, second serial (reprint) or simultaneous rights. Accepts simultaneous and previously published submissions. Send typed ms with rights for sale noted and information about when and where the article previously appeared. Pays 60% of their fee for an original article. Reports in 4 months, sometimes longer. Sample copy and writer's guidelines for 50¢. "We now work from a theme list, which is available on request with our guidelines." Guidelines only for #10 SASE.

Nonfiction: "Seeks stories about real people; items that are helpful in practical Christian living (how-to's); items that shed Biblical light on matters of contemporary controversy; and items that motivate, that lead the reader to ask, 'Why shouldn't I try that?' Articles should tell how real people are involved for Christ. In choosing topics, *The Lookout* considers timeliness, the church and national calendar, and the ability of the material to fit the above guidelines. Remember to aim at laymen." Submit complete ms. Length: 500-2,000 words. Pays 5-10¢/word. We also use inspirational short pieces. "About 400-700 words is a good length for these. Relate an incident that illustrates a point without preaching."

Fiction: "A short story is printed in many issues; it is usually between 1,200-2,000 words long and should be as true to life as possible while remaining inspirational and helpful. Use familiar settings and situations. Most often we use stories with a Christian slant." Pays 5-10¢/word.

Photos: Reviews b&w prints, 4 × 6 or larger. Pays $25-50. Pays $75-200 for color transparencies for covers and inside use. Needs photos of people, especially adults in a variety of settings. Send to Photo Editor, Standard Publishing, at the above address.

THE LUTHERAN, Magazine of the Evangelical Lutheran Church in America, Evangelical Lutheran Church in America, 8765 W. Higgins Rd., Chicago IL 60631-4183. (312)380-2540. Fax: (312)380-2751. E-mail: lutheran.partl@ecunet.org. Editor: Edgar R. Trexler. Managing Editor: Roger R. Kahle. 30% freelance written. Monthly magazine for "lay people in church. News and activities of the Evangelical Lutheran Church in America, news of the world of religion, ethical reflections on issues in society, personal Christian experience." Estab. 1988. Circ. 800,000. **Pays on acceptance.** Publishes ms an average of 3 months after acceptance. Byline given. Offers 50% kill fee. Buys first rights. Submit seasonal/holiday material 4 months in advance. Query required. Reports in 3 weeks. Free sample copy and writer's guidelines.

Nonfiction: David L. Miller. Inspirational, interview/profile, personal experience, photo feature, religious. "No articles unrelated to the world of religion." Buys 40 mss/year. Query with published clips. Length: 1,000-1,500 words. Pays $400-1,000 for assigned articles; $100-500 for unsolicited articles. Pays expenses of writers on assignment.

Photos: Send photos with submission. Reviews contact sheets, transparencies, prints. Offers $50-175/photo. Captions and identification of subjects required. Buys one-time rights.

Columns/Departments: Lite Side (humor—church, religious), In Focus, Living the Faith, Values & Society, In Our Churches, Our Church at Work, 25-100 words. Send complete ms. Length: 25-100 words. Pays $10.

Tips: "Writers have the best chance selling us feature articles."

THE LUTHERAN JOURNAL, 7317 Cahill Rd., Edina MN 55439-2081. Publisher: John W. Leykom. Editor: Rev. Armin U. Deye. Quarterly family magazine for Lutheran Church members, middle age and older. Estab. 1938. Circ. 136,000. Pays on publication. Byline given. Accepts simultaneous and previously published submissions. Send tearsheet or photocopy of article typed ms with rights for sale noted and information about when and where the article previously appeared. For reprints, pays 50% of the amount paid for an original article. Reports in 4 months. Sample copy for 9 × 12 SAE with 2 first-class stamps.

Nonfiction: Inspirational, religious, human interest, historical articles. Interesting or unusual church projects. Informational, how-to, personal experience, interview, humor, think articles. Buys 25-30 mss/year. Submit complete ms. Length: 1,500 words maximum; occasionally 2,000 words. Pays 1-4¢/word.

Photos: Send b&w and color photos with accompanying ms. Captions required.

Fiction: Mainstream, religious, historical. Must be suitable for church distribution. Length: 2,000 words maximum. Pays 1-2¢/word.

‡**THE LUTHERAN WITNESS**, The Lutheran Church—Missouri Synod, 1333 S. Kirkwood Rd., St. Louis MO 63122. (314)965-9000. Editor: Rev. David Mahsman. Contact: David Strand. 50% freelance written. Monthly magazine. "*The Lutheran Witness* provides Missouri Synod laypeople with stories and information that complement congregational life, foster personal growth in faith, and help interpret the contemporary world from a Christian perspective." Estab. 1882. Circ. 325,000. **Pays on acceptance.** Publishes ms an average of 6 months after acceptance. Byline given. Offers 50% kill fee. Buys first rights. Editorial lead time 4 months. Submit seasonal material 6 months in advance. Accepts simultaneous and previously published submissions. Reports in 2 months. Sample copy and writer's guidelines free on request.

Nonfiction: General interest, humor, inspirational, interview/profile, opinion, personal experience, religious. Buys 40-50 mss/year. Send complete ms. Length: 250-1,600. Pays $100-300. Pays expenses of writers on assignment.

Photos: Send photos with submission. Offers $50-200/photo. Captions required. Buys one-time rights.

Columns/Departments: Humor, Opinion, Bible Studies. Buys 60 mss/year. Send complete ms. Pays $50-100.

MENNONITE BRETHREN HERALD, 3-169 Riverton Ave., Winnipeg, Manitoba R2L 2E5 Canada. (204)669-6575. Fax: (204)654-1865. E-mail: 75061.3572@compuserve.com. Editor: Jim Coggins. Managing Editor: Susan Brandt. 25% freelance written. Biweekly family publication "read mainly by people of the Mennonite faith, reaching a wide cross section of professional and occupational groups, but also including many homemakers. Readership includes people from both urban and rural communities." Estab. 1962. Circ. 14,000. Pays on publication. Publishes ms an average of 6 months after acceptance. Not copyrighted. Byline given. Sample copy for $1 and 9 × 12 SAE with 2 IRCs. Reports in 6 months. Accepts previously published submissions. Send photocopy of article or typed ms with rights for sale noted and information about when and where the article previously appeared. For reprints, pays 75% of the amount paid for an original article.

Nonfiction: Articles with a Christian family orientation; youth directed, Christian faith and life, and current issues. Wants articles critiquing the values of a secular society, attempting to relate Christian living to the practical situations of daily living; showing how people have related their faith to their vocations. Length: 1,500 words. Pays $30-40. Pays the expenses of writers on assignment.

Photos: Photos purchased with ms. Pays $10.

THE MESSENGER OF THE SACRED HEART, Apostleship of Prayer, 661 Greenwood Ave., Toronto, Ontario M4J 4B3 Canada. (416)466-1195. Editor: Rev. F.J. Power, S.J. Monthly magazine for "Canadian and US Catholics interested in developing a life of prayer and spirituality; stresses the great value of our ordinary actions and lives." 20% freelance written. Estab. 1891. Circ. 17,000. Buys first rights only. Byline given. **Pays on acceptance.** Submit seasonal material 5 months in advance. Reports in 1 month. Sample copy for $1 and 7½ × 10½ SAE. Writer's guidelines for #10 SASE.

Fiction: Religious/inspirational. Stories about people, adventure, heroism, humor, drama. Buys 12 mss/year. Send complete ms with SAE and IRCs. Unsolicited mss, unaccompanied by return postage, will not be returned. Length: 750-1,500 words. Pays 4¢/word.

Tips: "Develop a story that sustains interest to the end. Do not preach, but use plot and characters to convey the message or theme. Aim to move the heart as well as the mind. Before sending, cut out unnecessary or unrelated words or sentences. If you can, add a light touch or a sense of humor to the story. Your ending should have impact, leaving a moral or faith message for the reader."

‡**MOODY MAGAZINE**, Moody Bible Institute, 820 N. LaSalle Blvd., Chicago IL 60610. (312)329-2164. Fax: (312)329-2149. Managing Editor: Andrew Scheer. 80% freelance written. Monthly magazine for evan-

gelical Christianity. "Our readers are conservative, evangelical Christians highly active in their churches and concerned about applying their faith in daily living." Estab. 1900. Circ. 135,000. **Pays on acceptance.** Publishes ms an average of 6-9 months after acceptance. Byline given. Buys first North American serial rights. Submit seasonal material 9 months in advance. Query for all submissions. Unsolicited mss will be returned unread. Reports in 2 months. Sample copy for 10×13 SASE with 3 first-class stamps. Writer's guidelines for #10 SASE.
Nonfiction: Personal narratives (on living the Christian life), a few reporting articles. Buys 80 mss/year. Query. Length: 750-2,000 words. Pays 15¢/word for queried articles; 20¢/word for assigned articles. Sometimes pays the expenses of writers on assignment.
Columns/Departments: First Person (the only article written for non-Christians; a personal conversion testimony written by the author [will accept 'as told to's']; the objective is to tell a person's testimony in such a way that the reader will understand the gospel and want to receive Christ as Savior), 800-1,000 words; and Just for Parents (provides practical anecdotal guidance for parents, solidly based on biblical principles), 1,500-1,600 words. Buys 22 mss/year. Query. Pays 15¢/word.

MY DAILY VISITOR, Our Sunday Visitor, Inc., 200 Noll Plaza, Huntington IN 46750. (219)356-8400. Editors: Catherine and William Odell. 99% freelance written. Bimonthly magazine of Scripture meditations based on the day's Catholic mass readings. Circ. 30,000. **Pays on acceptance.** Publishes ms an average of 6 months after acceptance. Byline given. Not copyrighted. Buys one-time rights. Reports in 2 months. Sample copy and writer's guidelines for #10 SAE with 2 first-class stamps. "Guest editors write on assignment basis only."
Nonfiction: Inspirational, personal experience, religious. Buys 12 mss/year. Query with published clips. Length: 150-160 words times number of days in month. Pays $500 for 1 month (28-31) of meditations. Pays writers 25 gratis copies.

‡NEW WORLD OUTLOOK, The Mission Magazine of the United Methodist Church, General Board of Global Ministries, 475 Riverside Dr., Room 1351, New York NY 10115. Editor: Alma Graham. Contact: Christie R. House. 40% freelance written. Bimonthly magazine covering United Methodist mission programs, projects, and personnel. "As the mission magazine of The United Methodist Church, we publish articles on or related to the mission programs, projects, institutions, and personnel of the General Board of Global Ministries, both in the United States and around the world." Estab. 1911. Circ. 30,000. Pays on publication. Publishes ms an average of 4 months after acceptance. Byline given. Offers 50% kill fee or $100. Buys all rights. Editorial lead time 4 months. Submit seasonal material 4 months in advance. No simultaneous or previously published submissions. Sample copy for $2.50.
Nonfiction: Inspirational, personal experience, photo feature, religious, mission reports, mission studies. Special issues: Hong Kong, Taiwan, and China; Living in a Multicultural Society. Buys 24 mss/year. Query. Length: 500-2,000 words. Pays $50-300. Sometimes pays expenses of writers on assignment.
Photos: State availability of photos with submission. Reviews transparencies, prints. Offers $25-150/photo. Captions, identification of subjects required.
Tips: "Write for a list of United Methodist mission institutions, projects, or personnel in the writer's geographic area or in an area of the country or the world to which the writer plans to travel (at writer's own expense). Photojournalists have a decided advantage."

OBLATES, Missionary Association of Mary Immaculate, 15 S. 59th St., Belleville IL 62223-4694. (618)233-2238. Managing Editor: Christine Portell. Manuscripts Editor: Mary Mohrman. 30-50% freelance written. Prefers to work with published writers. Bimonthly inspirational magazine for Christians; audience mainly older adults. Circ. 500,000. **Pays on acceptance.** Usually publishes ms within 2 years after acceptance. Byline given. Buys first North American serial rights. Submit seasonal material 8 months in advance. Reports in 6 months. Sample copy and writer's guidelines for 6×9 or larger SAE with 2 first-class stamps.
Nonfiction: Inspirational and personal experience with positive spiritual insights. No preachy, theological or research articles. Avoid current events and controversial topics. Send complete ms. Length: 500 words. Pays $80.
Poetry: Light verse—reverent, well written, perceptive, with traditional rhythm and rhyme. "Emphasis should be on inspiration, insight and relationship with God." Submit maximum 2 poems. Length: 8-16 lines. Pays $30.
Tips: "Our readership is made up mostly of mature Americans who are looking for comfort, encouragement, and a positive sense of applicable Christian direction to their lives. Focus on sharing of personal insight to problem (i.e. death or change), but must be positive, uplifting. We have well-defined needs for an established market, but are always on the lookout for exceptional work."

THE OTHER SIDE, 300 W. Apsley St., Philadelphia PA 19144-4285. (215)849-2178. Editor: Mark Olson. Managing Editor: Dee Dee Risher. Managing Editor: Doug Davidson. 50% freelance written. Prefers to work with published/established writers. Bimonthly magazine emphasizing "spiritual nurture, prophetic reflection, forgotten voices and artistic visions from a radical Christian perspective." Estab. 1965. Circ. 14,000. **Pays on acceptance.** Publishes ms an average of 6 months after acceptance. Byline given. Buys all or first serial rights. Query for electronic submissions. Reports in 3 months. Sample copy for $4.50. Writer's guidelines for #10 SASE.

Nonfiction: Doug Davidson, managing editor. Current social, political and economic issues in the US and around the world: personality profiles, interpretative essays, interviews, how-to's, personal experiences, spiritual reflections, biblical interpretation and investigative reporting. "Articles must be lively, vivid and down-to-earth, with a radical faith-based Christian perspective." Length: 500-3,500 words. Pays $25-300.

Photos: Cathleen Benberg, art director. Photos or photo essays illustrating current social, political, or economic reality in the US and Third World. Especially interested in creative original art offering spiritual insight and/or fresh perspectives on contemporary issues. Pays $15-75 for b&w and $50-300 for color.

Fiction: Michael Larson, fiction editor. "Short stories, humor and satire conveying insights and situations that will be helpful to Christians with a radical commitment to peace and justice." Length: 300-4,000 words. Pays $25-250.

Poetry: Rod Jellema, poetry editor. "Short, creative poetry that will be thought-provoking and appealing to radical Christians who have a strong commitment to spirituality, peace and justice." Length: 3-50 lines. No more than 4 poems may be submitted at one time by any one author. Pays $15-20.

Tips: "We're looking for tightly written pieces (1,000-1,500 words) on interesting and unusual Christians (or Christian groups) who are putting their commitment to peace and social justice into action in creative and useful ways. We're also looking for provocative analytical and reflective pieces (1,000-4,000 words) dealing with contemporary social issues in the US and abroad."

OUR FAMILY, Oblate Fathers of St. Mary's Province, P.O. Box 249, Battleford, Saskatchewan S0M 0E0 Canada. (306)937-7771. Fax: (306)937-7644. Editor: Nestor Gregoire. 60% freelance written. Prefers to work with published/established writers. Monthly magazine for average family men and women with high school and early college education. Estab. 1949. Circ. 14,265. **Pays on acceptance.** Publishes ms an average of 6 months after acceptance. Byline given. Offers 100% kill fee. Generally purchases first North American serial rights; also buys all, simultaneous, second serial (reprint) or one-time rights. Submit seasonal material 4 months in advance. Accepts simultaneous and previously published submissions. Send tearsheet or photocopy of article or typed ms with rights for sale noted and information about when and where the article previously appeared. Reports in 1 month. *Writer's Market* recommends allowing 2 months for reply. Sample copy for 9 × 12 SAE with $2.50 postage. Only Canadian postage or IRC useful in Canada. Writer's guidelines 50¢.

Nonfiction: Humor (related to family life or husband/wife relations), inspirational (anything that depicts people responding to adverse conditions with courage, hope and love), personal experience (with religious dimensions), photo feature (particularly in search of photo essays on human/religious themes and on persons whose lives are an inspiration to others). Accepts phone queries. Buys 72-88 unsolicited mss/year. Pays expenses of writers on assignment.

Photos: Photos purchased with or without accompanying ms. Pays $35 for 5 × 7 or larger b&w glossy prints and color photos (which are converted into b&w). Offers additional payment for photos accepted with ms (payment for these photos varies according to their quality). Free photo spec sheet for SASE.

Poetry: Avant-garde, free verse, haiku, light verse, traditional. Buys 4-10 poems/issue. Length: 3-30 lines. Pays 75¢-$1/line. Must have a religious dimension.

Fillers: Jokes, gags, anecdotes, short humor. Buys 2-10/issue.

Tips: "Writers should ask themselves whether this is the kind of an article, poem, etc. that a busy housewife would pick up and read when she has a few moments of leisure. We are particularly looking for articles on the spirituality of marriage. We will be concentrating more on recent movements and developments in the church to help make people aware of the new church of which they are a part."

OUR SUNDAY VISITOR MAGAZINE, 200 Noll Plaza, Huntington IN 46750. (219)356-8400. Publisher: Robert P. Lockwood. Editor: David Scott. 5% freelance written. Works with small number of new/unpublished writers each year. Weekly magazine for general Catholic audience. Circ. 120,000. **Pays on acceptance.** Publishes ms an average of 2 months after acceptance. Byline given. Submit seasonal material 2 months in advance. Query for electronic submissions. Reports in 1 month. Sample copy for #10 SASE.

Nonfiction: Catholic-related subjects. Should explain Catholic religious beliefs in articles of human interest, applying Catholic principles to current problems, Catholic profiles, etc. Payment varies depending on reputation of author, quality of work, and amount of research required. Buys 25 mss/year. Query. Length: 1,000-1,200 words. Minimum payment for features is $100. Pays expenses of writers on assignment.

Photos: Purchased with mss; with captions only. Reviews b&w glossy prints and transparencies. Pays minimum of $200/cover photo story; $125/b&w story; $25/color photo; $10/b&w photo.

THE PENTECOSTAL MESSENGER, Messenger Publishing House, P.O. Box 850, Joplin MO 64802-0850. (417)624-7050. Fax: (417)624-7102. Editor: Don Allen. Managing Editor: Peggy Lee Allen. 25% freelance written. Works with small number of new/unpublished writers each year. Bimonthly magazine covering Pentecostal Christianity. "*The Pentecostal Messenger* is the official organ of the Pentecostal Church of God. It goes to ministers and church members." Estab. 1919. Circ. 8,000. Pays on publication. Publishes ms an average of 6 months after acceptance. Byline given. Buys second serial (reprint) or simultaneous rights.

Submit seasonal material 4 months in advance. Accepts simultaneous and previously published submissions. Send tearsheet or photocopy of article or typed ms with rights for sale noted and information about when and where the article previously appeared. For reprints, pays 100% of the amount paid for an original article. Reports in 2 months. Sample copy for 9×12 SAE with 4 first-class stamps. Free writer's guidelines.

Nonfiction: Inspirational, personal experience, religious. Buys 35 mss/year. Send complete ms. Length: 1,800 words. Pays 1½¢/word.

Photos: Send photos with submission. Reviews 2¼×2¼ transparencies and prints. Offers $10-25/photo. Captions and model releases required. Buys one-time rights.

Tips: "Articles need to be inspirational, informative, written from a positive viewpoint, and not extremely controversial."

PIME WORLD, 17330 Quincy St., Detroit MI 48221-2765. (313)342-4066. Managing Editor: Paul Witte. 10% freelance written. Monthly (except July and August) magazine emphasizing foreign missionary activities of the Catholic Church in Burma, India, Bangladesh, the Philippines, Hong Kong, Africa, etc., for an adult audience, interested in current issues in the missions. Audience is largely high school educated, conservative in both religion and politics." Estab. 1954. Circ. 30,000. Pays on publication. Publishes ms an average of 3 months after acceptance. Buys all rights. Byline given. Submit seasonal material 4 months in advance. Accepts simultaneous submissions. Reports in 2 months.

Nonfiction: Informational and inspirational foreign missionary activities of the Catholic Church. Buys 5-10 unsolicited mss/year. Query or send complete ms. Length: 800-1,200 words. Pays 6¢/word.

Photos: Pays $10/color photo.

Tips: "Submit articles dealing with current issues of social justice, evangelization and pastoral work in Third World countries. Interviews of missionaries accepted. Good quality color photos greatly appreciated."

‡POWER FOR LIVING, Scripture Press Publications Inc., 1825 College Ave., Wheaton IL 60187. Editor: Don H. Alban, Jr. 100% freelance written. Quarterly Sunday School take-home paper with 13 weekly parts. **Pays on acceptance.** Publishes ms an average of 1 year after acceptance. Byline given. Buys one-time rights and second serial (reprint) rights. Editorial lead time 1 year. Submit seasonal material 1 year in advance. Accepts simultaneous and previously published submissions. Query for electronic submissions. Sample copy and writer's guidelines free on request.

Nonfiction: Inspirational, personal experience. Buys 150 mss/year. Send complete ms. Length: 1,500 words. Pays to 15¢/word for assigned articles; to 10¢/word for reprints.

Photos: State availability of photos with submission. Negotiates payment individually. Model releases, identification of subjects required. Buys one-time rights.

PRAIRIE MESSENGER, Catholic Journal, Benedictine Monks of St. Peter's Abbey, P.O. Box 190, Muenster, Saskatchewan S0K 2Y0 Canada. (306)682-1772. Fax: (306)682-5285. Editor: Rev. Andrew Britz, OSB. Associate Editor: Marian Noll and Maureen Weber. 10% freelance written. Weekly Catholic journal with strong emphasis on social justice, Third World and ecumenism. Estab. 1904. Circ. 8,400. Pays on publication. Publishes ms an average of 4 months after acceptance. Byline given. Offers 70% kill fee. Not copyrighted. Buys first North American serial, first, one-time, second serial (reprint) or simultaneous rights. Submit seasonal material 3 months in advance. Query for electronic submissions. Reports in 2 months. Sample copy and writers guidelines for 9×12 SAE with 90¢ Canadian postage or IRCs.

• The Canadian Church Press awarded *Prairie Messenger* first place for general excellence.

Nonfiction: Interview/profile, opinion, religious. "No articles on abortion or homosexuality." Buys 15 mss/year. Send complete ms. Length: 250-600 words. Pays $40-60. Sometimes pays expenses of writers on assignment.

Photos: Send photos with submission. Reviews 3×5 prints. Offers $10/photo. Captions required. Buys all rights.

PRESBYTERIAN RECORD, 50 Wynford Dr., North York, Ontario M3C 1J7 Canada. (416)444-1111. Fax: (416)441-2825. Editor: Rev. John Congram. 50% freelance written. Eager to work with new/unpublished writers. Monthly magazine for a church-oriented, family audience. Circ. 60,000. Pays on publication. Publishes ms an average of 4 months after acceptance. Buys first serial, one-time or simultaneous rights. Submit seasonal material 3 months in advance. Reports on ms accepted for publication in 2 months. Returns rejected material in 3 months. Sample copy and writer's guidelines for 9×12 SAE with $1 Canadian postage or IRCs.

Nonfiction: Material on religious themes. Check a copy of the magazine for style. Also personal experience, interview, inspirational material. No material solely or mainly American in context. When possible, photos should accompany manuscript; e.g., current events, historical events and biographies. Buys 15-20 unsolicited mss/year. Query. Length: 1,000-2,000 words. Pays $45-55 (Canadian). Sometimes pays expenses of writers on assignment.

Photos: Pays $15-20 for b&w glossy photos. Uses positive transparencies for cover. Pays $50. Captions required.

Tips: "There is a trend away from maudlin, first-person pieces redolent with tragedy and dripping with simplistic, pietistic conclusions."

‡PRESBYTERIANS TODAY, Presbyterian Church (U.S.A.), 100 Witherspoon St., Louisville KY 40202-1396. (502)569-5637. Fax: (502)569-8073. E-mail: survey@pcusa.org. Managing Editor: Catherine Cottingham. Associate Editor: Eva Stimson. Estab. 1867. 65% freelance written. Prefers to work with published/established writers. Denominational magazine published 10 times/year covering religion, denominational activities and public issues for members of the Presbyterian Church (U.S.A.). **Pays on acceptance** (commissioned articles) or on scheduling for publication. Publishes ms an average of 9 months after acceptance. Byline given. Occasionally publishes reprints; send typed ms with rights for sale noted and information about when and where article originally appeared. For reprints, pays 75% of amount paid for an original article. Buys first North American serial rights. Submit seasonal material 4 months in advance. Reports in 2 weeks on queries; 1 month on mss. *Writer's Market* recommends allowing 2 months for reply. Sample copy and writer's guidelines available upon request.
Nonfiction: Inspirational and Presbyterian programs, issues, people; any subject from a Christian viewpoint. Rarely uses secular subjects. Buys 20 mss/year. Send complete ms. Length: 800-1,500 words. Pays $75-300.
Photos: State availability of photos. Reviews color prints or transparencies and b&w prints. Pays $15-25 for b&w; $25-50 for color. Identification of subjects required. Buys one-time rights.

‡PRIMARY DAYS, Scripture Press Publications, Inc., 1825 College Ave., Wheaton IL 60187. Editor: Janice K. Burton. 75% freelance written. Quarterly Sunday School take-home paper with 13 weekly parts. "Our readers are 6-8 years old. All materials attempt to show God's working in the lives of children. Must have a true Christian slant, not just a moral implication." **Pays on acceptance.** Publishes ms an average of 1-2 years after acceptance. Byline given. Buys first North American serial rights, first rights, one-time rights, second serial (reprint) rights and all rights. Editorial lead time 1 year. Submit seasonal material 1 year in advance. Accepts previously published submissions. Reports in 2 months on mss. Sample copy and writer's guidelines for #10 SASE.
Nonfiction: Inspirational (stories), interview/profile. "All stories, etc. must have a spiritual perspective. Show God at work in a child's life. Buys 10-20 mss/year. Send complete ms. Length: 300-350 words. Pays 7-10¢/word.
Fiction: Adventure, ethnic, religious. Buys 10-15 mss/year. Send complete ms. Length: 300-350 words. Pays 7-10¢/word.
Fillers: Buys 8-12 puzzles, games, fun activities/year. Length: 150 words maximum. Pays 7-10¢/word.
Tips: "Show a real feel for the age level. Know your readers and what is age-appropriate in terms of concepts and vocabulary. Submit only best quality manuscripts."

‡PRISM, ESA, 10 Lancaster Ave., Wynnewood PA 19096. (610)645-9391. Editor: Dwight Ozard. 50% freelance written. Bimonthly magazine. "*Prism* is the voice of the evangelical alternative—young, progressive, socially-active Christians, concerned for the poor, race-issues, simple living, environmental issues." Estab. 1993. Circ. 10,000. Pays on publication. Publishes ms an average of 5 months after acceptance. Byline sometimes given. Buys one-time rights. Submit seasonal material 5 months in advance. Accepts previously published submissions. Accepts electronic submissions by disk. Sample for $3. Writer's guidelines free on request.
Nonfiction: Essays, exposé, inspirational, interview/profile, new product, opinion, religious, review. Special issues: arts and faith. Buys 6 mss/year. Send complete ms. Length: 800-5,500 words. Pays $25-200 for assigned articles; $25-100 for unsolicited articles.
Photos: State availability of photos with submissions. Reviews contact sheets. Negotiates payment individually. Identification of subjects required.
Columns/Departments: Buys 3 mss/year. Query. Pays $25-200.
Fiction: Religious, slice-of-life vignettes. Buys 1 mss/year. Send comlete ms. Length: 800-4,000 words. Pays $25-200.
Fillers: Anecdotes, facts. Buys 4/year. Length: 50-400 words. Pays $10-50.

‡PROCLAIM, Baptist Sunday School Board, 127 Ninth Ave. N., Nashville TN 37234. (615)251-2874. Editor: Billy J. Chitwood. 75% freelance written. Quarterly magazine covering preaching-worship materials. "Material must be practical, theologically and biblically sound, and appeal to evangelical churches." Estab. 1975. Circ. 15,000. **Pays on acceptance.** Publishes ms an average of 3-6 months after acceptance. Byline given. Buys first rights or all rights. Editorial lead time 1 year. Submit seasonal material 6 months in advance. Accepts previously published submissions. Reports in 2 weeks on queries; 3 months on mss. Sample copy and writer's guidelines free on request.
Nonfiction: Inspirational, religious, sermons, sermon illustrations. Buys 50-60 mss/year. Query. Length: 600-4,000 words. Pays $5½¢/word; $8 minimum.

PURPOSE, 616 Walnut Ave., Scottdale PA 15683-1999. (412)887-8500. Editor: James E. Horsch. 95% freelance written. Weekly magazine "for adults, young and old, general audience with varied interests. My readership is interested in seeing how Christianity works in difficult situations." Estab. 1968. Circ. 16,000. **Pays on acceptance.** Publishes ms an average of 8 months after acceptance. Byline given, including city, state/province. Buys one-time rights. Submit seasonal material 6 months in advance. Accepts simultaneous and previously published submissions. Send tearsheet or photocopy of article or short story or typed ms with rights for sale noted and information about when and where the material previously appeared. Reports in 2 months. Sample copy and writer's guidelines for 6×9 SAE with 2 first-class stamps.

Nonfiction: Inspirational stories from a Christian perspective. "I want stories that go to the core of human problems in family, business, politics, religion, gender and any other areas—and show how the Christian faith resolves them. I want material that's upbeat. *Purpose* is a magazine which conveys truth either through quality fiction or through articles that use the best story techniques. Our magazine accents Christian discipleship. Christianity affects all of life, and we expect our material to demonstrate this. I would like to see story-type articles about individuals, groups and organizations who are intelligently and effectively working at some of the great human problems such as hunger, poverty, international understanding, peace, justice, etc., because of their faith." Buys 130 mss/year. Submit complete ms. Length: 900 words maximum. Pays 5¢/word maximum. Buys one-time rights only.

Photos: Photos purchased with ms. Pays $5-15 for b&w (less for color), depending on quality. Must be sharp enough for reproduction; requires prints in all cases. Captions desired.

Fiction: Humorous, religious, historical fiction related to discipleship theme. "Produce the story with specificity so that it appears to take place somewhere and with real people. It should not be moralistic. Essays and how-to-do-it pieces must include a lot of anecdotal, life exposure examples."

Poetry: Traditional poetry, blank verse, free verse, light verse. Buys 130 poems/year. Length: 12 lines maximum. Pays $5-15/poem depending on length and quality. Buys one-time rights only.

Fillers: Anecdotal items from 200-599 words. Pays 4¢/word maximum.

Tips: "We are looking for articles which show the Christian faith working at issues where people hurt; stories need to be told and presented professionally. Good photographs help place material with us."

REFORM JUDAISM, Union of American Hebrew Congregations, 838 5th Ave., New York NY 10021. (212)249-0100. Editor: Aron Hirt-Manheimer. Managing Editor: Joy Weinberg. 20% freelance written. Quarterly magazine of Reform Jewish issues. "*Reform Judaism* is the official voice of the Union of American Hebrew Congregations, linking the institutions and affiliates of Reform Judaism with every Reform Jew. RJ covers developments within the Movement while interpreting events and Jewish tradition from a Reform perspective." Pays on publication. Publishes ms an average of 3 months after acceptance. Byline given. Offers kill fee for commissioned articles. Buys first North American serial rights. Submit seasonal/holiday material 6 months in advance. Accepts photocopied and previously published submissions. Send tearsheet or photocopy of article or short story or typed ms with rights for sale noted and information about when and where the material previously appeared. Reports in 1 month on queries and mss. Sample copy for $3.50.

Nonfiction: Book excerpt (reviews), exposé, general interest, historical/nostalgic, inspirational, interview/profile, opinion, personal experience, photo feature, travel. Buys 50 mss/year. Submit complete ms. Length: 600-2,000 words. Pays 10-30¢/word. Sometimes pays expenses of writers on assignment.

Photos: Send photos with ms. Prefers 8×10/color or slides and b&w prints. Pays $25-75. Identification of subjects required. Buys one-time rights.

Fiction: Ethnic, humorous, mainstream, religious. Buys 4 mss/year. Send complete ms. Length: 600-1800 words. Pays 10-30¢/word. Publishes novel excerpts.

REVIEW FOR RELIGIOUS, 3601 Lindell Blvd., Room 428, St. Louis MO 63108-3393. (314)977-7363. Fax: (314)977-7362. Editor: David L. Fleming, S.J. 100% freelance written. Bimonthly magazine for Roman Catholic priests, brothers and sisters. Estab. 1942. Pays on publication. Publishes ms an average of 9 months after acceptance. Byline given. Buys first North American serial rights; rarely buys second serial (reprint) rights. Reports in 2 months.

Nonfiction: Articles on spiritual, liturgical, canonical matters only; not for general audience. Length: 2,000-8,000 words. Pays $6/page.

Tips: "The writer must know about religious life in the Catholic Church and be familiar with prayer, vows, community life and ministry."

ST. ANTHONY MESSENGER, 1615 Republic St., Cincinnati OH 45210-1298. Fax: (513)241-0399. Editor-in-Chief: Norman Perry. 55% freelance written. "Willing to work with new/unpublished writers if their writing is of a professional caliber." Monthly magazine for a national readership of Catholic families, most of which have children in grade school, high school or college. Circ. 325,000. **Pays on acceptance.** Publishes ms an average of 9 months after acceptance. Byline given. Buys first North American serial rights. Submit seasonal material 6 months in advance. Query for electronic submissions. Reports in 2 months. Sample copy and writer's guidelines for 9×12 SAE with 4 first-class stamps.

● The editor says he is short on seasonal, special occasion pieces. He also informs us that *St. Anthony Messenger* won first place for general excellence in the Catholic Press Association.

Nonfiction: How-to (on psychological and spiritual growth, problems of parenting/better parenting, marriage problems/marriage enrichment), humor, informational, inspirational, interview, personal experience (if pertinent to our purpose), personal opinion (limited use; writer must have special qualifications for topic), profile. Buys 35-50 mss/year. Length: 1,500-3,000 words. Pays 14¢/word. Sometimes pays the expenses of writers on assignment.

Fiction: Mainstream, religious. Buys 12 mss/year. Submit complete ms. Length: 2,000-3,000 words. Pays 14¢/word.

Tips: "The freelancer should ask why his or her proposed article would be appropriate for us, rather than for *Redbook* or *Saturday Review.* We treat human problems of all kinds, but from a religious perspective. Articles should reflect Catholic theology, spirituality and employ a Catholic terminology and vocabulary. We need more articles on prayer, scripture, Catholic worship. Get authoritative information (not merely library research); we want interviews with experts. Write in popular style; use lots of examples, stories and personal quotes. Word length is an important consideration."

ST. JOSEPH'S MESSENGER & ADVOCATE OF THE BLIND, Sisters of St. Joseph of Peace, St. Joseph's Home, P.O. Box 288, Jersey City NJ 07303-0288. Editor-in-Chief: Sister Ursula Maphet. 30% freelance written. Eager to work with new/unpublished writers. Quarterly magazine. Estab. 1898. Circ. 20,000. **Pays on acceptance.** Publishes ms an average of 3 months after acceptance. Buys first serial and second serial (reprint) rights; reassigns rights back to author after publication in return for credit line in next publication. Submit seasonal material 3 months in advance (no Christmas issue). Accepts simultaneous and previously published submissions. Send typed ms with rights for sale noted and information about when and where the article previously appeared. Pays 100% of their fee for an original article. Reports in 1 month. Sample copy and writer's guidelines for 9×12 SAE with 2 first-class stamps.

Nonfiction: Humor, inspirational, nostalgia, personal opinion, personal experience. Buys 24 mss/year. Submit complete ms. Length: 300-1,500 words. Pays $3-15.

Fiction: Romance, suspense, mainstream, religious. Buys 30 mss/year. Submit complete ms. Length: 600-1,600 words. Pays $6-25.

Poetry: Light verse, traditional. Buys 25 poems/year. Submit maximum 10 poems. Length: 50-300 words. Pays $5-20.

Tips: "It's rewarding to know that someone is waiting to see freelancers' efforts rewarded by 'print'. It's annoying, however, to receive poor copy, shallow material or inane submissions. Human interest fiction, touching on current happenings, is what is most needed. We look for social issues woven into story form. We also seek non-preaching articles that carry a message that is positive."

SCP JOURNAL AND SCP Newsletter, Spiritual Counterfeits Project, P.O. Box 4308, Berkeley CA 94704-4308. (510)540-0300. Fax: (510)540-1107. Editor: Tal Brooke. Co-editor: Brooks Alexander. 5% freelance written. Prefers to work with published/established writers. "The *SCP Journal* and *SCP Newsletter* are quarterly publications "geared to reach demanding non-believers while giving Christians authentic insight into the very latest spiritual and cultural trends." Their targeted audience is the educated lay reader. Estab. 1975. Circ. 18,000. Pays on publication. Publishes ms an average of 6 months after acceptance. Byline given. Rights negotiable. Accepts simultaneous and previously published submissions after telephone inquiry. Send photocopy of article. Reprint payment is negotiable. Reports in 3 months. Sample copy for $5. Writer's guidelines for SASE.

Nonfiction: Book excerpts, essays, exposé, interview/profile, opinion, personal experience, religious. Query by telephone. Length: 2,500-3,500 words. Pay negotiated by phone.

• Less emphasis on book reviews and more focus on specialized "single issue" topics.

Photos: State available photos. Reviews contact sheets and prints or slides. Offers no additional payment for photos accepted with ms. Captions, model releases, identification of subjects required. Buys one-time rights.

Tips: "The area of our publication most open to freelancers is specialized topics covered by *SCP.* Send samples of work that are relevant to *SCP*'s area of interest only after telephone inquiry."

‡SEEK, Standard Publishing, 8121 Hamilton Ave., Cincinnati OH 45231. (513)931-4050, ext. 365. Editor: Eileen H. Wilmoth. 98% freelance written. Prefers to work with published/established writers. Quarterly Sunday school paper, in weekly issues for young and middle-aged adults who attend church and Bible classes. Circ. 45,000. **Pays on acceptance.** Publishes ms an average of 1 year after acceptance. Byline given. Buys first serial and second serial (reprint) rights. Submit seasonal material 1 year in advance. Accepts previously published submissions. Send tearsheet of article or typed ms with rights for sale noted. For reprints, pays 50% of amount paid for an original article. Reports in 3 months. Sample copy and writer's guidelines for 6×9 SAE with 2 first-class stamps.

Nonfiction: "We look for articles that are warm, inspirational, devotional, of personal or human interest; that deal with controversial matters, timely issues of religious, ethical or moral nature, or first-person testimonies, true-to-life happenings, vignettes, emotional situations or problems; communication problems and examples of answered prayers. Article must deliver its point in a convincing manner but not be patronizing or preachy. It must appeal to either men or women, must be alive, vibrant, sparkling and have a title that demands the article be read. We always need stories about families, marriages, problems on campus and life testimonies." Buys 150-200 mss/year. Submit complete ms. Length: 400-1,200 words. Pays 5¢/word.

Photos: B&w photos purchased with or without mss. Pays $20 minimum for good 8×10 glossy prints.
Fiction: Religious fiction and religiously slanted historical and humorous fiction. No poetry. Length: 400-1,200 words. Pays 5¢/word.
Tips: "Submit mss which tell of faith in action or victorious Christian living as central theme. We select manuscripts as far as one year in advance of publication. Complimentary copies are sent to our published writers immediately following printing."

‡SHAMBHALA SUN, Creating Enlightened Society, 1345 Spruce St., Boulder CO 80302-4886. (303)440-8849. Editor: Melvin McLeod. Managing Editor: Molly DeShong. 95% freelance written. Bimonthly magazine covering Buddhism, contemplative spiritual life, western/eastern thought, arts, lifestyles. "A contemplative arts and philosophy magazine covering Buddhism, and spiritual issues of the Western world. Audience: spiritual seekers, artists, those interested in health/well-being issues; no special slant required." Estab. 1978. Circ. 20,000. Pays on publication. Publishes ms an average of 2 months after acceptance. Byline given. Buys first North American serial, first, second serial and simultaneous rights or makes work-for-hire assignments. Editorial lead time 2 months. Submit seasonal material 2 months in advance. Accepts simultaneous and previously published submissions. Reports in 1 week on queries; 1 month on mss.
Nonfiction: Book excerpts, essays, exposé, general interest, historical/nostalgic, how-to (meditation, disciplines of arts, science, cooking, etc.), humor, inspirational, interview/profile, new product, opinion, personal experience, photo feature, religious, technical, travel. Buys 4-5 mss/year. Query. Length: 600-4,000 words. Pays $400. Pays expenses of writers in assignment.
Photos: State availability of photos with submissions. Reviews 3×4 prints. Negotiates payment individually. Identification of subjects required.
Columns/Departments: Cooking, 3,000 words; Travel, book and film reviews, 1,000 words; political/philosophical (spirituality, world issues, community issues), 1-3,000 words. Buys 4-5 mss/year. Query. Pays $40-400.
Fiction: Adventure, condensed novels, confession, erotica, ethnic, experimental, fantasy, historical, horror, humorous, mainstream, mystery, novel excerpts, religious, science fiction, slice-of-life vignettes, suspense. Buys 2-3 mss/year. Query. Length: 600-3,000 words. Pays $0-400.
Poetry: Avant-garde, free verse, haiku, light verse, traditional. Buys 1-2 poems/year. Submit maximum 5 poems. Pays $0-100.
Fillers: Anecdotes, facts, gags to be illustrated by cartoonist, newsbreaks, short humor. Buys 1-2/year. Length: 0-1,000 words. Pays $0-400.

SHARING THE VICTORY, Fellowship of Christian Athletes, 8701 Leeds Rd., Kansas City MO 64129. (816)921-0909. Fax: (816)921-8755. Editor: John Dodderidge. Assistant Editor: Will Greer. Managing Editor: Don Hilkemeier. 60% freelance written. Prefers to work with published/established writers, but works with a growing number of new/unpublished writers each year. Monthly (September-May) magazine. "We seek to encourage and enable athletes and coaches at all levels to take their faith seriously on and off the 'field'." Estab. 1959. Circ. 50,000. Pays on publication. Publishes ms an average of 4 months after acceptance. Byline given. Buys first rights. Submit seasonal/holiday material 3 months in advance. Accepts previously published submissions. Send photocopy of article. For reprints, pays 50% of the amount paid for an original article. Reports in 1 month on queries; 2 months on mss. *Writer's Market* recommends allowing 2 months for reply. Sample copy for $1 and 9×12 SAE with 3 first-class stamps. Free writer's guidelines for #10 SASE.
Nonfiction: Humor, inspirational, interview/profile (with "name" athletes and coaches solid in their faith), personal experience, photo feature. No "sappy articles on 'I became a Christian and now I'm a winner.'" Buys 5-20 mss/year. Query. Length: 500-1,000 words. Pays $100-200 for unsolicited articles, more for the exceptional profile.
Photos: State availability of photos with submission. Reviews contact sheets. Pay depends on quality of photo but usually a minimum $100. Model releases required for "name" individuals. Buys one-time rights.
Poetry: Free verse. Buys 3 poems/year. Pays $50.
Tips: "Profiles and interviews of particular interest to coed athlete, primarily high school and college age. Our graphics and editorial content appeal to youth. The area most open to freelancers is profiles on or interviews with well-known athletes or coaches (male, female, minorities) and offbeat but interscholastic team sports."

SIGNS OF THE TIMES, Pacific Press Publishing Association, P.O. Box 7000, Boise ID 83707. (208)465-2500. Fax: (208)465-2531. Editor: Marvin Moore. 40% freelance written. Works with a small number of new/unpublished writers each year. Monthly magazine on religion. "We are a Seventh-day Adventist publication encouraging the general public to practice the principles of the Bible." Estab. 1874. Circ. 245,000. Pays on publication. Publishes ms an average of 8 months after acceptance. Byline given. Offers kill fee. Buys first North American serial rights. Submit seasonal material 8 months in advance. Accepts previously published submissions. Send tearsheet or photocopy of article or typed ms with rights for sale noted and information about when and where the article previously appeared. Pays 50% of their fee for an original article. Reports in 1 month on queries; 2 months on mss. *Writer's Market* recommends allowing 2 months for reply. Sample copy and writer's guidelines for 9×12 SAE with 3 first-class stamps.

Nonfiction: General interest, how-to, inspirational, interview/profile. "We want writers with a desire to share the good news of reconciliation with God. Articles should be people-oriented, well-researched and should have a sharp focus." Buys 75 mss/year. Query with or without published clips or send complete ms. Length: 650-2,500 words. Pays $100-400. Sometimes pays the expenses of writers on assignment.

Photos: Merwin Stewart, photo editor. Send photos with query or ms. Reviews b&w contact sheets, 35mm color transparencies, 5×7 or 8×10 b&w prints. Pays $35-300 for transparencies; $20-50 for prints. Model releases and identification of subjects required (captions helpful). Buys one-time rights.

Tips: "Don't write for us unless you've read us and are familiar with Adventist beliefs."

SPIRITUAL LIFE, 2131 Lincoln Rd. NE, Washington DC 20002-1199. (202)832-8489. Fax: (202)832-8967. E-mail: edodonnell@aol.com. Editor: Br. Edward O'Donnell, O.C.D. 80% freelance written. Prefers to work with published/established writers. Quarterly. "Largely Catholic, well-educated, serious readers. A few are non-Catholic or non-Christian." Circ. 12,000. **Pays on acceptance.** Publishes ms an average of 1 year after acceptance. Buys first North American serial rights. Reports in 2 months. Sample copy and writer's guidelines for 7×10 or larger SASE with 5 first-class stamps.

 • In 1994, this magazine won First Place: Catholic Press Association Award for General Excellence in Prayer and Spirituality.

Nonfiction: Serious articles of contemporary spirituality. High quality articles about our encounter with God in the present day world. Language of articles should be college level. Technical terminology, if used, should be clearly explained. Material should be presented in a positive manner. Sentimental articles or those dealing with specific devotional practices not accepted. Buys inspirational and think pieces. "Brief autobiographical information (present occupation, past occupations, books and articles published, etc.) should accompany article." No fiction or poetry. Buys 20 mss/year. Length: 3,000-5,000 words. Pays $50 minimum. "Five contributor's copies are sent to author on publication of article." Book reviews should be sent to Br. Edward O'Donnell, O.C.D.

STANDARD, Nazarene International Headquarters, 6401 The Paseo, Kansas City MO 64131. (816)333-7000. Editor: Everett Leadingham. 100% freelance written. Works with a small number of new/unpublished writers each year. Weekly inspirational paper with Christian reading for adults. Estab. 1936. Circ. 160,000. **Pays on acceptance.** Publishes ms an average of 15-18 months after acceptance. Byline given. Buys one-time rights and second serial (reprint) rights. Submit seasonal material 6 months in advance. Accepts previously published submissions. Send tearsheet of short story. Reports in 8-10 weeks. Free sample copy. Writer's guidelines for SAE with 2 first-class stamps.

 • *Standard* no longer publishes nonfiction but prefers fiction or fiction-type stories. Does not want how-to, inspiration/devotionals or social issues pieces.

Fiction: Prefers fiction-type stories *showing* Christianity in action. Send complete ms; no queries. Length: 500-1,500 words. Pays 3½¢/word for first rights; 2¢/word for reprint rights.

Poetry: Free verse, haiku, light verse, traditional. Buys 50 poems/year. Submit maximum 5 poems. Length: 50 lines maximum. Pays 25¢/line.

Tips: "Stories should express Christian principles without being preachy. Setting, plot and characterization must be realistic. Fiction articles should be labeled 'Fiction' on the manuscript. True experience articles may be first person, 'as told to,' or third person."

SUNDAY DIGEST, Cook Communications Ministries, 850 N. Grove Ave., Elgin IL 60120-2892. Editor: Sharon Stultz. 75% freelance written. Prefers to work with established writers. Issued weekly to Christian adults in Sunday school. "*Sunday Digest* provides a combination of original articles and reprints, selected to help adult readers better understand the Christian faith, to keep them informed of issues within the Christian community, and to challenge them to a deeper personal commitment to Christ." Estab. 1886. **Pays on acceptance.** Publishes ms an average of 15 months after acceptance. Buys first or reprint rights. Accepts previously published submissions. Send tearsheet or photocopy of article or short story, or preferably typed ms with rights for sale noted and information about when and where the material previously appeared. Reports in 3 months. Sample copy and writer's guidelines for 6×9 SAE with 2 first-class stamps.

Nonfiction: Needs articles applying the Christian faith to personal and social problems, articles on family life and church relationships, inspirational self-help, personal experience, how-to, interview articles preferred over fiction. Length: 400-1,700 words. Pays $50-225.

Fiction: Publishes inspirational fiction.

Tips: "It is crucial that the writer is committed to quality Christian communication with a crisp, clear writing style. Christian message should be woven in, not tacked on. We receive many stories about personal

---

For explanation of symbols, see the Key to Symbols and Abbreviations. For unfamiliar words, see the Glossary.

experiences but not nearly enough missionary stories, interviews with people of interest, profiles of small ministries, and Christians in other countries."

TEACHERS INTERACTION, Concordia Publishing House, 3558 S. Jefferson Ave., St. Louis MO 63118-3968. Fax: (314)268-1329. Editor: Jane Haas. 20% freelance written. Quarterly magazine of practical, inspirational, theological articles for volunteer church school teachers. Material must be true to the doctrines of the Lutheran Church—Missouri Synod. Estab. 1960. Circ. 20,400. Pays on publication. Publishes ms an average of 1 year after acceptance. Byline given. Buys all rights. Submit seasonal material 1 year in advance. Reports in 3 months on mss. Sample copy for $2.75. Writer's guidelines for #10 SASE.

Nonfiction: How-to (practical help/ideas used successfully in own classroom), inspirational (to the church school worker—must be in accordance with LCMS doctrine), personal experience (of a Sunday school classroom nature—growth). No theological articles. Buys 6 mss/year. Send complete ms. Length: 750-1,500 words.

Fillers: "*Teachers Interaction* buys short Interchange items—activities and ideas planned and used successfully in a church school classroom." Buys 48/year. Length: 200 words maximum. Pays $20.

Tips: "Practical, or 'it happened to me' experiences articles would have the best chance. Also short items—ideas used in classrooms; seasonal and in conjunction with our Sunday school material, Our Life in Christ. Our format includes *all* volunteer church school teachers, Sunday school teachers, Vacation Bible School, and midweek teachers, as well as teachers of adult Bible studies."

TEEN LIFE, Gospel Publishing House, 1445 Boonville Ave., Springfield MO 65802-1894. (417)862-2781, ext. 4357. Editor: Tammy Bicket. Mostly freelance written. Eager to work with new/unpublished writers. Weekly magazine of Assemblies of God denomination of Christian fiction and articles for church-oriented teenagers, ages 12-17. Circ. 85,000. **Pays on acceptance.** Publishes ms an average of 15 months after acceptance. Byline given. Buys first North American serial, one-time, simultaneous and second serial (reprint) rights. Submit seasonal material 18 months in advance. Accepts simultaneous and previously published submissions. Send tearsheet or photocopy of article or typed ms with rights for sale noted and information about when and where the article previously appeared. Response time varies. Sample copy for 9×12 SAE with 2 first-class stamps. Writer's guidelines for #10 SASE.

Nonfiction: Interviews with Christian athletes, musicians, missionaries, authors, or others with notable and helpful Christian testimonies or helpful experiences; transcriptions of discussion sessions where a group of teens talk about a particular issue; information on a topic or issue of interest gathered from experts in those fields (i.e. a doctor talks about teens' sexuality, a psychologist talks about dysfunctional families, a police officer talks about the dangers of gangs, etc.). Book excerpts, church history, general interest, how-to (deal with various life problems), humor, inspirational, personal experience, world issues, apologetics, prayer, devotional life, the occult, angels, church. Buys 80-100 mss/year. Send complete ms. Length: 500-1,200 words. Pays 2-3¢/word.

Photos: Photos purchased with accompanying ms. Pays $35 for 8×10 b&w glossy print; $50 for 35mm slide.

Fiction: Adventure, humorous, mystery, romance, suspense. Buys 80-100 mss/year. Send complete ms. Length: 500-1,200 words. Pays 2-3¢/word.

Tips: "We need more male-oriented stories, articles, etc. Also need more stories or articles about life in the city and about people of diverse races. Avoid stereotypes. Avoid clichéd or trite situations with pat Christian answers and easy solutions. Avoid stories or articles without a Christian slant or emphasis, or those with a moral just tacked on at the end."

‡TEEN POWER, Scripture Press Publications, Inc., Box 632, Glen Ellyn IL 60138. Editor: Amy J. Cox. 90% freelance written. Quarterly Sunday School take-home paper with weekly parts. "*Teen Power* is a Sunday School take-home paper for young teens (ages 11-15). Its purpose is to show readers how biblical principles for Christian living can be applied to everyday life." **Pays on acceptance.** Publishes ms an average of 1-2 years after acceptance. Byline given. Buys one-time rights. Editorial lead time 1 year. Submit seasonal material 6 months in advance. Accepts simultaneous and previously published submissions. Reports in 3 months on mss. Sample copy and writer's guidelines for #10 SASE.

Nonfiction: Humor, inspirational, interview/profile, personal experience, religious. Buys 75 mss/year. Send complete ms. Length: 300-1,000 words. Pays $25-120.

Photos: State availability of photos with submissions. Negotiates payment individually. Model releases required. Buys one-time rights.

A bullet introduces comments by the editors of Writer's Market *indicating special information about the listing.*

Fiction: Humorous, religious, slice-of-life vignettes. Buys 75 mss/year. Send complete ms. Length: 600-1,200 words. Pays $45-120.

Tips: "We are looking for fresh, creative true stories, true-to-life fiction, and nonfiction articles. All must show how God and the Bible are relevant in the lives of today's teens. All manuscripts *must* have a clear, spiritual emphasis or 'take away value.' We don't use stories which merely have a good moral. Be careful not to preach or talk down to kids. Also, be realistic. Dialogue should be natural. Resolutions should not be too easy or tacked on. We are a specialized market with a distinct niche, but we do rely heavily on freelance writers. We are open to any new writer who grasps the purpose of our publication."

‡THE UNITED CHURCH OBSERVER, 84 Pleasant Blvd., Toronto, Ontario M4J 2Z8 Canada. (416)960-8500. Fax: (416)960-8477. Editor: Muriel Duncan. 20% freelance written. Prefers to work with published/established writers. Monthly newsmagazine for people associated with The United Church of Canada. Deals primarily with events, trends and policies having religious significance. Most coverage is Canadian, but reports on international or world concerns will be considered. Pays on publication. Publishes ms an average of 4 months after acceptance. Byline usually given. Buys first serial rights and occasionally all rights.

Nonfiction: Occasional opinion features only. Extended coverage of major issues usually assigned to known writers. No opinion pieces or poetry. Submissions should be written as news, no more than 1,200 words length, accurate and well-researched. Queries preferred. Rates depend on subject, author and work involved. Pays expenses of writers on assignment "as negotiated."

Photos: Buys photographs with mss. Black & white should be 5×7 minimum; color 35mm or larger format. Payment varies.

Tips: "The writer has a better chance of breaking in at our publication with short articles; this also allows us to try more freelancers. Include samples of previous *news* writing with query. Indicate ability and willingness to do research, and to evaluate that research. The most frequent mistakes made by writers in completing an article for us are organizational problems, lack of polished style, short on research, and a lack of inclusive language."

‡UNITY MAGAZINE, Unity School of Christianity, 1901 NW Blue Parkway, Unity Village MO 64065. Editor: Philip White. Associate Editor: Janet McNamara. 25% freelance written. Interested in working with authors who are skilled at writing in the metaphysical Christian/New Thought/spiritual development persuasion. Estab. 1889. Circ. 120,000. **Pays on acceptance.** Publishes ms an average of 1 year after acceptance. Byline given. Buys first North American serial rights. Sometimes publishes reprints of previously published articles. Send photocopy of article and information about when and where the article previously appeared. Submit seasonal material 9 months in advance. Query for electronic submissions. Reports in 2 months on queries; 3 months on mss. Free sample copy and writer's guidelines upon request.

Nonfiction: *Spiritual* self-help and personal experience, holistic health, prosperity, biblical interpretation, religious, inspirational. Buys 200 mss/year. Send complete ms. Length: 1,000-1,800 words. Pays 20¢/word.

Photos: State availability of photos with submission. Reviews transparencies and prints. Offers $35-200/photo. Model releases and identification of subjects required. Buys one-time rights.

Poetry: Inspirational, religious and seasonal. Buys 40 poems/year. Submit maximum 5 poems. Length: 30 lines maximum. Pays $20 minimum.

THE UPPER ROOM, Daily Devotional Guide, P.O. Box 189, Nashville TN 37202-0189. (615)340-7252. Fax: (615)340-7006. Editor and Publisher: Janice T. Grana. Managing Editor: Mary Lou Redding. 95% freelance written. Eager to work with new/unpublished writers. Bimonthly magazine "offering a daily inspirational message which includes a Bible reading, text, prayer, 'Thought for the Day,' and suggestion for further prayer. Each day's meditation is written by a different person and is usually a personal witness about discovering meaning and power for Christian living through scripture study which illuminates daily life." Circ. 2.2 million (US); 385,000 outside US Pays on publication. Publishes ms an average of 1 year after acceptance. Byline given. Buys first North American serial rights and translation rights. Submit seasonal material 14 months in advance. Manuscripts are not returned. If writers include a stamped, self addressed postcard, we will notify them that their writing has reached us. This does not imply acceptance or interest in purchase. Sample copy and writer's guidelines with a 4×6 SAE and 2 first-class stamps.

● This market does not respond unless material is accepted for publication.

Nonfiction: Inspirational, personal experience, Bible-study insights. No poetry, lengthy "spiritual journey" stories. Buys 365 unsolicited mss/year. Send complete ms. Length: 250 words maximum. Pays $15.

Tips: "The best way to break into our magazine is to send a well-written manuscript that looks at the Christian faith in a fresh way. Standard stories and sermon illustrations are immediately rejected. We very much want to find new writers and welcome good material. We are particularly interested in meditations based on Old Testament characters and stories. Good repeat meditations can lead to work on longer assignments for our other publications, which pay more. A writer who can deal concretely with everyday situations, relate them to the Bible and spiritual truths, and write clear, direct prose should be able to write for *The Upper Room*. We want material that provides for more interaction on the part of the reader—meditation suggestions, journaling suggestions, space to reflect and link personal experience with the meditation for the day."

VIRTUE, The Christian Magazine for Women, P.O. Box 36630, Colorado Springs CO 80936-3663. (719)531-7776. Fax: (719)535-0172. Editor: Nancie Carmichael. Managing Editor: Jeanette Thomason. 75% freelance written. Works with small number of new/unpublished writers each year. Bimonthly magazine that "shows through features and columns the depth and variety of expression that can be given to women and faith." Estab. 1978. Circ. 175,000. Pays on acceptance or publication. Publishes ms an average of 4 months after acceptance. Byline given. Buys first North American serial rights. Submit seasonal material 9 months in advance. Accepts previously published submissions. Send photocopy of article or short story or typed ms with rights for sale noted and information about when and where the article previously appeared. Reports in 2 months. Sample copy for 9×12 SAE with 7 first-class stamps. Writer's guidelines for #10 SASE.
Nonfiction: Book excerpts, how-to, humor, inspirational, interview/profile, opinion, personal experience, religious. Buys 60 mss/year. Query. Length: 600-1,800 words. Pays 15-25¢/word.
Photos: State availability of photos with submission.
Columns/Departments: In My Opinion (reader editorial); One Woman's Journal (personal experience); Equipped for Ministry (Christian service potpourri); Real Men (women from a man's viewpoint). Buys 25 mss/year. Query. Length: 1,000-1,500. Pays 15-25¢/word.
Fiction: Humorous, religious. Buys 4-6 mss/year. Send complete ms. Length: 1,500-1,800 words. Pays 15-25¢/word.
Poetry: Free verse, traditional. Buys 7-10 poems/year. Submit maximum 3 poems. Length: 3-30 lines. Pays $15-50.

‡VITAL CHRISTIANITY, Warner Press, Inc., P.O. Box 2499, Anderson IN 46018-2499. (317)644-7721. E-mail: sb128@aol.com. Editor-in-Chief: David C. Shultz. Managing Editor: Steven A. Beverly. 20-25% freelance written. Prefers to work with published/established writers. Monthly magazine covering Christian living for people attending local Church of God congregations. Estab. 1881. Circ. 26,000. **Pays on acceptance.** Byline given. Buys one-time rights. Submit seasonal material 6 months in advance. Query for electronic submissions. Reports in 6 weeks. Accepts previously published submissions. Send typed ms with rights for sale noted and information about when and where the article previously appeared. For reprints, pays 100% of their fee for an original article. Sample copy and writer's guidelines for 9×12 SASE and 7 first-class stamps.
Nonfiction: Humor (with religious point); inspirational (religious—not preachy); and personal experience (related to putting one's faith into practice). Buys 125 mss/year. Length: 1,000 words maximum. Pays $10-140.
Tips: "Fillers, personal experience and good holiday articles are areas of our magazine open to freelancers. Writers should request our guidelines and list of upcoming topics of interest to determine if they have interest or expertise in writing for us. Always send SASE."

THE WESLEYAN ADVOCATE, The Wesleyan Publishing House, P.O. Box 50434, Indianapolis IN 46250-0434. (317)576-8156. Fax: (317)842-1649. Executive Editor: Dr. Norman G. Wilson. 50% freelance written. Monthly magazine of The Wesleyan Church. Estab. 1842. Circ. 20,000. Pays on publication. Publishes ms an average of 1 year after acceptance. Byline given. Buys first rights or simultaneous rights (prefers first rights). Submit seasonal material 6 months in advance. Accepts simultaneous and previously published submissions. Send photocopy of article and typed ms with rights for sale noted and information about when and where the article previously appeared. Pays 50% of their fee for an original article. Query for electronic submissions. Reports in 2 weeks. Sample copy for $2. Writer's guidelines for #10 SASE.
Nonfiction: Humor, inspirational, religious. Buys 50 mss/year. Send complete ms. Length: 250-650 words. Pays $10-40 for assigned articles; $5-25 for unsolicited articles.
Photos: Send photos with submission. Reviews transparencies. Buys one-time rights.
Tips: "Write for a guide."

‡WHEREVER, In The World For Jesus' Sake, The Evangelical Alliance Mission, P.O. Box 969, Wheaton IL 60189. Editor: Jack Kilgore. Contact: Dana Felmly. 70% freelance written. Triannual magazine covering missionary activities. "*Wherever* is a thematic magazine which helps people decide if overseas missions is for them. Our audience is mostly college students, grad and seminary students, young professionals." Estab. 1976. Circ. 7,700. Pays on publication. Publishes ms an average of 8 months after acceptance. Byline given. Buys all rights unless other arrangements are made. Editorial lead time 9 months. No simultaneous submissions. Reports in 1 month on queries. Sample copy for 9×12 SAE with 3 first-class stamps. Writer's guidelines for #10 SASE.
Nonfiction: Book excerpts, humor, inspirational, interview/profile, personal experience. Buys 13 mss/year. Write for guidelines. Length: 500-1,000 words. Pays $75-125. Sometimes pays expenses of writers on assignment.
Photos: Send photos with submission. Reviews transparencies, prints. Offers no additional payment for photos accepted with ms. Captions, identification of subjects required. Buys first and reprint rights.
Fiction: Missions themes. Buys 1 mss/year. Write for guidelines. Length: 500-1,000 words. Pays $75-125.
Poetry: Avant-garde, free verse, Haiku, light verse, traditional. Buys 1 poem/year. Submit maximum 1 poem. Pays $75.

Tips: "Because of our focus, we have very specific needs. Write to us to get on our author mail list. Three times a year, we will send guidelines, story ideas, and the theme for the particular issue. After reading the guidelines, query us with your proposals. Authors are encouraged to go beyond our guides, suggesting more creative approaches to the theme."

‡THE WITNESS, Episcopal Church Publishing Co., 1249 Washington Blvd., #3115, Detroit MI 48226. (313)962-2650. Editor: Jeanie Wylie-Kellermann. Managing Editor: Julie A. Wortman. Contact: Marianne Arbogast. 20% freelance written. Monthly magazine covering religion and politics from a left perspective. "Our readers are people of faith who are interested in wrestling with scripture and current events with the goal of serving God and effecting change that diminishes the privilege of the rich." Estab. 1917. Circ. 4,000. Pays on publication. Publishes ms an average of 3 months after acceptance. Byline given. Offers 50% kill fee. Buys first rights. Editorial lead time 6 weeks. Submit seasonal material 3 months in advance. Accepts simultaneous submissions. Query for electronic submissions. Responds only to material accepted for publication. Sample copy and writer's guidelines free on request.

Nonfiction: Exposé, general interest, historical/nostalgic, humor, interview/profile, personal experience, photo feature, religious. Buys 10 mss/year. Query with or without published clips, or send complete ms. Length: 250-1,800 words. Pays $50-250 for assigned articles; $50-100 for unsolicited articles; and 1-year subscription. Sometimes pays expenses of writers on assignment.

Photos: State availability of photos with submissions. Reviews prints. Offers $0-30/photo. Captions, identification of subjects required. Buys one-time rights.

Poetry: Buys 10 poems/year. Submit maximum 5 poems. Pays $0-30.

Tips: "We're eager for *short* news pieces that relate to racial-, gender- and eco-justice. Our issues are thematic which makes queries advisable. We don't publish material written in a dry academic style, we like stories that allow marginalized people to speak in their own words."

WOMAN'S TOUCH, Assemblies of God Women's Ministries Department (GPH), 1445 Boonville, Springfield MO 65802-1894. (417)862-2781. Fax: (417)862-0503. Editor: Peggy Musgrove. Associate Editor: Aleda Swartzendruber. 75-90% freelance written. Willing to work with new/unpublished writers. Bimonthly inspirational magazine for women. "Articles and contents of the magazine should be compatible with Christian teachings as well as human interests. The audience is women, both homemakers and those who are career-oriented." Estab. 1977. Circ. 21,000. **Pays on acceptance.** Byline given. Buys one-time rights. Submit seasonal/holiday material 8 months in advance. Accepts previously published submissions. Send photocopy of article and information about when and where the article previously appeared. Reports in 3 months. Sample copy for 9½ × 11 SAE with 3 first-class stamps. Writer's guidelines for #10 SASE.

Nonfiction: General interest, how-to, inspirational, personal experience, religious, travel. Buys 60 mss/year. Send complete ms. Length: 500-800 words. Pays $10-35 for unsolicited articles.

Photos: State availability of photos with submission. Reviews negatives, transparencies, 4 × 6 prints. Offers no additional payment for photos accepted with ms. Identification of subjects required. Buys one-time rights.

Columns/Departments: 'A Final Touch' for short human interest articles—home and family or career-oriented." Buys 6 mss/year. Query with published clips. Length: 80-500 words. Pays $20-35.

Poetry: Free verse, light verse, traditional. Buys 6 poems/year. Submit maximum 3 poems. Length: 4-50 lines. Pays $5-20.

Fillers: Facts. Buys 5/year. Length: 50-200. Pays $5-15.

THE WORLD, Unitarian Universalist Association, 25 Beacon St., Boston MA 02108-2800. (617)742-2100. Fax: (617)367-3237. E-mail: worldmag@uua.org. Editor-in-Chief: Linda Beyer. 50% freelance written. Bimonthly magazine covering religious education, spirituality, social consciousness, UUA projects and news, church communities, and personal philosophies of interesting people. "Purpose: to promote and inspire denominational self-reflection; to inform readers about the wide range of UU values, purposes, activities, aesthetics, and spiritual attitudes, and to educate readers about the history, personalities, and congregations that comprise UUism; to enhance its dual role of leadership and service to member congregations." Estab. 1987. Circ. 110,000. **Pays on acceptance.** Publishes mss an average of 1 year after acceptance. Byline given. Buys one-time rights. Editorial lead time 3 months. Submit seasonal material 3 months in advance. Pay varies. Query for electronic submissions. Reports in 2 months on queries; 3 months on mss. Sample copy and writer's guidelines for 9 × 12 SASE.

Nonfiction: All articles must have a UU angle. Essays, historical/nostalgic (Unitarian or Universalist focus), inspirational, interview/profile (with UU individual or congregation), commentary, photo feature (of UU congregation or project), religious and travel. No unsolicited poetry or fiction. Buys 10 mss/year. Query with published clips. Length: 1,500-3,500 words. Pays $400 minimum for assigned feature articles. Sometimes pays expenses of writers on assignment.

Photos: State availability of photos with submission. Reviews contact sheets. Offers no additional payment for photos accepted with ms. Captions, model releases and identification of subjects required. Buys one-time rights.

Columns/Departments: Among Ourselves (news, profiles, inspirational reports), 300-700 words; Book Reviews (liberal religion, social issues, politics), 600-800 words. Buys 15 mss/year. Query (profiles, book reviews) or send complete mss (news). Pays $75-250 for assigned articles and book reviews.

Tips: "Get to know your local congregation, find its uniqueness, tell its story. We don't have enough congregational profiles."

Retirement

Retirement magazines have changed to meet the active lifestyles of their readers and editors dislike the kinds of stereotypes people have of the over-50 age group. More people are retiring in their 50s, while others are starting a business or traveling and pursuing hobbies. These publications give readers specialized information on health and fitness, medical research, finances and other topics of interest, as well as general articles on travel destinations and recreational activities.

‡ACTIVE TIMES MAGAZINE, 417 Main St., Carbondale CO 81623. Editor: Chris Kelly. 80% freelance written. Quarterly magazine covering over-50 market. "We target active, adults over-50. We emphasize the positive, enjoyable aspects of aging." Estab. 1992. Circ. 7 million. **Pays on acceptance.** Publishes ms an average of 3-6 months after acceptance. Byline given. Offers 50% kill fee. Buys first North American serial rights. Editorial lead time 3 months. Submit seasonal material 6-9 months in advance. Query for electronic submissions. Reports in 3 weeks on queries. Sample copy for 9×12 SAE and 5 first-class stamps. Writer's guidelines for #10 SASE.
Nonfiction: General interest, historical/nostalgic, interview/profile, travel. Buys 50 mss/year. Query with published clips. Length: 500-2,000 words. Pays $75-1,000 for assigned articles; $50-250 for unsolicited articles. Sometimes pays expenses of writers on assignment.
Photos: State availability of photos with submission. Reviews contact sheets, 35mm transparencies, prints. Negotiates payment individually. Identification of subjects required. Buys one-time rights.
Columns/Departments: Profile (interesting over-50), 700 words. Buys 4-8 mss/year. Query with published clips. Pays $150-400.
Tips: "Write a detailed query, with substantiating clips. Query should show how story will appeal to active over-50 reader."

‡A BETTER TOMORROW, Celebrating the Prime of Your Life, Royal Magazine Group, 404 BNA Dr., Suite 508, Bldg. 200, Nashville TN 37217. (615)872-8080. Editor: Vicki Huffman. 60% freelance written. Bimonthly magazine "offering encouragement and information to aging baby boomers, those in transition from raising children to exploring the future. Articles will entertain, inspire and instruct people to plan for the future while motivating them to celebrate Christian living." Estab. 1992. Circ. 20,000. **Pays on acceptance.** Publishes ms an average of 6 months after acceptance. Byline given. Offers 20% kill fee. Buys first North American serial rights. Editorial lead time 4 months. Submit seasonal material 6 months in advance. Accepts simultaneous submissions. Query for electronic submissions. Reports in 2 months. Sample copy for $3. Writer's guidelines for #10 SASE.
Nonfiction: Book excerpts, humor, inspirational, interview/profile, religious, travel. Buys 50 mss/year. Query with published clips. Length: 800-3,000 words. Pays $60-400 for assigned articles; $50-350 for unsolicited articles.
Photos: State availability of photos with submission. Negotiates payment individually. Identification of subjects required. Buys one-time rights.
Columns/Departments: Dollars & Sense (financial advice for seniors), 1,200 words; Good Sports (sports for seniors), 1,000 words; Laugh Lines (humorous anecdotes), 800 words. Buys 10-15 mss/year. Query with published clips. Pays $80-200.
Fillers: Anecdotes concerning grandchildren. Buys 30/year. Length: 40-120 words. Pays $20.
Tips: "Know our audience—the active person over 50 who is involved in life."

‡CANADIAN SENIORITY, 2506 Linwood St., Pickering, Ontario L1X 1E5 Canada. Editor: David Todd. 80% freelance written. Bimonthly magazine covering mature audience interests, i.e., travel, finances, nutrition, etc. Estab. 1985. Circ. 150,000. Pays on publication. Publishes ms 3 months after acceptance. Byline given. Buys one-time use, no preferred rights. Editorial lead time 2 months. Submit seasonal material 3 months in advance. Accepts simultaneous and previously published submissions. Query for electronic submissions. Sample copy for 9×12 SAE and IRCs. Writer's guidelines printed in masthead of magazine only.
Nonfiction: Book excerpts, general interest, how-to, inspirational, interview/profile, new product, religious. Buys 18 mss/year. Send complete ms. Length: 200-1,200 words. Pays $25-300. Sometimes pays other than cash payment if negotiated prior to printing.
Photos: State availability of photos with submission. Reviews photocopies unless otherwise requested. Negotiates payment individually. Captions required. Buys one-time use.
Columns/Departments: Book reviews, Canadian financial strategies. Buys 18 mss/year. Send complete ms. Pays $25-200.

Fiction: Humorous, novel excerpts, romance. Buys 6 mss/year. Send complete ms. Length: 500-1,200 words. Pays $25-100.
Fillers: Facts, newsbreaks. Buys 18/year. Length: 100-500 words. Pays $25-200.

FLORIDA RETIREMENT LIFESTYLES, Housing • Travel • Leisure, Gidder House Publishing, Inc., P.O. Box 161848, Altamonte Springs FL 32714-1848. Editor: Kerry Smith. 20% freelance written. Monthly magazine directed toward Florida or Florida-bound retirees in an upbeat manner—unusual as well as typical Florida places, people, etc. Estab. 1946. Circ. 35,000. Pays on publication. Publishes ms an average of 3 months after acceptance. No kill fee. Buys first North American serial, first, one-time, second serial (reprint), simultaneous rights, all rights and/or makes work-for-hire assignments. Submit seasonal material 3 months in advance. Accepts previously published submissions. Send tearsheet or photocopy of article and information about when and where the article previously appeared. 50% of the amount paid for an original article. Query for electronic submissions. Reports in 3 weeks on queries. Free writer's guidelines. Sample copy for $2.
Nonfiction: Hobbies, new careers, transition how to's, how-to (learn new skill as senior), humor, inspirational, interview/profile, new product, personal experience, photo feature, travel. Editorial calendar available on request. No negative or health related articles. Buys 30 mss/year. Query with or without published clips or send complete ms. Length: 800-1,500 words. Pays 10¢/word up to $100. Sometimes pays expenses of writers on assignment.
Photos: Send photos with submissions. Reviews transparencies and prints. Offers $5-25/photo. Model releases and identification of subjects required. Buys one-time rights or all rights.
Tips: "Look for the unusual, little known but interesting aspects of Florida living that seniors want or need to know about. Housing, finance and real estate are of primary interest."

KEY HORIZONS, The Magazine For Your Best Years, Emmis Publishing Corp., 950 N. Meridian St., Suite 1200, Indianapolis IN 46204. Editor: Deborah Paul. Managing Editor: Joan Todd. 75% freelance written. Quarterly magazine for older adults, age 55 and older. "*Key Horizons* takes a positive approach to life, stressing ways to improve quality of life." Estab. 1988. Circ. 260,000 (controlled circulation—sent to certain Blue Cross/Blue Shield policy holders in several states). Pays on publication. Publishes ms an average of 2 months after acceptance. Byline given. Offers $50 kill fee. Buys first North American serial rights. Submit seasonal material 6 months in advance. Query for electronic submissions. Reports in 1 month on queries; 2 months on mss. Free writer's guidelines with SASE.
Nonfiction: General interest, tips for better living, health, money, travel (domestic only). No first person, domestic humor, puzzles. Buys 25-35 mss/year. Query with published clips or send complete ms. Length: 1,500 words. Pays $250-500. SASE required for response.
Photos: State availability of photos with submission. Reviews 2¼×2¼ transparencies and 8×10 prints. Offers $25/photo. Captions and identification of subjects required. Buys one-time rights. Payment negotiable.
Columns/Departments: Health, money, travel, food. (1,200 words). Like tips and sidebars. No nostalgia. Buys 12-16 mss/year. Query with published clips or send complete ms. Pays $300. SASE required for response.
Tips: "Take an upbeat approach. View older adults as vital, productive, active people. We appreciate detailed, well-written query letters that show some preliminary research."

MATURE LIVING, A Christian Magazine for Senior Adults, Sunday School Board of the Southern Baptist Convention, 127 Ninth Ave. N., Nashville TN 37234. (615)251-2274. Editor: Al Shackleford. 70% freelance written. Monthly leisure reading magazine for senior adults 50 and older. Estab. 1977. Circ. 350,000. **Pays on acceptance.** Byline given. Buys one-time rights. Submit seasonal material 12 months in advance. Reports in 3 months. Sample copy for 9×12 SAE with 4 first-class stamps. Writer's guidelines for #10 SASE.
Nonfiction: General interest, historical/nostalgic, how-to, humor, inspirational, interview/profile, personal experience, photo feature, crafts, travel. No pornography, profanity, occult, liquor, dancing, drugs, gambling. No book reviews. Buys 100 mss/year. Send complete ms. Length: 1,200 words maximum; prefers 950 words. Pays 5½¢/word (accepted). $75 minimum.
Photos: State availability of photos with submission. Offers $10-25/photo. Pays on publication. Buys one-time rights.
Fiction: Humorous, mainstream, slice-of-life vignettes. No reference to liquor, dancing, drugs, gambling; no pornography, profanity or occult. Buys 12 mss/year. Send complete ms. Length: 900-1,200 words. Pays 5½¢/word. $75 minimum.
Poetry: Light verse, traditional. Buys 30 poems/year. Submit maximum 5 poems. Length: open. Pays $13-20.
Fillers: Anecdotes, facts, short humor. Buys 10/issue. Length: 50 words maximum. Pays $10.

MATURE OUTLOOK, Meredith Corp., 1912 Grand Ave., Des Moines IA 50309-3379. Associate Editor: Peggy Person. 80% freelance written. Bimonthly magazine on travel, health, nutrition, money and garden for over-50 audience. They may or may *not* be retired. Circ. 925,000. **Pays on acceptance.** Publishes ms an average 7 months after acceptance. Byline given. Offers 20% kill fee. Buys all rights or makes work-for-hire assignments. Submit all material 9 months in advance. Query for electronic submissions. Reports in 2 weeks. Sample copy for $1. Writer's guidelines for #10 SASE.

Nonfiction: How-to, travel, health, fitness. No personal experience or poetry. Buys 50-60 mss/year. Query with published clips. Length: 150-1,000 words. Pays $100-750 for assigned articles. Pays telephone expenses of writers on assignment.

Photos: State availability of photos with submission.

Tips: "Please query. Please don't call."

MATURE YEARS, The United Methodist Publishing House, 201 Eighth Ave. S., Nashville TN 37202-0801. Fax: (615)749-6512. Editor: Marvin W. Cropsey. 50% freelance written. Prefers to work with published/established writers. Quarterly magazine covering interests of older adults and Bible study. "*Mature Years* is designed to help persons in and nearing the retirement years understand and appropriate the resources of the Christian faith in dealing with specific problems and opportunities related to aging. Estab. 1954. Circ. 70,000. **Pays on acceptance.** Publishes ms an average of 12 months after acceptance. Buys first North American serial rights. Submit seasonal material 14 months in advance. Accepts previously published articles. Send photocopy or typed ms with rights for sale noted and information about when and where the article previously appeared. For reprints, pays 100% of the amount paid for an original article. Query for electronic submissions. Reports in 2 weeks on queries; 2 months for mss. Sample copy for $3.50 and 9 × 12 SAE. Writer's guidelines for #10 SASE.

Nonfiction: How-to (hobbies), inspirational, religious, travel (special guidelines), older adult health, finance issues. Buys 75-80 mss/year. Send complete ms. Length: 900-2,500 words. Pays $45-125. Sometimes pays expenses of writers on assignments.

Photos: Send photos with submission. Negotiates payment individually. Captions, model releases required. Buys one-time rights.

Columns/Departments: Health Hints (retirement, health), 900-1,200 words; Going Places (travel, pilgrimmage), 1,000-1,500 words; Fragments of Life (personal inspiration), 250-600 words; Modern Revelations (religious/inspirational), 900-1,100 words; Money Matters (personal finance), 1,200-1,800 words; Puzzle Time (religioius puzzles, crosswords). Buys 4 mss/year each. Send complete ms. Pays $45-125.

Fiction: Religious, slice-of-life vignettes, retirement years. Buys 4 mss/year. Send complete ms. Length: 1,000-2,500 words. Pays $60-125.

Poetry: Free verse, haiku, light verse, traditional. Buys 24 poems/year. Submit 6 poems maximum. Length: 3-16 lines. Pays $5-20.

MODERN MATURITY, American Association of Retired Persons, 3200 E. Carson St., Lakewood CA 90712. (310)496-2277. Editor: J. Henry Fenwick. 50% freelance written. Prefers to work with published/established writers. Bimonthly magazine for readership of persons 50 years of age and over. Circ. 22.6 million. **Pays on acceptance.** Publishes ms an average of 6 months after acceptance. Byline given. Buys first North American serial rights. Submit seasonal material 6 months in advance. Query for electronic submissions. Reports in 2-3 months. Free sample copy and writer's guidelines.

Nonfiction: Careers, workplace, practical information in living, financial and legal matters, personal relationships, consumerism. Query first. *No unsolicited mss.* Length: up to 2,000 words. Pays up to $3,000. Sometimes pays expenses of writers on assignment.

Photos: Photos purchased with or without accompanying ms. Pays $250 and up for color; $150 and up for b&w.

Fiction: Very occasional short fiction.

Tips: "The most frequent mistake made by writers in completing an article for us is poor follow-through with basic research. The outline is often more interesting than the finished piece. We do not accept unsolicited mss."

‡SENIOR HIGHLIGHTS, Senior Highlights, Inc., 26081 Merit Circle, Suite 101, Laguna Hills CA 92653. (714)367-0776. Fax: (714)367-1006. Publisher/Editor: Lee McCamon. Contact: Julie Puckett. 30% freelance written. Monthly magazine covering active, older adults over 50 years old. "*Senior Highlights* is a monthly magazine designed to enrich the lifestyle for persons 50 and older. It features interesting and inspiring stories relative to this age group. Our objective is 'Making Your Next Years Your Best Years.' *Senior Highlights* informs more than one million monthly readers throughout Central and Southern California. Five separate editions reach Greater Los Angeles, Orange and San Diego counties as well as the Inland Empire (Riverside and San Bernardino counties) and the San Fernando Valley (including Ventura county)." Estab. 1983. Circ. 444,000. Pays on publication. Publishes ms an average of 3 months after acceptance. Byline given. Buys first, second serial (reprint) rights and simultaneous rights. Editorial lead time 2 months. Submit seasonal material 3 months in advance. Accepts simultaneous submissions. Reports in 3 months. Sample copy for $3. Writer's guidelines for #10 SASE.

Nonfiction: General interest, historical/nostalgic, humor, inspirational, interview/profile, opinion/commentary, personal experience, travel (domestic and international), breakthroughs in science and medicine, health, exercise and nutrition, arts and entertainment (film, stage, art, music, literature, restaurants), hobbies, gardening and sports, retirement living/housing, personal finance, consumer protection & information. Special issues: editorial calendar available. "Do not send articles that discuss how to 'cure' old age. Do not send articles that talk 'about' seniors rather than 'to' seniors. Recognize who you are talking to: active, talented and intelligent older people." Buys 60 mss/year. Query or send complete ms. Length: 300-800 words. Pays $0-100 for assigned articles; $0-25 for unsolicited articles.

Photos: State availability of or send photos with submission. Reviews color slides or transparencies, b&w prints. Offers no additional payment for photos accepted with ms. Captions are required.

Columns/Departments: Celebrity Feature (high profile, easily recognizable celebrities that are still actively involved), 800 words; Letters to the Editor (publish one per month; must be clearly written), 300 words; Health (nutrition/fitness; medical breakthroughs), 800 words; Lifestyles (housing, food/recipes, restaurants, gardening, hobbies, sports and legislation), 800 words; Moneywise (consumer issues, personal finance and investing), 800 words; Travel (domestic and international), 800 words; Who's to Say (outstanding, extraordinary seniors), 800 words. Buys 120 mss/year. Query or send complete ms. Pays $0-50.

Tips: "We are looking for articles that tie in to our editorial calendar topics in exciting and innovative ways. We have a special need for upbeat health articles that avoid stereotyping our readers as sickly and emphasize prevention. Talk directly to our readers and stick with subjects that directly impact their lives. Keep in mind our readers' needs and interests differ dramatically from 50 to over 100 years old. No telephone queries. Unorganized thoughts and materials are tossed."

SENIOR MAGAZINE, 3565 S. Higuera St., San Luis Obispo CA 93401. (805)544-8711. Fax: (805)544-4450. Editor/Publisher: Gary D. Suggs. 90% freelance written. Monthly magazine covering seniors to inform and entertain the "over-50" audience. Estab. 1981. Circ. 240,000. Pays on publication. Byline given. Publishes ms an average of 1 month after acceptance. Not copyrighted. Buys first or second rights. Submit seasonal material 2 months in advance. Reports in 1 month. *Writer's Market* recommends allowing 2 months for reply. Sample copy for 9×12 SAE with 6 first-class stamps. Writer's guidelines for SASE.

Nonfiction: Historical/nostalgic, humor, inspirational, personal experience, travel. Special issues: War Years (November); Christmas (December); Travel (October, March). Buys 30-75 mss/year. Query. Length: 300-900 words. Pays $1.50/inch.

Photos: Send photos with submission. Reviews 8×10 b&w prints only. Offers $10-25/photo. Captions and identification of subjects required. Buys one-time rights.

Columns/Departments: Finance (investment), Taxes, Auto, Health. Length: 300-900 words. Pays $1.50/inch.

SENIOR WORLD NEWSMAGAZINE, Kendell Communications, Inc., 71000 Pioneer Way, P.O. Box 1565, El Cajon CA 92020-1565. (619)593-2910. Executive Editor: Laura Impastato. Travel Editor: Jerry Goodrum. Entertainment Editor: Iris Neal. Health Editor: Wendy Worrall. Feature Editor: Carolyn Pantier. 5% freelance written. Prefers to work with published/established writers. Monthly tabloid newspaper for active older adults living in San Diego, Orange, Los Angeles, Riverside and San Bernardino counties. Estab. 1973. Circ. 500,000. Pays on publication. Buys first serial rights. Accepts simultaneous submissions. Reports in 2 months. Sample copy for $3. Free writer's guidelines.

• *Senior World* is using little freelance material right now.

Nonfiction: "We are looking for stories on health, stressing wellness and prevention; travel—international, domestic and how-to; profiles of senior celebrities and remarkable seniors; finance and investment tips for seniors; and interesting hobbies." Send query or complete ms. Length: 500-1,000 words. Pays $50-100.

Photos: State availability of photos with submission. Needs b&w with model release.

Columns/Departments: Most of our columns are local or staff-written. We will consider a query on a column idea accompanied by a sample column.

Tips: "No pity the poor seniors material. Remember that we are primarily a news publication and that our content and style reflect that. Our readers are active, vital adults 55 years of age and older." No telephone queries.

SPECTRUM NEWSPAPERS, (formerly *Senior Spectrum*), 1624 22nd St., West Sacramento CA 95816. Fax: (916)321-5219. Editor: Julie Howard. 45% freelance written. Weekly tabloid. "Sacramento newspaper for seniors emphasizing legislation, local, state and national news, features and local calendar aimed at over-55 community." Estab. 1972. Circ. 25,000. Pays on publication. Publishes ms an average of 2 months after acceptance. Byline given. Buys first North American serial rights and simultaneous rights. Submit seasonal material 3 months in advance. Reports immediately.

Nonfiction: Travel. Does not want "anything aimed at less than age 50-plus market; anything patronizing or condescending to seniors." Buys 3-6 mss/year. Query with or without published clips or send complete ms. Length: 50-1,000 words. Pays $5-30 for assigned articles; $5-25 for unsolicited articles.

Photos: Send photos with submission (or photocopies of available pictures). Offers $3-10/photo. Identification of subjects required. Buys one-time rights.

Tips: Area most open to freelancers is travel. We will not promote any product or business unless it is the only one in existence. Must be applicable to senior lifestyle.

SUCCESSFUL RETIREMENT, Grass Roots Publishing, 950 Third Ave., 16th Floor, New York NY 10022. Editor: Marcia Vickers. 90% freelance written. Bimonthly magazine covering retirement. "Fun, upbeat, a youthful approach to retirement. No fuddy-duddyness. Our audience consists of "pretirees and retirees—average age 65. (No 'little old lady from Pasadena' stories)." Estab. 1993. Circ. 100,000. Pays on publication. Publishes ms an average of 6 months after acceptance. Byline given. Buys all rights. Editorial lead time 6 months. Submit seasonal material 6 months in advance. Query for electronic submissions. Occasionally accepts previously published submissions. Send tearsheet of article and information about when and where the article previously appeared with rights for sale noted. Reports in 3 months. Sample copy for $3.50 (plus postage and handling). Writer's guidelines free on request.
• Circulation of *Successful Retirement* was increased from 20,000 to 100,000.
Nonfiction: Health, how-to, humor, motivational, interview/profile, older celebrity profiles, relationships, travel, retirement locales, second careers, profiles of retirees doing unusual, interesting things and retirement life. "No lengthy, essay-type pieces or opinion pieces. Nothing negative or drab. Must pertain to retirement or aging." Buys 60 mss/year. Query with published clips. For humor pieces, send entire ms. Length: 500-1,000 words. Pays $150 minimum.
Photos: State availability of photos with submission or send photos with submission. Identification of subjects required.
Columns/Departments: "Columns are written by staff writers. Query *only* if you have new column idea." Query with published clips. Pays $150-200.

Romance and Confession

Listed here are publications that need stories of romance ranging from ethnic and adventure to romantic intrigue and confession. Each magazine has a particular slant; some are written for young adults, others to family-oriented women. Some magazines also are interested in general interest nonfiction on related subjects.

BLACK SECRETS, Sterling/McFadden, 233 Park Ave. S., 5th Floor, New York NY 10003. (212)780-3500. Fax: (212)780-3555. Editor: Marcia Mahan. Accepts previously published submissions. Send short story or typed ms with rights for sale noted and information about when and where story previously appeared. See *Intimacy/Black Romance*.
Fiction: "This is our most romantic magazine of the five. We use one longer story between 20-24 pages for this book, and sometimes we feature it on the cover. Save your harsh, sleazy stories for another magazine. Give us your softest, dreamiest, most imaginative, most amorous story with a male love interest we can't help but fall in love with. Make sure your story has body and not just bodies. Our readers love romance, but they also require substance."
Tips: "Please request a sample and guidelines before submitting. Enclose a 9×12 SASE with 5 first-class stamps."

BRONZE THRILLS, Sterling/McFadden, 233 Park Ave. S., 5th Floor, New York NY 10003. (212)780-3500. Fax: (212)780-3522. Editor: Marcia Mahan. Estab. 1982. See *Intimacy/Black Romance*.
Fiction: "Stories can be a bit more extraordinary and uninhibited than in the other magazines but still they have to be romantic. For example, we might buy a story about a woman who finds out her husband is a transsexual in *Bronze Thrills*, but not for *Jive* (our younger magazine). The stories for this magazine tend to have a harder, more adult edge of reality than the others."

INTIMACY/BLACK ROMANCE, Sterling/McFadden, 233 Park Ave. S., 5th Floor, New York NY 10003. (212)780-3500. Fax: (212)780-3522. Editor: Marcia Mahan. 100% freelance written. Eager to work with new/unpublished writers. Bimonthly magazine of romance and love. Estab. 1982. Circ. 100,000. Pays on publication. Publishes ms an average of 2 months after acceptance. Byline given on articles only. Buys all rights. Submit seasonal material 6 months in advance. Reports in 2 months. Sample copy for 9×12 SAE with 5 first-class stamps. Writer's guidelines for #10 SASE.
Nonfiction: How-to (relating to romance and love) and feature articles on any aspect of relationships. Buys 100 mss/year. Query with published clips or send complete ms. Length: 3-5 pages. Pays $100.
Photos: Send photos with submission. Reviews contact sheets, negatives, transparencies.
Fiction: Confession and romance. "Stories that are too graphic in content and lack romance are unacceptable." Buys 300 mss/year. Accepts stories which are a bit more romantic than those written for *Jive*, *Black Confessions* or *Bronze Thrills*. Send complete ms (4,000-5,000 words). Pays $75-100.
Tips: "I still get excited when I read a ms by an unpublished writer whose use of language is magical and fresh. I'm always looking for that diamond in the fire. Send us your *best* shot. Writers who are careless, sloppy and ungrammatical are an immediate turn-off for me. Please do your homework first. Is it the type of story we buy? Is it written in ms format? Does it make one want to read it?"

JIVE, Sterling/McFadden, 233 Park Ave. S., 5th Floor, New York NY 10003. (212)780-3500. Fax: (212)780-3555. Editor: Marcia Mahan. 100% freelance written. Eager to work with new/unpublished writers. Bimonthly magazine of romance and love. Estab. 1982. Circ. 100,000. Pays on publication. Publishes ms an average of 2 months after acceptance. Byline given on articles only. Buys all rights. Submit seasonal material 6 months in advance. Reports in 2 months on queries; 6 months on mss. Sample copy for 9×12 SASE with 5 first-class stamps. Free writer's guidelines.

Nonfiction: How-to (relating to romance and love) and feature articles on any aspect of relationships. "We like our articles to have a down-to-earth flavor. They should be written in the spirit of sisterhood, fun and creativity. Come up with an original idea our readers may not have thought of but will be dying to try out." Buys 100 mss/year. Query with published clips or send complete ms. Length: 3-5 typed pages. Pays $100.

Columns/Departments: Fashion, health, beauty articles accepted. Length: 3-5 pages.

Fiction: Confession and romance. "Stories that are too graphic and lack romance are unacceptable. However, all stories must contain one or two love scenes. Love scenes should allude to sex—romantic, not lewd." Buys 300 mss/year. Send complete ms (4,000-5,000 words). Pays $75-100.

Tips: "We are leaning toward more romantic writing styles as opposed to the more graphic stories of the past. Our audience is largely black teenagers. The stories should reinforce Black pride and should be geared toward teenage issues. Our philosophy is to show our experiences in as positive a light as possible without promoting any of the common stereotypes that are associated with Black men, lovemaking prowess, penile size, etc. Stereotypes of any kind are totally unacceptable. The fiction section which accepts romance stories and confession stories is most open to freelancers. Also, our special features section is very open. We would also like to see stories that are set outside the US (perhaps they could be set in the Caribbean, Europe, Africa, etc.) and themes that are reflective of things happening around us in the 90s—abortion, AIDS, alienation, surrogate mothers, etc. But we also like to see stories that transcend our contemporary problems and can give us a moment of pleasure, warmth, joy and relief. The characters should be anywhere from teenage to 30s but not the typical 'country bumpkin girl who was turned out by a big city pimp' type story. Please, writers who are not Black, research your story to be sure that it depicts Black people in a positive manner. Do not make a Black character a caricature of a non-Black character. Read contemporary Black fiction to ensure that your dialogue and speech idioms are natural to the Black vernacular."

MODERN ROMANCES, Sterling/Macfadden Partnership, 233 Park Ave. S., New York NY 10003. (212)979-4800. Fax: (212)979-7342. Editor: Eileen Fitzmaurice. 100% freelance written. Monthly magazine for family-oriented working women, ages 18-65 years old. Circ. 200,000. Pays the last week of the month of issue. Buys all rights. Submit seasonal material at least 6 months in advance. Reports in 9-11 months. Writer's guidelines for #10 SASE.

• This editor is especially in need of short, well-written stories (approximately 3,000-5,000 words).

Nonfiction: Confession stories with reader identification and a strong emotional tone; a strong emphasis on characterization and well-defined plots. Should be realistic and compelling. No query letters. No third-person material. Buys 10 mss/issue. Submit complete ms. Length: 2,500-10,000 words. Pays 5¢/word. Buys all rights.

Poetry: Light, romantic poetry and seasonal/holiday subjects. Length: 24 lines maximum. Pays $2/line. Look at poetry published in previous issues before submitting.

TRUE CONFESSIONS, Macfadden Women's Group, 233 Park Ave. S., New York NY 10003. (212)979-4800. Editor: Pat Byrdsong. 100% freelance written. Eager to work with new/unpublished writers. Monthly magazine for high-school-educated, blue-collar women, teens through maturity. Circ. 280,000. Buys all rights. Byline given on featured columns: My Man, The Feminine Side, Incredible But True, My Moment With God and You and Your Pet. Pays during the last week of month of issue. Publishes ms an average of 4 months after acceptance. Submit seasonal material 6 months in advance. Reports in 6 months.

Nonfiction: Timely, exciting, true emotional first-person stories on the problems that face today's women. The narrators should be sympathetic, and the situations they find themselves in should be intriguing, yet realistic. Many stories may have a strong romantic interest and a high moral tone; however, personal accounts or "confessions," no matter how controversial the topic, are encouraged and accepted. Careful study of a current issue is suggested. Length: 4,000-7,000 words; also book lengths of 8,000-10,000 words. Pays 5¢/word. Also publishes humor, poetry and mini-stories (3,000 words maximum). Submit complete ms. No simultaneous submissions. SASE required. Buys all rights.

• Always looking for topical material.

TRUE EXPERIENCE, The Sterling/MacFadden Partnership, 233 Park Ave. S., New York NY 10003. (212)979-4800. Editor: Claire Cloutier LeBlanc. Associate Editor: Alison M. Way. 100% freelance written. Monthly magazine covering women's confession stories. "*True Experience* is a women's confession magazine which publishes first-person short stories on actual occurrences. Our stories cover such topics as love, romance, crime, family problems and social issues. The magazine's primary audience consists of working-class women in the South, Midwest and rural West. Our stories aim to portray the lives and problems of 'real women.' " Estab. 1928. Circ. 100,000. Pays on publication. Publishes ms an average of 4 months after acceptance. No byline. Buys all rights. Editorial lead time 4 months. Submit seasonal material 6 months in advance. Query for electronic submissions. Reports in 2 weeks on queries; 4 months on mss. Sample copy for $1.69. Writer's guidelines for #10 SASE.

Nonfiction: Confession, humorous, mystery, romance, slice-of-life vignettes. Buys 125 mss/year. Send complete ms. Length: 1,000-10,000 words. Pays 3¢/word.

Columns/Departments: Woman Talk (brief stories covering rites of passage in women's lives), 500-1,500 words; How We Met (anecdotes describing a couple's first meeting), 300-1,000 words. Buys 24 mss/year. Send complete ms. Pays $50-75.

Poetry: Light verse, traditional. Buys 5 poems/year. Submit maximum 10 poems. Length: 4-50 lines. Pays $2/line.

Tips: "The best way to break into our publication is to send us a well-written, interesting story with sympathetic characters. Stories focusing on topical subjects like sexual harassment, crime, AIDS, or natural disasters are most likely to receive serious considerations. No special submission methods are called for. All stories must be written in first person."

TRUE LOVE, Macfadden Women's Group, 233 Park Ave. S., New York NY 10003. (212)979-4800. Fax: (212)979-7342. Editor: Kristina Kracht. 100% freelance written. Monthly magazine for young, blue-collar women, 22-55. Confession stories based on true happenings, with reader identification and a strong emotional tone. Circ. 200,000. Pays the last week of the month of the issue. Buys all rights. Submit seasonal material 6 months in advance. No simultaneous submissions. Reports in 8 months. Sample copy for $2 and 9×12 SAE. Writer's guidelines for #10 SASE.

● *True Love* needs more romance stories.

Nonfiction: Confessions, true love stories, problems and solutions, health problems, marital and child-rearing difficulties. Avoid graphic sex. Stories dealing with reality, current problems, everyday events, with emphasis on emotional impact. No stories written in third person. Buys 10 stories/issue. Buy all rights. Submit complete ms; returned only with SAE and sufficient postage. Length: 2,000-10,000 words. Pays 3¢/word.

Columns/Departments: The Life I Live, $100; How I Know I'm In Love, 700 words or less; $75; Pet Shop, $50; Kids Will Be Kids, $50; Here Comes The Bride, $50.

Poetry: Light romantic poetry. Length: 24 lines maximum. Pay $2/line.

Tips: "The story must appeal to the average blue-collar woman. It must deal with her problems and interests. Characters—especially the narrator—must be sympathetic. Focus is especially on young working women."

TRUE ROMANCE, Sterling/Macfadden Partnership, 233 Park Ave. S., New York NY 10003. (212)979-4800. Fax: (212)979-7342. Editor: Pat Vittuci. Monthly magazine. 100% freelance written. Readership primarily young, working class women, teens through retired. Confession stories based on true happenings, with reader identification and strong emotional tone. No third-person material; no simultaneous submissions. Estab. 1923. Circ. 225,000. Pays 1 month after publication. Buys all rights. Submit seasonal/holiday material at least 6 months in advance. Reports in 5 months.

Nonfiction: Confessions, true love stories; problems and solutions; dating and marital and child-rearing difficulties. Realistic stories dealing with current problems, everyday events, with strong emotional appeal. Buys 12 stories/issue. Submit complete ms. Length 1,500-7,500 words. Pays 3¢/word; slightly higher rates for short-shorts.

Poetry: Light romantic poetry. Buys 100/year. Length: 24 lines maximum. Pay depends on merit.

Tips: "A timely, well-written story that is told by a sympathetic narrator who sees the central problem through to a satisfying resolution is *all* important to break into *True Romance*. We are always looking for good emotional, identifiable stories."

TRUE STORY, Sterling/Macfadden Partnership, 233 Park Ave. S., New York NY 10003. (212)979-4800. Editor: Lisa Rabidoux Finn. 80% freelance written. Monthly magazine for young married, blue-collar women, 20-35; high school education; increasingly broad interests; home-oriented, but looking beyond the home for personal fulfillment. Circ. 1.7 million. Buys all rights. Byline given "on articles only." Pays 1 month after publication. Submit seasonal material 1 year in advance. Reports in approximately 8-12 months.

Nonfiction: "First-person stories covering all aspects of women's interests: love, marriage, family life, careers, social problems, etc. The best direction a new writer can be given is to carefully study several issues of the magazine; then submit a fresh, exciting, well-written true story. We have no taboos. It's the handling and believability that make the difference between a rejection and an acceptance." Buys about 125 full-length mss/year. Submit only complete mss for stories. Length: 1,500-10,000 words. Pays 5¢/word; $150 minimum. Pays a flat rate for columns or departments, as announced in the magazine. Query for fact articles.

Rural

These publications draw readers interested in rural lifestyles. Surprisingly, many readers are from urban centers who dream of or plan to build a house in the country.

‡CAROLINA COUNTRY, North Carolina Association of Electric Cooperatives, 3400 Summer Blvd,, Raleigh NC 27604. Editor: Michael E.C. Gery. 30% freelance written. Monthly magazine for members of North Carolina's electric cooperatives. General interest material concerning North Carolina's culture, business, history, people. Estab. 1952. Circ. 340,000. **Pays on acceptance.** Publishes ms an average of 3 months after acceptance. Byline given. Offers 50% kill fee. Buys all rights. Editorial lead time 3 months. Submit seasonal material 3 months in advance. Accepts simultaneous and previously published submissions (if outside North Carolina). Reports in 1 month on queries; 2 months on mss.
Nonfiction: General interest, historical/nostalgic, humor, photo feature. Buys 12 mss/year. Send complete ms. Length: 600-1,500 words. Pays $100-400.
Photos: Send photos with submission. Reviews transparencies, prints. Negotiates payment individually. Captions, identification of subjects required. Buys one-time rights.
Columns/Departments: Focus (useful resource news in North Carolina), 100 words. Buys 10 mss/year. Send complete ms. Pays $20-100.
Tips: "Interested in North Carolina information that would not likely appear in local newspapers. Our readers are rural and suburban residents."

‡THE COUNTRY CONNECTION, The Magazine for Country Folk, Pinecone Publishing, P.O. Box 100, Boulter, Ontario K0L 1G0 Canada. (613)332-3651. Editor: Gus Zylstra. 75% freelance written. Semiannual magazine covering country life and tourism. *"The Country Connection* is a magazine for country folk and those who wish they were. Building on our commitment to heritage, cultural, artistic, and outdoor themes, we continually add new topics to illuminate the country experience of people living within nature. Our goal is to chronicle rural life in its many aspects, giving 'voice' to the countryside." Estab. 1989. Circ. 15,000. Pays on publication. Publishes ms an average of 6 months after acceptance. Byline given. Buys first rights. Editorial lead time 4 months. Submit seasonal material 4 months in advance. Query for electronic submissions. Sample copy $3.95. Writer's guidelines for #10 SAE and IRC.
Nonfiction: General interest, historical/nostalgic, humor, personal experience, photo feature, travel. No hunting and fishing articles. Buys 20 mss/year. Send complete ms. Length: 500-2,000 words. Pays 7-10¢/word. Sometimes pays expenses of writers on assignment.
Photos: Send photos with submission. Reviews transparencies and prints. Offers $10-50/photo. Captions required. Buys one-time rights.
Columns/Departments: Pays 7-10¢/word.
Fiction: Adventure, fantasy, historical, humorous, slice-of-life vignettes, country living. Buys 4 mss/year. Send complete ms. Length: 500-1,500 words. Pays 7-10¢/word.
Tips: "Send (original content) manuscript with appropriate support material such as photos, illustrations, maps, etc."

COUNTRY JOURNAL, 4 High Ridge Park, Standford CT 06905. (203)321-1778. Fax: (203)322-1966. Editor: Peter V. Fossel. Managing Editor: Valerie Kanter. Editorial Assistant: Cristin Marandino. 90% freelance written. Works with a small number of new/unpublished writers each year. Bimonthly magazine "that is the authoritative resource on rural life, providing practical advise for the country dweller. Readership aimed to middle and upper income levels." Estab. 1974. Circ. 150,000. **Pays on acceptance.** Rates range from 20-40¢/word. Byline given. Buys first North American serial rights. Submit seasonal material 1 year in advance. Accepts previously published submissions. Send photocopy of article. For reprints, pays 10% of the amount paid for an original article. Reports in 4 months. Sample copy for $4. Writer's guidelines for SASE.
Nonfiction: Conservation, gardening, nature, projects, small-scale farming, how-to, issues affecting rural areas. Query with published clips and SASE. Length: 1,500-2,000 words. Pays 20-40¢/word.
Photos: Art director. State availability of photos. Reviews b&w contact sheets, 5×7 and 8×10 b&w glossy prints and 35mm or larger transparencies with SASE. Captions, model release, identification of subjects required. Buys one-time rights.
Columns/Departments: Sentinel (brief articles on country topics, how-tos, current events and updates). Buys 5 mss/issue. Query with published clips and SASE. Length: 200-400 words. Pays approximately $75.
Poetry: Free verse, light verse, traditional. Buys 1 poem/issue. Pays $50/poem. Include SASE.
Tips: "Be as specific in your query as possible and explain why you are qualified to write the piece (especially for how-to's and controversial subjects). The writer has a better chance of breaking in at our publication with short articles."

THE COUNTRYMAN, Sheep St., Burford, Oxon Ox184L UK. 01993 822258. Editor: Christopher Hall. 75% freelance written. Bimonthly magazine covering rural life and affairs. Estab. 1927. Circ. 60,000. Pays on publication. Publishes ms an average of 6-12 months after acceptance. Byline given. Buys first rights (photos and drawings) or all rights (mss). Editorial lead time 2 months. Submit seasonal material 6 months in advance. Reports in 2 weeks on queries.
Nonfiction: Historical/nostalgic, personal experience, photo feature, rural. Buys 60-70 mss/year. Send complete ms. Length: 1,800 words maximum. Pays £60 minimum.

Photos: Send photos with submission. Reviews ½ plate b&w. Negotiates payment individually. Captions required. Buys one-time rights.

Poetry: Free verse, traditional. Buys 50 poems/year. Submit maximum 3 poems. Length: 4-40 lines. Pays £5-25.

Fillers: Anecdotes. Buys 40/year. Length: 100 words maximum. Pays £5-20.

Tips: "Reading the magazine is best."

ELECTRIC CONSUMER, Indiana Statewide Association of Rural Electric Cooperatives, Inc., P.O. Box 24517, Indianapolis IN 46224. (317)487-2220. Editor: Emily Born. Associate Editor: Richard G. Biever. Monthly tabloid covering rural electric cooperatives (relevant issues affecting members). News/feature format for electric cooperative members in Indiana. "Our readers are rural/suburban, generally conservative and have the common bond of electric cooperative membership." Estab. 1951. Circ. 275,480. Pays on publication. Byline given. Buys one-time rights. Submit seasonal material 3 months in advance. Accepts simultaneous and previously published submissions. Send photocopy of article (not necessary, but helpful) or typed ms with rights for sale noted and information about when and where the article previously appeared. Reports in 2 months. Free sample copy and writer's guidelines.

Nonfiction: General interest and humor, gardening, Indiana history, how to save money. "We are looking for upbeat, concise articles that offer tips on ways to save energy, or general interest articles with 'news readers can use.' Sidebars with bulleted information a big plus, as is original artwork to accompany article." Buys 12 mss/year. Send complete ms. Considers lengths up to 1,200 words. Pays $40-150.

Photos: State availability of photos with submission. Price commensurate to quality and use. Captions, model releases, identification of subjects required. Buys one-time rights.

Columns/Departments: Humor (personal experiences usually, always "clean" family-oriented), 750-1,000 words. Buys 8 mss/year. Send complete ms. Pays $45.

Tips: "We have redesigned, downsized our publication. Our 10×12¼ publication is now stitched and trimmed. We now, though, have less space for freelance articles. They need to be concise and *useful* for our readers, tips, how-to's, etc., preferred over humor. We no longer use *fiction* or poetry."

FARM & RANCH LIVING, Reiman Publications, 5400 S. 60th St., Greendale WI 53129. (414)423-0100. E-mail: 76150.162@compuserve.com. Editor: Nick Pabst. 80% freelance written. Eager to work with new/unpublished writers. Bimonthly lifestyle magazine aimed at families that farm or ranch full time. "*F&RL* is *not* a 'how-to' magazine—it focuses on people rather than products and profits." Estab. 1968. Circ. 380,000. **Pays on acceptance.** Publishes ms an average of 6 months after acceptance. Byline given. Buys first serial rights and one-time rights. Submit seasonal material 6 months in advance. Accepts previously published submissions. Send tearsheet of article or typed ms with rights for sale noted. Reports in 6 weeks. Sample copy for $2. Writer's guidelines for #10 SASE.

Nonfiction: Interview/profile, photo feature, nostalgia, humor, inspirational, personal experience. No how-to articles or stories about "hobby farmers" (doctors or lawyers with weekend farms); no issue-oriented stories (pollution, animal rights, etc.). Buys 30 mss/year. Submit query or finished ms. Length: 600-1,200 words. Pays $150-300 for text-and-photos package. Accepts previously published submissions. Send tearsheet of article or typed ms with rights for sale noted.

Photos: Scenic. State availability of photos with query. Pays $75-200 for 35mm color slides. Buys one-time rights.

Fillers: Jokes, anecdotes, short humor with farm or ranch slant. Buys 50/year. Length: 50-150 words. Pays $20.

Tips: "Our readers enjoy stories and features that are upbeat and positive. A freelancer must see *F&RL* to fully appreciate how different it is from other farm publications—ordering a sample is strongly advised (not available on newsstands). Photo features (about interesting farm or ranch families) and personality profiles are most open to freelancers. We can make separate arrangements for photography if writer is unable to provide photos."

FARM FAMILY AMERICA, Fieldhagen Publishing, Inc., 190 Fifth St. E., Suite 121, St. Paul MN 55101. (612)292-1747. Editor: George Ashfield. 75% freelance written. Five issues per year. Published by American Cyanamid and written to the lifestyle, activities and travel interests of American farm families. Circ. 300,000. **Pays on acceptance.** Publishes ms an average of 2 months after acceptance. Byline given. Offers 25% kill fee. Buys first rights or second serial (reprint) rights. Submit seasonal material 6 months in advance. Accepts simultaneous submissions. Reports in 6 weeks. Writer's guidelines for #10 SASE.

Nonfiction: General interest and travel. Buys 30 mss/year. Query with published clips. Length: 1,000-1,800 words. Pays $400-650.

Photos: State availability of photos with submission. Reviews 35mm transparencies and prints. Offers $160-700/photo. Model releases and identification of subjects required. Buys one-time rights.

FARM TIMES, P.O. Box 158, Rupert ID 83350. (208)436-1111. Fax: (208)436-9455. Editor: Eric Goodell. 50% freelance written. Monthly tabloid for agriculture-farming/ranching. "*Farm Times* is 'dedicated to rural living.' Stories related to farming and ranching in the states of Idaho, Nevada, Utah, Wyoming and Oregon are our mainstay, but farmers and ranchers do more than just work. General, or human interest articles that appeal to rural readers, are often used." Estab. 1987. Pays on publication. Byline given. Offers 100% kill fee "if submitted in acceptable form—writer's notes won't do it." Buys first rights. Editorial lead time 1 month. Submit seasonal material 3 months in advance. Accepts previously published submissions. Send photocopy of article and information about when and where the article previously appeared. Pays 100% of the amount paid for an original article. Reports in 2 months on queries. Sample copy and writer's guidelines free on request.

Nonfiction: Exposé, general interest, historical/nostalgic, how-to, interview/profile, new product (few), opinion, late breaking ag news. No humor, inspirational, essay, first person, personal experience or book excerpts. Buys 200 mss/year. Query with published clips. Send complete ms. Length: 600-800 words. Pays $1.25/column inch.

Photos: Send photos with submission. Reviews contact sheets with negatives, 35mm or larger transparencies and 5×7 or larger prints. Offers $5/b&w inside, $35/color cover. Captions, model releases, identification of subjects required. Buys one-time rights.

Column/Departments: Hoof Beats (horse care [technical]), 500-600 words; B Section Cover (winter months—travel [anywhere]), 600-1,200 words; B Section Cover (summer months—photo/essay [interesting people/places]) 600-800 words; Rural Religion (interesting churches/missions/religious activities) 600-800 words. Buys 12 mss/year. Query. Send complete ms. Pays $1.25/column inch.

Tips: "Query with a well-thought-out idea that will appeal to rural readers. Of special interest is how environmental issues will affect farmers/ranchers, endangered species act, EPA, etc. We are also interested in features on specialty farming—mint, seed crops, unusual breeds of animals. All of *Farm Times* is a good market for freelancers, but Rural Religion is the best place to get started. Write tightly. Be sure of facts and names."

HARROWSMITH COUNTRY LIFE, Ferry Road, Charlotte VT 05445. (802)425-3961. Fax: (802)425-3307. E-mail: harrowedit@aol.com. Managing Editor: Karan Davis Cutler. Contact: Lisa Rathke. Bimonthly magazine covering country living, gardening, shelter, food and environmental issues. "*Harrowsmith Country Life* readers are generally college educated country dwellers, looking for good information." Estab. 1986. Circ. 200,000. Pays 45 days after acceptance. Byline given. Offers 25% kill fee. Buys first North American serial rights. Occasionally accepts previously published submissions. Send tearsheet, photocopy or typed submission with rights for sale noted along with information about when and where the article previously appeared. Reports in 2 months. Sample copy for $4. Writer's guidelines for #10 SASE.

Nonfiction: Book excerpts, essays, environmental issues, how-to (gardening/cooking building), humor, interview/profile, opinion. Buys 36 mss/year. Query with published clips. Length: 500-5,000 words. Pays $500-2,000. Pays expenses of writers on assignment.

Photos: State availability of photos with submission. Reviews 35mm transparencies. Offers $100-325/photo. Model releases and identification of subjects required. Buys one-time rights.

Columns/Departments: Sourcebank (ideas, tips, tools, techniques relating to gardening, the environment, food, health), 50-400 words; Gazette (brief news items). Buys 30 mss/year. Query with published clips. Length: 40-400 words. Pays $25-150.

Tips: "While main feature stories are open to freelancers, a good way for us to get to know the writer is through our Sourcebank (tips, products and ideas) and Gazette (brief news items) departments. Articles should contain examples, quotations and anecdotes. They should be detailed and factual. Please submit material to Lisa Rathke, assistant editor."

HARROWSMITH COUNTRY LIFE MAGAZINE, Telemedia Communications, Inc., 25 Sheppard Ave. W, North York Ontario M2N 6S7 Canada. (416)733-7600. Fax: (416)733-7981. Editor: Arlene Stacey. 75% freelance written. Published 6 times/year "for those interested in country living, organic gardening, family, food and country homes. Estab. 1976. Circ. 360,000. **Pays on acceptance.** Publishes ms an average of 4 months after acceptance. Byline given. Buys first North American serial rights. Submit seasonal material 6 months in advance. Reports in 6 weeks. Sample copy for $5. Free writer's guidelines.

● This publication won the National Magazine Awards for Humor.

Nonfiction: Country living, how-to, general interest, gardening, homes, country famiy activities, environmental, profile. "We are always in need of quality gardening articles geared to northern conditions. No how-to articles written by people who are not totally familiar with their subject. We feel that in this field simple research does not compensate for lack of long-time personal experience." Buys 10 mss/issue. Query. Length: 500-2,000 words. Pays $150-1,200.

Photos: State availability of photos with query. Captions required. Buys one-time rights.

Tips: "We have high standards of excellence. We welcome and give thorough consideration to all freelance submissions. Our magazine is read by North Americans who live in rural areas or who hope to make the urban to rural transition. They want to know about the realities of country life as well as the dreams."

THE MOTHER EARTH NEWS, Dept. WM, 24 E. 23rd St., 5th Floor, New York NY 10010. (212)260-7210. Fax: (212)260-7445. E-mail: mearthnews@aol.com. Editor: Owen Lipstein. Managing Editor: Sunny Edmonds. Assistant Editor: Molly Miller. Mostly freelance written. Bimonthly magazine emphasizing "country living and country skills, for both long-time and would-be ruralites." Circ. 350,000. **Pays on acceptance.** Byline given. Submit seasonal material 5 months in advance. No handwritten mss. Rarely accepts previously published submissions. Send information about when and where the article previously appeared. Reports within 3 months. Publishes ms an average of 6 months after acceptance. Sample copy for $5. Writer's guidelines for #10 SASE with 2 first-class stamps.

Nonfiction: How-to, home business, alternative energy systems, home building, home retrofit and home maintenance, energy-efficient structures, seasonal cooking, gardening, crafts. Buys 100-150 mss/year. Query. "A short, to-the-point paragraph is often enough. If it's a subject we don't need at all, we can answer immediately. If it tickles our imagination, we'll ask to take a look at the whole piece. No phone queries, please." Length: 300-3,000 words. Publishes nonfiction book excerpts.

Photos: Purchased with accompanying ms. Send prints or transparencies. Uses 8×10 b&w glossies or any size color transparencies. Include type of film, speed and lighting used. Total purchase price for ms includes payment for photos. Captions and credits required.

Tips: "Probably the best way to break in is to study our magazine, digest our writer's guidelines, and send us a concise article illustrated with color transparencies that we can't resist. When folks query and we give a go-ahead on speculation, we often offer some suggestions. Failure to follow those suggestions can lose the sale for the author. We want articles that tell what real people are doing to take charge of their own lives. Articles should be well-documented and tightly written treatments of topics we haven't already covered. The critical thing is length, and our payment is by space, not word count. *No phone queries.*"

RURAL HERITAGE, 281 Dean Ridge Lane, Gainesboro TN 38562-5039. (615)268-0655. Editor: Gail Damerow. Publisher: Allan Damerow. 98% freelance written. Willing to work with a small number of new/unpublished writers. Bimonthly magazine devoted to the training and care of draft animals, and other traditional country skills. Estab. 1975. Circ. 3,000. Pays on publication. Publishes ms an average of 6 months after acceptance. Byline given. Buys first English language rights. Submit seasonal material 6 months in advance. Accepts previously published submissions, but only if previous publication had limited or regional circulation. Send tearsheet or photocopy of article, typed ms with rights for sale noted and information about when and where the article previously appeared. For reprints, pays 100% of the amount paid for an original article. Reports in 3 months. Sample copy for $6. Writer's guidelines #10 SASE.

Nonfiction: How-to (crafting and farming); interview/profile (people using draft animals); photo feature. No articles on *mechanized* farming. Buys 100 mss/year. Query or send complete ms. Length: 750-1,500 words. Pays 5¢/word.

Photos: Send photos with ms. Pays $10. Captions and identification of subjects required. Buys one-time rights. Six covers/year (color transparency or 5×7 horizontal print), animals in harness $50; back covers, humorous rural scene (same size, format) $25. Photo guidelines for #10 SASE.

Columns/Departments: Self-sufficiency (modern people preserving traditional American lifestyle), 750-1,500 words; Drafter's Features (draft animals used for farming, shows and pulls—their care), 750-1,500 words; Crafting (implement designs and patterns), 750-1,500 words; Country Kids (descriptions of rural youngsters who have done [or are doing] remarkable things), 750 words; Humor, 750-900 words. Pays 5¢/word.

Poetry: Traditional. Pays $5-25.

Tips: "Always welcome are: 1) Detailed descriptions and photos of horse-drawn implements 2) Prices and other details of draft animal auctions and sales."

‡THE RURAL VOICE, North Huron Publishing Company, Inc., P.O. Box 429, Blyth Ontario N0M 1H0 Canada. (519)523-4311. Editor: Keith Roulston. 25% freelance written. Monthly magazine covering agriculture and rural life. Estab. 1975. Circ. 15,000. Byline given. Buys first North American serial rights. Editorial lead time 3 months. Submit seasonal material 3 months in advance. Accepts simultaneous and previously published submissions. Reports in 2 weeks on queries; 2 months on mss. Sample copy for $2. Writer's guidelines free on request.

Nonfiction: How-to, humor, interview/profile, personal experience. Buys 12 mss/year. Query. Length: 1,000-2,500 words. Pays $120-300.

Photos: Send photos with submission. Reviews negatives, 5×7 prints. Offers $7-10/photo. Identification of subjects required. Buys one-time rights.

Fiction: Buys 4 mss/year. Query. Length: 1,000-2,500 words. Pays $120-300.

RURALITE, P.O. Box 558, Forest Grove OR 97116-0558. (503)357-2105. Fax: (503)357-8615. Editor-in-Chief: Curtis Condon. Associate Editor: Walt Wentz. 80% freelance written. Works with new, unpublished writers "who have mastered the basics of good writing." Monthly magazine aimed at members of consumer-owned electric utilities throughout 9 western states, including Alaska. Publishes 52 regional editions. Estab. 1954. Circ. 265,000. Buys first rights, sometimes reprint rights. Accepts previously published submissions. Send photocopy of article or typed ms with rights for sale noted and information about when and where the article previously appeared. For reprints, pays 50% of "*our* regular freelance rates." Rights may be reassigned. Byline given. **Pays on acceptance**. Query first; unsolicited manuscripts submitted without request rarely read by editors. Reports in 1 month. Sample copy and writer's guidelines for 10×13 SAE with 4 first-class stamps.

Nonfiction: Looking for well-written nonfiction, (occasional fiction piece) dealing primarily with human interest topics. Must have strong Northwest perspective and be sensitive to Northwest issues and attitudes. Wide range of topics possible, from energy-related subjects to little-known travel destinations to unusual businesses located in areas served by consumer-owned electric utilities. "About half of our readers are rural and small town residents; others are urban and suburban. Topics with an obvious 'big-city' focus not accepted. Family-related issues, Northwest history (no encyclopedia rewrites), people and events, unusual tidbits that tell the Northwest experience are best chances for a sale. Nostalgic, dripping sentimental pieces rejected out of hand." Buys 50-60 mss/yr. Length 800-2,000 words. Pays $140-400, quality photos may increase upper pay limit for "polished stories with impact."

Photos: "Illustrated stories are the key to a sale. Stories without art rarely make it, with the exception of humor pieces. Black and white prints, color slides, all formats, accepted with 'razor-sharp' focus. Fuzzy, low-contrast photos may lose the sale."

Tips: "Study a recent copy. Follow directions when given an assignment. Be able to deliver a complete package (story and photos). We're looking for regular contributors to whom we can assign topics from our story list after they've proven their ability to deliver quality mss."

‡**YIPPY YI YEA™ MAGAZINE**, Long Publications, 8393 E. Holly Rd., Holly MI 48442. Editor: Cheryl Anderson. Contact: Judith Karns. 80% freelance written. Quarterly magazine covering western lifestyle. "We cater to those who have an interest in western lifestyles, clothing, history, art, decorating." Estab. 1991. Circ. 70,000. **Pays on acceptance.** Photography paid on publication. Publishes ms an average of 8-10 months after acceptance. Byline given. Buys first North American serial rights. Editorial lead time 6 months. Submit seasonal material 1 year in advance. Query for electronic submissions. Sample copy and writer's guidelines free on request.

Nonfiction: Historical/nostalgic, interview/profile, photo feature, home decorating. Buys 40 mss/year. Query with published clips, Length: 700-1,000 words. Pays $75-300.

Photos: State availability of or send photos with submission. Reviews transparencies (35mm, 2¼, 4×5). Offers $25/photo. Captions, identification of subjects required. Buys one-time rights.

Fiction: Short-short stories. Buys 4 mss/year. Send complete ms. Length: 700 words. Pays $75-250.

Poetry: Cowboy. Buys 2-3 poems/year. Submit maximum 1 poem. Length: 32 lines. Pays $75-200.

Tips: "Solid writing background is preferred. Be prepared to work with editor for clean, concise copy."

Science

These publications are published for laymen interested in technical and scientific developments and discoveries, applied science and technical or scientific hobbies. Publications of interest to the personal computer owner/user are listed in the Personal Computers section. Journals for scientists and engineers are listed in Trade in various sections.

ARCHAEOLOGY, Archaeological Institute of America, 135 William St., New York NY 10038. (212)732-5154. Fax: (212)732-5707. Editor-in-Chief: Peter A. Young. 5% freelance written. "We generally commission articles from professional archaeologists." Bimonthly magazine on archaeology. "The only magazine of its kind to bring worldwide archaeology to the attention of the general public." Estab. 1948. Circ. 175,000. Pays on publication. Byline given. Offers 25% kill fee. Buys first North American serial rights. Submit seasonal material 6 months in advance. Accepts simultaneous submissions. Query preferred. Free sample copy and writer's guidelines.

Nonfiction: Essays, general interest. Buys 6 mss/year. Length: 1,000-3,000 words. Pays $750 maximum. Sometimes pays expenses of writers on assignment.

Photos: Send photos with submission.

ASTRONOMY, Kalmbach Publishing, P.O. Box 1612, Waukesha WI 53187-1612. (414)796-8776. Fax: (414)796-1142. E-mail: 72000.2704@compuserve.com. Editor: Robert Burnham. Managing Editor: Rhoda I. Sherwood. 75% freelance written. Monthly magazine covering astronomy—the science and hobby of. "Half of our magazine is for hobbyists (who may have little interest in the heavens in a scientific way); the other half is directed toward armchair astronomers who may be intrigued by the science." Estab. 1973. Circ. 170,000. **Pays on acceptance.** "We are governed by what is happening in the space program and the heavens. It can be up to a year before we publish a manuscript." Byline given. Buys first North American serial, one-time and all rights. Query for electronic submissions. Reports in 1 month on queries; 2 months on mss. Writer's guidelines for SASE.

Nonfiction: Book excerpts, space and astronomy, how-to for astro hobbyists, humor (in the viewpoints column and about astro), new product, photo feature, technical. Buys 100-200 mss/year. Query. Length: 500-4,500 words. Pays $50-500.

Photos: Send photos with submission. Reviews transparencies and prints. Pays $25/photo. Captions, model releases and identification of subjects required.

Tips: "Submitting to *Astronomy* could be tough. (Take a look at how technical astronomy is.) But if someone is a physics teacher (or math or astronomy), he or she might want to study the magazine for a year to see the sorts of subjects and approaches we use and then submit a proposal."

THE ELECTRON, CIE Publishing, 1776 E. 17th St., Cleveland OH 44114-3679. (216)781-9400. Fax: (216)781-0331. Managing Editor: Denise M. Zakrajsek. 80% freelance written. Bimonthly tabloid on electronics and high technology. Estab. 1934. Circ. 25,000. Pays on publication. Publishes ms an average of 2 months after acceptance. Byline given. Buys all rights. Accepts simultaneous queries and previously published submissions. Reports as soon as possible. Sample copy and writer's guidelines for 8½×11 SASE.

Nonfiction: Technical (tutorial and how-to), technology news and feature, photo feature and career/educational. All submissions must be electronics/technology-related. Query with letter/proposal and published clips. Pays $50-500.

Photos: State availability of photos. Reviews 8×10 and 5×7 b&w prints. Captions and identification of subjects required.

Tips: "We would like to receive educational electronics/technical articles. They must be written in a manner understandable to the beginning-intermediate electronics student. We are also seeking news/feature-type articles covering timely developments in high technology."

‡OMNI, Omni International, Ltd., 277 Park Ave., 4th Floor, New York NY 10172-0003. This magazine of science and science fiction has recently moved to an online format, and the print version has become a quarterly. Query before submitting.

POPULAR SCIENCE, 2 Park Ave., New York NY 10016. (212)779-5000. Fax: (212)779-5468. Editor-in-Chief: Fred Abatemarco. Executive Editor: Richard Stepler. 50% freelance written. Prefers to work with published/established writers. Monthly magazine for the well-educated adult, interested in science, technology, new products. Estab. 1872. Circ. 1.8 million. **Pays on acceptance.** Publishes ms an average of 4 months after acceptance. Byline given. Buys first North American serial rights only. Pays negotiable kill fee. Any electronic submission OK. Reports in 4 weeks. Query. Writer's guidelines for #10 SASE.

Nonfiction: "*Popular Science* is devoted to exploring (and explaining) to a nontechnical but knowledgeable readership the technical world around us. We cover all of the sciences, engineering and technology, and above all, products. We are largely a 'thing'-oriented publication: things that fly or travel down a turnpike, or go on or under the sea, or cut wood, or reproduce music, or build buildings, or make pictures. We are especially focused on the new, the ingenious and the useful. Contributors should be as alert to the possibility of selling us pictures and short features as they are to major articles. Freelancers should study the magazine to see what we want and avoid irrelevant submissions." Buys several hundred mss/year. Uses mostly color photos. Pays expenses of writers on assignment.

Tips: "Probably the easiest way to break in here is by covering a news story in science and technology that we haven't heard about yet. We need people to be acting as scouts for us out there and we are willing to give the most leeway on these performances. We are interested in good, sharply focused ideas in all areas we cover. We prefer a vivid, journalistic style of writing, with the writer taking the reader along with him, showing the reader what he saw, through words. Please query first."

SCIENTIFIC AMERICAN, 415 Madison Ave., New York NY 10017. Monthly publication covering developments and topics of interest in the world of science. This magazine did not respond to our request for information. Query before submitting.

21ST CENTURY SCIENCE & TECHNOLOGY, 21st Century Science Associates, P.O. Box 16285, Washington DC 20041. (703)777-7473. Fax: (703)777-8853. Editor: Carol White. Managing Editor: Marjorie Mazel Hecht. 10-20% freelance written. Quarterly magazine that covers frontier science and technology and science history. "We are interested in material that deals with progress." Estab. 1988. Circ. 30,000. Pays on publication. Byline given. Buys one-time rights and makes work-for-hire assignments. Accepts simultaneous and previously published submissions. Send photocopy of article and information about when and where the article previously appeared. Query for electronic submissions. Reports in 6 weeks on queries. Sample copy for 9×12 SAE with 5 first-class stamps.

Nonfiction: Book excerpts, exposé (environmental hoaxes), historical, interview/profile, new product, technical (new scientific research, astronomy, cold fusion, fusion, space exploration, biophysics and advanced nuclear). Buys 5-6 mss/year. Query. Length: 500-6,000 words. Pays up to $100. We supply copies of issue in quantity.

Photos: State availability of photos with submission. Reviews contact sheets, transparencies and prints. Offers $25 minimum/photo. Captions, model releases and identification of subjects required. Buys one-time rights.

Science Fiction, Fantasy and Horror

These publications often publish experimental fiction and many are open to new writers. More information on these markets can be found in the Contests and Awards section under the Fiction heading.

‡**ABERRATIONS**, Sirius Fiction, P.O. Box 460430, San Francisco CA 94146-0430. (415) 777-3909. Editor: Richard Blair. Monthly magazine of science fiction, fantasy, and horror aimed at a mature audience. "We're looking for speculative stories that run the gamut from the pulp-era science fiction, fiction, horror of the 30s and 40s to the experimental and literary work of today." Estab. 1992. Circ. 1,500. Pays on publication. Publishes ms. an average of 1 year after acceptance. Byline given. Buys first English language serial and one-time rights. Submit seasonal material 8 months in advance. Electronic submissions only after acceptance. Reports in 4 months max. Sample copy for $4.50 postpaid. Writer's guidelines for #10 SASE.
Nonfiction: Anything with a science fiction, fiction, horror tie-in. "However, please keep in mind that we're not interested in the paranormal, UFOs, nor are we looking for 'how to write science fiction' pieces." Send complete ms. Length: 3,000 words (query for longer). Pays ¼¢/word.
Poetry: No longer a poetry market.
Fiction: Science fiction, fantasy, and horror. "We use a variety of 'types' of stories within the speculative genres. Whether it's humorous horror or cerebral sci-fi, we want character-driven, plot intensive storylines. From sword and sorcery to space opera to psychological horror, however and whatever your muse is trying to beat out of you send it our way." Buys 120 mss/year. Send complete ms. Length: 8,000 words max. Pays ¼¢/word.
Tips: "While there are still no restrictions on language and subject matter, we're seeking to expand the scope of stories within the magazine, and are therefore no longer looking exclusively for shock or splatter science fiction, fiction, horror fiction. Stories that do possess graphically violent/sexual scenes should have these aspects be crucial to the plot. Under *no* circumstances are we interested in stories dealing with the violent/sexual abuse of children. All that said, we're very open to stories that take chances (whether this be through characterization, plotting, or structuring) as well as those that take more traditional approaches to science fiction, fiction, horror. Both fiction and nonfiction are wide open."

‡**ABSOLUTE MAGNITE, The Magazine of Science Fiction Adventures**, (formerly *Harsh Mistress*), DNA Publications, P.O. Box 13, Greenfield MA 01302. Editor: Warren Lapine. 95% freelance written. Quarterly science fiction magazine covering science fiction short stories. "We specialize in action/adventure science fiction with an emphasis on hard science. Interested in tightly-plotted, character-driven stories." Estab. 1993. Circ. 6,000. Pays on publication. Publishes ms an average of 6 months after acceptance. Byline given. Buys first North American serial rights, first rights and second serial (reprint) rights. Editorial lead time 1 month. Submit seasonal material 6 months in advance. Accepts simultaneous and previously published submissions. Send typed ms with rights for sale noted and information about when and where the article previously appeared. For reprints, pays 33% of the amount paid for an original article. Reports in 2 weeks on queries; 1 month on mss. Sample copy for $5. Writer's guidelines for #10 SASE.
 • This editor is still looking for tightly plotted stories that are character driven. He is now purchasing more short stories than before.
Fiction: Science fiction. Buys 30 mss/year. Send complete ms. Length: 1,000-25,000 words. Pays 3¢/word.
Poetry: Narrative verse. Buys 2 poems/year. Submit maximum 3 poems. 1,000-25,000 words. Pays 1.5¢/word.
Tips: "We are not interested in 'drawer-cleaning' exercises. There is no point in sending less than your best effort if you are interested in a career in writing. Stories between 10,000 and 18,000 words have the best chance of selling to us as we don't buy that many short manuscripts."

ANALOG SCIENCE FICTION & FACT, Dell Magazines Fiction Group, 1540 Broadway, New York NY 10036. Editor: Dr. Stanley Schmidt. 100% freelance written. Eager to work with new/unpublished writers. For general future-minded audience. Monthly. Estab. 1930. Buys first North American serial and nonexclusive foreign serial rights. **Pays on acceptance.** Publishes ms an average of 10 months after acceptance. Byline given. Reports in 1 month. Sample copy for $3 and 6×9 SASE with 5 first-class stamps. Writer's guidelines for #10 SASE.
 • *Analog* has won one Nebula and two Hugo awards.
Nonfiction: Illustrated technical articles dealing with subjects of not only current but future interest, i.e., topics at the present frontiers of research whose likely future developments have implications of wide interest. Buys about 13 mss/year. Query. Length: 5,000 words. Pays 6¢/word.
Fiction: "Basically, we publish science fiction stories. That is, stories in which some aspect of future science or technology is so integral to the plot that, if that aspect were removed, the story would collapse. The science can be physical, sociological or psychological. The technology can be anything from electronic engineering to biogenetic engineering. But the stories must be strong and realistic, with believable people doing believable things—no matter how fantastic the background might be." Buys 60-100 unsolicited mss/year. Send complete

ms of short fiction; query about serials. "We don't publish novel excerpts as such, though we occasionally do one that can stand on its own as an independent story." Length: 2,000-80,000 words. Pays 4¢/word for novels; 5-6¢/word for novelettes; 6-8¢/word for shorts under 7,500 words; $450-600 for intermediate lengths.

Tips: "In query give clear indication of central ideas and themes and general nature of story line—and what is distinctive or unusual about it. We have no hard-and-fast editorial guidelines, because science fiction is such a broad field that I don't want to inhibit a new writer's thinking by imposing 'Thou Shalt Not's.' Besides, a really good story can make an editor swallow his preconceived taboos. I want the best work I can get, regardless of who wrote it—and I need new writers. So I work closely with new writers who show definite promise, but of course it's impossible to do this with *every* new writer. No occult or fantasy."

ASIMOV'S SCIENCE FICTION, Dell Magazines Fiction Group, 1540 Broadway, New York NY 10036. (212)856-6400. Fax: (212)782-8309 (for correspondence only, no submissions). E-mail: 71154.662@compuserve.com. Editor: Gardner Dozois. Executive Editor: Sheila Williams. 98% freelance written. Works with a small number of new/unpublished writers each year. Published 13 times a year, including 2 double issues. Estab. 1977. Circ. 100,000. **Pays on acceptance.** Buys first North American serial and nonexclusive foreign serial rights; reprint rights occasionally. No simultaneous submissions. Reports in 2 months. Sample copy for $3 and 6½×9½ SAE. Writer's guidelines for #10 SASE.
 • This publication has won Hugo, Nebula and *Locus* Awards.
Nonfiction: No longer uses freelance nonfiction.
Fiction: Science fiction primarily. Some fantasy and poetry. "It's best to read a great deal of material in the genre to avoid the use of some *very* old ideas." Buys 10 mss/issue. Submit complete ms and SASE with *all* submissions. Length: 100-20,000 words. Pays 5-8¢/word except for novel serializations at 4¢/word.
Tips: "We prefer stories which contain good character development."

MARION ZIMMER BRADLEY'S FANTASY MAGAZINE, P.O. Box 249, Berkeley CA 94701-0249. Editor: Mrs. Marion Z. Bradley. 100% freelance written. Quarterly magazine of fantasy fiction. Estab. 1988. **Pays on acceptance.** Publishes ms an average of 1 year after acceptance. Byline given. Buys first North American serial rights. Reports in 3 months. Sample copy for $4.
Fiction: Fantasy. No science fiction, very little horror. Buys 55-60 mss/year. Send complete ms. Length: 300-7,500 words. Pays 3-10¢/word.
Tips: "Do not submit without first reading guidelines."

‡CENTURY, Century Publishing, Inc., P.O. Box 150510, Brooklyn NY 11215. Editor: Robert K.J. Killheffer. 100% freelance written. Bimonthly 6×9 magazine covering speculative fiction (science fiction, fantasy, horror). "We're looking for speculative fiction with a high degree of literary accomplishment—ambitious work which can appeal not only to the genre's regular audience but to readers outside the genre as well." Estab. 1994. Circ. 5,000. **Pays on acceptance.** Publishes ms an average of 6 months after acceptance. Byline given. Buys first world English rights, non-exclusive reprint rights. Reports in 3 months on mss. Sample copy for $5.95. Writer's guidelines for #10 SASE.
Fiction: Experimental, fantasy, horror, science fiction. Buys 65 mss/year. Send complete ms. Length: 1,000-20,000 words. Pays 4-6¢/word.

DEAD OF NIGHT MAGAZINE, Dead of Night Publications, 916 Shaker Rd., Suite 228, Longmeadow MA 01106-2416. Editor: Lin Stein. 90% freelance written. Quarterly magazine (July/October/January/April). "Our readers enjoy horror, mystery, fantasy and sci-fi, and they also don't mind an 'old-fashioned' vampire or ghost story on occasion. Because of the genre mix in our magazine, we appeal to a wide readership." Estab. 1989. Circ. 3,200. Pays on publication. Publishes ms an average of 6-12 months after acceptance. Byline given. Offers 10% kill fee. Buys 1st North American serial rights or one-time rights. Editorial lead time 3 months. Submit seasonal material 6 months in advance. Reports in 3 weeks on queries; 2 months on mss. Sample copy for $5 (current issue); $2.50 (back issue subject to availability). Writer's guidelines for #10 SASE.
Nonfiction: Book excerpts, interview/profile, book/film reviews. Buys 8-10 mss/year. Send complete ms. Length: 350-2,800 words. Pays 2¢/word minimum.
Fiction: Fantasy, horror, mystery, novel excerpts, science fiction. Nothing non-genre. Buys 7-15 mss/year. Send complete ms. Length: 500-3,000 words (occasionally longer, to 4,200 words). Pays 4-7¢/word. Publishes novel excerpts.
Poetry: Used occasionally. Pays $7/poem.
Tips: "We are most open to fiction. (Most of our reviews are written by our contributing editors—on a regular basis, but freelancers may query.) For tips or hints, the best, of course, is to read the magazine! The second best is to at least read our guidelines, and the last tip is to try to present us with a horror/mystery/fantasy or science fiction story that is fresh, original, and entertaining. If the story entertains the editors here, we'll buy it so our *readers* can enjoy it and be entertained by it as well."

HOBSON'S CHOICE, The Starwind Press, P.O. Box 98, Ripley OH 45167-0098. (513)392-4549. Editors: David F. Powell and Susannah C. West. Contact: Susannah C. West. 75% freelance written. Eager to work with new/unpublished writers. Bimonthly magazine "for older teenagers and adults who have an interest in science and technology, and who also enjoy reading well-crafted science fiction and fantasy." Estab. 1974. Circ. 2,500. Pays on publication. Publishes ms an average of 1 year after acceptance. Byline given. Rights vary with author and material; negotiated with author. Usually first serial rights and second serial reprint rights (nonfiction). Query for electronic submissions. "We encourage disposable submissions; easier for us and easier for the author. Just enclose SASE for our response." Accepts previously published submissions. Send photocopy of article or short story and information about when and where material previously appeared. Pays 30% of amount paid for an original article." We prefer non-simultaneous submissions." Reports in 3 months. Sample copy $2.25 for 9×12 SAE. Writer's guidelines for #10 SASE. "Tipsheet package for $1.50; contains all guidelines, tipsheets on science fiction writing, nonfiction science writing and submission etiquette."

  • *Hobson's Choice* is often overstocked with fiction; their needs for nonfiction are greater than for fiction.

Nonfiction: How-to (technological interest, e.g., how to build a robot eye, building your own radio receiver, etc.), interview/profile (of leaders in science and technology fields), technical ("did you know" articles dealing with development of current technology). "No speculative articles, dealing with topics such as the Abominable Snowman, Bermuda Triangle, etc. Query. Length: 1,000-7,000 words. Pays 1-4¢/word.

Photos: Send photos with accompanying query or ms. Reviews b&w contact sheets and prints. Model releases and identification of subjects required. "If photos are available, we prefer to purchase them as part of the written piece." Buys negotiable rights.

Fiction: Fantasy, science fiction. "No stories whose characters were created by others (e.g. Lovecraft, *Star Trek*, *Star Wars* characters, etc.)." Buys 15-20 mss/year. Send complete ms. Length: 2,000-10,000 words. Pays 1-4¢/word. "We prefer previously unpublished fiction. No query necessary. We don't publish horror, poetry, novel excerpts or serialized novels."

Tips: "Our need for nonfiction is greater than for fiction at present. Almost all our fiction and nonfiction is unsolicited. We rarely ask for rewrites, because we've found that rewrites are often disappointing; although the writer may have rewritten it to fix problems, he/she frequently changes parts we liked, too."

‡**PULPHOUSE**, Pulphouse Publishing Inc., Box 1227, Eugene OR 97442. Editor: Dean Wesley Smith. All freelance written. Quarterly magazine covering science fiction, fantasy, mystery, horror and mainstream fiction short stories. Estab. 1987. Circ. 10,000. Pays after return of contract. Publishes ms an average of 1 year after acceptance. Byline given. Buys first North American serial rights. Editorial lead time 1 year. Submit seasonal material 1 year in advance. Reports in 2 months on mss. Sample copy for $4.95. Writer's guidelies for #10 SASE.

Photos: Photos for covers. Send photos with submission.

Fiction: Adventure, erotica, experimental, fantasy, historical, horror, humorous, mainstream, mystery, romance, science fiction, slice-of-life vignettes, suspense, western. Buys 50 mss/year. Send complete ms. Length: 50-7,000 words. Pays 4-7¢/word.

Poetry: Avant-garde, free verse, haiku, light verse, traditional. Buys 20/year. Submit maximum 3 poems. Length: 5-50 lines. Pays $10-50.

Tips: Include a SASE.

‡**REALMS OF FANTASY**, Sovereign Media, P.O. Box 527, Rumson NJ 07760. Editor: Shawna McCarthy. 100% freelance written. Bimonthly magazine covering heroic, contemporary, traditional, feminist, dark, light and unclassifiable fantasy. Estab. 1994. Circ. 53,000. **Pays on acceptance**, 30 days after contract. Publishes ms an average of 3 months after acceptance. Byline given. Offers 20% kill fee. Buys first world rights. Editorial lead time 2 months. Submit seasonal material 3 months in advance. Accepts simultaneous and previously published submissions. Reports in 2 months. Sample copy for $4.50. Writer's guidelines for #10 SASE.

Nonfiction: Interview/profile, new product (games), book reviews. Buys 24 mss/year. Query with published clips. Length: 2,500. Pays $150-300. Sometimes pays expenses of writers on assignment.

Photos: State availability of photos with submission. Reviews contact sheets. Offers no additional payment for photos accepted with ms. Identification of subjects required. Buys one-time rights.

Columns/Departments: Book Reviews (newest fantasy book review), 200-2,500 words; Games (newest fantasy games), 200-2,500 words. Buys 12 mss/year. Query with published clips. Pays $50-200.

Fiction: Adventure, fantasy. Buys 36 mss/year. Send complete ms. Length: 600-10,000 words. Pays 3-5¢/word.

‡**SCIENCE FICTION AGE**, Sovereign Media, P.O. Box 369, Damascus MD 20872-0369. Editor: Scott Edelman. 100% freelance written. Bimonthly magazine. Hard, soft science fiction, new wave, old guard, magic, cyberpunk, literary science fiction. Estab. 1992. Circ. 68,000. **Pays on acceptance.** Publishes ms an average of 4 months after acceptance. Byline given. Offers 10% kill fee. Buys first North American serial rights, with an option on first world rights. Editorial lead time 3 months. Submit seasonal material 3 months in advance. Reports in 2 months. Sample copy for $5. Writer's guidelines for #10 SASE.

Nonfiction: Essays, interview/profile, new product, opinion. Buys 24 mss/year. Query with published clips. Length: 200-2,500 words. Pays 3-5¢/word. Sometimes pays expenses of writers on assignment.
Photos: State availability of photos with submission. Reviews contact sheets. Offers no additional payment for photos accepted with ms. Identification of subjects required. Buys one-time rights.
Columns/Departments: Book Reviews, 800-1,200 words; Game Reviews, 1,750 words; Comics Review, 300 words; Essay, 2,000 words. Science, 2,500 words. Buys 30 mss/year. Query with published clips. Pays 3-5¢/word.
Fiction: Fantasy, science fiction. Buys 42 mss/year. Send complete ms. Length: 1,000-21,000 words. Pays 5-8¢/word.

THE SCREAM FACTORY, The Magazine of Horrors, Past, Present, and Future, Deadline Press, P.O. Box 2808, Apache Junction AZ 85217. Editors: Peter Enfantino, Bob Morrish and John Scoleri. Contact: Peter Enfantino. 75% freelance written. Quarterly literary magazine about horror in films and literature. Estab. 1988. Circ. 2,500. Pays on publication. Publishes ms an average of 6 months after acceptance. Buys first North American serial rights. Submit seasonal material 6 months in advance. No simultaneous submissions or reprints. Reports in 2 weeks on queries, 1 month on ms. Sample copy for $7 (please make checks payable to *The Scream Factory*). Writer's guidelines for #10 SASE.
 • Does *not* accept fiction.
Nonfiction: Essays, historical/nostalgic, interview/profile, new product, personal experience. Buys 35-50 mss/year. Query or send complete ms. Pays ½¢/word.
Photos: Send photos with submission. Reviews prints. Offers no additional payment for photos accepted with ms. Captions required. Buys one-time rights.
Columns/Departments: Book reviews of horror novels/collections; Writer's Writing (what horror authors are currently working on).
Fillers: Facts, newsbreaks. Pays ½¢/word. Also small reviews (150-200 words). "Please query on these."
Tips: "Looking for reviews of horror fiction, especially the lesser known authors. News on the horror genre, interviews with horror authors and strong opinion pieces. No unsolicited fiction accepted."

THE SILVER WEB, A Magazine of the Surreal, Buzzcity Press, P.O. Box 38190, Tallahassee FL 32315. (904)385-8948. Publisher/Editor: Ann Kennedy. 100% freelance written. Semiannual literary magazine that features science fiction, dark fantasy and horror. Estab. 1988. Circ. 1,000. **Pays on acceptance.** Byline given. Buys first North American serial, or one-time or second serial (reprint) rights. Accepts simultaneous and previously published submissions. Send information before submitting ms about when and where material previously appeared. For reprints, pays standard rate. Reports in 2 months. Query for electronic submissions. Sample copy for $5.95. Writer's guidelines for #10 SASE.
 • *The Silver Webb* payment rates have gone up. The editor is looking for well-written character-driven plots that are unique, original and strange, preferably surreal.
Nonfiction: Essays, interview/profile, opinion. Buys 4-8 mss/year. Query. Length: 500-8,000 words. Pays 2-3¢/word.
Photos: State availability of photos with submission. Reviews prints. Offers no additional payment for photos accepted with ms. Identification of subjects required. Buys one-time rights.
Fiction: Experimental, horror, science fiction. "We do not want to see typical storylines, endings or predictable revenge stories." Buys 20-25 mss/year. Send complete ms. Length: 500-8,000 words. Pays 2-3¢/word. Publishes novel excerpts but query first.
Poetry: Avant-garde, free verse, haiku. Buys 10-15/year. Submit maximum 5 poems. Pays $5-20.
Fillers: Art fillers. Buys 10/year. Pays $2-5.
Tips: "Give us an unusual unpredictable story with strong, believable characters that we can care about. Surprise us with something unique. We do look for interviews with people in the field (writers, artists, filmmakers)."

‡SPACE AND TIME, 138 W. 70th St., 4B, New York NY 10023-4468. Editor-in-chief: Gordon Linzner. 100% freelance written. Biannual magazine of science fiction and fantasy. "We feature a mix of fiction and poetry in all aspects of the fantasy genre—science fiction, supernatural horror, sword & sorcery, mixed genre, unclassifiable. Its variety makes it stand out from more narrowly focused magazines. Our readers enjoy quality material that surprises and provokes." Estab. 1966. Circ. 2,000. **Pays on acceptance.** Publishes ms an average of 6 months after acceptance. Byline given. Buys first North American serial rights. Editorial lead time 6 months. Query for electronic submissions. Reports in 1 month on mss. Sample copy $5 plus $1.25 handling charge. Writer's guidelines for #10 SASE.
Nonfiction: Essays on fantasy, science fiction, science, etc. "No so-called 'true' paranormal." Buys 1-2 mss/year. Send complete ms. Length: 1,000 words maximum. Pays 1¢/word plus 2 contributor copies.
Photos/Artwork: Claudia Carlson, art editor. Artwork (could include photos). Send nonreturnable photocopies. Reviews prints. Pays $10 for interior illustration, $25 for cover, plus 2 contributor copies. Model releases required. Buys one-time rights.
Fiction: Tom Piccirilli, fiction editor. Fantasy, horror, science fiction, mixed genre (i.e., science-fiction-mystery, western-horror, etc.) and unclassifiable; "anything that falls outside of fantasy/science fiction (but

that leaves a lot)." Buys 15-20 mss/year. Send complete ms. Length: 10,000 words maximum. Pays 1¢/word plus 2 contributor copies.

Poetry: Lawrence Greenberg, poetry editor. Avant-garde, free verse, haiku, light verse, traditional; "anything that cannot conceivably fit into fantasy/science fiction/horror." Buys 10-15 poems/year. Submit maximum 3 poems. Length: no limits. Pays 1¢/word ($5 minimum) plus 2 contributor copies.

Tips: "Avoid cliches and standard plots unless you have something new to add."

STARLOG MAGAZINE, The Science Fiction Universe, Starlog Group, 475 Park Ave. S., 8th Floor, New York NY 10016-1689. (212)689-2830. Fax: (212)889-7933. Editor: David McDonnell. 90% freelance written. Eager to work with new/unpublished writers. Monthly magazine covering "the science fiction-fantasy genre: its films, TV, books, art and personalities." Estab. 1976. "We concentrate on interviews with actors, directors, writers, producers, special effects technicians and others. Be aware that 'sci-fi' and 'Trekkie' are seen as derogatory terms by our readers and by us." Pays on publication. Publishes ms an average of 4 months after acceptance. Byline given. Offers kill fee "only to manuscripts *written* or interviews *done for us*." Buys all rights. No simultaneous submissions. Reports in 6 weeks. "We provide an assignment sheet and contract to *all* writers with deadline and other info, authorizing a queried piece." Sample copy for $5. Writer's guidelines for #10 SASE.

Nonfiction: Interview/profile (actors, directors, screenwriters who've made science fiction films and science fiction novelists); photo features; retrospectives of famous science fiction films and TV series; coverage of science fiction fandom, etc. "We also sometimes cover science fiction/fantasy animation and comics." No personal opinion think pieces/essays. *No* first person. Avoids articles on horror films/creators. "We prefer article format as opposed to Q&A interviews." Buys 175 mss/year. Query first with published clips. "We accept queries by mail *only*, by fax if there's a critical time factor. No phone calls. Ever! Unsolicited phone calls *cannot* be returned." Length: 500-3,000 words. Pays $35 (500-word pieces); $50-75 (sidebars); $125-250 (1,000-word plus pieces).

Photos: State availability of photos. Pays $10-25 for slide transparencies and $8×10 b&w prints depending on quality. "No separate payment for photos provided by film studios." Captions, model releases, identification of subjects and credit line on photos required. Photo credit given. Buys all rights.

Columns/Departments: Fanlog (articles on fandom and its aspects—mostly staff-written); Booklog (book reviews, $15 each, by assignment only); Medialog (news of upcoming science fiction films and TV projects); Videolog (videocassette and disk releases of genre interest, staff-written); Gamelog (video, computer, role-playing games). Buys 80-100 reviews/year. Query with published clips. Book review, 200 words maximum; multi-article, 300-500 words. No kill fee.

Tips: "Absolutely *no fiction*. We do *not* publish it and we throw away fiction manuscripts from writers who also *can't* be bothered to include SASES. Nonfiction only please! A writer can best break in to *Starlog* by getting an unusual interview or by *out-thinking* us and coming up with something *new* on a current film or book. We are always looking for *new* angles on *Star Trek: The Next Generation, Voyager, Deep Space Nine, Star Wars*, the original *Star Trek, Doctor Who* and seeking features on such series as *Starman, Beauty & the Beast, Lost in Space, Space: 1999, Battlestar Galactica, The Twilight Zone, The Outer Limits*. Know your subject before you try us. Most full-length major assignments go to freelancers with whom we're already dealing. But if we like your clips and ideas, we'll be happy to give *you* a chance. We are looking for new freelancers who act professional—and they are *harder* to find. If a letter isn't good enough to pitch your story, we don't *need* that story. I'd rather see how you write (in a letter), than listen to your chit-chatty powers of persuasion on the phone."

2 AM MAGAZINE, P.O. Box 6754, Rockford IL 61125-1754. E-mail: p.anderson21@genie.geis.com. Editor: Gretta M. Anderson. 95% freelance written. Quarterly magazine of fiction, poetry, articles and art for readers of fantasy, horror and science fiction. Estab. 1986. Circ. 2,000. **Pays on acceptance.** Publishes ms an average of 9 months after acceptance. Byline given. Buys first North American serial rights. Submit seasonal material 1 year in advance. Reports in 1 month on queries; 3 months on mss. Sample copy for $5.95. Writer's guidelines for #10 SASE.

Nonfiction: How-to, interview/profile, opinion, also book reviews of horror, fantasy or SF recent releases. "No essays originally written for high school or college courses." Buys 5 mss/year. Query with or without published clips or send complete ms. Length: 500-2,000 words. Pay ½-1¢/word.

Photos: State availability of photos with submission. Offers no additional payment for photos accepted with ms. Identification of subjects required. Buys one-time rights.

Fiction: Fantasy, horror, mystery, science fiction, suspense. Buys 50 mss/year. Send complete ms. Length: 500-5,000 words. Pays ½-1¢/word.

Poetry: Free verse, traditional. "No haiku/zen or short poems without imagery." Buys 20 poems/year. Submit up to 5 poems at one time. Length: 5-100 lines. Pays $1-5.

Tips: "We are looking for taut, imaginative fiction. We need more reviews of horror novels. Please use proper manuscript format; all manuscripts must include a SASE to be considered. We suggest to Canadian and foreign writers that they send disposable manuscripts with one IRC and #10 SAE for response, if US postage stamps are unavailable to them."

‡**THE URBANITE, Surreal & Lively & Bizarre**, Urban Legend Press, P.O. Box 4737, Davenport IA 52808. Editor: Mark McLaughlin. 95% freelance written. Triannual magazine covering surreal fiction and poetry. "We look for quality fiction in an urban setting with a surrealistic tone. . . We prefer character-driven storylines. Our audience is urbane, culture-oriented, and hard to please!" Estab. 1991. Circ. 500. **Pays on acceptance.** Publishes ms an average of 6 months after acceptance. Byline given. Offers 100% kill fee. Buys first North American serial rights and non-exclusive rights for public readings (we hold readings of the magazine at various venues—like libraries). Accepts previously published submissions (but query first). Reports in 1 month on queries; 3-5 months on mss. Sample copy for $5. Writer's guidelines for #10 SASE.
Fiction: Experimental, fantasy (contemporary), slipstream/cross genre, horror, humorous, science fiction (but not "high-tech"), surrealism of all sorts. Buys 45 mss/year. Send complete ms. Length: 500-3,000 words. Pays $10-60 (2¢/word).
Poetry: Avant-garde, free verse, traditional, narrative poetry. Buys 15 poems/year. Submit maximum 3 poems. No length limits. Pays $10/poem.
Tips: "Writers should familiarize themselves with surrealism in literature: too often, we receive stories filled with genre clichés. Also: we prefer character-driven stories."

Sports

A variety of sports magazines, from general interest to sports medicine, are covered in this section. For the convenience of writers who specialize in one or two areas of sport and outdoor writing, the publications are subcategorized by the sport or subject matter they emphasize. Publications in related categories (for example, Hunting and Fishing; Archery and Bowhunting) often buy similar material. Writers should read through this entire section to become familiar with the subcategories. Publications on horse breeding and hunting dogs are classified in the Animal section, while horse racing is listed here. Publications dealing with automobile or motorcycle racing can be found in the Automotive and Motorcycle category. Markets interested in articles on exercise and fitness are listed in the Health and Fitness section. Outdoor publications that promote the preservation of nature, placing only secondary emphasis on nature as a setting for sport, are in the Nature, Conservation and Ecology category. Regional magazines are frequently interested in sports material with a local angle. Camping publications are classified in the Travel, Camping and Trailer category.

Archery and Bowhunting

‡**AMERICAN BOWHUNTER MAGAZINE**, (formerly *International Bowhunter Magazine*), P.O. Box 67, Pillager MN 56473-0067. (218)746-3333. Fax: (218)746-3307. Editor: Johnny E. Boatner. 95% freelance written. Bimonthly magazine on bowhunting. "We are interested in any kind of articles that deal with bowhunting. We pride ourselves as a magazine written by hunter/writers, rather than writer/hunters. We are not interested in articles that just fill pages, we like each paragraph to say something." Estab. 1982. Circ. 65,000. Pays on publication. Publishes ms an average of 6 months after acceptance. Byline sometimes given. Buys first rights. Submit seasonal/holiday material 4 months in advance. Reports in 2 months. Free sample copy and writer's guidelines.
Nonfiction: Historical/nostalgic, how-to, humor, interview/profile, new product, personal experience, photo feature, technical and travel; all bowhunting and archery related. "No commercials of writers' pet products; no articles including bad ethics or gore, target archery." Buys 75 mss/year. Send complete ms. Length: 600-3,500 words. Pays $25 minimum for assigned articles; $25-250 for unsolicited articles. Sometimes pays in contributor copies or other premiums. Sometimes pays expenses of writers on assignments.
Photos: Send photos with submission. Reviews transparencies and prints. Don't send slides. Offers no additional payment for photos accepted with ms. Captions and identification of subjects required. Buys one-time rights.

Market conditions are constantly changing! If this is 1997 or later, buy the newest edition of Writer's Market *at your favorite bookstore or order directly from* Writer's Digest Books.

Fiction: Adventure (bowhunting related) and historical (bowhunting), novel excerpts. Send complete ms. Length: 600-3,500 words. Pays $25-250.

Fillers: Anecdotes, facts, gags to be illustrated by cartoonist, newsbreaks and short humor. Buys 10/year. Length: 100-500 words. Pays $10-50.

Tips: "We do mainly first person accounts as long as they relate to hunting with the bow and arrow. If you have a bowhunting story you want to tell, then type it up and send it in. We publish more first time writers than any other bowhunting magazine. Keep the articles clean, entertaining and informative. We do a few how-tos, but mainly want articles about bowhunting and the great outdoors that relate to bowhunting."

BOWHUNTER, The Number One Bowhunting Magazine, Cowles Magazines, 6405 Flank Dr., Harrisburg PA 17112-8200. (717)657-9555. Fax: (717)657-9552. Editor/Founder: M.R. James. Publisher/Editorial Director: David Canfield. Contact: Richard Cochran, Managing Editor. 85% freelance written. Bimonthly magazine (with two special issues) on hunting big and small game with bow and arrow. "We are a special interest publication, produced by bowhunters for bowhunters, covering all aspects of the sport. Material included in each issue is designed to entertain and inform readers, making them better bowhunters." Estab. 1971. Circ. 180,000. **Pays on acceptance.** Publishes ms an average of 10-12 months after acceptance. Byline given. Kill fee varies. Buys first North American serial and one-time rights. Submit seasonal material 8 months in advance. Reports in 1 month on queries; 5 weeks on mss. *Writer's Market* recommends allowing 2 months for reply. Sample copy for $2. Free writer's guidelines.

Nonfiction: General interest, how-to, interview/profile, opinion, personal experience, photo feature. "We publish a special 'Big Game' issue each Fall (September) but need all material by mid-March. Our other annual publication, *Whitetail Bowhunter*, is staff written or by assignment only. We don't want articles that graphically deal with an animal's death. And, please, no articles written from the animal's viewpoint." Buys 100 plus mss/year. Query. Length: 250-2,000 words. Pays $500 maximum for assigned articles; $75-500 for unsolicited articles. Sometimes pays expenses of writers on assignment.

Photos: Send photos with submission. Reviews 35mm and 2¼×2¼ transparencies and 5×7 and 8×10 prints. Offers $50-250/photo. Captions required. Buys one-time rights.

Tips: "A writer must know bowhunting and be willing to share that knowledge. Writers should anticipate *all* questions a reader might ask, then answer them in the article itself or in an appropriate sidebar. Articles should be written with the reader foremost in mind; we won't be impressed by writers seeking to prove how good they are—either as writers or bowhunters. We care about the reader and don't need writers with 'I' trouble. Features are a good bet because most of our material comes from freelancers. The best advice is: Be yourself. Tell your story the same as if sharing the experience around a campfire. Don't try to write like you think a writer writes."

PETERSEN'S BOWHUNTING, Petersen Publishing Company, 6420 Wilshire Blvd., Los Angeles CA 90048-5515. (213)782-2000. Editor: Greg Tinsley. 70% freelance written. Magazine published 8 times/year covering bowhunting. "Very equipment oriented. Our readers are 'superenthusiasts,' therefore our writers must have an advanced knowledge of hunting archery." Circ. 115,000. **Pays on acceptance.** Byline given. Buys all rights. Editorial lead time 6 months. Submit seasonal material 6 months in advance. Query for electronic submissions. Reports in 1 month. Sample copy for #10 SASE. Writer's guidelines free on request.

Nonfiction: How-to, humor, interview/profile, new product, opinion, personal experience, photo feature. Buys 40 mss/year. Send complete ms. Length: 2,000-2,500 words. Pays $300. Sometimes pays expenses of writers on assignment.

Photos: Send photos with submission. Reviews contact sheets, 35mm transparencies, 5×7 prings. Offers $35-250/photo. Captions and model releases required. Buys one-time rights.

Columns/Departments: Query. Pays $200-300.

Fillers: Facts, newsbreaks. Buys 12/year. Length: 150-400 words. Pays $25-75.

Tips: Feature articles must be supplied to *Petersen's Bowhunting* in either 5.25 IBM (or compatible) or 3.50 MacIntosh floppy disks.

Baseball and Softball

USA SOFTBALL MAGAZINE, (formerly *Balls and Strikes*), Amateur Softball Association, 2801 NE 50th St., Oklahoma City OK 73111. (405)424-5266. Fax: (405)424-3855. 20% freelance written. Works with a small number of new/unpublished writers each year. "Only national bimonthly magazine covering amateur softball." Circ. 300,000. Pays on publication. Publishes ms an average of 2 months after acceptance. Buys first rights. Byline given. Reports in 3 weeks. Sample copy for SASE.

Nonfiction: General interest, historical/nostalgic, interview/profile, technical. Query. Length: 2-3 pages. Pays $100-200.

Photos: Pays $50.
Tips: "We generally like shorter features because we try to get as many different features as possible in each issue."

Bicycling

ADVENTURE CYCLIST, Adventure Cycling Assn., Box 8308, Missoula MT 59807. (406)721-1776. Fax: (406)721-8754. Editor: Daniel D'Ambrosio. 75% freelance written. Bicycle touring magazine for Adventure Cycling members published 9 times yearly. Circ. 30,000. Pays on publication. Byline given. Include short bio with manuscript. Buys first serial rights. Submit seasonal/holiday material 3 months in advance. Query for electronic submissions. Sample copy and guidelines for 9×12 SAE with 4 first-class stamps.
Nonfiction: Historical/nostalgic; how-to; humor; interview/profile; personal experience ("my favorite tour"); photo feature; technical; and travel. Buys 20-25 mss/year. Query with published clips or send complete ms. Length: 800-2,500 words. Pay negotiable.
Photos: Bicycle, scenery and portraits. State availability of photos. Model releases and identification of subjects required.
Fiction: Adventure, experimental, historical and humorous. Not interested in anything that doesn't involve bicycles. Query with published clips or send complete ms. Length: 800-2,500 words. Pay negotiable.

BICYCLING, Rodale Press, Inc., 33 E. Minor St., Emmaus PA 18098. (610)967-5171. Fax: (610)967-8960. Editor and Publisher: James C. McCullagh. Managing Editor: Bill Strickland. 20-25% freelance written. Prefers to work with published/established writers. Publishes 11 issues/year (10 monthly, 1 bimonthly); 96-188 pages. Estab. 1961. Circ. 360,000. **Pays on acceptance**. Byline given. Buys all rights. Submit seasonal/holiday material 6 months in advance. Query for electronic submissions. Reports in 2 months. Sample copy for $2.50. Writer's guidelines for #10 SASE.
Nonfiction: How-to (on all phases of bicycle touring, repair, maintenance, commuting, new products, clothing, riding technique, nutrition for cyclists, conditioning); fitness is more important than ever; also travel (bicycling must be central here); photo feature (on cycling events of national significance); and technical (component review—query). "We are strictly a bicycling magazine. We seek readable, clear, well-informed pieces. We rarely run articles that are pure humor or inspiration but a little of either might flavor even our most technical pieces. No poetry or fiction." Buys 1-2 unsolicited mss/issue. Send complete ms. Length: 1,500 words average. Pays $25-1,200. Sometimes pays expenses of writers on assignment.
Photos: State availability of photos with query letter or send photo material with ms. Pays $15-50 for b&w prints and $35-250 for transparencies. Captions preferred; model release required.
Fillers: Anecdotes and news items for Paceline section.
Tips: "We're alway seeking interesting accounts of cycling as a lifestyle."

CRANKMAIL, Cycling in Northern Ohio, P.O. Box 110236, Cleveland OH 44111-0236. Editor: James Guilford. Magazine published 10 times/year covering bicycling in all aspects. "Our publication serves the interests of bicycle enthusiasts . . . established, accomplished adult cyclists. These individuals are interested in reading about the sport of cycling, bicycles as transportation, ecological tie-ins, sports nutrition, the history and future of bicycles and bicycling." Estab. 1977. Circ. 1,000. Pays on publication. Byline given. Publication not copyrighted. Buys one-time or second serial (reprint) rights. Editorial lead time 1 month. Submit seasonal material 3 months in advance. Accepts previously published submissions. Sample copy for $1. Writer's guidelines for #10 SASE.
Nonfiction: Essays, historical/nostalgic, how-to, humor, interview/profile, new product, personal experience, technical. "No articles encouraging folks to start or get involved in bicycling—our readers are already cyclists." Send complete ms. "Don't query." Length: 2,500 words maximum. Pays $10 minimum for unsolicited articles.
Fillers: Cartoons. Pays $5-10.

CYCLING USA, The Official Publication of the U.S. Cycling Federation, One Olympic Plaza, Colorado Springs CO 80909. (719)578-4581. Fax: (719)578-4596. E-mail: usacycling@aol.com. Editor: Jason Anderson. 50% freelance written. Monthly magazine covering reportage and commentary on American bicycle racing, personalities and sports physiology, for USCF licensed cyclists. Circ. 35,000. Pays on publication. Publishes ms an average of 2 months after acceptance. Byline given. Accepts simultaneous queries and previously published submissions. Send photocopy of article. For reprints, pays 100% of the amount paid for an original article. Reports in 2 weeks. Sample copy for 10×12 SAE with 2 first-class stamps.
  • *Cycling USA* is looking for longer, more in-depth features (1,000-1,500 words).
Nonfiction: How-to (train, prepare for a bike race), interview/profile, opinion, personal experience, photo feature, technical and race commentary on major cycling events. No comparative product evaluations. Buys 15 mss/year. Query with published clips. Length: 800-1,200 words. Pays 15¢/word.
Photos: State availability of photos. Pays $15-50 for 5×7 b&w prints; $100 for transparencies used as cover. Captions required. Buys one-time rights.

Tips: "A background in bicycle racing is important because the sport is somewhat insular, technical and complex. Most major articles are generated inhouse. Race reports are most open to freelancers. Be concise, informative and anecdotal. Our format is more compatible with 800-1,200 word articles than longer features."

VELONEWS, The Journal of Competitive Cycling, 1830 55th St., Boulder CO 80301-2700. (303)440-0601. Fax: (303)444-6788. Managing Editor: Tim Johnson. 60% freelance written. Monthly tabloid September-February, biweekly March-August covering bicycle racing. Estab. 1972. Circ. 48,000. Pays on publication. Publishes ms an average of 1 month after acceptance. Byline given. Buys one-time rights. Accepts simultaneous submissions. Query for electronic submissions. Reports in 3 weeks. Sample copy for 9×12 SAE with 7 first-class stamps.
Nonfiction: In addition to race coverage, opportunities for freelancers include reviews (book and videos) and health-and-fitness departments. Buys 100 mss/year. Query. Length: 300-1,200 words. Pays 10¢/word minimum.
Photos: State availability of photos. Pays $16.50-50 for b&w prints. Pays $150 for color used on cover. Captions and identification of subjects required. Buys one-time rights.

Boating

BOAT PENNSYLVANIA, Pennsylvania Fish and Boat Commission, P.O. Box 67000, Harrisburg PA 17106-7000. (717)657-4518. Editor: Art Michaels. 80% freelance written. Quarterly magazine covering motorboating, sailing, canoeing, water skiing, kayaking and rafting in Pennsylvania. Prefers to work with published/established contributors, but works with a few unpublished writers and photographers every year. Pays 2 months after acceptance. Publishes ms an average of 8 months after acceptance. Byline given. Buys variable rights. Submit seasonal/holiday material 8 months in advance. Prefers electronic or diskette submission. Reports in 2 weeks on queries; 2 months on mss. Sample copy for 9×12 SAE with 4 first-class stamps. Writer's guidelines for #10 SASE.
Nonfiction: How-to, technical, historical/nostalgic, all related to water sports in Pennsylvania. No fishing material. Buys 40 mss/year. Query. Length: 300-3,000 words. Pays $25-300.
Photos: Send photos with submission. Also reviews photos separately. Rights purchased and rates vary. Reviews 35mm and larger color transparencies and 8×10 b&w prints. Captions, model releases, identification of subjects required.

CANOE & KAYAK MAGAZINE, Canoe Associates, P.O. Box 3146, Kirkland WA 98083. (206)827-6363. Fax: (206)827-1893. Editor: Nancy Harrison Hill. Managing Editor: Dennis Stuhaug. 80-90% freelance written. Bimonthly magazine on canoeing, whitewater kayaking and sea kayaking. Estab. 1972. Circ. 80,000. Pays on publication. Publishes ms an average of 9-12 months after acceptance. Byline given. Buys right to reprint in annuals; author retains copyright. Submit seasonal/holiday material 4 months in advance. Accepts previously published submissions. Send tearsheet of article or typed ms with rights for sale noted and information about where and when it previously appeared. For reprints, pays $5/column inch. Query for electronic submissions. Reports in 1 month. Sample copy and writer's guidelines for 9×12 SASE with 5 first-class stamps.
Nonfiction: Essays, general interest, historical/nostalgic, how-to, humor, interview/profile, new product, opinion, personal experience, photo feature, technical, travel. Plans a special entry-level guide to canoeing and kayaking. No "trip diaries." Buys 60 mss/year. Query with or without published clips or send complete ms. Length: 500-2,200 words. Pays $5/column inch. Pays the expenses of writers on assignment.
Photos: State availability of or send photos with submission. "Good photos help sell a story." Reviews contact sheets, negatives, transparencies and prints. "Some activities we cover are canoeing, kayaking, canoe fishing, camping, canoe sailing or poling, backpacking (when compatible with the main activity) and occasionally inflatable boats. We are not interested in groups of people in rafts, photos showing disregard for the environment, gasoline-powered, multi-horsepower engines unless appropriate to the discussion, or unskilled persons taking extraordinary risks." Offers $50-150/photo. Model releases and identification of subjects occasionally required. Buys one-time rights.
Columns/Departments: Continuum (essay); Counter Currents (environmental) both 1,500 words; Put-In (short interesting articles); Short Strokes (destinations), 1,000-1,500 words. Buys 60 mss/year. Pays $5/column inch.
Fiction: Uses very little fiction.
Fillers: Anecdotes, facts, newsbreaks. Buys 20/year. Length: 500-1,000 words. Pays $5/column inch.
Tips: "Start with Put-In articles (short featurettes) of approximately 500 words, book reviews, or short, unique equipment reviews. Or give us the best, most exciting article we've ever seen—with great photos. Short Strokes is also a good entry forum focusing on short trips on good waterways accessible to lots of people. Focusing more on technique and how-to articles."

CURRENTS, Voice of the National Organization for River Sports, 212 W. Cheyenne Mountain Blvd., Colorado Springs CO 80906. (719)579-8759. Fax: (719)576-6238. Editor: Greg Moore. 25% freelance written. Quarterly magazine covering whitewater river running (kayaking, rafting, river canoeing). Estab. 1979. Circ. 5,000. Pays on publication. Publishes ms an average of 6 months after acceptance. Byline given. Offers 25% kill fee. Buys first North American serial, first and one-time rights. Submit seasonal/holiday material 2 months in advance. Accepts simultaneous and previously published submissions. "Please let us know if this is a simultaneous submission or if the article has been previously published." Reports in 2 weeks on queries; 1 month on mss. *Writer's Market* recommends allowing 2 months for reply. Sample copy for $1 and 9×12 SAE with 3 first-class stamps. Writer's guidelines for #10 SASE.

Nonfiction: How-to (run rivers and fix equipment), in-depth reporting on river conservation and access issues and problems, humor (related to rivers), interview/profile (any interesting river runner), opinion, personal experience, technical, travel (rivers in other countries). "We tell river runners about river conservation, river access, river equipment, how to do it, when, where, etc." No trip accounts without originality; no stories about "my first river trip." Buys 20 mss/year. Query with or without clips of published work. Length: 500-2,500 words. Pays $35-150.

Photos: State availability of photos. Pays $35-50. Reviews b&w or color prints or slides; b&w preferred. Captions and identification of subjects (if racing) required. Buys one-time rights. Captions must include names of the river and rapid.

Columns/Departments: Book and film reviews (river-related). Buys 5 mss/year. Query with or without clips of published work or send complete ms. Length: 100-500 words. Pays $25.

Fiction: Adventure (river). Buys 2 mss/year. Query. Length: 1,000-2,500 words. Pays $35-75. "Must be well-written, on well-known river and beyond the realm of possibility."

Fillers: Clippings, jokes, gags, anecdotes, short humor, newsbreaks. Buys 5/year. Length: 25-100 words. Pays $5-10.

Tips: "We need more material on river news—proposed dams, wild and scenic river studies, accidents, etc. If you can provide brief (300-500 words) on these subjects, you will have a good chance of being published. Material must be on whitewater rivers. Go to a famous river and investigate it; find out something we don't know—especially about rivers that are *not* in Colorado or adjacent states—we already know about the ones near us."

HEARTLAND BOATING, Inland Publications, Inc., P.O. Box 1067, Martin TN 38237-1067. (901)587-6791. Fax: (901)587-6893. Editor: Molly Lightfoot Blom. Estab. 1988. 50% freelance written. Published 7 times per year during boating season "devoted to both power and sail boating enthusiasts throughout middle America; houseboats are included. The focus is on the freshwater inland rivers and lakes of the Heartland; primarily the Tennessee, Cumberland, Ohio and Mississippi rivers and the Tennessee-Tombigbee Waterway. No Great Lakes or salt water material will be considered unless it applies to our area." Circ. 16,000. Pays on publication. Publishes ms an average of 3 months after acceptance. Byline given. Buys first North American serial and sometimes second serial (reprint) rights. Submit seasonal/holiday material 6 months in advance. Accepts simultaneous and previously published submissions. Send tearsheet or photocopy of article and information about where and when it previously appeared. Pays 50% of the amount paid for an original article. Query for electronic submissions. Reports in 4 months. Sample copy for $5. Free writer's guidelines.

Nonfiction: General interest, historical/nostalgic, how-to, humor, interview/profile, new product, personal experience, photo feature, technical, travel. Buys 20-40 mss/year. Prefers queries to unsolicited mss with or without published clips. Length: 800-2,000 words. Negotiates payment.

Photos: Send photos with query. Reviews contact sheets, transparencies. Buys one-time rights.

Columns/Departments: Buys 50 mss/year. Query. Negotiates payment.

HOT BOAT, LFP Publishing, 9171 Wilshire Blvd., Suite 300, Beverly Hills CA 90210. (310)858-7155. Fax: (310)274-7985. E-mail: boatchic@aol.com. Editor: Kevin Spaise. Senior Editor: Cheryl Newman. 50% freelance written. A monthly magazine on performance boating (16-35 feet), water skiing and water sports in general. "We're looking for concise, technically oriented 'how-to' articles on performance modifications; personality features on interesting boating-oriented personalities, and occasional event coverage." Circ. 90,000. Pays upon publication. Publishes ms an average of 2 months after acceptance. Byline given. Offers 40% kill fee. Buys all rights; also reprint rights occasionally. Submit seasonal/holiday material 3 months in advance. Reports in 3 weeks on queries; 1 month on mss. Sample copy for $3 and 9×12 SAE with $1.35 postage.

Nonfiction: How-to (increase horsepower, perform simple boat related maintenance), humor, interview/profile (racers and manufacturers), new product, personal experience, photo feature, technical. "Absolutely no sailing—we deal strictly in powerboating." Buys 30 mss/year. Query with published clips. Length: 500-2,000 words. Pays $75-450. Sometimes pays expenses of writers on assignment.

Photos: Send photos with submission. Reviews transparencies. Captions, model releases, identification of subjects required. Buys all rights.

Tips: "We're always open to new writers. If you query with published clips and we like your writing, we can keep you on file even if we reject the particular query. It may be more important to simply establish contact. Once we work together there will be much more work to follow."

LAKELAND BOATING, The magazine for Great Lakes boaters, O'Meara-Brown Publications, 1560 Sherman Ave., Suite 1220, Evanston IL 60201-4802. (708)869-5400. Fax: (708)869-5989. Editor: John Wooldridge. Managing Editor: Randy Hess. 50% freelance written. Monthly magazine covering Great Lakes boating. Estab. 1945. Circ. 60,000. Pays on publication. Byline given. Buys first North American serial rights. Query for electronic submissions. Reports in 4 months. Sample copy for $5.50 and 9×12 SAE with 6 first-class stamps. Writer's guidelines for #10 SASE.

Nonfiction: Book excerpts, historical/nostalgic, how-to, interview/profile, personal experience, photo feature, technical, travel. No inspirational, religious, expose or poetry. Must relate to boating in Great Lakes. Buys 20-30 mss/year. Query. Length: 800-3,500 words. Pays $100-600 for assigned articles.

Photos: State availability of photos. Reviews transparencies; prefers 35mm. Captions required. Buys one-time rights.

Columns/Departments: Bosun's Locker (technical or how-to pieces on boating), 100-1,000 words. Buys 40 mss/year. Query. Pays $30-100.

MOTOR BOATING & SAILING, 250 W. 55th St., New York NY 10019. (212)649-4099. Fax: (212)489-9258. Editor and Publisher: Peter A. Janssen. Monthly magazine covering powerboats and sailboats for people who own their own boats and are active in a yachting lifestyle. Estab. 1907. Circ. 135,056. **Pays on acceptance.** Byline given. Buys one-time rights. Reports in 2 months.

Nonfiction: General interest (navigation, adventure, cruising), how-to (maintenance). Buys 5-6 mss/issue. Average issue includes 8-10 feature articles. Query. Length: 2,000 words.

Photos: Reviews 5×7 b&w glossy prints and 35mm or larger color transparencies. Offers no additional payment for photos accepted with ms. Captions and model releases required.

NOR'WESTING, Nor'westing Publications, Inc., 6044 Seaview Ave. NW, Seattle WA 98107. (206)783-8939. Fax: (206)783-9011. Editor: Gloria Kruzner. 95% freelance written. Monthly magazine covering Pacific Northwest boating, cruising destinations. "We want to pack our pages with cruising articles, special Northwest destinations, local boating personalities. How to get to a destination, what's there when you arrive, etc." Estab. 1964. Circ. 8,500 paid; 9,000 total. Pays approximately 2 months after publication. Publishes ms an average of 2 months after acceptance. Byline given. Buys first North American serial rights and makes work-for-hire assignments. Editorial lead time 3 months. Submit seasonal material 3 months in advance. Accepts simultaneous submissions (Please note where else it's being submitted). Reports in 2 months. Sample copy and writer's guidelines for #10 SASE.

Nonfiction: How-to (boat outfitting, electronics, fish, galley), interview/profile (boater personalities), new product, personal experience (cruising), photo feature, technical, travel (local destinations). Special issues: Boat shows (Seattle) (January); Spring outfitting (March/April); Cruising destinations (June/August); Rough water boating (November/December). Buys 35-40 mss/year. Send complete ms. Length: 900-2,000 words. Pays $100-150. Sometimes pays expenses of writers on assignment.

Photos: Send photos with submission. Reviews transparencies, 3×5 prints. Negotiates payment individually. Identification of subjects required. Normally buys one-time rights.

Columns/Departments: Trailerboating (small craft boating—tech/destination), 900; Galley Ideas (cooking afloat—recipes/ideas), 900; Hardwired (Boating Electronics), 1,000; Cruising Fisherman (Fishing tips, destinations), 1,000. Buys 36-40 mss/year. Query with published clips. Pays $50-100.

Fillers: Anecdotes, gags to be illustrated by cartoonist. Buys 5-10/year. Length: 100-500 words. Pays $25-75.

Tips: "Include specific information on destination—how many moorage buoys, cost for showers, best time to visit. Any hazards to watch for while approaching? Why bother going if excitement for area/boating doesn't shine through in piece?"

OFFSHORE, Boating Magazine of the Northeast, Offshore Publications, Inc., 220-9 Reservoir St., Needham MA 02194. (617)449-6204. Fax: (617)449-9702. E-mail: oshore@aol.com. Editor: Jack Goodman, Jr. Estab. 1976. 80% freelance written. Eager to work with new/unpublished writers. Monthly magazine covering boating and the coast from Maine to New Jersey. Circ. 35,000. **Pays on acceptance.** Publishes ms an average of 2 months after acceptance. Byline given. Offers negotiable kill fee. Buys first North American serial rights. Submit seasonal/holiday material 3 months in advance. Accepts simultaneous and previously published submissions. Send tearsheet or photocopy of article or short story or typed ms with rights for sale noted and information about when and where the article previously appeared. Pays $100 for reprints. Query for electronic submissions. Reports in 2 weeks. *Writer's Market* recommends allowing 2 months for reply. Sample copy for 10×13 SAE with 6 first-class stamps. Writer's guidelines for #10 SASE.

Nonfiction: Articles on boats, boating, New York, New Jersey and New England coastal places and people. Coastal history of NJ, NY, CT, RI, MA, NH and ME. Thumbnail and/or outline of topic will elicit immediate response. Buys 90 mss/year. Query with writing sample or send complete ms. Length: 1,000-3,000 words. Pays 15¢/word and up.

Fiction: Boat-related fiction.

Photos: Reviews 35mm slides only. For covers, pays $200 and up. Identification of subjects required. Buys one-time rights.

Tips: "Demonstrate familiarity with boats or region and ability to recognize subjects of interest to regional boat owners. Those subjects need not be boats. *Offshore* is serious but does not take itself as seriously as most national boating magazines. The most frequent mistake made by writers in completing an article for us is failing to build on a theme (what is the point of the story?)."

POWER BOATING CANADA, 2585 Skymark Ave., Unit 306, Mississauga, Ontario L4W 4L5 Canada. (905)624-8218. Fax: (905)624-6764. Editor: Pam Cottrell. 40% freelance written. Bimonthly magazine covering power boating. Estab. 1984. Circ. 50,000. Pays on publication. Publishes ms an average of 3 months after acceptance. Byline given. Not copyrighted. Buys first North American serial rights in English and French or second serial (reprint) rights. Accepts simultaneous and previously published submissions. Send photocopy of article or typed ms with rights for sale noted and information about when and where the article previously appeared. Query for electronic submissions.

Nonfiction: "Any articles related to the sport of power boating, especially boat tests." Travel (boating destinations). No personal anecdotes. Buys 20 mss/year. Query. Length: 1,000-2,500 words. Pays $150-300.

Photos: State availability of photos with submission. Send photos with submission. Reviews contact sheets, negatives, transparencies, prints. Offers no additional payment for photos accepted with ms. Identification of subjects required. Buys one-time rights.

Fiction: Publishes novel excerpts.

SAIL, 275 Washington St., Newton MA 02158-1630. (617)964-3030. Fax: (617)630-3737. Editor: Patience Wales. Managing Editor: Amy Ullrich. 50% freelance written. Works with a small number of new/unpublished writers each year. Monthly magazine for audience that is "strictly sailors, average age 42, above average education." Estab. 1970. **Pays on acceptance.** Publishes ms an average of 10 months after acceptance. Buys first North American rights. Submit seasonal or special material at least 6 months in advance. Accepts previously published submissions. Send tearsheet or photocopy of article with information about when and where it previously appeared. Pays 50% of amount paid for an original article. Reports in 10 weeks. Writer's guidelines for 1 first-class stamp.

Nonfiction: Amy Ullrich, managing editor. Wants "articles on sailing: technical, techniques and feature stories." Interested in how-to, personal experience, distance cruising, destinations, technical aspects of boat construction, systems. "Generally emphasize the excitement of sail and the human, personal aspect. No logs." Special issues: "Cruising, chartering, fitting-out, special race (e.g., America's Cup), boat show." Buys 100 mss/year (freelance and commissioned). Length: 1,000-2,800 words. Pays $200-800. Sometimes pays the expenses of writers on assignment.

Photos: Offers additional payment for photos. Uses b&w glossy prints or Fujichrome transparencies. Pays $600 if photo is used on the cover.

Tips: "Request an articles specification sheet."

SAILING MAGAZINE, 125 E. Main St., Port Washington WI 53074-0249. (414)284-3494. Fax: (414)284-7764. E-mail: 75553.3666@compuserv.com. Editor: Micca Leffingwell Hutchins. Publisher: William F. Schanen, III. Monthly magazine. Estab. 1966. Circ. 52,000. Pays on publication. **Does not** accept simultaneous or previously published submissions. Prefer text in Word on disk for Mac or to E address. Reports in 2 months.

Nonfiction: "Experiences of sailing—cruising, racing or learning." Must be written to AP Stylebook. Buys 8 mss/year. Length: 750-1,500 words. Must be accompanied by photos, and maps if applicable. Payment dependent length of article and use in the magazine.

Photos: Color photos (transparencies) purchased with or without accompanying text. Captions are required.

SEA KAYAKER, Sea Kayaker, Inc., P.O. Box 17170, Seattle WA 98107-0870. (206)789-1326. Fax: (206)781-1141. Editor: Karen Reed. Managing Editor: Christopher Cunningham. 80% freelance written. Works frequently with new/unpublished writers each year. Bimonthly magazine on the sport of sea kayaking. Estab. 1984. Circ. 20,000. Pays on publication. Publishes ms an average of 6 months after acceptance. Byline given. Offers 10% kill fee. Buys first North American serial or second serial (reprint) rights. Submit seasonal material 6 months in advance. Reports in 2 months. Sample copy for $5.30. Free writer's guidelines with SASE.

Nonfiction: Essays, historical, how-to (on making equipment), humor, profile, opinion, personal experience, technical, travel. Buys 40 mss/year. Query with or without published clips or send complete ms. Length: 750-4,000 words. Pays about 10¢/word. Sometimes pays the expenses of writers on assignment.

Photos: Send photos with submission. Reviews contact sheets. Offers $25-100/photo. Captions requested. Buys one-time rights.

Columns/Departments: History, Safety, Environment, Journey. Length: 750-4,000 words. Pays 10¢/word, minimum.

Fiction: Kayak related adventure, fantasy, historical, humorous, mainstream, slice-of-life vignettes. Send complete ms. Length: 750-4,000 words. Pays about 10¢/word.

Tips: "We consider unsolicited mss that include a SASE, but we give greater priority to brief (several paragraphs) descriptions of proposed articles accompanied by at least two samples—published or unpublished—of your writing. Enclose a statement as to why you're qualified to write the piece and indicate whether photographs or illustrations are available to accompany the piece."

‡TRAILER BOATS MAGAZINE, Poole Publications, Inc., 20700 Belshaw Ave., Carson CA 90746-3510. (310)537-6322. Fax: (310)537-8735. Editor: Randy Scott. 30-40% freelance written. Works with a small number of new/unpublished writers each year. Monthly magazine (November/December issue combined). Emphasizes legally trailerable boats and related powerboating activities. Circ. 85,000. **Pays on acceptance.** Publishes ms 2-6 months after acceptance. Byline given. Buys all rights. Submit seasonal/holiday material 5 months in advance. Query for electronic submissions. Reports in 1 month. Sample copy $1.25; writer's guidelines for #10 SASE.
Nonfiction: General interest (trailer boating activities); historical (places, events, boats); how-to (repair boats, installation, etc.); humor (almost any boating-related subject); nostalgia (same as historical); personal experience; photo feature; profile; technical; and travel (boating travel on water or highways). No "How I Spent My Summer Vacation" stories, or stories not even remotely connected to trailerable boats and related activities. Buys 18-30 unsolicited mss/year. Query or send complete ms. Length: 500-2,000 words. Pays expenses of writers on assignment.
Photos: Send photos with ms. Pays $10-75 for 8 × 10 b&w prints; $25-350 for color transparencies. Captions required.
Columns/Departments: Boaters Bookshelf (boating book reviews); Over the Transom (funny or strange boating photos). Buys 2/issue. Query. Length: 100-500 words. Mini-Cruise (short enthusiastic approach to a favorite boating spot). Need map and photographs. Length: 500-750 words. Pays $250. Open to suggestions for new columns/departments.
Fiction: Adventure, experimental, historical, humorous and suspense. "We do not use many fiction stories but we will consider them if they fit the general editorial guidelines." Query or send complete ms. Length: 500-1,500 words. Pays $150-450.
Tips: "Query should contain short general outline of the intended material; what kind of photos; how the photos illustrate the piece. Write with authority covering the subject like an expert. Frequent mistakes are not knowing the subject matter or the audience. Use basic information rather than prose, particularly in travel stories. The writer may have a better chance of breaking in at our publication with short articles and fillers if they are typically hard to find articles. We do most major features inhouse."

WATERFRONT NEWS, SOUTHERN CALIFORNIA, Your Local Boating News, Duncan McIntosh Co., Inc., 17782 Cowan, Suite C, 2nd Floor, Irvine CA 92714. (714)660-6150. Fax: (714)660-6172. Associate Editor: Erin McNiff. 10% freelance written. Monthly news magazine covering recreational boating, sailing, sportfishing and lifestyles in Southern California. Articles are aimed at owners of pleasureboats with an emphasis on where to go, what to do with their vessel, locally. Est. 1993. Circ. 40,000. Pays on publication. Publishes ms an average of 1 month after submission. Byline given. Buys first North American rights. Query for all submissions. Reports in 1 month on queries. Sample copy and writer's guidelines for SASE.
Nonfiction: Sportfishing how-to, cruising destinations, spot news of interest to boaters. Length: 150-1,000 words. Pays $25-150. No fiction. Some shipping expenses covered if requested in advance, in writing.
Photos: State availability of photos with query or send photos with submission. Reviews any size prints and transparencies, color or b&w. Offers $15-50/photo. Identification of subjects required. Buys one-time rights.
Columns/Departments: News (including changes, developments in state and federal law that affect local boaters, personality profile on a local boater who cruises somewhere outside Southern California, or a how-to piece on a Southern California port of call, or an interview/profile about a unique cruiser who is visiting Southern California during a long-range voyage aboard his own boat); Racing (covers major regattas in Southern California, both power and sail, and local racers who travel to compete at the highest levels around the world); Sportfishing (short how-to articles for catching fish in Southern California with your own boat); Business (new developments in boating accessories and services of interest to Southern California boat owners.) Query with published clips.

WATERWAY GUIDE, Argus Business, Inc., 6151 Powers Ferry Rd. NW, Atlanta GA 30339-2941. (404)618-0313. Fax: (404)618-0349. Associate Publisher: Judith Powers. 90% freelance written. Quarterly magazine on intracoastal waterway travel for recreational boats. "Writer must be knowledgable about navigation and the areas covered by the guide." Estab. 1947. Circ. 45,000. Pays on publication. Publishes ms an average of 3 months after acceptance. Byline given sometimes. Kill fee varies. Buys all rights. Reports in 3 months on queries; 4 months on mss. Sample copy for $33.95 with $3 postage.
Nonfiction: Historical/nostalgic, how-to, photo feature, technical, travel. "No personal boating experiences." Buys 25 mss/year. Query with or without published clips or send complete ms. Length: 200 words minimum. Pays $50-3,000 for assigned articles. Pays in contributor copies or other premiums for helpful tips and useful information.
Photos: Send photos with submission. Reviews 3 × 5 prints. Offers $25/b&w photo, $600/color photos used on the cover. Identification of subjects required. Buys one-time rights.

Fillers: Facts. Buys 6/year. Length: 250-1,000 words. Pays $50-150.

Tips: "Must have on-the-water experience and be able to provide new and accurate information on geographic areas covered by *Waterway Guide*."

WOODENBOAT MAGAZINE, The Magazine for Wooden Boat Owners, Builders, and Designers, WoodenBoat Publications, Inc., P.O. Box 78, Brooklin ME 04616. (207)359-4651. Fax: (207)359-8920. Editor-in-Chief: Jonathan A. Wilson. Editor: Matthew P. Murphy. Senior Editor: Mike O'Brien. 50% freelance written. Works with a small number of new/unpublished writers each year. Bimonthly magazine for wooden boat owners, builders and designers. "We are devoted exclusively to the design, building, care, preservation, and use of wooden boats, both commercial and pleasure, old and new, sail and power. We work to convey quality, integrity and involvement in the creation and care of these craft, to entertain, inform, inspire, and to provide our varied readers with access to individuals who are deeply experienced in the world of wooden boats." Estab. 1974. Circ. 106,000. Pays on publication. Publishes ms an average of 1 year after acceptance. Byline given. Offers variable kill fee. Buys first North American serial rights. Accepts simultaneous and previously published submissions (with notification). Send tearsheet or photocopy of article or typed ms with rights for sale noted with information about when and where the article previously appeared. Query for electronic submissions. Reports in 3 weeks on queries; 2 months on mss. Sample copy for $4.50. Writer's guidelines for SASE.

Nonfiction: Technical (repair, restoration, maintenance, use, design and building wooden boats). No poetry, fiction. Buys 50 mss/year. Query with published clips. Length: 1,500-5,000 words. Pays $150-200/1,000 words. Sometimes pays expenses of writers on assignment.

Photos: Send photos with query. Negatives must be available. Pays $15-75 for b&w; $25-350 for color. Identification of subjects required. Buys one-time rights.

Columns/Departments: On the Waterfront pays for information on wooden boat-related events, projects, boatshop activities, etc. Buys 25/year. "We use the same columnists for each issue." Send complete information. Length: 250-1,000 words. Pays $5-50 for information.

Tips: "We appreciate a detailed, articulate query letter, accompanied by photos, that will give us a clear idea of what the author is proposing. We appreciate samples of previously published work. It is important for a prospective author to become familiar with our magazine first. It is extremely rare for us to make an assignment with a writer with whom we have not worked before. Most work is submitted on speculation. The most common failure is not exploring the subject material in enough depth."

YACHTING, Times Mirror Magazines Inc., 2 Park Ave., 5th Floor, New York NY 10016-5695. (212)779-5300. Fax: (212)725-1035. Associate Publisher: Mary Ann Cox. Executive Editor: Charles Barthold. 50% freelance written. "The magazine is written and edited for experienced, knowledgeable yachtsmen." Estab. 1907. Circ. 132,000. Pays on publication. Byline given. Buys first rights. Submit seasonal/holiday material 6 months in advance. Reports in 1 month.

Nonfiction: Book excerpts, personal experience, photo feature, travel. No cartoons, fiction, poetry. Query with published clips. Length: 250-2,000 words. Pays $250-1,000 for assigned articles. Pays expenses of writers on assignment.

Photos: Send photos with submission. Reviews 35mm transparencies. Offers some additional payment for photos accepted with ms. Captions, model releases and identification of subjects required.

Columns/Departments: Cruising Yachtsman (stories on cruising; contact Cynthia Taylor, senior editor); Racing Yachtsman (stories about sail or power racing; contact Lisa Ken Wooten); Yacht Yard (how-to and technical pieces on yachts and their systems; contact Dennis Caprio, Senior editor). Buys 30 mss/year. Send complete ms. Length: 750 words maximum. Pays $250-500.

Tips: "We require considerable expertise in our writing because our audience is experienced and knowledgeable. Vivid descriptions of quaint anchorages and quainter natives are fine, but our readers want to know how the yachtsmen got there, too. They also want to know how their boats work."

Bowling

BOWLING, Dept. WM, 5301 S. 76th St., Greendale WI 53129. (414)421-6400, ext. 230. Editor: Bill Vint. 15% freelance written. Bimonthly, official publication of the American Bowling Congress. Estab. 1934. Circ. 135,000. **Pays on acceptance.** Publishes ms an average of 2 months after acceptance. Byline given. Rights purchased vary with author and material; usually buys all rights. Reports in 1 month. Sample copy for $2.50.

Nonfiction: "This is a specialized field and the average writer attempting the subject of bowling should be well-informed. However, anyone is free to submit material for approval." Wants articles about unusual ABC sanctioned leagues and tournaments, personalities, etc., featuring male bowlers. Nostalgia articles also considered. No first-person articles or material on history of bowling. Length: 500-1,200 words. Pays $100-300 per article. No poems, songs or fiction.

Photos: Pays $10-15/photo.

Tips: "Submit feature material on bowlers, generally amateurs competing in local leagues, or special events involving the game of bowling. Should have connection with ABC membership. Queries should be as detailed as possible so that we may get a clear idea of what the proposed story would be all about. It saves us time and the writer time. Samples of previously published material in the bowling or general sports field would help. Once we find a talented writer in a given area, we're likely to go back to him in the future. We're looking for good writers who can handle assignments professionally and promptly." No articles on professionals.

Football

NFL EXCLUSIVE, The Official Magazine of the NFL Season Ticket holder, SportsImage, Inc., Suite 302, 2107 Elliott Ave., Seattle WA 98121. (206)728-7200. Editor: Mike Olson. 100% freelance written. Annual magazine covering NFL football. Estab. 1991. Circ. 427,350. Pays on publications. Byline given. Offers 100% kill fee. Buys all rights. Editorial lead time 3 months. Submit seasonal material 2 months in advance. Accepts previously published submissions. Sample copy for 8½×11 SAE with 5 first-class stamps.
Nonfiction: Historical/nostalgic, interview/profile. Buys 15 mss/year. Query with published clips. Length: 1,000 words. Pays $200. Sometimes pays expenses of writers on assignment.
Photos: Send photos with submission. Reviews transparencies. Negotiates payment individually. Identification of subjects required. Buys one-time rights.
Tips: "Come up with ideas, trends or concepts that revolve around a historical look at the NFL. Not so much the famous moments (i.e. Super Bowl), rather, the hidden, yet significant, events that shaped the league."

Gambling

‡CHICAGO'S CASINO REVIEW, Hyde Park Media, 635 Chicago Ave., #250, Evanston IL 60202. Contact: Articles Editor. 80% freelance written. Bimonthly covering casino and other legal gambling. Estab. 1994. Circ. 30,000. Pays on publication. Publishes ms an average of 2-4 months after acceptance. Byline given. Buys first rights, one-time rights, second serial (reprint) rights, simultaneous rights and all rights. Editorial lead time 2-4 months. Submit seasonal material 4 months in advance. Accepts simultaneous and previously published submissions. Reports in 1 month on queries; 2 months on mss. Sample copy for $5 and 10×13 SAE with 4 first-class stamps.
Nonfiction: Book excerpts, historical/nostalgic, how-to, humor, inspirational, interview/profile, opinion, personal experience, photo feature, travel (all with a gambling hook). Buys 75-100 mss/year. Query. Send complete ms. Length: 800-2,000 words. Pays $50-250 for assigned articles; $25-100 for unsolicited articles.
Photos: State availability of photos with submission. Reviews 5×7 prints. Negotiates payment individually. Captions, model releases, identification of subjects required. Buys all rights.
Tips: "Detailed queries and having quality art to go along with any proposed articles. We're always looking for highly stylized, quality art, i.e., photos and line art."

WIN, Gambling Times Incorporated, 120 S. San Fernando Blvd., Suite 439, Burbank CA 91502. Fax: (818)845-0325 (9-5 p.m. weekdays, Pacific Time). No voice calls. Editor: Joey Sinatra. Monthly magazine for gambling, entertainment, computers. Estab. 1979. Circ. 56,000. Pays on publication. Publishes ms an average of 3 months after acceptance. Byline given. Buys first North American serial rights. Editorial lead time 3 months. Submit seasonal material 3 months in advance. Accepts simultaneous submissions. Query for electronic submissions. Reports in 6 weeks on queries, 2 months on mss. Writer's guidelines with SASE.
Nonfiction: Book excerpts, essays, historical/nostalgic, how-to (casino games), interview/profile, new product, photo feature, technical. Buys 6 mss/year. Send complete ms. Length: 1,600-2,000 words. Pays $75 minimum for assigned articles. Sometimes "pays" contributors with travel, hotel rooms.
Photos: Send photos with submission. Reviews 4×5 transparencies and prints. Negotiates payment individually. Captions, model releases and identification of subjects required. Buys all rights.
Fiction: Gambling subplots. No previously published fiction. Buys 12 mss/year. Send complete ms. Length: 1,200-2,500 words. Pay negotiable.
Fillers: Facts, newsbreaks. Buys 30/year. Length: 250-600 words. Pays $25 minimum.

General Interest

EXPLORE, Canada's Outdoor Adventure Magazine, Thompson & Gordon Publishing Co. Ltd., 301-14 St. NW, Suite 420, Calgary Alberta T2N 2A1 Canada. (403)270-8890. Editor: Marion Harrison. 30% freelance written. Bimonthly magazine covering Outdoor Recreation "for those who seek some form of adventure in their travels. The magazine covers popular activities such as backpacking, bicycling, canoeing, and backcountry skiing featuring Canadian and international destinations. Other topics covered include ecotourism, the environment, outdoor photography, sports medicine, equipment, and new products for the outdoor recreationist." Estab. 1981. Circ. 30,000. Pays on publication. Byline given. Offers 50% kill fee on assigned stories. Buys first North American serial rights. Editorial lead time 6-12 months. Submit seasonal material

6 months in advance. Accepts simultaneous submissions. Query for electronic submissions. Reports in 2 months. Sample copy for $5. Writer's guidelines for #10 SASE—IRCs required from outside Canada.

• *Explore* was nominated for Magazine of the Year at the Western Canada Magazine Awards in Vancouver.

Nonfiction: Personal experience, travel. Query with published clips. Length: 1,500-2,500 words. Pays $250-500 (Canadian).

Photos: Send photos with submission. Reviews contact sheets, transparencies and prints. Offers no additional payment for photos accepted with ms. Captions required. Buys one-time rights.

Columns/Departments: Gearing Up (clothing, equipment for outdoor recreation). 1,800; Photography (outdoor photography tips), 1,200. Buys 5 mss/year. Query. Pays $275.

Tips: "Remember *Explore* is a *Canadian* magazine with 95% Canadian readership that wants to read about Canada! We buy three articles *per year* which feature U.S. destinations. Submit manuscript and photos for fastest response. Feature articles are required more often than departments. Features are first-person narratives that are exciting and interesting. We are using fewer travel pieces, more researched issue-oriented articles. Quality photos are a must."

ROCKY MOUNTAIN SPORTS MAGAZINE, Sports & Fitness Publishing, 2025 Pearl St., Boulder CO 80302. (303)440-5111. Publisher: Will Gadd. Editor: Don Silver. 50% freelance written. Monthly magazine of sports in the Rocky Mountain States and Canada. "*Rocky* is a magazine for sports-related lifestyles and activities. Our mission is to reflect and inspire the active lifestyle of Rocky Mountain residents." Estab. 1987. Circ. 45,000. Pays on publication. Publishes ms an average of 2 months after acceptance. Byline given. Offers 25% kill fee. Buys second serial (reprint) rights. Editorial lead time 1½ months. Submit seasonal material 2 months in advance. Accepts previously published submissions. Send photocopy of article or short story. For reprints, pays 20-50% of the amount paid for an original article. Query for electronic submissions. Reports in 3 weeks on queries; 2 months on mss. Sample copy and writer's guidelines for #10 SASE.

• The editor of this publication says he wants to see mountain outdoor sports writing **only**. No ball sports, no hunting, no fishing.

Nonfiction: Book excerpts, essays, exposé, how-to: (no specific sports, trips, adventures), humor, inspirational, interview/profile, new product, opinion, personal experience, photo feature, travel. Special issues: Photo Annual (August); snowboarding (December); Alpine and Nordic (January and February); Mountain biking (April). No articles on football, baseball, basketball or other sports covered in-depth by newspapers. Buys 24 mss/year. Query with published clips. Length: 2,500 maximum words. Pays $150 minimum for assigned articles. Sometimes pays expenses of writers on assignment.

Photos: State availability of photos with submission. Reviews transparencies and prints. Offers $25-250/photo. Captions and identification of subjects required. Buys one-time rights.

Columns/Departments: Scree (short newsy items), 50-800 words; Photo Gallery (photos depicting nature and the spirit of sport); and High Altitude (essay on quirky topics related to Rockies). Buys 20 mss/year. Query. Pays $25-200.

Fiction: Adventure, experimental, humorous. "Nothing that isn't sport-related." Buys 5 mss/year. Query. Length: 250-1,500 words. Pays $50-200. Publishes novel excerpts.

Fillers: Anecdotes, facts, gags to be illustrated by cartoonist, newsbreaks, short humor. Buys 20/year. Length: 10-200 words. Pays $25-75.

Tips: "Submit stories for the Scree section first."

SPORT, Petersen Publishing Co., 6420 Wilshire Blvd., Los Angeles CA 90048-5515. (213)782-2828. Editor: Cam Benty. 80% freelance written. Monthly magazine. **Pays on acceptance**. Publishes ms an average of 3 months after acceptance. Offers 25% kill fee. Buys first North American serial or all rights. Reports in 2 months.

Nonfiction: "Prefers to see articles on professional, big-time sports: basketball, football, baseball, with some boxing. The articles we buy must be contemporary pieces, not a history of sports or a particular sport." Query with published clips. Length: News briefs, 200-300 words; Departments, 1,400 words; Features, 1,500-3,000 words. Averages 50¢/word for articles.

SPORTS ILLUSTRATED, Time & Life Bld., Rockefeller Center, New York NY 10020-1393. Senior Editor: Chris Hunt. Weekly publication covering sports of all kinds. Query before submitting.

WINDY CITY SPORTS MAGAZINE, Chicago Sports Resources, 1450 W. Randolph, Chicago IL 60607. (312)421-1551. Fax: (312)421-1454. Editor: Jeff Banowetz. 75% freelance written. Monthly magazine covering amateur, participatory sports. Estab. 1987. Circ. 100,000 (Chicago and suburbs). **Pays on acceptance**; pays on publication for blind submissions. Offers 25% kill fee. Buys one-time rights. Editorial lead time 2 months. Submit seasonal material 2-12 months in advance. Accepts simultaneous and previously published submissions. Reports in 1 month on queries. Sample copy for $2 or SASE. Writer's guidelines free on request.

Nonfiction: Essays (re: sports controversial issues), how-to (do sports), inspirational (profiles of accomplished athletes), interview/profile, new product, opinion, personal experience, photo feature (in Chicago), travel. No articles on professional sports. Buys 120 mss/year. Query with clips. Length: 500-1,200 words. Pays 10¢/word. Sometimes pays expenses of writers on assignment.

Photos: State availability or send photos with submission. Reviews contact sheets and prints. Negotiates payment individually. Captions and identification of subjects required. Buys one-time rights.

Columns/Departments: "We run the following columns (750-900 words) every month: running, cycling, fitness centers, nutrition, sports medicine, women's, road trip (adventure travel) and in-line skating." Buys 70 mss/year. Query with published clips. Send complete ms. Pays $75-125.

Fillers: Anecdotes, facts, gags to be illustrated by cartoonist, short humor. Buys 10/year. Length: 20-500 words. Pays $25-100.

Tips: "Best way to get assignment: ask for writer's guidelines, editor's schedule and sample copy ($2 SASE). *Read magazine!* Query me with story ideas for a column (I run columns every month and am always looking for ideas) or query on features using editorial schedule. Always try to target Chicago looking Midwest."

WOMEN'S SPORTS & FITNESS MAGAZINE, Women's Sports & Fitness, Inc., 2025 Pearl St., Boulder CO 80302-5323. (303)440-5111. Senior Editors: Daryn Eller and Lisa Peters O'Brien. Assistant Editor: Janet Lee. 90% freelance written. Works with a small number of new/unpublished writers each year. Magazine published 8 times/year emphasizing women's sports, fitness and health. Estab. 1974. Circ. 165,000. Pays on publication. Publishes ms an average of 3 months after acceptance. Buys first North American serial rights. Submit seasonal/holiday material 3 months in advance. Sometimes accepts previously published submissions. Send photocopy of article or typed ms with rights for sale noted and information about when and where the article previously appeared. For reprints, payment varies. Reports in 3 months. Sample copy for $5 and 9×12 SAE. Writer's guidelines for #10 SASE.

Nonfiction: Profile, service piece, interview, how-to, historical, personal experience, new product. "All articles should have the latest information from knowledgeable sources. All must be of national interest to athletic women." Buys 4 mss/issue. Length: 500-1,500 words. Query with published clips. Pays $500-2,000 for features, including expenses.

Photos: State availability of photos. Pays about $50-300 for b&w prints; $50-500 for 35mm color transparencies. Buys one-time rights.

Columns/Departments: Buys 5-8/issue. Query with published clips. Length: 200-750 words. Pays $100-400.

Tips: "If the writer doesn't have published clips, best advice for breaking in is to concentrate on columns and departments (the Beat and Source) first. Query letters should tell why our readers—active women (with an average age in the mid-thirties) who partake in sports or fitness activities six times a week—would want to read the article. We're especially attracted to articles with a new angle, fresh or difficult-to-get information. We go after the latest in health, nutrition and fitness research, or reports about lesser-known women in sports who are on the threshold of greatness. We also present profiles of the best athletes and teams. We want the profiles to give insight into the person as well as the athlete. We have a cadre of writers whom we've worked with regularly, but we are always looking for new writers."

Golf

GOLF MAGAZINE, Times Mirror Magazines, 2 Park Ave., New York NY 10016-5695. (212)779-5000. Fax: (212)779-5522. Editor: James A. Frank. Senior Editors: David Barrett and Mike Purkey. 40% freelance written. Monthly magazine on golf, professional and amateur. Circ. 1.275 million. **Pays on acceptance.** Publishes ms an average of 4 months after acceptance. Byline sometimes given. Offers 20% kill fee. Buys first North American serial rights. Submit seasonal/holiday material 4 months in advance. Query for electronic submissions. Reports in 1 month on queries. *Writer's Market* recommends allowing 2 months for reply. Free writer's guidelines.

Nonfiction: General interest, historical/nostalgic, how-to, humor, interview/profile. Buys 10-20 mss/year. Query or query with published clips. Length: 100-2,500 words. Pays $100-2,500. Sometimes pays expenses of writers on assignment.

Photos: State availability of photos with submission or send photos with submission. Offers standard page rate. Captions, model releases, identification of subjects required. Buys one-time rights.

Columns/Departments: Buys 5-10 mss/year. Query with or without published clips or send complete ms. Length: 100-1,200 words. Pays $100-1,000.

Fillers: Newsbreaks, short humor. Buys 5-10/year. Length: 50-100 words. Pays $50-150.

Tips: "Be familiar with the magazine and with the game of golf."

‡GOLF TIPS, The Game's Most In-Depth Instruction & Equipment Magazine, Werner Publishing Corp., 12121 Wilshire Blvd., Suite 1220, Los Angeles CA 90025. (310)820-1500. Editor: Nick Mastroni. Contact: Scott Smith, Managing Editor. 40% freelance written. Magazine published 9 times/year covering golf instruction and equipment. "Our readers are devoted golfers, usually in the middle to medium-high income range, who first and foremost are interested in improving their golf games." Estab. 1989. Circ. 215,000. Pays on publication. Publishes ms an average of 3 months after acceptance. Byline given. Editorial lead time 5 months. Submit seasonal material 5 months in advance. Accepts simultaneous submissions. Reports in 2 months on queries; 1 month on mss. Sample copy and writer's guidelines free on request.

Nonfiction: Book excerpts, how-to (golf instruction), humor, new product, travel. Buys 25 mss/year. Query with published clips. Length: 200-1,800 words. Pays $100-750. Sometimes pays expenses of writers on assignment.

Photos: State availability of photos with submission. Reviews contact sheets, transparencies. Negotiates payment individually.

Columns/Departments: Club Fitting & Design (written by people with technical knowledge on various facets of golf club design), 800-1,000 words. Buys 9 mss/year. Query with published clips. Pays $300.

Tips: "Talk to local golf teaching professionals. What are some succinct, visually-reproducible teaching tenets that are fresh and to their knowledge have not appeared in instruction magazines before? Good, clear, one- and two-page instruction articles are best break-in bets. Attending golf merchandise shows is also a good source of article ideas."

‡METROLINA GOLF MAGAZINE, Tayside Publishing Co. Inc., P.O. Box 9122, Hickory NC 28603-9122. (704)327-4332. Editor: Gil Capps. 20% freelance written. Tabloid published 8 times/year. "*Metrolina Golf Magazine* is edited for golfers in the Charlotte metropolitan area of North and South Carolina. It features profiles of local players; coverage of regional tournaments; and reviews of courses, travel destinations and equipment." Estab. 1992. Circ. 25,000. Pays on publication. Publishes ms an average of 3 months after acceptance. Byline given. Offers $25 kill fee. Buys all rights. Editorial lead time 3 months. Submit seasonal material 6 months in advance. Sample copy for 9×12 SAE and 3 first-class stamps. Writer's guidelines for #10 SASE.

Nonfiction: Essays, exposé, general interest, historical/nostalgic, how-to, humor, interview/profile, new product, opinion, personal experience, photo feature, technical, travel (all pertaining to golf). Buys 15 mss/year. Query with published clips. Length: 400-1,200 words. Pays $25-100 for assigned articles; $0-75 for unsolicited articles. Sometimes pays expenses of writers on assignment.

Photos: State availability of photos with submission. Reviews 5×7 prints. Negotiates payment individually. Identification of subjects required. Buys one-time rights.

Fillers: Anecdotes, facts, gags to be illustrated by cartoonist, newsbreaks, short humor. Buys 2/year. Length: 1-300 words. Pays $5-50.

SCORE, Canada's Golf Magazine, Canadian Controlled Media Communications, 287 MacPherson Ave., Toronto, Ontario M4V 1A4 Canada. (416)928-2909. Fax: (416)928-1357. Managing Editor: Bob Weeks. 70% freelance written. Works with a small number of new/unpublished writers each year. Magazine published 7 times/year covering golf. "*Score* magazine provides seasonal coverage of the Canadian golf scene, professional, amateur, senior and junior golf for men and women golfers in Canada, the US and Europe through profiles, history, travel, editorial comment and instruction." Estab. 1982. Circ. 140,000 audited. **Pays on acceptance.** Byline given. Offers negotiable kill fee. Buys all rights and second serial (reprint) rights. Submit seasonal/holiday material 8 months in advance. Reports in 8 months. Sample copy for $2.50 (Canadian) and 9×12 SAE with IRCs. Writer's guidelines for #10 SAE and IRC.

Nonfiction: Book excerpts (golf); historical/nostalgic (golf and golf characters); interview/profile (prominent golf professionals); photo feature (golf); travel (golf destinations only). The yearly April/May issue includes tournament results from Canada, the US, Europe, Asia, Australia, etc., history, profile, and regular features. "No personal experience, technical, opinion or general-interest material. Most articles are by assignment only." Buys 25-30 mss/year. Query with published clips. Length: 700-3,500 words. Pays $200-1,500.

Photos: Send photos with query or ms. Pays $50-100 for 35mm color transparencies (positives) or $30 for 8×10 or 5×7 b&w prints. Captions, model release (if necessary), and identification of subjects required. Buys all rights.

Columns/Departments: Profile (historical or current golf personalities or characters); Great Moments ("Great Moments in Canadian Golf"—description of great single moments, usually game triumphs); New Equipment (Canadian availability only); Travel (golf destinations, including "hard" information such as greens fees, hotel accommodations, etc.); Instruction (by special assignment only; usually from teaching golf professionals); The Mental Game (psychology of the game, by special assignment only); History (golf equipment collections and collectors, development of the game, legendary figures and events). Buys 17-20 mss/year. Query with published clips or send complete ms. Length: 700-1,700 words. Pays $140-400.

Tips: "Only writers with an extensive knowledge of golf and familiarity with the Canadian golf scene should query or submit in-depth work to *Score*. Many of our features are written by professional people who play the game for a living or work in the industry. All areas mentioned under Columns/Departments are open to freelancers. Most of our *major* features are done on assignment only."

Guns

‡AMERICAN RIFLEMAN, National Rifle Association of America, 11250 Waples Mill Rd., Fairfax VA 22030. (703)267-1336. Fax: (703)267-3971. Editor: E.G. Bell, Jr. 25% freelance written. Monthly magazine covering firearms. "We are a member magazine devoted to the history, use, manufacturing, development and care of all types of portable small arms. We have a relatively sophisticated audience and international readership in this subject area." Estab. 1871. Circ. 1.8 million. **Pays on acceptance.** Publishes ms an average of 3-5 months after acceptance. Byline given. No kill fee. Buys first North American serial rights. Submit seasonal/holiday material 3 months in advance. Query for electronic submissions. Reports in 1 week on queries; 3 weeks on mss. Free writer's guidelines.

Nonfiction: Historical/nostalgic (firearms), how-to (firearms making/repair), technical (firearms related). "No fiction, poetry, essays, pure hunting tales or anything unrelated to firearms." Buys 30-35 mss/year. Query. Length: 5,000 words maximum. Pays $500 maximum. Sometimes pays expenses of writers on assignment.

Photos: Send photos with submission. Offers no additional payment for photos accepted with ms. Captions and identification of subjects required. Buys one-time rights.

Columns/Departments: From The Bench (articles on reloading ammunition or how-to firearms-related pieces), 2-3,000 words. Buys 12 mss/year. Query. Pays $400 maximum.

Tips: "For starters, it is unlikely that any of our potential authors are unfamiliar with this magazine. Well illustrated, high-quality gunsmithing articles are needed, as well as innovative material on reloading, any of the shooting sports, historical topics, etc. We have an abundance of scholarly material on the gun control issue, but we have bought the occasional thoughtful piece. Aside from our 'From The Bench' column we purchase only feature articles. We do accept unpaid submissions called 'In My Experience' that might introduce authors to us, but most are from long-time readers."

GUN DIGEST, DBI Books, Inc., 4092 Commercial Ave., Northbrook IL 60062. (312)272-6310. Editor-in-Chief: Ken Warner. 50% freelance written. Prefers to work with published/established writers but works with a small number of new/unpublished writers each year. Annual journal covering guns and shooting. Estab. 1944. **Pays on acceptance.** Publishes ms an average of 20 months after acceptance. Byline given. Buys all rights. Reports in 1 month.

Nonfiction: Buys 50 mss/issue. Query. Length: 500-5,000 words. Pays $100-600; includes photos or illustration package from author.

Photos: State availability of photos with query letter. Reviews 8×10 b&w prints. Payment for photos included in payment for ms. Captions required.

Tips: Award of $1,000 to author of best article (juried) in each issue.

GUNS & AMMO, Petersen Publishing Co., 6420 Wilshire Blvd., Los Angeles CA 90048. (213)782-2160. Fax: (213)782-2477. Editor: Kevin E. Steele. Managing Editor: Christine Potvin. 10% freelance written. Monthly magazine covering firearms. "Our readers are enthusiasts of handguns, rifles, shotguns and accessories." Circ. 600,000. **Pays on acceptance.** Publishes ms 6 months after acceptance. Byline given. Buys all rights. Submit seasonal material 6 months in advance. Accepts previously published submissions. Send typed ms with rights for sale noted along with information about when and where the article previously appeared. Query for electronic submissions. Writer's guidelines for #10 SASE.

Nonfiction: Opinion. Buys 24 mss/year. Send complete ms. Length: 800-2,500 words. Pays $125-500.

Photos: Send photos with submissions. Review 7×9 prints. Offers no additional payment for photos accepted with ms. Captions, model releases, identification of subjects required. Buys all rights.

Columns/Departments: RKBA (opinion column on right to keep and bear arms). Send complete ms. Length: 800-1,200 words. Pays $125-500.

GUNS & AMMO ANNUAL, Petersen Publishing Co., 6420 Wilshire Blvd., Los Angeles CA 90048. (213)782-2160. Fax: (213)782-2477. Editor: Bill O'Brien. Managing Editor: Christine Skaglund. 20% freelance written. Annual magazine covering firearms. "Our audience consists of enthusiasts of firearms, shooting sports and accessories." **Pays on acceptance.** Publishes ms an average of 9-12 months after acceptance. Byline given. Buys all rights. Reports in 1 month.

Nonfiction: Buys 10 mss/year. Send complete ms. Length: 2,000-4,000 words. Pays $250-500.

Photos: Send photos with submission. Reviews 8×10 prints. Offers no additional payment for photos accepted with ms. Captions, model releases, identification of subjects required. Buys all rights.

Fiction: Publishes novel excerpts.

Tips: "We need feature articles on firearms and accessories. See current issue for examples."

‡HANDGUNS, (formerly *Petersen's Handguns*), Petersen Publishing Co., 6420 Wilshire Blvd., Los Angeles CA 90048. (213)782-2868. Editor: Mr. Jan M. Libourel. Managing Editor: Chris Potvin. 60% freelance written. Monthly magazine covering handguns and handgun accessories. Estab. 1986. Circ. 150,000. **Pays on acceptance.** Byline given. No kill fee. Buys all rights. Reporting time varies. Free sample copy and writer's guidelines.

Nonfiction: General interest, historical, how-to, profile, new product and technical. "No articles not germane to established topics of magazine." Buys 50 mss/year. Send complete ms. Pays $300-500.

Photos: Send photos with submission. Reviews contact sheets and 5×7 prints. Offers no additional payment for photos accepted with ms. Captions, model releases and identification of subjects required. Buys all rights.

Tips: "Send manuscript after querying editor by telephone and establishing acceptability. We are most open to feature stories. Be guided by published examples appearing in the magazine."

MUZZLE BLASTS, National Muzzle Loading Rifle Association, P.O. Box 67, Friendship IN 47021. (812)667-5131. Fax: (812)667-5137. Editor: Robert H. Wallace. 65% freelance written. Monthly association magazine covering muzzleloading. "Articles must relate to muzzleloading or the muzzleloading era of American history." Estab. 1939. Circ. 25,000. Pays on publication. Publishes ms an average of 6 months after acceptance. Byline given. Offers $50 kill fee. Buys first North American serial rights, one-time rights and second serial (reprint) rights. Editorial lead time 4 months. Submit seasonal material 6 months in advance. Reports in 1 month on mss. Sample copy and writer's guidelines free on request.

● *Muzzle Blasts* now accepts manuscripts on 5.25 or 3.5 DOS diskettes in most major wordprocessing programs; they prefer any of the Word Perfect™ formats.

Nonfiction: Book excerpts, general interest, historical/nostalgic, how-to, humor, interview/profile, new product, personal experience, photo feature, technical, travel. "No subject matter that does not pertain to muzzleloading." Buys 80 mss/year. Query. Length: 2,500 words. Pays $300 minimum for assigned articles; $50 minimum for unsolicited articles.

Photos: Send photos with submission. Reviews 5×7 prints. Negotiates payment individually. Captions and model releases required. Buys one-time rights.

Columns/Departments: Buys 96 mss/year. Query. Pays $50-200.

Fiction: Adventure, historical, humorous. Must pertain to muzzleloading. Buys 6 mss/year. Query. Length: 2,500 words. Pays $50-300.

Fillers: Facts. Pays $50.

Tips: Please contact the NMLRA for writer's guidelines.

Horse Racing

THE BACKSTRETCH, 19899 W. Nine Mile Rd., Southfield MI 48075-3960. (810)354-3232. Fax: (810)354-3157. Editor-in-Chief/Publisher: Harriet Dalley. 85% freelance written. Works with a small number of new/unpublished writers each year. Bimonthly magazine for thoroughbred horse trainers, owners, breeders, farm managers, track personnel, jockeys, grooms and racing fans who span the age range from very young to very old. Publication of United Thoroughbred Trainers of America, Inc. Estab. 1962. Circ. 12,000. Publishes ms an average of 3 months after acceptance. Accepts previously published material. Send tearsheet or photocopy or typed ms with rights for sale noted and information about when and where the article previously appeared. For reprints, pays 50% of the amount paid for an original article. Reports in 3 months. Sample copy $3 for 9×12 SAE with 7 first-class stamps.

● This year, a larger percent of *The Backstretch* is being written by freelancers.

Nonfiction: "*Backstretch* contains mostly general information. Articles deal with biographical material on trainers, owners, jockeys, horses, issues and trends within the industry, historical track articles, etc. Unless writer's material is related to Thoroughbreds and Thoroughbred racing, it should not be submitted. Opinion on Thoroughbreds should be qualified with expertise on the subject. Articles accepted on speculation basis—payment made after material is used. If not suitable, articles are returned if SASE is included. Articles that do not require printing by a specified date are preferred. There is no special length requirement and amount paid depends on material. It is advisable to include photos, if possible. Articles should be original copies and should state whether presented to any other magazine, or whether previously printed in any other magazine. Submit complete ms. We do not buy crossword puzzles, cartoons, newspaper clippings, poetry."

‡HOOF BEATS, United States Trotting Association, 750 Michigan Ave., Columbus OH 43215. (614)224-2291. Fax: (614)228-1385. Editor: Dean A. Hoffman. 35% freelance written. Works with a small number of new/unpublished writers each year. Monthly magazine covering harness racing for the participants of the sport of harness racing. "We cover all aspects of the sport—racing, breeding, selling, etc." Estab. 1933. Circ. 18,000. Pays on publication. Publishes ms an average of 3 months after acceptance. Byline given. Buys negotiable rights. Submit seasonal/holiday material 3 months in advance. Reports in 1 month. Free sample copy, postpaid. Accepts previously published submissions. Send photocopy of article or short story. For reprints, pay is negotiable.

Nonfiction: General interest, historical/nostalgic, humor, inspirational, interview/profile, new product, personal experience, photo feature. Buys 15-20 mss/year. Query. Length: open. Pays $100-400. Pays the expenses of writers on assignment "with approval."

Photos: State availability of photos. Pays variable rates for 35mm transparencies and prints. Identification of subjects required. Buys one-time rights.

Fiction: Historical, humorous, novel excerpts, interesting fiction with a harness racing theme. Buys 2-3 mss/year. Query. Length: open. Pays $100-400.

‡THE MARYLAND HORSE, Mid-Atlantic Thoroughbred, Maryland Horse Breeders Association., Box 427, Timonium MD 21094. (410)252-2100. Editor: Richard W. Wilcke. Contact: Lucy Acton. 50% freelance written. Bimonthly magazine covering thoroughbred racing/racing and other horse sports in Maryland. **Pays on acceptance.** Publishes ms an average of 2 months after acceptance. Byline given. Buys all rights. Editorial lead time 4 months. No simultaneous or previously published submissions. Query for electronic submissions. Reports in 1 week on queries. Sample copy free on request.

Nonfiction: Book excerpts, essays, general interest, historical/nostalgic, how-to, humor, inspirational, interview/profile, new product, opinion, personal experience, photo feature—topics must all be related to horses. Buys 24 mss/year. Query. Length: 1,000-3,000 words. Pays $100-350. Sometimes pays expenses of writers on assignment.

Photos: State availability of photos with submission. Reviews contact sheets, prints. Offers $15/photo.

Columns/Departments: Pays $100-350.

THE QUARTER RACING JOURNAL, American Quarter Horse Association, P.O. Box 32470, Amarillo TX 79120. (806)376-4811. Fax: (806)376-8364. Editor-in-Chief: Jim Jennings. Executive Editor: Audie Rackley. 10% freelance written. Monthly magazine. "The official racing voice of The American Quarter Horse Association. We promote quarter horse racing. Articles include training, breeding, nutrition, sports medicine, health, history, etc." Estab. 1988. Circ. 12,000. **Pays on acceptance.** Publishes ms an average of 3 months after acceptance. Buys first North American serial rights. Submit seasonal/holiday material 3 months in advance. Reports in 1 month on queries. Free sample copy and writer's guidelines.

Nonfiction: Historical (must be on quarter horses or people associated with them), how-to (training), nutrition, health, breeding and opinion. "We welcome submissions year-round. No fiction." Query. Length: 700-2,500 words. Pays $150-300.

Photos: Send photos with submission. Offers no additional payment for photos accepted with ms. Captions and identification of subjects required.

Tips: "Query first—must be familiar with quarter horse racing and be knowledgeable of the sport. If writing on nutrition, it must be applicable. Most open to features covering nutrition, health care. Use a knowledgable source with credentials."

Hunting and Fishing

ALABAMA GAME & FISH, Game & Fish Publications, Inc., P.O. Box 741, Marietta GA 30061. Editor: Jimmy Jacobs. See *Game & Fish Publications*.

AMERICAN HUNTER, 11250 Waples Mill Rd., Fairfax VA 22030-7400. Editor: Tom Fulgham. For hunters who are members of the National Rifle Association. Circ. 1.5 million. Buys first North American serial rights. Byline given. Writer's guidelines for #10 SASE.

Nonfiction: Factual material on all phases of hunting. Not interested in material on fishing or camping. Prefers queries. Length: 1,000-2,000 words. Pays $250-450.

Photos: No additional payment made for photos used with mss. Pays $25 for b&w photos purchased without accompanying mss. Pays $50-300 for color.

ARKANSAS SPORTSMAN, Game & Fish Publications, Inc., P.O. Box 741, Marietta GA 30061. (404)953-9222. Editor: Bob Borgwat. See *Game & Fish Publications*.

‡BAIT FISHERMAN, Beaver Pond Publishing, P.O. Box 224, Greenville PA 16125. Editor: Randy Ferguson. 95% freelance written. Bimonthly magazine covering natural bait fishing, fresh and saltwater. "We are concerned with fishing for all species of fresh and saltwater fish. We are slanted exclusively toward bait fishing. We are not concerned with the use of artificial lures." Estab. 1995. Circ. 5,000. Pays on publication. Publishes ms an average of 6 months after acceptance. Byline given. Buys first rights, one-time rights or second serial (reprint) rights. Editorial lead time 4 months. Submit seasonal material 4-6 months in advance. Accepts simultaneous and previously published submissions. Accepts electronic submissions by disk but hard copy preferred. Reports in 2 months on queries; 3 months on mss. Writer's guidelines free on request.

Nonfiction: General interest, how-to (bait collection, presentation, maintenance, etc.), interview/profile, personal experience (with bait fishing specific slant), travel ("hot spot" locations). Buys 40-50 mss/year. Query. Length: 1,000-2,000 words. Pays $30-100 plus 3 copies.

Photos: Send photos with submission. Reviews contact sheets, negatives, 35mm transparencies, 5×7 prints (preferred). Offers no additional payment for photos accepted with ms. Captions, identification of subjects required. Buys one-time rights.

Fillers: Anecdotes, facts, newsbreaks, bait-specific legislation pieces, how-tos and hints. Buys 10-20/year. Length: 50-500 words. Pays $10-30.

Tips: "Query with detailed description of what you can provide our readers. State availability of photos, graphics and sidebars. We want detailed how-to, where-to and natural history pieces regarding all facets of bait fishing."

BASSIN', 15115 S. 76th E. Ave., Bixby OK 74008. (918)366-4441. Fax: (918)491-9424. E-mail: 73172.2054@compuserve.com. Managing Editor: Simon McCaffery. Executive Editor: Mark Chesnut. 90% freelance written. Magazine published 8 times/year covering freshwater fishing with emphasis on black bass. Estab. 1985. Circ. 220,000. Publishes ms an average of 8 months after acceptance. Pays within 30 days of acceptance. Byline given. Buys first North American rights. Submit seasonal material 8 months in advance. Prefers queries. Submit electronic queries through e-mail. Reports in 5 weeks. Sample copy for $3. Writer's guidelines for #10 SASE.
Nonfiction: How-to and where-to stories on bass fishing. Prefers completed ms. Length: up to 1,200 words. Pays $200-500 on acceptance.
Photos: Send photos with ms. Pays $500 for color cover. Send b&w prints or transparencies. Buys one-time rights. Photo payment on publication.
Tips: "Reduce the common fishing slang terminology when writing for *Bassin'*. This slang is usually regional and confuses anglers in other areas of the country. Good strong features will win me over more quickly than short articles or fillers. Absolutely no poetry. We also need stories on fishing tackle and techniques for catching all species of freshwater bass."

BASSMASTER MAGAZINE, B.A.S.S. Publications, 5845 Carmichael Pkwy., Montgomery AL 36141-0900. (205)272-9530. Fax: (205)279-9530. Editor: Dave Precht. 80% freelance written. Prefers to work with published/established writers. Magazine published 10 issues/year about largemouth, smallmouth and spotted bass for dedicated beginning and advanced bass fishermen. Circ. 550,000. **Pays on acceptance.** Publication date of ms after acceptance "varies—seasonal material could take years"; average time is 8 months. Byline given. Buys all rights. Submit seasonal material 6 months in advance. Reports in 2 months. Sample copy for $2. Writer's guidelines for #10 SASE.
Nonfiction: Historical, interview (of knowledgeable people in the sport), profile (outstanding fishermen), travel (where to go to fish for bass), how-to (catch bass and enjoy the outdoors), new product (reels, rods and bass boats), conservation related to bass fishing. "No 'Me and Joe go fishing' type articles." Query. Length: 400-2,100 words. Pays 20¢/word.
• Needs destination stories (how to fish a certain area) for the Northwest and Northeast.
Columns/Departments: Short Cast/News & Views (upfront regular feature covering news-related events such as new state bass records, unusual bass fishing happenings, conservation, new products and editorial viewpoints); 250-400 words.
Photos: "We want a mixture of b&w and color photos." Pays $50 minimum for b&w prints. Pays $300-350 for color cover transparencies. Captions required; model releases preferred. Buys all rights.
Fillers: Anecdotes, short humor, newsbreaks. Buys 4-5 mss/issue. Length: 250-500 words. Pays $50-100.
Tips: "Editorial direction continues in the short, more direct how-to article. Compact, easy-to-read information is our objective. Shorter articles with good graphics, such as how-to diagrams, step-by-step instruction, etc., will enhance a writer's articles submitted to *Bassmaster Magazine*. The most frequent mistakes made by writers in completing an article for us are poor grammar, poor writing, poor organization and superficial research."

BC OUTDOORS, OP Publishing, 202-1132 Hamilton St., Vancouver, British Columbia V6B 2S2 Canada. (604)687-1581. Fax: (604)687-1925. Editor: Karl Bruhn. 80% freelance written. Works with a small number of new/unpublished writers each year. Magazine published 8 times/year covering fishing, camping, hunting and the environment of outdoor recreation. Estab. 1946. Circ. 42,000. Pays on publication. Publishes ms an average of 3 months after acceptance. Byline given. Offers negotiable kill fee. Buys first North American serial rights. Query for electronic submissions. Reports in 1 month. Sample copy and writer's guidelines for 8×10 SAE with 7 first-class stamps.
Nonfiction: How-to (new or innovative articles on outdoor subjects), personal experience (outdoor adventure), outdoor topics specific to British Columbia. "We would like to receive how-to, where-to features dealing with hunting and fishing in British Columbia and the Yukon." Buys 80-90 mss/year. Query. Length: 1,500-2,000 words. Pays $300-500. Sometimes pays the expenses of writers on assignment.
• Wants in-depth, informative, professional writing only.
Photos: State availability of photos with query. Pays $25-75 on publication for 5×7 b&w prints; $35-150 for color contact sheets and 35mm transparencies. Captions and identification of subjects required. Buys one-time rights.
Tips: "Emphasis on environmental issues. Those pieces with a conservation component have a better chance of being published. Subject must be specific to British Columbia. We receive many manuscripts written by people who obviously do not know the magazine or market. The writer has a better chance of breaking in at our publication with short, lesser-paying articles and fillers, because we have a stable of regular writers in constant touch who produce most main features."

‡BUGLE, Journal of Elk and the Hunt, Rocky Mountain Elk Foundation, 2291 W. Broadway, Missoula MT 59802. (406)523-4568. Editor: Dan Crockett. Contact: Jan Brocci, assistant editor. 50% freelance written. Quarterly magazine covering conservation and hunting. "*Bugle* is the membership publication of the Rocky Mountain Elk Foundation, a nonprofit wildlife conservation group; it also sells on newsstands. Our readers are predominantly hunters, many of them naturalists who care deeply about protecting wildlife habitat. Hunting stories and essays should celebrate the hunting experience, demonstrating respect for wildlife, the land and the hunt. Articles on elk behavior or elk habitat should include personal observations and entertain as well as educate." Estab. 1984. Circ. 150,000. **Pays on acceptance**. Publishes ms 6-9 months after acceptance. Byline given. Offers variable kill fee. Buys one-time rights. Editorial lead time 6 months. Submit seasonal material 6 months in advance. Accepts previously published submissions. Query for electronic submissions. Reports in 1 month on queries; 2 months on mss. Sample copy $5. Writer's guidelines for #10 SASE.

Nonfiction: Book excerpts, essays, general interest (elk related), historical/nostalgic, humor, opinion, personal experience, photo feature. No how-to, where-to. Buys 2 mss/year. Query with or without published clips or send complete ms. Length: 1,500-4,500 words. Pays 15-25¢/word and 3 contributor copies; more issues at cost. Pays expenses of writers on assignment.

Columns/Departments: Situation Ethics, 1,000-2,000 words; Thoughts & Themes, 1,500-4,000 words; Women in the Outdoors, 1,000-3,000 words. Buys 12 mss/year. Query with or without published clips or send complete ms. Pays 15-25¢/word.

Fiction: Adventure, historical, humorous, slice-of-life vignettes, western. No fiction that doesn't pertain to elk or elk hunting. Buys 4 mss/year. Query with or without published clips or send complete ms. Length: 1,500-4,500 words. Pays 15-25¢/word.

Poetry: Free verse, haiku, light verse, traditional. Buys 1-2 poems/year. Submit maximum 6 poems. Pays $50-200.

Tips: "Creative queries (250-500 words) that showcase your concept and your style remain the most effective approach. We're hungry for submissions for two specific columns: Situation Ethics and Women in the Outdoors. Send a SASE for guidelines. We also welcome strong well-reasoned opinion pieces on topics pertinent to hunting and wildlife conservation, and humorous pieces about elk behavior or encounters with elk (hunting or otherwise)."

CALIFORNIA GAME & FISH, Game & Fish Publications, Inc., Box 741, Marietta GA 30061. Editor: Burt Carey. See *Game & Fish Publications*.

FIELD & STREAM, 2 Park Ave., New York NY 10016-5695. Editor: Duncan Barnes. 50% freelance written. Eager to work with new/unpublished writers. Monthly. "Broad-based service magazine for the hunter and fisherman. Editorial content ranges from very basic how-to stories detailing a useful technique or a device that sportsmen can make, to articles of penetrating depth about national hunting, fishing, and related activities. Also humor and personal essays, nostalgia and 'mood pieces' on the hunting or fishing experience." Estab. 1895. **Pays on acceptance.** Buys first rights. Byline given. Occasionally accepts previously published submissions if suitable. Send photocopy of article and information about when and where it previously appeared. Reports in 2 months. Query. Writer's guidelines for #10 SASE.

Nonfiction: Length: 1,500-2,000 words for features. Payment varies depending on the quality of work, importance of the article. Pays $800 and up for major features. *Field & Stream* also publishes regional sections with feature articles on hunting and fishing in specific areas of the country. The sections are geographically divided into East, Midwest, West and South, and appear 12 months/year.

Photos: Prefers color slides to b&w. Query first with photos. When photos purchased separately, pays $450 minimum for color. Buys first rights to photos.

Fillers: Buys short "how it's done" fillers for "By the Way." Must be unusual or helpful subjects. Also buys "Field Guide" pieces, short articles on natural phenomena as specifically related to hunting and fishing; "Myths and Misconceptions," short pieces debunking a commonly held belief about hunting and fishing, and short "Outdoor Basics" of "Sportsmen's Project" articles.

FLORIDA GAME & FISH, Game & Fish Publications, Inc., Box 741, Marietta GA 30061. (404)953-9222. Editor: Jimmy Jacobs. See *Game & Fish Publications*.

FLORIDA SPORTSMAN, Wickstrom Publishers Inc., 5901 SW 74 St., Miami FL 33143. (305)661-4222. Fax: (305)284-0277. Editor: Biff Lampton. 30% freelance written. Works with new/unpublished writers. Monthly magazine covering fishing, boating and related sports—Florida and Caribbean only. Circ. 100,000. **Pays on acceptance**. Publishes ms an average of 6 months after acceptance. Byline given. Offers 50% kill fee. Buys first North American serial rights. Submit seasonal/holiday material 6 months in advance. Reports in 1 week on queries; 1 month on mss. *Writer's Market* recommends allowing 2 months for reply. Free sample copy. Writer's guidelines for #10 SASE.

Nonfiction: Essays (environment or nature), how-to (fishing, hunting, boating), humor (outdoors angle), personal experience (in fishing, etc.), technical (boats, tackle, etc., as particularly suitable for Florida specialties). "We use reader service pieces almost entirely—how-to, where-to, etc. One or two environmental pieces per issue as well. Writers *must* be Florida based, or have lengthy experience in Florida outdoors. All articles must have strong Florida emphasis. We do not want to see general how-to-fish-or-boat pieces which might well appear in a national or wide-regional magazine." Buys 40-60 mss/year. Query. Length: 2,000-3,000 words. Pays $300-400. Sometimes pays expenses of writers on assignment.

Photos: Send photos with submission. Reviews 35mm transparencies and 4×5 and larger prints. Offers no additional payment for photos accepted with ms. Buys one-time rights.

Tips: "Feature articles are most open to freelancers; however there is little chance of acceptance unless contributor is an accomplished and avid outdoorsman *and* a competent writer-photographer with considerable experience in Florida."

FLORIDA WILDLIFE, Florida Game & Fresh Water Fish Commission, 620 S. Meridian St., Tallahassee FL 32399-1600. (904)488-5563. Fax: (904)488-6988. Editor: Dick Sublette. Associate Editor: Janisse Ray. About 30% freelance written. Bimonthly 4-color state magazine covering hunting, natural history, fishing, endangered species and wildlife conservation. "In outdoor sporting articles we seek themes of wholesome recreation. In nature articles we seek accuracy and conservation purpose." Estab. 1947. Circ. 26,000. Pays on publication. Byline given. Buys first North American serial and occasionally second serial (reprint) rights. Submit seasonal/holiday material 6 months in advance. Accepts simultaneous and previously published submissions. Send tearsheet of article or typed ms with rights for sale noted. "Inform us if it is previously published work." Reports in 2 months (acknowledgement of receipt of materials); up to 2 years for acceptance, usually less for rejections. Prefers photo/ms packages. Sample copy for $2.95. Writer's/photographer's guidelines for SASE.

Nonfiction: General interest (bird watching, hiking, camping, boating), how-to (hunting and fishing), humor (wildlife related; no anthropomorphism), inspirational (conservation oriented), personal experience (wildlife, hunting, fishing, outdoors), photo feature (Florida species: game, nongame, botany), technical (rarely purchased, but open to experts). "We buy general interest hunting, fishing and nature stories. No stories that humanize animals, or opinionated stories not based on confirmable facts." Buys 30-40 mss/year. Send slides/ms. Length: 500-1,500 words. Generally pays $50/published page.

Photos: State availability of photos with story query. Prefer 35mm color slides of hunting, fishing, and natural science series of Florida wildlife species. Pays $20-50 for inside photos; $100 for front cover photos, $50 for back cover. "We like short, specific captions." Buys one-time rights.

Fiction: "We rarely buy fiction, and then only if it is true to life and directly related to good sportsmanship and conservation. No fairy tales, erotica, profanity or obscenity." Buys 2-3 mss/year. Send complete mss and label "fiction." Length: 500-1,200 words. Generally pays $50/published page.

Tips: "Read and study recent issues for subject matter, style and examples of our viewpoint, philosophy and treatment. We look for wholesome recreation, ethics, safety, and good outdoor experience more than bagging the game in our stories. We usually need well-written hunting and freshwater fishing articles that are entertaining and informative and that describe places to hunt and fish in Florida."

FLY FISHERMAN, Cowles Magazines Inc., P.O. Box 8200, Harrisburg PA 17105-8200. (717)657-9555. Fax: (717)657-9526. Editor and Publisher: John Randolph. Managing Editor: Philip Hanyok. 85-90% freelance written. Bimonthly magazine on fly fishing. Estab. 1969. Circ. 130,000. Reports in 2 months. Sample copy for 9×12 SAE with 7 first-class stamps.

‡FLY FISHING IN SALT WATERS, Hook and Release Publications, Inc., 2001 Western Ave., Suite 210, Seattle WA 98121. (206)443-3273. Editor: R.P. Van Gytenbeek. 90% freelance written. Bimonthly magazine covering fly fishing in salt waters. Estab. 1994. Circ. 44,000. **Pays on acceptance.** Publishes ms an average of 1-12 months after acceptance. Byline given. Kill fee negotiable. Buys first North American serial rights and electronic storage and retrieval. Editorial lead time 2 months. Submit seasonal material at least 2 months in advance. No simultaneous or previously published submissions. Query for electronic submissions. Prefers 3.5 disk with text in ASCII format only. Reports in 1 month on queries; 2 months on mss. Sample copy for $6. Writer's guidelines for #10 SASE.

Nonfiction: Book excerpts, essays, historical/nostalgic, how-to, interview/profile, new product, personal experience, photo feature, technical, travel, resource issues (conservation). Buys 40-50 mss/year. Query. Length: 1,500-2,500 words. Pays $400-500.

Photos: Send photos with submission. Reviews transparencies (35mm color only). Negotiates payment individually. Captions, identification of subjects required. Buys one-time rights.

Columns/Departments: Legends/Reminiscences (history-profiles-nostalgia), 2,000-2,500 words; Resource (conservation issues), 1,500 words; Fly Tier's Bench (how to tie saltwater flies), 1,000-1,200 words, photos critical; Tackle & Technique (technical how-to), 1,500 words, photos or illustrations critical; Boating (technical how-to), 2,000-2,500 words; (Other departments are mostly staff written or by assignment only). Buys 25-30 mss/year. Query. Pays $400-500.

Fiction: Adventure, humorous, mainstream. Send complete ms. Length: 2,000-3,000 words. Pays $500.

Fillers: Most fillers are staff written.

FUR-FISH-GAME, 2878 E. Main, Columbus OH 43209-9947. Editor: Mitch Cox. 65% freelance written. Works with a small number of new/unpublished writers each year. Monthly magazine for outdoorsmen of all ages who are interested in hunting, fishing, trapping, dogs, camping, conservation and related topics. Estab. 1900. Circ. 105,000. **Pays on acceptance.** Publishes ms an average of 7 months after acceptance.

Byline given. Buys first serial rights or all rights. Reports in 2 months. Query. Sample copy for $1 and 9×12 with SAE. Writer's guidelines for #10 SASE.

Nonfiction: "We are looking for informative, down-to-earth stories about hunting, fishing, trapping, dogs, camping, boating, conservation and related subjects. Nostalgic articles are also used. Many of our stories are 'how-to' and should appeal to small-town and rural readers who are true outdoorsmen. Some recent articles have told how to train a gun dog, catch big-water catfish, outfit a bowhunter and trap late-season muskrat. We also use personal experience stories and an occasional profile, such as an article about an old-time trapper. 'Where-to' stories are used occasionally if they have broad appeal." Length: 500-3,000 words. Pays $75-150 depending upon quality, photo support, and importance to magazine. Short filler stories pay $35-80.

Photos: Send photos with ms. Photos are part of ms package and receive no additional payment. Prefers color prints or transparencies. Prints can be 5×7 or 8×10. Captions required.

Tips: "We are always looking for quality articles that tell how to hunt or fish for game animals or birds that are popular with everyday outdoorsmen but often overlooked in other publications, such as catfish, bluegill, crappie, squirrel, rabbit, crows, etc. We also use articles on standard seasonal subjects such as deer and pheasant, but like to see a fresh approach or new technique. Trapping articles, especially instructional ones based on personal experience, are useful all year. Articles on gun dogs, ginseng and do-it-yourself projects are also popular with our readers. An assortment of photos and/or sketches greatly enhances any manuscript, and sidebars, where applicable, can also help."

GAME & FISH PUBLICATIONS, INC., 2250 Newmarket Pkwy., Suite 110, Marietta GA 30067. (404)953-9222. Fax: (404)933-9510. Editorial Director: Ken Dunwoody. Publishes 30 different monthly outdoor magazines, each one covering the fishing and hunting opportunities in a particular state or region (see individual titles and editors). 90% freelance written. Estab. 1975. Total circ. 500,000. Pays 75 days prior to cover date of issue. Publishes ms an average of 6 months after acceptance. Byline given. Offers negotiable kill fee. Buys first North American serial rights. Submit seasonal material at least 8 months in advance. Editors prefer to hold queries until that season's material is assigned. Reports in 3 months on mss. Sample copy for $2.50 and 9×12 SASE. Writer's guidelines for #10 SASE.

Nonfiction: Prefer queries over unsolicited ms. Article lengths either 1,500 or 2,500 words. Pays separately for articles and accompanying photos. Manuscripts pay $125-300, cover photos $250, inside color $75 and b&w $25. Reviews transparencies and b&w prints. Prefers captions and identification of species/subjects. Buys one-time rights to photos.

Fiction: Buys some humor and nostalgia stories pertaining to hunting and fishing. Pays $125-250. Length 1,500-2,500 words.

Tips: "Our readers are experienced anglers and hunters, and we try to provide them with useful, entertaining articles about where, when and how to enjoy the best hunting and fishing in their state or region. We also cover topics concerning game and fish management, conservation and environmental issues. Most articles should be aimed at outdoorsmen in one particular state. After familiarizing themselves with our magazine(s), writers should query the appropriate state editor (see individual listings) or send to Ken Dunwoody."

GEORGIA SPORTSMAN, Game & Fish Publications, Box 741, Marietta GA 30061. (404)953-9222. Editor: Jimmy Jacobs. See *Game & Fish Publications*.

GRAY'S SPORTING JOURNAL, P.O. Box 1207, Augusta GA 30903-1207. Editor: David C. Foster. Contact: Leslie Nelson. 100% freelance written. Bimonthly magazine covering hunting and fishing. "Engage discerning audience with high quality literature (fiction and nonfiction), poetry, beautiful photography and original art." Estab. 1976. Circ. 30,000. Pays on publication. Publishes ms an average of 1 year after acceptance. Byline given. Buys first North American serial rights. Editorial lead time 2 months. Submit seasonal material 1 year in advance. Accepts simultaneous submissions. Query for electronic submissions. Sample copy for $3. Writer's guidelines free on request.

Nonfiction: Historical/nostalgic, humor, personal experience, photo feature, travel. Special issues: Expeditions & Guides Book (December), travel-related book for hunters and anglers. Buys 70 mss/year. Send complete ms. Pays $125-1,500. Sometimes pays expenses of writers on assignment.

Photos: Freelancers should state availability of photos with submission. Reviews transparencies. Offers $75-250/photo. Identification of subjects required. Buys one-time rights.

Fiction: Adventure, sporting life. Buys 30 mss/year. Send complete ms. Pays $500-2500.

Poetry: Contact: Leslie Nelson. Free verse, light verse, traditional. Buys 6 poems/year. Submit maximum 3 poems. Pays $250.

GREAT PLAINS GAME & FISH, Game & Fish Publications, Box 741, Marietta GA 30061. (404)953-9222. Editor: Nick Gilmore. See *Game & Fish Publications*.

ILLINOIS GAME & FISH, Game & Fish Publications, Inc., Box 741, Marietta GA 30061. (404)953-9222. Editor: Bill Hartlage. See *Game & Fish Publications*.

INDIANA GAME & FISH, Game & Fish Publications, Inc., Box 741, Marietta GA 30061. (404)953-9222. Editor: Ken Freel. See *Game & Fish Publications*.

IOWA GAME & FISH, Game & Fish Publications, Inc., Box 741, Marietta GA 30061. (404)953-9222. Editor: Bill Hartlage. See *Game & Fish Publications*.

KENTUCKY GAME & FISH, Game & Fish Publications, Inc., Box 741, Marietta GA 30061. (404)953-9222. Editor: Bill Hartlage. See *Game & Fish Publications*.

LOUISIANA GAME & FISH, Game & Fish Publications, Inc., Box 741, Marietta GA 30061. (404)953-9222. Editor: Bob Borgwat. See *Game & Fish Publications*.

‡THE MAINE SPORTSMAN, P.O. Box 365, Augusta ME 04330. Editor: Harry Vanderweide. 80% freelance written. "Eager to work with new/unpublished writers, but because we run over 30 regular columns, it's hard to get into *The Maine Sportsman* as a beginner." Monthly tabloid. Estab. 1972. Circ. 30,000. Pays "during month of publication." Buys first rights. Publishes ms an average of 3 months after acceptance. Byline given. Reports in 2 weeks. Accepts previously published submissions. Send typed ms with rights for sale. For reprints, pays 100% of amount paid for an original article.
Nonfiction: "We publish only articles about Maine hunting and fishing activities. Any well-written, researched, knowledgeable article about that subject area is likely to be accepted by us." Mostly wants Maine-specific where-to-go articles. Buys 25-40 mss/issue. Submit complete ms. Length: 200-2,000 words. Pays $20-300. Sometimes pays the expenses of writers on assignment.
Photos: "We can have illustrations drawn, but prefer 1-3 b&w photos." Submit photos with accompanying ms. Pays $5-50 for b&w print.
Tips: "It's rewarding finding a writer who has a fresh way of looking at ordinary events. Specific where-to-go about Maine is needed."

MARLIN, The International Sportfishing Magazine, Marlin Magazine, a division of World Publications, Inc., P.O. Box 2456, Winter Park FL 32790. (407)628-4802. Editor: David Ritchie. 90% freelance written. Bimonthly magazine on big game fishing. "*Marlin* covers the sport of big game fishing (billfish, tuna, sharks, dorado and wahoo). Our readers are sophisticated, affluent and serious about their sport—they expect a high-class, well-written magazine that provides information and practical advice." Estab. 1982. Circ. 30,000. **Pays on acceptance for text**, on publication for photos. Publishes ms an average of 3 months after acceptance. Byline given. Buys first North American serial rights. Submit seasonal/holiday material 2-3 months in advance. Query for electronic submissions. Sample copy and writer's guidelines for $2.90 and SAE.
Nonfiction: General interest, how-to (bait-rigging, tackle maintenance, etc.), new product, personal experience, photo feature, technical, travel. "No freshwater fishing stories. No 'me & Joe went fishing' stories, unless top quality writing." Buys 30-50 mss/year. Query with published clips. Length: 800-2,200 words. Pays $250-500.
Photos: State availability of photos with submission. Original slides, please. Offers $25-300/photo. $500 for a cover. Buys one-time rights.
Columns/Departments: Tournament Reports (reports on winners of major big game fishing tournaments), 300-600 words; Blue Water Currents (news features), 300-900 words. Buys 25 mss/year. Query. Pays $100-250. Accepts previously published articles in news section only. Send photocopy of article, including information about when and where the article previously appeared. For reprints, pays 50-75% of the amount paid for an original article.
Tips: "Tournament reports are a good way to break in to *Marlin*. Make them short but accurate, and provide photos of fishing action (*not* dead fish hanging up at the docks!). We always need how-tos and news items. Our destination pieces (travel stories) emphasize where and when to fish, but include information on where to stay also. For features: crisp, high action stories—nothing flowery or academic. Technical/how-to: concise and informational—specific details. News: Again, concise with good details—watch for legislation affecting big game fishing, outstanding catches, new clubs and organizations, new trends and conservation issues."

MICHIGAN OUT-OF-DOORS, P.O. Box 30235, Lansing MI 48909. (517)371-1041. Fax: (517)371-1505. Editor: Kenneth S. Lowe. 50% freelance written. Works with a small number of new/unpublished writers each year. Monthly magazine emphasizing outdoor recreation, especially hunting and fishing, conservation and environmental affairs. Estab. 1947. Circ. 130,000. **Pays on acceptance.** Publishes ms an average of 6 months after acceptance. Byline given. Buys first North American serial rights. Phone queries OK. Submit seasonal/holiday material 6 months in advance. Reports in 1 month. *Writer's Market* recommends allowing 2 months for reply. Sample copy for $2. Free writer's guidelines.

> *Always check the most recent copy of a magazine for the address and editor's name before you send in a query or manuscript.*

Nonfiction: Exposé, historical, how-to, informational, interview, nostalgia, personal experience, personal opinion, photo feature, profile. No humor or poetry. "Stories *must* have a Michigan slant unless they treat a subject of universal interest to our readers." Buys 8 mss/issue. Send complete ms. Length: 1,000-3,000 words. Pays $75 minimum for feature stories. Pays expenses of writers on assignment.

Photos: Purchased with or without accompanying ms. Pays $15 minimum for any size b&w glossy prints; $150 maximum for color (for cover). Offers no additional payment for photos accepted with accompanying ms. Buys one-time rights. Captions preferred.

Tips: "Top priority is placed on true accounts of personal adventures in the out-of-doors—well-written tales of very unusual incidents encountered while hunting, fishing, camping, hiking, etc. The most rewarding aspect of working with freelancers is realizing we had a part in their development. But it's annoying to respond to queries that never produce a manuscript."

MICHIGAN SPORTSMAN, Game & Fish Publications, Inc., Box 741, Marietta GA 30061. (404)953-9222. Editor: Dennis Schmidt. See *Game & Fish Publications*.

MID WEST OUTDOORS, Mid West Outdoors, Ltd., 111 Shore Drive, Hinsdale (Burr Ridge) IL 60521-5885. (708)887-7722. Fax: (708)887-1958. Editor: Gene Laulunen. Monthly tabloid emphasizing fishing, hunting, camping and boating. 100% freelance written. Estab. 1967. Circ. 50,000. Pays on publication. Buys simultaneous rights. Byline given. Submit seasonal material 2 months in advance. Accepts simultaneous and previously published submissions. Send tearsheet of article. Reports in 3 weeks. Publishes ms an average of 3 months after acceptance. Sample copy for $1. Writer's guidelines for #10 SASE.

Nonfiction: How-to (fishing, hunting, camping in the Midwest) and where-to-go (fishing, hunting, camping within 500 miles of Chicago). "We do not want to see any articles on 'my first fishing, hunting or camping experiences,' 'cleaning my tackle box,' 'tackle tune-up,' or 'catch and release.' " Buys 1,800 unsolicited mss/year. Send complete ms or story on 3.5 diskette with ms included. Length: 1,000-1,500 words. Pays $15-30.

Photos: Offers no additional payment for photos accompanying ms unless used as covers; uses b&w prints. Buys all rights. Captions required.

Columns/Departments: Fishing, Hunting. Open to suggestions for columns/departments. Send complete ms. Pays $25.

Tips: "Break in with a great unknown fishing hole or new technique within 500 miles of Chicago. Where, how, when and why. Know the type of publication you are sending material to."

MID-ATLANTIC GAME & FISH, Game & Fish Publications, Inc., Box 741, Marietta GA 30061. (404)953-9222. Editor: Ken Freel. See *Game & Fish Publications*.

MINNESOTA SPORTSMAN, Game & Fish Publications, Inc., Box 741, Marietta GA 30061. (404)953-9222. Editor: Dennis Schmidt. See *Game & Fish Publications*.

MISSISSIPPI GAME & FISH, Game & Fish Publications, Inc., Box 741, Marietta GA 30061. (404)953-9222. Editor: Bob Borgwat. See *Game & Fish Publications*.

MISSOURI GAME & FISH, Game & Fish Publications, Inc., Box 741, Marietta GA 30061. (404)953-9222. Editor: Bob Borgwat. See *Game & Fish Publications*.

MUSKY HUNTER MAGAZINE, Outlook Publishing, P.O. Box 147, Minocqua WI 54548. (715)356-6301. Fax: (715)358-2807. Editor: Jim Saric. 90% freelance written. Bimonthly magazine on musky fishing. "Serves the vertical market of musky fishing enthusiasts. We're interested in how-to where-to articles." Estab. 1988. Circ. 18,000. Pays on publication. Publishes ms an average of 4 months after acceptance. Byline given. Buys first or one-time rights. Submit seasonal/holiday material 4 months in advance. Reports in 2 months. Sample copy for 9×12 SAE with 5 first-class stamps. Writer's guidelines for #10 SASE.

Nonfiction: Historical/nostalgic (related only to musky fishing), how-to (modify lures, boats and tackle for musky fishing), personal experience (must be musky fishing experience), technical (fishing equipment), travel (to lakes and areas for musky fishing). Buys 50 mss/year. Send complete ms. Length: 1,000-2,000 words. Pays $100-200 for assigned articles; $50-200 for unsolicited articles. Payment of contributor copies or other premiums negotiable.

Photos: Send photos with submission. Reviews 35mm transparencies and 3×5 prints. Offers no additional payment for photos accepted with ms. Identification of subjects required. Buys one-time rights.

NEW ENGLAND GAME & FISH, Game & Fish Publications, Inc., Box 741, Marietta GA 30061. (404)953-9222. Editor: Steve Carpenteri. See *Game & Fish Publications*.

NEW YORK GAME & FISH, Game & Fish Publications, Inc., Box 741, Marietta GA 30061. (404)953-9222. Editor: Steve Carpenteri. See *Game & Fish Publications*.

NORTH AMERICAN FISHERMAN, Official Publication of North American Fishing Club, 12301 Whitewater Dr., Suite 260, Minnetonka MN 55343. (612)936-0555. Publisher: Mike Edison. Editor: Steve Pennaz. 75% freelance written. Magazine published 7 times a year on fresh- and saltwater fishing across North America. Estab. 1987. Circ. 475,000. **Pays on acceptance.** Publishes ms an average of 4 months after acceptance. Offers $150 kill fee. Buys first North American serial, one-time and all rights. Submit seasonal/holiday material 6 months in advance. Reports in 1 month. Sample copy for $5 and 9×12 SAE with 6 first-class stamps. Prefers written queries; no longer accepts phone queries.
Nonfiction: How-to (species-specific information on how-to catch fish), news briefs on fishing from various state agencies, travel (where to information on first class fishing lodges). Buys 35-40 mss/year. Query by mail. Length: 700-2,100. Pays $100-500.
Photos: Send photos with submission. Additional payment made for photos accepted with ms. Captions and identification of subjects required. Buys one-time rights. Pays up to $200 for inside art, $500 for cover.
Fillers: Facts, newsbreaks. Buys 60/year. Length: 50-100. Pays $35-50.
Tips: "We are looking for news briefs on important law changes, new lakes, etc. Areas most open for freelancers are: full-length features, cover photos and news briefs. Know what subject you are writing about. Our audience of avid fresh and saltwater anglers know how to fish and will see through weak or dated fishing information. Must be on cutting edge for material to be considered."

‡NORTH AMERICAN HUNTER, Official Publication of the North American Hunting Club, North American Hunting Club, P.O. Box 3401, Minnetonka MN 55343. (612)936-9333. Fax: (612)936-9755. Publisher: Russ Nolan. Editor: Bill Miller. 60% freelance written. A bimonthly magazine for members of the North American Hunting Club covering strictly North American hunting. "The purpose of the NAHC is to enhance the hunting skill and enjoyment of its 665,000 members." Estab. 1978. Circ. 665,000. **Pays on acceptance.** Publishes ms an average of 6-10 months after acceptance. Byline given. Buys first North American serial rights, first rights, one-time rights, second serial (reprint) rights or all rights. Submit seasonal/holiday material 1 year in advance. Query for electronic submissions. Reports in 2 months. Accepts previously published submissions. Send typed ms with rights for sale noted. For reprints, pays 50% of amount paid for an original article. Sample copy $5; writer's guidelines for #10 SASE.
Nonfiction: Exposé (on hunting issues); how-to (on hunting); humor; interview/profile; new product; opinion; personal experience; photo feature and where-to-hunt. No fiction or "Me and Joe." Buys 18-24 mss/year. Query. Length: 1,000-2,500 words. Pays $200-325 for assigned articles; pays $25-325 for unsolicited articles. Bonus for mss submitted on computer disks.
Photos: Send photos with submissions. Reviews transparencies and 5×7 or 8×10 prints. Offers no additional payment for photos accepted with ms. Captions and identification of subjects required. Buys one-time rights.
Tips: "Write stories as if they are from one hunting friend to another."

NORTH AMERICAN WHITETAIL, The Magazine Devoted to the Serious Trophy Deer Hunter, Game & Fish Publications, Inc., 2250 Newmarket Pkwy., Suite 110, Marietta GA 30067. (404)953-9222. Fax: (404)933-9510. Editor: Gordon Whittington. 70% freelance written. Magazine published 8 times/year about hunting trophy-class white-tailed deer in North America, primarily the US. "We provide the serious hunter with highly sophisticated information about trophy-class whitetails and how, when and where to hunt them. We are not a general hunting magazine or a magazine for the very occasional deer hunter." Estab. 1982. Circ. 170,000. Pays 75 days prior to cover date of issue. Publishes ms an average of 6 months after acceptance. Byline given. Offers negotiable kill fee. Buys first North American serial rights. Submit seasonal/holiday material 10 months in advance. Reports in 3 months on mss. Editor prefers to keep queries on file, without notification, until the article can be assigned or author informs of prior sale. Sample copy for $3 and 9×12 SAE with 7 first-class stamps. Writer's guidelines for #10 SASE.
Nonfiction: How-to interview/profile. Buys 50 mss/year. Query. Length: 1,000-3,000 words. Pays $150-400.
Photos: Send photos with submission. Reviews 2×2 transparencies and 8×10 prints. Offers no additional payment for photos accepted with ms. Captions and identification of subjects required. Buys one-time rights.
Columns/Departments: Trails and Tails (nostalgic, humorous or other entertaining styles of deer-hunting material, fictional or nonfictional), 1,400 words. Buys 8 mss/year. Send complete ms. Pays $150.
Tips: "Our articles are written by persons who are deer hunters first, writers second. Our hard-core hunting audience can see through material produced by non-hunters or those with only marginal deer-hunting expertise. We have a continual need for expert profiles/interviews. Study the magazine to see what type of hunting expert it takes to qualify for our use, and look at how those articles have been directed by the writers. Good photography of the interviewee and his hunting results must accompany such pieces."

NORTH CAROLINA GAME & FISH, Game & Fish Publications, Inc., Box 741, Marietta GA 30061. (404)953-9222. Fax: (419)394-7405. Editor: Jeff Samsel. See *Game & Fish Publications.*

OHIO GAME & FISH, Game & Fish Publications, Inc., Box 741, Marietta GA 30061. (404)953-9222. Editor: Steve Carpenteri. See *Game & Fish Publications.*

OHIO OUT-OF-DOORS, Redbird Publications, P.O. Box 117, St. Marys OH 45885. (419)394-3226. Fax: (419)394-7405. Publisher/Managing Editor: John Andreoni. 40-50% freelance written. Monthly magazine that covers outdoor activities and conservation issues. "We cover outdoors-related topics; the wise use of game and fish management; appreciation of the outdoors. Our readers are hunters, fishermen and conservationists." Estab. 1991. Circ. 4,000. Pays on publication. Byline given. Not copyrighted. Buys first North American serial rights. Submit seasonal/holiday material 4 months in advance. Accepts previously published submissions. Send typed ms or legible photocopy or tearsheet with rights for sale noted and information about when and where the article previously appeared. Pays 100% of the amount paid for an original article. Query for electronic submissions. Reports in 1 month on queries. Sample copy for 11 × 13 SAE with 4 first-class stamps.

Nonfiction: Essays, general interest, historical/nostalgic, how-to (catch fish, make rods, learn to shoot or do anything outdoor oriented), humor, interview/profile, new product, opinion, photo feature, technical, travel. "We are looking for material on spring fishing, upland game, wildlife hunting, fishing for specifics, turkey hunting, deer hunting, boats, mushroom hunting, ice fishing and black powder guns. No 'Bob and me' or 'me and Joe' articles focusing on kill or catch." Buys 20 mss/year. *Query* only. Length: 500-2,000 words. Pays $25-50 for assigned articles.

Photos: State availability of photos or send photos with submission. Reviews 35mm vertical transparencies, 5 × 7 prints. Offers $5 for b&w, $10 for color and $25 for cover (one-time use vertical shot).

Columns/Departments: Buys 36 mss/year. *Query.* Length: 500-800 words. Pays $25 minimum.

Fiction: Adventure (outdoor slant), historical (outdoor slant), humorous. Buys few mss/year. Query. Length: 500-2,000 words.

Tips: "Writers must sell publisher/editor with a query. Query should reflect writing style. Writers will have the best luck submitting material for features. Pick a specific topic, research well, quote authorities when possible and include a powerful, well-written lead.

OKLAHOMA GAME & FISH, Game & Fish Publications, Box 741, Marietta GA 30061. (404)953-9222. Fax: (404)933-9510. Editor: Nick Gilmore. See *Game & Fish Publications.*

PENNSYLVANIA GAME & FISH, Game & Fish Publications, Inc., Box 741, Marietta GA 30061. (404)953-9222. Editor: Steve Carpenteri. See *Game & Fish Publications.*

PETERSEN'S HUNTING, Petersen's Publishing Co., 8490 Sunset Blvd., Los Angeles CA 90069. (310)854-2184. Editor: Todd Smith. Managing Editor: Denise LaSalle. 40% freelance written. Works with a small number of new/unpublished writers each year. Monthly magazine covering sport hunting. "We are a 'how-to' magazine devoted to all facets of sport hunting, with the intent to make our readers more knowledgeable, more successful and safer hunters." Circ. 325,000. **Pays on acceptance.** Publishes ms an average of 9 months after acceptance. Byline given. Offers $50 kill fee. Buys all rights. Submit seasonal/holiday queries 9 months in advance. Reports in 2 weeks. Free sample copy and writer's guidelines covering format, sidebars and computer disks available on request.

Nonfiction: General interest, historical/nostalgic, how-to (on hunting techniques), travel. Special issues: Hunting Annual (August). Buys 30 mss/year. Query. Length: 2,000 words. Pays $350 minimum.

Photos: Send photos with submission. Reviews 35mm transparencies and 8 × 10 b&w prints. Offers no additional payment for b&w photos accepted with ms; offers $50-250/color photo. Captions, model releases, identification of subjects required. Buys one-time rights.

ROCKY MOUNTAIN GAME & FISH, Game & Fish Publications, Inc., Box 741, Marietta GA 30061. Editor: Burt Carey. See *Game & Fish Publications.*

SAFARI MAGAZINE, The Journal of Big Game Hunting, Safari Club International, 4800 W. Gates Pass Rd., Tucson AZ 85745. (520)620-1220. Fax: (520)622-1205. Director of Publications/Editor: William R. Quimby. 90% freelance written. Bimonthly club journal covering international big game hunting and wildlife conservation. Circ. 23,000. Pays on publication. Publishes ms an average of 12-18 months after acceptance. Byline given. Offers $100 kill fee. Buys all rights. Submit seasonal/holiday material 1 year in advance. Reports in 2 weeks on queries; 6 weeks on mss. Sample copy for $4. Writer's guidelines for SASE.

Nonfiction: Photo feature (wildlife), technical (firearms, hunting techniques, etc.). Buys 48 mss/year. Query or send complete ms. Length: 1,500-2,500 words. Pays $200 for professional writers, lower rates if not professional.

Photos: State availability of photos with query or ms, or send photos with query or ms. Payment depends on size in magazine. Pays $45 for b&w; $50-150 color. Captions, model releases, identification of subjects required. Buys one-time rights.

Tips: "Study the magazine. Send manuscripts and photo packages with query. Make it appeal to knowledgeable, world-travelled big game hunters. Features on conservation contributions from big game hunters around the world are open to freelancers. We have enough stories on first-time African safaris and North American hunting. We need South American and Asian hunting stories, plus stories dealing with hunting and conservation."

SALT WATER SPORTSMAN MAGAZINE, 77 Franklin St., Boston MA 02110. (617)338-2300. Fax: (617)338-2309. Editor: Barry Gibson. Emphasizes saltwater fishing. 85% freelance written. Works with a small number of new/unpublished writers each year. Monthly magazine. Circ. 150,000. **Pays on acceptance.** Publishes ms an average of 5 months after acceptance. Byline given. Buys first North American serial rights. Offers 100% kill fee. Submit seasonal material 8 months in advance. Accepts previously published submissions. Send tearsheet of article and information about when and where the article previously appeared. Pays negotiable. Reports in 1 month. Sample copy and writer's guidelines for 9 × 12 SAE with 10 first-class stamps.

Nonfiction: How-to, personal experience, technical, travel (to fishing areas). "Readers want solid how-to, where-to information written in an enjoyable, easy-to-read style. Personal anecdotes help the reader identify with the writer." Prefers new slants and specific information. Query. "It is helpful if the writer states experience in salt water fishing and any previous related articles. We want one, possibly two well-explained ideas per query letter—not merely a listing. Good pictures with query often help sell the idea." Buys 100 mss/year. Length: 1,200-1,500 words. Pays $350 and up. Sometimes pays the expenses of writers on assignment. "A good way to break in with us is to submit short (800-1,000 words) where-to/how-to pieces for one of our three regional editions (Atlantic, Southern and Pacific) with a couple of b&w photos. Write Whit Griswold for regional guidelines."

Photos: Purchased with or without accompanying ms. Captions required. Uses 5 × 7 or 8 × 10 b&w prints and color slides. Pays $1,000 minimum for 35mm, 2¼ × 2¼ or 8 × 10 transparencies for cover. Offers additional payment for photos accepted with accompanying ms.

Columns/Departments: Sportsman's Workbench (how to make fishing or fishing-related boating equipment), 100 or more words.

Tips: "There are a lot of knowledgeable fishermen/budding writers out there who could be valuable to us with a little coaching. Many don't think they can write a story for us, but they'd be surprised. We work with writers. Shorter articles that get to the point which are accompanied by good, sharp photos are hard for us to turn down. Having to delete unnecessary wordage—conversation, clichés, etc.—that writers feel is mandatory is annoying. Often they don't devote enough attention to specific fishing information."

SOUTH CAROLINA GAME & FISH, Game & Fish Publications, Inc., Box 741, Marietta GA 30061. (404)953-9222. Editor: Jeff Samsel. See *Game & Fish Publications*.

SOUTH CAROLINA WILDLIFE, P.O. Box 167, Rembert Dennis Bldg., Columbia SC 29202-0167. (803)734-3972. Editor: John Davis. Managing Editor: Linda Renshaw. Bimonthly magazine for South Carolinians interested in wildlife and outdoor activities. 75% freelance written. Estab. 1954. Circ. 69,000. Byline given. **Pays on acceptance.** Publishes ms an average of 6 months after acceptance. Buys first rights. Free sample copy. Reports in 2 months.

Nonfiction: Articles on outdoor South Carolina with an emphasis on preserving and protecting our natural resources. "Realize that the topic must be of interest to South Carolinians and that we must be able to justify using it in a publication published by the state department of natural resources—so if it isn't directly about outdoor recreation, a certain plant or animal, it must be somehow related to the environment and conservation. Readers prefer a broad mix of outdoor related topics (articles that illustrate the beauty of South Carolina's outdoors and those that help the reader get more for his/her time, effort, and money spent in outdoor recreation). These two general areas are the ones we most need. Subjects vary a great deal in topic, area and style, but must all have a common ground in the outdoor resources and heritage of South Carolina. Review back issues and query with a one-page outline citing sources, giving ideas for photographs, explaining justification and giving an example of the first two paragraphs." Does not need any column material. Generally does not seek photographs. The publisher assumes no responsibility for unsolicited material. Buys 25-30 mss/year. Length: 1,000-3,000 words. Pays an average of $200-400/article depending upon length and subject matter.

Tips: "We need more writers in the outdoor field who take pride in the craft of writing and put a real effort toward originality and preciseness in their work. Query on a topic we haven't recently done. The most frequent mistakes made by writers in completing an article are failure to check details and go in-depth on a subject."

SOUTHERN OUTDOORS MAGAZINE, B.A.S.S. Publications, 5845 Carmichael Rd., Montgomery AL 36117. (205)277-3940. Editor: Larry Teague. Magazine published 9 times/year covering Southern outdoor activities, including hunting, fishing, boating, shooting and camping. 90% freelance written. Prefers to work with published/established writers. Estab. 1952. Circ. 257,000. **Pays on acceptance.** Publishes ms an average of 6 months to 1 year after acceptance. Buys all rights. Reports in 2 months. Sample copy for $2.50 and 9 × 12 SAE with 5 first-class stamps.

Nonfiction: Articles should be service-oriented, helping the reader excel in outdoor sports. Emphasis is on techniques, trends and conservation. Some "where-to" features purchased on Southern hunting and fishing destinations. Buys 120 mss/year. Length: 2,500 words maximum. Sidebars are a selling point. Pays 15-20¢/word.

Photos: Usually purchased with mss. Pays $75 for 35mm transparencies without ms, $400 for covers.

Fillers: Humorous or thought-provoking pieces (1,500 words) appear in each issue's S.O. Essay department.

Tips: "It's easiest to break in with short articles. We buy very little first-person. Stories most likely to sell: outdoor medicine, bass fishing, deer hunting, other freshwater fishing, inshore saltwater fishing, bird and small-game hunting, shooting, camping and boating."

‡**SPORTING CLAYS MAGAZINE**, Patch Communications, 5211 S. Washington Ave., Titusville FL 32780. (407)268-5010. Editor: George Conrad. Contact: Jill Martello, assistant editor. Monthly magazine covering sporting clays. "*Sporting Clays* reports on shooting activities with instructional columns, equipment reviews and range listings, and is the official publication of the National Sporting Clays Association." Estab. 1987. Circ. 30,000. Pays on publication. Publishes ms an average of 6 months after acceptance. Byline given. Buys first North American serial rights. Editorial lead time 4 months. Submit seasonal material 6 months in advance. No simultaneous or previously published submissions. Reports in 1 month on queries.

Nonfiction: Historical/nostalgic, how-to (technique), interview/profile, new product, personal experience, photo feature, technical, travel. Buys 5 mss/year. Query with published clips and SASE. Length: 700-1,000 words.

Photos: Send photos with submission. Reviews transparencies, prints. Negotiates payment individually. Captions, identification of subjects required. Buys one-time rights.

SPORTS AFIELD, 250 W. 55th St., New York NY 10019-5201. (212)649-4000. Editor-in-Chief: Terry McDonell. Executive Editor: Fred Kesting. 20% freelance written. Monthly magazine for people of all ages whose interests are centered around the out-of-doors (hunting and fishing) and related subjects. Estab. 1887. Circ. 506,011. Buys first North American serial rights for features. **Pays on acceptance.** Publishes ms an average of 6 months after acceptance. Byline given. "Our magazine is seasonal and material submitted should be in accordance. Fishing in spring and summer; hunting in the fall." Submit seasonal material 9 months in advance. Reports in 2 months. Query or submit complete ms. Writer's guidelines for 1 first-class stamp.

Nonfiction: "Informative how-to articles with emphasis on product and service and personal experiences with good photos on hunting, fishing, camping, conservation, and environmental issues (limited where-to-go) related to hunting and fishing. We want first-class writing and reporting." Buys 15-17 unsolicited mss/year. Length: 500-2,500 words.

Photos: "For photos without ms, duplicates of 35mm color transparencies preferred."

Fiction: Adventure, humor, nostalgia (if related to hunting and fishing).

Fillers: Send to *Almanac* editor. For outdoor tips specifically for hunters, fishermen and campers, unusual, how-to and nature items. Payment on publication. Buys all rights.

Tips: "Read a recent copy of *Sports Afield* so you know the market you're writing for. Manuscript *must* be available on disk."

TENNESSEE SPORTSMAN, Game & Fish Publications, Box 741, Marietta GA 30061. (404)953-9222. Editor: Jeff Samsel. See *Game & Fish Publications*.

TEXAS SPORTSMAN, Game & Fish Publications, Inc., Box 741, Marietta GA 30061. (404)953-9222. Editor: Nick Gilmore. See *Game & Fish Publications*.

‡**TIDE MAGAZINE**, Coastal Conservation Association, 220-W, 4801 Woodway, Houston TX 77056. (713)626-4222. Fax: (713)961-3801. Editor: Doug Pike. Bimonthly magazine on saltwater fishing and conservation of marine resources. Estab. 1977. Circ. 40,000. Pays on publication. Byline given. Buys one-time rights. Submit seasonal material 6 months in advance. Reports in 1 month.

Nonfiction: Essays, exposé, general interest, historical/nostalgic, humor, opinion, personal experience and travel. Buys 30 mss/year. Query with published clips. Length: 1,200-1,500 words. Pays $250 for ms/photo package.

Photos: Reviews 35mm transparencies and 8×10 b&w prints. Offers no additional payment for photos accepted with ms. Captions required. Buys one-time rights. Pays $25 for b&w, $50 for color inside.

Fiction: Slice-of-life vignettes. Buys 1 mss/year. Query or send complete ms. Length: 1,200-1,500 words. Pays $250.

‡**TRAPPER & PREDATOR CALLER**, Krause Publications Inc., 700 E. State St., Iola WI 54990. (715)445-2214. Fax: (715)445-4087. Editor: Gordy Krahn. 90% freelance written. Monthly tabloid covers trapping, predator calling and muzzleloading. "Our editorial goal is to entertain and educate our readers with national and regional articles that promote trapping." Estab. 1975. Circ. 35,000. Pays on publication. Offers $50 kill fee. Buys first North American serial rights. Submit seasonal material 6 months in advance. Reports in 2 weeks. *Writer's Market* recommends allowing 2 months for reply. Free sample copy and writer's guidelines.

Nonfiction: How-to, humor, interview/profile, new product, opinion and personal experience. Buys 60 mss/year. Query with or without published clips or send complete ms. Length: 1,200-2,500 words. Pays $80-250 for assigned articles; $40-200 for unsolicited articles.

Photos: Send photos with submission. Reviews prints. Offers no additional payment for photos accepted with ms. Captions and identification of subjects required. Buys one-time rights.

Fillers: Facts, gags to be illustrated by cartoonist, newsbreaks and short humor. Buys 60/year. Length: 200-800 words. Pays $25-80.

Tips: "We are always looking for new ideas and fresh material on trapping, predator calling and black powder hunting."

TURKEY & TURKEY HUNTING, Krause Publications, 800 E. State St., Iola WI 54900. Editors: Jim Casada and Gerry Blair. Managing Editor: Gordy Krahn. 80% freelance written. Covers turkey hunting and other issues related to wild turkeys. Published February, March, April, Spring, Fall, Winter. "It is imperative that contributors be well versed in the lure and lore of hunting wild turkeys." Estab. 1991. **Pays on acceptance.** Publishes ms an average of 4 months after acceptance. Byline given. Buys first North American serial rights. Editorial lead time 4 months. Query for electronic submissions. Reports in 6 weeks on queries; 2 months on mss. Prefer queries first. Writer's guidelines for #10 SASE.

Nonfiction: Books excerpts (rarely), historical/nostalgic, how-to, humor (rarely), interview/profile, new product, personal experience, photo feature, travel. "We normally do one or two theme issues a year. Examples from the past include calling tactics, destinations and A Turkey Hunter's Christmas. No advertorials or poetry. Buys 40-50 mss/year. Query with or without published clips. Length: 1,500-3,000. Pays $150-300.

Photos: Send photos with submission. Reviews contact sheets, negatives, transparencies. Offers $40-250/cover photo. Captions required. Buys one-time rights.

Tips: "We have the most trouble in getting good submissions on turkey biology and behavior, along with management principles and practices. These subjects *must* be covered in a fashion which is interesting and informative for the average reader. Feature articles are your best bet. Tight, bright pieces which are well-written and well-researched are most likely to be accepted. Queries with an unusual slant or touching on a subject we have not recently covered in detail are good opportunities for first-time writers. We tend to work regularly with a stable of 20 or so writers but are always looking for new talent."

TURKEY CALL, Wild Turkey Center, P.O. Box 530, Edgefield SC 29824-0530. (803)637-3106. Fax: (803)637-0034. Editor: Gene Smith. 50-60% freelance written. Eager to work with new/unpublished writers and photographers. Bimonthly educational magazine for members of the National Wild Turkey Federation. Estab. 1973. Circ. 90,000. Buys one-time rights. Byline given. **Pays on acceptance.** Publishes ms an average of 6 months after acceptance. Reports in 1 month. No queries necessary. Submit complete package. Wants original mss only. Sample copy for $3 and 9×12 SAE. Writer's guidelines for #10 SASE.

Nonfiction: Feature articles dealing with the hunting and management of the American wild turkey. Must be accurate information and must appeal to national readership of turkey hunters and wildlife management experts. No poetry or first-person accounts of unremarkable hunting trips. May use some fiction that educates or entertains in a special way. Length: up to 3,000 words. Pays $35 for items, $65 for short fillers of 600-700 words, $200-350 for illustrated features.

Photos: "We want quality photos submitted with features." Art illustrations also acceptable. "We are using more and more inside color illustrations." For b&w, prefer 8×10 glossies, but 5×7 OK. Transparencies of any size are acceptable. No typical hunter-holding-dead-turkey photos or setups using mounted birds or domestic turkeys. Photos with how-to stories must make the techniques clear (example: how to make a turkey call; how to sculpt or carve a bird in wood). Pays $20 minimum for one-time rights on b&w photos and simple art illustrations; up to $75 for inside color, reproduced any size; $2 for covers.

Tips: "The writer should simply keep in mind that the audience is 'expert' on wild turkey management, hunting, life history and restoration/conservation history. He/she *must know the subject*. We are buying more third-person, more fiction, more humor—in an attempt to avoid the 'predictability trap' of a single subject magazine."

VIRGINIA GAME & FISH, Game & Fish Publications, Inc., Box 741, Marietta GA 30061. (404)953-9222. Editor: Jeff Samsel. See *Game & Fish Publications*.

WASHINGTON-OREGON GAME & FISH, Game & Fish Publications, Inc., Box 741, Marietta GA 30061. Editor: Burt Carey. See *Game & Fish Publications*.

WEST VIRGINIA GAME & FISH, Game & Fish Publications, Inc., Box 741, Marietta GA 30061. (404)953-9222. Editor: Ken Freel. See *Game & Fish Publications*.

WESTERN OUTDOORS, 3197-E Airport Loop, Costa Mesa CA 92626. (714)546-4370. Editor: Jack Brown. 60% freelance written. Works with a small number of new/unpublished writers each year. Emphasizes fishing, boating for California, Oregon, Washington, Baja California, and Alaska. Publishes 9 issues/year. Estab. 1961. Circ. 128,000. **Pays on acceptance.** Publishes ms an average of 6 months after acceptance. Buys first North American serial rights. Submit seasonal material 6 months in advance. Reports in 1 month. Sample copy for $2. Writer's guidelines for #10 SASE.

- *Western Outdoors* now emphasizes freshwater and saltwater fishing and boating exclusively. Area of coverage is limited to far west states and Baja California.

Nonfiction: Where-to (catch more fish, improve equipment, etc.), how-to informational, photo feature. "We do not accept fiction, poetry." Buys 45-55 assigned mss/year. Query in writing. Length: 1,000-1,500 words. Pays average $450.

Photos: Purchased with accompanying ms. Captions required. Prefers professional quality 35mm slides. Offers no additional payment for photos accepted with accompanying ms. Pays $250 for covers.

Tips: "Provide a complete package of photos, map, trip facts and manuscript written according to our news feature format. Excellence of color photo selections make a sale more likely. The most frequent mistake made by writers in completing an article for us is that they don't follow our style. Our guidelines are quite clear."

WESTERN SPORTSMAN, P.O. Box 737, Regina, Saskatchewan S4P 3A8 Canada. (306)352-2773. Fax: (306)565-2440. Editor: Brian Bowman. 90% freelance written. Bimonthly magazine for fishermen, hunters, campers and others interested in outdoor recreation. "Note that our coverage area is Alberta, Saskatchewan and Manitoba." Estab. 1968. Circ. 29,000. Rights purchased vary with author and material. Usually buys first North American serial or second serial (reprint) rights. Accepts previously published submissions. Send typed ms with rights for sale noted and information about when and where the article previously appeared. For reprints, pays 100% of the amount paid for an original article. Byline given. Pays on publication. Publishes ms an average of 6 months after acceptance. "We try to include as much information as possible on all subjects in each edition. Therefore, we often publish fishing articles in our winter issues along with a variety of winter stories. If material is dated, we would like to receive articles 4 months in advance of our publication date." Reports in 1 month. Sample copy for $4 and 9×12 SAE with 4 IRCs (US). Free writer's guidelines with SASE.

- *Western Sportsman* now accepts articles and news items relating to British Colombia hunting and fishing.

Nonfiction: "It is necessary that all articles can identify with our coverage area. We are interested in manuscripts from writers who have experienced an interesting fishing or hunting experience. We also publish other informational pieces as long as they relate to our coverage area. We are more interested in articles which tell about the average guy living on beans, guiding his own boat, stalking his game and generally doing his own thing in our part of Western Canada than a story describing a well-to-do outdoorsman traveling by motorhome, staying at an expensive lodge with guides doing everything for him except catching the fish or shooting the big game animal. The articles that are submitted to us need to be prepared in a knowledgeable way and include more information than the actual fish catch or animal or bird kill. Discuss the terrain, the people involved on the trip, the water or weather conditions, the costs, the planning that went into the trip, the equipment and other data closely associated with the particular event. We're always looking for new writers." Buys 60 mss/year. Submit complete ms and SASE or IRCs. Length: 1,500-2,000 words. Pays up to $300 (Canadian). Sometimes pays the expenses of writers on assignment.

Photos: Photos purchased with ms with no additional payment. Also purchased without ms. Pays $30-50 for 5×7 or 8×10 b&w print; $175-250 for 35mm or larger transparency for front cover.

WISCONSIN SPORTSMAN, Game & Fish Publications, Inc., Box 741, Marietta GA 30061. Editor: Dennis Schmidt. See *Game & Fish Publications.*

Martial Arts

BLACK BELT, Rainbow Publications, Inc., 24715 Ave. Rockefeller, Valencia CA 91355. (805)257-4066. Fax: (805)257-3028. Executive Editor: Jim Coleman. 80-90% freelance written. Works with a small number of new/unpublished writers each year. Monthly magazine emphasizing martial arts for both practioner and layman. Estab. 1961. Circ. 100,000. Pays on publication. Publishes ms an average of 5 months after acceptance. Buys first North American serial rights, retains right to republish. Submit seasonal/holiday material 6 months in advance. Reports in 3 weeks.

Nonfiction: Exposé, how-to, informational, interview, new product, personal experience, profile, technical, travel. Buys 8-9 mss/issue. Query or send complete ms. Length: 1,200 words minimum. Pays $100-300.

Photos: Very seldom buys photos without accompanying mss. Captions required. Total purchase price for ms includes payment for photos. Model releases required.

Fiction: Historical, modern day. Buys 1-2 mss/year. Query. Pays $100-150.

Tips: "We also publish an annual yearbook and special issues periodically. The yearbook includes our annual 'Black Belt Hall of Fame' inductees."

‡INSIDE KARATE, The Magazine for Today's Total Martial Artist, Unique Publications, 4201 Vanowen Place, Burbank CA 91505. (818)845-2656. Fax: (818)845-7761. Editor: John Steven Soet. 90% freelance written. Works with a number of new/unpublished writers each year. Monthly magazine covering the martial arts. Circ. 120,000. Publishes ms an average of 3 months after acceptance. Byline given. Buys first North

American serial rights. Reports in 3 weeks on queries; 6 weeks on mss. Sample copy $2.50 for 9×12 SAE with 5 first-class stamps. Writer's guidelines for #10 SASE.

Nonfiction: Book excerpts, exposé (of martial arts), historical/nostalgic, humor, interview/profile (with approval only), opinion, personal experience, photo feature and technical (with approval only). "*Inside Karate* seeks a balance of the following in each issue: tradition, history, glamour, profiles and/or interviews (both by assignment only), technical, philosophical and think pieces. Not interested in 'tough guys,' self-serving pieces, or movie-star wannabes." Buys 70 mss/year. Query. Length: 1,000-2,500 words; prefers 10-12 page mss. Pays $25-125.

Photos: Send photos with ms. Prefers 3×5 bordered b&w. Captions and identification of subjects required. Buys one-time rights.

Tips: "In our publication, writing style and/or expertise is not the determining factor. Beginning writers with martial arts expertise may submit. Trends in magazine publishing that freelance writers should be aware of include the use of less body copy, better (and interesting) photos to be run large with 'story' caps. If the photos are poor and the reader can't grasp the whole story by looking at photos and copy, forget it."

INSIDE KUNG-FU, The Ultimate In Martial Arts Coverage!, Unique Publications, 4201 Vanowen Place, Burbank CA 91505. (818)845-2656. Fax: (818)845-7761. Editor: Dave Cater. 75% freelance written. Monthly magazine covering martial arts for those with "traditional, modern, athletic and intellectual tastes. The magazine slants toward little-known martial arts, and little-known aspects of established martial arts." Estab. 1973. Circ. 100,000. Pays on publication date on magazine cover. Publishes ms an average of 6 months after acceptance. Byline given. Buys first North American serial rights. Submit seasonal/holiday material 4 months in advance. Accepts simultaneous and previously published submissions. Send tearsheet of article or short story or typed ms with rights for sale noted and information about when and where the article previously appeared. No payment for reprints. Reports in 1 month on queries; 2 months on mss. Sample copy for $2.95 and 9×12 SAE with 5 first-class stamps. Writer's guidelines for #10 SASE.

Nonfiction: Exposé (topics relating to the martial arts), historical/nostalgic, how-to (primarily technical materials), cultural/philosophical, interview/profile, personal experience, photo feature, technical. "Articles must be technically or historically accurate." No "sports coverage, first-person articles or articles which constitute personal aggrandizement." Buys 120 mss/year. Query or send complete ms. Length: 8-10 pages, typewritten and double-spaced.

• *Inside Kung-Fu* is looking for external-type articles (fighting, weapons, multiple hackers).

Photos: Send photos with accompanying ms. Reviews b&w contact sheets, b&w negatives, 5×7 or 8×10 b&w prints. Offers no additional payment for photos. Captions and model release required.

Fiction: Adventure, historical, humorous, mystery, suspense. "Fiction must be short (1,000-2,000 words) and relate to the martial arts. We buy very few fiction pieces." Publishes novel excerpts. Buys 2-3 mss/year.

Tips: "The writer may have a better chance of breaking in at our publication with short articles and fillers since smaller pieces allow us to gauge individual ability, but we're flexible—quality writers get published, period. The most frequent mistakes made by writers in completing an article for us are ignoring photo requirements and model releases (always number one—and who knows why? All requirements are spelled out in writer's guidelines)."

JOURNAL OF ASIAN MARTIAL ARTS, Via Media Publishing Co., 821 W. 24th St., Erie PA 16502-2523. (814)455-9517. Fax: (814)838-7811. Editor: Michael A. DeMarco. 90% freelance written. Quarterly magazine covering "all historical and cultural aspects related to Asian martial arts, offering a mature, well-rounded view of this uniquely fascinating subject. Although the journal treats the subject with academic accuracy (references at end), writing need not lose the reader!" Estab. 1991. Pays on publication. Publishes ms an average of 1 year after acceptance. Byline given. Buys first rights and second serial (reprint) rights. Submit seasonal/holiday material 6 months in advance. Query for electronic submissions. Accepts previously published submissions. Send photocopy of article and information about when and where the article previously appeared. Reports in 1 month on queries; 2 months on mss. Sample copy for $10. Writer's guidelines for #10 SASE.

Nonfiction: Essays, exposé, historical/nostalgic, how-to (martial art techniques and materials, e.g., weapons, symbols), interview/profile, personal experience, photo feature (place or person), religious, technical, travel. "All articles should be backed with solid, reliable reference material. No articles overburdened with technical/foreign/scholarly vocabulary, or material slanted as indirect advertising or for personal aggrandizement." Buys 30 mss/year. Query. Length: 2,000-10,000 words. Pays $150-500 for unsolicited articles.

Photos: State availability of photos with submission. Reviews contact sheets, negatives, transparencies, prints. Offers no additional payment for photos accepted with ms. Model releases and identification of subjects required. Buys one-time and reprint rights.

Columns/Departments: Location (city, area, specific site, Asian or Non-Asian, showing value for martial arts, researchers, history); Media Review (film, book, stamps, music for aspects of academic and artistic interest). Buys 16 mss/year. Query. Length: 1,000-2,500 words. Pays $50-200.

Fiction: Adventure, historical, humorous, slice-of-life vignettes, translation. "We are not interested in material that does not focus on martial arts culture." Buys 2 mss/year. Query. Length: 2,000-10,000 words. Pays $100-500.

Poetry: Avant-garde, free verse, haiku, light verse, traditional, translation. "No poetry that does not focus on martial art culture." Buys 4 poems/year. Submit maximum 10 poems. Pays $10-100.

Fillers: Anecdotes, facts, gags to be illustrated by cartoonist, newsbreaks, short humor. Buys 10/year. Length: 25-500 words. Pays $1-50.

Tips: "Always query before sending a manuscript. We are open to varied types of articles; most however require a strong academic grasp of Asian culture. For those not having this background, we suggest trying a museum review, or interview, where authorities can be questioned, quoted and provide supportive illustrations. We especially desire articles/reports from Asia, with photo illustrations, particularly of a martial art style, so readers can visually understand the unique attributes of that style, its applications, evolution, etc. 'Location' and media reports are special areas that writers may consider, especially if they live in a location of martial art significance."

KARATE/KUNG FU ILLUSTRATED, Rainbow Publications, Inc., P.O. Box 918, Santa Clarita CA 91380. (805)257-4066. Fax: (805)257-3028. Executive Editor: Robert Young. 70% freelance written. Bimonthly consumer magazine covering martial arts. "KKI presents factual historical accounts of the development of the martial arts, along with technical pieces on self-defense. We use only material from which readers can learn." Estab. 1969. Circ. 35,000. Pays on publication. Publishes ms an average of 6 months after acceptance. Byline given. Buys all rights. Editorial lead time 3 months. Submit seasonal material 4 months in advance. Accepts simultaneous submissions. Reports in 2 weeks on queries; 1 month on mss. Sample copy for 9 × 12 SAE and 5 first-class stamps. Writer's guidelines free on request.

Nonfiction: Book excerpts, general interest (martial arts), historical/nostalgic (martial arts development), how-to (technical articles on specific kicks, punches, etc.), interview/profile (only with *major* martial artist), new products (for annual product review), travel (to Asian countries for martial arts training/research), comparisons of various styles and techniques. "No fiction or self-promotional pieces." Buys 30 mss/year. Query. Length: 1,000-3,000 words. Pays $100-150.

Photos: Freelancers should send photos with submission. Reviews contact sheets, negatives and 5 × 7 prints. Offers no additional payment for photos accepted with ms. Captions, model releases and identification of subjects required.

Columns/Departments: Bushido Book (essays explaining martial arts philosophy), 1,000-1,500 words; Martial Spirit (personal experience that must apply to all readers) 1,000 words. Buys 12 mss/year. Query. Pays $0-75.

Tips: "You need not be an expert in a specific martial art to write about it. But if you are not an expert, find one and use his knowledge to support your statements. Also, references to well-known books can help lend credence to the work of unknown writers. Inexperienced writers should begin by writing about a subject they know well. For example, if you study karate, start by writing about karate. Don't study karate for one year, then try to break in to a martial arts magazine by writing about Kung fu, because we already have Kung fu practitioners who write about that."

MARTIAL ARTS TRAINING, Rainbow Publications, P.O. Box 918, Santa Clarita CA 91380-9018. (805)257-4066. Fax: (805)257-3028. Executive Editor: Douglas Jeffrey. 75% freelance written. Works with many new/unpublished writers each year. Bimonthly magazine about martial arts training. Estab. 1961. Circ. 60,000. Pays on publication. Publishes ms an average of 6 months after acceptance. Buys all rights. Submit seasonal material 4 months in advance, but best to send query letter first. Reports in 2 months. Writer's guidelines for #10 SASE.

Nonfiction: How-to (training related features). Buys 30-40 unsolicited mss/year. Send query or complete ms. Length: 1,500-2,500 words. Pays $100-175.

Photos: State availability of photos. Most ms should be accompanied by photos. Reviews 5 × 7 and 8 × 10 b&w glossy prints. Can reproduce prints from negatives. Offers no additional payment for photos accepted with ms. Model releases required. Buys all rights. Photos not purchased without accompanying mss.

Tips: "I'm looking for how-to, nuts-and-bolts training stories that are martial arts related. Our magazine covers fitness and conditioning, not the martial arts techniques themselves."

T'AI CHI, Leading International Magazine of T'ai Chi Ch'uan, Wayfarer Publications, P.O. Box 26156, Los Angeles CA 90026. (213)665-7773. Fax: (213)665-1627. Editor/Publisher: Marvin Smalheiser. 90% freelance written. Bimonthly consumer magazine covering T'ai Chi Ch'uan as a martial art and for Health & Fitness. "Covers T'ai Chi Ch'uan and other internal martials, plus qigong and Chinese health, nutrition and philosophical disciplines. Readers are practitioners or laymen interested in developing skills and insight for self-defense, health and self-improvement." Estab. 1977. Circ. 30,000. Pays on publication. Publishes ms an average of 3-5 months after acceptance. Byline given. Buys first North American serial rights. Editorial lead time 3 months. Submit seasonal material 6 months in advance. Reports in 3 weeks on queries; 3 months on mss. Sample copy for $3.50. Writer's guidelines for #10 SASE.

● This publication needs more material but it must be related to the needs of its readers.

Nonfiction: Book excerpts, essays, how-to (on T'ai Chi Ch'uan, qigong and related Chinese disciplines), interview/profile, personal experience. "Do not want articles promoting an individual, system or school." Buys 50-60 mss/year. Query or send complete ms. Length: 1,200-4,500 words. Pays $60-500 for assigned

articles; $60-500 for unsolicited articles. Sometimes pays expenses of writers on assignment.
Photos: Send photos with submission. Reviews transparencies and 3×5 prints. Offers no additional payment for photos accepted with ms. Captions, model releases and identification of subjects required. Buys one-time rights and reprint.
Poetry: Free verse, light verse, traditional. "No poetry unrelated to our content." Buys 6 poems/year. Submit maximum 3 poems. Length: 12-30 lines. Pays $25-50.
Tips: "Think and write for practitioners and laymen who want information and insight and who are trying to work through problems to improve skills and their health. No promotional material."

Miscellaneous

‡**AMERICAN HIKER**, American Hiking Society, P.O. Box 20160, Washington DC 20041-2160. (703)255-9304. Editor: David Lillard. 50% freelance written. Bimonthly magazine. "*American Hiker* covers the recreation opportunities on America's trails and focuses on the people who work to protect them." Estab. 1988. Circ. 10,000. Pays on publication. Publishes ms 3 months after acceptance. Byline given. Offers $25 kill fee. Buys first rights. Editorial lead time 3 months. Submit seasonal material 6 months in advance. Accepts simultaneous and previously published submissions. Query for electronic submissions. Reports in 2 weeks on queries; 2 months on mss. Sample copy for $1. Writer's guidelines for #10 SASE.
Nonfiction: Book excerpts, essays, interview/profile, travel. Buys 18 mss/year. Query with published clips. Length: 250-1,400 words. Pays $25-150 for assigned articles; $25-75 for unsolicited articles.
Photos: State availability of photos with submission. Reviews transparencies. Offers $25/photo. Buys one-time rights.
Columns/Departments: Hiking Family (family tips), Soft Wear (low-impact camping), Hiker's Access (book reviews), all 800 words. Buys 12 mss/year. Query with published clips. Pays $75-125.
Tips: "Focus on people who are building and protecting trails—not accounts of travel."

NEW YORK OUTDOORS, 51 Atlantic Ave., Floral Park NY 11001. Fax: (516)437-6841. Editor: John Tsaousis. 100% freelance written. Estab. 1992. Buys first North American serial rights. Publishes ms an average of 6 months after acceptance. Accepts previously published submissions. Send photocopy of article and information about where and when article previously appeared. For reprints, pays 45% of the amount paid for an original article. Reports in 1 month on queries. Writer's guidelines for #10 SASE.
Nonfiction: "*New York Outdoors* is dedicated to providing information to its readers about all outdoor participatory activities in New York and its surrounding states. Paddlesports, camping, hiking, cycling, 'adventure' sports, etc." Query. Length: 1,500-2,000 words. A good selection of transparencies must accompany submissions. Pays $250. Lead time 4 months. "Aside from accurate and interesting writing, provide source material for our readers who may wish to try the activity. We also have use for shorter pieces (to 500 words) on the same type of topics, but focusing on a single event, person, place or occurrence. Query. These pay $50."
Tips: Would like to see more queries on camping, hiking, in line, climbing, mountain biking topic areas.

OUTSIDE, Mariah Media Inc., Outside Plaza, 400 Market St., Santa Fe, NM 87501. (505)989-7100. Editor: Mark Bryant. Managing Editor: Tish Hamilton. 90% freelance written. Monthly magazine on outdoor recreation and travel. "*Outside* is a monthly national magazine for active, educated, upscale adults who love the outdoors and are concerned about its preservation." Estab. 1977. Circ. 475,000. **Pays on acceptance.** Publishes ms an average of 3 months after acceptance. Byline given. Offers 25% kill fee. Buys first North American serial rights. Submit seasonal/holiday material 4-5 months in advance. Electronic submission OK for solicited materials; not for unsolicited. Reports in 6 weeks on queries; 2 months on mss. Sample copy for $4 for 9×12 SAE with 9 first-class stamps. Writer's guidelines for SASE.
Nonfiction: Book excerpts; essays; reports on the environment; outdoor sports and expeditions; general interest; how-to; humor; inspirational; interview/profile (major figures associated with sports, travel, environment, outdoor); opinion, personal experience (expeditions; trying out new sports); photo feature (outdoor photography); technical (reviews of equipment, how-to); travel (adventure, sports-oriented travel). All should pertain to the outdoors: Bike section; Downhill Skiing; Cross-country Skiing; Adventure Travel. Do not want to see articles about sports that we don't cover (basketball, tennis, golf, etc.). Buys 40 mss/year. Query with published clips and SASE. Length: 1,500-4,000 words. Negotiates payment. Pays expenses of writers on assignment.
Photos: "Do not send photos; if we decide to use a freelancer's story, we may request to see the writer's photos." Reviews transparencies. Offers $180/photo minimum. Captions and identification of subjects required. Buys one-time rights.
Columns/Departments: Dispatches, contact Brad Wetzler (news, events, short profiles relevant to outdoors), 200-1,000 words; Destinations, contact Leslie Weeden, (places to explore, news, and tips for adventure travelers), 250-400 words; Review, contact Andrew Tilin, (evaluations of products), 200-1,500 words. Buys 180 mss/year. Query with published clips. Length: 200-2,000 words. Payment varies.

Tips: "Prospective writers should study the magazine before querying. Look at the magazine for our style, subject matter and standards." The departments are the best areas for freelancers to break in.

PRIME TIME SPORTS & FITNESS, GND Prime Time Publishing, P.O. Box 6097, Evanston IL 60204. (312)869-6434. Fax: (708)864-1206. Editor: Dennis A. Dorner. Managing Editor: Steven Ury. 80% freelance written. Eager to work with new/unpublished writers. Monthly magazine covering seasonal pro sports and racquet and health club sports and fitness. Estab. 1974. Circ. 35,000. Pays on publication. Publishes ms an average of 6 months after acceptance. Byline given. Buys all rights; will assign back to author in 85% of cases. Submit seasonal/holiday material 6 months in advance. Accepts simultaneous and previously published submissions. Send photocopy of article or short story or typed ms with rights for sale noted and information about when and where the article previously appeared. For reprints, pays 20% of the amount paid for an original article. Reports in 2-6 months. Sample copy for 10×12 SAE with 7 first-class stamps.
 • The editor is especially looking for writers who understand that the publication needs authoritative shorter articles.
Nonfiction: Book excerpts (fitness and health), exposé (in tennis, fitness, racquetball, health clubs, diets), adult (slightly risqué and racy fitness), how-to (expert instructional pieces on any area of coverage), humor (large market for funny pieces on health clubs and fitness), inspirational (on how diet and exercise combine to bring you a better body, self), interview/profile, new product, opinion (only from recognized sources who know what they are talking about), personal experience (definitely—humor), photo feature (on related subjects); technical (on exercise and sport), travel (related to fitness, tennis camps, etc.), news reports (on racquetball, handball, tennis, running events). Special issues: Swimsuit and Resort Issue (March); Baseball Preview (April); Summer Fashion (July); Pro Football Preview (August); Fall Fashion (October); Ski Issue (November); Christmas Gifts and related articles (December). "We love short articles that get to the point. Nationally oriented big events and national championships. No articles on local only tennis and racquetball tournaments without national appeal." Buys 150 mss/year. Length: 2,000 words maximum. Pays $20-150. Sometimes pays the expenses of writers on assignment.
Photos: Nancy Thomas, photo editor. Specifically looking for fashion photo features. Send photos with ms. Pays $5-75 for b&w prints. Captions, model releases, identification of subjects required. Buys all rights, "but returns 75% of photos to submitter."
Columns/Departments: George Thomas, column/department editor. New Products; Fitness Newsletter; Handball Newsletter; Racquetball Newsletter; Tennis Newsletter; News & Capsule Summaries; Fashion Spot (photos of new fitness and bathing suits and ski equipment); related subjects. Buys 100 mss/year. Send complete ms. Length: 50-250 words ("more if author has good handle to cover complete columns"). Pays $5-25.
Fiction: Judy Johnson, fiction editor. Erotica (if related to fitness club), fantasy (related to subjects), humorous (definite market), religious ("no God-is-my shepherd, but Body-is-God's-temple OK"), romance (related subjects). "Upbeat stories are needed." Buys 20 mss/year. Send complete ms. Length: 500-2,500 words maximum. Pays $20-150.
Poetry: Free verse, haiku, light verse, traditional on related subjects. Length: up to 150 words. Pays $10-25.
Tips: "Send us articles dealing with court club sports, exercise and nutrition that exemplify an upbeat 'you can do it' attitude. Pro sports previews 3-4 months ahead of their seasons are also needed. Good short fiction or humorous articles can break in. Expert knowledge of any related subject can bring assignments; any area is open. We consider everything as a potential article, but are turned off by credits, past work and degrees. We have a constant demand for well-written articles on instruction, health and trends in both. Other articles needed are professional sports training techniques, fad diets, tennis and fitness resorts, photo features with aerobic routines. A frequent mistake made by writers is length—articles are too long. When we assign an article, we want it newsy if it's news and opinion if opinion."

RACQUETBALL MAGAZINE, American Amateur Racquetball Association, 1685 W. Uintah, Colorado Springs CO 80904. (719)635-5396. Fax: (719)535-9648. Director of Communications: Linda Mojer. 20-30% freelance written. Bimonthly magazine "geared toward a readership of informed, active enthusiasts who seek entertainment, instruction and accurate reporting of events." Estab. 1990. Circ. 45,000. Pays on publication. Publishes ms an average of 2 months after acceptance. Buys one-time rights. Editorial lead time 3 months. Submit seasonal material 3 months in advance. Accepts simultaneous and previously published submissions. Send typed ms with rights for sale noted and information about when and where the article previously appeared. Query for electronic submissions. Reports in 2 months. Sample copy for $4. Writer's guidelines free on request.
Nonfiction: How-to (instructional racquetball tips), humor, interview/profile (personalities who play racquetball). Buys 2-3 mss/year. Send complete ms. Length: 1,500-3,000 words. Pays $100. Sometimes pays expenses of writers on assignment.
Photos: Send photos with submission. Reviews 3×5 prints. Negotiates payment individually. Model releases, identification of subjects required. Buys one-time rights.
Fiction: Humorous (racquetball related). Buys 1-2 mss/year. Send complete ms. Length: 1,500-3,000 words. Pays $100-250.

REFEREE, Referee Enterprises, Inc., P.O. Box 161, Franksville WI 53126-9987. (414)632-8855. Fax: (414)632-5460. Editor: Tom Hammill. 20-25% freelance written. Works with a small number of new/unpublished writers each year. Monthly magazine for well-educated, mostly 26- to 50-year-old male sports officials. Estab. 1975. Circ. 35,000. Pays on acceptance of completed ms. Publishes ms an average of 4 months after acceptance. Rights purchased varies. Submit seasonal/holiday material 4-6 months in advance. Accepts previously published submissions. Send tearsheet or photocopy of article or typed ms with rights for sale noted and information about when and where it previously appeared. Pays 50% of their fee for an original article. Reports in 2 weeks. Sample copy for 10×13 SAE with 7 first-class stamps. Writer's guidelines for #10 SASE.

Nonfiction: How-to, informational, humor, interview, profile, personal experience, photo feature, technical. Buys 54 mss/year. Query. Length: 700-3,000 words. Pays 4-10¢/word. "No general sports articles."

Photos: Purchased with or without accompanying ms or on assignment. Captions preferred. Send contact sheet, prints, negatives or transparencies. Pays $20 for each b&w used; $35 for each color used; $100 for color cover, $75 for b&w cover.

Columns/Departments: Law (legal aspects); Take Care (fitness, medical); Between the Lines (anecdotes); Heads Up (psychology). Buys 24 mss/year. Query. Length: 200-800 words. Pays 4¢/word up to $100 maximum for regular columns.

Fillers: Jokes, gags, anecdotes, puzzles, referee shorts. Query. Length: 50-200 words. Pays 4¢/word in some cases; others offer only author credit lines.

Tips: "Queries with a specific idea appeal most to readers. Generally, we are looking more for feature writers, as we usually do our own shorter/filler-type material. It is helpful to obtain suitable photos to augment a story. Don't send fluff—we need hard-hitting, incisive material tailored just for our audience. Anything smacking of public relations is a no sale. Don't gloss over the material too lightly or fail to go in-depth looking for a quick sale (taking the avenue of least resistance)."

SIGNPOST FOR NORTHWEST TRAILS MAGAZINE, 1305 Fourth Ave., Suite 512, Seattle WA 98101-2401. E-mail: dnelson@dnelson.seanet.com. Publisher: Washington Trails Association. Executive Editor: Dan A. Nelson. 10% freelance written. "We will consider working with both previously published and unpublished freelancers." Monthly magazine about hiking, backpacking and similar trail-related activities, strictly from a Pacific Northwest viewpoint. Estab. 1966. Will consider any rights offered by author. Publishes ms an average of 6 months after acceptance. Reports in 2 months. Accepts previously published submissions. Include information about when and where the article previously appeared. Query or submit complete ms. Writer's guidelines for #10 SASE.

Nonfiction and Photos: "Most material is donated by subscribers or is staff-written. Payment for purchased material is low, but a good way to break in to print and share your outdoor experiences."

Tips: "We cover only *self-propelled* backcountry sports and won't consider manuscripts about trail bikes, snowmobiles or power boats. We *are* interested in articles about modified and customized equipment, food and nutrition, and personal experiences in the Pacific Northwest backcountry."

SILENT SPORTS, Waupaca Publishing Co., P.O. Box 152, Waupaca WI 54981-9990. (715)258-5546. Fax: (715)258-8162. Editor: Greg Marr. 75% freelance written. Eager to work with new/unpublished writers. Monthly magazine on running, cycling, cross-country skiing, canoeing, in-line skating, camping, backpacking and hiking aimed at people in Wisconsin, Minnesota, northern Illinois and portions of Michigan and Iowa. "Not a coffee table magazine. Our readers are participants from rank amateur weekend athletes to highly competitive racers." Estab. 1984. Circ. 10,000. Pays on publication. Publishes ms an average of 3 months after acceptance. Byline given. Offers 20% kill fee. Buys one-time rights. Submit seasonal/holiday material 4 months in advance. Accepts previously published submissions. Send typed ms with rights for sale noted and information about when and where the article previously appeared. Pay negotiated. Reports in 3 months. Sample copy and writer's guidelines for 10×13 SAE with 6 first-class stamps.

• The editor needs local angles on in-line skating and recreation bicycling.

Nonfiction: General interest, how-to, interview/profile, opinion, technical, travel. All stories/articles must focus on the Upper Midwest. First-person articles discouraged. Buys 25 mss/year. Query. Length: 2,500 words maximum. Pays $15-100. Sometimes pays expenses of writers on assignment.

Tips: "Where-to-go, how-to and personality profiles are areas most open to freelancers. Writers should keep in mind that this is a regional, Midwest-based publication."

SKYDIVING, 1725 N. Lexington Ave., DeLand FL 32724. (904)736-4793. Fax: (904)736-9786. Editor: Michael Truffer. 25% freelance written. Works with a small number of new/unpublished writers each year. Monthly tabloid featuring skydiving for sport parachutists, worldwide dealers and equipment manufacturers. Circ. 10,400. Average issue includes 3 feature articles and 3 columns of technical information. Pays on publication. Publishes ms an average of 3 months after acceptance. Byline given. Buys one-time rights. Accepts simultaneous and previously published submissions, if so indicated. Query for electronic submissions. Reports in 1 month. *Writer's Market* recommends allowing 2 months for reply. Sample copy for $2. Writer's guidelines for 9×12 SAE with 4 first-class stamps.

Nonfiction: "Send us news and information on equipment, techniques, events and outstanding personalities who skydive. We want articles written by people who have a solid knowledge of parachuting." No personal experience or human-interest articles. Query. Length: 500-1,000 words. Pays $25-100. Sometimes pays the expenses of writers on assignment.

Photos: State availability of photos. Reviews 5×7 and larger b&w glossy prints. Offers no additional payment for photos accepted with ms. Captions required.

Fillers: Newsbreaks. Length: 100-200 words. Pays $25 minimum.

Tips: "The most frequent mistake made by writers in completing articles for us is that the writer isn't knowledgeable about the sport of parachuting."

TRUCKIN', World's Leading Sport Truck Publication, McMullen & Yee Publishing, 774 S. Placentia Ave., Placentia CA 92670. (714)572-2255. Editor: Steve Stillwell. 15% freelance written. Monthly magazine covering customized sport trucks. "Materials we purchase are events coverage, technical articles and truck features, all having to be associated with customized —½-ton pickups and mini-trucks." Estab. 1975. Circ. 200,000. Pays on publication. Buys all rights unless previously agreed upon. Editorial lead time 3 months. Submit seasonal material 6 months in advance. Query for electronic submissions. Reports in 2 weeks on queries; 1 month on mss. Sample copy for $4.50.Writer's guidelines free on request.

Nonfiction: How-to, new product, photo feature, technical, events coverage. Buys 50 mss/year. Query. Length: 1,000 words minimum. Pay negotiable. Sometimes pays expenses of writers on assignment.

Photos: Send photos with submission. Reviews contact sheets and transparencies. Captions, model releases and identification of subjects required. Buys all rights unless previously agreed upon.

Columns/Departments: Bill Blankenship. Insider (latest automotive/truck news), 2,000 words. Buys 70 mss/year. Send complete ms. Pays $25 minimum.

Fillers: Bill Blankenship. Anecdotes, facts, newsbreaks. Buys 50/year. Length: 600-1,000 words. Pay negotiable.

Tips: "Send all queries and submissions in envelopes larger than letter size to avoid being detained with a mass of reader mail. Send complete packages with transparencies and contact sheets (with negatives). Submit hard copy and a computer disc when possible. Editors purchase the materials that are the least complicated to turn into magazine pages! All materials have to be fresh/new and primarily outside of California."

VOLLEYBALL MAGAZINE, Avcom Publishing, Ltd., 21700 Oxnard St., Suite 1600, Woodland Hills CA 91367. (818)593-3900. Fax: (818)593-2274. Editor: Rick Hazeltine. Executive Editor: Don Patterson. Managing Editor: David Kraft. 50% freelance written. Monthly magazine covering the sport of volleyball. Estab. 1990. Circ. 75,000. Pays on publication. Publishes ms an average of 3 months after acceptance. Byline given. Offers 50% kill fee. Buys first North American serial rights. Editorial lead time 3 months. Submit seasonal material 3 months in advance. Query for electronic submissions.

Nonfiction: Historical/nostalgic, how-to (skills instruction, nutrition strategy, fitness), humor, interview/ profile, technical. No event coverage. Buys 72 mss/year. Query with published clips. Length: 250-3,000 words. Pays $100. Sometimes pays expenses of writers on assignment.

Photos: Send photos with submission. Reviews transparencies—no duplicates. Offers $40-225/photo. Captions, model releases and identification of subjects requried. Buys one-time rights.

Columns/Departments: Fitness (must relate specifically to volleyball); Nutrition (for athletes); Mental (mental side of sports). Length: 1,000-1,200 words. Buys 36 mss/year. Query with published clips. Pays $200-250.

Olympic Sports

INSIDE TRIATHLON, Inside Communications, 1830 N. 55th St., Boulder CO 80301. (303)440-0601. Fax: (303)444-6788. E-mail: insidetri@aol.com. Editor: Chris Newbound. 70% freelance written. Monthly tabloid covering triathlon/duathlon. Estab. 1993. Circ. 20,000. Pays on publication. Byline given. Offers 33% kill fee. Editorial lead time 2 months. Submit seasonal material 2 months in advance. Accepts simultaneous submissions. Submit tearsheet of article. Query for electronic submissions. Reports in 1 month on queries. Sample copy and writer's guidelines free on request.

Nonfiction: Query with published clips. Length: 1,000-2,500 words. Pays $300-400.

Columns/Departments: Body Shop (training articles), 750-1,000 words; At the Races (Race Reports), 500 words. Query with published clips.

Tips: "Query with clips. Know the magazine. Suggest useful articles our readers would be interested in. Transition area/At the Races/Body Shop most open to freelancers."

INTERNATIONAL OLYMPIC LIFTER, IOL Publications, 3602 Eagle Rock, P.O. Box 65855, Los Angeles CA 90065. (213)257-8762. Editor: Bob Hise. 20% freelance written. Bimonthly magazine covering the Olympic sport of weightlifting. Estab. 1973. Circ. 10,000. Pays on publication. Publishes ms an average of 3 months after acceptance. Byline given. Offers $25 kill fee. Buys one-time rights or negotiable rights. Submit seasonal/holiday material 5 months in advance. Accepts previously published submissions. Send photocopy of article and information about when and where the article previously appeared. For reprints, payment is negotiated. Reports in 3 months. Sample copy for $4. Writer's guidelines for 9×12 SAE with 5 first-class stamps.

• *International Olympic Lifter* needs more biographies and training routines on the *Olympic* weightlifting top names.

Nonfiction: Training articles, contest reports, diet—all related to Olympic weightlifting. Buys 4 mss/year. Query. Length: 250-2,000 words. Pays $25-100.

Photos: Action (competition and training). State availability of photos. Pays $1-5 for 5×7 b&w prints. Identification of subjects required.

Poetry: Dale Rhoades, poetry editor. Light verse, traditional—related to Olympic lifting. Buys 6-10 poems/year. Submit maximum 3 poems. Length: 12-24 lines. Pays $10-20.

Tips: "A writer must be acquainted with Olympic-style weightlifting. Since we are an international publication we do not tolerate ethnic, cultural, religious or political inclusions. Articles relating to AWA are readily accepted."

‡**OLYMPIAN MAGAZINE**, U.S. Olympic Committee, One Olympic Plaza, Colorado Springs CO 80909. (719)578-4529. Fax: (719)578-4677. Managing Editor: Frank Zang. 50% freelance written. Bimonthly magazine covering olympic sports and athletes. Estab. 1974. Circ. 120,000. Pays on publication. Byline given. Offers 100% kill fee. Query for electronic submissions. Accepts previously published submissions. Send photocopy of article. For reprints, pay 50% of the amount paid for an original article. Free writer's guidelines.

Nonfiction: Photo feature, feature/profiles of athletes in Olympic sports. Query. Length: 1,200-2,000 words. Pays $300 for assigned articles.

Photos: State availability of photos with submission. Reviews transparencies and prints. Offers $50-250/photo. Captions, model releases and identification of subjects required. Buys one-time rights.

USA GYMNASTICS, 201 S. Capitol Ave., Suite 300, Pan American Plaza, Indianapolis IN 46225. (317)237-5050. Fax: (317)237-5069. Editor: Luan Peszek. 20% freelance written. Bimonthly magazine covering gymnastics—national and international competitions. Designed to educate readers on fitness, health, safety, technique, current topics, trends and personalities related to the gymnastics/fitness field. Readers are ages of 7-18, parents and coaches. Estab. 1981. Circ. 63,000. Pays on publication. Publishes ms an average of 4 months after acceptance. Byline given. Buys all rights. Submit seasonal/holiday material 4 months in advance. Accepts simultaneous and previously published submissions. Reports in 2 months. Sample copy for $5.

Nonfiction: General interest, how-to (related to fitness, health, gymnastics), inspirational, interview/profile, new product, opinion (Open Floor section), photo feature. Buys 3 mss/year. Query. Length: 1,500 words maximum. Payment negotiated.

Photos: Send photos with submission. Offers no additional payment for photos accepted with ms. Identification of subjects required. Buys all rights.

Tips: "Any articles of interest to gymnasts (men, women and rhythmic gymnastics) coaches, judges and parents, are what we're looking for. This includes nutrition, toning, health, safety, current trends, gymnastics techniques, timing techniques etc."

Running

NEW YORK RUNNING NEWS, New York Road Runners Club, 9 E. 89th St., New York NY 10128. (212)860-2280. Fax: (212)860-9754. Editor: Raleigh Mayer. Managing Editor: Don Mogelefsky. 75% freelance written. Bimonthly regional sports magazine covering running, racewalking, nutrition and fitness. Material should be of interest to members of the New York Road Runners Club. Estab. 1958. Circ. 45,000. Pays on publication. Time to publication varies. Byline given. Offers 33% kill fee. Buys first North American serial rights. Submit seasonal/holiday material 4 months in advance. Accepts simultaneous and previously published submissions. Send photocopy of article with information about when and where it previously appeared. Pays 25-50% of their fee for an original article. Reports in 2 months. Sample copy for $3. Writer's guidelines for #10 SASE.

Nonfiction: Running and marathon articles. Special issues: N.Y.C. Marathon (submissions in by August 1). No non-running stories. Buys 25 mss/year. Query. Length: 750-1,750 words. Pays $50-250. Pays documented expenses of writers on assignment.

Photos: Send photos with submission. Reviews 8×10 b&w prints. Offers $35-300/photo. Captions, model releases, identification of subjects required. Buys one-time rights.

Columns/Departments: Essay (running-related topics). Query. Length: 750 words. Pays $50-125.

Tips: "Be knowledgeable about the sport of running. Write like a runner."

RUNNER'S WORLD, Rodale Press, 33 E. Minor St., Emmaus PA 18098. (215)967-5171. Senior Editor: Bob Wischnia. 10% freelance written. Monthly magazine on running, mainly long-distance running. "The magazine for and about distance running, training, health and fitness, injury precaution, race coverage, personalties of the sport." Estab. 1966. Circ. 450,000. Pays on publication. Publishes ms an average of 6 months after acceptance. Byline given. Buys one-time rights. Submit seasonal/holiday material 6 months in advance. Query for electronic submissions. Reports in 2 months. Writer's guideline requests to Pat Erickson for #10 SASE.

Nonfiction: How-to (train, prevent injuries), interview/profile, personal experience. No "my first marathon" stories. No poetry. Buys 10 mss/year. Query. Pays the expenses of writers on assignment.

Photos: State availability of photos with submission. Identification of subjects required. Buys one-time rights.

Columns/Departments: Christina Negron. Finish Line (personal experience—humor); Training Log (training of well-known runner). Buys 15 mss/year. Query.

Skiing and Snow Sports

AMERICAN SKATING WORLD, Independent Publication of the American Ice Skating Community, Business Communications Inc., 1816 Brownsville Rd., Pittsburgh PA 15210-3908. (412)885-7600. Fax: (412)885-7617. Editor: Robert A. Mock. Managing Editor: H. Kermit Jackson. 70% freelance written. Eager to work with new/unpublished writers. Monthly tabloid on figure skating. Estab. 1979. Circ. 15,000. Pays following publication. Publishes ms an average of 3 months after acceptance. Byline given. Buys first North American serial rights and occasionally second serial (reprint) rights. Submit seasonal/holiday material 3 months in advance. Occasionally accepts previously published submissions. Send tearsheet of article. For reprints, payment is negotiable. Reports in 3 months. Sample copy and writer's guidelines for $3.50.

• The increased activity and interest in figure skating have increased demands on *American Skating World*'s contributor network. New writers from nontraditional areas (i.e., outside of East Coast, Upper Midwest, California) are particularly welcome.

Nonfiction: Exposé, historical/nostalgic, how-to (technique in figure skating), humor, inspirational, interview/profile, new product, opinion, personal experience, photo feature, technical, travel. Special issues: annual fashion issue (September); Industry (May). Rarely accepts fiction. AP Style Guidelines are the basic style source, but we are not bound by that convention. Short, snappy paragraphs desired. Buys 150 mss/year. Send complete ms. "Include phone number; response time longer without it." Length: 600-1,000 words. Pays $25-100.

Photos: Send photos with query or ms. Reviews transparencies and b&w prints. Pays $5 for b&w; $15 for color. Identification of subjects required. Buys all rights for b&w; one-time rights for color.

Columns/Departments: Buys 30 mss/year. Send complete ms. Length: 500-750 words. Pays $25-50.

Fillers: Clippings, anecdotes. No payment for fillers.

Tips: "Event coverage is most open to freelancers; confirm with managing editor to ensure event has not been assigned. We are drawing more extensively from non-U.S. based writers. Questions are welcome; call managing editor EST, 10-4, Monday-Friday."

SKATING, United States Figure Skating Association, 20 1st St., Colorado Springs CO 80906-3697. (719)635-5200. Fax: (719)635-9548. Editor: Jay Miller. Monthly magazine official publication of the USFSA. Estab. 1923. Circ. 40,000. Pays on publication. Publishes ms an average of 3 months after acceptance. Buys all rights. Byline given. Accepts previously published submissions. Send photocopy of article and information about when and where the article previously appeared. For reprints, pay varies.

Nonfiction: Historical, informational, interview, photo feature, historical biographies, profile (background and interests of national-caliber amateur skaters), technical and competition reports. Buys 4 mss/issue. All work by assignment. Length: 400-800 words. Pay varies.

Photos: Photos purchased with or without accompanying ms. Pays $15 for 8×10 or 5×7 b&w glossy prints and $35 for color prints or transparencies. Query.

Columns/Departments: Ice Breaker (news briefs), Foreign National Reports, Center Ice (guest), Letters to Editor, People. Buys 4 mss/issue. All work by assignment. Length: 500-2,000 words.

Tips: "We want writing by experienced persons knowledgeable in the technical and artistic aspects of figure skating with a new outlook on the development of the sport. Knowledge and background in technical aspects of figure skating are essential to the quality of writing expected. We would also like to receive articles on former competitive skaters. No professional skater material."

SKI TRIPPER, P.O. Box 20305, Roanoke VA 24018. (703)772-7644. Editor: Tom Gibson. 50% freelance written Consumer newsletter published monthly November-April covering snow skiing in mid-Atlantic region. "Need reports on trips taken to regional ski resorts and to long-distance resorts (western US/Canada, Europe, New Zealand, South America) from the region. Trip reports are written from an unbiased viewpoint and tell good and bad things other people making the trip in the future should look out for. Also need informational pieces on resorts, skiers and skiing-related activities. Estab. 1993. Circ. 1,000. **Pays on acceptance**. Publishes ms an average of 3 months after acceptance. Buys first North American serial rights. Editorial lead time 1 month. Submit seasonal material 2 months in advance. Query for electronic submissions. Reports in 3 weeks on queries; 1 month on mss. Sample copy and writer's guidelines free on request.

Nonfiction: Personal experience, travel. "No articles on ski shops and ski equipment." Buys 12 mss/year. Query. Length: 750-2,000 words. Pays $30-90.

Tips: "If you're going on a ski trip to or from the mid-Atlantic region, let us know—it may be one we'd like to cover."

SKIING, Times Mirror Magazines, Inc., 2 Park Ave., New York NY 10016. Editor-in-Chief: Rick Knoll. Covers skiing equipment, fashion and news. Query before submitting. No personal stories, previously published articles or poetry.

SNOW COUNTRY, The Year-Round Magazine of Mountain Sports & Living, New York Times Magazine Group, 5520 Park Ave., Trumbull CT 06611. (203)323-7038. Fax: (203)373-7111. Editor: John Fry. Managing Editor: Robert LaMarche. 85% freelance written. Monthly (September-January) and Spring, Summer Preview and Summer issues). Focuses on mountain lifestyles and recreation at and around ski resorts. "Because we publish year-round, we cover a broader range of subjects than ski-only publications. Besides skiing, topics include scenic drives, mountain biking, hiking, rollerblading, real estate, etc." Estab. 1988. Circ. 465,000. **Pays on acceptance.** Publishes ms an average of 6 months after acceptance. Byline given. Kill fee varies. Buys first North American serial rights and foreign affiliates. Submit seasonal material 6 months in advance. Reports in 1 month. Free writer's guidelines.

• *Snow Country* was rated among "Top-10 Up and Coming" magazines by *Adweek* in 1994.

Nonfiction: General interest, historical/nostalgic, how-to, humor, interview/profile, new product, photo feature, technical and travel. Buys 45 mss/year. Query with published clips. Length: 250-1,200 words. Pays $200-1,000. Pays expenses of writers on assignment.

Photos: State availability of photos with submission. Reviews transparencies. Identification of subjects required. Buys one-time rights.

Columns/Departments: Follow Me (instructional items on skiing, mountain biking, photography, hiking), 200 words; Snow Country Store (items on mountain artisans, craftsmen and their products), 250 words. Buys 35 mss/year. Query with published clips. Pays $200-300.

Tips: "Area most open to freelancers: short articles on people who've moved to snow country and are making a living there."

Soccer

‡SOCCER MAGAZINE, Patch Communications, 5211 S. Washington Ave., Titusville FL 32780. (407)268-5010. Editor: Michael Lewis. Contact: Jill Martello, assistant editor. Magazine published 9 times/year covering "the sport at every level for players, coaches, referees and parents, offering tournament and league coverage as well as player profiles and coaching, nutrition, youth/women's development and training tips columns." Estab. 1993. Circ. 20,000. Pays on publication. Publishes ms an average of 6 months after acceptance. Byline given. Buys first North American serial rights. Editorial lead time 4 months. Submit seasonal material 6 months in advance. No simultaneous or previously published submissions. Query for electronic submissions. Reports in 1 month on queries. Writer's guidelines for #10 SASE.

Nonfiction: How-to (coaching), interview/profile, new product, personal experience, photo feature, technical (nutrition). Buys 6 mss/year. Query with published clips and SASE. Length: 600-1,200 words.

Photos: Send photos with submission. Reviews transparencies, prints. Negotiates payment individually. Captions, identification of subjects required. Buys one-time rights.

‡SOCCER NOW, Official Publication of the American Youth Soccer Organization, American Youth Soccer Organization, 5403 W. 138th St., Hawthorne CA 90250. (800)USA-AYSO. Editor: Sean Hilferty. 35% freelance written. Quarterly magazine covering soccer (AYSO and professional). "For AYSO members, both players (age 5-18) and their parents. We want to focus mostly on the 6-12 age group. Human interest about AYSO players and adult volunteers, or professional players (especially if they played in AYSO as kids)." Estab. 1976. Circ. 370,000. Pays on publication. Publishes ms an average of 2-3 months after acceptance. Byline given. Makes work-for-hire assignments. Editorial lead time 1-3 months. Query for electronic submissions. Reports in 1 month on queries. Sample copy free on request.

Nonfiction: General interest (soccer), historical/nostalgic, how-to (playing tips subject to approval by Director of Coaching), interview/profile, personal experience, photo feature. Buys 12 mss/year. Query. Length: 400-2,000 words. Pays $50-200. Sometimes pays expenses of writers on assignment.

Photos: Send photos with submission. Reviews contact sheets, transparencies, prints. Offers $0-50/photo. Identification of subjects required. Buys one-time rights.

Columns/Departments: Hot Shots (profile of AYSO player who is a standout in something *other* than soccer), 750 words; On The Spot (interview (Q&A format) with pro player), 1,300 words. Buys 8 mss/year. Query. Pays $100-200.

Tennis

TENNIS WEEK, Tennis News, Inc., 341 Madison Ave., 6th Floor, New York NY 10017. (212)808-4750. Fax: (212)983-6302. Managing Editors: Cherry V. Masih, Kim Kodl. 10% freelance written. Biweekly magazine covering tennis. "For readers who are either tennis fanatics or involved in the business of tennis." Estab. 1974. Circ. 80,000. Pays on publication. Byline given. Buys all rights. Editorial lead time 1 month. Submit seasonal material 1 month in advance. Query for electronic submissions. Reports in 1 month on queries. Sample copy for $3.

Nonfiction: Buys 15 mss/year. Query with or without published clips. Length: 1,000-2,000 words. Pays $300.

Water Sports

DIVER, Seagraphic Publications, Ltd., 10991 Shellbridge Way, Suite 295, Richmond, British Columbia V6X 3C6 Canada. (604)273-4333. Fax: (604)273-0813. Editor/Publisher: Peter Vassilopoulos. Contact: Stephanie Bold, assistant editor. Magazine published 9 times/year emphasizing scuba diving, ocean science and technology (commercial and military diving) for a well-educated, outdoor-oriented readership. Circ. 17,500. Payment "follows publication." Buys first North American serial rights. Byline given. Submit seasonal/holiday material July-September for consideration for following year. Send SAE with IRCs. Reports in up to 3 months. Publishes ms up to 1 year after acceptance. "Articles are subject to being accepted for use in supplement issues on tabloid." Travel features considered only in September/October for use following year. Buys only 6 freelance travel items a year.

Nonfiction: How-to (underwater activities such as photography, etc.), general interest (underwater oriented), humor, historical (shipwrecks, treasure artifacts, archeological), interview (underwater personalities in all spheres—military, sports, scientific or commercial), personal experience (related to diving), photo feature (marine life), technical (related to oceanography, commercial/military diving, etc.), travel (dive resorts). No subjective product reports. Buys 25 mss/year. Submit complete ms. Length: 800-1,500 words. Pays $2.50/column inch.

Photos: "Features are mostly those describing dive sites, experiences, etc. Photo features are reserved more as specials, while almost all articles must be well illustrated with color or b&w prints supplemented by color transparencies." Submit original photo material with accompanying ms. Pays $7 minimum for 5×7 or 8×10 b&w glossy prints; $15 minimum for 35mm color transparencies. Captions and model releases required. Buys one-time rights.

Columns/Departments: Book reviews. Submit complete ms. Length: 200 words maximum. No payment.

Fillers: Anecdotes, newsbreaks, short humor. Buys 8-10/year. Length: 50-150 words. No payment for news items.

Tips: "No phone calls inquiring about status of manuscript. Write if no response within reasonable time. Only brief, to-the-point correspondence will be answered. Lengthy communications will probably result in return of work unused. Publisher assumes no liability to use material even after lengthy waiting period. Acceptances only subject to final and actual use."

SCUBA TIMES, The Active Diver's Magazine, GBP, Inc., 14110 Perdido Key Dr., Pensacola FL 32507. (904)492-7805. Fax: (904)492-7805. Managing Editor: Fred D. Garth. Editor: Gary Nichols. 90% freelance written. Bimonthly magazine on scuba diving. Estab. 1979. Circ. 43,000. Pays on publication. Publishes ms an average of 6 months after acceptance. Byline given. Buys first North American serial rights. Accepts previously published submissions. Send information about when and where the article previously appeared. For reprints, pays 100% of the amount paid for an original article. Submit seasonal material 1 year in advance. Query for electronic submissions. Reports in 6 weeks. Sample copy for $3. Writer's guidelines for #10 SASE.

Nonfiction: How-to (advanced diving techniques such as technical, very deep, mixed gases, cave diving, wreck diving); humor; interview/profile (colorful characters in diving); personal experience (only if it is astounding); photo feature (creatures, places to dive); technical (physics, biology, medicine as it relates to diving); travel (dive destinations). No beginner-level dive material. Buys 75 mss/year. Query with published clips or send complete ms. Length: 150 words for sidebars, 1,500 for major destination features. Pays $75/published page. Sometimes pays expenses of writers on assignment.

Photos: Send photos with submission. Reviews transparencies. Offers $25-75/page; $150/front cover photo. Captions and identification of subjects required. Buys one-time rights.

Columns/Departments: What a Wreck (informative guide to any wreck, old or new), 750 words; Creature Feature (one knock-out photo of a mysterious sea creature plus story of life cycle and circumstances that led to photo), 500 words; Last Watering Hole, (great photos, usually topside, and story about a dive site so remote most divers will never go), 500 words; Advanced Diving (how-to and advanced techniques for expanding dive adventure), 750 words. Buys 60 mss/year. Query with published clips. Length; 500-1,000 words. Pays $25-75/page.

Fillers: " 'Free Flowing' sections allows writers to be creative, thought provoking as they contemplate diver's relationship to the marine world." Anecdotes, short humor. Buys 10/year. Length: 300-900 words. Pays $25-75/page.

Tips: "Be a diver. Everyone tries for the glamorous destination assignments, but it is easier to break into the columns, especially, 'Last Watering Hole,' 'What a Wreck' and 'Creature Feature.' Outstanding photos are a must. We will coax a good article out of a great photographer whose writing skills are not developed.

Very little is written in-house. Diving freelancers are the heart and soul of *STM*. Unknowns receive as much consideration as the big names. Know what you are talking about and present it with a creative flair. Divers are often technical or scientific by profession or disposition and their writing lacks flow, power and grace. Make us *feel* those currents and *smell* the diesel from the yacht."

SURFER, Surfer Publications, P.O. Box 1028, Dana Point CA 92629. (714)496-5922. Fax: (714)496-7849. E-mail: 73061.2324@compuserve.com. Editor: Steve Hawk. Assistant Editor: Lisa Boelter. 75% freelance written. Monthly magazine "aimed at experts and beginners with strong emphasis on action surf photography." Estab. 1960. Circ. 110,000. Pays on publication. Byline given. Buys first North American serial rights. Submit seasonal/holiday material 6 months in advance. Accepts simultaneous submissions. Query for electronic submissions. Reports in 2 months. Sample copy for $3.95 with 9 × 12 SASE. Writer's guidelines for #10 SASE.

Nonfiction: How-to (technique in surfing), humor, inspirational, interview/profile, opinion, personal experience (all surf-related), photo feature (action surf and surf travel), technical (surfboard design), travel (surf exploration and discovery—photos required). Buys 30-50 mss/year. Query with or without published clips or send complete ms. Length: 500-2,500 words. Pays 20-25¢/word. Sometimes pays the expenses of writers on assignment.

Photos: Send photos with submission. Reviews 35mm negatives and transparencies. Buys 12-24 illustrations/year. Prices vary. Used for columns: Environment, Surf Docs and sometimes features. Send samples with SASE to Art Director. Offers $25-250/photo. Identification of subjects required. Buys one-time and reprint rights.

Columns/Departments: Environment (environmental concerns to surfers), 1,000-1,500 words; Surf Stories (personal experiences of surfing), 1,000-1,500 words; Reviews (surf-related movies, books), 500-1,000 words; Sections (humorous surf-related items with b&w photos), 100-500 words. Buys 25-50 mss/year. Send complete ms. Pays 20-25¢/word.

Fiction: Surf-related adventure, fantasy, horror, humorous, science fiction. Buys 10 mss/year. Send complete ms. Length: 750-2,000 words. Pays 15-20¢/word.

Tips: "All sections are open to freelancers but interview/profiles are usually assigned. Try 'People Who Surf'—a good way to get a foot in the door. Stories must be authoritative and oriented to the hardcore surfer."

SWIM MAGAZINE, Sports Publications, Inc., P.O. Box 2025, Sedona AZ 86339-2025. (602)282-4799. Fax: (602)282-4697. Editor: Dr. Phillip Whitten. 50% freelance written. Prefers to work with published/selected writers. Bimonthly magazine. "*Swim Magazine* is for adults interested in swimming for fun, fitness and competition. Readers are fitness-oriented adults from varied social and professional backgrounds who share swimming as part of their lifestyle. Readers are well-educated, affluent and range in age from 20-100 with most in the 30-49 age group; about 50% female, 50% male." Estab. 1984. Circ. 39,100. Pays approximately 1 month after publication. Publishes ms an average of 4 months after acceptance. Byline given. Submit seasonal/holiday material 4 months in advance. Accepts previously published submissions. Send tearsheet or photocopy of article or typed ms with rights for sale noted along with information about when and where the article previously appeared. Reports in 1 month on queries; 3 months on mss. Sample copy for $3 (prepaid) and 9 × 12 SAE with 5 first-class stamps. Free writer's guidelines.

Nonfiction: How-to (training plans and techniques), interview/profile (people associated with fitness and competitive swimming), inspirational, general health, new product (articles describing new products for fitness and competitive training). "Articles need to be informative as well as interesting. In addition to fitness and health articles, we are interested in exploring fascinating topics dealing with swimming for the adult reader." Send complete ms. Length: 500-3,000 words. Pays $3/published column inch. "No payment for articles about personal experiences."

• Using shorter articles.

Photos: Send photos with ms. Offers no additional payment for photos accepted with ms. Captions, model releases, identification of subjects required.

Tips: "Our how-to articles and physiology articles best typify *Swim Magazine*'s projected style for fitness and competitive swimmers. *Swim Magazine* will accept medical guidelines and exercise physiology articles only by M.D.s and Ph.Ds."

WATERSKI MAGAZINE, The World's Leading Water Skiing Magazine, World Publications, 330 W. Canton Ave., Winter Park FL 32789. (407)628-4082. Fax: (407)628-7061. Editor: Rob May. Managing Editor: Barb McCarter. 25% freelance written. Magazine published 10 times/year for water skiing and related watersports. "*WaterSki* instructs, advises, enlightens, informs *and* creates an open forum for skiers around the world. It provides definitive information on instruction, products, people and travel destinations." Estab. 1978. Circ. 105,000. **Pays on acceptance**. Publishes ms an average of 4 months after acceptance. Offers 25% kill fee. Buys first North American serial and second serial (reprint) rights. Editorial lead time 2 months. Submit seasonal material 2 months in advance. Query for electronic submissions. Reports in 1 month on queries; 2 months on mss. Sample copy for 8½ × 11 SAE with 4 first-class stamps. Writer's guidelines for #10 SASE.

Nonfiction: General interest, historical/nostalgic, how-to (water ski instruction boating-related), interview/profile, new product, photo feature, technical, travel. Does not want to see anything not directly related to the sport of water skiing. Buys 10 mss/year. Query with published clips. Length: 1,750-3,000 words. Pays $200 minimum for assigned articles. Pays other upon inability to meet author's pay request. Sometimes pays expenses of writers on assignment.

• Continues to accept more stories that are not necessarily hard-core water skiing, especially travel.

Photos: Send photos with submission. Reviews 2¼×2¼ transparencies, all slides. Negotiates payment individually. Identification of subjects required. Buys one-time rights on color, all rights on b&w.

Columns/Departments: Shortline (interesting news of the sport), 300 words; Quick Tips (short instruction on water skiing and 500 words. Buys 10 mss/year. Query with published clips. Pays $75-125.

Fiction: Adventure, experimental, historical, humorous. Does not want to see anything not directly related to water skiing. Buys 10 mss/year. Query with published clips. Length: 1,750-4,000 words. Pays $200-500.

Fillers: Anecdotes, facts, gags to be illustrated by cartoonist, newsbreaks, short humor. Buys 15/year. Length: 200-500 words. Pays $75-125.

Tips: "I recommend a query call to see if there are any immediate openings in the calendar. Follow-up with a published submission (if applicable). Writers should have some interest in the sport, and understand its people, products and lifestyle. The features sections offer the most opportunity for freelancers. One requirement: It must have a positive, strong water skiing slant, whether it be personality, human interest, or travel."

Wrestling

‡**WRESTLING WORLD**, Sterling/MacFadden, 233 Park Ave. S., New York NY 10003. (212)780-3500. Fax: (212)780-3555. Editor: Stephen Ciacciarelli. 100% freelance written. Bimonthly magazine for professional wrestling fans. We run profiles of top wrestlers and managers and articles on current topics of interest on the mat scene." Circ. 100,000. **Pays on acceptance.** Byline given. Buys first North American serial rights. Reports in 2 weeks. Sample copy $3 for SAE with 3 first-class stamps.

Nonfiction: Interview/profile and photo feature. "No general think pieces." Buys 100 mss/year. Query with or without published clips or send complete ms. Length: 1,500-2,500 words. Pays $75-125.

Photos: State availability of photos with submission. Reviews 35mm transparencies and prints. Offers $25-50/photo package. Pays $50-150 for transparencies. Identification of subjects required. Buys one-time rights.

Tips: "Anything topical has the best chance of acceptance. Articles on those hard-to-reach wrestlers stand an excellent chance of acceptance."

Teen and Young Adult

The publications in this category are for young people ages 13-19. Publications for college students are listed in Career, College and Alumni. Those for younger children are listed in the Juvenile category.

CHALLENGE, Baptist Brotherhood Commission, 1548 Poplar Ave., Memphis TN 38104-2493. (901)272-2461. Editor: Jene Smith. Contact: Shelley Smith, Assistant Editor. 5% freelance written. Monthly magazine for "boys age 12-18 who are members of a missions organization in Southern Baptist churches." Circ. 28,500. Byline given. Pays on publication. Publishes ms an average of 6-8 months after acceptance. Buys simultaneous rights. Submit seasonal/holiday material 8 months in advance. Accepts simultaneous and previously published submissions. Send tearsheet or photocopy of article and information about where and when the article previously appeared. For reprints, pays 90% of the amount paid for an original article. Reports in 1 month. *Writer's Market* recommends allowing 2 months for reply. Sample copy and writer's guidelines for 9×12 SAE with 3 first-class stamps. Writer's guidelines only for #10 SASE.

Nonfiction: How-to (crafts, hobbies), informational (youth), inspirational (sports/entertainment personalities); photo feature (sports, teen subjects). No "preachy" articles, fiction or excessive dialogue. Submit complete ms. Length: 500-800 words. Pays $20-50.

Photos: Purchased with accompanying ms or on assignment. Captions required. Query. Pays $10 for 8×10 b&w glossy prints.

Tips: "The writer has a better chance of breaking in at our publication with youth related articles (youth issues, and sports figures). Most topics are set years in advance. The most frequent mistake made by writers is sending us preachy articles. Aim for the mid- to older-teen instead of younger teen."

EXPLORING MAGAZINE, Boy Scouts of America, P.O. Box 152079, Irving TX 75015-2079. (214)580-2365. Fax: (214)580-2079. Executive Editor: Scott Daniels. 85% freelance written. Prefers to work with published/established writers. Magazine published 4 times/year—Winter (January), Spring (April), Summer (June), Fall (November)—covering the co-ed teen-age Exploring program of the BSA. Estab. 1970. Circ. 350,000. **Pays on acceptance.** Publishes ms an average of 8 months after acceptance. Byline given. Buys first rights. Submit seasonal/holiday material 6 months in advance. Reports in 1 month. *Writer's Market* recommends allowing 2 months for reply. Sample copy for 9×12 SAE with 5 first-class stamps. Writer's guidelines for #10 SASE. Write for guidelines and "What is Exploring?" fact sheet.

Nonfiction: General interest: teenage popular culture, music, films, health, fitness, fashion, cars, computers, how-to (organize trips, meetings, etc.); interview/profile (of outstanding Explorer), travel (backpacking or canoeing with Explorers). Buys 15-20 mss/year. Query with clips. Length: 800-1,600 words. Pays $350-500. Pays expenses of writers on assignment.

Photos: Brian Payne, photo editor. State availability of photos with query letter or ms. Reviews b&w contact sheets and 35mm transparencies. Captions required. Buys one-time rights.

Tips: "Contact the local Exploring Director in your area (listed in phone book white pages under Boy Scouts of America). Find out if there are some outstanding post activities going on and then query magazine editor in Irving, Texas. Strive for shorter texts, faster starts and stories that lend themselves to dramatic photographs."

FLORIDA LEADER (for high school students), Oxendine Publishing, Inc., P.O. Box 14081, Gainesville FL 32604-2081. (904)373-6907. Editor: W.H. "Butch" Oxendine Jr. Managing Editor: Kay Quinn King. Quarterly magazine covering high school and pre-college youth. Estab. 1983. Circ. 50,000. Pays on publication. Publishes ms an average of 2-3 months after acceptance. Buys all rights. Submit seasonal material 4 months in advance. Accepts simultaneous and previously published submissions. Query for electronic submissions. Reports in 1-2 months on queries. Sample copy for 8×11 with 3 first-class stamps. For query response and/or writer's guidelines send #10 SASE.

Nonfiction: How-to, humor, new product, opinion. "No lengthy individual profiles or articles without primary and secondary sources of attribution." Length: 250-1,000 words. Pays $35 maximum. Pays students or first-time writers with contributor's copies.

Photos: Send photos with submission. Reviews contact sheets, negatives, transparencies. Offers $50/photo maximum. Captions, model releases, identification of subjects required. Buys all rights.

Columns/Departments: College Living (various aspects of college life, general short humor oriented to high school or college students), 250-1,000 words. Buys 10 mss/year. Query. Length: 250-1,000 words. Pays $35 maximum.

Fillers: Facts, newsbreaks, short humor. Buys 10/year. Length: 100-500 words. Pays $35 maximum.

Tips: "Read other high school and college publications for current issues, interests. Send manuscripts or outlines for review. All sections open to freelance work. Always looking for lighter, humorous articles as well as features on Florida colleges and universities, careers, jobs. Multi-sourced (5-10) articles are best."

GUIDE, 55 W. Oak Ridge Dr., Hagerstown MD 21740. Fax: (301)790-9734. Editor: Carolyn Rathbun. 50% freelance written. Works with a small number of new/unpublished writers each year. Weekly magazine journal for junior youth and early teens. "Its content reflects Christian beliefs and standards." Estab. 1953. Circ. 40,000. Buys first serial, simultaneous and second serial (reprint) rights. **Pays on acceptance.** Publishes ms an average of 6-9 months after acceptance. Byline given. Submit seasonal/holiday material 6 months in advance. Accepts previously published submissions. Send typed ms with rights for sale noted and information about when and where the material previously appeared. For reprints, pays 50% of amount paid for an original article. Reports in 3 weeks. Free sample copy.

Nonfiction: We are especially interested in *true* stories that show God's involvement in 10- to 14-year-olds' lives. True adventure that illustrates a spiritual principle is high priority.

Fiction: Wants stories of character-building and spiritual value. Should emphasize the positive aspects of living, obedience to parents, perseverance, kindness, etc. "*We can always use Christian humor* and 'drama in real life' stories that show God's protection, and seasonal stories—Christmas, Thanksgiving, special holidays. We do not use stories of hunting, fishing, trapping or spiritualism. Many authors miss the mark by not setting forth a *clear application* of Biblical principles to everyday situations." Buys about 300 mss/year. Send complete ms (include word count and Social Security number). Length: up to 1,200 words. Pays 3-6¢/word. Length: 1,200 words maximum.

• *Guide* is still looking for sparkling humor and adventure stories, filled with mystery, action, discovery, dialogue.

Tips: "Typical topics we cover in a yearly cycle include choices (music, clothes, friends, diet); friend-making skills; school problems (cheating, peer pressure, new school); self-esteem; changes; sibling relationships; divorce; step-families; drugs; and communication. We often buy short fillers, and an author who does not fully understand our needs is more likely to sell with a short-short. Our target age is 10-14. Our most successful writers are those who present stories from the viewpoint of a young teen-ager, written in the active voice. Stories that sound like an adult's sentiments passing through a young person's lips are *not* what we're looking for. Use believable dialogue."

‡INSIGHT, A Spiritual Lift for Teens, The Review and Herald Publishing Association, 55 W. Oak Ridge Dr., Hagerstown MD 21740. (301)791-7000. Editor: Lori Peckham. 80% freelance written. Weekly magazine covering spiritual life of teenagers. "*INSIGHT* publishes true dramatic stories, interviews, and community and mission service features that relate directly to the lives of Christian teenagers, particularly those with a

Seventh-day Adventist background." Estab. 1970. Circ. 20,000. Pays on publication. Publishes ms an average of 4 months after acceptance. Byline given. Offers 50% kill fee. Buys first rights and second serial (reprint) rights. Editorial lead time 3 months. Submit seasonal material 6 months in advance. Accepts previously published submissions. Query for electronic submissions. Reports in 1 month. Sample copy for $2 and #10 SASE. Writer's guidelines free on request.

Nonfiction: How-to (teen relationships and experiences), humor, interview/profile, personal experience, photo feature, religious. Buys 120 mss/year. Send complete ms. Length: 500-2,000 words. Pays $25-150 for assigned articles; $25-125 for unsolicited articles.

Photos: State availability of photos with submission. Reviews contact sheets, negatives, transparencies, prints. Negotiates payment individually. Model releases required. Buys one-time rights.

Columns/Departments: Interviews (Christian culture figures, esp. musicians), 2,000 words; Service With a Smile (teens contributing to community or church), 1,000 words; On the Edge (dramatic true stories about Christians), 2,000 words. Buys 80 mss/year. Send complete ms. Pays $40-125.

Tips: "Skim two months of *INSIGHT*. Write about your teen experiences. Use informed, contemporary style and vocabulary. Become a Christian if you're not already."

THE NEW ERA, 50 E. North Temple, Salt Lake City UT 84150. (801)240-2951. Fax: (801)240-5997. Managing Editor: Richard M. Romney. 60% freelance written. "We work with both established writers and newcomers." Monthly magazine for young people of the Church of Jesus Christ of Latter-day Saints (Mormon), their church leaders and teachers. Estab. 1971. Circ. 230,000. **Pays on acceptance.** Publishes ms an average of 1 year after acceptance. Byline given. Buys all rights. Rights reassigned upon written request. Submit seasonal material 1 year in advance. Query for electronic submissions. Reports in 2 months. Sample copy for $1 and 9×12 SAE with 2 first-class stamps. Writer's guidelines for SASE.

Nonfiction: Material that shows how the Church of Jesus Christ of Latter-day Saints is relevant in the lives of young people today. Must capture the excitement of being a young Latter-day Saint. Special interest in the experiences of young Mormons in other countries. No general library research or formula pieces without the *New Era* slant and feel. Uses informational, how-to, personal experience, interview, profile, inspirational, humor, historical, think pieces, travel, spot news. Query preferred. Length: 150-2,000 words. Pays 3-12¢/word. *For Your Information* (news of young Mormons around the world). Pays expenses of writers on assignment.

Photos: Uses b&w photos and transparencies with mss. Payment depends on use, $10-125 per photo. Individual photos used for *Photo of the Month*.

Fiction: Adventure, science fiction, humorous. Must relate to young Mormon audience. Pays minimum 3¢/word.

Poetry: Traditional forms, blank verse, free verse, light verse, all other forms. Must relate to editorial viewpoint. Pays minimum 25¢/line.

Tips: "The writer must be able to write from a Mormon point of view. We're especially looking for stories about successful family relationships. We anticipate using more staff-produced material. This means freelance quality will have to improve."

SEVENTEEN, 850 Third Ave., New York NY 10022. Editor-in-Chief: Caroline Miller. Managing Editor: Kelly Crouch. 80% freelance written. Works with a small number of new/unpublished writers each year. Monthly. Circ. 1.9 million. Buys one-time rights for nonfiction and fiction by adult writers and work by teenagers. Pays 25% kill fee. **Pays on acceptance.** Publishes ms an average of 6 months after acceptance. Byline given. Reports in up to 3 months.

Nonfiction: Articles and features of general interest to young women who are concerned with the development of their lives and the problems of the world around them; strong emphasis on topicality and helpfulness. Send brief outline and query, including a typical lead paragraph, summing up basic idea of article. Also likes to receive articles and features on speculation. Query with tearsheets or copies of published articles. Length: 1,200-2,000 words. Pays $50-150 for articles written by teenagers but more to established adult freelancers. Articles are commissioned after outlines are submitted and approved. Fees for commissioned articles $650-1,500. Sometimes pays the expenses of writers on assignment.

Photos: Margaret Kemp, art director. Photos usually by assignment only.

Fiction: Joe Bargmann, fiction editor. Thoughtful, well-written stories on subjects of interest to young women between the ages of 12 and 20. Avoid formula stories—"My sainted Granny," "My crush on Brad," etc.—no heavy moralizing or condescension of any sort. Humorous stories and mysteries are welcomed. Best lengths are 1,000-3,000 words. Pays $500-1,500.

Poetry: Contact Voice editor. By teenagers only. Pays $50. Submissions are nonreturnable unless accompanied by SASE.

Tips: "Writers have to ask themselves whether or not they feel they can find the right tone for a *Seventeen* article—a tone which is empathetic yet never patronizing; lively yet not superficial. Not all writers feel comfortable with, understand or like teenagers. If you don't like them, *Seventeen* is the wrong market for you. The best way for beginning teenage writers to crack the *Seventeen* lineup is for them to contribute suggestions and short pieces to the Voices section, a literary format which lends itself to just about every kind of writing: profiles, essays, exposes, reportage and book reviews."

STRAIGHT, Standard Publishing Co., 8121 Hamilton Ave., Cincinnati OH 45231-2323. (513)931-4050. Fax: (513)931-0904. Editor: Carla J. Crane. 90% freelance written. Estab. 1950. Weekly magazine (published quarterly) for "teens, age 13-19, from Christian backgrounds who generally receive this publication in their Sunday School classes or through subscriptions." **Pays on acceptance.** Publishes ms an average of 1 year after acceptance. Buys first rights, second serial (reprint) rights or simultaneous rights. Byline given. Submit seasonal/holiday material 9-12 months in advance. Accepts previously published submissions. Send tearsheet of article or story. Reports in 2 months. Sample copy free. Writer's guidelines for #10 SAE with 2 first-class stamps.

Nonfiction: Religious-oriented topics, teen interest (school, church, family, dating, sports, part-time jobs), humor, inspirational, personal experience. "We want articles that promote Christian values and ideals." No puzzles. Query or submit complete ms. Include Social Security number on ms. "We're buying more short pieces these days; 12 pages fill up much too quickly." Length: 800-1,500 words.

Fiction: Adventure, humorous, religious, suspense. "All fiction should have some message for the modern Christian teen. Fiction should deal with all subjects in a forthright manner, without being preachy and without talking down to teens. No tasteless manuscripts that promote anything adverse to the Bible's teachings." Submit complete ms. Length: 1,000-1,500 words. Pays 3-7¢/word.

Photos: May submit photos with ms. Pays $25-50 for 8×10 b&w glossy prints and $75-125 for color slides. Model releases should be available. Buys one-time rights.

Tips: "Don't be trite. Use unusual settings or problems. Use a lot of illustrations, a good balance of conversation, narration, and action. Style must be clear, fresh—no sermonettes or sickly-sweet fiction. Take a realistic approach to problems. Be willing to submit to editorial policies on doctrine; knowledge of the *Bible* a must. Also, be aware of teens today, and what they do. Language, clothing, and activities included in mss should be contemporary. We need more fillers and stories on real teens doing something positive in their school/community, standing up for their faith. These pieces should be no longer than 800 words."

'TEEN, Petersen Publishing Co., 6420 Wilshire Blvd., Los Angeles CA 90048. (213)782-2950. Editor: Roxanne Camron. 40% freelance written. Monthly magazine covering teenage girls ages 12-19. " *'Teen* is edited for high school girls. We include all topics that are of interest to females aged 12-19. Our readers want articles on heavy hitting subjects like drugs, sex, teen pregnancy, etc., and we also devote a significant number of pages each month to health, beauty and fashion." Estab. 1957. Circ. 1,143,653. **Pays on acceptance.** Byline sometimes given. Buys all rights. Editorial lead time 6 months. Submit seasonal material 6 months in advance. Accepts simultaneous submissions. Reports in 10 weeks. Sample copy for $2.50. Writer's guidelines for #10 SASE.

Nonfiction: General interest, how-to (geared for teen market), humor, inspirational, personal experience. Buys 35 mss/year. Query with or without published clips. Length: 250-750 words. Payment varies depending on length of research required.

Fiction: Karle Dickerson. Adventure, condensed novels, fantasy, horror, mainstream, mystery, romance. Buys 12 mss/year. Send complete ms. Length: 2,500-3,500 words. Pays $250.

‡VENTURE, Christian Service Brigade, P.O. Box 150, Wheaton IL 60189. (708)665-0630. Editor: Deborah Christensen. 50% freelance written. Bimonthly magazine "for boys 8-11 years old. Most of them are involved in Christian Service Brigade." Estab. 1959. Circ. 21,000. Pays on publication. Publishes ms an average of 6-12 months after acceptance, "sometimes longer." Byline given. Offers $35 kill fee. Buys first rights or second serial (reprint) rights. Editorial lead time 3 months. Submit seasonal material 4-6 months in advance. Accepts previously published submissions. Sample copy for $1.85 and 10×13 SAE with 4 first-class stamps. Writer's guidelines for #10 SASE.

Nonfiction: Interview/profile, photo feature, religious, nature, science. Buys 6 mss/year. Send complete ms. Length: 500-1,000 words (prefer shorter). Pays $45-100 for assigned articles; $25-80 for unsolicited articles.

Photos: State availability of photos with submission. Reviews transparencies. Buys one-time rights.

Fiction: Adventure, humorous, mystery, religious, suspense. Buys 6 mss/year. Send complete ms. Length: 500-1,000 words. Pays $25-100.

Tips: "Know boys, know biblical Christianity and know how to write."

WITH, The Magazine for Radical Christian Youth, Faith and Life Press, 722 Main St., P.O. Box 347, Newton KS 67114-0347. (316)283-5100. Coeditors: Eddy Hall, Carol Duerksen. 60% freelance written. Magazine for teenagers published 8 times/year. "We are the magazine for Mennonite, Brethren, and Mennonite Brethren Youth. Our purpose is to disciple youth within congregations." Circ. 5,700. **Pays on acceptance.** Byline given. Buys one-time rights. Submit seasonal/holiday material 6 months in advance. Accepts simultaneous and previously published submissions. Send typed ms with rights for sale noted, including information about when and where the material previously appeared. Pays 60% of the amount paid for original material. Reports in 1 month on queries; 2 months on mss. Sample copy for 9×12 SAE with 4 first-class stamps. Writer's guidelines and theme list for #10 SASE. Additional detailed guidelines for first person stories and/or how-to articles available for #10 SASE.

Nonfiction: Humor, personal experience, religious, how-to, youth. Buys 15 mss/year. Send complete ms. Length: 400-1,800 words. Pays 5¢/word for simultaneous rights; 3¢/word for reprint rights for unsolicited

articles. Higher rates for first person stories and how-to articles written on assignment. (Query on these.)
Photos: Sometimes pays the expenses of writers on assignment. Send photos with submission. Reviews 8×10 b&w prints. Offers $10-50/photo. Identification of subjects required. Buys one-time rights.
Fiction: Humorous, religious, youth, parables. Buys 15 mss/year. Send complete ms. Length: 500-2,000 words. Payment same as nonfiction.
Poetry: Avant-garde, free verse, haiku, light verse, traditional. Buys 4-6 poems. Pays $10-25.
Tips: "We're looking for more wholesome humor, not necessarily religious—fiction, nonfiction, cartoons, light verse. Christmas and Easter material has a good chance with us because we receive so little of it."

YM, Gruner & Jahr, 685 Third Ave., New York NY 10017. (212)878-8644. Editor: Sally Lee. Senior Editor: Jane Katz. 25% freelance written. Magazine covering teenage girls/dating. "We are a national magazine for young women ages 15-24. They're bright, enthusiastic and inquisitive. Our goal is to guide them—in effect, to be a 'best friend' and help them through the many exciting, yet often challenging, experiences of young adulthood." Estab. 1940s. Circ. 1.9 million. **Pays on acceptance.** Byline given. Offers 25% kill fee. Buys all rights. Editorial lead time 4 months. Submit seasonal material 5 months in advance. Accepts simultaneous submissions. Sample copy for $2.50. Writer's guidelines free on request.
Nonfiction: How-to, interview/profile, personal experience, first-person stories. "*YM* publishes two special issues a year. One is a self-discovery issue, the other is a love issue filled with articles on relationships." Buys 20 mss/year. Query with published clips. Length: 2,000 words maximum. Pays 75¢/word for assigned articles; 50-75¢/word for unsolicited articles. Pays expenses of writers on assignment.
Tips: "Our relationship articles are loaded with advice from psychologists and real teenagers. Areas most open to freelancers are: 2,000 word first-person stories covering a personal triumph over adversity—incorporating a topical social/political problem; 2,000 word relationship stories; 1,200 word relationship articles."

YOUNG SALVATIONIST, The Salvation Army, P.O. Box 269, Alexandria VA 22313-0269. (703)684-5500. Fax: (703)684-5539. Address all correspondence to Youth Editor. 75% freelance written. Works with a small number of new/unpublished writers each year. Monthly Christian magazine for high school teens. "Only material with a definite Christian emphasis or from a Christian perspective will be considered." Circ. 50,000. **Pays on acceptance.** Publishes ms an average of 10 months after acceptance. Byline given. Buys first North American serial, first, one-time or second serial (reprint) rights. Accepts previously published submissions. Send tearsheet, photocopy of article or typed ms with rights for sale noted and information about when and where the article previously appeared. For reprints, pays 100% of the amount paid for an original article. Submit seasonal/holiday material 6 months in advance. Reports in 2 months. Sample copy for 9×12 SAE with 3 first-class stamps. Writer's guidelines for #10 SASE.
Nonfiction: Inspirational, how-to, humor, interview/profile, personal experience, photo feature, religious. "Articles should deal with issues of relevance to teens (high school students) today; avoid 'preachiness' or moralizing." Buys 60 mss/year. Send complete ms. Length: 500-1,200 words. Pays 10¢/word.
Fiction: Adventure, fantasy, humorous, religious, romance, science fiction—all from a Christian perspective. Length: 500-1,200 words. Pays 10¢/word. Occasionally publishes novel excerpts.
Tips: "Study magazine, familiarize yourself with the unique 'Salvationist' perspective of *Young Salvationist*; learn a little about the Salvation Army; media, sports, sex and dating are strongest appeal."

YOUTH UPDATE, St. Anthony Messenger Press, 1615 Republic St., Cincinnati OH 45210-1298. (513)241-5615. Editor: Carol Ann Morrow. 90% freelance written. Monthly newsletter of faith life for teenagers, "designed to attract, instruct, guide and challenge Catholics of high school age by applying the Gospel to modern problems/situations." Circ. 30,000. **Pays on acceptance.** Publishes ms an average of 6 months after acceptance. Byline given. Reports in 3 months. Sample copy and writer's guidelines for #10 SASE.
Nonfiction: Inspirational, practical self-help, spiritual. "Adults who pay for teen subs want more church-related and curriculum-related topics." Buys 12 mss/year. Query. Length: 2,200-2,300 words. Pays $350-400. Sometimes pays expenses of writers on assignment. No reprints.
Tips: "Query first!"

ZELOS, (formerly *Freeway*), P.O. Box 632, Glen Ellyn IL 60138-0632. Editor: Amy J. Cox. 50% freelance written. Eager to work with new/unpublished writers. Quarterly notebook. Estab. 1973. Prefers one-time rights but buys some reprints. Purchases 52 mss/year. Byline given. Accepts previously published submissions. Send tearsheet or photocopy of article or typed ms with rights for sale noted and information about when and where the article previously appeared. For reprints, pays 100% of the amount paid for an original article. Reports on material accepted for publication in 3 months. Publishes ms an average of 1 year after acceptance. Returns rejected material in 2 months. Free photocopy of sample material and writer's guidelines with SASE. Sample copies for $4.99.
• *Zelos* has gone from a weekly take-home paper to a quarterly, spiral-bound Christian Life Notebook. The book includes monthly and weekly calendars, staff-written devotionals and journaling activities, an advice column and a freelance-written feature to correlate with each weekly section. It is trying to publish more personal experience, profile, and "as told to to" stories. All material needs to be 1,000 words or less.

Nonfiction: "*Zelos*'s greatest need is for personal experience stories showing how God has worked in teens' lives. Stories are best written in first-person, 'as told to' author. Incorporate specific details, anecdotes, and dialogue. Show, don't tell, how the subject thought and felt. Weave spiritual conflicts and prayers into entire manuscript; avoid tacked-on sermons and morals. Stories should show how God has helped the person resolve a problem or how God helped save a person from trying circumstances (1,000 words or less). Avoid stories about accident and illness; focus on events and emotions of everyday life. We also need self-help or how-to articles with practical Christian advice on daily living, and trend articles addressing secular fads from a Christian perspective. We do not use devotional material, or fictionalized Bible stories." Pays 6-10¢/word. Some poetry ($20-50).

Photos: Whenever possible, provide clear 8×10 or 5×7 b&w photos to accompany mss (or any other available photos). Payment is $5-30.

Fiction: "We use true-to-life and humorous fiction."

Tips: "Study our 'Tips to Writers' pamphlet and sample copy, then send complete ms. In your cover letter, include information about who you are, writing qualifications, and experience working with teens. Include SASE."

Travel, Camping and Trailer

Travel magazines give travelers indepth information about destinations, detailing the best places to go, attractions in the area and sites to see—but they also keep them up-to-date about potential negative aspects of these destinations. Publications in this category tell tourists and campers the where-tos and how-tos of travel. This category is extremely competitive, demanding quality writing, background information and professional photography. Each has its own slant and should be studied carefully before sending submissions.

‡AAA GOING PLACES, Magazine for Today's Traveler, AAA Auto Club South, 1515 N. Westshore Blvd., Tampa FL 33607. (813)289-5923. Editor: Phyllis Zeno. 50% freelance written. Bimonthly magazine on auto news, driving trips, cruise travel, tours. Estab. 1982. Circ. 980,000. Pays on publication. Publishes ms an average of 6 months after acceptance. Byline given. Buys one-time rights. Submit seasonal/holiday material 9 months in advance. Simultaneous submissions OK. Publishes reprints of previously published articles or short stories. Send tearsheet of article or short story, photocopy of article or typed ms with rights for sale noted and information about when and where the article previously appeared. Reports in 2 months. Sample copy for 8×10 SAE and 4 first-class stamps. Free writer's guidelines.

Nonfiction: Historical/nostalgic, how-to, humor, interview/profile, personal experience, photo feature, travel. Special issues include Cruise Guide and Europe Issue. Buys 15 mss/year. Send complete ms. Length: 500-1,500 words. Pays $15 per printed page.

Photos: State availability of photos with submission. Reviews 2×2 transparencies. Offers no additional payment for photos accepted with ms. Captions required.

Columns/Departments: AAAway We Go (local attractions in Florida, Georgia or Tennessee).

ADVENTURE WEST, America's Guide to Discovering the West, Ski West Publications, Inc., P.O. Box 3210, Incline Village NV 89450. (702)832-3700,. Editor: Marianne Porter. Managing Editor: Brian Beffort. 80% freelance written. Bimonthly magazine covering adventure travel in the West. Estab. 1992. Circ. 155,000. Pays on publication. Publishes ms an average of 4-6 months after acceptance. Byline given. Offers 15% kill fee. Buys first North American serial rights. Editorial lead time 4 months. Submit seasonal material 6 months in advance. Accepts simultaneous submissions. Occasionally accepts previously published submissions. Send tearsheet of article or short story and information about when and where the article previously appeared. Reports in 2 months; 2 months on mss. Sample copy for $3.50 and 10×13 SASE with 9 first-class stamps. Writer's guidelines free on request with SASE.

• *Adventure West* has gone from quarterly to bimonthly publication and consequently has doubled its requests for nonfiction manuscripts and column/department material.

Nonfiction: Historical/nostalgic, humor, interview/profile, personal experience, photo feature, travel. "We only publish adventure travel done in the West, including Alaska, Hawaii, western Canada and western Mexico." Buys 80 mss/year. Query with published clips. Length: 1,000-2,500 words. Pays $150-500. Sometimes pays expenses of writers on assignment.

Photos: Send photos with submission. Reviews transparencies and slides. Negotiates payment individually. Captions and identification of subjects required. "We need itemized list of photos submitted." Buys one-time rights.

Columns/Departments: Buys 80 mss/year. Query with published clips. Pays $150-450.

Fiction: Humorous, western. "We publish humorous experiences in the West; that is the only fiction we accept." Buys 4 mss/year. Query with published clips. Length: 1,000-1,500 words. Pays $270-450.

Tips: "We like exciting, inspirational first-person stories on adventure. If the query or the unsolicited ms grabs us, we will use it. Our writer's guidelines are comprehensive. Follow them."

ARUBA NIGHTS, Nights Publications, 1831 Rene Levesque Blvd. West, Montreal, Quebec H3H 1R4 Canada. Fax: (514)931-6273. Editor: Stephen Trotter. Managing Editor: Zelly Zuskin. Annual magazine covering the Aruban vacation lifestyle experience. Estab. 1988. Circ. 200,000. **Pays on acceptance.** Publishes ms an average of 6-10 months after acceptance. Offers 15% kill fee. Buys first North American serial and first Caribbean rights. Editorial lead time 2 months. Query for electronic submissions. Reports in 2 weeks on queries; 1 months on mss. *Writer's Market* recommends allowing 2 months for reply. Sample copy for $5. Writer's guidelines free on request.
Nonfiction: General interest, historical/nostalgic, how-to features relative to Aruba vacationers, humor, inspirational, interview/profile, eco-tourism, opinion, personal experience, photo feature, travel, Aruban culture, art, activities, entertainment, topics relative to vacationers in Aruba. "No negative pieces or stale rewrites." Buys 5-10 mss/year. Query with published clips. Length: 250-750 words. Pays $125-350 for assigned articles; $100-250 for unsolicited articles.
Photos: State availability with submission. Offers $25-100/photo. Captions, model releases, identification of subjects required. Buys one-time rights.
Tips: "Demonstrate your voice in your query letter. Focus on individual aspects of the Aruban lifestyle and vacation experience (e.g., art, gambling tips, windsurfing, a colorful local character, a personal experience, etc.), rather than generalized overviews. Provide an angle that will be entertaining to both vacationers and Arubans."

‡ASU TRAVEL GUIDE, ASU Travel Guide, Inc., 1525 Francisco Blvd. E., San Rafael CA 94901. (415)459-0300. Fax: (415)459-0494. Managing Editor: Christopher Gil. 80% freelance written. Quarterly guidebook covering international travel features and travel discounts for well-traveled airline employees. Estab. 1970. Circ. 60,000. Publishes ms an average of 4 months after acceptance. Byline given. Buys first North American serial rights, first and second rights to the same material, and second serial (reprint) rights to material originally published elsewhere; also makes work-for-hire assignments. Submit seasonal/holiday material 6 months in advance. Accepts simultaneous and previously published submissions. Send tearsheet of article with information about when and where the article previously appeared. For reprints, pays 100% of the amount paid for an original article. Reports in 1 year. Sample copy available for 6½ × 9 SAE with 5 first-class stamps. Writer's guidelines for #10 SASE.
Nonfiction: International travel articles "similar to those run in consumer magazines. Not interested in amateur efforts from inexperienced travelers or personal experience articles that don't give useful information to other travelers." Buys 16 ms/year. Destination pieces only; no "Tips On Luggage" articles. Unsolicited mss or queries without SASE will not be acknowledged. No telephone queries. Length: 1,800 words. Pays $200.
Photos: "Interested in clear, high-contrast photos." Reviews 5 × 7 and 8 × 10 b&w or color prints. "Payment for photos is included in article price; photos from tourist offices are acceptable."
Tips: "Query with samples of travel writing and a list of places you've recently visited. We appreciate clean and simple style. Keep verbs in the active tense and involve the reader in what you write. Avoid 'cute' writing, coined words and stale cliches. The most frequent mistakes made by writers in completing an article for us are: 1) Lazy writing—using words to describe a place that could describe any destination such as 'there is so much to do in (fill in destination) that whole guidebooks have been written about it'; 2) Including fare and tour package information—our readers make arrangements through their own airline."

BACKPACKER, Rodale Press, Inc., 33 E. Minor St., Emmaus PA 18098-0099. (610)967-8296. Fax: (610)967-8181. E-mail: bpeditor@aol.com. Editor: John Viehman. Managing Editor: Tom Shealey. 50% freelance written. Magazine published 9 times/year covering wilderness travel. Estab. 1973. Circ. 210,000. **Pays on acceptance.** Byline given. Offers 25% kill fee. Buys one-time rights or all rights. Rarely accepts previously published submissions. Send tearsheet of article including information about when and where the article previously appeared. Reports in 2 months. Writer's guidelines for #10 SASE.
• *Backpacker* tells us better writers are applying; competition is getting *tougher*.
Nonfiction: Essays, exposé, historical/nostalgic, how-to (expedition planner), humor, inspirational, interview/profile, new product, opinion, personal experience, technical, travel. No step-by-step accounts of what you did on your summer vacation—stories that chronicle every rest stop and gulp of water. Query with published clips and SASE. Length: 750-3,000 words. Pays $400-2,000. Sometimes pays (pre-determined) expenses of writers on assignment. "What we want are features that let us and the readers 'feel' the place, and experience your wonderment, excitement, disappointment or other emotions encountered 'out there.' If we feel like we've been there after reading your story, you've succeeded."
Photos: State availability of photos with submission. Amount varies—depends on size of photo used. Buys one-time rights.
Columns/Departments: Footnotes "News From All Over" (adventure, environment, wildlife, trails, techniques, organizations, special interests—well-written, entertaining, short, newsy item), 50-500 words; Body Language (in-the-field column), 750-1,200 words; Moveable Feast (food-related aspects of wilderness: nutri-

tion, cooking techniques, recipes, products and gear), 500-750 words; Weekend Wilderness (brief but detailed guides to wilderness areas, providing thorough trip-planning information, only enough anecdote to give a hint, then the where/when/hows), 500-750 words; Technique (ranging from beginner to expert focus, written by people with solid expertise, details ways to improve performance, how-to-do-it instructions, information on equipment manufacturers and places readers can go), 750-1,500 words; and Backcountry (personal perspectives, quirky and idiosyncratic, humorous critiques, manifestos and misadventures, interesting angle, lesson, revelation or moral), 750-1,200 words. Buys 25-50 mss/year. Query with published clips. Pays $200-600. No phone calls regarding story ideas. Written queries only.

Tips: "Our best advice is to read the publication—most freelancers don't know the magazine at all. The best way to break in is with an article for the Backcountry, Weekend Wilderness or Footnotes Department."

BONAIRE NIGHTS, Nights Publications, 1831 René Lévesque Blvd. W., Montreal, Quebec H3H 1R4 Canada. Fax: (514)931-6273. Editor: Stephen Trotter. 80% freelance written. Annual magazine covering Bonaire vacation experience. "Upbeat entertaining lifestyle articles: colorful profiles of locals, eco-tourism; lively features on culture, activities (particularly scuba and snorkeling), special events, historical attractions, how-to features. Audience is North American tourist." Estab. 1993. Circ. 60,000. **Pays on acceptance.** Publishes ms an average of 6-10 months after acceptance. Byline given. Offers 15% kill fee. Buys first North American serial rights and first Caribbean rights. Editorial lead time 2 months. Query for electronic submissions. Reports in 2 weeks on queries; 1 month on mss. Sample copy for $5. Writer's guidelines for #10 SASE.

Nonfiction: General interest, historical/nostalgic, how-to, humor, inspirational, interview/profile, opinion, personal experience, photo feature, travel, local culture, art, activities, especially scuba diving, snorkeling, eco-tourism. Buys 6-9 mss/year. Query with published clips. Length: 250-750 words. Pays $125-350 for assigned articles; $100-250 for unsolicited articles.

Photos: State availability of photos with submission. Reviews transparencies. Offers $25-100/slide. Captions, model releases, identification of subjects required. Buys one-time or first rights.

Tips: "Demonstrate your voice in your query letter. Focus on the Bonaire lifestyle, what sets it apart from other islands. We want personal experience, not generalized overviews. Be positive and provide an angle that will appeal to residents as well as visitors."

‡BUON GIORNO, The Port Magazine of Costa Cruises, On-Board Media, Inc. 777 Arthur Godfrey Rd., Suite 300, Miami Beach FL 33140. (305)673-0400. Fax: (305)674-9396. Managing Editor: Lynn Ulivieri. 95% freelance written. Annual magazine covering Caribbean region. "This bilingual (English/French, English/Italian) in-cabin magazine reaches French, Italian and American cruise passengers travelling to various Caribbean port destinations. Stories must appeal to a multi-national readership." Estab. 1992. Circ. 69,950. Pays half on acceptance, half on publication for features; on publication for fillers. Publishes ms an average of 4 months after acceptance. Byline given. Offers 50% kill fee. Buys first rights or second serial (reprint) rights. Editorial lead time 4-6 months. Accepts previously published submissions, if so noted. Reports in 1 month. Sample copy free on written request. Writer's guidelines for #10 SASE.

Nonfiction: Book excerpts, essays, general interest, humor, interview/profile, new product, photo feature, travel. Does not want politics, sex, religion, general history, shopping information or advertorials, no personal experience. Buys 12 features/year, plus assigned editorial covering ports-of-call and numerous fillers. Query with published clips. Length: 800-2,000 words. Pays $150-1,000, negotiable per assignment. Sometimes pays expenses of writers on assignment.

Photos: State availability of photos with submission. Negotiates payment individually. Captions, model releases, identification of subjects required. Buys one-time and reprint rights.

Fillers: Anecdotes, facts, newsbreaks, short humor. Buys 50/year. Length: 50-500 words. Pays $25-100.

Tips: "Do not send any general overviews on port destinations or editorial on shopping or long-standing attractions that can be found in any travel guide. Focus on unique aspects of island culture, colorful local personalities, new twists on the themes of ecology/wildlife, food, folklore, festivals, etc. A first-hand knowledge of the subject matter is a must. News-oriented material is always welcomed. Demonstrate your voice in your query letter, send a selection of writing samples that reveal your range, and include a list of subjects and regions of expertise."

CAMPERS MONTHLY, Northeast Edition–Maine to New York; Mid Atlantic Edition—New York to Virginia; Mid-Central Edition—Western Pennsylvania, Western New York; West Virginia, Eastern Ohio, P.O. Box 260, Quakertown PA 18951. (215)536-6420. Fax: (215)536-6509. E-mail: wer v2@aol.com. Editor: Paula Finkbeiner. 50% freelance written. Monthly (except December) tabloid covering tenting and recreational vehicle camping and travel. "With the above emphasis, we want to encourage our readers to explore all forms of outdoor recreation using a tent or recreational vehicle as a 'home away from home.' Travel-places to go, things to do and see." Estab. 1991 (Mid-Atlantic), 1993 (Northeast), 1995 (Mid-Central). Circ. 35,000 (Mid-Atlantic), 25,000 (Northeast), 20,000 (Mid-Central). Pays on publication. Publishes ms an average of 2 months after acceptance. Byline given. Buys simultaneous rights. Editorial lead time 2 months. Submit seasonal material 3-4 months in advance. Accepts simultaneous and previously published submissions. Send photocopy of article or typed ms with rights for sale noted and information about when and where the article previously appeared. For reprints, pays 80% of amount paid for original article. Query for electronic submissions. Reports in 1 month. Sample copy and writer's guidelines free on request.

Nonfiction: Historical/nostalgic (tied into a camping trip), how-to (selection, care, maintenance of RV's, tents, accessories, etc.) humor, personal experience, travel (camping in the Mid-Atlantic or Northeast region). Special issue: Snowbird Issue (October)—geared towards campers heading South. This is generally the only time we accept articles on areas outside our coverage area. Buys 15-20 mss/year. Send complete ms. Length: 800-1,500 words. Pays $70 for assigned articles; $50 for unsolicited articles. Sometimes pays expenses of writers on assignment.

Photos: Send photos with submission. Reviews 5×7 or 8×10 glossy b&w prints. Offers $3-5/photo. Don't send snapshots or polaroids. Avoid slides.

Columns/Departments: Campground Cook (Ideas for cooking in RV's, tents and over campfires, should include recipes), 500-1,000 words; Tales From The Road (humorous stories of "on-the-road" travel), 350-800 words; Tech Tips (technical pieces on maintenance and enhanced usage of RV-related equipment), 350-1,800 words. Buys 15 mss/year. Send complete ms. Pays $40-60.

Fiction: Humorous, slice-of-life vignettes. Buys 10 mss/year. Query. Length: 300-1,000 words. Pays $60-75.

Fillers: Facts, short humor. Buys 8/year. Length: 30-350. Pays $20-35.

Tips: Most open to freelancers are "destination pieces focusing on a single attraction or activity or closely clustered attractions are always needed. General interest material, technical or safety ideas (for RVs and tents) is an area we're always looking for pieces on. Off the beaten track destinations always get priority."

CAMPING TODAY, Official Publication of the Family Campers & RVers, 126 Hermitage Rd., Butler PA 16001-8509. (412)283-7401. Editors: DeWayne Johnston and June Johnston. 30% freelance written. Prefers to work with published/established writers. Monthly official membership publication of the FCRV, "the largest nonprofit family camping and RV organization in the United States and Canada. Members are heavily oriented toward RV travel, both weekend and extended vacations. Concentration is on member activities in chapters. Group is also interested in conservation and wildlife. The majority of members are retired." Estab. 1983. Circ. 25,000. Pays on publication. Publishes ms an average of 6 months after acceptance. Byline given. Buys one-time rights. Submit seasonal/holiday material 3 months in advance. Accepts simultaneous and previously published submissions. Send typed ms with rights for sale noted and information about when and where the article previously appeared. Pays 35-50% of their fee for an original article. Reports in 60 days. Sample copy and guidelines for 4 first-class stamps. Writer's guidelines only for #10 SASE.

Nonfiction: Travel (interesting places to visit by RV, camping), humor (camping or travel related, please, no "our first campout stories"), interview/profile (interesting campers), new products, technical (RVs related). Buys 10-15 mss/year. Send complete ms with photos. Length: 750-2,000 words. Pays $50-150.

Photos: Send photos with ms. Need b&w or sharp color prints inside (we can make prints from slides) and vertical transparencies for cover. Captions required.

Tips: "Freelance material on RV travel, RV maintenance/safety, and items of general camping interest throughout the United States and Canada will receive special attention."

CANCÚN NIGHTS, Nights Publications, 1831 Rene Levesque Blvd. West, Montreal, Quebec H3H 1R4 Canada. Fax: (514)931-6273. Editor: Stephen Trotter. Managing Editor: Zelly Zuskin. 80% freelance written. Destination lifestyle magazine. Semiannual magazine covering the Cancún vacation experience. Seeking "upbeat, entertaining lifestyle articles: colorful profiles of locals; lively features on culture, activities, night life, special events, historical attractions, Mayan achievements; how-to features; humor. Our audience is the North American vacationer." Estab. 1991. Circ. 550,000. **Pays on acceptance.** Publishes ms an average of 6-10 months after acceptance. Offers 15% kill fee. Buys first North American serial rights and first Mexican rights. Editorial lead time 2 months. Query for electronic submissions. Reports 2 weeks on queries; 1 month on mss. *Writer's Market* recommends allowing 2 months for reply. Sample copy for $5. Writer's guidelines free on request.

Nonfiction: General interest, historical/nostalgic, how-to let vacationers get the most from their holiday, humor, inspirational, eco-tourism, interview/profile, opinion, personal experience, photo feature, travel, local culture, art, activities, night life, topics relative to vacationers in Cancún. Does not want to see negative pieces, stale rewrites. Buys 8-12 mss/year. Query with published clips. Length: 250-750 words. Pays $125-350 for assigned articles; $100-250 for unsolicited articles.

Photos: State availability of photos with submission. Reviews transparencies. Offers $25-100/photo. Captions, model releases, identification of subjects required. Buys one-time rights.

Tips: "Demonstrate your voice in your query letter. Focus on individual aspects of the Cancún lifestyle and vacation experience (e.g., art, history, snorkeling, fishing, a colorful local character, a personal experience, etc.), entertaining to both vacationers and residents."

CARIBBEAN TRAVEL AND LIFE, 8403 Colesville Rd., Suite 830, Silver Spring MD 20910. (301)588-2300. Editor-in-Chief: Veronica Gould Stoddart. 90% freelance written. Prefers to work with published/established writers. Bimonthly magazine covering travel to the Caribbean, Bahamas and Bermuda. Estab. 1985. Circ.

130,000. Pays on publication. Publishes ms an average of 3 months after acceptance. Byline given. Offers 25% kill fee. Buys first North American serial rights. Submit seasonal/holiday material 6 months in advance. Reports in 2 months. Sample copy for 9×12 SAE with 9 first-class stamps. Writer's guidelines for #10 SASE.

Nonfiction: General interest, how-to, interview/profile, culture, personal experience, travel. No "guidebook rehashing; superficial destination pieces or critical exposes." Buys 30 mss/year. Query with published clips. Length: 2,000-2,500 words. Pays $550.

Photos: Send photos with submission. Reviews 35mm transparencies. Offers $75-400/photo. Captions and identification of subjects required. Buys one-time rights.

Columns/Departments: Resort Spotlight (in-depth review of luxury resort); Tradewinds (focus on one particular kind of water sport or sailing/cruising); Island Buys (best shopping for luxury goods, crafts, duty-free); Island Spice (best cuisine and/or restaurant reviews with recipes); Money Matters (dollar-wise travel, bargain destinations, how to save money); EcoWatch (conservation efforts and projects); all 1,000-1,500 words; Postcards from Paradise (short items on great finds in travel, culture, and special attractions), 500 words. Buys 36 mss/year. Query with published clips or send complete ms. Length: 500-1,250 words. Pays $75-200.

Tips: "We are especially looking for stories with a personal touch and lively, entertaining anecdotes, as well as strong insight into people and places being covered. Writer should demonstrate why he/she is the best person to do that story based on extensive knowledge of the subject, frequent visits to destination, residence in destination, specialty in field."

‡CARLSON VOYAGEUR, Magazine of Radisson Hotels, Radisson Seven Seas Cruises and Country Inns & Suites By Carlson, Pace Communications Inc., 1301 Carolina St., Greensboro NC 27401. Editor: Melinda L. Stovall. 90% freelance written. Quarterly guest-room magazine. "*Carlson Voyageur* presents articles with travel angles to convey the adventure and action in which its upscale guests can get involved." Circ. 150,000. **Pays on acceptance.** Publishes ms an average of 3 months after acceptance. Byline given. Offers 25% kill fee. Buys first North American serial rights. Editorial lead time 3 months. Submit seasonal material 4 months in advance. No simultaneous or previously published submissions. Reports in 6 weeks on queries; 2 months on mss. Sample copy for $3. Writer's guidelines for #10 SASE.

Nonfiction: Travel, sports, arts/cultural, celebrity profiles as relates to travel. Buys 12 mss/year. Query with published clips. Length: 600-1,900 words. Pays $300-800. Sometimes pays limited expenses of writers on assignment.

Photos: State availability of photos with submission. Reviews transparencies. Negotiates payment individually. Identification of subjects required. Buys one-time rights.

Columns/Departments: Cultural Stopover (cultural slant to travel destination served by Radisson, personal travel experience), 1,500 words; Broad Horizons (destination served by Radisson), 600 words. Buys 8 mss/year. Query with published clips. Pays $300-500.

Tips: "Please know destinations/ports served."

COAST TO COAST MAGAZINE, A Publication for the Members of Coast to Coast Magazine, 3601 Calle Tecate, Camarillo CA 93012. Editor: Valerie Rogers. 80% freelance written. magazine published 8 times/year for members of Coast to Coast Resorts. Estab. 1972. Circ. 300,000. **Pays on acceptance.** Publishes ms an average of 3 months after acceptance. Byline given. Offers 33% kill fee. Buys first North American serial rights. Submit seasonal/holiday material 5 months in advance. Query for electronic submissions. Accepts previously published submissions. Send photocopy of article, information about when and where the article previously appeared. Pays 50% of the amount paid for an original article. Reports in 1 month on queries; 2 months on mss. Sample copy for $2 and 9×12 SASE.

Nonfiction: Book excerpts, essays, general interest, historical/nostalgic, how-to, humor, inspirational, interview/profile, new product, opinion, personal experience, photo feature, technical, travel. Buys 50 mss/year. Query with published clips or send complete ms. Length: 500-2,500 words. Pays $75-600.

Photos: Send photos with submission. Reviews transparencies. Offers $50-600/photo. Identification of subjects required. Buys one-time rights.

Tips: "Send published clips with queries, or story ideas will not be considered."

CONDÉ NAST TRAVELER, The Condé Nast Publications, 360 Madison Ave., New York NY 10017. (212)880-8800. Editor: Thomas J. Wallace. Managing Editor: Dee Aldrich. 75% freelance written. Monthly magazine covering travel. "Our motto, Truth in Travel, sums up our editorial philosophy: to present travel destinations, news and features in a candid, journalistic style. Our writers do not accept complimentary tickets, hotel rooms, gifts, or the like. While our departments present service information in a tipsheet or newsletter manner, our destination stories are literary in tone. Our readers are affluent, well-educated, and sophisticated about travel." Estab. 1987. Circ. 1 million. **Pays on acceptance.** Publishes ms 3-6 months after acceptance. Byline given. Offers 25% kill fee. Buys all rights. Editorial lead time 3 months. Submit seasonal material 4-6 months in advance. Reports in 2 months on queries.

Nonfiction: Alison Humes, features editor. Travel. No humor. Query. Length: 500-5,000 words. Pays $1/word. Pays expenses of writers on assignment.

Columns/Departments: Stop Press, edited by Cliff Hopkinson, executive editor/news (travel news items—keep in mind that we are a monthly magazine with a long lead time), 500 words; Word of Mouth, edited by Catherine Kelley, arts editor (timely and hip items on new, trendy restaurants, shops, bars, exhibits around the world—will not consider annual events or subjects that receive much publicity elsewhere), 25-50 words (no byline). Following departments "tend not to use unsolicited ideas, but those who insist should be careful to contact the correct editor: Great Drives, As Others See Us: Peter Frank; Food in Review: Gully Wells; Gear in Review: Jason Nixon; Shopping: Catherine Kelley. Other departments are staff-generated and do not accept freelance submissions." Buys 10-20 mss/year. Query. Pays $1/word.

Tips: "Please keep in mind that we very rarely assign stories based on unsolicited queries because (1) our inventory of unused stories (features and departments) is very large, and (2) most story ideas are generated inhouse by the editors, as it is very difficult for outsiders to anticipate the needs of our inventory. To submit story ideas, send a brief (one paragraph) description of the idea(s) to the appropriate editor. Please do not send clips, resumes, photographs, itineraries, or abridged or full-length manuscripts. Due to our editorial policy, we *do not* purchase completed manuscripts. Telephone calls are not accepted."

THE COOL TRAVELER, The Rome Cappucino Review, P.O. Box 273, Selins Grove PA 17870-1813. Editor/Publisher: Bob Moore. Managing Editor: MaryBeth Feeney. 100% freelance written. Bimonthly publication covering travel. "We do not emphasize affluence but rather the experiences one has while traveling: romance, adventure, thrills, chills, etc. We have even published excerpts from diaries!" Estab. 1988. Circ. 750-1,250. Pays on publication. Publishes ms an average of 2-3 months after acceptance. Byline given. Send bio. Buys one-time rights. Submit seasonal/holiday material 4 months in advance. Accepts simultaneous and previously published submissions. Send information about when and where the article previously appeared. For reprints, payment is negotiable. Query for electronic submissions. Reports in 6 weeks "unless we like it—then it could be 4-6 months." Sample copy for $3. Free writer's guidelines with SASE.

● *The Cool Traveler* would like more information-based material and would like to hear from travelers on journeys lasting over six months: on-the-scene information.

Nonfiction: Personal experience, travel, art history. Special issues: Christmas and International Festival. "We don't want a listing of names and prices but personal experiences and unusual experiences. Writers should have a sense of humor." Buys 15 mss/year. Send complete ms. Length: 1,000 words maximum. Pays $5-20 for unsolicited articles.

Columns/Departments: News items pertaining to particular countries. ("Really need these!") Seasonal (material pertaining to a certain time of year: like a winter festival or summer carnival), 1,500 words maximum. Women travel. Pays $5-20. Big need for tidbits.

Poetry: Free verse, light verse, traditional. No poetry that is too sentimental. Buys 3 poems/year. Submit maximum 3 poems. Length: 5-75 lines. Pays $5-20.

Tips: "We would strongly like some strictly news-oriented material."

‡CROWN & ANCHOR, The Port Magazine of Royal Caribbean Cruise Line, On-Board Media, Inc. 777 Arthur Godfrey Rd., Suite 300, Miami Beach FL 33140. (305)673-0400. Fax: (305)674-9396. Managing Editor: Lynn Ulivieri. 95% freelance written. Annual magazine covering Caribbean Far East, Mexican Riviera, the Bahamas and Alaska. "This publication reaches cruise vacationers on board RCCL ships on 3-11 night Caribbean, Bahamas, Mexican Riviera, Alaska and Far East itineraries. Culture, art, architecutre, natural wonders, food, folklore, legends, lingo/idioms, festivals, literature, eco-systems, local wares of these regions. Current themese such as celebrity retreats, hit recordings and hot artists and writers are welcomed." Estab. 1992. Circ. 792,184. Pays half on acceptance, half on publication for features; on publication for fillers. Publishes ms an average of 4 months after acceptance. Byline given. Offers 50% kill fee. Buys first rights or second serial (reprint) rights. Editorial lead time 6 months. Accepts previously published submissions, if so noted. Reports in 1 month. Sample copy free on written request. Writer's guidelines for #10 SASE.

Nonfiction: Book excerpts, essays, general interest, humor, interview/profile, new product, photo feature, travel. Does not want politics, sex, religion, general history, shopping information or advertorials, no personal experience. Buys 12 features/year, plus assigned editorial covering ports-of-call and numerous fillers. Query with published clips. Length: 800-2,000 words. Pays $150-1,000, negotiable per assignment. Sometimes pays expenses of writers on assignment.

Photos: State availability of photos with submission. Negotiates payment individually. Captions, model releases, identification of subjects required. Buys one-time and reprint rights.

Fillers: Anecdotes, facts, newsbreaks, short humor. Buys 50/year. Length: 50-500 words. Pays $25-100.

Tips: "Do not send any general overviews on port destinations or editorial on shopping or long-standing attractions that can be found in any travel guide. Focus on unique aspects of island culture, colorful local personalities, new twists on the themes of ecology/wildlife, food, folklore, festivals, etc. A first-hand knowledge of the subject matter is a must. News-oriented material is always welcomed. Demonstrate your voice in your query letter, send a selection of writing samples that reveal your range, and include a list of subjects and regions of expertise."

CRUISE TRAVEL MAGAZINE, World Publishing Co., 990 Grove St., Evanston IL 60201-4370. (708)491-6440. Editor: Robert Meyers. Contact: Charles Doherty, managing editor. 95% freelance written. Bimonthly magazine on cruise travel. "This is a consumer-oriented travel publication covering the world of pleasure cruising on large cruise ships (with some coverage of smaller ships), including ports, travel tips, roundups." Estab. 1979. **Pays on acceptance.** Publishes ms an average of 6 months after acceptance. Byline given. Offers 50% kill fee. Buys first North American serial, one-time or second serial (reprint) rights. Accepts simultaneous and previously published submissions. Send tearsheet or photocopy of article and typed ms with rights for sale noted. Reports in 1 month. *Writer's Market* recommends allowing 2 months for reply. Sample copy for $5 and 9×12 SAE with 6 first-class stamps. Writer's guidelines for #10 SASE.

Nonfiction: General interest, historical/nostalgic, interview/profile, personal experience, photo feature, travel. "No daily cruise 'diary', My First Cruise, etc." Buys 72 mss/year. Query with or without published clips or send complete ms. Length: 500-1,500 words. Pays $100-400.

Photos: Send photos with submission. Reviews transparencies and prints. "Must be color, 35m preferred (other format OK); color prints second choice." Offers no additional payment for photos accepted with ms "but pay more for well-illustrated ms." Captions and identification of subjects required. Buys one-time rights.

Fillers: Anecdotes, facts. Buys 3 mss/year. Length: 300-700 words. Pays $75-200.

Tips: "Do your homework. Know what we do and what sorts of things we publish. Know the cruise industry—we can't use novices. Good, sharp, bright color photography opens the door fast. We still need good pictures—we are not interested in developing any new contributors who cannot provide color support to manuscripts."

‡CRUISING IN STYLE, The Port Magazine of Crystal Cruises, On-Board Media, Inc. 777 Arthur Godfrey Rd., Suite 300, Miami Beach FL 33140. (305)673-0400. Fax: (305)674-9396. Managing Editor: Lynn Ulivieri. 95% freelance written. Annual magazine covering Caribbean, Panama Canal, Mexican Riviera. "This in-cabin magazine reaches sophisticated cruise passengers seeking a vacation/learning experience. We are looking for well-researched original material on interesting aspects of the port destination." Estab. 1992. Circ. 792,184. Pays half on acceptance, half on publication for features; on publication for fillers. Publishes ms an average of 4 months after acceptance. Byline given. Offers 50% kill fee. Buys first rights or second serial (reprint) rights. Editorial lead time 6 months. Accepts previously published submissions, if so noted. Reports in 1 month. Sample copy free on written request. Writer's guidelines for #10 SASE.

Nonfiction: Book excerpts, essays, general interest, humor, interview/profile, new product, photo feature, travel. Does not want politics, sex, religion, general history, shopping information or advertorials, no personal experience. Buys 12 features/year, plus assigned editorial covering ports-of-call and numerous fillers. Query with published clips. Length: 800-2,000 words. Pays $150-1,000, negotiable per assignment. Sometimes pays expenses of writers on assignment.

Photos: State availability of photos with submission. Negotiates payment individually. Captions, model releases, identification of subjects required. Buys one-time and reprint rights.

Fillers: Anecdotes, facts, newsbreaks, short humor. Buys 50/year. Length: 50-500 words. Pays $25-100.

Tips: "Do not send any general overviews on port destinations or editorial on shopping or long-standing attractions that can be found in any travel guide. Focus on unique aspects of island culture, colorful local personalities, new twists on the themes of ecology/wildlife, food, folklore, festivals, etc. A first-hand knowledge of the subject matter is a must. News-oriented material is always welcomed. Demonstrate your voice in your query letter, send a selection of writing samples that reveal your range, and include a list of subjects and regions of expertise."

CURAÇAO NIGHTS, Nights Publications, 1831 Rene Levesque Blvd. West, Montreal, Quebec H3H 1R4 Canada. Fax: (514)931-6273. Editor: Stephen Trotter. Managing Editor: Zelly Zuskin. 80% freelance written. Annual magazine covering the Curaçao vacation experience. "We are seeking upbeat, entertaining lifestyle articles; colorful profiles of locals; lively features on culture, activities, night life, eco-tourism, special events, gambling; how-to features; humor. Our audience is the North American vacationer." Estab. 1989. Circ. 155,000. **Pays on acceptance.** Publishes ms an average of 6-10 months after acceptance. Byline given. Offers 15% kill fee. Buys first North American serial and first Caribbean rights. Editorial lead time 2 months. Query for electronic submissions. Reports in 2 weeks on queries; 1 month on mss. *Writer's Market* recommends allowing 2 months for reply. Sample copy for $5. Writer's guidelines free on request.

Nonfiction: General interest, historical/nostalgic, how-to help a vacationer get the most from their vacation, eco-tourism, humor, inspirational, interview/profile, opinion, personal experience, photo feature, travel, local culture, art, activities, night life, topics relative to vacationers in Curaçao. "No negative pieces or stale rewrites." Buys 5-10 mss/year. Query with published clips. Length: 250-750 words. Pays $125 minimum, $350 maximum for assigned articles; $100 minimum, $250 maximum for unsolicited articles.

Photos: State availability of photos with submission. Reviews transparencies. Offers $25-100/photo. Captions, model releases, identification of subjects required. Buys one-time rights.

Tips: "Demonstrate your voice in your query letter. Focus on individual aspects of the island lifestyle and vacation experience (e.g., art, gambling tips, windsurfing, a colorful local character, a personal experience, etc.), rather than generalized overviews. Provide an angle that will be entertaining to both vacationers and Curaçaoans."

‡DESTINATIONS, The Port Magazine of Celebrity Cruises, On-Board Media, Inc. 777 Arthur Godfrey Rd., Suite 300, Miami Beach FL 33140. (305)673-0400. Fax: (305)674-9396. Managing Editor: Lynn Ulivieri. 95% freelance written. Annual magazine covering Caribbean, Panama Canal, Bahamas regions. "This in-cabin magazine reaches cruise passengers traveling to various Caribbean ports of call. We are looking for original material on interesting aspects of the island destination. We are not interested in articles on cruising, per se, or anything related to the cruise ship." Estab. 1992. Circ. 792,184. Pays half on acceptance, half on publication for features; on publication for fillers. Publishes ms an average of 4 months after acceptance. Byline given. Offers 50% kill fee. Buys first rights or second serial (reprint) rights. Editorial lead time 6 months. Accepts previously published submissions, if so noted. Reports in 1 month. Sample copy free on written request. Writer's guidelines for #10 SASE.

Nonfiction: Book excerpts, essays, general interest, humor, interview/profile, new product, photo feature, travel. Does not want politics, sex, religion, general history, shopping information or advertorials, no personal experience. Buys 12 features/year, plus assigned editorial covering ports-of-call and numerous fillers. Query with published clips. Length: 800-2,000 words. Pays $150-1,000, negotiable per assignment. Sometimes pays expenses of writers on assignment.

Photos: State availability of photos with submission. Negotiates payment individually. Captions, model releases, identification of subjects required. Buys one-time and reprint rights.

Fillers: Anecdotes, facts, newsbreaks, short humor. Buys 50/year. Length: 50-500 words. Pays $25-100.

Tips: "Do not send any general overviews on port destinations or editorial on shopping or long-standing attractions that can be found in any travel guide. Focus on unique aspects of island culture, colorful local personalities, new twists on the themes of ecology/wildlife, food, folklore, festivals, etc. A first-hand knowledge of the subject matter is a must. News-oriented material is always welcomed. Demonstrate your voice in your query letter, send a selection of writing samples that reveal your range, and include a list of subjects and regions of expertise."

ENDLESS VACATION, Endless Vacation, P.O. 80260, Indianapolis IN 46280-0260. (317)871-9504. Fax: (317)871-9507. Associate Editor: Jackson Mahaney. Prefers to work with published/established writers. Bimonthly magazine covering travel destinations, activities and issues that enhance the lives of vacationers. Estab. 1974. Circ. 907,609. **Pays on acceptance.** Publishes ms an average of 6 months after acceptance. Byline given. Buys first North American serial rights. Accepts simultaneous and previously published submissions. Send photocopy of article and typed ms with rights for sale noted and information about when and where the article previously appeared. For reprints, pays 25% of the amount paid for an original article. Publishes novel excerpts. Reports in 1 month. *Writer's Market* recommends allowing 2 months for reply. Sample copy for $5 and 9×12 SAE with 3 first-class stamps. Writer's guidelines for #10 SASE.

Nonfiction: Contact: Manuscript Editor. Buys 24 mss/year (approximately). Most are from established writers already published in *Endless Vacation. Accepts very few unsolicited pieces.* Query with published clips. Length: 1,000-2,000 words. Pays $500-1,000 for assigned articles; $250-800 for unsolicited articles. Sometimes pays the expenses of writers on assignment.

Photos: Reviews 4×5 transparencies and 35mm slides. Offers $100-500/photo. Model releases and identification of subjects required. Buys one-time rights.

Columns/Departments: Compleat Traveler (on travel news and service-related information); Weekender (on domestic weekend vacation travel). Query with published clips. Length: 800-1,000 words. Pays $150-600. Sometimes pays the expenses of writers on assignment. Also news items for Facts, Fads and Fun Stuff column on travel news, products or problems. Length: 100-200 words. Pays $100/item.

Tips: "We will continue to focus on travel trends and resort destinations. Articles must be packed with pertinent facts and applicable how-tos. Information—addresses, phone numbers, dates of events, costs—must be current and accurate. We like to see a variety of stylistic approaches, but in all cases the lead must be strong. A writer should realize that we require first-hand knowledge of the subject and plenty of practical information. For further understanding of *Endless Vacation*'s direction, the writer should study the magazine and guidelines for writers."

FAMILY MOTOR COACHING, Official Publication of the Family Motor Coach Association, 8291 Clough Pike, Cincinnati OH 45244-2796. (513)474-3622. Fax: (513)474-2332. Editor: Pamela Wisby Kay. Associate Editor: Robbin Maue. 80% freelance written. "We prefer that writers be experienced RVers." Monthly magazine emphasizing travel by motorhome, motorhome mechanics, maintenance and other technical information. Estab. 1963. Circ. 99,000. **Pays on acceptance.** Publishes ms an average of 8 months after acceptance. Buys first North American serial rights. Byline given. Submit seasonal/holiday material 4 months in advance. Reports in 2 months. Sample copy for $2.50. Writer's guidelines for #10 SASE.

Nonfiction: Motorhome travel (various areas of country accessible by motor coach), how-to (do it yourself motor home projects and modifications), bus conversions, humor, interview/profile, new product, technical, nostalgia. Buys 15-20 mss/issue. Query with published clips . Length: 1,000-2,000 words. Pays $100-500.

Photos: State availability of photos with query. Offers no additional payment for b&w contact sheets, 35mm or 2¼×2¼ color transparencies. Captions and model releases required. Prefers first North American serial rights but will consider one-time rights on photos only.

Tips: "The greatest number of contributions we receive are travel; therefore, that area is the most competitive. However, it also represents the easiest way to break in to our publication. Articles should be written for those traveling by self-contained motor home. The destinations must be accessible to motor home travelers and any peculiar road conditions should be mentioned."

‡GO MAGAZINE, AAA Carolinas, 720 E. Morehead St., Charlotte NC 28230. (704)377-3600. Editor: Tom Crosby. Contact: Donna Emmary. 20% freelance written. Bimonthly newspaper covering travel, automotive, safety (traffic) and insurance."Consumer oriented membership publication providing information on complex or expensive subjects—car buying, vacations, traffic safety problems, etc." Estab. 1928. Circ. 400,000. **Pays on acceptance.** Publishes ms an average of 2 months after acceptance. No kill fee. Buys second serial (reprint) rights, simultaneous rights or makes work-for-hire assignments. Editorial lead time 6 weeks. Submit seasonal material 6 weeks in advance. Accepts previously published submissions. Query for electronic submissions. Reports in 2 weeks on queries; 2 months on mss. Sample copy for SAE with 4 first-class stamps. Writer's guidelines for #10 SASE.
Nonfiction: How-to (fix auto, travel safety, etc.), humor, travel, automotive insurance, traffic safety. Buys 12-14 mss/year. Query with published clips. Length: 600-900 words. Pays 15¢/word. Sometimes pays expenses of writers on assignment.
Photos: Send photos with submission. Offers no additional payment for photos accepted with ms. Buys one-time rights.

THE INTERNATIONAL RAILWAY TRAVELER, Hardy Publishing Co., Inc., Editorial offices: P.O. Box 3747, San Diego CA 92163. (619)260-1332. Fax: (619)296-4220. 100% freelance written. Bimonthly newsletter covering rail travel. Estab. 1983. Circ. 3,500. Pays on publication. Byline given. Offers 25% kill fee. Buys first North American serial rights. Editorial lead time 4 months. Submit seasonal material 6 months in advance. Query for electronic submissions. Reports in 1 month on queries; 2 months on mss. Sample copy for $7. Writer's guidelines for #10 SASE.
Nonfiction: Book excerpts, essays, general interest, how-to, interview/profile, new product, opinion, personal experience, photo feature, travel. Buys 12 mss/year. Query with published clips or send complete ms. Include SASE for return of ms. Length: 800-1,200 words. Pays $1.50 per column inch.
Photos: Send photos with submission. Include SASE for return of photos. Reviews contact sheets, negatives, transparencies, prints (8×10 preferred; will accept 5×7). Offers $10-20/photo. Costs of converting slides and negatives to prints are deducted from payment. Captions and identification of subjects required. Buys one-time rights.
Tips: "We want factual articles concerning world rail travel which would not appear in the mass-market travel magazines. IRT readers and editors love stories and photos on off-beat train trips as well as more conventional train trips covered in unconventional ways. With IRT, the focus is on the train travel experience, not the description. Be sure to include details (prices, passes, schedule info, etc.) for readers who might want to take the trip."

ISLANDS, An International Magazine, Islands Publishing Company, 3886 State St., Santa Barbara CA 93105-3112. Fax: (805)569-0349. Editor: Joan Tapper. 95% freelance written. Works with established writers. Bimonthly magazine covering islands throughout the world. "We cover accessible and once-in-a-lifetime islands from many different perspectives: travel, culture, lifestyle. We ask our authors to give us the essence of the island and do it with literary flair." Estab. 1981. Circ. 185,000. **Pays on acceptance.** Publishes ms an average of 8 months after acceptance. Byline given. Buys all rights. Query for electronic submissions. Reports in 1 month on queries; 6 weeks on ms. Sample copy for $5.50. Writer's guidelines for #10 SASE.
Nonfiction: General interest, personal experience, photo feature, any island-related material. No service stories. "Each issue contains 3-4 feature articles of roughly 2,000-4,000 words, and 4-5 departments, each of which runs approximately 750-1,500 words. Any authors who wish to be commissioned should send a detailed proposal for an article, an estimate of costs (if applicable) and samples of previously published work." Buys 25 feature mss/year. "The majority of our feature manuscripts are commissioned." Query with published clips or send complete ms. Feature length: 2,000-4,000 words. Pays $800-3,000. Pays expenses of writers on assignment.
Photos: State availability or send photos with query or ms. Pays $75-300 for 35mm transparencies. "Fine color photography is a special attraction of *Islands*, and we look for superb composition, technical quality and editorial applicability." Label slides with name and address, include captions, and submit in protective plastic sleeves. Identification of subjects required. Buys one-time rights.
Columns/Departments: "Arts, Profiles, Nature, Sports, Lifestyle, Food, Encounters, Island Hopping featurettes—all island related. Brief Logbook items should be highly focused on some specific aspect of islands." Buys 50 mss/year. Query with published clips. Length: 500-1,500 words. Pays $100-700.
Tips: "A freelancer can best break in to our publication with short (500-1,000 word) departments or Logbooks that are highly focused on some aspect of island life, history, people, etc. Stay away from general, sweeping articles. We are always looking for topics for our Islanders and Logbook pieces. We will be using big name writers for major features; will continue to use newcomers and regulars for columns and departments."

‡JOURNAL OF CHRISTIAN CAMPING, Christian Camping International, P.O. Box 62189, Colorado Springs CO 80962-2189. (719)260-9400. Fax: (719)260-6398. E-mail: cciusa@aol.com. Editor: Dean Ridings. 75% freelance written. Prefers to work with published/established writers. Bimonthly magazine emphasizing the broad scope of organized camping with emphasis on Christian camping. "Leaders of youth camps and adult conferences read our magazine to get practical help in ways to run their camps." Estab. 1963. Circ. 6,500. Pays on publication. Publishes ms an average of 4 months after acceptance. Rights negotiable. Byline given. Accepts previously published submissions. Send photocopy of article and information about when and where the article previously appeared. For reprints, pays 50% of amount paid for an original article. Reports in 1 month. Sample copy $2.25 plus 9×12 SASE. Writer's guidelines for #10 SASE.

Nonfiction: General interest (trends in organized camping in general and Christian camping in particular); how-to (anything involved with organized camping from motivating staff, to programming, to record keeping, to camper follow-up); inspirational (limited use, but might be interested in practical applications of Scriptural principles to everyday situations in camping, no preaching); interview (with movers and shakers in camping and Christian camping in particular; submit a list of basic questions first); and opinion (write a letter to the editor). Buys 20-30 mss/year. Query required. Length: 600-1,200 words. Pays 6¢/word.

Photos: Send photos with ms. Pays $25-150 for 5×7 b&w contact sheet or print; price negotiable for 35mm color transparencies. Rights negotiable.

Tips: "The most frequent mistake made by writers is that they send articles unrelated to our readers. Ask for our publication guidelines first."

THE MATURE TRAVELER, Travel Bonanzas for 49ers-Plus, GEM Publishing Group, Box 50400, Reno NV 89513-0400. (702)786-7419. Editor: Gene E. Malott. 30% freelance written. Monthly newsletter on senior citizen travel. Estab. 1984. Circ. 2,500. **Pays on acceptance.** Publishes ms an average of 3 months after acceptance. Byline given. Offers 25% kill fee. Buys one-time rights. Submit seasonal/holiday material 3 months in advance. Accepts simultaneous and previously published submissions, if so noted. Send tearsheet or photocopy of article and information about when and where the article previously appeared. Pays 50% of their fee for an original article. Reports in 1 month. Sample copy and guidelines for $1 and #10 SAE with 2 first-class stamps. Writer's guidelines only for #10 SASE.

Nonfiction: Travel for seniors. "General travel and destination pieces should be senior-specific, aimed at 49ers and older." Query. Length: 600-1,200 words. Pays $50-100.

Photos: State availability of photos with submission. Reviews contact sheets and b&w (only) prints. Captions required. Buys one-time rights.

Tips: "Read the guidelines and write stories to our readers' needs—not to the general public."

MEXICO EVENTS & DESTINATIONS, A traveler's guide, Travel Mexico Magazine Group, P.O. Box 188037, Carlsbad CA 92009-0801, (619)929-0707. Fax: (619)929-0714. Group Editor: Gabriela Flores. Bimonthly magazine covering tourism and travel to Mexico. "*MEXICO Events & Destinations* focuses on promoting Mexico as a travel destination to readers in the United States and Canada. Our interest is in the many worlds of Mexico. We cover the people and cultures of Mexico with regular sections on food, history, ecotourism, language, walking tours, shopping guides, outdoor recreation, driving, business, real estate and luxury travel." Estab. 1992. Circ. 100,000. Pays 1 month after publication. Publishes ms an average of 2 months after acceptance. Byline given. Buys first rights. Editorial lead time 3 months. Submit seasonal material 5 months in advance. Accepts previously published submissions. Send tearsheet or photocopy of article and information about when and where the article previously appeared. For reprints, pays 30% of the amount paid for an original article. Query for electronic submissions. Reports in 2 months on queries; 1 month on mss. Sample copy for 10×13 SAE with 6 first-class stamps. Writer's guidelines for #10 SASE.

Nonfiction: Travel—Mexico only. "We do not want articles that focus on other countries. We cover Mexico exclusively." Buys 75 mss/year. Query with published clips. Length: 400-1,200 words. Pays 25¢/word.

Photos: Send photos with submission. Reviews transparencies, slides. Offers $20-200/photo. Captions and identification of subjects required. Buys one-time rights.

Tips: "We are looking for writers who know Mexico and who have experience writing about that country. A positive attitude about Mexico is a plus. We do not recommend sending mss, but rather prefer that writers send query with published clips (that will be kept on file unless SASE enclosed) along with list of their area(s) of expertise with regard to Mexico. Our features and columns are all open to freelancers. We are most interested in new discoveries or new twists on familiar destinations in Mexico. But keep in mind that most of our articles are on assignment basis."

THE MIDWEST MOTORIST, AAA Auto Club of Missouri, 12901 N. 40 Dr., St. Louis MO 63141. (314)523-7350. Editor: Michael J. Right. Managing Editor: Deborah M. Klein. 80% freelance written. Bimonthly magazine focusing on travel and auto-related topics. "We feature articles on regional and world travel, area history, auto safety, highway and transportation news." Estab. 1971. Circ. 398,173. **Pays on acceptance.** Byline given. Not copyrighted. Buys first North American serial rights, second serial (reprint) rights. Accepts simultaneous and previously published submissions. Send typed ms with rights for sale noted and information about when and where the article previously appeared. For reprints, pays 40% of the amount paid for an original article. Reports in 1 month with SASE enclosed. Sample copy for 12½×9½ SAE with 3 first-class stamps. Writer's guidelines for #10 SASE.

Nonfiction: Buys 40 mss/year. Query. Length: 2,000 words maximum. Pays $350 (maximum).

Photos: State availability of photos with submission. Reviews transparencies. Offers no additional payment for photos accepted with ms. Captions required. Buys one-time rights.

Tips: "Editorial schedule set 18 months in advance. Request a copy. Serious writers ask for media kit to help them target their piece. Some stories available throughout the year. Travel destinations and tips are most open to freelancers; auto-related topics handled by staff. Make the story bright and quick to read. We see too many 'Here's a recount of our family vacation' manuscripts. Go easy on first-person accounts."

NEW YORK DAILY NEWS, Travel Section, 220 E. 42 St., New York NY 10017. (212)210-1699. Fax: (212)210-2203. Travel Editor: Gunna Biteé Dickson. 30% freelance written. Prefers to work with published/established writers. Weekly tabloid. Circ. 1.8 million. "We are the largest circulating newspaper travel section in the country and take all types of articles ranging from experiences to service oriented pieces that tell readers how to make a certain trip." Pays on publication. Publishes ms an average of 3 months after acceptance. Byline given. Submit seasonal/holiday material 4 months in advance. Query for electronic submissions. Reports "as soon as possible." Writer's guidelines for #10 SASE.

Nonfiction: General interest, historical/nostalgic, humor, inspirational, personal experience, travel. "Most of our articles involve practical trips that the average family can afford—even if it's one you can't afford every year. We also run stories for the Armchair Traveler, an exotic and usually expensive trip. We are looking for professional quality work from professional writers who know what they are doing. The pieces have to give information and be entertaining at the same time. No 'How I Spent My Summer Vacation' type articles. No PR hype." Buys 60 mss/year. Query with SASE. Length: 1,000 words maximum. Pays $75-200.

Photos: "Good pictures always help sell good stories." State availability of photos with ms. Reviews contact sheets and negatives. Captions and identification of subjects required. Buys all rights.

Columns/Departments: Short Hops is based on trips to places within a 300-mile radius of New York City. Length: 700-800 words. Weekly staff columns: Dollar Wise and Business Travel Tips.

Tips: "A writer might have some luck gearing a specific destination to a news event or date: In Search of Irish Crafts in March, for example, but do it well in advance."

NEWSDAY, *New York Newsday*, 235 Pinelawn Rd., Melville NY 11747. (516)843-2980. Travel Editor: Marjorie K. Robins. 20% freelance written. For general readership of Sunday newspaper travel section. Estab. 1940. Circ. 700,000. Buys all rights for New York area only. Buys 45-60 mss/year. Pays on publication. Prefer typewritten manuscripts. Simultaneous submissions considered if others are being made outside the New York area.

Nonfiction: No assignments to freelancers. No query letters. Only completed mss accepted on spec. All trips must be paid for in full by writer. Proof required. Service stories preferred. Destination pieces must be for the current year. Length: 1,200 words maximum. Pays $75-350, depending on space allotment. Fax submissions not encouraged.

- At press time it was announced that *New York Newsday* will cease publication.

NORTHEAST OUTDOORS, Northeast Outdoors, Inc., P.O. Box 2180, Waterbury CT 06722-2180. (203)755-0158. Fax: (203)755-3480. Editorial Director: John Florian. 50% freelance written. Works with a small number of new/unpublished writers each year. Monthly tabloid covering family camping in the Northeastern US. Estab. 1968. Circ. 14,000. Pays on publication. Publishes ms an average of 8 months after acceptance. Byline given. Buys first rights and regional rights. Submit seasonal/holiday material 5 months in advance. Accepts previously published submissions "if articles were published outside Northeast region." Send typed ms with rights for sale noted and information about when and where the article previously appeared. Pays 50% of their fee for an original article. Query for electronic submissions. Reports in 2 weeks. Sample copy for 9×12 SAE with 6 first-class stamps. Writer's guidelines for #10 SASE.

- At this publication there is less freelance need since more is done now by staff.

Nonfiction: How-to (camping), humor, new product (company and RV releases only), recreation vehicle and camping experiences in the Northeast, features about private (only) campgrounds and places to visit in the Northeast while RVing, personal experience, photo feature, travel. "No diaries of trips, dog or fishing-only stories, or anything not camping and RV related." Length: 300-1,500 words. Pays $40-80 for articles with b&w photos; pays $30-75 for articles without art.

Photos: Send photos with submission. Reviews contact sheets and 5×7 prints or larger. Captions and identification of subjects required. Buys one-time rights.

ALWAYS enclose a self-addressed, stamped envelope (SASE) with all your queries and correspondence.

Columns/Departments: Mealtime (campground cooking), 300-900 words. Buys 12 mss/year. Query or send complete ms. Length: 750-1,000 words. Pays $25-50.
Tips: "We most often need material on private campgrounds and attractions in New England. We are looking for upbeat, first-person stories about where to camp, what to do or see, and how to enjoy camping."

NORTHWEST TRAVEL, Northwest Regional Magazines, 1525 12th St., P.O. Box 18000, Florence OR 97439-0130. (800)348-8401. Editor: Dave Peden. Managing Editor: Judy Fleagle. 75% freelance written. Bimonthly magazine of Northwest living. Estab. 1991. Circ. 50,000. Pays after publication. Publishes ms an average of 6-12 months after acceptance. Byline given. Offers 33% kill fee. Buys first North American serial rights. Submit seasonal/holiday material 6 months in advance. Query for electronic submissions. Occasionally accepts previously published submissions. Send tearsheet or photocopy of article or typed ms with rights for sale noted and information about when and where the article previously appeared. Pays approximately 65% of the amount paid for an original article. Reports in 1 month on queries; 3 months on mss. Sample copy for $4.50. Writer's guidelines for #10 SASE.
Nonfiction: Travel as pertains to Pacific Northwest. "Any article not related to the Pacific Northwest will be returned." Query with published clips. Length: 500-2,000 words. Pays $50-350. "Along with payment comes 2-5 copies."
Photos: Send photos with submission. Preferred 35mm or larger transparencies, 3×5 or larger prints with negatives, if possible. Captions and identification of subjects required as well as who to credit. Buys one-time rights.
Fillers: Newsbreaks (no-fee basis), short articles. Buys 30/year. Byline given. Length: 300-500 words. Pays $35-65.
Tips: "Slant article for readers who do not live in the Pacific Northwest. We try to use at least one historical article and at least two travel articles in each issue. City and town profiles, special out-of-the-way places to visit, will also be used in each issue. An occasional restaurant feature will be used. Short articles with photos (transparencies preferred) will be easiest to fit in. Query first. After go-ahead, send cover letter with manuscript/photo package. Photos often make the difference in deciding which article gets published."

ONTARIO MOTOR COACH REVIEW, Naylor Communications Ltd., 920 Yonge St., 6th Floor, Toronto, Ontario M4W 3C7 Canada. (416)961-1028. Fax: (416)924-4408. Editor: Lori Knowles. 50% freelance written. Annual magazine on travel and tourist destinations. Estab 1970. Circ. 3,000. Pays 30 days from deadline. Byline given. Offers 33% kill fee. Buys first North American serial rights and all rights. Submit seasonal/holiday material 2 months in advance. Accepts simultaneous and previously published submissions. Send typed ms with rights for sale noted and information about when and where the article previously appeared. Pays 80% of their fee for an original article. Query for electronic submissions. Reports in 6 weeks. *Writer's Market* recommends allowing 2 months for reply. Free sample copy and writer's guidelines.
   • *Review* is a destination guide for bus tour operators and organizers; does NOT refer to RV travel.
Nonfiction: General interest, historical, interview/profile, new product, personal experience related to motor coach bus, travel, photo feature, technical, travel. Buys 5-10 mss/year. Query with published clips. Length: 500-3,000 words. Pays 20-25¢/word. Pays expenses of writers on assignment.
Photos: State availability of photos with submission. Reviews transparencies and prints. Offers $25-200/photo. Identification of subjects required.

OUTDOOR TRAVELER, Mid-Atlantic, WMS Publications, 1 Morton Dr., Suite 102, P.O. Box 2748, Charlottesville VA 22902. (804)984-0655. Fax: (804)984-0656. Editor: Marianne Marks. Associate Editor: Scott Clark. 85% freelance written. Quarterly magazine. "*Outdoor Traveler* is designed to help readers (well-educated, active adults) enjoy the Mid-Atlantic outdoors through year-round seasonal coverage of outdoor recreation, travel, adventure and nature." Estab. 1993. Circ. 30,000. Pays on publication. Byline given. Offers 25% kill fee. Buys first North American serial rights. Editorial lead time 6 months. Submit seasonal material 6-8 months in advance. Accepts simultaneous submissions. Reports in 2 months. Sample copy for $4. Writer's guidelines for #10 SASE.
   • This publication needs more short features (1-2 pages), as well as more profiles, humor pieces and service/informational articles.
Nonfiction: Travel, nature, personal experience, humor, interview/profile, essays, book excerpts, how-to (outdoor sports technique), photo feature, historic/nostalgic (related to outdoor sports or travel). No "What I did on my vacation" articles; no golf or tennis. Buys 35 mss/year. Query with published clips. Length: 300-2,000 words. Pays 20¢/word. Sometimes pays expenses of writers on assignment.
Photos: Send photos with submission. Reviews transparencies. Offers $50/photo minimum. Captions, model releases and identification of subjects required. Buys one-time rights.
Columns/Departments: Lodging (seasonal pieces, with outdoor slant), 600-800 words; Destinations (brief but detailed guides to outdoor sports destinations), 600 words; Book Reviews (reviews of interest to readers), 100-150 words. Buys 35 mss/year. Query with published clips. Pays 20¢/word.
Fillers: Anecdotes, facts, newsbreaks, short humor. Length: 300 words.
Tips: "Freelancers should query with clips that reveal strong writing skills, a professional style, and knowledge of our region and subject matter."

PASSENGER TRAIN JOURNAL, Pentrex, P.O. Box 379, Waukesha WI 53187. (414)542-4900. Fax: (414)542-7595. E-mail: 76307.1175@compuserve.com. Editor: Carl Swanson. 90% freelance written. Monthly magazine covering passenger railroading news and info. "*Passenger Train Journal* covers news and travel topics related to rail travel. Readers tend to be relatively affluent, well-educated and well-traveled." Estab. 1968. Circ. 15,000. Pays on publication. Publishes ms an average of 6 months after acceptance. Byline given. Buys all rights. Editorial lead time 2 months. Submit seasonal material 6 months in advance. Accepts previously published submissions. Query for electronic submissions. Reports in 2 months. Sample copy for $3.50. Writer's guidelines free on request.

Nonfiction: Historical/nostalgic (rail travel), travel (rail). Buys 40 mss/year. Send complete ms. Length: 1,500-3,500 words. Pays 5¢/word.

Photos: Send photos with submission. Reviews prints and transparencies. Offers $10-50/photo. Captions required. Buys one-time rights.

Columns/Departments: Rail Travel (descriptions of rail travel and destinations), 2,000 words. Buys 12 mss/year. Send complete ms. Pays 5¢/word.

Tips: "The majority of *Passenger Train Journal* is produced by freelancers and we pride ourselves on being open to new authors. Our job is easier if freelancers send complete stories and photo illustrations with their package. We particularly need stories for our 'Rail Travel' section. Stories should be slanted toward describing one train trip with the emphasis on helping readers plan a similar journey. Photo illustrations and a map of the route often tip the balance in favor of a submissions."

RV TIMES MAGAZINE, 1100 Welborne Dr., Suite 204, Richmond VA 23229. (804)741-5376. Editor: Alice P. Supple. 75% freelance written. Prefers to work with published/established writers; works with a small number of new/unpublished writers each year. Monthly except December. "We supply the camping public with articles and information on outdoor activities related to camping. Our audience is primarily families that own recreational vehicles." Estab. 1973. Circ. 35,000. Pays on publication. Publishes ms an average of 4-6 months after acceptance. Byline given. Buys one-time, second serial (reprint) or simultaneous rights. Submit seasonal/holiday material 2 months in advance. Accepts simultaneous and previously published submissions. Send typed ms with rights for sale noted and information about when and where the article previously appeared. Pays 100% of the amount paid for an original article. Query for electronic submissions. Sample copy and writer's guidelines for 9×12 SAE with 7 first-class stamps. Reports only on acceptance. Allow 2 months for reply, if one is to come.

Nonfiction: How-to, travel, information on places to camp, "tourist related articles, places to go, things to see. Does not have to be camping related." Buys 80 mss/year. Query with or without published clips or send complete ms. Length: 500-2,000 words.

Photos: Always prefers "people" pictures as opposed to scenic. Buys one-time rights. Black and white, color prints, slides; prefer vertical format.

● Looking for more *quality* color slides, preferably with people in active pursuit of outdoor activities (verticle format).

Tips: "All areas of *RV Times* are open to freelancers. We will look at all articles and consider for publication. Return of unsolicited mss is not guaranteed; however, every effort is made to return photos."

RV WEST MAGAZINE, Vernon Publications Inc., 3000 Northup Way, Suite 200, Bellevue WA 98004. (800)700-6962. Fax: (206)822-9372. Publisher: Geoffrey P. Vernon. 85% freelance written. Works with a small number of new/unpublished writers each year. Monthly magazine for Western recreational vehicle owners. Estab. 1977. Circ. 75,000. Pays on publication. Byline given. Buys one-time rights. Submit seasonal/ holiday material at least 3 months in advance of best month for publication. Accepts simultaneous submissions. Submit complete ms. Reports in several months on mss. Free writer's guidelines.

Nonfiction: Historical/nostalgic, new product, personal experience (particularly travel), travel (Western destinations for RVs), events of interest to RVers. No non-RV travel articles. Query with or without published clips. Length: 750-1,750 words. Pays $1.50/inch.

● No longer accepting how-to articles.

Photos: Send photos with submissions. Color slides and b&w prints preferred. Offers $5 for each published photo. Identification of subjects required.

Tips: "RV travel/destination stories are most open to freelancers. Include all information of value to RVers, and reasons why they would want to visit the location (13 Western states). Short items of interest may also be submitted, including tips, humorous anecdotes and jokes related to RVing. Indicate best time frame for publication."

ST. MAARTEN NIGHTS, Nights Publications, 1831 Rene Levesque Blvd. West, Montreal, Quebec H3H 1R4 Canada. Fax: (514)931-6273. Editor: Stephen Trotter. Managing Editor: Zelly Zuskin. 80% freelance written. Annual magazine covering the St. Maarten/St. Martin vacation experience seeking "upbeat entertaining lifestyle articles: colorful profiles of islanders; lively features on culture, activities, night life, eco-tourism, special events, gambling; how-to features; humor. Our audience is the North American vacationer." Estab. 1981. Circ. 225,000. **Pays on acceptance.** Publishes ms an average of 6-10 months after acceptance. Byline given. Offers 15% kill fee. Buys first North American serial and first Caribbean rights. Editorial lead time

2 months. Query for electronic submissions. Reports in 2 weeks on queries; 1 month on mss. *Writer's Market* recommends allowing 2 months for reply. Sample copy for $5. Writer's guidelines free on request.

Nonfiction: General interest, historical/nostalgia, how-to (gamble), sail, etc., humor, inspirational, interview/ profile, opinion, ecological (eco-tourism), personal experience, photo feature, travel, local culture, art, activities, entertainment, topics relative to vacationers in St. Maarten/St. Martin. "No negative pieces or stale rewrites." Buys 5-10 mss/year. Query with published clips. Length: 250-750 words. Pays $125-350 for assigned articles; $100-250 for unsolicited articles.

Photos: State availability of photos with submission. Reviews transparencies. Offers $25-100/photo. Captions, model releases, identification of subjects required. Buys one-time rights.

‡TEXAS HIGHWAYS, Official Travel Magazine of Texas, Texas Department of Transportation, Box 141009, Austin TX 78714-1009. (512)483-3675. Fax: (512)483-3672. Editor: Jack Lowry. Managing Editor: Jill Lawless. 85% freelance written. Prefers to work with published/established writers. Monthly tourist magazine covering travel and history for Texas only. **Pays on acceptance.** Publishes ms an average of 10 months after acceptance. Byline given. Offers $100 kill fee. Buys one-time rights. Submit seasonal/holiday material 1 year in advance. No simultaneous queries. Reports in 1 month on queries. Sample copy and writer's guidelines for 9×12 SAE with 3 first-class stamps.

Nonfiction: Historical/nostalgic, photo feature and travel. Must be concerned with travel in Texas. Send material on "what to see, what to do, where to go in *Texas*." Material must be tourist-oriented. "No disaster features." Buys 75 mss/year. Query with published clips. Length: 1,000-2,000 words. Pays $400-1,000. Sometimes pays expenses of writers on assignment "after we have worked with them awhile."

Photos: Michael A. Murphy, photo editor. Send photos with query or ms. Pays upon publication $80 for less than half a page, $120 for half page, $170 for a full page, $400 for front cover, $300 for back cover. Accepts 35mm and large original color transparencies. Captions and identification of subjects required. Buys one-time rights.

TIMES OF THE ISLANDS, The International Magazine of the Turks & Caicos Islands, Times Publications Ltd., P.O. Box 234, Caribbean Place, Providenciales Turks & Caicos Islands, British West Indies. (809)946-4788. Fax: (809)946-4703. Editor: Kathy Matusik. 80% freelance written. Quarterly magazine covering The Turks & Caicos Islands. "*Times of the Islands* is used by the public and private sector to attract visitors and potential investors/developers to the Islands. It strives to portray the advantages of the Islands and their friendly people. It is also used by tourists, once on-island, to learn about services, activities and accommodations available." Estab. 1988. Circ. 5,500-8,000. Pays on publication. Publishes ms an average of 6 months after acceptance. Byline given. Buys second serial (reprint) rights and publication rights for 6 months with respect to other publications distributed in Caribbean. Editorial lead time 4 months. Submit seasonal material 4 months in advance. Accepts simultaneous and previously published submissions. Send photocopy of article along with information about when and where it previously appeared. Query for electronic submissions. Reports in 6 weeks on queries; 2 months on mss. "Keep in mind, mail to Islands is SLOW. Faxing can speed response time." Sample copy for $4 and postage between Miami and your destination. Writer's guidelines for #10 SASE.

Nonfiction: Book excerpts or reviews, essays, general interest (Caribbean art, culture, cooking, crafts), historical/nostalgic, humor, interview/profile (locals), personal experience (trips to the Islands), photo feature, technical (island businesses), travel, nature, ecology, business (offshore finance), watersports. Special issues: Diving Guide to the Turks & Caicos Islands (1995). Buys 30 mss/year. Query. Length: 500-3,000 words. Pays $50-150.

Photos: Send photos with submission—slides preferred. Reviews 3×5 prints. Offers no additional payment for photos accepted with ms. Pays $15-100/photo. Identification of subjects required.

Columns/Departments: Profiles from Abroad (profiles of T&C Islanders who are doing something outstanding internationally), 500 words. Buys 4 mss/year. Query. Pays $50-100. "Also, please query with new column ideas!"

Fiction: Adventure (sailing, diving), ethnic (Caribbean), historical (Caribbean), humorous (travel-related), mystery, novel excerpts. Buys 1 ms/year. "Would buy three to four if available." Query. Length: 1,000-2,000 words. Pays $100-200.

Tips: "Make sure that the query/article specifically relates to the Turks and Caicos Islands. The theme can be general (ecotourism, for instance), but the manuscript should contain specific and current references to the Islands. We're a high-quality magazine, with a small budget and staff and are very open-minded to ideas (and manuscripts). Writers who have visited the Islands at least once would probably have a better perspective from which to write. Query well ahead of time and let me know when you plan to visit."

TOURING AMERICA, Travel in the USA, Canada and Mexico, Fancy Publications, Inc., Box 6050, Mission Viejo CA 92690. (714)855-8822, ext. 406. Editor: Bob Carpenter. Bimonthly magazine covering travel in North America. Estab. 1991. Pays on receipt of contract signed by author. Publishes ms an average of 3 months after acceptance. Byline given. Buys first North American serial and anthology rights. Editorial lead time 4 months. Submit seasonal material 6 months in advance ("after receiving go-ahead to write it.")

Does not consider unsolicited mss. Sample copy for $5.50 from Back Issue Dept. Writer's guidelines free on request for #10 SASE.

● *Touring America*'s 1996 editorial calendar is filled.

Nonfiction: "We have become an 'assignment-only' publication for almost all of our published material. Query letters are still marginally welcome if they identify specific topics; have a specific, well-focused story slant; are accompanied by a proposed opening paragraph and emphasize: 1) a hitherto completely undiscovered travel destination within the North American continent or 2) a completely original way of treating known destinations. Unsolicited manuscripts are not welcome."

TRANSITIONS ABROAD, P.O. Box 1300, Amherst MA 01004-1300. (413)256-3414. Editor/Publisher: Clay Hubbs. 80-90% freelance written. Eager to work with new/unpublished writers. Magazine resource for low-budget international travel with an educational or work component. Estab. 1977. Circ. 15,000. Pays on publication. Buys first rights and second (reprint) rights. Byline given. Written queries only. Reports in 2 months. Sample copy for $5. Writer's guidelines and topics schedule for #10 SASE. Manuscript returned only with SASE.

Nonfiction: Lead articles (up to 2,000 words) provide first-hand practical information on independent travel to featured country or region (see topics schedule). Pays $75-150. Also, how-to (find educational and specialty travel opportunities), practical information (evaluation of courses, special interest and study tours, economy travel), travel (new learning and cultural travel ideas). Foreign travel only. Few destination ("tourist") pieces. *Transitions Abroad* is a resource magazine for educated and adventurous travelers, not for travel novices or armchair travelers. Emphasis on information—which must be usable by readers—and on interaction with people in host country. Buys 20 unsolicited mss/issue. Query with credentials. Length: 500-1,500 words. Pays $25-150. Include author's bio with submissions. Buys longer information features for resource guides. Length: 1,000-5,000 words. Pays $75-150.

● *Transitions Abroad* now publishes an *Alternative Travel Directory* annually. Best articles from the magazine may be reprinted in *Directory* and *Educational Travel Resource Guides*.

Photos: Send photos with ms. Pays $10-45 for prints (color acceptable, b&w preferred), $125 for covers (b&w only). Photos increase likelihood of acceptance. Buys one-time rights. Captions and ID on photos required.

Columns/Departments: Worldwide Travel Bargains (destinations, activities and accomodations for budget travelers—featured in every issue); Tour and Program Notes (new courses or travel programs); Travel Resources (new information and ideas for independent travel); Working Traveler (how to find jobs and what to expect); Activity Vacations (travel opportunities that involve action and learning, usually by direct involvement in host culture); Responsible Travel (information on community-organized tours). Buys 10/issue. Send complete ms. Length: 1,000 words maximum. Pays $20-50.

Fillers: Info Exchange (information, preferably first-hand—having to do with travel, particularly offbeat educational travel and work or study abroad). Buys 10/issue. Length: 750 words maximum. Pays $20.

Tips: "We like nuts and bolts stuff, practical information, especially on how to work, live and cut costs abroad. Our readers want usable information on planning their own travel itinerary. Be specific: names, addresses, current costs. We are particularly interested in educational and long-stay travel and study abroad for adults and senior citizens. *Educational Travel Resource Guide* published each year in July provides best information sources on work, study, and independent travel abroad. Each bimonthly issue contains a worldwide directory of educational and specialty travel programs. (Topics schedule included with writers' guidelines.)

TRAVEL À LA CARTE, 136 Walton St., Port Hope, Ontario L1A 1N5 Canada. (905)885-7948. Fax: (905)885-7202. Editor: Donna Carter. 70% freelance written. Bimonthly travel magazine. "Lighthearted entertaining articles on travel destinations worldwide, with a focus on the places and people visited. Our audience is travellers, airline, train and car." Pays on publication. Byline given. Offers no kill fee. Not copyrighted. Buys first North American and one-time rights. Submit seasonal/holiday material 4 months in advance. Accepts simultaneous submissions. Reports in 1 month. Free sample copy and writer's guidelines with SASE.

Nonfiction: Travel. Buys 12-15 mss/year. Query with published clips. Length: 1,500-2,000 words. Pays $125-275.

Photos: Send transparencies or slides with submission. Offers no additional payment for photos accepted with ms. Identification of subjects required. Buys one-time rights.

Tips: "Send a list of travel destinations and samples of writing and photography. Do not send off-the-beaten path articles for destinations that require flight changes followed by train, canoe and treks to remote areas."

TRAVEL & LEISURE, American Express Publishing Corp., 1120 Avenue of the Americas, New York NY 10036. (212)382-5600. Editor-in-Chief: Nancy Novogrod. Executive Editor: Stephen Drucker. Managing Editor: Mark Orwoll. 80% freelance written. Monthly magazine. Circ. 900,000. **Pays on acceptance.** Byline given. Offers 25% kill fee. Buys first world rights. Reports in 6 weeks. *Writer's Market* recommends allowing 2 months for reply. Sample copy for $5. Writer's guidelines for #10 SASE.

● There is no single editorial contact for *Travel & Leisure*. It is best to find the name of the editor of each section, as appropriate for your submission.

Nonfiction: Travel. Buys 200 mss/year. Query. Length open. Payment varies. Pays the expenses of writers on assignment.
Photos: Discourages submission of unsolicited transparencies. Payment varies. Captions required. Buys one-time rights.
Tips: "Read the magazine. There are 2 regional editions: East and West. Regional sections are best places to start."

TRAVELER PUBLICATIONS, (formerly *Sea Mass Traveler*), Publishers of *Sea Mass Traveler, Mystic Traveler* and *Newport Traveler*, 174 Bellevue Ave., Suite 207, Newport RI 02840. (401)847-0226. Managing Editor: Joanne Blake. 100% freelance written. Monthly regional tabloid covering places of interest in southern Massachusetts, southern Connecticut and all of Rhode Island. "Stories that get the reader to "do, see, or act upon." Estab. 1992. Circ. 120,000 winter 240,000 summer. Pays on publication. Byline given. Buys all rights. Editorial lead time 2 months. Submit seasonal material 2 months in advance. Accepts simultaneous and previously published submissions. Query for electronic submissions. Reports in 2 months on mss. Sample copy and writer's guidelines free on request.
• Three magazines (above) are published by one editorial office. Send only one manuscript and it will be circulated between magazines.
Nonfiction: Essays, general interest, historical/nostalgic, photo feature (travel). Buys 60 mss/year. Send complete ms. Length: 700-1,200 words. Pays 5¢/word. Sometimes pays expenses of writers on assignment.
Photos: Send photos with submission. Reviews prints. Negotiates payment individually. Buys one-time rights.
Fillers: Facts. Buys 30/year. Length: 50-200 words. Pays 5¢/word.
Tips: "We are very interested in tours that cover an entire area. It could be a tour of wineries, a certain kind of shop, golf courses, etc. Always include address, phone, hour, admissions prices."

WESTERN RV NEWS, 56405 Cascade View Lane, Warren OR 97053-9736. (503)222-1255. Fax: (503)222-1255. E-mail: wruneph@aol.com. Editor: Elsie Hathaway. 75% freelance written. Monthly magazine for owners of recreational vehicles. Estab. 1966. Pays on publication. Publishes ms an average of 3-6 months after acceptance. Byline given. Buys first rights and second serial (reprint) rights. Accepts simultaneous and previously published submissions. Send photocopy and typed ms with rights for sale noted and information about when and where the article previously appeared and photocopy of article if available. For reprints, pays 60% of amount paid for an original article. Reports in 1 month. *Writer's Market* recommends allowing 2 months for reply. Sample copy and writer's guidelines for 9 × 12 SAE with 5 first-class stamps. Guidelines for #10 SASE. Request to be put on free temporary mailing list for publication.
Nonfiction: How-to (RV oriented, purchasing considerations, maintenance), humor (RV experiences), new product (with ancillary interest to RV lifestyle), personal experiences (varying or unique RV lifestyles) technical (RV systems or hardware), travel. "No articles without an RV slant." Buys 100 mss/year. Submit complete ms. Length: 250-1,200 words. Pays $15-100.
Photos: Send photos with submission. Prefer b&w. Offers $5-10/photo. Captions, model releases, identification of subjects required. Buys one-time rights.
Fillers: Encourage anecdotes, RV related tips and short humor. Length: 50-250 words. Pays $5-25.
Tips: "Highlight the RV lifestyle! Western travel (primarily NW destinations) articles should include information about the availability of RV sites, dump stations, RV parking and accessibility. Thorough research and a pleasant, informative writing style are paramount. Technical, how-to, and new product writing is also of great interest to us. Photos definitely enhance the possibility of article acceptance."

Women's

Women have an incredible variety of publications available to them—about 50 appear on newsstands in an array of specialties. A number of titles in this area have been redesigned during the past year to compete in the crowded marketplace. Many have stopped publishing fiction and are focusing more on short, human interest nonfiction articles. Magazines that also use material slanted to women's interests can be found in the following categories: Business and Finance; Child Care and Parental Guidance; Contemporary Culture; Food and Drink; Gay and Lesbian Interest; Health and Fitness; Hobby and Craft; Home and Garden; Relationships; Religious; Romance and Confession; and Sports.

ALLURE, Condé Nast, 360 Madison Ave., New York NY 10017. Articles Editor: Tom Prince. Monthly publication covering beauty, lifestyle and culture. Query before submitting. Call or write for guidelines, include SASE. Most beauty articles are written inhouse. Reflections section most open to freelancers. "Read and become *very* familiar with the magazine."

‡AMBIENCE, P.O. Box 12134, Berkeley CA 94712. Editor: Deborah Fleischman. Estab. 1995. Quarterly magazine for women aged 20 and older. 100% freelance written. Works with new, unpublished as well as established writers. "*Ambience* premiers as a unique and overdue magazine designed to explore, women's vision of romance and sensuality and offer a full scale appreciation of the ways in which sexuality impacts our lives." Pays on publication. Payment negotiable. Byline given. Reports in 2 months on ms, 1 month on queries. Publishes an average of 6 months after acceptance. Accepts simultaneous and previously published submissions. Send tearsheet or photocopy of article or short story, typed ms with rights for sale noted and information about when and where the article previously appeared. Writers guidelines for #10 SASE. "No phone calls please."

Nonfiction: Query first with published clips or send complete ms. Buys average 30 mss/year. General interest, travel book/music/video reviews, exposé, humor, interview/profile, personal experience—all related to women's sexuality. Length 1,000-5,000 words. Buys first North American serial rights and/or reprint rights. Especially interested in feature articles dealing with international themes, women's sexual health and interviews/profiles of celebrities/authors/artists who have dealt with sexuality in their work. Prefer in-depth, well researched material that is both lively and entertaining. No superficial, advice oriented or "relationship" topics that are usually covered in other women's magazines.

Fiction: "We invite erotic fiction, which like a good aphrodisiac will leave a woman drunk with anticipation and in blunter terms 'turn us on.' Focus is heterosexual but we appreciate diversity." Query or send complete ms. Buys average of 100 mss/year. Buys first, one time and/or second serial rights. Use for promotional and/ or other rights arranged. Prefer visceral stories, subtle and emotionally intriguing themes, lustful entanglements and multicultural tales. All themes considered: humor, farce, fantasy, serious, dark, taboo, romance, porn, erotic—real and imagined. Your story should set the mood and leave room for the imagination. Excerpts of larger works OK. Focus on *women's* sexual experiences and fantasies."

Photos: *Ambience* is interested in presenting a cornucopia of shapes, faces and colors to reflect the wondrous variety of our species and our sexual relations. Make sure your photos capture the essence of a woman's sexual experience or fantasy—ie. the mood that precedes and provokes desire. Especially interested in nostalgia, romance, and *interaction* between the sexes. Captions, model releases and identification of subjects required. See photographers market for more specifications. Send 8 × 10 glossy prints or 35mm, 2¼ × 2¼, 4 × 5, 8 × 10 transparencies. SASE #10 for guidelines. Buys one-time rights. Use for promotional and/or other rights arranged. Work primarily assignment oriented.

Poetry: Accepts free verse, light verse. 250 word maximum. Buys approximately 20 poems/year.

Tips: "Submissions from both sexes welcome but we emphasize women's sexual/sensual experience. Our focus is heterosexual but we appreciate diversity. This is not a "literary" erotic mgazine but a mainstream one aimed at women who want sexuality to be treated honestly, seriously, and provocatively."

AMERICAN WOMAN, GCR Publishing, 1700 Broadway, 34th Floor, New York NY 10019-5905. (212)541-7100. Fax: (212)245-1241. Editor-in-Chief: Lynn Varacalli. Managing Editor: Sandy Kosherick. 50% freelance written. Bimonthly magazine for "women in their 20s, 30s, 40s, mostly single, dealing with relationships and self-help." Estab. 1990. Circ. 200,000. Pays on publication. Publishes ms an average of 2 months after acceptance. Byline given. Offers 25% kill fee. Buys one-time and second serial (reprint) rights. Submit seasonal/holiday material 5 months in advance. Accepts simultaneous and previously published submissions. Send photocopy of article and information about when and where the article previously appeared. For reprints, pays 25% of the amount paid for an original article. Reports in 1 month. Sample copy for $2.50. Writer's guidelines for #10 SASE.

Nonfiction: Book excerpts, self-help, inspirational, interview/profile, personal experience. "No poetry, recipes or fiction." Buys 40 mss/year. Query with published clips. Length: 700-1,500 words. Pays $250-800 for assigned articles; $200-700 for unsolicited articles. Pays for phone, mailings, faxes, transportation costs of writers on assignment.

Photos: State availability of photos with submission. Reviews contact sheets, transparencies, prints. Offers $75-150/photo. Captions, model releases, identification of subjects required. Buys one-time rights.

Tips: "We are interested in true-life stories and stories of inspiration—women who have overcome obstacles in their lives, trends (new ideas in dating, relationships, places to go, new hot spots for meeting men), articles about women starting businesses on a shoestring and money-saving articles (on clothes, beauty, vacations, mail order, entertainment)."

BRIDAL GUIDE, Globe Communications Corp., 441 Lexington Ave., New York NY 10017. (212)949-4040. Fax: (212)286-0072. Editor-in-Chief: Stephanie Wood. Travel Editor: Cherylann Coutts. Assistant Editor: Monica Bernstein. 50% freelance written. Prefer to work with experienced/published writers. A bimonthly magazine covering relationships, sexuality, health and nutrition, psychology, finance, travel. Please do not send queries concerning wedding planning articles, beauty, and fashion, since we produce them in-house. We do not accept personal wedding essays, fiction, or poetry. Reports in 3 months. Sample copy for $4.95 and SASE with 4 first-class stamps; writer's guidelines available.

Nonfiction: We prefer queries rather than actual manuscript submissions. All correspondence accompanied by an SASE will be answered (response time is within 6 weeks). Length: 1,500-3,000 words. Pays on acceptance. Buys 100 mss/year.

Photos: Ed Melnitsky, art director. Photography and illustration submissions should be sent to the art department.
Columns/Departments: Regular columns include finance, sex and health, new products, etiquette, relationships, travel.

BRIDE'S, Condé Nast, 350 Madison Ave., New York NY 10017. (212)880-2518. Managing Editor: Sally Kiobridge. Editor-in-Chief: Millie Martini-Bratten. 40% freelance written. Eager to work with new/unpublished writers. Bimonthly magazine for the first- or second-time bride, her family and friends, the groom and his family and friends. Circ. 400,000. **Pays on acceptance.** Publishes ms an average of 2 months after acceptance. Buys all rights. Also buys first and second serial rights for book excerpts on marriage, communication, finances. Offers 20% kill fee, depending on circumstances. Buys 40 unsolicited mss/year. Byline given. Reports in 2 months. Address mss to Features Department. Writer's guidelines for #10 SASE.
Nonfiction: "We want warm, personal articles, optimistic in tone, with help offered in a clear, specific way. All issues should be handled within the context of marriage. How-to features on all aspects of marriage: communications, in-laws, careers, money, sex, housing, housework, family planning, marriage after having a baby, religion, interfaith marriage, step-parenting, second marriage, reaffirmation of vows; informational articles on the realities of marriage, the changing roles of men and women, the kind of troubles in engagement that are likely to become big issues in marriage; stories from couples or marriage authorities that illustrate marital problems and solutions to men and women; book excerpts on marriage, communication, finances, sex; and how-to features on wedding planning that offer expert advice. Also success stories of marriages of long duration. We use first-person pieces and articles that are well researched, relying on quotes from authorities in the field, and anecdotes and dialogues from real couples. We publish first-person essays on provocative topics unique to marriage." Query or submit complete ms. Article outline preferred. Length: 800-1,000 words. Pays $300-800.
Columns/Departments: The Love column accepts reader love poems, for $25 each. The Something New section accepts reader wedding planning and craft ideas, pays $25.
Tips: "Since marriage rates are up, large, traditional weddings, personalized to reflect the couples' lifestyles, are back in style, and more women work than ever before, do *not* query us on just living together or becoming a stay-at-home wife after marriage. Send us a query or a well-written article that is both easy to read and offers real help for the bride or groom as she/he adjusts to her/his new role. No first-person narratives on wedding and reception planning, home furnishings, cooking, fashion, beauty, travel. We're interested in unusual ideas, experiences, and lifestyles. No 'I used baby pink rose buds' articles."

COMPLETE WOMAN, For All The Women You Are, Associated Publications, Inc., 875 N. Michigan Ave., Chicago IL 60611-1901. (312)266-8680. Editor: Bonnie L. Krueger. Associate Editor: Martha Carlson. 90% freelance written. Bimonthly magazine of general interest for women. Areas of concern are love life, health, fitness, emotions, etc. Estab. 1980. Circ. 350,000. Pays on publication. Publishes ms an average of 5 months after acceptance. Byline given. Buys first North American serial, second serial (reprint) and simultaneous rights. Submit seasonal/holiday material 5 months in advance. Accepts simultaneous and previously published submissions. Send tearsheet or photocopy of article or short story or send typed ms with rights for sale noted and information about when and where the article previously appeared. Reports in 2 months. Writer's guidelines for #10 SASE.
Nonfiction: Book excerpts, general interest, how-to, humor, inspirational, interview/profile, new product, personal experience, photo feature. "We want self-help articles written for today's woman. Articles that address dating, romance, sexuality and relationships are an integral part of our editorial mix, as well as inspirational and motivational pieces." Buys 60-100 mss/year. Query with published clips, or send complete ms. Length: 800-2,000 words. Pays $80-400. Sometimes pays expenses of writers on assignment.
Photos: Send photos with submission. Reviews 2¼ or 35mm transparencies and 5×7 prints. Offers $35-75/photo. Captions, model releases, identification of subjects required. Buys one-time rights.
Poetry: Avant-garde, free verse, light verse, traditional. Nothing over 30 lines. Buys 50 poems/year. Submit maximum 5 poems. Pays $10.

COSMOPOLITAN, The Hearst Corp., 224 W. 57th St., New York NY 10019. (212)649-2000. Executive Editor: Roberta Ashley. 90% freelance written. Monthly magazine for 18- to 35-year-old single, married, divorced women—all working. **Pays on acceptance.** Byline given. Offers 10-15% kill fee. Buys all magazine rights and occasionally negotiates first North American rights. Submit seasonal/holiday material 6 months in advance. Accepts previously published submissions appearing in minor publications. Send tearsheet of article, typed ms with rights for sale noted and information about when and where the article previously appeared. For reprints, pays 100% of the amount paid for an original article. Reports in 1 week on queries; 3 weeks on mss. *Writer's Market* recommends allowing 2 months for reply. Sample copy for $2.50. Writer's guidelines for #10 SASE.
Nonfiction: Book excerpts, how-to, humor, opinion, personal experience and anything of interest to young women. Buys 350 mss/year. Query with published clips or send complete ms. Length: 500-3,500 words. Pays expenses of writers on assignment.

Fiction: Betty Kelly. Condensed novels, humorous, novel excerpts, romance and original short stories with romantic plots. Buys 18 mss/year. Query. Length: 750-3,000 words.
Poetry: Free verse, light verse. Buys 30 poems/year. No maximum number. Length: 4-30 lines.
Fillers: Irene Copeland. Facts. Buys 240/year. Length: 300-1,000 words.

COUNTRY WOMAN, Reiman Publications, P.O. Box 643, Milwaukee WI 53201. (414)423-0100. Managing Editor: Kathy Pohl. 75-85% written by readers. Willing to work with new/unpublished writers. Bimonthly magazine on the interests of country women. "*Country Woman* is for contemporary rural women of all ages and backgrounds and from all over the US and Canada. It includes a sampling of the diversity that makes up rural women's lives—love of home, family, farm, ranch, community, hobbies, enduring values, humor, attaining new skills and appreciating present, past and future all within the context of the lifestyle that surrounds country living." Estab. 1970. **Pays on acceptance.** Byline given. Buys first North American serial, one-time and second serial (reprint) rights. Submit seasonal/holiday material 5 months in advance. Accepts previously published submissions (on occasion). Send typed ms with rights for sale noted and information about when and where the material previously appeared. Reprint payment varies. Reports in 2 months on queries; 3 months on mss. Sample copy for $2. Writer's guidelines for #10 SASE.
Nonfiction: General interest, historical/nostalgic, how-to (crafts, community projects, decorative, antiquing, etc.), humor, inspirational, interview/profile, personal experience, photo/feature packages profiling interesting country women—all pertaining to a rural woman's interest. Articles must be written in a positive, light and entertaining manner. Query. Length: 1,000 words maximum.
Photos: Send color photos with query or ms. Reviews 35mm or 2¼ transparencies or excellent-quality color prints. Uses only excellent quality color photos. No b&w. "We pay for photo/feature packages." Captions, model releases and identification of subjects required. Buys one-time rights.
Columns/Departments: Why Farm Wives Age Fast (humor), I Remember When (nostalgia) and Country Decorating. Buys 10-12 mss/year (maximum). Query or send complete ms. Length: 500-1,000 words. Pays $75-125.
Fiction: Main character *must* be a country woman. All fiction must have a country setting. Fiction must have a positive, upbeat message. Includes fiction in every issue. Would buy more fiction if stories suitable for our audience were sent our way. Query or send complete ms. Length: 750-1,000 words. Pays $90-125.
Poetry: Traditional, light verse. "Poetry must have rhythm and rhyme! It must be country-related. Always looking for seasonal poetry." Buys 30 poems/year. Submit maximum 6 poems. Length: 5-24 lines. Pays $10-25.
Tips: "We have recently broadened our focus to include 'country' women, not just women on farms and ranches. This allows freelancers a wider scope in material. Write as clearly and with as much zest and enthusiasm as possible. We love good quotes, supporting materials (names, places, etc.) and strong leads and closings. Readers relate strongly to where they live and the lifestyle they've chosen. They want to be informed and entertained, and that's just exactly why they subscribe. Readers are busy—not too busy to read—but when they do sit down, they want good writing, reliable information and something that feels like a reward. How-to, humor, personal experience and nostalgia are areas most open to freelancers. Profiles, to a certain degree, are also open. Be accurate and fresh in approach."

DAUGHTERS OF SARAH, The Magazine for Christian Feminists, Daughters of Sarah, 2121 Sheridan Rd., Evanston IL 60201. (708)866-3882. Editor: Elizabeth Anderson. Associate Editor: Cathi Falsani. 85% freelance written. Quarterly Christian feminist magazine published by women calling for justice, mutuality, and reconciliation in the church and the world. We are a forum for a wide variety of viewpoints that are both Christian and feminist." Estab. 1974. Circ. 5,000. Pays on publication. Publishes ms an average of 3-4 months after acceptance. Byline given. Buys first North American and one-time rights. Editorial lead time 3 months. Submit seasonal material 3 months in advance. Accepts previously published submissions. Send photocopy of article or short story or typed ms with rights for sale noted and information about when and where the article previously appeared. For reprints, pays 100% of the amount paid for an original article. Reports in 4 months. Sample copy for $4. Writer's guidelines for #10 SASE.
 • Upcoming themes include, Contemplative Life/Worship (fall 1995), Women and Money (winter 1996).
Nonfiction: Essays, exposé, general interest, historical/nostalgic, humor, inspirational, interview/profile, opinion, personal experience, religious. "We are a thematic magazine. Each issue focuses on a specific theme. It is essential to send for a theme list. We don't want to see anything *not* relating to women or women's issues and anything without Biblical or feminist perspective." Query. Length: 500-2,100 words. Pays $15/printed page minimum plus 2 copies.
Photos: Send photos with submission. Reviews 8 × 10 prints. Negotiates payment individually. Identification of subjects required. Buys one-time rights. Address art submissions to Emile Ferrris, art director.
Columns/Departments: Elizabeth Anderson, editor. Segue (feminist women in conservative/mainline churches), 800 words; Feminist Pilgrim (Biblical exegesis/theological discourse), 1,000 words; Women in Ministry (clergy women and lay women in ministry tell personal stories), 1,000 words. Buys 6 mss/year. Query. Pays $15-80.

Fiction: Confession, historical, humorous, religious. Buys 2 mss/year. Query. Length: 600-2,000 words. Pays $15-80.

Poetry: Free verse, light verse. Buys 6/year. Submit maximum 2 poems. Length: 4-50 lines. Pays $15-45.

Tips: "Query, query, query! Our writer's guidelines are very helpful and speak to specific areas (and pet peeves) that will help you get published in *Daughters of Sarah*. Use inclusive language. Use a personal approach and avoid 'preachy' academic-ese, and issues not relating to women, feminism and Christianity. Our nonfiction area is most open. My greatest advice is to send for our guidelines and themes and then please query first before sending a manuscript. Stick to issues relating to a specific theme."

ESSENCE, 1500 Broadway, New York NY 10036. (212)642-0600. Editor-in-Chief: Susan L. Taylor. Executive Editor: Linda Villarosa. Editor-at-Large: Valerie Wilson Wesley. Monthly magazine. Estab. 1970. Circ. 1 million. **Pays on acceptance.** Makes assignments on one-time serial rights basis. 3 month lead time. Pays 25% kill fee. Byline given. Submit seasonal/holiday material 6 months in advance. Accepts previously published submissions. Send tearsheet of article, information about when and where the article previously appeared. Pays 50% of the amount paid for an original article. Reports in 2 months. Sample copy for $2. Free writer's guidelines.

Nonfiction: Valerie Wilson Wesley. "We're looking for articles that inspire and inform Black women. The topics we include in each issue are provocative. Every article should move the *Essence* woman emotionally and intellectually. We welcome queries from good writers on a wide range of topics; general interest, health and fitness, historical, how-to, humor, self-help, relationships, work, personality interview, personal experience, political issues, business and finances, personal opinion." Buys 200 mss/year. Query only; word length will be given upon assignment. Pays $500 minimum. Also publishes novel and nonfiction book excerpts.

Photos: Janice Wheele, art director. State availability of photos with query. Pays $100 for b&w page; $300 for color page. Captions and model release required. "We particularly would like to see photographs for our travel section that feature Black travelers."

Columns/Departments: Query department editors: Contemporary Living (home, food, lifestyle, travel, consumer information): Corliss Hill and Cara Roberts Arts: Gordon Chambers; Health & Fitness: Tonya Adam; Travel: Cara Roberts. Query ;only; word length will be given upon assignment. Pays $100 minimum.

Tips: "Please note that *Essence* no longer accepts unsolicited mss for fiction, poetry or nonfiction, except for the Brothers, Windows, Back Talk and Interiors columns. So please only send query letters for nonfiction story ideas."

FAMILY CIRCLE MAGAZINE, 110 Fifth Ave., New York NY 10011. (212)463-1000. Fax: (212)463-1808. Editor-in-Chief: Susan Ungaro. 70% freelance written. Magazine published 17 times/year. Usually buys all print rights. Offers 20% kill fee. Byline given. **Pays on acceptance.** "We are a national women's magazine which offers advice, fresh information and entertaining features to women. Query should stress the unique aspects of an article and expert sources; we want articles that will help our readers or make a difference in how they live." Reports in 6 weeks.

Nonfiction: Nancy Clark, deputy editor. Women's interest subjects such as family and personal relationships, children, physical and mental health, nutrition, self-improvement and profiles of ordinary women doing extraordinary things for her community or the nation for 'Women Who Make a Difference' series. "We look for well-written, well-reported stories told through interesting anecdotes and insightful writing. We want well-researched service journalism on all subjects." Query. Length: 1,000-2,500 words. Pays $1/word.

Tips: "Query letters should be concise and to the point. Also, writers should keep close tabs on *Family Circle* and other women's magazines to avoid submitting recently run subject matter."

FIRST FOR WOMEN, Bauer Publishing Co., P.O. Box 1648, 270 Sylvan Ave., Englewood Cliffs NJ 07632. Magazine pubilshed every 3 weeks. Executive Editor. Teresa Hagen. Query before submitting. Feature sections more open to freelancers over service sections. "Be familiar with the magazine."

GLAMOUR, Condé Nast, 350 Madison Ave., New York NY 10017. (212)880-8800. Fax: (212)880-6922. E-mail: glamourmag@aol.com. Editor-in-Chief: Ruth Whitney. 75% freelance written. Works with a small number of new/unpublished writers each year. Monthly magazine for college-educated women, 18-35 years old. Estab. 1939. Circ. 2.3 million. **Pays on acceptance.** Offers 20% kill fee. Publishes ms an average of 1 year after acceptance. Byline given. Accepts previously published submissions. Send information about when and where the article previously appeared. For reprints, payment varies. Reports in 3 months. Writer's guidelines for #10 SASE.

 A bullet introduces comments by the editors of **Writer's Market** *indicating special information about the listing.*

Nonfiction: Pamela Erens, articles editor. "Editorial approach is 'how-to' with articles that are relevant in the areas of careers, health, psychology, interpersonal relationships, etc. We look for queries that are fresh and include a contemporary, timely angle. Fashion, beauty, travel, food and entertainment are all staff-written. We use 1,000-word opinion essays for our Viewpoint section. Our His/Hers column features generally stylish essays on relationships or comments on current mores by male and female writers in alternate months." Pays $1,000 for His/Hers mss; $500 for Viewpoint mss. Buys first North American serial rights. Buys 10-12 mss/ issue. Query "with letter that is detailed, well-focused, well-organized, and documented with surveys, statistics and research; personal essays excepted." Short articles and essays (1,500-2,000 words) pay $1,000 and up; longer mss (2,500-3,000 words) pay $1,500 minimum. Sometimes pays the expenses of writers on assignment.

Tips: "We're looking for sharply focused ideas by strong writers and are constantly raising our standards. We are interested in getting new writers, and we are approachable, mainly because our range of topics is so broad. We've increased our focus on male-female relationships."

GOOD HOUSEKEEPING, Hearst Corp., 959 Eighth Ave., New York NY 10019. (212)649-2000. Editor-in-Chief: Ellen Levine. Executive Editor: Janet Chan. Managing Editor: Sarah Scrymser. Prefers to work with published/established writers. Monthly magazine. Circ. 5 million. **Pays on acceptance.** Buys all rights. Pays 25% kill fee. Byline given. Submit seasonal/holiday material 6 months in advance. Reports in 6 weeks. *Writer's Market* recommends allowing 2 months for reply. Sample copy for $2. Writer's guidelines for #10 SASE.

Nonfiction: Joan Thursh, articles editor. Phyllis Levy, book editor. Shirley Howard, regional editor. Medical informational, investigative, inspirational, interview, nostalgia, personal experience, profile. Buys 4-6 mss/ issue. Query. Length: 1,500-2,500 words. Pays $1,500+ on acceptance for full articles from new writers. Pays $250-350 for local interest and travel pieces of 2,000 words. Pays the expenses of writers on assignment.

Photos: Herbert Bleiweiss, art director. Photos purchased on assignment mostly. Some short photo features with captions. Pays $100-350 for b&w; $200-400 for color photos. Query. Model releases required.

Columns/Departments: Light Housekeeping & Fillers, edited by Rosemary Leonard. Humorous short-short prose and verse. Jokes, gags, anecdotes. Pays $25-50. The Better Way, edited by Erika Mark. Ideas and in-depth research. Query. Pays $250-500. "Mostly staff written; only outstanding ideas have a chance here."

Fiction: Lee Quarfoot, fiction editor. Uses romance fiction and condensations of novels that can appear in one issue. Looks for reader identification. "We get 1,500 unsolicited mss/month—includes poetry; a freelancer's odds are overwhelming—but we do look at all submissions." Send complete mss. Manuscripts will not be returned. Only responds on acceptance. Length: 1,500 words (short-shorts); novel according to merit of material; average 5,000-word short stories. Pays $1,000 minimum for fiction short-shorts; $1,250 for short stories.

Poetry: Arleen Quarfoot, poetry editor. Light verse and traditional. "Presently overstocked." Poems used as fillers. Pays $5/line for poetry on acceptance.

Tips: "Always send a SASE. We prefer to see a query first. Do not send material on subjects already covered in-house by the Good Housekeeping Institute—these include food, beauty, needlework and crafts."

‡HORIZONS, Women's News & Feminist Views, Horizons Inc., P.O. Box 128 Station Main, Winnipeg, Manitoba B3C 2G1 Canada. (204)779-3665. Coordinating Editor: Penni Mitchell. 50% freelance written. Quarterly magazine covering women's issues. Estab. 1991. Circ. 4,000. Pays on publication. Publishes ms an average of 2-3 months after acceptance. Byline given. Buys second serial (reprint) rights. Editorial lead time 3 months. Query for electronic submissions. Sample copy $5.50. Writer's guidelines for #10 SAE and IRC.

Nonfiction: Interview/profile, opinion, personal experience. Query. Length: 600-2,000 words. Pays $100-300.

Photos: State availability of photos with submission. Offers $25-50/photo. Captions required. Buys one-time rights.

Columns/Departments: Query. Pays $100-200.

LADIES' HOME JOURNAL, Meredith Corporation, 100 Park Ave., New York NY 10017-5516. (212)953-7070. Publishing Director and Editor-in-Chief: Myrna Blyth. 50% freelance written. Monthly magazine focusing on issues of concern to women. Circ. 5 million. **Pays on acceptance.** Offers 25% kill fee. Rights bought vary with submission. Reports on queries within 3 months with SASE. Writer's guidelines for #10 SASE, attention: writer's guidelines.

Nonfiction: Submissions on the following subjects should be directed to the editor listed for each: investigative reports, news-related features, psychology/relationships/sex (Pam O'Brien, features editor); medical/ health (Deborah Pike, health editor); celebrities/entertainment (Melanie Gerasa, entertainment editor); travel stories (Sharlene Johnson, associate editor). Query with published clips. Length: 1,500-3,000 words. Fees vary. Pays expenses of writers on assignment.

Photos: State availability of photos with submission. Offers variable payment for photos accepted with ms. Captions, model releases and identification of subjects required. Rights bought vary with submission. (*LHJ* arranges for its own photography almost all the time.)
Columns/Departments: Query the following editor or box for column ideas. A Woman Today (Box WT); Woman to Woman (Box WW); Parents' Journal (Mary Mohler, senior editor); Pet News (Shana Aborn, associate features editor).
Fiction: Mary Mohler, editor, books and fiction. Only short stories and novels submitted by an agent or publisher will be considered. Buys 12 mss/year. Does not accept poetry of any kind.

McCALL'S, 110 Fifth Ave., New York NY 10011-5603. (212)463-1000. Editor: Sally Koslow. Executive Editor: Cathy Cavender. 90% freelance written. "Study recent issues. Our publication carefully and conscientiously serves the needs of the woman reader—concentrating on matters that directly affect her life and offering information and understanding on subjects of personal importance to her." Monthly. Circ. 5 million. **Pays on acceptance.** Publishes ms an average of 6 months after acceptance. Offers 20% kill fee. Byline given. Buys exclusive or First North American rights. Reports in 2 months. Writer's guidelines for #10 SASE.
Nonfiction: The editors are seeking meaningful stories of personal experience, fresh slants for self-help and relationship pieces, and well-researched action-oriented articles and narratives dealing with social problems concerning readers. Topics must have broad appeal, but they must be approached in a fresh, new, you-haven't-read-this-elsewhere way. *McCall's* buys 200-300 articles/year, many in the 1,500-2,000-word length. Pays variable rates for nonfiction. These are on subjects of interest to women: health, personal narratives, celebrity biographies and autobiographies, etc. Almost all features on food, fashion, beauty and decorating are staff-written. Sometimes pays the expenses of writers on assignment.
Tips: Query first. Use the tone and format of our most recent issues as your guide. Preferred length: 1,500-2,000 words. Address submissions to executive editor unless otherwise specified.

MADEMOISELLE, Condé Nast, 350 Madison Ave., New York NY 10017. Managing Editor: Faye Haun. Contact: Katherine Brown Weissman, executive editor. 95% freelance written. Prefers to work with published/established writers. Columns are written by columnists; "sometimes we give new writers a 'chance' on shorter, less complex assignments." Monthly magazine for women age 21-31. Circ 1.2 million. Buys first North American serial rights. **Pays on acceptance**; rates vary.
Nonfiction: Particular concentration on articles of interest to the intelligent young woman, including personal relationships, health, careers, trends, and current social problems. Send health queries to Dana Points, associate editor. Send entertainment queries to Jeanie Pyun, entertainment editor. Query with published clips and SAE. Length: 1,000 words.
Photos: Cindy Searight, art director. Commissioned work assigned according to needs. Photos of fashion, beauty, travel. Payment ranges from no-charge to an agreed rate of payment per shot, job series or page rate. Buys all rights. Pays on publication for photos.
Tips: "We are looking for timely, well-researched manuscripts."

MIRABELLA, Hachette Filipacchi, 1633 Broadway, New York NY 10019. Monthly publication covering fashion and culture. This magazine was recently sold. Query before submitting.

MODERN BRIDE, 249 W. 17th St., New York NY 10011. (212)337-7096. Editor: Cele Lalli. Executive Editor: Mary Ann Cavlin. **Pays on acceptance.** Offers 25% kill fee. Buys first periodical rights. Accepts previously published submissions. Reports in 1 month.
Nonfiction: Book excerpts, general interest, how-to, personal experience. Buys 60 mss/year. Query with published clips. Length: 500-2,000 words. Pays $600-1,200.
Columns/Departments: Geri Bain, editor. Travel.
Poetry: Free verse, light verse and traditional. Buys very few. Submit maximum 6 poems.

PLAYGIRL, 801 Second Ave., New York NY 10017. (212)661-7878. Editor-in-Chief: Laurie Sue Brockway. Contact: Judy Cole, managing editor. 75% freelance written. Prefers to work with published/established writers. Monthly entertainment magazine for 18- to 55-year-old females. Circ. 500,000. Average issue 3 articles; 1 celebrity interview. Pays within 6 weeks of acceptance. Publishes ms an average of 3 months after acceptance. Byline given. Offers 20% kill fee. Buys all rights. Submit seasonal material 6 months in advance. Accepts simultaneous submissions, if so indicated. Reports in 1 month on queries; 3 months on mss. Writer's guidelines for #10 SASE.
Nonfiction: Humor for the modern woman/man, exposés (related to women's issues), interview (Q&A format with major show business celebrities), articles on sexuality, medical breakthroughs, relationships, coping, careers, insightful, lively articles on current issues, investigative pieces particularly geared to *Playgirl*. Buys 6 mss/issue. Query with clips of previously published work. Length: 1,000-2,500 words. Pays $300-1,000. Sometimes pays the expenses of writers on assignment.
Tips: "Best bets for first-time writers: Men's Room/Women's Room (humor) and Fantasy Forum. No phone calls please."

RADIANCE, The Magazine for Large Women, Box 30246, Oakland CA 94604. (510)482-0680. Editor: Alice Ansfield. 95% freelance written. Quarterly magazine "that encourages and supports women *all* sizes of large to live fully now, to stop putting their lives on hold until they lose weight." Estab. 1984. Circ. 10,000. Pays on publication. Publishes ms an average of 10 months after acceptance. Byline given. Offers $25 kill fee. Buys one-time and second serial (reprint) rights. Submit seasonal/holiday material at least 8-10 months in advance. Accepts previously published submissions. Query for electronic submissions. Reports in 4 months. Sample copy for $3.50. Writer's guidelines for #10 SASE.

Nonfiction: Book excerpts (related to large women), essays, exposé, general interest, historical/nostalgic, how-to (on health/well-being/fashion/fitness, etc.), humor, inspirational, interview/profile, opinion, personal experience, photo feature, travel. "No diet successes or articles condemning people for being fat." Query with published clips. Length: 1,000-2,500 words. Pays $35-100. Sometimes pays writers with contributor copies or other premiums.

Photos: State availability of photos with submission. Offers $15-50/photo. Captions and identification of subjects preferred. Buys one-time rights.

Columns/Departments: Up Front and Personal (personal profiles of women from all areas of life); Health and Well-Being (physical/emotional well-being, self care, research); Expressions (features on artists who celebrate the full female figure); Images (designer interviews, color/style/fashion, features); Inner Journeys (spirituality, personal experiences, interviews); Perspectives (cultural and political aspects of being in a larger body); and On the Move (women active in all kinds of sports, physical activities) and Travel. Buys 60 mss/ year. Query with published clips. Length: 1,000-2,500 words. Pays $50-100.

Fiction: Condensed novels, ethnic, fantasy, historical, humorous, mainstream, novel excerpts, romance, science fiction, serialized novels, slice-of-life vignettes relating somehow to large women. "No woman-hates-self-till-meets-man'-type fiction!" Buys 15 mss/year. Query with published clips. Length: 800-1,500 words. Pays $35-100.

Poetry: Reflective, empowering, experiential. Related to women's feelings and experience, re: their bodies, self-esteem, acceptance. Buys 30 poems/year. Length: 4-45 lines. Pays $10-30.

Tips: "We welcome talented, sensitive, responsible, open-minded writers. We profile women from all walks of life who are all sizes of large, of all ages and from all ethnic groups and lifestyles. We welcome writers' ideas on interesting large women from across the US and abroad. We're an open, light-hearted magazine that's working to help women feel good about themselves now, whatever their body size. *Radiance* is one of the major forces working for size acceptance. We want articles to address all areas of vital importance in women's lives. Please read a copy of *Radiance* before writing for us."

REDBOOK MAGAZINE, 224 W. 57th St., New York NY 10019. Senior Editors: Harriet Lyons and Toni Gerber Hope. Health Editor: Toni Hope. Fiction Editor: Dawn Raffel. Contact: Any of editorial assistants listed on masthead. 90% freelance written. Monthly magazine. Estab. 1903. Circ. 3.2 million. **Pays on acceptance.** Publishes ms an average of 4-6 months after acceptance. Rights purchased vary with author and material. Reports in 3 months. Writer's guidelines for #10 SASE.

Nonfiction: "*Redbook* addresses young mothers between the ages of 25 and 44. Most of our readers are married with children 12 and under; over 60 percent work outside the home. The articles entertain, educate and inspire our readers to confront challenging issues. Each article must be timely and relevant to *Redbook* readers' lives. Article subjects of interest: social issues, parenting, sex, marriage, news profiles, true crime, dramatic narratives, money, psychology, health. Please enclose sample of previously published work with articles or unsolicited manuscripts. Length: articles, 2,500-3,000 words; short articles, 1,000-1,500 words.

Columns/Departments: "We are interested in stories for the 'A Mother's Story' series offering the dramatic retelling of an experience involving you, your husband or child. (Also done "as told to.") For each 1,500-2,000 words accepted for publication as A Mother's Story, we pay $750. Manuscripts accompanied by a 9×12 SASE, must be signed, and mailed to: A Mother's Story, c/o *Redbook Magazine*. Reports in 6 months. We also need stories for the back page 'Happy Endings' column, stories of about 800 words that, just as the title suggests, end happily. See past issues for samples."

Fiction: "Of the 20,000 unsolicited manuscripts that we receive annually, we buy about 10 or more stories/ year. We also find many more stories that are not necessarily suited to our needs but are good enough to warrant our encouraging the author to send others. *Redbook* looks for fresh, well-crafted stories that reflect some aspect of the experiences and interests of our readers; it's a good idea to read several issues to get a feel for what we buy. No unsolicited novels or novellas, please." Payment begins at $1,000 for short stories.

Tips: "Shorter, front-of-the-book features are usually easier to develop with first-time contributors, especially A Mother's Story and Happy Endings. We also buy short takes (250 words) for our You & Your Child opening page—succinct, charming advice-driven items. Most *Redbook* articles require solid research, well-developed anecdotes from on-the-record sources, and fresh, insightful quotes from established experts in a field that pass our 'reality check' test."

REVIEW, A Publication of North American Benefit Association, 1338 Military St., P.O. Box 5020, Port Huron MI 48061-5020. (313)985-5191, ext. 29. Fax: (810)985-6970. Editor: Janice U. Whipple. Director of Communications: Patricia J. Samar. 30% freelance written. Works only with published/established writers. Quarterly magazine published for NABA's primarily women-membership to help them care for themselves and their families. Estab. 1892. Circ. 36,000. Pays on publication. Publishes ms an average of 1 year after acceptance. Byline given. Not copyrighted. Buys one-time, simultaneous and second serial (reprint) rights. Submit seasonal/holiday material 6 months in advance. Accepts simultaneous and previously published submissions. Send photocopy of article or send typed ms with rights for sale noted and information about when and where ms previously appeared. For reprints, pays 15% of the amount paid for an original article. Reports in 1 year (usually less). Sample copy for 9×12 SAE with 4 first-class stamps. Writer's guidelines for #10 SASE.

Nonfiction: The cover of this publication states: "Key Information Vital to Every Woman's Fiscal and Physical Health." Looking primarily for general interest stories for women aged 25-44 regarding physical, mental and emotional health and fitness; and financial/fiscal health and fitness. "We would like to see more creative financial pieces that are directed at women. Also interested in creative interesting stories about marketing life insurance and annuities to the women's market." Buys 4-10 mss/year. Send complete ms. Length: 1,000-2,000 words. Pays $150-500/ms.

Photos: Not interested in photos at this time, unless accompanied by a ms. Model release and identification of subjects required.

Tips: "We have begun more clearly defining the focus of our magazine. We receive FAR TOO MANY stories from people who clearly ignore the information this listing and/or our writer's guidelines. No more stories about Tippy the Spotted Pig, please!"

SAGEWOMAN, Celebrating the Goddess in Every Woman, P.O. Box 641, Point Arena CA 95468. (707)882-2052. Fax: (707)882-2793. Editor: Anne Newkirk Niven. 60% freelance written. Quarterly consumer magazine covering Goddess spirituality. "*SageWoman* is a quarterly magazine of women's spirituality. Our readers are people (primarily but not exclusively women) who identify positively with the term 'Goddess.' This does not mean that they are necessarily self-identified Goddess worshippers, Pagans, or Wiccans, although a majority of our readers would probably be comfortable with those terms. Our readers include women of a variety of religious faiths, ranging from Roman Catholic to Lesbian Separatist Witch and everywhere in between. The majority of every issue is created from the contributions of our readers, so your creativity and willingness to share is vital to *SageWoman*'s existence!" Estab. 1988. Circ. 12,000. Pays on publication. Publishes ms an average of 3 months after acceptance. Byline given. Offers 100% kill fee. Buys first North American serial rights and second serial (reprint) rights. Editorial lead time 5 months. Submit seasonal material 5 months in advance. Query for electronic submissions. Reports in 2 weeks on queries; 1 month on mss. Sample copy for $6. Writer's guidelines free on request.

Nonfiction: Book excerpts, essays, personal experience, religious. "No material not related to our subject matter. We do not publish fiction, or poetry." Buys 50 mss/year. Query with published clips. Length: 200-6,000 words. Pays $20 minimum for assigned articles, $5 minimum for unsolicited articles. Sometimes pays expenses of writers on assignment.

Photos: State availability of photos with submission. Reviews contact sheets and any size prints. Offers $5-20/photo. Model releases required. Buys one-time rights.

Tips: "Send for a sample copy first—our subject matter is very specific and if we are not on the same path, submitting material will be a waste of energy and time. Writers should ask about upcoming themes."

TODAY'S CHRISTIAN WOMAN, 465 Gundersen Dr., Carol Stream IL 60188-2498. (708)260-6200. Fax: (708)260-0114. E-mail: tcwedit@aol.com. Queries only. Editor: Ramona Cramer Tucker. Assistant Editor: Camerin Courtney. 25% freelance written. Works with a small number of new/unpublished writers each year. Bimonthly magazine for Christian women of all ages, single and married, homemakers and career women. Estab. 1979. Circ. 408,000. **Pays on acceptance.** Publishes ms an average of 6 months after acceptance. Byline given. Buys first rights only. Submit seasonal/holiday material 9 months in advance. Reports in 2 months. Sample copy for $5. Writer's guidelines for #10 SASE.

Nonfiction: How-to, narrative, inspirational. Query only; no unsolicited mss. "The query should include article summary, purpose and reader value, author's qualifications, suggested length and date to send. Pays 15¢/word.

Tips: "Articles focus on the following relationships: marriage, parenting, self, spiritual life and friendship. All articles should be highly anecdotal, personal in tone, and universal in appeal."

VANITY FAIR, Condé Nast, 350 Madison Ave., New York NY 10017. Monthly publication covering contemporary culture. Call Editorial Department first to explain nature of work. All submissions must include SASE. Don't send photos. No longer publishes fiction or poetry. Features sections usually have assigned writers. "Be familiar with editorial content of magazine."

VICTORIA, Hearst Corp., 224 W. 57th St., New York NY 10019. "Specialized copywriting needs and visual nature of this magazine make it an unsuitable candidate for freelance submissions."

VOGUE, Condé Nast, 350 Madison Ave., New York NY 10017. Managing Editor: Laurie Jones. Monthly publication covering style, fashion and current culture. Query with résumés and/or published clips. Call for guidelines.

WEST COAST WOMAN, LMB Media, Inc., P.O. Box 819, Sarasota FL 34230-0819. (813)954-3300. Fax: (813)954-3300. Editor: Louise Bruderle. 50% freelance written. Monthly tabloid for women on the west coast of Florida. "*West Coast Woman* is a lifestyle publication." Estab. 1988. Circ. 30,000. Pays on publication. Byline given. Offers 50% kill fee. Buys first or one-time rights. Submit seasonal/holiday material 2 months in advance. Sample copy for $3.50. Writer's guidelines for #10 SASE.
  • *West Coast Woman* is focusing less on fashion, beauty, women-only editorial, and more on first-person stories.
Nonfiction: Real estate, gardening, how-to, health, beauty, book reviews, seniors, car care, home design, fitness, photo feature, technical, travel, sports, fashion, money/finance, nutrition, cooking, food/wine. No humor, slice-of-life, essays, poems, poetry or comics/cartoons." Buys 130 mss/year. Query with published clips. Length: 750-3,000 words. Pays $35-65 for 750 words. Also makes ad trades for promotional tie-ins.
Photos: State availability of photos with submission. Reviews contact sheets, 35mm transparencies. Model releases required. Buys one-time rights.
Columns/Departments: Money/Finance. Buys 130 mss/year. Query with published clips. Length: 750-3,000 words. Pays $35-65 for 750 words.

WOMAN, Woman's Magazine Network of Connecticut, Inc., (formerly *Fairfield County Woman*), 15 Bank St., Stamford CT 06901. (203)323-3105. Fax: (203)323-4112. Editor: Rita Papazian. 75% freelance written. A women's regional monthly tabloid focusing on careers, education, health, relationships and family life. Connecticut writers and Connecticut stories of interest to women only. Intern opportunities available. Estab. 1982. Circ. 65,000. Pays 60 days after publication. Byline given. Buys first rights. Submit seasonal/holiday material 3 months in advance. Query for electronic submissions. Reports in 6 months. Sample copy for 10×13 SAE with 6 first-class stamps.
  • *Woman* only publishes Connecticut writers.
Nonfiction: Essays, how-to, humor, local interview/profile. Buys 50 mss/year. Query with published clips. Length: 800-2,000 words. Pays $35-100 for assigned articles; $25-75 for unsolicited articles. Sometimes pays expenses of writers on assignment.
Photos: State availability of photos with submission. Reviews 5×7 prints. Offers no additional payment with ms. Buys one-time rights.

WOMAN'S DAY, 1633 Broadway, New York NY 10019. (212)767-6000. Senior Articles Editor: Rebecca Greer. 75% or more of articles freelance written. 17 issues/year. Circ. 6 million. Pays negotiable kill fee. Byline given. **Pays on acceptance.** Reports in 1 month or less on queries. Submit detailed queries.
Nonfiction: Uses articles on all subjects of interest to women—marriage, family life, childrearing, education, homemaking, money management, careers, family health, work and leisure activities. Also interested in fresh, dramatic narratives of women's lives and concerns. "These must be lively and fascinating to read." Length: 500-2,500 words, depending on material. Payment varies depending on length, type, writer, and whether it's for regional or national use, but rates are high. Pays the expenses of writers on confirmed assignment. "We no longer accept unsolicited manuscripts—and can not return or be responsible for those that are sent to us."
Fillers: Neighbors columns also pay $75/each for brief practical suggestions on homemaking, childrearing and relationships. Address to the editor of the section.
Tips: "Our primary need is for ideas with broad appeal that can be featured on the cover. We're buying more short pieces. Writers should consider Quick section which uses factual pieces of 100-300 words."

THE WOMAN'S JOURNAL, 3 Sisters' Press, Inc., P.O. Box 156, Beaverton OR 97075-0156. Editor: Wendy Waller Heromin. 90% freelance written. Monthly tabloid covering professional women's issues. "We are a regional publication for professional women who are seeking career advancement, sideline money-making opportunities and/or are in business for themselves. We focus on success stories. Other topics include health and fitness, home and garden, book reviews, family issues." Estab. 1986. Circ. 10,000. Pays on publication. Publishes ms an average of 2 months after acceptance. Byline given. Buys first North American serial rights. Editorial lead time 2 months. Submit seasonal material 3 months in advance. Accepts simultaneous submissions. Reports in 1 month on queries. Sample copy for 11×17 SAE with 3 first-class stamps. Writer's guidelines for #10 SASE.
Nonfiction: Humor, interview/profile, opinion (on women's issues), photo feature, travel. Buys 120 mss/year. Query with published clips or send complete ms. Length: 250-500 words. Pays 3-4¢/word for assigned articles; 2-3¢/word for unsolicited articles. Sometimes pays expenses of writers on assignment.
Photos: Send photos with submission. Reviews 4×5 prints. Negotiates payment individually. Captions, model releases, identification of subjects required. Buys one-time rights or all rights.
Columns/Departments: Contact: Dianne Perry. "Women's Eye View" (short personal opinion piece on any topic of interest to women), 500 words; Guest editorial (discuss policies, issues or recent news developments that affect women), 500 words; Book Reviews (books that touch on topics ranging from health, wealth, relationships to travel), 500 words. Buys 40 mss/year. Send complete ms. Pays $15-25.
Tips: "We are looking for crisp, professional stories with heart. Our publication strives to enrich thought, show new possibilities and remove self-imposed limitations, without being sentimental or dipping into pop-

psychology. Submit stories which support our approach. Send clips or manuscript and SASE. No telephone calls, please. We need material on career and finance, success stories of side-line businesses and at-home businesses and contributors for our 'Woman's Eye View' column. We welcome and encourage new writers."

WOMAN'S WORLD, The Woman's Weekly, Heinrich Bauer North America Inc., 270 Sylvan Ave., Englewood Cliffs NJ 07632. Fax: (201)569-3584. Editor-in-Chief: Stephanie Saible. 95% freelance written. Weekly magazine covering "human interest and service pieces of interest to family-oriented women across the nation." **Pays on acceptance.** Publishes ms an average of 4 months after acceptance. Buys first North American serial rights for 6 months. Submit seasonal/holiday material 4 months in advance. Reports in 6 weeks on queries; 2 months on mss. Writer's guidelines for #10 SASE.

Nonfiction: Dramatic personal women's stories and articles on self-improvement, medicine and health topics; pays $500 for 1,000 words. Features include Emergency (real life drama); My Story; Turning Point (in a woman's life); One Woman's Battle; Happy Ending; Women Are Talking About (topics readers can relate to); Relationships (pop psychology or coping). Queries to Andrea Florczak.

Fiction: Jeanne Muchnick, fiction editor. Short story, romance and mainstream of 1,900 words and mini-mysteries of 1,200 words. "Each of our stories has a light romantic theme with a protagonist no older than 40. Each can be written from either a masculine or feminine point of view. Women characters may be single, married or divorced. Plots must be fast moving with vivid dialogue and action. The problems and dilemmas inherent in them should be contemporary and realistic, handled with warmth and feeling. The stories must have a positive resolution." Not interested in science fiction, fantasy, historical romance or foreign locales. No explicit sex, graphic language or seamy settings. Specify "short story" on envelope. Always enclose SASE. Reports in 2 months. No phone queries. Pays $1,000 on acceptance for North American serial rights for 6 months. "The 1,200 word mini-mysteries may feature either a 'whodunnit' or 'howdunnit' theme. The mystery may revolve around anything from a theft to murder. However, we are not interested in sordid or grotesque crimes. Emphasis should be on intricacies of plot rather than gratuitous violence. The story must include a resolution that clearly states the villain is getting his or her come-uppance." Submit complete mss. Specify "mini mystery" on envelope. Enclose SASE. Stories slanted for a particular holiday should be sent at least 6 months in advance. No phone queries.

Tips: "Come up with good queries. Short queries are best. We have a strong emphasis on well-researched material. Writers must send research with ms including book references and phone numbers for double checking. The most frequent mistakes made by writers in completing an article for us are sloppy, incomplete research, not writing to the format, and not studying the magazine carefully enough beforehand."

WOMEN'S CIRCLE, P.O. Box 299, Lynnfield MA 01940-0299. Editor: Marjorie Pearl. 100% freelance written. Bimonthly magazine for women of all ages. Usually buys first rights for ms. Buys all rights for craft and needlework projects. **Pays on acceptance.** Byline given. Publishes ms an average of 6-12 months after acceptance. Submit seasonal material 8 months in advance. Reports in 3 months. Sample copy for $2. Writer's guidelines for #10 SASE.

● *Women's Circle* does not use fiction or poetry.

Nonfiction: Especially interested in stories about successful, home-based female entrepreneurs with b&w photos or transparencies. Length: 1,000-2,000 words. Also interesting and unusual money-making ideas. Welcomes good quality crafts, needlework, how-to directions in any media—crochet, fabric, etc.

‡YOU, Family Communications, 37 Hanna Ave., Suite #1, Toronto Ontario M6K 1X1 Canada. (416)537-2604. Editor: Bettie Bradley. Contact: Shirley-Anne Ohannessian. 15% freelance written. Quarterly magazine covering health, food, beauty. "*You* magazine's editorial focus is on health, food, beauty with a 'how to' improve yourself slant. Articles are helpful and upbeat." Estab. 1982. Circ. 225,000. **Pays on acceptance.** Publishes ms an average of 6-12 months after acceptance. Byline given. Buys first rights. Editorial lead time 6 months. Submit seasonal material 6 months in advance. Reports in 1 month on queries. Sample copy for #10 SASE.

Nonfiction: General interest, how-to (improve oneself physically, mentally, emotionally), humor. Buys 12-15 mss/year. Query. Length: 800-1,2000 words. Pays $250.

Photos: State availability of photos with submission. Negotiates payment individually. Identification of subjects required. Buys one-time rights.

Columns/Departments: Male Point of View (male-authored opinion feature), 1,000 words. Buys 4 mss/year. Query. Pays $250.

Consumer Magazines/Changes '95-'96

The following consumer publications were listed in the 1995 edition but do not have listings in this edition. The majority did not respond to our request to update their listings. If a reason was given for their exclusion, we have included it in parentheses after the listing.

A Better Life for You
A Positive Approach
AAA World
Aboard Magazine
Aboriginal Science Fiction
Accent
Affaire de Coeur
African Continent News
African-American Heritage
Alabama Heritage
Alberta Farm & Ranch
Alive!
Amazing Computing
Amazing Stories (ceased publication)
America
American Citizen Italian Press
American Collector's Journal
American Farriers Journal (removed by request)
American Photo
Amoco Traveler
Ancestry Journal
Antiques & Auction News
Ararat (unable to contact)
Archipelago
Asia-Pacific Defense Forum
Audience
Baby Connection News Journal
Baja Times (ceased publication)
Bam
Banjo Newsletter
Beacon Magazine (no freelance)
Berkshire Magazine
Better Health
Biblical Illustrator
BK News
Blackjack Forum
Block Island Magazine & Travel Guide
Borealis
Boston Business Journal
Bow & Arrow Hunting
Bowhunting World
Bowlers Journal
Bridal Trends
Business
Business New Hampshire
California Bicyclist
Campus Life
Canadian West (ceased publication)
Career Pilot
Careers & Colleges
Caribbean Digest
Caribbean Sports & Travel
Casino Player
CD-ROM Reporter
Centerstage
Changes (ceased publication)
Charlotte Magazine
Chesapeake Bay Magazine
Chevy Outdoors
Chicago Studies

Chicago Tribune travel section
Child Stars
Christian Century
Christian Reader
Christian Response
Christian Social Action
Christianity Today
Cineaste
Civil War Times Illustrated
Classic Car Digest (unable to contact)
Classical Music
Clubhouse
Clubmex
Colaborer
Collector's Sportslook
College Monthly (unable to contact)
Comedy Magazine
Comments
Corporate Cleveland
Crafts Magazine
Crafts 'n' Things
Craftworks
Creative Woodworks & Crafts
Crime Prevention
Crochet Fantasy
Cross Stitch Sampler (ceased publication)
Crosswalk
Cruising World
Current World Leaders
Dallas Life (ceased publication)
Darkroom & Creative Camera Techniques
Destination Discovery (unable to contact)
Detroit Monthly
The Diamond
Dirt Rag
Discovery YMCA (removed by request)
Diver
Divorced Parents X-Change
The Door
Drummer
Earthkeeper
East Bay Monthly
Economic Monitor
Edges
Emerge
Environment
Episcopal Life
European Car
Family Living
Fangoria
Fiberfest
Fifty-Something
Film Quarterly
The Fisherman
Fishing World
Florida Travel & Life
Flying
Folio Weekly

Fordham Magazine (no freelance)
France Today
Freedom (no longer pays)
Fury
Futurific
Genealogical Computing
Gibbons-Humms Guide
Golf Digest
Grand Rapids Magazine
Great Expeditions
Gulf Coast Fisherman
Gulf Coast Golfer
Gun World
Guns
Heart Dance (no longer pays)
High Society Magazine
Hinduism Today
Hispanic Business
Home & Studio Recording (now Recording)
Home Office Opportunities
Homes
Houston Life
Ideals
In Context
Inland Sea
Inner-View
Inside Texas Running
Insider
International Examiner
Int'l Gymnast
Island Life
Jet Sports
Jewish News of Greater Phoenix
Jewish Weekly News
Joe Bob Report
Juggler's World
Junior Trails
Ladies' Home Journal Parent's Digest
Leisureways
Linchpin
Loose Change
Lottoworld
Lotus
Lutheran Forum
MacLine
Magazine for Christian Youth (ceased publication)
Mail Call
Manuscripts
Marine Corps Gazette
Maryland
Media History Digest
Metro
Metro Singles Lifestyles
Metro Sports
Metropolis
Michigan Living
Micropendium
Mid-Atlantic Country
Midstream
Military Lifestyle (ceased publication)

Minneapolis St. Paul Magazine
Miraculous Medal
Mississippi Magazine
Mississippi Rag
Mississippi State Alumnus
Missouri Magazine
Monarchy Canada
Mondo 2000
Mopar Muscle
Motor Trend
Motorhome
Motorland
Mountain States Collector
Ms.
Muir's Original Log Home Guide
Muscle Mag International
Mustang Monthly
Muzzleloader
Mystic Traveler
Nation's Business
National Christian Reporter
National Review (removed by request)
Nautilus (removed by request)
New Haven Advocate
New Jersey Outdoors
New Living
New Woman
Night Owl's Newsletter
Noah's Ark
North Texas Golfer
North-South
Northwest Airlines World Traveler (unable to contact)
Norway At Your Service
Nostalgia
Novascope
Now and Then
Numismatist
Ocean State Traveler (removed by request)
Old Mill News
Old West
On the Scene
On Track (unable to contact)
One Shot (ceased publication)
Open Wheel
Oregon Business
Oregon Stater
Ottawa Magazine
Outdoor America
Outdoor Life
Overseas!
Pacific Northwest (ceased publication)
Paintworks
Palm Beach Illustrated
Palm Springs Life
Pandora
Paper Collectors Marketplace
Parent Care
PCM
Pediatrics for Parents
Pen and Quill
Penn Stater
Pennsylvania Angler

Pentecostal Evangel
Peoplenet
Performing Arts
Pet Focus
Pets
Phoenix
Plumpers & Big Women
Polish American Journal
Polo
Poor Katy's Almanac (no longer pays)
Postcard Collector
Pragmatist
Profit
Proscenium
Public
Publish
Pulse!
Queen of All Hearts
Queen's Mystery Magazine, Ellery
Quick & Easy Crafts
Quick 'n Easy Country Cooking
Quilt World
Quilting International
Racquet
Reader's Review
Regardies (ceased publication)
The Reporter
Retired Officer
Rhode Island Monthly
Rugby
Sailing World
San Diego Home/Garden Lifestyles
San Francisco Bay Guardian
San Gabriel Valley Magazine
Satellite Orbit
Scorecard (no freelance)
Scott Stamp Monthly
Screw
Sea
Sea's Waterfront Northwest News
$ensible Sound
Shipmate
Singlelife
Sisters Today
Slo-Pitch News
Smartkids
Snowboarder
Snowy Egret
Soap Opera Update
Soccer America
Social Justice Review
South Florida Parenting
Speakers Idea File (removed by request)
Spin-Off
Spirit
Sport Fishing
Sporting News (no freelance)
Sports International
Sproutletter
Spur
Star*Line
STL (no freelance)

Student Leadership Journal
Sugah
Super Cycle
Tallahassee
Team Penning USA
Technology Review
'Teen
Teen Dream
Texas Alcalde (removed by request for 1 year)
Texas Bicyclist
Theater of Blood
This People
Threads
3-2-1 Contact (no freelance)
Today's Times
Total Health
Tradition
Travel America
Travel News
Travel Smart
Treasure
Trumpeter
Tucson Lifestyle
UFO
United Methodist Reporter
Vegetarian Journal
Vermont Times
Videomania
Vikinship
Virginia Cavalcade
Vista
Washington Flyer
Washington Monthly
Washington Post Magazine
Water Skier
Waterfront News
Weekend Woodcrafts
Western & Eastern Treasures
Western People
Western Producer
Western Tales
Wildlife Art News
Wilson Quarterly
Windy City Sports
Winning!
Wisconsin Trails
Women & Guns
Women With Wheels (no longer pays)
Wonderful West Virginia
Woodmen (no freelance)
Worcester Magazine
Working at Home
World Coin News (no freelance)
World Policy Journal
WPI Journal
Yesterday's Magazette
Yesteryear
You!
Young Scholar
Your Home
Youth Soccer News
Zoo Life (ceased publication)

Trade, Technical and Professional Journals......681

Trade, Technical and Professional Journals

Many writers who pick up a *Writer's Market* for the first time do so with the hope of selling an article or story to one of the popular, high-profile consumer magazines likely to be found on newsstands and in bookstores. Many of those writers are surprised to find an entire world of magazine publishing that exists outside the realm of commercial magazines and that they may have never known about—trade journals. Writers who *have* discovered trade journals have found a market that offers the chance to publish regularly in subject areas they find interesting, editors who are typically more accessible than their commercial counterparts and pay rates that rival those of the big-name magazines.

Trade journal is the general term for any publication focusing on a particular occupation or industry. Other terms used to describe the different types of trade publications are business, technical and professional journals. They are read by truck drivers, brick layers, farmers, commercial fishermen, heart surgeons—let's not forget butchers, bakers, and candlestick makers—and just about everyone else working in a trade or profession. Trade periodicals are sharply angled to the specifics of the professions they report on. They offer business-related news, features and service articles that will foster their readers' professional development. A surgeon reads *Cardiology World News* to keep up with developments in cardiac disease and treatment. Readers of *Roofer Magazine* are looking for the latest news and information about the roofing industry.

Trade magazine editors tell us their readers are a knowledgeable and highly interested audience. Writers for trade magazines have to either possess knowledge about the field in question or be able to report it accurately from interviews with those who do. Writers who have or can develop a good grasp of a specialized body of knowledge will find trade magazine editors who are eager to hear from them. And since good writers with specialized knowledge are a somewhat rare commodity, trade editors tend, more than typical consumer magazine editors, to cultivate ongoing relationships with writers. If you can prove yourself as a writer who "delivers," you will be paid back with frequent assignments and regular paychecks.

An ideal way to begin your foray into trade journals is to write for those that report on your present profession. Whether you've been selling real estate, managing a grocery store or performing bypass surgery, begin by familiarizing yourself with the magazines that serve your occupation. After you've read enough issues to have a feel for the kinds of pieces they run, approach the editors with your own article ideas. If you don't have experience in a profession but can demonstrate an ability to understand (and write about) the intricacies and issues of a particular trade that interests you, editors will still be willing to hear from you.

Photographs help increase the value of most stories for trade journals. If you can provide photos, mention that in your query or send copies. Since selling photos with a story usually means a bigger paycheck, it is worth any freelancer's time to develop basic camera skills.

Query a trade journal as you would a consumer magazine. Most trade editors like to discuss an article with a writer first and will sometimes offer names of helpful sources. Mention any direct experience you may have in the industry in your cover letter. Send a resume and clips if they show you have some background or related experience in the subject area. Read each listing carefully for additional submission guidelines.

To stay abreast of new trade magazines starting up, watch for news in *Folio* and *Advertising Age* magazines. Another source for information about trade publications is the *Business Publication Advertising Source*, published by Standard Rate and Data Service (SRDS) and available in most libraries. Designed primarily for people who buy ad space, the volume provides names and addresses of thousands of trade journals, listed by subject matter.

For information on additional trade publications not listed in *Writer's Market*, see Trade, Technical and Professional Journals/Changes '95-'96 at the end of this section.

Advertising, Marketing and PR

Trade journals for advertising executives, copywriters and marketing and public relations professionals are listed in this category. Those whose main focus is the advertising and marketing of specific products, such as home furnishings, are classified under individual product categories. Journals for sales personnel and general merchandisers can be found in the Selling and Merchandising category.

ADVERTISING AGE, Dept. WM, 740 N. Rush, Chicago IL 60611-2590. (312)649-5200. Fax: (312)649-5331. Managing Editor: Melanie Rigney. Executive Editor/Features: Larry Edwards. Editor: Steve Yahn. Interactive Media and Marketing Editor: Scott Donston. Deputy Editor: Larry Doherty. New York office: 220 E. 42nd St., New York NY 10017. (212)210-0100. Bureau Chief: Pat Sloan. Primarily staff-produced. Includes weekly sections devoted to one topic (i.e., marketing to consumer segments, TV syndication trends). Freelance work is done on assignment only. Pays kill fee "based on hours spent plus expenses." Byline given "except short articles or contributions to a roundup."
  ● *Advertising Age* reports that it is increasingly interested in consumer marketing trends, and in technology/new media stories.

AMERICAN ADVERTISING, The American Advertising Federation, 1101 Vermont Ave. NW, Suite 500, Washington DC 20005. E-mail: aafjpfal@iia.org. Editor: Jenny Pfalzgraf. 50% freelance written. Quarterly association magazine covering advertising and marketing issues. "*American Advertising* is a nonprofit publication of the American Advertising Federation, covering trends in marketing, advertising and media and the activities of the AAF." Estab. 1984. Circ. 50,000. **Pays on acceptance.** Publishes ms an average of 1 month after acceptance. Byline given. Buys first rights or second serial (reprint) rights. Editorial lead time 3 months. Accepts simultaneous and previously published submissions. Send photocopy of article. Negotiates payment. Query for electronic submissions. Reports in 1 month on queries. "Do not send manuscripts cold." Sample copy for 9×12 SAE with 4 first-class stamps.
  ● *American Advertising* is offering more coverage of interactive media/new technology.
Nonfiction: Book excerpts, how-to (marketing/advertising strategies), humor, interview/profile (leaders in ad business). "Not interested in negative stories about the ad business." Buys 4 mss/year. Query with published clips. Length: 500-2,000 words. Pays 25¢/word or negotiates rates. All articles are assigned.
Photos: State availability of photos with submission. Reviews contact sheets. Negotiates payment individually. Captions required. Buys one-time rights.
Columns/Departments: Ad Club Spotlight (features unique programs of AAF-member ad clubs), 500 words; Legislative Watch (focuses on legislative developments affecting ad business), 500 words; People (profiles top dogs in advertising and media), 500 words. Buys 1 mss/year. Query with published clips. Pays 25¢/word.
Tips: "Because we are nonprofit, a lot of work is commissioned pro bono from industry experts. All stories must have some tie-in to the AAF's membership and activities. Please familiarize yourself with the magazine before submitting."

AMERICAN DEMOGRAPHICS, American Demographics, Inc., P.O. Box 68, Ithaca NY 14851-0068. (607)273-6343. Fax: (607)273-3196. Editor-in-Chief: Brad Edmondson. Managing Editor: Nancy Ten Kate. Contact: Diane Crispell, executive editor. 25% freelance written. Works with a small number of new/unpublished writers each year. Monthly magazine for business executives, market researchers, media and communications people, public policymakers. Estab. 1978. Circ. 35,000. Pays on publication. Publishes ms an average of 4 months after acceptance. Buys all rights. Submit seasonal material 6 months in advance. Query for electronic submissions. Reports in 6 months. Include self-addressed stamped postcard for return word that ms arrived safely. Sample copy for $5 and 9 × 11 SAE. Writer's guidelines for #10 SASE.

Nonfiction: General interest (on demographic trends, implications of changing demographics, profile of business using demographic data); how-to (on the use of demographic techniques, psychographics, understand projections, data, apply demography to business and planning). No anecdotal material. Sometimes pays the expenses of writers on assignment.

Tips: "Writer should have clear understanding of specific population trends and their implications for business and planning. The most important thing a freelancer can do is to read the magazine and be familiar with its style and focus."

ART DIRECTION, Advertising Trade Publications, Inc., 10 E. 39th St., 6th Floor, New York NY 10016. (212)889-6500. Fax: (212)889-6504. Editor: Dan Barron. 10% freelance written. Prefers to work with published/established writers. Monthly magazine emphasizing advertising design for art directors of ad agencies (corporate, in-plant, editorial, freelance, etc.). Circ. 10,250. Pays on publication. Buys one-time rights. Reports in 3 months. Sample copy for $4.50.

Nonfiction: How-to articles on advertising campaigns. Pays $100 minimum.

MEDIA INC., Pacific Northwest Media, Marketing and Creative Services News, P.O. Box 24365, Seattle WA 98124-0365. (206)382-9220. Fax: (206)382-9437. Publisher: Richard K. Wottjer. 75% freelance written. Monthly tabloid covering Northwest US media, advertising, marketing and creative-service industries. Audience is Northwest ad agencies, marketing professionals, media and creative-service professionals. Estab. 1987. Circ. 10,000. Byline given. Reports in 1 month. Sample copy for 9 × 12 SAE with 6 first-class stamps.

Tips: "It is best if writers live in the Pacific Northwest and can report on local news and events in Media Inc.'s areas of business coverage."

‡MORE BUSINESS, 11 Wimbledon Court, Jericho NY 11753. Editor: Trudy Settel. 50% freelance written. Monthly magazine "selling publications material to business for consumer use (incentives, communication, public relations)—look for book ideas and manuscripts." Estab. 1975. Circ. 10,000. **Pays on acceptance.** Publishes ms an average of 1 month after acceptance. Buys all rights. Reports in 3 months. Sample copy for 9 × 12 SAE with first class stamps.

Nonfiction: General interest, how-to, vocational techniques, nostalgia, photo feature, profile and travel. Reviews new computer software. Buys 10-20 mss/year. Word length varies with article. Payment negotiable. Query. Pays $4,000-7,000 for book mss.

QUIRK'S MARKETING RESEARCH REVIEW, P.O. Box 23536, Minneapolis MN 55423. (612)861-8051. Editor: Joseph Rydholm. 25% freelance written. Monthly magazine covering market research. "Our readers are marketing researchers in a variety of industries, from consumer products to financial services. Unlike the academic marketing research journals, we focus on the practical, hands-on experiences of researchers through case histories of research projects and articles on specific research techniques." Estab. 1986. Circ. 16,000. Pays on publication. Byline given. Buys one-time rights. Editorial lead time 3 months. Accepts simultaneous and previously published submissions. Send photocopy of article or typed ms with rights for sale noted and information about when and where the article previously appeared. Pays 50% of the amount paid for an original article. Query for electronic submissions. Prefers PC: ASCII/Macintosh: Microsoft Word. Reports in 3 months on queries, 1 month on mss. Sample copy and writer's guidelines free on request.

Nonfiction: Interview/profile, technical. "Writers assume we want marketing-related articles. We do, but only if *marketing research* is part of it. Articles on direct marketing or telemarketing aren't of interest." Buys 10 mss/year. Query with published clips. Length: 1,500-2,500 words. Pays $200 minimum. Sometimes pays expenses of writers on assignment.

Photos: State availability of photos with submission. Reviews contact sheets and 35mm transparencies. Offers $25-75/photo. Identification of subjects required. Buys one-time rights.

Tips: "The key is to focus on *research*—telephone surveys, focus groups, mall intercepts, etc. We don't want telemarketing/direct mail, etc. articles. Make sure you know how to use research terms. We write for a broad audience because people come to the marketing research field from so many backgrounds—some know a lot, some know a little about the techniques. We're most interested in 'research in action,' application-based articles that show readers how others are using research. Our greatest need is for case history-style articles on successful marketing research projects. In these stories, the writer interviews a research user and

---

***ALWAYS** enclose a self-addressed, stamped envelope (SASE) with all your queries and correspondence.*

their supplier—usually a research company—to profile the project and explain how marketing research was used, what the goals were for the research, and why certain research techniques were used. I would also like to retain stringers to attend various research conventions/gatherings and write reports on them for our magazine."

RESPONSE TV, The First Magazine of Direct Response Television, Advanstar Communications, 201 E. Sandpointe, Suite 600, Santa Ana CA 92707. (714)513-8400. Fax: (714)513-8483. E-mail: rtvdave@aol.com. Managing Editor: David Nagel. 30% freelance written. Monthly magazine covering direct response television. "We look for business writers with experience in advertising, marketing, direct marketing, telemarketing, TV production, cable TV industry and home shopping." Estab. 1992. Circ. 21,000. **Pays on acceptance.** Byline given. Offers 50% kill fee. Buys all rights. Editorial lead time 2 months. Accepts previously published submissions. Reports in 2 weeks on queries, 1 month on mss. Sample copy for $6.
Nonfiction: General interest, interview/profile, opinion, technical, case studies. Buys 25 mss/year. Query with published clips. Length: 1,200-2,000 words. Pays $300-500. Sometimes pays expenses of writers on assignment.
Photos: State availability of photos with submission. Reviews contact sheets, negatives, transparencies. Negotiates payment individually. Model releases, identification of subjects required. Buys one-time rights.
Columns/Departments: New media (interactive advertising and merchandising), 200 words; Support Services (telemarketing, fulfillment), 200 words; Legal (advertising and marketing law), 800 words. Buys 12 mss/year. Query with published clips. Pays $300.
Tips: "Familiarity with topics such as home shopping, direct response TV, interactive TV and infomercials. General interest in advertising and marketing."

SIGNCRAFT, The Magazine for the Commercial Sign Shop, SignCraft Publishing Co., Inc., P.O. Box 06031, Fort Myers FL 33906. (813)939-4644. Editor: Tom McIltrot. 10% freelance written. Bimonthly magazine of the sign industry. "Like any trade magazine, we need material of direct benefit to our readers. We can't afford space for material of marginal interest." Estab. 1980. Circ. 19,500. Pays on publication. Publishes ms an average of 9 months after acceptance. Byline given. Offers negotiable kill fee. Buys first North American serial or all rights. Accepts previously published submissions. Reports in 1 month. Sample copy and writer's guidelines for $3.
Nonfiction: Interviews, profiles. "All articles should be directly related to quality commercial signs. If you are familiar with the sign trade, we'd like to hear from you." Buys 20 mss/year. Query with or without published clips. Length: 500-2,000 words. Pays up to $250.

Art, Design and Collectibles

The businesses of art, art administration, architecture, environmental/package design and antiques/collectibles are covered in these listings. Art-related topics for the general public are located in the Consumer Art and Architecture category. Antiques and collectibles magazines for enthusiasts are listed in Consumer Hobby and Craft. (Listings of markets looking for freelance artists to do artwork can be found in *Artist's and Graphic Designer's Market*, Writer's Digest Books).

‡**ANTIQUEWEEK**, Mayhill Publications Inc., P.O. Box 90, Knightstown IN 46148-0090. (317)345-5133. Fax: (800)695-8153. Central Edition Editor: Tom Hoepf. Eastern Edition Editor: Connie Swaim. Genealogy Editor: Diana Hoy. 80% freelance written. Weekly tabloid on antiques, collectibles and genealogy. *AntiqueWeek* publishes two editions: Eastern and Central. "*AntiqueWeek* has a wide range of readership from dealers and auctioneers to collectors, both advanced and novice. Our readers demand accurate information presented in an entertaining style." Estab. 1968. Circ. 60,000. Pays on publication. Byline given. Buys first and second serial (reprint) rights. Submit seasonal material 1 month in advance. Accepts previously published submissions. Send typed ms with rights for sale noted and information about when and where the article previously appeared. For reprints, pays 50% of the amount paid for an original article. Free sample copy. Writer's guidelines for #10 SASE.
Nonfiction: Historical/nostalgic, how-to, interview/profile, opinion, personal experience, antique show and auction reports, feature articles on particular types of antiques and collectibles. Buys 400-500 mss/year. Query with or without published clips or send complete ms. Length: 1,000-2,000 words. Pays $50-150.
Photos: Send photos with submission. Identification of subjects required.
Columns/Departments: Insights (opinions on buying, selling and collecting antiques), 500-1,000 words; Your Ancestors (advice, information on locating sources for genealogists). Buys 150 mss/year. Query. Length: 500-1,500 words. Pays $25-50.
Tips: "Writers should know their topics thoroughly. Feature articles must be well-researched and clearly written. An interview and profile article with a knowledgeable collector might be the break for a first-time

contributor. As we move toward the year 2000, there is much more interest in 20th-century collectibles. *Antiqueweek* also seeks articles that reflect the lasting popularity of traditional antiques."

APPLIED ARTS, 885 Don Mills Rd., Suite 324, Toronto, Ontario M3C 1V9 Canada. (416)510-0909. Fax: (416)510-0913. E-mail: elink@interlog.com. Editor: Peter Giffen. 70% freelance written. Magazine published 5 times/year covering graphic design, advertising, photography and illustration. Estab. 1986. Circ. 12,000. **Pays on acceptance.** Byline given. Buys first North American serial rights. Query for electronic submissions. Reports in 2 months on queries. Sample copy for 10×13 SAE with $1.70 Canadian postage or 4 IRCs.
Nonfiction: Interview/profile, opinion, photo feature, technical (computers and the applied arts) and trade articles about graphic design, advertising, photography and illustration. Buys 20-30 mss/year. Query with published clips. Length: 500-2,500 words. Pays 60¢ (Canadian)/word.
Photos: Offers no additional payment for photos accepted with ms. Buys one-time rights.
Tips: "It helps if writers have some familiarity with the communication arts field. Writers should include a solid selection of published articles. Writers have the best chance selling articles on graphic design and advertising. Take time to read back issues of the magazine before querying."

THE APPRAISERS STANDARD, New England Appraisers Assocation, 5 Gill Terrace, Ludlow VT 05149-1003. (802)228-7444. Publisher/Editor: Linda L. Tucker. 50% freelance written. Works with a small number of new/unpublished writers each year. Bimonthly publication on the appraisals of antiques, art, collectibles, jewelry, coins, stamps and real estate. "The writer should be extremely knowledgeable on the subject, and the article should be written with appraisers in mind, with prices quoted for objects, good pictures and descriptions of articles being written about." Estab. 1980. Circ. 1,300. Pays on publication. Publishes ms an average of 4-6 months after acceptance. Byline given, with short bio to establish writer's credibility. Buys first and simultaneous rights. Accepts simultaneous and previously published submissions. Send typed ms with rights for sale noted and information about when and where the article previously appeared. For reprints, pays 100% of the amount paid for an original article. Submit seasonal material 2 months in advance. Reports in 1 month on queries, 2 months on mss. Sample copy for 9×12 SAE with 2 first-class stamps. Writer's guidelines for #10 SASE.
Nonfiction: Interview/profile, personal experience, technical, travel. "All articles must be geared toward professional appraisers." Query with or without published clips, or send complete ms. Length: 700 words. Pays $50.
Photos: Send photos with submission. Reviews negatives and prints. Offers no additional payment for photos accepted with ms. Identification of subjects required. Buys one-time rights.
Tips: "Interviewing members of the association for articles, reviewing, shows and large auctions are all ways for writers who are not in the field to write articles for us."

ARTS MANAGEMENT, 408 W. 57th St., New York NY 10019. (212)245-3850. Editor: A.H. Reiss. Magazine published 5 times/year for cultural institutions. 2% freelance written. Estab. 1962. Circ. 6,000. Pays on publication. Byline given. Buys all rights. Query. Reports in 2 months. Writer's guidelines for #10 SASE.
  ● Mostly staff-written; uses very little outside material.
Nonfiction: Short articles, 400-900 words, tightly written, expository, explaining how art administrators solved problems in publicity, fund raising and general administration; actual case histories emphasizing the how-to. Also short articles on the economics and sociology of the arts and important trends in the nonprofit cultural field. Must be fact-filled, well-organized and without rhetoric. Pays 2-4¢/word. No photographs or pictures.

‡CONTEMPORARY STONE DESIGN, Business News Publishing Co., 1 Kalisa Way, Suite 205, Paramus NJ 07652. (201)599-0136. Fax: (201)599-2378. Publisher: Alex Bachrach. Editor: Michael Reis. Quarterly magazine covering the full range of stone design and architecture—from classic and historic spaces to current projects. Estab. 1995. Circ. 14,000. Pays on publication. Publishes ms an average of 3 months after acceptance. Byline given. Buys first rights only. Submit seasonal material 6 months in advance. Reports in 2-3 weeks. Sample copy for $10.
Nonfiction: Overall features on a certain aspect of stone design or specific articles on individual architectural projects. Interview/profile of a prominent architect/designer or firm. Photo feature, technical, architectural design. Buys 8 mss/year. Query with published clips. Length: 1,500-3,000 words. Pays $6/column inch. Pays expenses of writers on assignment.
Photos: State availability of photos with submission. Reviews transparencies and prints. Pays $10/photo accepted with ms. Captions and identification of subjects required. Buys one-time rights.
Columns/Departments: Upcoming Events (for the architecture and design community); Stone Classics (featuring historic architecture); question and answer session with a prominent architect or designer. 1,500-2,000 words. Pays $6/inch.
Tips: "The visual aspect of the magazine is key, so architectural photography is a must for any story. Cover the entire project, but focus on the stonework and how it relates to the rest of the space. Architects are very helpful in describing their work and often provide excellent quotes. As a new magazine, we are looking for

freelance submissions and are open to new feature topics. This is a narrow subject, however, so it's a good idea to speak with an editor before submitting anything."

‡**COREL MAGAZINE**, Omray Inc., 9801 Anderson Mill Rd., Suite 207, Austin TX 78730. (512)250-1700. Editor: Scott Campbell. Contact: Jennifer Campbell, managing editor. 80-90% freelance written. Monthly magazine covering computer graphic design software and hardware. "*Corel Magazine* is edited for users of CorelDraw, Photo-Paint, and other graphics software from Corel Corp. and third parties. Focus is on step-by-step tutorials, technical and product solutions, and real-world graphic design. Targeted to graphic design professionals and business presentation graphics users." Byline given. Offers $50 kill fee. Buys first North American serial rights. Editorial lead time 10 weeks. Submit seasonal material 3 months in advance. Query for electronic submissions. Reports in 2 weeks on queries; 1 month on mss. Sample copy free on request.
Nonfiction: How-to (step-by-step graphics and text explaining how to create image or effect using any Corel software), new product, personal experience, technical, product reviews, tips and tricks. Buys 180 mss/year. Query. Length: 500-2,500 words. Pays $150-750 for assigned articles; $50-500 for unsolicited articles. Sometimes pays expenses of writers on assignment.
Photos: Most artwork will be computer-generated. Send photos with submission. Offers no additional payment for photos accepted with ms.
Columns/Departments: In the Box (review/how-to), 1,500 words plus art. Query. Pays $150-500.

HOW, The Bottomline Design Magazine, F&W Publications, Inc., 1507 Dana Ave., Cincinnati OH 45207-1005. (513)531-2222. Contact: Editor. 75% freelance written. Bimonthly graphic design and illustration business journal. "*HOW* gives a behind-the-scenes look at not only *how* the world's best graphic artists and illustrators conceive and create their work, but *why* they did it that way. We also focus on the *business* side of design—how to run a profitable studio." Estab. 1985. Circ. 37,000. **Pays on acceptance.** Byline given. Buys first North American serial rights. Query for electronic submissions. Reports in 6 weeks. Sample copy for $8.50. Writer's guidelines for #10 SASE.
 • *HOW* recently won the *Folio Magazine* gold Ozzie Award for outstanding design.
Nonfiction: Interview/profile, business tips, new products. Special issues: Self-Promotion Annual (September/October); Business Annual (November/December). No how-to articles for beginning artists or fine-art-oriented articles. Buys 40 mss/year. Query with published clips and samples of subject's work (artwork or design). Length: 1,200-1,500 words. Pays $250-600. Sometimes pays expenses of writers on assignment.
Photos: State availability of artwork with submission. Reviews 35mm or larger transparencies. May reimburse mechanical photo expenses. Captions are required. Buys one-time rights.
Columns/Departments: Marketplace (focuses on lucrative fields for designers/illustrators); Production (ins, outs and tips on production); Applications (behind the scenes of electronically produced design projects). Buys 20 mss/year. Query with published clips. Length: 1,000-2,000 words. Pays $150-400.
Tips: "We look for writers who can recognize graphic designers on the cutting-edge of their industry, both creatively and business-wise. Writers must have an eye for detail, and be able to relay *HOW*'s step-by-step approach in an interesting, concise manner—without omitting any details. Showing you've done your homework on a subject—and that you can go beyond asking 'those same old questions'—will give you a big advantage."

LETTER ARTS REVIEW, (formerly *Lettering Arts Review*), 1624 24th Ave. SW, Norman OK 73072. (405)364-8794. Fax: (405)364-8914. Publisher/Editor: Karyn L. Gilman. 98% freelance written. Eager to work with new/unpublished writers with calligraphic expertise and language skills. Quarterly magazine on lettering and related book arts, both historical and contemporary in nature. Estab. 1982. Circ. 5,500. Pays on publication. Publishes ms an average of 9 months after acceptance. Byline given. Offers 20% kill fee. Buys first rights. Query for electronic submissons. Reports in 3 months. Sample copy for 9×12 SAE with 7 first-class stamps. Free writer's guidelines.
 • The emphasis here is on articles of a critical nature specifically for this audience.
Nonfiction: Interview/profile, opinion, contemporary, historical. Buys 50 mss/year. Query with or without published clips or send complete ms. Length: 1,000-2,000 words. Pays $50-200 for assigned articles; $25-200 for unsolicited articles. Sometimes pays the expenses of writers on assignment.
Photos: State availability of photos with submission. Reviews contact sheets, negatives, transparencies and prints. Pays agreed upon cost. Captions and identification of subjects required. Buys one-time rights.
Columns/Departments: Book Reviews, Viewpoint (critical), 500-1,500 words; Ms. (discussion of manuscripts in collections), 1,000-2,000 words; Profile (contemporary calligraphic figure), 1,000-2,000 words. Query. Pays $50-200.
Tips: "*Letter Arts Review*'s primary objective is to encourage the exchange of ideas on lettering and the lettering arts, its past and present as well as trends for the future. Historical research, typography, graphic design, fine press and artists' books, and other related aspects of the lettering arts are welcomed. Third person is preferred, however first person will be considered if appropriate. Writer should realize that this is a specialized audience."

MANHATTAN ARTS INTERNATIONAL MAGAZINE, Renée Phillips Associates, 200 E. 72nd St., Suite 26L, New York NY 10021. (212)472-1660. Fax: (212)794-0343. Editor-in-Chief: Renée Phillips. Managing Editor: Michael Jason. 100% freelance written. Monthly magazine covering fine art. Audience is comprised of art professionals, artists and collectors. Educational, informative, easy-to-read style, making art more accessible. Highly promotional of new artists. Estab. 1983. Circ. 50,000. Pays on publication. Publishes ms an average of 1 month after acceptance. Byline given. Makes work for hire assignments. Submit seasonal material 3 months in advance. Accepts simultaneous submissions. Reports in 3 months. Sample copy for $4, payable to Renée Phillips Associates (no postage or envelope required).

Nonfiction: Book excerpts (art), essays (art world), general interest (collecting art), inspirational (artists success stories), interview/profile (major art leaders), new product (art supplies), technical (art business). Buys 100 mss/year. Query with published clips; all articles are assigned. Length: 150-500 words. Pays $25-50. New writers receive byline and promotion, art books. Sometimes pays expenses of writers on assignment.

Photos: Send photos with submission. Offers no additional payment for photos accepted with ms. Captions, model releases and identification of subjects required.

Columns/Departments: Reviews/Previews (art critiques of exhibitions in galleries and museums), 150-250 words; Artists/Profiles (features on major art leaders), 250-500 words; The New Collector (collectibles, interviews with dealers, collectors), 250-500 words; Artopia (inspirational features, success stories), 250-500 words; Art Books, Art Services, 150-500 words. Buys 100 mss/year. Query with published clips. Pays $25-50.

Tips: "A knowledge of the current, contemporary art scene is a must. An eye for emerging talent is an asset."

THE MIDATLANTIC ANTIQUES MAGAZINE, Monthly Guide to Antiques, Art, Auctions & Collectibles, Henderson Newspapers, Inc., P.O. Box 908, Henderson NC 27536-0908. (919)492-4001. Fax: (919)430-0125. Editor: Lydia Stainback. 65% freelance written. Monthly tabloid covering antiques, art, auctions and collectibles. "The *MidAtlantic* reaches dealers, collectors, antique shows and auction houses primarily on the East Coast, but circulation includes 48 states and Europe." Estab. 1984. Circ. 14,000. Pays on publication. Byline given. Buys first rights. Submit seasonal material 6 months in advance. Reports in 1 month on queries; 2 months on mss. Sample copy and writer's guidelines for 10×13 SAE with 10 first-class stamps.

Nonfiction: Book excerpts, historical/nostalgic, how-to (choose an antique to collect; how to sell your collection; how to identify market trends), interview/profile, personal experience, photo feature, technical. Buys 60-75 mss/year. Query. Length: 800-2,000 words. Pays $50-125. Trade for advertising space. Rarely pays expenses of writers on assignment.

●*Midlantic Antiques* received the Mid-Atlantic Newspaper Advertising marketing Executives Best "Niche" Publication.

Photos: Send photos with submission. Offers no additional payment for photos accepted with ms. Identification of subjects required. Buys one-time rights.

Tips: "Please contact by mail first, but a writer may call with specific ideas after initial contact. Looking for writers who have extensive knowledge in specific areas of antiques. Articles should be educational in nature. We are also interested in how-to articles, i.e., how to choose antiques to collect; how to sell your collection and get the most for it; looking for articles that focus on future market trends. We want writers who are active in the antiques business and can predict good investments. (Articles with photographs are given preference.) We are looking for people who are not only knowledgeable, but can write well."

‡NOSTALGIA WORLD, For Collectors & Fans, Northeast International, P.O. Box 231, North Haven, CT 06473. Managing Editor: Richard A. Mason Jr. 50% freelance written. Bimonthly magazine of collectibles. Estab. 1978. Circ. 5,000. Pays on publication. Publishes ms an average of 6 months after acceptance. Byline sometimes given. Buys all rights. Editorial lead time 6 months. Submit seasonal material 9 months in advance. Accepts simultaneous and previously published submissions. Send typed ms with rights for sale noted and information about when and where the article previously appeared. For reprints, pay varies. Reports in 1 month on queries; 6 months on mss. Sample copy for $6. Writer's guidelines for $1 and #10 SASE.

Nonfiction: Historical/nostalgic, how to get started in collecting, biographies/profiles of celebrities or knowledgeable collectors, and entertainment collectibles (records, gum cards, toys, sheet music, movie and TV memorabilia, personality items, comics, sports memorabilia, etc.). "No furniture, glassware or other non-entertaining collectibles, and no reminiscing." Buys 20 mss/year. Send complete ms. Length: 250-1,500. Pays $25 for assigned articles; $15 for unsolicited articles. Sometimes pays expenses of writers on assignment.

Photos: Send photos with submission. Reviews prints. Negotiates payment individually. Captions and identification of subjects required. Buys all rights.

Columns/departments: Collector's Corner (a specific collectible); Step Into the Attic (antique collectibles); Flash Back! (an anniversary or other date in history). Length: 500-1,500 words. Buys 10 mss/year. Send complete ms. Pays $15-25.

Tips: "Most readers are curious to discover the value of their collectibles. *Nostalgia World* provides a place to buy, sell and trade their collectibles. We also list conventions, showings and fan club news across the country. Read a copy of the magazine before submitting."

PROGRESSIVE ARCHITECTURE, Dept. WM, P.O. Box 1361, Stamford CT 06904. Fax: (203)348-4023. Editor: John M. Dixon. Editorial Director: Thomas Fisher. 5-10% freelance written. Prefers to work with published/established writers. Monthly. Estab. 1920. **Pays on acceptance.** Publishes ms an average of 4 months after acceptance. Buys all rights for use in architectural press. Query for electronic submissions. Reports in 4 months.

    • *Progressive Architecture* has received a Citation of Merit from the Jesse H. Near Awards for investigative reporting.

Nonfiction: "Articles of technical, professional interest devoted to architecture, interior design, and urban design and planning, and illustrated by photographs and architectural drawings. We also use technical articles which are prepared by technical authorities and would be beyond the scope of the lay writer. Practically all the material is professional, and most of it is prepared by writers in the field who are approached by the magazine for material." Pays $150-400. Sometimes pays the expenses of writers on assignment.

Photos: Buys one-time reproduction rights to b&w and color photos.

SUCCESS NOW! FOR ARTISTS, The Fine Artists Monthly Guide To Success and Self-Empowerment, Renée Phillips Associates, 200 E. 72nd St., #26L, New York NY 10021. (212)472-1660. Contact: Michael Jason, executive editor. Monthly newsletter for fine artists. "Practical solutions for today's challenges faced by fine artists. Motivational style wanted. Special opportunities for artists wanted." Estab. 1992. Circ. 2,000. **Pays on acceptance.** Publishes ms an average of 2 months after acceptance. Byline given. Offers $25-50. Buys one-time rights or makes work-for-hire assignments. Editorial lead time 1-2 months. Submit seasonal material 3 months in advance. Sample copy for $4.

Nonfiction: Book excerpts, how-to (career advice), new product, personal experience (success story). Send complete ms. Length: up to 150 words. Pays in copies. Sometimes pays expenses of writers on assignment.

Columns/Departments: What's New (new products, organizations, services, books), 50-150 words. Send outline or short description.

Tips: "We seek advice from professionals in the field or interviews and observations about critical aspects concerning fine artists' careers. Artists themselves are welcome to submit success stories. We require concise, factual and comprehensive articles."

Auto and Truck

These publications are geared to automobile, motorcycle and truck dealers; professional truck drivers; service department personnel; or fleet operators. Publications for highway planners and traffic control experts are listed in the Government and Public Service category.

AUTO GLASS JOURNAL, Grawin Publications, Inc., 303 Harvard E., Suite 101, P.O. Box 12099, Seattle WA 98102-0099. (206)322-5120. Editor: Jeff Martin. 10% freelance written. Prefers to work with published/established writers. Monthly magazine on auto glass replacement. International publication for the auto glass replacement industry. Includes step-by-step glass replacement procedures for current model cars and business management, industry news and trends. Estab. 1953. Circ. 5,700. **Pays on acceptance.** Publishes ms an average of 5 months after acceptance. No byline given. Buys all rights. Query for electronic submissions. Reports in 5 months. Sample copy for 6×9 SAE with 3 first-class stamps. Writer's guidelines for #10 SASE.

Nonfiction: Articles relating to auto glass and general business management. Buys 12-20 mss/year. Query with published clips. Length: 1,000-3,000 words. Pays $50-200, with photos.

Photos: State availability of photos. Reviews b&w contact sheets and negatives. Payment included with ms. Captions required. Buys all rights.

‡**AUTOMOTIVE COOLING JOURNAL**, National Automotive Radiator Service Association, P.O. Box 97, E. Greenville PA 18041. (215)541-4500. Editor: Wayne Juchno. Contact: Richard Krisher. Monthly managing editor. 20% freelance written. Monthly magazine covering cooling system and mobile A/C service. "The *ACJ* is targeted to the cooling system and air conditioning service shop owner and operator. Its mission is to provide these independent business people with information they need about service, management, marketing, regulation, environment and industry trends." Estab. 1956. Circ. 10,500. Pays on publication. Publishes ms an average of 3 months after acceptance. Byline given. Editorial lead time 3 months. Submit seasonal material 6 months in advance. Accepts simultaneous and previously published submissions. Query for electronic submissions. Reports in 2 months on mss; 1 month on queries.

Nonfiction: Interview/profile, new product, photo feature, technical. Buys 12 mss/year. Query with published clips. Length: 1,000-5,000 words. Pays $100-500 for assigned articles; $100-300 for unsolicited articles. Sometimes pays expenses of writers on assignment.

Photos: State availability of photos with submission. Reviews contact sheets. Negotiates payment individually. Captions, model releases, identification of subjects required. Buys one-time rights.

‡O&A MARKETING NEWS, KAL Publications Inc., 1037 N. Lake Ave., Pasadena CA 91104. Editor: Kathy Laderman. 10% freelance written. Bimonthly tabloid covering petroleum marketing industry. "*O&A Marketing News* is editorially directed to people engaged in the distribution, merchandising, installation and servicing of gasoline, oil, TBA alternative fuel and automotive aftermarket products in the 13 Western states." Estab. 1966. Circ. 8,000. Pays on publication. Publishes ms an average of 0-3 months after acceptance. Byline sometimes given. Not copyrighted. Buys one-time rights. Editorial lead time 0-1 month. Accepts simultaneous submissions. Reports in 1 month on mss. Sample copy for $3.

Nonfiction: Exposé, interview/profile, photo feature, industry news. Buys 20 mss/year. Send complete ms. Length: 100-10,000 words. Pays per column inch typeset.

Photos: State availability of photos with submission. Reviews contact sheets, prints (5 × 7 preferred). Offers $5/photo. Identification of subjects required. Buys one-time rights.

Fillers: Gags to be illustrated by cartoonist, short humor. Buys 7/year. Length: 1-200 words. Pays per column inch.

Tips: "Seeking Western industry news. We're always seeking more stories covering the more remote states such as Montana, Idaho, and Hawaii—but any timely, topical *news* oriented stories will be considered."

OVERDRIVE, The Magazine for the American Trucker, Randall Publishing Co./Overdrive, Inc., P.O. Box 3187, Tuscaloosa AL 35403-3187. (205)349-2990. Fax: (205)750-8070. Editorial Director: G.C. Skipper. Managing Editor: Deborah Lockridge. 25% freelance written. Monthly magazine for independent truckers. Estab. 1961. Circ. 115,800. Pays on publication. Publishes ms an average of 2 months after acceptance. Byline given. 10% kill fee. Buys all North American rights. Reports in 2 months. Sample copy and writers' guidelines for 9 × 12 SASE.

Nonfiction: Essays, exposé, how-to (truck maintainance and operation), interview/profile (successful independent truckers), personal experience, photo feature, technical. All must be related to independent trucker interest. Query with or without published clips or send complete ms. Length: 500-2,000 words. Pays $100-600 for assigned articles; $50-500 for unsolicited articles.

Photos: Send photos with submission. Reviews transparencies and 5 × 7 prints. Offers $25-50/photo. Identification of subjects required. Buys all rights.

Tips: "Talk to independent truckers. Develop a good knowledge of their concerns as small business owners, truck drivers and individuals. We prefer articles that quote experts, people in the industry and truckers to first-person expositions on a subject. Get straight facts. Look for good material on truck safety, on effects of government regulations, and on rates and business relationships between independent truckers, brokers, carriers and shippers."

SUCCESSFUL DEALER, Kona-Cal, Inc., 707 Lake Cook Rd., Suite 300, Deerfeld IL 60015-4933. (708)498-3180. Fax: (708)498-3197. E-mail: 75572.677@compuserve.com or truckparts@aol.com. Editor: David Zaritz. Contact: Denise L. Rondini, Editorial Director. 10% freelance written. Bimonthly magazine for heavy-duty truck dealers. "*Successful Dealer*'s primary readers are the principal owners of medium- and heavy-duty truck dealerships. Additional readers are the executives, managers and sales personnel employed by these dealerships." Estab. 1978. Circ. 17,500. Pays on publication. Publishes ms an average of 4 months after acceptance. Byline given. Buys first North American serial or second (reprint) rights. Editorial lead time 3 months. Reports in 2-3 weeks on queries. Sample copy and writer's guidelines free on request.

Nonfiction: General interest (industry trends/developments), how-to (operate more profitably), interview/profile (industry leaders), technical (new developments in truck componentry). "We do not want single new product features; no opinion pieces." Buys 8 mss/year. Query. Length: 1,000-1,500 words. Pays $400 minimum for assigned articles or departments; $350 minimum for unsolicited articles. Sometimes pays expenses of writers on assignment.

Photos: Send photos with submission. Reviews contact sheets, negatives, transparencies and prints. Offers no additional payment for photos accepted with ms. Captions, model releases and identification of subjects required.

Tips: "It helps for the writer to be familiar with the industry."

TOW-AGE, Kruza Kaleidoscopix, Inc., P.O. Box 389, Franklin MA 02038-0389. Editor: J. Kruza. For readers who run their own towing service business. 5% freelance written. Prefers to work with published/established writers. Published every 6 weeks. Estab. 1960. Circ. 18,000. Buys all rights; usually reassigns rights. **Pays on acceptance.** Accepts simultaneous submissions. Reports in 1 month. Sample copy for $3. Writer's guidelines for #10 SASE.

Nonfiction: Articles on business, legal and technical information for the towing industry. "Light reading material; short, with punch." Informational, how-to, personal, interview, profile. Buys about 18 mss/year. Query or submit complete ms. Length: 600-800 words. Pays $50-150. Spot news and successful business operations. Length: 300-800 words. Technical articles. Length: 400-1,000 words. Pays expenses of writers on assignment.

Photos: Black and white 8 × 10 photos purchased with or without mss, or on assignment. Pays $25 for first photo; $10 for each additional photo in series. Captions required.

TRUCK PARTS AND SERVICE, Kona Communications, Inc., S707 Lake Cook Rd., uite 300, Deerfield IL 60015-4909. Fax: (708)498-3197. E-mail: truckprts@aol.com or 75572.677@compuserve.com. Editor: David Zaritz. Managing Editor: Denise L. Rondini. Contact: David Zaritz. 10% freelance written. Monthly magazine for repair shops and distributors in heavy-duty trucking. *"Truck Parts and Service*'s primary readers are owners of truck parts distributorships and independent repair shops. Both types of businesses sell parts and repair service to fleet and individual owners of medium- to heavy-duty trucks, buses and trailers. Other readers include the executives, managers and sales personnel employed by the parts distributors and repair shops." Estab. 1966. Circ. 17,500. **Pays on acceptance.** Publishes ms an average of 4 months after acceptance. Byline given. Buys first North American serial or second serial (reprint) rights. Editorial lead time 3 months. Reports in 2-3 weeks on queries. Sample copy and writer's guidelines free on request.
Nonfiction: General interest (industry trends or developments); how-to (operate more profitably); interview/profile (industry leaders); technical (new developments in truck components or repair and maintenance procedures). "We do not want single new product features; no opinion pieces." Buys 12 mss/year. Query. Length: 1,000-1,500 words. Pays $400 minimum for assigned articles; $350 for unsolicited articles. Sometimes pays expenses of writers on assignment.
Photos: Send photos with submission. Reviews contact sheets, negatives, transparencies and prints. Captions, model releases and identification of subjects required.
Tips: "It helps for the writer to be very familiar with the industry."

Aviation and Space

In this section are journals for aviation business executives, airport operators and aviation technicians. Publications for professional and private pilots can be found in the Consumer Aviation section.

AG-PILOT INTERNATIONAL MAGAZINE, Graphics Plus, P.O. Box 1607, Mt. Vernon WA 98273-1607. (206)336-9737. Fax: (206)336-2506. Editor Publisher: Tom J. Wood. Monthly magazine emphasizing agricultural aerial application (crop dusting). "This is intended to be a fun-to-read, technical, as well as humorous, and serious publication for the ag pilot and operator. They are our primary target." 20% freelance written. Estab. 1978. Circ. 6,872. Pays on publication. Publishes ms an average of 3 months after acceptance. Buys all rights. Byline given unless writer requests name withheld. Accepts previously published submissions. Reports in 1 month. Sample copy for 9 × 12 SAE with 7 first-class stamps. Writer's guidelines for #10 SASE.
Nonfiction: Exposé (of EPA, OSHA, FAA, NTSB or any government function concerned with this industry), general interest, historical, interview (of well-known ag/aviation person); nostalgia, personal opinion, new product, personal experience, photo feature. "If we receive an article, in any area we have solicited, it is quite possible this person could contribute intermittently. Industry-related material is a must. *No newspaper clippings.*" Send complete ms. Length: 800-1,500 words. Pays $50-200.
Photos: "We would like one color or b&w (5 × 7 preferred) with the manuscript, if applicable—it will help increase your chance of publication." Offers no additional payment for photos accepted with ms. Captions preferred, model release required.
Columns/Departments: International (of prime interest, crop dusting-related); Embryo Birdman (should be written, or appear to be written, by a beginner spray pilot); The Chopper Hopper (by anyone in the helicopter industry); Trouble Shooter (ag aircraft maintenance tips); Catchin' The Corner (written by a person obviously skilled in the crop dusting field of experience or other interest-capturing material related to the industry); Old Pro's Nest. Send complete ms. Length: 800-1,500 words. Pays $25-100.
Poetry: Interested in all ag-aviation related poetry. Buys 1 poem/issue. Submit no more than 2 at one time. Maximum length: 20 inch × 48 picas. Pays $10-50.
Fillers: Short jokes, short humor and industry-related newsbreaks. Length: 10-100 words. Pays $5-20.
Tips: "Writers should be witty and knowledgeable about the crop dusting aviation world. Material *must* be agricultural/aviation-oriented. *Crop dusting or nothing!*"

GSE TODAY, P.O. Box 480, Hatch NM 87937. Editor: G.C. Prill. Contact: Dixie Binning. 70% freelance written. Bimonthly magazine covering aviation ground support world wide. "Our readers are those aviation professionals who are involved in ground support—the equipment manufacturers, the suppliers, the ramp operators, ground handlers, airport and airline manager. We cover issues of interest to this community—deicing, ramp safety, equipment technology, pollution, etc." Estab. 1993. Circ. 15,000. Pays on publication. Publishes ms an average of 2 months after acceptance. Buys all rights. Editorial lead time 2 months. Accepts unsolicited mss. Query for electronic submissions. Accepts previously published submissions. Send photocopy or typed ms with rights for sale noted and information about when and where the article previously appeared. For reprints, pays 50% of the amount paid for an original article. Reports in 3 weeks on queries; 3 months on mss. Sample copy for 9 × 11 SAE with 5 first-class stamps.
Nonfiction: How-to (use or maintain certain equipment), interview/profile, new products, personal experience (from ramp operators), technical aspects of ground support equipment and issues, industry events,

meetings, new rules and regulations. Buys 12-20 mss/year. Send complete ms. Length: 400-3,000 words. Pays 25¢/published word.

Photos: Send photos with submissions. Reviews 5×7 prints. Offers no additional payment for photos accepted with ms. Identification of subjects required. Buys all rights.

Tips: "Write about subjects that relate to ground services. Write in clear and simple terms—personal experience is always welcome. If you have an aviation background or ground support experience, let us know."

WINGS WEST, 7009 S. Potomac St., Englewood CO 80112-4209. (303)397-7600. Fax: (303)397-7619. Publisher/Editor: Edward D. Huber. 50% freelance written. Bimonthly magazine on mountain flying performance, aviation and aerospace in the West. Estab. 1985. Circ. 15,000. Pays on publication. Publishes ms an average of 1 year after acceptance. Byline given. Offers $25 kill fee. Buys all rights. Submit seasonal/holiday material 6 months in advance. Accepts previously published submissions. Send tearsheet or photocopy of article or short story and information about when and where the article previously appeared. Query for electronic submissions. Sample copy available. Send cover letter with copy of ms, Mac or DOS file saved as text only, unformed ASCII, or in QuarkXPress (Mac) on 3½-inch floppy diskette (telephonic submissions (303)397-6987), author's bio and photo. Writing and photographic guidelines available.

Nonfiction: General interest illustrative of people, how to fly, flying experiences, mountain flying, humor, new products, opinion, opportunities, challenges, cultures, and special places. Buys 18-35 mss/year. Length: 800-2,000 words. Pay starts at $50/published page (includes text and photos).

Fiction: Interested in new ideas. Query.

Photos: Send photos with submission (copies acceptable for evaluation). Credit line given.

Columns/Departments: Medical (aeromedical factors), legal (FARs, enforcement, legal problems), mountain flying, travel, safety, product news and reviews, industry news. *Wings West* purchases first serial rights. May consider second serial reprint rights, query.

Beauty and Salon

‡**COSMETICS, Canada's business magazine for the cosmetics, fragrance, toiletry and personal care industry**, Maclean Hunter Publishing Ltd., 227 Front St. E., Suite 100, Toronto, Ontario M5A 1E8 Canada. (416)865-9362. Editor: Ronald A. Wood. 35% freelance written; "99.9% of freelance articles are assigned by the editor to writers whose work he is familiar with and who have a broad knowledge of this industry as well as contacts, etc." Bimonthly. "Our main reader segment is the retail trade—department stores, drugstores, salons, estheticians—owners and cosmeticians/beauty advisors; plus manufacturers, distributors, agents and suppliers to the industry." Estab. 1972. Circ. 13,000. **Pays on acceptance.** Publishes ms an average of 3 months after acceptance. Byline given. Offers 50% kill fee. Buys all rights. Editorial lead time 4 months. Submit seasonal material 4 months in advance. Query for electronic submissions. Reports in 1 month. Sample copy for $6 (Canadian) and 8% GST.

Nonfiction: General interest, interview/profile, photo feature. Buys 60 mss/year. Query. Length: 250-1,200 words. Pays 30¢/word. Sometimes pays expenses of writers on assignment.

Photos: Send photos with submission. Reviews transparencies (2½ up to 8×10) and prints (4×6 up to 8×10). Offers no additional payment for photos accepted with ms. Captions, model releases and identification of subjects required. Buys all rights.

Columns/Departments: Behind the Scenes (brief profile of person not directly involved with major industry firms), 300 words and portrait photo. Buys 28 mss/year, "all assigned on a regular basis from correspondents and columnists that we know personally from the industry." Pays 30¢/word.

Tips: "Must have broad and intense knowledge of the Canadian cosmetics, fragrance and toiletries industry and retail business."

NAILPRO, The Magazine for Nail Professionals, Creative Age Publications, 7628 Densmore Ave., Van Nuys CA 91406. Fax: (818)782-7450. Editor: Linda Lewis. 75% freelance written. Monthly magazine "written for manicurists and nail technicians working in full-service salons or nails-only salons. It covers technical and business aspects of working in and operating a nail-care service, as well as the nail-care industry in general." Estab. 1989. Circ. 47,000. **Pays on acceptance.** Publishes ms 4-6 months after acceptance. Byline given. Offers 50% kill fee. Buys one-time, second serial (reprint), simultaneous or all rights. Editorial lead time 3 months. Submit seasonal material 3 months in advance. Accepts simultaneous and previously published submissions. Send typed ms with rights for sale noted and information about when and where the article previously appeared. For reprints, pays 50-75% of the amount paid for an original article. Query for electronic submissions. Reports in 6 weeks. Sample copy for $2 and 8½×11 SASE.

Nonfiction Book excerpts, how-to, humor, inspirational, interview/profile, personal experience, photo feature, technical. No general interest articles or business articles not geared to the nail-care industry. Buys 50 mss/year. Query. Length: 1,000-3,000 words. Pays $150-350.

Photos: Send photos with submission. Reviews transparencies and prints. Negotiates payment individually. Model releases and identification of subjects required. Buys one-time rights.

Columns/Departments: Building Business (articles on marketing nail services/products), 1,500-3,000 words; Shop Talk (aspects of operating a nail salon), 1,500-3,000 words; Hollywood File (nails in the news, movies or TV), 1,000-1,500 words. Buys 50 mss/year. Query. Pays $150-250.

NAILS, Bobit Publishing, 2512 Artesia Blvd., Redondo Beach CA 90278-3296. (310)376-8788. Fax: (310)376-9043. Editor: Cyndy Drummey. Managing Editor: Suzette Hill. 10% freelance written. Monthly magazine for the nail care industry. "*NAILS* seeks to educate its readers on new techniques and products, nail anatomy and health, customer relations, working safely with chemicals, salon sanitation, and the business aspects of working in or running a salon." Estab. 1983. Circ. 52,000. **Pays on acceptance.** Byline given. Buys all rights. Submit seasonal material 4 months in advance. Accepts previously published submissions. Send tearsheet of article and information about when and where the article previously appeared. Query for electronic submissions. Reports in 3 months on queries. Free sample copy. No writer's guidelines available.
 • *Nails* was a 1993 WPA Maggie Award Winner in the category of Best Special Interest/Trade Magazine.
Nonfiction: Historical/nostalgic, how-to, inspirational, interview/profile, personal experience, photo feature, technical. "No articles on one particular product, company profiles or articles slanted towards a particular company or manufacturer." Buys 20 mss/year. Query with published clips. Length: 1,200-3,000 words. Pays $100-400. Sometimes pays expenses of writers on assignment.
Photos: State availability of photos with submission. Reviews contact sheets, transparencies and prints (any standard size acceptable). Offers $50-200/photo. Captions, model releases and identification of subjects required. Buys all rights.
Tips: "Send clips and query; *do not send unsolicited manscripts*. We would like to see ideas for articles on a unique salon or a business article that focuses on a specific aspect or problem encountered when working in a salon. The Modern Nail Salon section, which profiles nail salons and full-service salons, is most open to freelancers. Focus on an innovative business idea or unique point of view. Articles from experts on specific business issues—insurance, handling difficult employees, cultivating clients—are encouraged."

‡SKIN INC. MAGAZINE, The Business Magazine for Skin Care Professionals, Allured Publishing Corp., 362 S. Schmale Rd., Carol Stream IL 60188. (708)653-2155. Publisher/Editor: Marian Raney. Contact: Melinda Taschetta-Millane, associate editor. 30% freelance written. Bimonthly magazine covering the skin care industry. "Manuscripts are considered for publication that contain original and new information in the general fields of skin care and makeup, dermatological, plastic and reconstructive surgical techniques. The subject may cover the science of skin, the business of skin care and makeup and plastic surgeons on healthy (i.e. non-diseased) skin. Subjects may also deal with raw materials, formulations and regulations concerning claims for products and equipment." Estab. 1988. Circ. 8,000. Pays on publication. Publishes ms an average of 4-6 months after acceptance. Byline given. No kill fee. Buys all rights. Editorial lead time 6 months. Submit seasonal material 6-12 months in advance. Accepts simultaneous submissions. Reports in 1 week on queries; 1 month on mss. Sample copy and writer's guidelines free on request.
Nonfiction: General interest, how-to, interview/profile, personal experience, technical. Buys 6 mss/year. Query with published clips. Length: 2,000 words. Pays $100-350 for assigned articles; $50-250 for unsolicited articles.
Photos: State availability of photos with submission. Reviews 3×5 prints. Offers no additional payment for photos accepted with ms. Captions, model releases, identification of subjects required. Buys one-time rights.
Columns/Departments: Dollars & Sense (tips and solutions for managing money), 2,000-2,500 words; Person to Person (managing personnel), 2,000-2,500 words; Marketing for the 90s (marketing tips for salon owners), 2,000-2,500 words. Query with published clips. Pays $50-250.
Fillers: Facts, newsbreaks. Buys 6 mss/year. Length: 250-500 words. Pays $50-100.
Tips: Have an understanding of the skin care industry.

Beverages and Bottling

Manufacturers, distributors and retailers of soft drinks and alcoholic beverages read these publications. Publications for bar and tavern operators and managers of restaurants are classified in the Hotels, Motels, Clubs, Resorts and Restaurants category.

AMERICAN BREWER, P.O. Box 510, Hayward CA 94543-0510. (415)538-9500 (a.m. only). Fax: (510)538-9500. Publisher: Bill Owens. 100% freelance written. Quarterly magazine covering micro-breweries. Estab. 1986. Circ. 10,000. Pays on publication. Publishes ms an average of 4 months after acceptance. Byline given. Buys one-time rights. Accepts previously published submissions. Send tearsheet or photocopy of article. For reprints, pays 30% of the amount paid for an original article. Reports in 2 weeks on queries. Sample copy for $5.
Nonfiction: Humor, opinion, travel. Query. Length: 1,500-2,500 words. Pays $50-250 for assigned articles.

MID-CONTINENT BOTTLER, 8575 W. 110th, Suite 218, Overland Park KS 66210. (913)469-8611. Fax: (913)469-8626. Publisher: Floyd E. Sageser. 5% freelance written. Prefers to work with published/established writers. Bimonthly magazine for "soft drink bottlers in the 20-state Midwestern area." Estab. 1970. Not copyrighted. **Pays on acceptance.** Publishes ms an average of 2 months after acceptance. Buys first rights only. Reports "immediately." Sample copy for 9×12 SAE with 10 first-class stamps. Guidelines for #10 SASE.
Nonfiction: "Items of specific soft drink bottler interest with special emphasis on sales and merchandising techniques. Feature style desired." Buys 2-3 mss/year. Length: 2,000 words. Pays $50-200. Sometimes pays the expenses of writers on assignment.
Photos: Photos purchased with mss.

‡MODERN BREWERY AGE, Business Journals, Inc., 50 Day St., Norwalk CT 06854. Editor: Peter V.K. Reid. 10% freelance written. Bimonthly magazine covering brewing and beer wholesaling. "*Modern Brewery Age* has a readership made up of brewers, beer industry suppliers and beer wholesalers. They are seeking information that will assist them in doing business." Estab. 1938. Circ. 6,000. Pays on publication. Publishes ms an average of 2 months after acceptance. Byline given. Editorial lead time 2-3 months. Submit seasonal material 2-3 months in advance. No simultaneous or previously published submissions. Query for electronic submissions. Reports in 1 month on queries; 2 months on mss. Sample copy for $6.
Nonfiction: Historical/nostalgic (on brewing industry), how-to (on brewing), interview/profile (with brewing figure). Buys 6-10 mss/year. Query with published clips. Pays $200-400. Sometimes pays expenses of writers on assignment.
Photos: Send photos with submission. Negotiates payment individually.

VINEYARD & WINERY MANAGEMENT, P.O. Box 231, Watkins Glen NY 14891-0231. (607)535-7133. Fax: (607)535-2998. E-mail: vandwm@aol.com. Editor: J. William Moffett. 80% freelance written. Bimonthly trade magazine of professional importance to grape growers, winemakers and winery sales and business people. Estab. 1975. Circ. 4,500. Pays on publication. Byline given. Buys first North American serial rights and occasionally simultaneous rights. Query for electronic submissions. Reports in 3 weeks on queries; 1 month on mss. *Writer's Market* recommends allowing 2 months for reply. Sample copy free. Writer's guidelines for #10 SASE.
Nonfiction: How-to, interview/profile, technical. Subjects are technical in nature and explore the various methods people in these career paths use to succeed, and also the equipment and techniques they use successfully. Business articles and management topics are also featured. The audience is national with western dominance. Buys 30 mss/year. Query. Length: 300-5,000 words. Pays $30-1,000. Pays some expenses of writers on some assignments.
Photos: State availability of photos with submission. Reviews contact sheets, negatives and transparencies. Identification of subjects required. "Black and white often purchased for $20 each to accompany story material; 35mm and/or 4×5 transparencies for $50 and up; 6/year of vineyard and/or winery scene related to story. Query."
  ● This publication no longer considers short fiction.
Tips: "We're looking for long-term relationships with authors who know the business and write well. Electronic submissions preferred; query for formats."

Book and Bookstore

Publications for book trade professionals from publishers to bookstore operators are found in this section. Journals for professional writers are classified in the Journalism and Writing category.

BLOOMSBURY REVIEW, A Book Magazine, Dept. WM, Owaissa Communications Co., Inc., 1028 Bannock, Denver CO 80204-4037. (303)892-0620. Fax: (303)892-5620. Publisher/Editor-in-chief: Tom Auer. Editor/Associate Publisher: Marilyn Auer. 75% freelance written. Bimonthly tabloid covering books and book-related matters. "We publish book reviews, interviews with writers and poets, literary essays and original poetry. Our audience consists of educated, literate, *non-specialized* readers." Estab. 1980. Circ. 50,000. Pays on publication. Publishes ms an average of 4 months after acceptance. Byline given. Buys first or one-time rights. Reports in 4 months. Reprints considered but not encouraged. Send photocopy of article and information about when and where the article previously appeared. For reprints, pays 100% of amount paid for an original article. Sample copy for $4 and 9×12 SASE. Writer's guidelines for #10 SASE.
Nonfiction: Essays, interview/profile, book reviews. "Summer issue features reviews, etc. about the American West. *We do not publish fiction.*" Buys 60 mss/year. Query with published clips or send complete ms. Length 800-1,500 words. Pays $10-20. Sometimes pays writers with contributor copies or other premiums "if writer agrees."
Photos: State availability of photos with submissions. Reviews prints. Offers no additional payment for photos accepted with ms. Buys one-time rights.

Columns/Departments: Book reviews and essays. Buys 6 mss/year. Query with published clips or send complete ms. Length: 500-1,500 words. Pays $10-20.

Poetry: Ray Gonzalez, poetry editor. Avant-garde, free verse, haiku, light verse, traditional. Buys 20 poems/year. Submit up to 5 poems at one time. Pays $5-10.

Tips: "We appreciate receiving published clips and/or completed manuscripts. Please—no rough drafts. Book reviews should be of new books (within 6 months of publication)."

THE HORN BOOK MAGAZINE, The Horn Book, Inc., 11 Beacon St., Suite 1000, Boston MA 02108. (617)227-1555. Editor: Anita Silvey. 10% freelance written. Prefers to work with published/established writers. Bimonthly magazine covering children's literature for librarians, booksellers, professors, teachers and students of children's literature. Estab. 1924. Circ. 22,500. Pays on publication. Publishes ms an average of 4 months after acceptance. Byline given. Submit seasonal material 6 months in advance. Accepts simultaneous submissions. Reports in 2 weeks on queries; 1 month on mss. Writer's guidelines available upon request.

Nonfiction: Interview/profile (children's book authors and illustrators); topics of interest to the children's bookworld. Writers should be familiar with the magazine and its contents. Buys 20 mss/year. Query or send complete ms. Length: 1,000-2,800 words. Honorarium paid upon publication.

Tips: "Writers have a better chance of breaking in to our publication with a query letter on a specific article they want to write."

THE WOMEN'S REVIEW OF BOOKS, The Women's Review, Inc., Wellesley College, Wellesley MA 02181-8259. (617)283-2500. Editor: Linda Gardiner. Monthly newspaper. "Feminist review of recent trade and academic writing by and about women. Reviews recent nonfiction books, primarily." Estab. 1983. Circ. 16,000. Pays on publication. Publishes ms an average of 2 months after acceptance. Byline given. Offers $50 kill fee. Buys first North American serial rights. Editorial lead time 2 months. Query for electronic submissions. Reports in 2 months. Sample copy free on request.

Nonfiction: Book reviews only. No articles considered; no unsolicited mss. Only book review queries. Buys 200 mss/year. Query with published clips. Pays 12¢/word. Sometimes pays expenses of writers on assignment.

Tips: "Only experienced reviewers for national media are considered. Reviewers must have expertise in subject of book under review. Never send unsolicited manuscripts."

Brick, Glass and Ceramics

These publications are read by manufacturers, dealers and managers of brick, glass and ceramic retail businesses. Other publications related to glass and ceramics are listed in the Consumer Art and Architecture and Consumer Hobby and Craft sections.

STAINED GLASS, Stained Glass Association of America, 6 SW Second St., #7, Lee's Summit MO 64063. Contact: Katei Gross. 70% freelance written. Quarterly magazine covering stained glass and glass art. "Since 1906, *Stained Glass* has been the official voice of the Stained Glass Association of America. As the oldest, most respected stained glass publication in North America, *Stained Glass* preserves the techniques of the past as well as illustrates the trends of the future. This vital information, of significant value to the professional stained glass studio, is also of interest to those for whom stained glass is an avocation or hobby." Estab. 1906. Circ. 5,000. Pays on publication. Publishes ms an average of 6 months after acceptance. Byline given. Buys one-time rights. Editorial lead time 3 months. Submit seasonal material 6 months in advance. Accepts simultaneous and previously published submissions. Reports in 3 months. Sample copy and writer's guidelines free on request.

Nonfiction: How-to, humor, interview/profile, new product, opinion, photo feature, technical. Strong need for technical and how to create architectural type stained glass. Glass etching, use of etched glass in stained glass compositions, framing. Buys 9 mss/year. Query or send complete ms but must include photos or slides—very heavy on photos. Pays $25/page. Sometimes pays expenses of writers on assignment.

Photos: Send photos with submission. Reviews 4×5 transparencies. Negotiates payment individually. Identification of subjects required. Buys one-time rights.

Columns/Departments: Teknixs (technical, how-to, stained and glass art), word length varies by subject. Buys 4 mss/year. Query or send complete ms, but must be illustrated.

Tips: "Writers should be extremely well versed in the glass arts. Photographs are extremely important and must be of very high quality. Very sight-oriented magazine. Submissions without photographs or illustrations are seldom considered unless something special and writer states that photos are available. However, prefer to see with submission."

‡US GLASS, METAL & GLAZING, Key Communications Inc., P.O. Box 569, Garrisonville VA 22463. Editor: Debra Levy. 25% freelance written. Monthly magazine for companies involved in the auto glass and flat glass trades. Estab. 1966. Circ. 20,000. Pays on publication. Publishes ms an average of 3 months after acceptance. Byline given. Offers 25% kill fee. Buys all rights. Editorial lead time 3 months. Submit seasonal

material 2 months in advance. Accepts simultaneous submissions. Query for electronic submissions. Reports in 1 month on queries; 2 months on mss. Sample copy and writer's guidelines for $10.
Nonfiction: Sandi Thornley. How-to, new product, technical. Buys 12 mss/year. Query with published clips. Pays $300-600 for assigned articles. Sometimes pays expenses of writers on assignment.
Photos: State availability of photos with submission. Reviews contact sheets. Offers no additional payment for photos accepted with ms. Captions, identification of subjects required. Buys first North American rights.

Building Interiors

Owners, managers and sales personnel of floor covering, wall covering and remodeling businesses read the journals listed in this category. Interior design and architecture publications may be found in the Consumer Art, Design and Collectibles category. For journals aimed at other construction trades see the Construction and Contracting section.

PWC, Painting & Wallcovering Contractor, Finan Publishing Co. Inc., 8730 Big Bend Blvd., St. Louis MO 63119-3730. (314)961-6644. Fax: (314)961-4809. Editor: Jeffery Beckner. 90% freelance written. Bimonthly magazine for painting and wallcovering contracting. "*PWC* provides news you can use: information helpful to the painting and wallcovering contractor in the here and now." Estab. 1928. Circ. 30,000. Pays 30 days after acceptance. Publishes an average of 1 month after acceptance. Byline given. Kill fee determined on individual basis. Buys first North American serial rights. Editorial lead time 2 months. Submit seasonal material 2 months in advance. Accepts simultaneous and previously published submissions. Send photocopy of article and information about when and where the article previously appeared. For reprints, negotiates payment. Query for electronic submissions; hard copy required. Reports in 2 weeks. Sample copy free on request.
Nonfiction: Essays, exposé, how-to (painting and wallcovering), interview/profile, new product, opinion personal experience. Buys 40 mss/year. Query with published clips. Length: 1,500-2,500 words. Pays $300 minimum. Pays expenses of writers on assignment.
Photos: State availability of or send photos with submission. Reviews contact sheets, negatives, transparencies and prints. Offers no additional payment for photos accepted with ms. Identification of subjects required. Buys one-time and all rights.
Columns/Departments: Anything of interest to the small businessman, 1,250 words. Buys 2 mss/year. Query with published clips. Pays $50-100.
Tips: "We almost always buy on an assignment basis. The way to break in is to send good clips, and I'll try and give you work."

REMODELING, Hanley-Wood, Inc., One Thomas Circle NW, Suite 600, Washington DC 20005. (202)452-0800. Fax: (202)785-1974. Editor: Wendy Jordan. 5% freelance written. Monthly magazine covering residential and light commercial remodeling. "We cover the best new ideas in remodeling design, business, construction and products." Estab. 1985. Circ. 98,000. Pays on publication. Publishes ms an average of 3 months after acceptance. Byline given. Offers 5¢/word kill fee. Buys first North American serial rights. Query for electronic submissions. Reports in 1 month. Free sample copy and writer's guidelines.
Nonfiction: Interview/profile, small business trends, new product, technical. Buys 4 mss/year. Query with published clips. Length: 250-1,000 words. Pays 20¢/word. Sometimes pays the expenses of writers on assignment.
Photos: State availability of photos with submission. Reviews slides, 4×5 transparencies and 8×10 prints. Offers $25-100/photo. Captions, model releases and identification of subjects required. Buys one-time rights.
Tips: "The areas of our publication most open to freelancers are news and new product news."

Business Management

These publications cover trends, general theory and management practices for business owners and top-level business executives. Publications that use similar material but have a less technical slant are listed in the Consumer Business and Finance section. Journals for middle management, including supervisors and office managers, appear in the Management and Supervision section. Those for industrial plant managers are listed under Industrial Operations and under sections for specific industries, such as Machinery and Metal. Publications for office supply store operators are included in the Office Environment and Equipment section.

‡**ACCOUNTING TECHNOLOGY**, Faulkner & Gray (Division of Thompson Professional Publishing), 11 Penn Plaza, New York NY 10001. (212)967-7000. Editor: Ted Needleman. Contact: Larry Zuckerman.

40% freelance written. Magazine published 11 times/year covering hardware and software for accountants. "*Accounting Technology* is a high quality magazine dedicated to a simple editorial charter. We show our readers how to make more money by applying technology. Our writers must have a background in technology or accounting and a clear readable writing style." Estab. 1984. Circ. 25,000. Pays on publication. Publishes ms an average of 2-3 months after acceptance. Offers 25% kill fee. Buys first North American and second serial (reprint) rights. Editorial lead time 3 months. No simultaneous or previously published submissions. Reports in 4-6 weeks. Sample copy and writer's guidelines free on request.

Nonfiction: How-to, review. Buys 50 mss/year. No unsolicited ms. Query with published clips. Pays $150-3,000.

Columns/Departments: By assignment only, 2,000 words. Buys 40 mss/year. Query with published clips. Pays $400.

‡ACROSS THE BOARD, The Conference Board Magazine, The Conference Board, 845 Third Ave., New York NY 10022. 60-70% freelance written. Monthly magazine covering general management. "Our audience is primarily senior executives of large American companies." Estab. 1976. Circ. 30,000. Pays on publication. Publishes ms an average of 3 months after acceptance. Byline given. Offers 33% kill fee. Buys first North American serial rights. Editorial lead time 2-3 months. Accepts simultaneous and previously published submissions. Reports in 3 weeks on queries; 2 weeks on mss. Sample copy and writer's guidelines free on request.

Nonfiction: Book excerpts, essays, how-to, opinion, personal experience. Buys 40 mss/year. Query with or without published clips, or send complete ms. Length: 2,500-3,500 words. Pays $800-1,000. Sometimes pays expenses of writers on assignment.

Photos: State availability of photos with submission.

Columns/Departments: Commentary (strong opinions on subjects of pertinence to our readers), 1,200-1,500 words. Pays $250-400.

‡BUSINESS ETHICS MAGAZINE, The Magazine of Socially Responsible Business, Mavis Publishing, 52 S. 10th St., Suite 110, Minneapolis MN 55403-2001. (612)962-4701. Senior Editor: Mary Scott. Contact: Dale Kurschner, editor. 70% freelance written. Bimonthly magazine. "*Business Ethics* is the only magazine focused on socially responsible capitalism—the art of making money ethically, and in a socially responsible manner. It covers socially responsible investing, business news, trends and issues. We present insightful interviews with major business leaders, news features and timely analysis stories, charts tracking socially responsible businesses, and fresh perspectives on life and work. Issues covered include progressive personnel management, truth in marketing, employee ownership, environmental protection, corporate ethics, workplace diversity, philanthropy, and more." Estab. 1987. Circ. 30,000. Pays on publication. Publishes ms 3 months after acceptance. Byline given. Offers 15-20% kill fee. Buys first North American serial rights and second serial (reprint) rights. Editorial lead time 2 months. Accepts previously published submissions. Query for electronic submissions. Reports in 1 month. Sample copy for 8×10 SAE with 5 first-class stamps. Writer's guidelines for #10 SASE.

● Last fall, *Business Ethics* broke the story questioning the integrity of the Body Shop's product claims.

Nonfiction: Essays, expose, general interest, humor, inspirational, interview/profile, opinion, personal experience. Special issue: Year-End Annual on trends, news, "best-of." Buys 120 mss/year. Query with published clips. Length: 200-2,000 words. Pays $50-700. Sometimes pays in contributor copies; depends on situation. Sometimes pays expenses of writers on assignment.

Photos: State availability of photos or send photos with submission. Reviews contact sheets, negatives, transparencies, prints. Negotiates payment individually. Identification of subjects required. Buys one-time rights.

Columns/Departments: Commentary (opinion piece), Perspectives (essay on work life), Book Review Essays; 400-800 words. Query with published clips.

Fillers: Newsbreaks, short humor. Buys 60/year. Length: 100-300 words. Pays $50-100.

Tips: "Cater submissions to one of our sections, such as Trend Watch, Working Ideas, Perspectives and Commentary. Please send in published clips along with the idea."

‡BUSINESS MARKETING, Crain Communications Inc., 740 N. Rush St., Chicago IL 60611-2525. (312)649-5260. Editor: Chuck Paustian. Contact: Char Kosek, Managing Editor. 80% freelance written. Monthly

---

Market conditions are constantly changing! If this is 1997 or later, buy the newest edition of Writer's Market at your favorite bookstore or order directly from Writer's Digest Books.

magazine covering business-to-business marketing. Readers are senior-level marketing professionals, business-to-business marketing. Estab. 1916. Circ. 30,000. Pays on publication. Byline given. Buys all rights. Editorial lead time 2 months. Submit seasonal material 2 months in advance. Query for electronic submissions. Sample copy and writer's guidelines free on request.
Nonfiction: Interview/profile, opinion. Query. Sometimes pays expenses of writers on assignment.
Photos: State availability of photos with submission. Negotiates payment individually. Buys all rights.
Columns/Departments: Query.

‡CONSUMER GOODS MANUFACTURER, Partnering with Retail through Technology, Edgell Communications, 1 W. Hanover Ave., Randolph NJ 07869. Editor: Mark Frantz. 60% freelance written. Bimonthly tabloid covering suppliers to retailers. "Readers are the functional managers/executives in all types of retail and consumer goods firms. They are making major improvements in company operations and in alliances with customers/suppliers." Estab. 1991. Circ. 26,000. Pays on publication. Byline sometimes given. Buys first rights and second serial (reprint) rights. Editorial lead time 2-3 months. Submit seasonal material 3 months in advance. Query for electronic submissions. Sample copy for 11×15 SAE with 6 first-class stamps. Writer's guidelines for #10 SASE.
Nonfiction: How-to, interview/profile, technical. Buys 100 mss/year. Query with published clips. Length: 1,200-2,400 words. Pays $500 maximum for assigned articles. Sometimes pays contributor copies as negotiated. Sometimes pays expenses of writers on assignment.
Photos: Send photos with submission. Reviews contact sheets, negatives, transparencies and prints. Offers no additional payment for photos accepted with ms. Identification of subjects required. Buys one-time rights plus reprint, if applicable.
Tips: "Case histories about companies achieving substantial results using advanced management practices and/or advanced technology are best intro."

CONVENTION SOUTH, Covey Communications Corp., 2001 W. First St., P.O. Box 2267, Gulf Shores AL 36547-2267. (334)968-5300. Fax: (334)968-4532. Editor: J.Talty O'Connor. 50% freelance written. Trade journal on planning meetings and conventions in the South. Estab. 1983. Circ. 10,000. Pays on publication. Byline given. Buys first rights or second serial (reprint) rights. Submit seasonal/holiday material 2 months in advance. Accepts simultaneous and previously published submissions. Query for electronic submissions. Reports in 2 months on queries. Free sample copy.
Nonfiction: How-to (relative to meeting planning/travel), photo feature, travel. Buys 20 mss/year. Query. Length: 1,250-3,000 words. Pays $75-150. Pays in contributor copies or other premiums if arranged in advance. Sometime pays expenses of writers on assignment.
Photos: Send photos with submission. Reviews 5×7 prints. Offers no additional payment for photos accepted with ms. Captions and identification of subjects required. Buys one-time rights.

FINANCIAL EXECUTIVE, Financial Executives Institute, 10 Madison Ave., Morristown NJ 07962-1938. Fax: (201)267-4031. Editor: Robin Couch Cardillo. 2% freelance written. Bimonthly magazine for corporate financial management. "*Financial Executive* is published for senior financial executives of major corporations and explores corporate accounting and treasury related issues." Circ. 20,000. Pays on publication. Buys all rights. Sample copy for $5 and 9×12 SAE with 6 first-class stamps. Writer's guidelines for #10 SASE.
Nonfiction: Interviews of senior financial executives involved in issues listed above. Also, pieces ghostwritten for financial executives. Query with published clips. Length: 1,500-2,500 words. Pays $500-1,000.
Tips: "The query approach is best. (Address correspondence to Robin Couch Cardillo.) We use business or financial articles that follow a *Wall Street Journal* approach—a fresh idea, with its significance (to financial executives), quotes, anecdotes and an interpretation or evaluation. Our content will follow developments in treasury management, information management, regulatory changes, tax legislation, Congressional hearings/legislation, business and financial reporting. There is also interest in employee benefits, international business and impact of technology. We have very high journalistic standards."

‡FORECAST, The Magazine of Demographics and Business Statistics, Faulkner & Gray (Division of Thomson Professional Publishing), 11 Penn Plaza, New York NY 10001. (212)631-1420. Editor: Caitlin Kelly. 80% freelance written. Bimonthly magazine covering statistical information of use to business decision-makers. "A strong understanding of the relevance and practical application in business, of statistical and demographic information is required (i.e., Bureau of Labor Statistics, Census, etc.). The audience is 30% Fortune 500 companies, 60% midsize, often entrepreneurial; 10% consultants; 70% are CEO's or senior VP's, often of marketing; 75% are in manufacturing consumer goods; 25% business to business." Estab. 1992. Circ. 25,000. **Pays on acceptance.** Publishes ms an average of 1 month after acceptance. Byline given. Offers 25% kill fee. Buys first North American serial rights. Editorial lead time 1 month. No simultaneous submissions. Accepts previously published submissions. Query for electronic submissions. Reports in 2-3 weeks on queries; 1 month on mss. Sample copy for #10 SASE.
Nonfiction: Book excerpts, essays, interview/profile, new product, technical. Buys 30 mss/year. Query with published clips. Length: 1,500 words. Pays 35-50¢/word. Sometimes pays expenses of writers on assignment.

Photos: State availability of photos with submission. Reviews contact sheets, negatives, transparencies. Negotiates payment individually. Identification of subjects required. Buys one-time rights.

Columns/Departments: Book Reviews (business), 700-1,000 words; World/Region (business), 1,200-1,500 words. Buys 10 mss/year. Query with published clips. Pays 30-50¢/word.

Tips: "1) Send letter and résumé with clips. 2) Get a copy of the magazine and read it *carefully*. 3) Send us specific ideas."

HR MAGAZINE, Society for Human Resource Management, 606 N. Washington St., Alexandria VA 22314. (703)548-3440. Editor: Michelle Martinez. Monthly magazine covering human resource profession "with special focus on business news that affects the workplace including court decisions, legislative actions and government regulations." Estab. 1950. Circ. 56,000. **Pays on acceptance.** Publishes ms an average of 6 months after acceptance. Byline given. Offers $200 kill fee. Buys first North American, first, one-time, all or world rights or makes work-for-hire assignments. Query for electronic submissions. Prefers IBM compatible 3.5 or 5.25 disk. Sample copy for $7.50. Writer's guidelines free on request.

Nonfiction: Interview/profile, new product, opinion, personal experience, technical. Buys 6 mss/year. Query. Length: 700-2,200 words. Pays $200 minimum. Pays expenses of writers on assignment.

Photos: State availability of photos with submission. Reviews contact sheets. Offers no additional payment for photos accepted with ms. Model releases and identification of subjects required.

HR NEWS, Society for Human Resource Management, 606 N. Washington St., Alexandria VA 22314. (703)548-3440. Editor: Michelle Martinez. Monthly tabloid covering human resource profession "with special focus on business news that affects the workplace including court decisions, legislative actions and government regulations." Estab. 1982. Circ. 52,000. Pays on publication. Publishes ms an average of 1 month after acceptance. Byline given. Buys first or one-time rights or makes work-for-hire assignments. Editorial lead time 1-2 months. Query for electronic submissions. Prefers most DOS or Windows software or ASCII. Reports in 1 month on queries. Sample copy and writer's guidelines free.

Nonfiction: Interview/profile, personal experience. Buys 6 mss/year. Query with published clips. Length: 300-1,000 words. Pays 40¢/word. Sometimes pays expenses of writers on assignment.

Photos: State availability of photos with submission. Reviews contact sheets, any prints. Negotiates payment individually. Captions and identification of subjects required. Buys one-time rights.

Tips: "Experienced business/news writers should send some clips and story ideas for our file of potential writers in various regions and for various subjects. Local/state business news or government actions affecting HR management of potentially national interest is an area open to freelancers."

‡INSIDE SELF-STORAGE, Virgo Publishing Inc., 4141 N. Scottsdale Rd., Suite 316, Scottsdale AZ 85251. (602)990-1101. Editor: Drew Whitney. 60-70% freelance written. Monthly magazine covering the self-storage industry with regard to owners and operators. "Articles must be thoroughly researched, and we prefer that the author have some experience or expertise in the industry." Estab. 1990. Circ. 15,000. Pays on publication. Publishes ms an average of 2 months after acceptance. Byline given. Buys first North American serial rights. Editorial lead time 4 months. Submit seasonal material 3-6 months in advance. Query for electronic submissions. Reports in 2 weeks on queries; 1 month on mss. Sample copy for 9×12 SASE.

Nonfiction: Book excerpts, interview/profile, new product, technical. Buys 30 mss/year. Query with or without published clips. Length: 850-3,500 words. Pays $200 maximum for assigned articles. Pays expenses of writers on assignment.

Photos: Reviews 3×5 prints. Negotiates payment individually. Model releases and identification of subjects required. Buys one-time rights.

Columns/Departments: Managers' World, Marketing, Straight Talk; 1,000 words. Buys 24 mss/year. Query with published clips. Pays $200 maximum.

Tips: "Demonstrate a knowledge and understanding of the self-storage industry. Submit story ideas in writing."

MAY TRENDS, George S. May International Company, 303 S. Northwest Hwy., Park Ridge IL 60068-4255. (708)825-8806. Fax: (708)825-7937. Editor: Rosalind J. Angell. 20% freelance written. Works with a small number of new/unpublished writers each year. Free magazine published 1-2 times/year for owners and managers of small and medium-sized businesses, hospitals and nursing homes, trade associations, Better Business Bureaus, educational institutions and newspapers. Estab. 1966. Circ. 30,000. Buys all rights. Byline given. Pays on publication. Publishes ms an average of 6 months after acceptance. Returns rejected material immediately. Reports in 2 months. Sample copy for 9×12 SAE with 4 first-class stamps.

Nonfiction: "We prefer articles dealing with how to solve problems of specific industries (manufacturers, wholesalers, retailers, service businesses, small hospitals and nursing homes) where contact has been made with key executives whose comments regarding their problems may be quoted. We want problem solving articles, *not* success stories that laud an individual company. We like articles that give the business manager concrete suggestions on how to deal with specific problems—i.e., 'five steps to solve . . .,' 'six key questions to ask when . . .,' and 'four tell-tale signs indicating . . .' Focus is on marketing, economic and technological trends that have an impact on medium- and small-sized businesses, not on the 'giants'; automobile dealers coping with existing dull markets; and contractors solving cost-inventory problems. Will consider material on successful business operations and merchandising techniques." Buys up to 10 mss/year. Query or submit complete ms. Length: 2,000-3,000 words. Pays $150-250.

Tips: Query letter should tell "type of business and problems the article will deal with. We specialize in the problems of small (20-100 employees, $800,000-10,000,000 volume) businesses (manufacturing, wholesale, retail and service), plus medium and small healthcare facilities. We are now including nationally known writers in each issue—writers like the Vice Chairman of the Federal Reserve Bank, the US Secretary of the Treasury; names like George Bush and Malcolm Baldrige; titles like the Chairman of the Joint Committee on Accreditation of Hospitals; and Canadian Minister of Export. This places extra pressure on freelance writers to submit very good articles. Frequent mistakes: 1) writing for big business, rather than small, and 2) using language that is too academic."

RECORDS MANAGEMENT QUARTERLY, Association of Records Managers and Administrators, Inc., P.O. Box 4580, Silver Spring MD 20914-4580. Editor: Ira A. Penn, CRM, CSP. 10% freelance written. Eager to work with new/unpublished writers. Quarterly professional journal covering records and information management. Estab. 1967. Circ. 12,000. Pays on publication. Publishes ms an average of 6 months after acceptance. Byline given. Buys all rights. Accepts simultaneous submissions. Reports in 1 month on mss. *Writer's Market* recommends allowing 2 months for reply. Sample copy for $14. Free writer's guidelines.

Nonfiction: Professional articles covering theory, case studies, surveys, etc., on any aspect of records and information management. Buys 20-24 mss/year. Send complete ms. Length: 2,500 words minimum. Pays $50-300 "stipend"; no contract.

Photos: Send photos with ms. Offers no additional payment for photos accepted with ms. Prefers b&w prints. Captions required.

Tips: "A writer *must* know our magazine. Most work is written by practitioners in the field. We use very little freelance writing, but we have had some and it's been good. A writer must have detailed knowledge of the subject he/she is writing about. Superficiality is not acceptable."

‡RETAIL INFO SYSTEMS NEWS, Where retail management shops for technology, Edgell Communications, 1 W. Hanover Ave., Randolph NJ 07869. Editor: Mark Frantz. 60% freelance written. Monthly magazine covering retailers. "Readers are the functional managers/executives in all types of retail and consumer goods firms. They are making major improvements in company operations and in alliances with customers/suppliers." Estab. 1982. Circ. 18,500. Pays on publication. Byline sometimes given. Buys first rights and second serial (reprint) rights. Editorial lead time 2-3 months. Submit seasonal material 3 months in advance. Query for electronic submissions. Sample copy for 11 × 15 SAE with 6 first-class stamps. Writer's guidelines for #10 SAE.

Nonfiction: How-to, interview/profile, technical. Buys 100 mss/year. Query with published clips. Length: 1,200-2,400 words. Pays $500 maximum for assigned articles. Sometimes pays in contributor copies as negotiated. Sometimes pays expenses of writers on assignment.

Photos: Send photos with submission. Reviews contact sheets, negatives, transparencies and prints. Offers no additional payment for photos accepted with ms. Identification of subjects required. Buys one-time rights plus reprint, if applicable.

Tips: "Case histories about companies achieving substantial results using advanced management practices and/or advanced technology are best intro."

SIGN BUSINESS, National Business Media Inc., 1008 Depot Hill Rd., P.O. Box 1416, Broomfield CO 80038-1416. (303)469-0424. Fax: (303)469-5730. Editor: Terence Wike. 25% freelance written. Trade journal on the sign industry—electric, commercial, architectural. "This is business-to-business writing; we try to produce news you can use, rather than human interest." Estab. 1985. Circ. 20,500. Pays on publication. Publishes ms an average of 2 months after acceptance. Byline given. Buys first North American serial rights. Accepts previously published submissions. Send photocopy of article. For reprints, pays 50% of the amount paid for an original article. Submit seasonal material 4 months in advance. Query for electronic submissions. Reports in 1 month. Sample copy for $5. Writer's guidelines for #10 SASE.

Nonfiction: How-to (sign-painting techniques, new uses for computer cutters, lettering styles), etc.; interview/profile (sign company execs, shop owners with *unusual* work etc.), other (news on sign codes, legislation, unusual signs, etc.). "No humor, human interest, generic articles with 'sign' replacing another industry, no first-person writing, no profiles of a sign shop just because someone nice runs the business." Buys 20 mss/year. Query with published clips. Length: 500-3,000 words. Pays $85-250.

Photos: Send photos with submission. Reviews 3 × 5 transparencies and prints. Offers $5-10/photo. Identification of subjects required. Buys one-time rights and/or reprint rights.

Tips: "Find a sign shop, or sign company, and take some time to learn the business. The sign business is easily a $5 billion-plus industry every year in the US, and we treat it like a business, not a hobby. If you see a sign that stops you in your tracks, find out who made it; if it's a one-in-10,000 kind of sign, chances are good we'll want to know more. Writing should be factual and avoid polysyllabic words that waste a reader's time."

THE SMALL BUSINESS GAZETTE, America's Small Business Newspaper, Bovan Publishing Group, Inc., P.O. Box 1147, Buckingham PA 18912. (215)794-3826. E-mail: bizgazette@aol.com. or 71141.1331@compuserve.com. Managing Editor: Jim Donovan. 80% freelance written. Monthly newspaper covering small business. "Easy to implement, useful techniques and how to articles pertaining to running a successful small business." Estab. 1993. Circ. 50,000. Pays on publication. Publishes ms an average of 2 months after acceptance. Byline given. Buys first North American serial, one-time or simultaneous rights. Editorial lead time 2 months. Submit seasonal material 4 months in advance. Accepts simultaneous and previously published submissions. Send typed ms with rights for sale noted. Reports in 2 months on queries. Sample copy for $2. Writer's guidelines free on request.

Nonfiction: Book excerpts, how-to (business), humor, inspirational, interview/profile, new product, photo feature. Length: 700-1,000 words. Pays $50 and up. Sometimes pays expenses of writers on assignment.

Photos: State availability of photos with submission. Reviews 4×5 prints. Negotiates payment individually. Captions, model releases and identification of subjects required. Buys one-time rights.

Columns/Departments: Computers (small business computing), 1,000 words; Sales/Marketing (selling and marketing your business), 1,000 words. Buys 60 mss/year. Query with published clips. Pays $50.

Tips: "Submission on Compuserve or America Online preferred. Reader should learn something that will help them grow their business. No fluff!"

‡**U.S. ASSOCIATION EXECUTIVE, USAE Newspaper**, Custom News, 4341 Montgomery Ave., Bethesda MD 20814. (301)951-1881. Managing Editor: Diane Kirsh. 15% freelance written. Weekly tabloid covering association management, business travel, meetings and conventions, hotel news. "Our readers are top executives at associations, hotels, convention and visitor bureaus who want to know the latest news in their industry. We have a full-time staff, so we are interested in features from freelancers on associations, executives, new trends in technology, that affects associations, hotels, etc." Estab. 1982. Pays on publication. Publishes ms an average of 2 weeks after acceptance. Buys first North American serial rights. Editorial lead time 1 month. Submit seasonal material 2 months in advance. Accepts simultaneous submissions. Query for electronic submissions. Reports in 3 weeks on queries; 3 months on mss. Sample copy for $2. Writer's guidelines free on request.

Nonfiction: Book excerpts, general interest, interview/profile, new product, travel. Buys 30 mss/year. Query. Length: 700-1,500 words. Pays $100-200. Sometimes pays expenses of writers on assignment.

Photos: State availability of photos with submission. Reviews 3×5 prints. Offers no additional payment for photos accepted with ms. Identification of subjects required. Buys one-time rights.

Columns/Departments: Hot Off The Press (reviews of books on management, tourism, sales and marketing), 500-750 words. Buys 3 mss/year. Send complete ms. Pays $100-200.

‡**WORLD TRADE MAGAZINE**, Freedom Magazines, Inc., 17702 Cowan, Irvine CA 92714. (714)798-3500. Editor: Lawrence Delaney Jr.. 90% freelance written. Monthly magazine covering world trade. "*World Trade Magazine* is written for the up to 100,000 people who run America's growing midsize ($10 million to $300 million total sales) global companies. They are looking for entertaining, nuts-and-bolts articles that help them become more savvy global players." Estab. 1989. Circ. 62,000. Pays on publication. Publishes ms an average of 2 months after acceptance. Byline given. No kill fee. Buys first North American serial rights. Editorial lead time 3 months. Accepts simultaneous submissions. Query for electronic submissions. Reports in 2 weeks on queries; 1 month on mss. Sample copy and writer's guidelines free on request.

Nonfiction: Essays, how-to, interview/profile, personal experience, travel. Buys 50 mss/year. Query. Length: 750-2,500 words. Pays $500-1,200. Sometimes pays expenses of writers on assignment.

Photos: State availability of photos with submission. Negotiates payment individually. Buys one-time rights.

Church Administration and Ministry

Publications in this section are written for clergy members, church leaders and teachers. Magazines for lay members and the general public are listed in the Consumer Religious section.

‡**CHILDREN'S MINISTRY**, Group Publishing Inc., 2890 N. Monroe Ave., Loveland CO 80538. (303)669-3836. Editor: Christine Yount. Contact: Barbara Beach, departments editor. 73% freelance written. Bimonthly magazine of practical articles for Christian adults who work with children from birth to sixth grade. "The magazine's purpose is to supply practical ideas to help adults encourage children to grow spiritually." Estab. 1991. Circ. 50,000. **Pays on acceptance.** Byline given. Offers $25 kill fee. Buys all rights. Editorial lead time 5-6 months. Submit seasonal material 5 months in advance. Query for electronic submissions. Reports in 2 months. Sample copy for $2 and 9×12 SAE. Writer's guidelines for #10 SASE.

Nonfiction: How-to (practical, quick teaching ideas—games, crafts, devotional). No "preachy" articles. Query with or without published clips. Length: 50-1,200 words. Pays $25-100. Sometimes pays other than cash payments to reviewers. Sometimes pays expenses of writers on assignment.

Photos: State availability of photos with submission. Reviews contact sheets and prints. Offers $50-75/photo. Buys one-time rights.

Columns/Departments: Preschool Page (hints, songs, Bible activities), 50-125 words; Group Games, 125 words; Seasonal Specials, 125 words; Nursery Notes (help for nursery workers), 125 words; 5-Minute Messages (Scripture based, fun), 125 words; For Parents Only (ideas for parent self-help, communication with children), 125 words. Buys 50 mss/year. Send complete ms. Pays $25.

Tips: "Potential authors should be familiar with children's ministry and its style. Most successful authors are ones who have experience working with children in the church. We like new ideas with 'ah-hahs.' "

‡CREATOR MAGAZINE, Bimonthly Magazine of Balanced Music Ministries, Church Music Association Inc., 4631 Cutwater Lane, Hilliard OH 43026. (614)777-7774. Editor: Marshall Sanders. 35% freelance written. Bimonthly magazine covering Protestant music ministry and worship. "All readers are church music choir directors. Content focuses on the spectrum of worship styles from praise and worship to traditional to liturgical. All denominations subscribe. Articles on worship, choir rehearsal, handbells, children's/youth choirs, technique, relationships, etc." Estab. 1978. Circ. 6,000. Pays on publication. Publishes ms an average of 4 months after acceptance. Byline given. Buys first rights, one-time roghts or second serial (reprint) rights; occasionally buys no rights. Editorial lead time 3 months. Submit seasonal material 4 months in advance. Accepts simultaneous and previously published submissions if notified. Query for electronic submissions. Sample copy for 9×12 SAE with 5 first-class stamps. Writer's guidelines free on request.

Nonfiction: Essays, how-to (be a better church musician, choir director, rehearsal technician, etc.), humor (short personal perspectives), inspirational, interview/profile (call first), new product (call first), opinion, personal experience, photo feature, religious, technical (choral technique). Special issues: July/August is directed toward adult choir members, rather than directors. Buys 20 mss/year. Query or send complete ms. Length: 1,000-10,000 words. Pays $30-75 for assigned articles; $30-60 for unsolicited articles. Pays expenses of writers on assignment.

Photos: State availability of or send photos with submission. Reviews negatives, 8×10 prints. Offers no additional payment for photos accepted with ms. Captions appreciated. Buys one-time rights.

Columns/Departments: Hints & Humor (music ministry short ideas, anecdotes [cute] ministry experience), 75-250 words; Inspiration (motivational ministry stories), 200-500 words; Children/Youth (articles about specific choirs), 1,000-5,000 words. Buys 15 mss/year. Query or send complete ms. Pays $20-60.

Tips: "Request article guidelines and stick to it. If theme is relevant and guidelines are followed, we will probably publish."

‡THE JOURNAL OF ADVENTIST EDUCATION, General Conference of SDA, 12501 Old Columbia Pike, Silver Spring MD 10904-6600. (301)680-5075. Editor: Beverly J. Rumble. Bimonthly (except skips issue in summer) professional journal covering teachers and administrators in SDA school system. Estab. 1939. Circ. 7,500. Pays on publication. Publishes ms 3-12 months after acceptance. Byline given. Buys first rights. Editorial lead time 3 months. Accepts previously published submissions. Reports in 6 weeks on queries; 4 months on mss. Sample copy for 10×12 SAE with 5 first-class stamps. Writer's guidelines free on request.

Nonfiction: Book excerpts, essays, how-to, personal experience, photo feature, religious, education. Theme issues have assigned authors. "No brief first-person stories about Sunday Schools." Query. Length: 1,000-1,500 words. Pays $25-100.

Photos: State availability of photos or send photos with submission. Reviews prints. Negotiates payment individually. Captions required. Buys one-time rights.

LEADERSHIP, A Practical Journal for Church Leaders, Christianity Today, Inc., 465 Gundersen Dr., Carol Stream IL 60188. (708)260-6200. E-mail: LeaderJ@aol.com. Editor: Kevin A. Miller. 75% freelance written. Works with a small number of new/unpublished writers each year. Quarterly magazine covering church leadership. Writers must have a "knowledge of and sympathy for the unique expectations placed on pastors and local church leaders. Each article must support points by illustrating from real life experiences in local churches." Estab. 1980. Circ. 75,000. **Pays on acceptance.** Publishes ms an average of 6 months after acceptance. Byline given. Buys first North American serial rights. Submit seasonal material 6 months in advance. Accepts previously published submissions. Send photocopy of article and information about when and where the article previously appeared. For reprints, pays 50% of the amount paid for an original article. Reports in 6 weeks on queries; 2 months on mss. Sample copy for $3. Free writer's guidelines.

Nonfiction: How-to, humor, personal experience. "No articles from writers who have never read our journal." Buys 50 mss/year. Send complete ms. Length: 100-5,000 words. Pays $50-350. Sometimes pays the expenses of writers on assignment.

Photos: State availability of photos with submission. Offers no additional payment for photos accepted with ms. Identification of subjects required. Buys one-time rights.

Columns/Departments: To Illustrate (short stories or analogies that illustrate a biblical principle), 100 words. Buys 25 mss/year. Send complete ms. Pays $25-50.

PASTORAL LIFE, Society of St. Paul, P.O. Box 595, Route 224, Canfield OH 44406-0595. Fax: (216)533-1076. Editor: Anthony Chenevey, SSP. 66% freelance written. Works with new/unpublished writers. Monthly magazine emphasizing priests and those interested in pastoral ministry. Estab. 1953. Circ. 2,800. Buys first rights only. Byline given. Pays on publication. Publishes ms an average of 6 months after acceptance. Query with outline before submitting ms. "New contributors are expected to include, in addition, a few lines of personal data that indicate academic and professional background." Reports in 1 month. Sample copy and writer's guidelines for 6×9 SAE with 4 first-class stamps.
Nonfiction: "*Pastoral Life* is a professional review, principally designed to focus attention on current problems, needs, issues and important activities related to all phases of pastoral work and life." Buys 30 unsolicited mss/year. Length: 2,000-3,000 words. Pays 4¢/word minimum.

THE PREACHER'S MAGAZINE, Nazarene Publishing House, E. 10814 Broadway, Spokane WA 99206-5003. Editor: Randal E. Denny. Assistant Editor: Cindy Osso. 15% freelance written. Works with a small number of new/unpublished writers each year. Quarterly magazine of seasonal/miscellaneous articles. "A resource for ministers; Wesleyan-Arminian in theological persuasion." Circ. 18,000. Pays on publication. Publishes ms an average of 9 months after acceptance. Byline given. Buys first serial, second serial (reprint) and simultaneous rights. Submit seasonal material 9 months in advance. Accepts previously published submissions. Send photocopy of article or typed ms with rights for sale noted and information about when and where the article previously appeared. For reprints, pays 100% of the amount paid for an original article. Writer's guidelines for #10 SASE.
Nonfiction: How-to, humor, inspirational, opinion, personal experience, all relating to aspects of ministry. No articles that present problems without also presenting answers to them; things not relating to pastoral ministry. Buys 48 mss/year. Send complete ms. Length: 700-2,500 words. Pays 3½¢/word.
Photos: Send photos with ms. Reviews 35mm transparencies and b&w prints. Model release and identification of subjects required. Buys one-time rights.
Columns/Departments: Stories Preachers Tell Each Other (humorous).
Fiction: Publishes novel excerpts.
Fillers: Anecdotes, short humor. Buys 10/year. Length: 400 words maximum. Pays 3½¢/word.
Tips: "Writers for the *Preacher's Magazine* should have insight into the pastoral ministry, or expertise in a specialized area of ministry. Our magazine is a highly specialized publication aimed at the minister. Our goal is to assist, by both scholarly and practical articles, the modern-day minister in applying Biblical theological truths."

THE PRIEST, Our Sunday Visitor, Inc., 200 Noll Plaza, Huntington IN 46750-4304. (219)356-8400. Fax: (219)356-8472. Editor: Father Owen F. Campion. Associate Editor: George P. Foster. 80% freelance written. Monthly magazine for the priesthood. "We run articles that will aid priests in their day-to-day ministry. Includes items on spirituality, counseling, administration, theology, personalities, the saints, etc." **Pays on acceptance.** Byline given. Not copyrighted. Buys first North American serial rights. Editorial lead time 3 months. Submit seasonal material at least 4 months in advance. Query for electronic submissions. Reports in 2 weeks on queries; 1 month on mss. Sample copy and writer's guidelines free on request.
Nonfiction: Essays, historical/nostalgic, humor, inspirational, interview/profile, opinion, personal experience, photo feature, religious. Buys 96 mss/year. Send complete ms. Length: 1,500-5,000 words. Pays $300 minimum for assigned articles; $50 minimum for unsolicited articles.
Photos: Send photos with submission. Reviews transparencies and prints. Negotiates payment individually. Captions and identification of subjects required. Buys one-time rights.
Columns/Departments: Viewpoint (whatever applies to priests and the Church), 1,000 words. Buys 36 mss/year. Send complete ms. Pays $50-100.
Tips: "Say what you have to say in an interesting and informative manner and stop. Freelancers are most often published in 'Viewpoints.' Please do not stray from the magisterium of the Catholic Church."

YOUR CHURCH, Helping You With the Business of Ministry, Christianity Today, Inc., 465 Gundersen Dr., Carol Stream IL 60188. (708)260-6200. E-mail: YCEditor@aol.com. Managing Editor: Richard Doebler. 70% freelance written. Bimonthly magazine for the business of today's church. "Articles pertain to the business aspects of ministry pastors are called upon to perform: administration, purchasing, management, technology, building, etc." Estab. 1955. Circ. 200,000. **Pays on acceptance.** Publishes ms an average of 4 months after acceptance. Byline given. Buys one-time rights. Submit seasonal material 5 months in advance. Accepts simultaneous and previously published submissions. Send photocopy of article and information about when and where the article previously appeared. For reprints, pays 30% of the amount paid for an original article. Reports in 1 month on queries; 2 months on mss. Sample copy and writer's guidelines for 9×12 SAE with 5 first-class stamps.
Nonfiction: How-to, new product, technical. Buys 12 mss/year. Send complete ms. Length: 900-1,500 words. Pays about 10¢/word.
Photos: State availability of photos with submission. Reviews 4×5 transparencies and 5×7 or 8×10 prints. Offers no additional payment for photos accepted with ms. Captions, model releases and identification of subjects required. Buys one-time rights.

Tips: "The editorial is generally geared toward brief and helpful articles dealing with some form of church business. Concise, bulletted points from experts in the field are typical for our articles."

‡YOUTH AND CHRISTIAN EDUCATION LEADERSHIP, Pathway Press, P.O. Box 2250, Cleveland TN 37320-2250. Editor: Lance Colkmire. 15% freelance written. Quarterly magazine covering Christian education. "*Leadership* is written for teachers, youth pastors, children's pastors, and other local church Christian education leaders." Estab. 1976. Circ. 9,700. **Pays on acceptance.** Publishes ms an average of 6 months after acceptance. Not copyrighted. Buys first North American serial, first, one-time, second serial (reprint) or simultaneous rights. Editorial lead time 6 months. Submit seasonal material 6 months in advance. Accepts simultaneous and previously published submissions. Reports in 1 month on queries; 3 months on mss. Sample copy for $1. Writer's guidelines free on request.
Nonfiction: How-to (for church teachers), inspirational, interview/profile. Buys 10 mss/year. Send complete ms. Length: 400-1,200 words. Pays $25-55 for assigned articles; $20-45 for unsolicited articles.
Photos: State availability of photos with submission. Reviews contact sheets, transparencies. Negotiates payment individually. Buys one-time rights.
Columns/Departments: Sunday School Leadership, 500 words; Reaching Out (creative evangelism), 500 words; The Pastor and Christian Education, 500 words. Send complete ms. Pays $20-40.

‡THE YOUTH LEADER, General Council of the Assemblies of God, 1445 Boonville Ave., Springfield MO 65802. (417)862-2781. Editor: Rich Percifield. Contact: Chuck Goldberg, Managing Editor. 75% freelance written. Published 8 times/year covering Assemblies of God and Pentecostal Youth Ministry. "We're dedicated to providing practical helps for the busy pentecostal youth minister in need of material that will minister to his group." Estab. 1975. Circ. 3,000. Pays on publication. Publishes ms 6 months after acceptance. Byline given. Buys one-time rights. Editorial lead time 5 months. Submit seasonal material 5 months in advance. Accepts simultaneous and previously published submissions. Reports in 2 weeks on queries; 1 month on mss. Sample copy and writer's guidelines free on request.
Nonfiction: How-to (aspects of youth ministry), inspirational, interview/profile, religious. "We do not want general religious material that is not youth-ministry specific. We're geared to equipping youth ministers with helps." Buys 20 mss/year. Send complete ms. Length: 1,000-1,500 words. Pays expenses of writers on assignment. "We work primarily through assignments, though we don't discourage unsolicited material."
Photos: State availability or send photos with submission. Offers no additional payment for photos accepted with ms. Captions required. Buys one-time rights.
Columns/Departments: Brainstorms (youth meeting idea starters), 100-500 words; Program Plans (youth meeting outlines), 500 words. Buys 98 mss/year. Send complete ms. Pays 4¢/word.
Tips: "Request magazine and study thoroughly. Submit a tightly written, spiritually compelling Program Plan or Brainstorm exhibiting slavish devotion to format. Once one has arrested our attention with this, an article assignment should eventually follow, if the writer's credentials are there."

Clothing

ATI, America's Textiles International, Billian Publishing Co., 2100 Powers Ferry Rd., Atlanta GA 30339. (404)955-5656. Fax: (404)952-0669. Editor: Monte G. Plott. Associate Editor: Rolf Viertel. 10% freelance written. Monthly magazine covering "the business of textile, apparel and fiber industries with considerable technical focus on products and processes. No puff pieces pushing a particular product." Estab. 1887. Pays on publication. Byline sometimes given. Buys first North American serial rights. Query for electronic submissions.
Nonfiction: Technical, business. "No PR, just straight technical reports." Buys 10 mss/year. Query. Length: 500 words minimum. Pays $100/published page. Sometimes pays expenses of writers on assignment.
Photos: Send photos with submission. Reviews prints. Offers no additional payment for photos accepted with ms. Captions required. Buys one-time rights.

BOBBIN, Bobbin Blenheim Media, 1110 Shop Rd., P.O. Box 1986, Columbia SC 29202-1986. (803)771-7500. Fax: (803)799-1461. Editor-in-Chief: Susan Black. 25% freelance written. Monthly magazine for CEO's and top management in apparel and sewn products manufacturing companies. Circ. 9,788. Pays on publication. Byline given. Buys all rights. Reports in 6 weeks. Free sample copy and writer's guidelines.
Columns/Departments: Trade View, R&D, Network News, Partnerships, Personnel Management, Labor Forum, NON-Apparel Highlights, Fabric Notables.
Tips: "Articles should be written in a style appealing to busy top managers and should in some way foster thought or new ideas, or present solutions/alternatives to common industry problems/concerns. CEOs are most interested in quick read pieces that are also informative and substantive. Articles should not be based on opinions but should be developed through interviews with industry manufacturers, retailers or other experts, etc. Sidebars may be included to expand upon certain aspects within the article. If available, illustrations, graphs/charts, or photographs should accompany the article."

IMPRINTING BUSINESS, WFC, Inc., 3000 Hadley Rd., South Plainfield NJ 07080. (908)769-1160. Fax: (908)769-1171. Editor: Bruce Sachenski. Monthly magazine for persons in imprinted garment industry and screen printing. Circ. 27,000. Pays on publication. Publishes ms an average of 3 months after acceptance. Byline given. Buys one-time rights. Submit seasonal/holiday material 3 months in advance. Accepts previously published submissions. Reports in 2 months. Sample copy for $10.
Nonfiction: How-to, new product, photo feature, technical, business. Buys 3 mss/year. Send complete ms. Length: 1,500-3,500 words. Pays $200-500 for assigned articles.
Photos: Send photos with submission. Reviews contact sheets. Offers no additional payment for photos accepted with ms. Identification of subjects required.
Tips: "We need general business stories, advertising, store management, etc."

‡MR MAGAZINE, The Magazine of Menswear Retailing, Business Journals, Inc., 50 Day St., Norwalk CT 06854. (203)853-6015. Editor: Karen Alberg Grossman. Contact: Katherine Grayson. 20% freelance written. Magazine published 8 times/year covering "up-to-the-minute coverage of menswear industry and retailers." Estab. 1990. Circ. 30,000. Pays on publication. Publishes ms an average of 2 months after acceptance. Byline given. Buys all rights. Editorial lead time 2 months. Submit seasonal material 2 months in advance. No simultaneous or previously published submissions. Query for electronic submissions. Reports in 1 month. Sample copy for $3.50 (if available). Writer's guidelines free on request.
Nonfiction: Humor, interview/profile, new product, opinion, personal experience (all dealing with men and menswear). Editorial calendar available. Buys 25-30 mss/year. Query with published clips or send complete ms. Length: 500-2,000 words. Pays $150-750. Sometimes pays expenses of writers on assignment.
Photos: Send photos with submission. Reviews transparencies or prints. Offers no additional payment for photos accepted with ms. Identification of subjects required. Buys all rights.

‡TEXTILE RENTAL, Uniform and Linen Service Management Trends, Textile Rental Services Association of America, 1130 E. Hallandale Beach Blvd., Suite B, Hallandale FL 33009. (305)457-7555. Editor: Christine Seaman. Contact: Steven R. Biller, managing editor. 25% freelance written. Monthly magazine covering management, information and trends for uniform and linen rental executives. *"Textile Rental* covers government, environment, labor, workplace safety, regulatory compliance, computer technology, the economy, plant operations, marketing, sales and service." Byline sometimes given. Offers negotiable kill fee. Editorial lead time 2 months. Submit seasonal material 4 months in advance. Accepts previously published submissions. Query for electronic submissions. Reports in 3-4 weeks on queries; 2-3 months on mss. Sample copy free on request. Writer's guidelines for #10 SASE.
Nonfiction: Historical/nostalgic, how-to, inspirational, interview/profile, new product, technical. Buys 10-12 mss/year. Query with published clips. Length: 1,000-5,000 words. Pays $50-400. Pays writers with contributor copies at writer's request. Sometimes pays expenses of writers on assignment.
Photos: Reviews contact sheets. Negotiates payment individually. Captions and identification of subjects preferred. Buys one-time rights.
Fillers: Anecdotes, facts, gags to be illustrated by cartoonist, newsbreaks, short humor. Buys 25-30/year. Length: 150-500 words. Pays $35-100.

Coin-Operated Machines

VENDING TIMES, 1375 Broadway, New York NY 10018. (212)302-4700. Fax: (212)221-3311. Editor: Arthur E. Yohalem. Monthly magazine for operators of vending machines. Estab. 1960. Circ. 15,450. Pays on publication. Buys all rights. "We will discuss in detail the story requirements with the writer." Sample copy for $4.
Nonfiction: Feature articles and news stories about vending operations; practical and important aspects of the business. "We are always willing to pay for good material." Query.

Confectionery and Snack Foods

These publications focus on the bakery, snack and candy industries. Journals for grocers, wholesalers and other food industry personnel are listed in Groceries and Food Products.

PACIFIC BAKERS NEWS, 180 Mendell St., San Francisco CA 94124-1740. (415)826-2664. Publisher: C.W. Soward. 30% freelance written. Eager to work with new/unpublished writers. Monthly business newsletter for commercial bakeries in the western states. Estab. 1961. Pays on publication. No byline given; uses only 1-paragraph news items.
Nonfiction: Uses bakery business reports and news about bakers. Buys only brief "boiled-down news items about bakers and bakeries operating only in Alaska, Hawaii, Pacific Coast and Rocky Mountain states. We welcome clippings. We need monthly news reports and clippings about the baking industry and the donut

business. No pictures, jokes, poetry or cartoons." Length: 10-200 words. Pays 10¢/word for news and 6¢ for clips (words used).

Construction and Contracting

Builders, architects and contractors learn the latest industry news in these publications. Journals targeted to architects are also included in the Consumer Art and Architecture category. Those for specialists in the interior aspects of construction are listed under Building Interiors.

‡**ABERDEEN'S CONCRETE CONSTRUCTION**, The Aberdeen Group, 426 S. Westgate St., Addison IL 60101. (708)543-0870. Managing Editor: Anne Balogh. 20% freelance written. Monthly magazine covering concrete construction, "a how-to magazine for concrete contractors. It also covers job stories and new equipment in the industry." Estab. 1956. Circ. 85,000. **Pays on acceptance.** Publishes ms an average of 3 months after acceptance. Byline given. Editorial lead time 2 months. Submit seasonal material 3 months in advance. Query for electronic submissions. Reports in 2 weeks on queries; 1 month on mss. Sample copy free on request.
Nonfiction: How-to, new product, personal experience, photo feature, technical, job stories. Buys 7-10 mss/ year. Query. Length varies. Pays $250 for assigned articles; $200 minimum for unsolicited articles. Sometimes pays expenses of writers on assignment.
Photos: State availability of photos with submission. Reviews contact sheets, negatives, transparencies, prints. Negotiates payment individually. Captions required. Buys one-time rights.
Tips: "Must have a good understanding of the concrete construction industry. How-to stories only accepted from industry experts. Job stories must cover the procedures, materials, and equipment used as well as the scope of the project."

AUTOMATED BUILDER, CMN Associates, Inc., P.O. Box 120, Cartinteria CA 93014-0120. (805)684-7659. Fax: (805)684-1765. Editor-in-Chief: Don Carlson. 15% freelance written. Monthly magazine specializing in management for industrialized (manufactured) housing and volume home builders. Estab. 1964. Circ. 25,000. **Pays on acceptance.** Publishes ms an average of 3 months after acceptance. Buys first North American serial rights. Phone queries OK. Reports in 2 weeks. Free sample copy and writer's guidelines.
 • *Automated Builder* reports that their freelance writing needs have increased since last year.
Nonfiction: Case history articles on successful home building companies which may be 1) production (big volume) home builders; 2) mobile home manufacturers; 3) modular home manufacturers; 4) prefabricated (panelized) home manufacturers; 5) house component manufacturers; or 6) special unit (in-plant commercial building) manufacturers. Also uses interviews, photo features and technical articles. "No architect or plan 'dreams'. Housing projects must be built or under construction." Buys 15 mss/year. Query. Length: 500-1,000 words maximum. Pays $300 minimum.
Photos: Purchased with accompanying ms. Query. No additional payment. Wants 4×5, 5×7 or 8×10 glossies or 35mm or larger color transparencies (35mm preferred). Captions required.
Tips: "Stories often are too long, too loose; we prefer 500 to 750 words. We prefer a phone query on feature articles. If accepted on query, article usually will not be rejected later."

CAM MAGAZINE, Construction Association of Michigan, 500 Stephenson Hwy., Suite 400, Troy MI 48083. (810)585-1000. Fax: (810)585-9785. Editor: Marla S. Janness. 5% freelance written. Monthly magazine covering all facets of the construction industry. "*CAM Magazine* is devoted to the growth and progress of individuals and companies serving and servicing the construction industry. It provides a forum on new construction industry technology and practices, current information on new construction projects, products and services, and publishes information on industry personnel changes and advancements." Estab. 1978. Circ. 4,000. Pays on publication. Byline given. Buys all rights. Editorial lead time 2 months. Submit seasonal material 3 months in advance. Query for electronic submissions. Sample copy free on request.
Nonfiction: Construction-related only. Buys 3 mss/year. Query with published clips. Length: 1,000-5,000 words. Pays $50.
Photos: Send photos with submission. Reviews contact sheets, negatives, transparencies and prints. Offers no additional payment for photos accepted with ms. Buys one-time rights.
Tips: "Anyone having *current* knowledge or expertise on some of our featured topics is welcomed to submit articles. Recent experience or information on a construction-related issue or new trends and innovations, is also helpful."

CONSTRUCTION COMMENT, Naylor Communications Ltd., 920 Yonge St., 6th Floor, Suite 600, Toronto, Ontario M4W 3C7 Canada. (416)961-1028. Fax: (416)924-4408. Editor: Lori Knowles. 80% freelance written. Semiannual magazine on construction industry in Ottawa. "*Construction Comment* reaches all members of the Ottawa Construction Association and most senior management of firms relating to the industry."

Estab. 1970. Circ. 3,000. Pays 30 days after deadline. Byline given. Offers 33% kill fee. Buys first North American serial rights. Submit seasonal material 2 months in advance. Accepts simultaneous and previously published submissions. Send tearsheet or photocopy of article and information about when and where the article previously appeared. For reprints, pays 80% of amount paid for an original article. Query for electronic submissions. Reports in 6 weeks.

Nonfiction: General interest, historical, interview/profile, new product, photo feature, technical. "We publish a spring/summer issue and a fall/winter issue. Submit correspondingly or inquire two months ahead of these times." Buys 10 mss/year. Query with published clips. Length: 500-2,500 words. Pays 25¢/word. Pays expenses of writers on assignment.

Photos: State availability of photos with submission. Reviews transparencies and prints. Offers $25-200/photo. Identification of subjects required.

Tips: "Please send copies of work and a general query. I will respond as promptly as my deadlines allow."

CONSTRUCTION MARKETING TODAY, The Aberdeen Group, 426 S. Westgate St., Addison IL 60101. (708)543-0870. Editor: Diana Granitto. 25% freelance written. Monthly tabloid covering marketing equipment or materials to the construction industry. "Our readers are manufacturers of construction equipment and building materials. Specifically, our readers are marketing people and top execs at those companies. The magazine carries business news, marketing case studies and marketing how-to articles. The magazine does not have heavily technical content, so writers need not be knowledgeable of the industry. Business writing and company profile writing experience is a plus." Estab. 1990. Circ. 4,000. Pays on publication. Byline given. Buys first rights and simultaneous rights. Editorial lead time 2 months. Query for electronic submissions. Occasionally accepts previously published articles. Send tearsheet, photocopy of article or typed ms with rights for sale noted and information about when and where the article previously appeared. Pay varies. Reports in 5 weeks on queries; 2 months on mss. Sample copy free on request.

Nonfiction: Exposé, how-to (marketing), interview/profile, opinion, personal experience, business news, marketing trends. "No stories aimed at contractors or stories that show no relevancy to the industry." Buys 15 mss/year. Query with published clips. Length: 800-3,000 words. Pays $200. Pays in contributor's copies if "author is an industry consultant or has a service he is trying to sell to our readers, or he works for a manufacturing company." Sometimes pays expenses of writers on assignment.

Photos: State availability of photos with submission. Reviews contact sheets. Negotiates payment individually. Captions and identification of subjects required. Buys all rights.

Tips: "Show that you have a grasp of what the magazine is about. We are not a technical how-to magazine geared to contractors, as most construction publications are. We have a unique niche. We are targeted to manufacturers marketing to contractors. We are looking for stories that have a fresh and intriguing look, that are entertaining to read, that are relevant to our readers, that are informative and that show an attention to detail in the reporting. Page 1 news, inside features, company profiles, industry marketing trends and marketing how-to stories are most open to freelancers. Stories should be tailored to our industry."

CONSTRUCTION SPECIFIER, 601 Madison St., Alexandria VA 22314-1791. (703)684-0300. Fax: (703)684-0465. E-mail: 72113.1665@compuserve.com. Publisher: Jack Reeder. 50% freelance written. Works with a small number of new/unpublished writers each year. Monthly professional society magazine for architects, engineers, specification writers and project managers. Monthly. Estab. 1949. Circ. 19,000. Pays on publication. Publishes ms an average of 4 months after acceptance. Deadline: 60 days preceding publication on the 1st of each month. Buys world serial rights. Accepts previously published submissions. Send information about when and where the article previously appeared. Does not pay for reprints. Query for electronic submissions. "Call or write first." Model release, author copyright transferral requested. Reports in 3 weeks. Sample copy for 9×12 SAE with 6 first-class stamps. Writer's guidelines for #10 SASE.

Nonfiction: Articles on selection and specification of products, materials, practices and methods used in commercial (non-residential) construction projects, specifications as related to construction design, plus legal and management subjects. Query. Length: 2,500-3,500 words maximum. Pays up to 15¢/published word (negotiable), plus art. Pays minor expenses of writers on assignment, to an agreed upon limit.

Photos: Photos desirable in consideration for publication; line art, sketches, diagrams, charts and graphs also desired. Full color transparencies may be used; 8×10 glossies, 3¼ slides preferred. Payment negotiable.

Tips: "We need more good technical articles."

COST CUTS, The Enterprise Foundation, American City Bldg., 10227 Wincopin Circle, Suite 500, Columbia MD 21044-3400. (410)964-1230. Fax: (410)964-1918. Editor: Peggy Armstrong. 25% freelance written. Quarterly newsletter on rehabilitation of low-income housing. "*Cost Cuts* seeks ways to reduce the cost of rehabbing and constructing low-income housing and also informs of changes in federal policy, local and state efforts in low-income housing and pro bono work in this area. *Cost Cuts* is distributed nationally to rehab specialists, agencies and others involved in the production of low-income housing." Estab. 1983. Circ. 7,000. Pays on publication. Byline given. Buys one-time rights. Submit seasonal material 3 months in advance. Accepts previously published submissions. Send tearsheet of article, typed ms with rights for sale noted and information about when and where the article previously appeared. Query for electronic submissions. Reports in 1 month. Sample copy for 9×12 SAE with 2 first-class stamps. Writer's guidelines for #10 SASE.

Nonfiction: How-to, interview/profile, technical, international. "No personal experience of do-it-yourselfers in single-family homes. We want articles concerning high production of low-income housing." Buys 10-15 mss/year. Query with published clips. Length: 100-1,500 words. Pays $50-200 for assigned articles; $200 maximum for unsolicited articles. Sometimes pays expenses of writers on assignment.

Photos: Send photos with submission. Reviews contact sheets and 3×5 and 5×7 prints. Captions and identification of subjects required. Buys one-time rights.

Fillers: Facts, newsbreaks. Buys 20/year. Length: 100-500 words. Pays $25-50.

Tips: "The Foundation's mission is to see that all low-income people in the United States have the opportunity for fit and affordable housing and to move up and out of poverty into the mainstream of American life. Freelancers must be conscious of this context. Articles must include case studies of specific projects where costs have been cut. Charts of cost comparisons to show exactly where cuts were made are most helpful."

INDIANA BUILDER, Pro Tec Publishing & Printing, 500 S. Cory Lane, Bloomington IN 47403. (812)332-1639. Editor: C. Dale Risch. 40% freelance written. Monthly magazine covering residential construction. "Our readers are professional builders and remodelers." Estab. 1989. Circ. 12,500. **Pays on acceptance.** Byline given. Buys one-time rights. Editorial lead time 1 month. Submit seasonal material 3 months in advance. Accepts simultaneous and previously published submissions. Query for electronic submissions. Sample copy free on request.

Nonfiction: How-to (construction). Buys 60 mss/year. Query with published clips. Length: 500-2,000 words. Pays 5¢/word. Sometimes pays expenses of writers on assignment.

Photos: State availability of or send photos with submission. Reviews contact sheets. Negotiates payment individually. Captions required. Buys one-time rights.

INLAND ARCHITECT, The Midwestern Building Arts Magazine, Inland Architect Press, 3525 W. Peterson Ave., Suite 103, Chicago IL 60659. (312)465-5151. (312)866-9906. Contact: Steven Polydoris. 80% freelance written. Bimonthly magazine covering architecture and urban planning. "*Inland Architect* is a critical journal covering architecture and design in the Midwest for an audience primarily of architects. *Inland* is open to all points of view, providing they are intelligently expressed and of relevance to architecture." Estab. 1883. Circ. 8,000. Pays on publication. Publishes ms an average of 2 months after acceptance. Byline given. Offers 30% kill fee. Buys first rights. Reports in 2 months. Sample copy for $15 (includes shipping and handling).

Nonfiction: Book excerpts, essays, historical/nostalgic, interview/profile, criticism, photo feature of architecture. Every summer *Inland* focuses on a Midwestern city, its architecture and urban design; call to find out 1996 city. No new products, "how to run your office," or technical pieces. Buys 40 mss/year. Query with published clips or send complete ms. Length: 750-3,500 words. Pay varies for assigned articles. Sometimes pays the expenses of writers on assignment.

Photos: Send photos with submission. Reviews 4×5 transparencies, slides and 8×10 prints. Offers no additional payment for photos accepted with ms. Identification of subjects required. Buys one-time rights.

Columns/Departments: Books (reviews of new publications on architecture, design, and occasionally, art), 250-1,000 words. Buys 10 mss/year. Query. Pays $50. Space (interiors), pay varies; Inlandscape (news of new/under construction projects), pay varies; Earth (design projects with an emphasis on their environmental implications), pay varies.

Tips: "Propose to cover a lecture, to interview a certain architect, etc. Articles must be written for an audience primarily consisting of well-educated architects. If an author feels he has a 'hot' timely idea, a phone call is appreciated."

MASONRY, 1550 Spring Rd., Oak Brook IL 60521. (708)782-6767. Editor: Gene Adams. 20% freelance written. Bimonthly magazine covering masonry contracting. "*Masonry Magazine* for masonry contractors and other members of the masonry industry, who are engaged in commercial, residential, institutional, governmental, industrial and renovation building projects. Readers include architects, engineers, specifiers, project manufacturers and others." Estab. 1961. Circ. 12,000. **Pays on acceptance.** Byline given. Buys first North American serial, first, one-time, second serial (reprint), simultaneous or all rights or makes work-for-hire assignments. Editorial lead time 2 months. Submit seasonal material 3 months in advance. Accepts simultaneous and previously published submissions. Send tearsheet or typed ms with rights for sale noted and information about when and where the article previously appeared. For reprints, negotiates payment. Reports in 3 weeks on queries; 8 months on mss. Sample copy and writer's guidelines free on request.

Nonfiction: Book excerpts, historical/nostalgic, how-to (contracting problems), interview/profile, new product, personal experience, photo feature, technical. Buys 12-18 mss/year. Query. Length: 500-4,000 words. Pays $150-250 for assigned articles; $25-50 for unsolicited articles.

Photos: Send photos with submission. Reviews contact sheets. Offers $10-50/photo or negotiates payment individually. Captions and identification of subjects required. Buys one-time and/or all rights.

PACIFIC BUILDER & ENGINEER, Vernon Publications Inc., 3000 Northup Way, Suite 200, Bellevue WA 98004. (206)827-9900. Fax: (206)822-9372. Editor: Carl Molesworth. Editorial Director: Michele Andrus Dill. 44% freelance written. Biweekly magazine covering non-residential construction in the Northwest and Alaska. "Our readers are construction contractors in Washington, Oregon, Idaho, Montana and Alaska. The feature stories in *PB&E* focus on ongoing construction projects in our coverage area. They address these questions: What is the most significant challenge to the general contractor? What innovative construction techniques or equipment are being used to overcome the challenges?" Estab. 1902. Circ. 14,500. Pays on publication. Publishes ms an average of 2 months after acceptance. Byline given. Buys first North American serial and second serial (reprint) rights. Editorial lead time 6 weeks. Submit seasonal material 2 months in advance. Query for electronic submissions. Reports in 2 months on queries; 6 weeks on mss. Sample copy for $7. Writer's guidelines for #10 SASE.
Nonfiction: How-to, new product, photo feature. "No non-construction stories; no residential construction articles; no construction stories without a Northwest or Alaska angle." Buys 18 mss/year. Query with published clips. Length: 750-2,000 words. Pays $100. Sometimes pays expenses of writers on assignment.
Photos: State availability of photos with submission. Reviews contact sheets, transparencies. Offers $15-125/photo. Captions and identification of subjects and equipment required. Buys one-time rights.
Tips: "Find an intriguing, ongoing construction project in our five-state region. Talk to the general contractor's project manager to see what he/she thinks is unusual, innovative or exciting about the project to builders. Then go ahead and query us. If we haven't already covered the project, there's a possibility that we may assign a feature. Be prepared to tour the site, put on a hard hat and get your boots dirty."

PIPELINE & UTILITIES CONSTRUCTION, Oildom Publishing Co. of Texas, Inc., P.O. Box 219368, Houston TX 77218-9368. (713)558-6930. Editor: Robert Carpenter. 5% freelance written. Monthly magazine covering underground oil and gas pipeline, water and sewer pipeline, cable construction for contractors and owning companies. Circ. 29,000. Buys first North American serial rights. Publishes ms an average of 3 months after acceptance. Reports in 1 month. Sample copy for SASE.
Nonfiction: How-to, job stories. Query with published clips. Length: 1,000-2,000 words. Pays $100/printed page "unless unusual expenses are incurred in getting the story." Sometimes pays the expenses of writers on assignment.
Photos: Send photos with ms. Reviews color prints and slides. Captions required. Buys one-time rights.
Tips: "We supply guidelines outlining information we need." The most frequent mistake made by writers in completing articles is unfamiliarity with the field.

ROOFER MAGAZINE, Construction Publications, Inc., 12734 Kenwood Lane, #73, Ft. Myers FL 33907. (813)489-2929. Editor: Angela Hutto. 10% freelance written. Eager to work with new/unpublished writers. Monthly magazine covering the roofing industry for roofing contractors. Estab. 1981. Circ. 22,000. Pays on publication. Publishes ms an average of 5 months after acceptance. Byline given. Buys first and second serial (reprint) rights. Submission must be exclusive to our field. Submit seasonal material 4 months in advance. Reports in 2 months. Sample copy and writer's guidelines for SAE with 6 first-class stamps.
   ● With an influx of material and reduction in staff, reporting times may run longer than stated.
Nonfiction: Profiles of roofing contractors (explicit guidelines available), humorous pieces; other ideas welcome. Buys 5-10 mss/year. Query in writing. Length: approximately 1,500 words. Pays $125-250 (average: $175).
Photos: Send photos with completed mss; color slides are preferred. Identification of subjects required. "We purchase photographs for specific needs, but those that accompany an article are not purchased separately. The price we pay in the article includes the use of the photos. Always searching for photos of unusual roofs or those with a humorous slant."
Tips: "Contractor profiles are our most frequent purchase from freelance writers and a favorite to our readers. Our guidelines explain exactly what we are looking for and should help freelancers select the right person to interview. We provide sample questions to ask about the topics we would like discussed the most. For those submitting queries about other articles, we prefer substantial articles (no fillers please). Slant articles toward roofing contractors. We have little use for generic articles that can appear in any business publication and give little consideration to such material submitted."

‡RSI, Roofing/Siding/Insulation, Advanstar Communications, 7500 Old Oak Blvd., Cleveland OH 44130. (216)243-8100. Fax: (216)891-2675. Editor: Michael Russo. 15% freelance written. Monthly magazine about roofing, siding and insulation fields. "Our audience is comprised almost entirely of contractors in the roofing, siding and/or insulation fields. The publication's goal is to help them improve their business, with heavy emphasis on application techniques." Estab. 1945. Circ. 20,000. Pays on publication. Publishes ms an average of 3 months after acceptance. Byline sometimes given. Buys all rights. Free sample copy.
Nonfiction: How-to (application of RSI products), new product, technical (on roofing, siding and/or insulation) and business articles directed at subcontractors. "No consumer-oriented articles. Our readers sell to consumers and building owners." Buys 6 mss/year. Query. Length: 1,000-3,000 words. Pays $100-800 for assigned articles; $50-400 for unsolicited articles. Sometimes pays the expenses of writers on assignment.

Photos: State availability of photos with submission. Reviews 2¼×2¼ transparencies and 5×7 prints. Offers no additional payment for photos accepted with ms. Captions and identification of subjects required.

SHOPPING CENTER WORLD, Argus Business, 6151 Powers Ferry Rd., Atlanta GA 30339-2941. (404)955-2500. Fax: (404)955-0400. Editor: Teresa DeFranks. 75% freelance written. Prefers to work with published/established writers. Monthly magazine covering the shopping center industry. "Material is written with the shopping center developer, owner, manager and shopping center tenant in mind." Estab. 1972. Pays on publication. Publishes ms an average of 3 months after acceptance. Byline given. Buys all rights. Query for electronic submissions. Reports in 2 months. Sample copy for $9.50.
Nonfiction: Interview/profile, new product, opinion, photo feature, technical. Buys 50 mss/year. Query with published clips or send complete ms. Length: 750-3,000 words. Pays $75-500. Sometimes pays expenses of writers on assignment.
Photos: State availability of photos with submission. Reviews 4×5 transparencies and 35mm slides. Offers no additional payment for photos accepted with ms. Model releases and identification of subjects required. Buys one-time rights.
Tips: "We are always looking for talented writers to work on assignment. Writers with real estate writing and business backgrounds have a better chance. Industry trends and state reviews are all freelance written on an assignment basis. Most assignments are made to those writers who are familiar with the magazine's subject matter and have already reviewed our editorial calendar of future topics."

‡**SOUTHWEST CONTRACTOR**, The McGraw Hill Companies, #1, 2050 E. University, Phoenix AZ 85034. (602)258-1641. Fax: (602)495-9407. Editor: Teresa Verbout. 20% freelance written. Monthly magazine about construction industry/engineering and mining. "Problem-solving case histories of projects in AZ, NM, NV and west TX emphasizing engineering, equipment, materials and people." Estab. 1938. Circ. 6,200. Pays on publication. Byline given. Buys first rights and makes work-for-hire assignments. Submit seasonal material 3 months in advance. Accepts previously published submissions. Send typed ms with rights for sale noted and information about when and where the article previously appeared. Does not pay for reprints. Reports in 2 months. Sample copy for $3 and 9×12 SAE with 5 first-class stamps. Writer's guidelines for #10 SASE.
Nonfiction: Interview/profile, technical. Buys 24 mss/year. Query. Length: 1,000-3,000 words. Pays $4/column inch at 14 picas wide. Sometimes pays expenses of writers on assignment.
Photos: State availability of photos with submission. Reviews 3×5 prints. Offers $10/b&w maximum; photos; $75 color. Captions and identification of subjects required. Buys one-time rights.
Columns/Departments: People, Around Southwest (general construction activities), Association News (all associations involved with industry), Manufacturer's News, Legal News (construction only). Contracts awarded (construction only), Mining News.

Dental

PROOFS, The Magazine of Dental Sales and Marketing, PennWell Publishing Co., P.O. Box 3408, Tulsa OK 74101-3400. (918)835-3161. Fax: (918)831-9804. Editor: Mary Elizabeth Good. 5% freelance written. Magazine published 10 times/year covering dental trade. "*Proofs* is the only publication of the dental trade for dental dealers, sales forces and key marketing personnel of manufacturers. It publishes news of the industry (not the profession), personnel changes and articles on how to sell dental equipment and merchandise and services that can be provided to the dentist-customer." Estab. 1917. Circ. 7,000. Pays on publication. Byline given. Buys first North American serial rights. Editorial lead time 1 month. Query for electronic submissions. Reports in 2 weeks on queries. Sample copy and writer's guidelines free on request.
Nonfiction: General interest, historical/nostalgic, how-to, interview/profile, opinion, personal experience. "No articles written for dentist-readers." Buys 15 mss/year. Query or send complete ms. Length: 400-1,250. Pays $100-200.
Photos: Either state availability of photos with submission or send photos with submission. Reviews minimum size 3½×5 prints. Offers no additional payment for photos accepted with ms. Identification of subjects required. Buys one-time rights.
Tips: "Learn something about the dental industry and how it operates. We have no interest in manufacturers who sell only direct. We do not want information on products and how they work, but will take news items on manufacturers' promotions involving products. Most interested in stories on how to sell *in the dental industry*; industry personnel feel they are 'unique' and not like other industries. In many cases, this is true, but not entirely. We are most open to feature articles on selling, supply-house operations, providing service."

Drugs, Health Care and Medical Products

THE APOTHECARY, Health Care Marketing Services, P.O. Box AP, Los Altos CA 94023. (415)941-3955. Fax: (415)941-2303. Editor: Jerold Karabensh. Publication Director: Janet Goodman. Managing Editor: Dale

C. Osborne. Contact: Vicki Cooper. 100% freelance written. Prefers to work with published/established writers who possess some knowledge of pharmacy and business/management topics. Quarterly magazine providing practical information to community retail pharmacists." Estab. 1888. Circ. 60,000. **Pays on acceptance.** Publishes ms an average of 5 months after acceptance. Byline given. Buys all rights. Submit seasonal material 8 months in advance. Reports in up to 6 months. Sample copy for 9×12 SAE with 4 first-class stamps. Writer's guidelines for #10 SASE.

Nonfiction: How-to (e.g., manage a pharmacy), opinion (of registered pharmacists), health-related feature stories. "We publish only those general health articles with some practical application for the pharmacist as business person. No general articles not geared to our pharmacy readership; no fiction." Buys 4 mss/year. Query with published clips. Length: 750-3,000 words. Pays $100-300.

Columns/Departments: Commentary (views or issues relevant to the subject of pharmacy or to pharmacists). Send complete ms. Length: 750-1,000 words. "This section is unpaid; we will take submissions with byline."

Tips: "Submit material geared to the *pharmacist* as *business person*. Write according to our policy, i.e., business articles with emphasis on practical information for a community pharmacist. We suggest reading several back issues and following general feature story tone, depth, etc. Stay away from condescending use of language. Though our articles are written in simple style, they must reflect knowledge of the subject and reasonable respect for the readers' professionalism and intelligence."

CONSULTANT PHARMACIST, American Society of Consultant Pharmacists, 1321 Duke St., Alexandria VA 22314-3563. (703)739-1300. Fax: (703)739-1500. Editor: L. Michael Posey. Production Manager: Billy Stroemer. 10% freelance written. Monthly journal on consultant pharmacy. "We do not promote drugs or companies but rather ideas and information." Circ. 11,200. **Pays on acceptance.** Publishes ms an average of 4 months after acceptance. Byline given. Buys first North American serial rights. Send disk with accepted article. Reports in 2 weeks. Sample copy for 9×12 SAE with 6 first-class stamps. Writer's guidelines for #10 SASE.

Nonfiction: How-to (related to consultant pharmacy), interview/profile, technical. Buys 10 mss/year. Query with published clips. Length: 750-2,000 words. Pays $300-1,200. Sometimes pays expenses of writers on assignment.

Photos: Send photos with submission. Offers $100/photo session. Captions, model releases and identification of subjects required. Buys one-time rights.

Tips: "This journal is devoted to consultant pharmacy, so articles must relate to this field."

‡PHARMACY PRACTICE, The Professional Journal for Canada's Pharmacists, Thomson Healthcare Communications, 1120 Birchmount Rd., Suite 200, Scarborough, Ontario M1K 5G4 Canada. (416)750-8900. Editor: Anne Bokma. 80% freelance written. Magazine published 10 times/year covering pharmacy. "We look for clinical and professional topics of interest to retail pharmacists. Most articles and columns are written by pharmacists." **Pays on acceptance.** Publishes ms an average of 2 months after acceptance. Byline given. Offers 50% kill fee. Buys first rights. Editorial lead time 4 months. Submit seasonal material 4 months in advance. Query for electronic submissions. Reports in 2 weeks on queries. Sample copy free on request.

Nonfiction: Pays telephone expenses of writers on assignment.

Photos: Reviews contact sheets, negatives, transparencies and prints. Negotiates payment individually. Buys one-time rights.

Education and Counseling

Professional educators, teachers, coaches and counselors—as well as other people involved in training and education—read the journals classified here. Many journals for educators are nonprofit forums for professional advancement; writers contribute articles in return for a byline and contributor's copies. *Writer's Market* includes only educational journals that pay freelancers for articles. Education-related publications for students are included in the Consumer Career, College and Alumni; and Teen and Young Adult sections. Listings in the Childcare and Parental Guidance and Psychology and Self-Improvement sections of Consumer Magazines may also be of interest.

ARTS & ACTIVITIES, Publishers' Development Corporation, Dept. WM, 591 Camino de la Reina, Suite 200, San Diego CA 92108-3104. (619)297-5352. Fax: (619)297-5353. Editor: Maryellen Bridge. 95% freelance written. Eager to work with new/unpublished writers. Monthly (except July and August) art education magazine covering art education at levels from preschool through college for educators and therapists engaged in arts and crafts education and training. Estab. 1932. Circ. 24,000. Pays on publication. Publishes ms an average of 9-12 months after acceptance. Byline given. Buys first North American serial rights. Submit seasonal material 6 months in advance. Reports in 3 months. Sample copy for 9×12 SAE with 8 first-class stamps. Writer's guidelines for #10 SASE.

Nonfiction: Historical/nostalgic (arts, activities, history); how-to (classroom art experiences, artists' techniques); interview/profile (of artists); opinion (on arts activities curriculum, ideas on how to do things better, philosophy of art education); personal experience in the art classroom ("this ties in with the how-to, we like it to be *personal*, no recipe style"); articles on exceptional art programs. Buys 80-100 mss/year. Length: 200-2,000 words. Pays $35-150.

   ● Editors here are seeking more materials for upper elementary and secondary levels on printmaking, ceramics, 3-dimensional design, weaving, fiber arts (stitchery, tie-dye, batik, etc.), crafts, painting and multicultural art.

Tips: "Frequently in unsolicited manuscripts, writers obviously have not studied the magazine to see what style of articles we publish. Send for a sample copy to familiarize yourself with our style and needs. The best way to find out if his/her writing style suits our needs is for the author to submit a manuscript on speculation. We prefer an anectdotal style of writing, so that readers will feel as though they are there in the art room as the lesson/project is taking place. Also, good quality photographs of student artwork are important. We are a *visual* art magazine!"

‡THE ATA MAGAZINE, The Alberta Teachers' Association, 11010 142nd St., Edmonton, Alberta T5N 2R1 Canada. (403)453-2411. Editor: Tim Johnston. Contact: Raymond Gariepy, Managing Editor. 50% freelance written. Quarterly magazine covering education. Estab. 1920. Circ. 39,500. Pays on publication. Publishes ms an average of 2 months after acceptance. Byline given. Offers kill fee of $75. Buys one-time rights. Editorial lead time 2 months. Submit seasonal material 2 months in advance. Accepts simultaneous submissions and previously published submissions. Reports in 2 months. Sample copy and writer's guidelines free on request.

Nonfiction: Education-related topics. Buys 12 mss/year. Query with published clips. Length: 250-1,000 words. Pays $75-150. Sometimes pays expenses of writers on assignment.

Photos: Send photos with submission. Reviews 4×6 prints. Negotiates payment individually. Captions required. Negotiates rights.

CLASS ACT, Class Act, Inc., P.O. Box 802, Henderson KY 42420. Editor: Susan Thurman. 75% freelance written. Educational newsletter published 9 times/year covering English/language arts education. "Our writers must know English as a classroom subject and should be familiar with writing for teens. If you can't make your manuscript interesting to teenagers, we're not interested." Estab. 1993. Circ. 300. **Pays on acceptance.** Publishes ms an average of 3 months after acceptance. Byline given. Offers 100% kill fee. Buys all rights. Editorial lead time 2 months. Submit seasonal material 3 months in advance. Accepts simultaneous submissions. Reports in 1 month. Sample copy for $3. Writer's guidelines for #10 SASE.

Nonfiction: How-to (games, puzzles, assignments relating to English education). "NO Masters theses; no esoteric articles; no poetry; no educational theory or jargon." Buys 15 mss/year. Send complete ms. Length: 100-2,000 words. Pays $10-40.

Columns/Departments: Writing assignments (innovative, thought-provoking for teens) 500 words; Puzzles, games (English education oriented) 200 words; Teacher tips (bulletin boards, time-saving devices), 100 words. Send complete ms. Pays $10-40.

Fillers: Teacher tips. Pays $10.

Tips: "Please know the kind of language used by junior/senior high students. Don't speak above them. Also, it helps to know what these students *don't* know, in order to explain or emphasize the concepts. Clip art is sometimes used but is not paid extra for. We like material that's slightly humorous while still being educational. Especially open to innovative writing assignments; educational puzzles and games and instructions on basics. Again, be familiar with this age group."

DANCE TEACHER NOW, The Practical Magazine of Dance, SMW Communications, Inc., 3101 Poplarwood Court, #310, Raleigh NC 27604-1010. Fax: (919)872-6888. E-mail: dancenow@aol.com. Editor: K.C. Patrick. 80% freelance written. Our readers are professional dance educators, business persons and related professionals in all forms of dance. Estab. 1979. Circ. 8,000. **Pays on acceptance.** Publishes ms an average of 2-3 months after acceptance. Byline given. Negotiates rights and permission to reprint on request. Submit seasonal/holiday material 6 months in advance. Query. Prefers PC disks. Reports in 2 months. Sample copy for 9×12 SAE with 6 first-class stamps. Free writer's guidelines.

A bullet introduces comments by the editors of Writer's Market *indicating special information about the listing.*

Nonfiction: How-tos (teach, business), interview/profile, new product, personal experience, photo feature. Special issues: Summer Programs (February); Music & More; (July/August); Costumes and Production Preview (November); College/Training Schools (December). No PR or puff pieces. All articles must be well researched. Buys 50 mss/year. Query. Length: 1,500-3,500 words. Pays $100-400 for unsolicited articles.

Photos: Send photos with submission. Reviews contact sheets, negatives, transparencies and prints. Limited photo budget.

Columns/Departments: Practical Tips (how-tos or updates, 100-350 words. Pays $25/published tip. Free Calendar Listings (auditions/competitions/workshops), 50 words.

Tips: Read several issues—particularly seasonal. Stay within writers guidelines.

EDUCATION IN FOCUS, Books for All Times, Inc., Box 2, Alexandria VA 22313. (703)548-0457. Editor: Joe David. Semiannual newsletter covering educational issues. Pays on publication. Buys first, one-time and second serial (reprint) rights. Negotiates rights to include articles in books. Accepts simultaneous submissions. Reports in 1 month. *Writer's Market* recommends allowing 2 months for reply. Please include SASE with all submissions.

Nonfiction: "We are looking for articles that expose the failures and discuss the successes of education."

LEARNING, 1607 Battleground Ave., Greensboro NC 27408. Fax: (910)272-8020. Editor/Publisher: Charlene F. Gaynor. 45% freelance written. Monthly magazine (during school year) covering elementary and junior high school education topics. Estab. 1972. Circ. 220,000. **Pays on acceptance.** Buys all rights. Submit seasonal material 9 months in advance. Reports in up to 6 months. Sample copy for $3. Free writer's guidelines.

• This magazine has become more selective; submissions must meet the format.

Nonfiction: "We publish manuscripts that describe innovative, practical teaching strategies." How-to (classroom management, specific lessons or units or activities for children—all at the elementary and junior high level—and hints for teaching in all curriculum areas); personal experience (from teachers in elementary and junior high schools); profile (with teachers who are in unusual or innovative teaching situations). Strong interest in articles that deal with discipline, teaching strategy, motivation and working with parents. Buys 250 mss/year. Query. Length: 500-3,500 words. Pays $75-300.

Tips: "We're looking for practical, teacher-tested ideas and practices as well as first-hand personal accounts of dramatic successes—or failures—with a lesson to be drawn. No theoretical or academic papers. We're also interested in examples of especially creative classrooms and teachers. Emphasis on professionalism will increase: top teachers telling what they do best and how."

MEDIA & METHODS, American Society of Educators, 1429 Walnut St., Philadelphia PA 19102. (215)563-3501. Fax: (215)587-9706. Editorial Director: Michele Sokoloff. Bimonthly trade journal published during the school year about educational products, media technologies and programs for schools and universities. Readership: Librarians and media specialists. Estab. 1963. Circ. 42,000. Pays on publication. Publishes ms an average of 3 months after acceptance. Byline given. Buys first North American serial rights. Free sample copy and writer's guidelines.

Nonfiction: How-to, practical, new product, personal experience, technical. Must send query letter, outline or call editor. Do not send ms. Length: 600-1,200 words. Pays $75-200.

Photos: State availability of photos with submission. Reviews 3×5 prints. Offers no additional payment for photos accepted with ms. Captions and identification of subjects required. Buys one-time rights.

MEDIA PROFILES: The Health Sciences Edition, Olympic Media Information, P.O. Box 190, West Park NY 12493-0190. (914)384-6563. E-mail: medprofile@aol.com. Publisher: Walt Carroll. 100% freelance written. Consists entirely of signed reviews of videos, CAI, CD-ROMs, etc. plus articles on medical and nursing sites on the Internet for health care education (no editorials or "articles"). Subscribers are medical and nursing libraries, colleges and universities where health sciences are taught. Journal magazine format, published quarterly. Estab. 1967. Circ. 1,000. Pays on publication. Publishes ms an average of 4 months after acceptance. Buys all rights. Buys 160 mss/year. Word processing (IBM or Mac) disk submissions preferred. "Sample copies and writer's guidelines sent on receipt of résumé, background, and mention of subject areas you are interested (most qualified) in reviewing. Enclose $5 for writer's guidelines and sample issue. (Refunded with first payment upon publication)." Accepts previously published submissions. Send photocopy of article. For reprints, pays negotiable amount. Reports in 1 month. Query.

Nonfiction: "We are the only review publication devoted exclusively to evaluation of films, videos, CAI and CD-ROMs for medical and health training. We have a highly specialized, definite format that must be followed in all cases. Samples should be seen by all means. Our writers should first have a background in health sciences; second, have some experience with audiovisuals; and third, follow our format precisely. Writers with advanced degrees and teaching affiliations with colleges and hospital education departments given preference. We are interested in reviews of media materials for nursing education, in-service education, continuing education, personnel training, patient education, patient care and medical problems. Currently seeking MDs, RNs, PhDs with clinical and technical expertise. Unsolicited mss not welcome. We will have videos sent directly to reviewers who accept the assignments." Pays $15/review.

SCHOOL ARTS MAGAZINE, 50 Portland St., Worcester MA 01608-9959. Fax: (508)753-3834. Editor: Eldon Katter. 85% freelance written. Monthly magazine (September-May), serving arts and craft education profession, K-12, higher education and museum education programs written by and for art teachers. Estab. 1901. Pays on publication. Publishes ms an average of 3 months "if timely; if less pressing, can be 1 year or more" after acceptance. Buys all rights. Reports in 3 months. Free sample copy and writer's guidelines.
Nonfiction: Articles on art and craft activities in schools. Should include description and photos of activity in progress, as well as examples of finished artwork. Query or send complete ms. Length: 600-1,400 words. Pays $30-150.
Tips: "We prefer articles on actual art projects or techniques done by students in actual classroom situations. Philosophical and theoretical aspects of art and art education are usually handled by our contributing editors. Our articles are reviewed and accepted on merit and each is tailored to meet our needs. Keep in mind that art teachers want practical tips, above all—more hands-on information than academic theory. Write your article with the accompanying photographs in hand." The most frequent mistakes made by writers are "bad visual material (photographs, drawings) submitted with articles, or a lack of complete descriptions of art processes; and no rationale behind programs or activities. Familiarity with the field of art education is essential."

TEACHING THEATRE, Educational Theatre Association, 3368 Central Pkwy., Cincinnati OH 45225. (513)559-1996. Editor: James Palmarini. 75% freelance written. Membership benefit of Teachers Education Association (part of ETA). Quarterly magazine covering education theater K-12, primary emphasis on secondary level education. "*Teaching Theatre* emphasizes the teaching, theory, philosophy issues that are of concern to teachers at the elementary, secondary, and—as they relate to teaching K-12 theater—college levels. We publish work that explains specific approaches to teaching (directing, acting, curriculum development and management, etc.); advocates curriculum reform; or offers theories of theater education." Estab. 1989. Circ. 2,000. **Pays on acceptance.** Publishes ms an average of 1-3 months after acceptance. Byline given. Buys one-time rights. Editorial lead time 2 months. Submit seasonal material 3 months in advance. Accepts simultaneous and previously published submissions. Query for electronic submissions. Reports in 1 month on queries; 3 months on mss. Sample copy for $2. Writer's guidelines for #10 SASE.
Nonfiction: Book excerpts, essays, how-to, interview/profile, opinion, technical theater. "*Teaching Theatre*'s audience is well-educated and most have considerable experience in their field; while *generalist* articles are not discouraged, it should be assumed that readers already *possess* basic skills." Buys 15 mss/year. Query. Pays $100-300 for published articles. "We generally pay cash and 5 copies of issue."
Photos: State availability of photos with submission. Reviews contact sheets, 5×7 and 8×10 transparencies and prints. Offers no additional payment for photos accepted with ms.

TEACHING TOLERANCE, The Southern Poverty Law Center, 400 Washington Ave., Montgomery AL 36104. (205)264-0286. Fax: (205)264-3121. Assistant Editor: David Aronson. 50% freelance written. Semi-annual magazine covering education for diversity. "*Teaching Tolerance* is dedicated to helping K-12 teachers promote tolerance and understanding between widely diverse groups of students. Includes articles, teaching ideas, and reviews of other resources available to educators." Estab. 1991. Circ. 225,000. **Pays on acceptance.** Byline given. Buys first North American serial rights. Editorial lead time 6 months. Submit seasonal material 6 months in advance. Query for electronic submissions. Sample copy and writer's guidelines free on request.
Nonfiction: Essays, how-to (classroom techniques), interview/profile, personal experience, photo feature, multicultural education. "No jargon, rhetoric or academic analysis. No theoretical discussions on the pros/cons of multicultural education." Buys 6-8 mss/year. Query with published clips. Length: 1,000-3,000 words. Pays $500-3,000 maximum. Sometimes pays expenses of writers on assignment.
Photos: State availability of photos with submission. Reviews contact sheets and transparencies. Offers no additional payment for photos accepted with ms. Captions and identification of subjects required. Buys one-time rights.
Columns/Departments: Essays (personal reflection, how-to, school program) 400-800 words; Idea Exchange (special projects, other school activities) 100 words; Interview/profile (usually features nationally known figure) 1,000-2,500 words; Student Writings (Short essays dealing with diversity, tolerance & justice) 300-500 words. Buys 8-12 mss/year. Pays $100-1,000. Query with published clips.
Fillers: Elsie Williams, editorial assistant. Anecdotes, facts, gags to be illustrated by cartoonist. newsbreaks, short humor. Buys 10/year. Length: 25-250 words. Pays $10-25.
Tips: "We want lively, simple, concise writing. The writing style should be descriptive and reflective, showing the strength of programs dealing successfully with diversity by employing clear descriptions of real scenes and interactions, and by using quotes from teachers and students. We ask that prospective writers study previous issues of the magazine and writer's guidelines before sending a query with ideas. Most open to articles that have a strong classroom focus. We are interested in approaches to teaching tolerance and promoting understanding that really work—approaches we might not have heard of. We want to inform our readers; we also want to inspire and encourage them. We know what's happening nationally; we want to know what's happening in your neighborhood classroom."

TEACHING/K-8, The Professional Magazine, Early Years, Inc., 740 Richards Ave., 7th Floor, Norwalk CT 06854-2319. (203)855-2650. Fax: (203)855-2656. Editor: Allen Raymond. Editorial Director: Patricia Broderick. 90% freelance written. "We prefer material from classroom teachers." Monthly magazine covering teaching of K-8. Estab. 1970. Pays on publication. Publishes ms an average of 7 months after acceptance. Byline given. Buys all rights. Submit seasonal material 6 months in advance. Reports in 2 months. Sample copy for $3 and 9×12 SAE with 10 first-class stamps. Writer's guidelines for #10 SASE.
Nonfiction: Classroom curriculum material. Send complete ms. Length: 1,200-1,500 words. Pays $50 maximum.
Photos: Offers no additional payment for photos accepted with ms. Model releases and identification of subjects required.
Tips: "Manuscripts should be specifically oriented to a successful teaching strategy, idea, project or program. Broad overviews of programs or general theory manuscripts are not usually the type of material we select for publication. Because of the definitive learning level we cover (pre-school through grade eight) we try to avoid presenting general groups of unstructured ideas. We prefer classroom tested ideas and techniques."

TECH DIRECTIONS, Prakken Publications, Inc., P.O. Box 8623, Ann Arbor MI 48107-8623. (313)769-1211. Fax: (313)769-8383. Managing Editor: Paul J. Bamford. 100% freelance written. Eager to work with new/unpublished writers. Monthly magazine (except June and July) covering issues, trends and projects of interest to industrial, vocational, technical and technology educators at the secondary and postsecondary school levels. Estab. 1934. Circ. 45,000. Buys all rights. Pays on publication. Publishes ms an average of 8-12 months after acceptance. Byline given. Prefers authors who have direct connection with the field of industrial and/or technical education. No simultaneous submissions. Accepts previously published submissions. Send photocopy of article and information about when and where the article previously appeared. For reprints, pays 100% of amount paid for an original article. Reports in 2 months. Sample copy and writer's guidelines for 9×12 SAE with 3 first-class stamps.
Nonfiction: Uses articles pertinent to the various teaching areas in industrial and technology education (woodwork, electronics, drafting, machine shop, graphic arts, computer training, etc.). "The outlook should be on innovation in educational programs, processes or projects that directly apply to the industrial/technical education area." Buys general interest, how-to, opinion, personal experience, technical and think pieces, interviews, humor, and coverage of new products. Buys 135 unsolicited mss/year. Length: 200-2,000 words. Pays $25-150.
Photos: Send photos with accompanying query or ms. Reviews b&w and color prints. Payment for photos included in payment for ms.
Columns/Departments: Tech-Niques (brief items which describe short-cuts or special procedures relevant to the technology or vocational education). Buys 30 mss/year. Send complete ms. Length: 20-100 words. Pays $25 minimum.
Tips: "We are most interested in articles written by industrial, vocational and technical educators about their class projects and their ideas about the field. We need more and more technology-related articles, especially written for the community college level."

TODAY'S CATHOLIC TEACHER, 330 Progress Rd., Dayton OH 45449-2386. (513)847-5900. Fax: (513)847-5910. Editor: Mary C. Noschang. 40% freelance written. Works with a small number of new/unpublished writers each year. For administrators, teachers and parents concerned with Catholic schools and education in general. Estab. 1967. Circ. 60,000. Pays after publication. Publishes ms an average of 3 months after acceptance. Byline given. Buys all rights. Phone queries OK. Submit seasonal material 3 months in advance. Reports in 4 months. Sample copy for $3. Writer's guidelines for #10 SASE; mention *Writer's Market* in request.
Nonfiction: How-to (based on experience, particularly for teachers to use in the classroom to supplement curriculum, philosophy with practical applications); interview (of practicing educators, educational leaders); personal experience (classroom happenings other educators can learn from); a few profiles (of educational leaders). Buys 40-50 mss/year. Submit complete ms. Length: 800-2,000 words. Pays $150-250.
Photos: State availability of photos with ms. Offers no additional payment for 8×10 b&w glossy prints. Buys one-time rights. Captions preferred; model releases required.
Tips: "We prefer articles that are of interest or practical help to educators—educational trends, teaching ideas, curriculum-related material, administration suggestions, articles teachers can use in classroom to teach current topics, etc."

UNIVERSITY AFFAIRS, Association of Universities and Colleges of Canada, 600-350 Albert St., Ontario K1R 1B1 Canada. (613)563-1236. Fax: (613)563-9745. E-mail: pberkowi@aucc.ca. Editor: Christine Tausig Ford. Associate Editor: Peggy Berkowitz. 25% freelance written. Tabloid published 10 times/year covering Canadian higher education. "Targeted to university faculty and administrators across Canada, *University Affairs* contains news, issues and commentary about higher education and research." Estab. 1959. Circ. 27,000. **Pays on acceptance.** Byline given. Buys first or all rights. Editorial lead time 3 months. Submit seasonal material 3 months in advance. Query for electronic submissions. Reports in 6 weeks on queries; 2 months on mss. Sample copy free on request.

• *University Affairs* is looking for greater analysis and more issues-oriented articles related to "hot" topics in higher education.

Nonfiction: Essays, general interest, interview/profile, opinion, photo feature. Buys 25 mss/year. Query with published clips. Length: 1,000-1,800 words. Pays $125-750 (Canadian).

Photos: State availability of photos with submission. Reviews contact sheets, negatives, transparencies, prints. Negotiates payment individually. Captions, model releases, identification of subjects required. Buys all rights.

Columns/Departments: Around the Universities (short, feature articles about research or teaching achievements or "firsts"), 200 words. Query with published clips. Pay $125-200 (Canadian).

Tips: "Read the publication before contacting me. Have a solid understanding of both my needs and the subject matter involved. Be accurate, check facts, and make sure your writing is high quality. Look for the human interest angle. Put yourself in place of the readers—what makes your story meaningful for them."

‡**WONDERFUL IDEAS**, P.O. Box 64691, Burlington VT 05406-4691. 1-(800)92-IDEAS. Editor: Nancy Segal Janes. 40% freelance written. Newsletter published 8 times/year covering elementary and middle school mathematics. "*Wonderful Ideas* provides elementary and middle school teachers with creative and thought-provoking math activities, games, and lessons, with a focus on manipulatives and problem solving. Teacher-written and classroom-tested, these activities are designed to challenge students, while drawing strong connections between mathematical concepts and concrete problems. Book reviews and relationships of activities to NCTM Standards are also included." Estab. 1989. Circ. 1,600. Pays on publication. Publishes ms an average of 6 months after acceptance. Byline given. Buys all rights. Editorial lead time 2 months. Submit seasonal material 2 months in advance. Accepts simultaneous submissions. Query for electronic submissions. Reports in 1 month on queries; 3 months on mss. Sample copy and writer's guidelines free on request.

Nonfiction: Ideas for teaching elementary and middle school mathematics. Buys 10-15 mss/year. Query. Length: 900 words. Pays $20-60.

Columns/Departments: Wonderful Materials (review of new math materials and books), 700 words. Buys 3 mss/year. Query. Pays $20-60.

Electronics and Communication

These publications are edited for broadcast and telecommunications technicians and engineers, electrical engineers and electrical contractors. Included are journals for electronic equipment designers and operators who maintain electronic and telecommunication systems. Publications for appliance dealers can be found in Home Furnishings and Household Goods.

BROADCAST TECHNOLOGY, P.O. Box 420, Bolton, Ontario L7E 5T3 Canada. (905)857-6076. Fax: (905)857-6045. Editor-in-Chief: Doug Loney. 50% freelance written. Monthly (except August, December) magazine covering Canadian broadcasting industry. Estab. 1975. Circ. 8,000. Pays on publication. Byline given. Buys all rights. Phone queries OK.

Nonfiction: Technical articles on developments in broadcast engineering, especially pertaining to Canada. Query. Length: 500-1,500 words. Pays $100-300.

Photos: Purchased with accompanying ms. Black and white or color. Captions required.

Tips: "Most of our outside writing is by regular contributors, usually employed fulltime in broadcasting. The specialized nature of our magazine requires a specialized knowledge on the part of a writer."

‡**CD-ROM PROFESSIONAL**, Pemberton Press/Online Inc., 649 Massachusetts Ave., Suite 10, Cambridge MA 02139. (617)492-0268. Fax: (617)492-3159. Editor: David R. Guenette. 70% freelance written. Monthly magazine covering CD-ROM, multimedia, electronic publishing. Practical business, professional orientation. Estab. 1987. Circ. 22,000. Pays on publication. Publishes ms an average of 3 months after acceptance. Byline given. Kill fee varies. Buys first North American serial and second serial (reprint) rights. Editorial lead time 3-4 months. Accepts previously published submissions. Query for electronic submissions. Reports in 1-2 months. Sample copy and writer's guidelines free on request.

Nonfiction: Interview/profile, new product, technical. Buys 108 mss/year. Length: 1,500-4,500 words. Pays $300-1,500.

Photos: State availability of photos with submissions. Reviews transparencies, prints. Offers no additional payment for photos accepted with ms. Captions required. Buys one-time rights.

Columns/Departments: Steve Nathens, assistant editor. Pays $300-1,500.

COMMUNICATIONS QUARTERLY, P.O. Box 465, Barrington NH 03825-0465. Phone/Fax: (603)664-2515. E-mail: commquart@aol.com or 72127.745@compuserve.com. Publisher: Richard Ross. Editor: Terry Littlefield. 80% freelance written. Quarterly publication on theoretical and technical aspects of amateur radio and communication industry technology. Estab. 1990. Circ. 10,000. Pays on publication. Publishes ms an average of 6 months after acceptance. Byline given. Buys first rights. Query for electronic submissions. Reports in 1 month. Sometimes accepts previously published submissions. Send photocopy of article and information about when and where the article previously appeared. For reprints, pays 100% of the amount paid for an original article. Writer's guidelines for #10 SASE.

Nonfiction: "Interested in technical and theory pieces on all aspects of amateur radio and the communications industry. State-of-the-art developments are of particular interest to our readers. No human interest stories." Query or send complete ms. Pays $40/published page.

Photos: Send photos with submission. Reviews 5×7 b&w prints. Offers no additional payment for photos accepted with ms. Captions and identification of subjects required. Buys one-time rights.

Tips: "We are looking for writers with knowledge of the technical or theoretical aspects of the amateur radio and communication industries. Our readers are interested in state-of-the-art developments, high-tech construction projects and the theory behind the latest technologies."

ELECTRONIC SERVICING & TECHNOLOGY, CQ Communications, 76 N. Broadway, Hicksville NY 11801. (516)681-2922. Fax: (516)681-2926. Editorial Office: P.O. Box 12487, Overland Park KS 66212. Phone/Fax: (913)492-4857. Editor: Conrad Persson. 80% freelance written. Monthly magazine for professional servicers and electronic enthusiasts who are interested in buying, building, installing and repairing consumer electronic equipment (audio, TV, video, microcomputers, electronic games, etc.). Estab. 1951. Circ. 38,000. Pays on publication. Publishes ms an average of 4 months after acceptance. Byline given. Buys one-time rights. Accepts previously published submissions. Send typed ms with rights for sale noted and information about when and where the article previously appeared. Reports in 1 month on queries; 2 months on mss. Sample copy and writer's guidelines for 9×12 SAE with 5 first-class stamps.

Nonfiction: How-to (service, build, install and repair home entertainment; electronic testing and servicing equipment); new product; technical. "Explain the techniques used carefully so that even hobbyists can understand a how-to article." Buys 50 mss/year. Query with complete ms. Length: 1,500 words minimum. Pays $100-300.

Photos: Send photos with ms. Reviews transparencies and prints. Captions required. Buys one-time rights. Payment included in total ms package.

Columns/Departments: Business Corner, 1,000 words; Successful Servicing, 2,000 words; Computer Corner, 1,000 words. Buys 36 mss/year. Query with complete ms. Pays $50-150.

Tips: "In order to write for *ES&T* it is almost essential that a writer have an electronics background: technician, engineer or serious hobbyist. Our readers want nuts-and-bolts information on electronics."

THE INDEPENDENT Film & Video Monthly, Foundation for Independent Video & Film, 625 Broadway, 9th Floor, New York NY 10012-2611. (212)473-3400. Fax: (212)677-8732. E-mail: aivf@tmn.com. Editor: Patricia Thomson. 60% freelance written. Works with a small number of new/unpublished writers each year. Monthly magazine of practical information for producers of independent film and video with focus on low budget, art and documentary work. Estab. 1979. Circ. 18,000. Pays on publication. Publishes ms an average of 4 months after acceptance. Byline given. Buys first serial rights. Submit seasonal material 4 months in advance. Accepts previously published submissions. Send tearsheet or photocopy of article or typed ms with rights for sale noted, and information about when and where the article previously appeared. For reprints, pay varies. Query for electronic submissions. Reports in 3 months. Pay varies. Sample copy for 9×12 SASE with 5 first-class stamps.

Nonfiction: Book excerpts ("in our area"), how-to, technical (low-tech only), theoretical/critical articles. No reviews. Buys 60 mss/year. Query with published clips. Length: 1,200-3,500 words. Pays $50-200.

Tips: "Since this is a specialized publication, we prefer to work with writers on short pieces first. Writers should be familiar with specific practical and theoretical issues concerning independent film and video."

PRO SOUND NEWS, International News Magazine for the Professional Sound Production Industry, 2 Park Ave., Suite 1820, New York NY 10016. (212)213-3444. Fax: (212)213-3484. Editor: Debra A. Pagan. Managing Editor: Andrea M. Rotondo. 30% freelance written. Works with a small number of new/unpublished writers each year. Monthly tabloid covering the music recording, concert sound reinforcement, TV and film sound industry. Circ. 30,000. Pays on publication. Publishes ms an average of 1 month after acceptance. Byline given. Buys first serial rights. Accepts previously published submissions. Query for electronic submissions. Reports in 2 weeks.

Nonfiction: Query with published clips. Length: 1,000 words. Pays $200-300 for assigned articles.

RADIO WORLD INTERNATIONAL, Industrial Marketing Advisory Services, 5827 Columbia Pike, 3rd Floor, Falls Church VA 22041-9811. (703)998-7600. Fax: (703)998-2966. Editor: Alan Carter. Managing Editor: Rogelio Ocampo. Associate Editor (Articles Editor): T. Carter Ross. 50% freelance written. Monthly trade newspaper for radio broadcasting "covering radio station technology, regulatory news, business and management developments outside the US. Articles should be geared toward engineers, producers and managers." Estab. 1990. Circ. 20,000. Pays on publication. Byline given. Offers 50% kill fee. Buys worldwide serial rights. Query for electronic submissions. Reports in 3 weeks. Free sample copy and writer's guidelines.

Nonfiction: New products, technical, regulatory and management news, programming trend pieces. Buys 100 mss/year. Query with published clips. Length: 750-1,000 words. Pays 20¢/word. Sometimes pays expenses of writers on assignment.

Photos: Send photos with submission. Captions and identification of subjects required. Buys all rights.

Columns/Departments: User reports (field reports from engineers on specific equipment); radio management; studio/audio issues, 750-1,000 words. Buys 50/year. Query. Pays 20¢/word.

Fillers: Newsbreaks. Buys 50/year. Length: 100-500 words.

Tips: "Our news and feature sections are the best bets for freelancers. Focus on radio station operations and the state of the industry worldwide."

SATELLITE RETAILER, Triple D Publishing, Inc., Dept. WM, P.O. Box 2384, Shelby NC 28151-2384. (704)482-9673. Fax: (704)484-8558. E-mail: HomTheater@aol.com. Editor: David B. Melton. 75% freelance written. Monthly magazine covering home satellite TV. "We look for technical, how-to, marketing, sales, new products, product testing, and news for the satellite television dealer." Estab. 1981. Circ. 12,000. Pays on publication. Byline given. Offers 30% kill fee. Buys all rights. Submit seasonal material 3 months in advance. Accepts simultaneous submissions. Query for electronic submissions. Reports in 2 months. Free sample copy and writer's guidelines.

Nonfiction: How-to, new product, personal experience, photo feature, technical. Buys 24 mss/year. Query with or without published clips or send complete ms. Length: 1,800-3,600 words. Pays $150-400. Sometimes pays expenses of writers on assignment.

Photos: Send photos with submission. Reviews contact sheets, transparencies (35mm or 4×5). Captions, model releases and identification of subjects required. Buys all rights.

Tips: "Familiarity with electronics and television delivery systems is a definite plus."

Energy and Utilities

People who supply power to homes, businesses and industry read the publications in this section. This category includes journals covering the electric power, natural gas, petroleum, solar and alternative energy industries.

ALTERNATIVE ENERGY RETAILER, Zackin Publications, Inc., P.O. Box 2180, Waterbury CT 06722-2180. (203)755-0158. Fax: (203)755-3480. Editorial Director: John Florian. 5% freelance written. Prefers to work with published/established writers. Monthly magazine on selling home hearth products—chiefly solid fuel and gas-burning appliances. "We seek detailed how-to tips for retailers to improve business. Most freelance material purchased is about retailers and how they succeed." Estab. 1980. Circ. 10,000. Pays on publication. Publishes ms an average of 2 months after acceptance. Buys first North American serial rights. Submit seasonal material 4 months in advance. Reports in 2 weeks on queries. Sample copy for 9×12 SAE with 4 first-class stamps. Writer's guidelines for #10 SASE.

  • Submit articles that focus on hearth market trends and successful sales techniques.

Nonfiction: How-to (improve retail profits and business know-how), interview/profile (of successful retailers in this field). No "general business articles not adapted to this industry." Buys 10 mss/year. Query. Length: 1,000 words. Pays $200.

Photos: State availability of photos. Pays $25-125 maximum for 5×7 b&w prints. Reviews color transparencies. Identification of subject required. Buys one-time rights.

Tips: "A freelancer can best break into our publication with features about readers (retailers). Stick to details about what has made this person a success."

‡ELECTRIC PERSPECTIVES, Edison Electric Institute, 701 Pennsylvania Ave. NW, Washington DC 20004. (202)508-5714. E-mail: blume.e@geis.eel.com. Editor: Eric R. Blume. 20% freelance written. Bimonthly magazine for executives and managers in investor-owned electric utilities. Estab. 1976. Circ. 20,000. **Pays on acceptance of final draft.** Publishes ms an average of 3 months after acceptance. Byline given. Offers 20% kill fee. Buys first rights or makes work-for-hire assignments. Editorial lead time 4 months. Submit seasonal material 4 months in advance. Accepts simultaneous submissions. Reports in 6 weeks on queries; 2 months on mss. Sample copy for $5. Writer's guidelines free on request.

Nonfiction: Business, essays, historical/nostalgic, photo feature, technical. Buys 5 mss/year. Query. Length: 2,000-5,000 words. Pays $750 for assigned articles; $500 for unsolicited articles. Does not pay expenses of writers on assignment.

Photos: Send photos with submission. Reviews transparencies, 3×5 prints. Negotiates payment individually. Model releases, identification of subjects required. Buys one-time rights.

Columns/Departments: End-Use Technology Review (electrotechnologies at work), 2,000 words; Regulatory Review (utility regulation), 2,000 words; Financial Review (financial subjects), 2,000 words; Statistical Review (utility statistics and analysis). Buys 2 mss/year. Pays $400-1,000.

Tips: "Must develop idea and have a style that will hold the interest of intelligent electric-utility decision maker—CEO or chief engineer or vice president of customer service or corporate pilot. Send abstract or outline first. We're looking for feature articles on hot topics for the electric-utility industry. New angles, rather than restatements of basic utility themes."

ELECTRICAL APPARATUS, The Magazine of Electromechanical & Electronic Application & Maintenance, Barks Publications, Inc., 400 N. Michigan Ave., Chicago IL 60611-4198. (312)321-9440. Editorial Director: Elsie Dickson. Senior Editor: Kevin N. Jones. Managing Editor: Ann Coles. Monthly magazine for persons working in electrical and electronic maintenance, chiefly in industrial plants, who install and service electrical motors, transformers, generators, controls and related equipment. Estab. 1967. Circ. 17,000. **Pays on acceptance.** Publishes ms an average of 3 months after acceptance. Byline given. Buys all rights unless other arrangements made. Reports in 1 week on queries; 1 month on mss. *Writer's Market* recommends allowing 2 months for reply. Query for electronic submissions. Sample copy for $4.
Nonfiction: Technical. Length: 1,500-2,500. Pays $250-500 for assigned articles plus authorized expenses.
   • Columns are now all staff-written.
Tips: "All feature articles are assigned to staff and contributing editors and correspondents. Professionals interested in appointments as contributing editors and correspondents should submit résumé and article outlines, including illustration suggestions. Writers should be competent with a camera, which should be described in résumé. Technical expertise is absolutely necessary, preferably an E.E. degree, or practical experience. We are also book publishers and some of the material in *EA* is now in book form, bringing the authors royalties. Also publishes an annual directory, subtitled *ElectroMechanical Bench Reference.*"

NATIONAL PETROLEUM NEWS, 25 Northwest Point Blvd., Suite 800, Elk Grove Village IL 60007. (708)427-9512. Fax: (708)427-2041. Editor: Don Smith. 3% freelance written. Prefers to work with published/established writers. Monthly magazine for decision-makers in the oil marketing and convenience store industry. Estab. 1909. Circ. 14,000. Rights purchased vary with author and material. Usually buys all rights. Pays on acceptance if done on assignment. Publishes ms an average of 2 months after acceptance. "The occasional freelance copy we use is done on assignment." Query. Accepts previously published submissions. Send typed ms with rights for sale noted (on disk) and information about when and where the article previously appeared.
   • This magazine is particularly interested in articles on international industry-related material.
Nonfiction: Material related directly to developments and issues in the oil marketing and convenience store industry and "how-to" and "what-with" case studies. "No unsolicited copy, especially with limited attribution regarding information in story." Buys 3-4 mss/year. Length: 2,000 words maximum. Pays $50-150/printed page. Sometimes pays the expenses of writers on assignment.
Photos: Pays $150/printed page. Payment for b&w photos "depends upon advance understanding."

PUBLIC POWER, Dept. WM, 2301 M St. NW, Washington DC 20037-1484. (202)467-2948. Fax: (202)467-2910. Editor/Publisher: Jeanne Wickline LaBella. 60% freelance written. Prefers to work with published/established writers. Bimonthly. Estab. 1942. **Pays on acceptance.** Publishes ms an average of 3 months after acceptance. Byline given. Query for electronic submissions. Reports in 6 months. Free sample copy and writer's guidelines.
Nonfiction: Features on municipal and other local publicly owned electric utilities. Pays 20¢/word on edited ms.
Photos: Uses b&w glossy and color slides.

RELAY MAGAZINE, Florida Municipal Electric Association, P.O. Box 10114, Tallahassee FL 32302-2114. (904)224-3314. Editor: Stephanie Wolanski. 5% freelance written. Monthly trade journal. "Must be electric utility-oriented, or must address legislative issues of interest to us." Estab. 1942. Circ. 1,900. Pays on publication. Byline given. Publication not copyrighted. Buys first North American serial, one-time and second serial (reprint) rights. Accepts simultaneous and previously published submissions. Send photocopy of article or typed ms with rights for sale noted and information about when and where article previously appeared. Query for electronic submissions. Reports in 3 months. Free sample copy.
Nonfiction: Interview/profile, technical and electric innovations. No articles that haven't been pre-approved by query. Length: 3-6 pages double spaced. Pays $50.
Photos: State availability of photos with submission. Pay and rights purchased vary. Captions and identification of subjects required.

UTILITY AND TELEPHONE FLEETS, Practical Communications, Inc., 321 Cary Point Dr., P.O. Box 183, Cary IL 60013-0183. (708)639-2200. Fax: (708)639-9542. Editor/Associate Publisher: Alan Richter. 10% freelance written. Magazine published 8 times/year for fleet managers and maintenance supervisors for electric gas and water utilities, telephone, interconnect and cable TV companies, public works departments and related contractors. "Case history/application features are also welcome." Estab. 1987. Circ. 18,000. Pays on publication. Publishes ms an average of 1 month after acceptance. Byline given. Offers 20% kill fee. Buys all rights. Submit seasonal material 2 months in advance. Accepts previously published submissions.

Send photocopy of article or typed ms with rights for sale noted and information about when and where the article previously appeared. For reprints, pays 50% of amount paid for an original article. Reports in 2 months. Free sample copy and writer's guidelines.

Nonfiction: How-to (ways for performing fleet maintenance/improving management skills/vehicle tutorials), technical, case history/application features. No advertorials in which specific product or company is promoted. Buys 2-3 mss/year. Query with published clips. Length: 1,000-2,800 words. Pays $50/page.

Photos: Send photos with submission. Reviews contact sheets, negatives, 3×5 transparencies and prints. Offers no additional payment for photos accepted with ms. Captions required. Buys one-time rights.

Tips: "Working with a utility or telephone company and gathering information about a construction, safety or fleet project is the best approach for a freelancer."

Engineering and Technology

Engineers and professionals with various specialties read the publications in this section. Publications for electrical, electronics and telecommunications engineers are classified separately under Electronics and Communication. Magazines for computer professionals are in the Information Systems section.

GRADUATING ENGINEER, Peterson's/COG Publishing, 16030 Ventura Blvd., Suite 560, Encino CA 91436. (818)789-5371. Editor-in-Chief: Charlotte Chandler Thomas. 40% freelance written. Prefers to work with published/established writers. Magazine published September-March "to help graduating engineers make the transition from campus to the working world." Estab. 1979. Circ. 83,000. Pays 30 days after acceptance. Publishes ms an average of 2 months after acceptance. Byline given. Buys first North American serial rights. Accepts previously published submissions. Send or photocopy of article, or typed ms with rights for sale noted and information about when and where the article previously appeared. For reprints, pays 40% of the amount paid for an original article. Writer's guidelines available.

• *Graduating Engineer* is using fewer freelance writers, and more inhouse and reprints.

Nonfiction: General interest (on management, human resources), career entry, interpersonal skills, job markets, careers, career trends. Special issues: Minority, Women and Engineers and scientists with disabilities. Buys 30 mss/year. Query. Length: 2,000-3,000 words. Pays $300-700.

Photos: State availability of photos, illustrations or charts. Reviews 35mm color transparencies, 8×10 b&w glossy prints. Captions and model release required.

Tips: "We're generating new types of editorial. We closely monitor economy here and abroad so that our editorial reflects economic, social and global trends."

‡LASER FOCUS WORLD MAGAZINE, Pennwell Publishing, 10 Tara Blvd., #5FL, Nashua NH 03062-2801. (603)891-0123. Fax: (603)891-0574. E-mail: lfworld@mcimail.com. Publisher: Florence Oreiro. Editorial Director: Jeffrey N. Bairstow. Executive Editor: Heather W. Messenger. Managing Editor: Barbara Murray. Less than 1% freelance written. Monthly magazine for physicists, scientists and engineers involved in the research and development, design, manufacturing and applications of lasers, laser systems and all other segments of electro-optical technologies. Estab. 1968. Circ. 60,000. Publishes ms an average of 6 months after acceptance. Byline given unless anonymity requested. Retains all rights. Query for electronic submissions. Reports in 2 months. Free sample copy and writer's guidelines.

Nonfiction: Lasers, laser systems, fiberoptics, optics, detectors, sensors, imaging and other electro-optical materials, components, instrumentation and systems. "Each article should serve our reader's need by either stimulating ideas, increasing technical competence or improving design capabilities in the following areas: natural light and radiation sources, artificial light and radiation sources, light modulators, optical materials and components, image detectors, energy detectors, information displays, image processing, information storage and processing, subsystem and system testing, support equipment and other related areas. No flighty prose, material not written for our readership or irrelevant material. Query first with a clear statement and outline of why the article would be important to our readers."

Photos: Send photos with ms. Reviews 8×10 b&w glossies or 4×5 color transparencies. Drawings: Rough drawings acceptable, are finished by staff technical illustrator.

Tips: "The writer has a better chance of breaking in at our publication with short articles because shorter articles are easier to schedule, but must address more carefully our requirements for technical coverage. Most of our submitted materials come from technical experts in the areas we cover. The most frequent mistake made by writers in completing articles for us is that the articles are too commercial, i.e., emphasize a given product or technology from one company. Also articles are not the right technical depth, too thin or too scientific."

MINORITY ENGINEER, An Equal Opportunity Career Publication for Professional and Graduating Minority Engineers, Equal Opportunity Publications, Inc., 150 Motor Pkwy., Suite 420, Hauppauge NY 11788-5145. (516)273-0066. Fax: (516)273-8936. Editor: James Schneider. 60% freelance written. Prefers to work with published/established writers. Triannual magazine covering career guidance for minority engineering students and minority professional engineers. Estab. 1969. Circ. 16,000. Pays on publication. Publishes ms an average of 6 months after acceptance. Byline given. Buys first rights. Deadline dates: Fall (June 1); Winter (September 15); Spring (January 15). Accepts simultaneous and previously published submissions. Sample copy and writer's guidelines for 9×12 SAE with 5 first-class stamps.

Nonfiction: Book excerpts; articles (on job search techniques, role models); general interest (on specific minority engineering concerns); how-to (land a job, keep a job, etc.); interview/profile (minority engineer role models); new product (new career opportunities); opinion (problems of ethnic minorities); personal experience (student and career experiences); technical (on career fields offering opportunities for minority engineers). "We're interested in articles dealing with career guidance and job opportunities for minority engineers." Query or send complete ms. Length: 1,000-1,500 words. Sometimes pays the expenses of writers on assignment. Pays 10¢/word.

Photos: Prefers 35mm color slides but will accept b&w. Captions and identification of subjects required. Buys all rights. Pays $15. Cartoons accepted. Pays $25.

Tips: "Articles should focus on career guidance, role model and industry prospects for minority engineers. Prefer articles related to careers, not politically or socially sensitive."

NATIONAL DEFENSE, American Defense Preparedness Association, Dept. WM, 2101 Wilson Blvd., Arlington VA 22201-3061. (703)522-1820. Fax: (703)522-1885. Editor: Robert Williams. Executive Editor: Sandra I. Meadows. Magazine published 10 times/year covering all facets of the North American defense industrial base. "Interest is on articles offering a sound analysis of new and ongoing patterns in procurement, research and development of new technology, and budgeting trends." Estab. 1920. Circ. 40,000. Byline given. Buys all rights. Requires electronic submission. Reports in 1 month on queries. Free sample copy and writer's guidelines for SASE.

Nonfiction: Feature and photos. Buys 12-15 mss/year. Query first. Length: 1,500-2,000 words. Pays negotiated fees. Pays expenses of writers on assignment "with prior arrangement."

Photos: Send photos with submission. Reviews contact sheets, negatives, transparencies and prints. Offers no additional payment for photos accepted with ms. Captions required. Buys all rights.

SENSORS, The Journal of Applied Sensor Technology, Helmers Publishing, Inc., 174 Concord St., Peterborough NH 03458. (603)924-9631. Fax: (603)924-2076. Editor: Dorothy Rosa. 5% freelance written. Monthly magazine covering electrical and mechanical engineering. "To provide timely, authoritative technical information on the integration of sensors—via data acquisition hardware and software—into subassemblies, manufacturing and process control systems, and products." Estab. 1984. Circ. 65,000. **Pays on acceptance.** Publishes ms an average of 6 months after acceptance. Byline given. Buys first North American serial rights, all rights or makes work-for-hire assignments. Editorial lead time 6 months. Query for electronic submissions. Reports in 1 month on queries; 2 months on mss. Sample copy and writer's guidelines free on request.

Nonfiction: Technical, new product, opinion. Special issue: Data acquisition (June). Buys 3 mss/year. Query. Length: 800-2,400 words. Pay negotiable. Sometimes pays expenses of writers on assignment.

Photos: Send photos with submission. Reviews prints. Offers no additional payment for photos accepted with ms. Caption, model releases and identification of subjects required. Buys one-time rights.

WOMAN ENGINEER, An Equal Opportunity Career Publication for Graduating Women and Experienced Professionals, Equal Opportunity Publications, Inc., 150 Motor Pkwy., Suite 420, Hauppauge NY 11788-5145. (516)273-8743. Fax: (516)273-8936. Editor: Anne Kelly. 60% freelance written. Works with a small number of new/unpublished writers each year. Triannual magazine covering career guidance for women engineering students and professional women engineers. Estab. 1968. Circ. 16,000. Pays on publication. Publishes ms an average of 3-12 months after acceptance. Byline given. Buys First North American serial rights. Reports in 3 months. Free sample copy and writer's guidelines.

Nonfiction: "Interested in articles dealing with career guidance and job opportunities for women engineers. Looking for manuscripts showing how to land an engineering position and advance professionally. Wants features on job-search techniques, engineering disciplines offering career opportunities to women; companies with career advancement opportunities for women; problems facing women engineers and how to cope with such problems; and role-model profiles of successful women engineers, especially in government, military and defense-related industries." Query. Length: 1,000-2,500 words. Pays 10¢/word.

Photos: Prefers color slides but will accept b&w. Captions and identification of subjects required. Buys all rights. Pays $15.

Tips: "We will be looking for shorter manuscripts (800-1,000 words) on job-search techniques and first-person 'As I See It.' "

Entertainment and the Arts

The business of the entertainment/amusement industry in arts, film, dance, theater, etc.

is covered by these publications. Journals that focus on the people and equipment of various music specialties are listed in the Music section, while art and design business publications can be found in Art, Design and Collectibles. Entertainment publications for the general public can be found in the Consumer Entertainment section.

BOXOFFICE MAGAZINE, RLD Publishing Corp., Suite 100, 6640 Sunset Blvd., Hollywood CA 90028-7159. (213)465-1186. Fax: (213)465-5049. Editor-in-Chief: Ray Greene. 5% freelance written. Monthly business magazine about the motion picture industry for members of the film industry: theater owners, film producers, directors, financiers and allied industries. Estab. 1920. Circ. 10,000. Pays on publication. Publishes ms an average of 2-4 months after acceptance. Byline given. Buys all rights, including electronic publishing. Submit seasonal material 2 months in advance. Reports in 3 months. Send typed ms with rights for sale noted. Sample copy for 9×12 SAE with 6 first-class stamps.
Nonfiction: Investigative, interview, profile, new product, photo feature, technical. "We are a general news magazine about the motion picture industry and are looking for stories about trends, developments, problems or opportunities facing the industry. Almost any story will be considered, including corporate profiles, but we don't want gossip or celebrity stuff." Query with published clips. Length: 1,500-2,500 words. Pays $100-150.
Photos: State availability of photos. Pays $10 maximum for 8×10 b&w prints. Captions required.
Tips: "Request a sample copy, indicating you read about *Boxoffice* in *Writer's Market*. Write a clear, comprehensive outline of the proposed story and enclose a résumé and clip samples. We welcome new writers but don't want to be a classroom. Know how to write. We look for 'investigative' articles."

CALLBOARD, Monthly Theatre Trade Magazine, Theatre Bay Area, 657 Mission St., #402, San Francisco CA 94105. (415)957-1557. Fax: (415)957-1556. Editor: Belinda Taylor. 50% freelance written. Monthly magazine for theater. "We publish news, views, essays and features on the Northern California theater industry. We also include listings, audition notices and job resources." Estab. 1976. Circ. 5,000. Pays on publication. Publishes ms an average of 3-4 months after acceptance. Byline given. Offers 50% kill fee. Buys first rights. Editorial lead time 1 month. Submit seasonal material 2 months in advance. Accepts simultaneous and previously published submissions. Send tearsheet of article or typed ms with rights for sale noted and information about when and where the article previously appeared. For reprints, pays 50% of amount paid for an original article. Query for electronic submissions. Reports in 1 month on queries. Sample copy for $4.75.
Nonfiction: Book excerpts, essays, opinion, personal experience, technical (theater topics only). *No profiles of actors.* Buys 12-15 mss/year. Query with published clips. Length: 800-2,000 words. Pays $100 minimum for assigned articles. Pays other for unsolicited articles. Sometimes pays expenses of writers on assignment (phone calls and some travel).
Photos: State availability of photos with submission. Reviews contact sheets or 5×7 prints. Offers no additional payment for photos accepted with ms. Identification of subjects required. Buys one-time rights.

CLUB MODÈLE, (formerly *Model & Performer*), Aquino Productions, P.O. Box 15760, Stamford CT 06901. (203)967-9952. Editor: Andres Aquino. 40% freelance written. Monthly magazine on fashion modeling, entertainment (video, film). "*Club Modèle* covers the business of modeling entertainment and fashion, including: performers, entertainers, dancers, actors, models, celebrities, agents, producers and managers, photographers; casting, TV, film, video, theater and show productions; fashion industries, trade shows and exhibits." Estab. 1991. Circ. 100,000. Pays on publication. Publishes ms an average of 2 months after acceptance. Byline given sometimes. Offers 50% kill fee. Buys first North American serial or all rights. Editorial lead time 3 months. Submit seasonal material 3 months in advance. Accepts simultaneous submissions. Reports in 6 weeks on queries; 2 months on mss. Sample copy for $4. Writer's guidelines for 9×12 SAE with 6 first-class stamps.
Nonfiction: General interest, how-to, interview/profile, photo feature and travel. Buys 24 mss/year. Send complete ms. Length:300-1,500 words. Pays 10¢/word minimum for unsolicited articles.
Photos: Send photos with submission. Reviews 2×2 transparencies and 8×10 prints. Offers $10-25/photo. Captions, model release and identification of subjects required. Buys one-time rights or all rights.
Columns/Departments: Pays $25-50.
Tips: "Covers how-to articles: how to succeed in film, video, modeling. How to break into any aspect of the fashion and entertainment industries. Be specific. Send $4 for a sample and specific guidelines. Know the content of *Club Modèle*. We are most open to interviews with celebrities (with photos), and how-to articles."

FUNWORLD, International Association of Amusement Parks & Attractions, 1448 Duke St., Alexandria VA 22314-3464. (703)836-4800. Fax: (703)836-4801. Executive Editor: Rick Henderson. 50% freelance written. Monthly trade journal covering the amusement park submissions. "Articles should be written for amusement park executives, not the public." Estab. 1985. Circ. 7,500. Pays on publication. Publishes ms an average of 2 months after acceptance. Byline given. Offers 30% kill fee. Buys first serial rights. Submit seasonal material

4 months in advance. Accepts previously published submissions. Send tearsheet or photocopy of article or typed ms with rights for sale noted and information about when and where the article previously appeared. Query for electronic submissions. Reports in 2 months on queries. Free sample copy and writer's guidelines.
Nonfiction: How-to, interview/profile, photo feature, technical. "No articles about industry suppliers." Buys 48 mss/year. Query with published clips. Length: 1,000-3,000 words. Pays $200-600 for assigned articles; $150-450 for unsolicited articles. Sometimes pays expenses of writers on assignment.
Photos: State availability of photos with query or send photos with submission. Reviews color 3×5 prints, slides. Captions, model releases and identification of subjects required. Buys one-time rights.
Tips: "Writers should visit a small- to medium-sized park in their area and look for unique features or management styles that other park managers might like to read about. We want less fluff, more substance."

THE HOLLYWOOD REPORTER, 5055 Wilshire Blvd., Los Angeles CA 90036-4396. (213)525-2000. Fax: (213)525-2377. Publisher/Editor-in-Chief: Robert J. Dowling. Editor: Alex Ben Block. Editorial Director of Special Issues: Randall Tierney. Daily is 25% freelance written. Specials are 90% freelance written. Daily entertainment trade publication emphasizing indepth analysis and news coverage of creative and business aspects of film, TV, theater and music production. Estab. 1930. Circ. 23,000. Publishes ms an average of 1 week after acceptance for daily, 1 month for special issues. Query first.
Tips: "Short articles fit our format best. The most frequent mistake made by writers in completing an article for us is that they are not familiar with our publication. We are a business publication; we don't want celebrity gossip."

OPPORTUNITIES FOR ACTORS & MODELS, A Guide to Working in Cable TV-Radio-Print Advertising, Copy Group, 1900 N. Vine St., Suite 315, Hollywood CA 90068-3980. Fax: (213)464-4575. Editor: Len Miller. 50% freelance written. Works with a small number of new/unpublished writers each year. Monthly newsletter "serving the interests of those people who are (or would like to be) a part of the cable-TV, radio, and print advertising industries." Estab. 1969. Circ. 10,000. **Pays on acceptance.** Publishes ms an average of 3 months after acceptance. Byline given. Buys all rights. Reports in 1 month. Free sample copy and writer's guidelines for #10 SASE.
Nonfiction: How-to, humor, inspirational, interview/profile, local news, personal experience, photo feature, technical (within cable TV). Coverage should include the model scene, little theatre, drama groups, comedy workshops and other related events and places. "Detailed information about your local cable TV station should be an important part of your coverage. Get to know the station and its creative personnel." Buys 120 mss/year. Query. Length: 100-950 words. Pays $50 maximum.
Photos: State availability of photos. Model release and identification of subjects required. Buys one-time or all rights.
Columns/Departments: "We will consider using your material in a column format with your byline." Buys 60 mss/year. Query. Length: 150-450 words. Pays $50 maximum.
Tips: "Good first person experiences, interviews and articles, all related to modeling, acting, little theater, photography (model shots) and other interesting items are needed."

STAGE DIRECTIONS, For and About Regional Community and Academic Theater, *SMW* Communications, Inc., 3101 Poplarwood, Suite 310, Raleigh NC 27604. Fax: (919)872-6888. E-mail: stagedir@aol.com. Editor: Stephen Peithman. 25% freelance written. Magazine published 10 times/year covering theater: community, regional and academic. "*Stage Directions* covers a full range of theater-productions, design, management and marketing. Articles are based on problem-solving." Estab. 1988. Circ. 4,500. Pays on publication. Publishes ms an average of 2-3 months after acceptance. Byline given. Buys all rights. Editorial lead time 4-6 months. Submit seasonal material 6 months in advance. Accepts simultaneous and previously published submissions, if so noted. Send typed ms with rights for sale noted and information about when and where the article previously appeared. For reprints, pays 50% of the amount paid for an original article. Query for electronic submissions. Reports in 2-3 weeks on queries. Sample copy for 9×12 SAE with 2 first-class stamps. Writer's guidelines free on request.
Nonfiction: Stephen Peithman. How-to, new product, personal experience, photo feature, technical. Buys 24 mss/year. Prefers query or send complete ms. Length: 350-1,000 words. Pays 10¢/word. Sometimes pays expenses of writers on assignment.
Photos: State availability of photos with submission and describe. Reviews contact sheets, 2×2 transparencies and 5×7 prints. Offers $20/photo. Captions, model releases and identification of subjects required. Buys one-time rights.
Tips: "We are very receptive to new writers, but they must give evidence of quality writing and ability to follow through. Keep story focused and upbeat as you describe a theatrical problem-solving experience or situation. Use quotes from participants/experts."

WORLD'S FAIR, World's Fair, Inc., P.O. Box 339, Corte Madera CA 94976-0339. (415)924-6035. Editor: Alfred Heller. Less than 75% freelance written. Quarterly magazine exploring the people, politics, pageantry and planning of world's fairs and thematic exhibitions, with emphasis on current and upcoming events. Also looks at science museums and theme parks; investigates high-tech exhibit techniques. Mostly slanted toward exposition and amusement industry professionals. Estab. 1981. Circ. 5,000. **Pays on acceptance.** Publishes ms an average of 3 months after acceptance. Byline given. Offers 50% kill fee. Buys all rights. Reports in 1 month. Sample copy and writer's guidelines for 9×12 SAE with 3 first-class stamps.

Nonfiction: Informative articles, interview/profiles, photo features related to international fairs and world's-fair-caliber exhibits and exhibit technology. Buys 8-10 mss/year. Query with published clips. Length: 500-2,500 words. Pays $50-350. Sometimes pays expenses of writers on assignment.

Photos: State availability of photos or line drawings with submission. Reviews contact sheets and 8×10 b&w prints. Identification of subjects required. Buys one-time rights.

Tips: Looking for "correspondents in cities planning major expositions, in the US and abroad."

Farm

The successful farm writer focuses on the business side of farming. For technical articles, editors feel writers should have a farm background or agricultural training, but there are opportunities for the general freelancer too. The following farm publications are divided into six categories, each specializing in a different aspect of farming: crops and soil management; dairy farming; livestock; management; miscellaneous; and regional.

Crops and Soil Management

CITRUS & VEGETABLE MAGAZINE, 7402 N. 56th St., Suite 560, Tampa FL 33617-7737. (813)980-6386. Fax: (813)980-2871. Editor: Gordon Smith. Monthly magazine on the citrus and vegetable industries. Estab. 1938. Circ. 12,000. Pays on publication. Publishes ms an average of 1 month after acceptance. Byline given. Kill fee varies. Buys exclusive first rights. Query first. Reports in 2 months on queries. Free sample copy and writer's guidelines.

Nonfiction: Book excerpts (if pertinent to relevant agricultural issues); how-to (grower interest—cultivation practices, etc.); new product (of interest to Florida citrus or vegetable growers); personal experience; photo feature. Buys 20 mss/year. Query with published clips or send complete ms. Length: approx. 1,200 words. Pays about $200.

Photos: Send photos with submission. Reviews 5×7 prints. Prefers color slides. Offers $15 minimum/photo. Captions and identification of subjects required. Buys first rights.

Columns/Departments: Citrus Summary (news to citrus industry in Florida: market trends, new product lines), Vegetable Vignettes (new cultivars, anything on trends or developments within vegetable industry of Florida). Send complete ms.

Tips: "Show initiative—don't be afraid to call whomever you need to get your information for story together—accurately and with style. Submit ideas and/or completed ms well in advance. Focus on areas that have not been widely written about elsewhere in the press. Looking for fresh copy. Have something to sell and be convinced of its value. Become familiar with the key issues, key players in the citrus industry in Florida. Have a specific idea in mind for a news or feature story and try to submit manuscript at least one month in advance of publication."

GRAIN JOURNAL, Grain Publications, Inc., 2490 N. Water St., Decatur IL 62526. (217)877-8660. Fax: (217)877-6647. Editor: Ed Zdrojewski. 10% freelance written. Bimonthly magazine covering grain handling and merchandising. "*Grain Journal* serves the North American grain industry, from the smallest country grain elevators and feed mills to major export terminals." Estab. 1972. Circ. 11,444. Pays on publication. Publishes ms an average of 2 months after acceptance. Byline sometimes given. Buys first rights. Editorial lead time 2 months. Submit seasonal material 2 months in advance. Accepts simultaneous submissions. Query for electronic submissions. Sample copy free on request.

Nonfiction: How-to, interview/profile, new product, technical. Query. Length: 750 words maximum. Pays $100.

Photos: Send photos with submission. Reviews contact sheets, negatives, transparencies and 3×5 prints. Offers $50-100/photo. Captions and identification of subjects required. Buys one-time rights.

Tips: "Call with your idea. We'll let you know if it is suitable for our publication."

‡**THE GROWER**, Vance Publishing Corp., 10901 W. 84th St., Lenexa KS 66214. (913)438-0708. Editor: Pat Mosher. 40-50% freelance written. Monthly magazine covering commercial fruit and vegetable growers. "*The Grower* is designed to meet marketing and (production) management needs of high-volume commercial fruit and vegetable growers. This is not a magazine for small growers who grow for roadside markets or for backyard gardners." Estab. 1967. Circ. 27,500. **Pays on acceptance.** Publishes ms an average of 1-2 months after acceptance. Byline given. Offers 30% kill fee. Buys all rights. Editorial lead time 2 months. Submit

seasonal material 3 months in advance. Query for electronic submissions. Reports in 3 weeks on queries; 2 months on mss. Sample copy and writer's guidelines free on request.

Nonfiction: How-to (production techniques, marketing strategies), interview/profile (successful growers), new product, technical (production techniques), marketing. Buys 25-35 mss/year. Query with published clips. Length: 500-1,200 words. Pays $275-375 for assigned articles; $200-300 for unsolicited articles.

Photos: Send photos with submission. Reviews 4×5 transparencies, 4×5 prints. Captions required. Buys all rights.

Columns/Departments: Tree Fruit (production techniques, marketing strategies, exporting, new varieties), 750-1,000 words; Row Crops (production techniques, marketing), 750-1,000 words; Packing & Shipping (new equipment, new packaging), 750-1,000 words. Buys 12-15 mss/year. Query with published clips. Pays $200-375.

Tips: "Know the audience: Commercial fruit and vegetable growers are sophisticated businessmen. Have a genuine interest in agriculture and farming. Discuss trends with university researchers. Understand that we are a trade publication and our readers are very busy. We want articles that contain information that is beneficial to our readers vs. information that is 'nice to know.' "

Dairy Farming

DAIRY GOAT JOURNAL, W. 2997 Markert Rd., Helenville WI 53137. (414)593-8385. Fax: (414)593-8384. Editor: Dave Thompson. 50% freelance written. Monthly. "We are looking for clear and accurate articles about dairy goat owners, their herds, cheesemaking, and other ways of marketing products. Some readers own two goats; others own 1,500 and are large commercial operations." Estab. 1917. Circ. 8,000, including copies to more than 70 foreign countries. Pays on publication. Makes assignments. Query first.

Nonfiction: Information on personalities and on public issues affecting dairy goats and their owners. How-to articles with plenty of practical information. Health and husbandry articles should be written with appropriate experience or academic credentials. Buys 100 mss/year. Query with published clips or send complete ms. Length: 750-2,500 words. Pays $50-150. Pays expenses of writers on assignment.

Photos: Black and white or color. Vertical or horizontal for cover. Goats and/or people. Pays $100 max for 35mm slides for covers; $20 to $70 for inside use or for b&w. Accurate identification of all subjects acquired.

Tips: "We love good articles about dairy goats and will work with beginners, if you are cooperative."

THE WESTERN DAIRYMAN, (formerly *The Dairyman*), Dept. WM, P.O. Box 819, Corona CA 91718-0819. (909)735-2730. Fax: (909)735-2460. Editor: Dennis Halladay. 10% freelance written. Prefers to work with published/established writers. Monthly magazine dealing with large herd commercial dairy industry. Estab. 1922. Circ. 19,000. Pays on acceptance or publication. Publishes ms an average of 2-3 months after acceptance. Byline given. Buys first North American serial rights. Submit seasonal material 3 months in advance. Seldom accepts previously published submissions. Send information about when and where the article previously appeared. For reprints, pays 50% of amount paid for an original article. Reports in 1 month. Sample copy for 9×12 SAE with 4 first-class stamps.

Nonfiction: Interview/profile, new product, opinion, industry analysis. Special issues: Computers (February); Herd Health (August); Feeds and Feeding (May); Barns and Equipment (November). "No religion, nostalgia, politics or 'mom and pop' dairies." Query or send complete ms. Length: 300-5,000 words. Pays $100-300.

Photos: Send photos with query or ms. Reviews b&w contact sheets and 35mm or 2¼×2¼ transparencies. Pays $25 for b&w; $50-100 for color. Captions and identification of subjects required. Buys one-time rights.
  ● Photos are now a more critical part of story packages.

Tips: "Pretend you're an editor for a moment; would you want to buy a story without any artwork? Neither would I. Writers often don't know modern commercial dairying and they forget they're writing for an audience of *dairymen*. Publications are becoming more and more specialized. You've really got to know who you're writing for and why they're different."

Livestock

LLAMAS MAGAZINE, The International Camelid Journal, Clay Press, Inc., P.O. Box 100, Herald CA 95638. (209)223-0469. Fax: (209)223-0466. Editor: cheryl Dal Porto. Magazine published 7 times/year covering llamas, alpacas, camels, vicunas and guanacos. Estab. 1979. Circ. 6,000. Pays on publication. Publishes ms an average of 4 months after acceptance. Byline given. Buys first rights, second serial (reprint) rights and makes work-for-hire assignments. Submit seasonal material 6 months in advance. Accepts previously published submissions. Send tearsheet of article and information about when and where the article previously appeared. Reports in 1 month. Free sample copy. Writer's guidelines for 8½×11 SAE with $2.90 postage.

Nonfiction: How-to (on anything related to raising llamas), humor, interview/profile, opinion, personal experience, photo feature, travel (to countries where there are camelids). "All articles must have a tie-in to one of the camelid species." Buys 30 mss/year. Query with published clips. Length: 1,000-5,000 words. Pays $50-300 for assigned articles; $50-250 for unsolicited articles. May pay new writers with contributor copies. Sometimes pays the expenses of writers on assignment.

Photos: State availability of or send duplicates with submission. Reviews transparencies, 5×7 prints. Offers $25-100/photo. Captions, model releases and identification of subjects required. Buys one-time rights.

Fillers: Anecdotes, gags, short humor. Buys 25/year. Length: 100-500 words. Pays $25-50.

Tips: "Get to know the llama folk in your area and query us with an idea. We are open to any and all ideas involving llamas, alpacas and the rest of the camelids. We are always looking for good photos. You must know about camelids to write for us."

NATIONAL LAMB WOOL GROWER, (formerly *National Wool Grower*), American Sheep Industry Association, Inc., 6911 S. Yosemite St., Englewood CO 80112-1414. (303)771-3500. Editor: Janice Grauberger. 5% freelance written. Monthly trade journal covering sheep industry news. Estab. 1911. Circ. 20,000. Pays on publication. Byline sometimes given. Buys first rights and makes work-for-hire assignments. Submit seasonal material 3 months in advance. Free sample copy.

Nonfiction: How-to, interview/profile. Buys 9 mss/year. Query with or without published clips or send complete ms. Length: 1,000-5,000 words. Pays $150-200 for unsolicited articles.

Photos: Send photos with submission. Reviews transparencies and prints. Offers no additional payment for photos accepted with ms. Captions required. Buys one-time rights.

‡RATITE MARKETPLACE, Morgan Printing Co., P.O. Box 1613, 114 N. Mason, Bowie TX 76230. (817)872-6189. Fax: (817)872-3559. Editor: Judy Morgan. Managing Editor: Carol Johnson. 30% freelance written. Biweekly magazine covering ostrich, emu, rhea. "Covers the ratite industry nationwide. Articles need to pertain to the industry." Estab. 1989. Circ. 12,000. Pays on publication. Publishes ms an average of 2 months after acceptance. Byline given sometimes. Buys all rights. Editorial lead time 2 months. Submit seasonal material 3 months in advance. Accepts simultaneous and previously published submissions. Query for electronic submissions.

Nonfiction: How-to, new product, personal experience, photo feature, technical, travel. Buys 6 mss/year. Query with published clips. Length: 500-1,000 words. Pays $10-50 for assigned articles; $10-30 for unsolicited articles; also pays in contributor copies.

Photos: State availability of photos with submission. Reviews contact sheets. Negotiates payment individually. Captions, identification of subjects required. Buys all rights.

Columns/Departments: Buys 6 mss/year. Query with published clips. Pays $10-50.

Fiction: Historical, slice-of-life vignettes.

Fillers: Facts, newsbreaks, short humor. Length: 500-1,000 words.

Tips: "Learn by reading and researching about the industry."

SHEEP! MAGAZINE, W2997 Markert Rd., Helenville WI 53137. (414)593-8385. Fax: (414)593-8384. Editor: Dave Thompson. 50% freelance written. Prefers to work with published/established writers. Monthly magazine. "We're looking for clear, concise, useful information for sheep raisers who have a few sheep to a 1,000 ewe flock." Estab. 1980. Circ. 15,000. Pays on publication. Byline given. Offers $30 kill fee. Buys all rights. Makes work-for-hire assignments. Submit seasonal material 3 months in advance. Accepts previously published submissions. Send tearsheet or photocopy of article. For reprints, pays 40% of the amount paid for an original article. Free sample copy and writer's guidelines.

Nonfiction: Book excerpts; information (on personalities and/or political, legal or environmental issues affecting the sheep industry); how-to (on innovative lamb and wool marketing and promotion techniques, efficient record-keeping systems or specific aspects of health and husbandry). Health and husbandry articles should be written by someone with extensive experience or appropriate credentials (i.e., a veterinarian or animal scientist); profiles (on experienced sheep producers who detail the economics and management of their operation); features (on small businesses that promote wool products and stories about local and regional sheep producer's groups and their activities); new products (of value to sheep producers; should be written by someone who has used them); technical (on genetics, health and nutrition); first person narratives. Buys 80 mss/year. Query with published clips or send complete ms. Length: 750-2,500 words. Pays $45-150. Pays the expenses of writers on assignment.

Photos: Color—vertical compositions of sheep and/or people—for cover. Use only b&w inside magazine. Black and white, 35mm photos or other visuals improve chances of a sale. Pays $100 maximum for 35mm color transparencies; $20-50 for 5×7 b&w prints. Identification of subjects required. Buys all rights.

Tips: "Send us your best ideas and photos! We love good writing!"

Management

AGRI-NEWS, Western Livestock Reporter Inc., P.O. Box 30755, Billings MT 59107. (406)259-5406. Senior Editor: Chuck Rightmire. 5% freelance written. Weekly newspaper covering agriculture. "*Agri-News* follows a generally conservative slant on news and features for agricultural producers and businesses in Montana and northern Wyoming. We focus on general agricultural interests—farming and ranching—in those areas." Estab. 1968. Circ. 17,000. Pays on 1st of month after publication. Publishes ms an average of 1 month after acceptance. Byline given. Buys first rights. Editorial lead time 1 month. Submit seasonal material 1 month in advance. Accepts simultaneous and previously published submissions. Reports in 1 week on queries; 1 month on mss.

Nonfiction: Exposé, general interest, historical/nostalgic, how-to, humor, inspirational, interview/profile, new product, personal experience, (all from agricultural and area viewpoint), photo feature. Buys 24 mss/ year. Send complete ms. Length: 1,000 words maximum. Pays $50 for assigned articles; $35 for unsolicited articles. Sometimes pays expenses of writers on assignment.

Photos: Send photos with submission. Reviews prints. Offers $7.50/photo. Identification of subjects required. Buys one-time rights.

Tips: "Contact the editor with an idea, submit a final piece, or send a resume with clips to set up a freelance relationship. Unless assigned, all articles, etc., must be submitted on speculation."

AGWAY COOPERATOR, P.O. Box 4933, Syracuse NY 13221-4933. (315)449-6117. Editor: Sue Zarins. 2% freelance written. Bimonthly magazine for farmers. Estab. 1964. **Pays on acceptance.** Publishes ms an average of 6 months after acceptance. Time between acceptance and publication varies considerably. Usually reports in 1 month. Free sample copy.

Nonfiction: Should deal with topics of farm or rural interest in the Northeastern US. Length: 1,200 words maximum. Pays $150-300, depending on length, illustrations.

Tips: "We prefer an Agway tie-in, if possible. Fillers don't fit into our format. Occasionally assigns freelance articles. We will be acquiring more outside articles on topics of importance to progressive commercial farmers."

‡FARM & COUNTRY, Ontario's Commercial Farmer Trade Journal, Agricultural Publishing Co., 100 Broadview Ave., #402, Toronto, Ontario M4M 3H3 Canada. (416)463-8080. Managing Editor: John Muggeridge. 25% freelance written. Tabloid published 18 times/year covering agriculture. Estab. 1935. Circ. 52,000. Pays on publication. Publishes ms an average of 1 month after acceptance. Not copyrighted. Buys first rights and one-time rights. Editorial lead time 2 weeks. Submit seasonal material 1 month in advance. Accepts previously published submissions. Query for electronic submissions. Reports in 1 month. Sample copy and writer's guidelines free on request.

Nonfiction: Book excerpts, essays, exposé, general interest, historical/nostalgic, how-to, humor, interview/ profile, new product, opinion, personal experience, photo feature, technical, travel. Buys 200 mss/year. Query with published clips. Length: 500-1,000 words. Pays $100-400 (Canadian).

Photos: Send photos with submission. Reviews 2¼×2¼ transparencies and 4×5 prints. Offers $10-300 (Canadian)/photo. Captions, identification of subjects required. Buys one-time rights.

Columns/Departments: Opinion, humour, how-to (all dealing with agriculture), 700 words. Buys 75 mss/ year. Query with published clips. Pays $100-200 (Canadian).

FARM JOURNAL, Dept. WM, 230 W. Washington Square, Philadelphia PA 19106. (215)829-4700. Editor: Earl Ainsworth. Magazine published 13 times/year with many regional editions. Material bought for one or more editions depending upon where it fits. Buys all rights. Byline given "except when article is too short or too heavily rewritten to justify one." **Pays on acceptance.** Payment is the same regardless of editions in which the piece is used.

Nonfiction: Timeliness and seasonableness are very important. Material must be highly practical and should be helpful to as many farmers as possible. Farmers' experiences should apply to one or more of these 8 basic commodities: corn, wheat, milo, soybeans, cotton, dairy, beef and hogs. Technical material must be accurate. No farm nostalgia. Query to describe a new idea that farmers can use. Length: 500-1,500 words. Pays 10-20¢/published word.

Photos: Much in demand either separately or with short how-to material in picture stories and as illustrations for articles. Warm human-interest-pix for covers—activities on modern farms. For inside use, shots of home-made and handy ideas to get work done easier and faster, farm news photos, and pictures of farm people with interesting sidelines. In b&w, 8×10 glossies are preferred; color submissions should be 2¼×2¼ for the cover and 35mm for inside use. Pays $50 and up for b&w shot; $75 and up for color.

Tips: "*Farm Journal* now publishes in hundreds of editions reflecting geographic, demographic and economic sectors of the farm market."

FARM SUPPLY RETAILING, Quirk Enterprises, Inc., P.O. Box 23536, 6607 18th Ave. S., Minneapolis MN 55423-0536. (612)861-8051. Fax: (612)861-1836. Editor: Joseph Rydholm. 50% freelance written. Monthly magazine for owners and managers of stores that sell farm hardware and supplies. "Our readers are the owners and managers of stores that sell feed, seed, fertilizer, farm supplies and hardware and related items. Our editorial goal is to give them practical information they can use to make their stores better and more profitable. The main stories are case history profiles of successful dealers and marketing-related articles tailored to farm store owners." Estab. 1993. Circ. 22,000. Pays on publication. Publishes ms an average of

3 months after acceptance. Byline given. Buys one-time rights. Editorial lead time 3 months. Submit seasonal material 4 months in advance. Accepts simultaneous and previously published submissions. Send typed ms with rights for sale noted and information about when and where the article previously appeared. Query for electronic submissions. Reports in 1 month on queries; 2 months on mss. Sample copy and writer's guidelines free on request.

• *Farm Supply Retailing* reports that it is using more freelance writing.

Nonfiction: How-to, interview/profile (with successful agribusiness dealers), opinion (on controversial industry issues). Subjects must be business-oriented (taxes, credit, inventory, employee relations, etc.). "No self-serving pieces by motivational speakers/consultants or articles that don't pertain to our editorial focus." Buys 35 mss/year. Query with published clips. Length: 1,000-2,500 words. Pays $200 minimum for assigned articles, $150 minimum for unsolicited articles. Sometimes pays expenses of writers on assignment.

Photos: State availability of photos with submission. Reviews contact sheets, transparencies and prints. Offers $25-75/photo. Identification of subjects required. Buys one-time rights.

Tips: "We welcome articles from freelancers. Our greatest need is for profiles of successful dealers. Submit several color slides with the article. Length between 1,500-2,000 words. Our readers are curious about how other dealers run their operations. Articles should discuss the dealer's selling philosophies, the farming sectors (hog farming, soybean, corn, etc.) his or her customers work in, any companies or product lines he or she has had success with, and any promotional or marketing efforts (advertising, direct mail) that have been successful. We also need articles on various business-related topics such as store layout, displays, store appearance, customer relations, employee management. We will consider articles of a general business nature but the most desirable are those tailored to farm supply dealers."

FORD NEW HOLLAND NEWS, P.O. Box 1895, New Holland PA 17557-0903. Fax: (717)355-3600. Editor: Gary Martin. 50% freelance written. Works with a small number of new/unpublished writers each year. Magazine published 8 times/year on agriculture; designed to entertain and inform farm families. Estab. 1960. **Pays on acceptance.** Publishes ms an average of 6 months after acceptance. Byline given. Offers negotiable kill fee. Buys first North American serial, one-time and second serial (reprint) rights. Submit seasonal material 6 months in advance. Accepts previously published submissions. Reports in 2 months. Sample copy and writer's guidelines for 9 × 12 SAE with 2 first-class stamps.

Nonfiction: "We need strong photo support for articles of 1,200-1,700 words on farm management and farm human interest." Buys 40 mss/year. Query. Pays $500-700. Sometimes pays the expenses of writers on assignment.

Photos: Send photos with query when possible. Reviews color transparencies. Pays $50-300, $500 for cover shot. Captions, model release and identification of subjects required. Buys one-time rights.

Tips: "We thrive on good article ideas from knowledgeable farm writers. The writer must have an emotional understanding of agriculture and the farm family and must demonstrate in the article an understanding of the unique economics that affect farming in North America. We want to know about the exceptional farm managers, those leading the way in agriculture. We want new efficiencies and technologies presented through the real-life experiences of farmers themselves. Use anecdotes freely. Successful writers keep in touch with the editor as they develop the article."

SMALL FARM TODAY, The How-to Magazine of Alternative Crops, Livestock, and Direct Marketing, Missouri Farm Publishing, Inc., Ridge Top Ranch, 3903 W. Ridge Trail Rd., Clark MO 65243-9900. (314)687-3525. Fax: (314)687-3148. Editor: Ron Macher. Bimonthly magazine "for small farmers and small-acreage landowners interested in diversification, direct marketing, alternative crops, horses, draft animals, small livestock, exotic and minor breeds, home-based businesses, gardening, vegetable and small fruit crops." Estab. 1984 as *Missouri Farm Magazine*. Circ. 12,000. Pays 30 days after publication. Publishes ms an average of 6 months after acceptance. Byline given. Buys first serial and nonexclusive reprint rights (right to reprint article in an anthology). Submit seasonal/holiday material 4 months in advance. Accepts previously published submissions. Send information about when and where the article previously appeared. For reprints, pays 58% of amount paid for an original article. Reports in 3 months. Sample copy for $3. Writer's guidelines available.

• In the past this magazine concentrated on articles that applied to Missouri farms. Now they have a national audience and need articles from all over the US.

Nonfiction: Practical and how-to (small farming, gardening, alternative crops/livestock). Query letters recommended. Length: 500-2,000 words. Pays 3½¢/word.

Photos: Send photos with submission. Offers $6 for inside photos and $10 for cover photos. Captions required. Pays $4 for negatives or slides. Buys one-time rights and nonexclusive reprint rights (for anthologies).

Tips: "Topic must apply to the small farm or acreage. It helps to provide more practical and helpful information without the fluff."

Miscellaneous

‡FOREST FARMERS, Forest Farmers Association, P.O. Box 95385, Atlanta GA 30347. (404)325-2954. Editor: Steve Newton. Contact: Jack Warren. Bimonthly magazine covering forestry, private property rights, environmental issues. Estab. 1950. Circ. 6,000. Pays on publication. Publishes ms an average of 4 months after acceptance. No kill fee. Not copyrighted. Busy all rights or makes work-for-hire assignments. Editorial lead time 4 months. Submit seasonal material 2 months in advance. Accepts simultaneous submissions. Query for electronic submissions. Reports in months on queries. Sample copy for $5. Writer's guidelines free on request.

Nonfiction: Book excerpts, exposé, general interest, humor, inspirational, technical. Buys 4 mss/year. Query. Length: 2,000-3,000 words. Pays $500 for assigned articles; $250 for unsolicited articles.

Photos: State availability of photos with submissions. Reviews 5×7 prints. Offers no additional payment for photos accepted with ms. Buys one-time rights.

Tips: Best approach to break in would be "articles about how forest landowners can generate more timber or wildlife on their property and how US congressional actions affect the value or management of private property."

Regional

‡ARKANSAS FARMER, (formerly *Arkansas Farm & Country*), Box 150001, Raleigh NC 27615. Editor: Eva Ann Donnis. 20% freelance written. Monthly tabloid covering agriculture, commercial farmers and ranchers doing business in Arkansas. Estab. 1985. Circ. 11,700. Pays on publication. Byline given. Negotiable kill fee. Buys one-time rights. Submit seasonal/holiday material 1 month in advance. Query for electronic submissions. Reports in 3 weeks on queries; 1 month on mss. Sample copy for 9×13 SAE with 3 first class stamps.

Nonfiction: How-to (farming or ranching only), interview/profile (farmer, rancher, agribusiness or legislator), new product, technical (farm oriented products or method). No general interest pieces without relevance to farming or country living. Buys 15-20 mss/year. Query with or without published clips, or send complete ms. Length: 500-1,000 words. Pays $75 plus expenses.

Photos: State availability of photos with submission. Reviews contact sheets and 3×5 or larger prints. Offers $5-20/photo. Captions and identification of subjects required. Buys one-time rights.

Tips: "Query with good ideas that will be of interest to Arkansas farmers and ranchers. We serve their interests *only*. Keep manuscripts short (15-30 inches maximum). Photos are helpful."

IOWA REC NEWS, 8525 Douglas, Suite 48, Urbandale IA 50322-2992. (515)276-5350. Editor: Jody Garlock. 15% freelance written. Monthly magazine emphasizing energy issues and human interest features for residents of rural Iowa. Estab. 1946. Circ. 116,000. Pays on publication. Publishes ms an average of 3 months after acceptance. Buys first serial and second serial (reprint) rights. Accepts simultaneous and previously published submissions. Send tearsheet of article and information about when and where the article previously appeared. For reprints, pay varies. Reports in 2 months.

Nonfiction: General interest, historical, humor, rural lifestyle trends, energy awareness features, photo feature. Send complete ms.

Tips: "The easiest way to break into our magazine is: research a particular subject well, include appropriate attributions to establish credibility, authority and include a couple paragraphs about the author. Reading and knowing about rural people is important. Stories that touch the senses or can improve the lives of the readers are highly considered, as are those with a strong Iowa angle. We're also looking for good humor articles. Freelancers have the advantage of offering subject matter that existing staff may not be able to cover. Inclusion of nice photos is also a plus. The most frequent mistakes made by writers are: story too long or too biased; no attribution to any source of info; and not relevant to electric consumers, rural living."

THE LAND, Minnesota's Ag Publication, Free Press Co., P.O. Box 3169, Mankato MN 56002-3169. Editor: Randy Frahm. 50% freelance written. Weekly tabloid covering Minnesota agriculture. "We are interested in articles on farming in Minnesota. Although we're not tightly focused on any one type of farming, our articles must be of interest to farmers. In other words, will your article topic have an impact on people who live and work in rural areas?" Estab. 1976. Circ. 40,000. **Pays on acceptance.** Publishes ms an average of 3 months after acceptance. Byline given. Buys first North American serial rights. Editorial lead time 1 month. Submit seasonal material 2 months in advance. Reports in 3 weeks on queries; 2 months on mss. Sample copy free on request. Writer's guidelines for #10 SASE.

Nonfiction: General interest (ag), how-to, interview/profile, personal experience, technical. Buys 15-40 mss/year. Query. Length: 500-1,500 words. Pays $25 minimum for assigned articles. Pays expenses of writers on assignment.

Photos: State availability of photos with submission. Reviews contact sheets. Negotiates payment individually. Buys one-time rights.

Tips: "Be enthused about rural Minnesota life and agriculture and be willing to work with our editors. We try to stress relevance." Most open to feature articles.

MAINE ORGANIC FARMER & GARDENER, Maine Organic Farmers & Gardeners Association, RR 2, Box 594, Lincolnville ME 04849. (207)763-3043. Editor: Jean English. 40% freelance written. Prefers to work with published/established local writers. Quarterly magazine covering organic farming and gardening for urban and rural farmers and gardeners and nutrition-oriented, environmentally concerned readers. "*MOF&G* promotes and encourages sustainable agriculture and environmentally sound living. Our primary focus is organic farming, gardening and forestry, but we also deal with local, national and international agriculture, food and environmental issues." Estab. 1976. Circ. 10,000. Pays on publication. Publishes ms an average of 8 months after acceptance. Byline and bio given. Buys first North American serial, one-time, first serial or second serial (reprint) rights. Submit seasonal material 1 year in advance. Accepts simultaneous and previously published submissions. Send typed ms with rights for sale noted and information about when and where the article previously appeared. Pays 50% of amount paid for an original article. Reports in 2 months. Sample copy for $2 and SAE with 7 first-class stamps. Free writer's guidelines.

Nonfiction: Book reviews; how-to based on personal experience, research reports, interviews. Profiles of farmers, gardeners, plants. Information on renewable energy, recycling, nutrition, health, non-toxic pest control, organic farm management and marketing. "We use profiles of New England organic farmers and gardeners and news reports (500-1,000 words) dealing with US/international sustainable ag research and development, rural development, recycling projects, environmental and agricultural problems and solutions, organic farms with broad impact, cooperatives and community projects." Buys 30 mss/year. Query with published clips or send complete ms. Length: 1,000-3,000 words. Pays $20-150.

Photos: State availability of b&w photos with query; send 3×5 b&w photos with ms. Captions, model releases and identification of subjects required. Buys one-time rights.

Tips: "We are a nonprofit organization. Our publication's primary mission is to inform and educate, but we also want readers to enjoy the articles."

N.D. REC/RTC MAGAZINE, N.D. Association of RECs, P.O. Box 727, Mandan ND 58554-0727. (701)663-6501. Fax: (701)663-3745. Editor: Kent Brick. 10% freelance written. Prefers to work with published/established writers. Monthly magazine covering rural electric program and rural North Dakota lifestyle. "Our magazine goes to the 70,000 North Dakota families who get their electricity from rural electric cooperatives. We cover rural lifestyle, energy conservation, agriculture, farm family news and other features of importance to this predominantly agrarian state. Of course, we represent the views of our statewide association." Estab. 1954. Circ. 78,000. Pays on publication; **pays on acceptance for assigned features**. Publishes ms average of 6 months after acceptance. Byline given. Buys first North American serial rights. Accepts previously published submissions. Send photocopy of article or short story, or typed ms with rights for sale noted. Pays 25% of the amount paid for an original article. Submit seasonal material 6 months in advance. Reports in 2 months. Sample copy for 9×12 SAE with 6 first-class stamps.

● *N.D. REC/RTC* reports a need for articles with greater emphasis on matters pertaining to equipment for the home and family issues related to money, parenting, personal health, small business and telecommunications.

Nonfiction: Exposé (subjects of ND interest dealing with rural electric, rural enterprises, rural lifestyle); historical/nostalgic (ND events or people only); how-to (save energy, weatherize homes, etc.); interview/profile (on great leaders of the rural electric program, rural and small town America); opinion. Buys 10-12 mss/year. Pays $100-500. Pays expenses of writers on assignment.

Photos: "Good quality photos accompanying ms improve chances for sale."

Fiction: Historical. "No fiction that does not relate to our editorial goals." Buys 2-3 mss/year. Length: 400-1,200 words. Pays $35-150. Reprints novel excerpts.

Tips: "Write about a North Dakotan—one of our rural residents who has done something notable in the ag/energy/rural electric/rural lifestyle areas."

OHIO FARMER, 1350 W. Fifth Ave., Columbus OH 43212. (614)486-9637. Editor: Tim White. 10% freelance written. Magazine for Ohio farmers and their families published 15 issues/year (monthly April-December; biweekly January-March). Estab. 1848. Circ. 77,000. Usually buys all rights. Pays on publication. Publishes ms an average of 2 months after acceptance. Reports in 2 months. Query for electronic submissions. Sample copy for $1 and SAE with 4 first-class stamps. Free writer's guidelines.

● This magazine is part of Farm Progress Co. State Farm magazine group.

Nonfiction: Technical and on-the-farm stories. Buys informational, how-to and personal experience. Buys 10 mss/year. Submit complete ms. Length: 600-700 words. Pays $200.

Photos: Offers no additional payment for photos purchased with ms. Pays $5-25 for b&w; $35-100 for color. Send 4×5 b&w glossies and transparencies or 8×10 color prints.

Tips: "Freelance submissions must be of a technical agricultural nature."

PENNSYLVANIA FARMER, Farm Progress Publications, P.O. Box 4475, Gettysburg PA 17325. (717)334-4300. Editor: John Vogel. 20% freelance written. Monthly farm business magazine "oriented to providing readers with ideas to help their businesses and personal lives." Estab. 1877. Circ. 57,000. Pays on publication. Publishes ms an average of 3 months after acceptance. Buys first-time rights. Submit seasonal material 3 months in advance. Accepts simultaneous submissions. Reports in 1 month. Writer's guidelines for #10 SASE.

Nonfiction: Humor, inspirational, technical. No stories without a strong tie to Mid-Atlantic farming. Buys 15 mss/year. Query. Length: 500-1,000 words. Pays $50-150. Sometimes pays the expenses of writers on assignment.

Photos: Send photos with submission. Reviews 35mm transparencies. Pays $25-300 for each color photo accepted with ms. Captions and identification of subjects required.

TODAY'S FARMER, MFA Incorporated, 615 Locust, Columbia MO 65201. (314)876-5252. Editor: Chuck Lay. Managing Editor: Tom Montgomery. Contact: Chuck Lay. 50% freelance written. Company publication. Magazine published 10 times/year covering agriculture. "We are owned and published by MFA Incorporated, an agricultural cooperative. We examine techniques and issues that help farmers and ranchers better meet the challenges of the present and future." Estab. 1908. Circ. 46,000. **Pays on acceptance.** Publishes ms an average of 2 months after acceptance. Byline given. Offers 100% kill fee. Publication not copyrighted. Buys first North American serial rights. Editorial lead time 2 months. Submit seasonal material at least 3 months in advance. Query for electronic submissions. Sample copy for $1. Writer's guidelines available by phone.

Nonfiction: How-to (ag technical), interview/profile, photo feature, technical. "No fiction, articles on MFA competitors, or subjects outside our trade territory (Missouri, Iowa, Arkansas)." Buys 30 mss/year. Query with published clips. Length: 1,000-2,000 words. Pays $200 minimum (features). Sometimes pays expenses of writers on assignment.

Photos: Send photos with submission. Reviews contact sheets. Negotiates payment individually. Identification of subjects required. Buys one-time rights.

Tips: "Freelancers can best approach us by knowing our audience (farmers/ranchers who are customers of MFA) and knowing their needs. We publish traditional agribusiness information that helps farmers do their jobs more effectively. Know the audience. We edit for length, AP style."

Finance

These magazines deal with banking, investment and financial management. Publications that use similar material but have a less technical slant are listed under the Consumer Business and Finance section.

CA MAGAZINE, 277 Wellington St. W., Toronto, Ontario M5V 3H2 Canada. Editor: Nelson Luscombe. Managing Editor: Ruby Andrew. 10% freelance written. Works with a small number of writers each year. Magazine published 10 times/year for accountants and financial managers. Estab. 1911. Circ. 67,000. Pays on publication for the article's copyright. Buys all rights. Publishes ms an average of 4 months after acceptance. Reports in 1 month. Free sample copy.

● *CA Magazine* won a gold National Magazine Award for Service Journalism.

Nonfiction: Accounting, business, finance, management, taxation. Also, subject-related humor pieces and cartoons. "We accept whatever is relevant to our readership, no matter the origin as long as it meets our standards." Length: 1,500-3,000 words. Payment varies with qualification of writers. Sometimes pays the expenses of writers on assignment.

EQUITIES MAGAZINE INC., 145 E. 49th St., Suites 5B and 5C, New York NY 10017. (212)832-7800. Editor: Robert J. Flaherty. 50% freelance written. Monthly magazine covering publicly owned middle market and emerging growth companies. "We are a financial magazine covering the fastest-growing companies in the world. We study the management of companies and act as critics reviewing their performances. We aspire to be 'The Shareholder's Friend'. We want to be a bridge between quality public companies and sophisticated investors." Estab. 1951. Circ. 15,000. Pays on publication. Publishes ms an average of 2 months after acceptance. Byline given. Buys first and reprint rights. Sample copy for 9 × 12 SAE with 5 first-class stamps.

Nonfiction: New product, technical. Buys 30 mss/year. "We must know the writer first as we are careful about whom we publish. A letter of introduction with résumé and clips is the best way to introduce yourself. Financial writing requires specialized knowledge and a feel for people as well, which can be a tough combination to find." Query with published clips. Length: 300-1,500 words. Pays $150-750 for assigned articles, more for very difficult or investigative pieces. Carries guest columns by famous money managers who are not writing for cash payments, but to showcase their ideas and approach. Pays expenses of writers on assignment.

Photos: Send photos with submission. Reviews contact sheets, negatives, transparencies and prints. Offers no additional payment for photos accepted with ms. Identification of subjects required.

Columns/Departments: Pays $25-75 for assigned items only.

Tips: "Anyone who enjoys analyzing a business and telling the story of the people who started it, or run it today, is a potential *Equities* contributor. But to protect our readers and ourselves, we are careful about who writes for us. Business writing is an exciting area and our stories reflect that. If a writer relies on numbers and percentages to tell his story, rather than the individuals involved, the result will be numbingly dull."

THE FEDERAL CREDIT UNION, National Association of Federal Credit Unions, P.O. Box 3769, Washington DC 20007-0269. (703)522-4770. Fax: (703)524-1082. Editor: Patrick M. Keefe. Managing Editor: Robin Johnston. 25% freelance written. "Looking for writer with financial, banking or credit union experience, but will work with inexperienced (unpublished) writers based on writing skill." Bimonthly magazine covering credit unions. Estab. 1967. Circ. 8,200. Pays on publication. Publishes ms an average of 3 months after acceptance. Byline given. Buys first North American serial rights. Submit seasonal material 5 months in advance. Accepts simultaneous submissions. Send ms with rights for sale noted and information about when and where the article previously appeared. Query for electronic submissions. Reports in 2 months. Sample copy for 10×13 SAE with 5 first-class stamps. Writer's guidelines for #10 SASE.
Nonfiction: Query with published clips and SASE. Length: 1,200-2,000 words. Pays $200-800 for assigned articles.
Photos: Send photos with submission. Reviews 35mm transparencies and 5×7 prints. Offers no additional payment for photos accepted with ms. Model releases and identification of subjects required. Buys all rights.
Tips: "Provide résumé or listing of experience pertinent to subject. Looking only for articles that focus on events in Congress and regulatory agencies."

ILLINOIS BANKER, Illinois Bankers Association, 111 N. Canal St., Suite 1111, Chicago IL 60606-7204. (312)876-9900. Fax: (312)876-3826. Editor: Ashley Couch. Monthly magazine covering commercial banking. "*Illinois Banker* publishes articles that directly relate to commercial banking. Our audience is approximately 3,000 bankers and vendors related to the banking industry. The purpose of the publication is to educate and inform readers on major public policy issues affecting banking today, as well as provide new ideas that can be applied to day-to-day operations and management. Writers may not sell or promote a product or service." Estab. 1891. Circ. 2,500. **Pays on acceptance.** Publishes ms an average of 3 months after acceptance. Reports in 3 months. Byline given. Buys first North American serial rights. Editorial lead time 6 weeks. Accepts simultaneous and previously published submissions. Send tearsheet of article or short story or typed ms with rights for sale noted and information about when and where the article previously appeared. Query for electronic submissions. Reports in 3 months. Sample copy and writer's guidelines free on request.
Nonfiction: Essays, historical/nostalgic, humor, inspirational, interview/profile, new product, opinion, personal experience, financially related. "It is *IBA* policy that writers do not sell or promote a particular product, service or organization within the content of an article written for publication." Buys 3-5 mss/year. Query. Length: 500-1,000 words. Pays $50 minimum for unsolicited articles.
Photos: State availability of photos with submission. Reviews contact sheets, negatives, transparencies and prints. Offers $25-50/photo. Captions and identification of subjects required. Buys one-time rights.
Fiction: Historical, humorous, mainstream, slife-of-life vignettes (financial). Buys 3 mss/year. Query. Length: 500-1,000 words. Pays $50-100.
Tips: "We appreciate that authors contact the editor before submitting articles to discuss topics. Articles published in *Illinois Banker* address current issues of key importance to the banking industry in Illinois. Our intention is to keep readers informed of the latest industry news, developments and trends, as well as provide necessary technical information. We publish articles on any topic that affects the banking industry, provided the content is in agreement with Association policy and position. Because we are a trade association, most articles need to be reviewed by an advisory committee before publication; therefore, the earlier they are submitted the better. Some recent topics include: agriculture, bank architecture, commercial and consumer credit, marketing, operations/cost control, security and technology. In addition, articles are also considered on the topics of economic development and business/banking trends in Illinois and the Midwest region."

INDEPENDENT BANKER, Independent Bankers Association of America, P.O. Box 267, Sauk Centre MN 56378-0267. (612)352-6546. Editor: David C. Bordewyk. 25% freelance written. Works with a number of new/unpublished writers each year. Monthly magazine targeting the CEOs of the nation's community banks. Estab. 1950. Circ. 9,500. Pays on publication. Publishes ms an average of 4 months after acceptance. Byline given. Not copyrighted. Buys first serial rights. Reports in 6 weeks. Sample copy and writer's guidelines for 9×12 SAE with 6 first-class stamps.
Nonfiction: Features: interview/profile (example: a community bank's innovative success at marketing, strategic planning), banking trends, how-to articles on bank operation and marketing issues. "Our editorial approach is predicated on two things: quality writing and an ability to give readers a sense of the people interviewed for a particular story. People enjoy reading about other people." Buys 15 mss/year. Sidebars welcome. No fiction. Query. Length: 1,500-2,500 words. Pays $400 maximum.
Photos: State availability of photos with submission. Uses color transparencies, color prints or b&w prints. Pays $25/photo. Identification of subjects required. Buys one-time rights.
Columns/Departments: "Newslines," short general-interest items about banking and finance; "Update," short pieces about community banks and bankers, such as a bank's unique home mortgage marketing program or an interesting personality in community banking. Length: 75-175 words. Byline given. Pays $50.
Tips: "The best way to get acquainted with us is by writing a short piece (75-175 words) for either our 'Newslines' or 'Update' departments. Since they are often read first, the accent is on crisp, clean writing that packs a punch. Our editorial content seeks to convey the strength of locally owned, locally managed community banks, and the need to protect America's diversified financial system. We are working to position

Independent Banker as a writer's magazine that provides solid information for community bank CEOs in a creative, entertaining manner."

NAPFA ADVISOR, The Newsletter for Fee-Only Financial Advisors, (formerly *NAPFA News*), National Association of Personal Financial Advisors, 1130 W. Lake Cook Rd., Suite 150, Buffalo Grove IL 60089. (708)537-7723. Editor: Margery Wasserman. 60% freelance written. Monthly newsletter covering financial planning. "*NAPFA News* publishes practice management and investment strategy articles targeted to fee-only financial advisors. Topics that relate to comprehensive financial planning geared to the practitioner are desired. Readers range from sole practitioners to members of larger firms." Estab. 1985. Circ. 1,000. Pays on publication. Publishes ms an average of 3 months after acceptance. Byline given. Buys first North American serial, first, one-time or second serial (reprint) rights. Editorial lead time 2 months. Submit seasonal material 3 months in advance. Accepts simultaneous and previously published submissions. Send tearsheet of article. Query for electronic submissions. Reports in 2-3 months on queries. Sample copy for 9×12 SAE with 4 first-class stamps.
Nonfiction: Reviews of financial planning books and software programs, financial planning issues, practice management tips. Buys 50 mss/year. Query. Length: 750-2,000 words. Pays 20¢/word up to $300.
Photos: State availability of photos with submission. Reviews 5×7 prints. Offers no additional payment for photos accepted with ms. Captions, model releases, identification of subjects required. Buys one-time rights.
Columns/Departments: Practice Profile (assigned), 1,700-2,000 words; Book Reviews (fee-only planning perspective), 750-1,500 words; Software Reviews (fee-only planning perspective), 750-1,500 words. Pays 20¢/word up to $300.
Tips: "All writing must be directed to the financial practitioner, not the consumer. Freelancers who are interested in writing for *NAPFA Advisor* will have a strong background in financial planning, investment, and practice management issues and will understand the differences between fee-only, fee-based, fee and commission, and commission-based financial planning."

RESEARCH MAGAZINE, Ideas for Today's Investors, Research Services, 2201 Third St., San Francisco CA 94107. (415)621-0220. Fax: (415)620-0735. Editor: Rebecca McReynolds. 50% freelance written. Monthly business magazine of corporate profiles and subjects of interest to stockbrokers. Estab. 1977. Circ. 80,000. Pays on publication. Publishes ms an average of 2 months after acceptance. Byline given. Offers 20% kill fee. Buys first North American serial or second serial (reprint) rights. Query for electronic submissions. Reports in 1 month. Sample copy for 9×12 SAE with 4 first-class stamps. Writer's guidelines for #10 SASE.
Nonfiction: How-to (sales tips), interview/profile, new product, financial products. Buys approximately 50 mss/year. Query with published clips. Length: 1,000-3,000 words. Pays $300-900. Sometimes pays expenses of writers on assignment.
Tips: "Only submit articles that fit our editorial policy and are appropriate for our audience. *Only the non-corporate profile section is open to freelancers.* We use local freelancers on a regular basis for corporate profiles."

SECONDARY MARKETING EXECUTIVE, LDJ Corporation, P.O. Box 2330, Waterbury CT 06722. (203)755-0158. Fax: (203)755-3480. Editorial Director: John Florian. 20% freelance written. Monthly tabloid on secondary marketing. "The magazine is read monthly by executives in financial institutions who are involved with secondary marketing, which is the buying and selling of mortgage loans and servicing rights. The editorial slant is toward how-to and analysis of trends, rather than spot news." Estab. 1986. Circ. 22,000. **Pays on acceptance.** Publishes ms an average of 1 month after acceptance. Byline given. Offers 30% kill fee. Buys first rights. Submit seasonal material 4 months in advance. Query for electronic submissions. Reports in 2 weeks. *Writer's Market* recommends allowing 1 month for reply. Sample copy and writer's guidelines for 9×12 SAE with 6 first-class stamps.
Nonfiction: How-to (improve secondary marketing operations and profits), opinion. Buys 20 mss/year. Query. Length: 800-1,200 words. Pays $200-400.
Photos: State availability of photos with submission. Reviews contact sheets. Offers $25/photo. Captions, model releases and identification of subjects required. Buys one-time rights.

Fishing

‡AQUACULTURE MAGAZINE, Achill River Corp., P.O. Box 2329, Asheville NC 28802. (704)254-7334. Editor: Greg Gallagher. 50% freelance written. Bimonthly magazine covering aquaculture, mariculture and fish farming. "*Aquaculture Magazine* serves aquaculturists engaged in the production processing and marketing of finfish, shellfish, crustaceans, and aquatic plants. It is read by fish farmers, scientists, academicians, local, state, and federal government aquaculture program personnel. Feature articles include stories on individual operations, research and trends related to various species and legislative and commercial developments."

Pays on acceptance. Publishes ms an average of 4 months after acceptance. Byline given. Buys first rights. Editorial lead time 3 months. Submit seasonal material 3 months in advance. Query for electronic submissions. Sample copy for $4. Writer's guidelines free on request.

Nonfiction: How-to, technical. Length: 2,000 words. Pays 10¢/word.

Photos: Send photos with submission. Reviews contact sheets. Offers $5-25/photo. Captions required. Buys all rights.

Columns/Departments: Newsreels (trade show events, government info), 1,000 words; Features (fish farming operations), 2,000-3,000 words; Headliners (fish farming operations), 1,000 words. Buys 30 mss/ year. Pays 10¢/word.

Fillers: Newbreaks. Buys 10/year. Length: 250-500 words. Pays 10¢/word.

Tips: "Call the editor and propose your ideas. Write *Aquaculture Magazine* with your proposed idea for an article."

NORTHERN AQUACULTURE, Harrison House Publishers, 4611 William Head Rd., Victoria, British Columbia V9B 5T7 Canada. (604)478-9209. Fax: (604)478-1184. Editor: Peter Chettleburgh. 50% freelance written. Works with a small number of new/unpublished writers each year. Bimonthly magazine covering aquaculture in Canada and the northern US. Estab. 1985. Circ. 4,000. Pays on publication. Publishes ms an average of 3 months after acceptance. Byline given. Buys first North American serial rights. Submit seasonal material 5 months in advance. Reports in 3 weeks. Free sample copy for 9×12 SAE with $2 IRCs. Free writer's guidelines.

Nonfiction: How-to, interview/profile, new product, opinion, photo feature. Buys 20-24 mss/year. Query. Length: 200-1,500 words. Pays 10-20¢/word for assigned articles; 10-15¢/word for unsolicited articles. May pay writers with contributor copies if writer requests. Sometimes pays the expenses of writers on assignment.

Photos: Send photos with submission. Reviews 5×7 prints. Captions required. Buys one-time rights.

WESTCOAST FISHERMAN, Westcoast Publishing Ltd., 1496 West 72 Ave., Vancouver, British Columbia V6P 3C8 Canada. (604)266-8611. Fax: (604)266-6437. E-mail: wcoast@wimsey.com. Editor: Peter A. Robson. 40% freelance written. Monthly trade journal covering commercial fishing in British Columbia. "We're a non-aligned magazine dedicated to the people in the B.C. commercial fishing industry. Our publication reflects and celebrates the individuals and communities that collectively constitute B.C. fishermen." Estab. 1986. Pays on publication. Publishes ms an average of 2-3 months after acceptance. Byline given. Buys first and one-time rights. Accepts previously published submissions. Send photocopy of article or typed ms with rights for sale noted and information about when and where the article previously appeared. For reprints, pays 100% of amount paid for an original article. Reports in 2 months.

Nonfiction: Interview/profile, photo feature, technical. Buys 30-40 mss/year. Query with or without published clips or send complete ms. Length: 250-2,500 words. Pays $25-450.

Photos: Send photos with submission. Reviews contact sheets, negatives, transparencies and 5×7 prints. Offers $5-100/photo. Identification of subjects required. Buys one-time rights.

Poetry: Avant-garde, free verse, haiku, light verse, traditional. "We use poetry written by or for West Coast fishermen." Buys 6 poems/year. Length: 1 page. Pay is $25.

Florists, Nurseries and Landscapers

Readers of these publications are involved in growing, selling or caring for plants, flowers and trees. Magazines geared to consumers interested in gardening are listed in the Consumer Home and Garden section.

FLORIST, The FTD Association, 29200 Northwestern Hwy., P.O. Box 2227, Southfield MI 48037-2227. (313)355-9300. Editor-in-Chief: William P. Golden. Managing Editor: Barbara Koch. 5% freelance written. Monthly magazine for retail flower shop owners, managers and floral designers. Other readers include floriculture growers, wholesalers, researchers and teachers. Circ. 28,000. **Pays on acceptance.** Publishes ms an average of 2 months after acceptance. Buys one-time rights. Pays 10-25% kill fee. Reports in 1 month.

Nonfiction: Articles should pertain to marketing, merchandising, financial management or personnel management in a retail flower shop. Also, giftware, floral and interior design trends. No general interest, fiction or personal experience. Buys 5 unsolicited mss/year. Query with published clips. Length: 1,200-2,500 words. Pays $200-400.

Photos: State availability of photos with query. Pays $10-25 for 5×7 b&w photos or color transparencies. Buys one-time rights.

Tips: "Business management articles must deal specifically with retail flower shops and their unique merchandise and concerns. Send samples of published work with query. Suggest several ideas in query letter."

GROWERTALKS, Ball Publishing, 335 N. River St., P.O Box 9, Batavia IL 60510. (708)208-9080. Managing Editor: Chris Beytes. 50% freelance written. Monthly magazine covering ornamental horticulture—primarily greenhouse flower growers. "*GrowerTalks* serves the commercial greenhouse grower. Editorial emphasis is on floricultural crops: bedding plants, potted floral crops, foliage and fresh cut flowers. Our readers are growers, managers and owners. We're looking for writers who've had experience in the greenhouse industry." Estab. 1937. Circ. 10,500. Pays on publication. Publishes ms an average of 6 months after acceptance. Byline given. Buys first North American serial rights. Editorial lead time 4 months. Submit seasonal material 6 months in advance. Query for electronic submissions. Reports in 1 month. Sample copy and writer's guidelines free on request.

Nonfiction: How-to (time- or money-saving projects for professional flower/plant growers); interview/ profile (ornamental horticulture growers); personal experience (of a grower); technical (about growing process in greenhouse setting). "No articles that promote only one product." Buys 36 mss/year. Query. Length: 1,200-1,600 words. Pays $125 minimum for assigned articles; $75 minimum for unsolicited articles. Sometimes pays in other premiums or contributor copies.

Photos: State availability of photos with submission. Reviews 2½×2½ slides and 3×5 prints. Negotiates payment individually. Captions, model releases and identification of subjects required. Buys one-time rights.

Tips: "Discuss magazine with ornamental horticulture growers to find out what topics that have or haven't appeared in the magazine interest them."

THE GROWING EDGE, New Moon Publishing Inc., 215 SW Second, Suite 201, P.O. Box 1027, Corvallis OR 97339-1027. (503)757-2511. Fax: (503)757-0028. E-mail: talexan@peak.org. Editor: Trisha Coene. 85% freelance written. Eager to work with new or unpublished writers. Quarterly magazine signature covering indoor and outdoor high-tech gardening techniques and tips. Estab. 1980. Circ. 40,000. Pays on publication. Publishes ms an average of 3 months after acceptance. Byline given. Buys first serial and reprint rights. Submit seasonal material at least 6 months in advance. Query for electronic submissions. Reports in 3 months. Sample copy for $6.50. Writer's guidelines for #10 SASE.

Nonfiction: Book excerpts and reviews relating to high-tech gardening, general interest, how-to, interview/ profile, personal experience, technical. Query first. Length: 500-2,500 words. Pays 10¢/word.

Photos: Pays $175/color cover photos; $25-50/inside photo. Pays on publication. Credit line given. Buys first and reprint rights.

Tips: Looking for information which will give the reader/gardener/farmer the "growing edge" in high-tech gardening and farming on topics such as hydroponics, high intensity grow lights, water conservation, drip irrigation, advanced organic fertilizers, new seed varieties and greenhouse cultivation.

ORNAMENTAL OUTLOOK, The Professional Magazine for the Professional Grower, FGR, Inc., 1331 N. Mills Ave., Orlando FL 32803-2598. (407)894-6522. Fax: (407)894-6511. Editor: Kris Sweet. 50% freelance written. Bimonthly magazine covering ornamental horticulture. "*Ornamental Outlook* is written for commercial growers of ornamental plants in Florida. Our goal is to provide interesting and informative articles on such topics as production, legislation, safety, technology, pest control, water management and new varieties as they apply to Florida growers." Estab. 1991. Circ. 12,500. Pays 30 days after publication. Publishes ms an average of 4 months after acceptance. Byline given. Buys all rights. Editorial lead time 2 months. Submit seasonal material 3 months in advance. Query for electronic submissions. Reports in 1-3 months. Sample copy for 9×12 SAE with 5 first-class stamps. Writer's guidelines free on request.

Nonfiction: Interview/profile, photo feature, technical. "No first-person articles. No word-for-word meeting transcripts or all-quote articles." Query with published clips. Length: 750-1,000 words. Pays 12¢/word.

Photos: Send photos with submission. Reviews contact sheets, transparencies and prints. Offers $10-30/ photo. Captions and identification of subjects required. Buys one-time rights.

Columns/Departments: Management (news that helps wholesale growers manage nurseries), 750 words. Query with published clips. Pays 12¢/word.

Tips: "I am most impressed by written queries that address specific subjects of interest to our audience, which is the *Florida* grower of *commercial* horticulture. Our biggest demand is for features, about 1,000 words, that follow subjects listed on our editorial calendar (which is sent with guidelines). Please do not send articles of national or consumer interest."

‡TREE CARE INDUSTRY MAGAZINE, National Arborist Association, P.O. Box 1094, Amherst NH 03031-1094. (800)733-2622. Editor: Peter Gerstenberger. 50% freelance written. Monthly magazine covering tree care and landscape maintenance. Estab. 1990. Circ. 23,000. Pays on publication. Publishes ms an average of 3 months after acceptance. Byline given. Buys first North American serial rights. Editorial lead time 10 weeks. Submit seasonal material 3 months in advance. Reports in 2 weeks on queries; 2 months on mss. Sample copy for 9×12 SAE with 6 first-class stamps. Writer's guidelines free on request.

Nonfiction: Book excerpts, general interest, historical/nostalgic, humor, interview/profile, new product, personal expeience, technical. Buys 10 mss/year. Query with published clips Length: 900-3,500 words. Payment negotiable. Sometimes pays expenses of writers on assignment.

Photos: Send photos with submission. Reviews prints. Negotiates payment individually. Captions, identification of subjects required. Buys one-time rights.

Columns/Departments: Management Exchange (business management-related), 1,200-1,800 words; Industry Innovations (inventions), 1,200 words; From The Field (OP/ED from practioners), 1,200 words. Buys 40 mss/year. Send complete ms. Pays $100 and up.

Tips: "Preference is given to writers with background and knowledge of the tree care industry; our focus is relatively narrow. Preference is also given to photojournalists willing to work on speculation."

Government and Public Service

Listed here are journals for people who provide governmental services at the local, state or federal level or for those who work in franchised utilities. Journals for city managers, politicians, bureaucratic decision makers, civil servants, firefighters, police officers, public administrators, urban transit managers and utilities managers are listed in this section.

THE CALIFORNIA HIGHWAY PATROLMAN, California Association of Highway Patrolmen, 2030 V Street, Sacramento CA 95818-1730. (916)452-6751. Editor: Carol Perri. 70% freelance written. Monthly magazine covering CHP info, California history, history of vehicles and/or transportation. "Our readers are either uniformed officers or pro-police oriented." Estab. 1937. Circ. 20,000. Pays on publication. Publishes ms an average of 6-9 months after acceptance. No kill fee. Byline given. Buys one-time rights. Submit seasonal material 3-6 months in advance. Accepts simultaneous and previously published submissions. Send tearsheet or photocopy of article or typed ms and information on when and where the article previously appeared. No telephone queries. Reports in 1 month on queries, up to 3 months on mss. Sample copy for 9×12 SAE with 5 first-class stamps. Writer's guidelines for #10 SASE.

Nonfiction: General interest, historical/nostalgic, humor, interview/profile, photo feature, technical, travel. "No 'how you felt when you received a ticket (or survived an accident)!' No fiction." Buys 80-100 mss/year. Query with or without published clips or send complete ms. Length: 750-3,000 words. Pays 5¢/word or $50 minimum.

Photos: State availability of photos with submission. Send photos (or photocopies of available photos) with submission. Reviews prints. Offers $5/photo. Captions and identification of subjects required. Returns all photos. Buys one-time rights.

    ● Articles with accompanying photos receive preference.

‡CAMPAIGNS AND ELECTIONS, 1020 1511 K St., NW, Washington DC 20005. (202)638-7788. Editor: Ron Faucheux. 30% freelance written. Magazine published 10 times/year covering US campaigns and elections; political professionals. Estab. 1980. Circ. 64,000. Publishes ms an average of 2 months after acceptance. Byline given. Offers negotiable kill fee. Buys first North American serial rights. Query for electronic submissions. Reports in 2 weeks on queries; 3 weeks on mss. *Writer's Market* recommends allowing 2 months for reply. Accepts previously published submissions. Send typed ms with rights for sale noted. Sample copy for 9×12 SAE with 5 first class stamps. Free writer's guidelines.

Nonfiction: Political campaign case studies, local news, how-to, humor/political, interview/profile/political, new product campaign industry, personal experience/political and technical/political-campaign industry. "Does not want to see anything not related to campaign industry. No policy 'issues,' i.e. abortion, health care, etc." Query with or without published clips or send complete ms. Length: 400-2,800 words.

Photos: Send photos with submission. Reviews contact sheets, negatives, transparencies and 5×7 prints. Offers no additional payment for photos accepted with ms. Captions and identification of subjects required. Buys one-time rights.

Columns/Departments: Inside Politics (tales involving political professionals—unpublished information), 400 words; From the Field (from the campaign trail-hard, fast, unpublished), 200 words. Buys 15 mss/year. Query. Length: 200-400 words.

Fillers: Anecdotes, short humor "must be political, true, unpublished." Buys 6 items/year. Length: 100-250 words.

Tips: "Call—discuss a topic. Understand we write for candidates, elected officials and the political professionals who support them, with how-to help, and case studies (always sought). Also information on corporate public affairs and grassroots lobbying."

CHIEF OF POLICE MAGAZINE, National Association of Chiefs of Police, 3801 Biscayne Blvd., Miami FL 33137. (305)573-0070. Editor-in-Chief: Jim Gordon. Bimonthly trade journal for law enforcement commanders (command ranks). Circ. 13,500. **Pays on acceptance.** Publishes ms an average of 4-6 months after acceptance. Byline given. Buys first rights. Submit seasonal material 6 months in advance. Accepts simultaneous and previously published submissions. Reports in 2 weeks. Sample copy for $3 and 9×12 SAE with 5 first-class stamps. Writer's guidelines for #10 SASE.

Nonfiction: General interest, historical/nostalgic, how-to, humor, inspirational, interview/profile, new product, personal experience, photo feature, religious, technical. "We want stories about interesting police cases and stories on any law enforcement subject or program that is positive in nature. No exposé types. Nothing anti-police." Buys 50 mss/year. Send complete ms. Length: 600-2,500 words. Pays $25-75 for assigned articles; $10-50 for unsolicited articles. Sometimes (when pre-requested) pays the expenses of writers on assignment.

Photos: Send photos with submission. Reviews 5×6 prints. Pays $5-10 for b&w; $10-25 for color. Captions required. Buys one-time rights.

Columns/Departments: New Police (police equipment shown and tests), 200-600 words. Buys 6 mss/year. Send complete ms. Pays $5-25.

Fillers: Anecdote, short humor, law-oriented cartoons. Buys 100/year. Length: 100-1,600 words. Pays $5-25.

Tips: "Writers need only contact law enforcement officers right in their own areas and we would be delighted. We want to recognize good commanding officers from sergeant and above who are involved with the community. Pictures of the subject or the department are essential and can be snapshots. We are looking for interviews with police chiefs and sheriffs on command level with photos."

‡**CORRECTIONS FORUM**, Partisan Publishing Inc., 320 Broadway, Bethpage NY 11714. Editor: Ken Distler. 60% freelance written. Magazine published 8 times/year covering prison and jail management. Estab. 1992. Circ. 11,000. Pays on publication. Publishes ms an average of 2 months after acceptance. Byline given. No kill fee. Editorial lead time 3 months. Submit seasonal material 3 months in advance. Accepts simultaneous and previously published submissions. Query for electronic submissions. Reports in 3-4 weeks on queries; 4-6 months on mss (unsolicited). Sample copy for 9×12 SAE with $1.47 postage.

Nonfiction: How-to (as done by peers successfully), humor, interview/profile, new product, technical. Buys 10 mss/year. Query. Length: 750-2,000 words. Pays $200-300 for assigned articles; $150-200 for unsolicited articles. Sometimes pays expenses of writers on assignment.

Photos: Send photos with submission. Offers no additional payment for photos accepted with ms. Captions, identification of subjects required. Buys all rights.

Filler: Anecdotes, gags to be illustrated by cartoonist, newsbreaks, short humor. Buys 3/year. Length: 500-750 words. Pays $100-150.

Tips: Looking for interesting treatment of common themes, in-depth technology treatment for layman, brief, thorough coverage of complex topics.

‡**FIRE CHIEF**, Argus Business, 35 E. Wacker Dr., Suite 700, Chicago IL 60601. (312)726-7277. Editor: Scott Baltic. 90% freelance written. Monthly magazine covering fire department management and leadership. "*Fire Chief* is the management magazine of the fire service, addressing the administrative, personnel, training, prevention/education, professional development and operational issues faced by chiefs and other fire officers, whether in paid, volunteer or combination departments." Estab. 1956. Circ. 44,000. Pays on publication. Publishes ms an average of 3-6 months after acceptance. Byline given. Offers 50% kill fee. Buys first, one-time, second serial (reprint) or all rights. Editorial lead time 2 months. Submit seasonal material 4 months in advance. Query for electronic submissions. Reports in 1 month on queries; 2 months on mss. Sample copy and writer's guidelines free on request.

Nonfiction: How-to, technical. Buys 50-60 mss/year. Query with published clips. Length: 1,500-8,000 words. Pays $50-400. Sometimes pays expenses of writers on assignment.

Photos: State availability of photos with submissions. Reviews transparencies, prints. Negotiates payment individually. Captions, identification of subjects required. Buys one-time rights.

Tips: "Writers who are unfamiliar with the fire service are very unlikely to place anything with us. Many pieces that we reject are either too unfocused or too abstract. We want articles that help keep fire chiefs well informed and effective at their jobs."

FIREHOUSE MAGAZINE, PTN Publishing, 445 Broad Hollow Rd., Suite 21, Melville NY 11747. (516)845-2700. Fax: (516)845-7109. Editor-in-Chief: Harvey Eisner. 85% freelance written. Works with a small number of new/unpublished writers each year. Monthly magazine covering fire service. "*Firehouse* covers major fires nationwide, controversial issues and trends in the fire service, the latest firefighting equipment and methods of firefighting, historical fires, firefighting history and memorabilia. Fire-related books, fire safety education, hazardous materials incidents and the emergency medical services are also covered." Estab. 1976. Circ. 127,000. Pays on publication. Byline given. Exclusive submissions only. Query for electronic submissions. Sample copy for 9×12 SAE with 7 first-class stamps. Writer's guidelines free.

Nonfiction: Book excerpts (of recent books on fire, EMS and hazardous materials); historical/nostalgic (great fires in history, fire collectibles, the fire service of yesteryear); how-to (fight certain kinds of fires, buy and maintain equipment, run a fire department); technical (on almost any phase of firefighting, techniques, equipment, training, administration); trends (controversies in the fire service). No profiles of people or departments that are not unusual or innovative, reports of nonmajor fires, articles not slanted toward firefighters' interests. No poetry. Buys 100 mss/year. Query with or without published clips or send complete ms. Length: 500-3,000 words. Pays $50-400 for assigned articles; $50-300 for unsolicited articles. Sometimes pays the expenses of writers on assignment.

Photos: Send photos with query or ms. Pays $15-45 for b&w prints; $20-200 for transparencies and color prints. Cannot accept negatives. Captions and identification of subjects required.

Columns/Departments: Training (effective methods); Book Reviews; Fire Safety (how departments teach fire safety to the public); Communicating (PR, dispatching); Arson (efforts to combat it). Buys 50 mss/year. Query or send complete ms. Length: 750-1,000 words. Pays $100-300.

Tips: "Read the magazine to get a full understanding of the subject matter, the writing style and the readers before sending a query or manuscript. Send photos with manuscript or indicate sources for photos. Be sure to focus articles on firefighters."

FOREIGN SERVICE JOURNAL, Dept. WM, 2101 E St. NW, Washington DC 20037-2990. (202)338-8244. Fax: (202)338-6820. Editor: Karen Krebsbach. 75% freelance written. Monthly magazine for Foreign Service personnel and others interested in foreign affairs and related subjects. Estab. 1924. Pays on publication. Publishes ms an average of 3 months after acceptance. Byline given. Buys first North American serial rights. Reports in 1 month. Sample copy for $3.50 and 10×12 SAE with 6 first-class stamps. Writer's guidelines for SASE.

• A new column is Postcards from Abroad.

Nonfiction: Uses articles on "diplomacy, professional concerns of the State Department and Foreign Service, diplomatic history and articles on Foreign Service experiences. Much of our material is contributed by those working in the profession. Informed outside contributions are welcomed, however." Query. Buys 15-20 unsolicited mss/year. Length: 1,000-4,000 words. Offers honoraria.

Fiction: Publishes short stories about foreign service life in the annual August fiction issue.

Tips: "We're more likely to want your article if it has something to do with diplomacy or diplomats."

LAW AND ORDER, Hendon Co., 1000 Skokie Blvd., Wilmette IL 60091. (708)256-8555. Fax: (708)256-8574. E-mail: 71171.1344@compuserve.com. Editor: Bruce W. Cameron. 90% freelance written. Prefers to work with published/established writers. Monthly magazine covering the administration and operation of law enforcement agencies, directed to police chiefs and supervisors. Estab. 1952. Circ. 38,000. Pays on publication. Publishes ms an average of 6 months after acceptance. Byline given. Buys first North American serial rights. Submit seasonal material 3 months in advance. No simultaneous queries. Query for electronic submissions. Can accept mss via CompuServe. Reports in 1 month. Sample copy for 9×12 SAE. Free writer's guidelines.

Nonfiction: General police interest; how-to (do specific police assignments); new product (how applied in police operation); technical (specific police operation). Special issues: Buyers Guide (January); Communications (February); Training (March); International (April); Administration (May); Small Departments (June); Mobile Patrol (July); Equipment (August); Weapons (September); Police Science (November); Community Relations (December). No articles dealing with courts (legal field) or convicted prisoners. No nostalgic, financial, travel or recreational material. Buys 150 mss/year. Length: 2,000-3,000 words. Pays 10¢/word for professional writers; 5¢/word for others.

Photos: Send photos with ms. Reviews transparencies and prints. Identification of subjects required. Buys all rights.

Tips: "*L&O* is a respected magazine that provides up-to-date information that chiefs can use. Writers must know their subject as it applies to this field. Case histories are well received. We are upgrading editorial quality—stories *must* show some understanding of the law enforcement field. A frequent mistake is not getting photographs to accompany article."

‡LAW ENFORCEMENT TECHNOLOGY, PTN Publishing Co., 445 Broad Hollow Rd., #21, Melville NY 11747. Editor: Donna Rogers. 50% freelance written. Monthly magazine covering police management and technology. Estab. 1974. Circ. 35,000. Pays on publication. Publishes ms an average of 6 months after acceptance. Byline given. Offers 25% kill fee. Buys first North American serial rights. Editorial lead time 4-6 months. Submit seasonal material 4-6 months in advance. Reports in 3-4 weeks on queries; 2 months on mss. Sample copy for SAE and 6 first-class stamps. Writer's guidelines for #10 SASE.

Nonfiction: Book excerpts, how-to, humor, interview/profile, photo feature, police management and training. Buys 15 mss/year. Query. Length: 800-1,800 words. Pays $75-300 for assigned articles.

Photos: Send photos with submission. Reviews contact sheets, transparencies, 5×7 or 8×10 prints. Offers no additional payment for photos accepted with ms. Captions required. Buys one-time rights.

Fiction: Adventure, condensed novels, historical, humorous, mystery, novel excerpts, slice-of-life vignettes, suspense, (all must be police oriented). Buys 4 mss/year. Send complete ms. Length: 1,000-2,000 words. Pays $150-300.

For explanation of symbols, see the Key to Symbols and Abbreviations. For unfamiliar words, see the Glossary.

Tips: "Writer should have background in police work or currently work for a police agency. Most of our articles are technical or supervisory in nature. Please query first after looking at a sample copy."

NATIONAL MINORITY POLITICS, 13555 Bammel N. Houston, Suite 227, Houston TX 77066. (713)444-4265. Editor: Gwenevere Daye Richardson. 10-15% freelance written. Monthly opinion and news magazine taking a moderate to conservative political approach. Estab. 1988. Circ. 15,000. Pays on publication. Publishes ms an average of 1 month after acceptance. Byline given. Buys one-time rights. Editorial lead time 2 months. Submit seasonal material 2 months in advance. Accepts simultaneous submissions. No previously published material. Query for electronic submissions. Reports in 3-4 weeks on queries. Sample copy and writer's guidelines on request for $2.
  • *National Minority Politics* received the 1994 Outstanding Publication Award from the Conservative Political Action Conference.
Nonfiction: Exposé, interview/profile, commentary and features on national political topics. "These topics can be, but are not limited to, those which are considered traditionally 'minority' concerns. But prefer those which give a broad view or analysis of national or regional political elections, trends, issues, and economic issues as well." Buys approximately 24 mss/year. Query with published clips. Length: 750-1,000 words. Pays standard rate of $100 for unsolicited mss, usually more for assigned articles.
Columns/Departments: The Nation (commentaries on national issues), 750-1,000 words; features, 1,000-1,500 words; "Speaking Out," personal commentary, 750-1,000 words.
Fillers: Political cartoons. Pays $25.
Tips: "Submissions must be well-written, timely, have depth and take an angle not generally available in national newspapers and magazines. Since our magazine takes a moderate to conservative approach, we prefer not to receive commentaries which do not fall in either of these categories."

9-1-1 MAGAZINE, Official Publications, Inc., 18201 Weston Place, Tustin CA 92680-2251. (714)544-7776. Fax: (714)838-9233. E-mail: magazn911@aol.com. Editor: Randall Larson. 85% freelance written. Bimonthly magazine for knowledgeable public safety communications and response personnel and those associated with those respective professions. "*9-1-1 Magazine* is published to provide information valuable to all those interested in this exciting and rewarding profession." Estab. 1947. Circ. 20,000. Pays on publication. Publishes ms an average of 2 months after acceptance. Byline given. Offers 20% kill fee. Buys one-time and second serial (reprint) rights. Submit seasonal material well in advance. Accepts simultaneous submissions. Query for electronic submissions. Reports in 2 months on queries; 3 months on mss. Must be accompanied by SASE if to be returned. Sample copy for 9×12 SAE with 5 first-class stamps. Writer's guidelines for #10 SASE.
Nonfiction: Incident report, new product, photo feature, technical. Buys 10 mss/year. Send complete ms. "We prefer queries, but will look at manuscripts on speculation. Most positive responses to queries are considered on spec, but occasionally we will make assignments." Length: 1,000-2,500 words. Pays $100-300 for unsolicited articles.
Photos: Send photos with submission. Reviews color transparencies and prints. Offers $25-300/photo. Captions and identification of subjects required. Buys one-time rights.
Fillers: Cartoons. Buys 10/year. Pays $25-50.
Tips: "What we don't need are 'my first call' articles, or photography of a less-than-excellent quality. We seldom use poetry or fiction. *9-1-1 Magazine* is published for a knowledgeable, up-scale professional. Our primary considerations in selecting material are: quality, appropriateness of material, brevity, knowledge of our readership, accuracy, accompanying photography, originality, wit and humor, a clear direction and vision, and proper use of the language."

PLANNING, American Planning Association, 1313 E. 60th St., Chicago IL 60637-2891. (312)955-9100. Editor: Sylvia Lewis. 25% freelance written. Monthly magazine emphasizing urban planning for adult, college-educated readers who are regional and urban planners in city, state or federal agencies or in private business or university faculty or students. Estab. 1972. Circ. 30,000. Pays on publication. Publishes ms an average of 3 months after acceptance. Buys all rights. Byline given. Reports in 2 months. Sample copy and writer's guidelines for 9×12 SAE with 5 first-class stamps.
Nonfiction: Exposé (on government or business, but topics related to planning, housing, land use, zoning); general interest (trend stories on cities, land use, government); how-to (successful government or citizen efforts in planning, innovations, concepts that have been applied); technical (detailed articles on the nitty-gritty of planning, zoning, transportation but no footnotes or mathematical models). Also needs news stories up to 400 words. "It's best to query with a fairly detailed, one-page letter. We'll consider any article that's well written and relevant to our audience. Articles have a better chance if they are timely and related to planning and land use and if they appeal to a national audience. All articles should be written in magazine feature style." Buys 2 features and 1 news story/issue. Length: 500-2,000 words. Pays $100-900. "We pay freelance writers and photographers only, not planners."
Photos: "We prefer that authors supply their own photos, but we sometimes take our own or arrange for them in other ways." State availability of photos. Pays $25 minimum for 8×10 matte or glossy prints and $200 for 4-color cover photos. Captions required. Buys one-time rights.

POLICE, Hare Publications, 6300 Yarrow Dr., Carlsbad CA 92009-1597. (619)438-2511. Fax: (619)931-5809. Editor: John Molnar. 90% freelance written. Monthly magazine covering topics related to law enforcement officers. "Our audience is primarily law enforcement personnel such as patrol officers, detectives and security police." Estab. 1968. Circ. 58,000. **Pays on acceptance.** Publishes ms an average of 6 months after acceptance. Buys all rights (returned to author 45 days after publication). Submit theme material 6 months in advance. Reports in 3 months. Sample copy for $2. Writer's guidelines for #10 SAE with 2 first-class stamps.

Nonfiction: General interest, interview/profile, new product, personal experience, technical. Buys 30 mss/year. Query only. Length: 2,000-3,000 words. Pays $250-350.

Photos: Send photos with submission. Reviews color transparencies. Captions required. Buys all rights.

Columns/Departments: The Beat (entertainment section—humor, fiction, first-person drama, professional tips); The Arsenal (weapons, ammunition and equipment used in the line of duty); Fit For Duty (fitness, nutrition, mental health life style changes); Officer Survival (theories, skills and techniques used by officers for street survival). Buys 50 mss/year. Query only. Length: 1,000-2,500 words. Pays $75-250.

Tips: "You are writing for police officers—people who live a dangerous and stressful life. Study the editorial calendar—yours for the asking—and come up with an idea that fits into a specific issue. We are actively seeking talented writers."

POLICE AND SECURITY NEWS, DAYS Communications, Inc., 15 Thatcher Rd., Quakertown PA 18951-2503. (215)538-1240. Fax: (215)538-1208. Editor: James Devery. 40% freelance written. Bimonthly tabloid on public law enforcement and private security. "Our publication is designed to provide educational and entertaining information directed toward management level. Technical information written for the expert in a manner that the non-expert can understand." Estab. 1985. Circ. 20,964. Pays on publication. Publishes ms an average of 2 months after acceptance. Byline given. Buys first North American serial rights. Accepts simultaneous and previously published submissions. Free sample copy and writer's guidelines for 9 × 12 SAE with $1.93 postage.

Nonfiction: Al Menear, articles editor. Exposé, historical/nostalgic, how-to, humor, interview/profile, opinion, personal experience, photo feature, technical. Buys 12 mss/year. Query. Length: 200-4,000 words. Pays 10¢/word. Sometimes pays in trade-out of services.

Photos: State availability of photos with submission. Reviews 3 × 5 prints. Offers $10-50/photo. Buys one-time rights.

Fillers: Facts, newsbreaks, short humor. Buys 6/year. Length: 200-2,000 words. Pays 10¢/word.

POLICE TIMES, American Federation of Police, 3801 Biscayne Blvd., Miami FL 33137. (305)573-0070. Fax: (305)573-9819. Editor-In-Chief: Jim Gordon. 80% freelance written. Eager to work with new/unpublished writers. Bimonthly tabloid covering "law enforcement (general topics) for men and women engaged in law enforcement and private security, and citizens who are law and order concerned." Circ. 55,000. **Pays on acceptance.** Publishes ms an average of 3-6 months after acceptance. Byline given. Buys second serial (reprint) rights. Submit seasonal material 4 months in advance. Accepts simultaneous and previously published submissions. Sample copy for $2.50 and 9 × 12 SAE with 3 first-class stamps. Writer's guidelines for #10 SASE.

Nonfiction: Book excerpts; essays (on police science); exposé (police corruption); general interest; historical/nostalgic; how-to; humor; interview/profile; new product; personal experience (with police); photo feature; technical—all police-related. "We produce a special edition on police killed in the line of duty. It is mailed May 15 so copy must arrive six months in advance. Photos required." No anti-police materials. Buys 50 mss/year. Send complete ms. Length: 200-4,000 words. Pays $5-50 for assigned articles; $5-25 for unsolicited articles.

Photos: Send photos with submission. Reviews 5 × 6 prints. Offers $5-25/photo. Identification of subjects required. Buys all rights.

Columns/Departments: Legal Cases (lawsuits involving police actions); New Products (new items related to police services); Awards (police heroism acts). Buys variable number of mss/year. Send complete ms. Length: 200-1,000 words. Pays $5-25.

Fillers: Anecdotes, facts, newsbreaks, cartoons, short humor. Buys 100/year. Length: 50-100 words. Pays $5-10. Fillers are usually humorous stories about police officer and citizen situations. Special stories on police cases, public corruptions, etc. are most open to freelancers.

SUPERINTENDENT'S PROFILE & PRODUCE-SERVICE DIRECTORY, Profile Publications, 5986 Sturgen Dr., LaFayette NY 13084. (315)677-3555. Editor/Publisher: Jim Cropper. Prefers to work with published/established writers. Monthly magazine specifically published for every highway superintendent, public works director, and D.O.T. official in New York State, including every village, city, town and county. Estab. 1978. Circ. 2,600. Bylines given for excellent material. Pays up to $100 for appropriate nonfiction articles with topic matter relating to our readership's interests. Send tearsheet of previously published article, or ms for consideration. Submit seasonal material 3 months in advance. Sample copy for $2 and 9 × 12 SASE with 5 first-class stamps.

Nonfiction: Interview/Profiles of Highway Superintendents or Public Works Directors in NYS highlighting their departmental operations, and any innovative techniques used in a variety of municipal tasks. Length: 2 full, 8½ × 11, pages typed single space in 10 point type. Pays $150 for full length ms. All ms edited to fit magazine format. Sometimes pays the expenses of writers on assignment.

Photos: Subject matter must pertain to highway or public works. Reviews b&w 5 × 7s or contact sheets. Pays $5-10. Captions and identification of subjects required. All rights for use of photos granted to publisher if accepted.

Tips: "We are New York State's most widely read publication among highway, public works and D.O.T. professionals. Although we can't pay high rates, we will only consider high quality work. Articles should be written as objectively as possible, and should provide thorough reliable source identification, and content specifically suited to the highway and public works industry."

TRANSACTION/SOCIETY, Bldg. 4051, Rutgers University, New Brunswick NJ 08903. (908)445-2280 ext. 83. Fax: (908)445-3138. Editor: Irving Louis Horowitz. Publisher: Mary E. Curtis. 10% freelance written. Prefers to work with published/established writers. Bimonthly magazine for social scientists (policymakers with training in sociology, political issues and economics). Estab. 1962. Circ. 45,000. Buys all rights. Byline given. Pays on publication. Publishes ms an average of 6 months after acceptance. No simultaneous submissions. Query for electronic submissions; "manual provided to authors." Reports in 3 months. Sample copy and writer's guidelines for 9 × 12 SAE with 5 first-class stamps.

Nonfiction: Brigitte M. Goldstein, managing editor. "Articles of wide interest in areas of specific interest to the social science community. Must have an awareness of problems and issues in education, population and urbanization that are not widely reported. Articles on overpopulation, terrorism, international organizations. No general think pieces." Query. Payment for articles is made only if done on assignment. *No payment for unsolicited articles.*

Photos: Douglas Harper, photo editor. Pays $200 for photographic essays done on assignment or accepted for publication.

Tips: "Submit an article on a thoroughly unique subject, written with good literary quality. Present new ideas and research findings in a readable and useful manner. A frequent mistake is writing to satisfy a journal, rather than the intrinsic requirements of the story itself. Avoid posturing and editorializing."

YOUR VIRGINIA STATE TROOPER MAGAZINE, Virginia State Police Association, 6944 Forest Hill Ave., Richmond VA 23225. Editor: Rebecca V. Jackson. 60% freelance written. Triannual magazine covering police topics for troopers (state police), non-sworn members of the department and legislators. Estab. 1974. Circ. 5,000. **Pays on acceptance.** Publishes ms an average of 3 months after acceptance. Byline given. Buys first North American serial and all rights on assignments. Submit seasonal material 4 months in advance. Accepts simultaneous and previously published submissions. Send typed ms with rights for sale noted and information about when and where the article previously appeared. For reprints, pays 20% of amount paid for an original article. Reports in 2 months.

Nonfiction: Exposé (consumer or police-related); general interest; fitness/health; tourist (VA sites); financial planning (tax, estate planning tips); historical/nostalgic; how-to; book excerpts/reports (law enforcement related); humor, interview/profile (notable police figures); technical (radar); other (recreation). Buys 55-60 mss/year. Query with clips or send complete ms. Length: 2,500 words. Pays $250 maximum/article (10¢/word). Sometimes pays expenses of writers on assignment. Does not send sample copies.

Photos: Send photos with ms. Pays $50 maximum for several 5 × 7 or 8 × 10 b&w glossy prints to accompany ms. Cutlines and model releases required. Buys one-time rights.

Cartoons: Send copies. Pays $20. Buys one-time rights. Buys 20 cartoons/year.

Fiction: Adventure, humorous, mystery, novel excerpts, suspense. Buys 3 mss/year. Send complete ms. Length: 2,500 words minimum. Pays $250 maximum (10¢/word) on acceptance.

Tips: In addition to items of interest to the VA State Police, general interest is stressed.

Groceries and Food Products

In this section are publications for grocers, food wholesalers, processors, warehouse owners, caterers, institutional managers and suppliers of grocery store equipment. See the section on Confectionery and Snack Foods for bakery and candy industry magazines.

CANADIAN GROCER, Maclean-Hunter Ltd., Maclean Hunter Building, 777 Bay St., Toronto, Ontario M5W 1A7 Canada. (416)596-5772. Fax: (416)593-3162. Editor: George H. Condon. Managing Editor: Simone Collier. 40% freelance written. Prefers to work with published/established writers. Monthly magazine about supermarketing and food retailing for Canadian chain and independent food store managers, owners, buyers, executives, food brokers, food processors and manufacturers. Estab. 1886. Circ 18,500. **Pays on acceptance.** Publishes an average of 2 months after acceptance. Byline given. Buys first Canadian rights. Accepts previously published submissions. Send typed ms with rights for sale noted and information about when and where the article previously appeared. For reprints, pays 50% of the amount paid for an original article. Phone queries OK. Submit seasonal material 2 months in advance. Reports in 2 months. Sample copy for $5.

Nonfiction: Interview (Canadian trendsetters in marketing, finance or food distribution); technical (store operations, equipment and finance); news features on supermarkets. "Freelancers should be well versed on the supermarket industry. We don't want unsolicited material. Writers with business and/or finance expertise are preferred. Know the retail food industry and be able to write concisely and accurately on subjects relevant to our readers: food store managers, senior corporate executives, etc. A good example of an article would be 'How a dairy case realignment increased profits while reducing prices, inventory and stock-outs.' " Query with clips of previously published work. Pays 30¢/word. Pays the expenses of writers on assignment.

Photos: State availability of photos. Pays $10-25 for prints or slides. Captions preferred. Buys one-time rights.

Tips: "Suitable writers will be familiar with sales per square foot, merchandising mixes and direct product profitability."

FLORIDA GROCER, Florida Grocer Publications, Inc., P.O. Box 430760, South Miami FL 33243-0760. (305)441-1138. Fax: (305)661-6720. Editor: Dennis Kane. 5% freelance written. "*Florida Grocer* is a 16,000-circulation monthly trade newspaper, serving members of the Florida food industry. Our publication is edited for chain and independent food store owners and operators as well as members of allied industries." Estab. 1956. **Pays on acceptance.** Byline given. Buys all rights. Submit seasonal material 3 months in advance. Reports in 2 months. Sample copy for 10×14 SAE with 10 first-class stamps.

Nonfiction: Book excerpts, exposé, general interest, humor, features on supermarkets and their owners, new product, new equipment, photo feature, video. Buys variable number of mss/year. Query with or without published clips or send complete ms. Payment varies. Sometimes pays the expenses of writers on assignment.

Photos: State availability of photos with submission. Terms for payment on photos "included in terms of payment for assignment."

Tips: "We prefer feature articles on new stores (grand openings, etc.), store owners, operators; Florida-based food manufacturers, brokers, wholesalers, distributors, etc. We also publish a section in Spanish and also welcome the above types of materials in Spanish (Cuban)."

THE FOOD CHANNEL, America's Source For Food Trends, Noble & Associates, 515 N. State, 29th Floor, Chicago IL 60610. (312)644-4600. E-mail: foodchan@interaccess.com. Editor: John Scroggins. 30% freelance written. Biweekly newsletter covering food trends. "*The Food Channel* is published by Noble & Associates, a food-focused advertising, promotional marketing and new product development company. *The Food Channel* provides insight into emerging trends in the food and beverage industries and the implications for manufacturers, suppliers and consumers." Estab. 1988. Circ. 2,500. Pays on publication. Publishes ms an average of 2 months after acceptance. Byline given. Editorial lead time 2 months. Query for electronic submissions. Reports in 1 month. Sample copy and writer's guidelines free on request.

Nonfiction: Trends in food marketing, consumer behavior, future of food. Length: 500-1,100 words. Pays 50¢/word.

Columns/Departments: Buys 15 mss/year. Query.

Tips: "We are most open to 500-1,100-word articles covering food marketing trends. Using freelancers for very focused articles on legislation, specialty foods and demographics as related to food."

FOOD DISTRIBUTION MAGAZINE, Products and Promotions for Mainstream Distribution, National Food Distribution Network, 406 Water St., Warren RI 02885. Editor: Dara Wilson Chadwick. 30% freelance written. Monthly magazine covering the specialty food industry. "We are looking for pieces of interest to supermarket buyers, food distributors, and gourmet and specialty food stores. Quality writing, interesting and informative articles." Estab. 1958. Circ. 35,000. Pays on publication. Publishes ms an average of 2 months after acceptance. Byline given. Buys all rights. Editorial lead time 2-4 months. Submit seasonal material 4 months in advance. Accepts previously published submissions. Send information about when and where the article appeared. For reprints, pays negotiable rate. Query for electronic submissions. Reports in 1-2 months. Sample copy for $5.

● *Food Distribution* is looking to use more freelancers from across the nation, and is particularly interested in retailer profile features and indepth looks at specialty food retail operations.

Nonfiction: Humor, new product, photo feature. Buys 3-10 mss/year. Query with published clips. Length: 1,000-3,000 words. Pay negotiable. Sometimes pays expenses of writers on assignment.

For information on setting your freelance fees, see How Much Should I Charge?

Photos: Send photos with submission. Reviews transparencies, prints. Negotiates payment individually. Buys one-time rights or all rights.
Tips: Query first.

‡**FRESH CUT MAGAZINE, The Magazine for Value-added Produce**, Columbia Publishing, P.O. Box 1467, Yakima WA 98907. (509)248-2452. Editor: Ken Hodge. 40% freelance written. Magazine published 9 times/year covering minimally processed fresh fruits and vegetables, packaged salads, etc. "We want informative articles about processing produce. We also want stories about how these products are sold at retail, in restaurants, etc." Estab. 1993. Circ. 6,900. Pays on publication. Publishes ms an average of 1-2 months after acceptance. Byline given. Buys all rights. Editorial lead time 1-2 months. Submit seasonal material 3 months in advance. Query for electronic submissions. Reports in 1 month on queries; 2 months on mss. Sample copy for 9×12 SASE. Writer's guidelines for #10 SASE.
Nonfiction: Historical/nostalgic, new product, opinion, technical. Buys 20-40 mss/year. Query with published clips. Pays $125-200 for assigned articles; $75-125 for unsolicited articles.
Photos: Send photos with submission. Reviews transparencies. Offers no additional payment for photos accepted with ms. Identification of subjects required. Buys one-time rights.
Columns/Departments: Packaging; Food Safety; Processing/engineering. Buys 10-12 mss/year. Query. Pays $125-200.
Fillers: Facts. Length: 300 words maximum. Pays $25-50.

‡**GOURMET NEWS**, United Publications, 38 Lafayette St., Box 1056, Yarmouth ME 04096. (207)846-0600. Editor: Clarke Canfield. 10-20% freelance written. Monthly tabloid covering gourmet and specialty food industry. "We are a business newspaper covering the gourmet food industry. Our readers are gourmet food retailers and distributors and articles should be written with them in mind. We do not write about gourmet restaurants." Estab. 1991. Circ. 22,000. Pays on publication. Publishes ms an average of 1-2 months after acceptance. Byline given. Offers $50 kill fee. Buys first rights. Editorial lead time 2 months. Query for electronic submissions. Reports in 3-4 months on queries.
Nonfiction: General interest, news articles, such as trends and issues. Buys 12-20 mss/year. Query. Length: 800-2,000 words. Pays $100-500. No unsolicited mss. Sometimes pays expenses of writers on assignment.
Photos: State availability of photos with submissions. Reviews transparencies, prints. Offers no additional payment for photos accepted with ms.
Tips: "If you are a proven writer with proven skills, I will consider assigning articles to you. If you are relatively new in journalism, be prepared to pitch a specific story with a news angle. There must be a news angle, such as a trend in gourmet foods (growth of teas, organic foods, the growing influence of men in buying food) or an issue."

THE GOURMET RETAILER, 3301 Ponce De Leon Blvd., #300, Coral Gables FL 33134-7273. (305)446-3388. Fax: (305)446-2868. Executive Editor: Michael Keighley. 30% freelance written. Monthly magazine covering specialty foods and housewares. "Our readers are owners and managers of specialty food and upscale housewares retail units. Writers must know the trade exceptionally well and be research-oriented." Estab. 1979. Circ. 21,000. Pays on publication. Publishes ms an average of 3 months after acceptance. Byline sometimes given. No kill fee. Buys all rights. Submit seasonal material 6 months in advance. Query for electronic submissions. Reports in 2 months on queries. Free sample copy and writer's guidelines.
Nonfiction: Interview/profile (retail stores, manufacturers). Query. No unsolicited mss. Buys 12 mss/year. Query with published clips. Length: 1,500-2,200 words.
Photos: State availability of photos with submission. Reviews negatives, 5×7 transparencies, 8×10 prints. Offers $15-25/photo. Identification of subjects required. Buys one-time rights.
Tips: "I enjoy hearing from established business writers. I am looking for upmarket food/housewares news; and for profiles of specialty retailers. We are extremely stringent on editorial quality."

‡**GROCERY DISTRIBUTION MAGAZINE, The Magazine for Physical Distribution and Plant Development for the Food Industry**, Grocery Market Publication, 455 S. Frontage Rd., #116, Burr Ridge IL 60521. Editor: Richard W. Mulville. 35% freelance written. Bimonthly magazine covering food distribution. "Edited for executives responsible for food warehousing/transportation functions." Estab. 1975. Circ. 15,000. **Pays on acceptance.** Publishes ms an average of 2 months after acceptance. No byline. Offers 100% kill fee. Buys all rights. Editorial lead time 1 month. Query for electronic submissions. Reports in 1-2 weeks on queries. Writer's guidelines free on request.
Nonfiction: How-to (emphasize case history articles detailing use of systems or equipment by distributors). Buys 4-5 mss/year. Query with published clips. Length: 1,500-3,000. Pays $150-300/400 (more if photos submitted by writer). Sometimes pays expenses of writers on assignment (if overnight travel required).
Photos: State availability of photos with submissions. Reviews contact sheets, negatives, 3×5 transparencies or prints. "All forms acceptable, usually make agreement before hand." Negotiates payment individually. Captions, identification of subjects required. Buys all rights.

Tips: "Write advising us of availability to do articles. If indicated, we send form for freelancer to complete and return to us (gives us information on territory covered, experience, payment expected, photographic abilities, etc."

‡HEALTH FOODS BUSINESS, PTN Publishing Co., 2 University Plaza, Suite 11, Hackensack NJ 07601. (516)845-2700. Editor: Gina Geslewitz. 70% freelance written. Monthly magazine covering health foods. "The business magazine for natural products retailers." Estab. 1953. Circ. 11,500. Pays on publication. Publishes ms an average of 3 months after acceptance. Byline given. Buys first North American serial rights. Editorial lead time 3-4 months. Submit seasonal material 3 months in advance. Query for electronic submissions. Reports in 2-4 weeks on queries. Sample copy for $3. Writer's guidelines free on requesst.
Nonfiction: Store profile. Query. Pays $100-150.
Photos: State availability of photos with submissions.
Tips: "We are always looking for well-written store profiles with lots of detailed information, but new writers should always query first to receive writer's guidelines and other directions."

MEAT BUSINESS MAGAZINE, 109 W. Washington, Millstadt IL 62260. (800)451-0914 or (314)621-0170. Fax: (618)476-1616. Editor: Jerome P. Curry. Staff produced or on assignment to established freelancer. Monthly magazine for meat processors, retailers, locker plant operators, freezer provisioners, portion control packers, meat dealers and food service (food plan) operators. **Pays on acceptance.** Queries with SASE welcome.

MINNESOTA GROCER, Serving the Upper Midwest Retail Food Industry, Minnesota Grocers Council, Inc., 533 St. Clair Ave., St. Paul MN 55102-2859. (612)228-0973. Fax: (612)228-1949. Director of Communications: Ronelle Ewing. 25% freelance written. Bimonthly magazine on the retail grocery industry in Minnesota. Estab. 1951. Circ. 4,200. Pays on publication. Publishes ms an average of 2-4 months after acceptance. Buys all rights. Submit seasonal material 3 months in advance. Accepts previously published submissions. Send tearsheet of article or typed ms with rights for sale noted. Does not pay for reprints. Reports in 2 months. Sample copy and writer's guidelines for 9×12 SAE with 4 first-class stamps.
Nonfiction: How-to better market, display and sell food and other items in a grocery store; how to find new markets; interview/profile; and new products. Special issue: economic forecast (January/February). Buys 6 mss/year. Query with published clips. Length: 300-1,500 words. Pays $200-800 for assigned articles. Sometimes pays expenses of writers on assignment.
Photos: State availability of photos with submission. Reviews contact sheets and 5×7 prints. Captions, model releases and identification of subjects required. Buys all rights.
Columns/Departments: Query with published clips.
Tips: "The best way to be considered for a freelance assignment is first and foremost to have a crisp, journalistic writing style on clips. Second it is very helpful to have a knowledge of the issues and trends in the grocery industry. Third, because we are a regional trade publication, it is crucial that articles be localized to Minnesota or the Upper Midwest."

‡PACKER/SHIPPER, Columbia Publishing, P.O. Box 1467, Yakima WA 98907. (509)248-2457. Editor: Ken Hodge. 25% freelance written. Magazine published 8 times/year covering packing, shipping and marketing fresh fruit and vegetables. Estab. 1992. Circ. 8,900. Pays on publication. Publishes ms an average of 2 months after acceptance. Byline given. Buys all rights. Editorial lead time 2 months. Submit seasonal material 3 months in advance. Accepts simultaneous submissions. Reports in 2 weeks on queries; 2 months on mss. Sample copy for 9×12 SASE.
Nonfiction: Historical/nostalgic, interview/profile, new product, opinion, technical. Buys 10-12 mss/year. Query. Length: 750-1,200 words. Pays $125-300 for assigned articles; $75-125 for unsolicited articles.
Photos: State availability of photos with submissions. Reviews contact sheets, transparencies, prints. Offers no additional payment for photos accepted with ms. Captions, identification of subjects required. Buys one-time rights.
Columns/Departments: Machinery; Sanitation/food safety; Marketing/packaging. Buys 8 mss/year. Query. Pays $125-200.
Fillers: Facts. Length: 100-300 words. Pays $25-50.

PRODUCE NEWS, 2185 Lemoine Ave., Fort Lee NJ 07024-6003. Fax: (201)592-0809. Editor: Gordon Hochberg. 10-15% freelance written. Works with a small number of new/unpublished writers each year. Weekly magazine for commercial growers and shippers, receivers and distributors of fresh fruits and vegetables, including chain store produce buyers and merchandisers. Estab. 1897. Circ. 10,000. Pays on publication. Publishes ms an average of 2 weeks after acceptance. Deadline is Monday afternoon before Thursday press day. Reports in 1 month. Sample copy and writer's guidelines for 10×13 SAE with 4 first-class stamps.
   • This publication looks for stringers in specific areas of the country to cover the produce business.
Nonfiction: News stories (about the produce industry). Buys profiles, spot news, coverage of successful business operations and articles on merchandising techniques. Query. Pays $1/column inch minimum for original material. Sometimes pays the expenses of writers on assignment.

Photos: Black and white glossies. Pays $8-10/photo.

Tips: "Stories should be trade-oriented, not consumer-oriented. As our circulation grows in the next year, we are interested in stories and news articles from all fresh fruit-growing areas of the country."

‡**SEAFOOD LEADER**, Waterfront Press Co., 1115 NW 46th St., Seattle WA 98107. (206)547-6030. Fax: (206)548-9346. Editor: Peter Redmayne. Managing Editor: Rob Lovitt. 20% freelance written. Works with a small number of new/unpublished writers each year. Bimonthly journal on the seafood business. Estab. 1980. Circ. 15,000. Pays on publication. Publishes ms an average of 3 months after acceptance. Byline given. Buys first rights and second serial (reprint) rights. Accepts simultaneous and previously published submissions. Send tearsheet or photocopy of article, typed ms with rights for sale noted and information about when and where the article previously appeared. For reprints, pays 50% of the amount paid for an original article. Query for electronic submissions. Reports in 1 month on queries; 2 months on mss. Sample copy for $4 with 9×12 SAE.

Nonfiction: General seafood interest, marketing/business, historical/nostalgic, interview/profile, opinion, photo feature. Each of *Seafood Leader's* six issues has a slant: Retail/Aquaculture (January/February), Buyer's Guide (March/April), International (May/June), Foodservice/Restaurant (July/August), Whole Seafood Catalog (September/October) and Shrimp/Alaska (November/December). Each issue also includes stories outside of the particular focus, particularly shorter features and news items. No recreational fishing; no first person articles. Buys 12-15 mss/year. Query with or without published clips or send complete ms. Length: 1,000-2,500 words. Pays 15-25¢/word published depending upon amount of editing necessary. Sometimes pays the expenses of writers on assignment.

Photos: State availability of photos with submission. Reviews contact sheets and transparencies. Offers $50/inside color photo, $100 for cover. Buys one-time rights.

Fillers: Newsbreaks. Buys 10-15/year. Length: 100-250 words. Pays $50-100.

Tips: "*Seafood Leader* is steadily increasing in size and has a growing need for full-length feature stories and special sections. Articles on innovative, unique and aggressive people or companies involved in seafood are needed. Writing should be colorful, tight and fact-filled, always emphasizing the subject's formula for increased seafood sales. Readers should feel as if they have learned something applicable to their business."

Home Furnishings and Household Goods

Readers rely on these publications to learn more about new products and trends in the home furnishings and appliance trade. Magazines for consumers interested in home furnishings are listed in the Consumer Home and Garden section.

APPLIANCE SERVICE NEWS, 110 W. Saint Charles Rd., P.O. Box 789, Lombard IL 60148-0789. Fax: (708)932-9552. Editor: William Wingstedt. Monthly "newspaper style" publication for professional service people whose main interest is repairing major and/or portable household appliances—service shop owner, service manager or service technician. Estab. 1950. Circ. 42,000. Buys all rights. Byline given. Pays on publication. Considers simultaneous submissions. Reports in 1 month. Sample copy for $3.

Nonfiction: James Hodl, associate editor. "Our main interest is in technical articles about appliances and their repair. Material should be written in a straightforward, easy-to-understand style. It should be crisp and interesting, with high informational content. Our main interest is in the major and portable appliance repair field. We are not interested in retail sales." Query. Pays $200-300/feature.

Photos: Pays $20 for b&w photos used with ms. Captions required.

CHINA GLASS & TABLEWARE, Doctorow Communications, Inc., P.O. Box 2147, Clifton NJ 07015. (201)779-1600. Fax: (201)779-3242. Editor-in-Chief: Amy Stavis. 60% freelance written. Works with a small number of new/unpublished writers each year. Monthly magazine for buyers, merchandise managers and specialty store owners who deal in tableware, dinnerware, glassware, flatware and other tabletop accessories. Estab. 1892. Pays on publication. Publishes ms an average of 3-4 months after acceptance. Buys one-time rights. Byline given. Phone queries OK. Submit seasonal material 3 months in advance. Reports in 3 months. Sample copy and writer's guidelines for 9×12 SAE; mention *Writer's Market* in request.

Nonfiction: General interest (on store successes, reasons for a store's business track record); interview (personalities of store owners, how they cope with industry problems, why they are in tableware); technical (on the business aspects of retailing china, glassware and flatware). "Bridal registry material always welcomed." No articles on how-to or gift shops. Buys 2-3 mss/issue. Query. Length: 1,500-3,000 words. Pays $60/page. Sometimes pays the expenses of writers on assignment.

Photos: State availability of photos with query. No additional payment for b&w or color contact sheets. Captions required. Buys first serial rights.

Tips: "Show imagination in the query; have a good angle on a story that makes it unique from the competition's coverage and requires less work on the editor's part for rewriting a snappy beginning."

‡FLOORING MAGAZINE, 114 Elkton Lane, North Babylon NY 11703. (516)254-3719. Fax: (516)667-4129. Editor: Greg Valero. 20% freelance written. Prefers to work with published/established writers. Monthly magazine for floor covering retailers, wholesalers, contractors, specifiers and designers. Estab. 1931. Circ. 25,000. Pays on publication. Publishes ms an average of 3 months after acceptance. Byline given. Buys all rights. Query for electronic submissions. "Send letter with writing sample to be placed in our freelance contact file." Editorial calendar available for #10 SASE.

Nonfiction: "Mostly staff written. Buys a small number of manuscripts throughout the year. Needs writers with 35mm photography skills for local assignments. Study our editorial calender and send a concise query."

HAPPI, (Household and Personal Products Industry), 17 S. Franklin Turnpike, P.O. Box 555, Ramsey NJ 07446-0555. Fax: (201)825-0553. Editor: Tom Branna. 5% freelance written. Magazine for "manufacturers of soaps, detergents, cosmetics and toiletries, waxes and polishes, insecticides, and aerosols." Estab. 1964. Circ. 18,000. Not copyrighted. Pays on publication. Publishes ms an average of 2 months after acceptance. Submit seasonal material 2 months in advance. Reports in 1 month.

Nonfiction: "Technical and semi-technical articles on manufacturing, distribution, marketing, new products, plant stories, etc., of the industries served. Some knowledge of the field is essential in writing for us." Buys informational interview, photo feature, spot news, coverage of successful business operations, new product articles, coverage of merchandising techniques and technical articles. No articles slanted toward consumers. Query with published clips. Buys 3-4 mss/year. Length: 500-2,000 words. Pays $25-300. Sometimes pays expenses of writers on assignment.

Photos: Black and white 5×7 or 8×10 glossies purchased with mss. Pays $10.

Tips: "The most frequent mistakes made by writers are unfamiliarity with our audience and our industry; slanting articles toward consumers rather than to industry members."

‡HOME LIGHTING & ACCESSORIES, P.O. Box 2147, Clifton NJ 07015. (201)779-1600. Fax: (201)779-3242. Editor: Linda Longo. 25% freelance written. Prefers to work with published/established writers. Monthly magazine for lighting showrooms/department stores. Estab. 1923. Circ. 10,000. Pays on publication. Publishes ms an average of 4-6 months after acceptance. Buys first rights. Submit seasonal material 6 months in advance. Reports in 2 months. Accepts previously published submissions. Send tearsheet of article and information about when and where the article previously appeared. Sample copy for 9×12 SAE with 4 first class stamps.

Nonfiction: Interview (with lighting retailers); personal experience (as a businessperson involved with lighting); profile (of a successful lighting retailer/lamp buyer); technical (concerning lighting or lighting design). Buys less than 6 mss/year. Query. Pays $60/published page. Sometimes pays the expenses of writers on assignment.

Photos: State availability of photos with query. Offers no additional payment for 5×7 or 8×10 b&w glossy prints. Pays additional $90 for color transparencies used on cover. Captions required.

Tips: "We don't need fillers—only features."

WINDOW FASHIONS, Design and Education Magazine, G&W McNamara Publishing, Inc., 4225 White Bear Pkwy., Suite 400, St. Paul MN 55110. (612)293-1544. Fax: (612)653-4308. Editor: Linnéa C. Addison. 50% freelance written. Monthly magazine covering custom window fashions—interior design. "Dedicated to the advancement of the window fashions industry, *Window Fashions* magazine provides comprehensive information on design and business principles, window fashion aesthetics and product applications. The magazine serves the window treatment industry, including designers, retailers, dealers, specialty stores, workrooms, manufacturers, fabricators and others associated with the field of interior design." Estab. 1981. Circ. 22,000. Pays on publication. Publishes ms an average of 3 months after acceptance. Byline given. Offers 25% kill fee. Buys all rights. Editorial lead time 2-3 months. Submit seasonal material at least 3 months in advance. Query for electronic submissions. Reports in 2 months on queries if SASE is included. Sample copy for $5.

Nonfiction: How-to (window fashion installation), interview/profile (of designers), new product, photo feature, technical, and other specific topics within the field. "No broad topics not specific to the window fashions industry." Buys 24 mss/year. Query with published clips. Length: 800-1,500 words. Pays $150 minimum for assigned articles.

Photos: State availability of photos with submission. Reviews 4×6 or 8×10 transparencies and prints (at least 4×6). Offers no additional payment for photos accepted with ms. Captions required. Buys all rights and release for publication, anthology, promotional use, etc.

Columns/Departments: Buys 24-36 mss/year. Query with published clips.

Tips: "The most helpful experience is if a writer has knowledge of interior design or, specifically, window treatments. We already have a pool of generalists, although we welcome clips from writers who would like to be considered for assignments. Our style is professional business writing—no flowery prose. Articles tend to be to the point as our readers are busy professionals who read for information, not for leisure. Most of all we need creative ideas and approaches to topics in the field of window treatments and interior design. A writer needs to be knowledgeable in the field because our readers would know if information was inaccurate."

Hospitals, Nursing and Nursing Homes

In this section are journals for medical and nonmedical nursing home personnel, clinical and hospital staffs and medical laboratory technicians and managers. Journals publishing technical material on medical research and information for physicians in private practice are listed in the Medical category.

AMERICAN JOURNAL OF NURSING, 555 W. 57th St., New York NY 10019-2961. (212)582-8820. Fax: (212)586-5460. E-mail: martin.d@ajn.org. Editorial Director: Martin DiCarlantonio. Eager to work with new/unpublished nurse-authors. Monthly magazine covering nursing and health care. Estab. 1900. Circ. 239,000. Pays on publication. Publishes ms an average of 3-4 months after acceptance. Byline given. Reports in 2 weeks on queries, 4-6 weeks on mss. Sample copy for $4. Writer's guidelines free.
Nonfiction: Practical, hands-on clinical articles of interest to hospital staff nurses; professional issues; personal experience. No material other than nursing care and nursing issues. Nurse-authors only accepted for publication.
Photos: Karliese Greiner, art director. Reviews b&w and color transparencies and prints. Model release and identification of subjects required. Buys variable rights.
Tips: "Everything we publish is written by nurses and edited inhouse."

HEALTHCARE RISK MANAGEMENT, (formerly *Hospital Risk Management*), American Health Consultants, P.O. Box 740056, Atlanta GA 30374. (404)262-7436. Fax: (404)261-3964. Managing Editor: Linda Morningstar. 10% freelance written. Monthly newsletter on health care risk management. Estab. 1977. Circ. 2,500. Pays on publication. Publishes ms an average of 2 months after acceptance. Buys all rights. Reports in 3 months. Free sample copy.
Nonfiction: How-to (pertaining to hospitals' legal liability management). "We need informative articles written by experts in the field that aren't boring, on topics concerning hospital safety, insurance for hospitals and reducing legal risk. Nothing analytical." Buys 10-12 mss/year. Query required. Length: 1,500 words. Pays under $100.

‡JOURNAL OF CHRISTIAN NURSING, Nurses Christian Fellowship, a division of Inter-Varsity Christian Fellowship, 430 E. Plaza Dr., Westmont IL 60559. (708)887-2500. Editor: Judith Allen Shelly. Contact: Melodee Yohe, Managing Editor. 30-40% freelance written. Quarterly professional journal/magazine covering spiritual care, ethics, crosscultural issues, etc. "Our target audience is Christian nurses in the US and is nondenominational in character. We are prolife in position. We strive to help Christian nurses view nursing practice through the eyes of faith. Articles must be relevant to Christian nursing and consistent with our statement of faith." Estab. 1984. Circ. 10,000. Pays on publication. Publishes ms 3-24 months after acceptance. Byline given unless subject matter requires pseudonym. Offers 50% kill fee. Not copyrighted. Buys first rights; second serial (reprint) rights, rarely; all rights, only multiple-authored case studies. Editorial lead time 6-24 months. Submit seasonal material 1 year in advance. Occasionally accepts previously published submissions. Reports in 1 month on queries; 2 months on mss. Sample copy for $4 and SAE with 4 first-class stamps. Writers guidelines for #10 SASE.
Nonfiction: How-to, humor, inspirational, interview/profile, opinion, personal experience, photo feature, religious. All must be appropriate for Christian nurses. No purely academic articles, subjects not appropriate for Christian nurses, devotionals, Bible study. Buys 20-30 mss/year. Send complete ms. Length: 6-12 pages (typed, double spaced). Pays $25-80 and up to 8 complimentary copies.
Photos: State availability of photos or send photos with submission. Reviews prints. Offers no additional payment for photos accepted with ms. Model releases and identification of subjects required. No rights purchased; all photos returned.
Columns/Departments: The Last Word (personal opinion), 750-900 words; Book Reviews (Resources). Buys 2-3 mss/year. Send complete ms. Pays $25-50 (Last Word); no payment for Book Reviews.
Tips: "Unless an author is a nurse, it will be unlikely that he/she will have an article accepted—unless they write a very interesting story about a nurse who is involved in creative ministry with a strong faith dimension."

JOURNAL OF NURSING JOCULARITY, The Humor Magazine for Nurses, JNJ Publishing, Inc., P.O. Box 40416, Mesa AZ 85274. (602)835-6165. E-mail: 73314.3032@compuserve.com. Editor: Fran London, RN, MS. 75% freelance written. Quarterly magazine covering nursing and medical humor. "*Journal of Nursing Jocularity* is read by health care professionals. Published manuscripts pertain to the lighter side of health care, predominantly from the perspective of the health care provider." Estab. 1990. Circ. 20,000. Pays on publication. Publishes ms an average of 1 year after acceptance. Offers 100% kill fee. Buys one-time rights. Editorial lead time 6-12 months. Submit seasonal material 9-12 months in advance. Accepts simultaneous and previously published submissions. Send typed ms with rights for sale noted and information about when and where the article previously appeared. Query for electronic submissions. Reports in 2 months on queries; 3 months on mss. Sample copy for $2. Writer's guidelines for 9×10 SAE with 2 first-class stamps.

Nonfiction: Essays, historical/nostalgic, humor, interview/profile, opinion, personal experience, *current* research on therapeutic use of humor. "Our readers are primarily active nurses. Our focus is *insider humor.*" Buys 4-8 mss/year. Length: 500-1,500 words. Pays $5. Sometimes pays expenses of writers on assignment.
Photos: State availability of photos with submission. Model releases required. Buys one-time rights.
Columns/Departments: Stories from the Floor (anecdotes—true nursing experiences), 16-200 words; Call Lites (health care jokes with insider edge), 16-200 words; Student Nurse Cut-Ups (anecdotes—true student nurse experiences), 16-150 words. Pays *JNJ* T-shirt.
Fiction: Humorous, slice-of-life vignettes. Buys 30 mss/year. Query or send complete ms. Length: 500-1,500 words. Pays $5.
Poetry: Avant-garde, free verse, haiku, light verse, traditional, songs and cheers. Buys 4-6 poems/year. Submit maximum 3 poems. Pays $5.
Fillers: Anecdotes, gags to be illustrated by cartoonist, short humor. Length: 16-200 words. Pays T-shirt.
Tips: "Our readers are primarily working nurses. *JNJ*'s focus is insider humor—the kind only a health care provider understands. *Very few* non-health care providers have been able to submit material that rings true. We do not publish material written from a patient's point of view."

NURSING96, Springhouse Corporation, 1111 Bethlehem Pike, P.O. Box 908, Springhouse PA 19477-0908. (215)646-8700. Fax: (215)653-0826. E-mail: 73751.42@compuserve.com. Contact: Pat Wolf, Editorial Dept. Administrator. Clinical Director: Patricia Nornhold. Managing Editor: Jane Benner. 100% freelance written by nurses. Monthly magazine on the nursing field. "Our articles are written by nurses for nurses; we look for practical advice for the working nurse that reflects the author's experience." Estab. 1971. Circ. 424,000. Pays on publication. Publishes ms an average of 18 months after acceptance. Byline given. Offers 50% kill fee. Buys all rights. Submit seasonal material 6-8 months in advance. Accepts previously published submissions. "Any form acceptable, but focus must be nursing." Prefers submissions on disk in any program. Reports in 2 weeks on queries; 3 months on mss. Sample copy for $4 with 9×12 SAE. Call 800-617-1717, ext. 300 for free writers' guidelines.
Nonfiction: Book excerpts, exposé, how-to (specifically as applies to nursing field), inspirational, new product, opinion, personal experience, photo feature. No articles from patients' point of view, humor articles, poetry, etc. Buys 100 mss/year. Query. Length: 100 words minimum. Pays $50-400 for feature articles.
Photos: State availability of photos with submission. Offers no additional payment for photos accepted with ms. Model releases required. Buys all rights.

Hotels, Motels, Clubs, Resorts and Restaurants

These publications offer trade tips and advice to hotel, club, resort and restaurant managers, owners and operators. Journals for manufacturers and distributors of bar and beverage supplies are listed in the Beverages and Bottling section.

BARTENDER MAGAZINE, Foley Publishing, P.O. Box 158, Liberty Corner NJ 07938. (908)766-6006. Fax: (908)766-6607. Publisher: Raymond P. Foley. Editor: Jaclyn M. Wilson. Quarterly magazine emphasizing liquor and bartending for bartenders, tavern owners and owners of restaurants with full-service liquor licenses. 100% freelance written. Prefers to work with published/established writers; eager to work with new/unpublished writers. Circ. 147,000. Pays on publication. Publishes ms an average of 3 months after acceptance. Buys first serial, first North American serial, one-time, second serial (reprint), all or simultaneous US rights. Byline given. Submit seasonal material 3 months in advance. Accepts simultaneous and previously published submissions. Send tearsheet of article and information about when and where the article previously appeared. For reprints, pays 60% of the amount paid for an original article. Reports in 2 months. Sample copies for 9×12 SAE with 4 first-class stamps.
Nonfiction: General interest, historical, how-to, humor, interview (with famous bartenders or ex-bartenders), new products, nostalgia, personal experience, unique bars, opinion, new techniques, new drinking trends, photo feature, profile, travel, bar sports or bar magic tricks. Send complete ms. Length: 100-1,000 words.
Photos: Send photos with ms. Pays $7.50-50 for 8×10 b&w glossy prints; $10-75 for 8×10 color glossy prints. Caption preferred and model release required.
Columns/Departments: Bar of the Month; Bartender of the Month; Drink of the Month; Creative Cocktails; Bar Sports; Quiz; Bar Art; Wine Cellar; Tips from the Top (from prominent figures in the liquor industry); One For The Road (travel); Collectors (bar or liquor-related items); Photo Essays. Query. Length: 200-1,000 words. Pays $50-200.
Fillers: Clippings, jokes, gags, anecdotes, short humor, newsbreaks, anything relating to bartending and the liquor industry. Length: 25-100 words. Pays $5-25.
Tips: "To break in, absolutely make sure that your work will be of interest to all bartenders across the country. Your style of writing should reflect the audience you are addressing. The most frequent mistake made by writers in completing an article for us is using the wrong subject."

‡**BED & BREAKFAST, The Journal for Innkeepers**, Virgo Publishing Inc., 4141 N. Scottsdale Rd., Suite 316, Scottsdale AZ 85251. (602)990-1101. Editor: Drew Whitney. Managing Editor: Valerie Demetros. 60-70% freelance written. Bimonthly magazine covering the bed-and-breakfast and innkeeping industries with regard to innkeepers. "Articles must be thoroughly researched, and we prefer that the author have some experience or expertise in the industry." Estab. 1994. Circ. 15,000. Pays on publication. Publishes ms 2-4 months after acceptance. Byline given. Buys first North American serial rights. Editorial lead time 4 months. Submit seasonal material 4-6 months in advance. Query for electronic submissions. Reports in 2 weeks on queries; 1 month on mss. Sample copy for 9×12 SASE.

Nonfiction: Book excerpts, interview/profile, new product, personal experience, technical. Buys 12 mss/year. Query with or without published clips. Length: 800-3,500 words. Pays $200 maximum for assigned articles. Pays expenses of writers on assignment.

Photos: Send photos with submission. Reviews 3×5 prints. Negotiates payment individually. Model releases and identification of subjects required. Buys one-time rights.

Columns/Departments: Buys 6 mss/year. Pays $200 maximum.

‡**CULINARY TRENDS, Dedicated to the World of Culinary Arts**, Culinary Publication, Inc., 6285 E. Spring St., Long Beach CA 90808. (310)496-2558. Editor: Tim Linden. 50% freelance written. Quarterly magazine covering food, restaurant, hotel industry. "Our primary audience is chefs, restaurant owners, caters, hotel managers, and anyone interested in cooking and food!" Pays on publication. Publishes ms an average of 4 months after acceptance. Byline given. Buys first or one-time rights. Editorial lead time 4 months. Query for electronic submissions (disk only). Sample copy for $7.

Nonfiction: How-to (cooking techniques), humor, interview/profile, opinion, photo feature, articles on restaurants must include photos and recipes. Buys 12 mss/year. Query with published clips. Length: 700-3,000 words. Pays $100-300.

Photos: Send photos with submission. Reviews transparencies, prints. Offers no additional payment for photos accepted with ms. Captions required. Buys one-time rights.

Columns/Departments: Wine (selling wine), 700 words. Buys 4 mss/year. Query with published clips. Pays $0-100.

Tips: "We like to get stories about restaurants with the focus on the chef and the food. Quality color or transparencies or slides are essential along with recipes."

FLORIDA HOTEL & MOTEL JOURNAL, The Official Publication of the Florida Hotel & Motel Association, Accommodations, Inc., P.O. Box 1529, Tallahassee FL 32302-1529. (904)224-2888. Editorial Associate: Janet Litherland. Editor: Mrs. Jayleen Woods. 10% freelance written. Prefers to work with published/established writers. Monthly magazine for managers in the lodging industry (every licensed hotel, motel and resort in Florida). Estab. 1978. Circ. 7,000. Pays on publication. Publishes ms an average of 2 months after acceptance. Byline given. Offers $50 kill fee. Buys all rights and makes work-for-hire assignments. Submit seasonal material 2 months in advance. Accepts previously published submissions. Send tearsheet of article and information about when and where the article previously appeared. For reprints, pays flat fee of $55. Reports in 4-6 weeks. Sample copy and writer's guidelines for 9×12 SAE with 7 first-class stamps.

Nonfiction: General interest (business, finance, taxes); historical/nostalgic (old Florida hotel reminiscences); how-to (improve management, housekeeping procedures, guest services, security and coping with common hotel problems); humor (hotel-related anecdotes); inspirational (succeeding where others have failed); interview/profile (of unusual hotel personalities); new product (industry-related and non brand preferential); photo feature (queries only); technical (emerging patterns of hotel accounting, telephone systems, etc.); travel (transportation and tourism trends only—no scenics or site visits); property renovations and maintenance techniques. "We would like to run more humorous anecdotes on hotel happenings than we're presently receiving." Buys 10-12 mss/year. Query with proposed topic and clips of published work. Length: 750-2,500 words. Pays $75-250 "depending on type of article and amount of research." Sometimes pays the expenses of writers on assignment.

Photos: Send photos with ms. Pays $25-100 for 4×5 color transparencies; $10-15 for 5×7 b&w prints. Captions, model release and identification of subjects required.

Tips: "We prefer feature stories on properties or personalities holding current membership in the Florida Hotel and Motel Association. Membership and/or leadership brochures are available (SASE) on request. We're open to articles showing how hotel management copes with energy systems, repairs, renovations, new guest needs and expectations. The writer may have a better chance of breaking in at our publication with short articles and fillers because the better a writer is at the art of condensation, the better his/her feature articles are likely to be."

FLORIDA RESTAURATEUR, Florida Restaurant Association, 2441 Hollywood Blvd., Hollywood FL 33020-6623. (305)921-6300. Fax: (305)925-6381. Editor: Hugh P. (Mickey) McLinden. 15% freelance written. Monthly magazine for food service and restaurant owners and managers dealing with trends, legislation, training, sanitation, new products, spot news. Estab. 1946. Circ. 32,141. Pays on publication. Publishes ms an average of 1 month after acceptance. Byline given. Buys one-time rights. Submit seasonal material 3 months in advance. Accepts simultaneous and previously published submissions. Send tearsheet or photocopy of article or typed ms with rights for sale noted and information about when and where the article previously appeared. For reprints, pays 35% of the amount paid for an original article. Reports in 1 month on queries; 2 months on mss.

Nonfiction: How-to, general interest, interview/profile, new product, personal experience, management techniques, operational procedures, technical. Query. Length: 500-1,500 words. Pays $200-300 for assigned articles; $150-200 for unsolicited articles.

Photos: State availability of photos with submission. Reviews transparencies and 5×7 prints. Offers $50-250/photo. Model releases and identification of subjects required. Buys one-time rights.

FOOD & SERVICE, Texas Restaurant Association, P.O. Box 1429, Austin TX 78767-1429. (512)472-3666 (in Texas, 1-800-395-2872). Fax: (512)472-2777. Editor: Julie Stephen Sherrier. 50% freelance written. Magazine published 10 times/year providing business solutions to Texas restaurant owners and operators. Estab. 1941. Circ. 6,000. **Pays on acceptance.** Written queries required. Reports in 1 month. Byline given. Not copyrighted. Buys first rights. Accepts previously published submissions. Send tearsheet or photocopy of article. Pay varies. Query for electronic submissions. Sample copy and editorial calendar for 11×14 SAE with 6 first-class stamps. Free writer's guidelines.

Nonfiction: Features must provide business solutions to problems in the restaurant and food service industries. Topics vary but always have business slant; usually particular to Texas. No restaurant critiques, human interest stories or seasonal copy. Quote members of the Texas Restaurant Association; substantiate with facts and examples. Query. Length: 1,500-2,500 words, features; shorter articles sometimes used; product releases, 300-word maximum. Payment rates vary.

Photos: State availability of photos, but photos usually assigned.

INNKEEPING WORLD, P.O. Box 84108, Seattle WA 98124. Fax: (206)362-7847. Editor/Publisher: Charles Nolte. 75% freelance written. Eager to work with new/unpublished writers. Magazine published 10 times/year emphasizing the hotel industry worldwide. Estab. 1979. Circ. 2,000. **Pays on acceptance.** Publishes ms an average of 2 months after acceptance. Buys all rights. No byline. Submit seasonal material 1 month in advance. Reports in 1 month. Sample copy and writer's guidelines for 9×12 SAE with 3 first-class stamps.

Nonfiction: Managing—interviews with successful hotel managers of large and/or famous hotels/resorts (600-1,200 words); Marketing—interviews with hotel marketing executives on successful promotions/case histories (300-1,000 words); Sales Promotion—innovative programs for increasing business (100-600 words); Food Service—outstanding hotel restaurants, menus and merchandising concepts (300-1,000 words); and Guest Relations—guest service programs, management philosophies relative to guests (200-800 words). Pays $100 minimum or 20¢/word (whichever is greater) for main topics. Other topics—advertising, cutting expenses, guest comfort, hospitality, ideas, reports and trends, special guestrooms, staff relations. Length: 50-500 words. Pays 20¢/word. "If a writer asks a hotel for a complimentary room, the article will not be accepted, nor will *Innkeeping World* accept future articles from the writer."

Tips: "We need more in-depth reporting on successful sales promotions—results-oriented information."

‡PIZZA & PASTA MAGAZINE, Talcott Communications Corp., 20 N. Wacker Dr., Suite 3230, Chicago IL 60015. (312)849-2220. Editor: Joseph Declan Moran. 5% freelance written. Monthly magazine covering Italian American foodservice in America. "*Pizza & Pasta Magazine* is the business publication for the Italian American foodservice industy. An informative, how-to magazine that helps operators of pizza and pasta restaurants improve their business." Estab. 1988. Circ. 35,000. Pays on publication. Publishes ms an average of 1 month after acceptance. Byline given. Buys one-time rights. Editorial lead time 2 months. Submit seasonal material 4 months in advance. Sample copy free on request.

Nonfiction: How-to, interview/profile, new product, technical, news briefs, promotions. "We do not accept unsolicited stories. If a writer has an idea or a suggestion for a story, please call the editor first." Buys 4 mss/year. Length: 1,000-2,000 words. Pays $150-250.

Photos: State availability of photos with submissions. Reviews transparencies. Negotiates payment individually. Captions required. Buys one-time rights.

Columns/Departments: Independent Spotlight (mom & pop pizza, pasta restaurant), 800 words; Franchise Spotlight (profile of franchise/franchisor), 800-1,000 words. Buys 2 mss/year. Query with published clips. Pays $150-250.

Fillers: Facts, newsbreaks. Buys 2/year. Length: 100-300 words. Does not pay for fillers.

Tips: "Always call me first. Everyone has a great story idea, but call and ask what we have on our editorial calendar so that we can determine if your idea will fit in with an upcoming issue. Do not call more than once a week. There are a lot of people with great story ideas, but only so much space each month."

PIZZA TODAY, The Monthly Professional Guide To Pizza Profits, ProTech Publishing and Communications, Inc., P.O. Box 1347, New Albany IN 47151. (812)949-0909. Fax: (812)941-9711. Editor: James E. Reed. 30% freelance written. Prefers to work with published/established writers. Monthly magazine for the pizza industry, covering trends, features of successful pizza operators, business and management advice, etc. Estab. 1983. Circ. 55,000. Pays on publication. Publishes ms an average of 2 months after acceptance. Byline given. Offers 10-30% kill fee. Buys all and negotiable rights. Submit seasonal/holiday material 3 months in advance. Accepts simultaneous and previously published submissions. Query for electronic submissions. "All articles must be supplied on a 3½-inch disk and accompanied by a hard copy. Most major wordprocessor formats accepted; else submit in ASCII format." Reports in 2 months on queries; 3 weeks on mss. Sample copy and writer's guidelines for 10×13 SAE with 6 first-class stamps. No phone calls, please.

Nonfiction: Interview/profile, new product, entrepreneurial slants, time management, pizza delivery, employee training. No fillers, fiction, humor or poetry. Buys 40-60 mss/year. Query with published clips. Length: 750-2,500 words. Pays $50-125/page. Sometimes pays the expenses of writers on assignment.

Photos: Send photos with submission. Reviews contact sheets, negatives, 4×5 transparencies, color slides and 5×7 prints. Offers $5-25/photo. Captions required.

Tips: "We would like to receive nutritional information for low-cal, low-salt, low-fat, etc. pizza. Writers must have strong pizza business and foodservice background."

‡RESTAURANT DIGEST, Panagos Publishing, Inc., 15215 Shady Grove Rd., Suite 305, Rockville MD 20850. (301)921-0388. Editor: Larisa Lomacky. 40% freelance written. Monthly tabloid covering foodservice industry of MD, VA, DC. "*Restaurant Digest* is for owners/managers of restaurants, cafeterias and catering services in Maryland, Virginia and Washington, DC and for the suppliers who serve them. We are a business journal: We do *not* publish restaurant reviews." Estab. 1986. Circ. 18,000. Publishes ms an average of 1 month after acceptance. Byline given. Offers 50% kill fee. Buys first rights. Editorial lead time 1 month. Submit seasonal material 2 months in advance. Query for electronic submissions. Reports in 2 weeks on queries; 1 month on mss. Sample copy and writer's guidelines free on request.

Nonfiction: Interview/profile. Query with published clips. Length: 500-1,500 words. Pays $75-100. Pays long-distance phone bills of writers on assignment.

Photos: State availability of photos with submissions. Reviews prints. Offers no additional payment for photos accepted with ms. Identification of subjects required. Buys one-time rights.

Columns/Departments: Technology (use of technology in foodservice), 750-1,000 words. Query. Pays $0-75.

Tips: "Please query before submitting; we prefer to assign articles. The articles should provide helpful advice to our readers on how they can become as successful as the chef or restaurant profiled. We also prefer *local* writers (from Maryland, Virginia or Washington DC). Many become regular correspondents."

RESTAURANT HOSPITALITY, Penton Publishing, 1100 Superior Ave., Cleveland OH 44114. (216)696-7000. Fax: (216)696-0836. Editor-in-Chief: Michael DeLuca. Managing Editor: Michael Sanson. 10% freelance written. Works exclusively with published/established writers. Monthly magazine covering the foodservice industry for owners and operators of independent restaurants, hotel foodservices, executives of national and regional restaurant chains. Estab. 1919. Circ. 100,000. Average issue includes 5-10 features. **Pays on acceptance.** Publishes ms an average of 3 months after acceptance. Byline given. Buys first North American serial rights. Reports in 2 months. Sample copy for 9×12 SAE with 10 first-class stamps.

• *Restaurant Hospitality* is accepting fewer stories.

Nonfiction: General interest (articles that advise operators how to run their operations profitably and efficiently), interview (with operators), profile. Stories on psychology, consumer behavior, managerial problems and solutions, design elements. No restaurant reviews. Buys 20-30 mss/year. Query with clips of previously published work and a short bio. Length: 500-1,500 words. Pays $125/published page. Pays the expenses of writers on assignment.

Photos: Send color photos with ms. Captions required.

Tips: "We would like to receive queries for articles on food and management trends. More how-to articles wanted. We need new angles on old stories, and we like to see pieces on emerging trends and technologies in the restaurant industry. Our readers don't want to read how to open a restaurant or why John Smith is so successful."

VACATION INDUSTRY REVIEW, Interval International, P.O. Box 431920, South Miami FL 33243-1920. (305)666-1861, ext. 7022. Fax: (305)667-4495. E-mail: leposkyg@servax.fiu.edu. Editor: George Leposky. 30% freelance written. Prefers to work with published/established writers. Quarterly magazine covering leisure lodgings (timeshare resorts, fractionals, and other types of vacation-ownership properties). Estab. 1982. Circ. 15,000. Pays on publication. Publishes ms an average of 3-6 months after acceptance. Byline given. Buys all rights and makes work-for-hire assignments. Submit seasonal material at least 6 months in advance. Query for electronic submissions. Reports in 1 month. Writer's guidelines for #10 SASE.

Nonfiction: How-to, interview/profile, new product, opinion, personal experience, technical, travel. No consumer travel or non-vacation real-estate material. Buys 10-12 mss/year. Query with published clips. Length: 1,000-1,500 words. Pays 25¢/word. Pays expenses of writers on assignment, if previously arranged.

Photos: Send photos with submission. Reviews contact sheets, 35mm transparencies, and 5×7 or larger prints. Offers no additional payment for photos accepted with ms. Captions and identification of subjects required. Buys one-time rights.

Tips: "We want articles about the business aspects of the vacation ownership industry: entrepreneurship, project financing, design and construction, sales and marketing, operations, management—in short, anything that will help our readers plan, build, sell, and run a quality vacation ownership property that satisfies the owners/guests and earns a profit for the developer and marketer. Our destination pieces are trade-oriented, reporting the status of tourism and the development of various kinds of vacation-ownership facilities in a city, region, or country. You can discuss things to see and do in the context of a resort located near an attraction, but that shouldn't be the main focus or reason for the article. We're also interested in owner associations at vacation-ownership resorts (not residential condos). Prefers electronic submissions. Query for details."

Industrial Operations

Industrial plant managers, executives, distributors and buyers read these journals. Some industrial management journals are also listed under the names of specific industries. Publications for industrial supervisors are listed in Management and Supervision.

COMPRESSED AIR, 253 E. Washington Ave., Washington NJ 07882-2495. Editor/Publications Manager: S.M. Parkhill. 75% freelance written. Magazine published 8 times/year emphasizing applied technology and industrial management subjects for engineers and managers. Estab. 1896. Circ. 145,000. Buys all rights. Publishes ms an average of 6 months after acceptance. Reports in 2 months. Free sample copy; mention *Writer's Market* in request.
Nonfiction: "Articles must be reviewed by experts in the field." Buys 56 mss/year. Query with published clips. Pays negotiable fee. Sometimes pays expenses of writers on assignment.
Photos: State availability of photos in query. Payment for slides, transparencies and glossy prints is included in total purchase price. Captions required. Buys all rights.
Tips: "We are presently looking for freelancers with a track record in industrial/technology/management writing. Editorial schedule is developed in the summer before the publication year and relies heavily on article ideas from contributors. Résumé and samples help. Writers with access to authorities preferred; and prefer interviews over library research. The magazine's name doesn't reflect its contents. We suggest writers request sample copies."

INDUSTRIAL FABRIC PRODUCTS REVIEW, Industrial Fabrics Association International, 345 Cedar St., Suite 800, St. Paul MN 55101-1088. (612)222-2508. Fax: (612)222-8215. Senior Editor: Sue Zorichak. 90% staff- and industry-written. Monthly magazine covering industrial textiles and products made from them for company owners, salespeople and researchers in a variety of industrial textile areas. Estab. 1915. Circ. 11,000. Pays on publication. Publishes ms an average of 2 months after acceptance. Byline given. Buys all rights. Reports in 1 month.
Nonfiction: Technical, marketing and other topics related to any aspect of industrial fabric industry from fiber to finished fabric product. Special issues: new products, industrial products and equipment. No historical or apparel-oriented articles. Buys 8-10 mss/year. Query with phone number. Length: 1,200-3,000 words.
Tips: "We encourage freelancers to learn our industry and make regular, solicited contributions to the magazine. We do not buy photography."

‡LUBRICANTS WORLD, The Oil Daily Co., 1401 New York Ave., NW, Washington DC 20005. (202)662-0715. Editor: John A. Moore. 35% freelance written. Monthly magazine covering lubricants and their markets. "Every month we cover: additives, automotive lubricants, lubricating grease, industrial lubricants, lubricant manufacturing and marketing, metalworking fluids, packaging, quick lube operations, testing and analysis, and used oil and recycling." Estab. 1991. Circ. 13,000. Pays on publication. Publishes ms an average of 1 month after acceptance. Byline given. Buys all rights unless otherwise agreed. Editorial lead time 1-2 months. Submit seasonal material 1-2 months in advance. Query for electronic submissions. Sample copy and writer's guidelines free on request.
Nonfiction: Historical/nostalgic, new product, opinion, photo feature, technical, business. Query. Length: 1,000 words maximum. Pays $400 maximum for assigned articles; $200 maximum for unsolicited articles. Sometimes pays expenses of writers on assignment.
Photos: State availability of photos with submissions. Reviews prints. Offers $5-200/photo. Identification of subjects required. Buys one-time rights.
Tips: "Get a copy of magazine. Read it. Then contact us with story ideas."

> ***Always check the most recent copy of a magazine for the address and editor's name before you send in a query or manuscript.***

PLANT, Dept. WM, 777 Bay St., Toronto, Ontario M5W 1A7 Canada. (416)596-5776. Fax: (416)596-5552. Editor: Ron Richardson. 10% freelance written. Prefers to work with published/established writers. Bimonthly magazine for Canadian plant managers and engineers. Estab. 1940. Circ. 42,000. **Pays on acceptance.** Publishes ms an average of 2 months after acceptance. Buys first Canadian rights. Reports in 3 weeks. Free sample copy.
Nonfiction: How-to, technical and management technique articles. Must have Canadian slant. No generic articles that appear to be rewritten from textbooks. Buys fewer than 20 unsolicited mss/year. Query. Pays 31¢/word minimum. Pays the expenses of writers on assignment.
  • *Plant* is seeking submissions which display greater technical knowledge about computers in industry.
Photos: State availability of photos with query. Pays $60 for b&w prints; $100 for 2¼×2¼ or 35mm transparencies. Captions required. Buys one-time rights.
Tips: "Increased emphasis on the use of computers and programmable controls in manufacturing will affect the types of freelance material we buy. Read the magazine. Know the Canadian readers' special needs. Case histories and interviews only—no theoretical pieces. We have a tabloid-size format, and this means shorter (about 800-word) features."

QUALITY MANAGEMENT, (formerly *Quality Assurance Bulletin*), Bureau of Business Practice, 24 Rope Ferry Rd., Waterford CT 06386-0001. (800)243-0876. Fax: (203)434-3078. Contact: Editor. 80% freelance written. Biweekly newsletter for quality assurance supervisors and managers and general middle to top management. **Pays on acceptance.** No byline given. Buys all rights. Reports in 2 weeks on queries; 1 month on mss. *Writer's Market* recommends allowing 2 months for reply. Free sample copy and writer's guidelines.
Nonfiction: Interview and articles with a strong how-to slant that make use of direct quotes whenever possible. Query before writing your article. Length: 800-1,500 words. Pays 10-15¢/word.
Tips: "Write for freelance guidelines and follow them closely."

WEIGHING & MEASUREMENT, Key Markets Publishing Co., P.O. Box 5867, Rockford IL 61125. (815)636-7739. Fax: (815)636-7741. Editor: David M. Mathieu. Bimonthly magazine for users of industrial scales and meters. Estab. 1914. Circ. 15,000. **Pays on acceptance.** Buys all rights. Offers 20% kill fee. Byline given. Reports in 2 weeks. Sample copy for $2.
Nonfiction: Interview (with presidents of companies); personal opinion (guest editorials on government involvement in business, etc.); profile (about users of weighing and measurement equipment); technical. Buys 25 mss/year. Query on technical articles; submit complete ms for general interest material. Length: 750-1,500 words. Pays $125-200.

Information Systems

These publications give computer professionals more data about their field. Consumer computer publications are listed under Personal Computers.

ACCESS TO WANG, The Independent Magazine for Wang System Users, New Media Publications, 10711 Burnet Rd., Suite 305, Austin TX 78758. Fax: (512)873-7782. E-mail: 75730.2465@compuserve.com. Editor: Patrice Sarath. 75% freelance written. Monthly magazine covering Wang computers, providing how-to articles for users of Wang computer systems, Wang office automation software and coexistence and migration applications. Estab. 1984. Circ. 10,000. Pays 30 days after publication. Publishes ms an average of 2 months after acceptance. Byline given. Offers $25 kill fee. Buys first North American serial rights. Editorial lead time 3 months. Submit seasonal material 4 months in advance. Query for electronic submissions. Sample copy and writer's guidelines free on request.
Nonfiction: How-to, new product, technical, computer reviews, computer product reviews. Buys 50 mss/year. Query. Length: 1,500-2,000 words. Pays $150 for assigned articles; $100 for unsolicited articles.
Photos: Send photos with submissions. Reviews 3×5 transparencies and prints. Offers no additional payment for photos accepted with ms. Captions, model releases and identification of subjects required. Buys all rights.
Columns/Departments: Special Report (varies from month to month), 2,000-2,500. Buys 12 mss/year. Query. Pays $150.
Tips: "Writer must have computer experience specific to Wang computers. Also must have networking, Unix, programming, or similar experience. First step: call for the editorial calendar."

ADVANCED SYSTEMS/SUN WORLD, Client/Server Products for Unix Professionals, IDG, 501 Second St., San Francisco CA 94107. (415)267-1727. Fax: (415)267-1732. E-mail: michael.mccarthy@advanced.com. (Prefers correspondence by e-mail.) Editor: Michael McCarthy. 20% freelance written. Monthly magazine covering Unix-on-Risc. "We are a product magazine—product news, product reviews. Our readers want reliable, knowledgeable, honest analysis of products, their capabilities and shortcomings. *Advanced*

Systems is written to be accessible to a semi-technical audience." Estab. 1989. Circ. 85,000. **Pays on acceptance.** Publishes ms an average of 2 months after acceptance. Byline given. Offers 50% kill fee. Buys first North American serial rights and nonexclusive all other and international rights. Editorial lead time 3 months. Submit seasonal material 3 months in advance. Query for electronic submissions. Reports in 3-4 weeks on queries; 1 month on mss.

Nonfiction: Technical, reviews, technical features. Buys 15 mss/year. Query. Length: 600-2,000 words. Pays $250-2,000. Sometimes pays expenses of writers on assignment.

Photos: State availability of photos with submission. Negotiates payment individually. Captions required. Buys all rights.

Columns/Departments: Seek columnists with hands-on experience. Query. Pays $500-1,000.

Tips: "We need reviewers of Unix products who have Risc workstations, work experience/expertise in a particular field relevant to the products being reviewed, who can write a well organized, readable review, meet a deadline, and know what they're talking about."

‡ATUNC NEWSLETTER, Apple Three Users of Northern California, P.O. Box 16427, San Francisco CA 94116. (415)731-0829. Editor: Li Kung Shaw. 50% freelance written. Monthly newsletter of AIII technology, life and stories of all users. Technical and human aspects of AIII and its users in the world. Estab. 1984. Circ. 150. Pays on publication. Buys first rights. Submit seasonal material 2 months in advance. Accepts simultaneous and previously published material. Query for electronic submissions. Reports in 1 month. Free sample copy.

Nonfiction: Anything related to AIII or its users. Buys 12 mss/year. Query. Length: 500-3,000 words. Pays $10-100. Pays in contributor copies or other premiums under mutual agreement.

Photos: Send photos with submission. Reviews contact sheets. Offers no additional payment for photos accepted with ms. Buys one-time rights.

Fiction: "No fiction except those related to AIII and its users."

Poetry: "No poems except those related to AIII or its users."

Fillers: "No fillers except those related to AIII or its users."

‡AUTOCAD WORLD, The New Product Newspaper for the AutoCAD Professional, Publications/Communications Inc., 12416 Hymeadow Dr., Austin TX 78729. (512)250-9023. Editor: Larry Storer. Contact: Tara Ross. 50% freelance written. Monthly tabloid covering AutoCAD software. "*AutoCAD World* is designed for the AutoCAD user who wants to find out the latest product news and what's happening in the market." Estab. 1992. Circ. 30,000. Pays on publication. Publishes ms an average of 3 months after acceptance. Byline given. No kill fee. Editorial lead time 2 months. Submit seasonal material 3 months in advance. Query for electronic submissions. Writer's guidelines free on request.

Nonfiction: Book excerpts, general interest, how-to, interview/profile, new product, opinion, technical. Buys 10 mss/year. Send complete ms. Length: 300-2,000 words. Pays $0-250.

Photos: State availability of photos with submissions. Reviews transparencies, prints. Offers no additional payment for photos accepted with ms. Captions required.

Columns/Departments: Pays $0-250.

THE C/C++ USERS JOURNAL, R&D Publications, Inc., 1601 W. 23rd, Suite 200, Lawrence KS 66046. (913)841-1631. Editor: P.J. Plauger. Contact: Marc Briand. 90% freelance written. Monthly magazine covering C and C++ programming. "*CUJ* is written for professional C and C++ programmers. Articles are practical, advanced, and code-intensive. Authors are *always* professional C and C++ programmers." Estab. 1988. Circ. 43,000. Pays on publication. Publishes ms an average of 5 months after acceptance. Byline given. Offers $150 kill fee. Buys all rights. Editorial lead time 4 months. Query for electronic submissions. Reports in 2 weeks on queries. Accepts previously published submissions. Send typed ms with rights for sale noted. Sample copy and writer's guidelines free on request.

Nonfiction: Technical. Buys 90-110 mss/year. Query. Length: 500 minimum. Pay varies.

CIRCUIT CELLAR INK, The Computer Applications Journal, 4 Park St., Vernon CT 06066. (203)875-2199. E-mail: ken.davidson@circellar.com. Editor: Kenneth Davidson. 99% freelance written. Monthly magazine covering design of embedded controllers. "Most of our articles are written by engineers for engineers. They deal with the lower level details of computer hardware and software design. Most articles deal with dedicated, embedded processors rather than desktop computers." Estab. 1988. Circ. 45,000. Pays on publication. Publishes ms an average of 6 months after acceptance. Byline given. Offers $100 kill fee. Buys first rights. Editorial lead time 2 months. Submit seasonal material 3 months in advance. Accepts simultaneous submissions. Query for electronic submissions. Reports in 1 month. Sample copy and writer's guideline free on request.

Nonfiction: New product, technical. Buys 40 mss/year. Send complete ms. Length: 1,000-5,000 words. Pays $100.

Photos: Send photos with submissions. Reviews transparencies, slides and 3×5 prints. Offers no additional payment for photos accepted with ms. Captions required. Buys one-time rights.

Tips: "Contact editor with address, phone number, fax number, e-mail address, and article subject interests. Will send an author's guide."

DATABASE, The Magazine of Electronic Database Reviews, Online Inc., 10 Mountain View Dr., Somers NY 10589. E-mail: phane@well.sf.ca.us. Editor: Paula Hane. 40% freelance written. Bimonthly magazine covering information industry. "Authors and readers are information professionals at libraries and information centers in business, universities and government—who use databases in online, CD-ROM, disk and tape formats and resources on the Internet." Estab. 1978. Circ. 4,000. Pays on publication. Publishes ms an average of 4-6 months after acceptance. Byline given. Buys first rights, second serial (reprint) rights. Editorial lead time 4 months. Submit seasonal material 4-5 months in advance. Query for electronic submissions. Reports in 3 weeks on queries. Sample copy free on request—call 1(800)248-8466. Writer's guidelines free on request.

• *Database* received the 1994 IAC authorship Award for Best Article on an Online Topic.

Nonfiction: How-to (online search techniques), interview/profile, new product, opinion, technical, product reviews. Buys 40 mss/year. Query. Length: 1,000 words. Payment varies. Sometimes pays expenses of writers on assignment.

Photos: State availability of photos with submission. Negotiates payment individually. Captions required. Buys one-time rights and reprint rights.

Tips: "We are only interested in submissions from working information professionals. Inquire with an article idea or outline proposal before submitting a completed manuscript." Database reviews and comparisons are most open to freelancers.

EASY APPROACH, Solutions for Lotus Approach users, Pinnacle Publishing, Inc., P.O. Box 888, Kent WA 98035-0888. (206)251-1900. Editor: Linda L. Briggs. 95% freelance written. Monthly newsletter covering Lotus approach. "This hands-on newsletter provides helpful advice and tips for getting more use out of this Windows-based database manager." Estab. 1994. Pays on publication. Publishes ms an average of 3 months after acceptance. Byline given. Offers 25% kill fee. Buys all rights. Editorial lead time 4 months. Query for electronic submissions. Reports in 2 months on queries; 3 months on mss. Sample copy and writer's guidelines free on request.

Nonfiction: Book excerpts, how-to, new product, technical. "Please! No general interest articles about software use. Must be targeted to the product the newsletter covers." Buys 72 mss/year. Send complete ms. Length: 500-5,000 words. Pays $100 and up. Sometimes pays expenses of writers on assignment.

Tips: "Start with tips! Figure out ways to do something easier or faster and share that in a brief write-up. We pay $25 and a pound of coffee per tip and we use scads of them!"

FOCUS, The Magazine of the North American Data General Users Group, Turnkey Publishing, Inc., P.O. Box 200549, Austin TX 78720. (512)335-2286. Fax: (512)335-3083. E-mail: gfarman@zilker.net. Editor: Doug Johnson. 80% freelance written. Monthly trade journal covering Data General computers. Technical and practical information specific to the use of Data General computers. Estab. 1985. Circ. 8,000. Pays on publication. Publishes ms an average of 2 months after acceptance. Buys first North American serial rights. Reports in 1 month. Sample copy and writer's guidelines for 9×12 SAE with 6 first-class stamps.

Nonfiction: How-to (programming techniques, macros), technical. Query. Length: 1,000-3,000 words. Pays $50 minimum for assigned articles. Pays in contributor copies or other premiums if the writer works for a company that sells hardware or software to the Data General marketplace.

• *Focus* reports an increased need for articles about the commercial Unix market, applicable to Data General.

Photos: State availability of photos with submission. Reviews contact sheets, transparencies and prints. Offers no additional payment for photos accepted with ms. Model releases and identification of subjects required. Buys one-time rights.

FOXTALK, Making Microsoft FoxPro development easier, Pinnacle Publishing, Inc., P.O. Box 888, Kent WA 98035-0888. (206)251-1900. Editor: Bob Grommes. 95% freelance written. Monthly trade newsletter covering FoxPro development. "*FoxTalk* shows professional developers how to create more effective, more efficient software applications using FoxPro, a Microsoft development tool." Estab. 1989. Circ. 10,000. Pays on publication. Publishes ms an average of 3 months after acceptance. Byline given. Offers 25% kill fee. Buys all rights. Editorial lead time 4 months. Query for electronic submissions. Reports in 2 months on queries; 3 months on mss. Sample copy and writer's guidelines free on request.

Nonfiction: Book excerpts, how-to, new product, technical, technical tips. "Please! No general interest articles about software use. Must be targeted to the product the newsletter covers." Buys 72 mss/year. Send complete ms. Length: 500-5,000 words. Pays $25-600. Sometimes pays expenses of writers on assignment.

Tips: "Use the software product the newsletter covers. Be an expert in it! Develop a specific technique that other users would want to try out and explain it thoroughly in your article. Start with tips! Figure out ways to do something easier or faster and share that in a brief write-up. We pay $25 and a pound of coffee each and we use scads of them!"

‡**HUM-THE GOVERNMENT COMPUTER MAGAZINE**, Hum Communications Ltd., 202-557 Cambridge St. S., Ottawa Ontario K1S 4J4 Canada. (613)237-4862. Editor: Tim Lougheed. 60% freelance written. Monthly magazine covering use and management of computers in Canadian public sector. Estab. 1991. Circ. 13,500. Pays on publication. Publishes ms an average of 10 weeks after acceptance. Byline given. Offers 10% kill fee. Buys first rights or second serial (reprint) rights. Editorial lead time 3 months. Accepts previously published submissions. Query for electronic submissions. Reports in 3 weeks on queries; 2 months on mss. Sample copy for 10×12 SASE.
Nonfiction: Book excerpts, essays, how-to, humor, interview/profile, new product, opinion, personal experience, technical. Buys 30 mss/year. Query with published clips. Length: 750-3,000 words. Pays $75-500. Sometimes pays expenses of writers on assignment.
Photos: State availability of photos with submissions. Negotiates payment individually. Captions, identification of subjects required. Buys one-time rights.

‡**ID SYSTEMS, The Magazine of Automatic Data Collection**, Helmers Publishing, Inc.. 174 Concord St., Peterborough NH 03458. (603)924-9631. Fax: (603)924-7408. Editor: Mary Langen. Managing Editor: Martha Gouse. 20% freelance written. Monthly magazine about automatic identification technologies. Circ. 73,500. **Pays on acceptance.** Byline given. Buys all rights. Query for electronic submissions. Reports in 2 months on queries. Free sample copy and writer's guidelines.
Nonfiction: Application stories, technical tutorials. "We want articles we have assigned, not spec articles." Buys 20/year. Query with published clips. Length: 1,200 words. Pays $300.
Photos: Send photos with submission. Reviews contact sheets, transparencies (35mm) and prints. Offers no additional payment for photos accepted with ms. Identification of subjects required. Rights vary article to article.
Tips: "Send letter, résumé and clips. If background is appropriate, we will contact writer as needed. We give detailed instructions."

INFORMATION TODAY, Learned Information Inc., 143 Old Marlton Pike, Medford NJ 08055-8750. (609)654-6266. Fax: (609)654-4309. Publisher: Thomas H. Hogan. Editor: David Hoffman. 30% freelance written. Tabloid published 11 times/year for the users and producers of electronic information services. Estab. 1979. Circ. 10,000. Pays on publication. Publishes ms an average of 1-3 months after acceptance. Byline given. Buys first North American serial rights. Submit seasonal material 2 months in advance. Reports in 2 weeks. Sample copy and writer's guidelines for 9×12 SAE with 6 first-class stamps.
● *Information Today* reports that hot topics include the Internet, multimedia, virtual libraries and new technologies in electronic delivery.
Nonfiction: Book reviews; interview/profile and new product; technical (dealing with computerized information services); articles on library technology, artificial intelligence, online databases and services, and integrated online library systems. Also covers software and optical publishing (CD-ROM and multimedia). Buys approximately 25 mss/year. Query with published clips or send complete ms on speculation. Length: 500-1,500 words. Pays $90-220.
Photos: State availability of photos with submission.
Tips: "We look for clearly-written, informative articles dealing with the electronic delivery of information. Writing style should not be jargon-laden or heavily technical."

JOURNAL OF INFORMATION ETHICS, McFarland & Co., Inc., Publishers, Box 611, Jefferson NC 28640. (910)246-4460. Fax: (910)246-5018. Editor: Robert Hauptman, LRS, 720 Fourth Ave. S., St. Cloud State University, St. Cloud MN 56301. (612)255-4822. Fax: (612)255-4778. All ms queries to Editor. 90% freelance written. Semiannual magazine covering information sciences, ethics. "Addresses ethical issues in all of the information sciences with a deliberately interdisciplinary approach. Topics range from electronic mail monitoring to library acquisition of controversial material. The journal's aim is to present thoughtful considerations of ethical dilemmas that arise in a rapidly evolving system of information exchange and dissemination." Estab. 1992. Circ. 500. Pays on publication. Publishes ms an average of 6-9 months after acceptance. Byline given. Buys all rights. Submit seasonal material 8 months in advance. Query for electronic submissions. Sample copy for $21. Writer's guidelines free on request.
Nonfiction: Essays, opinion, book reviews. Buys 10 mss/year. Send complete ms. Length: 500-3,500 words. Pays $25.
Tips: "Familiarize yourself with the many areas subsumed under the rubric of information ethics, e.g., privacy, scholarly communication, errors, peer review, confidentiality, e-mail, etc."

NETWORK ADMINISTRATOR, R&D Publications, Inc., Suite 200, 1601 W. 23rd., Lawrence KS 66046. (913)841-1631. Fax: (913)841-2624. E-mail: joe@rdpub.com. Editor: Robert Ward. Managing Editor: Joe Casad. 90% freelance written. Bimonthly trade magazine covering PC LAN administration. "Network Administrator is written for PC LAN administrators. Articles are technical and practical. Articles are written by practicing administrators." Estab. 1994. Circ. 10,000. Pays on publication. Byline given. Offers $150 kill fee. Buys all rights. Editorial lead time 4 months. Query for electronic submissions. Reports in 3 weeks on queries. Sample and writer's guidelines free on request.

Nonfiction: Book excerpts, technical. "No *non*-technical articles." Buys 20-40 mss/year. Query. Length: 1,000 words.

NETWORK WORLD, Network World Publishing, Dept. WM, 161 Worcester Rd., Framingham MA 01701. (508)875-6400. Fax: (508)820-3467. Editor: John Gallant. Features Editor: Charles Bruno. 25% freelance written. Weekly tabloid covering data, voice and video communications networks (including news and features on communications management, hardware and software, services, education, technology and industry trends) for senior technical managers at large companies. Estab. 1986. Circ. 150,000. **Pays on acceptance.** Byline given. Offers negotiable kill fee. Buys all rights. Submit all material 2 months in advance. Query for electronic submissions. Reports in 5 months. Free sample copy and writer's guidelines.
Nonfiction: Exposé, general interest, how-to (build a strong communications staff, evaluate vendors, choose a value-added network service), humor, interview/profile, opinion, technical. Editorial calendar available. "Our readers are users: avoid vendor-oriented material." Buys 100-150 mss/year. Query with published clips. Length: 500-2,500 words. Pays $600 minimum for assigned or unsolicited articles.
Photos: Send photos with submission. Reviews 35mm, 2¼ and 4×5 transparencies and b&w prints (prefers 8×10 but can use 5×7). Captions, model releases and identification of subjects required. Buys one-time rights.
Tips: "We look for accessible treatments of technological, managerial or regulatory trends. It's OK to dig into technical issues as long as the article doesn't read like an engineering document. Feature section is most open to freelancers. Be informative, stimulating, controversial and technically accurate."

ONLINE, The Magazine of Online Information Systems, P.O. Box 17507, Fort Mitchell KY 41017. (606)331-6345. E-mail: ngarman@well.sf.ca.us. Editor: Nancy Garman. 95% freelance written. Bimonthly magazine covering online information and industry. "*Online* is edited and written for the 'information professional'—librarians or subject specialists who routinely use online and Internet services. *Online* stresses practical, how-to advice on the effective, efficient use of online databases. It emphasizes innovative tips and techniques and new technologies and products." Estab. 1977. Circ. 5,500. Pays on publication. Publishes ms 3-6 months after acceptance. Byline given. Negotiable kill fee. Buys first rights. Editorial lead time 3-6 months. Submit seasonal material 6 months in advance. Query for electronic submissions. Reports in 2 weeks on queries; 1 month on mss. Sample copy and writer's guidelines free on request.
Nonfiction: How-to, new product, opinion, personal experience, technical, software/hardware/feature reviews. Buys 35 mss/year. Query with published clips. Length: 1,500-4,000 words. Sometimes pays expenses of writers on assignment.
Photos: Send photos with submission. Reviews contact sheets, negatives, transparencies, prints. Negotiates payment individually. Captions required. Buys one-time rights.
Columns/Departments: Columnists are long-term authors. Buys 40 mss/year. Query.
Tips: "All areas open, but must know about online searching, online industry, the Internet—have some technical know-how or understanding of library/information professional market."

OPEN COMPUTING, McGraw-Hill's Magazine for Managers of Information Services and Technology, 1900 O'Farrell St., San Mateo CA 94403. (415)513-6800. Fax: (415)513-6986. E-mail: rusty@ uworld.com. Feature Editor: Rusty Weston. 30% freelance written. Monthly magazine directed to people who use, make or sell open computing products, particularly in a commercial environment. Most readers are Information Services Managers or Chief Information Officers of corporations. Estab. 1984. Circ. 105,000. **Pays on acceptance.** A rewrite is usually required. Publishes ms an average of 4 months after acceptance. Byline given. Offers kill fee. Buys all rights. Electronic submissions only. Reports in 1 month. Sample copy for $3. Writer's guidelines sent. Ask for editorial calendar so query can be tailored to the magazine's need; send SASE with 2 first-class stamps.
• *Open Computing* is now written exclusively for managers of information services.
Nonfiction: Increasingly looks for articles on how end-users are using UNIX and open computing as business solutions. Also needs well-written articles on emerging technologies and trends. Query by phone or with cover letter and published clips. Length: 1,000-3,000 words. Pays $100-2,000. Sometimes pays the expenses of writers on assignment.
Tips: "We have shifted more toward a business and commercial focus. The best way to get an acceptance on an article is to consult our editorial calendar and tailor a pitch to a particular story."

THE QUICK ANSWER, The Independent Monthly Guide to Q&A Expertise, Pinnacle Publishing, Inc., P.O. Box 888, Kent WA 98035-0888. (206)251-1900 ext. 3060. Editor: Tom Marcellus. 95% freelance written. Monthly newsletter covering working with Symantec's Q&A database manager. "This hands-on newsletter provides readers with helpful advice and tips for getting more use out of Q&A, a database manager and word processor from Symantec Corp." Estab. 1990. Circ. 7,000. Pays on publication. Publishes ms an average of 3 months after acceptance. Byline given. Offers 25% kill fee. Buys all rights. Editorial lead time 4 months. Query for electronic submissions. Reports in 2 months on queries; 3 months on mss. Sample copy and writer's guidelines free on request.

Nonfiction: Book excerpts, how-to, new product, technical. Buys 72 mss/year. Send complete ms. Length: 500-5,000 words. Pays $100 and up.

Tips: "Use the software product the newsletter covers. Be an expert in it! Develop a specific technique that other users would want to try out and explain it thoroughly in your article."

REFERENCE CLIPPER, Making CA-Clipper Development Easier, Pinnacle Publishing, Inc., P.O. Box 888, Kent WA 98035-0888. (206)251-1900. Editor: Savannah Brentnall. 95% freelance written. Monthly trade newsletter covering application development with CA Clipper. "*Reference Clipper* provides hands-on advice, techniques, and tips for creating more effective software applications using Clipper. Estab. 1988. Circ. 5,000. Pays on publication. Publishes ms an average of 3 months after acceptance. Byline given. Offers 25% kill fee. Buys all rights. Editorial lead time 4 months. Query for electronic submissions. Reports in 2 months on queries; 3 months on mss. Writer's guidelines free on request.

Nonfiction: Book excerpts, how-to, new product, technical. "Please! No general interest articles about software use. Must be targeted to the product the newsletter covers." Buys 72 mss/year. Send complete ms. Length: 500-5,000 words. Pays $100 and up.

Tips: "Use the software product the newsletter covers. Be an expert in it! Develop a specific technique that other users would want to try out and explain it thoroughly in your article. Start with tips! Figure out ways to do something easier or faster and share that in a brief write-up. We pay $25 and a pound of coffee each and we use scads of them!"

SMART ACCESS, Solutions for Microsoft Access Developers and Power Users, Pinnacle Publishing, Inc., P.O. Box 888, Kent WA 98035-0888. (206)251-1900. Editor: Paul Litwin. 95% freelance written. Monthly trade newsletter covering software development with access. "Smart Access provides hands-on advice, techniques, and tips for creating more effective software applications—faster—using Microsoft Access." Estab. 1993. Circ. 9,000. Pays on publication. Publishes ms an average of 3 months after acceptance. Byline given. Offers 25% kill fee. Buys all rights. Editorial lead time 4 months. Query for electronic submissions. Reports in 2 months on queries; 3 months on mss. Sample copy and writer's guideline free on request.

Nonfiction: Book excerpts, how-to, new product, technical. "Please! No general interest articles about software use. Must be targeted to the product the newsletter covers." Buys 72 mss/year. Send complete ms. Length: 500-5,000 words. Pays $100 and up.

Tips: "Use the software product the newsletter covers. Be an expert in it! Develop a specific technique that other users would want to try out and explain it thoroughly in your article. Start with tips! Figure out ways to do something easier or faster and share that in a brief write-up. We pay $25 and a pound of coffee each and we use scads of them!"

‡SOFTWARE DEVELOPMENT, Products & Practices For the Corporate Developer, Miller Freeman Inc., 600 Harrison St., San Francisco CA 94107. (415)905-2200. Editor: Larry O'Brien. Contact: Deborah Sommers. 50% freelance written. Monthly magazine covering computer programming. Estab. 1993. Circ. 72,000. Pays on publication. Publishes ms an average of 2 months after acceptance. Byline given. Offers $125 kill fee. Buys all rights. Editorial lead time 4-5 months. Submit seasonal material 5 months in advance. Query for electronic submissions. Sample copy and writer's guidelines free on request.

Nonfiction: How-to, new product, technical. Buys 30 mss/year. Query with published clips. Length: 1,500-3,000 words. Pays $300-1,000 for assigned articles; $300-600 for unsolicited articles.

3X/400 SYSTEMS MANAGEMENT, Adams/Hunter Publishing, 25 Northwest Point Blvd., Suite 800, Elk Grove Village IL 60007. (708)427-9512. Fax: (708)427-2006. E-mail: 71333.730@compuserve.com. Editor: Wayne Rhodes. 10% freelance written. Works with a small number of new/unpublished writers each year. Monthly magazine covering applications of IBM minicomputers (S/36/38/ and AS/400) in business. Estab. 1973. Circ. 55,000. Pays on publication. Publishes ms an average of 3 months after acceptance. Byline given. Buys all rights. Submit seasonal material 4 months in advance. Electronic submissions may be made via CompuServe. Reports in 3 months on queries. Sample copy for 9 × 12 SAE with 4 first-class stamps. Writer's guidelines for #10 SASE.

Nonfiction: How-to (use the computer in business), technical (organization of a data base or file system). "A writer who submits material to us should be an expert in computer applications. No material on large-scale computer equipment." No poetry. Buys 8 mss/year. Query. Length: 2,000-4,000 words. Sometimes pays expenses of writers on assignment.

Tips: "Frequent mistakes are not understanding the audience and not having read past issues of the magazine."

Insurance

FLORIDA UNDERWRITER, National Underwriter Co., 9887 Fourth St., N., Suite 230, St. Petersburg FL 33702-2488. (813)576-1101. Editor: James E. Seymour. Editorial Director: Ian Mackenzie. 20% freelance

written. Monthly magazine about insurance. "*Florida Underwriter* covers insurance for Florida insurance professionals: producers, executives, risk managers, employee benefit administrators. We want material about any insurance line, Life & Health or Property & Casualty, but *must* have a Florida tag—Florida authors preferred." Estab. 1984. Circ. 10,000. Pays on publication. Publishes ms an average of 2-3 months after acceptance. Byline given. Buys all rights. Submit seasonal material 3 months in advance. Accepts simultaneous and previously published submissions. Send tearsheet or photocopy of article or typed ms with rights for sale noted and information about when and where the article previously appeared. For reprints, pays 25% of the amount paid for an original article. Query for electronic submissions. Reports in 1 month. Free sample copy and writer's guidelines.
Nonfiction: Essay, exposé, historical/nostalgic, how-to, interview/profile, new product, opinion, technical. "We don't want articles that aren't about insurance for insurance people or those that lack Florida angle. No puff pieces. Note: Most non-inhouse pieces are contributed gratis by industry experts." Buys 6 mss/year. Query with or without published clips or send complete ms. Length: 500-1,500 words. Pays $50-150 for assigned articles; $25-100 for unsolicited articles. "Industry experts contribute in return for exposure." Sometimes pays expenses of writers on assignment.
Photos: State availability of photos with submission. Send photos with submission. Reviews 5×7 prints. Offers no additional payment for photos accepted with ms. Identification of subjects required.

GEICO DIRECT, K.L. Publications, 2001 Killebrew Dr., Suite 105, Bloomington MN 55425-1879. Editor: Mary Lou Brooks. 60% freelance written. Semiannual magazine published for the Government Employees Insurance Company (GEICO) policyholders. Estab. 1988. Circ. 1.5 million. **Pays on acceptance** by client. Byline given. Buys first North American serial rights. Query for electronic submissions. Reports in 2 months.
Nonfiction: Americana, home and auto safety, car care, financial, lifestyle, travel. Query with published clips. Length: 1,000 words. Pays $350-500.
Photos: Reviews 35mm transparencies. Payment varies.
Columns/Departments: Moneywise, 50+, Your Car. Query with published clips. Length: 500-600 words. Pays $175-350.
Tips: "We prefer work from published/established writers, especially those with specialized knowledge of the insurance industry, safety issues and automotive topics."

THE LEADER, Fireman's Fund Insurance Co., 777 San Marin Dr., Novato CA 94998-0000. (415)899-2109. Fax: (415)899-2126. Editor/Communications Manager: Jim Toland. 70% freelance written. Quarterly magazine on insurance. "*The Leader* contains articles and information for Fireman's Fund employees and retirees about special projects, meetings, events, employees and offices nationwide—emphasizing the business of insurance and the unique people who work for the company. Some travel and lifestyle features." Estab. 1863. **Pays on acceptance.** Publishes ms an average of 3 months after acceptance. Buys one-time rights. Accepts simultaneous and previously published submissions. Send photocopy of article and typed ms with rights for sale noted. For reprints, pays 100% of amount paid for an original article. Reports in 1 month or less on mss. Free sample copy with SASE.
  • *The Leader* received the International Association of Business Communicators (IABC) Silver Six Award for Best News Writing in 10 Western states.
Nonfiction: Interview/profile, new products, employees involved in positive activities in the insurance industry and in the communities where company offices are located. Query with published clips. Length: 200-2,500 words. Pays $100-500.
Photos: Reviews contact sheets and prints. Sometimes buys color slides. Offers $50-100/photo for b&w, up to $250 for color. Buys one-time rights.
Tips: "It helps to work in the insurance business and/or know people at Fireman's Fund. Writers with business reporting experience are usually most successful—though we've published many first-time writers. Research the local Fireman's Fund branch office (not sales agents who are independents). Look for newsworthy topics. Strong journalism and reporting skills are greatly appreciated."

Jewelry

THE DIAMOND REGISTRY BULLETIN, 580 Fifth Ave., #806, New York NY 10036. (212)575-0444. Fax: (212)575-0722. Editor-in-Chief: Joseph Schlussel. 50% freelance written. Monthly newsletter. Estab. 1969. Pays on publication. Buys all rights. Submit seasonal material 1 month in advance. Accepts simultaneous and previously published submissions. Reports in 3 weeks. Sample copy for $5.
Nonfiction: Prevention advice (on crimes against jewelers); how-to (ways to increase sales in diamonds, improve security, etc.); interview (of interest to diamond dealers or jewelers). Submit complete ms. Length: 50-500 words. Pays $75-150.
Tips: "We seek ideas to increase sales of diamonds. We have more interest in diamond mining."

FASHION ACCESSORIES, S.C.M. Publications, Inc., 65 W. Main St., Bergenfield NJ 07621-1696. (201)384-3336. Fax: (201)384-6776. Managing Editor: Samuel Mendelson. Monthly newspaper covering costume or fashion jewelry. "Serves the manufacturers, manufacturers' sales reps, importers and exporters of ladies' fashion jewlery, men's jewelry, gifts and boutiques and related novelties." Estab. 1951. Circ. 10,000. **Pays on acceptance.** Byline given. Not copyrighted. Buys first rights. Submit seasonal material 3 months in advance. Sample copy for $2 and 9×12 SAE with 4 first-class stamps.

Nonfiction: Essays, general interest, historical/nostalgic, how-to, humor, interview/profile, new product, travel. Buys 20 mss/year. Query with published clips. Length: 1,000-2,000 words. Pays $100-300. Sometimes pays the expenses of writers on assignment.

Photos: Send photos with submission. Reviews 4×5 prints. Offers no additional payment for photos accepted with ms. Identification of subjects required. Buys one-time rights.

Columns/Departments: Fashion Report (interviews and reports of fashion news), 1,000-2,000 words.

Tips: "We are interested in anything that will be of interest to costume jewelry buyers."

Journalism and Writing

Journalism and writing magazines cover both the business and creative sides of writing. Writing publications offer inspiration and support for professional and beginning writers. Although there are many valuable writing publications that do not pay, we list those that pay for articles.

AMERICAN JOURNALISM REVIEW, 8701 Adelphi Rd., Adelphi MD 20783. (301)431-4771. Fax: (301)431-0097. E-mail: editor@ajr.umd.edu. Managing Editor: Jean Cobb. 90% freelance written. Magazine published 10 times/year covering print and broadcast journalism. "*AJR* reports on the business, ethics and problems of the news media." Estab. 1977. Circ. 25,000. Pays on publication. Byline given. Offers 25% kill fee. Buys first North American serial rights. Editorial lead time 2-3 months. Submit seasonal material 3-4 months in advance. Query for electronic submissions. Reports in 1 month. Please read a copy before sending queries. Sample copy for $4.50.

Nonfiction: Analysis of media coverage, examination of ethical issues, stories on trends in print and broadcast journalism, essays, exposé, humor, interview/profile. Buys 100 mss/year. Query with published clips. Length: 500-5,000 words. Pays 20¢/word minimum. Pays expenses of writers on assignment.

Photos: "We only use commissioned photos."

Fillers: Suzan Revah, associate editor. Buys 100/year. Length: 5-30 words. Pays $25. "*AJR*'s 'Take 2' column prints humorous headlines and short excerpts from articles."

BOOK DEALERS WORLD, North American Bookdealers Exchange, P.O. Box 606, Cottage Grove OR 97424. Phone/fax: (503)942-7455. Editorial Director: Al Galasso. Senior Editor: Michelle M. Jerin. 50% freelance written. Quarterly magazine covering writing, self-publishing and marketing books by mail. Circ. 20,000. Pays on publication. Publishes ms an average of 3 months after acceptance. Byline given. Buys first serial and second serial (reprint) rights. Accepts simultaneous and previously published submissions. Send typed ms with rights for sale noted and information about when and where the article previously appeared. For reprints, pays 80% of the amount paid for an original article. Reports in 1 month. Sample copy for $3.

Nonfiction: Book excerpts (writing, mail order, direct mail, publishing); how-to (home business by mail, advertising); interview/profile (of successful self-publishers). Positive articles on self-publishing, new writing angles, marketing, etc. Buys 10 mss/year. Send complete ms. Length: 1,000-1,500 words. Pays $25-50.

Columns/Departments: Print Perspective (about new magazines and newsletters); Self-Publisher Profile (on successful self-publishers and their marketing strategy). Buys 20 mss/year. Send complete ms. Length: 250-1,000 words. Pays $5-20.

Fillers: Fillers concerning writing, publishing or books. Buys 6/year. Length: 100-250 words. Pays $3-10.

Tips: "Query first. Get a sample copy of the magazine."

BYLINE, P.O. Box 130596, Edmond OK 73013-0001. (405)348-5591. Editor/Publisher: Marcia Preston. Managing Editor: Kathryn Fanning. 80-90% freelance written. Eager to work with new/unpublished writers. Monthly magazine for writers and poets. "We stress encouragement of beginning writers." Estab. 1981. **Pays on acceptance**. Publishes ms an average of 3 months after acceptance. Byline given. Buys first North American serial rights. Reports in 2 months or less. Sample copy for $4 postpaid. Writer's guidelines for #10 SASE.

Nonfiction: How-to, humor, inspirational, personal experience, *all* connected with writing and selling. Read magazine for special departments. Buys approximately 100 mss/year. Prefers queries; will read complete mss. Length: 1,500-1,800 words. Usual rate for features is $50. Needs short humor on writing (300-600 words). Pays $15-25 on acceptance.

Fiction: General fiction of high quality. Send complete ms: 2,000-3,000 words preferred. Pays $100.

Poetry: Betty Shipley, poetry editor. Any style, on a writing theme. Preferred length: 4-30 lines. Pays $5-10 on acceptance, plus free issue.

Tips: "We'd like to see more 1,500-1,800 word features on how to write better, market better, etc."

‡CANADIAN AUTHOR, Canadian Authors Association, 275 Slater St., Suite 500, Ottawa, Ontario K1P 5H9 Canada. Contact: Editor. 95% freelance written. Prefers to work with published/established writers. Quarterly magazine "for writers—all ages, all levels of experience." Estab. 1919. Circ. 3,000. Pays on publication. Publishes ms an average of 6 months after acceptance. Buys first Canadian rights. Byline given. Written queries only. Sample copy for $5. Writer's guidelines for #10 SAE and IRC.

Nonfiction: How-to (on writing, selling; the specifics of the different genres—what they are and how to write them); informational (the writing scene—who's who and what's what); interview (with writers, mainly leading ones, but also those with a story that can help others write and sell more often); and opinion. No personal, lightweight writing experiences; no fillers. Query with immediate pinpointing of topic, length (if ms is ready) and writer's background. Length: 1,000-2,500 words. Pays $30/printed page.

Photos: "We're after an interesting-looking magazine, and graphics are a decided help." State availability of photos with query. Offers $10/photo for b&w photos accepted with ms. Buys one-time rights.

Poetry: High quality. "Major poets publish with us—others need to be as good." Buys 60 poems/year. Pays $15.

Tips: "We dislike material that condescends to its reader and articles that advocate an adversarial approach to writer/editor relationships. We agree that there is a time and place for such an approach, but good sense should prevail. If the writer is writing to a Canadian freelance writer, the work will likely fall within our range of interest."

CANADIAN WRITER'S JOURNAL, Gordon M. Smart Publications, P.O. Box 6618, Depot 1, Victoria, British Columbia V8P 5N7 Canada. (604)477-8807. Editor: Gordon M. Smart. Accepts well-written articles by inexperienced writers. Quarterly magazine for writers. Estab. 1985. Circ. 350. 75% freelance written. Pays on publication. Publishes ms an average of 3-9 months after acceptance. Byline given. Accepts previously published submissions. Send typed ms with rights for sale noted and information about when and where the article previously appeared. For reprints, pays 100% of amount paid for an original article. Reports in 2 months. Sample copy for $3 and $1 postage. Writer's guidelines for #10 SAE and IRC.

Nonfiction: How-to articles for writers. Buys 50-55 mss/year. Query optional. Length: 500-1,200 words. Pays about $5/published magazine page.

Fiction: Requirements currently being met by annual contest.

Poetry: Short poems or extracts used as part of articles on the writing of poetry. Annual poetry contest. Wind Song Column uses some short poems. Consult guidelines for details.

Tips: "We prefer short, tightly written, informative how-to articles. US writers note that US postage cannot be used to mail from Canada. Obtain Canadian stamps, use IRCs or send small amounts in cash."

EDITOR & PUBLISHER, 11 W. 19th St., New York NY 10011-4234. Fax: (212)929-1259. Editor: Robert U. Brown. Managing Editor: John Consoli. 10% freelance written. Weekly magazine for newspaper publishers, editors, executives, employees and others in communications, marketing, advertising, etc. Estab. 1884. Circ. 25,000. Pays on publication. Publishes ms an average of 1 month after acceptance. Buys first serial rights. Reports in 2 months. Sample copy for $1.75.

Nonfiction: Uses newspaper business articles and news items; also newspaper personality features and printing technology. Query.

THE EDITORIAL EYE, Focusing on Publications Standards and Practices, EEI, 66 Canal Center Plaza, Suite 200, Alexandria VA 22314-5507. (703)683-0683. Fax: (703)683-4915. Editor: Linda B. Jorgensen. 5-15% range freelance written. Prefers to work with published, established and working professional editors and writers. Monthly professional newsletter on editorial subjects: writing, editing, graphic design, production, quality control and language usage. "Our readers are professional publications people. Use journalistic style but avoid overly general topics and facile prescriptions. Our review process is vigorous." Circ. 5,000. **Pays on acceptance.** Publishes ms an average of 3-6 months after acceptance. Byline given. Buys first North American serial rights. "We retain the right to use articles in our training division and in an anthology of collected articles." Reports in 3 months. Sample copy for #10 SAE with 2 first-class stamps. Guidelines tailored to the article following a proposal or outline.

● *The Editorial Eye* reports a need for articles on multimedia, electronic and workgroup publishing, and online editing.

Nonfiction: Editorial and production problems, issues, standards, practices and techniques; publication management; publishing technology; writing, style, grammar and usage, and neologisms. No word games, vocabulary building, language puzzles or poetry. Buys about 24 mss/year. "Would buy more if quality were higher. *Must* look at sample issue." Query. Length: 500-1,500. Pays $50-200.

Tips: "We seek mostly lead articles written by people in the publications field about the practice of editing or writing. Our style is journalistic with a light touch (not cute). We are interested in submissions on the craft of editing, levels of editing, writing and editing aided by computer, publications management, lexicography, usages, quality control, resources, and interviews with nonfiction writers and editors. Our back issue list provides a good idea of the kinds of articles we run. Do not send articles without looking at a sample. Do not expect an extensive critique. Do not send a vilification of editors and expect me to print it. Welcome repeat work from a roster of writers I'm developing, and always looking for new voices."

‡EXCHANGE, A newsletter for writers who are Christian, Exchange Publishing, 15 Torrance Rd., #104, Scarborough, Ontario M1J 3K2 Canada. (416)439-4320 (evenings & weekends). Editor: Audrey Dorsch. 70% freelance written. Quarterly newsletter on the craft of writing. "A vehicle for Christian writers to exchange information and ideas, and receive professional development." Estab. 1991. Circ. 300. Pays on publication. Byline given. Offers 30-50% kill fee. Not copyrighted. Buys one-time rights. Editorial lead time 2 months. Query for electronic submissions. Reports in 1 month.

Nonfiction: How-to, humor, opinion, personal experience. All must be related to writing. Buys 20 mss/ year. Send complete ms. Length: 300-500 words. Pays 8¢/word. Sometimes pays copies or other premiums to foreign contributors who cannot exchange Canadian currency. Sometimes pays expenses of writers on assignment.

Tips: "Think about what writing help you would have liked. Now that you are past that hurdle, write about it to help other writers."

FICTION WRITER'S GUIDELINE, The Newsletter of Fiction Writer's Connection (FWC), P.O. Box 4065, Deerfield Beach FL 33442-4065. (305)426-4705. Editor: Blythe Camenson. 20% freelance written. Monthly newsletter covering how-to for fiction writers. "*Fiction Writer's Guideline* takes an upbeat approach to encourage writers, but doesn't shy away from the sometimes harsh realities of the publishing industry." Estab. 1993. Circ. 1,000. Pays on publication. Publishes ms an average of 3 months after acceptance. Byline given. Buys first, one-time or second serial (reprint) rights. Editorial lead time 1 month. Submit seasonal material 3 months in advance. Accepts simultaneous and previously published submissions. Send typed ms with rights for sale noted and information about when and where the article previously appeared. Reports in 2 weeks on queries; 1 month on mss. Sample copy for #10 SAE with 55¢ postage. Writer's guidelines for #10 SASE.

Nonfiction: General interest, how-to (the business and craft of writing fiction), humor, inspirational, interview/profile (of agents, editors, and authors), new product, personal experience (on getting published), short book reviews (how-to books for writers). Buys 30 mss/year. Query. Length: 200-1,500 words. Pays $10-25. Sometimes pays expenses of writers on assignment. Send complete ms.

Columns/Departments: Advice From An Agent/Editor (how to approach, what they're looking for, advice to fiction writers), 1,500 words; "Writing Tips" (specific advice on style and structure), 400 words. Buys 12 mss/year. Query. Pays $10-100.

Fillers: Anecdotes, facts, newsbreaks, short humor; all to do with the business or craft of writing fiction. Buys 50/year. Length: 20-100 words. Pays $1-10.

Tips: Looking for "interviews with agents or editors. Our guidelines include specific questions to ask. Query or call first to make sure your choice has not already been interviewed. We also need a cover article each month on some aspect of writing fiction, from specific tips for different categories/genres, to handling viewpoint, characterization, or dialogue etc. Also fillers. Request a sample copy to see the newsletter's format."

FREELANCE, Saskatchewan Writers Guild, Box 3986, Regina, Saskatchewan S4P 3R9. Editor: April Davies. 25% freelance written. Literary magazine published 10 times/year covering writing. "*FreeLance* is the membership newsmagazine of the Saskatchewan Writers Guild. It publishes literary news, news about members, a Saskatchewan literary events calendar, markets and resources information, news on new books by members, updates on SWG programs, articles on the craft or business of writing and literary issues, and comments on these." No poetry or fiction. Estab. 1969. Circ. 800. Pays on publication. Publishes ms an average of 1-2 months after acceptance. Byline given. Buys first North American serial or second serial (reprint) rights. Editorial lead time 1 month. Accepts previously published submissions. Reports in 3 weeks on queries; 2 months on mss. Sample copy and writer's guidelines free on request.

Nonfiction: Essays (on the craft of writing); how-to (craft or business of writing); interview/profile (writers); new product (writing-related); opinion (literary issues); technical (craft of writing); reports on writers' conferences, colonies, workshops, etc. Buys 25 mss/year. Send complete ms. Length: 600-1,000 words. Pays $40/ published page.

Photos: Send photos with submissions. Reviews prints. Offers $10 (based on publication size). Captions required. Buys one-time rights.

FREELANCE WRITER'S REPORT, CNW Publishing, Maple Ridge Rd., North Sandwich NH 03259. (603)284-6367. Fax: (603)284-6648. Editor: Dana K. Cassell. 35% freelance written. Prefers to work with published/established writers. Monthly newsletter covering writing and marketing advice for established freelance writers. Estab. 1982. Pays on publication. Publishes ms an average of 6 months after acceptance. Byline given. Buys one-time rights. Submit seasonal material 2 months in advance. Accepts simultaneous and previously published submissions. Reports in 1 month. Sample of older copy for 9×12 SAE with 2 first-class stamps; current copy for $4. No writer's guidelines; refer to this listing.

Nonfiction: Book excerpts (on writing profession); how-to (market, write, research); new product (only those pertaining to writers); photojournalism; promotion and administration of a writing business. No humor, fiction or poetry. Buys 100 mss/year. Send complete ms. Length: 500 words maximum. Pays 10¢/edited word to subscribers; non-subscribers receive a trade-out subscription equal to 10¢/edited word.

Tips: "Write in terse newsletter style, eliminate flowery adjectives and edit mercilessly. Send something that will help writers increase profits from writing output—must be a proven method. We're targeting more to the established writer, less to the beginner."

GOTTA WRITE NETWORK LITMAG, Maren Publications, 612 Cobblestone Circle, Glenview IL 60025. Fax: (708)296-7631. Editor: Denise Fleischer. 80% freelance written. Semiannual literary magazine covering writer's techniques, markets. "Any article should be presented as if openly speaking to the reader. It should inform from the first paragraph to the last." Estab. 1988. Circ. 200. Pays before publication. Publishes ms an average of 2-12 months after acceptance. Byline given. Buys first North American serial rights or makes work-for-hire assignments. Editorial lead time 6 months. Reports in 2-4 months. Sample copy for $5. Writer's guidelines for #10 SASE.

Nonfiction: Articles (on writing), how-to (on writing techniques), interview/profile (for Behind the Scenes section), new product (books, software, computers), photo feature (on poets/writers/editors big and small press). "Don't want to see 'My first sale,' 'When I Can't Write,' 'Dealing With Rejection,' 'Writer's Block,' a speech from a writers convention, an article published 10 times by other editors." Buys 25 mss/year. Query with published clips. Send complete ms. Length: 3-5 pages. Pays $5 and contributor's copy.

Photos: State availability of photos with submission. Reviews contact sheets and prints. Offers $10 ($20 for cover art). Captions, model releases and identification of subjects required. Buys one-time rights.

Columns/Departments: Poetry Scene (focus on poetry groups, slams, publications), 3 pages maximum; In Print (writing books—reviews), 2 pages. Buys 50 mss/year. Pays $5.

Fiction: Adventure, ethnic, experimental, fantasy, historical, horror, humorous, mainstream, mystery, romance, science fiction, slice-of-life vignettes, suspense, western. No dark fantasy. Buys 15 and up mss/year. Query with published clips. Send complete ms. Page length: 5-10. Pays $10 maximum.

Poetry: Avant-garde, free verse, haiku, beat—experimental. No poetry no can understand or that has no meaning.

Fillers: Anecdotes, facts, newsbreaks, tips. Buys 100/year. Length: 100-250 words. Pays in contributor's copies. Open to editor's releases, feature ideas and product information from the manufacturer.

HOUSEWIFE-WRITER'S FORUM, P.O. Box 780, Lyman WY 82937-0780. (307)782-7003. Editor: Emma Bluemel. 90% freelance written. Bimonthly newsletter and literary magazine for women writers. "We are a support network and writer's group on paper directed to the unique needs of women who write and juggle home life." Estab. 1988. Circ. 2,000. **Pays on acceptance.** Publishes ms an average of 6-12 months after acceptance. Byline given. Buys first North American serial rights. Submit seasonal material 6 months in advance. Simultaneous and previously published submissions sometimes used. Send typed ms with rights for sale noted and information about when and where the article previously appeared. For reprints, pays 50-75% of the amount paid for an original article. Reports in 1 month on queries; 3 months on mss. Sample copy for $3. Writer's guidelines for #10 SASE.

Nonfiction: Essays, how-to, humor, interview/profile, opinion, personal experience. Buys 60-100 mss/year. Query with or without published clips. Length: 2,000 words maximum, 1,000-1,500 words preferred. Pays 1¢/word.

Columns/Departments: Confessions of Housewife-Writers (essays pertaining to our lives as women and writers). Buys 30-40 mss/year. Send complete ms. Length: 250-750 words. Pays 1¢/word. Share a book, tape, video, helpful hint—anything that has made your life as a writer easier, more profitable or more fun. Length: 150-250 words. Pays $3.

Fiction: Edward Wahl, fiction editor. Experimental, fantasy, historical, humorous, mainstream, mystery, romance, science fiction, and suspense. No pornography. Buys 12-15 mss/year. Send complete ms. Length: 2,000 words maximum. Pays 1¢/word.

Poetry: Avant-garde, free verse, light verse, traditional and humorous. Buys 30-60 poems/year. Submit maximum 5 poems at one time. 45 lines maximum. Pays $2 maximum.

Tips: "Our tone is warm, nurturing and supportive to writers in all stages of their writing careers. We favor how-to articles on writing and getting published and would like to see more interviews with writers who have achieved some degree of success. Our 'Confessions' department is for all the fun, interesting, funny, tragic, unbelievable things that happen to you as a Housewife-Writer."

‡MAINE IN PRINT, Maine Writers and Publishers Alliance, 12 Pleasant St., Brunswick ME 04011. (207)729-6333. Editor: Lisa Holbrook. Monthly newsletter for writers, editors, teachers, librarians, etc. focusing on Maine literature and the craft of writing. Estab. 1975. Circ. 4,000. Pays on publication. Publishes ms an average of 2 months after acceptance. Byline given. Offers 50% kill fee. Buys one-time rights. Editorial lead time 1 month. Accepts simultaneous and previously published submissions. Query for electronic submissions. Reports in 2 weeks on queries; 1 month on mss. Sample copy and writer's guidelines free.

Nonfiction: Essays, how-to (writing), interview/profile, technical writing. No creative writing, fiction or poetry. Buys 24 mss/year. Query with published clips. Length: 400-1,800 words. Pays $25-75 for assigned articles.

Photos: State availability of photos with submission. Offers no additional payment for photos accepted with ms.

Columns/Departments: Front-page articles (writing related), 500-1,800 words. Sounding Board (opinion pieces on writing or the arts). Buys 12 mss/year. Query. Pays $25 minimum.
Tips: "Become a member of Maine Writers & Publishers Alliance. Become familiar with Maine literary scene."

NEW WRITER'S MAGAZINE, Sarasota Bay Publishing, P.O. Box 5976, Sarasota FL 34277-5976. (813)953-7903. Editor: George J. Haborak. 95% freelance written. Bimonthly magazine for new writers. *"New Writer's Magazine* believes that *all* writers are *new* writers in that each of us can learn from one another. So, we reach pro and non-pro alike." Estab. 1986. Circ. 5,000. Pays on publication. Byline given. Buys first rights. Reports in 2 weeks on queries; 1 month on mss. *Writer's Market* recommends allowing 2 months for reply. Sample copy for $3. Writer's guidelines for #10 SASE.
Nonfiction: General interest, how-to (for new writers), humor, interview/profile, opinion, personal experience (with pro writer). Buys 50 mss/year. Send complete ms. Length: 700-1,000 words. Pays $10-50 for assigned and unsolicited articles.
Photos: Send photos with submission. Reviews 5×7 prints. Offers no additional payment for photos accepted with ms. Captions required.
Fiction: Experimental, historical, humorous, mainstream, slice-of-life vignettes. "Again, we do *not* want anything that does not have a tie-in with the writing life or writers in general." Buys 2-6 mss/year. "We offer a special fiction contest held each year with cash prizes." Send complete ms. Length: 700-800 words. Pays $20-40.
Poetry: Free verse, light verse, traditional. Does not want anything *not* for writers. Buys 10-20 poems/year. Submit maximum 3 poems. Length: 8-20 lines. Pays $5 maximum.
Fillers: Anecdotes, facts, newsbreaks, short humor. Buys 5-15/year. Length: 20-100 words. Pays $5 maximum. Cartoons, writing lifestyle slant. Buys 20-30/year. Pays $10 maximum.
Tips: "Any article *with photos* has a good chance, especially an *up close & personal* interview with an established professional writer offering advice, etc."

OHIO WRITER, Poets League of Greater Cleveland, P.O. Box 528, Willoughby OH 44094. Editor: Linda Rome. 90% freelance written. Bimonthly covering writing and Ohio writers. Estab. 1987. Pays on publication. Publishes ms an average of 4 months after acceptance. Byline given. Buys one-time rights and second serial (reprint) rights. Editorial lead time 4 months. Submit seasonal material 4 months in advance. Accepts previously published submissions. Send photocopy of article or typed ms with rights for sale noted and information about when and where the article previously appeared. For reprints, pays 50% of amount paid for an original article. Reports in 1 month. Sample copy for $2. Writer's guidelines for SASE.
Nonfiction: Essays, how-to, humor, inspirational, interview/profile, opinion, personal experience—"all must relate to the writing life or Ohio writers, or Ohio publishing scene." Buys 24 mss/year. Send complete ms. Length: 1,000-2,000 words. Pays $25 minimum, up to $50 for lead article; other payment under arrangement with writer.
Columns/Departments: Subjectively Yours (opinions, controversial stance on writing life), 1,500 words; Reviews (Ohio writers, publishers or publishing), 500 words; Focus On (Ohio publishing scene, how to write/publish certain kind of writing (e.g., travel). Buys 6 mss/year. Send complete ms. Pays $25-50; $5/book review.
Tips: "Profiles and interviews of writers who live in Ohio are always needed."

POETS & WRITERS, 72 Spring St., 3rd Floor,New York NY 10012. Managing Editor: Jane Ludlam. 100% freelance written. Bimonthly professional trade journal for poets and fiction writers. No original poetry or fiction. Estab. 1973. Circ. 53,000. **Pays on acceptance** of finished draft. Publishes ms an average of 4 months after acceptance. Byline given. Offers 20% kill fee. Buys first North American serial and first rights or makes work-for-hire assignments. Editorial lead time 1 year. Submit seasonal material 1 year in advance. Query for electronic submissions. Reports in 6 weeks on mss. Sample copy for $3.95 to Circulation Dept. Writer's guidelines for #10 SASE.
Nonfiction: Personal essays about literature, how-to (craft of poetry or fiction writing), interview/profile with poets or fiction writers (no Q&A), regional reports of literary activity, reports on small presses, service pieces about publishing trends. Buys 35 mss/year. Query with published clips or send complete ms. Length: 1,500-3,600 words.
Photos: State availability of photos with submission. Reviews b&w prints. Offers no additional payment for photos accepted with ms.
Columns/Departments: Literary and publishing news, 500-600 words; profiles of emerging and established poets and fiction writers, 2,400-3,600 words; regional reports (literary activity in US), 1,800-3,600 words. Buys 24 mss/year. Query with published clips. Send complete ms. Pays $100-300.

‡THE PROLIFIC WRITER'S MAGAZINE, The Inkwell of Ideas, BSK Communications and Associates, P.O. Box 554, Oradell NJ 07649. (201)262-3277. Editor: Brian S. Konradt. Managing Editor: Rick Ahrens. 95% freelance written. Quarterly magazine covering professional freelancers. "Our audience is aspiring and professional freelance writers interested in the writing craft and pursuing freelance careers." Estab. 1992.

Circ. 4,000. Pays on publication. Publishes ms an average of 4 months after acceptance. Byline given. Buys first North American serial rights, second serial (reprint) rights. Editorial lead time 4 months. Submit seasonal material 4 months in advance. Accepts simultaneous submissions. Query for electronic submissions. Reports in 2 weeks on queries; 1 month on mss. Sample copy for $4. Writer's guidelines for #10 SASE.

Nonfiction: Essays, historical/nostalgic, how-to (writing; literary), humor, inspirational, interview/profile, opinion, photo feature, technical. Buys 35 mss/year. Send complete ms. Length: 100-3,000 words. Pays $40 minimum for assigned articles; $20 minimum for unsolicited articles. Sometimes pays expenses of writers on assignment.

Photos: Send photos with submission. Reviews contact sheets. Offers no additional payment for photos accepted with ms. Captions and identification of subjects required. Buys one-time rights.

Columns/Departments: Contact: Editorial staff. Profile on a Poet (biography of a successful poet), 1,000-2,000 words; Careet Path of a Freelance Writer (interview with a professional freelance writer), 2,000-3,000 words; The Paperless Planet (articles on electronic publishing), 500-3,000 words. Buys 30 mss/year. Send complete ms. Pays $5-50.

Fiction: Adventure, confession, ethnic, experimental, historical, humorous, mainstream, romance, slice-of-life vignettes. No science fiction and fantasy. Buys 10 mss/year. Send complete ms. Length: 50-300 words. Pays contributor's copies.

Poetry: Shamrock Greenleaf, poetry editor. Avant-garde, free verse, haiku, light verse, traditional. No greeting-card type. Buys 40 poems/year. Submit maximum 4 poems. Length: 4-50 lines. Pays contributor's copies.

Fillers: Contact: Editorial staff. Anecdotes, facts, gags to be illustrated by cartoonist, newsbreaks, short humor. Buys 16/year. Length: 10-250 words. Pays contributor's copies.

Tips: "We are most open to nonfiction articles, including how-to, interviews, profiles, reviews and essay."

RISING STAR, 47 Byledge Rd., Manchester NH 03104. (603)623-9796. Editor: Scott E. Green. 50% freelance written. Bimonthly newsletter on science fiction and fantasy markets for writers and artists. Estab. 1980. Circ. 150. Pays on publication. Publishes ms an average of 3 months after acceptance. Byline given. Not copyrighted. Buys first rights. Accepts simultaneous and previously published submissions. Send tearsheet or typed ms with rights for sale noted and information about when and where the article previously appeared. For reprints, pays $5. Reports in 1 month on queries. Sample copy for $1.50 and #10 SASE. Free writer's guidelines. Subscription $7.50 for 6 issues, payable to Scott Green.

Nonfiction: Book excerpts, essays, interview/profile, opinion. Buys 8 mss/year. Query. Length: 500-900 words. Pays $3 minimum.

ST. LOUIS JOURNALISM REVIEW, 8380 Olive Blvd., St. Louis MO 63132. (314)991-1699. Fax: (314)997-1898. Editor/Publisher: Charles L. Klotzer. 50% freelance written. Prefers to work with published/established writers. Monthly tabloid newspaper critiquing St. Louis media, print, broadcasting, TV and cable primarily by working journalists and others. Also covers issues not covered adequately by dailies. Occasionally buys articles on national media criticism. Estab. 1970. Circ. 5,500. Buys all rights. Byline given. Sample copy for $2.50.

Nonfiction: "We buy material which analyzes, critically, St. Louis metro area media and, less frequently, national media institutions, personalities or trends." No taboos. Pays the expenses of writers on assignment subject to prior approval.

SCAVENGER'S NEWSLETTER, 519 Ellinwood, Osage City KS 66523-1329. (913)528-3538. Editor: Janet Fox. 15% freelance written. Eager to work with new/unpublished writers. Monthly newsletter covering markets for science fiction/fantasy/horror/mystery materials especially with regard to the small press. Estab. 1984. Circ. 1,000. Publishes ms an average of 8 months after acceptance. Byline given. Not copyrighted. Places copyright symbol on title page; rights revert to contributor on publication. Buys one-time rights. Accepts simultaneous and previously published submissions. Send information about when and where the article previously appeared. For reprints, pays 100% of amount paid for an original article. Reports in 1 month if SASE included. Sample copy for $2. Writer's guidelines for #10 SASE.

• *Scavenger's Newsletter* recently was awarded the Small Press Genre Association Award for outstanding achievement in the small press.

Nonfiction: Essays, general interest, how-to (write, sell, publish science fiction/fantasy/horror/mystery), humor, interview/profile (writers, artists in the field), opinion. Buys 12-15 mss/year. Send complete ms. Length: 1,000 words maximum. **Pays on acceptance**, $4.

Poetry: Avant-garde, free verse, haiku, traditional. All related to science fiction/fantasy/horror/mystery genres. Buys 36 poems/year. Submit maximum 3 poems. Length: 10 lines maximum. **Pays on acceptance**, $2.

Tips: "Because this is a small publication, it has occasional overstocks. We're especially looking for science fiction/fantasy/horror/mystery commentary as opposed to writer's how-tos."

SMALL PRESS REVIEW, P.O. Box 100, Paradise CA 95967. Editor: Len Fulton. Monthly for "people interested in small presses and magazines, current trends and data; many libraries." Circ. 3,500. Byline given. Reports in 2 months. Free sample copy.

Nonfiction: News, short reviews, photos, short articles on small magazines and presses. Uses how-to, personal experience, interview, profile, spot news, historical, think, photo, and coverage of merchandising techniques. Accepts 50-200 mss/year. Length: 100-200 words. "Query if you're unsure."

THE WRITER, 120 Boylston St., Boston MA 02116-4615. Editor-in-Chief/Publisher: Sylvia K. Burack. 20-25% freelance written. Prefers to buy work of published/established writers. Monthly. Estab. 1887. **Pays on acceptance.** Publishes ms an average of 6-8 months after acceptance. Buys first serial rights. Sample copy for $3.50.
Nonfiction: Practical articles for writers on how to write for publication, and how and where to market manuscripts in various fields. Considers all submissions promptly. No assignments. Length: 2,000 words maximum.
Tips: "New types of publications and our continually updated market listings in all fields will determine changes of focus and fact."

WRITER'S DIGEST, 1507 Dana Ave., Cincinnati OH 45207. (513)531-2222. Submissions Editor: Paul Singer. 90% freelance written. Monthly magazine about writing and publishing. "Our readers write fiction, poetry, nonfiction, plays and all kinds of creative writing. They're interested in improving their writing skills, improving their sales ability, and finding new outlets for their talents." Estab. 1921. Circ. 225,000. **Pays on acceptance.** Publishes ms an average of 1 year after acceptance. Buys first North American serial rights for one-time editorial use, possible electronic posting, microfilm/microfiche use and magazine promotional use. Pays 20% kill fee. Byline given. Submit seasonal material 8 months in advance. Accepts previously published submissions from noncompeting markets. Send tearsheet or photocopy of article, noting rights for sale and when and where the article previously appeared. Query for electronic submissions. "We're able to use electronic submissions only for accepted pieces and will discuss details if we buy your work. We'll accept computer printout submissions, of course—but they *must* be readable. We strongly recommend letter-quality. If you don't want your manuscript returned, indicate that on the first page of the manuscript or in a cover letter." Reports in 3-6 weeks. Sample copy for $3.50 ($3.70 in Ohio). Writer's guidelines for #10 SASE.
Nonfiction: "Our mainstay is the how-to article—that is, an article telling how to write and sell more of what you write. For instance, how to write compelling leads and conclusions, how to improve your character descriptions, how to become more efficient and productive. We like plenty of examples, anecdotes and $$$ in our articles—so other writers can actually see what's been done successfully by the author of a particular piece. We like our articles to speak directly to the reader through the use of the first-person voice. Don't submit an article on what five book editors say about writing mysteries. Instead, submit an article on how you cracked the mystery market and how our readers can do the same. But don't limit the article to your experiences; include the opinions of those five editors to give your article increased depth and authority." General interest (about writing); how-to (writing and marketing techniques that work); humor (short pieces); inspirational; interview and profile (query first); new product; personal experience (marketing and freelancing experiences). "We can always use articles on fiction and nonfiction technique, and solid articles on poetry or scriptwriting are always welcome. No articles titled 'So You Want to Be a Writer,' and no first-person pieces that ramble without giving a lesson or something readers can learn from in the sharing of the story." Buys 90-100 mss/year. Queries are preferred, but complete mss OK. Length: 500-3,000 words. Pays 10¢/ word minimum. Sometimes pays expenses of writers on assignment.
Photos: Used only with interviews and profiles. State availability of photos or send contact sheet with ms. Captions required.
Columns/Departments: Chronicle (first-person narratives about the writing life; length: 1,200-1,500 words); The Writing Life (length: 50-800 words); and Tip Sheet (short items that offer solutions to writing and freelance business-related problems that writers commonly face). Buys approximately 150 articles/year for Writing Life and Tip Sheet sections. Send complete ms.
Poetry: Light verse about "the writing life"—joys and frustrations of writing. "We are also considering poetry other than short light verse—but related to writing, publishing, other poets and authors, etc." Buys an average of 1 an issue. Submit poems in batches of 1-8. Length: 2-20 lines. Pays $10-50/poem.
Fillers: Anecdotes and short humor, primarily for use in The Writing Life column. Uses up to 4/issue. Length: 50-250 words.

WRITER'S FORUM, Writer's Digest School, 1507 Dana Ave., Cincinnati OH 45207. (513)531-2222. Editor: Amanda Boyd. 100% freelance written. Quarterly newsletter covering writing techniques, marketing and inspiration for students enrolled in fiction and nonfiction writing courses offered by Writer's Digest School. Estab. 1970. Circ. 13,000. **Pays on acceptance.** Publishes ms an average of 6 months after acceptance. Byline given. Buys first serial or second serial (reprint) rights. Submit seasonal/holiday material 4 months in advance. Accepts simultaneous and previously published submissions. Query for electronic submissions. Reports in 4-6 weeks. Free sample copy.
Nonfiction: How-to (write or market short stories, or articles, novels and nonfiction books) and inspirational articles that will motivate beginning writers. Buys 12 mss/year. Prefers complete mss to queries. "If you prefer to query, please do so by mail, not phone." Length: 500-1,000 words. Pays $10-25.

WRITER'S GUIDELINES: A Roundtable for Writers and Editors, Box 608, Pittsburg MO 65724. Fax: (417)993-5544. Editor: Susan Salaki. 97% freelance written. Bimonthly roundtable forum and market news reports for writers and editors. "We are interested in what writers on both sides of the desk have to say about the craft of writing." Estab. 1988. Circ. 1,000. Pays on publication. Byline given. Rights to the original work revert to contributors after publication. Reports in 1 week. Sample copy for $4. Writer's guidelines for #10 SASE.

Nonfiction: General interest, historical articles on writers/writing, psychological aspects of being a writer, how-to, interview/profile, personal experience, humor, fillers. Buys 20 mss/year. Prefer disposable photocopy submissions complete with SASE. May use both sides of each sheet of paper to save postage costs. Include SASE with all correspondence. Length: 800-1,000 words. Pay varies from copies to up to $25.

Fillers: Facts about writing or writers, short humor and cartoons, "wide-open to any facts of interest to writers or editors." No payment for fillers.

Tips: "If you believe what you have to say about writing or editing has needed to be said for some time now, then I'm interested. If you say it well, I'll buy it. This is a unique publication in that we offer original guidelines for over 300 magazine and book publishers and because of this service, writers and editors are linked in a new and exciting way—as correspondents. Articles that help to bridge the gap which has existed between these two professions have the best chance of being accepted. Publishing background does not matter. Include a short biography and cover letter with your submissions."

‡WRITERS INFORMATION NETWORK, The Professional Association for Christian Writers, P.O. Box 11337, Bainbridge Island, WA 98110. (206)842-9103. Editor: Elaine Wright Colvin. 33⅓% freelance written. Bimonthly newsletter covering religious publishing industry. Estab. 1983. Circ. 1,000. **Pays on acceptance.** Publishes ms 1 month after acceptance. Byline given. Buys first North American serial rights. Editorial lead time 2 months. Submit seasonal material 2 months in advance. Reports in 1 month. Sample copy for 9×12 SAE with $1.01 postage. Writer's guidelines for #10 SASE.

Nonfiction: How-to (writing), humor, inspirational, personal experience. Send complete ms. Pays $5-250; sometimes pays other than cash. Sometimes pays expenses of writers on assignment.

Columns/Departments: Bulletin Board, Speakers' Platform, Computer Corner. Send complete ms.

WRITERS INTERNATIONAL FORUM, Bristol Services International, P.O. Box 516, Tracyton WA 98393-0516. Editorial Director: Sandra E. Haven. 90% freelance written. Bimonthly publication designed to publish aspiring writers' stories and to forward resulting responses from readers. Estab. 1990. Buys first rights. Byline and brief bio given. No poetry. Also offers a column of tips from readers, a markets listing, lessons on writing, Tips of the Trade, and features about the writing craft. Submit mss with SASE, cover letter, clear copies (not originals as notations may be made prior to return). No multiple or simultaneous submissions. Reports in 6 weeks. Guidelines, contest information and details on upcoming themes or special Junior and Senior editions available for SASE. Sample copy for $3,50, Special Editions $5; subscription $14.

Columns/Departments: Writer to Writer: tips on writing sent in by writers (maximum 300 words), pays 1 copy; Perspectives: 1 essay published per issue that offers a writer's personal, philosophic and/or humorous perspective (maximum 500 words), pays $5 and 3 contributor copies. Send complete ms; mark for intended column.

Fiction: Any genre (no slice-of-life, violence, graphic sex or experimental formats). "We also publish 2 special editions. Stories written for and/or by those aged 6-18 can be submitted for our Juniors edition (mark manuscript accordingly). Stories that concern the lives of seniors as well as manuscripts written by seniors can be submitted for our Seniors edition (mark manuscript accordingly). Stories published will be open to responses by readers; some responses published. Send complete ms. Book excerpts considered if they are so marked and within our fiction limits (include brief overview of book). Length: 2,000 words maximum, 600-1,200 preferred. **Pays on acceptance**, $5 minimum, plus 3 contributor's copies.

Tips: "We specialize in traditional fiction with definite plots and resolutions resulting from the main character's action and/or decision. Always include a cover letter that says something about you and your manuscript's intended audience (children's story, mystery, whatever). We are a friendly magazine and we make every effort to treat writers on a personal level, however, we insist that all of our requirements be met. Please read our guidelines and follow them carefully. All submissions will receive a complimentary critique."

WRITER'S JOURNAL, Minnesota Ink, Inc., 3585 N. Lexington Ave., Suite 328, Arden Hills MN 55126. (612)486-7818. Publisher/Managing Editor: Valerie Hockert. Poetry Editor: Esther M. Leiper. 40% freelance written. Bimonthly. Circ. 52,000. Pays on publication. Publishes ms an average of 4 months after acceptance. Byline given. Buys first North American serial rights. Submit seasonal material 6 months in advance. Query for electronic submissions. Reports in 1 month on queries; 6 weeks on mss. Sample copy for $4. Writer's guidelines for #10 SASE.

Nonfiction: How-to (on the business and approach to writing), motivational, interview/profile, opinion. "*Writer's Journal* publishes articles on style, technique, editing methods, copy writing, research, writing of news releases, writing news stories and features, creative writing, grammar reviews, marketing, the business aspects of writing, copyright law and legal advice for writers/editors, independent book publishing, interview techniques, and more." Also articles on the use of computers by writers and a book review section. Buys

30-40 mss/year. Send complete ms. Length: 700-1,000 words. Pays to $50.

Poetry: Avant-garde, free verse, haiku, light verse, traditional. "The *Writer's Journal* runs two poetry contests each year in the spring and fall: Winner, 2nd, 3rd place and 10 honorable mentions." Buys 20-30 poems/year. Submit maximum 5 poems. Length: 25 lines maximum. Pays 25¢ line.

Tips: "Articles must be *well* written and slanted toward the business (or commitment) of writing and/or being a writer. Interviews with established writers should be in-depth, particularly reporting interviewee's philosophy on writing, how he or she got started, etc." The *Writer's Journal* now incorporates Minnesota Ink. Minnesota Ink is 100% freelance written and contains fiction and poetry.

WRITER'S YEARBOOK, 1507 Dana Ave., Cincinnati OH 45207. Submissions Editor: Paul Singer. 90% freelance written. Newsstand annual for freelance writers, journalists and teachers of creative writing. "Please note that the *Yearbook* is currently using a 'best of' format. That is, we are reprinting the best writing about writing published in the last year: articles, fiction and book excerpts. The *Yearbook* now uses little original material, so do not submit queries or original manuscripts. We will, however, consider already-published material for possible inclusion." Estab. 1929. Buys reprint rights. Accepts previously published submissions. Send tearsheet or photocopy of article, noting rights for sale and when and where the article previously appeared. Pays 20% kill fee. Byline given. **Pays on acceptance.** Publishes ms an average of 6 months after acceptance. "If you don't want your manuscript returned, indicate that on the first page of the manuscript or in a cover letter."

Nonfiction: "In reprints, we want articles that reflect the current state of writing in America: trends, inside information, and money-saving and money-making ideas for the freelance writer. We try to touch on the various facets of writing in each issue of the *Yearbook*—from fiction to poetry to playwriting, and any other endeavor a writer can pursue. How-to articles—that is, articles that explain in detail how to do something—are very important to us. For example, you could explain how to establish mood in fiction, how to improve interviewing techniques, how to write for and sell to specialty magazines, or how to construct and market a good poem. We are also interested in the writer's spare time—what she/he does to retreat occasionally from the writing wars, where and how to refuel and replenish the writing spirit. 'How Beats the Heart of a Writer' features interest us, if written warmly, in the first person, by a writer who has had considerable success. We also want interviews or profiles of well-known bestselling authors, always with good pictures. Articles on writing techniques that are effective today are always welcome. We provide how-to features and information to help our readers become more skilled at writing and successful at selling their writing." Buys 15-20 mss (reprints only)/year. Length: 750-4,500 words. Pays 2½¢/word minimum.

Photos: Interviews and profiles must be accompanied by high-quality photos. Reviews b&w photos only, depending on use. Captions required.

WRITING CONCEPTS, The Business Communications Report, 7481 Huntsman Blvd., Suite 720, Springfield VA 22153-1648. Editor/Publisher: John De Lellis. Monthly business newsletter on writing, editing, publication management and production, communications and publications technology, public relations and marketing. "Our readers are experienced staff professionals responsible for communications and publications in businesses, corporations and nonprofit organizations. They need specific, practical advice on how to do their job better." Estab. 1983. Pays within 45 days of acceptance. Publishes ms an average of 2 months after acceptance. Byline sometimes given. Buys all rights. Editorial lead time 2 months. Need submissions on 3.5″ disk in both ASCII and word processing format. Reports in 6 weeks on queries. Two sample copies and writer's guidelines for $3.00 and #10 SASE.

- *Writing Concepts* does *not* use material on how to get published or on the business side of freelance writing/editing.

Nonfiction: "Practical, short, well-researched, how-to articles geared to organizational staff communications/publications managers. We need source and ordering information for each article. See sample issues for style. No humor, opinion, inspirational items. All articles must be *interviews* of leading experts in the communications field. No long articles, except special reports. We are open to ideas for 2,000 word special reports in the communications management and publication production field." Buys 20 mss/year. Length: 500-600 words. Pays $80-125.

Photos: State availability of photos with submission. Offers no additional payment for photos accepted with ms.

Column/Departments: Publications Management, Quick Takes (useful sources, tips on publications, communications, writing and editing, PR and marketing, and communications/publications technology); Writing Techniques (*business* writing for organization staffers); Style Matters (business editing for organization staffers); PR and Marketing; Technology Watch (technology trends/issues relating to communications and publications work in organizations).

Tips: "Read sample issues and editorial guidelines *before* you query."

WRITING FOR MONEY, P.O. Box 1144, Hendersonville NC 28793. (704)696-9708. Fax: (704)696-2379. E-mail: wfmoney@aol.com. Editor: John Clausen. 25% freelance written. Newsletter published every 3 weeks covering freelance writing opportunities. "Our newsletter covers writing opportunities for freelance magazine writers and copywriters, authors, script writers, screenplay writers, playwrights, catalog copywriters, greeting card writers, and just about every kind of writer looking to make a buck." Estab. 1993. Circ. 6,000. Pays on publication. Publishes ms an average of 3 months after acceptance. Byline given. Buys first North American serial and non-exclusive reprint rights. Editorial lead time 2 months (sometimes shorter). Submit seasonal material 3 months in advance. Query for electronic submissions. Reports in 6 weeks on queries; 6 months on mss. Sample copy for $5. Writer's guidelines for #10 SASE.

Columns/Departments: First Person (personal success stories from freelancers), 500-900 words; Business Tactics (ways for freelancers to handle the "business side" of writing), 500-900 words; Other Markets (new, innovative ways for freelancers to make money writing), 500-900 words. Buys 50 mss/year. Query with published clips or send completed mss. Pays $50.

Tips: "Study the back issues to see what we are buying."

‡THE WRITING SELF, Journeys Into The Act of Writing, P.O. Box 245, Lenox Hill Station NY 10021. Editors: Julia Nourok, Helen Gorenstein. Contact: Scot Nourok, managing editor. 80% freelance written. Quarterly magazine covering trade/journalism and writing for nonfiction, fiction and poetry. "We're interested in a broad range of subjects that share with our readers the writing life. We look for manuscripts that will stimulate our readers to keep on writing even when the refrigerator breaks down, the computer won't save, or the book gets published. We're partial to pieces that are honestly written, intimate, or that make us laugh." Estab. 1992. Circ. 800. **Pays on acceptance.** Publishes ms an average of 2-3 months after acceptance. Byline given. Buys one-time rights. Editorial lead time 6 months. Accepts simultaneous submissions. Reports in 1-2 months on queries; 3-6 months on mss. Sample copy for $3. Writer's guidelines for #10 SASE.

Nonfiction: Book excerpts, essays, humor, opinion, personal experience. Buys 25-35 mss/year. Send complete ms. Length: 500-1,200 words. Pays $5-20 plus 3 copies of journal.

Columns/Departments: Book Review (writers' journals, diaries, letters, memoirs, essays), 750-1,000 words; Short Short Inner Voices (writers' personal experiences—coping with isolation), 500-1,000 words; Workshop Beat (impressions/insights gained in attending writers' conference), 750-1,000 words. Buys 15-20 mss/year. Send complete ms. Pays $10-20 plus 3 copies of journal.

Fiction: Humorous, novel excerpts, slice-of-life vignettes. Buys 1-2 mss/year. Send complete ms. Length: 500-1,000 words. Pays $10-20.

Poetry: Buys 2-3 poems/year. Submit maximum 4 poems. Length: 5-25 lines. Pays $5-10.

Fillers: Short humor, anecdotes. Buys 2-3/year. Length: 50-250 words. Pays $5.

Tips: "We're interested in pieces that examine the hazardous and uplifting experiences of the writing life in a personal way. We buy manuscripts that share your joys, conflicts, and survival techniques with other writers. No how-to articles with an instructional tone, please. Send for a sample issue and guidelines. Read the journal. We always like hearing from our readers."

Law

While all of these publications deal with topics of interest to attorneys, each has a particular slant. Be sure that your subject is geared to a specific market—lawyers in a single region, law students, paralegals, etc. Publications for law enforcement personnel are listed under Government and Public Service.

THE ALTMAN WEIL PENSA REPORT TO LEGAL MANAGEMENT, Altman Weil Pensa Publications, 1100 Commerce Dr., Racine WI 53406. (414)886-1304. Fax: (414)886-1139. Editor: James Wilber. 15-20% freelance written. Works with a small number of new/unpublished writers each year. Monthly newsletter covering law office management, purchases (equipment, insurance services, space, etc.) and technology. Estab. 1974. Circ. 2,200. Pays on publication. Publishes ms an average of 3-6 months after acceptance. Byline given. Buys all rights; sometimes second serial (reprint) rights. Accepts previously published material. Send photocopy of article or typed ms with rights for sale noted plus diskette, and information about when and where the article previously appeared. For reprints, pays 50% of the amount paid for an original article. Query for electronic submissions. Reports in 1 month on queries; 2-3 months on mss. Sample copy for #10 SASE.

Nonfiction: How-to (buy, use, repair), interview/profile, new product. "Looking especially for practical, "how-to" articles on law office management and technology." Buys 12 mss/year. Query. Submit a sample of previous writing. Length: 500-2,500 words. Pays $125/published page.

BENCH & BAR OF MINNESOTA, Minnesota State Bar Association, 514 Nicollet Ave., Suite 300, Minneapolis MN 55402-1021. (612)333-1183. Fax: (612)333-4927. Editor: Judson Haverkamp. 10% freelance written. Magazine published 11 times/year covering the law/legal profession. "Audience is mostly Minnesota lawyers. *Bench & Bar* seeks reportage, analysis, and commentary on trends and issues in the law and the legal profession, especially in Minnesota. Preference to items of practical/human interest to professionals in law." Estab. 1931. Circ. 14,000. **Pays on acceptance.** Publishes ms an average of 3 months after acceptence. Byline given. Buys first North American serial rights and makes work-for-hire assignments. Reports in 1 month. Sample copy for 9×12 SAE with 4 first-class stamps. Writer's guidelines free.

Nonfiction: General interest, historical/nostalgic, how-to (how to handle particular types of legal, ethical problems in office management, representation, etc.), humor, interview/profile, technical/legal. "We do not want one-sided opinion pieces or advertorial." Buys 4-5 mss/year. Query with published clips or send complete ms. Length: 1,500-3,000 words. Pays $300-800. Sometimes pays expenses of writers on assignment.

Photos: State availability of photos with submission. Reviews 5×7 or larger prints. Offers $25-100/photo upon publication. Model releases and identification of subjects required. Buys one-time rights.

CALIFORNIA LAWYER, Dept. WM, 1210 Fox Plaza, 1390 Market St., San Francisco CA 94102. (415)252-0500. Editor: Jane Goldman. Managing Editor: Michael Lester. 80% freelance written. Monthly magazine of law-related articles and general interest subjects of appeal to lawyers and judges. Estab. 1928. Circ. 135,000. **Pays on acceptance.** Publishes ms an average of 3 months after acceptance. Byline given. Buys first rights; publishes only original material. Accepts simultaneous submissions. Reports in 2 weeks on queries; 3 weeks on mss. *Writer's Market* recommends allowing 2 months for reply. Sample copy and writer's guidelines on request with SASE.

Nonfiction: General interest, news and feature articles on law-related topics. "We are interested in concise, well-written and well-researched articles on issues of current concern, as well as well-told feature narratives with a legal focus. We would like to see a description or outline of your proposed idea, including a list of possible sources." Buys 36 mss/year. Query with published clips if available. Length: 500-3,000 words. Pays $200-1,500.

Photos: Jamison Chandler, photo editor. State availability of photos with query letter or ms. Reviews prints. Identification of subjects and releases required.

Columns/Departments: Legal Technology, Short News, Legal Culture, Books. Query with published clips if available. Length: 750-1,500 words. Pays $200-600.

LAW PRACTICE MANAGEMENT—the Magazine of the Section of Law Practice Management of the American Bar Association, P.O. Box 11418, Columbia SC 29211-1418. Managing Editor/Art Director: Delmar L. Roberts. Editorial contact for freelance submissions: John C. Tredennick, Esq., articles editor; Holland & Hart, P.O. Box 8749, Denver CO 80201. 10% freelance written. Magazine published 8 times/year for the practicing lawyer and law practice administrator. Estab. 1975. Circ. 22,005 (BPA). Rights purchased vary with author and material. Usually buys all rights. Byline given. Pays on publication. Publishes ms an average of 8 months after acceptance. Query. Sample copy for $7 (make check payable to American Bar Association). Free writer's guidelines. Returns rejected material in 3 months, if requested.

Nonfiction: "We assist the practicing lawyer in operating and managing his or her office by providing relevant articles and departments written in a readable and informative style. Editorial content is intended to aid the lawyer by conveying management methods that will allow him or her to provide legal services to clients in a prompt and efficient manner at reasonable cost. Typical topics of articles include fees and billing; client/lawyer relations; computer hardware/software; mergers; retirement/disability; marketing; compensation of partners and associates; legal data base research; and use of paralegals." No elementary articles on a whole field of technology, such as, "why you need computers in the law office." Pays $100-400.

Photos: Pays $50-60 for b&w photos purchased with mss; $50-100 for color; $200-300 for cover transparencies.

Tips: "We have a theme for each issue with two to three articles relating to the theme. We also publish thematic issues occasionally in which an entire issue is devoted to a single topic. The March and November/December issues each year are devoted to law practice technology."

THE LAWYER'S PC, A Newsletter for Lawyers Using Personal Computers, Shepard's/McGraw-Hill, Inc., P.O. Box 1108, Lexington SC 29071-1108. (803)359-9941. Editor: Robert P. Wilkins. Managing Editor: Daniel E. Harmon. 50% freelance written. Biweekly newsletter covering computerized law firms. "Our readers are lawyers who want to be told how a particular microcomputer program or type of program is being applied to a legal office task, such as timekeeping, litigation support, etc." Estab. 1983. Circ. 3,500. Pays end of the month of publication. Publishes ms an average of 2 months after acceptance. Byline given. Buys first North American serial rights and the right to reprint. Submit seasonal material 5 months in advance. Accepts previously published submissions. Send tearsheet or photocopy of article or typed ms with rights for sale noted and information about when and where the articl eprevoiusly appeared. For reprints, pays 100% of the amount paid for an original article. Query for electronic submissions. Reports in 1 month on queries; 4 months on mss. Sample copy for 9×12 SAE with 3 first-class stamps. Free writer's guidelines.

Nonfiction: How-to (applications articles on law office computerization) and software reviews written by lawyers who have no compromising interests. No general articles on why lawyers need computers or reviews of products written by public relations representatives or vending consultants. Buys 30-35 mss/year. Query. Length: 500-2,500 words. Pays $50-500. Sometimes pays the expenses of writers on assignment.

Tips: "Most of our writers are lawyers. If you're not a lawyer, you need to at least understand why general business software may not work well in a law firm. If you understand lawyers' specific computer problems, write an article describing how to solve one of those problems, and we'd like to see it."

THE LAWYERS WEEKLY, The Newspaper for the Legal Profession in Canada, Butterworth (Canada) Inc., 75 Clegg Rd., Markham, Ontario L6G IA1 Canada. (905)479-2665. Fax: (905)479-3758. Editor: Don Brillinger. 30% freelance written. "We will work with any *talented* writer of whatever experience level." Tabloid published 48 times/year covering Canadian law and legal affairs for a "sophisticated up-market readership of lawyers." Estab. 1983. Circ. 8,000/week; 22,500 once per month. Pays on publication. Publishes ms within 1 month after acceptance. Byline given. Offers 50% kill fee. Usually buys all rights. Submit seasonal material 6 weeks in advance. Accepts simultaneous submissions. Query for electronic submissions. Reports in 1 month. Sample copy for $8 (Canadian) with 9 × 12 SAE.

Nonfiction: Exposé, general interest (law), how-to (professional), humor, interview/profile (Canadian lawyers and judges), opinion, technical, news, case comments. "We try to wrap up the week's legal events and issues in a snappy informal package. We especially like news stories with photos or illustrations. We are always interested in feature or newsfeature articles involving current legal issues, but contributors should keep in mind our audience is trained in *English/Canadian common law*—not US law. That means most US-focused stories will generally not be accepted. No routine court reporting or fake news stories about commercial products. Buys 200-300 mss/year. Query or send complete ms. Length: 700-1,500 words. Payment negotiable. Payment in Canadian dollars. Sometimes pays the expenses of writers on assignment.

Photos: State availability of photos with query letter or ms. Reviews b&w and color contact sheets, negatives and 5 × 7 prints. Identification of subjects required. Buys one-time rights.

Fillers: Clippings, newsbreaks. Length: 50-200 words. Pays $10 minimum.

Tips: "Freelancers can best break into our publication by submitting news, features, and accounts of unusual or bizarre legal events. A frequent mistake made by writers is forgetting that our audience is intelligent and learned in law. They don't need the word 'plaintiff' explained to them." No unsolicited mss returned without SASE (or IRC to US or non-Canadian destinations). "No US postage on SASEs, please!"

‡LEGAL ASSISTANT TODAY, James Publishing, Inc., 3520 Cadillac Ave., Suite E, Costa Mesa CA 92626. (714)755-5450. Fax: (714)751-5508. Editor-in-Chief: Gina Farrell Gladwell. Executive Editor: Leanne Cazares. Bimonthly magazine covering information for paralegals/legal assistants. "Our magazine is geared toward all legal assistants/paralegals throughout the country, regardless of specialty (litigation, corporate, bankruptcy, environmental law, etc.). How-to articles to help paralegals do their jobs more effectively are most in demand, as is career and salary information, and timely news and trends pieces." Estab. 1983. Circ. 17,000. **Pays on acceptance.** Publishes ms an average of 3 months after acceptance. Byline given. Usually buys all rights. Editorial lead time 10 weeks. Submit seasonal material 3 months in advance. Accepts simultaneous submissions. Reports in 1 month on queries; 2 months on mss. Sample copy free on request. Writer's guidelines free on request.

● *Legal Assistant Today* needs much more practitioner, "how-to" articles, noting that readers want articles on how to do their jobs better and faster.

Nonfiction: How-tos for paralegals, issues affecting the paralegal profession, profiles of new products for law office, opinion on legal topics (paralegal), personal experience of paralegals on the job. "Each issue has a theme: litigation support, research and discovery, corporate services. Since ours is a national magazine, we limit regional or local stories (except for the news)." Buys 36 mss/year. Query with published clips. Length: 2,000-4,000 words. (News, profiles shorter.) Pays $100 minimum. "Pay is negotiated per assignment; pay can be *substantially* more depending on experience and length and quality of manuscript." Pays expenses of writers on assignment.

Photos: Send photos with submission. Reviews prints. Negotiates payment individually. Identification of subjects required. Buys one-time rights.

Columns/Departments: "Last Laugh"—humorous piece on legal world; 1,000-1,200 words. Pays $75-100.

Fillers: Anecdotes, facts, newsbreaks and short humor "pertaining to paralegals." Pay negotiated.

Tips: "We prefer writers with previous experience working in a law office or writing for legal publications who have some understanding of what paralegals would find interesting or useful. Writers must understand our audience. There is some opportunity for investigative journalism as well as the usual features, profiles and news. How-to articles are especially desired. If you are a great writer who can interview effectively, and really dig into the topic to grab the readers' attention, we need you! We are open to ideas (queries), but also assign selected topics: News: brief, hard news topics regarding paralegals (or trend pieces on the profession.); Profiles: paralegals who've worked on fascinating cases, etc.; Features: presents information to help paralegals advance in their careers."

THE PENNSYLVANIA LAWYER, Pennsylvania Bar Association, P.O. Box 186, 100 South St., Harrisburg PA 17108-0186. (717)238-6715. Executive Editor: Marcy Carey Mallory. Editorial Director: Donald C. Sarvey. Managing Editor: Sherri Kimmel. 25% freelance written. Prefers to work with published/established writers. Bimonthly magazine published as a service to the legal profession. Estab. 1895. Circ. 27,000. **Pays on acceptance.** Publishes ms an average of 3-6 months after acceptance. Byline given. Buys first rights generally, occasionally one-time rights or second serial (reprint) rights. Submit seasonal material 6 months in advance. Simultaneous submissions discouraged. Reports in 6 weeks. Sample copy and writer's

guidelines for #10 SAE with 3 first-class stamps.
Nonfiction: General interest, how-to, interview/profile, new product, law-practice management, personal experience. All features *must* relate in some way to Pennsylvania lawyers or the practice of law in Pennsylvania. Buys 10-12 mss/year. Query. Length: 600-1,500 words. Pays $75-350. Sometimes pays the expenses of writers on assignment.

THE PERFECT LAWYER, A Newsletter for Lawyers Using WordPerfect Products, Shepard's/McGraw-Hill Inc., P.O. Box 1108, Lexington SC 29071-1108. (803)359-9941. Editor: Robert P. Wilkins. Associate Editor: Daniel E. Harmon. 50% freelance written. Monthly newsletter covering the use of WordPerfect Corporation-related products in law offices. Estab. 1990. Circ. 3,500. Pays at end of the month after publication. Publishes ms an average of 2-3 months after acceptance. Byline given. Buys first North American serial rights, electronic rights and the right to reprint. Submit seasonal material 5 months in advance. Accepts previously published submissions. Send tearsheet or photocopy of article or typed ms with rights for sale noted and information about when and where the article previously appeared. For reprints, pays 100% of the amount paid for an original article. Query for electronic submissions. Reports in 4 months. Sample copy for 9 × 12 SAE with 4 first-class stamps. Free writer's guidelines.
Nonfiction: How-to computer articles, must be law office-specific. Occasional reviews of WordPerfect-related products for law firms. Buys 25-35 mss/year. Query. Length: 500-2,500 words. Pays $25-200. Sometimes pays expenses of writers on assignment.
Tips: "Writers should understand the specific computer needs of law firms. Our readers are interested in how to solve office automation problems with computers and WordPerfect or related software products."

SHEPARD'S ELDER CARE/LAW NEWSLETTER, Shepard's/McGraw-Hill, Inc., P.O. Box 1108, Lexington SC 29071-1108. (803)359-9941. Fax: (803)857-8226. Editor: Robert P. Wilkins. Managing Editor: Daniel E. Harmon. Associate Editor: Aida Rogers. 40% freelance written. Monthly newsletter for lawyers and other professionals who work with older clients, focusing on legal and related issues of concern to the aging community. Estab. 1991. Pays end of the month of publication. Publishes ms an average of 2 months after acceptance. Byline given. Buys first North American serial rights, electronic rights and reprint rights. Submit seasonal material 5 months in advance. Accepts previously published submissions. Send tearsheet or photocopy of article or typed ms with rights for sale noted and information about when and where the article previously appeared. For reprints, pays 100% of the amount paid for an original article. Query for electronic submissions. Reports in 1 month on queries; 2 months on mss. Pay negotiable. Sample copy for 9 × 12 SAE with 3 first-class stamps. Writer's guidelines free.
Nonfiction: Informational articles about legal issues, pending and new legislation, organizations and other resources of interest to lawyers who work with aging clients and their families. Query. Pays $25-200. Does not pay phone expenses.

STUDENT LAWYER, American Bar Association, 750 N. Lake Shore Dr., Chicago IL 60611. (312)988-6048. Editor: Sarah Hoban. 95% freelance written. Works with a small number of new/unpublished writers each year. Monthly (September-May) magazine. Estab. 1972. Circ. 33,000. Pays on publication. Buys first serial and second serial (reprint) rights. Accepts previously published submissions. Send tearsheet or typed ms with rights for sale noted and information about when and where the article previously appeared. For reprints, pays 25-50% of the amount paid for an original article. Pays negotiable kill fee. Byline given. Submit seasonal material 4 months in advance. Reports in 6 weeks. Publishes ms an average of 3 months after acceptance. Sample copy for $4. Free writer's guidelines.
Nonfiction: Features cover legal education and careers and social/legal subjects. Also profiles (prominent persons in law-related fields); opinion (on matters of current legal interest); essays (on legal affairs); interviews; photo features. Query. Length: 3,000-5,000 words. Pays $300-900 for main features. Covers some writer's expenses.
Columns/Departments: Briefly (short stories on unusual and interesting developments in the law); Legal Aids (unusual approaches and programs connected to teaching law students and lawyers); Esq. (brief profiles of people in the law); End Note (short pieces on a variety of topics; can be humorous, educational, outrageous); Pro Se (opinion slot for authors to wax eloquent on legal issues); Et Al. (column for short features that fit none of the above categories). Buys 4-8 mss/issue. Length: 250-1,000 words. Pays $100-350.
Fiction: "We buy fiction only when it is very good and deals with issues of law in the contemporary world or offers insights into the inner workings of lawyers. No mystery, poetry or science fiction accepted."
Tips: "*Student Lawyer* actively seeks good new writers. Legal training definitely not essential; writing talent is. The writer should not think we are a law review; we are a feature magazine with the law (in the broadest sense) as the common denominator. Past articles concerned family law, copyright law, violence against lawyers, and many aspects of legal education. Find issues of national scope and interest to write about; be aware of subjects the magazine—and other media—have already covered and propose something new. Write clearly and well."

Leather Goods

SHOE SERVICE, SSIA Service Corp., 5024-R Campbell Blvd., Baltimore MD 21236-5974. (410)931-8100. Fax: (410)931-8111. Editor: Mitchell Lebovic. 25% freelance written. "We want well-written articles, whether they come from new or established writers." Monthly magazine for business people who own and operate small shoe repair shops. Estab. 1921. Circ. 8,000. Pays on publication. Publishes ms an average of 3 months after acceptance. Byline given. Buys first serial, first North American serial and one-time rights. Submit seasonal material 3 months in advance. Accepts simultaneous and previously published submissions. Reports in 6 weeks. Sample copy for $2 and 9×12 SAE.
Nonfiction: How-to (run a profitable shop); interview/profile (of an outstanding or unusual person on shoe repair); business articles (particularly about small business practices in a service/retail shop). Buys 12-24 mss/year. Query with published clips or send complete ms. Length: 500-2,000 words. Pays 5¢/word.
Photos: "Quality photos will help sell an article." State availability of photos. Pays $10-30 for 8×10 b&w prints. Uses some color photos, but mostly b&w glossies. Captions, model release and identification of subjects required.
Tips: "Visit some shoe repair shops to get an idea of the kind of person who reads *Shoe Service*. Profiles are the easiest to sell to us if you can find a repairer we think is unusual."

Library Science

Librarians read these journals for advice on promotion and management of libraries, library and book trade issues and information access and transfer. Be aware of current issues such as censorship, declines in funding and government information policies. For journals on the book trade see Book and Bookstore.

AMERICAN LIBRARIES, 50 E. Huron St., Chicago IL 60611. (312)280-4216. Fax: (312)440-0901. E-mail: u56747@uicvm.uic.edu. Acting Editor: Leonard Kniffel. Acting Senior Editor: Gordon Flagg. 10-20% freelance written. Works with a small number of new/unpublished writers each year. Magazine published 11 times/year for librarians. "A highly literate audience. They are for the most part practicing professionals with a down-to-earth interest in people and current professional trends." Estab. 1907. Circ. 56,000. Buys first North American serial rights. Publishes ms an average of 4 months after acceptance. Pays negotiable kill fee. Byline given. Submit seasonal material 6 months in advance. Reports in 10 weeks with SASE.
Nonfiction: "Material reflecting the special and current interests of the library profession. Nonlibrarians should browse recent journals in the field, available on request in medium-sized and large libraries everywhere. Topic and/or approach must be fresh, vital or highly entertaining. Library memoirs and stereotyped stories about old maids, overdue books, fines, etc., are unacceptable. Our first concern is with the American Library Association's activities and how they relate to the 55,000 reader/members. Tough for an outsider to write on this topic, but not to supplement it with short, offbeat or significant library stories and features." No fillers. Buys 2-6 freelance mss/year. Pays $15 for news tips used, $25-300 for briefs and articles.
Photos: "Will look at color transparencies and bright color prints for inside and cover use." Pays $50-200 for photos.
Tips: "You can break in with a sparkling, 300-word report on a true, offbeat library event, use of new technology, or with an exciting color photo and caption. Though stories on public libraries are always of interest, we especially need arresting material on academic and school libraries."

CHURCH MEDIA LIBRARY MAGAZINE, 127 Ninth Ave. N., Nashville TN 37234. (615)251-2752. Editor: Floyd B. Simpson. Quarterly magazine for adult leaders in church organizations and people interested in library work (especially church library work). Estab. 1891. Circ. 30,000. Pays on publication. Buys all, first serial and second serial (reprint) rights. Byline given. Accepts previously published submissions. Send photocopy of article. For reprints, pays 75% of the amount paid for an original article. Reports in 1 month. Free sample copy and writer's guidelines.
Nonfiction: "We are primarily interested in articles that relate to the development of church libraries in providing media and services to support the total program of a church and in meeting individual needs. We publish how-to accounts of services provided, promotional ideas, exciting things that have happened as a result of implementing an idea or service; human interest stories that are library-related; and media training (teaching and learning with a media mix). Articles should be practical for church library staffs and for teachers and other leaders of the church." Buys 10-15 mss/issue. Query. Pays 5½¢/word.

EMERGENCY LIBRARIAN, Dyad Services, Box C34069, Dept. 284, Seattle WA 98124-1069. (604)925-0266. Fax: (604)925-0566. E-mail: rockland@mindlink.bc.ca. Editor: Ken Haycock. Publishes 5 issues/year. Estab. 1979. Circ. 7,500. Pays on publication. No multiple submissions. Reports in 6 weeks. Free writer's guidelines.

Nonfiction: Emphasis is on improvement of library service for children and young adults in school and public libraries. Also annotated bibliographies. Buys 3 mss/issue. Query. Length: 1,000-3,500 words. Pays $50.
Columns/Departments: Five regular columnists. Also Book Reviews (of professional materials in education, librarianship). Query. Length: 100-300 words. Payment consists of book reviewed.

THE LIBRARY IMAGINATION PAPER, Carol Bryan Imagines, 1000 Byus Dr., Charleston WV 25311-1310. (304)345-2378. 30% freelance written. Quarterly newspaper covering public relations education for librarians. Clip art included in each issue. Estab. 1978. Circ. 3,000. Pays on publication. Publishes ms an average of 6 months after acceptance. Byline given. Buys one-time rights. Submit seasonal material 3 months in advance. Accepts simultaneous and previously published submissions. Send tearsheet or photocopy of article and information about when and where the article previously appeared. Reports in 2 months. Sample copy for $5. Writer's guidelines for SASE.
Nonfiction: How-to (on "all aspects of good library public relations—both mental tips and hands-on methods. We need how-to and tips pieces on all aspects of PR, for library subscribers—both school and public libraries. In the past we've featured pieces on taking good photos, promoting an anniversary celebration, working with printers, and producing a slide show.") No articles on "what the library means to me." Buys 4-6 mss/year. Query with or without published clips, or send complete ms. Length: 600 or 2,200 words. Pays $25 or $50.
Photos: Send photos with submission. Reviews 3×5, 5×7 or 8×10 prints. Offers $5/photo. Captions required. Buys one-time rights.
Tips: "Someone who has worked in the library field and has first-hand knowledge of library PR needs, methods and processes will do far better with us. Our readers are people who cannot be written down to—but their library training has not always incorporated enough preparation for handling promotion, publicity and the public."

WILSON LIBRARY BULLETIN, Dept. WM, 950 University Ave., Bronx NY 10452-4221. (718)588-8400 ext. 2245. Fax: (718)681-1511. E-mail: graceann@wlb.hwwilson.com. Editor: GraceAnne A. DeCandido. 75% freelance written. Monthly (September-June) for professional librarians and those interested in the book and library worlds. Estab. 1914. Circ. 13,000. Pays on publication. Publishes ms an average of 3 months after acceptance. Buys first North American serial rights, electronic rights. Sample copies may be seen on request in most libraries. "Manuscript must be original copy, double-spaced." Deadlines are a minimum 2 months before publication. Reports in 3 months. Free sample copy and writer's guidelines.
Nonfiction: Uses articles "of interest to librarians and information professionals throughout the nation and around the world. Style must be lively, readable and sophisticated, with appeal to modern professionals; facts must be thoroughly researched. Subjects range from the political to the comic in the world of media and libraries, with an emphasis on the human as well as the technical aspects of any story. No condescension: no library stereotypes." Prefers material from practicing librarians; "we rarely accept submissions from freelancers who are not librarians." Buys 20-30 mss/year. Send complete ms. Length: 1,000-3,500 words. Pays $100-400. Sometimes pays the expenses of writers on assignment.
Tips: "Libraries have changed. You'd better first discover how."

Lumber

NORTHERN LOGGER AND TIMBER PROCESSOR, Northeastern Loggers' Association, Dept WM, P.O. Box 69, Old Forge NY 13420. (315)369-3078. Fax: (315)369-3736. Editor: Eric A. Johnson. 40% freelance written. Monthly magazine of the forest industry in the northern US (Maine to Minnesota and south to Virginia and Missouri). "We are not a purely technical journal, but are more information oriented." Estab. 1952. Circ. 13,600. Pays on publication. Publishes ms an average of 3 months after acceptance. Byline given. Buys all rights. Submit seasonal material 3 months in advance. Accepts previously published submissions. Reports in 2 weeks. Free sample copy and writer's guidelines.
Nonfiction: Exposé, general interest, historical/nostalgic, how-to, interview/profile, new product, opinion. "We only buy feature articles, and those should contain some technical or historical material relating to the forest products industry." Buys 12-15 mss/year. Query. Length: 500-2,500 words. Pays $50-250.
Photos: Send photos with ms. Pays $35 for 35mm color transparencies; $15 for 5×7 b&w prints. Captions and identification of subjects required.
Tips: "We accept most any subject dealing with this part of the country's forest industry, from historical to logging, firewood and timber processing."

SOUTHERN LUMBERMAN, Greysmith Publishing, Inc., P.O. Box 681629, Franklin TN 37068-1629. (615)791-1961. Fax: (615)790-6188. Editor: Nanci P. Gregg. 20-30% freelance written. Works with a small number of new/unpublished writers each year. Monthly trade journal for the sawmill industry. Estab. 1881. Circ. 12,000. Pays on publication. Publishes ms an average of 3 months after acceptance. Byline given. Not copyrighted. Buys first North American rights. Submit seasonal material 6 months in advance. Query for electonic submissions. Accepts previously published submissions. Send tearsheet or photocopy of article and information about when and where the article previously appeared. For reprints, pays 25-50% of amount paid for an original article. Reports in 1 month on queries; 2 months on mss. Sample copy for $3 and 9×12 SAE with 5 first-class stamps. Writer's guidelines for #10 SASE.

Nonfiction: How to sawmill better, interview/profile, equipment analysis, technical. Sawmill features. Buys 10-15 mss/year. Query with or without published clips, or send complete ms. Length: 500-2,000 words. Pays $150-350 for assigned articles; $100-250 for unsolicited articles. Sometimes pays the expenses of writers on assignment.

Photos: Send photos with submission. Reviews transparencies and 4×5 b&w prints. Offers $10-25/photo. Captions and identification of subjects required.

Tips: "Like most, we appreciate a clearly-worded query listing merits of suggested story—what it will tell our readers they need/want to know. We want quotes, we want opinions to make others discuss the article. Best hint? Find an interesting sawmill operation owner and start asking questions—I bet a story idea develops. We need b&w photos too. Most open is what we call the Sweethart Mill stories. We publish at least one per month, and hope to be printing two or more monthly in the immediate future. Find a sawmill operator and ask questions—what's he doing bigger, better, different. We're interested in new facilities, better marketing, improved production."

Machinery and Metal

AMERICAN METAL MARKET, Chilton Publications, A Unit of Capital Cities/ABC, Inc., 825 Seventh Ave., New York NY 10019. (212)887-8550. Fax: (212)887-8520. Editor: Michael G. Botta. Contact: Peter Kelton, international news editor. 5% freelance written. Daily newspaper covering metals production and trade. "Bible of the metals industry. Covers production and trade of ferrous, nonferrous, and scrap metals. Read by senior executives. Focus on *breaking* news and price information." Estab. 1882. Circ. 11,000. Pays on publication per inch used in publication. Publishes ms an average of 0-1 months after acceptance. Byline given. Buys all rights and electronic rights. Editorial lead time 0-1 months. Query for electronic submissions. Reports in 0-1 weeks on queries. Sample copy and writer's guidelines free on request.

Nonfiction: Publishes roughly 45 special issues/year. Query. Pays $7/in.

Photos: Send photos with submission. Reviews 5×7 prints. Negotiates payment individually. Identification of subjects required. Buys all rights.

Tips: "Contact Peter Kelton, or Christopher Munford, managing editor, directly with story ideas. Primarily we are interested in purchasing *breaking* news items. Clear all stories with news desk (Kelton or Munford) in advance. Unsolicited articles submitted at writer's risk. Contact Bob Manas, Senior Editor, special issues, to discuss upcoming topics."

FABRICATOR, Ornamental & Miscellaneous Metal, National Ornamental & Miscellaneous Metals Association, 804-10 Main St., #E, Forest Park GA 30050. Editor: Todd Daniel. 20% freelance written. Bimonthly magazine covering ornamental metalwork. "Any business stories published must contain an angle specific to our industry." Estab. 1959. Circ. 8,000. **Pays on acceptance.** Byline given. Publication not copyrighted. Buys one-time rights. Editorial lead time 2 months. Accepts simultaneous and previously published submissions. Send typed ms with rights for sale noted. Electronic submissions OK. Reports in 6 weeks on queries. Sample copy for SASE. Writer's guidelines for $1.

Nonfiction: How-to, humor, interview/profile, personal experience, photo feature, technical. "Nothing in a Q&A format." Buys 6-7 mss/year. Query. Length: 1,200-2,000 words. Pays $150 minimum for assigned articles; $125 minimum for unsolicited articles. "Many write for publicity." Pays expenses of writers on assignment.

Photos: State availability of photos with submission. Reviews contact sheets, negatives, transparencies and prints. Offers no additional payment for photos acepted with ms. Model releases required. Buys one-time rights.

Tips: "Don't write articles in passive voice."

MODERN MACHINE SHOP, 6600 Clough Pike, Cincinnati OH 45244-4090. (513)231-8020. Fax: (513)231-2818. Executive Editor: Mark Albert. 25% freelance written. Monthly. Estab. 1928. Pays 1 month following acceptance. Publishes ms an average of 6 months after acceptance. Byline given. Query for electronic submissions. Reports in 1 month. Call for sample copy. Writer's guidelines for #10 SASE.

Nonfiction: Uses articles dealing with all phases of metalworking, manufacturing and machine shop work, with photos. No general articles. "Ours is an industrial publication, and contributing authors should have a working knowledge of the metalworking industry. "We regularly use contributions from machine shop owners, engineers, other technical experts, and suppliers to the metalworking industry. Almost all of these contributors pursue these projects to promote their own commercial interests. " Buys 10 unsolicited mss/year. Query. Length: 1,000-3,500 words. Pays current market rate.

Tips: "Articles that review basic metalworking/machining processes, especially if they include a rethinking or re-evaluation of these processes in light of today's technical trends, are always welcome."

NICKEL, The Magazine Devoted to Nickel and Its Applications, Nickel Development Institute, 214 King St. W., Suite 510, Toronto, Ontario M5H 3S6 Canada. (416)591-7999. Fax: (416)591-7987. Editor: James S. Borland. 30% freelance written. Quarterly magazine covering the metal nickel and all of its applications. Estab. 1985. Circ. 34,000. **Pays on acceptance**. Publishes ms an average of 3 months after acceptance. Byline given. Buys first rights. Accepts previously published submissions. Send tearsheet of article or typed ms with rights for sale noted and information about when and where the article previously appeared. For reprints, pays 50% of the amount paid for an original article. Reports in 1 month. Sample copies and writer's guidelines free from Nickel Development Institute Librarian.

Nonfiction: Semi-technical. Buys 20 mss/year. Query. Length: 50-1,000 words. Pays competitive rates, by negotiation. Sometimes pays expenses of writers on assignment.

Photos: State availability of photos with submission. Offers competitive rates by negotiation. Captions, model releases and identification of subjects required.

Tips: "Write to Librarian, Nickel Development Institute, for two free copies of *Nickel* and study them. Know something about nickel's 300,000 end uses. Be at home in writing semitechnical material. Then query the editor with a story idea in a one-page letter—no fax queries or phone calls. Complete magazine is open, except Technical Literature column."

‡33 METALPRODUCING, Penton Publishing Inc., 1100 Superior Ave., Cleveland OH 44114. (216)696-7000. Editor: Wallace D. Huskonen. 50% freelance written. Monthly magazine covering producing metal mill products from ore/scrap. "The mission of *33 Metalproducing* is to provide timely, authoritative and useful information on domestic and global trends in the metalproducing industry (SIC 33) for operating management engineers, and other management personnel." Estab. 1962. Circ. 18,000. Pays on publication. Publishes ms an average of 1 month after acceptance. Byline given. Editorial lead time 2 months. Query for electronic submissions. Reports in 2 weeks on queries; 1 month on mss. Sample copy and writer's guidelines free on request.

Nonfiction: Book excerpts, interview/profile, technical. Buys 20 mss/year. Query with published clips. Length: 750-3,000 words. Pays $100-1,000.

Photos: State availability of photos with submissions. Reviews contact sheets, negatives, transparencies, prints. Offers no additional payment for photos accepted with ms. Captions, identification of subjects required. Buys all rights.

Tips: "A freelance writer should demonstrate ability to use the language of metal producing in producing features for *33MP*."

Maintenance and Safety

ADC, Animal Damage Control, Beaver Pond Publishing, P.O. Box 224, Greenville PA 16125. (412)588-3492. Editor: Rich Faler. 80% freelance written. Bimonthly magazine covering resolution of human/animal conflicts. "We want human, cost-effective how-to information written for the full- or part-time professional." Estab. 1993. Circ. 2,000. Pays on publication. Publishes ms an average of 6 months after acceptance. Byline given. Buys first rights, one-time rights or second serial (reprint) rights. Editorial lead time 4 months. Submit seasonal material 4 months in advance. Accepts simultaneous and previously published submissions. Reports in 6 weeks on queries; 2 months on mss. Sample copy for $3. Writer's guidelines free on request.

Nonfiction How-to, interview/profile, new product, personal experience, photo feature, technical. Buys 40 mss/year. Query. Length: 500-2,500 words. Pays $30 minimum.

Photos: Send photos with submission. Reviews contact sheets, negatives, transparencies and prints. Offers no additional payment for photos accepted with ms. Captions required. Buys one-time rights.

Fillers: Anecdotes, facts, newsbreaks, short humor. Buys 20/year. Length 50-500 words. Pays $5-30.

Tips: "Select as narrow a topic as possible in the ADC field, then give a lot of meat on that one specific."

‡BRUSHWARE, Centaur, Inc., Route 3, Box 165, Huddleston VA 24104. (703)297-1517. Editor: Tom Goldberg. Publisher: Carl H. Wurzer. 100% freelance written. Bimonthly magazine covering brush, applicator, mop industry. "General management articles are what we look for. Writers who can do plant profiles of our industry." Estab. 1898. Circ. 1,200. **Pays on acceptance**. Publishes ms an average of 3-4 months after acceptance. Byline given. Offers 100% kill fee. Buys second serial (reprint) rights or makes work-for-hire assignments. Editorial lead time 4 months. Accepts simultaneous and previously published submissions.

Nonfiction General interest, plant profiles with photos. Buys 20 mss/year. Query with or without published clips. Length: 800-2,000 words. Pays $500-1,000 for assigned articles; $25-100 for unsolicited articles. Pays expenses of writers on assignment.

Photos: State availability of photos with submission. Reviews 4 × 6 prints. Negotiates payment individually. Captions, identification of subjects required. Buys one-time rights.

CLEANING AND MAINTENANCE MANAGEMENT, The Magazine for Today's Building Cleaning Maintenance/Housekeeping Executive, (formerly *Cleaning Management*), National Trade Publications, Inc., 13 Century Hill Dr., Latham NY 12110-2197. (518)783-1281. Fax: (518)783-1386. Managing Editor: Anne Dantz. Monthly national trade magazine covering building cleaning maintenance/housekeeping operations in larger institutions such as hotels, schools, hospitals, office buildings, industrial plants, recreational and religious buildings, shopping centers, airports, etc. Articles must be aimed at managers of on-site building/facility cleaning staffs or owners/managers of contract cleaning companies. Estab. 1963. Circ. 42,000. Pays on publication, with invoice. Byline given. Buys all rights. Reports in 2 weeks. Sample copy and writer's guidelines for 9 × 12 SAE with 8 first-class stamps.

Nonfiction: Articles on: discussions of facility-wide systems for custodial operations/cleaning tasks; system-wide analysis of custodial task cost-effectiveness and staffing levels; the organization of cleaning tasks on an institution-wide basis; recruitment, training, motivation and supervision of building cleaning employees; the cleaning of buildings or facilities of unusual size, type, design, construction or notoriety; interesting case studies; or advice for the successful operation of a contract cleaning business. Buys 6-12 mss/year. Length: 500-1,500 words. Pays $50-200. Please query.

Photos: State availability of photos. Prefer color or b&w prints, rates negotiable. Captions, model releases and identification of subjects required.

Tips: Chances of acceptance are directly proportional to the article's relevance to the professional, on-the-job needs and interests of facility/custodial managers or contract building cleaners.

CLEANING BUSINESS, 1512 Western Ave., P.O. Box 1273, Seattle WA 98111. (206)622-4241. Fax: (206)622-6876. Publisher: William R. Griffin. Associate Editor: Jim Saunders. 80% freelance written. Quarterly magazine covering technical and management information relating to cleaning and self-employment. "We cater to those who are self-employed in any facet of the cleaning and maintenance industry and seek to be top professionals in their field. *Cleaning Business* is published for self-employed cleaning professionals, specifically carpet, upholstery and drapery cleaners; janitorial and maid services; window washers; odor, water and fire damage restoration contractors. Our readership is small but select. We seek concise, factual articles, realistic but definitely upbeat." Circ. 6,000. Pays 1 month after publication. Publishes ms an average of 3 months after acceptance. Byline given. Buys first serial, second serial (reprint) and all rights or makes work-for-hire assignments. Submit seasonal material 6 months in advance. Reports in 3 months. Sample copy for $3 and 8 × 10 SAE with 3 first-class stamps. Writer's guidelines for #10 SASE.

Nonfiction: Exposé (safety/health business practices); how-to (on cleaning, maintenance, small business management); humor (clean jokes, cartoons); interview/profile; new product (must be unusual to rate full article—mostly obtained from manufacturers); opinion; personal experience; technical. Special issues: "What's New?" (February). No "wordy articles written off the top of the head, obviously without research, and needing more editing time than was spent on writing." Buys 40 mss/year. Query with or without published clips. Length: 500-3,000 words. Pays $5-80. ("Pay depends on amount of work, research and polishing put into article much more than on length.") Pays expenses of writers on assignment with prior approval only.

Photos: State availability of photos or send photos with ms. Pays $5-25 for "smallish" b&w prints. Captions, model release and identification of subjects required. Buys one-time rights and reprint rights. "Magazine size is 8½ × 11—photos need to be proportionate. Also seeks full-color photos of relevant subjects for cover."

Columns/Departments: "Ten regular columnists now sell four columns per year to us. We are interested in adding Safety & Health and Fire Restoration columns (related to cleaning and maintenance industry). We are also open to other suggestions—send query." Buys 36 columns/year; department information obtained at no cost. Query with or without published clips. Length: 500-1,500 words. Pays $15-85.

Fillers: Jokes, gags, anecdotes, short humor, newsbreaks, cartoons. Buys 40/year. Length: 3-200 words. Pays $1-20.

Tips: "We are constantly seeking quality freelancers from all parts of the country. A freelancer can best break in to our publication with fairly technical articles on how to do specific cleaning/maintenance jobs; interviews with top professionals covering this and how they manage their business; and personal experience. Our readers demand concise, accurate information. Don't ramble. Write only about what you know and/or have researched. Editors don't have time to rewrite your rough draft. Organize and polish before submitting."

‡LAUNDRY NEWS, The Newspaper of Record for Institutional Launderers, 19 W. 21st St., New York NY 10010. (212)741-2095. Editor-in-Chief: Richard Merli. 10-15% freelance written. Monthly newspaper covering institutional laundries. "The newspaper is addressed to 16,000 managers of laundries in hotels, hospitals, prisons and other institutions." Estab. 1975. Circ. 16,000. Pays on publication. Publishes ms an average of 2-3 months after acceptance. Byline given. No kill fee. Buys first North American, first, or one-time rights or makes work-for-hire assignments. Editorial lead time 3 months. Submit seasonal material 3 months in advance. No simultaneous or previously published submissions. Query for electronic submissions. Reports in 1 week on queries. Sample copy and writer's guidelines for #10 SAE with 3 first-class stamps.

Nonfiction: Book excerpts, exposé, interview/profile, new product, photo feature, technical, hard news. Monthly special reports on technical subjects. Buys 15-20 mss/year. Query with published clips. Length: 600-2,000 words. Pays $300-400. Sometimes pays expenses of writers on assignment.

Photos: State availability of or send photos with submission. Reviews 5×7 prints. Negotiates payment individually. Captions, identification of subjects required. Buys all rights.

Columns/Departments: Film of Book Reviews (news), 500-750 words. Buys 6 mss/year or less. Query with published clips. Pays $300.

Tips: "Writers should have a sense of urgency and determination to ferret out the hard news angle on a story and to provide our readers with the critical information needed to make intelligent, informed decisions."

PEST CONTROL MAGAZINE, 7500 Old Oak Blvd., Cleveland OH 44130. (216)243-8100. Fax: (216)891-2675. Editor: Jerry Mix. Monthly magazine for professional pest control operators and sanitarians. Estab. 1933. Circ. 20,000. Buys all rights. Buys 12 mss/year. Pays on publication. Submit seasonal material 2 months in advance. Reports in 1 month. Query or submit complete ms.

Nonfiction: Business tips, unique control situations, personal experience (stories about pest control operations and their problems). Must have trade or business orientation. No general information type of articles desired. Buys 3 unsolicited mss/year. Length: 1,000 words. Pays $150-500 minimum. Regular columns use material oriented to this profession. Length: 2,000 words.

Photos: No additional payment for photos used with mss. Pays $50-150 for 8×10 color or transparencies.

PEST MANAGEMENT, National Pest Control Association, Inc., 8100 Oak St., Dunn Loring VA 22027-1097. (703)573-8330. Fax: (703)573-4116. Editor: Kathleen H. Bova. Assistant Editor: Joe Vallina. 30% freelance written. Monthly, except combined November/December issue trade journal. "Our readers are members of the structural pest control industry. They include owners/operators of large corporations and one-man operations, and professional entomologists. Our style is in between Barry and Buckley—not informal, but not high-brow." Estab. 1981. Circ. 5,500. Pays on publication. Publishes ms an average of 2 months after acceptance. Byline given. Buys all rights. Submit seasonal material 3 months in advance. Accepts simultaneous and previously published submissions. Send photocopy of article with rights for sale noted and information about when and where the article previously appeared. For reprints, pays 15¢/word. Electronic submissions formatted for Macintosh Microsoft Word or QuarkXpress. Reports in 2 months. Free sample copy and writer's guidelines.

Nonfiction: Book excerpts, how-to, interview/profile, opinion, personal experience, photo feature, technical, travel. Special issues planned on public relations, office equipment and office automation, safety, add-on business opportunities, ant, fleas, rodents, spiders and termites. No articles about specific products, general information articles. Buys 12 mss/year. Query with or without published clips, or send complete ms. Length: 1,500-5,000 words. Pays $150-500.

Photos: State availability of photos with submission. Reviews any size prints. Offers no additional payment for photos accepted with ms. Identification of subjects required.

Tips: "Tailor articles to our readership; leave technical articles to staff; concentrate on special issues; don't be afraid to contact us with innovative ideas."

SAFETY COMPLIANCE LETTER, with OSHA Highlights, Bureau of Business Practice, 24 Rope Ferry Rd., Waterford CT 06386. (203)442-4365. Fax: (203)434-3078. Editor: Michele Rubin. Publishers: James O'Shea. 80% freelance written. Bimonthly newsletter covering occupational safety and health. Publishes interview-based how-to and success stories for personnel in charge of safety and health in manufacturing/industrial environments. Circ. 15,000. Pays on acceptance after editing. Publishes ms an average of 3-6 months after acceptance. No byline given. Buys all rights. Submit seasonal material 4 months in advance. Reports in 1 month. Sample copy and writer's guidelines for SASE.

Nonfiction: How-to implement a particular occupational safety/health program, changes in OSHA regulations, and examples of exceptional safety/health programs. Only accepts articles that are based on an interview with a safety manager, safety consultant, occupational physician, or OSHA expert. Buys 48 mss/year. Query. Length: 750-1,200 words. Pays 10-15¢/word.

SECURITY SALES, Management Resource for the Professional Installing Dealer, Bobit Publishing, 2512 Artesia Blvd., Redondo Beach CA 90278-3296. (310)376-8788. Fax: (310)376-9043. Editor/Associate Publisher: Jason Knott. Senior Editor: Amy K. Jones. 5% freelance written. Monthly magazine that covers the security industry. "Editorial covers technology, management and marketing designed to help installing security dealers improve their businesses. Closed-circuit TV, burglary and fire equipment, and access control systems are main topics." Estab. 1979. Circ. 22,800. Pays on publication. Publishes ms an average of 3-6 months after acceptance. Byline sometimes given. Buys all rights. Editorial lead time 2 months. Submit seasonal material 4 months in advance. Query for electronic submissions. Accepts simultaneous submissions. Sample copy free on request.

Nonfiction: How-to, technical. "No generic business operations articles. Submissions must be specific to security and contain interviews with installing dealers." Buys 3-6 mss/year. Send complete ms. Length: 800-1,500 words. Pays $50 minimum.

Photos: Send photos with submission. Reviews prints. Offers no additional payment for photos accepted with ms. Captions, model releases and identification of subjects required.

Tips: "Case studies of specific security installations with photos and diagrams are needed. Interview dealers who installed system and ask how they solved specific problems, why they chose certain equipment, cost of job, etc."

Management and Supervision

This category includes trade journals for middle management business and industrial managers, including supervisors and office managers. Journals for business executives and owners are classified under Business Management. Those for industrial plant managers are listed in Industrial Operations.

‡COMPENSATION AND BENEFIT MANAGER'S REPORT, Bureau of Business Practice, 24 Rope Ferry Rd., Waterford CT 06386. Editor: Beth Stemple. 30% freelance written. Biweekly newsletter covering compensation and benefits. Estab. 1987. Circ. 4,000. **Pays on acceptance.** Publishes ms an average of 4 months after acceptance. No byline. Buys all rights. Editorial lead time 2 months. Submit seasonal material 6 months in advance. Accepts simultaneous submissions, if so noted. Query for electronic submissions. Reports in 3 weeks on queries, 2 months on mss. Sample copy and writer's guidelines free on request.
Nonfiction: How-to (compensation and benefits policy and practice). Buys 24 mss/year. Query. Length: 800-1,400 words. Pays 14-18¢/word plus one copy.
Tips: "Interview a compensatoin and benefits manager to find out how he or she has solved a problem, and then itemize the steps it takes to implement the problem-solving policy and practice."

EMPLOYEE RELATIONS AND HUMAN RESOURCES BULLETIN, Bureau of Business Practice, 24 Rope Ferry Rd., Waterford CT 06386. Fax: (203)434-3078. E-mail: 70303.2324@compuserve.com. Senior Editor: Beth Stemple. 40% freelance written. Works with a small number of new/unpublished writers each year. Semimonthly newsletter for personnel, human resource and employee relations managers on the executive level. Estab. 1940. Circ. 8,000. **Pays on acceptance.** Publishes ms an average of 3 months after acceptance. Buys all rights. No byline. Phone queries OK. Submit seasonal material 6 months in advance. Reports in 1 month. Sample copy and writer's guidelines free.
Nonfiction: Interviews about all types of business and industry such as banks, insurance companies, public utilities, airlines, consulting firms, etc. Interviewee should be a high level company officer—human resources executive, president, industrial relations manager, etc. Writer must get signed release from person interviewed showing that article has been read and approved by him/her, before submission. Some subjects for interviews might be productivity improvement, communications, compensation, labor relations, safety and health, grievance handling, human relations techniques and problems, etc. No general opinions and/or philosophy of good employee relations or general good motivation/morale material. Buys 1-2 mss/issue. Query is mandatory. Length: 800-2,000 words. Pays 14-18¢/word after editing. Sometimes pays the telephone expenses of writers on assignment. Modem transmission available by prior arrangement with editor.
Tips: "We are outsourcing more, which means we're looking for a wider variety of freelancers with solid knowledge of various business fields."

‡HR BRIEFING, (formerly *Personnel Manager's Letter*), Bureau of Business Practice, 24 Rope Ferry Rd., Waterford CT 06386. (203)442-4365, ext. 778. Editor: Jill Whitney. 75% freelance written. Eager to work with new/unpublished writers. Semimonthly newsletter emphasizing all aspects of personnel practices for personnel managers in all types and sizes of companies, both white collar and industrial. **Pays on acceptance.** Publishes ms an average of 5 months after acceptance. Buys all rights. Submit seasonal material 4 months in advance. Reports in 1 month. Sample copy and writer's guidelines for 10×13 SAE with 2 first class stamps; send request to Public Relations Department.
Nonfiction: Interviews with personnel managers or human resource professionals on topics of current interest in the personnel field. Buys 30 mss/year. Query with brief, specific outline. Length: 800-1,500 words.
Tips: "We're looking for concrete, practical material on how to solve problems. We're providing information about trends and developments in the field. We don't want filler copy. It's very easy to break in. Include your phone number with your query so we can discuss the topic. Send for guidelines first, though, so we can have a coherent conversation."

‡HUMAN RESOURCE EXECUTIVE, Axon Group, 747 Dresher Rd., P.O. Box 980, Dept. 500, Dresher PA 19044. (215)784-0860. E-mail: 75372.436@compuserve.com. Editor: David Shadovitz. 30% freelance written. Monthly magazine serving the information needs of chief human resource professionals/executives in companies, government agencies and nonprofit institutions with 500 or more employees." Estab. 1987. Circ. 45,000. **Pays on acceptance.** Publishes ms an average of 2 months after acceptance. Byline given. Offers 50% kill fee on assigned stories. Buys first and all rights including reprint rights. Query for electronic submissions. Reports in 1 month. Sample copy for 10×13 SAE with 2 first-class stamps. Writer's guidelines for #10 SAE with 1 first-class stamp.

Nonfiction: Book excerpts, interview/profile. Buys 16 mss/year. Query with published clips. Length: 1,700-2,400 words. Pays $200-700. Sometimes pays expenses of writers on assignment.

Photos: State availability of photos with submission. Reviews contact sheets. Offers no additional payment for photos accepted with ms. Identification of subjects required. Buys first and repeat rights.

‡PRODUCTION MANAGEMENT BULLETIN, Bureau of Business Practice, 24 Rope Ferry Rd., Waterford CT 06386. (800)243-0876. Fax: (203)434-3078. 75% freelance written. Biweekly newsletter for production/manufacturing managers primarily. "Articles are meant to address a common workplace issue faced by such managers (absenteeism, low productivity, improving quality, ensuring safety, etc.) and explain how readers may deal with the issue. **Pays on acceptance.** Publishes ms an average of 4 months after acceptance. Byline not given. Buys all rights. Reports in 2 weeks on queries; 3 weeks on mss. *Writer's Market* recommends allowing 2 months for reply. Free sample copy and writer's guidelines.

Nonfiction: How-to (on managing people, solving workplace problems, improving productivity). No high-level articles aimed at upper management. Buys 60-70 mss/year. Query. Length: 800-1,500 words. Pays 9-15¢/word.

Tips: Freelancers may call the editor at (800)243-0876. Prospective writers are strongly urged to send for writer's guidelines. Sections of publication most open to freelancers are lead story; inside stories (generally 3-4 per issue); and Production Management Clinic (in every other issue). Include concrete, how-to steps for dealing effectively with the topic at hand.

SALES MANAGER'S BULLETIN, The Bureau of Business Practice, 24 Rope Ferry Rd., Waterford CT 06386-0001. Fax: (203)434-3078. Editor: Paulette S. Kitchens. 33% freelance written. Prefers to work with published/established writers. Semimonthly newsletter for sales managers and salespeople interested in getting into sales management. Estab. 1917. **Pays on acceptance.** Publishes ms an average of 3-6 months after acceptance. Written queries only except from regulars. Submit seasonal material 6 months in advance. Original interview-based material only. Buys all rights. Reports in 1 month. Sample copy and writer's guidelines only when request is accompanied by SAE with 2 first-class stamps.

Nonfiction: How-to (motivate salespeople, cut costs, create territories, etc.); interview (with working sales managers who use innovative techniques); technical (marketing stories based on interviews with experts). No articles on territory management, saving fuel in the field, or public speaking skills. Break into this publication by reading the guidelines and sample issue. Follow the directions closely and chances for acceptance go up dramatically. One easy way to start is with an interview article ("Here's what sales executives have to say about . . ."). Query is vital to acceptance: "Send a simple note explaining briefly the subject matter, the interviewees, slant, length, and date of expected completion, accompanied by a SASE. Does not accept unqueried mss. Length: 800-1,000 words. Pays 10-15¢/word, edited copy.

Tips: "Freelancers should always request samples and writer's guidelines, accompanied by SASE. Requests without SASE are discarded immediately. Examine the sample, and don't try to improve on our style. Write as we write. Don't 'jump around' from point to point and don't submit articles that are too chatty and with not enough real information. The more time a writer can save the editors, the greater his or her chance of a sale and repeated sales, when queries may no longer be necessary. We will focus more on selling more product, meeting intense competition, customer relations/partnerships, and sales forecasting."

SECURITY MANAGEMENT BULLETIN: Protecting People, Property & Assets, Bureau of Business Practice, 24 Rope Ferry Rd., Waterford CT 06386. Editor: Alex Vaughn. 75% freelance written. Eager to work with new/unpublished writers. Semi-monthly newsletter emphasizing security for industry. "All material should be slanted toward security directors, primarily industrial, retail and service businesses, but others as well." Circ. 3,000. Pays when article assigned to future issue. Buys all rights. Phone queries OK. Free sample copy and writer's guidelines.

Nonfiction: Interview (with security professionals only). "Articles should be tight and specific. They should deal with new security techniques or new twists on old ones." Buys 2-5 mss/issue. Query. Length: 750-1,000 words. Pays 15¢/word.

TODAY'S LEADER, (formerly *Supervisor's Bulletin*), Bureau of Business Practice, 24 Rope Ferry Rd., Waterford CT 06386-0001. (203)442-4365, ext. 783. Fax: (203)434-3078. Editor: Phred Mileski. 50-75% freelance written. "We work with both new and established writers, and are always looking for fresh talent." Monthly newsletter for mid-level, blue collar supervisors/managers in the manufacturing and service industries who wish to improve their leadership skills. Estab. 1915. **Pays on acceptance.** Publishes ms an average of 3 months after acceptance. No byline given. Buys all rights. Reports in 2 weeks on queries; 6 weeks on mss. Free sample copy and writer's guidelines.

ALWAYS enclose a self-addressed, stamped envelope (SASE) with all your queries and correspondence.

Nonfiction: How-to (solve a supervisory problem on the job or avoid litigation); interview (of top-notch supervisors or experts who can give advice on supervisory issues). Sample topics could include: how to increase productivity, cut costs, achieve better teamwork, and step-by-step approaches to problem-solving. No filler or non-interview based copy. Buys 36 mss/year. Query first. "Strongly urge writers to study guidelines and samples." Length: 750 words. Pays 12-18¢/word.

Tips: "We need interview-based articles that emphasize direct quotes. Define a problem and show how the supervisor solved it. Write in a light, conversational style, talking directly to supervisors who can benefit from putting the interviewee's tips into practice."

TRAINING MAGAZINE, Lakewood Publications, 50 S. Ninth St., Minneapolis MN 55402. (612)333-0471. Fax: (612)333-6526. Editor: Jack Gordon. Managing Editor: Chris Lee. 10% freelance written. Monthly magazine covering training and employee development in the business world. "Our core readers are managers and professionals who specialize in employee training and development (e.g., corporate training directors, VP-human resource development, etc.). We have a large secondary readership among managers of all sorts who are concerned with improving human performance in their organizations. We take a businesslike approach to training and employee education." Estab. 1964. Circ. 56,000. **Pays on acceptance.** Publishes ms an average of 3 months after acceptance. Byline given. Buys first North American serial and second serial (reprint) rights. Accepts simultaneous submissions. Reports in 2 weeks on queries; 6 weeks on mss. Sample copy for 9×12 SAE with 4 first-class stamps. Writer's guidelines for #10 SASE.

Nonfiction: Essay; exposé; how-to (on training, management, sales, productivity improvement, etc.); humor; interview/profile; new product; opinion; photo feature; technical (use of audiovisual aids, computers, etc.). "No puff, no 'testimonials' or disguised ads in any form, no 'gee-whiz' approaches to the subjects." Buys 10-12 mss/year. Query with or without published clips, or send complete ms. Length: 200-3,000 words. Pays $50-750.

Photos: State availability of photos or send with submission. Reviews contact sheets and prints. Offers no additional payment for photos accepted with ms. Identification of subjects required. Buys one-time rights and reprint rights.

Columns/Departments: Training Today (news briefs, how-to tips, reports on pertinent research, trend analysis, etc.), 200-800 words. Buys 6 mss/year. Query or send complete ms. Pays $50-125.

Tips: "We almost never give firm assignments to unfamiliar writers, so you have to be willing to hit us with one or two on spec to break in. Short pieces for our Training Today section involve least investment on your part, but also are less likely to convince us to assign you a feature. When studying the magazine, freelancers should look at our staff-written articles for style, approach and tone. Do not concentrate on articles written by people identified as consultants, training directors, etc."

WAREHOUSE MANAGEMENT SOLUTIONS, (formerly *Warehousing Supervisor's Bulletin*), Bureau of Business Practice, 24 Rope Ferry Rd., Waterford CT 06386-0001. (203)442-4365. Fax: (203)434-2546. Editor: Peter Hawkins. 50-75% freelance written. "We work with a variety of writers, and we are always looking for fresh talent." Biweekly newsletter for warehouse managers and supervisors interested in becoming more effective on the job. **Pays on acceptance.** Publishes ms an average of 3 months after acceptance. No byline given. Buys all rights. No simultaneous submissions. Reports in 2 weeks on queries; 6 weeks on mss. Free sample copy and writer's guidelines.

Nonfiction: How-to (increase efficiency, control or cut costs, cut absenteeism or tardiness, increase productivity, raise morale); interview (of warehouse supervisors or managers who have solved problems on the job). No noninterview articles, textbook-like descriptions, union references or advertising of products. Buys 50 mss/year. Query. Length: 1,000-1,600 words. Pays 12-17¢/word.

Tips: "All articles must be interview-based and emphasize how-to information. They should also include a reference to the interviewee's company (location, size, products, function of the interviewee's department, and number of employees). Focus articles on one problem, and get the interviewee to pinpoint the best way to solve it. Appropriate artwork (charts, forms, photos) helpful. Write in a light, conversational style, talking directly to the reader who will benefit from putting the interviewee's tips into practice."

Marine and Maritime Industries

CHARTER INDUSTRY, The Management Magazine for the Charter Industry, Charter Industry Services, Inc., 43 Kindred St., P.O. Box 375, Stuart FL 34995-0375. (407)288-1066. Fax: (407)288-5015. Editor: Paul McElroy. 50% freelance written. Bimonthly trade journal that covers legislative and industry issues. "*CI* is not a consumer 'Let's go on a fishing trip' publication, but is a business publication for people in the charter business, including sportfishing, diving, excursion and sailing charters." Estab. 1985. Circ. 10,750. Pays on publication. Byline given. Buys all rights and makes work-for-hire assignments. Accepts previously published submissions. Send tearsheet of article or typed ms with rights for sale noted and information about when and where the article previously appeared. For reprints, pays 25% of the amount paid for an original article. Reports in 2 weeks on queries. Sample copy for 9×12 SAE with 6 first-class stamps. Writer's guidelines for #10 SAE with 2 first-class stamps.

Nonfiction: Historical/nostalgic, how-to, humor, inspirational, interview/profile, opinion. No fishing stories. Buys 24 mss/year. Query with published clips. Length: 800-2,000 words. Pays $75-150. Sometimes pays expenses of writers on assignment.

Photos: State availability of photos with submission or send photos with submission. Reviews 5×7 prints. Offers no additional payment for photos accepted with ms. Captions, model releases and identification of subjects required. Buys one-time rights.

Columns/Departments: Taxes, Legal, Photography. Buys 12 mss/year. Query. Length: 600 words.

Tips: "Writers should know that the readers are professional captains who depend upon their boats and the sea to make their living. They demand the writer know the subject and the application to the industry. Those without knowledge of the industry should save their postage." Areas most open to freelancers are "personal profiles of sucessful charter captains and charter ports. We have guidelines for articles on both subjects. Most freelancer submissions are rejected because they don't do their homework properly. Our readers are tough taskmasters. Don't try to fool them!"

MARINE BUSINESS JOURNAL, The Voice of the Marine Industries Nationwide, 1766 Bay Rd., Miami Beach FL 33139. (305)538-0700. Fax: (305)532-8657. Editorial Director: Andree Conrad. Contact: Jim Murphy. 25% freelance written. Bimonthly tabloid that covers the recreational boating industry. *"The Marine Business Journal* is aimed at boating dealers, distributors and manufacturers, naval architects, yacht brokers, marina owners and builders, marine electronics dealers, distributors and manufacturers, and anyone involved in the US marine industry. Articles cover news, new product technology and public affairs affecting the industry." Estab. 1986. Circ. 26,000. Pays on publication. Publishes ms an average of 1 month after acceptance. Byline given. Buys first North American serial, one-time or second serial (reprint rights). Query for electronic submissions. Reports in 2 weeks on queries. Sample copy for $2.50 and 9×12 SAE with 7 first-class stamps. Writer's guidelines for #10 SASE.

Nonfiction: Buys 20 mss/year. Query with published clips. Length: 500-2,000 words. Pays $100-200 for assigned articles. Sometimes pays expenses of writers on assignment.

Photos: State availability of photos with submission. Reviews 35mm or larger transparencies and 5×7 prints. Offers $25-50/photo. Captions, model releases and identification of subjects required. Buys one-time rights.

Tips: "Query with clips. It's a highly specialized field, written for professionals by professionals, almost all on assignment or by staff."

OCEAN NAVIGATOR, Marine Navigation & Ocean Voyaging, Navigator Publishing Corp., 18 Danforth St., Portland ME 04101. (207)772-2466. Editor: Tim Queeney. Bimonthly magazine covering marine navigation and ocean voyaging. Estab. 1985. Circ. 40,600. Pays on publication. Byline given. Accepts simultaneous and previously published submissions. Send typed ms with rights for sale noted and information about when and where the article previously appeared. Electronic submissions recommended. Writer's guidelines available on request.

Nonfiction: How-to, personal experience, technical. No racing (except navigational challenges); no travel logs/diaries. Query or send complete ms. Pays 15¢/word up to $500.

Photos: Send photos with submission. Offers $50-75/photo; $400 for cover photo.

Medical

Through these journals physicians, therapists and mental health professionals learn how other professionals help their patients and manage their medical practices. Publications for nurses, laboratory technicians and other medical personnel are listed in the Hospitals, Nursing and Nursing Home section. Publications for drug store managers and drug wholesalers and retailers, as well as hospital equipment suppliers, are listed with Drugs, Health Care and Medical Products. Publications for consumers that report trends in the medical field are found in the Consumer Health and Fitness categories.

‡ALTERNATIVE THERAPIES IN HEALTH AND MEDICINE, InnoVision Communications, 101 Columbia, Aliso Viejo CA 92656. (800)899-1712. Publisher: Bonnie Horrigan. Managing Editor: Michael Villaire. Contact: Editorial Assistant. 10% freelance written. Bimonthly magazine covering alternative/complementary health care for the practitioner. *"AT* is a forum for sharing information concerning the practical use of alternative therapies in preventing and treating disease, healing illness and promoting health. We publish a variety of disciplined inquiry methods, including high quality scientific research. We encourage the integration of alternative therapies with conventional medical practices. Our audience is primary care physicians and nurses, and alternative health care practitioners. Stories should provide useful information for them." Estab. 1994. Circ. 20,000. **Pays on acceptance.** Publishes ms an average of 3 months after acceptance. Offers 50% kill fee. Buys first North american serial and second serial (reprint) rights. Editorial lead time 3 months. Submit seasonal material 6 months in advance. Query for electronic submissions. Reports in 1 month on queries; 2 months on mss. Sample copy for $10. Writer's guidelines for #10 SASE.

Nonfiction: News of interest to practitioner. No consumer-oriented articles, weight-loss plans, personal experiences. Buys 6 mss/year. Query with published clips. Length: 500-1,200 words. Pays $500-750.

Photos: State availability of photos with submissions. Reviews contact sheets. Negotiates payment individually. Model releases, identification of subjects required. Buys one-time and reprint rights.

Fillers: Newsbreaks, short humor. Buys 6-12/year. Length: 100-250 words. Pays $25-100.

Tips: "Remember who our audience is—health care practitioners. Spot, and report thoroughly and responsibly on trends in the field that would interest and be of use to our audience. A recent issue had stories on insurance programs that cover alternative therapies, and medical school that teach courses on alternative medicine to students."

AMERICAN MEDICAL NEWS, American Medical Association, Dept. WM, 515 N. State St., Chicago IL 60610. (312)464-4429. Fax: (312)464-4445. Editor: Barbara Bolsen. Contact Topic Editor: Ronni Scheier, Public Health and Physician Well-Being; Howard Larkin, Health Systems Finance & Delivery (edits business section, which publishes service features intended to help doctors run their medical practices more effectively); Bill Silberg, Professional Issues; Mary O'Connell, Health Systems Trends/Health System Reform. 5-10% freelance written. "Prefers writers experienced at covering health policy and public health issues—not clinical medicine." Weekly tabloid providing physician readers with news, information and analysis of issues and trends affecting the practice of medicine. "The aim is to help them understand and react effectively to events and trends. This is a well-educated, highly sophisticated physician audience." Circ. 375,000 physicians. **Pays on acceptance.** Publishes ms an average of 2 months after acceptance. Offers variable kill fee. Buys first North American rights. Reports in 1 month. Sample copy for 9×12 SAE with 2 first-class stamps. Free writer's guidelines.

Tips: "An understanding of our publication and its needs is crucial for the successful query."

CARDIOLOGY WORLD NEWS, Medical Publishing Enterprises, P.O. Box 1548, Marco Island FL 33969. (813)394-0400. Fax: (813)394-0400. Editor: John H. Lavin. 75% freelance written. Prefers to work with published/established writers. Monthly magazine covering cardiology and the cardiovascular system. "We need short news articles *for doctors* on any aspect of our field—diagnosis, treatment, risk factors, etc." Estab. 1985. **Pays on acceptance.** Publishes ms an average of 2 months after acceptance. Byline given "for special reports and feature-length articles." Offers 20% kill fee. Buys first North American serial rights. Query for electronic submissions. Reports in 2 months. Sample copy for $1. Free writer's guidelines with #10 SASE.

Nonfiction: New product and technical (clinical). No fiction, fillers, profiles of doctors or poetry. Query with published clips. Length: 250-1,200 words. Pays $50-300; $50/column for news articles. Pays expenses of writers on assignment.

Photos: State availability of photos with query. Pays $50/published photo. Rough captions, model release and identification of subjects required. Buys one-time rights.

Tips: "Submit written news articles of 250-500 words on speculation with basic source material (not interview notes) for fact-checking. We demand clinical or writing expertise for full-length feature. Clinical cardiology conventions/symposia are the best source of news and feature articles."

‡CINCINNATI MEDICINE, Academy of Medicine, 320 Broadway, Cincinnati OH 45234-9506. (513)421-7010. Fax: (513)721-4378. Associate Editor: Pamela G. Fairbanks. Editor: Rhonda Tepe. One freelance article/issue. Works with a small number of new/unpublished writers each year. Monthly membership newspaper for the Academy of Medicine of Cincinnati covering socio-economic and political factors that affect the practice of medicine in Cincinnati. For example: Effects of Medicare changes on local physicians and patients. (99% of readers are Cincinnati physicians.) Estab. 1978. Circ. 3,000. **Pays on acceptance.** Publishes ms an average of 1 month after acceptance. Byline given. Makes work-for-hire assignments. Reports in 6 weeks on queries; 3 months on mss. Accepts simultaneous submissions. Send photocopy of article and information about when and where the article previously appeared. For reprints, pays not more than $400. Sample copy for $3 and 9×12 SAE with 9 first-class stamps. Writer's guidelines for #10 SASE.

● *Cincinnati Medicine* reports that in January 1995 they switched to a tabloid newspaper format, making stories shorter and newsier.

Nonfiction: Historical/nostalgic (history of, or reminiscences about, medicine in Cincinnati); interview/profile (of medical leaders in Cincinnati); opinion (opinion pieces on controversial medico-legal and medico-ethical issues). "We do not accept scientific/research articles." Buys 12 mss/year. Query with published clips or send complete ms. Length: 500-750 words. Pays $125-400.

Photos: State availability of photos with query or ms. Captions and identification of subjects required. Buys one-time rights.

Tips: Send published clips. "We emphasize solid reporting and accurate, well-balanced analysis."

EMERGENCY, The Journal of Emergency Services, 6300 Yarrow Dr., Carlsbad CA 92009-1597. (619)438-2511. Fax: (619)931-5809. Editor: Doug Fiske. 100% freelance written. Works with a small number of new/unpublished writers each year. Monthly magazine covering prehospital emergency care. "Our readership is primarily composed of EMTs, paramedics and other EMS personnel. We prefer a professional, semi-technical approach to prehospital subjects." Estab. 1969. Circ. 30,000. **Pays on acceptance.** Publishes ms an average of 4 months after acceptance. Byline given. Buys all rights (revert to author after 3 months). Submit seasonal material 6 months in advance. Reports in 2-3 months. Sample copy for $3. Writer's guidelines for #10 SASE.

Nonfiction: Semi-technical exposé, how-to (on treating prehospital emergency patients), interview/profile, new techniques, opinion, photo feature. "We do not publish cartoons, term papers, product promotions disguised as articles or overly technical manuscripts." Buys 60 mss/year. Query with published clips. Length 1,500-3,000 words. Pays $100-400.

Photos: Send photos with submission. Reviews color transparencies and b&w prints. Photos accepted with mss increase payment. Offers $30/photo without ms; $100 for cover photos. Captions and identification of subjects required. All medics pictured must be using universal precautions (gloves, etc.).

Columns/Departments: Open Forum (opinion page for EMS professionals), 750-800 words; Skills Primer (basic skills, how-to with photos), 1,000-2,000 words; Rescue Call (cover a specific rescue or technique); Drug Watch (focus on one particular drug a month). Buys 10 mss/year. Query first. Pays $50-250.

Fillers: Facts, newsbreaks. Buys 10/year. Length: no more than 500 words. Pays $0-75.

Tips: "Writing style for features and departments should be knowledgeable and lively with a clear theme or story line to maintain reader interest and enhance comprehension. The biggest problem we encounter is dull, lifeless term-paper-style writing with nothing to pique reader interest. Keep in mind we are not a textbook, but all technical articles must be well referenced with footnotes within the text. We follow AP style. Accompanying photos are a plus.We appreciate a short, one paragraph biography on the author."

FACETS, American Medical Association Alliance, Inc., 515 N. State St., Chicago IL 60610. (312)464-4470. Fax: (312)464-5839. Editor: Kathleen T. Jordan. 25% freelance written. Work with both established and new writers. Bimonthly magazine for physicians' spouses. Estab. 1965. Circ. 65,000. **Pays on acceptance.** Publishes ms an average of 6 months after acceptance. Buys first rights. Accepts simultaneous and previously published submissions. Reports in 2 months. Sample copy and writer's guidelines for 9 × 12 SAE with 2 first-class stamps.

Nonfiction: All articles must be related to the experiences of physicians' spouses. Current health issues; financial topics, physicians' family circumstances, business management and volunteer leadership how-to's. Buys 10 mss/year. Query with clear outline of article—what points will be made, what conclusions drawn, what sources will be used. No personal experience or personality stories. Length: 1,000-2,500 words. Pays $300-800. Pays expenses of writers on assignment.

Photos: State availability of photos with query. Uses 8 × 10 glossy b&w prints and 2¼ × 2¼ transparencies.

Tips: Uses "articles only on specified topical matter with good sources, not hearsay or personal opinion. Since we use only nonfiction and have a limited readership, we must relate factual material."

HMO, Group Health Association of America, 1129 20th St. NW, Suite 600, Washington DC 20036. (202)778-3250. Fax: (202)331-7487. Editor: Susan Pisano. Contact: Diana Madden. 35% freelance written. Bimonthly magazine for news and analysis of the health maintenance organization (HMO) industry. "*HMO* magazine is geared toward senior administrative and medical managers in HMOs. Articles must succinctly and clearly define issues of concern or news to the HMO industry. Articles must ask 'why' and 'how' and answer with examples. Articles should inform and generate interest and discussion about topics on anything from medical management to regulatory issues." Estab. 1990. Circ. 6,000. Pays 30 days within acceptance of article in final form. Publishes ms an average of 2 months after acceptance. Byline given. Offers 30% kill fee. Buys all rights. Editorial lead time 2 months. Submit seasonal material 2 months in advance. Accepts simultaneous submissions. Query for electronic submissions. Reports in 1 month on queries. Sample copy and writer's guidelnes free on request.

Nonfiction: How-to (how industry professionals can better operate their health plans), opinion. "We do not accept any articles relating to clinical health issues, such as nutrition or any general health topics that do not address issues of concern to HMO administrators; nor do we accept stories that promote products." Buys 20 mss/year. Query. Length: 1,800-2,500 words. Pays 40¢/word minimum for assigned articles; 35¢/word minimum for unsolicited articles. Pays phone expenses of writers on assignment.

Photos: State availability of photos with submission. Reviews contact sheets. Offers no additional payment for photos accepted with ms. Buys all rights.

Columns/Departments: Washington File (health policy issues relating to HMOs and managed health care), 1,800 words; Preventive Care (case study or discussion of public health HMOs), 1,800 words; The Market (market niches for HMOs—with examples), 1,800 words. Buys 6 mss/year. Query with published clips. Pays 35-50¢/word.

Tips: "Follow the current health care debate. Look for HMO success stories in your community; we like to include case studies on everything from medical management to regulatory issues so that our readers can learn from their colleagues. Our readers are members of our trade association and look for advice and news. Topics relating to the quality and cost benefits of HMOs are the ones most frequently assigned to writers, whether a feature or department. For example, a recent story on 'The High Price of Compliance' relating to costs associated with not complying with prescription advice, got a lot of reader interest. The writer interviewed a number of experts inside and outside the HMO field."

JEMS, The Journal of Emergency Medical Services, Jems Communications, Suite 200, 1947 Camino Vida Roble, Carlsbad CA 92008-2789. (619)431-9797. Fax: (619)431-8176. Executive Editor: Keith Griffiths. Senior Editor: Nancy Hays. 25% freelance written. Monthly magazine for emergency medical services—all phases. The journal is directed to the personnel who serve the emergency medicine industry: paramedics, EMTs, emergency physicians and nurses, administrators, EMS consultants, etc. Estab. 1980. Circ. 35,000. Pays on publication. Publishes ms an average of 3-6 months after acceptance. Byline given. Buys all North American serial rights. Submit seasonal material 6 months in advance. Query for electronic submissions. Reports in 2 months. Free sample copy and writer's guidelines.
Nonfiction: Essays, general interest, how-to (prehospital care), continuing education, humor, interview/profile, new product, opinion, photo feature, technical. Buys 18 mss/year. Query. Length: 900-3,600 words. Pays $150-400.
  • *JEMS* has an increased need for investigative reporters who can cover system politics, trends and product concerns and have a strong EMS knowledge base.
Photos: State availability of photos with submission. Offers no additional payment for photos accepted with ms. Buys one-time rights.
Columns/Departments: Teacher Talk (directed toward EMS instructors), 2,400 words; Manager's Forum (EMS administrators), 1,500-2,000 words; First Person (personal accounts of life in EMS); Law and Policy (legislative reports).
Tips: "Feature articles are most open to freelancers. We have guidelines available upon request and, of course, manuscripts must be geared toward our specific EMS audience."

‡MANAGED CARE, A Guide for Physicians, Stezzi Communications, Inc., 301 Oxford Valley Rd., Suite 1105A, Yardley PA 19067. (215)321-5480. Editor: Patrick Mullen. Contact: Timothy Kelley. 75% freelance written. Monthly magazine covering primary care physicians who are involved in managed care. "We emphasize practical, usable information that helps the family physician, internist or other physician cope with the ever more complex array of options, challenges and hazards that accompanies the rapidly changing health care industry. Our regular readers understand that "health care reform" isn't a piece of legislation; it's an evolutionary process that's already well under way. But we hope to help our readers also keep the faith that led them to medicine in the first place." Estab. 1992. Circ. 78,000. **Pays on acceptance.** Publishes ms an average of 1 month after acceptance. Byline given. Offers 20% kill fee. Buys all rights. Editorial lead time 3 months. Submit seasonal material 4 months in advance. Reports in 3 weeks on queries; 2 months on mss. Sample copy free.
Nonfiction: Book excerpts, general interest, how-to (deal with requisites of managed care, such as contracts with health plans, affiliation arrangements, relationships with staffers, computer needs, etc.), humor, interview/profile, opinion, personal experience, technical. Buys 35 mss/year. Query. Length: 1,000-3,000 words. Pays $1,000-1,500 for assigned articles; $100-1,000 for unsolicited articles. Pays expenses of writers on assignment.
Photos: State availability of photos with submissions. Reviews contact sheets, negatives, transparencies, prints. Negotiates payment individually. Buys one-time rights.
Columns/Departments: Paul Wynn. News/Commentary (usually staff-written, but regional editions, may increase needs in 95). 100-300 words. Pays $50-100.
Tips: "We're looking for reliable freelancers who can write for our audience with our approach, so 'breaking in' may yield assignments. Do this by writing impeccably and with flair, and try to reflect the practicing physician's interests and perspective. (Cardinal rule: That physician is busy, with many things vying for his/her reading time. Be sprightly, but don't waste our readers' time.)"

MANAGED HEALTHCARE, Advanstar Communications, 7500 Old Oak Blvd., Cleveland OH 44130. (216)891-2703. Fax: (216)891-2683. Editor: Margaret Mulligan. Managing Editor: Timothy N. Troy. 75% freelance written. Monthly trade magazine covering managed health care industry. "We cover the spectrum of managed health care, including news, finance, technology and in-depth analysis of buyer and provider issues." Estab. 1991. Circ. 42,500. **Pays on acceptance.** Publishes ms an average of 2 months after acceptance. Byline given. Editorial lead time 2 months. Query for electronic submissions. Sample copy not available.
Nonfiction: Buys 85 mss/year. Query by mail. Length: 750-3,000 words. Fee negotiated. Sometimes pays expenses of writers on assignment.
Photos: State availability of photos or send photos with submission. Reviews prints. Negotiates payment individually. Identification of subjects required. Buys one-time North American rights.
Columns/Departments: Margaret Mulligan, editor. Commentary (expert opinion on managed care issues), 750-1,000 words. Query.
Tips: News section is most open to freelancers.

MEDICAL IMAGING, The Business Magazine for Technology Management, 10 Risho Ave, East Providence RI 02916. (401)434-1050. Fax: (401)434-1090. Editor: Jack Spears. Contact: Mary Tierney, news and business editor. 5% freelance written. Monthly magazine covering diagnostic imaging equipment. "Our editorial statement is to provide cost-effective solutions to the maintenance and management of diagnostic imaging equipment. Articles should address this." Estab. 1986. Circ. 18,000. **Pays on acceptance.** Publishes ms an average of 2 months after acceptance. Byline given. Offers 50% kill fee. Buys all rights. Editorial lead time 2 months. Responds to query letters, "as soon as possible." Sample copy for $10 prepaid. Writer's guidelines for #10 SASE.
Nonfiction: Interview/profile, technical. "No general interest/human interest stories about healthcare. Articles *must* deal with our industry-diagnostic imaging." Buys 6 mss/year. Query with published clips. Length: 1,500-2,500 words. Pays approximately 25¢/word. Sometimes pays expenses of writers on assignment.
Photos: State availability of photos with submission. Reviews negatives. Offers no additional payment for photos accepted with ms "unless assigned separately." Model releases and identification of subjects required. Buys all rights.
Tips: "Send a letter with an interesting story idea that is applicable to our industry, diagnostic imaging. Then follow up with a phone call. Areas most open to freelancers are feature and technology. You don't have to be an engineer or doctor but you have to know how to talk and listen to them."

THE NEW PHYSICIAN, 1890 Preston White Dr., Reston VA 22091-4325. Editor: Laura Milani. 40% freelance written. Magazine published 9 times/year for medical students, interns, residents and educators. Circ. 30,000. **Pays on acceptance.** Publishes an average of 3 months after acceptance. Accepts simultaneous and previously published submissions. Send photocopy of article and information about when and where the article previously appeared. For reprints, pay varies. Publishes novel excerpts. Reports in 2 months. Sample copy for 10×13 SAE with 5 first-class stamps. Writer's guidelines for SASE.
Nonfiction: Articles on social, political, economic issues in medical education/health care. Buys about 12 features/year. Query or send complete ms. Length: 800-3,500 words. Pays 25-50¢/word with higher fees for selected pieces. Pays expenses of writers on assignment.
Tips: "Although we are published by an association (the American Medical Student Association), we are not a 'house organ.' We are a professional magazine for readers with a progressive view on health care issues and a particular interest in improving medical education and the health care system. Our readers demand sophistication on the issues we cover. Freelancers should be willing to look deeply into the issues in question and not be satisfied with a cursory review of those issues."

‡OPTICAL PRISM, VezCom Inc., 31 Hastings Dr., Unionville Ontario L3R 4Y5 Canada. (905)475-9343. Editor: Allan K. Vezina. 50% freelance written. Magazine published 9 times/year covering a wide variety of material including contact lens fitting, eyeglass and contact lens dispensing, practice management, marketing and merchandising articles, as well as wholesale and retail 'success stories.' " Estab. 1983. Circ. 7,883. **Pays on acceptance.** Publishes ms an average of 4 months after acceptance. Offers 100% kill fee. Buys first, one-time and second serial (reprint) rights. Editorial lead time 4 months. Submit seasonal material 5 months in advance. Accepts simultaneous and previously published submissions. For reprints, pays 3¢/word to a maximum of $200 (Canadian). Reports in 2 weeks on story outlines; 1 month on mss. Sample copy free on request.
Nonfiction: Essays, exposé, general interest, historical/nostalgic, how-to (fit contact lens types, fit eyeglasses, grind lenses, etc.), humor, inspirational, interview/profile, new product (full article only), personal experience, photo feature, technical. Buys 15-20 mss/year. Send complete ms, story outline. Length: 1,500-10,000 words. Pays 10¢/word to a maximum of $500 (Canadian).
Photos: Send photos with submission. Reviews transparencies. Offers no additional payment for photos accepted with ms. Captions, model releases, identification of subjects required. Buys one-time rights.
Tips: "Writers should remember they are writing for doctors of optometry and doctors of medicine—therefore, standards should be very high to reflect the educational backgrounds of the readers."

‡OPTOMETRIC ECONOMICS, American Optometric Association, 243 N. Lindbergh Blvd., St. Louis MO 63141. (314)991-4100. Contact: Gene Mitchell, managing editor. 90% freelance written. Quarterly magazine covering practice management for optometrists. "Feature articles with strong 'how-to' slant that cover nuts and bolts of specific issues: business/financial management, marketing, staff management, dispensing, patient communication, managed care, comanagement of refractive surgery, insurance payor issues, computers, computerized equipment and other technology, office management, office design, etc. Articles should offer practical resources/information. Style is conversational, not stuffy or overly clinical. Stories that promote products not accepted." Estab. 1991. Circ. 29,000. **Pays on acceptance.** Publishes ms an average of 3 months after acceptance. Buys first, second serial (reprint and all rights, or makes work-for-hire assignments. Editorial lead time 3 months. Submit seasonal material 5 months in advance. Query for electronic submissions. Reports in 2 weeks on queries; 1 month on mss. Sample copy for $5. Writer's guidelines for #10 SASE.
Nonfiction: How-to (practice/business management, opinion, photo feature, technical. Buys 30 mss/year. Query with published clips. Length: 1,200-3,000 words. Pays $200-600 for assigned articles; $80-250 for unsolicited articles. Sometimes pays expenses of writers on assignment.

Photos: State availability of photos with submissions. Reviews contact sheets, transparencies, prints. Captions, model releases, identification of subjects required. Buys one-time or all rights.
Columns/Departments: Computing (software and computerized ophthalmic equipment), 500-1,200 words. Query with published clips. Pays $100-250.
Fillers: Anecdotes, facts, gags to be illustrated by cartoonist, short humor. Buys 3/year. Length: 10-50 words. Pays $0-25.
Tips: "Our readers are practicing professionals who need in-depth exploration of specific practice management topics. Avoid overly general or elementary articles, e.g., "Top Ten Ways to Market your Practice." We usually avoid 'generalist' freelancers in favor of writers who've specialized in a given area or areas. Submit letter of inquiry and/or article outline. Show that you've read the magazine and have made an effort to understand readers' needs and the profession of optometry."

‡THE PHYSICIAN AND SPORTSMEDICINE, McGraw-Hill, 4530 W. 77th St., Edina MN 55435. (612)835-3222. Managing Editor: Terry Monahan. 15% freelance written. Prefers to work with published/established writers. Monthly magazine covering medical aspects of sports and exercise. "We publish articles that are of practical, clinical interest to our physician audience." Estab. 1973. Circ. 130,000. **Pays on acceptance.** Publishes ms an average of 4 months after acceptance. Byline given. Generally buys all rights. Reports in 2 months. Sample copy for $8. Writer's guidelines for #10 SASE.
  ● This publication is relying more heavily on the clinical component of the journal, meaning review articles written by physicians who have expertise in a specific specialty.
Nonfiction: New developments and issues in sports medicine. Query. Length: 250-2,500 words. Pays $150-1,200.
Photos: Carol Johnson, photo editor. State availability of photos. Buys one-time rights.

PHYSICIAN'S MANAGEMENT, Advantar Communications, 7500 Old Oak Blvd., Cleveland OH 44130. (216)243-8100. Fax: (216)891-2683. Editor-in-Chief: Bob Feigenbaum. Prefers to work with published/ established writers. Monthly magazine emphasizing finances, investments, malpractice, socioeconomic issues, estate and retirement planning, small office administration, practice management, computers and taxes for primary care physicians in private practice. Estab. 1960. Circ. 120,000. **Pays on acceptance.** Publishes ms an average of 2-6 months after acceptance. Submit seasonal material 5 months in advance. Query for electronic submissions. Reports in 1 month. Sample copy for $10. Writer's guidelines for #10 SASE.
Nonfiction: *"Physician's Management* is a practice management/economic publication, not a clinical one." Publishes how-to articles (limited to medical practice management); informational (when relevant to audience); personal experience articles (if written by a physician). No fiction, clinical material or satire that portrays MD in an unfavorable light; or soap opera, "real-life" articles. Length: 2,000-2,500 words. Query with SASE. Pays $125/3-column printed page. Use of charts, tables, graphs, sidebars and photos strongly encouraged. Sometimes pays expenses of writers on assignment.
Tips: "Talk to doctors first about their practices, financial interests, and day-to-day nonclinical problems and then query us. Also, the ability to write a concise, well-structured and well-researched magazine article is essential. Freelancers who think like patients fail with us. Those who can think like MDs are successful."

PHYSICIAN'S PRACTICE DIGEST, 100 S. Charles St., 13th Floor, Baltimore MD 21201. (410)539-3100. Fax: (410)539-3188. Editor: Bruce Goldfarb. 75% freelance written. Quarterly magazine covering the business side of medical practice. "Magazine is about physician practice management, the business of medicine and health care. Readers are primarily in solo practice or small groups. Not a clinical publication." Estab. 1990. Circ. 30,000. Pays on publication. Publishes ms an average of 2 months after acceptance. Byline given. Offers 25% kill fee. Buys one-time rights. Editorial lead time 3 months. Submit seasonal material 6 months in advance. Accepts previously published submissions. Send typed ms with rights for sale noted and information about when and where the article previously appeared. Query for electronic submissions. Sample copy and writer's guidelines free on request.
Nonfiction: How-to, interview/profile, opinion. "Anything related to health reform is hot now—managed care, reimbursement. No clinical articles." Buys 40 mss/year. Query with published clips. Length: 500-2,500 words. Pays 25¢/word minimum for assigned articles. Sometimes pays expenses of writers on assignment.
Photos: State availability of photos with submission. Reviews transparencies. Negotiates payment individually. Captions, model releases and identification of subjects required. Buys one-time rights.
Columns/Departments: Office Technology (computers, software, simulators, etc.), 500 words; Malpractice (reform, arbitration, etc.), 500 words; Managed Care (contracting, UR, guidelines, etc.), 500 words. Query with published clips. Pays 25-50¢/word.
Tips: "It's absolutely essential to read the magazine. We *do not* run clinical articles. We're trying to help our readers cope while the health care industry undergoes radical transformation. We welcome ideas and information that will help the physician better manage the practice. Read the magazine! Think about what the reader *needs to know.* Look for health care trends and find the angle that affects physicians."

‡PHYSICIANS' TRAVEL & MEETING GUIDE, Excerpta Media, Inc., Reed-Elsevier, 105 Raider Blvd., Belle Mead NJ 08052. Editor: Bea Riemschneider. Managing Editor: Susann Tepperberg. 50% freelance

written. Monthly magazine covering travel for physicians and their families. *Physicians' Travel & Meeting Guide* supplies continuing medical education events listings and extensive travel coverage of international and national destinations. Circ. 153,000. **Pays on acceptance.** Byline given. Buys first North American serial rights. Submit seasonal material 4-6 months in advance. Reports in 3 months.
Nonfiction: Photo feature, travel. Buys 20-25 mss/year. Query with published clips. Length: 450-3,000 words. Pays $150-1,000 for assigned articles.
Photos: State availability of photos with submission. Send photos with submission. Reviews 35mm or 4×5 transparencies. Captions and identification of subjects required. Buys one-time rights.

PODIATRY MANAGEMENT, P.O. Box 750129, Forest Hills NY 11375. (718)897-9700. Fax: (718)896-5747. E-mail: gcfg37a@prodigy.com. Publisher: Scott C. Borowsky. Editor: Barry Block, DPM, J.D. Managing Editor: Martin Kruth. Magazine published 9 times/year for practicing podiatrists. "Aims to help the doctor of podiatric medicine to build a bigger, more successful practice, to conserve and invest his money, to keep him posted on the economic, legal and sociological changes that affect him." Estab. 1982. Circ. 13,000. Pays on publication. Byline given. Buys first North American serial and second serial (reprint) rights. Submit seasonal material 4 months in advance. Accepts simultaneous and previously published submissions. Send photocopy of article. For reprints, pays 33% of amount paid for an original article. Reports in 2 weeks. Sample copy for $3 and 9×12 SAE. Writer's guidelines for #10 SASE.
Nonfiction: General interest (taxes, investments, estate planning, recreation, hobbies); how-to (establish and collect fees, practice management, organize office routines, supervise office assistants, handle patient relations); interview/profile about interesting or well-known podiatrists; and personal experience. "These subjects are the mainstay of the magazine, but offbeat articles and humor are always welcome." Send tax and financial articles to Martin Kruth, 5 Wagon Hill Lane, Avon, CT 06001. Buys 25 mss/year. Query. Length: 1,000-2,500 words. Pays $150-600.
Photos: State availability of photos. Pays $15 for b&w contact sheet. Buys one-time rights.

‡STITCHES, The Journal of Medical Humour, 16787 Warden Ave., R.R. #3, Newmarket, Ontario L3Y 4W1 Canada. Editor: Simon Hally. 90% freelance written. Magazine published 10 times/year covering humor for physicians. "*Stitches* is read primarily by physicians in Canada. Stories with a medical slant are particularly welcome, but we also run a lot of non-medical material. It must be funny and, of course, brevity is the soul of wit." Estab. 1990. Circ. 41,000. Pays on publication. Publishes ms 2-6 months after acceptance. Byline given. Offers 50% kill fee. Buys first North American serial rights. Editorial lead time 2 months. Submit seasonal material 3 months in advance. Query for electronic submissions. Reports in 6 weeks on queries; 2 months on mss. Sample copy free on request.
Nonfiction: Humor, personal experience. Buys 20 mss/year. Send complete ms. Length: 100-2,000 words. Pays $35-750 (Canadian).
Fiction: Humorous. Buys 30 mss/year. Send complete ms. Length: 100-2,000 words. Pays $35-750 (Canadian).
Poetry: Humorous. Buys 5 poems/year. Submit maximum 5 poems. Length: 2-20 lines. Pays $20-100.
Fillers: Gags to be illustrated by cartoonist, short humor. Pay negotiable.
Tips: "Due to the nature of humorous writing, we have to see a completed manuscript, rather than a query, to determine if it is suitable for us. Along with a short cover letter, that's all we require."

STRATEGIC HEALTH CARE MARKETING, Health Care Communications, 11 Heritage Lane, P.O. Box 594, Rye NY 10580. (914)967-6741. Editor: Michele von Dambrowski. 75% freelance written. Prefers to work with published/established writers. "Will only work with unpublished writer on a 'stringer' basis initially." Monthly newsletter covering health care marketing and management in a wide range of settings including hospitals and medical group practices, home health services and managed care organizations. Emphasis is on strategies and techniques employed within the health care field and relevant applications from other service industries. Estab. 1984. Pays on publication. Publishes ms an average of 2 months after acceptance. Byline given. Offers 25% kill fee. Buys first North American serial rights. Reports in 1 month. Sample copy for 9×12 SAE with 3 first-class stamps. Guidelines sent with sample copy only.
● *Strategic Health Care Marketing* is specifically seeking writers with expertise/contacts in managed care and integrated delivery systems.
Nonfiction: How-to, interview/profile, new product, technical. Buys 45 mss/year. Query with published clips. No unsolicited mss accepted. Length: 700-3,000 words. Pays $100-450. Sometimes pays the expenses of writers on assignment with prior authorization.
Photos: State availability of photos with submissions. (Photos, unless necessary for subject explanation, are rarely used.) Reviews contact sheets. Offers $10-30/photo. Captions and model releases required. Buys one-time rights.
Tips: "Writers with prior experience on business beat for newspaper or newsletter will do well. We require a sophisticated, indepth knowledge of health care reform issues and impact. This is not a consumer publication—the writer with knowledge of both health care and marketing will excel. Interviews or profiles are most open to freelancers. Absolutely no unsolicited manuscripts; any received will be returned or discarded unread."

UNIQUE OPPORTUNITIES, The Physician's Resource, U O Inc., Suite 817, 455 S. Fourth Ave., Louisville KY 40202. Fax: (502)587-0848. E-mail: Bettoo@aol.com. Editor: Mollie Vento Hudson. Contact: Bett Coffman, assistant editor. 45% freelance written. Bimonthly magazine covering physician relocation, "published for physicians interested in a new career opportunity. It offers physicians useful information and first-hand experiences to guide them in making informed decisions concerning their first or next career opportunity. It provides regular features and columns about specific aspects of the search process." Estab. 1991. Circ. 80,000 physicians. **Pays on acceptance.** Publishes ms an average of 2 months after acceptance. Byline given. Offers 33% kill fee. Buys first North American serial rights. Editorial lead time 3 months. Submit seasonal material 6 months in advance. Query for electronic submissions. Reports in 2 months on queries. Sample copy for 9×12 SAE with 6 first-class stamps. Writer's guidelines for #10 SASE.

Nonfiction: Opinion (on issues relating to physician recruitment), practice options and information of interest to relocating physicians. Buys 12 mss/year. Query with published clips. Length: 1,500-3,500 words. Pays $750-1,500. Sometimes pays expenses of writers on assignment.

Photos: State availability of photos with submission. Negotiates payment individually. Model releases and identification of subjects required. Buys one-time rights.

Columns/Departments: Remarks (opinion from industry experts on physician relocation), 500 words. Buys 6 mss/year. Query with published clips. Pays $250-500.

Tips: "Submit queries via letter with ideas for articles that directly pertain to physician career issues, such as specific or unusual practice opportunities, relocation or practice establishment subjects, etc. Feature articles are most open to freelancers. Physician sources are most important, with tips and advice from both the physicians and business experts. Physicians like to know what other physicians think and are doing, but also appreciate the suggestions of other business people."

Music

Publications for musicians and for the recording industry are listed in this section. Other professional performing arts publications are classified under Entertainment and the Arts. Magazines featuring music industry news for the general public are listed in the Consumer Entertainment and Music sections. (Markets for songwriters can be found in *Songwriter's Market*, Writer's Digest Books.)

‡**THE CHURCH MUSICIAN**, 127 Ninth Ave. N., Nashville TN 37234. (615)251-2961. Fax: (615)251-3866 or 5951. Editor: Jere Adams. Estab. 1950. 20% freelance written. Works with a small number of new/unpublished writers each year; eager to work with new/unpublished writers. Quarterly publication for Southern Baptist church music leaders. Estab. 1950. Circ. 16,000. Buys all rights. **Pays on acceptance.** Publishes ms an average of 1 year after acceptance. No query required. Reports in 2 months. Accepts previously published articles. Send photocopy of article or typed ms with rights for sale noted and information about when and where the article previously appeared. For reprints, pays 50% of the amount paid for an original article. Sample copy for 9×12 SAE with 3 first-class stamps.

Nonfiction: Leadership and how-to features, success stories and articles on Protestant church music. "We reject material when the subject of an article doesn't meet our needs. And they are often poorly written, or contain too many 'glittering generalities' or lack creativity. We're interested in success stories; a 'this-worked-for-me' type of story." Length: maximum 1,300 words. Pays up to 5½¢/word.

Photos: Purchased with mss; related to mss content only. "We can use color photos."

Fiction: Inspiration, guidance, motivation and morality with Protestant church music slant. Length: to 1,300 words. Pays up to 5½¢/word.

Poetry: Church music slant, inspirational. Length: 8-24 lines. Pays $5-15.

Fillers: Short humor. Church music slant. No clippings. Pays $5-15.

Tips: "I'd advise a beginning writer to write about his or her experience with some aspect of church music; the social, musical and spiritual benefits from singing in a choir; a success story about their instrumental group; a testimonial about how they were enlisted in a choir—especially if they were not inclined to be enlisted at first. A writer might speak to hymn singers—what turns them on and what doesn't. Some might include how music has helped them to talk about Jesus as well as sing about Him. We would prefer most of these experiences be related to the church, of course, although we include many articles by freelance writers whose affiliation is other than Baptist. A writer might relate his experience with a choir of blind or deaf members. Some people receive benefits from working with unusual children—retarded, or culturally deprived, emotionally unstable, and so forth."

‡**INTERNATIONAL BLUEGRASS**, International Bluegrass Music Association, 207 E. Second St., Owensboro KY 42303. (502)684-9025. Editor: Dan Hays. 10% freelance written. Bimonthly newsletter covering bluegrass music industry. "We are the business publication for the bluegrass music industry. IBMA believes that our music has growth potential. We are interested in hard news and features concerning how to reach that potential and how to conduct business more effectively." Estab. 1985. Circ. 3,000. Pays on publication.

Publishes ms an average of 2 months after acceptance. Byline given. Not copyrighted. Buys one-time rights. Submit seasonal/holiday material 4 months in advance. Accepts simultaneous and previously published submissions. Send photocopy of article and information about when and where the article previously appeared. Does not pay for reprints. Query for electronic submissions. Reports in 1 month on queries. Sample copy for 6×9 SAE with 2 first-class stamps.

Nonfiction: Book excerpts, essays, how-to (conduct business effectively within bluegrass music), new product and opinion. No interview/profiles of performers (rare exceptions) or fans. Buys 6 mss/year. Query with or without published clips. Length: 300-1,200 words. Unsolicited mss are not accepted, but unsolicited news about the industry is accepted. Pays up to $150/article for assigned pieces. Buys 1-2 mss/issue.

Photos: Send photos with submission. Reviews 5×8 prints. Offers no additional payment for photos accepted with ms. Captions and identification of subjects required. Buys one-time rights.

Columns/Departments: Staff written.

Fillers: Anecdotes, facts, newsbreaks.

Tips: "The easiest break-in is to submit an article about an organizational member of IBMA—such as a bluegrass associate, instrument manufacturer or dealer, or performing venue. We're interested in a slant strongly toward the business end of bluegrass music. We're especially looking for material dealing with audience development and how to book bluegrass bands outside of the existing market."

‡MIX MAGAZINE, Cardinal Business Media Inc., 6400 Hollis St., Suite 12, Emeryville CA 94608. Editor: George Petersen. Contact: Blair Jackson. 50% freelance written. Monthly magazine covering pro audio. "*Mix* is a trade publication geared toward professionals in the music/sound production recording and post-production industries. We include stories about music production, sound for picture, live sound, audio and multimedia, etc. We prefer pieces that are applications-oriented." Estab. 1977. Circ. 50,000. Pays on publication. Publishes ms an average of 3 months after acceptance. Byline given. Offers 50% kill fee. Buys first North American serial rights. Editorial lead time 10 weeks. Submit seasonal material 3 months in advance. No simultaneous or previously published submissions. Query for electronic submissions. Reports in 2 weeks on queries; 1 month on mss. Sample copy for $6. Writer's guidelines free on request.

Nonfiction: How-to, interview/profile, new product, technical, project/studio spotlights. Special issues: Sound for picture supplement (April and September), Design issue (August). Buys 60 mss/year. Query. Length 500-2,000 words. Pays $100-400 for assigned articles; $100-300 for unsolicited articles.

Photos: State availability of photos with submissions. Reviews 4×5 transparencies, prints. Negotiates payment individually. Captions, identification of subjects required. Buys one-time rights.

Columns/Departments: Insider Audio (an industry bio on his/her specialty), 1,500 words. Buys 12 mss/year. Query. Pays $250 maximum.

Tips: "Send a letter outlining the article, including a description of the topic, information sources, what qualifies writers for the story, and mention of available graphics. A writing sample is also helpful."

OPERA NEWS, Metropolitan Opera Guild, Inc., 70 Lincoln Center Plaza, New York NY 10023-6593. (212)769-7080. Fax: (212)769-7007. Editor: Patrick J. Smith. Managing Editor: Brian Kellow. 75% freelance written. Monthly magazine (May-November, biweekly December-April), for people interested in opera; the opera professional as well as the opera audience. Estab. 1936. Circ. 120,000. Pays on publication. Publishes ms an average of 4 months after acceptance. Byline given. Buys first serial rights only. Query for electronic submissions. Sample copy for $4.

Nonfiction: Most articles are commissioned in advance. Monthly issues feature articles on various aspects of opera worldwide; biweekly issues contain articles related to the broadcasts from the Metropolitan Opera. Emphasis is on high quality writing and an intellectual interest to the opera-oriented public. Informational, personal experience, interview, profile, historical, think pieces, personal opinion, opera reviews. "Also willing to consider quality fiction and poetry on opera-related themes though acceptance is rare." Query by mail. Length: 1,500-2,800 words. Pays $450-1,000. Sometimes pays the expenses of writers on assignment.

Photos: State availability of photos with submission. Buys one-time rights.

Columns/Departments: Buys 24 mss/year.

STUDIO SOUND, and Broadcast Engineering, Spotlight Publications, Ludgate House, 245 Blackfriars Rd., London SE1 9UR United Kingdom. (+)71-620-3636. Fax: (+)44 71-401-8036. Editor: Tim Goodyer. 80% freelance written. Monthly magazine covering professional audio and recording—"all matters relating to pro audio—music recording, music for picture, post production—reviews and feature articles." Estab. 1959. Circ. 20,000 worldwide. Pays on publication. Byline given. Offers 20% kill fee. Buys first rights. Editorial lead time 3 months. Accepts simultaneous submissions. Query for electronic submissions.

Nonfiction: Historical/nostalgic, how-to, interview/profile, new product, opinion, personal experience, photo feature. No company profiles. Buys 80 mss/year. Send complete ms. Length: 850-4,000 words. Pays $150 minimum. Sometimes pays expenses of writers on assignment.

Photos: State availability of photos with submission. Reviews 35mm transparencies and 5×7 prints. Negotiates payment individually. Identification of subjects required. Buys one-time rights.

Office Environment and Equipment

‡**MANAGING OFFICE TECHNOLOGY**, Penton Publishing, 1100 Superior Ave., Cleveland OH 44114. (216)696-7000. Editor: Lura Romei. 20% freelance written. Monthly magazine covering office technology. Estab. 1956. Circ. 120,000. **Pays on acceptance.** Editorial lead time 5-6 months after acceptance. Byline given. Buys first North American serial rights. Editorial lead time 6 months. Query for electronic submissions. Reports in 2 months. Sample copy and writer's guidelines free on request.
Nonfiction: How-to. Buys 10 mss/year. Query. Length: 1,200-2,500 words. Pays $300-600 for assigned articles; $100-400 for unsolicited articles. Sometimes pays expenses of writers on assignment.
Photos: State availability of photos with submissions. Reviews contact sheets, transparencies, prints. Offers no additional payment for photos accepted with ms. Captions, identification of subjects required. Buys one-time rights.

MODERN OFFICE TECHNOLOGY, Penton Publishing, Dept. WM, 1100 Superior Ave., Cleveland OH 44114-2501. (216)696-7000. Fax: (216)696-7648. E-mail: luraromei@aol.com. Editor: Lura K. Romei. Production Manager: Gina Runyon. 5-10% freelance written. Monthly magazine covering office automation for corporate management and personnel, financial management, administrative and operating management, systems and information management, managers and supervisors of support personnel and purchasing. Estab. 1956. Circ. 128,000. **Pays on acceptance.** Publishes ms an average of 6 months after acceptance. Byline given. Buys first and one-time rights. Query for electronic submissions. Reports in 3 months. Accepts previously published submissions. Send photocopy of article and information about when and where the article previously appeared. Sample copy and writer's guidelines for 9×12 SAE with 4 first-class stamps.
Nonfiction: New product, opinion, technical. Query with or without published clips or send complete ms. Length: open. Pays $300-600 for assigned articles; $250-400 for unsolicited articles. Pays expenses of writers on assignment.
Photos: Send photos with submission. Reviews contact sheets, 4×5 transparencies and prints. Consult editor. Captions and identification of subjects required. Buys one-time rights.
Tips: "Submitted material should alway present topics and ideas, on issues that are clearly and concisely defined. Material should describe problems and solution. Writer should describe benefits to reader in tangible results whenever possible."

‡**OFFICE RELOCATION MAGAZINE**, 600 Haverford Rd., Haverford PA 19041. (610)649-6565. Contact: Lawrence Dillon. 100% freelance written. Bimonthly magazine covering office relocation. "Our readers are relocating their offices. Most have never done this before. We try to summarize industry information so it makes sense to them." Estab. 1992. Circ. 40,000. Pays on publication. Publishes ms an average of 2 months after acceptance. Offers 50% kill fee or $175. Buys all rights. Editorial lead time 3 months. Submit seasonal material 3 months in advance. Accepts simultaneous submissions. Query for electronic submissions. Sample copy and writer's guidelines free on request.
Nonfiction: How-to, new product, photo feature, technical, computer industry. Buys 30 mss/year. Query with published clips. Length: 1,000-2,000 words. Pays $350-550 for assigned articles; $300-500 for unsolicited articles. Pays expenses of writers on assignment (long distance charges).
Photos: State availability of photos with submissions. Reviews transparencies. Offers no additional payment for photos accepted with ms. Captions required. Buys all rights.
Columns/Departments: Computers (computer issues when moving office), 1,000 words. Query with or without published clips. Pays $350-550.
Tips: "Our publication is a how-to magazine. Industries that our readers need to be updated on: computer, telephones, business equipment, office furniture, office design, networks, software, carpeting, new site selection, long distance, healthy workplace, interior design, ergonomics, lighting. We look for articles in all of these industries as they pertain to moving your office. Especially computers!"

THE SECRETARY®, Stratton Publishing & Marketing, Inc., 2800 Shirlington Rd., Suite 706, Arlington VA 22206. Publisher: Debra J. Stratton. Managing Editor: Tracy Fellin Savidge. 90% freelance written. Magazine published 9 times/year covering the secretarial profession. Estab. 1946. Circ. 44,000. Pays on publication or "mostly unpaid." Publishes ms an average of 6-18 months after acceptance. Byline given. Kill fee negotiable. Buys first rights. Editorial lead time 3 months. Submit seasonal material 5 months in advance. Accepts simultaneous and previously published submissions. Send tearsheet of article or typed ms with rights for sale noted (on disk, preferred) and information about when and where the article previously appeared. Query for electronic submissions. For electronic (IBM) PC-compatible, Word Perfect or ASCII on disk. Reports in 2-3 months. Sample copy $3 through (816)891-6600 ext. 235. Writer's guidelines free on request through publishing office.
Nonfiction: Book excerpts, general interest, how-to (buy and use office equipment, advance career, etc.), interview/profile, new product, personal experience. Buys 6-10 mss/year. Query. Length: 2,000 words. Pays $250 minimum for assigned articles; $0-75 minimum for unsolicited articles. Pays expenses of writers on assignment.

Photos: Send photos with submission. Reviews transparencies and prints. Negotiable payment for photos accepted with ms. Identification of subjects required. Buys one-time rights.
Columns/Departments: Product News (new office products, non promotional), 500 words maximum; Random Input (general interest—career, woman's, workplace issues), 500 words maximum; First Person (first-hand experiences from secretaries), 800 words. Send complete ms.
Tips: "We're in search of articles addressing travel; meeting and event-planning; office recycling programs; computer hardware and software; workplace issues; international business topics. Must be appropriate to secretaries."

Paper

‡THE PAPER STOCK REPORT, News and Trends of the Paper Recycling Markets, McEntee Media Corp., 13727 Holland Rd., Cleveland OH 44142. (216)362-7979. Editor: Ken McEntee. Biweekly newsletter covering "market trends, news in the paper recycling industry. Audience is interested in new innovative markets, applications for recovered scrap paper as well as new laws and regulations impacting recycling." Estab. 1990. Circ. 2,000. Pays on publication. Publishes ms an average of 1 month after acceptance. Byline given. Buys first or all rights. Editorial lead time 2 months. Submit seasonal material 2 months in advance. Accepts simultaneous and previously published submissiosn. Query for electronic submissions. Reports in 1 month on queries. Sample copy for #10 SAE with 55¢ postage.
Nonfiction: Book excerpts, essays, exposé, general interest, historical/nostalgic, interview/profile, new product, opinion, technical, all related to paper recycling. Buys 0-13 mss/year. Send complete ms. Length: 250-1,000 words. Pays $50-250 for assigned articles; $25-250 for unsolicited articles. Pays expenses of writers on assignment.
Photos: State availability of photos with submissions. Reviews contact sheets. Negotiates payment individually. Identification of subjects required.
Tips: "Article must be valuable to readers in terms of presenting new market opportunities or cost-saving measures."

PULP & PAPER CANADA, Southam Inc., Suite 410, 3300 Côte Vertu, St. Laurent, Quebec H4R 2B7 Canada. (514)339-1399. Fax: (514)339-1396. Publisher: Mark Yerbary. Editor: Graeme Rodden. 5% freelance written. Prefers to work with published/established writers. Monthly magazine. Estab. 1903. Circ. 10,361. **Pays on acceptance.** Publishes ms "as soon as possible" after acceptance. Byline given. Offers kill fee according to prior agreement. Buys first North American serial rights. Reports in 1 month. Free sample copy.
Nonfiction: How-to (related to processes and procedures in the industry); interview/profile (of Canadian leaders in pulp and paper industry); technical (relevant to modern pulp and/or paper industry). No fillers, short industry news items, or product news items. Buys 10 mss/year. Query first with published clips or send complete ms. Articles with photographs (b&w glossy) or other good quality illustrations will get priority review. Length: maximum 1,500 words (with photos). Pays $160 (Canadian)/published page including photos, graphics, charts, etc.
Tips: "Any return postage must be in either Canadian stamps or International Reply Coupons *only*."

Pets

Listed here are publications for professionals in the pet industry—pet product wholesalers, manufacturers, suppliers, and retailers, and owners of pet specialty stores, grooming businesses, aquarium retailers and those interested in the pet fish industry. Publications for pet owners are listed in the Consumer Animal section.

PET BUSINESS, 5400 NW 84th Ave., Miami FL 33166-3333. (305)592-9890. Editorial Director: Elizabeth McKey. 30% freelance written. "Our monthly news magazine reaches retailers, distributors and manufacturers of pet products. Groomers, veterinarians and serious hobbyists are also represented." Estab. 1973. Circ. 18,000. Pays on publication. Publishes ms an average of 2 months after acceptance. Byline given. Buys first rights. Submit seasonal/holiday material 3 months in advance. Reports in 3-4 months. Sample copy for $3. Writer's guidelines for SASE.
Nonfiction: "Articles must be well-researched and pertain to major business trends in the pet industry. Research, legislative and animal behavior reports are of interest. All data must be attributed. Articles should be business-oriented, not intended for the pet owner market. Send query or complete ms. Length: 250-2,000 words. Pays 12¢/word.
Photos: Send color slides, transparencies or prints with submission. Offers $20/photo. Buys one-time rights.
Tips: "We are open to national and international news of the pet industry written in standard news format, or well-researched, business- or trend-oriented feature articles."

THE PET DEALER, PTN Publishing Co., 445 Broad Hollow Rd., Melville NY 11747. (516)845-2700. Fax: (516)845-7109. Editor: Jean Miller. 70% freelance written. Prefers to work with published/established writers, but works with new/published writers. "We want writers who are good reporters and clear communicators with a fine command of the English language." Monthly magazine emphasizing merchandising, marketing and management for owners and managers of pet specialty stores, departments, and pet groomers and their suppliers. Estab. 1949. Circ. 18,500. Pays on publication. "May be many months between acceptance of a manuscript and publication." Byline given. Submit seasonal material 4 months in advance. Accepts previously published submissions. Send typed ms with rights for sale noted and information about when and where the article previously appeared. For reprints, pays 1-10% of amount paid for an original article. Reports in 3 months. Sample copy for $5 and 8×10 SAE with 10 first-class stamps. Queries without SASE will not be answered.

Nonfiction: How-to (store operations, administration, merchandising, marketing, management, promotion and purchasing). Consumer pet articles—lost pets, best pets, humane themes—*not* welcome. "We *are* interested in helping—dog, cat, monkey, whatever stories tie in with the human/animal bond. Emphasis is on *trade* merchandising and marketing of pets and supplies." Buys 2-4 unsolicited mss/year. Length: 1,000-2,000 words. Pays $50-125.

Photos: Submit undeveloped photo material with ms. No additional payment for 5×7 b&w glossy prints. Buys one-time rights. Will give photo credit for photography students. Also seeking cover art: original illustrated animal portraits (paid).

Fillers: Publishes poetry and cartoons (unpaid) as fillers.

Tips: "We're interested in store profiles outside the New York, New Jersey, Connecticut and Pennsylvania metro areas. Photos are of key importance and should include a storefront shot. Articles focus on new techniques in merchandising or promotion, and overall trends in the Pet Industry. Want to see more articles from retailers and veterinarians with retail operations. Submit query letter first, with writing background summarized; include samples. We seek one-to-one, interview-type features on retail pet store merchandising. Indicate the availability of the proposed article, and your willingness to submit on exclusive or first-in-the-trade-field basis."

PET PRODUCT NEWS, Fancy Publications, P.O. Box 6050, Mission Viejo CA 92690. (714)855-8822. Fax: (714)855-3045. Managing Editor: Jack Sweet. 80% freelance written. Monthly magazine for retail pet stores. "*Pet Product News* covers business/legal and economic issues of importance to pet product retailers, suppliers and distributors, as well as product information and animal care issues. We're looking for straightforward articles on the proper care of dogs, cats, birds, fish and exotics (reptiles, hamsters, etc.) as information the retailers can pass on to new pet owners." Estab. 1947. Circ. 25,000. Pays on publication. Byline given. Offers $50 kill fee. Buys first North American serial rights. Editorial lead time 3 months. Submit seasonal material 4 months in advance. Query for electronic submissions. No multiple submissions. Reports in 2 weeks on queries. Sample copy for $4.50. Writer's guidelines free on request.

• *Pet Product News* stories are taking a more news-oriented approach; fewer profiles and "how-tos" for Mom & Pop retailers and more coverage of business developments at multi-store chains and mass merchants.

Nonfiction: General interest, interview/profile, new product, photo feature, technical. "No cute animal stories or those directed at the pet owner." Buys 150 mss/year. Query. Length: 500-1,500 words. Pays $175-350.

Columns/Departments: "Retail News" (timely news stories about business issues affecting pet retailers), 800-1,000 words; "Industry News" (news articles representing coverage of pet product suppliers, manufacturers, distributors and associations), 800-1,000 words; Dog & Cat (products and care of), 1,000-1,500 words; Fish & Bird (products and care of), 1,800-1,500 words; Exotics (products and care of), 1,500-2,000 words. Buys 120 mss/year. Query. Send complete ms. Pays $175-350.

Tips: "Be more than just an animal lover. You have to know about health, nutrition and care. Product and business articles are told in both an informative and entertaining style. Go into pet stores, talk to the owners and see what they need to know to be better business people in general, who have to deal with everything from balancing the books, free trade agreements and animal right activists. All sections are open, but you have to be extremely knowledgeable on the topic, be it taxes, management, profit building, products, nutrition, animal care or marketing."

Photography Trade

Journals for professional photographers are listed in this section. Magazines for the general public interested in photography techniques are in the Consumer Photography section. (For listings of markets for freelance photography use *Photographer's Market*, Writer's Digest Books.)

‡**THE COMMERCIAL IMAGE**, PTN Publishing Co., 445 Broad Hollow Rd., Melville NY 11747. (516)845-2700. Editor: Steven Shaw. Contact: Susan E. Stegemann. 50% freelance written. Monthly tabloid covering

commercial photography. Pays on publication. Byline given. Buys one-time rights. Editorial lead time 3 months. Submit seasonal material 3 months in advance. Query for electronic submissions. Sample copy and writer's guidelines free on request.

Nonfiction: Interview/profile, technical. Buys 10 mss/year. Query with published clips. Length: 1,000-2,000 words. Pays $75/printed page.

Photos: Send photos with submission. Reviews 8×10 transparencies and prints. Offers no additional payment for photos accepted with ms. Captions, model releases, identification of subjects required. Buys one-time rights.

‡PHOTO EDITORS REVIEW, 1201 Montego, #4, Walnut Creek CA 94598-2819. Phone/fax: (510)935-7406. Publisher: Robert Shepherd. Bimonthly journal for photo editors. Audience is mostly professional photo editors and magazine photographers. Estab. 1994. Circ. 4,200. **Pays on acceptance.** Byline given. Offers 25% kill fee. Buys first North American serial, first, one-time or simultaneous rights. Editorial lead time 3 months. Submit seasonal material 4 months in advance. Accepts simultaneous and previously published submissions. Reports in 1 month on queries; 2 months on mss. Sample copy for $3 and 9×12 SAE with 4 first-class stamps. Writer's guidelines for #10 SASE on request.

Nonfiction: Photo critiques from the editor's point of view and how-to photo features; legal and photo editing advice from professional photo editors. Buys 12-18 mss/year. Query. Length: 750-1,500 words. Pays up to $200 for assigned articles; up to $100 for unsolicited articles.

Photos: Send photos with submission. Reviews contact sheets and 3½×5 to 8×10 prints. Offers $50/photo. Captions, model releases and identification of subjects required. Buys one-time rights.

Columns/Departments: Photo critiques, 750-1,500 words; legal (the photo editor and the law), 750-1,500 words; how-to photo features, 750-1,500 words. Buys 12-18 mss/year. Query. Pays $100-200.

Tips: "We are a trade publication that caters to the needs of professional photo editors; therefore, marketable photos that exhibit universal themes will be given top priority. We look for five characteristics by which we judge photographic materials: Sharp exposure (unless the image was intended as a soft-focus shot), impact, easily identifiable theme or subject, emphasis of the theme or subject, and simplicity."

PHOTO MARKETING, Photo Marketing Assocation Intl., 3000 Picture Place, Jackson MI 49201-8853. (517)788-8100. Fax: (517)788-8371. Director, Publications: Gary Pageau. 2% freelance written. Monthly magazine for photo industry retailers, finishers and suppliers. "Articles must be specific to the photo industry and cannot be authored by anyone who writes for other magazines in the photo industry. We provide management information on a variety of topics as well as profiles of successful photo businesses and analyses of current issues in the industry." Estab. 1925. Circ. 22,000. **Pays on acceptance.** Publishes ms an average of 2 months after acceptance. Byline given. Buys one-time rights and exclusive photo magazine rights. Accepts simultaneous submissions. Reports in 2 months. Free sample copy. Writer's guidelines for #10 SASE.

• *Photo Marketing* is placing more emphasis on case studies.

Nonfiction: Interview/profile (anonymous consumer shops for equipment); personal experience (interviews with photo retailers); technical (photofinishing lab equipment); new technology (still electronic video). Buys 5 mss/year. Send complete ms. Length: 1,000-2,300 words. Pays $150-350.

Photos: State availability of photos with submission. Reviews negatives, 5×7 transparencies and prints. Offers $25-35/photo. Buys one-time rights.

Columns/Departments: Anonymous Consumer (anonymous shopper shops for equipment at photo stores), 1,800 words. Buys 5 mss/year. Query with published clips. Length: 1,800 words. Pays up to $200.

Tips: "All main sections use freelance material: business tips, promotion ideas, employee concerns, advertising, co-op, marketing. But they must be geared to and have direct quotes from members of the association."

THE PHOTO REVIEW, 301 Hill Ave., Langhorne PA 19047-2819. (215)757-8921. Editor: Stephen Perloff. 50% freelance written. Quarterly magazine on photography with reviews, interviews and articles on art photography. Estab. 1976. Circ. 2,500. Pays on publication. Publishes ms an average of 3 months after acceptance. Byline given. Buys one-time rights. Accepts simultaneous and previously published submissions. Reports in 1 month on queries; 2 months on mss. Sample copy for 9×12 SAE with 6 first-class stamps. Writer's guidelines for #10 SASE.

Nonfiction: Essays, historical/nostalgic, interview/profile, opinion. No how-to articles. Buys 10-15 mss/year. Query. Pays $25-200.

Photos: Send photos with submission. Reviews 8×10 prints. Offers no additional payment for photos accepted with ms. Captions and identification of subjects required. Buys one-time rights.

‡PHOTOGRAPHIC PROCESSING, PTN Publishing Co., 445 Broad Hollow Rd., Melville NY 11747. (516)845-2700. Editor: Bill Schiffner. 30-40% freelance written. Monthly magazine covering photographic (commercial/minilab) and electronic processing markets. Estab. 1965. Circ. 23,000. Pays on publication. Publishes ms an average of 3-4 months after acceptance. Byline given. Offers $75 kill fee. Editorial lead time 2-3 months. Submit seasonal material 2-3 months in advance. Accepts simultaneous submissions. Sample copy and writer's guidelines free on request.

Nonfiction: How-to, interview/profile, new product, photo feature. Buys 30-40 mss/year. Query with published clips. Length: 1,500-2,200 words. Pays $250-325 for assigned articles; $200-250 for unsolicited articles.

Photos: Send photos with submission. Reviews 4×5 transparencies, 4×6 prints. Offers no additional payment for photos accepted with ms. Captions required. Buys one-time rights.

Columns/Departments: Surviving in the 90s (business articles offering tips to labs on how make their businesses run better), 1,500-1,800 words; Productivity Focus (getting more productivity out of your lab). Buys 10 mss/year. Query with published clips. Pays $150-200.

Plumbing, Heating, Air Conditioning and Refrigeration

‡DISTRIBUTOR, The Voice of Wholesaling, Technical Reporting Corp., Dept. WM, 651 Washington St., #300, Chicago IL 60661. (312)993-0929. Fax: (312)993-0960. Editor: Robert J. Heselbarth. 30% freelance written. Prefers to work with published/established writers. Bimonthly magazine for heating, ventilating, air conditioning and refrigeration wholesalers. "Editorial material shows executive wholesalers how they can run better businesses and cope with personal and business problems." Circ. 17,000. Pays on publication. Publishes ms an average of 1 month after acceptance. Byline sometimes given. Buys one-time rights. Submit seasonal material 3 months in advance. "We want material exclusive to the field (industry)." Query for information on electronic submissions. Reports in 1 month. Sample copy for $4.

Nonfiction: How-to (run a better business, cope with problems), interview/profile (the wholesalers). No flippant or general approaches. Buys 6 mss/year. Query with or without published clips or send complete ms. Length: 1,000-2,000 words. Pays $100-200 (10¢/word). Sometimes pays the expenses of writers on assignment.

Photos: State availability of or send photos with query or ms. Pays $5 minimum. Captions and identification of subjects required.

Tips: "Know the industry—come up with a different angle on an industry subject (one we haven't dealt with in a long time). Wholesale ideas and top-quality business management articles are most open to freelancers."

HEATING, PLUMBING, AIR CONDITIONING, 1370 Don Mills Rd., Suite 300, Don Mills, Ontario M3B 3N7 Canada. (416)759-2500. Fax: (416)759-6979. Publisher: Bruce Meacock. Editor: Bruce Cole. 20% freelance written. Monthly magazine for mechanical contractors; plumbers; warm air and hydronic heating, refrigeration, ventilation, air conditioning and insulation contractors; wholesalers; architects; consulting and mechanical engineers who are in key management or specifying positions in the plumbing, heating, air conditioning and refrigeration industries in Canada. Estab. 1923. Circ. 16,500. Pays on publication. Publishes ms an average of 3 months after acceptance. Accepts previously published submissions. Send tearsheet or photocopy of article or typed ms with rights for sale noted and information about when and where article appeared. Reports in 2 months. For a prompt reply, "enclose a sheet on which is typed a statement either approving or rejecting the suggested article which can either be checked off, or a quick answer written in and signed and returned." Sample copy free.

Nonfiction: News, technical, business management and "how-to" articles that will inform, educate, motivate and help readers to be more efficient and profitable who design, manufacture, install, sell, service, maintain or supply all mechanical components and systems in residential, commercial, institutional and industrial installations across Canada. Length: 1,000-1,500 words. Pays 25¢/word. Sometimes pays expenses of writers on assignment.

Photos: Photos purchased with ms. Prefers 4×5 or 5×7 glossies.

Tips: "Topics must relate directly to the day-to-day activities of *HPAC* readers in Canada. Must be detailed, with specific examples, quotes from specific people or authorities—show depth. We specifically want material from other parts of Canada besides southern Ontario. Not really interested in material from US unless specifically related to Canadian readers' concerns. We primarily want articles that show *HPAC* readers how they can increase their sales and business step-by-step based on specific examples of what others have done."

‡SERVICE REPORTER, The Total Publication for the Comfort Industry, Palmer Publishing Co., 651 W. Washington St., Suite 300, Chicago IL 60661. Editor: Edwin G. Schwenn. 25% freelance written. Monthly tabloid covering HVAC industry. "Latest news, developments, articles and features of interest to HVAC/R contractors." Estab. 1968. Circ. 53,000. Pays on publication. Publishes ms an average of 3 months after acceptance. Byline given. Offers 50% kill fee. Buys first North American serial and second serial (reprint) rights. Editorial lead time 6 weeks. Submit seasonal material 3 months in advance. No simultaneous or previously published submissions. Reports in 1 month on mss. Sample copy for $3.

Nonfiction: How-to, interview/profile, new product, photo feature, technical. Buys a couple mss/year. Query. Length: 1,000-2,000 words. Pays $100-350 for assigned articles; $50-250 for unsolicited articles.

Photos: State availability of or send photos with submission. Reviews transparencies, prints. Offers $25-50/photo. Captions, identification of subjects required. Buys first and second publication rights.
Columns/Departments: Buys very few mss/year. Query. Pays $10-25.
Fillers: Anecdotes, facts, gags to be illustrated by cartoonist, newsbreaks, humor. Buys 12/year. Length: 25-50 words. Pays $25-50.

SNIPS MAGAZINE, 1949 N. Cornell Ave., Melrose Park IL 60160. (708)544-3870. Fax: (708)544-3884. Editor: Nick Carter. 2% freelance written. Monthly magazine for sheet metal, warm air heating, ventilating, air conditioning and roofing contractors. Estab. 1932. Publishes ms an average of 3 months after acceptance. Buys all rights. "Write for detailed list of requirements before submitting any work."
Nonfiction: Material should deal with information about contractors who do sheet metal, warm air heating, air conditioning, ventilation and metal roofing work; also about successful advertising campaigns conducted by these contractors and the results. Length: less than 1,000 words unless on special assignment. Pays 5¢/word for first 500 words, 2¢/word thereafter.
Photos: Pays $5 each for small snapshot pictures, $10 each for usable 8×10 pictures.

Printing

CANADIAN PRINTER, Maclean Hunter Ltd., 777 Bay St., Toronto, Ontario M5W 1A7 Canada. (416)596-5781. Fax: (416)596-5965. Editor: Nick Hancock. Assistant Editor: Stephen Forbes. 20% freelance written. Monthly magazine for printing and the allied industries. "*Canadian Printer* wants technical matter on graphic arts, printing, binding, typesetting, specialty production and trends in technology." Circ. 13,000. Pays on publication. Publishes ms an average of 1-3 months after acceptance. Byline given. Buys first North American serial rights. Reports in 6 months. Sample copy for 9×12 SAE with 2 IRCs.
Nonfiction: Technical. "We do not want US plant articles—this is a Canadian magazine." Buys 5-10 mss/year. Query or send complete ms. Length: 400-1,600 words. Pays 30¢/word (Canadian). Pays expenses of writers on assignment "on prior arrangement."
Photos: Send photos with submission. Reviews 4×5 prints. Offers $50 (Canadian)/photo. Captions and identification of subjects required. Buys one-time rights.

MODERN REPROGRAPHICS, Marion Street Press, Inc., P.O. Box 577339, Chicago IL 60657. (312)868-1238. Fax: (312)868-1052. E-mail: edba8767@aol.com. Editor: Ed Avis. 60% freelance written. Bimonthly magazine covering large-format reproduction (blueprints, etc.). "Modern Reprographics is for people who do large-format reproduction, such as blueprints, color posters, etc. Articles are geared towards blueprint shops, service bureaus, and in-plant repro departments and help them find new markets and do their work better." Estab. 1993. Circ. 6,000. Pays on publication. Publishes ms an average of 1 month after acceptance. Byline given. Offers 25% kill fee. Buys first North American serial rights. Editorial lead time 2 months. Accepts previously published submissions. Send typed ms with rights for sale noted and information about when and where the article previously appeared. For reprints, pays 75% of the amount paid for an original article. Query for electronic submissions. Reports in 3 weeks on queries; 1 month on mss. Sample copy for 11×14 SAE with 5 first-class stamps.
Nonfiction: How-to, interview/profile (blueprint shop owner, e.g.), new product, personal experience, technical, new markets. Buys 15 mss/year. Query with published clips. Length: 800-2,000 words. Pays $150. Sometimes pays expenses of writers on assignment.
Photos: State availability of photos with submission. Captions and identification of subjects required. Buys one-time rigths.
Tips: "Writers can best break in with a profile of an interesting, innovative reprographics shop or department. Profiles should have a 'hook,' and some historical background on the shop or department. We are picky about technical articles, so please query first. All articles are written in language that non-reprographers can understand."

PERSPECTIVES, In-Plant Management Association (IPMA), 1205 W. College St., Liberty MO 64068-3733. (816)781-1111. Editor: Barbara Schaaf Petty. 25% freelance written. Monthly trade newsletter covering inhouse print and mail operations. "Inhouse print/mail departments are faced with competition from commer-

---

Market conditions are constantly changing! If this is 1997 or later, buy the newest edition of Writer's Market *at your favorite bookstore or order directly from* Writer's Digest Books.

cial printers and facilities management companies. Writers must be pro-insourcing and reflect that this industry is a profitable profession." Estab. 1986. Circ. 2,300; twice a year it reaches 5,000. Pays on publication. Publishes ms an average of 2 months after acceptance. Byline given. Buys all rights. Editorial lead time 2 months. Accepts previously published submissions. Send photocopy of article and information about when and where the article previously appeared. Reports in 1 month. Sample copy for 9×12 SAE.

Nonfiction: Interview/profile, new product, technical, general management. Payment negotiated individually. Sometimes pays expenses of writers on assignment.

Photos: State availability of photos with submission. Reviews contact sheets and 5×7 prints. Offers no additional payment for photos accepted with ms. Captions required. Buys one-time rights.

Columns/Departments: Executive Insight (management, personnel how-tos, employment law), 650-1,500 words. Buys 12 mss/year. Query with published clips.

Tips: "A knowledge of the printing industry is helpful. Articles with concrete examples or company/individual profiles work best."

PRINT & GRAPHICS, 1432 Duke St., Alexandria VA 22314-3436. (703)683-8800. Fax: (703)683-8801. Editor: Carole Anne Turner. Publisher: Geoff Lindsay. 10% freelance written. Eager to work with new/ unpublished writers. Monthly tabloid of the commercial printing industry for owners and executives of graphic arts firms. Estab. 1980. Circ. 20,000. **Pays on acceptance.** Publishes ms an average of 2 months after acceptance. Byline given. Buys one-time rights. Accepts simultaneous and previously published submissions. Send photocopy of article and information about when and where the article previously appeared. Pays $150 flat fee. Publishes trade book excerpts. Electronic submissions OK via standard protocols, but requires hard copy also. Reports in 2 months. Sample copy for $2.

Nonfiction: Book excerpts, historical/nostalgic, how-to, interview/profile, new product, opinion, personal experience, photo feature, technical. "All articles should relate to graphic arts management or production." Buys 20 mss/year. Query with published clips. Length: 750-2,000 words. Pays $100-250.

Photos: State availability of photos. Pays $25-75 for 5×7 b&w prints. Captions and identification of subjects required.

‡PRINTING NEWS EAST, The Newsweekly for Imaging to Finishing, PTN Publishing Co., 445 Broad Hollow Rd., Suite 21, Melville NY 11747. (516)845-2700. Editor: Heidi Tolliver. 25% freelance written. Weekly tabloid covering graphic arts and printing-related industries. "Stories should be tight, and information presented in a way that has practical applications for the readers." Estab. 1928. Circ. 9,000. Pays on publication. Publishes ms an average of 1-3 months after acceptance. Byline given. Kill fee negotiable. Buys first North American serial rights or makes work-for-hire assignments. Editorial lead time 1 month. Submit seasonal material 1 month in advance. Query for electronic submissions. Reports in 1-2 weeks on queries; 1 month on mss. Sample copy free on request.

Nonfiction: Interview/profile, technical, hard news/feature. "We are a regional publication (NY, NJ, PA, CT). Buys 100-150 mss/year. Query. Length: 500-1,200 words. Pays $500 maximum for assigned articles; $300 maximum for unsolicited articles. Sometimes pays expenses of writers on assignment.

Photos: Send photos with submission. Reviews transparencies, prints. Offers no additional payment for photos accepted with ms. Captions, identification of subjects required. Buys one-time rights.

Columns/Departments: Prepress, press, postpress (technical/how-to), 500-1,000 words; Business/management (technical/how-to), 500-1,000 words. Buys 1-10 mss/year. Query. Pays $300 maximum.

Fillers: Newsbreaks. Buys 1-10/year. Length: 50-500 words. Pays $25-100.

Tips: "Call me with a breaking news story—companies merging, closing, partnering, launching innovative programs, etc.—or with a particular aspect of its business. We have a small staff and four states to cover, so I rely on a network of writers to keep me up-to-date. Hot topics are legislation, environmental compliance, marketing, cost containment, use of technology. I welcome short articles (500 words or less) as fillers; we don't buy more of these simply because we don't receive them. In particular, I need stringers who can cover meetings for me in the New York/New Jersey metropolitan area, as well as in Philadelphia, and I would welcome inquiries from available writers."

SCREEN PRINTING, 407 Gilbert Ave., Cincinnati OH 45202-2285. (513)421-2050. Fax: (513)421-5144. Editor: Steve Duccilli. 30% freelance written. Works with a small number of new/unpublished writers each year. Monthly magazine for the screen printing industry, including screen printers (commercial, industrial and captive shops), suppliers and manufacturers, ad agencies and allied professions. Estab. 1953. Circ. 15,000. Pays on publication. Publishes ms an average of 3-4 months after acceptance. Byline given. Buys all rights. Reporting time varies. Sample copies available for sale through circulation department. Writer's guidelines for SAE.

● There's an increasing emphasis here on personality features and coverage of fine art screen printers.

Nonfiction: "Because the screen printing industry is a specialized but diverse trade, we do not publish general interest articles with no pertinence to our readers. Subject matter is open, but should fall into one of four categories—technology, management, profile, or news. Features in all categories must identify the relevance of the subject matter to our readership. Technology articles must be informative, thorough, and objective—no promotional or 'advertorial' pieces accepted. Management articles may cover broader business or industry specific issues, but they must address the screen printer's unique needs. Profiles may cover serigraphers, outstanding shops, unique jobs and projects, or industry personalities; they should be in-depth features, not PR puff pieces, that clearly show the human interest or business relevance of the subject. News pieces should be timely (reprints from non-industry publications will be considered) and must cover an event or topic of industry concern." Buys 6-10 mss/year. Query. Unsolicited mss not returned. Length: 1,500-3,500 words. Pays $200 minimum for major features. Sometimes pays the expenses of writers on assignment.

Photos: Cover photos negotiable; b&w or color. Published material becomes the property of the magazine.

Tips: "If the author has a working knowledge of screen printing, assignments are more readily available. General management articles are rarely used."

Real Estate

BUSINESS FACILITIES, Group C Communications, Inc., 121 Monmouth St., P.O. Box 2060, Red Bank NJ 07701. (908)842-7433. Fax: (908)758-6634. Editor: Eric Peterson. Managing Editor: Mary Ellen McCandless. 20% freelance written. Prefers to work with published/established writers. Monthly magazine covering corporate expansion, economic development and commercial and industrial real estate. "Our audience consists of corporate site selectors and real estate people; our editorial coverage is aimed at providing news and trends on the plant location and corporate expansion field." Estab. 1967. Circ. 40,000. Pays on publication. Publishes ms an average of 2 months after acceptance. Byline given. Buys all rights. Reports in 2 weeks. Sample copy and writer's guidelines for SASE.

● Magazine is currently overstocked, and will be accepting fewer pieces for the near future.

Nonfiction: General interest, how-to, interview/profile, personal experience. No news shorts or clippings; feature material only. Buys 12-15 mss/year. Query. Length: 1,000-3,000 words. Pays $200-1,000 for assigned articles; $200-600 for unsolicited articles. Sometimes pays the expenses of writers on assignment.

Photos: State availability of photos with submission. Reviews contact sheets, transparencies and 8×10 prints. Payment negotiable. Captions and identification of subjects required. Buys one-time rights.

Tips: "First, remember that our reader is a corporate executive responsible for his company's expansion and/or relocation decisions and our writers have to get inside that person's head in order to provide him with something that's helpful in his decision-making process. And second, the biggest turnoff is a telephone query. We're too busy to accept them and must require that all queries be put in writing. Submit major feature articles only; all news departments, fillers, etc., are staff prepared. A writer should be aware that our style is not necessarily dry and business-like. We tend to be more casual and a writer should look for that aspect of our approach."

FINANCIAL FREEDOM REPORT QUARTERLY, 4505 S. Wasatch Blvd., Salt Lake City UT 84124. (801)272-3500. Fax: (801)273-5423. Chairman of the Board: Mark O. Haroldsen. Managing Editor: Carolyn Tice. 25% freelance written. Eager to work with new/unpublished writers. Quarterly magazine for "professional and nonprofessional investors and would-be investors in real estate—real estate brokers, insurance companies, investment planners, truck drivers, housewives, doctors, architects, contractors, etc. The magazine's content is presently expanding to interest and inform the readers about other ways to put their money to work for them." Estab. 1976. Circ. 50,000. Pays on publication. Publishes ms an average of 3 months after acceptance. Buys all rights. Phone queries OK. Accepts simultaneous submissions. Query for electronic submissions. Reports in 3 months. Sample copy for $5.

Nonfiction: How-to (find real estate bargains, finance property, use of leverage, managing property, developing market trends, goal setting, motivational); interviews (success stories of those who have relied on own initiative and determination in real estate market or related fields). Buys 10 unsolicited mss/year. Query with clips of published work or submit complete ms. Length: 1,500-3,000 words. Pays 5-10¢/word. Sometimes pays the expenses of writers on assignment.

Photos: Send photos with ms. Uses 8×10 b&w or color matte prints. Captions required.

Tips: "We would like to find several specialized writers in our field of real estate investments. A writer must have had some hands-on experience in the real estate field."

‡FLORIDA REAL ESTATE JOURNAL, Real Estate Network International, 441 E. Central Ave., Winter Haven FL 33880. (800)274-2812. Editor: Larry Thornberry. Managing Editor: Ron Starner. 50% freelance written. Real estate newspaper covering commercial real estate in Florida. "Our readers are developers, brokers, property managers, bankers, architects, engineers, construction types, lawyers, investors and others concerned with all phases of the industry and issues of concern to people in the industry." Estab. 1993. Circ. 15,000. Pays on publication. Publishes ms an average of 1 month after acceptance; "articles are timely, nothing sits around." Byline given. Offers 100% kill fee if events make story unusable; no kill fee "if story not up to standards." Buys all rights; will reassign to writer on request. Editorial lead time 1 month. Accepts previously published submissions. Query for electronic submissions. Reports in 2 weeks on queries; 1 month on mss. Sample copy free on request.

Nonfiction: How-to, interview/profile, new product, market analysis/trend stories. No articles on residential real estate. Buys 35-50 mss/year. Query with published clips or call. Length: 700-2,000 words. Pays $100-

300 for assigned articles; $100-200 for unsolicited articles. Pays expenses of writers on assignment.

Photos: Reviews contact sheets, negatives, transparencies and prints; prefer prints, any size. Offers no additional payment for photos accepted with ms. Negotiates payment individually. Identification of subjects required. "Usually get photos from subjects covered; will return if requested."

Tips: "Know the commercial real estate industry in your area and what the people in the industry want to read. We strive to publish information real estate practitioners can use in their businesses."

‡INTERNATIONAL REAL ESTATE INVESTOR, Real Estate Network International, 441 E. Central Ave., Winter Haven FL 33880. (800)274-2812. Editor: Larry Thornberry. Managing Editor: Ron Starner. 50% freelance written. Monthly newspaper covering international real estate topics of interest to investors in real estate. "Our readers are international investors, developers, brokers, government officials, lenders, insurers and others concerned with real estate. We do macro and micro stories; trends; individual or company profiles; stories on regulations, or about cultural or political trends that could affect real estate." Estab. 1995. Circ. 5,000. Pays on publication. Publishes ms an average of 1 month after acceptance; "quick turnaround—subjects are timely." Byline given. Offers 100% kill fee if events make story not usable; no kill fee "if story not up to standards." Buys all rights; can reassign to writer on request. Editorial lead time 1 month. Accepts previously published submissions. Query for electronic submissions. Reports in 2 weeks on queries; 1 month on mss. Sample copy free on request.

Nonfiction: How-to, interview/profile, new product, technical, market analysis/trends. Buys 25-30 mss/year. Query with published clips or call. Length: 800-2,000 words. Pays $100-300 for assigned articles; $100-200 for unsolicited articles. Pays expenses of writers on assignment.

Photos: Send photos with submission. Reviews contact sheets, negatives, transparencies and prints; prefers prints, any size. Offers no additional payment for photos accepted with ms; "usually get photos from subject covered."

Tips: "Understand the kind of information real estate investors and practitioners need to be successful and be able to provide it."

JOURNAL OF PROPERTY MANAGEMENT, Institute of Real Estate Management, P.O. Box 109025, Chicago IL 60610-9025. (312)329-6058. Fax: (312)661-0217. Executive Editor: Mariwyn Evans. 30% freelance written. Bimonthly magazine covering real estate management and development. "The *Journal* has a feature/information slant designed to educate readers in the application of new techniques and to keep them abreast of current industry trends." Circ. 20,300. **Pays on acceptance.** Publishes ms an average of 3 months after acceptance. Byline given. Buys all rights. Query for electronic submissions. Reports in 6 weeks on queries; 1 month on mss. *Writer's Market* recommends allowing 2 months for reply. Free sample copy and writer's guidelines.

• This journal wants more "nuts-and-bolts" articles.

Nonfiction: How-to, interview, technical (building systems/computers), demographic shifts in business employment and buying patterns, marketing. "No non-real estate subjects, personality or company, humor." Buys 8-12 mss/year. Query with published clips. Length: 1,500-2,500 words. Sometimes pays the expenses of writers on assignment.

Photos: State availability of photos with submission. Reviews contact sheets. May offer additional payment for photos accepted with ms. Model releases and identification of subjects required. Buys one-time rights.

Columns/Departments: Katherine Anderson, associate editor. Insurance Insights, Tax Issues, Investment and Finance Insights, Legal Issues. Buys 6-8 mss/year. Query. Length: 750-1,500 words.

‡MIDWEST REAL ESTATE NEWS, Argus Business, 35 E. Wacker Dr., Chicago IL 60601. (312)726-7277. Editor: Roger A. Nadolny. 70% freelance written. Monthly tabloid covering commercial real estate. "We cover all aspects of commercial real estate including office, industrial, retail, hotel and multifamily. We cover the sttes of OH, MI, IN, IL, WI, MN, MO, NE, KS and IA." Estab. 1987. Circ. 18,000. Pays on publication. Publishes ms an average of 2-4 months after acceptance. Byline given. Buys all rights. Editorial lead time 3 months. Submit seasonal material 3 months in advance. Accepts simultaneous and previously published submissions. Query for electronic submissions. Sample copy and writer's guidelines free on request.

Nonfiction: Essays, general interest, how-to (perform and succeed in commercial real estate), area real estate reports, interview/profile, personal experience, technical. "We do a special pull-out section in September and October on Detroit and Chicago." Buys 50 mss/year. Query. Length: 2,000-4,000 words. Pays $300-500.

Photos: Send photos with submission. Offers no additional payment for photos accepted with ms. Captions required. Buys one-time rights.

Tips: "Freelancers should call me and get a copy of our editorial calendar. Determine what topics are of interest and then call me to discuss how to go about writing the article."

PLANTS SITES & PARKS, The Corporate Advisor for Relocation Strategies, BPI Communications Inc., 10100 W. Sample Rd., Suite 201, Coral Springs FL 33065. (800)753-2660. Fax: (305)752-2995. Editor: Ken Ibold. 35% freelance written. Bimonthly magazine covering business, especially as it involves site locations. Estab. 1974. Circ. 40,500. **Pays on acceptance.** Publishes ms an average of 1 month after acceptance. Byline given. Negotiable kill fee. Buys all rights. Editorial lead time 3-4 months. Reports in 1 month on queries. Sample copy and writer's guidelines free on request.

Nonfiction: Book excerpts, real estate, labor, industry, finance topics geared toward manufacturing executives. Buys 25-30 mss/year (total for features *and* columns/departments). Query with published clips. Length: 1,000-7,000 words. Pays $300 minimum for assigned articles. Pays expenses of writers on assignment.

Photos: State availability of photos with submission. Negotiates payment individually. Captions required. Rights negotiable.

Columns/Departments: Regional Review (profile business climate of each state), 1,000-5,000 words; Industry Outlook (trend stories on specific industries), 5,000-7,500 words; Global Market (business outlook for specific overseas areas), 2,000-5,000 words. Buys 25-30 mss/year (total for columns/departments and features). Query with published clips. Pays $300-2,000.

Resources and Waste Reduction

EROSION CONTROL, The Journal for Erosion and Sediment Control Professionals, Forester Communications, Inc., 5638 Hollister Ave., Suite 301, Santa Barbara CA 93117. (805)681-1300. Fax: (805)681-1312. E-mail: msw@rain.org. Editor: John Trotti. 70% freelance written. Bimonthly magazine covering all aspects of erosion prevention and sediment control. "*Erosion Control* is a practical, hands-on, 'how-to' professional journal, and is the official journal of the International Erosion Control Association. Our readers are civil engineers, landscape architects, builders, developers, public works officials, road and highway construction officials and engineers, soils specialists, farmers, landscape contractors and others involved with any activity that disturbs significant areas of surface vegetation. We ask all writers to tailor what they submit to this audience." Estab. 1994. Circ. 17,000. Pays on publication. Publishes ms an average of 3 months after acceptance. Byline given. Offers 10% or $10 kill fee. Buys all rights. Editorial lead time 3 months. Submit seasonal material 4 months in advance. Query for electronic submissions. Reports in 6 weeks on queries; 2 months on mss. Sample copy and writer's guidelines free on request.

Nonfiction: Book excerpts, interview/profile, personal experience, photo feature, technical. "No rudimentary, basic articles written for the average layperson. Our readers are experienced professionals with years of technical, practical experience in the field. Anything submitted that is judged by us to be speaking beneath the readers will be rejected." Buys 20 mss/year. Query with published clips. Length: 1,800-3,200 words. Pays $400. Sometimes pays expenses of writers on assignment.

Photos: Send photos with submission. Reviews transparencies and 5×7 or 8×10 prints. Negotiates payment individually. Captions, model releases and identification of subjects required. Buys all rights.

Columns/Departments: Field Report (news from the readers), 500-2,000 words. Buys 12 mss/year. Query. Pays $50-150.

Fillers: Anecdotes, facts, gags to be illustrated by cartoonist. Buys 30/year. Pays $25-250.

Tips: "We're a small company and easy to reach. We're open to any and all ideas as to editorial topics to cover. We strive to provide the reader with usable material, and present it in full color with graphic embellishment whenever possible. Dry, highly technical material is edited to make it more palatable and concise for the reader. Most of our feature articles come from freelancers. Interviews and quotes should be from the readers—the professionals working in the field—*not* manufacturers, *not* professional PR firms. Strive to write material that is 'over the heads' of our readers. If anything, attempt to make them 'reach.' Anything submitted that is too rudimentary, fundamental, elementary, etc., cannot be accepted for publication."

MSW MANAGEMENT, The Journal for Municipal Solid Waste Professionals, Forester Communications, Inc., 5638 Hollister Ave., Suite 301, Santa Barbara CA 93117. (805)681-1300. Fax: (805)681-1312. E-mail: msw@rain.org. Editor: John Trotti. 70% freelance written. Bimonthly magazine covering solid waste management—landfilling, composting, recycling, incineration. "*MSW Management* is written for *public sector* solid waste professionals—the people working for the local counties, cities, towns, boroughs and provinces. They run the landfills, recycling programs, composting, incineration. They are responsible for all aspects of garbage collection and disposal; buying and maintaining the associated equipment; and designing, engineering and building the waste processing facilities, transfer stations and landfills." Estab. 1991. Circ. 24,000. Pays on publication. Byline given. Offers 10% or $100 kill fee. Buys all rights. Editorial lead time 3 months. Submit seasonal material 4 months in advance. Query for electronic submissions. Reports in 6 weeks on queries; 2 months on mss. Sample copy free on request.

Nonfiction: Book excerpts, interview/profile, personal experience, photo feature, technical. *Elements of Integral Solid Waste Management*, published every October, includes articles and essays on *all* aspects of solid waste management. "No rudimentary, basic articles written for the average person on the street. Our readers are experienced professionals with years of practical, in-the-field experience. Any material submitted that we judge as too fundamental will be rejected." Buys 27 mss/year. Query. Length: 1,800-3,500 words. Pays $400. Sometimes pays expenses of writers on assignment.

Photos: Send photos with submission. Reviews transparencies and 5×7 or 8×10 prints. Negotiates payment individually. Captions, model releases and identification of subjects required. Buys all rights.

Columns/Departments: Field Report (news from the readers), 2,000 words; Washington Watch (news from DC), 1,500 words; Contracting (negotiating with the private sector). Buys 18 mss/year. Query. Pays $50-250.

Fillers: Anecdotes, facts, gags to be illustrated by cartoonist. Buys 30/year. Pays $25-250.

Tips: "We're a small company, easy to reach. We're open to any and all ideas as to possible editorial topics. We endeavor to provide the reader with usable material, and present it in full color with graphic embellishment whenever possible. Dry, highly technical material is edited to make it more palatable and concise. Most of our feature articles come from freelancers. Interviews and quotes should be from public sector solid waste managers and engineers—*not* PR people, *not* manufacturers. Strive to write material that is 'over the heads' of our readers. If anything, attempt to make them 'reach.' Anything submitted that is too basic, elementary, fundamental, rudimentary, etc. cannot be accepted for publication."

‡**THE PUMPER**, COLE Publishing Inc., Drawer 220, Three Lakes WI 54562-0220. (715)546-3347. President: Robert J. Kendall. Production Manager: Ken Lowther. 50% freelance written. Eager to work with new/unpublished writers. Monthly tabloid covering the liquid waste hauling industry (portable toilet renters, septic tank pumpers, industrial waste haulers, chemical waste haulers, oil field haulers, and hazardous waste haulers). "Our publication is read by companies that handle liquid waste and manufacturers of equipment." Estab. 1979. Circ. 15,000. Pays on publication. Publishes ms an average of 1 month after acceptance. Byline given. Buys first serial rights. Free sample copy and writer's guidelines.

Nonfiction: Exposé (government regulations, industry problems, trends, public attitudes, etc.); general interest (state association meetings, conventions, etc.); how-to (related to industry, e.g., how to incorporate septage or municipal waste into farm fields, how to process waste, etc.); humor (related to industry, especially septic tank pumpers or portable toilet renters); interview/profile (including descriptions of business statistics, type of equipment, etc.); new product; personal experience; photo feature; and technical (especially reports on research projects related to disposal). "We are looking for quality articles that will be of interest to our readers; length is not important. We publish trade journals. We need articles that deal with the trade. Studies on land application of sanitary waste are of great interest." Query or send complete ms. Pays 7½¢/word.

Photos: Send photos with query or ms. Pays $15 for b&w and color prints that are used. No negatives. "We need good contrast." Captions "suggested" and model release required. Buys one-time rights.

Tips: "Material must pertain to liquid waste-related industries listed above. We hope to expand the editorial content of our monthly publications. We also have publications for sewer and drain cleaners with the same format as *The Pumper*; however, *The Cleaner* has a circulation of 18,000. We are looking for the same type of articles and pay is the same."

RESOURCE RECYCLING, North America's Recycling Journal, Resource Recycling, Inc., Dept. WM, P.O. Box 10540, Portland OR 97210-0540. (503)227-1319. Fax: (503)227-6135. Editor-in-Chief: Jerry Powell. Editor: Meg Lynch. 5% freelance written. Eager to work with new/unpublished writers. Monthly trade journal covering post-consumer recycling of paper, plastics, metals, glass and other materials. Estab. 1982. Circ. 16,000. Pays on publication. Publishes ms an average of 3-9 months after acceptance. Byline given. Buys first rights. Accepts simultaneous and previously published submissions. Send photocopy of article and information about when and where the article previously appeared. For reprints, pays 100% of amount paid for an original article. Query for electronic submissions. Reports in 2-3 months on queries. Sample copy and writer's guidelines for 9×12 SAE with 7 first-class stamps.

Nonfiction: "No non-technical pieces." Buys 2-4 mss/year. Query with published clips. Length: 1,200-1,800 words. Pays $300-350. Pays with contributor copies "if writers are more interested in professional recognition than financial compensation." Sometimes pays the expenses of writers on assignment.

Photos: State availability of photos with submission. Reviews contact sheets, negatives and prints. Offers $5-50. Identification of subjects required. Buys one-time rights.

Tips: "Overviews of one recycling aspect in one state (e.g., oil recycling in Alabama) will receive attention. We will increase coverage of source reduction and yard waste composting."

Selling and Merchandising

Sales personnel and merchandisers interested in how to sell and market products successfully consult these journals. Publications in nearly every category of Trade also buy sales-related materials if they are slanted to the product or industry with which they deal.

‡**ANSOM, Army Navy Store and Outdoor Merchandiser**, PTN Publishing Co., 445 Broad Hollow Rd., Melville NY 11747. (516)845-2700. Editor: Paul Bubny. 10% freelance written. Monthly tabloid covering army/navy and outdoor product retailing (camping, hunting, fishing and related outdoor sports). Estab. 1949. Circ. 10,400. Pays on publication. Publishes ms an average of 2 months after acceptance. Byline given. Buys one-time rights. Editorial lead time 6 weeks. Submit seasonal material 3 months in advance. Accepts

previously published submissions, if not published in competing magazine. Accept electronic submissions by disk. Reports in 1 week on queries; 1 month on mss. Writer's guidelines free on request.

Nonfiction: Book excerpts, how-to (merchandise various products manage a retail operation), interview/profile, new product, technical. Buys 6-9 mss/year. Send complete ms. Length: 800-4,000 words. Pays $125-200 for assigned articles; $75-125 for unsolicited articles. Sometimes pays expenses of writers on assignment.

Photos: Send photos with submission. Reviews 5×8 prints, color slides. Negotiates payment individually. Captions, identification of subjects required. Buys one-time rights.

Columns/Departments: Legal Advisor (legal issues for small business owners), 1,000-1,200 words; Business Insights (general management topics of interest to small business owners), 1,000-1,500 words. Buys 12-18 mss/year. Send complete ms. Pays $75-125.

Tips: "Approach the editor either with subject matter that fits in with the magazine's specific area of concern, or with willingness to take on assignments that fit magazine's editorial scope."

ASD/AMD TRADE NEWS, Associated Surplus Dealers/Associated Merchandise Dealers, 2525 Ocean Park Blvd., Santa Monica CA 90405-5201. (310)396-6006. Fax: (310)399-2662. Editor: Roger Backlar. 80% freelance written. Monthly trade newspaper on topics of interest to small retailers, wholesalers, merchandise dealers, swap meat vendors etc. "Many of our readers have small, family-owned businesses." Estab. 1967. Circ. 90,000. Pays on publication. Publishes ms an average of 1-2 months after acceptance. Byline given. Offers 25% kill fee. Buys one-time rights. Submit seasonal material 3 months in advance. Accepts simultaneous and previously published submissions. Send hardcopy ms and computer disk with rights for sale noted and information about when and where the article previously appeared. For reprints, pays 100% of the amount paid for an original article. Reports in 2 weeks on queries; 2 months on mss. Free sample copy and writer's guidelines.

Nonfiction: How-to (merchandise a store more effectively, buy and sell products), product/category specific (query first), interview/profile (dealers/owners), personal experience (of dealers and merchandisers), photo feature (ASD/AMD trade shows), general small business articles of interest. "February and August are the largest issues of the year. We generally need more freelance material for those two issues. No articles that are solely self-promotion pieces or straight editorials. We also need articles that tell a small business owner/manager how to handle legal issues, home business topics, import/export, personnel questions and business matters, such as accounting." Buys 100 mss/year. Query with or without published clips, or send complete ms. Length: 1,000-1,500 words. Pays $125-200. Pays expenses of writers on assignment.

Photos: State availability of photos with submission. Reviews 3½×5 prints. Payment depends on whether photos were assigned or not. Identification of subjects required. Buys one-time rights.

Columns/Departments: Business & News Briefs (summarizes important news/business news affecting small businesses/dealers/merchandisers), 500 words; ASD Profile (interview with successful dealer), 1,000 words; Merchandising Tips (how to better merchandise a business), 1,000 words; Legal, Finance, Marketing, Advertising, Personnel sections, 1,000 words; Merchandise/business specific features, 1,500 words. Buys 70 mss/year. Query or send complete ms. Pays $125-200.

Tips: "Talk to retailers. Find out what their concerns are, and the types of wholesalers/merchandisers they deal with. Write articles to meet those needs. It's as simple as that. The entire publication is open to freelance writers who can write good articles. We're now more sectionalized. We especially need articles that are of use or interest to very small businesses (1-10 employees). We need new looks at the cities in which we hold trade shows (Las Vegas, Atlantic City, Reno, and New York.)"

BALLOONS AND PARTIES TODAY MAGAZINE, The Original Balloon Magazine of New-Fashioned Ideas, Festivities Publications, 1205 W. Forsyth St., Jacksonville FL 32204. (904)634-1902. Fax: (904)633-8764. Publisher: Debra Paulk. Editor: April Anderson. 10% freelance written. Monthly international trade journal for professional party decorators and for gift delivery businesses. Estab. 1986. Circ. 10,000. Pays on publication. Publishes ms an average of 3 months after acceptance. Byline given. Buys one-time rights. Submit seasonal material 6 months in advance. Query for electronic submissions. Reports in 6 weeks. Sample copy for 9×12 SAE.

Nonfiction: Interview/profile, photo feature, technical, craft. Buys 12 mss/year. Query with or without published clips or send complete ms. Length: 500-1,500 words. Pays $100-300 for assigned articles; $50-200 for unsolicited articles. Sometimes pays expenses of writers on assignment.

Photos: Send photos with submission. Reviews 2×2 transparencies and 3×5 prints. Pays $10/photo accepted with ms (designs, arrangements, decorations only—no payment for new products). Captions, model releases and identification of subjects required. Buys one-time rights.

Columns/Departments: Great Ideas (craft projects using balloons, large scale decorations), 200-500 words. Send full manuscript with photos. Pays $10/photo.

Tips: "Show unusual, lavish, and outstanding examples of balloon sculpture, design and decorating. Offer specific how-to information. Be positive and motivational in style."

CHRISTIAN RETAILING, Strang Communications, 600 Rinehart Road, Lake Mary FL 32746. (407)333-0600. Fax: (407)333-9753. Managing Editor: Carol Chapman Stertzer. 60% freelance written. Trade journal featuring 18 issues/year covering issues and products of interest to Christian vendors and retail stores. "Our editorial is geared to help retailers run a successful business. We do this with product information, industry news and feature articles." Estab. 1958. Circ. 9,500. Pays on publication. Publishes ms an average of 5 months after acceptance. Bylines sometimes given. Kill fee varies. Buys all rights. Submit seasonal material 5 months in advance. Accepts previously published submissions. Send photocopy of article and information about when and where the article previously appeared. Reports in 2 months. Sample copy for $3. Writer's guidelines for #10 SASE.

Nonfiction: How-to (any articles on running a retail business—books, gifts, music, video, clothing of interest to Christians), new product, religious, technical. Buys 36 mss/year. Send complete ms. Length: 700-2,000 words. Pays $200-340. Sometimes pays expenses of writers on assignment.

Photos: State availability of photos with submission. Reviews contact sheets, transparencies and prints. Usually offers no additional payment for photos accepted with ms. Captions required. Buys one-time rights.

Columns/Departments: Industry News; Book News; Music News; Video Update; Product Spectrum; Gift News.

Fillers: Cartoon, illustrations, graphs/charts.

Tips: "Visit Christian bookstores and see what they're doing—the products they carry, the issues that concern them. Then write about it!"

COLLEGE STORE, (formerly *College Store Journal*), National Association of College Stores, 500 E. Lorain, Oberlin OH 44074. (216)775-7777. Editor: Ronald D. Stevens. 50% freelance written. Bimonthly association magazine covering college bookstore operations (retailing). "*College Store* is the journal of record for the National Association of College Stores and serves its members by publishing information and expert opinion on all phases of college store retailing." Estab. 1928. Circ. 7,200. Pays on publication or special arrangement. Byline given. Buys first rights. Editorial lead time 2 months. Submit seasonal material 6 months in advance. Accepts simultaneous submissions. Query for electronic submissions. Reports in 1 month. Sample copy free on request. Writer's guidelines not available.

Nonfiction: Historical/nostalgic, how-to, interview/profile, personal experience, technical (unique attributes of college stores/personnel). "Articles must have clearly defined connection to college stores and collegiate retailing." Buys 24 mss/year. Query with published clips. Length: 1,500-3,000 words. Pays $400 minimum for assigned articles; $200 minimum for unsolicited articles. Sometimes pays expenses of writers on assignment.

Photos: Send photos with submission. Reviews 2¼ × 2¼ transparencies and 5 × 7 prints. Negotiates payment individually. Captions and identification of subjects required. Buys one-time rights.

Columns/Departments: Buys 12 mss/year. Query with published clips. Pays $200-400.

Tips: "It's best if writers work (or have worked) in a college store. Articles on specific retailing successes are most open to freelancers—they should include information on how well an approach worked and the reasons for it, whether they are specific to a campus or region, etc."

‡COMICS RETAILER, Business Management for the Comics Industry, Krause Publications, 700 E. State St., Iola WI 54990. Editor: John Jackson Miller. 50% freelance written. Monthly magazine covering comic-book store retail topics; product news; "how-to sell"; commentary. "We try to help our readers apply 'real-world' retailing techniques to the flourishing, but still very young, comic-book retail industry. Reader knowledge of technical retailing techniques varies widely, so articles must be useful to novice and sophisticated retailers alike." Estab. 1992. Circ. 6,000. Pays on publication. Publishes ms an average of 6 months after acceptance. Byline given. Buys one-time rights or perpetual but non-exclusive rights. Editorial lead time 1 month. Submit seasonal material 3 months in advance. Accepts simultaneous submissions, if so noted. Reports in 3 months. Sample copy for $5.

Nonfiction: How-to (retail management), interview/profile, new product, photo feature. Buys 30 mss/year. Send complete ms. Length: 2,500 words maximum. Pays $50-250 for assigned articles; $25-225 for unsolicited articles.

Photos: State availability of photos with submissions. Reviews 5 × 7 prints. Negotiates payment individually. Captions, identification of subjects required. Buys one-time rights.

Tips: "We want to help our readers prosper in an industry that's grown out of a hobby in just a few short years. We don't expect outsiders to be familiar with the very special nature of the comics retail field—in fact, so much is unique to the field that readers will recognize a fumbled attempt to relate to them right away. Rather, our audience desires nuts-and-bolts information that'll help them run more efficient, successful stores. Writers who can teach without talking down and who stay abreast of retailing issues do well with us."

‡ELECTRONIC RETAILING, The Magazine for the New Age of Marketing, Creative Age Publications, 7628 Densmore Ave., Van Nuys CA 91406-2088. (818)782-7328. Executive Editor: Kathy St. Louis. 80% freelance written. Bimonthly magazine covering electronic retailing applications for marketers. "Writing for our readers requires knowledge of basic marketing (advertising principles), familiarity with emerging fields of computer-based selling (online shopping, CD-ROM, CDi), direct response television, television shopping, cable television industry." Estab. 1994. Circ. 21,500. **Pays on acceptance**. Publishes ms 1-2 months after acceptance. Byline given. Offers 50% kill fee. Buys first rights and one-time rights. Editorial lead time 2 months. Submit seasonal material 4-6 months in advance. Considers simultaneous submissions. Query for electronic submisions. Sample copy free.

Nonfiction: How-to (market or sell product or service using new electronic media), interview/profile, opinion. No previously published or general business articles. Buys 20-30 mss/year. Query with published clips. Length: 500-2,000 words. Pays $150-400 for assigned articles; $100-300 for unsolicited articles. Sometimes pays expenses of writers on assignment.

Photos: Send photos with submission. Offers no additional payment for photos accepted with ms. Identification of subjects required. Buys one-time rights.

Columns/Departments: On the Air (new TV advertising), 500 words; Channel News (new cable TV channels), 500 words; New Media (new marketing applications in CD-ROM, on-line services, interactive TV, kiosks), 500-750 words; Book Review (new-age marketing related), 500-750 words. Buys 20 mss/year. Query with published clips. Pays $50-100 per item.

Tips: "Provide summary of similar writing experience, business background, areas of expertise. Fax or mail, then follow up with phone call to discuss with editor."

EVENTS BUSINESS NEWS, S.E.N. Inc., (formerly *Special Events Business News*), 523 Route 38, Suite 207, Cherry Hill NJ 08002. (609)488-5255. Contact: Maria King. 20% freelance written. Monthly tabloid covering special events across North America, including festivals, fairs, auto shows, home shows, trade shows, etc. Covers 21 categories of shows/events. Byline given. Buys first rights. Submit seasonal material 3 months in advance. Accepts previously published submissions. Send photocopy of article and information about when and where the article previously appeared. Sample copy and writers guidelines free.

Nonfiction: How-to, interview/profile, event review, new product. Special issues: annual event directory, annual flea market directory. No submissions unrelated to selling at events. Query. Length: 400-750 words. Pays $2.50/column inch.

Photos: Send photos with submission. Reviews contact sheets. Offers $10/photo. Captions required. Buys one-time rights.

Columns/Departments: Five columns monthly (must deal with background of event, vendors or unique facets of industry in North America). Query with published clips. Length: 400-700 words. Pays $3/column inch.

INCENTIVE, Bill Communications, Dept. WM, 355 Park Ave., New York NY 10010. (212)986-4800. Fax: (212)867-4395. Editor: Jennifer Juergens. Executive Editor: Judy Quinn. Monthly magazine covering sales promotion and employee motivation: managing and marketing through motivation. Estab. 1905. Circ. 41,000. **Pays on acceptance.** Publishes ms an average of 3 months after acceptance. Byline always given. Buys all rights. Accepts previously published submissions. Send tearsheet and information about when and where the article previously appeared. For reprints, pays 50% of the amount paid for an original article. Query for electronic submissions. Reports in 1 month on queries; 2 months on mss. Sample copy for 9×12 SAE.

• *Incentive* won the *Folio* Award of Excellence in 1994.

Nonfiction: General interest (motivation, demographics), how-to (types of sales promotion, buying product categories, using destinations), interview/profile (sales promotion executives); corporate case studies; travel (incentive-oriented). Buys up to 48 mss/year. Query with 2 published clips. Length: 1,000-2,000 words. Pays $250-700 for assigned articles; does not pay for unsolicited articles. Pays expenses of writers on assignment.

Photos: Send photos with submission. Reviews contact sheets and transparencies. Offers no additional payment for photos accepted with ms. Identification of subjects required.

Tips: "Read the publication, then query."

‡INFO FRANCHISE NEWSLETTER, P.O. Box 670, 9 Duke St., St. Catharines, Ontario L2R 6W8 Canada. (905)688-2665. Fax: (905)688-7728. Also P.O. Box 550, 728 Center St., Lewiston NY 14092-0550. (716)754-4669. Editor-in-Chief: E.L. Dixon, Jr. Assistant Editor: Heather Maguire. Monthly newsletter. Estab. 1977. Circ. 4,000. Pays on publication. Buys all rights. Reports in 1 month.

Nonfiction: Exposè, how-to, informational, interview, profile, new product, personal experience, technical. "We are particularly interested in receiving articles regarding franchise legislation, franchise litigation, franchise success stories, and new franchises. Both American and Canadian items are of interest. We do not want to receive any information which is not fully documented or articles which could have appeared in any newspaper or magazine in North America. An author with a legal background who could comment upon such things as arbitration and franchising or class actions and franchising, would be of great interest to us."

NICHE, The Magazine For Progressive Retailers, The Rosen Group, 3000 Chestnut Ave., Suite 300, Baltimore MD 21211. (410)889-3093. Editor: Hope Daniels. 10% freelance written. Quarterly magazine covering contemporary art and craft retailers. "*NICHE* centers on creative answers to the various problems and dilemmas retailers face daily. Minimal coverage of product. Audience is 80% independent retailers of contemporary craft and unique products designed and made in the US, other 20% are professional craftspeople." Estab. 1988. Circ. 20,000. Pays on publication. Publishes ms an average of 4 months after acceptance. Byline given. Buys second serial (reprint) or all rights. Editorial lead time 2 months. Submit seasonal material 6 months in advance. Accepts previously published submissions. Query for electronic submissions.

Reports in 1 month on queries; 6 weeks on mss. Sample copy for $3. Writer's guidelines for #10 SASE.
• *Niche* is looking for in-depth articles on store security, innovative merchandising/display or marketing and promotion. Stories of interest to independent retailers, such as gallery owners, may be submitted.

Nonfiction: Interview/profile, opinion, photo feature, and articles targeted to independent retailers and small business owners. Buys 6-10 mss/year. Query with published clips. Length: 500-3,000 words. Pays $100. Sometimes pays expenses of writers on assignment.

Photos: Send photos with submission. Reviews 4×5 transparencies or slides. Negotiates payment individually. Identification of subjects required. Buys all rights.

Columns/Departments: Retail Details (general retail information), 350 words; Artist Profiles (biographies of American Craft Artists), 450 words; Resources (book/video/seminar reviews pertaining to retailers), 200 words. Buys 6 mss/year. Query with published clips. Pays $40-300.

PARTY & PAPER RETAILER, 4Ward Corp, 70 New Canaan Ave., Norwalk CT 06850. (203)845-8020. Editor: Trisha McMahon Drain. 90% freelance written. Monthly magazine for party goods and fine stationery industry covering "every aspect of how to do business better for owners of party and fine stationery shops. Tips and how-tos on display, marketing, success stories, advertising, operating costs, etc." Estab. 1985. Circ. 25,000. Pays on publication. Offers 10% kill fee. Buys first North American serial rights. Editorial lead time 6 months. Submit seasonal material 6 months in advance. Accepts previously published submissions. Send tearsheet or photocopy of article and information about when and where the article previously appeared. Query for electronic submissions. Reports in 2 months. Sample copy for $4.50

Nonfiction: Book excerpts, how-to (retailing related). No articles written in the first person. Buys 100 mss/year. Query with published clips. Length: 800-1,800 words. Pay "depends on topic, word count expertise, deadline." Pays telephone expenses of writers on assignment.

Photos: State availability of photos with submission. Reviews transparencies. Negotiates payment individually. Captions and identification of subjects required. Buys one-time rights.

Columns/Departments: Shop Talk (successful party/stationery store profile), 1,800 words; Storekeeping (selling, employees, market, running store), 800 words; Cash Flow (anything finance related), 800 words; On Display (display ideas and how-to). Buys 30 mss/year. Query with published clips. Pay varies.

PROFESSIONAL SELLING, 24 Rope Ferry Rd., Waterford CT 06386-0001. (203)442-4365. Fax: (203)434-3078. Editor: Paulette S. Kitchens. 33% freelance written. Prefers to work with published/established writers. Bimonthly newsletter in 2 sections for sales professionals covering industrial, wholesale, high-tech and financial services sales. "*Professional Selling* provides field sales personnel with both the basics and current information that can help them better perform the sales function." Estab. 1917. **Pays on acceptance.** Publishes ms an average of 4-6 months after acceptance. No byline given. Buys all rights. Submit seasonal material 6 months in advance. Reports in 1 month. Sample copy and writer's guidelines for #10 SAE with 2 first-class stamps.

Nonfiction: How-to (successful sales techniques); interview/profile (interview-based articles). "We buy only interview-based material." Buys 12-15 mss/year. No unsolicited mss; written queries only. Length: 800-1,000 words.

Tips: "*Professional Selling* includes a 4-page "Sales Spotlight" devoted to a single topic of major importance to sales professionals. Only the lead article for each section is open to freelancers. Lead article must be based on an interview with an actual sales professional. Freelancers may occasionally interview sales managers, but the slant must be toward field sales, *not* management."

‡**SALES AND MARKETING STRATEGIES & NEWS**, Hughes Communications, 211 W. State St., Rockford IL 61101. Managing Editor: Bruce Ericson. Contact: Kristi Nelson, Associate Editor. Tabloid published 8 times/year covering brand, promotion, incentives, sales automation, sales training, marketing, meetings, p.o.p., trade shows. Estab. 1991. Circ. 72,000. Pays on publication. Publishes ms 2-3 months after acceptance. Byline given. Offers 15% kill fee. Buys first North American serial rights. Editorial lead time 4 months. Query for electronic submissions. Sample copy and writer's guidelines free on request.

Nonfiction: How-to, technical. Buys 120 mss/year. Query. Length: 500-900 words. Pays $150-300 for assigned articles. "Expert writers are given a bio at end of story." Sometimes pays expenses of writers on assignment.

Photos: Send photos with submission. Reviews transparencies and prints. Offers no additional payment for photos accepted with ms. Identification of subjects requried.

Sport Trade

Retailers and wholesalers of sports equipment and operators of recreation programs read these journals. Magazines about general and specific sports are classified in the Consumer Sports section.

AMERICAN FIREARMS INDUSTRY, AFI Communications Group, Inc., 2455 E. Sunrise Blvd., 9th Floor, Ft. Lauderdale FL 33304-3118. Fax: (305)561-4129. 10% freelance written. Works with writers specifically in the firearms trade. Monthly magazine specializing in the sporting arms trade. Estab. 1973. Circ. 30,000. Pays on publication. Publishes ms an average of 1 month after acceptance. Buys all rights. Reports in 2 weeks.

Nonfiction: R.A. Lesmeister, articles editor. Publishes informational, technical and new product articles. No general firearms subjects. Query. Length: 900-1,500 words. Pays $150-300. Sometimes pays the expenses of writers on assignment.

Photos: Reviews 8×10 color glossy prints. Manuscript price includes payment for photos.

AMERICAN FITNESS, 15250 Ventura Blvd., Suite 200, Sherman Oaks CA 91403. (818)905-0040. Fax: (818)990-5468. Editor-at-Large: Peg Jordan, R.N. Managing Editor: Rhonda J. Wilson. 75% freelance written. Eager to work with new/unpublished writers. Bimonthly magazine covering exercise and fitness, health and nutrition. "We need timely, in-depth, informative articles on health, fitness, aerobic exercise, sports nutrition, age-specific fitness and outdoor activity." Circ. 29,000. Pays 4-6 weeks after publication. Publishes ms an average of 6 months after acceptance. Byline given. Buys all rights. Submit seasonal material 4 months in advance. Accepts simultaneous and previously published submissions. Query for electronic submissions. Reports in 6 weeks. Sample copy for $1 and SAE with 6 first-class stamps. Writer's guidelines for SAE.

Nonfiction: Women's health and fitness issues (pregnancy, family, pre- and post-natal, menopause and eating disorders); exposé (on nutritional gimmickry); historical/nostalgic (history of various athletic events); inspirational (sports leader's motivational pieces); interview/profile (fitness figures); new product (plus equipment review); personal experience (successful fitness story); photo feature (on exercise, fitness, new sport); youth and senior fitness; travel (spas that cater to fitness industry). No articles on unsound nutritional practices, popular trends or unsafe exercise gimmicks. Buys 18-25 mss/year. Query. Length: 800-1,500 words. Pays $80-140. Sometimes pays expenses of writers on assignment.

Photos: Sports, action, fitness, aquatic aerobics, aerobic competitions and exercise classes. "We are especially interested in photos of high-adrenalin sports like rock climbing and mountain biking." Pays $10 for b&w prints; $35 for transparencies. Captions, model release and identification of subjects required. Usually buys all rights; other rights purchased depend on use of photo.

Columns/Departments: Adventure (treks, trails and global challenges); strength (the latest breakthroughs in weight training) and clubscene (profiles and highlights of the fitness club industry). Query with published clips or send complete ms. Length: 800-1,000 words. Pays $80-100.

Fillers: Cartoons, clippings, jokes, short humor, newsbreaks. Buys 12/year. Length: 75-200 words. Pays $35.

Tips: "Cover a unique aerobics or fitness angle, provide accurate and interesting findings, and write in a lively, intelligent manner. We are looking for new health and fitness reporters and writers. *AF* is a good place for first-time authors or for regularly published authors who want to sell spin-offs or reprints."

AQUA, The Business Magazine for Spa and Pool Professionals, Athletic Business Publications, 1846 Hoffman St., Madison WI 53704. (608)249-0186. Fax: (608)249-1153. Editor: Alan E. Sanderfoot. Managing Editor: Elissa Sard Pollack. Contact: Alan E. Sanderfoot. 20% freelance written. Monthly magazine covering swimming pools and spas. "*AQUA* is a business magazine for swimming pool and spa retailers, builders and service communities." Estab. 1975. Circ. 16,000. Pays on publication. Byline given. Publishes ms an average of 2 months after acceptance. Offers 25% kill fee. Buys first North American serial rights. Editorial lead time 4 months. Submit seasonal material 4 months in advance. Accepts simultaneous and previously published submissions. Send photocopy of article or typed ms with rights for sale noted and information about when and where the article previously appeared. Query for electronic submissions. Reports in 1 month on queries; 3 months on mss. Sample copy for 8½×11 SAE with 6 first-class stamps.

Nonfiction: How-to (store design, advertising, promotion, personnel management), interview/profile (dealer). No personal anecdotes. Buys 40 mss/year. Query with published clips. Length: 1,200-2,500 words. Pays $50-500 for assigned articles, $0-50 for unsolicited articles. Sometimes pays expenses of writers on assignment (limit agreed upon in advance).

Photos: Send photos with submission. Reviews transparencies, prints. Offers no additional payment for photos accepted with ms. Captions and identification of subjects required. Buys rights.

Columns/Departments: Sales (retail sales), 1,000 words; Management (retail), 1,000 words; Finance (retail), 1,000 words. Buys 30 mss/year. Query with published clips. Pays $0-100.

Tips: "Read the magazine, learn about pool and spa construction, and understand retailing. We are most open to profiles—find pool/spa dealers with a unique approach to retailing and highlight that in a query."

BOWLING PROPRIETOR, Bowling Proprietors' Association of America, P.O. Box 5802, Arlington TX 76017. (817)649-5105. Editor: Daniel W. Burgess. 5% freelance written. Monthly magazine covering bowling industry. "We cover the business of bowling, from the perspective of the owners and operators of bowling *centers* (not alleys)." Estab. 1954. Circ. 5,000. Pays on publication. Publishes ms an average of 2 months after acceptance. Byline sometimes given. Offers 50% kill fee. Buys first North American serial rights. Editorial lead time 2 months. Submit seasonal material 4 months in advance. Accepts simultaneous and previously published submissions. Send tearsheet or photocopy of article and information about when and where the article previously appeared. For reprints, pays 25% of the amount paid for an original article. Query for electronic submissions. Reports in 6 weeks on queries. Sample copy free on request.

Nonfiction: Book excerpts, how-to, interview/profile, new product, opinion, technical and business angles, i.e., marketing, customer service. "No 50s, 60s nostalgia pieces." Buys 2 mss/year. Query with published clips. Length: 500-1,200 words. Pays $300 minimum for assigned articles; $100 minimum for unsolicited articles. Sometimes pays in contributor copies or other premiums for "unsolicited, mutually beneficial articles." Sometimes pays expenses of writers on assignment (limit agreed upon in advance).

Photos: State availability of photos with submission. Reviews contact sheets, 35mm transparencies, 5×7 or 8×10 prints. Negotiates payment individually. Captions and identification of subjects required. Buys one-time rights.

Columns/Departments: News Notes (regular news items of the industry), 250 words. Buys 1 ms/year. Send complete ms. Pays $10-50.

FITNESS MANAGEMENT, Issues and Solutions for Fitness Services, Leisure Publications, Inc., 215 S. Highway 101, Suite 110, P.O. Box 1198, Solana Beach CA 92075-0910. (619)481-4155. Fax: (619)481-4228. E-mail: fitmgt@cts.com. Editor: Edward H. Pitts. Managing Editor: Ronale McClure. 50% freelance written. Monthly magazine covering commercial, corporate and community fitness centers. "Readers are owners, managers and program directors of physical fitness facilities. *FM* helps them run their enterprises safely, efficiently and profitably. Ethical and professional positions in health, nutrition, sports medicine, management, etc., are consistent with those of established national bodies." Estab. 1985. Circ. 26,000. Pays on publication. Publishes ms an average of 5 months after acceptance. Byline given. Pays 50% kill fee. Buys all rights. Submit seasonal material 6 months in advance. Query for electronic submissions. Reports in 3 months. Sample copy for $5. Writer's guidelines for #10 SASE.

Nonfiction: Book excerpts (prepublication), how-to (manage fitness center and program), new product (no pay), photo feature (facilities/programs), technical and other (news of fitness research and major happenings in fitness industry). No exercise instructions or general ideas without examples of fitness businesses that have used them successfully. Buys 50 mss/year. Query. Length: 750-2,000 words. Pays $60-300 for assigned articles; up to $300 for unsolicited articles. Pays expenses of writers on assignment.

Photos: Send photos with submission. Reviews contact sheets, 2×2 and 4×5 transparencies; prefers glossy prints, 5×7 to 8×10. Offers $10-25/photo. Captions and model releases required.

Tips: "We seek writers who are expert in a business or science field related to the fitness-service industry or who are experienced in the industry. Be current with the state of the art/science in business and fitness and communicate it in human terms (avoid intimidating academic language; tell the story of how this was learned and/or cite examples of quotes of people who have applied the knowledge successfully)."

GOLF COURSE NEWS, The Newspaper for the Golf Course Industry, United Publications Inc., P.O. Box 997, 38 Lafayette St., Yarmouth ME 04096. (207)846-0600. Fax: (207)846-0657. Managing Editor: Mark Leslie. 15% freelance written. Monthly tabloid covering golf course maintenance, design, construction and management. "Articles should be written with the golf course superintendent in mind. Our readers are superintendents, course architects and builders, owners and general managers." Estab. 1989. Circ. 25,000. **Pays on acceptance.** Publishes ms an average of 2 months after acceptance. Byline given. Buys first North American serial rights. Editorial lead time 1 month. Submit seasonal material 2 months in advance. Accepts simultaneous submissions. Query for electronic submissions. Reports in 2 weeks on queries; 2 months on mss. Free sample copy and writer's guidelines.

Nonfiction: Book excerpts, general interest, interview/profile, new product, opinion, photo feature. "No how-to articles." Buys 24 mss/year. Query with published clips. Length: 500-1,500 words. Pays $200. Sometimes pays expenses of writers on assignment.

Photos: Send photos with submission. Reviews negatives, transparencies and prints. Offers no additional payment for photos accepted with ms. Identification of subjects required. Buys one-time rights.

Columns/Departments: On the Green (innovative ideas in the industry), 1,000 words. Buys 4 mss/year. Query with published clips. Pays $200-500.

Tips: "Keep your eye out for news affecting the golf industry. Then contact us with your story ideas. We are a national paper and accept both national and regional interest articles. We are interested in receiving features on development of golf projects. We also have an edition covering the golf industry in the Asia-Pacific retion—aptly called *Golf Course News Asia-Pacific* published four times per year—April, June, September and November. Contact person is Editor Hal Phillips."

‡IDEA TODAY, The International Association of Fitness Professionals, Dept. WM, 6190 Cornerstone Court E., Suite 204, San Diego CA 92121. (619)535-8979. Assistant Editor: Therese Hannon. Editor: Patricia A. Ryan. Executive Editor: Mary Monroe. 70% freelance written. Magazine published 10 times/year for the dance-exercise and personal training industry. "All articles must be geared to fitness professionals—aerobics instructors, one-to-one trainers and studio and health club owners—covering topics such as aerobics, nutrition, injury prevention, entrepreneurship in fitness, fitness-oriented research and exercise programs." Estab. 1984. Circ. 20,000. **Pays on acceptance.** Publishes ms an average of 4 months after acceptance. Byline given. Buys all rights. Accepts simultaneous submissions. Reports in 2 months on queries. Sample copy for $4.

Nonfiction: How-to, technical. No general information on fitness; our readers are pros who need detailed information. Buys 15 mss/year. Query. Length: 1,000-3,000 words. Pays $100-300.

Photos: State availability of photos with submission. Offers no additional payment for photos with ms. Model releases required. Buys all rights.

Columns/Departments: Exercise Science (detailed, specific info; must be written by expert), 750-1,500 words; Industry News (short reports on research, programs and conferences), 150-300 words; Fitness Handout (exercise and nutrition info for participants), 750 words. Buys 80 mss/year. Query. Length: 150-1,500 words. Pays varies.

Tips: "We don't accept fitness information for the consumer audience on topics such as why exercise is good for you. Writers who have specific knowledge of, or experience working in the fitness industry have an edge."

INLINE RETAILER & INDUSTRY NEWS, Sports & Fitness Publishing, 2025 Pearl St., Boulder CO 80302. (303)440-5111. Fax: (303)440-3313. E-mail: Mshafran@aol.com. Editor: Michael W. Shafran. 15% freelance written. Monthly tabloid covering the in-line skating industry. "*InLine Retailer* is a business magazine dedicated to spotting new trends, products and procedures that will help in-line retailers and manufacturers keep a competitive edge." Estab. 1992. Circ. 6,000. Pays on publication. Publishes ms an average of 1 month after acceptance. Byline given. Offers 30% kill fee. Buys first North American serial rights. Editorial lead time 2 months. Submit seasonal material 3-4 months in advance. Query for electronic submissions. Prefers Macintosh compatible. Reports in 2 weeks on queries. Sample copy for $5.

● *Inline Retailer* reports that it is looking for more writers with a background in business, particularly sporting goods, to help write news pieces providing insight or analysis into the in-line industry.

Nonfiction: How-to, interview/profile, new product, technical. Buys 30 mss/year. Query with published clips. Length: 500-2,000 words. Pays 15¢/word minimum for assigned articles; 10¢/word for unsolicited articles. Sometimes pays expenses of writers on assignment.

Columns/Departments: Retailer Corner (tips for running an in-line retail store), 1,000-1,200 words; Industry Interview (insights from high-level industry figures), 1,200-1,500 words. Buys 10 mss/year. Query with published clips or send complete ms. Pays 10-15¢/word.

Tips: "It's best to write us and explain your background in either the sporting goods business or in-line skating. Mail several clips and also send some ideas that you think would be suitable for our readers. The features and Retailer Corner sections are the ones we typically assign to freelancers. Writers should have solid reporting skills, particularly when it comes to getting subjects to disclose technology, news or tips that they may be willing to do without some prodding."

THE INTERNATIONAL SADDLERY AND APPAREL JOURNAL, EEMG, Inc., P.O. Box 3039, Berea KY 40403-3039. (606)986-4644. Fax: (606)986-1770. Editor: Janet Buell. 25% freelance written. Bimonthly magazine "serving the business and marketing needs of the equine trade industry. Feature departments present articles which address the current business and marketing issues, trends, and practices in the equestrian and equine goods industries. Monthly news and products sections are also included." Estab. 1987. Circ. 8,000. Pays on publication. Byline given. Offers negotiable kill fee. Buys first North American serial rights. Accepts previously published submissions. Send photocopy of article or typed ms with rights for sale noted and information about when and where the article previously appeared. Reports in 2 months on queries..

Nonfiction: Exposé (business-oriented), how-to (should be usable business information), interview/profile (with industry people). We are not a "backyard," casual interest horse magazine. No fiction. Buys 60 mss/year. Query with published clips. Length: 1,000-2,500 words. Payment based on piece and the information and value of the article. Rarely pays expenses of writers on assignment.

Photos: State availability of or send photos with submissions. Reviews 3½×5 prints. Offers $5-15/photo (negotiable). Captions or model releases required. Buys one-time rights.

Columns/Departments: International (overseas, business interest pieces), 1,000 words; Retail Marketing (articles that give tack shop retailers information about marketing products), 1,000 words. Buys 10 mss/year. Query with published clips.

Tips: "Read *ISAJ* and other trade publications. Understand that we serve the professional business community, including: tack shops, feed stores, gift shops, and manufacturers. People in the equine trade are like other business-people; they have employees, need insurance, travel, own computers, advertise and want pertinent business information."

ISIA NEWSLETTER, Ice Skating Institute of America, 355 W. Dundee Rd., Buffalo Grove IL 60089. Managing Editor: Lara Lowery. 20% freelance written. Bimonthly newsletter covering ice skating industry. "News-

The double dagger before a listing indicates that the listing is new in this edition. New markets are often more receptive to freelance submissions.

oriented articles on rink/facility management, coaching issues, health, industry business news." Estab. 1961. Circ. 4,500. Pays on publication. Publishes ms an average of 2 months after acceptance. Byline given. Buys one-time rights, second serial (reprint) rights or makes work-for-hire assignments. Editorial lead time 2 months. Submit seasonal material 6 months in advance. Accepts simultaneous and previously published submissions. Send tearsheet of article. Query for electronic submissions. Reports in 1 month on queries; 2 months on mss. Sample copy free on request.

Nonfiction: Book excerpts, how-to, interview/profile, technical, ice skating industry issues, news. Query with published clips. Length: 250-500 words. Pays $75. Sometimes pays expenses of writers on assignment.

Photos: State availability of or send photos with submission. Reviews contact sheets, 5×7 prints. Offers $10-35/photo. Captions, model releases and identification of subjects required. Buys one-time rights or all rights if work-for-hire assignment.

Columns/Departments: WORD (What Other Rinks Are Doing—marketing their program/facility), 250 words or less; Safety (product/air quality/facility safety), 250-500 words; News (industry issues/news), 250-500 words. Buys 6-8 mss/year. Query with published clips. Pays $75-150 depending on extent of research needed for work.

NSGA RETAIL FOCUS, National Sporting Goods Association, 1699 Wall St., Suite 700, Mt. Prospect IL 60056-5780. (708)439-4000. Fax: (708)439-0111. E-mail: nsga1699@aol.com. Publisher: Thomas G. Drake. Associate Publisher: Larry Weindruch. Editor: Bob Nieman. 75% freelance written. Works with a small number of new/unpublished writers each year. "*NSGA Retail Focus* serves as a monthly trade journal for presidents, CEOs and owners of more than 22,000 retail sporting goods firms." Estab. 1948. Circ. 9,000. Pays on publication. Publishes ms an average of 1 month after acceptance. Byline given. Offers 50% kill fee. Buys first rights and second serial (reprint) rights. Submit seasonal material 3 months in advance. Query for electronic submissions. Sample copy for 9×12 SAE with 5 first-class stamps.

Nonfiction: Essays, interview/profile, photo feature. "No articles written without sporting goods retail businesspeople in mind as the audience. In other words, no generic articles sent to several industries." Buys 50 mss/year. Query with published clips. Pays $75-500. Sometimes pays the expenses of writers on assignment.

Photos: State availability of photos with submission. Reviews contact sheets, negatives, transparencies and 5×7 prints. Payment negotiable. Buys one-time rights.

Columns/Departments: Personnel Management (succinct tips on hiring, motivating, firing, etc.); Tax Advisor (simplified explanation of how tax laws affect retailer); Sales Management (in-depth tips to improve sales force performance); Retail Management (detailed explanation of merchandising/inventory control); Advertising (case histories of successful ad campaigns/ad critiques); Legal Advisor; Computers; Store Design; Visual Merchandising; all 1,500 words. Buys 50 mss/year. Query. Length: 1,000-1,500 words. Pays $75-300.

POOL & SPA NEWS, Leisure Publications, 3923 W. Sixth St., Los Angeles CA 90020-4290. (213)385-3926. Fax: (213)383-1152. Editor-in-Chief: Jim McCloskey. 15-20% freelance written. Semimonthly magazine emphasizing news of the swimming pool and spa industry for pool builders, pool retail stores and pool service firms. Estab. 1960. Circ. 17,000. Pays on publication. Publishes ms an average of 1-2 months after acceptance. Buys all rights. Query for electronic submissions. Reports in 2 weeks. Sample copy for $5 and 9×12 SAE with 10 first-class stamps.

Nonfiction: Interview, profile, technical. Phone queries OK. Length: 500-2,000 words. Pays 5-14¢/word. Pays expenses of writers on assignment.

Photos: Pays $10 per b&w photo used.

PROFESSIONAL BOATBUILDER MAGAZINE, WoodenBoat Publications Inc., P.O. Box 78, Naskeag Rd., Brooklin ME 04616-0078. (207)359-4651. Fax: (207)359-8920. Editor: Paul Lazarus. 75% freelance written. Bimonthly magazine for boat building companies, repair yards, naval architects, and marine surveyors. Estab. 1989. Circ. 21,000 (BPA audited). Pays 45 days after acceptance. Byline given. Buys first North American serial rights. Accepts previously published submissions. Send typed ms with rights for sale noted and information about when and where article previously appeared. Reports in 2 months. Free sample copy and writer's guidelines.

Nonfiction: How-to, new product, opinion, technical. "We are now looking for more articles on marine systems (electrical, hydraulic, propulsion, etc.) and accessory equipment (deck hardware, engine controls, etc.)" No information better directed to boating consumers. Buys 30 mss/year. Query with or without published clips or send complete ms. Length: 1,000-4,000 words. Pays 20¢/word. Sometimes pays expenses of writers on assignment.

Photos: State availability of photos with submission. Reviews transparencies and 8×10 b&w prints. Offers $15-200/photo; $350 for color cover. Identification of subjects and full captions required. Buys one-time rights.

Columns/Departments: Judy Robbins, managing editor. Tools of the Trade (new tools/materials/machinery of interest to boatbuilders), 100-500 words. Buys 10 mss/year. Query with published clips. Pays $25-100.

THOROUGHBRED TIMES, Thoroughbred Times Company, Inc., 496 Southland Dr., P.O. Box 8237, Lexington KY 40533. (606)260-9800. Editor: Mark Simon. 10% freelance written. Weekly tabloid covering thoroughbred racing and breeding. "Articles are written for professionals who breed and/or race thoroughbreds at tracks in the US. Articles must help owners and breeders understand racing to help them realize a profit." Estab. 1985. Circ. 15,000. Pays on publication. Publishes ms an average of 1 month after acceptance. Byline given. Offers 50% kill fee. Buys all rights. Submit seasonal material 2 months in advance. Query for electronic submissions. Reports in 2 weeks.
Nonfiction: General interest, historical/nostalgic, interview/profile, technical. Buys 52 mss/year. Query. Length: 500-2,500 words. Pays 10-20¢/word. Sometimes pays expenses of writers on assignment.
Photos: State availability of photos with submission. Reviews prints. Offers $25/photo. Identification of subjects required. Buys one-time rights.
Tips: "We are looking for farm stories and profiles of owners, breeders, jockeys and trainers."

WOODALL'S CAMPGROUND MANAGEMENT, Woodall Publications Corp., 13975 W. Polo Trail Dr., Lake Forest IL 60045. (708)362-6700. Editor: Mike Byrnes. 10% freelance written. Monthly tabloid covering campground management and operation for managers of private and public campgrounds throughout the US. Estab. 1970. Circ. 10,000. Pays after publication. Publishes ms an average of 8 months after acceptance. Byline given. Buys all rights. Reassigns rights to author upon written request. Submit seasonal material 4 months in advance. Reports in 1 month on queries; 2 months on mss. Free sample copy and writer's guidelines.
Nonfiction: How-to, interview/profile, technical. "Our articles tell our readers how to maintain their resources, manage personnel and guests, market, develop new campground areas and activities, and interrelate with the major tourism organizations within their areas. 'Improvement' and 'profit' are the two key words." Buys 14 mss/year. Query. Length: 500 words minimum. Pays $50-200.
Photos: Send contact sheets and negatives. "We pay for each photo used."
Tips: "The best type of story to break in with is a case history approach about how a campground improved its maintenance, physical plant or profitability."

Stone, Quarry and Mining

‡COAL MAGAZINE, Intertec Publishing, 29 N. Wacker Dr., Chicago IL 60606. (312)726-2802. Editor: Arthur P. Sanda. 10% freelance written. Monthly magazine covering US and world coal industry, addressing a "technically-oriented audience along with typical senior level company and corporate offices." Estab. 1900. Circ. 22,000. Pays on publication. Publishes ms an average of 2 months after acceptance. Byline given. No kill fee. Buys all rights. Editorial lead time 1 month. Submit seasonal material 3 months in advance. No simultaneous or previously published submissions. Query for electronic submissions. Reports in 1 month on queries; 2 months on mss. Sample copy and writer's guidelines free on request.
Nonfiction: How-to (reduce costs, improve productivity), interview/profile, new product, technical. Buys 6 mss/year. Send complete ms. Length: 1,000-3,000 words. Pays $100-300. Sometimes pays expenses of writers on assignment.
Photos: Send photos with submission. Reviews transparencies, prints. Offers no additional payment for payment for photos accepted with ms. Captions, identification of subjects required. Buys all rights.
Columns/Departments: Steve Fiscor, managing editor. Developments to Watch (new technology, methods), 1,000 words; Operating Ideas (new technology, methods), 1,000 words; Blasting Concepts (explosives in mining), 1,000 words. Query. Pays $100-300.

COAL PEOPLE MAGAZINE, Al Skinner Inc., Dept. WM, 629 Virginia St. W., P.O. Box 6247, Charleston WV 25362. (304)342-4129. Fax: (304)343-3124. Editor/Publisher: Al Skinner. Managing Editor: Christina Karawan. 50% freelance written. Monthly magazine with stories about coal people, towns and history. "Most stories are about people or historical—either narrative or biographical on all levels of coal people, past and present—from coal execs down to grass roots miners. Most stories are upbeat—showing warmth of family or success from underground up!" Estab. 1976. Circ. 11,000. Pays on publication. Publishes ms an average of 3 months after acceptance. Byline given. Buys first rights, second serial (reprint) rights and makes work-for-hire assignments. Accepts previously published submissions. Send photocopy of article and information about when and where the article previously appeared. Submit seasonal material 2 months in advance. Reports in 3 months. Sample copy for 9×12 SAE with 10 first-class stamps.
Nonfiction: Book excerpts (and film if related to coal), historical/nostalgic (coal towns, people, lifestyles), humor (including anecdotes and cartoons), interview/profile (for coal personalities), personal experience (as relates to coal mining), photo feature (on old coal towns, people, past and present). Special issues: calendar issue for more than 300 annual coal shows, association meetings, etc. (January); surface mining/reclamation award (July); Christmas in Coal Country (December). No poetry, no fiction or environmental attacks on the coal industry. Buys 32 mss/year. Query with published clips. Length: 5,000 words. Pays $75.
Photos: Send photos with submission. Reviews contact sheets, transparencies, and 5×7 prints. Captions and identification of subjects required. Buys one-time rights and one-time reprint rights.

Columns/Departments: Editorials—anything to do with current coal issues (non-paid); Mine'ing Our Business (bull pen column—gossip—humorous anecdotes), Coal Show Coverage (freelance photojournalist coverage of any coal function across the US). Buys 10 mss/year. Query. Length: 300-500 words. Pays $15.

Fillers: Anecdotes. Buys 10/year. Length: 300 words. Pays $15.

Tips: "We are looking for good feature articles on coal people, towns, companies—past and present, color slides (for possible cover use) and b&w photos to complement stories. Could also use a few news writers to take photos and do journalistic coverage on coal events across the country. Slant stories more toward people and less on historical. More faces and names than old town, company store photos. Include more quotes from people who lived these moments!" The following geographical areas are covered: Eastern Canada; Mexico; Europe; China; Russia; Poland; Australia; as well as US states Alabama, Tennessee, Virginia, Washington, Oregon, North and South Dakota, Arizona, Colorado, Alaska and Wyoming.

‡GOLD PROSPECTOR, Gold Prospectors Association of America, Dept. WM, P.O. Box 891509, Temecula CA 92589-1509. (909)699-4749. Executive Editor: Perry Massie. Publications Editor: Tom Kraak. 60% freelance written. Eager to work with new/unpublished writers. Bimonthly magazine covering gold prospecting and mining. "*Gold Prospector* magazine is the official publication of the Gold Prospectors Association of America. The GPAA is an international organization of 100,000 members who are interested in recreational prospecting and mining. Our primary audience is people of all ages who like to take their prospecting gear with them on their weekend camping trips, and fishing and hunting trips. Our readers are interested in all types of prospecting methods (panning, sluicing, high banking, dry washing, metal detecting, etc. Also travel to gold prospecting "ghost towns" and historical sites. We try to carry stories in each issue pertaining to these subjects." Estab. 1965. Circ. 150,000. Pays on publication. Publishes ms an average of 9 months after acceptance. Byline given. Buys first North American serial and second serial (reprint) rights. Submit seasonal/holiday material 1 year in advance. Accepts previously published submissions. Reports in 6 weeks. Sample copy for $2. Writer's guidelines for #10 SASE.

Nonfiction: Historical/nostalgic, how-to (prospecting techniques, equipment building, etc.), humor, new product, personal experience, technical, travel. "One of our publishing beliefs is that our audience would rather experience life than watch it on television—that they would like to take a rough and tumble chance with the sheer adventure of taking gold from the ground or river after it has perhaps lain there for a million years. Even if they don't, they seem to enjoy reading about those who do in the pages of *Gold Prospector* magazine." Buys 75-100 mss/year. Query with or without published clips or send complete ms. Length: 1,000-3,000 words. Pays 75¢/column inch (photos and illustrations are measured the same as type).

Photos: State availability of photos with query or ms. Pays 75¢/column inch for photos, transparencies or reflective art. Buys all rights.

Tips: "Articles must be slanted to interest a prospector, miner, or treasure hunter. For example, a first-aid article could address possible prospecting accidents. Any subject can be so tailored."

STONE REVIEW, National Stone Association, 1415 Elliot Place NW, Washington DC 20007. (202)342-1100. Fax: (202)342-0702. E-mail: fatlee@cais.com. Editor: Frank Atlee. Bimonthly magazine covering quarrying and supplying of crushed stone, "designed to be a communications forum for the crushed stone industry. Publishes information on industry technology, trends, developments and concerns. Audience are quarry operations/management, and manufacturers of equipment, suppliers of services to the industry." Estab. 1985. Circ. 4,000. Pays on publication. Publishes ms an average of 3 months after acceptance. Byline given. Negotiable kill fee. Buys one-time rights. Accepts simultaneous and previously published submissions. Send tearsheet, photocopy or typed ms with information about when and where the article previously appeared. Payment negotiable. Reports in 1 month. Sample copy for 9×12 SAE with 3 first-class stamps.

Nonfiction: Technical. Query with or without published clips or send complete ms. Length: 1,000-2,500 words. "Note: We have no budget for freelance material, but I'm willing to secure payment for right material."

Photos: State availability of photos with query, then send photos with submission. Reviews contact sheets, negatives, transparencies and prints. Offers no additional payment for photos accepted with ms. Identification of subjects required. Buys one-time rights.

Tips: "At this point, most features are written by contributors in the industry, but I'd like to open it up. Articles on unique equipment, applications, etc. are good, as are those reporting on trends (e.g., there is a strong push on now for environmentally sound operations). Also interested in stories on family-run operations involving three or more generations."

STONE WORLD, Business News Publishing Company, 1 Kalisa Way, Suite 205, Paramus NJ 07652. (201)599-0136. Fax: (201)599-2378. Publisher/Editorial Director: John Sailer. Editor: Michael Reis. Monthly magazine on natural building stone for producers and users of granite, marble, limestone, slate, sandstone, onyx and other natural stone products. Estab. 1984. Circ. 18,000. Pays on publication. Publishes ms an average of 6 months after acceptance. Byline given. Buys first rights or second serial (reprint) rights. Submit seasonal material 6 months in advance. Accepts previously published submissions. Send photocopy of article or typed ms with rights for sale noted and information about when and where the article previously appeared. For reprints, pays 50% of the amount paid for an original article. Publishes technical book excerpts. Reports in 2 months. Sample copy for $10.

Nonfiction: How-to (fabricate and/or install natural building stone), interview/profile, photo feature, technical, architectural design, artistic stone uses, statistics, factory profile, equipment profile, trade show review. Buys 10 mss/year. Query with or without published clips or send complete ms. Length: 600-3,000 words. Pays $4/column inch. Pays the expenses of writers on assignment.

Photos: State availability of photos with submission. Reviews transparencies and prints. Pays $10/photo accepted with ms. Captions and identification of subjects required. Buys one-time rights.

Columns/Departments: News (pertaining to stone or design community); New Literature (brochures, catalogs, books, videos, etc. about stone); New Products (stone products); New Equipment (equipment and machinery for working with stone); Calendar (dates and locations of events in stone and design communities). Query or send complete ms. Length: 300-600 words. Pays $4/inch.

Tips: "Articles about architectural stone design accompanied by professional color photographs and quotes from designing firms are often published, especially when one unique aspect of the stone selection or installation is highlighted. We are also interested in articles about new techniques of quarrying and/or fabricating natural building stone."

Toy, Novelty and Hobby

Publications focusing on the toy and hobby industry are listed in this section. For magazines for hobbyists see the Consumer Hobby and Craft section.

THE STAMP WHOLESALER, P.O. Box 706, Albany OR 97321-0006. (503)928-4484. Fax: (503)967-7262. Editor: Ken Palke. 60% freelance written. Newspaper published 28 times/year for philatelic businesspeople; many are part-time and/or retired from other work. Estab. 1937. Circ. 4,700. Pays on publication. Byline given. Buys all rights. Reports in 1 month. Accepts previously published submissions. Send information about when and where the article previously appeared. Free sample copy and writer's guidelines.

Nonfiction: "Focus on how-to, general business techniques, computer how-to for business, stamp business trends and history, specialty aspects of the stamp business i.e., auctions, catalogs, postal history, cinderellas, approvals, mail order, opinion pieces. The articles must be directed specifically to stamp dealers. Many of our writers are stamp dealers themselves. We are beginning to cover phone cards as well as stamps." Buys 120 ms/year. Submit complete ms. Length: 1,000-2,000 words. Pays $25 and up/article.

Tips: "Send queries on business stories or stamp dealer profiles. We need stories to help dealers make and save money. We also buy cartoons on stamp dealer topics. We especially need business profiles of stamp dealers located in various parts of the country. We pay $175 for these, but we expect an in-depth, facts and figures business article with color pictures in return."

‡TOY BUSINESS MAGAZINE, New Media Publications, 10711 Burnet Rd., Suite 305, Austin TX 78758. Editor: Kathleen M. Carson. 40% freelance written. Monthly magazine covering toy industry, focusing on retailing, manufacturing and licensing issues. "Industry analysis is important. Particularly looking for toy expertise as it relates to retailing." Estab. 1995. Circ. 17,000. Pays on publication. Publishes ms an average of 1 month after acceptance. Byline given. Buys all rights. Editorial lead time 2-3 months. Query for electronic submissions. Reports in 2 weeks. Sample copy and writer's guidelines free on request.

Nonfiction: How-to, interview/profile. Buys 60 mss/year. Query with published clips and resume. Length: 900-2,200 words. Pays $350 maximum for assigned articles (1,000 words minimum); 15-20¢/word negotiated with editor for unsolicited articles.

Transportation

These publications are for professional movers and people involved in transportation of goods. For magazines focusing on trucking see also Auto and Truck.

BUS WORLD, Magazine of Buses and Bus Systems, Stauss Publications, P.O. Box 39, Woodland Hills CA 91365-0039. (818)710-0208. E-mail: mgpg68a@prodigy.com. Editor: Ed Stauss. 25% freelance written. Quarterly trade journal covering the transit and intercity bus industries. Estab. 1978. Circ. 5,000. Pays on publication. Reports in 1 month. Sample copy with writer's guidelines for $2.

Photos: Buys photos with mss.

Fillers: Cartoons. Buys 4-6/year. Pays $10.

Tips: "No tourist or travelog viewpoints. Be employed in or have a good understanding of the bus industry. Be enthusiastic about buses—their history and future. Acceptable material will be held until used and will not be returned unless requested by sender. Unacceptable and excess material will be returned only if accompanied by suitable SASE."

‡CANADIAN TRANSPORTATION LOGISTICS, Canadian Warehousing Logistics, Southam Inc., 1450 Don Mills Rd., Don Mills (Toronto), Ontario M3B 2X7 Canada. Editor: Bonnie Toews. 20% freelance written. Monthly magazine covering transportation, distribution and integrated logistics. "We like crisp, easy-to-read stories. Even though our readers are often engineers or business executives, their reading time is compacted with an overload of information daily. We write for logistics managers in charge of total supply chain movement of cargo and technology. This includes economic conditions worldwide that affect shipping. Our emphasis is on 'how-to' and leading edge trends." Estab. 1898. Circ. 17,000. **Pays on acceptance.** Publishes ms an average of 3 months after acceptance. Byline given. Buys first North American serial rights. Editorial lead time 3 months. Submit seasonal material 2 months in advance. Accepts simultaneous submissions. Query for electronic submissions. Reports in 1 week on queries. Sample copy and writer's guidelines free on request.

Nonfiction: How-to (do their jobs better), interview/profile, new product, technical. Special issues: Presidents' Issue (November—Help logistics managers with information they can use in presentations to chief executives to affect change in their operating process). Buys 12 mss/year. Query with published clips. Length: 750-1,500 words. Pays $250-500.

Photos: State availability of photos with submissions. Reviews negatives, 3×5 transparencies. Offers no additional payment for photos accepted with ms. Captions, model releases, identification of subjects required. Buys one-time rights.

Tips: "No puff pieces! Nor product promos! We take problems our readers have in the workplace and go to suppliers to find out how they or other technical experts would show readers how to solve their situation."

‡DISTRIBUTION, The Transportation & Business Logistics Magazine, Chilton Co., One Chilton Way, Radnor PA 19089. (610)964-4244. Editor: Jim Thomas. Contact: Jodi Melbin. 50% or more freelance written. Monthly magazine covering transportation and logistics. "Our audience are the companies that require transportation professionals. Stories revolve around ways—or programs—that improve distribution logistics processes within industries, as well as the use of carriers, forwarders and third-party companies." Estab. 1901. Circ. 70,000. **Pays on acceptance.** Publishes ms an average of 1-3 months after acceptance. Buys one-time rights. Editorial lead time 2 months. Query for electronic submissions. Sample copy for #10 SASE.

Nonfiction: General interest, how-to, interview/profile, technical, travel (to see departments). Buys 36 mss/year. Query with published clips. Length: 1,200-1,500 words. Pays $300-650.

Photos: Send photos with submissions. Reviews contact sheets, transparencies, prints. Negotiates payment individually. Identification of subjects required.

Columns/Departments: Global Report (global ports, DCs etc.), 500-750 words. Buys 12-20 mss/year. Query. Pays $300-650.

Tips: "Query letter with background and already published articles related to field. Most articles are assigned, so we are interested in getting writers experienced in business writing. We are developing writer's guidelines."

INBOUND LOGISTICS, Thomas Publishing Co., 5 Penn Plaza, 8th Floor, New York NY 10001. (212)629-1560. Fax: (212)629-1565. Publisher: Keith Biondo. Editor: Felecia Stratton. 50% freelance written. Prefers to work with published/established writers. Monthly magazine covering the transportation industry. *"Inbound Logistics* is distributed to people who buy, specify, or recommend inbound freight transportation services and equipment. The editorial matter provides basic explanations of inbound freight transportation, directory listings, how-to technical information, trends and developments affecting inbound freight movements, and expository, case history feature stories." Estab. 1980. Circ. 52,500. Pays on publication. Publishes ms an average of 3 months after acceptance. Byline given. Buys all rights. Accepts simultaneous and previously published submissions. Send tearsheet of article and information about when and where the article previously appeared. For reprints, pays 20% of amount paid for an original article. Reports in 2 months. Sample copy and writer's guidelines for 9×12 SAE with 5 first-class stamps.

Nonfiction: How-to (basic help for purchasing agents and traffic managers), interview/profile (purchasing and transportation professionals). Buys 20 mss/year. Query with published clips. Length: 750-1,000 words. Pays $100-400. Pays expenses of writers on assignment.

Photos: Marilyn Giannakouros, photo editor. State availability of photos with query. Pays $100-500 for b&w contact sheets, negatives, transparencies and prints; $250-500 for color contact sheets, negative transparencies and prints. Captions and identification of subjects required.

Columns/Departments: Viewpoint (discusses current opinions on transportation topics). Query with published clips.

Tips: "Have a sound knowledge of the transportation industry; educational how-to articles get our attention."

NATIONAL BUS TRADER, The Magazine of Bus Equipment for the United States and Canada, 9698 W. Judson Rd., Polo IL 61064-9015. (815)946-2341. Fax: (815)946-2347. Editor: Larry Plachno. 25% freelance written. Eager to work with new/unpublished writers. Monthly magazine for manufacturers, dealers and owners of buses and motor coaches. Estab. 1977. Circ. 8,500. Pays either on acceptance or publication. Publishes ms an average of 3 months after acceptance. Byline given. Not copyrighted. Buys rights "as required by writer." Accepts simultaneous and previously published submissions. Reports in 1 month. Sample copy for 9×12 SAE.

Nonfiction: Historical/nostalgic (on old buses); how-to (maintenance repair); new products; photo feature; technical (aspects of mechanical operation of buses). "We are finding that more and more firms and agencies are hiring freelancers to write articles to our specifications. We are more likely to run them if someone else pays." No material that does *not* pertain to bus tours or bus equipment. Buys 3-5 unsolicited mss/year. Query. Length varies. Pays variable rate. Sometimes pays the expenses of writers on assignment.

Photos: State availability of photos. Reviews 5×7 or 8×10 prints and 35mm transparencies. Captions, model release and identification of subjects required.

Columns/Departments: Bus Maintenance; Buses and the Law; Regulations; Bus of the Month. Buys 20-30 mss/year. Query. Length: 250-400 words. Pays variable rate.

Tips: "We are a very technical publication. Submit qualifications showing extensive background in bus vehicles. We're very interested in well-researched articles on older bus models and manufacturers, or current converted coaches. We would like to receive history of individual bus models prior to 1953 and history of GMC 'new look' models. Write or phone editors with article concept or outline for comments and approval."

SHIPPING DIGEST, The National Shipping Weekly of Export Transportation, Geyer McAllister Publications Inc., 51 Madison Ave., New York NY 10010. (212)689-4411. Fax: (212)683-7929. Editor: Maria Reines. 20% freelance written. Weekly magazine covering ocean, surface, air transportation, ports, intermodal and EDI. "Read by executives responsible for exporting US goods to foreign markets. Emphasis is on services offered by ocean, surface and air carriers, their development and trends; port developments; trade agreements; government regulation; electronic data interchange." Pays on publication. Publishes ms an average of 1 month after acceptance. Byline given. Buys first rights. Reports in 2 months. Free sample copy and writer's guidelines.

Nonfiction: Interview/profile. Query. Length: 800-1,500 words. Pays $150-350.

Photos: State availability of photos with submission. Reviews contact sheets and 5×7 prints. Offers no payment for photos accepted with ms. Identification of subjects required. Buys one-time rights.

Travel

Travel professionals read these publications to keep up with trends, tours and changes in transportation. Magazines about vacations and travel for the general public are listed in the Consumer Travel section.

‡**CORPORATE MEETINGS & INCENTIVES**, Adams/Laux Publishing, 63 Great Rd., Maynard MA 01754. (508)897-5552. Editor: Connie Goldstein. Contact: Barbara Scofidio. 75% freelance written. Monthly magazine covering meetings and incentive travel. "Our cover stories focus on issues of interest to senior execs—from building a horizontal organization to encouraging innovation—and the integral role meetings play in achieving these goals." Circ. 36,000. Pays 30 days after acceptance. Offers 33% kill fee. Buys first North American serial rights. Editorial lead time 3 months. Submit seasonal material 4 months in advance. Accepts simultaneous submissions. Query for electronic submissions. Sample copy for SAE with $1.50 postage. Writer's guidelines for #10 SASE.

Nonfiction: Interview/profile, travel with a meetings angle. Special issue: Golf (April). Buys 30 mss/year. Query with published clips. Length: 2,000-4,000 words. Pays 50¢/word. Sometimes pays expenses of writers on assignment.

Photos: State availability of photos with submissions. Reviews contact sheets, transparencies, prints. Negotiates payment individually. Identification of subjects required. Buys one-time rights.

Columns/Departments: Buys 24 mss/year. Query. Pays $250-500.

Tips: "Looking for strong business writers with experience writing about employee motivation, quality programs, incentive programs—ways that companies improve productivity. Best to send relevant clips with a letter after taking a look at the magazine."

THE ROAD EXPLORER, (formerly *Ontario Motor Coach Review*), Naylor Communications Ltd., 920 Yonge St., Suite 600, Toronto, Ontario M4W 3C7 Canada. (416)961-1028. Fax: (416)924-4408. Editor: Lori Knowles. 80% freelance written. *Explorer* is published biannually (spring and fall) for the Ontario Motor Coach Association (OMCA). The magazine both reviews events and issues of the OMCA, and serves as a destination guide for motor coach (bus) tour operators.

Nonfiction: Looking for material directed at bus tours in the following areas: Canadian and US destinations (including provinces, states, cities, and towns), auto routes, road tours, major events, attractions, sporting attractions and historical sites. Query with published clips and SASE. Length: 500-2,500 words. Byline given. Rates will be negotiated. Offers 33% kill fee. Accepts simultaneous and previously published submissions. Reports in 6 weeks.

Photos: State availability of photos with submission. Reviews transparencies and prints. Offers $25-200/photo. Identification of subjects required.

Tips: "This is a publication for bus tour operators. We do not accept submissions directed at RV owners. Please send copies of work, a query, and SASE. We will respond as promptly as deadlines allow."

RV BUSINESS, TL Enterprises, Inc., 3601 Calle Tecate, Camarillo CA 93012. (805)389-0300. Fax: (805)389-0484. Senior Managing Editor: Stephen Boilon. 60% freelance written. Prefers to work with published/established writers. Monthly magazine covering the recreational vehicle and allied industries for people in the RV industry—dealers, manufacturers, suppliers and finance experts. Estab. 1950. Circ. 19,000. **Pays on acceptance.** Publishes ms an average of 2 months after acceptance. Byline given. Offers 50% kill fee. Buys first North American serial rights. Submit seasonal material 6 months in advance. Query for electronic submissions. Reports in 2 months. Sample copy for 9 × 12 SAE with 5 first-class stamps.
Nonfiction: Technical, financial, legal or marketing issues; how-to (deal with any specific aspect of the RV business); specifics and verification of statistics required—must be factual; technical (photos required, 4-color preferred). Buys 50 mss/year. Query with published clips. Send complete ms—"but only read on speculation." Length: 1,000-1,500 words. Pays variable rate up to $500. Sometimes pays expenses of writers on assignment.
Photos: State availability of photos with query or send photos with ms. Reviews 35mm transparencies and 8 × 10 b&w prints. Captions, model release, and identification of subjects required. Buys one-time or all rights; unused photos returned.
Columns/Departments: Guest editorial; News (50-500 words maximum, b&w photos appreciated); RV People (color photos/4-color transparencies; this section lends itself to fun, upbeat copy). Buys 100-120 mss/year. Query or send complete ms. Pays $25-200 "depending on where used and importance."
Tips: "Query. Phone OK; letter preferable. Send one or several ideas and a few lines letting us know how you plan to treat it/them. We are always looking for good authors knowledgeable in the RV industry or related industries. Change of editorial focus requires more articles that are brief, factual, hard hitting, business oriented and in-depth. Will work with promising writers, published or unpublished."

SPECIALTY TRAVEL INDEX, Alpine Hansen, 305 San Anselmo Ave., #313, San Anselmo CA 94960. (415)459-4900. Editor: C. Steen Hansen. Contact: C. Steen Hansen. 90% freelance written. Semiannual magazine covering adventure and special interest travel. Estab. 1980. Circ. 45,000. Pays on publication. Byline given. Buys one-time rights. Editorial lead time 3 months. Submit seasonal material 3 months in advance. Accepts previously published submissions. Send tearsheet of article. For reprints, pays 100% of the amount paid for an original article. Query for electronic submissions. Writer's guidelines on request.
Nonfiction: How-to, new product, personal experience, photo feature, travel. Buys 15 mss/year. Query. Length: 1,000 words. Pays $200 minimum.
Photos: State availability of photos with submission. Reviews 35mm transparencies and 5 × 7 prints. Negotiates payment individually. Captions and identification of subjects required.

STAR SERVICE, Reed Travel Group, 500 Plaza Dr., Secaucus NJ 07096-3602. (201)902-2000. Fax: (201)319-1797. Publisher: Steven R. Gordon. "Eager to work with new/unpublished writers as well as those working from a home base abroad, planning trips that would allow time for hotel reporting, or living in major ports for cruise ships." Worldwide guide to accommodations and cruise ships founded in 1960 (as *Sloane Travel Agency Reports*) and sold to travel agencies on subscription basis. Pays 15 days after publication. Buys all rights. Query should include details on writer's experience in travel and writing, clips, specific forthcoming travel plans, and how much time would be available for hotel or ship inspections. Buys 5,000 reports/year. Pays $18/report used. Sponsored trips are acceptable. General query should precede electronic submission. Reports in 3 months. Writer's guidelines and list of available assignments for #10 SASE.
Nonfiction: Objective, critical evaluations of hotels and cruise ships suitable for international travelers, based on personal inspections. Freelance correspondents ordinarily are assigned to update an entire state or country. "Assignment involves on-site inspections of all hotels and cruise ships we review; revising and updating published reports; and reviewing new properties. Qualities needed are thoroughness, precision, perseverance and keen judgment. Solid research skills and powers of observation are crucial. Travel and travel writing experience are highly desirable. Reviews must be colorful, clear, and documented with hotel's brochure, rate sheet, etc. We accept no advertising or payment for listings, so reviews should dispense praise and criticism where deserved."
Tips: "We may require sample hotel or cruise reports on facilities near freelancer's hometown before giving the first assignment. No byline because of sensitive nature of reviews."

Trade, Technical and Professional Journals/ Changes '95-'96

The following trade publications were listed in the 1995 edition but do not have listings in this edition of *Writer's Market*. The majority did not respond to our request to update their listings or return a questionnaire for a new listing. If a reason was given for their exclusion, we have included it after the listing.

ABA Journal	Aftermarket Business	Alumi-News
Action Sports Retailer	Agri-Times Northwest	American Cinematographer

American Coin-op
American Glass Review
American Salesman
Amusement Business
Apparel Industry
Area Development
Art Business News;Crafts Report
Automatic Machining
Barrister
Battery Man
Bee Culture
Beef
Beverage World
Bicycle Business Journal
Billboard
Bottom Line
Boxboard Containers
Brahman Journal
Bus Tours Magazine
Bus World (no longer pays)
Business & Health
Business Radio
Cable Communications
California Pharmacist (no longer pays)
Canadian Defence Quarterly
Canadian Pharmaceutical Journal
Candy Industry
Candy Wholesaler
Casino Journal
Chemical Business (ceased publication)
Chief Executive
China Business & Economic Update
Christian Ministry
Church Educator
Comics Journal
Communication Briefings
Computer Graphics World
Contractor
Convene
Corporate Legal Times
Custom Applicator
DBMS
Dealer Communicator
Deca Dimensions
Dental Economics
Digital Systems Journal
Dimensional Stone
Docket
Early Childhood News
Earshot Jazz
Eastern Aftermarket Journal
Editors' Forum
Education Center, Inc.
Educational Retailer
Engravers Journal
Farm Futures
Farm Pond Harvest
Farmweek
Feminist Bookstore News (no longer pays)

FFA New Horizons
Fine Homebuilding
Flowers
Foodservice Director
Foreign Trade
Foundation News
Future, Now
Futures
Gift Basket Review
Giftware News
Glass Magazine
Groom & Board
Ground Water Age
Hardware Age
Health Systems Review (removed by request)
High Technology Careers
High Volume Printing
Home Furnishings Executive
HP/Apollo Workstation
Identity
Illinois Legal Times
Imprint
Industry Week
Inform
Instructor
Insurance Journal
Journal of Light Construction
Juornal of Career Planning & Employment (no longer pays)
Lawyers Weekly USA
Leader
Library Journal
Link Magazine
Location Update
Lodging Hospitality
Los Angeles Times Book Review
Manage
Management Review
Managers Report
Manufacturing Systems
MD Magazine
Mechanical Engineering
Medical Economics
Members (removed by request)
Mexico Update
Mine Regulation Reporter
Momentum
NADTP Journal
National Cattleman
Occupational Health & Safety
Onion World
Ornamental and Miscellaneous Metal Fabricator
Outside Plant
Pacific Fishing
Pension World (now Pension Management)
Pet Age
Pharmacy Times
Photo Lab Management
Photostocknotes
Play Meter

Playthings
Polled Hereford World (no freelance)
Preaching
Proceedings
Professional Agent
Professional Mariner
Progressive Farmer
Prorodea Sports News
Quality Digest
Quick Frozen Foods Int'l
Quick Printing
Rangefinder
RDH
Realtors
Recycling Today
Remodeling News
Rescue
Sanitary Maintenance
Savings & Community Banker
Security Dealer
Self-employed America
Shoe Retailing Today
Shooter's Rag
Signs of the Times
Small Business News (no freelance)
Southern Beverage Journal
Souvenirs & Novelties
Supervision
Swimming Pool/Spa Age
SYS Admin
Tea & Coffee Trade Journal
Teaching Today
Technology & Learning
Texas Architect
Tile Design & Installation
Transportation Builder
Travelage West
Turf
Uniform Monthly
Utility Construction and Maintenance
Utility Fleet Management
Vehicle Leasing Today
Veterinary Economics
Victimology
Video Business
Virginia Town & City
Walls & Ceilings
Western Hay
Windows/DOS Developer's Journal
Wines & Vines
Wisconsin Grocer
Wisconsin Restaurateur
Women in Business (no freelance)
Woodwind Quarterly
Writers Connection
Writer's Nook News
Writers Open Forum
Writers' Report
Wyoming Rural Electric News

Scriptwriting

Everyone has a story to tell, something to say. In telling that story as a play, movie, TV show or educational video you have selected that form over other possibilities. Scriptwriting makes some particular demands, but one thing remains the same for authors of novels, nonfiction books and scripts: you'll learn to write by rewriting. Draft after draft your skills improve until, hopefully, someone likes your work enough to hire you.

Whether you are writing a video to train doctors in a new surgical technique, alternative theater for an Off-Broadway company or you want to see your name on the credits of the next Arnold Schwarzenegger movie, you must perfect both writing and marketing skills. A successful scriptwriter is a talented artist and a savvy businessperson. But marketing must always be secondary to writing. A mediocre pitch for a great script will still get you farther than a brilliant pitch for a mediocre script. The art and craft of scriptwriting lies in successfully executing inspiration.

Writing a script is a private act. Polishing it may involve more people as you ask friends and fellow writers to take a look at it. Marketing takes your script public in an effort to find the person willing to give the most of what you want, whether it's money, exposure or control, in return for your work.

There are accepted ground rules to presenting and marketing scripts. Following those guidelines will maximize your chances of getting your work before an audience.

Presenting your script professionally earns a serious consideration of its content. Certain types of scripts have a definite format and structure. An educational video written in a one-column format, a feature film much longer than 120 pages or an hour-long TV show that peaks during the first 20 minutes indicates an amateur writer. There are several sources for correct formats, including *The Writer's Digest Book of Manuscript Formats*, by Buchman and Groves and *The Complete Guide to Script Formats*, by Cole and Haig.

Submission guidelines are similar to those for other types of writing. The initial contact is a one-page query letter, with a brief synopsis and a few lines as to your credits or experience relevant to the subject of your script. Never send a complete manuscript until it is requested. Almost every script sent to a producer, studio, or agent must be accompanied by a release form. Ask the producer or agent for his form when invited to submit the complete script. Always include a self-addressed stamped envelope if you want your work returned; a self-addressed stamped postcard will do for acknowledgement or reply if you do not need your script returned.

Most writers break in with spec scripts, written "for free," which serve as calling cards to show what they can do. These scripts plant the seeds of your professional reputation by making the rounds of influential people looking to hire writers, from advertising executives to movie moguls. Good writing is more important than a specific plot. Make sure you are sending out your best work; a first draft is not a finished product. Have several spec scripts completed, as a producer will often decide that a story is not right for him, or a similar work is already in production, but want to know what else you have. Be ready for that invitation.

Writing a script is a matter of learning how to refine your writing so that the work reads as a journey, not a technical manual. The best scripts have concise, visceral scenes that demand to be presented in a specific order and accomplish definite goals.

Educational videos have a message that must be expressed economically and directly, engaging the audience in an entertaining way while maintaining interest in the topic. Theatrical plays are driven by character and dialogue that expose a thematic core and engender enthusiasm or involvement in the conflict. Cinematic screenplays, while more visually-oriented, are a series of discontinuous scenes stacked to illuminate the characters, the obstacles confronting them and the resolution they reach.

A script is a difficult medium—written words that sound natural when spoken, characters that are original yet resonate with the audience, believable conflicts and obstacles in tune with the end result. One theater added to their listing the following tip: "Don't write plays. Write novels, short stories, anything but plays. But if you *must* write plays. . . . " If you are compelled to present your story visually, be aware of the intense competition it will face. Hone it, refine it, keep working on it until it can be no better, then look for the best home you can find. That's success.

Business and Educational Writing

"It's no longer the plankton of the filmmaking food chain," says Kirby Timmons, creative director of the video production company CRM Films. Scripts for corporate training, business management and education videos have become as sophisticated as those designed for TV and film, and they carry the additional requirement of conveying specific content. With an audience that is increasingly media literate, anything that looks and feels like a "training film" will be dead in the water. The trick is to produce a script that engages, compels *and* informs about the topic, whether it's customer relations, listening skills or effective employee management, while staying on a tight budget.

This can create its own challenges, but is an excellent way to increase your skills and exercise your craft. Good scriptwriters are in demand in this field. There is a strong emphasis on producing a polished complete script before filming begins, and a writer's involvement doesn't end until the film is "in the can."

A remarkably diverse industry, educational and corporate video is a $18-25 billion business, compared to theatrical films and TV, estimated at $5 billion. And there is the added advantage that opportunities are widespread, from large local corporations to small video production houses in your area. Larger companies often have inhouse video production companies, but others rely on freelance writers. Your best bet would be to find work with companies that specialize in making educational and corporate video while at the same time making yourself known to the creative directors of inhouse video staffs in large corporations. Advertising agencies are also a good source of work, as they often are asked by their clients for help in creating films and use freelance writers and producers.

Business and educational video is a market-driven industry, with material created either in response to a general need or a specific demand. The production company usually identifies a subject and finds the writer. As such, there is a perception that a spec script will not work in this media. While it is true that, as in TV and theatrical films, a writer's spec script is rarely produced, it is a good résumé of qualifications and sample of skills. It can get you other work even though it isn't produced. Your spec script should demonstrate a knowledge of this industry's specific format. For the most part video scripts are written in two-columns, video on the left, audio on the right. Computer software is available to format the action and dialogue; *The Writer's Digest Guide to Manuscript Formats* also covers the basics of video script format.

Aside from the original script, another opportunity for the writer is the user's guide that often accompanies a video. If you are hired to create the auxiliary material you'll receive a copy of the finished video and write a concurrent text for the teacher or implementor to use.

Networking is very important. There is no substitute for calling companies and finding out what is in your area. Contact local training and development companies and find out who they serve and what they need. It pays to join professional organizations such as the Association of Visual Communicators and the Association for Training and Development, which offer seminars and conventions. Making the rounds at a business convention of video producers with your business card could earn you a few calls and invitations to submit writing samples.

Budgets are tighter for educational or corporate videos than for theatrical films. You'll want to work closely with the producer to make sure your ideas can be realized within the budget. Your fee will vary with each job, but generally a script written for a production house such as CRM in a subject area with broad marketability will pay $5,000-7,000. A custom-produced video for a specific company will usually pay less. The pay does not increase exponentially with your experience; large increases come if you choose to direct and produce as well as write.

With the expansion of cable TV-based home shopping opportunities, direct response TV (infomercials) is an area with increasing need for writers to create the scripts that sell the products. Production companies are located across the country, and more are popping up as the business grows. Pay can range from $5,000-18,000, depending on the type, length and success of the program. *The Hollywood Scriptwriter* (1625 N. Wilcox, #385, Hollywood CA 90028; (805)495-5447) published a three-part series on direct response scriptwriting, discussing structure, format and marketing, which is available for $8.

The future of business and educational video lies in interactive media or multimedia. Interactive media combines computer and video technology to create a product that doesn't have to progress along a linear path. Videos that offer the viewer the opportunity to direct the course of events hold exciting possibilities for corporate training and educational applications. Writers will be in high demand as stories offer dozens of choices in storylines. Interactive video will literally eat up pages of script as quickly as a good writer produces them. A training session may last only 20 minutes, but the potential untapped story lines could add up to hours worth of script that must be written, realized and made available. From training salespeople to doctors, or teaching traffic rules to issues in urbanization, corporate and educational video is about to undergo a tremendous revolution.

For information on more business and educational scriptwriting markets, see Scriptwriting Markets/Changes '95-'96 at the end of the Screenwriting section.

☐**ABS ENTERPRISES**, P.O. Box 5127, Evanston IL 60204-5127. (708)982-1414. Fax: (708)982-1418. President: Alan Soell. "We produce material for all levels of corporate, medical, cable and educational institutions for the purposes of training and development, marketing and meeting presentations. We also are developing programming for the broadcast areas." 75% freelance written. "We work with a core of three to five freelance writers from development to final drafts." All scripts published are unagented submissions. Buys all rights. Accepts previously produced material. Reports in 2 weeks on queries.
Needs: Videotape, multimedia, realia, slides, tapes and cassettes, television shows/series. Currently interested in "sports instructional series that could be produced for the consumer market on tennis, gymnastics, bowling, golf, aerobics, health and fitness, cross-country skiing and cycling. Also motivational and self-improvement type videos and film ideas to be produced. These could cover all ages '6-60'; and from professional to blue collar jobs. These two areas should be 30 minutes and be timeless in approach for long shelf life. Sports audience, age 25-45; home improvement, 25-65. Cable TV needs include the two groups of programming detailed here. We are also looking for documentary work on current issues, nuclear power, solar power, urban development, senior citizens—but with a new approach." Query or submit synopsis/outline and résumé. Pays by contractual agreement.
Tips: "I am looking for innovative approaches to old problems that just don't go away. The approach should be simple and direct so there is immediate audience identification with the presentation. I also like to see

a sense of humor used. Trends in the audiovisual field include interactive video with disk—for training purposes."

ADVANTAGE MEDIA INC., 21356 Nordhoff St., Suite 102, Chatsworth CA 91311. (818)700-0504. Fax: (818)700-0612. Vice President: Susan Cherno. Estab. 1983. Audience is "all employees, including supervisory and management staff; generic audiences; medium-large companies, educational institutions, government, healthcare, insurance, financial." Works with 1-2 writers/year. Buys exclusive rights for distribution. Accepts previously produced material (exclusive distribution only). Reports in 1 month on queries. Catalog free. Submit synopsis/outline, completed script or résumé. Usually pays flat fee for writing; negotiable by project.
Needs: Videotapes. "Generic settings, rainbow mix of characters. Topics: change, motivation, diversity, quality, safety, customer service. 20 minutes maximum. Documentary if points are clear or skill-building 'how to'. Must make a point for teaching purposes."
Tips: "Training programs must appeal to a diverse audience but be 'TV quality'. They must teach, as well as be somewhat entertaining. Must hold interest. Should present the problem, but solve it and not leave the audience hanging or to solve it themsvles. Must stay realistic, believable and be fast-paced. I think there will be a need for even more types of video-based materials for a growing need for training within organizations."

‡ASSOCIATED AUDIO/VIDEO & DIGITAL, 914 Arctic St., Bridgeport CT 06608. President: Richard Kraus. Estab. 1971. Audience is childrens educational and corporate training and corporate meeting multimedia. Buys 5 scripts/year. Works with 2 writers/year. Buys first rights. Accepts previously produced material. Reports in 3 months on queries. Query with synopsis and résumé. Payment to be negotiated.
Needs: Multimedia kits, filmstrips (sound), tapes and cassettes. "We are starting to sell CD-ROM educational topics to schools, and training materials."

A/V CONCEPTS CORP., 30 Montauk Blvd., Oakdale NY 11769-1399. (516)567-7227. Fax: (516)567-8745. Contact: P. Solimene or L. Solimene. Produces material for elementary-high school students, either on grade level or in remedial situations. Estab. 1971. 100% freelance written. Buys 25 scripts/year from unpublished/unproduced writers. Employs video, book and personal computer media. Reports in 1 month on outline, 6 weeks on final scripts. Buys all rights. Sample copy for 9×12 SAE with 5 first-class stamps.
Needs: Interested in original educational computer (disk-based) software programs for Apple +, 48k. Main concentration in language arts, mathematics and reading. "Manuscripts must be written using our lists of vocabulary words and meet our readability formula requirements. Specific guidelines are devised for each level. Length of manuscript and subjects will vary according to grade level for which material is prepared. Basically, we want material that will motivate people to read." Pays $300 and up.
Tips: "Writers must be highly creative and highly disciplined. We are interested in high interest/low readability materials."

SAMUEL R. BLATE ASSOCIATES, 10331 Watkins Mill Dr., Gaithersburg MD 20879-2935. (301)840-2248. Fax: (301)840-2248. President: Samuel R. Blate. Produces audiovisual and educational material for business, education, institutions, state and federal governments. "We work with 2 *local* writers per year on a per project basis—it varies as to business conditions and demand." Buys first rights when possible. Query for electronic submissions. Reports in 1 month. SASE for return.
Needs: Scripts on technical and outdoor subjects. Query with samples. SASE for return. Payment "depends on type of contract with principal client." Pays some expenses of writers on assignment.
Tips: "Writers must have a strong track record of technical and aesthetic excellence. Clarity is not next to divinity—it is above it."

BOSUSTOW MEDIA GROUP, 7655 Sunset Blvd., Suite 114, Hollywood CA 90046-2700. (213)874-7613. Owner: Tee Bosustow. Estab. 1983. Produces material for corporate, TV and home video clients. Reports in 2 weeks on queries.
Needs: Tapes, cassettes, videotapes. "Unfortunately, no one style, etc. exists. We produce a variety of products, a good deal of it children's programming." Submit synopsis/outline and résumé only. Pays agreed upon fee.

CAMBRIDGE EDUCATIONAL, 90 MacCorkle Ave. SW, South Charleston WV 25303. Production Staff: Charlotte Angel. Estab. 1983. Audience is junior high/high schools, vocational schools, libraries, guidance centers. Buys 18-24 scripts/year. Works with 12-18 writers/year. Buys all rights. "Samples are kept for file reference." Reports only if interested. Free catalog. Query with synopsis, résumé or writing sample ("excerpt from a previous script, preferably"). Makes outright purchase of $2,000-4,000.
Needs: Videotapes. Educational programming suitable for junior high and high school age groups (classroom viewing and library reference). "Programs range from 20-35-minutes in length. Each should have a fresh approach for how-tos, awareness, and introductions to various subject matters. Subjects range from guidance, home economics, parenting, health, and vocational to social studies, fine arts, music, science and business."
• This company is looking for authors to write non-linear programs for multimedia CD-ROM.

Tips: "We are looking for a new slant on some standard educational topics, as well as more contemporary issues. Currently focusing on job search and parenting issues."

CLEARVUE/eav, INC., Dept. WM, 6465 N. Avondale Ave., Chicago IL 60631-1909. (312)775-9433. Fax: (312)775-9844. President: Mark Ventling. Contact: Mary Watanabe. Produces material for educational market—grades K-12. 75% freelance written. Prefers to work with published/established writers. Buys 5 scripts/year, also some teaching materials. Buys all rights. Accepts previously produced material. Query for electronic submissions. Reports in 2 weeks on queries; 3 weeks on submissions. Free catalog.
Needs: Videos, multimedia kits, CD-ROM. "Our videos are 8-30 minutes for all curriculum areas." Query. Makes outright purchase, $500-1,000. Sometimes pays the expenses of writers on assignment.
Tips: "Our interests are in video and CD-ROM for the elementary and high school markets on all subjects."

‡CONTINENTAL FILM PRODUCTIONS CORPORATION, P.O. Box 5126, 4220 Amnicola Hwy., Chattanooga TN 37406. (615)622-1193. Fax: (615)629-0853. President: James L. Webster. Estab. 1951. Produces "AV and video presentations for businesses and nonprofit organizations for sales, training, public relations, documentation, motivation, etc." Works with many writers annually. Buys all rights. No previously produced material. Unsolicited submissions not returned. Reports in 1 week.
Needs: "We do need new writers of various types. Please contact us by mail with samples and résumé." Produces slides, motion pictures, multi-image presentations, interactive programs and videos. Query with samples and résumé. Outright purchase: $250 minimum.
Tips: Looks for writers whose work shows " technical understanding, humor, common sense, practicality, simplicity, creativity, etc. Important for writers to adapt script to available production budget." Suggests writers "increase use of humor in training films." Also seeking scripts on "human behavior in industry."

CRM FILMS, 1801 Avenue of the Stars, #715, Los Angeles CA 90067-5802. Fax: (310)789-5392. Creative Director: Kirby Timmons. Estab. 1960. Material for business and organizational training departments. Buys 2-4 scripts/year. Works with 6-8 writers/year. Buys all rights and interactive training rights. No previously produced material. Reports in 1 month. Catalog for 10×13 SAE with 4 first-class stamps. Query with résumé and script sample of writer's work in informational or training media. Makes outright purchase of $4,000-7,000, or in accordance with Writers Guild standard. "We accept WGA standard one-page informational/interactive agreement which stipulates *no* minimum but qualifies writer for pension and health coverage."
  • See the interview with Creative Director Kirby Timmons in the 1994 *Writer's Market*.
Needs: Videotapes, multimedia kits. "CRM is looking for short (10-20 minute) scripts on management topics such as communication, decision making, team building and customer service. No 'talking heads,' prefer drama-based, awareness approach as opposed to 'how-to' style, but will on occasion produce either."
Tips: "Know the *specific* training need which your idea or script fulfills! Total quality management will influence product line for forseeable future—learn about 'TQM' before submitting."

EDUCATIONAL INSIGHTS, Editorial Dept., 19560 S. Rancho Way, Dominguez Hills CA 90220. (310)637-2131. Fax: (310)605-5048. Submissions Editor: Livian Perez. Estab. 1962. Produces material for elementary schools and retail "home-learning" markets. Works with 5 writers/year. Buys all rights or exclusive licensing agreements. Accepts previously produced material. Reports in 2-4 weeks. Catalog for 9×12 SAE with 2 first-class stamps.
Needs: Charts, models, multimedia kits, study prints, tapes and cassettes, teaching machine programs. Query with samples. Pays varied royalties or makes outright purchase.
Tips: "Keep up-to-date information on educational trends in mind. Study the market before starting to work. We receive 20 manuscripts per week—all reviewed and returned, if rejected."

EDUCATIONAL VIDEO NETWORK, 1401 19th St., Huntsville TX 77340. (409)295-5767. President: Dr. Kenneth L. Russell. Executive Editor: Gary Edmondson. Estab. 1953. Produces material for junior high, senior high, college and university audiences. Buys "perhaps 20 scripts/year." Buys all rights or pays royalty on gross retail and wholesale. Accepts previously produced material. Reports in 1-2 months. Free catalog and writer's guidelines.
Needs: Video for educational purposes. Query. Royalty varies.
Tips: "Educational video productions fall into two basic divisions. First, are the curriculum-oriented programs that teachers in the various academic disciplines can use to illustrate or otherwise enhance textbook material in their subjects. Such programs should either be introductory overviews or concentrate on specific segments of lesson plans. Recent titles: *The New Food Guide Pyramid, Air Pollution, Smog and Acid Rain*, and *Africa: Continent of Contrasts*. The second type of educational program deals with guidance and personal development areas. These programs need to reflect enough edutainment values to keep visually-sophisticated teens engaged while providing the real and valuable information that could help students with school and life. Recent titles: *Efficient Time Management,, Making the Grade, Developing Your Self Esteem*, and *Dealing with Anger*. EVN is always looking for writers/producers who can write and illustrate for educational purposes."

EFFECTIVE COMMUNICATION ARTS, INC., P.O. Box 250, Wilton CT 06897-0250. (203)761-8787. (203)761-0568. President: David Jacobson. Estab. 1965. Produces films, videotapes and interactive multimedia for physicians, nurses and medical personnel. Prefers to work with published/established writers. 80% freelance written. Buys approximately 20 scripts/year. Query for electronic submissions. Buys all rights. Reports in 1 month.
Needs: Multimedia kits, television shows/series, videotape presentations, interactive videodisks, CD-ROM multimedia. Currently producing about 15 videotapes for medical audiences; 6 interactive disks for medical audience; 3 interactive disks for point-of-purchase. Submit complete script and résumé. Makes outright purchase. Pays expenses of writers on assignment.
Tips: "Interactive design skills are increasingly important."

‡THE FILM HOUSE INC., 130 E. Sixth St., Cincinnati OH 45202. (513)381-2211. President: Ken Williamson. Estab. 1973. Audience is corporate communications and television commercials. Buys 5 scripts/year. Works with 3 writers/year. Buys all rights. No previously published material. Reoprts in 1 month on queries. Query with résumé.
Needs: Films, videotapes. Corporate, training and new product video. Writing assignments on a project basis only.
Tips: "We hire only seasonal, experienced writers on a freelance, per project basis. If interested send only a résumé."

HAYES SCHOOL PUBLISHING CO., INC., 321 Pennwood Ave., Wilkinsburg PA 15221-3398. (412)371-2373. Fax: (412)371-6408. President: Clair N. Hayes III. Estab. 1940. Produces material for school teachers and principals, elementary through high school. Also produces charts, workbooks, teacher's handbooks, posters, bulletin board material and reproducible blackline masters (grades K-12). 25% freelance written. Prefers to work with published/established writers. Buys 5-10 scripts/year from unpublished/unproduced writers. 100% of scripts produced are unagented submissions. Buys all rights. Query for electronic submissions. Reports in 3 months. Catalog for SAE with 3 first-class stamps. Writer's guidelines for #10 SAE with 2 first-class stamps.
Needs: Educational material only. Particularly interested in educational material for elementary school level. Query. Pays $25 minimum.

‡INFORMEDIA®, P.O. Box 13287, Austin TX 78711-3287. Contact: M. Sidoric. Estab. 1970. Audience is corporate sales/marketing meetings, general professional audiences, client specific presentations. Buys 3-4 scripts/year. Works with 5-6 writers/year. Buys all rights, but will negotiate. No previously published material. Reports in 1 month on queries and submissions. Query with résumé and samples. Makes outright purchase of $1,500.
Needs: Videotapes, multimedia kits, slides. AV modules 5-10 minutes in length; usually client specific in nature. Show openers—grand—bold. Topics: innovation/technology/teamwork.
Tips: Sees "less emphasis on staid productions. Solid, selling information in memorable format."

‡INTERACTIVE ARTS, 3200 Airport Ave., Santa Monica CA 90405. (213)390-9466. Vice President: David Schwartz. Estab. 1985. Audience is general public; theme parks; museums; college and high school students; corporate and industrial clients. Buys 4-5 scripts and 10 treatments/year. Works with 5-6 writers/year. Buys all rights. Reports in 2 weeks.
Needs: Multimedia (computer), interactive videodiscs, videotapes, educational/science documentaries, theme park films. "Our needs vary from consumer multimedia titles to museum projects and from educational/scientific documentaries to theme park projects." Queries desired from California residents only.

JIST WORKS, INC., 720 N. Park Ave., Indianapolis IN 46202. (317)264-3767. Video Production Manager: Jeff Heck. Estab. 1981. Produces career counseling, motivational materials (youth to adult) that encourage good planning and decision making for a successful future. Buys 7-10 scripts/year. Works with 2-3 writers/year. Buys all rights. Accepts previously produced material. Reports in 2 months. Catalog free. Query with synopsis. Makes outright purchase of $500 minimum.
Needs: Videotapes, multimedia kits. 15-30 minute video VHS tapes on job search materials and related markets.

‡PAUL S. KARR PRODUCTIONS, 2925 W. Indian School Rd., Box 11711, Phoenix AZ 85017. Phone/fax: (602)266-4198. Fax: (602)266-4198. Utah Division: 1024 N. 250 E., Box 1254, Orem UT 84057. (801)226-8209. Produces films and videos for industry, business, education, TV spots and entertainment. *Do not submit material unless requested.* Works on co-production ventures that have been funded.
Needs: Produces 16mm films and videos. Query. Payment varies.
Tips: "One of the best ways for a writer to become a screenwriter is to come up with a client that requires a film or video. He can take the project to a production company, such as we are, assume the position of an associate producer, work with an experienced professional producer in putting the production into being, and in that way learn about video and filmmaking, chalk up some meaningful credits, and share in the profits.

Direct consumer TV spots (that is, 800-number sales spots) have become a big business in the Phoenix market the last few years. Our company is set up to handle all facets of this area of television marketing."

‡MOTIVATION MEDIA, INC., 1245 Milwaukee Ave., Glenview IL 60025-2499. (708)297-4740. Fax: (708)297-6829. Senior Creative Director: Kevin Kivikko. Produces customized meeting, training and marketing material for presentation to salespeople, customers, shareholders, corporate/industrial employees and distributors. 90% freelance written. Buys 50 scripts/year. Prefers to work with published/established writers. All scripts produced are unagented submissions. Buys all rights. Reports in 1 month.
Needs: Material for all audiovisual media—particularly marketing-oriented (sales training, sales promotional, sales motivational) material. Produces sales meeting programs, videotapes, print collateral, audio programs and interactive multimedia. Software should be AV oriented. Query with samples and résumé. Pays $150-5,000. Pays the expenses of writers on assignment.

OMNI PRODUCTIONS, 655 W. Carmel Dr., Carmel IN 46032-2500. (317)844-6664. Vice President: Dr. Sandra M. Long. Estab. 1976. Produces commercial, training, educational and documentary material. Buys all rights.
Needs: Educational, documentary, commercial, training, motivational. Produces slides, video shows, multi-image, videotapes. Query. Makes outright purchase.
Tips: "Must have experience as writer and have examples of work. Examples need to include print copy and finished copy of videotape if possible. A résumé with educational background, general work experience and experience as a writer must be included. Especially interested in documentary-style writing. Writers' payment varies, depending on amount of research needed, complexity of project, length of production and other factors."

PALARDO PRODUCTIONS, 1807 Taft Ave., Suite 4, Hollywood CA 90028. Phone/fax: (213)469-8991. Director: Paul Ardolino. Estab. 1971. Produces material for youth ages 13-35. Buys 3-4 scripts/year. Buys all rights. Reports in 2 weeks on queries; 1 month on scripts.
Needs: Multimedia kits, tapes and cassettes, videotapes. "We are seeking ideas relating to virtual reality, comedy scripts involving technology and coming of age; rock'n'roll bios." Submit synopsis/outline and résumé. Pays in accordance with Writers Guild standards.
Tips: "Do not send a complete script—only synopsis of four pages or less *first.*"

PHOTO COMMUNICATION SERVICES, INC., 6055 Robert Dr., Traverse City MI 49684. (616)943-8800. President: M'Lynn Hartwell. Produces commercial, industrial, sales, training material etc. 95% freelance written. No scripts from unpublished/unproduced writers. 100% of scripts produced are unagented submissions. Buys all rights and first serial rights. Query for electronic submissions. Reports in 1 month.
Needs: Multimedia kits, slides, tapes and cassettes, video presentations. Primarily interested in 35mm multimedia and video. Query with samples or submit completed script and résumé. Pays by agreement.

‡ROUSER COMPANY PRESENTATION RESOURCES, 208 W. Magnolia Ave., Knoxville TN 37917. General Manager: Martin Rouser. Estab. 1932. Audience is corporate dealer network, end users. Buys 3 scripts/year. Works with 2 writers/year. Buys first rights. Accepts previously produced material. Reports in 1 month on queries and submissions. Query. Makes outright purchase.
Needs: Charts, videotapes, filmstrips (silent and sound), overhead transparencies, slides, tapes and cassettes. Corporate meeting opener multi-image module for the marine industry.

PATRICIA RUST PRODUCTIONS, Suite 924, 12021 Wilshire Blvd., Los Angeles CA 90025. President: Patricia Rust. Estab. 1984. "Company spans poetry publication to childrens to humor. While it encompasses a wide range, it is highly selective and tries to be visionary and ahead of the pack in scope, originality and execution." Buys variable rights depending on the situation and goals. Reports in 2 months on queries. Query. "Our production includes publishing, audio-video and theatrical and each project is carefully conceived and executed to influence and entertain in a meaningful way. Our standards are extremely high with regard to quality, message and meaning."
Needs: Film loops, films, videotapes, tapes and cassettes.
Tips: "While we are in the business of entertainment, we look for projects that provide answers and elevate thinking. We work with only top industry professionals and strive to represent quality and commerciality."

‡PETER SCHLEGER COMPANY, 200 Central Park S., 27-B, New York NY 10019-1415. Phone/fax: (212)245-4973. President: Peter R. Schleger. Produces material primarily for employee populations in corporations and non-profit organizations. Buys all rights, "most work is for a one-time use, and that piece may have no life beyond one project." Accepts previously produced material. Reports in 1 month. "Typical programs are customized workshops or specific individual programs from subjects such as listening and presentation skills to medical benefits communication. No program is longer than 10 minutes. If they need to be, they become shorter modules."

Needs: Produces sound filmstrips, video and printed manuals and leader's guides. Send completed script and résumé. Makes outright purchase; payment "depends on script length."

Tips: "We are looking to receive and keep on file a résumé and short, completed script sample of a program not longer than 10 minutes. The shorter the better to get a sense of writing style and the ability to structure a piece. We would also like to know the fees the writer expects for his/her work. Either per-diem, by project budget or by finished script page. We want communicators with a training background or who have written training programs, modules and the like. We want to know of people who have written print material, as well. We do not want to see scripts that have been written and are looking for a producer/director. We will look at queries for possible workshops or new approaches for training, but these must be submitted as longshots only; it is not our primary business. As we also produce video and audio media, we will work with writers who have clients needing these services."

SPENCER PRODUCTIONS, INC., 234 Fifth Ave., New York NY 10001. (212)865-8829. General Manager: Bruce Spencer. Executive Producer: Alan Abel. Produces material for high school students, college students and adults. Occasionally uses freelance writers with considerable talent. Reports in 1 month. Catalog for #10 SASE.
Needs: Prerecorded tapes and cassettes. Satirical material only. Query. Pay is negotiable.

‡STIEGLER GROUP, INC., 148 Patty Bowker, Tabernacle NJ 08088. President: Gary Stiegler. Estab. 1991. Audience is corporate/broadcast. Buys 6-8 scripts/year. Works with 2-3 writers/year. Buys all rights. No previously produced material. Makes outright purchase of $500-5,000.
Needs: Videotapes. Aviation, travel, environmental, corporate promotions.

TALCO PRODUCTIONS, 279 E. 44th St., New York NY 10017-4354. (212)697-4015. Fax: (212)697-4827. President: Alan Lawrence. Vice President: Marty Holberton. Estab. 1968. Produces variety of material for TV, radio, business, trade associations, nonprofit organizations, public relations (chiefly political and current events), etc. Audiences range from young children to senior citizens. 20-40% freelance written. Buys scripts from published/produced writers only. Buys all rights. No previously published material. Reports in 3 weeks on queries. *Does not accept unsolicited mss.*
  • Talco reports that it is doing more public relations oriented work: print, videotape and radio.
Needs: Films (16, 35mm), slides, radio tapes and cassettes, videotape. "We maintain a file of writers and call on those with experience in the same general category as the project in production. We do not accept unsolicited manuscripts. We prefer to receive a writer's résumé listing credits. If his/her background merits, we will be in touch when a project seems right." Makes outright purchase/project and in accordance with Writers Guild standards (when appropriate). Sometimes pays the expenses of writers on assignment.
Tips: "Concentration is now in TV productions. Production budgets will be tighter."

ED TAR ASSOCIATES, INC., 230 Venice Way, Venice CA 90291. (310)306-2195. Fax: (310)306-0654. Estab. 1972. Audience is dealers, salespeople, public. Buys all rights. No previously produced material. Makes outright purchase.
Needs: Films (16, 35mm), videotapes, slides, tapes, business theater and live shows. "We are constantly looking for *experienced* writers of corporate, product and live show scripts. Send résumé and samples. Track record of proven writing for a variety of corporate clients a must."

TEL-AIR INTERESTS, INC., 1755 NE 149th St., Miami FL 33181. (305)944-3268. Fax: (305)944-1143. President: Grant H. Gravitt. Produces material for groups and theatrical and TV audiences. Buys all rights. Submit résumé.
Needs: Documentary films on education, travel and sports. Produces films and videotape. Makes outright purchase.

ULTITECH, INC., Foot of Broad St., Stratford CT 06497. (203)375-7300. Fax/BBS: (203)375-6699. E-mail: comcowic@world.std.com. Estab. 1993. Designs, develops and produces interactive communications programs including video, multimedia, expert systems, software tools, computer-based training and audience response meetings. Specializes in medicine, science and technology. Prefers to work with published/estab-lished writers with video, multimedia and medical experience. 90% freelance written. Buys writing for approximately 15-20 programs/year. Electronic submissions onto BBS. Buys all rights. Reports in 1 month.
Needs: Currently producing about 10 interactive programs for medical audiences. Submit résumé and com-plete script. Makes outright purchase. Pays expenses of writers on assignment.

ALWAYS enclose a self-addressed, stamped envelope (SASE) with all your queries and correspondence.

Tips: "Interactive media for learning and entertainment is a growing outlet for writers—acquiring skills for interactive design and development will pay back in assignments."

‡**VIDEO RESOURCES**, Box 18642, Irvine CA 92713. Contact: Brad Hagen. Produces material for corporate executives. Buys 10 scripts/year. Buys all rights. No previously produced material. SASE. Reports in 1 month.
Needs: Films, home video market (special interest, dramatic, comedy, kid-vid), videotapes, multimedia kits, slides, tapes and cassettes. Query with samples. Makes outright purchase.

VISUAL HORIZONS, 180 Metro Park, Rochester NY 14623. (716)424-5300. Fax: (716)424-5313. President: Stanley Feingold. Produces material for general audiences. Buys 5 programs/year. Reports in 5 months. Free 64 page catalog.
Needs: Business, medical and general subjects. Produces silent and sound filmstrips, multimedia kits, slide sets, videotapes. Query with samples. Payment negotiable.

‡**WIDGET PRODUCTIONS, LTD.**, 120 Duane St., #8, New York NY 10007. (212)285-1447. Contact: Terry Krueger. Audience is US/international TV. Buys 6 scripts/year. Works with 10 writers/year. Buys all rights. Accepts previously produced material. Reports in 1 month on queries and submissions. Query with synopsis. Makes outright purchase of $500-3,000, dependent on 30, 60, 120 second format.
Needs: Films (16mm), videotapes, tapes and cassettes. 30, 60, 120 second Direct Response TV commercials. Occasionally 30 minute (28-30 minute).
Tips: "DR is increasing slant toward direct selling and simple story."

‡**WILLOW ASSOCIATES**, 4061 Glendenning Rd., Downers Grove IL 60515-2228. (708)969-1982. Principal: William H. Holt, Jr. Estab. 1988. Audience is corporate communications. Buys 1 script/year. Works with 4 writers/year. Submissions will not be returned. Reports in 2 months on queries and submissions. Query.
Needs: Films (16mm), videotapes, slides, tapes and cassettes. Short, corporate communications, training topics.

Playwriting

TV and movies are visual media where the words are often less important than the images. Writing plays uses different muscles, different techniques. Plays are built on character and dialogue—words put together to explore and examine characters.

The written word is respected in the theater by producer, cast, director and even audience, to a degree unparalleled in other formats. While any work involving so many people to reach its final form is in essence a collaboration, it is presided over by the playwright and changes can be made only with her approval, a power many screenwriters can only envy. If a play is worth producing, it will be produced "as is."

Counterbalancing the greater freedom of expression are the physical limitations inherent in live performance: a single stage, smaller cast, limited sets and lighting and, most importantly, a strict, smaller budget. These conditions affect not only what but also how you write.

Start writing your play by reading. Your local library has play anthologies. Check the listings in this section for play publishers such as Aran Press, Baker's Plays and Samuel French. Reading gives you a feel for how characters are built, layer by layer, word by word, how each interaction presents another facet of a character. Exposition must mean something to the character, and the story must be worth telling for a play to be successful.

There are plenty of books, seminars and workshops to help you with the writing of your play. The development of character, setting, dialogue and plot are skills that will improve with each draft. The specific play format is demonstrated in *The Complete Book of Script Formats*, by Cole and Haig and *The Writer's Digest Book of Manuscript Formats*, by Buchman and Groves.

Once the final draft of your play is finished you begin marketing it, which can take as long (or longer) than writing it. Before you begin you must have your script bound (three brads and a cover are fine) and copyrighted at the Copyright Office of the Library of Congress or registered with the Writers Guild of America. Write either agency and ask for information and an application.

Your first goal will be to get at least a reading of your play. You might be lucky and get a small production. Community theaters or smaller regional houses are good places to start. Volunteer at a local theater. As prop mistress or spotlight operator you will get a sense of how a theater operates, the various elements of presenting a play and what can and cannot be done, physically as well as dramatically. Personal contacts are important. Get to know the literary manager or artistic director of local theaters, which is the best way to get your script considered for production. Find out about any playwrights' groups in your area through local theaters or the drama departments of nearby colleges and universities. Use your creativity to connect with people that might be able to push your work higher.

Contests can be a good way to get noticed. Many playwriting contests offer as a prize at least a staged reading and often a full production. Once you've had a reading or workshop production, set your sights on a small production. Use this as a learning experience. Seeing your play on stage can help you view it more objectively and give you the chance to correct any flaws or inconsistencies. Incorporate any comments and ideas from the actors, director or even audience that you feel are on the mark into revisions of your script.

Use a small production also as a marketing tool. Keep track of all the press reviews, any interviews with you, members of the cast or production and put together a "press kit" for your play that can make the rounds with the script.

After you've been produced you have several directions to take your play. You can aim for a larger commercial production; you can try to get it published; you can seek artistic grants. After you have successfully pursued at least one of those avenues you can look for an agent. Choosing one direction does not rule out pursuing others at the same time. *The Dramatists Sourcebook*, published annually by Theatre Communications Group (355 Lexington Ave., New York NY 10017) lists opportunities in all these areas. The Dramatists Guild (234 W. 45th St., New York NY 10036) has three helpful publications: a bimonthly newsletter with articles, news and up-to-date information and opportunities, a quarterly journal, and an annual directory, a resource book for playwrights listing theaters, agents, workshops, grants, contests, etc.

Good reviews in a smaller production can get you noticed by larger theaters paying higher royalties and doing more ambitious productions. To submit your play to larger theaters you'll put together a submission package. This will include a one-page query letter to the literary manager or dramaturg briefly describing the play. Mention any reviews and give the number of cast members and sets. You will also send a two- to three-page synopsis, a ten-page sample of the most interesting section of your play, your résumé and the press kit you've assembled. Do not send your complete manuscript until it is requested.

You can also explore publishing your play. *Writer's Market* lists many play publishers. When your script is published your play will make money while someone else does the marketing. You'll be listed in a catalog that is sent out to hundreds or thousands of potential performance spaces—high schools, experimental companies, regional and community theaters—for possible production. You'll receive royalty checks for both performance fees and book sales. In contacting publishers you'll want to send your query letter with the synopsis and reviews.

There are several sources for grants. Some are federal or state, but don't overlook sources closer to home. The category "Arts Councils and Foundations" in Contests and Awards in this book lists a number of sources. On the national level contact the NEA Theater Program Fellowship for Playwrights (1100 Pennsylvania Ave. NW, Washington DC 20506). State arts commissions are another possible source, and also offer opportunities for involvement in programs where you can meet fellow playwrights. Some cities have arts and cultural commissions that offer grants for local artists. PEN publishes a comprehensive annual book, *Grants and Awards Available to American Writers* that also includes a section for Canadian writers. The latest edition is available from the PEN American Center (568 Broadway, New York NY 10012).

Once you have been produced on a commercial level, your play has been published or you have won an important grant, you can start pursuing an agent. This is not always easy. Fewer agents represent playwrights alone—there's more money in movies and TV. No agent will represent an unknown playwright. Having an agent does *not* mean you can sit back and enjoy the ride. You will still need to get out there and network, establishing ties with theaters, directors, literary managers, other writers, producers, state art agencies and publishers, trying to get your work noticed. What it does mean is that you'll have some help. A good agent will have personal contacts that can place your work for consideration at a higher level than your efforts alone might.

There is always the possibility of moving from plays to TV and movies. There is a certain cachet in Hollywood surrounding successful playwrights. The writing style will be different—more visually oriented, less dependent on your words. The money is better, but you will have less command over the work once you've sold that copyright. It seems to be easier for a playwright to cross over to movies than for a screenwriter to cross over to plays.

Writing a script can make you feel isolated, even when your characters are so real to you they seem to be in the room as you write. Sometimes the experience and companionship of other playwrights is what you need to get you over a particular hurdle in your play. Membership and service organizations such as The Dramatists Guild, The International Women's Writing Guild and local groups such as the Playwright's Center in Minneapolis and the Northwest Playwright's Guild in Seattle can help you feel still a part of this world as you are off creating your own.

For information on more playwriting markets, see Scriptwriting Markets/ Changes '95-'96 at the end of the Screenwriting section.

A.D. PLAYERS, 2710 W. Alabama, Houston TX 77098-2106. (713)526-2721. Fax: (713)522-5475. Artistic Director: Jeannette Clift George. Estab. 1967. Produces 3 full-length plays/year plus numerous one-act special events and repertory productions. Professional Christian theater company. "Productions include 5 Grace Theater Series shows and 5 Nancy Calhoun Paulson Children's Theatre Series shows, 2-3 staged readings and 10-12 Repertory Series shows on tour. The mainstage performance area is a proscenium stage with minimal wing space and no fly space; the children's theater space is in the round. Tour performance arenas vary from auditoriums and theaters to gymnasiums/cafetoriums and churches. Audiences for each series include adults and children, some with church affiliation." Query with synopsis only. Send materials to Literary Manager. Reports in 2-12 months. Payment terms negotiable.
Needs: "One-act and full-length plays, any style, reflecting God's reality in everyday life. Seasonal plays, any length, and short pieces (up to one hour) especially needed." Write to the Literary Manager for specific script submittal guidelines. No unsolicited scripts.
   ● A.D. Players is interested in seeing more children's material with small casts (4-6 actors).
Tips: "Because of our specific signature as a Christian repertory company we would not be interested in plays that have no reference to the reality of God or man's search for spiritual significance in his world."

ACTORS' STOCK COMPANY, 3884 Van Ness Lane, Dallas TX 75220. (214)353-9916. Artistic Director: Keith Oncale. Estab. 1988. Produces 3-4 plays/year. "We stage semi-professional productions to a young adult to middle-aged general audience." Query with synopsis. Reports in 3 months. Purchases reading privileges. Pays royalty.
   ● Actors Stock Company reports that two scripts by *Writer's Market* readers have received staged readings, one of which also had a full production.
Needs: Two- and three-act plays, covering a wide variety of styles, but with fewer than 12 cast members. Average staging facilities are 100-seat houses or smaller.
Tips: "Trends today reflect a return to comic realism that comments on our society without commenting on the play itself."

ACTORS THEATRE OF LOUISVILLE, 316 W. Main St., Louisville KY 40202-4218. (502)584-1265. Producing Director: Jon Jory. Estab. 1964. Produces approximately 20 new plays of varying lengths/year. Professional productions are performed for subscription audience from diverse backgrounds. Agented submissions only for full-length plays; open submissions to National Ten-Minute Play Contest (plays 10 pages or less). Reports in 6-9 months on submissions, mostly in the fall. Buys variable rights. Offers variable royalty.
Needs: "We are interested in full-length, one-act and ten-minute plays and in plays of ideas, language, humor, experiment and passion."

ALABAMA SHAKESPEARE FESTIVAL, 1 Festival Dr., Montgomery AL 36117-4605. Artistic Director: Kent Thompson. Produces 14 plays/year. Inhouse productions, tours, general audience, children audience. Reports in 6-8 months. Pays royalty.
Needs: "ASF develops works by Southern writers, works that deal with the South and/or African-American themes, works that deal with Southern and/or African-American history."

‡ALLEYWAY THEATRE, 1 Curtain Up Alley, Buffalo NY 14202-1911. Dramaturg: Joyce Stilson. Estab. 1980-competition 1990. Produces 5 full-length, 10-15 short plays/year. Submit complete ms. Reports in 4-6 months. Buys first production, credit rights. Pays 7% royalty plus travel and accomodations for opening.
● Alleyway Theatre also sponsors the Maxim Mazumdar New Play Competition. See the Contest & Award section for more information.
Needs: "Theatrical" work as opposed to mainstream TV.
Tips: Sees a trend toward social-issue-oriented works.

AMELIA MAGAZINE, 329 "E" St., Bakersfield CA 93304. (805)323-4064. Editor: Frederick A. Raborg, Jr. Estab. 1983. Publishes 1 play/year. Submit complete ms. Reports in 2 months. Buys first North American serial rights only. Pays $150 plus publication as winner of annual Frank McClure One-Act Play Award.
Needs: "Plays with virtually any theme or concept. We look for excellence within the one-act, 45 minutes running time format. We welcome the avant-garde and experimental. We do not object to the erotic, though not pornographic. Fewer plays are being produced on Broadway, but the regionals seem to be picking up the slack. That means fewer equity stages and more equity waivers."

‡AMERICAN MUSIC FESTIVAL, 123 S. Broad St., Suite 2515, Philadelphia PA 19109. (215)893-1570. Artistic Director: Ben Levit. Estab. 1983. Produces 4 musicals/year. Professional productions for young minded audiences 20s-60s. Submit script and tape of music. Reports in 6 months. Pays royalty.
Needs: Music-driven music theater/opera pieces, varied musical styles, experimental work. Seven in orchestra, 10-14 cast, 28×40 stage.
Tips: Innovative topics and use of media, music, technology a plus. Sees trends of arts in technology (interactive theater, virtual reality, sound design); works are shorter in length (1-1½ hours with no intermissions or 2 hours with intermission).

‡AMERICAN STAGE, 211 3rd St. South, P.O. Box 1560, St. Petersburg FL 33731. (813)823-1600. Artistic Director: Victoria Holloway. Estab. 1978. Produces 5 plays/year. Plays performed on "our mainstage, in the park (Shakespeare) or on tour in schools." Submit query and synopsis. Reports in 4 months. Payment varies.
Needs: New American plays for small cast. No musicals.

AN CLAIDHEAMH SOLUIS/CELTIC ARTS CENTER, P.O. Box 861778, Los Angeles CA 90086-1778. (213)462-6844. Artistic Director: Sean Walsh. Estab. 1985. Produces 6 plays/year. Equity 99-seat plan. Query with synopsis. Reports in 6 months. Rights acquired vary. Pays $25-50.
Needs: Scripts of Celtic interest (Scottish, Welsh, Irish, Cornish, Manx, Breton). "This can apply to writer's background or subject matter. We are particularly concerned with works that relate to the survival of ethnic cultures and traditions, especially those in danger of extinction."

ARAN PRESS, 1320 S. Third St., Louisville KY 40208-2306. (502)636-0115. Fax: (502)634-8001. Editor/Publisher: Tom Eagan. Estab. 1983. Audience is professional, community, college, university, summer stock and dinner theaters. Query. Reports in 1-2 weeks on submissions. Contracts for publication and production rights. Pays 10% book royalty and 50% production royalty.
● Aran Press would like to see more comedies.
Tips: No children's plays. "Tip to writers of plays: don't. Write novels, nonfiction, whatever, but don't write plays. If you *must* write plays, and you can't get published by one of the other publishers, send us an inquiry. If you care for what we have to offer, welcome aboard."

ARDEN THEATRE COMPANY, P.O. Box 779, Philadelphia PA 19105. (215)829-8900. Artistic Directors: Terrence J. Arden, Aaron Pogner. Estab. 1988. Produces 5 plays/year. Query with synopsis. Reports in 6 months. Pays 5% royalty.
Needs: Full-length, adaptations and musicals. Flexible in terms of cast size.

ARKANSAS REPERTORY THEATRE, P.O. Box 110, Little Rock AR 72203-0110. (501)378-0445. Fax: (501)378-0012. Literary Manager: Brad Mooy. Estab. 1976. Produces 11 full productions each season (7 on the MainStage, 3 on the SecondStage and 1 Educational Tour). We also produce staged readings and Celebrity Playreadings plus workshop productions. One MainStage show tours the country and the Educational Tour is regional. Query with synopsis. Reports in up to 3 months. Rights purchased vary. Pays royalty or per performance; "this also varies per show."
Needs: "We produce an ecclectic season, with musicals, comedies, dramas and at least one original premiere per season."

ART CRAFT PUBLISHING CO., 233 Dows Bldg., Box 1058, Cedar Rapids IA 52406-1058. (319)364-6311. Fax: (319)364-1771. Publisher: C. McMullen. Estab. 1928. Publishes plays and musicals for the junior and senior high school market. Query with synopsis or submit complete script. Reports in 2 months. Purchases amateur rights only. Makes outright purchase or pays royalty.
Needs: "Our current need is for full-length productions, two- and three-act plays and musicals, preferably comedy or mystery-comedy with a large number of characters. We sell almost exclusively to junior and smaller senior high school groups, thus we are unable to publish material that may contain controversial or offensive subject matter."

‡**ARTISTS REPERTORY THEATRE**, 1111 S.W. Tenth, Portland OR 97205. (503)242-2436. Contact: Allen Nause. Est. 1987. Produces 8 plays/year. Plays performed in professional regional theater. Submit complete ms. Reports in 6 months. Pays royalty.
Needs: Full-length plays. "The 110-seat Wilson Center where we perform is very intimate, thus requiring fairly small casts, approximtely 10 maximum."
Tips: "We tend to be attracted to hard-hitting material that focuses on emotional development."

‡**ARTREACH TOURING THEATRE**, 3074 Madison Rd., Cincinnati OH 45209. (513)871-2300. Fax: (513)871-2501. Director: Kathryn Schultz Miller. Produces 6 plays/year to be performed nationally in theaters and schools. "We are a professional company. Our audience is primarily young people in schools and their families." Submit complete ms. Reports in 5 months. Buys exclusive right to produce for 9 months. Pays $10/show (approximately 1,000 total performances through the year).
Needs: Plays for children and adolescents. Serious, intelligent plays about contemporary life or history/ legend. "Limited sets and props. Scripts must use only 3 actors, 45 minutes long. Should be appropriate for touring." No clichéd approaches, camp or musicals.
Tips: "We look for opportunities to create innovative stage effects using few props, and we like scripts with good acting opportunities."

ASOLO THEATRE COMPANY, 5555 N. Tamiami Tr., Sarasota FL 34243-2141. (813)351-9010. Fax: (813)351-5796. Contact: Associate Artistic Director. Estab. 1960. Produces 8 plays/year. 20% freelance written. A LORT theater with an intimate performing space. Works with 2-4 unpublished/unproduced writers annually. No unsolicited scripts. Send a letter with 1 page synopsis, 1 page of dialogue and SAE. Reports in 8 months. Negotiates rights and payment.
Needs: Play must be *full length*. "We do not restrict ourselves to any particular genre or style—generally we do a good mix of classical and modern works."

‡**BAILIWICK REPERTORY**, 1229 W. Belmont Ave., Chicago IL 60657-3205. (312)883-1090. Artistic Director: Cecilia D. Keenan. Executive Director: David Sak. Pride Series Curator: Kerry Riffle. Estab. 1982. Produces 5 mainstage plays (classic and newly comissioned) each year (submit by November 1); 5 new full-length in New Directions series; 50 1-acts in annual Directors Festival (submit by December 1); pride performance series (gay and lesbian plays, poetry), includes one acts, poetry, workshops, and staged adaptations of prose. Submit by October 1. "Our audience is a typical Chicago market. Our plays are highly theatrical and politically aware." One acts should be submitted *before* April 1. (One-act play fest runs August-September). Reports in 3 months. Pays 6% royalty.
Needs: We need daring scripts that break the mold. Large cast or musicals are OK. Creative staging solutions are a must.
Tips: "Know the rules, then break them creatively and *boldly! Please send SASE for manuscript submission guidelines before you submit.*"

BAKER'S PLAYS PUBLISHING CO., Dept. WM, 100 Chauncy St., Boston MA 02111-1783. (617)482-1280. Fax: (617)482-7613. Editor: John B. Welch. Contact: Raymond Pape. Estab. 1845. 80% freelance written. Plays performed by amateur groups, high schools, children's theater, churches and community theater groups. 75% of scripts unagented submissions. Works with 2-3 unpublished/unproduced writers annually. Submit complete script with news clippings, résumé. Submit complete cassette of music with musical submissions. Publishes 18-25 straight plays and musicals, all originals. Pay varies; makes outright purchase price to split in production fees; 10% book royalty. Reports in 2-6 months.

Needs: "We are finding strong support in our new division—plays from young authors featuring contemporary pieces for high school production."
- Send SASE for information on Baker's Plays High School Playwriting Contest.

‡**MARY BALDWIN COLLEGE THEATRE**, Mary Baldwin College, Staunton VA 24401. (703)887-7192. Artistic Director: Terry K. Southerington. Estab. 1842. Produces 5 plays/year. 10% freelance written. 75% of scripts are unagented submissions. Works with 0-1 unpublished/unproduced writer annually. An undergraduate women's college theater with an audience of students, faculty, staff and local community (adult, conservative). Query with synopsis. Query for electronic submissions. Reports in 1 year. Buys performance rights only. Pays $10-50/performance.
Needs: Full-length and short comedies, tragedies, musical plays, particularly for young women actresses, dealing with women's issues both contemporary and historical. Experimental/studio theater not suitable for heavy sets. Cast should emphasize women. No heavy sex; minimal explicit language.
Tips: "A perfect play for us has several roles for young women, few male roles, minimal production demands, a concentration on issues relevant to contemporary society, and elegant writing and structure."

BARTER THEATRE, P.O. Box 867, Abingdon VA 24210-0867. (703)628-2281. Fax: (703)628-4551. Artistic Director: Richard Rose. Estab. 1933. Produces 14 plays/year. Play performed in residency at 2 facilities, a 400-seat proscenium theater and a smaller 150-seat flexible theater. "Our plays are intended for diversified audiences of all ages." Submit synopsis and dialogue sample only to: Richard Rose, artistic director. Reports in 3-6 months. Royalty negotiable.
- Barter Theatre has premiered four new works over the last two years. One of the premieres has been optioned for Broadway for the 1995-96 season. (Also looking for freelance publication and PR writers for feature articles.)
Needs: "We are looking for good plays, comedies and dramas, that entertain and are relevant; plays that comment on the times and mankind; plays that are universal. We prefer casts of 4-12, single or unit set. Hard language can be a factor."

‡**BERKELEY REPERTORY THEATRE**, 2025 Addison, Berkeley CA 94704. (510)204-8901. Artistic Director: Sharon Ott. Produces 6 plays/year. Agented submissions or a brief description of the play—an account of what the play is about; a production and publication history of the play; a list of other works with production and publication history; an account of other recognition (grants, awards, etc.); the first 20 pages of the script; a SASE if material is to be returned; a self-addressed stamped postcard if acknowledgement of receipt of script is desired.
Tips: "We are attracted to plays that explore the complexity of contemporary society, that demand the theater as their form of expression, and that compel our audience toward a significant examination of how and why we live our lives as we do. We are partial toward work in which the language is used for expressing complex ideas in a complex way rather than simply as a vehicle for human psychology. Plays need not be large or small in terms of cast-size or setting, but should be expansive in their theatrical vision of the world."

‡**BERKSHIRE PUBLIC THEATRE**, 30 Union St., P.O. Box 860, Pittsfield MA 01202-0860. (413)445-4631. Fax: (413)445-4640. Artistic Director: Frank Bessell. Literary Manager: Linda Austin. Estab. 1976. Produces 10 plays/year. Year-round regional theater. Professional, non-Equity. Special interests: Contemporary issues; works dealing with ethics and morality; global concerns. Send résumé, production history of the work, character break-down, synopsis, ten pages of dialogue, and self-addressed, stamped postcard for our response. Reports in 2 months on queries; 1 year on ms. Various payment arrangements.

‡**BERKSHIRE THEATRE FESTIVAL, INC.**, E. Main St., Stockbridge MA 01262. Artistic Director: Arthur Storch. 25% original scripts. Produces 7-8 plays a year (4 are mainstage and 4 are second spaces). Submissions by agents only.

BILINGUAL FOUNDATION OF THE ARTS, 421 North Ave., #19, Los Angeles CA 90031. (213)225-4044. Fax: (213)225-1250. Artistic Director: Margarita Galban. Dramaturg/Literary Manager: Guillermo Reyes. Estab. 1973. Produces 3-5 plays plus 9-10 staged readings/year. "Productions are presented at home theater in Los Angeles, California. Our audiences are largely Hispanic and all productions are performed in English and Spanish. The Bilingual Foundation of the Arts produces plays in order to promote the rich heritage of Hispanic history and culture. Though our plays must be Hispanic in theme, we reach out to the entire community." Submit complete script. Reports in 3-6 months. Rights negotiable. Pays royalty.
Needs: "Plays must be Hispanic in theme. Comedy, drama, light musical, children's theater, etc. are accepted for consideration. Theater is 99-seater, no flies."
- More plays in Spanish are needed.

BOARSHEAD THEATER, 425 S. Grand Ave., Lansing MI 48933. (517)484-7800. Artistic Director: John Peakes. Estab. 1966. Produces 8 plays/year (6 mainstage, 2 young peoples theater productions inhouse). Mainstage Actors' Equity Association company; also Youth Theater—touring to schools by our intern com-

pany. Query with synopsis, cast list (with descriptions), 5-10 pages of representative dialogue, SASP. Reports on query and synopsis in 1 week. Full scripts (when requested) in 4-8 months. Pays royalty.
Needs: Thrust stage. Cast usually 8 or less; ocassionally up to 12-14. Prefer staging which depends on theatricality rather than multiple sets. Send plays re Young people's Theater % Education Director. No musicals considered. One acts only for Young People's Theater.

BRISTOL RIVERSIDE THEATRE, P.O. Box 1250, Bristol PA 19007. (215)785-6664. Producing Artistic Director: Susan D. Atkinson. Estab. 1986. "Due to a backlog of submitted scripts, we will not be accepting any new scripts until summer, 1995."

CALIFORNIA THEATER CENTER, P.O. Box 2007, Sunnyvale CA 94087. (408)245-2978. Fax: (408)245-0235. Literary Manager: Will Huddleston. Estab. 1976. Produces 15 plays/year. Plays are for young audiences in both our home theater and for tour. Query with synopsis. Reports in 6 months. "We negotiate a set fee."
Needs: All plays must be suitable for young audiences, must be around 1 hour in length. Cast sizes vary. Many shows require touring sets.

CENTER STAGE, 700 N. Calvert St., Baltimore MD 21202-3686. (410)685-3200. Resident Dramaturg: James Magruder. Estab. 1963. Produces 6-8 plays/year. "LORT 'B' and LORT 'C' theaters; audience is both subscription and single-ticket. Wide-ranging audience profile." Query with synopsis, 10 sample pages and résumé, or submit through agent. Reports in 3 months. Rights and payment negotiated.
Needs: Produces dramas and comedies, musical theater works. No one-act plays. "Casts over 12 would give us pause. Be inventive, theatrical, not precious; we like plays with vigorous language and stage image. Domestic naturalism is discouraged; strong political or social interests are encouraged. Plays about bourgeois adultery, life in the suburbs, Amelia Earhart, Alzheimer's, midlife crises, 'wacky southerners' fear of intimacy, Hemingway, backstage life, are not acceptable, as are spoofs and mysteries."
Tips: "We are interested in reading adaptations and translations as well as original work."

CENTER THEATER, 1346 W. Devon Ave., Chicago IL 60660. (312)508-0200. Artistic Director: Daniel S. LaMorte. Estab. 1984. Produces approximately 8 plays/year. "We run professional productions in our Chicago 'off-Loop' theaters for a diverse audience. We also hold an international play contest annually. For more info send SASE to Dale Calandra, Literary Manager." *Agented submissions only.* Reports in 3 months.
 • This theater has recently established a playwright-in-residence program and professional seminars in playwriting and screenwriting.

THE CHANGING SCENE THEATER, 1527½ Champa St., Denver CO 80202. Director: Alfred Brooks. Contact: Maxine Munt. Year-round productions in theater space. Cast may be made up of both professional and amateur actors. For public audience; age varies, but mostly youthful and interested in taking a chance on new and/or experimental works. No limit to subject matter or story themes. Emphasis is on the innovative. "Also, we require that the playwright be present for at least one performance of his work, if not for the entire rehearsal period. We have a small stage area, but are able to convert to round, semi-round or environmental. Prefer to do plays with limited sets and props." Two and three acts only.
Needs: Produces 8-10 nonmusicals a year; all are originals. 90% freelance written. 65% of scripts produced are unagented submissions. Works with 3-4 unpublished/unproduced writers annually. "We do not pay royalties or sign contracts with playwrights. We function on a performance-share basis of payment. Our theater seats 76; the first 50 seats go to the theater; the balance is divided among the participants in the production. The performance-share process is based on the entire production run and not determined by individual performances. We do not copyright our plays." Send complete script. Reporting time varies; usually several months.
Recent Production: *Plague Song*, by David Nuss.
Tips: "We are experimental: open to young artists who want to test their talents and open to experienced artists who want to test new ideas/explore new techniques. Dare to write 'strange and wonderful' well-thought-out scripts. We want upbeat ones. Consider that we have a small performance area (24′ × 31′) when submitting."

CHARLOTTE REPERTORY THEATRE, 2040 Charlotte Plaza, Charlotte NC 28244. (704)375-4796. Fax: (704)375-9462. Literary Manager: Claudia Carter Covington. Literary Associate: Carol Bellamy. Estab. 1976. Produces 13 plays/year. "We are a not-for-profit regional theater." Submit complete script with SASE. Reports in 2-3 months. Writers receive free plane fare and housing for festival.
Needs: "Need full-length, not previously produced professionally, scripts. No limitations in cast, props, staging, etc."

CHILDREN'S STORY SCRIPTS, Baymax Productions, 2219 W. Olive Ave., Suite 130, Burbank CA 91506-2648. (818)563-6105. Fax: (818)563-2968. Editor: Deedra Bebout. Estab. 1990. "Our audience consists of children, grades K-8 (5-13-year-olds)." Send complete script with SASE. Reports in 1 month. Licenses all rights to story; author retains copyright. Pays graduated royalty based on sales.

Needs: "We are adding new titles now and will continue to do so as we find appropriate stories. We look for stories which are fun for kids to read, involve a number of readers throughout, and dovetail with school subjects."
Tips: "The scripts are not like theatrical scripts. They combine dialogue and prose narration, a la Readers Theatre. If a writer shows promise, we'll work with him. Our most important goal is to benefit children. Send #10 SASE for guidelines with samples. We do not respond to submissions without SASE."

‡**CINCINNATI PLAYHOUSE IN THE PARK**, Dept. WM, P.O. Box 6537, Cincinnati OH 45206-0537. (513)345-2242. Fax: (513)345-2254. Contact: Artistic Associate. Estab. 1960. Produces original works and previously produced plays. "Nonprofit LORT theater, producing 11 plays annually in two spaces—a 629-seat thrust stage and a 220-seat three/sided arena. The audience is a broad cross-section of people from all over the Ohio, Kentucky and Indiana areas, from varied educational and financial bases." Write for the guidelines for Lois and Richard Rosenthal New Play Prize to submit previously unproduced, new plays for consideration.

CIRCUIT PLAYHOUSE/PLAYHOUSE ON THE SQUARE, 51 S. Cooper, Memphis TN 38104. (901)725-0776. Artistic Director: Jackie Nichols. Produces 16 plays/year. 100% freelance written. Professional plays performed for the Memphis/Mid-South area. Member of the Theatre Communications Group. 100% of scripts unagented submissions. Works with 1 unpublished/unproduced writer annually. Play contest held each fall. Submit complete script. Reports in 6 months. Buys percentage of royalty rights for 2 years. Pays $500.
Needs: All types; limited to single or unit sets. Cast of 20 or fewer.
Tips: "Each play is read by three readers through the extended length of time a script is kept. Preference is given to scripts for the southeastern region of the US."

‡**CITIARTS THEATRE**, 1975 Diamond Blvd., A-20, Concord CA 94520. (510)798-1300. Contact: Richard Elliott. Estab. 1974. Produces 6 plays/year. Query with synopsis. Reports in 3 months. Pays standard royalty.
Needs: Small plays and musicals that are popular, rarely produced, or new. Certain "stylized plays or musicals which have a contemporary edge to them (e.g., *Les Liasons Dangereuses, La Bete, Candide*)." Cast size no larger than 13; most casts around 5-7. "We are not interested in one-character pieces. If work is a musical, we do not recommend those requiring a band of larger than 7 pieces."
Tips: "Our audiences want light entertainment, comedies and musicals."

‡**CITY THEATRE COMPANY**, 57 S. 13th St., Pittsburgh PA 15203. Fax: (412)431-5535. Producing Director: Marc Masterson. Literary Manager: Gwen Orel. Produces 5 full productions/year. "We are a small professional theater, operating under an Equity contract, and committed to plays of ideas and substance relevant to contemporary American values and cultures. Our seasons are innovative and challenging, both artistically and socially. We perform in a 225-seat thrust or proscenium stage, playing usually 7 times a week, each production running 1 month or more. We have a committed audience following." Query with synopsis or submit through agent. Obtains no rights. Pays 5-6% royalty. Reports in 6 months.
Needs: "No limits on style or subject, but we are most interested in theatrical plays that have something to say about the way we live. No light comedies or TV-issue dramas." Normal cast limit is 7. Plays must be appropriate for small space without flies.
Tips: "Our emphasis is on new and recent American plays."

I.E. CLARK, PUBLISHER, Saint John's Rd., P.O. Box 246, Schulenburg TX 78956-0246. (409)743-3232. Contact: Donna Cozzaglio. Estab. 1956. Publishes 15 plays/year for educational theater, children's theater, religious theater, regional professional theater and amateur community theater. 20% freelance written. Publishes 3-4 scripts/year unagented submissions. Submit complete script, one at a time. Script will not be returned without SASE. Reports in 3-6 months. Buys all available rights; "We serve as an agency as well as a publisher." Pays standard book and performance royalty, "amount and percentages dependent upon type and marketability of play." Catalog for $2. Writer's guidelines for #10 SASE.
Needs: "We are interested in plays of all types—short or long. Audiotapes of music or videotapes of a performance are requested with submissions of musicals. We require that a play has been produced (directed by someone other than the author); photos, videos, and reviews of the production are helpful. No limitations in cast, props, staging, etc. Plays with only one or two characters are difficult to sell. We insist on literary quality. We like plays that give new interpretations and understanding of human nature. Correct spelling, punctuation and grammar (befitting the characters, of course) impress our editors."
Tips: "Entertainment value and a sense of moral responsibility seem to be returning as essential qualities of a good play script. The era of glorifying the negative elements of society seems to be fading rapidly. Literary quality, entertainment value and good craftsmanship rank in that order as the characteristics of a good script in our opinion. 'Literary quality' means that the play must—in beautiful, distinctive, and un-trite language—say something; preferably something new and important concerning man's relations with his fellow man or God; and these 'lessons in living' must be presented in an intelligent, believable and creative manner. Plays for children's theater are tending more toward realism and childhood problems, but fantasy and dramatization of fairy tales are also needed."

‡CLEVELAND PUBLIC THEATRE, 6415 Detroit Ave., Cleveland OH 44102. (216)631-2727. Fax: (216)631-2575. Artistic Director: James A. Levin. Estab. 1982. Produces 6 (full production) plays/year. Also sponsors Festival of New Plays. 150-seat alternative performance space. "Our audience believes that art touches your heart and your nerve endings." Query with synopsis for full season. Rights negotiable. Pays $15-100/performance.
Needs: Poetic, experimental, avant-garde, political, multicultural works that need a stage (not a camera); interdisciplinary cutting-edge work (dance/performance art/music/visual); works that stretch or explode the imagination and conventional boundaries. "We are a 150-seat black box with no fly space. We are low-budget—imagination must substitute for dollars."
Tips: "No conventional comedies, musicals, adaptations, children's plays—if you think Samuel French would love it, we probably won't. No TV sitcoms or soaps masquerading as theater. Theater is *not* TV or films. Learn the impact of what live bodies do to an audience in the same room. We are particularly interested in artists from our region who can grow with us on a longterm basis."

COAST TO COAST THEATER COMPANY, P.O. Box 3855, Hollywood CA 90078. (818)782-1212. Artistic Director: Bryan W. Simon. Estab. 1989. Produces 2-3 plays/year. Equity and equity waiver theater. Query and synopsis. Responds if interested. Buys West Coast, Midwest or East Coast rights, depending on location of production. Pays 5% royalty or makes outright purchase $100-250 or pays per performance.
Needs: Full-length off-beat comedies or dramas with small cast, simple sets.

COLONY STUDIO THEATRE, 1944 Riverside Dr., Los Angeles CA 90039. New play selection committee: Judith Goldstein. Produces 4 mainstage productions and 4 workshop productions/year. Professional 99-seat theater with thrust stage. Casts from a resident company of professional actors. No unsolicited scripts. Submission guidelines for SASE. Reports in up to 1 year. Negotiated rights. Pays royalties for each performance.
Needs: Full length (90-120 minutes) with a cast of 2-10. No musicals or experimental works.
Tips: "A polished script is the mark of a skilled writer. Submissions should be in professional (centered) format."

CONTEMPORARY DRAMA SERVICE, Meriwether Publishing Ltd., P.O. Box 7710, Colorado Springs CO 80933. (303)594-4422. Fax: (719)594-9916. Editor-in-Chief: Arthur Zapel. Associate Editors: Theodore Zapel and Rhonda Wray. Estab. 1969. Publishes 50-60 plays/year. "We publish for the secondary school market and colleges. We also publish for mainline liturgical churches—drama activities for church holidays, youth activities and fundraising entertainments. These may be plays or drama-related books." Query with synopsis or submit complete script. Reports in 6 weeks or less. Obtains either amateur or all rights. Pays 10% royalty or makes outright negotiated purchase.
   ● Contemporary Drama Service is looking for a creative book on "Writing Your Own Wedding Vows" and/or other trade book candidates on planning a wedding.
Needs: "Most of the plays we publish are one-acts, 15-45 minutes in length. We occasionally publish full-length two-act or three-act plays. We prefer comedies in the longer plays. Musical plays must have name appeal either by prestige author, prestige title adaptation or performance on Broadway or TV. Comedy sketches, monologues and 2-character plays are welcomed. We prefer simple staging appropriate to high school, college or church performance. We like playwrights who see the world positively and with a sense of humor. Offbeat themes and treatments are accepted if the playwright can sustain a light touch and not take himself or herself too seriously. In documentary or religious plays we look for good research and authenticity. We are publishing many scenebooks or special themes and textbooks on the theatrical arts. We are especially interested in authority-books on costuming, acting, set design and lighting and related subjects."

THE COTERIE, 2450 Grand Ave., Kansas City MO 64108-2520. (816)474-6785. Fax: (816)474-6785. Artistic Director: Jeff Church. Estab. 1979. Produces 7-8 plays/year. "Plays produced at Hallmark's Crown Center in downtown Kansas City in the Coterie's resident theater (capacity 240). A typical performance run is one month in length." Query with synopsis; submit complete script only if an established playwright in youth theater field. Reports in 2-4 months. "We retain some rights on commissioned plays." Pays royalty per performance and flat fee.
Needs: "We produce plays which are universal in appeal; they may be original or adaptations of classic or contemporary literature. Typically, not more than 12 in a cast—prefer 5-9 in size. No fly space or wing space."
Tips: "No couch plays. Prefer plays by seasoned writers who have established reputations. Groundbreaking and exciting scripts from the youth theater field welcome. It's prefectly fine if your play is a little off-center." Trends in the field that writers should be mindful of: "Make certain your submitted play to us is *very* theatrical and not cinematic. Writers need to see how far the field of youth and family theater has come—the interesting new areas we're going—before sending us your query or manuscript."

CREATIVE PRODUCTIONS, INC., 2 Beaver Place, Aberdeen NJ 07747. (908)566-6985. Artistic Director: Walter L. Born. Produces 2 musicals/year. Non-equity, year-round productions. "We use musicals with folks with disabilities and older performers in addition to 'normal' performers, for the broad spectrum of viewers." Query with synopsis. Reports in 2 weeks. Buys rights to perform play for specified number of performances. Pay negotiable.

Needs: Original musicals with upbeat themes adaptable to integrated company of traditional and non-traditional performers. Maximum cast of 12, sets can't "fly," facilities are schools, no mammoth sets and multiple scene changes, 90 minutes maximum run time.

Tips: No blue material, pornographic, obscene language. Submit info on any performances. Demo tape (musicals) plus vocal/piano score list of references on users of their material to confirm bio info.

CREEDE REPERTORY THEATRE, P.O. Box 269, Creede CO 81130-0269. (719)658-2541. Director: Richard Baxter. Estab. 1966. Produces 6 plays/year. Plays performed for a summer audience. Query with synopsis. Reports in 1 year. Royalties negotiated with each author—paid on a per performance basis.

Needs: One-act children's scripts. Special consideration given to plays focusing on the cultures and history of the American West and Southwest.

Tips: "We seek new adaptations of classical or older works as well as original scripts."

‡CROSSLEY THEATRE/ACTORS CO-OP, 1760 N. Gower, Hollywood CA 90028. (213)462-8460. Artistic Director: Robin Strand. Main Stage: AEA 99 seat theater plan; September-June, 4-5 plays; Second Stage: AEA 99 seat theater plan, primarily for developing new material including full-length plays, one acts, readings, musical revues. Query with synopsis. Reports in 8-10 weeks. Pays per performance.

Needs: "We seek material with large themes written with intelligence. No abuse stories (substance, family, etc.) unless moral or philosophical dilemma is investigated (i.e., Equus); no family dramas unless dramatic conflict transcends mere venting of hurt feelings (i.e., 1918)." Prefer casts of 12 or less (doubling is OK). Prefer minimum set changes.

Tips: "The Crossley Theatre and the Crossley Terrace Theatre are located on church grounds so there are some language restrictions. The Actors Co-op has received much critical acclaim including 42 Drama-Logue Awards and three Drama Critics Circle Awards in the last four years."

DELAWARE THEATRE COMPANY, 200 Water St., Wilmington DE 19801-5030. (302)594-1104. Artistic Director: Cleveland Morris. Estab. 1978. Produces 5 plays/year. 10% freelance written. "Plays are performed as part of a five-play subscription season in a 300-seat auditorium. Professional actors, directors and designers are engaged. The season is intended for a general audience." 10% of scripts are unagented submissions. Works with 1 unpublished/unproduced writer every 2 years. Query with synopsis and an excerpt of 5-10 pages. Reports in 6 months. Buys variable rights. Pays 5% (variable) royalty.

Needs: "We present comedies, dramas, tragedies and musicals. All works must be full length and fit in with a season composed of standards and classics. All works have a strong literary element. Plays showing a flair for language and a strong involvement with the interests of classical humanism are of greatest interest. Single-set, small-cast works are likeliest for consideration." Recent trend toward "more economical productions."

‡DETROIT REPERTORY THEATRE, 13103 Woodrow Wilson, Detroit MI 48238-3686. (313)868-1347. Artistic Director: Bruce Millan. Estab. 1957. Produces 4 plays/year. Professional theater, 194 seats operating on A.E.A. SPT contract Detroit metropolitan area. Submit complete ms. Reports in 3-6 months. "Should the play be accepted for production, we ask that no other theater within 100 miles of the city produce the for 6 months prior and after our production dates. Pays 6% royalty.

Needs: Cast limited to no more than 7 characters.

Tips: Wants issue-oriented works. No musicals or one-act plays.

DORSET THEATRE FESTIVAL, Box 519, Dorset VT 05251-0519. (802)867-2223. Fax: (802)867-0144. Artistic Director: Jill Charles. Estab. 1976. Produces 5 plays/year, 1 a new work. "Our plays will be performed in our Equity summer stock theatre and are intended for a sophisticated community." Agented submissions only. Reports in 3-6 months. Rights and compensation arranged on an individual basis.

Needs: "Looking for full-length contemporary American comedy or drama. Limited to a cast of six."

Tips: "Language and subject matter appropriate to general audience."

DRAMATICS MAGAZINE, Dept. WM, 3368 Central Pkwy., Cincinnati OH 45225. (513)559-1996. Editor: Don Corathers. Estab. 1929. Publishes 5 plays/year. For high school theater students and teachers. Submit complete ms. Reports in 3 months. Buys first North American serial rights only. Accepts previously published plays. Send tearsheet, photocopy or typed ms with rights for sale noted and information about when and

---

☐ *Open box preceding a listing indicates a cable TV market.*

where the work previously appeared. For reprints, pays 50% of the amount paid for an original piece. Purchases one-time publication rights only for $100-400.

Needs: "We are seeking one-acts to full-lengths that can be produced in an educational theater setting. We don't publish musicals."

Tips: "No melodrama, farce, children's theater, or cheap knock-offs of TV sitcoms or movies. Fewer writers are taking the time to learn the conventions of theater—what makes a piece work on stage, as opposed to film and television—and their scripts show it."

ELDRIDGE PUBLISHING CO., P.O. Box 1595, Venice FL 34284. (813)496-4679. Fax: (813)493-9680. Editor: Nancy Vorhis. Estab. 1906. Publishes 50-60 new plays/year for middle school, junior high, senior high, church and community audience. Query with synopsis (acceptable) or submit complete ms (preferred). Please send cassette tapes with any operettas. Reports in 2 months. Buys all rights. Pays 50% royalties and 10% copy sales. Makes outright purchase from $200-500. Writer's guidelines for #10 SASE.

- For 1995-1996 Eldridge Publishing will be looking for more community theater plays. These plays will have smaller casts and more meaningful subject matter. They will still continue to publish large cast plays for high schools.

Needs: "We are most interested in full-length plays and musicals for our school and community theater market. Prefers large, flexible casts, if possible. Nothing lower than junior high level, please. We always love comedies but also look for serious, high caliber plays reflective of today's sophisticated students. We also need one-acts and plays for children's theater. In addition, in our religious market we're always searching for Christmas and Easter plays."

Tips: "Submissions are welcomed at any time but during our fall season; response will definitely take 2 months. Authors are paid royalties twice a year. They receive complimentary copies of their published plays, the annual catalog and 50% discount if buying additional copies."

THE EMPTY SPACE, 3509 Fremont Ave. N., Seattle WA 98103-8813. (206)547-7633. Artistic Director: Eddie Levi Lee. Estab. 1970. Produces 5-10 plays/year. 100% freelance written. Professional plays for subscriber base and single ticket Seattle audience. One script/year is unagented submission. Works with 5-6 unpublished/unproduced writers annually. Query with synopsis before sending script. Response in 2 months. LOA theater.

Needs: "We are interested in full-length plays and small musicals, especially works that break the fourth wall, or give the audience a unique live experience in some way."

ENCORE PERFORMANCE PUBLISHING, P.O. Box 692, Orem UT 84059-4554. (801)225-0605. Editor: Michael C. Perry. Estab. 1979. Publishes 20-50 plays/year. "Our audience consists of all ages with emphasis on the family; educational institutions from elementary through college/university, community theaters and professional theaters." No unsolicited mss. Query with synopsis. Reports in 1 month on queries; 3 months on scripts. Pays 50% performance royalty; 10% book royalty. Submit from May-August.

Needs: "We are looking for plays with strong message about or for families, plays with young actors among cast, any length, all genres. We prefer scripts with at least close or equal male/female roles, could lean to more female roles." Plays must have had at least 2 fully staged productions. Unproduced plays can be read with letter of recomendation accompanying the query.

Tips: "No performance art pieces or plays with overtly sexual themes or language. Looking for adaptations of Twain and other American authors."

‡THE ENSEMBLE STUDIO THEATRE, 549 W. 52nd St., New York NY 10019. (212)247-4982. Fax: (212)664-0041. Artistic Director: Curt Dempster. Estab. 1971. Produces 250 projects/year for off-off Broadway developmental theater. 100-seat house, 60-seat workshop space. Do not fax mss or résumés. Submit complete ms. Reports in 3 months. Standard production contract: mini contract with Actors' Equity Association or letter of agreement. Pays $80-1,000.

Needs: Full-length plays and one acts with strong dramatic actions and situations. No musicals, versedramas or elaborate costume dramas.

Tips: Submit work September-April. "We are dedicated to developing new American plays."

‡EUREKA THEATRE COMPANY, 330 Townsend, Suite 210, San Francisco CA 94107. (415)243-9899. Contact: David Parr. Estab. 1972. Produces 3-5 fully-staged plays/year. Plays performed in professional-AEA, year-round for socially involved adult audiences. Query with synopsis. "We prefer a synopsis and

The double dagger before a listing indicates that the listing is new in this edition. New markets are often more receptive to freelance submissions.

sample scenes and self-addressed, stamped postcard, not a whole unsolicited script." Reports in 3 months. Rights negotiated. Pays negotiable royalty/commission.

Needs: "The mission of the Eureka Theatre Company continues to be to present productions of plays of honesty and integrity which address the concerns and realities of the time and place in which we live. We want to continue the Eureka tradition of entertaining and provoking our audiences as we present them with the urgency of dealing with the diversity and the opportunities of the society in which we live and work. In these final years of the twentieth century, we see it as an imperative to sum up this waning millenium even as we examine and question the next."

Tips: "No one-acts (although we would consider a collection and short works by a single writer or collective); no light-hearted musicals. We are tired of being told 'this is the next *Angels in America*.' We want plays which reflect the cultural diversity of the area in which we live and work. Remember, you are writing for the live stage, *not* for film or TV."

‡EXTRA VIRGIN PERFORMANCE COOPERATIVE, P.O. Box 224832, Dallas TX 75222. (214)941-3664. Artistic Director: Gretchen Sween. Estab. 1992. Produces 3 plays/year. "Plays are professional, low-tech productions for largely adult, intellectual and daring audiences." Submit complete ms with synopsis. Reports in 2 months. Pays writer's travel expenses and board for attending production.

Needs: "Previously unproduced, low-tech, experimental plays that are intellectually challenging, socially conscious, and mythological in scope." Prefers single set and small casts.

Tips: No old-fashioned "well-made plays," sit-coms, or those which are exceedingly technologically demanding. "We see a trend toward the resurgence of poetic language and non-materialistic environments and stagings."

‡FLORIDA STUDIO THEATRE, 1241 N. Palm Ave., Sarasota FL 34236. (813)366-9017. New plays director: Chris Angermann. Produces 4 established and 3 new plays/year. "FST is a professional not-for-profit theater." Plays are produced in 165-seat theater for a subscription audience (primarily). FST operates under a small professional theater contract of Actor's Equity. Query with synopsis. Reports in 2 months on queries; 7 months on mss. Pays $200 for workshop production of new script.

Needs: Contemporary plays ("courageous and innovative"). Prefers casts of no more than 8 and single sets.

THE FOOTHILL THEATRE COMPANY, P.O. Box 1812, Nevada City CA 95959. (916)265-9320. Artistic Director: Philip Charles Sneed. Estab. 1977. Produces 7-9 plays/year. "We are a professional theater company operating under an Actors' Equity Association contract for part of the year, and performing in the historic 246-seat Nevada Theatre (built in 1865) and in a converted space in a nearby cultural center (70-seat black box). The audience is a mix of locals and tourists." Query with synopsis or submit complete script. Reports in 6 months or less. Buys negotiable rights. Pay varies.

Needs: "We are most interested in plays which speak to the region and its history, as well as to its current concerns. No melodramas. Theatrical, above all." No limitations.

Tips: "Avoid the cliché at all costs, and don't be derivative; we're interested in a unique and unassailable vision."

FOUNTAIN THEATRE, 5060 Fountain Ave., Los Angeles CA 90029. (213)663-2235. Artistic Directors: Deborah Lawlor, Stephen Sachs. Estab. 1990. Produces 6 plays/year. Produced at Fountain Theatre (99-seat equity plan). Query through agent or recommendation of theater professional. Query with synopsis to: Jay Alan Quantrill, Producint Director/Dramaturg. Reports in 6 months. Rights acquired vary. Pays royalty.

Needs: Original plays, adaptations of American literature, "material that incorporates dance of language into text with unique use and vision."

‡THE FREELANCE PRESS, P.O. Box 548, Dover MA 02030-2207. (508)785-1260. Managing Editor: Narcissa Campion. Estab. 1984. Publishes 4 plays/year for children/young adults. Submit complete ms with SASE. Reports in 3-4 months. Pays 2-3% royalty. Pays 10% of the price of each script and score.

Needs: "Publish original musical theater for young people, dealing with issues of importance to them, also adapt 'classics' into musicals for 8-16-year-old age groups to perform." Large cast; flexible, simple staging and props.

GEORGE STREET PLAYHOUSE, 9 Livingston Ave., New Brunswick NJ 08901. (908)846-2895. Producing Director: Gregory Hurst. Literary Manager: Tricia Roche. Produces 7 plays/year. Professional regional theater (LORT C). No unsolicited scripts. Professional recommendation only. Reports on scripts in 6-8 months.

Needs: Full-length dramas, comedies and musicals that present a fresh perspective on society and challenge expectations of theatricality. Prefers cast size under 9. Also presents 40-minute social issue-plays appropriate for touring to school-age children; cast size limited to 4 actors.

Tips: "We produce up to four new plays and one new musical each season. We have a strong interest in receiving work from minority writers whose voices are not traditionally heard on America's main stages."

THE GOODMAN THEATRE, 200 S. Columbus Ave., Chicago IL 60603. (312)443-3811. Artistic Director: Robert Falls. Literary Manager: Susan V. Booth. Estab. 1925. Produces 9 plays/year. "The Goodman is a professional, not-for-profit theater producing both a mainstage and studio series for its subscription-based audience. The Goodman does not accept unsolicited scripts from playwrights or agents, nor will it respond to synopses of plays submitted by playwrights, unless accompanied by a stamped, self-addressed postcard. The Goodman may request plays to be submitted for production consideration after receiving a letter of inquiry or telephone call from recognized literary agents or producing organizations." Reports in 6 months. Buys variable rights. Pay is variable.

Needs: Full-length plays, translations, musicals; special interest in social or political themes.

GREAT AMERICAN HISTORY THEATRE, 30 E. Tenth St., St. Paul MN 55101. (612)292-4323. Fax: (612)292-4322. Interim Artistic Director: Ron Peluso. Estab. 1978. Produces 6-7 plays/year. Thrust stage; 597 seats. "Our performances are intended for mainstream audiences." Query with synopsis. Reports in 2 weeks on synopsis; 2 months on scripts. Buys production rights. Pays variable royalty. "We commission new works, amount to be negotiated."

Needs: "We provide audiences with a mirror to the lives of the people of Minnesota and the Midwest, and a window to other people and times. We do this by commissioning, producing and touring plays that dramatize the history, folklore and social issues of its own region and other locales. We limit our cast sizes to no larger than ten and we prefer pieces that can be staged simply."

THE GROUP (Seattle Group Theatre), 305 Harrison St., Seattle WA 98109. (206)441-9480. Fax: (206)441-9839. Artistic Director: Tim Bond. (Submit to Talvin Wilks, Literary Manager). Estab. 1978. Produces 5 plays and 1-3 workshop productions/year. "Plays are performed in our 197-seat theater—The Carlton Playhouse. Intended for a multiethnic audience. Professional, year-round theater." Query with synopsis, sample pages of dialogue and SASE for reply. Reports in 6-8 weeks. Rights obtained varies per production. Royalty varies.

Needs: "We look for scripts suitable for multiethnic casting that deal with social, cultural and political issues relevant to the world today."

Tips: *No phone calls.*

‡HARTFORD STAGE COMPANY, 50 Church St., Hartford CT 06103. (203)525-5601. Artistic Director: Mark Lamos. Estab. 1963. Produces 6 plays/year. Regional theater productions with a wide range in audience. Agented submissions only; "for unsolicited scripts, we accept only synopsis, 10-page dialogue sample, and SASE." Reports in 3-4 weeks for synopsis; 3-4 months for ms. Rights bought varies. Pays royalty.

Needs: Classics, new plays, musicals, "open to almost anything. Looking more for small to medium casts (1-12) but larger casts are also looked at."

Tips: Does not want typical Broadway fare, i.e., Phantom of the Opera, Cats.

HEUER PUBLISHING CO., 233 Dows Bldg., Box 248, Cedar Rapids IA 52406-0248. (319)364-6311. Fax: (319)364-1771. Owner/Editor: C. Emmett McMullen. Estab. 1928. Publishes plays and musicals for junior and senior high school and church groups. Query with synopsis or submit complete script. Reports in 2 months. Purchases amateur rights only. Pays royalty or makes outright purchase.

Needs: "One- and three-act plays suitable for school production. Preferably comedy or mystery/comedy. All material should be of the capabilities of high school actors. We prefer material with one set. No special day material or material with controversial subject matter."

‡HIPPODROME STATE THEATRE, 25 SE Second Place, Gainesville FL 32601. (904)373-5968. Dramaturg: David Boyce. Estab. 1973. Produces 4 productions. Plays are performed on one main stage (266 seats) for a subscriber audience. Professional recommendation and agent submission only. Response: 6-10 months.

Needs: "We accept plays of any genre or subject matter. We're looking for *good writing* and fresh, original voices." Cast should not exceed 8; staging flexible, but should be appropriate for thrust stage.

HONOLULU THEATRE FOR YOUTH, 2846 Ualena St., Honolulu HI 96819-1910. (808)839-9885. Fax: (808)839-7018. Produces 6 plays/year. 50% freelance written. Plays are professional productions in Hawaii, primarily for young audiences (ages 2-20). 80% of scripts unagented submissions. Works with 2 unpublished/unproduced writers annually. Reports in 4 months. Buys negotiable rights.

Needs: Contemporary subjects of concern/interest to young people; adaptations of literary classics; fantasy including space, fairy tales, myth and legend. "HTY wants well-written plays, 60-90 minutes in length, that have something worthwhile to say and that will stretch the talents of professional adult actors. Cast not exceeding 8; *no* technical extravaganzas; *no* full-orchestra musicals; simple sets and props, costumes can be elaborate. No plays to be enacted by children or camp versions of popular fairytales." Query with synopsis. Pays $1,000-2,500.

Tips: "Young people are intelligent and perceptive; if anything, more so than lots of adults, and if they are to become fans and eventual supporters of good theater, they must see good theater while they are young. Trends on the American stage that freelance writers should be aware of include a growing awareness that we are living in a world community. We must learn to share and understand other people and other cultures."

WILLIAM E. HUNT, 801 West End Ave., New York NY 10025. Estab. 1947. Producer/Director: William E. Hunt. Interested in reading scripts for stock production, off-Broadway and even Broadway production. "Small cast, youth-oriented, meaningful, technically adventuresome; serious, funny, far-out. Must be about people first, ideas second. No political or social tracts." No one-act, anti-Black, anti-Semitic or anti-gay plays. "I do not want 1920, 1930 or 1940s plays disguised as modern by 'modern' language. I do not want plays with 24 characters or 150 costumes, plays about symbols instead of people. I do not want plays that are really movie or TV scripts." Works with 2-3 unpublished/unproduced writers annually. Pays royalties on production: Off-Broadway, 5%; on Broadway, 5%, 7½% and 10%, based on gross. No royalty paid if play is selected for a showcase production. Reports in "a few weeks." Must have SASE or script will not be returned.

Tips: "Production costs and weekly running costs in the legitimate theater are so high today that no play (or it is the very rare play) with more than six characters and more than one set, by a novice playwright, is likely to be produced unless that playwright will either put up or raise the money him or herself for the production."

‡INTAR HISPANIC AMERICAN ARTS CENTER, 420 W. 42nd St., New York NY 10036. (212)695-6134. Artistic Director: Max Ferra. Estab. 1969. Produces 3 plays/year. "We are an off-Broadway theater. Our productions are intended for the general theater-going audience. They are always reviewed by all the major critics in New York City." Submit complete ms. Reports in 2 months. Makes outright purchase from $1,000-3,000.

Needs: "We produce plays by Hispanic-Americans or translations/adaptations of works by Latin-American or Spanish authors. Prefer smaller cast. No wing space."

Tips: "Please address manuscript to my name and title, in care of our organization."

‡INTIMAN THEATRE COMPANY, P.O. Box 19760, Seattle WA 98109. (206)626-0775. Artistic Director: Warner Shook. Estab. 1972. Produces 6 plays/year. Lort C Regional Theater in Seattle. Query with synopsis and sample pages. Reports in 4 months.

Needs: Well-crafted dramas and comedies by playwrights who fully utilize the power of language and character relationships to explore enduring themes.

Needs: Prefers character-driven plays.

‡J.D. PRODUCTIONS, 3649 Warner Ave., Louisville KY 40207. (502)893-2942. Artistic Director: Jolene DeLory. Estab. 1994. Produces 6-8 plays/year for community, semiprofessional, professional, dinner theater, possibly traveling troupe for short plays. All audiences, including children. Query with synopsis or submit complete ms. Reports in 6 weeks. Obtains all rights. Pays negotiable royalty, 50% minimum, depending on type of material.

Needs: Short plays, musical revues, full-length (2 hours). Open to all subjects at this time, directed toward all audiences, including children.

Tips: "Audiences are gravitating back toward classics, or plays that resemble classics. They like the older plays especially mystery and comedy and older musicals (or shows with that tone). I am also looking for short plays and musical revues for a particular theater group with the third oldest continuous running theater in the country. I am the director of the group."

JEWEL BOX THEATRE, 3700 N. Walker, Oklahoma City OK 73118-7099. (405)521-1786. Artistic Director: Charles Tweed. Estab. 1986. Produces 6 plays/year. Amateur productions. For 3,000 season subscribers and general public. Submit complete script. Reports in 4 months. Pays $500 contest prize.

Needs: "Write theater for entry form during September-October. We produce dramas, comedies and musicals. Only two- or three-act plays can be accepted. Our theater is in-the-round, so we adapt plays accordingly." Deadline: mid-January.

JEWISH REPERTORY THEATRE, 1395 Lexington Ave., New York NY 10128. (212)415-5550. Artistic Director: Ran Avni. Estab. 1974. Produces 4 plays, 15 readings/year. New York City professional off-Broadway production. Submit complete script with SASE. Reports in 1 month. First production/option to move to Broadway or off-Broadway. Pays royalty.

Needs: Full-length only. Straight plays and musicals. Must have some connection to Jewish life, characters, history. Maximum 7 characters. Limited technical facilities.

Tips: No biblical plays.

KUMU KAHUA, 46 Merchant St., Honolulu HI 96813. (808)737-4161. Fax: (808)536-4222. Artistic Director: Dennis Carroll. Estab. 1971. Produces 5 productions, 3-4 public readings/year. "Plays performed at new Kumu Kahua Theatre, flexible 120-seat theater, for community audiences." Submit complete script. Reports in 4 months. Pays royalty of $35/performance; usually 14 performances of each production.

Needs: "Plays must have some interest for local audiences, preferably by being set in Hawaii or dealing with some aspect of the Hawaiian experience. Prefer small cast, with simple staging demands."

Tips: "We need time to evaluate scripts (our response time is four months)."

LAGUNA PLAYHOUSE, P.O. Box 1747, Laguna Beach CA 92652-1747. (714)497-5900, ext. 206. Fax: (714)497-6948. Artistic Director: Andrew Barnicle. Estab. 1920. Produces 10 plays/year. Amateur with Equity Guest Artists: 5 mainstage (9,000 subscribers); Amateur: 5 youth theater (1,500 subscribers). Submit complete script. Reports in 2-12 months. Royalty negotiable.
Needs: Seeking full-length plays: comedy, drama, classical, musical, youth theater.
Recent Production: *Teachers' Lounge*, by John Twomey. (world premiere, full production).
Tips: "We are committed to one full production of an original play every other season."
  ● Laguna Playhouse has opened a second theater venue and expects to mount full productions of original works more regularly than in the past. However, limited staff to read and process original works can mean a long response time.

LILLENAS PUBLISHING CO., P.O. Box 419527, Kansas City MO 64141-6527. (816)931-1900. Fax: (816)753-4071. Editor: Paul M. Miller. Estab. 1926. "We publish on two levels: (1) Program Builders—seasonal and topical collections of recitations, sketches, dialogues and short plays; (2) Drama Resources. These assume more than one format: (a) full-length scripts, (b) one-acts, shorter plays and sketches all by one author, (c) collection of short plays and sketches by various authors. All program and play resources are produced with local church and Christian school in mind. Therefore there are taboos." Queries are encouraged, but synopses and complete scripts are read. "First rights are purchased for Program Builder scripts. For our line of Drama Resources, we purchase all print rights, but this is negotiable." Writer's guidelines for #10 SASE. Reports in 3 months
  ● This publisher is more interested in full-length scripts—both religious and secular. Monologs are of lesser interest than previously.
Needs: 98% of Program Builder materials are freelance written. Scripts selected for these publications are outright purchases; verse is minimum of 25 cents/line, prose (play scripts) are minimum of $5/double-spaced page. "Lillenas Drama Resources is a line of play scripts that are, for the most part, written by professionals with experience in production as well as writing. However, while we do read unsolicited scripts, more than half of what we publish is written by experienced authors whom we have already published." Drama Resources (whether full-length scripts, one-acts, or sketches) are paid on a 10% royalty. There are no advances.
Tips: "All plays need to be presented in standard play script format. We welcome a summary statement of each play. Purpose statements are always desirable. Approximate playing time, cast and prop lists, etc. are important to include. We are interested in fully scripted traditional plays, reader's theater scripts, choral speaking pieces. Contemporary settings generally have it over Biblical settings. Christmas and Easter scripts must have a bit of a twist. Secular approaches to these seasons (Santas, Easter bunnies, and so on), are not considered. We sell our product in 10,000 Christian bookstores and by catalog. We are probably in the forefront as a publisher of religious drama resources."

LIVE OAK THEATRE, 200 Colorado St., Austin TX 78701. (512)472-5143. Fax: (512)472-7199. Artistic Director: Don Toner. Literary Manager: Tom Byrne. Estab. 1982. Professional theater produces 6 plays/season. "Live Oak has a history of producing works of Texan and Southern topics. Well-crafted, new American plays that are strongly theatrical." Pays royalty. Reports in 10 days with SASE. Late summer for scripts.
Needs: Full length, translations, adaptations, musicals. Guidelines for #10 SASE.
Tips: Also sponsors annual new play awards. Guidelines for #10 SASE.
  ● Ask for guidelines to the Live Oak Theatre Harvest Festival of New American Plays.

‡MANHATTAN THEATRE CLUB, 453 W. 16th St., New York NY 10011-5896. Director of Play Development: Kate Loewald. Produces 8 plays/year. Two-theater performing arts complex classified as off-Broadway, using professional actors. No unsolicited scripts. No queries. Reports in 6 months..
Needs: "We present a wide range of new work, from this country and abroad, to a subscription audience. We want plays about contemporary problems and people. Comedies are welcome. Multiple set shows are discouraged.Average cast is 8."

‡MERRIMACK REPERTORY THEATRE, Dept. WM, P.O. Box 228, Lowell MA 01853-0228. (508)454-6324. Fax: (508)934-0166. Artistic Director: David G. Kent. Estab. 1979. Produces 7 plays/year. Professional LORT D. Agented submissions and letters of inquiry only. Reports in 6 months.
Needs: All styles and genres. "We are a small 386-seat theater—with a modest budget. Plays should be good stories, with strong dialogue, real situations and human concerns. Especially interested in plays about American life and culture."

‡MERRY-GO-ROUND PLAYHOUSE, INC., P.O. Box 506, Auburn NY 13021. (315)255-1305. Artistic Director: Edward Sayles. Estab. 1958. Produces 10 plays/year. Childrens touring company—throughout US and Canada. Summer Musical—refurbished carousel; seating 325. Submit complete ms. Reports in 3 months. Rights negotiable. Pays 8-15% royalty or $20-35/performance.
Needs: Childrens musicals, fairy tales, educational and social minded plays, adult play readings, musical theater. Prefers cast of no more than 4, props and staging needs to be flexible for touring.
Tips: "We look at and consider any and all material—particularly self-esteem and multicultural themes."

‡MILWAUKEE REPERTORY THEATER, 108 E. Wells St., Milwaukee WI 53202. (414)224-1761. Artistic Director: Joseph Hanreddy. Estab. 1954. Produces 14 plays/year. "The 1995-96 season is set. Submission is through agent only."

‡MIXED BLOOD THEATRE COMPANY, 1501 S. Fourth St., Minneapolis MN 55454. (612)338-0937. Artistic Director: Jack Reuler. Estab. 1975. Produces 5 plays/year. Equity productions in 200-seat theatre. "Professional main stage production for adult audiences." Query with synopsis only. No unsolicited scripts unless intended for "Mixed Blood Versus America Annual Playwriting Contest." "We pay for production and retain no rights beyond that. Payment varies. Playwright receives a guaranteed fee plus a percentage of the gate. Our payments to writers are competitive."
Needs: Seeking "well-written stories with characters we care about."
Tips: "Don't be shy. Send us a script for our contest or a query for produced work. Be concise."

MODERN INTERNATIONAL DRAMA, Theater Dept., SUNY, P.O. Box 6000, Binghamton NY 13902-6000. (607)777-2704. Managing Editor: George E. Wellwarth. Estab. 1967. Publishes 5-6 plays/year. "Audience is academic and professional." Query with synopsis or submit complete script. Reports in 3 months. "Rights remain with author and translator." Pays 3 complimentary copies.
Needs: Publishes plays of ideas; 20th century; any style and any length; *translations from any language of previously untranslated plays only.*
Tips: "No popular theater."

‡THE MUNY STAGE 2, (formerly The Muny/Student Theatre), 634 N. Grand, Suite 1118, St. Louis MO 63130-1002. (314)652-5213. Fax: (314)533-3345. Artistic Director: Christopher Limber. Estab. 1979. The Independent Educational outreach program for the Muny; the oldest and largest outdoor summer theater in the country. The Muny Stage 2 offers a mainstage season of 2-4 productions and a touring company which reaches 170 venues over an 8-month touring season. MST is one of the most comprehensive theater education programs in the Midwest. Main artistic focus—development of new work. MST is willing to consider scenarios and concept sketches as well as completed plays.
Needs: 45-60 minute plays. New adaptations of classic literature; plays that explore contemporary issues. Plays with young protagonists. Socially relevant themes, enhancement of academic curriculum helpful, though not always a requirement.

MUSICAL THEATRE WORKS, INC., Dept. WM, 4th Floor, 440 Lafayette St., New York NY 10003-6919. (212)677-0040. Fax: (212)598-0105. Artistic Director: Anthony Stimac. Estab. 1983. "MTW develops scripts from informal to staged readings. When the project is deemed ready for the public, a showcase is set up for commercial interest. MTW musicals are professionally produced and presented in an off-Broadway New York City theater and intended for a well-rounded, sophisticated, theater-going audience. Additionally, 50% of all MTW MainStage productions have gone on to engagements on Broadway and in 12 states across the country." Submit complete script with audiotape. Reports in 2-4 months. Buys 1% future gross; on fully-produced works. Pays negotiable royalty. SASE required to return script and tape.
Needs: "MTW only produces full-length works of musical theater and is interested not only in those classically written, but has a keen interest in works which expand the boundaries and subject matter of the artform. MTW is a small, but prolific, organization with a limited budget. It is, therefore, necessary to limit production costs."
Tips: "The dramatic stage of recent years has successfully interpreted social problems of the day, while the musical theater has grown in spectacle and foregone substance. Since the musical theater traditionally incorporated large themes and issues it is imperative that we now marry these two ideas—large themes and current issues—to the form. Send a neat, clean, typewritten script with a well marked, clear audiotape, produced as professionally as possible, to the attention of the Literary Manager."

NECESSARY ANGEL THEATRE, 490 Adelaide St. W., Suite #201, Toronto, Ontario M5V 1T2 Canada. (416)703-0406. Fax: (416)504-8702. Artistic Director: Richard Rose. Estab. 1978. Produces 2 plays/year. Plays are Equity productions in various Toronto theaters and performance spaces for an urban audience between 20-55 years of age. Submit synopsis only. Does not return submissions. Reports in 6 months. Pays 10% royalty.
Needs: "We are open to new theatrical ideas, environmental pieces, unusual acting styles and large casts. The usual financial constraints exist, but they have never eliminated a work to which we felt a strong commitment. No TV-influenced sitcoms or melodramas."

‡THE NEW AMERICAN THEATER CENTER, 118 N. Main St., Rockford IL 61101. (815)963-9454. Produces a spectrum of American and international work in 10-month season. "The New American Theater Center is a professional equity theater company performing on two stages, a thrust stage with 282-seat house and a 100-seat house theater in the round. It is located in a predominantly middle-class Midwestern town." Submit synopsis with SASE. *No* full scripts. Pays royalty based on number of performances.

Needs: No limitations, prefer contemporary pieces. Open to format, etc. No opera.
Tips: "We look for new work that addresses contemporary issues; we do not look for work of any one genre or production style."

THE NEW CONSERVATORY CHILDREN'S THEATRE COMPANY AND SCHOOL, New Conservatory Theatre Center, 25 Van Ness, Lower Level, San Francisco CA 94102. (415)861-4814. Fax: (415)861-6988. Artistic Director: Ed Decker. Produces 4-5 plays/year. "The New Conservatory is a children's theater school (ages 4-19) and operates year-round. Each year we produce several plays, for which the older students (usually 10 and up) audition. These are presented to the general public at the New Conservatory Theatre Center in San Francisco (50-150 seats). Our audience is approximately age 5-adult." Query with synopsis. Reports in 3 months. Royalty negotiable.
Needs: "We emphasize works in which children play *children*, and prefer relevant and controversial subjects, although we also do musicals. We have a commitment to new plays. Examples of our shows are: Mary Gail's *Nobody Home* (world premiere; about latchkey kids); Brian Kral's *Special Class* (about disabled kids); and *The Inner Circle*, by Patricia Loughrey (commissioned scripts about AIDS prevention for kids). As we are a nonprofit group on limited budget, we tend not to have elaborate staging; however, our staff is inventive—includes choreographer and composer. Write innovative theater that explores topics of concern/interest to young people, that takes risks. We concentrate more on ensemble than individual roles, too. We do *not* want to see fairy tales or trite rehashings of things children have seen/heard since the age of two. See theater as education, rather than 'children being cute.' "
Tips: "It is important for young people and their families to explore and confront issues relevant to growing up in the 90s. Theater is a marvelous teaching tool that can educate while it entertains."

NEW PLAYS INCORPORATED, Dept. WM, P.O. Box 5074, Charlottesville VA 22905-5074. (804)979-2777. Publisher: Patricia Whitton. Estab. 1964. Publishes an average of 4 plays/year. Publishes for producers of plays for young audiences and teachers in college courses on child drama. Query with synopsis. Reports in 2 months. Agent for amateur and semi-professional productions, exclusive agency for script sales. Pays 50% royalty on productions; 10% on script sales. Free catalog.
Needs: Plays for young audiences with something innovative in form and content. Length: usually 45-90 minutes. "Should be suitable for performance by adults for young audiences." No skits, assembly programs, improvisations or unproduced scripts.

NEW PLAYWRIGHTS' PROGRAM, The University of Alabama, P.O. Box 870239, Tuscaloosa AL 35487-0239. (205)348-9032. Fax: (205)348-9048. E-mail: pcastagn@roso.as.ua.edu. Director/Dramaturg: Dr. Paul C. Castagno. Endowed by Gallaway Fund, estab. 1982. Produces at least 1 new play/year. Mainstage and second stage, University Theatre, The University of Alabama. Submit synopsis or complete ms. Playwrights may submit potential workshop ideas for consideration. Reports in 3-6 months. Accepts scripts in various forms: new dramaturgy to traditional. Recent MFA playwriting graduates (within 1 year) may be given consideration for ACTF productions. Send SASE. Stipends competitive with or exceed most contests.

‡NEW STAGE THEATRE, 1100 Carlisle, Jackson MS 39202. (601)948-0143. Artistic Director: Steven David Martin. Estab. 1965. Produces 9 plays/year. "Professional productions, 8 mainstage, 1 in our 'second space.' We play to an audience comprised of Jackson, the state of Mississippi and the Southeast." Query with synopsis. Reports in 6 weeks. Exclusive premiere contract upon acceptance of play for mainstage production. Pays royalty of 5-8% or $25-60/performance.
Needs: Southern themes, contemporary issues, small casts (5-8), and single set plays are desirable.
Tips: Does not want historical dramas, one-acts, one person plays, melodramas. "My biggest complaint about modern plays is that most seem to really be screenplays, with short scenes, and a multitude of settings. We seem to be getting away from the theater's strength. I'm looking for plays that illuminate the human condition. Strong character relationships, surprise in the unfolding of the story and strong character development."

THE NEW THEATRE GUILD, 321 S. Van Ness Ave., Los Angeles CA 90020-4612. Artistic Director: George Hale. Estab. 1987. Produces 2-3 plays/year. USA (Los Angeles/New York) and Western Europe. Query with synopsis; submit complete script or agented submissions. Reports in 2 months. Negotiable.
Needs: Full length plays—comedies and dramas. No musicals. Accepts one-act plays.

NEW TUNERS THEATRE, 1225 W. Belmont Ave., Chicago IL 60657. (312)929-7287. Artistic Director Projects:Allan Chambers. Produces 1-3 new musicals/year. 66% developed in our New Tuners workshop. "Some scripts produced are unagented submissions. Plays performed in a small off-Loop theater seating 148 for a general theater audience, urban/suburban mix. Submit synopsis, cover letter and cassette selections of the score, if available. Reports in 3 months. Next step is script and score (reports in 6 months). "Submit first, we'll negotiate later." Pays 6-10% of gross. "Authors are given a stipend to cover a residency of at least two weeks."

Needs: "We're interested in all forms of musical theater including more innovative styles. Our production capabilities are limited by the lack of space, but we're very creative and authors should submit anyway. The smaller the cast, the better. We are especially interested in scripts using a younger (35 and under) ensemble of actors. We mostly look for authors who are interested in developing their script through workshops, rehearsals and production. No casts over 12. No one-man shows."

Tips: "We would like to see the musical theater articulating something about the world around us, rather than merely diverting an audience's attention from that world."

‡NEW YORK THEATRE WORKSHOP, 79 E. Fourth St., New York NY 10003. (212)302-7737. Fax: (212)391-9875. Artistic Director: James C. Nicola. Literary Manager: Gerard Manning. Estab. 1979. Produces 3-4 full productions; approximately 50 readings/year. Plays are performed off-Broadway, Equity LOA contract theater. Audience is New York theater-going audience and theater professionals. Query with synopsis and 10 page sample scene. Reports in 5 months. Option to produce commercially; percentage of box office gross from commercial and percentage of author's net subsidiary rights within specified time limit from our original production. Pays fee because of limited run, with additional royalty payments; for extensions; $1,500-2,000 fee range.

Needs: Full-length plays, one acts, translations/adaptations, music theater pieces; proposals for performance projects. Large issues, socially relevant issues, innovative form and language, minority issues. Plays utilizing more than 8 actors usually require outside funding.

Tips: No overtly commercial, traditional, Broadway-type musicals.

NINE O'CLOCK PLAYERS, 1367 N. St. Andrews Place, Los Angeles CA 90028. (213)469-1973. Estab. 1928. Contact: Artistic Director. Produces 2 plays/year. "Plays produced at Assistance League Playhouse by resident amateur and semi-professional company. All plays are musical adaptations of classical children's literature. Plays must be appropriate for children ages 4-12." Query with synopsis. Reports in 1 month. Pays negotiable royalty or per performance.

Needs: "Plays must have at least 9-15 characters and be 75 minutes long. Productions are done on a proscenium stage in classical theater style. All plays must have humor, music and good moral values. No audience participation improvisational plays."

‡THE NORTH CAROLINA BLACK REPERTORY COMPANY, Dept. WM, P.O. Box 95, Winston-Salem NC 27102. (919)723-2266. Fax: (919)723-2223. Artistic Director: Larry Leon Hamlin. Estab. 1979. Produces 4-6 plays/year. Plays produced primarily in North Carolina, New York City, the North and Southeast. Submit complete ms. Reports in 5 months. Obtains negotiable rights. Negotiable payment.

Needs: "Full-length plays and musicals: mostly African-American with special interest in historical or contemporary *statement* genre. A cast of 10 would be a comfortable limit; we discourage multiple sets."

Tips: "The best time to submit manuscripts is between September and February."

NORTHLIGHT THEATRE, 600 Davis St., Evanston IL 60201. (708)869-7732. Artistic Director: Russell Vandenbroucke. Estab. 1975. Produces 5 plays/year. "We are a professional, Equity theater, LORT D. We have a subscription base of 5,000, and have a significant number of single ticket buyers." Query with synopsis. Reports in 3 months. Buys production rights plus royalty on future mountings. Pays royalty and fee to playwright that is a guarantee against royalties.

Needs: "Full-length plays, translations, adaptations, musicals. Interested in plays of 'ideas,' plays that are passionate and/or hilarious, stylistic exploration and complexity. Generally looking for cast size of eight or less, but there are always exceptions made for the right play."

Tips: "Please, do not try to do what television and film do better! Also, no domestic realism."

ODYSSEY THEATRE ENSEMBLE, 2055 S. Sepulveda Blvd., Los Angeles CA 90025. (310)477-2055. Fax: (310)444-0455. Literary Manager: Jan Lewis. Estab. 1965. Produces 9 plays/year. Plays performed in a 3-theater facility. "All three theaters are Equity 99-seat theater plan. We have a subscription audience of 4,000 for a nine-play main season, and they are offered a discount on our rentals and co-productions. Remaining seats are sold to the general public." Query with résumé, synopsis, cast breakdown and 8-10 pages of sample dialogue and cassette if a musical. Scripts must be securely bound. Reports in 1 month on queries; 6 months on scripts. Buys negotiable rights. Pays 5-7% royalty. Does *not* return scripts without SASE.

Needs: "Full-length plays only with either an innovative form and/or provocative subject matter. We desire highly theatrical pieces that explore possibilities of the live theater experience. We are seeking full-length musicals and some plays with smaller casts (2-4). We are not reading one-act plays or light situation comedies. We are seeking Hispanic material for our resident Hispanic unit as well as plays from all cultures and ethnicities."

OLD GLOBE THEATRE, P.O. Box 2171, San Diego CA 92112-2171. (619)231-1941. Literary Manager: Raúl Moncada. Produces 12 plays/year. "We are a LORT B+ institution with three theaters: 581-seat mainstage, 225-seat arena, 621-seat outdoor. Our plays are produced for a single-ticket and subscription audience of 250,000 patrons from a large cross-section of southern California, including visitors from through-

out the US." Submit complete script through agent only. One-page synopsis if not represented. Reports in 3-10 months. Buys negotiable rights. Royalty varies.
Needs: "We are looking for plays of strong literary and theatrical merit, works that display an accomplished sense of craft, and pieces that present a detailed cultural vision. Submissions must be full-length plays."

‡**OLDCASTLE THEATRE COMPANY**, Box 1555, Bennington VT 05201-1555. (802)447-0564. Artistic Director: Eric Peterson. Produces 7 plays/year. Plays are performed in the new Bennington Center for the Arts, by a professional Equity theater company (in a April-October season) for general audiences, including residents of a three-state area and tourists during the vacation season. Submit complete ms. Reports in 6 months. Pays by negotiation with the playwright. A not-for-profit theater company.
Needs: Produces classics, musicals, comedy, drama, most frequently American works. Usual performance time is 2 hours. "With a small stage, we limit to small cast."

‡**OMAHA THEATER COMPANY FOR YOUNG PEOPLE**, (formerly Emmy Gifford Children's Theater), 3504 Center St., Omaha NE 68105. (402)345-4849. Artistic Director: James Larson. Produces 6 plays/year. "Our target audience is children, preschool-high school and their parents." Query with synopsis and SASE. Reports in 9 months. Royalty negotiable.
Needs: "Plays must be geared to children and parents (PG rating). Titles recognized by the general public have a stronger chance of being produced." Cast limit: 25 (8-10 adults). No adult scripts.
Tips: "Unproduced plays may be accepted only after a letter of inquiry (familiar titles only!)."

EUGENE O'NEILL THEATER CENTER'S NATIONAL PLAYWRIGHTS CONFERENCE and NEW DRAMA FOR MEDIA PROJECT, 234 W. 44th St., Suite 901, New York NY 10036-3909. (212)382-2790. Fax: (212)921-5538. Artistic Director: Lloyd Richards. Estab. 1965. Develops staged readings of 9-12 stage plays, 2-3 screenplays or teleplays/year. "We accept unsolicited scripts with no prejudice toward either represented or unrepresented writers. Our theater is located in Waterford, Connecticut, and we operate under an Equity LORT contract. We have three theaters: Barn—250 seats, Amphitheater—300 seats, Instant Theater—150 seats. Submission guidelines for #10 SASE in the fall. Complete bound, unproduced, original plays are eligible (no adaptations). Decision by late April. Pays stipend plus room, board and transportation. We accept script submissions September 15-December 1 of each year. Conference takes place during July each summer."
• Scripts are selected on the basis of talent, not commercial potential.
Needs: "We use modular sets for all plays, minimal lighting, minimal props and no costumes. We do script-in-hand readings with professional actors and directors. Our focus is on new play/playwright development."

THE OPEN EYE THEATER, P.O. Box 204, Denver NY 12421. Phone/fax: (607)326-4986. Producing Artistic Director: Amie Brockway. The Open Eye is a not-for-profit professional theater company working in New York City since 1972, in the rural villages of Delaware County, NY since 1991, and on tour. The theater specializes in the development of new plays for multi-generational audiences (children ages 8 and up, and adults of all ages). Ensemble plays with music and dance, culturally diverse and historical material, myth, folklore, and stories with universal themes are of interest. Program includes readings, developmental workshops, and fully staged productions.
• The Open Eye Theater is not accepting unsolicited scripts.
Tips: Send one-page letter with one paragraph plot synopsis, cast breakdown and setting, résumé and SAE. "We will provide the stamp and contact you *if we want to see the script*."

OREGON SHAKESPEARE FESTIVAL ASSOCIATION, P.O. Box 158, Ashland OR 97520. (503)482-2111. Fax: (503)482-0446. Associate Director/Play Development: Cynthia White. Estab. 1935. Produces 11 plays/year. The Angus Bowmer Theater has a thrust stage and seats 600. The Black Swan is an experimental space and seats 150. The Elizabethan Outdoor Theatre seats 1,200 (stages almost exclusively Shakespearean productions there, mid-June-September). Query with synopsis, résumé and 10 pages of dialogue from unsolicited sources. Complete scripts from agents only. Reports in 6-18 months. Negotiates individually for rights with the playwright's agent. "Most plays run within our ten-month season for 6-10 months, so royalties are paid accordingly."
Needs: "A broad range of classic and contemporary scripts. One or two fairly new scripts/season. Also a play readings series which focuses on new work. Plays must fit into our ten-month rotating repertory season. Black Swan shows usually limited to ten actors." No one acts or musicals. Submissions from women and minority writers are strongly encouraged.
Tips: "Send your work through an agent if possible. Send the best examples of your work rather than all of it. Don't become impatient or discouraged if it takes six months or more for a response. Don't expect detailed critiques with rejections. I want to see plays with heart and soul, intelligence, humor and wit. We're seeking plays with characters that *live*—that exist as living beings, not simply mouthpieces for particular positions. Try to avoid TV writing (i.e., cliché situations, dialogue, characters), unless it's specifically for broad comic purposes. I also think theater is a place for the *word*. So, the word first, then spectacle and high-tech effects."

ORGANIC THEATER COMPANY, 3319 N. Clark, Chicago IL 60657. (312)327-2427. Artistic Director: Paul Frellick. Estab. 1969. AEA, CAT and non-equity productions and workshops. Query with synopsis and 10 page sample. Reports in 1 month on queries. Negotiable royalty. Send inquiries to Literary Manager.
Needs: "We are seeking full-length or long one-acts—challenging plays that fully explore the theatrical medium; strong visual and physical potential (unproduced works only)."

‡THE PASSAGE THEATRE COMPANY, P.O. Box 967, Trenton NJ 08605-0967. Artistic Director: Stephen Stout. Estab. 1985. Produces 3 plays/year. "Passage is a professional theater celebrating the new American play." Please submit synopsis and ten page sample only. Reports in 3 months. Pays royalty.
Needs: "We consider 1-3-act plays dealing with social, cultural and artistic issues. We also do workshops and readings of plays. We work actively with the writers in developing their work. Passage Theatre has a strong propensity towards plays with multi-ethnic themes and utilizing inter-racial casting."

‡PENNSYLVANIA STAGE COMPANY, Dept. WM, 837 Linden St., Allentown PA 18101. (215)437-6110. Artistic Director: Charles Richter. Estab. 1980. Produces 5 plays and musicals/year. "We are a LORT D theater and our season runs from October through June. The large majority of our audience comes from the Lehigh Valley. Our audience consists largely of adults. We also offer special student and senior citizen matinees." Query with synopsis, cast list, 10 pages of dialogue and SASE. Reports in 3 months for scripts; 1 month for synopsis.
Needs: "The PSC produces full-length plays and musicals that are innovative and imaginative and that broaden our understanding of ourselves and society. Looking for wide range of styles and topics." Prefers 8 characters or fewer for plays and musicals.
Tips: "Works presented at the Stage Company have a passion for being presented now, should be entertaining and meaningful to our local community, and perpetuate our theatrical and literary heritage. We do not want to limit our options in achieving this artistic mission. Special programs: We have a staged reading program (New Evolving Works) where a director, actors and the playwright work together during an intensive 3-day rehearsal period. A discussion with the audience follows the staged reading."

PEOPLE'S LIGHT & THEATRE COMPANY, 39 Conestoga Rd., Malvern PA 19355. (610)647-1900. Co-Artistic Directors: Abigail Adams, Stephen Novelli. Estab. 1974. Produces 5-6 plays/year. LORT theater, general audience. Query with synopsis with 10 page dialogue sample. Reports in 6 months. Pays negotiable royalty.
Needs: Full length, sometime one acts, no musicals. Cast of 8-10 maximum. Prefers single set.

PIER ONE THEATRE, P.O. Box 894, Homer AK 99603. (907)235-7333. Artistic Director: Lance Petersen. Estab. 1973. Produces 5-8 plays/year. "Plays to various audiences for various plays—e.g. children's, senior citizens, adult, family, etc. Plays are produced on Kemai Peninsula." Submit complete script. Reports in 3 months. Pays $25-125/performance.
Needs: "No restrictions—willing to read *all* genres. However, for the near future, we are going to present work by Alaskan playwrights, and work of specific Alaskan interest."
Tips: "We prefer to have the whole script to evaluate."

‡PILLSBURY HOUSE THEATRE, 3501 Chicago Ave. S., Minneapolis MN 55405. (612)824-0708. Artistic Director: Ralph Remington. Estab. 1980. Produces 4 plays/year. Multicultural audience. Accepts unsolicited submissions. Reports in 3 months. Rights are negotiable. Pays royalty or makes outright purchase from $400-1,000.
Needs: "Only works that speak to issues of socio-political change; works that address marginalized groups, eg. people of color, women, lesbians/gays, the disabled and the economically disenfranchised. 120 seat intimate theater. No fly space. Proscenium/black box."
Tips: Does not want fluffy musicals and comedies.

PIONEER DRAMA SERVICE, INC., P.O. Box 4267, Englewood CO 80155-4267. (303)779-4035. Fax: (303)779-4315. Publisher: Steven Fendrich. Estab. 1963. 10% freelance written. Plays are performed by high school, junior high and adult groups, colleges, churches and recreation programs for audiences of all ages. "We are one of the largest full-service play publishers in the country in that we handle straight plays, musicals, children's theater and melodrama." Publishes 15 plays/year; 20% musicals and 80% straight plays. Query preferred; unsolicited scripts accepted. Retains all rights. Reports in 2 months. Pays on royalty basis with some outright purchase. All submissions automatically entered in Shubert Fendrich Memorial Playwriting Contest. Contest guidelines for SASE.
Needs: "We use the standard two-act format: two-act musicals, comedies, mysteries, drama, melodrama and plays for children's theater (plays to be done by adult actors for children). We are looking for more plays dealing with the problems of teens." Length: two-act musicals and comedies, up to 90 minutes; children's theater, 1 hour. Prefer many female roles, 1 simple set. Currently overstocked on one-act plays.

□PLAYERS PRESS, INC., P.O. Box 1132, Studio City CA 91614-0132. Senior Editor: Robert W. Gordon. "We deal in all entertainment areas and handle publishable works for film and television as well as theater.

Performing arts books, plays and musicals. All plays must be in stage format for publication." Also produces scripts for video and material for cable television. 80% freelance written. 20-30 scripts/year unagented submissions; 5-15 books also unagented. Works with 1-10 unpublished/unproduced writers annually. Query. "Include #10 SASE, reviews and proof of production. All play submissions must have been produced and should include a flier and/or program with dates of performance." Reports in 1 month on queries; 1 year on mss. Buys negotiable rights. "We prefer all area rights." Pays variable royalty according to area; approximately 10-75% of gross receipts. Also makes outright purchase of $100-25,000 or $5-5,000/performance.

Needs: "We prefer comedies, musicals and children's theater, but are open to all genres. We will rework the script after acceptance. We are interested in the quality, not the format. Performing Arts Books that deal with theater how-to are of strong interest."

Tips: "Send only material requested. Do not telephone."

PLAYS, The Drama Magazine for Young People, 120 Boylston St., Boston MA 02116-4615. Editor: Sylvia K. Burack. Estab. 1941. Publishes approximately 75 one-act plays and dramatic program material each school year to be performed by junior and senior high, middle grades, lower grades. "Scripts should follow the general style of *Plays*. Stage directions should not be typed in capital letters or underlined. No incorrect grammar or dialect." Desired lengths are: junior and senior high—15-20 double-spaced pages (20-30 minutes playing time); middle grades—10-15 pages (15-20 minutes playing time); lower grades—6-10 pages (8-15 minutes playing time). Pays "good rates on acceptance." Query first for adaptations. Reports in 2-3 weeks. Sample copy $3.50. Send SASE for specification sheet.

Needs: "Can use comedies, farces, melodramas, skits, mysteries and dramas, plays for holidays and other special occasions, such as Book Week; adaptations of classic stories and fables; historical plays; plays about black history and heroes; puppet plays; folk and fairy tales; creative dramatics; and plays for conservation, ecology or human rights programs."

‡PLAYWRIGHTS HORIZONS, 416 W. 42nd St., New York NY 10036. (212)564-1235. Artistic Director: Don Scardino. Estab. 1971. Produces 7 plays/year. Plays performed off-Broadway. Send complete ms with résumé. Send plays to Tim Sannford, Literary Director; musicals to Dana Williams, Musical Theatre Program Director. Reports in 5 months. Negotiates for future rights. Pays outright sum, and then percentage after a certain run.

Needs: "We are looking for recent, full-length plays, and musicals by American authors. There is limited stage space."

Tips: "No adaptations, children's theater, biographical or historical plays, psychological family dramas or relationship sit-coms. We look for plays with a strong sense of language and a clear dramatic action that truly use the resources of the theater. Minority authors are encouraged."

‡PLAYWRIGHTS THEATRE OF NEW JERSEY, 33 Green Village Rd., Madison NJ 07940. (201)514-1787. Artistic Director: John Pietrowski. Associate Artistic Director: Joseph Megel. Literary Associate: Kate Mc-Ateer. Estab. 1986. Produces 1-3 productions, 5 staged readings and sit-down readings/year. "We operate under a letter of agreement (LOA with LORT Rules) with Actors' Equity Association for all productions. Readings are held under a staged reading code." Submit complete ms. Short bio and production history required. Reports in 3 months. "For productions we ask the playwright to sign an agreement that gives us exclusive rights to the play for the production period and for 30 days following. After the 30 days we give the rights back with no strings attached, except for commercial productions. We ask that our developmental work be acknowledged in any other professional productions." Pays $250 for productions, $150 for staged readings. Scripts accepted September 1-April 30 only.

Needs: Any style or length; full length, one acts, musicals.

Tips: "We are looking for plays in the early stages of development—plays that take on important personal and social issues in a theatrical manner."

POPE THEATRE COMPANY, 262 S. Ocean Blvd., Manalapan FL 33462. (407)585-3404. Producing Artistic Director: Louis Tyrrell. Estab. 1987. Produces 7 plays/year (5 during the regular season, 2 in the summer). "We are a fully professional (LOA) theater. We attract an audience comprised of both local residents and seasonal visitors. Many, but by no means all, of our subscribers are retirees." Agented submissions only. Reports in 6 months. Buys production rights only. Pays 6-10% royalty. "A SASE is required if a playwright wants a script returned."

Needs: "We produce new American plays. We prefer to do Florida premieres of thought-provoking, socially-conscious, challenging plays. Our stage is relatively small, which prevents us from producing works with a large cast."

PORTLAND REPERTORY THEATER, 815 NW 12th, Portland OR 97209. (503)224-2403. Fax: (503)224-0710. Producing Artistic Director: Geoffrey Sherman. Literary Manager: Kit Koenig. Estab. 1980. Produces 6-9 plays/year. "Small, professional, not-for-profit, regional theater. Two stages: Mainstage—230 seat, proscenium with long-time subscriber base (age 30-70s); Stage II—160 seat thrust, new, for new plays/experimental works and a staged reading series." Query with synopsis, first 10-15 pages, character breakdown, set

description and SASE. Agented submissions. Reports in 2-6 months. Pays percentage of gross.
Needs: Comedies, thriller, drama, small musicals; with smaller casts, no more than 2 sets to run approximately 2 hours. Cast not to exceed 8; no more than 2 sets.
Tips: "No puppet shows, mime, melodrama or children's shows."

PRIMARY STAGES COMPANY, INC., 584 Ninth Ave., New York NY 10036. (212)333-7471. Contact: Andrew Leynse, literary manager. Artistic Director: Casey Childs. Estab. 1983. Produces 4 plays, 6 workshops/year. All plays are produced professionally off-Broadway at Primary Stages Theatre, 354 W. 45th St. Query with synopsis. Reports in 3 months. "If Primary Stages produces the play, we ask for the right to move it for up to six months after the closing performance." Writers paid $1,155 for production.
Needs: We are looking for highly theatrical works that were written exclusively with the stage in mind. We do not want TV scripts or strictly realistic plays."
Tips: No "living room plays, disease-of-the-week plays, back-porch plays, father/son work-it-all-out-plays, etc."

‡THE PURPLE ROSE THEATRE CO., P.O. Box 220, Chelsea MI 48118. (313)475-5817. Artistic Director: T. Newell Kring. Estab. 1990. Produces 4 plays/year. Plays produced at P.R.T.C. (a regional theater with S.P.T. Equity contract), are intended for Midwest/Middle America audiences. Query with synopsis. Reports in 1-2 months. Pays 5-6% royalty.
Needs: Modern, topical 2 acts, 90-120 minutes. Prefer scripts that use comedy to deal with serious subjects. Prefer continuous action (no blackouts). 8-10 cast maximum. No fly space; unit set preferable but not required. Small 119 seat ¾ thrust house.
Tips: No period pieces, lavish musicals, related one-acts, large casts, children's plays. Submit script queries and synopses to Literary Coordinator.

THE QUARTZ THEATRE, 392 Taylor, Ashland OR 97520-3058. (503)482-8119. Artistic Director: Dr. Robert Spira. Estab. 1973. Produces several video films/year. Send 3 pages of dialogue and personal bio. Reports in 2 weeks. Pays 5% royalty after expenses.
Needs: "Any length, any subject, with or without music. We seek playwrights with a flair for language and theatrical imagination."
Tips: "We look at anything. We do not do second productions unless substantial rewriting is involved. Our theater is a stepping stone to further production. Our playwrights are usually well-read in comparative religion, philosophy, psychology, and have a comprehensive grasp of human problems. We seek the 'self-indulgent' playwright who pleases him/herself first of all."

THE ROAD COMPANY, P.O. Box 5278 EKS, Johnson City TN 37603-5278. (615)926-7726. E-mail: road co@aol.com. Literary Manager: Christine Murdock. Estab. 1975. Produces 3 plays/year. "Our professional productions are intended for a general adult audience." Query with synopsis. Reports in 4 months. Pays royalty. "When we do new plays we generally try to have the playwright in residence during rehearsal for 3-4 weeks for about $1,000 plus room and board."
Needs: "We like plays that experiment with form, that challenge, inform and entertain. We are a small ensemble based company. We look for smaller cast shows of 4-6."
Tips: "We are always looking for 2-character (male/female) plays. We are interested in plays set in the South. We are most interested in new work that deals with new forms. We write our own plays using improvisational techniques which we then tour throughout the Southeast. When funding permits, we include one of our own new plays in our home season."

RUBBERTREE PRODUCTIONS, 11301 W. Olympic Blvd., #511, Los Angeles CA 90064. (213)939-6747. Estab. 1992. Produces 1 play/year. Equity-waiver/Los Angeles smaller (99 seat) theaters—audience: twenty something crowd. Query letter only—no phone calls. Reports in 2 weeks. Pay varies according to arrangement with writers.
Needs: Full length only—prefer plays targeted to "Generation X" audience.

‡SAN JOSÉ REPERTORY THEATRE, P.O. Box 2399, San Jose CA 95109. (408)291-2266. Artistic Director: Ms. Timothy Near. Estab. 1980. Produces 6 plays/year. Professional Lort C theater. Query with synopsis. Reports in 6 months. Pays royalty.
Needs: Small cast musicals (no more than 8 including musicians) multicultural plays.

‡SEATTLE CHILDREN'S THEATRE, P.O. Box 9640, Seattle WA 98109. (206)443-0807. Artistic Director: Linda Hartzell. Queries to: Deborah L. Frockt, literary manager/dramaturg. Produces 6 plays/year. Professional (adult actors) performing for young audiences, families and school groups. Resident company—not touring. Query with synopsis, 10 pages of sample dialogue, résumé or bio. Reports on query in 3-6 months; mss in 6-12 months. Pay varies.
Needs: Challenging, imaginative, sophisticated full-length work for young audiences—both adapted and original material. We produce one musical/year. No turntable, no traps.

Tips: "We welcome queries by all populations and encourage queries by women and minorities. We prefer sophisticated material (we have many adults in our audience). All shows produced by SCT are multiracially cast."

‡**SEATTLE REPERTORY THEATRE**, 155 Mercer St., Seattle WA 98109. (206)443-2210. Artistic Director: Dan Sullivan. Estab. 1963. Produces 9 plays/year: 6 mainstage, 3 second stage. Plays performed in Seattle, with occasional transfers elsewhere. Agented submissions only. Reports in 2-3 months. Buys percentage of future royalties. Pays royalty.
Needs: "The Seattle Repertory Theatre produces eclectic programming. We rarely produce plays with more than 15 people in the cast! We welcome a wide variety of writing."

‡**SHAW FESTIVAL THEATRE**, P.O. Box 774, Niagara-on-the-Lake, Ontario L0S 1J0 Canada. Fax: (905)468-5438. Artistic Director: Christopher Newton. Estab. 1962. Produces 10 plays/year. "Professional summer festival operating three theaters (Festival: 861 seats; Court House: 349 seats; and Royal George: 328 seats). We also host some music and some winter rentals. Mandate is based on the works of G.B. Shaw and his contemporaries. We prefer to hold rights for Canada and northeastern US, also potential to tour." Pays 5-6% royalty. Submit with SASE or SAE and IRCs, depending on country of origin.
Needs: "We operate an acting ensemble of up to 75 actors; this includes 14 actor/singers and we have sophisticated production facilities. During the summer season (April-October) the Academy of the Shaw Festival organizes several workshops of new Canadian plays."

SHENANDOAH INTERNATIONAL PLAYWRIGHTS RETREAT, Rt. 5, Box 167F, Staunton VA 24401. (703)248-1868. Program Director: Robert Graham Small. Estab. 1976. Produces in workshop 11 plays/year. Submit complete script. Obtains no rights. Writers are provided fellowships, room and board to Shenandoah.
Tips: "We are looking for *good* material, not derivative; from writers who enjoy exploration with dedicated theater professionals. Live theater *must* be theatrical! Consider global issues. Look beyond and explore connections that will lift characters/conflicts to a universal plane."

SILVERHAWK L.L.C., P.O. Box 1640, Escondido CA 92033. Publishes 25-30 plays/year. Professional, community and college theaters. Submit complete script that can be written on. Reports in 3 months. Buys all rights. Pays 50% production royalty and 10% of script sales.
Needs: "We will look at all plays, but would particularly like to see one-act plays of literary and artistic merit that are suitable for one-act competitions. Also we'd like groups of three one acts that can use the same stage set, and groups of one acts with a common theme, including seasonal. We have a youth and children's editor looking for children's plays of real merit. We will also consider unusual works and literary works that some publishers would consider to be not sufficiently commercial."
Tips: "Please don't send us children's plays that assume children are real morons. The same for amateur plays. Please be sure your story line is original. Mark children's plays Attn: Mary Jo Leap."

AUDREY SKIRBALL-KENIS THEATRE, 9478 W. Olympic Blvd., Suite 304, Beverly Hills CA 90212. (310)284-8965. Fax: (310)203-8067. E-mail: mead.hunter@cabin.com. Director of Literary Programs:Mead Hunter. Estab. 1989. Produces 18-22 stage readings and 3-4 workshop productions/year. "We utilize three theater facilities in the Los Angeles area with professional directors and casts. Our rehearsed readings and workshop productions are offered year-round. Our audience is the general public *and* theater professionals." Query with synopsis and sample pages. Reports in 3-4 months. Obtains no rights. Pays $150 for staged readings; $500 for workshop productions. Workshops are selected from plays previously presented in the reading series.
●	ASK now publishes a biannual magazine, *Parabasis*, which focuses on news and issues surrounding the art, business and craft of contemporary playwriting. Playwrights are asked to query about proposed articles.
Needs: "We need full-length original plays that have not yet had full productions, and which would benefit from a rehearsed reading as a means of further developing the play."
Tips: "We are a nonprofit organization dedicated to new plays and playwrights. We do not produce plays for commercial runs, nor do we request any future commitment from the playwright should their play find a production through our reading or workshop programs."

SOUTH COAST REPERTORY, P.O. Box 2197, Costa Mesa CA 92628-1197. (714)957-2602. Fax: (714)545-0391. Dramaturg: Jerry Patch. Literary Manager: John Glore. Estab. 1964. Produces 6 plays/year on mainstage, 5 on second stage. Professional nonprofit theater; a member of LORT and TCG. "We operate in our own facility which houses a 507-seat mainstage theater and a 161-seat second stage theater. We have a combined subscription audience of 21,000." Query with synopsis; scripts considered if submitted by agent. Reports in 4 months. Acquires negotiable rights. Pays negotiable royalty.
Needs: "We produce full lengths. We prefer well-written plays that address contemporary concerns and are dramaturgically innovative. A play whose cast is larger than 15-20 will need to be extremely compelling and its cast size must be justifiable."

Tips: "We don't look for a writer to write for us—he or she should write for him or herself. We look for honesty and a fresh voice. We're not likely to be interested in writers who are mindful of *any* trends. Originality and craftsmanship are the most important qualities we look for."

SOUTHERN APPALACHIAN REPERTORY THEATRE (SART), Mars Hill College, P.O. Box 620, Mars Hill NC 28754-0620. (704)689-1384. Artistic Director: James W. Thomas. Asst. Managing Director: Gaynelle Caldwell. Estab. 1975. Produces 6 plays/year. "Since 1975 the Southern Appalachian Repertory Theatre has produced 951 performances of 103 plays and played to over 131,000 patrons in the 152-seat Owen Theatre on the Mars Hill College campus. The theater's goals are quality, adventurous programming and integrity, both in artistic form and in the treatment of various aspects of the human condition. SART is a professional summer theater company whose audiences range from students to senior citizens." Reports in 6-12 months. Also conducts an annual Southern Appalachian Playwrights' Conference in which 5 playwrights are invited for informal readings of their new scripts. Deadline for submission is October 1 and conference is held the last weekend in January. If script is selected for production during the summer season, an honorarium is paid to the playwright in the amount of $500. Enclose SASE for return of script.
Needs: Since 1975, one of SART's goals has been to produce at least one original play each summer season. To date, 34 original scripts have been produced. Plays by southern Appalachian playwrights or about southern Appalachia are preferred, but by no means exclusively. Complete new scripts welcomed.

STAGE ONE: The Louisville Children's Theatre, 425 W. Market St., Louisville KY 40202-3300. (502)589-5946. Fax: (502)589-5779. Producing Director: Moses Goldberg. Estab. 1946. Produces 6-7 plays/ year. 20% freelance written; 15-20% unagented submissions (excluding work of playwright-in-residence). Plays performed by an Equity company for young audiences ages 4-18; usually does different plays for different age groups within that range. Submit complete script. Reports in 4 months. Pays negotiable royalty or $25-75/performance.
Needs: "Good plays for young audiences of all types: adventure, fantasy, realism, serious problem plays about growing up or family entertainment. Cast: ideally, ten or less. Honest, visual potentiality, worthwhile story and characters are necessary. An awareness of children and their schooling is a plus. No campy material or anything condescending to children. No musicals unless they are fairly limited in orchestration."

STAGE WEST, P.O. Box 2587, Fort Worth TX 76113. (817)924-9454. Artistic Director: Jerry Russell. Estab. 1979. Produces 8 plays/year. "We stage professional productions at our own theater for a mixed general audience." Query with synopsis. Reports in 3-6 months. Rights are negotiable. Pays 7% royalty.
Needs: "We want full-length plays that are accessible to a mainstream audience but possess traits that are highly theatrical. Cast size of ten or less and single or unit set are desired."

CHARLES STILWILL, Managing Artistic Director, Community Playhouse, P.O. Box 433, Waterloo IA 50704-0433. (319)235-0367. Estab. 1917. Plays performed by Waterloo Community Playhouse with a volunteer cast. Produces 11 plays (6 adult, 5 children's); 1-2 musicals and 9-10 nonmusicals/year; 1-3 originals. 17% freelance written; most unagented submissions. Works with 1-3 unpublished/unproduced writers annually. "We are one of few community theaters with a commitment to new scripts. We do at least one and have done as many as four a year. We have 4,300 season members. Average attendance is 3,300. We do a wide variety of plays. Our public isn't going to accept nudity, too much sex, too much strong language. We don't have enough Black actors to do all-Black shows. Theater has done plays with as few as 2 characters, and as many as 98. On the main stage, we usually pay between $400 and $500. We also produce children's theater. Submit complete script. Please, no loose pages. Reports negatively within 1 year, but acceptance sometimes takes longer because we try to fit a wanted script into the balanced season. We sometimes hold a script longer than a year if we like it but cannot immediately find the right slot for it. Last year we did the world premiere of *The Ninth Step* which was written in 1989 and the year before we did the world premiere of *Grace Under Pressure*, written in 1984. We are currently doing the world premiere of *First Child*."
Needs: "For our Children's Theater and our Adult Biannual Holiday (Christmas) show, we are looking for good adaptations of name children's stories or very good shows that don't necessarily have a name. We produce children's theater with both adult and child actors."

‡SYRACUSE STAGE, 820 E. Genesee, Syracuse NY 13210. (315)443-4008. Artistic Director: Tazewell Thompson. Estab. 1974. Produces 7 plays/year. Professional LORT productions. Query with synopsis and an excerpt of 10 pages. Reports in weeks on queries. Rights defined in contracts.
Needs: Full-length plays—one-person shows. All styles of theater—clever, language oriented plays preferred.
Tips: No sitcom-like plays.

TACOMA ACTORS GUILD, 901 Broadway, 6th Floor, Tacoma WA 98402-4404. (206)272-3107. Fax: (206)272-3358. Artistic Director: Bruce K. Sevy. Estab. 1978. Produces 6-7 plays/year. Plays perfomed at Theatre On The Square. Audience consists of playgoers in the south Puget Sound region. Query with synopsis.

Reports in 2-4 months on queries; 1 year on scripts. Rights negotiable. Pays negotiable royalty or makes outright purchase of $500 minimum.
Needs: Full length. Single or simple set. Modest cast (2-7). Comedy, drama, musical. "Our budgets are modest."
Tips: "No extreme language, violence, nudity, sexual situations. We don't do a *lot* of new work so opportunities are limited."

TADA!, 120 W. 28th St., New York NY 10001. (212)627-1732. Fax: (212)243-6736. Artistic Director: Janine Nina Trevens. Estab. 1984. Produces 2-4 plays/year. "TADA! produces original musicals and plays performed by children at our 95-seat theater. Productions are for family audiences." Submit complete script and tape, if musical. Reports in 6 months. Pays 5% royalty or commission fee (varies).
- TADA! also sponsors a one-act play competition for their Spring Staged Reading Series. Works must be original, unproduced and unpublished one-acts. Plays may be geared toward teen audiences. Call for deadlines.
Needs: "Generally pieces run from 45-70 minutes. Must be enjoyed by children and adults and performed by a cast of children ages 6-17."
Tips: "No redone fairy tales or pieces where children are expected to play adults. Be careful not to condescend when writing for children's theater."

THE TEN-MINUTE MUSICALS PROJECT, P.O. Box 461194, West Hollywood CA 90046. (213)656-8751. Producer: Michael Koppy. Estab. 1987. Produces 1-10 plays/year. "Plays performed in Equity regional theaters in the US and Canada." Submit complete script, lead sheets and cassette. Deadline August 31; notification by December 15 annually. Buys performance rights. Pays $250 royalty advance upon selection, against equal share of performance royalties when produced. Submission guidelines for #10 SASE.
Needs: Looking for complete short stage musicals playing between 7-14 minutes. Limit cast to 10 (5 women, 5 men).

THEATER ARTISTS OF MARIN, P.O. Box 150473, San Rafael CA 94915. (415)454-2380. Artistic Director: Charles Brousse. Estab. 1980. Produces 3 plays/year. Professional showcase productions for a general adult audience. Submit complete script. Reports in 6 months. Assists in marketing to other theaters and offers script development assistance.
Needs: "All types of scripts: comedy, drama, farce. Prefers contemporary setting, with some relevance to current issues in American society. Will also consider 'small musicals,' reviews or plays with music." No children's shows, domestic sitcoms, one-man shows or commercial thrillers.

‡THEATER LUDICRUM, INC., 64 Charlesgate E., Suite 83, Boston MA 02215. (617)424-6831. President: George Bistransin. Estab. 1985. Produces 2-3 plays/year. Plays are performed in a small, non-equity theater in Boston. "Our audience includes minority groups (people of color, gays, women)." Submit complete ms. Reports in 6 months. Rights revert to author after production. Pays $15-30/performance.
Needs: "As a small theater with a small budget, we look for scripts with minimal sets, costumes, props and expense in general. We are interested in scripts that emphasize the word and acting."

THE THEATER OF NECESSITY, 11702 Webercrest, Houston TX 77048. (713)733-6042. Artistic Director: Philbert Plumb. Estab. 1981. Produces 4 plays/year. Plays are produced in a small professional theater. Submit complete script. Reports in 1 year. Buys performance rights. Pays standard royalties based on size of house for small productions or individual contracts for large productions (average $500/run). "We usually keep script on file unless we are certain we will never use it." Send SASE with script and #10 SASE for response.
Needs: "Any play in a recognizable genre must be superlative in form and intensity. Experimental plays are given an easier read. We move to larger venue if the play warrants the expense."

‡THEATER OF THE FIRST AMENDMENT, George Mason University, Fairfax VA 22030. (703)993-1122. Contact: Rick Davis. Estab. 1990. Produces 3 plays/year. Professional productions performed in an Equity LOA 150-seat theater. Query with synopsis. Reports in 3 months. Pays combination of percentage of box office gross against a guaranteed minimum royalty.

THEATRE & COMPANY, 20 Queen St. N., Kitchener, Ontario N2H 2G8 Canada. Artistic Director: Stuart Scadron-Wattles. Literary Manager: Wes Wikkerink. Estab. 1988. Produces 4 plays/year. Semi-professional productions for a general audience. Query with synopsis and SAE with IRCs. Reports in 3 months. Pays $50-100/performance.
Needs: "One act or full length; comedy or drama; musical or straight; written from or compatible with a biblical world view." No cast above 10; prefers unit staging. Looking for small cast (less than 5) ensemble comedies.
Tips: Looks for "non-religious writing from a biblical world view for an audience which loves the theater. Avoid current trends toward shorter scenes. Playwrights should be aware that they are writing for the stage— not television. We encourage audience interaction, using an acting ensemble trained in improvisation."

‡THEATRE AT LIME KILN, P.O. Box 663, Lexington VA 24450. (703)463-7088. Artistic Director: Barry Mines. Estab. 1983. Produces 7 plays/year. Professional outdoor summer theater. Audience is family oriented. Query with synopsis or submit complete ms. Reports in 4 months. Rights vary. Pay varies.
Needs: Full length, musical or straight. Material should reflect culture/issues/concerns of Appalachian region. Outdoor theater, limited sets. Cast of 9 or less preferred.
Tips: No urban angst. Smaller cast shows have a better chance of being produced.

‡THEATRE CALGARY, 220 Ninth Ave. SE, Calgary, Alberta T2G 5C4 Canada. (403)294-7440. Fax: (403)294-7493. Executive Producer: Brian Rintoul. Estab. 1970. Produces 6-8 plays/year. Professional productions. Reports in 3 months. Buys production rights usually, "but it can vary with specific contracts." Payments and commissions negotiated under individual contracts.
Needs: "Theatre Calgary is a major Canadian regional theater."
Tips: "Theatre Calgary still accepts unsolicited scripts, but does not have a significant script development program at the present time. We cannot guarantee a quick return time, and we will not return scripts without pre-paid envelopes. Please use IRCs"

THEATRE DE LA JEUNE LUNE, 105 N. First St., Minneapolis MN 55401-1411. (612)332-3968. Fax: (612)332-0048. Artistic Directors: Barbra Berlovitz Desbois, Vincent Garcieux, Robert Rosen, Dominique Serrand. Estab. 1979. Produces 2-3 plays/year. Professional nonprofit company producing September-May for general audience. Query with synopsis. Reports in 3 months. Pays royalty or per performance. No unsolicited scripts, please.
Needs: "All subject matter considered, although plays with universal themes are desired; plays that concern people of today. We are constantly looking for plays with large casts. Generally *not* interested in plays with 1-4 characters. No psychological drama or plays that are written alone in a room without the input of outside vitality and life."
Tips: "We are an acting company that takes plays and makes them ours; this could mean cutting a script or not heeding a writer's stage directions. We are committed to the performance in front of the audience as the goal of all the contributing factors; therefore, the actors' voice is extremely important."

THEATRE WEST, 3333 Cahuenga W., Los Angeles CA 90068-1365. Contact: Arden Lewis or Doug Haverty. Estab. 1962. Produces 6 plays or one acts/year. "99-seat waiver productions in our theater. Audiences are primarily young urban professionals." Submit script, résumé and letter requesting membership. Reports in 2 months. Requires 5% of writer's share of sale to another media. Pays royalty "based on gross box office—equal to all other participants."
Needs: Uses minimalistic scenery.
Tips: "TW is a dues-paying membership company. Only members can submit plays for production. So you must seek membership prior to action for a production."

THEATREWORKS/USA, 890 Broadway, New York NY 10003. (212)677-5959. Artistic Director: Jay Harnick. Literary Manager: Barbara Pasternack. Produces 3 new musicals/plays with music season. Produces professional musicals and plays that primarily tour (TYA contract) but also play at an off-Broadway theater for a young audience. Query with synopsis or sample show. Reports in 8 months. Buys all rights. Pays 6% royalty. Offers $1,500 advance against future royalties for new, commissioned plays.
Needs: Musicals and plays with music for children. Historical/biographical themes (ages 8-15), classic literature, fairy tales, and issue-oriented themes and material suitable for young people ages 5-12. Five person cast, minimal lighting. "We like well-crafted shows with good dramatic structure—a protagonist who wants something specific, an antagonist, a problem to be solved—character development, tension, climax, etc. No Saturday Afternoon Special-type shows, shows with nothing to say or 'kiddie' theater shows or fractured fairy tales. We do not address high school audiences."
Tips: "Writing for kids is just like writing for adults—only better (clearer, cleaner). Kids will not sit still for unnecessary exposition and overblown prose. Long monologues, soliloquies and 'I Am' songs and ballads should be avoided. Television, movies and video make the world of entertainment highly competitive. We've noticed lately how well popular children's titles, contemporary and in public domain, sell. We are very interested in acquiring adaptations of this type of material."

STEVE TYLER, 6915 Fountain Ave., Los Angeles CA 90028. Estab. 1991. Produces 2 plays/year. "Mostly 99 AEA seat plan theater—with hopes to move to a larger venue." Query with synopsis. Reports in months. Royalty varies.

For information on setting your freelance fees, see How Much Should I Charge?

Needs: Full-length plays that are topical, political or gay-themed political. Prefers smaller casts (less than 8) and plays that are written to be plays not movies.

UNICORN THEATRE, 3820 Main St., Kansas City MO 64111. (816)531-PLAY. Fax: (816)531-0421. Producing Artistic Director: Cynthia Levin. Produces 6-8 plays/year. "We are a professional Equity Theatre. Typically, we produce plays dealing with contemporary issues." Send full script. Reports in 2 months.
Needs: Prefers contemporary (post-1950) scripts. Does not accept musicals, one-acts, or historical plays. Query with script, brief synopsis, bio, character breakdown, SASE if script is to be returned, SASP for acknowledgement of receipt is desired. A royalty/prize of $1,000 will be awarded the playwright of any play selected through this process, The National Playwright Award. This script receives production as part of the Unicorn's regular season.

VIRGINIA STAGE COMPANY, P.O. Box 3770, Norfolk VA 23514-3770. (804)627-6988. Fax: (804)628-5958. Literary Manager: Jefferson H. Lindquist. Estab. 1979. VSC is a LORT C-1 theatre serving southeastern Virginia audiences. Performing spaces are mainstage (700-seat) theatre with proscenium stage and a 99-seat second stage. Produces 4-6 plays/year. Send letter, synopsis, SASE, and sample pages only. Submission time: January-April. Responds in 6 months. Scripts returned to author or agent only if postage is included.
Needs: Full-length plays, and musicals with tapes only.

WALNUT STREET THEATRE, 9th and Walnut Streets, Philadelphia PA 19107. (215)574-3550. Executive Director: Bernard Havard. Literary Manager: Beverly Elliott. Estab. 1809. Produces 5 mainstage and 5 studio plays/year. "Our plays are performed in our own space. WST has 3 theaters—a proscenium (mainstage), 1,052 seats; 2 studios, 79-99 seats. We have a subscription audience, second largest in the nation." Query with synopsis and 10 pages. Writer's must be members of the Dramatists' Guild. Reports in 5 months. Rights negotiated per project. Pays royalty (negotiated per project) or outright purchase.
Needs: "Full-length dramas and comedies, musicals, translations, adaptations and revues. The studio plays must have a cast or no more than four, simple sets."
Tips: "Bear in mind that on the mainstage we look for plays with mass appeal, Broadway-style. The studio spaces are our off-Broadway. No children's plays. Our mainstage audience goes for work that is entertaining and light. Our studio season is where we look for plays that have bite and are more provocative." Include SASE for return of materials.

WEST COAST ENSEMBLE, P.O. Box 38728, Los Angeles CA 90038. (213)871-8673. Artistic Director: Les Hanson. Estab. 1982. Produces 6 plays/year. Plays performed in 1 of 2 theaters in Hollywood. Submit complete script. Reports in 6-9 months. Obtains exclusive rights in southern California to present the play for the period specified. All ownership and rights remain with the playwright. Pays $25-45/performance. Writers guidelines for #10 SASE.
Needs: Prefers a cast of 6-12.
Tips: "Submit the script in acceptable dramatic script format."

THE WOMEN'S PROJECT AND PRODUCTIONS, 10 Columbus Circle, #2270, New York NY 10019. (212)765-1706. Artistic Director: Julia Miles. Estab. 1978. Produces 3 plays/year. Professional Off-Broadway productions. Query with synopsis and 10 sample pages of dialogue. Reports in 1 month on queries.
Needs: "We are looking for full-length plays, written by women."

WOOLLY MAMMOTH THEATRE COMPANY, 1401 Church St. NW, Washington DC 20005-1903. (202)393-3939. Artistic Director: Howard Shalwitz. Literary Manager: Jim Byrnes. Produces 5 plays/year. 50% freelance written. Produces professional productions for the general public in Washington, DC 2-3 scripts/year unagented submissions. Works with 1-2 unpublished/unproduced writers annually. Accepts unsolicited scripts. Reports in 3 months on scripts; very interesting scripts often take much longer. Buys first- and second- class production rights. Pays 5% royalty.
Needs: "We look only for plays that are highly unusual in some way. Also interested in multicultural projects. Apart from an innovative approach, there is no formula. One-acts are not used." Cast limit of 8.

‡WORCESTER FOOTHILLS THEATRE COMPANY, 074 Worcester Center, 110 Front St., Suite 137, Worcester MA 01608. (508)754-3314. Fax: (508)767-0676. Artistic Director: Marc P. Smith. Estab. 1974. Produces 7 plays/year. Full time professional theater, general audience. Query with synopsis. Reports in 3 weeks. Pays royalty.
Needs: "Produce plays for general audience. No gratuitous violence, sex or language. Prefer cast under 10 and single set. 30' proscenium with apron but no fly space."

Screenwriting

Practically everyone you meet in Los Angeles, from your airport cabbie on, is writing a script. It might be a feature film, movie of the week, TV series or documentary, but the sheer amount of competition can seem overwhelming. Some will never make a sale, while others make a decent living on sales and options without ever having any of their work produced. But there are those writers who make a living doing what they love and see their names roll by on the credits. How do they get there? How do *you* get there?

First, work on your writing. You'll improve with each script, so there is no way of getting around the need to write and write some more. It's a good idea to read as many scripts as you can get your hands on. Check your local bookstores and libraries. Script City (Suite 1500, 8033 Sunset Blvd., Hollywood CA 90046, (800)676-2522) carries thousands of movie and TV scripts, classics to current releases, as well as books, audio/video seminars and software in their $2 catalog. Book City (Dept. 101, 308 N. San Fernando Blvd., Burbank CA 91502, (800)4-CINEMA) has film and TV scripts in all genres and a large selection of movie books in their $2.50 catalog.

There are lots of books that will give you the "rules" of format and structure for writing for TV or film. Samuel French (7623 Sunset Blvd., Hollywood CA 90046 (213)876-0570) carries a number of how-to books and reference materials on these subjects. The correct format marks your script as a professional submission. Most successful scriptwriters will tell you to learn the correct structure, internalize those rules—and then throw them away and write intuitively.

Writing for TV

To break into TV you must have spec scripts—work written for free that serves as a calling card and gets you in the door. A spec script showcases your writing abilities and gets your name in front of influential people. Whether a network has invited you in to pitch some ideas, or a movie producer has contacted you to write a first draft for a feature film, the quality of writing in your spec script got their attention and that may get you the job.

It's a good idea to have several spec scripts, perhaps one each for three of the top five shows in the format you prefer to work in, whether it's sitcom (half-hour comedies), episodic (one hour series) or movie of the week (two hour dramatic movies). Perhaps you want to showcase the breadth of your writing ability; some writers have a portfolio of a few eight o'clock type shows (i.e., *Mad About You*, *Home Improvement*), a few nine-o'clock shows (i.e., *Friends*, *Ellen*, *Seinfeld*) and one or two episodics (i.e., *Homicide*, *Law and Order*, *NYPD Blue*). These are all "hot" shows for writers and can demonstrate your abilities to create believable dialogue for characters already familiar to your intended readers. For TV and cable movies you should have completed original scripts (not sequels to existing movies) and you might also have a few for episodic TV shows.

In choosing the shows you write spec scripts for you must remember one thing: don't write a script for a show you want to work on. If you want to write for *NYPD Blue*, for example, you'll send a *Law and Order* script and vice versa. It may seem contradictory, but it is standard practice. It reduces the chances of lawsuits, and writers and producers can feel very proprietary about their show and their stories. They may not be objective enough to fairly evaluate your writing. In submitting another similar type of show you'll avoid those problems while demonstrating comparable skills.

In writing your TV script you must get *inside* the show and understand the characters' internal motivations. You must immerse yourself in how the characters speak, think and interact. Don't introduce new characters in a spec script for an existing show—write believable dialogue for the characters as they are portrayed. Be sure to choose a show that you like—you'll be better able to demonstrate your writing ability through characters you respond to.

You must also understand the external factors. How the show is filmed bears on how you write. Most sitcoms are shot on videotape with three cameras, on a sound stage with a studio audience. Episodics are often shot on film with one camera and include on-location shots. *Mad About You* has a flat, evenly-lit look and takes place in a limited number of locations. *Law and Order* has a gritty realism with varying lighting and a variety of settings from McCord's office to outside a bodega on East 135th.

Another important external influence in writing for TV is the timing of commercials in conjunction with the act structure. There are lots of sources detailing the suggested content and length of acts, but generally a sitcom has a teaser (short opening scene), two acts and a tag (short closing scene), and an episodic has a teaser, four acts and a tag. Each act closes with a turning point. Watching TV analytically and keeping a log of events will reveal some elements of basic structure. *Successful Scriptwriting*, by Wolff & Cox (Writer's Digest Books), offers detailed discussions of various types of shows.

Writing for the movies

With feature films you may feel at once more liberated and more bound by structure. An original movie script contains characters you have created, with storylines you design, allowing you more freedom than you have in TV. However, your writing must still convey believable dialogue and realistic characters, with a plausible plot and high-quality writing carried through the roughly 120 pages. The characters must have a problem that involves the audience. When you go to a movie you don't want to spend time watching the *second* worst night of a character's life. You're looking for the big issue that crystallizes a character, that portrays a journey with important consequences.

At the same time you are creating, you should also be constructing. Be aware of the basic three act structure for feature films. Scenes can be of varying lengths, but are usually no longer than three to three and a half pages. Some writers list scenes that must occur, then flesh them out from beginning to end, writing with the structure of events in mind. The beginning and climactic scenes are the easiest; it's how they get there from here that's difficult.

Many novice screenwriters tend to write too many visual cues and camera directions into their scripts. Your goal should be to write something readable, like a "compressed novella." Write succinct resonant scenes and leave the camera technique to the director and producer. In action/adventure movies, however, there needs to be a balance since the script demands more visual direction.

It seems to be easier for TV writers to cross over to movies. Cable movies bridge the two, and are generally less derivative and more willing to take chances with a higher quality show designed to attract an audience not interested in network offerings. Cable is also less susceptible to advertiser pullout, which means it can tackle more controversial topics.

Feature films and TV are very different and writers occupy different positions. TV is a medium for writers and producers; directors work for them. Many TV writers are also producers. In feature films the writers and producers work for the director and often have little or no say about what happens to the work once the script has been sold. For TV the writer pitches the idea; for feature films generally the producer pitches the idea and then finds a writer.

Marketing your scripts

If you intend to make writing your profession you must act professionally. Accepted submission practices should become second nature.

● The initial pitch is made through a query letter, which is no longer than one page with a one paragraph synopsis and brief summary of your credits if they are relevant to the subject of your script.

● Never send a complete manuscript until it is requested.

● Almost every script sent to a producer, studio or agent must be accompanied by a release form. Ask for that company's form when you receive an invitation to submit the whole script. Mark your envelope "release form enclosed" to prevent it being returned unread.

● Always include a self-addressed stamped envelope if you want your work returned; a disposable copy may be accompanied by a self-addressed stamped postcard for reply.

● Allow four to six weeks from receipt of your manuscript before writing a follow-up letter.

When your script is requested, be sure it's written in the appropriate format. Unusual binding, fancy covers or illustrations mark an amateur. Three brass brads with a plain or black cover indicate a pro.

There are a limited number of ideas in the world, so it's inevitable that similar ideas occur to more than one person. Hollywood is a buyers' market and a release form states that pretty clearly. An idea is not copyrightable, so be careful about sharing premises. The written expression of that idea, however, can be protected and it's a good idea to do so. The Writers Guild of America can register scripts for television and theatrical motion pictures, series formats, storylines and step outlines. You need not be a member of the WGA to use this service. Copyrighting your work with the Copyright Office of the Library of Congress also protects your work from infringement. Contact either agency for more information and an application form.

If you are a writer, you should write—all the time. When you're not writing, read. There are numerous books on the art, craft and business of screenwriting. See the Publications of Interest at the end of *Writer's Market* for a few or check the catalogs of companies previously mentioned. The different trade papers of the industry such as *Daily Variety* and *Hollywood Reporter* can keep you in touch with the day to day doings and upcoming events. Specialty newsletters such as *Hollywood Scriptwriter, Creative Screenwriting* and *New York Scriptwriter* offer tips from successful scriptwriters and agents. The *Hollywood Creative Directory* is an extensive list of production companies, studios and networks that also lists companies and talent with studio deals.

Computer services, such as America Online, have various bulletin boards and chat hours for scriptwriters that provide contact with other writers and a chance to share information and encouragement.

It may take years of work before you come up with a script someone is willing to take a chance on. Those years need to be spent learning your craft and understanding the business. Polishing scripts, writing new material, keeping current with the industry and networking constantly will keep you busy. When you do get that call you'll be confident in your abilities and know that your hard work is beginning to pay off.

For information on more screenwriting markets, see Scriptwriting Markets/ Changes '95-'96 at the end of the Screenwriting section.

ALLIED ARTISTS, INC., 859 N. Hollywood Way, Suite 377, Burbank CA 91505. (818)594-4089. Vice President, Development: John Nichols. Estab. 1990. Produces material for broadcast and cable television, home video and film. Buys 3-5 scripts/year. Works with 10-20 writers/year. Buys first rights or all rights. Accepts previously produced material. Reports in 2 months on queries; 3 months on scripts. Submit synopsis/outline. Pays in accordance with Writers Guild standards (amount and method negotiable). Written queries only—no phone pitches.
Needs: Films (16, 35mm), videotapes. Social issue TV special (30-60 minutes); special interest home video topics; instruction and entertainment; positive values feature screenplays.

Tips: "We are looking for positive, up-lifting dramatic stories involving real people situations. Future trend is for more reality-based programming, as well as interactive television programs for viewer participation."

‡**THE AMERICAN MOVING PICTURE COMPANY INC.**, 838 N. Doheny Dr., #904, Los Angeles CA 90069. (310)273-3838. C.E.O., President: William A. Levey. Estab. 1979. Theatrical motion picture audience. Buys screenplay rights and ancillaries. No previously produced material. Does not return submissions. Reports in 1 month. Query with synopsis. Pays in accordance with Writers Guild standards or more.
Needs: Films (35mm), commercial.

ANGEL FILMS, 967 Highway 40, New Franklin MO 65274-9778. (314)698-3900. Fax: (314)698-3900. Vice President Production: Matthew Eastman. Estab. 1980. Produces material for feature films, television. Buys 10 scripts/year. Works with 20 writers/year. Buys all rights. Accepts previously published material (if rights available). Reports in 1 months on queries; 1-2 months on scripts. Query with synopsis. Makes outright purchase "depending upon budget for project. Our company is a low-budget producer which means people get paid fairly, but don't get rich."
- This company is looking for writers for a new science fiction television series, *The Chronicles of Erick Uttland.*
Needs: Films (35mm), videotapes. "We are looking for projects that can be used to produce feature film and television feature film and series work. These would be in the areas of action adventure, comedy, horror, thriller, science fiction, animation for children."
Tips: "Don't copy others. Try to be original. Don't overwork your idea. As far as trends are concerned, don't pay attention to what is 'in.' By the time it gets to us it will most likely be on the way 'out.' And if you can't let your own grandmother read it, don't send it. If you wish material returned, enclose proper postage with all submissions. Send SASE for response to queries and return of scripts."

ANGEL'S TOUCH PRODUCTIONS, 1055 Allen Ave., Suite B, Glendale CA 91201-1654. Director of Development: Phil Nemy. Estab. 1986. Professional screenplays and teleplays. Send synopsis. Reports in 6 months. Rights negotiated between production company and author. Payment negotiated.
Needs: All types, all genres, only full-length teleplays and screenplays—no one-acts.
Tips: "We are now only seeking feature film screenplays, television screenplays, and episodic teleplays."

BARNSTORM FILMS, 73 Market St., Venice CA 90291. (310)396-5937. Contact: Denise Stewart. Estab. 1969. Produces feature films. Has an overall deal with MGM Studios. Buys 2-3 scripts/year. Works with 4-5 writers/year. No query letters accepted; submissions by WGA signatory agents only.

☐**BIG STAR MOTION PICTURES LTD.**, 13025 Yonge St., #201, Richmond Hill, Ontario L4E 1Z5 Canada. (416)720-9825. Contact: Frank A. Deluca. Estab. 1991. Buys 5 scripts/year. Works with 5-10 writers/year. Reports in 1 month on queries; 2 months on scripts. Submit synopsis. "We deal with each situation differently and work on a project-by-project basis."
Needs: Films (35mm). "We are very active in all medias, but are primarily looking for television projects, cable, network, etc. True life situations are of special interest for MOW."

‡**C.A. MANAGEMENT & PRODUCTIONS**, 1875 Century Park E., #2707, Los Angeles CA 90067. Acquisition/Development: Ramon Burdeos. Estab. 1988. Feature film market. Buys 3-4 scripts/year. Works with 5-6 writers/year. Buys option to purchase. Reports in 1 month on queries; 2 months on submissions. Query with synopsis and résumé. Individual contractual agreement.
Needs: Films (35mm). Feature length (120 page) narrative screenplays, both narrative and comedic.

‡**CANVAS HOUSE FILMS**, 3671 Bear St., #E, Santa Ana CA 92704. (714)850-1964. Producer: Mitch Teemley. Estab. 1994. General audience. Buys 2-3 scripts/year. Works with 10-15 writers/year. Buys first rights, all rights. Accepts previously produced material. Reports in 1 month on queries; 4 months on submissions. Query with synopsis and résumé. Pays in accordance with Writers Guild standards.
Needs: Films (35mm). "Quality feature-length filmscripts—all types, but no lurid, 'hard-R'-rated material."
Tips: "Know proper formatting and story structure. There is a need for 'family' material that can appeal to *grown-ups* as well as children."

CAREY-IT-OFF PRODUCTIONS, % 14925 Magnolia, Suite 205, Sherman Oaks CA. (818)789-0954. Fax: (818)789-5967. President: Kathi Carey. Estab. 1984. Works with 1-2 writers/year. Buys all rights. No pre-

☐ ***Open box preceding a listing indicates a cable TV market.***

viously produced material. Reports in 6 months on queries; 6 months on scripts.

Needs: Looking for true stories to develop for MOWs—(you must own the rights to the story). Stories can be written as teleplays or not. Please do *not* send unsolicited scripts; all unsolicited scripts will be returned. Query with synopsis or treatment. Always enclose SASE. Makes outright purchase in accordance with Writers Guild standards.

Tips: "Please do not send articles by registered or certified mail. Do *not* call. You will be notified of any interest in your work."

CINE/DESIGN FILMS, INC., P.O. Box 6495, Denver CO 80206. (303)777-4222. Producer/Director: Jon Husband. Produces educational material for general, sales-training and theatrical audiences. 75% freelance written; 90% unagented submissions. "Original, solid ideas are encouraged." Rights purchased vary.

Needs: Films (16, 35mm). "Motion picture outlines in the theatrical and documentary areas. We are seeking theatrical scripts in the low-budget area that are possible to produce for under $1 million. We seek flexibility and personalities who can work well with our clients." FSend 8-10-page outline before submitting ms. Pays $100-200/screen minute on 16mm productions. Theatrical scripts negotiable.

Tips: "Understand the marketing needs of film production today. Materials will not be returned."

CINEQUANON PICTURES INTERNATIONAL, 8489 W. Third St., Los Angeles CA 90048. Director, Acquisitions and Legal Affairs: Stacey Kivel. Estab. 1993. Interested in scripts with attachments, either a cast, a director, or financing. Also looking for finished or nearly finished feature length, color films seeking distribution. May provide completion financing. Science fiction, martial arts, high-tech, action, hip youth oriented projects. All terms and conditions are negotiable.

Recent Releases: *Hits*, (Martin Sheen), *Kissing Miranda*, produced by Tom Taylor (*Fried Green Tomatoes*), *Desperate Measures*, (Timothy Bottoms).

CLARK FILM PRODUCTION CHARITY, INC., P.O. Box 773, Balboa CA 92661. President: Mr. Clark. Estab. 1987. General audience. Buys 1 script/year. Works with 4 writers/year. Buys first rights. Accepts previously produced material. Reports in 6 months. Submit synopsis/outline. Pays in accordance with Writers Guild of America west standards.

Needs: "We will rewrite existing screenplay (owned)."

Recent Production: *The Ralph DePalma Story* (full-length motion picture)."

□**CRONUS INTERNATIONAL ENTERTAINMENT, INC.**, 5110 Tujunga Ave., #4, North Hollywood CA 91601-4925. (818)763-1977. Producing Director: Herb Rodgers. "The company was formed in 1990 for the purpose of selecting screenplays and developing them for production, either as movies of the week for network/cable, or for production for feature length films for distribution internationally. All scripts should follow professional format and be 95-110 pages in length. Authors of selected scripts will be contacted about options to produce. Only scripts with SASE will be returned."

‡**CUTTING EDGE PRODUCTIONS**, 2026 Federal Ave., Los Angeles CA 90025. (310)478-8700. President: Tom Forsythe. Estab. 1982. Looking for full-length feature film scripts for theatrical release. Buys 5 scripts/year. Buys film, TV and allied rights. Reports in 1 month on mss.

Needs: Screenplays should be in standard format, approximately 120 pages. Query with synopsis. Pays in accordance with Writers Guild standards.

Tips: "Recognize that film distribution is becoming centralized by the major studios who only buy screenplays that are $20 million ideas. Before starting a script ask yourself: Is this a $20 million idea? Always ask yourself if you would watch the story you're telling. The smash hit mentality dominates feature production. Despite films like *Driving Miss Daisy*, hard-edged films continue to be the rule. We only respond to submissions accompanied by SASE."

DAKOTA NORTH ENTERTAINMENT, Hollywood TV Studios, Bldg. 11, 5800 Sunset Blvd., Los Angeles CA 90028. Fax: (213)871-8429. Producer/Director: Troy Miller. Estab. 1987. Works with 4-8 writers/year. No previously produced material. Reports in 1 month. Query with synopsis. Pay varies.

Needs: Films (16, 35mm), videotapes, multimedia kits. Looking for "theatrical: original screenplays for production (broad comedy, action, adventure); multimedia: event-oriented day and date or self-contained properties for network specials."

EARTH TRACKS PRODUCTIONS, 4809 Avenue N, Suite 286, Brooklyn NY 11234. Contact: David Krinsky. Estab. 1985. Produces material for "major and independent studios." Buys 1-3 scripts/year. Buys all rights. No books, no treatments, no articles. *Only* completed movie and TV movie scripts. Reports in 6 weeks on queries.

● This producer notes a high rate of inappropriate submissions. Please read and follow guidelines carefully.

Needs: Commercial, well-written, high concept scripts in the drama, comedy, action and thriller genres. No other scripts. Query with 1-page synopsis and SASE. No treatments. *Do not send any scripts unless requested.*

Tips: "Can always use a *good* comedy. Writers should be flexible and open to suggestions. Material with interest (in writing) from a known actor/director is a *major plus* in the consideration of the material. We also need sexy thrillers. Any submissions of more than two pages will *not* be read or returned."

EAST EL LAY FILMS, 12041 Hoffman St., Studio City CA 91604. (818)769-4565. (818)769-1917. President: Daniel Kuhn. Estab. 1992. Low-budget feature films for television markets. Buys 2 scripts/year. Works with many writers/year. Buys first rights and options for at least 1 year with refusal rights. Accepts previously produced material. Reports in 3-4 weeks on queries. Query with synopsis and résumé. Pays royalty, makes outright purchase or option fee.
Needs: Film loops (35mm), videotapes.

ECLECTIC FILMS, INC., 5750 Wilshire Blvd., Suite 580, Los Angeles CA 90036. Principals: Robert Schaffel, Youssef Vahabzadeh. Vice President, Creative Affairs: Sharon Roesler. Feature film audience—worldwide. Reports in 1-2 months on script. Call or write to request permission to submit completed screenplays.

ENTERTAINMENT PRODUCTIONS, INC., 2118 Wilshire Blvd., Suite 744, Santa Monica CA 90403. (310)456-3143. Producer: Edward Coe. Contact: Story Editor. Estab. 1971. Produces films for theatrical and television (worldwide) distribution. Reports in 1 month (only if SASE is enclosed for reply and/or return of material).
Needs: Screenplays. Only unencumbered originals. Query with synopsis. Makes outright purchase for all rights. Price negotiated on a project-by-project basis. Writer's release in any form will be acceptable.
Tips: "State why script has great potential."

FINE ART PRODUCTIONS, 67 Maple St., Newburgh NY 12550. (914)561-5866. Contact: Richie Suraci. Estab. 1992. Produces material for all genres. Buys variable number of scripts/year. Works with variable number of writers/year. Buys first rights, all rights, "varies with project. Negotiable." Accepts previously produced material. Reports in 3-6 months. Catalog for 8½ × 11 SAE with 52¢ postage. Query with synopsis, outline, script and résumé. "Everything is negotiable by project, varies per project."
• Fine Art Productions is looking for sci-fi, adult erotica, comedy; adventures to India Tantric Shiva/ Shakti Temples, adventures to Africa.
Needs: Charts, film loops (all formats), films (all formats), kinescopes, microfilm, videotapes, multimedia kits, phonograph records, silent and sound filmstrips, teaching machine programs, overhead transparencies, slides, study prints, tapes and cassettes, models. "Looking for all genres. Submit or we won't know it exists."

‡GAMARA PICTURES, 6943 Hazeltine, #14, Van Nuys CA 91405. Producer/Director: Dali Moyzes. Intended for all audiences. Buys 4 scripts/year. Works with 4-8 writers/year. Buys all rights. Reports in 2 months. Catalog for #10 SASE. Query with complete script, résumé and SASE. Pays in accordance with Writer's Guild standards.
Needs: Films (35mm). Feature film screenplays and TV sitcoms—any subject—for future possible production.
Tips: "Please send by special 4th class mail (printed matter)—about $1.50."

‡GOLDEN QUILL, 202 E. 42nd St., New York NY 10017. Executuve Vice President: Hassan Ildari. Estab. 1991. Buys 3 scripts/year. Works with 6 writers/year. Accepts previously produced material. Reports in 3 weeks. Query with synopsis. Outright purchase.
Needs: Films (35mm).

INTERNATIONAL HOME ENTERTAINMENT, 1440 Veteran Ave., Suite 650, Los Angeles CA 90024. (213)460-4545. Assistant to the President: Jed Leland, Jr. Estab. 1976. Buys first rights. Reports in 2 months. Query. Pays in accordance with Writers Guild standards. *No unsolicited scripts.*
• Looking for material that is international in scope.

‡JEF FILMS, 143 Hickory Hill Circle, Osterville MA 02655. (508)428-7198. President: Jeffrey H. Aikman. Estab. 1973. Feature films primarily geared for teens through adults. Buys 12 scripts/year. Buys all rights. Accepts previously published material. Reports in 3 months. Catalog for #10 SASE. Query with synopsis. Makes outright purchase, "amount dependent on style, length, budget of project, experience of writer."
Needs: Films (35mm), videotapes. Feature films in the dramatic, science fiction, erotic thriller, screwball comedy fields.
Tips: "Keep trying. We get 75-100 scripts/week, we will work with first-time writers, especially for quirky/ offbeat materials. More needs for erotic thrillers, good dramatic stories featuring strong character actors."

‡THE JEWISH TELEVISION COMMISSION, 1 South Franklin St., Chicago IL 60606-4694. (312)444-2896. Fax: (312)855-2474. Director of Programming and Syndication: Mindy Soble. "Television scripts are requested for *The Magic Door*, a children's program produced in conjunction with CBS's WBBM-TV 2 in

Chicago." four scripts/television season. Buys all rights. Reports in 1 month. Writers guidelines for #10 SASE.

Needs: "*Magic Door Television Theatre* is an anthology series of 4 specials/year designed for broadcast on weekends around the 5 p.m. hour. The target audience is 12 years of age, however the material should be viable for the whole family to enjoy. It is Jewish in content, yet universal in scope. Each episode should be built on an idea anchored in a Jewish value. While the perspective is Jewish, such topics as family, education, adversity, tradition, etc. are obviously not exclusive to the Jewish purview. We seek material rooted in Jewish thought, yet characterized by a 'pro-social' message. This anthology series is television theater. It is designed to look like theater and we hope to capitalize on the elements characteristic of theater such as focused use of language, interior space, condensed time and vivid characterizations. The series is produced on videotape in a TV studio which lends itself to this style. We want scripts that are highly stylized and expressionistic. For the young target audience humor is an important element in each script. Each half hour episode stands on its own and is wholly unrelated to other episodes in the series." Submit synopsis/outline, résumé or a complete ms with the right to reject. Makes outright purchase of $1,000.

Tips: "A Judaic background is helpful, yet not critical. Writing for children is key. We prefer to use Chicago writers, as script rewrites are paramount and routine."

KJD TELEPRODUCTIONS, 30 Whyte Dr., Voorhees NJ 08043. (609)751-3500. Fax: (609)751-7729. E-mail: mactoday@ios.com. President: Larry Scott. Estab. 1989. Broadcast audience. Buys 6 scripts/year. Works with 3 writers/year. Buys all rights. No previously produced material. Reports in 1 month. Catalog free. Query. Makes outright purchase.

Needs: Films, videotapes, multimedia kits.

KN'K PRODUCTIONS INC., 5230 Shira Dr., Valley Village CA 91607-2300. (818)760-3106. Fax: (818)788-6606 or (818)760-3106. Creative Director: Katharine Kramer. Contact: Martin Shapiro. Estab. 1992. "Looking for film material with strong roles for mature women (ages 40-55 etc.). Also roles for young women and potential movie musicals, message movies." Buys 3 scripts/year. Works with 5 writers/year. Buys all rights. No previously produced material. Reports in 2-3 months. Catalog for #10 SASE. Submit synopsis, complete script and résumé. Pays in accordance with Writers Guild standards or partnership.

● Kn'K is looking particularly for female-driven vehicles for mature actresses, 45-55.

Needs: Multimedia kits. "Doing more partnerships with writers as opposed to just Writers Guild minimum. Concentration on original vehicles for the mature actress to fill the gap that's missing from mainstream cinema."

Tips: "We are seeking inspirational true/life stories such as women overcoming obstacles, human growth, movie musicals."

‡LAKE-DAYS ENTERTAINMENT, 7060 Hollywood Blvd., #1025, Los Angeles CA 90028. Contact: George Bailey. Estab. 1992. Film and television production; family-oriented subject matter and good thrillers. Buys 25-50 scripts/year. Buys all rights. No previously produced material. Reports in 5 days on queries; 2 months on submissions. Query with synopsis or completed script. Pays in accordance with Writer's Guild stardard.

Needs: Films. Looking for feature length scripts dealing with family subject matter. Must have story, interesting characters. Also interested in very good thrillers.

Tips: "Scripts should have a great narrative flow, interesting characters, and not to rehash old and tired themes. Please be creative with the thrillers and with the family-oriented material."

DAVID LANCASTER PRODUCTIONS, 3356 Bennett Dr, Los Angeles CA 90068-1704. Story Editor: Scott Fort. Estab. 1985. Feature films audience. Buys 8-10 scripts/year. Works with 18-25 writers/year. Buys film and TV rights. No previously produced material. Reports in 2-3 weeks on queries; 2 weeks on scripts. Query with synopsis.

Needs: Action oriented screenplays, dramas with an edge.

Tips: "We will accept nothing without a release on outside of envelope. Please do not call us. We will reply only to queries accompanied by a SASE. Absolutely no unrequested screenplays accepted—we will refuse delivery on all unsolicited material."

RON LEVINSON PRODUCTIONS, 7201 Raintree Circle, Culver City CA 90230. (310)559-2470. Fax: (310)559-7244. TV and film material. Buys first and all rights. Submissions through agents or with release.

LIGHTVIEW ENTERTAINMENT, 11901 Santa Monica Blvd., Suite 571, Los Angeles CA 90025. Fax: (310)820-3670. E-mail: lightview@aol.com. Producer: Laura McCorkindale. Estab. 1991. Options 20 scripts/year. Option includes purchase price which incorporates all rights. Purchase price negotiable. Options include purchase price which incorporates all rights. Send 1-2 page detailed synopsis with SASE to the attention of Dana Shelbourne. "We will respond via mail within 1 month to let you know if we want to see your screenplay. If we request your screenplay after reading synopsis, please allow 3 months for a second response."

Needs: Feature film screenplays. "Our films range from smaller budget intelligent, artistic independent films to big budget commercial studio films. All genres."
Tips: "Take time writing your synopses and be detailed! Synopsis should be as well written as your screenplay. Be sure it is at least one page—but not more than two! Although we are looking for all types of screenplays, we are especially drawn to inspirational stories that enlighten and entertain. *We do not accept unsolicited phone calls,* so please correspond only through the mail."

LOCKWOOD FILMS (LONDON) INC., 365 Ontario St., London, Ontario N5W 3W6 Canada. (519)434-6006. Fax: (519)645-0507. President: Nancy Johnson. Contact: Christina Young, program development. Estab. 1974. Audience is entertainment and general broadcast for kids 9-12, adults and family viewing. Works with 5-6 writers/year. Buys all rights. No previously produced material. Reports in 2 months on queries. Submit query with synopsis, résumé or sample scripts. "Submissions will not be considered unless a proposal submission agreement is signed. We will send one upon receiving submissions." Negotiated fee.
Needs: Family entertainment: series, seasonal specials, mini-series, and movies of the week. Also feature films.
Tips: "Potential contributors should have a fax machine and should be prepared to sign a 'proposal submission agreement.' "

‡□**LEE MAGID PRODUCTIONS,** P.O. Box 532, Malibu CA 90265. (213)463-5998. President: Lee Magid. Produces material for all markets: adult, commercial—even musicals. 90% freelance written. 70% of scripts produced are unagented submissions. Works with many unpublished/unproduced writers. Buys all rights or will negotiate. No previously produced material. Does not return unsolicited material.
Needs: Films, sound filmstrips, phonograph records, television shows/series and videotape presentations. Currently interested in film material, either for video (television) or theatrical. "We deal with cable networks, producers, live-stage productions, etc." Works with musicals for cable TV. Prefers musical forms for video comedy. Submit synopsis/outline and résumé. Pays royalty, in accordance with Writers Guild standards, makes outright purchase or individual arrangement depending on author.
Tips: "We're interested in comedy material. Forget drug-related scripts."

MARS PRODUCTIONS CORPORATION, 10215 Riverside Dr., Toluca Lake CA 91602. (818)980-8011. Fax: (818)980-1900. Producer: Mark Delo. Estab. 1969. Produces family and action films. Buys 3 scripts/year. Works with 5 writers/year. Buys all rights, options. No previously produced material. Reports in 3 months. Query with synopsis/outline and SASE. Makes outright purchase "depending on the project."
Needs: Film (35mm).
Tips: "Follow the standard script format. I do not like too much detail of action or camera angles."

□**MEDIACOM DEVELOPMENT CORP.,** P.O. Box 6331, Burbank CA 91510-6331. (818)594-4089. Director/Program Development: Felix Girard. Estab. 1978. 80% freelance written. Buys 8-12 scripts annually from unpublished/unproduced writers. 50% of scripts produced are unagented submissions. Query with samples. Reports in 1 month. Buys all rights or first rights. Written query only. Please do not call.
Needs: Produces films, multimedia kits, tapes and cassettes, slides and videotape with programmed instructional print materials, broadcast and cable television programs. Publishes software ("programmed instruction training courses"). Negotiates payment depending on project. Looking for new ideas for CD-ROM titles.
Tips: "Send short samples of work. Especially interested in flexibility to meet clients' demands, creativity in treatment of precise subject matter. We are looking for good, fresh projects (both special and series) for cable and pay television markets. A trend in the audiovisual field that freelance writers should be aware of is the move toward more interactive video disc/computer CRT delivery of training materials for corporate markets."

‡**MERIWETHER PUBLISHING LTD. (Contemporary Drama Service),** Dept. WM, 885 Elkton Dr., Colorado Springs CO 80907-3557. President: Mark Zapel. Executive Editor: Arthur L. Zapel. Estab. 1969. "We publish how-to materials in book and video formats. We are interested in materials for high school and college level students only. Our Contemporary Drama Service division publishes 60-70 plays/year." 80% written by unpublished writers. Buys 40-60 scripts/year from unpublished/unproduced writers. 90% of scripts are unagented submissions. Reports in 1 month on queries; 2 months on full-length mss. Query with synopsis/outline, résumé of credits, sample of style and SASE. Catalog available for $2 postage. Offers 10% royalty or makes outright purchase.
Needs: Book mss on theatrical arts subjects especially books of short scenes for amateur and professional actors. "We are now looking for scenebooks with special themes: 'scenes for young women,' 'comedy scenes for two actors' etc. These scenebooks need not be original provided the compiler can get letters of permission from the original copyright owner. We are interested in all textbook candidates for theater arts subjects. Christian children's activity book mss also accepted. We will consider elementary level religious materials and plays, but no elementary level children's secular plays. Query. Pays royalty; sometimes makes outright purchase.

Tips: "We publish a wide variety of speech contest materials for high school students. We are publishing more reader's theater scripts and musicals based on classic literature or popular TV shows, provided the writer includes letter of clearance from the copyright owner. Our educational books are sold to teachers and students at college and high school levels. Our religious books are sold to youth activity directors, pastors and choir directors. Our trade books are directed at the public with a sense of humor. Another group of buyers is the professional theater, radio and TV category."

THE MERRYWOOD STUDIO, 137 E. 38th St., #75, New York NY 10016-2650. Creative Director: Raul daSilva. Estab. 1984. Produces animated motion pictures for entertainment audiences. "We are planning to severely limit but not close out freelance input. Will be taking roughly 5-7%. However, we might be seeking a few *experienced* top writers for new children's animation business (ages 2-5, 10 and above/crossover to adult)."
  ● The Merrywood Studio has expanded the range of writing to the pre-school child.
Needs: Proprietary material only. Human potential themes woven into highly entertaining drama, high adventure, comedy. This is a new market for animation with only precedent in the illustrated novels published in France and Japan. Cannot handle unsolicited mail/scripts and will not return mail. Open to *agented* submissions of credit sheets, concepts and synopses only. Profit sharing depending upon value of concept and writer's following. Pays at least Writers Guild levels or better, plus expenses.
Tips: "This is *not a market for beginning writers*. Established, professional work with highly unusual and original themes is sought. If you love writing, it will show and we will recognize it and reward it in every way you can imagine. We are not a 'factory' and work on a very high level of excellence."

MILWAUKEE FILMWORKS, 9595 Wilshire Blvd., #610, Beverly Hills CA 90212. Fax: (310)278-2632. Contact: Douglas. Estab. 1991. Film and television audience. Buys 2 scripts/year. Works with 6 writers/year. Buys screenplays-option. Accepts previously produced material. Returns submissions on a case to case basis. Reports in 2 months. Query with complete script. Pay varies in accordance with Writers Guild standards.
Needs: Films (35mm).

MONAREX HOLLYWOOD CORPORATION, 9421½ W. Pico Blvd., Los Angeles CA 90035. (310)552-1069. Fax: (310)552-1724. President: Chris D. Nebe. Estab. 1978. Producers of theatrical and television motion pictures and miniseries; also international distributors. Buys 5-6 scripts/year. Buys all rights. Reports in 2 months.
Needs: "We are seeking action, adventure, comedy and character-oriented love stories, dance, horror and dramatic screenplays." First submit synopsis/outline with SASE. After review of the synopsis/outline, the screenplay will be requested. Pays in accordance with Writers Guild standards.
Tips: "We look for exciting visuals with strong characters and a unique plot."

MONTIVAGUS PRODUCTIONS, 6310 Hazeltine Ave., Suite 212, Van Nuys CA 91401. (818)782-1212. Estab. 1990. Buys 3 scripts/year. Works with 3-4 writers/year. Buys all rights. Responds if interested on queries; 1 month on scripts. Query with synopsis only. Pays in accordance with Writers Guild standards.
Needs: Films (35mm), videotapes.

‡MUSE OF FIRE PRODUCTIONS, 1277 Barry Ave., #5, Los Angeles CA 90025. Contact: Alex Epstein. Estab. 1992. Film audience. Works with 5 writers/year. Buys all rights. No previously produced material. Reports in 1 month on queries, 2 months on submissions. Query with synopsis. Pay negotiable per industry standards—non WGA.
Needs: Films. "Scripts with great hooks and decent writing; scripts without hooks with awesome roles actors will kill to play; no gangster/lowlife/world-is-horrible downers."
Tips: "Don't write for a low budget. Write what you'd pay money to see with someone you love!"

NEW & UNIQUE VIDEOS, 2336 Sumac Dr., San Diego CA 92105. (619)282-6126. Creative Director: Candace Love. Estab. 1982. General TV and videotape audiences. Buys 10-15 scripts/year. Buys first rights, all rights. No previously produced material. Reports in 1-2 months. Catalog for #10 SASE. Query with synopsis. Makes outright purchase, negotiable.
Needs: Videotapes.
Tips: "We are seeking unique slants on interesting topics in 60-90 minute special-interest videotape format. Imagination and passion, not to mention humor are pluses. Titles produced include 'Massage for Relaxation'; 'Ultimate Mountain Biking' and 'Full Cycle: World Odyssey.' No threatical titles. Please study the genre and get an understanding of what 'special interest' means." We are heading towards moving pictures (i.e. video, computers, CD-ROM, etc.) in a big way as book sales diminish. If writers can adapt to the changes, their work will always be in demand."

OCEAN PARK PICTURES, 220 Main St., Venice CA 90291. (310)450-1220. Executive Producer: Tim Goldberg. Estab. 1989. All audiences. Buys 5 scripts/year. Works with 10 writers/year. Buys first or all rights.

Accepts previously produced material. Reports in 1 month on queries; 2 months on scripts. Query with synopsis, complete script and résumé. Pay varies.
Needs: Film (35mm).

ODYSSEY INTERNATIONAL, P.O. Box 230902, Encinitas CA 92023. Contact: Gary Schmad. Estab. 1983. General, mature/adult audience. Buys 2-3 scripts/year. Works with 2-3 writers/year. Buys all rights. Reports in 2 months on queries. Catalog for #10 SASE. Query with synopsis. Pays 2-6% royalty or will consider outright purchase.
Needs: Films (16, 35mm), videotapes. Sitcom—"Flannigan's Last Resort"—Cheers in a topless bar (22½-28½ minutes); Feature—"R" exotic adventure (90-115 mintues); Video—Playboy style with Shakespearean ploys (58 minutes); Travelog—"On the Road"—off-beat travel series (22½ minutes).
Tips: "Our venue is comedic and sexy, but tasteful. No sleaze, please."

PACE FILMS, INC., PHC, 411 E. 53rd St., New York NY 10022. (212)755-5486. President: R. Vanderbes. Estab. 1965. Produces material for a general theatrical audience. Buys all rights. Reports in 2 months.
Needs: Theatrical motion pictures. Produces and distributes 35mm motion pictures for theatrical, TV and videocassettes. Query with synopsis/outline and writing background/credits. Submit complete script, outline and SASE. Pays in accordance with Writers Guild standards.

PAPILLON PRODUCTIONS, (formerly Sceneries Productions), 1712 Anacapa St., Santa Barbara CA 93101. Phone/fax: (805)569-0733. Head of Acquisitions: Diane Itier. Estab. 1989. Produces material for any audience. Buys 5 scripts/year. Works with 4 writers/year. Buys all rights. Accepts previously produced material. Reports in 1 month. Submit complete script and résumé. Pays in accordance with Writers Guild standards.
Needs: Films. "We are seeking any screenplay for full-length motion pictures."
Tips: "Be patient but aggressive enough to keep people interested in your screenplay."

☐ **TOM PARKER MOTION PICTURES**, 3941 S. Bristol, #285, Santa Ana CA 92704. (714)545-2887. Fax: (714)545-9775. President: Tom Parker. Produces and distributes feature-length motion pictures worldwide for theatrical, home video, pay and free TV. Also produces short subject special interest films (30, 45, 60 minutes). Works with 5-10 scripts/year. Previously produced and distributed "Amazing Love Secret" (R), "Amorous Adventures of Ricky D." (R), and "The Sturgis Story" (R). Reports in 3-6 months. "Follow the instructions herein and do not phone for info or to inquire about your script."
Needs: "Complete script *only* for low budget (under $1 million) "R" or "PG" rated action/thriller, action/adventure, comedy, adult romance (R), sex comedy (R), family action/adventure to be filmed in 35mm film for the theatrical and home video market. (Do not send TV movie scripts, series, teleplays, stage plays). *Very limited dialogue.* Scripts should be action-oriented and fully described. Screen stories or scripts OK, but no camera angles please. No heavy drama, documentaries, social commentaries, dope stories, weird or horror. Violence or sex OK, but must be well motivated with strong story line." Submit synopsis and description of characters with finished scripts. Makes outright purchase: $5,000-25,000. Will consider participation, co-production.
Tips: "Absolutely will not return scripts or report on rejected scripts unless accompanied by SASE."

PICTURE ENTERTAINMENT CORPORATION, 9595 Wilshire Blvd., Suite 505, Beverly Hills CA 90212. (310)858-8300. President/CEO: Lee Caplin. Vice President Development: Sonia Mintz. Produces feature films for theatrical audience and TV audience. Buys 2 scripts/year. Works with 10 writers/year. Buys all rights. Reports on submissions in 2 months.
Needs: Films (35mm); videotapes. Feature scripts 100-120 pages. Submit completed script. "Pays on a deal by deal basis; some WGA, some not."
Tips: "Don't send derivitive standard material. Emphasis on unique plot and characters, realistic dialogue. *Discourage* period pieces, over-the-top comedy, graphic sex/violence, SciFi. *Encourage* action, action/comedy, thriller, thriller/comedy."

THE PUPPETOON STUDIOS, P.O. Box 80141, Las Vegas NV 89180. Producer/Director: Arnold Leibovit. Estab. 1987. "Broad audience." Works with 5 writers/year. Reports in 1 month on queries; 2 months on scripts. Query with synopsis. Submit complete script. A Submission Release *must* be included with all queries. Produced and directed "The Puppetoon Movie." SASE required for return of all materials. Pays in accordance with Writers Guild standards. No novels, plays, poems, treatments; no submissions on computer disk. No unsolicited unagented material. Must include release form.
Needs: Films (35mm). "We are seeking animation properties including presentation drawings and character designs. The more detailed drawings with animation scripts the better."

‡**RED HOTS ENTERTAINMENT**, 634 N. Glen Oaks Blvd., #374, Burbank CA 91502-1024. Director of Development: Chip Miller/Chip Miller. Estab. 1990. Buys 1 script/year. Works with 3-5 writers/year. Buys first rights, all rights, "short and long term options, as well." No previously produced material. Reports in 2-3 weeks on queries; 1-2 months on mss. Query with synopsis or submit complete ms ("writer's choice").

Pays in accordance with Writer's Guild standards. "Negotiable on writer's previous credits, etc."
Needs: Film loops (16mm), films (35mm), videotapes. "We are a feature film and television production company and have no audiovisual material needs."
Tips: "Best advice possible: originality, uniqueness, write from your instincts and *don't* follow trends."

ROCKET PICTURES, 9536 Wilshire Blvd., #410, Beverly Hills CA 90212. (310)247-7600. Director of Creative Affairs: Irwin M. Rappaport. Audience encompasses all ages, emphasis on teenage, political, thriller and comedy themes. Buys 20-25 scripts/year. Buys first or all rights. No previously produced material. Reports in 1-2 months. Query with synopsis. Pays in accordance with Writers Guild standards.
Needs: Films (35mm), videotapes, multimedia (CD-ROM).

ROSSHEIM PRODUCTIONS, 2441 Beverly Ave., #15, Santa Monica CA 90405. President: Phyllis Caroll. Estab. 1991. TV and feature film audience. Buys several scripts/year. Works with several writers/year. Buys TV and movie/feature rights. Produced 1993 ABC TV movie "For Their Own Good." Reports in 3 months. Query with synopsis of story and complete script. "I am also looking for true stories for TV MOWs. I prefer news articles or some documentation to accompany material." Pay varies in accordance with Writers Guild standards. Must include SASE for return of materials.

RUSH STREET PRODUCTIONS, 8881 W. Pico Blvd., Suite 200, Los Angeles CA 90035. (310)550-0824. Producer/Writer: Jordan Rush. Head of Development: Suzanne Fenton. Estab. 1990. Film and TV audience. Interested in high concept comedies and high concept thrillers. Works with unlimited writers/year. Buys all rights. Produced "Club Fed" and "Never Talk to Strangers" (feature) and "Coach" (TV). Reports in 2 weeks on queries. Send résumé.

THE SHELDON/POST COMPANY, 1437 Rising Glen Rd., Los Angeles CA 90069. Producers: David Sheldon, Ira Post. Estab. 1989. Produces theatrical motion pictures, movies and series for television. Have contract with Twentieth Century-Fox. Options and acquires all rights. Reports in 1 month. Query with 2-3 page synopsis, 2-3 sample pages and SASE. "Do not send scripts or books. If the synopsis is of interest you will be sent a release form to send with your manuscript." Pays in accordance with Writers Guild standards. No advance payments.
● The Sheldon/Post Company reports that it is expanding into children's and family stories.
Needs: "We look for all types of material, including women's stories, suspense dramas, family stories, horror, sci-fi, thrillers, action-adventure—scripts or treatments." True stories should include news articles or other documentation.
Tips: "Write realistic stories with strong characters with whom the viewer can identify."

SHORELINE PICTURES, 1901 Avenue of the Stars, #1774, Los Angeles CA 90067. (310)551-2060. Director of Development: Peter Soby, Jr. Estab. 1993. Mass audiences. Buys 8 scripts/year. Works with 8 writers/year. Buys all rights. Reports in 1 month on submissions. Query.
Needs: Films (35, 70mm). Looking for "character-driven films that are very commercial. No exploitation or horror. Comedies and dramas, yes. Completed screenplays only. We are especially keen to find a comedy. Note, there is an audience for adult films as reflected in films like *The Piano*, *The Player*, *Crying Game*, *Joy Luck Club*, etc. Principal of our company co-produced *Glengarry Glen Ross*."

‡SKYLARK FILMS, 1123 Pacific St., Santa Monica CA 90405. (310)396-5753. Contact: Brad Pollack. Estab. 1990. Buys 6 scripts/year. Buys first or all rights. Accepts previously produced material. Reports in 2-4 weeks on queries; 1-2 months on submissions. Query with synopsis. Option or other structures depending on circumstances. Pays in accordance with Writer's Guild standards.
Needs: Films (TV, cable, feature).

‡SNOWBIRD ENTERTAINMENT, P.O. Box 1172, Burbank CA 91507. Producer: Peter Jackson. Audience is all ages. G, PG, PG-13 and R. Buys 1-2 scripts/year. Works with 1-2 writers/year. Buys all rights. Reports in 1-2 weeks on queries; 2-3 months on submissions. Query with complete script and résumé. Makes outright purchase or in accordance with Writer's Guild standards,. depending on the script and budget.
Needs: Films (35mm). "Snowbird Entertainment is looking for feature length screenplays in the following genres: action, action-adventure, mystery thriller, political thriller, suspense thriller or docu-dramas (true-life stories)."
Tips: "Writers need their scripts to have excellent story telling, good complex characters. There are no trends in feature films. (Trends is a Hollywood word.) It's all about stories. Is it a story the film audience wants to see. When it's all said and done it all comes down to what your 'gut' tells you. To quote Harry Cohn of Columbia Pictures 'If my ass moves, it's a winner.' "

SOUTH FORK PRODUCTIONS, P.O. Box 1935, Santa Monica CA 90406-1935. Producer: Jim Sullivan. Estab. 1980. Produces material for TV and film. Buys 2 scripts/year. Works with 4 writers/year. Buys all rights. No previously produced material. Send synopsis/outline and motion picture treatments, plus previous

credits, with SASE. No complete scripts. Pays in accordance with Writers Guild Standards.
Needs: Films (16, 35mm), videotapes.
Tips: "Follow established formats for treatments. SASE for return."

☐**STONEROAD PRODUCTIONS, INC.**, 11288 Ventura Blvd., #909, Studio City CA 91604. Contact: Story Department. Estab. 1992. Produces feature films for theaters, cable TV and home video. PG, R, and G-rated films. Buys/options 15-25 scripts/year. Works with 10 writers/year. Buys all rights; if published material, subsidiary rights. Accepts previously produced material. Reports in 1 month on queries if interested; 2 months on submissions. Query with synopsis. Pay varies greatly: option, outright purchase, wide range.
Needs: Films (35mm). All genres. Looking for good material from writers who have taken the time to learn the unique and difficult craft of scriptwriting.
Tips: "Interesting query letters intrigue us—and tell us something about the writer. Query letter should include a short 'Log Line' or 'Pitch' encapsulating 'what this story is about' and the genre in just a few sentences. We look for strong stories and strong characters. We make movies that we would like to see. Producers are known for encouraging new (e.g. unproduced) screenwriters and giving real consideration to their scripts."

TALKING RINGS ENTERTAINMENT, P.O. Box 80141, Las Vegas NV 89180. President and Artistic Director: Arnold Leibovit. Estab. 1988. "Produces material for motion pictures and television. Works with 5 writers/year. Reports on submissions in 2 months. Only send complete scripts. No treatments, novels, poems or plays, no submissions on computer disk. Query with synopsis. A Submission Release must be included with all queries. Produced and directed "The Fantasy Film Worlds of George Pal," "The Puppetoon Movie." Currently producing "The Time Machine Returns" and a remake of "The Seven Faces of Dr. Lao." SASE required for return of all materials. Pays in accordance with Writers Guild Standards.
Needs: Films (35mm), videotapes. No unsolicited unagented material. Must include release form.

UNIFILMS, INC., 22931 Sycamore Creek Dr., Valencia CA 91354-2050. (805)297-2000. Vice President, Development: Jack Adams. Estab. 1984. Buys 0-5 scripts/year. Reports in 2 weeks on queries.
Needs: Feature films *only*. Looking for feature film screenplays, current format, 100-120 pages long; commercial but not stupid, dramatic but not "artsy," funny but not puerile. Query with synopsis and SASE. "If you don't include a SASE, we won't reply. We do not accept unsolicited scripts. Save your postage; if you send us a script we'll return it unopened."
Tips: "If you've taken classes, read books, attended seminars and writers' workshops all concerned with scriptwriting and read hundreds of produced studio screenplays *prior* to seeing the film and you're still convinced you've got a wonderful script, we might want to see it. But desire and enthusiasm are not enough; you have to have independent corroboration that your work is as good as you think it is. If you've got someone else in the entertainment industry to recommend your script, we might be more interested in seeing it. But if you waste our time with a project that's not yet ready to be seen, we're not going to react well. Your first draft is not usually the draft you're going to show to the industry. *Get a professional opinion first*, then rewrite before you submit to us. Very few people care about synopses, outlines or treatments for sales consideration. THE SCRIPT is the basic blueprint, and everyone in the country is working on a script. Ideas are a dime a dozen. If you can *execute* that idea well and get people *excited* about that idea, you've got something. But most writers are wanna-bes, who submit scripts that need a lot more work just to get to the 'promising' stage. Scripts are *always* rewritten. If you can't convince us you're a *writer*, we don't care. But if you *can* write and you've got a *second* wonderful script we might talk. But don't send a 'laundry list' of your scripts; pick the best one and pitch it to us. If it's not for us, then maybe come back with project number two. More than one project at a time confuses Hollywood; make it easy for us and you'll make it easy for yourself. And if you do it in a professional manner, you'll convince us sooner. Good luck, and keep writing. (Rewriting.)"

VANGUARD PRODUCTIONS, 12111 Beatrice St., Culver City CA 90230. Contact: Terence M. O'Keefe. Estab. 1985. Buys 1 script/year. Buys all rights or options rights. Accepts previously produced material. Reports in 3 months on queries; 6 months on scripts. Query with synopsis, résumé and SASE. Pays in accordance with Writers Guild standards or negotiated option.
Needs: Films (35mm), videotapes.

ZACHARY ENTERTAINMENT, 273 S. Swall Dr., Beverly Hills CA 90211-2612. Development Associate: Lois Gore. Estab. 1981. Audience is film goers of all ages, television viewers. Buys 8-10 scripts/year. Works with 50 writers/year. Rights purchased vary. Produced *The Tie That Binds*, feature film for Hollywood Picture, a division of Walt Disney Studios. Reports in 2 weeks on queries; 3 months on submissions. Query with synopsis. Pay varies.
Needs: Films.

ZENITH ENTERTAINMENT, (formerly Blacktail Productions), P.O. Box 462061, Los Angeles CA 90046. President: Michael Valdes. Estab. 1993. Audience concentration is low-budget action films. Buys 5 scripts/

year. Works with 10-15 writers/year. Buys all rights. No previously produced material. Reports in 2-3 months on queries; 3-5 months on scripts. Catalog for #10 SASE. Query with synopsis, complete script, résumé, SASE and contact numbers. Pay varies.

Needs: Films (16, 35mm), videotapes. Looking for "action films—well-written, character driven—overall budget $200,000-300,000; script $ accordingly. Also character-driven scripts for $1-5 million range."

ZETA ENTERTAINMENT LTD., 8315 Beverly Blvd., Los Angeles CA 90048. Estab. 1988. Buys 3-6 scripts/ year. Works with over 12 writers/year. Buys all rights. No previously produced material. Reports in 1 month on queries; up to 6 months on scripts. Query with synopsis and SASE for completed scripts only. Pays in accordance with Writers Guild standards.

Needs: Films (35mm)

Recent Productions: *Guncrazy, Fist of the North Star, One Good Turn.*

THE ZVEJNIEKS GROUP, INC., 187 Cocohatchee St., Naples FL 33963. Contact: Ingrida Sylvia. Estab. 1983. "Emphasis is placed on quality of original written work for major motion picture production. Good writing creates its own audience." Limited to 15 projects in development at any given time. Rights negotiated on an individual basis. Accepts previously produced material. Reports in 1-2 months. Submit 1-page synopsis of story and characters. Pay negotiated on individual basis.

Needs: "As a producer of major motion pictures, our primary goal is to entertain audiences with quality movies. We are always looking for fresh, interesting, well-written stories with good character development. The script should elicit some sort of emotion from the reader/audience."

Tips: "According to Chairman Eric S. Zvejnieks, a serious problem facing the industry is a lack of genuine original creative material which would allow for greater diversity in films. Writing talent is often overlooked, an unfortunate reality partially attributable to the system within which writers work. The underlying philosophy of the company is that every great movie starts with a great story, a simple yet often forgotten concept."

Scriptwriting Markets/Changes '95-'96

The following scriptwriting markets were listed in the 1995 edition but do not have listings in this edition of *Writer's Market*. The majority did not respond to our request to update their listing or return a questionnaire for a new listing. If a reason was given for their exclusion, we have included it in parentheses after the listing name.

All American Communications
American Inside Theatre (not accepting mss)
Arnold & Associates Productions
Aska Film Productions
Blue Rider Pictures (removed by request due to inappropriate submissions)
Bolder Multimedia
Boz Productions
Breakneck Featuers
Brooklyn Bridge People
Carronade Group
Charles Rapp Enterprises
Childsplay
Compro Productions
Cornerstone Productions
Creative Edge Films
Delta Max Productions
Diner Theatre
Discovery (cancelled)
Educational Images
Edward D. Hansen
Encore Theatre
Francis Teri, Independent Prod.

Gessler Publishing
Gretna Theatre
Hokus Pokus Productions
Horizon Theatre Company
Image Innovations
Jacoby/Storm Productions
JAG Entertainment
Kolmor Visions
Mad River Theater Works (no freelance)
Mediacom Development
Mirimar Enterprises
MNC Films
Moxie Pictures
Nat'l Music Theater Conference
Never A Dull Moment Productions
New Line Productions
No Mas Entertainment
One on One Computer Training
Parallel Pictures
Perseverance Theatre
Pittsburgh Public Theater
Playwrights Preview Productions
Plotpoint (removed by request)

Quaigh Theatre
Rainmaker Productions
Rhythms Productions (not accepting mss)
Riverside Theatre
Rust St. Productions
Sceneries Productions
Second Stage Theatre
Silhouette Pictures
Southwest Pictures
Tapestry Films
Target Canada Productions
Television Production Services
Theatre Virginia
Theatreworks
Troll Associates
Unusual Cabaret (out of business)
Vanguard Films
Vecchio Entertainment
Video-Visions
Vigilante Theatre Company
Vision Films
Westbeth Theatre Center
Wilma Theatre

Syndicates

Newspaper syndicates distribute columns, cartoons and other written material to newspapers around the country—and sometimes around the world. Competition for syndication slots is stiff. Coveted spots in general interest, humor and political commentary are held by big-name columnists such as Bob Greene, Molly Ivins and William Raspberry. And multitudes of aspiring writers wait in the wings, hoping one of these heavy hitters will move on to something else and leave the spotlight open.

Although this may seem discouraging, there are in fact many areas in which less-known writers are syndicated. As consumer interests and lifestyles change, new doors are being opened for innovative writers capable of covering emerging trends.

Most syndicates distribute a variety of columns, cartoons and features. Although the larger ones are usually only interested in running ongoing material, smaller ones often accept short features and one-shots in addition to continuous columns. Specialized syndicates—those that deal with a single area such as business—often sell to magazines, trade journals and other business publications as well as to newspapers.

The winning combination

In presenting yourself and your work, note that most syndicated columnists start out writing for local newspapers. Many begin as staff writers, develop a following in a particular area, and are then picked up by a syndicate. Before approaching a syndicate, write for a paper in your area. Be sure to develop a good collection of clips that you feel is representative of your best writing.

New ideas are paramount to syndication. Sure, you'll want to study the popular columnists to see how their pieces are structured (most are short—from 500-750 words—and really pack a punch), but don't make the mistake of imitating a well-known columnist. Syndicates are looking for original material that is timely, saleable and original. Do not submit a column to a syndicate on a subject it already covers. The more unique the topic, the greater your chances of having it picked up. Most importantly, be sure to choose a topic that interests you and one you know well.

Approaching markets

Most syndicates prefer a query letter and about six sample columns or writing samples and a SASE. You may also want to include a client list and business card if available. If you have a particular area of expertise pertinent to your submission, mention this in your letter and back it up by sending related material. For highly specialized or technical matter, provide credentials to show you are qualified to handle the topic.

In essence, syndicates act as agents or brokers for the material they handle. Writing material is usually sold as a package. The syndicate will promote and market the work to newspapers (and sometimes to magazines) and keep careful records of sales. Writers usually receive 40-60% of gross receipts. Some syndicates may also pay a small salary or flat fee for one-shot items.

Syndicates usually acquire all rights to accepted material, although a few are now offering writers and artists the option of retaining ownership. In selling all rights, writers give up ownership and future use of their creations. Consequently, sale of all rights is not the best deal for writers, and has been the reason many choose to work with syndicates that buy less restrictive rights. Before signing a contract with a syndicate, you may want to go over the terms with an attorney or with an agent who has a background in law. The best contracts will usually offer the writer a percentage of gross receipts (as opposed to net receipts) and will not bind the writer for longer than five years.

The self-syndication option

Many writers choose to self-syndicate. This route allows you to retain all rights, and gives you the freedom of a business owner. But as a self-syndicated writer, you must also act as your own manager, marketing team and sales force. You must develop mailing lists, and a pricing, billing and collections structure.

Payment is usually negotiated on a case-by-case basis. Small newspapers may offer only $10-20 per column, but larger papers may pay much more (for more information on pay rates, see How Much Should I Charge? on page 44). The number of papers you deal with is only limited by your marketing budget and your tenacity.

If you self-syndicate, be aware that some newspapers are not copyrighted, so you should copyright your own material. It's less expensive to copyright columns as a collection than individually. For more information on copyright procedures, see Copyrighting Your Writing in the Business of Writing section.

Additional information on newspaper markets can be found in *The Gale Directory of Publications* (available in most libraries). The *Editor & Publisher Syndicate Directory* (11 W. 19th St., New York NY 10011) has a list of syndicates, contact names and features; the weekly magazine, *Editor & Publisher*, also has news articles about syndicates and can provide you with information about changes and events in the industry.

For information on syndicates not included in *Writer's Market*, see Syndicates/ Changes '95-'96 at the end of this section.

ADVENTURE FEATURE SYNDICATE, 329 Harvery Dr., Glendale CA 91206. (818)551-0077. Editor: Vicky D. Letcher. Estab. 1976. Reports in 1 month. Buys all rights, first North American serial rights and second serial (reprint) rights.
Needs: Fiction (spies), fillers (adventure/travel), action/adventure comic strips and graphic novels. Submit complete ms.

ALLIED FEATURE SYNDICATE, P.O. Drawer 48, Joplin MO 64802-0048. (417)673-2860. Fax: (800)628-1705. Editor: Robert J. Blanset. Contact: Irene Blanset. Estab. 1944. 70% freelance written on contract; 30% on a one-time basis. Works with 36 writers/year. Works with 30 previously unpublished writers/year. Syndicates to newspapers (60%); magazines (30%); inhouse organs (10%). Submissions will be returned "only on request." Reports in 6 weeks. Buys all rights.
Needs: Buys news articles, cartoon strips, panels and features. Must be directly related to business, electronics, human resources, computers or quality and test design. All other non-related materials will be rejected and returned to sender if SASE is included. Query with clips of published work. Pays 50% author's percentage "after production costs" or 5¢/word. Currently syndicates "A Little Prayer," by Mary Alice Bennett (religious filler); "Murphy's Law of Electronics," by Nic Frising (cartoon panel).
Tips: "Allied Feature Syndicate is one of very few agencies syndicating electronics manufacturing targeted materials and information."

‡AMERICAN CROSSWORD FEDERATION, P.O. Box 69, Massapequa Park NY 11762. Contact: Stanley Newman. Estab. 1983. 100% freelance written by writers on a one-time basis. Buys 400 features/year. Works with 50 writers/year. Works with 20 new previously unpublished writers/year. Syndicates to magazines, newspapers. Query for electronic submissions. Reports in 2 months. Buys all rights. Writer's guidelines for #10 SASE. Submit complete ms.
Needs: Crosswords. Pays $40-300. Currently syndicates *Newsday Crossword* and *Tough Cryptics*, by Stanley Newman.
Tips: Send for style sheet *first*.

‡AMERIPRESS/AMERIPRENSA (Latin America And Spain), P.O. Box 6363, Virginia Beach VA 23450-8443. Editors: Russ Mathena and Marjorie Leon de Mathena. Estab. 1991. 100% from freelancers, 50% by writers on a one-time basis. 20% photos. Syndicates to magazines and newspapers. Send all material on IBM

ASCII diskettes with hard copy. Reports in 1-2 months. All rights, first North American serial or second (reprints) rights.

Needs: Magazine and newspaper features, news items and sexuality articles considered. Single (one-shot) features and article series on spec only. Spanish and English (translations 10% less). Query or submit complete ms on IBM ASCII diskette with hard copy. If you want your material returned, send SASE. Pays 50% author's percentage for articles with all expenses from syndicate share. 60% for photos. "We are working more closely with foreign as well as the domestic market. We have good relations with European, Japanese and New Zealand syndicates as well."

AMPERSAND COMMUNICATIONS, 2311 S. Bayshore Dr., Miami FL 33133-4728. (305)285-2200. Editor: George Leposky. Estab. 1982. 100% written by writers on contract. "We syndicate only our own material at present, but we will consider working with others whose material is exceptionally good. Novices need not contact us." Syndicates to magazines and newspapers. Query for electronic submissions. Reports in up to 4 months. Buys all rights. Writer's guidelines $2 for SASE.

Needs: Newspaper columns, travel, business, science and health, regional cuisine, natural foods, environment; typically 500-750 words, rarely up to 1,500 words. Material from other writers must complement, not compete with, our own travel, business, environment, health and home improvement columns. Query with clips of published work and complete ms—samples of proposal columns. Pays 50% of net after production. "Note: For columns requiring photos, the writer must supply to us the required number of images and quantity of each image at his/her expense. We are not in the photo duplication business and will not provide this service." Currently syndicates Traveling the South, by George and Rosalie Leposky (travel); Business Insights, by Lincoln Avery (business); Food for Thought (cooking) by Rosalie Leposky; HealthScan, by George Leposky (health); EnviroScan, by George Leposky (environment); House and Home, by Lynne Avery (home improvement).

Tips: "Be an *excruciatingly* good writer; good alone isn't enough. Find a niche that doesn't seem to be covered. Do research to cover your topics in-depth, but in few words. The reader's attention span is shriveling, and so are ad lineage and column inches available for syndicated features."

ARKIN MAGAZINE SYNDICATE INC., 500 Bayview Dr., Suite F, N. Miami Beach FL 33160-4747. Editorial Director: Joseph Arkin. Estab. 1958. 20% freelance written by writers on contract; 80% freelance written on a one-time basis. "We regularly purchase articles from several freelancers for syndication in trade and professional magazines." Accepts previously published submissions, "if all rights haven't been sold." Reports in 3 weeks. Buys all North American magazine and newspaper rights.

Needs: Magazine articles (nonfiction, 750-2,200 words), directly relating to business problems common to several different types of businesses and photos (purchased with written material). "We are in dire need of the 'how-to' business article." Will not consider article series or columns. Submit complete ms; "SASE required with all submissions." Pays 3-10¢/word; $5-10 for photos; "actually, line drawings are preferred instead of photos." **Pays on acceptance.**

Tips: "Study a representative group of trade magazines to learn style, needs and other facets of the field."

ARTHUR'S INTERNATIONAL, 2613 High Range Dr., Las Vegas NV 89134. (702)228-3731. Editor: Marvin C. Arthur. Syndicates to newspapers and magazines. Reports in 1 week. "SASE must be enclosed." Buys all rights.

Needs: Fillers, magazine columns, magazine features, newspaper columns, newspaper features and news items. "We specialize in timely nonfiction and historical stories, and columns, preferably the unusual. We utilize humor. Travel stories utilized in 'World Traveler.' " Buys one-shot features and article series. "Since the majority of what we utilize is column or short story length, it is better to submit the article so as to expedite consideration and reply. Do not send any lengthy manuscripts." Pays 50% of net sales, salary on some contracted work and flat rate on commissioned work. Currently syndicates "Marv," by Marvin C. Arthur (informative, humorous, commentary); "Humoresque," by Don Alexander (humorous); and "World Spotlight," by Don Kampel (commentary).

Tips: "We do not use cartoons but we are open for fine illustrators."

BUDDY BASCH FEATURE SYNDICATE, 771 West End Ave., New York NY 10025-5572. (212)666-2300. Editor/Publisher: Buddy Basch. Estab. 1965. 10% written on contract; 2% freelance written by writers on a one-time basis. Buys 10 features/year. Works with 3-4 previously unpublished writers annually. Syndicates to print media: newspapers, magazines, giveaways, house organs, etc. Reports in 3 weeks. Buys first North American serial rights.

• Most stories are done inhouse.

Needs: Magazine features, newspaper features, and one-shot ideas that are really different. "Try to make them unusual, unique, real 'stoppers,' not the usual stuff." Will consider one-shots and article series on travel, entertainment, human interest—"the latter, a wide umbrella that makes people stop and read the piece. Different, unusual and unique are the key words, not what the *writer* thinks is, but which have been done nine million times before." Query. Pays 20-50% commission. Additional payment for photos $10-50. Currently syndicates It Takes a Woman, by Frances Scott (woman's feature), Travel Whirl, Scramble Steps (puzzle) and others.

Tips: "Never mind what your mother, fiancé or friend thinks is good. If it has been done before and is old hat, it has no chance. Do some research and see if there are a dozen similar items in the press. Don't just try a very close 'switch' on them. You don't fool anyone with this. There are fewer and fewer newspapers, with more and more people vying for the available space. But there's *always* room for a really good, *different* feature or story. Trouble is few writers (amateurs especially) know a good piece, I'm sorry to say. Read *Writer's Market*, carefully, noting which syndicate might be interested in the type of feature you are submitting. That will save you time and money and get you better results."

BLACK PRESS SERVICE, INC., 166 Madison Ave., New York NY 10016. (212)686-6850. Editor: Roy Thompson. Estab. 1966. 10% written on contract; 10% freelance written on a one-time basis. Buys hundreds of features/year. Works with hundreds of writers/year. Syndicates to magazines, newspapers and radio. Reports in 2 months. Buys all rights. Submit complete ms.
Needs: Magazine and newspaper columns; news items; magazine and newspaper features; radio broadcast material. Purchases single (one shot) features and articles series (current events oriented). Pays variable flat rate. Currently syndicates Bimonthly Report, by staff (roundup of minority-oriented news).

‡BOOTSTRAPS, 249 W. 21st St., New York NY 10011. Editor: William Neal. Estab. 1979. 100% freelance written by writers on a one-time basis. Buys 12 features/year. Works with 3 writers/year. Works with 3 new previously unpublished writers/year. Syndicates to newspapers. Reports in 1 month. Buys first North American serial rights. Writer's guidelines for #10 SASE. Query only.
Needs: Newspaper columns. Purchase single (one shot) features. Pays author's percentage 50%.

‡CENTRE ICE COMMUNICATIONS, 43½ Sentinel Rd., Lake Placid NY 12946. (518)523-4289. Managing Editor: Kyle Woodlief. Estab. 1992. Syndicates to magazines, newspapers. Query for electronic submissions. Reports in 2 months. Buys all rights. Writer's guidelines for #10 SASE. Query with clips of published work.

‡CHICAGO SUN-TIMES FEATURES SYNDICATE, 401 N. Wabash, Suite 532A, Chicago IL 60611. (312)321-2890. Contact: Elizabeth Owens-Schiele. 20% written by writers on contract. Works with 10 writers/year. Works with 10 new previously unpublished writers/year. Syndicates to newspapers. Query for electronic submissions. Reports in 2-3 months. Buys all rights. Writer's guidelines for #10 SASE. Submit complete ms or query with clips of published work.
Needs: Newspaper columns and features, comics, editorial cartoons, "unique" columns. Does not purchase either single (one shot) features or articles series. Pays 50% author's percentage. Currently syndicates All That Zazz, by Jeffrey Zaslow (advice column); Sports Columns, by various authors (sports features); Gaming, by John Grochowski (gambling advice). Sportswriters: Tim Weigel, Rick Telander. Cartoons: Dick Clark's Rock, Roll and Remember; Pling; the chidren's cartoon; Batch, the single's cartoon.
Tips: "The market is highly competitive. Before you pursue syndication check the E&P syndicate directory for the number of similar columns. Send complete packages of published/unpublished clips to syndicates. Recognize that newsprint costs are up almost 40% and sales are down. Remember money in syndication is made in volume."

CLEAR CREEK FEATURES, Box 3303, Grass Valley CA 95945. Editor: Mike Drummond. Estab. 1988. 50% written on contract; no one shots. Buys 0 features/year. Works with 5 writers/year. Works with 2 previously unpublished writers/year. Syndicates to magazines and newspapers. Query for electronic submissions. Reports in 1 month. Buys first North American serial, all and second serial (reprint) rights. Submit clips of published work.
Needs: Fiction, magazine and newspaper columns, magazine features. Pays 50% author's percentage. Currently syndicates Coping in the Country, by Mike Drummond (humor); The Voice of Experience, by various (humor/commentary), This Old Klutz, by various (humor).
Tips: "Identify a niche and dig in!"

‡COMMUNITY PRESS SERVICE, 300 Strathmore, P.O. Box 639, Frankfort KY 40602. (502)223-1736. Contact: Phyllis Cornett. Estab. 1990. 30% written by writers on contract; 10% freelance written by writers on a one-time basis. Buys 600 features/year. Works with 10-15 writers/year. Syndicates to newspapers. Query for electronic submissions. Reports in 1-2 months. Buys all rights. Writer's guidelines for free. Query with clips of published work.
Needs: Fillers, newspaper columns and features. Purchases single panel cartoons. Pays flat rate depending on length of article. Currently syndicates P.C. Primer, by Roger Creighton (computer column); The Bible Speaks, by Rev. Lawrence Althouse (religious); Calling Colleen, by Linette Wheeler (advice).

‡COMPUTER USER NEWS BUREAU, 220 S. Sixth St., Suite 500, Minneapolis MN 55402. (612)336-9286. Contact: Krista Havenstein. Estab. 1982. 100% written by writers on contract. Buys 150 features/year. Works with 40 writers/year. Syndicates to magazines, newspapers. Query for electronic submissions. Reports in 1-

4 months. Buys all rights. No writer's guidelines. Submit complete ms or query with clips of published work.

Needs: Magazine features (high technology/computing only, business end-user orientation). Pays 10% author's percentage or minimum guarantee of $50-300. Currently syndicates Computer Pursuits, by Nelson King (industry observation and predictions); Down to Business, by Steve Deyo (industry and Human-factors observations); CD-ROM, by various authors (CD-ROM reviews).

Tips: "We cover the whole computer industry, all platforms from a business user perspective. We take 80% of our material from longstanding board of contributing editors. Spots are limited and often winnowed for contributing writers. We are journalists, not technical writers or PC hacks. Send samples or finished piece with SASE and don't waste our time. We will respond."

CONTINENTAL FEATURES/CONTINENTAL NEWS SERVICE, 341 W. Broadway, Suite 265, San Diego CA 92101-3802. (619)492-8696. Editor-in-Chief: Gary P. Salamone. Estab. 1981. 100% written on contract. "Writers who offer the kind and quality of writing we seek stand an equal chance regardless of experience." Syndicates to the print media. Reports in 1 month. Writer's guidelines for #10 SASE.

Needs: Magazine and newspaper features. "Feature material should fit the equivalent of one-quarter to one-half standard newspaper page, and Continental News considers an ultra-liberal or ultra-conservative slant inappropriate." Query. Pays 70% author's percentage. Currently syndicates News and Comment, by Charles Hampton Savage (general news commentary/analysis); Continental Viewpoint, by staff; Portfolio, (cartoon/caricature art); Travelers Checks, by Ann Hattes; Middle East Cable, by Mike Maggio; and InVideo, by Harley Lond; over 50 features in all.

● This syndicate is considering fewer proposals for one-time projects. Virtually all of their new feature creators are signed to work on a continuing basis.

Tips: "Continental News seeks country profiles/background articles that pertain to foreign countries. Writers who possess such specific knowledge/personal experience stand an excellent chance of acceptance, provided they can focus the political, economic and social issues. We welcome them to submit their proposals. We foresee the possibility of diversifying our feature package by representing writers and feature creators through a team-marketing network nationwide. We have plans to introduce 40 new text features alone."

COPLEY NEWS SERVICE, P.O. Box 190, San Diego CA 92112. (619)293-1818. Fax: (619)293-2322. Editorial Manager: Glenda Winders. 85% written by stringers on contract; 15% freelance written on a one-time basis. Offers 200 features/week. Sells to newspapers and online services. Reports in 1-2 months. Buys first rights.

Needs: Fillers, newspaper columns and features. Looking for video, food, travel, opinion, new ideas. Subjects include interior design, outdoor recreation, fashion, antiques, real estate, pets, gardening. Query with clips of published work. Pays $50-100 flat rate or $400 salary/month.

‡CRAFT PATTERNS, INC., 3545 Stern Ave., St. Charles IL 60174. (708)584-3334. Marketing Rep: Marsha Sidmore. Estab. 1940. 25% written by writers on contract. Buys 1 feature/year. Works with 2 writers/year. Syndicates to newspapers. Query for electronic submissions. Reports in 2 months. Buys all rights. Query with clips of published work.

Needs: Fillers and newspaper features. Pay negotiable. Currently syndicates "Project-of-the-Week," by Woodley Smith (woodworking project feature); "Home Design-of-the-Week," by M. Sidmore (home plan feature).

CREATE-A-CRAFT, P.O. Box 330008, Ft. Worth TX 76163. (817)292-1855. Contact: Editor. Estab. 1967. 5% written by writers on contract; 50% freelance written. Buys 5 features/year. Works with 3 writers/year. Works with 3 previously unpublished writers/year. Syndicates to magazines and newspapers. Reports in 4 months. Submissions will not be returned. Buys all rights. Writer's guidelines $2.50 for #10 SASE. Prefers agented submissions only (submit complete ms).

Needs: Magazine and newspaper columns and features. "Looking for material on appraising, art, decorative arts, politics (how politics affect art only); 400-2,000 words. Comics must be in strip form only." Pays $6-10 flat hourly rate (depending on project). All work is work-for-hire. Currently syndicates Appraisals by Abramson (appraisal column); Those Characters from Cowtown (cartoon); Rojo (cartoon); Golden Gourmets (cartoon); Gallant Gators (cartoon). Author is always listed as Create-A-Craft (no byline given).

Tips: "Know the market you are writing for."

CREATIVE SYNDICATION SERVICES, P.O. Box 40, Eureka MO 63025-0040. (314)587-7126. Editor: Debra Holly. Estab. 1977. 10% written on contract; 50% freelance written on a one-time basis. Syndicates to magazines, newspapers and radio. Query for electronic submissions. Reports in 1 month. Buys all rights. Currently syndicates The Weekend Workshop, by Ed Baldwin; Woodcrafting, by Ed Baldwin; and Classified Clippers, a feature exclusive for the Classified Section of newspapers.

Tips: "We are looking for writers who do crafts, woodworking, needle-crafts and sewing."

CRICKET COMMUNICATIONS, INC., P.O. Box 527, Ardmore PA 19003-0527. (610)789-2480 or (215)747-6684. Fax: (215)747-7082. Editor: J.D. Krickett. Estab. 1975. 10% written on contract; 10% freelance written on a one-time basis. Works with 2-3 previously unpublished writers/year. Syndicates to trade magazines and newspapers. Reports in 1 month. Buys all rights.

Needs: Magazine and newspaper columns and features, news items—all tax and financial-oriented (700-1,500 words); also newspaper columns, features and news items directed to small business. Query with clips of published work. Pays $50-500. Currently syndicates Hobby/Business, by Mark E. Battersby (tax and financial); Farm Taxes, by various authors; and Small Business Taxes, by Mark E. Battersby.

DANY NEWS SERVICE, 22 Lesley Dr., Syosset NY 11791. Editor: David Nydick. Estab. 1966. Buys 10% from freelancers. Buys 30 features/year (from freelancers). Syndicates to newspapers. Reports in 1 month. Buys all rights. Submit complete ms.

Needs: Newspaper columns and features, how-to (help your child). Pays $50 minimum guarantee. Currently syndicates You, Your Child and School; You, Your Child and Sports; and You, Your Child and Entertainment, (how-to help your child).

EDITORIAL CONSULTANT SERVICE, P.O. Box 524, West Hempstead NY 11552-1206. (516)481-5487. Editorial Director: Arthur A. Ingoglia. Estab. 1964. 40% written on contract; 25% freelance written on a one-time basis. "We work with 75 writers in the US and Canada." Adds about 10 new columnists/year. Syndicates material to an average of 60 newspapers, magazines, automotive trade and consumer publications, and radio stations with circulation of 50,000-575,000. Buys all rights. Writer's guidelines for #10 SASE. Reports in 1-2 months.

Needs: Magazine and newspaper columns and features, news items, radio broadcast material. Prefers carefully documented material with automotive slant. Also considers automotive trade features. Will consider article series. No horoscope, child care, lovelorn or pet care. Query. Author's percentage varies; usually averages 50%. Additional payment for 8×10 b&w and color photos accepted with ms. Submit 2-3 columns. Currently syndicates Let's Talk About Your Car, by R. Hite.

Tips: "Emphasis is placed on articles and columns with an automotive slant. We prefer consumer-oriented features, how to save money on your car, what every woman should know about her car, how to get more miles per gallon, etc."

‡EUROPA PRESS NEWS SERVICE, Clasificador 5, Tajamar Providencia, Santiago, Chile. (562)235-2902 or (562)235-1584. Fax: (562)235-1731. Editor: Maria Marta Raggio. Estab. 1963. 50% freelance written by writers on a one-time basis. Syndicates to magazines and newspapers. Reports in 3 months. Buys second serial rights for Latin America and other customers in Europe, Far East. Publishes reprints of previously published articles. Send tearsheet of article. For reprints, pays 50% of the amount paid for an original article.

Needs: Magazine features (science, technology, celebrities: interviews with candid shots), newspaper features, recipes, handiworks, etc., with color photos. Buys one-shot features and article series. "Travel, adventure, human-interest stories with pictures. Query with clips of published work or submit complete ms. Pays 50% author's percentage. Currently syndicates Moda al dia, by Claudia Moda (color photo with captions); Household Advice, by Penny Orchard (column with illustrations); and The World Today, by London Express (articles with b&w pictures).

Tips: "We are seeking good, up-to-date articles about technology, science, medicine, business, marketing; also, interviews with celebrities in show business, politics, sports preferably with color photos. Do not submit travel articles unless with color transparencies."

FOTOPRESS, INDEPENDENT NEWS SERVICE INTERNATIONAL, Box 1268, Station Q, Toronto, Ontario M4T 2P4 Canada. (905)935-2887. Fax: (905)935-2770. Executive Editor: John Milan Kubik. Estab. 1983. 50% written on contract; 25% freelance written on a one-time basis. Works with 30% previously unpublished writers. Syndicates to domestic and international magazines, newspapers, radio, TV stations and motion picture industry. Reports in 2 months. Buys variable rights. Writer's guidelines for $3 money order, SAE with IRC.

Needs: Fillers, magazine and newspaper columns and features, news items, radio broadcast material, documentary, the environment, travel and art. Buys one-shot and article series for international politics, scientists, celebrities and religious leaders. Query or submit complete ms. Pays 50-75% author's percentage. Offers $5-150 for accompanying ms.

Tips: "We need all subjects from 500-3,000 words. Photos are purchased with or without features. All writers are regarded respectfully—their success is our success."

GLENMOOR MEDIA GROUP, 733 Main St., Suite 173, Willits CA 95490. (707)459-6027. General Manager: R.C. Moorhead. Estab. 1989. 25% written on contract; 25% freelance written on a one-time basis. Buys 10-15 features/year. Works with 10 writers/year. Works with 0 previously unpublished writers/year. Syndicates to magazines and newspapers. Reports in 3 months. Buys first North American serial rights. Query with clips of published work.

Needs: Newspaper columns, magazine and single features. Pays 50% author's percentage. Pays $5-50 for photos. Currently syndicates On The Road with Ron Moorhead, by Ron Moorhead (automotive road tests); Women & Wheels, by G.A. Blake (automotive topics for women); Automobiles & Questions, by Ron

Moorhead (automotive Q&A); Road Warriors, by Tom Lankard and Ron Moorhead (automotive-related subjects).

‡GRIFFITH NEWS FEATURE SERVICE WORLDWIDE, 234 Fifth Ave., New York NY 10001. Editor-in-Chief: Bill Griffith. Estab. 1980. Syndicates to magazines, newspapers, radio, TV, world-wide syndicates. Submissions not returned. Buys first North American serial or second serial (reprint) rights. "Will look at anything, good! Open. Previously published works not required or necessary.
Needs: Fiction, magazine columns and features, newspaper columns and features, film format. Special interest: documented angel encounters and healing. Length: 800-1,000 words. Pays only if and when sold. Currently syndicates Feature Story, by Bill Griffith (all subjects); Feature Story, by Vickie and Bill (all subjects); Fix It, by Jim Griffith (housing construction and repairs).

‡GSM FEATURES, P.O. Box 104, Oradell NJ 07649-0104. (201)385-2000. Editorial Director: Bob Nesoff. Estab. 1968. 100% written by writers on contract. Buys 300 pieces/year. Syndicates to newspapers. Reports in 1 month. Buys first North American serial rights. Writer's guidelines for SASE.
Needs: Newspaper columns and features. Does not purchase single (one-shot) features. Query only with SASE. Pays flat rate $25-100. Currently syndicates Traveling, by Bob and Sandy Nesoff (weekly travel column); Cooking, by Janine Draizin (recipes); Powder Trails, by Wendy Naimaister and Barbara Thorson (18-30 year old audience ski column); Books, by Ross Warren (book review column); Skiing by Bob Nesoff (weekly ski column); The Scene, by Karen Michelle (weekly youth column 17-25 year old audience); Wine & Dine, by Gail Gerson (weekly restaurant column); Stage & Screen, by Ed Curtis, Hollywood & Broadway Insider Info Reviews of Movies & Stage, (weekly column).
Tips: "Trend toward more family-oriented and less expensive activities."

‡THE HARLEM VALLEY HUMOR FACTORY, P.O. Box 822, Pawling NY 12564. Editor/Publisher: Robert J. Lee. Estab. 1995. 100% freelance written by writers on a one-time basis. Buys 40+ features/year. Works with 40+ writers/year. Works with 10-30+ new previously unpublished writers/year. Syndicates to magazines. Reports in 1 month. Buys first North American serial rights or will negotiate second serial (reprint) rights. Writer's guidelines for #10 SASE. Query only.
Needs: Fillers, poems/song lyrics, cartoons. Buys single (one-shot) features. "Good quality work will always be considered regardless of topic or length. We prefer humor and (or) topical material of liberal slant. We will publish controversial material often unacceptable to other markets." Pays $5-15/outlet (price determined by length and originality). "Presently developing several regular features, each of which will be done by various freelance authors."
Tips: "We offer opportunities for previously unpublished writers—particularly those doing work unsuited for the mainstream press."

HISPANIC LINK NEWS SERVICE, 1420 N St. NW, Washington DC 20005. (202)234-0280. Fax: (202)234-4090. Publisher: Charles A. Ericksen. Editor: Jonathan Higuera. Estab. 1980. 50% freelance written on contract; 50% freelance written on a one-time basis. Buys 156 columns and features/year. Works with 50 writers/year; 5 previously unpublished writers. Syndicates to 100 newspapers and magazines with circulations ranging from 5,000 to 300,000. Reports in up to 1 month. Buys second serial (reprint) or negotiable rights. For reprints, send photocopy of article. Pays 100% of the amount paid for an original article ($25 for guest columns). Free writer's guidelines.
Needs: Newspaper columns and features. One-shot features and article series. "We prefer 650-700 word op/ed analysis or new features geared to a general national audience, but focus on issue or subject of particular interest to Hispanic Americans. Some longer pieces accepted occasionally." Query or submit complete ms. Pays $25-100. Currently syndicates Hispanic Link, by various authors (opinion and/or feature columns).
Tips: "We would especially like to get topical material and vignettes relating to Hispanic presence and progress in the United States. Provide insights on Hispanic experience geared to a general audience. Of the columns we accept, 85 to 90% are authored by Hispanics; the Link presents Hispanic viewpoints and showcases Hispanic writing talent through its subscribing newspapers and magazines. Copy should be submitted in English. We syndicate in English and Spanish."

HOLLYWOOD INSIDE SYNDICATE, P.O. Box 49957, Los Angeles CA 90049-0957. (909)678-6237. Fax: (909)678-6237. Editor: John Austin. Estab. 1968. 10% written on contract; 40% freelance written on a one-time basis. Purchases entertainment-oriented mss for syndication to newspapers in San Francisco, Philadelphia, Detroit, Montreal, London, Sydney, Manila, South Africa, etc. Accepts previously published submissions, if published in the US and Canada only. Reports in 3 months.
Needs: News items (column items concerning entertainment—motion picture—personalities and jet setters for syndicated column; 750-800 words). Also considers series of 1,500-word articles; "suggest descriptive query first. We are also looking for off-beat travel pieces (with pictures) but not on areas covered extensively in the Sunday supplements; not luxury cruise liners but lower cost cruises. We also syndicate nonfiction book subjects—sex, travel, etc., to overseas markets. No fiction. Must have b&w photos with submissions if possible." Also require 1,500-word celebrity profiles on internationally recognized celebrities. We stress

internationally." Query or submit complete ms. Currently syndicates Books of the Week column and "Cele-bri-Quotes," "Movie Trivia Quiz," "Hollywood Inside."

Tips: "Study the entertainment pages of Sunday (and daily) newspapers to see the type of specialized material we deal in. Perhaps we are different from other syndicates, but we deal with celebrities. No 'I' journalism such as 'when I spoke to Cloris Leachman.' Many freelancers submit material from the 'dinner theater' and summer stock circuit of 'gossip type' items from what they have observed about the 'stars' or featured players in these productions—how they act off stage, who they romance, etc. We use this material."

‡HYDE PARK MEDIA, Chicago Metro News Services, 1314 Howard St., Suite 2, Chicago IL 60626-1425. 10% freelance written by writers on a one-time basis. Syndicates to midwestern newspapers and magazines. Reports in 1 month. Buys first and second serial rights.

Needs: Unusual, off-beat magazine features (1,500-3,000 words) and newspaper features with a regional hook (750-1,500 words). Buys single (one-shot) features only. Send SASE with query. Pays 50% commission on sale.

Tips: "Please read 'Needs' paragraph above before sending material. Why waste anyone's time?"

‡INTERNATIONAL PHOTO NEWS, 193 Sandpiper Ave., Royal Palm Beach FL 33411-2937. (407)793-3424. Editor: Elliott Kravetz. Estab. 1974. 10% written by freelance writers under contract. Buys 52 features/year. Works with 25 previously unpublished writers/year. Syndicates to newspapers. Query for electronic submissions. Reports in up to 3 months. Buys second serial (reprint) rights. Writer's guidelines for SASE.

Needs: Magazine columns and features (celebrity), newspaper columns and features (political or celebrity), news items (political). Buys one-shot features. Query with clips of published work. Pays 50% author's percentage. Pays $5 for photos accepted with ms. Currently syndicates Celebrity Interview, by Jay and Elliott Kravetz.

Tips: "Go after celebrities who are on the cover on major magazines."

INTERNATIONAL PUZZLE FEATURES, 740 Van Rensselaer Ave., Niagara Falls NY 14305. Contact: Pat Battaglia. Estab. 1990. 0% written on contract; 5-10% freelance written on a one-time basis. Buys 10 features/year. Works with 0 writers/year. Works with all new previously unpublished writers. Syndicates to newspapers. Reports in 1 month. Writer's guidelines for #10 SASE. Submit complete ms.

Needs: Concisely written, entertaining word puzzles. Pays $5 flat rate/puzzle. Currently syndicates If You're So Smart . . ., by Pat Battaglia (word puzzles).

Tips: "We are not interested in crossword, word search, cryptogram, mathematical or trivia puzzles."

INTERPRESS OF LONDON AND NEW YORK, 400 Madison Ave., New York NY 10017-1909. (212)832-2839. Editor: Jeffrey Blyth. Estab. 1971. 50% freelance written on contract; 50% freelance written on a one-time basis. Works with 3-6 previously unpublished writers/year. Buys British and European rights mostly, but can handle world rights. Accepts previously published submissions "for overseas." Pays on publication or agreement of sale. Reports in 3 weeks.

Needs: "Unusual nonfiction stories and photos for British and European press. Picture stories, for example, on such 'Americana' as a 5-year-old evangelist; the 800-pound 'con-man'; the nude-male calendar; tallest girl in the world; interviews with pop celebrities such as Madonna, Michael Jackson, Bill Cosby, Tom Selleck, Cher, Priscilla Presley, Bette Midler, Eddie Murphy, Liza Minelli; also news of stars on top TV shows; cult subjects such as voodoo; college fads; anything amusing or offbeat. Extracts from books such as Earl Wilson's *Show Business Laid Bare*, inside-Hollywood type series ('Secrets of the Stuntmen'). Real life adventure dramas ('Three Months in an Open Boat,' 'The Air Crash Cannibals of the Andes'). No length limits—short or long, but not too long. Query or submit complete ms. Payment varies; depending on whether material is original, or world rights. Pays top rates, up to several thousand dollars, for exclusive material."

Photos: Purchased with or without features. Captions required. Standard size prints. Pay $50-100, but no limit on exclusive material.

Tips: "Be alert to the unusual story in your area—the sort that interests the American tabloids (and also the European press)."

M GROUP FEATURES SYNDICATE, P.O. Box 12486, San Antonio TX 78212-0486. Fax: (210)(210)737-1404. E-mail: mgroupfs@aol.com. Contact: Randall Sherman. Estab. 1994. Syndicates to publications in lesbian, bisexual, gay and transgendered communities. Query for electronic submissions. Reports in 2 months. Buys first North American serial rights, all rights, second serial (reprint) rights. Guidelines for SASE. Submit complete ms.

Needs: Fiction (500-1,000 words); magazine columns (500-1,000 words); Newspaper columns (500-1,000 words); fillers (100-500 words); magazine features (500-1,800 words); newspaper features (500-1,800 words); cartoon strips and panels; word puzzles; trivia quizzes. Pays 35-50% authors percentage or flat rate $5-25. Pays $5-100 for photos.

Tips: "Writing about the positive aspects of alternative lifestyles is most important, because raising the consciousness of the lesbian, bisexual, gay and transgendered communities will promote a higher level of self-respect. These are 'uncharted waters' that should excite new talents."

JERRY D. MEAD ENTERPRISES, P.O. Box 2796, Carson City NV 89702. (702)884-2648. Fax: (702)884-2484. E-mail: winetrader@aol.com. Contact: Jerry D. Mead. Estab. 1969. 70% written on contract; 30% freelance written on a one-time basis. Syndicates to magazines and newspapers. Query for electronic submissions. Reports immediately or not at all. Buys first North American serial rights or second serial (reprint) rights. Query only.

Needs: Magazine and newspaper columns and features; single features. Pays 50% author's percentage. Currently syndicates Mead on Wine, by Jerry D. Mead (weekly/newspaper); The Travel Trader, by E. Edward Boyd (monthly/travel); The Lodging Report, by Sandra Wechsler (monthly/travel).

MEGALO MEDIA, P.O. Box 678, Syosset NY 11791. (212)535-6811. Editor: J. Baxter Newgate. Estab. 1972. 50% written on contract; 50% freelance written on a one-time basis. Works with 5 previously unpublished writers/year. Syndicates to newspapers. Query for electronic submissions. Reports in 1 month. Buys all rights. Free writer's guidelines.

Needs: Crossword puzzles. Buys one-shot features. Submit complete ms. Pays flat rate of $150 for Sunday puzzle. Currently syndicates National Challenge, by J. Baxter Newgate (crossword puzzle); Crossword Puzzle, by J. Baxter Newgate.

MIDWEST FEATURES INC., P.O. Box 9907, Madison WI 53715-0907. Contact: Mary Bergin. Estab. 1991. 80% written on contract; 20% freelance written on a one-time basis. Buys 2-3 features/year. Works with 10-12 writers/year. Syndicates to newspapers. Query for electronic submissions. Reports in 2 months. Buys second serial (reprint) rights. Query with clips of published work.

Needs: Newspaper columns and features. Material must have a Wisconsin emphasis. Length: 500-1,000 words. Purchases single (one shot) features. Ideal length: 750 words. Series in past have been book excerpts ("Nathan's Christmas") and seasonal material (spring gardening, Milwaukee Brewer spring training). Pays authors 50% when reprints of previously published work are sold. Currently syndicates: Cross Country, by John Oncken (farming); Midwest Gardening, by Jan Riggenbagh (gardening); Beyond Hooks & Bullets, by Pat Durkin (outdoor sports).

NEW LIVING, P.O. Box 1519, Stony Brook NY 11790. (516)981-7232. Publisher: Christine Lynn Harvey. Estab. 1991. 20% written under contract; 5% freelance written on one-time basis. Buys 20 features/year. Works with 20 writers/year. Works with 5 previously unpublished writers/year. Syndicates to magazines, newspapers, radio, 900 phone lines. Query for electronic submissions. Reports in 6 months. Buys all rights. Query with clips of published work. Writer's guidelines for #10 SASE.

Needs: Magazine and newspaper columns and features, news items, fillers, radio broadcast material. Purchases single (one shot) features and articles series. "Looking for articles on health and fitness (nutrition, healthy recipes, sports medicine, exercise tips, running, tennis, golf, bowling, aerobics, cycling, swimming, cross-training, watersports, travel, medical advice)." Also offers to list author's business affiliation, address, and phone number in article.

Photos: Offers $25-100 for photos accepted with ms.

Tips: "Be highly qualified in the area that you are writing about. If you are going to write a medical column, you must be a doctor, or at least affiliated with a nationally recognized medical organization."

NEW YORK TIMES SYNDICATION SALES CORP., 122 E. 42nd St., New York NY 10168. (212)449-3300. Executive Editor: Gloria Brown Anderson. Syndicates only select one-shot articles. Buys second serial (reprint) rights.

Needs: Previously published magazine and newspaper features of between 750 and 1,500 words. Primarily trend, holiday and lifestyle features; and interviews with celebrities or notable personalities. Submission must have been published within the previous year. Payment to author is varied. Send tearsheets of article. Photos are welcome with articles. Enclose a self-addressed stamped envelope.

Tips: "Topics should cover universal markets and either be by a well-known writer or have an off-beat quality."

NEWS FLASH INTERNATIONAL, INC., Division of the Observer Newspapers, 2262 Centre Ave., Bellmore NY 11710-3400. (516)679-9888. Fax: (516)731-0338. Editor: Jackson B. Pokress. Estab. 1960. 25% written on contract; 25% freelance written on a one-time basis. Supplies material to Observer newspapers and overseas publications. Works with 10-20 previously unpublished writers annually. "Contact editor prior to submission to allow for space if article is newsworthy." Pays on publication. Reports in 2 months.

Nonfiction: "We have been supplying a 'ready-for-camera' sports page (tabloid size) complete with column and current sports photos on a weekly basis to many newspapers on Long Island, as well as pictures and written material to publications in England and Canada. Payment for assignments is based on the article. Payments vary from $20 for a feature of 800 words. Our sports stories feature in-depth reporting as well as book reviews on this subject. We are always in the market for good photos, sharp and clear, action photos of boxing, wrestling, football, baseball and hockey. We cover all major league ball parks during the baseball and football seasons. We are accredited to the Mets, Yanks, Jets and Giants. During the winter we cover basketball and hockey and all sports events at the Nassau Coliseum."

Photos: Purchased on assignment; captions required. Uses "good quality 8×10 b&w glossy prints; good choice of angles and lenses." Pays $7.50 minimum for b&w photos.

Tips: "Submit articles which are fresh in their approach on a regular basis with good quality black and white glossy photos if possible; include samples of work. We prefer well-researched, documented stories with quotes where possible. We are interested in profiles and bios on woman athletes. There is a big interest in this in the foreign market. Women's boxing, volleyball and basketball are major interests."

NEWSPAPER ENTERPRISE ASSOCIATION, INC., Dept. WM, 200 Park Ave., New York NY 10166-0079. (212)692-3700. Editorial Director: Diana Loevy. 100% written by writers on contract. "We provide a comprehensive package of features to mostly small- and medium-sized newspapers." Reports in 6 weeks. Buys all rights.

Needs: "Columns purchased must fill a need in our feature lineup and must appeal to a wide variety of people in all parts of the country. We are most interested in lively writing. We are also interested in features that are not merely copies of other features already on the market. The writer must know his or her subject. Any writer who has a feature that meets all of those requirements should send a few copies of the feature to us, along with his or her plans for the column and some background material on the writer." Current columnists include Hodding Carter, III, Dr. Peter Gott, Ben Wattenberg and William Rusher. Current comics include Born Loser, Frank & Ernest, Eek & Meek, Kit 'n' Carlyle, Berry's World, Arlo and Janis, and Snafu.

Tips: "We get enormous numbers of proposals for first person columns—slice of life material with lots of anecdotes. While many of these columns are big successes in local newspapers, it's been our experience that they are extremely difficult to sell nationally. Most papers seem to prefer to buy this sort of column from a talented local writer."

SENIOR WIRE, Clear Mountain Communications, 2377 Elm St., Denver CO 80207. (303)355-3882. Fax: (303)355-2720. E-mail: 72370.3520@compuserve.com. Editor/Publisher: Allison St. Claire. Estab. 1988. 100% freelance written. Monthly news, information and feature syndication service to various senior publications, and companies interested in senior market. Circulation nationwide, varies per article depending on which articles are bought for publication. Pays 50% of fee for each use of ms (fees range from $5-30). Pays on publication. Buys first North American serial and simultaneous rights. Submit seasonal/holiday material 3 months in advance. Prefers mss; queries only with SASE. No payment for photos but they help increase sales. Reports in up to 3 months. Writer's guidelines $1 with SASE. Query for electronic submissions. Please indicate on top of ms if available on 3.5″ or 5.25″ floppy disk or by modem.

Needs: Does not want "anything aimed at less than age 55-plus market; anything patronizing or condescending to seniors." Manuscripts requested include: seasonal features, especially those with a nostalgic angle (750-800 words); travel tips (no more than 500-750 words); personal travel experiences as a mature traveler (700-1,000 words); personal essays and commentary (500-750 words). The following topics currently are covered by assigned columnists and similar material has little chance of immediate acceptance: national legislation; professional health, psychological, sexual, financial and legal advice; recommendations for those with physical limitations; golf; food; gardening; collectibles; and Q&A on relationships, pets, and beauty tips after 50. Accepts 12 mss in each category/year.

Tips: "That quintessential sweet little old lady in the rocking chair, Whistler's mother, was just 50 years old when she posed for that painting. Today, the average age of the Rolling Stones is 54. Most of our client papers like to emphasize active, thoughtful, concerned seniors and are currently picking up material that shows seniors living in the 'real,' i.e., contemporary, world. For example, do you have your own personal fax yet; how has a computer changed your life; what kind of new cars are you looking at? What adventures have you been involved in? What impact are you/seniors having on the world around them—and vice versa?"

‡THE SOUND OF WRITING, P.O. Box 15452, Washington DC 20003. Associate Producer: Dallas Hudgens. Estab. 1987. 100% freelance written on a one-time basis. Buys 40-50 short stories/year (short fiction of 2,500 words or fewer, preferably fewer). Packages stories for half-hour show broadcast on NPR. Receives submissions September-May *only*. Buys audio and print/audio anthology rights for 3 years. Reports in 2 months. Parent institution: The Center for the Book in the Library of Congress. (Formerly produced by the Syndicated Fiction Project.)

Needs: Fiction (short stories of 2,500 words or fewer). Submit complete mss. Pays flat rate of $300 for purchase of rights, $100 if used in print or audio anthology.

Tips: "We're looking for stories of exceptional quality that have a 'high narrative profile' (i.e., that would work well on radio)."

‡SYNDICATION ASSOCIATES, INC., P.O. Box 400, Jenks OK 74037. Contact: Ann M. Wayland. Estab. 1986. 25% written by writers on contract. Buys 0 features/year. Works with 2 writers/year. Works with 2 new previously unpublished writers/year. Syndicates to newspapers. Returns material only if requested. Buys all rights. No writer's guidelines. "Submit material at our request."

Needs: Fillers, newspaper features, craft-oriented features used for fillers and also for editorial feature. Purchases articles series. Considers woodworking, quilting, cross-stitch, fabric craft; general crafting must be complete project/pattern with instructions and illustration. Length will vary depending on project. Pays a flat rate based on the feature submitted. Will vary by project depending on length and detail. Currently syndicates Classified Crafts, by staff authors (woodworking, PVC and general craft); Toys-U-Build, by staff authors (toys; primarily woodcraft); The Woodwright, by Bob Sawyer (woodworking column).

UNITED CARTOONIST SYNDICATE, P.O. Box 7081, Corpus Christi TX 78415. (512)850-2930. Fax: (512)857-2424. Art Director: Pedro Moreno. Estab. 1975. 40% written on contract; 10% freelance written on a one-time basis. Buys 25 features/year. Works with 25 writers/year. Works with 10 new previously unpublished writers/year. Syndicates to magazines, newspapers and book stores. Buys all rights. Writer's guidelines for $10. Submit $10 first (check or money order) for guidelines, then material to Pedro Moreno.

Needs: Fiction, fillers, magazine and newspaper columns and features, news items, comic strips and panels and single features (500 words or less with brief illustration, comic strip or comic panel). Pays $25-100 for photos. Currently syndicates Ten Commandments, by James Rodriguez (comic book); Comic Guidelines, by Pedro Moreno (guidelines); Caricatures, by Pedro Moreno (caricatures).

Tips: "Do not submit handwritten material or bad copies. Send clean typewritten material."

WHITEGATE FEATURES SYNDICATE, 71 Faunce Dr., Providence RI 02906. (401)274-2149. Contact: Eve Green. Editor: Ed Isaac. Estab. 1987. Buys 100% of material from freelance writers. Syndicates to newspapers; planning to begin selling to magazines and radio. Query for electronic submissions. Reports in 3 months. Buys all rights.

Needs: Fiction for Sunday newspaper magazines; magazine and newspaper columns and features, cartoon strips. Buys one-shots and article series. Query with clips of published work. For cartoon strips, submit samples. Pays 50% author's percentage on columns. Additional payment for photos accepted with ms. Currently syndicates Indoor Gardening, by Jane Adler; Looking Great, by Gloria Lintermans; Strong Style, by Hope Strong.

Tips: "Please aim for a topic that is fresh. Newspapers seem to want short text pieces, 400-800 words. We do *not* return materials. We like to know a little about author's or cartoonist's background. We prefer people who have already been published. Please send material to Eve Green."

● Whitegate Features is looking for more gardening, travel, medical and food text columns.

WORLD NEWS SYNDICATE, LTD., P.O. Box 419, Hollywood CA 90078-0419. Phone/fax: (213)469-2333 (do not use to submit samples). Managing Editor: Laurie Williams. Estab. 1965. Syndicates to newspapers. Reports in 1 month. Buys first North American serial rights. Query with *published* clips. Looking for short columns, featurettes, home, medical, entertainment-interest, music, TV, films, 500-600 words."

● The managing editor says they only accept material already published regularly in writer's own living area. They accept no "new" ideas.

Needs: Fillers and newspaper columns. Pays 45-50% author's percentage.

Syndicates/Changes '95-'96

The following syndicates were listed in the 1995 edition but do not have listings in this edition of *Writer's Market*. The majority did not respond to our request to update their listings or return a questionnaire for a new listing. If a reason was given for their exclusion, we have included it in parentheses after the listing name.

America Int'l Syndicate
Columbia Company
Comic Art Therapy
Creators Syndicate
Crown Syndicate
Entertainment News Syndicate
Feature Enterprises (out of business)
(Gabriel) Graphics News Bureau

Interstate News Service
Jodi Jill Features
King Features
Landmark Designs
Lew Little Enterprises
Los Angeles Times Syndicate
Royal Features
Singer Media Corp.
Special Features Syndicate

Sports Network
Syndicated Fiction Project (cancelled due to NEA cuts)
Syndicated News Service
United Feature Syndicate
Universal Press Syndicate
Washington Post Writers Group (removed by request)

Greeting Cards & Gift Ideas

How many greeting cards showed up in your mailbox last year? If you are in line with the national average, you received 31 cards, seven of them for your birthday. That's according to figures published by The Greeting Card Association, a national trade organization representing the multi-billion dollar greeting card industry.

In fact, nearly 50% of all first class mail now consists of greeting cards. And, of course, card manufacturers rely on writers to supply them with enough skillfully crafted sentiments to meet the demand. The perfect greeting card verse is one that will appeal to a large audience, yet will make each buyer feel that the card was written exclusively for him or her.

Three greeting card companies continue to dominate this industry; together, American Greetings, Hallmark and Gibson Greetings supply about 80% of all cards sold. The other 20% are published by hundreds of companies who have found success mainly by not competing head to head with the big three but by choosing instead to pursue niche markets—regional and special-interest markets that the big three either cannot or do not supply.

A professional approach to markets

As markets become more focused, it's important to keep current on specific company needs. Familiarize yourself with the differences among lines of cards by visiting card racks. Ask retailers which lines are selling best. You may also find it helpful to read trade magazines such as *Greetings* and *Party and Paper Retailer*. These publications will keep you apprised of changes and events within the field, including seminars and trade shows.

Once you find a card line that appeals to you, write to the company and request its market list, catalog or submission guidelines (usually available for a SASE or a small fee). This information will help you determine whether or not your ideas are appropriate for that market.

Submission procedures vary among greeting card publishers, depending on the size and nature of the company. Keep in mind that many companies (especially the large ones) will not review your writing samples until you've signed and returned their disclosure contract or submission agreement, assuring them that your material is original and has not been submitted elsewhere.

Some editors prefer to see individual card ideas on 3×5 cards, while others prefer to receive a number of complete ideas on $8\frac{1}{2} \times 11$ bond paper. Be sure to put your best pieces at the top of the stack. Most editors do not want to see artwork unless it is professional, but they do appreciate conceptual suggestions for design elements. If your verse depends on an illustration to make its point or if you have an idea for a unique card shape or foldout, include a dummy card with your writing samples.

The usual submission includes from 5 to 15 card ideas and an accompanying cover letter, plus mechanical dummy cards, if necessary. Some editors also like to receive a résumé, client list and business card. Some do not. Be sure to check the listings and the company's writer's guidelines for such specifications before submitting material.

Payment for greeting card verse varies, but most firms pay per card or per idea; a handful pay small royalties. Some companies prefer to test a card first and will pay a small fee for a test card idea. In some instances, a company may even purchase an idea and never use it.

Greeting card companies will also buy ideas for gift products and may plan to use card material for a number of subsequent items. Licensing—the sale of rights to a particular character for a variety of products from mugs to T-shirts—is a growing part of the greetings industry. Because of this, however, note that most card companies buy all rights. We now include in this section markets for licensed product lines such as mugs, bumper stickers, buttons, posters and the like.

Information of interest to writers wishing to know more about working with the greeting card industry is available from the Greeting Card Creative Network. Write to them at 1200 G Street NW, Suite 760, Washington, DC 20005.

Managing your submissions

Because you will be sending out many samples, you may want to label each sample. Establish a master card for each verse idea and record where and when each was sent and whether it was rejected or purchased. Keep all cards sent to one company in a batch and give each batch a number. Write this number on the back of your return SASE to help you match up your verses as they are returned.

For more information on greeting card companies not listed in *Writer's Market*, see Greeting Card & Gift Ideas/Changes '95-'96 at the end of this section.

‡**ALASKA MOMMA INC.**, 303 Fifth Ave., New York NY 10016. (212)679-4404. Contact: Shirley Henschel. Estab. 1979. Receives 200 submissions/year; bought 12 ideas/samples last year. Submit seasonal/holiday material 10 months in advance. Reports in 1 month. Material copyrighted. Pays on signing the license.
Needs: Juvenile, studio. Submit 20 ideas/batch.
Other Product Lines: Calendars, gift books, plaques, posters, puzzles. Pays royalties on sales.
Tips: "Need strong themes."

‡**ALEF JUDAICA INC.**, 8440 Warner Dr., Culver City CA 90232. (310)202-0024. President: Guy Orner. Estab. 1977. 10% freelance written. Receives 130 submissions/year; bought 65 ideas/samples last year. Submit seasonal/holiday material 8 months in advance. Reports in 2 months. Pays on publication.
Needs: Judaica. Prefers unrhymed verse ideas. Submit 12 ideas/batch.

‡**ALL STAR PAPER CO.**, 1500 Old Deerfield Rd., #19-20, Highland Park IL 60035. (708)831-5811. Contact: Fran Greenspon. Estab. 1978. Submit seasonal/holiday material 9 months in advance. Material copyrighted. Pays on publication.
Needs: Judaic—Hanukkah, Rosh Hashana, Bar/Bat Mitzvah. Prefers unrhymed verse.

AMBERLEY GREETING CARD CO., 11510 Goldcoast Dr., Cincinnati OH 45249-1695. (513)489-2775. Editor: Dave McPeek. Estab. 1966. 90% freelance written. Bought 200 freelance ideas/samples last year. Reports in 1 month. Material copyrighted. Buys all rights. **Pays on acceptance.** Writer's guidelines for #10 SASE. Market list regularly revised.
● This company is now accepting alternative humor.
Needs: "Original, easy to understand, belly-laugh or outrageous humor. We sell to the 'masses, not the classes' so keep it simple and to the point. Humor accepted in all captions, including general birthday, family birthday, get well, anniversary, thank you, friendship, etc. No non-humorous material needed or considered this year. Pays $150/card idea." Submit maximum 10 ideas/batch.
Tips: "Send SASE for our writer's guidelines before submitting. Amberley publishes humorous specialty lines in addition to a complete conventional line that is accented with humor. Since humor is our specialty, we are highly selective. Be sure that a SASE with the correct US postage is included with your material. Otherwise it will not be returned."

ARGUS COMMUNICATIONS, 200 E. Bethany, Allen TX 75002-3804. (214)390-6300. Editorial Coordinator: Beth Davis. 90% freelance written. Primarily interested in material for posters. Reports in 2 months. **Pays on acceptance.** Submission guidelines available for #10 SASE for each market you are interested in. Please indicate the market your submission is for on the outside of your envelope.
● Argus Communications has expanded its markets and is focusing on three specific groups: education, general and Christian. By describing more clearly its specific targets, freelance writers should

be able to select and write for the market(s) where they feel their strengths are. In return, Argus hopes it will be able to get better use out of the submissions it receives.

Needs: "We have three specific markets for which we buy editorial: (1) Education market: poster editorial for teachers to place in their classrooms that is positive, motivational, inspirational, thought-provoking and success-oriented. Also, poster editorial that encourages teamwork and conflict resolution, and editorial that reflects basic values such as honesty, integrity, kindness, trust, etc. (2) General market: poster editorial for teenagers through adults that is bright, timely and funny. The editorial should reflect current trends, lifestyles and attitudes. Humor and light sarcasm are the emphasis for this market. (3) Christian market: poster editorial for teenagers through adults that is positive, inspirational, motivational, encouraging or even humorous. The editorial should express basic Christian faith, beliefs and values.

Other Product Lines: Greeting cards, postcards, calendars.

Tips: "Poster editorial is an at-a-glance, brief message that makes an impression, whether it is thought-provoking, humorous or inspirational. Our posters capture your attention with a creative mixture of humorous, dynamic and motivational editorial. Keep in mind that postcard editorial should express a simple 'me to you' message. Think of a new way to express a friendly hi, thinking of you, miss you, thank you or what's new."

‡BEDOL INTERNATIONAL GROUP INC., P.O. Box 2847, Rancho Cucamonga CA 91729. Contact: Mark A. Bedol. Estab. 1982. 100% freelance written. Receives 50 submissions/year; bought 20 ideas/samples last year. Submit seasonal/holiday material 1 year in advance. Does not return submissions. Buys all rights. Pays on publication.

Needs: Conventional, humorous, inspirational, studio. Prefers rhymed verse ideas. Submit 20 ideas/batch.

Tips: "Market to the mass (general) market."

BLUE MOUNTAIN ARTS, INC., Dept. WM, P.O. Box 1007, Boulder CO 80306-1007. E-mail: bma@rmii. com. Contact: Editorial Staff. Estab. 1971. Buys 100 items/year. Reports in 3-6 months. Pays on publication.

Needs: "We are interested in reviewing poetry and writings that would be appropriate for greeting cards, which means that they should reflect a message, feeling, or sentiment that one person would want to share with another. We'd like to receive sensitive, original submissions about love relationships, family members, friendships, philosophies, and any other aspect of life. Poems and writings for specific holidays (Christmas, Valentine's Day, etc.) and special occasions, such as graduation, birthdays, anniversary, and get well are also considered." Submit seasonal material at least 4 months in advance. Buys worldwide, exclusive rights, $200/poem; anthology rights $25.

Other Product Lines: Calendars, gift books, prints, mugs.

Tips: "We strongly suggest that you familiarize yourself with our products before submitting material, although we caution you not to study them too hard. We do *not* need more poems that sound like something we've already published. We're looking for poetry that expresses real emotions and feelings, so we suggest that you have someone specific in mind (a friend, relative, etc.) as you write. The majority of the poetry we publish *does not rhyme*. We do not wish to receive books, unless you are interested in having portions excerpted for greeting cards; nor do we wish to receive artwork or photography. We prefer that submissions be typewritten, one poem per page. Only a small portion of the freelance material we receive is selected each year, either for publication on a notecard or in a gift anthology, and the review process can also be lengthy, but please be assured that every manuscript is given serious consideration."

BRILLIANT ENTERPRISES, 117 W. Valerio St., Santa Barbara CA 93101-2927. President: Ashleigh Brilliant. Estab. 1967. Buys all rights. Submit words and art in black on 3½×3½ horizontal, thin white paper in batches of no more than 15. Reports "usually in 2 weeks." Catalog and sample set for $2.

Needs: Postcards. Messages should be "of a highly original nature, emphasizing subtlety, simplicity, insight, wit, profundity, beauty and felicity of expression. Accompanying art should be in the nature of oblique commentary or decoration rather than direct illustration. Messages should be of universal appeal, capable of being appreciated by all types of people and of being easily translated into other languages. Because our line of cards is highly unconventional, it is essential that freelancers study it before submitting. No topical references or subjects limited to American culture or puns." Limit of 17 words/card. Pays $50 for "complete ready-to-print word and picture design."

‡BURGOYNE, INC., 2030 E. Byberry Rd., Philadelphia PA 19116. Creative Director: Jeanna Lane. Estab. 1907. 2% freelance written. Receives 15 submissions/year; bought 2 ideas/samples last year. Submit seasonal/holiday material 6 months in advance. Buys greeting card rights. **Pays on acceptance**.

Needs: Inspirational, juvenile, sensitivity, soft line. Prefers rhymed or unrhymed verse ideas. Submit 5 ideas/batch.

THE CALLIGRAPHY COLLECTION INC., 2604 NW 74th Place, Gainesville FL 32653. (904)375-8530. Fax: (904)374-9957. Editor: Katy Fischer. Reports in 6 months. Buys all rights. Pays on publication.

Needs: "Ours is a line of framed prints of watercolors with calligraphy." Conventional, humorous, informal, inspirational, sensitivity, soft line. Prefers unrhymed verse, but will consider rhymed. Submit 3 ideas/batch. Pays $50-100/framed print idea.

Other Product Lines: Gift books, greeting books, plaques.
Tips: "Sayings for friendship are difficult to get. Bestsellers are humorous, sentimental and inspirational ideas—such as for wedding and family and friends. Our audience is women 20 to 50 years of age. Write something they would like to give or receive as a lasting gift."

COMSTOCK CARDS, 600 S. Rock, Suite 15, Reno NV 89502-4115. Fax: (702)856-9406. Owner: Patti P. Wolf. Production Manager: David Delacroix. Estab. 1986. 35% freelance written. Receives 500 submissions/year; bought 150 freelance ideas/samples last year. Submit seasonal/holiday material 1 year in advance. Reports in 5 weeks. Buys all rights. **Pays on acceptance.** Writer's guidelines/market list for SASE. Market list issued one time only.
Needs: Humorous, informal, invitations, "puns, put-downs, put-ons, outrageous humor aimed at a sophisticated, adult female audience. Also risqué cartoon cards. No conventional, soft line or sensitivity hearts and flowers, etc." Pays $50-75/card idea, cartoons negotiable.
Other Product Lines: Notepads, cartoon cards, invitations.
Tips: "Always keep holiday occasions in mind and personal me-to-you expressions that relate to today's occurrences. Ideas must be simple and concisely delivered. A combination of strong image and strong gag line make a successful greeting card. Consumers relate to themes of work, sex and friendship combined with current social, political and economic issues."

CONTEMPORARY DESIGNS, 213 Main St., Gilbert IA 50105. (515)232-5188. Fax: (515)232-3380. Editor: Sallie Abelson. Estab. 1977. 90% freelance written. Submit seasonal/holiday material 1 year in advance. Reports in 1-2 months. Buys all rights. **Pays on acceptance.**
Needs: Short positive humorous copy for memo pads, mugs, etc. Themes: music, sports, age, diet, the working world, camp and Judaica.
Other Product Lines: Quote and gift books, mugs, tote bags, aprons and pillow cases, memo pads..

CONTENOVA GIFTS, 735 Park North Blvd., Suite 114, Clarkston GA 30021. (404)292-4676. Fax: (404)292-4684. Director of Marketing: Vicki Boynton. Estab. 1965. 100% freelance written. Receives an estimated 15,000 submissions/year. Submit ideas on 3×5 cards or small mock-ups in batches of 10-15. Buys world rights. **Pays on acceptance.** Current needs list for SASE.
Needs: Humorous for mugs, magnets and other gifts, but no greeting cards. "Short gags with good punch work best." Birthday, belated birthday, get well, anniversary, thank you, congratulations, miss you, new job, etc. Seasonal ideas needed for Christmas, Valentine's Day, Mother's Day, Father's Day. Pays $35.
Tips: "No longer using drinking themes. Put together your best ideas and submit them. One great idea sent is much better than 20 poor ideas filling an envelope. We are always searching for new writers who can produce quality work. You need not be previously published. Our audience is 18-65—the full mug consumers. We do *not* use poetry."

CREATE-A-CRAFT, P.O. Box 330008, Fort Worth TX 76163-0008. (817)292-1855. Estab. 1967. 5% freelance written. Receives 300 submissions/year; bought 2 freelance ideas/samples last year. Submit seasonal/holiday material 1 year in advance. "No phone calls from freelancers accepted. We deal through agents only. Submissions not returned even if accompanied by SASE—not enough staff to take time to package up returns." Buys all rights. Sample greeting cards $2.50 for #10 SASE.
Needs: Announcements, conventional, humorous, juvenile, studio. "Payment depends upon the assignment, amount of work involved, and production costs involved in project."
Tips: No unsolicited material. "Send letter of inquiry describing education and experience, or résumé with one sample first. We will screen applicants and request samples from those who interest us."

DESIGN DESIGN INC., P.O. Box 2266, Grand Rapids MI 49501-2266. Fax: (616)774-2448. Creative Director: Tom Vituj. Estab. 1985. 100% freelance written. Receives 450 submissions/year. Submit seasonal/holiday material 1 year in advance. Reports in 2 months. Buys all rights. Pays on publication. Free writer's guidelines on request.
Needs: Announcements, informal, juvenile, conventional, sensitivity, seasonal, humorous, invitations. Prefers unrhymed verse. Submit 12 ideas/batch. Also looking for traditional, sentimental, beautiful.

DISKOTECH INC., 7930 State Line, Suite 210, Prairie Village KS 66208. (913)432-8606. Fax: (913)432-8606*51. E-mail: 72754.2773@compuserve.com. Publisher/Editor: John Slegman. Estab. 1989. Publishes PCcards™ which are multimedia greeting cards that come on computer diskettes and run on PCs. PCcards™ are for all seasons, ages and tastes. Looking for short, exciting computer animations, better if they include music or sound effects. Also looking for freelance writers with ideas/sentiments. Need all types of humor. Enclose SASE with submissions. Reports in 2 months. Recent PCcards™ include 3-D, interactive 4-D and virtual reality.

‡DUCK AND COVER PRODUCTIONS, P.O. Box 21640, Oakland CA 94609. Contact: Jim Buser. Estab. 1990. 50% freelance written. Receives 200 submissions/year. Bought 80 ideas/samples last year. Reports in 2-3 weeks. Buys all rights on novelty products. Pays on publication. Guidelines for #10 SAE with 2 first-class stamps. Market list available on request.
Other Product Lines: Novelty buttons and magnets. Pays $25/idea.
Tips: "We do best with original, intelligent statements that make fun of life in the neurotic '90s. Our target audience would be educated, aware, yet skeptical and anxious young adults; however, anyone with an offbeat sense of humor can enjoy our line. We sell to novelty stores, head shops, record stores, bookstores, sex shops, comic stores, etc. There are no taboos for our writers; we encourage them to be as weird and/or rude as possible. We feel buttons and magnets are commercial cousins to graffiti and there is a definite psychological spin to our line. Cerebral material that makes use of contemporary pop vocabulary is a plus. We do *not* want to see old clichés or slogans already in the market."

‡EPCONCEPTS, P.O. Box 363, Piermont NY 10968. (914)359-7137. Contact: Steve Epstein. Estab. 1983. 95% freelance written. Receives 1,200 submissions/year; bought 15 ideas/samples last year. Submit seasonal/holiday material 2 months in advance. Reports in 2-3 months. Buys one-time greeting card rights. Pays ½ on acceptance; ½ on publication. Writer's guidelines for #10 SASE.
Needs: Announcements, conventional, humorous, informal, inspirational, invitations, juvenile, studio, all holidays. Prefers unrhymed verse ideas. Submit 20 ideas/batch on 8½×11 paper; no index cards.
Other Product Lines: Post cards, buttons, mugs, work (jotting down ideas) pads.
Tips: "Humorous sells best; especially birthdays, anniversaries, friendship/love and light risqué. Target audience is ages 20-50, upscale and appreciative of photography, antiques, illustrations and cartoons. Trends can always include certain social and political phenomenons, e.g., Presidents, first ladies, etc."

EPHEMERA, INC., P.O. Box 490, Phoenix OR 97535. Contact: Editor. Estab. 1979. 90% freelance written. Receives 2,000 submissions/year; bought 200 ideas/samples last year. Reports in 10 weeks. Buys all rights. Pays on publication. Writer's guidelines/market list for #10 SASE. Market list issued one time only.
Needs: "Original, provocative, irreverent and outrageously funny slogans for novelty buttons and magnets sold in card and gift shops, bookstores, record shops, political and gay shops, adult stores, amusement parks etc.!" Pays $25/slogan.

‡FINE ART PRODUCTIONS, 67 Maple St., Newburgh NY 12550-4034. Contact: Richie Suraci. Estab. 1994. 80% freelance written. Receives 12-30 submissions/year; bought 12 ideas/samples last year. Submit seasonal/holiday material 6-12 months in advance. Reports in 3-8 months. **Pays on acceptance** or publication. Writer's guidelines/market list free for SAE and 72¢ postage.
Needs: Announcements, humorous, inspirational, invitations, sensitivity, soft line, erotic, sci-fi, adult, fantasy, romance. Prefers rhymed or unrhymed verse verse.

FOTOFOLIO, INC., 536 Broadway, New York NY 10012. (212)226-0923. Fax: (212)226-0072. Editors: Julie Galan, Ron Schick, JoAnne Seador. Estab. 1976. Submit seasonal/holiday material 1 year in advance (visuals only). Reports in 1 month. Pays on publication.
Other Product Lines: Postcards, notecards, posters.
Tips: "We specialize in high quality fine art photography."

‡GALLANT GREETINGS, Dept. WM, 4300 United Pkwy., Schiller Park IL 60176. Vice President, Sales and Marketing: Chris Allen. 90% freelance written. Bought 500 freelance ideas/samples last year. Reports in 3 months. Buys world greeting card rights. Pays 60-90 days after acceptance. Writer's guidelines for SASE.
Needs: Announcements, conventional, humorous, informal, inspirational, invitations, juvenile. Submit 20 cards/batch.
Tips: "Greeting cards should and do move with the times, and sometimes writers don't. Keep aware of what is going on around you."

GIBSON GREETINGS, 2100 Section Rd., Cincinnati OH 45237.
 • At press time, Gibson was looking to sell the company. Query before submitting.

‡KATE HARPER DESIGNS, P.O. Box 2112, Berkeley CA 94702. Contact: Art Director. Estab. 1993. Submit seasonal/holiday material 1 year in advance. Reports in 1 month. Pays flat fee for usage, not exclusive, $25 plus author's name on front of card. **Pays on acceptance**. Writer's guidelines/market list for SASE.
Needs: Humorous, informal, inspirational, everyday cards. "Quotes needed about work, family, love, kids, career, technology and marriage with a twist of humor. Something a working mom would laugh at and/or

tips on how to have it all and still live to tell about it. Be adventurous and say what you really think in first person. Nothing cute or sweet, please. Avoid traditional ideas of card quotes. Serious quotes also considered. Quotes must be 20 words or less." Prefers unrhymed verse ideas. Submit 10 ideas/batch.

‡INFINITY COLLECTIONS, P.O. Box 41201, Washington DC 20018. President: Karmen A. Booker. Estab. 1990. 10% freelance written. Submit seasonal/holiday material 2 months in advance. Reports in 2 months. Purchases exclusive rights to sentiment, a flat fee with no further royalties. Pays on publication. Writer's guidelines/market list for $2.
Needs: Inspirational. Submit 5-8 ideas/batch.
Tips: "Cards that sell best are Happy Birthday, Friendship, Thank You, Graduation and Mother's Day cards. Card buyers look for a personal touch in verse. Therefore, please have someone in mind (a friend, relative, etc.) as you write."

KIMBERLEY ENTERPRISES, INC., 15029 S. Figueroa St., Gardena CA 90248-1721. (310)538-1331. Fax: (310)538-2045. Vice President: M. Hernandez. Estab. 1979. 15% freelance written. Receives less than 100 submissions/year; bought 12 ideas/samples last year. Submit seasonal material 9 months in advance. Reports in up to 3 months. Material not copyrighted. Pays on acceptance. Market list available on mailing list basis.
Needs: Announcements, conventional, inspirational, invitations. Send 12 ideas maximum.
Other Product Lines: Plaques. Pays $10-250.
Tips: "The primary future interest for the company is in the plaque line, with an emphasis on inspirational or conventional appeal."

KOGLE CARDS, INC., 1498 S. Lipan St., Denver CO 80223. (303)698-9007. President: Patricia Koller. Please send submissions Attn: Art Director. Estab. 1982. 40% freelance written. Receives 100 submissions/year; bought 80 ideas/samples last year. Submit seasonal/holiday material 18 months in advance. Reports in 1 month. Buys all rights. Pays on publication.
Needs: Humorous, business related. Rhymed or unrhymed verse ideas.
Tips: "We produce cards designed for the business community, in particular salespeople, real estate, travel, hairdresser, insurance and chiropractic."

‡L&H MAHAR ART PUBLISHERS, 945 Murray Rd., Middle Grove NY 12850. Contact: Larry Mahar. Estab. 1982. 5% freelance written. Receives 20 submissions/year; bought 4 ideas/samples last year. No seasonal material. Reports in 1 week. Our use only; writer retains ownership. Pays on publication. Writer's guidelines/market list for #10 SASE. Market list issued one time only.
Needs: "Verses averaging 8 lines non-rhyming prose—poem style of type that could be put on a plaque (mother, love, family, friendship). No humor. Basically serious social expression."

LOVE GREETING CARDS, INC., 1717 Opa Loca Blvd., Opa-Locka FL 33054. (305)685-5683. Contact: Anita Drittel. Estab. 1984. 75% freelance written. Receives 200-300 submissions/year; bought 400 ideas/samples last year. Submit seasonal/holiday material 6 months in advance. Reports in 1 month. Buys all rights. **Pays on acceptance**. Market list regularly revised.
Needs: Informal, juvenile, humorous, general.
Other Product Lines: Greeting books ($100-300), posters ($200-500).
Tips: "There's a great demand for animal cards."

‡THE LOVELACE FAMILY LTD., 2824 International Circle, Colorado Springs CO 80910. (719)475-7100. Administrative Assistant/Art & Product Development: Susannah Nix. Estab. 1990. 15% freelance written. Submit seasonal/holiday material 11 months in advance. Reports 1-2 months. Pays on publication. Writer's guidelines/market list free. Market list regularly revised.
Needs: Conventional and humorous cards featuring wildlife subjects. Prefers unrhymed verse ideas. Submit 20 ideas/batch.
Tips: "Simple, conventional cards sell best. We prefer greetings that are not too long and humor should be kept tasteful. Our cards feature photographs and illustrations of wildlife and nature and are targeted at animal and environmental enthusiasts."

MAILAWAYS, P.O. Box 782, Tavares FL 32778-0782. (904)742-8196. Editor: Gene Chambers. Estab. 1992. Submit seasonal/holiday material 3 months in advance. Reports in 1 month. Material "not yet copyrighted, but will be." Rights negotiable. **Pays on acceptance.** Writer's guidelines for #10 SASE. Market list issued one time only.
Needs: Inspirational, sensitivity, experimental poetry. Submit 5 ideas/batch.
Other Product Lines: Gift books and greeting books ($10, negotiable).
Tips: "What sells best is the *short*, inspirational verse, rhymed or not, upbeat but with an emotional *jolt* of familiar feeling. Audience is both the average person *and* the *sensitive soul*."

‡NORTHERN EXPOSURE GREETING CARDS, 461 Sebastopol Ave., Santa Rosa CA 95401. (707)546-2153. Contact: Bruce Henson, Jack Freed. Estab. 1991. 100% freelance written. Receives 100 or more submissions/year; bought 50 ideas/samples last year. Submit seasonal/holiday material 6 months in advance. Reports in 1 month. Material copyrighted. Pays on publication. Writer's guidelines/market list for 8½×11 SAE with 4 first-class stamps. Market list available on mailing list basis.
Needs: Humorous, everyday cards. Unrhymed verse ideas. Submit 5-15 ideas/batch.
Tips: "We produce high quality photographic greeting cards that sell in many upper scale retail stores. Because our photographic images are generally humorous it's important that the verse be humorous in most instances."

OATMEAL STUDIOS, P.O. Box 138W3, Rochester VT 05767. (802)767-3171. Creative Director: Helene Lehrer. Estab. 1979. 85% freelance written. Buys 200-300 greeting card lines/year. **Pays on acceptance.** Reports within 6 weeks. Current market list for #10 SASE.
Needs: Birthday, friendship, anniversary, get well cards, etc. Also Christmas, Chanukah, Mother's Day, Father's Day, Easter, Valentine's Day, etc. Will review concepts. Humorous material (clever and *very* funny) year-round. "Humor, conversational in tone and format, sells best for us." Prefers unrhymed contemporary humor. Current pay schedule available with guidelines.
Other Product Lines: Notepads, stick-on notes.
Tips: "The greeting card market has become more competitive with a greater need for creative and original ideas. We are looking for writers who can communicate situations, thoughts, and relationships in a funny way and apply them to a birthday, get well, etc., greeting and we are willing to work with them in targeting our style. We will be looking for material that says something funny about life in a new way."

‡PAINTED HEARTS & FRIENDS, 1222 N. Fair Oaks Ave., Pasadena CA 91103. Contact: Kathy Nusbaum. 20% freelance written. Receives 500-1,000 submissions/year. Submit seasonal/holiday material 3 months in advance. Pays on publication. Writer's guidelines/market list for 4×9 SASE. Market list regularly revised.
Needs: Announcements, conventional, humorous, inspirational, realistic, invitations, juvenile. Submit 12 ideas/batch.
Other Product Lines: Gift books, post cards, poster.
Tips: Watercolor cards sell best for this company.

‡PALM PROJECTS INC., P.O. Box 1770, Canal St., Station, New York NY 10013-1770. (718)788-8296. Contact: Paul Ketley. Estab. 1989. 25% freelance written. Bought 2 ideas/samples last year. Submit seasonal/holiday material 1 year in advance. Reports in 1-2 months. Material copyrighted. Pays on publication.
Needs: Humorous.
Other Product Lines: Calendars, post cards, posters.
Tips: "We currently only offer contemporary humorous cards of an environmental nature under the Revenge Cards Trademark."

‡PANDA INK GREETING CARDS, P.O. Box 5129, West Hills CA 91308-5129. (818)340-8061. Contact: Ruth Ann or Irwin Epstein. Estab. 1981. 10-20% freelance written. Receives 100 submissions/year; bought 50 ideas/samples last year. Submit seasonal/holiday material 6 months in advance. Reports in 1 month. Buys first rights. **Pays on acceptance**. Writer's guidelines free.
Needs: Conventional, humorous, juvenile, soft line, Judaic, ethnic. Prefers rhymed and unrhymed verse ideas. Submit 10 ideas/batch.
Tips: "No risqué, sarcasm, insulting. Need Jewish/Yiddish language in most cases."

PARAMOUNT CARDS INC., Dept. WM, P.O. Box 6546, Providence RI 02940-6546. (401)726-0800. Contact: Editorial Freelance Coordinator. Estab. 1906. Buys 100s of ideas/year. Submit seasonal material 1 month in advance. Reports in 1 month. Buys all rights. **Pays on acceptance.** Writer's guidelines for SASE.
Needs: All types of conventional verses. Fresh, inventive humorous verses, especially family birthday cards. Would also like to see more conversational prose, especially in family titles such as Mother, Father, Sister, Husband, Wife, etc. Submit 10-15/batch. No tired, formulaic rhymes.
Tips: "Study the market! Go to your local card shops and analyze what you see. Ask the storekeepers which cards are selling. Then apply what you've learned to your own writing. The best cards (and we buy only the best) will have mass appeal and yet, in the consumer's eyes, will read as though they were created exclusively for her. A feminine touch is important, as 90% of all greeting cards are purchased by women."

C.M. PAULA COMPANY, 7773 School Rd., Cincinnati OH 45249. Contact: Editorial Supervisor. Estab. 1958. 10% freelance written. "Looking for humor *only* from previously published social-expression writers. Seasoned writers should submit published writing samples. If there is a match in style, we will then contact writers with assignments." Reports in 2-3 months. Buys all rights. **Pays on acceptance**.
Product Lines: Coffee mugs, key rings, stationery pads, magnets, dimensional statues and awards.
Tips: "Our needs are light humor—nothing risqué. A writer can get a quick idea of the copy we use by looking over our store displays. Please note—we do not publish greeting cards."

PLUM GRAPHICS INC., P.O. Box 136, Prince Station, New York NY 10012. (212)966-2573. President: Yvette Cohen. Estab. 1983. 100% freelance written. Bought 21 samples last year. Does not return samples unless accompanied by SASE. Reports in 3-4 months. Buys greeting card and stationery rights. Pays on publication. Guidelines sheet for SASE. "Sent out about twice a year in conjunction with the development of new cards."
Needs: Humorous. "We don't want general submissions. We want them to relate to our next line." Prefers unrhymed verse. Greeting cards pay $40.
Tips: "Sell to all ages. Humor is always appreciated. We want short, to-the-point lines."

QUALITY ARTWORKS, 2262 N. Penn Rd., P.O. Box 369, Hatfield PA 19440-0369. Creative Director: Linda Tomezsko Morris. Estab. 1985. 10% freelance written. Reports in 2 months. Buys all rights. **Pays on acceptance.** Writer's guidelines/market list for #10 SASE. Market list issued one time only.
Needs: Conventional, inspirational, juvenile, sensitivity, soft line. Prefers unrhymed verse.
Other Product Lines: Bookmarks, scrolls, stationery, blank books. Payment is negotiable.
Tips: "We are looking for sophisticated yet inspirational verse (directed toward women). The main emphasis of our business is bookmarks."

RESTAURANT GREETING CARDS, 8440 Runford Dr., Boynton Beach FL 33437-2723. (407)392-8985. Fax: (407)392-4174. Contact: Michael Tomasso. Estab. 1975. 75% freelance written. Receives 100 submissions/year; bought 10 ideas/samples last year. Submit seasonal/holiday material 8 months in advance. Reports in 3 months. Pays on publication. Market list available on mailing list basis.
Needs: Humorous (must be restaurant related). Prefers unrhymed verse.
Tips: "Target market is restaurants. Humorous greeting, birthday, thank you, sells well. Pizza delivery, Chinese delivery, bagel, bakery, deli. Be sure not to offend ethnicity of card subject."

ROCKSHOTS, INC., 632 Broadway, New York NY 10012. (212)420-1400. Fax: (212)353-8756. Editor: Bob Vesce. Estab. 1979. Buys 75 greeting card verse (or gag) lines/year. Submit seasonal/holiday material 1 year in advance. Reports in 2 months. Buys rights for greeting-card use. Writer's guidelines for SASE.
Needs: Humorous ("should be off-the-wall, as outrageous as possible, preferably for sophisticated buyer"); soft line; combination of sexy and humorous come-on type greeting ("sentimental is not our style"); and insult cards ("looking for cute insults"). No sentimental or conventional material. "Card gag can adopt a sentimental style, then take an ironic twist and end on an off-beat note." Submit no more than 10 card ideas/samples per batch. Send to attention: Submissions. Pays $50/gagline. Prefers gag lines on 8×11 paper with name, address, and phone and social security numbers in right corner, or individually on 3×5 cards.
Tips: "Think of a concept that would normally be too outrageous to use, give it a cute and clever wording to make it drop-dead funny and you will have commercialized a non-commercial message. It's always good to mix sex and humor. Our emphasis is definitely on the erotic. Hard-core eroticism is difficult for the general public to handle on greeting cards. The trend is toward 'light' sexy humor, even cute sexy humor. 'Cute' has always sold cards, and it's a good word to think of even with the most sophisticated, crazy ideas. 80% of our audience is female. Remember that your gag line will be illustrated by a photographer. So try to think visually. If no visual is needed, the gag line *can* stand alone, but we generally prefer some visual representation. It is a very good idea to preview our cards at your local store if this is possible to give you a feeling of our style."

‡RUSS BERRIE & COMPANY, INC., 111 Bauer Dr., Oakland NJ 07436. Contact: Angelica Berrie. Estab. 1963. 50% freelance written. Receives thousands of submissions/year; bought hundreds of ideas last year. Submit seasonal/holiday material 2 years in advance. Reports in 2-4 months. **Pays on acceptance.** Writer's guidelines/market list for #10 SAE with 2 first-class stamps. Market list regularly revised.
Needs: Conventional, humorous, inspirational, juvenile, sensitivity, soft line. Submit 10-25 ideas/batch.
Other Product Lines: Payment varies according to each product and length of copy, as well as the number of pieces purchased, but ranges between $25-100/piece. Calendars (undated-perpetual), gift books, greeting books, plaques, post cards, promotions, bookmarks, pocket cards, magnets, mugs, key rings.
Tips: "Humorous cards for women, florals, inspirational—but we are always looking for new concepts that can also be adapted to gift products and other paper products."

SANGAMON, INC., P.O. Box 410, Taylorville IL 62568. (217)824-2261. Fax: (217)824-2300. Contact: Editorial Department. Estab. 1931. 90% freelance written. Reports in 3 months. Buys all rights. **Pays on acceptance.** Writer's guidelines for SASE.
Needs: Conventional, humorous, inspirational, juvenile, sensitivity, studio. "We offer a balance of many styles. We'd like to see more conversational prose styles for the conventional lines." Submit 15 ideas maximum/batch.
Other Product Lines: Calendars, promotions.
Tips: "We only request submissions based on background and writing experience. We work 12-18 months ahead of a season and only accept material on assignment."

MARCEL SCHURMAN CO., INC., 2500 N. Watney Way, Fairfield CA 94533. Editor: Meg Schutte. Estab. 1950. 20% freelance written. Receives 500 submissions/year; bought 50 freelance ideas/samples last year. Reports in 1 month. **Pays on acceptance.** Writer's guidelines for #10 SASE.
Needs: Sentimental, contemporary, inspirational/support, seasonal and everyday categories. Prefers unrhymed verse, but on juvenile cards rhyme is OK. Submit 10-15 cards in single batch.
Tips: "Historically, our nostalgic and art museum cards sell best. However, we are moving toward more contemporary cards and humor. Target market: upscale, professional, well-educated; average age 40; more female."

TRISAR, INC., 121 Old Springs Rd., Anaheim CA 92808. (714)282-2626. Editor: Randy Harris. Estab. 1979. 50% freelance written. Receives 1,000 submissions/year; bought 25 ideas/samples last year. Submit seasonal/holiday material 1 year in advance. Reports in 3 months. Buys all rights. **Pays on acceptance**. Writer guidelines for #10 SASE.
Needs: Humorous, studio, age-related feelings about turning 40, 50, 60; seasonal oriented themes including Love, Mom, Dad, Grad, Halloween, Christmas. Unrhymed verse and one-liners only. Submit ideas on 3×5 cards.
Other Product Lines: T-shirts, boxers, mugs, greeting cards, buttons. Also gift bags and paper party goods. Current pay scale available with guidelines.
Tips: "Best-selling lines capture current lifestyle, witty thoughts on growing older. We do not accept risqué statements. Up-beat statements that appeal to a broad range of people are best. Especially looking for humor about turning 50 and retirement. Fresh puns for graduation and holidays such as Halloween are important."

‡UNIQUE GREETINGS, INC., P.O. Box 5783, Manchester NH 03108. (603)647-6777. Contact: Michael Normand. Estab. 1988. 10% freelance written. Receives 15 submissions/year. Submit seasonal/holiday material 1 year in advance. Reports in 6 weeks. Buys all rights. Writer's guidelines/market list for SASE. Market list regularly revised.
Needs: Watercolors, cute animals, flower scenes, etc. Prefers unrhymed verse. Submit 12 ideas/batch.
Tips: "General and Happy Birthday sell the best."

VAGABOND CREATIONS, INC., 2560 Lance Dr., Dayton OH 45409. (513)298-1124. Editor: George F. Stanley, Jr. 10% freelance written. Bought 10-15 ideas/samples last year. Submit seasonal/holiday material 6 months in advance. Reports in 1 week. Buys all rights. Ideas sometimes copyrighted. **Pays on acceptance.** Writer's guidelines for #10 SASE. Market list issued one time only.
Needs: Cute, humorous greeting cards (illustrations and copy) often with animated animals or objects in people-situations with short, subtle tie-in message on inside page only. No poetry. Pays $15-25/card idea.

WARNER PRESS, PUBLISHERS, 1200 E. Fifth St., P.O. Box 2499, Anderson IN 46018-9988. Product Editor: Robin Fogle. Estab. 1880. 50% freelance written. Reports in 2 months. Buys all rights. **Pays on acceptance.** Must send #10 SASE for guidelines before submitting.
Needs: Religious themes; sensitive prose and inspirational verse for boxed cards, posters, calendars. Pays $20-35. Also accepts ideas for coloring and activity books.

WEST GRAPHICS, 385 Oyster Point Blvd., #7, South San Francisco CA 94080. (800)648-9378. Fax: (415)588-5552. Contact: Production Department. Estab. 1980. 80% freelance written. Receives 20,000 submissions/year; bought 200 freelance ideas/samples last year. Reports in 6 weeks. Buys greeting card rights. Pays 30 days after publication. Writer's guidelines/market list for #10 SASE.
Needs: "We are looking for outrageous contemporary humor that is on the cutting edge." Prefers unrhymed verse. Submit 10-30 ideas/batch. Pays $100.
Tips: "West Graphics is an alternative greeting card company which offers a diversity of humor from 'off the wall' to 'tastefully tasteless'. Our goal is to publish cards that challenge the limits of taste and keep people laughing. The majority of our audience is women in their 30s and 40s, ideas should be targeted to issues they care about: relationships, sex, aging, success, money, crime, etc."

CAROL WILSON FINE ARTS, INC., P.O. Box 17394, Portland OR 97217-1810. (503)261-1860. President: Gary Spector. Estab. 1983. 90% freelance written. Receives thousands of submissions/year; bought less than 10 freelance ideas/samples last year. Submit seasonal/holiday material 6-12 months in advance. Reports in 2 months. Buys negotiable rights. Pays on acceptance or publication depending on type of agreement. Writer's guidelines/market list for #10 SASE. Market list regularly revised.
Needs: Humorous, unrhymed. Pays $50-100/idea. "Royalties could be considered for a body of work."
Tips: "The majority of our humor customers are educated women, age 30-50. It is important that the humor be not only personal and funny, but also 'sendable;' meaning appropriate to send to the intended recipient. This seems obvious but is often overlooked. Our fine arts customers are similar, but include an older range. We need messages that are personal and positive for all occasions."

Greeting Cards & Gift Ideas/Changes '95-'96

The following greeting card publishers were listed in the 1995 edition but do not have listings in this edition of *Writer's Market*. The majority did not respond to our request to update their listings or return a questionnaire for a new listing. If a reason was given for their exclusion, we have included it in parentheses after the listing name.

Allport Editions
American Greetings
Branches
Brighton Publications
Current (removed by request for 1 year)
Digressions
Flavia Studios

C.R. Gibson Co. (removed by request)
Gifted Line (no freelance)
Hallmark Cards
Imagine (removed by request for 1 year)
Paper Moon Graphics
Peacock Papers

Portal Publications
Scott Cards (removed by request)
Silver Visions
Snafu Designs
Sunrise Publications
TLC Greetings
Vintage Images

Resources

Contests and Awards

The contests and awards listed in this section are arranged by subject. Nonfiction writers can turn immediately to nonfiction awards listed alphabetically by the name of the contest or award. The same is true for fiction writers, poets, playwrights and screenwriters, journalists, children's writers and translators. You'll also find general book awards, miscellaneous awards, arts council and foundation fellowships, and multiple category contests.

New contests and awards are announced in various writer's publications nearly every day. However, many lose their funding or fold—and sponsoring magazines go out of business just as often. We have contacted the organizations whose contests and awards are listed here with the understanding that they are valid through 1996. If you are using this section in 1997 or later, keep in mind that much of the contest information listed here will not be current. Requirements such as entry fees change, as do deadlines, addresses and contact names.

To make sure you have all the information you need about a particular contest, always send a self-addressed, stamped, business-sized envelope (#10 SASE) to the contact person in the listing before entering a contest. The listings in this section are brief, and many contests have lengthy, specific rules and requirements that we could not include in our limited space. And many contests have specific entry forms that must accompany your submission. A response with rules and guidelines will not only provide specific instructions, it will also confirm that the award is still being offered.

When you receive a set of guidelines, you will see that some contests are not for some writers. The writer's age, previous publication, geographic location and the length of the work are common matters of eligibility. Read the requirements carefully to ensure you don't enter a contest for which you are not qualified. You should also be aware that every year, more and more contests, especially those sponsored by "little" literary magazines, are charging entry fees.

Contest and award competition is very strong. While a literary magazine may publish ten short stories in an issue, only one will win the prize in a contest. Give yourself the best chance of winning by sending only your best work. There is always a percentage of manuscripts a contest judge or award director casts off immediately as unpolished, amateurish or wholly unsuitable for the competition.

To avoid first-round rejection, make certain that you and your work qualify in every way for the award. Some contests are more specific than others. There are many contests and awards for a "best poem," but some award only the best lyric poem, sonnet or haiku.

Winning a contest or award can launch a successful writing career. Take a professional approach by doing a little extra research. Find out who the previous winner of the award was by investing in a sample copy of the magazine in which the prize-winning article, poem or short story appeared. Attend the staged reading of an award-winning play. Your extra effort will be to your advantage in competing with writers who simply submit blindly.

If a contest or award requires nomination by your publisher, ask your publisher to nominate you. Many welcome the opportunity to promote a work (beyond their own, conventional means) they've published. Just be sure the publisher has plenty of time before the deadline to nominate your work.

Further information on funding for writers is available at most large public libraries. See the *Annual Register of Grant Support* (National Register Publishing Co., 3004 Glenview Rd., Wilmette IL 60091); *Foundations and Grants to Individuals* (Foundation Center, 79 Fifth Ave., New York NY 10003) and *Grants and Awards Available to American Writers* (PEN American Center, 568 Broadway, New York NY 10012). For more listings of contests and awards for fiction writers, see *Novel & Short Story Writer's Market* (Writer's Digest Books). *Poet's Market* (Writer's Digest Books) lists contests and awards available to poets. *Children's Writer's & Illustrator's Market* (Writer's Digest Books) has a section of contests and awards, as well. Two more good sources for literary contests are *Poets & Writers* (72 Spring St., New York NY 10012), and the *Associated Writing Programs Newsletter* (Old Dominion University, Norfolk VA 23529). Journalists should look into the annual Journalism Awards Issue of *Editor & Publisher* magazine (11 W. 19th St., New York NY 10011), published in the last week of December. Playwrights should be aware of the newsletter put out by The Dramatists Guild, (234 W. 44th St., New York NY 10036).

For more information on contests and awards not listed in *Writer's Market*, see Contests and Awards/Changes '95-'96 at the end of this section.

General

THE CHRISTOPHER AWARD, The Christophers, 12 E. 48th St., New York NY 10017. (212)759-4050. Award Director: Peggy Flanagan. Estab. 1949. Outstanding books published during the calendar year that "affirm the highest values of the human spirit."

COMMONWEALTH CLUB OF CALIFORNIA BOOK AWARDS, (formerly California Literature Award), 595 Market St., San Francisco CA 94105. (415)597-6700. Fax: (415)597-6729. Contest/Award Director: Jim Coplan. Estab. 1931. Offered annually for previously published submissions appearing in print January 1-December 31 of the previous year. "Purpose of award is the encouragement and production of literature in California. Categories include: fiction, nonfiction, poetry, first novel, juvenile ages up to 10, juvenile 11-16, notable contribution to publishing and California." Deadline: January 1. Guidelines for SASE. Can be nominated by publisher as well. Prize: Medals to be awarded at publicized event. Judged by jury of 8-10 academics and peers selected by the club's Board of Governors. "Work must be authored by California resident (or must have been a resident at time of publication)."

‡CRAFT OF WRITING MANUSCRIPT CONTEST, Greater Dallas Writers Association and Center for Continuing Education, University of Texas at Dallas, P.O. Box 833688, M/S CN1.1, Richardson TX 75083. (214)883-2204. Fax: (214)883-2995. Contact: Janet Harris. Offered annually for unpublished work. "The Manuscript Contest is held in conjunction with the annual Craft of Writing Conference, September 22 and 23, 1995. Manuscripts must be accompanied by the registration fee ($195) for the conference. All information concerning both contest and conference will be mailed to interested parties upon request." Guidelines upon request. Charges $195 fee for contest and conference.

‡FULBRIGHT SCHOLAR PROGRAM, Council for International Exchange of Scholars, 3007 Tilden St. NW, Suite 5M, Washington DC 20008-3009. (202)686-7877. Fax: (202)362-3442. Contact: Steven A. Blodgett. Offered annually for previously published or unpublished submissions. One thousand awards to conduct research, lecture, or for combined research and lecturing in 140 countries worldwide. Awards are available for writers both in and out of academia. Grants range from 2 months to an academic year. Virtually all disciplines participate. Deadline: August 1. Application materials available in March by mail or phone. "Benefits vary by country, but generally include international travel and living expenses abroad." Judged by peer review panels plus Fulbright organization abroad (selection). "Scholars in all academic ranks are eligible to apply, from junior faculty to professor emeriti. Applications are also encouraged from professionals outside academia, as well as from faculty at all types of institutions. Basic eligibility requirements are U.S. citizenship and the Ph.D. or comparable professional qualifications (for certain fields such as the fine arts or TEFL, the terminal degree in the field may be sufficient). For lecturing awards, university or college teaching experience is expected. Language skills are needed for some countries."

HOOSIER HORIZON WRITING CONTEST, Write-On, Hoosiers, Inc., P.O. Box 51, Crown Point IN 46307. (219)663-707. Contact: Sharon Palmeri. Offered annually for unpublished work to build an awareness of Indiana talent. Deadline: July. Guidelines for SASE. Charges $1 fee per poem or story (check or money order only). Prize: 1st-$15 and publication; 2nd-$10, certificate and ribbon; 3rd-$5, certificate and ribbon. Open to all Indiana writers.

‡LOUISIANA LITERARY AWARD, Louisana Library Association, P.O. Box 3058, Baton Rouge LA 70821. (504)342-4928. Fax: (504)342-3547. Contact: Literary Award Committee. Estab. 1909. Offered annually for work published during the preceding year related to Louisiana. Guidelines for SASE.

‡MATURE WOMEN'S GRANTS, National League of American Pen Women, 1300 17th St., Washington DC 20036. (202)785-1997. Contact: Shirley Holden Helberg. Offered every 2 years to further the 35+ age woman and her creative purposes in art, music and letters. Deadline: January 15, even numbered years. Award announced by July 15. Send letter stating age, background and purpose for the money. Send SASE by August 1 in odd-numbered years for information. Charges $8 fee. Prize: $1,000 for art, letters and music.

MINNESOTA VOICES PROJECT COMPETITION, New Rivers Press, 420 N. Fifth St., #910, Minneapolis MN 55401. (612)339-7114. Editor/Publisher: C.W. Truesdale. Offered annually for new and emerging writers of poetry, prose, essays, and memoirs (as well as other forms of creative prose) from Wisconsin, Minnesota, Iowa and the Dakotas, to be published in book form for the first time. Deadline: April 1. Guidelines for SASE.

MODERN LANGUAGE ASSOCIATION PRIZE FOR A FIRST BOOK, Modern Language Association, 10 Astor Place, New York NY 10003-6981. (212)475-9500. Fax: (212)477-9863. Contact: Richard Brod. Offered annually for the first book-length publication by a current member of the association. To qualify, a book must be a literary or linguistic study, a critical edition of an important work, or a critical biography. Studies dealing with literary theory, media, cultural history and writer disciplinary topics are eligible. Deadline: May 1. Guidelines for SASE. Prize: $1,000 and certificate.

‡NATIONAL BOOK AWARDS, National Book Foundation, Attn: National Book Awards, 260 Fifth Ave., Room 904, New York NY 10001. (212)685-0261. Executive Director: Neil Baldwin. Awards Coordinator: Kevin La Follette. Fiction, nonfiction and poetry—books by American authors. "Publishers must enter the books." Deadlines: July 15 (entry forms); July 31 (books). Charges $100 fee.

NEW WRITING AWARD, New Writing, Box 1812, Amherst NY 14226-7812. Contact: Sam Meade. Offered annually for unpublished work "to award the best of *new* writing. We accept short stories, poems, plays, novels, essays, films and emerging forms. All entries are considered for the award based on originality." Charges $10 reading fee for first entry; $5 per additional entry—no limit. Guidelines and form for SASE. Prize: Monetary award (up to $3,000 in cash and prizes) and possible publication. Judged by editors. "We are looking for new, interesting work."

OHIOANA BOOK AWARDS, Ohioana Library Association, 65 S. Front St., Room 1105, Columbus OH 43215. Phone/fax: (614)466-3831. Editor: Barbara Maslekoff. Estab. 1929. Books published within the past year by Ohioans or about Ohio and Ohioans. Submit 2 copies of book on publication.

‡PEN CENTER WEST LITERARY AWARDS, PEN Center West, 672 S. Lafayette Park Place, #41, Los Angeles CA 90057. (213)365-8500. Fax: (213)365-9616. Estab. 1952. Awards and $500 cash prizes offered for work published in previous calendar year. Deadline: 4 copies must be received by December 31. Open to writers living west of the Mississippi River. Award categories: fiction, nonfiction, poetry, drama, children's literature, screenplay, teleplay, journalism, criticism, translation.

PULITZER PRIZES, The Pulitzer Prize Board, 702 Journalism, Columbia University, New York NY 10027. (212)854-3841. Estab. 1917. Journalism in US newspapers (published daily or weekly), and in letters, drama and music by Americans. Deadline: February 1 (journalism); March 1 (music and drama); July 1 and November 1 (letters).

ROCKY MOUNTAIN ARTIST'S/ECCENTRIC BOOK COMPETITION, Hemingway Western Studies Center, Boise State University, 1910 University Dr., Boise ID 83725. (208)385-1999. Fax: (208)385-4373. E-mail: rentrusk@idbsu.idbsu.edu. Contest Director: Tom Trusky. Offered annually "to publish multiple edition artist's or eccentric books of special interest to Rocky Mountain readers. Topics must be public issues (race, gender, environment, etc.). Authors may hail from Topeka or Ulan Bator, but their books must initially have regional appeal." Deadline: September 1-December 1. Guidelines for SASE. Prize: $500, publication, standard royalties. Judged by: First round: 5 regional judges; semi-finalists are evaluated by four judges from a national board. First rights to Hemingway Center. Open to any writer.

THE CARL SANDBURG LITERARY ARTS AWARDS, The Friends of the Chicago Public Library, 400 S. State St., 10S-7, Chicago IL 60605. (312)747-4907. Estab. 1979. Chicago (and metropolitan area) writers of published fiction, nonfiction, poetry and children's literature. Deadline for submission: August 1.

SMALL PRESS PUBLISHER OF THE YEAR, Quality Books Inc., 1003 W. Pines Rd., Oregon IL 61061. (815)732-4450. Fax: (815)732-4499. Contact: Michael Huston. Estab. 1964. "Each year a publisher is named that publishes titles we stock and has demonstrated ability to produce a timely and topical title, suitable for libraries. This publisher attains 'quality bestseller status and supports their distributor.' " Title must have been selected for stocking by Quality Books Inc. QBI is the principal nationwide distributor of small press titles to libraries.

SOCIETY OF MIDLAND AUTHORS AWARD, Society of Midland Authors, % Ford-Choyke, 29 E. Division St., Chicago IL 60610. (312)337-1482. President: Phyllis Ford-Choyke. Offered annually for work published between January 1 and December 31. "Award for best work by writers of the 12 Midwestern states: Illinois, Indiana, Iowa, Kansas, Michigan, Minnesota, Missouri, Nebraska, North Dakota, South Dakota, Wisconsin, Ohio and the stimulation of creative literary effort. Seven categories: poetry, adult fiction, adult nonfiction, biography, juvenile fiction, juvenile nonfiction, drama." Deadline: January 15, 1996. Guidelines for SASE. Money and plaque given at annual dinner in Chicago, in May.

TOWSON STATE UNIVERSITY PRIZE FOR LITERATURE, College of Liberal Arts, Towson State University, Towson MD 21204-7097. (410)830-2128. Award Director: Dean Annette Chappell. Estab. 1979. Book or book-length ms that has been accepted for publication, written by a Maryland author of no more than 40 years of age. Deadline: May 15.

‡UNIVERSITY OF ARIZONA SUMMER RESIDENCY PROGRAM, University of Arizona Poetry Center, 1216 N. Cherry Ave., Tucson AZ 85719. (602)321-7760. Fax: (602)621-5566. Contact: Alison Deming. Offered annually to provide an individual writer with a place to create in a quiet neighborhood. Deadline: February 15-March 15. Guidelines for SASE.

SAUL VIENER PRIZE, American Jewish Historical Society, 2 Thornton Rd., Waltham MA 02154. Editor: Marc Lee Raphael. Estab. 1985. Offered every 2 years for work published within previous 2 years. "Award for outstanding scholarly work in American Jewish history." Deadline: February 15. Write/call Marc Lee Raphael. Prize: $500. Open to any writer.

‡WESTERN STATES BOOK AWARDS, Western States Arts Federation, 236 Montezuma Ave., Santa Fe NM 87501. (505)988-1166. Estab. 1984. Unpublished fiction, poetry or creative nonfiction, that has been accepted for publication in the award year, by a press in a Western States Arts Federation member state: Alaska, Arizona, California, Colorado, Idaho, Montana, Nevada, New Mexico, Oregon, Utah, Washington, and Wyoming. Manuscript duplication and return postage fee of $10. Send #10 SASE for deadline. Prize: $5,000.

WHITING WRITERS' AWARDS, Mrs. Giles Whiting Foundation, 1133 Avenue of the Americas, New York NY 10036. Director: Gerald Freund. "The Foundation gives annually $30,000 each to up to ten writers of poetry, fiction, nonfiction and plays. The awards place special emphasis on exceptionally promising emerging talent." Direct applications and informal nominations are not accepted by the Foundation.

WORLD FANTASY AWARDS ASSOCIATION, 5 Winding Brook Dr., #1B, Guilderland NY 12084-9719. President: Peter Dennis Pautz. Estab. 1975. Previously published work recommended by previous convention attendees in several categories, including life achievement, novel, novella, short story, anthology, collection, artist, special award-pro and special award non-pro. Deadline: July 1. Works are recommended by attendees of current and previous 2 years' conventions, and a panel of judges. Winners determined by vote of panel.

Nonfiction

HERBERT BAXTER ADAMS PRIZE, American Historical Association, 400 A St. SE, Washington DC 20003. Fax: (202)544-8307. Contact: Executive Assistant. Offered annually for a US or Canadian author's first substantial book in the field of modern European history from 1815 to the present. Guidelines for #10 SASE. Prize: $1,000. Deadline: May 15.

‡AIP SCIENCE WRITING AWARDS IN PHYSICS & ASTRONOMY, American Institute of Physics, One Physics Ellipse, College Park MD 20740. (301)209-3090. Fax: (301)209-0846. Contact: Joan Wrather. Offered annually for previously published work "to recognize and stimulate distinguished writing that improves the general public's understanding and appreciation of physics and astronomy." Deadlines: Articles, Booklets or Books by Professional Journalists published between January 1-December 31 due February 6; Articles, Booklets or Books intended for Children up to 15 years published between July 1-June 30 due July 24; Articles, Booklets or Books by physicists or astronomers published between May 1-April 30 due May 19. Guidelines for SASE. Prize: $3,000, inscribed Windsor chair, certificate and certificate to publisher.

ANNUAL PERSONAL ESSAY CONTEST, Belles Lettres: A Review of Books by Women, 11151 Captain's Walk Ct., North Potomac MD 20878-0441. (301)294-0278. Contest Director: Renee Shea. Estab. 1993. Offered annually for unpublished work "to promote excellence in personal essay writing." Entries accepted January 1-August 31 of each year. Contest rules and entry forms available for SASE. Charges $20 fee. "This entitles writer to one year's subscription to *Belles Lettres*. Current subscribers may enter for free." Prize: $500. "Rights revert to author after piece is published, except for anthology inclusions." Open to women only.

‡APSA BOOK AWARDS, American Political Science Association, 1527 New Hampshire Ave. NW, Washington DC 20036. (202)483-2512. Fax: (202)483-2657. Contact: Sean Twombly. Offered annually for work published in the previous 2 years. Four awards: Ralph J. Bunche Award (for the best scholarly work in political science which explores the phenomenon of ethnic and cultural pluralism); Gladys M. Kammerer Award (for the best political science publication in the field of US national policy); Victoria Schuck Award (for the best book published on women and politics); Woodrow Wilson Foundation Award (for the best book published in the United States in the field of government, politics and international affairs). Deadline: February 15. Guidelines for SASE.

‡VINCENT ASTOR MEMORIAL LEADERSHIP ESSAY CONTEST, US Naval Institute, 118 Maryland Ave., Annapolis MD 21402-5035. (410)268-6110. Fax: (410)269-7940. Award Director: James A. Barber, Jr. Essays on the topic of leadership in the sea services (junior officers and officer trainees). Deadline: February 15.

MRS. SIMON BARUCH UNIVERSITY AWARD, United Daughters of the Confederacy, 328 N. Boulevard, Richmond VA 23220-4057. (404)255-0549. Offered biannually in even-numbered years for unpublished work for the purpose of encouraging research in Southern history, the United Daughters of the Confederacy offers as a grant-aid of publication the Mrs. Simon Baruch University Award of $2,000. Deadline: May 1. Authors and publishers interested in the Baruch Award contest should ask for a copy of these rules. All inquiries should be addressed to the Chairman of the Mrs. Simon Baruch University Award Committee at the above address. Award: $2,000 and $500 author's award. Invitation to participate in the contest is extended (1) to anyone who has received a Master's, Doctoral, or other advanced degree within the past fifteen years, from a university in the United States: and (2) to any graduate student whose thesis or dissertation has been accepted by such an institution. Manuscripts must be accompanied by a statement from the registrar giving dates of attendance, and by full biographical data together with passport photograph of the authors.

GEORGE LOUIS BEER PRIZE, American Historical Association, 400 A St. SE, Washington DC 20003. Fax: (202)544-8307. Contact: Executive Assistant. Offered annually for the best work on European international history since 1895. Prize: $1,000. Deadline: May 15.

THE PAUL BIRDSALL PRIZE IN EUROPEAN MILITARY & STRATEGIC HISTORY, American Historical Association, 400 A. St. SE, Washington DC 20003. Fax: (202)544-8307. Contact: Executive Assistant. Offered biannually for a major work in European military and strategic history. Guidelines for SASE. Prize: $1,000. Deadline: May 15. Next award year is 1996.

JAMES HENRY BREASTED PRIZE, American Historical Association, 400 A St. SE, Washington DC 20003. Fax: (202)544-8307. Contact: Executive Assistant. Offered annually in a 4-year chronological cycle for an outstanding book in any field of history prior to 1000 A.D. Prize: $1,000. Deadline: May 15. In 1995, books in African, North American and Latin American history will be eligible.

‡THE BROSS PRIZE, Lake Forest College, 555 N. Sheridan, Lake Forest IL 60045. (708)735-5169. Fax: (708)735-6291. Contact: Professor Ron Miller. Offered every 10 years for unpublished work "to award the best book or treatise on the relation between any discipline or topic of investigation and the Christian religion." Deadline: September 1, 2000. Guidelines for SASE. Prize: Award varies depending on interest earned. Manuscripts awarded prizes become property of the college. Open to any writer.

‡ARLEIGH BURKE ESSAY CONTEST, US Naval Institute, 118 Maryland Ave., Annapolis MD 21402-5035. (410)268-6110. Fax: (410)269-7940. Award Director: James A. Barber, Jr. Estab. 1873. Essay that advances professional, literary or scientific knowledge of the naval and maritime services. Deadline: December 1.

CLIFFORD PRIZE, American Society for 18th Century Studies, Computer Center 108, Utah State University, Logan UT 84322-3730. Phone/fax: (801)797-4065. E-mail: uthomp@gibbs.oit.unc.edu. Executive Secretary: Dr. Jeffrey Smitten. Contact: James Thompson, Mary Sheriff (UNC-Chapel Hill), Bernadette Fort (Northwestern University). Offered annually for previously published work, "the best nominated article, an outstanding study of some aspect of 18th-century culture, interesting to any 18th-century specialist, regardless of discipline." Guidelines for SASE. Must submit 8 copies of the article. Prize: $500, certificate from ASECS. Judged by committee of distinguished members. Winners must be society members ($30-50 dues).

‡COAST GUARD ESSAY CONTEST, Naval Institute Essay and Photo Contests, 118 Maryland Ave., Annapolis MD 21402-5035. (410)268-6110. Fax: (410269-7940. Contact: Bert Hubinger. Offered annually for original, analytical and/or interpretative, unpublished essays; maximum 3,000 words. Essays must discuss current issues and new directions for the Coast Guard. Deadline: June 1. Guidelines available. Prizes: $1,000, $750 and $500. Winning essays are published in December *Proceedings*. Open to anyone.

MORTON N. COHEN AWARD, Modern Language Association of America, 10 Astor Place, New York NY 10003-6981. (212)475-9500. Fax: (212)477-9863. Contact: Richard Brod. Estab. 1989. Awarded in odd-numbered years for a previously published distinguished edition of letters. At least 1 volume of the edition must have been published during the previous 2 years. Prize: $1,000. Guidelines for #10 SASE. Deadline: May 1.

DE LA TORRE BUENO PRIZE, Dance Perspectives Foundation, % 85 Ford Ave., Fords NJ 08863-1652. (908)738-7598. Fax: (908)548-2642. Contact: Barbara Palfy. Estab. 1973. Open to writers or their publishers who have published an original book of dance scholarship within the previous year. Deadline: January 15.

THE PREMIO DEL REY PRIZE, American Historical Association, 400 A St. SE, Washington DC 20003. Fax: (202)544-8307. Contact: Executive Assistant. Offered biannually for a distinguished book in English in the field of early Spanish and Hispanic history and culture (prior to 1516). Guidelines for SASE. Prize: $1,000. Deadline: May 15. Next award year is 1996.

DEXTER PRIZE, Society for the History of Technology, Dept. of Social Sciences, Michigan Tech University, 1400 Townsend Dr., Houghton MI 49931-1295. (906)487-2459. Fax: (906)487-2468. Contact: Society Secretary. Estab. 1968. For work published in the previous 3 years: for 1996—1993 to 1995. "Award given to the best book in the history of technology." Deadline: April 15. Guidelines for SASE. Prize: $2,000 and a plaque from the Dexter Chemical Company.

‡GORDON W. DILLON/RICHARD C. PETERSON MEMORIAL ESSAY PRIZE, American Orchid Society, Inc., 6000 S. Olive Ave., West Palm Beach FL 33405-9974. (407)585-8666. Fax: (407)585-0654. Contact: Jane Mengel. Estab. 1985. "To honor the memory of two outstanding former editors of the *American Orchid Society Bulletin*. Annual themes of the essay competitions are announced by the Editor of the *A.O.S. Bulletin* in the May issue. Themes in past years have included Orchid Culture, Orchids in Nature and Orchids in Use. The contest is open to all individuals with the exception of A.O.S. employees and their immediate families."

JOHN H. DUNNING PRIZE IN AMERICAN HISTORY, Executive Assistant, American Historical Association, 400 A St. SE, Washington DC 20003. Fax: (202)544-8307. Offered biannually in odd-numbered years for any topic in US history. Prize: $1,000. Deadline: May 5.

THE RALPH WALDO EMERSON AWARD, The Phi Beta Kappa Society, 1811 Q St. NW, Washington DC 20009-1696. (202)265-3808. Fax: (202)986-1601. Contact: Administrator, Phi Beta Kappa Book Awards. Estab. 1960. Studies of the intellectual and cultural condition of man published in the US during the 12-month period preceding the entry deadline, and submitted by the publisher. Books must have been published May 1, 1994-April 30, 1995. Deadline: April 30. Author must be a US citizen or resident.

DAVID W. AND BEATRICE C. EVANS BIOGRAPHY AWARD, Mountain West Center for Regional Studies, Utah State University, University Hill, Logan UT 84322-0735. (801)750-3630. Fax: (801)750-3899. Contact: F. Ross Peterson, Shannon R. Hoskins. Estab. 1983. Offered to encourage the writing of biography about people who have played a role in Mormon Country. (Not the religion, the country: Intermountain West with parts of Southwestern Canada and Northwestern Mexico.) Deadline: December 31, 1995. Publishers or author may nominate book. Criteria for consideration: Work must be a biography or autobiography on "Mormon Country"; must be submitted for consideration for publication year's award; new editions or reprints are not eligible; mss are accepted. Submit 6 copies.
• The award continues to be $10,000, but this may change in the near future.

JOHN K. FAIRBANK PRIZE IN EAST ASIAN HISTORY, American Historical Association, 400 A St. SE, Washington DC 20003. Fax: (202)544-8307. Contact: Executive Assistant. Offered annually for an outstanding book on the history of China proper, Vietnam, Chinese central Asia, Mongolia, Manchuria, Korea or Japan since the year 1800. Guidelines for #10 SASE. Prize: $1,000. Deadline: May 15.

HERBERT FEIS AWARD FOR NONACADEMICALLY-AFFILIATED HISTORIANS, American Historical Association, 400 A St. SE, Washington DC 20003. Contact: Executive Assistant. Estab. 1984. Offered annually for the best book, article/articles, or policy paper by an historian not affiliated with academe. Prize: $1,000, Funded by a grant from the Rockefeller Foundation. Deadline: May 15.

‡FIRST SERIES AWARD FOR CREATIVE NONFICTION, Mid-List Press, 4324 12th Ave. S., Minneapolis MN 55407-3218. Open to any writer who has never published a book of creative nonfiction. Submit either a collection of essays or a single book-length work; minimum length 50,000 words. Charges $10 fee. Submit entire ms begining after March 31; must be *received* (not postmarked) by July 1. No ms returned without SASE. Manuscripts without SASE *must* include #10 SASE for notification. Will acknowledge receipt of ms only if self-addressed stamped postcard enclosed. Only 1 submission/person/award. Accepts simultaneous submissions. Guidelines and entry form for SASE. Awards include publication and an advance against royalties.

THE CHRISTIAN GAUSS AWARD, The Phi Beta Kappa Society, 1811 Q St. NW, Washington DC 20009-1696. (202)265-3808. Fax: (202)986-1601. Contact: Administrator, Phi Beta Kappa Book Awards. Estab. 1950. Works of literary criticism or scholarship published in the US during the 12-month period preceding the entry deadline, and submitted by the publisher. Books must have been published May 1, 1994-April 30, 1995. Deadline: April 30. Author must be a US citizen or resident.

LEO GERSHOY AWARD, American Historical Association, 400 A St. SE, Washington DC 20003. Fax: (202)544-8307. Contact: Executive Assistant. Offered annually to the author of the most outstanding work in English on any aspect of the field of 17th and 18th-century Western European history. Prize: $1,000. Deadline: May 15.

‡LOUIS GOTTSCHALK PRIZE 1996, American Society for 18th Century Studies, Computer Center 108, Utah State University, Logan UT 84322-3730. Phone/fax: (801)797-4065. E-mail: uthomp@gibbs.oit .unc.edu. Executive Secretary: Jeffrey Smitten. Contact: James Thompson, Mary Sheriff (UNC-Chapel Hill), Bernadette Fort (Northwestern University). Offered annually for previously published (between Jan. 1993 and Dec. 1993) work. Purpose is "to award outstanding historical or critical study on the 18th century. Louis Gottschalk (1899-1975), second president of ASECS, President of the American Historical Association and for many years Distinguished Service Professor at the University of Chicago, exemplified in his scholarship the humanistic ideals which this award is meant to encourage." Deadline: November 15, 1995. Guidelines and form available for SASE. Publisher must send in 5 copies for contest. Prize: $1,000 and certificate from ASECS. Judged by committee of distinguished members. Winners must be society members ($30-50 dues).

CLARENCE HARING PRIZE, American Historical Association, 400 A St. SE, Washington DC 20003. Fax: (202)544-8307. Contact: Executive Assistant. Offered every 4 years for the best work by a Latin American scholar in Latin American history. Prize: $500. Deadline: May 15. Next award year is 1996.

‡INTERNATIONAL NAVIES ESSAY CONTEST, Naval Institute Essay and Photo Contests, 118 Maryland Ave., Annapolis MD 21402-5035. (410)268-6110. Fax: (410269-7940. Contact: Bert Hubinger. Offered annually for original, analytical and/or interpretative, unpublished essays; maximum 3,000 words. Essays must discuss strategic, geographic, and cultural influences on individual or regional navies, their commitments and capabilities, and relationships with other navies. Deadline: August 1. Guidelines available. Prizes: $1,000, $750 and $500. Open to authors of all nationalities.

‡ANSON JONES, M.D. AWARD, % Texas Medical Association, 401 W. 15th St., Austin TX 78701-1680. (512)370-1392. Contact: Jean Pietrobono. Estab. 1957. Health (Texas newspaper, magazine—trade, commercial, association, chamber or company—radio, TV and Spanish language). Deadline: January 15.

JOAN KELLY MEMORIAL PRIZE IN WOMEN'S HISTORY, American Historical Association, 400 A St. SE, Washington DC 20003. Fax: (202)544-8307. Contact: Executive Assistant. Estab. 1984. Offered annually for the best work in women's history and/or feminist theory. Prize: $1,000. Deadline: May 15.

KATHERINE SINGER KOVACS PRIZE, Modern Language Association of America, 10 Astor Place, New York NY 10003-6981. (212)475-9500. Fax: (212)477-9863. Contact: Richard Brod. Estab. 1990. Offered annually for book in English on Latin American or Spanish literatures and cultures published in previous year. Guidelines for #10 SASE. Prize: $1,000. Deadline: May 1.

THE LINCOLN PRIZE AT GETTYSBURG COLLEGE, Lincoln & Soldiers Institute, Gettysburg College, Campus Box 435, Gettysburg PA 17325. (717)337-6590. Fax: (717)337-6596. Chairman of the Board: Gabor

S. Boritt. Offered annually for works appearing in print January 1-December 31 each year, "to recognize annually the finest scholarly work on Abraham Lincoln, the Civil War soldier, or on the American Civil War. All things being equal, preference will be given to work on Lincoln, the Civil War soldier and work that addresses the literate general public. In rare instances the Prize may go to a work of fiction, poetry, drama and beyond." Deadline: December 1, July 1 (for spring publications). Guidelines for #10 SASE. Prize: $50,000 cash award and sculpture. Prize awarded April of the following year. Ten copies of the published entry must be submitted by the appropriate deadline, accompanied by a brief letter stating the author, title of work and publication date.

LITTLETON-GRISWOLD PRIZE, American Historical Association, 400 A St. SE, Washington DC 20003. Fax: (202)544-8307. Contact: Executive Assistant. Estab. 1985. Offered annually for the best book in any subject on the history of American law and society. Deadline: May 15. Prize: $1,000.

LOFT CREATIVE NONFICTION RESIDENCY PROGRAM, The Loft, Pratt Community Center, 66 Malcolm Ave. SE, Minneapolis MN 55414-3551. Contact: Program Director. Estab. 1974. Opportunity to work in month-long seminar with resident writer and cash award to 6 creative nonfiction writers. "Must live close enough to Minneapolis to participate fully." Deadline: November (subject to change). Guidelines for SASE.

JAMES RUSSELL LOWELL PRIZE, Modern Language Association of America, 10 Astor Place, New York NY 10003-6981. (212)475-9500. Fax: (212)477-9863. Contact: Richard Brod. Offered annually for literary or linguistic study, or critical edition or biography published in previous year. Open to MLA members only. Guidelines for #10 SASE. Prize: $1,000. Deadline: March 1.

‡McLEMORE PRIZE, Mississippi Historical Society, P.O. Box 571, Jackson MS 39205-0571. (601)359-6850. Fax: (601)359-6905. Managing Editor: Christine Wilson. Estab. 1902. Scholarly book on a topic in Mississippi history/biography published in the year of competition (year previous to January 1 deadline). Deadline: January 1.

‡MARINE CORPS ESSAY CONTEST, Naval Institute Essay and Photo Contests, 118 Maryland Ave., Annapolis MD 21402-5035. (410)268-6110. Fax: (410)269-7940. Contact: Bert Hubinger. Offered annually for original, analytical and/or interpretative, unpublished essays; maximum 3,000 words. Essays must discuss current issues and new directions for the Marine Corps. Deadline: May 1. Guidelines available. Prizes: $1,000, $750 and $500. Winning essays published in November *Proceedings*. Open to anyone.

HOWARD R. MARRARO PRIZE, American Historical Association, 400 A St. SE, Washington DC 20003. Fax: (202)544-8307. Contact: Executive Assistant. Offered annually for the best work in any epoch of Italian history, Italian cultural history, or Italian-American relations. Prize: $500. Deadline: May 15.

HOWARD R. MARRARO PRIZE, Modern Language Association of America, 10 Astor Place, New York NY 10003-6981. (212)475-9500. Fax: (212)477-9863. Contact: Richard Brod. Offered in even-numbered years for books or essays on any phase of Italian literature or comparative literature involving Italian, published in previous 2 years. Open to MLA members only. Guidelines for #10 SASE. Prize: $750. Deadline: May 1.

‡THE MAYFLOWER SOCIETY CUP COMPETITION, North Carolina Literary and Historical Association, 109 E. Jones St., Raleigh NC 27601-2807. (919)733-7305. Contact: Award Director. Previously published nonfiction by a North Carolina resident. Deadline: July 15.

MELCHER BOOK AWARD, Unitarian Universalist Association, 25 Beacon St., Boston MA 02108-2800. Fax: (617)367-3237. Staff Liaison: Patricia Frevert. Estab. 1964. Previously published book on religious liberalism. Deadline: December 31.

KENNETH W. MILDENBERGER PRIZE, Modern Language Association of America, 10 Astor Place, New York NY 10003-6981. (212)475-9500. Fax: (212)477-9863. Contact: Richard Brod. Offered annually for previously published research in the field of teaching foreign languages and literatures. Guidelines for #10 SASE. Prize: $500. Deadline: May 1.

MLA PRIZE FOR INDEPENDENT SCHOLARS, Modern Language Association of America, 10 Astor Place, New York NY 10003-6981. (212)475-9500. Fax: (212)477-9863. Contact: Richard Brod. Offered annually for book in the field of English or another modern language literature published in previous year. Authors who hold tenure or tenure-track positions in higher education are not eligible. Guidelines and application form for SASE. Prize: $1,000. Deadline: May 1.

GEORGE JEAN NATHAN AWARD FOR DRAMATIC CRITICISM, Cornell University, Department of English, Goldwin Smith Hall, Ithaca NY 14853. (607)255-6801. Fax: (607)255-6661. E-mail: ww22@cor nell.edu. Contact: Chair, Dept. of English. Offered annually to the American "who has written the best piece of drama criticism during the theatrical year (July 1-June 30), whether it is an article, an essay, treatise or book." Guidelines for SASE. Prize: $5,000 and a silver medallion. Only published work may be submitted, and the author must be an American citizen.

‡**NATIONAL JEWISH BOOK AWARD—AUTOBIOGRAPHY/MEMOIR**, Sandra Brand and Arik Weintraub Award, Jewish Book Council, 15 E. 26th St., New York NY 10010. (212)532-4949. Director: Carolyn Starman Hessel. Offered annually to an author of an autobiography or a memoir of the life of a Jewish person.

‡**NATIONAL JEWISH BOOK AWARD—CONTEMPORARY JEWISH LIFE**, The Jewish Book Council, 15 E. 26th St., New York NY 10010. (212)532-4949. Contact: Carolyn Starman Hessel. Offered annually for a nonfiction work dealing with the sociology of modern Jewish life.

‡**NATIONAL JEWISH BOOK AWARD—HOLOCAUST**, Leon Jolson Award, Jewish Book Council, 15 E. 26th St., New York NY 10010. (212)532-4949. Contact: Carolyn Starman Hessel. Offered annually for a nonfiction book concerning the Holocaust. Deadline: September 1.

‡**NATIONAL JEWISH BOOK AWARD—ISRAEL**, Morris J. and Betty Kaplun Memorial Award, Jewish Book Council, 15 E. 26th St., New York NY 10010. (212)532-4949 ext. 297. President: Arthur Kurzweil. Executive Director: Carolyn Starman Hessel. Offered annually for a nonfiction work about Zionism and/or the State of Israel. Deadline: September 1.

NATIONAL JEWISH BOOK AWARD—JEWISH HISTORY, Gerrard and Ella Berman Award, Jewish Book Council, 15 E. 26th St., New York NY 10010. (212)532-4949 ext. 297. Director: Carolyn Starman Hessel. Offered annually for a book of Jewish history. Deadline: September 1.

‡**NATIONAL JEWISH BOOK AWARD—JEWISH THOUGHT**, Jewish Book Council, 15 E. 26th St., New York NY 10010. (212)532-4949. Director: Carolyn Starman Hessel. Offered annually for a book dealing with some aspect of Jewish thought, past or present. Deadline: September 1.

‡**NATIONAL JEWISH BOOK AWARD—SCHOLARSHIP**, Sarah H. and Julius Kushner Memorial Award, Jewish Book Council, 15 E. 26th St., New York NY 10010. (212)532-4949. Director: Carolyn Starman Hessel. Offered annually for a book which makes an original contribution to Jewish learning. Deadline: September 1.

‡**NATIONAL JEWISH BOOK AWARD—VISUAL ARTS**, Anonymous Award, Jewish Book Council, 15 E. 26th St., New York NY 10010. (212)532-4949. Director: Carolyn Starman Hessel. Offered annually for a book about Jewish art. Deadline: September 1.

THE FREDERIC W. NESS BOOK AWARD, Association of American Colleges and Universities, 1818 R St. NW, Washington DC 20009. (202)387-3760. Fax: (202)265-9532. Director For Membership: Peggy Neal. Offered annually for work previously published July 1-June 30 of the year in which it is being considered. "Each year the Frederic W. Ness Book Award Committee of the Association of American Colleges and Universities recognizes books which contribute to the understanding and improvement of liberal education." Deadline: August 15. Guidelines and entry forms for SASE. "Writers may nominate their own work; however, we send letters of invitation to publishers to nominate qualified books." Prize: Presentation at the association's annual meeting and $1,000. Transportation and one night hotel for meeting are also provided.

ALLAN NEVINS PRIZE, Society of American Historians, 2 Butler Library, Columbia University, New York NY 10027. Executive Secretary: Professor Mark Carnes. Offered for American history (nominated doctoral dissertations on arts, literature, science and American biographies). Deadline: January 15. Prize: $1,000, certificate and publication.

NEW JERSEY COUNCIL FOR THE HUMANITIES BOOK AWARD, New Jersey Council for the Humanities (NJCH), 28 W. State St., 6th Floor, New Brunswick NJ 08608. (609)695-4838. Fax: (609)695-4929. Coordinator: Erica Mosner. Offered annually for work previously published January 1-December 31 to honor a New Jersey author by virtue of birth, residence, or occupation, and to bring more exposure to humanities books that stimulate curiosity and enrich the general public's understanding of their world. Deadline: Usually February 1. Guidelines for SASE. "Publisher only must nominate the book, but author can call us and we will send the information directly to their publisher." Prize: $1,000 for the author, $2,000 pro forma marketing award to publisher, and title distributed to up to 100 libraries throughout New Jersey. Judged by NJCH's Book Award Committee.

‡**NORTH AMERICAN INDIAN PROSE AWARD, University of Nebraska Press**, 327 Nebraska Hall, Lincoln NE 68588-0520. Contact: Award Director. Offered for the best new work by an American Indian writer. Prize: publication by the University of Nebraska Press with $1,000 advance. Guidelines for #10 SASE. Deadline: July 1.

‡**ELI M. OBOLER MEMORIAL AWARD**, American Library Association's Intellectual Freedom Round Table, 50 E. Huron St., Chicago IL 60611. (312)280-4224. Contact: Chairman. "Offered every 2 years" to the author of an article (including a review), a series of thematically connected articles, a book, or a manual published on the local, state or national level, in English or in English translation. The works to be considered must have as their central concern one or more issues, events, questions or controversies in the area of intellectual freedom, including matters of ethical, political, or social concern related to intellectual freedom. The work for which the award is granted must have been published within the *two-year* period ending the December prior to the ALA Annual Conference at which it is granted." Deadline: December 1, 1997.

FRANK LAWRENCE AND HARRIET CHAPPELL OWSLEY AWARD, Southern Historical Association, Department of History, University of Georgia, Athens GA 30602-1602. (706)542-8848. Fax: (706)542-2455. Managing Editor: John B. Boles. Estab. 1934. Offered in odd-numbered years for recognition of a distinguished book in Southern history published in even-numbered years. Publishers usually submit the books. Deadline: March 1.

‡**FRANCIS PARKMAN PRIZE**, Society of American Historians, 2 Butler Library, Columbia University, New York NY 10027. (212)854-2221. Contact: Professor Mark Carnes. Offered annually for Colonial or national US history book. Deadline: January 15. Prize: $1,000, bronze medal and certificates to author and publisher.

PEN/JERARD FUND, PEN American Center, 568 Broadway, New York NY 10012. (212)334-1660. Fax: (212)334-2181. Contact: John Morrone. Estab. 1986. Biennial grant of $4,000 for American woman writer of nonfiction for a booklength work in progress in odd-numbered years. Guidelines for #10 SASE. Next award: 1997. Deadline: January 2.

PEN/MARTHA ALBRAND AWARD FOR NONFICTION, PEN American Center, 568 Broadway, New York NY 10012. (212)334-1660. Fax: (212)334-2181. Coordinator: John Morrone. Offered annually for a first-published book of general nonfiction distinguished by qualities of literary and stylistic excellence. Eligible books must have been published in the calendar year under consideration. Authors must be American citizens or permanent residents. Although there are no restrictions on the subject matter of titles submitted, non-literary books will not be considered. Books should be of adult nonfiction for the general or academic reader. Deadline: December 23. Publishers, agents and authors themselves must submit *3* copies of each eligible title. Prize: $1,000, and a residence at the Johnson Studio Center, Johnson, Vermont.

PEN/SPIELVOGEL-DIAMONSTEIN AWARD, PEN American Center, 568 Broadway, New York NY 10012. (212)334-1660. Fax: (212)334-2181. Coordinator: John Morrone. Offered for the best previously unpublished collection of essays on any subject by an American writer. "The $5,000 prize is awarded to preserve the dignity and esteem that the essay form imparts to literature." Authors must be American citizens or permanent residents. The essays included in books submitted may have been previously published in magazines, journals or anthologies, but must not have collectively appeared before in book form. Books will be judged on the basis of the literary character and distinction of the writing. Publishers, agents, or the authors themselves must submit 4 copies of each eligible title. Deadline: December 23.

PHI BETA KAPPA AWARD IN SCIENCE, The Phi Beta Kappa Society, 1811 Q St. NW, Washington DC 20009-1696. (202)265-3808. Fax: (202)986-1601. Contact: Book Awards Administrator. Estab. 1959. Offered annually for interpretations of the physical or biological sciences or mathematics published in the US May 1, 1995-April 30, 1996 and submitted by the publisher. Books that are exclusively histories of science are *not* eligible, nor are biographies of scientists in which a narrative emphasis predominates. Works of fiction are not eligible. Deadline: April 30. Author must be a US citizen or resident.

PHI BETA KAPPA BOOK AWARDS, The Phi Beta Kappa Society, 1811 Q St. NW, Washington DC 20009-1696. (202)265-3808. Fax: (202)986-1601. Contact: Book Awards Administrator. Estab. 1776. Offered annually to recognize and honor outstanding scholarly books published in the US May 1, 1995-April 30, 1996 in the fields of the humanities, the social sciences, and the natural sciences and mathematics. Deadline: April 30. "Authors may request information, however books must be submitted by the publisher." Entries must be the works of authors who are US citizens or residents.

‡**COLIN L. POWELL JOINT WARFIGHTING ESSAY CONTEST**, Naval Institute Essay and Photo Contests, 118 Maryland Ave., Annapolis MD 21402-5035. (410)268-6110. Fax: (410)269-7940. Contact: Bert Hubinger. Offered annually for original, analytical and/or interpretative, unpublished essays; maximum 3,000 words. Essays must discuss combat readiness in a joint context (key issues involving two or more services).

Essays may be heavy in uni-service detail, but must have joint application in terms of tactics, strategy, weaponry, combat training, force structure, doctrine, operations, organization for combat, or interoperability of hardware, software and procedures. Deadline: April 1. Guidelines available. Prizes: $2,500, $2,000 and $1,000. Winning essays published in July *Proceedings*. Open to military professionals and civilians.

THE BARBARA SAVAGE "MILES FROM NOWHERE" MEMORIAL AWARD, The Mountaineers Books, 1011 SW Klickitat Way, Suite 107, Seattle WA 98134. (206)223-6303. Award Director: Margaret Foster. Offered in even-numbered years for previously unpublished book-length nonfiction personal adventure narrative. Narrative must be based on an outdoor adventure involving hiking, mountain climbing, bicycling, paddle sports, skiing, snowshoeing, nature, conservation, ecology, or adventure travel not dependent upon motorized transport. Subjects *not* acceptable include hunting, fishing, or motorized or competitive sports. Guidelines for 9×12 SASE. Prize: $3,000 cash award, a $12,000 guaranteed advance against royalties and publication by The Mountaineers. Next submission deadline is October 1, 1996.
● More regional and conservation-oriented titles are preferred.

‡ALDO AND JEANNE SCAGLIONE PRIZE FOR STUDIES IN GERMANIC LANGUAGES, Modern Language Association of America, 10 Astor Place, New York NY 10003-6981. (212)475-9500. Fax: (212)477-9863. Contact: Richard Brod. Offered in even-numbered years for previously published outstanding scholarly work appearing in print in 1994 or 1995 and written by a member of the MLA, on the linguistics or literatures of the Germanic languages. Deadline: May 1, 1996. Guidelines for SASE. Prize: $1,000 and certificate presented at association's annual convention in December. "Works of literary history, literary criticism, and literary theory are elibible. Books that are primarily translations are not."

ALDO AND JEANNE SCAGLIONE PRIZE FOR STUDIES IN SLAVIC LANGUAGES AND LITERATURES, Modern Language Association, 10 Astor Place, New York NY 10003-6981. (212)475-9500. Fax: (212)477-9863. Contact: Richard Brod. Offered biannually for books published in the previous 2 years. Books published in 1995 or 1996 are eligible. Membership in the MLA is not required. Works of literary history, literary criticism, philology and literary theory are eligible. Deadline: May 1. Guidelines for SASE. Prize: $1,000 and a certificate.

ALDO AND JEANNE SCAGLIONE PRIZE IN COMPARATIVE LITERARY STUDIES, Modern Language Association of America, 10 Astor Place, New York NY 10003-6981. (212)614-6406. Contact: Richard Brod. Offered annually for work published in the preceding year that is outstanding scholarly work in the field of comparative literary studies involving at least 2 literatures. Prize: $1,000 and certificate. Judged by committee of the MLA. Writer must be a member of the MLA. Works of scholarship, literary history, literary criticism and literary theory are eligible. Books that are primarily translations are not.

ALDO AND JEANNE SCAGLIONE PRIZE IN FRENCH AND FRANCOPHONE STUDIES, 10 Astor Place, New York NY 10003-6981. (212)614-6406. Contact: Richard Brod. Offered annually for work published in the preceding year that is an outstanding scholarly work in the field of French or francophone linguistic or literary studies. Prize: $1,000 and certificate. Judged by a committee of the MLA. Writer must be a member of the MLA. Works of scholarship, literary history, literary criticism and literary theory are eligible; books that are primarily translations are not. Deadline: May 1.

‡SCIENCE IN SOCIETY BOOK AWARDS, Canadian Science Writers' Association, P.O. Box 75, Station A, Toronto, Ontario M5W 1A2 Canada. (416)928-0624. Fax: (416)960-0528. Director: Andy F. Visser-deVries. Offered annually for work published January 1-December 31 of previous year. Two awards: Children's Book Award and General Science Book Award, available for and to the general public with value in promoting greater understanding of science. Deadline: December 15. Guidelines for SASE. Prize: $1,000 and a plaque. Works entered become property of CSWA. Open to Canadian citizens or resident of Canada. Material published in Canada.

‡SERGEANT KIRKLAND'S PRIZE IN CONFEDERATE HISTORY, Sergeant Kirkland's Museum and Historical Society, Inc., 912 Lafayette Blvd., Fredericksburg VA 22401-5617. (703)899-5565. Fax: (703)899-7643. Offered annually for the best research work focusing on an individual Confederate soldier or regimental unit. Text must have been in publication during the 12 months prior to the June 1 deadline. Studies should be in scholarly form and based, in part, on primary sources, with the usual documentation and bibliography. Must be at least 65,000 words. Prize: $500 and engraved plaque.

MINA P. SHAUGHNESSY PRIZE, Modern Language Association of America, 10 Astor Place, New York NY 10003-6981. (212)475-9500. Fax: (212)477-9863. Contact: Richard Brod. Offered annually for research publication (book or article) in the field of teaching English language and literature published during preceding year. Guidelines for #10 SASE. Prize: $500. Deadline: May 1.

FRANCIS B. SIMKINS AWARD, Southern Historical Association, Department of History, University of Georgia, Athens GA 30602-1602. (706)542-8848. Fax: (706)542-2455. Managing Editor: John B. Boles.

Estab. 1934. Offered in odd-numbered years for recognition of the best first book by an author in the field of Southern history over a 2-year period. The award is sponsored jointly with Longwood College. Longwood College supplies the cash amount and the certificate to the author(s) for this award. The SHA furnishes a certificate to the publisher. Deadline: March 1.

C.L. SONNICHSEN BOOK AWARD, Texas Western Press of the University of Texas at El Paso, El Paso TX 79968-0633. (915)747-5688. Press Director: John Bristol. Estab. 1952. Offered for previously unpublished nonfiction ms dealing with the history, literature or cultures of the Southwest. Deadline: March 1.

BRYANT SPANN MEMORIAL PRIZE, History Department, Indiana State University, Terre Haute IN 47809. Estab. 1980. Social criticism in the tradition of Eugene V. Debs. Deadline: April 30. Guidelines for SASE. SASE also required with submissions. Prize: $1,000.

‡CHARLES S. SYDNOR AWARD, Southern Historical Association, Department of History, University of Georgia, Athens GA 30602. (706)542-8848. Offered in even-numbered years for recognition of a distinguished book in Southern history published in odd-numbered years. Deadline: March 1.

Fiction

AIM MAGAZINE SHORT STORY CONTEST, P.O. Box 20554, Chicago IL 60620-0554. (312)874-6184. Managing Editor: Dr. Myron Apilado. Estab. 1974. Unpublished short stories (4,000 words maximum) "promoting brotherhood among people and cultures." Deadline: August 15.
 • *Aim* is a nonprofit publication; its staff is volunteer.

AKC GAZETTE FICTION CONTEST, (formerly Pure-Bred Dogs American Kennel Gazette Fiction Contest), The American Kennel Club, 51 Madison Ave., New York NY 10010. Associate Editor: David Savage. Estab. 1885. 1st-Prize: $350 and publication; cash prize to top 3 winners, . Guidelines for #10 SASE.

NELSON ALGREN SHORT STORY AWARDS, *Chicago Tribune*, 435 N. Michigan Ave., Chicago IL 60611. Contact: Larry Kart. Offered annually for previously unpublished stories between 2,500-10,000 words by American writers. Deadline: February 1. Guidelines for SASE. Prize: 1st-$5,000; $1,000 each to 3 runners-up. No phone calls please.

ANVIL PRESS INTERNATIONAL 3-DAY NOVEL WRITING CONTEST, Anvil Press, 204-A 175 E. Broadway, Vancouver, British Columbia V5T 1W2 Canada. (604)876-8710. Fax: (604)879-2667. Contact: Brian Kaufman. Estab. 1988. Offered annually for the best novel written in 3 days (Labor Day weekend). Entrants return finished novels to Anvil Press for judging. Registration deadline: Friday before Labor Day weekend. Send SASE (IRC if from the US) for details. Charges $15 fee.

‡CANADIAN AUTHORS ASSOCIATION, Metropolitan Toronto Branch, 33 Springbank Ave., Scarborough, Ontario M1N 1G2 Canada. Phone/fax: (416)698-8687. Cross-Canada contest offered annually to encourage writing of new short story fiction (under 3,000 words) and to help new Canadian authors publish. Deadline: November 30. Winners and 10 honorary mentions published in top quality Winners' Circle Short Story Anthology. Also 5 cash prizes. Charges $15 fee. Send SASE for entry form and free brochure, "How Best to Write for a Short Story Contest."

‡CANADIAN FICTION MAGAZINE, Contributor's Prize. P.O. Box 1061, Kingston, Ontario K7L 4Y5 Canada. Contact: Editor-in-Chief. Estab. 1971. Best story of year in French or English. Canadian citizens only. Deadline: September 15. Prize: $500.

RAYMOND CARVER SHORT STORY CONTEST, English Department, Humboldt State University, Arcata CA 95521. Contact: Coordinator. Offered annually for unpublished work. Deadline: November 1. Guidelines available for SASE. Charges $10/story fee. Prize: 1st-$500 plus publication in *Toyon*, Humboldt State University's literary magazine. 2nd-$250. Previous year's judges include Ann Beattie, Deena Metzger, James D. Houston, Gary Fisketjon. Contest open to any writer living in the US.

JAMES FENIMORE COOPER PRIZE, Society of American Historians, Box 2, Butler Library, Columbia University, New York NY 10027. (212)854-2221. Executive Secretary: Professor Mark Carnes. Offered annually for historical novel on an American theme. Deadline: January 15. Prize: $1,000 and certificates to author or publisher.

‡THE WILLIAM FAULKNER LITERARY COMPETITION, The Pirate's Alley Faulkner Society, 632 Pirate's Alley, New Orleans LA 70116-3254. (504)586-1609. Fax: (504)522-9725. Contest Director: Joseph J. DeSalvo, Jr.. Offered annually for unpublished mss to encourage publisher interest in a promising writer's novel, novella, short story or short story by a Louisiana high school student. Deadline: April 15. Guidelines for SASE. Charges entry fee: novel $35, novella $30, short story $25, high school short story $10. Prize: novel-$7,500, novella-$2,500; short story-$1,500, high school-$1,000; and expenses for trip to New Orleans for Faulkner Celebration. Excerpts published in Society's Literary Quarterly. The Society retains the right to publish excerpts. Open to all US residents.

‡FC2/ILLINOIS STATE UNIVERSITY, National Fiction Competition, PC2- Unit for Contemporary Literature, Illinois State University, Normal IL 61790-4242. (309)438-3582. Fax: (309)438-3523. Contact: Curtis White. Offered annually for unpublished book-length work of fiction chosen by a nationally distinguished judge. Deadline: November 15. Guidelines for SASE. Charges $15 fee. Prize: Publication and visit to campus. Open to any writer.

‡FIRST SERIES FOR SHORT FICTION, Mid-List Press, 4324 12th Ave. S., Minneapolis MN 55407-3218. Open to any writer who has never published a book-length collection of short fiction (short stories, novellas); minimum 50,000 words. Submit entire ms beginning *after* March 31, and must be *received* (not postmarked) by July 1. Only 1 submission/person/award. Accepts simultaneous submissions. Charges $10 fee. No ms returned without SASE. Mss submitted without return envelope *must* include #10 SASE for notification. Will acknowledge receipt of ms only if self-addressed stamped postcard enclosed. Guidelines and entry form for SASE. Awards include publication and an advance against royalties.

ROBERT L. FISH MEMORIAL AWARD, Mystery Writers of America, Inc., 17 E. 47th St., 6th Floor, New York NY 10017. (212)888-8171. (212)888-8107. Contact: Priscilla Ridgway. Offered annually for the best first mystery or suspense short story published during the previous year. Deadline: December 1.

GLIMMER TRAIN'S SHORT STORY AWARD FOR NEW WRITERS, Glimmer Train Press, Inc., 812 SW Washington St., Suite 1205, Portland OR 97205. (503)221-0836. Fax: (503)221-0837. Contest Director: Linda Davies. Offered 2 times/year for any writer whose fiction hasn't appeared in a nationally-distributed publication with a circulation over 5,000. "Send original, unpublished short (1,200-8,000 words) story with $11 reading fee (covers up to two stories sent together in same envelope) during the months of February/March and August/September. Title page must include name, address, phone, and 'Short-Story Award for New Writers' must be written on outside of envelope. No need for SASE as materials will not be returned. We cannot acknowledge receipt or provide status of any particular manuscript. Winners notified by July 1 (for February/March entrants) and January 1 (for August/September entrants). Winner receives $1,200 and publication in *Glimmer Train Stories*. First/second runners-up receive $500/$300, respectively, and honorable mention. All applicants receive a copy of the issue in which winning entry is published and runners-up announced."

HEEKIN GROUP FOUNDATION WRITING FELLOWSHIPS PROGRAM, The Heekin Group Foundation, P.O. Box 1534, Sisters OR 97759. (503)548-4147. Contest/Award Director: Sarah Heekin Redfield. Offered annually for unpublished works. James J. Fellowship for the Novel in Progress (2), Tara Fellowship for Short Fiction (2); Mary Molloy Fellowship for Children's Working Novel (1); Siobhan Fellowship for Nonfiction Essay (1). These 6 fellowships are awarded to beginning career writers for assistance in their literary pursuits. Deadline: December 1. Guidelines for SASE. Charges $20 fellowship application fee. Prize: James Fellowship: $3,000; Tara Fellowship: $1,500; Mary Molloy Fellowship: $2,000; Siobhan Fellowship: $2,000. Roster of finalist judges include Graywolf Press, SOHO Press, Dalkey Archive Press. Fellowships are available to those writers who are unpublished in the novel, short fiction and essay.

‡THE JANET HEIDINGER KAFKA PRIZE, English Department, Susan B. Anthony Center for Women's Studies, 538 Lattimore Hall, University of Rochester, Rochester NY 14627. Attention: Director SBA Center. Book-length fiction (novel, short story or experimental writing) by US woman citizen. Publishers must submit 4 copies. Deadline: May 1.

DRUE HEINZ LITERATURE PRIZE, University of Pittsburgh Press, 127 N. Bellefield Ave., Pittsburgh PA 15260. (412)624-4110. Fax: (412)624-7380. Series Editor: Ed Ochester. Estab. 1936. Collection of short fiction. Offered annually to writers who have published a book-length collection of fiction or a minimum of 3 short stories or novellas in commercial magazines or literary journals of national distribution. Does not return manuscripts. Guidelines for SASE. Submit: July-August.

‡HEMINGWAY DAYS FIRST NOVEL CONTEST, Hemingway Days Festival, P.O. Box 4045, Key West FL 33041. (305)294-4440. Contact: Michael Whalton. Offered annually for unpublished work to help an aspiring novelist get his or her book in print. Deadline: May 1. Guidelines for SASE. Charges $20 fee. Prize: $1,000 plus literary representation. Restricted to writers who have not had a novel published.

ERNEST HEMINGWAY FOUNDATION AWARD, PEN American Center, 568 Broadway, New York NY 10012. Contact: John Morrone. First-published novel or short story collection by an American author. Submit 3 copies. Deadline: December 23.

HEMINGWAY SHORT STORY COMPETITION, Hemingway Days Festival, P.O. Box 4045, Key West FL 33041-4045. (305)294-4440. Coordinator: Lorian Hemingway. Estab. 1981. Unpublished short stories. Deadline: June 1. Charges $10 fee. Guidelines for SASE. Prize: 1st-$1,000; 2nd and 3rd-$500 runner-up awards.
• A new contest has been created for first novels. Write for guidelines.

L. RON HUBBARD'S WRITERS OF THE FUTURE CONTEST, P.O. Box 1630C, Los Angeles CA 90078. (213)466-3310. Estab. 1983. Contest Administrator: Joni Labaqui. Unpublished science fiction, fantasy and horror. Guidelines for #10 SASE. Prize: $2,250 quarterly prizes; $4,000 annual Grand Prize, with 5-day workshop and publication in major anthology. Authors retain all rights.

INTERNATIONAL IMITATION HEMINGWAY COMPETITION, PEN Center West, 672 S. La Fayette Park Place, Suite 41, Los Angeles CA 90057. (213)365-8500. Unpublished one-page (500 words) parody of Hemingway. Must mention Harry's Bar and must be funny. Deadline: March 1. Winner receives round trip transportation for 2 to Florence, Italy and dinner at Harry's Bar & American Grill in Florence.

AGA KHAN PRIZE FOR FICTION, Box 5, 541 E. 72nd St., New York NY 10021. Estab. 1953. Fax: (212)861-0018. Contact: Fiction Editor. Offered annually for the best previously unpublished short story published in *The Paris Review* that year. Manuscripts must be a minimum of 1,000-10,000 words. All fiction mss submitted will be considered. Prize: $1,000.

LAWRENCE FOUNDATION AWARD, *Prairie Schooner*, 201 Andrews, University of Nebraska, Lincoln NE 68588-0334. (402)472-0911. Editor: Hilda Raz. Estab. 1978. Offered annually for the best short story published in *Prairie Schooner*. Winner announced in the spring issue of the following year. Manuscripts read September-May. Prize: $1,000. The Lawrence Foundation is a charitable trust located in New York City.

‡**LIBIDO SHORT FICTION CONTEST**, *Libido*, 5318 N. Paulina St., Chicago IL 60640. Erotic short fiction, 1,000-4,000 words. Deadline: Entries must be postmarked by no later than September 1. Only entries with SASE will be returned. Entries must clearly say "contest" on the envelope. Charges $15 fee. Prizes: 1st, $1,000 and publication in *Libido*; 2nd, $200; 3rd through 5th, 1-year subscriptions to *Libido*. Winners chosen by *Libido* editors. "Open to all sexual orientations, but winning stories will fit the general tone and style of *Libido*. Bonus points are awarded for accuracy of characterization, sense of style and humor, generally the darker side."

LINES IN THE SAND SHORT FICTION CONTEST, LeSand Publications, 1252 Terra Nova Blvd., Pacifica CA 94044. (415)355-9069. Associate Editor: Barbara J. Less. Estab. 1992. Offered annually to encourage the writing of good, short fiction. Deadline: October 31. Guidelines for #10 SASE. Charges $5 fee. Prizes: 1st-$50; 2nd-$25; 3rd-$10; plus publication in January/February Awards edition.

‡**LONG FICTION CONTEST**, White Eagle Coffee Store Press, P.O. Box 383, Fox River Grove IL 60021. (708)639-9200. Offered annually for unpublished work to recognize long short stories 8,000-14,000 words (about 30-50 pages). Deadline: December 15. Guidelines for SASE. Charges $10 fee. A.E. Coppard Prize: $200 and publication plus 25 copies of chapbook. Open to any writer, no restrictions on materials.

‡**MAGIC-REALISM-MAGAZINE SHORT-FICTION AWARD**, c/o Pyx Press, P.O. Box 92648, Sylmar CA 91392. Award for works published in 1995. Entries must be original works of magic realism in English of less than 20,000 words. Only stories which first appeared in the 1995 calendar year can be considered. Reprint rights must be available. Submit tearsheets/photocopies or published material; nothing in ms format will be considered. Entries cannot be acknowledged or returned. Deadline: February 15, 1996. Winning entry will be announced in fall 1996 issue of *Magic Realism*. No limit on number of entries per author or publisher. Winning story will be published in chapbook form by Pyx Press. Winning author and publisher each receive $25. Any individual may nominate own or another's published work.

MID-LIST PRESS FIRST SERIES AWARD FOR THE NOVEL, Mid-List Press, 4324-12th Ave. S., Minneapolis MN 55407-3218. (612)822-3733. Contact: Lane Stiles, senior editor. Offered annually for unpublished novels to locate and publish quality mss by first-time writers, particularly those mid-list titles that major publishers may be rejecting. Deadline February 1. guidelines for SASE. *Applicants should write, not call, for guidelines.* Charges $10 fee. Prize: $1,000 advance against royalties, plus publication. Judged by ms readers and editors of Mid-List Press: editors and publishers make final decisions. Open to any writer who has never published a *novel*.

MINNESOTA INK FICTION CONTEST, Minnesota Ink, Inc., 3585 N. Lexington Ave., Suite 328, Arden Hills MN 55126. (612)486-7818. Contact: Valerie Hockert. Offered annually for previously unpublished fiction. Deadline: December 31. Charges $5 fee.

NATIONAL JEWISH BOOK AWARD—FICTION, The Arete Foundation Award, Jewish Book Council, 15 E. 26th St., New York NY 10010. (212)532-4949, ext. 297. Fax: (212)481-4174. President Arthur Kurzweil. Executive Director: Carolyn Starman Hessel. Offered for Jewish fiction (novel or short story collection). Deadline: September 1.

NEW RIVERS PRESS AMERICAN FICTION CONTEST, New Rivers Press, English Department, Moorhead State University, Moorhead MN 56563-2996. Fax: (218236-2168. E-mail: davisa@mhdl.moorhead.msus.edu. Contest Director: Alan Davis. Estab. 1987. Offered annually to promote established and emerging writers. Submissions cannot be previously published. Prize: $1,000, $500, $250. (20-25 finalists published.) All finalists also receive a free copy of publication. Submit January 1-May 1. Guidelines for #10 SASE. Charges $7.50/story fee. Multiple and simultaneous submissions acceptable. Buys first North American serial rights to winning stories.

THE FLANNERY O'CONNOR AWARD FOR SHORT FICTION, The University of Georgia Press, 330 Research Dr., Athens GA 30602-4901. (706)369-6140. Fax: (706)369-6131. Series Editor: Charles East. Editorial Assistant: Jane Kobres. Estab. 1981. Submission period: June-July 31. Charges $10 fee. Does not return mss. Manuscripts must be 200-275 pages long. Authors do not have to be previously published. Guidelines for SASE. Prize: $1,000 and publication by Press under standard book contract.

FRANK O'CONNOR PRIZE FOR FICTION, *Descant*, Texas Christian University, P.O. Box 32872, Fort Worth TX 76129-1000. (817)921-7240. Estab. 1984. Offered annually for the best short story in the *Descant* volume. Prize: $500 given through the magazine by an anonymous donor.

‡PENNY DREADFUL SHORT STORY CONTEST, sub-TERRAIN Magazine, 2041-175 East Broadway, Vancouver, Ontario V5T 1W2 Canada. (604)876-8710. Fax: (604)879-2667. Offered annually to foster new and upcoming writers. Deadline May 15. Guidelines for SASE. Charges $15 fee for first story, $5 for additional entries. Prize: $250 (Canadian), publication in summer issue and 4-issue subscription to sub-TERRAIN.

EDGAR ALLAN POE AWARD, Mystery Writers of America, Inc., 17 E. 47th St., New York NY 10017. (212)888-8171. Contact: Priscilla Ridgway. Entries must be copyrighted or produced/published in the year they are submitted. Deadline: December 1. Entries for the book categories are usually submitted by the publisher but may be submitted by the author or his agent.

PRISM INTERNATIONAL FICTION CONTEST, *Prism International*, University of British Columbia, Buch E462, 1866 Main Mall, Vancouver, British Columbia V6T 1Z1 Canada. (604)822-2514. Fax: (604)822-3616. E-mail: prism@unixg.ubc.ca. Offered annually for previously unpublished fiction. Deadline: December 1. Guidelines for #10 SASE with Canadian postage or #10 SAE with 1 IRC. Entry fee includes 1 year subscription. Prizes: 1st-$2,000; 5 honorable mentions of $200 each, plus publication payment.

QUARTERLY WEST NOVELLA COMPETITION, *Quarterly West*, 317 Olpin Union, University of Utah, Salt Lake City UT 84112. (801)581-3938. Estab. 1976. Offered biannually for 2 unpublished novellas. Charges fee. Guidelines for SASE. Deadline: December 31 of even-numbered years.

SIR WALTER RALEIGH AWARD, North Carolina Literary and Historical Association, 109 E. Jones St., Raleigh NC 27601-2807. (919)733-7305. Awards Coordinator: Freda Brittain. Previously published fiction by a North Carolina resident. Deadline: July 15.

HAROLD U. RIBALOW AWARD, Hadassah WZOA, 50 W. 58th St., New York NY 10019. Editor: Alan Tigay. Offered annually for an English-language book of fiction on a Jewish theme published January 1-December 31 in a calendar year. Deadline: April. Prize: $1,000. Books should be submitted by the publisher.

‡SEVENTEEN MAGAZINE FICTION CONTEST, 850 Third Ave., New York NY 10022. Estab. 1948. Previously unpublished short stories from writers 13-21 years old. Deadline: April 30. Guidelines for SASE.

SFWA NEBULA® AWARDS, Science-fiction and Fantasy Writers of America, Inc., 5 Winding Brook Dr., #1B, Guilderland NY 12084-9719. Estab. 1966. Science fiction or fantasy in the categories of novel, novella, novelette and short story recommended by members. Final ballot and awards decided by ballot of the active members for works professionally published during the previous calendar year.

SHORT STORY CONTEST, *Japanophile*, P.O. Box 223, Okemos MI 48864-0223. (517)669-2109. Contact: Earl Snodgrass. Estab. 1974. Offered annually for unpublished short stories that lead to a better understanding of Japanese culture. "We prefer a setting in Japan and at least one Japanese and one non-Japanese character." Charges $5 fee. Deadline: December 31.

JOHN SIMMONS SHORT FICTION AWARD and IOWA SHORT FICTION AWARDS, Department of English, University of Iowa. English-Philosophy Building, Iowa City IA 52242-1408. Offered annually for previously unpublished fiction. Prize: publication. Guidelines for #10 SASE. Deadline: August 1-September 30.

THE SOUTHERN REVIEW/LOUISIANA STATE UNIVERSITY SHORT FICTION AWARD, Louisiana State University, 43 Allen Hall, Baton Rouge LA 70803. (504)388-5108. Selection Committee Chairman: Dave Smith. First collection of short stories by an American published in the US during previous year. Deadline: January 31. A publisher or an author may submit an entry by mailing 2 copies of the collection.

THE STAND MAGAZINE SHORT STORY COMPETITION, *Stand Magazine*, 179 Wingrove Rd., Newcastle on Tyne, NE4 9DA United Kingdom. (091)-2733280. Contact: Editors of *Stand Magazine*. "This biennial competition is an open international contest for unpublished writing in the English language intended to foster a wider interest in the short story as a literary form and to promote and encourage excellent writing in it." Deadline: March 31. "Please note that intending entrants enquiring from outside the UK should send International Reply Coupons, not stamps from their own countries. In lieu of an entry fee we ask for a minimum donation of £4 or $8 US per story entered." Editorial inquiries should be made with SASE to: Daniel Schenker and Amanda Kay, 122 Morris Road, Lacey's Spring AL 35754.

‡THE VIRTUAL PRESS ANNUAL WRITER'S CONTEST, The Virtual Press, 408 Division St., Shawano WI 54166. Publisher: William Stanek. Offered annually for unpublished work to promote the writing of quality short fiction, fantasy, mystery and science fiction. Deadline: November 1. Guidelines for SASE. "Writers could also send requests via e-mail or check or World Wide Web site http://www.gloha.com/william/uphp. html. Charges $10 fee. Prize: 12 cash awards (4 per category): 1st-$75, 2nd-$50, 3rd-$25, 4th-$10, plus publication in annual anthology.

EDWARD LEWIS WALLANT BOOK AWARD, Mrs. Irving Waltman, 3 Brighton Rd., West Hartford CT 06117. Estab. 1963. Offered for fiction with significance for the American Jew (novel or short stories) by an American writer (one who was born or educated in the United States) published during current year. Deadline: December 31.

WASHINGTON PRIZE FOR FICTION, Larry Kaltman Literary Agency, 1301 S. Scott St., Arlington VA 22204-4656. (703)920-3771. Estab. 1989. Offered for previously unpublished fiction of at least 65,000 words. Deadline: November 30. Charges $30 fee. Prize: 1st-$3,000; 2nd-$2,000, 3rd-$1,000; and literary representation if desired.

WELLSPRING'S SHORT FICTION CONTEST, 770 Tonkawa Rd., Long Lake MN 55356-9233. (612)471-9259. Contest Director: Maureen LaJoy. Estab. 1988. Offered 2 times/year for previously unpublished short fiction to encourage the writing of well-crafted and plotted, meaningful short fiction. Deadlines: January 1, July 1. Guidelines for #10 SASE. Charges $10 fee. Prize: 1st-$100; 2nd-$75; 3rd-$25.

‡WINNERS' CIRCLE SHORT STORY CONTEST, Canadian Authors Association, Metropolitan Toronto Branch, 33 Springbank Ave., Scarborough, Ontario M1N 1G2 Canada. (416)698-8687. Fax: (416)698-8687. Contact: Bill Belfontaine. Contest to encourage writing of new short stories (2,500-3,500 words) which help Canadian authors to get published. Opens July 1 annually, closes November 30. Guidelines, entry form and free brochure, "How Best to Write for a Short Story Contest," for SASE (SAE/IRC). No mss returned, but winner's list available for separate SASE (SAE/IRC). Winners announced to local and national media soon after judging, usually March of following year. Prizes: 5 cash winners (1st, $500; 4 others, $100 each). 10 or more Honorary Mentions. Winners and honorary mentions published in *Winners' Circle Anthology* and also receive official contest certificate. Entry fee $15/story, multiple submissions encouraged. All entrants receive free copy of professionally published *1995 Winners' Circle Anthology*.

‡THOMAS WOLFE FICTION PRIZE, North Carolina Writers' Network, P.O. Box 954, Carrboro NC 27510. Fax: (919)929-0535. Contact: Rachel Hunsinger. Offered annually for unpublished work "to recognize a notable work of fiction—either short story or novel excerpt—while honoring one of North Carolina's best writers—Thomas Wolfe." Deadline: August 31. Guidelines for SASE. Charges $5 fee. Prize: $500 and potential publication. Past judges have included Anne Tyler and Barbara Kingsolver.

WRITERS' JOURNAL ANNUAL SHORT STORY CONTEST, Minnesota Ink, Inc., 3585 N. Lexington Ave., Suite 328, Arden Hills MN 55126. (612)486-7818. Contact: Valerie Hockert. Estab. 1987. Previously unpublished short stories. Deadline: May 31. Charges $5 fee.

Poetry

JOHN WILLIAMS ANDREWS NARRATIVE POETRY CONTEST, *Poet Lore*, The Writer's Center, 4508 Walsh St., Bethesda MD 20815. (301)654-8664. Directors: Phillip Jason, Geraldine Connolly. Estab. 1889.

Offered annually for unpublished narrative poems of 100 lines or more. Deadline: November 30. Prize: $350 and publication in *Poet Lore*. "*Poet Lore* has first publication rights for poems submitted. All rights revert to the author after publication in *Poet Lore*."

ANHINGA PRIZE FOR POETRY, Anhinga Press, P.O. Box 10595, Tallahassee FL 32302. (904)575-5592. Fax: (904)442-6323. Contact: Rick Campbell. Offered annually for a book-length collection of poetry by an author who has not published more than one book of poetry. "We use a well-known independent judge." Submit January 1-March 1. Guidelines for #10 SASE. Charges $15 fee. Prize: $1,000 and publication. Open to any writer writing in English.

ANNUAL INTERNATIONAL NARRATIVE POETRY CONTEST, Poets and Patrons, Inc., 2820 W. Birchwood, Chicago IL 60645. Contact: Robert Mills. Unpublished poetry. Deadline: September 1. Prizes: 1st-$75; 2nd-$25.

ANNUAL POETRY CONTEST, National Federation of State Poetry Societies, 3520 State Rt. 56, Mechanicsburg OH 43044. (513)834-2666. Chairman: Amy Jo Zook. Estab. 1959. Previously unpublished poetry. "There are 50 categories. Entrant must have flier to see them all." Deadline: March 15. Guidelines for #10 SASE. Charges fees. See guidelines for fees and prizes.
  • All awards are announced in June and published in August.

‡ARKANSAS POETRY AWARD, The University of Arkansas Press, 201 Ozark Ave., Fayetteville AR 72701. (501)575-3246. Fax: (501)575-6044. Award Director: Carolyn Brt. Estab. 1990. Offered for previously unpublished full-length poetry ms to recognize living US poets whose works have not been previously published or accepted for publication in book form and thus forward the Press's stated mission of "disseminating the fruits of creative activity." Deadline May 1. Charges $15 fee. Guidelines for #10 SASE. Award: publication of the collection by the University of Arkansas Press.

GORDON BARBER MEMORIAL AWARD, Poetry Society of America, 15 Gramercy Park S., New York NY 10003. (212)254-9628. Contact: Award Director. Offered for a poem of exceptional merit or character. Guidelines for #10 SASE. Guidelines subject to change. Deadline: December 22. Open to members only. Prize: $200.

GEORGE BOGIN MEMORIAL AWARD, Poetry Society of America, 15 Gramercy Park S., New York NY 10003. (212) 254-9628. Contact: Award Director. Offered for a selection of 4-5 poems that reflects the encounter of the ordinary and the extraordinary, uses language in an original way, and takes a stand against oppression in any of its forms. Guidelines for #10 SASE. Guidelines subject to change. Deadline: December 22. Charges $5 fee for nonmembers. Prize: $500.

BRITTINGHAM PRIZE IN POETRY, FELIX POLLAK PRIZE IN POETRY, University of Wisconsin Press, 114 N. Murray St., Madison WI 53715. Contest Director: Ronald Wallace. Estab. 1985. Unpublished book-length mss of original poetry. Submissions must be *received* by the press *during* the month of September (postmark is irrelevant) and must be accompanied by a SASE for contest results. Prizes: $1,000 each and publication of winning mss. Guidelines for #10 SASE. Manuscripts will *not* be returned. Charges $15 fee, payable to University of Wisconsin Press. Results in February.

BUCKNELL SEMINAR FOR YOUNGER POETS, Stadler Center for Poetry, Bucknell University, Lewisburg PA 17837. (717)524-1853. Contact: John Wheatcroft. Offered annually. "The Seminar provides an extended opportunity for undergraduates to write and to be guided by established poets. It balances private time for writing, disciplined learning, and camaraderie among the 10 Fellows selected." Deadline: March 1. Guidelines for SASE. Prize: 10 fellowships provide tuition, room, board, and spaces for writing during 4-week long seminar. Fellows are responsible for their own transportation. Only students from American colleges who have completed their sophomore, junior, or senior years are eligible to apply.

GERALD CABLE POETRY COMPETITION, Silverfish Review Press, P.O. Box 3541, Eugene OR 97403-0541. (503)344-5060. Editor: Rodger Moody. To publish a poetry book by a deserving author. Submit September and October. Guidelines for SASE. Charges $15 fee. Prize: $1,000 and 25 copies (press run of 1,200).

GERTRUDE B. CLAYTOR MEMORIAL AWARD, Poetry Society of America, 15 Gramercy Park S., New York NY 10003. (212)254-9628. Contact: Award Director. Offered for poem in any form on the American scene or character. Guidelines for #10 SASE. Guidelines subject to change. Deadline: December 22. Members only. Prize: $250.

CLEVELAND STATE UNIVERSITY POETRY CENTER PRIZE, Cleveland State University Poetry Center, Cleveland OH 44115. (216)687-3986. Fax: (216)687-6943. Contact: Editor. Estab. 1962. Offered to identify, reward and publish the best unpublished book-length poetry ms submitted. Submissions accepted only December-February. Deadline: Postmarked on or before March 1. Charges $15 fee. "Submission implies willingness to sign contract for publication if manuscript wins." $1,000 prize for best ms. Two of the other finalist mss are also published for standard royalty (no prize). Guidelines for SASE.

COMPUWRITE, The Writers Alliance, 12 Skylark Lane, Stony Brook NY 11790. Contest Director: Kiel Stuart. Estab. 1982. Offered for previously unpublished poems. "We want an expressive, clever poem (up to 15 lines) on the act of writing with a personal computer." Deadline: January 15. Guidelines for #10 SASE. Prize: publication plus software package with at least $100 retail value.

THE BERNARD F. CONNERS PRIZE FOR POETRY, *The Paris Review*, 541 E. 72nd St., Box 5, New York NY 10021. Fax: (212)861-0018. Poetry Editor: Richard Howard. Estab. 1953. Offered for unpublished poetry over 200 lines published in *The Paris Review* that year. Prize: $1,000. Winner selected from among the eligible regular submissions. There is no special application or deadline. Must include SASE.

‡CONTEMPORARY POETRY SERIES, University of Georgia Press, 330 Research Dr., Athens GA 30602. (706)369-6140. Coordinator: Jane Kobres. Offered 2 times/year. Two awards: for poets who have not had a full-length book of poems published (deadline in September), and poets with at least one full-length publication (deadline in January). Guidelines for SASE. Charges $10 fee.

MARY CAROLYN DAVIES MEMORIAL AWARD, Poetry Society of America, 15 Gramercy Park S., New York NY 10003. (212)254-9628. Contact: Award Director. Unpublished poem suitable for setting to music. Guidelines for #10 SASE. Guidelines subject to change. Deadline: December 22. Prize: $250. Members only.

BILLEE MURRAY DENNY POETRY CONTEST, Lincoln College, 300 Keokuk St., Lincoln IL 62656. Contest Administrator: Janet Overton. Estab. 1981. Unpublished poetry. Deadline: May 31. Prizes: $1,000, $500, $250. Charges $10/poem fee (limit 3). Entry form for SASE.

ALICE FAY DI CASTAGNOLA AWARD, Poetry Society of America, 15 Gramercy Park S., New York NY 10003. (212)254-9628. Contact: Award Director. Manuscript in progress: poetry, prose or verse-drama. Guidelines for #10 SASE. Guidelines subject to change. Deadline: December 22. Prize: $1,000. Members only.

"DISCOVERY"/THE NATION, The Joan Leiman Jacobson Poetry Prizes, The Unterberg Poetry Center of the 92nd Street YM-YWHA, 1395 Lexington Ave., New York NY 10128. Estab. 1973. Open to poets who have not published a book of poems (chapbooks, self-published books included). Deadline: early February. Do not call. Write for competition guidelines.

MILTON DORFMAN POETRY PRIZE, Rome Art & Community Center, 308 W. Bloomfield St., Rome NY 13440. (315)336-1040. Contact: Leo G. Crandall. Estab. 1990. "The purpose of the Milton Dorfman Poetry Prize is to offer poets an outlet for their craft. All submissions must be previously unpublished." Entries accepted: July 1-November 1, postmarked. Guidelines for #10 SASE. Charges $3 fee. Prize: 1st-$500; 2nd-$200; 3rd-$100. Open to any writer.

THE EIGHTH MOUNTAIN POETRY PRIZE, The Eighth Mountain Press, 624 SE 29th Ave., Portland OR 97214-3026. (503)233-3936. Contact: Ruth Gundle. Estab. 1987. "Biennial prize for a book-length manuscript by a woman writer. Poems may be considered if submission is termed 'collected' or 'selected'. Award is judged by a nationally recognized woman poet." Buys all rights. Entries must be postmarked in January of even-numbered years. Guidelines for #10 SASE. Charges $15 fee. Prize: $1,000 advance against royalties and publication in the prize series.

‡VERNA EMERY POETRY PRIZE, Purdue University Press, 1532 S. Campus Courts, Bldg. E, West Lafayette IN 47907-1532. (317)494-2038. Fax: (317)496-2442. Offered annually for a single-authored book of poetry. No translations. Deadline: January 31. Guidelines for SASE. Charges $10 fee.

NORMA FARBER FIRST BOOK AWARD, Poetry Society of America, 15 Gramercy Park S., New York NY 10003. (212)254-9628. Contact: Award Director. First book of original poetry submitted by the publisher. Deadline: December 22. Charges $10/book fee. Guidelines for #10 SASE. Guidelines subject to change. Prize: $1,000.

CONSUELO FORD AWARD, Poetry Society of America, 15 Gramercy Park S., New York NY 10003. (212)254-9628. Contact: Award Director. Unpublished lyric. Guidelines for #10 SASE. Guidelines subject to change. Deadline: December 22. Members only. Prize: $250.

THE 49th PARALLEL POETRY CONTEST, The Signpost Press Inc., M.S. 9055, Western Washington University, Bellingham WA 98225. (206)734-9781. Contest Director: Robin Hemley. Estab. 1977. Unpublished poetry. Submit September 15-December 1. Charges $3/poem fee. Anyone submitting 3 or more poems will receive a complimentary 1-year subscription to *The Bellingham Review*. Awards: 1st-$150; 2nd-$100; 3rd-$50.

‡GREEN LAKE CHAPBOOK PRIZE, Owl Creek Press, 1620 N. 45th St., Seattle WA 98103. Any combination of published and unpublished poems under 40 pages in length as long as the work has not previously appeared in book form (except anthologies). Guidelines for SASE. Include SASE for return of ms. Deadline: August 15. Charges $10 fee. Prize: Publication and $500 advance against royalties.

GROLIER POETRY PRIZE, Grolier Poetry Book Shop, Inc. & Ellen LaForge Memorial Poetry Foundation, Inc., 6 Plympton St., Cambridge MA 02138. (617)547-4648. Contact: Ms. Louisa Solano. Estab. 1973. For previously unpublished work to encourage and recognize developing writers. Open to all poets who have not published with either a vanity, small press, trade, or chapbook of poetry. Opens January 15; deadline: May 1. Guidelines must be followed; send SASE. Charges $6 fee. Prize: honorarium of $150 for two poets. Also poems of each winner and 4 runners-up will be published in the Grolier Poetry Prize Annual.

CECIL HEMLEY MEMORIAL AWARD, Poetry Society of America, 15 Gramercy Park S., New York NY 10003. (212)254-9628. Contact: Award Director. Unpublished lyric poem on a philosophical theme. Guidelines for #10 SASE. Deadline: December 22. Members only. Prize: $300.

INTERNATIONAL TANKA SPLENDOR AWARDS, (formerly Mirrors International Tanka Award), AHA Books, P.O. Box 1250, Gualala CA 95445-1250. (707)882-2226. Editor: Jane Reichhold. Estab. 1988. "The purpose of the contest is to acquaint writers with the Japanese poetry form, tanka. By choosing 31 winners for publication in a chapbook, it is hoped that standards and examples will be set, re-evaluated, changed and enlarged. The genre is one of Japan's oldest, but the newest to English." Deadline: September 30. Guidelines for #10 SASE. Maximum 10 entries. No fee. Send SASE for winners list. 31 winning entries published in *Tanka Splendor*, which is given to the winners and then goes on sale for up to 3 years by AHA Books distribution.

IOWA POETRY PRIZES, University of Iowa Press, 119 W. Park Rd., Iowa City IA 52242. "The awards were initiated to encourage mature poets and their work." Manuscripts received in February and March. Send SASE. No reader's fee. Two $1,000 prizes are awarded annually. Final judging is performed by press editorial staff. Competition open to writers of English (whether citizens of US or not) who have published at least 1 previous book. No member of the faculty, staff or student body of University of Iowa is eligible.

‡RANDALL JARRELL POETRY PRIZE, North Carolina Writers' Network, 3501 Highway 54 West, Studio C, Chapel Hill NC 27516. Offered annually for unpublished work "to honor Randall Jarrell and his life at UNC-Greensboro by recognizing the best poetry submitted." Deadline: November 1. Guidelines for SASE. Charges $5 fee. Prize: $500, a public reading and reception and publication in *Parnassus: Poetry in Review*.

THE CHESTER H. JONES FOUNDATION NATIONAL POETRY COMPETITION, P.O. Box 498, Chardon OH 44024-9996. Estab. 1982. Offered annually for persons in the US, Canada and US citizens living abroad. Winning poems plus others, called "commendations," are published in a chapbook available from the foundation. Deadline: March 31. Charges $2 fee for first poem, $1 for each succeeding poem up to 10. Maximum 10 entries, no more than 32 lines each; must be unpublished. Prize: 1st-$1,000; 2nd-$750; 3rd-$500; 4th-$250; several honorable mentions $50. All commendations, which are printed in the winners book receive $10. Winners receive the book free.

‡THE JUNIPER PRIZE, University of Massachusetts, Amherst MA 01003. (413)545-2217. Fax: (413)545-1226. Contact: Bruce Wilcox. Estab. 1964. First book of poetry. Deadline: September 30. Charges $10 fee.

‡KALLIOPE'S ANNUAL SUE SANIEL ELKIND POETRY CONTEST, *Kalliope, a journal of women's art*, 3939 Roosevelt Blvd., Jacksonville FL 32205. (904)381-3511. Contact: Mary Sue Koeppel. Offered annually for unpublished work. "Poetry may be in any style and on any subject. Maximum poem length is 50 lines. Only unpublished peoms and poems not submitted elsewhere are eligible." Deadline: October 15, 1995. Guidelines for SASE. Charges entry fee: $3/poem or 4 poems for $10. No limit on number of poems entered by any one poet. Prize: $1,000, publication of poem in *Kalliope*. The winning poem is published as are the finalists' poems. Copyright then returns to the authors.

‡(HELEN AND LAURA KROUT) MEMORIAL OHIOANA POETRY AWARD, Ohioana Library Association, 65 S. Front St., Suite 1105, Columbus OH 43215. (614)466-3831. Contact: Linda R. Hengst. Offered annually "to an individual whose body of work has made, and continues to make, a significant contribution to the poetry of Ohio, and through whose work, interest in poetry has been developed." Deadline: December

31. Guidelines for SASE. Recipieint must have been born in Ohio or lived in Ohio at least 5 years.

‡LAST POEMS POETRY CONTEST, sub-TERRAIN Magazine, 204A-175 E. Broadway, Vancouver, British Columbia V5T 1W2 Canada. (604)876-8710. Fax: (604)879-2667. Offered annually for unpublished poetry that encapsulates the North American experience at the close of the 20th Century. Deadline: January 31. Guidelines for SASE. Charges $15 fee, 4 poem maximum. Prize: $100, publication in spring issue and 4-issue subscription to sub-TERRAIN Magazine.

LEAGUE OF CANADIAN POETS AWARDS, National Poetry Contest, Gerald Lampert Award, and Pat Lowther Award, 3rd Floor, 54 Wolseley St., Toronto, Ontario M5T 1A5 Canada. (416)504-1657. Fax: (416)947-0159. Estab. 1966. Offered annually to promote new Canadian poetry/poets and also to recognize exceptional work in each category. Submissions to be published in the preceding year (awards), or previously unpublished (poetry contest). Deadline: January 31. Enquiries from publishers welcome. Charge: $6/poem fee for contest *only*. Open to Canadians living at home and abroad. The candidate must be a Canadian citizen or landed immigrant, although publisher need not be Canadian. For complete contest and awards rules, contact Edita Petrauskaite at address above.

ELIAS LIEBERMAN STUDENT POETRY AWARD, Poetry Society of America, 15 Gramercy Park S., New York NY 10003. (212)254-9628. Contact: Award Director. Unpublished poem by student (grades 9-12). Poet must reside in the US or its territories. Guidelines for #10 SASE. Guidelines subject to change. Deadline: December 22. Charges $1 fee. Prize: $100.

THE RUTH LILLY POETRY PRIZE, The Modern Poetry Association, 60 W. Walton St., Chicago IL 60610-3305. Contact: Joseph Parisi. Estab. 1986. Offered annually to poet whose accomplishments in the field of poetry warrant extraordinary recognition. No applicants or nominations are accepted. Deadline varies.

LOCAL 7's ANNUAL NATIONAL POETRY COMPETITION, Santa Cruz/Monterey Local 7, National Writers Union, P.O. Box 2409, Aptos CA 95001-2409. (408)728-2855. Coordinator: Don Monkerud. Offered annually for previously unpublished poetry to encourage the writing of poetry and to showcase unpublished work of high quality. Proceeds support the work of Local 7 of the National Writers Union. Deadline varies. Guidelines for #10 SASE. Charges $3/poem fee. Prize: 1st-$200; 2nd-$100; 3rd-$50.

LOUISIANA LITERATURE PRIZE FOR POETRY, *Louisiana Literature*, SLU—Box 792, Southeastern Louisiana University, Hammond LA 70403. (504)549-5021. Contest Director: Dr. David Hanson. Estab. 1984. Unpublished poetry. Deadline: February 15. Rules for SASE. Prize: $400. Entries considered for publication.

‡AMY LOWELL POETRY TRAVELING SCHOLARSHIP, % Choate, Hall & Stewart, Exchange Place, 35th Floor, Boston MA 02109-2891. (617)248-5000. Fax: (617)248-4000. Award Director: F. Davis Dassori, Jr., Trustee. Offered annually to support an American-born poet whose work would benefit from a year spent outside of North America." Deadline: Oct. 15. Requests for applications must be received by October 1. Applications may be requested by fax but cannot be supplied by fax. Guidelines for #10 SASE. Prize: $29,000 (amount varies as it is a portion of income of a portfolio) to be paid in quarterly installments.

JOHN MASEFIELD MEMORIAL AWARD, Poetry Society of America, 15 Gramercy Park S., New York NY 10003. (212)254-9628. Contact: Award Director. Unpublished narrative poem in English. No translations. Guidelines for SASE. Guidelines subject to change. Deadline: December 22. Charges $5 fee for nonmembers. Award $500.

LUCILLE MEDWICK MEMORIAL AWARD, Poetry Society of America, 15 Gramercy Park S., New York NY 10003. (212)254-9628. Contact: Award Director. Original poem in any form or freedom on a humanitarian theme. Guidelines for #10 SASE. Guidelines subject to change. Prize: $500. Deadline: December 22. Members only.

MID-LIST PRESS FIRST SERIES AWARD FOR POETRY, Mid-List Press, 4324 12th Ave. S., Minneapolis MN 55407-3218. (612)822-3733. Contact: Lane Stiles, senior editor. Estab. 1989. Offered annually for unpublished book of poetry to encourage new poets. Deadline: February 1. Guidelines for SASE. Charges $10 fee. Prize: publication and an advance against royalties $500. Judged by Mid-List's editors and ms readers. Winners are offered a contract at the conclusion of the judging. Contest is open to any writer who has never published a book of poetry. ("We do not consider a chapbook to be a book of poetry.")

MINNESOTA INK SEMI-ANNUAL POETRY CONTEST, Minnesota Ink, Inc., 3585 N. Lexington Ave., Suite 328, Arden Hills MN 55126. (612)486-7818. Contact: Glenda Olsen. Offered winter and summer for unpublished poets. Deadline: February 28, August 15. Charges $2 fee for first poem; $1 each poem thereafter.

MISSISSIPPI VALLEY NON-PROFIT POETRY CONTEST, P.O. Box 3188, Rock Island IL 61204-3188. (309)259-1057. Director: Max Molleston. Estab. 1972. Unpublished poetry: adult general, student division, Mississippi Valley, senior citizen, religious, rhyming, jazz, humorous, haiku, history and ethnic. Deadline: 1996. Charges $5 fee, $3 for students. Up to 5 poems may be submitted with a limit of 50 lines/poem.

MORSE POETRY PRIZE, Northeastern University English Deptment, 406 Holmes Hall, Boston MA 02115. (617)437-2512. Contact: Guy Rotella. Previously published poetry, book-length mss of first or second books. Charges $10/fee. Prize: Publication by Northeastern University Press and a $500 cash award.

NATIONAL LOOKING GLASS AWARD FOR A SINGLE POEM, *Pudding Magazine: The International Journal of Applied Poetry*, 60 N. Main St., Johnstown OH 43031. (614)967-6060. Contest Director: Jennifer Bosveld. Estab. 1979. Previously unpublished poems. "To identify and publish the finest work reflecting the editorial slant of *Pudding Magazine: The International Journal of Applied Poetry.* We recommend subject matter in the area of social justice, ecology and human impact, human relations, popular culture and *artistic* work from a theraputic process." Deadline: September 30. Guidelines for #10 SASE. Charges $2/poem fee. Number of entries unlimited. Prize: $250 total in cash prizes.

NATIONAL LOOKING GLASS POETRY CHAPBOOK COMPETITION, *Pudding Magazine: The International Journal of Applied Poetry*, 60 N. Main St., Johnstown OH 43031. (614)967-6060. Contest Director: Jennifer Bosveld. "To publish a collection of poems that represents our magazine's editorial slant: popular culture, social justice, psychological, etc. Poems might be themed or not." Deadline: June 30. Guidelines for #10 SASE. Charges $9 fee. Prize: publication of the book and 20 copies to the author plus wholesale rights.

‡HOWARD NEMEROV SONNET AWARD, *The Formalist: A Journal of Metrical Poetry*, 320 Hunter Dr., Evansville IN 47711. Contact: Mona Baer. Offered annually for unpublished work to encourage poetic craftsmanship and to honor the memory of the late Howard Nemerov, third US Poet Laureate and a masterful writer of sonnets. Deadline: May 15. Guidelines for SASE. Charges $2/sonnet fee. Prize: $1,000 cash and publication in *The Formalist*; 11 other finalists also published. Acquires first North American serial rights for those sonnets chosen for publication. Upon publication all rights revert to the author. Open to the international community of writers.

GUY OWEN POETRY PRIZE, *Southern Poetry Review*, English Dept. UNCC, Charlotte NC 28223. (704)547-4336. Award Director: Ken McLaurin. Estab. 1985. Offered annually for the best unpublished poem submitted in an open competition. Given in memory of Guy Owen, a poet, fiction writer and founder of *Southern Poetry Review*. Submit in April only—3-5 previously unpublished poems and SASE. Charges $8 fee that includes one year subscription to *SPR* to begin with the Fall issue, containing the winning poem. Prize: $500 and publication in *SPR*.

‡OWL CREEK POETRY PRIZE, Owl Creek Press, 1620 N. 45th St., Seattle WA 98103. Any combination of published and unpublished poems over 50 pages in length as long as the work has not previously appeared in book form (except anthologies). Guidelines for SASE. Include SASE for return of ms. Deadline: February 15. Charges $15 fee. Prize: Publication and $750 advance against royalties.

‡PAUMANOK POETRY AWARD, Visiting Writers Program, SUNY Farmingdale, Knapp Hall SUNY Farmingdale, Farmingdale NY 11735. Offered annually for published or unpublished poems. Send cover letter, 1-paragraph bio, 5-7 poems (name and address on each poem). Include SASE for notification of winners. (Send photocopies only; mss will not be returned.) Deadline: September 15. Charges $10 fee, payable to SUNY Farmingdale VWP. Prize: 1st-$750 plus expenses for a reading in 1995-96 series; 2 runners-up—$300 plus expenses for a reading in series.

THE RICHARD PHILLIPS POETRY PRIZE, The Phillips Publishing Co., P.O. Box 121, Watts OK 74964. Contact: Richard Phillips, Jr. Offered annually to give a modest financial reward to emerging poets who have

ALWAYS submit unsolicited manuscripts or queries with a self-addressed, stamped envelope (SASE) within your country or a self-addressed envelope with International Reply Coupons (IRC) purchased from the post office for other countries.

not yet established themselves sufficiently to generate appropriate compensation for their work. Deadline: September 5. Guidelines for SASE. Charges $10 fee. Prize: $1,000 and publication. Open to all poets. "There are no anthologies to buy. No strings attached. Simply put, the poet who enters the best manuscript will win the prize of $1,000 and will receive a check in that amount within 30 days of the deadline."

THE POETRY CENTER BOOK AWARD, The Poetry Center, San Francisco State University, 1600 Holloway Ave., San Francisco CA 94132-9901. (415)338-2227. Fax: (415)338-2493. Award Director: Melissa Black. Estab. 1980. Offered annually for previously published books of poetry and chapbooks, appearing in year of the prize. "Prize given for an extraordinary book of American poetry." Deadline December 31. Guidelines for #10 SASE. Charges $10/book fee. Prize: $500 and an invitation to read in The Poetry Center Reading Series. Please include a cover letter noting author name, book title(s), name of person issuing check, and check number.

POETRY MAGAZINE POETRY AWARDS, 60 W. Walton St., Chicago IL 60610. (312)255-3703. Editor: Joseph Parisi. Estab. 1912. All poems already published in *Poetry* during the year are automatically considered for annual prizes.

POETRY PUBLICATION, The PEN (Poetry Explosion Newsletter), The Poet Band Co., P.O. Box 2648, Newport News VA 23609-0648. Editor: Arthur C. Ford. Estab. 1984. Send maximum of 5 poems. Enclose $1 for reading fee. Use rhyme and non-rhyming verse. Maximum lines: 40. Prose maximum: 200-300 words. Allow 1 month for response. Sample copy $4. Send SASE for more information. Quarterly newsletter (*The Pen*) issued March, June, September and December. Subscriptions are $15 (yearly) or $28 for 2 years.

‡POETS AND PATRONS, INC. INTERNATIONAL NARRATIVE POETRY CONTEST, 2820 W. Birchwood, Chicago IL 60045. Chairperson: Robert Mills. Deadline: September 1. *Must* send for rules after March 1.

POETS CLUB OF CHICAGO INTERNATIONAL SHAKESPEAREAN/PETRARCHAN SONNET CONTEST, 130 Windsor Park Dr. C-323, Carol Stream IL 60188. Chairman: Lavone Holt. Estab. 1954. Deadline: September 1. Guidelines for SASE after March 1.
 • The Petrarchan Sonnet form has been added to this contest.

FELIX POLLAK PRIZE IN POETRY, University of Wisconsin Press, 114 N. Murray St., Madison WI 53715. Contest Director: Ronald Wallace. Estab. 1994. Unpublished book length ms of original poetry. Submissions must be received by the press during the month of September (postmark is irrelevant) and must be accompanied by SASE for contest results. Prize: $1,000 and publication. Guidelines for #10 SASE. Does not return mss. Charges $15 fee, payable to University of Wisconsin Press. Notification in February.

PRAIRIE SCHOONER STROUSSE AWARD, *Prairie Schooner*, 201 Andrews, University of Nebraska, Lincoln NE 68588-0334. (402)472-0911. Editor: Hilda Raz. Estab. 1977. Offered annually for the best poem or group of poems published in *Prairie Schooner*. Manuscripts read September-May. Winner announced in the spring issue of the following year. Prize: $500.

QUARTERLY REVIEW OF LITERATURE POETRY SERIES, 26 Haslet Ave., Princeton NJ 08540. (609)921-6976. "QRL Poetry Series is a book publishing series chosen from an open competition." Publishes 4-6 titles/year. Prize: $1,000, publication and 100 copies to each winner for a book of miscellaneous poems, a single long poem, a poetic play or a book of translations. Guidelines for SASE. Submission May and October *only*.

THE BYRON HERBERT REECE INTERNATIONAL POETRY AWARDS, Georgia State Poetry Society, Inc., 1590 Riderwood Court, Decatur GA 30033-1531. (404)633-1647. Contact: Betty Lou Gore. Estab. 1987. Offered annually for previously unpublished poetry to honor the late Georgia poet, Byron Herbert Reece. Deadline in January. Guidelines for #10 SASE. Charges entry fee of $5/first poem; $1/additional poem. Prize: 1st-$250; 2nd-$100; 3rd-$50.

ROANOKE-CHOWAN AWARD FOR POETRY, North Carolina Literary and Historical Association, 109 E. Jones St., Raleigh NC 27601-2807. (919)733-7305. Previously published poetry by a resident of North Carolina. Deadline: July 15.

NICHOLAS ROERICH POETRY PRIZE, Story Line Press, Three Oaks Farm, Brownsville OR 97327-9718. (503)466-5352. Fax: (503)466-3200. Contact: Michele Thompson. Estab. 1988. First full-length book of poetry. Any writer who has not published a full-length collection of poetry (48 pages or more) in English is eligible to apply. Deadline: October 15. Charges $15 fee. Prize: $1,000, publication, a reading at the Nicholas Roerich Museum in New York.

‡ANNA DAVIDSON ROSENBERG AWARD FOR POEMS ON THE JEWISH EXPERIENCE, Judah L. Magnes Museum, 2911 Russell St., Berkeley CA 94705. (510)549-6950. Fax: (510)849-3650. Contact: Paula Friedman. Offered annually for unpublished work to encourage poetry of/on/from the Jewish experience. Deadline for requesting entry forms is July 15; deadline for receipt of poems is August 31. Guidelines and entry form for SASE. Submissions must include entry form. Charges $2 fee for up to 4 poems. Prize: 1st-$100; 2nd-$50; 3rd-$25; $25-New/Emerging Poet Prize; $25-Youth Award also, Senior Award and Honorable Mentions. All winners receive certificate, and winning poems are read in an Awards Reading here. Open to any writer.

SHELLEY MEMORIAL AWARD, Poetry Society of America, 15 Gramercy Park S., New York NY 10003. (212)254-9628. Contact: Award Director. Deadline: December 22. By nomination only to a living American poet. Prize: $2,000-6,000.

THE SOW'S EAR CHAPBOOK PRIZE, *The Sow's Ear Poetry Review*, 19535 Pleasant View Dr., Abingdon VA 24211-6827. (703)628-2651. Contest Director: Larry K. Richman. Estab. 1988. 24-26 pages of poetry. Submit March-April. Guidelines for #10 SASE. Charges $10 fee. Prize: 1st-$500, 50 copies and distribution to subscribers; 2nd-$100; 3rd-$100.

THE SOW'S EAR POETRY PRIZE, The Sow's Ear Poetry Review, 19535 Pleasant View Dr., Abingdon VA 24211-6827. (703)628-2651. Contest Director: Larry K. Richman. Estab. 1988. Previously unpublished poetry. Submit September-October. Guidelines for #10 SASE. Charges $2 fee/poem. Prizes: $500, $100, $50 and publication, plus publication for 20-25 finalists. All submissions considered for publication.

‡ANN STANFORD POETRY PRIZE, Southern California Anthology, % Master of Professional Writing Program, WPH 404, U.S.C., Los Angeles CA 90089-4034. (213)740-3252. Contest Director: James Ragan. Estab. 1988. Previously unpublished poetry to honor excellence in poetry in memory of poet and teacher Ann Stanford. Include cover sheet with name, address and titles of the 5 poems entered. Deadline: April 15. Guidelines for #10 SASE. Charges $10 fee. Prize: 1st-$750; 2nd-$250; 3rd-$100. Winning poems are published in *The Southern California Anthology* and all entrants receive a free issue.

EDWARD STANLEY AWARD, *Prairie Schooner*, 201 Andrews, University of Nebraska, Lincoln NE 68588-0334. (402)472-0911. Fax: (402)472-4636. Editor: Hilda Raz. Offered annually for poems published in *Prairie Schooner*. Manuscripts read September-May. Winner announced in the spring issue of the following year. Prize: $300.

THE AGNES LYNCH STARRETT POETRY PRIZE, University of Pittsburgh Press, 127 N. Bellefield Ave., Pittsburgh PA 15260. (412)624-4110. Fax: (412)624-7380. Series Editor: Ed Ochester. Estab. 1936. First book of poetry for poets who have not had a full-length book published. Deadline: March and April only. Guidelines for SASE.

ELIZABETH MATCHETT STOVER MEMORIAL AWARD, *Southwest Review*, 307 Fondren Library W., P.O. Box 374, Southern Methodist University, Dallas TX 75275-0374. (214)373-7440. For the best poem or group of poems that appeared in the magazine during the previous year. Prize: $150.

TROIKA COMPETITION, Thorntree Press, 547 Hawthorn Lane, Winnetka IL 60093. (708)446-8099. Contact: Eloise Bradley Fink. Estab. 1985. Imagery is important. Manuscripts considered January 1-February 14, in *odd-numbered years*. "We will be selecting three poets for our next *Troika*. Contestants are asked to submit a stapled group of ten pages of *un*published poetry, single or double spaced, photocopied, with a $4 reader's fee. Manuscripts will not be returned."

KATE TUFTS DISCOVERY AWARD FOR POETRY, The Claremont Graduate School, 160 E. Tenth St., Claremont CA 91711. (909)621-8974. Award Director: Murray M. Schwartz. Offered annually for poetry published in book form in English during the previous year. Guidelines and form for SASE. Entry form must accompany submission. Deadline: December 15. Prize: $5,000. Entrants must agree to reproduction rights and to be present at award ceremony.

KINGSLEY TUFTS POETRY AWARD AT THE CLAREMONT GRADUATE SCHOOL, The Claremont Graduate School, 160 E. Tenth St., Claremont CA 91711. (909)621-8974. Award Director: Murray M. Schwartz. Offered annually for poetry published in book form in English during the previous year. Also open to book-length mss that have not been published but were created in the year prior to the award. In that case, poet must have publication credits. Guidelines and form for SASE. Entry form must accompany submission. Deadline: December 15. Prize: $50,000. Entrants must agree to reproduction rights and to be present at award ceremony and week's residency the Claremont Graduate School.

VERVE POETRY CONTEST, *VERVE* Magazine, P.O. Box 3205, Simi Valley CA 93093. Contest Director: Ron Reichick. Estab. 1989. Offered 2 times/year for previously unpublished poetry. "Fund raiser for *VERVE*

Magazine which receives no grants and has no ties with any institutions." Deadlines: April 1 and October 1. Guidelines for #10 SASE. Charges $2/poem. Prizes: 1st-$100; 2nd-$50; 3rd-$25.

CELIA B. WAGNER AWARD, Poetry Society of America, 15 Gramercy Park St. S., New York NY 10003. (212)254-9628. Contact: Award Director. Unpublished poem worthy of the art in any style. Guidelines for #10 SASE. Guidelines subject to change. Deadline: December 22. Charges $5 fee for nonmembers.

‡THE WALT WHITMAN AWARD, The Academy of American Poets, 584 Broadway, Suite 1208, New York NY 10012. (212)274-0343. Fax: (212)274-9427. Contact: Matthew Brogan. Annual award for original poetry, in English, by one poet. No limitations on the kind of poetry or subject matter, though translations are not eligible. Contestants must be living citizens of U.S. who have neither published, nor committed to publish, a volume of poetry 40 pages or more in length and in an edition of 500 or more copies, either in the U.S. or abroad. Deadline: November 15. Guidelines for SASE. Charges $20 fee. Prize: $1,000 and publication of ms by Louisiana State University Press. Judged by eminent poets, selected each year.

WILLIAM CARLOS WILLIAMS AWARD, Poetry Society of America, 15 Gramercy Park S., New York NY 10003. (212)254-9628. Contact: Award Director. Small press, nonprofit, or university press book of poetry submitted by publisher. Deadline: December 22. Guidelines and form for SASE. Guidelines subject to change. Charges $10/book fee. Prize: $500-2,000.

ROBERT H. WINNER MEMORIAL AWARD, Poetry Society of America, 15 Gramercy Park S., New York NY 10003. (212)254-9628. Contact: Award Director. "For a poet whose first book appeared when he was almost 50, recognizing and rewarding the work of someone in midlife. Open to poets over 40, still unpublished or with one book." Guidelines for #10 SASE. Guidelines subject to change. Charges $5 fee for nonmembers. Deadline: December 22. Prize: $2,500.

WINTER POETRY COMPETITION, Still Waters Press, 112 W. Duerer St., Galloway NJ 08201-9402. Contest Director: Shirley A. Warren. Estab. 1989. Guidelines for #10 SASE. Charges $10 fee. Deadline: September 30. Sample winning chapbook: $5.

WOMEN'S WORDS POETRY COMPETITION, Still Waters Press, 112 W. Duerer St., Galloway NJ 08201-9402. Contest Director: Shirley A. Warren. Guidelines for #10 SASE.Charges $10 fee. Deadline: February 28.

THE WRITER MAGAZINE/EMILY DICKINSON AWARD, Poetry Society of America, 15 Gramercy Park S., New York NY 10003. (212)254-9628. Contact: Award Director. Poem inspired by Emily Dickinson, though not necessarily in her style. Guidelines for #10 SASE. Guidelines subject to change. Deadline: December 22. Members only. Prize: $100.

WRITERS' JOURNAL SEMI-ANNUAL POETRY CONTEST, Minnesota Ink, Inc., 3585 N. Lexington Ave., Suite 328, Arden Hills MN 55126. (612)486-7818. Contact: Esther M. Leiper. Previously unpublished poetry. Deadline: November 30, April 15. Charges $2 fee first poem; $1 each thereafter.

YALE SERIES OF YOUNGER POETS, Yale University Press, P.O. Box 209040, New Haven CT 06520-9040. Contact: Richard Miller. First book of poetry by poet under the age of 40. Submit during February. Guidelines for #10 SASE. Charges $15 fee. Winning manuscript is published by Yale University Press. The author receives the usual royalties.

ZUZU'S PETALS POETRY CONTEST, *Zuzu's Petals Annual*, P.O. Box 4476, Allentown PA 18105-4476. (610)821-1324. Editor: T. Dunn. Offered 2 times/year for previously unpublished poetry. Deadline: March 1, September 1. Guidelines for #10 SASE. Charges $2 fee/poem. Prize: top 3 winners share 40% of the contest's proceeds. All entries automatically considered for publication.

Playwriting and Scriptwriting

AMERICAN SHORTS, Florida Studio Theater, 1241 N. Palm Ave., Sarasota FL 34236. (813)366-9017. Fax: (813)955-4137. Offered annually for unpublished plays no more than 5 pages long on a theme that changes every year. 1994 theme was "men and women, not necessarily in that order." Deadline: varies: send inquiry to above address. Prize: $500.

‡ANNUAL ONE-ACT PLAY COMPETITION, TADA!, 120 W. 28th St., New York NY 10001. (212)627-1732. Fax: (212)243-6736. Contact: Nina Trevens. Offered annually for unpublished work to encourage playwrights, composers and lyricists to develop new plays for young audiences. Deadline: varies each year, usually in early spring/late winter. For guidelines call Nina Trevens at (212)627-1732. Prize: cash prize and staged readings of winners. Must be material with a cast composed predominantly of children.

THE MARGARET BARTLE PLAYWRITING AWARD, Community Children's Theatre of Kansas City, 8021 E. 129th Terrace, Grandview MO 64030-2114. (816)761-5775. Award Director: E. Blanche Sellens. Estab. 1951. Offered annually for unpublished plays for elementary school audiences. "Our purpose is two-fold: to award a deserving author of a good, well-written play, and to produce the play royalty-free by one of our trouping units." Deadline: January 31. Guidelines for SASE. Prize: $500.

THE BEVERLY HILLS THEATRE GUILD-JULIE HARRIS PLAYWRIGHT AWARD COMPETITION, 2815 N. Beachwood Drive, Los Angeles CA 90068. (213)465-2703. Playwright Award Coordinator: Marcella Meharg. Estab. 1978. Original full-length plays, unpublished, unproduced and not currently under option. Application required, available upon request with SASE. Submissions accepted with applications from August 1-November 1.

‡WALDO M. AND GRACE C. BONDERMAN IUPUI NATIONAL YOUTH THEATRE PLAYWRITING COMPETITION, Indiana University-Purdue University at Indianapolis, 525 N. Blackford St., Indianapolis IN 46202. (317)274-2095. Fax: (317)278-1025. Contact: Dr. Dorothy Webb. Offered every 2 years for unpublished work. Deadline: September 1 in even-numbered years. Guidelines for SASE. Prize: $1,000 and professionally staged reading to top 4 playwrights.

CALIFORNIA YOUNG PLAYWRIGHTS CONTEST, The Playwright Project, 1450 Frazee Rd., Suite 215, San Diego CA 92108. (619)298-9242. Fax: (619)298-9244. Contest Director: Deborah Salzer. Offered annually for previously unpublished plays by young writers to stimulate young people to create dramatic works, and to nurture promising young writers (under age 19). Deadline: April 1. Guidelines for 9×12 SASE. Award consists of "professional production of 3-5 winning plays at the Old Globe Theatre in San Diego, plus royalty. All entrants receive detailed evaluation letter." Judged by theater professionals in the Southern California area. Scripts must be a minimum of 10 standard typewritten pages. Writers must be California residents under age 19 as of the deadline date.

CEC JACKIE WHITE MEMORIAL NATIONAL CHILDREN'S PLAYWRITING CONTEST, Columbia Entertainment Company, 309 Parkade Blvd., Columbia MO 65202. (314)874-5628. Contact: Betsy Phillips. Estab. 1988. Offered annually for "top notch unpublished scripts for theater school use, to challenge and expand the talents of our students, ages 10-15. The entry should be a full length play with speaking roles for 20-30 characters of all ages and with at least 10 roles developed in some detail." Deadline: May 30. Production and some travel expenses for 1st and 2nd place winners, plus cash award for 1st place. Guidelines for SASE. Entrants receive written evaluation of work. Charges $10 fee.

JANE CHAMBERS PLAYWRITING AWARD, Women and Theatre Program of Association for Theatre in Higher Education (WTP/ATHE), % Tori Haring-Smith, English Department, Box 1852, Brown University, Providence RI 02912. (401)247-2911. Director: Tori Haring-Smith. Estab. 1983. "To recognize a woman playwright who has written a play with a feminist perspective, a majority of roles for women, and which experiments with the dramatic form." Deadline: February 15. Notification: May 31. Guidelines for #10 SASE. Prize: $1,000, plus travel expenses, and reading at the WTP/ATHE national conference in August. Student award: $250. "Writer must be female. A recommendation from a theatre professional is helpful, but not required."

‡CLAUDER COMPETITION, in Playwriting Excellence, P.O. Box 383259, Cambridge MA 02238. (617)322-3189. Contact: Betsy Carpenter. Offered every 2 years for unproduced plays to encourage *New England* playwrights. Deadline: June 30, 1997. Guidelines for SASE. Prize: $3,000 and full production.

CLEVELAND PUBLIC THEATRE NEW PLAYS FESTIVAL, Cleveland Public Theatre, 6415 Detroit Ave., Cleveland OH 44102. (216)631-2727. Fax: (216)631-2575. Festival Director: Terrence Cranendonk. Estab. 1983. Annual festival of staged readings of 10-15 alternative, experimental, poetic, political work, and plays by women, people of color, gays/lesbians. Deadline: September 1. Guidelines for SASE. Charges $10 fee.

COE COLLEGE PLAYWRITING FESTIVAL, Coe College, 1220 First Ave. NE., Cedar Rapids IA 52402-5092. (319)399-8689. Fax: (319)399-8748. Contact: Susan Wolverton. Estab. 1993. Offered 2 times/year for unpublished work to provide a venue for new works for the stage. "There is usually a theme for the festival. We are interested in full-length productions, *not* one acts or musicals." Next festival: 1996-97. Guidelines for SASE. Prize: $325, plus 1-week residency as guest artist with airfare, room and board provided. Judges are a select committee of professionals. "There are no specific criteria although a current résumé is requested."

THE CHRISTOPHER COLUMBUS SCREENPLAY DISCOVERY AWARDS, 433 N. Camden Dr., #600, Beverly Hills CA 90210. (310)288-1988. Fax: (310)288-0257. Monthly and annual contest "to discover new screenplay writers." Deadline: December 1. Charges $45 fee. Prize: options up to $10,000, plus professional development guidance and access to agents, producers, and studios. Judged by reputable industry professionals (producers, development executives, story analysts). Writer must give option to purchase if selected.

CUNNINGHAM PRIZE FOR PLAYWRITING, The Theatre School, DePaul University, 2135 N. Kenmore, Chicago IL 60614. (312)325-7938. Fax: (312)325-7920. Contact: Lara Goetsch. Offered annually for published or unpublished work "to recognize and encourage the writing of dramatic works which affirm the centrality of religion, broadly defined, and the human quest for meaning, truth and community." Deadline: December 1. Guidelines for SASE. Prize: $5,000. Judged by "a panel of distinguished citizens including members of the faculty of DePaul University, representatives of the Cunningham Prize Advisory Commitee, critics and others from the theater professions, chaired by John Ransford Watts, dean of the Theatre School." Open to writers whose usual residence or base of operations is in the Chicago area.

DFAP ONE-ACT PLAYWRITING CONTEST, Dubuque Fine Arts Players, 569 S. Grandview, Dubuque IA 52003. (319)582-5558. Contest Director: Sally T. Ryan. Offered annually for unpublished work to encourage playwrights. Deadline: January 31. Guidelines for SASE. Charges $10 fee. Prize: staged productions and money: $600, $300, $200. Acquires right to produce for 4 performances. Must be original, unproduced. Submit 2 copies plus entry fee.

‡**WALT DISNEY STUDIOS FELLOWSHIP PROGRAM**, Walt Disney Studios, 500 S. Buena Vista St., Burbank CA 91521-0880. (818)560-6894. Contact: Brenda Vangsness. Offered annually to discover new creative talent to work full-time developing their craft at Disney in feature film and television writing. Deadline: March 13-April 7. Guidelines for SASE. "Writing samples are required, as well as a résumé, completed application form and notarized standard letter agreement (available from the Program Administrator." Prize: $30,000 salary for 1 year period beginning mid-October. Fellows outside of LA area will be provided with airfare and 1 month's accommodations. Open to all writers. Those with WGA credits should apply through the Guild's Employment Access program.

DRAMARAMA, Playwrights' Center of San Francisco, P.O. Box 460466, San Francisco CA 94146-0466. (415)626-4603. Offered annually for unproduced, unpublished plays. No musicals or childrens' plays. Deadline: March 15. Guidelines for SASE. Must send for guidelines before submitting script. Include SASP with submission for list of winners. Charges $25 fee. Staged reading for all finalists. Prize: $500.

DRURY COLLEGE ONE-ACT PLAY CONTEST, Drury College, 900 N. Benton Ave., Springfield MO 65802-3344. (417)873-7430. Contact: Sandy Asher. Estab. 1986. Offered in even-numbered years for unpublished and professionally unproduced plays. One play per playwright. Deadline: December 1. Guidelines for SASE. Winning plays receive special recommendation to The Open Eye: New Stagings, an Off-Broadway theater in New York City.

DUBUQUE FINE ARTS PLAYERS ANNUAL ONE-ACT PLAYWRITING CONTEST, 569 S. Grandview, Dubuque IA 52003. (319)582-5558. Contest Coordinator: Sally T. Ryan. Annual competition since 1977 for previously unpublished, unproduced plays. Adaptations must be of playwright's own work or of a work in the public domain. No children's plays or musicals. No scripts over 35 pages or 40 minutes performance time. Two copies of ms required. Script Readers' review sheets available. "Concentrate on character, relationships, and a good story." Deadline: January 31. Guidelines for #10 SASE. Charges $10 fee. Prizes: $600, $300, $200, plus possible full production of play. Buys rights to first full-stage production and subsequent local video rights. Reports by June 30.

SAM EDWARDS DEAF PLAYWRIGHTS COMPETITION, New York Deaf Theatre, Ltd., 305 Seventh Ave., 11th Floor, New York NY 10001-6008. Voice: (212)924-9491. TTY: (212)924-9535. Contest Director: Jackie Roth. Offered annually for unpublished and unproduced work. "Established in 1989 to honor the memory of a founding member of the New York Deaf Theatre, the competition seeks to encourage deaf writers to create their unique stories for the stage. Keenly aware of the void which exists of plays written by deaf playwrights, the competition is the only opportunity of its kind that nurtures deaf writers in the development of their play writing skills. Unproduced scripts by deaf playwrights are accepted in two categories: full-length and one act plays." Deadline: September 1. Guidelines for SASE. Charges $10 US/Canadian and $15 foreign countries. Prize: $400 for full-length play, $200 for one-act play. "New York Deaf Theatre exercises the right to produce the winning plays, within a two-year period, as a staged reading, workshop production or full production. The competition is open to deaf writers only. It should be noted that while NYDT's mission is to create opportunities for American Sign Language Theatre for deaf theater artists and, in doing so, fosters a better understanding of Deaf Culture, the competition will accept scripts from all deaf people no matter what their primary mode of communication. However, we will only produce scripts that are in harmony with our mission."

‡**DAVID JAMES ELLIS MEMORIAL AWARD**, Theatre Americana, Box 245, Altadena CA 91001. (818)397-1740. Director: Hertha Donato, Playreading Committee. Offered annually for previously unpub-

lished work to produce original plays of Americana background and history or by American authors. Deadline: January 31. "No entry necessary but we will send guidelines on request with SASE." Prize: $500.

EMERGING PLAYWRIGHT AWARD, Playwrights Preview Productions, 17 E. 47th St., New York NY 10017. Phone/fax: (212)289-2168. Contact: Pamela Faith Jackson. Submissions required to be unpublished and unproduced in New York City. Send script, letter of introduction, production history, author's name résumé and SASE. Submissions accepted year-round. Plays selected in August and January for award consideration. Estab. 1983. Prize: $500 and New York showcase production.
  • Playwrights Preview Productions has added a new award, the Urban Stages Award.

‡LAWRENCE S. EPSTEIN PLAYWRITING AWARD, 115 HaHeras Rd., Barnegat NJ 08005-2814. Contact: Lawrence Epstein. Unpublished submissions. Deadline: October. Published in Dramatist's Guild and other newsletters.

THE FESTIVAL OF EMERGING AMERICAN THEATRE, The Phoenix Theatre, 749 N. Park Ave., Indianapolis IN 46202. (317)635-7529. Contact: Bryan Fonseca. Annual playwriting competition. Deadline: February 15.

FUND FOR NEW AMERICAN PLAYS, American Express & President's Committee on Arts & Humanities, J.F. Kennedy Center, Washington DC 20566. (202)416-8024. Fax: (202)416-8026. Manager: Sophy Burnham. Estab. 1988. Previously unproduced work. "Program objectives: to encourage playwrights to write, and nonprofit professional theaters to produce new American plays; to ease the financial burdens of nonprofit professional theater organizations producing new plays; to provide a playwright with a better production of the play than the producing theater would normally be able to accomplish." Deadline: March 15 (date changes from year to year). "Nonprofit theater organizations can mail in name and address to be placed on the mailing list." Prize: $10,000 for playwrights plus grants to theaters based on scripts submitted by producing theaters. A few encouragement grants of $2,500 are given to promising playwrights chosen from the submitted proposals. Submissions and funding proposals only through the producing theater.

JOHN GASSNER MEMORIAL PLAYWRITING AWARD, The New England Theatre Conference, Department of Theatre, Northeastern University, 360 Huntington Ave., Boston MA 02115. (617)424-9275. Estab. 1952. Unpublished full-length plays. Guidelines for #10 SASE. Deadline: April 15. Charges $10 fee; free for members of New England Theatre Conference.

GILMAN & GONZALEZ-FALLA THEATER FOUNDATION AWARD, 109 E. 64th St., New York NY 10021. (212)734-8011. Offered annually for previously produced work to encourage the creative elements in the American musical theater. Deadline August 31. Guidelines for SASE. Prize: $25,000. The script or lyrics must have been part of a musical theater work produced in the US in either a commercial theater, professional not-for-profit theater or an accredited university or college theater program.

‡GILMORE CREEK PLAYWRITING COMPETITION, Saint Mary's College of Minnesota, Campus Box 78, Winona MN 55987. (507)457-1606. Fax: (507)457-1633. Contest Director: Robert R. Pevitts. Offered every 2 years for unpublished work providing an opportunity for new works to be produced. Accept full-length plays, translations, adaptations, musicals, children's plays. Prize: $2,500 and production.

‡GEORGE HAWKINS PLAYWRIGHTING CONTEST, The Ensemble Theatre, 3535 Main St., Houston TX 77002-9529. (713)520-0055. Fax: (713)520-1269. Contact: Eileen J. Morris. Offered annually for previously unproduced short plays or musicals for young African-American audiences. Deadline: March 20 (deadline varies depending on the beginning and end of production season). Guidelines for SASE. Prize: $500 plus round-trip transportation to Houston. "Any writer may submit material that illuminates the African-American experience for children 6 to 16. Scenery must be simple, cast of no more than 5 adults and maximum playing time of 45 minutes."

HBO NEW WRITERS PROJECT, HBO and Wavy Line Productions, 2049 Century Park E., Suite 4200, Los Angeles CA 90067. Award Director: Steve Kaplan. Offered annually. "The HBO New Writers Project is designed to encourage and cultivate emerging multicultural writers and performing talent. We are seeking submissions of one-act plays, solo performance pieces or original ½ hour teleplays. Plays should be no more than 60 pages in length. We are seeking to discover a new generation of comic voices, who reflect the multicultural world in which we live." Deadline: February 1. Guidelines for SASE. "The Project will select 25 plays for participation in a Writers Workshop sponsored by HBO, in conjunction with Wavy Line Productions, Inc., with the intention that these works will be nurtured for possible stage, TV or film development."

HENRICO THEATRE COMPANY ONE-ACT PLAYWRITING COMPETITION, Henrico Theatre Co., P.O. Box 27032, Richmond VA 23273. (804)672-5100. Fax: (804)672-5284. Contest/Award Director: J. Larkin Brown. Offered annually for previously unpublished plays to produce new dramatic works in one-act form.

Award also for plays/musicals with a Christmas theme. Deadline: July 1. Guidelines for SASE. Prize: one-act $250; runner-up $125; Christmas show $250. All winning entries are produced; videotape sent to author. Judged by H.T.C. Playreading Committee. "Scripts with small casts and simpler sets given preference. Controversial themes should be avoided."

HIGH SCHOOL PLAYWRITING CONTEST, Baker's Plays, 100 Chauncy St., Boston MA 02111-1783. Phone/fax: (617)482-1280. Contest Director: Raymond Pape. Offered annually for previously unpublished plays. "Open to any high school student. Plays must be accompanied by the signature of a sponsoring high school drama or English teacher, and it is recommended that the play receive a production or a public reading prior to the submission." Deadline: postmarked by January 31. Guidelines for #10 SASE. Prize: 1st-$500 and the play published by Baker's Plays; 2nd-$250 and Honorable Mention; 3rd-$100 and Honorable Mention. Write for more information.

‡JOSEPH E. HUSTON DISTINGUISHED PLAYWRIGHTS AWARD, TORCHLIGHT PRODUCTIONS, 405 W. Howard St., Muncie IN 47305. (317)281-0941. Contact: Tim Kowalsky. Offered annually to assist new playwrights with their unpublished work. Deadline: October 15. Guidelines for SASE. Also contact TPSecretary@aol.com or Tylonius@eworld.com. Charges $10 entry fee. Prizes: 1st $100; 2nd $50; 3rd $25; plus production of 1st place winner. Acquires rights to produce one or all of the winning plays without royalty fees.

INNER CITY CULTURAL CENTER'S NATIONAL SHORT PLAY COMPETITION, Inner City Cultural Center, 1605 N. Ivar St., Los Angeles CA 90028. (213)962-2102. Contact: C. Bernard Jackson. Offered annually for unpublished work. Deadline: July. Charges $45 fee. "All entries are presented live before an audience and jurors who are professionals in the arts and entertainment industry. Writer is responsible for preparation of submission for presentation."

‡INTERNATIONAL ONE-PAGE PLAY COMPETITION, *Lamia Ink!*, P.O. Box 202, Prince St. Station, New York NY 10012. Contact: Cortland Jessup. Offered annually to encourage and promote performance writers and to challenge all interested writers. Interested in all forms of theater and performance writing in one page format. Deadline: March 15. No phone calls. Guidelines for SASE. Charges $1/one-page play. Maximum of 3 plays per author per competition. Prize: 1st-$200. Public reading given for top 12 in NYC. Publication in *Lamia Ink!*. If play has been previously published, playwright must have retained copyright. Prize: 1st-$200.

INTERNATIONAL PLAY CONTEST, Center Theater, 1346 W. Devon, Chicago IL 60660. (312)508-0200. Contact: Dale Calandra. Offered annually for unpublished work to foster and encourage the growth of playwrights. Deadline: end of February. Guidelines for SASE. Charges $15 fee. Prize: 1st-$300 cash award and production. "We do not accept unsolicited manuscripts. We will look at a one-page synopsis/character breakdown with a cover letter and résumé. Responses will only be given to those inquiries that include a SASE.

JEWEL BOX THEATRE PLAYWRIGHTING COMPETITION, Jewel Box Theatre, 3700 N. Walker, Oklahoma City OK 73118-7099. (405)521-1786. Contact: Charles Tweed. Estab. 1982. Only two- or three-acts accepted or one-acts comprising an evening of theater. Deadline: January 15. Prize: $500.

‡GEORGE R. KERNODLE ONE-ACT PLAYWRITING COMPETITION, University of Arkansas, Department of Drama, 619 Kimpel Hall, Fayetteville AR 72701. (501)575-2953. Fax: (501)575-7602. Director: Kent R. Brown. Submissions to be unpublished and unproduced (workshop productions acceptable). Deadline: June 1. Charges $3 fee per submission. Submission limit: 3. Open to all playwrights residing in the United States and Canada.

‡THE LARRY L. KING OUTSTANDING TEXAS PLAYWRIGHT AWARD, Live Oak Theatre, 200 Colorado St., Austin TX 78701. (512)472-5143. Fax: (512)472-7199. Contact: Tom Byrne. Offered annually for unpublished work to discover and produce exciting new Texas plays. (Texas themes and/or authors.) Deadline: November 1. Plays received after November 1 are included in the following years contest. Guidelines for SASE. Prize: $500 and a staged reading. "We expect authors to negotiate a production contact after the award is presented." Open to Texas residents.

MARC A. KLEIN PLAYWRITING AWARD FOR STUDENTS, Department of Theater Arts, Case Western Reserve University, 10900 Euclid Ave., Cleveland OH 44106-7077. (216)368-2858. Fax: (216)368-5184. E-mail: jmo3@po.cwru.edu. Chair, Reading Committee: John Orlock. Estab. 1975. Unpublished, professionally unproduced full-length play, or evening of related short plays by student in American college or university. Prize: $1,000, which includes $500 to cover residency expenses; production. Deadline: May 15.

LEE KORF PLAYWRITING AWARDS, The Original Theatre Works, Cerritos College, 11110 Alondra, Norwalk CA 90650. (310)860-2451, ext. 2638. Fax: (310)467-5005. Contact: Gloria Manriquez. Estab.

1984. Previously unproduced plays. Deadline: January 1. "All plays—special attention paid to plays with multicultural theme." Guidelines for SASE. Prize: ranges from $250 for workshop production to $750 royalty award and full-scale production during summer theater.

‡**KUMU KAHUA/UHM THEATRE DEPARTMENT PLAYWRITING CONTEST**, Kumu Kahua Theatre Inc./University of Hawaii at Manoa, Department of Theatre and Dance, 1770 East-West Rd., Honolulu HI 96822. (808)956-2588. Fax: (808)956-4234. Contact: Dennis Carroll. Offered annually for unpublished work to honor full-length and short plays, both about Hawaii (for international or local writers) or about other locations/themes (local residents only). Deadline: January 1. Guidelines available every September. Prize: $500, $250, Division I, full-length and short; $200, $100 Division II full-length and short.

‡**L.A. DESIGNERS' THEATRE-COMMISSIONS**, L.A. Designers' Theatre, P.O. Box 1883, Studio City CA 91614-0883. (213)650-9600. Fax: (818)9085-9200. (818)769-9000 T.D.D. Contact: Richard Niederberg. Quarterly contest "to promote new work and push it onto the conveyor belt to filmed or videotaped entertainment." All submissions must be registered with copyright office and be unpublished by "major" publishers. Material will *not* be returned. Deadline: February 15, May 15, August 15, November 15. "No rules, no fees, no entry forms. Just present an idea that can be commissioned into a full work." Prize: A production or publication of the work in the Los Angeles market. Judged by staff members from organization (anonymous to writer). "We only want 'first refusal.' If you are picked, we negotiate royalties with the writer." Open to any writer.

LIVE OAK THEATRE'S HARVEST FESTIVAL OF NEW AMERICAN PLAYS, (formerly Live Oak Theatre New Play Awards), Live Oak Theatre, 200 Colorado St., Austin TX 78701-3923. (512)472-5143. Fax: (512)472-7199. Contact: Tom Byrne. Annual awards for previously unpublished, unproduced, full-length plays. Deadline: November 1. Guidelines for #10 SASE. Prize: $1,000, $500 and possible production.

LOVE CREEK ANNUAL SHORT PLAY FESTIVAL, Love Creek Productions, % Granville, 75 Liberty Place, Weehawken NJ 07087-7012. Festival Manager: Cynthia Granville. Estab. 1985. Annual festival for unpublished plays, unproduced in New York in the previous year. "We believe that a script is incomplete as a work of art until it is performed. As an encouragement to playwrights and an enrichment opportunity for Love Creek's over 300 member artists, administrators and technicians, we have therefore established the Festival as a playwriting competition in which scripts are judged on their merits in performance." Deadline: September 30. Guidelines for #10 SASE. All entries must specify "festival" on envelope and must include letter giving permission to produce script, if chosen and stating whether equity showcase is acceptable.
 • Love Creek is now able to produce more small cast full-length plays if they require simple sets and run under 100 minutes. Larger cast full-length are still preferred. These are not part of festival competitions.

LOVE CREEK MINI FESTIVALS, Love Creek Productions, % Granville, 75 Liberty Place, Weehawken NJ 07087-7012. Festival Literary Manager: Cynthia Granville. "The Mini Festivals are an outgrowth of our annual Short Play Festival in which we produce scripts concerning a particular issue or theme which our artistic staff selects according to current needs, interests and concerns of our members, audiences and playwrights submitting to our Short Play Festival throughout the year." Guidelines for #10 SASE. Submissions must list name of festival on envelope and must include letter giving permission to produce script, if chosen, and stating whether equity showcase is acceptable. Finalists receive a mini-showcase production in New York City. Winner receives a $200 prize. Write for upcoming themes, deadlines usually end of March, May, July, October; Fear of God: Religion in the 90s will be presented again in 1995-96 along with others TBA.

‡**McLAREN MEMORIAL COMEDY PLAYWRITING COMPETITION**, Midland Community Theatre, 2000 W. Wadley, Midland TX 79705. (915)682-2544. Fax: (915)682-6136. Contact: Mary Lou Cassidy. Estab. 1946. Offered annually for unpublished work. "Entry must be a comedy. Can be one- or two-act. Number of characters or subject is not limited. Make us laugh." Deadline: January 31. Charges $5 fee. Guidelines and form for #10 SASE. Prize: $400, Reader's Theatre Performance, airfare and hotel for 1 week rehearsal and performance.

MAXIM MAZUMDAR NEW PLAY COMPETITION, Alleyway Theatre, One Curtain Up Alley, Buffalo NY 14202-1911. (716)852-2600. Dramaturg: Joyce Stilson. Estab. 1990. Annual competition. Full Length: not less than 90 minutes, no more than 10 performers. One-Act: less than 60 minutes, no more than 6 performers. Deadline: September 1. Finalists announced January 1. "Playwrights may submit work directly. There is no entry form. Annual playwright's fee $5. Please specify if submission is to be included in competition." Prize: full length—$400, travel plus lodging, production and royalties; one-act—$100, production plus royalties. "Alleyway Theatre must receive first production credit in subsequent printings and productions."

MILL MOUNTAIN THEATRE NEW PLAY COMPETITION, Mill Mountain Theatre, Center in the Square, 1 Market Square, 2nd Floor, Roanoke VA 24011-1437. (703)342-5730. Literary Manager: Jo Weinstein.

Estab. 1985. Previously unpublished and unproduced plays for up to 10 cast members. Deadline: January 1. Guidelines for SASE.

MIXED BLOOD VERSUS AMERICA, Mixed Blood Theatre Company, 1501 S. Fourth St., Minneapolis MN 55454. (612)338-0984. Contact: David B. Kunz. Estab. 1983. Theater company estab. 1975. "Mixed Blood Versus America encourages and seeks out the emerging playwright. Mixed Blood is not necessarily looking for scripts that have multi-racial casts, rather good scripts that will be cast with the best actors available." Open to all playwrights who have had at least one of their works produced or workshopped (either professionally or educationally). Only unpublished, unproduced plays are eligible for contest. Limit 2 submissions per playwright. No translations or adaptations. Guidelines for SASE. Deadline: March 15.

MRTW ANNUAL RADIO SCRIPT CONTEST, Midwest Radio Theatre Workshop, 915 E. Broadway, Columbia MO 65201. (314)874-5676. Contact: Steve Donofrio. Estab. 1979. "The purpose of the award is to encourage the writing of radio scripts and to showcase both established and emerging radio playwrights. Some winning works are produced for radio and all winning works are published in the annual MRTW Scriptbook. Our scriptbook is the only one of it's kind in this country." Deadline: November 15. Guidelines for SASE. "A cash award of $800 is split among the top 2-4 entries, depending on recommendation of the jurors. Winners receive free workshop registration. Those who receive honorable mention, as well as award-winning plays, are included in the scriptbook; a total of 10-16 are published annually. We acquire the right to publish the script in the scriptbook, which is distributed at cost, and the right to produce the script for air; all other rights retained by the author."

MULTICULTURAL THEATRE WORKS SERIES, Seattle Group Theatre, 305 Harrison St., Seattle WA 98109. (206)441-9480. Estab. 1984. Full-length translations, adaptations and plays for young audiences. Musicals are not eligible. "New works, by culturally diverse playwrights, focusing on contemporary social, political and cultural issues relevant to the world community. Submission packet should include query, sample pages of dialogue, synopsis and an SASE for reply. Full manuscript submitted by solicitation only." Honorarium, airfare and housing. Submission period: ongoing.

NANTUCKET SHORT PLAY COMPETITION AND FESTIVAL, Nantucket Theatrical Productions, Box 2177, Nantucket MA 02584. (508)228-5002. Contest Director: Jim Patrick. Offered annually for unpublished work to seek out quality new short plays. Deadline: March 1. Guidelines for SASE. Charges $5 fee. Prize: $200 grand prize to overall winner. Staged readings to several runners-up. Possible publishers referral. Acquires right to give staged readings at our festival. Open to any writer. No special criteria. Running time 1 hour or less.

NATIONAL CANADIAN ONE-ACT PLAYWRITING COMPETITION, Ottawa Little Theatre, 400 King Edward Ave., Ottawa, Ontario K1N 7M7 Canada. (613)233-8948. Fax: (613)233-8027. Director: George Stonyk. Estab. 1913. "To encourage literary and dramatic talent in Canada." Submit January-May. Guidelines for #10 SASE with Canadian postage or #10 SAE with 1 IRC. Prize: $1,000, $700, $500.

NATIONAL ONE-ACT PLAYWRITING COMPETITION, Little Theatre of Alexandria, 600 Wolfe St., Alexandria VA 22314. (703)683-5778. Contact: Chairman Playwriting Competition. Estab. 1978. To encourage original writing for theatre. Submissions must be original, unpublished, unproduced one-act stage plays. Deadline: March 31. Guidelines for SASE. Submit scripts after November 1. Charges $5 fee. Prize: 1st-$350; 2nd-$250; 3rd-$150.

NATIONAL PLAYWRIGHTS' AWARD, Unicorn Theatre, 3820 Main St., Kansas City MO 64111. (816)531-7529. Offered annually for previously unproduced work. "We produce contemporary original scripts, preferring scripts that deal with social concerns. However, we accept (and have produced) comedies." Guidelines for SASE. Prize: $1,000 in royalty/prize fee and mainstage production at the Unicorn as part of its regular season.

NATIONAL TEN-MINUTE PLAY CONTEST, Actors Theatre of Louisville, 316 W. Main St., Louisville KY 40202-4218. (502)584-1265. Fax: (502)561-3300. Literary Manager: Michael Bigelow Dixon. Estab. 1964. Previously unproduced (professionally) ten-minute plays (10 pages or less). "Entries must *not* have had an Equity or Equity-waiver production." Deadline: December 1. Prize: $1,000. Please write or call for submission guidelines.

‡NEW AMERICAN COMEDY FESTIVAL, Ukiah Players Theatre, 1041 Low Gap Rd., Ukiah CA 95482. (707)462-1210. Contact: Kate Magruder. Offered every 2 years for unpublished work to help playwrights develop their full-length comedies into funnier, stronger scripts. Deadline: December 31 of odd-numbered years. Guidelines for SASE. Prize $1,000 each for 2 winning playwrights, also travel (up to $400) to Ukiah for 2-week festival, lodging and per diem.

NEW ENGLAND NEW PLAY COMPETITION AND SHOWCASE, The Vineyard Playhouse Co., Inc., Box 2452, Vineyard Haven MA 02568. (508)693-6450. Contact: Eileen Wilson. Offered annually for unpublished, unproduced full-length, non-musical works suitable for a cast of 10 or fewer. Deadline: June 30. Notification: September 10. Guidelines for SASE. Charges $5 fee. Prize: 4 finalists receive transportation to Martha's Vineyard from a New England location and up to 3 nights accommodation to attend staged reading and consideration for full stage production. Grand prize winner also receives $500.

‡NEW PLAYS STAGED READING CONTEST, TADA! 120 W. 28th St., New York NY 10001, (212)627-1732. Fax: (212)243-6736. Contest Director: Janine Nina Trevins. Offered annually for unpublished and unproduced work to introduce the playwriting process to family audiences in a staged reading series featuring the winning entries. The cast must be predominantly children, the children are cast from the TADA! company and adult actors will be hired. The plays must be appropriate for children and teenage audiences. Deadline: February 1. Please send cover letter and play with SASE for return. If the play is a musical, include a tape of the music. No application form necessary. Prize: $200-500 and staged reading held in TADA!'s theater. Grand Prize is a workshopped production. Contest is open.

‡NEW PLAYWRIGHTS COMPETITION, The White-Willis Theatre, 5266 Gate Lake Road, Ft. Lauderdale FL 33319. (305)722-4371. Director: Ann White. Offered annually for previously unpublished full-length play scripts. Award: $500 and production by the White-Willis Theatre. Competition opens June 1. Deadline September 1.
- 1995 marked the twelfth year of this competition.

DON AND GEE NICHOLL FELLOWSHIPS IN SCREENWRITING, Academy of Motion Picture Arts & Sciences, 8949 Wilshire Blvd., Beverly Hills CA 90211-1972. (310)247-3059. Director: Greg Beal. Estab. 1985. Offered annually for unproduced screenplays to identify talented new screenwriters. Deadline: May 1. Charges $30 fee. Guidelines for SASE. Prize: $25,000 fellowships (up to 5/year). Recipients announced late October. Open to writers who have not earned more than $1,000 writing for films or TV.

OFF-OFF-BROADWAY ORIGINAL SHORT PLAY FESTIVAL, 45 W. 25th St., New York NY 10010. Fax: (212)206-1429. Contact: William Talbot. Offered annually for unpublished work. "The Festival was developed in 1976 to bolster those theater companies and schools offering workshops, programs and instruction in playwriting. It proposes to encourage them by offering them and their playwrights the opportunity of having their plays seen by new audiences and critics, and of having them reviewed for publication." Deadline: late winter. Guidelines for SASE. Prize: "Presentation on NY stage before NY audiences and critics. Publication of selected plays by Samuel French Inc." Judged by members of NYC critics' circles. "No individual writer may enter on his/her own initiative. Entries must come from theater companies, professional schools or colleges which foster playwriting by conducting classes, workshops or similar programs of assistance to playwrights."

OGLEBAY INSTITUTE TOWNGATE THEATRE PLAYWRITING CONTEST, Oglebay Institute, Stifel Fine Arts Center, 1330 National Rd., Wheeling WV 26003. (304)242-7700. Fax: (304)242-4203. Director, Performing Arts Dept. Estab. 1976. Offered annually for unpublished works. Deadline: January 1. Guidelines for SASE. Prize: $300, limited-run production of play. "All full-length *non-musical* plays that have never been professionally produced or published are eligible." Winner announced March 1.

‡OPUS MAGNUM DISCOVERY AWARD, Christopher Columbus Society, 433 N. Camden Dr., #600, Beverly Hills CA 90210. (310)288-1881. Fax: (310)288-0257. Contact: Carlos de Abreu. Annual award to discover new authors with books/manuscripts that can be optioned for features or TV movies. Deadline: December 1. Guidelines for SASE. Charges $75 fee. Prize: Option moneys to winner, up to $10,000. Judged by entertainment industry story analysts and producers.

‡ORIGINAL PLAYWRITING AWARD COMPETITION, Theatre Department of Elmira College, Elmira NY 14901. (607)735-1981. Contact: Professor Fred Goodson. Offered in even-numbered years for unpublished work to encourage the development of quality plays for the theater. "Also provides students with the opportunity to mount an original work." Deadline: June 1, 1996. Guidelines for SASE. Prize: $1,000 cash and a full-scale production at Elmira College. Judged by screening committee headed by Fred Goodson, program director, Elmira College or Theatre Department. "With the exception of a World Premiere Production at Elmira College, no other rights are acquired." Open to any writer.

‡MILDRED & ALBERT PANOWSKI PLAYWRITING AWARD, (formerly Shiras Institute/Mildred & Albert Panowski Playwriting Award), Forest A. Roberts Theatre, Northern Michigan University, Marquette MI 49855-5364. (906)227-2553. Award Director: Dr. James A. Panowski. Estab. 1978. Unpublished, unproduced, full-length plays. Scripts must be *received* on or before Nov. 20. Guidelines and application for SASE.

ROBERT J. PICKERING AWARD FOR PLAYWRIGHTING EXCELLENCE, Coldwater Community Theater, % 89 Division, Coldwater MI 49036. (517)279-7963. Committee Chairperson: J. Richard Colbeck. Estab.

1982. Previously unproduced monetarily. "To encourage playwrights to submit their work, to present a previously unproduced play in full production." Deadline: end of year. Guidelines for SASE. Submit script with SASE. Prize: 1st-$200, 2nd-$100, 3rd-$50. "We reserve right to produce winning script."

PLAYWRIGHTS' THEATER OF DENTON NEW PLAY COMPETITION, Playwrights' Theater of Denton, P.O. Box 732, Denton TX 76202-0732. Contact: Mark Pearce. Offered annually for stage plays of any length. Deadline: December 15. Guidelines for SASE. Charges $15 fee, payable to Sigma Corporation. Prize: $1,000, possible production. Open to any writer.

PLAYWRITING COMPETITION FOR YOUNG AUDIENCES, Indiana University-Purdue University at Indianapolis, Young Audiences Playwriting Competition, 525 N. Blackford St., Indianapolis IN 46202-3120. (317)274-2095. Fax: (317)278-1025. E-mail: wmccrear@indycms.iupui.edu. Assistant to the Director: W. Mark McCreary. Estab. 1983. Offered in even-numbered years for previously unpublished plays for young audiences through high school. Guidelines for SASE.

FRANCESCA PRIMUS SOUTHERN PLAYWRITING COMPETITION, (formerly Southern Playwriting Competition), Southern Festival Theatre, Department of Theatre Arts, University of Mississippi, University MS 38677. (601)232-5816. Contact: Scott McCoy. Estab. 1985. Competition for unpublished and unproduced original full-length scripts for the theatre by a Southern writer or a work with a markedly Southern theme. Deadline: December 1. Up to 3 winners annually are awarded $1,500 each and full professional production. Selections announced February 15.

RIVERFRONT PLAYHOUSE SCRIPTWRITING COMPETITION, Riverfront Playhouse, P.O. Box 105, Palo Cedro CA 96073; Playhouse: 1620 E. Cypress, Redding, CA 96002. (916)547-4801. Contest Director: Paul Robeson. "Offered annually for unpublished scripts to broaden the appreciation, awareness, and understanding of live theater by providing the environment for local talent to act, direct and creatively express themselves in the arts of the stage.The competition is designed to encourage and stimulate artistic growth among community playwrights. It provides playwrights the unique opportunity to mount and produce an original work at the *Riverfront Playhouse*." Deadline: December 2. Guidelines for SASE. Charges $25 fee. Prize: a reading, workshop and/or a full production of the winning entry. Cash prizes, as determined by the Board of Directors of the *Riverfront Playhouse*. Judged by college instructors and professional writers.

THE LOIS AND RICHARD ROSENTHAL NEW PLAY PRIZE, Cincinnati Playhouse in the Park, Box 6537, Cincinnati OH 45206. (513)345-2242. Contact: Madeleine Pabis, artistic associate. Unpublished full-length plays only. Complete scripts will not be accepted. Query first for guidelines. Scripts must not have received a full-scale professional production. Deadline: October 15-February 1.

MORTON R. SARETT NATIONAL PLAYWRITING COMPETITION, University of Nevada Las Vegas Theatre Arts, P.O. Box 455036, Las Vegas NV 89154-5036. (702)895-3666. Contact: Corrine A. Bonate. Offered biannually for unpublished, unproduced original, innovative, full-length plays in English on any subject. Deadline: mid-December. Guidelines for SASE. Prize: $3,000 and production by UNLV Theatre Arts. Open to any writer.

SHENANDOAH INTERNATIONAL PLAYWRIGHTS RETREAT, ShenanArts, Inc., Rt. 5, Box 167F, Staunton VA 24401. (540)248-1868. Fax: (540)248-1868. Program Director: Robert Graham Small. Estab. 1976. Offered annually. "Shenandoah exists to provide young and established playwrights with a challenging, stimulating environment to test and develop new work." Deadline: March 1. Award application form available for SASE. "The writers, each on fellowship, work in close and intensive collaboration with dramaturgs, directors and the acting company. What occurs is a simultaneous 'on-the-feet/on-the-page' exploration of each play, culminating in a staged reading and company response."

SHUBERT FENDRICH MEMORIAL PLAYWRITING CONTEST, Pioneer Drama Service, P.O. Box 4267, Englewood CO 80155-4267. (303)779-4035. Fax: (303)779-4315. Contest Director: Steven Fendrich. Assistant Editor: Terri Smolensky-Johnson. Offered annually for previously produced, but unpublished plays. Deadline: March 1. Estab. 1990. Prize: publication with $1,000 advance in royalty. "All rights to work are obtained by Pioneer. All submitted work must be produced prior to submission."

DOROTHY SILVER PLAYWRITING COMPETITION, Jewish Community Center, 3505 Mayfield Rd., Cleveland Heights OH 44118. (216)382-4000, ext. 275. Fax: (216)382-5401. Contact: Elaine Rembrandt. Estab. 1948. All entries must be original works, not previously produced, suitable for a full-length presentation; directly concerned with the Jewish experience. Deadline: December 15. Cash award plus staged reading.

SILVERHAWKE ONE-ACT PLAY COMPETITION, P.O. Box 1640, Escondido CA 92033. Contact: Ms. Chris Watkins. Offered annually for previously unpublished plays in 4 categories: student writer, teacher, open, plays for children. Deadline: July 1. Notification: December 1. Prize: publication and inclusion in Silverhawke catalog. SASE for return of materials.

SILVERHAWKE PLAYWRIGHT'S COMPETITION, P.O. Box 1640, Escondido CA 92023. Contact: Ms. Chris Watkins. Offered annually for previously unpublished plays in 4 categories: student writer, teacher, open, plays for children. Deadline: July 1. Notification: December 1. Prize: publication and inclusion in Silverhawke catalog. SASE for return of materials.

SUSAN SMITH BLACKBURN PRIZE, 3239 Avalon Place, Houston TX 77019. (713)654-4484. Fax: (713)654-8184. Director: Emilie S. Kilgore. Offered annually for women playwrights for full-length plays written in English. Prize: 1st-$5,000 and signed de Kooning print; 2nd-$2,000; other finalists $500 each. Deadline: September 20. Nomination by artistic directors or theater professionals invited to submit.

SOUTH CAROLINA PLAYWRIGHTS FESTIVAL, Trustus Theatre, P.O. Box 11721, Columbia SC 29211. (803)771-9153. Assistant Artistic Director/Literary Manager: Jayce T. Tromsness. Estab. 1989. Offered annually for previously unpublished work. "Full-length plays accepted. No musicals, children's shows, translations or adaptations." Cast limit 8. Submit January 1-March 1. Contact by phone between 1-6 pm. Guidelines for SASE. Prize: 1st-$500, full production, travel and housing for tech week; 2nd-$250 plus staged reading; one acts $50 and late night readings.

SOUTHEASTERN THEATRE CONFERENCE NEW PLAY PROJECT, P.O. Box 2250, Mississippi State University MS 39762. (601)325-7952. Contact: Jeff Elwell. Offered annually for the discovery, development and publicizing of worthy new unproduced plays and playwrights. Eligibility limited to members of 10 state SETC Region: AL, FL, GA, KY, MS, NC, SC, TN, VA, WV. Submit March 1-June 1. Bound full-length or related one acts under single cover (one submission only). Does not return scripts. Guidelines available upon request. Prize: $1,000, staged reading at SETC Convention, expenses paid trip to convention and preferred consideration for National Playwrights Conference.

SOUTHERN PLAYWRIGHTS COMPETITION, Center for Southern Studies/Jacksonville State University, Pelham Rd., Jacksonville AL 36265-9982. (205)782-5411. Fax: (205)782-5689. Contact: Steven J. Whitton. Estab. 1988. Offered annually. "The Center for Southern Studies seeks to identify and encourage the best of Southern Playwrighting." Deadline: February 15. Guidelines for SASE. Prize: $1,000 and a production of the play. Playwrights must be native to or resident of AL, AR, FL, GA, KY, LA, MS, NC, SC, TN, TX, VA or WV.

‡SOUTHWEST THEATRE ASSOCIATION NEW PLAY CONTEST, Southwest Theatre Association, School of Drama, University of Oklahoma, 563 Elm, Norman OK 73019. (405)325-4021. Fax: (405)325-0400. Contact: Ray Paolino. Annual contest for unpublished work to promote the writing and production of new plays in the Southwest region. Deadline: March 31. Guidelines for SASE. Charges $10. Prize: $200 honorarium, a staged reading at the annual SWTA convention, possible publication in *Theatre Southwest*. Judged by the New Plays Committee of the Southwest Theatre Association. Open to all writers. No musicals or children's plays. Letter of recommendation suggested.

SPRING STAGED READING PLAY CONTEST, TADA!, 120 W. 28th St., New York NY 10001. (212)627-1732. Fax: (212)727-3611. Contest Director: Janine Nina Trevens. Offered annually for unpublished work to introduce the playwriting process to family audiences in a staged reading series featuring the winning entries. One-act plays to be appropriate for children or teenage or family audiences, cast to be mostly children up to age 17. Deadline: January 15. Please send a cover letter and play with SASE for return, no application form necessary. Prize: $200 and a staged reading held in TADA!'s theater with TADA! cast and others hired by TADA! Contest is open. Plays must be appropriate for children or family audiences.

MARVIN TAYLOR PLAYWRITING AWARD, Sierra Repertory Theatre, P.O. Box 3030, Sonora CA 95370-3030. (209)532-3120. Producing Director: Dennis Jones. Estab. 1981. Full-length plays. Deadline: August 31.

‡THEATER AT LIME KILN REGIONAL PLAYWRITING CONTEST, Theater at Lime Kiln, 14 S. Randolph St., Lexington VA 24450. (703)463-7088. Fax: (703)463-1083. Contact: Eleanor Connor. Offered annually for unpublished work. "With this contest Lime Kiln seeks to encourage playwrights to create works about our region of the country. Material should be limited geographically to Appalachia (Virginia, Western North Carolina, West Virginia, Eastern Kentucky, Eastern Tennesee). Plays with music encouraged." Submit August 1-September 30. Guidelines for SASE. Prize: 1st-$1,000; 2nd-$500; possibility of staged reading. Open to all writers.

THEATRE MEMPHIS NEW PLAY COMPETITION, Theatre Memphis, P.O. Box 240117, Memphis TN 38124-0117. (901)682-8323. Fax: (901)763-4096. Estab. 1981. Chairman, New Play Competition: Kim Ford.

Offered every 3 years to promote new playwrights' works and new works by established playwrights. No musicals or one acts. Bound scripts only. Deadline: July 1, 1996. Include SASE if scripts are to be returned.
● This competition runs in a 3-year cycle. Do not submit before January 1, 1996.

UNIVERSITY OF ALABAMA NEW PLAYWRIGHTS PROGRAM, P.O. Box 870239, Tuscaloosa AL 35487-0239. (205)348-9032. Fax: (205)348-9048. E-mail: pcastagn@roso.as.ua.edu. Director/Dramaturg: Dr. Paul C. Castagno. Estab. 1982. Full-length plays for mainstage; experimental plays for B stage. Workshops and small musicals can be proposed. Queries responded to quickly. Stipends competitive with, or exceed most contests. Development process includes readings, visitations, and possible complete productions with faculty director and dramaturg. Guidelines for SASE. Up to 6 months assessment time.

‡URBAN STAGES AWARD, Playwrights' Preview Productions, 17 E. 47th St., New York NY 10017. (212)289-2168. Fax: (212)289-2168. Contact: Pamela Faith Jackson. Audience development program of radio-style staged readings that tour the libraries throughout the boroughs of New York City. Ethnically diverse encouraged. Plays between 30-60 minutes. Cast maximum of 5 (doubling encouraged). Submissions must be unpublished and unproduced in New York City. Send script, letter of introduction, production or reading history, author's résumé and SASE. Submissions accepted February 1-June 15. Selections by September 15. Prize: $200; air fare for out-of-town playwrights.

‡US WEST THEATREFEST, Denver Center Theatre Company, 1050 13th St., Denver CO 80204. (303)825-2117. Fax: (303)825-2117. Program Director: Tom Szentgyorgyi, associate artistic director for new play development. Offered annually for unproduced, full-length work. "The US West TheatreFest is a new play program. Up to eight scripts are selected for developmental readings during the season; up to four of these scripts are then chosen for production the following year." There is no submission deadline, but interested writers should send SASE for submission guidelines before mailing their work. Playwrights chosen for readings are given transportation to and from the theater, housing, and a stipend.

VERMONT PLAYWRIGHT'S AWARD, The Valley Players, % RD 167, Waitsfield VT 05673. Award Director: Tony Egan. Offered annually for unpublished nonmusical, full-length play suitable for production by a community theater group to encourage development of playwrights in Vermont, New Hampshire and Maine. Deadline: October 1. SASE. Prize: $1,000. Judged by resident professionals in theater, journalism, publishing or public relations or broadcasting. Must be a resident of VT, NH or ME.

THEODORE WARD PRIZE FOR PLAYWRITING, Columbia College Theater/Music Center, 72 E. 11th St., Chicago IL 60605-1996. Fax: (312)663-9591. Contact: Chuck Smith. Estab. 1985. "To uncover and identify new unpublished African-American plays that are promising and produceable." Deadline: August 1. All rights for music or biographies must be secured prior to submission. All entrants must be of African-American descent and residing within the US. Only 1 complete script per playwright will be accepted.

L. ARNOLD WEISSBERGER PLAYWRITING COMPETITION, New Dramatists, Inc., 424 W. 44th St., New York NY 10036-5205. (212)757-6960. Fax: (212)265-4738. Contact: Literary Associate. Estab. 1984. Offered annually for previously unproduced plays. "The L. Arnold Weissberger Award is a cash prize that recognizes a previously unproduced new play by a playwright with any level of experience. The $5,000 prize is awarded annually, and the competition is judged by professional theater critics. The selection criteria was established by L. Arnold Weissberger, a theatrical attorney, who sought to discover a 'well-made play.' " Deadline: May 31. Applications accepted between December 31 of the previous year and May 31, the deadline, for an award announcement the following May. Guidelines for SASE. Prize: $5,000 and a public staged reading of the prize-winning play. Plays must be submitted by nomination only. Nominators may include artistic directors or literary managers of non-rofit theaters; literary agents; dramaturgs affiliated with university drama departments or professional producing theater companies; chairpersons and accredited university theater or playwriting programs. Nominations will be limited to one script per nominator. Nomination letters are recommended but not required. All scripts must include name, address, phone number and title of nominator, in addition to playwrite.
● New Dramatists Inc. is a service organization offering playwrights time, space and tools (at no charge). Write for membership information.

WEST COAST ENSEMBLE FULL-PLAY COMPETITION, West Coast Ensemble, P.O. Box 38728, Los Angeles CA 90038. Artistic Director: Les Hanson. Estab. 1982. Unpublished (in Southern California) plays. No musicals or children's plays for full-play competition. No restrictions on subject matter. Deadline: December 31 for full-length plays.

‡WHITE BIRD ANNUAL PLAYWRITING CONTEST, White Bird Productions, Inc., P.O. Box 20233 Columbus Circle Station, New York NY 10023. (718)788-5984. Contact: Kathryn Dickinson. Offered annually for the two best unpublished one-act or full-length plays (non-musical) that best deal with an environmental theme, topic or event. Deadline: February 15, 1996. Guidelines and entry form for SASE. Prize: "For 1996

$200 honorarium and a NYC staged reading." Judged by literary committee. Contest open to all playwrights.

WICHITA STATE UNIVERSITY PLAYWRITING CONTEST, University Theatre, Wichita State University, Wichita KS 67260-0153. (316)689-3185. Fax: (316)689-3951. Contest Director: Professor Leroy Clark. Estab. 1974. Unpublished, unproduced full-length or 2-3 short plays of at least 90 minutes playing time. No musicals or children's plays. Deadline: February 15. Guidelines for SASE. Prize: production of winning play (ACTF) and expenses paid trip for playwright to see final rehearsals and/or performances. Contestants must be graduate or undergraduate students in a US college or university.

‡WOMEN'S PLAYWRITING FESTIVAL, Perishable Theatre, P.O. Box 23132, Providence RI 02903. (401)331-2695. Contact: Kathleen Jenkins. Offered annually for unpublished/unproduced one acts by women, 10-45 minutes in length, 2 submissions per author. Deadline: December 31. Guidelines for SASE. Prize: 3 winners of $250 each.

‡WRITERS GUILD AWARDS, Writers Guild of America west, 8955 Beverly Blvd., West Hollywood CA 90048. Scripts (screen, TV and radio). Members only. Submission deadline TV and radio: September; submissions not required for screen.

Y.E.S. NEW PLAY FESTIVAL, Northern Kentucky University, 207FA, Department of Theatre, Highland Heights KY 41099-1007. (606)572-6303. Fax: (606)572-5566. Project Director: Mike King. Offered every 2 years for unproduced plays to encourage the development of playwrights and to bring previously unproduced works to the stage. Estab. 1981. Deadline: May 1-October 15 for scripts. Full-length plays, adaptations and musicals. Guidelines for SASE. No application fee. Prize: $400 and expense-paid visit to NKU to see their play in production.

Journalism

AAAS SCIENCE JOURNALISM AWARDS, American Association for the Advancement of Science, 1333 H St. NW, Washington DC 20005. (202)326-6440. Fax: (202)789-0455. Contact: Ellen Cooper. Offered annually for previously published work July 1, 1994-June 30, 1995 to reward excellence in reporting on science and its applications in daily newspapers with circulation over 100,000; newspapers with circulation under 100,000; general circulation magazines; radio; television." Deadline: August 1. Award: $2,500, plaque, trip to AAAS Annual Meeting. Sponsored by the Whitaker Foundation.

AMY WRITING AWARDS, The Amy Foundation, P.O. Box 16091, Lansing MI 48901. (517)323-6233. President: James Russell. Estab. 1985. Articles communicating Biblical truth published in the secular media. Deadline: January 31, for those from previous calendar year. Prize: $10,000, $5,000, $4,000, $3,000, $2,000 and 10 prizes of $1,000.

‡CANADIAN FOREST SERVICE-ONTARIO JOURNALISM AWARD, Canadian Forest Service Ontario/ Natural Resources Canada, % CSWA, P.O. Box 75, Station A, Toronto, Ontario M5W 1A2 Canada. (416)928-9624. Fax: (416)960-0528. Contact: Andy F. Visser-deVries. Offered annually for work published January 1-December 31 of the previous year to recognize outstanding journalism that promotes public awareness of forests and issues surrounding forests in Ontario. Deadline: February 15. Guidelines for SASE. Prize: $1,000 and plaque. Material becomes property of Canadian Forest Service. Does not return mss. Open to writers who have published in an Ontario publication.

‡CATHOLIC PRESS ASSOCIATION JOURNALISM AWARDS, Catholic Press Association, 119 N. Park Ave., Rockville Centre NY 11570. (516)471-4730. Fax: (516)471-4804. Contact: Owen McGovern. To recognize quality work published January-December of previous year by journalists who work for a Catholic publication. There are numerous categories for newspapers and magazines. Deadline: Mid-February. Charges $30 fee. Only journalists who are published in Catholic publications are eligible.

RUSSELL L. CECIL ARTHRITIS MEDICAL JOURNALISM AWARDS, Arthritis Foundation, 1314 Spring St. NW, Atlanta GA 30309-9901. (404)872-7100. Fax: (404)872-0457. E-mail: lnewbern@arthritis.org. Contact: Lisa M. Newbern. Estab. 1956. News stories, articles and radio/TV scripts on the subject of arthritis and the Arthritis Foundation published or broadcast for general circulation during the previous calendar year. Deadline: February 15.

HARRY CHAPIN MEDIA AWARDS, World Hunger Year, 505 Eighth Ave., 21st Floor, New York NY 10018-6582. (212)629-8850. Fax: (212)465-9274. E-mail: whyria@aol.com. Coordinator: Peter Mann. Estab. 1982. Critical issues of domestic and world hunger, poverty and development (newspaper, periodical, TV, radio, photojournalism, books). Prizes: $1,000-2,500. Deadline: February 15.

‡GREG CLARK OUTDOOR WRITING AWARD, Ontario Ministry of Natural Resources, % CSWA, P.O. Box 75, Station A, Toronto, Ontario M5W 1A2 Canada. (416)928-9624. Fax: (416)960-0528. Contact: Andy F. Visser-deVries. Offered annually for work published January 1-December 31 of the previous year to recognize outstanding journalism that increases public awareness of Ontario's natural resources. Deadline: February 15. Guidelines for SASE. Prize: $500 and plaque. Entries become property of Ontario Ministry of Natural Resources. Does not return mss. Open to writers who have published in an Ontario publication that is about natural resources of Ontario.

FOURTH ESTATE AWARD, American Legion National Headquarters, 700 N. Pennsylvania, Indianapolis IN 46206. (317)630-1253. Contact: Lew Wood. Estab. 1919. Offered annually for excellence in journalism in a published or broadcast piece on an issue of national concern during the previous calendar year. Deadline: January 31.

THE GREAT AMERICAN TENNIS WRITING AWARDS, *Tennis Week*, 341 Madison Ave., New York NY 10017. (212)808-4750. Fax: (212)983-6302. Publisher: Eugene L. Scott. Estab. 1986. Category 1: unpublished ms by an aspiring journalist with no previous national byline. Category 2: unpublished ms by a non-tennis journalist. Category 3: unpublished ms by a tennis journalist. Categories 4-6: published articles and one award to a book. Deadline: December 15.

THE ROY W. HOWARD AWARDS, Scripps Howard Foundation, P.O. Box 5380, Cincinnati OH 45201-5380. (513)977-3035. Estab. 1972. Public service reporting by a daily newspaper in the US or its territories. Fact sheet available in fall of year.

INTERNATIONAL READING ASSOCIATION PRINT MEDIA AWARD, International Reading Association, P.O. Box 8139, Newark DE 19714-8139. (302)731-1600 ext. 215. Fax: (302)731-1057. Contact: Janet Butler. Estab. 1956. Recognizes outstanding reporting on reading and literacy by professional journalists. Deadline: January 15.

DONALD E. KEYHOE JOURNALISM AWARD, Fund for UFO Research, P.O. Box 277, Mt. Rainier MD 20712. (703)684-6032. Fax: (703)684-6032. Chairman: Richard Hall. Estab. 1979. Offered annually for the best article or story published or broadcast in a newspaper, magazine, TV or radio news outlet during the previous calendar year. Separate awards for print and broadcast media. Also makes unscheduled cash awards for published works on UFO phenomena research or public education.

‡LOUIS M. LYONS AWARD, Nieman Foundation at Harvard University, 1 Francis Ave., Cambridge MA 02138. (617)495-2237. Fax: (617)495-8976. Contact: Chair, Lyons Award Committee. "Annual award for previously published print or broadcast material." Previously published entries must have appeared in print between January and December of the previous calendar year. "The Award, which recognizes conscience and integrity in journalism, is named in honor of the late Louis M. Lyons, Curator of the Nieman Foundation for 25 years. To be eligible for nomination, nominees must be full-time print or broadcast journalists (domestic or foreign)." Deadline: March 1. "Nominations must be made by third parties, whether individuals or organizations. News organizations may nominate one of their own employees. Applications must contain the following: an official letter of nomination, one-page biography of the nominee, two letters of recommendation and three samples of the nominee's work. The Lyons Award carries a $1,000 honorarium."

THE EDWARD J. MEEMAN AWARDS, Scripps Howard Foundation, P.O. Box 5380, Cincinnati OH 45201-5380. (513)977-3035. Estab. 1967. Environmental reporting by a daily newspaper in the US or its territories. Fact sheet available in fall of the year.

MENCKEN AWARDS, Free Press Association, P.O. Box 63, Port Hadlock WA 98339. FPA Executive Director: Bill Bradford. Estab. 1981. Honoring defense of human rights and individual liberties, or exposés of governmental abuses of power. Categories: News Story or Investigative Report, Feature Story or Essay/Review, Editorial or Op-Ed Column, Editorial Cartoon, Book, and Defense of First Amendment. Entries *must* have been published or broadcast during previous calendar year. Deadline: April 1 (for work from previous year). Guidelines and form for SASE. Charges $5 fee. Late deadline: May 1 with extra fee.

NATIONAL AWARDS FOR EDUCATION REPORTING, Education Writers Association, 1331 H St. NW, #307, Washington DC 200056. (202)637-9700. Fax: (202)637-9707. Executive Director: Lisa Walker. Estab. 1980. Offered annually for submissions published during the previous year. Categories are: 1) newspapers under 100,000 circulation; 2) newspapers over 100,000 circulation; 3) magazines excluding trade and institutional journals that are circulated to the general public; 4) special interest, institutional and trade publications; 5) television; and 6) radio. Write for more information. Deadline: mid-January. Charges $35 fee.

‡ALICIA PATTERSON JOURNALISM FELLOWSHIP, Alicia Patterson Foundation, 1730 Pennsylvania Ave. NW, Suite 850, Washington DC 20006. (202)393-5995. Fax: (301)951-8512. E-mail: apfengel@charm.net.

Contact: Margaret Engel. Offered annually for previously published submissions to give 5-7 print journalists a year of in-depth research and reporting. Applicants must have 5 years of professional print journalism experience and be U.S. citizens. Fellows write 4 magazine-length pieces for the *Alicia Patterson Reporter*, a quarterly magazine, during their fellowship year. Fellows must take a year's leave from their jobs, but may do other freelance articles during the year. Deadline: October 1. Write, call or fax for applications. Prize: $30,000 stipend for calendar year.

ERNIE PYLE AWARD, Scripps Howard Foundation, P.O. Box 5380, Cincinnati OH 45201-5380. (513)977-3035. Estab. 1953. Human interest reporting by a newspaper man or woman for work published in a daily newspaper in the US or its territories. Fact sheet available in fall of the year.

WILLIAM B. RUGGLES JOURNALISM SCHOLARSHIP, National Right to Work Committee, Suite 500, 8001 Braddock Rd., Springfield VA 22160-0999. (703)321-9820. Fax: 7143. Contact: Linda Staukup. Estab. 1974. "To honor the late William B. Ruggles, editor emeritas of the Dallas Morning News, who coined the phrase 'Right to Work.' " Deadline: January 1-March 31. Prize: $2,000 scholarship. "We do reserve the right to reprint the material/excerpt from the essay in publicizing the award. Applicant must be a graduate or undergraduate student majoring in journalism in institutions of higher learning throughout the US."

THE CHARLES M. SCHULZ AWARD, Scripps Howard Foundation, P.O. Box 5380, Cincinnati OH 45201-5380. (513)977-3035. Estab. 1980. For a student cartoonist at a college newspaper or magazine. Fact sheet available in fall of the year.

SCIENCE IN SOCIETY JOURNALISM AWARDS, National Association of Science Writers, Box 294, Greenlawn NY 11740. (516)757-5664. Contact: Diane McGurgan. Newspaper, magazine and broadcast science writing. Deadline: (postmarked) July 1 for work published June 1-May 31 of previous year.

‡SCIENCE IN SOCIETY JOURNALISM AWARDS, Canadian Science Writers' Association, P.O. Box 75, Station A, Toronto, Ontario M5W 1A2 Canada. (416)928-9624. Fax: (416)928-0528. Contact: Andy F. Visser-deVries. Offered annually for work published/aired January 1-December 31 of previous year to recognize outstanding contributions to science journalism in all media. Two newspaper, 2 magazine, 2 TV, 2 radio, 1 trade publications 1 student science writing award. Deadline: February 15. Guidelines for SASE. Prize: $1,000 and a plaque. Material becomes property of CSWA. Does not return mss. Open to Canadian citizens or residents of Canada.

CHARLES E. SCRIPPS AWARD, Scripps Howard Foundation, P.O. Box 5380, Cincinnati OH 45201-5380. (513)977-3035. Estab. 1986. Combatting illiteracy, by a daily newspaper, television, cable and/or radio station in the US or its territories. Fact sheet available in fall of the year.

THE EDWARD WILLIS SCRIPPS AWARD, Scripps Howard Foundation, P.O. Box 5380, Cincinnati OH 45201. (513)977-3035. Estab. 1976. Service to the First Amendment by a daily newspaper in the US or its territories. Fact sheet available in fall of the year.

‡SOVEREIGN AWARD OUTSTANDING NEWSPAPER STORY, OUTSTANDING FEATURE STORY, The Jockey Club of Canada, P.O. Box 156, Rexdale, Ontario M9W 5L2 Canada. (416)675-7756. Fax: (416)675-6378. Contact: Gary Loschke. Estab. 1975. Offered annually to recognize outstanding achievement in the area of Canadian thoroughbred racing journalism published November 1-October 31 of the previous year. Newspaper Story: Appeared in a newspaper by a racing columnist on Canadian Racing subject matter. Outstanding Feature Story: Appeared in a magazine book or newspaper, written as feature story on Canadian Racing subject matter. Deadline: October 31. There is no nominating process other than the writer submit no more than 1 entry per category. Special Criteria: Must be of Canadian racing content. A copy of the newspaper article or magazine story must be provided along with a 3¼" disk containing the story in an ASCII style format. Any Apple formated articles must be converted in IBM compatible disks.

I.F. STONE AWARD FOR STUDENT JOURNALISM, The Nation Institute, 72 Fifth Ave., New York NY 10011. (212)242-8400. Director: Peter Meyer. Offered annually to recognize excellence in student journalism. Open to undergraduate students in US colleges. Award: $1,000, plus publication. Deadline: June 30.

THE WALKER STONE AWARD, Scripps Howard Foundation, P.O. Box 5380, Cincinnati OH 45201-5380. (513)977-3035. Estab. 1973. Editorial writing by a newspaper man or woman published in a daily newspaper in the US or its territories. Fact sheet available in fall of the year.

THE TEN BEST "CENSORED" STORIES OF 1995, Project Censored—Sonoma State University, Rohnert Park CA 94928. (707)664-2500. Fax: (707)664-2505. Assistant Director: Mark Lowenthal. Estab. 1976.

Current published, nonfiction stories of national social significance that have been overlooked or under-reported by the news media. Deadline: November 1.

• Carl Jensen and Project Censored choose 25 stories that have been underreported to make up *Censored: The News That Didn't Make the News and Why*, published by Four Walls Eight Windows.

TRAVEL JOURNALISM AWARDS, Hawaii Visitors Bureau, Suite 801, 2270 Kalakaua Ave., Honolulu HI 96815. (808)924-0213. Fax: (808)924-2120. Contact: Gail Ann Chew. Offered annually for travel journalism. Deadline: March.

Writing for Children and Young Adults

‡JANE ADDAMS CHILDREN'S BOOK AWARD, Jane Addams Peace Association and Women's International League for Peace and Freedom, 2015 Bluebell Ave., Boulder CO 80302. Award Director: Judith Volc. Estab. 1953. Book published previous year that promotes peace, social justice, and the equality of the sexes and races. Deadline: April 1.

AMERICAN ASSOCIATION OF UNIVERSITY WOMEN AWARD, NORTH CAROLINA DIVISION, North Carolina Literary and Historical Association, 109 E. Jones St., Raleigh NC 27601-2807. (919)733-7305. Awards Coordinator: Freda Brittain. Previously published juvenile literature by a North Carolina resident. Deadline: July 15.

IRMA S. AND JAMES H. BLACK AWARD, Bank Street College of Education, 610 W. 112th St., New York NY 10025. (212)875-4452. Fax: (212)875-4759. Award Director: Linda Greengrass. Estab. 1972. Offered annually for a book for young children, published in the previous year, for excellence of both text and illustrations. Entries must have been published during the previous calendar year. Deadline for entries: January after book is published.

BOSTON GLOBE-HORN BOOK AWARD, *The Boston Globe*, 135 Morrissey Blvd, P.O. Box 2378, Boston MA 02107. Offered annually for previously published work in children's literature. One award for each category: original fiction or poetry, picture book, and nonfiction. Publisher submits entry. Prize: $500 in each category.

‡CHILDREN'S WRITER WRITING CONTESTS, *Children's Writer* Newsletter, 95 Long Ridge Rd., West Redding CT 06896. (203)792-8600. Fax: (203)792-8406. Publisher: Prescott Kelly. Offered 3 times/year to promote higher quality children's literature. "Each contest has its own theme. Our last three were (1) An animal story for ages 4 to 6; to 500 words. (2) A history article for ages 8 to 12; to 750 words. (3) A humor story for ages 8 to 12; to 900 words." Submissions must be unpublished. Deadline: Last Friday in February, June and October. Guidelines for SASE; put "Contest Request" in lower left of envelope. Charges $10 fee for nonsubscribers only, which is applicable against a subscription to *Children's Writer*. Prize: 1st place—$100 or $1,000, a certificate and publication in *Children's Writer*; 2nd place—$50 or $500, and certificate; 3rd-5th places—$25 or $250 and certificates. One or two contests each year with the higher cash prizes also include $100 prizes plus certificates for 6th-12th places. Judged by selected members of faculty and staff of Institute of Children's Literature. Acquires first North American serial rights for grand prize winners only.

MARGUERITE DE ANGELI PRIZE, Bantam Doubleday Dell Books for Young Readers, 1540 Broadway, New York NY 10036. (212)354-6500. Fax: (212)782-9698. Offered annually for unpublished fiction manuscript suitable for readers 7-10 years of age that concerns the diversity of the American experience, either contemporary or historical. Guidelines for SASE. Prize includes a book contract with a cash advance. Judged by editors at Bantam Doubleday Dell.

‡JOAN FASSLER MEMORIAL BOOK AWARD, Association for the Care of Children's Health (ACCH), 7910 Woodmont Ave., #300, Bethesda MD 20814. (301)654-6549. Fax: (301)986-4553. Contact: Trish McClean, membership manager. Offered annually for work published in 1994 and 1995 to the author(s) of the trade book that makes the most distinguished contribution to a child's or young person's understanding of hospitalization, illness, disabling conditions, dying and death, and preventive care. Deadline: December 31. Guidelines for SASE. Prize: $1,000 and a plaque.

DON FREEMAN MEMORIAL GRANT-IN-AID, Society of Children's Book Writers and Illustrators (SCBWI), 22736 Vanowen St., #106, West Hills CA 91307. To enable picture-book artists to further their understanding, training and/or work. Members only. Deadline: February 15. Grants: $1,000 and $500 runner-up.

GOLDEN KITE AWARDS, Society of Children's Book Writers and Illustrators (SCBWI), Suite 106, 22736 Vanowen St., West Hills CA 91307. (818)888-8760. Coordinator: Sue Alexander. Estab. 1973. Calendar year published children's fiction, nonfiction and picture illustration books by a SCBWI member. Deadline: December 15.

HIGHLIGHTS FOR CHILDREN FICTION CONTEST, *Highlights for Children*, 803 Church St., Honesdale PA 18431-1824. Manuscript Coordinator: Beth Troop. Estab. 1946. Stories for children ages 2-12; category varies each year. Guidelines for SASE. Stories should be limited to 900 words for older readers, 600 words for younger readers. No crime or violence, please. Specify that ms is a contest entry. All entries must be postmarked January 1-February 28.

INTERNATIONAL READING ASSOCIATION CHILDREN'S BOOK AWARD, International Reading Association, P.O. Box 8139, 800 Barksdale Rd., Newark DE 19714-8139. (302)731-1600 ext. 221. First or second book by an author who shows unusual promise in the children's book field. Categories: younger readers, ages 4-10; older readers, ages 10-16 and over, and informational book (ages 4-16). Deadline: December 1.

MILKWEED PRIZE FOR CHILDREN'S LITERATURE, Milkweed Editions, First Ave. N., Suite 400, Minneapolis MN 55401. (612)332-3192. First Reader: Elisabeth Fitz. Annual prize for unpublished works. Estab. 1993. "Milkweed is looking for a novel or biography intended for readers aged 8-14. Manuscripts should be of high literary quality and must be double-spaced, 110-350 pages in length. The Milkweed Prize for Children's Literature will be awarded to the best manuscript for children ages 8-14 that Milkweed accepts for publication during each calendar year by a writer not previously published by Milkweed Editions. Prize: $2,000 over and above any advance and royalties agreed upon at the time of acceptance. Must SASE for guidelines, both for regular children's submission policies and for the announcement of the restructured contest. Catalog for $1 postage.

‡THE MARY MOLLOY FELLOWSHIP IN CHILDREN'S WORKING FICTION, The Heekin Group Foundation, Children's Literature Div., P.O. Box 209, Middlebury VT 05753. (802)388-8651. Contact: Deirdre Heekin. Offered annually for unpublished work. Purpose is "to support beginning and emerging writers in the children's literature field." Deadline: December 1. Guidelines for SASE. Charges $20 fee. Prize: $1,500. Judges for 1996: Hyperion Books for Children. Applicants may not have published in the middle readers category, ages 8-12.

‡NATIONAL JEWISH BOOK AWARD—CHILDREN'S LITERATURE, Jewish Book Council, 15 E. 26th St., New York NY 10010. (212)532-4949. Director: Carolyn Starman Hessel. Children's book on Jewish theme. Deadline: September 1.

SCOTT O'DELL AWARD FOR HISTORICAL FICTION, 1418 E. 57th St., Chicago IL 60637. (312)752-7880. Director: Zena Sutherland. Estab. 1981. Historical fiction book for children set in the Americas. Entries must have been published during previous year. Deadline: December 31.
 • Graham Salisbury was the 1995 winner of this award for *Under the Blood Red Sun*, published by Delacorte.

PEN/NORMA KLEIN AWARD, PEN American Center, 568 Broadway, New York NY 10012. (212)334-1660. Fax: (212)334-2181. Contact: John Morrone. Offered in odd-numbered years to recognize an emerging voice of literary merit among American writers of children's fiction. *Candidates may not nominate themselves.* Next award is 1997. Deadline: December 15, 1995. Guidelines for #10 SASE. Award: $3,000.

SILVER BAY AWARDS FOR CHILDREN'S LITERATURE, The Writer's Voice of the Silver Bay Association, Silver Bay NY 12874. (518)543-8833. Fax: (518)543-6733. Contact: Sharon Ofner. Offered annually for best unpublished children's ms set in the Adirondack Mountains, illustrated or non-illustrated. Deadline: February 1. Charges $25 fee. Prize: $1,000.

‡(ALICE WOOD MEMORIAL) OHIOANA FOR CHILDREN'S LITERATURE, Ohioana Library Association, 65 Front St., Suite 1105, Columbus OH 43215. (614)466-3831. Contact: Linda R. Hengst. Offered "to an author whose body of work has made, and continues to make, a significant contribution to literature for children or young adults." Deadline: December 31. Recipient must have been born in Ohio or lived in Ohio at least 5 years.

WORK-IN-PROGRESS GRANT, Society of Children's Book Writers and Illustrators (SCBWI) and Judy Blume, #106, 22736 Vanowen St., West Hills CA 91307. Two grants—one designated specifically for a contemporary novel for young people—to assist SCBWI members in the completion of a specific project. Deadline: June 1. Guidelines for SASE.

Translation

‡AMERICAN TRANSLATORS ASSOCIATION HONORS AND AWARDS, American Translators Association, 1800 Diagonal Rd., Suite 220, Alexandria VA 22314. (703)683-6100. Fax: (703)683-6122. Contact:

Walter Bacak. Student award offered annually; other awards offered every two years. Categories: best student translation; best literary translation in German; and best literary translation in any language but German. Guidelines for SASE. Prize varies—usually $500 and a trip to annual conference.

‡FELLOWSHIPS FOR TRANSLATORS, National Endowment for the Arts Literature Program, 1100 Pennsylvania Ave. NW, Washington DC 20506. (202)682-5451. Award Director: Gigi Bradford. Published translators of exceptional talent.

LEWIS GALANTIÈRE PRIZE FOR LITERARY TRANSLATION, American Translators Association, % Professor Breon Mitchell, Wells Scholars Program, 1331 E. Tenth St., Indiana University, Bloomington IN 47405. (812)855-9491. Offered in even-numbered years to recognize the outstanding translation of a previously published work from languages other than German published in the United States. Deadline: April 15.

‡GERMAN PRIZE FOR LITERARY TRANSLATION, American Translators Association, Wells Scholars Program, 1331 E. Tenth St., Bloomington IN 47405. Chair: Breon Mitchell. Offered in odd-numbered years for previously published book translated from German to English. In even-numbered years, the Lewis Galantière Prize is awarded for translations other than German to English. Deadline April 15.

JOHN GLASSCO TRANSLATION PRIZE, Literary Translators' Association of Canada, Association des traducteurs et traductrices littéraires du Canada, 3492, av. Laval, Montreal, Quebec H2X 3C8 Canada. Estab. 1981. Offered annually for a translator's *first* book-length literary translation into French or English, published in Canada during the previous calendar year. The translator must be a Canadian citizen or landed immigrant. Eligible genres include fiction, creative nonfiction, poetry, published plays, children's books. Deadline: January 15. Write for application form. Award: $500.

‡LOCKERT LIBRARY OF POETRY IN TRANSLATION, Princeton University Press, 41 William St., Princeton NJ 08540. (609)452-4900. E-mail: rebrown@pupress.princeton.edu. Editor: Robert E. Brown. Book-length poetry translation of a single poet.

PEN/BOOK-OF-THE-MONTH CLUB TRANSLATION PRIZE, PEN American Center, 568 Broadway, New York NY 10012. Contact: John Morrone. One award of $3,000 to a literary book-length translation into English published in the calendar year under consideration. (No technical, scientific or reference.) Deadline: December 31.

PEN/RALPH MANHEIM MEDAL FOR TRANSLATION, PEN American Center, 568 Broadway, New York NY 10012. (212)334-1660. Fax: (212)334-2181. Contact: John Morrone. Translators nominated by the PEN Translation Committee. Given every 3 years. Next award: 1997.

‡ALDO AND JEANNE SCAGLIONE PRIZE FOR LITERARY TRANSLATION, Modern Language Association of America, 10 Astor Place, New York NY 10003-6981. (212)475-9500. Fax: (212)477-9863. Director of Special Projects: Richard Brod. Offered in even-numbered years for a translation of book-length literary work and in odd-numbered years for a book-length work of literary history, literary criticism, philology or literary theory appearing in print in 1994 or 1995. Deadline: May 1, 1996. Guidelines for SASE. Prize: $1,000 and a certificate presented at the association's annual convention in December.

STUDENT TRANSLATION PRIZE, American Translators Association, % Prof. Breon Mitchell, Wells Scholars Program, 1331 E. Tenth St., Indiana University, Bloomington IN 47405 (812)855-9491. Support is granted for a promising project to an unpublished student enrolled in a translation program at a US college or university. Deadline: April 15. Must be sponsored by a faculty member.

‡TRANSLATION PRIZE, The American-Scandinavian Foundation, 725 Park Ave., New York NY 10021. (212)879-9779. Fax: (212)249-3444. Offered annually for unpublished outstanding translations of poetry, fiction, drama or literary prose originally written in Danish, Finnish, Icelandic, Norwegian or Swedish. Deadline: 1st weekday in June. Guidelines for SASE. Prize: $2,000 (honorable mention gets $500 Inger Sjöberg Prize) and bronze medallion; publication of an excerpt in *Scandinavian Review*, ASF's magazine.

Multiple Writing Areas

AKRON MANUSCRIPT CLUB WRITER'S CONTEST, Akron Manuscript Club & Akron University, P.O. Box 1101, Cuyahoga Falls OH 44223-0101. (216)923-2094. Contact: M.M. LoPiccolo. Estab. 1929. Offered annually for previously unpublished stories to provide critique, encouragement and some financial help to authors in 3 categories. Deadline is always some time in March. Guidelines for #10 SASE. Charges $20 entry/critique fee. Prize: 1st-certificate to $50, according to funding; 2nd and 3rd-certificates.

AMELIA STUDENT AWARD, *Amelia Magazine*, 329 E St., Bakersfield CA 93304. (805)323-4064. Editor: Frederick A. Raborg, Jr. Previously unpublished poems, essays and short stories by high school students, 1 entry per student; each entry should be signed by parent, guardian *or* teacher to verify originality. Deadline: May 15.

ANNUAL FICTION AND POETRY CONTEST, Rambunctious Press, 1221 W. Pratt, Chicago IL 60626-4329. Contest Director: Mary Alberts. Estab. 1982. Unpublished short stories and poems. Deadline varies. Charges $3/story, $2/poem.

ARIZONA AUTHORS' ASSOCIATION ANNUAL NATIONAL LITERARY CONTEST, Arizona Authors' Association, 3509 E. Shea Blvd., #117, Phoenix AZ 85028-3339. (602)867-9001. Contact: Iva Martin. Previously unpublished poetry, short stories, essays. Deadline: July 29. Charges $5 fee for poetry; $7 fee for short stories and essays.

AWP ANNUAL AWARD SERIES, Associated Writing Programs, Tallwood House, Mail Stop, George Mason University/IE3, Fairfax VA 22030. (703)993-4301. Fax: (703)993-4302. Contact: Beth Jarock. Estab. 1967. Offered annually for book length mss in poetry, short fiction, nonfiction and novel. Deadline: February 28. Charges $10/ms for AWP members; $15/ms for nonmembers.

EMILY CLARK BALCH AWARD, *Virginia Quarterly Review*, 1 West Range, Charlottesville VA 22903. (804)924-3124. Fax:(804)924-1397. E-mail: jco7e@virginia.edu. Editor: Staige D. Blackford. Best short story/poetry accepted and published by the *Virginia Quarterly Review* during a calendar year. No deadline.

BEST OF HOUSEWIFE-WRITER'S FORUM: THE CONTESTED WILLS TO WRITE, *Housewife-Writer's Forum*, P.O. Box 780, Lyman WY 82937-0780. (307)782-7003. Contact: Emma Bluemel. Estab. 1988. Unpublished prose and poetry categories. Deadline: June 1. Charges $4 for prose; $2 for poetry. Also sponsors Rejection Revenge contest for most rejection slips collected in contest year. No entry fee. Contest runs June 1-May 31.

BYLINE MAGAZINE CONTESTS, P.O. Box 130596, Edmond OK 73013. (405)348-5591. Publisher: Marcia Preston. Estab. 1981. Unpublished short stories, poems and other categories. Several categories offered each month which are open to anyone. Deadline on annual award, which is for subscribers only, November 1. Guidelines for #10 SASE. Charges $5 for short story; $3 for poems on annual award. Similar small fees for monthly contests.

CALIFORNIA WRITERS' CLUB CONFERENCE CONTEST, 4913 Marlborough Way, Carmichael CA 95608. (916)488-7094. Unpublished adult fiction (short stories), adult fiction (novels), adult nonfiction, juvenile fiction, poetry and scripts. "Our conference is biennial, next being in 1995." Deadline: varies in spring. Charges fee.

‡CANADIAN AUTHORS ASSOCIATION ANNUAL CREATIVE WRITING AWARDS FOR HIGH SCHOOL, COLLEGE AND UNIVERSITY STUDENTS, (formerly Canadian Author Student Creative Writing Awards), Canadian Authors Association, Box 32219, 250 Harding Blvd. W, Richmond Hill, Ontario L4C 9R0 Canada. To encourage creative writing of unpublished fiction, nonfiction and poetry at the secondary school level. Deadline: March 27, 1995. Must use tearsheet entry form. Must be secondary school, college or university student. Prizes of $500 and 4 honorable mentions in each category (best poem, best story, best article). Send SAE and 1 IRC for guidelines.

THE CHELSEA AWARDS FOR POETRY AND SHORT FICTION, % Richard Foerster, Editor, P.O. Box 1040, York Beach ME 03910. Estab. 1958. Previously unpublished submissions. "Two prizes awarded for the best work of short fiction and for the best group of 4-6 poems selected by the editors in anonymous competitions." Deadline: June 15 for fiction; December 15 for poetry. Guidelines for SASE. Charges $10 fee (includes free subscription to *Chelsea*). Checks made payable to Chelsea Associates, Inc. Prize: $500, winning entries published in *Chelsea*. Include SASE for notification of competition results. Does not return mss. *Note:* General submissions and other business should be addressed to the editor at *Chelsea*, P.O. Box 773, Cooper Station, New York, NY 10276.

CHICANO/LATINO LITERARY CONTEST, Department of Spanish and Portuguese, University of California-Irvine, Irvine CA 92717. (714)824-5702. Contact: Alejandro Morales or Ruth M. Gratzer. Estab. 1974. "To promote the dissemination of unpublished Chicano/Latino literature, and to encourage its development. The call for entries will be genre specific, rotating through four categories: novel (1995), short story (1996), poetry (1997) and drama (1998)." Deadline: April 30. "Interested parties may write for entry procedures." The contest is open to all citizens or permanent residents of the US.

‡THE DANCING JESTER PRESS "ONE NIGHT IN PARIS SHOULD BE ENOUGH" CONTEST, The Dancing Jester Press, 3411 Garth Rd., Suite 208, Baytown TX 77521. (713)427-9560. Fax: (713)428-8685.

Contact: Shiloh Daniel for fiction/poetry; Glenda Daniel for nonfiction. Offered annually for unpublished work. For the nonfiction "Letters-of-Conscience Contest" letters must have been written during the previous year. "The Dancing Jester Prizes 1995: *Poetry*—the purpose of this contest is to recognize excellence in poetics. *Fiction*—The purpose of this contest is to recognize excellence in the practice of fiction. *Nonfiction Letters-of-Conscience Award*—This competition recognizes those writers of letters sent in hopes of securing the release of prisoners held in captivity because the free expression of art or thought. Anyone (including the author) may submit a ms that is eligible. Send for entry and details. 1st-place—Poetry: The night of 4/1/96 in Paris, France all expenses paid; Fiction: the night of 4/1/96 in Paris, Texas plus publication of short story in *Dancing Jester Best Fiction of 1995*; Nonfiction: the Jester Medallion. 2nd-place—Poetry/Fiction: the Jester Medallion. Nonfiction: publication in the annual anthology of Letters-of-Conscience. 3rd-place: all—a pair of "One Night in Paris Should Be Enough" tee-shirts.

DEEP SOUTH WRITERS CONTEST, Deep South Writers Conference, P.O. Box 44691, University of Southwestern Louisiana, Lafayette LA 70504-4691. (318)231-6908. Contact: Contest Clerk. Estab. 1960. Deadline: July 15. Guidelines for SASE. Charges $15 fee for novels and full-length plays; $10 for other submissions. Does not return mss.

‡EDITORS' PRIZE, Missouri Review, 1507 Hillcrest Hall, University of Missouri, Columbia MO 65211. (314)882-4474. Contact: Speer Morgan, Greg Michalson. Offered annually for unpublished fiction, essays or poetry. Deadline: October 15. Guidelines for SASE. Charges $15/entry. Prize: Fiction—$1,000 and publication; Essay—$1,000 and publication; Poetry—$500 and publication. Open to any writer.

VIRGINIA FAULKNER AWARD FOR EXCELLENCE IN WRITING, *Prairie Schooner*, 201 Andrews, University of Nebraska, Lincoln NE 68588-0334. (402)472-0911. Editor: Hilda Raz. Estab. 1988. All genres eligible for consideration. The winning piece must have been published in *Prairie Schooner* during the previous calendar year. Manuscripts read September-May. Prize: $1,000.

FEMINIST WRITERS' CONTEST, Dept WM, 648 N. Northwest Hwy., #258, Park Ridge IL 60068. Contact: Pamela Sims. Estab. 1990. Categories: Fiction and nonfiction (5,000 or fewer words). Work should reflect feminist perspectives (should not endorse or promote sexism, racism, ageism, anti-lesbianism, etc.) Guidelines for SASE. Deadline: August 31. Charge $10 fee. Cash awards.

‡FOLIO, Department of Literature, American University, Washington DC 20016. Estab. 1984. Fiction, poetry, essays, interviews and b&w artwork. "We look for quality work and award an annual prize for best poem and best story published per year." Published twice annually. Manuscripts read September-March 15.

FOSTER CITY ANNUAL WRITERS CONTEST, Foster City Committee for the Arts, 650 Shell Blvd., Foster City CA 94404. Unpublished fiction, poetry, humor and childrens' stories. $2,500 in prizes. Deadline: November 1. Guidelines for SASE.

MILES FRANKLIN LITERARY AWARD, Arts Management Pty. Ltd., 180 Goulburn St., Darlinghurst, NSW 2010 Australia. Fax: 61-2-2648201. Offered annually for work published for the first time the year preceding award. "The award is for a novel or play which presents Australian life in any of its phases. Biographies, collections of short stories or children's books are *not* eligible for the award." Deadline: January 31. Guidelines for #10 SAE with 1 IRC. Prize: $25,000 (Australian). "This award is open to writers of any nationality. However, the novel or play must be about Australian life."

‡GEORGETOWN REVIEW SHORT STORY AND POETRY CONTEST, Georgetown College, 400 E. College St., Georgetown KY 40324. (502)863-8000. Fax: (502)868-8888. Contact: Steve Carter. Deadline: August 1. Guidelines for SASE. Charges fee: $5/short story; $2.50/poem. Prize: $150 for winning story and poem. Runner ups receive publication and 1 year's subscription to *Georgetown Review*.

THE GREENSBORO REVIEW LITERARY AWARD IN FICTION AND POETRY, *The Greensboro Review*, English Department, University of North Carolina-Greensboro, Greensboro NC 27412-5001. (910)334-5459. Fax: (910)334-3281. E-mail: clarks@fagan.uncg.edo. Contact: Fiction or Poetry Editor. Estab. 1984. Annual award for fiction and poetry recognizing the best work published in the winter issue of *The Greensboro Review*. Deadline: September 15. Sample copy for $4.

HACKNEY LITERARY AWARDS, *Writing Today*, Box A-3/Birmingham-Southern College, Birmingham AL 35254. (205)226-4921. Contact: Special Events Office. Estab. 1969. Offered annually for unpublished novel, short story and poetry. Deadline: September 30 for novels, December 31 for short stories and poetry. Guidelines for SASE.

‡HOPEWELL REVIEW, Arts Indiana, Inc., 47 S. Pennsylvania St., Suite 701, Indianapolis IN 46204. (317)632-7894. Publisher/CEO: Ann M. Stack. Editor: Joseph F. Trimmer. Annual collection of poetry, short fiction and personal essays published by Arts Indiana, Inc. It is distributed to select Arts Indiana members, sold in bookstores and newsstands, and is used as a text for university-level classes. Approximately seven short stories and essays and 25 poems by Indiana writers are featured. Three $500 Awards of Excellence are given in the categories of poetry, short fiction, and personal essay. The jurors for the 1995 anthology were: Poetry Juror: Neal Bowers, Editor, *Poet and Critic*; Short Story Juror: Katrina Kenison, Series Editor, *Best American Short Stories*; and Personal Essay Juror: Stan Lindberg, Editor, *Georgia Review*. Deadline: March 1. Guidelines for SASE. Prize: $150 for each accepted short story and $35 for each poem. Writers must be Indiana residents and at least 18 years of age.

‡**KINETICS-ANNUAL AFRICAN-AMERICAN WRITING CONTEST**, Kinetics, P.O. Box 132067, Columbus OH 43213. Contact: Sharon Washington. Offered annually; unpublished submissions only. "The contest encourages fiction and nonfiction writing of an African-American bent. There are three categories: poetry, fiction and essay." Deadline: the day before Thanksgiving. Guidelines for SASE. Prizes: $75 first place; $50 second place; $25 third place. Judged by a panel of eductors and writers; panel varies according to availability of judges. "Kinetics reserves the right to publish winners and other noted pieces in the *Kinetics Journal*. Kinetics also reserves editing rights." Open to any unpublished writer.

ROSE LEFCOWITZ PRIZES, *Poet Lore*, The Writer's Center, 4508 Walsh St., Bethesda MD 20815. (301)654-8664. Executive Editors: Philip Jason, Geraldine Connolly. Offered annually for previously unpublished poetry or criticism. The prizes go to the single best poem and piece of critical prose to appear in a given volume of *Poet Lore*. Guidelines for #10 SASE. Prizes include $150 for each winner (1 winner for poetry, 1 for prose). Rights revert to the author after first publication in *Poet Lore*. "Only poems and prose that appear in a volume of *Poet Lore* are considered. A poem or piece of critical prose must first appear in the magazine before it will be considered for the prize."

‡**LETRAS DE ORO SPANISH LITERARY PRIZES**, Iberian Studies, University of Miami, P.O. Box 248123, Coral Gables FL 33124. (305)284-3266. Fax: (305)284-4406. Contact: Dr. Joaquin Roy. Offered annually for unpublished work. "The Spanish Literary contest Letras de Oro now in its tenth year, has received national and international prestige for recognizing the excellent contribution of authors who write in Spanish and reside in the US. There are prizes in five categories: novel, short story, theater, essay and poetry. The prize awards include $2,500 cash for the winning entries and the publication of the winning manuscripts in the Letras de Oro literary collection." Deadline: October 12. Guidelines available by mail, phone or fax. Contest is open to any writer who writes in Spanish and reside in the US. Poems and short stories should contain enough material to create a book. Essays require a minimum of 100 pages.

HUGH J. LUKE AWARD, *Prairie Schooner*, 201 Andrews, University of Nebraska, Lincoln NE 68588-0334. (402)472-0911. Editor: Hilda Raz. Offered annually for work published in *Prairie Schooner*. Winner announced in the spring issue of the following year. Manuscripts read September-May. Prize: $250.

MASTERS LITERARY AWARDS, Center Press, P.O. Box 16452, Encino CA 91416-6452. (818)377-4301. Contact: Gabriella Stone. Offered annually and quarterly for work published within 2 years (preferred) and unpublished work (accepted). Fiction: 15 page, maximum; Poetry: 5 pages or 150 lines, maximum; Nonfiction: 10 page, maximum. Deadlines: March 15, June 15th, August 15th, December 15. Guidelines for SASE. Charges $15 reading/administration fee. Prizes: 5 quarterly honorable mentions from which is selected one yearly Grand Prize of $1,000. "A selection of all winning entries will appear in our national literary publication" judged by "three anonymous experts chosen yearly from literary and publishing field." Center Press retains one time publishing rights to selected winners. Open to all writers.

THE MENTOR AWARD, *Mentor Newsletter*, P.O. Box 4382, Overland Park KS 66204-0382. Award Director: Maureen Waters. Estab. 1989. Offered annually to promote and encourage mentoring through feature articles, essays, book/movie reviews, interviews or short stories about mentoring-related subjects. Guidelines for #10 SASE. Charges $4 fee. Prize: $100. Writer must be at least 16 years old.

MIDLAND AUTHORS AWARD, Society of Midland Authors, % Ford-Choyke, 29 E. Division St., Chicago IL 60610. (312)337-1482. Estab. 1915. Annual awards for published or produced drama, fiction, nonfiction, poetry, biography, children's fiction and children's nonfiction. Authors must reside in the states of Illinois, Indiana, Iowa, Kansas, Michigan, Minnesota, Missouri, Nebraska, North Dakota, South Dakota, Wisconsin or Ohio. Guidelines for SASE. Deadline: January 15, 1996.

‡**THE MILTON CENTER POST-GRADUATE FELLOWSHIP**, The Milton Center, 3200 McCormick Ave., Wichita KS 67213. (316)942-4291, ext. 326. Fax: (316)942-9658. Contact: Virginia Stern Owens. Offered annually for unpublished submissions "to provide new writers of Christian commitment with the opportunity to complete their first book-length manuscript of fiction or poetry with a supportive community of writers." Deadline: January 31. Guidelines for SASE. Charges $15 fee. Award: $6,000 stipend, plus living expenses

for one (married applicants welcome, although expenses are only provided for one). Judged by The Fellows of the Milton Center. Two fellowships are awarded/year.

THE NEBRASKA REVIEW AWARDS IN FICTION AND POETRY, *The Nebraska Review*, ASH 215, University of Nebraska-Omaha, Omaha NE 68182-0324. (402)554-2771. (402)554-3436. E-mail: ncreview@fa cpacs.unomaha.edu. Contact: Susan Aizenberg (poetry), James Reed (fiction). Estab. 1973. Previously unpublished fiction and a poem or group of poems. Deadline: November 30.

NEUSTADT INTERNATIONAL PRIZE FOR LITERATURE, 110 Monnet Hall, Norman OK 73019. (405)325-4531. Estab. 1969. Previously published fiction, poetry and drama. Nominations are made only by members of the jury, which changes every 2 years.

NEW LETTERS LITERARY AWARDS, University of Missouri-Kansas City, Kansas City MO 64110-2499. Fax: (816)235-2611. Awards Coordinator: Glenda McCrary. Estab. 1986. Unpublished fiction, poetry and essays. Deadline: May 15. Finalists are notified the middle of August; winners announced the third week in September. Charges $10 fee. Guidelines for SASE.

NIMROD, ARTS AND HUMANITIES COUNCIL OF TULSA PRIZES, 2210 S. Main, Tulsa OK 74114. (918)584-3333. Fax: (918)582-2787. Editor: Francine Ringold. Unpublished fiction (Katherine Anne Porter prize) and poetry (Pablo Neruda Prize). Deadline: April 15. Charges $15 fee, includes an issue of *Nimrod*. (Writers entering both fiction and poetry contest need only pay once.) Guidelines for #10 SASE. Sample copies $6.95 for an older issue, $8 for a recent issue.

‡PEN CENTER USA WEST ANNUAL LITERARY AWARDS, PEN Center USA West, 672 S. Lafayette Park Place, #41, Los Angeles CA 90057. (213)365-8500. Fax: (213)365-9616. Contact: Shannon Bellemare. Offered annually for fiction, nonfiction, poetry, children's literature, translation, drama, screenplay, teleplay published January 1-December 31 of the current year. Deadline: December 31. Guidelines for SASE. Prize: $500. Open to authors west of the Mississippi River.

PRAIRIE SCHOONER BERNICE SLOTE AWARD, *Prairie Schooner*, 201 Andrews, University of Nebraska, Lincoln NE 68588-0334. (402)472-0911. Editor: Hilda Raz. Estab. 1984. Offered annually for the best work by a beginning writer published in *Prairie Schooner*. Winner announced in the spring issue of the following year. Manuscripts read September-May. Prize: $500.

PRAIRIE SCHOONER READERS' CHOICE AWARDS, *Prairie Schooner*, 201 Andrews, University of Nebraska, Lincoln NE 68588-0334. (402)472-0911. Editor: Hilda Raz. Offered annually for work published in *Prairie Schooner*. Winners announced in the spring issue of the following year. Manuscripts read September-May. Prize: $250 each. Several Readers' Choice Awards are given each year.

THE PRESIDIO LA BAHIA AWARD, Sons of the Republic of Texas, 5942 Abrams Rd., #222, Dallas TX 75231. Offered annually "to promote suitable preservation of relics, appropriate dissemination of data, and research into our Texas heritage, with particular attention to the Spanish Colonial period." Deadline: June 1-September 30. Guidelines for SASE. Prize: $2,000 total; 1st prize a minimum of $1,200, 2nd and 3rd prizes at the discretion of the judges.

QUINCY WRITER'S GUILD ANNUAL CREATIVE WRITING CONTEST, Quincy Writer's Guild, c/o Natalie Miller Rotunda, P.O. Box 433, Quincy IL 62306-0433. Categories include: poetry, short story, fiction. Deadline: January 1-April 15. Charges $2/poem; $4/short story or article. "No identification should appear on manuscripts, but should be on a separate 3×5 card attached to the entry with name, address, phone number, word count, and title of work." Previously unpublished work. Cash prizes. Guidelines for SASE.

RHYME TIME CREATIVE WRITING COMPETITION, *Rhyme Time*, P.O. Box 2907, Decatur IL 62524. Award Director: Linda Hutton. Estab. 1981. Annual no-fee contest. Submit 1 typed poem, any style, any length. One winner will receive $25; one runner-up will receive a year's subscription to *Rhyme Time*. No poems will be published. Include SASE. Deadline: November 1.

MARY ROBERTS RINEHART FUND, MSN 3E4 English Department, George Mason University, 4400 University Dr., Fairfax VA 22030-4444. (703)993-1185. Contact: William Miller. Grants by nomination to unpublished creative writers for fiction, poetry, drama, biography, autobiography or history with a strong narrative quality. Submissions are accepted for fiction and poetry in odd years, and nonfiction and drama in even years. Deadline: Nov. 30.

SUMMERFIELD G. ROBERTS AWARD, Sons of the Republic of Texas, 5942 Abrams Rd., #222, Dallas TX 75231. Offered annually for submissions published during the previous calendar year "to encourage literary effort and research about historical events and personalities during the days of the Republic of Texas,

1836-1846, and to stimulate interest in the period." Deadline: January 15. Guidelines for SASE. Prize: $2,500. Judges are 3 previous winners of the award.

‡ROM/CON, (formerly Reader Riter Poll), 1555 Washington Ave., San Leandro CA 94577. (415)357-5665. Director: Barbara N. Keenan. Awards for previously published material in 12 categories appearing in *Affaire de Coeur* magazine. Deadline: March 15. "Rom-Con Awards are given at the annual conference and are presented for the highest quality of writing in the Romance genre. The 1994 awards were given September 7-9, 1995 at Rom-Con '95 in Reno, Nevada."

SCHOLASTIC WRITING AWARDS, 555 Broadway, New York NY 10012. (212)343-6890. Estab. 1923. Fiction, nonfiction, poetry, essay, drama essay and portfolio (for students in grades 7-12 only). Write for complete information. Cash prizes, grants and scholarships. Deadline: December to mid-January.

‡SONORA REVIEW ANNUAL LITERARY AWARDS, *Sonora Review*, English Department, University of Arizona, Tucson AZ 85721. $500 Fiction Award given each Spring to the best previously unpublished short story. Deadline: December 1. Charges $10 fee. $500 Poetry Award given each Fall to the best previously unpublished poem. Four poems/5 page maximum submission. Deadline: July 1. Charges $10 fee. For both awards, all entrants receive a copy of the issue in which the winning entry appears. No formal application form is required; regular submission guidelines apply. Guidelines for #10 SASE. For samples, send $6.

SOUTHWEST REVIEW AWARDS, Southern Methodist University, 307 Fondren Library West, P.O. Box 0374, Dallas TX 75275-0374. (214)768-1036. Contact: Rose Torres. Offered annually for fiction, nonfiction and poetry published in the magazine. "The $1,000 John H. McGinnis Memorial Award is given each year for fiction and nonfiction that has been published in the *Southwest Review* in the previous year. Stories or articles are not submitted directly for the award, but simply for publication in the magazine. The Elizabeth Matchett Stover Award, an annual prize of $150, is awarded to the author of the best poem or group of poems published in the magazine during the preceding year."

‡TENNESSEE WRITERS ALLIANCE LITERARY COMPETITION, Tennessee Writers Alliance, P.O. Box 120396, Nashville TN 37212. (615)383-0227. Contact: Literary Competition Director. Offered annually for unpublished short fiction, poetry, nonfiction (personal essay). Deadline: varies. Guidelines for SASE. Charges $5 fee for members, $10 fee for non-member Tennessee residents. Prize: 1st-$500; 2nd-$250; 3rd-$100 and publication. Right to publish once. Open to any member of The Tennessee Writers Alliance and Tennessee residents. Membership is open to all, regardless of residence, for $20/year. $10/year for students.

‡TMWC LITERARY CONTEST, Tennessee Mountain Writers' Conference, P.O. Box 4895, Oak Ridge TN 37831. (615)482-1307. Fax: (615)483-1992. Contact: Patricia Hope. Offered annually for unpublished work to give beginning writers an outlet for their work. Deadline: March 31. Guidelines for SASE. Charges $5 fee only to those not attending conference, otherwise it's free. Prize: 1st-$50 and plaque; 2nd-$30 and plaque; 3rd-$20 and plaque; Honorable Mention certificates.

FRANK WATERS SOUTHWEST WRITERS AWARD, Martin Foundation/Frank Waters Foundation, P.O. Box 1357, Ranchos De Taos NM 87557. (505)758-9869. Offered annually for unpublished works of fiction giving recognition and monetary grants to 3 Western writers from 6 Western states. Top prize winner will be published. Guidelines for SASE. Submit 2 complete copies of ms with no name attached (relevant information included in query letter. Word limit: 10,000. Deadline: May 31. Charges $10 fee. Prize: 1st-$5,000; 2nd-$3,000; 3rd-$1,000. Judges are 3 panels of writers, editors, publishers, etc. including: Rudolfo Anaya, John Nichols, Frank Waters. Open to writers from the 6 western states of CO, NM, UT, AZ, NV, TX.

WESTERN MAGAZINE AWARDS, Western Magazine Awards Foundation, 3898 Hillcrest Ave., North Vancouver, British Columbia V7R 4B6 Canada. (604)984-7525. Fax: (604)985-6262. Contact: Tina Baird. Offered annually for magazine work published January 1-December 31 of previous calendar year. Entry categories include business, culture, science, technology and medicine, entertainment, fiction, political issues, and much more. Write or phone for rules and entry forms. Deadline: February 1. Entry fee: $22 for work in magazines with circulation under 20,000; $28 for work in magazines with circulation over 20,000. $500 award. Applicant must be a Canadian citizen, landed immigrant, or a fulltime resident of Canada. The work must have been published in a magazine whose main editorial office is in Western Canada, the NW Territories and Yukon.

WRITERS AT WORK FELLOWSHIP COMPETITION, Writers at Work, P.O. Box 1146, Centerville UT 84014-5146. (801)292-9285. Contact: Dawn Marano or Shelley Hunt-Camoin. Offered annually for unpublished short stories, novel excerpts and poetry. Deadline: March 15. Guidelines for SASE. Call (801)292-9285. Charges $12 fee. "Only the fee is required for consideration. Short stories or novel excerpts must be no longer than 20 double-spaced pages (one story per entry only). Poetry submissions are limited to 6 poems, 10 pages maximum." Prize: $1,500, publication and conference tuition; $500, conference tuition.

WRITER'S DIGEST WRITING COMPETITION, *Writer's Digest* Magazine, 1507 Dana Ave., Cincinnati OH 45207-9966. (513)531-2690, ext. 633. Fax: (513)531-1843. Contest Director: Rachel Johnson. Contest in 65th year. Categories: Personal Essays, Feature Articles, Literary Short Stories, Mainstream/Genre Short Stories, Rhyming Poems, Non-Rhyming Poems, Stage Plays and Television/Movie Scripts. Submissions must be unpublished. Guidelines for #10 SASE. Deadline: May 31.

‡PHYLLIS SMART YOUNG/CHRIS O'MALLEY PRIZES IN POETRY AND FICTION, (formerly Felix Pollak/Chris O'Malley Prizes in Poetry and Fiction), *The Madison Review*, Dept. of English, 600 N. Park St., Madison WI 53706. (608)263-3374. Director: Ronald Kuka. Offered annually for previously unpublished work. "The Phyllis Smart Young contest awards $500 to the best poems submitted, out of a field of around 500 submissions yearly. The purpose of the prize is to award good poets. Submissions must consist of three poems. The Chris O'Malley prize in fiction is awarded to the best piece of fiction." Deadline: September 30. Prize: poetry $500; fiction $500; plus publication in the spring issue of *The Madison Review*. All contest entries are considered as submissions to *The Madison Review*, the literary journal sponsoring the contest. No simultaneous submissions to other publications. There is a reading fee of $3 for each entry in both the Young and O'Malley contests.

Arts Councils and Foundations

‡ARTIST ASSISTANCE FELLOWSHIP, Minnesota State Arts Board, 432 Summit Ave., St. Paul MN 55102. (612)297-2603. Fax: (612)297-4304. E-mail: msab@maroon.tc.umn.edu. Artist Assistance Program Associate: Karen Mueller. Annual fellowships of $6,000 to be used for time, materials, living expenses. Literary categories include prose, poetry and theater arts (playwriting and screenwriting). Applicants must be Minnesota residents. Deadline: October.

ARTISTS FELLOWSHIP, Japan Foundation, 39th Floor, 152 W. 57th St., New York NY 10019. (212)489-0299. Fax: (212)489-0409. Contact: Program Assistant. Offered annually. Deadline: December 1. "Contact us around September. Write or fax interest. Judged by committee in Japan Foundation headquarters in Tokyo. Keep in mind that this is an international competition. Due to the breadth of the application pool only four artists are selected for awards in the US. Applicants need not submit a writing sample, but if one is submitted it must be brief. Three letters of recommendation must be submitted from peers. One letter will double as a letter of affiliation, which must be submitted by a *Japan-based* (not necessarily an ethnic Japanese) peer artist. The applicant must present have a concise and cogent project objective and must be a professional writer/artist with accessible qualifications, i.e., a list of major works or publications."

ARTS RECOGNITION AND TALENT SEARCH, National Foundation for Advancement in the Arts, 800 Brickell Ave., Suite 500, Miami FL 33131. (305)377-1140 or (800)970-ARTS. Fax: (305)377-1149. Contact: Sherry Thompson, Programs Officer. Estab. 1981. For achievements in dance, music, photography, theater, visual arts and writing. Students fill in and return the application, available at every public and private high school around the nation, for cash awards of up to $3,000 each and scholarship opportunities worth more than $3 million. Deadline: early-June 1, regular-October 1. Charges $25 registration fee for June; $35 for October.

ASSISTANCE TO ESTABLISHED WRITERS, Nova Scotia Department of Education and Cultural Cultural Affairs Division, P.O. Box 578, Halifax, Nova Scotia B3J 2S9 Canada. (902)424-6389. Fax: (902)424-0710. Offered twice annually for unpublished submissions to assist the professional writer with the costs of completing the research or manuscript preparation for a project in which a trade publisher has expressed serious interest." Deadline: April 1 and October 1. Prize: Maximum of $2,000 (Canadian). Applicant must be a Canadian citizen or landed immigrant and must have had their principal residence in Nova Scotia for 12 consecutive months at the time of application. Applicant must be an experienced writer who writes for print or broadcast media, film or stage, who has been consistently published and/or produced in the media.

GEORGE BENNETT FELLOWSHIP, Phillips Exeter Academy, 20 Main St., Exeter NH 03833-2460. Coordinator, Selection Committee: Charles Pratt. Estab. 1968. Annual award of stipend, room and board "to provide time and freedom from material considerations to a person seriously contemplating or pursuing a career as a writer. Applicants should have a manuscript in progress which they intend to complete during the fellowship period." Guidelines for SASE. "Telephone inquiries strongly discouraged." Deadline: December 1. Charges $5 fee. Residence at the Academy during the Fellowship period required.

BRODY ARTS FUND FELLOWSHIP, California Community Foundation, 606 S. Olive St., Suite 2400, Los Angeles CA 90014-1526. (213)413-4042. Estab. 1985. "The Brody Arts Fund is designed to serve the needs of emerging artists and arts organizations, especially those rooted in the diverse, multicultural communities of Los Angeles. The fellowship program rotates annually between three main subsections of the arts. Literary artists will be considered in 1997; and again in 2000. Applications are available and due in the first quarter of the year. Applicants must reside in Los Angeles County. Students not eligible."

BUSH ARTIST FELLOWSHIPS, The Bush Foundation, E-900 First National Bank Bldg., 332 Minnesota St., St. Paul MN 55101. (612)227-5222. Contact: Sally F. Dixon. Estab. 1976. Award for Minnesota, North Dakota, South Dakota, and western Wisconsin residents "to buy 6-18 months of time for the applicant to do his/her own work." Up to 15 fellowships/year. $26,000 stipend each plus additional $7,000 for production and travel. Deadline: mid-November.

‡CAREER OPPORTUNITY GRANTS, Minnesota State Arts Board, 432 Summit Ave., St. Paul MN 55102. (612)297-2603. Fax: (612)297-4304. Artist Assistance Program Associate: Karen Mueller. Offered 3 times/year. "Career Opportunity grants ranging from $100 to $1,000 may be used to support unique, concrete opportunities that may significantly enhance an artist's work or career." Applications accepted in fiction, creative nonfiction, poetry, playwriting, screenwriting. Applicants must be Minnesota residents. Deadlines in September, January, May.

COLORADO VISIONS (COVISIONS) PROJECT GRANTS, Colorado Council on the Arts, 750 Pennsylvania St., Denver CO 80203-3699. (303)894-2619. Director: Daniel Salazar. Annual grants to support innovative projects of high artistic merit in all disciplines, including literature. Open to Colorado residents only. Deadline: June 15.

COLORADO VISIONS (COVISIONS) RECOGNITION AWARDS IN LITERATURE, Colorado Council on the Arts, 750 Pennsylvania St., Denver CO 80203-3699. (303)894-2619. Director: Daniel Salazar. Offered annually to "acknowledge outstanding accomplishment among individual arts as well as encourage public accessiblity to their work." Deadline: December 15.

COMMONWEALTH OF PENNSYLVANIA COUNCIL ON THE ARTS LITERATURE FELLOWSHIPS, 216 Finance Bldg., Harrisburg PA 17120. (717)787-6883. Award Director: Marcia D. Salvatore. Estab. 1966. Fellowships for Pennsylvania writers of fiction and poetry. Deadline: August 1.

CREATIVITY FELLOWSHIP, Northwood University, Alden B. Dow Creativity Center, Midland MI 48640-2398. (517)837-4478. Award Director: Carol B. Coppage. Estab. 1979. Eight-week summer residency for individuals in any field who wish to pursue new and creative ideas that have potential impact in their fields. No accommodations for family/pets. Deadline: December 31.

DORLAND MOUNTAIN ARTS COLONY RESIDENCIES, Dorland Mountain Arts Colony, P.O. Box 6, Temecula CA 92593. (909)676-5039. Contact: Admissions Secretary. "Dorland Mountain Colony's Artist residencies are awarded semiannually to writers, artists, composers whose work passes review by a committee of established artists in the appropriate discipline." Deadline: March 1, September 1. Guidelines and entry forms for SASE. Residencies 1-2 months. "Small cabin donations are asked of accepted artists."

‡FELLOWSHIP-LITERATURE, Alabama State Council on the Arts, One Dexter Ave., Montgomery AL 36130. (205)242-4076. Fax: (205)240-3269. Contact: Becky Mullen. Literature Fellowship offered on alternate, even-numbered years for previously published or unpublished work to set aside time to create and to improve skills. Two year Alabama residency requirement. Deadline: May 1. Guidelines available. Prize: $10,000 or $5,000.

FELLOWSHIP/NEW JERSEY STATE COUNCIL ON THE ARTS, CN306, Trenton NJ 08625. (609)292-6130. Contact: Grants Office. Annual prose, poetry, playwriting in literature awards for New Jersey residents. Applications available in September. Deadline: December.

‡FELLOWSHIPS FOR CREATIVE WRITERS, National Endowment for the Arts Literature Program, 1100 Pennsylvania Ave. NW, Washington DC 20506. (202)682-5451. Award Director: Gigi Bradford. Published creative writers of exceptional talent. Deadline: Poetry, March 3; Fiction/Creative Nonfiction, May 26.

‡FELLOWSHIPS IN LITERATAURE & THEATRE, Pennsylvania Council on the Arts, 216 Finance Bldg., Harrisburg PA 17120. (717)787-6883. Fax: (717)783-2538. Contact: Marcia D. Salvatore. Offered biennially to allow writers to set aside time for creative work. Literature Program: Fellowships in poetry or fiction. Theatre Program: Fellowships in playwriting. Deadline: August 1. Phone and request "The Guide to the

ALWAYS enclose a self-addressed, stamped envelope (SASE) with all your queries and correspondence.

Fellowship Programs." Prize: $5,000. Artists retain rights to their work. Two year Pennsylvania residency requirement.

‡**FELLOWSHIPS TO ASSIST RESEARCH AND ARTISTIC CREATION**, John Simon Guggenheim Memorial Foundation, 90 Park Ave., New York NY 10016. (212)687-4470. Offered annually to assist scholars and artists to engage in research in any field of knowledge and creation in any of the arts, under the freest possible conditions and irrespective of race, color, or creed. Application for SASE.

WILLIAM FLANAGAN MEMORIAL CREATIVE PERSONS CENTER, Edward F. Albee Foundation, 14 Harrison St., New York NY 10013. (212)226-2020. Foundation Secretary: David Briggs. Annual one-month residency at "The Barn" in Montauk, New York offers writers privacy and a peaceful atmosphere in which to work. Deadline: April 1. Prize: room only, writers pay for food and travel expenses. Judging by panel of qualified professionals.

FLORIDA INDIVIDUAL ARTIST FELLOWSHIPS, Florida Department of State, Division of Cultural Affairs, The Capitol, Tallahassee FL 32399-0250. (904)487-2980. Fax: (904)922-5259. Director: Peyton Fearington. Fellowship for Florida writers only. Prize: $5,000 each for fiction, poetry and children's literature. Deadline: January.

‡**GOVERNOR GENERAL'S LITERARY AWARDS**, Canada Council, Writing and Publishing Section, 350 Albert St., P.O. Box 1047, Ottawa, Ontario K1P 5V8 Canada. (613)566-4376. Fax: (613)566-4410. Contact: Writing and Publishing Officer. "Awards are given annually to the best English-language and French-language work in each of the seven categories of fiction, nonfiction, poetry, drama, translation children's literature (text) and children's literature (illustration). Books must be first-edition trade books which have been written, translated or illustrated by Canadian citizens or permanent residents of Canada and published in Canada or abroad during the previous year. In the case of translation, the original work must also be a Canadian-authored title. Books must be submitted by publishers and accompanied by a Publisher's Submission Form, which is available from the Writing and Publishing Section." Deadline: August 31.

‡**IDAHO WRITER-IN-RESIDENCE**, Idaho Commission on the Arts, Box 83720, Boise ID 83720-0008. (208)334-2119. Program Coordinator: Diane Josephy Peavey. Estab. 1982. Offered every 2 years for previously published (within previous 5 years) or unpublished work. Award of $10,000 for an Idaho writer, who over the two-year period reads his/her work throughout the state to increase the appreciation for literature. Deadline: spring, 1997; dates change. Guidelines for SASE. Open to any Idaho writer.

ILLINOIS ARTS COUNCIL ARTISTS FELLOWSHIP, James R. Thompson Center, 100 W. Randolph, Suite 10-500, Chicago IL 60601. (312)814-6750. Contact: Director of Communication Arts. Offered every 2 years for previously published or unpublished work. "Submitted work must have been completed no more than four years prior to deadline. Artists fellowships are awarded to Illinois artists of exceptional talent to enable them to pursue their artistic goals; fellowships are offered in poetry and prose (fiction and creative nonfiction)." Deadline: September 1. "Interested Illinois writers should write or call for information." Prize: $500 Finalist Award; $5,000 or $10,000 Artist's Fellowship. "Writer must be Illinois resident and not a degree-seeking student. Applicants for Poetry Fellowship can submit up to 15 pages of work in manuscript; prose fellowship applicants can submit up to 30 pages of work in manuscript."

‡**INDIVIDUAL ARTIST FELLOWSHIP AWARD**, Montana Arts Council, 316 N. Park Ave., Suite 252, Helena MT 59620. (406)444-6430. Contact: Fran Morrow. Offered annually to *Montana Residents only*. Deadline: April 30.

INDIVIDUAL ARTIST PROGRAM, Wisconsin Arts Board, 101 E. Wilson St., 1st Floor, Madison WI 53702. Grant Coordinator: Elizabeth Malner. Estab. 1990. (608)266-0190. Annual fellowships and grants for Wisconsin residents. Call for more information.

INDIVIDUAL ARTISTS FELLOWSHIPS, Nebraska Arts Council, 3838 Davenport St., Omaha NE 68131-2329. (402)595-2122. Fax: (402)595-2334. Contact: Suzanne Wise. Estab. 1991. Offered biannually (literature alternates with performing arts) to recognize exemplary achievements by originating artists in their fields of endeavor and supports the contributions made by Nebraska artists to the quality of life in this state. Deadline: October 1. "Generally, master awards are $3,000-4,000 and merit awards are $1,000-2,000. Funds available are announced in September prior to the deadline." Must be a resident of Nebraska for at least 2 years prior to submission date; 18 years of age; not enrolled in an undergraduate, graduate or certificate-granting program in English, creative writing, literature, or related field.

ISLAND LITERARY AWARDS, Prince Edward Island Council of the Arts, P.O. Box 2234, Charlottetown, Prince Edward Island C1A 8B9 Canada. (902)368-4410. Award Director: Judy K. MacDonald. Offers 6 awards for previously unpublished poetry, short fiction, playwriting feature article, children's literature and student writing. Deadline: February 15. Guidelines for #10 SAE with 1 IRC. Charges $6 fee. *Available to residents of PEI only.*

JOSEPH HENRY JACKSON/JAMES D. PHELAN LITERARY AWARDS, The San Francisco Foundation, Administered by Intersection for the Arts, 446 Valencia St., San Francisco CA 94103. (415)626-2787. Contact: Awards Coordinator. Estab. 1965. Jackson Award: unpublished, work-in-progress fiction (novel or short story), nonfiction or poetry by author age 20-35, with 3-year consecutive residency in northern California or Nevada prior to submission. Phelan: unpublished, work-in-progress fiction, nonfiction, short story, poetry or drama by California-born author age 20-35. Deadline: January 31.

EZRA JACK KEATS MEMORIAL FELLOWSHIP, Ezra Jack Keats Foundation (funding) awarded through Kerlan Collection, University of Minnesota, 109 Walter Library, 117 Pleasant St. SE., Minneapolis MN 55455. (612)624-4576. Fax: (612)625-5525. Curator, Kerlan Collection: Karen Hoyle. To award a talented writer and/or illustrator of children's books who wishes to use Kerlan Collection for the furtherance of his or her artistic development." Deadline: early May. Guidelines for SASE. Prize: $1,500 for travel to study at Kerlan Collection. Judged by a committee of 4-5 members from varying colleges at University of Minnesota and outside the University. "Special consideration will be given to someone who would find it difficult to finance the visit to the Kerlan Collection."

‡KENTUCKY ARTS COUNCILS FELLOWSHIPS IN WRITING, Kentucky Arts Council, 31 Fountain Place, Frankfort KY 40601. (502)564-3757. Fax: (502)564-2839. Contact: Irwin Pickett. Offered in even-numbered years for development/artist's work. Deadline: September 1996. Guidelines for SASE (3 months before deadline). Award: $5,000. Must be Kentucky resident.

LITERARY ARTS PROGRAMS, Arts Branch, Department of Municipalities, Culture and Housing, P.O. Box 6000, Fredericton, New Brunswick E3B 5H1 Canada. (506)453-2555. Fax: (506)453-2416. Contact: Bruce Dennis, Literary Arts Officer, Arts Branch. Grant and awards programs: Development Travel, Promotional Travel. Excellence Awards, Creation, Artist-in-Residence, Arts Scholarships and New Brunswick Arts Abroad programs. *Available to New Brunswick residents only. (Must have resided in NB 2 of past 4 years.)*

THE GERALD LOEB AWARDS, The John E. Anderson Graduate School of Management at UCLA, 405 Hilgard Ave., Los Angeles CA 90024-1481. (310)206-1877. Fax: (310)206-9830. Contact: Office of Communications. Consideration is limited to articles published in the previous calendar year. "To recognize writers who make significant contributions to the understanding of business, finance and the economy." Deadline: February 15 "unless it lands on a holiday." Charges $20 fee. Winners in each category receive $1,000. Honorable mentions, when awarded, receive $500.

LOFT-McKNIGHT WRITERS AWARD, The Loft, Pratt Community Center, 66 Malcolm Ave. SE, Minneapolis MN 55414-3551. Contact: Program Coordinator. Eight awards of $7,500 and two awards of distinction at $10,500 each for *Minnesota* writers of poetry and creative prose. Deadline: November. Guidelines for SASE.

LOFT-MENTOR SERIES, The Loft, Pratt Community Center, 66 Malcolm Ave. SE, Minneapolis MN 55414-3551. Contact: Program Coordinator. Estab. 1974. Opportunity to work with 4 nationally known writers and small stipend available to 8 winning poets and fiction writers. "Must live close enough to Minneapolis to participate fully in the series." Deadline: May. Guidelines for SASE.

WALTER RUMSEY MARVIN GRANT, Ohioana Library Association, 65 S. Front St., Suite 1105, Columbus OH 43215. (614)466-3831. Director: Linda Hengst. Offered in even-numbered years. Applicant must have been born in Ohio or have lived in Ohio for 5 years or more, must be 30 years of age or younger, and not have published a book. Deadline: January 31. Entries submitted may consist of up to 6 pieces of prose. No submission may total more than 60 pages or less than 10. No entries will be returned.

MONEY FOR WOMEN, Barbara Deming Memorial Fund, Inc., P.O. Box 40-1043, Brooklyn NY 11240-1043. Contact: Pam McAllister. "Small grants to individual feminists in the arts (musicians, artists, writers, poets, photographers) whose work addresses women's concerns and/or speaks for peace and justice from a feminist perspective." Deadline: December 31-June 30. Guidelines for SASE. Prize: grants up to $1,000: "The Fund does *not* give educational assistance, monies for personal study or loans, monies for dissertation or research projects, grants for group projects, business ventures, or emergency funds for hardships." Open to individual feminists in the arts. Applicants must be citizens of the US or Canada.
- The fund also offers two awards, the "Gerty, Gerty, Gerty in the Arts, Arts, Arts" for outstanding works by a lesbian and the "Fannie Lou Hamer Award" for work which combats racism and celebrates women of color.

NANTUCKET PLAYWRIGHT'S RETREAT, Nantucket Theatrical Productions, Box 2171, Nantucket MA 02584. (508)228-5002. Director: Jim Patrick. Offered annually for "opportunities to have works in progress read; discussion and criticism by directors, actors, and peers; workshops and seminars; and a relatively inexpensive chance to write and visit the historic and beautiful island of Nantucket. We anticipate offering weekend seminars and weeklong increments at our retreat at an affordable price with a loosely structured program to facilitate an author's work in progress. Likely dates January through March. Write for more information."

NATIONAL ENDOWMENT FOR THE ARTS: ARTS ADMINISTRATION FELLOWS PROGRAM/FEL-LOWSHIP, National Endowment for the Arts, 1100 Pennsylvania Ave. NW, Washington DC 20506. (202)682-5786. Fax: (202)682-5610. Contact: Anya Nykyforiak. Estab. 1973. Offered in spring, summer and fall for arts managers and administrators including those in the nonprofit literary publishing field or writers' centers. Fellows come from all arts disciplines to the NEA for an 11-week residency to acquire an overview of this Federal agency's operations. Deadline: January, April, July. Guidelines may be requested by letter or telephone.

NEW HAMPSHIRE INDIVIDUAL ARTISTS' FELLOWSHIPS, New Hampshire State Council on the Arts, 40 N. Main St., Concord NH 03301-4974. (603)271-2789. Fax: (603)271-3584. Coordinator: Audrey V. Sylvester. Estab. 1982. "To recognize artistic excellence and professional commitment." Deadline: July 1. Guidelines for SASE or call for application. Prize: up to $3,000. Applicant must be over 18; not enrolled as fulltime student; be a New Hampshire resident and may not have been a fellow in preceding year.

‡NJ STATE COUNCIL ON THE ARTS FELLOWSHIP, New Jersey State Council on the Arts, CN 306, Trenton NJ 08625. (609)292-6130. Fax: (609)989-1440. Contact: Steven R. Runk, Grants Coordinator. Offered annually to enable artists and writers to continue producing new work categories are offered in prose (fiction and nonfiction), poetry and playwriting. Deadline: mid-December. Guidelines for SASE. Prize: grant ranging between $5,000-$12,000. Persons eligible for fellowships are: a) Artists who are permanent residents of the State of New Jersey (all awards are subject to verification of New Jersey residency); b) Artists who have NOT received a fellowship since Fiscal Year 1990-91 (recipients may not re-apply for four years); c) Artists who are NOT matriculated students in a graduate, undergraduate or high school program at the time of application. (Fellowships may not provide funding for scholarships or academic study in pursuit of any college degree.)

NEW YORK STATE WRITER IN RESIDENCE PROGRAM, New York State Council on the Arts, 915 Broadway, New York NY 10010. (212)387-7028. Contact: Literature Program Director. Offered in odd-numbered years to reward writers' work and give writers a chance to work with a nonprofit organization in a community setting." Deadline: March 1, 1997. Award: $8,000 stipend for a 3 month residency. Applications are judged by a panel of writers, administrators, and translators. Applicant must be nominated by a New York state nonprofit organization.

PALENVILLE INTERARTS COLONY RESIDENCY PROGRAM, 2 Bond St., New York NY 10012, (212)254-4614. Contact: Joanna Sherman, Patrick Sciarratta. Offered annually offering room or cabin for writers to work in a creative, unpressured environment free from distractions. Residencies, partially or fully subsidized, available May 1-September 30. Deadline: April 1. Guidelines for SASE. Charges $10 application fee. Prize: partially or fully subsidized residencies. Judged by panel of artists in each discipline. "Writing panel is one person, changes every other year. Writer should have three years professional experience—but acceptance is primarily based on quality of submitted sample writing. Open to playwrights, poets, etc. etc. Emerging writers welcome to apply."

RESIDENCY, Millay Colony for the Arts, P.O. Box 3, Austerlitz NY 12017. (518)392-3103. Executive Director: Ann-Ellen Lesser. Offered to fiction and nonfiction writers, poets and playwrights of talent. In-office deadlines: February 1 for June-September; May 1 for October-January, September 1 for February-May. Write (include SASE) or call for brochure and application form. One-month residency, room and board and studio. Open to writers, composers and visual artists.

STEGNER FELLOWSHIP, Stanford Creative Writing Program, Stanford University, Stanford CA 94305-2087. (415)723-2637. Fax: (415)725-0755. Contact: Gay Pierce. Estab. 1940. Annual fellowships (5 fiction, 5 poetry) include all tuition costs and a living stipend of $13,000/year for writers to come to Stanford for 2 years to attend workshop to develop their particular writing. Deadline: first working day after New Years.

‡UTAH ORIGINAL WRITING COMPETITION, Utah Arts Council, 617 E. S. Temple, Salt Lake City UT 84102-1177. (801)533-5895. Fax: (801)533-6196. Contact: G. Barnes, Literary Coordinator. Offered annually for unpublished work to recognize merits of literary writing of Utahns by national judges. Deadline: mid-June. Write, phone or fax for guidelines. Prize: certificate and cash prizes of $200-1,000. Open to Utah citizens only.

WALDEN RESIDENCY FELLOWSHIPS, Northwest Writing Institute, Campus Box 100, Lewis & Clark College, Portland OR 97219-7899. (503)768-7745. Fax: (503)768-7715. Offered annually to provide a quiet, remote work space for Oregon writers who are working on a project. Deadline: late November. Guidelines for SASE. Prize: 6- to 8-week residencies (3 per year) in a cabin in Southern Oregon. Utilities and partial board are included. The sponsor and 2 other writers form a committee to judge the applications and select recipients. Writer must be from Oregon.

‡WRITERS' SCHOLARSHIP, North Carolina Arts Council, Department of Cultural Resources, Raleigh NC 27601-2807. (919)733-2111. Literature Director: Deborah McGill. Competitive grants available on 6 weeks' notice July 1-March 30 to provide writers of fiction, poetry and literary nonfiction who have a record of literary accomplishment with opportunities for research or enrichment. Deadline: April 1. Write for guidelines. "We budget $1,500 each year for grants of up to $500." Writer must have been a resident of NC for at least a year, and may not be enrolled in any degree-granting program at the time of application.

‡WYOMING ARTS COUNCIL LITERARY FELLOWHIPS, Wyoming Arts Council, 2320 Capitol Ave. Cheyenne WY 82002. (307)777-7742. Literature Coordinator: Guy Lebeda. Estab. 1986. Fellowships to honor the most outstanding previously published or unpublished new work by Wyoming writers (all genres: poetry, fiction, nonfiction, drama). Deadline: July1, subject to change subsequent years. Writers may call WAC office; guidelines are also printed in monthly *All Arts Newsletter*. Applicants must have been Wyoming residents for 1 year prior to entry deadline—and must remain so for 1 year following—and may not be fulltime students.

Miscellaneous

‡AJL REFERENCE BOOK AWARD, Association of Jewish Libraries, National Foundation for Jewish Culture, 330 Seventh Ave., 21st Floor, New York NY 10001. (216)381-6440. Offered annually for outstanding reference book published during the previous year in the field of Jewish studies.

AMWA MEDICAL BOOK AWARDS COMPETITION, American Medical Writers Association, 9650 Rockville Pike, Bethesda MD 20814. (301)493-0003. Contact: Book Awards Committee. Honors the best medical book published in the previous year in each of 3 categories: Books for Physicians, Books for Allied Health Professionals and Trade Books. Deadline April 1. Charges $20 fee.

ANIMAL RIGHTS WRITING AWARD, 421 S. State St., Clarks Summit PA 18411. Chairperson: Helen Jones. Offered annually to the author of an exceptionally meritorious book or article which advances the cause of animal rights. "Works will be judged for content and literary excellence." Prize: $500 and plaque. If 2 awards are made in 1 year, each author will receive $250 and a plaque. "Nominations may be made by anyone providing the work has been published in the English language. Suggested divisions are: novel, book length nonfiction, children's book, article. Three copies of the work shall be submitted to the ISAR, with a cover letter stating author, date of publication, and name of person or entity submitting. If no submission is considered deserving, an award will not be given in that division. Special awards may be given at the discretion of the judges."

BOWLING WRITING COMPETITION, American Bowling Congress Publications, 5301 S. 76th St., Greendale WI 53129-1127. Fax: (414)421-7977. Editor: Bill Vint. Estab. 1935. Feature, editorial and news all relating to the sport of bowling. Deadline: December 1. Prize: 1st-$300 in each category; additional awards of $225, $200, $175, $150, $75 and $50.

GOLF WRITER'S CONTEST, Golf Course Superintendents Association of America, GCSAA, 1421 Research Park Dr., Lawrence KS 66049-3859. Fax: (913)832-4433. Contact: Terry Ostmeyer. Previously published work pertaining to golf course superintendents. Must be a member of Golf Writers Association of America.

HARVARD OAKS CAREER GUIDANCE AWARD, 208 S. LaSalle, #1681, Chicago IL 60604. Award Director: William A. Potter. Quarterly award to writers of published articles covering relevant topics in career selection and job search strategies. Deadline: March 31, June 30, September 30, December 31. Guidelines for #10 SASE.

STEPHEN LEACOCK MEMORIAL AWARD FOR HUMOUR, Stephen Leacock Associates, P.O. Box 854, Orillia, Ontario L3V 6K8 Canada. (705)325-6546. Contest Director: Jean Dickson. Estab. 1947. For a book of humor published in previous year by a Canadian author. Include 10 copies of each entry and a b&w photo with bio. Deadline: December 31. Charges $25 fee. Prize: Stephen Leacock Memorial Medal and Manulife Bank of Canada Award of $5,000.

LOUDEST LAF! LAUREL, *Laf!* Scher Maihem Publishing Ltd., P.O. Box 313, Avilla IN 46710-0313. Contact: Fran Glass. "To encourage the writing of excellent short humor (600 words or less), and to develop great humorists in the tradition of Mark Twain." Deadline: June 1, 1996. Guidelines for #10 SASE. Charges $8—

includes a one-year subscription to *Laf!*, a bimonthly humor tabloid. Prize: $100 grand prize. Winner and exceptional entries will be published in January/February awards edition of *Laf!*

‡**NMMA DIRECTORS AWARD**, National Marine Manufacturers Association, 600 Third Ave., New York NY 10016. (212)922-1212. Fax: (212)922-9581. Contribution to boating and allied water sports through newspaper, magazine, radio, television, film or book as a writer, artist, broadcaster, editor or photographer. Nomination must be submitted by a representative of a member company of National Marine Manufacturers Association. Deadline: Nov. 30.

‡**REUBEN AWARD**, National Cartoonists Society, P.O. Box 20267, New York NY 10023. (212)627-1550. "Outstanding Cartoonist of the Year" chosen from National Cartoonists Society membership.

‡**WESTERN HERITAGE AWARD**, National Cowboy Hall of Fame & Western Heritage Center, 1700 NE 63rd, Oklahoma City OK 73111. (405)478-2250 ext. 221. Contact: Dana Sullivant. Offered annually for excellence in representation of great stories of the American West published January 1-December 31 in a calendar year. Competition includes 7 literary categories: Nonfiction; Western Novel; Juvenile Book; Art Book; Short Story; Poetry Book; and Magazine Article. Deadline for entries: November 31.

Contests and Awards/Changes '95-'96

The following contests were listed in the 1995 edition but do not have listings in this edition of *Writer's Market*. The majority did not respond to our request to update their listings or return a questionnaire for a new listing. If a reason was given for their exclusion, we have included it in a parentheses after the listing name.

Aaron's All Star Poetry Awards
Alberta New Fiction Competition
Alberta Writing for Youth Competition
American Speech-Language-Hearing Association, National Media Awards
Annual Associateship
Anthem Essay Contest
Arroz Con Leche
Artist Projects
Artist's Fellowships (NY)
Athe Playwright's Prize
Athenaeum of Philadelphia Literary Award
Albert J. Beveridge Award
Black Warrior Review Literary Awards
Howard W. Blakeslee Awards
Heywood Broun Award
Witter Bynner Foundation for Poetry, Inc. Grants
Pierre-Francois Caille Memorial Medal
California Playwrights Competition
Melville Cane Award (cancelled)
Karel Čapek Translation Award
Celebration of One-Acts
Chicago Sun-Times/Friends of Literature Awards
Collegiate Poetry Contest (cancelled)
Cornerstone Dramaturgy and Development Project
Creative Artists Grant
Gustav Davidson Memorial Award
Dayton Playhouse Future Fest
Delacorte Press Prize for a First Young Adult Novel
Marie Louise D'Esternaux Poetry Contest

Diverse Visions Interdisciplinary Grants Program
David Dornstein Memorial Creative Writing Contest for Young Adult Writers
Eaton Literary Associates Literary Awards Program
Editors' Book Award
Excalibur Book Award
Eyster Prize
Florida State Writing Competition
FMCT's Biennial Playwrights Competition (Mid-West)
Foray Awards
Fountainhead Essay Contest
GAP: Fellowship
Gavel Awards
Great Lakes Colleges Association New Writers Award
Great Platte River Playwrights Festival
Sidney Hillman Prize Award
Individual Artist Fellowships (OR)
Int'l Play Competition
Jerusalem Prize
Kansas Quarterly/Kansas Arts Commission Awards
Lamont Poetry Selection
Peter I.B. Lavan Younger Poets Award
Literature Fellowships
Dennis McIntyre Playwriting Award
Marin Individual Artists Grants
Lenore Marshall/Nation Prize for Poetry
Military Lifestyle Fiction Contest (cancelled)
Milkweed National Fiction Prize
Robert T. Morse Writers Award
Frank Luther Mott-Kappa Tau

Alpha Research Award in Journalism
National Theater Translation Fund Commissioning Grants (cancelled)
National Writers Association Articles and Essays Contest
National Writers Association Novel Writing Contest
National Writers Association Poetry Contest
National Writers Association Short Story Contest
New Works Competition
New York State Historical Association Manuscript Award
Charles J. and N. Mildred Nilon Excellence in Minority Fiction Award
Olga "Ollie" Tschirley Nordhaus Feature Writing Competition
Panhandler Poetry Chapbook Competition
William Peden Prize in Fiction
Pen Writing Awards for Prisoners
Peterloo Poets Open Poetry Competition
Playboy College Fiction Contest
Playhouse on the Square New Play Competition
Renato Poggioli Translation Award
Porter's Quarterly Poetry Contest
Prometheus Award/Hall of Fame
Promising Playwright Award
Radio Script Writers Competition
Saint Louis Literary Award
Science-Writing Award;Siena College Playwrights' Competition
Sierra Repertory Theatre
Snake Nation Press's Annual Poetry Contest

John Ben Snow Award
Sonomo Country Playwrights
    Festival
Special Libraries Association
    Media Award
Sucarnochee Review
Amaury Talbot Prize Fund for African Anthropology
Tennessee Williams One-Act Play
    Contest

Texas Bluebonnet Award
Theatre in Process Playwriting
    Award
Theatre Library Association
    Award
Translation Commissions
Ucross Foundation Residency
Undergraduate Annual Paper
    Competition in Cryptology
Vermont Council on the Arts

Very Special Arts Young Playwrights Program
H.W. Wilson Library Periodical
    Award
Writer's Film Project
Young Playwrights Festival
Anna Zornio Memorial Theatre
    for Youth Playwriting Award

Organizations of Interest

Professional organizations, both local and national, can be very helpful in helping writers build contacts. They often provide valuable opportunities for networking, information about new developments in the industry, and guidance in business or legal matters.

The majority of organizations listed here publish newsletters and other materials that can provide you with useful information for your writing career. Some even provide opportunities such as conferences and referral services.

Keep in mind that numerous local organizations and writers' clubs also exist, and can provide occasions for networking in your own area. You can usually find information about such groups in your local library or through an area college writing program.

Some of the following national organizations have branches or chapters in different cities across the country. Write to the organization for information about its membership requirements, individual chapters and programs for writers.

American Book Producers Association
160 Fifth Ave., Suite 625
New York NY 10010-7000
(212)645-2368

American Medical Writers Association
9650 Rockville Pike
Bethesda MD 20814-3998
(301)493-0003

American Society of Journalists & Authors, Inc.
1501 Broadway, Suite 302
New York NY 10036
(212)997-0947

American Translators Association
1800 Diagonal Rd., Suite 220
Alexandria, VA 22314-0214
(703)683-6100

Associated Writing Programs
Tallwood House MSIE3
George Mason University
Fairfax VA 22030
(703)993-4301

Association of Authors Representatives
10 Astor Pl., 3rd Floor
New York NY 10003
(212)353-3709

Association of Desk-Top Publishers
4507 30th St., Suite 800
San Diego CA 92116-4239
(619)563-9714

The Authors Guild
330 W. 42nd St., 29th Floor
New York NY 10036
(212)563-5904

The Authors League of America, Inc.
330 W. 42nd St.
New York NY 10036
(212)564-8350

Copywriters Council of America, Freelance
Linick Bldg. 102, 7 Putter Lane
Middle Island NY 11953-0102
(516)924-8555

Council of Literary Magazines & Presses
154 Christopher St., Suite 3C
New York NY 10014
(212)741-9110

The Dramatists Guild
234 W. 44th St., 11th Floor
New York NY 10036
(212)398-9366

Editorial Freelancers Association
71 W. 23rd St., Suite 1504
New York NY 10010
(212)929-5400

Education Writers Association
1331 H. NW, Suite 307
Washington DC 20036
(202)637-9700

Freelance Editorial Association
P.O. Box 38035
Cambridge MA 02238
(617)643-8626

International Association of Business Communicators
1 Hallidie Plaza, Suite 600
San Francisco CA 94102
(415)433-3400

International Association of Crime Writers Inc., North American Branch
JAF Box 1500
New York NY 10116
(212)757-3915

International Television Association
6311 N. O'Connor Rd., Suite 230
Irving TX 75039
(214)869-1112

International Women's Writing Guild
Box 810, Gracie Station
New York NY 10028-0082
(212)737-7536

Mystery Writers of America
17 E. 47th St., 6th Floor
New York NY 10017
(212)888-8171

National Association of Science Writers
Box 294
Greenlawn NY 11740
(516)757-5664

National Writers Association
1450 S. Havana, Suite 424
Aurora CO 80012
(303)751-7844

National Writers Union
873 Broadway, Suite 203
New York NY 10003
(212)254-0279

PEN American Center
568 Broadway
New York NY 10012
(212)334-1660

Poetry Society of America
15 Grammercy Park
New York NY 10003
(212)254-9628

Poets & Writers
72 Spring St.
New York NY 10012
(212)226-3586

Publication Services Guild
P.O. Box 720082
Atlanta GA 30358-2082
(404)951-4721

Public Relations Society of America
33 Irving Place
New York NY 10003
(212)995-2230

Romance Writers of America
13700 Veterans Memorial Dr., Suite 315
Houston TX 77014
(713)440-6885

Science-Fiction Fantasy Writers of America
Suite 1B, 5 Winding Brook Dr.
Guilderland NY 12084
(518)869-5361

Society of American Business Editors & Writers
% Janine Latus-Musick
University of Missouri
School of Journalism
76 Jannett Hall
Columbia MO 65211
(314)882-7862

Society of American Travel Writers
4101 Lake Boone Trail, Suite 201
Raleigh NC 27607
(919)787-5181

Society of Children's Book Writers and Illustrators
22736 Vanowen St., Suite 106
West Hills CA 91307
(818)888-8760

Society of Professional Journalists
16 S. Jackson
Greencastle IN 46135
(317)653-3333

Volunteer Lawyers for the Arts
1 E. 53rd St., 6th Floor
New York NY 10022
(212)319-2787

Women in Communications, Inc.
Suite 417, 2101 Wilson Blvd.
Arlington VA 22201

Writers Alliance
12 Skylark Lane
Stoney Brook NY 11790
(516)751-7080

Writers Guild of America (East)
555 W. 57th St.
New York NY 10019
(212)767-7800

Writers Guild of America (West)
8955 Beverly Blvd.
West Hollywood CA 90048
(310)550-1000

Publications of Interest

In addition to newsletters and publications from local and national organizations, there are trade publications, books, and directories which offer valuable information about writing and about marketing your manuscripts and understanding the business side of publishing. Some also list employment agencies that specialize in placing publishing professionals, and some announce actual freelance opportunities.

Trade magazines

ADVERTISING AGE, Crain Communications Inc., 740 N. Rush St., Chicago IL 60611. (312)649-5200. *Weekly magazine covering advertising in magazines, trade journals and business.*

AMERICAN JOURNALISM REVIEW, 8701 Adelphi Rd., Adelphi MD 20783. (301)431-4771. *10 issues/year magazine for journalists and communications professionals.*

DAILY VARIETY, Daily Variety Ltd./Cahners Publishing Co., 5700 Wilshire Blvd., Los Angeles CA 90036. (213)857-6600. *Trade publication on the entertainment industry, with helpful information for screenwriters.*

EDITOR & PUBLISHER, The Editor & Publisher Co., 11 W. 19th St., New York NY 10011. (212)675-4380. *Weekly magazine covering the newspaper publishing industry.*

FOLIO, Cowles Business Media, 911 Hope St., Stamford CT 06907-0949. (203)358-9900. *Monthly magazine covering the magazine publishing industry.*

GREETINGS MAGAZINE, MacKay Publishing Corp., 307 Fifth Ave., 16th Floor, New York NY 10016. (212)679-6677. *Monthly magazine covering the greeting card industry.*

HORN BOOK MAGAZINE, 11 Beacon St., Boston MA 02108. (617)227-1555. *Bimonthly magazine that covers children's literature.*

PARTY & PAPER RETAILER, 4 Ward Corp., 70 New Canaan Ave., Norwalk CT 06850. (203)845-8020. *Monthly magazine covering the greeting card and gift industry.*

POETS & WRITERS INC., 72 Spring St., New York NY 10012. (212)226-3586. *Monthly magazine, primarily for literary writers and poets.*

PUBLISHERS WEEKLY, Bowker Magazine Group, Cahners Publishing Co., 249 W. 17th St., 6th Floor, New York NY 10011. (212)645-0067. *Weekly magazine covering the book publishing industry.*

SCIENCE FICTION CHRONICLE, P.O. Box 022730, Brooklyn NY 11202-0056. (718)643-9011. *Monthly magazine for science fiction, fantasy and horror writers.*

THE WRITER, 120 Boylston St., Boston MA 02116. (617)423-3157. *Monthly writers' magazine.*

WRITER'S DIGEST, 1507 Dana Ave., Cincinnati OH 45207. (513)531-2222. *Monthly writers' magazine.*

Books and directories

AV MARKET PLACE, R.R. Bowker, A Reed Reference Publishing Co., 121 Chanlon Rd., New Providence NJ 07974. (908)464-6800.

THE COMPLETE GUIDE TO SELF PUBLISHING, by Marilyn and Tom Ross, Writer's

Digest Books, 1507 Dana Ave., Cincinnati OH 45207. (513)531-2222.

COPYRIGHT HANDBOOK, R.R. Bowker, A Reed Reference Publishing Co., 121 Chanlon Rd., New Providence NJ 07974. (908)464-6800.

DIRECTORY OF EDITORIAL RESOURCES, 66 Canal Center Plaza, Suite 200, Alexandria VA 22314-5507. (703)683-0683.

DRAMATISTS SOURCEBOOK, edited by Gillian Richards and Linda MacColl, Theatre Communications Group, Inc., 355 Lexington Ave., New York NY 10017. (212)697-5230.

GUIDE TO LITERARY AGENTS, edited by Kirsten Holm, Writer's Digest Books, 1507 Dana Ave., Cincinnati OH 45207. (513)531-2222.

THE GUIDE TO WRITERS CONFERENCES, ShawGuides Inc. Educational Publishers, Box 1295, New York NY 10023. (212)799-6464.

HOW TO WRITE IRRESISTIBLE QUERY LETTERS, by Lisa Collier Cool, Writer's Digest Books, 1507 Dana Ave., Cincinnati OH 45207. (513)531-2222.

THE INSIDER'S GUIDE TO BOOK EDITORS, PUBLISHERS & LITERARY AGENTS, by Jeff Herman, Prima Publishing, Box 1260, Rocklin CA 95677-1260. (916)786-0426.

INTERNATIONAL DIRECTORY OF LITTLE MAGAZINES & SMALL PRESSES, edited by Len Fulton, Dustbooks, P.O. Box 100, Paradise CA 95967. (916)877-6110.

LITERARY MARKET PLACE and INTERNATIONAL LITERARY MARKET PLACE, R.R. Bowker, A Reed Reference Publishing Co., 121 Chanlon Rd., New Providence NJ 07974. (908)464-6800.

PROFESSIONAL WRITER'S GUIDE, edited by Donald Bower and James Lee Young, National Writers Press, Suite 424, 1450 S. Havana, Aurora CO 80012. (303)751-7844.

STANDARD DIRECTORY OF ADVERTISING AGENCIES, National Register Publishing, A Reed Reference Publishing Co., 121 Chanlon Rd., New Providence NJ 07974. (908)464-6800.

SUCCESSFUL SCRIPTWRITING, by Jurgen Wolff and Kerry Cox, Writer's Digest Books, 1507 Dana Ave., Cincinnati OH 45207. (513)531-2222.

THE WRITER'S GUIDE TO SELF-PROMOTION AND PUBLICITY, by Elane Feldman, Writer's Digest Books, 1507 Dana Ave., Cincinnati OH 45207. (513)531-2222.

THE WRITER'S LEGAL COMPANION, by Brad Bunnin and Peter Beren, Addison-Wesley Publishing Co., 1 Jacob Way, Reading MA 01867. (617)944-3000.

WRITING TOOLS: Essential Software for Anyone Who Writes with a PC, by Hy Bender, Random House Electronic Publishing, 201 E. 50 St., New York NY 10022. (212)572-8700.

Glossary

Key to symbols and abbreviations is on page 63.

Advance. A sum of money a publisher pays a writer prior to the publication of a book. It is usually paid in installments, such as one-half on signing the contract; one-half on delivery of a complete and satisfactory manuscript. The advance is paid against the royalty money that will be earned by the book.

Advertorial. Advertising presented in such a way as to resemble editorial material. Information may be the same as that contained in an editorial feature, but it is paid for or supplied by an advertiser and the word "advertisement" appears at the top of the page.

All rights. See Rights and the Writer in the Minding the Details article.

Anthology. A collection of selected writings by various authors or a gathering of works by one author.

Assignment. Editor asks a writer to produce a specific article for an agreed-upon fee.

Auction. Publishers sometimes bid for the acquisition of a book manuscript that has excellent sales prospects. The bids are for the amount of the author's advance, advertising and promotional expenses, royalty percentage, etc. Auctions are conducted by agents.

B&W. Abbreviation for black and white photographs.

Backlist. A publisher's list of its books that were not published during the current season, but that are still in print.

Belles lettres. A term used to describe fine or literary writing—writing more to entertain than to inform or instruct.

Bimonthly. Every two months. See also *semimonthly*.

Bionote. A sentence or brief paragraph about the writer. Also called a "bio," it can appear at the bottom of the first or last page of a writer's article or short story or on a contributor's page.

Biweekly. Every two weeks.

Boilerplate. A standardized contract. When an editor says "our standard contract," he means the boilerplate with no changes. Writers should be aware that most authors and/or agents make many changes on the boilerplate.

Book packager. Draws all elements of a book together, from the initial concept to writing and marketing strategies, then sells the book package to a book publisher and/or movie producer. Also known as book producer or book developer.

Business size envelope. Also known as a #10 envelope, it is the standard size used in sending business correspondence.

Byline. Name of the author appearing with the published piece.

Category fiction. A term used to include all various labels attached to types of fiction. See also *genre*.

CD-ROM. Compact Disc-Read Only Memory. A computer information storage medium capable of holding enormous amounts of data. Information on a CD-ROM cannot be deleted. A computer user must have a CD-ROM drive to access a CD-ROM..

Chapbook. A small booklet, usually paperback, of poetry, ballads or tales.

Clean copy. A manuscript free of errors, cross-outs, wrinkles or smudges.

Clips. Samples, usually from newspapers or magazines, of your *published* work.

Coffee table book. An oversize book, heavily illustrated.

Column inch. The amount of space contained in one inch of a typeset column.

Commercial novels. Novels designed to appeal to a broad audience. These are often broken down into categories such as western, mystery and romance. See also *genre*.

Commissioned work. See *assignment*.

Concept. A statement that summarizes a screenplay or teleplay—before the outline or treatment is written.

Contributor's copies. Copies of the issues of magazines sent to the author in which the author's work appears.

Cooperative publishing. See *co-publishing*.

Co-publishing. Arrangement where author and publisher share publication costs and profits of a book. Also known as *cooperative publishing*. See also *subsidy publisher*.

Copyediting. Editing a manuscript for grammar, punctuation and printing style, not subject content.

Copyright. A means to protect an author's work. See Copyright in the Minding the Details section.

Cover letter. A brief letter, accompanying a complete manuscript, especially useful if responding to an editor's request for a manuscript. A cover letter may also accompany a book proposal. A cover letter is *not* a query letter; see Targeting Your Ideas in the Getting Published section.

Derivative works. A work that has been translated, adapted, abridged, condensed, annotated or otherwise produced by altering a previously created work. Before producing a derivative work, it is necessary to secure the written permission of the copyright owner of the original piece.

Desktop publishing. A publishing system designed for a personal computer. The system is capable of typesetting, some illustration, layout, design and printing—so that the final piece can be distributed and/or sold.

Disk. A round, flat magnetic plate on which computer data may be stored.

Docudrama. A fictional film rendition of recent newsmaking events and people.

Dot-matrix. Printed type where individual characters are composed of a matrix or pattern of tiny dots. Near letter quality (see *NLQ*) dot-matrix submissions are generally acceptable to editors.

Electronic submission. A submission made by modem or on computer disk.

El-hi. Elementary to high school.

E-mail. Electronic mail. Mail generated on a computer and delivered over a computer network to a specific individual or group of individuals. To send or receive e-mail, a user must have an account with an online service, which provides an e-mail address and electronic mailbox.

Epigram. A short, witty sometimes paradoxical saying.

Erotica. Fiction or art that is sexually oriented.

Fair use. A provision of the copyright law that says short passages from copyrighted material may be used without infringing on the owner's rights.

Fax (facsimile machine). A communication system used to transmit documents over telephone lines.

Feature. An article giving the reader information of human interest rather than news. Also used by magazines to indicate a lead article or distinctive department.

Filler. A short item used by an editor to "fill" out a newspaper column or magazine page. It could be a timeless news item, a joke, an anecdote, some light verse or short humor, puzzle, etc.

First North American serial rights. See Rights and the Writer in the Minding the Details article.

Formula story. Familiar theme treated in a predictable plot structure—such as boy meets girl, boy loses girl, boy gets girl.

Frontlist. A publisher's list of its books that are new to the current season.

Galleys. The first typeset version of a manuscript that has not yet been divided into pages.

Genre. Refers either to a general classification of writing, such as the novel or the poem, or to the categories within those classifications, such as the problem novel or the sonnet. Genre fiction describes commercial novels, such as mysteries, romances and science fiction. Also called category fiction.

Ghostwriter. A writer who puts into literary form an article, speech, story or book based on another person's ideas or knowledge.

Glossy. A black and white photograph with a shiny surface as opposed to one with a non-shiny matte finish.

Gothic novel. A fiction category or genre in which the central character is usually a beautiful young girl, the setting an old mansion or castle, and there is a handsome hero and a real menace, either natural or supernatural.

Graphic novel. An adaptation of a novel in graphic form, long comic strip or heavily illustrated story, of 40 pages or more, produced in paperback form.

Hard copy. The printed copy of a computer's output.

Hardware. All the mechanically-integrated components of a computer that are not software. Circuit boards, transistors and the machines that are the actual computer are the hardware.

Home page. The first page of a World Wide Web document.

Honorarium. Token payment—small amount of money, or a byline and copies of the publication.

Hypertext. Words or groups of words in an electronic document that are linked to other text, such as a definition or a related document. Hypertext can also be linked to illustrations..

Illustrations. May be photographs, old engravings, artwork. Usually paid for separately from the manuscript. See also *package sale*.

Imprint. Name applied to a publisher's specific line or lines of books (e.g., Anchor Books is an imprint of Doubleday).

Interactive. A type of computer interface that takes user input, such as answers to computer-generated questions, and then acts upon that input.

Interactive fiction. Works of fiction in book or computer software format in which the reader determines the path the story will take. The reader chooses from several alternatives at the end of a "chapter," and thus determines the structure of the story. Interactive fiction features multiple plots and endings.

Internet. A worldwide network of computers that offers access to a wide variety of electronic resources. Originally a US Department of Defense project, begun in 1969.

Invasion of privacy. Writing about persons (even though truthfully) without their consent.

Kill fee. Fee for a complete article that was assigned but which was subsequently cancelled.

Lead time. The time between the acquisition of a manuscript by an editor and its actual publication.

Letter-quality submission. Computer printout that looks typewritten.

Libel. A false accusation or any published statement or presentation that tends to expose another to public contempt, ridicule, etc. Defenses are truth; fair comment on a matter of public interest; and privileged communication—such as a report of legal proceedings or client's communication to a lawyer.

List royalty. A royalty payment based on a percentage of a book's retail (or "list") price. Compare *net royalty*.

Little magazine. Publications of limited circulation, usually on literary or political subject matter.

LORT. An acronym for League of Resident Theatres. Letters from A to D follow LORT and designate the size of the theater.

Magalog. Mail order catalog with how-to articles pertaining to the items for sale.

Mainstream fiction. Fiction that transcends popular novel categories such as mystery, romance and science fiction. Using conventional methods, this kind of fiction tells stories about people and their conflicts with greater depth of characterization, background, etc., than the more narrowly focused genre novels.

Mass market. Nonspecialized books of wide appeal directed toward a large audience. Smaller and more cheaply produced than trade paperbacks, they are found in many non-bookstore outlets, such as drug stores, supermarkets, etc.

Microcomputer. A small computer system capable of performing various specific tasks with data it receives. Personal computers are microcomputers.

Midlist. Those titles on a publisher's list that are not expected to be big sellers, but are expected to have limited sales. Midlist books are mainstream, not literary, scholarly or genre, and are usually written by new or unknown writers.

Model release. A paper signed by the subject of a photograph (or the subject's guardian, if a juvenile) giving the photographer permission to use the photograph, editorially or for advertising purposes or for some specific purpose as stated.

Modem. A device used to transmit data from one computer to another via telephone lines.

Monograph. A detailed and documented scholarly study concerning a single subject.

Multimedia. Computers and software capable of integrating text, sound, photographic-quality images, animation and video.

Multiple submissions. Sending more than one poem, gag or greeting card idea at the same time. This term is often used synonymously with simultaneous submission.

Net royalty. A royalty payment based on the amount of money a book publisher receives on the sale of a book after booksellers' discounts, special sales discounts and returns. Compare list royalty.

Network. A group of computers electronically linked to share information and resources.

Newsbreak. A brief, late-breaking news story added to the front page of a newspaper at press time or a magazine news item of importance to readers.

NLQ. Near letter-quality print required by some editors for computer printout submissions. See also *dot-matrix*.

Novelette. A short novel, or a long short story; 7,000 to 15,000 words approximately. Also known as a novella.

Novelization. A novel created from the script of a popular movie, usually called a movie "tie-in" and published in paperback.

Offprint. Copies of an author's article taken "out of issue" before a magazine is bound and given to the author in lieu of monetary payment. An offprint could be used by the writer as a published writing sample.

On spec. An editor expresses an interest in a proposed article idea and agrees to consider the finished piece for publication "on speculation." The editor is under no obligation to buy the finished manuscript.

One-shot feature. As applies to syndicates, single feature article for syndicate to sell; as contrasted with article series or regular columns syndicated.

One-time rights. See Rights and the Writer in the Minding the Details article.

Online Service. Computer networks accessed via modem. These services provide users with various resources, such as electronic mail, news, weather, special interest groups and shopping. Examples of such providers include America Online and CompuServe.

Outline. A summary of a book's contents in five to 15 double-spaced pages; often in the form of chapter headings with a descriptive sentence or two under each one to show the scope of the book. A screenplay's or teleplay's outline is a scene-by-scene narrative description of the story (10-15 pages for a ½-hour teleplay; 15-25 pages for a 1-hour teleplay; 25-40 pages for a 90-minute teleplay; 40-60 pages for a 2-hour feature film or teleplay).

Over-the-transom. Describes the submission of unsolicited material by a freelance writer.

Package sale. The editor buys manuscript and photos as a "package" and pays for them with one check.

Page rate. Some magazines pay for material at a fixed rate per published page, rather than per word.

Parallel submission. A strategy of developing several articles from one unit of research for submission to similar magazines. This strategy differs from simultaneous or multiple submission, where the same article is marketed to several magazines at the same time.

Payment on acceptance. The editor sends you a check for your article, story or poem as soon as he decides to publish it.

Payment on publication. The editor doesn't send you a check for your material until it is published.

Pen name. The use of a name other than your legal name on articles, stories or books when you wish to remain anonymous. Simply notify your post office and bank that you are using the name so that you'll receive mail and/or checks in that name. Also called a pseudonym.

Photo feature. Feature in which the emphasis is on the photographs rather than on accompanying written material.

Plagiarism. Passing off as one's own the expression of ideas and words of another writer.

Potboiler. Refers to writing projects a freelance writer does to "keep the pot boiling" while working on major articles—quick projects to bring in money with little time or effort. These may be fillers such as anecdotes or how-to tips, but could be short articles or stories.

Proofreading. Close reading and correction of a manuscript's typographical errors.

Proscenium. The area of the stage in front of the curtain.

Prospectus. A preliminary written description of a book or article, usually one page in length.

Pseudonym. See *pen name*.

Public domain. Material that was either never copyrighted or whose copyright term has expired.

Query. A letter to an editor intended to raise interest in an article you propose to write.

Release. A statement that your idea is original, has never been sold to anyone else and that you are selling the negotiated rights to the idea upon payment.

Remainders. Copies of a book that are slow to sell and can be purchased from the publisher at a reduced price. Depending on the author's book contract, a reduced royalty or no royalty is paid on remainder books.

Reporting time. The time it takes for an editor to report to the author on his/her query or manuscript.

Reprint rights. See Rights and the Writer in the Minding the Details article.

Round-up article. Comments from, or interviews with, a number of celebrities or experts on a single theme.

Royalties, standard hardcover book. 10% of the retail price on the first 5,000 copies sold; 12½% on the next 5,000; 15% thereafter.

Royalties, standard mass paperback book. 4 to 8% of the retail price on the first 150,000 copies sold.

Royalties, standard trade paperback book. No less than 6% of list price on the first 20,000 copies; 7½% thereafter.

Scanning. A process through which letter-quality printed text (see *NLQ*) or artwork is read by a computer scanner and converted into workable data.

Screenplay. Script for a film intended to be shown in theaters.

Self-publishing. In this arrangement, the author keeps all income derived from the book, but he pays for its manufacturing, production and marketing.

Semimonthly. Twice per month.

Semiweekly. Twice per week.

Serial. Published periodically, such as a newspaper or magazine.

Sidebar. A feature presented as a companion to a straight news report (or main magazine article) giving sidelights on human-interest aspects or sometimes elucidating just one aspect of the story.

Similar submission. See *parallel submission*.

Simultaneous submissions. Sending the same article, story or poem to several publishers at the same time. Some publishers refuse to consider such submissions. No simultaneous submissions should be made without stating the fact in your letter.

Slant. The approach or style of a story or article that will appeal to readers of a specific magazine. For example, a magazine may always use stories with an upbeat ending.

Slice-of-life vignette. A short fiction piece intended to realistically depict an interesting moment of everyday living.

Slides. Usually called transparencies by editors looking for color photographs.

Slush pile. The stack of unsolicited or misdirected manuscripts received by an editor or book publisher.

Software. The computer programs that control computer hardware, usually run from a disk drive of some sort. Computers need software in order to run. These can be word processors, games, spreadsheets, etc.

Speculation. The editor agrees to look at the author's manuscript with no assurance that it will be bought.

Style. The way in which something is written—for example, short, punchy sentences or flowing narrative.

Subsidiary rights. All those rights, other than book publishing rights included in a book contract—such as paperback, book club, movie rights, etc.

Subsidy publisher. A book publisher who charges the author for the cost to typeset and print his book, the jacket, etc. as opposed to a royalty publisher who pays the author.

Synopsis. A brief summary of a story, novel or play. As part of a book proposal, it is a comprehensive summary condensed in a page or page and a half, single-spaced. See also *outline*.

Tabloid. Newspaper format publication on about half the size of the regular newspaper page, such as the *National Enquirer*.

Tagline. A caption for a photo or a comment added to a filler.

Tearsheet. Page from a magazine or newspaper containing your printed story, article, poem or ad.

Trade. Either a hardcover or paperback book; subject matter frequently concerns a special interest. Books are directed toward the layperson rather than the professional.

Transparencies. Positive color slides; not color prints.

Treatment. Synopsis of a television or film script (40-60 pages for a 2-hour feature film or teleplay).

Unsolicited manuscript. A story, article, poem or book that an editor did not specifically ask to see.

User friendly. Easy to handle and use. Refers to computer hardware and software designed with the user in mind.

Vanity publisher. See *subsidy publisher*.

Word processor. A computer program, used in lieu of a typewriter, that allows for easy, flexible manipulation and output of printed copy.

World Wide Web (WWW). An Internet resource that utilizes hypertext to access information. It also supports formatted text, illustrations and sounds, depending on the user's computer capabilities.

Work-for-hire. See Copyright in the Minding the Details article.

YA. Young adult books.

Book Publishers
Subject Index

This index will help you find publishers that consider books on specific subjects—the subjects you choose to write about. Remember that a publisher may be listed here under a general subject category such as Art and Architecture, while the company publishes *only* art history or how-to books. Be sure to consult each company's detailed individual listing, its book catalog and several of its books before you send your query or proposal. The page number of the detailed listing is provided for your convenience.

Fiction

Adventure. Aqua Quest 80; Ariadne Press 253; Armstrong Publishing Corp. 81; Atheneum Books For Young Readers 82; Avanyu 83; Avon 83; Avon Flare 84; Baldwin & Knowlton 84; Bantam 86; Bethel 88; Black Heron 254; Black Tie 254; Bookcraft 92; Borealis Press 232; Caitlin Press 232; Camelot 96; Carol 97; Cave 99; Clarion 103; Comic Art 105; Compass Productions 270; Covenant Communications 281; Dan River 111; Dancing Jester 111; Davenport, May 112; Dial Books For Young Readers 115; Discus Press 116; Down The Shore 256; Dutton Children's Books 117; E.M. Press 281; Fiesta City 257; Fine, Donald I. 122; Floricanto Press 123; Fort Dearborn 124; Grandin 128; Guild Bindery Press 283; Harian Creative Books 283; HarperCollins 131; Hendrick-Long 133; Holiday House 136; ICS Books, Inc. 139; Just Us Books 147; Kar-Ben Copies 147; Lion Press 259; Little, Brown, Children's Book Division 152; Lodestar 154; Mayhaven 286; Mountaineers Books 164; New Victoria 168; Ozark 175; Paradigm 288; Path Press 288; Playground Books 182; Prep Publishing 183; Presidio Press 184; Purple Finch 263; Random House 188; Shoestring Press 246; Sierra Club 195; Soho Press 197; Starburst 200; Tudor Publishers 210; Turnstone Press 248; Univ. Press of Georgia 292; Vandamere Press 219; Vista Publishing Inc. 293; Weiss Associates, Daniel 275; Whispering Coyote Press 223; Wilde Publishing 225; Willowisp Press, Inc. 226; Windflower Communications 294; Wordstorm 251; Worldwide Library 251; Write Way 227; Zebra and Pinnacle 228.

Confession. Acropolis South 72; Carol 97; Dan River 111; Discus Press 116; Fort Dearborn 124; Random House 188; Univ. Press of Georgia 292.

Erotica. Baldwin & Knowlton 84; Black Tie 254; Blue Moon 90; Circlet Press 103; Dan River 111; Dancing Jester 111; Discus Press 116; Éditions Logiques/Logical Publishing 235; Ekstasis Editions 235; Floricanto Press 123; Fort Dearborn 124; Gay Sunshine Press and Leyland Publications 126; HMS Press 237; New Falcon 287; New Victoria 168; Permeable Press 262; Press Gang 243; Spectrum Press 199; Univ. Press of Georgia 292; Vandamere Press 219; Zebra and Pinnacle 228.

Ethnic. Another Chicago 79; Arcade Publishing 80; Arsenal Pulp 229; Asian Humanities Press 82; Atheneum Books For Young Readers 82; Avalon 83; Avon Flare 84; Baldwin & Knowlton 84; Blue Dolphin 90; Borealis Press 232; Branden. 93; Canadian Inst. of Ukrainian Studies 233; Champion Bookss 100; Charlesbridge 100; China Books & Periodicals, Inc. 101; Clarity Press 255; Coffee House 105; Colonial Press 280; Confluence Press 107; Coteau Books 234; Covenant Communications 281; Cuff Publications, Harry 234; Dancing Jester 111; Discus Press 116; Ecco Press 118; Faber & Faber 121; Fine, Donald I. 122; Floricanto Press 123; Fort Dearborn 124; Four Walls Eight Windows 124; Gay Sunshine Press and Leyland Publications 126; Guernica Editions 236; Herald Press Canada 237; Holiday House 136; Interlink Publishing Group 142; Just Us Books 147; Kar-Ben Copies 147; Lincoln Springs 259; Mayhaven 286; Media Bridge 160; Mercury House 160; Northland 169; Oolichan Books 241; Path Press 288; Polychrome 183; QED Press 187; Reed Books Canada 244; Royal Fireworks Press 191; Shoestring Press 246; Soho Press 197; Span Press 198; Shoreline 246; Spectrum Press 199; Spinsters Ink 199; Third World Press 207; Tudor Publishers 210; Turnstone Press 248; Univ. Of Illinois 213; Univ. of Texas 217; Univ. Press of Georgia 292; Weigl Educational 250; White Pine 224.

Experimental. Another Chicago 79; Arsenal Pulp 229; Atheneum Books For Young Readers 82;

Baldwin & Knowlton 84; Black Heron 254; China Books & Periodicals, Inc. 101; Dan River 111; Dancing Jester 111; Depth Charge 255; Discus Press 116; Éditions Logiques/Logical Publishing 235; Ekstasis Editions 235; Empyreal Press 235; Fort Dearborn 124; Four Walls Eight Windows 124; Gay Sunshine Press and Leyland Publications 126; Goose Lane Editions 236; Harian Creative Books 283; Livingston Press 153; McClelland & Stewart 239; Mercury House 160; New Falcon 287; Oolichan Books 241; Permeable Press 262; Quarry Press 243; Random House 188; Ronsdale Press 245; Scots Plaid 264; Shoestring Press 246; Smith 197; Spectrum Press 199; Stone Bridge 201; Third Side Press 207; Turnstone Press 248; Ultramarine 211; Univ. Of Illinois 213; Wilde Publishing 225; Xenos Books 267; York Press 251.

Fantasy. Ace Science Fiction 72; Atheneum Books For Young Readers 82; Avon 83; Baen 84; Baldwin & Knowlton 84; Bantam 86; Blue Star 91; Camelot 96; Carol 97; Circlet Press 103; Comic Art 105; Compass Productions 270; Covenant Communications 281; Crossway 110; Dan River 111; DAW 113; Del Rey 114; Dial Books For Young Readers 115; Discus Press 116; Dutton Children's Books 117; Éditions Logiques/Logical Publishing 235; Fort Dearborn 124; HarperCollins 131; HMS Press 237; Holiday House 136; Hollow Earth 136; Just Us Books 147; Kar-Ben Copies 147; Lion Press 259; Little, Brown, Children's Book Division 152; Lodestar 154; Naiad Press 165; New Falcon 287; New Victoria 168; Overlook Press 174; Playground Books 182; Random House 188; Shoestring Press 246; Starburst 200; Stone Bridge 201; TOR Books 209; TSR 210; Univ. Press of Georgia 292; Virtual Press 292; Windflower Communications 294; Worldwide Library 251; Write Way 227; Zebra and Pinnacle 228.

Feminist. Another Chicago 79; Ariadne Press 253; Arsenal Pulp 229; Baldwin & Knowlton 84; Black Tie 254; Calyx Books 254; Champion Bookss 100; Circlet Press 103; Cleis Press 104; Coteau Books 234; Dancing Jester 111; Discus Press 116; Empyreal Press 235; Firebrand 122; Fort Dearborn 124; Four Walls Eight Windows 124; Goose Lane Editions 236; HMS Press 237; Interlink Publishing Group 142; Lincoln Springs 259; Little, Brown, Children's Book Division 152; Mercury House 160; Mercury Press 240; Mother Courage 164; Naiad Press 165; Negative Capability 166; New Falcon 287; Oolichan Books 241; Papier-Mache Press 176; Path Press 288; Permeable Press 262; Press Gang 243; Quarry Press 243; Reed Books Canada 244; Smith 197; Soho Press 197; Spectrum Press 199; Spinsters Ink 199; Stone Bridge 201; Third Side Press 207; Third World Press 207; Turnstone Press 248; Vista Publishing Inc. 293.

Gay/Lesbian. Alyson 75; Arsenal Pulp 229; Baldwin & Knowlton 84; Bantam 86; Calyx Books 254; Champion Bookss 100; Circlet Press 103; Cleis Press 104; Dancing Jester 111; Firebrand 122; Fort Dearborn 124; Gay Sunshine Press and Leyland Publications 126; HMS Press 237; Little, Brown, Children's Book Division 152; Madwoman Press 260; Mercury House 160; Mother Courage 164; Naiad Press 165; New Falcon 287; New Victoria 168; Permeable Press 262; Press Gang 243; Quarry Press 243; Reed Books Canada 244; Rising Tide 190; Spectrum Press 199; Spinsters Ink 199; Starbooks Press 291; Stone Bridge 201; Third Side Press 207.

Gothic. Atheneum Books For Young Readers 82; Baldwin & Knowlton 84; Dan River 111; Discus Press 116; Ekstasis Editions 235; HarperCollins 131; Lincoln Springs 259; Mayhaven 286; Mercury House 160; Purple Finch 263; TSR 210; Zebra and Pinnacle 228.

Hi-Lo. China Books & Periodicals, Inc. 101.

Historical. Arcade Publishing 80; Archives Publications 80; Ariadne Press 253; Atheneum Books For Young Readers 82; Avanyu 83; Ballantine 85; Bantam 86; Barbour and Co. 86; Beacon Hill Press 87; Bear Flag 269; Berkley Publishing Group, The 88; Borealis Press 232; Branden. 93; Brassey's 93; Caitlin Press 232; Carolrhoda 98; Cave 99; Center For Western Studies 279; Chapel Street 255; China Books & Periodicals, Inc. 101; Colonial Press 280; Covenant Communications 281; Cuff Publications, Harry 234; Dan River 111; Dial Books For Young Readers 115; Down The Shore 256; Ecco Press 118; Éditions La Liberté 235; Fine, Donald I. 122; Fort Dearborn 124; Friends United 125; Gay Sunshine Press and Leyland Publications 126; Goose Lane Editions 236; Grandin 128; Greenleaf Press 129; HarperCollins 131; Harvest House 132; Hendrick-Long 133; Herald Press Canada 237; Hiller Box Manufacturing 271; HMS Press 237; Holiday House 136; Howells House 137; ICS Books, Inc. 139; Ithaca Press 259; Just Us Books 147; Kar-Ben Copies 147; Leisure Books 151; Lincoln Springs 259; LiLittle, Brown, Children's Book Division 152; Lodestar 154; McClelland & Stewart 239; Mayhaven 286; Mercury House 160; Michaelis Medical 287; Nautical & Aviation 166; Negative Capability 166; New Victoria 168; Ozark 175; Path Press 288; Pelican 177; Permeable Press 262; Philomel Books 180; Pineapple Press 181; Playground Books 182; Prep Publishing 183; Presidio Press 184; Purple Finch 263; Random House 188; Scots Plaid 264; Servant 194; Shoestring Press 246; Sierra Club 195; Signature 195; Silver Moon 274; Soho Press 197; Sunflower Univ. 291; Third World Press 207; TOR Books 209; Tudor Publishers 210; Tyndale House Publishers 210; Univ. Press of Georgia 292; Wilderness Adventure 225; Windflower Communications 294; Write Way 227; Ye Galleon 294; Zebra and Pinnacle 228.

Horror. Atheneum Books For Young Readers 82; Baldwin & Knowlton 84; Bantam 86; Black Tie 254; Carol 97; Compass Productions 270; Cool Hand 107; Dan River 111; Discus Press 116; Fine, Donald I. 122; Fort Dearborn 124; Gryphon 130; HMS Press 237; ICS Books, Inc. 139; New Falcon 287; Parachute Press, Inc. 273; Prep Publishing 183; Random House 188; TOR Books 209; Zebra and Pinnacle 228.

Humor. Absey & Co. 70; Acme Press 253; American Atheist 76; Arcade Publishing 80; Ariadne Press 253; Armstrong Publishing Corp. 81; Atheneum Books For Young Readers 82; Avon Flare 84; Baldwin & Knowlton 84; Caitlin Press 232; Camelot 96; Carol 97; Catbird Press 98; Center Press 100; Clarion 103; Colonial Press 280; Compass Productions 270; Coteau Books 234; Covenant Communications 281; Cuff Publications, Harry 234; Dan River 111; Dial Books For Young Readers 115; Discus Press 116; E.M. Press 256; E.M. Press 281; Fort Dearborn 124; Grandin 128; Harian Creative Books 283; Herald Press Canada 237; Hiller Box Manufacturing 271; HMS Press 237; Holiday House 136; ICS Books, Inc. 139; Just Us Books 147; Key Porter Books 238; Lion Press 259; Little, Brown, Children's Book Division 152; Lodestar 154; McClelland & Stewart 239; Mayhaven 286; New Victoria 168; Oolichan Books 241; Ozark 175; Paradigm 288; Path Press 288; Pelican 177; Playground Books 182; Prep Publishing 183; Signature 195; SJL 196; TSR 210; Tudor Publishers 210; Turnstone Press 248; Vandamere Press 219; Weiss Associates, Daniel 275; Willowisp Press, Inc. 226; Wordstorm 251; Write Way 227; Zebra and Pinnacle 228.

Juvenile. Absey & Co. 70; Advocacy Press 253; African American Images 73; Archway Paperbacks/Minstrel Books 81; Armstrong Publishing Corp. 81; Atheneum Books For Young Readers 82; Bantam 86; Bear Flag 269; Bookcraft 92; Borealis Press 232; Boyds Mills 93; Camelot 96; Carolrhoda 98; Chapel Street 255; Christian Education Publishers 102; Christian Publications, Inc. 102; Chronicle 102; Cobblehill 105; Colonial Press 280; Compass Productions 270; Concordia 106; Consortium 281; Cool Kids 108; Coteau Books 234; Covenant Communications 281; Crossway 110; Dancing Jester 111; Denison & Co., T.S. 115; Discus Press 116; Dorling Kindersley 116; Down The Shore 256; Dutton Children's Books 117; E.M. Press 256; Eakin Press/Sunbelt Media, Inc. 118; Éditions La Liberté 235; Ekstasis Editions 235; Fiesta City 257; Fort Dearborn 124; Free Spirit 125; Friends United 125; Grandin 128; Grosset & Dunlap 129; Hendrick-Long 133; Herald Press 134; Herald Press Canada 237; Hiller Box Manufacturing 271; Holiday House 136; Houghton Mifflin 137; ICS Books, Inc. 139; Ideals Children's Books 140; Interlink Publishing Group 142; Jones Univ. Press, Bob 146; Lee & Low 151; Lerner 151; Little, Brown, Children's Book Division 152; Lodestar 154; Lorimer & Co., James 239; Lothrop, Lee & Shepard 155; McClelland & Stewart 239; Mayhaven 286; Media Bridge 160; Mega-Books 273; Morehouse 163; Morrow Junior Books 164; Northland 169; Orca Book Publishers Ltd. 241; Orchard Books 172; Ozark 175; Pacific Educational Press 242; Parachute Press, Inc. 273; Pauline Books & Media 176; Peachtree 177; Peguis 242; Pelican 177; Philomel Books 180; Pippin Press 181; Playground Books 182; Polychrome 183; Prep Publishing 183; Purple Finch 263; Random House, Juvenile Books 188; Ronsdale Press 245; Roussan 245; Royal Fireworks Press 191; Scholastic Canada 245; Shoestring Press 246; Silver Moon 274; SJL 196; Soundprints 198; Speech Bin 199; Stoddard Publishing 246; Támbourine Books 204; Third World Press 207; Tidewater 208; Tree Frog 247; Tudor Publishers 210; Walker and Co. 221; Ward Hill 221; Weigl Educational 250; Weiss Associates, Daniel 275; Whispering Coyote Press 223; Willowisp Press, Inc. 226; Windflower Communications 294.

Literary. Absey & Co. 70; Another Chicago 79; Arcade Publishing 80; Archives Publications 80; Ariadne Press 253; Arsenal Pulp 229; Baker Book House 84; Baldwin & Knowlton 84; Bantam 86; Black Heron 254; Black Tie 254; Blue Dolphin 90; Bookcraft 92; Borealis Press 232; Cadmus Editions 254; Calyx Books 254; Carol 97; Carter Press 255; Catbird Press 98; Cave 99; Center Press 100; Champion Bookss 100; China Books & Periodicals, Inc. 101; Cleis Press 104; Coffee House 105; Confluence Press 107; Coteau Books 234; Covenant Communications 281; Creative Arts 281; Dan River 111; Dancing Jester 111; Depth Charge 255; Down The Shore 256; E.M. Press 256; E.M. Press 281; Ecco Press 118; Éditions La Liberté 235; Éditions Logiques/Logical Publishing 235; Ekstasis Editions 235; Empyreal Press 235; Eriksson, Paul S. 120; Fine, Donald I. 122; Floricanto Press 123; Fort Dearborn 124; Four Walls Eight Windows 124; Godine, David R. 127; Goose Lane Editions 236; Grandin 128; Guild Bindery Press 283; Gutter Press 236; HarperCollins 131; Heaven Bone 258; Herald Press Canada 237; HMS Press 237; Hollow Earth 136; Houghton Mifflin 137; Hounslow Press 238; Howells House 137; ICS Books, Inc. 139; Lincoln Springs 259; Little, Brown 153; Livingston Press 153; Longstreet Press 155; McClelland & Stewart 239; MacMurray & Beck 158; Mercury House 160; Mercury Press 240; Mount Olive 287; Negative Capability 166; Netherlandic Press 240; New Falcon 287; New Rivers Press 168; NeWest 240; Nightshade Press 261; Norton Co., W.W. 170; Oolichan Books 241; Orca Book Publishers Ltd. 241; Overlook Press 174; Path Press 288; Peachtree 177; Permanent Press/Second Chance Press, The 178; Permeable Press 262; Pineapple Press 181; Prep Publishing 183; Press Gang 243; Puckerbrush Press 263; Purple Finch 263; QED Press 187; Quarry Press 243; Random House Of Canada 244; Reed Books Canada 244; Ronsdale Press 245; Scots Plaid 264; Shoestring Press 246; Shoreline 246; Smith 197; Soho Press 197; Somerville House 274; Southern Methodist Univ. 198; Spectrum Press 199; Stone Bridge 264; Stormline Press 265; Sunk Island 246; Third Side Press 207; Third World Press 207; Thistledown Press 247; Three Continents Press 207; Turnstone Press 248; Tuttle, Charles E. 248; UCLA-American Indian Studies Center 266; Ultramarine 211; Univ. of Arkansas, The 213; Univ. of North Texas 216; Univ. of Pittsburgh 216; Univ. Press of Georgia 292; White Pine 224; Wilde Publishing 225; Willowisp Press, Inc. 226; Zebra and Pinnacle 228; Zoland Books 228.

Mainstream/Contemporary. Absey & Co. 70; Academy Chicago 71; Arcade Publishing 80; Ariadne Press 253; Atheneum Books For Young Readers 82; Avon Flare 84; Baldwin & Knowlton 84; Bantam 86; Berkley Publishing Group, The 88; Blue Dolphin 90; Bookcraft 92; Caitlin Press 232; Camelot 96; Citadel Press 103; Confluence Press 107; Cool Hand 107; Coteau Books 234; Covenant Communications 281; Crossway 110; Cuff Publications, Harry 234; Dan River 111; Dancing Jester 111; Delancey Press 255; Dell Publishers 114; Dickens Publications 256; Discus Press 116; Down East 117; Down The Shore 256; Dutton 117; E.M. Press 256; E.M. Press 281; Edicones Universal 282; Éditions La Liberté 235; Éditions Logiques/Logical Publishing 235; Ekstasis Editions 235; Fawcett Juniper 122; Fine, Donald I. 122; Fort Dearborn 124; Guild Bindery Press 283; Harian Creative Books 283; HMS Press 237; Ithaca Press 259; Key Porter Books 238; Lerner 151; Lincoln Springs 259; Lion Press 259; Little, Brown 153; Lodestar 154; Longstreet Press 155; McClelland & Stewart 239; Mayhaven 286; Morrow, William 163; Mount Olive 287; Orca Book Publishers Ltd. 241; Pantheon Books 175; Paper Chase Press 175; Papier-Mache Press 176; Path Press 288; Peachtree 177; Permanent Press/Second Chance Press, The 178; Perspectives Press 179; Pineapple Press 181; Prep Publishing 183; Quarry Press 243; Random House 188; Reed Books Canada 244; Scots Plaid 264; Shoreline 246; Sierra Club 195; Simon & Schuster 196; Soho Press 197; Spectrum Press 199; Starburst 200; Stoddard Publishing 246; Third World Press 207; Tudor Publishers 210; Turnstone Press 248; Univ. Of Illinois 213; Univ. of Iowa 214; Univ. Press of Mississippi 218; Villard Books 220; Vista Publishing Inc. 293; Ward Hill 221; Wilde Publishing 225; Willowisp Press, Inc. 226; Wordstorm 251; Write Way 227; Zebra and Pinnacle 228.

Military/War. Fort Dearborn 124; Naval Institute 166; Presidio Press 184; Sunflower Univ. 291.

Multicultural. Serendipity Systems 194.

Mystery. Academy Chicago 71; Accord Communications 72; Arcade Publishing 80; Atheneum Books For Young Readers 82; Avalon 83; Avon 83; Avon Flare 84; Baker Book House 84; Baldwin & Knowlton 84; Bantam 86; Berkley Publishing Group, The 88; Bookcraft 92; Camelot 96; Carol 97; Cave 99; Chapel Street 255; Clarion 103; Comic Art 105; Compass Productions 270; Cool Hand 107; Countryman Press 109; Covenant Communications 281; Dan River 111; Dancing Jester 111; Dial Books For Young Readers 115; Dickens Publications 256; Discus Press 116; Doubleday 116; E.M. Press 281; Earth-Love 256; Fine, Donald I. 122; Fort Dearborn 124; Four Walls Eight Windows 124; Gay Sunshine Press and Leyland Publications 126; Godine, David R. 127; Gryphon 130; HarperCollins 131; Harvest House 132; Hendrick-Long 133; HMS Press 237; Holiday House 136; Hollow Earth 136; Lincoln Springs 259; Lion Press 259; Little, Brown, Children's Book Division 152; Lodestar 154; McClelland & Stewart 239; Mayhaven 286; Mega-Books 273; Mysterious Press 165; Naiad Press 165; New Victoria 168; Paradigm 288; Permanent Press/Second Chance Press, The 178; Planning/Communications 182; Platinum Press 289; Playground Books 182; Pocket Books 183; Prep Publishing 183; Presidio Press 184; Purple Finch 263; QED Press 187; Random House 188; Reed Books Canada 244; Royal Fireworks Press 191; Scholastic 194; Silver Moon 274; Soho Press 197; Spinsters Ink 199; Stone Bridge 201; Tudor Publishers 210; Turnstone Press 248; Vandamere Press 219; Virtual Press 292; Vista Publishing Inc. 293; Walker and Co. 221; Willowisp Press, Inc. 226; Wordstorm 251; Write Way 227; Zebra and Pinnacle 228.

Nostalgia. Fort Dearborn 124.

Occult. Archives Publications 80; Baldwin & Knowlton 84; Colonial Press 280; Dan River 111; Discus Press 116; Floricanto Press 123; Fort Dearborn 124; Llewellyn 153; New Falcon 287; Sunk Island 246; Wilde Publishing 225; Write Way 227; Zebra and Pinnacle 228.

Picture Books. Armstrong Publishing Corp. 81; Boyds Mills 93; Center Press 100; Charlesbridge 100; Chronicle 102; Cobblehill 105; Colonial Press 280; Compass Productions 270; Concordia 106; Cool Kids 108; Dancing Jester 111; Down The Shore 256; Farrar, Straus and Giroux 121; Gold'n' Honey Books 127; Grosset & Dunlap 129; Herald Press Canada 237; Hiller Box Manufacturing 271; Holiday House 136; ICS Books, Inc. 139; Ideals Children's Books 140; Interlink Publishing Group 142; Key Porter Books 238; Little, Brown, Children's Book Division 152; Lodestar 154; Lothrop, Lee & Shepard 155; Mayhaven 286; Media Bridge 160; Michaelis Medical 287; Morehouse 163; Orca Book Publishers Ltd. 241; Orchard Books 172; Owen, Richard C. 174; Owl

Books 273; Ozark 175; Philomel Books 180; Pippin Press 181; Playground Books 182; Polychrome 183; Random House, Juvenile Books 188; Shoestring Press 246; Tambourine Books 204; Third World Press 207; Unity Books 211; Whispering Coyote Press 223; Willowisp Press, Inc. 226.

Plays. Anchorage Press 79; Chicago Plays 100; Colonial Press 280; Compass Productions 270; Coteau Books 234; Dan River 111; Dancing Jester 111; Discus Press 116; Drama Book Publishers 117; Ecco Press 118; Ekstasis Editions 235; Fiesta City 257; Fort Dearborn 124; French, Samuel 125; HMS Press 237; Media Bridge 160; Meriwether 161; Mount Olive 287; Pacific Educational Press 242; Players Press 182; Playwrights Canada 242; Scots Plaid 264; Spectrum Press 199; Tambra Publishing 265; Third World Press 207; Wilde Publishing 225.

Poetry. Absey & Co. 70; Adastra Press 253; Ahsahta Press 253; Another Chicago 79; Asian Humanities Press 82; Black Ball 254; Black Tie 254; Blue Dolphin 90; Boyds Mills 93; Cadmus Editions 254; Caitlin Press 232; Calyx Books 254; Center Press 100; Champion Bookss 100; Christopher Publishing House 280; Cleveland State Univ. Poetry Center 104; Colonial Press 280; Confluence Press 107; Copper Canyon 108; Dante Univ. Of America 112; Depth Charge 255; Dusty Dog Reviews 256; Ecco Press 118; Ecrits Des Forges 234; Edicones Universal 282; Ekstasis Editions 235; Gaff Press 257; Guernica Editions 236; Gutter Press 236; Heaven Bone 258; High Plains 135; Hippopotamus Press 237; HMS Press 237; Intertext 259; Inverted-A 259; Jewish Publication Society 145; Louisiana State Univ. 155; Mercury Press 240; Mid-List Press 161; Morrow, William 163; Mortal Press 260; Mount Olive 287; Negative Capability 166; Netherlandic Press 240; New Rivers Press 168; Nightshade Press 261; Northwoods Press 170; Oberlin College 261; Oolichan Books 241; Orchard Books 172; Orchises Press 173; Papier-Mache Press 176; Paragon House 288; Press Gang 243; Puckerbrush Press 263; QED Press 187; Quarry Press 243; Royal Fireworks Press 191; Scots Plaid 264; Signature 195; Smith 197; Sono Nis 246; Spectrum Press 199; Starbooks Press 291; Sunk Island 246; Texas Tech Univ. 206; Third World Press 207; Thistledown Press 247; Three Continents Press 207; Tia Chucha Press 208; Tilbury House 291; Turnstone Press 248; Tuttle, Charles E. 248; UCLA-American Indian Studies Center 266; Univ. of Arkansas, The 213; Univ. of California 213; Univ. of Iowa 214; Univ. of Massachusetts 214; Univ. of North Texas 216; Univ. of Pittsburgh 216; Univ. of Scranton 217; Vehicule Press 250; Vista Publishing Inc. 293; Whispering Coyote Press 223; White Pine 224; Whole Notes 266; Xenos Books 267.

Regional. Blair, John F. 89; Borealis Press 232; Cuff Publications, Harry 234; Down East 117; Faber & Faber 121; Fort Dearborn 124; Interlink Publishing Group 142; New England Press 167; Nightshade Press 261; Northland 169; Peachtree 177; Pelican 177; Philomel Books 180; Pineapple Press 181; Sunstone Press 203; Texas Christian Univ. 205; Thistledown Press 247; Tidewater 208; Univ. of Maine 214; Univ. Press of Colorado 217; Univ. Press of New England 218; Vista Publications 266; Windflower Communications 294.

Religious. ACTA Publications 72; Archives Publications 80; Barbour and Co. 86; Beacon Hill Press 87; Bell Tower 87; Bethel 88; Blue Dolphin 90; Blue Star 91; Branden. 93; Bridge Publishing 278; Broadman & Holman 94; Christian Education Publishers 102; Christian Publications, Inc. 102; College Press, Inc. 280; Compass Productions 270; Concordia 106; Covenant Communications 281; Crossway 110; Discus Press 116; Fort Dearborn 124; Friends United 125; Gold'n' Honey Books 127; Grandin 128; Hensley, Virgil 134; Herald Press 134; Herald Press Canada 237; Hiller Box Manufacturing 271; HMS Press 237; Kar-Ben Copies 147; Media Bridge 160; Morehouse 163; Mount Olive 287; Nelson, Thomas 167; New Falcon 287; Pauline Books & Media 176; Prep Publishing 183; Resource Publications 290; Revell, Fleming H. 189; Shaw, Harold 195; Shoestring Press 246; Signature 195; Standard 200; Tyndale House Publishers 210; Unity Books 211; Victor Books 219; Windflower Communications 294.

Romance. Atheneum Books For Young Readers 82; Avalon 83; Avon 83; Avon Flare 84; Baldwin & Knowlton 84; Bantam 86; Barbour and Co. 86; Berkley Publishing Group, The 88; Bookcraft 92; Borealis Press 232; Covenant Communications 281; Dan River 111; Dial Books For Young Readers 115; Discus Press 116; Doubleday 116; Floricanto Press 123; Flower Valley 257; Fort Dearborn 124; Harian Creative Books 283; Herald Press Canada 237; HMS Press 237; Leisure Books 151; Lincoln Springs 259; Mayhaven 286; New Victoria 168; Paradigm 288; Pocket Books 183; Prep Publishing 183; Purple Finch 263; Scholastic 194; Shoestring Press 246; Silhouette 196; Starburst 200; Tudor Publishers 210; Univ. Press of Georgia 292; Weiss Associates, Daniel 275; Wilde Publishing 225; Willowisp Press, Inc. 226; Zebra and Pinnacle 228.

Science Fiction. Ace Science Fiction 72; Atheneum Books For Young Readers 82; Avon 83; Baen 84; Baldwin & Knowlton 84; Bantam 86; Black Heron 254; Carol 97; Circlet Press 103; Compass Productions 270; Covenant Communications 281; Crossway 110; Dan River 111; DAW 113; Del Rey 114; Discus Press 116; E.M. Press 281; Éditions Logiques/Logical Publishing 235; Ekstasis Editions 235; Fine, Donald I. 122; Fort Dearborn 124; Gay Sunshine Press and Leyland Publications 126; Gryphon 130; HarperCollins 131; HMS Press 237; Hollow Earth 136; Inverted-A 259; Just

Us Books 147; Lion Press 259; Little, Brown, Children's Book Division 152; Lodestar 154; Mayhaven 286; New Falcon 287; New Victoria 168; Paradigm 288; Permeable Press 262; Playground Books 182; Pocket Books 183; Prep Publishing 183; Purple Finch 263; Quarry Press 243; Royal Fireworks Press 191; Shoestring Press 246; SJL 196; Stone Bridge 201; Swan-Raven & Co. 203; TOR Books 209; TSR 210; Tudor Publishers 210; Ultramarine 211; Univ. Press of Georgia 292; Virtual Press 292; Willowisp Press, Inc. 226; Write Way 227.

Short Story Collections. Absey & Co. 70; Another Chicago 79; Arcade Publishing 80; Arsenal Pulp 229; Baldwin & Knowlton 84; Bookcraft 92; Borealis Press 232; Caitlin Press 232; Calyx Books 254; Center For Western Studies 279; Champion Bookss 100; Chapel Street 255; Chronicle 102; Circlet Press 103; Coffee House 105; Colonial Press 280; Confluence Press 107; Coteau Books 234; Dan River 111; Dancing Jester 111; Discus Press 116; Down The Shore 256; Dutton Children's Books 117; E.M. Press 256; Ecco Press 118; Éditions La Liberté 235; Ekstasis Editions 235; Empyreal Press 235; Faber & Faber 121; Floricanto Press 123; Fort Dearborn 124; Gay Sunshine Press and Leyland Publications 126; Godine, David R. 127; Goose Lane Editions 236; Harian Creative Books 283; Herald Press Canada 237; HMS Press 237; ICS Books, Inc. 139; Indiana Historical Society 259; Interlink Publishing Group 142; Inverted-A 259; Lincoln Springs 259; Livingston Press 153; McClelland & Stewart 239; Mercury House 160; Mercury Press 240; Naiad Press 165; Negative Capability 166; Netherlandic Press 240; New Rivers Press 168; NeWest 240; Oolichan Books 241; Ozark 175; Papier-Mache Press 176; Path Press 288; Permeable Press 262; Playground Books 182; Press Gang 243; Purple Finch 263; Quarry Press 243; Resource Publications 290; Ronsdale Press 245; Scots Plaid 264; Shoreline 246; Somerville House 274; Southern Methodist Univ. 198; Spectrum Press 199; Stone Bridge 201; Third World Press 207; TSR 210; Tudor Publishers 210; Turnstone Press 248; Univ. Of Illinois 213; Univ. of Arkansas, The 213; Univ. of Missouri 215; Univ. of North Texas 216; Univ. Press of Georgia 292; Virtual Press 292; Vista Publishing Inc. 293; White Pine 224; Willowisp Press, Inc. 226; Wordstorm 251; Zebra and Pinnacle 228; Zoland Books 228.

Spiritual (New Age, Etc.). Wilshire Book Co. 226.

Sports. Fort Dearborn 124.

Suspense. Accord Communications 72; Arcade Publishing 80; Atheneum Books For Young Readers 82; Avon 83; Avon Flare 84; Baldwin & Knowlton 84; Bantam 86; Berkley Publishing Group, The 88; Bethel 88; Bookcraft 92; Camelot 96; Clarion 103; Comic Art 105; Covenant Communications 281; Dan River 111; Dancing Jester 111; Dial Books For Young Readers 115; Discus Press 116; Doubleday 116; Fine, Donald I. 122; Fort Dearborn 124; Gryphon 130; HarperCollins 131; HMS Press 237; Holiday House 136; Hounslow Press 238; Ivy League 259; Just Us Books 147; Little, Brown, Children's Book Division 152; Lodestar 154; Mayhaven 286; Mysterious Press 165; Paradigm 288; Path Press 288; Permanent Press/Second Chance Press, The 178; Playground Books 182; Pocket Books 183; Prep Publishing 183; Presidio Press 184; Purple Finch 263; QED Press 187; Random House 188; Soho Press 197; TOR Books 209; Vandamere Press 219; Vista Publishing Inc. 293; Walker and Co. 221; Willowisp Press, Inc. 226; Wordstorm 251; Write Way 227; Zebra and Pinnacle 228.

Western. Atheneum Books For Young Readers 82; Avalon 83; Avanyu 83; Avon 83; Baldwin & Knowlton 84; Bantam 86; Berkley Publishing Group, The 88; Bookcraft 92; Center For Western Studies 279; Comic Art 105; Covenant Communications 281; Creative Arts 281; Dan River 111; Dancing Jester 111; Discus Press 116; Doubleday 116; Evans and Co., M. 120; Fine, Donald I. 122; Fort Dearborn 124; Grandin 128; HarperCollins 131; Hendrick-Long 133; Lodestar 154; Mayhaven 286; New Victoria 168; Playground Books 182; Pocket Books 183; Prep Publishing 183; Shoestring Press 246; Starburst 200; Sunflower Univ. 291; Walker and Co. 221; Zebra and Pinnacle 228.

Young Adult. Archway Paperbacks/Minstrel Books 81; Baldwin & Knowlton 84; Bantam 86; Bethel 88; Blue Heron 90; Bookcraft 92; Borealis Press 232; Boyds Mills 93; Caitlin Press 232; Chapel Street 255; Cobblehill 105; Colonial Press 280; Commune-A-Key 105; Concordia 106; Covenant Communications 281; Crossway 110; Dancing Jester 111; Discus Press 116; E.M. Press 281; Éditions La Liberté 235; Eriako Assoc. 271; Fort Dearborn 124; Farrar, Straus and Giroux 121; Godine, David R. 127; Greenleaf Press 129; Herald Press 134; Herald Press Canada 237; Houghton Mifflin 137; Jones Univ. Press, Bob 146; Lerner 151; Lion Press 259; Little, Brown, Children's Book Division 152; Lodestar 154; Lorimer & Co., James 239; McClelland & Stewart 239; McElderry Books, Margaret K. 157; Mayhaven 286; Media Bridge 160; Mega-Books 273; Morehouse 163; Morrow, William 163; Nelson, Thomas 167; Orchard Books 172; Ozark 175; Pacific Educational Press 242; Parachute Press, Inc. 273; Philomel Books 180; Pippin Press 181; Polychrome 183; Prep Publishing 183; Purple Finch 263; Random House, Juvenile Books 188; Roussan 245; Scholastic Canada 245; Scholastic 194; Shoreline 246; Tambourine Books 204; Texas

Christian Univ. 205; Third World Press 207; Thistledown Press 247; Tree Frog 247; Walker and Co. 221; Ward Hill 221; Weiss Associates, Daniel 275; Willowisp Press, Inc. 226; Zebra and Pinnacle 228.

Nonfiction

Agriculture/Horticulture. ACRES U.S.A. 72; Bright Mountain 254; Camino 96; Chelsea Green 279; Discus Press 116; Dorling Kindersley 116; Hartley & Marks 131; Haworth Press 132; HMS Press 237; Hoard & Sons, W.D. 258; Idyll Arbor 140; Interstate 285; Iowa State Univ. Press 144; Lyons & Burford, Publishers, Inc. 156; McClelland & Stewart 239; Natural Heritage/Natural Heritage 240; Purdue Univ. 186; Purich Publishing 243; Stipes 201; Story Communications/Garden Way 201; Sunflower Univ. 291; Tilbury House 291; Timber Press 208; Univ. of Alaska 212; Univ. of Nebraska 215; Univ. of North Texas 216; Weidner & Sons 222; Wilde Publishing 225; Windward 226; Woodbridge Press 227.

Alternative Lifestyles. Luramedia 156; Sterling 200.

Americana. Addicus Books 73; Alaska Northwest 73; Ancestry Inc. 79; Ardsley House Publishers, Inc. 81; Atheneum Books For Young Readers 82; Avanyu 83; Baldwin & Knowlton 84; B&B 85; Bantam 86; Berkshire House 88; Blair, John F. 89; Boston Mills Press 232; Bowling Green State Univ. 92; Branden. 93; Brevet 94; Camino 96; Carol 97; Cave 99; Caxton 99; Charles River 255; Christopher Publishing House 280; Clarion 103; Clear Light 103; Compass Productions 270; Confluence Press 107; Covenant Communications 281; Dancing Jester 111; Denali Press 114; Discus Press 116; Down East 117; Down The Shore 256; E.M. Press 281; Eakin Press/Sunbelt Media, Inc. 118; Ecco Press 118; Éditions La Liberté 235; Elliott & Clark 119; EPM 120; Eriksson, Paul S. 120; Faber & Faber 121; Filter Press 257; Fort Dearborn 124; Glenbridge 126; Godine, David R. 127; Golden West 127; Harian Creative Books 283; HarperCollins 131; Herald Publishing House 134; Heyday 135; High Plains 135; HMS Press 237; Howells House 137; International Publishers 143; JSA Publications 272; Kurian Reference Books, George 272; Laing Communications 272; Layla Productions 272; Lehigh Univ. Press 151; Lerner 151; Library Research Assoc. 286; Lincoln Springs 259; Lion Books 152; Longstreet Press 155; Lorien House 260; Lyons & Burford, Publishers, Inc. 156; McDonald & Woodward 157; Mayhaven 286; Meyerbooks 260; Michigan State Univ. 161; Mosaic Press Miniature Books 260; Mountain Press 164; Mustang Publishing 165; Mystic Seaport Museum 261; New England Press 167; Nova Science 170; Oldbuck Press 171; Oregon Historical Society Press 173; Path Press 288; Pelican 177; PHB 180; Picton Press 180; Prep Publishing 183; Pruett 185; Purdue Univ. 186; Quill Driver Books/Word Dancer Press 187; Rawhide Western 188; Royal Fireworks Press 191; Rutgers Univ. Press 191; Sachem Publishing Assoc. 274; Sand River 264; Sarpedon 193; Schiffer 193; Scholastic Canada 245; Sergeant Kirkland's 194; Shoreline 246; Signature 195; Silver Burdett Press 196; Spectrum Press 199; Storm Peak 264; Sunflower Univ. 291; Texas Christian Univ. 205; Texas Tech Univ. 206; Thorson & Assoc. 275; Transaction 292; Tudor Publishers 210; Univ. Of Idaho 213; Univ. Of Illinois 213; Univ. of Alaska 212; Univ. of Arizona 212; Univ. of Arkansas, The 213; Univ. of Nebraska 215; Univ. of North Carolina 215; Univ. of North Texas 216; Univ. of Oklahoma 216; Univ. of Pennsylvania 216; Univ. of Tennessee 217; Univ. Press of Georgia 292; Univ. Press of Mississippi 218; Univ. Press of New England 218; Utah State Univ. Press 218; Vandamere Press 219; Vanderbilt Univ. Press 219; Viking Studio Books 220; Washington State Univ. Press 222; Watts, Franklin 222; Wayfinder Press 222; Westernlore Press 223; Wieser & Wieser 275; Wilde Publishing 225; Wilderness Adventure 225; Ye Galleon 294.

Animals. Alpine 75; Archway Paperbacks/Minstrel Books 81; Armstrong Publishing Corp. 81; Atheneum Books For Young Readers 82; Baldwin & Knowlton 84; Ballantine 85; Barron's Educational Series, Inc. 86; Bergh 88; Blackbirch Press 89; Boxwood Press 278; Carol 97; Carolrhoda 98; Cave 99; Christopher Publishing House 280; Compass Productions 270; Countrysport Press 109; Creative Spark 270; Dawn 113; Discus Press 116; Doral 116; Dorling Kindersley 116; Dutton Children's Books 117; E.M. Press 281; Éditions La Liberté 235; Epicenter Press 119; Eriksson, Paul S. 120; Faber & Faber 121; Fort Dearborn 124; Half Halt 130; Harmony House 283; HarperCollins 131; HMS Press 237; Homestead 137; Hounslow Press 238; ICS Books, Inc. 139; Iowa State Univ. Press 144; Jones Univ. Press, Bob 146; Kesend Publishing, Ltd., Michael 148; Key Porter Books 238; Learning Works 150; Lerner 151; Little, Brown, Children's Book Division 152; Lone Pine 239; Lyons & Burford, Publishers, Inc. 156; McClelland & Stewart 239; McDonald & Woodward 157; Mayhaven 286; Millbrook Press 162; Mosaic Press Miniature Books 260; Natural Heritage/ Natural Heritage 240; Northland 169; Optimum 241; Owen, Richard C. 174; Owl Books 273; Ozark 175; Parachute Press, Inc. 273; Parrot Press 262; Pineapple Press 181; Plexus 182; Raincoast Book Distribution 244; Republic Of Texas Press 189; Rocky Top 190; Soundprints 198; Southfarm Press 198; Sterling 200; Story Communications/Garden Way 201; Texas Tech Univ. 206; Trafalgar

Square 265; Univ. of Alaska 212; Viking Studio Books 220; Warren 221; Weidner & Sons 222; Wheetley Co. 275; Whitecap Books 250; Wilderness Adventure 225; Willowisp Press, Inc. 226; Wilshire Book Co. 226; Windward 226.

Anthropology/Archaeology. Alaska Northwest 73; Archives Publications 80; Avanyu 83; Baywood 86; Beacon 87; Blackbirch Press 89; Blue Dolphin 90; Cambridge Univ. 96; Caratzas, Aristide D. 279; Cave 99; Center For Afro-American Studies 255; Center For Western Studies 279; Clear Light 103; Dancing Jester 111; Denali Press 114; Eagle's View 118; Éditions La Liberté 235; Filter Press 257; Floricanto Press 123; Fort Dearborn 124; HMS Press 237; Horsdale & Schubart 237; Howells House 137; Humanics Publishing 138; Inner Traditions Int'l 142; Insight Books 142; Int'l Resources 272; Johnson Books 146; Kent State Univ. 147; Knowledge, Ideas & Trends (KIT) 148; Kodansha America 149; Learning Works 150; Lerner 151; Lone Pine 239; Louisiana State Univ. 155; McDonald & Woodward 157; Marketscope Books 159; Mayfield 159; Millbrook Press 162; Minnesota Historical Society 162; Natural Heritage/Natural Heritage 240; Nelson-Hall 167; New Falcon 287; Northland 169; Nova Science 170; Oxford Univ. Press 174; Paideia Press 262; Pax Publishing 262; Pendaya 262; Pennsylvania Historical and Museum Commission 178; Phi Delta Kappa Educational Foundation 180; Pickwick 288; Platinum Press 289; Plenum 182; Quest Books 187; Rhombus 263; Routledge 190; Rutgers Univ. Press 191; Schenkman 290; Scots Plaid 264; Sergeant Kirkland's 194; Spectrum Press 199; Stanford Univ. Press 200; Sunflower Univ. 291; Third World Press 207; Thorson & Assoc. 275; Tyrone Press, The 211; UCLA-American Indian Studies Center 266; Univ. Of Idaho 213; Univ. Of Montreal 249; Univ. of Alabama 212; Univ. of Alaska 212; Univ. of Arizona 212; Univ. of Iowa 214; Univ. of Michigan 214; Univ. of Nevada 215; Univ. of New Mexico 215; Univ. of Pennsylvania 216; Univ. of Pittsburgh 216; Univ. of Tennessee 217; Univ. of Texas 217; Univ. of Toronto 249; Univ. Press of America 217; Vanderbilt Univ. Press 219; Vista Publications 266; Weatherhill 293; Westernlore Press 223; Wheetley Co. 275; White Cliffs Media 223.

Art/Architecture. ABC-CLIO 70; Aberdeen Group 70; ACA Books 71; Alaska Northwest 73; Allworth Press 74; Architectural Book Publishing Co., Inc. 80; Archives Publications 80; Ashgate 278; Asian Humanities Press 82; Atheneum Books For Young Readers 82; Avanyu 83; Barron's Educational Series, Inc. 86; Beil, Frederic C. 87; Black Ball 254; Bowling Green State Univ. 92; Branden. 93; Bucknell Univ. 95; Calyx Books 254; Cambridge Univ. 96; Camino 96; Caratzas, Aristide D. 279; Carol 97; Carolrhoda 98; Center For Afro-American Studies 255; Center For Western Studies 279; Center Press 100; China Books & Periodicals, Inc. 101; Christopher Publishing House 280; Chronicle 102; Clear Light 103; Consultant Press 107; Crisp Publications 110; Da Capo 111; Dancing Jester 111; Davenport, May 112; Davis Publications 113; Discus Press 116; Distinctive Publishing 116; Dorling Kindersley 116; Dundurn Press 234; Ecco Press 118; Elliott & Clark 119; EPM 120; Eriksson, Paul S. 120; Excalibur Publishing 256; Fairleigh Dickinson Univ. 121; Family Album 256; Fitzhenry & Whiteside 236; Flower Valley 257; Fort Dearborn 124; Four Walls Eight Windows 124; Godine, David R. 127; Goose Lane Editions 236; Guernica Editions 236; Gutter Press 236; HarperCollins 131; Hartley & Marks 131; High Plains 135; HMS Press 237; Hollow Earth 136; Holmes & Meier 136; Homestead 137; Horsdale & Schubart 237; Hounslow Press 238; Howells House 137; Hudson Hill 138; Inner Traditions Int'l 142; Insight Books 142; Interlink Publishing Group 142; Italica Press 144; Kent State Univ. 147; Lang, Peter 285; Learning Works 150; Lehigh Univ. Press 151; Lerner 151; Little, Brown, Children's Book Division 152; Locust Hill Press 154; Lone Pine 239; Louisiana State Univ. 155; Loyola Univ. 156; Lyons & Burford, Publishers, Inc. 156; McClelland & Stewart 239; McFarland & Co. 157; McGraw-Hill Companies 157; Mayfield 159; Mayhaven 286; Mercury Press 240; Meriwether 161; Minnesota Historical Society 162; Morrow, William 163; Mosaic Press Miniature Books 260; Mount Ida 261; Mystic Seaport Museum 261; Natural Heritage/Natural Heritage 240; North Light 169; Northland 169; Optimum 241; Oregon Historical Society Press 173; Overlook Press 174; Oxford Univ. Press 174; Pacific Educational Press 242; PBC Int'l 177; Pendaya 262; Pennsylvania Historical and Museum Commission 178; Pickwick 288; Pincushion Press 289; PMN Publishing 289; Pogo Press, Incorporated 183; Princeton Architectural Press 289; Professional Publications 185; Pruett 185; Quarry Press 243; Quest Books 187; Raincoast Book Distribution 244; Random House 188; Resource Publications 290; Schiffer 193; Shoestring Press 246; Shoreline 246; Simon & Schuster 196; 16th Century Journal 264; Sound View 264; Sourcebooks 198; Spectrum Press 199; Sterling 200; Stone Bridge 201; Sunstone Press 203; TAB Books 204; Tenth Avenue 274; Texas Tech Univ. 206; Thorson & Assoc. 275; Tuttle, Charles E. 248; Univ. of Alaska 212; Univ. of Alberta 248; Univ. of California 213; Univ. of Massachusetts 214; Univ. of Missouri 215; Univ. of New Mexico 215; Univ. of Pennsylvania 216; Univ. of Pittsburgh 216; Univ. of Scranton 217; Univ. of Tennessee 217; Univ. of Texas 217; Univ. Press of America 217; Univ. Press of New England 218; Vanderbilt Univ. Press 219; Visions Communications 266; Walch, Publisher, J. Weston 221; Warren 221;

Washington State Univ. Press 222; Weatherhill 293; Western Book/Journal 293; Wheetley Co. 275; Whitson 224; Williamson 225; Zoland Books 228.

Astrology/Psychic/New Age. ACS Publications 277; American Federation of Astrologers 78; ASTRO Communications Services 82; Bantam 86; Bear and Co. 87; Blue Star 91; Cassandra Press 98; Crossing Press 110; Delphi Press 114; Hampton Roads 283; Harper San Francisco 131; In Print 259; Llewellyn 153; Mercury House 160; New Falcon 287; Quest Books 187; Somerville House 274; Sterling 200; Sunk Island 246; Swan-Raven & Co. 203; Theosophical Publishing House 206; Thorsons 247; Valley of the Sun 219; Whitford Press 224; Wild Flower 224.

Audiocassettes. Bantam 86; Schirmer Books 193; Walch, Publisher, J. Weston 221.

Autobiography. Diskotech 256; E.M. Press 256; Pantheon Books 175; Permanent Press/Second Chance Press, The 178; Soho Press 197; Trilogy Books 209; Zondervan 228.

Bibliographies. Borgo Press 92; Confluence Press 107; Family Album 256; Gryphon 130; Klein, B. 148; Locust Hill Press 154; Scarecrow Press 193; Ultramarine 211; Whitson 224.

Biography. Academy Chicago 71; Acropolis South 72; Amadeus Press 75; American Atheist 76; Arcade Publishing 80; Architectural Book Publishing Co., Inc. 80; Archives Publications 80; Arden Press Inc. 81; Arden Press Inc. 81; Atheneum Books For Young Readers 82; Avanyu 83; Avon 83; Baldwin & Knowlton 84; Bantam 86; Barbour and Co. 86; Beil, Frederic C. 87; Bergh 88; Berkshire House 88; Blackbirch Graphics 269; Blackbirch Press 89; Bliss 254; Blue Dove 90; Bonus Books 91; Bookcraft 92; Borealis Press 232; Borgo Press 92; Bowling Green State Univ. 92; Boxwood Press 278; Branden. 93; Brassey's 93; Bridge Publishing 278; Bright Mountain 254; Caitlin Press 232; Cambridge Univ. 96; Cambridge Univ. 96; Camino 96; Canadian Plains Research Center 233; Carolrhoda 98; Catholic Univ. of America 99; Cave 99; Center For Western Studies 279; Charles River 255; Chelsea Green 279; China Books & Periodicals, Inc. 101; Christian Publications, Inc. 102; Christopher Publishing House 280; Citadel Press 103; Clarion 103; Clear Light 103; Colonial Press 280; Consortium 281; Contemporary Books 107; Cool Hand 107; Covenant Communications 281; Creative Arts 281; Creative Spark 270; Cross Cultural 110; Cuff Publications, Harry 234; Da Capo 111; Dan River 111; Dancing Jester 111; Dante Univ. Of America 112; Davidson, Harlan 113; Dawson, W.S. 113; Dee, Ivan R. 114; Discipleship Resources 115; Discus Press 116; Diskotech 256; Dundurn Press 234; Dutton 117; Dutton Children's Books 117; E.M. Press 256; E.M. Press 281; Eakin Press/Sunbelt Media, Inc. 118; Ecco Press 118; ECW Press 234; Edicones Universal 282; Éditions La Liberté 235; Éditions Logiques/Logical Publishing 235; Ekstasis Editions 235; Elliott & Clark 119; Enslow 119; Eriksson, Paul S. 120; Faber & Faber 121; Family Album 256; Fine, Donald I. 122; Fitzhenry & Whiteside 236; Floricanto Press 123; Friends United 125; Gardner Press 282; Gaslight 126; Giniger Co., K S 271; Godine, David R. 127; Goose Lane Editions 236; Grandin 128; Great Ocean 258; Greenleaf Press 129; Guernica Editions 236; Guild Bindery Press 283; Gutter Press 236; Hancock House 131; Harper San Francisco 131; HarperCollins 131; Hastings House 132; Hendrick-Long 133; High Plains 135; Hive 136; HMS Press 237; Hoard & Sons, W.D. 258; Holmes & Meier 136; Homestead 137; Honor Books 284; Horsdale & Schubart 237; Houghton Mifflin 137; Hounslow Press 238; Howells House 137; Huntington House 139; I.A.A.S. Publishers 258; In Print 259; Indiana Historical Society 259; Indiana Historical Society 259; International Publishers 143; Italica Press 144; Jones Univ. Press, Bob 146; Just Us Books 147; Kent State Univ. 147; Kesend Publishing, Ltd., Michael 148; Key Porter Books 238; Kindred Productions 238; Knowledge, Ideas & Trends (KIT) 148; Kodansha America 149; Kregel Publications 149; Laing Communications 272; Lake View Press 149; Lamppost Press 272; Lang, Peter 285; LAWCO Ltd. 259; Lawrence Books, Merloyd 150; Lee & Low 151; Lehigh Univ. Press 151; Lerner 151; Library Research Assoc. 286; Limelight Editions 152; Lion Press 259; Little, Brown 153; Lone Pine 239; Longstreet House 286; Longstreet Press 155; Louisiana State Univ. 155; Loyola Univ. 156; McClelland & Stewart 239; McDonald & Woodward 157; McGuinn & McGuire 158; Macmillan Canada 240; Madison Books 158; Maisonneuve Press 158; Marketscope Books 159; MasterMedia 286; Masters Press 159; Mercury House 160; Mercury Press 240; Mid-List Press 161; Minnesota Historical Society 162; Morrow, William 163; Mosaic Press Miniature Books 260; Mount Olive 287; Mystic Seaport Museum 261; National Press 165; Naval Institute 166; New England Press 167; New Falcon 287; New Victoria 168; Nodin Press 169; North Country 287; Norton Co., W.W. 170; Nova Science 170; Oolichan Books 241; Optimum 241; Orca Book Publishers Ltd. 241; Orchises Press 173; Oregon Historical Society Press 173; Oregon State Univ. 173; Overlook Press 174; Oxford Univ. Press 174; Pandora Press 242; Pantheon Books 175; Paragon House 288; Partners in Publishing 262; Path Press 288; Pauline Books & Media 176; Pelican 177; Pennsylvania Historical and Museum Commission 178; Permanent Press/Second Chance Press, The 178; Pineapple Press 181; Platinum Press 289; Plexus 182; Pocket Books 183; Prep Publishing 183; Press Gang 243; Press of MacDonald & Reinecke 274; Prima 184; Pruett 185; Publicom 274; Purdue Univ. 186; QED Press 187; Quest Books 187; Quill Driver Books/Word Dancer Press 187; Ragged Edge 290;

Random House 188; Random House Of Canada 244; Regnery 189; Republic Of Texas Press 189; Revell, Fleming H. 189; Rhombus 263; Ronsdale Press 245; Royal Fireworks Press 191; Rutgers Univ. Press 191; Rutledge Hill Press 191; Safari Press 192; Sarpedon 193; Schirmer Books 193; Scots Plaid 264; Shoestring Press 246; Shoreline 246; Signature 195; Simon & Schuster 196; Skinner House 196; Soho Press 197; Soho Press 197; Sono Nis 246; Spectrum Press 199; Stoddard Publishing 246; Storm Peak 264; Sunflower Univ. 291; Swedenborg Found. 203; Taylor 204; Tenth Avenue 274; Texas State Historical Association 205; Thunder's Mouth Press 207; Tilbury House 291; Times Books 208; Titan Books 247; Transaction 292; Trilogy Books 209; Tudor Publishers 210; 2M Communications 275; United Church Publishing House 248; Univ. Of Idaho 213; Univ. Of Illinois 213; Univ. of Alabama 212; Univ. of Alaska 212; Univ. of Arkansas, The 213; Univ. of Massachusetts 214; Univ. of Nebraska 215; Univ. of Nevada 215; Univ. of New Mexico 215; Univ. of North Texas 216; Univ. of Pittsburgh 216; Univ. Press of Georgia 292; Univ. Press of Kentucky 218; Univ. Press of Mississippi 218; Univ. Press of New England 218; Utah State Univ. Press 218; Vandamere Press 219; Vanderbilt Univ. Press 219; Vanwell 249; Vehicule Press 250; Virtual Press 292; Vista Publishing Inc. 293; Walker and Co. 221; Ward Hill 221; Washington State Univ. Press 222; Watts, Franklin 222; Wayfinder Press 222; Weatherhill 293; Western Book/Journal 293; Western Tanager 266; Westernlore Press 223; White Cliffs Media 223; Whitecap Books 250; Wilde Publishing 225; Wilderness Adventure 225; Wiley & Sons, John 225; Winch & Associates/Jalmar Press, B.L. 293; Windflower Communications 294; Write Way 227; Ye Galleon 294; Zebra and Pinnacle 228; Zoland Books 228; Zondervan 228.

Business/Economics. Abbott, Langer & Assoc. 70; Adams Publishing 73; Adams-Blake 73; Addicus Books 73; Aegis 253; Allen 74; Almar 74; Amacom 75; America West 76; American Hospital Publishing 78; Ashgate 278; ASQC 82; Atheneum Books For Young Readers 82; Avery 83; Avon 83; Baldwin & Knowlton 84; Bantam 86; Barron's Educational Series, Inc. 86; Benjamin Co., The 269; Berkley Publishing Group, The 88; Betterway 89; BNA 91; Bonus Books 91; Brevet 94; Brighton 94; Business McGraw-Hill 95; Butterworth-Heinemann 95; Cambridge Univ. 96; Canadian Plains Research Center 233; Caradium 97; Career Advancement Center 279; Carol 97; Carswell Thomson 233; Cato Institute 99; Center For Afro-American Studies 255; Cerier Book Development, Alison Brown 270; China Books & Periodicals, Inc. 101; Christopher Publishing House 280; Cleaning Consultant Services 280; Colonial Press 280; Consultant Press 107; Contemporary Books 107; Crisp Publications 110; Cypress 111; Davidson, Harlan 113; Dearborn Financial 113; Desktop Grafx 270; Discus Press 116; Drama Book Publishers 117; Eakin Press/Sunbelt Media, Inc. 118; Eriako Assoc. 271; Eriksson, Paul S. 120; Facts On File 121; Fairleigh Dickinson Univ. 121; Fort Dearborn 124; Forum 124; Gardner Press 282; Garrett 126; Giniger Co., K S 271; Glenbridge 126; Globe Pequot 127; Great Quotations 129; Guild Bindery Press 283; HarperCollins 131; Hastings House 132; Haworth Press 132; Health Administration Press 133; Hive 136; HMS Press 237; Holmes & Meier 136; Honor Books 284; Hounslow Press 238; Howells House 137; HRD Press 138; I.A.A.S. Publishers 258; ILR Press 141; Info Net 284; Insight Books 142; Intercultural Press 142; International Foundation Of Employee Benefit Plans 143; Int'l Information Assoc. 143; International Publishers 143; Int'l Resources 272; Iowa State Univ. Press 144; Jamenair 259; Jewish Lights Publishing 145; Jewish Lights Publishing 145; Jist Works 145; Jist Works 145; Key Porter Books 238; Klein, B. 148; Knowledge, Ideas & Trends (KIT) 148; Kodansha America 149; Kurian Reference Books, George 272; Laing Communications 272; Lang, Peter 285; LAWCO Ltd. 259; Lerner 151; Lexington Books 151; Library Research Assoc. 286; Lifetime Books 152; Lion Books 152; Locust Hill Press 154; Lone Pine 239; Lorimer & Co., James 239; McClelland & Stewart 239; McFarland & Co. 157; McGraw-Hill Companies 157; Macmillan Canada 240; Markowski Int'l 273; MasterMedia 286; Menasha Ridge 273; Metamorphous Press 161; Michaelis Medical 287; Michigan State Univ. 161; Mid-List Press 161; Mosaic Press Miniature Books 260; National Press 165; National Textbook 166; Neal-Schuman 166; New World Library 168; Nova Science 170; Noyes Data 171; NTECHNICAL Publishing Group 171; Oceana 171; Oregon Historical Society Press 173; Oryx Press 173; Oxford Univ. Press 174; Pacific View 262; Paper Chase Press 175; Paradigm 176; Path Press 288; Pax Publishing 262; Pelican 177; PennWell Books 178; Peterson's 179; Peterson's 179; Pfeiffer & Co. 180; Piccadilly Books 180; Pilot Books 181; Planning/Communications 182; PMN Publishing 289; Precept Press 183; Prentice-Hall Canada 243; Prep Publishing 183; Prima 184; Productive Publications 243; PSI Research 186; Publicom 274; QED Press 187; Random House 188; Reed Books Canada 244; Regnery 189; Resolution Business 263; Routledge 190; Roxbury 191; Royal Fireworks Press 191; Russian Information Services 191; Schaum 193; Schenkman 290; Self-Counsel 245; SJL 196; Solution 291; Sourcebooks 198; Starburst 200; Stipes 201; Stoddard Publishing 246; Stone Bridge 201; Stone Bridge 264; Success 202; Sulzburger & Graham 202; Summers Press 202; Sunflower Univ. 291; Systems 204; TAB Books 204; Ten Speed 205; Texas A&M Univ. 205; Third Side Press 207; Thompson Educational 247;

Thorsons 247; Times Books 208; Todd 209; Transaction 292; Tuttle, Charles E. 248; Univ. of Michigan 214; Univ. of Pennsylvania 216; Univ. of Pittsburgh 216; Univ. Press of America 217; Univ. Press of Georgia 292; Verso 250; Visions Communications 266; Vista Publishing Inc. 293; Walch, Publisher, J. Weston 221; Walker and Co. 221; Washington State Univ. Press 222; Weatherhill 293; Weidner & Sons 222; Wheetley Co. 275; Wiley & Sons, John 225; Wilshire Book Co. 226; Zebra and Pinnacle 228.

Child Guidance/Parenting. Active Parenting Publishers 72; Armstrong Publishing Corp. 81; Avery 83; Baker Book House 84; Baldwin & Knowlton 84; Ballantine 85; Bantam 86; Barron's Educational Series, Inc. 86; Blue Bird 89; Bookcraft 92; Cambridge Educational 96; Camino 96; Cerier Book Development, Alison Brown 270; Chicago Review Press 100; Child Welfare League Of America 101; Cline/Fay 104; College Board 105; Compass Productions 270; Concordia 106; Consortium 281; Covenant Communications 281; Creative Spark 270; Discipleship Resources 115; Distinctive Publishing 116; Éditions La Liberté 235; Elder Books 119; EPM 120; Focus on the Family 123; Fort Dearborn 124; Free Spirit 125; Gardner Press 282; Great Quotations 129; Gylantic 130; Harvard Common 131; Health Communications 133; Hensley, Virgil 134; Herald Press Canada 237; HMS Press 237; Home Education Press 137; Honor Books 284; Hounslow Press 238; Human Services Institute 138; Humanics Publishing 138; I.A.A.S. Publishers 258; Insight Books 142; Interlink Publishing Group 142; ones Publishing 146; Lamppost Press 272; Lawrence Books, Merloyd 150; Learning Works 150; Lexington Books 151; Lifetime Books 152; Love and Logic Press, Inc. 155; Luramedia 156; McBooks 260; McClelland & Stewart 239; Marketscope Books 159; Marlor Press 159; MasterMedia 286; Mayfield 159; Meadowbrook Press 160; Michaelis Medical 287; Mills & Sanderson 260; National Press 165; Neal-Schuman 166; New Harbinger 167; New Hope 167; Nova Science 170; Optimum 241; Our Child 262; Ozark 175; Pauline Books & Media 176; Peterson's 179; Phi Delta Kappa Educational Foundation 180; Publicom 274; Purple Finch 263; Reed Books Canada 244; Revell, Fleming H. 189; Royal Fireworks Press 191; St. John's Publishing 264; Shaw, Harold 195; Sourcebooks 198; Starburst 200; Stoddard Publishing 246; Student College Aid Publishing Division 265; Sulzburger & Graham 202; Summit 202; Taylor 204; Times Books 208; Tudor Publishers 210; 2M Communications 275; Tyndale House Publishers 210; Vandamere Press 219; Victor Books 219; Volcano Press 266; Walker and Co. 221; Warren 221; Waterfront Books 266; Weidner & Sons 222; Westport Publishers, Inc. 223; Wheetley Co. 275; Whitecap Books 250; Wiley & Sons, John 225; Williamson 225; Winch & Associates/Jalmar Press, B.L. 293.

Coffeetable Book. Alpine 75; American & World Geographic 76; Bentley, Robert 88; Bookcraft 92; Brassey's 93; Bridge Publishing 278; Caxton 99; Center For Western Studies 279; CFC Productions 255; China Books & Periodicals, Inc. 101; Chronicle 102; Clear Light 103; Countrysport Press 109; Dancing Jester 111; Dorling Kindersley 116; Down The Shore 256; Dundurn Press 234; Ecco Press 118; Éditions Logiques/Logical Publishing 235; Elliott & Clark 119; Epicenter Press 119; Eriako Assoc. 271; Flower Valley 257; Fort Dearborn 124; Giniger Co., K S 271; Godine, David R. 127; Guild Bindery Press 283; Harian Creative Books 283; Harmony House 283; Hastings House 132; Herald Press Canada 237; Hiller Box Manufacturing 271; Homestead 137; Honor Books 284; Hounslow Press 238; ICS Books, Inc. 139; Interlink Publishing Group 142; Key Porter Books 238; Laing Communications 272; Lark Books 149; Layla Productions 272; Longstreet Press 155; McBooks 260; McClelland & Stewart 239; McDonald & Woodward 157; Michaelis Medical 287; Minnesota Historical Society 162; Mount Olive 287; Natural Heritage/Natural Heritage 240; North Country 287; NorthWord Press 170; Optimum 241; Pelican 177; Pendaya 262; Pincushion Press 289; Raincoast Book Distribution 244; Reed Books Canada 244; Revell, Fleming H. 189; Schiffer 193; Stoddard Publishing 246; Texas State Historical Association 205; Texas Tech Univ. 206; 2M Communications 275; Viking Studio Books 220; Voyageur Press 220; Weatherhill 293; Whitecap Books 250; Wieser & Wieser 275; Wilde Publishing 225.

Communications. Baywood 86; Butterworth-Heinemann 95; Computer Science Press 106; Mayfield 159; Mayfield 159; Michigan State Univ. 161; Oak Knoll Press 171; Paradigm 176; TAB Books 204; Tiare 208; Univelt, Inc. 212; Univ. of Alabama 212; Wadsworth 220.

Community/Public Affairs. Houghton Mifflin 137; Kumarian Press 285; Madison Books 158; Pfeiffer & Co. 180; Univ. of Alabama 212; Univ. of Massachusetts 214; Univ. of Nevada 215; Watts, Franklin 222.

Computers/Electronic. Adams-Blake 73; Amacom 75; Baywood 86; Branden. 93; Butterworth-Heinemann 95; Career 97; Carol 97; Computer Science Press 106; Consumertronics-Top Secret 107; CSLI Publications, Stanford Univ. 110; Cypress 111; Desktop Grafx 270; Duke Press 117; Eckert & Co., J.K. 270; Éditions Logiques/Logical Publishing 235; Fort Dearborn 124; Gleason Group 271; Grapevine 128; HMS Press 237; Hollow Earth 136; Index Publishing Group 141; Jamenair 259; Jewish Lights Publishing 145; Jewish Lights Publishing 145; Laing Communications

272; Lerner 151; McGraw-Hill Companies 157; MasterMedia 286; Mayhaven 286; MIS Press 162; Neal-Schuman 166; North Light 169; Nova Science 170; Noyes Data 171; One On One Computer Training 172; Oxford Univ. Press 174; Paradigm 176; Peachpit Press 177; PROMPT Publications 185; PSI Research 186; Resolution Business 263; Royal Fireworks Press 191; San Francisco Press 192; Schaum 193; Serendipity Systems 194; SJL 196; Sulzburger & Graham 202; Sybex 203; Systemsware 265; TAB Books 204; Teachers College 204; Thorson & Assoc. 275; Tiare 208; Virtual Press 292; Visions Communications 266; Waite Group 220; Walch, Publisher, J. Weston 221; Weidner & Sons 222; Wheetley Co. 275; White Cliffs Media 223; Wilde Publishing 225; Wiley & Sons, John 225; Williamson 225; Wilshire Book Co. 226.

Consumer Affairs. Almar 74; Benjamin Co., The 269; Consumer Reports Books 107; International Foundation Of Employee Benefit Plans 143; Oryx Press 173.

Cooking/Foods/Nutrition. Absey & Co. 70; Alaska Northwest 73; Arcade Publishing 80; Archives Publications 80; Archives Publications 80; Atheneum Books For Young Readers 82; Avery 83; Ballantine 85; Bantam 86; Barron's Educational Series, Inc. 86; Benjamin Co., The 269; Bergh 88; Berkley Publishing Group, The 88; Berkshire House 88; Blue Dolphin 90; Bonus Books 91; Briarcliff Press 278; Bright Mountain 254; Bristol 94; Caitlin Press 232; Cambridge Educational 96; Camino 96; Carol 97; Cassandra Press 98; Cerier Book Development, Alison Brown 270; Chapelle 270; China Books & Periodicals, Inc. 101; Christopher Publishing House 280; Chronicle 102; Clear Light 103; Colonial Press 280; Contemporary Books 107; Cool Hand 107; Countryman Press 109; Countrywoman's Press 270; Creative Book 109; Crossing Press 110; Dancing Jester 111; David, Jonathan 112; Dawn 113; Discus Press 116; Discus Press 116; Dorling Kindersley 116; Eakin Press/Sunbelt Media, Inc. 118; Ecco Press 118; Edicones Universal 282; Éditions La Liberté 235; Éditions Logiques/Logical Publishing 235; EPM 120; Eriksson, Paul S. 120; Evans and Co., M. 120; Explorer's Guide 120; Facts On File 121; Fiesta City 257; Filter Press 257; Fine, Donald I. 122; Fisher 123; Floricanto Press 123; Fort Dearborn 124; Four Walls Eight Windows 124; Glenbridge 126; Globe Pequot 127; Godine, David R. 127; Harian Creative Books 283; Harmony House 283; HarperCollins 131; Harvard Common 131; Hastings House 132; Hawkes 283; Haworth Press 132; Herald Press Canada 237; Hiller Box Manufacturing 271; HMS Press 237; Hoffman Press 258; Hounslow Press 238; Howell Press 137; Humanics Publishing 138; ICS Books, Inc. 139; Info Net 284; Interlink Publishing Group 142; Interweave Press 144; Iowa State Univ. Press 144; Jewish Lights Publishing 145; Jewish Lights Publishing 145; Key Porter Books 238; Kodansha America 149; Lamppost Press 272; Lark Books 149; Layla Productions 272; Lerner 151; Lifetime Books 152; Little, Brown, Children's Book Division 152; Little, Brown 153; Longstreet Press 155; Lyons & Burford, Publishers, Inc. 156; McBooks 260; McClelland & Stewart 239; Macmillan Canada 240; Maverick 159; Mayhaven 286; Media Bridge 160; Menasha Ridge 273; Meyerbooks 260; Michaelis Medical 287; Minnesota Historical Society 162; Morrow, William 163; Mosaic Press Miniature Books 260; Mount Olive 287; National Press 165; New World Library 168; Northland 169; Nova Science 170; Optimum 241; Parachute Press, Inc. 273; Peachtree 177; PigOut Publications 263; Platinum Press 289; Pocket Books 183; Pollard Press 263; Prentice-Hall Canada 243; Prima 184; Pruett 185; Purple Finch 263; Ragged Mountain Press 187; Raincoast Book Distribution 244; Raincoast Book Distribution 244; Random House 188; Random House Of Canada 244; RedBrick Press 263; Reed Books Canada 244; Republic Of Texas Press 189; Rutledge Hill Press 191; Shoestring Press 246; SJL 196; Starburst 200; Story Communications/Garden Way 201; Summit 202; Systems 204; Ten Speed 205; Tidewater 208; Times Books 208; Tudor Publishers 210; Tuttle, Charles E. 292; Tuttle, Charles E. 248; Two Lane 265; 2M Communications 275; Univ. of North Carolina 215; Viking Studio Books 220; Voyageur Press 220; Warren 221; Weatherhill 293; Westport Publishers, Inc. 223; Wheetley Co. 275; Whitecap Books 250; Wieser & Wieser 275; Williamson 225; Woodbridge Press 227.

Counseling/Career Guidance. Adams Publishing 73; Advocacy Press 253; Almar 74; American Counseling 77; Career 97; Dorling Kindersley 116; Ferguson, J.G. 257; Flores, J. 123; Graduate Group 283; Jamenair 259; Jist Works 145; Markowski Int'l 273; Morehouse 163; NASW Press 165; National Textbook 166; Octameron 171; Peterson's 179; Pilot Books 181; Planning/Communications 182; Resource Publications 290; Rosen 190; Shaw, Harold 195; Starburst 200; Teachers College 204; Vandamere Press 219.

Crafts. Barron's Educational Series, Inc. 86; Briarcliff Press 278; Chapelle 270; Countrywoman's Press 270; Davis Publications 113; Down East 117; Eagle's View 118; Interweave Press 144; Kodansha America 149; Lark Books 149; Learning Works 150; Naturegraph 261; North Light 169; Owl Books 273; Stackpole Books 199; Standard 200; Sterling 200; Story Communications/Garden Way 201; Sunstone Press 203; Tenth Avenue 274.

Educational. ABC-CLIO 70; Absey & Co. 70; ACA Books 71; Accent Publications 71; Active Parenting Publishers 72; African American Images 73; Amacom 75; American Catholic Press 253;

American Counseling 77; Anchorage Press 79; Armstrong Publishing Corp. 81; ASQC 82; Baldwin & Knowlton 84; Barron's Educational Series, Inc. 86; Baywood 86; Benjamin Co., The 269; Blue Bird 89; Blue Dolphin 90; Caddo Gap 96; Cambridge Educational 96; Canadian Inst. of Ukrainian Studies 233; Carol 97; Cato Institute 99; Charles River 255; Chicago Review Press 100; Church Growth 102; Cline/Fay 104; College Board 105; Colonial Press 280; Comic Art 105; Communication/Therapy 106; Compass Productions 270; Consortium 281; Corwin Press 108; Cottonwood Press 108; Creative Spark 270; Crisp Publications 110; Dancing Jester 111; Davidson, Harlan 113; Davis Publications 113; Denison & Co., T.S. 115; Discipleship Resources 115; Discovery Enterprises 281; Discus Press 116; Distinctive Publishing 116; Duquesne Univ. Press 117; Éditions La Liberté 235; Education Center 118; Elder Books 119; EPM 120; ETC 120; Fitzhenry & Whiteside 236; Fort Dearborn 124; Free Spirit 125; Front Row Experience 257; Gardner Press 282; Great Ocean 258; Greenleaf Press 129; Group Publishing 129; Gryphon House Inc. 258; Gutter Press 236; Harcourt Brace Jovanovich Canada 237; Harian Creative Books 283; Harmony House 283; Hay House 132; Health Press 133; Herald Press Canada 237; Highsmith Press 135; Hiller Box Manufacturing 271; HMS Press 237; Home Education Press 137; Howells House 137; Humanics Publishing 138; Hunter House 139; I.A.A.S. Publishers 258; Insight Books 142; Intercultural Press 142; Interstate 285; Jamenair 259; Kent State Univ. 147; Kurian Reference Books, George 272; Leadership Publishers 150; Learning Works 150; Lifetime Books 152; Love and Logic Press, Inc. 155; McClelland & Stewart 239; Maisonneuve Press 158; Masefield 260; Media Bridge 160; Meriwether 161; Metamorphous Press 161; Michaelis Medical 287; Milkweed Editions 162; Modern Language Association of America 162; Morehouse 163; Mount Olive 287; Natural Heritage/Natural Heritage 240; Naturegraph 261; Neal-Schuman 166; Negative Capability 166; New Falcon 287; New Hope 167; New Society 168; Noble Press 169; Nova Press 170; Nova Science 170; Octameron 171; Oise Press 241; Open Court 172; Oryx Press 173; Ozark 175; Pacific Educational Press 242; Paideia Press 262; Partners in Publishing 262; Path Press 288; Pax Publishing 262; Peguis 242; Peterson's 179; Pfeiffer & Co. 180; Phi Delta Kappa Educational Foundation 180; Planning/Communications 182; Pollard Press 263; Prakken 183; PSI Research 186; Publicom 274; Purple Finch 263; Quarry Press 243; Reference Service Press 188; Regnery 189; Reidmore Books 244; Religious Education Press 189; Resource Publications 290; Routledge 190; Royal Fireworks Press 191; Rutgers Univ. Press 191; Schenkman 290; Scholastic Professional Books 194; Shoreline 246; Silver Moon 274; Social Science Education Consortium 197; Span Press 198; Speech Bin 199; Standard 200; Starburst 200; Sugar Hill 265; Sulzburger & Graham 202; TAB Books 204; Teachers College 204; Third World Press 207; Thompson Educational 247; Tudor Publishers 210; UCLA-American Indian Studies Center 266; Univ. Of Montreal 249; Univ. of Alaska 212; Univ. of Ottawa 249; Univ. Press of America 217; Univ. Press of Georgia 292; Vandamere Press 219; Vanderbilt Univ. Press 219; Verso 250; Walch, Publisher, J. Weston 221; Wall & Emerson 250; Warren 221; Waterfront Books 266; Weidner & Sons 222; Wheetley Co. 275; White Cliffs Media 223; Wilde Publishing 225; Winch & Associates/Jalmar Press, B.L. 293.

Entertainment/Games. Baseline II 86; Borgo Press 92; Broadway 95; Cardoza 97; Chess Enterprises 100; Citadel Press 103; Devyn Press 115; Drama Book Publishers 117; Faber & Faber 121; Facts On File 121; Focal Press 123; McFarland & Co. 157; Speech Bin 199; Standard 200; Sterling 200; Univ. of Nevada 215.

Ethnic. African American Images 73; Alaska Northwest 73; Arsenal Pulp 229; Avanyu 83; Beacon 87; Black Ball 254; Blackbirch Graphics 269; Bowling Green State Univ. 92; Calyx Books 254; Camino 96; Canadian Inst. of Ukrainian Studies 233; Carol 97; Center For Afro-American Studies 255; Center For Western Studies 279; Charles River 255; China Books & Periodicals, Inc. 101; Clarity Press 255; Clear Light 103; Colonial Press 280; Confluence Press 107; Covenant Communications 281; Creative Book 109; Creative Spark 270; Dancing Jester 111; Davidson, Harlan 113; Denali Press 114; Discipleship Resources 115; Discus Press 116; Eagle's View 118; Eakin Press/Sunbelt Media, Inc. 118; Eriako Assoc. 271; Evras Press 256; Fairleigh Dickinson Univ. 121; Feminist Press at the City Univ. of NY 122; Filter Press 257; Fitzhenry & Whiteside 236; Floricanto Press 123; Fort Dearborn 124; Guernica Editions 236; Herald Press 134; Herald Press Canada 237; HMS Press 237; Holmes & Meier 136; Humanics Publishing 138; Hunter House 139; Hyperion Press, 238; I.A.A.S. Publishers 258; Indiana Univ. 141; Inner Traditions Int'l 142; Insight Books 142; Interlink Publishing Group 142; International Publishers 143; Italica Press 144; Judson Press 146; Just Us Books 147; Kar-Ben Copies 147; Knowledge, Ideas & Trends (KIT) 148; Kodansha America 149; Kurian Reference Books, George 272; Learning Works 150; Lee & Low 151; Lerner 151; Lincoln Springs 259; Lion Books 152; Little, Brown, Children's Book Division 152; Locust Hill Press 154; Louisiana State Univ. 155; Luramedia 156; McDonald & Woodward 157; Maisonneuve Press 158; Maverick 159; Media Bridge 160; Mercury House 160; Michigan State Univ. 161; Middle Passage 260; Millbrook Press 162; Minnesota Historical Society 162; Natural Heritage/

Natural Heritage 240; Naturegraph 261; Netherlandic Press 240; New World Library 168; NeWest 240; Noble Press 169; Nodin Press 169; Oolichan Books 241; Oregon Historical Society Press 173; Pacific Educational Press 242; Pacific View 262; Path Press 288; Pelican 177; Polychrome 183; Pruett 185; Purich Publishing 243; Reference Service Press 188; Reidmore Books 244; Routledge 190; Royal Fireworks Press 191; Rutgers Univ. Press 191; Salina Bookshelf 192; Scots Plaid 264; Shoestring Press 246; Shoreline 246; Span Press 198; Spectrum Press 199; Stanford Univ. Press 200; Sunflower Univ. 291; Texas Tech Univ. 206; Theosophical Publishing House 206; Third World Press 207; Three Continents Press 207; Tilbury House 291; Todd 209; 2M Communications 275; Tyrone Press, The 211; UCLA-American Indian Studies Center 266; Univ. Of Idaho 213; Univ. of Alaska 212; Univ. of Arizona 212; Univ. of California Los Angeles Center for Afro-American Studies Publications 266; Univ. of Manitoba 249; Univ. of Massachusetts 214; Univ. of Michigan 214; Univ. of Nebraska 215; Univ. of Nevada 215; Univ. of New Mexico 215; Univ. of North Texas 216; Univ. of Oklahoma 216; Univ. of Pittsburgh 216; Univ. of Tennessee 217; Univ. of Texas 217; Univ. Press of America 217; Univ. Press of Georgia 292; Univ. Press of Mississippi 218; Warren 221; Washington State Univ. Press 222; Weigl Educational 250; White Cliffs Media 223; White Pine 224; Williamson 225; Windflower Communications 294.

Feminism. Feminist Press at the City Univ. of NY 122; Firebrand 122; New Victoria 168; Pandora Press 242; Publishers Assoc. 186; Publishers Assoc. 186; Spinsters Ink 199; Times Change 265; Vehicule Press 250.

Film/Cinema/Stage. Ardsley House Publishers, Inc. 81; Baseline II 86; Borgo Press 92; Broadway 95; Chicago Plays 100; Citadel Press 103; Dee, Ivan R. 114; Drama Book Publishers 117; Fairleigh Dickinson Univ. 121; Focal Press 123; French, Samuel 125; Gaslight 126; Guernica Editions 236; Indiana Univ. 141; Knowledge Industry 148; Limelight Editions 152; Lone Eagle 154; McFarland & Co. 157; Mayfield 159; Mayfield 159; Meriwether 161; Overlook Press 174; Piccadilly Books 180; Players Press 182; Scarecrow Press 193; Schirmer Books 193; Teachers College 204; Titan Books 247; Univ. of Texas 217; Univ. Press of America 217; Vestal Press 219.

Gardening. Briarcliff Press 278; Camino 96; Chelsea Green 279; Chicago Review Press 100; China Books & Periodicals, Inc. 101; Chronicle 102; Countrywoman's Press 270; Discus Press 116; Dorling Kindersley 116; Elliott & Clark 119; EPM 120; Fisher 123; Fort Dearborn 124; Globe Pequot 127; Godine, David R. 127; Graber Productions 271; Hartley & Marks 131; Hay House 132; Herbal Studies 258; HMS Press 237; Holmes & Meier 136; Howell Press 137; Interlink Publishing Group 142; Interweave Press 144; Jones Univ. Press, Bob 146; Kodansha America 149; Lamppost Press 272; Lark Books 149; Layla Productions 272; Lone Pine 239; Longstreet Press 155; Lyons & Burford, Publishers, Inc. 156; McClelland & Stewart 239; Naturegraph 261; Optimum 241; Ortho Information Services 173; Peachtree 177; Peter Pauper Press 179; Pineapple Press 181; Random House Of Canada 244; Reed Books Canada 244; Sierra Club 195; SJL 196; Stackpole Books 199; Starburst 200; Sterling 200; Stoddard Publishing 246; Story Communications/Garden Way 201; Taylor 204; Ten Speed 205; Timber Press 208; Univ. of North Carolina 215; Van Patten 266; Viking Studio Books 220; Warren 221; Weatherhill 293; Weidner & Sons 222; Whitecap Books 250; Wieser & Wieser 275; Williamson 225; Windward 226; Woodbridge Press 227.

Gay/Lesbian. Alyson 75; Arsenal Pulp 229; Baldwin & Knowlton 84; Bantam 86; Beacon 87; Calyx Books 254; Carol 97; Cleis Press 104; Crossing Press 110; Da Capo 111; Dancing Jester 111; Feminist Press at the City Univ. of NY 122; Firebrand 122; Fort Dearborn 124; Gay Sunshine Press and Leyland Publications 126; Gutter Press 236; Gylantic 130; Harper San Francisco 131; Haworth Press 132; HMS Press 237; Hunter House 139; Ide House 140; Insight Books 142; Lexington Books 151; Liberal Press 152; Little, Brown, Children's Book Division 152; McClelland & Stewart 239; Madwoman Press 260; Maisonneuve Press 158; Mercury House 160; Monument Press 163; Neal-Schuman 166; New Falcon 287; New Victoria 168; Oxford Univ. Press 174; Paradigm 288; Press Gang 243; Publishers Assoc. 186; Quarry Press 243; Rising Tide 190; Routledge 190; Rutgers Univ. Press 191; Skinner House 196; Spectrum Press 199; Starbooks Press 291; Third Side Press 207; 2M Communications 275; Univ. of Michigan 214; Viking Studio Books 220; Volcano Press 266; Wiley & Sons, John 225.

General Nonfiction. American Atheist 76; Arcade Publishing 80; Asian Humanities Press 82; Avon Flare 84; B&B 268; Beacon 87; Beil, Frederic C. 87; Biddle 254; Brett Books 254; Charles River 255; Delancey Press 255; Dell Publishers 114; Dutton 117; Evans and Co., M. 120; Fawcett Juniper 122; Glenbridge 126; Harcourt Brace 131; Haworth Press 132; Houghton Mifflin 137; Index Publishing Group 141; Indiana Univ. 141; Inverted-A 259; Johnson Books 146; Kent State Univ. 147; Knopf, Alfred A. 148; Lang, Peter 285; Leisure Books 151; Lothrop, Lee & Shepard 155; Marlor Press 159; Mills & Sanderson 260; Morrow, William 163; New England Publishing Assoc. 273; Norton Co., W.W. 170; Pantheon Books 175; Peachtree 177; Pocket Books 183; Potentials Developments Inc. 263; Quill Driver Books/Word Dancer Press 187; Republic Of Texas

Press 189; Scholastic 194; Sierra Club 195; Silvercat 264; Starburst 200; Taylor 204; Tiare 208; Time-Life Books 208; Tyrone Press, The 211; Univ. of Calgary 249; Verso 250; Villard Books 220; Writer's Digest Books 227.

Gift Books. American & World Geographic 76; Bell Tower 87; Blue Dolphin 90; Carol 97; Chronicle 102; Commune-A-Key 105; Elder Books 119; Epicenter Press 119; EPM 120; Fort Dearborn 124; Health Communications 133; ICS Books, Inc. 139; Jewish Lights Publishing 145; Morehouse 163; Natural Heritage/Natural Heritage 240; New World Library 168; Oldbuck Press 171; Papier-Mache Press 176; Peachtree 177; Peter Pauper Press 179; Quarry Press 243; Raincoat Book Distribution 244; Reed Books Canada 244; Sibyl 195; Sourcebooks 198; Summit 202; Viking Studio Books 220.

Government/Politics. ABC-CLIO 70; ACA Books 71; Acropolis South 72; America West 76; American Atheist 76; Arcade Publishing 80; Ashgate 278; ASQC 82; Atheneum Books For Young Readers 82; Avon 83; Bantam 86; Bergh 88; Black Ball 254; Bliss 254; Bonus Books 91; Borealis Press 232; Borgo Press 92; Branden. 93; Brassey's 93; Bucknell Univ. 95; Business McGraw-Hill 95; C Q Inc. 95; C Q Press 95; Camino 96; Canadian Inst. of Ukrainian Studies 233; Canadian Plains Research Center 233; Caratzas, Aristide D. 279; Carol 97; Catholic Univ. of America 99; Cato Institute 99; Center For Afro-American Studies 255; China Books & Periodicals, Inc. 101; Christopher Publishing House 280; Cleis Press 104; Colonial Press 280; Consumertronics-Top Secret 107; Creative Spark 270; Cross Cultural 110; Cuff Publications, Harry 234; Da Capo 111; Dancing Jester 111; Davidson, Harlan 113; Dee, Ivan R. 114; Denali Press 114; Discus Press 116; Dutton 117; Ecco Press 118; Edicones Universal 282; Éditions La Liberté 235; Ekstasis Editions 235; Eriksson, Paul S. 120; Fairleigh Dickinson Univ. 121; Feminist Press at the City Univ. of NY 122; Fort Dearborn 124; Four Walls Eight Windows 124; Glenbridge 126; Guernica Editions 236; Gutter Press 236; HarperCollins 131; Health Administration Press 133; HMS Press 237; Horsdale & Schubart 237; Howells House 137; Humanities Press 138; Humanities Press Int'l 284; Huntington House 139; I.A.A.S. Publishers 258; ICS Books, Inc. 139; Ide House 140; ILR Press 141; Indiana Univ. 141; Insight Books 142; Intercultural Press 142; Interlink Publishing Group 142; International Publishers 143; Key Porter Books 238; Kurian Reference Books, George 272; Lake View Press 149; Lang, Peter 285; Lerner 151; Liberal Press 152; Library Research Assoc. 286; Lincoln Springs 259; Lion Books 152; Lone Pine 239; Loompanics 155; Lorimer & Co., James 239; Louisiana State Univ. 155; McClelland & Stewart 239; Maisonneuve Press 158; Masefield 260; MasterMedia 286; Mercury House 160; Mercury Press 240; Michigan State Univ. 161; Milkweed Editions 162; Millbrook Press 162; Monument Press 163; National Press 165; Neal-Schuman 166; Nelson-Hall 167; New Falcon 287; NeWest 240; Noble Press 169; Northern Illinois Univ. 169; Nova Science 170; Oolichan Books 241; Oregon Historical Society Press 173; Oryx Press 173; Oxford Univ. Press 174; Pantheon Books 175; Path Press 288; Pelican 177; Pennsylvania Historical and Museum Commission 178; Planners Press 181; Planning/Communications 182; Prentice-Hall Canada 243; Prima 184; Publishers Assoc. 186; Purdue Univ. 186; Purich Publishing 243; Rawhide Western 188; Reed Books Canada 244; Regnery 189; Reidmore Books 244; Republic Of Texas Press 189; Rhombus 263; Routledge 190; Rutgers Univ. Press 191; Sachem Publishing Assoc. 274; Sarpedon 193; Schaum 193; Shoestring Press 246; SJL 196; Social Science Education Consortium 197; Solution 291; Spectrum Press 199; Stanford Univ. Press 200; Stoddard Publishing 246; Stone Bridge 201; Summit 202; Sunflower Univ. 291; Teachers College 204; Temple 205; Third World Press 207; Thompson Educational 247; Thunder's Mouth Press 207; Transaction 292; Tuttle, Charles E. 248; UCLA-American Indian Studies Center 266; Univ. Of Illinois 213; Univ. of Alabama 212; Univ. of Alabama 212; Univ. of Alaska 212; Univ. of Arkansas, The 213; Univ. of Michigan 214; Univ. of Missouri 215; Univ. of North Carolina 215; Univ. of North Texas 216; Univ. of Ottawa 249; Univ. of Pittsburgh 216; Univ. Press of America 217; Univ. Press of Mississippi 218; Univ. Press of New England 218; Utah State Univ. Press 218; Vanderbilt Univ. Press 219; Vehicule Press 250; Verso 250; Vista Publications 266; Walch, Publisher, J. Weston 221; Washington State Univ. Press 222; Watts, Franklin 222; Wayfinder Press 222; Weatherhill 293; Western Book/Journal 293; Wheetley Co. 275; Wilde Publishing 225; Wiley & Sons, John 225; Write Way 227; Abbott, Langer & Assoc. 70; Baywood 86; BNA 91; Brevet 94; Drama Book Publishers 117; Hamilton Institute, Alexander 130; Health Administration Press 133; ILR Press 141; Intercultural Press 142; International Publishers 143; Jewish Lights Publishing 145; Pfeiffer & Co. 180; Temple 205

Health/Medicine. Abelexpress 252; Acropolis South 72; Adams-Blake 73; Addicus Books 73; Almar 74; America West 76; American Counseling 77; American Hospital Publishing 78; ASQC 82; Atheneum Books For Young Readers 82; Avery 83; Avon 83; Baldwin & Knowlton 84; Ballantine 85; Bantam 86; Barron's Educational Series, Inc. 86; Baywood 86; Benjamin Co., The 269; Berkley Publishing Group, The 88; Blackbirch Press 89; Blue Dolphin 90; Blue Poppy 90; Bonus Books 91; Branden. 93; Briarcliff Press 278; Butterworth-Heinemann 95; Cambridge Educational

96; Cambridge Univ. 96; Cardoza 97; Carol 97; Cassandra Press 98; Cato Institute 99; Cerier Book Development, Alison Brown 270; Charles Press 279; Christopher Publishing House 280; Chronicle 102; Cleaning Consultant Services 280; Cline/Fay 104; Commune-A-Key 105; Consortium 281; Consumer Reports Books 107; Consumertronics-Top Secret 107; Contemporary Books 107; Cool Hand 107; Crisp Publications 110; Crossing Press 110; Dawn 113; Discus Press 116; Distinctive Publishing 116; Dorling Kindersley 116; E.M. Press 281; Eastland Press 118; Elder Books 119; Elysium Growth 119; Eriksson, Paul S. 120; Evans and Co., M. 120; Facts On File 121; Feminist Press at the City Univ. of NY 122; Ferguson, J.G. 257; Fisher 123; Floricanto Press 123; Fort Dearborn 124; Free Spirit 125; Gardner Press 282; Giniger Co., K S 271; Government Institutes 127; Graber Productions 271; Gylantic 130; Hampton Roads 283; HarperCollins 131; Hartley & Marks 131; Hastings House 132; Hawkes 283; Haworth Press 132; Hay House 132; Health Administration Press 133; Health Press 133; Henry, Joseph 134; Herbal Studies 258; HMS Press 237; Hounslow Press 238; Humanics Publishing 138; Hunter House 139; I.A.A.S. Publishers 258; ICS Books, Inc. 139; Idyll Arbor 140; Information Resources 141; Inner Traditions Int'l 142; Insight Books 142; International Foundation Of Employee Benefit Plans 143; Int'l Information Assoc. 143; International Medical 143; Ivy League 259; Jewish Lights Publishing 145; Jones Univ. Press, Bob 146; Kesend Publishing, Ltd., Michael 148; Key Porter Books 238; Kumarian Press 285; Laing Communications 272; Lamppost Press 272; Lawrence Books, Merloyd 150; Learning Works 150; Lerner 151; Lifetime Books 152; Llewellyn 153; Love and Logic Press, Inc. 155; Luramedia 156; McClelland & Stewart 239; McFarland & Co. 157; Macmillan Canada 240; MacMurray & Beck 158; Maradia Press 260; Marcus Books 240; Marketscope Books 159; Markowski Int'l 159; Markowski Int'l 273; MasterMedia 286; Masters Press 159; Mayfield 159; Metamorphous Press 161; Meyerbooks 260; Michaelis Medical 287; Mid-List Press 161; Millbrook Press 162; Monument Press 163; Mosaic Press Miniature Books 260; NASW Press 165; Natural Heritage/ Natural Heritage 240; Naturegraph 261; Neal-Schuman 166; Negative Capability 166; New Falcon 287; New Harbinger 167; New Joy Press 261; New Readers Press 168; Nova Science 170; Olson & Co., C. 261; Optimum 241; Oryx Press 173; Oxford Univ. Press 174; Pacific View 262; Parthenon Publishing Group 288; Pax Publishing 262; Pelican 177; PennWell Books 178; Perspectives Press 179; Platinum Press 289; Plenum 182; Popular Medicine 263; Precept Press 183; Prentice-Hall Canada 243; Press Gang 243; Prima 184; Productive Publications 243; QED Press 187; Quest Books 187; Random House 188; Regnery 189; Rocky Top 190; Rutgers Univ. Press 191; San Francisco Press 192; Skidmore-Roth Publishing, Inc. 290; Slack 197; Society 197; Southern Methodist Univ. 198; Speech Bin 199; Starburst 200; Sterling 200; Stillpoint 200; Stoddard Publishing 246; Storm Peak 264; Sulzberger & Graham 202; Summit 202; Sunflower Univ. 291; Swan-Raven & Co. 203; Systems 204; Taylor 204; Temple 205; Ten Speed 205; Texas Tech Univ. 206; Theosophical Publishing House 206; Third Side Press 207; Third World Press 207; Thorsons 247; Times Books 208; Todd 209; Transaction 292; Tuttle, Charles E. 292; 2M Communications 275; Ulysses Press 211; Unity Books 211; Univ. Of Montreal 249; Univ. of Alaska 212; Univ. of Pittsburgh 216; Vanderbilt Univ. Press 219; Viking Studio Books 220; Vista Publishing Inc. 293; Volcano Press 266; Walch, Publisher, J. Weston 221; Walker and Co. 221; Wall & Emerson 250; Waterfront Books 266; Weidner & Sons 222; Weiser, Inc., Samuel 223; Westport Publishers, Inc. 223; Wheetley Co. 275; Wilde Publishing 225; Wiley & Sons, John 225; Williamson 225; Woodbine House 227; Woodbridge Press 227; Woodland Health Books 227; WRS 228; YMAA Publication Center 267; Zebra and Pinnacle 228.

Hi-Lo. Cambridge Educational 96; National Textbook 166; New Readers Press 168.

History. ABC-CLIO 70; Academy Chicago 71; Accord Communications 72; African American Images 73; Alaska Northwest 73; American Atheist 76; Ancestry Inc. 79; Appalachian Mountain Club Books 79; Arcade Publishing 80; Architectural Book Publishing Co., Inc. 80; Arden Press Inc. 81; Ardsley House Publishers, Inc. 81; Aronson, Inc., Jason 81; Arsenal Pulp 229; Atheneum Books For Young Readers 82; Avanyu 83; Avery 83; Avon 83; Aztex 84; Baldwin & Knowlton 84; Bandanna 85; B&B 85; Beachway Press 254; Bear Flag 269; Beil, Frederic C. 87; Berkshire House 88; Black Ball 254; Blackbirch Press 89; Bookcraft 92; Borgo Press 92; Boston Mills Press 232; Bowling Green State Univ. 92; Boxwood Press 278; Branden. 93; Brassey's 93; Brevet 94; Bright Mountain 254; Bucknell Univ. 95; Caitlin Press 232; Cambridge Univ. 96; Cambridge Univ. 96; Camino 96; Canadian Inst. of Ukrainian Studies 233; Canadian Plains Research Center 233; Caratzas, Aristide D. 279; Carol 97; Carolrhoda 98; Catholic Univ. of America 99; Cave 99; Center For Afro-American Studies 255; Center For Western Studies 279; Charles River 255; Chicago Review Press 100; China Books & Periodicals, Inc. 101; Christopher Publishing House 280; Citadel Press 103; Clarion 103; Clear Light 103; Colonial Press 280; Confluence Press 107; Countryman Press 109; Creative Spark 270; Cross Cultural 110; Crossway 110; Cuff Publications, Harry 234; Da Capo 111; Dante Univ. Of America 112; Davidson, Harlan 113; Dawson, W.S. 113; Dee, Ivan

R. 114; Denali Press 114; Discipleship Resources 115; Discovery Enterprises 281; Discus Press 116; Down East 117; Down The Shore 256; Drama Book Publishers 117; Dundurn Press 234; Dutton Children's Books 117; Eagle's View 118; Eakin Press/Sunbelt Media, Inc. 118; Ecco Press 118; Éditions La Liberté 235; Eerdmans, William B. 282; Elliott & Clark 119; EPM 120; Eriksson, Paul S. 120; Excalibur Publications 256; Faber & Faber 121; Facts On File 121; Fairleigh Dickinson Univ. 121; Family Album 256; Feminist Press at the City Univ. of NY 122; Fine, Donald I. 122; Fitzhenry & Whiteside 236; Flores, J. 123; Floricanto Press 123; Fort Dearborn 124; Four Walls Eight Windows 124; Friedlander, Joel 257; Giniger Co., K S 271; Glenbridge 126; Goose Lane Editions 236; Grandin 128; Greenleaf Press 129; Guernica Editions 236; Guild Bindery Press 283; Gutter Press 236; Hancock House 131; HarperCollins 131; Hawkes 283; Heart Of The Lakes 283; Helm Publishing 271; Herald Press Canada 237; Herald Publishing House 134; Heyday 135; High Plains 135; Hippocrene 135; Hive 136; HMS Press 237; Holmes & Meier 136; Homestead 137; Horsdale & Schubart 237; Hounslow Press 238; Howell Press 137; Howells House 137; Humanities Press 138; Humanities Press Int'l 284; I.A.A.S. Publishers 258; ICS Publications 140; Ide House 140; ILR Press 141; Indiana Univ. 141; Info Net 284; Inner Traditions Int'l 142; Interlink Publishing Group 142; International Marine Co. 143; International Publishers 143; Int'l Resources 272; Iowa State Univ. Press 144; Italica Press 144; Jewish Publication Society 145; Johnson Books 146; Jones Univ. Press, Bob 146; JSA Publications 272; Kent State Univ. 147; Kesend Publishing, Ltd., Michael 148; Kinseeker 148; Knowledge, Ideas & Trends (KIT) 148; Kodansha America 149; Kurian Reference Books, George 272; Laing Communications 272; Lake View Press 149; Lang, Peter 285; Layla Productions 272; Learning Works 150; Lehigh Univ. Press 151; Lerner 151; Liberal Press 152; Library Research Assoc. 286; Lifetime Books 152; Lincoln Springs 259; Lion Books 152; Little, Brown, Children's Book Division 152; Little, Brown 153; Lone Pine 239; Longstreet House 286; Longstreet Press 155; Lorien House 260; Lorimer & Co., James 239; Louisiana State Univ. 155; Loyola Univ. 156; M.A.P. Productions 239; McClelland & Stewart 239; McDonald & Woodward 157; McFarland & Co. 157; McGuinn & McGuire 158; Macmillan Canada 240; Madison Books 158; Maisonneuve Press 158; Masefield 260; Maverick 159; Mayhaven 286; Mercury Press 240; Meyerbooks 260; Michigan State Univ. 161; Milkweed Editions 162; Millbrook Press 162; Minnesota Historical Society 162; Morehouse 163; Morrow, William 163; Mosaic Press Miniature Books 260; Mountain Press 164; Mystic Seaport Museum 261; National Press 165; Natural Heritage/Natural Heritage 240; Nautical & Aviation 166; Naval Institute 166; Netherlandic Press 240; New England Press 167; New Victoria 168; NeWest 240; Noble Press 169; Nodin Press 169; Northern Illinois Univ. 169; Northland 169; Norton Co., W.W. 170; Nova Science 170; Oldbuck Press 171; Oolichan Books 241; Orca Book Publishers Ltd. 241; Oregon Historical Society Press 173; Oregon State Univ. 173; Overlook Press 174; Oxford Univ. Press 174; Pacific Boating Almanac 288; Pantheon Books 175; Paragon House 288; Peachtree 177; Pelican 177; Pennsylvania Historical and Museum Commission 178; Permanent Press/Second Chance Press, The 178; PHB 180; Pickwick 288; Picton Press 180; Pineapple Press 181; Platinum Press 289; Pogo Press, Incorporated 183; Prairie Oak 263; Presidio Press 184; Press of MacDonald & Reinecke 274; Primer Publishers 263; Pruett 185; Publishers Assoc. 186; Publishers Syndication Int'l 263; Purdue Univ. 186; Purich Publishing 243; QED Press 187; Quarry Press 243; Ragged Edge 290; Raincoast Book Distribution 244; Random House 188; Random House Of Canada 244; Rawhide Western 188; Reed Books Canada 244; Regnery 189; Reidmore Books 244; Republic Of Texas Press 189; Rockbridge 263; Routledge 190; Royal Fireworks Press 191; Rutgers Univ. Press 191; Sachem Publishing Assoc. 274; St. Anthony Messenger Press 192; St. Bede's Publications 192; San Francisco Press 192; Sarpedon 193; Schaum 193; Schiffer 193; Scholastic Canada 245; Scots Plaid 264; Sergeant Kirkland's 194; Shoestring Press 246; Shoreline 246; Signature 195; Silver Burdett Press 196; Silver Moon 274; Simon & Schuster 196; 16th Century Journal 264; Skinner House 196; Social Science Education Consortium 197; Sono Nis 246; Southern Methodist Univ. 198; Southfarm Press 198; Spectrum Press 199; Stackpole Books 199; Stanford Univ. Press 200; Stoddard Publishing 246; Storm Peak 264; Sunflower Univ. 291; Sunstone Press 203; Teachers College 204; Temple 205; Texas A&M Univ. 205; Texas State Historical Association 205; Texas Tech Univ. 206; Texas Western Press 206; Third World Press 207; Thorson & Assoc. 275; Three Continents Press 207; Tidewater 208; Tilbury House 291; Times Books 208; Transaction 292; Transportation Trails 209; Tree Frog 247; Tudor Publishers 210; Tuttle, Charles E. 248; Tyrone Press, The 211; UCLA-American Indian Studies Center 266; United Church Publishing House 248; Univ. Of Idaho 213; Univ. Of Illinois 213; Univ. Of Montreal 249; Univ. of Alabama 212; Univ. of Alaska 212; Univ. of Alberta 248; Univ. of Arkansas, The 213; Univ. of California 213; Univ. of Iowa 214; Univ. of Maine 214; Univ. of Manitoba 249; Univ. of Massachusetts 214; Univ. of Michigan 214; Univ. of Missouri 215; Univ. of Nebraska 215; Univ. of Nevada 215; Univ. of New Mexico 215; Univ. of North Carolina 215; Univ. of North Texas 216; Univ. of Oklahoma 216; Univ. of Ottawa 249; Univ.

of Pennsylvania 216; Univ. of Pittsburgh 216; Univ. of Tennessee 217; Univ. of Texas 217; Univ. Press of America 217; Univ. Press of Mississippi 218; Univ. Press of New England 218; Utah State Univ. Press 218; Vandamere Press 219; Vanderbilt Univ. Press 219; Vehicule Press 250; Vestal Press 219; Vista Publications 266; Wadsworth 220; Walch, Publisher, J. Weston 221; Washington State Univ. Press 222; Watts, Franklin 222; Wayfinder Press 222; Weatherhill 293; Western Book/Journal 293; Western Tanager 266; Westernlore Press 223; Wheetley Co. 275; Whitecap Books 250; Wiener, Markus 224; Wieser & Wieser 275; Wilde Publishing 225; Wilderness Adventure 225; Wiley & Sons, John 225; Windflower Communications 294; Write Way 227; Ye Galleon 294; Zondervan 228.

Hobby. Accord Communications 72; Almar 74; Ancestry Inc. 79; Atheneum Books For Young Readers 82; Bale 85; Benjamin Co., The 269; Berkshire House 88; Betterway 89; Bookworks 269; Brewers 94; Carol 97; Carstens 98; Chapelle 270; Chicago Review Press 100; Comic Art 105; Consumertronics-Top Secret 107; Countrysport Press 109; Cypress 111; Discus Press 116; Dorling Kindersley 116; Dundurn Press 234; E.M. Press 256; Eagle's View 118; Éditions La Liberté 235; EPM 120; Eriksson, Paul S. 120; Filter Press 257; Fort Dearborn 124; Gem Guides 126; Gryphon 130; Hawkes 283; HMS Press 237; Index Publishing Group 141; Info Net 284; Interweave Press 144; ones Publishing 146; JSA Publications 272; Kalmbach 147; Kesend Publishing, Ltd., Michael 148; Klein, B. 148; Lark Books 149; Lifetime Books 152; Little, Brown, Children's Book Division 152; Lyons & Burford, Publishers, Inc. 156; McClelland & Stewart 239; Marketscope Books 159; Markowski Int'l 159; Markowski Int'l 273; Maverick 159; Mayhaven 286; Millbrook Press 162; Mosaic Press Miniature Books 260; Mustang Publishing 165; Owl Books 273; Paper Chase Press 175; Pincushion Press 289; Pollard Press 263; Productive Publications 243; Rocky Top 190; Schiffer 193; Scholastic Canada 245; Sono Nis 246; Stackpole Books 199; Sterling 200; Story Communications/Garden Way 201; Success 202; Sulzburger & Graham 202; Thorson & Assoc. 275; Tudor Publishers 210; Univ. of North Carolina 215; Vestal Press 219; Virtual Press 292; Warren 221; Weidner & Sons 222; Wieser & Wieser 275.

House And Home. Brighton 94; Pantheon Books 175; Sterling 200; Taylor 204.

How-To. Abbott, Langer & Assoc. 70; Aberdeen Group 70; Absey & Co. 70; ACA Books 71; Accent On Living 71; Accent Publications 71; Accord Communications 72; Acropolis South 72; Adams-Blake 73; Addicus Books 73; Allen 74; Allworth Press 74; Almar 74; Alpine 75; Alpine Inc. 277; Amacom 75; American Association for State and Local History 76; American Correctional 77; Amherst Media 78; Amigadget 253; Ancestry Inc. 79; Andrews and McMeel 79; Appalachian Mountain Club Books 79; Aqua Quest 80; Archives Publications 80; Arman, M. 277; ASQC 82; Atheneum Books For Young Readers 82; Auto Book 253; Avery 83; Avon 83; Aztex 84; Baldwin & Knowlton 84; Ballantine 85; Bantam 86; Bell Tower 87; Benjamin Co., The 269; Bentley, Robert 88; Berkley Publishing Group, The 88; Betterway 89; Bicycle Books 89; Blackbirch Graphics 269; Blue Bird 89; Blue Dolphin 90; Bonus Books 91; Bookcraft 92; Bookworks 269; Briarcliff Press 278; Brick House 94; Bright Mountain 254; Brighton 94; Business McGraw-Hill 95; Butterworth-Heinemann 95; Cambridge Educational 96; Camino 96; Caradium 97; Cardoza 97; Career Advancement Center 279; Carol 97; Cassandra Press 98; CCC 99; Center Press 100; Cerier Book Development, Alison Brown 270; Chapelle 270; Charles Press 279; Chelsea Green 279; Chicago Review Press 100; China Books & Periodicals, Inc. 101; Chosen Books 101; Christian Publications, Inc. 102; Christopher Publishing House 280; Church Growth 102; Cleaning Consultant Services 280; College Board 105; Comic Art 105; Communication/Therapy 106; Concordia 106; Consultant Press 107; Consumer Reports Books 107; Consumertronics-Top Secret 107; Contemporary Books 107; Cool Hand 107; Corkscrew Press 255; Cornell Maritime 108; Countryman Press 109; Countrywoman's Press 270; Craftsman Book 109; Creative Book 109; Crisp Publications 110; Crossing Press 110; Cypress 111; Dancing Jester 111; David, Jonathan 112; Dearborn Financial 113; Desktop Grafx 270; Devyn Press 115; Dickens Publications 256; Discus Press 116; Diskotech 256; Distinctive Publishing 116; Doral 116; Dorling Kindersley 116; Duke Press 117; E.M. Press 256; Eagle's View 118; Éditions Logiques/Logical Publishing 235; Elder Books 119; EPM 120; Eriksson, Paul S. 120; Fiesta City 257; Filter Press 257; Fisherman Library 123; Flores, J. 123; Flower Valley 257; Focal Press 123; Focus on the Family 123; Fort Dearborn 124; Gambling Times 257; Garrett 126; Gay Sunshine Press and Leyland Publications 126; Globe Pequot 127; Grapevine 128; Graphic Arts 258; Graphic Arts Technical Foundation 128; Great Ocean 258; Group Publishing 129; Gryphon HouseHalf Halt 130; Hamilton Institute, Alexander 130; Harper San Francisco 131; HarperCollins 131; Hartley & Marks 131; Hastings House 132; Hawkes 283; Herbal Studies 258; Heritage 134; Heyday 135; HMS Press 237; Hoffman Press 258; Hollow Earth 136; Home Education Press 137; Hounslow Press 238; Humanics Publishing 138; I.A.A.S. Publishers 258; ICS Books, Inc. 139; In Print 259; Info Net 284; Insight Books 142; Intercultural Press 142; Interlink Publishing Group 142; Int'l Resources 272; International Wealth Success 144; Interweave Press

144; Jamenair 259; Jelmar 259; Jewish Lights Publishing 145; Jewish Lights Publishing 145; Jist Works 145; ones Publishing 146; JSA Publications 272; Kalmbach 147; Kesend Publishing, Ltd., Michael 148; Klein, B. 148; Knowledge, Ideas & Trends (KIT) 148; Laing Communications 272; Lamppost Press 272; Lark Books 149; LAWCO Ltd. 259; Layla Productions 272; Library Research Assoc. 286; Lifetime Books 152; Lion Books 152; Little, Brown 153; Llewellyn 153; Lone Eagle 154; Lone Pine 239; Loompanics 155; Lorien House 260; McBooks 260; McClelland & Stewart 239; McDonald & Woodward 157; McGraw-Hill Companies 157; Marketscope Books 159; Markowski Int'l 159; Markowski Int'l 273; MasterMedia 286; Masters Press 159; Maverick 159; Meadowbrook Press 160; Media Bridge 160; Menasha Ridge 273; Meriwether 161; Metamorphous Press 161; Michaelis Medical 287; Mid-List Press 161; Morrow, William 163; Mother Courage 164; Mount Olive 287; Mountaineers Books 164; Mustang Publishing 165; Mystic Seaport Museum 261; Naturegraph 261; Neal-Schuman 166; New Falcon 287; New Hope 167; North Light 169; Nova Press 170; Oak Knoll Press 171; Oldbuck Press 171; Olson & Co., C. 261; One On One Computer Training 172; Optimum 241; Orchises Press 173; Ortho Information Services 173; Owl Books 273; Pacific Learning Council 262; Paladin Press 175; Paper Chase Press 175; Paradigm 288; Parrot Press 262; Partners in Publishing 262; Peachpit Press 177; Perspectives Press 179; Piccadilly Books 180; Pineapple Press 181; PMN Publishing 289; Prima 184; PROMPT Publications 185; ProStar 289; PSI Research 186; Publicom 274; QED Press 187; Quill Driver Books/Word Dancer Press 187; Ragged Mountain Press 187; Rainbow 188; Reed Books Canada 244; Revell, Fleming H. 189; Rocky Mountain 245; Rocky Top 190; Royal Fireworks Press 191; Safari Press 192; Schiffer 193; Scots Plaid 264; Self-Counsel 245; Solution 291; Sourcebooks 198; Speech Bin 199; Starburst 200; Sterling 200; Stoddard Publishing 246; Stoeger 201; Stone Bridge 201; Stoneydale Press 201; Story Communications/Garden Way 201; Success 202; Sulzburger & Graham 202; Summit 202; Sunstone Press 203; Systems 204; TAB Books 204; Tambra Publishing 265; Taylor 204; Technical Books for the Layperson 265; Ten Speed 205; Tenth Avenue 274; Thomas Investigative 207; Tiare 208; Time-Life Books 208; Titan Books 247; Todd 209; Tudor Publishers 210; Turtle Press 265; Tuttle, Charles E. 248; 2M Communications 275; UCLA-American Indian Studies Center 266; Van Patten 266; Virtual Press 292; Visions Communications 266; Vista Publishing Inc. 293; Voyageur Press 220; Waite Group 220; Wasatch Publishers 266; Waterfront Books 266; Weatherhill 293; Weiser, Inc., Samuel 223; Whitehorse Press 266; Whitford Press 224; Wilde Publishing 225; Wilderness Adventure 225; Wilderness Press 225; Wiley & Sons, John 225; Williamson 225; Wilshire Book Co. 226; Writer's Digest Books 227; Writer's Resources 267; Zebra and Pinnacle 228.

Humanities. Asian Humanities Press 82; Borgo Press 92; Dante Univ. Of America 112; Duquesne Univ. Press 117; Feminist Press at the City Univ. of NY 122; Indiana Univ. 141; Lang, Peter 285; Roxbury 191; Stanford Univ. Press 200; Univ. of Arkansas, The 213; Whitson 224; Zondervan 228.

Humor. Acme Press 253; Andrews and McMeel 79; Arsenal Pulp 229; Atheneum Books For Young Readers 82; Baldwin & Knowlton 84; Ballantine 85; Bantam 86; Barbour and Co. 86; Black Ball 254; Black Tooth 254; Carol 97; Catbird Press 98; CCC 99; Center Press 100; Chicago Plays 100; Citadel Press 103; Clarion 103; Clear Light 103; Colonial Press 280; Commune-A-Key 105; Compass Productions 270; Contemporary Books 107; Cool Hand 107; Corkscrew Press 255; Creative Book 109; Cuff Publications, Harry 234; Dancing Jester 111; Dawson, W.S. 113; Discus Press 116; Distinctive Publishing 116; E.M. Press 281; Edicones Universal 282; Éditions Logiques/Logical Publishing 235; Epicenter Press 119; EPM 120; Eriksson, Paul S. 120; Fiesta City 257; Fort Dearborn 124; Friends United 125; Gardner Press 282; Great Quotations 129; Gutter Press 236; Harian Creative Books 283; HarperCollins 131; Hastings House 132; HMS Press 237; Hoard & Sons, W.D. 258; Honor Books 284; Horsdale & Schubart 237; Hounslow Press 238; Hyperion Press 238; ICS Books, Inc. 139; ones Publishing 146; JSA Publications 272; Key Porter Books 238; Knowledge, Ideas & Trends (KIT) 148; Lamppost Press 272; Layla Productions 272; Limelight Editions 152; Longstreet Press 155; McClelland & Stewart 239; Macmillan Canada 240; Marketscope Books 159; Mayhaven 286; Menasha Ridge 273; Meriwether 161; Mosaic Press Miniature Books 260; Mustang Publishing 165; Orchises Press 173; Paladin Press 175; Paradigm 288; Pax Publishing 262; Peachtree 177; Pelican 177; Piccadilly Books 180; Pollard Press 263; Prep Publishing 183; Press Gang 243; Price Stern Sloan 184; Quarry Press 243; Ragged Mountain Press 187; Raincoast Book Distribution 244; Random House 188; Reed Books Canada 244; Royal Fireworks Press 191; Rutledge Hill Press 191; Scots Plaid 264; Shoreline 246; Signature 195; Sterling 200; Stoddard Publishing 246; Success 202; Summit 202; Titan Books 247; Tuttle, Charles E. 248; 2M Communications 275; Weatherhill 293; Wordstorm 251; Zebra and Pinnacle 228.

Illustrated Book. Advocacy Press 253; Alpine 75; American & World Geographic 76; Atheneum Books For Young Readers 82; Avanyu 83; Ballantine 85; Bandanna 85; Bantam 86; Bear and Co.

87; Beil, Frederic C. 87; Bergh 88; Betterway 89; Black Ball 254; Blackbirch Graphics 269; Blackbirch Press 89; Bliss 254; Boston Mills Press 232; Branden. 93; Canadian Plains Research Center 233; Charlesbridge 100; Cleaning Consultant Services 280; Colonial Press 280; Comic Art 105; Compass Productions 270; Consumertronics-Top Secret 107; Countrysport Press 109; Cypress 111; Dancing Jester 111; Davis Publications 113; Dial Books For Young Readers 115; Dorling Kindersley 116; Down The Shore 256; Éditions Logiques/Logical Publishing 235; Elysium Growth 119; EPM 120; Eriako Assoc. 271; Flores, J. 123; Fort Dearborn 124; Giniger Co., K S 271; Godine, David R. 127; Gold'n' Honey Books 127; Goose Lane Editions 236; Graphic Arts Center 128; Great Ocean 258; Great Quotations 129; Harmony House 283; Herald Press Canada 237; Hiller Box Manufacturing 271; Holiday House 136; Homestead 137; Hounslow Press 238; Howell Press 137; Howells House 137; Humanics Publishing 138; I.A.A.S. Publishers 258; ICS Books, Inc. 139; Indiana Historical Society 259; Interlink Publishing Group 142; ones Publishing 146; Just Us Books 147; Kesend Publishing, Ltd., Michael 148; Key Porter Books 238; Laing Communications 272; Lamppost Press 272; Lark Books 149; Layla Productions 272; Limelight Editions 152; Longstreet Press 155; Lothrop, Lee & Shepard 155; M.A.P. Productions 239; McBooks 260; McClelland & Stewart 239; McDonald & Woodward 157; Mayhaven 286; Meadowbrook Press 160; Metamorphous Press 161; Minnesota Historical Society 162; Mosaic Press Miniature Books 260; Mountain Automation 261; New England Press 167; NorthWord Press 170; Oldbuck Press 171; Optimum 241; Orca Book Publishers Ltd. 241; Ozark 175; Pelican 177; Pendaya 262; Pennsylvania Historical and Museum Commission 178; Peter Pauper Press 179; Philomel Books 180; Pincushion Press 289; Playground Books 182; Pogo Press, Incorporated 183; Press Gang 243; Press of MacDonald & Reinecke 274; Princeton Architectural Press 289; Publicom 274; Raincoast Book Distribution 244; Random House 188; Reed Books Canada 244; Royal Fireworks Press 191; Schiffer 193; Shoestring Press 246; Shoreline 246; Soundprints 198; Sourcebooks 198; Speech Bin 199; Stoddard Publishing 246; Sunflower Univ. 291; Tenth Avenue 274; Texas State Historical Association 205; Texas Tech Univ. 206; Third World Press 207; Thorson & Assoc. 275; Tidewater 208; Titan Books 247; Tuttle, Charles E. 248; 2M Communications 275; UAHC Press 292; Univ. of New Mexico 215; Vanderbilt Univ. Press 219; Viking Studio Books 220; Warren 221; Wayfinder Press 222; Weatherhill 293; Wilderness Adventure 225; Willowisp Press, Inc. 226; Windward 226; Zephyr Press 267.

Juvenile Books. Abingdon Press 70; Absey & Co. 70; Advocacy Press 253; African American Images 73; Aqua Quest 80; Archives Publications 80; Archway Paperbacks/Minstrel Books 81; Armstrong Publishing Corp. 81; Atheneum Books For Young Readers 82; Baker Book House 84; B&B 85; Barbour and Co. 86; Barron's Educational Series, Inc. 86; Bear Flag 269; Behrman House 87; Beil, Frederic C. 87; Bergh 88; Blackbirch Graphics 269; Blackbirch Press 89; Bookcraft 92; Borealis Press 232; Boyds Mills 93; Branden. 93; Bridge Publishing 278; Camino 96; Carolrhoda 98; Chapelle 270; Charlesbridge 100; China Books & Periodicals, Inc. 101; Clarion 103; Cobblehill 105; Comic Art 105; Compass Productions 270; Concordia 106; Cool Kids 108; Covenant Communications 281; Creative Spark 270; Dancing Jester 111; Davenport, May 112; Dawn 113; Denison & Co., T.S. 115; Dial Books For Young Readers 115; Dickens Publications 256; Discovery Enterprises 281; Discus Press 116; Doral 116; Down The Shore 256; Dundurn Press 234; Dutton Children's Books 117; E.M. Press 281; Eakin Press/Sunbelt Media, Inc. 118; Éditions La Liberté 235; Éditions Logiques/Logical Publishing 235; Eerdmans, William B. 282; Enslow 119; Eriako Assoc. 271; Explorer's Guide 120; Farrar, Straus and Giroux 121; Feminist Press at the City Univ. of NY 122; Fiesta City 257; Fitzhenry & Whiteside 236; Focus on the Family 123; Fort Dearborn 124; Free Spirit 125; Friends United 125; Godine, David R. 127; Gold'n' Honey Books 127; Graber Productions 271; Grandin 128; Great Quotations 129; Greenhaven Press 129; Greenleaf Press 129; Grosset & Dunlap 129; Gryphon House 258; Hendrick-Long 133; Herald Press 134; Herald Press Canada 237; Hiller Box Manufacturing 271; HMS Press 237; Holiday House 136; Homestead 137; Houghton Mifflin 137; Houghton Mifflin 137; Humanics Publishing 138; Huntington House 139; Hyperion Press, 238; I.A.A.S. Publishers 258; ICS Books, Inc. 139; Ideals Children's Books 140; Interlink Publishing Group 142; Jewish Lights Publishing 145; Jewish Publication Society 145; Jones Univ. Press, Bob 146; Just Us Books 147; Kar-Ben Copies 147; Key Porter Books 238; Kindred Productions 238; Laing Communications 272; Lamppost Press 272; Lark Books 149; Layla Productions 272; Learning Works 150; Lee & Low 151; Lerner 151; Lerner 151; Liguori 152; Little, Brown, Children's Book Division 152; Lodestar 154; Lone Pine 239; Lorimer & Co., James 239; Lothrop, Lee & Shepard 155; Lucent Books 156; McClelland & Stewart 239; McElderry Books, Margaret K. 157; Marlor Press 159; MasterMedia 286; Mayhaven 286; Meadowbrook Press 160; Media Bridge 160; Michaelis Medical 287; Millbrook Press 162; Morehouse 163; Morrow, William 163; Morrow Junior Books 164; Mount Olive 287; Natural Heritage/Natural Heritage 240; New Hope 167; North Country 287; NorthWord Press 170; Optimum 241; Orca Book Publishers

Ltd. 241; Orchard Books 172; Oregon Historical Society Press 173; Owen, Richard C. 174; Owl Books 273; Oxford Univ. Press 174; Ozark 175; Pacific Educational Press 242; Pacific View 262; Parachute Press, Inc. 273; Pauline Books & Media 176; Peachtree 177; Pelican 177; Perspectives Press 179; Philomel Books 180; Pippin Press 181; Players Press 182; Playground Books 182; Polychrome 183; Prep Publishing 183; Press of MacDonald & Reinecke 274; Price Stern Sloan 184; Publicom 274; Purple Finch 263; Quarry Press 243; Raincoast Book Distribution 244; Random House, Juvenile Books 188; Reed Books Canada 244; Ronsdale Press 245; Rosen 190; Royal Fireworks Press 191; Salina Bookshelf 192; Scholastic Canada 245; Scholastic Professional Books 194; Shoestring Press 246; Sierra Club 195; Silver Burdett Press 196; Silver Moon 274; SJL 196; Skinner House 196; Soundprints 198; Speech Bin 199; Standard 200; Starburst 200; Sterling 200; Stoddard Publishing 246; Storm Peak 264; Story Communications/Garden Way 201; TAB Books 204; Tambourine Books 204; Tenth Avenue 274; Texas Christian Univ. 205; Third World Press 207; Thorson & Assoc. 275; Tidewater 208; Tilbury House 291; Tudor Publishers 210; Twenty-First Century Books 210; UAHC Press 292; Unity Books 211; Victor Books 219; Visions Communications 266; Volcano Press 266; Walker and Co. 221; Ward Hill 221; Warren 221; Waterfront Books 266; Whitecap Books 250; Wiley & Sons, John 225; Williamson 225; Willowisp Press, Inc. 226; Winch & Associates/Jalmar Press, B.L. 293; Windflower Communications 294; Windward 226; Zondervan 228.

Language and Literature. ABC-CLIO 70; Anchorage Press 79; Archives Publications 80; Arsenal Pulp 229; Asian Humanities Press 82; Baldwin & Knowlton 84; Bandanna 85; Bantam 86; Barron's Educational Series, Inc. 86; Beil, Frederic C. 87; Borealis Press 232; Bowling Green State Univ. 92; Calyx Books 254; Canadian Inst. of Ukrainian Studies 233; Caratzas, Aristide D. 279; Carol 97; Catholic Univ. of America 99; Center Press 100; China Books & Periodicals, Inc. 101; Clarion 103; College Board 105; Colonial Press 280; Communication/Therapy 106; Confluence Press 107; Consortium 281; Coteau Books 234; Cottonwood Press 108; Creative Arts 281; CSLI Publications, Stanford Univ. 110; Dancing Jester 111; Dante Univ. Of America 112; Davidson, Harlan 113; Dee, Ivan R. 114; Discus Press 116; Dundurn Press 234; Ecco Press 118; Éditions La Liberté 235; Education Center 118; EPM 120; Facts On File 121; Family Album 256; Feminist Press at the City Univ. of NY 122; Floricanto Press 123; Fort Dearborn 124; Four Walls Eight Windows 124; Goose Lane Editions 236; Gryphon 130; Guernica Editions 236; Gutter Press 236; Harian Creative Books 283; Herald Press Canada 237; Highsmith Press 135; Hippocrene 135; Hippopotamus Press 237; HMS Press 237; Insight Books 142; Interlink Publishing Group 142; Italica Press 144; Jewish Publication Society 145; Kent State Univ. 147; Kodansha America 149; Lake View Press 149; Lang, Peter 285; Langenscheidt 149; Learning Works 150; Lehigh Univ. Press 151; Lerner 151; Les Editions La Lignée 238; Lincoln Springs 259; Livingston Press 153; Locust Hill Press 154; Longstreet Press 155; Louisiana State Univ. 155; M.A.P. Productions 239; McClelland & Stewart 239; Maisonneuve Press 158; Mayfield 159; Mercury House 160; Mercury Press 240; Michigan State Univ. 161; Milkweed Editions 162; Modern Language Association of America 162; Mount Olive 287; National Textbook 166; Neal-Schuman 166; Negative Capability 166; Netherlandic Press 240; New England Publishing Assoc. 273; New Readers Press 168; Nightshade Press 261; NTC Publishing Group 171; Oolichan Books 241; Oregon State Univ. 173; Oryx Press 173; Oxford Univ. Press 174; Peguis 242; Press Gang 243; Purdue Univ. 186; Purple Finch 263; QED Press 187; Quarry Press 243; Reed Books Canada 244; Ronsdale Press 245; Roxbury 191; Royal Fireworks Press 191; Russian Information Services 191; Rutgers Univ. Press 191; Sand River 264; Schaum 193; Schenkman 290; Scots Plaid 264; Serendipity Systems 194; Sierra Club 195; 16th Century Journal 264; Smith 197; Spectrum Press 199; Stanford Univ. Press 200; Stone Bridge 201; Stone Bridge 264; Sunflower Univ. 291; Sunk Island 246; Texas Tech Univ. 206; Third Side Press 207; Third World Press 207; Three Continents Press 207; Tuttle, Charles E. 248; UCLA-American Indian Studies Center 266; Univ. Of Idaho 213; Univ. Of Illinois 213; Univ. Of Montreal 249; Univ. of Alabama 212; Univ. of Alaska 212; Univ. of California 213; Univ. of Iowa 214; Univ. of Michigan 214; Univ. of Nebraska 215; Univ. of Nevada 215; Univ. of North Carolina 215; Univ. of North Texas 216; Univ. of Oklahoma 216; Univ. of Ottawa 249; Univ. of Pennsylvania 216; Univ. of Pittsburgh 216; Univ. of Tennessee 217; Univ. of Texas 217; Univ. Press of America 217; Univ. Press of Kentucky 218; Univ. Press of Mississippi 218; Utah State Univ. Press 218; Vanderbilt Univ. Press 219; Vehicule Press 250; Verso 250; Vista Publications 266; Wadsworth 220; Walch, Publisher, J. Weston 221; Warren 221; Weatherhill 293; Weidner & Sons 222; Weigl Educational 250; Wheatley Co. 275; White Pine 224; Wilde Publishing 225; Wiley & Sons, John 225; Writer's Digest Books 227; York Press 251; Zephyr Press 267; Zoland Books 228.

Law. Allworth Press 74; Almar 74; American Bar Association, Publications Planning & Marketing 77; American Correctional 77; Banks-Baldwin 85; BNA 91; Carswell Thomson 233; Catbird Press 98; Garrett 126; Government Institutes 127; Hamilton Institute, Alexander 130; Lawyers & Judges

150; Oceana 171; Planners Press 181; Purich Publishing 243; Self-Counsel 245; Summer Press 202; Temple 205; Transaction 292; Transnational Publishers 209; Univ. of North Carolina 215; Univ. of Pennsylvania 216.

Literary Criticism. Accord Communications 72; Barron's Educational Series, Inc. 86; Borgo Press 92; Bucknell Univ. 95; Dundurn Press 234; ECW Press 234; Fairleigh Dickinson Univ. 121; Gaslight 126; Godine, David R. 127; Guernica Editions 236; Gutter Press 236; Holmes & Meier 136; Lang, Peter 285; M.A.P. Productions 239; Maisonneuve Press 158; NeWest 240; Northern Illinois Univ. 169; Purdue Univ. 186; Routledge 190; Smith 197; Stanford Univ. Press 200; Texas Christian Univ. 205; Third World Press 207; Three Continents Press 207; Univ. of Alabama 212; Univ. of Arkansas, The 213; Univ. of Massachusetts 214; Univ. of Missouri 215; Univ. of Pennsylvania 216; Univ. of Tennessee 217; Univ. of Texas 217; Univ. Press of Mississippi 218; York Press 251.

Marine Subjects. Cornell Maritime 108; Helm Publishing 271; International Marine Co. 143; McGraw-Hill Companies 157; Marlor Press 159; Maverick 159; Mystic Seaport Museum 261; ProStar 289; Sono Nis 246; TAB Books 204; Transportation Trails 209.

Military/War. Avery 83; Aviation Book 254; Avon 83; Blair, John F. 89; Brassey's 93; Carol 97; Combined Books 105; Consumertronics-Top Secret 107; Da Capo 111; Discus Press 116; Eakin Press/Sunbelt Media, Inc. 118; EPM 120; Excalibur Publications 256; Fairleigh Dickinson Univ. 121; Fine, Donald I. 122; Flores, J. 123; Fort Dearborn 124; Harmony House 283; Hippocrene 135; HMS Press 237; Howell Press 137; Howells House 137; I.A.A.S. Publishers 258; ones Publishing 146; Key Porter Books 238; Kurian Reference Books, George 272; Lincoln Springs 259; Longstreet House 286; Louisiana State Univ. 155; McClelland & Stewart 239; Macmillan Canada 240; Maisonneuve Press 158; Michigan State Univ. 161; Monument Press 163; Natural Heritage/ Natural Heritage 240; Nautical & Aviation 166; Naval Institute 166; Oldbuck Press 171; Optimum 241; Paladin Press 175; Platinum Press 289; PMN Publishing 289; Presidio Press 184; Publishers Syndication Int'l 263; Random House Of Canada 244; Reference Service Press 188; Regnery 189; Sachem Publishing Assoc. 274; Sarpedon 193; Schiffer 193; Shoestring Press 246; Southfarm Press 198; Stackpole Books 199; Stoddard Publishing 246; Sunflower Univ. 291; Texas A&M Univ. 205; Thorson & Assoc. 275; Thorson & Assoc. 275; Tudor Publishers 210; Tyrone Press, The 211; Univ. of Alaska 212; Univ. of Nebraska 215; Univ. of North Texas 216; Vandamere Press 219; Vanwell 249; Viking Studio Books 220; Wieser & Wieser 275; Wiley & Sons, John 225; Zebra and Pinnacle 228.

Money/Finance. Adams-Blake 73; Allen 74; Almar 74; Ashgate 278; ASQC 82; Baldwin & Knowlton 84; Bale 85; Bonus Books 91; Briarcliff Press 278; Brick House 94; Business McGraw-Hill 95; Cambridge Educational 96; Caradium 97; Career Advancement Center 279; Carol 97; Cato Institute 99; Center Press 100; Consumer Reports Books 107; Consumertronics-Top Secret 107; Contemporary Books 107; Crisp Publications 110; Cypress 111; Dearborn Financial 113; Discus Press 116; Elder Books 119; Eriako Assoc. 271; Flores, J. 123; Focus on the Family 123; Fort Dearborn 124; Forum 124; Garrett 126; Globe Pequot 127; Hay House 132; Hensley, Virgil 134; Herald Press Canada 237; HMS Press 237; Honor Books 284; Hounslow Press 238; I.A.A.S. Publishers 258; Insight Books 142; International Wealth Success 144; Jewish Lights Publishing 145; Jewish Lights Publishing 145; Key Porter Books 238; Lamppost Press 272; Lerner 151; Lexington Books 151; McClelland & Stewart 239; McGraw-Hill Companies 157; Macmillan Canada 240; Marketscope Books 159; Markowski Int'l 273; MasterMedia 286; Michaelis Medical 287; National Press 165; Neal-Schuman 166; New Society 168; New World Library 168; Nova Science 170; Pax Publishing 262; Pilot Books 181; Planning/Communications 182; PMN Publishing 289; Prentice-Hall Canada 243; Prep Publishing 183; PSI Research 186; Reed Books Canada 244; Schaum 193; Sourcebooks 198; Starburst 200; Stoddard Publishing 246; Success 202; Sulzburger & Graham 202; Summit 202; Sunflower Univ. 291; Systems 204; Ten Speed 205; Todd 209; Tuttle, Charles E. 248; ULI 211; Univ. Press of Georgia 292; Wheetley Co. 275; Zebra and Pinnacle 228.

Multicultural. ABC-CLIO 70; Facts On File 121; Feminist Press at the City Univ. of NY 122; Guernica Editions 236; Highsmith Press 135; Humanics Publishing 138; Intercultural Press 142; Jewish Lights Publishing 145; Judson Press 146; Lee & Low 151; Lerner 151; Luramedia 156; Media Bridge 160; Oolichan Books 241; Oryx Press 173; Polychrome 183; Rutgers Univ. Press 191; Tilbury House 291; Univ. of Pennsylvania 216; Ward Hill 221; Weigl Educational 250.

Multimedia. Dancing Jester 111; Drama Book Publishers 117; Elder Books 119; Hartwick Electronic 258; McGraw-Hill Companies 157; Media Bridge 160; Paideia Press 262; ProStar 289; Reed Books Canada 244; Serendipity Systems 194; Sunk Island 246; Virtual Press 292; Wadsworth 220.

Music/Dance. Amadeus Press 75; American Catholic Press 253; Archives Publications 80; Ardsley House Publishers, Inc. 81; Atheneum Books For Young Readers 82; Baldwin & Knowlton 84; Betterway 89; Black Ball 254; Bliss 254; Bold Strummer Ltd., The 91; Branden. 93; Bucknell Univ. 95; Cambridge Univ. 96; Carol 97; Carolrhoda 98; Center For Afro-American Studies 255;

Centerstream 100; Colonial Press 280; Consortium 281; Creative Arts 281; Da Capo 111; Dance Horizons 111; Dancing Jester 111; Discipleship Resources 115; Distinctive Publishing 116; Drama Book Publishers 117; Ecco Press 118; Éditions La Liberté 235; Faber & Faber 121; Fairleigh Dickinson Univ. 121; Feminist Press at the City Univ. of NY 122; Fort Dearborn 124; Glenbridge 126; Guernica Editions 236; HarperCollins 131; HMS Press 237; Humanics Publishing 138; Indiana Univ. 141; Inner Traditions Int'l 142; JSA Publications 272; Lang, Peter 285; Lerner 151; Limelight Editions 152; Locust Hill Press 154; Louisiana State Univ. 155; McClelland & Stewart 239; McFarland & Co. 157; Mayfield 159; Media Bridge 160; Mercury Press 240; Meriwether 161; Mosaic Press Miniature Books 260; Nelson-Hall 167; Norton Co., W.W. 170; Oxford Univ. Press 174; Pacific Educational Press 242; Pelican 177; Prima 184; Purple Finch 263; Quarry Press 243; Random House 188; Resource Publications 290; San Francisco Press 192; Scarecrow Press 193; Schaum 193; Schirmer Books 193; Stipes 201; Sunflower Univ. 291; Tenth Avenue 274; Texas Tech Univ. 206; Tiare 208; Tilbury House 291; Timber Press 208; Titan Books 247; Transaction 292; Univ. Of Illinois 213; Univ. of Iowa 214; Univ. of Pittsburgh 216; Univ. Press of America 217; Univ. Press of New England 218; Vestal Press 219; Viking Studio Books 220; Wadsworth 220; Walch, Publisher, J. Weston 221; Walker and Co. 221; Warren 221; Weiser, Inc., Samuel 223; Wheetley Co. 275; White Cliffs Media 223; Wilde Publishing 225; Writer's Digest Books 227.

Nature/Environment. ABC-CLIO 70; Alaska Northwest 73; Amwell Press 79; Appalachian Mountain Club Books 79; Aqua Quest 80; Arcade Publishing 80; Atheneum Books For Young Readers 82; Avery 83; Baldwin & Knowlton 84; B&B 85; Bantam 86; Baywood 86; Beachway Press 254; Beacon 87; Bear and Co. 87; Berkshire House 88; Blackbirch Graphics 269; Blackbirch Press 89; Blair, John F. 89; Bliss 254; Blue Dolphin 90; BNA 91; Boxwood Press 278; Brick House 94; Canadian Plains Research Center 233; Carol 97; Carolrhoda 98; Cave 99; Chapel Street 255; Charlesbridge 100; Chelsea Green 279; ChemTec 233; China Books & Periodicals, Inc. 101; Chronicle 102; Clarion 103; Clear Light 103; Confluence Press 107; Consumertronics-Top Secret 107; Countryman Press 109; Countrysport Press 109; Dancing Jester 111; Dawn 113; Discipleship Resources 115; Discus Press 116; Dorling Kindersley 116; Down East 117; Down The Shore 256; Dutton Children's Books 117; Eakin Press/Sunbelt Media, Inc. 118; Éditions La Liberté 235; Ekstasis Editions 235; Elliott & Clark 119; Elysium Growth 119; Epicenter Press 119; EPM 120; Eriksson, Paul S. 120; Explorer's Guide 120; Facts On File 121; Fitzhenry & Whiteside 236; Foghorn Press 124; Fort Dearborn 124; Four Walls Eight Windows 124; Gardner Press 282; Gem Guides 126; Godine, David R. 127; Goose Lane Editions 236; Government Institutes 127; Great Quotations 129; Grosset & Dunlap 129; Hancock House 131; Harmony House 283; Harper San Francisco 131; HarperCollins 131; Hartley & Marks 131; Hay House 132; Helm Publishing 271; Herald Press Canada 237; Heyday 135; High Plains 135; HMS Press 237; Homestead 137; Horsdale & Schubart 237; Houghton Mifflin 137; ICS Books, Inc. 139; Inner Traditions Int'l 142; Insight Books 142; Interlink Publishing Group 142; Iowa State Univ. Press 144; Johnson Books 146; Jones Univ. Press, Bob 146; Kesend Publishing, Ltd., Michael 148; Key Porter Books 238; Kodansha America 149; Kumarian Press 285; Lark Books 149; Lawrence Books, Merloyd 150; Learning Works 150; Lerner 151; Little, Brown, Children's Book Division 152; Little, Brown 153; Llewellyn 153; Lone Pine 239; Longstreet Press 155; Lorien House 260; Luramedia 156; Lyons & Burford, Publishers, Inc. 156; M.A.P. Productions 239; McClelland & Stewart 239; McDonald & Woodward 157; Marketscope Books 159; MasterMedia 286; Maverick 159; Mayhaven 286; Mercury House 160; Meyerbooks 260; Milkweed Editions 162; Millbrook Press 162; Mosaic Press Miniature Books 260; Mountain Press 164; Mountaineers Books 164; Natural Heritage/Natural Heritage 240; Naturegraph 261; New England Cartographics 261; New England Press 167; New Society 168; New World Library 168; Nightshade Press 261; Noble Press 169; North Country 287; Northland 169; NorthWord Press 170; Nova Science 170; Noyes Data 171; Olson & Co., C. 261; Orca Book Publishers Ltd. 241; Oregon Historical Society Press 173; Oregon State Univ. 173; Owen, Richard C. 174; Owl Books 273; Oxford Univ. Press 174; Ozark 175; Pacific Educational Press 242; Peter Pauper Press 179; Picton Press 180; Pineapple Press 181; Plexus 182; Primer Publishers 263; Pruett 185; PSI Research 186; Ragged Mountain Press 187; Raincoast Book Distribution 244; Rawhide Western 188; Reed Books Canada 244; Regnery 189; Rhombus 263; Rocky Mountain 245; Rocky Top 190; Ronsdale Press 245; Rutgers Univ. Press 191; Schenkman 290; Scholastic Canada 245; Scots Plaid 264; Shoestring Press 246; Sierra Club 195; Silver Burdett Press 196; Soundprints 198; Stackpole Books 199; Stanford Univ. Press 200; Starburst 200; Sterling 200; Stillpoint 200; Stipes 201; Stoddard Publishing 246; Story Communications/Garden Way 201; Sunflower Univ. 291; Systems 204; Ten Speed 205; Texas A&M Univ. 205; Texas Tech Univ. 206; Thorsons 247; Tilbury House 291; Timber Press 208; Times Change 265; Univ. Of Idaho 213; Univ. of Alaska 212; Univ. of Alberta 248; Univ. of Arizona 212; Univ. of Arkansas, The 213; Univ. of California 213; Univ. of Iowa 214; Univ. of Massachusetts 214; Univ. of Michigan 214; Univ. of Nebraska 215; Univ.

of Nevada 215; Univ. of North Carolina 215; Univ. of North Texas 216; Univ. of Ottawa 249; Univ. of Texas 217; Univ. Press of Colorado 217; Univ. Press of Mississippi 218; Univ. Press of New England 218; Vanderbilt Univ. Press 219; Verso 250; Visions Communications 266; Voyageur Press 220; Walker and Co. 221; Warren 221; Wasatch Publishers 266; Washington State Univ. Press 222; Waterfront Books 266; Watts, Franklin 222; Wayfinder Press 222; Weatherhill 293; Weidner & Sons 222; Weigl Educational 250; Wheetley Co. 275; Whitecap Books 250; Wieser & Wieser 275; Wilde Publishing 225; Wilderness Adventure 225; Wilderness Press 225; Williamson 225; Willowisp Press, Inc. 226; Windward 226; Zoland Books 228.

Philosophy. American Atheist 76; Ardsley House Publishers, Inc. 81; Aronson, Inc., Jason 81; Ashgate 278; Asian Humanities Press 82; Atheneum Books For Young Readers 82; Baldwin & Knowlton 84; Bandanna 85; Bantam 86; Beacon 87; Bell Tower 87; Black Ball 254; Blue Star 91; Boxwood Press 278; Bucknell Univ. 95; Carol 97; Cassandra Press 98; Catholic Univ. of America 99; Center Press 100; Christopher Publishing House 280; Clear Light 103; Colonial Press 280; Consumertronics-Top Secret 107; Cross Cultural 110; Dancing Jester 111; Davidson, Harlan 113; Discus Press 116; Edicones Universal 282; Eerdmans, William B. 282; Elysium Growth 119; Eriako Assoc. 271; Facts On File 121; Fairleigh Dickinson Univ. 121; Fort Dearborn 124; Friedlander, Joel 257; Glenbridge 126; Godine, David R. 127; Guernica Editions 236; Gutter Press 236; Harper San Francisco 131; HarperCollins 131; Hay House 132; HMS Press 237; Humanics Publishing 138; Humanities Press 138; Humanities Press Int'l 284; I.A.A.S. Publishers 258; Indiana Univ. 141; Inner Traditions Int'l 142; Intercultural Press 142; International Publishers 143; Int'l Resources 272; Italica Press 144; Jewish Lights Publishing 145; Kodansha America 149; Lang, Peter 285; Larson Publications/PBPF 150; Locust Hill Press 154; Louisiana State Univ. 155; McClelland & Stewart 239; MacMurray & Beck 158; Maisonneuve Press 158; Maisonneuve Press 158; Mayfield 159; Mercury House 160; Michigan State Univ. 161; New Falcon 287; Nicolas-Hays 261; Noble Press 169; Northern Illinois Univ. 169; Nova Science 170; Open Court 172; Oxford Univ. Press 174; Paideia Press 262; Paragon House 288; Path Press 288; Paulist Press 176; Pax Publishing 262; Prep Publishing 183; Purdue Univ. 186; Regnery 189; Rocky Top 190; Routledge 190; St. Bede's Publications 192; Schaum 193; Scots Plaid 264; Simon & Schuster 196; Spectrum Press 199; Stone Bridge 201; Swan-Raven & Co. 203; Swedenborg Found. 203; Teachers College 204; Theosophical Publishing House 206; Third World Press 207; Thorsons 247; Transaction 292; Turtle Press 265; Tuttle, Charles E. 292; Tuttle, Charles E. 248; Unity Books 211; Univ. Of Illinois 213; Univ. Of Montreal 249; Univ. of Alberta 248; Univ. of Massachusetts 214; Univ. of Michigan 214; Univ. of Ottawa 249; Univ. of Pittsburgh 216; Univ. of Scranton 217; Univ. Press of America 217; Vanderbilt Univ. Press 219; Verso 250; Wadsworth 220; Wall & Emerson 250; Weatherhill 293; Weiser, Inc., Samuel 223; Wheetley Co. 275; Wilde Publishing 225; Wisdom 226; Writer's Resources 267.

Photography. Allworth Press 74; Amherst Media 78; Atheneum Books For Young Readers 82; Avanyu 83; Branden. 93; Butterworth-Heinemann 95; Caitlin Press 232; Carstens 98; Cave 99; Center Press 100; Chronicle 102; Clarion 103; Clear Light 103; Consultant Press 107; Cuff Publications, Harry 234; Dancing Jester 111; Dorling Kindersley 116; Elliott & Clark 119; Elysium Growth 119; Epicenter Press 119; Focal Press 123; Fort Dearborn 124; Harmony House 283; Hollow Earth 136; Homestead 137; Hounslow Press 238; Howells House 137; Hudson Hill 138; ICS Books, Inc. 139; Key Porter Books 238; Layla Productions 272; Lone Pine 239; Lone Pine 239; Longstreet Press 155; Louisiana State Univ. 155; McClelland & Stewart 239; Minnesota Historical Society 162; Natural Heritage/Natural Heritage 240; New England Press 167; Northland 169; NTC Publishing Group 171; Oregon Historical Society Press 173; Pendaya 262; PHB 180; Quarry Press 243; Random House 188; Shoreline 246; Stormline Press 265; Sunflower Univ. 291; Temple 205; Tenth Avenue 274; Tilbury House 291; Univ. of Alberta 248; Univ. of Iowa 214; Univ. of Nebraska 215; Univ. of New Mexico 215; Viking Studio Books 220; Voyageur Press 220; Wayfinder Press 222; Weatherhill 293; Wieser & Wieser 275; Writer's Digest Books 227; Zoland Books 228; HMS Press 237.

Psychology. Active Parenting Publishers 72; Addicus Books 73; African American Images 73; American Counseling 77; Archives Publications 80; Aronson, Inc., Jason 81; Asian Humanities Press 82; Asian Humanities Press 82; Atheneum Books For Young Readers 82; Avon 83; Baldwin & Knowlton 84; Bantam 86; Baywood 86; Bell Tower 87; Blue Dolphin 90; Boxwood Press 278; Bucknell Univ. 95; Cambridge Univ. 96; Carol 97; Cassandra Press 98; Center For Afro-American Studies 255; Cerier Book Development, Alison Brown 270; CFC Productions 255; Charles Press 279; Christopher Publishing House 280; Citadel Press 103; Cline/Fay 104; Colonial Press 280; Commune-A-Key 105; Conari Press 106; Consortium 281; Contemporary Books 107; Cypress 111; Da Capo 111; Dancing Jester 111; Dawn 113; Discus Press 116; Distinctive Publishing 116; Dutton 117; E.M. Press 281; Edicones Universal 282; Éditions La Liberté 235; Eerdmans, William B. 282;

Ekstasis Editions 235; Elder Books 119; Elysium Growth 119; Eriksson, Paul S. 120; Facts On File 121; Fairleigh Dickinson Univ. 121; Floricanto Press 123; Fort Dearborn 124; Free Spirit 125; Friedlander, Joel 257; Gardner Press 282; Glenbridge 126; Guernica Editions 236; Harper San Francisco 131; HarperCollins 131; Hartley & Marks 131; Hastings House 132; Hawkes 283; Haworth Press 132; Hay House 132; Health Communications 133; Herald Press Canada 237; Human Services Institute 138; Humanics Publishing 138; Hunter House 139; I.A.A.S. Publishers 258; Inner Traditions Int'l 142; Insight Books 142; Intercultural Press 142; Int'l Information Assoc. 143; Int'l Resources 272; Knowledge, Ideas & Trends (KIT) 148; Kodansha America 149; Lang, Peter 285; Larson Publications/PBPF 150; Lawrence Books, Merloyd 150; Lexington Books 151; Libra 286; Lion Press 259; Llewellyn 153; Locust Hill Press 154; Lorien House 260; Love and Logic Press, Inc. 155; Luramedia 156; McClelland & Stewart 239; MacMurray & Beck 158; Maisonneuve Press 158; Markowski Int'l 273; Masefield 260; MasterMedia 286; Mayfield 159; Metamorphous Press 161; Michaelis Medical 287; Mother Courage 164; National Press 165; Nelson-Hall 167; New Falcon 287; New Harbinger 167; New World Library 168; Nicolas-Hays 261; Norton Co., W.W. 170; Nova Science 170; Oxford Univ. Press 174; Paper Chase Press 175; Paradigm 176; Pauline Books & Media 176; Pax Publishing 262; Perspectives Press 179; Peter Pauper Press 179; Plenum 182; Prep Publishing 183; Prima 184; Professional Resource 185; QED Press 187; Quest Books 187; Routledge 190; Schenkman 290; Scots Plaid 264; Sibyl 195; Society 197; Sourcebooks 198; Stanford Univ. Press 200; Starburst 200; Stoddard Publishing 246; Sulzburger & Graham 202; Sunk Island 246; Swedenborg Found. 203; Theosophical Publishing House 206; Third Side Press 207; Third World Press 207; Thorsons 247; Transaction 292; Tudor Publishers 210; 2M Communications 275; Unity Books 211; Univ. Of Montreal 249; Univ. of Nebraska 215; Univ. Press of America 217; Univ. Press of Georgia 292; Univ. Press of New England 218; Victor Books 219; Vista Publishing Inc. 293; Walch, Publisher, J. Weston 221; Weidner & Sons 222; Weiser, Inc., Samuel 223; Westport Publishers, Inc. 223; Wheetley Co. 275; Wiley & Sons, John 225; Williamson 225; Wilshire Book Co. 226; Winch & Associates/Jalmar Press, B.L. 293; Wisdom 226; Woodbridge Press 227; WRS 228.

Real Estage. Contemporary Books 107; Dearborn Financial 113; Government Institutes 127; PMN Publishing 289; Starburst 200; ULI 211.

Recreation. Accord Communications 72; Alaska Northwest 73; American & World Geographic 76; Appalachian Mountain Club Books 79; Atheneum Books For Young Readers 82; Berkshire House 88; Betterway 89; Bicycle Books 89; Bliss 254; Bonus Books 91; Carol 97; Cave 99; Chronicle 102; Compass Productions 270; Countryman Press 109; Dancing Jester 111; Denali Press 114; Discipleship Resources 115; Discus Press 116; Dorling Kindersley 116; Down East 117; Elysium Growth 119; Enslow 119; Epicenter Press 119; EPM 120; Eriksson, Paul S. 120; Explorer's Guide 120; Facts On File 121; Foghorn Press 124; Gem Guides 126; Globe Pequot 127; Harian Creative Books 283; Hay House 132; Herald Press Canada 237; Heyday 135; HMS Press 237; Horsdale & Schubart 237; ICS Books, Inc. 139; Info Net 284; Johnson Books 146; Layla Productions 272; Lerner 151; Lion Books 152; Little, Brown, Children's Book Division 152; Lone Pine 239; McClelland & Stewart 239; McFarland & Co. 157; Macmillan Canada 240; Marketscope Books 159; Masters Press 159; Maverick 159; Menasha Ridge 273; Meriwether 161; Mountaineers Books 164; Mustang Publishing 165; Natural Heritage/Natural Heritage 240; Neal-Schuman 166; New England Cartographics 261; New York Niche Press 169; Nova Science 170; Orca Book Publishers Ltd. 241; Paper Chase Press 175; Peachtree 177; Pelican 177; Pollard Press 263; ProStar 289; Pruett 185; Raincoast Book Distribution 244; Reed Books Canada 244; Republic Of Texas Press 189; Rocky Mountain 245; Scholastic Canada 245; Starburst 200; Sterling 200; Stipes 201; Stoddard Publishing 246; Sulzburger & Graham 202; Sunflower Univ. 291; Ten Speed 205; Univ. Of Idaho 213; Vandamere Press 219; Voyageur Press 220; Wasatch Publishers 266; Wayfinder Press 222; Western Tanager 266; Wheetley Co. 275; Whitecap Books 250; Wieser & Wieser 275; Wilde Publishing 225; Wilderness Press 225; Windward 226; World Leisure 267.

Reference. Abbott, Langer & Assoc. 70; ABC-CLIO 70; ACA Books 71; Accord Communications 72; Adams Publishing 73; Allworth Press 74; Alpine 75; Alta Mira 253; Amacom 75; Amadeus Press 75; American Association for State and Local History 76; American Atheist 76; American Correctional 77; American Counseling 77; American Hospital Publishing 78; Ancestry Inc. 79; Andrews and McMeel 79; Appalachian Mountain Club Books 79; Architectural Book Publishing Co., Inc. 80; Archives Publications 80; Arden Press Inc. 81; Arman, M. 277; Ashgate 278; Asian Humanities Press 82; Avanyu 83; Avery 83; Baker Book House 84; Baldwin & Knowlton 84; Ballantine 85; B&B 85; Banks-Baldwin 85; Baseline II 86; Behrman House 87; Beil, Frederic C. 87; Bethel 88; Betterway 89; Blackbirch Graphics 269; Blackbirch Press 89; Bliss 254; Blue Bird 89; BNA 91; Bookcraft 92; Borealis Press 232; Borgo Press 92; Bowling Green State Univ. 92; Branden. 93; Brassey's 93; Brick House 94; Broadway 95; Business McGraw-Hill 95; Butterworth-

Group 220; Walker and Co. 221; Wall & Emerson 250; Wayfinder Press 222; Weatherhill 293; Weidner & Sons 222; Whitehorse Press 266; Whitford Press 224; Wiley & Sons, John 225; Wisdom 226; Woodbine House 227; Writer's Resources 267; York Press 251; Zondervan 228.

Regional. Addicus Books 73; Alaska Northwest 73; Almar 74; American & World Geographic 76; Appalachian Mountain Club Books 79; Arsenal Pulp 229; Avanyu 83; Baldwin & Knowlton 84; Beachway Press 254; Bear Flag 269; Beil, Frederic C. 87; Berkshire House 88; Blair, John F. 89; Bliss 254; Borealis Press 232; Boston Mills Press 232; Bowling Green State Univ. 92; Boxwood Press 278; Brick House 94; Bright Mountain 254; Caddo Gap 96; Caitlin Press 232; Camino 96; Canadian Plains Research Center 233; Carol 97; Cave 99; Caxton 99; Center For Western Studies 279; Chapel Street 255; Chicago Review Press 100; Chronicle 102; Clear Light 103; Colonial Press 280; Compass Productions 270; Confluence Press 107; Coteau Books 234; Countryman Press 109; Covenant Communications 281; Creative Arts 281; Cuff Publications, Harry 234; Davidson, Harlan 113; Dawson, W.S. 113; Denali Press 114; Desktop Grafx 270; Discus Press 116; Distinctive Publishing 116; Down East 117; Down The Shore 256; Dundurn Press 234; Eakin Press/Sunbelt Media, Inc. 118; Ecco Press 118; ECW Press 234; Eerdmans, William B. 282; Epicenter Press 119; EPM 120; Explorer's Guide 120; Faber & Faber 121; Family Album 256; Filter Press 257; Fitzhenry & Whiteside 236; Fort Dearborn 124; Gem Guides 126; Globe Pequot 127; Golden West 127; Goose Lane Editions 236; Guernica Editions 236; Guild Bindery Press 283; Hancock House 131; Harian Creative Books 283; Heart Of The Lakes 283; Helm Publishing 271; Hemingway Western Studies Series 258; Hendrick-Long 133; Herald Publishing House 134; Heyday 135; High Plains 135; HMS Press 237; Hoard & Sons, W.D. 258; Horsdale & Schubart 237; Hunter Publishing 139; Indiana Historical Society 259; Indiana Univ. 141; Johnson Books 146; Kent State Univ. 147; Kinseeker 148; Lahontan Images 259; Laing Communications 272; Livingston Press 153; Longstreet House 286; Longstreet Press 155; Louisiana State Univ. 155; M.A.P. Productions 239; McBooks 260; Marketscope Books 159; Maverick 159; Mayhaven 286; Menasha Ridge 273; Minnesota Historical Society 162; Moon Publications 163; Mountain Press 164; Natural Heritage/Natural Heritage 240; New England Cartographics 261; New England Press 167; New York Niche Press 169; Nightshade Press 261; Nodin Press 169; North Country 287; Northern Illinois Univ. 169; Northland 169; Oldbuck Press 171; Oolichan Books 241; Orca Book Publishers Ltd. 241; Oregon Historical Society Press 173; Oregon State Univ. 173; Overlook Press 174; Pelican 177; Penguin Books Canada, 242; Pennsylvania Historical and Museum Commission 178; Pineapple Press 181; Prairie Oak 263; Prentice-Hall Canada 243; Prep Publishing 183; Primer Publishers 263; Pruett 185; Purdue Univ. 186; Quarry Press 243; Quill Driver Books/Word Dancer Press 187; Raincoast Book Distribution 244; Renaissance House 189; Republic Of Texas Press 189; Resolution Business 263; Rhombus 263; Ronsdale Press 245; Rutgers Univ. Press 191; Sand River 264; Schiffer 193; Scots Plaid 264; Shoestring Press 246; Shoreline 246; Signature 195; Sono Nis 246; Southern Methodist Univ. 198; Stoddard Publishing 246; Stormline Press 265; Sunflower Univ. 291; Sunstone Press 203; Syracuse Univ. 203; Tamarack Books 265; Temple 205; Texas A&M Univ. 205; Texas Christian Univ. 205; Texas Tech Univ. 206; Texas Western Press 206; Third World Press 207; Tidewater 208; Tilbury House 291; Timber Press 208; Tree Frog 247; Tudor Publishers 210; Tuttle, Charles E. 248; Two Lane 265; Umbrella Books 211; Univ. Of Idaho 213; Univ. of Alaska 212; Univ. of Alberta 248; Univ. of Arizona 212; Univ. of Maine 214; Univ. of Manitoba 249; Univ. of Michigan 214; Univ. of Missouri 215; Univ. of Nevada 215; Univ. of North Texas 216; Univ. of Oklahoma 216; Univ. of Ottawa 249; Univ. of Pittsburgh 216; Univ. of Scranton 217; Univ. of Tennessee 217; Univ. of Texas 217; Univ. Press of Colorado 217; Univ. Press of Georgia 292; Univ. Press of Mississippi 218; Univ. Press of New England 218; Utah State Univ. Press 218; Valiant Press 266; Vandamere Press 219; Vanderbilt Univ. Press 219; Vanwell 249; Vehicule Press 250; Vestal Press 219; Vista Publications 266; Voyageur Press 220; Walker and Co. 221; Wasatch Publishers 266; Washington State Univ. Press 222; Wayfinder Press 222; Western Book/Journal 293; Western Tanager 266; Westernlore Press 223; Wheetley Co. 275; Whitecap Books 250; Wilde Publishing 225; Wilderness Adventure 225; Zoland Books 228.

Religion. Abingdon Press 70; Accent Publications 71; ACTA Publications 72; Alban Institute 74; American Atheist 76; American Catholic Press 253; American Counseling 77; Asian Humanities Press 82; Atheneum Books For Young Readers 82; Baker Book House 84; Bantam 86; Barbour and Co. 86; Beacon Hill Press 87; Beacon 87; Bear and Co. 87; Behrman House 87; Beil, Frederic C. 87; Bell Tower 87; Berkley Publishing Group, The 88; Bethel 88; Black Ball 254; Blue Dolphin 90; Blue Dove 90; Blue Star 91; Bookcraft 92; Bridge Publishing 278; Broadman & Holman 94; Bucknell Univ. 95; Canadian Inst. of Ukrainian Studies 233; Caratzas, Aristide D. 279; Cassandra Press 98; Catholic Univ. of America 99; China Books & Periodicals, Inc. 101; Chosen Books 101; Christian Education Publishers 102; Christian Publications, Inc. 102; Christopher Publishing House 280; Church Growth 102; College Press 105; College Press, Inc. 280; Compass Productions 270;

Concordia 106; Covenant Communications 281; Creation House 109; Cross Cultural 110; Crossway 110; Dancing Jester 111; David, Jonathan 112; Delphi Press 114; Discipleship Resources 115; E.M. Press 281; Eerdmans, William B. 282; Elder Books 119; Facts On File 121; Fort Dearborn 124; Forward Movement Publications 124; Franciscan Press 257; Franciscan Univ. Press 125; Friends United 125; Gold'n' Honey Books 127; Grandin 128; Great Quotations 129; Group Publishing 129; Guernica Editions 236; Harper San Francisco 131; HarperCollins 131; Harvest House 132; Haworth Press 132; Hay House 132; Hensley, Virgil 134; Herald Press 134; Herald Press Canada 237; Herald Publishing House 134; Hiller Box Manufacturing 271; HMS Press 237; Hollow Earth 136; Honor Books 284; Humanics Publishing 138; Humanities Press 138; Huntington House 139; ICS Publications 140; Idyll Arbor 140; Indiana Univ. 141; Inner Traditions Int'l 142; Interlink Publishing Group 142; Italica Press 144; Jewish Lights Publishing 145; Jewish Publication Society 145; Judson Press 146; Kindred Productions 238; Kodansha America 149; Kregel Publications 149; Kurian Reference Books, George 272; Lang, Peter 285; Larson Publications/PBPF 150; Liguori 152; Locust Hill Press 154; Loyola Univ. 156; Luramedia 156; McClelland & Stewart 239; Marketscope Books 159; Markowski Int'l 273; MasterMedia 286; Mayfield 159; Media Bridge 160; Meriwether 161; Michigan State Univ. 161; Monument Press 163; Morehouse 163; Morrow, William 163; Mount Olive 287; National 261; Nelson, Thomas 167; New Falcon 287; New Hope 167; New World Library 168; Nicolas-Hays 261; Nova Science 170; Oldbuck Press 171; Oolichan Books 241; Open Court 172; Orbis Books 172; Our Sunday Visitor 174; Oxford Univ. Press 174; Paideia Press 262; Paragon House 288; Pauline Books & Media 176; Paulist Press 176; Pelican 177; Pickwick 288; PMN Publishing 289; Prep Publishing 183; Publishers Assoc. 186; Purple Finch 263; Quarry Press 243; Quest Books 187; Ragged Edge 290; Rainbow 188; Random House 188; Rawhide Western 188; Regnery 189; Religious Education Press 189; Resource Publications 290; Resurrection Press 189; Revell, Fleming H. 189; St. Anthony Messenger Press 192; St. Bede's Publications 192; St. Vladimir's Seminary 290; Servant 194; Shaw, Harold 195; Shoreline 246; Sibyl 195; Signature 195; 16th Century Journal 264; Skinner House 196; Somerville House 274; Standard 200; Starburst 200; Stillpoint 200; Sunflower Univ. 291; Sunk Island 246; Swedenborg Found. 203; Theosophical Publishing House 206; Third World Press 207; Thorsons 247; Triumph Books 209; Tuttle Co., Charles E. 292; Tuttle, Charles E. 248; Tyndale House Publishers 210; Tyrone Press, The 211; UAHC Press 292; United Church Publishing House 248; Unity Books 211; Univ. Of Montreal 249; Univ. of Alabama 212; Univ. of Manitoba 249; Univ. of North Carolina 215; Univ. of Ottawa 249; Univ. of Scranton 217; Univ. of Tennessee 217; Univ. Press of America 217; Vanderbilt Univ. Press 219; Victor Books 219; Visions Communications 266; Wadsworth 220; Weiser, Inc., Samuel 223; Wheetley Co. 275; Wilshire Book Co. 226; Windflower Communications 294; Wisdom 226; Writer's Resources 267; Zondervan 228.

Scholarly. Baywood 86; BNA 91; Cambridge Univ. 96; Canadian Inst. of Ukrainian Studies 233; Canadian Plains Research Center 233; Cross Cultural 110; Dante Univ. Of America 112; Fairleigh Dickinson Univ. 121; Focal Press 123; Hemingway Western Studies Series 258; Humanities Press Int'l 284; Indiana Univ. 141; Kent State Univ. 147; Knopf, Alfred A. 148; Lang, Peter 285; Lehigh Univ. Press 151; McFarland & Co. 157; Michigan State Univ. 161; Modern Language Association of America 162; Nelson-Hall 167; Oise Press 241; Oregon State Univ. 173; Paragon House 288; Phi Delta Kappa Educational Foundation 180; Pickwick 288; Publishers Assoc. 186; Purdue Univ. 186; Religious Education Press 189; Routledge 190; St. Vladimir's Seminary 290; Scarecrow Press 193; Schirmer Books 193; Stanford Univ. Press 200; Texas Christian Univ. 205; Texas Tech Univ. 206; Texas Western Press 206; Three Continents Press 207; Transaction 292; Univ. Of Illinois 213; Univ. of Alabama 212; Univ. of Alaska 212; Univ. of Alberta 248; Univ. of Arizona 212; Univ. of Calgary 249; Univ. of California Los Angeles Center for Afro-American Studies Publications 266; Univ. of California 213; Univ. of Maine 214; Univ. of Manitoba 249; Univ. of Michigan 214; Univ. of Missouri 215; Univ. of New Mexico 215; Univ. of North Carolina 215; Univ. of Ottawa 249; Univ. of Pennsylvania 216; Univ. of Pittsburgh 216; Univ. of Scranton 217; Univ. of Tennessee 217; Univ. of Texas 217; Univ. of Toronto 249; Univ. Press of America 217; Univ. Press of Colorado 217; Univ. Press of Kentucky 218; Univ. Press of Mississippi 218; Utah State Univ. Press 218; Vanderbilt Univ. Press 219; Verso 250; Westernlore Press 223; Whitson 224; York Press 251.

Science/Technology. ABC-CLIO 70; Abelexpress 252; Aegis 253; Alaska Northwest 73; American Astronautical Society 76; American Chemical 77; Amherst Media 78; B&B 85; Bantam 86; Bear and Co. 87; Blackbirch Press 89; Boxwood Press 278; Cambridge Univ. 96; Carol 97; Cave 99; Charlesbridge 100; ChemTec 233; College Board 105; Colonial Press 280; Consortium 281; Consumertronics-Top Secret 107; Da Capo 111; Dancing Jester 111; Discovery Enterprises 281; Discus Press 116; Dutton 117; Dutton Children's Books 117; Éditions La Liberté 235; Enslow 119; Facts On File 121; Focal Press 123; Fort Dearborn 124; Four Walls Eight Windows 124; Graber Productions 271; Grapevine 128; Grosset & Dunlap 129; HarperCollins 131; Hay House 132; Helm

Publishing 271; Henry, Joseph 134; HMS Press 237; Houghton Mifflin 137; Howells House 137; HRD Press 138; Insight Books 142; Int'l Information Assoc. 143; Interstate 285; Iowa State Univ. Press 144; Johnson Books 146; Kalmbach 147; Kodansha America 149; Learning Works 150; Lehigh Univ. Press 151; Lerner 151; Little, Brown, Children's Book Division 152; Little, Brown 153; Locust Hill Press 154; Lorien House 260; Lyons & Burford, Publishers, Inc. 156; McClelland & Stewart 239; McDonald & Woodward 157; McGraw-Hill Companies 157; Metamorphous Press 161; Michaelis Medical 287; Mid-List Press 161; Millbrook Press 162; Mountain Press 164; Nace Int'l 287; Naturegraph 261; New Falcon 287; New Readers Press 168; Nova Science 170; Noyes Data 171; Oregon State Univ. 173; Owl Books 273; Oxford Univ. Press 174; Pacific Educational Press 242; Parthenon Publishing Group 288; PennWell Books 178; Plenum 182; Plexus 182; Precept Press 183; PROMPT Publications 185; Purdue Univ. 186; Quest Books 187; Regnery 189; Rocky Top 190; Rutgers Univ. Press 191; San Francisco Press 192; Schaum 193; Schenkman 290; Scholastic Canada 245; Shoestring Press 246; Silver Burdett Press 196; Silver Moon 274; Simon & Schuster 196; SJL 196; Solution 291; Stanford Univ. Press 200; Sterling 200; Stipes 201; Sulzburger & Graham 202; Sunflower Univ. 291; Systems 204; TAB Books 204; Ten Speed 205; Texas Tech Univ. 206; Theosophical Publishing House 206; Thorson & Assoc. 275; Times Books 208; Transaction 292; Tudor Publishers 210; Univelt, Inc. 212; Univ. of Alaska 212; Univ. of Arizona 212; Univ. of Maine 214; Univ. of Michigan 214; Univ. of Texas 217; Univ. Press of Georgia 292; Univ. Press of New England 218; Verso 250; Viking Studio Books 220; Virtual Press 292; Visions Communications 266; Wadsworth 220; Walch, Publisher, J. Weston 221; Walker and Co. 221; Wall & Emerson 250; Warren 221; Watts, Franklin 222; Weidner & Sons 222; Weigl Educational 250; Western Book/Journal 293; Wheetley Co. 275; Wilde Publishing 225; Wiley & Sons, John 225; Williamson 225; Willowisp Press, Inc. 226; Windward 226.

Self-Help. Accent Publications 71; Acropolis South 72; ACS Publications 277; Active Parenting Publishers 72; Adams Publishing 73; Addicus Books 73; Advocacy Press 253; Aegis 253; Allen 74; Almar 74; Alta Mira 253; Amacom 75; American Counseling 77; Arcus 253; Atheneum Books For Young Readers 82; Avon 83; Baker Book House 84; Baldwin & Knowlton 84; Ballantine 85; Bantam 86; Bell Tower 87; Benjamin Co., The 269; Betterway 89; Blackbirch Graphics 269; Blue Dolphin 90; Blue Poppy 90; Bookcraft 92; Bridge Publishing 278; Business McGraw-Hill 95; Caradium 97; Career Advancement Center 279; Carol 97; Cassandra Press 98; CCC 99; Cerier Book Development, Alison Brown 270; CFC Productions 255; Charles Press 279; China Books & Periodicals, Inc. 101; Chosen Books 101; Christian Publications, Inc. 102; Christopher Publishing House 280; Cleaning Consultant Services 280; Cliffs Notes 104; Cline/Fay 104; College Board 105; Colonial Press 280; Commune-A-Key 105; Conari Press 106; Consortium 281; Consumer Reports Books 107; Consumertronics-Top Secret 107; Contemporary Books 107; Cool Hand 107; Creative Spark 270; Crisp Publications 110; Cypress 111; Dancing Jester 111; David, Jonathan 112; Desktop Grafx 270; Devyn Press 115; Discus Press 116; Distinctive Publishing 116; Dutton 117; E.M. Press 281; Earth-Love 256; Éditions Logiques/Logical Publishing 235; Elder Books 119; Elliott & Clark 119; Elysium Growth 119; EPM 120; Eriksson, Paul S. 120; Fine, Donald I. 122; Fisher 123; Flores, J. 123; Focus on the Family 123; Fort Dearborn 124; Free Spirit 125; Friedlander, Joel 257; Gambling Times 257; Gardner Press 282; Garrett 126; Giniger Co., K S 271; Graber Productions 271; Grandin 128; Great Ocean 258; Great Quotations 129; Hampton Roads 283; Harian Creative Books 283; Harper San Francisco 131; HarperCollins 131; Hartley & Marks 131; Harvest House 132; Hastings House 132; Hawkes 283; Hay House 132; Health Communications 133; Herald Press 134; Herald Press Canada 237; Herald Publishing House 134; Herbal Studies 258; HMS Press 237; Hounslow Press 238; Human Services Institute 138; Humanics Publishing 138; Hunter House 139; Huntington House 139; Info Net 284; Insight Books 142; Intercultural Press 142; International Wealth Success 144; Ivy League 259; Jamenair 259; Jewish Lights Publishing 145; Jist Works 145; Kesend Publishing, Ltd., Michael 148; Key Porter Books 238; Klein, B. 148; Knowledge, Ideas & Trends (KIT) 148; Lamppost Press 272; Lifetime Books 152; Liguori 152; Limelight Editions 152; Llewellyn 153; Loompanics 155; Love and Logic Press, Inc. 155; Luramedia 156; McClelland & Stewart 239; McDonald & Woodward 157; McGraw-Hill Companies 157; Macmillan Canada 240; Marketscope Books 159; Markowski Int'l 159; Markowski Int'l 273; MasterMedia 286; Masters Press 159; Media Bridge 160; Metamorphous Press 161; Meyerbooks 260; Michaelis Medical 287; Mid-List Press 161; Mills & Sanderson 260; Mother Courage 164; Mustang Publishing 165; National Press 165; Negative Capability 166; Nelson, Thomas 167; New Falcon 287; New Harbinger 167; New Joy Press 261; New World Library 168; Nicolas-Hays 261; Nova Press 170; Nova Science 170; One On One Computer Training 172; Pacific Learning Council 262; Paper Chase Press 175; Parrot Press 262; Partners in Publishing 262; Path Press 288; Pauline Books & Media 176; Paulist Press 176; Pax Publishing 262; Peachtree 177; Pelican 177; Perspectives Press 179; Peter Pauper Press 179; Planning/Communications 182; PMN Publishing

289; Prep Publishing 183; Press Gang 243; Prima 184; Productive Publications 243; Publicom 274; Purple Finch 263; QED Press 187; Quest Books 187; Ragged Edge 290; Random House 188; Reed Books Canada 244; Resurrection Press 189; Revell, Fleming H. 189; Rocky Top 190; Rosen 190; Royal Fireworks Press 191; Rutledge Hill Press 191; Schaum 193; Schenkman 290; Self-Counsel 245; Servant 194; Shaw, Harold 195; Sibyl 195; SJL 196; Skinner House 196; Society 197; Solution 291; Sourcebooks 198; Starburst 200; Stillpoint 200; Stoddard Publishing 246; Success 202; Sulzburger & Graham 202; Summit 202; Sunk Island 246; Swedenborg Found. 203; Systems 204; Tambra Publishing 265; Technical Books for the Layperson 265; Ten Speed 205; Theosophical Publishing House 206; Third Side Press 207; Third World Press 207; Thorsons 247; Todd 209; Trilogy Books 209; Triumph Books 209; Tudor Publishers 210; Turtle Press 265; Tuttle Co., Charles E. 292; Tyndale House Publishers 210; United Church Publishing House 248; Unity Books 211; Valley of the Sun 219; Victor Books 219; Virtual Press 292; Visions Communications 266; Vista Publishing Inc. 293; Volcano Press 266; Waite Group 220; Walker and Co. 221; Weiser, Inc., Samuel 223; Weiss Associates, Daniel 275; Western Book/Journal 293; Whitford Press 224; Wiley & Sons, John 225; Williamson 225; Wilshire Book Co. 226; Winch & Associates/Jalmar Press, B.L. 293; Windflower Communications 294; Wisdom 226; Woodbridge Press 227; World Leisure 267; Writer's Resources 267; WRS 228; Zondervan 228.

Social Sciences. Borgo Press 92; C Q Press 95; Duquesne Univ. Press 117; Eerdmans, William B. 282; Feminist Press at the City Univ. of NY 122; Indiana Historical Society 259; Indiana Univ. 141; International Publishers 143; Lang, Peter 285; Nelson-Hall 167; New Readers Press 168; Northern Illinois Univ. 169; Open Court 172; Oryx Press 173; Plenum 182; Routledge 190; Roxbury 191; Social Science Education Consortium 197; Stanford Univ. Press 200; Teachers College 204; Univ. of California 213; Univ. of Missouri 215; Verso 250; Wadsworth 220; Walch, Publisher, J. Weston 221; Weigl Educational 250; Whitson 224.

Sociology. American Counseling 77; Ashgate 278; Atheneum Books For Young Readers 82; Avanyu 83; Baldwin & Knowlton 84; Bantam 86; Baywood 86; Blue Bird 89; Branden. 93; Bucknell Univ. 95; Canadian Inst. of Ukrainian Studies 233; Canadian Plains Research Center 233; Cato Institute 99; Center For Afro-American Studies 255; Charles Press 279; Child Welfare League Of America 101; China Books & Periodicals, Inc. 101; Christopher Publishing House 280; Cleis Press 104; Cline/Fay 104; Colonial Press 280; Consortium 281; Creative Spark 270; Cross Cultural 110; Cuff Publications, Harry 234; Dancing Jester 111; Davidson, Harlan 113; Discus Press 116; Distinctive Publishing 116; Edicones Universal 282; Éditions La Liberté 235; Eerdmans, William B. 282; Elysium Growth 119; Enslow 119; Eriksson, Paul S. 120; Faber & Faber 121; Fairleigh Dickinson Univ. 121; Feminist Press at the City Univ. of NY 122; Fort Dearborn 124; Free Spirit 125; Gardner Press 282; Glenbridge 126; HarperCollins 131; Haworth Press 132; Hay House 132; Health Administration Press 133; HMS Press 237; Howells House 137; Humanics Publishing 138; Humanities Press 138; Humanities Press Int'l 284; I.A.A.S. Publishers 258; ILR Press 141; Insight Books 142; Intercultural Press 142; Int'l Resources 272; Knowledge, Ideas & Trends (KIT) 148; Kodansha America 149; Lake View Press 149; Lang, Peter 285; Lexington Books 151; Libra 286; Lincoln Springs 259; Lorimer & Co., James 239; Louisiana State Univ. Press 155; Love and Logic Press, Inc. 155; McClelland & Stewart 239; McFarland & Co. 157; MacMurray & Beck 158; Maisonneuve Press 158; Marketscope Books 159; Markowski Int'l 273; Masefield 260; Mayfield 159; Mercury Press 240; Metamorphous Press 161; Mother Courage 164; NASW Press 165; Nelson-Hall 167; New Falcon 287; Noble Press 169; Nova Science 170; Oxford Univ. Press 174; Perspectives Press 179; Planning/Communications 182; Plenum 182; Purdue Univ. 186; Ragged Edge 290; Random House 188; Rawhide Western 188; Regnery 189; Roxbury 191; Rutgers Univ. Press 191; Schenkman 290; Scots Plaid 264; Spectrum Press 199; Stanford Univ. Press 200; Stoddard Publishing 246; Sunflower Univ. 291; Teachers College 204; Temple 205; Third World Press 207; Thomas Investigative 207; Thompson Educational 247; Transaction 292; Tyrone Press, The 211; UCLA-American Indian Studies Center 266; United Church Publishing House 248; Univ. Of Illinois 213; Univ. Of Montreal 249; Univ. of Alberta 248; Univ. of Arkansas, The 213; Univ. of Massachusetts 214; Univ. of Michigan 214; Univ. of North Carolina 215; Univ. of Ottawa 249; Univ. of Pittsburgh 216; Univ. of Scranton 217; Univ. of Toronto 249; Univ. Press of America 217; Univ. Press of New England 218; Vehicule Press 250; Verso 250; Wadsworth 220; Walch, Publisher, J. Weston 221; Wayfinder Press 222; Wheetley Co. 275; White Cliffs Media 223; Wiley & Sons, John 225; Winch & Associates/Jalmar Press, B.L. 293; Windflower Communications 294.

Software. Adams-Blake 73; ASQC 82; Baseline II 86; Branden. 93; Career 97; Cliffs Notes 104; Communication/Therapy 106; Consumertronics-Top Secret 107; Covenant Communications 281; Cypress 111; Dancing Jester 111; Desktop Grafx 270; Eckert & Co., J.K. 270; Family Album 256; Fort Dearborn 124; Grapevine 128; HMS Press 237; Hollow Earth 136; HRD Press 138; Jamenair 259; Jist Works 145; Laing Communications 272; McGraw-Hill Companies 157; MIS Press 162;

198; Sterling 200; Stipes 201; Sulzburger & Graham 202; Summers Press 202; Sybex 203; Systems 204; Systemsware 265; TAB Books 204; Technical Books for the Layperson 265; Texas Tech Univ. 206; Texas Western Press 206; Thorson & Assoc. 275; Tiare 208; Transaction 292; Tudor Publishers 210; ULI 211; Univelt, Inc. 212; Univ. Of Idaho 213; Univ. of Alaska 212; Univ. Press of Georgia 292; Vestal Press 219; Virtual Press 292; Visions Communications 266; Waite Group 220; Weidner & Sons 222; Western Book/Journal 293; Wheetley Co. 275; Wilde Publishing 225; Wiley & Sons, John 225.

Textbook. Abingdon Press 70; ACA Books 71; Active Parenting Publishers 72; Advocacy Press 253; Amacom 75; American Association for State and Local History 76; American Correctional 77; American Counseling 77; American Hospital Publishing 78; Anchorage Press 79; Arden Press Inc. 81; Ardsley House Publishers, Inc. 81; Arman, M. 277; Ashgate 278; Asian Humanities Press 82; Avery 83; Baker Book House 84; Bandanna 85; Barron's Educational Series, Inc. 86; Baseline II 86; Beacon Hill Press 87; Behrman House 87; Bliss 254; Blue Poppy 90; Bowling Green State Univ. 92; Boxwood Press 278; Branden. 93; Brassey's 93; Bridge Publishing 278; Butterworth-Heinemann 95; C Q Press 95; Cambridge Univ. 96; Canadian Plains Research Center 233; Caratzas, Aristide D. 279; Career 97; Center For Afro-American Studies 255; Center For Western Studies 279; Charlesbridge 100; ChemTec 233; China Books & Periodicals, Inc. 101; Christian Education Publishers 102; Christopher Publishing House 280; Church Growth 102; Cleaning Consultant Services 280; Cliffs Notes 104; Colonial Press 280; Comic Art 105; Computer Science Press 106; Consortium 281; Corwin Press 108; Cottonwood Press 108; CSLI Publications, Stanford Univ. 110; Cuff Publications, Harry 234; Cypress 111; Dancing Jester 111; Dearborn Financial 113; Desktop Grafx 270; Discus Press 116; Distinctive Publishing 116; Drama Book Publishers 117; Duke Press 117; Eastland Press 118; Eckert & Co., J.K. 270; Éditions Logiques/Logical Publishing 235; Eerdmans, William B. 282; Elysium Growth 119; ETC 120; Fire Engineering Books & Videos 122; Fitzhenry & Whiteside 236; Focal Press 123; Fort Dearborn 124; Friends United 125; Gardner Press 282; Grapevine 128; Graphic Arts 258; Graphic Arts Technical Foundation 128; Group Publishing 129; Harcourt Brace Jovanovich Canada 237; Haworth Press 132; Health Administration Press 133; Herald Press Canada 237; Hiller Box Manufacturing 271; Hive 136; HMS Press 237; Hoard & Sons, W.D. 258; Holt, Rinehard & Winston 136; Howells House 137; Humanities Press 138; I.A.A.S. Publishers 258; Idyll Arbor 140; Information Resources 141; Intercultural Press 142; International Foundation Of Employee Benefit Plans 143; Int'l Information Assoc. 143; International Medical 143; International Publishers 143; Interstate 285; Jewish Lights Publishing 145; Jist Works 145; Kregel Publications 149; Laing Communications 272; Lang, Peter 285; Leadership Publishers 150; Les Editions La Lignée 238; Liberal Press 152; Loyola Univ. 156; McClelland & Stewart 239; Mayfield 159; Media Bridge 160; Medical Physics 160; Meriwether 161; Metal Powder Industries Fed. 260; Metamorphous Press 161; Michaelis Medical 287; Monument Press 163; Nace Int'l 287; NASW Press 165; National Textbook 166; Neal-Schuman 166; Nelson-Hall 167; New Falcon 287; New Harbinger 167; Nova Science 170; NTC Publishing Group 171; Ohio Biological Survey 261; Oise Press 241; Open Court 172; Orchises Press 173; Oxford Univ. Press 174; Pacific Educational Press 242; Paideia Press 262; Paradigm 176; Paragon House 288; Parthenon Publishing Group 288; Partners in Publishing 262; Paulist Press 176; Picton Press 180; PMN Publishing 289; Precept Press 183; Press Gang 243; Princeton Architectural Press 289; Professional Publications 185; Professional Resource 185; ProStar 289; PSI Research 186; Publicom 274; Publishers Assoc. 186; Purich Publishing 243; Ragged Edge 290; Rainbow 188; Reidmore Books 244; Religious Education Press 189; Rosen 190; Routledge 190; Roxbury 191; Royal Fireworks Press 191; St. Bede's Publications 192; Salina Bookshelf 192; San Francisco Press 192; Schaum 193; Schenkman 290; Schiffer 193; Schirmer Books 193; Scots Plaid 264; Skidmore-Roth Publishing, Inc. 290; Slack 197; Sourcebooks 198; Speech Bin 199; Stanford Univ. Press 200; Stipes 201; Stone Bridge 264; Sulzburger & Graham 202; Systems 204; Systemsware 265; Technical Books for the Layperson 265; Third World Press 207; Thomas Investigative 207; Thompson Educational 247; Transaction 292; Transnational Publishers 209; Tudor Publishers 210; Tyrone Press, The 211; UAHC Press 292; Univ. Of Idaho 213; Univ. Of Montreal 249; Univ. of Alaska 212; Univ. of Alberta 248; Univ. of Michigan 214; Univ. of Ottawa 249; Univ. of Pittsburgh 216; Univ. Press of America 217; Univ. Press of Georgia 292; Utah State Univ. Press 218; Vanderbilt Univ. Press 219; Visions Communications 266; Vista Publishing Inc. 293; Wadsworth 220; Wall & Emerson 250; Weidner & Sons 222; Weigl Educational 250; Wheetley Co. 275; White Cliffs Media 223; White Pine 224; Wiener, Markus 224; Wilde Publishing 225; Wiley & Sons, John 225; Wisdom 226; York Press 251; Zondervan 228.

Translation. Alaska Northwest 73; Alyson 75; American Chemical 77; Architectural Book Publishing Co., Inc. 80; Arman, M. 277; Aronson, Inc., Jason 81; Aztex 84; Briarcliff Press 278; Calyx Books 254; Canadian Inst. of Ukrainian Studies 233; Center For Western Studies 279; China Books

& Periodicals, Inc. 101; Citadel Press 103; Cleis Press 104; Colonial Press 280; Confluence Press 107; Dante Univ. Of America 112; Davis Publications 113; Desktop Grafx 270; Ecco Press 118; ETC 120; Evras Press 256; Feminist Press at the City Univ. of NY 122; Fort Dearborn 124; Goose Lane Editions 236; Guernica Editions 236; Hartley & Marks 131; Hippopotamus Press 237; HMS Press 237; Holmes & Meier 136; Hounslow Press 238; Howells House 137; Indiana Univ. 141; Intercultural Press 142; Iowa State Univ. Press 144; Italica Press 144; Johnson Books 146; Kodansha America 149; Lang, Peter 285; M.A.P. Productions 239; McClelland & Stewart 239; Maisonneuve Press 158; Mercury House 160; Oberlin College 261; Oolichan Books 241; Paulist Press 176; Pickwick 288; QED Press 187; Resource Publications 290; Rutgers Univ. Press 191; St. Bede's Publications 192; Scots Plaid 264; Spectrum Press 199; Stoddard Publishing 246; Stone Bridge 201; Stone Bridge 264; Theosophical Publishing House 206; Three Continents Press 207; Timber Press 208; Transaction 292; Univ. of Alabama 212; Univ. of Alaska 212; Univ. of California 213; Univ. of Massachusetts 214; Univ. of Nebraska 215; Univ. of Ottawa 249; Univ. of Texas 217; Vanderbilt Univ. Press 219; Wheetley Co. 275; White Pine 224; Wisdom 226; Zephyr Press 267; Zoland Books 228.

Transportation. Auto Book 253; Aviation Book 254; Aztex 84; Bentley, Robert 88; Boston Mills Press 232; Career 97; Carstens 98; Golden West 127; Howell Press 137; Iowa State Univ. Press 144; Markowski Int'l 159; Maverick 159; Schiffer 193; Sono Nis 246; TAB Books 204; Thorson & Assoc. 275; Transportation Trails 209; New England Press 167.

Travel. Academy Chicago 71; Alaska Northwest 73; Almar 74; Appalachian Mountain Club Books 79; Aqua Quest 80; Arcade Publishing 80; Atheneum Books For Young Readers 82; Barron's Educational Series, Inc. 86; Beachway Press 254; Bear Flag 269; Bicycle Books 89; Blair, John F. 89; Briarcliff Press 278; Camino 96; Caratzas, Aristide D. 279; Cardoza 97; Carol 97; Carousel Press 255; Cave 99; China Books & Periodicals, Inc. 101; Christopher Publishing House 280; Chronicle 102; Compass Productions 270; Cool Hand 107; Countryman Press 109; Dancing Jester 111; Discus Press 116; Dorling Kindersley 116; Down The Shore 256; Ecco Press 118; Ekstasis Editions 235; Elysium Growth 119; Epicenter Press 119; EPM 120; Eriako Assoc. 271; Eriksson, Paul S. 120; Evras Press 256; Explorer's Guide 120; Filter Press 257; Fort Dearborn 124; Four Walls Eight Windows 124; Gem Guides 126; Giniger Co., K S 271; Globe Pequot 127; Graber Productions 271; HarperCollins 131; Harvard Common 131; Hastings House 132; Helm Publishing 271; Heyday 135; High Plains 135; Hippocrene 135; HMS Press 237; Hollow Earth 136; Homestead 137; Horsdale & Schubart 237; Hounslow Press 238; Hunter Publishing 139; ICS Books, Inc. 139; Info Net 284; Intercultural Press 142; Interlink Publishing Group 142; Int'l Resources 272; Italica Press 144; Jewish Lights Publishing 145; Jewish Lights Publishing 145; Johnson Books 146; Johnston Associates, Int'l 259; Kesend Publishing, Ltd., Michael 148; Kodansha America 149; Kumarian Press 285; Kurian Reference Books, George 272; Learning Works 150; Lone Pine 239; Lonely Planet 154; Lyons & Burford, Publishers, Inc. 156; McClelland & Stewart 239; McDonald & Woodward 157; Marlor Press 159; Maverick 159; Menasha Ridge 273; Mercury House 160; Moon Publications 163; Mosaic Press Miniature Books 260; Mount Olive 287; Mountain Press 164; Mountaineers Books 164; Mustang Publishing 165; Neal-Schuman 166; New Joy Press 261; New York Niche Press 169; Nodin Press 169; NTC Publishing Group 171; Open Road 172; Orca 241; Paradise 262; Passport Press 176; Pelican 177; Pendaya 262; Pennsylvania Historical and Museum Commission 178; Pilot Books 181; Prairie Oak 263; Prima 184; Primer Publishers 263; ProStar 289; Pruett 185; Quarry Press 243; Raincoast Book Distribution 244; RedBrick Press 263; Reed Books Canada 244; Renaissance House 189; Rockbridge 263; Rocky Mountain 245; Russian Information Services 191; Scots Plaid 264; Shoestring Press 246; Shoreline 246; Soho Press 197; Stoddard Publishing 246; Stone Bridge 201; Stone Bridge 264; Storm Peak 264; Sulzburger & Graham 202; Todd 209; Tuttle, Charles E. 248; Two Lane 265; Ulysses Press 211; Umbrella Books 211; Univ. Of Montreal 249; Univ. of Michigan 214; Univ. Press of Georgia 292; Verso 250; Vista Publications 266; Voyageur Press 220; Wasatch Publishers 266; Wayfinder Press 222; Weatherhill 293; Whitecap Books 250; Whitehorse Press 266; Wieser & Wieser 275; Wilde Publishing 225; Wilderness Adventure 225; World Leisure 267; Zephyr Press 267; Zoland Books 228.

Women's Issues/Studies. ABC-CLIO 70; American Counseling 77; Arden Press Inc. 81; Baker Book House 84; Baldwin & Knowlton 84; Bandanna 85; Bantam 86; Baywood 86; Beacon 87; Blackbirch Graphics 269; Blackbirch Press 89; Blue Dolphin 90; Bonus Books 91; Bowling Green State Univ. 92; Calyx Books 254; Carol 97; Center For Afro-American Studies 255; Charles River 255; China Books & Periodicals, Inc. 101; Cleis Press 104; Commune-A-Key 105; Conari Press 106; Contemporary Books 107; Creative Spark 270; Crossing Press 110; Dancing Jester 111; Davidson, Harlan 113; Delphi Press 114; Discus Press 116; Elder Books 119; Epicenter Press 119; EPM 120; Fairleigh Dickinson Univ. 121; Feminist Press at the City Univ. of NY 122; Floricanto Press 123; Focus on the Family 123; Fort Dearborn 124; Franciscan Univ. Press 125; Gardner Press

282; Goose Lane Editions 236; Great Quotations 129; Gylantic 130; Harper San Francisco 131; Harvest House 132; Haworth Press 132; Hay House 132; Health Communications 133; Hensley, Virgil 134; HMS Press 237; Holmes & Meier 136; Honor Books 284; Human Services Institute 138; Humanics Publishing 138; Hunter House 139; ICS Books, Inc. 139; Ide House 140; ILR Press 141; Indiana Univ. 141; Inner Traditions Int'l 142; Insight Books 142; Interlink Publishing Group 142; International Publishers 143; Jewish Lights Publishing 145; Jewish Publication Society 145; Key Porter Books 238; Knowledge, Ideas & Trends (KIT) 148; Kumarian Press 285; Lake View Press 149; Lamppost Press 272; Lexington Books 151; Liberal Press 152; Lincoln Springs 259; Llewellyn 153; Locust Hill Press 154; Longstreet Press 155; Lorimer & Co., James 239; Luramedia 156; M.A.P. Productions 239; McClelland & Stewart 239; McFarland & Co. 157; MacMurray & Beck 158; Maisonneuve Press 158; MasterMedia 286; Mayfield 159; Mercury House 160; Mercury Press 240; Michaelis Medical 287; Milkweed Editions 162; Minnesota Historical Society 162; Monument Press 163; Negative Capability 166; New Falcon 287; New Hope 167; New Joy Press 261; New Society 168; New World Library 168; Nicolas-Hays 261; Noble Press 169; Open Court 172; Oregon Historical Society Press 173; Oxford Univ. Press 174; Paideia Press 262; Pandora Press 242; Paper Chase Press 175; Papier-Mache Press 176; Path Press 288; Prep Publishing 183; Press Gang 243; Press of MacDonald & Reinecke 274; Publicom 274; Publishers Assoc. 186; Random House Of Canada 244; Reed Books Canada 244; Reference Service Press 188; Routledge 190; Royal Fireworks Press 191; Rutgers Univ. Press 191; Scarecrow Press 193; Schenkman 290; Sibyl 195; Signature 195; Skinner House 196; Sourcebooks 198; Spectrum Press 199; Spinsters Ink 199; Stone Bridge 201; Sulzburger & Graham 202; Sunflower Univ. 291; Swan-Raven & Co. 203; Teachers College 204; Temple 205; Tenth Avenue 274; Texas A&M Univ. 205; Third Side Press 207; Third Side Press 207; Third World Press 207; Thompson Educational 247; Tilbury House 291; Times Books 208; Times Change 265; Transnational Publishers 209; Trilogy Books 209; Triumph Books 209; Tudor Publishers 210; Turtle Press 265; 2M Communications 275; United Church Publishing House 248; Univ. Of Idaho 213; Univ. of Arizona 212; Univ. of Manitoba 249; Univ. of Massachusetts 214; Univ. of Michigan 214; Univ. of Oklahoma 216; Univ. of Ottawa 249; Univ. of Pennsylvania 216; Univ. of Tennessee 217; Univ. of Texas 217; Vanderbilt Univ. Press 219; Verso 250; Victor Books 219; Viking Studio Books 220; Vista Publishing Inc. 293; Volcano Press 266; White Pine 224; Wiley & Sons, John 225; Windflower Communications 294; Writer's Resources 267; Zoland Books 228.

World Affairs. ABC-CLIO 70; Biddle 254; Clarity Press 255; Family Album 256; Interlink Publishing Group 142; Kumarian Press 285; McFarland & Co. 157; Stillpoint 200; Times Books 208; Univ. of Arizona 212; Univ. Press of America 217; Univ. Press of Kentucky 218.

Young Adult. Bantam 86; Archway Paperbacks/Minstrel Books 81; Atheneum Books For Young Readers 82; Barron's Educational Series, Inc. 86; Bridge Publishing 278; Cambridge Educational 96; Cliffs Notes 104; Cobblehill 105; College Board 105; Davenport, May 112; Dial Books For Young Readers 115; Dundurn Press 234; Enslow 119; Fitzhenry & Whiteside 236; Greenhaven Press 129; Group Publishing 129; Hendrick-Long 133; Houghton Mifflin 137; Just Us Books 147; Lucent Books 156; McElderry Books, Margaret K. 157; Partners in Publishing 262; Philomel Books 180; Pippin Press 181; Price Stern Sloan 184; Random House, Juvenile Books 188; Rosen 190; Silver Burdett Press 196; Tyndale House Publishers 210; Walker and Co. 221; Ward Hill 221.

Can't find a listing in the General Index? Check the Changes '95-'96 at the end of each section: Book Publishers, page 296; Consumer Publications, page 678; Trade Journals, page 814; Scriptwriting Markets, page 863; Syndicates, page 884; Greeting Card Publishers, page 884; and Contests, page 936.

General Index

Can't find a listing in the General Index? Check the Changes '95-'96 at the end of each section: Book Publishers, page 296; Consumer Publications, page 678; Trade Journals, page 814; Scriptwriting Markets, page 863; Syndicates, page 884; Greeting Card Publishers, page 884; and Contests, page 936.

More Great Books For Writers!

The Writer's Ultimate Research Guide—Save research time and frustration with the help of this guide. 352 information-packed pages will point you straight to the information you need to create better, more accurate fiction and nonfiction. With hundreds of listings of books and databases, each entry reveals how current the information is, what the content and organization are like, and much more! *#10447/$19.99/352 pages/available October 1, 1995*

Queries and Submissions—Sell your articles again and again! Discover proven strategies for writing attention-grabbing query and cover letters, craft dynamic opening paragraphs, brainstorm article ideas, earn an editor's trust, and much more! *#10426/$15.99/176 pages*

Description—Discover how to use detailed description to awaken the reader's senses; advance the story using only relevant description; create original word depictions of people, animals, places, weather; and much more! *#10451/$15.99/176 pages*

How to Write Like an Expert About Anything—Find out how to use new technology and traditional research methods to get the information you need, envision new markets and write proposals that sell, find and interview experts on any topic, and much more! *#10449/$17.99/224 pages*

How to Write Fast (While Writing Well)—Discover what makes a story and what it takes to research and write one. Then, learn, step-by-step how to cut wasted time and effort by planning interviews for maximum results, beating writer's block with effective plotting, getting the most information from traditional library research and on-line computer bases, and much more! Plus, a complete chapter loaded with tricks and tips for faster writing. *#10473/$15.99/208 pages/paperback/available September 1, 1995*

The Writer's Digest Guide to Good Writing—In one book, you'll find the best in writing instruction gleaned from the past 75 years of *Writer's Digest* magazine! Successful authors like Vonnegut, Steinbeck, Oates, Michener, and over a dozen others share their secrets on writing technique, idea generation, inspiration, and getting published. *#10391/$18.99/352 pages*

Thesaurus of Alternatives to Worn-Out Words and Phrases—Rid your work of trite clichés and hollow phrases for good! Alphabetical entries shed light on the incorrect, the bland and the overused words that plague so many writers. Then you'll learn how to vivify your work with alternative, lively and original words! *#10408/$17.99/304 pages*

Voice & Style—Discover how to create character and story voices! You'll learn to write with a spellbinding narrative voice, create original character voices, write dialogue that conveys personality, control tone of voice to create mood, and make the story's voices harmonize into a solid style. *#10452/ $15.99/176 pages*

Writing for Money—Discover where to look for writing opportunities—and how to make them pay off. You'll learn how to write for magazines, newspapers, radio and TV, newsletters, greeting cards, and a dozen other hungry markets! *#10425/$17.99/256 pages*

The Writer's Digest Guide to Manuscript Formats—Don't take chances with your hard work! Learn how to prepare and submit books, poems, scripts, stories and more with the professional look editors expect from a good writer. *#10025/$19.99/200 pages*

Roget's Superthesaurus—For whenever you need just the right word! You'll find "vocabulary builder" words with pronunciation keys and sample sentences, quotations that double as synonyms, plus the only word-find reverse dictionary in any thesaurus—all in alphabetical format! *#10424/ $22.99/624 pages*